Major Canadian Cities:
Compared & Ranked

Comparaison et classement des principales villes canadiennes

Additional Publications

For more detailed information or to place an order, see the back of the book.

CANADIAN PARLIAMENTARY GUIDE 2013
Guide parlementaire canadien

1266 pages, 6 x 9, Hardcover
ISBN 978-1-61925-148-9
ISSN 0315-6168

Published annually since before Confederation, this indispensable guide to government in Canada provides information on federal and provincial governments, with biographical sketches of government members, descriptions of government institutions, and historical text and charts. With significant bilingual sections, the Guide covers elections from Confederation to the present, including the most recent provincial elections.

FINANCIAL SERVICES CANADA 2013-2014
Services financiers au Canada

1684 pages, 8 1/2 x 11, Softcover
16th edition, April 2013
ISBN 978-1-61925-146-5
ISSN 1484-2408

This directory of Canadian financial institutions and organizations includes banks and depository institutions, non-depository institutions, investment management firms, financial planners, insurance companies, accountants, major law firms, government and regulatory agencies, and associations. Fully indexed.

CANADIAN ALMANAC & DIRECTORY 2013
Répertoire et almanach canadien

2366 pages, 8 1/2 x 11, Hardcover
166th edition, November 2012
ISBN 978-1-59237-988-0
ISSN 0068-8193

A combination of textual material, charts, colour photographs and directory listings, the Canadian Almanac & Directory provides the most comprehensive picture of Canada, from physical attributes to economic and business summaries to leisure and recreation.

GOVERNMENTS CANADA SUMMER/FALL 2013
Gouvernements du Canada

1042 pages, 8 1/2 x 11, Softcover
Summer/Fall 2013
ISBN 978-1-61925-149-6
ISSN 1493-3918

Governments Canada provides a solution to finding the departments and people that you are searching for within our federal and provincial political system.

ASSOCIATIONS CANADA 2013
Associations du Canada

2104 pages, 8 1/2 x 11, Hardcover
33th edition, February 2013
ISBN 978-1-61925-145-8
ISSN 1186-9798

Nearly 20,000 entries profile Canadian and international organizations active in Canada. Over 2,000 subject classifications index activities, professions and interests served by associations. Includes listings of NGOs, institutes, coalitions, social agencies, federations, foundations, trade unions, fraternal orders, political parties. Fully indexed by subject, geographic location, electronic addresses, executive name, acronym, mailing list availability, conferences and publications.

LIBRARIES CANADA 2013-2014
Bibliothèques Canada

1000 pages, 8 1/2 x 11, Softcover
28th edition, May 2013
ISBN 978-1-61925-147-2
ISSN 1920-2849

Libraries Canada offers comprehensive information on Canadian libraries, resource centres, business information centres, professional associations, regional library systems, archives, library schools, government libraries, and library technical programs.

HEALTH GUIDE CANADA 2013-2014
Guide canadien de la santé

944 pages, 8 1/2 x 11, Softcover
1st edition, May 2013
ISBN: 978-1-61925-185-4

Health Guide Canada contains thousands of ways to deal with the many aspects of chronic or mental health disorder. It includes associations, government agencies, libraries and resource centres, educational facilities, hospitals and publications.

CANADIAN ENVIRONMENTAL RESOURCE GUIDE 2013-2014
Guide des ressources environnementales canadiennes

2-vol. set, 1552 pages, 8 1/2 x 11, Softcover
18th Edition, August 2013
ISBN 978-1-61925-144-1
ISSN 1920-2725

Canada's most complete national listing of environmental associations and organizations, governmental regulators and purchasing groups, product and service companies, special libraries and more! All indexed and categorized for quick and easy reference. Also included are companies registered by ISO 9001, 9002, 9003 and 14001.

1st Edition

Major Canadian Cities:
Compared & Ranked

Comparaison et classement des principales villes canadiennes

Grey House Publishing Canada

PUBLISHER: Leslie Mackenzie
GENERAL MANAGER: Bryon Moore

Grey House Publishing

EDITORIAL DIRECTOR: Laura Mars
MARKETING DIRECTOR: Jessica Moody
COMPOSITION: David Garoogian

Grey House Publishing Canada
555 Richmond Street West, Suite 301
Toronto, ON M5V 3B1
866-433-4739
FAX 416-644-1904
www.greyhouse.ca
e-mail: info@greyhouse.ca

Grey House Publishing Canada, Inc. is a wholly owned subsidiary of Grey House Publishing, Inc. USA.

While every effort has been made to ensure the reliability of the information presented in this publication, Grey House Publishing Canada, Inc. neither guarantees the accuracy of the data contained herein nor assumes any responsibility for errors, omissions or discrepancies. Grey House accepts no payment for listing; inclusion in the publication of any organization, agency, institution, publication, service or individual does not imply endorsement of the editors or publisher.

Errors brought to the attention of the publisher and verified to the satisfaction of the publisher will be corrected in future editions.

Except by express prior written permission of the Copyright Proprietor no part of this work may be copied by any means of publication or communication now known or developed hereafter including, but not limited to, use in any directory or compilation or other print publication, in any information storage and retrieval system, in any other electronic device, or in any visual or audio-visual device or product.

This publication is an original and creative work, copyrighted by Grey House Publishing, Inc. and is fully protected by all applicable copyright laws, as well as by laws covering misappropriation, trade secrets and unfair competition.

Grey House Publishing has added value to the underlying factual material through one or more of the following efforts: unique and original selection; expression; arrangement; coordination; and classification.

Grey House Publishing, Inc. will defend its rights in this publication.

Copyright © 2013 Grey House Publishing Canada, Inc.
All rights reserved

Printed in Canada by Webcom, Inc.

ISBN: 978-1-61925-260-8

Cataloguing in Publication Data is available from Libraries and Archives Canada.

TABLE OF CONTENTS

PROFILES

Abbotsford, British Columbia . . . 1
Population Growth and Density . . . 2
Gender . . . 2
Marital Status . . . 2
Age Characteristics: 0 to 49 Years . . . 3
Age Characteristics: 50 Years and Over, and Median Age . . . 3
Private Households by Household Size . . . 4
Dwelling Type . . . 4
Shelter Costs . . . 4
Occupied Private Dwellings by Period of Construction . . . 4
Educational Attainment . . . 5
Household Income Distribution . . . 5
Median and Average Household and Economic Family Income . . . 5
Individual Income Distribution . . . 6
Labour Force Status . . . 6
Labour Force by Industry (NAICS Codes 11-52) . . . 7
Labour Force by Industry (NAICS Codes 53-91) . . . 7
Occupation . . . 8
Place of Work Status . . . 8
Mode of Transportation to Work . . . 9
Visible Minority Population Characteristics . . . 9
Aboriginal Population . . . 10
Ethnic Origin . . . 10
Religion . . . 11
Religion-Christian Denominations . . . 11
Immigrant Status and Period of Immigration . . . 12
Mother Tongue . . . 12
Language Spoken Most Often at Home . . . 13
Knowledge of Official Languages . . . 13

Ajax, Ontario . . . 15
Population Growth and Density . . . 16
Gender . . . 16
Marital Status . . . 16
Age Characteristics: 0 to 49 Years . . . 17
Age Characteristics: 50 Years and Over, and Median Age . . . 17
Private Households by Household Size . . . 18
Dwelling Type . . . 18
Shelter Costs . . . 18
Occupied Private Dwellings by Period of Construction . . . 18
Educational Attainment . . . 19
Household Income Distribution . . . 19
Median and Average Household and Economic Family Income . . . 19
Individual Income Distribution . . . 20
Labour Force Status . . . 20
Labour Force by Industry (NAICS Codes 11-52) . . . 21
Labour Force by Industry (NAICS Codes 53-91) . . . 21
Occupation . . . 22
Place of Work Status . . . 22
Mode of Transportation to Work . . . 23
Visible Minority Population Characteristics . . . 23
Aboriginal Population . . . 24
Ethnic Origin . . . 24
Religion . . . 25
Religion-Christian Denominations . . . 25
Immigrant Status and Period of Immigration . . . 26
Mother Tongue . . . 26
Language Spoken Most Often at Home . . . 27
Knowledge of Official Languages . . . 27

Barrie, Ontario . . . 29
Population Growth and Density . . . 30
Gender . . . 30
Marital Status . . . 30
Age Characteristics: 0 to 49 Years . . . 31
Age Characteristics: 50 Years and Over, and Median Age . . . 31
Private Households by Household Size . . . 32
Dwelling Type . . . 32
Shelter Costs . . . 32
Occupied Private Dwellings by Period of Construction . . . 32
Educational Attainment . . . 33
Household Income Distribution . . . 33
Median and Average Household and Economic Family Income . . . 33
Individual Income Distribution . . . 34
Labour Force Status . . . 34
Labour Force by Industry (NAICS Codes 11-52) . . . 35
Labour Force by Industry (NAICS Codes 53-91) . . . 35
Occupation . . . 36
Place of Work Status . . . 36
Mode of Transportation to Work . . . 37
Visible Minority Population Characteristics . . . 37
Aboriginal Population . . . 38
Ethnic Origin . . . 38
Religion . . . 39
Religion-Christian Denominations . . . 39
Immigrant Status and Period of Immigration . . . 40
Mother Tongue . . . 40
Language Spoken Most Often at Home . . . 41
Knowledge of Official Languages . . . 41

Brampton, Ontario . . . 43
Population Growth and Density . . . 44
Gender . . . 44
Marital Status . . . 44
Age Characteristics: 0 to 49 Years . . . 45
Age Characteristics: 50 Years and Over, and Median Age . . . 45
Private Households by Household Size . . . 46
Dwelling Type . . . 46
Shelter Costs . . . 46
Occupied Private Dwellings by Period of Construction . . . 46
Educational Attainment . . . 47
Household Income Distribution . . . 47
Median and Average Household and Economic Family Income . . . 47
Individual Income Distribution . . . 48
Labour Force Status . . . 48
Labour Force by Industry (NAICS Codes 11-52) . . . 49
Labour Force by Industry (NAICS Codes 53-91) . . . 49
Occupation . . . 50
Place of Work Status . . . 50
Mode of Transportation to Work . . . 51
Visible Minority Population Characteristics . . . 51
Aboriginal Population . . . 52
Ethnic Origin . . . 52
Religion . . . 53
Religion-Christian Denominations . . . 53
Immigrant Status and Period of Immigration . . . 54
Mother Tongue . . . 54
Language Spoken Most Often at Home . . . 55
Knowledge of Official Languages . . . 55

Burlington, Ontario . . . 57
Population Growth and Density . . . 58
Gender . . . 58
Marital Status . . . 58
Age Characteristics: 0 to 49 Years . . . 59
Age Characteristics: 50 Years and Over, and Median Age . . . 59
Private Households by Household Size . . . 60
Dwelling Type . . . 60
Shelter Costs . . . 60
Occupied Private Dwellings by Period of Construction . . . 60
Educational Attainment . . . 61
Household Income Distribution . . . 61
Median and Average Household and Economic Family Income . . . 61
Individual Income Distribution . . . 62
Labour Force Status . . . 62
Labour Force by Industry (NAICS Codes 11-52) . . . 63
Labour Force by Industry (NAICS Codes 53-91) . . . 63
Occupation . . . 64

Table of Contents

- Place of Work Status 64
- Mode of Transportation to Work 65
- Visible Minority Population Characteristics 65
- Aboriginal Population 66
- Ethnic Origin 66
- Religion 67
- Religion-Christian Denominations 67
- Immigrant Status and Period of Immigration ... 68
- Mother Tongue 68
- Language Spoken Most Often at Home 69
- Knowledge of Official Languages 69

Burnaby, British Columbia 71
- Population Growth and Density 72
- Gender 72
- Marital Status 72
- Age Characteristics: 0 to 49 Years 73
- Age Characteristics: 50 Years and Over, and Median Age 73
- Private Households by Household Size 74
- Dwelling Type 74
- Shelter Costs 74
- Occupied Private Dwellings by Period of Construction 74
- Educational Attainment 75
- Household Income Distribution 75
- Median and Average Household and Economic Family Income ... 75
- Individual Income Distribution 76
- Labour Force Status 76
- Labour Force by Industry (NAICS Codes 11-52) 77
- Labour Force by Industry (NAICS Codes 53-91) 77
- Occupation 78
- Place of Work Status 78
- Mode of Transportation to Work 79
- Visible Minority Population Characteristics 79
- Aboriginal Population 80
- Ethnic Origin 80
- Religion 81
- Religion-Christian Denominations 81
- Immigrant Status and Period of Immigration ... 82
- Mother Tongue 82
- Language Spoken Most Often at Home 83
- Knowledge of Official Languages 83

Calgary, Alberta 85
- Population Growth and Density 86
- Gender 86
- Marital Status 86
- Age Characteristics: 0 to 49 Years 87
- Age Characteristics: 50 Years and Over, and Median Age 87
- Private Households by Household Size 88
- Dwelling Type 88
- Shelter Costs 88
- Occupied Private Dwellings by Period of Construction 88
- Educational Attainment 89
- Household Income Distribution 89
- Median and Average Household and Economic Family Income ... 89
- Individual Income Distribution 90
- Labour Force Status 90
- Labour Force by Industry (NAICS Codes 11-52) 91
- Labour Force by Industry (NAICS Codes 53-91) 91
- Occupation 92
- Place of Work Status 92
- Mode of Transportation to Work 93
- Visible Minority Population Characteristics 93
- Aboriginal Population 94
- Ethnic Origin 94
- Religion 95
- Religion-Christian Denominations 95
- Immigrant Status and Period of Immigration ... 96
- Mother Tongue 96
- Language Spoken Most Often at Home 97
- Knowledge of Official Languages 97

Cambridge, Ontario 99
- Population Growth and Density 100
- Gender 100
- Marital Status 100
- Age Characteristics: 0 to 49 Years 101
- Age Characteristics: 50 Years and Over, and Median Age 101
- Private Households by Household Size 102
- Dwelling Type 102
- Shelter Costs 102
- Occupied Private Dwellings by Period of Construction 102
- Educational Attainment 103
- Household Income Distribution 103
- Median and Average Household and Economic Family Income ... 103
- Individual Income Distribution 104
- Labour Force Status 104
- Labour Force by Industry (NAICS Codes 11-52) 105
- Labour Force by Industry (NAICS Codes 53-91) 105
- Occupation 106
- Place of Work Status 106
- Mode of Transportation to Work 107
- Visible Minority Population Characteristics 107
- Aboriginal Population 108
- Ethnic Origin 108
- Religion 109
- Religion-Christian Denominations 109
- Immigrant Status and Period of Immigration ... 110
- Mother Tongue 110
- Language Spoken Most Often at Home 111
- Knowledge of Official Languages 111

Chatham-Kent, Ontario 113
- Population Growth and Density 114
- Gender 114
- Marital Status 114
- Age Characteristics: 0 to 49 Years 115
- Age Characteristics: 50 Years and Over, and Median Age 115
- Private Households by Household Size 116
- Dwelling Type 116
- Shelter Costs 116
- Occupied Private Dwellings by Period of Construction 116
- Educational Attainment 117
- Household Income Distribution 117
- Median and Average Household and Economic Family Income ... 117
- Individual Income Distribution 118
- Labour Force Status 118
- Labour Force by Industry (NAICS Codes 11-52) 119
- Labour Force by Industry (NAICS Codes 53-91) 119
- Occupation 120
- Place of Work Status 120
- Mode of Transportation to Work 121
- Visible Minority Population Characteristics 121
- Aboriginal Population 122
- Ethnic Origin 122
- Religion 123
- Religion-Christian Denominations 123
- Immigrant Status and Period of Immigration ... 124
- Mother Tongue 124
- Language Spoken Most Often at Home 125
- Knowledge of Official Languages 125

Coquitlam, British Columbia 127
- Population Growth and Density 128
- Gender 128
- Marital Status 128
- Age Characteristics: 0 to 49 Years 129
- Age Characteristics: 50 Years and Over, and Median Age 129
- Private Households by Household Size 130
- Dwelling Type 130
- Shelter Costs 130
- Occupied Private Dwellings by Period of Construction 130
- Educational Attainment 131
- Household Income Distribution 131
- Median and Average Household and Economic Family Income ... 131
- Individual Income Distribution 132

Labour Force Status	132
Labour Force by Industry (NAICS Codes 11-52)	133
Labour Force by Industry (NAICS Codes 53-91)	133
Occupation	134
Place of Work Status	134
Mode of Transportation to Work	135
Visible Minority Population Characteristics	135
Aboriginal Population	136
Ethnic Origin	136
Religion	137
Religion-Christian Denominations	137
Immigrant Status and Period of Immigration	138
Mother Tongue	138
Language Spoken Most Often at Home	139
Knowledge of Official Languages	139

Edmonton, Alberta … 141
Population Growth and Density	142
Gender	142
Marital Status	142
Age Characteristics: 0 to 49 Years	143
Age Characteristics: 50 Years and Over, and Median Age	143
Private Households by Household Size	144
Dwelling Type	144
Shelter Costs	144
Occupied Private Dwellings by Period of Construction	144
Educational Attainment	145
Household Income Distribution	145
Median and Average Household and Economic Family Income	145
Individual Income Distribution	146
Labour Force Status	146
Labour Force by Industry (NAICS Codes 11-52)	147
Labour Force by Industry (NAICS Codes 53-91)	147
Occupation	148
Place of Work Status	148
Mode of Transportation to Work	149
Visible Minority Population Characteristics	149
Aboriginal Population	150
Ethnic Origin	150
Religion	151
Religion-Christian Denominations	151
Immigrant Status and Period of Immigration	152
Mother Tongue	152
Language Spoken Most Often at Home	153
Knowledge of Official Languages	153

Gatineau, Québec … 155
Population Growth and Density	156
Gender	156
Marital Status	156
Age Characteristics: 0 to 49 Years	157
Age Characteristics: 50 Years and Over, and Median Age	157
Private Households by Household Size	158
Dwelling Type	158
Shelter Costs	158
Occupied Private Dwellings by Period of Construction	158
Educational Attainment	159
Household Income Distribution	159
Median and Average Household and Economic Family Income	159
Individual Income Distribution	160
Labour Force Status	160
Labour Force by Industry (NAICS Codes 11-52)	161
Labour Force by Industry (NAICS Codes 53-91)	161
Occupation	162
Place of Work Status	162
Mode of Transportation to Work	163
Visible Minority Population Characteristics	163
Aboriginal Population	164
Ethnic Origin	164
Religion	165
Religion-Christian Denominations	165
Immigrant Status and Period of Immigration	166
Mother Tongue	166

Language Spoken Most Often at Home	167
Knowledge of Official Languages	167

Greater Sudbury, Ontario … 169
Population Growth and Density	170
Gender	170
Marital Status	170
Age Characteristics: 0 to 49 Years	171
Age Characteristics: 50 Years and Over, and Median Age	171
Private Households by Household Size	172
Dwelling Type	172
Shelter Costs	172
Occupied Private Dwellings by Period of Construction	172
Educational Attainment	173
Household Income Distribution	173
Median and Average Household and Economic Family Income	173
Individual Income Distribution	174
Labour Force Status	174
Labour Force by Industry (NAICS Codes 11-52)	175
Labour Force by Industry (NAICS Codes 53-91)	175
Occupation	176
Place of Work Status	176
Mode of Transportation to Work	177
Visible Minority Population Characteristics	177
Aboriginal Population	178
Ethnic Origin	178
Religion	179
Religion-Christian Denominations	179
Immigrant Status and Period of Immigration	180
Mother Tongue	180
Language Spoken Most Often at Home	181
Knowledge of Official Languages	181

Guelph, Ontario … 183
Population Growth and Density	184
Gender	184
Marital Status	184
Age Characteristics: 0 to 49 Years	185
Age Characteristics: 50 Years and Over, and Median Age	185
Private Households by Household Size	186
Dwelling Type	186
Shelter Costs	186
Occupied Private Dwellings by Period of Construction	186
Educational Attainment	187
Household Income Distribution	187
Median and Average Household and Economic Family Income	187
Individual Income Distribution	188
Labour Force Status	188
Labour Force by Industry (NAICS Codes 11-52)	189
Labour Force by Industry (NAICS Codes 53-91)	189
Occupation	190
Place of Work Status	190
Mode of Transportation to Work	191
Visible Minority Population Characteristics	191
Aboriginal Population	192
Ethnic Origin	192
Religion	193
Religion-Christian Denominations	193
Immigrant Status and Period of Immigration	194
Mother Tongue	194
Language Spoken Most Often at Home	195
Knowledge of Official Languages	195

Halifax, Nova Scotia … 197
Population Growth and Density	198
Gender	198
Marital Status	198
Age Characteristics: 0 to 49 Years	199
Age Characteristics: 50 Years and Over, and Median Age	199
Private Households by Household Size	200
Dwelling Type	200
Shelter Costs	200
Occupied Private Dwellings by Period of Construction	200

Table of Contents

Educational Attainment 201
Household Income Distribution. 201
Median and Average Household and Economic Family Income . . 201
Individual Income Distribution. 202
Labour Force Status 202
Labour Force by Industry (NAICS Codes 11-52). 203
Labour Force by Industry (NAICS Codes 53-91). 203
Occupation 204
Place of Work Status 204
Mode of Transportation to Work 205
Visible Minority Population Characteristics 205
Aboriginal Population. 206
Ethnic Origin 206
Religion. 207
Religion-Christian Denominations 207
Immigrant Status and Period of Immigration 208
Mother Tongue 208
Language Spoken Most Often at Home 209
Knowledge of Official Languages. 209

Hamilton, Ontario **211**
Population Growth and Density 212
Gender 212
Marital Status. 212
Age Characteristics: 0 to 49 Years 213
Age Characteristics: 50 Years and Over, and Median Age 213
Private Households by Household Size 214
Dwelling Type 214
Shelter Costs. 214
Occupied Private Dwellings by Period of Construction 214
Educational Attainment 215
Household Income Distribution. 215
Median and Average Household and Economic Family Income . . 215
Individual Income Distribution. 216
Labour Force Status 216
Labour Force by Industry (NAICS Codes 11-52). 217
Labour Force by Industry (NAICS Codes 53-91). 217
Occupation 218
Place of Work Status 218
Mode of Transportation to Work 219
Visible Minority Population Characteristics 219
Aboriginal Population. 220
Ethnic Origin 220
Religion. 221
Religion-Christian Denominations 221
Immigrant Status and Period of Immigration 222
Mother Tongue 222
Language Spoken Most Often at Home 223
Knowledge of Official Languages. 223

Kelowna, British Columbia. **225**
Population Growth and Density 226
Gender 226
Marital Status. 226
Age Characteristics: 0 to 49 Years 227
Age Characteristics: 50 Years and Over, and Median Age 227
Private Households by Household Size 228
Dwelling Type 228
Shelter Costs. 228
Occupied Private Dwellings by Period of Construction 228
Educational Attainment 229
Household Income Distribution. 229
Median and Average Household and Economic Family Income . . 229
Individual Income Distribution. 230
Labour Force Status 230
Labour Force by Industry (NAICS Codes 11-52). 231
Labour Force by Industry (NAICS Codes 53-91). 231
Occupation 232
Place of Work Status 232
Mode of Transportation to Work 233
Visible Minority Population Characteristics 233
Aboriginal Population. 234
Ethnic Origin 234

Religion. 235
Religion-Christian Denominations 235
Immigrant Status and Period of Immigration 236
Mother Tongue 236
Language Spoken Most Often at Home 237
Knowledge of Official Languages. 237

Kingston, Ontario **239**
Population Growth and Density 240
Gender 240
Marital Status. 240
Age Characteristics: 0 to 49 Years 241
Age Characteristics: 50 Years and Over, and Median Age 241
Private Households by Household Size 242
Dwelling Type 242
Shelter Costs. 242
Occupied Private Dwellings by Period of Construction 242
Educational Attainment 243
Household Income Distribution. 243
Median and Average Household and Economic Family Income . . 243
Individual Income Distribution. 244
Labour Force Status 244
Labour Force by Industry (NAICS Codes 11-52). 245
Labour Force by Industry (NAICS Codes 53-91). 245
Occupation 246
Place of Work Status 246
Mode of Transportation to Work 247
Visible Minority Population Characteristics 247
Aboriginal Population. 248
Ethnic Origin 248
Religion. 249
Religion-Christian Denominations 249
Immigrant Status and Period of Immigration 250
Mother Tongue 250
Language Spoken Most Often at Home 251
Knowledge of Official Languages. 251

Kitchener, Ontario. **253**
Population Growth and Density 254
Gender 254
Marital Status. 254
Age Characteristics: 0 to 49 Years 255
Age Characteristics: 50 Years and Over, and Median Age 255
Private Households by Household Size 256
Dwelling Type 256
Shelter Costs. 256
Occupied Private Dwellings by Period of Construction 256
Educational Attainment 257
Household Income Distribution. 257
Median and Average Household and Economic Family Income . . 257
Individual Income Distribution. 258
Labour Force Status 258
Labour Force by Industry (NAICS Codes 11-52). 259
Labour Force by Industry (NAICS Codes 53-91). 259
Occupation 260
Place of Work Status 260
Mode of Transportation to Work 261
Visible Minority Population Characteristics 261
Aboriginal Population. 262
Ethnic Origin 262
Religion. 263
Religion-Christian Denominations 263
Immigrant Status and Period of Immigration 264
Mother Tongue 264
Language Spoken Most Often at Home 265
Knowledge of Official Languages. 265

Langley, British Columbia. **267**
Population Growth and Density 268
Gender 268
Marital Status. 268
Age Characteristics: 0 to 49 Years 269
Age Characteristics: 50 Years and Over, and Median Age 269

Private Households by Household Size	270	Mode of Transportation to Work	303
Dwelling Type	270	Visible Minority Population Characteristics	303
Shelter Costs	270	Aboriginal Population	304
Occupied Private Dwellings by Period of Construction	270	Ethnic Origin	304
Educational Attainment	271	Religion	305
Household Income Distribution	271	Religion-Christian Denominations	305
Median and Average Household and Economic Family Income	271	Immigrant Status and Period of Immigration	306
Individual Income Distribution	272	Mother Tongue	306
Labour Force Status	272	Language Spoken Most Often at Home	307
Labour Force by Industry (NAICS Codes 11-52)	273	Knowledge of Official Languages	307
Labour Force by Industry (NAICS Codes 53-91)	273		
Occupation	274	**Longueuil, Québec**	**309**
Place of Work Status	274	Population Growth and Density	310
Mode of Transportation to Work	275	Gender	310
Visible Minority Population Characteristics	275	Marital Status	310
Aboriginal Population	276	Age Characteristics: 0 to 49 Years	311
Ethnic Origin	276	Age Characteristics: 50 Years and Over, and Median Age	311
Religion	277	Private Households by Household Size	312
Religion-Christian Denominations	277	Dwelling Type	312
Immigrant Status and Period of Immigration	278	Shelter Costs	312
Mother Tongue	278	Occupied Private Dwellings by Period of Construction	312
Language Spoken Most Often at Home	279	Educational Attainment	313
Knowledge of Official Languages	279	Household Income Distribution	313
		Median and Average Household and Economic Family Income	313
Laval, Québec	**281**	Individual Income Distribution	314
Population Growth and Density	282	Labour Force Status	314
Gender	282	Labour Force by Industry (NAICS Codes 11-52)	315
Marital Status	282	Labour Force by Industry (NAICS Codes 53-91)	315
Age Characteristics: 0 to 49 Years	283	Occupation	316
Age Characteristics: 50 Years and Over, and Median Age	283	Place of Work Status	316
Private Households by Household Size	284	Mode of Transportation to Work	317
Dwelling Type	284	Visible Minority Population Characteristics	317
Shelter Costs	284	Aboriginal Population	318
Occupied Private Dwellings by Period of Construction	284	Ethnic Origin	318
Educational Attainment	285	Religion	319
Household Income Distribution	285	Religion-Christian Denominations	319
Median and Average Household and Economic Family Income	285	Immigrant Status and Period of Immigration	320
Individual Income Distribution	286	Mother Tongue	320
Labour Force Status	286	Language Spoken Most Often at Home	321
Labour Force by Industry (NAICS Codes 11-52)	287	Knowledge of Official Languages	321
Labour Force by Industry (NAICS Codes 53-91)	287		
Occupation	288	**Lévis, Québec**	**323**
Place of Work Status	288	Population Growth and Density	324
Mode of Transportation to Work	289	Gender	324
Visible Minority Population Characteristics	289	Marital Status	324
Aboriginal Population	290	Age Characteristics: 0 to 49 Years	325
Ethnic Origin	290	Age Characteristics: 50 Years and Over, and Median Age	325
Religion	291	Private Households by Household Size	326
Religion-Christian Denominations	291	Dwelling Type	326
Immigrant Status and Period of Immigration	292	Shelter Costs	326
Mother Tongue	292	Occupied Private Dwellings by Period of Construction	326
Language Spoken Most Often at Home	293	Educational Attainment	327
Knowledge of Official Languages	293	Household Income Distribution	327
		Median and Average Household and Economic Family Income	327
London, Ontario	**295**	Individual Income Distribution	328
Population Growth and Density	296	Labour Force Status	328
Gender	296	Labour Force by Industry (NAICS Codes 11-52)	329
Marital Status	296	Labour Force by Industry (NAICS Codes 53-91)	329
Age Characteristics: 0 to 49 Years	297	Occupation	330
Age Characteristics: 50 Years and Over, and Median Age	297	Place of Work Status	330
Private Households by Household Size	298	Mode of Transportation to Work	331
Dwelling Type	298	Visible Minority Population Characteristics	331
Shelter Costs	298	Aboriginal Population	332
Occupied Private Dwellings by Period of Construction	298	Ethnic Origin	332
Educational Attainment	299	Religion	333
Household Income Distribution	299	Religion-Christian Denominations	333
Median and Average Household and Economic Family Income	299	Immigrant Status and Period of Immigration	334
Individual Income Distribution	300	Mother Tongue	334
Labour Force Status	300	Language Spoken Most Often at Home	335
Labour Force by Industry (NAICS Codes 11-52)	301	Knowledge of Official Languages	335
Labour Force by Industry (NAICS Codes 53-91)	301		
Occupation	302	**Markham, Ontario**	**337**
Place of Work Status	302	Population Growth and Density	338

MAJOR CANADIAN CITIES: COMPARED AND RANKED

Table of Contents

Gender 338
Marital Status 338
Age Characteristics: 0 to 49 Years 339
Age Characteristics: 50 Years and Over, and Median Age 339
Private Households by Household Size 340
Dwelling Type 340
Shelter Costs 340
Occupied Private Dwellings by Period of Construction 340
Educational Attainment 341
Household Income Distribution 341
Median and Average Household and Economic Family Income .. 341
Individual Income Distribution 342
Labour Force Status 342
Labour Force by Industry (NAICS Codes 11-52) 343
Labour Force by Industry (NAICS Codes 53-91) 343
Occupation 344
Place of Work Status 344
Mode of Transportation to Work 345
Visible Minority Population Characteristics 345
Aboriginal Population 346
Ethnic Origin 346
Religion 347
Religion-Christian Denominations 347
Immigrant Status and Period of Immigration 348
Mother Tongue 348
Language Spoken Most Often at Home 349
Knowledge of Official Languages 349

Mississauga, Ontario 351
Population Growth and Density 352
Gender 352
Marital Status 352
Age Characteristics: 0 to 49 Years 353
Age Characteristics: 50 Years and Over, and Median Age 353
Private Households by Household Size 354
Dwelling Type 354
Shelter Costs 354
Occupied Private Dwellings by Period of Construction 354
Educational Attainment 355
Household Income Distribution 355
Median and Average Household and Economic Family Income .. 355
Individual Income Distribution 356
Labour Force Status 356
Labour Force by Industry (NAICS Codes 11-52) 357
Labour Force by Industry (NAICS Codes 53-91) 357
Occupation 358
Place of Work Status 358
Mode of Transportation to Work 359
Visible Minority Population Characteristics 359
Aboriginal Population 360
Ethnic Origin 360
Religion 361
Religion-Christian Denominations 361
Immigrant Status and Period of Immigration 362
Mother Tongue 362
Language Spoken Most Often at Home 363
Knowledge of Official Languages 363

Montréal, Québec 365
Population Growth and Density 366
Gender 366
Marital Status 366
Age Characteristics: 0 to 49 Years 367
Age Characteristics: 50 Years and Over, and Median Age 367
Private Households by Household Size 368
Dwelling Type 368
Shelter Costs 368
Occupied Private Dwellings by Period of Construction 368
Educational Attainment 369
Household Income Distribution 369
Median and Average Household and Economic Family Income .. 369
Individual Income Distribution 370
Labour Force Status 370

Labour Force by Industry (NAICS Codes 11-52) 371
Labour Force by Industry (NAICS Codes 53-91) 371
Occupation 372
Place of Work Status 372
Mode of Transportation to Work 373
Visible Minority Population Characteristics 373
Aboriginal Population 374
Ethnic Origin 374
Religion 375
Religion-Christian Denominations 375
Immigrant Status and Period of Immigration 376
Mother Tongue 376
Language Spoken Most Often at Home 377
Knowledge of Official Languages 377

Oakville, Ontario 379
Population Growth and Density 380
Gender 380
Marital Status 380
Age Characteristics: 0 to 49 Years 381
Age Characteristics: 50 Years and Over, and Median Age 381
Private Households by Household Size 382
Dwelling Type 382
Shelter Costs 382
Occupied Private Dwellings by Period of Construction 382
Educational Attainment 383
Household Income Distribution 383
Median and Average Household and Economic Family Income .. 383
Individual Income Distribution 384
Labour Force Status 384
Labour Force by Industry (NAICS Codes 11-52) 385
Labour Force by Industry (NAICS Codes 53-91) 385
Occupation 386
Place of Work Status 386
Mode of Transportation to Work 387
Visible Minority Population Characteristics 387
Aboriginal Population 388
Ethnic Origin 388
Religion 389
Religion-Christian Denominations 389
Immigrant Status and Period of Immigration 390
Mother Tongue 390
Language Spoken Most Often at Home 391
Knowledge of Official Languages 391

Oshawa, Ontario 393
Population Growth and Density 394
Gender 394
Marital Status 394
Age Characteristics: 0 to 49 Years 395
Age Characteristics: 50 Years and Over, and Median Age 395
Private Households by Household Size 396
Dwelling Type 396
Shelter Costs 396
Occupied Private Dwellings by Period of Construction 396
Educational Attainment 397
Household Income Distribution 397
Median and Average Household and Economic Family Income .. 397
Individual Income Distribution 398
Labour Force Status 398
Labour Force by Industry (NAICS Codes 11-52) 399
Labour Force by Industry (NAICS Codes 53-91) 399
Occupation 400
Place of Work Status 400
Mode of Transportation to Work 401
Visible Minority Population Characteristics 401
Aboriginal Population 402
Ethnic Origin 402
Religion 403
Religion-Christian Denominations 403
Immigrant Status and Period of Immigration 404
Mother Tongue 404
Language Spoken Most Often at Home 405

Knowledge of Official Languages . . . 405

Ottawa, Ontario . . . 407
Population Growth and Density . . . 408
Gender . . . 408
Marital Status . . . 408
Age Characteristics: 0 to 49 Years . . . 409
Age Characteristics: 50 Years and Over, and Median Age . . . 409
Private Households by Household Size . . . 410
Dwelling Type . . . 410
Shelter Costs . . . 410
Occupied Private Dwellings by Period of Construction . . . 410
Educational Attainment . . . 411
Household Income Distribution . . . 411
Median and Average Household and Economic Family Income . . 411
Individual Income Distribution . . . 412
Labour Force Status . . . 412
Labour Force by Industry (NAICS Codes 11-52) . . . 413
Labour Force by Industry (NAICS Codes 53-91) . . . 413
Occupation . . . 414
Place of Work Status . . . 414
Mode of Transportation to Work . . . 415
Visible Minority Population Characteristics . . . 415
Aboriginal Population . . . 416
Ethnic Origin . . . 416
Religion . . . 417
Religion-Christian Denominations . . . 417
Immigrant Status and Period of Immigration . . . 418
Mother Tongue . . . 418
Language Spoken Most Often at Home . . . 419
Knowledge of Official Languages . . . 419

Québec, Québec . . . 421
Population Growth and Density . . . 422
Gender . . . 422
Marital Status . . . 422
Age Characteristics: 0 to 49 Years . . . 423
Age Characteristics: 50 Years and Over, and Median Age . . . 423
Private Households by Household Size . . . 424
Dwelling Type . . . 424
Shelter Costs . . . 424
Occupied Private Dwellings by Period of Construction . . . 424
Educational Attainment . . . 425
Household Income Distribution . . . 425
Median and Average Household and Economic Family Income . . 425
Individual Income Distribution . . . 426
Labour Force Status . . . 426
Labour Force by Industry (NAICS Codes 11-52) . . . 427
Labour Force by Industry (NAICS Codes 53-91) . . . 427
Occupation . . . 428
Place of Work Status . . . 428
Mode of Transportation to Work . . . 429
Visible Minority Population Characteristics . . . 429
Aboriginal Population . . . 430
Ethnic Origin . . . 430
Religion . . . 431
Religion-Christian Denominations . . . 431
Immigrant Status and Period of Immigration . . . 432
Mother Tongue . . . 432
Language Spoken Most Often at Home . . . 433
Knowledge of Official Languages . . . 433

Regina, Saskatchewan . . . 435
Population Growth and Density . . . 436
Gender . . . 436
Marital Status . . . 436
Age Characteristics: 0 to 49 Years . . . 437
Age Characteristics: 50 Years and Over, and Median Age . . . 437
Private Households by Household Size . . . 438
Dwelling Type . . . 438
Shelter Costs . . . 438
Occupied Private Dwellings by Period of Construction . . . 438
Educational Attainment . . . 439
Household Income Distribution . . . 439
Median and Average Household and Economic Family Income . . 439
Individual Income Distribution . . . 440
Labour Force Status . . . 440
Labour Force by Industry (NAICS Codes 11-52) . . . 441
Labour Force by Industry (NAICS Codes 53-91) . . . 441
Occupation . . . 442
Place of Work Status . . . 442
Mode of Transportation to Work . . . 443
Visible Minority Population Characteristics . . . 443
Aboriginal Population . . . 444
Ethnic Origin . . . 444
Religion . . . 445
Religion-Christian Denominations . . . 445
Immigrant Status and Period of Immigration . . . 446
Mother Tongue . . . 446
Language Spoken Most Often at Home . . . 447
Knowledge of Official Languages . . . 447

Richmond, British Columbia . . . 449
Population Growth and Density . . . 450
Gender . . . 450
Marital Status . . . 450
Age Characteristics: 0 to 49 Years . . . 451
Age Characteristics: 50 Years and Over, and Median Age . . . 451
Private Households by Household Size . . . 452
Dwelling Type . . . 452
Shelter Costs . . . 452
Occupied Private Dwellings by Period of Construction . . . 452
Educational Attainment . . . 453
Household Income Distribution . . . 453
Median and Average Household and Economic Family Income . . 453
Individual Income Distribution . . . 454
Labour Force Status . . . 454
Labour Force by Industry (NAICS Codes 11-52) . . . 455
Labour Force by Industry (NAICS Codes 53-91) . . . 455
Occupation . . . 456
Place of Work Status . . . 456
Mode of Transportation to Work . . . 457
Visible Minority Population Characteristics . . . 457
Aboriginal Population . . . 458
Ethnic Origin . . . 458
Religion . . . 459
Religion-Christian Denominations . . . 459
Immigrant Status and Period of Immigration . . . 460
Mother Tongue . . . 460
Language Spoken Most Often at Home . . . 461
Knowledge of Official Languages . . . 461

Richmond Hill, Ontario . . . 463
Population Growth and Density . . . 464
Gender . . . 464
Marital Status . . . 464
Age Characteristics: 0 to 49 Years . . . 465
Age Characteristics: 50 Years and Over, and Median Age . . . 465
Private Households by Household Size . . . 466
Dwelling Type . . . 466
Shelter Costs . . . 466
Occupied Private Dwellings by Period of Construction . . . 466
Educational Attainment . . . 467
Household Income Distribution . . . 467
Median and Average Household and Economic Family Income . . 467
Individual Income Distribution . . . 468
Labour Force Status . . . 468
Labour Force by Industry (NAICS Codes 11-52) . . . 469
Labour Force by Industry (NAICS Codes 53-91) . . . 469
Occupation . . . 470
Place of Work Status . . . 470
Mode of Transportation to Work . . . 471
Visible Minority Population Characteristics . . . 471
Aboriginal Population . . . 472
Ethnic Origin . . . 472
Religion . . . 473

Table of Contents

Religion-Christian Denominations . . . 473
Immigrant Status and Period of Immigration . . . 474
Mother Tongue . . . 474
Language Spoken Most Often at Home . . . 475
Knowledge of Official Languages . . . 475

Saanich, British Columbia . . . 477
Population Growth and Density . . . 478
Gender . . . 478
Marital Status . . . 478
Age Characteristics: 0 to 49 Years . . . 479
Age Characteristics: 50 Years and Over, and Median Age . . . 479
Private Households by Household Size . . . 480
Dwelling Type . . . 480
Shelter Costs . . . 480
Occupied Private Dwellings by Period of Construction . . . 480
Educational Attainment . . . 481
Household Income Distribution . . . 481
Median and Average Household and Economic Family Income . . 481
Individual Income Distribution . . . 482
Labour Force Status . . . 482
Labour Force by Industry (NAICS Codes 11-52) . . . 483
Labour Force by Industry (NAICS Codes 53-91) . . . 483
Occupation . . . 484
Place of Work Status . . . 484
Mode of Transportation to Work . . . 485
Visible Minority Population Characteristics . . . 485
Aboriginal Population . . . 486
Ethnic Origin . . . 486
Religion . . . 487
Religion-Christian Denominations . . . 487
Immigrant Status and Period of Immigration . . . 488
Mother Tongue . . . 488
Language Spoken Most Often at Home . . . 489
Knowledge of Official Languages . . . 489

Saguenay, Québec . . . 491
Population Growth and Density . . . 492
Gender . . . 492
Marital Status . . . 492
Age Characteristics: 0 to 49 Years . . . 493
Age Characteristics: 50 Years and Over, and Median Age . . . 493
Private Households by Household Size . . . 494
Dwelling Type . . . 494
Shelter Costs . . . 494
Occupied Private Dwellings by Period of Construction . . . 494
Educational Attainment . . . 495
Household Income Distribution . . . 495
Median and Average Household and Economic Family Income . . 495
Individual Income Distribution . . . 496
Labour Force Status . . . 496
Labour Force by Industry (NAICS Codes 11-52) . . . 497
Labour Force by Industry (NAICS Codes 53-91) . . . 497
Occupation . . . 498
Place of Work Status . . . 498
Mode of Transportation to Work . . . 499
Visible Minority Population Characteristics . . . 499
Aboriginal Population . . . 500
Ethnic Origin . . . 500
Religion . . . 501
Religion-Christian Denominations . . . 501
Immigrant Status and Period of Immigration . . . 502
Mother Tongue . . . 502
Language Spoken Most Often at Home . . . 503
Knowledge of Official Languages . . . 503

Saskatoon, Saskatchewan . . . 505
Population Growth and Density . . . 506
Gender . . . 506
Marital Status . . . 506
Age Characteristics: 0 to 49 Years . . . 507
Age Characteristics: 50 Years and Over, and Median Age . . . 507
Private Households by Household Size . . . 508
Dwelling Type . . . 508
Shelter Costs . . . 508
Occupied Private Dwellings by Period of Construction . . . 508
Educational Attainment . . . 509
Household Income Distribution . . . 509
Median and Average Household and Economic Family Income . . 509
Individual Income Distribution . . . 510
Labour Force Status . . . 510
Labour Force by Industry (NAICS Codes 11-52) . . . 511
Labour Force by Industry (NAICS Codes 53-91) . . . 511
Occupation . . . 512
Place of Work Status . . . 512
Mode of Transportation to Work . . . 513
Visible Minority Population Characteristics . . . 513
Aboriginal Population . . . 514
Ethnic Origin . . . 514
Religion . . . 515
Religion-Christian Denominations . . . 515
Immigrant Status and Period of Immigration . . . 516
Mother Tongue . . . 516
Language Spoken Most Often at Home . . . 517
Knowledge of Official Languages . . . 517

Sherbrooke, Québec . . . 519
Population Growth and Density . . . 520
Gender . . . 520
Marital Status . . . 520
Age Characteristics: 0 to 49 Years . . . 521
Age Characteristics: 50 Years and Over, and Median Age . . . 521
Private Households by Household Size . . . 522
Dwelling Type . . . 522
Shelter Costs . . . 522
Occupied Private Dwellings by Period of Construction . . . 522
Educational Attainment . . . 523
Household Income Distribution . . . 523
Median and Average Household and Economic Family Income . . 523
Individual Income Distribution . . . 524
Labour Force Status . . . 524
Labour Force by Industry (NAICS Codes 11-52) . . . 525
Labour Force by Industry (NAICS Codes 53-91) . . . 525
Occupation . . . 526
Place of Work Status . . . 526
Mode of Transportation to Work . . . 527
Visible Minority Population Characteristics . . . 527
Aboriginal Population . . . 528
Ethnic Origin . . . 528
Religion . . . 529
Religion-Christian Denominations . . . 529
Immigrant Status and Period of Immigration . . . 530
Mother Tongue . . . 530
Language Spoken Most Often at Home . . . 531
Knowledge of Official Languages . . . 531

St. Catharines, Ontario . . . 533
Population Growth and Density . . . 534
Gender . . . 534
Marital Status . . . 534
Age Characteristics: 0 to 49 Years . . . 535
Age Characteristics: 50 Years and Over, and Median Age . . . 535
Private Households by Household Size . . . 536
Dwelling Type . . . 536
Shelter Costs . . . 536
Occupied Private Dwellings by Period of Construction . . . 536
Educational Attainment . . . 537
Household Income Distribution . . . 537
Median and Average Household and Economic Family Income . . 537
Individual Income Distribution . . . 538
Labour Force Status . . . 538
Labour Force by Industry (NAICS Codes 11-52) . . . 539
Labour Force by Industry (NAICS Codes 53-91) . . . 539
Occupation . . . 540
Place of Work Status . . . 540
Mode of Transportation to Work . . . 541

Table of Contents

    Visible Minority Population Characteristics 541
    Aboriginal Population. 542
    Ethnic Origin 542
    Religion. 543
    Religion-Christian Denominations 543
    Immigrant Status and Period of Immigration 544
    Mother Tongue 544
    Language Spoken Most Often at Home 545
    Knowledge of Official Languages. 545

St. John's, Newfoundland and Labrador **547**
    Population Growth and Density 548
    Gender 548
    Marital Status. 548
    Age Characteristics: 0 to 49 Years 549
    Age Characteristics: 50 Years and Over, and Median Age 549
    Private Households by Household Size 550
    Dwelling Type 550
    Shelter Costs. 550
    Occupied Private Dwellings by Period of Construction 550
    Educational Attainment 551
    Household Income Distribution. 551
    Median and Average Household and Economic Family Income . . 551
    Individual Income Distribution. 552
    Labour Force Status 552
    Labour Force by Industry (NAICS Codes 11-52). 553
    Labour Force by Industry (NAICS Codes 53-91). 553
    Occupation 554
    Place of Work Status 554
    Mode of Transportation to Work 555
    Visible Minority Population Characteristics 555
    Aboriginal Population. 556
    Ethnic Origin 556
    Religion. 557
    Religion-Christian Denominations 557
    Immigrant Status and Period of Immigration 558
    Mother Tongue 558
    Language Spoken Most Often at Home 559
    Knowledge of Official Languages. 559

Surrey, British Columbia. **561**
    Population Growth and Density 562
    Gender 562
    Marital Status. 562
    Age Characteristics: 0 to 49 Years 563
    Age Characteristics: 50 Years and Over, and Median Age 563
    Private Households by Household Size 564
    Dwelling Type 564
    Shelter Costs. 564
    Occupied Private Dwellings by Period of Construction 564
    Educational Attainment 565
    Household Income Distribution. 565
    Median and Average Household and Economic Family Income . . 565
    Individual Income Distribution. 566
    Labour Force Status 566
    Labour Force by Industry (NAICS Codes 11-52). 567
    Labour Force by Industry (NAICS Codes 53-91). 567
    Occupation 568
    Place of Work Status 568
    Mode of Transportation to Work 569
    Visible Minority Population Characteristics 569
    Aboriginal Population. 570
    Ethnic Origin 570
    Religion. 571
    Religion-Christian Denominations 571
    Immigrant Status and Period of Immigration 572
    Mother Tongue 572
    Language Spoken Most Often at Home 573
    Knowledge of Official Languages. 573

Terrebonne, Québec **575**
    Population Growth and Density 576
    Gender 576

    Marital Status. 576
    Age Characteristics: 0 to 49 Years 577
    Age Characteristics: 50 Years and Over, and Median Age 577
    Private Households by Household Size 578
    Dwelling Type 578
    Shelter Costs. 578
    Occupied Private Dwellings by Period of Construction 578
    Educational Attainment 579
    Household Income Distribution. 579
    Median and Average Household and Economic Family Income . . 579
    Individual Income Distribution. 580
    Labour Force Status 580
    Labour Force by Industry (NAICS Codes 11-52). 581
    Labour Force by Industry (NAICS Codes 53-91). 581
    Occupation 582
    Place of Work Status 582
    Mode of Transportation to Work 583
    Visible Minority Population Characteristics 583
    Aboriginal Population. 584
    Ethnic Origin 584
    Religion. 585
    Religion-Christian Denominations 585
    Immigrant Status and Period of Immigration 586
    Mother Tongue 586
    Language Spoken Most Often at Home 587
    Knowledge of Official Languages. 587

Thunder Bay, Ontario **589**
    Population Growth and Density 590
    Gender 590
    Marital Status. 590
    Age Characteristics: 0 to 49 Years 591
    Age Characteristics: 50 Years and Over, and Median Age 591
    Private Households by Household Size 592
    Dwelling Type 592
    Shelter Costs. 592
    Occupied Private Dwellings by Period of Construction 592
    Educational Attainment 593
    Household Income Distribution. 593
    Median and Average Household and Economic Family Income . . 593
    Individual Income Distribution. 594
    Labour Force Status 594
    Labour Force by Industry (NAICS Codes 11-52). 595
    Labour Force by Industry (NAICS Codes 53-91). 595
    Occupation 596
    Place of Work Status 596
    Mode of Transportation to Work 597
    Visible Minority Population Characteristics 597
    Aboriginal Population. 598
    Ethnic Origin 598
    Religion. 599
    Religion-Christian Denominations 599
    Immigrant Status and Period of Immigration 600
    Mother Tongue 600
    Language Spoken Most Often at Home 601
    Knowledge of Official Languages. 601

Toronto, Ontario **603**
    Population Growth and Density 604
    Gender 604
    Marital Status. 604
    Age Characteristics: 0 to 49 Years 605
    Age Characteristics: 50 Years and Over, and Median Age 605
    Private Households by Household Size 606
    Dwelling Type 606
    Shelter Costs. 606
    Occupied Private Dwellings by Period of Construction 606
    Educational Attainment 607
    Household Income Distribution. 607
    Median and Average Household and Economic Family Income . . 607
    Individual Income Distribution. 608
    Labour Force Status 608
    Labour Force by Industry (NAICS Codes 11-52). 609

Table of Contents

Labour Force by Industry (NAICS Codes 53-91) . . . 609
Occupation . . . 610
Place of Work Status . . . 610
Mode of Transportation to Work . . . 611
Visible Minority Population Characteristics . . . 611
Aboriginal Population . . . 612
Ethnic Origin . . . 612
Religion . . . 613
Religion-Christian Denominations . . . 613
Immigrant Status and Period of Immigration . . . 614
Mother Tongue . . . 614
Language Spoken Most Often at Home . . . 615
Knowledge of Official Languages . . . 615

Trois-Rivières, Québec . . . 617
Population Growth and Density . . . 618
Gender . . . 618
Marital Status . . . 618
Age Characteristics: 0 to 49 Years . . . 619
Age Characteristics: 50 Years and Over, and Median Age . . . 619
Private Households by Household Size . . . 620
Dwelling Type . . . 620
Shelter Costs . . . 620
Occupied Private Dwellings by Period of Construction . . . 620
Educational Attainment . . . 621
Household Income Distribution . . . 621
Median and Average Household and Economic Family Income . . 621
Individual Income Distribution . . . 622
Labour Force Status . . . 622
Labour Force by Industry (NAICS Codes 11-52) . . . 623
Labour Force by Industry (NAICS Codes 53-91) . . . 623
Occupation . . . 624
Place of Work Status . . . 624
Mode of Transportation to Work . . . 625
Visible Minority Population Characteristics . . . 625
Aboriginal Population . . . 626
Ethnic Origin . . . 626
Religion . . . 627
Religion-Christian Denominations . . . 627
Immigrant Status and Period of Immigration . . . 628
Mother Tongue . . . 628
Language Spoken Most Often at Home . . . 629
Knowledge of Official Languages . . . 629

Vancouver, British Columbia . . . 631
Population Growth and Density . . . 632
Gender . . . 632
Marital Status . . . 632
Age Characteristics: 0 to 49 Years . . . 633
Age Characteristics: 50 Years and Over, and Median Age . . . 633
Private Households by Household Size . . . 634
Dwelling Type . . . 634
Shelter Costs . . . 634
Occupied Private Dwellings by Period of Construction . . . 634
Educational Attainment . . . 635
Household Income Distribution . . . 635
Median and Average Household and Economic Family Income . . 635
Individual Income Distribution . . . 636
Labour Force Status . . . 636
Labour Force by Industry (NAICS Codes 11-52) . . . 637
Labour Force by Industry (NAICS Codes 53-91) . . . 637
Occupation . . . 638
Place of Work Status . . . 638
Mode of Transportation to Work . . . 639
Visible Minority Population Characteristics . . . 639
Aboriginal Population . . . 640
Ethnic Origin . . . 640
Religion . . . 641
Religion-Christian Denominations . . . 641
Immigrant Status and Period of Immigration . . . 642
Mother Tongue . . . 642
Language Spoken Most Often at Home . . . 643
Knowledge of Official Languages . . . 643

Vaughan, Ontario . . . 645
Population Growth and Density . . . 646
Gender . . . 646
Marital Status . . . 646
Age Characteristics: 0 to 49 Years . . . 647
Age Characteristics: 50 Years and Over, and Median Age . . . 647
Private Households by Household Size . . . 648
Dwelling Type . . . 648
Shelter Costs . . . 648
Occupied Private Dwellings by Period of Construction . . . 648
Educational Attainment . . . 649
Household Income Distribution . . . 649
Median and Average Household and Economic Family Income . . 649
Individual Income Distribution . . . 650
Labour Force Status . . . 650
Labour Force by Industry (NAICS Codes 11-52) . . . 651
Labour Force by Industry (NAICS Codes 53-91) . . . 651
Occupation . . . 652
Place of Work Status . . . 652
Mode of Transportation to Work . . . 653
Visible Minority Population Characteristics . . . 653
Aboriginal Population . . . 654
Ethnic Origin . . . 654
Religion . . . 655
Religion-Christian Denominations . . . 655
Immigrant Status and Period of Immigration . . . 656
Mother Tongue . . . 656
Language Spoken Most Often at Home . . . 657
Knowledge of Official Languages . . . 657

Whitby, Ontario . . . 659
Population Growth and Density . . . 660
Gender . . . 660
Marital Status . . . 660
Age Characteristics: 0 to 49 Years . . . 661
Age Characteristics: 50 Years and Over, and Median Age . . . 661
Private Households by Household Size . . . 662
Dwelling Type . . . 662
Shelter Costs . . . 662
Occupied Private Dwellings by Period of Construction . . . 662
Educational Attainment . . . 663
Household Income Distribution . . . 663
Median and Average Household and Economic Family Income . . 663
Individual Income Distribution . . . 664
Labour Force Status . . . 664
Labour Force by Industry (NAICS Codes 11-52) . . . 665
Labour Force by Industry (NAICS Codes 53-91) . . . 665
Occupation . . . 666
Place of Work Status . . . 666
Mode of Transportation to Work . . . 667
Visible Minority Population Characteristics . . . 667
Aboriginal Population . . . 668
Ethnic Origin . . . 668
Religion . . . 669
Religion-Christian Denominations . . . 669
Immigrant Status and Period of Immigration . . . 670
Mother Tongue . . . 670
Language Spoken Most Often at Home . . . 671
Knowledge of Official Languages . . . 671

Windsor, Ontario . . . 673
Population Growth and Density . . . 674
Gender . . . 674
Marital Status . . . 674
Age Characteristics: 0 to 49 Years . . . 675
Age Characteristics: 50 Years and Over, and Median Age . . . 675
Private Households by Household Size . . . 676
Dwelling Type . . . 676
Shelter Costs . . . 676
Occupied Private Dwellings by Period of Construction . . . 676
Educational Attainment . . . 677
Household Income Distribution . . . 677
Median and Average Household and Economic Family Income . . 677

Individual Income Distribution	678
Labour Force Status	678
Labour Force by Industry (NAICS Codes 11-52)	679
Labour Force by Industry (NAICS Codes 53-91)	679
Occupation	680
Place of Work Status	680
Mode of Transportation to Work	681
Visible Minority Population Characteristics	681
Aboriginal Population	682
Ethnic Origin	682
Religion	683
Religion-Christian Denominations	683
Immigrant Status and Period of Immigration	684
Mother Tongue	684
Language Spoken Most Often at Home	685
Knowledge of Official Languages	685

Winnipeg, Manitoba — 687

Population Growth and Density	688
Gender	688
Marital Status	688
Age Characteristics: 0 to 49 Years	689
Age Characteristics: 50 Years and Over, and Median Age	689
Private Households by Household Size	690
Dwelling Type	690
Shelter Costs	690
Occupied Private Dwellings by Period of Construction	690
Educational Attainment	691
Household Income Distribution	691
Median and Average Household and Economic Family Income	691
Individual Income Distribution	692
Labour Force Status	692
Labour Force by Industry (NAICS Codes 11-52)	693
Labour Force by Industry (NAICS Codes 53-91)	693
Occupation	694
Place of Work Status	694
Mode of Transportation to Work	695
Visible Minority Population Characteristics	695
Aboriginal Population	696
Ethnic Origin	696
Religion	697
Religion-Christian Denominations	697
Immigrant Status and Period of Immigration	698
Mother Tongue	698
Language Spoken Most Often at Home	699
Knowledge of Official Languages	699

RANKINGS

Cities Ranked by Population, Population Growth, and Population Density	701
Cities Ranked by Median Age	702
Cities Ranked by Household Size: 1 Person	703
Cities Ranked by Household Size: 2 Persons	704
Cities Ranked by Household Size: 3 Persons	705
Cities Ranked by Household Size: 4 Persons	706
Cities Ranked by Household Size: 5 Persons	707
Cities Ranked by Household Size: 6 or More Persons	708
Cities Ranked by Average Number of Persons in Private Households	709
Cities Ranked by Shelter Costs	710
Cities Ranked by Highest Level of Education: High School Diploma	711
Cities Ranked by Highest Level of Education: Bachelor's Degree	713
Cities Ranked by Highest Level of Education: University Certificate or Diploma above Bachelor Level	715
Cities Ranked by Median Economic Family Income	717
Cities Ranked by Occupation: Management	718
Cities Ranked by Occupation: Business, Finance & Administration	720
Cities Ranked by Occupation: Natural/Applied Sciences & Related	722
Cities Ranked by Occupation: Health	724
Cities Ranked by Occupation: Education, Law & Social, Community & Government Services	726
Cities Ranked by Occupation: Art, Culture, Recreation & Sport	728
Cities Ranked by Occupation: Sales & Service	730
Cities Ranked by Occupation: Trades, Transport & Equipment Operators & Related	732
Cities Ranked by Occupation: Natural Resources, Agriculture & Related Production	734
Cities Ranked by Occupation: Manufacturing & Utilities	736
Cities Ranked by Mode of Transportation to Work: Car, Truck or Van, as Driver	738
Cities Ranked by Mode of Transportation to Work: Public Transit	740
Cities Ranked by Mode of Transportation to Work: Walked	742
Cities Ranked by Visible Minority Population: Total Minority	744
Cities Ranked by Visible Minority Population: South Asian	746
Cities Ranked by Visible Minority Population: Chinese	748
Cities Ranked by Visible Minority Population: Black	750
Cities Ranked by Visible Minority Population: Filipino	752
Cities Ranked by Visible Minority Population: Latin American	754
Cities Ranked by Visible Minority Population: Arab	756
Cities Ranked by Visible Minority Population: Southeast Asian	758
Cities Ranked by Visible Minority Population: West Asian	760
Cities Ranked by Visible Minority Population: Korean	762
Cities Ranked by Visible Minority Population: Japanese	764
Cities Ranked by Visible Minority Population: Multiple Visible Minorities	766
Cities Ranked by Religion: Buddhist	768
Cities Ranked by Religion: Christian	770
Cities Ranked by Religion: Hindu	772
Cities Ranked by Religion: Jewish	774
Cities Ranked by Religion: Muslim	776
Cities Ranked by Religion: Sikh	778
Cities Ranked by Religion: Traditional (Aboriginal) Spirituality	780
Cities Ranked by Religion: Other Religions	782
Cities Ranked by Religion: No Religious Affiliation	784
Cities Ranked by Mother Tongue: English	786
Cities Ranked by Mother Tongue: French	788
Cities Ranked by Mother Tongue: Non-official Language	790

Sources for City Backgrounds — 793

INTRODUCTION

This first edition of *Major Canadian Cities: Compared and Ranked* provides an in-depth comparison and analysis of the 50 most populated cities in Canada. Each 14-page city chapter incorporates information from dozens of resources to create the following major sections:

- **Background:** Lively narrative of significant facts covering the geography, history, industries and culture of a city, emphasizing Canada's diversity.

- **Study Rankings:** A number of study results from sources such as Statistics Canada, Economic Development Offices, *fDi Magazine* and Canada Survey of Giving, in a number of categories—smartest, most generous, safest, most visionary—marking the city's place in the spectrum of cities across Canada.

- **Statistical Tables:** Tables on 28 topics, including age, marital status, housing, ethnicity, labour force, language, income, transportation, and more, with city, provincial and national data. Statistics are taken from the *National Household Survey of 2011* and the *2011 Census*.

City chapters are followed by **Ranking Tables** that rank each city and answer such questions as:

- Which cities in Canada have the youngest population?
- Where is the economic growth the strongest in Canada?
- Which cities have the most university graduates?
- Which cities have the best labour statistics?

A detailed Table of Contents is your guide to not only the city chapters, which are listed in alphabetical order, but also to the specific statistic or ranking table you are interested in.

Major Canadian Cities is designed for a wide variety of readers: private individuals considering relocation; professionals considering expansion of their business or changing careers; corporations considering relocation, opening up additional offices, or creating new divisions; government agencies; general and market researchers; real estate consultants; human resource personnel; urban planners; and investors.

If you wish to conduct unique searches and comparisons and make your own analytical tables, sorting by specific characteristics, we recommend you check out **Canada's Information Resource Centre (CIRC)**, where subscribers have full access to this rich database. Trial subscriptions are available by calling 866-433-4739. You can also reach us online at **www.greyhouse.ca**.

Abbotsford, British Columbia

Background

Abbotsford is located in the centre of the Fraser Valley, 68 kilometres east of the City of Vancouver in British Columbia and approximately five kilometres from the U.S. border. The city is situated on the flatlands between the Coast and Cascade mountain ranges.

Abbotsford's rich agricultural lands have served the Sto:lo First Nations, the Gold Rush settlers and later, the Canadian Pacific Railway workers who built Abbotsford's train station in 1891. By 1910, Abbotsford was providing nearby New Westminster and Vancouver with crops of tobacco, farm produce and dairy products. Abbotsford has been a breadbasket to Vancouver ever since and is known as a "City in the Country." The Fraser Valley's high-quality soils, moderate climate and water accessibility produce a range of vegetables, nursery products, field and cereal crops, sod and pasture.

Throughout the year, Abbotsford hosts more than 200 festivals and events, such as the Abbotsford AgriFair and Rodeo, the Abbotsford International Airshow and the Abbotsford Multicultural Festival. The city's vibrant agri-tourism industry offers dairy farm tours, u-pick apple orchards and pumpkin farms, gold honey and meadery (honey) wines, and a trout hatchery run by the Freshwater Fisheries Society of BC.

The main campus of the University of the Fraser Valley is located in Abbotsford. Two Christian colleges, Columbia Bible College and Summit Pacific College, are also located in the city. Abbotsford has one of the largest South Asian populations in British Columbia and is considered the third most culturally diverse city in the province.

Abbotsford has summer highs of plus 22.5 degrees Celsius, winter lows of minus 0.03 degrees Celsius, and an average rainfall just over 1507 mm per year.

Rankings

- In 2011, Abbotsford was ranked Canada's most generous community in terms of charitable donations. The Abbotsford-Mission census metropolitan area (CMA) has ranked #1 across Canada for nine consecutive years. Statistics Canada reported that in 2010 residents gave a median donation of $620 to charities. There were 25,650 donors in Abbotsford (tax filers who claimed a donation) who gave a total of almost $74 million, a 5.1% increase from 2009. Tied for second place were Calgary and Victoria with median donations of $390. *Statistics Canada, Charitable Donors, 2010 with files from Abbotsford News, December 5, 2011*
- Community involvement and a police crackdown on gang violence decreased the Abbotsford-Mission CMA homicide rate to 0.56 per 100,000 population in 2011, a drop of 930% from the 5.21 rate of 2009. *Statistics Canada, Crime Severity Index, 2008-2011*
- The Abbotsford-Mission CMA ranked #4 out of 25 BC CMAs for population growth. Between 2006 and 2011, the area grew by 7.4% compared to the national growth of 5.9%. The City of Abbotsford has more than doubled since 1981, growing at a rate of 126% between 1981 and 2006. *Statistics Canada. 2012. Focus on Geography Series, 2011 Census with files from Abbotsford Community Profile 2010, City of Abbotsford Economic Development and Planning Services, January 2010*

PROFILES / Abbotsford, British Columbia

Population Growth and Density

Area	Population in 2001	Population in 2006	Population in 2011	Population Change 2001–2006	Population Change 2006–2011	Land Area (sq. km)	Population Density per sq. km
Abbotsford	115,494	124,258	133,497	7.2	7.4	375.55	355.5
British Columbia	3,907,738	4,113,487	4,400,057	5.3	7.0	922,509.29	4.8
Canada	30,007,094	31,612,897	33,476,688	5.4	5.9	8,965,121.42	3.7

Source: Statistics Canada. 2012. Census Profile. 2011 Census. Statistics Canada Catalogue no. 98-316-XWE. Ottawa. Released October 24 2012. http://www12.statcan.gc.ca/census-recensement/2011/dp-pd/prof/index.cfm?Lang=E;
Statistics Canada 2007. 2006 Community Profiles. 2006 Census. Statistics Canada Catalogue no. 92-591-XWE. Ottawa. Released March 13 2007. http://www12.statcan.ca/census-recensement/2006/dp-pd/prof/92-591/index.cfm?Lang=E

Gender

Area	Males	Females
	Number	
Abbotsford	65,870	67,625
British Columbia	2,156,600	2,243,455
Canada	16,414,225	17,062,460
	Percent of Population	
Abbotsford	49.3	50.7
British Columbia	49.0	51.0
Canada	49.0	51.0

Source: Statistics Canada. 2012. Census Profile. 2011 Census. Statistics Canada Catalogue no. 98-316-XWE. Ottawa. Released October 24 2012.
http://www12.statcan.gc.ca/census-recensement/2011/dp-pd/prof/index.cfm?Lang=E

Marital Status

Area	Married[1]	Living Common-law	Single[2]	Separated	Divorced	Widowed
			Number			
			Total			
Abbotsford	59,735	5,940	27,335	2,925	6,075	6,150
British Columbia	1,832,605	321,965	1,014,270	102,040	246,515	205,300
Canada	12,941,960	3,142,525	7,816,045	698,240	1,686,035	1,584,530
			Males			
Abbotsford	29,840	2,990	15,070	1,205	2,405	1,200
British Columbia	913,430	161,530	550,830	43,570	98,130	41,550
Canada	6,470,300	1,575,495	4,206,320	299,655	680,415	310,940
			Females			
Abbotsford	29,895	2,950	12,265	1,720	3,675	4,950
British Columbia	919,175	160,435	463,435	58,470	148,385	163,750
Canada	6,471,660	1,567,035	3,609,730	398,585	1,005,620	1,273,590
			Percent of Population			
			Total			
Abbotsford	55.2	5.5	25.3	2.7	5.6	5.7
British Columbia	49.2	8.6	27.2	2.7	6.6	5.5
Canada	46.4	11.3	28.0	2.5	6.0	5.7
			Males			
Abbotsford	56.6	5.7	28.6	2.3	4.6	2.3
British Columbia	50.5	8.9	30.4	2.4	5.4	2.3
Canada	47.8	11.6	31.1	2.2	5.0	2.3
			Females			
Abbotsford	53.9	5.3	22.1	3.1	6.6	8.9
British Columbia	48.0	8.4	24.2	3.1	7.8	8.6
Canada	45.2	10.9	25.2	2.8	7.0	8.9

Note: (1) and not separated, (2) never legally married
Source: Statistics Canada. 2012. Census Profile. 2011 Census. Statistics Canada Catalogue no. 98-316-XWE. Ottawa. Released October 24 2012.
http://www12.statcan.gc.ca/census-recensement/2011/dp-pd/prof/index.cfm?Lang=E

Age Characteristics: 0 to 49 Years

Area	0 to 4 Years	5 to 9 Years	10 to 14 Years	15 to 19 Years	20 to 24 Years	25 to 29 Years	30 to 34 Years	35 to 39 Years	40 to 44 Years	45 to 49 Years
					Number					
					Total					
Abbotsford	8,530	8,245	8,550	9,475	9,175	9,280	8,720	8,435	9,045	9,390
British Columbia	219,665	218,915	238,780	275,165	279,825	288,780	275,985	280,870	313,765	350,600
Canada	1,877,095	1,809,895	1,920,355	2,178,135	2,187,450	2,169,590	2,162,905	2,173,930	2,324,875	2,675,130
					Males					
Abbotsford	4,380	4,310	4,465	4,810	4,655	4,670	4,265	4,155	4,465	4,785
British Columbia	112,885	112,200	122,465	141,670	142,290	143,475	135,220	135,455	151,430	170,580
Canada	961,150	925,965	983,995	1,115,845	1,108,775	1,077,275	1,058,810	1,064,200	1,141,720	1,318,715
					Females					
Abbotsford	4,150	3,930	4,090	4,665	4,520	4,610	4,455	4,280	4,580	4,605
British Columbia	106,775	106,715	116,315	133,500	137,535	145,305	140,755	145,415	162,335	180,020
Canada	915,945	883,935	936,360	1,062,295	1,078,670	1,092,315	1,104,095	1,109,735	1,183,155	1,356,420
					Percent of Population					
					Total					
Abbotsford	6.4	6.2	6.4	7.1	6.9	7.0	6.5	6.3	6.8	7.0
British Columbia	5.0	5.0	5.4	6.3	6.4	6.6	6.3	6.4	7.1	8.0
Canada	5.6	5.4	5.7	6.5	6.5	6.5	6.5	6.5	6.9	8.0
					Males					
Abbotsford	6.6	6.5	6.8	7.3	7.1	7.1	6.5	6.3	6.8	7.3
British Columbia	5.2	5.2	5.7	6.6	6.6	6.7	6.3	6.3	7.0	7.9
Canada	5.9	5.6	6.0	6.8	6.8	6.6	6.5	6.5	7.0	8.0
					Females					
Abbotsford	6.1	5.8	6.0	6.9	6.7	6.8	6.6	6.3	6.8	6.8
British Columbia	4.8	4.8	5.2	6.0	6.1	6.5	6.3	6.5	7.2	8.0
Canada	5.4	5.2	5.5	6.2	6.3	6.4	6.5	6.5	6.9	7.9

Source: Statistics Canada. 2012. Census Profile. 2011 Census. Statistics Canada Catalogue no. 98-316-XWE. Ottawa. Released October 24 2012.
http://www12.statcan.gc.ca/census-recensement/2011/dp-pd/prof/index.cfm?Lang=E

Age Characteristics: 50 Years and Over, and Median Age

Area	50 to 54 Years	55 to 59 Years	60 to 64 Years	65 to 69 Years	70 to 74 Years	75 to 79 Years	80 to 84 Years	85 Years and Over	Median Age
				Number					
				Total					
Abbotsford	9,285	8,180	7,485	5,700	4,430	3,635	2,960	2,975	37.9
British Columbia	354,610	323,335	291,040	210,900	160,715	127,480	96,945	92,675	41.9
Canada	2,658,965	2,340,635	2,052,670	1,521,715	1,153,065	922,700	702,070	645,515	40.6
				Males					
Abbotsford	4,610	3,935	3,540	2,790	2,055	1,685	1,265	1,025	36.7
British Columbia	172,060	157,455	142,645	103,785	77,350	60,720	42,745	32,150	41.1
Canada	1,309,030	1,147,300	1,002,690	738,010	543,435	417,945	291,085	208,300	39.6
				Females					
Abbotsford	4,680	4,245	3,945	2,910	2,370	1,950	1,700	1,950	38.9
British Columbia	182,550	165,880	148,395	107,115	83,360	66,760	54,200	60,520	42.7
Canada	1,349,940	1,193,335	1,049,985	783,705	609,630	504,755	410,985	437,215	41.5
				Percent of Population					
				Total					
Abbotsford	7.0	6.1	5.6	4.3	3.3	2.7	2.2	2.2	—
British Columbia	8.1	7.3	6.6	4.8	3.7	2.9	2.2	2.1	—
Canada	7.9	7.0	6.1	4.5	3.4	2.8	2.1	1.9	—
				Males					
Abbotsford	7.0	6.0	5.4	4.2	3.1	2.6	1.9	1.6	—
British Columbia	8.0	7.3	6.6	4.8	3.6	2.8	2.0	1.5	—
Canada	8.0	7.0	6.1	4.5	3.3	2.5	1.8	1.3	—
				Females					
Abbotsford	6.9	6.3	5.8	4.3	3.5	2.9	2.5	2.9	—
British Columbia	8.1	7.4	6.6	4.8	3.7	3.0	2.4	2.7	—
Canada	7.9	7.0	6.2	4.6	3.6	3.0	2.4	2.6	—

Source: Statistics Canada. 2012. Census Profile. 2011 Census. Statistics Canada Catalogue no. 98-316-XWE. Ottawa. Released October 24 2012.
http://www12.statcan.gc.ca/census-recensement/2011/dp-pd/prof/index.cfm?Lang=E

PROFILES / Abbotsford, British Columbia

Private Households by Household Size

Area	1 Person	2 Persons	3 Persons	4 Persons	5 Persons	6 or More Persons	Average Number of Persons in Private Households
			Households				
Abbotsford	10,950	14,660	6,635	6,990	3,720	3,495	2.8
British Columbia	498,925	613,270	264,135	237,725	91,600	58,985	2.5
Canada	3,673,310	4,544,820	2,081,900	1,903,300	724,405	392,885	2.5
			Percent of Households				
Abbotsford	23.6	31.6	14.3	15.0	8.0	7.5	–
British Columbia	28.3	34.8	15.0	13.5	5.2	3.3	–
Canada	27.6	34.1	15.6	14.3	5.4	2.9	–

Source: Statistics Canada. 2012. Census Profile. 2011 Census. Statistics Canada Catalogue no. 98-316-XWE. Ottawa. Released October 24 2012.
http://www12.statcan.gc.ca/census-recensement/2011/dp-pd/prof/index.cfm?Lang=E

Dwelling Type

Area	Single-detached House	Semi-detached House	Row House	Apartment: Building with Five or More Storeys	Apartment: Building with Fewer Than Five Storeys	Duplex Apartment	Movable Dwelling	Other Single-attached House
				Number				
Abbotsford	20,265	1,360	3,870	900	11,115	8,385	495	60
British Columbia	842,120	52,825	130,365	143,970	361,150	184,355	46,960	2,885
Canada	7,329,150	646,245	791,600	1,234,770	2,397,550	704,485	183,510	33,310
				Percent of Dwellings				
Abbotsford	43.6	2.9	8.3	1.9	23.9	18.1	1.1	0.1
British Columbia	47.7	3.0	7.4	8.2	20.5	10.4	2.7	0.2
Canada	55.0	4.9	5.9	9.3	18.0	5.3	1.4	0.3

Source: Statistics Canada. 2012. Census Profile. 2011 Census. Statistics Canada Catalogue no. 98-316-XWE. Ottawa. Released October 24 2012.
http://www12.statcan.gc.ca/census-recensement/2011/dp-pd/prof/index.cfm?Lang=E

Shelter Costs

	Owned Dwellings					Rented Dwellings		
Area	Number	Median Value[1] ($)	Average Value[1] ($)	Median Monthly Costs[2] ($)	Average Monthly Costs[2] ($)	Number	Median Monthly Costs[3] ($)	Average Monthly Costs[3] ($)
Abbotsford	33,535	393,600	405,802	1,204	1,266	11,910	801	866
British Columbia	1,202,000	448,835	543,635	1,023	1,228	519,855	903	989
Canada	9,013,410	280,552	345,182	978	1,141	4,060,385	784	848

Note: All figures cover non-farm, non-reserve private dwellings; (1) Refers to the dollar amount expected by the owner if the dwelling were to be sold; (2) Includes all shelter expenses paid by households that own their dwellings, such as the mortgage payment and the costs of electricity, heat, water and other municipal services, property taxes and condominium fees; (3) Includes all shelter expenses paid by households that rent their dwellings, such as the monthly rent and the costs of electricity, heat and municipal services.
Source: Statistics Canada. 2013. 2011 National Household Survey. Statistics Canada Catalogue no. 99-004-XWE. Ottawa. Released September 11, 2013.

Occupied Private Dwellings by Period of Construction

Area	1960 or Before	1961 to 1980	1981 to 1990	1991 to 2000	2001 to 2005	2006 to 2011
			Number			
Abbotsford	2,590	13,025	11,920	11,290	3,805	3,820
British Columbia	282,675	551,655	308,450	329,780	133,235	158,845
Canada	3,273,105	4,152,715	2,112,110	1,707,880	1,031,020	1,042,430
			Percent of Dwellings			
Abbotsford	5.6	28.0	25.7	24.3	8.2	8.2
British Columbia	16.0	31.3	17.5	18.7	7.6	9.0
Canada	24.6	31.2	15.9	12.8	7.7	7.8

Note: Figures cover non-farm, non-reserve private dwellings and includes data up to May 10, 2011.
Source: Statistics Canada. 2013. 2011 National Household Survey. Statistics Canada Catalogue no. 99-004-XWE. Ottawa. Released September 11, 2013.

Educational Attainment

Area	No Certificate, Diploma or Degree	High School Diploma or Equivalent[1]	Apprenticeship or Trades Certificate or Diploma[2]	College, CEGEP or Other Non-University Certificate or Diploma	University Certificate or Diploma Below the Bachelor Level[3]	Bachelor's Degree	University Certificate, Diploma or Degree Above Bachelor Level[4]
				Number			
				Total			
Abbotsford	23,225	32,865	11,650	16,090	6,635	8,870	6,295
British Columbia	607,655	1,009,400	387,455	628,115	208,245	511,240	294,725
Canada	5,485,400	6,968,935	2,950,685	4,970,020	1,200,130	3,634,425	2,049,930
				Males			
Abbotsford	11,425	15,925	7,600	6,500	2,735	3,880	3,420
British Columbia	305,040	475,670	262,245	260,580	86,995	235,620	149,300
Canada	2,742,875	3,305,415	1,928,970	2,118,430	513,235	1,643,080	1,043,350
				Females			
Abbotsford	11,810	16,940	4,050	9,590	3,895	4,990	2,870
British Columbia	302,620	533,735	125,210	367,535	121,250	275,625	145,425
Canada	2,742,520	3,663,515	1,021,715	2,851,595	686,890	1,991,345	1,006,585
				Percent of Population			
				Total			
Abbotsford	22.0	31.1	11.0	15.2	6.3	8.4	6.0
British Columbia	16.7	27.7	10.6	17.2	5.7	14.0	8.1
Canada	20.1	25.6	10.8	18.2	4.4	13.3	7.5
				Males			
Abbotsford	22.2	30.9	14.8	12.6	5.3	7.5	6.6
British Columbia	17.2	26.8	14.8	14.7	4.9	13.3	8.4
Canada	20.6	24.9	14.5	15.9	3.9	12.4	7.8
				Females			
Abbotsford	21.8	31.3	7.5	17.7	7.2	9.2	5.3
British Columbia	16.2	28.5	6.7	19.6	6.5	14.7	7.8
Canada	19.6	26.2	7.3	20.4	4.9	14.3	7.2

Note: Figures cover total population aged 15 years and over by highest certificate, diploma or degree; (1) Includes persons who have graduated from a secondary school or equivalent. It excludes persons with a postsecondary certificate, diploma or degree; (2) Includes Registered Apprenticeship certificates (including Certificate of Qualification, Journeyperson's designation) and other trades certificates or diplomas such as pre-employment or vocational certificates and diplomas from brief trade programs completed at community colleges, institutes of technology, vocational centres, and similar institutions; (3) Comparisons with other data sources suggest that the category 'University certificate or diploma below the bachelor's level' was over-reported in the NHS. This category likely includes some responses that are actually college certificates or diplomas, bachelor's degrees or other types of education (e.g., university transfer programs, bachelor's programs completed in other countries, incomplete bachelor's programs, non-university professional designations). We recommend users interpret the results for the 'University certificate or diploma below the bachelor's level' category with caution; (4) 'University certificate or diploma above bachelor level' includes the categories: 'Degree in medicine, dentistry, veterinary medicine or optometry,' 'Master's degree' and 'Earned doctorate.'
Source: Statistics Canada. 2013. 2011 National Household Survey. Statistics Canada Catalogue no. 99-004-XWE. Ottawa. Released September 11, 2013.

Household Income Distribution

Area	Less than $10,000	$10,000 to $19,999	$20,000 to $29,999	$30,000 to $39,999	$40,000 to $49,999	$50,000 to $59,999	$60,000 to $79,999	$80,000 to $99,999	$100,000 to $124,999	$125,000 to $149,999	$150,000 and Over
					Households						
Abbotsford	1,875	3,680	3,940	4,630	4,475	3,600	6,680	5,380	4,900	2,860	4,435
British Columbia	96,465	156,565	157,605	167,220	158,400	140,340	246,720	193,180	167,415	106,325	174,385
Canada	626,705	1,141,945	1,193,925	1,271,675	1,206,800	1,102,120	1,865,280	1,458,240	1,260,770	802,555	1,389,240
					Percent of Households						
Abbotsford	4.0	7.9	8.5	10.0	9.6	7.7	14.4	11.6	10.5	6.2	9.5
British Columbia	5.5	8.9	8.9	9.5	9.0	8.0	14.0	10.9	9.5	6.0	9.9
Canada	4.7	8.6	9.0	9.5	9.1	8.3	14.0	10.9	9.5	6.0	10.4

Note: Household income is the sum of the total incomes of all members of that household. Total income refers to monetary receipts from certain sources, before income taxes and deductions, during calendar year 2010.
Source: Statistics Canada. 2013. 2011 National Household Survey. Statistics Canada Catalogue no. 99-004-XWE. Ottawa. Released September 11, 2013.

Median and Average Household and Economic Family Income

Area	Median Household Income ($)	Average Household Income ($)	Median After-tax Household Income ($)	Average After-tax Household Income ($)	Median Economic Family Income ($)	Average Economic Family Income ($)	Median After-tax Economic Family Income ($)	Average After-tax Economic Family Income ($)
Abbotsford	62,350	76,973	56,876	67,409	75,807	88,468	68,020	77,409
British Columbia	60,333	77,378	54,379	66,264	75,797	91,967	67,915	78,580
Canada	61,072	79,102	54,089	66,149	76,511	94,125	67,044	78,517

Note: Figures cover household and economic familiy income in 2010. A household is defined as a person or a group of persons (other than foreign residents) who occupy the same private dwelling and do not have a usual place of residence elsewhere in Canada. Every person is a member of one and only one household. An economic family is defined as a group of two or more persons who live in the same dwelling and are related to each other by blood, marriage, common-law, adoption or a foster relationship. A couple may be of opposite or same sex.
Source: Statistics Canada. 2013. 2011 National Household Survey. Statistics Canada Catalogue no. 99-004-XWE. Ottawa. Released September 11, 2013.

PROFILES / Abbotsford, British Columbia

Individual Income Distribution

Area	Less than $10,000	$10,000 to $19,999	$20,000 to $29,999	$30,000 to $39,999	$40,000 to $49,999	$50,000 to $59,999	$60,000 to $79,999	$80,000 to $99,999	$100,000 to $124,999	$125,000 and Over
Number										
Total										
Abbotsford	18,430	21,430	14,850	12,000	9,360	7,045	8,900	4,130	2,195	1,900
British Columbia	645,915	666,060	470,255	404,860	338,595	253,215	330,590	169,190	89,520	96,055
Canada	4,492,040	4,835,710	3,670,020	3,180,360	2,603,520	1,921,650	2,437,440	1,302,045	693,580	782,135
Males										
Abbotsford	7,860	8,030	6,430	5,735	5,005	4,200	6,015	2,785	1,705	1,575
British Columbia	275,815	263,170	201,000	186,285	167,400	143,765	206,400	112,525	65,050	74,260
Canada	1,936,365	1,864,880	1,588,260	1,522,190	1,333,510	1,079,780	1,473,145	823,720	492,905	599,905
Females										
Abbotsford	10,575	13,405	8,425	6,265	4,360	2,840	2,885	1,350	485	330
British Columbia	370,100	402,880	269,255	218,575	171,190	109,445	124,195	56,670	24,470	21,795
Canada	2,555,675	2,970,825	2,081,760	1,658,170	1,270,010	841,870	964,300	478,330	200,680	182,230
Percent of Population										
Total										
Abbotsford	18.4	21.4	14.8	12.0	9.3	7.0	8.9	4.1	2.2	1.9
British Columbia	18.6	19.2	13.6	11.7	9.8	7.3	9.5	4.9	2.6	2.8
Canada	17.3	18.7	14.2	12.3	10.0	7.4	9.4	5.0	2.7	3.0
Males										
Abbotsford	15.9	16.3	13.0	11.6	10.1	8.5	12.2	5.6	3.5	3.2
British Columbia	16.3	15.5	11.9	11.0	9.9	8.5	12.2	6.6	3.8	4.4
Canada	15.2	14.7	12.5	12.0	10.5	8.5	11.6	6.5	3.9	4.7
Females										
Abbotsford	20.8	26.3	16.6	12.3	8.6	5.6	5.7	2.7	1.0	0.6
British Columbia	20.9	22.8	15.2	12.4	9.7	6.2	7.0	3.2	1.4	1.2
Canada	19.4	22.5	15.8	12.6	9.6	6.4	7.3	3.6	1.5	1.4

Note: Figures cover individuals aged 15 years and over with income. Income refers to monetary receipts from certain sources, before income taxes and deductions, during calendar year 2010.
Source: Statistics Canada. 2013. 2011 National Household Survey. Statistics Canada Catalogue no. 99-004-XWE. Ottawa. Released September 11, 2013.

Labour Force Status

Area	In the Labour Force - All	Employed	Unemployed	Not in the Labour Force
Number				
Total				
Abbotsford	70,535	64,515	6,020	35,100
British Columbia	2,354,245	2,171,465	182,775	1,292,595
Canada	17,990,080	16,595,035	1,395,045	9,269,445
Males				
Abbotsford	37,435	34,375	3,065	14,045
British Columbia	1,223,375	1,124,590	98,785	552,070
Canada	9,388,570	8,634,310	754,255	3,906,785
Females				
Abbotsford	33,095	30,135	2,955	21,055
British Columbia	1,130,870	1,046,875	83,990	740,530
Canada	8,601,515	7,960,725	640,790	5,362,660
Percent of Labour Force				
Total				
Abbotsford	66.8	61.1	8.5	33.2
British Columbia	64.6	59.5	7.8	35.4
Canada	66.0	60.9	7.8	34.0
Males				
Abbotsford	72.7	66.8	8.2	27.3
British Columbia	68.9	63.3	8.1	31.1
Canada	70.6	64.9	8.0	29.4
Females				
Abbotsford	61.1	55.7	8.9	38.9
British Columbia	60.4	55.9	7.4	39.6
Canada	61.6	57.0	7.4	38.4

Note: Figures are based on total population 15 years and over
Source: Statistics Canada. 2013. 2011 National Household Survey. Statistics Canada Catalogue no. 99-004-XWE. Ottawa. Released September 11, 2013.

Labour Force by Industry (NAICS Codes 11–52)

Area	Agriculture, forestry, fishing & hunting	Mining, quarrying, & oil & gas extraction	Utilities	Construction	Manufacturing	Wholesale Trade	Retail Trade	Transportation & warehousing	Information & cultural industries	Finance & insurance
					Number					
					Total					
Abbotsford	5,285	220	205	6,710	6,350	2,900	7,635	4,720	920	2,025
British Columbia	61,210	25,450	13,215	181,510	148,810	90,560	266,265	118,675	62,235	91,790
Canada	437,650	261,050	149,940	1,215,380	1,619,295	733,445	2,031,665	827,780	420,830	767,960
					Males					
Abbotsford	2,595	215	190	5,995	4,665	2,060	3,255	3,870	520	705
British Columbia	40,810	21,175	9,650	159,605	108,480	61,730	121,750	89,155	37,250	35,375
Canada	307,370	211,690	110,765	1,068,710	1,167,680	494,545	933,850	617,305	235,875	296,995
					Females					
Abbotsford	2,685	0	20	720	1,685	840	4,385	855	400	1,325
British Columbia	20,405	4,275	3,560	21,910	40,335	28,820	144,515	29,520	24,980	56,415
Canada	130,285	49,360	39,175	146,670	451,615	238,900	1,097,820	210,475	184,955	470,960
					Percent of Labour Force					
					Total					
Abbotsford	7.7	0.3	0.3	9.7	9.2	4.2	11.1	6.8	1.3	2.9
British Columbia	2.7	1.1	0.6	7.9	6.5	3.9	11.6	5.1	2.7	4.0
Canada	2.5	1.5	0.9	6.9	9.2	4.2	11.6	4.7	2.4	4.4
					Males					
Abbotsford	7.1	0.6	0.5	16.3	12.7	5.6	8.9	10.5	1.4	1.9
British Columbia	3.4	1.8	0.8	13.3	9.0	5.1	10.1	7.4	3.1	2.9
Canada	3.3	2.3	1.2	11.6	12.7	5.4	10.2	6.7	2.6	3.2
					Females					
Abbotsford	8.3	0.0	0.1	2.2	5.2	2.6	13.6	2.7	1.2	4.1
British Columbia	1.8	0.4	0.3	2.0	3.6	2.6	13.1	2.7	2.3	5.1
Canada	1.6	0.6	0.5	1.7	5.4	2.8	13.1	2.5	2.2	5.6

Note: Figures are based on total experienced labour force 15 years and over. Experienced labour force refers to persons who, during the week of Sunday, May 1 to Saturday, May 7, 2011, were employed and the unemployed who had last worked for pay or in self-employment in either 2010 or 2011.
Source: Statistics Canada. 2013. 2011 National Household Survey. Statistics Canada Catalogue no. 99-004-XWE. Ottawa. Released September 11, 2013.

Labour Force by Industry (NAICS Codes 53–91)

Area	Real estate & rental & leasing	Profess., scientific & tech. services	Mgmt of companies & enterprises	Admin. & support, waste mgmt & remed. services	Educational services	Health care & social assistance	Arts, entertain. & recreation	Accomm. & food services	Other services (except public admin.)	Public admin.
					Number					
					Total					
Abbotsford	1,380	3,290	25	2,890	4,790	6,565	1,015	4,525	3,715	3,750
British Columbia	54,840	179,355	2,440	98,890	167,875	249,030	56,915	179,625	112,745	143,875
Canada	321,895	1,240,850	17,460	728,330	1,301,435	1,949,650	363,405	1,130,750	807,800	1,261,050
					Males					
Abbotsford	675	1,700	0	1,630	1,550	1,150	565	1,445	1,915	1,995
British Columbia	29,790	98,760	1,320	55,745	55,635	47,020	29,750	73,570	49,130	74,040
Canada	179,090	688,625	9,380	411,250	424,915	349,430	188,270	469,990	372,940	652,510
					Females					
Abbotsford	710	1,590	25	1,260	3,245	5,415	445	3,080	1,800	1,755
British Columbia	25,055	80,590	1,120	43,145	112,235	202,010	27,175	106,055	63,615	69,840
Canada	142,805	552,225	8,075	317,085	876,515	1,600,220	175,135	660,760	434,865	608,535
					Percent of Labour Force					
					Total					
Abbotsford	2.0	4.8	0.0	4.2	7.0	9.5	1.5	6.6	5.4	5.4
British Columbia	2.4	7.8	0.1	4.3	7.3	10.8	2.5	7.8	4.9	6.2
Canada	1.8	7.1	0.1	4.1	7.4	11.1	2.1	6.4	4.6	7.2
					Males					
Abbotsford	1.8	4.6	0.0	4.4	4.2	3.1	1.5	3.9	5.2	5.4
British Columbia	2.5	8.2	0.1	4.6	4.6	3.9	2.5	6.1	4.1	6.2
Canada	1.9	7.5	0.1	4.5	4.6	3.8	2.0	5.1	4.1	7.1
					Females					
Abbotsford	2.2	4.9	0.1	3.9	10.1	16.8	1.4	9.6	5.6	5.4
British Columbia	2.3	7.3	0.1	3.9	10.2	18.3	2.5	9.6	5.8	6.3
Canada	1.7	6.6	0.1	3.8	10.4	19.1	2.1	7.9	5.2	7.2

Note: Figures are based on total experienced labour force 15 years and over. Experienced labour force refers to persons who, during the week of Sunday, May 1 to Saturday, May 7, 2011, were employed and the unemployed who had last worked for pay or in self-employment in either 2010 or 2011.
Source: Statistics Canada. 2013. 2011 National Household Survey. Statistics Canada Catalogue no. 99-004-XWE. Ottawa. Released September 11, 2013.

PROFILES / Abbotsford, British Columbia

Occupation

Area	Mgmt	Business, Finance & Admin.	Natural/ Applied Sciences & Related	Health	Education, Law & Social, Community & Government Services	Art, Culture, Recreation & Sport	Sales & Service	Trades, Transport & Equip. Operators & Related	Natural Resources, Agri. & Related Production	Mfg & Utilities
Number										
Total										
Abbotsford	6,875	9,790	2,790	4,030	7,530	1,605	15,275	13,020	4,560	3,450
British Columbia	263,685	368,980	154,055	147,620	265,910	78,565	554,345	337,140	60,295	74,720
Canada	1,963,600	2,902,045	1,237,775	1,107,200	2,064,675	503,415	4,068,170	2,537,775	397,930	805,040
Males										
Abbotsford	4,740	2,405	2,340	920	2,710	645	5,830	12,405	2,205	2,475
British Columbia	162,365	104,285	122,570	32,490	89,645	38,300	233,065	317,385	45,155	54,470
Canada	1,229,460	854,190	966,355	217,520	676,550	232,535	1,745,705	2,385,615	318,945	564,300
Females										
Abbotsford	2,130	7,385	445	3,110	4,815	960	9,450	610	2,360	975
British Columbia	101,320	264,690	31,480	115,125	176,265	40,270	321,285	19,755	15,135	20,250
Canada	734,140	2,047,855	271,415	889,675	1,388,130	270,875	2,322,465	152,165	78,980	240,740
Percent of Labour Force										
Total										
Abbotsford	10.0	14.2	4.0	5.8	10.9	2.3	22.2	18.9	6.6	5.0
British Columbia	11.4	16.0	6.7	6.4	11.5	3.4	24.0	14.6	2.6	3.2
Canada	11.2	16.5	7.0	6.3	11.7	2.9	23.1	14.4	2.3	4.6
Males										
Abbotsford	12.9	6.6	6.4	2.5	7.4	1.8	15.9	33.8	6.0	6.7
British Columbia	13.5	8.7	10.2	2.7	7.5	3.2	19.4	26.5	3.8	4.5
Canada	13.4	9.3	10.5	2.4	7.4	2.5	19.0	26.0	3.5	6.1
Females										
Abbotsford	6.6	22.9	1.4	9.6	14.9	3.0	29.3	1.9	7.3	3.0
British Columbia	9.2	23.9	2.8	10.4	15.9	3.6	29.1	1.8	1.4	1.8
Canada	8.7	24.4	3.2	10.6	16.5	3.2	27.7	1.8	0.9	2.9

Note: Figures are based on total experienced labour force 15 years and over
Source: Statistics Canada. 2013. 2011 National Household Survey. Statistics Canada Catalogue no. 99-004-XWE. Ottawa. Released September 11, 2013.

Place of Work Status

Area	Worked at Home	Worked Outside Canada	No Fixed Workplace Address	Worked at Usual Place
Number				
Total				
Abbotsford	5,020	260	10,585	48,650
British Columbia	174,000	12,480	304,465	1,680,525
Canada	1,142,640	66,460	1,868,245	13,517,690
Males				
Abbotsford	2,440	190	8,315	23,425
British Columbia	84,015	9,210	225,840	805,525
Canada	582,150	47,355	1,400,485	6,604,325
Females				
Abbotsford	2,580	65	2,265	25,225
British Columbia	89,990	3,270	78,620	875,000
Canada	560,490	19,100	467,760	6,913,370
Percent of Labour Force				
Total				
Abbotsford	7.8	0.4	16.4	75.4
British Columbia	8.0	0.6	14.0	77.4
Canada	6.9	0.4	11.3	81.5
Males				
Abbotsford	7.1	0.6	24.2	68.1
British Columbia	7.5	0.8	20.1	71.6
Canada	6.7	0.5	16.2	76.5
Females				
Abbotsford	8.6	0.2	7.5	83.7
British Columbia	8.6	0.3	7.5	83.6
Canada	7.0	0.2	5.9	86.8

Note: Figures are based on total employed labour force 15 years and over.
Source: Statistics Canada. 2013. 2011 National Household Survey. Statistics Canada Catalogue no. 99-004-XWE. Ottawa. Released September 11, 2013.

Mode of Transportation to Work

Area	Car; Truck; Van; as Driver	Car; Truck; Van; as Passenger	Public Transit	Walked	Bicycled	All Other Modes
			Number			
			Total			
Abbotsford	50,215	4,720	1,135	1,605	500	1,055
British Columbia	1,415,745	110,695	250,450	132,205	42,260	33,635
Canada	11,393,140	867,050	1,851,525	880,815	201,780	191,625
			Males			
Abbotsford	27,560	2,095	540	695	410	435
British Columbia	773,160	47,425	107,645	57,000	26,595	19,535
Canada	6,238,835	349,530	788,290	387,580	135,840	104,725
			Females			
Abbotsford	22,655	2,630	600	910	90	615
British Columbia	642,580	63,270	142,810	75,205	15,665	14,100
Canada	5,154,305	517,520	1,063,235	493,230	65,940	86,900
			Percent of Labour Force			
			Total			
Abbotsford	84.8	8.0	1.9	2.7	0.8	1.8
British Columbia	71.3	5.6	12.6	6.7	2.1	1.7
Canada	74.0	5.6	12.0	5.7	1.3	1.2
			Males			
Abbotsford	86.8	6.6	1.7	2.2	1.3	1.4
British Columbia	75.0	4.6	10.4	5.5	2.6	1.9
Canada	77.9	4.4	9.8	4.8	1.7	1.3
			Females			
Abbotsford	82.4	9.6	2.2	3.3	0.3	2.2
British Columbia	67.4	6.6	15.0	7.9	1.6	1.5
Canada	69.8	7.0	14.4	6.7	0.9	1.2

Note: Figures are based on total employed labour force 15 years and over.
Source: Statistics Canada. 2013. 2011 National Household Survey. Statistics Canada Catalogue no. 99-004-XWE. Ottawa. Released September 11, 2013.

Visible Minority Population Characteristics

Area	Total Minority	South Asian[1]	Chinese	Black	Filipino	Latin American	Arab	SE Asian[2]	West Asian[3]	Korean	Japanese	Multiple[4]
						Number						
						Total						
Abbotsford	38,700	29,725	1,805	1,120	895	755	250	1,110	130	1,470	510	575
British Columbia	1,180,870	313,440	438,140	33,260	126,040	35,465	14,090	51,970	38,960	53,770	38,120	31,160
Canada	6,264,750	1,567,400	1,324,750	945,665	619,310	381,280	380,620	312,075	206,840	161,130	87,270	171,935
						Males						
Abbotsford	19,330	14,845	890	645	425	360	135	530	60	675	215	310
British Columbia	565,965	157,135	208,175	17,365	53,715	16,985	8,010	25,055	19,420	25,325	16,295	15,255
Canada	3,043,010	790,755	632,325	453,005	268,885	186,355	203,485	154,035	105,620	77,165	38,270	83,335
						Females						
Abbotsford	19,370	14,880	915	470	470	400	115	580	65	795	290	270
British Columbia	614,905	156,300	229,960	15,895	72,320	18,480	6,080	26,920	19,540	28,440	21,820	15,905
Canada	3,221,745	776,650	692,420	492,660	350,425	194,925	177,140	158,045	101,220	83,965	48,990	88,600
						Percent of Population						
						Total						
Abbotsford	29.6	22.7	1.4	0.9	0.7	0.6	0.2	0.8	0.1	1.1	0.4	0.4
British Columbia	27.3	7.2	10.1	0.8	2.9	0.8	0.3	1.2	0.9	1.2	0.9	0.7
Canada	19.1	4.8	4.0	2.9	1.9	1.2	1.2	0.9	0.6	0.5	0.3	0.5
						Males						
Abbotsford	29.9	23.0	1.4	1.0	0.7	0.6	0.2	0.8	0.1	1.0	0.3	0.5
British Columbia	26.6	7.4	9.8	0.8	2.5	0.8	0.4	1.2	0.9	1.2	0.8	0.7
Canada	18.8	4.9	3.9	2.8	1.7	1.2	1.3	1.0	0.7	0.5	0.2	0.5
						Females						
Abbotsford	29.2	22.4	1.4	0.7	0.7	0.6	0.2	0.9	0.1	1.2	0.4	0.4
British Columbia	28.0	7.1	10.5	0.7	3.3	0.8	0.3	1.2	0.9	1.3	1.0	0.7
Canada	19.3	4.7	4.1	3.0	2.1	1.2	1.1	0.9	0.6	0.5	0.3	0.5

Note: The Employment Equity Act defines visible minorities as 'persons, other than Aboriginal peoples, who are non-Caucasian in race or non-white in colour';
(1) Includes 'East Indian,' 'Pakistani,' 'Sri Lankan,' etc.; (2) Includes 'Vietnamese,' 'Cambodian,' 'Malaysian,' 'Laotian,' etc.; (3) Includes 'Iranian,' 'Afghan,' etc.; (4) Includes respondents who reported more than one visible minority group by checking two or more mark-in circles, e.g., 'Black' and 'South Asian.'
Source: Statistics Canada. 2013. 2011 National Household Survey. Statistics Canada Catalogue no. 99-004-XWE. Ottawa. Released September 11, 2013.

PROFILES / Abbotsford, British Columbia

Aboriginal Population

Area	Aboriginal Identity[1]	First Nations (North American Indian) Single Identity[2]	Métis Single Identity	Inuk (Inuit) Single Identity	Multiple Aboriginal Identities[3]	Aboriginal Identities Not Included Elsewhere
Number — Total						
Abbotsford	4,460	2,200	2,065	55	95	45
British Columbia	232,290	155,020	69,475	1,570	2,480	3,745
Canada	1,400,685	851,560	451,795	59,440	11,415	26,475
Males						
Abbotsford	2,040	920	1,020	40	45	0
British Columbia	113,080	75,400	33,940	820	1,190	1,735
Canada	682,190	411,785	223,335	29,495	5,525	12,055
Females						
Abbotsford	2,420	1,280	1,045	0	50	30
British Columbia	119,215	79,620	35,540	750	1,290	2,015
Canada	718,500	439,775	228,460	29,950	5,890	14,420
Percent of Population — Total						
Abbotsford	3.4	1.7	1.6	0.0	0.1	0.0
British Columbia	5.4	3.6	1.6	0.0	0.1	0.1
Canada	4.3	2.6	1.4	0.2	0.0	0.1
Males						
Abbotsford	3.2	1.4	1.6	0.1	0.1	0.0
British Columbia	5.3	3.5	1.6	0.0	0.1	0.1
Canada	4.2	2.5	1.4	0.2	0.0	0.1
Females						
Abbotsford	3.6	1.9	1.6	0.0	0.1	0.0
British Columbia	5.4	3.6	1.6	0.0	0.1	0.1
Canada	4.3	2.6	1.4	0.2	0.0	0.1

Note: (1) Includes persons who reported being an Aboriginal person, that is, First Nations (North American Indian), Métis or Inuk (Inuit) and/or those who reported Registered or Treaty Indian status, that is registered under the Indian Act of Canada, and/or those who reported membership in a First Nation or Indian band. Aboriginal peoples of Canada are defined in the Constitution Act, 1982, section 35-2 as including the Indian, Inuit and Métis peoples of Canada; (2) Users should be aware that the estimates associated with this variable are more affected than most by the incomplete enumeration of certain Indian reserves and Indian settlements in the National Household Survey (NHS); (3) Includes persons who reported being any two or all three of the following: First Nations (North American Indian), Métis or Inuk (Inuit).
Source: Statistics Canada. 2013. 2011 National Household Survey. Statistics Canada Catalogue no. 99-004-XWE. Ottawa. Released September 11, 2013.

Ethnic Origin

Area	North American Aboriginal	Other North American	European	Caribbean	Latin, Central and South American	African	Asian	Oceania
Number — Total								
Abbotsford	5,230	27,150	83,760	500	1,705	1,285	36,145	925
British Columbia	267,085	884,490	2,812,935	20,035	52,725	47,185	1,122,445	35,770
Canada	1,836,035	11,070,455	20,157,965	627,590	544,375	766,735	5,011,225	74,875
Males								
Abbotsford	2,370	13,495	41,125	280	805	680	17,830	545
British Columbia	128,880	440,920	1,387,940	10,225	25,605	23,575	535,825	17,425
Canada	885,675	5,462,685	9,913,150	291,640	264,635	387,360	2,435,540	37,490
Females								
Abbotsford	2,855	13,650	42,630	225	900	600	18,315	380
British Columbia	138,205	443,570	1,424,990	9,810	27,120	23,610	586,620	18,340
Canada	950,360	5,607,770	10,244,820	335,945	279,740	379,380	2,575,680	37,385
Percent of Population — Total								
Abbotsford	4.0	20.7	64.0	0.4	1.3	1.0	27.6	0.7
British Columbia	6.2	20.5	65.0	0.5	1.2	1.1	26.0	0.8
Canada	5.6	33.7	61.4	1.9	1.7	2.3	15.3	0.2
Males								
Abbotsford	3.7	20.9	63.7	0.4	1.2	1.1	27.6	0.8
British Columbia	6.1	20.7	65.3	0.5	1.2	1.1	25.2	0.8
Canada	5.5	33.8	61.3	1.8	1.6	2.4	15.1	0.2
Females								
Abbotsford	4.3	20.6	64.2	0.3	1.4	0.9	27.6	0.6
British Columbia	6.3	20.2	64.8	0.4	1.2	1.1	26.7	0.8
Canada	5.7	33.6	61.4	2.0	1.7	2.3	15.4	0.2

Note: The sum of the ethnic groups in this table is greater than the total population estimate because a person may report more than one ethnic origin in the NHS.
Source: Statistics Canada. 2013. 2011 National Household Survey. Statistics Canada Catalogue no. 99-004-XWE. Ottawa. Released September 11, 2013.

Religion

Area	Buddhist	Christian	Hindu	Jewish	Muslim	Sikh	Traditional (Aboriginal) Spirituality	Other Religions	No Religious Affiliation
Number									
Total									
Abbotsford	720	65,055	1,955	210	715	26,145	25	665	35,465
British Columbia	90,620	1,930,415	45,795	23,130	79,310	201,110	10,295	35,500	1,908,285
Canada	366,830	22,102,745	497,965	329,495	1,053,945	454,965	64,935	130,835	7,850,605
Males									
Abbotsford	335	30,380	960	100	400	13,020	0	205	19,135
British Columbia	40,175	883,680	22,945	11,255	39,780	100,610	5,085	14,680	1,007,420
Canada	168,465	10,497,775	250,435	161,265	540,555	229,435	31,805	57,745	4,225,645
Females									
Abbotsford	380	34,675	995	115	315	13,125	0	465	16,325
British Columbia	50,440	1,046,735	22,845	11,880	39,530	100,500	5,210	20,820	900,865
Canada	198,365	11,604,975	247,525	168,235	513,395	225,530	33,135	73,090	3,624,965
Percent of Population									
Total									
Abbotsford	0.5	49.7	1.5	0.2	0.5	20.0	0.0	0.5	27.1
British Columbia	2.1	44.6	1.1	0.5	1.8	4.7	0.2	0.8	44.1
Canada	1.1	67.3	1.5	1.0	3.2	1.4	0.2	0.4	23.9
Males									
Abbotsford	0.5	47.1	1.5	0.2	0.6	20.2	0.0	0.3	29.6
British Columbia	1.9	41.6	1.1	0.5	1.9	4.7	0.2	0.7	47.4
Canada	1.0	64.9	1.5	1.0	3.3	1.4	0.2	0.4	26.1
Females									
Abbotsford	0.6	52.2	1.5	0.2	0.5	19.8	0.0	0.7	24.6
British Columbia	2.3	47.6	1.0	0.5	1.8	4.6	0.2	0.9	41.0
Canada	1.2	69.5	1.5	1.0	3.1	1.4	0.2	0.4	21.7

Note: Religion refers to the person's self-identification as having a connection or affiliation with any religious denomination, group, body, sect, cult or other religiously defined community or system of belief. Religion is not limited to formal membership in a religious organization or group. Persons without a religious connection or affiliation can self-identify as atheist, agnostic or humanist, or can provide another applicable response.
Source: Statistics Canada. 2013. 2011 National Household Survey. Statistics Canada Catalogue no. 99-004-XWE. Ottawa. Released September 11, 2013.

Religion—Christian Denominations

Area	Anglican	Baptist	Catholic	Christian Orthodox	Lutheran	Pentecostal	Presbyterian	United Church	Other Christian
Number									
Total									
Abbotsford	3,875	2,720	10,885	605	1,960	3,180	1,160	4,660	36,015
British Columbia	213,975	91,575	650,360	39,845	71,470	58,300	44,635	222,230	538,030
Canada	1,631,845	635,840	12,810,705	550,690	478,185	478,705	472,385	2,007,610	3,036,780
Males									
Abbotsford	1,785	1,260	5,130	275	940	1,425	530	1,795	17,240
British Columbia	94,330	41,565	303,300	19,475	32,205	26,590	19,925	94,020	252,270
Canada	752,945	293,905	6,167,290	270,205	221,525	217,850	218,955	912,545	1,442,550
Females									
Abbotsford	2,090	1,460	5,750	330	1,015	1,755	630	2,865	18,775
British Columbia	119,645	50,010	347,060	20,375	39,270	31,710	24,710	128,210	285,770
Canada	878,900	341,940	6,643,415	280,485	256,660	260,850	253,430	1,095,065	1,594,230
Percent of Population									
Total									
Abbotsford	3.0	2.1	8.3	0.5	1.5	2.4	0.9	3.6	27.5
British Columbia	4.9	2.1	15.0	0.9	1.7	1.3	1.0	5.1	12.4
Canada	5.0	1.9	39.0	1.7	1.5	1.5	1.4	6.1	9.2
Males									
Abbotsford	2.8	2.0	7.9	0.4	1.5	2.2	0.8	2.8	26.7
British Columbia	4.4	2.0	14.3	0.9	1.5	1.3	0.9	4.4	11.9
Canada	4.7	1.8	38.2	1.7	1.4	1.3	1.4	5.6	8.9
Females									
Abbotsford	3.1	2.2	8.7	0.5	1.5	2.6	0.9	4.3	28.3
British Columbia	5.4	2.3	15.8	0.9	1.8	1.4	1.1	5.8	13.0
Canada	5.3	2.0	39.8	1.7	1.5	1.5	1.6	6.6	9.6

Note: Religion refers to the person's self-identification as having a connection or affiliation with any religious denomination, group, body, sect, cult or other religiously defined community or system of belief. Religion is not limited to formal membership in a religious organization or group. Persons without a religious connection or affiliation can self-identify as atheist, agnostic or humanist, or can provide another applicable response.
Source: Statistics Canada. 2013. 2011 National Household Survey. Statistics Canada Catalogue no. 99-004-XWE. Ottawa. Released September 11, 2013.

PROFILES / Abbotsford, British Columbia

Immigrant Status and Period of Immigration

Area	Non-Immigrants[1]	Immigrants All	Before 1971	1971 to 1980	1981 to 1990	1991 to 2000	2001 to 2005	2006 to 2011	Non-Permanent Residents[3]
Number									
Total									
Abbotsford	95,345	33,930	6,330	3,830	4,115	8,940	5,290	5,425	1,675
British Columbia	3,067,590	1,191,875	223,215	161,335	156,445	305,655	160,100	185,115	64,995
Canada	25,720,175	6,775,765	1,261,055	870,775	949,890	1,539,050	992,070	1,162,915	356,385
Males									
Abbotsford	47,415	16,305	3,145	1,900	2,080	4,325	2,480	2,385	820
British Columbia	1,533,255	561,490	109,510	76,865	72,625	140,985	74,395	87,110	30,880
Canada	12,753,235	3,231,370	605,430	416,670	454,570	724,905	474,545	555,245	178,515
Females									
Abbotsford	47,925	17,625	3,180	1,930	2,035	4,615	2,815	3,045	855
British Columbia	1,534,330	630,385	113,710	84,470	83,820	164,675	85,710	98,005	34,115
Canada	12,966,935	3,544,400	655,625	454,105	495,325	814,145	517,530	607,670	177,870
Percent of Population									
Total									
Abbotsford	72.8	25.9	4.8	2.9	3.1	6.8	4.0	4.1	1.3
British Columbia	70.9	27.6	5.2	3.7	3.6	7.1	3.7	4.3	1.5
Canada	78.3	20.6	3.8	2.7	2.9	4.7	3.0	3.5	1.1
Males									
Abbotsford	73.5	25.3	4.9	2.9	3.2	6.7	3.8	3.7	1.3
British Columbia	72.1	26.4	5.2	3.6	3.4	6.6	3.5	4.1	1.5
Canada	78.9	20.0	3.7	2.6	2.8	4.5	2.9	3.4	1.1
Females									
Abbotsford	72.2	26.5	4.8	2.9	3.1	6.9	4.2	4.6	1.3
British Columbia	69.8	28.7	5.2	3.8	3.8	7.5	3.9	4.5	1.6
Canada	77.7	21.2	3.9	2.7	3.0	4.9	3.1	3.6	1.1

Note: (1) Non-immigrant refers to a person who is a Canadian citizen by birth; (2) Immigrant refers to a person who is or has ever been a landed immigrant/permanent resident. This person has been granted the right to live in Canada permanently by immigration authorities. Some immigrants have resided in Canada for a number of years, while others have arrived recently. Some immigrants are Canadian citizens, while others are not. Most immigrants are born outside Canada, but a small number are born in Canada. In the 2011 National Household Survey, 'Immigrants' includes immigrants who landed in Canada prior to May 10, 2011; (3) Non-permanent resident refers to a person from another country who has a work or study permit, or who is a refugee claimant, and any non-Canadian-born family member living in Canada with them.
Source: Statistics Canada. 2013. 2011 National Household Survey. Statistics Canada Catalogue no. 99-004-XWE. Ottawa. Released September 11, 2013.

Mother Tongue

Area	English	French	Non-official Language	English & French	English & Non-official Language	French & Non-official Language	English, French & Non-official Language
Number							
Total							
Abbotsford	86,660	1,095	41,670	185	2,085	75	40
British Columbia	3,062,435	57,275	1,154,215	8,600	68,800	3,345	1,530
Canada	18,858,980	7,054,975	6,567,680	144,685	396,330	74,430	24,095
Males							
Abbotsford	43,000	555	20,280	85	1,065	35	20
British Columbia	1,526,350	28,315	543,395	4,065	32,875	1,520	725
Canada	9,345,225	3,452,380	3,157,785	69,975	192,000	36,535	11,965
Females							
Abbotsford	43,670	540	21,390	100	1,025	40	25
British Columbia	1,536,085	28,965	610,825	4,535	35,925	1,830	805
Canada	9,513,750	3,602,590	3,409,895	74,710	204,330	37,890	12,130
Percent of Population							
Total							
Abbotsford	65.7	0.8	31.6	0.1	1.6	0.1	0.0
British Columbia	70.3	1.3	26.5	0.2	1.6	0.1	0.0
Canada	56.9	21.3	19.8	0.4	1.2	0.2	0.1
Males							
Abbotsford	66.1	0.9	31.2	0.1	1.6	0.1	0.0
British Columbia	71.4	1.3	25.4	0.2	1.5	0.1	0.0
Canada	57.5	21.2	19.4	0.4	1.2	0.2	0.1
Females							
Abbotsford	65.4	0.8	32.0	0.1	1.5	0.1	0.0
British Columbia	69.2	1.3	27.5	0.2	1.6	0.1	0.0
Canada	56.4	21.4	20.2	0.4	1.2	0.2	0.1

Note: Figures cover total population excluding institutional residents.
Source: Statistics Canada. 2012. Census Profile. 2011 Census. Statistics Canada Catalogue no. 98-316-XWE. Ottawa. Released October 24 2012.
http://www12.statcan.gc.ca/census-recensement/2011/dp-pd/prof/index.cfm?Lang=E

Language Spoken Most Often at Home

Area	English	French	Non-official Language	English & French	English & Non-official Language	French & Non-official Language	English, French & Non-official Language
			Number				
			Total				
Abbotsford	99,815	205	26,365	110	5,245	30	55
British Columbia	3,506,595	16,685	670,100	4,700	155,065	930	2,130
Canada	21,457,075	6,827,865	3,673,865	131,205	875,135	109,700	46,330
			Males				
Abbotsford	49,270	90	12,960	60	2,620	10	20
British Columbia	1,733,775	8,015	317,670	2,240	74,155	435	940
Canada	10,585,620	3,348,235	1,767,310	63,475	425,370	53,010	22,845
			Females				
Abbotsford	50,545	110	13,405	50	2,625	15	35
British Columbia	1,772,820	8,665	352,430	2,460	80,905	495	1,185
Canada	10,871,455	3,479,625	1,906,555	67,730	449,765	56,690	23,485
			Percent of Population				
			Total				
Abbotsford	75.7	0.2	20.0	0.1	4.0	0.0	0.0
British Columbia	80.5	0.4	15.4	0.1	3.6	0.0	0.0
Canada	64.8	20.6	11.1	0.4	2.6	0.3	0.1
			Males				
Abbotsford	75.8	0.1	19.9	0.1	4.0	0.0	0.0
British Columbia	81.1	0.4	14.9	0.1	3.5	0.0	0.0
Canada	65.1	20.6	10.9	0.4	2.6	0.3	0.1
			Females				
Abbotsford	75.7	0.2	20.1	0.1	3.9	0.0	0.1
British Columbia	79.9	0.4	15.9	0.1	3.6	0.0	0.1
Canada	64.5	20.6	11.3	0.4	2.7	0.3	0.1

Note: Figures cover total population excluding institutional residents.
Source: Statistics Canada. 2012. Census Profile. 2011 Census. Statistics Canada Catalogue no. 98-316-XWE. Ottawa. Released October 24 2012.
http://www12.statcan.gc.ca/census-recensement/2011/dp-pd/prof/index.cfm?Lang=E

Knowledge of Official Languages

Area	English Only	French Only	English & French	Neither English nor French
		Number		
		Total		
Abbotsford	118,290	40	5,860	7,625
British Columbia	3,912,950	2,045	296,645	144,555
Canada	22,564,665	4,165,015	5,795,570	595,920
		Males		
Abbotsford	59,065	10	2,625	3,325
British Columbia	1,943,760	950	132,940	59,590
Canada	11,222,185	1,925,340	2,876,560	241,790
		Females		
Abbotsford	59,225	30	3,235	4,300
British Columbia	1,969,190	1,095	163,705	84,965
Canada	11,342,485	2,239,680	2,919,005	354,135
		Percent of Population		
		Total		
Abbotsford	89.7	0.0	4.4	5.8
British Columbia	89.8	0.0	6.8	3.3
Canada	68.1	12.6	17.5	1.8
		Males		
Abbotsford	90.8	0.0	4.0	5.1
British Columbia	90.9	0.0	6.2	2.8
Canada	69.0	11.8	17.7	1.5
		Females		
Abbotsford	88.7	0.0	4.8	6.4
British Columbia	88.7	0.0	7.4	3.8
Canada	67.3	13.3	17.3	2.1

Note: Figures cover total population excluding institutional residents.
Source: Statistics Canada. 2012. Census Profile. 2011 Census. Statistics Canada Catalogue no. 98-316-XWE. Ottawa. Released October 24 2012.
http://www12.statcan.gc.ca/census-recensement/2011/dp-pd/prof/index.cfm?Lang=E

Ajax, Ontario

Background

Ajax is located in the Durham Region of southern Ontario, on the shore of Lake Ontario. The municipality is bordered by the communities of Pickering to the west and Whitby to the east. The City of Ajax is part of the eastern portion of the Greater Toronto Area (GTA) and is situated 45 minutes from downtown Toronto.

In 1939, upon the declaration of World War II, what is now known as Ajax was a farming community in Pickering Township. A few years later, acres of farmland had been converted into a shell filing plant employing over 9,000 people. Defence Industries Limited built nearly 100 kilometres of railway and roads through the region. The City of Ajax was named after the HMS Ajax, a Royal Navy cruiser that was renowned for an early Second World War victory against a German battleship.

Today, Ajax's street names honour wartime history. Harwood Avenue, the city's main street, is named after Commodore Henry H. Harwood, commander of HMS Ajax. The community's waterfront is the longest undeveloped waterfront property in the GTA; it offers six kilometres of walking and cycling trails. Greenwood Conservation Area consists of nearly 40 kilometres of trails as well as two leash-free areas for dogs and a creek popular for rainbow trout fishing.

Ajax was the first fully registered municipality in North America to receive an ISO 9001-2000 distinction. The area has nearly 2,000 businesses, a local labour force of almost 85,000 people and access to a regional workforce of over 2 million in the GTA.

Popular attractions such as the McLean Community Centre and Town Hall, the Ajax Public Library, the Cultural Expressions Gallery and St. Francis Centre host community events throughout the year.

Ajax has summer highs of plus 23.87 degrees Celsius, winter lows of minus 10.13 degrees Celsius, and an average rainfall just over 815 mm per year.

Rankings

- In 2011, *fDi Magazine* ranked Ajax as a top City of the Future. The magazine, owned by The Financial Times Business Group, ranked 405 cities across North and South America. Ajax ranked in the Top 10 in three categories: economic potential (#10); cost effectiveness (#7) and infrastructure (#7). Out of the four categories for city size, Ajax was classified as a micro-city and competed against cities with populations of less than 100,000. *fDi Intelligence, "American Cities of the Future, 2011/12," released April 8, 2011*
- In 2011, Real Estate Investment Network, a real estate research organization, ranked hundreds of towns and cities across Ontario for real estate investment and found Ajax to be one of the best. The City of Ajax and its region, Durham (including regional cities Whitby and Pickering), ranked #7 overall. Evaluation factors included population growth, new infrastructure, employment rate, political leadership and access to major transportation routes. The City of Hamilton ranked #1 and Toronto ranked #8. *Real Estate Investment Network (REIN), "Top Ontario Investment Towns 2011-2015," May 10, 2011*

PROFILES / Ajax, Ontario

Population Growth and Density

Area	Population in 2001	Population in 2006	Population in 2011	Population Change 2001–2006	Population Change 2006–2011	Land Area (sq. km)	Population Density per sq. km
Ajax	73,753	90,167	109,600	22.3	21.6	67.07	1,634.2
Ontario	11,410,046	12,160,282	12,851,821	6.6	5.7	908,607.67	14.1
Canada	30,007,094	31,612,897	33,476,688	5.4	5.9	8,965,121.42	3.7

Source: Statistics Canada. 2012. Census Profile. 2011 Census. Statistics Canada Catalogue no. 98-316-XWE. Ottawa. Released October 24 2012. http://www12.statcan.gc.ca/census-recensement/2011/dp-pd/prof/index.cfm?Lang=E;
Statistics Canada 2007. 2006 Community Profiles. 2006 Census. Statistics Canada Catalogue no. 92-591-XWE. Ottawa. Released March 13 2007. http://www12.statcan.ca/census-recensement/2006/dp-pd/prof/92-591/index.cfm?Lang=E

Gender

Area	Males	Females
	Number	
Ajax	52,890	56,705
Ontario	6,263,140	6,588,685
Canada	16,414,225	17,062,460
	Percent of Population	
Ajax	48.3	51.7
Ontario	48.7	51.3
Canada	49.0	51.0

Source: Statistics Canada. 2012. Census Profile. 2011 Census. Statistics Canada Catalogue no. 98-316-XWE. Ottawa. Released October 24 2012. http://www12.statcan.gc.ca/census-recensement/2011/dp-pd/prof/index.cfm?Lang=E

Marital Status

Area	Married[1]	Living Common-law	Single[2]	Separated	Divorced	Widowed
			Number			
			Total			
Ajax	46,060	5,380	25,590	2,540	4,120	3,280
Ontario	5,367,400	791,210	2,985,020	319,805	593,730	613,880
Canada	12,941,960	3,142,525	7,816,045	698,240	1,686,035	1,584,530
			Males			
Ajax	22,960	2,680	12,855	955	1,330	555
Ontario	2,681,320	397,620	1,583,760	133,790	231,160	117,980
Canada	6,470,300	1,575,495	4,206,320	299,655	680,415	310,940
			Females			
Ajax	23,095	2,695	12,735	1,585	2,790	2,725
Ontario	2,686,075	393,590	1,401,260	186,015	362,570	495,905
Canada	6,471,660	1,567,035	3,609,730	398,585	1,005,620	1,273,590
			Percent of Population			
			Total			
Ajax	53.0	6.2	29.4	2.9	4.7	3.8
Ontario	50.3	7.4	28.0	3.0	5.6	5.8
Canada	46.4	11.3	28.0	2.5	6.0	5.7
			Males			
Ajax	55.5	6.5	31.1	2.3	3.2	1.3
Ontario	52.1	7.7	30.8	2.6	4.5	2.3
Canada	47.8	11.6	31.1	2.2	5.0	2.3
			Females			
Ajax	50.6	5.9	27.9	3.5	6.1	6.0
Ontario	48.6	7.1	25.4	3.4	6.6	9.0
Canada	45.2	10.9	25.2	2.8	7.0	8.9

Note: (1) and not separated, (2) never legally married
Source: Statistics Canada. 2012. Census Profile. 2011 Census. Statistics Canada Catalogue no. 98-316-XWE. Ottawa. Released October 24 2012. http://www12.statcan.gc.ca/census-recensement/2011/dp-pd/prof/index.cfm?Lang=E

Age Characteristics: 0 to 49 Years

Area	0 to 4 Years	5 to 9 Years	10 to 14 Years	15 to 19 Years	20 to 24 Years	25 to 29 Years	30 to 34 Years	35 to 39 Years	40 to 44 Years	45 to 49 Years
					Number					
					Total					
Ajax	7,300	7,310	8,025	8,950	7,415	6,545	7,380	8,120	8,650	9,940
Ontario	704,260	712,755	763,755	863,635	852,910	815,120	800,365	844,335	924,075	1,055,880
Canada	1,877,095	1,809,895	1,920,355	2,178,135	2,187,450	2,169,590	2,162,905	2,173,930	2,324,875	2,675,130
					Males					
Ajax	3,735	3,725	4,095	4,525	3,725	3,135	3,295	3,785	4,055	4,755
Ontario	360,590	365,290	391,630	443,680	432,490	400,045	383,340	405,845	447,920	517,510
Canada	961,150	925,965	983,995	1,115,845	1,108,775	1,077,275	1,058,810	1,064,200	1,141,720	1,318,715
					Females					
Ajax	3,565	3,585	3,930	4,425	3,690	3,415	4,085	4,335	4,595	5,185
Ontario	343,670	347,465	372,125	419,950	420,415	415,075	417,030	438,485	476,155	538,370
Canada	915,945	883,935	936,360	1,062,295	1,078,670	1,092,315	1,104,095	1,109,735	1,183,155	1,356,420
					Percent of Population					
					Total					
Ajax	6.7	6.7	7.3	8.2	6.8	6.0	6.7	7.4	7.9	9.1
Ontario	5.5	5.5	5.9	6.7	6.6	6.3	6.2	6.6	7.2	8.2
Canada	5.6	5.4	5.7	6.5	6.5	6.5	6.5	6.5	6.9	8.0
					Males					
Ajax	7.1	7.0	7.7	8.6	7.0	5.9	6.2	7.2	7.7	9.0
Ontario	5.8	5.8	6.3	7.1	6.9	6.4	6.1	6.5	7.2	8.3
Canada	5.9	5.6	6.0	6.8	6.8	6.6	6.5	6.5	7.0	8.0
					Females					
Ajax	6.3	6.3	6.9	7.8	6.5	6.0	7.2	7.6	8.1	9.1
Ontario	5.2	5.3	5.6	6.4	6.4	6.3	6.3	6.7	7.2	8.2
Canada	5.4	5.2	5.5	6.2	6.3	6.4	6.5	6.5	6.9	7.9

Source: Statistics Canada. 2012. Census Profile. 2011 Census. Statistics Canada Catalogue no. 98-316-XWE. Ottawa. Released October 24 2012.
http://www12.statcan.gc.ca/census-recensement/2011/dp-pd/prof/index.cfm?Lang=E

Age Characteristics: 50 Years and Over, and Median Age

Area	50 to 54 Years	55 to 59 Years	60 to 64 Years	65 to 69 Years	70 to 74 Years	75 to 79 Years	80 to 84 Years	85 Years and Over	Median Age
				Number					
				Total					
Ajax	8,875	6,445	5,065	3,280	2,325	1,830	1,240	905	36.2
Ontario	1,006,140	864,620	765,655	563,485	440,780	356,150	271,510	246,400	40.4
Canada	2,658,965	2,340,635	2,052,670	1,521,715	1,153,065	922,700	702,070	645,515	40.6
				Males					
Ajax	4,335	3,150	2,430	1,570	1,035	805	460	280	35.3
Ontario	492,560	418,755	370,370	270,875	206,350	161,345	113,620	80,925	39.4
Canada	1,309,030	1,147,300	1,002,690	738,010	543,435	417,945	291,085	208,300	39.6
				Females					
Ajax	4,535	3,295	2,640	1,710	1,285	1,025	780	625	36.9
Ontario	513,580	445,865	395,275	292,610	234,435	194,805	157,890	165,475	41.3
Canada	1,349,940	1,193,335	1,049,985	783,705	609,630	504,755	410,985	437,215	41.5
				Percent of Population					
				Total					
Ajax	8.1	5.9	4.6	3.0	2.1	1.7	1.1	0.8	–
Ontario	7.8	6.7	6.0	4.4	3.4	2.8	2.1	1.9	–
Canada	7.9	7.0	6.1	4.5	3.4	2.8	2.1	1.9	–
				Males					
Ajax	8.2	6.0	4.6	3.0	2.0	1.5	0.9	0.5	–
Ontario	7.9	6.7	5.9	4.3	3.3	2.6	1.8	1.3	–
Canada	8.0	7.0	6.1	4.5	3.3	2.5	1.8	1.3	–
				Females					
Ajax	8.0	5.8	4.7	3.0	2.3	1.8	1.4	1.1	–
Ontario	7.8	6.8	6.0	4.4	3.6	3.0	2.4	2.5	–
Canada	7.9	7.0	6.2	4.6	3.6	3.0	2.4	2.6	–

Source: Statistics Canada. 2012. Census Profile. 2011 Census. Statistics Canada Catalogue no. 98-316-XWE. Ottawa. Released October 24 2012.
http://www12.statcan.gc.ca/census-recensement/2011/dp-pd/prof/index.cfm?Lang=E

PROFILES / Ajax, Ontario

Private Households by Household Size

Area	1 Person	2 Persons	3 Persons	4 Persons	5 Persons	6 or More Persons	Average Number of Persons in Private Households
Households							
Ajax	5,055	8,815	7,125	8,305	3,660	2,075	3.1
Ontario	1,230,975	1,584,415	803,030	783,925	310,860	174,305	2.6
Canada	3,673,310	4,544,820	2,081,900	1,903,300	724,405	392,885	2.5
Percent of Households							
Ajax	14.4	25.2	20.3	23.7	10.4	5.9	–
Ontario	25.2	32.4	16.4	16.0	6.4	3.6	–
Canada	27.6	34.1	15.6	14.3	5.4	2.9	–

Source: Statistics Canada. 2012. Census Profile. 2011 Census. Statistics Canada Catalogue no. 98-316-XWE. Ottawa. Released October 24 2012.
http://www12.statcan.gc.ca/census-recensement/2011/dp-pd/prof/index.cfm?Lang=E

Dwelling Type

Area	Single-detached House	Semi-detached House	Row House	Apartment: Building with Five or More Storeys	Apartment: Building with Fewer Than Five Storeys	Duplex Apartment	Movable Dwelling	Other Single-attached House
Number								
Ajax	23,100	2,000	5,075	2,145	1,435	1,270	0	10
Ontario	2,718,880	279,470	415,225	789,970	498,160	160,460	15,800	9,540
Canada	7,329,150	646,245	791,600	1,234,770	2,397,550	704,485	183,510	33,310
Percent of Dwellings								
Ajax	65.9	5.7	14.5	6.1	4.1	3.6	0.0	0.0
Ontario	55.6	5.7	8.5	16.2	10.2	3.3	0.3	0.2
Canada	55.0	4.9	5.9	9.3	18.0	5.3	1.4	0.3

Source: Statistics Canada. 2012. Census Profile. 2011 Census. Statistics Canada Catalogue no. 98-316-XWE. Ottawa. Released October 24 2012.
http://www12.statcan.gc.ca/census-recensement/2011/dp-pd/prof/index.cfm?Lang=E

Shelter Costs

	Owned Dwellings					Rented Dwellings		
Area	Number	Median Value[1] ($)	Average Value[1] ($)	Median Monthly Costs[2] ($)	Average Monthly Costs[2] ($)	Number	Median Monthly Costs[3] ($)	Average Monthly Costs[3] ($)
Ajax	30,460	333,633	357,867	1,650	1,615	4,570	1,050	1,061
Ontario	3,446,650	300,862	367,428	1,163	1,284	1,385,535	892	926
Canada	9,013,410	280,552	345,182	978	1,141	4,060,385	784	848

Note: All figures cover non-farm, non-reserve private dwellings; (1) Refers to the dollar amount expected by the owner if the dwelling were to be sold; (2) Includes all shelter expenses paid by households that own their dwellings, such as the mortgage payment and the costs of electricity, heat, water and other municipal services, property taxes and condominium fees; (3) Includes all shelter expenses paid by households that rent their dwellings, such as the monthly rent and the costs of electricity, heat and municipal services.
Source: Statistics Canada. 2013. 2011 National Household Survey. Statistics Canada Catalogue no. 99-004-XWE. Ottawa. Released September 11, 2013.

Occupied Private Dwellings by Period of Construction

Area	1960 or Before	1961 to 1980	1981 to 1990	1991 to 2000	2001 to 2005	2006 to 2011
Number						
Ajax	2,630	6,115	9,165	5,330	5,810	5,995
Ontario	1,330,235	1,420,570	763,430	609,310	414,795	348,310
Canada	3,273,105	4,152,715	2,112,110	1,707,880	1,031,020	1,042,430
Percent of Dwellings						
Ajax	7.5	17.5	26.2	15.2	16.6	17.1
Ontario	27.2	29.1	15.6	12.5	8.5	7.1
Canada	24.6	31.2	15.9	12.8	7.7	7.8

Note: Figures cover non-farm, non-reserve private dwellings and includes data up to May 10, 2011.
Source: Statistics Canada. 2013. 2011 National Household Survey. Statistics Canada Catalogue no. 99-004-XWE. Ottawa. Released September 11, 2013.

PROFILES / Ajax, Ontario

Educational Attainment

Area	No Certificate, Diploma or Degree	High School Diploma or Equivalent[1]	Apprenticeship or Trades Certificate or Diploma[2]	College, CÉGEP or Other Non-University Certificate or Diploma	University Certificate or Diploma Below the Bachelor Level[3]	Bachelor's Degree	University Certificate, Diploma or Degree Above Bachelor Level[4]
				Number			
				Total			
Ajax	12,655	25,245	5,565	20,050	4,960	12,300	5,770
Ontario	1,954,520	2,801,805	771,140	2,070,875	427,150	1,515,075	933,100
Canada	5,485,400	6,968,935	2,950,685	4,970,020	1,200,130	3,634,425	2,049,930
				Males			
Ajax	6,145	12,175	3,700	8,925	2,235	5,140	2,925
Ontario	957,040	1,337,055	520,390	894,235	193,355	692,345	470,290
Canada	2,742,875	3,305,415	1,928,970	2,118,430	513,235	1,643,080	1,043,350
				Females			
Ajax	6,510	13,070	1,865	11,125	2,720	7,165	2,845
Ontario	997,475	1,464,755	250,750	1,176,640	233,790	822,730	462,805
Canada	2,742,520	3,663,515	1,021,715	2,851,595	686,890	1,991,345	1,006,585
				Percent of Population			
				Total			
Ajax	14.6	29.2	6.4	23.2	5.7	14.2	6.7
Ontario	18.7	26.8	7.4	19.8	4.1	14.5	8.9
Canada	20.1	25.6	10.8	18.2	4.4	13.3	7.5
				Males			
Ajax	14.9	29.5	9.0	21.6	5.4	12.5	7.1
Ontario	18.9	26.4	10.3	17.7	3.8	13.7	9.3
Canada	20.6	24.9	14.5	15.9	3.9	12.4	7.8
				Females			
Ajax	14.4	28.9	4.1	24.6	6.0	15.8	6.3
Ontario	18.4	27.1	4.6	21.8	4.3	15.2	8.6
Canada	19.6	26.2	7.3	20.4	4.9	14.3	7.2

Note: Figures cover total population aged 15 years and over by highest certificate, diploma or degree; (1) Includes persons who have graduated from a secondary school or equivalent. It excludes persons with a postsecondary certificate, diploma or degree; (2) Includes Registered Apprenticeship certificates (including Certificate of Qualification, Journeyperson's designation) and other trades certificates or diplomas such as pre-employment or vocational certificates and diplomas from brief trade programs completed at community colleges, institutes of technology, vocational centres, and similar institutions; (3) Comparisons with other data sources suggest that the category 'University certificate or diploma below the bachelor's level' was over-reported in the NHS. This category likely includes some responses that are actually college certificates or diplomas, bachelor's degrees or other types of education (e.g., university transfer programs, bachelor's programs completed in other countries, incomplete bachelor's programs, non-university professional designations). We recommend users interpret the results for the 'University certificate or diploma below the bachelor's level' category with caution; (4) 'University certificate or diploma above bachelor level' includes the categories: 'Degree in medicine, dentistry, veterinary medicine or optometry,' 'Master's degree' and 'Earned doctorate.'
Source: Statistics Canada. 2013. 2011 National Household Survey. Statistics Canada Catalogue no. 99-004-XWE. Ottawa. Released September 11, 2013.

Household Income Distribution

Area	Less than $10,000	$10,000 to $19,999	$20,000 to $29,999	$30,000 to $39,999	$40,000 to $49,999	$50,000 to $59,999	$60,000 to $79,999	$80,000 to $99,999	$100,000 to $124,999	$125,000 to $149,999	$150,000 and Over
						Households					
Ajax	900	1,330	1,450	1,920	2,050	2,675	5,035	5,175	4,645	3,545	6,310
Ontario	201,780	354,530	405,725	425,410	425,720	398,705	680,850	552,660	497,970	331,460	611,840
Canada	626,705	1,141,945	1,193,925	1,271,675	1,206,800	1,102,120	1,865,280	1,458,240	1,260,770	802,555	1,389,240
						Percent of Households					
Ajax	2.6	3.8	4.1	5.5	5.9	7.6	14.4	14.8	13.3	10.1	18.0
Ontario	4.1	7.3	8.3	8.7	8.7	8.2	13.9	11.3	10.2	6.8	12.5
Canada	4.7	8.6	9.0	9.5	9.1	8.3	14.0	10.9	9.5	6.0	10.4

Note: Household income is the sum of the total incomes of all members of that household. Total income refers to monetary receipts from certain sources, before income taxes and deductions, during calendar year 2010.
Source: Statistics Canada. 2013. 2011 National Household Survey. Statistics Canada Catalogue no. 99-004-XWE. Ottawa. Released September 11, 2013.

Median and Average Household and Economic Family Income

Area	Median Household Income ($)	Average Household Income ($)	Median After-tax Household Income ($)	Average After-tax Household Income ($)	Median Economic Family Income ($)	Average Economic Family Income ($)	Median After-tax Economic Family Income ($)	Average After-tax Economic Family Income ($)
Ajax	88,262	100,305	75,662	83,770	96,573	108,414	82,904	90,553
Ontario	66,358	85,772	58,717	71,523	80,987	100,152	71,128	83,322
Canada	61,072	79,102	54,089	66,149	76,511	94,125	67,044	78,517

Note: Figures cover household and economic familiy income in 2010. A household is defined as a person or a group of persons (other than foreign residents) who occupy the same private dwelling and do not have a usual place of residence elsewhere in Canada. Every person is a member of one and only one household. An economic family is defined as a group of two or more persons who live in the same dwelling and are related to each other by blood, marriage, common-law, adoption or a foster relationship. A couple may be of opposite or same sex.
Source: Statistics Canada. 2013. 2011 National Household Survey. Statistics Canada Catalogue no. 99-004-XWE. Ottawa. Released September 11, 2013.

PROFILES / Ajax, Ontario

Individual Income Distribution

Area	Less than $10,000	$10,000 to $19,999	$20,000 to $29,999	$30,000 to $39,999	$40,000 to $49,999	$50,000 to $59,999	$60,000 to $79,999	$80,000 to $99,999	$100,000 to $124,999	$125,000 and Over
					Number					
					Total					
Ajax	15,510	11,885	8,080	8,540	8,265	7,140	9,890	6,060	2,820	2,515
Ontario	1,780,355	1,748,060	1,361,710	1,136,730	980,790	746,360	964,280	574,710	293,865	330,285
Canada	4,492,040	4,835,710	3,670,020	3,180,360	2,603,520	1,921,650	2,437,440	1,302,045	693,580	782,135
					Males					
Ajax	6,950	4,365	3,425	3,970	3,735	3,315	5,425	3,680	1,820	1,945
Ontario	781,095	669,815	580,990	535,255	491,125	407,005	569,205	341,160	201,125	244,500
Canada	1,936,365	1,864,880	1,588,260	1,522,190	1,333,510	1,079,780	1,473,145	823,720	492,905	599,905
					Females					
Ajax	8,560	7,525	4,650	4,575	4,530	3,830	4,465	2,375	1,000	575
Ontario	999,265	1,078,245	780,720	601,475	489,665	339,360	395,075	233,550	92,740	85,790
Canada	2,555,675	2,970,825	2,081,760	1,658,170	1,270,010	841,870	964,300	478,330	200,680	182,230
					Percent of Population					
					Total					
Ajax	19.2	14.7	10.0	10.6	10.2	8.8	12.3	7.5	3.5	3.1
Ontario	18.0	17.6	13.7	11.5	9.9	7.5	9.7	5.8	3.0	3.3
Canada	17.3	18.7	14.2	12.3	10.0	7.4	9.4	5.0	2.7	3.0
					Males					
Ajax	18.0	11.3	8.9	10.3	9.7	8.6	14.0	9.5	4.7	5.0
Ontario	16.2	13.9	12.1	11.1	10.2	8.4	11.8	7.1	4.2	5.1
Canada	15.2	14.7	12.5	12.0	10.5	8.5	11.6	6.5	3.9	4.7
					Females					
Ajax	20.3	17.9	11.0	10.9	10.8	9.1	10.6	5.6	2.4	1.4
Ontario	19.6	21.2	15.3	11.8	9.6	6.7	7.8	4.6	1.8	1.7
Canada	19.4	22.5	15.8	12.6	9.6	6.4	7.3	3.6	1.5	1.4

Note: Figures cover individuals aged 15 years and over with income. Income refers to monetary receipts from certain sources, before income taxes and deductions, during calendar year 2010.
Source: Statistics Canada. 2013. 2011 National Household Survey. Statistics Canada Catalogue no. 99-004-XWE. Ottawa. Released September 11, 2013.

Labour Force Status

| | In the Labour Force | | | Not in the |
Area	All	Employed	Unemployed	Labour Force
		Number		
		Total		
Ajax	63,065	57,570	5,495	23,475
Ontario	6,864,990	6,297,005	567,985	3,608,685
Canada	17,990,080	16,595,035	1,395,045	9,269,445
		Males		
Ajax	31,175	28,590	2,585	10,075
Ontario	3,542,030	3,249,165	292,865	1,522,690
Canada	9,388,570	8,634,310	754,255	3,906,785
		Females		
Ajax	31,890	28,980	2,910	13,405
Ontario	3,322,955	3,047,840	275,120	2,085,990
Canada	8,601,515	7,960,725	640,790	5,362,660
		Percent of Labour Force		
		Total		
Ajax	72.9	66.5	8.7	27.1
Ontario	65.5	60.1	8.3	34.5
Canada	66.0	60.9	7.8	34.0
		Males		
Ajax	75.6	69.3	8.3	24.4
Ontario	69.9	64.2	8.3	30.1
Canada	70.6	64.9	8.0	29.4
		Females		
Ajax	70.4	64.0	9.1	29.6
Ontario	61.4	56.3	8.3	38.6
Canada	61.6	57.0	7.4	38.4

Note: Figures are based on total population 15 years and over
Source: Statistics Canada. 2013. 2011 National Household Survey. Statistics Canada Catalogue no. 99-004-XWE. Ottawa. Released September 11, 2013.

Labour Force by Industry (NAICS Codes 11–52)

Area	Agriculture, forestry, fishing & hunting	Mining, quarrying, & oil & gas extraction	Utilities	Construction	Manufacturing	Wholesale Trade	Retail Trade	Transportation & warehousing	Information & cultural industries	Finance & insurance
Number – Total										
Ajax	105	95	1,310	3,430	5,040	3,095	6,695	2,825	2,560	6,240
Ontario	101,280	29,985	57,035	417,900	697,565	305,030	751,200	307,405	178,720	364,415
Canada	437,650	261,050	149,940	1,215,380	1,619,295	733,445	2,031,665	827,780	420,830	767,960
Males										
Ajax	55	90	805	2,985	3,520	1,885	3,225	2,140	1,420	2,520
Ontario	66,485	25,650	42,685	369,300	493,305	197,770	344,480	225,245	98,835	153,125
Canada	307,370	211,690	110,765	1,068,710	1,167,680	494,545	933,850	617,305	235,875	296,995
Females										
Ajax	50	0	510	445	1,515	1,210	3,470	680	1,135	3,715
Ontario	34,800	4,340	14,350	48,595	204,260	107,260	406,720	82,160	79,885	211,290
Canada	130,285	49,360	39,175	146,670	451,615	238,900	1,097,820	210,475	184,955	470,960
Percent of Labour Force – Total										
Ajax	0.2	0.2	2.1	5.6	8.3	5.1	11.0	4.6	4.2	10.2
Ontario	1.5	0.4	0.9	6.3	10.4	4.6	11.2	4.6	2.7	5.5
Canada	2.5	1.5	0.9	6.9	9.2	4.2	11.6	4.7	2.4	4.4
Males										
Ajax	0.2	0.3	2.7	9.9	11.6	6.2	10.7	7.1	4.7	8.3
Ontario	1.9	0.7	1.2	10.7	14.3	5.7	10.0	6.5	2.9	4.4
Canada	3.3	2.3	1.2	11.6	12.7	5.4	10.2	6.7	2.6	3.2
Females										
Ajax	0.2	0.0	1.7	1.4	4.9	3.9	11.3	2.2	3.7	12.1
Ontario	1.1	0.1	0.4	1.5	6.3	3.3	12.6	2.5	2.5	6.5
Canada	1.6	0.6	0.5	1.7	5.4	2.8	13.1	2.5	2.2	5.6

Note: Figures are based on total experienced labour force 15 years and over. Experienced labour force refers to persons who, during the week of Sunday, May 1 to Saturday, May 7, 2011, were employed and the unemployed who had last worked for pay or in self-employment in either 2010 or 2011.
Source: Statistics Canada. 2013. 2011 National Household Survey. Statistics Canada Catalogue no. 99-004-XWE. Ottawa. Released September 11, 2013.

Labour Force by Industry (NAICS Codes 53–91)

Area	Real estate & rental & leasing	Profess., scientific & tech. services	Mgmt of companies & enterprises	Admin. & support, waste mgmt & remed. services	Educational services	Health care & social assistance	Arts, entertain. & recreation	Accomm. & food services	Other services (except public admin.)	Public admin.
Number – Total										
Ajax	1,170	4,590	45	2,805	3,605	6,615	960	3,450	2,410	3,910
Ontario	133,980	511,020	6,525	309,630	499,690	692,130	144,065	417,675	296,340	458,665
Canada	321,895	1,240,850	17,460	728,330	1,301,435	1,949,650	363,405	1,130,750	807,800	1,261,050
Males										
Ajax	600	2,260	0	1,620	1,060	955	540	1,550	1,170	1,830
Ontario	72,835	281,420	3,540	172,475	162,765	120,165	75,035	177,240	133,795	236,655
Canada	179,090	688,625	9,380	411,250	424,915	349,430	188,270	469,990	372,940	652,510
Females										
Ajax	565	2,330	30	1,190	2,545	5,655	420	1,895	1,240	2,080
Ontario	61,145	229,600	2,990	137,155	336,925	571,965	69,030	240,430	162,550	222,015
Canada	142,805	552,225	8,075	317,085	876,515	1,600,220	175,135	660,760	434,865	608,535
Percent of Labour Force – Total										
Ajax	1.9	7.5	0.1	4.6	5.9	10.9	1.6	5.7	4.0	6.4
Ontario	2.0	7.6	0.1	4.6	7.5	10.4	2.2	6.3	4.4	6.9
Canada	1.8	7.1	0.1	4.1	7.4	11.1	2.1	6.4	4.6	7.2
Males										
Ajax	2.0	7.5	0.0	5.4	3.5	3.2	1.8	5.1	3.9	6.1
Ontario	2.1	8.2	0.1	5.0	4.7	3.5	2.2	5.1	3.9	6.9
Canada	1.9	7.5	0.1	4.5	4.6	3.8	2.0	5.1	4.1	7.1
Females										
Ajax	1.8	7.6	0.1	3.9	8.3	18.4	1.4	6.2	4.0	6.8
Ontario	1.9	7.1	0.1	4.2	10.4	17.7	2.1	7.4	5.0	6.9
Canada	1.7	6.6	0.1	3.8	10.4	19.1	2.1	7.9	5.2	7.2

Note: Figures are based on total experienced labour force 15 years and over. Experienced labour force refers to persons who, during the week of Sunday, May 1 to Saturday, May 7, 2011, were employed and the unemployed who had last worked for pay or in self-employment in either 2010 or 2011.
Source: Statistics Canada. 2013. 2011 National Household Survey. Statistics Canada Catalogue no. 99-004-XWE. Ottawa. Released September 11, 2013.

Occupation

Area	Mgmt	Business, Finance & Admin.	Natural/ Applied Sciences & Related	Health	Education, Law & Social, Community & Government Services	Art, Culture, Recreation & Sport	Sales & Service	Trades, Transport & Equip. Operators & Related	Natural Resources, Agri. & Related Production	Mfg & Utilities
					Number					
					Total					
Ajax	7,890	12,965	5,050	3,630	6,270	1,615	13,685	6,750	625	2,470
Ontario	770,580	1,138,330	494,500	392,695	801,465	206,420	1,550,260	868,515	106,810	350,685
Canada	1,963,600	2,902,045	1,237,775	1,107,200	2,064,675	503,415	4,068,170	2,537,775	397,930	805,040
					Males					
Ajax	4,810	3,650	3,875	650	1,810	710	6,185	6,285	535	1,735
Ontario	474,655	352,505	384,345	78,330	264,570	96,055	673,880	812,280	82,610	233,565
Canada	1,229,460	854,190	966,355	217,520	676,550	232,535	1,745,705	2,385,615	318,945	564,300
					Females					
Ajax	3,075	9,310	1,180	2,980	4,465	905	7,505	465	85	730
Ontario	295,920	785,825	110,150	314,370	536,895	110,370	876,380	56,230	24,200	117,115
Canada	734,140	2,047,855	271,415	889,675	1,388,130	270,875	2,322,465	152,165	78,980	240,740
					Percent of Labour Force					
					Total					
Ajax	12.9	21.3	8.3	6.0	10.3	2.6	22.5	11.1	1.0	4.1
Ontario	11.5	17.0	7.4	5.9	12.0	3.1	23.2	13.0	1.6	5.2
Canada	11.2	16.5	7.0	6.3	11.7	2.9	23.1	14.4	2.3	4.6
					Males					
Ajax	15.9	12.1	12.8	2.1	6.0	2.3	20.5	20.8	1.8	5.7
Ontario	13.7	10.2	11.1	2.3	7.7	2.8	19.5	23.5	2.4	6.8
Canada	13.4	9.3	10.5	2.4	7.4	2.5	19.0	26.0	3.5	6.1
					Females					
Ajax	10.0	30.3	3.8	9.7	14.5	2.9	24.4	1.5	0.3	2.4
Ontario	9.2	24.3	3.4	9.7	16.6	3.4	27.2	1.7	0.7	3.6
Canada	8.7	24.4	3.2	10.6	16.5	3.2	27.7	1.8	0.9	2.9

Note: Figures are based on total experienced labour force 15 years and over
Source: Statistics Canada. 2013. 2011 National Household Survey. Statistics Canada Catalogue no. 99-004-XWE. Ottawa. Released September 11, 2013.

Place of Work Status

Area	Worked at Home	Worked Outside Canada	No Fixed Workplace Address	Worked at Usual Place
		Number		
		Total		
Ajax	2,785	105	6,050	48,625
Ontario	423,790	31,390	670,835	5,170,980
Canada	1,142,640	66,460	1,868,245	13,517,690
		Males		
Ajax	1,275	80	4,380	22,855
Ontario	216,900	21,150	486,560	2,524,555
Canada	582,150	47,355	1,400,485	6,604,325
		Females		
Ajax	1,515	25	1,670	25,775
Ontario	206,895	10,240	184,275	2,646,420
Canada	560,490	19,100	467,760	6,913,370
		Percent of Labour Force		
		Total		
Ajax	4.8	0.2	10.5	84.5
Ontario	6.7	0.5	10.7	82.1
Canada	6.9	0.4	11.3	81.5
		Males		
Ajax	4.5	0.3	15.3	79.9
Ontario	6.7	0.7	15.0	77.7
Canada	6.7	0.5	16.2	76.5
		Females		
Ajax	5.2	0.1	5.8	88.9
Ontario	6.8	0.3	6.0	86.8
Canada	7.0	0.2	5.9	86.8

Note: Figures are based on total employed labour force 15 years and over.
Source: Statistics Canada. 2013. 2011 National Household Survey. Statistics Canada Catalogue no. 99-004-XWE. Ottawa. Released September 11, 2013.

Mode of Transportation to Work

Area	Car; Truck; Van; as Driver	Car; Truck; Van; as Passenger	Public Transit	Walked	Bicycled	All Other Modes
			Number			
			Total			
Ajax	40,440	3,355	8,710	1,335	180	655
Ontario	4,235,315	357,110	818,270	299,095	69,885	62,145
Canada	11,393,140	867,050	1,851,525	880,815	201,780	191,625
			Males			
Ajax	22,065	1,135	3,095	540	125	280
Ontario	2,316,680	143,410	340,995	131,765	47,635	30,635
Canada	6,238,835	349,530	788,290	387,580	135,840	104,725
			Females			
Ajax	18,380	2,220	5,615	800	55	370
Ontario	1,918,640	213,700	477,275	167,325	22,250	31,515
Canada	5,154,305	517,520	1,063,235	493,230	65,940	86,900
			Percent of Labour Force			
			Total			
Ajax	74.0	6.1	15.9	2.4	0.3	1.2
Ontario	72.5	6.1	14.0	5.1	1.2	1.1
Canada	74.0	5.6	12.0	5.7	1.3	1.2
			Males			
Ajax	81.0	4.2	11.4	2.0	0.5	1.0
Ontario	76.9	4.8	11.3	4.4	1.6	1.0
Canada	77.9	4.4	9.8	4.8	1.7	1.3
			Females			
Ajax	67.0	8.1	20.5	2.9	0.2	1.3
Ontario	67.8	7.5	16.9	5.9	0.8	1.1
Canada	69.8	7.0	14.4	6.7	0.9	1.2

Note: Figures are based on total employed labour force 15 years and over.
Source: Statistics Canada. 2013. 2011 National Household Survey. Statistics Canada Catalogue no. 99-004-XWE. Ottawa. Released September 11, 2013.

Visible Minority Population Characteristics

Area	Total Minority	South Asian[1]	Chinese	Black	Filipino	Latin American	Arab	SE Asian[2]	West Asian[3]	Korean	Japanese	Multiple[4]
					Number							
					Total							
Ajax	49,995	15,025	2,555	17,510	4,820	1,065	1,165	645	1,770	205	305	2,135
Ontario	3,279,565	965,990	629,140	539,205	275,380	172,560	151,645	137,875	122,530	78,290	29,085	96,735
Canada	6,264,750	1,567,400	1,324,750	945,665	619,310	381,280	380,620	312,075	206,840	161,130	87,270	171,935
					Males							
Ajax	23,850	7,400	1,205	8,390	2,115	440	665	255	900	95	120	1,050
Ontario	1,582,480	484,355	301,575	251,295	116,825	83,205	79,620	67,645	62,515	38,045	13,345	46,765
Canada	3,043,010	790,755	632,325	453,005	268,885	186,355	203,485	154,035	105,620	77,165	38,270	83,335
					Females							
Ajax	26,145	7,625	1,350	9,115	2,710	625	500	390	870	110	190	1,090
Ontario	1,697,085	481,635	327,570	287,915	158,555	89,360	72,025	70,230	60,010	40,250	15,740	49,970
Canada	3,221,745	776,650	692,420	492,660	350,425	194,925	177,140	158,045	101,220	83,965	48,990	88,600
					Percent of Population							
					Total							
Ajax	45.8	13.8	2.3	16.0	4.4	1.0	1.1	0.6	1.6	0.2	0.3	2.0
Ontario	25.9	7.6	5.0	4.3	2.2	1.4	1.2	1.1	1.0	0.6	0.2	0.8
Canada	19.1	4.8	4.0	2.9	1.9	1.2	1.2	0.9	0.6	0.5	0.3	0.5
					Males							
Ajax	45.2	14.0	2.3	15.9	4.0	0.8	1.3	0.5	1.7	0.2	0.2	2.0
Ontario	25.6	7.8	4.9	4.1	1.9	1.3	1.3	1.1	1.0	0.6	0.2	0.8
Canada	18.8	4.9	3.9	2.8	1.7	1.2	1.3	1.0	0.7	0.5	0.2	0.5
					Females							
Ajax	46.3	13.5	2.4	16.2	4.8	1.1	0.9	0.7	1.5	0.2	0.3	1.9
Ontario	26.2	7.4	5.1	4.4	2.5	1.4	1.1	1.1	0.9	0.6	0.2	0.8
Canada	19.3	4.7	4.1	3.0	2.1	1.2	1.1	0.9	0.6	0.5	0.3	0.5

Note: The Employment Equity Act defines visible minorities as 'persons, other than Aboriginal peoples, who are non-Caucasian in race or non-white in colour';
(1) Includes 'East Indian,' 'Pakistani,' 'Sri Lankan,' etc.; (2) Includes 'Vietnamese,' 'Cambodian,' 'Malaysian,' 'Laotian,' etc.; (3) Includes 'Iranian,' 'Afghan,' etc.; (4) Includes respondents who reported more than one visible minority group by checking two or more mark-in circles, e.g., 'Black' and 'South Asian.'
Source: Statistics Canada. 2013. 2011 National Household Survey. Statistics Canada Catalogue no. 99-004-XWE. Ottawa. Released September 11, 2013.

PROFILES / Ajax, Ontario

Aboriginal Population

Area	Aboriginal Identity[1]	First Nations (North American Indian) Single Identity[2]	Métis Single Identity	Inuk (Inuit) Single Identity	Multiple Aboriginal Identities[3]	Aboriginal Identities Not Included Elsewhere
Number						
Total						
Ajax	1,080	710	315	15	15	25
Ontario	301,430	201,100	86,020	3,355	2,910	8,040
Canada	1,400,685	851,560	451,795	59,440	11,415	26,475
Males						
Ajax	525	340	165	0	0	0
Ontario	145,020	96,620	41,755	1,475	1,420	3,750
Canada	682,190	411,785	223,335	29,495	5,525	12,055
Females						
Ajax	555	370	150	0	0	20
Ontario	156,410	104,485	44,260	1,880	1,490	4,295
Canada	718,500	439,775	228,460	29,950	5,890	14,420
Percent of Population						
Total						
Ajax	1.0	0.7	0.3	0.0	0.0	0.0
Ontario	2.4	1.6	0.7	0.0	0.0	0.1
Canada	4.3	2.6	1.4	0.2	0.0	0.1
Males						
Ajax	1.0	0.6	0.3	0.0	0.0	0.0
Ontario	2.3	1.6	0.7	0.0	0.0	0.1
Canada	4.2	2.5	1.4	0.2	0.0	0.1
Females						
Ajax	1.0	0.7	0.3	0.0	0.0	0.0
Ontario	2.4	1.6	0.7	0.0	0.0	0.1
Canada	4.3	2.6	1.4	0.2	0.0	0.1

Note: (1) Includes persons who reported being an Aboriginal person, that is, First Nations (North American Indian), Métis or Inuk (Inuit) and/or those who reported Registered or Treaty Indian status, that is registered under the Indian Act of Canada, and/or those who reported membership in a First Nation or Indian band. Aboriginal peoples of Canada are defined in the Constitution Act, 1982, section 35-2 as including the Indian, Inuit and Métis peoples of Canada; (2) Users should be aware that the estimates associated with this variable are more affected than most by the incomplete enumeration of certain Indian reserves and Indian settlements in the National Household Survey (NHS); (3) Includes persons who reported being any two or all three of the following: First Nations (North American Indian), Métis or Inuk (Inuit).
Source: Statistics Canada. 2013. 2011 National Household Survey. Statistics Canada Catalogue no. 99-004-XWE. Ottawa. Released September 11, 2013.

Ethnic Origin

Area	North American Aboriginal	Other North American	European	Caribbean	Latin, Central and South American	African	Asian	Oceania
Number								
Total								
Ajax	1,875	23,340	58,700	16,435	4,970	4,705	29,845	375
Ontario	441,395	3,059,480	8,231,410	396,485	271,545	331,460	2,604,595	19,410
Canada	1,836,035	11,070,455	20,157,965	627,590	544,375	766,735	5,011,225	74,875
Males								
Ajax	815	11,560	28,150	7,770	2,210	2,375	14,285	240
Ontario	210,490	1,507,105	4,019,885	181,805	130,035	160,940	1,265,540	9,855
Canada	885,675	5,462,685	9,913,150	291,640	264,635	387,360	2,435,540	37,490
Females								
Ajax	1,055	11,780	30,550	8,665	2,755	2,335	15,560	140
Ontario	230,905	1,552,380	4,211,525	214,675	141,510	170,515	1,339,050	9,555
Canada	950,360	5,607,770	10,244,820	335,945	279,740	379,380	2,575,680	37,385
Percent of Population								
Total								
Ajax	1.7	21.4	53.7	15.0	4.6	4.3	27.3	0.3
Ontario	3.5	24.2	65.1	3.1	2.1	2.6	20.6	0.2
Canada	5.6	33.7	61.4	1.9	1.7	2.3	15.3	0.2
Males								
Ajax	1.5	21.9	53.3	14.7	4.2	4.5	27.0	0.5
Ontario	3.4	24.4	65.0	2.9	2.1	2.6	20.5	0.2
Canada	5.5	33.8	61.3	1.8	1.6	2.4	15.1	0.2
Females								
Ajax	1.9	20.9	54.2	15.4	4.9	4.1	27.6	0.2
Ontario	3.6	24.0	65.1	3.3	2.2	2.6	20.7	0.1
Canada	5.7	33.6	61.4	2.0	1.7	2.3	15.4	0.2

Note: The sum of the ethnic groups in this table is greater than the total population estimate because a person may report more than one ethnic origin in the NHS.
Source: Statistics Canada. 2013. 2011 National Household Survey. Statistics Canada Catalogue no. 99-004-XWE. Ottawa. Released September 11, 2013.

Religion

Area	Buddhist	Christian	Hindu	Jewish	Muslim	Sikh	Traditional (Aboriginal) Spirituality	Other Religions	No Religious Affiliation
				Number					
				Total					
Ajax	785	72,775	6,490	410	7,550	590	0	250	20,365
Ontario	163,750	8,167,295	366,720	195,540	581,950	179,765	15,905	53,080	2,927,790
Canada	366,830	22,102,745	497,965	329,495	1,053,945	454,965	64,935	130,835	7,850,605
				Males					
Ajax	350	34,375	3,055	180	3,760	285	0	130	10,680
Ontario	75,355	3,839,925	183,580	95,795	293,925	90,515	7,600	23,555	1,571,195
Canada	168,465	10,497,775	250,435	161,265	540,555	229,435	31,805	57,745	4,225,645
				Females					
Ajax	435	38,405	3,440	235	3,790	305	0	120	9,680
Ontario	88,395	4,327,365	183,140	99,740	288,025	89,250	8,310	29,525	1,356,600
Canada	198,365	11,604,975	247,525	168,235	513,395	225,530	33,135	73,090	3,624,965
				Percent of Population					
				Total					
Ajax	0.7	66.6	5.9	0.4	6.9	0.5	0.0	0.2	18.6
Ontario	1.3	64.6	2.9	1.5	4.6	1.4	0.1	0.4	23.1
Canada	1.1	67.3	1.5	1.0	3.2	1.4	0.2	0.4	23.9
				Males					
Ajax	0.7	65.1	5.8	0.3	7.1	0.5	0.0	0.2	20.2
Ontario	1.2	62.1	3.0	1.5	4.8	1.5	0.1	0.4	25.4
Canada	1.0	64.9	1.5	1.0	3.3	1.4	0.2	0.4	26.1
				Females					
Ajax	0.8	68.1	6.1	0.4	6.7	0.5	0.0	0.2	17.2
Ontario	1.4	66.9	2.8	1.5	4.5	1.4	0.1	0.5	21.0
Canada	1.2	69.5	1.5	1.0	3.1	1.4	0.2	0.4	21.7

Note: Religion refers to the person's self-identification as having a connection or affiliation with any religious denomination, group, body, sect, cult or other religiously defined community or system of belief. Religion is not limited to formal membership in a religious organization or group. Persons without a religious connection or affiliation can self-identify as atheist, agnostic or humanist, or can provide another applicable response.
Source: Statistics Canada. 2013. 2011 National Household Survey. Statistics Canada Catalogue no. 99-004-XWE. Ottawa. Released September 11, 2013.

Religion—Christian Denominations

Area	Anglican	Baptist	Catholic	Christian Orthodox	Lutheran	Pentecostal	Presbyterian	United Church	Other Christian
				Number					
				Total					
Ajax	6,565	2,030	34,105	3,005	865	4,600	2,435	6,240	12,940
Ontario	774,560	244,650	3,976,610	297,710	163,460	213,945	319,585	952,465	1,224,300
Canada	1,631,845	635,840	12,810,705	550,690	478,185	478,705	472,385	2,007,610	3,036,780
				Males					
Ajax	3,070	945	16,430	1,495	365	1,950	1,235	2,635	6,250
Ontario	355,175	112,285	1,895,940	145,825	75,225	94,955	148,535	435,255	576,730
Canada	752,945	293,905	6,167,290	270,205	221,525	217,850	218,955	912,545	1,442,550
				Females					
Ajax	3,495	1,085	17,680	1,505	500	2,645	1,200	3,605	6,695
Ontario	419,390	132,370	2,080,665	151,885	88,230	118,990	171,050	517,210	647,570
Canada	878,900	341,940	6,643,415	280,485	256,660	260,850	253,430	1,095,065	1,594,230
				Percent of Population					
				Total					
Ajax	6.0	1.9	31.2	2.8	0.8	4.2	2.2	5.7	11.8
Ontario	6.1	1.9	31.4	2.4	1.3	1.7	2.5	7.5	9.7
Canada	5.0	1.9	39.0	1.7	1.5	1.5	1.4	6.1	9.2
				Males					
Ajax	5.8	1.8	31.1	2.8	0.7	3.7	2.3	5.0	11.8
Ontario	5.7	1.8	30.7	2.4	1.2	1.5	2.4	7.0	9.3
Canada	4.7	1.8	38.2	1.7	1.4	1.3	1.4	5.6	8.9
				Females					
Ajax	6.2	1.9	31.3	2.7	0.9	4.7	2.1	6.4	11.9
Ontario	6.5	2.0	32.2	2.3	1.4	1.8	2.6	8.0	10.0
Canada	5.3	2.0	39.8	1.7	1.5	1.6	1.5	6.6	9.6

Note: Religion refers to the person's self-identification as having a connection or affiliation with any religious denomination, group, body, sect, cult or other religiously defined community or system of belief. Religion is not limited to formal membership in a religious organization or group. Persons without a religious connection or affiliation can self-identify as atheist, agnostic or humanist, or can provide another applicable response.
Source: Statistics Canada. 2013. 2011 National Household Survey. Statistics Canada Catalogue no. 99-004-XWE. Ottawa. Released September 11, 2013.

PROFILES / Ajax, Ontario

Immigrant Status and Period of Immigration

Area	Non-Immigrants[1]	Immigrants All	Before 1971	1971 to 1980	1981 to 1990	1991 to 2000	2001 to 2005	2006 to 2011	Non-Permanent Residents[3]
				Number Total					
Ajax	71,365	37,315	5,770	6,635	7,160	9,500	5,245	3,010	540
Ontario	8,906,000	3,611,365	723,030	464,380	538,285	866,220	518,405	501,060	134,425
Canada	25,720,175	6,775,765	1,261,055	870,775	949,890	1,539,050	992,070	1,162,915	356,385
				Males					
Ajax	34,915	17,660	2,760	3,195	3,375	4,480	2,475	1,375	235
Ontario	4,410,240	1,706,385	341,820	217,990	258,095	408,270	245,850	234,360	64,825
Canada	12,753,235	3,231,370	605,430	416,670	454,570	724,905	474,545	555,245	178,515
				Females					
Ajax	36,450	19,655	3,010	3,435	3,785	5,020	2,770	1,630	305
Ontario	4,495,765	1,904,985	381,210	246,390	280,190	457,950	272,550	266,695	69,600
Canada	12,966,935	3,544,400	655,625	454,105	495,325	814,145	517,530	607,670	177,870
				Percent of Population Total					
Ajax	65.3	34.2	5.3	6.1	6.6	8.7	4.8	2.8	0.5
Ontario	70.4	28.5	5.7	3.7	4.3	6.8	4.1	4.0	1.1
Canada	78.3	20.6	3.8	2.7	2.9	4.7	3.0	3.5	1.1
				Males					
Ajax	66.1	33.4	5.2	6.0	6.4	8.5	4.7	2.6	0.4
Ontario	71.3	27.6	5.5	3.5	4.2	6.6	4.0	3.8	1.0
Canada	78.9	20.0	3.7	2.6	2.8	4.5	2.9	3.4	1.1
				Females					
Ajax	64.6	34.8	5.3	6.1	6.7	8.9	4.9	2.9	0.5
Ontario	69.5	29.4	5.9	3.8	4.3	7.1	4.2	4.1	1.1
Canada	77.7	21.2	3.9	2.7	3.0	4.9	3.1	3.6	1.1

Note: (1) Non-immigrant refers to a person who is a Canadian citizen by birth; (2) Immigrant refers to a person who is or has ever been a landed immigrant/permanent resident. This person has been granted the right to live in Canada permanently by immigration authorities. Some immigrants have resided in Canada for a number of years, while others have arrived recently. Some immigrants are Canadian citizens, while others are not. Most immigrants are born outside Canada, but a small number are born in Canada. In the 2011 National Household Survey, 'Immigrants' includes immigrants who landed in Canada prior to May 10, 2011; (3) Non-permanent resident refers to a person from another country who has a work or study permit, or who is a refugee claimant, and any non-Canadian-born family member living in Canada with them.
Source: Statistics Canada. 2013. 2011 National Household Survey. Statistics Canada Catalogue no. 99-004-XWE. Ottawa. Released September 11, 2013.

Mother Tongue

Area	English	French	Non-official Language	English & French	English & Non-official Language	French & Non-official Language	English, French & Non-official Language
			Number Total				
Ajax	83,200	1,580	21,680	325	2,335	115	70
Ontario	8,677,040	493,300	3,264,435	46,605	219,425	13,645	7,615
Canada	18,858,980	7,054,975	6,567,680	144,685	396,330	74,430	24,095
			Males				
Ajax	40,330	710	10,375	160	1,130	60	30
Ontario	4,276,970	232,785	1,562,190	21,805	106,790	6,285	3,495
Canada	9,345,225	3,452,380	3,157,785	69,975	192,000	36,535	11,965
			Females				
Ajax	42,865	875	11,305	160	1,205	60	40
Ontario	4,400,065	260,510	1,702,240	24,795	112,635	7,365	4,115
Canada	9,513,750	3,602,590	3,409,895	74,710	204,330	37,890	12,130
			Percent of Population Total				
Ajax	76.1	1.4	19.8	0.3	2.1	0.1	0.1
Ontario	68.2	3.9	25.7	0.4	1.7	0.1	0.1
Canada	56.9	21.3	19.8	0.4	1.2	0.2	0.1
			Males				
Ajax	76.4	1.3	19.7	0.3	2.1	0.1	0.1
Ontario	68.9	3.7	25.2	0.4	1.7	0.1	0.1
Canada	57.5	21.2	19.4	0.4	1.2	0.2	0.1
			Females				
Ajax	75.8	1.5	20.0	0.3	2.1	0.1	0.1
Ontario	67.6	4.0	26.1	0.4	1.7	0.1	0.1
Canada	56.4	21.4	20.2	0.4	1.2	0.2	0.1

Note: Figures cover total population excluding institutional residents.
Source: Statistics Canada. 2012. Census Profile. 2011 Census. Statistics Canada Catalogue no. 98-316-XWE. Ottawa. Released October 24 2012.
http://www12.statcan.gc.ca/census-recensement/2011/dp-pd/prof/index.cfm?Lang=E

Language Spoken Most Often at Home

Area	English	French	Non-official Language	English & French	English & Non-official Language	French & Non-official Language	English, French & Non-official Language
			Number				
			Total				
Ajax	93,430	760	10,030	265	4,660	45	110
Ontario	10,044,810	284,115	1,827,870	37,955	509,105	6,370	11,845
Canada	21,457,075	6,827,865	3,673,865	131,205	875,135	109,700	46,330
			Males				
Ajax	45,195	370	4,800	110	2,245	20	45
Ontario	4,930,610	133,495	872,860	17,250	248,050	2,855	5,225
Canada	10,585,620	3,348,235	1,767,310	63,475	425,370	53,010	22,845
			Females				
Ajax	48,230	395	5,235	155	2,415	25	65
Ontario	5,114,200	150,620	955,010	20,705	261,055	3,520	6,620
Canada	10,871,455	3,479,625	1,906,555	67,730	449,765	56,690	23,485
			Percent of Population				
			Total				
Ajax	85.5	0.7	9.2	0.2	4.3	0.0	0.1
Ontario	79.0	2.2	14.4	0.3	4.0	0.1	0.1
Canada	64.8	20.6	11.1	0.4	2.6	0.3	0.1
			Males				
Ajax	85.6	0.7	9.1	0.2	4.3	0.0	0.1
Ontario	79.4	2.1	14.1	0.3	4.0	0.0	0.1
Canada	65.1	20.6	10.9	0.4	2.6	0.3	0.1
			Females				
Ajax	85.3	0.7	9.3	0.3	4.3	0.0	0.1
Ontario	78.5	2.3	14.7	0.3	4.0	0.1	0.1
Canada	64.5	20.6	11.3	0.4	2.7	0.3	0.1

Note: Figures cover total population excluding institutional residents.
Source: Statistics Canada. 2012. Census Profile. 2011 Census. Statistics Canada Catalogue no. 98-316-XWE. Ottawa. Released October 24 2012.
http://www12.statcan.gc.ca/census-recensement/2011/dp-pd/prof/index.cfm?Lang=E

Knowledge of Official Languages

Area	English Only	French Only	English & French	Neither English nor French
		Number		
		Total		
Ajax	100,430	80	7,655	1,140
Ontario	10,984,360	42,980	1,395,805	298,920
Canada	22,564,665	4,165,015	5,795,570	595,920
		Males		
Ajax	49,130	35	3,250	370
Ontario	5,445,050	18,805	627,725	118,765
Canada	11,222,185	1,925,340	2,876,560	241,790
		Females		
Ajax	51,300	40	4,405	775
Ontario	5,539,310	24,175	768,085	180,155
Canada	11,342,485	2,239,680	2,919,005	354,135
		Percent of Population		
		Total		
Ajax	91.9	0.1	7.0	1.0
Ontario	86.3	0.3	11.0	2.3
Canada	68.1	12.6	17.5	1.8
		Males		
Ajax	93.1	0.1	6.2	0.7
Ontario	87.7	0.3	10.1	1.9
Canada	69.0	11.8	17.7	1.5
		Females		
Ajax	90.8	0.1	7.8	1.4
Ontario	85.1	0.4	11.8	2.8
Canada	67.3	13.3	17.3	2.1

Note: Figures cover total population excluding institutional residents.
Source: Statistics Canada. 2012. Census Profile. 2011 Census. Statistics Canada Catalogue no. 98-316-XWE. Ottawa. Released October 24 2012.
http://www12.statcan.gc.ca/census-recensement/2011/dp-pd/prof/index.cfm?Lang=E

Barrie, Ontario

Background

Located on the western shores of Lake Simcoe and overlooking Kempenfelt Bay, Barrie is one hour north of the Greater Toronto Area (GTA) and is considered the "Gateway to Cottage Country." Although Barrie is situated within Simcoe County, a popular cottage region, the city is politically independent.

Barrie was first inhabited by First Nations peoples who rested on the western shores of Kempenfelt Bay before portaging Lake Simcoe and the Nottawasage River toward Lake Huron. Settlers and former British soldiers arrived shortly after the War of 1812. The railway built in 1865, and later Highway 400 in 1950, linked Barrie to the City of York (Toronto).

Attractions in Barrie include the MacLaren Art Centre, the Georgian Theatre, Simcoe County Museum and the Barrie Speedway. Boat cruises and dragon boat races on Lake Simcoe and treetop trekking through hardwood forests are popular summer activities. Barrie's Snowbelt location offers some of Central Ontario's best skiing conditions.

Barrie's primary resources are advanced manufacturing and automotive technology. Growing industries include traditional manufacturing, such as packaging, and industrial automation. The city's emerging industry is geo-synthetic biosciences. One of the world's largest industrial engineering facilities, the Industrial Research and Development Institute Facility, is located 40 minutes outside Barrie. In 2012, IBM opened the IBM Canada Leadership Data Centre, a $175-million-dollar computing facility, the first of its kind in Canada.

Annual festivals and events include Winterfest, the Spring Tonic Maple Syrup Festival, Jazz by the Bay and the Inter-Tribal Competition Pow Wow.

Barrie has summer highs of plus 24.73 degrees Celsius, winter lows of minus 10.93 degrees Celsius, and an average rainfall just over 700 mm per year.

Rankings

- Barrie was identified as one of Canada's "Smartest Cities" by the Canadian Council on Learning. Barrie ranked #10 out of more than 4,500 Canadian cities and communities. Criteria: formal education, skills acquisition, city social values and cultural opportunities per capita. Barrie tied with Gatineau, Windsor and Kelowna. The top 3 "Smartest Cities" were Victoria, Saskatoon and Calgary. *Canadian Council on Learning, 2010 Composite Learning Index with files from Maclean's "Canada's Smartest Cities 2010: Overall Rankings," March 20, 2010*
- Barrie's crime rate was identified as reflective of Canada's overall crime in 2011. Statistics Canada's crime severity index (CSI) ranked Barrie #29 out of the 33 census metropolitan areas (CMAs) in Canada (the lower a city ranks on the index, the safer the city). In Barrie and across Canada, crime had decreased by 3%, and was now the lowest crime rate since the early 1970s. *Statistics Canada, Canadian Centre for Justice Statistics, Uniform Crime Reporting Survey, July 24, 2012*
- Barrie was ranked as one of Canada's most caring communities. The City of Barrie ranked #14 out of 37 Canadian cities in terms of local volunteer rates. Just over 50% of Barrie residents (over the age of 15) volunteered their time in 2004. Canadians volunteered nearly 2.1 billion hours in 2010. *The Canadian Council on Learning with files from Statistics Canada: Canada Survey of Giving, Volunteering and Participation 2004 and March 21st, 2012*

PROFILES / Barrie, Ontario

Population Growth and Density

Area	Population in 2001	Population in 2006	Population in 2011	Population Change 2001–2006	Population Change 2006–2011	Land Area (sq. km)	Population Density per sq. km
Barrie	103,710	128,430	135,711	23.8	5.7	77.39	1,753.6
Ontario	11,410,046	12,160,282	12,851,821	6.6	5.7	908,607.67	14.1
Canada	30,007,094	31,612,897	33,476,688	5.4	5.9	8,965,121.42	3.7

Source: Statistics Canada. 2012. Census Profile. 2011 Census. Statistics Canada Catalogue no. 98-316-XWE. Ottawa. Released October 24 2012. http://www12.statcan.gc.ca/census-recensement/2011/dp-pd/prof/index.cfm?Lang=E;
Statistics Canada 2007. 2006 Community Profiles. 2006 Census. Statistics Canada Catalogue no. 92-591-XWE. Ottawa. Released March 13 2007. http://www12.statcan.ca/census-recensement/2006/dp-pd/prof/92-591/index.cfm?Lang=E

Gender

Area	Males	Females
	Number	
Barrie	65,675	70,035
Ontario	6,263,140	6,588,685
Canada	16,414,225	17,062,460
	Percent of Population	
Barrie	48.4	51.6
Ontario	48.7	51.3
Canada	49.0	51.0

Source: Statistics Canada. 2012. Census Profile. 2011 Census. Statistics Canada Catalogue no. 98-316-XWE. Ottawa. Released October 24 2012. http://www12.statcan.gc.ca/census-recensement/2011/dp-pd/prof/index.cfm?Lang=E

Marital Status

Area	Married[1]	Living Common-law	Single[2]	Separated	Divorced	Widowed
			Number			
			Total			
Barrie	50,565	11,180	30,340	4,215	7,130	6,015
Ontario	5,367,400	791,210	2,985,020	319,805	593,730	613,880
Canada	12,941,960	3,142,525	7,816,045	698,240	1,686,035	1,584,530
			Males			
Barrie	25,235	5,575	16,170	1,700	2,605	1,035
Ontario	2,681,320	397,620	1,583,760	133,790	231,160	117,980
Canada	6,470,300	1,575,495	4,206,320	299,655	680,415	310,940
			Females			
Barrie	25,335	5,605	14,170	2,515	4,525	4,975
Ontario	2,686,075	393,590	1,401,260	186,015	362,570	495,905
Canada	6,471,660	1,567,035	3,609,730	398,585	1,005,620	1,273,590
			Percent of Population			
			Total			
Barrie	46.2	10.2	27.7	3.9	6.5	5.5
Ontario	50.3	7.4	28.0	3.0	5.6	5.8
Canada	46.4	11.3	28.0	2.5	6.0	5.7
			Males			
Barrie	48.2	10.7	30.9	3.2	5.0	2.0
Ontario	52.1	7.7	30.8	2.6	4.5	2.3
Canada	47.8	11.6	31.1	2.2	5.0	2.3
			Females			
Barrie	44.3	9.8	24.8	4.4	7.9	8.7
Ontario	48.6	7.1	25.4	3.4	6.6	9.0
Canada	45.2	10.9	25.2	2.8	7.0	8.9

Note: (1) and not separated, (2) never legally married
Source: Statistics Canada. 2012. Census Profile. 2011 Census. Statistics Canada Catalogue no. 98-316-XWE. Ottawa. Released October 24 2012. http://www12.statcan.gc.ca/census-recensement/2011/dp-pd/prof/index.cfm?Lang=E

Age Characteristics: 0 to 49 Years

Area	0 to 4 Years	5 to 9 Years	10 to 14 Years	15 to 19 Years	20 to 24 Years	25 to 29 Years	30 to 34 Years	35 to 39 Years	40 to 44 Years	45 to 49 Years
Number										
Total										
Barrie	8,265	8,645	9,345	10,330	9,140	8,810	9,160	9,740	10,365	11,735
Ontario	704,260	712,755	763,755	863,635	852,910	815,120	800,365	844,335	924,075	1,055,880
Canada	1,877,095	1,809,895	1,920,355	2,178,135	2,187,450	2,169,590	2,162,905	2,173,930	2,324,875	2,675,130
Males										
Barrie	4,210	4,420	4,725	5,270	4,530	4,330	4,445	4,760	5,010	5,690
Ontario	360,590	365,290	391,630	443,680	432,490	400,045	383,340	405,845	447,920	517,510
Canada	961,150	925,965	983,995	1,115,845	1,108,775	1,077,275	1,058,810	1,064,200	1,141,720	1,318,715
Females										
Barrie	4,055	4,230	4,615	5,065	4,610	4,485	4,715	4,980	5,350	6,045
Ontario	343,670	347,465	372,125	419,950	420,415	415,075	417,030	438,485	476,155	538,370
Canada	915,945	883,935	936,360	1,062,295	1,078,670	1,092,315	1,104,095	1,109,735	1,183,155	1,356,420
Percent of Population										
Total										
Barrie	6.1	6.4	6.9	7.6	6.7	6.5	6.7	7.2	7.6	8.6
Ontario	5.5	5.5	5.9	6.7	6.6	6.3	6.2	6.6	7.2	8.2
Canada	5.6	5.4	5.7	6.5	6.5	6.5	6.5	6.5	6.9	8.0
Males										
Barrie	6.4	6.7	7.2	8.0	6.9	6.6	6.8	7.2	7.6	8.7
Ontario	5.8	5.8	6.3	7.1	6.9	6.4	6.1	6.5	7.2	8.3
Canada	5.9	5.6	6.0	6.8	6.8	6.6	6.5	6.5	7.0	8.0
Females										
Barrie	5.8	6.0	6.6	7.2	6.6	6.4	6.7	7.1	7.6	8.6
Ontario	5.2	5.3	5.6	6.4	6.4	6.3	6.3	6.7	7.2	8.2
Canada	5.4	5.2	5.5	6.2	6.3	6.4	6.5	6.5	6.9	7.9

Source: Statistics Canada. 2012. Census Profile. 2011 Census. Statistics Canada Catalogue no. 98-316-XWE. Ottawa. Released October 24 2012.
http://www12.statcan.gc.ca/census-recensement/2011/dp-pd/prof/index.cfm?Lang=E

Age Characteristics: 50 Years and Over, and Median Age

Area	50 to 54 Years	55 to 59 Years	60 to 64 Years	65 to 69 Years	70 to 74 Years	75 to 79 Years	80 to 84 Years	85 Years and Over	Median Age
Number									
Total									
Barrie	9,925	7,525	6,285	4,680	3,615	3,165	2,490	2,490	37.2
Ontario	1,006,140	864,620	765,655	563,485	440,780	356,150	271,510	246,400	40.4
Canada	2,658,965	2,340,635	2,052,670	1,521,715	1,153,065	922,700	702,070	645,515	40.6
Males									
Barrie	4,910	3,625	2,955	2,155	1,575	1,405	935	730	36.0
Ontario	492,560	418,755	370,370	270,875	206,350	161,345	113,620	80,925	39.4
Canada	1,309,030	1,147,300	1,002,690	738,010	543,435	417,945	291,085	208,300	39.6
Females									
Barrie	5,015	3,900	3,330	2,530	2,040	1,760	1,555	1,760	38.3
Ontario	513,580	445,865	395,275	292,610	234,435	194,805	157,890	165,475	41.3
Canada	1,349,940	1,193,335	1,049,985	783,705	609,630	504,755	410,985	437,215	41.5
Percent of Population									
Total									
Barrie	7.3	5.5	4.6	3.4	2.7	2.3	1.8	1.8	–
Ontario	7.8	6.7	6.0	4.4	3.4	2.8	2.1	1.9	–
Canada	7.9	7.0	6.1	4.5	3.4	2.8	2.1	1.9	–
Males									
Barrie	7.5	5.5	4.5	3.3	2.4	2.1	1.4	1.1	–
Ontario	7.9	6.7	5.9	4.3	3.3	2.6	1.8	1.3	–
Canada	8.0	7.0	6.1	4.5	3.3	2.5	1.8	1.3	–
Females									
Barrie	7.2	5.6	4.8	3.6	2.9	2.5	2.2	2.5	–
Ontario	7.8	6.8	6.0	4.4	3.6	3.0	2.4	2.5	–
Canada	7.9	7.0	6.2	4.6	3.6	3.0	2.4	2.6	–

Source: Statistics Canada. 2012. Census Profile. 2011 Census. Statistics Canada Catalogue no. 98-316-XWE. Ottawa. Released October 24 2012.
http://www12.statcan.gc.ca/census-recensement/2011/dp-pd/prof/index.cfm?Lang=E

PROFILES / Barrie, Ontario

Private Households by Household Size

Area	1 Person	2 Persons	3 Persons	4 Persons	5 Persons	6 or More Persons	Average Number of Persons in Private Households
			Households				
Barrie	10,960	15,975	8,925	9,025	3,530	1,525	2.7
Ontario	1,230,975	1,584,415	803,030	783,925	310,860	174,305	2.6
Canada	3,673,310	4,544,820	2,081,900	1,903,300	724,405	392,885	2.5
			Percent of Households				
Barrie	21.9	32.0	17.9	18.1	7.1	3.1	–
Ontario	25.2	32.4	16.4	16.0	6.4	3.6	–
Canada	27.6	34.1	15.6	14.3	5.4	2.9	–

Source: Statistics Canada. 2012. Census Profile. 2011 Census. Statistics Canada Catalogue no. 98-316-XWE. Ottawa. Released October 24 2012.
http://www12.statcan.gc.ca/census-recensement/2011/dp-pd/prof/index.cfm?Lang=E

Dwelling Type

Area	Single-detached House	Semi-detached House	Row House	Apartment: Building with Five or More Storeys	Apartment: Building with Fewer Than Five Storeys	Duplex Apartment	Movable Dwelling	Other Single-attached House
				Number				
Barrie	31,045	2,245	5,015	3,650	4,930	2,915	115	25
Ontario	2,718,880	279,470	415,225	789,970	498,160	160,460	15,800	9,540
Canada	7,329,150	646,245	791,600	1,234,770	2,397,550	704,485	183,510	33,310
				Percent of Dwellings				
Barrie	62.2	4.5	10.0	7.3	9.9	5.8	0.2	0.1
Ontario	55.6	5.7	8.5	16.2	10.2	3.3	0.3	0.2
Canada	55.0	4.9	5.9	9.3	18.0	5.3	1.4	0.3

Source: Statistics Canada. 2012. Census Profile. 2011 Census. Statistics Canada Catalogue no. 98-316-XWE. Ottawa. Released October 24 2012.
http://www12.statcan.gc.ca/census-recensement/2011/dp-pd/prof/index.cfm?Lang=E

Shelter Costs

		Owned Dwellings					Rented Dwellings	
Area	Number	Median Value[1] ($)	Average Value[1] ($)	Median Monthly Costs[2] ($)	Average Monthly Costs[2] ($)	Number	Median Monthly Costs[3] ($)	Average Monthly Costs[3] ($)
Barrie	37,550	276,279	292,021	1,413	1,391	12,395	1,001	1,032
Ontario	3,446,650	300,862	367,428	1,163	1,284	1,385,535	892	926
Canada	9,013,410	280,552	345,182	978	1,141	4,060,385	784	848

Note: All figures cover non-farm, non-reserve private dwellings; (1) Refers to the dollar amount expected by the owner if the dwelling were to be sold; (2) Includes all shelter expenses paid by households that own their dwellings, such as the mortgage payment and the costs of electricity, heat, water and other municipal services, property taxes and condominium fees; (3) Includes all shelter expenses paid by households that rent their dwellings, such as the monthly rent and the costs of electricity, heat and municipal services.
Source: Statistics Canada. 2013. 2011 National Household Survey. Statistics Canada Catalogue no. 99-004-XWE. Ottawa. Released September 11, 2013.

Occupied Private Dwellings by Period of Construction

Area	1960 or Before	1961 to 1980	1981 to 1990	1991 to 2000	2001 to 2005	2006 to 2011
			Number			
Barrie	5,310	9,500	8,365	13,115	9,750	3,915
Ontario	1,330,235	1,420,570	763,430	609,310	414,795	348,310
Canada	3,273,105	4,152,715	2,112,110	1,707,880	1,031,020	1,042,430
			Percent of Dwellings			
Barrie	10.6	19.0	16.7	26.3	19.5	7.8
Ontario	27.2	29.1	15.6	12.5	8.5	7.1
Canada	24.6	31.2	15.9	12.8	7.7	7.8

Note: Figures cover non-farm, non-reserve private dwellings and includes data up to May 10, 2011.
Source: Statistics Canada. 2013. 2011 National Household Survey. Statistics Canada Catalogue no. 99-004-XWE. Ottawa. Released September 11, 2013.

Educational Attainment

Area	No Certificate, Diploma or Degree	High School Diploma or Equivalent[1]	Apprenticeship or Trades Certificate or Diploma[2]	College, CÉGEP or Other Non-University Certificate or Diploma	University Certificate or Diploma Below the Bachelor Level[3]	Bachelor's Degree	University Certificate, Diploma or Degree Above Bachelor Level[4]
				Number			
				Total			
Barrie	19,915	32,115	8,880	26,830	3,415	10,355	5,450
Ontario	1,954,520	2,801,805	771,140	2,070,875	427,150	1,515,075	933,100
Canada	5,485,400	6,968,935	2,950,685	4,970,020	1,200,130	3,634,425	2,049,930
				Males			
Barrie	10,120	15,480	6,075	11,605	1,410	4,425	2,325
Ontario	957,040	1,337,055	520,390	894,235	193,355	692,345	470,290
Canada	2,742,875	3,305,415	1,928,970	2,118,430	513,235	1,643,080	1,043,350
				Females			
Barrie	9,795	16,635	2,805	15,225	2,005	5,935	3,125
Ontario	997,475	1,464,755	250,750	1,176,640	233,790	822,730	462,805
Canada	2,742,520	3,663,515	1,021,715	2,851,595	686,890	1,991,345	1,006,585
				Percent of Population			
				Total			
Barrie	18.6	30.0	8.3	25.1	3.2	9.7	5.1
Ontario	18.7	26.8	7.4	19.8	4.1	14.5	8.9
Canada	20.1	25.6	10.8	18.2	4.4	13.3	7.5
				Males			
Barrie	19.7	30.1	11.8	22.6	2.7	8.6	4.5
Ontario	18.9	26.4	10.3	17.7	3.8	13.7	9.3
Canada	20.6	24.9	14.5	15.9	3.9	12.4	7.8
				Females			
Barrie	17.6	30.0	5.1	27.4	3.6	10.7	5.6
Ontario	18.4	27.1	4.6	21.8	4.3	15.2	8.6
Canada	19.6	26.2	7.3	20.4	4.9	14.3	7.2

Note: Figures cover total population aged 15 years and over by highest certificate, diploma or degree; (1) Includes persons who have graduated from a secondary school or equivalent. It excludes persons with a postsecondary certificate, diploma or degree; (2) Includes Registered Apprenticeship certificates (including Certificate of Qualification, Journeyperson's designation) and other trades certificates or diplomas such as pre-employment or vocational certificates and diplomas from brief trade programs completed at community colleges, institutes of technology, vocational centres, and similar institutions; (3) Comparisons with other data sources suggest that the category 'University certificate or diploma below the bachelor's level' was over-reported in the NHS. This category likely includes some responses that are actually college certificates or diplomas, bachelor's degrees or other types of education (e.g., university transfer programs, bachelor's programs completed in other countries, incomplete bachelor's programs, non-university professional designations). We recommend users interpret the results for the 'University certificate or diploma below the bachelor's level' category with caution; (4) 'University certificate or diploma above bachelor level' includes the categories: 'Degree in medicine, dentistry, veterinary medicine or optometry,' 'Master's degree' and 'Earned doctorate.'
Source: Statistics Canada. 2013. 2011 National Household Survey. Statistics Canada Catalogue no. 99-004-XWE. Ottawa. Released September 11, 2013.

Household Income Distribution

Area	Less than $10,000	$10,000 to $19,999	$20,000 to $29,999	$30,000 to $39,999	$40,000 to $49,999	$50,000 to $59,999	$60,000 to $79,999	$80,000 to $99,999	$100,000 to $124,999	$125,000 to $149,999	$150,000 and Over
						Households					
Barrie	1,645	3,005	3,910	4,005	4,870	4,015	7,445	6,275	5,810	3,790	5,165
Ontario	201,780	354,530	405,725	425,410	425,720	398,705	680,850	552,660	497,970	331,460	611,840
Canada	626,705	1,141,945	1,193,925	1,271,675	1,206,800	1,102,120	1,865,280	1,458,240	1,260,770	802,555	1,389,240
						Percent of Households					
Barrie	3.3	6.0	7.8	8.0	9.8	8.0	14.9	12.6	11.6	7.6	10.3
Ontario	4.1	7.3	8.3	8.7	8.7	8.2	13.9	11.3	10.2	6.8	12.5
Canada	4.7	8.6	9.0	9.5	9.1	8.3	14.0	10.9	9.5	6.0	10.4

Note: Household income is the sum of the total incomes of all members of that household. Total income refers to monetary receipts from certain sources, before income taxes and deductions, during calendar year 2010.
Source: Statistics Canada. 2013. 2011 National Household Survey. Statistics Canada Catalogue no. 99-004-XWE. Ottawa. Released September 11, 2013.

Median and Average Household and Economic Family Income

Area	Median Household Income ($)	Average Household Income ($)	Median After-tax Household Income ($)	Average After-tax Household Income ($)	Median Economic Family Income ($)	Average Economic Family Income ($)	Median After-tax Economic Family Income ($)	Average After-tax Economic Family Income ($)
Barrie	69,471	80,928	61,159	68,598	80,247	91,073	69,539	76,973
Ontario	66,358	85,772	58,717	71,523	80,987	100,152	71,128	83,322
Canada	61,072	79,102	54,089	66,149	76,511	94,125	67,044	78,517

Note: Figures cover household and economic familiy income in 2010. A household is defined as a person or a group of persons (other than foreign residents) who occupy the same private dwelling and do not have a usual place of residence elsewhere in Canada. Every person is a member of one and only one household. An economic family is defined as a group of two or more persons who live in the same dwelling and are related to each other by blood, marriage, common-law, adoption or a foster relationship. A couple may be of opposite or same sex.
Source: Statistics Canada. 2013. 2011 National Household Survey. Statistics Canada Catalogue no. 99-004-XWE. Ottawa. Released September 11, 2013.

Individual Income Distribution

Area	Less than $10,000	$10,000 to $19,999	$20,000 to $29,999	$30,000 to $39,999	$40,000 to $49,999	$50,000 to $59,999	$60,000 to $79,999	$80,000 to $99,999	$100,000 to $124,999	$125,000 and Over
					Number					
					Total					
Barrie	17,650	17,350	14,420	11,895	10,235	7,215	10,595	6,270	3,170	2,390
Ontario	1,780,355	1,748,060	1,361,710	1,136,730	980,790	746,360	964,280	574,710	293,865	330,285
Canada	4,492,040	4,835,710	3,670,020	3,180,360	2,603,520	1,921,650	2,437,440	1,302,045	693,580	782,135
					Males					
Barrie	7,180	6,185	5,590	5,265	5,025	4,330	6,825	4,025	2,460	1,965
Ontario	781,095	669,815	580,990	535,255	491,125	407,005	569,205	341,160	201,125	244,500
Canada	1,936,365	1,864,880	1,588,260	1,522,190	1,333,510	1,079,780	1,473,145	823,720	492,905	599,905
					Females					
Barrie	10,470	11,170	8,830	6,625	5,210	2,885	3,770	2,245	715	430
Ontario	999,265	1,078,245	780,720	601,475	489,665	339,360	395,075	233,550	92,740	85,790
Canada	2,555,675	2,970,825	2,081,760	1,658,170	1,270,010	841,870	964,300	478,330	200,680	182,230
					Percent of Population					
					Total					
Barrie	17.4	17.1	14.2	11.8	10.1	7.1	10.5	6.2	3.1	2.4
Ontario	18.0	17.6	13.7	11.5	9.9	7.5	9.7	5.8	3.0	3.3
Canada	17.3	18.7	14.2	12.3	10.0	7.4	9.4	5.0	2.7	3.0
					Males					
Barrie	14.7	12.7	11.4	10.8	10.3	8.9	14.0	8.2	5.0	4.0
Ontario	16.2	13.9	12.1	11.1	10.2	8.4	11.8	7.1	4.2	5.1
Canada	15.2	14.7	12.5	12.0	10.5	8.5	11.6	6.5	3.9	4.7
					Females					
Barrie	20.0	21.3	16.9	12.7	10.0	5.5	7.2	4.3	1.4	0.8
Ontario	19.6	21.2	15.3	11.8	9.6	6.7	7.8	4.6	1.8	1.7
Canada	19.4	22.5	15.8	12.6	9.6	6.4	7.3	3.6	1.5	1.4

Note: Figures cover individuals aged 15 years and over with income. Income refers to monetary receipts from certain sources, before income taxes and deductions, during calendar year 2010.
Source: Statistics Canada. 2013. 2011 National Household Survey. Statistics Canada Catalogue no. 99-004-XWE. Ottawa. Released September 11, 2013.

Labour Force Status

Area	In the Labour Force - All	In the Labour Force - Employed	In the Labour Force - Unemployed	Not in the Labour Force
		Number		
		Total		
Barrie	74,420	68,275	6,145	32,535
Ontario	6,864,990	6,297,005	567,985	3,608,685
Canada	17,990,080	16,595,035	1,395,045	9,269,445
		Males		
Barrie	38,210	35,280	2,930	13,230
Ontario	3,542,030	3,249,165	292,865	1,522,690
Canada	9,388,570	8,634,310	754,255	3,906,785
		Females		
Barrie	36,215	33,000	3,215	19,310
Ontario	3,322,955	3,047,840	275,120	2,085,990
Canada	8,601,515	7,960,725	640,790	5,362,660
		Percent of Labour Force		
		Total		
Barrie	69.6	63.8	8.3	30.4
Ontario	65.5	60.1	8.3	34.5
Canada	66.0	60.9	7.8	34.0
		Males		
Barrie	74.3	68.6	7.7	25.7
Ontario	69.9	64.2	8.3	30.1
Canada	70.6	64.9	8.0	29.4
		Females		
Barrie	65.2	59.4	8.9	34.8
Ontario	61.4	56.3	8.3	38.6
Canada	61.6	57.0	7.4	38.4

Note: Figures are based on total population 15 years and over
Source: Statistics Canada. 2013. 2011 National Household Survey. Statistics Canada Catalogue no. 99-004-XWE. Ottawa. Released September 11, 2013.

Labour Force by Industry (NAICS Codes 11–52)

Area	Agriculture, forestry, fishing & hunting	Mining, quarrying, & oil & gas extraction	Utilities	Construction	Manufacturing	Wholesale Trade	Retail Trade	Transportation & warehousing	Information & cultural industries	Finance & insurance
Number										
Total										
Barrie	200	185	800	5,120	7,860	3,355	9,885	3,740	1,625	2,395
Ontario	101,280	29,985	57,035	417,900	697,565	305,030	751,200	307,405	178,720	364,415
Canada	437,650	261,050	149,940	1,215,380	1,619,295	733,445	2,031,665	827,780	420,830	767,960
Males										
Barrie	130	135	580	4,565	5,960	2,340	4,545	2,815	850	955
Ontario	66,485	25,650	42,685	369,300	493,305	197,770	344,480	225,245	98,835	153,125
Canada	307,370	211,690	110,765	1,068,710	1,167,680	494,545	933,850	617,305	235,875	296,995
Females										
Barrie	75	55	220	555	1,905	1,015	5,335	925	770	1,445
Ontario	34,800	4,340	14,350	48,595	204,260	107,260	406,720	82,160	79,885	211,290
Canada	130,285	49,360	39,175	146,670	451,615	238,900	1,097,820	210,475	184,955	470,960
Percent of Labour Force										
Total										
Barrie	0.3	0.3	1.1	7.0	10.8	4.6	13.6	5.1	2.2	3.3
Ontario	1.5	0.4	0.9	6.3	10.4	4.6	11.2	4.6	2.7	5.5
Canada	2.5	1.5	0.9	6.9	9.2	4.2	11.6	4.7	2.4	4.4
Males										
Barrie	0.3	0.4	1.6	12.2	16.0	6.3	12.2	7.5	2.3	2.6
Ontario	1.9	0.7	1.2	10.7	14.3	5.7	10.0	6.5	2.9	4.4
Canada	3.3	2.3	1.2	11.6	12.7	5.4	10.2	6.7	2.6	3.2
Females										
Barrie	0.2	0.2	0.6	1.6	5.4	2.9	15.1	2.6	2.2	4.1
Ontario	1.1	0.1	0.4	1.5	6.3	3.3	12.6	2.5	2.5	6.5
Canada	1.6	0.6	0.5	1.7	5.4	2.8	13.1	2.5	2.2	5.6

Note: Figures are based on total experienced labour force 15 years and over. Experienced labour force refers to persons who, during the week of Sunday, May 1 to Saturday, May 7, 2011, were employed and the unemployed who had last worked for pay or in self-employment in either 2010 or 2011.
Source: Statistics Canada. 2013. 2011 National Household Survey. Statistics Canada Catalogue no. 99-004-XWE. Ottawa. Released September 11, 2013.

Labour Force by Industry (NAICS Codes 53–91)

Area	Real estate & rental & leasing	Profess., scientific & tech. services	Mgmt of companies & enterprises	Admin. & support, waste mgmt & remed. services	Educational services	Health care & social assistance	Arts, entertain. & recreation	Accomm. & food services	Other services (except public admin.)	Public admin.
Number										
Total										
Barrie	1,500	3,820	30	3,735	5,445	8,255	1,695	5,740	2,610	4,655
Ontario	133,980	511,020	6,525	309,630	499,690	692,130	144,065	417,675	296,340	458,665
Canada	321,895	1,240,850	17,460	728,330	1,301,435	1,949,650	363,405	1,130,750	807,800	1,261,050
Males										
Barrie	755	2,000	25	1,970	1,695	1,030	775	2,315	1,180	2,705
Ontario	72,835	281,420	3,540	172,475	162,765	120,165	75,035	177,240	133,795	236,655
Canada	179,090	688,625	9,380	411,250	424,915	349,430	188,270	469,990	372,940	652,510
Females										
Barrie	740	1,820	0	1,765	3,755	7,225	920	3,430	1,430	1,950
Ontario	61,145	229,600	2,990	137,155	336,925	571,965	69,030	240,430	162,550	222,015
Canada	142,805	552,225	8,075	317,085	876,515	1,600,220	175,135	660,760	434,865	608,535
Percent of Labour Force										
Total										
Barrie	2.1	5.3	0.0	5.1	7.5	11.4	2.3	7.9	3.6	6.4
Ontario	2.0	7.6	0.1	4.6	7.5	10.4	2.2	6.3	4.4	6.9
Canada	1.8	7.1	0.1	4.1	7.4	11.1	2.1	6.4	4.6	7.2
Males										
Barrie	2.0	5.4	0.1	5.3	4.5	2.8	2.1	6.2	3.2	7.2
Ontario	2.1	8.2	0.1	5.0	4.7	3.5	2.2	5.1	3.9	6.9
Canada	1.9	7.5	0.1	4.5	4.6	3.8	2.0	5.1	4.1	7.1
Females										
Barrie	2.1	5.2	0.0	5.0	10.6	20.5	2.6	9.7	4.0	5.5
Ontario	1.9	7.1	0.1	4.2	10.4	17.7	2.1	7.4	5.0	6.9
Canada	1.7	6.6	0.1	3.8	10.4	19.1	2.1	7.9	5.2	7.2

Note: Figures are based on total experienced labour force 15 years and over. Experienced labour force refers to persons who, during the week of Sunday, May 1 to Saturday, May 7, 2011, were employed and the unemployed who had last worked for pay or in self-employment in either 2010 or 2011.
Source: Statistics Canada. 2013. 2011 National Household Survey. Statistics Canada Catalogue no. 99-004-XWE. Ottawa. Released September 11, 2013.

Occupation

Area	Mgmt	Business, Finance & Admin.	Natural/ Applied Sciences & Related	Health	Education, Law & Social, Community & Government Services	Art, Culture, Recreation & Sport	Sales & Service	Trades, Transport & Equip. Operators & Related	Natural Resources, Agri. & Related Production	Mfg & Utilities
					Number					
					Total					
Barrie	8,145	10,280	3,845	4,645	9,045	2,210	19,105	10,440	735	4,195
Ontario	770,580	1,138,330	494,500	392,695	801,465	206,420	1,550,260	868,515	106,810	350,685
Canada	1,963,600	2,902,045	1,237,775	1,107,200	2,064,675	503,415	4,068,170	2,537,775	397,930	805,040
					Males					
Barrie	5,205	2,925	3,275	635	3,000	1,025	7,770	9,775	535	3,170
Ontario	474,655	352,505	384,345	78,330	264,570	96,055	673,880	812,280	82,610	233,565
Canada	1,229,460	854,190	966,355	217,520	676,550	232,535	1,745,705	2,385,615	318,945	564,300
					Females					
Barrie	2,940	7,355	570	4,010	6,040	1,185	11,335	665	200	1,025
Ontario	295,920	785,825	110,150	314,370	536,895	110,370	876,380	56,230	24,200	117,115
Canada	734,140	2,047,855	271,415	889,675	1,388,130	270,875	2,322,465	152,165	78,980	240,740
					Percent of Labour Force					
					Total					
Barrie	11.2	14.2	5.3	6.4	12.5	3.0	26.3	14.4	1.0	5.8
Ontario	11.5	17.0	7.4	5.9	12.0	3.1	23.2	13.0	1.6	5.2
Canada	11.2	16.5	7.0	6.3	11.7	2.9	23.1	14.4	2.3	4.6
					Males					
Barrie	14.0	7.8	8.8	1.7	8.0	2.7	20.8	26.2	1.4	8.5
Ontario	13.7	10.2	11.1	2.3	7.7	2.8	19.5	23.5	2.4	6.8
Canada	13.4	9.3	10.5	2.4	7.4	2.5	19.0	26.0	3.5	6.1
					Females					
Barrie	8.3	20.8	1.6	11.4	17.1	3.4	32.1	1.9	0.6	2.9
Ontario	9.2	24.3	3.4	9.7	16.6	3.4	27.2	1.7	0.7	3.6
Canada	8.7	24.4	3.2	10.6	16.5	3.2	27.7	1.8	0.9	2.9

Note: Figures are based on total experienced labour force 15 years and over
Source: Statistics Canada. 2013. 2011 National Household Survey. Statistics Canada Catalogue no. 99-004-XWE. Ottawa. Released September 11, 2013.

Place of Work Status

Area	Worked at Home	Worked Outside Canada	No Fixed Workplace Address	Worked at Usual Place
		Number		
		Total		
Barrie	4,010	220	8,025	56,020
Ontario	423,790	31,390	670,835	5,170,980
Canada	1,142,640	66,460	1,868,245	13,517,690
		Males		
Barrie	1,930	165	5,850	27,335
Ontario	216,900	21,150	486,560	2,524,555
Canada	582,150	47,355	1,400,485	6,604,325
		Females		
Barrie	2,085	60	2,170	28,680
Ontario	206,895	10,240	184,275	2,646,420
Canada	560,490	19,100	467,760	6,913,370
		Percent of Labour Force		
		Total		
Barrie	5.9	0.3	11.8	82.0
Ontario	6.7	0.5	10.7	82.1
Canada	6.9	0.4	11.3	81.5
		Males		
Barrie	5.5	0.5	16.6	77.5
Ontario	6.7	0.7	15.0	77.7
Canada	6.7	0.5	16.2	76.5
		Females		
Barrie	6.3	0.2	6.6	86.9
Ontario	6.8	0.3	6.0	86.8
Canada	7.0	0.2	5.9	86.8

Note: Figures are based on total employed labour force 15 years and over.
Source: Statistics Canada. 2013. 2011 National Household Survey. Statistics Canada Catalogue no. 99-004-XWE. Ottawa. Released September 11, 2013.

Mode of Transportation to Work

Area	Car; Truck; Van; as Driver	Car; Truck; Van; as Passenger	Public Transit	Walked	Bicycled	All Other Modes
			Number			
			Total			
Barrie	51,540	4,855	3,600	2,745	520	785
Ontario	4,235,315	357,110	818,270	299,095	69,885	62,145
Canada	11,393,140	867,050	1,851,525	880,815	201,780	191,625
			Males			
Barrie	27,575	2,085	1,420	1,215	415	480
Ontario	2,316,680	143,410	340,995	131,765	47,635	30,635
Canada	6,238,835	349,530	788,290	387,580	135,840	104,725
			Females			
Barrie	23,960	2,770	2,180	1,530	110	310
Ontario	1,918,640	213,700	477,275	167,325	22,250	31,515
Canada	5,154,305	517,520	1,063,235	493,230	65,940	86,900
			Percent of Labour Force			
			Total			
Barrie	80.5	7.6	5.6	4.3	0.8	1.2
Ontario	72.5	6.1	14.0	5.1	1.2	1.1
Canada	74.0	5.6	12.0	5.7	1.3	1.2
			Males			
Barrie	83.1	6.3	4.3	3.7	1.3	1.4
Ontario	76.9	4.8	11.3	4.4	1.6	1.0
Canada	77.9	4.4	9.8	4.8	1.7	1.3
			Females			
Barrie	77.7	9.0	7.1	5.0	0.4	1.0
Ontario	67.8	7.5	16.9	5.9	0.8	1.1
Canada	69.8	7.0	14.4	6.7	0.9	1.2

Note: Figures are based on total employed labour force 15 years and over.
Source: Statistics Canada. 2013. 2011 National Household Survey. Statistics Canada Catalogue no. 99-004-XWE. Ottawa. Released September 11, 2013.

Visible Minority Population Characteristics

Area	Total Minority	South Asian[1]	Chinese	Black	Filipino	Latin American	Arab	SE Asian[2]	West Asian[3]	Korean	Japanese	Multiple[4]
						Number						
						Total						
Barrie	10,095	1,760	975	2,525	815	1,105	325	640	125	535	280	500
Ontario	3,279,565	965,990	629,140	539,205	275,380	172,560	151,645	137,875	122,530	78,290	29,085	96,735
Canada	6,264,750	1,567,400	1,324,750	945,665	619,310	381,280	380,620	312,075	206,840	161,130	87,270	171,935
						Males						
Barrie	5,090	970	455	1,430	305	425	200	340	70	255	135	280
Ontario	1,582,480	484,355	301,575	251,295	116,825	83,205	79,620	67,645	62,515	38,045	13,345	46,765
Canada	3,043,010	790,755	632,325	453,005	268,885	186,355	203,485	154,035	105,620	77,165	38,270	83,335
						Females						
Barrie	5,005	785	520	1,095	510	680	120	305	50	285	150	210
Ontario	1,697,085	481,635	327,570	287,915	158,555	89,360	72,025	70,230	60,010	40,250	15,740	49,970
Canada	3,221,745	776,650	692,420	492,660	350,425	194,925	177,140	158,045	101,220	83,965	48,990	88,600
						Percent of Population						
						Total						
Barrie	7.6	1.3	0.7	1.9	0.6	0.8	0.2	0.5	0.1	0.4	0.2	0.4
Ontario	25.9	7.6	5.0	4.3	2.2	1.4	1.2	1.1	1.0	0.6	0.2	0.8
Canada	19.1	4.8	4.0	2.9	1.9	1.2	1.2	0.9	0.6	0.5	0.3	0.5
						Males						
Barrie	7.9	1.5	0.7	2.2	0.5	0.7	0.3	0.5	0.1	0.4	0.2	0.4
Ontario	25.6	7.8	4.9	4.1	1.9	1.3	1.3	1.1	1.0	0.6	0.2	0.8
Canada	18.8	4.9	3.9	2.8	1.7	1.2	1.3	1.0	0.7	0.5	0.2	0.5
						Females						
Barrie	7.3	1.1	0.8	1.6	0.7	1.0	0.2	0.4	0.1	0.4	0.2	0.3
Ontario	26.2	7.4	5.1	4.4	2.5	1.4	1.1	1.1	0.9	0.6	0.2	0.8
Canada	19.3	4.7	4.1	3.0	2.1	1.2	1.1	0.9	0.6	0.5	0.3	0.5

Note: The Employment Equity Act defines visible minorities as 'persons, other than Aboriginal peoples, who are non-Caucasian in race or non-white in colour';
(1) Includes 'East Indian,' 'Pakistani,' 'Sri Lankan,' etc.; (2) Includes 'Vietnamese,' 'Cambodian,' 'Malaysian,' 'Laotian,' etc.; (3) Includes 'Iranian,' 'Afghan,' etc.; (4) Includes respondents who reported more than one visible minority group by checking two or more mark-in circles, e.g., 'Black' and 'South Asian.'
Source: Statistics Canada. 2013. 2011 National Household Survey. Statistics Canada Catalogue no. 99-004-XWE. Ottawa. Released September 11, 2013.

PROFILES / Barrie, Ontario

Aboriginal Population

Area	Aboriginal Identity[1]	First Nations (North American Indian) Single Identity[2]	Métis Single Identity	Inuk (Inuit) Single Identity	Multiple Aboriginal Identities[3]	Aboriginal Identities Not Included Elsewhere
Number — Total						
Barrie	3,440	1,800	1,550	10	60	20
Ontario	301,430	201,100	86,020	3,355	2,910	8,040
Canada	1,400,685	851,560	451,795	59,440	11,415	26,475
Males						
Barrie	1,610	870	705	0	25	0
Ontario	145,020	96,620	41,755	1,475	1,420	3,750
Canada	682,190	411,785	223,335	29,495	5,525	12,055
Females						
Barrie	1,830	925	845	0	35	0
Ontario	156,410	104,485	44,260	1,880	1,490	4,295
Canada	718,500	439,775	228,460	29,950	5,890	14,420
Percent of Population — Total						
Barrie	2.6	1.4	1.2	0.0	0.0	0.0
Ontario	2.4	1.6	0.7	0.0	0.0	0.1
Canada	4.3	2.6	1.4	0.2	0.0	0.1
Males						
Barrie	2.5	1.3	1.1	0.0	0.0	0.0
Ontario	2.3	1.6	0.7	0.0	0.0	0.1
Canada	4.2	2.5	1.4	0.2	0.0	0.1
Females						
Barrie	2.7	1.4	1.2	0.0	0.1	0.0
Ontario	2.4	1.6	0.7	0.0	0.0	0.1
Canada	4.3	2.6	1.4	0.2	0.0	0.1

Note: (1) Includes persons who reported being an Aboriginal person, that is, First Nations (North American Indian), Métis or Inuk (Inuit) and/or those who reported Registered or Treaty Indian status, that is registered under the Indian Act of Canada, and/or those who reported membership in a First Nation or Indian band. Aboriginal peoples of Canada are defined in the Constitution Act, 1982, section 35-2 as including the Indian, Inuit and Métis peoples of Canada; (2) Users should be aware that the estimates associated with this variable are more affected than most by the incomplete enumeration of certain Indian reserves and Indian settlements in the National Household Survey (NHS); (3) Includes persons who reported being any two or all three of the following: First Nations (North American Indian), Métis or Inuk (Inuit).
Source: Statistics Canada. 2013. 2011 National Household Survey. Statistics Canada Catalogue no. 99-004-XWE. Ottawa. Released September 11, 2013.

Ethnic Origin

Area	North American Aboriginal	Other North American	European	Caribbean	Latin, Central and South American	African	Asian	Oceania
Number — Total								
Barrie	6,600	46,650	104,400	2,555	1,680	1,195	7,385	240
Ontario	441,395	3,059,480	8,231,410	396,485	271,545	331,460	2,604,595	19,410
Canada	1,836,035	11,070,455	20,157,965	627,590	544,375	766,735	5,011,225	74,875
Males								
Barrie	3,055	23,030	50,330	1,355	770	630	3,575	130
Ontario	210,490	1,507,105	4,019,885	181,805	130,035	160,940	1,265,540	9,855
Canada	885,675	5,462,685	9,913,150	291,640	264,635	387,360	2,435,540	37,490
Females								
Barrie	3,545	23,615	54,070	1,200	915	570	3,810	105
Ontario	230,905	1,552,380	4,211,525	214,675	141,510	170,515	1,339,050	9,555
Canada	950,360	5,607,770	10,244,820	335,945	279,740	379,380	2,575,680	37,385
Percent of Population — Total								
Barrie	5.0	35.0	78.4	1.9	1.3	0.9	5.5	0.2
Ontario	3.5	24.2	65.1	3.1	2.1	2.6	20.6	0.2
Canada	5.6	33.7	61.4	1.9	1.7	2.3	15.3	0.2
Males								
Barrie	4.7	35.5	77.7	2.1	1.2	1.0	5.5	0.2
Ontario	3.4	24.4	65.0	2.9	2.1	2.6	20.5	0.2
Canada	5.5	33.8	61.3	1.8	1.6	2.4	15.1	0.2
Females								
Barrie	5.2	34.5	79.0	1.8	1.3	0.8	5.6	0.2
Ontario	3.6	24.0	65.1	3.3	2.2	2.6	20.7	0.1
Canada	5.7	33.6	61.4	2.0	1.7	2.3	15.4	0.2

Note: The sum of the ethnic groups in this table is greater than the total population estimate because a person may report more than one ethnic origin in the NHS.
Source: Statistics Canada. 2013. 2011 National Household Survey. Statistics Canada Catalogue no. 99-004-XWE. Ottawa. Released September 11, 2013.

PROFILES / Barrie, Ontario

Religion

Area	Buddhist	Christian	Hindu	Jewish	Muslim	Sikh	Traditional (Aboriginal) Spirituality	Other Religions	No Religious Affiliation
Number									
Total									
Barrie	600	88,365	410	665	1,405	140	40	355	41,275
Ontario	163,750	8,167,295	366,720	195,540	581,950	179,765	15,905	53,080	2,927,790
Canada	366,830	22,102,745	497,965	329,495	1,053,945	454,965	64,935	130,835	7,850,605
Males									
Barrie	230	41,345	235	355	760	80	20	115	21,665
Ontario	75,355	3,839,925	183,580	95,795	293,925	90,515	7,600	23,555	1,571,195
Canada	168,465	10,497,775	250,435	161,265	540,555	229,435	31,805	57,745	4,225,645
Females									
Barrie	365	47,015	165	305	645	60	15	240	19,610
Ontario	88,395	4,327,365	183,140	99,740	288,025	89,250	8,310	29,525	1,356,600
Canada	198,365	11,604,975	247,525	168,235	513,395	225,530	33,135	73,090	3,624,965
Percent of Population									
Total									
Barrie	0.5	66.3	0.3	0.5	1.1	0.1	0.0	0.3	31.0
Ontario	1.3	64.6	2.9	1.5	4.6	1.4	0.1	0.4	23.1
Canada	1.1	67.3	1.5	1.0	3.2	1.4	0.2	0.4	23.9
Males									
Barrie	0.4	63.8	0.4	0.5	1.2	0.1	0.0	0.2	33.4
Ontario	1.2	62.1	3.0	1.5	4.8	1.5	0.1	0.4	25.4
Canada	1.0	64.9	1.5	1.0	3.3	1.4	0.2	0.4	26.1
Females									
Barrie	0.5	68.7	0.2	0.4	0.9	0.1	0.0	0.4	28.7
Ontario	1.4	66.9	2.8	1.5	4.5	1.4	0.1	0.5	21.0
Canada	1.2	69.5	1.5	1.0	3.1	1.4	0.2	0.4	21.7

Note: Religion refers to the person's self-identification as having a connection or affiliation with any religious denomination, group, body, sect, cult or other religiously defined community or system of belief. Religion is not limited to formal membership in a religious organization or group. Persons without a religious connection or affiliation can self-identify as atheist, agnostic or humanist, or can provide another applicable response.
Source: Statistics Canada. 2013. 2011 National Household Survey. Statistics Canada Catalogue no. 99-004-XWE. Ottawa. Released September 11, 2013.

Religion—Christian Denominations

Area	Anglican	Baptist	Catholic	Christian Orthodox	Lutheran	Pentecostal	Presbyterian	United Church	Other Christian
Number									
Total									
Barrie	11,955	3,760	36,590	1,230	1,455	2,085	5,135	12,315	13,830
Ontario	774,560	244,650	3,976,610	297,710	163,460	213,945	319,585	952,465	1,224,300
Canada	1,631,845	635,840	12,810,705	550,690	478,185	478,705	472,385	2,007,610	3,036,780
Males									
Barrie	5,515	1,795	17,535	600	695	905	2,255	5,505	6,530
Ontario	355,175	112,285	1,895,940	145,825	75,225	94,955	148,535	435,255	576,730
Canada	752,945	293,905	6,167,290	270,205	221,525	217,850	218,955	912,545	1,442,550
Females									
Barrie	6,435	1,965	19,055	630	760	1,175	2,880	6,805	7,300
Ontario	419,390	132,370	2,080,665	151,885	88,230	118,990	171,050	517,210	647,570
Canada	878,900	341,940	6,643,415	280,485	256,660	260,850	253,430	1,095,065	1,594,230
Percent of Population									
Total									
Barrie	9.0	2.8	27.5	0.9	1.1	1.6	3.9	9.2	10.4
Ontario	6.1	1.9	31.4	2.4	1.3	1.7	2.5	7.5	9.7
Canada	5.0	1.9	39.0	1.7	1.5	1.5	1.4	6.1	9.2
Males									
Barrie	8.5	2.8	27.1	0.9	1.1	1.4	3.5	8.5	10.1
Ontario	5.7	1.8	30.7	2.4	1.2	1.5	2.4	7.0	9.3
Canada	4.7	1.8	38.2	1.7	1.4	1.3	1.4	5.6	8.9
Females									
Barrie	9.4	2.9	27.8	0.9	1.1	1.7	4.2	9.9	10.7
Ontario	6.5	2.0	32.2	2.3	1.4	1.8	2.6	8.0	10.0
Canada	5.3	2.0	39.8	1.7	1.5	1.6	1.5	6.6	9.6

Note: Religion refers to the person's self-identification as having a connection or affiliation with any religious denomination, group, body, sect, cult or other religiously defined community or system of belief. Religion is not limited to formal membership in a religious organization or group. Persons without a religious connection or affiliation can self-identify as atheist, agnostic or humanist, or can provide another applicable response.
Source: Statistics Canada. 2013. 2011 National Household Survey. Statistics Canada Catalogue no. 99-004-XWE. Ottawa. Released September 11, 2013.

PROFILES / Barrie, Ontario

Immigrant Status and Period of Immigration

Area	Non-Immigrants[1]	Immigrants All	Before 1971	1971 to 1980	1981 to 1990	1991 to 2000	2001 to 2005	2006 to 2011	Non-Permanent Residents[3]
Number – Total									
Barrie	116,080	16,685	5,675	2,355	2,305	2,540	1,935	1,865	475
Ontario	8,906,000	3,611,365	723,030	464,380	538,285	866,220	518,405	501,060	134,425
Canada	25,720,175	6,775,765	1,261,055	870,775	949,890	1,539,050	992,070	1,162,915	356,385
Males									
Barrie	56,835	7,720	2,520	1,095	1,130	1,160	855	965	260
Ontario	4,410,240	1,706,385	341,820	217,990	258,095	408,270	245,850	234,360	64,825
Canada	12,753,235	3,231,370	605,430	416,670	454,570	724,905	474,545	555,245	178,515
Females									
Barrie	59,245	8,965	3,155	1,265	1,175	1,380	1,080	905	215
Ontario	4,495,765	1,904,985	381,210	246,390	280,190	457,950	272,550	266,695	69,600
Canada	12,966,935	3,544,400	655,625	454,105	495,325	814,145	517,530	607,670	177,870
Percent of Population – Total									
Barrie	87.1	12.5	4.3	1.8	1.7	1.9	1.5	1.4	0.4
Ontario	70.4	28.5	5.7	3.7	4.3	6.8	4.1	4.0	1.1
Canada	78.3	20.6	3.8	2.7	2.9	4.7	3.0	3.5	1.1
Males									
Barrie	87.7	11.9	3.9	1.7	1.7	1.8	1.3	1.5	0.4
Ontario	71.3	27.6	5.5	3.5	4.2	6.6	4.0	3.8	1.0
Canada	78.9	20.0	3.7	2.6	2.8	4.5	2.9	3.4	1.1
Females									
Barrie	86.6	13.1	4.6	1.8	1.7	2.0	1.6	1.3	0.3
Ontario	69.5	29.4	5.9	3.8	4.3	7.1	4.2	4.1	1.1
Canada	77.7	21.2	3.9	2.7	3.0	4.9	3.1	3.6	1.1

Note: (1) Non-immigrant refers to a person who is a Canadian citizen by birth; (2) Immigrant refers to a person who is or has ever been a landed immigrant/permanent resident. This person has been granted the right to live in Canada permanently by immigration authorities. Some immigrants have resided in Canada for a number of years, while others have arrived recently. Some immigrants are Canadian citizens, while others are not. Most immigrants are born outside Canada, but a small number are born in Canada. In the 2011 National Household Survey, 'Immigrants' includes immigrants who landed in Canada prior to May 10, 2011; (3) Non-permanent resident refers to a person from another country who has a work or study permit, or who is a refugee claimant, and any non-Canadian-born family member living in Canada with them.
Source: Statistics Canada. 2013. 2011 National Household Survey. Statistics Canada Catalogue no. 99-004-XWE. Ottawa. Released September 11, 2013.

Mother Tongue

Area	English	French	Non-official Language	English & French	English & Non-official Language	French & Non-official Language	English, French & Non-official Language
Number – Total							
Barrie	117,135	3,120	12,410	435	960	50	30
Ontario	8,677,040	493,300	3,264,435	46,605	219,425	13,645	7,615
Canada	18,858,980	7,054,975	6,567,680	144,685	396,330	74,430	24,095
Males							
Barrie	57,065	1,420	5,945	190	485	25	20
Ontario	4,276,970	232,785	1,562,190	21,805	106,790	6,285	3,495
Canada	9,345,225	3,452,380	3,157,785	69,975	192,000	36,535	11,965
Females							
Barrie	60,065	1,705	6,470	250	475	25	15
Ontario	4,400,065	260,510	1,702,240	24,795	112,635	7,365	4,115
Canada	9,513,750	3,602,590	3,409,895	74,710	204,330	37,890	12,130
Percent of Population – Total							
Barrie	87.3	2.3	9.3	0.3	0.7	0.0	0.0
Ontario	68.2	3.9	25.7	0.4	1.7	0.1	0.1
Canada	56.9	21.3	19.8	0.4	1.2	0.2	0.1
Males							
Barrie	87.6	2.2	9.1	0.3	0.7	0.0	0.0
Ontario	68.9	3.7	25.2	0.4	1.7	0.1	0.1
Canada	57.5	21.2	19.4	0.4	1.2	0.2	0.1
Females							
Barrie	87.0	2.5	9.4	0.4	0.7	0.0	0.0
Ontario	67.6	4.0	26.1	0.4	1.7	0.1	0.1
Canada	56.4	21.4	20.2	0.4	1.2	0.2	0.1

Note: Figures cover total population excluding institutional residents.
Source: Statistics Canada. 2012. Census Profile. 2011 Census. Statistics Canada Catalogue no. 98-316-XWE. Ottawa. Released October 24 2012.
http://www12.statcan.gc.ca/census-recensement/2011/dp-pd/prof/index.cfm?Lang=E

PROFILES / Barrie, Ontario

Language Spoken Most Often at Home

Area	English	French	Non-official Language	English & French	English & Non-official Language	French & Non-official Language	English, French & Non-official Language
			Number				
			Total				
Barrie	126,090	1,160	4,555	270	2,020	15	40
Ontario	10,044,810	284,115	1,827,870	37,955	509,105	6,370	11,845
Canada	21,457,075	6,827,865	3,673,865	131,205	875,135	109,700	46,330
			Males				
Barrie	61,305	510	2,235	110	965	5	15
Ontario	4,930,610	133,495	872,860	17,250	248,050	2,855	5,225
Canada	10,585,620	3,348,235	1,767,310	63,475	425,370	53,010	22,845
			Females				
Barrie	64,785	655	2,325	160	1,055	5	25
Ontario	5,114,200	150,620	955,010	20,705	261,055	3,520	6,620
Canada	10,871,455	3,479,625	1,906,555	67,730	449,765	56,690	23,485
			Percent of Population				
			Total				
Barrie	94.0	0.9	3.4	0.2	1.5	0.0	0.0
Ontario	79.0	2.2	14.4	0.3	4.0	0.1	0.1
Canada	64.8	20.6	11.1	0.4	2.6	0.3	0.1
			Males				
Barrie	94.1	0.8	3.4	0.2	1.5	0.0	0.0
Ontario	79.4	2.1	14.1	0.3	4.0	0.0	0.1
Canada	65.1	20.6	10.9	0.4	2.6	0.3	0.1
			Females				
Barrie	93.9	0.9	3.4	0.2	1.5	0.0	0.0
Ontario	78.5	2.3	14.7	0.3	4.0	0.1	0.1
Canada	64.5	20.6	11.3	0.4	2.7	0.3	0.1

Note: Figures cover total population excluding institutional residents.
Source: Statistics Canada. 2012. Census Profile. 2011 Census. Statistics Canada Catalogue no. 98-316-XWE. Ottawa. Released October 24 2012.
http://www12.statcan.gc.ca/census-recensement/2011/dp-pd/prof/index.cfm?Lang=E

Knowledge of Official Languages

Area	English Only	French Only	English & French	Neither English nor French
		Number		
		Total		
Barrie	124,345	135	9,120	550
Ontario	10,984,360	42,980	1,395,805	298,920
Canada	22,564,665	4,165,015	5,795,570	595,920
		Males		
Barrie	60,860	60	3,980	240
Ontario	5,445,050	18,805	627,725	118,765
Canada	11,222,185	1,925,340	2,876,560	241,790
		Females		
Barrie	63,480	70	5,140	310
Ontario	5,539,310	24,175	768,085	180,155
Canada	11,342,485	2,239,680	2,919,005	354,135
		Percent of Population		
		Total		
Barrie	92.7	0.1	6.8	0.4
Ontario	86.3	0.3	11.0	2.3
Canada	68.1	12.6	17.5	1.8
		Males		
Barrie	93.4	0.1	6.1	0.4
Ontario	87.7	0.3	10.1	1.9
Canada	69.0	11.8	17.7	1.5
		Females		
Barrie	92.0	0.1	7.4	0.4
Ontario	85.1	0.4	11.8	2.8
Canada	67.3	13.3	17.3	2.1

Note: Figures cover total population excluding institutional residents.
Source: Statistics Canada. 2012. Census Profile. 2011 Census. Statistics Canada Catalogue no. 98-316-XWE. Ottawa. Released October 24 2012.
http://www12.statcan.gc.ca/census-recensement/2011/dp-pd/prof/index.cfm?Lang=E

Brampton, Ontario

Background

Brampton is located north of Toronto's Lester B. Pearson International Airport. The City of Brampton is part of the northern Greater Toronto Area (GTA) and is situated 30 minutes from downtown Toronto.

The Brampton area was originally settled by farmers in the early 1800s. In 1834, Methodist settlers named the area after their British home. Brampton was officially incorporated into a farming village of more than 500 people in 1853. Prosperity, manufacturing and population growth accompanied the building of Brampton's rail line and station in 1856. With the creation of the Region of Peel, Brampton became a city in 1974.

Brampton residents speak more than 70 languages and represent more than 170 different cultures. It was the youngest community in the Toronto census metropolitan area (CMA) in 2011. The city offers a variety of libraries, educational facilities, places of worship and health services.

Every weekday more than 100,000 vehicles pass through Brampton's major transportation routes and increase the city's daytime employment population by almost 10,000 people. Key industries include manufacturing, the city's largest employer, and retail and wholesale trade. Brampton has more than 8,000 businesses and was given a Triple A credit rating by Standard and Poor's. Recently the Province of Ontario designated Brampton an urban growth area and predicted the city's population will grow to 725,000 by 2031.

Brampton hosts community-minded events throughout the year such as the Farmers' Market, Gage Park Skating Trail, Rib 'n' Roll, Classic Cars and Legendary Stars, Shakespeare in the Garden Square and the Flower City Parade. Because of its tidiness, landscaping, environmental action, forestry and floral displays, Brampton was awarded the International Communities in Bloom title in 2008 and is considered "Canada's Flower City." Brampton has over 6,000 acres of parkland and green space.

Brampton has summer highs of plus 25.37 degrees Celsius, winter lows of minus 8.97 degrees Celsius, and an average rainfall just over 684 mm per year.

Rankings

- Brampton was identified as the best city for homeowners selling their homes without a real estate agent. The PropertySold.ca poll ranked 10 of Ontario's largest cities. Brampton was praised for a high number of monthly listings and new housing developments. Kitchener-Waterloo and Mississauga ranked #2 and #3, respectively. *Real Estate News, "Top 10 for Sale By Owner Cities in Ontario: Brampton Ranks Number 1," September 7th, 2011*
- Brampton ranked #2 in population growth when compared to other Canadian cities with populations greater than 100,000. The 2011 Census showed that Brampton grew by 20.8% between 2006 and 2011. The city has the lowest median age among Canada's largest cities. *Statistics Canada. 2012. Focus on Geography Series, 2011 Census, September 19th, 2012*

PROFILES / Brampton, Ontario

Population Growth and Density

Area	Population in 2001	Population in 2006	Population in 2011	Population Change 2001–2006	Population Change 2006–2011	Land Area (sq. km)	Population Density per sq. km
Brampton	325,428	433,806	523,911	33.3	20.8	266.34	1,967.1
Ontario	11,410,046	12,160,282	12,851,821	6.6	5.7	908,607.67	14.1
Canada	30,007,094	31,612,897	33,476,688	5.4	5.9	8,965,121.42	3.7

Source: Statistics Canada. 2012. Census Profile. 2011 Census. Statistics Canada Catalogue no. 98-316-XWE. Ottawa. Released October 24 2012. http://www12.statcan.gc.ca/census-recensement/2011/dp-pd/prof/index.cfm?Lang=E;
Statistics Canada 2007. 2006 Community Profiles. 2006 Census. Statistics Canada Catalogue no. 92-591-XWE. Ottawa. Released March 13 2007. http://www12.statcan.ca/census-recensement/2006/dp-pd/prof/92-591/index.cfm?Lang=E

Gender

Area	Males	Females
Number		
Brampton	258,710	265,200
Ontario	6,263,140	6,588,685
Canada	16,414,225	17,062,460
Percent of Population		
Brampton	49.4	50.6
Ontario	48.7	51.3
Canada	49.0	51.0

Source: Statistics Canada. 2012. Census Profile. 2011 Census. Statistics Canada Catalogue no. 98-316-XWE. Ottawa. Released October 24 2012.
http://www12.statcan.gc.ca/census-recensement/2011/dp-pd/prof/index.cfm?Lang=E

Marital Status

Area	Married[1]	Living Common-law	Single[2]	Separated	Divorced	Widowed
Number — Total						
Brampton	230,605	17,950	115,260	11,280	17,205	17,285
Ontario	5,367,400	791,210	2,985,020	319,805	593,730	613,880
Canada	12,941,960	3,142,525	7,816,045	698,240	1,686,035	1,584,530
Males						
Brampton	115,245	8,980	61,100	4,360	6,355	3,360
Ontario	2,681,320	397,620	1,583,760	133,790	231,160	117,980
Canada	6,470,300	1,575,495	4,206,320	299,655	680,415	310,940
Females						
Brampton	115,360	8,970	54,165	6,920	10,850	13,925
Ontario	2,686,075	393,590	1,401,260	186,015	362,570	495,905
Canada	6,471,660	1,567,035	3,609,730	398,585	1,005,620	1,273,590
Percent of Population — Total						
Brampton	56.3	4.4	28.1	2.8	4.2	4.2
Ontario	50.3	7.4	28.0	3.0	5.6	5.8
Canada	46.4	11.3	28.0	2.5	6.0	5.7
Males						
Brampton	57.8	4.5	30.6	2.2	3.2	1.7
Ontario	52.1	7.7	30.8	2.6	4.5	2.3
Canada	47.8	11.6	31.1	2.2	5.0	2.3
Females						
Brampton	54.9	4.3	25.8	3.3	5.2	6.6
Ontario	48.6	7.1	25.4	3.4	6.6	9.0
Canada	45.2	10.9	25.2	2.8	7.0	8.9

Note: (1) and not separated, (2) never legally married
Source: Statistics Canada. 2012. Census Profile. 2011 Census. Statistics Canada Catalogue no. 98-316-XWE. Ottawa. Released October 24 2012.
http://www12.statcan.gc.ca/census-recensement/2011/dp-pd/prof/index.cfm?Lang=E

Age Characteristics: 0 to 49 Years

Area	0 to 4 Years	5 to 9 Years	10 to 14 Years	15 to 19 Years	20 to 24 Years	25 to 29 Years	30 to 34 Years	35 to 39 Years	40 to 44 Years	45 to 49 Years
					Number					
					Total					
Brampton	37,380	38,100	38,835	39,260	35,180	36,335	39,025	41,350	41,460	41,070
Ontario	704,260	712,755	763,755	863,635	852,910	815,120	800,365	844,335	924,075	1,055,880
Canada	1,877,095	1,809,895	1,920,355	2,178,135	2,187,450	2,169,590	2,162,905	2,173,930	2,324,875	2,675,130
					Males					
Brampton	19,335	19,705	20,270	20,345	17,960	17,225	17,935	19,645	20,270	20,685
Ontario	360,590	365,290	391,630	443,680	432,490	400,045	383,340	405,845	447,920	517,510
Canada	961,150	925,965	983,995	1,115,845	1,108,775	1,077,275	1,058,810	1,064,200	1,141,720	1,318,715
					Females					
Brampton	18,050	18,390	18,570	18,915	17,220	19,105	21,090	21,705	21,190	20,390
Ontario	343,670	347,465	372,125	419,950	420,415	415,075	417,030	438,485	476,155	538,370
Canada	915,945	883,935	936,360	1,062,295	1,078,670	1,092,315	1,104,095	1,109,735	1,183,155	1,356,420
					Percent of Population					
					Total					
Brampton	7.1	7.3	7.4	7.5	6.7	6.9	7.4	7.9	7.9	7.8
Ontario	5.5	5.5	5.9	6.7	6.6	6.3	6.2	6.6	7.2	8.2
Canada	5.6	5.4	5.7	6.5	6.5	6.5	6.5	6.5	6.9	8.0
					Males					
Brampton	7.5	7.6	7.8	7.9	6.9	6.7	6.9	7.6	7.8	8.0
Ontario	5.8	5.8	6.3	7.1	6.9	6.4	6.1	6.5	7.2	8.3
Canada	5.9	5.6	6.0	6.8	6.8	6.6	6.5	6.5	7.0	8.0
					Females					
Brampton	6.8	6.9	7.0	7.1	6.5	7.2	8.0	8.2	8.0	7.7
Ontario	5.2	5.3	5.6	6.4	6.4	6.3	6.3	6.7	7.2	8.2
Canada	5.4	5.2	5.5	6.2	6.3	6.4	6.5	6.5	6.9	7.9

Source: Statistics Canada. 2012. Census Profile. 2011 Census. Statistics Canada Catalogue no. 98-316-XWE. Ottawa. Released October 24 2012.
http://www12.statcan.gc.ca/census-recensement/2011/dp-pd/prof/index.cfm?Lang=E

Age Characteristics: 50 Years and Over, and Median Age

Area	50 to 54 Years	55 to 59 Years	60 to 64 Years	65 to 69 Years	70 to 74 Years	75 to 79 Years	80 to 84 Years	85 Years and Over	Median Age
				Number					
				Total					
Brampton	34,955	28,705	24,770	17,455	12,200	8,170	5,355	4,300	34.7
Ontario	1,006,140	864,620	765,655	563,485	440,780	356,150	271,510	246,400	40.4
Canada	2,658,965	2,340,635	2,052,670	1,521,715	1,153,065	922,700	702,070	645,515	40.6
				Males					
Brampton	17,655	13,900	11,975	8,525	5,815	3,750	2,270	1,450	34.1
Ontario	492,560	418,755	370,370	270,875	206,350	161,345	113,620	80,925	39.4
Canada	1,309,030	1,147,300	1,002,690	738,010	543,435	417,945	291,085	208,300	39.6
				Females					
Brampton	17,300	14,805	12,795	8,930	6,390	4,420	3,085	2,855	35.3
Ontario	513,580	445,865	395,275	292,610	234,435	194,805	157,890	165,475	41.3
Canada	1,349,940	1,193,335	1,049,985	783,705	609,630	504,755	410,985	437,215	41.5
				Percent of Population					
				Total					
Brampton	6.7	5.5	4.7	3.3	2.3	1.6	1.0	0.8	–
Ontario	7.8	6.7	6.0	4.4	3.4	2.8	2.1	1.9	–
Canada	7.9	7.0	6.1	4.5	3.4	2.8	2.1	1.9	–
				Males					
Brampton	6.8	5.4	4.6	3.3	2.2	1.4	0.9	0.6	–
Ontario	7.9	6.7	5.9	4.3	3.3	2.6	1.8	1.3	–
Canada	8.0	7.0	6.1	4.5	3.3	2.5	1.8	1.3	–
				Females					
Brampton	6.5	5.6	4.8	3.4	2.4	1.7	1.2	1.1	–
Ontario	7.8	6.8	6.0	4.4	3.6	3.0	2.4	2.5	–
Canada	7.9	7.0	6.2	4.6	3.6	3.0	2.4	2.6	–

Source: Statistics Canada. 2012. Census Profile. 2011 Census. Statistics Canada Catalogue no. 98-316-XWE. Ottawa. Released October 24 2012.
http://www12.statcan.gc.ca/census-recensement/2011/dp-pd/prof/index.cfm?Lang=E

PROFILES / Brampton, Ontario

Private Households by Household Size

Area	1 Person	2 Persons	3 Persons	4 Persons	5 Persons	6 or More Persons	Average Number of Persons in Private Households
			Households				
Brampton	18,050	31,520	27,825	35,720	18,590	17,570	3.5
Ontario	1,230,975	1,584,415	803,030	783,925	310,860	174,305	2.6
Canada	3,673,310	4,544,820	2,081,900	1,903,300	724,405	392,885	2.5
			Percent of Households				
Brampton	12.1	21.1	18.6	23.9	12.5	11.8	–
Ontario	25.2	32.4	16.4	16.0	6.4	3.6	–
Canada	27.6	34.1	15.6	14.3	5.4	2.9	–

Source: Statistics Canada. 2012. Census Profile. 2011 Census. Statistics Canada Catalogue no. 98-316-XWE. Ottawa. Released October 24 2012.
http://www12.statcan.gc.ca/census-recensement/2011/dp-pd/prof/index.cfm?Lang=E

Dwelling Type

Area	Single-detached House	Semi-detached House	Row House	Apartment: Building with Five or More Storeys	Apartment: Building with Fewer Than Five Storeys	Duplex Apartment	Movable Dwelling	Other Single-attached House
				Number				
Brampton	78,975	20,240	17,215	17,005	6,805	8,970	30	35
Ontario	2,718,880	279,470	415,225	789,970	498,160	160,460	15,800	9,540
Canada	7,329,150	646,245	791,600	1,234,770	2,397,550	704,485	183,510	33,310
				Percent of Dwellings				
Brampton	52.9	13.6	11.5	11.4	4.6	6.0	0.0	0.0
Ontario	55.6	5.7	8.5	16.2	10.2	3.3	0.3	0.2
Canada	55.0	4.9	5.9	9.3	18.0	5.3	1.4	0.3

Source: Statistics Canada. 2012. Census Profile. 2011 Census. Statistics Canada Catalogue no. 98-316-XWE. Ottawa. Released October 24 2012.
http://www12.statcan.gc.ca/census-recensement/2011/dp-pd/prof/index.cfm?Lang=E

Shelter Costs

	Owned Dwellings					Rented Dwellings		
Area	Number	Median Value[1] ($)	Average Value[1] ($)	Median Monthly Costs[2] ($)	Average Monthly Costs[2] ($)	Number	Median Monthly Costs[3] ($)	Average Monthly Costs[3] ($)
Brampton	121,975	359,741	398,374	1,666	1,606	27,255	1,022	1,047
Ontario	3,446,650	300,862	367,428	1,163	1,284	1,385,535	892	926
Canada	9,013,410	280,552	345,182	978	1,141	4,060,385	784	848

Note: All figures cover non-farm, non-reserve private dwellings; (1) Refers to the dollar amount expected by the owner if the dwelling were to be sold; (2) Includes all shelter expenses paid by households that own their dwellings, such as the mortgage payment and the costs of electricity, heat, water and other municipal services, property taxes and condominium fees; (3) Includes all shelter expenses paid by households that rent their dwellings, such as the monthly rent and the costs of electricity, heat and municipal services.
Source: Statistics Canada. 2013. 2011 National Household Survey. Statistics Canada Catalogue no. 99-004-XWE. Ottawa. Released September 11, 2013.

Occupied Private Dwellings by Period of Construction

Area	1960 or Before	1961 to 1980	1981 to 1990	1991 to 2000	2001 to 2005	2006 to 2011
			Number			
Brampton	7,415	35,155	28,510	25,540	31,485	21,165
Ontario	1,330,235	1,420,570	763,430	609,310	414,795	348,310
Canada	3,273,105	4,152,715	2,112,110	1,707,880	1,031,020	1,042,430
			Percent of Dwellings			
Brampton	5.0	23.6	19.1	17.1	21.1	14.2
Ontario	27.2	29.1	15.6	12.5	8.5	7.1
Canada	24.6	31.2	15.9	12.8	7.7	7.8

Note: Figures cover non-farm, non-reserve private dwellings and includes data up to May 10, 2011.
Source: Statistics Canada. 2013. 2011 National Household Survey. Statistics Canada Catalogue no. 99-004-XWE. Ottawa. Released September 11, 2013.

PROFILES / Brampton, Ontario

Educational Attainment

Area	No Certificate, Diploma or Degree	High School Diploma or Equivalent[1]	Apprenticeship or Trades Certificate or Diploma[2]	College, CÉGEP or Other Non-University Certificate or Diploma	University Certificate or Diploma Below the Bachelor Level[3]	Bachelor's Degree	University Certificate, Diploma or Degree Above Bachelor Level[4]
				Number			
				Total			
Brampton	81,505	118,630	26,145	75,595	23,060	50,370	31,605
Ontario	1,954,520	2,801,805	771,140	2,070,875	427,150	1,515,075	933,100
Canada	5,485,400	6,968,935	2,950,685	4,970,020	1,200,130	3,634,425	2,049,930
				Males			
Brampton	38,610	58,495	17,425	33,570	11,165	23,810	15,260
Ontario	957,040	1,337,055	520,390	894,235	193,355	692,345	470,290
Canada	2,742,875	3,305,415	1,928,970	2,118,430	513,235	1,643,080	1,043,350
				Females			
Brampton	42,895	60,135	8,720	42,020	11,895	26,550	16,345
Ontario	997,475	1,464,755	250,750	1,176,640	233,790	822,730	462,805
Canada	2,742,520	3,663,515	1,021,715	2,851,595	686,890	1,991,345	1,006,585
				Percent of Population			
				Total			
Brampton	20.0	29.2	6.4	18.6	5.7	12.4	7.8
Ontario	18.7	26.8	7.4	19.8	4.1	14.5	8.9
Canada	20.1	25.6	10.8	18.2	4.4	13.3	7.5
				Males			
Brampton	19.5	29.5	8.8	16.9	5.6	12.0	7.7
Ontario	18.9	26.4	10.3	17.7	3.8	13.7	9.3
Canada	20.6	24.9	14.5	15.9	3.9	12.4	7.8
				Females			
Brampton	20.6	28.8	4.2	20.1	5.7	12.7	7.8
Ontario	18.4	27.1	4.6	21.8	4.3	15.2	8.6
Canada	19.6	26.2	7.3	20.4	4.9	14.3	7.2

Note: Figures cover total population aged 15 years and over by highest certificate, diploma or degree; (1) Includes persons who have graduated from a secondary school or equivalent. It excludes persons with a postsecondary certificate, diploma or degree; (2) Includes Registered Apprenticeship certificates (including Certificate of Qualification, Journeyperson's designation) and other trades certificates or diplomas such as pre-employment or vocational certificates and diplomas from brief trade programs completed at community colleges, institutes of technology, vocational centres, and similar institutions; (3) Comparisons with other data sources suggest that the category 'University certificate or diploma below the bachelor's level' was over-reported in the NHS. This category likely includes some responses that are actually college certificates or diplomas, bachelor's degrees or other types of education (e.g., university transfer programs, bachelor's programs completed in other countries, incomplete bachelor's programs, non-university professional designations). We recommend users interpret the results for the 'University certificate or diploma below the bachelor's level' category with caution; (4) 'University certificate or diploma above bachelor level' includes the categories: 'Degree in medicine, dentistry, veterinary medicine or optometry,' 'Master's degree' and 'Earned doctorate.'
Source: Statistics Canada. 2013. 2011 National Household Survey. Statistics Canada Catalogue no. 99-004-XWE. Ottawa. Released September 11, 2013.

Household Income Distribution

Area	Less than $10,000	$10,000 to $19,999	$20,000 to $29,999	$30,000 to $39,999	$40,000 to $49,999	$50,000 to $59,999	$60,000 to $79,999	$80,000 to $99,999	$100,000 to $124,999	$125,000 to $149,999	$150,000 and Over
						Households					
Brampton	4,370	6,330	7,935	10,625	11,360	12,655	23,900	20,350	19,750	12,535	19,455
Ontario	201,780	354,530	405,725	425,410	425,720	398,705	680,850	552,660	497,970	331,460	611,840
Canada	626,705	1,141,945	1,193,925	1,271,675	1,206,800	1,102,120	1,865,280	1,458,240	1,260,770	802,555	1,389,240
						Percent of Households					
Brampton	2.9	4.2	5.3	7.1	7.6	8.5	16.0	13.6	13.2	8.4	13.0
Ontario	4.1	7.3	8.3	8.7	8.7	8.2	13.9	11.3	10.2	6.8	12.5
Canada	4.7	8.6	9.0	9.5	9.1	8.3	14.0	10.9	9.5	6.0	10.4

Note: Household income is the sum of the total incomes of all members of that household. Total income refers to monetary receipts from certain sources, before income taxes and deductions, during calendar year 2010.
Source: Statistics Canada. 2013. 2011 National Household Survey. Statistics Canada Catalogue no. 99-004-XWE. Ottawa. Released September 11, 2013.

Median and Average Household and Economic Family Income

Area	Median Household Income ($)	Average Household Income ($)	Median After-tax Household Income ($)	Average After-tax Household Income ($)	Median Economic Family Income ($)	Average Economic Family Income ($)	Median After-tax Economic Family Income ($)	Average After-tax Economic Family Income ($)
Brampton	77,787	89,010	68,782	76,816	82,935	93,817	73,450	81,066
Ontario	66,358	85,772	58,717	71,523	80,987	100,152	71,128	83,322
Canada	61,072	79,102	54,089	66,149	76,511	94,125	67,044	78,517

Note: Figures cover household and economic familiy income in 2010. A household is defined as a person or a group of persons (other than foreign residents) who occupy the same private dwelling and do not have a usual place of residence elsewhere in Canada. Every person is a member of one and only one household. An economic family is defined as a group of two or more persons who live in the same dwelling and are related to each other by blood, marriage, common-law, adoption or a foster relationship. A couple may be of opposite or same sex.
Source: Statistics Canada. 2013. 2011 National Household Survey. Statistics Canada Catalogue no. 99-004-XWE. Ottawa. Released September 11, 2013.

MAJOR CANADIAN CITIES: COMPARED AND RANKED

PROFILES / Brampton, Ontario

Individual Income Distribution

Area	Less than $10,000	$10,000 to $19,999	$20,000 to $29,999	$30,000 to $39,999	$40,000 to $49,999	$50,000 to $59,999	$60,000 to $79,999	$80,000 to $99,999	$100,000 to $124,999	$125,000 and Over
Number — Total										
Brampton	75,810	67,840	51,905	45,760	40,110	29,920	34,405	16,615	7,480	5,565
Ontario	1,780,355	1,748,060	1,361,710	1,136,730	980,790	746,360	964,280	574,710	293,865	330,285
Canada	4,492,040	4,835,710	3,670,020	3,180,360	2,603,520	1,921,650	2,437,440	1,302,045	693,580	782,135
Males										
Brampton	33,210	26,860	24,305	21,630	20,365	16,585	21,760	10,595	5,280	4,000
Ontario	781,095	669,815	580,990	535,255	491,125	407,005	569,205	341,160	201,125	244,500
Canada	1,936,365	1,864,880	1,588,260	1,522,190	1,333,510	1,079,780	1,473,145	823,720	492,905	599,905
Females										
Brampton	42,600	40,985	27,595	24,130	19,750	13,335	12,640	6,025	2,195	1,570
Ontario	999,265	1,078,245	780,720	601,475	489,665	339,360	395,075	233,550	92,740	85,790
Canada	2,555,675	2,970,825	2,081,760	1,658,170	1,270,010	841,870	964,300	478,330	200,680	182,230
Percent of Population — Total										
Brampton	20.2	18.1	13.8	12.2	10.7	8.0	9.2	4.4	2.0	1.5
Ontario	18.0	17.6	13.7	11.5	9.9	7.5	9.7	5.8	3.0	3.3
Canada	17.3	18.7	14.2	12.3	10.0	7.4	9.4	5.0	2.7	3.0
Males										
Brampton	18.0	14.6	13.2	11.7	11.0	9.0	11.8	5.7	2.9	2.2
Ontario	16.2	13.9	12.1	11.1	10.2	8.4	11.8	7.1	4.2	5.1
Canada	15.2	14.7	12.5	12.0	10.5	8.5	11.6	6.5	3.9	4.7
Females										
Brampton	22.3	21.5	14.5	12.6	10.3	7.0	6.6	3.2	1.2	0.8
Ontario	19.6	21.2	15.3	11.8	9.6	6.7	7.8	4.6	1.8	1.7
Canada	19.4	22.5	15.8	12.6	9.6	6.4	7.3	3.6	1.5	1.4

Note: Figures cover individuals aged 15 years and over with income. Income refers to monetary receipts from certain sources, before income taxes and deductions, during calendar year 2010.
Source: Statistics Canada. 2013. 2011 National Household Survey. Statistics Canada Catalogue no. 99-004-XWE. Ottawa. Released September 11, 2013.

Labour Force Status

Area	In the Labour Force — All	Employed	Unemployed	Not in the Labour Force
Number — Total				
Brampton	281,250	254,595	26,650	125,655
Ontario	6,864,990	6,297,005	567,985	3,608,685
Canada	17,990,080	16,595,035	1,395,045	9,269,445
Males				
Brampton	147,965	135,440	12,525	50,385
Ontario	3,542,030	3,249,165	292,865	1,522,690
Canada	9,388,570	8,634,310	754,255	3,906,785
Females				
Brampton	133,285	119,160	14,125	75,275
Ontario	3,322,955	3,047,840	275,120	2,085,990
Canada	8,601,515	7,960,725	640,790	5,362,660
Percent of Labour Force — Total				
Brampton	69.1	62.6	9.5	30.9
Ontario	65.5	60.1	8.3	34.5
Canada	66.0	60.9	7.8	34.0
Males				
Brampton	74.6	68.3	8.5	25.4
Ontario	69.9	64.2	8.3	30.1
Canada	70.6	64.9	8.0	29.4
Females				
Brampton	63.9	57.1	10.6	36.1
Ontario	61.4	56.3	8.3	38.6
Canada	61.6	57.0	7.4	38.4

Note: Figures are based on total population 15 years and over
Source: Statistics Canada. 2013. 2011 National Household Survey. Statistics Canada Catalogue no. 99-004-XWE. Ottawa. Released September 11, 2013.

Labour Force by Industry (NAICS Codes 11–52)

Area	Agriculture, forestry, fishing & hunting	Mining, quarrying, & oil & gas extraction	Utilities	Construction	Manufacturing	Wholesale Trade	Retail Trade	Transportation & warehousing	Information & cultural industries	Finance & insurance
					Number Total					
Brampton	950	265	1,235	14,560	44,465	19,700	31,935	31,520	6,470	13,640
Ontario	101,280	29,985	57,035	417,900	697,565	305,030	751,200	307,405	178,720	364,415
Canada	437,650	261,050	149,940	1,215,380	1,619,295	733,445	2,031,665	827,780	420,830	767,960
					Males					
Brampton	575	205	880	12,905	28,020	11,155	14,825	23,245	3,705	5,445
Ontario	66,485	25,650	42,685	369,300	493,305	197,770	344,480	225,245	98,835	153,125
Canada	307,370	211,690	110,765	1,068,710	1,167,680	494,545	933,850	617,305	235,875	296,995
					Females					
Brampton	380	55	350	1,650	16,445	8,540	17,110	8,275	2,770	8,195
Ontario	34,800	4,340	14,350	48,595	204,260	107,260	406,720	82,160	79,885	211,290
Canada	130,285	49,360	39,175	146,670	451,615	238,900	1,097,820	210,475	184,955	470,960
					Percent of Labour Force Total					
Brampton	0.3	0.1	0.5	5.4	16.4	7.3	11.8	11.6	2.4	5.0
Ontario	1.5	0.4	0.9	6.3	10.4	4.6	11.2	4.6	2.7	5.5
Canada	2.5	1.5	0.9	6.9	9.2	4.2	11.6	4.7	2.4	4.4
					Males					
Brampton	0.4	0.1	0.6	9.0	19.5	7.8	10.3	16.2	2.6	3.8
Ontario	1.9	0.7	1.2	10.7	14.3	5.7	10.0	6.5	2.9	4.4
Canada	3.3	2.3	1.2	11.6	12.7	5.4	10.2	6.7	2.6	3.2
					Females					
Brampton	0.3	0.0	0.3	1.3	12.9	6.7	13.4	6.5	2.2	6.4
Ontario	1.1	0.1	0.4	1.5	6.3	3.3	12.6	2.5	2.5	6.5
Canada	1.6	0.6	0.5	1.7	5.4	2.8	13.1	2.5	2.2	5.6

Note: Figures are based on total experienced labour force 15 years and over. Experienced labour force refers to persons who, during the week of Sunday, May 1 to Saturday, May 7, 2011, were employed and the unemployed who had last worked for pay or in self-employment in either 2010 or 2011.
Source: Statistics Canada. 2013. 2011 National Household Survey. Statistics Canada Catalogue no. 99-004-XWE. Ottawa. Released September 11, 2013.

Labour Force by Industry (NAICS Codes 53–91)

Area	Real estate & rental & leasing	Profess., scientific & tech. services	Mgmt of companies & enterprises	Admin. & support, waste mgmt & remed. services	Educational services	Health care & social assistance	Arts, entertain. & recreation	Accomm. & food services	Other services (except public admin.)	Public admin.
					Number Total					
Brampton	5,155	15,610	300	15,925	12,830	20,410	3,110	13,015	9,560	10,790
Ontario	133,980	511,020	6,525	309,630	499,690	692,130	144,065	417,675	296,340	458,665
Canada	321,895	1,240,850	17,460	728,330	1,301,435	1,949,650	363,405	1,130,750	807,800	1,261,050
					Males					
Brampton	3,025	8,190	145	8,825	3,425	2,850	1,645	4,675	4,970	5,215
Ontario	72,835	281,420	3,540	172,475	162,765	120,165	75,035	177,240	133,795	236,655
Canada	179,090	688,625	9,380	411,250	424,915	349,430	188,270	469,990	372,940	652,510
					Females					
Brampton	2,130	7,415	150	7,105	9,410	17,560	1,470	8,335	4,585	5,575
Ontario	61,145	229,600	2,990	137,155	336,925	571,965	69,030	240,430	162,550	222,015
Canada	142,805	552,225	8,075	317,085	876,515	1,600,220	175,135	660,760	434,865	608,535
					Percent of Labour Force Total					
Brampton	1.9	5.8	0.1	5.9	4.7	7.5	1.1	4.8	3.5	4.0
Ontario	2.0	7.6	0.1	4.6	7.5	10.4	2.2	6.3	4.4	6.9
Canada	1.8	7.1	0.1	4.1	7.4	11.1	2.1	6.4	4.6	7.2
					Males					
Brampton	2.1	5.7	0.1	6.1	2.4	2.0	1.1	3.2	3.5	3.6
Ontario	2.1	8.2	0.1	5.0	4.7	3.5	2.2	5.1	3.9	6.9
Canada	1.9	7.5	0.1	4.5	4.6	3.8	2.0	5.1	4.1	7.1
					Females					
Brampton	1.7	5.8	0.1	5.6	7.4	13.8	1.2	6.5	3.6	4.4
Ontario	1.9	7.1	0.1	4.2	10.4	17.7	2.1	7.4	5.0	6.9
Canada	1.7	6.6	0.1	3.8	10.4	19.1	2.1	7.9	5.2	7.2

Note: Figures are based on total experienced labour force 15 years and over. Experienced labour force refers to persons who, during the week of Sunday, May 1 to Saturday, May 7, 2011, were employed and the unemployed who had last worked for pay or in self-employment in either 2010 or 2011.
Source: Statistics Canada. 2013. 2011 National Household Survey. Statistics Canada Catalogue no. 99-004-XWE. Ottawa. Released September 11, 2013.

PROFILES / Brampton, Ontario

Occupation

Area	Mgmt	Business, Finance & Admin.	Natural/ Applied Sciences & Related	Health	Education, Law & Social, Community & Government Services	Art, Culture, Recreation & Sport	Sales & Service	Trades, Transport & Equip. Operators & Related	Natural Resources, Agri. & Related Production	Mfg & Utilities
Number — Total										
Brampton	23,540	51,505	18,140	11,415	21,425	4,425	61,540	50,210	2,035	27,215
Ontario	770,580	1,138,330	494,500	392,695	801,465	206,420	1,550,260	868,515	106,810	350,685
Canada	1,963,600	2,902,045	1,237,775	1,107,200	2,064,675	503,415	4,068,170	2,537,775	397,930	805,040
Males										
Brampton	14,345	17,370	14,380	1,725	5,725	2,140	25,820	46,300	1,690	14,440
Ontario	474,655	352,505	384,345	78,330	264,570	96,055	673,880	812,280	82,610	233,565
Canada	1,229,460	854,190	966,355	217,520	676,550	232,535	1,745,705	2,385,615	318,945	564,300
Females										
Brampton	9,190	34,140	3,760	9,685	15,700	2,280	35,725	3,905	345	12,780
Ontario	295,920	785,825	110,150	314,370	536,895	110,370	876,380	56,230	24,200	117,115
Canada	734,140	2,047,855	271,415	889,675	1,388,130	270,875	2,322,465	152,165	78,980	240,740
Percent of Labour Force — Total										
Brampton	8.7	19.0	6.7	4.2	7.9	1.6	22.7	18.5	0.7	10.0
Ontario	11.5	17.0	7.4	5.9	12.0	3.1	23.2	13.0	1.6	5.2
Canada	11.2	16.5	7.0	6.3	11.7	2.9	23.1	14.4	2.3	4.6
Males										
Brampton	10.0	12.1	10.0	1.2	4.0	1.5	17.9	32.2	1.2	10.0
Ontario	13.7	10.2	11.1	2.3	7.7	2.8	19.5	23.5	2.4	6.8
Canada	13.4	9.3	10.5	2.4	7.4	2.5	19.0	26.0	3.5	6.1
Females										
Brampton	7.2	26.8	2.9	7.6	12.3	1.8	28.0	3.1	0.3	10.0
Ontario	9.2	24.3	3.4	9.7	16.6	3.4	27.2	1.7	0.7	3.6
Canada	8.7	24.4	3.2	10.6	16.5	3.2	27.7	1.8	0.9	2.9

Note: Figures are based on total experienced labour force 15 years and over
Source: Statistics Canada. 2013. 2011 National Household Survey. Statistics Canada Catalogue no. 99-004-XWE. Ottawa. Released September 11, 2013.

Place of Work Status

Area	Worked at Home	Worked Outside Canada	No Fixed Workplace Address	Worked at Usual Place
Number — Total				
Brampton	9,625	905	29,615	214,450
Ontario	423,790	31,390	670,835	5,170,980
Canada	1,142,640	66,460	1,868,245	13,517,690
Males				
Brampton	4,750	735	22,555	107,400
Ontario	216,900	21,150	486,560	2,524,555
Canada	582,150	47,355	1,400,485	6,604,325
Females				
Brampton	4,870	175	7,065	107,050
Ontario	206,895	10,240	184,275	2,646,420
Canada	560,490	19,100	467,760	6,913,370
Percent of Labour Force — Total				
Brampton	3.8	0.4	11.6	84.2
Ontario	6.7	0.5	10.7	82.1
Canada	6.9	0.4	11.3	81.5
Males				
Brampton	3.5	0.5	16.7	79.3
Ontario	6.7	0.7	15.0	77.7
Canada	6.7	0.5	16.2	76.5
Females				
Brampton	4.1	0.1	5.9	89.8
Ontario	6.8	0.3	6.0	86.8
Canada	7.0	0.2	5.9	86.8

Note: Figures are based on total employed labour force 15 years and over.
Source: Statistics Canada. 2013. 2011 National Household Survey. Statistics Canada Catalogue no. 99-004-XWE. Ottawa. Released September 11, 2013.

Mode of Transportation to Work

Area	Car; Truck; Van; as Driver	Car; Truck; Van; as Passenger	Public Transit	Walked	Bicycled	All Other Modes
			Number			
			Total			
Brampton	192,050	16,425	28,765	4,015	685	2,135
Ontario	4,235,315	357,110	818,270	299,095	69,885	62,145
Canada	11,393,140	867,050	1,851,525	880,815	201,780	191,625
			Males			
Brampton	109,630	5,805	11,785	1,380	505	855
Ontario	2,316,680	143,410	340,995	131,765	47,635	30,635
Canada	6,238,835	349,530	788,290	387,580	135,840	104,725
			Females			
Brampton	82,420	10,620	16,985	2,630	185	1,280
Ontario	1,918,640	213,700	477,275	167,325	22,250	31,515
Canada	5,154,305	517,520	1,063,235	493,230	65,940	86,900
			Percent of Labour Force			
			Total			
Brampton	78.7	6.7	11.8	1.6	0.3	0.9
Ontario	72.5	6.1	14.0	5.1	1.2	1.1
Canada	74.0	5.6	12.0	5.7	1.3	1.2
			Males			
Brampton	84.4	4.5	9.1	1.1	0.4	0.7
Ontario	76.9	4.8	11.3	4.4	1.6	1.0
Canada	77.9	4.4	9.8	4.8	1.7	1.3
			Females			
Brampton	72.2	9.3	14.9	2.3	0.2	1.1
Ontario	67.8	7.5	16.9	5.9	0.8	1.1
Canada	69.8	7.0	14.4	6.7	0.9	1.2

Note: Figures are based on total employed labour force 15 years and over.
Source: Statistics Canada. 2013. 2011 National Household Survey. Statistics Canada Catalogue no. 99-004-XWE. Ottawa. Released September 11, 2013.

Visible Minority Population Characteristics

Area	Total Minority	South Asian[1]	Chinese	Black	Filipino	Latin American	Arab	SE Asian[2]	West Asian[3]	Korean	Japanese	Multiple[4]
						Number						
						Total						
Brampton	346,230	200,220	8,035	70,290	17,905	11,405	4,125	8,630	3,485	525	675	7,385
Ontario	3,279,565	965,990	629,140	539,205	275,380	172,560	151,645	137,875	122,530	78,290	29,085	96,735
Canada	6,264,750	1,567,400	1,324,750	945,665	619,310	381,280	380,620	312,075	206,840	161,130	87,270	171,935
						Males						
Brampton	170,860	100,775	3,980	33,005	8,490	5,735	2,165	4,240	1,735	220	425	3,680
Ontario	1,582,480	484,355	301,575	251,295	116,825	83,205	79,620	67,645	62,515	38,045	13,345	46,765
Canada	3,043,010	790,755	632,325	453,005	268,885	186,355	203,485	154,035	105,620	77,165	38,270	83,335
						Females						
Brampton	175,380	99,445	4,055	37,285	9,415	5,670	1,960	4,390	1,755	310	250	3,705
Ontario	1,697,085	481,635	327,570	287,915	158,555	89,360	72,025	70,230	60,010	40,250	15,740	49,970
Canada	3,221,745	776,650	692,420	492,660	350,425	194,925	177,140	158,045	101,220	83,965	48,990	88,600
						Percent of Population						
						Total						
Brampton	66.4	38.4	1.5	13.5	3.4	2.2	0.8	1.7	0.7	0.1	0.1	1.4
Ontario	25.9	7.6	5.0	4.3	2.2	1.4	1.2	1.1	1.0	0.6	0.2	0.8
Canada	19.1	4.8	4.0	2.9	1.9	1.2	1.2	0.9	0.6	0.5	0.3	0.5
						Males						
Brampton	66.4	39.1	1.5	12.8	3.3	2.2	0.8	1.6	0.7	0.1	0.2	1.4
Ontario	25.6	7.8	4.9	4.1	1.9	1.3	1.3	1.1	1.0	0.6	0.2	0.8
Canada	18.8	4.9	3.9	2.8	1.7	1.2	1.3	1.0	0.7	0.5	0.2	0.5
						Females						
Brampton	66.5	37.7	1.5	14.1	3.6	2.1	0.7	1.7	0.7	0.1	0.1	1.4
Ontario	26.2	7.4	5.1	4.4	2.5	1.4	1.1	1.1	0.9	0.6	0.2	0.8
Canada	19.3	4.7	4.1	3.0	2.1	1.2	1.1	0.9	0.6	0.5	0.3	0.5

Note: The Employment Equity Act defines visible minorities as 'persons, other than Aboriginal peoples, who are non-Caucasian in race or non-white in colour';
(1) Includes 'East Indian,' 'Pakistani,' 'Sri Lankan,' etc.; (2) Includes 'Vietnamese,' 'Cambodian,' 'Malaysian,' 'Laotian,' etc.; (3) Includes 'Iranian,' 'Afghan,' etc.; (4) Includes respondents who reported more than one visible minority group by checking two or more mark-in circles, e.g., 'Black' and 'South Asian.'
Source: Statistics Canada. 2013. 2011 National Household Survey. Statistics Canada Catalogue no. 99-004-XWE. Ottawa. Released September 11, 2013.

PROFILES / Brampton, Ontario

Aboriginal Population

Area	Aboriginal Identity[1]	First Nations (North American Indian) Single Identity[2]	Métis Single Identity	Inuk (Inuit) Single Identity	Multiple Aboriginal Identities[3]	Aboriginal Identities Not Included Elsewhere
Number						
Total						
Brampton	3,430	1,980	1,115	60	50	220
Ontario	301,430	201,100	86,020	3,355	2,910	8,040
Canada	1,400,685	851,560	451,795	59,440	11,415	26,475
Males						
Brampton	1,470	845	465	25	20	110
Ontario	145,020	96,620	41,755	1,475	1,420	3,750
Canada	682,190	411,785	223,335	29,495	5,525	12,055
Females						
Brampton	1,965	1,135	650	35	30	110
Ontario	156,410	104,485	44,260	1,880	1,490	4,295
Canada	718,500	439,775	228,460	29,950	5,890	14,420
Percent of Population						
Total						
Brampton	0.7	0.4	0.2	0.0	0.0	0.0
Ontario	2.4	1.6	0.7	0.0	0.0	0.1
Canada	4.3	2.6	1.4	0.2	0.0	0.1
Males						
Brampton	0.6	0.3	0.2	0.0	0.0	0.0
Ontario	2.3	1.6	0.7	0.0	0.0	0.1
Canada	4.2	2.5	1.4	0.2	0.0	0.1
Females						
Brampton	0.7	0.4	0.2	0.0	0.0	0.0
Ontario	2.4	1.6	0.7	0.0	0.0	0.1
Canada	4.3	2.6	1.4	0.2	0.0	0.1

Note: (1) Includes persons who reported being an Aboriginal person, that is, First Nations (North American Indian), Métis or Inuk (Inuit) and/or those who reported Registered or Treaty Indian status, that is registered under the Indian Act of Canada, and/or those who reported membership in a First Nation or Indian band. Aboriginal peoples of Canada are defined in the Constitution Act, 1982, section 35-2 as including the Indian, Inuit and Métis peoples of Canada; (2) Users should be aware that the estimates associated with this variable are more affected than most by the incomplete enumeration of certain Indian reserves and Indian settlements in the National Household Survey (NHS); (3) Includes persons who reported being any two or all three of the following: First Nations (North American Indian), Métis or Inuk (Inuit).
Source: Statistics Canada. 2013. 2011 National Household Survey. Statistics Canada Catalogue no. 99-004-XWE. Ottawa. Released September 11, 2013.

Ethnic Origin

Area	North American Aboriginal	Other North American	European	Caribbean	Latin, Central and South American	African	Asian	Oceania
Number								
Total								
Brampton	5,850	64,425	172,180	58,400	20,655	27,975	254,115	460
Ontario	441,395	3,059,480	8,231,410	396,485	271,545	331,460	2,604,595	19,410
Canada	1,836,035	11,070,455	20,157,965	627,590	544,375	766,735	5,011,225	74,875
Males								
Brampton	2,760	32,190	84,810	26,890	10,135	13,635	127,200	265
Ontario	210,490	1,507,105	4,019,885	181,805	130,035	160,940	1,265,540	9,855
Canada	885,675	5,462,685	9,913,150	291,640	264,635	387,360	2,435,540	37,490
Females								
Brampton	3,090	32,230	87,365	31,505	10,520	14,340	126,920	195
Ontario	230,905	1,552,380	4,211,525	214,675	141,510	170,515	1,339,050	9,555
Canada	950,360	5,607,770	10,244,820	335,945	279,740	379,380	2,575,680	37,385
Percent of Population								
Total								
Brampton	1.1	12.4	33.0	11.2	4.0	5.4	48.7	0.1
Ontario	3.5	24.2	65.1	3.1	2.1	2.6	20.6	0.2
Canada	5.6	33.7	61.4	1.9	1.7	2.3	15.3	0.2
Males								
Brampton	1.1	12.5	32.9	10.4	3.9	5.3	49.4	0.1
Ontario	3.4	24.4	65.0	2.9	2.1	2.6	20.5	0.2
Canada	5.5	33.8	61.3	1.8	1.6	2.4	15.1	0.2
Females								
Brampton	1.2	12.2	33.1	11.9	4.0	5.4	48.1	0.1
Ontario	3.6	24.0	65.1	3.3	2.2	2.6	20.7	0.1
Canada	5.7	33.6	61.4	2.0	1.7	2.3	15.4	0.2

Note: The sum of the ethnic groups in this table is greater than the total population estimate because a person may report more than one ethnic origin in the NHS.
Source: Statistics Canada. 2013. 2011 National Household Survey. Statistics Canada Catalogue no. 99-004-XWE. Ottawa. Released September 11, 2013.

Religion

Area	Buddhist	Christian	Hindu	Jewish	Muslim	Sikh	Traditional (Aboriginal) Spirituality	Other Religions	No Religious Affiliation
Number									
Total									
Brampton	6,715	263,385	63,390	830	36,960	97,790	0	1,340	50,885
Ontario	163,750	8,167,295	366,720	195,540	581,950	179,765	15,905	53,080	2,927,790
Canada	366,830	22,102,745	497,965	329,495	1,053,945	454,965	64,935	130,835	7,850,605
Males									
Brampton	3,355	125,860	31,760	380	18,430	49,345	0	585	27,730
Ontario	75,355	3,839,925	183,580	95,795	293,925	90,515	7,600	23,555	1,571,195
Canada	168,465	10,497,775	250,435	161,265	540,555	229,435	31,805	57,745	4,225,645
Females									
Brampton	3,365	137,520	31,630	450	18,530	48,445	0	755	23,155
Ontario	88,395	4,327,365	183,140	99,740	288,025	89,250	8,310	29,525	1,356,600
Canada	198,365	11,604,975	247,525	168,235	513,395	225,530	33,135	73,090	3,624,965
Percent of Population									
Total									
Brampton	1.3	50.5	12.2	0.2	7.1	18.8	0.0	0.3	9.8
Ontario	1.3	64.6	2.9	1.5	4.6	1.4	0.1	0.4	23.1
Canada	1.1	67.3	1.5	1.0	3.2	1.4	0.2	0.4	23.9
Males									
Brampton	1.3	48.9	12.3	0.1	7.2	19.2	0.0	0.2	10.8
Ontario	1.2	62.1	3.0	1.5	4.8	1.5	0.1	0.4	25.4
Canada	1.0	64.9	1.5	1.0	3.3	1.4	0.2	0.4	26.1
Females									
Brampton	1.3	52.1	12.0	0.2	7.0	18.4	0.0	0.3	8.8
Ontario	1.4	66.9	2.8	1.5	4.5	1.4	0.1	0.5	21.0
Canada	1.2	69.5	1.5	1.0	3.1	1.4	0.2	0.4	21.7

Note: Religion refers to the person's self-identification as having a connection or affiliation with any religious denomination, group, body, sect, cult or other religiously defined community or system of belief. Religion is not limited to formal membership in a religious organization or group. Persons without a religious connection or affiliation can self-identify as atheist, agnostic or humanist, or can provide another applicable response.
Source: Statistics Canada. 2013. 2011 National Household Survey. Statistics Canada Catalogue no. 99-004-XWE. Ottawa. Released September 11, 2013.

Religion—Christian Denominations

Area	Anglican	Baptist	Catholic	Christian Orthodox	Lutheran	Pentecostal	Presbyterian	United Church	Other Christian
Number									
Total									
Brampton	15,975	7,820	135,555	4,985	1,745	22,545	6,750	13,070	54,940
Ontario	774,560	244,650	3,976,610	297,710	163,460	213,945	319,585	952,465	1,224,300
Canada	1,631,845	635,840	12,810,705	550,690	478,185	478,705	472,385	2,007,610	3,036,780
Males									
Brampton	7,095	3,895	67,055	2,660	755	10,310	3,350	5,715	25,025
Ontario	355,175	112,285	1,895,940	145,825	75,225	94,955	148,535	435,255	576,730
Canada	752,945	293,905	6,167,290	270,205	221,525	217,850	218,955	912,545	1,442,550
Females									
Brampton	8,875	3,925	68,500	2,320	990	12,230	3,400	7,360	29,910
Ontario	419,390	132,370	2,080,665	151,885	88,230	118,990	171,050	517,210	647,570
Canada	878,900	341,940	6,643,415	280,485	256,660	260,850	253,430	1,095,065	1,594,230
Percent of Population									
Total									
Brampton	3.1	1.5	26.0	1.0	0.3	4.3	1.3	2.5	10.5
Ontario	6.1	1.9	31.4	2.4	1.3	1.7	2.5	7.5	9.7
Canada	5.0	1.9	39.0	1.7	1.5	1.5	1.4	6.1	9.2
Males									
Brampton	2.8	1.5	26.0	1.0	0.3	4.0	1.3	2.2	9.7
Ontario	5.7	1.8	30.7	2.4	1.2	1.5	2.4	7.0	9.3
Canada	4.7	1.8	38.2	1.7	1.4	1.3	1.4	5.6	8.9
Females									
Brampton	3.4	1.5	26.0	0.9	0.4	4.6	1.3	2.8	11.3
Ontario	6.5	2.0	32.2	2.3	1.4	1.8	2.6	8.0	10.0
Canada	5.3	2.0	39.8	1.7	1.5	1.6	1.5	6.6	9.6

Note: Religion refers to the person's self-identification as having a connection or affiliation with any religious denomination, group, body, sect, cult or other religiously defined community or system of belief. Religion is not limited to formal membership in a religious organization or group. Persons without a religious connection or affiliation can self-identify as atheist, agnostic or humanist, or can provide another applicable response.
Source: Statistics Canada. 2013. 2011 National Household Survey. Statistics Canada Catalogue no. 99-004-XWE. Ottawa. Released September 11, 2013.

PROFILES / Brampton, Ontario

Immigrant Status and Period of Immigration

Area	Non-Immigrants[1]	Immigrants All	Before 1971	1971 to 1980	1981 to 1990	1991 to 2000	2001 to 2005	2006 to 2011	Non-Permanent Residents[3]
Number									
Total									
Brampton	253,110	263,670	22,340	31,600	43,675	76,240	49,110	40,700	4,535
Ontario	8,906,000	3,611,365	723,030	464,380	538,285	866,220	518,405	501,060	134,425
Canada	25,720,175	6,775,765	1,261,055	870,775	949,890	1,539,050	992,070	1,162,915	356,385
Males									
Brampton	128,215	126,815	10,890	14,655	21,795	37,170	23,605	18,710	2,430
Ontario	4,410,240	1,706,385	341,820	217,990	258,095	408,270	245,850	234,360	64,825
Canada	12,753,235	3,231,370	605,430	416,670	454,570	724,905	474,545	555,245	178,515
Females									
Brampton	124,890	136,850	11,450	16,950	21,885	39,065	25,510	21,995	2,110
Ontario	4,495,765	1,904,985	381,210	246,390	280,190	457,950	272,550	266,695	69,600
Canada	12,966,935	3,544,400	655,625	454,105	495,325	814,145	517,530	607,670	177,870
Percent of Population									
Total									
Brampton	48.6	50.6	4.3	6.1	8.4	14.6	9.4	7.8	0.9
Ontario	70.4	28.5	5.7	3.7	4.3	6.8	4.1	4.0	1.1
Canada	78.3	20.6	3.8	2.7	2.9	4.7	3.0	3.5	1.1
Males									
Brampton	49.8	49.3	4.2	5.7	8.5	14.4	9.2	7.3	0.9
Ontario	71.3	27.6	5.5	3.5	4.2	6.6	4.0	3.8	1.0
Canada	78.9	20.0	3.7	2.6	2.8	4.5	2.9	3.4	1.1
Females									
Brampton	47.3	51.9	4.3	6.4	8.3	14.8	9.7	8.3	0.8
Ontario	69.5	29.4	5.9	3.8	4.3	7.1	4.2	4.1	1.1
Canada	77.7	21.2	3.9	2.7	3.0	4.9	3.1	3.6	1.1

Note: (1) Non-immigrant refers to a person who is a Canadian citizen by birth; (2) Immigrant refers to a person who is or has ever been a landed immigrant/permanent resident. This person has been granted the right to live in Canada permanently by immigration authorities. Some immigrants have resided in Canada for a number of years, while others have arrived recently. Some immigrants are Canadian citizens, while others are not. Most immigrants are born outside Canada, but a small number are born in Canada. In the 2011 National Household Survey, 'Immigrants' includes immigrants who landed in Canada prior to May 10, 2011; (3) Non-permanent resident refers to a person from another country who has a work or study permit, or who is a refugee claimant, and any non-Canadian-born family member living in Canada with them.
Source: Statistics Canada. 2013. 2011 National Household Survey. Statistics Canada Catalogue no. 99-004-XWE. Ottawa. Released September 11, 2013.

Mother Tongue

Area	English	French	Non-official Language	English & French	English & Non-official Language	French & Non-official Language	English, French & Non-official Language
Number							
Total							
Brampton	269,790	4,375	225,065	940	20,410	735	375
Ontario	8,677,040	493,300	3,264,435	46,605	219,425	13,645	7,615
Canada	18,858,980	7,054,975	6,567,680	144,685	396,330	74,430	24,095
Males							
Brampton	133,185	2,055	111,165	440	10,360	340	160
Ontario	4,276,970	232,785	1,562,190	21,805	106,790	6,285	3,495
Canada	9,345,225	3,452,380	3,157,785	69,975	192,000	36,535	11,965
Females							
Brampton	136,605	2,325	113,900	500	10,050	400	210
Ontario	4,400,065	260,510	1,702,240	24,795	112,635	7,365	4,115
Canada	9,513,750	3,602,590	3,409,895	74,710	204,330	37,890	12,130
Percent of Population							
Total							
Brampton	51.7	0.8	43.1	0.2	3.9	0.1	0.1
Ontario	68.2	3.9	25.7	0.4	1.7	0.1	0.1
Canada	56.9	21.3	19.8	0.4	1.2	0.2	0.1
Males							
Brampton	51.7	0.8	43.1	0.2	4.0	0.1	0.1
Ontario	68.9	3.7	25.2	0.4	1.7	0.1	0.1
Canada	57.5	21.2	19.4	0.4	1.2	0.2	0.1
Females							
Brampton	51.7	0.9	43.1	0.2	3.8	0.2	0.1
Ontario	67.6	4.0	26.1	0.4	1.7	0.1	0.1
Canada	56.4	21.4	20.2	0.4	1.2	0.2	0.1

Note: Figures cover total population excluding institutional residents.
Source: Statistics Canada. 2012. Census Profile. 2011 Census. Statistics Canada Catalogue no. 98-316-XWE. Ottawa. Released October 24 2012.
http://www12.statcan.gc.ca/census-recensement/2011/dp-pd/prof/index.cfm?Lang=E

Language Spoken Most Often at Home

Area	English	French	Non-official Language	English & French	English & Non-official Language	French & Non-official Language	English, French & Non-official Language
\multicolumn{8}{c}{Number}							
\multicolumn{8}{c}{Total}							
Brampton	325,005	2,020	142,575	850	50,120	420	690
Ontario	10,044,810	284,115	1,827,870	37,955	509,105	6,370	11,845
Canada	21,457,075	6,827,865	3,673,865	131,205	875,135	109,700	46,330
\multicolumn{8}{c}{Males}							
Brampton	160,205	960	70,090	370	25,555	205	320
Ontario	4,930,610	133,495	872,860	17,250	248,050	2,855	5,225
Canada	10,585,620	3,348,235	1,767,310	63,475	425,370	53,010	22,845
\multicolumn{8}{c}{Females}							
Brampton	164,805	1,065	72,485	475	24,570	215	375
Ontario	5,114,200	150,620	955,010	20,705	261,055	3,520	6,620
Canada	10,871,455	3,479,625	1,906,555	67,730	449,765	56,690	23,485
\multicolumn{8}{c}{Percent of Population}							
\multicolumn{8}{c}{Total}							
Brampton	62.3	0.4	27.3	0.2	9.6	0.1	0.1
Ontario	79.0	2.2	14.4	0.3	4.0	0.1	0.1
Canada	64.8	20.6	11.1	0.4	2.6	0.3	0.1
\multicolumn{8}{c}{Males}							
Brampton	62.2	0.4	27.2	0.1	9.9	0.1	0.1
Ontario	79.4	2.1	14.1	0.3	4.0	0.0	0.1
Canada	65.1	20.6	10.9	0.4	2.6	0.3	0.1
\multicolumn{8}{c}{Females}							
Brampton	62.4	0.4	27.5	0.2	9.3	0.1	0.1
Ontario	78.5	2.3	14.7	0.3	4.0	0.1	0.1
Canada	64.5	20.6	11.3	0.4	2.7	0.3	0.1

Note: Figures cover total population excluding institutional residents.
Source: Statistics Canada. 2012. Census Profile. 2011 Census. Statistics Canada Catalogue no. 98-316-XWE. Ottawa. Released October 24 2012.
http://www12.statcan.gc.ca/census-recensement/2011/dp-pd/prof/index.cfm?Lang=E

Knowledge of Official Languages

Area	English Only	French Only	English & French	Neither English nor French
\multicolumn{5}{c}{Number}				
\multicolumn{5}{c}{Total}				
Brampton	471,625	375	25,500	24,190
Ontario	10,984,360	42,980	1,395,805	298,920
Canada	22,564,665	4,165,015	5,795,570	595,920
\multicolumn{5}{c}{Males}				
Brampton	237,310	150	11,135	9,105
Ontario	5,445,050	18,805	627,725	118,765
Canada	11,222,185	1,925,340	2,876,560	241,790
\multicolumn{5}{c}{Females}				
Brampton	234,315	225	14,365	15,080
Ontario	5,539,310	24,175	768,085	180,155
Canada	11,342,485	2,239,680	2,919,005	354,135
\multicolumn{5}{c}{Percent of Population}				
\multicolumn{5}{c}{Total}				
Brampton	90.4	0.1	4.9	4.6
Ontario	86.3	0.3	11.0	2.3
Canada	68.1	12.6	17.5	1.8
\multicolumn{5}{c}{Males}				
Brampton	92.1	0.1	4.3	3.5
Ontario	87.7	0.3	10.1	1.9
Canada	69.0	11.8	17.7	1.5
\multicolumn{5}{c}{Females}				
Brampton	88.8	0.1	5.4	5.7
Ontario	85.1	0.4	11.8	2.8
Canada	67.3	13.3	17.3	2.1

Note: Figures cover total population excluding institutional residents.
Source: Statistics Canada. 2012. Census Profile. 2011 Census. Statistics Canada Catalogue no. 98-316-XWE. Ottawa. Released October 24 2012.
http://www12.statcan.gc.ca/census-recensement/2011/dp-pd/prof/index.cfm?Lang=E

Burlington, Ontario

Background

The City of Burlington is located in southern Ontario on the north shore of Lake Ontario. Burlington is the western part of the Greater Toronto Area (GTA) and is also included as part of the nearby Hamilton Census Metropolitan Area (CMA).

European settlers first came to the Burlington region in the late 1700s. In recognition of his loyalty to the Crown during the American Revolution, Captain Joseph Brant was granted tracts of land in 1784, which he sold to Loyalist settlers. By 1900, Burlington was a prosperous and growing farming community.

The geography of Burlington is shaped by the Niagara Escarpment, Lake Ontario and the sloping plain where the city is situated. There are just over 580 hectares (1,433 acres) of parkland throughout the region and nine golf courses. Local attractions include the Royal Botanical Gardens, Bronte Creek Provincial Park and the Burlington Performing Arts Centre.

Burlington is central to the Golden Horseshoe and offers access to three international airports as well as major highway routes. With five post-secondary institutions in Burlington and schools in nearby Hamilton, Oakville, Toronto, St. Catharines and Waterloo, Burlington's economy is primarily knowledge-based.

Recent construction projects in the city include the Waterfront Regeneration Trust, a $17.4 million renewal project linking 740 kilometres of waterfront trails between Brockville and Niagara-on-the-Lake. The redevelopment and expansion of the city's Joseph Brant Memorial Hospital is projected at $312 million.

Popular local festivals and events include the city's Winter Carnival, Women's Show, KidsDay, the Kite Festival and Joseph Brant Day.

Burlington has summer highs of plus 26.53 degrees Celsius, winter lows of minus 7.03 degrees Celsius, and an average rainfall just over 770 mm per year.

Rankings

- Burlington was ranked #2 out of 190 Canadian cities in terms of "Best Places to Live 2012." *Money Sense Magazine* evaluated each city using 22 different criteria categories and point systems, such as affordable housing, population growth, air quality and walk/bike to work ratios. The City of Burlington also ranked #2 for "Best Places for Kids." *Money Sense, Canada's Best Places to Live, March 20, 2012*
- Burlington was ranked as one of Ontario's best cities for festivals and events. In 2012, three of the city's largest festivals were ranked in the province's Top 100 festival listings: the Sound of Music festival, Burlington's Canada Day festivities and the Children's Festival. The city's Sound of Music Festival has ranked in the Top 100 since 2000. *Festivals and Events Ontario (FEO), 2012 Top Festivals and Events Ontario, March 5, 2012*

PROFILES / Burlington, Ontario

Population Growth and Density

Area	Population in 2001	Population in 2006	Population in 2011	Population Change 2001–2006	Population Change 2006–2011	Land Area (sq. km)	Population Density per sq. km
Burlington	150,836	164,415	175,779	9.0	6.9	185.66	946.8
Ontario	11,410,046	12,160,282	12,851,821	6.6	5.7	908,607.67	14.1
Canada	30,007,094	31,612,897	33,476,688	5.4	5.9	8,965,121.42	3.7

Source: Statistics Canada. 2012. Census Profile. 2011 Census. Statistics Canada Catalogue no. 98-316-XWE. Ottawa. Released October 24 2012. http://www12.statcan.gc.ca/census-recensement/2011/dp-pd/prof/index.cfm?Lang=E;
Statistics Canada 2007. 2006 Community Profiles. 2006 Census. Statistics Canada Catalogue no. 92-591-XWE. Ottawa. Released March 13 2007. http://www12.statcan.ca/census-recensement/2006/dp-pd/prof/92-591/index.cfm?Lang=E

Gender

Area	Males	Females
	Number	
Burlington	84,520	91,255
Ontario	6,263,140	6,588,685
Canada	16,414,225	17,062,460
	Percent of Population	
Burlington	48.1	51.9
Ontario	48.7	51.3
Canada	49.0	51.0

Source: Statistics Canada. 2012. Census Profile. 2011 Census. Statistics Canada Catalogue no. 98-316-XWE. Ottawa. Released October 24 2012.
http://www12.statcan.gc.ca/census-recensement/2011/dp-pd/prof/index.cfm?Lang=E

Marital Status

Area	Married[1]	Living Common-law	Single[2]	Separated	Divorced	Widowed
			Number			
			Total			
Burlington	78,900	10,110	35,230	4,305	8,435	8,880
Ontario	5,367,400	791,210	2,985,020	319,805	593,730	613,880
Canada	12,941,960	3,142,525	7,816,045	698,240	1,686,035	1,584,530
			Males			
Burlington	39,375	5,015	18,485	1,700	2,815	1,710
Ontario	2,681,320	397,620	1,583,760	133,790	231,160	117,980
Canada	6,470,300	1,575,495	4,206,320	299,655	680,415	310,940
			Females			
Burlington	39,520	5,090	16,745	2,600	5,615	7,170
Ontario	2,686,075	393,590	1,401,260	186,015	362,570	495,905
Canada	6,471,660	1,567,035	3,609,730	398,585	1,005,620	1,273,590
			Percent of Population			
			Total			
Burlington	54.1	6.9	24.2	3.0	5.8	6.1
Ontario	50.3	7.4	28.0	3.0	5.6	5.8
Canada	46.4	11.3	28.0	2.5	6.0	5.7
			Males			
Burlington	57.0	7.3	26.7	2.5	4.1	2.5
Ontario	52.1	7.7	30.8	2.6	4.5	2.3
Canada	47.8	11.6	31.1	2.2	5.0	2.3
			Females			
Burlington	51.5	6.6	21.8	3.4	7.3	9.3
Ontario	48.6	7.1	25.4	3.4	6.6	9.0
Canada	45.2	10.9	25.2	2.8	7.0	8.9

Note: (1) and not separated, (2) never legally married
Source: Statistics Canada. 2012. Census Profile. 2011 Census. Statistics Canada Catalogue no. 98-316-XWE. Ottawa. Released October 24 2012.
http://www12.statcan.gc.ca/census-recensement/2011/dp-pd/prof/index.cfm?Lang=E

Age Characteristics: 0 to 49 Years

Area	0 to 4 Years	5 to 9 Years	10 to 14 Years	15 to 19 Years	20 to 24 Years	25 to 29 Years	30 to 34 Years	35 to 39 Years	40 to 44 Years	45 to 49 Years
					Number					
					Total					
Burlington	9,455	10,125	10,350	11,195	9,935	9,415	10,655	12,090	13,160	14,455
Ontario	704,260	712,755	763,755	863,635	852,910	815,120	800,365	844,335	924,075	1,055,880
Canada	1,877,095	1,809,895	1,920,355	2,178,135	2,187,450	2,169,590	2,162,905	2,173,930	2,324,875	2,675,130
					Males					
Burlington	4,925	5,215	5,275	5,775	5,020	4,620	5,055	5,785	6,350	6,945
Ontario	360,590	365,290	391,630	443,680	432,490	400,045	383,340	405,845	447,920	517,510
Canada	961,150	925,965	983,995	1,115,845	1,108,775	1,077,275	1,058,810	1,064,200	1,141,720	1,318,715
					Females					
Burlington	4,525	4,910	5,070	5,420	4,915	4,800	5,595	6,300	6,815	7,515
Ontario	343,670	347,465	372,125	419,950	420,415	415,075	417,030	438,485	476,155	538,370
Canada	915,945	883,935	936,360	1,062,295	1,078,670	1,092,315	1,104,095	1,109,735	1,183,155	1,356,420
					Percent of Population					
					Total					
Burlington	5.4	5.8	5.9	6.4	5.7	5.4	6.1	6.9	7.5	8.2
Ontario	5.5	5.5	5.9	6.7	6.6	6.3	6.2	6.6	7.2	8.2
Canada	5.6	5.4	5.7	6.5	6.5	6.5	6.5	6.5	6.9	8.0
					Males					
Burlington	5.8	6.2	6.2	6.8	5.9	5.5	6.0	6.8	7.5	8.2
Ontario	5.8	5.8	6.3	7.1	6.9	6.4	6.1	6.5	7.2	8.3
Canada	5.9	5.6	6.0	6.8	6.8	6.6	6.5	6.5	7.0	8.0
					Females					
Burlington	5.0	5.4	5.6	5.9	5.4	5.3	6.1	6.9	7.5	8.2
Ontario	5.2	5.3	5.6	6.4	6.4	6.3	6.3	6.7	7.2	8.2
Canada	5.4	5.2	5.5	6.2	6.3	6.4	6.5	6.5	6.9	7.9

Source: Statistics Canada. 2012. Census Profile. 2011 Census. Statistics Canada Catalogue no. 98-316-XWE. Ottawa. Released October 24 2012.
http://www12.statcan.gc.ca/census-recensement/2011/dp-pd/prof/index.cfm?Lang=E

Age Characteristics: 50 Years and Over, and Median Age

Area	50 to 54 Years	55 to 59 Years	60 to 64 Years	65 to 69 Years	70 to 74 Years	75 to 79 Years	80 to 84 Years	85 Years and Over	Median Age
				Number					
				Total					
Burlington	13,505	11,130	10,600	8,490	6,780	5,755	4,625	4,070	41.8
Ontario	1,006,140	864,620	765,655	563,485	440,780	356,150	271,510	246,400	40.4
Canada	2,658,965	2,340,635	2,052,670	1,521,715	1,153,065	922,700	702,070	645,515	40.6
				Males					
Burlington	6,610	5,220	4,885	3,950	3,090	2,540	1,960	1,315	40.5
Ontario	492,560	418,755	370,370	270,875	206,350	161,345	113,620	80,925	39.4
Canada	1,309,030	1,147,300	1,002,690	738,010	543,435	417,945	291,085	208,300	39.6
				Females					
Burlington	6,890	5,915	5,715	4,545	3,690	3,215	2,660	2,760	43.0
Ontario	513,580	445,865	395,275	292,610	234,435	194,805	157,890	165,475	41.3
Canada	1,349,940	1,193,335	1,049,985	783,705	609,630	504,755	410,985	437,215	41.5
				Percent of Population					
				Total					
Burlington	7.7	6.3	6.0	4.8	3.9	3.3	2.6	2.3	—
Ontario	7.8	6.7	6.0	4.4	3.4	2.8	2.1	1.9	—
Canada	7.9	7.0	6.1	4.5	3.4	2.8	2.1	1.9	—
				Males					
Burlington	7.8	6.2	5.8	4.7	3.7	3.0	2.3	1.6	—
Ontario	7.9	6.7	5.9	4.3	3.3	2.6	1.8	1.3	—
Canada	8.0	7.0	6.1	4.5	3.3	2.5	1.8	1.3	—
				Females					
Burlington	7.6	6.5	6.3	5.0	4.0	3.5	2.9	3.0	—
Ontario	7.8	6.8	6.0	4.4	3.6	3.0	2.4	2.5	—
Canada	7.9	7.0	6.2	4.6	3.6	3.0	2.4	2.6	—

Source: Statistics Canada. 2012. Census Profile. 2011 Census. Statistics Canada Catalogue no. 98-316-XWE. Ottawa. Released October 24 2012.
http://www12.statcan.gc.ca/census-recensement/2011/dp-pd/prof/index.cfm?Lang=E

PROFILES / Burlington, Ontario

Private Households by Household Size

Area	1 Person	2 Persons	3 Persons	4 Persons	5 Persons	6 or More Persons	Average Number of Persons in Private Households
			Households				
Burlington	16,940	23,610	11,025	11,825	3,880	1,500	2.5
Ontario	1,230,975	1,584,415	803,030	783,925	310,860	174,305	2.6
Canada	3,673,310	4,544,820	2,081,900	1,903,300	724,405	392,885	2.5
			Percent of Households				
Burlington	24.6	34.3	16.0	17.2	5.6	2.2	–
Ontario	25.2	32.4	16.4	16.0	6.4	3.6	–
Canada	27.6	34.1	15.6	14.3	5.4	2.9	–

Source: Statistics Canada. 2012. Census Profile. 2011 Census. Statistics Canada Catalogue no. 98-316-XWE. Ottawa. Released October 24 2012.
http://www12.statcan.gc.ca/census-recensement/2011/dp-pd/prof/index.cfm?Lang=E

Dwelling Type

Area	Single-detached House	Semi-detached House	Row House	Apartment: Building with Five or More Storeys	Apartment: Building with Fewer Than Five Storeys	Duplex Apartment	Movable Dwelling	Other Single-attached House
				Number				
Burlington	36,075	3,115	12,915	10,600	5,220	790	15	60
Ontario	2,718,880	279,470	415,225	789,970	498,160	160,460	15,800	9,540
Canada	7,329,150	646,245	791,600	1,234,770	2,397,550	704,485	183,510	33,310
				Percent of Dwellings				
Burlington	52.4	4.5	18.8	15.4	7.6	1.1	0.0	0.1
Ontario	55.6	5.7	8.5	16.2	10.2	3.3	0.3	0.2
Canada	55.0	4.9	5.9	9.3	18.0	5.3	1.4	0.3

Source: Statistics Canada. 2012. Census Profile. 2011 Census. Statistics Canada Catalogue no. 98-316-XWE. Ottawa. Released October 24 2012.
http://www12.statcan.gc.ca/census-recensement/2011/dp-pd/prof/index.cfm?Lang=E

Shelter Costs

	Owned Dwellings					Rented Dwellings		
Area	Number	Median Value[1] ($)	Average Value[1] ($)	Median Monthly Costs[2] ($)	Average Monthly Costs[2] ($)	Number	Median Monthly Costs[3] ($)	Average Monthly Costs[3] ($)
Burlington	53,935	399,402	431,943	1,328	1,392	14,810	1,056	1,091
Ontario	3,446,650	300,862	367,428	1,163	1,284	1,385,535	892	926
Canada	9,013,410	280,552	345,182	978	1,141	4,060,385	784	848

Note: All figures cover non-farm, non-reserve private dwellings; (1) Refers to the dollar amount expected by the owner if the dwelling were to be sold; (2) Includes all shelter expenses paid by households that own their dwellings, such as the mortgage payment and the costs of electricity, heat, water and other municipal services, property taxes and condominium fees; (3) Includes all shelter expenses paid by households that rent their dwellings, such as the monthly rent and the costs of electricity, heat and municipal services.
Source: Statistics Canada. 2013. 2011 National Household Survey. Statistics Canada Catalogue no. 99-004-XWE. Ottawa. Released September 11, 2013.

Occupied Private Dwellings by Period of Construction

Area	1960 or Before	1961 to 1980	1981 to 1990	1991 to 2000	2001 to 2005	2006 to 2011
			Number			
Burlington	11,180	23,525	10,980	10,475	7,270	5,350
Ontario	1,330,235	1,420,570	763,430	609,310	414,795	348,310
Canada	3,273,105	4,152,715	2,112,110	1,707,880	1,031,020	1,042,430
			Percent of Dwellings			
Burlington	16.3	34.2	16.0	15.2	10.6	7.8
Ontario	27.2	29.1	15.6	12.5	8.5	7.1
Canada	24.6	31.2	15.9	12.8	7.7	7.8

Note: Figures cover non-farm, non-reserve private dwellings and includes data up to May 10, 2011.
Source: Statistics Canada. 2013. 2011 National Household Survey. Statistics Canada Catalogue no. 99-004-XWE. Ottawa. Released September 11, 2013.

Educational Attainment

Area	No Certificate, Diploma or Degree	High School Diploma or Equivalent[1]	Apprenticeship or Trades Certificate or Diploma[2]	College, CÉGEP or Other Non-University Certificate or Diploma	University Certificate or Diploma Below the Bachelor Level[3]	Bachelor's Degree	University Certificate, Diploma or Degree Above Bachelor Level[4]
Number							
Total							
Burlington	17,850	37,775	8,655	33,275	6,700	25,500	13,760
Ontario	1,954,520	2,801,805	771,140	2,070,875	427,150	1,515,075	933,100
Canada	5,485,400	6,968,935	2,950,685	4,970,020	1,200,130	3,634,425	2,049,930
Males							
Burlington	8,850	17,245	5,750	14,115	3,380	12,190	6,900
Ontario	957,040	1,337,055	520,390	894,235	193,355	692,345	470,290
Canada	2,742,875	3,305,415	1,928,970	2,118,430	513,235	1,643,080	1,043,350
Females							
Burlington	8,995	20,530	2,905	19,160	3,325	13,305	6,860
Ontario	997,475	1,464,755	250,750	1,176,640	233,790	822,730	462,805
Canada	2,742,520	3,663,515	1,021,715	2,851,595	686,890	1,991,345	1,006,585
Percent of Population							
Total							
Burlington	12.4	26.3	6.0	23.2	4.7	17.8	9.6
Ontario	18.7	26.8	7.4	19.8	4.1	14.5	8.9
Canada	20.1	25.6	10.8	18.2	4.4	13.3	7.5
Males							
Burlington	12.9	25.2	8.4	20.6	4.9	17.8	10.1
Ontario	18.9	26.4	10.3	17.7	3.8	13.7	9.3
Canada	20.6	24.9	14.5	15.9	3.9	12.4	7.8
Females							
Burlington	12.0	27.3	3.9	25.5	4.4	17.7	9.1
Ontario	18.4	27.1	4.6	21.8	4.3	15.2	8.6
Canada	19.6	26.2	7.3	20.4	4.9	14.3	7.2

Note: Figures cover total population aged 15 years and over by highest certificate, diploma or degree; (1) Includes persons who have graduated from a secondary school or equivalent. It excludes persons with a postsecondary certificate, diploma or degree; (2) Includes Registered Apprenticeship certificates (including Certificate of Qualification, Journeyperson's designation) and other trades certificates or diplomas such as pre-employment or vocational certificates and diplomas from brief trade programs completed at community colleges, institutes of technology, vocational centres, and similar institutions; (3) Comparisons with other data sources suggest that the category 'University certificate or diploma below the bachelor's level' was over-reported in the NHS. This category likely includes some responses that are actually college certificates or diplomas, bachelor's degrees or other types of education (e.g., university transfer programs, bachelor's programs completed in other countries, incomplete bachelor's programs, non-university professional designations). We recommend users interpret the results for the 'University certificate or diploma below the bachelor's level' category with caution; (4) 'University certificate or diploma above bachelor level' includes the categories: 'Degree in medicine, dentistry, veterinary medicine or optometry,' 'Master's degree' and 'Earned doctorate.'
Source: Statistics Canada. 2013. 2011 National Household Survey. Statistics Canada Catalogue no. 99-004-XWE. Ottawa. Released September 11, 2013.

Household Income Distribution

Area	Less than $10,000	$10,000 to $19,999	$20,000 to $29,999	$30,000 to $39,999	$40,000 to $49,999	$50,000 to $59,999	$60,000 to $79,999	$80,000 to $99,999	$100,000 to $124,999	$125,000 to $149,999	$150,000 and Over
Households											
Burlington	1,560	2,800	4,265	4,925	5,005	5,385	9,185	8,585	7,715	6,085	13,250
Ontario	201,780	354,530	405,725	425,410	425,720	398,705	680,850	552,660	497,970	331,460	611,840
Canada	626,705	1,141,945	1,193,925	1,271,675	1,206,800	1,102,120	1,865,280	1,458,540	1,260,770	802,555	1,389,240
Percent of Households											
Burlington	2.3	4.1	6.2	7.2	7.3	7.8	13.4	12.5	11.2	8.8	19.3
Ontario	4.1	7.3	8.3	8.7	8.7	8.2	13.9	11.3	10.2	6.8	12.5
Canada	4.7	8.6	9.0	9.5	9.1	8.3	14.0	10.9	9.5	6.0	10.4

Note: Household income is the sum of the total incomes of all members of that household. Total income refers to monetary receipts from certain sources, before income taxes and deductions, during calendar year 2010.
Source: Statistics Canada. 2013. 2011 National Household Survey. Statistics Canada Catalogue no. 99-004-XWE. Ottawa. Released September 11, 2013.

Median and Average Household and Economic Family Income

Area	Median Household Income ($)	Average Household Income ($)	Median After-tax Household Income ($)	Average After-tax Household Income ($)	Median Economic Family Income ($)	Average Economic Family Income ($)	Median After-tax Economic Family Income ($)	Average After-tax Economic Family Income ($)
Burlington	82,494	105,503	70,781	85,444	98,995	122,561	84,225	98,935
Ontario	66,358	85,772	58,717	71,523	80,987	100,152	71,128	83,322
Canada	61,072	79,102	54,089	66,149	76,511	94,125	67,044	78,517

Note: Figures cover household and economic familiy income in 2010. A household is defined as a person or a group of persons (other than foreign residents) who occupy the same private dwelling and do not have a usual place of residence elsewhere in Canada. Every person is a member of one and only one household. An economic family is defined as a group of two or more persons who live in the same dwelling and are related to each other by blood, marriage, common-law, adoption or a foster relationship. A couple may be of opposite or same sex.
Source: Statistics Canada. 2013. 2011 National Household Survey. Statistics Canada Catalogue no. 99-004-XWE. Ottawa. Released September 11, 2013.

Individual Income Distribution

Area	Less than $10,000	$10,000 to $19,999	$20,000 to $29,999	$30,000 to $39,999	$40,000 to $49,999	$50,000 to $59,999	$60,000 to $79,999	$80,000 to $99,999	$100,000 to $124,999	$125,000 and Over
					Number					
					Total					
Burlington	20,885	19,010	16,270	15,040	13,435	11,605	15,885	11,110	6,355	8,225
Ontario	1,780,355	1,748,060	1,361,710	1,136,730	980,790	746,360	964,280	574,710	293,865	330,285
Canada	4,492,040	4,835,710	3,670,020	3,180,360	2,603,520	1,921,650	2,437,440	1,302,045	693,580	782,135
					Males					
Burlington	8,585	6,375	6,195	6,595	6,005	5,600	9,075	6,775	4,515	6,360
Ontario	781,095	669,815	580,990	535,255	491,125	407,005	569,205	341,160	201,125	244,500
Canada	1,936,365	1,864,880	1,588,260	1,522,190	1,333,510	1,079,780	1,473,145	823,720	492,905	599,905
					Females					
Burlington	12,300	12,635	10,075	8,445	7,430	6,005	6,810	4,340	1,845	1,865
Ontario	999,265	1,078,245	780,720	601,475	489,665	339,360	395,075	233,550	92,740	85,790
Canada	2,555,675	2,970,825	2,081,760	1,658,170	1,270,010	841,870	964,300	478,330	200,680	182,230
					Percent of Population					
					Total					
Burlington	15.2	13.8	11.8	10.9	9.7	8.4	11.5	8.1	4.6	6.0
Ontario	18.0	17.6	13.7	11.5	9.9	7.5	9.7	5.8	3.0	3.3
Canada	17.3	18.7	14.2	12.3	10.0	7.4	9.4	5.0	2.7	3.0
					Males					
Burlington	13.0	9.6	9.4	10.0	9.1	8.5	13.7	10.3	6.8	9.6
Ontario	16.2	13.9	12.1	11.1	10.2	8.4	11.8	7.1	4.2	5.1
Canada	15.2	14.7	12.5	12.0	10.5	8.5	11.6	6.5	3.9	4.7
					Females					
Burlington	17.1	17.6	14.0	11.8	10.4	8.4	9.5	6.0	2.6	2.6
Ontario	19.6	21.2	15.3	11.8	9.6	6.7	7.8	4.6	1.8	1.7
Canada	19.4	22.5	15.8	12.6	9.6	6.4	7.3	3.6	1.5	1.4

Note: Figures cover individuals aged 15 years and over with income. Income refers to monetary receipts from certain sources, before income taxes and deductions, during calendar year 2010.
Source: Statistics Canada. 2013. 2011 National Household Survey. Statistics Canada Catalogue no. 99-004-XWE. Ottawa. Released September 11, 2013.

Labour Force Status

Area	In the Labour Force - All	Employed	Unemployed	Not in the Labour Force
		Number		
		Total		
Burlington	98,785	93,030	5,755	44,725
Ontario	6,864,990	6,297,005	567,985	3,608,685
Canada	17,990,080	16,595,035	1,395,045	9,269,445
		Males		
Burlington	50,730	47,690	3,040	17,700
Ontario	3,542,030	3,249,165	292,865	1,522,690
Canada	9,388,570	8,634,310	754,255	3,906,785
		Females		
Burlington	48,055	45,340	2,710	27,025
Ontario	3,322,955	3,047,840	275,120	2,085,990
Canada	8,601,515	7,960,725	640,790	5,362,660
		Percent of Labour Force		
		Total		
Burlington	68.8	64.8	5.8	31.2
Ontario	65.5	60.1	8.3	34.5
Canada	66.0	60.9	7.8	34.0
		Males		
Burlington	74.1	69.7	6.0	25.9
Ontario	69.9	64.2	8.3	30.1
Canada	70.6	64.9	8.0	29.4
		Females		
Burlington	64.0	60.4	5.6	36.0
Ontario	61.4	56.3	8.3	38.6
Canada	61.6	57.0	7.4	38.4

Note: Figures are based on total population 15 years and over
Source: Statistics Canada. 2013. 2011 National Household Survey. Statistics Canada Catalogue no. 99-004-XWE. Ottawa. Released September 11, 2013.

Labour Force by Industry (NAICS Codes 11–52)

Area	Agriculture, forestry, fishing & hunting	Mining, quarrying, & oil & gas extraction	Utilities	Construction	Manufacturing	Wholesale Trade	Retail Trade	Transportation & warehousing	Information & cultural industries	Finance & insurance
					Number					
					Total					
Burlington	435	185	610	5,085	9,995	6,525	11,800	3,905	2,865	7,075
Ontario	101,280	29,985	57,035	417,900	697,565	305,030	751,200	307,405	178,720	364,415
Canada	437,650	261,050	149,940	1,215,380	1,619,295	733,445	2,031,665	827,780	420,830	767,960
					Males					
Burlington	215	130	450	4,425	7,260	4,250	5,310	2,695	1,665	3,450
Ontario	66,485	25,650	42,685	369,300	493,305	197,770	344,480	225,245	98,835	153,125
Canada	307,370	211,690	110,765	1,068,710	1,167,680	494,545	933,850	617,305	235,875	296,995
					Females					
Burlington	215	55	165	665	2,740	2,275	6,490	1,205	1,195	3,620
Ontario	34,800	4,340	14,350	48,595	204,260	107,260	406,720	82,160	79,885	211,290
Canada	130,285	49,360	39,175	146,670	451,615	238,900	1,097,820	210,475	184,955	470,960
					Percent of Labour Force					
					Total					
Burlington	0.4	0.2	0.6	5.2	10.3	6.7	12.2	4.0	3.0	7.3
Ontario	1.5	0.4	0.9	6.3	10.4	4.6	11.2	4.6	2.7	5.5
Canada	2.5	1.5	0.9	6.9	9.2	4.2	11.6	4.7	2.4	4.4
					Males					
Burlington	0.4	0.3	0.9	8.9	14.5	8.5	10.6	5.4	3.3	6.9
Ontario	1.9	0.7	1.2	10.7	14.3	5.7	10.0	6.5	2.9	4.4
Canada	3.3	2.3	1.2	11.6	12.7	5.4	10.2	6.7	2.6	3.2
					Females					
Burlington	0.5	0.1	0.3	1.4	5.8	4.8	13.8	2.6	2.5	7.7
Ontario	1.1	0.1	0.4	1.5	6.3	3.3	12.6	2.5	2.5	6.5
Canada	1.6	0.6	0.5	1.7	5.4	2.8	13.1	2.5	2.2	5.6

Note: Figures are based on total experienced labour force 15 years and over. Experienced labour force refers to persons who, during the week of Sunday, May 1 to Saturday, May 7, 2011, were employed and the unemployed who had last worked for pay or in self-employment in either 2010 or 2011.
Source: Statistics Canada. 2013. 2011 National Household Survey. Statistics Canada Catalogue no. 99-004-XWE. Ottawa. Released September 11, 2013.

Labour Force by Industry (NAICS Codes 53–91)

Area	Real estate & rental & leasing	Profess., scientific & tech. services	Mgmt of companies & enterprises	Admin. & support, waste mgmt & remed. services	Educational services	Health care & social assistance	Arts, entertain. & recreation	Accomm. & food services	Other services (except public admin.)	Public admin.
					Number					
					Total					
Burlington	2,195	8,850	115	3,815	7,705	8,850	1,830	6,125	3,855	5,280
Ontario	133,980	511,020	6,525	309,630	499,690	692,130	144,065	417,675	296,340	458,665
Canada	321,895	1,240,850	17,460	728,330	1,301,435	1,949,650	363,405	1,130,750	807,800	1,261,050
					Males					
Burlington	1,065	5,115	55	2,145	2,135	1,365	900	2,680	1,810	2,770
Ontario	72,835	281,420	3,540	172,475	162,765	120,165	75,035	177,240	133,795	236,655
Canada	179,090	688,625	9,380	411,250	424,915	349,430	188,270	469,990	372,940	652,510
					Females					
Burlington	1,135	3,735	55	1,670	5,565	7,485	935	3,440	2,035	2,515
Ontario	61,145	229,600	2,990	137,155	336,925	571,965	69,030	240,430	162,550	222,015
Canada	142,805	552,225	8,075	317,085	876,515	1,600,220	175,135	660,760	434,865	608,535
					Percent of Labour Force					
					Total					
Burlington	2.3	9.1	0.1	3.9	7.9	9.1	1.9	6.3	4.0	5.4
Ontario	2.0	7.6	0.1	4.6	7.5	10.4	2.2	6.3	4.4	6.9
Canada	1.8	7.1	0.1	4.1	7.4	11.1	2.1	6.4	4.6	7.2
					Males					
Burlington	2.1	10.2	0.1	4.3	4.3	2.7	1.8	5.4	3.6	5.6
Ontario	2.1	8.2	0.1	5.0	4.7	3.5	2.2	5.1	3.9	6.9
Canada	1.9	7.5	0.1	4.5	4.6	3.8	2.0	5.1	4.1	7.1
					Females					
Burlington	2.4	7.9	0.1	3.5	11.8	15.9	2.0	7.3	4.3	5.3
Ontario	1.9	7.1	0.1	4.2	10.4	17.7	2.1	7.4	5.0	6.9
Canada	1.7	6.6	0.1	3.8	10.4	19.1	2.1	7.9	5.2	7.2

Note: Figures are based on total experienced labour force 15 years and over. Experienced labour force refers to persons who, during the week of Sunday, May 1 to Saturday, May 7, 2011, were employed and the unemployed who had last worked for pay or in self-employment in either 2010 or 2011.
Source: Statistics Canada. 2013. 2011 National Household Survey. Statistics Canada Catalogue no. 99-004-XWE. Ottawa. Released September 11, 2013.

PROFILES / Burlington, Ontario

Occupation

Area	Mgmt	Business, Finance & Admin.	Natural/ Applied Sciences & Related	Health	Education, Law & Social, Community & Government Services	Art, Culture, Recreation & Sport	Sales & Service	Trades, Transport & Equip. Operators & Related	Natural Resources, Agri. & Related Production	Mfg & Utilities
Number										
Total										
Burlington	14,965	17,700	7,810	5,520	11,880	2,725	23,105	9,280	995	3,125
Ontario	770,580	1,138,330	494,500	392,695	801,465	206,420	1,550,260	868,515	106,810	350,685
Canada	1,963,600	2,902,045	1,237,775	1,107,200	2,064,675	503,415	4,068,170	2,537,775	397,930	805,040
Males										
Burlington	9,880	5,805	6,125	1,005	3,720	1,260	10,380	8,630	805	2,295
Ontario	474,655	352,505	384,345	78,330	264,570	96,055	673,880	812,280	82,610	233,565
Canada	1,229,460	854,190	966,355	217,520	676,550	232,535	1,745,705	2,385,615	318,945	564,300
Females										
Burlington	5,085	11,895	1,680	4,515	8,160	1,460	12,720	650	190	835
Ontario	295,920	785,825	110,150	314,370	536,895	110,370	876,380	56,230	24,200	117,115
Canada	734,140	2,047,855	271,415	889,675	1,388,130	270,875	2,322,465	152,165	78,980	240,740
Percent of Labour Force										
Total										
Burlington	15.4	18.2	8.0	5.7	12.2	2.8	23.8	9.6	1.0	3.2
Ontario	11.5	17.0	7.4	5.9	12.0	3.1	23.2	13.0	1.6	5.2
Canada	11.2	16.5	7.0	6.3	11.7	2.9	23.1	14.4	2.3	4.6
Males										
Burlington	19.8	11.6	12.3	2.0	7.5	2.5	20.8	17.3	1.6	4.6
Ontario	13.7	10.2	11.1	2.3	7.7	2.8	19.5	23.5	2.4	6.8
Canada	13.4	9.3	10.5	2.4	7.4	2.5	19.0	26.0	3.5	6.1
Females										
Burlington	10.8	25.2	3.6	9.6	17.3	3.1	27.0	1.4	0.4	1.8
Ontario	9.2	24.3	3.4	9.7	16.6	3.4	27.2	1.7	0.7	3.6
Canada	8.7	24.4	3.2	10.6	16.5	3.2	27.7	1.8	0.9	2.9

Note: Figures are based on total experienced labour force 15 years and over
Source: Statistics Canada. 2013. 2011 National Household Survey. Statistics Canada Catalogue no. 99-004-XWE. Ottawa. Released September 11, 2013.

Place of Work Status

Area	Worked at Home	Worked Outside Canada	No Fixed Workplace Address	Worked at Usual Place
Number				
Total				
Burlington	6,625	365	8,155	77,880
Ontario	423,790	31,390	670,835	5,170,980
Canada	1,142,640	66,460	1,868,245	13,517,690
Males				
Burlington	3,440	260	5,775	38,220
Ontario	216,900	21,150	486,560	2,524,555
Canada	582,150	47,355	1,400,485	6,604,325
Females				
Burlington	3,190	110	2,385	39,660
Ontario	206,895	10,240	184,275	2,646,420
Canada	560,490	19,100	467,760	6,913,370
Percent of Labour Force				
Total				
Burlington	7.1	0.4	8.8	83.7
Ontario	6.7	0.5	10.7	82.1
Canada	6.9	0.4	11.3	81.5
Males				
Burlington	7.2	0.5	12.1	80.1
Ontario	6.7	0.7	15.0	77.7
Canada	6.7	0.5	16.2	76.5
Females				
Burlington	7.0	0.2	5.3	87.5
Ontario	6.8	0.3	6.0	86.8
Canada	7.0	0.2	5.9	86.8

Note: Figures are based on total employed labour force 15 years and over.
Source: Statistics Canada. 2013. 2011 National Household Survey. Statistics Canada Catalogue no. 99-004-XWE. Ottawa. Released September 11, 2013.

Mode of Transportation to Work

Area	Car; Truck; Van; as Driver	Car; Truck; Van; as Passenger	Public Transit	Walked	Bicycled	All Other Modes
			Number			
			Total			
Burlington	68,900	4,925	7,560	3,165	550	940
Ontario	4,235,315	357,110	818,270	299,095	69,885	62,145
Canada	11,393,140	867,050	1,851,525	880,815	201,780	191,625
			Males			
Burlington	36,270	2,040	3,560	1,130	485	500
Ontario	2,316,680	143,410	340,995	131,765	47,635	30,635
Canada	6,238,835	349,530	788,290	387,580	135,840	104,725
			Females			
Burlington	32,625	2,885	4,000	2,035	70	435
Ontario	1,918,640	213,700	477,275	167,325	22,250	31,515
Canada	5,154,305	517,520	1,063,235	493,230	65,940	86,900
			Percent of Labour Force			
			Total			
Burlington	80.1	5.7	8.8	3.7	0.6	1.1
Ontario	72.5	6.1	14.0	5.1	1.2	1.1
Canada	74.0	5.6	12.0	5.7	1.3	1.2
			Males			
Burlington	82.4	4.6	8.1	2.6	1.1	1.1
Ontario	76.9	4.8	11.3	4.4	1.6	1.0
Canada	77.9	4.4	9.8	4.8	1.7	1.3
			Females			
Burlington	77.6	6.9	9.5	4.8	0.2	1.0
Ontario	67.8	7.5	16.9	5.9	0.8	1.1
Canada	69.8	7.0	14.4	6.7	0.9	1.2

Note: Figures are based on total employed labour force 15 years and over.
Source: Statistics Canada. 2013. 2011 National Household Survey. Statistics Canada Catalogue no. 99-004-XWE. Ottawa. Released September 11, 2013.

Visible Minority Population Characteristics

Area	Total Minority	South Asian[1]	Chinese	Black	Filipino	Latin American	Arab	SE Asian[2]	West Asian[3]	Korean	Japanese	Multiple[4]
						Number						
						Total						
Burlington	20,785	6,325	2,845	2,830	1,600	1,660	1,600	670	785	895	435	845
Ontario	3,279,565	965,990	629,140	539,205	275,380	172,560	151,645	137,875	122,530	78,290	29,085	96,735
Canada	6,264,750	1,567,400	1,324,750	945,665	619,310	381,280	380,620	312,075	206,840	161,130	87,270	171,935
						Males						
Burlington	10,110	3,150	1,350	1,340	700	735	870	370	405	430	215	385
Ontario	1,582,480	484,355	301,575	251,295	116,825	83,205	79,620	67,645	62,515	38,045	13,345	46,765
Canada	3,043,010	790,755	632,325	453,005	268,885	186,355	203,485	154,035	105,620	77,165	38,270	83,335
						Females						
Burlington	10,675	3,180	1,500	1,485	900	930	730	295	390	460	220	455
Ontario	1,697,085	481,635	327,570	287,915	158,555	89,360	72,025	70,230	60,010	40,250	15,740	49,970
Canada	3,221,745	776,650	692,420	492,660	350,425	194,925	177,140	158,045	101,220	83,965	48,990	88,600
						Percent of Population						
						Total						
Burlington	12.0	3.6	1.6	1.6	0.9	1.0	0.9	0.4	0.5	0.5	0.3	0.5
Ontario	25.9	7.6	5.0	4.3	2.2	1.4	1.2	1.1	1.0	0.6	0.2	0.8
Canada	19.1	4.8	4.0	2.9	1.9	1.2	1.2	0.9	0.6	0.5	0.3	0.5
						Males						
Burlington	12.1	3.8	1.6	1.6	0.8	0.9	1.0	0.4	0.5	0.5	0.3	0.5
Ontario	25.6	7.8	4.9	4.1	1.9	1.3	1.3	1.1	1.0	0.6	0.2	0.8
Canada	18.8	4.9	3.9	2.8	1.7	1.2	1.3	1.0	0.7	0.5	0.2	0.5
						Females						
Burlington	11.9	3.5	1.7	1.7	1.0	1.0	0.8	0.3	0.4	0.5	0.2	0.5
Ontario	26.2	7.4	5.1	4.4	2.5	1.4	1.1	1.1	0.9	0.6	0.2	0.8
Canada	19.3	4.7	4.1	3.0	2.1	1.2	1.1	0.9	0.6	0.5	0.3	0.5

Note: The Employment Equity Act defines visible minorities as 'persons, other than Aboriginal peoples, who are non-Caucasian in race or non-white in colour';
(1) Includes 'East Indian,' 'Pakistani,' 'Sri Lankan,' etc.; (2) Includes 'Vietnamese,' 'Cambodian,' 'Malaysian,' 'Laotian,' etc.; (3) Includes 'Iranian,' 'Afghan,' etc.; (4) Includes respondents who reported more than one visible minority group by checking two or more mark-in circles, e.g., 'Black' and 'South Asian.'
Source: Statistics Canada. 2013. 2011 National Household Survey. Statistics Canada Catalogue no. 99-004-XWE. Ottawa. Released September 11, 2013.

PROFILES / Burlington, Ontario

Aboriginal Population

Area	Aboriginal Identity[1]	First Nations (North American Indian) Single Identity[2]	Métis Single Identity	Inuk (Inuit) Single Identity	Multiple Aboriginal Identities[3]	Aboriginal Identities Not Included Elsewhere
Number — Total						
Burlington	1,510	900	530	25	20	35
Ontario	301,430	201,100	86,020	3,355	2,910	8,040
Canada	1,400,685	851,560	451,795	59,440	11,415	26,475
Males						
Burlington	655	375	250	0	0	20
Ontario	145,020	96,620	41,755	1,475	1,420	3,750
Canada	682,190	411,785	223,335	29,495	5,525	12,055
Females						
Burlington	860	525	280	0	15	10
Ontario	156,410	104,485	44,260	1,880	1,490	4,295
Canada	718,500	439,775	228,460	29,950	5,890	14,420
Percent of Population — Total						
Burlington	0.9	0.5	0.3	0.0	0.0	0.0
Ontario	2.4	1.6	0.7	0.0	0.0	0.1
Canada	4.3	2.6	1.4	0.2	0.0	0.1
Males						
Burlington	0.8	0.4	0.3	0.0	0.0	0.0
Ontario	2.3	1.6	0.7	0.0	0.0	0.1
Canada	4.2	2.5	1.4	0.2	0.0	0.1
Females						
Burlington	1.0	0.6	0.3	0.0	0.0	0.0
Ontario	2.4	1.6	0.7	0.0	0.0	0.1
Canada	4.3	2.6	1.4	0.2	0.0	0.1

Note: (1) Includes persons who reported being an Aboriginal person, that is, First Nations (North American Indian), Métis or Inuk (Inuit) and/or those who reported Registered or Treaty Indian status, that is registered under the Indian Act of Canada, and/or those who reported membership in a First Nation or Indian band. Aboriginal peoples of Canada are defined in the Constitution Act, 1982, section 35-2 as including the Indian, Inuit and Métis peoples of Canada; (2) Users should be aware that the estimates associated with this variable are more affected than most by the incomplete enumeration of certain Indian reserves and Indian settlements in the National Household Survey (NHS); (3) Includes persons who reported being any two or all three of the following: First Nations (North American Indian), Métis or Inuk (Inuit).
Source: Statistics Canada. 2013. 2011 National Household Survey. Statistics Canada Catalogue no. 99-004-XWE. Ottawa. Released September 11, 2013.

Ethnic Origin

Area	North American Aboriginal	Other North American	European	Caribbean	Latin, Central and South American	African	Asian	Oceania
Number — Total								
Burlington	3,100	44,830	138,475	2,590	2,620	2,920	17,270	440
Ontario	441,395	3,059,480	8,231,410	396,485	271,545	331,460	2,604,595	19,410
Canada	1,836,035	11,070,455	20,157,965	627,590	544,375	766,735	5,011,225	74,875
Males								
Burlington	1,455	21,500	66,900	1,280	1,265	1,505	8,455	270
Ontario	210,490	1,507,105	4,019,885	181,805	130,035	160,940	1,265,540	9,855
Canada	885,675	5,462,685	9,913,150	291,640	264,635	387,360	2,435,540	37,490
Females								
Burlington	1,645	23,325	71,585	1,310	1,360	1,420	8,810	175
Ontario	230,905	1,552,380	4,211,525	214,675	141,510	170,515	1,339,050	9,555
Canada	950,360	5,607,770	10,244,820	335,945	279,740	379,380	2,575,680	37,385
Percent of Population — Total								
Burlington	1.8	25.8	79.8	1.5	1.5	1.7	10.0	0.3
Ontario	3.5	24.2	65.1	3.1	2.1	2.6	20.6	0.2
Canada	5.6	33.7	61.4	1.9	1.7	2.3	15.3	0.2
Males								
Burlington	1.7	25.7	79.9	1.5	1.5	1.8	10.1	0.3
Ontario	3.4	24.4	65.0	2.9	2.1	2.6	20.5	0.2
Canada	5.5	33.8	61.3	1.8	1.6	2.4	15.1	0.2
Females								
Burlington	1.8	26.0	79.8	1.5	1.5	1.6	9.8	0.2
Ontario	3.6	24.0	65.1	3.3	2.2	2.6	20.7	0.1
Canada	5.7	33.6	61.4	2.0	1.7	2.3	15.4	0.2

Note: The sum of the ethnic groups in this table is greater than the total population estimate because a person may report more than one ethnic origin in the NHS.
Source: Statistics Canada. 2013. 2011 National Household Survey. Statistics Canada Catalogue no. 99-004-XWE. Ottawa. Released September 11, 2013.

Religion

Area	Buddhist	Christian	Hindu	Jewish	Muslim	Sikh	Traditional (Aboriginal) Spirituality	Other Religions	No Religious Affiliation
Number									
Total									
Burlington	760	121,505	1,995	660	3,435	1,655	0	425	43,045
Ontario	163,750	8,167,295	366,720	195,540	581,950	179,765	15,905	53,080	2,927,790
Canada	366,830	22,102,745	497,965	329,495	1,053,945	454,965	64,935	130,835	7,850,605
Males									
Burlington	315	56,185	1,025	330	1,710	815	0	160	23,195
Ontario	75,355	3,839,925	183,580	95,795	293,925	90,515	7,600	23,555	1,571,195
Canada	168,465	10,497,775	250,435	161,265	540,555	229,435	31,805	57,745	4,225,645
Females									
Burlington	440	65,315	965	335	1,730	840	0	265	19,850
Ontario	88,395	4,327,365	183,140	99,740	288,025	89,250	8,310	29,525	1,356,600
Canada	198,365	11,604,975	247,525	168,235	513,395	225,530	33,135	73,090	3,624,965
Percent of Population									
Total									
Burlington	0.4	70.0	1.1	0.4	2.0	1.0	0.0	0.2	24.8
Ontario	1.3	64.6	2.9	1.5	4.6	1.4	0.1	0.4	23.1
Canada	1.1	67.3	1.5	1.0	3.2	1.4	0.2	0.4	23.9
Males									
Burlington	0.4	67.1	1.2	0.4	2.0	1.0	0.0	0.2	27.7
Ontario	1.2	62.1	3.0	1.5	4.8	1.5	0.1	0.4	25.4
Canada	1.0	64.9	1.5	1.0	3.3	1.4	0.2	0.4	26.1
Females									
Burlington	0.5	72.8	1.1	0.4	1.9	0.9	0.0	0.3	22.1
Ontario	1.4	66.9	2.8	1.5	4.5	1.4	0.1	0.5	21.0
Canada	1.2	69.5	1.5	1.0	3.1	1.4	0.2	0.4	21.7

Note: Religion refers to the person's self-identification as having a connection or affiliation with any religious denomination, group, body, sect, cult or other religiously defined community or system of belief. Religion is not limited to formal membership in a religious organization or group. Persons without a religious connection or affiliation can self-identify as atheist, agnostic or humanist, or can provide another applicable response.
Source: Statistics Canada. 2013. 2011 National Household Survey. Statistics Canada Catalogue no. 99-004-XWE. Ottawa. Released September 11, 2013.

Religion—Christian Denominations

Area	Anglican	Baptist	Catholic	Christian Orthodox	Lutheran	Pentecostal	Presbyterian	United Church	Other Christian
Number									
Total									
Burlington	17,370	2,950	54,685	3,970	2,185	1,955	6,420	16,010	15,965
Ontario	774,560	244,650	3,976,610	297,710	163,460	213,945	319,585	952,465	1,224,300
Canada	1,631,845	635,840	12,810,705	550,690	478,185	478,705	472,385	2,007,610	3,036,780
Males									
Burlington	7,755	1,465	25,640	1,825	1,030	865	3,040	7,150	7,410
Ontario	355,175	112,285	1,895,940	145,825	75,225	94,955	148,535	435,255	576,730
Canada	752,945	293,905	6,167,290	270,205	221,525	217,850	218,955	912,545	1,442,550
Females									
Burlington	9,610	1,490	29,040	2,145	1,155	1,085	3,385	8,860	8,550
Ontario	419,390	132,370	2,080,665	151,885	88,230	118,990	171,050	517,210	647,570
Canada	878,900	341,940	6,643,415	280,485	256,660	260,850	253,430	1,095,065	1,594,230
Percent of Population									
Total									
Burlington	10.0	1.7	31.5	2.3	1.3	1.1	3.7	9.2	9.2
Ontario	6.1	1.9	31.4	2.4	1.3	1.7	2.5	7.5	9.7
Canada	5.0	1.9	39.0	1.7	1.5	1.5	1.4	6.1	9.2
Males									
Burlington	9.3	1.7	30.6	2.2	1.2	1.0	3.6	8.5	8.8
Ontario	5.7	1.8	30.7	2.4	1.2	1.5	2.4	7.0	9.3
Canada	4.7	1.8	38.2	1.7	1.4	1.3	1.4	5.6	8.9
Females									
Burlington	10.7	1.7	32.4	2.4	1.3	1.2	3.8	9.9	9.5
Ontario	6.5	2.0	32.2	2.3	1.4	1.8	2.6	8.0	10.0
Canada	5.3	2.0	39.8	1.7	1.5	1.6	1.5	6.6	9.6

Note: Religion refers to the person's self-identification as having a connection or affiliation with any religious denomination, group, body, sect, cult or other religiously defined community or system of belief. Religion is not limited to formal membership in a religious organization or group. Persons without a religious connection or affiliation can self-identify as atheist, agnostic or humanist, or can provide another applicable response.
Source: Statistics Canada. 2013. 2011 National Household Survey. Statistics Canada Catalogue no. 99-004-XWE. Ottawa. Released September 11, 2013.

PROFILES / Burlington, Ontario

Immigrant Status and Period of Immigration

Area	Non-Immigrants[1]	Immigrants All	Before 1971	1971 to 1980	1981 to 1990	1991 to 2000	2001 to 2005	2006 to 2011	Non-Permanent Residents[3]
				Number Total					
Burlington	134,560	37,865	12,325	5,660	5,060	6,640	4,485	3,690	1,070
Ontario	8,906,000	3,611,365	723,030	464,380	538,285	866,220	518,405	501,060	134,425
Canada	25,720,175	6,775,765	1,261,055	870,775	949,890	1,539,050	992,070	1,162,915	356,385
				Males					
Burlington	65,540	17,690	5,550	2,770	2,435	3,105	2,140	1,685	515
Ontario	4,410,240	1,706,385	341,820	217,990	258,095	408,270	245,850	234,360	64,825
Canada	12,753,235	3,231,370	605,430	416,670	454,570	724,905	474,545	555,245	178,515
				Females					
Burlington	69,020	20,175	6,770	2,885	2,620	3,540	2,350	2,005	560
Ontario	4,495,765	1,904,985	381,210	246,390	280,190	457,950	272,550	266,695	69,600
Canada	12,966,935	3,544,400	655,625	454,105	495,325	814,145	517,530	607,670	177,870
				Percent of Population Total					
Burlington	77.6	21.8	7.1	3.3	2.9	3.8	2.6	2.1	0.6
Ontario	70.4	28.5	5.7	3.7	4.3	6.8	4.1	4.0	1.1
Canada	78.3	20.6	3.8	2.7	2.9	4.7	3.0	3.5	1.1
				Males					
Burlington	78.3	21.1	6.6	3.3	2.9	3.7	2.6	2.0	0.6
Ontario	71.3	27.6	5.5	3.5	4.2	6.6	4.0	3.8	1.0
Canada	78.9	20.0	3.7	2.6	2.8	4.5	2.9	3.4	1.1
				Females					
Burlington	76.9	22.5	7.5	3.2	2.9	3.9	2.6	2.2	0.6
Ontario	69.5	29.4	5.9	3.8	4.3	7.1	4.2	4.1	1.1
Canada	77.7	21.2	3.9	2.7	3.0	4.9	3.1	3.6	1.1

Note: (1) Non-immigrant refers to a person who is a Canadian citizen by birth; (2) Immigrant refers to a person who is or has ever been a landed immigrant/permanent resident. This person has been granted the right to live in Canada permanently by immigration authorities. Some immigrants have resided in Canada for a number of years, while others have arrived recently. Some immigrants are Canadian citizens, while others are not. Most immigrants are born outside Canada, but a small number are born in Canada. In the 2011 National Household Survey, 'Immigrants' includes immigrants who landed in Canada prior to May 10, 2011; (3) Non-permanent resident refers to a person from another country who has a work or study permit, or who is a refugee claimant, and any non-Canadian-born family member living in Canada with them.
Source: Statistics Canada. 2013. 2011 National Household Survey. Statistics Canada Catalogue no. 99-004-XWE. Ottawa. Released September 11, 2013.

Mother Tongue

Area	English	French	Non-official Language	English & French	English & Non-official Language	French & Non-official Language	English, French & Non-official Language
			Number Total				
Burlington	140,590	3,080	28,025	455	1,945	95	55
Ontario	8,677,040	493,300	3,264,435	46,605	219,425	13,645	7,615
Canada	18,858,980	7,054,975	6,567,680	144,685	396,330	74,430	24,095
			Males				
Burlington	68,285	1,320	13,280	200	920	40	20
Ontario	4,276,970	232,785	1,562,190	21,805	106,790	6,285	3,495
Canada	9,345,225	3,452,380	3,157,785	69,975	192,000	36,535	11,965
			Females				
Burlington	72,305	1,760	14,745	250	1,030	55	35
Ontario	4,400,065	260,510	1,702,240	24,795	112,635	7,365	4,115
Canada	9,513,750	3,602,590	3,409,895	74,710	204,330	37,890	12,130
			Percent of Population Total				
Burlington	80.7	1.8	16.1	0.3	1.1	0.1	0.0
Ontario	68.2	3.9	25.7	0.4	1.7	0.1	0.1
Canada	56.9	21.3	19.8	0.4	1.2	0.2	0.1
			Males				
Burlington	81.2	1.6	15.8	0.2	1.1	0.0	0.0
Ontario	68.9	3.7	25.2	0.4	1.7	0.1	0.1
Canada	57.5	21.2	19.4	0.4	1.2	0.2	0.1
			Females				
Burlington	80.2	2.0	16.4	0.3	1.1	0.1	0.0
Ontario	67.6	4.0	26.1	0.4	1.7	0.1	0.1
Canada	56.4	21.4	20.2	0.4	1.2	0.2	0.1

Note: Figures cover total population excluding institutional residents.
Source: Statistics Canada. 2012. Census Profile. 2011 Census. Statistics Canada Catalogue no. 98-316-XWE. Ottawa. Released October 24 2012.
http://www12.statcan.gc.ca/census-recensement/2011/dp-pd/prof/index.cfm?Lang=E

Language Spoken Most Often at Home

Area	English	French	Non-official Language	English & French	English & Non-official Language	French & Non-official Language	English, French & Non-official Language
			Number				
			Total				
Burlington	157,500	1,045	11,115	295	4,170	20	90
Ontario	10,044,810	284,115	1,827,870	37,955	509,105	6,370	11,845
Canada	21,457,075	6,827,865	3,673,865	131,205	875,135	109,700	46,330
			Males				
Burlington	76,075	465	5,345	130	2,010	10	30
Ontario	4,930,610	133,495	872,860	17,250	248,050	2,855	5,225
Canada	10,585,620	3,348,235	1,767,310	63,475	425,370	53,010	22,845
			Females				
Burlington	81,430	580	5,775	165	2,160	5	60
Ontario	5,114,200	150,620	955,010	20,705	261,055	3,520	6,620
Canada	10,871,455	3,479,625	1,906,555	67,730	449,765	56,690	23,485
			Percent of Population				
			Total				
Burlington	90.4	0.6	6.4	0.2	2.4	0.0	0.1
Ontario	79.0	2.2	14.4	0.3	4.0	0.1	0.1
Canada	64.8	20.6	11.1	0.4	2.6	0.3	0.1
			Males				
Burlington	90.5	0.6	6.4	0.2	2.4	0.0	0.0
Ontario	79.4	2.1	14.1	0.3	4.0	0.0	0.1
Canada	65.1	20.6	10.9	0.4	2.6	0.3	0.1
			Females				
Burlington	90.3	0.6	6.4	0.2	2.4	0.0	0.1
Ontario	78.5	2.3	14.7	0.3	4.0	0.1	0.1
Canada	64.5	20.6	11.3	0.4	2.7	0.3	0.1

Note: Figures cover total population excluding institutional residents.
Source: Statistics Canada. 2012. Census Profile. 2011 Census. Statistics Canada Catalogue no. 98-316-XWE. Ottawa. Released October 24 2012.
http://www12.statcan.gc.ca/census-recensement/2011/dp-pd/prof/index.cfm?Lang=E

Knowledge of Official Languages

Area	English Only	French Only	English & French	Neither English nor French
		Number		
		Total		
Burlington	157,725	115	15,170	1,235
Ontario	10,984,360	42,980	1,395,805	298,920
Canada	22,564,665	4,165,015	5,795,570	595,920
		Males		
Burlington	77,230	55	6,305	480
Ontario	5,445,050	18,805	627,725	118,765
Canada	11,222,185	1,925,340	2,876,560	241,790
		Females		
Burlington	80,495	60	8,865	755
Ontario	5,539,310	24,175	768,085	180,155
Canada	11,342,485	2,239,680	2,919,005	354,135
		Percent of Population		
		Total		
Burlington	90.5	0.1	8.7	0.7
Ontario	86.3	0.3	11.0	2.3
Canada	68.1	12.6	17.5	1.8
		Males		
Burlington	91.9	0.1	7.5	0.6
Ontario	87.7	0.3	10.1	1.9
Canada	69.0	11.8	17.7	1.5
		Females		
Burlington	89.3	0.1	9.8	0.8
Ontario	85.1	0.4	11.8	2.8
Canada	67.3	13.3	17.3	2.1

Note: Figures cover total population excluding institutional residents.
Source: Statistics Canada. 2012. Census Profile. 2011 Census. Statistics Canada Catalogue no. 98-316-XWE. Ottawa. Released October 24 2012.
http://www12.statcan.gc.ca/census-recensement/2011/dp-pd/prof/index.cfm?Lang=E

Burnaby, British Columbia

Background

Burnaby is located immediately east of Vancouver, British Columbia, within the centre of the Metro Vancouver area. Burnaby residents can travel to downtown Vancouver within 25 minutes by car or take the SkyTrain, the world's first fully automated, driverless, rapid transit system.

The area was first inhabited by First Nations such as the Musqueam and Tseil-Waututh. When the Gold Rush began in 1858, the region was surveyed by Robert Burnaby, after whom the city and Burnaby Lake are named. In 1891, a new Vancouver–New-Westminster tram line was built through Burnaby, creating a working-class suburb by the early 20th century.

Today, Burnaby is the third largest city in BC (pop: 223,218 in 2011) and is expected to grow 20% over the next decade. The district includes 41 elementary schools, eight secondary schools and two post-secondary institutions, Simon Fraser University and British Columbia Institute of Technology. In Burnaby, 25% of city land is designated as parks and open space. The Playgrounds of the Gods is located next to Simon Fraser University and features more than 50 wooden sculptures dedicated to the people of Burnaby.

Burnaby was one of the first cities in Canada to cultivate international "sister city" and "friendship city" relationships with cities from around the world. By 2012, Burnaby shared sister city relationships with Kushiro, Japan (1965); Mesa, Arizona (1998); Hwaseong, Korea (2010); and Zhongshan City, China (2011). More than half of Burnaby's population identifies as an immigrant or visible minority.

Burnaby has summer highs of plus 21.67 degrees Celsius, winter lows of plus 1.27 degrees Celsius, and an average rainfall just over 1833 mm per year.

Rankings

- Burnaby was ranked as the first city in Canada to become a Blue Community. According to the Council of Canadians, a Blue Community is a municipality that recognizes water as a human right; promotes public water and wastewater service; and bans the sale of bottled water in public facilities and at municipal events. In 2011, more than 10 Canadian cities were designed as Blue Communities. The majority of municipalities are located in British Columbia. *Council of Canadians, "Win! Burnaby Becomes a Blue Community," March 21st, 2011*
- *Maclean's Magazine* ranked Burnaby as "The Best-Run City" in Canada in 2009. The survey ranked municipal governments across Canada based on performance in areas such as socio-economic status, crime, fire services, transportation, road and sewer conditions, economic development, recreation spending and civic engagement indictors like voter turnout and library use. Burnaby was praised for being debt-free and having outstanding public services. Saskatoon, Saskatchewan, ranked #2 and British Columbia cities Surrey and Vancouver ranked #3 and #4, respectively. *Maclean's, "The Best-Run City in Canada," July 22nd, 2009*
- Burnaby was ranked as one of the few cities not affected by Canada's aging demographic (residents over 65). The median age in Burnaby was 39.1 in 2006 and remained almost the same at 39.8 in 2011. Nationally, the percentage of people aged 65 and over increased from 13.7% to 14.8%. Burnaby's aging demographic did not change and remained at 13.9% from 2006 to 2011. *Statistics Canada, "The Canadian Population in 2011: Age and Sex" with files from Burnaby Now.com, June 13th, 2012*

PROFILES / Burnaby, British Columbia

Population Growth and Density

Area	Population in 2001	Population in 2006	Population in 2011	Population Change 2001–2006	Population Change 2006–2011	Land Area (sq. km)	Population Density per sq. km
Burnaby	193,954	202,799	223,218	4.6	10.1	90.61	2,463.5
British Columbia	3,907,738	4,113,487	4,400,057	5.3	7.0	922,509.29	4.8
Canada	30,007,094	31,612,897	33,476,688	5.4	5.9	8,965,121.42	3.7

Source: Statistics Canada. 2012. Census Profile. 2011 Census. Statistics Canada Catalogue no. 98-316-XWE. Ottawa. Released October 24 2012.
http://www12.statcan.gc.ca/census-recensement/2011/dp-pd/prof/index.cfm?Lang=E;
Statistics Canada 2007. 2006 Community Profiles. 2006 Census. Statistics Canada Catalogue no. 92-591-XWE. Ottawa. Released March 13 2007.
http://www12.statcan.ca/census-recensement/2006/dp-pd/prof/92-591/index.cfm?Lang=E

Gender

Area	Males	Females
Number		
Burnaby	109,245	113,970
British Columbia	2,156,600	2,243,455
Canada	16,414,225	17,062,460
Percent of Population		
Burnaby	48.9	51.1
British Columbia	49.0	51.0
Canada	49.0	51.0

Source: Statistics Canada. 2012. Census Profile. 2011 Census. Statistics Canada Catalogue no. 98-316-XWE. Ottawa. Released October 24 2012.
http://www12.statcan.gc.ca/census-recensement/2011/dp-pd/prof/index.cfm?Lang=E

Marital Status

Area	Married[1]	Living Common-law	Single[2]	Separated	Divorced	Widowed
Number — Total						
Burnaby	95,525	11,290	60,135	4,575	11,005	9,560
British Columbia	1,832,605	321,965	1,014,270	102,040	246,515	205,300
Canada	12,941,960	3,142,525	7,816,045	698,240	1,686,035	1,584,530
Males						
Burnaby	47,485	5,695	32,275	1,820	4,120	1,850
British Columbia	913,430	161,530	550,830	43,570	98,130	41,550
Canada	6,470,300	1,575,495	4,206,320	299,655	680,415	310,940
Females						
Burnaby	48,040	5,595	27,860	2,755	6,885	7,710
British Columbia	919,175	160,435	463,435	58,470	148,385	163,750
Canada	6,471,660	1,567,035	3,609,730	398,585	1,005,620	1,273,590
Percent of Population — Total						
Burnaby	49.7	5.9	31.3	2.4	5.7	5.0
British Columbia	49.2	8.6	27.2	2.7	6.6	5.5
Canada	46.4	11.3	28.0	2.5	6.0	5.7
Males						
Burnaby	50.9	6.1	34.6	2.0	4.4	2.0
British Columbia	50.5	8.9	30.4	2.4	5.4	2.3
Canada	47.8	11.6	31.1	2.2	5.0	2.3
Females						
Burnaby	48.6	5.7	28.2	2.8	7.0	7.8
British Columbia	48.0	8.4	24.2	3.1	7.8	8.6
Canada	45.2	10.9	25.2	2.8	7.0	8.9

Note: (1) and not separated, (2) never legally married
Source: Statistics Canada. 2012. Census Profile. 2011 Census. Statistics Canada Catalogue no. 98-316-XWE. Ottawa. Released October 24 2012.
http://www12.statcan.gc.ca/census-recensement/2011/dp-pd/prof/index.cfm?Lang=E

Age Characteristics: 0 to 49 Years

Area	0 to 4 Years	5 to 9 Years	10 to 14 Years	15 to 19 Years	20 to 24 Years	25 to 29 Years	30 to 34 Years	35 to 39 Years	40 to 44 Years	45 to 49 Years
					Number					
					Total					
Burnaby	10,800	9,905	10,415	13,130	17,625	18,105	16,410	15,910	17,240	18,270
British Columbia	219,665	218,915	238,780	275,165	279,825	288,780	275,985	280,870	313,765	350,600
Canada	1,877,095	1,809,895	1,920,355	2,178,135	2,187,450	2,169,590	2,162,905	2,173,930	2,324,875	2,675,130
					Males					
Burnaby	5,615	5,050	5,335	6,810	9,075	9,135	8,145	7,640	8,145	8,785
British Columbia	112,885	112,200	122,465	141,670	142,290	143,475	135,220	135,455	151,430	170,580
Canada	961,150	925,965	983,995	1,115,845	1,108,775	1,077,275	1,058,810	1,064,200	1,141,720	1,318,715
					Females					
Burnaby	5,190	4,850	5,080	6,320	8,555	8,965	8,265	8,270	9,095	9,480
British Columbia	106,775	106,715	116,315	133,500	137,535	145,305	140,755	145,415	162,335	180,020
Canada	915,945	883,935	936,360	1,062,295	1,078,670	1,092,315	1,104,095	1,109,735	1,183,155	1,356,420
					Percent of Population					
					Total					
Burnaby	4.8	4.4	4.7	5.9	7.9	8.1	7.4	7.1	7.7	8.2
British Columbia	5.0	5.0	5.4	6.3	6.4	6.6	6.3	6.4	7.1	8.0
Canada	5.6	5.4	5.7	6.5	6.5	6.5	6.5	6.5	6.9	8.0
					Males					
Burnaby	5.1	4.6	4.9	6.2	8.3	8.4	7.5	7.0	7.5	8.0
British Columbia	5.2	5.2	5.7	6.6	6.6	6.7	6.3	6.3	7.0	7.9
Canada	5.9	5.6	6.0	6.8	6.8	6.6	6.5	6.5	7.0	8.0
					Females					
Burnaby	4.6	4.3	4.5	5.5	7.5	7.9	7.3	7.3	8.0	8.3
British Columbia	4.8	4.8	5.2	6.0	6.1	6.5	6.3	6.5	7.2	8.0
Canada	5.4	5.2	5.5	6.2	6.3	6.4	6.5	6.5	6.9	7.9

Source: Statistics Canada. 2012. Census Profile. 2011 Census. Statistics Canada Catalogue no. 98-316-XWE. Ottawa. Released October 24 2012.
http://www12.statcan.gc.ca/census-recensement/2011/dp-pd/prof/index.cfm?Lang=E

Age Characteristics: 50 Years and Over, and Median Age

Area	50 to 54 Years	55 to 59 Years	60 to 64 Years	65 to 69 Years	70 to 74 Years	75 to 79 Years	80 to 84 Years	85 Years and Over	Median Age
					Number				
					Total				
Burnaby	16,970	15,005	12,535	8,705	7,335	6,050	4,530	4,280	39.8
British Columbia	354,610	323,335	291,040	210,900	160,715	127,480	96,945	92,675	41.9
Canada	2,658,965	2,340,635	2,052,670	1,521,715	1,153,065	922,700	702,070	645,515	40.6
					Males				
Burnaby	8,155	7,230	6,055	4,250	3,375	2,850	2,010	1,590	38.6
British Columbia	172,060	157,455	142,645	103,785	77,350	60,720	42,745	32,150	41.1
Canada	1,309,030	1,147,300	1,002,690	738,010	543,435	417,945	291,085	208,300	39.6
					Females				
Burnaby	8,820	7,775	6,480	4,460	3,960	3,205	2,515	2,690	40.8
British Columbia	182,550	165,880	148,395	107,115	83,360	66,760	54,200	60,520	42.7
Canada	1,349,940	1,193,335	1,049,985	783,705	609,630	504,755	410,985	437,215	41.5
					Percent of Population				
					Total				
Burnaby	7.6	6.7	5.6	3.9	3.3	2.7	2.0	1.9	–
British Columbia	8.1	7.3	6.6	4.8	3.7	2.9	2.2	2.1	–
Canada	7.9	7.0	6.1	4.5	3.4	2.8	2.1	1.9	–
					Males				
Burnaby	7.5	6.6	5.5	3.9	3.1	2.6	1.8	1.5	–
British Columbia	8.0	7.3	6.6	4.8	3.6	2.8	2.0	1.5	–
Canada	8.0	7.0	6.1	4.5	3.3	2.5	1.8	1.3	–
					Females				
Burnaby	7.7	6.8	5.7	3.9	3.5	2.8	2.2	2.4	–
British Columbia	8.1	7.4	6.6	4.8	3.7	3.0	2.4	2.7	–
Canada	7.9	7.0	6.2	4.6	3.6	3.0	2.4	2.6	–

Source: Statistics Canada. 2012. Census Profile. 2011 Census. Statistics Canada Catalogue no. 98-316-XWE. Ottawa. Released October 24 2012.
http://www12.statcan.gc.ca/census-recensement/2011/dp-pd/prof/index.cfm?Lang=E

PROFILES / Burnaby, British Columbia

Private Households by Household Size

Area	1 Person	2 Persons	3 Persons	4 Persons	5 Persons	6 or More Persons	Average Number of Persons in Private Households
			Households				
Burnaby	23,650	26,860	15,580	12,930	4,710	3,110	2.5
British Columbia	498,925	613,270	264,135	237,725	91,600	58,985	2.5
Canada	3,673,310	4,544,820	2,081,900	1,903,300	724,405	392,885	2.5
			Percent of Households				
Burnaby	27.2	30.9	17.9	14.9	5.4	3.6	–
British Columbia	28.3	34.8	15.0	13.5	5.2	3.3	–
Canada	27.6	34.1	15.6	14.3	5.4	2.9	–

Source: Statistics Canada. 2012. Census Profile. 2011 Census. Statistics Canada Catalogue no. 98-316-XWE. Ottawa. Released October 24 2012.
http://www12.statcan.gc.ca/census-recensement/2011/dp-pd/prof/index.cfm?Lang=E

Dwelling Type

Area	Single-detached House	Semi-detached House	Row House	Apartment: Building with Five or More Storeys	Apartment: Building with Fewer Than Five Storeys	Duplex Apartment	Movable Dwelling	Other Single-attached House
				Number				
Burnaby	21,355	2,735	7,775	19,055	23,180	12,670	15	50
British Columbia	842,120	52,825	130,365	143,970	361,150	184,355	46,960	2,885
Canada	7,329,150	646,245	791,600	1,234,770	2,397,550	704,485	183,510	33,310
				Percent of Dwellings				
Burnaby	24.6	3.1	9.0	21.9	26.7	14.6	0.0	0.1
British Columbia	47.7	3.0	7.4	8.2	20.5	10.4	2.7	0.2
Canada	55.0	4.9	5.9	9.3	18.0	5.3	1.4	0.3

Source: Statistics Canada. 2012. Census Profile. 2011 Census. Statistics Canada Catalogue no. 98-316-XWE. Ottawa. Released October 24 2012.
http://www12.statcan.gc.ca/census-recensement/2011/dp-pd/prof/index.cfm?Lang=E

Shelter Costs

		Owned Dwellings				Rented Dwellings		
Area	Number	Median Value[1] ($)	Average Value[1] ($)	Median Monthly Costs[2] ($)	Average Monthly Costs[2] ($)	Number	Median Monthly Costs[3] ($)	Average Monthly Costs[3] ($)
Burnaby	55,120	600,941	648,217	1,030	1,281	31,710	966	1,029
British Columbia	1,202,000	448,835	543,635	1,023	1,228	519,855	903	989
Canada	9,013,410	280,552	345,182	978	1,141	4,060,385	784	848

Note: All figures cover non-farm, non-reserve private dwellings; (1) Refers to the dollar amount expected by the owner if the dwelling were to be sold; (2) Includes all shelter expenses paid by households that own their dwellings, such as the mortgage payment and the costs of electricity, heat, water and other municipal services, property taxes and condominium fees; (3) Includes all shelter expenses paid by households that rent their dwellings, such as the monthly rent and the costs of electricity, heat and municipal services.
Source: Statistics Canada. 2013. 2011 National Household Survey. Statistics Canada Catalogue no. 99-004-XWE. Ottawa. Released September 11, 2013.

Occupied Private Dwellings by Period of Construction

Area	1960 or Before	1961 to 1980	1981 to 1990	1991 to 2000	2001 to 2005	2006 to 2011
			Number			
Burnaby	14,555	26,350	15,445	13,955	6,380	10,150
British Columbia	282,675	551,655	308,450	329,780	133,235	158,845
Canada	3,273,105	4,152,715	2,112,110	1,707,880	1,031,020	1,042,430
			Percent of Dwellings			
Burnaby	16.8	30.3	17.8	16.1	7.3	11.7
British Columbia	16.0	31.3	17.5	18.7	7.6	9.0
Canada	24.6	31.2	15.9	12.8	7.7	7.8

Note: Figures cover non-farm, non-reserve private dwellings and includes data up to May 10, 2011.
Source: Statistics Canada. 2013. 2011 National Household Survey. Statistics Canada Catalogue no. 99-004-XWE. Ottawa. Released September 11, 2013.

Educational Attainment

Area	No Certificate, Diploma or Degree	High School Diploma or Equivalent[1]	Apprenticeship or Trades Certificate or Diploma[2]	College, CÉGEP or Other Non-University Certificate or Diploma	University Certificate or Diploma Below the Bachelor Level[3]	Bachelor's Degree	University Certificate, Diploma or Degree Above Bachelor Level[4]
				Number			
				Total			
Burnaby	25,945	47,740	14,745	30,700	13,905	37,320	18,880
British Columbia	607,655	1,009,400	387,455	628,115	208,245	511,240	294,725
Canada	5,485,400	6,968,935	2,950,685	4,970,020	1,200,130	3,634,425	2,049,930
				Males			
Burnaby	11,675	22,665	9,280	14,000	6,550	18,155	9,645
British Columbia	305,040	475,670	262,245	260,580	86,995	235,620	149,300
Canada	2,742,875	3,305,415	1,928,970	2,118,430	513,235	1,643,080	1,043,350
				Females			
Burnaby	14,270	25,070	5,460	16,705	7,360	19,170	9,230
British Columbia	302,620	533,735	125,210	367,535	121,250	275,625	145,425
Canada	2,742,520	3,663,515	1,021,715	2,851,595	686,890	1,991,345	1,006,585
				Percent of Population			
				Total			
Burnaby	13.7	25.2	7.8	16.2	7.3	19.7	10.0
British Columbia	16.7	27.7	10.6	17.2	5.7	14.0	8.1
Canada	20.1	25.6	10.8	18.2	4.4	13.3	7.5
				Males			
Burnaby	12.7	24.6	10.1	15.2	7.1	19.7	10.5
British Columbia	17.2	26.8	14.8	14.7	4.9	13.3	8.4
Canada	20.6	24.9	14.5	15.9	3.9	12.4	7.8
				Females			
Burnaby	14.7	25.8	5.6	17.2	7.6	19.7	9.5
British Columbia	16.2	28.5	6.7	19.6	6.5	14.7	7.8
Canada	19.6	26.2	7.3	20.4	4.9	14.3	7.2

Note: Figures cover total population aged 15 years and over by highest certificate, diploma or degree; (1) Includes persons who have graduated from a secondary school or equivalent. It excludes persons with a postsecondary certificate, diploma or degree; (2) Includes Registered Apprenticeship certificates (including Certificate of Qualification, Journeyperson's designation) and other trades certificates or diplomas such as pre-employment or vocational certificates and diplomas from brief trade programs completed at community colleges, institutes of technology, vocational centres, and similar institutions; (3) Comparisons with other data sources suggest that the category 'University certificate or diploma below the bachelor's level' was over-reported in the NHS. This category likely includes some responses that are actually college certificates or diplomas, bachelor's degrees or other types of education (e.g., university transfer programs, bachelor's programs completed in other countries, incomplete bachelor's programs, non-university professional designations). We recommend users interpret the results for the 'University certificate or diploma below the bachelor's level' category with caution; (4) 'University certificate or diploma above bachelor level' includes the categories: 'Degree in medicine, dentistry, veterinary medicine or optometry,' 'Master's degree' and 'Earned doctorate.'
Source: Statistics Canada. 2013. 2011 National Household Survey. Statistics Canada Catalogue no. 99-004-XWE. Ottawa. Released September 11, 2013.

Household Income Distribution

Area	Less than $10,000	$10,000 to $19,999	$20,000 to $29,999	$30,000 to $39,999	$40,000 to $49,999	$50,000 to $59,999	$60,000 to $79,999	$80,000 to $99,999	$100,000 to $124,999	$125,000 to $149,999	$150,000 and Over
						Households					
Burnaby	7,015	7,745	8,085	8,135	7,990	6,790	11,420	8,820	7,705	4,895	8,245
British Columbia	96,465	156,565	157,605	167,220	158,400	140,340	246,720	193,180	167,415	106,325	174,385
Canada	626,705	1,141,945	1,193,925	1,271,675	1,206,800	1,102,120	1,865,280	1,458,240	1,260,770	802,555	1,389,240
						Percent of Households					
Burnaby	8.1	8.9	9.3	9.4	9.2	7.8	13.2	10.2	8.9	5.6	9.5
British Columbia	5.5	8.9	8.9	9.5	9.0	8.0	14.0	10.9	9.5	6.0	9.9
Canada	4.7	8.6	9.0	9.5	9.1	8.3	14.0	10.9	9.5	6.0	10.4

Note: Household income is the sum of the total incomes of all members of that household. Total income refers to monetary receipts from certain sources, before income taxes and deductions, during calendar year 2010.
Source: Statistics Canada. 2013. 2011 National Household Survey. Statistics Canada Catalogue no. 99-004-XWE. Ottawa. Released September 11, 2013.

Median and Average Household and Economic Family Income

Area	Median Household Income ($)	Average Household Income ($)	Median After-tax Household Income ($)	Average After-tax Household Income ($)	Median Economic Family Income ($)	Average Economic Family Income ($)	Median After-tax Economic Family Income ($)	Average After-tax Economic Family Income ($)
Burnaby	56,136	72,238	51,123	62,680	71,511	85,237	64,587	73,929
British Columbia	60,333	77,378	54,379	66,264	75,797	91,967	67,915	78,580
Canada	61,072	79,102	54,089	66,149	76,511	94,125	67,044	78,517

Note: Figures cover household and economic familiy income in 2010. A household is defined as a person or a group of persons (other than foreign residents) who occupy the same private dwelling and do not have a usual place of residence elsewhere in Canada. Every person is a member of one and only one household. An economic family is defined as a group of two or more persons who live in the same dwelling and are related to each other by blood, marriage, common-law, adoption or a foster relationship. A couple may be of opposite or same sex.
Source: Statistics Canada. 2013. 2011 National Household Survey. Statistics Canada Catalogue no. 99-004-XWE. Ottawa. Released September 11, 2013.

PROFILES / Burnaby, British Columbia

Individual Income Distribution

Area	Less than $10,000	$10,000 to $19,999	$20,000 to $29,999	$30,000 to $39,999	$40,000 to $49,999	$50,000 to $59,999	$60,000 to $79,999	$80,000 to $99,999	$100,000 to $124,999	$125,000 and Over
					Number					
					Total					
Burnaby	41,265	34,930	22,310	20,540	16,280	11,695	15,800	8,060	4,090	3,645
British Columbia	645,915	666,060	470,255	404,860	338,595	253,215	330,590	169,190	89,520	96,055
Canada	4,492,040	4,835,710	3,670,020	3,180,360	2,603,520	1,921,650	2,437,440	1,302,045	693,580	782,135
					Males					
Burnaby	18,375	15,005	10,270	9,520	7,830	6,465	9,285	5,220	2,880	2,700
British Columbia	275,815	263,170	201,000	186,285	167,400	143,765	206,400	112,525	65,050	74,260
Canada	1,936,365	1,864,880	1,588,260	1,522,190	1,333,510	1,079,780	1,473,145	823,720	492,905	599,905
					Females					
Burnaby	22,900	19,920	12,040	11,015	8,455	5,230	6,510	2,840	1,210	940
British Columbia	370,100	402,880	269,255	218,575	171,190	109,445	124,195	56,670	24,470	21,795
Canada	2,555,675	2,970,825	2,081,760	1,658,170	1,270,010	841,870	964,300	478,330	200,680	182,230
					Percent of Population					
					Total					
Burnaby	23.1	19.6	12.5	11.5	9.1	6.5	8.8	4.5	2.3	2.0
British Columbia	18.6	19.2	13.6	11.7	9.8	7.3	9.5	4.9	2.6	2.8
Canada	17.3	18.7	14.2	12.3	10.0	7.4	9.4	5.0	2.7	3.0
					Males					
Burnaby	21.0	17.1	11.7	10.9	8.9	7.4	10.6	6.0	3.3	3.1
British Columbia	16.3	15.5	11.9	11.0	9.9	8.5	12.2	6.6	3.8	4.4
Canada	15.2	14.7	12.5	12.0	10.5	8.5	11.6	6.5	3.9	4.7
					Females					
Burnaby	25.1	21.9	13.2	12.1	9.3	5.7	7.1	3.1	1.3	1.0
British Columbia	20.9	22.8	15.2	12.4	9.7	6.2	7.0	3.2	1.4	1.2
Canada	19.4	22.5	15.8	12.6	9.6	6.4	7.3	3.6	1.5	1.4

Note: Figures cover individuals aged 15 years and over with income. Income refers to monetary receipts from certain sources, before income taxes and deductions, during calendar year 2010.
Source: Statistics Canada. 2013. 2011 National Household Survey. Statistics Canada Catalogue no. 99-004-XWE. Ottawa. Released September 11, 2013.

Labour Force Status

Area	In the Labour Force - All	In the Labour Force - Employed	In the Labour Force - Unemployed	Not in the Labour Force
		Number		
		Total		
Burnaby	120,290	111,370	8,920	68,945
British Columbia	2,354,245	2,171,465	182,775	1,292,595
Canada	17,990,080	16,595,035	1,395,045	9,269,445
		Males		
Burnaby	62,625	57,980	4,645	29,335
British Columbia	1,223,375	1,124,590	98,785	552,070
Canada	9,388,570	8,634,310	754,255	3,906,785
		Females		
Burnaby	57,660	53,385	4,275	39,610
British Columbia	1,130,870	1,046,875	83,990	740,530
Canada	8,601,515	7,960,725	640,790	5,362,660
		Percent of Labour Force		
		Total		
Burnaby	63.6	58.9	7.4	36.4
British Columbia	64.6	59.5	7.8	35.4
Canada	66.0	60.9	7.8	34.0
		Males		
Burnaby	68.1	63.0	7.4	31.9
British Columbia	68.9	63.3	8.1	31.1
Canada	70.6	64.9	8.0	29.4
		Females		
Burnaby	59.3	54.9	7.4	40.7
British Columbia	60.4	55.9	7.4	39.6
Canada	61.6	57.0	7.4	38.4

Note: Figures are based on total population 15 years and over
Source: Statistics Canada. 2013. 2011 National Household Survey. Statistics Canada Catalogue no. 99-004-XWE. Ottawa. Released September 11, 2013.

Labour Force by Industry (NAICS Codes 11–52)

Area	Agriculture, forestry, fishing & hunting	Mining, quarrying, & oil & gas extraction	Utilities	Construction	Manufacturing	Wholesale Trade	Retail Trade	Transportation & warehousing	Information & cultural industries	Finance & insurance
Number										
Total										
Burnaby	490	275	915	6,930	7,250	5,980	13,260	5,410	5,265	6,485
British Columbia	61,210	25,450	13,215	181,510	148,810	90,560	266,265	118,675	62,235	91,790
Canada	437,650	261,050	149,940	1,215,380	1,619,295	733,445	2,031,665	827,780	420,830	767,960
Males										
Burnaby	285	155	570	6,070	4,855	3,875	6,495	4,210	3,385	2,810
British Columbia	40,810	21,175	9,650	159,605	108,480	61,730	121,750	89,155	37,250	35,375
Canada	307,370	211,690	110,765	1,068,710	1,167,680	494,545	933,850	617,305	235,875	296,995
Females										
Burnaby	195	125	350	860	2,400	2,100	6,765	1,200	1,875	3,675
British Columbia	20,405	4,275	3,560	21,910	40,335	28,820	144,515	29,520	24,980	56,415
Canada	130,285	49,360	39,175	146,670	451,615	238,900	1,097,820	210,475	184,955	470,960
Percent of Labour Force										
Total										
Burnaby	0.4	0.2	0.8	5.9	6.2	5.1	11.3	4.6	4.5	5.5
British Columbia	2.7	1.1	0.6	7.9	6.5	3.9	11.6	5.1	2.7	4.0
Canada	2.5	1.5	0.9	6.9	9.2	4.2	11.6	4.7	2.4	4.4
Males										
Burnaby	0.5	0.3	0.9	9.9	7.9	6.3	10.6	6.9	5.5	4.6
British Columbia	3.4	1.8	0.8	13.3	9.0	5.1	10.1	7.4	3.1	2.9
Canada	3.3	2.3	1.2	11.6	12.7	5.4	10.2	6.7	2.6	3.2
Females										
Burnaby	0.3	0.2	0.6	1.5	4.3	3.7	12.1	2.1	3.3	6.6
British Columbia	1.8	0.4	0.3	2.0	3.6	2.6	13.1	2.7	2.3	5.1
Canada	1.6	0.6	0.5	1.7	5.4	2.8	13.1	2.5	2.2	5.6

Note: Figures are based on total experienced labour force 15 years and over. Experienced labour force refers to persons who, during the week of Sunday, May 1 to Saturday, May 7, 2011, were employed and the unemployed who had last worked for pay or in self-employment in either 2010 or 2011.
Source: Statistics Canada. 2013. 2011 National Household Survey. Statistics Canada Catalogue no. 99-004-XWE. Ottawa. Released September 11, 2013.

Labour Force by Industry (NAICS Codes 53–91)

Area	Real estate & rental & leasing	Profess., scientific & tech. services	Mgmt of companies & enterprises	Admin. & support, waste mgmt & remed. services	Educational services	Health care & social assistance	Arts, entertain. & recreation	Accomm. & food services	Other services (except public admin.)	Public admin.
Number										
Total										
Burnaby	3,090	12,290	160	5,755	8,460	11,815	2,590	9,460	5,985	5,485
British Columbia	54,840	179,355	2,440	98,890	167,875	249,030	56,915	179,625	112,745	143,875
Canada	321,895	1,240,850	17,460	728,330	1,301,435	1,949,650	363,405	1,130,750	807,800	1,261,050
Males										
Burnaby	1,795	7,115	65	3,115	3,330	2,300	1,315	4,335	2,460	2,715
British Columbia	29,790	98,760	1,320	55,745	55,635	47,020	29,750	73,570	49,130	74,040
Canada	179,090	688,625	9,380	411,250	424,915	349,430	188,270	469,990	372,940	652,510
Females										
Burnaby	1,295	5,175	90	2,640	5,135	9,510	1,280	5,120	3,525	2,765
British Columbia	25,055	80,590	1,120	43,145	112,235	202,010	27,175	106,055	63,615	69,840
Canada	142,805	552,225	8,075	317,085	876,515	1,600,220	175,135	660,760	434,865	608,535
Percent of Labour Force										
Total										
Burnaby	2.6	10.5	0.1	4.9	7.2	10.1	2.2	8.1	5.1	4.7
British Columbia	2.4	7.8	0.1	4.3	7.3	10.8	2.5	7.8	4.9	6.2
Canada	1.8	7.1	0.1	4.1	7.4	11.1	2.1	6.4	4.6	7.2
Males										
Burnaby	2.9	11.6	0.1	5.1	5.4	3.8	2.1	7.1	4.0	4.4
British Columbia	2.5	8.2	0.1	4.6	4.6	3.9	2.5	6.1	4.1	6.2
Canada	1.9	7.5	0.1	4.5	4.6	3.8	2.0	5.1	4.1	7.1
Females										
Burnaby	2.3	9.2	0.2	4.7	9.2	17.0	2.3	9.1	6.3	4.9
British Columbia	2.3	7.3	0.1	3.9	10.2	18.3	2.5	9.6	5.8	6.3
Canada	1.7	6.6	0.1	3.8	10.4	19.1	2.1	7.9	5.2	7.2

Note: Figures are based on total experienced labour force 15 years and over. Experienced labour force refers to persons who, during the week of Sunday, May 1 to Saturday, May 7, 2011, were employed and the unemployed who had last worked for pay or in self-employment in either 2010 or 2011.
Source: Statistics Canada. 2013. 2011 National Household Survey. Statistics Canada Catalogue no. 99-004-XWE. Ottawa. Released September 11, 2013.

Occupation

Area	Mgmt	Business, Finance & Admin.	Natural/ Applied Sciences & Related	Health	Education, Law & Social, Community & Government Services	Art, Culture, Recreation & Sport	Sales & Service	Trades, Transport & Equip. Operators & Related	Natural Resources, Agri. & Related Production	Mfg & Utilities
					Number					
					Total					
Burnaby	12,495	22,120	12,630	7,235	12,220	4,000	30,155	12,400	900	3,180
British Columbia	263,685	368,980	154,055	147,620	265,910	78,565	554,345	337,140	60,295	74,720
Canada	1,963,600	2,902,045	1,237,775	1,107,200	2,064,675	503,415	4,068,170	2,537,775	397,930	805,040
					Males					
Burnaby	7,885	7,030	9,840	1,620	4,230	2,255	13,850	11,855	735	1,945
British Columbia	162,365	104,285	122,570	32,490	89,645	38,300	233,065	317,385	45,155	54,470
Canada	1,229,460	854,190	966,355	217,520	676,550	232,535	1,745,705	2,385,615	318,945	564,300
					Females					
Burnaby	4,605	15,095	2,790	5,615	7,985	1,745	16,300	545	160	1,235
British Columbia	101,320	264,690	31,480	115,125	176,265	40,270	321,285	19,755	15,135	20,250
Canada	734,140	2,047,855	271,415	889,675	1,388,130	270,875	2,322,465	152,165	78,980	240,740
					Percent of Labour Force					
					Total					
Burnaby	10.6	18.9	10.8	6.2	10.4	3.4	25.7	10.6	0.8	2.7
British Columbia	11.4	16.0	6.7	6.4	11.5	3.4	24.0	14.6	2.6	3.2
Canada	11.2	16.5	7.0	6.3	11.7	2.9	23.1	14.4	2.3	4.6
					Males					
Burnaby	12.9	11.5	16.1	2.6	6.9	3.7	22.6	19.4	1.2	3.2
British Columbia	13.5	8.7	10.2	2.7	7.5	3.2	19.4	26.5	3.8	4.5
Canada	13.4	9.3	10.5	2.4	7.4	2.5	19.0	26.0	3.5	6.1
					Females					
Burnaby	8.2	26.9	5.0	10.0	14.2	3.1	29.1	1.0	0.3	2.2
British Columbia	9.2	23.9	2.8	10.4	15.9	3.6	29.1	1.8	1.4	1.8
Canada	8.7	24.4	3.2	10.6	16.5	3.2	27.7	1.8	0.9	2.9

Note: Figures are based on total experienced labour force 15 years and over.
Source: Statistics Canada. 2013. 2011 National Household Survey. Statistics Canada Catalogue no. 99-004-XWE. Ottawa. Released September 11, 2013.

Place of Work Status

Area	Worked at Home	Worked Outside Canada	No Fixed Workplace Address	Worked at Usual Place
		Number		
		Total		
Burnaby	6,285	1,165	12,935	90,985
British Columbia	174,000	12,480	304,465	1,680,525
Canada	1,142,640	66,460	1,868,245	13,517,690
		Males		
Burnaby	3,215	830	9,245	44,690
British Columbia	84,015	9,210	225,840	805,525
Canada	582,150	47,355	1,400,485	6,604,325
		Females		
Burnaby	3,070	330	3,690	46,295
British Columbia	89,990	3,270	78,620	875,000
Canada	560,490	19,100	467,760	6,913,370
		Percent of Labour Force		
		Total		
Burnaby	5.6	1.0	11.6	81.7
British Columbia	8.0	0.6	14.0	77.4
Canada	6.9	0.4	11.3	81.5
		Males		
Burnaby	5.5	1.4	15.9	77.1
British Columbia	7.5	0.8	20.1	71.6
Canada	6.7	0.5	16.2	76.5
		Females		
Burnaby	5.8	0.6	6.9	86.7
British Columbia	8.6	0.3	7.5	83.6
Canada	7.0	0.2	5.9	86.8

Note: Figures are based on total employed labour force 15 years and over.
Source: Statistics Canada. 2013. 2011 National Household Survey. Statistics Canada Catalogue no. 99-004-XWE. Ottawa. Released September 11, 2013.

Mode of Transportation to Work

Area	Car; Truck; Van; as Driver	Car; Truck; Van; as Passenger	Public Transit	Walked	Bicycled	All Other Modes
			Number			
			Total			
Burnaby	63,525	4,475	29,240	4,490	750	1,435
British Columbia	1,415,745	110,695	250,450	132,205	42,260	33,635
Canada	11,393,140	867,050	1,851,525	880,815	201,780	191,625
			Males			
Burnaby	37,085	1,390	12,440	1,800	585	630
British Columbia	773,160	47,425	107,645	57,000	26,595	19,535
Canada	6,238,835	349,530	788,290	387,580	135,840	104,725
			Females			
Burnaby	26,435	3,085	16,800	2,690	170	810
British Columbia	642,580	63,270	142,810	75,205	15,665	14,100
Canada	5,154,305	517,520	1,063,235	493,230	65,940	86,900
			Percent of Labour Force			
			Total			
Burnaby	61.1	4.3	28.1	4.3	0.7	1.4
British Columbia	71.3	5.6	12.6	6.7	2.1	1.7
Canada	74.0	5.6	12.0	5.7	1.3	1.2
			Males			
Burnaby	68.8	2.6	23.1	3.3	1.1	1.2
British Columbia	75.0	4.6	10.4	5.5	2.6	1.9
Canada	77.9	4.4	9.8	4.8	1.7	1.3
			Females			
Burnaby	52.9	6.2	33.6	5.4	0.3	1.6
British Columbia	67.4	6.6	15.0	7.9	1.6	1.5
Canada	69.8	7.0	14.4	6.7	0.9	1.2

Note: Figures are based on total employed labour force 15 years and over.
Source: Statistics Canada. 2013. 2011 National Household Survey. Statistics Canada Catalogue no. 99-004-XWE. Ottawa. Released September 11, 2013.

Visible Minority Population Characteristics

Area	Total Minority	South Asian[1]	Chinese	Black	Filipino	Latin American	Arab	SE Asian[2]	West Asian[3]	Korean	Japanese	Multiple[4]
						Number						
						Total						
Burnaby	130,945	17,480	67,780	3,445	12,905	3,765	1,535	3,945	4,440	7,645	3,780	3,855
British Columbia	1,180,870	313,440	438,140	33,260	126,040	35,465	14,090	51,970	38,960	53,770	38,120	31,160
Canada	6,264,750	1,567,400	1,324,750	945,665	619,310	381,280	380,620	312,075	206,840	161,130	87,270	171,935
						Males						
Burnaby	62,590	8,850	32,375	1,705	5,490	1,780	895	1,900	2,160	3,730	1,745	1,805
British Columbia	565,965	157,135	208,175	17,365	53,715	16,985	8,010	25,055	19,420	25,325	16,295	15,255
Canada	3,043,010	790,755	632,325	453,005	268,885	186,355	203,485	154,035	105,620	77,165	38,270	83,335
						Females						
Burnaby	68,355	8,630	35,400	1,740	7,415	1,980	640	2,050	2,280	3,915	2,035	2,050
British Columbia	614,905	156,300	229,960	15,895	72,320	18,480	6,080	26,920	19,540	28,440	21,820	15,905
Canada	3,221,745	776,650	692,420	492,660	350,425	194,925	177,140	158,045	101,220	83,965	48,990	88,600
						Percent of Population						
						Total						
Burnaby	59.5	7.9	30.8	1.6	5.9	1.7	0.7	1.8	2.0	3.5	1.7	1.8
British Columbia	27.3	7.2	10.1	0.8	2.9	0.8	0.3	1.2	0.9	1.2	0.9	0.7
Canada	19.1	4.8	4.0	2.9	1.9	1.2	1.2	0.9	0.6	0.5	0.3	0.5
						Males						
Burnaby	57.9	8.2	30.0	1.6	5.1	1.6	0.8	1.8	2.0	3.5	1.6	1.7
British Columbia	26.6	7.4	9.8	0.8	2.5	0.8	0.4	1.2	0.9	1.2	0.8	0.7
Canada	18.8	4.9	3.9	2.8	1.7	1.2	1.3	1.0	0.7	0.5	0.2	0.5
						Females						
Burnaby	60.9	7.7	31.6	1.6	6.6	1.8	0.6	1.8	2.0	3.5	1.8	1.8
British Columbia	28.0	7.1	10.5	0.7	3.3	0.8	0.3	1.2	0.9	1.3	1.0	0.7
Canada	19.3	4.7	4.1	3.0	2.1	1.1	0.9	0.9	0.6	0.5	0.3	0.5

Note: The Employment Equity Act defines visible minorities as 'persons, other than Aboriginal peoples, who are non-Caucasian in race or non-white in colour';
(1) Includes 'East Indian,' 'Pakistani,' 'Sri Lankan,' etc.; (2) Includes 'Vietnamese,' 'Cambodian,' 'Malaysian,' 'Laotian,' etc.; (3) Includes 'Iranian,' 'Afghan,' etc.; (4) Includes respondents who reported more than one visible minority group by checking two or more mark-in circles, e.g., 'Black' and 'South Asian.'
Source: Statistics Canada. 2013. 2011 National Household Survey. Statistics Canada Catalogue no. 99-004-XWE. Ottawa. Released September 11, 2013.

PROFILES / Burnaby, British Columbia

Aboriginal Population

Area	Aboriginal Identity[1]	First Nations (North American Indian) Single Identity[2]	Métis Single Identity	Inuk (Inuit) Single Identity	Multiple Aboriginal Identities[3]	Aboriginal Identities Not Included Elsewhere
Number						
Total						
Burnaby	3,295	2,000	1,130	0	25	140
British Columbia	232,290	155,020	69,475	1,570	2,480	3,745
Canada	1,400,685	851,560	451,795	59,440	11,415	26,475
Males						
Burnaby	1,585	900	560	0	15	105
British Columbia	113,080	75,400	33,940	820	1,190	1,735
Canada	682,190	411,785	223,335	29,495	5,525	12,055
Females						
Burnaby	1,710	1,100	575	0	0	35
British Columbia	119,215	79,620	35,540	750	1,290	2,015
Canada	718,500	439,775	228,460	29,950	5,890	14,420
Percent of Population						
Total						
Burnaby	1.5	0.9	0.5	0.0	0.0	0.1
British Columbia	5.4	3.6	1.6	0.0	0.1	0.1
Canada	4.3	2.6	1.4	0.2	0.0	0.1
Males						
Burnaby	1.5	0.8	0.5	0.0	0.0	0.1
British Columbia	5.3	3.5	1.6	0.0	0.1	0.1
Canada	4.2	2.5	1.4	0.2	0.0	0.1
Females						
Burnaby	1.5	1.0	0.5	0.0	0.0	0.0
British Columbia	5.4	3.6	1.6	0.0	0.1	0.1
Canada	4.3	2.6	1.4	0.2	0.0	0.1

Note: (1) Includes persons who reported being an Aboriginal person, that is, First Nations (North American Indian), Métis or Inuk (Inuit) and/or those who reported Registered or Treaty Indian status, that is registered under the Indian Act of Canada, and/or those who reported membership in a First Nation or Indian band. Aboriginal peoples of Canada are defined in the Constitution Act, 1982, section 35-2 as including the Indian, Inuit and Métis peoples of Canada; (2) Users should be aware that the estimates associated with this variable are more affected than most by the incomplete enumeration of certain Indian reserves and Indian settlements in the National Household Survey (NHS); (3) Includes persons who reported being any two or all three of the following: First Nations (North American Indian), Métis or Inuk (Inuit).
Source: Statistics Canada. 2013. 2011 National Household Survey. Statistics Canada Catalogue no. 99-004-XWE. Ottawa. Released September 11, 2013.

Ethnic Origin

Area	North American Aboriginal	Other North American	European	Caribbean	Latin, Central and South American	African	Asian	Oceania
Number								
Total								
Burnaby	3,805	21,935	89,780	1,400	4,505	4,105	124,170	1,420
British Columbia	267,085	884,490	2,812,935	20,035	52,725	47,185	1,122,445	35,770
Canada	1,836,035	11,070,455	20,157,965	627,590	544,375	766,735	5,011,225	74,875
Males								
Burnaby	1,745	11,205	45,425	635	2,220	2,095	59,255	690
British Columbia	128,880	440,920	1,387,940	10,225	25,605	23,575	535,825	17,425
Canada	885,675	5,462,685	9,913,150	291,640	264,635	387,360	2,435,540	37,490
Females								
Burnaby	2,065	10,730	44,350	760	2,280	2,015	64,915	735
British Columbia	138,205	443,570	1,424,990	9,810	27,120	23,610	586,620	18,340
Canada	950,360	5,607,770	10,244,820	335,945	279,740	379,380	2,575,680	37,385
Percent of Population								
Total								
Burnaby	1.7	10.0	40.8	0.6	2.0	1.9	56.4	0.6
British Columbia	6.2	20.5	65.0	0.5	1.2	1.1	26.0	0.8
Canada	5.6	33.7	61.4	1.9	1.7	2.3	15.3	0.2
Males								
Burnaby	1.6	10.4	42.0	0.6	2.1	1.9	54.8	0.6
British Columbia	6.1	20.7	65.3	0.5	1.2	1.1	25.2	0.8
Canada	5.5	33.8	61.3	1.8	1.6	2.4	15.1	0.2
Females								
Burnaby	1.8	9.6	39.5	0.7	2.0	1.8	57.9	0.7
British Columbia	6.3	20.2	64.8	0.4	1.2	1.1	26.7	0.8
Canada	5.7	33.6	61.4	2.0	1.7	2.3	15.4	0.2

Note: The sum of the ethnic groups in this table is greater than the total population estimate because a person may report more than one ethnic origin in the NHS.
Source: Statistics Canada. 2013. 2011 National Household Survey. Statistics Canada Catalogue no. 99-004-XWE. Ottawa. Released September 11, 2013.

Religion

Area	Buddhist	Christian	Hindu	Jewish	Muslim	Sikh	Traditional (Aboriginal) Spirituality	Other Religions	No Religious Affiliation
				Number Total					
Burnaby	10,660	94,475	4,895	605	9,900	6,395	20	1,635	91,670
British Columbia	90,620	1,930,415	45,795	23,130	79,310	201,110	10,295	35,500	1,908,285
Canada	366,830	22,102,745	497,965	329,495	1,053,945	454,965	64,935	130,835	7,850,605
				Males					
Burnaby	4,615	43,345	2,385	295	4,935	3,275	0	720	48,515
British Columbia	40,175	883,680	22,945	11,255	39,780	100,610	5,085	14,680	1,007,420
Canada	168,465	10,497,775	250,435	161,265	540,555	229,435	31,805	57,745	4,225,645
				Females					
Burnaby	6,050	51,135	2,510	305	4,965	3,115	15	920	43,155
British Columbia	50,440	1,046,735	22,845	11,880	39,530	100,500	5,210	20,820	900,865
Canada	198,365	11,604,975	247,525	168,235	513,395	225,530	33,135	73,090	3,624,965
				Percent of Population Total					
Burnaby	4.8	42.9	2.2	0.3	4.5	2.9	0.0	0.7	41.6
British Columbia	2.1	44.6	1.1	0.5	1.8	4.7	0.2	0.8	44.1
Canada	1.1	67.3	1.5	1.0	3.2	1.4	0.2	0.4	23.9
				Males					
Burnaby	4.3	40.1	2.2	0.3	4.6	3.0	0.0	0.7	44.9
British Columbia	1.9	41.6	1.1	0.5	1.9	4.7	0.2	0.7	47.4
Canada	1.0	64.9	1.5	1.0	3.3	1.4	0.2	0.4	26.1
				Females					
Burnaby	5.4	45.6	2.2	0.3	4.4	2.8	0.0	0.8	38.5
British Columbia	2.3	47.6	1.0	0.5	1.8	4.6	0.2	0.9	41.0
Canada	1.2	69.5	1.5	1.0	3.1	1.4	0.2	0.4	21.7

Note: Religion refers to the person's self-identification as having a connection or affiliation with any religious denomination, group, body, sect, cult or other religiously defined community or system of belief. Religion is not limited to formal membership in a religious organization or group. Persons without a religious connection or affiliation can self-identify as atheist, agnostic or humanist, or can provide another applicable response.
Source: Statistics Canada. 2013. 2011 National Household Survey. Statistics Canada Catalogue no. 99-004-XWE. Ottawa. Released September 11, 2013.

Religion—Christian Denominations

Area	Anglican	Baptist	Catholic	Christian Orthodox	Lutheran	Pentecostal	Presbyterian	United Church	Other Christian
				Number Total					
Burnaby	4,730	3,640	43,190	4,965	2,040	1,800	2,840	5,810	25,460
British Columbia	213,975	91,575	650,360	39,845	71,470	58,300	44,635	222,230	538,030
Canada	1,631,845	635,840	12,810,705	550,690	478,185	478,705	472,385	2,007,610	3,036,780
				Males					
Burnaby	1,995	1,685	20,055	2,350	915	840	1,330	2,440	11,740
British Columbia	94,330	41,565	303,300	19,475	32,205	26,590	19,925	94,020	252,270
Canada	752,945	293,905	6,167,290	270,205	221,525	217,850	218,955	912,545	1,442,550
				Females					
Burnaby	2,735	1,960	23,140	2,615	1,125	960	1,505	3,375	13,720
British Columbia	119,645	50,010	347,060	20,375	39,270	31,710	24,710	128,210	285,770
Canada	878,900	341,940	6,643,415	280,485	256,660	260,850	253,430	1,095,065	1,594,230
				Percent of Population Total					
Burnaby	2.1	1.7	19.6	2.3	0.9	0.8	1.3	2.6	11.6
British Columbia	4.9	2.1	15.0	0.9	1.7	1.3	1.0	5.1	12.4
Canada	5.0	1.9	39.0	1.7	1.5	1.5	1.4	6.1	9.2
				Males					
Burnaby	1.8	1.6	18.6	2.2	0.8	0.8	1.2	2.3	10.9
British Columbia	4.4	2.0	14.3	0.9	1.5	1.3	0.9	4.4	11.9
Canada	4.7	1.8	38.2	1.7	1.4	1.3	1.4	5.6	8.9
				Females					
Burnaby	2.4	1.7	20.6	2.3	1.0	0.9	1.3	3.0	12.2
British Columbia	5.4	2.3	15.8	0.9	1.8	1.4	1.1	5.8	13.0
Canada	5.3	2.0	39.8	1.7	1.5	1.6	1.5	6.6	9.6

Note: Religion refers to the person's self-identification as having a connection or affiliation with any religious denomination, group, body, sect, cult or other religiously defined community or system of belief. Religion is not limited to formal membership in a religious organization or group. Persons without a religious connection or affiliation can self-identify as atheist, agnostic or humanist, or can provide another applicable response.
Source: Statistics Canada. 2013. 2011 National Household Survey. Statistics Canada Catalogue no. 99-004-XWE. Ottawa. Released September 11, 2013.

PROFILES / Burnaby, British Columbia

Immigrant Status and Period of Immigration

Area	Non-Immigrants[1]	Immigrants All	Before 1971	1971 to 1980	1981 to 1990	1991 to 2000	2001 to 2005	2006 to 2011	Non-Permanent Residents[3]
				Number Total					
Burnaby	101,740	111,170	12,510	13,680	13,355	33,580	18,510	19,525	7,345
British Columbia	3,067,590	1,191,875	223,215	161,335	156,445	305,655	160,100	185,115	64,995
Canada	25,720,175	6,775,765	1,261,055	870,775	949,890	1,539,050	992,070	1,162,915	356,385
				Males					
Burnaby	52,820	51,595	6,160	6,325	6,115	15,355	8,545	9,090	3,675
British Columbia	1,533,255	561,490	109,510	76,865	72,625	140,985	74,395	87,110	30,880
Canada	12,753,235	3,231,370	605,430	416,670	454,570	724,905	474,545	555,245	178,515
				Females					
Burnaby	48,920	59,580	6,350	7,360	7,240	18,230	9,965	10,440	3,670
British Columbia	1,534,330	630,385	113,710	84,470	83,820	164,675	85,710	98,005	34,115
Canada	12,966,935	3,544,400	655,625	454,105	495,325	814,145	517,530	607,670	177,870
				Percent of Population Total					
Burnaby	46.2	50.5	5.7	6.2	6.1	15.2	8.4	8.9	3.3
British Columbia	70.9	27.6	5.2	3.7	3.6	7.1	3.7	4.3	1.5
Canada	78.3	20.6	3.8	2.7	2.9	4.7	3.0	3.5	1.1
				Males					
Burnaby	48.9	47.7	5.7	5.9	5.7	14.2	7.9	8.4	3.4
British Columbia	72.1	26.4	5.2	3.6	3.4	6.6	3.5	4.1	1.5
Canada	78.9	20.0	3.7	2.6	2.8	4.5	2.9	3.4	1.1
				Females					
Burnaby	43.6	53.1	5.7	6.6	6.5	16.3	8.9	9.3	3.3
British Columbia	69.8	28.7	5.2	3.8	3.8	7.5	3.9	4.5	1.6
Canada	77.7	21.2	3.9	2.7	3.0	4.9	3.1	3.6	1.1

Note: (1) Non-immigrant refers to a person who is a Canadian citizen by birth; (2) Immigrant refers to a person who is or has ever been a landed immigrant/permanent resident. This person has been granted the right to live in Canada permanently by immigration authorities. Some immigrants have resided in Canada for a number of years, while others have arrived recently. Some immigrants are Canadian citizens, while others are not. Most immigrants are born outside Canada, but a small number are born in Canada. In the 2011 National Household Survey, 'Immigrants' includes immigrants who landed in Canada prior to May 10, 2011; (3) Non-permanent resident refers to a person from another country who has a work or study permit, or who is a refugee claimant, and any non-Canadian-born family member living in Canada with them.
Source: Statistics Canada. 2013. 2011 National Household Survey. Statistics Canada Catalogue no. 99-004-XWE. Ottawa. Released September 11, 2013.

Mother Tongue

Area	English	French	Non-official Language	English & French	English & Non-official Language	French & Non-official Language	English, French & Non-official Language
			Number Total				
Burnaby	93,425	1,680	119,440	355	6,140	305	115
British Columbia	3,062,435	57,275	1,154,215	8,600	68,800	3,345	1,530
Canada	18,858,980	7,054,975	6,567,680	144,685	396,330	74,430	24,095
			Males				
Burnaby	48,175	885	56,095	180	2,950	150	45
British Columbia	1,526,350	28,315	543,395	4,065	32,875	1,520	725
Canada	9,345,225	3,452,380	3,157,785	69,975	192,000	36,535	11,965
			Females				
Burnaby	45,250	795	63,340	180	3,195	155	65
British Columbia	1,536,085	28,965	610,825	4,535	35,925	1,830	805
Canada	9,513,750	3,602,590	3,409,895	74,710	204,330	37,890	12,130
			Percent of Population Total				
Burnaby	42.2	0.8	53.9	0.2	2.8	0.1	0.1
British Columbia	70.3	1.3	26.5	0.2	1.6	0.1	0.0
Canada	56.9	21.3	19.8	0.4	1.2	0.2	0.1
			Males				
Burnaby	44.4	0.8	51.7	0.2	2.7	0.1	0.0
British Columbia	71.4	1.3	25.4	0.2	1.5	0.1	0.0
Canada	57.5	21.2	19.4	0.4	1.2	0.2	0.1
			Females				
Burnaby	40.0	0.7	56.1	0.2	2.8	0.1	0.1
British Columbia	69.2	1.3	27.5	0.2	1.6	0.1	0.0
Canada	56.4	21.4	20.2	0.4	1.2	0.2	0.1

Note: Figures cover total population excluding institutional residents.
Source: Statistics Canada. 2012. Census Profile. 2011 Census. Statistics Canada Catalogue no. 98-316-XWE. Ottawa. Released October 24 2012.
http://www12.statcan.gc.ca/census-recensement/2011/dp-pd/prof/index.cfm?Lang=E

Language Spoken Most Often at Home

Area	English	French	Non-official Language	English & French	English & Non-official Language	French & Non-official Language	English, French & Non-official Language
			Number				
			Total				
Burnaby	128,910	610	75,750	260	15,640	95	200
British Columbia	3,506,595	16,685	670,100	4,700	155,065	930	2,130
Canada	21,457,075	6,827,865	3,673,865	131,205	875,135	109,700	46,330
			Males				
Burnaby	64,860	320	35,510	125	7,515	40	100
British Columbia	1,733,775	8,015	317,670	2,240	74,155	435	940
Canada	10,585,620	3,348,235	1,767,310	63,475	425,370	53,010	22,845
			Females				
Burnaby	64,050	290	40,235	135	8,125	50	100
British Columbia	1,772,820	8,665	352,430	2,460	80,905	495	1,185
Canada	10,871,455	3,479,625	1,906,555	67,730	449,765	56,690	23,485
			Percent of Population				
			Total				
Burnaby	58.2	0.3	34.2	0.1	7.1	0.0	0.1
British Columbia	80.5	0.4	15.4	0.1	3.6	0.0	0.0
Canada	64.8	20.6	11.1	0.4	2.6	0.3	0.1
			Males				
Burnaby	59.8	0.3	32.7	0.1	6.9	0.0	0.1
British Columbia	81.1	0.4	14.9	0.1	3.5	0.0	0.0
Canada	65.1	20.6	10.9	0.4	2.6	0.3	0.1
			Females				
Burnaby	56.7	0.3	35.6	0.1	7.2	0.0	0.1
British Columbia	79.9	0.4	15.9	0.1	3.6	0.0	0.1
Canada	64.5	20.6	11.3	0.4	2.7	0.3	0.1

Note: Figures cover total population excluding institutional residents.
Source: Statistics Canada. 2012. Census Profile. 2011 Census. Statistics Canada Catalogue no. 98-316-XWE. Ottawa. Released October 24 2012.
http://www12.statcan.gc.ca/census-recensement/2011/dp-pd/prof/index.cfm?Lang=E

Knowledge of Official Languages

Area	English Only	French Only	English & French	Neither English nor French
		Number		
		Total		
Burnaby	194,970	135	11,870	14,485
British Columbia	3,912,950	2,045	296,645	144,555
Canada	22,564,665	4,165,015	5,795,570	595,920
		Males		
Burnaby	97,070	55	5,480	5,865
British Columbia	1,943,760	950	132,940	59,590
Canada	11,222,185	1,925,340	2,876,560	241,790
		Females		
Burnaby	97,895	80	6,390	8,620
British Columbia	1,969,190	1,095	163,705	84,965
Canada	11,342,485	2,239,680	2,919,005	354,135
		Percent of Population		
		Total		
Burnaby	88.0	0.1	5.4	6.5
British Columbia	89.8	0.0	6.8	3.3
Canada	68.1	12.6	17.5	1.8
		Males		
Burnaby	89.5	0.1	5.1	5.4
British Columbia	90.9	0.0	6.2	2.8
Canada	69.0	11.8	17.7	1.5
		Females		
Burnaby	86.6	0.1	5.7	7.6
British Columbia	88.7	0.0	7.4	3.8
Canada	67.3	13.3	17.3	2.1

Note: Figures cover total population excluding institutional residents.
Source: Statistics Canada. 2012. Census Profile. 2011 Census. Statistics Canada Catalogue no. 98-316-XWE. Ottawa. Released October 24 2012.
http://www12.statcan.gc.ca/census-recensement/2011/dp-pd/prof/index.cfm?Lang=E

Calgary, Alberta

Background

Calgary is located in western Canada and is the largest city in Alberta. The city is in the foothills of the Canadian Rocky Mountains and is located 1,139 metres (3,740 feet) above sea level. Banff National Park is an hour's drive west of the city.

Calgary's Bow River Valley has been shaped by the migration patterns of the Blackfoot, Sarcee, Blood, Stoney and Shaganappi Nations for thousands of years. By the late 1870s, First Nations were trading with settlers, and the Hudson's Bay and North West trading companies soon set up trading posts. The North West Mounted Police built Fort Brisebois (renamed Fort Calgary) in 1875 as a way to maintain order in the region.

When the Canadian Pacific Railway began construction in 1881 and routed through the town of Calgary, the area was transformed from a remote frontier outpost into a gateway to Western settlement.

Since the City of Calgary was incorporated in 1894, Canada's frontier "Cow Town" has evolved into a major business and global energy centre. Calgary's oil-and-gas industry continues to boom. The city is the second largest head office city in Canada and has the youngest, best-educated workforce in the country. The city is also home to the highest number of technology start-up companies and has the strongest labour force participation rate in Canada.

The Calgary Stampede is an annual rodeo, exhibition and festival celebrating the city's cowboy culture and ranching lifestyle. Over a million spectators attend the 10-day event, which celebrated its 100th anniversary in 2012. Canada Olympic Park is a popular year-round attraction and the site of the XV Olympic Winter Games.

Calgary has summer highs of plus 21.87 degrees Celsius, winter lows of minus 13.5 degrees Celsius, and an average rainfall just over 320 mm per year.

Rankings

- Calgary was ranked #3 out of 24 global cities on the "Global Scorecard on Prosperity." For this study, the Conference Board of Canada for Toronto Trade measures liveability and economic performance. *Conference Board of Canada for Toronto Board of Trade, "Global Scorecard on Prosperity," 2011*
- Calgary was ranked #5 out of 140 cities worldwide in terms of the world's most liveable cities. The annual survey uses 30 factors ranking stability, health care, culture and environment, education and infrastructure. Vancouver and Toronto ranked #3 and #4 respectively. *Economist Intelligence Unit, "Liveability and Overview 2012," released August 14, 2012*
- *Maclean's Magazine* reported that, per capita, Calgary has the most millionaires in Canada. There are 215.8 millionaires in Calgary for every 100,000 people. The city also earned *Maclean's*/Canadian Council on Learning's "Smartest City in Canada" designation and was ranked #1 in Canada for highest level of Internet usage (Most Wired City). *Maclean's Magazine, "The real face of Calgary-young, cosmopolitan, confident," October 28th, 2010 with files from Avenue Magazine, May 2010*
- Calgary was ranked #1 in the "Best Place to Live by Population" category of cities with more than 1 million residents. It fell to #14 overall out of 190 Canadian cities and towns. *Money Sense Magazine, "Canada's Best Places to Live 2012," March 20, 2012*
- Calgary was ranked #1 by Environment Canada in three national climate categories: Sunniest Winter (366 hours); Most Sunny Days Year-Round (333 days); and Most Sunny Days in Cold Months (131.5 days). *Environment Canada, Canadian Cities are Weather Winners!, May 29, 2012*

PROFILES / Calgary, Alberta

Population Growth and Density

Area	Population in 2001	Population in 2006	Population in 2011	Population Change 2001–2006	Population Change 2006–2011	Land Area (sq. km)	Population Density per sq. km
Calgary	879,003	988,812	1,096,833	12.4	10.9	825.29	1,329.0
Alberta	2,974,807	3,290,350	3,645,257	10.6	10.8	640,081.87	5.7
Canada	30,007,094	31,612,897	33,476,688	5.4	5.9	8,965,121.42	3.7

Source: Statistics Canada. 2012. Census Profile. 2011 Census. Statistics Canada Catalogue no. 98-316-XWE. Ottawa. Released October 24 2012. http://www12.statcan.gc.ca/census-recensement/2011/dp-pd/prof/index.cfm?Lang=E;
Statistics Canada 2007. 2006 Community Profiles. 2006 Census. Statistics Canada Catalogue no. 92-591-XWE. Ottawa. Released March 13 2007. http://www12.statcan.ca/census-recensement/2006/dp-pd/prof/92-591/index.cfm?Lang=E

Gender

Area	Males	Females
Number		
Calgary	547,475	549,360
Alberta	1,827,815	1,817,440
Canada	16,414,225	17,062,460
Percent of Population		
Calgary	49.9	50.1
Alberta	50.1	49.9
Canada	49.0	51.0

Source: Statistics Canada. 2012. Census Profile. 2011 Census. Statistics Canada Catalogue no. 98-316-XWE. Ottawa. Released October 24 2012. http://www12.statcan.gc.ca/census-recensement/2011/dp-pd/prof/index.cfm?Lang=E

Marital Status

Area	Married[1]	Living Common-law	Single[2]	Separated	Divorced	Widowed
Number — Total						
Calgary	445,155	75,240	265,405	21,400	57,735	35,480
Alberta	1,484,700	272,155	823,935	70,860	177,375	131,440
Canada	12,941,960	3,142,525	7,816,045	698,240	1,686,035	1,584,530
Males						
Calgary	223,555	37,780	145,970	9,340	23,275	7,100
Alberta	745,670	136,180	460,575	31,685	75,875	26,745
Canada	6,470,300	1,575,495	4,206,320	299,655	680,415	310,940
Females						
Calgary	221,605	37,460	119,435	12,060	34,460	28,380
Alberta	739,035	135,980	363,355	39,170	101,500	104,695
Canada	6,471,660	1,567,035	3,609,730	398,585	1,005,620	1,273,590
Percent of Population — Total						
Calgary	49.4	8.4	29.5	2.4	6.4	3.9
Alberta	50.2	9.2	27.8	2.4	6.0	4.4
Canada	46.4	11.3	28.0	2.5	6.0	5.7
Males						
Calgary	50.0	8.5	32.7	2.1	5.2	1.6
Alberta	50.5	9.2	31.2	2.1	5.1	1.8
Canada	47.8	11.6	31.1	2.2	5.0	2.3
Females						
Calgary	48.9	8.3	26.3	2.7	7.6	6.3
Alberta	49.8	9.2	24.5	2.6	6.8	7.1
Canada	45.2	10.9	25.2	2.8	7.0	8.9

Note: (1) and not separated, (2) never legally married
Source: Statistics Canada. 2012. Census Profile. 2011 Census. Statistics Canada Catalogue no. 98-316-XWE. Ottawa. Released October 24 2012. http://www12.statcan.gc.ca/census-recensement/2011/dp-pd/prof/index.cfm?Lang=E

Age Characteristics: 0 to 49 Years

Area	0 to 4 Years	5 to 9 Years	10 to 14 Years	15 to 19 Years	20 to 24 Years	25 to 29 Years	30 to 34 Years	35 to 39 Years	40 to 44 Years	45 to 49 Years
					Number					
					Total					
Calgary	72,010	62,440	61,965	66,600	77,550	93,360	90,355	86,965	85,185	86,705
Alberta	244,880	218,990	220,920	238,205	258,475	288,735	274,390	260,135	258,515	280,635
Canada	1,877,095	1,809,895	1,920,355	2,178,135	2,187,450	2,169,590	2,162,905	2,173,930	2,324,875	2,675,130
					Males					
Calgary	37,105	31,700	31,645	34,175	38,980	46,835	45,230	43,620	43,350	43,585
Alberta	125,665	112,005	113,415	122,065	131,510	146,330	138,600	131,810	130,630	140,575
Canada	961,150	925,965	983,995	1,115,845	1,108,775	1,077,275	1,058,810	1,064,200	1,141,720	1,318,715
					Females					
Calgary	34,900	30,745	30,325	32,430	38,565	46,530	45,125	43,345	41,830	43,120
Alberta	119,210	106,990	107,505	116,145	126,965	142,405	135,795	128,325	127,890	140,060
Canada	915,945	883,935	936,360	1,062,295	1,078,670	1,092,315	1,104,095	1,109,735	1,183,155	1,356,420
					Percent of Population					
					Total					
Calgary	6.6	5.7	5.6	6.1	7.1	8.5	8.2	7.9	7.8	7.9
Alberta	6.7	6.0	6.1	6.5	7.1	7.9	7.5	7.1	7.1	7.7
Canada	5.6	5.4	5.7	6.5	6.5	6.5	6.5	6.5	6.9	8.0
					Males					
Calgary	6.8	5.8	5.8	6.2	7.1	8.6	8.3	8.0	7.9	8.0
Alberta	6.9	6.1	6.2	6.7	7.2	8.0	7.6	7.2	7.1	7.7
Canada	5.9	5.6	6.0	6.8	6.8	6.6	6.5	6.5	7.0	8.0
					Females					
Calgary	6.4	5.6	5.5	5.9	7.0	8.5	8.2	7.9	7.6	7.8
Alberta	6.6	5.9	5.9	6.4	7.0	7.8	7.5	7.1	7.0	7.7
Canada	5.4	5.2	5.5	6.2	6.3	6.4	6.5	6.5	6.9	7.9

Source: Statistics Canada. 2012. Census Profile. 2011 Census. Statistics Canada Catalogue no. 98-316-XWE. Ottawa. Released October 24 2012.
http://www12.statcan.gc.ca/census-recensement/2011/dp-pd/prof/index.cfm?Lang=E

Age Characteristics: 50 Years and Over, and Median Age

Area	50 to 54 Years	55 to 59 Years	60 to 64 Years	65 to 69 Years	70 to 74 Years	75 to 79 Years	80 to 84 Years	85 Years and Over	Median Age
				Number					
				Total					
Calgary	84,530	68,350	51,630	33,370	24,990	20,815	16,085	13,925	36.4
Alberta	279,705	233,785	182,160	125,700	94,775	76,040	57,725	51,485	36.5
Canada	2,658,965	2,340,635	2,052,670	1,521,715	1,153,065	922,700	702,070	645,515	40.6
				Males					
Calgary	42,755	34,705	25,770	16,150	11,475	9,325	6,600	4,475	35.9
Alberta	141,370	118,750	90,975	61,790	45,220	35,205	24,810	17,095	35.9
Canada	1,309,030	1,147,300	1,002,690	738,010	543,435	417,945	291,085	208,300	39.6
				Females					
Calgary	41,775	33,640	25,860	17,215	13,515	11,490	9,485	9,450	36.8
Alberta	138,335	115,030	91,185	63,905	49,555	40,835	32,915	34,390	37.1
Canada	1,349,940	1,193,335	1,049,985	783,705	609,630	504,755	410,985	437,215	41.5
				Percent of Population					
				Total					
Calgary	7.7	6.2	4.7	3.0	2.3	1.9	1.5	1.3	—
Alberta	7.7	6.4	5.0	3.4	2.6	2.1	1.6	1.4	—
Canada	7.9	7.0	6.1	4.5	3.4	2.8	2.1	1.9	—
				Males					
Calgary	7.8	6.3	4.7	2.9	2.1	1.7	1.2	0.8	—
Alberta	7.7	6.5	5.0	3.4	2.5	1.9	1.4	0.9	—
Canada	8.0	7.0	6.1	4.5	3.3	2.5	1.8	1.3	—
				Females					
Calgary	7.6	6.1	4.7	3.1	2.5	2.1	1.7	1.7	—
Alberta	7.6	6.3	5.0	3.5	2.7	2.2	1.8	1.9	—
Canada	7.9	7.0	6.2	4.6	3.6	3.0	2.4	2.6	—

Source: Statistics Canada. 2012. Census Profile. 2011 Census. Statistics Canada Catalogue no. 98-316-XWE. Ottawa. Released October 24 2012.
http://www12.statcan.gc.ca/census-recensement/2011/dp-pd/prof/index.cfm?Lang=E

PROFILES / Calgary, Alberta

Private Households by Household Size

Area	1 Person	2 Persons	3 Persons	4 Persons	5 Persons	6 or More Persons	Average Number of Persons in Private Households
			Households				
Calgary	110,005	136,260	70,975	66,935	25,145	14,100	2.6
Alberta	342,730	477,095	224,925	211,645	85,495	48,385	2.6
Canada	3,673,310	4,544,820	2,081,900	1,903,300	724,405	392,885	2.5
			Percent of Households				
Calgary	26.0	32.2	16.8	15.8	5.9	3.3	–
Alberta	24.7	34.3	16.2	15.2	6.1	3.5	–
Canada	27.6	34.1	15.6	14.3	5.4	2.9	–

Source: Statistics Canada. 2012. Census Profile. 2011 Census. Statistics Canada Catalogue no. 98-316-XWE. Ottawa. Released October 24 2012.
http://www12.statcan.gc.ca/census-recensement/2011/dp-pd/prof/index.cfm?Lang=E

Dwelling Type

Area	Single-detached House	Semi-detached House	Row House	Apartment: Building with Five or More Storeys	Apartment: Building with Fewer Than Five Storeys	Duplex Apartment	Movable Dwelling	Other Single-attached House
				Number				
Calgary	248,755	25,495	37,400	29,485	63,535	16,655	1,935	155
Alberta	883,265	71,845	97,865	58,205	197,940	33,505	46,590	1,060
Canada	7,329,150	646,245	791,600	1,234,770	2,397,550	704,485	183,510	33,310
				Percent of Dwellings				
Calgary	58.7	6.0	8.8	7.0	15.0	3.9	0.5	0.0
Alberta	63.5	5.2	7.0	4.2	14.2	2.4	3.4	0.1
Canada	55.0	4.9	5.9	9.3	18.0	5.3	1.4	0.3

Source: Statistics Canada. 2012. Census Profile. 2011 Census. Statistics Canada Catalogue no. 98-316-XWE. Ottawa. Released October 24 2012.
http://www12.statcan.gc.ca/census-recensement/2011/dp-pd/prof/index.cfm?Lang=E

Shelter Costs

		Owned Dwellings					Rented Dwellings		
Area	Number	Median Value[1] ($)	Average Value[1] ($)	Median Monthly Costs[2] ($)	Average Monthly Costs[2] ($)	Number	Median Monthly Costs[3] ($)	Average Monthly Costs[3] ($)
Calgary	306,700	400,697	455,691	1,366	1,386	116,675	1,093	1,123
Alberta	991,025	349,684	398,839	1,251	1,314	356,510	1,017	1,079
Canada	9,013,410	280,552	345,182	978	1,141	4,060,385	784	848

Note: All figures cover non-farm, non-reserve private dwellings; (1) Refers to the dollar amount expected by the owner if the dwelling were to be sold; (2) Includes all shelter expenses paid by households that own their dwellings, such as the mortgage payment and the costs of electricity, heat, water and other municipal services, property taxes and condominium fees; (3) Includes all shelter expenses paid by households that rent their dwellings, such as the monthly rent and the costs of electricity, heat and municipal services.
Source: Statistics Canada. 2013. 2011 National Household Survey. Statistics Canada Catalogue no. 99-004-XWE. Ottawa. Released September 11, 2013.

Occupied Private Dwellings by Period of Construction

Area	1960 or Before	1961 to 1980	1981 to 1990	1991 to 2000	2001 to 2005	2006 to 2011
			Number			
Calgary	49,480	135,660	61,840	73,245	56,180	47,015
Alberta	189,745	440,825	202,060	214,705	170,660	172,290
Canada	3,273,105	4,152,715	2,112,110	1,707,880	1,031,020	1,042,430
			Percent of Dwellings			
Calgary	11.7	32.0	14.6	17.3	13.3	11.1
Alberta	13.6	31.7	14.5	15.4	12.3	12.4
Canada	24.6	31.2	15.9	12.8	7.7	7.8

Note: Figures cover non-farm, non-reserve private dwellings and includes data up to May 10, 2011.
Source: Statistics Canada. 2013. 2011 National Household Survey. Statistics Canada Catalogue no. 99-004-XWE. Ottawa. Released September 11, 2013.

Educational Attainment

Area	No Certificate, Diploma or Degree	High School Diploma or Equivalent[1]	Apprenticeship or Trades Certificate or Diploma[2]	College, CÉGEP or Other Non-University Certificate or Diploma	University Certificate or Diploma Below the Bachelor Level[3]	Bachelor's Degree	University Certificate, Diploma or Degree Above Bachelor Level[4]
Number — Total							
Calgary	132,870	218,615	70,430	154,530	46,705	180,675	82,025
Alberta	550,465	764,390	318,280	530,100	122,465	418,180	184,860
Canada	5,485,400	6,968,935	2,950,685	4,970,020	1,200,130	3,634,425	2,049,930
Males							
Calgary	66,830	105,985	48,640	67,915	20,760	87,580	43,175
Alberta	283,115	365,625	233,190	225,215	51,345	190,245	97,085
Canada	2,742,875	3,305,415	1,928,970	2,118,430	513,235	1,643,080	1,043,350
Females							
Calgary	66,040	112,630	21,790	86,615	25,950	93,095	38,845
Alberta	267,350	398,765	85,095	304,885	71,120	227,930	87,775
Canada	2,742,520	3,663,515	1,021,715	2,851,595	686,890	1,991,345	1,006,585
Percent of Population — Total							
Calgary	15.0	24.7	8.0	17.4	5.3	20.4	9.3
Alberta	19.1	26.5	11.0	18.4	4.2	14.5	6.4
Canada	20.1	25.6	10.8	18.2	4.4	13.3	7.5
Males							
Calgary	15.2	24.0	11.0	15.4	4.7	19.9	9.8
Alberta	19.6	25.3	16.1	15.6	3.6	13.2	6.7
Canada	20.6	24.9	14.5	15.9	3.9	12.4	7.8
Females							
Calgary	14.8	25.3	4.9	19.5	5.8	20.9	8.7
Alberta	18.5	27.6	5.9	21.1	4.9	15.8	6.1
Canada	19.6	26.2	7.3	20.4	4.9	14.3	7.2

Note: Figures cover total population aged 15 years and over by highest certificate, diploma or degree; (1) Includes persons who have graduated from a secondary school or equivalent. It excludes persons with a postsecondary certificate, diploma or degree; (2) Includes Registered Apprenticeship certificates (including Certificate of Qualification, Journeyperson's designation) and other trades certificates or diplomas such as pre-employment or vocational certificates and diplomas from brief trade programs completed at community colleges, institutes of technology, vocational centres, and similar institutions; (3) Comparisons with other data sources suggest that the category 'University certificate or diploma below the bachelor's level' was over-reported in the NHS. This category likely includes some responses that are actually college certificates or diplomas, bachelor's degrees or other types of education (e.g., university transfer programs, bachelor's programs completed in other countries, incomplete bachelor's programs, non-university professional designations). We recommend users interpret the results for the 'University certificate or diploma below the bachelor's level' category with caution; (4) 'University certificate or diploma above bachelor level' includes the categories: 'Degree in medicine, dentistry, veterinary medicine or optometry,' 'Master's degree' and 'Earned doctorate.'
Source: Statistics Canada. 2013. 2011 National Household Survey. Statistics Canada Catalogue no. 99-004-XWE. Ottawa. Released September 11, 2013.

Household Income Distribution

Area	Less than $10,000	$10,000 to $19,999	$20,000 to $29,999	$30,000 to $39,999	$40,000 to $49,999	$50,000 to $59,999	$60,000 to $79,999	$80,000 to $99,999	$100,000 to $124,999	$125,000 to $149,999	$150,000 and Over
Households											
Calgary	17,970	20,550	24,055	28,370	29,350	30,290	57,375	50,120	47,220	33,990	84,140
Alberta	55,620	75,390	87,985	102,290	100,165	100,965	184,540	166,110	158,540	113,010	245,665
Canada	626,705	1,141,945	1,193,925	1,271,675	1,206,800	1,102,120	1,865,280	1,458,240	1,260,770	802,555	1,389,240
Percent of Households											
Calgary	4.2	4.9	5.7	6.7	6.9	7.2	13.6	11.8	11.2	8.0	19.9
Alberta	4.0	5.4	6.3	7.4	7.2	7.3	13.3	11.9	11.4	8.1	17.7
Canada	4.7	8.6	9.0	9.5	9.1	8.3	14.0	10.9	9.5	6.0	10.4

Note: Household income is the sum of the total incomes of all members of that household. Total income refers to monetary receipts from certain sources, before income taxes and deductions, during calendar year 2010.
Source: Statistics Canada. 2013. 2011 National Household Survey. Statistics Canada Catalogue no. 99-004-XWE. Ottawa. Released September 11, 2013.

Median and Average Household and Economic Family Income

Area	Median Household Income ($)	Average Household Income ($)	Median After-tax Household Income ($)	Average After-tax Household Income ($)	Median Economic Family Income ($)	Average Economic Family Income ($)	Median After-tax Economic Family Income ($)	Average After-tax Economic Family Income ($)
Calgary	81,256	109,698	70,098	89,223	97,790	128,841	83,669	104,490
Alberta	78,632	100,819	68,086	83,011	93,393	116,232	80,271	95,558
Canada	61,072	79,102	54,089	66,149	76,511	94,125	67,044	78,517

Note: Figures cover household and economic familiy income in 2010. A household is defined as a person or a group of persons (other than foreign residents) who occupy the same private dwelling and do not have a usual place of residence elsewhere in Canada. Every person is a member of one and only one household. An economic family is defined as a group of two or more persons who live in the same dwelling and are related to each other by blood, marriage, common-law, adoption or a foster relationship. A couple may be of opposite or same sex.
Source: Statistics Canada. 2013. 2011 National Household Survey. Statistics Canada Catalogue no. 99-004-XWE. Ottawa. Released September 11, 2013.

PROFILES / Calgary, Alberta

Individual Income Distribution

Area	Less than $10,000	$10,000 to $19,999	$20,000 to $29,999	$30,000 to $39,999	$40,000 to $49,999	$50,000 to $59,999	$60,000 to $79,999	$80,000 to $99,999	$100,000 to $124,999	$125,000 and Over
					Number					
					Total					
Calgary	137,735	116,835	97,335	89,225	84,200	66,610	92,485	59,575	37,305	60,100
Alberta	437,495	408,190	340,195	293,435	268,335	219,080	303,265	196,520	122,465	161,750
Canada	4,492,040	4,835,710	3,670,020	3,180,360	2,603,520	1,921,650	2,437,440	1,302,045	693,580	782,135
					Males					
Calgary	57,620	46,675	40,700	41,110	40,855	35,665	52,770	35,390	24,505	46,035
Alberta	176,040	152,740	137,535	132,145	130,180	120,865	188,080	127,695	89,525	131,500
Canada	1,936,365	1,864,880	1,588,260	1,522,190	1,333,510	1,079,780	1,473,145	823,720	492,905	599,905
					Females					
Calgary	80,115	70,170	56,635	48,115	43,350	30,945	39,715	24,190	12,800	14,065
Alberta	261,460	255,450	202,660	161,285	138,160	98,215	115,185	68,830	32,935	30,250
Canada	2,555,675	2,970,825	2,081,760	1,658,170	1,270,010	841,870	964,300	478,330	200,680	182,230
					Percent of Population					
					Total					
Calgary	16.4	13.9	11.6	10.6	10.0	7.9	11.0	7.1	4.4	7.1
Alberta	15.9	14.8	12.4	10.7	9.8	8.0	11.0	7.1	4.5	5.9
Canada	17.3	18.7	14.2	12.3	10.0	7.4	9.4	5.0	2.7	3.0
					Males					
Calgary	13.7	11.1	9.7	9.8	9.7	8.5	12.5	8.4	5.8	10.9
Alberta	12.7	11.0	9.9	9.5	9.4	8.7	13.6	9.2	6.5	9.5
Canada	15.2	14.7	12.5	12.0	10.5	8.5	11.6	6.5	3.9	4.7
					Females					
Calgary	19.1	16.7	13.5	11.5	10.3	7.4	9.5	5.8	3.0	3.3
Alberta	19.2	18.7	14.9	11.8	10.1	7.2	8.4	5.0	2.4	2.2
Canada	19.4	22.5	15.8	12.6	9.6	6.4	7.3	3.6	1.5	1.4

Note: Figures cover individuals aged 15 years and over with income. Income refers to monetary receipts from certain sources, before income taxes and deductions, during calendar year 2010.
Source: Statistics Canada. 2013. 2011 National Household Survey. Statistics Canada Catalogue no. 99-004-XWE. Ottawa. Released September 11, 2013.

Labour Force Status

| | In the Labour Force ||| Not in the |
Area	All	Employed	Unemployed	Labour Force
		Number		
		Total		
Calgary	656,545	617,040	39,505	229,305
Alberta	2,115,640	1,993,225	122,415	773,095
Canada	17,990,080	16,595,035	1,395,045	9,269,445
		Males		
Calgary	351,360	330,790	20,570	89,525
Alberta	1,143,840	1,078,370	65,470	301,975
Canada	9,388,570	8,634,310	754,255	3,906,785
		Females		
Calgary	305,185	286,250	18,935	139,780
Alberta	971,800	914,855	56,945	471,120
Canada	8,601,515	7,960,725	640,790	5,362,660
		Percent of Labour Force		
		Total		
Calgary	74.1	69.7	6.0	25.9
Alberta	73.2	69.0	5.8	26.8
Canada	66.0	60.9	7.8	34.0
		Males		
Calgary	79.7	75.0	5.9	20.3
Alberta	79.1	74.6	5.7	20.9
Canada	70.6	64.9	8.0	29.4
		Females		
Calgary	68.6	64.3	6.2	31.4
Alberta	67.3	63.4	5.9	32.7
Canada	61.6	57.0	7.4	38.4

Note: Figures are based on total population 15 years and over
Source: Statistics Canada. 2013. 2011 National Household Survey. Statistics Canada Catalogue no. 99-004-XWE. Ottawa. Released September 11, 2013.

Labour Force by Industry (NAICS Codes 11–52)

Area	Agriculture, forestry, fishing & hunting	Mining, quarrying, & oil & gas extraction	Utilities	Construction	Manufacturing	Wholesale Trade	Retail Trade	Transportation & warehousing	Information & cultural industries	Finance & insurance
					Number					
					Total					
Calgary	2,150	40,680	7,335	54,935	37,580	28,645	69,975	35,220	15,055	24,780
Alberta	61,165	136,500	22,035	195,905	123,465	89,000	229,225	104,770	35,465	68,760
Canada	437,650	261,050	149,940	1,215,380	1,619,295	733,445	2,031,665	827,780	420,830	767,960
					Males					
Calgary	1,340	24,335	4,370	46,640	27,705	19,845	33,015	25,080	8,250	10,430
Alberta	41,465	104,825	15,725	166,270	93,895	63,590	104,725	76,070	18,990	24,355
Canada	307,370	211,690	110,765	1,068,710	1,167,680	494,545	933,850	617,305	235,875	296,995
					Females					
Calgary	810	16,350	2,960	8,290	9,875	8,800	36,960	10,145	6,815	14,350
Alberta	19,700	31,670	6,305	29,635	29,570	25,415	124,500	28,700	16,470	44,410
Canada	130,285	49,360	39,175	146,670	451,615	238,900	1,097,820	210,475	184,955	470,960
					Percent of Labour Force					
					Total					
Calgary	0.3	6.3	1.1	8.5	5.8	4.4	10.8	5.4	2.3	3.8
Alberta	2.9	6.5	1.1	9.4	5.9	4.3	11.0	5.0	1.7	3.3
Canada	2.5	1.5	0.9	6.9	9.2	4.2	11.6	4.7	2.4	4.4
					Males					
Calgary	0.4	7.0	1.3	13.4	8.0	5.7	9.5	7.2	2.4	3.0
Alberta	3.7	9.3	1.4	14.7	8.3	5.6	9.3	6.7	1.7	2.2
Canada	3.3	2.3	1.2	11.6	12.7	5.4	10.2	6.7	2.6	3.2
					Females					
Calgary	0.3	5.5	1.0	2.8	3.3	2.9	12.3	3.4	2.3	4.8
Alberta	2.1	3.3	0.7	3.1	3.1	2.7	13.0	3.0	1.7	4.6
Canada	1.6	0.6	0.5	1.7	5.4	2.8	13.1	2.5	2.2	5.6

Note: Figures are based on total experienced labour force 15 years and over. Experienced labour force refers to persons who, during the week of Sunday, May 1 to Saturday, May 7, 2011, were employed and the unemployed who had last worked for pay or in self-employment in either 2010 or 2011.
Source: Statistics Canada. 2013. 2011 National Household Survey. Statistics Canada Catalogue no. 99-004-XWE. Ottawa. Released September 11, 2013.

Labour Force by Industry (NAICS Codes 53–91)

Area	Real estate & rental & leasing	Profess., scientific & tech. services	Mgmt of companies & enterprises	Admin. & support, waste mgmt & remed. services	Educational services	Health care & social assistance	Arts, entertain. & recreation	Accomm. & food services	Other services (except public admin.)	Public admin.
					Number					
					Total					
Calgary	14,335	76,625	1,080	26,350	40,025	61,070	14,545	40,135	28,880	27,055
Alberta	40,090	162,490	2,535	72,965	141,550	206,695	39,720	125,810	101,275	128,720
Canada	321,895	1,240,850	17,460	728,330	1,301,435	1,949,650	363,405	1,130,750	807,800	1,261,050
					Males					
Calgary	8,145	45,265	610	15,275	12,960	10,565	7,470	18,245	12,215	15,125
Alberta	22,305	91,715	1,270	40,320	44,045	33,030	19,510	50,795	49,330	69,075
Canada	179,090	688,625	9,380	411,250	424,915	349,430	188,270	469,990	372,940	652,510
					Females					
Calgary	6,190	31,355	470	11,075	27,065	50,500	7,080	21,890	16,665	11,935
Alberta	17,790	70,780	1,260	32,645	97,505	173,665	20,215	75,020	51,950	59,650
Canada	142,805	552,225	8,075	317,085	876,515	1,600,220	175,135	660,760	434,865	608,535
					Percent of Labour Force					
					Total					
Calgary	2.2	11.9	0.2	4.1	6.2	9.4	2.2	6.2	4.5	4.2
Alberta	1.9	7.8	0.1	3.5	6.8	9.9	1.9	6.0	4.8	6.2
Canada	1.8	7.1	0.1	4.1	7.4	11.1	2.1	6.4	4.6	7.2
					Males					
Calgary	2.3	13.0	0.2	4.4	3.7	3.0	2.2	5.3	3.5	4.4
Alberta	2.0	8.1	0.1	3.6	3.9	2.9	1.7	4.5	4.4	6.1
Canada	1.9	7.5	0.1	4.5	4.6	3.8	2.0	5.1	4.1	7.1
					Females					
Calgary	2.1	10.5	0.2	3.7	9.0	16.9	2.4	7.3	5.6	4.0
Alberta	1.9	7.4	0.1	3.4	10.2	18.1	2.1	7.8	5.4	6.2
Canada	1.7	6.6	0.1	3.8	10.4	19.1	2.1	7.9	5.2	7.2

Note: Figures are based on total experienced labour force 15 years and over. Experienced labour force refers to persons who, during the week of Sunday, May 1 to Saturday, May 7, 2011, were employed and the unemployed who had last worked for pay or in self-employment in either 2010 or 2011.
Source: Statistics Canada. 2013. 2011 National Household Survey. Statistics Canada Catalogue no. 99-004-XWE. Ottawa. Released September 11, 2013.

Occupation

Area	Mgmt	Business, Finance & Admin.	Natural/ Applied Sciences & Related	Health	Education, Law & Social, Community & Government Services	Art, Culture, Recreation & Sport	Sales & Service	Trades, Transport & Equip. Operators & Related	Natural Resources, Agri. & Related Production	Mfg & Utilities
					Number					
					Total					
Calgary	72,585	122,555	77,990	36,665	63,930	16,400	143,640	88,890	8,720	15,090
Alberta	248,520	347,880	168,725	125,125	211,945	45,140	438,865	367,650	69,950	64,345
Canada	1,963,600	2,902,045	1,237,775	1,107,200	2,064,675	503,415	4,068,170	2,537,775	397,930	805,040
					Males					
Calgary	46,650	38,045	60,295	7,060	20,815	7,215	64,825	83,255	7,275	11,455
Alberta	160,145	93,875	131,715	22,050	71,815	18,290	180,675	342,230	59,115	51,385
Canada	1,229,460	854,190	966,355	217,520	676,550	232,535	1,745,705	2,385,615	318,945	564,300
					Females					
Calgary	25,935	84,510	17,690	29,605	43,115	9,185	78,815	5,635	1,445	3,640
Alberta	88,370	254,005	37,005	103,070	140,135	26,855	258,190	25,425	10,835	12,960
Canada	734,140	2,047,855	271,415	889,675	1,388,130	270,875	2,322,465	152,165	78,980	240,740
					Percent of Labour Force					
					Total					
Calgary	11.2	19.0	12.1	5.7	9.9	2.5	22.2	13.8	1.3	2.3
Alberta	11.9	16.7	8.1	6.0	10.1	2.2	21.0	17.6	3.3	3.1
Canada	11.2	16.5	7.0	6.3	11.7	2.9	23.1	14.4	2.3	4.6
					Males					
Calgary	13.4	11.0	17.4	2.0	6.0	2.1	18.7	24.0	2.1	3.3
Alberta	14.2	8.3	11.6	1.9	6.3	1.6	16.0	30.3	5.2	4.5
Canada	13.4	9.3	10.5	2.4	7.4	2.5	19.0	26.0	3.5	6.1
					Females					
Calgary	8.7	28.2	5.9	9.9	14.4	3.1	26.3	1.9	0.5	1.2
Alberta	9.2	26.5	3.9	10.8	14.6	2.8	27.0	2.7	1.1	1.4
Canada	8.7	24.4	3.2	10.6	16.5	3.2	27.7	1.8	0.9	2.9

Note: Figures are based on total experienced labour force 15 years and over
Source: Statistics Canada. 2013. 2011 National Household Survey. Statistics Canada Catalogue no. 99-004-XWE. Ottawa. Released September 11, 2013.

Place of Work Status

Area	Worked at Home	Worked Outside Canada	No Fixed Workplace Address	Worked at Usual Place
		Number		
		Total		
Calgary	35,830	2,550	78,780	499,880
Alberta	147,245	6,620	292,055	1,547,305
Canada	1,142,640	66,460	1,868,245	13,517,690
		Males		
Calgary	16,710	1,925	59,540	252,610
Alberta	71,245	5,175	228,125	773,825
Canada	582,150	47,355	1,400,485	6,604,325
		Females		
Calgary	19,125	625	19,235	247,270
Alberta	76,005	1,445	63,930	773,480
Canada	560,490	19,100	467,760	6,913,370
		Percent of Labour Force		
		Total		
Calgary	5.8	0.4	12.8	81.0
Alberta	7.4	0.3	14.7	77.6
Canada	6.9	0.4	11.3	81.5
		Males		
Calgary	5.1	0.6	18.0	76.4
Alberta	6.6	0.5	21.2	71.8
Canada	6.7	0.5	16.2	76.5
		Females		
Calgary	6.7	0.2	6.7	86.4
Alberta	8.3	0.2	7.0	84.5
Canada	7.0	0.2	5.9	86.8

Note: Figures are based on total employed labour force 15 years and over.
Source: Statistics Canada. 2013. 2011 National Household Survey. Statistics Canada Catalogue no. 99-004-XWE. Ottawa. Released September 11, 2013.

PROFILES / Calgary, Alberta

Mode of Transportation to Work

Area	Car; Truck; Van; as Driver	Car; Truck; Van; as Passenger	Public Transit	Walked	Bicycled	All Other Modes
			Number			
			Total			
Calgary	403,475	31,330	99,445	29,260	7,400	7,750
Alberta	1,406,150	103,715	193,115	91,005	19,535	25,835
Canada	11,393,140	867,050	1,851,525	880,815	201,780	191,625
			Males			
Calgary	231,765	10,520	46,755	13,730	5,455	3,930
Alberta	798,140	43,990	91,260	40,550	13,950	14,055
Canada	6,238,835	349,530	788,290	387,580	135,840	104,725
			Females			
Calgary	171,705	20,805	52,695	15,530	1,950	3,820
Alberta	608,010	59,725	101,855	50,450	5,585	11,780
Canada	5,154,305	517,520	1,063,235	493,230	65,940	86,900
			Percent of Labour Force			
			Total			
Calgary	69.7	5.4	17.2	5.1	1.3	1.3
Alberta	76.4	5.6	10.5	4.9	1.1	1.4
Canada	74.0	5.6	12.0	5.7	1.3	1.2
			Males			
Calgary	74.2	3.4	15.0	4.4	1.7	1.3
Alberta	79.7	4.4	9.1	4.0	1.4	1.4
Canada	77.9	4.4	9.8	4.8	1.7	1.3
			Females			
Calgary	64.4	7.8	19.8	5.8	0.7	1.4
Alberta	72.6	7.1	12.2	6.0	0.7	1.4
Canada	69.8	7.0	14.4	6.7	0.9	1.2

Note: Figures are based on total employed labour force 15 years and over.
Source: Statistics Canada. 2013. 2011 National Household Survey. Statistics Canada Catalogue no. 99-004-XWE. Ottawa. Released September 11, 2013.

Visible Minority Population Characteristics

Area	Total Minority	South Asian[1]	Chinese	Black	Filipino	Latin American	Arab	SE Asian[2]	West Asian[3]	Korean	Japanese	Multiple[4]
						Number						
						Total						
Calgary	325,390	81,180	74,070	31,870	47,350	19,870	16,745	20,530	8,470	8,160	5,160	9,130
Alberta	656,325	156,665	133,390	74,435	106,035	41,305	34,920	41,025	16,030	15,000	12,415	18,840
Canada	6,264,750	1,567,400	1,324,750	945,665	619,310	381,280	380,620	312,075	206,840	161,130	87,270	171,935
						Males						
Calgary	161,190	41,835	35,805	16,710	21,100	10,445	8,615	10,095	4,565	3,960	2,230	4,455
Alberta	326,340	81,035	64,845	39,170	47,370	21,205	18,510	20,440	8,600	7,235	5,595	9,210
Canada	3,043,010	790,755	632,325	453,005	268,885	186,355	203,485	154,035	105,620	77,165	38,270	83,335
						Females						
Calgary	164,195	39,345	38,265	15,155	26,245	9,420	8,125	10,435	3,905	4,200	2,925	4,675
Alberta	329,985	75,630	68,550	35,265	58,660	20,095	16,415	20,585	7,425	7,765	6,820	9,630
Canada	3,221,745	776,650	692,420	492,660	350,425	194,925	177,140	158,045	101,220	83,965	48,990	88,600
						Percent of Population						
						Total						
Calgary	30.1	7.5	6.8	2.9	4.4	1.8	1.5	1.9	0.8	0.8	0.5	0.8
Alberta	18.4	4.4	3.7	2.1	3.0	1.2	1.0	1.1	0.4	0.4	0.3	0.5
Canada	19.1	4.8	4.0	2.9	1.9	1.2	1.2	0.9	0.6	0.5	0.3	0.5
						Males						
Calgary	29.8	7.7	6.6	3.1	3.9	1.9	1.6	1.9	0.8	0.7	0.4	0.8
Alberta	18.2	4.5	3.6	2.2	2.6	1.2	1.0	1.1	0.5	0.4	0.3	0.5
Canada	18.8	4.9	3.9	2.8	1.7	1.2	1.3	1.0	0.7	0.5	0.2	0.5
						Females						
Calgary	30.3	7.3	7.1	2.8	4.8	1.7	1.5	1.9	0.7	0.8	0.5	0.9
Alberta	18.6	4.3	3.9	2.0	3.3	1.1	0.9	1.2	0.4	0.4	0.4	0.5
Canada	19.3	4.7	4.1	3.0	2.1	1.2	1.1	0.9	0.6	0.5	0.3	0.5

Note: The Employment Equity Act defines visible minorities as 'persons, other than Aboriginal peoples, who are non-Caucasian in race or non-white in colour';
(1) Includes 'East Indian,' 'Pakistani,' 'Sri Lankan,' etc.; (2) Includes 'Vietnamese,' 'Cambodian,' 'Malaysian,' 'Laotian,' etc.; (3) Includes 'Iranian,' 'Afghan,' etc.; (4) Includes respondents who reported more than one visible minority group by checking two or more mark-in circles, e.g., 'Black' and 'South Asian.'
Source: Statistics Canada. 2013. 2011 National Household Survey. Statistics Canada Catalogue no. 99-004-XWE. Ottawa. Released September 11, 2013.

PROFILES / Calgary, Alberta

Aboriginal Population

Area	Aboriginal Identity[1]	First Nations (North American Indian) Single Identity[2]	Métis Single Identity	Inuk (Inuit) Single Identity	Multiple Aboriginal Identities[3]	Aboriginal Identities Not Included Elsewhere
Number						
Total						
Calgary	28,905	12,855	14,650	235	155	1,010
Alberta	220,695	116,670	96,870	1,985	1,870	3,300
Canada	1,400,685	851,560	451,795	59,440	11,415	26,475
Males						
Calgary	13,960	6,075	7,270	120	75	425
Alberta	108,295	56,470	48,345	1,035	965	1,480
Canada	682,190	411,785	223,335	29,495	5,525	12,055
Females						
Calgary	14,945	6,775	7,380	120	85	585
Alberta	112,400	60,200	48,525	950	905	1,815
Canada	718,500	439,775	228,460	29,950	5,890	14,420
Percent of Population						
Total						
Calgary	2.7	1.2	1.4	0.0	0.0	0.1
Alberta	6.2	3.3	2.7	0.1	0.1	0.1
Canada	4.3	2.6	1.4	0.2	0.0	0.1
Males						
Calgary	2.6	1.1	1.3	0.0	0.0	0.1
Alberta	6.0	3.1	2.7	0.1	0.1	0.1
Canada	4.2	2.5	1.4	0.2	0.0	0.1
Females						
Calgary	2.8	1.3	1.4	0.0	0.0	0.1
Alberta	6.3	3.4	2.7	0.1	0.1	0.1
Canada	4.3	2.6	1.4	0.2	0.0	0.1

Note: (1) Includes persons who reported being an Aboriginal person, that is, First Nations (North American Indian), Métis or Inuk (Inuit) and/or those who reported Registered or Treaty Indian status, that is registered under the Indian Act of Canada, and/or those who reported membership in a First Nation or Indian band. Aboriginal peoples of Canada are defined in the Constitution Act, 1982, section 35-2 as including the Indian, Inuit and Métis peoples of Canada; (2) Users should be aware that the estimates associated with this variable are more affected than most by the incomplete enumeration of certain Indian reserves and Indian settlements in the National Household Survey (NHS); (3) Includes persons who reported being any two or all three of the following: First Nations (North American Indian), Métis or Inuk (Inuit).
Source: Statistics Canada. 2013. 2011 National Household Survey. Statistics Canada Catalogue no. 99-004-XWE. Ottawa. Released September 11, 2013.

Ethnic Origin

Area	North American Aboriginal	Other North American	European	Caribbean	Latin, Central and South American	African	Asian	Oceania
Number								
Total								
Calgary	40,375	224,760	680,880	10,580	23,795	33,855	276,180	5,080
Alberta	263,720	830,700	2,506,665	25,035	54,650	78,580	551,715	12,985
Canada	1,836,035	11,070,455	20,157,965	627,590	544,375	766,735	5,011,225	74,875
Males								
Calgary	19,540	113,530	339,205	5,200	12,025	17,890	135,245	2,655
Alberta	129,275	424,805	1,254,145	12,420	27,550	41,680	271,145	6,620
Canada	885,675	5,462,685	9,913,150	291,640	264,635	387,360	2,435,540	37,490
Females								
Calgary	20,835	111,230	341,675	5,375	11,770	15,965	140,935	2,420
Alberta	134,445	405,895	1,252,520	12,620	27,105	36,895	280,570	6,360
Canada	950,360	5,607,770	10,244,820	335,945	279,740	379,380	2,575,680	37,385
Percent of Population								
Total								
Calgary	3.7	20.8	62.9	1.0	2.2	3.1	25.5	0.5
Alberta	7.4	23.3	70.3	0.7	1.5	2.2	15.5	0.4
Canada	5.6	33.7	61.4	1.9	1.7	2.3	15.3	0.2
Males								
Calgary	3.6	21.0	62.7	1.0	2.2	3.3	25.0	0.5
Alberta	7.2	23.7	69.9	0.7	1.5	2.3	15.1	0.4
Canada	5.5	33.8	61.3	1.8	1.6	2.4	15.1	0.2
Females								
Calgary	3.8	20.6	63.1	1.0	2.2	3.0	26.0	0.4
Alberta	7.6	22.9	70.6	0.7	1.5	2.1	15.8	0.4
Canada	5.7	33.6	61.4	2.0	1.7	2.3	15.4	0.2

Note: The sum of the ethnic groups in this table is greater than the total population estimate because a person may report more than one ethnic origin in the NHS.
Source: Statistics Canada. 2013. 2011 National Household Survey. Statistics Canada Catalogue no. 99-004-XWE. Ottawa. Released September 11, 2013.

Religion

Area	Buddhist	Christian	Hindu	Jewish	Muslim	Sikh	Traditional (Aboriginal) Spirituality	Other Religions	No Religious Affiliation
				Number Total					
Calgary	22,375	594,270	17,410	5,995	56,785	28,565	915	6,085	349,830
Alberta	44,410	2,152,200	36,845	10,900	113,445	52,335	15,100	16,605	1,126,130
Canada	366,830	22,102,745	497,965	329,495	1,053,945	454,965	64,935	130,835	7,850,605
				Males					
Calgary	10,265	280,400	9,080	2,925	29,225	14,620	435	2,775	191,330
Alberta	20,725	1,029,310	19,120	5,405	59,005	26,825	7,420	7,525	618,330
Canada	168,465	10,497,775	250,435	161,265	540,555	229,435	31,805	57,745	4,225,645
				Females					
Calgary	12,110	313,870	8,330	3,075	27,560	13,945	480	3,310	158,505
Alberta	23,680	1,122,890	17,725	5,495	54,435	25,510	7,680	9,080	507,800
Canada	198,365	11,604,975	247,525	168,235	513,395	225,530	33,135	73,090	3,624,965
				Percent of Population Total					
Calgary	2.1	54.9	1.6	0.6	5.2	2.6	0.1	0.6	32.3
Alberta	1.2	60.3	1.0	0.3	3.2	1.5	0.4	0.5	31.6
Canada	1.1	67.3	1.5	1.0	3.2	1.4	0.2	0.4	23.9
				Males					
Calgary	1.9	51.8	1.7	0.5	5.4	2.7	0.1	0.5	35.4
Alberta	1.2	57.4	1.1	0.3	3.3	1.5	0.4	0.4	34.5
Canada	1.0	64.9	1.5	1.0	3.3	1.4	0.2	0.4	26.1
				Females					
Calgary	2.2	58.0	1.5	0.6	5.1	2.6	0.1	0.6	29.3
Alberta	1.3	63.3	1.0	0.3	3.1	1.4	0.4	0.5	28.6
Canada	1.2	69.5	1.5	1.0	3.1	1.4	0.2	0.4	21.7

Note: Religion refers to the person's self-identification as having a connection or affiliation with any religious denomination, group, body, sect, cult or other religiously defined community or system of belief. Religion is not limited to formal membership in a religious organization or group. Persons without a religious connection or affiliation can self-identify as atheist, agnostic or humanist, or can provide another applicable response.
Source: Statistics Canada. 2013. 2011 National Household Survey. Statistics Canada Catalogue no. 99-004-XWE. Ottawa. Released September 11, 2013.

Religion—Christian Denominations

Area	Anglican	Baptist	Catholic	Christian Orthodox	Lutheran	Pentecostal	Presbyterian	United Church	Other Christian
				Number Total					
Calgary	41,285	17,200	263,805	17,540	23,465	14,385	13,375	65,925	137,300
Alberta	140,665	66,635	866,305	51,340	119,345	60,960	36,765	268,675	541,520
Canada	1,631,845	635,840	12,810,705	550,690	478,185	478,705	472,385	2,007,610	3,036,780
				Males					
Calgary	18,725	8,075	126,915	8,780	10,830	6,750	5,885	29,135	65,300
Alberta	65,130	31,645	422,160	25,145	56,120	28,580	16,835	123,255	260,440
Canada	752,945	293,905	6,167,290	270,205	221,525	217,850	218,955	912,545	1,442,550
				Females					
Calgary	22,560	9,125	136,890	8,760	12,630	7,635	7,485	36,790	71,995
Alberta	75,535	34,990	444,145	26,190	63,220	32,380	19,925	145,420	281,075
Canada	878,900	341,940	6,643,415	280,485	256,660	260,850	253,430	1,095,065	1,594,230
				Percent of Population Total					
Calgary	3.8	1.6	24.4	1.6	2.2	1.3	1.2	6.1	12.7
Alberta	3.9	1.9	24.3	1.4	3.3	1.7	1.0	7.5	15.2
Canada	5.0	1.9	39.0	1.7	1.5	1.5	1.4	6.1	9.2
				Males					
Calgary	3.5	1.5	23.5	1.6	2.0	1.2	1.1	5.4	12.1
Alberta	3.6	1.8	23.5	1.4	3.1	1.6	0.9	6.9	14.5
Canada	4.7	1.8	38.2	1.7	1.4	1.3	1.4	5.6	8.9
				Females					
Calgary	4.2	1.7	25.3	1.6	2.3	1.4	1.4	6.8	13.3
Alberta	4.3	2.0	25.0	1.5	3.6	1.8	1.1	8.2	15.8
Canada	5.3	2.0	39.8	1.7	1.5	1.6	1.5	6.6	9.6

Note: Religion refers to the person's self-identification as having a connection or affiliation with any religious denomination, group, body, sect, cult or other religiously defined community or system of belief. Religion is not limited to formal membership in a religious organization or group. Persons without a religious connection or affiliation can self-identify as atheist, agnostic or humanist, or can provide another applicable response.
Source: Statistics Canada. 2013. 2011 National Household Survey. Statistics Canada Catalogue no. 99-004-XWE. Ottawa. Released September 11, 2013.

PROFILES / Calgary, Alberta

Immigrant Status and Period of Immigration

Area	Non-Immigrants[1]	Immigrants All	Before 1971	1971 to 1980	1981 to 1990	1991 to 2000	2001 to 2005	2006 to 2011	Non-Permanent Residents[3]
				Number Total					
Calgary	760,940	298,820	32,125	35,160	40,525	62,985	59,620	68,400	22,470
Alberta	2,864,240	644,115	92,610	83,620	86,190	124,465	113,060	144,170	59,620
Canada	25,720,175	6,775,765	1,261,055	870,775	949,890	1,539,050	992,070	1,162,915	356,385
				Males					
Calgary	383,985	145,810	15,940	17,975	19,485	29,885	29,765	32,765	11,250
Alberta	1,449,740	313,170	45,390	41,910	41,145	58,970	56,395	69,360	30,765
Canada	12,753,235	3,231,370	605,430	416,670	454,570	724,905	474,545	555,245	178,515
				Females					
Calgary	376,960	153,005	16,180	17,190	21,040	33,105	29,860	35,635	11,220
Alberta	1,414,500	330,940	47,220	41,710	45,040	65,495	56,660	74,815	28,855
Canada	12,966,935	3,544,400	655,625	454,105	495,325	814,145	517,530	607,670	177,870
				Percent of Population Total					
Calgary	70.3	27.6	3.0	3.2	3.7	5.8	5.5	6.3	2.1
Alberta	80.3	18.1	2.6	2.3	2.4	3.5	3.2	4.0	1.7
Canada	78.3	20.6	3.8	2.7	2.9	4.7	3.0	3.5	1.1
				Males					
Calgary	71.0	26.9	2.9	3.3	3.6	5.5	5.5	6.1	2.1
Alberta	80.8	17.5	2.5	2.3	2.3	3.3	3.1	3.9	1.7
Canada	78.9	20.0	3.7	2.6	2.8	4.5	2.9	3.4	1.1
				Females					
Calgary	69.7	28.3	3.0	3.2	3.9	6.1	5.5	6.6	2.1
Alberta	79.7	18.7	2.7	2.4	2.5	3.7	3.2	4.2	1.6
Canada	77.7	21.2	3.9	2.7	3.0	4.9	3.1	3.6	1.1

Note: (1) Non-immigrant refers to a person who is a Canadian citizen by birth; (2) Immigrant refers to a person who is or has ever been a landed immigrant/permanent resident. This person has been granted the right to live in Canada permanently by immigration authorities. Some immigrants have resided in Canada for a number of years, while others have arrived recently. Some immigrants are Canadian citizens, while others are not. Most immigrants are born outside Canada, but a small number are born in Canada. In the 2011 National Household Survey, 'Immigrants' includes immigrants who landed in Canada prior to May 10, 2011; (3) Non-permanent resident refers to a person from another country who has a work or study permit, or who is a refugee claimant, and any non-Canadian-born family member living in Canada with them.
Source: Statistics Canada. 2013. 2011 National Household Survey. Statistics Canada Catalogue no. 99-004-XWE. Ottawa. Released September 11, 2013.

Mother Tongue

Area	English	French	Non-official Language	English & French	English & Non-official Language	French & Non-official Language	English, French & Non-official Language
			Number Total				
Calgary	752,525	16,900	292,540	2,705	21,230	995	515
Alberta	2,780,200	68,545	698,930	8,410	49,970	2,945	1,185
Canada	18,858,980	7,054,975	6,567,680	144,685	396,330	74,430	24,095
			Males				
Calgary	380,205	8,430	141,685	1,300	10,390	525	240
Alberta	1,405,655	35,355	340,125	4,045	24,210	1,500	565
Canada	9,345,225	3,452,380	3,157,785	69,975	192,000	36,535	11,965
			Females				
Calgary	372,315	8,470	150,855	1,400	10,845	475	275
Alberta	1,374,545	33,195	358,805	4,365	25,760	1,440	620
Canada	9,513,750	3,602,590	3,409,895	74,710	204,330	37,890	12,130
			Percent of Population Total				
Calgary	69.2	1.6	26.9	0.2	2.0	0.1	0.0
Alberta	77.0	1.9	19.4	0.2	1.4	0.1	0.0
Canada	56.9	21.3	19.8	0.4	1.2	0.2	0.1
			Males				
Calgary	70.0	1.6	26.1	0.2	1.9	0.1	0.0
Alberta	77.6	2.0	18.8	0.2	1.3	0.1	0.0
Canada	57.5	21.2	19.4	0.4	1.2	0.2	0.1
			Females				
Calgary	68.4	1.6	27.7	0.3	2.0	0.1	0.1
Alberta	76.4	1.8	19.9	0.2	1.4	0.1	0.0
Canada	56.4	21.4	20.2	0.4	1.2	0.2	0.1

Note: Figures cover total population excluding institutional residents.
Source: Statistics Canada. 2012. Census Profile. 2011 Census. Statistics Canada Catalogue no. 98-316-XWE. Ottawa. Released October 24 2012.
http://www12.statcan.gc.ca/census-recensement/2011/dp-pd/prof/index.cfm?Lang=E

Language Spoken Most Often at Home

Area	English	French	Non-official Language	English & French	English & Non-official Language	French & Non-official Language	English, French & Non-official Language
Number							
Total							
Calgary	857,565	6,730	173,595	1,610	46,715	460	730
Alberta	3,095,250	24,690	379,550	4,945	102,995	1,115	1,640
Canada	21,457,075	6,827,865	3,673,865	131,205	875,135	109,700	46,330
Males							
Calgary	430,055	3,355	85,030	820	22,925	220	365
Alberta	1,557,420	12,545	187,125	2,520	50,465	570	815
Canada	10,585,620	3,348,235	1,767,310	63,475	425,370	53,010	22,845
Females							
Calgary	427,515	3,375	88,565	795	23,790	235	360
Alberta	1,537,830	12,140	192,425	2,425	52,535	550	825
Canada	10,871,455	3,479,625	1,906,555	67,730	449,765	56,690	23,485
Percent of Population							
Total							
Calgary	78.9	0.6	16.0	0.1	4.3	0.0	0.1
Alberta	85.7	0.7	10.5	0.1	2.9	0.0	0.0
Canada	64.8	20.6	11.1	0.4	2.6	0.3	0.1
Males							
Calgary	79.2	0.6	15.7	0.2	4.2	0.0	0.1
Alberta	86.0	0.7	10.3	0.1	2.8	0.0	0.0
Canada	65.1	20.6	10.9	0.4	2.6	0.3	0.1
Females							
Calgary	78.5	0.6	16.3	0.1	4.4	0.0	0.1
Alberta	85.5	0.7	10.7	0.1	2.9	0.0	0.0
Canada	64.5	20.6	11.3	0.4	2.7	0.3	0.1

Note: Figures cover total population excluding institutional residents.
Source: Statistics Canada. 2012. Census Profile. 2011 Census. Statistics Canada Catalogue no. 98-316-XWE. Ottawa. Released October 24 2012.
http://www12.statcan.gc.ca/census-recensement/2011/dp-pd/prof/index.cfm?Lang=E

Knowledge of Official Languages

Area	English Only	French Only	English & French	Neither English nor French
Number				
Total				
Calgary	979,520	1,005	81,455	25,425
Alberta	3,321,810	3,205	235,565	49,600
Canada	22,564,665	4,165,015	5,795,570	595,920
Males				
Calgary	494,305	440	37,800	10,220
Alberta	1,679,330	1,430	110,485	20,210
Canada	11,222,185	1,925,340	2,876,560	241,790
Females				
Calgary	485,215	565	43,650	15,210
Alberta	1,642,480	1,780	125,075	29,395
Canada	11,342,485	2,239,680	2,919,005	354,135
Percent of Population				
Total				
Calgary	90.1	0.1	7.5	2.3
Alberta	92.0	0.1	6.5	1.4
Canada	68.1	12.6	17.5	1.8
Males				
Calgary	91.1	0.1	7.0	1.9
Alberta	92.7	0.1	6.1	1.1
Canada	69.0	11.8	17.7	1.5
Females				
Calgary	89.1	0.1	8.0	2.8
Alberta	91.3	0.1	7.0	1.6
Canada	67.3	13.3	17.3	2.1

Note: Figures cover total population excluding institutional residents.
Source: Statistics Canada. 2012. Census Profile. 2011 Census. Statistics Canada Catalogue no. 98-316-XWE. Ottawa. Released October 24 2012.
http://www12.statcan.gc.ca/census-recensement/2011/dp-pd/prof/index.cfm?Lang=E

Cambridge, Ontario

Background

The City of Cambridge is located in southern Ontario where the Grand River and Speed River meet. It is one hour west of downtown Toronto and 90 minutes from the U.S. border. Cambridge is part of the Regional Municipality of Waterloo and came from an amalgamation of three municipalities in 1973: the former City of Galt, the towns of Hespeler and Preston, and the hamlet of Blair.

Cambridge is situated in Canada's Technology Triangle (CTT), an area known for its concentration of science and technology companies. Three international airports are within an hour of Cambridge and rail service is provided by Canadian National and Canadian Pacific. The banks of the Grand River, one of Canada's Heritage Rivers, and the Speed River offer more than 50 kilometres of walking and cycling trails. City parkland covers more than 1,000 acres and 14 golf courses are nearby. Cambridge's Historic Farmers' Market is rated one of the best in Canada and the city's Antique Market is the largest in the country.

Over 33% of the labour force in Cambridge is employed in manufacturing. The manufacturing sector ranges from traditional textile to university-sponsored science-and-technology research, but the largest employer in the area is Toyota Motor Manufacturing. The city's diverse industrial base is shaped by the nearby colleges and universities in Kitchener, Waterloo and Guelph.

The city hosts Riverfest and the Cambridge Arts Festival every summer along with a Summer Concerts in the Park series.

Cambridge has summer highs of plus 25.23 degrees Celsius, winter lows of minus 9.30 degrees Celsius, and an average rainfall just over 787 mm per year.

Rankings

- *fDi Magazine* ranked Cambridge in the *Top 10 American Cities of the Future* list. Cambridge was ranked #8 out of 405 cities across North and South America. Cambridge was evaluated in the "Small Cities FDI Strategy" category and recognized for successfully attracting foreign direct investment (FDI). *fDi Intelligence, "American Cities of the Future, 2011/12," released April 8, 2011*
- The City of Cambridge and its region, Waterloo (including regional cities Kitchener and Waterloo) ranked #9 out of 27 mid-sized Canadian census metropolitan areas (CMAs) for its business competitiveness. Criteria: economy, health, society, housing, environment, innovation and education. Waterloo Region ranked in the Top 5 in these individual categories: number of innovations patented, quality of housing, low crime rate, household recycling population density, highest productivity, best employment rate and gross domestic product (GDP) per capital. *Conference Board of Canada, "City Magnets: Benchmarking the Attractiveness of Canada's CMAs," December 2007*
- *Best Health Magazine* ranked Cambridge Farmers' Market one of the best markets in Canada. The City of Cambridge was the only Ontario city to make the Top 10 list. The market was praised for its rich history (est. 1830) and assortment of produce, meats, cheeses and pastries. *Best Health Magazine, "Canada's Top Farmers' Markets 2008," Summer 2008*

PROFILES / Cambridge, Ontario

Population Growth and Density

Area	Population in 2001	Population in 2006	Population in 2011	Population Change 2001–2006	Population Change 2006–2011	Land Area (sq. km)	Population Density per sq. km
Cambridge	110,372	120,371	126,748	9.1	5.3	113.00	1,121.7
Ontario	11,410,046	12,160,282	12,851,821	6.6	5.7	908,607.67	14.1
Canada	30,007,094	31,612,897	33,476,688	5.4	5.9	8,965,121.42	3.7

Source: Statistics Canada. 2012. Census Profile. 2011 Census. Statistics Canada Catalogue no. 98-316-XWE. Ottawa. Released October 24 2012.
http://www12.statcan.gc.ca/census-recensement/2011/dp-pd/prof/index.cfm?Lang=E;
Statistics Canada 2007. 2006 Community Profiles. 2006 Census. Statistics Canada Catalogue no. 92-591-XWE. Ottawa. Released March 13 2007.
http://www12.statcan.ca/census-recensement/2006/dp-pd/prof/92-591/index.cfm?Lang=E

Gender

Area	Males	Females
Number		
Cambridge	62,245	64,500
Ontario	6,263,140	6,588,685
Canada	16,414,225	17,062,460
Percent of Population		
Cambridge	49.1	50.9
Ontario	48.7	51.3
Canada	49.0	51.0

Source: Statistics Canada. 2012. Census Profile. 2011 Census. Statistics Canada Catalogue no. 98-316-XWE. Ottawa. Released October 24 2012.
http://www12.statcan.gc.ca/census-recensement/2011/dp-pd/prof/index.cfm?Lang=E

Marital Status

Area	Married[1]	Living Common-law	Single[2]	Separated	Divorced	Widowed
Number						
Total						
Cambridge	51,595	9,240	26,675	3,715	5,685	5,480
Ontario	5,367,400	791,210	2,985,020	319,805	593,730	613,880
Canada	12,941,960	3,142,525	7,816,045	698,240	1,686,035	1,584,530
Males						
Cambridge	25,765	4,610	14,470	1,575	2,325	1,080
Ontario	2,681,320	397,620	1,583,760	133,790	231,160	117,980
Canada	6,470,300	1,575,495	4,206,320	299,655	680,415	310,940
Females						
Cambridge	25,830	4,625	12,200	2,140	3,360	4,400
Ontario	2,686,075	393,590	1,401,260	186,015	362,570	495,905
Canada	6,471,660	1,567,035	3,609,730	398,585	1,005,620	1,273,590
Percent of Population						
Total						
Cambridge	50.4	9.0	26.1	3.6	5.6	5.4
Ontario	50.3	7.4	28.0	3.0	5.6	5.8
Canada	46.4	11.3	28.0	2.5	6.0	5.7
Males						
Cambridge	51.7	9.3	29.0	3.2	4.7	2.2
Ontario	52.1	7.7	30.8	2.6	4.5	2.3
Canada	47.8	11.6	31.1	2.2	5.0	2.3
Females						
Cambridge	49.1	8.8	23.2	4.1	6.4	8.4
Ontario	48.6	7.1	25.4	3.4	6.6	9.0
Canada	45.2	10.9	25.2	2.8	7.0	8.9

Note: (1) and not separated, (2) never legally married
Source: Statistics Canada. 2012. Census Profile. 2011 Census. Statistics Canada Catalogue no. 98-316-XWE. Ottawa. Released October 24 2012.
http://www12.statcan.gc.ca/census-recensement/2011/dp-pd/prof/index.cfm?Lang=E

Age Characteristics: 0 to 49 Years

Area	0 to 4 Years	5 to 9 Years	10 to 14 Years	15 to 19 Years	20 to 24 Years	25 to 29 Years	30 to 34 Years	35 to 39 Years	40 to 44 Years	45 to 49 Years
Number										
Total										
Cambridge	7,960	8,160	8,250	8,855	8,170	8,040	8,345	9,265	9,575	10,675
Ontario	704,260	712,755	763,755	863,635	852,910	815,120	800,365	844,335	924,075	1,055,880
Canada	1,877,095	1,809,895	1,920,355	2,178,135	2,187,450	2,169,590	2,162,905	2,173,930	2,324,875	2,675,130
Males										
Cambridge	4,100	4,165	4,155	4,530	4,070	3,975	4,030	4,545	4,740	5,375
Ontario	360,590	365,290	391,630	443,680	432,490	400,045	383,340	405,845	447,920	517,510
Canada	961,150	925,965	983,995	1,115,845	1,108,775	1,077,275	1,058,810	1,064,200	1,141,720	1,318,715
Females										
Cambridge	3,860	3,995	4,100	4,325	4,100	4,070	4,315	4,725	4,830	5,295
Ontario	343,670	347,465	372,125	419,950	420,415	415,075	417,030	438,485	476,155	538,370
Canada	915,945	883,935	936,360	1,062,295	1,078,670	1,092,315	1,104,095	1,109,735	1,183,155	1,356,420
Percent of Population										
Total										
Cambridge	6.3	6.4	6.5	7.0	6.4	6.3	6.6	7.3	7.6	8.4
Ontario	5.5	5.5	5.9	6.7	6.6	6.3	6.2	6.6	7.2	8.2
Canada	5.6	5.4	5.7	6.5	6.5	6.5	6.5	6.5	6.9	8.0
Males										
Cambridge	6.6	6.7	6.7	7.3	6.5	6.4	6.5	7.3	7.6	8.6
Ontario	5.8	5.8	6.3	7.1	6.9	6.4	6.1	6.5	7.2	8.3
Canada	5.9	5.6	6.0	6.8	6.8	6.6	6.5	6.5	7.0	8.0
Females										
Cambridge	6.0	6.2	6.4	6.7	6.4	6.3	6.7	7.3	7.5	8.2
Ontario	5.2	5.3	5.6	6.4	6.4	6.3	6.3	6.7	7.2	8.2
Canada	5.4	5.2	5.5	6.2	6.3	6.4	6.5	6.5	6.9	7.9

Source: Statistics Canada. 2012. Census Profile. 2011 Census. Statistics Canada Catalogue no. 98-316-XWE. Ottawa. Released October 24 2012.
http://www12.statcan.gc.ca/census-recensement/2011/dp-pd/prof/index.cfm?Lang=E

Age Characteristics: 50 Years and Over, and Median Age

Area	50 to 54 Years	55 to 59 Years	60 to 64 Years	65 to 69 Years	70 to 74 Years	75 to 79 Years	80 to 84 Years	85 Years and Over	Median Age
Number									
Total									
Cambridge	9,330	7,955	6,725	4,775	3,600	2,880	2,080	2,105	38.0
Ontario	1,006,140	864,620	765,655	563,485	440,780	356,150	271,510	246,400	40.4
Canada	2,658,965	2,340,635	2,052,670	1,521,715	1,153,065	922,700	702,070	645,515	40.6
Males									
Cambridge	4,615	3,955	3,280	2,210	1,745	1,295	795	665	37.3
Ontario	492,560	418,755	370,370	270,875	206,350	161,345	113,620	80,925	39.4
Canada	1,309,030	1,147,300	1,002,690	738,010	543,435	417,945	291,085	208,300	39.6
Females									
Cambridge	4,715	4,000	3,445	2,570	1,855	1,585	1,285	1,440	38.7
Ontario	513,580	445,865	395,275	292,610	234,435	194,805	157,890	165,475	41.3
Canada	1,349,940	1,193,335	1,049,985	783,705	609,630	504,755	410,985	437,215	41.5
Percent of Population									
Total									
Cambridge	7.4	6.3	5.3	3.8	2.8	2.3	1.6	1.7	–
Ontario	7.8	6.7	6.0	4.4	3.4	2.8	2.1	1.9	–
Canada	7.9	7.0	6.1	4.5	3.4	2.8	2.1	1.9	–
Males									
Cambridge	7.4	6.4	5.3	3.6	2.8	2.1	1.3	1.1	–
Ontario	7.9	6.7	5.9	4.3	3.3	2.6	1.8	1.3	–
Canada	8.0	7.0	6.1	4.5	3.3	2.5	1.8	1.3	–
Females									
Cambridge	7.3	6.2	5.3	4.0	2.9	2.5	2.0	2.2	–
Ontario	7.8	6.8	6.0	4.4	3.6	3.0	2.4	2.5	–
Canada	7.9	7.0	6.2	4.6	3.6	3.0	2.4	2.6	–

Source: Statistics Canada. 2012. Census Profile. 2011 Census. Statistics Canada Catalogue no. 98-316-XWE. Ottawa. Released October 24 2012.
http://www12.statcan.gc.ca/census-recensement/2011/dp-pd/prof/index.cfm?Lang=E

PROFILES / Cambridge, Ontario

Private Households by Household Size

Area	1 Person	2 Persons	3 Persons	4 Persons	5 Persons	6 or More Persons	Average Number of Persons in Private Households
			Households				
Cambridge	10,040	14,730	8,400	8,460	3,265	1,570	2.7
Ontario	1,230,975	1,584,415	803,030	783,925	310,860	174,305	2.6
Canada	3,673,310	4,544,820	2,081,900	1,903,300	724,405	392,885	2.5
			Percent of Households				
Cambridge	21.6	31.7	18.1	18.2	7.0	3.4	—
Ontario	25.2	32.4	16.4	16.0	6.4	3.6	—
Canada	27.6	34.1	15.6	14.3	5.4	2.9	—

Source: Statistics Canada. 2012. Census Profile. 2011 Census. Statistics Canada Catalogue no. 98-316-XWE. Ottawa. Released October 24 2012.
http://www12.statcan.gc.ca/census-recensement/2011/dp-pd/prof/index.cfm?Lang=E

Dwelling Type

Area	Single-detached House	Semi-detached House	Row House	Apartment: Building with Five or More Storeys	Apartment: Building with Fewer Than Five Storeys	Duplex Apartment	Movable Dwelling	Other Single-attached House
				Number				
Cambridge	27,515	3,790	5,275	2,270	5,885	1,490	15	215
Ontario	2,718,880	279,470	415,225	789,970	498,160	160,460	15,800	9,540
Canada	7,329,150	646,245	791,600	1,234,770	2,397,550	704,485	183,510	33,310
				Percent of Dwellings				
Cambridge	59.2	8.2	11.4	4.9	12.7	3.2	0.0	0.5
Ontario	55.6	5.7	8.5	16.2	10.2	3.3	0.3	0.2
Canada	55.0	4.9	5.9	9.3	18.0	5.3	1.4	0.3

Source: Statistics Canada. 2012. Census Profile. 2011 Census. Statistics Canada Catalogue no. 98-316-XWE. Ottawa. Released October 24 2012.
http://www12.statcan.gc.ca/census-recensement/2011/dp-pd/prof/index.cfm?Lang=E

Shelter Costs

	Owned Dwellings				Rented Dwellings		
Area	Number	Median Value[1] ($)	Average Value[1] ($)	Median Monthly Costs[2] ($)	Average Monthly Costs[2] ($)	Number	Median Monthly Costs[3] ($)	Average Monthly Costs[3] ($)
Cambridge	33,855	269,837	293,854	1,284	1,259	12,595	805	850
Ontario	3,446,650	300,862	367,428	1,163	1,284	1,385,535	892	926
Canada	9,013,410	280,552	345,182	978	1,141	4,060,385	784	848

Note: All figures cover non-farm, non-reserve private dwellings; (1) Refers to the dollar amount expected by the owner if the dwelling were to be sold; (2) Includes all shelter expenses paid by households that own their dwellings, such as the mortgage payment and the costs of electricity, heat, water and other municipal services, property taxes and condominium fees; (3) Includes all shelter expenses paid by households that rent their dwellings, such as the monthly rent and the costs of electricity, heat and municipal services.
Source: Statistics Canada. 2013. 2011 National Household Survey. Statistics Canada Catalogue no. 99-004-XWE. Ottawa. Released September 11, 2013.

Occupied Private Dwellings by Period of Construction

Area	1960 or Before	1961 to 1980	1981 to 1990	1991 to 2000	2001 to 2005	2006 to 2011
			Number			
Cambridge	11,375	12,965	7,290	6,850	4,525	3,450
Ontario	1,330,235	1,420,570	763,430	609,310	414,795	348,310
Canada	3,273,105	4,152,715	2,112,110	1,707,880	1,031,020	1,042,430
			Percent of Dwellings			
Cambridge	24.5	27.9	15.7	14.7	9.7	7.4
Ontario	27.2	29.1	15.6	12.5	8.5	7.1
Canada	24.6	31.2	15.9	12.8	7.7	7.8

Note: Figures cover non-farm, non-reserve private dwellings and includes data up to May 10, 2011.
Source: Statistics Canada. 2013. 2011 National Household Survey. Statistics Canada Catalogue no. 99-004-XWE. Ottawa. Released September 11, 2013.

Educational Attainment

Area	No Certificate, Diploma or Degree	High School Diploma or Equivalent[1]	Apprenticeship or Trades Certificate or Diploma[2]	College, CÉGEP or Other Non-University Certificate or Diploma	University Certificate or Diploma Below the Bachelor Level[3]	Bachelor's Degree	University Certificate, Diploma or Degree Above Bachelor Level[4]
Number							
Total							
Cambridge	23,290	30,810	9,075	21,235	2,665	8,850	4,720
Ontario	1,954,520	2,801,805	771,140	2,070,875	427,150	1,515,075	933,100
Canada	5,485,400	6,968,935	2,950,685	4,970,020	1,200,130	3,634,425	2,049,930
Males							
Cambridge	11,230	14,965	6,385	9,045	1,300	4,055	2,275
Ontario	957,040	1,337,055	520,390	894,235	193,355	692,345	470,290
Canada	2,742,875	3,305,415	1,928,970	2,118,430	513,235	1,643,080	1,043,350
Females							
Cambridge	12,055	15,850	2,690	12,190	1,365	4,795	2,445
Ontario	997,475	1,464,755	250,750	1,176,640	233,790	822,730	462,805
Canada	2,742,520	3,663,515	1,021,715	2,851,595	686,890	1,991,345	1,006,585
Percent of Population							
Total							
Cambridge	23.1	30.6	9.0	21.1	2.6	8.8	4.7
Ontario	18.7	26.8	7.4	19.8	4.1	14.5	8.9
Canada	20.1	25.6	10.8	18.2	4.4	13.3	7.5
Males							
Cambridge	22.8	30.4	13.0	18.4	2.6	8.2	4.6
Ontario	18.9	26.4	10.3	17.7	3.8	13.7	9.3
Canada	20.6	24.9	14.5	15.9	3.9	12.4	7.8
Females							
Cambridge	23.5	30.8	5.2	23.7	2.7	9.3	4.8
Ontario	18.4	27.1	4.6	21.8	4.3	15.2	8.6
Canada	19.6	26.2	7.3	20.4	4.9	14.3	7.2

Note: Figures cover total population aged 15 years and over by highest certificate, diploma or degree; (1) Includes persons who have graduated from a secondary school or equivalent. It excludes persons with a postsecondary certificate, diploma or degree; (2) Includes Registered Apprenticeship certificates (including Certificate of Qualification, Journeyperson's designation) and other trades certificates or diplomas such as pre-employment or vocational certificates and diplomas from brief trade programs completed at community colleges, institutes of technology, vocational centres, and similar institutions; (3) Comparisons with other data sources suggest that the category 'University certificate or diploma below the bachelor's level' was over-reported in the NHS. This category likely includes some responses that are actually college certificates or diplomas, bachelor's degrees or other types of education (e.g., university transfer programs, bachelor's programs completed in other countries, incomplete bachelor's programs, non-university professional designations). We recommend users interpret the results for the 'University certificate or diploma below the bachelor's level' category with caution; (4) 'University certificate or diploma above bachelor level' includes the categories: 'Degree in medicine, dentistry, veterinary medicine or optometry,' 'Master's degree' and 'Earned doctorate.'
Source: Statistics Canada. 2013. 2011 National Household Survey. Statistics Canada Catalogue no. 99-004-XWE. Ottawa. Released September 11, 2013.

Household Income Distribution

Area	Less than $10,000	$10,000 to $19,999	$20,000 to $29,999	$30,000 to $39,999	$40,000 to $49,999	$50,000 to $59,999	$60,000 to $79,999	$80,000 to $99,999	$100,000 to $124,999	$125,000 to $149,999	$150,000 and Over
Households											
Cambridge	1,545	2,825	3,765	3,975	3,960	4,220	6,755	5,945	5,390	3,405	4,685
Ontario	201,780	354,530	405,725	425,410	425,720	398,705	680,850	552,660	497,970	331,460	611,840
Canada	626,705	1,141,945	1,193,925	1,271,675	1,206,800	1,102,120	1,865,280	1,458,240	1,260,770	802,555	1,389,240
Percent of Households											
Cambridge	3.3	6.1	8.1	8.6	8.5	9.1	14.5	12.8	11.6	7.3	10.1
Ontario	4.1	7.3	8.3	8.7	8.7	8.2	13.9	11.3	10.2	6.8	12.5
Canada	4.7	8.6	9.0	9.5	9.1	8.3	14.0	10.9	9.5	6.0	10.4

Note: Household income is the sum of the total incomes of all members of that household. Total income refers to monetary receipts from certain sources, before income taxes and deductions, during calendar year 2010.
Source: Statistics Canada. 2013. 2011 National Household Survey. Statistics Canada Catalogue no. 99-004-XWE. Ottawa. Released September 11, 2013.

Median and Average Household and Economic Family Income

Area	Median Household Income ($)	Average Household Income ($)	Median After-tax Household Income ($)	Average After-tax Household Income ($)	Median Economic Family Income ($)	Average Economic Family Income ($)	Median After-tax Economic Family Income ($)	Average After-tax Economic Family Income ($)
Cambridge	68,373	80,958	60,574	68,947	81,184	92,389	71,130	78,528
Ontario	66,358	85,772	58,717	71,523	80,987	100,152	71,128	83,322
Canada	61,072	79,102	54,089	66,149	76,511	94,125	67,044	78,517

Note: Figures cover household and economic familiy income in 2010. A household is defined as a person or a group of persons (other than foreign residents) who occupy the same private dwelling and do not have a usual place of residence elsewhere in Canada. Every person is a member of one and only one household. An economic family is defined as a group of two or more persons who live in the same dwelling and are related to each other by blood, marriage, common-law, adoption or a foster relationship. A couple may be of opposite or same sex.
Source: Statistics Canada. 2013. 2011 National Household Survey. Statistics Canada Catalogue no. 99-004-XWE. Ottawa. Released September 11, 2013.

Individual Income Distribution

Area	Less than $10,000	$10,000 to $19,999	$20,000 to $29,999	$30,000 to $39,999	$40,000 to $49,999	$50,000 to $59,999	$60,000 to $79,999	$80,000 to $99,999	$100,000 to $124,999	$125,000 and Over
					Number					
					Total					
Cambridge	15,415	15,775	14,280	12,280	11,215	7,895	9,225	5,165	2,060	2,255
Ontario	1,780,355	1,748,060	1,361,710	1,136,730	980,790	746,360	964,280	574,710	293,865	330,285
Canada	4,492,040	4,835,710	3,670,020	3,180,360	2,603,520	1,921,650	2,437,440	1,302,045	693,580	782,135
					Males					
Cambridge	6,585	5,580	5,700	5,740	5,645	4,745	6,050	3,625	1,520	1,800
Ontario	781,095	669,815	580,990	535,255	491,125	407,005	569,205	341,160	201,125	244,500
Canada	1,936,365	1,864,880	1,588,260	1,522,190	1,333,510	1,079,780	1,473,145	823,720	492,905	599,905
					Females					
Cambridge	8,825	10,195	8,580	6,535	5,575	3,145	3,170	1,545	535	460
Ontario	999,265	1,078,245	780,720	601,475	489,665	339,360	395,075	233,550	92,740	85,790
Canada	2,555,675	2,970,825	2,081,760	1,658,170	1,270,010	841,870	964,300	478,330	200,680	182,230
				Percent of Population						
					Total					
Cambridge	16.1	16.5	14.9	12.9	11.7	8.3	9.7	5.4	2.2	2.4
Ontario	18.0	17.6	13.7	11.5	9.9	7.5	9.7	5.8	3.0	3.3
Canada	17.3	18.7	14.2	12.3	10.0	7.4	9.4	5.0	2.7	3.0
					Males					
Cambridge	14.0	11.9	12.1	12.2	12.0	10.1	12.9	7.7	3.2	3.8
Ontario	16.2	13.9	12.1	11.1	10.2	8.4	11.8	7.1	4.2	5.1
Canada	15.2	14.7	12.5	12.0	10.5	8.5	11.6	6.5	3.9	4.7
					Females					
Cambridge	18.2	21.0	17.7	13.5	11.5	6.5	6.5	3.2	1.1	0.9
Ontario	19.6	21.2	15.3	11.8	9.6	6.7	7.8	4.6	1.8	1.7
Canada	19.4	22.5	15.8	12.6	9.6	6.4	7.3	3.6	1.5	1.4

Note: Figures cover individuals aged 15 years and over with income. Income refers to monetary receipts from certain sources, before income taxes and deductions, during calendar year 2010.
Source: Statistics Canada. 2013. 2011 National Household Survey. Statistics Canada Catalogue no. 99-004-XWE. Ottawa. Released September 11, 2013.

Labour Force Status

Area	In the Labour Force — All	Employed	Unemployed	Not in the Labour Force
		Number		
		Total		
Cambridge	70,050	64,215	5,835	30,595
Ontario	6,864,990	6,297,005	567,985	3,608,685
Canada	17,990,080	16,595,035	1,395,045	9,269,445
		Males		
Cambridge	36,640	33,655	2,990	12,620
Ontario	3,542,030	3,249,165	292,865	1,522,690
Canada	9,388,570	8,634,310	754,255	3,906,785
		Females		
Cambridge	33,410	30,560	2,850	17,980
Ontario	3,322,955	3,047,840	275,120	2,085,990
Canada	8,601,515	7,960,725	640,790	5,362,660
	Percent of Labour Force			
		Total		
Cambridge	69.6	63.8	8.3	30.4
Ontario	65.5	60.1	8.3	34.5
Canada	66.0	60.9	7.8	34.0
		Males		
Cambridge	74.4	68.3	8.2	25.6
Ontario	69.9	64.2	8.3	30.1
Canada	70.6	64.9	8.0	29.4
		Females		
Cambridge	65.0	59.5	8.5	35.0
Ontario	61.4	56.3	8.3	38.6
Canada	61.6	57.0	7.4	38.4

Note: Figures are based on total population 15 years and over
Source: Statistics Canada. 2013. 2011 National Household Survey. Statistics Canada Catalogue no. 99-004-XWE. Ottawa. Released September 11, 2013.

Labour Force by Industry (NAICS Codes 11–52)

Area	Agriculture, forestry, fishing & hunting	Mining, quarrying, & oil & gas extraction	Utilities	Construction	Manufacturing	Wholesale Trade	Retail Trade	Transportation & warehousing	Information & cultural industries	Finance & insurance
					Number					
					Total					
Cambridge	430	130	280	4,465	15,180	4,360	8,450	3,610	935	2,285
Ontario	101,280	29,985	57,035	417,900	697,565	305,030	751,200	307,405	178,720	364,415
Canada	437,650	261,050	149,940	1,215,380	1,619,295	733,445	2,031,665	827,780	420,830	767,960
					Males					
Cambridge	230	115	235	3,760	10,450	2,840	3,775	2,760	490	730
Ontario	66,485	25,650	42,685	369,300	493,305	197,770	344,480	225,245	98,835	153,125
Canada	307,370	211,690	110,765	1,068,710	1,167,680	494,545	933,850	617,305	235,875	296,995
					Females					
Cambridge	200	15	45	705	4,725	1,520	4,675	850	445	1,555
Ontario	34,800	4,340	14,350	48,595	204,260	107,260	406,720	82,160	79,885	211,290
Canada	130,285	49,360	39,175	146,670	451,615	238,900	1,097,820	210,475	184,955	470,960
					Percent of Labour Force					
					Total					
Cambridge	0.6	0.2	0.4	6.5	22.2	6.4	12.4	5.3	1.4	3.3
Ontario	1.5	0.4	0.9	6.3	10.4	4.6	11.2	4.6	2.7	5.5
Canada	2.5	1.5	0.9	6.9	9.2	4.2	11.6	4.7	2.4	4.4
					Males					
Cambridge	0.6	0.3	0.7	10.5	29.2	7.9	10.6	7.7	1.4	2.0
Ontario	1.9	0.7	1.2	10.7	14.3	5.7	10.0	6.5	2.9	4.4
Canada	3.3	2.3	1.2	11.6	12.7	5.4	10.2	6.7	2.6	3.2
					Females					
Cambridge	0.6	0.0	0.1	2.2	14.5	4.7	14.4	2.6	1.4	4.8
Ontario	1.1	0.1	0.4	1.5	6.3	3.3	12.6	2.5	2.5	6.5
Canada	1.6	0.6	0.5	1.7	5.4	2.8	13.1	2.5	2.2	5.6

Note: Figures are based on total experienced labour force 15 years and over. Experienced labour force refers to persons who, during the week of Sunday, May 1 to Saturday, May 7, 2011, were employed and the unemployed who had last worked for pay or in self-employment in either 2010 or 2011.
Source: Statistics Canada. 2013. 2011 National Household Survey. Statistics Canada Catalogue no. 99-004-XWE. Ottawa. Released September 11, 2013.

Labour Force by Industry (NAICS Codes 53–91)

Area	Real estate & rental & leasing	Profess., scientific & tech. services	Mgmt of companies & enterprises	Admin. & support, waste mgmt & remed. services	Educational services	Health care & social assistance	Arts, entertain. & recreation	Accomm. & food services	Other services (except public admin.)	Public admin.
					Number					
					Total					
Cambridge	1,345	3,230	30	3,190	3,640	6,100	1,195	4,055	2,685	2,740
Ontario	133,980	511,020	6,525	309,630	499,690	692,130	144,065	417,675	296,340	458,665
Canada	321,895	1,240,850	17,460	728,330	1,301,435	1,949,650	363,405	1,130,750	807,800	1,261,050
					Males					
Cambridge	610	1,575	25	1,505	915	695	630	1,620	1,265	1,545
Ontario	72,835	281,420	3,540	172,475	162,765	120,165	75,035	177,240	133,795	236,655
Canada	179,090	688,625	9,380	411,250	424,915	349,430	188,270	469,990	372,940	652,510
					Females					
Cambridge	735	1,655	0	1,680	2,730	5,405	560	2,435	1,420	1,195
Ontario	61,145	229,600	2,990	137,155	336,925	571,965	69,030	240,430	162,550	222,015
Canada	142,805	552,225	8,075	317,085	876,515	1,600,220	175,135	660,760	434,865	608,535
					Percent of Labour Force					
					Total					
Cambridge	2.0	4.7	0.0	4.7	5.3	8.9	1.7	5.9	3.9	4.0
Ontario	2.0	7.6	0.1	4.6	7.5	10.4	2.2	6.3	4.4	6.9
Canada	1.8	7.1	0.1	4.1	7.4	11.1	2.1	6.4	4.6	7.2
					Males					
Cambridge	1.7	4.4	0.1	4.2	2.6	1.9	1.8	4.5	3.5	4.3
Ontario	2.1	8.2	0.1	5.0	4.7	3.5	2.2	5.1	3.9	6.9
Canada	1.9	7.5	0.1	4.5	4.6	3.8	2.0	5.1	4.1	7.1
					Females					
Cambridge	2.3	5.1	0.0	5.2	8.4	16.6	1.7	7.5	4.4	3.7
Ontario	1.9	7.1	0.1	4.2	10.4	17.7	2.1	7.4	5.0	6.9
Canada	1.7	6.6	0.1	3.8	10.4	19.1	2.1	7.9	5.2	7.2

Note: Figures are based on total experienced labour force 15 years and over. Experienced labour force refers to persons who, during the week of Sunday, May 1 to Saturday, May 7, 2011, were employed and the unemployed who had last worked for pay or in self-employment in either 2010 or 2011.
Source: Statistics Canada. 2013. 2011 National Household Survey. Statistics Canada Catalogue no. 99-004-XWE. Ottawa. Released September 11, 2013.

PROFILES / Cambridge, Ontario

Occupation

Area	Mgmt	Business, Finance & Admin.	Natural/ Applied Sciences & Related	Health	Education, Law & Social, Community & Government Services	Art, Culture, Recreation & Sport	Sales & Service	Trades, Transport & Equip. Operators & Related	Natural Resources, Agri. & Related Production	Mfg & Utilities
Number – Total											
Cambridge	7,285	10,530	4,155	3,015	6,215	1,325	16,005	11,760	975	7,065
Ontario	770,580	1,138,330	494,500	392,695	801,465	206,420	1,550,260	868,515	106,810	350,685
Canada	1,963,600	2,902,045	1,237,775	1,107,200	2,064,675	503,415	4,068,170	2,537,775	397,930	805,040
Males											
Cambridge	4,480	3,030	3,215	380	1,715	590	6,205	10,980	705	4,480
Ontario	474,655	352,505	384,345	78,330	264,570	96,055	673,880	812,280	82,610	233,565
Canada	1,229,460	854,190	966,355	217,520	676,550	232,535	1,745,705	2,385,615	318,945	564,300
Females											
Cambridge	2,805	7,505	940	2,635	4,500	735	9,805	780	270	2,585
Ontario	295,920	785,825	110,150	314,370	536,895	110,370	876,380	56,230	24,200	117,115
Canada	734,140	2,047,855	271,415	889,675	1,388,130	270,875	2,322,465	152,165	78,980	240,740
Percent of Labour Force – Total											
Cambridge	10.7	15.4	6.1	4.4	9.1	1.9	23.4	17.2	1.4	10.3
Ontario	11.5	17.0	7.4	5.9	12.0	3.1	23.2	13.0	1.6	5.2
Canada	11.2	16.5	7.0	6.3	11.7	2.9	23.1	14.4	2.3	4.6
Males											
Cambridge	12.5	8.5	9.0	1.1	4.8	1.6	17.3	30.7	2.0	12.5
Ontario	13.7	10.2	11.1	2.3	7.7	2.8	19.5	23.5	2.4	6.8
Canada	13.4	9.3	10.5	2.4	7.4	2.5	19.0	26.0	3.5	6.1
Females											
Cambridge	8.6	23.1	2.9	8.1	13.8	2.3	30.1	2.4	0.8	7.9
Ontario	9.2	24.3	3.4	9.7	16.6	3.4	27.2	1.7	0.7	3.6
Canada	8.7	24.4	3.2	10.6	16.5	3.2	27.7	1.8	0.9	2.9

Note: Figures are based on total experienced labour force 15 years and over
Source: Statistics Canada. 2013. 2011 National Household Survey. Statistics Canada Catalogue no. 99-004-XWE. Ottawa. Released September 11, 2013.

Place of Work Status

Area	Worked at Home	Worked Outside Canada	No Fixed Workplace Address	Worked at Usual Place
Number – Total				
Cambridge	3,005	165	6,325	54,710
Ontario	423,790	31,390	670,835	5,170,980
Canada	1,142,640	66,460	1,868,245	13,517,690
Males				
Cambridge	1,450	135	4,725	27,345
Ontario	216,900	21,150	486,560	2,524,555
Canada	582,150	47,355	1,400,485	6,604,325
Females				
Cambridge	1,560	35	1,595	27,370
Ontario	206,895	10,240	184,275	2,646,420
Canada	560,490	19,100	467,760	6,913,370
Percent of Labour Force – Total				
Cambridge	4.7	0.3	9.8	85.2
Ontario	6.7	0.5	10.7	82.1
Canada	6.9	0.4	11.3	81.5
Males				
Cambridge	4.3	0.4	14.0	81.3
Ontario	6.7	0.7	15.0	77.7
Canada	6.7	0.5	16.2	76.5
Females				
Cambridge	5.1	0.1	5.2	89.6
Ontario	6.8	0.3	6.0	86.8
Canada	7.0	0.2	5.9	86.8

Note: Figures are based on total employed labour force 15 years and over.
Source: Statistics Canada. 2013. 2011 National Household Survey. Statistics Canada Catalogue no. 99-004-XWE. Ottawa. Released September 11, 2013.

Mode of Transportation to Work

Area	Car; Truck; Van; as Driver	Car; Truck; Van; as Passenger	Public Transit	Walked	Bicycled	All Other Modes
			Number			
			Total			
Cambridge	51,105	4,335	2,730	1,945	385	535
Ontario	4,235,315	357,110	818,270	299,095	69,885	62,145
Canada	11,393,140	867,050	1,851,525	880,815	201,780	191,625
			Males			
Cambridge	27,405	2,110	1,115	890	270	280
Ontario	2,316,680	143,410	340,995	131,765	47,635	30,635
Canada	6,238,835	349,530	788,290	387,580	135,840	104,725
			Females			
Cambridge	23,700	2,225	1,615	1,050	120	260
Ontario	1,918,640	213,700	477,275	167,325	22,250	31,515
Canada	5,154,305	517,520	1,063,235	493,230	65,940	86,900
			Percent of Labour Force			
			Total			
Cambridge	83.7	7.1	4.5	3.2	0.6	0.9
Ontario	72.5	6.1	14.0	5.1	1.2	1.1
Canada	74.0	5.6	12.0	5.7	1.3	1.2
			Males			
Cambridge	85.5	6.6	3.5	2.8	0.8	0.9
Ontario	76.9	4.8	11.3	4.4	1.6	1.0
Canada	77.9	4.4	9.8	4.8	1.7	1.3
			Females			
Cambridge	81.8	7.7	5.6	3.6	0.4	0.9
Ontario	67.8	7.5	16.9	5.9	0.8	1.1
Canada	69.8	7.0	14.4	6.7	0.9	1.2

Note: Figures are based on total employed labour force 15 years and over.
Source: Statistics Canada. 2013. 2011 National Household Survey. Statistics Canada Catalogue no. 99-004-XWE. Ottawa. Released September 11, 2013.

Visible Minority Population Characteristics

Area	Total Minority	South Asian[1]	Chinese	Black	Filipino	Latin American	Arab	SE Asian[2]	West Asian[3]	Korean	Japanese	Multiple[4]
					Number							
					Total							
Cambridge	15,775	6,520	1,135	2,320	830	1,265	700	1,300	390	175	245	385
Ontario	3,279,565	965,990	629,140	539,205	275,380	172,560	151,645	137,875	122,530	78,290	29,085	96,735
Canada	6,264,750	1,567,400	1,324,750	945,665	619,310	381,280	380,620	312,075	206,840	161,130	87,270	171,935
					Males							
Cambridge	7,800	3,320	520	1,170	345	655	365	660	180	115	85	180
Ontario	1,582,480	484,355	301,575	251,295	116,825	83,205	79,620	67,645	62,515	38,045	13,345	46,765
Canada	3,043,010	790,755	632,325	453,005	268,885	186,355	203,485	154,035	105,620	77,165	38,270	83,335
					Females							
Cambridge	7,975	3,200	615	1,155	490	610	335	640	205	60	160	205
Ontario	1,697,085	481,635	327,570	287,915	158,555	89,360	72,025	70,230	60,010	40,250	15,740	49,970
Canada	3,221,745	776,650	692,420	492,660	350,425	194,925	177,140	158,045	101,220	83,965	48,990	88,600
					Percent of Population							
					Total							
Cambridge	12.6	5.2	0.9	1.9	0.7	1.0	0.6	1.0	0.3	0.1	0.2	0.3
Ontario	25.9	7.6	5.0	4.3	2.2	1.4	1.2	1.1	1.0	0.6	0.2	0.8
Canada	19.1	4.8	4.0	2.9	1.9	1.2	1.2	0.9	0.6	0.5	0.3	0.5
					Males							
Cambridge	12.7	5.4	0.8	1.9	0.6	1.1	0.6	1.1	0.3	0.2	0.1	0.3
Ontario	25.6	7.8	4.9	4.1	1.9	1.3	1.3	1.1	1.0	0.6	0.2	0.8
Canada	18.8	4.9	3.9	2.8	1.7	1.2	1.3	1.0	0.7	0.5	0.2	0.5
					Females							
Cambridge	12.6	5.0	1.0	1.8	0.8	1.0	0.5	1.0	0.3	0.1	0.3	0.3
Ontario	26.2	7.4	5.1	4.4	2.5	1.4	1.1	1.1	0.9	0.6	0.2	0.8
Canada	19.3	4.7	4.1	3.0	2.1	1.2	1.1	0.9	0.6	0.5	0.3	0.5

Note: The Employment Equity Act defines visible minorities as 'persons, other than Aboriginal peoples, who are non-Caucasian in race or non-white in colour';
(1) Includes 'East Indian,' 'Pakistani,' 'Sri Lankan,' etc.; (2) Includes 'Vietnamese,' 'Cambodian,' 'Malaysian,' 'Laotian,' etc.; (3) Includes 'Iranian,' 'Afghan,' etc.; (4) Includes respondents who reported more than one visible minority group by checking two or more mark-in circles, e.g., 'Black' and 'South Asian.'
Source: Statistics Canada. 2013. 2011 National Household Survey. Statistics Canada Catalogue no. 99-004-XWE. Ottawa. Released September 11, 2013.

Aboriginal Population

Area	Aboriginal Identity[1]	First Nations (North American Indian) Single Identity[2]	Métis Single Identity	Inuk (Inuit) Single Identity	Multiple Aboriginal Identities[3]	Aboriginal Identities Not Included Elsewhere
Number						
Total						
Cambridge	2,470	1,510	715	185	0	50
Ontario	301,430	201,100	86,020	3,355	2,910	8,040
Canada	1,400,685	851,560	451,795	59,440	11,415	26,475
Males						
Cambridge	1,240	725	360	120	0	25
Ontario	145,020	96,620	41,755	1,475	1,420	3,750
Canada	682,190	411,785	223,335	29,495	5,525	12,055
Females						
Cambridge	1,230	780	350	65	0	25
Ontario	156,410	104,485	44,260	1,880	1,490	4,295
Canada	718,500	439,775	228,460	29,950	5,890	14,420
Percent of Population						
Total						
Cambridge	2.0	1.2	0.6	0.1	0.0	0.0
Ontario	2.4	1.6	0.7	0.0	0.0	0.1
Canada	4.3	2.6	1.4	0.2	0.0	0.1
Males						
Cambridge	2.0	1.2	0.6	0.2	0.0	0.0
Ontario	2.3	1.6	0.7	0.0	0.0	0.1
Canada	4.2	2.5	1.4	0.2	0.0	0.1
Females						
Cambridge	1.9	1.2	0.6	0.1	0.0	0.0
Ontario	2.4	1.6	0.7	0.0	0.0	0.1
Canada	4.3	2.6	1.4	0.2	0.0	0.1

Note: (1) Includes persons who reported being an Aboriginal person, that is, First Nations (North American Indian), Métis or Inuk (Inuit) and/or those who reported Registered or Treaty Indian status, that is registered under the Indian Act of Canada, and/or those who reported membership in a First Nation or Indian band. Aboriginal peoples of Canada are defined in the Constitution Act, 1982, section 35-2 as including the Indian, Inuit and Métis peoples of Canada; (2) Users should be aware that the estimates associated with this variable are more affected than most by the incomplete enumeration of certain Indian reserves and Indian settlements in the National Household Survey (NHS); (3) Includes persons who reported being any two or all three of the following: First Nations (North American Indian), Métis or Inuk (Inuit).
Source: Statistics Canada. 2013. 2011 National Household Survey. Statistics Canada Catalogue no. 99-004-XWE. Ottawa. Released September 11, 2013.

Ethnic Origin

Area	North American Aboriginal	Other North American	European	Caribbean	Latin, Central and South American	African	Asian	Oceania
Number								
Total								
Cambridge	4,060	37,505	93,340	1,885	2,280	1,320	12,665	115
Ontario	441,395	3,059,480	8,231,410	396,485	271,545	331,460	2,604,595	19,410
Canada	1,836,035	11,070,455	20,157,965	627,590	544,375	766,735	5,011,225	74,875
Males								
Cambridge	1,800	18,225	46,085	890	1,175	680	6,195	50
Ontario	210,490	1,507,105	4,019,885	181,805	130,035	160,940	1,265,540	9,855
Canada	885,675	5,462,685	9,913,150	291,640	264,635	387,360	2,435,540	37,490
Females								
Cambridge	2,260	19,280	47,255	995	1,105	640	6,470	70
Ontario	230,905	1,552,380	4,211,525	214,675	141,510	170,515	1,339,050	9,555
Canada	950,360	5,607,770	10,244,820	335,945	279,740	379,380	2,575,680	37,385
Percent of Population								
Total								
Cambridge	3.2	30.0	74.6	1.5	1.8	1.1	10.1	0.1
Ontario	3.5	24.2	65.1	3.1	2.1	2.6	20.6	0.2
Canada	5.6	33.7	61.4	1.9	1.7	2.3	15.3	0.2
Males								
Cambridge	2.9	29.6	74.8	1.4	1.9	1.1	10.1	0.1
Ontario	3.4	24.4	65.0	2.9	2.1	2.6	20.5	0.2
Canada	5.5	33.8	61.3	1.8	1.6	2.4	15.1	0.2
Females								
Cambridge	3.6	30.4	74.5	1.6	1.7	1.0	10.2	0.1
Ontario	3.6	24.0	65.1	3.3	2.2	2.6	20.7	0.1
Canada	5.7	33.6	61.4	2.0	1.7	2.3	15.4	0.2

Note: The sum of the ethnic groups in this table is greater than the total population estimate because a person may report more than one ethnic origin in the NHS.
Source: Statistics Canada. 2013. 2011 National Household Survey. Statistics Canada Catalogue no. 99-004-XWE. Ottawa. Released September 11, 2013.

Religion

Area	Buddhist	Christian	Hindu	Jewish	Muslim	Sikh	Traditional (Aboriginal) Spirituality	Other Religions	No Religious Affiliation
				Number Total					
Cambridge	1,050	86,170	1,850	145	3,760	1,430	10	280	30,355
Ontario	163,750	8,167,295	366,720	195,540	581,950	179,765	15,905	53,080	2,927,790
Canada	366,830	22,102,745	497,965	329,495	1,053,945	454,965	64,935	130,835	7,850,605
				Males					
Cambridge	535	40,800	895	75	2,010	670	0	155	16,480
Ontario	75,355	3,839,925	183,580	95,795	293,925	90,515	7,600	23,555	1,571,195
Canada	168,465	10,497,775	250,435	161,265	540,555	229,435	31,805	57,745	4,225,645
				Females					
Cambridge	520	45,370	950	70	1,745	765	0	130	13,870
Ontario	88,395	4,327,365	183,140	99,740	288,025	89,250	8,310	29,525	1,356,600
Canada	198,365	11,604,975	247,525	168,235	513,395	225,530	33,135	73,090	3,624,965
				Percent of Population Total					
Cambridge	0.8	68.9	1.5	0.1	3.0	1.1	0.0	0.2	24.3
Ontario	1.3	64.6	2.9	1.5	4.6	1.4	0.1	0.4	23.1
Canada	1.1	67.3	1.5	1.0	3.2	1.4	0.2	0.4	23.9
				Males					
Cambridge	0.9	66.2	1.5	0.1	3.3	1.1	0.0	0.3	26.7
Ontario	1.2	62.1	3.0	1.5	4.8	1.5	0.1	0.4	25.4
Canada	1.0	64.9	1.5	1.0	3.3	1.4	0.2	0.4	26.1
				Females					
Cambridge	0.8	71.5	1.5	0.1	2.8	1.2	0.0	0.2	21.9
Ontario	1.4	66.9	2.8	1.5	4.5	1.4	0.1	0.5	21.0
Canada	1.2	69.5	1.5	1.0	3.1	1.4	0.2	0.4	21.7

Note: Religion refers to the person's self-identification as having a connection or affiliation with any religious denomination, group, body, sect, cult or other religiously defined community or system of belief. Religion is not limited to formal membership in a religious organization or group. Persons without a religious connection or affiliation can self-identify as atheist, agnostic or humanist, or can provide another applicable response.
Source: Statistics Canada. 2013. 2011 National Household Survey. Statistics Canada Catalogue no. 99-004-XWE. Ottawa. Released September 11, 2013.

Religion—Christian Denominations

Area	Anglican	Baptist	Catholic	Christian Orthodox	Lutheran	Pentecostal	Presbyterian	United Church	Other Christian
				Number Total					
Cambridge	8,860	4,310	42,600	1,110	2,380	2,020	5,800	7,340	11,750
Ontario	774,560	244,650	3,976,610	297,710	163,460	213,945	319,585	952,465	1,224,300
Canada	1,631,845	635,840	12,810,705	550,690	478,185	478,705	472,385	2,007,610	3,036,780
				Males					
Cambridge	4,070	2,045	20,480	580	1,115	895	2,665	3,405	5,550
Ontario	355,175	112,285	1,895,940	145,825	75,225	94,955	148,535	435,255	576,730
Canada	752,945	293,905	6,167,290	270,205	221,525	217,850	218,955	912,545	1,442,550
				Females					
Cambridge	4,785	2,270	22,115	530	1,265	1,130	3,140	3,935	6,205
Ontario	419,390	132,370	2,080,665	151,885	88,230	118,990	171,050	517,210	647,570
Canada	878,900	341,940	6,643,415	280,485	256,660	260,850	253,430	1,095,065	1,594,230
				Percent of Population Total					
Cambridge	7.1	3.4	34.1	0.9	1.9	1.6	4.6	5.9	9.4
Ontario	6.1	1.9	31.4	2.4	1.3	1.7	2.5	7.5	9.7
Canada	5.0	1.9	39.0	1.7	1.5	1.5	1.4	6.1	9.2
				Males					
Cambridge	6.6	3.3	33.2	0.9	1.8	1.5	4.3	5.5	9.0
Ontario	5.7	1.8	30.7	2.4	1.2	1.5	2.4	7.0	9.3
Canada	4.7	1.8	38.2	1.7	1.4	1.3	1.4	5.6	8.9
				Females					
Cambridge	7.5	3.6	34.9	0.8	2.0	1.8	5.0	6.2	9.8
Ontario	6.5	2.0	32.2	2.3	1.4	1.8	2.6	8.0	10.0
Canada	5.3	2.0	39.8	1.7	1.5	1.6	1.5	6.6	9.6

Note: Religion refers to the person's self-identification as having a connection or affiliation with any religious denomination, group, body, sect, cult or other religiously defined community or system of belief. Religion is not limited to formal membership in a religious organization or group. Persons without a religious connection or affiliation can self-identify as atheist, agnostic or humanist, or can provide another applicable response.
Source: Statistics Canada. 2013. 2011 National Household Survey. Statistics Canada Catalogue no. 99-004-XWE. Ottawa. Released September 11, 2013.

PROFILES / Cambridge, Ontario

Immigrant Status and Period of Immigration

Area	Non-Immigrants[1]	Immigrants All	Before 1971	1971 to 1980	1981 to 1990	1991 to 2000	2001 to 2005	2006 to 2011	Non-Permanent Residents[3]
					Number Total				
Cambridge	99,490	25,295	7,000	5,325	3,755	4,000	3,075	2,135	270
Ontario	8,906,000	3,611,365	723,030	464,380	538,285	866,220	518,405	501,060	134,425
Canada	25,720,175	6,775,765	1,261,055	870,775	949,890	1,539,050	992,070	1,162,915	356,385
					Males				
Cambridge	49,225	12,295	3,325	2,600	1,885	1,965	1,565	950	105
Ontario	4,410,240	1,706,385	341,820	217,990	258,095	408,270	245,850	234,360	64,825
Canada	12,753,235	3,231,370	605,430	416,670	454,570	724,905	474,545	555,245	178,515
					Females				
Cambridge	50,270	12,995	3,665	2,720	1,870	2,040	1,515	1,185	165
Ontario	4,495,765	1,904,985	381,210	246,390	280,190	457,950	272,550	266,695	69,600
Canada	12,966,935	3,544,400	655,625	454,105	495,325	814,145	517,530	607,670	177,870
					Percent of Population Total				
Cambridge	79.6	20.2	5.6	4.3	3.0	3.2	2.5	1.7	0.2
Ontario	70.4	28.5	5.7	3.7	4.3	6.8	4.1	4.0	1.1
Canada	78.3	20.6	3.8	2.7	2.9	4.7	3.0	3.5	1.1
					Males				
Cambridge	79.9	20.0	5.4	4.2	3.1	3.2	2.5	1.5	0.2
Ontario	71.3	27.6	5.5	3.5	4.2	6.6	4.0	3.8	1.0
Canada	78.9	20.0	3.7	2.6	2.8	4.5	2.9	3.4	1.1
					Females				
Cambridge	79.3	20.5	5.8	4.3	2.9	3.2	2.4	1.9	0.3
Ontario	69.5	29.4	5.9	3.8	4.3	7.1	4.2	4.1	1.1
Canada	77.7	21.2	3.9	2.7	3.0	4.9	3.1	3.6	1.1

Note: (1) Non-immigrant refers to a person who is a Canadian citizen by birth; (2) Immigrant refers to a person who is or has ever been a landed immigrant/permanent resident. This person has been granted the right to live in Canada permanently by immigration authorities. Some immigrants have resided in Canada for a number of years, while others have arrived recently. Some immigrants are Canadian citizens, while others are not. Most immigrants are born outside Canada, but a small number are born in Canada. In the 2011 National Household Survey, 'Immigrants' includes immigrants who landed in Canada prior to May 10, 2011; (3) Non-permanent resident refers to a person from another country who has a work or study permit, or who is a refugee claimant, and any non-Canadian-born family member living in Canada with them.
Source: Statistics Canada. 2013. 2011 National Household Survey. Statistics Canada Catalogue no. 99-004-XWE. Ottawa. Released September 11, 2013.

Mother Tongue

Area	English	French	Non-official Language	English & French	English & Non-official Language	French & Non-official Language	English, French & Non-official Language
				Number Total			
Cambridge	100,075	1,705	21,940	265	1,580	40	40
Ontario	8,677,040	493,300	3,264,435	46,605	219,425	13,645	7,615
Canada	18,858,980	7,054,975	6,567,680	144,685	396,330	74,430	24,095
				Males			
Cambridge	49,410	815	10,615	120	790	20	20
Ontario	4,276,970	232,785	1,562,190	21,805	106,790	6,285	3,495
Canada	9,345,225	3,452,380	3,157,785	69,975	192,000	36,535	11,965
				Females			
Cambridge	50,665	885	11,320	150	795	20	20
Ontario	4,400,065	260,510	1,702,240	24,795	112,635	7,365	4,115
Canada	9,513,750	3,602,590	3,409,895	74,710	204,330	37,890	12,130
				Percent of Population Total			
Cambridge	79.7	1.4	17.5	0.2	1.3	0.0	0.0
Ontario	68.2	3.9	25.7	0.4	1.7	0.1	0.1
Canada	56.9	21.3	19.8	0.4	1.2	0.2	0.1
				Males			
Cambridge	80.0	1.3	17.2	0.2	1.3	0.0	0.0
Ontario	68.9	3.7	25.2	0.4	1.7	0.1	0.1
Canada	57.5	21.2	19.4	0.4	1.2	0.2	0.1
				Females			
Cambridge	79.4	1.4	17.7	0.2	1.2	0.0	0.0
Ontario	67.6	4.0	26.1	0.4	1.7	0.1	0.1
Canada	56.4	21.4	20.2	0.4	1.2	0.2	0.1

Note: Figures cover total population excluding institutional residents.
Source: Statistics Canada. 2012. Census Profile. 2011 Census. Statistics Canada Catalogue no. 98-316-XWE. Ottawa. Released October 24 2012.
http://www12.statcan.gc.ca/census-recensement/2011/dp-pd/prof/index.cfm?Lang=E

Language Spoken Most Often at Home

Area	English	French	Non-official Language	English & French	English & Non-official Language	French & Non-official Language	English, French & Non-official Language
Number							
Total							
Cambridge	110,780	435	10,540	170	3,640	20	55
Ontario	10,044,810	284,115	1,827,870	37,955	509,105	6,370	11,845
Canada	21,457,075	6,827,865	3,673,865	131,205	875,135	109,700	46,330
Males							
Cambridge	54,595	220	5,070	75	1,800	10	25
Ontario	4,930,610	133,495	872,860	17,250	248,050	2,855	5,225
Canada	10,585,620	3,348,235	1,767,310	63,475	425,370	53,010	22,845
Females							
Cambridge	56,185	215	5,470	95	1,840	10	30
Ontario	5,114,200	150,620	955,010	20,705	261,055	3,520	6,620
Canada	10,871,455	3,479,625	1,906,555	67,730	449,765	56,690	23,485
Percent of Population							
Total							
Cambridge	88.2	0.3	8.4	0.1	2.9	0.0	0.0
Ontario	79.0	2.2	14.4	0.3	4.0	0.1	0.1
Canada	64.8	20.6	11.1	0.4	2.6	0.3	0.1
Males							
Cambridge	88.4	0.4	8.2	0.1	2.9	0.0	0.0
Ontario	79.4	2.1	14.1	0.3	4.0	0.0	0.1
Canada	65.1	20.6	10.9	0.4	2.6	0.3	0.1
Females							
Cambridge	88.0	0.3	8.6	0.1	2.9	0.0	0.0
Ontario	78.5	2.3	14.7	0.3	4.0	0.1	0.1
Canada	64.5	20.6	11.3	0.4	2.7	0.3	0.1

Note: Figures cover total population excluding institutional residents.
Source: Statistics Canada. 2012. Census Profile. 2011 Census. Statistics Canada Catalogue no. 98-316-XWE. Ottawa. Released October 24 2012.
http://www12.statcan.gc.ca/census-recensement/2011/dp-pd/prof/index.cfm?Lang=E

Knowledge of Official Languages

Area	English Only	French Only	English & French	Neither English nor French
Number				
Total				
Cambridge	116,855	55	6,705	2,030
Ontario	10,984,360	42,980	1,395,805	298,920
Canada	22,564,665	4,165,015	5,795,570	595,920
Males				
Cambridge	57,970	25	2,980	810
Ontario	5,445,050	18,805	627,725	118,765
Canada	11,222,185	1,925,340	2,876,560	241,790
Females				
Cambridge	58,880	30	3,720	1,220
Ontario	5,539,310	24,175	768,085	180,155
Canada	11,342,485	2,239,680	2,919,005	354,135
Percent of Population				
Total				
Cambridge	93.0	0.0	5.3	1.6
Ontario	86.3	0.3	11.0	2.3
Canada	68.1	12.6	17.5	1.8
Males				
Cambridge	93.8	0.0	4.8	1.3
Ontario	87.7	0.3	10.1	1.9
Canada	69.0	11.8	17.7	1.5
Females				
Cambridge	92.2	0.0	5.8	1.9
Ontario	85.1	0.4	11.8	2.8
Canada	67.3	13.3	17.3	2.1

Note: Figures cover total population excluding institutional residents.
Source: Statistics Canada. 2012. Census Profile. 2011 Census. Statistics Canada Catalogue no. 98-316-XWE. Ottawa. Released October 24 2012.
http://www12.statcan.gc.ca/census-recensement/2011/dp-pd/prof/index.cfm?Lang=E

Chatham-Kent, Ontario

Background

Chatham-Kent is located in Southern Ontario and overlooks Lake Erie and Lake St. Clair. The region is comprised of 23 small cities, towns and villages. The majority of Chatham-Kent's communities are built along the banks of the historic Thames River. Over 1 million Canadians are within an hour from the region and the U.S. border is less than 100 kilometres away.

Chatham-Kent is the site of the Battle of the Thames, a rare American land victory during the War of 1812. British and First Nations loyalists fled American forces by following the region's Thames River, shortly after the death of Shawnee Chief Tecumseh. The Thames was also part of the Underground Railroad and the site of one of the largest and most successful Black settlements in Canada.

Half of the wind farm proposals in Ontario were awarded to Chatham-Kent in 2009. The municipality is home to internationally recognized companies such as Greenfield Ethanol and is the head office location of Union Gas and Pioneer Hi-Bred (a division of Dupont). Two post-secondary institutions are located within Chatham-Kent: the University of Guelph campus, which focuses on local agri-business research and innovation, including bio-fuels and renewable energy, and the St. Clair College of Applied Arts & Technology.

Chatham-Kent has the longest growing season in Canada and the municipality's bumper crops include corn, tomatoes, soybeans and other fruits and vegetables. Crop-based energies (ethanol) and wind farms are emerging industries. Others include the automotive manufacturing sector, which includes the International Truck and Engine's heavy truck assembly plant, and Canada's largest fresh water fishery.

The city's new YMCA opened in 2011, representing a portion of the $50-million investment in Chatham's tourism, culture, recreation and culture sectors. The municipality also recently finished building a new theatre, conference centre and recreation facility. The Classic (Car) Cruise, Culture Factory, Children's Water Festival and Retrofest are popular annual events and festivals in the area.

Chatam-Kent has summer highs of plus 26.43 degrees Celsius, winter lows of minus 5.77 degrees Celsius, and an average rainfall just over 807 mm per year.

Rankings

- Chatham-Kent was ranked #147 out of 190 Canadian cities in *Money Sense Magazine*'s "Best Places to Live." The city's best overall ratings were in weather (#13), affordable housing (#24) and a moderate crime rate (#88). Chatham-Kent's lower ratings were in culture (#163), population growth (#164) and access to doctors (#184). *Money Sense Magazine, "Canada's Best Places to Live 2012," March 20, 2012*
- *Reader's Digest* ranked Chatham-Kent as one of the best Canadian road trips. The city was ranked in the Top 10, and was praised for its scenic, historic roadways, eight motorcycle routes and annual bike rally in Port Dover. Other Top 10 destinations included Kelowna (BC), Jasper and Banff (AB), Pelee Island (ON) and the Eastern Townships in Québec. *Reader's Digest.ca, "Top 10 Best Canadian Road Trips," Spring 2012*

PROFILES / Chatham-Kent, Ontario

Population Growth and Density

Area	Population in 2001	Population in 2006	Population in 2011	Population Change 2001–2006	Population Change 2006–2011	Land Area (sq. km)	Population Density per sq. km
Chatham-Kent	107,341	108,177	103,671	0.8	-4.2	2,458.09	42.2
Ontario	11,410,046	12,160,282	12,851,821	6.6	5.7	908,607.67	14.1
Canada	30,007,094	31,612,897	33,476,688	5.4	5.9	8,965,121.42	3.7

Source: Statistics Canada. 2012. Census Profile. 2011 Census. Statistics Canada Catalogue no. 98-316-XWE. Ottawa. Released October 24 2012.
http://www12.statcan.gc.ca/census-recensement/2011/dp-pd/prof/index.cfm?Lang=E;
Statistics Canada 2007. 2006 Community Profiles. 2006 Census. Statistics Canada Catalogue no. 92-591-XWE. Ottawa. Released March 13 2007.
http://www12.statcan.ca/census-recensement/2006/dp-pd/prof/92-591/index.cfm?Lang=E

Gender

Area	Males	Females
Number		
Chatham-Kent	50,435	53,235
Ontario	6,263,140	6,588,685
Canada	16,414,225	17,062,460
Percent of Population		
Chatham-Kent	48.6	51.4
Ontario	48.7	51.3
Canada	49.0	51.0

Source: Statistics Canada. 2012. Census Profile. 2011 Census. Statistics Canada Catalogue no. 98-316-XWE. Ottawa. Released October 24 2012.
http://www12.statcan.gc.ca/census-recensement/2011/dp-pd/prof/index.cfm?Lang=E

Marital Status

Area	Married[1]	Living Common-law	Single[2]	Separated	Divorced	Widowed
Number						
Total						
Chatham-Kent	44,125	7,200	20,355	2,875	5,090	6,415
Ontario	5,367,400	791,210	2,985,020	319,805	593,730	613,880
Canada	12,941,960	3,142,525	7,816,045	698,240	1,686,035	1,584,530
Males						
Chatham-Kent	22,085	3,595	11,040	1,305	2,205	1,255
Ontario	2,681,320	397,620	1,583,760	133,790	231,160	117,980
Canada	6,470,300	1,575,495	4,206,320	299,655	680,415	310,940
Females						
Chatham-Kent	22,040	3,600	9,320	1,570	2,890	5,160
Ontario	2,686,075	393,590	1,401,260	186,015	362,570	495,905
Canada	6,471,660	1,567,035	3,609,730	398,585	1,005,620	1,273,590
Percent of Population						
Total						
Chatham-Kent	51.3	8.4	23.7	3.3	5.9	7.5
Ontario	50.3	7.4	28.0	3.0	5.6	5.8
Canada	46.4	11.3	28.0	2.5	6.0	5.7
Males						
Chatham-Kent	53.2	8.7	26.6	3.1	5.3	3.0
Ontario	52.1	7.7	30.8	2.6	4.5	2.3
Canada	47.8	11.6	31.1	2.2	5.0	2.3
Females						
Chatham-Kent	49.4	8.1	20.9	3.5	6.5	11.6
Ontario	48.6	7.1	25.4	3.4	6.6	9.0
Canada	45.2	10.9	25.2	2.8	7.0	8.9

Note: (1) and not separated, (2) never legally married
Source: Statistics Canada. 2012. Census Profile. 2011 Census. Statistics Canada Catalogue no. 98-316-XWE. Ottawa. Released October 24 2012.
http://www12.statcan.gc.ca/census-recensement/2011/dp-pd/prof/index.cfm?Lang=E

Age Characteristics: 0 to 49 Years

Area	0 to 4 Years	5 to 9 Years	10 to 14 Years	15 to 19 Years	20 to 24 Years	25 to 29 Years	30 to 34 Years	35 to 39 Years	40 to 44 Years	45 to 49 Years
					Number					
					Total					
Chatham-Kent	5,510	5,765	6,330	6,975	6,010	5,525	5,245	5,575	6,365	8,250
Ontario	704,260	712,755	763,755	863,635	852,910	815,120	800,365	844,335	924,075	1,055,880
Canada	1,877,095	1,809,895	1,920,355	2,178,135	2,187,450	2,169,590	2,162,905	2,173,930	2,324,875	2,675,130
					Males					
Chatham-Kent	2,770	2,985	3,195	3,505	3,080	2,730	2,675	2,670	3,125	4,050
Ontario	360,590	365,290	391,630	443,680	432,490	400,045	383,340	405,845	447,920	517,510
Canada	961,150	925,965	983,995	1,115,845	1,108,775	1,077,275	1,058,810	1,064,200	1,141,720	1,318,715
					Females					
Chatham-Kent	2,740	2,780	3,135	3,475	2,935	2,790	2,570	2,905	3,245	4,205
Ontario	343,670	347,465	372,125	419,950	420,415	415,075	417,030	438,485	476,155	538,370
Canada	915,945	883,935	936,360	1,062,295	1,078,670	1,092,315	1,104,095	1,109,735	1,183,155	1,356,420
					Percent of Population					
					Total					
Chatham-Kent	5.3	5.6	6.1	6.7	5.8	5.3	5.1	5.4	6.1	8.0
Ontario	5.5	5.5	5.9	6.7	6.6	6.3	6.2	6.6	7.2	8.2
Canada	5.6	5.4	5.7	6.5	6.5	6.5	6.5	6.5	6.9	8.0
					Males					
Chatham-Kent	5.5	5.9	6.3	6.9	6.1	5.4	5.3	5.3	6.2	8.0
Ontario	5.8	5.8	6.3	7.1	6.9	6.4	6.1	6.5	7.2	8.3
Canada	5.9	5.6	6.0	6.8	6.8	6.6	6.5	6.5	7.0	8.0
					Females					
Chatham-Kent	5.1	5.2	5.9	6.5	5.5	5.2	4.8	5.5	6.1	7.9
Ontario	5.2	5.3	5.6	6.4	6.4	6.3	6.3	6.7	7.2	8.2
Canada	5.4	5.2	5.5	6.2	6.3	6.4	6.5	6.5	6.9	7.9

Source: Statistics Canada. 2012. Census Profile. 2011 Census. Statistics Canada Catalogue no. 98-316-XWE. Ottawa. Released October 24 2012.
http://www12.statcan.gc.ca/census-recensement/2011/dp-pd/prof/index.cfm?Lang=E

Age Characteristics: 50 Years and Over, and Median Age

Area	50 to 54 Years	55 to 59 Years	60 to 64 Years	65 to 69 Years	70 to 74 Years	75 to 79 Years	80 to 84 Years	85 Years and Over	Median Age
				Number					
				Total					
Chatham-Kent	8,620	7,720	7,190	5,455	4,375	3,405	2,720	2,630	43.9
Ontario	1,006,140	864,620	765,655	563,485	440,780	356,150	271,510	246,400	40.4
Canada	2,658,965	2,340,635	2,052,670	1,521,715	1,153,065	922,700	702,070	645,515	40.6
				Males					
Chatham-Kent	4,205	3,820	3,520	2,630	2,075	1,525	1,110	760	42.6
Ontario	492,560	418,755	370,370	270,875	206,350	161,345	113,620	80,925	39.4
Canada	1,309,030	1,147,300	1,002,690	738,010	543,435	417,945	291,085	208,300	39.6
				Females					
Chatham-Kent	4,415	3,900	3,665	2,825	2,300	1,880	1,610	1,870	45.1
Ontario	513,580	445,865	395,275	292,610	234,435	194,805	157,890	165,475	41.3
Canada	1,349,940	1,193,335	1,049,985	783,705	609,630	504,755	410,985	437,215	41.5
				Percent of Population					
				Total					
Chatham-Kent	8.3	7.4	6.9	5.3	4.2	3.3	2.6	2.5	–
Ontario	7.8	6.7	6.0	4.4	3.4	2.8	2.1	1.9	–
Canada	7.9	7.0	6.1	4.5	3.4	2.8	2.1	1.9	–
				Males					
Chatham-Kent	8.3	7.6	7.0	5.2	4.1	3.0	2.2	1.5	–
Ontario	7.9	6.7	5.9	4.3	3.3	2.6	1.8	1.3	–
Canada	8.0	7.0	6.1	4.5	3.3	2.5	1.8	1.3	–
				Females					
Chatham-Kent	8.3	7.3	6.9	5.3	4.3	3.5	3.0	3.5	–
Ontario	7.8	6.8	6.0	4.4	3.6	3.0	2.4	2.5	–
Canada	7.9	7.0	6.2	4.6	3.6	3.0	2.4	2.6	–

Source: Statistics Canada. 2012. Census Profile. 2011 Census. Statistics Canada Catalogue no. 98-316-XWE. Ottawa. Released October 24 2012.
http://www12.statcan.gc.ca/census-recensement/2011/dp-pd/prof/index.cfm?Lang=E

Private Households by Household Size

Area	1 Person	2 Persons	3 Persons	4 Persons	5 Persons	6 or More Persons	Average Number of Persons in Private Households
			Households				
Chatham-Kent	12,010	16,155	6,180	5,460	1,980	1,060	2.4
Ontario	1,230,975	1,584,415	803,030	783,925	310,860	174,305	2.6
Canada	3,673,310	4,544,820	2,081,900	1,903,300	724,405	392,885	2.5
			Percent of Households				
Chatham-Kent	28.0	37.7	14.4	12.7	4.6	2.5	–
Ontario	25.2	32.4	16.4	16.0	6.4	3.6	–
Canada	27.6	34.1	15.6	14.3	5.4	2.9	–

Source: Statistics Canada. 2012. Census Profile. 2011 Census. Statistics Canada Catalogue no. 98-316-XWE. Ottawa. Released October 24 2012.
http://www12.statcan.gc.ca/census-recensement/2011/dp-pd/prof/index.cfm?Lang=E

Dwelling Type

Area	Single-detached House	Semi-detached House	Row House	Apartment: Building with Five or More Storeys	Apartment: Building with Fewer Than Five Storeys	Duplex Apartment	Movable Dwelling	Other Single-attached House
				Number				
Chatham-Kent	32,900	1,235	1,435	1,505	4,780	690	210	85
Ontario	2,718,880	279,470	415,225	789,970	498,160	160,460	15,800	9,540
Canada	7,329,150	646,245	791,600	1,234,770	2,397,550	704,485	183,510	33,310
				Percent of Dwellings				
Chatham-Kent	76.8	2.9	3.3	3.5	11.2	1.6	0.5	0.2
Ontario	55.6	5.7	8.5	16.2	10.2	3.3	0.3	0.2
Canada	55.0	4.9	5.9	9.3	18.0	5.3	1.4	0.3

Source: Statistics Canada. 2012. Census Profile. 2011 Census. Statistics Canada Catalogue no. 98-316-XWE. Ottawa. Released October 24 2012.
http://www12.statcan.gc.ca/census-recensement/2011/dp-pd/prof/index.cfm?Lang=E

Shelter Costs

		Owned Dwellings				Rented Dwellings		
Area	Number	Median Value[1] ($)	Average Value[1] ($)	Median Monthly Costs[2] ($)	Average Monthly Costs[2] ($)	Number	Median Monthly Costs[3] ($)	Average Monthly Costs[3] ($)
Chatham-Kent	29,955	149,775	167,643	738	875	11,525	654	656
Ontario	3,446,650	300,862	367,428	1,163	1,284	1,385,535	892	926
Canada	9,013,410	280,552	345,182	978	1,141	4,060,385	784	848

Note: All figures cover non-farm, non-reserve private dwellings; (1) Refers to the dollar amount expected by the owner if the dwelling were to be sold; (2) Includes all shelter expenses paid by households that own their dwellings, such as the mortgage payment and the costs of electricity, heat, water and other municipal services, property taxes and condominium fees; (3) Includes all shelter expenses paid by households that rent their dwellings, such as the monthly rent and the costs of electricity, heat and municipal services.
Source: Statistics Canada. 2013. 2011 National Household Survey. Statistics Canada Catalogue no. 99-004-XWE. Ottawa. Released September 11, 2013.

Occupied Private Dwellings by Period of Construction

Area	1960 or Before	1961 to 1980	1981 to 1990	1991 to 2000	2001 to 2005	2006 to 2011
			Number			
Chatham-Kent	19,210	13,555	4,205	3,540	1,380	945
Ontario	1,330,235	1,420,570	763,430	609,310	414,795	348,310
Canada	3,273,105	4,152,715	2,112,110	1,707,880	1,031,020	1,042,430
			Percent of Dwellings			
Chatham-Kent	44.8	31.6	9.8	8.3	3.2	2.2
Ontario	27.2	29.1	15.6	12.5	8.5	7.1
Canada	24.6	31.2	15.9	12.8	7.7	7.8

Note: Figures cover non-farm, non-reserve private dwellings and includes data up to May 10, 2011.
Source: Statistics Canada. 2013. 2011 National Household Survey. Statistics Canada Catalogue no. 99-004-XWE. Ottawa. Released September 11, 2013.

Educational Attainment

Area	No Certificate, Diploma or Degree	High School Diploma or Equivalent[1]	Apprenticeship or Trades Certificate or Diploma[2]	College, CÉGEP or Other Non-University Certificate or Diploma	University Certificate or Diploma Below the Bachelor Level[3]	Bachelor's Degree	University Certificate, Diploma or Degree Above Bachelor Level[4]
			Number				
			Total				
Chatham-Kent	22,045	25,990	7,115	18,950	1,670	5,610	2,750
Ontario	1,954,520	2,801,805	771,140	2,070,875	427,150	1,515,075	933,100
Canada	5,485,400	6,968,935	2,950,685	4,970,020	1,200,130	3,634,425	2,049,930
			Males				
Chatham-Kent	11,305	12,615	4,870	7,570	770	2,480	1,240
Ontario	957,040	1,337,055	520,390	894,235	193,355	692,345	470,290
Canada	2,742,875	3,305,415	1,928,970	2,118,430	513,235	1,643,080	1,043,350
			Females				
Chatham-Kent	10,735	13,375	2,240	11,380	910	3,135	1,510
Ontario	997,475	1,464,755	250,750	1,176,640	233,790	822,730	462,805
Canada	2,742,520	3,663,515	1,021,715	2,851,595	686,890	1,991,345	1,006,585
			Percent of Population				
			Total				
Chatham-Kent	26.2	30.9	8.5	22.5	2.0	6.7	3.3
Ontario	18.7	26.8	7.4	19.8	4.1	14.5	8.9
Canada	20.1	25.6	10.8	18.2	4.4	13.3	7.5
			Males				
Chatham-Kent	27.7	30.9	11.9	18.5	1.9	6.1	3.0
Ontario	18.9	26.4	10.3	17.7	3.8	13.7	9.3
Canada	20.6	24.9	14.5	15.9	3.9	12.4	7.8
			Females				
Chatham-Kent	24.8	30.9	5.2	26.3	2.1	7.2	3.5
Ontario	18.4	27.1	4.6	21.8	4.3	15.2	8.6
Canada	19.6	26.2	7.3	20.4	4.9	14.3	7.2

Note: Figures cover total population aged 15 years and over by highest certificate, diploma or degree; (1) Includes persons who have graduated from a secondary school or equivalent. It excludes persons with a postsecondary certificate, diploma or degree; (2) Includes Registered Apprenticeship certificates (including Certificate of Qualification, Journeyperson's designation) and other trades certificates or diplomas such as pre-employment or vocational certificates and diplomas from brief trade programs completed at community colleges, institutes of technology, vocational centres, and similar institutions; (3) Comparisons with other data sources suggest that the category 'University certificate or diploma below the bachelor's level' was over-reported in the NHS. This category likely includes some responses that are actually college certificates or diplomas, bachelor's degrees or other types of education (e.g., university transfer programs, bachelor's programs completed in other countries, incomplete bachelor's programs, non-university professional designations). We recommend users interpret the results for the 'University certificate or diploma below the bachelor's level' category with caution; (4) 'University certificate or diploma above bachelor level' includes the categories: 'Degree in medicine, dentistry, veterinary medicine or optometry,' 'Master's degree' and 'Earned doctorate.'
Source: Statistics Canada. 2013. 2011 National Household Survey. Statistics Canada Catalogue no. 99-004-XWE. Ottawa. Released September 11, 2013.

Household Income Distribution

Area	Less than $10,000	$10,000 to $19,999	$20,000 to $29,999	$30,000 to $39,999	$40,000 to $49,999	$50,000 to $59,999	$60,000 to $79,999	$80,000 to $99,999	$100,000 to $124,999	$125,000 to $149,999	$150,000 and Over
					Households						
Chatham-Kent	1,775	4,170	5,070	5,215	4,485	3,760	6,620	4,260	3,350	1,865	2,275
Ontario	201,780	354,530	405,725	425,410	425,720	398,705	680,850	552,660	497,970	331,460	611,840
Canada	626,705	1,141,945	1,193,925	1,271,675	1,206,800	1,102,120	1,865,280	1,458,240	1,260,770	802,555	1,389,240
					Percent of Households						
Chatham-Kent	4.1	9.7	11.8	12.2	10.5	8.8	15.5	9.9	7.8	4.4	5.3
Ontario	4.1	7.3	8.3	8.7	8.7	8.2	13.9	11.3	10.2	6.8	12.5
Canada	4.7	8.6	9.0	9.5	9.1	8.3	14.0	10.9	9.5	6.0	10.4

Note: Household income is the sum of the total incomes of all members of that household. Total income refers to monetary receipts from certain sources, before income taxes and deductions, during calendar year 2010.
Source: Statistics Canada. 2013. 2011 National Household Survey. Statistics Canada Catalogue no. 99-004-XWE. Ottawa. Released September 11, 2013.

Median and Average Household and Economic Family Income

Area	Median Household Income ($)	Average Household Income ($)	Median After-tax Household Income ($)	Average After-tax Household Income ($)	Median Economic Family Income ($)	Average Economic Family Income ($)	Median After-tax Economic Family Income ($)	Average After-tax Economic Family Income ($)
Chatham-Kent	51,851	63,843	47,333	55,664	64,670	75,925	58,692	65,998
Ontario	66,358	85,772	58,717	71,523	80,987	100,152	71,128	83,322
Canada	61,072	79,102	54,089	66,149	76,511	94,125	67,044	78,517

Note: Figures cover household and economic familiy income in 2010. A household is defined as a person or a group of persons (other than foreign residents) who occupy the same private dwelling and do not have a usual place of residence elsewhere in Canada. Every person is a member of one and only one household. An economic family is defined as a group of two or more persons who live in the same dwelling and are related to each other by blood, marriage, common-law, adoption or a foster relationship. A couple may be of opposite or same sex.
Source: Statistics Canada. 2013. 2011 National Household Survey. Statistics Canada Catalogue no. 99-004-XWE. Ottawa. Released September 11, 2013.

PROFILES / Chatham-Kent, Ontario

Individual Income Distribution

Area	Less than $10,000	$10,000 to $19,999	$20,000 to $29,999	$30,000 to $39,999	$40,000 to $49,999	$50,000 to $59,999	$60,000 to $79,999	$80,000 to $99,999	$100,000 to $124,999	$125,000 and Over
Number										
Total										
Chatham-Kent	14,100	16,200	14,350	11,185	7,655	5,405	6,085	3,235	1,280	1,035
Ontario	1,780,355	1,748,060	1,361,710	1,136,730	980,790	746,360	964,280	574,710	293,865	330,285
Canada	4,492,040	4,835,710	3,670,020	3,180,360	2,603,520	1,921,650	2,437,440	1,302,045	693,580	782,135
Males										
Chatham-Kent	6,000	6,030	6,320	5,790	4,370	3,435	3,760	1,870	930	845
Ontario	781,095	669,815	580,990	535,255	491,125	407,005	569,205	341,160	201,125	244,500
Canada	1,936,365	1,864,880	1,588,260	1,522,190	1,333,510	1,079,780	1,473,145	823,720	492,905	599,905
Females										
Chatham-Kent	8,095	10,170	8,030	5,395	3,280	1,975	2,320	1,365	350	190
Ontario	999,265	1,078,245	780,720	601,475	489,665	339,360	395,075	233,550	92,740	85,790
Canada	2,555,675	2,970,825	2,081,760	1,658,170	1,270,010	841,870	964,300	478,330	200,680	182,230
Percent of Population										
Total										
Chatham-Kent	17.5	20.1	17.8	13.9	9.5	6.7	7.6	4.0	1.6	1.3
Ontario	18.0	17.6	13.7	11.5	9.9	7.5	9.7	5.8	3.0	3.3
Canada	17.3	18.7	14.2	12.3	10.0	7.4	9.4	5.0	2.7	3.0
Males										
Chatham-Kent	15.2	15.3	16.1	14.7	11.1	8.7	9.6	4.8	2.4	2.1
Ontario	16.2	13.9	12.1	11.1	10.2	8.4	11.8	7.1	4.2	5.1
Canada	15.2	14.7	12.5	12.0	10.5	8.5	11.6	6.5	3.9	4.7
Females										
Chatham-Kent	19.7	24.7	19.5	13.1	8.0	4.8	5.6	3.3	0.8	0.5
Ontario	19.6	21.2	15.3	11.8	9.6	6.7	7.8	4.6	1.8	1.7
Canada	19.4	22.5	15.8	12.6	9.6	6.4	7.3	3.6	1.5	1.4

Note: Figures cover individuals aged 15 years and over with income. Income refers to monetary receipts from certain sources, before income taxes and deductions, during calendar year 2010.
Source: Statistics Canada. 2013. 2011 National Household Survey. Statistics Canada Catalogue no. 99-004-XWE. Ottawa. Released September 11, 2013.

Labour Force Status

Area	In the Labour Force - All	In the Labour Force - Employed	In the Labour Force - Unemployed	Not in the Labour Force
Number				
Total				
Chatham-Kent	50,695	45,535	5,160	33,425
Ontario	6,864,990	6,297,005	567,985	3,608,685
Canada	17,990,080	16,595,035	1,395,045	9,269,445
Males				
Chatham-Kent	26,480	23,475	3,005	14,365
Ontario	3,542,030	3,249,165	292,865	1,522,690
Canada	9,388,570	8,634,310	754,255	3,906,785
Females				
Chatham-Kent	24,215	22,060	2,160	19,060
Ontario	3,322,955	3,047,840	275,120	2,085,990
Canada	8,601,515	7,960,725	640,790	5,362,660
Percent of Labour Force				
Total				
Chatham-Kent	60.3	54.1	10.2	39.7
Ontario	65.5	60.1	8.3	34.5
Canada	66.0	60.9	7.8	34.0
Males				
Chatham-Kent	64.8	57.5	11.3	35.2
Ontario	69.9	64.2	8.3	30.1
Canada	70.6	64.9	8.0	29.4
Females				
Chatham-Kent	56.0	51.0	8.9	44.0
Ontario	61.4	56.3	8.3	38.6
Canada	61.6	57.0	7.4	38.4

Note: Figures are based on total population 15 years and over
Source: Statistics Canada. 2013. 2011 National Household Survey. Statistics Canada Catalogue no. 99-004-XWE. Ottawa. Released September 11, 2013.

Labour Force by Industry (NAICS Codes 11–52)

Area	Agriculture, forestry, fishing & hunting	Mining, quarrying, & oil & gas extraction	Utilities	Construction	Manufacturing	Wholesale Trade	Retail Trade	Transportation & warehousing	Information & cultural industries	Finance & insurance
					Number					
					Total					
Chatham-Kent	3,855	130	1,215	3,305	5,990	1,935	6,115	2,265	675	1,090
Ontario	101,280	29,985	57,035	417,900	697,565	305,030	751,200	307,405	178,720	364,415
Canada	437,650	261,050	149,940	1,215,380	1,619,295	733,445	2,031,665	827,780	420,830	767,960
					Males					
Chatham-Kent	2,735	130	705	3,020	4,590	1,495	2,425	1,830	420	340
Ontario	66,485	25,650	42,685	369,300	493,305	197,770	344,480	225,245	98,835	153,125
Canada	307,370	211,690	110,765	1,068,710	1,167,680	494,545	933,850	617,305	235,875	296,995
					Females					
Chatham-Kent	1,120	0	510	290	1,400	450	3,685	440	255	750
Ontario	34,800	4,340	14,350	48,595	204,260	107,260	406,720	82,160	79,885	211,290
Canada	130,285	49,360	39,175	146,670	451,615	238,900	1,097,820	210,475	184,955	470,960
					Percent of Labour Force					
					Total					
Chatham-Kent	7.8	0.3	2.5	6.7	12.2	3.9	12.4	4.6	1.4	2.2
Ontario	1.5	0.4	0.9	6.3	10.4	4.6	11.2	4.6	2.7	5.5
Canada	2.5	1.5	0.9	6.9	9.2	4.2	11.6	4.7	2.4	4.4
					Males					
Chatham-Kent	10.7	0.5	2.7	11.8	17.9	5.8	9.4	7.1	1.6	1.3
Ontario	1.9	0.7	1.2	10.7	14.3	5.7	10.0	6.5	2.9	4.4
Canada	3.3	2.3	1.2	11.6	12.7	5.4	10.2	6.7	2.6	3.2
					Females					
Chatham-Kent	4.7	0.0	2.2	1.2	5.9	1.9	15.6	1.9	1.1	3.2
Ontario	1.1	0.1	0.4	1.5	6.3	3.3	12.6	2.5	2.5	6.5
Canada	1.6	0.6	0.5	1.7	5.4	2.8	13.1	2.5	2.2	5.6

Note: Figures are based on total experienced labour force 15 years and over. Experienced labour force refers to persons who, during the week of Sunday, May 1 to Saturday, May 7, 2011, were employed and the unemployed who had last worked for pay or in self-employment in either 2010 or 2011.
Source: Statistics Canada. 2013. 2011 National Household Survey. Statistics Canada Catalogue no. 99-004-XWE. Ottawa. Released September 11, 2013.

Labour Force by Industry (NAICS Codes 53–91)

Area	Real estate & rental & leasing	Profess., scientific & tech. services	Mgmt of companies & enterprises	Admin. & support, waste mgmt & remed. services	Educational services	Health care & social assistance	Arts, entertain. & recreation	Accomm. & food services	Other services (except public admin.)	Public admin.
					Number					
					Total					
Chatham-Kent	715	1,545	0	2,550	3,095	5,930	790	3,400	2,350	2,310
Ontario	133,980	511,020	6,525	309,630	499,690	692,130	144,065	417,675	296,340	458,665
Canada	321,895	1,240,850	17,460	728,330	1,301,435	1,949,650	363,405	1,130,750	807,800	1,261,050
					Males					
Chatham-Kent	375	740	0	1,355	975	785	405	1,115	1,265	975
Ontario	72,835	281,420	3,540	172,475	162,765	120,165	75,035	177,240	133,795	236,655
Canada	179,090	688,625	9,380	411,250	424,915	349,430	188,270	469,990	372,940	652,510
					Females					
Chatham-Kent	335	805	0	1,195	2,125	5,145	380	2,285	1,095	1,335
Ontario	61,145	229,600	2,990	137,155	336,925	571,965	69,030	240,430	162,550	222,015
Canada	142,805	552,225	8,075	317,085	876,515	1,600,220	175,135	660,760	434,865	608,535
					Percent of Labour Force					
					Total					
Chatham-Kent	1.5	3.1	0.0	5.2	6.3	12.0	1.6	6.9	4.8	4.7
Ontario	2.0	7.6	0.1	4.6	7.5	10.4	2.2	6.3	4.4	6.9
Canada	1.8	7.1	0.1	4.1	7.4	11.1	2.1	6.4	4.6	7.2
					Males					
Chatham-Kent	1.5	2.9	0.0	5.3	3.8	3.1	1.6	4.3	4.9	3.8
Ontario	2.1	8.2	0.1	5.0	4.7	3.5	2.2	5.1	3.9	6.9
Canada	1.9	7.5	0.1	4.5	4.6	3.8	2.0	5.1	4.1	7.1
					Females					
Chatham-Kent	1.4	3.4	0.0	5.1	9.0	21.8	1.6	9.7	4.6	5.7
Ontario	1.9	7.1	0.1	4.2	10.4	17.7	2.1	7.4	5.0	6.9
Canada	1.7	6.6	0.1	3.8	10.4	19.1	2.1	7.9	5.2	7.2

Note: Figures are based on total experienced labour force 15 years and over. Experienced labour force refers to persons who, during the week of Sunday, May 1 to Saturday, May 7, 2011, were employed and the unemployed who had last worked for pay or in self-employment in either 2010 or 2011.
Source: Statistics Canada. 2013. 2011 National Household Survey. Statistics Canada Catalogue no. 99-004-XWE. Ottawa. Released September 11, 2013.

PROFILES / Chatham-Kent, Ontario

Occupation

Area	Mgmt	Business, Finance & Admin.	Natural/ Applied Sciences & Related	Health	Education, Law & Social, Community & Government Services	Art, Culture, Recreation & Sport	Sales & Service	Trades, Transport & Equip. Operators & Related	Natural Resources, Agri. & Related Production	Mfg & Utilities
Number										
Total										
Chatham-Kent	5,785	6,225	1,915	3,520	4,910	735	12,095	8,920	1,840	3,330
Ontario	770,580	1,138,330	494,500	392,695	801,465	206,420	1,550,260	868,515	106,810	350,685
Canada	1,963,600	2,902,045	1,237,775	1,107,200	2,064,675	503,415	4,068,170	2,537,775	397,930	805,040
Males										
Chatham-Kent	3,850	1,420	1,625	485	1,415	335	4,555	8,310	1,285	2,390
Ontario	474,655	352,505	384,345	78,330	264,570	96,055	673,880	812,280	82,610	233,565
Canada	1,229,460	854,190	966,355	217,520	676,550	232,535	1,745,705	2,385,615	318,945	564,300
Females										
Chatham-Kent	1,930	4,805	290	3,030	3,495	405	7,540	610	555	940
Ontario	295,920	785,825	110,150	314,370	536,895	110,370	876,380	56,230	24,200	117,115
Canada	734,140	2,047,855	271,415	889,675	1,388,130	270,875	2,322,465	152,165	78,980	240,740
Percent of Labour Force										
Total										
Chatham-Kent	11.7	12.6	3.9	7.1	10.0	1.5	24.5	18.1	3.7	6.8
Ontario	11.5	17.0	7.4	5.9	12.0	3.1	23.2	13.0	1.6	5.2
Canada	11.2	16.5	7.0	6.3	11.7	2.9	23.1	14.4	2.3	4.6
Males										
Chatham-Kent	15.0	5.5	6.3	1.9	5.5	1.3	17.7	32.4	5.0	9.3
Ontario	13.7	10.2	11.1	2.3	7.7	2.8	19.5	23.5	2.4	6.8
Canada	13.4	9.3	10.5	2.4	7.4	2.5	19.0	26.0	3.5	6.1
Females										
Chatham-Kent	8.2	20.4	1.2	12.8	14.8	1.7	31.9	2.6	2.4	4.0
Ontario	9.2	24.3	3.4	9.7	16.6	3.4	27.2	1.7	0.7	3.6
Canada	8.7	24.4	3.2	10.6	16.5	3.2	27.7	1.8	0.9	2.9

Note: Figures are based on total experienced labour force 15 years and over
Source: Statistics Canada. 2013. 2011 National Household Survey. Statistics Canada Catalogue no. 99-004-XWE. Ottawa. Released September 11, 2013.

Place of Work Status

Area	Worked at Home	Worked Outside Canada	No Fixed Workplace Address	Worked at Usual Place
Number				
Total				
Chatham-Kent	3,515	185	4,425	37,410
Ontario	423,790	31,390	670,835	5,170,980
Canada	1,142,640	66,460	1,868,245	13,517,690
Males				
Chatham-Kent	2,155	135	3,220	17,960
Ontario	216,900	21,150	486,560	2,524,555
Canada	582,150	47,355	1,400,485	6,604,325
Females				
Chatham-Kent	1,355	50	1,205	19,450
Ontario	206,895	10,240	184,275	2,646,420
Canada	560,490	19,100	467,760	6,913,370
Percent of Labour Force				
Total				
Chatham-Kent	7.7	0.4	9.7	82.2
Ontario	6.7	0.5	10.7	82.1
Canada	6.9	0.4	11.3	81.5
Males				
Chatham-Kent	9.2	0.6	13.7	76.5
Ontario	6.7	0.7	15.0	77.7
Canada	6.7	0.5	16.2	76.5
Females				
Chatham-Kent	6.1	0.2	5.5	88.2
Ontario	6.8	0.3	6.0	86.8
Canada	7.0	0.2	5.9	86.8

Note: Figures are based on total employed labour force 15 years and over.
Source: Statistics Canada. 2013. 2011 National Household Survey. Statistics Canada Catalogue no. 99-004-XWE. Ottawa. Released September 11, 2013.

PROFILES / Chatham-Kent, Ontario

Mode of Transportation to Work

Area	Car; Truck; Van; as Driver	Car; Truck; Van; as Passenger	Public Transit	Walked	Bicycled	All Other Modes
			Number			
			Total			
Chatham-Kent	36,310	2,190	545	2,030	425	345
Ontario	4,235,315	357,110	818,270	299,095	69,885	62,145
Canada	11,393,140	867,050	1,851,525	880,815	201,780	191,625
			Males			
Chatham-Kent	18,540	1,085	240	785	320	215
Ontario	2,316,680	143,410	340,995	131,765	47,635	30,635
Canada	6,238,835	349,530	788,290	387,580	135,840	104,725
			Females			
Chatham-Kent	17,770	1,105	310	1,245	100	125
Ontario	1,918,640	213,700	477,275	167,325	22,250	31,515
Canada	5,154,305	517,520	1,063,235	493,230	65,940	86,900
			Percent of Labour Force			
			Total			
Chatham-Kent	86.8	5.2	1.3	4.9	1.0	0.8
Ontario	72.5	6.1	14.0	5.1	1.2	1.1
Canada	74.0	5.6	12.0	5.7	1.3	1.2
			Males			
Chatham-Kent	87.5	5.1	1.1	3.7	1.5	1.0
Ontario	76.9	4.8	11.3	4.4	1.6	1.0
Canada	77.9	4.4	9.8	4.8	1.7	1.3
			Females			
Chatham-Kent	86.0	5.3	1.5	6.0	0.5	0.6
Ontario	67.8	7.5	16.9	5.9	0.8	1.1
Canada	69.8	7.0	14.4	6.7	0.9	1.2

Note: Figures are based on total employed labour force 15 years and over.
Source: Statistics Canada. 2013. 2011 National Household Survey. Statistics Canada Catalogue no. 99-004-XWE. Ottawa. Released September 11, 2013.

Visible Minority Population Characteristics

Area	Total Minority	South Asian[1]	Chinese	Black	Filipino	Latin American	Arab	SE Asian[2]	West Asian[3]	Korean	Japanese	Multiple[4]
						Number						
						Total						
Chatham-Kent	4,010	485	215	1,890	220	350	35	265	80	205	140	80
Ontario	3,279,565	965,990	629,140	539,205	275,380	172,560	151,645	137,875	122,530	78,290	29,085	96,735
Canada	6,264,750	1,567,400	1,324,750	945,665	619,310	381,280	380,620	312,075	206,840	161,130	87,270	171,935
						Males						
Chatham-Kent	2,040	250	85	995	65	185	25	125	20	125	80	55
Ontario	1,582,480	484,355	301,575	251,295	116,825	83,205	79,620	67,645	62,515	38,045	13,345	46,765
Canada	3,043,010	790,755	632,325	453,005	268,885	186,355	203,485	154,035	105,620	77,165	38,270	83,335
						Females						
Chatham-Kent	1,975	235	135	890	150	170	0	140	60	80	60	20
Ontario	1,697,085	481,635	327,570	287,915	158,555	89,360	72,025	70,230	60,010	40,250	15,740	49,970
Canada	3,221,745	776,650	692,420	492,660	350,425	194,925	177,140	158,045	101,220	83,965	48,990	88,600
						Percent of Population						
						Total						
Chatham-Kent	3.9	0.5	0.2	1.9	0.2	0.3	0.0	0.3	0.1	0.2	0.1	0.1
Ontario	25.9	7.6	5.0	4.3	2.2	1.4	1.2	1.1	1.0	0.6	0.2	0.8
Canada	19.1	4.8	4.0	2.9	1.9	1.2	1.2	0.9	0.6	0.5	0.3	0.5
						Males						
Chatham-Kent	4.1	0.5	0.2	2.0	0.1	0.4	0.1	0.3	0.0	0.3	0.2	0.1
Ontario	25.6	7.8	4.9	4.1	1.9	1.3	1.3	1.1	1.0	0.6	0.2	0.8
Canada	18.8	4.9	3.9	2.8	1.7	1.2	1.3	1.0	0.7	0.5	0.2	0.5
						Females						
Chatham-Kent	3.8	0.5	0.3	1.7	0.3	0.3	0.0	0.3	0.1	0.2	0.1	0.0
Ontario	26.2	7.4	5.1	4.4	2.5	1.4	1.1	1.1	0.9	0.6	0.2	0.8
Canada	19.3	4.7	4.1	3.0	2.1	1.2	1.1	0.9	0.6	0.5	0.3	0.5

Note: The Employment Equity Act defines visible minorities as 'persons, other than Aboriginal peoples, who are non-Caucasian in race or non-white in colour';
(1) Includes 'East Indian,' 'Pakistani,' 'Sri Lankan,' etc.; (2) Includes 'Vietnamese,' 'Cambodian,' 'Malaysian,' 'Laotian,' etc.; (3) Includes 'Iranian,' 'Afghan,' etc.; (4) Includes respondents who reported more than one visible minority group by checking two or more mark-in circles, e.g., 'Black' and 'South Asian.'
Source: Statistics Canada. 2013. 2011 National Household Survey. Statistics Canada Catalogue no. 99-004-XWE. Ottawa. Released September 11, 2013.

PROFILES / Chatham-Kent, Ontario

Aboriginal Population

Area	Aboriginal Identity[1]	First Nations (North American Indian) Single Identity[2]	Métis Single Identity	Inuk (Inuit) Single Identity	Multiple Aboriginal Identities[3]	Aboriginal Identities Not Included Elsewhere
Number						
Total						
Chatham-Kent	2,910	1,760	950	0	85	95
Ontario	301,430	201,100	86,020	3,355	2,910	8,040
Canada	1,400,685	851,560	451,795	59,440	11,415	26,475
Males						
Chatham-Kent	1,495	865	520	0	70	40
Ontario	145,020	96,620	41,755	1,475	1,420	3,750
Canada	682,190	411,785	223,335	29,495	5,525	12,055
Females						
Chatham-Kent	1,415	890	440	0	0	55
Ontario	156,410	104,485	44,260	1,880	1,490	4,295
Canada	718,500	439,775	228,460	29,950	5,890	14,420
Percent of Population						
Total						
Chatham-Kent	2.9	1.7	0.9	0.0	0.1	0.1
Ontario	2.4	1.6	0.7	0.0	0.0	0.1
Canada	4.3	2.6	1.4	0.2	0.0	0.1
Males						
Chatham-Kent	3.0	1.7	1.0	0.0	0.1	0.1
Ontario	2.3	1.6	0.7	0.0	0.0	0.1
Canada	4.2	2.5	1.4	0.2	0.0	0.1
Females						
Chatham-Kent	2.7	1.7	0.8	0.0	0.0	0.1
Ontario	2.4	1.6	0.7	0.0	0.0	0.1
Canada	4.3	2.6	1.4	0.2	0.0	0.1

Note: (1) Includes persons who reported being an Aboriginal person, that is, First Nations (North American Indian), Métis or Inuk (Inuit) and/or those who reported Registered or Treaty Indian status, that is registered under the Indian Act of Canada, and/or those who reported membership in a First Nation or Indian band. Aboriginal peoples of Canada are defined in the Constitution Act, 1982, section 35-2 as including the Indian, Inuit and Métis peoples of Canada; (2) Users should be aware that the estimates associated with this variable are more affected than most by the incomplete enumeration of certain Indian reserves and Indian settlements in the National Household Survey (NHS); (3) Includes persons who reported being any two or all three of the following: First Nations (North American Indian), Métis or Inuk (Inuit).
Source: Statistics Canada. 2013. 2011 National Household Survey. Statistics Canada Catalogue no. 99-004-XWE. Ottawa. Released September 11, 2013.

Ethnic Origin

Area	North American Aboriginal	Other North American	European	Caribbean	Latin, Central and South American	African	Asian	Oceania
Number								
Total								
Chatham-Kent	4,305	38,970	77,625	310	1,495	895	2,185	75
Ontario	441,395	3,059,480	8,231,410	396,485	271,545	331,460	2,604,595	19,410
Canada	1,836,035	11,070,455	20,157,965	627,590	544,375	766,735	5,011,225	74,875
Males								
Chatham-Kent	1,945	19,080	37,650	140	755	455	995	45
Ontario	210,490	1,507,105	4,019,885	181,805	130,035	160,940	1,265,540	9,855
Canada	885,675	5,462,685	9,913,150	291,640	264,635	387,360	2,435,540	37,490
Females								
Chatham-Kent	2,360	19,890	39,975	165	740	445	1,185	30
Ontario	230,905	1,552,380	4,211,525	214,675	141,510	170,515	1,339,050	9,555
Canada	950,360	5,607,770	10,244,820	335,945	279,740	379,380	2,575,680	37,385
Percent of Population								
Total								
Chatham-Kent	4.2	38.3	76.3	0.3	1.5	0.9	2.1	0.1
Ontario	3.5	24.2	65.1	3.1	2.1	2.6	20.6	0.2
Canada	5.6	33.7	61.4	1.9	1.7	2.3	15.3	0.2
Males								
Chatham-Kent	3.9	38.4	75.7	0.3	1.5	0.9	2.0	0.1
Ontario	3.4	24.4	65.0	2.9	2.1	2.6	20.5	0.2
Canada	5.5	33.8	61.3	1.8	1.6	2.4	15.1	0.2
Females								
Chatham-Kent	4.5	38.3	76.9	0.3	1.4	0.9	2.3	0.1
Ontario	3.6	24.0	65.1	3.3	2.2	2.6	20.7	0.1
Canada	5.7	33.6	61.4	2.0	1.7	2.3	15.4	0.2

Note: The sum of the ethnic groups in this table is greater than the total population estimate because a person may report more than one ethnic origin in the NHS.
Source: Statistics Canada. 2013. 2011 National Household Survey. Statistics Canada Catalogue no. 99-004-XWE. Ottawa. Released September 11, 2013.

Religion

Area	Buddhist	Christian	Hindu	Jewish	Muslim	Sikh	Traditional (Aboriginal) Spirituality	Other Religions	No Religious Affiliation
				Number Total					
Chatham-Kent	130	79,145	155	65	335	30	55	170	21,600
Ontario	163,750	8,167,295	366,720	195,540	581,950	179,765	15,905	53,080	2,927,790
Canada	366,830	22,102,745	497,965	329,495	1,053,945	454,965	64,935	130,835	7,850,605
				Males					
Chatham-Kent	75	37,525	80	0	165	25	30	80	11,715
Ontario	75,355	3,839,925	183,580	95,795	293,925	90,515	7,600	23,555	1,571,195
Canada	168,465	10,497,775	250,435	161,265	540,555	229,435	31,805	57,745	4,225,645
				Females					
Chatham-Kent	60	41,620	75	35	165	0	20	90	9,890
Ontario	88,395	4,327,365	183,140	99,740	288,025	89,250	8,310	29,525	1,356,600
Canada	198,365	11,604,975	247,525	168,235	513,395	225,530	33,135	73,090	3,624,965
				Percent of Population Total					
Chatham-Kent	0.1	77.8	0.2	0.1	0.3	0.0	0.1	0.2	21.2
Ontario	1.3	64.6	2.9	1.5	4.6	1.4	0.1	0.4	23.1
Canada	1.1	67.3	1.5	1.0	3.2	1.4	0.2	0.4	23.9
				Males					
Chatham-Kent	0.2	75.5	0.2	0.0	0.3	0.1	0.1	0.2	23.6
Ontario	1.2	62.1	3.0	1.5	4.8	1.5	0.1	0.4	25.4
Canada	1.0	64.9	1.5	1.0	3.3	1.4	0.2	0.4	26.1
				Females					
Chatham-Kent	0.1	80.1	0.1	0.1	0.3	0.0	0.0	0.2	19.0
Ontario	1.4	66.9	2.8	1.5	4.5	1.4	0.1	0.5	21.0
Canada	1.2	69.5	1.5	1.0	3.1	1.4	0.2	0.4	21.7

Note: Religion refers to the person's self-identification as having a connection or affiliation with any religious denomination, group, body, sect, cult or other religiously defined community or system of belief. Religion is not limited to formal membership in a religious organization or group. Persons without a religious connection or affiliation can self-identify as atheist, agnostic or humanist, or can provide another applicable response.
Source: Statistics Canada. 2013. 2011 National Household Survey. Statistics Canada Catalogue no. 99-004-XWE. Ottawa. Released September 11, 2013.

Religion—Christian Denominations

Area	Anglican	Baptist	Catholic	Christian Orthodox	Lutheran	Pentecostal	Presbyterian	United Church	Other Christian
				Number Total					
Chatham-Kent	6,505	4,105	34,005	325	495	1,980	3,520	12,815	15,395
Ontario	774,560	244,650	3,976,610	297,710	163,460	213,945	319,585	952,465	1,224,300
Canada	1,631,845	635,840	12,810,705	550,690	478,185	478,705	472,385	2,007,610	3,036,780
				Males					
Chatham-Kent	2,980	1,765	16,440	170	240	875	1,725	5,910	7,420
Ontario	355,175	112,285	1,895,940	145,825	75,225	94,955	148,535	435,255	576,730
Canada	752,945	293,905	6,167,290	270,205	221,525	217,850	218,955	912,545	1,442,550
				Females					
Chatham-Kent	3,525	2,340	17,560	155	250	1,100	1,795	6,910	7,975
Ontario	419,390	132,370	2,080,665	151,885	88,230	118,990	171,050	517,210	647,570
Canada	878,900	341,940	6,643,415	280,485	256,660	260,850	253,430	1,095,065	1,594,230
				Percent of Population Total					
Chatham-Kent	6.4	4.0	33.4	0.3	0.5	1.9	3.5	12.6	15.1
Ontario	6.1	1.9	31.4	2.4	1.3	1.7	2.5	7.5	9.7
Canada	5.0	1.9	39.0	1.7	1.5	1.5	1.4	6.1	9.2
				Males					
Chatham-Kent	6.0	3.5	33.1	0.3	0.5	1.8	3.5	11.9	14.9
Ontario	5.7	1.8	30.7	2.4	1.2	1.5	2.4	7.0	9.3
Canada	4.7	1.8	38.2	1.7	1.4	1.3	1.4	5.6	8.9
				Females					
Chatham-Kent	6.8	4.5	33.8	0.3	0.5	2.1	3.5	13.3	15.3
Ontario	6.5	2.0	32.2	2.3	1.4	1.8	2.6	8.0	10.0
Canada	5.3	2.0	39.8	1.7	1.5	1.6	1.5	6.6	9.6

Note: Religion refers to the person's self-identification as having a connection or affiliation with any religious denomination, group, body, sect, cult or other religiously defined community or system of belief. Religion is not limited to formal membership in a religious organization or group. Persons without a religious connection or affiliation can self-identify as atheist, agnostic or humanist, or can provide another applicable response.
Source: Statistics Canada. 2013. 2011 National Household Survey. Statistics Canada Catalogue no. 99-004-XWE. Ottawa. Released September 11, 2013.

PROFILES / Chatham-Kent, Ontario

Immigrant Status and Period of Immigration

Area	Non-Immigrants[1]	Immigrants All	Before 1971	1971 to 1980	1981 to 1990	1991 to 2000	2001 to 2005	2006 to 2011	Non-Permanent Residents[3]
				Number					
				Total					
Chatham-Kent	92,700	8,695	3,620	1,195	1,265	1,170	910	530	285
Ontario	8,906,000	3,611,365	723,030	464,380	538,285	866,220	518,405	501,060	134,425
Canada	25,720,175	6,775,765	1,261,055	870,775	949,890	1,539,050	992,070	1,162,915	356,385
				Males					
Chatham-Kent	45,390	4,190	1,660	620	595	620	415	265	150
Ontario	4,410,240	1,706,385	341,820	217,990	258,095	408,270	245,850	234,360	64,825
Canada	12,753,235	3,231,370	605,430	416,670	454,570	724,905	474,545	555,245	178,515
				Females					
Chatham-Kent	47,310	4,505	1,960	575	670	555	490	270	135
Ontario	4,495,765	1,904,985	381,210	246,390	280,190	457,950	272,550	266,695	69,600
Canada	12,966,935	3,544,400	655,625	454,105	495,325	814,145	517,530	607,670	177,870
				Percent of Population					
				Total					
Chatham-Kent	91.2	8.6	3.6	1.2	1.2	1.2	0.9	0.5	0.3
Ontario	70.4	28.5	5.7	3.7	4.3	6.8	4.1	4.0	1.1
Canada	78.3	20.6	3.8	2.7	2.9	4.7	3.0	3.5	1.1
				Males					
Chatham-Kent	91.3	8.4	3.3	1.2	1.2	1.2	0.8	0.5	0.3
Ontario	71.3	27.6	5.5	3.5	4.2	6.6	4.0	3.8	1.0
Canada	78.9	20.0	3.7	2.6	2.8	4.5	2.9	3.4	1.1
				Females					
Chatham-Kent	91.1	8.7	3.8	1.1	1.3	1.1	0.9	0.5	0.3
Ontario	69.5	29.4	5.9	3.8	4.3	7.1	4.2	4.1	1.1
Canada	77.7	21.2	3.9	2.7	3.0	4.9	3.1	3.6	1.1

Note: (1) Non-immigrant refers to a person who is a Canadian citizen by birth; (2) Immigrant refers to a person who is or has ever been a landed immigrant/permanent resident. This person has been granted the right to live in Canada permanently by immigration authorities. Some immigrants have resided in Canada for a number of years, while others have arrived recently. Some immigrants are Canadian citizens, while others are not. Most immigrants are born outside Canada, but a small number are born in Canada. In the 2011 National Household Survey, 'Immigrants' includes immigrants who landed in Canada prior to May 10, 2011; (3) Non-permanent resident refers to a person from another country who has a work or study permit, or who is a refugee claimant, and any non-Canadian-born family member living in Canada with them.
Source: Statistics Canada. 2013. 2011 National Household Survey. Statistics Canada Catalogue no. 99-004-XWE. Ottawa. Released September 11, 2013.

Mother Tongue

Area	English	French	Non-official Language	English & French	English & Non-official Language	French & Non-official Language	English, French & Non-official Language
			Number				
			Total				
Chatham-Kent	89,795	2,915	8,735	360	495	40	20
Ontario	8,677,040	493,300	3,264,435	46,605	219,425	13,645	7,615
Canada	18,858,980	7,054,975	6,567,680	144,685	396,330	74,430	24,095
			Males				
Chatham-Kent	43,925	1,390	4,260	165	235	20	10
Ontario	4,276,970	232,785	1,562,190	21,805	106,790	6,285	3,495
Canada	9,345,225	3,452,380	3,157,785	69,975	192,000	36,535	11,965
			Females				
Chatham-Kent	45,865	1,525	4,475	195	260	20	5
Ontario	4,400,065	260,510	1,702,240	24,795	112,635	7,365	4,115
Canada	9,513,750	3,602,590	3,409,895	74,710	204,330	37,890	12,130
			Percent of Population				
			Total				
Chatham-Kent	87.7	2.8	8.5	0.4	0.5	0.0	0.0
Ontario	68.2	3.9	25.7	0.4	1.7	0.1	0.1
Canada	56.9	21.3	19.8	0.4	1.2	0.2	0.1
			Males				
Chatham-Kent	87.8	2.8	8.5	0.3	0.5	0.0	0.0
Ontario	68.9	3.7	25.2	0.4	1.7	0.1	0.1
Canada	57.5	21.2	19.4	0.4	1.2	0.2	0.1
			Females				
Chatham-Kent	87.6	2.9	8.5	0.4	0.5	0.0	0.0
Ontario	67.6	4.0	26.1	0.4	1.7	0.1	0.1
Canada	56.4	21.4	20.2	0.4	1.2	0.2	0.1

Note: Figures cover total population excluding institutional residents.
Source: Statistics Canada. 2012. Census Profile. 2011 Census. Statistics Canada Catalogue no. 98-316-XWE. Ottawa. Released October 24 2012.
http://www12.statcan.gc.ca/census-recensement/2011/dp-pd/prof/index.cfm?Lang=E

Language Spoken Most Often at Home

Area	English	French	Non-official Language	English & French	English & Non-official Language	French & Non-official Language	English, French & Non-official Language
			Number				
			Total				
Chatham-Kent	97,030	640	3,590	195	875	5	15
Ontario	10,044,810	284,115	1,827,870	37,955	509,105	6,370	11,845
Canada	21,457,075	6,827,865	3,673,865	131,205	875,135	109,700	46,330
			Males				
Chatham-Kent	47,420	290	1,785	90	410	0	5
Ontario	4,930,610	133,495	872,860	17,250	248,050	2,855	5,225
Canada	10,585,620	3,348,235	1,767,310	63,475	425,370	53,010	22,845
			Females				
Chatham-Kent	49,610	350	1,800	110	460	5	10
Ontario	5,114,200	150,620	955,010	20,705	261,055	3,520	6,620
Canada	10,871,455	3,479,625	1,906,555	67,730	449,765	56,690	23,485
			Percent of Population				
			Total				
Chatham-Kent	94.8	0.6	3.5	0.2	0.9	0.0	0.0
Ontario	79.0	2.2	14.4	0.3	4.0	0.1	0.1
Canada	64.8	20.6	11.1	0.4	2.6	0.3	0.1
			Males				
Chatham-Kent	94.8	0.6	3.6	0.2	0.8	0.0	0.0
Ontario	79.4	2.1	14.1	0.3	4.0	0.0	0.1
Canada	65.1	20.6	10.9	0.4	2.6	0.3	0.1
			Females				
Chatham-Kent	94.8	0.7	3.4	0.2	0.9	0.0	0.0
Ontario	78.5	2.3	14.7	0.3	4.0	0.1	0.1
Canada	64.5	20.6	11.3	0.4	2.7	0.3	0.1

Note: Figures cover total population excluding institutional residents.
Source: Statistics Canada. 2012. Census Profile. 2011 Census. Statistics Canada Catalogue no. 98-316-XWE. Ottawa. Released October 24 2012.
http://www12.statcan.gc.ca/census-recensement/2011/dp-pd/prof/index.cfm?Lang=E

Knowledge of Official Languages

Area	English Only	French Only	English & French	Neither English nor French
		Number		
		Total		
Chatham-Kent	94,615	75	7,060	605
Ontario	10,984,360	42,980	1,395,805	298,920
Canada	22,564,665	4,165,015	5,795,570	595,920
		Males		
Chatham-Kent	46,490	25	3,215	270
Ontario	5,445,050	18,805	627,725	118,765
Canada	11,222,185	1,925,340	2,876,560	241,790
		Females		
Chatham-Kent	48,120	50	3,850	335
Ontario	5,539,310	24,175	768,085	180,155
Canada	11,342,485	2,239,680	2,919,005	354,135
		Percent of Population		
		Total		
Chatham-Kent	92.4	0.1	6.9	0.6
Ontario	86.3	0.3	11.0	2.3
Canada	68.1	12.6	17.5	1.8
		Males		
Chatham-Kent	93.0	0.0	6.4	0.5
Ontario	87.7	0.3	10.1	1.9
Canada	69.0	11.8	17.7	1.5
		Females		
Chatham-Kent	91.9	0.1	7.4	0.6
Ontario	85.1	0.4	11.8	2.8
Canada	67.3	13.3	17.3	2.1

Note: Figures cover total population excluding institutional residents.
Source: Statistics Canada. 2012. Census Profile. 2011 Census. Statistics Canada Catalogue no. 98-316-XWE. Ottawa. Released October 24 2012.
http://www12.statcan.gc.ca/census-recensement/2011/dp-pd/prof/index.cfm?Lang=E

Coquitlam, British Columbia

Background

Coquitlam is located in the Lower Mainland of British Columbia and is a member of Metro Vancouver, the province's largest city. The City of Coquitlam is 30 minutes from downtown Vancouver and 40 minutes from the U.S. border. Coquitlam is one of the fastest growing communities in the Metro Vancouver region and is expected to grow to 224,000 people by 2041.

The Coquitlam area was first inhabited by the Coast Salish First Nation. In 1891, the municipality was incorporated and became a lumber mill town attracting hundreds of French Canadian loggers from Québec. The loggers' Francophone neighbourhood, Maillardville, is still present today.

Coquitlam has more than 80 municipal parks and natural areas. The city also has access to provincial and regional parks such as Pinecone Burke Provincial Park (38,000 hectares) and Colony Farm Regional Park (404 hectares).

Professional services, retail/wholesale trade, manufacturing, technology, public administration, transportation and construction are Coquitlam's primary labour sectors. The construction of the Evergreen Rapid Transit Line linking Coquitlam to Vancouver in 2016 is expected to generate over 8,000 direct and indirect jobs for the region.

Coquitlam is home to diverse communities such as Kwikwetlem First Nation and Maillardville, the province's only Francophone neighbourhood. Large communities of Chinese, Korean and Iranian residents also live in Coquitlam. In 2009, Coquitlam was designated a Cultural Capital of Canada in recognition of the city's support for local diversity, culture and heritage.

Every year the city hosts more than 100 festivals and events such the Festival du Bois, Treefest, the BC Highland Games and the Korean Cultural Heritage Day Festival.

Coquitlam has summer highs of plus 21.03 degrees Celsius, winter lows of plus 1.03 degrees Celsius, and an average rainfall just over 1896 mm per year.

Rankings

- The Association of Consulting Engineering Companies (ACEC) and *Canadian Consulting Engineer Magazine* ranked Coquitlam's Poirier Sport and Leisure Complex as one of the most imaginative and innovative engineering projects in Canada. Out of 63 entries, the Poirier project won the 2011 Award of Excellence in the building category. The $62-million sports complex project was completed 10 months ahead of schedule and several million dollars under budget. *Association of Consulting Engineering Companies, 2011 Award Winners, November 1st, 2011*
- Statistics Canada ranked Coquitlam as one of the fastest growing cities in Canada. In 2011, Coquitlam (City) had a population of 126,456, representing growth of 10.4% from 2006. Coquitlam's growth is nearly double the national average of 5.9%. The 2011 Census also reported that the number of census families in Coquitlam increased by 11.5% since 2006, compared to the national average for Canada of 5.5%. *Statistics Canada. 2012. Focus on Geography Series, 2011 Census, September 19th, 2011*
- In 2009, the Department of Canadian Heritage ranked the City of Coquitlam one of Canada's "Cultural Capitals." Coquitlam was ranked in the 50,000 to 125,000 population category. The city was rewarded for supporting local arts, culture and cultural diversity. The city's success in preserving its Francophone heritage and the successful launch of the "Intercultural Celebrations: Past, Present and Future" project received special mention. Other 2009 Cultural Capitals of Canada winners in the same population category were Guelph (ON), Lethbridge (AB), Red Deer (AB) and Saint-Jean-Sur-Richelieu (QC). *Department of Canadian Heritage, Cultural Capitals of Canada national award program, 2009*

PROFILES / Coquitlam, British Columbia

Population Growth and Density

Area	Population in 2001	Population in 2006	Population in 2011	Population Change 2001–2006	Population Change 2006–2011	Land Area (sq. km)	Population Density per sq. km
Coquitlam	112,890	114,565	126,456	1.5	10.4	122.30	1,034.0
British Columbia	3,907,738	4,113,487	4,400,057	5.3	7.0	922,509.29	4.8
Canada	30,007,094	31,612,897	33,476,688	5.4	5.9	8,965,121.42	3.7

Source: Statistics Canada. 2012. Census Profile. 2011 Census. Statistics Canada Catalogue no. 98-316-XWE. Ottawa. Released October 24 2012.
http://www12.statcan.gc.ca/census-recensement/2011/dp-pd/prof/index.cfm?Lang=E;
Statistics Canada 2007. 2006 Community Profiles. 2006 Census. Statistics Canada Catalogue no. 92-591-XWE. Ottawa. Released March 13 2007.
http://www12.statcan.ca/census-recensement/2006/dp-pd/prof/92-591/index.cfm?Lang=E

Gender

Area	Males	Females
Number		
Coquitlam	62,100	64,355
British Columbia	2,156,600	2,243,455
Canada	16,414,225	17,062,460
Percent of Population		
Coquitlam	49.1	50.9
British Columbia	49.0	51.0
Canada	49.0	51.0

Source: Statistics Canada. 2012. Census Profile. 2011 Census. Statistics Canada Catalogue no. 98-316-XWE. Ottawa. Released October 24 2012.
http://www12.statcan.gc.ca/census-recensement/2011/dp-pd/prof/index.cfm?Lang=E

Marital Status

Area	Married[1]	Living Common-law	Single[2]	Separated	Divorced	Widowed
Number — Total						
Coquitlam	56,265	5,985	30,820	2,480	5,565	4,630
British Columbia	1,832,605	321,965	1,014,270	102,040	246,515	205,300
Canada	12,941,960	3,142,525	7,816,045	698,240	1,686,035	1,584,530
Males						
Coquitlam	27,925	2,995	16,690	945	2,050	835
British Columbia	913,430	161,530	550,830	43,570	98,130	41,550
Canada	6,470,300	1,575,495	4,206,320	299,655	680,415	310,940
Females						
Coquitlam	28,345	2,990	14,130	1,535	3,515	3,800
British Columbia	919,175	160,435	463,435	58,470	148,385	163,750
Canada	6,471,660	1,567,035	3,609,730	398,585	1,005,620	1,273,590
Percent of Population — Total						
Coquitlam	53.2	5.7	29.1	2.3	5.3	4.4
British Columbia	49.2	8.6	27.2	2.7	6.6	5.5
Canada	46.4	11.3	28.0	2.5	6.0	5.7
Males						
Coquitlam	54.3	5.8	32.4	1.8	4.0	1.6
British Columbia	50.5	8.9	30.4	2.4	5.4	2.3
Canada	47.8	11.6	31.1	2.2	5.0	2.3
Females						
Coquitlam	52.2	5.5	26.0	2.8	6.5	7.0
British Columbia	48.0	8.4	24.2	3.1	7.8	8.6
Canada	45.2	10.9	25.2	2.8	7.0	8.9

Note: (1) and not separated, (2) never legally married
Source: Statistics Canada. 2012. Census Profile. 2011 Census. Statistics Canada Catalogue no. 98-316-XWE. Ottawa. Released October 24 2012.
http://www12.statcan.gc.ca/census-recensement/2011/dp-pd/prof/index.cfm?Lang=E

Age Characteristics: 0 to 49 Years

Area	0 to 4 Years	5 to 9 Years	10 to 14 Years	15 to 19 Years	20 to 24 Years	25 to 29 Years	30 to 34 Years	35 to 39 Years	40 to 44 Years	45 to 49 Years
					Number					
					Total					
Coquitlam	6,490	6,710	7,500	9,170	9,090	7,935	7,445	8,200	10,415	11,175
British Columbia	219,665	218,915	238,780	275,165	279,825	288,780	275,985	280,870	313,765	350,600
Canada	1,877,095	1,809,895	1,920,355	2,178,135	2,187,450	2,169,590	2,162,905	2,173,930	2,324,875	2,675,130
					Males					
Coquitlam	3,240	3,535	3,880	4,745	4,760	4,055	3,620	3,800	4,815	5,410
British Columbia	112,885	112,200	122,465	141,670	142,290	143,475	135,220	135,455	151,430	170,580
Canada	961,150	925,965	983,995	1,115,845	1,108,775	1,077,275	1,058,810	1,064,200	1,141,720	1,318,715
					Females					
Coquitlam	3,250	3,170	3,620	4,425	4,325	3,880	3,830	4,400	5,600	5,765
British Columbia	106,775	106,715	116,315	133,500	137,535	145,305	140,755	145,415	162,335	180,020
Canada	915,945	883,935	936,360	1,062,295	1,078,670	1,092,315	1,104,095	1,109,735	1,183,155	1,356,420
					Percent of Population					
					Total					
Coquitlam	5.1	5.3	5.9	7.3	7.2	6.3	5.9	6.5	8.2	8.8
British Columbia	5.0	5.0	5.4	6.3	6.4	6.6	6.3	6.4	7.1	8.0
Canada	5.6	5.4	5.7	6.5	6.5	6.5	6.5	6.5	6.9	8.0
					Males					
Coquitlam	5.2	5.7	6.2	7.6	7.7	6.5	5.8	6.1	7.8	8.7
British Columbia	5.2	5.2	5.7	6.6	6.6	6.7	6.3	6.3	7.0	7.9
Canada	5.9	5.6	6.0	6.8	6.8	6.6	6.5	6.5	7.0	8.0
					Females					
Coquitlam	5.1	4.9	5.6	6.9	6.7	6.0	6.0	6.8	8.7	9.0
British Columbia	4.8	4.8	5.2	6.0	6.1	6.5	6.3	6.5	7.2	8.0
Canada	5.4	5.2	5.5	6.2	6.3	6.4	6.5	6.5	6.9	7.9

Source: Statistics Canada. 2012. Census Profile. 2011 Census. Statistics Canada Catalogue no. 98-316-XWE. Ottawa. Released October 24 2012.
http://www12.statcan.gc.ca/census-recensement/2011/dp-pd/prof/index.cfm?Lang=E

Age Characteristics: 50 Years and Over, and Median Age

Area	50 to 54 Years	55 to 59 Years	60 to 64 Years	65 to 69 Years	70 to 74 Years	75 to 79 Years	80 to 84 Years	85 Years and Over	Median Age
				Number					
				Total					
Coquitlam	11,110	9,160	6,985	4,755	3,740	2,820	1,960	1,800	40.3
British Columbia	354,610	323,335	291,040	210,900	160,715	127,480	96,945	92,675	41.9
Canada	2,658,965	2,340,635	2,052,670	1,521,715	1,153,065	922,700	702,070	645,515	40.6
				Males					
Coquitlam	5,350	4,600	3,440	2,355	1,720	1,325	840	600	39.3
British Columbia	172,060	157,455	142,645	103,785	77,350	60,720	42,745	32,150	41.1
Canada	1,309,030	1,147,300	1,002,690	738,010	543,435	417,945	291,085	208,300	39.6
				Females					
Coquitlam	5,755	4,560	3,540	2,400	2,020	1,485	1,115	1,200	41.2
British Columbia	182,550	165,880	148,395	107,115	83,360	66,760	54,200	60,520	42.7
Canada	1,349,940	1,193,335	1,049,985	783,705	609,630	504,755	410,985	437,215	41.5
				Percent of Population					
				Total					
Coquitlam	8.8	7.2	5.5	3.8	3.0	2.2	1.5	1.4	–
British Columbia	8.1	7.3	6.6	4.8	3.7	2.9	2.2	2.1	–
Canada	7.9	7.0	6.1	4.5	3.4	2.8	2.1	1.9	–
				Males					
Coquitlam	8.6	7.4	5.5	3.8	2.8	2.1	1.4	1.0	–
British Columbia	8.0	7.3	6.6	4.8	3.6	2.8	2.0	1.5	–
Canada	8.0	7.0	6.1	4.5	3.3	2.5	1.8	1.3	–
				Females					
Coquitlam	8.9	7.1	5.5	3.7	3.1	2.3	1.7	1.9	–
British Columbia	8.1	7.4	6.6	4.8	3.7	3.0	2.4	2.7	–
Canada	7.9	7.0	6.2	4.6	3.6	3.0	2.4	2.6	–

Source: Statistics Canada. 2012. Census Profile. 2011 Census. Statistics Canada Catalogue no. 98-316-XWE. Ottawa. Released October 24 2012.
http://www12.statcan.gc.ca/census-recensement/2011/dp-pd/prof/index.cfm?Lang=E

PROFILES / Coquitlam, British Columbia

Private Households by Household Size

Area	1 Person	2 Persons	3 Persons	4 Persons	5 Persons	6 or More Persons	Average Number of Persons in Private Households
			Households				
Coquitlam	9,750	13,400	8,610	9,075	3,065	1,655	2.7
British Columbia	498,925	613,270	264,135	237,725	91,600	58,985	2.5
Canada	3,673,310	4,544,820	2,081,900	1,903,300	724,405	392,885	2.5
			Percent of Households				
Coquitlam	21.4	29.4	18.9	19.9	6.7	3.6	–
British Columbia	28.3	34.8	15.0	13.5	5.2	3.3	–
Canada	27.6	34.1	15.6	14.3	5.4	2.9	–

Source: Statistics Canada. 2012. Census Profile. 2011 Census. Statistics Canada Catalogue no. 98-316-XWE. Ottawa. Released October 24 2012.
http://www12.statcan.gc.ca/census-recensement/2011/dp-pd/prof/index.cfm?Lang=E

Dwelling Type

Area	Single-detached House	Semi-detached House	Row House	Apartment: Building with Five or More Storeys	Apartment: Building with Fewer Than Five Storeys	Duplex Apartment	Movable Dwelling	Other Single-attached House
				Number				
Coquitlam	20,155	1,380	3,875	3,535	10,230	6,065	290	25
British Columbia	842,120	52,825	130,365	143,970	361,150	184,355	46,960	2,885
Canada	7,329,150	646,245	791,600	1,234,770	2,397,550	704,485	183,510	33,310
				Percent of Dwellings				
Coquitlam	44.2	3.0	8.5	7.8	22.5	13.3	0.6	0.1
British Columbia	47.7	3.0	7.4	8.2	20.5	10.4	2.7	0.2
Canada	55.0	4.9	5.9	9.3	18.0	5.3	1.4	0.3

Source: Statistics Canada. 2012. Census Profile. 2011 Census. Statistics Canada Catalogue no. 98-316-XWE. Ottawa. Released October 24 2012.
http://www12.statcan.gc.ca/census-recensement/2011/dp-pd/prof/index.cfm?Lang=E

Shelter Costs

	Owned Dwellings				Rented Dwellings		
Area	Number	Median Value[1] ($)	Average Value[1] ($)	Median Monthly Costs[2] ($)	Average Monthly Costs[2] ($)	Number	Median Monthly Costs[3] ($)	Average Monthly Costs[3] ($)
Coquitlam	33,875	599,465	588,265	1,310	1,421	11,675	949	1,035
British Columbia	1,202,000	448,835	543,635	1,023	1,228	519,855	903	989
Canada	9,013,410	280,552	345,182	978	1,141	4,060,385	784	848

Note: All figures cover non-farm, non-reserve private dwellings; (1) Refers to the dollar amount expected by the owner if the dwelling were to be sold; (2) Includes all shelter expenses paid by households that own their dwellings, such as the mortgage payment and the costs of electricity, heat, water and other municipal services, property taxes and condominium fees; (3) Includes all shelter expenses paid by households that rent their dwellings, such as the monthly rent and the costs of electricity, heat and municipal services.
Source: Statistics Canada. 2013. 2011 National Household Survey. Statistics Canada Catalogue no. 99-004-XWE. Ottawa. Released September 11, 2013.

Occupied Private Dwellings by Period of Construction

Area	1960 or Before	1961 to 1980	1981 to 1990	1991 to 2000	2001 to 2005	2006 to 2011
			Number			
Coquitlam	3,975	14,340	9,910	11,105	2,365	3,860
British Columbia	282,675	551,655	308,450	329,780	133,235	158,845
Canada	3,273,105	4,152,715	2,112,110	1,707,880	1,031,020	1,042,430
			Percent of Dwellings			
Coquitlam	8.7	31.5	21.8	24.4	5.2	8.5
British Columbia	16.0	31.3	17.5	18.7	7.6	9.0
Canada	24.6	31.2	15.9	12.8	7.7	7.8

Note: Figures cover non-farm, non-reserve private dwellings and includes data up to May 10, 2011.
Source: Statistics Canada. 2013. 2011 National Household Survey. Statistics Canada Catalogue no. 99-004-XWE. Ottawa. Released September 11, 2013.

Educational Attainment

Area	No Certificate, Diploma or Degree	High School Diploma or Equivalent[1]	Apprenticeship or Trades Certificate or Diploma[2]	College, CÉGEP or Other Non-University Certificate or Diploma	University Certificate or Diploma Below the Bachelor Level[3]	Bachelor's Degree	University Certificate, Diploma or Degree Above Bachelor Level[4]
				Number			
				Total			
Coquitlam	13,010	28,560	9,620	18,465	6,910	17,920	9,910
British Columbia	607,655	1,009,400	387,455	628,115	208,245	511,240	294,725
Canada	5,485,400	6,968,935	2,950,685	4,970,020	1,200,130	3,634,425	2,049,930
				Males			
Coquitlam	6,265	13,365	6,505	7,985	3,070	8,625	4,990
British Columbia	305,040	475,670	262,245	260,580	86,995	235,620	149,300
Canada	2,742,875	3,305,415	1,928,970	2,118,430	513,235	1,643,080	1,043,350
				Females			
Coquitlam	6,740	15,200	3,115	10,475	3,835	9,290	4,920
British Columbia	302,620	533,735	125,210	367,535	121,250	275,625	145,425
Canada	2,742,520	3,663,515	1,021,715	2,851,595	686,890	1,991,345	1,006,585
				Percent of Population			
				Total			
Coquitlam	12.5	27.4	9.2	17.7	6.6	17.2	9.5
British Columbia	16.7	27.7	10.6	17.2	5.7	14.0	8.1
Canada	20.1	25.6	10.8	18.2	4.4	13.3	7.5
				Males			
Coquitlam	12.3	26.3	12.8	15.7	6.0	17.0	9.8
British Columbia	17.2	26.8	14.8	14.7	4.9	13.3	8.4
Canada	20.6	24.9	14.5	15.9	3.9	12.4	7.8
				Females			
Coquitlam	12.6	28.4	5.8	19.6	7.2	17.3	9.2
British Columbia	16.2	28.5	6.7	19.6	6.5	14.7	7.8
Canada	19.6	26.2	7.3	20.4	4.9	14.3	7.2

Note: Figures cover total population aged 15 years and over by highest certificate, diploma or degree; (1) Includes persons who have graduated from a secondary school or equivalent. It excludes persons with a postsecondary certificate, diploma or degree; (2) Includes Registered Apprenticeship certificates (including Certificate of Qualification, Journeyperson's designation) and other trades certificates or diplomas such as pre-employment or vocational certificates and diplomas from brief trade programs completed at community colleges, institutes of technology, vocational centres, and similar institutions; (3) Comparisons with other data sources suggest that the category 'University certificate or diploma below the bachelor's level' was over-reported in the NHS. This category likely includes some responses that are actually college certificates or diplomas, bachelor's degrees or other types of education (e.g., university transfer programs, bachelor's programs completed in other countries, incomplete bachelor's programs, non-university professional designations). We recommend users interpret the results for the 'University certificate or diploma below the bachelor's level' category with caution; (4) 'University certificate or diploma above bachelor level' includes the categories: 'Degree in medicine, dentistry, veterinary medicine or optometry,' 'Master's degree' and 'Earned doctorate.'
Source: Statistics Canada. 2013. 2011 National Household Survey. Statistics Canada Catalogue no. 99-004-XWE. Ottawa. Released September 11, 2013.

Household Income Distribution

Area	Less than $10,000	$10,000 to $19,999	$20,000 to $29,999	$30,000 to $39,999	$40,000 to $49,999	$50,000 to $59,999	$60,000 to $79,999	$80,000 to $99,999	$100,000 to $124,999	$125,000 to $149,999	$150,000 and Over
						Households					
Coquitlam	2,790	3,185	3,535	3,715	3,615	3,335	6,000	5,010	5,000	3,270	6,090
British Columbia	96,465	156,565	157,605	167,220	158,400	140,340	246,720	193,180	167,415	106,325	174,385
Canada	626,705	1,141,945	1,193,925	1,271,675	1,206,800	1,102,120	1,865,280	1,458,240	1,260,770	802,555	1,389,240
						Percent of Households					
Coquitlam	6.1	7.0	7.8	8.2	7.9	7.3	13.2	11.0	11.0	7.2	13.4
British Columbia	5.5	8.9	8.9	9.5	9.0	8.0	14.0	10.9	9.5	6.0	9.9
Canada	4.7	8.6	9.0	9.5	9.1	8.3	14.0	10.9	9.5	6.0	10.4

Note: Household income is the sum of the total incomes of all members of that household. Total income refers to monetary receipts from certain sources, before income taxes and deductions, during calendar year 2010.
Source: Statistics Canada. 2013. 2011 National Household Survey. Statistics Canada Catalogue no. 99-004-XWE. Ottawa. Released September 11, 2013.

Median and Average Household and Economic Family Income

Area	Median Household Income ($)	Average Household Income ($)	Median After-tax Household Income ($)	Average After-tax Household Income ($)	Median Economic Family Income ($)	Average Economic Family Income ($)	Median After-tax Economic Family Income ($)	Average After-tax Economic Family Income ($)
Coquitlam	67,787	83,640	60,737	71,661	82,067	94,768	73,064	81,089
British Columbia	60,333	77,378	54,379	66,264	75,797	91,967	67,915	78,580
Canada	61,072	79,102	54,089	66,149	76,511	94,125	67,044	78,517

Note: Figures cover household and economic familiy income in 2010. A household is defined as a person or a group of persons (other than foreign residents) who occupy the same private dwelling and do not have a usual place of residence elsewhere in Canada. Every person is a member of one and only one household. An economic family is defined as a group of two or more persons who live in the same dwelling and are related to each other by blood, marriage, common-law, adoption or a foster relationship. A couple may be of opposite or same sex.
Source: Statistics Canada. 2013. 2011 National Household Survey. Statistics Canada Catalogue no. 99-004-XWE. Ottawa. Released September 11, 2013.

PROFILES / Coquitlam, British Columbia

Individual Income Distribution

Area	Less than $10,000	$10,000 to $19,999	$20,000 to $29,999	$30,000 to $39,999	$40,000 to $49,999	$50,000 to $59,999	$60,000 to $79,999	$80,000 to $99,999	$100,000 to $124,999	$125,000 and Over
					Number Total					
Coquitlam	21,245	16,500	11,940	10,440	9,135	7,180	9,865	5,595	2,780	2,825
British Columbia	645,915	666,060	470,255	404,860	338,595	253,215	330,590	169,190	89,520	96,055
Canada	4,492,040	4,835,710	3,670,020	3,180,360	2,603,520	1,921,650	2,437,440	1,302,045	693,580	782,135
					Males					
Coquitlam	9,080	6,440	5,120	4,945	4,205	3,895	6,190	3,560	2,065	2,250
British Columbia	275,815	263,170	201,000	186,285	167,400	143,765	206,400	112,525	65,050	74,260
Canada	1,936,365	1,864,880	1,588,260	1,522,190	1,333,510	1,079,780	1,473,145	823,720	492,905	599,905
					Females					
Coquitlam	12,170	10,065	6,825	5,495	4,935	3,285	3,675	2,040	710	580
British Columbia	370,100	402,880	269,255	218,575	171,190	109,445	124,195	56,670	24,470	21,795
Canada	2,555,675	2,970,825	2,081,760	1,658,170	1,270,010	841,870	964,300	478,330	200,680	182,230
					Percent of Population Total					
Coquitlam	21.8	16.9	12.2	10.7	9.4	7.4	10.1	5.7	2.9	2.9
British Columbia	18.6	19.2	13.6	11.7	9.8	7.3	9.5	4.9	2.6	2.8
Canada	17.3	18.7	14.2	12.3	10.0	7.4	9.4	5.0	2.7	3.0
					Males					
Coquitlam	19.0	13.5	10.7	10.4	8.8	8.2	13.0	7.5	4.3	4.7
British Columbia	16.3	15.5	11.9	11.0	9.9	8.5	12.2	6.6	3.8	4.4
Canada	15.2	14.7	12.5	12.0	10.5	8.5	11.6	6.5	3.9	4.7
					Females					
Coquitlam	24.5	20.2	13.7	11.0	9.9	6.6	7.4	4.1	1.4	1.2
British Columbia	20.9	22.8	15.2	12.4	9.7	6.2	7.0	3.2	1.4	1.2
Canada	19.4	22.5	15.8	12.6	9.6	6.4	7.3	3.6	1.5	1.4

Note: Figures cover individuals aged 15 years and over with income. Income refers to monetary receipts from certain sources, before income taxes and deductions, during calendar year 2010.
Source: Statistics Canada. 2013. 2011 National Household Survey. Statistics Canada Catalogue no. 99-004-XWE. Ottawa. Released September 11, 2013.

Labour Force Status

Area	In the Labour Force All	Employed	Unemployed	Not in the Labour Force
		Number Total		
Coquitlam	69,720	64,695	5,025	34,675
British Columbia	2,354,245	2,171,465	182,775	1,292,595
Canada	17,990,080	16,595,035	1,395,045	9,269,445
		Males		
Coquitlam	36,525	33,815	2,710	14,285
British Columbia	1,223,375	1,124,590	98,785	552,070
Canada	9,388,570	8,634,310	754,255	3,906,785
		Females		
Coquitlam	33,190	30,875	2,315	20,385
British Columbia	1,130,870	1,046,875	83,990	740,530
Canada	8,601,515	7,960,725	640,790	5,362,660
		Percent of Labour Force Total		
Coquitlam	66.8	62.0	7.2	33.2
British Columbia	64.6	59.5	7.8	35.4
Canada	66.0	60.9	7.8	34.0
		Males		
Coquitlam	71.9	66.6	7.4	28.1
British Columbia	68.9	63.3	8.1	31.1
Canada	70.6	64.9	8.0	29.4
		Females		
Coquitlam	61.9	57.6	7.0	38.0
British Columbia	60.4	55.9	7.4	39.6
Canada	61.6	57.0	7.4	38.4

Note: Figures are based on total population 15 years and over
Source: Statistics Canada. 2013. 2011 National Household Survey. Statistics Canada Catalogue no. 99-004-XWE. Ottawa. Released September 11, 2013.

Labour Force by Industry (NAICS Codes 11–52)

Area	Agriculture, forestry, fishing & hunting	Mining, quarrying, & oil & gas extraction	Utilities	Construction	Manufacturing	Wholesale Trade	Retail Trade	Transportation & warehousing	Information & cultural industries	Finance & insurance
					Number					
					Total					
Coquitlam	225	245	670	5,745	4,560	3,895	8,290	3,270	2,435	3,775
British Columbia	61,210	25,450	13,215	181,510	148,810	90,560	266,265	118,675	62,235	91,790
Canada	437,650	261,050	149,940	1,215,380	1,619,295	733,445	2,031,665	827,780	420,830	767,960
					Males					
Coquitlam	155	170	400	5,035	3,270	2,570	3,910	2,525	1,505	1,565
British Columbia	40,810	21,175	9,650	159,605	108,480	61,730	121,750	89,155	37,250	35,375
Canada	307,370	211,690	110,765	1,068,710	1,167,680	494,545	933,850	617,305	235,875	296,995
					Females					
Coquitlam	70	75	265	710	1,295	1,325	4,380	750	935	2,205
British Columbia	20,405	4,275	3,560	21,910	40,335	28,820	144,515	29,520	24,980	56,415
Canada	130,285	49,360	39,175	146,670	451,615	238,900	1,097,820	210,475	184,955	470,960
					Percent of Labour Force					
					Total					
Coquitlam	0.3	0.4	1.0	8.4	6.7	5.7	12.2	4.8	3.6	5.5
British Columbia	2.7	1.1	0.6	7.9	6.5	3.9	11.6	5.1	2.7	4.0
Canada	2.5	1.5	0.9	6.9	9.2	4.2	11.6	4.7	2.4	4.4
					Males					
Coquitlam	0.4	0.5	1.1	14.1	9.2	7.2	10.9	7.1	4.2	4.4
British Columbia	3.4	1.8	0.8	13.3	9.0	5.1	10.1	7.4	3.1	2.9
Canada	3.3	2.3	1.2	11.6	12.7	5.4	10.2	6.7	2.6	3.2
					Females					
Coquitlam	0.2	0.2	0.8	2.2	4.0	4.1	13.5	2.3	2.9	6.8
British Columbia	1.8	0.4	0.3	2.0	3.6	2.6	13.1	2.7	2.3	5.1
Canada	1.6	0.6	0.5	1.7	5.4	2.8	13.1	2.5	2.2	5.6

Note: Figures are based on total experienced labour force 15 years and over. Experienced labour force refers to persons who, during the week of Sunday, May 1 to Saturday, May 7, 2011, were employed and the unemployed who had last worked for pay or in self-employment in either 2010 or 2011.
Source: Statistics Canada. 2013. 2011 National Household Survey. Statistics Canada Catalogue no. 99-004-XWE. Ottawa. Released September 11, 2013.

Labour Force by Industry (NAICS Codes 53–91)

Area	Real estate & rental & leasing	Profess., scientific & tech. services	Mgmt of companies & enterprises	Admin. & support, waste mgmt & remed. services	Educational services	Health care & social assistance	Arts, entertain. & recreation	Accomm. & food services	Other services (except public admin.)	Public admin.
					Number					
					Total					
Coquitlam	1,700	6,015	90	2,545	5,310	6,455	1,170	4,470	3,585	3,660
British Columbia	54,840	179,355	2,440	98,890	167,875	249,030	56,915	179,625	112,745	143,875
Canada	321,895	1,240,850	17,460	728,330	1,301,435	1,949,650	363,405	1,130,750	807,800	1,261,050
					Males					
Coquitlam	790	3,340	50	1,480	1,675	1,155	670	1,995	1,480	2,005
British Columbia	29,790	98,760	1,320	55,745	55,635	47,020	29,750	73,570	49,130	74,040
Canada	179,090	688,625	9,380	411,250	424,915	349,430	188,270	469,990	372,940	652,510
					Females					
Coquitlam	910	2,675	35	1,060	3,640	5,295	500	2,475	2,105	1,650
British Columbia	25,055	80,590	1,120	43,145	112,235	202,010	27,175	106,055	63,615	69,840
Canada	142,805	552,225	8,075	317,085	876,515	1,600,220	175,135	660,760	434,865	608,535
					Percent of Labour Force					
					Total					
Coquitlam	2.5	8.8	0.1	3.7	7.8	9.5	1.7	6.6	5.3	5.4
British Columbia	2.4	7.8	0.1	4.3	7.3	10.8	2.5	7.8	4.9	6.2
Canada	1.8	7.1	0.1	4.1	7.4	11.1	2.1	6.4	4.6	7.2
					Males					
Coquitlam	2.2	9.3	0.1	4.1	4.7	3.2	1.9	5.6	4.1	5.6
British Columbia	2.5	8.2	0.1	4.6	4.6	3.9	2.5	6.1	4.1	6.2
Canada	1.9	7.5	0.1	4.5	4.6	3.8	2.0	5.1	4.1	7.1
					Females					
Coquitlam	2.8	8.3	0.1	3.3	11.2	16.4	1.5	7.6	6.5	5.1
British Columbia	2.3	7.3	0.1	3.9	10.2	18.3	2.5	9.6	5.8	6.3
Canada	1.7	6.6	0.1	3.8	10.4	19.1	2.1	7.9	5.2	7.2

Note: Figures are based on total experienced labour force 15 years and over. Experienced labour force refers to persons who, during the week of Sunday, May 1 to Saturday, May 7, 2011, were employed and the unemployed who had last worked for pay or in self-employment in either 2010 or 2011.
Source: Statistics Canada. 2013. 2011 National Household Survey. Statistics Canada Catalogue no. 99-004-XWE. Ottawa. Released September 11, 2013.

PROFILES / Coquitlam, British Columbia

Occupation

Area	Mgmt	Business, Finance & Admin.	Natural/ Applied Sciences & Related	Health	Education, Law & Social, Community & Government Services	Art, Culture, Recreation & Sport	Sales & Service	Trades, Transport & Equip. Operators & Related	Natural Resources, Agri. & Related Production	Mfg & Utilities
Number										
Total										
Coquitlam	8,245	12,695	5,875	4,085	7,235	2,060	16,300	9,135	520	1,955
British Columbia	263,685	368,980	154,055	147,620	265,910	78,565	554,345	337,140	60,295	74,720
Canada	1,963,600	2,902,045	1,237,775	1,107,200	2,064,675	503,415	4,068,170	2,537,775	397,930	805,040
Males										
Coquitlam	5,265	3,870	4,645	950	2,305	945	7,160	8,760	450	1,380
British Columbia	162,365	104,285	122,570	32,490	89,645	38,300	233,065	317,385	45,155	54,470
Canada	1,229,460	854,190	966,355	217,520	676,550	232,535	1,745,705	2,385,615	318,945	564,300
Females										
Coquitlam	2,980	8,825	1,225	3,135	4,930	1,120	9,135	375	75	575
British Columbia	101,320	264,690	31,480	115,125	176,265	40,270	321,285	19,755	15,135	20,250
Canada	734,140	2,047,855	271,415	889,675	1,388,130	270,875	2,322,465	152,165	78,980	240,740
Percent of Labour Force										
Total										
Coquitlam	12.1	18.6	8.6	6.0	10.6	3.0	23.9	13.4	0.8	2.9
British Columbia	11.4	16.0	6.7	6.4	11.5	3.4	24.0	14.6	2.6	3.2
Canada	11.2	16.5	7.0	6.3	11.7	2.9	23.1	14.4	2.3	4.6
Males										
Coquitlam	14.7	10.8	13.0	2.7	6.5	2.6	20.0	24.5	1.3	3.9
British Columbia	13.5	8.7	10.2	2.7	7.5	3.2	19.4	26.5	3.8	4.5
Canada	13.4	9.3	10.5	2.4	7.4	2.5	19.0	26.0	3.5	6.1
Females										
Coquitlam	9.2	27.3	3.8	9.7	15.2	3.5	28.2	1.2	0.2	1.8
British Columbia	9.2	23.9	2.8	10.4	15.9	3.6	29.1	1.8	1.4	1.8
Canada	8.7	24.4	3.2	10.6	16.5	3.2	27.7	1.8	0.9	2.9

Note: Figures are based on total experienced labour force 15 years and over
Source: Statistics Canada. 2013. 2011 National Household Survey. Statistics Canada Catalogue no. 99-004-XWE. Ottawa. Released September 11, 2013.

Place of Work Status

Area	Worked at Home	Worked Outside Canada	No Fixed Workplace Address	Worked at Usual Place
Number				
Total				
Coquitlam	4,595	470	8,365	51,260
British Columbia	174,000	12,480	304,465	1,680,525
Canada	1,142,640	66,460	1,868,245	13,517,690
Males				
Coquitlam	2,080	375	6,175	25,185
British Columbia	84,015	9,210	225,840	805,525
Canada	582,150	47,355	1,400,485	6,604,325
Females				
Coquitlam	2,515	95	2,190	26,080
British Columbia	89,990	3,270	78,620	875,000
Canada	560,490	19,100	467,760	6,913,370
Percent of Labour Force				
Total				
Coquitlam	7.1	0.7	12.9	79.2
British Columbia	8.0	0.6	14.0	77.4
Canada	6.9	0.4	11.3	81.5
Males				
Coquitlam	6.2	1.1	18.3	74.5
British Columbia	7.5	0.8	20.1	71.6
Canada	6.7	0.5	16.2	76.5
Females				
Coquitlam	8.1	0.3	7.1	84.5
British Columbia	8.6	0.3	7.5	83.6
Canada	7.0	0.2	5.9	86.8

Note: Figures are based on total employed labour force 15 years and over.
Source: Statistics Canada. 2013. 2011 National Household Survey. Statistics Canada Catalogue no. 99-004-XWE. Ottawa. Released September 11, 2013.

Mode of Transportation to Work

Area	Car; Truck; Van; as Driver	Car; Truck; Van; as Passenger	Public Transit	Walked	Bicycled	All Other Modes
			Number			
			Total			
Coquitlam	43,285	2,990	10,215	2,075	290	780
British Columbia	1,415,745	110,695	250,450	132,205	42,260	33,635
Canada	11,393,140	867,050	1,851,525	880,815	201,780	191,625
			Males			
Coquitlam	24,440	1,055	4,465	815	195	385
British Columbia	773,160	47,425	107,645	57,000	26,595	19,535
Canada	6,238,835	349,530	788,290	387,580	135,840	104,725
			Females			
Coquitlam	18,835	1,935	5,745	1,260	95	395
British Columbia	642,580	63,270	142,810	75,205	15,665	14,100
Canada	5,154,305	517,520	1,063,235	493,230	65,940	86,900
			Percent of Labour Force			
			Total			
Coquitlam	72.6	5.0	17.1	3.5	0.5	1.3
British Columbia	71.3	5.6	12.6	6.7	2.1	1.7
Canada	74.0	5.6	12.0	5.7	1.3	1.2
			Males			
Coquitlam	77.9	3.4	14.2	2.6	0.6	1.2
British Columbia	75.0	4.6	10.4	5.5	2.6	1.9
Canada	77.9	4.4	9.8	4.8	1.7	1.3
			Females			
Coquitlam	66.6	6.8	20.3	4.5	0.3	1.4
British Columbia	67.4	6.6	15.0	7.9	1.6	1.5
Canada	69.8	7.0	14.4	6.7	0.9	1.2

Note: Figures are based on total employed labour force 15 years and over.
Source: Statistics Canada. 2013. 2011 National Household Survey. Statistics Canada Catalogue no. 99-004-XWE. Ottawa. Released September 11, 2013.

Visible Minority Population Characteristics

Area	Total Minority	South Asian[1]	Chinese	Black	Filipino	Latin American	Arab	SE Asian[2]	West Asian[3]	Korean	Japanese	Multiple[4]
					Number							
					Total							
Coquitlam	54,750	5,245	21,575	1,265	4,865	1,895	995	1,550	6,380	7,830	1,310	1,615
British Columbia	1,180,870	313,440	438,140	33,260	126,040	35,465	14,090	51,970	38,960	53,770	38,120	31,160
Canada	6,264,750	1,567,400	1,324,750	945,665	619,310	381,280	380,620	312,075	206,840	161,130	87,270	171,935
					Males							
Coquitlam	26,460	2,565	10,460	660	2,075	850	530	770	3,160	3,770	670	845
British Columbia	565,965	157,135	208,175	17,365	53,715	16,985	8,010	25,055	19,420	25,325	16,295	15,255
Canada	3,043,010	790,755	632,325	453,005	268,885	186,355	203,485	154,035	105,620	77,165	38,270	83,335
					Females							
Coquitlam	28,285	2,685	11,120	600	2,790	1,040	465	780	3,220	4,060	645	770
British Columbia	614,905	156,300	229,960	15,895	72,320	18,480	6,080	26,920	19,540	28,440	21,820	15,905
Canada	3,221,745	776,650	692,420	492,660	350,425	194,925	177,140	158,045	101,220	83,965	48,990	88,600
					Percent of Population							
					Total							
Coquitlam	43.8	4.2	17.3	1.0	3.9	1.5	0.8	1.2	5.1	6.3	1.0	1.3
British Columbia	27.3	7.2	10.1	0.8	2.9	0.8	0.3	1.2	0.9	1.2	0.9	0.7
Canada	19.1	4.8	4.0	2.9	1.9	1.2	1.2	0.9	0.6	0.5	0.3	0.5
					Males							
Coquitlam	43.0	4.2	17.0	1.1	3.4	1.4	0.9	1.3	5.1	6.1	1.1	1.4
British Columbia	26.6	7.4	9.8	0.8	2.5	0.8	0.4	1.2	0.9	1.2	0.8	0.7
Canada	18.8	4.9	3.9	2.8	1.7	1.2	1.3	1.0	0.7	0.5	0.2	0.5
					Females							
Coquitlam	44.6	4.2	17.5	0.9	4.4	1.6	0.7	1.2	5.1	6.4	1.0	1.2
British Columbia	28.0	7.1	10.5	0.7	3.3	0.8	0.3	1.2	0.9	1.3	1.0	0.7
Canada	19.3	4.7	4.1	3.0	2.1	1.2	1.1	0.9	0.6	0.5	0.3	0.5

Note: The Employment Equity Act defines visible minorities as 'persons, other than Aboriginal peoples, who are non-Caucasian in race or non-white in colour';
(1) Includes 'East Indian,' 'Pakistani,' 'Sri Lankan,' etc.; (2) Includes 'Vietnamese,' 'Cambodian,' 'Malaysian,' 'Laotian,' etc.; (3) Includes 'Iranian,' 'Afghan,' etc.; (4) Includes respondents who reported more than one visible minority group by checking two or more mark-in circles, e.g., 'Black' and 'South Asian.'
Source: Statistics Canada. 2013. 2011 National Household Survey. Statistics Canada Catalogue no. 99-004-XWE. Ottawa. Released September 11, 2013.

PROFILES / Coquitlam, British Columbia

Aboriginal Population

Area	Aboriginal Identity[1]	First Nations (North American Indian) Single Identity[2]	Métis Single Identity	Inuk (Inuit) Single Identity	Multiple Aboriginal Identities[3]	Aboriginal Identities Not Included Elsewhere
Number						
Total						
Coquitlam	2,615	1,320	1,115	0	50	125
British Columbia	232,290	155,020	69,475	1,570	2,480	3,745
Canada	1,400,685	851,560	451,795	59,440	11,415	26,475
Males						
Coquitlam	1,185	545	555	0	20	65
British Columbia	113,080	75,400	33,940	820	1,190	1,735
Canada	682,190	411,785	223,335	29,495	5,525	12,055
Females						
Coquitlam	1,425	780	560	0	25	55
British Columbia	119,215	79,620	35,540	750	1,290	2,015
Canada	718,500	439,775	228,460	29,950	5,890	14,420
Percent of Population						
Total						
Coquitlam	2.1	1.1	0.9	0.0	0.0	0.1
British Columbia	5.4	3.6	1.6	0.0	0.1	0.1
Canada	4.3	2.6	1.4	0.2	0.0	0.1
Males						
Coquitlam	1.9	0.9	0.9	0.0	0.0	0.1
British Columbia	5.3	3.5	1.6	0.0	0.1	0.1
Canada	4.2	2.5	1.4	0.2	0.0	0.1
Females						
Coquitlam	2.2	1.2	0.9	0.0	0.0	0.1
British Columbia	5.4	3.6	1.6	0.0	0.1	0.1
Canada	4.3	2.6	1.4	0.2	0.0	0.1

Note: (1) Includes persons who reported being an Aboriginal person, that is, First Nations (North American Indian), Métis or Inuk (Inuit) and/or those who reported Registered or Treaty Indian status, that is registered under the Indian Act of Canada, and/or those who reported membership in a First Nation or Indian band. Aboriginal peoples of Canada are defined in the Constitution Act, 1982, section 35-2 as including the Indian, Inuit and Métis peoples of Canada; (2) Users should be aware that the estimates associated with this variable are more affected than most by the incomplete enumeration of certain Indian reserves and Indian settlements in the National Household Survey (NHS); (3) Includes persons who reported being any two or all three of the following: First Nations (North American Indian), Métis or Inuk (Inuit).
Source: Statistics Canada. 2013. 2011 National Household Survey. Statistics Canada Catalogue no. 99-004-XWE. Ottawa. Released September 11, 2013.

Ethnic Origin

Area	North American Aboriginal	Other North American	European	Caribbean	Latin, Central and South American	African	Asian	Oceania
Number								
Total								
Coquitlam	3,600	18,735	67,570	620	2,530	1,875	52,305	575
British Columbia	267,085	884,490	2,812,935	20,035	52,725	47,185	1,122,445	35,770
Canada	1,836,035	11,070,455	20,157,965	627,590	544,375	766,735	5,011,225	74,875
Males								
Coquitlam	1,625	9,405	33,495	270	1,160	1,040	25,275	285
British Columbia	128,880	440,920	1,387,940	10,225	25,605	23,575	535,825	17,425
Canada	885,675	5,462,685	9,913,150	291,640	264,635	387,360	2,435,540	37,490
Females								
Coquitlam	1,980	9,325	34,070	350	1,375	835	27,035	295
British Columbia	138,205	443,570	1,424,990	9,810	27,120	23,610	586,620	18,340
Canada	950,360	5,607,770	10,244,820	335,945	279,740	379,380	2,575,680	37,385
Percent of Population								
Total								
Coquitlam	2.9	15.0	54.0	0.5	2.0	1.5	41.8	0.5
British Columbia	6.2	20.5	65.0	0.5	1.2	1.1	26.0	0.8
Canada	5.6	33.7	61.4	1.9	1.7	2.3	15.3	0.2
Males								
Coquitlam	2.6	15.3	54.4	0.4	1.9	1.7	41.0	0.5
British Columbia	6.1	20.7	65.3	0.5	1.2	1.1	25.2	0.8
Canada	5.5	33.8	61.3	1.8	1.6	2.4	15.1	0.2
Females								
Coquitlam	3.1	14.7	53.7	0.6	2.2	1.3	42.6	0.5
British Columbia	6.3	20.2	64.8	0.4	1.2	1.1	26.7	0.8
Canada	5.7	33.6	61.4	2.0	1.7	2.3	15.4	0.2

Note: The sum of the ethnic groups in this table is greater than the total population estimate because a person may report more than one ethnic origin in the NHS.
Source: Statistics Canada. 2013. 2011 National Household Survey. Statistics Canada Catalogue no. 99-004-XWE. Ottawa. Released September 11, 2013.

Religion

Area	Buddhist	Christian	Hindu	Jewish	Muslim	Sikh	Traditional (Aboriginal) Spirituality	Other Religions	No Religious Affiliation
					Number Total				
Coquitlam	2,540	61,075	1,115	560	6,475	1,430	15	1,485	50,315
British Columbia	90,620	1,930,415	45,795	23,130	79,310	201,110	10,295	35,500	1,908,285
Canada	366,830	22,102,745	497,965	329,495	1,053,945	454,965	64,935	130,835	7,850,605
					Males				
Coquitlam	1,160	28,345	495	280	3,230	695	0	650	26,710
British Columbia	40,175	883,680	22,945	11,255	39,780	100,610	5,085	14,680	1,007,420
Canada	168,465	10,497,775	250,435	161,265	540,555	229,435	31,805	57,745	4,225,645
					Females				
Coquitlam	1,385	32,730	620	280	3,245	735	10	830	23,605
British Columbia	50,440	1,046,735	22,845	11,880	39,530	100,500	5,210	20,820	900,865
Canada	198,365	11,604,975	247,525	168,235	513,395	225,530	33,135	73,090	3,624,965
				Percent of Population Total					
Coquitlam	2.0	48.9	0.9	0.4	5.2	1.1	0.0	1.2	40.2
British Columbia	2.1	44.6	1.1	0.5	1.8	4.7	0.2	0.8	44.1
Canada	1.1	67.3	1.5	1.0	3.2	1.4	0.2	0.4	23.9
					Males				
Coquitlam	1.9	46.0	0.8	0.5	5.2	1.1	0.0	1.1	43.4
British Columbia	1.9	41.6	1.1	0.5	1.9	4.7	0.2	0.7	47.4
Canada	1.0	64.9	1.5	1.0	3.3	1.4	0.2	0.4	26.1
					Females				
Coquitlam	2.2	51.6	1.0	0.4	5.1	1.2	0.0	1.3	37.2
British Columbia	2.3	47.6	1.0	0.5	1.8	4.6	0.2	0.9	41.0
Canada	1.2	69.5	1.5	1.0	3.1	1.4	0.2	0.4	21.7

Note: Religion refers to the person's self-identification as having a connection or affiliation with any religious denomination, group, body, sect, cult or other religiously defined community or system of belief. Religion is not limited to formal membership in a religious organization or group. Persons without a religious connection or affiliation can self-identify as atheist, agnostic or humanist, or can provide another applicable response.
Source: Statistics Canada. 2013. 2011 National Household Survey. Statistics Canada Catalogue no. 99-004-XWE. Ottawa. Released September 11, 2013.

Religion—Christian Denominations

Area	Anglican	Baptist	Catholic	Christian Orthodox	Lutheran	Pentecostal	Presbyterian	United Church	Other Christian
				Number Total					
Coquitlam	4,025	2,630	26,750	2,935	1,880	1,505	1,840	4,970	14,540
British Columbia	213,975	91,575	650,360	39,845	71,470	58,300	44,635	222,230	538,030
Canada	1,631,845	635,840	12,810,705	550,690	478,185	478,705	472,385	2,007,610	3,036,780
					Males				
Coquitlam	1,755	1,160	12,535	1,505	850	770	840	2,130	6,805
British Columbia	94,330	41,565	303,300	19,475	32,205	26,590	19,925	94,020	252,270
Canada	752,945	293,905	6,167,290	270,205	221,525	217,850	218,955	912,545	1,442,550
					Females				
Coquitlam	2,265	1,470	14,215	1,430	1,030	745	1,005	2,830	7,735
British Columbia	119,645	50,010	347,060	20,375	39,270	31,710	24,710	128,210	285,770
Canada	878,900	341,940	6,643,415	280,485	256,660	260,850	253,430	1,095,065	1,594,230
				Percent of Population Total					
Coquitlam	3.2	2.1	21.4	2.3	1.5	1.2	1.5	4.0	11.6
British Columbia	4.9	2.1	15.0	0.9	1.7	1.3	1.0	5.1	12.4
Canada	5.0	1.9	39.0	1.7	1.5	1.5	1.4	6.1	9.2
					Males				
Coquitlam	2.9	1.9	20.4	2.4	1.4	1.3	1.4	3.5	11.1
British Columbia	4.4	2.0	14.3	0.9	1.5	1.3	0.9	4.4	11.9
Canada	4.7	1.8	38.2	1.7	1.4	1.3	1.4	5.6	8.9
					Females				
Coquitlam	3.6	2.3	22.4	2.3	1.6	1.2	1.6	4.5	12.2
British Columbia	5.4	2.3	15.8	0.9	1.8	1.4	1.1	5.8	13.0
Canada	5.3	2.0	39.8	1.7	1.5	1.6	1.5	6.6	9.6

Note: Religion refers to the person's self-identification as having a connection or affiliation with any religious denomination, group, body, sect, cult or other religiously defined community or system of belief. Religion is not limited to formal membership in a religious organization or group. Persons without a religious connection or affiliation can self-identify as atheist, agnostic or humanist, or can provide another applicable response.
Source: Statistics Canada. 2013. 2011 National Household Survey. Statistics Canada Catalogue no. 99-004-XWE. Ottawa. Released September 11, 2013.

PROFILES / Coquitlam, British Columbia

Immigrant Status and Period of Immigration

Area	Non-Immigrants[1]	Immigrants All	Before 1971	1971 to 1980	1981 to 1990	1991 to 2000	2001 to 2005	2006 to 2011	Non-Permanent Residents[3]
Number									
Total									
Coquitlam	70,420	52,080	4,845	5,455	6,340	17,495	9,595	8,345	2,515
British Columbia	3,067,590	1,191,875	223,215	161,335	156,445	305,655	160,100	185,115	64,995
Canada	25,720,175	6,775,765	1,261,055	870,775	949,890	1,539,050	992,070	1,162,915	356,385
Males									
Coquitlam	35,450	25,065	2,440	2,585	2,935	8,385	4,685	4,035	1,065
British Columbia	1,533,255	561,490	109,510	76,865	72,625	140,985	74,395	87,110	30,880
Canada	12,753,235	3,231,370	605,430	416,670	454,570	724,905	474,545	555,245	178,515
Females									
Coquitlam	34,975	27,015	2,400	2,870	3,405	9,115	4,905	4,315	1,455
British Columbia	1,534,330	630,385	113,710	84,470	83,820	164,675	85,710	98,005	34,115
Canada	12,966,935	3,544,400	655,625	454,105	495,325	814,145	517,530	607,670	177,870
Percent of Population									
Total									
Coquitlam	56.3	41.7	3.9	4.4	5.1	14.0	7.7	6.7	2.0
British Columbia	70.9	27.6	5.2	3.7	3.6	7.1	3.7	4.3	1.5
Canada	78.3	20.6	3.8	2.7	2.9	4.7	3.0	3.5	1.1
Males									
Coquitlam	57.6	40.7	4.0	4.2	4.8	13.6	7.6	6.6	1.7
British Columbia	72.1	26.4	5.2	3.6	3.4	6.6	3.5	4.1	1.5
Canada	78.9	20.0	3.7	2.6	2.8	4.5	2.9	3.4	1.1
Females									
Coquitlam	55.1	42.6	3.8	4.5	5.4	14.4	7.7	6.8	2.3
British Columbia	69.8	28.7	5.2	3.8	3.8	7.5	3.9	4.5	1.6
Canada	77.7	21.2	3.9	2.7	3.0	4.9	3.1	3.6	1.1

Note: (1) Non-immigrant refers to a person who is a Canadian citizen by birth; (2) Immigrant refers to a person who is or has ever been a landed immigrant/permanent resident. This person has been granted the right to live in Canada permanently by immigration authorities. Some immigrants have resided in Canada for a number of years, while others have arrived recently. Some immigrants are Canadian citizens, while others are not. Most immigrants are born outside Canada, but a small number are born in Canada. In the 2011 National Household Survey, 'Immigrants' includes immigrants who landed in Canada prior to May 10, 2011; (3) Non-permanent resident refers to a person from another country who has a work or study permit, or who is a refugee claimant, and any non-Canadian-born family member living in Canada with them.
Source: Statistics Canada. 2013. 2011 National Household Survey. Statistics Canada Catalogue no. 99-004-XWE. Ottawa. Released September 11, 2013.

Mother Tongue

Area	English	French	Non-official Language	English & French	English & Non-official Language	French & Non-official Language	English, French & Non-official Language
Number							
Total							
Coquitlam	68,700	1,420	51,790	235	2,890	105	75
British Columbia	3,062,435	57,275	1,154,215	8,600	68,800	3,345	1,530
Canada	18,858,980	7,054,975	6,567,680	144,685	396,330	74,430	24,095
Males							
Coquitlam	34,620	655	24,685	135	1,400	50	35
British Columbia	1,526,350	28,315	543,395	4,065	32,875	1,520	725
Canada	9,345,225	3,452,380	3,157,785	69,975	192,000	36,535	11,965
Females							
Coquitlam	34,075	765	27,100	105	1,495	55	40
British Columbia	1,536,085	28,965	610,825	4,535	35,925	1,830	805
Canada	9,513,750	3,602,590	3,409,895	74,710	204,330	37,890	12,130
Percent of Population							
Total							
Coquitlam	54.9	1.1	41.4	0.2	2.3	0.1	0.1
British Columbia	70.3	1.3	26.5	0.2	1.6	0.1	0.0
Canada	56.9	21.3	19.8	0.4	1.2	0.2	0.1
Males							
Coquitlam	56.2	1.1	40.1	0.2	2.3	0.1	0.1
British Columbia	71.4	1.3	25.4	0.2	1.5	0.1	0.0
Canada	57.5	21.2	19.4	0.4	1.2	0.2	0.1
Females							
Coquitlam	53.5	1.2	42.6	0.2	2.3	0.1	0.1
British Columbia	69.2	1.3	27.5	0.2	1.6	0.1	0.0
Canada	56.4	21.4	20.2	0.4	1.2	0.2	0.1

Note: Figures cover total population excluding institutional residents.
Source: Statistics Canada. 2012. Census Profile. 2011 Census. Statistics Canada Catalogue no. 98-316-XWE. Ottawa. Released October 24 2012.
http://www12.statcan.gc.ca/census-recensement/2011/dp-pd/prof/index.cfm?Lang=E

Language Spoken Most Often at Home

Area	English	French	Non-official Language	English & French	English & Non-official Language	French & Non-official Language	English, French & Non-official Language
			Number				
			Total				
Coquitlam	84,920	395	32,610	130	7,015	30	110
British Columbia	3,506,595	16,685	670,100	4,700	155,065	930	2,130
Canada	21,457,075	6,827,865	3,673,865	131,205	875,135	109,700	46,330
			Males				
Coquitlam	42,210	185	15,655	65	3,400	15	45
British Columbia	1,733,775	8,015	317,670	2,240	74,155	435	940
Canada	10,585,620	3,348,235	1,767,310	63,475	425,370	53,010	22,845
			Females				
Coquitlam	42,705	210	16,960	65	3,615	20	65
British Columbia	1,772,820	8,665	352,430	2,460	80,905	495	1,185
Canada	10,871,455	3,479,625	1,906,555	67,730	449,765	56,690	23,485
			Percent of Population				
			Total				
Coquitlam	67.8	0.3	26.0	0.1	5.6	0.0	0.1
British Columbia	80.5	0.4	15.4	0.1	3.6	0.0	0.0
Canada	64.8	20.6	11.1	0.4	2.6	0.3	0.1
			Males				
Coquitlam	68.5	0.3	25.4	0.1	5.5	0.0	0.1
British Columbia	81.1	0.4	14.9	0.1	3.5	0.0	0.0
Canada	65.1	20.6	10.9	0.4	2.6	0.3	0.1
			Females				
Coquitlam	67.1	0.3	26.7	0.1	5.7	0.0	0.1
British Columbia	79.9	0.4	15.9	0.1	3.6	0.0	0.1
Canada	64.5	20.6	11.3	0.4	2.7	0.3	0.1

Note: Figures cover total population excluding institutional residents.
Source: Statistics Canada. 2012. Census Profile. 2011 Census. Statistics Canada Catalogue no. 98-316-XWE. Ottawa. Released October 24 2012.
http://www12.statcan.gc.ca/census-recensement/2011/dp-pd/prof/index.cfm?Lang=E

Knowledge of Official Languages

Area	English Only	French Only	English & French	Neither English nor French
		Number		
		Total		
Coquitlam	111,635	60	8,025	5,490
British Columbia	3,912,950	2,045	296,645	144,555
Canada	22,564,665	4,165,015	5,795,570	595,920
		Males		
Coquitlam	55,785	25	3,525	2,245
British Columbia	1,943,760	950	132,940	59,590
Canada	11,222,185	1,925,340	2,876,560	241,790
		Females		
Coquitlam	55,850	35	4,500	3,250
British Columbia	1,969,190	1,095	163,705	84,965
Canada	11,342,485	2,239,680	2,919,005	354,135
		Percent of Population		
		Total		
Coquitlam	89.2	0.0	6.4	4.4
British Columbia	89.8	0.0	6.8	3.3
Canada	68.1	12.6	17.5	1.8
		Males		
Coquitlam	90.6	0.0	5.7	3.6
British Columbia	90.9	0.0	6.2	2.8
Canada	69.0	11.8	17.7	1.5
		Females		
Coquitlam	87.8	0.1	7.1	5.1
British Columbia	88.7	0.0	7.4	3.8
Canada	67.3	13.3	17.3	2.1

Note: Figures cover total population excluding institutional residents.
Source: Statistics Canada. 2012. Census Profile. 2011 Census. Statistics Canada Catalogue no. 98-316-XWE. Ottawa. Released October 24 2012.
http://www12.statcan.gc.ca/census-recensement/2011/dp-pd/prof/index.cfm?Lang=E

Edmonton, Alberta

Background

Edmonton is located on the North Saskatchewan River near the centre of the province of Alberta. Edmonton is the province's capital city and is often referred to as the "Gateway to the North." It is Canada's largest northern city. Edmonton is situated along the TransCanada Yellowhead Highway and offers easy and scenic access to northern Alberta's mountains, lakes and rivers.

Edmonton's physical landscape is rooted in Canadian history. The first fur-trading post in the Edmonton area was established in 1795 because of the region's abundance of building materials, beaver and bison. As the 19th century unfolded, Fort Edmonton grew to become the most powerful trading post west of present-day Winnipeg, Manitoba.

Today, Alberta's "boom times" translate into a growing economy for Edmonton. In 2011, Edmonton created 44,900 new jobs. The majority of jobs, particularly in accredited trades, offer incomes 26% higher than the national average. Edmonton is also facing a shortage in skilled labour, a trend affecting many of the city's industries and resource sectors.

Throughout the year, Edmonton celebrates its rich history through music, visual arts, dance, performing arts, sports and film. Edmonton is Canada's "Festival City" and offers more than 30 annual festivals such as the Canadian Finals Rodeo, Dreamspeakers (Aboriginal) Film Festival, Farmfair International and the Festival of Trees. The Edmonton Folk Music Festival in August is ranked as one of the best in the world.

Edmonton has average summer highs of plus 21.97 degrees Celsius, winter lows of minus 14.33 degrees Celsius, and an average rainfall just over 365 mm per year.

Rankings

- Edmonton was ranked #8 out of 190 Canadian cities for "Best Places to Live." *Money Sense Magazine* evaluated each city using 22 different criteria and point systems such as affordable housing, population growth, air quality and walk/bike to work ratios. *Money Sense, Canada's Best Places to Live, March 20, 2012*
- Edmonton's River Valley is Canada's largest urban green space. The city's "Ribbon of Green" consists of 27,400 acres of parkland (22 times larger than Central Park in New York) and offers Edmonton residents the highest area of green space in North America. *2011 Edmonton Economic Development Corporation*
- The Pembina Institute ranked Edmonton as having the most bike paths and on-street facilities per capita when compared to Vancouver, Calgary, Toronto, Ottawa and Montréal. Yet Edmonton commuters proved to be least likely to walk, cycle or use public transit. *Pembina Institute, Canada's Coolest Cities: Edmonton and CMA, May 26, 2010*
- Environment Canada ranked Edmonton #9 of the cities with the sunniest days per year in Canada. With an average of 321 days of bright sunshine annually, Edmonton was outranked by Calgary, a city with approximately 11 more days of sunshine (332 sunny days per year), the most in Canada. *Environment Canada, National Climate Data and Information Archive: Canadian Climate Normals or Averages 1971-2000*

PROFILES / Edmonton, Alberta

Population Growth and Density

Area	Population in 2001	Population in 2006	Population in 2011	Population Change 2001–2006	Population Change 2006–2011	Land Area (sq. km)	Population Density per sq. km
Edmonton	666,104	730,372	812,201	9.6	11.2	684.37	1,186.8
Alberta	2,974,807	3,290,350	3,645,257	10.6	10.8	640,081.87	5.7
Canada	30,007,094	31,612,897	33,476,688	5.4	5.9	8,965,121.42	3.7

Source: Statistics Canada. 2012. Census Profile. 2011 Census. Statistics Canada Catalogue no. 98-316-XWE. Ottawa. Released October 24 2012.
http://www12.statcan.gc.ca/census-recensement/2011/dp-pd/prof/index.cfm?Lang=E;
Statistics Canada 2007. 2006 Community Profiles. 2006 Census. Statistics Canada Catalogue no. 92-591-XWE. Ottawa. Released March 13 2007.
http://www12.statcan.ca/census-recensement/2006/dp-pd/prof/92-591/index.cfm?Lang=E

Gender

Area	Males	Females
Number		
Edmonton	404,875	407,325
Alberta	1,827,815	1,817,440
Canada	16,414,225	17,062,460
Percent of Population		
Edmonton	49.8	50.2
Alberta	50.1	49.9
Canada	49.0	51.0

Source: Statistics Canada. 2012. Census Profile. 2011 Census. Statistics Canada Catalogue no. 98-316-XWE. Ottawa. Released October 24 2012.
http://www12.statcan.gc.ca/census-recensement/2011/dp-pd/prof/index.cfm?Lang=E

Marital Status

Area	Married[1]	Living Common-law	Single[2]	Separated	Divorced	Widowed
Number — Total						
Edmonton	304,755	59,170	217,245	17,600	45,470	32,525
Alberta	1,484,700	272,155	823,935	70,860	177,375	131,440
Canada	12,941,960	3,142,525	7,816,045	698,240	1,686,035	1,584,530
Males						
Edmonton	153,165	29,635	120,135	7,700	18,645	6,195
Alberta	745,670	136,180	460,575	31,685	75,875	26,745
Canada	6,470,300	1,575,495	4,206,320	299,655	680,415	310,940
Females						
Edmonton	151,590	29,540	97,105	9,895	26,830	26,330
Alberta	739,035	135,980	363,355	39,170	101,500	104,695
Canada	6,471,660	1,567,035	3,609,730	398,585	1,005,620	1,273,590
Percent of Population — Total						
Edmonton	45.0	8.7	32.1	2.6	6.7	4.8
Alberta	50.2	9.2	27.8	2.4	6.0	4.4
Canada	46.4	11.3	28.0	2.5	6.0	5.7
Males						
Edmonton	45.7	8.8	35.8	2.3	5.6	1.8
Alberta	50.5	9.2	31.2	2.1	5.1	1.8
Canada	47.8	11.6	31.1	2.2	5.0	2.3
Females						
Edmonton	44.4	8.7	28.5	2.9	7.9	7.7
Alberta	49.8	9.2	24.5	2.6	6.8	7.1
Canada	45.2	10.9	25.2	2.8	7.0	8.9

Note: (1) and not separated, (2) never legally married
Source: Statistics Canada. 2012. Census Profile. 2011 Census. Statistics Canada Catalogue no. 98-316-XWE. Ottawa. Released October 24 2012.
http://www12.statcan.gc.ca/census-recensement/2011/dp-pd/prof/index.cfm?Lang=E

Age Characteristics: 0 to 49 Years

Area	0 to 4 Years	5 to 9 Years	10 to 14 Years	15 to 19 Years	20 to 24 Years	25 to 29 Years	30 to 34 Years	35 to 39 Years	40 to 44 Years	45 to 49 Years
	\multicolumn{10}{c|}{Number}									
	\multicolumn{10}{c|}{Total}									
Edmonton	50,560	42,320	42,555	48,950	67,850	75,695	65,365	57,450	55,955	60,100
Alberta	244,880	218,990	220,920	238,205	258,475	288,735	274,390	260,135	258,515	280,635
Canada	1,877,095	1,809,895	1,920,355	2,178,135	2,187,450	2,169,590	2,162,905	2,173,930	2,324,875	2,675,130
	\multicolumn{10}{c|}{Males}									
Edmonton	25,930	21,655	21,815	24,685	34,200	38,755	33,610	29,295	28,465	30,150
Alberta	125,665	112,005	113,415	122,065	131,510	146,330	138,600	131,810	130,630	140,575
Canada	961,150	925,965	983,995	1,115,845	1,108,775	1,077,275	1,058,810	1,064,200	1,141,720	1,318,715
	\multicolumn{10}{c|}{Females}									
Edmonton	24,630	20,665	20,745	24,265	33,650	36,935	31,750	28,150	27,490	29,945
Alberta	119,210	106,990	107,505	116,145	126,965	142,405	135,795	128,325	127,890	140,060
Canada	915,945	883,935	936,360	1,062,295	1,078,670	1,092,315	1,104,095	1,109,735	1,183,155	1,356,420
	\multicolumn{10}{c|}{Percent of Population}									
	\multicolumn{10}{c|}{Total}									
Edmonton	6.2	5.2	5.2	6.0	8.4	9.3	8.0	7.1	6.9	7.4
Alberta	6.7	6.0	6.1	6.5	7.1	7.9	7.5	7.1	7.1	7.7
Canada	5.6	5.4	5.7	6.5	6.5	6.5	6.5	6.5	6.9	8.0
	\multicolumn{10}{c|}{Males}									
Edmonton	6.4	5.3	5.4	6.1	8.4	9.6	8.3	7.2	7.0	7.4
Alberta	6.9	6.1	6.2	6.7	7.2	8.0	7.6	7.2	7.1	7.7
Canada	5.9	5.6	6.0	6.8	6.8	6.6	6.5	6.5	7.0	8.0
	\multicolumn{10}{c|}{Females}									
Edmonton	6.0	5.1	5.1	6.0	8.3	9.1	7.8	6.9	6.7	7.4
Alberta	6.6	5.9	5.9	6.4	7.0	7.8	7.5	7.1	7.0	7.7
Canada	5.4	5.2	5.5	6.2	6.3	6.4	6.5	6.5	6.9	7.9

Source: Statistics Canada. 2012. Census Profile. 2011 Census. Statistics Canada Catalogue no. 98-316-XWE. Ottawa. Released October 24 2012.
http://www12.statcan.gc.ca/census-recensement/2011/dp-pd/prof/index.cfm?Lang=E

Age Characteristics: 50 Years and Over, and Median Age

Area	50 to 54 Years	55 to 59 Years	60 to 64 Years	65 to 69 Years	70 to 74 Years	75 to 79 Years	80 to 84 Years	85 Years and Over	Median Age
	\multicolumn{9}{c|}{Number}								
	\multicolumn{9}{c|}{Total}								
Edmonton	60,290	51,205	39,255	26,640	21,515	18,365	14,820	13,320	36.0
Alberta	279,705	233,785	182,160	125,700	94,775	76,040	57,725	51,485	36.5
Canada	2,658,965	2,340,635	2,052,670	1,521,715	1,153,065	922,700	702,070	645,515	40.6
	\multicolumn{9}{c|}{Males}								
Edmonton	30,345	25,600	19,435	12,635	9,810	8,070	6,085	4,320	35.3
Alberta	141,370	118,750	90,975	61,790	45,220	35,205	24,810	17,095	35.9
Canada	1,309,030	1,147,300	1,002,690	738,010	543,435	417,945	291,085	208,300	39.6
	\multicolumn{9}{c|}{Females}								
Edmonton	29,945	25,605	19,820	14,005	11,700	10,295	8,740	9,000	36.9
Alberta	138,335	115,030	91,185	63,905	49,555	40,835	32,915	34,390	37.1
Canada	1,349,940	1,193,335	1,049,985	783,705	609,630	504,755	410,985	437,215	41.5
	\multicolumn{9}{c|}{Percent of Population}								
	\multicolumn{9}{c|}{Total}								
Edmonton	7.4	6.3	4.8	3.3	2.6	2.3	1.8	1.6	–
Alberta	7.7	6.4	5.0	3.4	2.6	2.1	1.6	1.4	–
Canada	7.9	7.0	6.1	4.5	3.4	2.8	2.1	1.9	–
	\multicolumn{9}{c|}{Males}								
Edmonton	7.5	6.3	4.8	3.1	2.4	2.0	1.5	1.1	–
Alberta	7.7	6.5	5.0	3.4	2.5	1.9	1.4	0.9	–
Canada	8.0	7.0	6.1	4.5	3.3	2.5	1.8	1.3	–
	\multicolumn{9}{c|}{Females}								
Edmonton	7.4	6.3	4.9	3.4	2.9	2.5	2.1	2.2	–
Alberta	7.6	6.3	5.0	3.5	2.7	2.2	1.8	1.9	–
Canada	7.9	7.0	6.2	4.6	3.6	3.0	2.4	2.6	–

Source: Statistics Canada. 2012. Census Profile. 2011 Census. Statistics Canada Catalogue no. 98-316-XWE. Ottawa. Released October 24 2012.
http://www12.statcan.gc.ca/census-recensement/2011/dp-pd/prof/index.cfm?Lang=E

PROFILES / Edmonton, Alberta

Private Households by Household Size

Area	1 Person	2 Persons	3 Persons	4 Persons	5 Persons	6 or More Persons	Average Number of Persons in Private Households
			Households				
Edmonton	94,910	105,815	51,940	43,960	17,635	10,495	2.5
Alberta	342,730	477,095	224,925	211,645	85,495	48,385	2.6
Canada	3,673,310	4,544,820	2,081,900	1,903,300	724,405	392,885	2.5
			Percent of Households				
Edmonton	29.2	32.6	16.0	13.5	5.4	3.2	–
Alberta	24.7	34.3	16.2	15.2	6.1	3.5	–
Canada	27.6	34.1	15.6	14.3	5.4	2.9	–

Source: Statistics Canada. 2012. Census Profile. 2011 Census. Statistics Canada Catalogue no. 98-316-XWE. Ottawa. Released October 24 2012.
http://www12.statcan.gc.ca/census-recensement/2011/dp-pd/prof/index.cfm?Lang=E

Dwelling Type

Area	Single-detached House	Semi-detached House	Row House	Apartment: Building with Five or More Storeys	Apartment: Building with Fewer Than Five Storeys	Duplex Apartment	Movable Dwelling	Other Single-attached House
				Number				
Edmonton	165,765	16,020	31,250	25,520	74,765	8,420	2,840	180
Alberta	883,265	71,845	97,865	58,205	197,940	33,505	46,590	1,060
Canada	7,329,150	646,245	791,600	1,234,770	2,397,550	704,485	183,510	33,310
				Percent of Dwellings				
Edmonton	51.0	4.9	9.6	7.9	23.0	2.6	0.9	0.1
Alberta	63.5	5.2	7.0	4.2	14.2	2.4	3.4	0.1
Canada	55.0	4.9	5.9	9.3	18.0	5.3	1.4	0.3

Source: Statistics Canada. 2012. Census Profile. 2011 Census. Statistics Canada Catalogue no. 98-316-XWE. Ottawa. Released October 24 2012.
http://www12.statcan.gc.ca/census-recensement/2011/dp-pd/prof/index.cfm?Lang=E

Shelter Costs

	Owned Dwellings					Rented Dwellings		
Area	Number	Median Value[1] ($)	Average Value[1] ($)	Median Monthly Costs[2] ($)	Average Monthly Costs[2] ($)	Number	Median Monthly Costs[3] ($)	Average Monthly Costs[3] ($)
Edmonton	210,655	349,154	379,968	1,222	1,278	114,090	1,003	1,055
Alberta	991,025	349,684	398,839	1,251	1,314	356,510	1,017	1,079
Canada	9,013,410	280,552	345,182	978	1,141	4,060,385	784	848

Note: All figures cover non-farm, non-reserve private dwellings; (1) Refers to the dollar amount expected by the owner if the dwelling were to be sold; (2) Includes all shelter expenses paid by households that own their dwellings, such as the mortgage payment and the costs of electricity, heat, water and other municipal services, property taxes and condominium fees; (3) Includes all shelter expenses paid by households that rent their dwellings, such as the monthly rent and the costs of electricity, heat and municipal services.
Source: Statistics Canada. 2013. 2011 National Household Survey. Statistics Canada Catalogue no. 99-004-XWE. Ottawa. Released September 11, 2013.

Occupied Private Dwellings by Period of Construction

Area	1960 or Before	1961 to 1980	1981 to 1990	1991 to 2000	2001 to 2005	2006 to 2011
			Number			
Edmonton	57,675	114,595	47,855	35,565	35,130	33,935
Alberta	189,745	440,825	202,060	214,705	170,660	172,290
Canada	3,273,105	4,152,715	2,112,110	1,707,880	1,031,020	1,042,430
			Percent of Dwellings			
Edmonton	17.8	35.3	14.7	11.0	10.8	10.4
Alberta	13.6	31.7	14.5	15.4	12.3	12.4
Canada	24.6	31.2	15.9	12.8	7.7	7.8

Note: Figures cover non-farm, non-reserve private dwellings and includes data up to May 10, 2011.
Source: Statistics Canada. 2013. 2011 National Household Survey. Statistics Canada Catalogue no. 99-004-XWE. Ottawa. Released September 11, 2013.

PROFILES / Edmonton, Alberta

Educational Attainment

Area	No Certificate, Diploma or Degree	High School Diploma or Equivalent[1]	Apprenticeship or Trades Certificate or Diploma[2]	College, CÉGEP or Other Non-University Certificate or Diploma	University Certificate or Diploma Below the Bachelor Level[3]	Bachelor's Degree	University Certificate, Diploma or Degree Above Bachelor Level[4]
				Number			
				Total			
Edmonton	115,630	172,970	62,650	116,090	32,345	105,925	55,205
Alberta	550,465	764,390	318,280	530,100	122,465	418,180	184,860
Canada	5,485,400	6,968,935	2,950,685	4,970,020	1,200,130	3,634,425	2,049,930
				Males			
Edmonton	56,335	83,415	46,375	50,650	14,090	48,300	29,150
Alberta	283,115	365,625	233,190	225,215	51,345	190,245	97,085
Canada	2,742,875	3,305,415	1,928,970	2,118,430	513,235	1,643,080	1,043,350
				Females			
Edmonton	59,295	89,550	16,275	65,435	18,255	57,625	26,060
Alberta	267,350	398,765	85,095	304,885	71,120	227,930	87,775
Canada	2,742,520	3,663,515	1,021,715	2,851,595	686,890	1,991,345	1,006,585
				Percent of Population			
				Total			
Edmonton	17.5	26.2	9.5	17.6	4.9	16.0	8.4
Alberta	19.1	26.5	11.0	18.4	4.2	14.5	6.4
Canada	20.1	25.6	10.8	18.2	4.4	13.3	7.5
				Males			
Edmonton	17.2	25.4	14.1	15.4	4.3	14.7	8.9
Alberta	19.6	25.3	16.1	15.6	3.6	13.2	6.7
Canada	20.6	24.9	14.5	15.9	3.9	12.4	7.8
				Females			
Edmonton	17.8	26.9	4.9	19.7	5.5	17.3	7.8
Alberta	18.5	27.6	5.9	21.1	4.9	15.8	6.1
Canada	19.6	26.2	7.3	20.4	4.9	14.3	7.2

Note: Figures cover total population aged 15 years and over by highest certificate, diploma or degree; (1) Includes persons who have graduated from a secondary school or equivalent. It excludes persons with a postsecondary certificate, diploma or degree; (2) Includes Registered Apprenticeship certificates (including Certificate of Qualification, Journeyperson's designation) and other trades certificates or diplomas such as pre-employment or vocational certificates and diplomas from brief trade programs completed at community colleges, institutes of technology, vocational centres, and similar institutions; (3) Comparisons with other data sources suggest that the category 'University certificate or diploma below the bachelor's level' was over-reported in the NHS. This category likely includes some responses that are actually college certificates or diplomas, bachelor's degrees or other types of education (e.g., university transfer programs, bachelor's programs completed in other countries, incomplete bachelor's programs, non-university professional designations). We recommend users interpret the results for the 'University certificate or diploma below the bachelor's level' category with caution; (4) 'University certificate or diploma above bachelor level' includes the categories: 'Degree in medicine, dentistry, veterinary medicine or optometry,' 'Master's degree' and 'Earned doctorate.'
Source: Statistics Canada. 2013. 2011 National Household Survey. Statistics Canada Catalogue no. 99-004-XWE. Ottawa. Released September 11, 2013.

Household Income Distribution

Area	Less than $10,000	$10,000 to $19,999	$20,000 to $29,999	$30,000 to $39,999	$40,000 to $49,999	$50,000 to $59,999	$60,000 to $79,999	$80,000 to $99,999	$100,000 to $124,999	$125,000 to $149,999	$150,000 and Over
						Households					
Edmonton	15,560	20,500	23,445	25,375	24,865	25,125	44,220	38,420	36,120	24,610	46,515
Alberta	55,620	75,390	87,985	102,290	100,165	100,965	184,540	166,110	158,540	113,010	245,665
Canada	626,705	1,141,945	1,193,925	1,271,675	1,206,800	1,102,120	1,865,280	1,458,240	1,260,770	802,555	1,389,240
						Percent of Households					
Edmonton	4.8	6.3	7.2	7.8	7.7	7.7	13.6	11.8	11.1	7.6	14.3
Alberta	4.0	5.4	6.3	7.4	7.2	7.3	13.3	11.9	11.4	8.1	17.7
Canada	4.7	8.6	9.0	9.5	9.1	8.3	14.0	10.9	9.5	6.0	10.4

Note: Household income is the sum of the total incomes of all members of that household. Total income refers to monetary receipts from certain sources, before income taxes and deductions, during calendar year 2010.
Source: Statistics Canada. 2013. 2011 National Household Survey. Statistics Canada Catalogue no. 99-004-XWE. Ottawa. Released September 11, 2013.

Median and Average Household and Economic Family Income

Area	Median Household Income ($)	Average Household Income ($)	Median After-tax Household Income ($)	Average After-tax Household Income ($)	Median Economic Family Income ($)	Average Economic Family Income ($)	Median After-tax Economic Family Income ($)	Average After-tax Economic Family Income ($)
Edmonton	72,248	90,340	62,877	75,566	89,252	107,644	77,447	89,901
Alberta	78,632	100,819	68,086	83,011	93,393	116,232	80,271	95,558
Canada	61,072	79,102	54,089	66,149	76,511	94,125	67,044	78,517

Note: Figures cover household and economic familiy income in 2010. A household is defined as a person or a group of persons (other than foreign residents) who occupy the same private dwelling and do not have a usual place of residence elsewhere in Canada. Every person is a member of one and only one household. An economic family is defined as a group of two or more persons who live in the same dwelling and are related to each other by blood, marriage, common-law, adoption or a foster relationship. A couple may be of opposite or same sex.
Source: Statistics Canada. 2013. 2011 National Household Survey. Statistics Canada Catalogue no. 99-004-XWE. Ottawa. Released September 11, 2013.

PROFILES / Edmonton, Alberta

Individual Income Distribution

Area	Less than $10,000	$10,000 to $19,999	$20,000 to $29,999	$30,000 to $39,999	$40,000 to $49,999	$50,000 to $59,999	$60,000 to $79,999	$80,000 to $99,999	$100,000 to $124,999	$125,000 and Over
					Number Total					
Edmonton	98,170	99,185	79,400	69,155	64,380	54,280	71,685	43,825	24,380	25,515
Alberta	437,495	408,190	340,195	293,435	268,335	219,080	303,265	196,520	122,465	161,750
Canada	4,492,040	4,835,710	3,670,020	3,180,360	2,603,520	1,921,650	2,437,440	1,302,045	693,580	782,135
					Males					
Edmonton	42,030	38,720	32,630	31,290	30,600	29,650	44,575	28,380	17,200	20,030
Alberta	176,040	152,740	137,535	132,145	130,180	120,865	188,080	127,695	89,525	131,500
Canada	1,936,365	1,864,880	1,588,260	1,522,190	1,333,510	1,079,780	1,473,145	823,720	492,905	599,905
					Females					
Edmonton	56,135	60,455	46,770	37,865	33,780	24,630	27,115	15,440	7,175	5,485
Alberta	261,460	255,450	202,660	161,285	138,160	98,215	115,185	68,830	32,935	30,250
Canada	2,555,675	2,970,825	2,081,760	1,658,170	1,270,010	841,870	964,300	478,330	200,680	182,230
					Percent of Population Total					
Edmonton	15.6	15.7	12.6	11.0	10.2	8.6	11.4	7.0	3.9	4.1
Alberta	15.9	14.8	12.4	10.7	9.8	8.0	11.0	7.1	4.5	5.9
Canada	17.3	18.7	14.2	12.3	10.0	7.4	9.4	5.0	2.7	3.0
					Males					
Edmonton	13.3	12.3	10.4	9.9	9.7	9.4	14.1	9.0	5.5	6.4
Alberta	12.7	11.0	9.9	9.5	9.4	8.7	13.6	9.2	6.5	9.5
Canada	15.2	14.7	12.5	12.0	10.5	8.5	11.6	6.5	3.9	4.7
					Females					
Edmonton	17.8	19.2	14.9	12.0	10.7	7.8	8.6	4.9	2.3	1.7
Alberta	19.2	18.7	14.9	11.8	10.1	7.2	8.4	5.0	2.4	2.2
Canada	19.4	22.5	15.8	12.6	9.6	6.4	7.3	3.6	1.5	1.4

Note: Figures cover individuals aged 15 years and over with income. Income refers to monetary receipts from certain sources, before income taxes and deductions, during calendar year 2010.
Source: Statistics Canada. 2013. 2011 National Household Survey. Statistics Canada Catalogue no. 99-004-XWE. Ottawa. Released September 11, 2013.

Labour Force Status

Area	In the Labour Force - All	Employed	Unemployed	Not in the Labour Force
		Number Total		
Edmonton	480,650	451,395	29,250	180,170
Alberta	2,115,640	1,993,225	122,415	773,095
Canada	17,990,080	16,595,035	1,395,045	9,269,445
		Males		
Edmonton	255,595	240,140	15,455	72,725
Alberta	1,143,840	1,078,370	65,470	301,975
Canada	9,388,570	8,634,310	754,255	3,906,785
		Females		
Edmonton	225,055	211,255	13,795	107,440
Alberta	971,800	914,855	56,945	471,120
Canada	8,601,515	7,960,725	640,790	5,362,660
		Percent of Labour Force Total		
Edmonton	72.7	68.3	6.1	27.3
Alberta	73.2	69.0	5.8	26.8
Canada	66.0	60.9	7.8	34.0
		Males		
Edmonton	77.8	73.1	6.0	22.2
Alberta	79.1	74.6	5.7	20.9
Canada	70.6	64.9	8.0	29.4
		Females		
Edmonton	67.7	63.5	6.1	32.3
Alberta	67.3	63.4	5.9	32.7
Canada	61.6	57.0	7.4	38.4

Note: Figures are based on total population 15 years and over
Source: Statistics Canada. 2013. 2011 National Household Survey. Statistics Canada Catalogue no. 99-004-XWE. Ottawa. Released September 11, 2013.

Labour Force by Industry (NAICS Codes 11–52)

Area	Agriculture, forestry, fishing & hunting	Mining, quarrying, & oil & gas extraction	Utilities	Construction	Manufacturing	Wholesale Trade	Retail Trade	Transportation & warehousing	Information & cultural industries	Finance & insurance
					Number					
					Total					
Edmonton	1,170	9,905	4,780	42,605	31,140	22,230	55,585	21,675	9,580	17,505
Alberta	61,165	136,500	22,035	195,905	123,465	89,000	229,225	104,770	35,465	68,760
Canada	437,650	261,050	149,940	1,215,380	1,619,295	733,445	2,031,665	827,780	420,830	767,960
					Males					
Edmonton	660	8,445	3,390	36,955	23,770	15,740	26,135	16,530	5,505	6,545
Alberta	41,465	104,825	15,725	166,270	93,895	63,590	104,725	76,070	18,990	24,355
Canada	307,370	211,690	110,765	1,068,710	1,167,680	494,545	933,850	617,305	235,875	296,995
					Females					
Edmonton	510	1,460	1,395	5,650	7,370	6,490	29,450	5,145	4,070	10,965
Alberta	19,700	31,670	6,305	29,635	29,570	25,415	124,500	28,700	16,470	44,410
Canada	130,285	49,360	39,175	146,670	451,615	238,900	1,097,820	210,475	184,955	470,960
					Percent of Labour Force					
					Total					
Edmonton	0.2	2.1	1.0	9.0	6.6	4.7	11.7	4.6	2.0	3.7
Alberta	2.9	6.5	1.1	9.4	5.9	4.3	11.0	5.0	1.7	3.3
Canada	2.5	1.5	0.9	6.9	9.2	4.2	11.6	4.7	2.4	4.4
					Males					
Edmonton	0.3	3.3	1.3	14.7	9.4	6.2	10.4	6.6	2.2	2.6
Alberta	3.7	9.3	1.4	14.7	8.3	5.6	9.3	6.7	1.7	2.2
Canada	3.3	2.3	1.2	11.6	12.7	5.4	10.2	6.7	2.6	3.2
					Females					
Edmonton	0.2	0.7	0.6	2.6	3.3	2.9	13.3	2.3	1.8	5.0
Alberta	2.1	3.3	0.7	3.1	3.1	2.7	13.0	3.0	1.7	4.6
Canada	1.6	0.6	0.5	1.7	5.4	2.8	13.1	2.5	2.2	5.6

Note: Figures are based on total experienced labour force 15 years and over. Experienced labour force refers to persons who, during the week of Sunday, May 1 to Saturday, May 7, 2011, were employed and the unemployed who had last worked for pay or in self-employment in either 2010 or 2011.
Source: Statistics Canada. 2013. 2011 National Household Survey. Statistics Canada Catalogue no. 99-004-XWE. Ottawa. Released September 11, 2013.

Labour Force by Industry (NAICS Codes 53–91)

Area	Real estate & rental & leasing	Profess., scientific & tech. services	Mgmt of companies & enterprises	Admin. & support, waste mgmt & remed. services	Educational services	Health care & social assistance	Arts, entertain. & recreation	Accomm. & food services	Other services (except public admin.)	Public admin.
					Number					
					Total					
Edmonton	9,505	35,035	385	17,590	37,330	53,370	8,495	32,915	23,690	38,695
Alberta	40,090	162,490	2,535	72,965	141,550	206,695	39,720	125,810	101,275	128,720
Canada	321,895	1,240,850	17,460	728,330	1,301,435	1,949,650	363,405	1,130,750	807,800	1,261,050
					Males					
Edmonton	5,095	20,020	175	9,745	13,980	10,340	4,415	13,745	11,250	19,670
Alberta	22,305	91,715	1,270	40,320	44,045	33,030	19,510	50,795	49,330	69,075
Canada	179,090	688,625	9,380	411,250	424,915	349,430	188,270	469,990	372,940	652,510
					Females					
Edmonton	4,410	15,015	215	7,845	23,350	43,030	4,080	19,170	12,440	19,025
Alberta	17,790	70,780	1,260	32,645	97,505	173,665	20,215	75,020	51,950	59,650
Canada	142,805	552,225	8,075	317,085	876,515	1,600,220	175,135	660,760	434,865	608,535
					Percent of Labour Force					
					Total					
Edmonton	2.0	7.4	0.1	3.7	7.9	11.3	1.8	7.0	5.0	8.2
Alberta	1.9	7.8	0.1	3.5	6.8	9.9	1.9	6.0	4.8	6.2
Canada	1.8	7.1	0.1	4.1	7.4	11.1	2.1	6.4	4.6	7.2
					Males					
Edmonton	2.0	7.9	0.1	3.9	5.5	4.1	1.8	5.5	4.5	7.8
Alberta	2.0	8.1	0.1	3.6	3.9	2.9	1.7	4.5	4.4	6.1
Canada	1.9	7.5	0.1	4.5	4.6	3.8	2.0	5.1	4.1	7.1
					Females					
Edmonton	2.0	6.8	0.1	3.5	10.6	19.5	1.8	8.7	5.6	8.6
Alberta	1.9	7.4	0.1	3.4	10.2	18.1	2.1	7.8	5.4	6.2
Canada	1.7	6.6	0.1	3.8	10.4	19.1	2.1	7.9	5.2	7.2

Note: Figures are based on total experienced labour force 15 years and over. Experienced labour force refers to persons who, during the week of Sunday, May 1 to Saturday, May 7, 2011, were employed and the unemployed who had last worked for pay or in self-employment in either 2010 or 2011.
Source: Statistics Canada. 2013. 2011 National Household Survey. Statistics Canada Catalogue no. 99-004-XWE. Ottawa. Released September 11, 2013.

PROFILES / Edmonton, Alberta

Occupation

Area	Mgmt	Business, Finance & Admin.	Natural/ Applied Sciences & Related	Health	Education, Law & Social, Community & Government Services	Art, Culture, Recreation & Sport	Sales & Service	Trades, Transport & Equip. Operators & Related	Natural Resources, Agri. & Related Production	Mfg & Utilities
Number										
Total										
Edmonton	46,670	80,795	38,230	33,870	53,090	12,180	108,655	79,900	6,710	13,100
Alberta	248,520	347,880	168,725	125,125	211,945	45,140	438,865	367,650	69,950	64,345
Canada	1,963,600	2,902,045	1,237,775	1,107,200	2,064,675	503,415	4,068,170	2,537,775	397,930	805,040
Males										
Edmonton	28,535	24,545	29,660	7,200	20,220	5,410	46,655	74,260	5,870	9,745
Alberta	160,145	93,875	131,715	22,050	71,815	18,290	180,675	342,230	59,115	51,385
Canada	1,229,460	854,190	966,355	217,520	676,550	232,535	1,745,705	2,385,615	318,945	564,300
Females										
Edmonton	18,135	56,250	8,565	26,675	32,865	6,770	61,995	5,635	840	3,355
Alberta	88,370	254,005	37,005	103,070	140,135	26,855	258,190	25,425	10,835	12,960
Canada	734,140	2,047,855	271,415	889,675	1,388,130	270,875	2,322,465	152,165	78,980	240,740
Percent of Labour Force										
Total										
Edmonton	9.9	17.1	8.1	7.2	11.2	2.6	23.0	16.9	1.4	2.8
Alberta	11.9	16.7	8.1	6.0	10.1	2.2	21.0	17.6	3.3	3.1
Canada	11.2	16.5	7.0	6.3	11.7	2.9	23.1	14.4	2.3	4.6
Males										
Edmonton	11.3	9.7	11.8	2.9	8.0	2.1	18.5	29.5	2.3	3.9
Alberta	14.2	8.3	11.6	1.9	6.3	1.6	16.0	30.3	5.2	4.5
Canada	13.4	9.3	10.5	2.4	7.4	2.5	19.0	26.0	3.5	6.1
Females										
Edmonton	8.2	25.4	3.9	12.1	14.9	3.1	28.0	2.5	0.4	1.5
Alberta	9.2	26.5	3.9	10.8	14.6	2.8	27.0	2.7	1.1	1.4
Canada	8.7	24.4	3.2	10.6	16.5	3.2	27.7	1.8	0.9	2.9

Note: Figures are based on total experienced labour force 15 years and over
Source: Statistics Canada. 2013. 2011 National Household Survey. Statistics Canada Catalogue no. 99-004-XWE. Ottawa. Released September 11, 2013.

Place of Work Status

Area	Worked at Home	Worked Outside Canada	No Fixed Workplace Address	Worked at Usual Place
Number				
Total				
Edmonton	20,125	1,170	57,660	372,445
Alberta	147,245	6,620	292,055	1,547,305
Canada	1,142,640	66,460	1,868,245	13,517,690
Males				
Edmonton	9,015	795	44,120	186,210
Alberta	71,245	5,175	228,125	773,825
Canada	582,150	47,355	1,400,485	6,604,325
Females				
Edmonton	11,105	375	13,545	186,235
Alberta	76,005	1,445	63,930	773,480
Canada	560,490	19,100	467,760	6,913,370
Percent of Labour Force				
Total				
Edmonton	4.5	0.3	12.8	82.5
Alberta	7.4	0.3	14.7	77.6
Canada	6.9	0.4	11.3	81.5
Males				
Edmonton	3.8	0.3	18.4	77.5
Alberta	6.6	0.5	21.2	71.8
Canada	6.7	0.5	16.2	76.5
Females				
Edmonton	5.3	0.2	6.4	88.2
Alberta	8.3	0.2	7.0	84.5
Canada	7.0	0.2	5.9	86.8

Note: Figures are based on total employed labour force 15 years and over.
Source: Statistics Canada. 2013. 2011 National Household Survey. Statistics Canada Catalogue no. 99-004-XWE. Ottawa. Released September 11, 2013.

Mode of Transportation to Work

Area	Car; Truck; Van; as Driver	Car; Truck; Van; as Passenger	Public Transit	Walked	Bicycled	All Other Modes
			Number			
			Total			
Edmonton	310,675	24,395	63,670	19,825	5,955	5,585
Alberta	1,406,150	103,715	193,115	91,005	19,535	25,835
Canada	11,393,140	867,050	1,851,525	880,815	201,780	191,625
			Males			
Edmonton	177,860	9,880	26,400	8,750	4,170	3,260
Alberta	798,140	43,990	91,260	40,550	13,950	14,055
Canada	6,238,835	349,530	788,290	387,580	135,840	104,725
			Females			
Edmonton	132,810	14,510	37,265	11,070	1,780	2,325
Alberta	608,010	59,725	101,855	50,450	5,585	11,780
Canada	5,154,305	517,520	1,063,235	493,230	65,940	86,900
			Percent of Labour Force			
			Total			
Edmonton	72.2	5.7	14.8	4.6	1.4	1.3
Alberta	76.4	5.6	10.5	4.9	1.1	1.4
Canada	74.0	5.6	12.0	5.7	1.3	1.2
			Males			
Edmonton	77.2	4.3	11.5	3.8	1.8	1.4
Alberta	79.7	4.4	9.1	4.0	1.4	1.4
Canada	77.9	4.4	9.8	4.8	1.7	1.3
			Females			
Edmonton	66.5	7.3	18.7	5.5	0.9	1.2
Alberta	72.6	7.1	12.2	6.0	0.7	1.4
Canada	69.8	7.0	14.4	6.7	0.9	1.2

Note: Figures are based on total employed labour force 15 years and over.
Source: Statistics Canada. 2013. 2011 National Household Survey. Statistics Canada Catalogue no. 99-004-XWE. Ottawa. Released September 11, 2013.

Visible Minority Population Characteristics

Area	Total Minority	South Asian[1]	Chinese	Black	Filipino	Latin American	Arab	SE Asian[2]	West Asian[3]	Korean	Japanese	Multiple[4]
					Number							
					Total							
Edmonton	238,755	57,500	49,660	30,355	36,565	13,330	13,800	15,480	6,610	4,565	2,080	6,665
Alberta	656,325	156,665	133,390	74,435	106,035	41,305	34,920	41,025	16,030	15,000	12,415	18,840
Canada	6,264,750	1,567,400	1,324,750	945,665	619,310	381,280	380,620	312,075	206,840	161,130	87,270	171,935
					Males							
Edmonton	118,865	29,630	24,190	15,600	16,695	6,680	7,440	7,820	3,490	2,040	845	3,300
Alberta	326,340	81,035	64,845	39,170	47,370	21,205	18,510	20,440	8,600	7,235	5,595	9,210
Canada	3,043,010	790,755	632,325	453,005	268,885	186,355	203,485	154,035	105,620	77,165	38,270	83,335
					Females							
Edmonton	119,890	27,870	25,470	14,755	19,865	6,645	6,365	7,665	3,115	2,525	1,235	3,370
Alberta	329,985	75,630	68,550	35,265	58,660	20,095	16,415	20,585	7,425	7,765	6,820	9,630
Canada	3,221,745	776,650	692,420	492,660	350,425	194,925	177,140	158,045	101,220	83,965	48,990	88,600
					Percent of Population							
					Total							
Edmonton	30.0	7.2	6.2	3.8	4.6	1.7	1.7	1.9	0.8	0.6	0.3	0.8
Alberta	18.4	4.4	3.7	2.1	3.0	1.2	1.0	1.1	0.4	0.4	0.3	0.5
Canada	19.1	4.8	4.0	2.9	1.9	1.2	1.2	0.9	0.6	0.5	0.3	0.5
					Males							
Edmonton	29.9	7.5	6.1	3.9	4.2	1.7	1.9	2.0	0.9	0.5	0.2	0.8
Alberta	18.2	4.5	3.6	2.2	2.6	1.2	1.0	1.1	0.5	0.4	0.3	0.5
Canada	18.8	4.9	3.9	2.8	1.7	1.2	1.3	1.0	0.7	0.5	0.2	0.5
					Females							
Edmonton	30.1	7.0	6.4	3.7	5.0	1.7	1.6	1.9	0.8	0.6	0.3	0.8
Alberta	18.6	4.3	3.9	2.0	3.3	1.1	0.9	1.2	0.4	0.4	0.4	0.5
Canada	19.3	4.7	4.1	3.0	2.1	1.2	1.1	0.9	0.6	0.5	0.3	0.5

Note: The Employment Equity Act defines visible minorities as 'persons, other than Aboriginal peoples, who are non-Caucasian in race or non-white in colour';
(1) Includes 'East Indian,' 'Pakistani,' 'Sri Lankan,' etc.; (2) Includes 'Vietnamese,' 'Cambodian,' 'Malaysian,' 'Laotian,' etc.; (3) Includes 'Iranian,' 'Afghan,' etc.; (4) Includes respondents who reported more than one visible minority group by checking two or more mark-in circles, e.g., 'Black' and 'South Asian.'
Source: Statistics Canada. 2013. 2011 National Household Survey. Statistics Canada Catalogue no. 99-004-XWE. Ottawa. Released September 11, 2013.

PROFILES / Edmonton, Alberta

Aboriginal Population

Area	Aboriginal Identity[1]	First Nations (North American Indian) Single Identity[2]	Métis Single Identity	Inuk (Inuit) Single Identity	Multiple Aboriginal Identities[3]	Aboriginal Identities Not Included Elsewhere
Number						
Total						
Edmonton	41,985	18,860	21,160	695	735	540
Alberta	220,695	116,670	96,870	1,985	1,870	3,300
Canada	1,400,685	851,560	451,795	59,440	11,415	26,475
Males						
Edmonton	19,825	8,355	10,545	335	320	265
Alberta	108,295	56,470	48,345	1,035	965	1,480
Canada	682,190	411,785	223,335	29,495	5,525	12,055
Females						
Edmonton	22,170	10,500	10,615	360	415	275
Alberta	112,400	60,200	48,525	950	905	1,815
Canada	718,500	439,775	228,460	29,950	5,890	14,420
Percent of Population						
Total						
Edmonton	5.3	2.4	2.7	0.1	0.1	0.1
Alberta	6.2	3.3	2.7	0.1	0.1	0.1
Canada	4.3	2.6	1.4	0.2	0.0	0.1
Males						
Edmonton	5.0	2.1	2.7	0.1	0.1	0.1
Alberta	6.0	3.1	2.7	0.1	0.1	0.1
Canada	4.2	2.5	1.4	0.2	0.0	0.1
Females						
Edmonton	5.6	2.6	2.7	0.1	0.1	0.1
Alberta	6.3	3.4	2.7	0.1	0.1	0.1
Canada	4.3	2.6	1.4	0.2	0.0	0.1

Note: (1) Includes persons who reported being an Aboriginal person, that is, First Nations (North American Indian), Métis or Inuk (Inuit) and/or those who reported Registered or Treaty Indian status, that is registered under the Indian Act of Canada, and/or those who reported membership in a First Nation or Indian band. Aboriginal peoples of Canada are defined in the Constitution Act, 1982, section 35-2 as including the Indian, Inuit and Métis peoples of Canada; (2) Users should be aware that the estimates associated with this variable are more affected than most by the incomplete enumeration of certain Indian reserves and Indian settlements in the National Household Survey (NHS); (3) Includes persons who reported being any two or all three of the following: First Nations (North American Indian), Métis or Inuk (Inuit).
Source: Statistics Canada. 2013. 2011 National Household Survey. Statistics Canada Catalogue no. 99-004-XWE. Ottawa. Released September 11, 2013.

Ethnic Origin

Area	North American Aboriginal	Other North American	European	Caribbean	Latin, Central and South American	African	Asian	Oceania
Number								
Total								
Edmonton	50,300	149,370	499,955	8,490	15,190	30,880	197,860	3,025
Alberta	263,720	830,700	2,506,665	25,035	54,650	78,580	551,715	12,985
Canada	1,836,035	11,070,455	20,157,965	627,590	544,375	766,735	5,011,225	74,875
Males								
Edmonton	23,905	75,775	248,260	4,070	7,630	16,205	97,855	1,620
Alberta	129,275	424,805	1,254,145	12,420	27,550	41,680	271,145	6,620
Canada	885,675	5,462,685	9,913,150	291,640	264,635	387,360	2,435,540	37,490
Females								
Edmonton	26,395	73,595	251,690	4,420	7,555	14,675	100,000	1,415
Alberta	134,445	405,895	1,252,520	12,620	27,105	36,895	280,570	6,360
Canada	950,360	5,607,770	10,244,820	335,945	279,740	379,380	2,575,680	37,385
Percent of Population								
Total								
Edmonton	6.3	18.8	62.8	1.1	1.9	3.9	24.9	0.4
Alberta	7.4	23.3	70.3	0.7	1.5	2.2	15.5	0.4
Canada	5.6	33.7	61.4	1.9	1.7	2.3	15.3	0.2
Males								
Edmonton	6.0	19.1	62.5	1.0	1.9	4.1	24.7	0.4
Alberta	7.2	23.7	69.9	0.7	1.5	2.3	15.1	0.4
Canada	5.5	33.8	61.3	1.8	1.6	2.4	15.1	0.2
Females								
Edmonton	6.6	18.5	63.1	1.1	1.9	3.7	25.1	0.4
Alberta	7.6	22.9	70.6	0.7	1.5	2.1	15.8	0.4
Canada	5.7	33.6	61.4	2.0	1.7	2.3	15.4	0.2

Note: The sum of the ethnic groups in this table is greater than the total population estimate because a person may report more than one ethnic origin in the NHS.
Source: Statistics Canada. 2013. 2011 National Household Survey. Statistics Canada Catalogue no. 99-004-XWE. Ottawa. Released September 11, 2013.

Religion

Area	Buddhist	Christian	Hindu	Jewish	Muslim	Sikh	Traditional (Aboriginal) Spirituality	Other Religions	No Religious Affiliation
				Number					
				Total					
Edmonton	16,840	444,560	14,865	3,445	43,645	19,555	1,240	4,375	247,150
Alberta	44,410	2,152,200	36,845	10,900	113,445	52,335	15,100	16,605	1,126,130
Canada	366,830	22,102,745	497,965	329,495	1,053,945	454,965	64,935	130,835	7,850,605
				Males					
Edmonton	8,065	210,590	7,630	1,695	22,755	10,050	490	1,850	133,785
Alberta	20,725	1,029,310	19,120	5,405	59,005	26,825	7,420	7,525	618,330
Canada	168,465	10,497,775	250,435	161,265	540,555	229,435	31,805	57,745	4,225,645
				Females					
Edmonton	8,775	233,970	7,230	1,750	20,890	9,510	755	2,525	113,365
Alberta	23,680	1,122,890	17,725	5,495	54,435	25,510	7,680	9,080	507,800
Canada	198,365	11,604,975	247,525	168,235	513,395	225,530	33,135	73,090	3,624,965
				Percent of Population					
				Total					
Edmonton	2.1	55.9	1.9	0.4	5.5	2.5	0.2	0.5	31.1
Alberta	1.2	60.3	1.0	0.3	3.2	1.5	0.4	0.5	31.6
Canada	1.1	67.3	1.5	1.0	3.2	1.4	0.2	0.4	23.9
				Males					
Edmonton	2.0	53.1	1.9	0.4	5.7	2.5	0.1	0.5	33.7
Alberta	1.2	57.4	1.1	0.3	3.3	1.5	0.4	0.4	34.5
Canada	1.0	64.9	1.5	1.0	3.3	1.4	0.2	0.4	26.1
				Females					
Edmonton	2.2	58.7	1.8	0.4	5.2	2.4	0.2	0.6	28.4
Alberta	1.3	63.3	1.0	0.3	3.1	1.4	0.4	0.5	28.6
Canada	1.2	69.5	1.5	1.0	3.1	1.4	0.2	0.4	21.7

Note: Religion refers to the person's self-identification as having a connection or affiliation with any religious denomination, group, body, sect, cult or other religiously defined community or system of belief. Religion is not limited to formal membership in a religious organization or group. Persons without a religious connection or affiliation can self-identify as atheist, agnostic or humanist, or can provide another applicable response.
Source: Statistics Canada. 2013. 2011 National Household Survey. Statistics Canada Catalogue no. 99-004-XWE. Ottawa. Released September 11, 2013.

Religion—Christian Denominations

Area	Anglican	Baptist	Catholic	Christian Orthodox	Lutheran	Pentecostal	Presbyterian	United Church	Other Christian
				Number					
				Total					
Edmonton	23,935	15,150	206,030	19,220	20,720	14,360	5,955	39,405	99,775
Alberta	140,665	66,635	866,305	51,340	119,345	60,960	36,765	268,675	541,520
Canada	1,631,845	635,840	12,810,705	550,690	478,185	478,705	472,385	2,007,610	3,036,780
				Males					
Edmonton	11,275	7,265	99,305	9,065	9,585	6,625	2,790	17,625	47,045
Alberta	65,130	31,645	422,160	25,145	56,120	28,580	16,835	123,255	260,440
Canada	752,945	293,905	6,167,290	270,205	221,525	217,850	218,955	912,545	1,442,550
				Females					
Edmonton	12,655	7,885	106,720	10,160	11,130	7,735	3,165	21,785	52,735
Alberta	75,535	34,990	444,145	26,190	63,220	32,380	19,925	145,420	281,075
Canada	878,900	341,940	6,643,415	280,485	256,660	260,850	253,430	1,095,065	1,594,230
				Percent of Population					
				Total					
Edmonton	3.0	1.9	25.9	2.4	2.6	1.8	0.7	5.0	12.5
Alberta	3.9	1.9	24.3	1.4	3.3	1.7	1.0	7.5	15.2
Canada	5.0	1.9	39.0	1.7	1.5	1.5	1.4	6.1	9.2
				Males					
Edmonton	2.8	1.8	25.0	2.3	2.4	1.7	0.7	4.4	11.9
Alberta	3.6	1.8	23.5	1.4	3.1	1.6	0.9	6.9	14.5
Canada	4.7	1.8	38.2	1.7	1.4	1.3	1.4	5.6	8.9
				Females					
Edmonton	3.2	2.0	26.8	2.5	2.8	1.9	0.8	5.5	13.2
Alberta	4.3	2.0	25.0	1.5	3.6	1.8	1.1	8.2	15.8
Canada	5.3	2.0	39.8	1.7	1.5	1.6	1.5	6.6	9.6

Note: Religion refers to the person's self-identification as having a connection or affiliation with any religious denomination, group, body, sect, cult or other religiously defined community or system of belief. Religion is not limited to formal membership in a religious organization or group. Persons without a religious connection or affiliation can self-identify as atheist, agnostic or humanist, or can provide another applicable response.
Source: Statistics Canada. 2013. 2011 National Household Survey. Statistics Canada Catalogue no. 99-004-XWE. Ottawa. Released September 11, 2013.

PROFILES / Edmonton, Alberta

Immigrant Status and Period of Immigration

Area	Non-Immigrants[1]	Immigrants All	Before 1971	1971 to 1980	1981 to 1990	1991 to 2000	2001 to 2005	2006 to 2011	Non-Permanent Residents[3]
				Number					
				Total					
Edmonton	570,290	205,445	26,355	27,400	30,155	40,560	34,905	46,075	19,940
Alberta	2,864,240	644,115	92,610	83,620	86,190	124,465	113,060	144,170	59,620
Canada	25,720,175	6,775,765	1,261,055	870,775	949,890	1,539,050	992,070	1,162,915	356,385
				Males					
Edmonton	286,880	99,015	12,700	13,495	14,295	18,905	17,440	22,175	11,010
Alberta	1,449,740	313,170	45,390	41,910	41,145	58,970	56,395	69,360	30,765
Canada	12,753,235	3,231,370	605,430	416,670	454,570	724,905	474,545	555,245	178,515
				Females					
Edmonton	283,405	106,430	13,655	13,900	15,860	21,655	17,470	23,905	8,930
Alberta	1,414,500	330,940	47,220	41,710	45,040	65,495	56,660	74,815	28,855
Canada	12,966,935	3,544,400	655,625	454,105	495,325	814,145	517,530	607,670	177,870
				Percent of Population					
				Total					
Edmonton	71.7	25.8	3.3	3.4	3.8	5.1	4.4	5.8	2.5
Alberta	80.3	18.1	2.6	2.3	2.4	3.5	3.2	4.0	1.7
Canada	78.3	20.6	3.8	2.7	2.9	4.7	3.0	3.5	1.1
				Males					
Edmonton	72.3	24.9	3.2	3.4	3.6	4.8	4.4	5.6	2.8
Alberta	80.8	17.5	2.5	2.3	2.3	3.3	3.1	3.9	1.7
Canada	78.9	20.0	3.7	2.6	2.8	4.5	2.9	3.4	1.1
				Females					
Edmonton	71.1	26.7	3.4	3.5	4.0	5.4	4.4	6.0	2.2
Alberta	79.7	18.7	2.7	2.4	2.5	3.7	3.2	4.2	1.6
Canada	77.7	21.2	3.9	2.7	3.0	4.9	3.1	3.6	1.1

Note: (1) Non-immigrant refers to a person who is a Canadian citizen by birth; (2) Immigrant refers to a person who is or has ever been a landed immigrant/permanent resident. This person has been granted the right to live in Canada permanently by immigration authorities. Some immigrants have resided in Canada for a number of years, while others have arrived recently. Some immigrants are Canadian citizens, while others are not. Most immigrants are born outside Canada, but a small number are born in Canada. In the 2011 National Household Survey, 'Immigrants' includes immigrants who landed in Canada prior to May 10, 2011; (3) Non-permanent resident refers to a person from another country who has a work or study permit, or who is a refugee claimant, and any non-Canadian-born family member living in Canada with them.
Source: Statistics Canada. 2013. 2011 National Household Survey. Statistics Canada Catalogue no. 99-004-XWE. Ottawa. Released September 11, 2013.

Mother Tongue

Area	English	French	Non-official Language	English & French	English & Non-official Language	French & Non-official Language	English, French & Non-official Language
			Number				
			Total				
Edmonton	545,840	16,180	219,195	2,110	16,525	945	410
Alberta	2,780,200	68,545	698,930	8,410	49,970	2,945	1,185
Canada	18,858,980	7,054,975	6,567,680	144,685	396,330	74,430	24,095
			Males				
Edmonton	275,805	8,425	105,940	1,000	7,915	460	190
Alberta	1,405,655	35,355	340,125	4,045	24,210	1,500	565
Canada	9,345,225	3,452,380	3,157,785	69,975	192,000	36,535	11,965
			Females				
Edmonton	270,035	7,750	113,255	1,110	8,605	490	215
Alberta	1,374,545	33,195	358,805	4,365	25,760	1,440	620
Canada	9,513,750	3,602,590	3,409,895	74,710	204,330	37,890	12,130
			Percent of Population				
			Total				
Edmonton	68.1	2.0	27.4	0.3	2.1	0.1	0.1
Alberta	77.0	1.9	19.4	0.2	1.4	0.1	0.0
Canada	56.9	21.3	19.8	0.4	1.2	0.2	0.1
			Males				
Edmonton	69.0	2.1	26.5	0.3	2.0	0.1	0.0
Alberta	77.6	2.0	18.8	0.2	1.3	0.1	0.0
Canada	57.5	21.2	19.4	0.4	1.2	0.2	0.1
			Females				
Edmonton	67.3	1.9	28.2	0.3	2.1	0.1	0.1
Alberta	76.4	1.8	19.9	0.2	1.4	0.1	0.0
Canada	56.4	21.4	20.2	0.4	1.2	0.2	0.1

Note: Figures cover total population excluding institutional residents.
Source: Statistics Canada. 2012. Census Profile. 2011 Census. Statistics Canada Catalogue no. 98-316-XWE. Ottawa. Released October 24 2012.
http://www12.statcan.gc.ca/census-recensement/2011/dp-pd/prof/index.cfm?Lang=E

Language Spoken Most Often at Home

Area	English	French	Non-official Language	English & French	English & Non-official Language	French & Non-official Language	English, French & Non-official Language
			Number				
			Total				
Edmonton	634,740	6,550	120,890	1,420	36,590	365	635
Alberta	3,095,250	24,690	379,550	4,945	102,995	1,115	1,640
Canada	21,457,075	6,827,865	3,673,865	131,205	875,135	109,700	46,330
			Males				
Edmonton	318,050	3,390	59,225	760	17,845	180	295
Alberta	1,557,420	12,545	187,125	2,520	50,465	570	815
Canada	10,585,620	3,348,235	1,767,310	63,475	425,370	53,010	22,845
			Females				
Edmonton	316,695	3,160	61,665	665	18,750	185	345
Alberta	1,537,830	12,140	192,425	2,425	52,535	550	825
Canada	10,871,455	3,479,625	1,906,555	67,730	449,765	56,690	23,485
			Percent of Population				
			Total				
Edmonton	79.2	0.8	15.1	0.2	4.6	0.0	0.1
Alberta	85.7	0.7	10.5	0.1	2.9	0.0	0.0
Canada	64.8	20.6	11.1	0.4	2.6	0.3	0.1
			Males				
Edmonton	79.6	0.8	14.8	0.2	4.5	0.0	0.1
Alberta	86.0	0.7	10.3	0.1	2.8	0.0	0.0
Canada	65.1	20.6	10.9	0.4	2.6	0.3	0.1
			Females				
Edmonton	78.9	0.8	15.4	0.2	4.7	0.0	0.1
Alberta	85.5	0.7	10.7	0.1	2.9	0.0	0.0
Canada	64.5	20.6	11.3	0.4	2.7	0.3	0.1

Note: Figures cover total population excluding institutional residents.
Source: Statistics Canada. 2012. Census Profile. 2011 Census. Statistics Canada Catalogue no. 98-316-XWE. Ottawa. Released October 24 2012.
http://www12.statcan.gc.ca/census-recensement/2011/dp-pd/prof/index.cfm?Lang=E

Knowledge of Official Languages

Area	English Only	French Only	English & French	Neither English nor French
		Number		
		Total		
Edmonton	725,920	1,075	58,210	15,995
Alberta	3,321,810	3,205	235,565	49,600
Canada	22,564,665	4,165,015	5,795,570	595,920
		Males		
Edmonton	365,425	465	27,580	6,260
Alberta	1,679,330	1,430	110,485	20,210
Canada	11,222,185	1,925,340	2,876,560	241,790
		Females		
Edmonton	360,495	605	30,630	9,730
Alberta	1,642,480	1,780	125,075	29,395
Canada	11,342,485	2,239,680	2,919,005	354,135
		Percent of Population		
		Total		
Edmonton	90.6	0.1	7.3	2.0
Alberta	92.0	0.1	6.5	1.4
Canada	68.1	12.6	17.5	1.8
		Males		
Edmonton	91.4	0.1	6.9	1.6
Alberta	92.7	0.1	6.1	1.1
Canada	69.0	11.8	17.7	1.5
		Females		
Edmonton	89.8	0.2	7.6	2.4
Alberta	91.3	0.1	7.0	1.6
Canada	67.3	13.3	17.3	2.1

Note: Figures cover total population excluding institutional residents.
Source: Statistics Canada. 2012. Census Profile. 2011 Census. Statistics Canada Catalogue no. 98-316-XWE. Ottawa. Released October 24 2012.
http://www12.statcan.gc.ca/census-recensement/2011/dp-pd/prof/index.cfm?Lang=E

Gatineau, Québec

Background

Gatineau is a city in western Québec located on the northern banks of the Ottawa River. The city is immediately across from Ottawa, the nation's capital in Ontario. Ottawa-Gatineau forms Canada's National Capital Region. In 2011, Gatineau was Québec's fourth largest city with a population of 265,349. Gatineau is the amalgamation of the former cities of Hull, Aylmer, Buckingham and Masson-Angers, which took place in 2002.

The region's written history dates back to Samuel de Champlain's first contact with Algonquin Aboriginals in 1631. However, the area did not significantly develop until after 1800. Early settlers cultivated Gatineau's abundant forests, which led to a booming wood and pulp-and-paper industry by 1875.

Today, Gatineau is considered a part of the Ottawa-Gatineau Census Metropolitan Area (CMA); the only CMA in Canada that crosses provincial boundaries. Compared to other big cities, commuters in the region are more likely to walk, bike or take public transit to work.

Gatineau's top attractions include the Canadian Museum of Civilization, the Casino du Lac-Leamy and the ByWard Market. The Gatineau Hot Air Balloon Festival in September is the fifth largest balloon festival in the world. Every February, Ottawa-Gatineau hosts Winterlude, the Capital's winter celebration, which was created in 1979 to celebrate Canada's northern climate and culture. It includes such festivities as ice sculpting, snow sliding and skating on the Rideau Canal. Winterlude's mascot is the Ice Hog Family.

Gatineau has average summer highs of plus 25.07 degrees Celsius, winter lows of minus 12.77 degrees Celsius, and an average rainfall just over 733 mm per year.

Rankings

- The Centre for the Study of Living Standards ranked Gatineau one of the happiest cities in Canada. The Top 4 happiest cities were in Québec: Québec City, Gatineau, Trois-Rivieres and Montréal. The 2012 study showed the largest increases in overall life satisfaction between 2003 and 2011 happened in the province of Québec and Yukon Territory. *The Centre for the Study of Living Standards, "Canadians Are Happy and Getting Happier: An Overview of Life Satisfaction in Canada: 2003-2011," released September 25, 2012*
- The 2011 Census showed that Ottawa-Gatineau outpaced the national growth between 2006 and 2011. The census metropolitan area (CMA) increased by 9.1%, while the national population grew by 5.9% and Ontario by 5.7%. *Statistics Canada, 2012. Focus on Geography Series, 2011 Census, September 19, 2012*

PROFILES / Gatineau, Québec

Population Growth and Density

Area	Population in 2001	Population in 2006	Population in 2011	Population Change 2001–2006	Population Change 2006–2011	Land Area (sq. km)	Population Density per sq. km
Gatineau	226,696	242,124	265,349	6.8	9.6	342.98	773.7
Québec	7,237,479	7,546,131	7,903,001	4.3	4.7	1,356,547.02	5.8
Canada	30,007,094	31,612,897	33,476,688	5.4	5.9	8,965,121.42	3.7

Source: Statistics Canada. 2012. Census Profile. 2011 Census. Statistics Canada Catalogue no. 98-316-XWE. Ottawa. Released October 24 2012.
http://www12.statcan.gc.ca/census-recensement/2011/dp-pd/prof/index.cfm?Lang=E;
Statistics Canada 2007. 2006 Community Profiles. 2006 Census. Statistics Canada Catalogue no. 92-591-XWE. Ottawa. Released March 13 2007.
http://www12.statcan.ca/census-recensement/2006/dp-pd/prof/92-591/index.cfm?Lang=E

Gender

Area	Males	Females
Number		
Gatineau	128,405	136,945
Québec	3,875,860	4,027,140
Canada	16,414,225	17,062,460
Percent of Population		
Gatineau	48.4	51.6
Québec	49.0	51.0
Canada	49.0	51.0

Source: Statistics Canada. 2012. Census Profile. 2011 Census. Statistics Canada Catalogue no. 98-316-XWE. Ottawa. Released October 24 2012.
http://www12.statcan.gc.ca/census-recensement/2011/dp-pd/prof/index.cfm?Lang=E

Marital Status

Area	Married[1]	Living Common-law	Single[2]	Separated	Divorced	Widowed
Number – Total						
Gatineau	78,775	42,610	65,640	4,710	16,190	11,150
Québec	2,353,770	1,391,550	1,942,090	105,195	463,830	387,945
Canada	12,941,960	3,142,525	7,816,045	698,240	1,686,035	1,584,530
Males						
Gatineau	39,320	21,275	34,100	2,010	6,000	2,225
Québec	1,177,720	697,695	1,045,540	46,465	188,265	77,430
Canada	6,470,300	1,575,495	4,206,320	299,655	680,415	310,940
Females						
Gatineau	39,460	21,335	31,540	2,695	10,190	8,925
Québec	1,176,050	693,850	896,545	58,720	275,565	310,515
Canada	6,471,660	1,567,035	3,609,730	398,585	1,005,620	1,273,590
Percent of Population – Total						
Gatineau	36.0	19.4	30.0	2.1	7.4	5.1
Québec	35.4	20.9	29.2	1.6	7.0	5.8
Canada	46.4	11.3	28.0	2.5	6.0	5.7
Males						
Gatineau	37.5	20.3	32.5	1.9	5.7	2.1
Québec	36.4	21.6	32.3	1.4	5.8	2.4
Canada	47.8	11.6	31.1	2.2	5.0	2.3
Females						
Gatineau	34.6	18.7	27.6	2.4	8.9	7.8
Québec	34.5	20.3	26.3	1.7	8.1	9.1
Canada	45.2	10.9	25.2	2.8	7.0	8.9

Note: (1) and not separated, (2) never legally married
Source: Statistics Canada. 2012. Census Profile. 2011 Census. Statistics Canada Catalogue no. 98-316-XWE. Ottawa. Released October 24 2012.
http://www12.statcan.gc.ca/census-recensement/2011/dp-pd/prof/index.cfm?Lang=E

Age Characteristics: 0 to 49 Years

Area	0 to 4 Years	5 to 9 Years	10 to 14 Years	15 to 19 Years	20 to 24 Years	25 to 29 Years	30 to 34 Years	35 to 39 Years	40 to 44 Years	45 to 49 Years
					Number					
					Total					
Gatineau	16,605	14,500	15,165	17,995	18,360	18,505	19,115	18,300	18,785	22,235
Québec	440,840	399,575	418,205	491,980	489,185	490,665	531,445	498,225	520,805	623,575
Canada	1,877,095	1,809,895	1,920,355	2,178,135	2,187,450	2,169,590	2,162,905	2,173,930	2,324,875	2,675,130
					Males					
Gatineau	8,525	7,445	7,510	9,040	9,045	9,065	9,375	8,980	9,105	10,755
Québec	225,525	203,675	213,540	249,960	246,850	245,695	264,980	249,610	261,120	311,320
Canada	961,150	925,965	983,995	1,115,845	1,108,775	1,077,275	1,058,810	1,064,200	1,141,720	1,318,715
					Females					
Gatineau	8,085	7,055	7,655	8,960	9,315	9,445	9,740	9,320	9,685	11,480
Québec	215,320	195,900	204,665	242,020	242,340	244,970	266,460	248,615	259,690	312,250
Canada	915,945	883,935	936,360	1,062,295	1,078,670	1,092,315	1,104,095	1,109,735	1,183,155	1,356,420
					Percent of Population					
					Total					
Gatineau	6.3	5.5	5.7	6.8	6.9	7.0	7.2	6.9	7.1	8.4
Québec	5.6	5.1	5.3	6.2	6.2	6.2	6.7	6.3	6.6	7.9
Canada	5.6	5.4	5.7	6.5	6.5	6.5	6.5	6.5	6.9	8.0
					Males					
Gatineau	6.6	5.8	5.8	7.0	7.0	7.1	7.3	7.0	7.1	8.4
Québec	5.8	5.3	5.5	6.4	6.4	6.3	6.8	6.4	6.7	8.0
Canada	5.9	5.6	6.0	6.8	6.8	6.6	6.5	6.5	7.0	8.0
					Females					
Gatineau	5.9	5.2	5.6	6.5	6.8	6.9	7.1	6.8	7.1	8.4
Québec	5.3	4.9	5.1	6.0	6.0	6.1	6.6	6.2	6.4	7.8
Canada	5.4	5.2	5.5	6.2	6.4	6.5	6.5	6.5	6.9	7.9

Source: Statistics Canada. 2012. Census Profile. 2011 Census. Statistics Canada Catalogue no. 98-316-XWE. Ottawa. Released October 24 2012.
http://www12.statcan.gc.ca/census-recensement/2011/dp-pd/prof/index.cfm?Lang=E

Age Characteristics: 50 Years and Over, and Median Age

Area	50 to 54 Years	55 to 59 Years	60 to 64 Years	65 to 69 Years	70 to 74 Years	75 to 79 Years	80 to 84 Years	85 Years and Over	Median Age
					Number				
					Total				
Gatineau	21,935	18,020	14,735	10,555	7,260	5,660	4,225	3,390	38.4
Québec	648,695	579,280	512,830	403,210	291,755	232,355	176,420	153,945	41.9
Canada	2,658,965	2,340,635	2,052,670	1,521,715	1,153,065	922,700	702,070	645,515	40.6
					Males				
Gatineau	10,595	8,735	7,100	5,000	3,225	2,380	1,565	960	37.3
Québec	320,695	285,295	250,675	194,305	135,830	101,675	69,170	45,945	40.7
Canada	1,309,030	1,147,300	1,002,690	738,010	543,435	417,945	291,085	208,300	39.6
					Females				
Gatineau	11,340	9,285	7,630	5,555	4,030	3,280	2,660	2,430	39.4
Québec	327,995	293,990	262,155	208,905	155,925	130,680	107,250	108,005	43.0
Canada	1,349,940	1,193,335	1,049,985	783,705	609,630	504,755	410,985	437,215	41.5
					Percent of Population				
					Total				
Gatineau	8.3	6.8	5.6	4.0	2.7	2.1	1.6	1.3	—
Québec	8.2	7.3	6.5	5.1	3.7	2.9	2.2	1.9	—
Canada	7.9	7.0	6.1	4.5	3.4	2.8	2.1	1.9	—
					Males				
Gatineau	8.3	6.8	5.5	3.9	2.5	1.9	1.2	0.7	—
Québec	8.3	7.4	6.5	5.0	3.5	2.6	1.8	1.2	—
Canada	8.0	7.0	6.1	4.5	3.3	2.5	1.8	1.3	—
					Females				
Gatineau	8.3	6.8	5.6	4.1	2.9	2.4	1.9	1.8	—
Québec	8.1	7.3	6.5	5.2	3.9	3.2	2.7	2.7	—
Canada	7.9	7.0	6.2	4.6	3.6	3.0	2.4	2.6	—

Source: Statistics Canada. 2012. Census Profile. 2011 Census. Statistics Canada Catalogue no. 98-316-XWE. Ottawa. Released October 24 2012.
http://www12.statcan.gc.ca/census-recensement/2011/dp-pd/prof/index.cfm?Lang=E

PROFILES / Gatineau, Québec

Private Households by Household Size

Area	1 Person	2 Persons	3 Persons	4 Persons	5 Persons	6 or More Persons	Average Number of Persons in Private Households
			Households				
Gatineau	34,830	37,905	18,445	14,885	4,825	1,870	2.3
Québec	1,094,410	1,181,240	496,140	421,080	142,555	59,920	2.3
Canada	3,673,310	4,544,820	2,081,900	1,903,300	724,405	392,885	2.5
			Percent of Households				
Gatineau	30.9	33.6	16.4	13.2	4.3	1.7	–
Québec	32.2	34.8	14.6	12.4	4.2	1.8	–
Canada	27.6	34.1	15.6	14.3	5.4	2.9	–

Source: Statistics Canada. 2012. Census Profile. 2011 Census. Statistics Canada Catalogue no. 98-316-XWE. Ottawa. Released October 24 2012.
http://www12.statcan.gc.ca/census-recensement/2011/dp-pd/prof/index.cfm?Lang=E

Dwelling Type

Area	Single-detached House	Semi-detached House	Row House	Apartment: Building with Five or More Storeys	Apartment: Building with Fewer Than Five Storeys	Duplex Apartment	Movable Dwelling	Other Single-attached House
				Number				
Gatineau	46,365	15,515	6,665	6,620	30,610	6,725	105	150
Québec	1,560,405	171,435	86,040	171,115	1,103,845	263,860	22,995	15,645
Canada	7,329,150	646,245	791,600	1,234,770	2,397,550	704,485	183,510	33,310
				Percent of Dwellings				
Gatineau	41.1	13.8	5.9	5.9	27.1	6.0	0.1	0.1
Québec	46.0	5.0	2.5	5.0	32.5	7.8	0.7	0.5
Canada	55.0	4.9	5.9	9.3	18.0	5.3	1.4	0.3

Source: Statistics Canada. 2012. Census Profile. 2011 Census. Statistics Canada Catalogue no. 98-316-XWE. Ottawa. Released October 24 2012.
http://www12.statcan.gc.ca/census-recensement/2011/dp-pd/prof/index.cfm?Lang=E

Shelter Costs

		Owned Dwellings				Rented Dwellings		
Area	Number	Median Value^1 ($)	Average Value^1 ($)	Median Monthly Costs^2 ($)	Average Monthly Costs^2 ($)	Number	Median Monthly Costs^3 ($)	Average Monthly Costs^3 ($)
Gatineau	72,450	219,283	235,739	1,070	1,069	40,275	733	770
Québec	2,056,665	214,537	249,427	841	936	1,308,465	643	685
Canada	9,013,410	280,552	345,182	978	1,141	4,060,385	784	848

Note: All figures cover non-farm, non-reserve private dwellings. (1) Refers to the dollar amount expected by the owner if the dwelling were to be sold; (2) Includes all shelter expenses paid by households that own their dwellings, such as the mortgage payment and the costs of electricity, heat, water and other municipal services, property taxes and condominium fees; (3) Includes all shelter expenses paid by households that rent their dwellings, such as the monthly rent and the costs of electricity, heat and municipal services.
Source: Statistics Canada. 2013. 2011 National Household Survey. Statistics Canada Catalogue no. 99-004-XWE. Ottawa. Released September 11, 2013.

Occupied Private Dwellings by Period of Construction

Area	1960 or Before	1961 to 1980	1981 to 1990	1991 to 2000	2001 to 2005	2006 to 2011
			Number			
Gatineau	17,930	34,390	20,420	17,770	10,350	11,895
Québec	946,900	1,115,455	533,790	353,355	206,035	239,685
Canada	3,273,105	4,152,715	2,112,110	1,707,880	1,031,020	1,042,430
			Percent of Dwellings			
Gatineau	15.9	30.5	18.1	15.8	9.2	10.5
Québec	27.9	32.9	15.7	10.4	6.1	7.1
Canada	24.6	31.2	15.9	12.8	7.7	7.8

Note: Figures cover non-farm, non-reserve private dwellings and includes data up to May 10, 2011.
Source: Statistics Canada. 2013. 2011 National Household Survey. Statistics Canada Catalogue no. 99-004-XWE. Ottawa. Released September 11, 2013.

Educational Attainment

Area	No Certificate, Diploma or Degree	High School Diploma or Equivalent[1]	Apprenticeship or Trades Certificate or Diploma[2]	College, CÉGEP or Other Non-University Certificate or Diploma	University Certificate or Diploma Below the Bachelor Level[3]	Bachelor's Degree	University Certificate, Diploma or Degree Above Bachelor Level[4]
				Number			
				Total			
Gatineau	45,430	47,370	26,480	37,615	9,495	30,325	18,970
Québec	1,436,025	1,404,755	1,049,470	1,075,855	305,330	766,100	437,050
Canada	5,485,400	6,968,935	2,950,685	4,970,020	1,200,130	3,634,425	2,049,930
				Males			
Gatineau	22,975	21,680	14,965	17,355	3,995	12,735	9,900
Québec	714,090	650,660	635,435	472,360	126,565	343,535	227,990
Canada	2,742,875	3,305,415	1,928,970	2,118,430	513,235	1,643,080	1,043,350
				Females			
Gatineau	22,455	25,695	11,510	20,260	5,495	17,590	9,070
Québec	721,930	754,095	414,035	603,495	178,765	422,565	209,065
Canada	2,742,520	3,663,515	1,021,715	2,851,595	686,890	1,991,345	1,006,585
				Percent of Population			
				Total			
Gatineau	21.1	22.0	12.3	17.4	4.4	14.1	8.8
Québec	22.2	21.7	16.2	16.6	4.7	11.8	6.8
Canada	20.1	25.6	10.8	18.2	4.4	13.3	7.5
				Males			
Gatineau	22.2	20.9	14.4	16.8	3.9	12.3	9.6
Québec	22.5	20.5	20.0	14.9	4.0	10.8	7.2
Canada	20.6	24.9	14.5	15.9	3.9	12.4	7.8
				Females			
Gatineau	20.0	22.9	10.3	18.1	4.9	15.7	8.1
Québec	21.9	22.8	12.5	18.3	5.4	12.8	6.3
Canada	19.6	26.2	7.3	20.4	4.9	14.3	7.2

Note: Figures cover total population aged 15 years and over by highest certificate, diploma or degree; (1) Includes persons who have graduated from a secondary school or equivalent. It excludes persons with a postsecondary certificate, diploma or degree; (2) Includes Registered Apprenticeship certificates (including Certificate of Qualification, Journeyperson's designation) and other trades certificates or diplomas such as pre-employment or vocational certificates and diplomas from brief trade programs completed at community colleges, institutes of technology, vocational centres, and similar institutions; (3) Comparisons with other data sources suggest that the category 'University certificate or diploma below the bachelor's level' was over-reported in the NHS. This category likely includes some responses that are actually college certificates or diplomas, bachelor's degrees or other types of education (e.g., university transfer programs, bachelor's programs completed in other countries, incomplete bachelor's programs, non-university professional designations). We recommend users interpret the results for the 'University certificate or diploma below the bachelor's level' category with caution; (4) 'University certificate or diploma above bachelor level' includes the categories: 'Degree in medicine, dentistry, veterinary medicine or optometry,' 'Master's degree' and 'Earned doctorate.'
Source: Statistics Canada. 2013. 2011 National Household Survey. Statistics Canada Catalogue no. 99-004-XWE. Ottawa. Released September 11, 2013.

Household Income Distribution

Area	Less than $10,000	$10,000 to $19,999	$20,000 to $29,999	$30,000 to $39,999	$40,000 to $49,999	$50,000 to $59,999	$60,000 to $79,999	$80,000 to $99,999	$100,000 to $124,999	$125,000 to $149,999	$150,000 and Over
						Households					
Gatineau	5,360	9,450	8,310	9,880	9,460	10,550	16,430	13,490	11,795	7,455	10,565
Québec	179,790	377,210	353,470	382,000	343,730	302,595	483,085	344,435	267,995	148,950	211,965
Canada	626,705	1,141,945	1,193,925	1,271,675	1,206,800	1,102,120	1,865,280	1,458,240	1,260,770	802,555	1,389,240
						Percent of Households					
Gatineau	4.8	8.4	7.4	8.8	8.4	9.4	14.6	12.0	10.5	6.6	9.4
Québec	5.3	11.1	10.4	11.3	10.1	8.9	14.2	10.1	7.9	4.4	6.2
Canada	4.7	8.6	9.0	9.5	9.1	8.3	14.0	10.9	9.5	6.0	10.4

Note: Household income is the sum of the total incomes of all members of that household. Total income refers to monetary receipts from certain sources, before income taxes and deductions, during calendar year 2010.
Source: Statistics Canada. 2013. 2011 National Household Survey. Statistics Canada Catalogue no. 99-004-XWE. Ottawa. Released September 11, 2013.

Median and Average Household and Economic Family Income

Area	Median Household Income ($)	Average Household Income ($)	Median After-tax Household Income ($)	Average After-tax Household Income ($)	Median Economic Family Income ($)	Average Economic Family Income ($)	Median After-tax Economic Family Income ($)	Average After-tax Economic Family Income ($)
Gatineau	63,911	75,880	54,223	62,011	82,580	92,376	69,226	75,331
Québec	51,842	66,205	45,968	55,121	68,344	82,045	59,560	68,091
Canada	61,072	79,102	54,089	66,149	76,511	94,125	67,044	78,517

Note: Figures cover household and economic familiy income in 2010. A household is defined as a person or a group of persons (other than foreign residents) who occupy the same private dwelling and do not have a usual place of residence elsewhere in Canada. Every person is a member of one and only one household. An economic family is defined as a group of two or more persons who live in the same dwelling and are related to each other by blood, marriage, common-law, adoption or a foster relationship. A couple may be of opposite or same sex.
Source: Statistics Canada. 2013. 2011 National Household Survey. Statistics Canada Catalogue no. 99-004-XWE. Ottawa. Released September 11, 2013.

PROFILES / Gatineau, Québec

Individual Income Distribution

Area	Less than $10,000	$10,000 to $19,999	$20,000 to $29,999	$30,000 to $39,999	$40,000 to $49,999	$50,000 to $59,999	$60,000 to $79,999	$80,000 to $99,999	$100,000 to $124,999	$125,000 and Over
Number										
Total										
Gatineau	29,505	35,205	24,535	24,005	22,880	21,635	25,575	11,955	6,005	4,135
Québec	1,005,600	1,309,515	941,630	866,290	653,400	449,185	515,815	211,070	109,975	120,915
Canada	4,492,040	4,835,710	3,670,020	3,180,360	2,603,520	1,921,650	2,437,440	1,302,045	693,580	782,135
Males										
Gatineau	13,525	14,170	10,955	11,465	11,455	10,210	13,330	7,015	3,975	3,010
Québec	441,455	516,150	427,295	432,625	345,950	256,700	313,880	143,785	80,000	91,475
Canada	1,936,365	1,864,880	1,588,260	1,522,190	1,333,510	1,079,780	1,473,145	823,720	492,905	599,905
Females										
Gatineau	15,980	21,040	13,580	12,540	11,425	11,425	12,250	4,940	2,025	1,125
Québec	564,150	793,365	514,335	433,670	307,455	192,485	201,935	67,275	29,980	29,440
Canada	2,555,675	2,970,825	2,081,760	1,658,170	1,270,010	841,870	964,300	478,330	200,680	182,230
Percent of Population										
Total										
Gatineau	14.4	17.1	11.9	11.7	11.1	10.5	12.4	5.8	2.9	2.0
Québec	16.3	21.2	15.2	14.0	10.6	7.3	8.3	3.4	1.8	2.0
Canada	17.3	18.7	14.2	12.3	10.0	7.4	9.4	5.0	2.7	3.0
Males										
Gatineau	13.6	14.3	11.1	11.6	11.6	10.3	13.5	7.1	4.0	3.0
Québec	14.5	16.9	14.0	14.2	11.3	8.4	10.3	4.7	2.6	3.0
Canada	15.2	14.7	12.5	12.0	10.5	8.5	11.6	6.5	3.9	4.7
Females										
Gatineau	15.0	19.8	12.8	11.8	10.7	10.7	11.5	4.6	1.9	1.1
Québec	18.0	25.3	16.4	13.8	9.8	6.1	6.4	2.1	1.0	0.9
Canada	19.4	22.5	15.8	12.6	9.6	6.4	7.3	3.6	1.5	1.4

Note: Figures cover individuals aged 15 years and over with income. Income refers to monetary receipts from certain sources, before income taxes and deductions, during calendar year 2010.
Source: Statistics Canada. 2013. 2011 National Household Survey. Statistics Canada Catalogue no. 99-004-XWE. Ottawa. Released September 11, 2013.

Labour Force Status

	In the Labour Force			Not in the
Area	All	Employed	Unemployed	Labour Force
Number				
Total				
Gatineau	151,065	142,395	8,675	64,615
Québec	4,183,445	3,880,425	303,020	2,291,145
Canada	17,990,080	16,595,035	1,395,045	9,269,445
Males				
Gatineau	76,500	71,645	4,855	27,105
Québec	2,188,555	2,014,810	173,745	982,080
Canada	9,388,570	8,634,310	754,255	3,906,785
Females				
Gatineau	74,570	70,745	3,825	37,510
Québec	1,994,885	1,865,610	129,275	1,309,065
Canada	8,601,515	7,960,725	640,790	5,362,660
Percent of Labour Force				
Total				
Gatineau	70.0	66.0	5.7	30.0
Québec	64.6	59.9	7.2	35.4
Canada	66.0	60.9	7.8	34.0
Males				
Gatineau	73.8	69.2	6.3	26.2
Québec	69.0	63.5	7.9	31.0
Canada	70.6	64.9	8.0	29.4
Females				
Gatineau	66.5	63.1	5.1	33.5
Québec	60.4	56.5	6.5	39.6
Canada	61.6	57.0	7.4	38.4

Note: Figures are based on total population 15 years and over
Source: Statistics Canada. 2013. 2011 National Household Survey. Statistics Canada Catalogue no. 99-004-XWE. Ottawa. Released September 11, 2013.

Labour Force by Industry (NAICS Codes 11–52)

Area	Agriculture, forestry, fishing & hunting	Mining, quarrying, & oil & gas extraction	Utilities	Construction	Manufacturing	Wholesale Trade	Retail Trade	Transportation & warehousing	Information & cultural industries	Finance & insurance
					Number					
					Total					
Gatineau	315	145	755	9,755	4,690	2,475	15,820	3,995	2,835	3,470
Québec	84,470	20,770	33,815	241,780	476,390	169,825	501,380	181,295	98,340	159,230
Canada	437,650	261,050	149,940	1,215,380	1,619,295	733,445	2,031,665	827,780	420,830	767,960
					Males					
Gatineau	240	90	660	8,750	3,780	2,060	7,745	3,215	1,600	1,240
Québec	61,540	18,035	24,560	213,605	343,345	113,545	234,725	137,745	56,455	56,930
Canada	307,370	211,690	110,765	1,068,710	1,167,680	494,545	933,850	617,305	235,875	296,995
					Females					
Gatineau	75	55	90	1,005	905	415	8,075	785	1,230	2,230
Québec	22,925	2,730	9,255	28,170	133,045	56,280	266,650	43,550	41,885	102,295
Canada	130,285	49,360	39,175	146,670	451,615	238,900	1,097,820	210,475	184,955	470,960
					Percent of Labour Force					
					Total					
Gatineau	0.2	0.1	0.5	6.6	3.2	1.7	10.7	2.7	1.9	2.3
Québec	2.1	0.5	0.8	5.9	11.7	4.2	12.3	4.4	2.4	3.9
Canada	2.5	1.5	0.9	6.9	9.2	4.2	11.6	4.7	2.4	4.4
					Males					
Gatineau	0.3	0.1	0.9	11.7	5.0	2.7	10.3	4.3	2.1	1.7
Québec	2.9	0.8	1.1	10.0	16.1	5.3	11.0	6.4	2.6	2.7
Canada	3.3	2.3	1.2	11.6	12.7	5.4	10.2	6.7	2.6	3.2
					Females					
Gatineau	0.1	0.1	0.1	1.4	1.2	0.6	11.0	1.1	1.7	3.0
Québec	1.2	0.1	0.5	1.4	6.8	2.9	13.7	2.2	2.2	5.3
Canada	1.6	0.6	0.5	1.7	5.4	2.8	13.1	2.5	2.2	5.6

Note: Figures are based on total experienced labour force 15 years and over. Experienced labour force refers to persons who, during the week of Sunday, May 1 to Saturday, May 7, 2011, were employed and the unemployed who had last worked for pay or in self-employment in either 2010 or 2011.
Source: Statistics Canada. 2013. 2011 National Household Survey. Statistics Canada Catalogue no. 99-004-XWE. Ottawa. Released September 11, 2013.

Labour Force by Industry (NAICS Codes 53–91)

Area	Real estate & rental & leasing	Profess., scientific & tech. services	Mgmt of companies & enterprises	Admin. & support, waste mgmt & remed. services	Educational services	Health care & social assistance	Arts, entertain. & recreation	Accomm. & food services	Other services (except public admin.)	Public admin.
					Number					
					Total					
Gatineau	1,715	7,405	75	6,515	11,710	16,210	3,795	8,835	5,680	42,010
Québec	61,365	282,115	3,965	156,130	301,425	496,125	78,795	253,145	189,290	295,480
Canada	321,895	1,240,850	17,460	728,330	1,301,435	1,949,650	363,405	1,130,750	807,800	1,261,050
					Males					
Gatineau	1,030	4,495	40	4,285	4,060	3,420	2,205	4,520	2,400	19,210
Québec	35,940	158,920	2,250	92,530	99,565	97,255	41,535	112,650	88,710	147,645
Canada	179,090	688,625	9,380	411,250	424,915	349,430	188,270	469,990	372,940	652,510
					Females					
Gatineau	690	2,910	40	2,230	7,650	12,795	1,585	4,315	3,280	22,800
Québec	25,425	123,205	1,715	63,605	201,860	398,870	37,260	140,495	100,585	147,835
Canada	142,805	552,225	8,075	317,085	876,515	1,600,220	175,135	660,760	434,865	608,535
					Percent of Labour Force					
					Total					
Gatineau	1.2	5.0	0.1	4.4	7.9	10.9	2.6	6.0	3.8	28.3
Québec	1.5	6.9	0.1	3.8	7.4	12.1	1.9	6.2	4.6	7.2
Canada	1.8	7.1	0.1	4.1	7.4	11.1	2.1	6.4	4.6	7.2
					Males					
Gatineau	1.4	6.0	0.1	5.7	5.4	4.6	2.9	6.0	3.2	25.6
Québec	1.7	7.4	0.1	4.3	4.7	4.5	1.9	5.3	4.2	6.9
Canada	1.9	7.5	0.1	4.5	4.6	3.8	2.0	5.1	4.1	7.1
					Females					
Gatineau	0.9	4.0	0.1	3.0	10.5	17.5	2.2	5.9	4.5	31.2
Québec	1.3	6.3	0.1	3.3	10.4	20.5	1.9	7.2	5.2	7.6
Canada	1.7	6.6	0.1	3.8	10.4	19.1	2.1	7.9	5.2	7.2

Note: Figures are based on total experienced labour force 15 years and over. Experienced labour force refers to persons who, during the week of Sunday, May 1 to Saturday, May 7, 2011, were employed and the unemployed who had last worked for pay or in self-employment in either 2010 or 2011.
Source: Statistics Canada. 2013. 2011 National Household Survey. Statistics Canada Catalogue no. 99-004-XWE. Ottawa. Released September 11, 2013.

Occupation

Area	Mgmt	Business, Finance & Admin.	Natural/ Applied Sciences & Related	Health	Education, Law & Social, Community & Government Services	Art, Culture, Recreation & Sport	Sales & Service	Trades, Transport & Equip. Operators & Related	Natural Resources, Agri. & Related Production	Mfg & Utilities
					Number					
					Total					
Gatineau	14,390	34,585	11,735	8,320	21,700	5,060	33,855	15,670	970	1,930
Québec	411,425	687,715	287,015	268,610	479,505	123,665	969,740	573,075	65,625	218,740
Canada	1,963,600	2,902,045	1,237,775	1,107,200	2,064,675	503,415	4,068,170	2,537,775	397,930	805,040
					Males					
Gatineau	8,445	10,320	9,030	1,755	8,065	2,350	17,625	14,995	865	1,590
Québec	261,620	207,545	221,430	53,480	148,715	58,150	436,370	542,055	53,640	154,485
Canada	1,229,460	854,190	966,355	217,520	676,550	232,535	1,745,705	2,385,615	318,945	564,300
					Females					
Gatineau	5,945	24,265	2,695	6,570	13,640	2,710	16,230	675	105	340
Québec	149,800	480,170	65,585	215,130	330,795	65,520	533,370	31,025	11,995	64,250
Canada	734,140	2,047,855	271,415	889,675	1,388,130	270,875	2,322,465	152,165	78,980	240,740
					Percent of Labour Force					
					Total					
Gatineau	9.7	23.3	7.9	5.6	14.6	3.4	22.8	10.6	0.7	1.3
Québec	10.1	16.8	7.0	6.6	11.7	3.0	23.7	14.0	1.6	5.4
Canada	11.2	16.5	7.0	6.3	11.7	2.9	23.1	14.4	2.3	4.6
					Males					
Gatineau	11.3	13.8	12.0	2.3	10.7	3.1	23.5	20.0	1.2	2.1
Québec	12.2	9.7	10.4	2.5	7.0	2.7	20.4	25.4	2.5	7.2
Canada	13.4	9.3	10.5	2.4	7.4	2.5	19.0	26.0	3.5	6.1
					Females					
Gatineau	8.1	33.2	3.7	9.0	18.6	3.7	22.2	0.9	0.1	0.5
Québec	7.7	24.7	3.4	11.0	17.0	3.4	27.4	1.6	0.6	3.3
Canada	8.7	24.4	3.2	10.6	16.5	3.2	27.7	1.8	0.9	2.9

Note: Figures are based on total experienced labour force 15 years and over
Source: Statistics Canada. 2013. 2011 National Household Survey. Statistics Canada Catalogue no. 99-004-XWE. Ottawa. Released September 11, 2013.

Place of Work Status

Area	Worked at Home	Worked Outside Canada	No Fixed Workplace Address	Worked at Usual Place
		Number		
		Total		
Gatineau	5,350	305	12,245	124,490
Québec	237,625	9,705	331,525	3,301,560
Canada	1,142,640	66,460	1,868,245	13,517,690
		Males		
Gatineau	2,540	215	9,550	59,340
Québec	122,060	7,055	249,535	1,636,165
Canada	582,150	47,355	1,400,485	6,604,325
		Females		
Gatineau	2,815	90	2,700	65,145
Québec	115,565	2,650	81,995	1,665,395
Canada	560,490	19,100	467,760	6,913,370
		Percent of Labour Force		
		Total		
Gatineau	3.8	0.2	8.6	87.4
Québec	6.1	0.3	8.5	85.1
Canada	6.9	0.4	11.3	81.5
		Males		
Gatineau	3.5	0.3	13.3	82.8
Québec	6.1	0.4	12.4	81.2
Canada	6.7	0.5	16.2	76.5
		Females		
Gatineau	4.0	0.1	3.8	92.1
Québec	6.2	0.1	4.4	89.3
Canada	7.0	0.2	5.9	86.8

Note: Figures are based on total employed labour force 15 years and over.
Source: Statistics Canada. 2013. 2011 National Household Survey. Statistics Canada Catalogue no. 99-004-XWE. Ottawa. Released September 11, 2013.

Mode of Transportation to Work

Area	Car; Truck; Van; as Driver	Car; Truck; Van; as Passenger	Public Transit	Walked	Bicycled	All Other Modes
			Number			
			Total			
Gatineau	93,800	9,320	23,720	6,165	2,670	1,070
Québec	2,713,295	136,490	484,600	215,210	48,870	34,620
Canada	11,393,140	867,050	1,851,525	880,815	201,780	191,625
			Males			
Gatineau	50,750	2,790	10,030	2,825	1,960	535
Québec	1,484,305	50,905	203,035	95,100	33,065	19,285
Canada	6,238,835	349,530	788,290	387,580	135,840	104,725
			Females			
Gatineau	43,050	6,525	13,690	3,340	710	535
Québec	1,228,995	85,585	281,565	120,110	15,800	15,335
Canada	5,154,305	517,520	1,063,235	493,230	65,940	86,900
			Percent of Labour Force			
			Total			
Gatineau	68.6	6.8	17.3	4.5	2.0	0.8
Québec	74.7	3.8	13.3	5.9	1.3	1.0
Canada	74.0	5.6	12.0	5.7	1.3	1.2
			Males			
Gatineau	73.7	4.0	14.6	4.1	2.8	0.8
Québec	78.7	2.7	10.8	5.0	1.8	1.0
Canada	77.9	4.4	9.8	4.8	1.7	1.3
			Females			
Gatineau	63.5	9.6	20.2	4.9	1.0	0.8
Québec	70.3	4.9	16.1	6.9	0.9	0.9
Canada	69.8	7.0	14.4	6.7	0.9	1.2

Note: Figures are based on total employed labour force 15 years and over.
Source: Statistics Canada. 2013. 2011 National Household Survey. Statistics Canada Catalogue no. 99-004-XWE. Ottawa. Released September 11, 2013.

Visible Minority Population Characteristics

Area	Total Minority	South Asian[1]	Chinese	Black	Filipino	Latin American	Arab	SE Asian[2]	West Asian[3]	Korean	Japanese	Multiple[4]
					Number							
					Total							
Gatineau	26,930	795	2,030	10,165	420	3,855	6,455	1,305	590	220	250	525
Québec	850,235	83,320	82,845	243,625	31,495	116,380	166,260	65,855	23,445	6,665	4,025	17,420
Canada	6,264,750	1,567,400	1,324,750	945,665	619,310	381,280	380,620	312,075	206,840	161,130	87,270	171,935
					Males							
Gatineau	13,225	380	880	4,730	180	1,875	3,575	680	310	85	150	220
Québec	418,545	43,410	37,295	116,605	12,435	56,940	89,505	32,940	12,070	3,135	1,565	8,315
Canada	3,043,010	790,755	632,325	453,005	268,885	186,355	203,485	154,035	105,620	77,165	38,270	83,335
					Females							
Gatineau	13,705	415	1,150	5,435	230	1,980	2,885	625	280	130	100	305
Québec	431,695	39,915	45,550	127,020	19,055	59,440	76,750	32,920	11,380	3,530	2,465	9,105
Canada	3,221,745	776,650	692,420	492,660	350,425	194,925	177,140	158,045	101,220	83,965	48,990	88,600
					Percent of Population							
					Total							
Gatineau	10.3	0.3	0.8	3.9	0.2	1.5	2.5	0.5	0.2	0.1	0.1	0.2
Québec	11.0	1.1	1.1	3.2	0.4	1.5	2.2	0.9	0.3	0.1	0.1	0.2
Canada	19.1	4.8	4.0	2.9	1.9	1.2	1.2	0.9	0.6	0.5	0.3	0.5
					Males							
Gatineau	10.4	0.3	0.7	3.7	0.1	1.5	2.8	0.5	0.2	0.1	0.1	0.2
Québec	11.0	1.1	1.0	3.1	0.3	1.5	2.3	0.9	0.3	0.1	0.0	0.2
Canada	18.8	4.9	3.9	2.8	1.7	1.2	1.3	1.0	0.7	0.5	0.2	0.5
					Females							
Gatineau	10.2	0.3	0.9	4.0	0.2	1.5	2.1	0.5	0.2	0.1	0.1	0.2
Québec	11.0	1.0	1.2	3.2	0.5	1.5	2.0	0.8	0.3	0.1	0.1	0.2
Canada	19.3	4.7	4.1	3.0	2.1	1.2	1.1	0.9	0.6	0.5	0.3	0.5

Note: The Employment Equity Act defines visible minorities as 'persons, other than Aboriginal peoples, who are non-Caucasian in race or non-white in colour'; (1) Includes 'East Indian,' 'Pakistani,' 'Sri Lankan,' etc.; (2) Includes 'Vietnamese,' 'Cambodian,' 'Malaysian,' 'Laotian,' etc.; (3) Includes 'Iranian,' 'Afghan,' etc.; (4) Includes respondents who reported more than one visible minority group by checking two or more mark-in circles, e.g., 'Black' and 'South Asian.'
Source: Statistics Canada. 2013. 2011 National Household Survey. Statistics Canada Catalogue no. 99-004-XWE. Ottawa. Released September 11, 2013.

PROFILES / Gatineau, Québec

Aboriginal Population

Area	Aboriginal Identity[1]	First Nations (North American Indian) Single Identity[2]	Métis Single Identity	Inuk (Inuit) Single Identity	Multiple Aboriginal Identities[3]	Aboriginal Identities Not Included Elsewhere
			Number			
			Total			
Gatineau	9,065	4,625	4,025	110	115	195
Québec	141,915	82,425	40,960	12,570	1,545	4,415
Canada	1,400,685	851,560	451,795	59,440	11,415	26,475
			Males			
Gatineau	4,490	2,270	2,050	15	60	85
Québec	70,205	40,105	21,300	6,265	720	1,815
Canada	682,190	411,785	223,335	29,495	5,525	12,055
			Females			
Gatineau	4,575	2,350	1,975	90	50	105
Québec	71,710	42,315	19,660	6,305	830	2,600
Canada	718,500	439,775	228,460	29,950	5,890	14,420
			Percent of Population			
			Total			
Gatineau	3.5	1.8	1.5	0.0	0.0	0.1
Québec	1.8	1.1	0.5	0.2	0.0	0.1
Canada	4.3	2.6	1.4	0.2	0.0	0.1
			Males			
Gatineau	3.5	1.8	1.6	0.0	0.0	0.1
Québec	1.8	1.1	0.6	0.2	0.0	0.0
Canada	4.2	2.5	1.4	0.2	0.0	0.1
			Females			
Gatineau	3.4	1.7	1.5	0.1	0.0	0.1
Québec	1.8	1.1	0.5	0.2	0.0	0.1
Canada	4.3	2.6	1.4	0.2	0.0	0.1

Note: (1) Includes persons who reported being an Aboriginal person, that is, First Nations (North American Indian), Métis or Inuk (Inuit) and/or those who reported Registered or Treaty Indian status, that is registered under the Indian Act of Canada, and/or those who reported membership in a First Nation or Indian band. Aboriginal peoples of Canada are defined in the Constitution Act, 1982, section 35-2 as including the Indian, Inuit and Métis peoples of Canada; (2) Users should be aware that the estimates associated with this variable are more affected than most by the incomplete enumeration of certain Indian reserves and Indian settlements in the National Household Survey (NHS); (3) Includes persons who reported being any two or all three of the following: First Nations (North American Indian), Métis or Inuk (Inuit).
Source: Statistics Canada. 2013. 2011 National Household Survey. Statistics Canada Catalogue no. 99-004-XWE. Ottawa. Released September 11, 2013.

Ethnic Origin

Area	North American Aboriginal	Other North American	European	Caribbean	Latin, Central and South American	African	Asian	Oceania
				Number				
				Total				
Gatineau	19,915	160,835	129,085	3,560	4,920	11,090	13,105	80
Québec	307,445	4,776,875	3,390,330	167,590	137,255	260,785	488,905	2,305
Canada	1,836,035	11,070,455	20,157,965	627,590	544,375	766,735	5,011,225	74,875
				Males				
Gatineau	9,335	77,800	63,175	1,630	2,395	5,545	6,595	35
Québec	146,725	2,345,180	1,678,310	77,665	67,195	135,740	241,515	1,135
Canada	885,675	5,462,685	9,913,150	291,640	264,635	387,360	2,435,540	37,490
				Females				
Gatineau	10,580	83,035	65,915	1,935	2,525	5,545	6,510	45
Québec	160,725	2,431,700	1,712,015	89,925	70,065	125,040	247,390	1,175
Canada	950,360	5,607,770	10,244,820	335,945	279,740	379,380	2,575,680	37,385
				Percent of Population				
				Total				
Gatineau	7.6	61.5	49.3	1.4	1.9	4.2	5.0	0.0
Québec	4.0	61.8	43.8	2.2	1.8	3.4	6.3	0.0
Canada	5.6	33.7	61.4	1.9	1.7	2.3	15.3	0.2
				Males				
Gatineau	7.3	61.2	49.7	1.3	1.9	4.4	5.2	0.0
Québec	3.8	61.5	44.0	2.0	1.8	3.6	6.3	0.0
Canada	5.5	33.8	61.3	1.8	1.6	2.4	15.1	0.2
				Females				
Gatineau	7.9	61.7	49.0	1.4	1.9	4.1	4.8	0.0
Québec	4.1	62.1	43.7	2.3	1.8	3.2	6.3	0.0
Canada	5.7	33.6	61.4	2.0	1.7	2.3	15.4	0.2

Note: The sum of the ethnic groups in this table is greater than the total population estimate because a person may report more than one ethnic origin in the NHS.
Source: Statistics Canada. 2013. 2011 National Household Survey. Statistics Canada Catalogue no. 99-004-XWE. Ottawa. Released September 11, 2013.

Religion

Area	Buddhist	Christian	Hindu	Jewish	Muslim	Sikh	Traditional (Aboriginal) Spirituality	Other Religions	No Religious Affiliation
					Number				
					Total				
Gatineau	1,085	209,910	295	210	7,190	25	60	600	42,300
Québec	52,390	6,356,880	33,540	85,100	243,430	9,275	2,025	12,340	937,545
Canada	366,830	22,102,745	497,965	329,495	1,053,945	454,965	64,935	130,835	7,850,605
					Males				
Gatineau	510	99,745	170	125	3,865	0	20	300	22,375
Québec	24,630	3,079,855	17,055	41,455	128,815	5,090	925	6,155	510,055
Canada	168,465	10,497,775	250,435	161,265	540,555	229,435	31,805	57,745	4,225,645
					Females				
Gatineau	575	110,165	125	80	3,325	20	35	300	19,920
Québec	27,760	3,277,020	16,480	43,645	114,615	4,185	1,100	6,175	427,485
Canada	198,365	11,604,975	247,525	168,235	513,395	225,530	33,135	73,090	3,624,965
				Percent of Population					
					Total				
Gatineau	0.4	80.2	0.1	0.1	2.7	0.0	0.0	0.2	16.2
Québec	0.7	82.2	0.4	1.1	3.1	0.1	0.0	0.2	12.1
Canada	1.1	67.3	1.5	1.0	3.2	1.4	0.2	0.4	23.9
					Males				
Gatineau	0.4	78.5	0.1	0.1	3.0	0.0	0.0	0.2	17.6
Québec	0.6	80.8	0.4	1.1	3.4	0.1	0.0	0.2	13.4
Canada	1.0	64.9	1.5	1.0	3.3	1.4	0.2	0.4	26.1
					Females				
Gatineau	0.4	81.9	0.1	0.1	2.5	0.0	0.0	0.2	14.8
Québec	0.7	83.6	0.4	1.1	2.9	0.1	0.0	0.2	10.9
Canada	1.2	69.5	1.5	1.0	3.1	1.4	0.2	0.4	21.7

Note: Religion refers to the person's self-identification as having a connection or affiliation with any religious denomination, group, body, sect, cult or other religiously defined community or system of belief. Religion is not limited to formal membership in a religious organization or group. Persons without a religious connection or affiliation can self-identify as atheist, agnostic or humanist, or can provide another applicable response.
Source: Statistics Canada. 2013. 2011 National Household Survey. Statistics Canada Catalogue no. 99-004-XWE. Ottawa. Released September 11, 2013.

Religion—Christian Denominations

Area	Anglican	Baptist	Catholic	Christian Orthodox	Lutheran	Pentecostal	Presbyterian	United Church	Other Christian
					Number				
					Total				
Gatineau	1,820	1,745	190,375	2,780	380	1,675	450	1,425	9,270
Québec	73,550	36,615	5,775,740	129,780	7,200	41,070	11,440	32,930	248,560
Canada	1,631,845	635,840	12,810,705	550,690	478,185	478,705	472,385	2,007,610	3,036,780
					Males				
Gatineau	900	785	90,410	1,435	180	825	250	675	4,285
Québec	34,815	16,585	2,802,920	63,960	3,425	18,640	5,265	14,945	119,305
Canada	752,945	293,905	6,167,290	270,205	221,525	217,850	218,955	912,545	1,442,550
					Females				
Gatineau	920	955	99,965	1,345	200	850	195	745	4,985
Québec	38,735	20,030	2,972,820	65,820	3,770	22,430	6,175	17,985	129,260
Canada	878,900	341,940	6,643,415	280,485	256,660	260,850	253,430	1,095,065	1,594,230
				Percent of Population					
					Total				
Gatineau	0.7	0.7	72.8	1.1	0.1	0.6	0.2	0.5	3.5
Québec	1.0	0.5	74.7	1.7	0.1	0.5	0.1	0.4	3.2
Canada	5.0	1.9	39.0	1.7	1.5	1.5	1.4	6.1	9.2
					Males				
Gatineau	0.7	0.6	71.1	1.1	0.1	0.6	0.2	0.5	3.4
Québec	0.9	0.4	73.5	1.7	0.1	0.5	0.1	0.4	3.1
Canada	4.7	1.8	38.2	1.7	1.4	1.3	1.4	5.6	8.9
					Females				
Gatineau	0.7	0.7	74.3	1.0	0.1	0.6	0.1	0.6	3.7
Québec	1.0	0.5	75.9	1.7	0.1	0.6	0.2	0.5	3.3
Canada	5.3	2.0	39.8	1.7	1.5	1.6	1.5	6.6	9.6

Note: Religion refers to the person's self-identification as having a connection or affiliation with any religious denomination, group, body, sect, cult or other religiously defined community or system of belief. Religion is not limited to formal membership in a religious organization or group. Persons without a religious connection or affiliation can self-identify as atheist, agnostic or humanist, or can provide another applicable response.
Source: Statistics Canada. 2013. 2011 National Household Survey. Statistics Canada Catalogue no. 99-004-XWE. Ottawa. Released September 11, 2013.

PROFILES / Gatineau, Québec

Immigrant Status and Period of Immigration

Area	Non-Immigrants[1]	Immigrants All	Before 1971	1971 to 1980	1981 to 1990	1991 to 2000	2001 to 2005	2006 to 2011	Non-Permanent Residents[3]
Number									
Total									
Gatineau	231,950	28,590	2,140	2,870	3,430	6,695	5,940	7,520	1,125
Québec	6,690,530	974,895	151,825	115,640	130,680	195,925	157,425	223,400	67,095
Canada	25,720,175	6,775,765	1,261,055	870,775	949,890	1,539,050	992,070	1,162,915	356,385
Males									
Gatineau	112,605	13,945	1,130	1,475	1,770	3,085	2,820	3,660	570
Québec	3,301,435	477,240	75,255	57,410	64,080	94,110	76,780	109,605	35,370
Canada	12,753,235	3,231,370	605,430	416,670	454,570	724,905	474,545	555,245	178,515
Females									
Gatineau	119,345	14,650	1,005	1,395	1,665	3,610	3,120	3,865	560
Québec	3,389,095	497,655	76,565	58,235	66,600	101,810	80,645	113,795	31,725
Canada	12,966,935	3,544,400	655,625	454,105	495,325	814,145	517,530	607,670	177,870
Percent of Population									
Total									
Gatineau	88.6	10.9	0.8	1.1	1.3	2.6	2.3	2.9	0.4
Québec	86.5	12.6	2.0	1.5	1.7	2.5	2.0	2.9	0.9
Canada	78.3	20.6	3.8	2.7	2.9	4.7	3.0	3.5	1.1
Males									
Gatineau	88.6	11.0	0.9	1.2	1.4	2.4	2.2	2.9	0.4
Québec	86.6	12.5	2.0	1.5	1.7	2.5	2.0	2.9	0.9
Canada	78.9	20.0	3.7	2.6	2.8	4.5	2.9	3.4	1.1
Females									
Gatineau	88.7	10.9	0.7	1.0	1.2	2.7	2.3	2.9	0.4
Québec	86.5	12.7	2.0	1.5	1.7	2.6	2.1	2.9	0.8
Canada	77.7	21.2	3.9	2.7	3.0	4.9	3.1	3.6	1.1

Note: (1) Non-immigrant refers to a person who is a Canadian citizen by birth; (2) Immigrant refers to a person who is or has ever been a landed immigrant/permanent resident. This person has been granted the right to live in Canada permanently by immigration authorities. Some immigrants have resided in Canada for a number of years, while others have arrived recently. Some immigrants are Canadian citizens, while others are not. Most immigrants are born outside Canada, but a small number are born in Canada. In the 2011 National Household Survey, 'Immigrants' includes immigrants who landed in Canada prior to May 10, 2011; (3) Non-permanent resident refers to a person from another country who has a work or study permit, or who is a refugee claimant, and any non-Canadian-born family member living in Canada with them.
Source: Statistics Canada. 2013. 2011 National Household Survey. Statistics Canada Catalogue no. 99-004-XWE. Ottawa. Released September 11, 2013.

Mother Tongue

Area	English	French	Non-official Language	English & French	English & Non-official Language	French & Non-official Language	English, French & Non-official Language
Number							
Total							
Gatineau	29,060	203,360	23,855	4,415	575	1,595	385
Québec	599,225	6,102,210	961,700	64,800	23,435	51,640	12,950
Canada	18,858,980	7,054,975	6,567,680	144,685	396,330	74,430	24,095
Males							
Gatineau	14,520	97,825	11,815	2,155	280	820	200
Québec	297,875	2,994,300	472,635	32,390	11,455	25,810	6,790
Canada	9,345,225	3,452,380	3,157,785	69,975	192,000	36,535	11,965
Females							
Gatineau	14,535	105,535	12,050	2,255	295	780	190
Québec	301,355	3,107,910	489,060	32,405	11,975	25,825	6,155
Canada	9,513,750	3,602,590	3,409,895	74,710	204,330	37,890	12,130
Percent of Population							
Total							
Gatineau	11.0	77.2	9.1	1.7	0.2	0.6	0.1
Québec	7.7	78.1	12.3	0.8	0.3	0.7	0.2
Canada	56.9	21.3	19.8	0.4	1.2	0.2	0.1
Males							
Gatineau	11.4	76.7	9.3	1.7	0.2	0.6	0.2
Québec	7.8	78.0	12.3	0.8	0.3	0.7	0.2
Canada	57.5	21.2	19.4	0.4	1.2	0.2	0.1
Females							
Gatineau	10.7	77.8	8.9	1.7	0.2	0.6	0.1
Québec	7.6	78.2	12.3	0.8	0.3	0.6	0.2
Canada	56.4	21.4	20.2	0.4	1.2	0.2	0.1

Note: Figures cover total population excluding institutional residents.
Source: Statistics Canada. 2012. Census Profile. 2011 Census. Statistics Canada Catalogue no. 98-316-XWE. Ottawa. Released October 24 2012.
http://www12.statcan.gc.ca/census-recensement/2011/dp-pd/prof/index.cfm?Lang=E

Language Spoken Most Often at Home

Area	English	French	Non-official Language	English & French	English & Non-official Language	French & Non-official Language	English, French & Non-official Language
			Number				
			Total				
Gatineau	35,180	205,710	12,965	4,840	1,100	2,530	925
Québec	767,415	6,249,080	554,400	71,555	43,765	100,110	29,625
Canada	21,457,075	6,827,865	3,673,865	131,205	875,135	109,700	46,330
			Males				
Gatineau	17,685	99,025	6,365	2,325	550	1,190	475
Québec	379,915	3,071,635	268,640	35,860	21,305	48,590	15,315
Canada	10,585,620	3,348,235	1,767,310	63,475	425,370	53,010	22,845
			Females				
Gatineau	17,500	106,685	6,595	2,515	550	1,345	450
Québec	387,500	3,177,450	285,760	35,695	22,460	51,525	14,310
Canada	10,871,455	3,479,625	1,906,555	67,730	449,765	56,690	23,485
			Percent of Population				
			Total				
Gatineau	13.4	78.1	4.9	1.8	0.4	1.0	0.4
Québec	9.8	80.0	7.1	0.9	0.6	1.3	0.4
Canada	64.8	20.6	11.1	0.4	2.6	0.3	0.1
			Males				
Gatineau	13.9	77.6	5.0	1.8	0.4	0.9	0.4
Québec	9.9	80.0	7.0	0.9	0.6	1.3	0.4
Canada	65.1	20.6	10.9	0.4	2.6	0.3	0.1
			Females				
Gatineau	12.9	78.7	4.9	1.9	0.4	1.0	0.3
Québec	9.7	79.9	7.2	0.9	0.6	1.3	0.4
Canada	64.5	20.6	11.3	0.4	2.7	0.3	0.1

Note: Figures cover total population excluding institutional residents.
Source: Statistics Canada. 2012. Census Profile. 2011 Census. Statistics Canada Catalogue no. 98-316-XWE. Ottawa. Released October 24 2012.
http://www12.statcan.gc.ca/census-recensement/2011/dp-pd/prof/index.cfm?Lang=E

Knowledge of Official Languages

Area	English Only	French Only	English & French	Neither English nor French
		Number		
		Total		
Gatineau	17,190	76,050	168,475	1,535
Québec	363,860	4,047,175	3,328,725	76,190
Canada	22,564,665	4,165,015	5,795,570	595,920
		Males		
Gatineau	9,005	33,160	84,765	690
Québec	180,175	1,871,500	1,758,410	31,175
Canada	11,222,185	1,925,340	2,876,560	241,790
		Females		
Gatineau	8,190	42,890	83,710	850
Québec	183,690	2,175,675	1,570,310	45,015
Canada	11,342,485	2,239,680	2,919,005	354,135
		Percent of Population		
		Total		
Gatineau	6.5	28.9	64.0	0.6
Québec	4.7	51.8	42.6	1.0
Canada	68.1	12.6	17.5	1.8
		Males		
Gatineau	7.1	26.0	66.4	0.5
Québec	4.7	48.7	45.8	0.8
Canada	69.0	11.8	17.7	1.5
		Females		
Gatineau	6.0	31.6	61.7	0.6
Québec	4.6	54.7	39.5	1.1
Canada	67.3	13.3	17.3	2.1

Note: Figures cover total population excluding institutional residents.
Source: Statistics Canada. 2012. Census Profile. 2011 Census. Statistics Canada Catalogue no. 98-316-XWE. Ottawa. Released October 24 2012.
http://www12.statcan.gc.ca/census-recensement/2011/dp-pd/prof/index.cfm?Lang=E

Greater Sudbury, Ontario

Background

Greater Sudbury/Grand Sudbury is a bilingual community located at the convergence of the Trans-Canada Highway in Northeastern Ontario, where the city serves as the regional capital. It is situated 390 kilometres north of Toronto and less than 300 kilometres east of Sault Ste. Marie. In 2001, Sudbury and its seven surrounding communities amalgamated into the City of Greater Sudbury.

The railway boom in 1883 signalled the area's mining boom with the discovery of rich copper deposits. Sudbury is now considered the mining industry capital of Canada because of its world-renowned nickel ore deposits and copper mines, and is known as "Nickel City." Sudbury's most famous landmark is the Big Nickel, a giant replica of Canada's five-cent piece, and the largest coin in the world.

Innovation in the science, technology, health and education sectors continues to increase. Laurentian University, Cambrian College, College Boreal and the recently opened Northern Ontario School of Medicine are based in Sudbury. The Neutrino Observatory is a $70 million astrophysics research project located two kilometres beneath Earth's surface.

Throughout the year, the City of Greater Sudbury hosts community-minded events such as the Blueberry Festival, Celtic Festival and Highland Games, Gem and Mineral Show and the Northern Lights Festival Boréal.

Greater Sudbury has summer highs of plus 23.3 degrees Celsius, winter lows of minus 16.37 degrees Celsius, and an average rainfall just over 656 mm per year.

Rankings

- Greater Sudbury was ranked in the top 100 best places to live in Canada. For the second consecutive year and third time in four years (2009 to 2012), Greater Sudbury came in at #76 out of 190 Canadian cities and towns with a population of more than 10,000. *Money Sense Magazine, "Canada's Best Places to Live 2012," March 20th, 2012 with files from 2009-2011*
- *Le Salon du livre du Grand Sudbury* was recognized by the Greater Sudbury Development Corporation for the growth of its literary festival into one of the largest literary festivals in Canada, ranked #4 after Montréal, Québec City and Ottawa. *Greater Sudbury Development Corporation, Quarterly Report: Growth and Development Highlights, June 25th, 2010*
- Greater Sudbury ranked as one of the best real estate investment cities in Canada. *Canadian Real Estate Magazine* noted that all classes of rental housing in the city increased between 3.5% and 5.9%. Sudbury was praised for diversifying from a mining to an administrative/service centre for Northern Ontario. *Canadian Real Estate Magazine, "Canada's Top 50 Rental Markets," March 16th, 2012*

PROFILES / Greater Sudbury, Ontario

Population Growth and Density

Area	Population in 2001	Population in 2006	Population in 2011	Population Change 2001–2006	Population Change 2006–2011	Land Area (sq. km)	Population Density per sq. km
Greater Sudbury	155,219	157,857	160,274	1.7	1.5	3,227.38	49.7
Ontario	11,410,046	12,160,282	12,851,821	6.6	5.7	908,607.67	14.1
Canada	30,007,094	31,612,897	33,476,688	5.4	5.9	8,965,121.42	3.7

Source: Statistics Canada. 2012. Census Profile. 2011 Census. Statistics Canada Catalogue no. 98-316-XWE. Ottawa. Released October 24 2012.
http://www12.statcan.gc.ca/census-recensement/2011/dp-pd/prof/index.cfm?Lang=E;
Statistics Canada 2007. 2006 Community Profiles. 2006 Census. Statistics Canada Catalogue no. 92-591-XWE. Ottawa. Released March 13 2007.
http://www12.statcan.ca/census-recensement/2006/dp-pd/prof/92-591/index.cfm?Lang=E

Gender

Area	Males	Females
	Number	
Greater Sudbury	78,225	82,050
Ontario	6,263,140	6,588,685
Canada	16,414,225	17,062,460
	Percent of Population	
Greater Sudbury	48.8	51.2
Ontario	48.7	51.3
Canada	49.0	51.0

Source: Statistics Canada. 2012. Census Profile. 2011 Census. Statistics Canada Catalogue no. 98-316-XWE. Ottawa. Released October 24 2012.
http://www12.statcan.gc.ca/census-recensement/2011/dp-pd/prof/index.cfm?Lang=E

Marital Status

Area	Married[1]	Living Common-law	Single[2]	Separated	Divorced	Widowed
			Number			
			Total			
Greater Sudbury	63,900	15,130	34,770	4,645	7,525	9,320
Ontario	5,367,400	791,210	2,985,020	319,805	593,730	613,880
Canada	12,941,960	3,142,525	7,816,045	698,240	1,686,035	1,584,530
			Males			
Greater Sudbury	31,930	7,560	18,875	2,080	3,185	1,800
Ontario	2,681,320	397,620	1,583,760	133,790	231,160	117,980
Canada	6,470,300	1,575,495	4,206,320	299,655	680,415	310,940
			Females			
Greater Sudbury	31,975	7,575	15,890	2,565	4,340	7,515
Ontario	2,686,075	393,590	1,401,260	186,015	362,570	495,905
Canada	6,471,660	1,567,035	3,609,730	398,585	1,005,620	1,273,590
			Percent of Population			
			Total			
Greater Sudbury	47.2	11.2	25.7	3.4	5.6	6.9
Ontario	50.3	7.4	28.0	3.0	5.6	5.8
Canada	46.4	11.3	28.0	2.5	6.0	5.7
			Males			
Greater Sudbury	48.8	11.6	28.8	3.2	4.9	2.8
Ontario	52.1	7.7	30.8	2.6	4.5	2.3
Canada	47.8	11.6	31.1	2.2	5.0	2.3
			Females			
Greater Sudbury	45.8	10.8	22.7	3.7	6.2	10.8
Ontario	48.6	7.1	25.4	3.4	6.6	9.0
Canada	45.2	10.9	25.2	2.8	7.0	8.9

Note: (1) and not separated, (2) never legally married
Source: Statistics Canada. 2012. Census Profile. 2011 Census. Statistics Canada Catalogue no. 98-316-XWE. Ottawa. Released October 24 2012.
http://www12.statcan.gc.ca/census-recensement/2011/dp-pd/prof/index.cfm?Lang=E

Age Characteristics: 0 to 49 Years

Area	0 to 4 Years	5 to 9 Years	10 to 14 Years	15 to 19 Years	20 to 24 Years	25 to 29 Years	30 to 34 Years	35 to 39 Years	40 to 44 Years	45 to 49 Years
					Number					
					Total					
Greater Sudbury	8,050	8,010	8,920	10,495	10,520	9,700	9,565	9,965	10,530	13,470
Ontario	704,260	712,755	763,755	863,635	852,910	815,120	800,365	844,335	924,075	1,055,880
Canada	1,877,095	1,809,895	1,920,355	2,178,135	2,187,450	2,169,590	2,162,905	2,173,930	2,324,875	2,675,130
					Males					
Greater Sudbury	4,130	4,110	4,555	5,375	5,215	4,840	4,710	4,975	5,170	6,665
Ontario	360,590	365,290	391,630	443,680	432,490	400,045	383,340	405,845	447,920	517,510
Canada	961,150	925,965	983,995	1,115,845	1,108,775	1,077,275	1,058,810	1,064,200	1,141,720	1,318,715
					Females					
Greater Sudbury	3,915	3,900	4,370	5,120	5,300	4,860	4,855	4,985	5,355	6,810
Ontario	343,670	347,465	372,125	419,950	420,415	415,075	417,030	438,485	476,155	538,370
Canada	915,945	883,935	936,360	1,062,295	1,078,670	1,092,315	1,104,095	1,109,735	1,183,155	1,356,420
					Percent of Population					
					Total					
Greater Sudbury	5.0	5.0	5.6	6.5	6.6	6.1	6.0	6.2	6.6	8.4
Ontario	5.5	5.5	5.9	6.7	6.6	6.3	6.2	6.6	7.2	8.2
Canada	5.6	5.4	5.7	6.5	6.5	6.5	6.5	6.5	6.9	8.0
					Males					
Greater Sudbury	5.3	5.3	5.8	6.9	6.7	6.2	6.0	6.4	6.6	8.5
Ontario	5.8	5.8	6.3	7.1	6.9	6.4	6.1	6.5	7.2	8.3
Canada	5.9	5.6	6.0	6.8	6.8	6.6	6.5	6.5	7.0	8.0
					Females					
Greater Sudbury	4.8	4.8	5.3	6.2	6.5	5.9	5.9	6.1	6.5	8.3
Ontario	5.2	5.3	5.6	6.4	6.4	6.3	6.3	6.7	7.2	8.2
Canada	5.4	5.2	5.5	6.2	6.3	6.4	6.5	6.5	6.9	7.9

Source: Statistics Canada. 2012. Census Profile. 2011 Census. Statistics Canada Catalogue no. 98-316-XWE. Ottawa. Released October 24 2012.
http://www12.statcan.gc.ca/census-recensement/2011/dp-pd/prof/index.cfm?Lang=E

Age Characteristics: 50 Years and Over, and Median Age

Area	50 to 54 Years	55 to 59 Years	60 to 64 Years	65 to 69 Years	70 to 74 Years	75 to 79 Years	80 to 84 Years	85 Years and Over	Median Age
					Number				
					Total				
Greater Sudbury	13,170	11,775	10,335	7,785	6,155	5,085	3,780	2,975	42.3
Ontario	1,006,140	864,620	765,655	563,485	440,780	356,150	271,510	246,400	40.4
Canada	2,658,965	2,340,635	2,052,670	1,521,715	1,153,065	922,700	702,070	645,515	40.6
					Males				
Greater Sudbury	6,335	5,660	5,170	3,720	2,840	2,185	1,590	975	41.1
Ontario	492,560	418,755	370,370	270,875	206,350	161,345	113,620	80,925	39.4
Canada	1,309,030	1,147,300	1,002,690	738,010	543,435	417,945	291,085	208,300	39.6
					Females				
Greater Sudbury	6,840	6,110	5,165	4,055	3,320	2,900	2,185	2,000	43.5
Ontario	513,580	445,865	395,275	292,610	234,435	194,805	157,890	165,475	41.3
Canada	1,349,940	1,193,335	1,049,985	783,705	609,630	504,755	410,985	437,215	41.5
					Percent of Population				
					Total				
Greater Sudbury	8.2	7.3	6.4	4.9	3.8	3.2	2.4	1.9	–
Ontario	7.8	6.7	6.0	4.4	3.4	2.8	2.1	1.9	–
Canada	7.9	7.0	6.1	4.5	3.4	2.8	2.1	1.9	–
					Males				
Greater Sudbury	8.1	7.2	6.6	4.8	3.6	2.8	2.0	1.2	–
Ontario	7.9	6.7	5.9	4.3	3.3	2.6	1.8	1.3	–
Canada	8.0	7.0	6.1	4.5	3.3	2.5	1.8	1.3	–
					Females				
Greater Sudbury	8.3	7.4	6.3	4.9	4.0	3.5	2.7	2.4	–
Ontario	7.8	6.8	6.0	4.4	3.6	3.0	2.4	2.5	–
Canada	7.9	7.0	6.2	4.6	3.6	3.0	2.4	2.6	–

Source: Statistics Canada. 2012. Census Profile. 2011 Census. Statistics Canada Catalogue no. 98-316-XWE. Ottawa. Released October 24 2012.
http://www12.statcan.gc.ca/census-recensement/2011/dp-pd/prof/index.cfm?Lang=E

PROFILES / Greater Sudbury, Ontario

Private Households by Household Size

Area	1 Person	2 Persons	3 Persons	4 Persons	5 Persons	6 or More Persons	Average Number of Persons in Private Households
				Households			
Greater Sudbury	19,165	24,685	10,735	9,310	2,775	930	2.3
Ontario	1,230,975	1,584,415	803,030	783,925	310,860	174,305	2.6
Canada	3,673,310	4,544,820	2,081,900	1,903,300	724,405	392,885	2.5
				Percent of Households			
Greater Sudbury	28.4	36.5	15.9	13.8	4.1	1.4	–
Ontario	25.2	32.4	16.4	16.0	6.4	3.6	–
Canada	27.6	34.1	15.6	14.3	5.4	2.9	–

Source: Statistics Canada. 2012. Census Profile. 2011 Census. Statistics Canada Catalogue no. 98-316-XWE. Ottawa. Released October 24 2012.
http://www12.statcan.gc.ca/census-recensement/2011/dp-pd/prof/index.cfm?Lang=E

Dwelling Type

Area	Single-detached House	Semi-detached House	Row House	Apartment: Building with Five or More Storeys	Apartment: Building with Fewer Than Five Storeys	Duplex Apartment	Movable Dwelling	Other Single-attached House
				Number				
Greater Sudbury	42,065	3,180	2,860	4,460	10,435	3,830	570	200
Ontario	2,718,880	279,470	415,225	789,970	498,160	160,460	15,800	9,540
Canada	7,329,150	646,245	791,600	1,234,770	2,397,550	704,485	183,510	33,310
				Percent of Dwellings				
Greater Sudbury	62.2	4.7	4.2	6.6	15.4	5.7	0.8	0.3
Ontario	55.6	5.7	8.5	16.2	10.2	3.3	0.3	0.2
Canada	55.0	4.9	5.9	9.3	18.0	5.3	1.4	0.3

Source: Statistics Canada. 2012. Census Profile. 2011 Census. Statistics Canada Catalogue no. 98-316-XWE. Ottawa. Released October 24 2012.
http://www12.statcan.gc.ca/census-recensement/2011/dp-pd/prof/index.cfm?Lang=E

Shelter Costs

		Owned Dwellings				Rented Dwellings		
Area	Number	Median Value[1] ($)	Average Value[1] ($)	Median Monthly Costs[2] ($)	Average Monthly Costs[2] ($)	Number	Median Monthly Costs[3] ($)	Average Monthly Costs[3] ($)
Greater Sudbury	45,855	225,236	250,513	1,002	1,112	21,660	750	753
Ontario	3,446,650	300,862	367,428	1,163	1,284	1,385,535	892	926
Canada	9,013,410	280,552	345,182	978	1,141	4,060,385	784	848

Note: All figures cover non-farm, non-reserve private dwellings; (1) Refers to the dollar amount expected by the owner if the dwelling were to be sold; (2) Includes all shelter expenses paid by households that own their dwellings, such as the mortgage payment and the costs of electricity, heat, water and other municipal services, property taxes and condominium fees; (3) Includes all shelter expenses paid by households that rent their dwellings, such as the monthly rent and the costs of electricity, heat and municipal services.
Source: Statistics Canada. 2013. 2011 National Household Survey. Statistics Canada Catalogue no. 99-004-XWE. Ottawa. Released September 11, 2013.

Occupied Private Dwellings by Period of Construction

Area	1960 or Before	1961 to 1980	1981 to 1990	1991 to 2000	2001 to 2005	2006 to 2011
			Number			
Greater Sudbury	22,575	25,295	8,810	6,735	1,685	2,495
Ontario	1,330,235	1,420,570	763,430	609,310	414,795	348,310
Canada	3,273,105	4,152,715	2,112,110	1,707,880	1,031,020	1,042,430
			Percent of Dwellings			
Greater Sudbury	33.4	37.4	13.0	10.0	2.5	3.7
Ontario	27.2	29.1	15.6	12.5	8.5	7.1
Canada	24.6	31.2	15.9	12.8	7.7	7.8

Note: Figures cover non-farm, non-reserve private dwellings and includes data up to May 10, 2011.
Source: Statistics Canada. 2013. 2011 National Household Survey. Statistics Canada Catalogue no. 99-004-XWE. Ottawa. Released September 11, 2013.

PROFILES / Greater Sudbury, Ontario

Educational Attainment

Area	No Certificate, Diploma or Degree	High School Diploma or Equivalent[1]	Apprenticeship or Trades Certificate or Diploma[2]	College, CÉGEP or Other Non-University Certificate or Diploma	University Certificate or Diploma Below the Bachelor Level[3]	Bachelor's Degree	University Certificate, Diploma or Degree Above Bachelor Level[4]
Number							
Total							
Greater Sudbury	28,095	32,555	14,060	34,060	3,070	13,210	7,555
Ontario	1,954,520	2,801,805	771,140	2,070,875	427,150	1,515,075	933,100
Canada	5,485,400	6,968,935	2,950,685	4,970,020	1,200,130	3,634,425	2,049,930
Males							
Greater Sudbury	13,685	15,255	10,075	15,200	1,125	5,635	3,420
Ontario	957,040	1,337,055	520,390	894,235	193,355	692,345	470,290
Canada	2,742,875	3,305,415	1,928,970	2,118,430	513,235	1,643,080	1,043,350
Females							
Greater Sudbury	14,410	17,295	3,985	18,865	1,940	7,580	4,130
Ontario	997,475	1,464,755	250,750	1,176,640	233,790	822,730	462,805
Canada	2,742,520	3,663,515	1,021,715	2,851,595	686,890	1,991,345	1,006,585
Percent of Population							
Total							
Greater Sudbury	21.2	24.6	10.6	25.7	2.3	10.0	5.7
Ontario	18.7	26.8	7.4	19.8	4.1	14.5	8.9
Canada	20.1	25.6	10.8	18.2	4.4	13.3	7.5
Males							
Greater Sudbury	21.3	23.7	15.6	23.6	1.7	8.8	5.3
Ontario	18.9	26.4	10.3	17.7	3.8	13.7	9.3
Canada	20.6	24.9	14.5	15.9	3.9	12.4	7.8
Females							
Greater Sudbury	21.1	25.4	5.8	27.7	2.8	11.1	6.1
Ontario	18.4	27.1	4.6	21.8	4.3	15.2	8.6
Canada	19.6	26.2	7.3	20.4	4.9	14.3	7.2

Note: Figures cover total population aged 15 years and over by highest certificate, diploma or degree; (1) Includes persons who have graduated from a secondary school or equivalent. It excludes persons with a postsecondary certificate, diploma or degree; (2) Includes Registered Apprenticeship certificates (including Certificate of Qualification, Journeyperson's designation) and other trades certificates or diplomas such as pre-employment or vocational certificates and diplomas from brief trade programs completed at community colleges, institutes of technology, vocational centres, and similar institutions; (3) Comparisons with other data sources suggest that the category 'University certificate or diploma below the bachelor's level' was over-reported in the NHS. This category likely includes some responses that are actually college certificates or diplomas, bachelor's degrees or other types of education (e.g., university transfer programs, bachelor's programs completed in other countries, incomplete bachelor's programs, non-university professional designations). We recommend users interpret the results for the 'University certificate or diploma below the bachelor's level' category with caution; (4) 'University certificate or diploma above bachelor level' includes the categories: 'Degree in medicine, dentistry, veterinary medicine or optometry,' 'Master's degree' and 'Earned doctorate.'
Source: Statistics Canada. 2013. 2011 National Household Survey. Statistics Canada Catalogue no. 99-004-XWE. Ottawa. Released September 11, 2013.

Household Income Distribution

Area	Less than $10,000	$10,000 to $19,999	$20,000 to $29,999	$30,000 to $39,999	$40,000 to $49,999	$50,000 to $59,999	$60,000 to $79,999	$80,000 to $99,999	$100,000 to $124,999	$125,000 to $149,999	$150,000 and Over
Households											
Greater Sudbury	2,425	6,230	6,125	5,505	6,330	5,685	9,820	7,960	6,940	4,235	6,350
Ontario	201,780	354,530	405,725	425,410	425,720	398,705	680,850	552,660	497,970	331,460	611,840
Canada	626,705	1,141,945	1,193,925	1,271,675	1,206,800	1,102,120	1,865,280	1,458,240	1,260,770	802,555	1,389,240
Percent of Households											
Greater Sudbury	3.6	9.2	9.1	8.1	9.4	8.4	14.5	11.8	10.3	6.3	9.4
Ontario	4.1	7.3	8.3	8.7	8.7	8.2	13.9	11.3	10.2	6.8	12.5
Canada	4.7	8.6	9.0	9.5	9.1	8.3	14.0	10.9	9.5	6.0	10.4

Note: Household income is the sum of the total incomes of all members of that household. Total income refers to monetary receipts from certain sources, before income taxes and deductions, during calendar year 2010.
Source: Statistics Canada. 2013. 2011 National Household Survey. Statistics Canada Catalogue no. 99-004-XWE. Ottawa. Released September 11, 2013.

Median and Average Household and Economic Family Income

Area	Median Household Income ($)	Average Household Income ($)	Median After-tax Household Income ($)	Average After-tax Household Income ($)	Median Economic Family Income ($)	Average Economic Family Income ($)	Median After-tax Economic Family Income ($)	Average After-tax Economic Family Income ($)
Greater Sudbury	62,481	76,772	55,437	64,788	80,084	93,061	69,972	78,151
Ontario	66,358	85,772	58,717	71,523	80,987	100,152	71,128	83,322
Canada	61,072	79,102	54,089	66,149	76,511	94,125	67,044	78,517

Note: Figures cover household and economic familiy income in 2010. A household is defined as a person or a group of persons (other than foreign residents) who occupy the same private dwelling and do not have a usual place of residence elsewhere in Canada. Every person is a member of one and only one household. An economic family is defined as a group of two or more persons who live in the same dwelling and are related to each other by blood, marriage, common-law, adoption or a foster relationship. A couple may be of opposite or same sex.
Source: Statistics Canada. 2013. 2011 National Household Survey. Statistics Canada Catalogue no. 99-004-XWE. Ottawa. Released September 11, 2013.

PROFILES / Greater Sudbury, Ontario

Individual Income Distribution

Area	Less than $10,000	$10,000 to $19,999	$20,000 to $29,999	$30,000 to $39,999	$40,000 to $49,999	$50,000 to $59,999	$60,000 to $79,999	$80,000 to $99,999	$100,000 to $124,999	$125,000 and Over
					Number					
					Total					
Greater Sudbury	20,115	21,590	17,110	15,955	14,955	10,735	12,400	7,105	3,680	3,300
Ontario	1,780,355	1,748,060	1,361,710	1,136,730	980,790	746,360	964,280	574,710	293,865	330,285
Canada	4,492,040	4,835,710	3,670,020	3,180,360	2,603,520	1,921,650	2,437,440	1,302,045	693,580	782,135
					Males					
Greater Sudbury	7,935	7,550	6,390	7,960	8,215	6,500	7,775	4,170	2,845	2,615
Ontario	781,095	669,815	580,990	535,255	491,125	407,005	569,205	341,160	201,125	244,500
Canada	1,936,365	1,864,880	1,588,260	1,522,190	1,333,510	1,079,780	1,473,145	823,720	492,905	599,905
					Females					
Greater Sudbury	12,180	14,045	10,720	7,995	6,735	4,230	4,630	2,940	840	690
Ontario	999,265	1,078,245	780,720	601,475	489,665	339,360	395,075	233,550	92,740	85,790
Canada	2,555,675	2,970,825	2,081,760	1,658,170	1,270,010	841,870	964,300	478,330	200,680	182,230
					Percent of Population					
					Total					
Greater Sudbury	15.8	17.0	13.5	12.6	11.8	8.5	9.8	5.6	2.9	2.6
Ontario	18.0	17.6	13.7	11.5	9.9	7.5	9.7	5.8	3.0	3.3
Canada	17.3	18.7	14.2	12.3	10.0	7.4	9.4	5.0	2.7	3.0
					Males					
Greater Sudbury	12.8	12.2	10.3	12.8	13.3	10.5	12.5	6.7	4.6	4.2
Ontario	16.2	13.9	12.1	11.1	10.2	8.4	11.8	7.1	4.2	5.1
Canada	15.2	14.7	12.5	12.0	10.5	8.5	11.6	6.5	3.9	4.7
					Females					
Greater Sudbury	18.7	21.6	16.5	12.3	10.4	6.5	7.1	4.5	1.3	1.1
Ontario	19.6	21.2	15.3	11.8	9.6	6.7	7.8	4.6	1.8	1.7
Canada	19.4	22.5	15.8	12.6	9.6	6.4	7.3	3.6	1.5	1.4

Note: Figures cover individuals aged 15 years and over with income. Income refers to monetary receipts from certain sources, before income taxes and deductions, during calendar year 2010.
Source: Statistics Canada. 2013. 2011 National Household Survey. Statistics Canada Catalogue no. 99-004-XWE. Ottawa. Released September 11, 2013.

Labour Force Status

Area	In the Labour Force - All	In the Labour Force - Employed	In the Labour Force - Unemployed	Not in the Labour Force
		Number		
		Total		
Greater Sudbury	83,630	77,095	6,535	48,970
Ontario	6,864,990	6,297,005	567,985	3,608,685
Canada	17,990,080	16,595,035	1,395,045	9,269,445
		Males		
Greater Sudbury	42,935	39,440	3,500	21,455
Ontario	3,542,030	3,249,165	292,865	1,522,690
Canada	9,388,570	8,634,310	754,255	3,906,785
		Females		
Greater Sudbury	40,695	37,655	3,035	27,510
Ontario	3,322,955	3,047,840	275,120	2,085,990
Canada	8,601,515	7,960,725	640,790	5,362,660
		Percent of Labour Force		
		Total		
Greater Sudbury	63.1	58.1	7.8	36.9
Ontario	65.5	60.1	8.3	34.5
Canada	66.0	60.9	7.8	34.0
		Males		
Greater Sudbury	66.7	61.2	8.2	33.3
Ontario	69.9	64.2	8.3	30.1
Canada	70.6	64.9	8.0	29.4
		Females		
Greater Sudbury	59.7	55.2	7.5	40.3
Ontario	61.4	56.3	8.3	38.6
Canada	61.6	57.0	7.4	38.4

Note: Figures are based on total population 15 years and over
Source: Statistics Canada. 2013. 2011 National Household Survey. Statistics Canada Catalogue no. 99-004-XWE. Ottawa. Released September 11, 2013.

Labour Force by Industry (NAICS Codes 11–52)

Area	Agriculture, forestry, fishing & hunting	Mining, quarrying, & oil & gas extraction	Utilities	Construction	Manufacturing	Wholesale Trade	Retail Trade	Transportation & warehousing	Information & cultural industries	Finance & insurance
					Number					
					Total					
Greater Sudbury	245	7,030	485	5,670	3,290	3,020	10,345	3,530	1,325	2,265
Ontario	101,280	29,985	57,035	417,900	697,565	305,030	751,200	307,405	178,720	364,415
Canada	437,650	261,050	149,940	1,215,380	1,619,295	733,445	2,031,665	827,780	420,830	767,960
					Males					
Greater Sudbury	170	6,545	430	4,805	2,820	2,365	4,570	2,710	655	600
Ontario	66,485	25,650	42,685	369,300	493,305	197,770	344,480	225,245	98,835	153,125
Canada	307,370	211,690	110,765	1,068,710	1,167,680	494,545	933,850	617,305	235,875	296,995
					Females					
Greater Sudbury	80	485	60	860	465	650	5,770	820	670	1,670
Ontario	34,800	4,340	14,350	48,595	204,260	107,260	406,720	82,160	79,885	211,290
Canada	130,285	49,360	39,175	146,670	451,615	238,900	1,097,820	210,475	184,955	470,960
					Percent of Labour Force					
					Total					
Greater Sudbury	0.3	8.6	0.6	6.9	4.0	3.7	12.6	4.3	1.6	2.8
Ontario	1.5	0.4	0.9	6.3	10.4	4.6	11.2	4.6	2.7	5.5
Canada	2.5	1.5	0.9	6.9	9.2	4.2	11.6	4.7	2.4	4.4
					Males					
Greater Sudbury	0.4	15.6	1.0	11.5	6.7	5.6	10.9	6.5	1.6	1.4
Ontario	1.9	0.7	1.2	10.7	14.3	5.7	10.0	6.5	2.9	4.4
Canada	3.3	2.3	1.2	11.6	12.7	5.4	10.2	6.7	2.6	3.2
					Females					
Greater Sudbury	0.2	1.2	0.2	2.2	1.2	1.6	14.4	2.1	1.7	4.2
Ontario	1.1	0.1	0.4	1.5	6.3	3.3	12.6	2.5	2.5	6.5
Canada	1.6	0.6	0.5	1.7	5.4	2.8	13.1	2.5	2.2	5.6

Note: Figures are based on total experienced labour force 15 years and over. Experienced labour force refers to persons who, during the week of Sunday, May 1 to Saturday, May 7, 2011, were employed and the unemployed who had last worked for pay or in self-employment in either 2010 or 2011.
Source: Statistics Canada. 2013. 2011 National Household Survey. Statistics Canada Catalogue no. 99-004-XWE. Ottawa. Released September 11, 2013.

Labour Force by Industry (NAICS Codes 53–91)

Area	Real estate & rental & leasing	Profess., scientific & tech. services	Mgmt of companies & enterprises	Admin. & support, waste mgmt & remed. services	Educational services	Health care & social assistance	Arts, entertain. & recreation	Accomm. & food services	Other services (except public admin.)	Public admin.
					Number					
					Total					
Greater Sudbury	1,455	4,035	20	2,575	7,525	11,355	1,560	5,410	3,645	7,090
Ontario	133,980	511,020	6,525	309,630	499,690	692,130	144,065	417,675	296,340	458,665
Canada	321,895	1,240,850	17,460	728,330	1,301,435	1,949,650	363,405	1,130,750	807,800	1,261,050
					Males					
Greater Sudbury	860	2,275	0	1,440	2,235	1,970	705	2,130	1,795	2,850
Ontario	72,835	281,420	3,540	172,475	162,765	120,165	75,035	177,240	133,795	236,655
Canada	179,090	688,625	9,380	411,250	424,915	349,430	188,270	469,990	372,940	652,510
					Females					
Greater Sudbury	600	1,760	0	1,135	5,290	9,390	850	3,280	1,850	4,240
Ontario	61,145	229,600	2,990	137,155	336,925	571,965	69,030	240,430	162,550	222,015
Canada	142,805	552,225	8,075	317,085	876,515	1,600,220	175,135	660,760	434,865	608,535
					Percent of Labour Force					
					Total					
Greater Sudbury	1.8	4.9	0.0	3.1	9.2	13.9	1.9	6.6	4.5	8.7
Ontario	2.0	7.6	0.1	4.6	7.5	10.4	2.2	6.3	4.4	6.9
Canada	1.8	7.1	0.1	4.1	7.4	11.1	2.1	6.4	4.6	7.2
					Males					
Greater Sudbury	2.1	5.4	0.0	3.4	5.3	4.7	1.7	5.1	4.3	6.8
Ontario	2.1	8.2	0.1	5.0	4.7	3.5	2.2	5.1	3.9	6.9
Canada	1.9	7.5	0.1	4.5	4.6	3.8	2.0	5.1	4.1	7.1
					Females					
Greater Sudbury	1.5	4.4	0.0	2.8	13.2	23.5	2.1	8.2	4.6	10.6
Ontario	1.9	7.1	0.1	4.2	10.4	17.7	2.1	7.4	5.0	6.9
Canada	1.7	6.6	0.1	3.8	10.4	19.1	2.1	7.9	5.2	7.2

Note: Figures are based on total experienced labour force 15 years and over. Experienced labour force refers to persons who, during the week of Sunday, May 1 to Saturday, May 7, 2011, were employed and the unemployed who had last worked for pay or in self-employment in either 2010 or 2011.
Source: Statistics Canada. 2013. 2011 National Household Survey. Statistics Canada Catalogue no. 99-004-XWE. Ottawa. Released September 11, 2013.

Occupation

Area	Mgmt	Business, Finance & Admin.	Natural/ Applied Sciences & Related	Health	Education, Law & Social, Community & Government Services	Art, Culture, Recreation & Sport	Sales & Service	Trades, Transport & Equip. Operators & Related	Natural Resources, Agri. & Related Production	Mfg & Utilities
Number											
Total											
Greater Sudbury	6,875	13,900	4,750	6,070	10,320	1,630	19,420	13,485	3,800	1,625
Ontario	770,580	1,138,330	494,500	392,695	801,465	206,420	1,550,260	868,515	106,810	350,685
Canada	1,963,600	2,902,045	1,237,775	1,107,200	2,064,675	503,415	4,068,170	2,537,775	397,930	805,040
Males											
Greater Sudbury	3,880	3,475	3,900	1,135	3,155	775	7,850	12,745	3,565	1,450
Ontario	474,655	352,505	384,345	78,330	264,570	96,055	673,880	812,280	82,610	233,565
Canada	1,229,460	854,190	966,355	217,520	676,550	232,535	1,745,705	2,385,615	318,945	564,300
Females											
Greater Sudbury	2,995	10,420	850	4,935	7,160	860	11,570	740	235	180
Ontario	295,920	785,825	110,150	314,370	536,895	110,370	876,380	56,230	24,200	117,115
Canada	734,140	2,047,855	271,415	889,675	1,388,130	270,875	2,322,465	152,165	78,980	240,740
Percent of Labour Force											
Total											
Greater Sudbury	8.4	17.0	5.8	7.4	12.6	2.0	23.7	16.5	4.6	2.0
Ontario	11.5	17.0	7.4	5.9	12.0	3.1	23.2	13.0	1.6	5.2
Canada	11.2	16.5	7.0	6.3	11.7	2.9	23.1	14.4	2.3	4.6
Males											
Greater Sudbury	9.3	8.3	9.3	2.7	7.5	1.8	18.7	30.4	8.5	3.5
Ontario	13.7	10.2	11.1	2.3	7.7	2.8	19.5	23.5	2.4	6.8
Canada	13.4	9.3	10.5	2.4	7.4	2.5	19.0	26.0	3.5	6.1
Females											
Greater Sudbury	7.5	26.1	2.1	12.4	17.9	2.2	29.0	1.9	0.6	0.5
Ontario	9.2	24.3	3.4	9.7	16.6	3.4	27.2	1.7	0.7	3.6
Canada	8.7	24.4	3.2	10.6	16.5	3.2	27.7	1.8	0.9	2.9

Note: Figures are based on total experienced labour force 15 years and over
Source: Statistics Canada. 2013. 2011 National Household Survey. Statistics Canada Catalogue no. 99-004-XWE. Ottawa. Released September 11, 2013.

Place of Work Status

Area	Worked at Home	Worked Outside Canada	No Fixed Workplace Address	Worked at Usual Place
Number				
Total				
Greater Sudbury	2,550	85	8,700	65,765
Ontario	423,790	31,390	670,835	5,170,980
Canada	1,142,640	66,460	1,868,245	13,517,690
Males				
Greater Sudbury	1,210	60	6,575	31,590
Ontario	216,900	21,150	486,560	2,524,555
Canada	582,150	47,355	1,400,485	6,604,325
Females				
Greater Sudbury	1,340	25	2,120	34,170
Ontario	206,895	10,240	184,275	2,646,420
Canada	560,490	19,100	467,760	6,913,370
Percent of Labour Force				
Total				
Greater Sudbury	3.3	0.1	11.3	85.3
Ontario	6.7	0.5	10.7	82.1
Canada	6.9	0.4	11.3	81.5
Males				
Greater Sudbury	3.1	0.2	16.7	80.1
Ontario	6.7	0.7	15.0	77.7
Canada	6.7	0.5	16.2	76.5
Females				
Greater Sudbury	3.6	0.1	5.6	90.7
Ontario	6.8	0.3	6.0	86.8
Canada	7.0	0.2	5.9	86.8

Note: Figures are based on total employed labour force 15 years and over.
Source: Statistics Canada. 2013. 2011 National Household Survey. Statistics Canada Catalogue no. 99-004-XWE. Ottawa. Released September 11, 2013.

Mode of Transportation to Work

Area	Car; Truck; Van; as Driver	Car; Truck; Van; as Passenger	Public Transit	Walked	Bicycled	All Other Modes
			Number			
			Total			
Greater Sudbury	60,090	5,215	3,370	3,950	520	1,310
Ontario	4,235,315	357,110	818,270	299,095	69,885	62,145
Canada	11,393,140	867,050	1,851,525	880,815	201,780	191,625
			Males			
Greater Sudbury	31,615	2,305	1,305	1,785	400	755
Ontario	2,316,680	143,410	340,995	131,765	47,635	30,635
Canada	6,238,835	349,530	788,290	387,580	135,840	104,725
			Females			
Greater Sudbury	28,470	2,915	2,060	2,165	120	560
Ontario	1,918,640	213,700	477,275	167,325	22,250	31,515
Canada	5,154,305	517,520	1,063,235	493,230	65,940	86,900
			Percent of Labour Force			
			Total			
Greater Sudbury	80.7	7.0	4.5	5.3	0.7	1.8
Ontario	72.5	6.1	14.0	5.1	1.2	1.1
Canada	74.0	5.6	12.0	5.7	1.3	1.2
			Males			
Greater Sudbury	82.8	6.0	3.4	4.7	1.0	2.0
Ontario	76.9	4.8	11.3	4.4	1.6	1.0
Canada	77.9	4.4	9.8	4.8	1.7	1.3
			Females			
Greater Sudbury	78.4	8.0	5.7	6.0	0.3	1.5
Ontario	67.8	7.5	16.9	5.9	0.8	1.1
Canada	69.8	7.0	14.4	6.7	0.9	1.2

Note: Figures are based on total employed labour force 15 years and over.
Source: Statistics Canada. 2013. 2011 National Household Survey. Statistics Canada Catalogue no. 99-004-XWE. Ottawa. Released September 11, 2013.

Visible Minority Population Characteristics

Area	Total Minority	South Asian[1]	Chinese	Black	Filipino	Latin American	Arab	SE Asian[2]	West Asian[3]	Korean	Japanese	Multiple[4]
						Number						
						Total						
Greater Sudbury	4,200	630	795	935	195	290	455	325	90	175	25	225
Ontario	3,279,565	965,990	629,140	539,205	275,380	172,560	151,645	137,875	122,530	78,290	29,085	96,735
Canada	6,264,750	1,567,400	1,324,750	945,665	619,310	381,280	380,620	312,075	206,840	161,130	87,270	171,935
						Males						
Greater Sudbury	2,255	355	455	520	90	120	245	170	55	80	0	125
Ontario	1,582,480	484,355	301,575	251,295	116,825	83,205	79,620	67,645	62,515	38,045	13,345	46,765
Canada	3,043,010	790,755	632,325	453,005	268,885	186,355	203,485	154,035	105,620	77,165	38,270	83,335
						Females						
Greater Sudbury	1,945	275	345	410	105	170	210	150	30	100	15	105
Ontario	1,697,085	481,635	327,570	287,915	158,555	89,360	72,025	70,230	60,010	40,250	15,740	49,970
Canada	3,221,745	776,650	692,420	492,660	350,425	194,925	177,140	158,045	101,220	83,965	48,990	88,600
						Percent of Population						
						Total						
Greater Sudbury	2.7	0.4	0.5	0.6	0.1	0.2	0.3	0.2	0.1	0.1	0.0	0.1
Ontario	25.9	7.6	5.0	4.3	2.2	1.4	1.2	1.1	1.0	0.6	0.2	0.8
Canada	19.1	4.8	4.0	2.9	1.9	1.2	1.2	0.9	0.6	0.5	0.3	0.5
						Males						
Greater Sudbury	2.9	0.5	0.6	0.7	0.1	0.2	0.3	0.2	0.1	0.1	0.0	0.2
Ontario	25.6	7.8	4.9	4.1	1.9	1.3	1.3	1.1	1.0	0.6	0.2	0.8
Canada	18.8	4.9	3.9	2.8	1.7	1.2	1.3	1.0	0.7	0.5	0.2	0.5
						Females						
Greater Sudbury	2.4	0.3	0.4	0.5	0.1	0.2	0.3	0.2	0.0	0.1	0.0	0.1
Ontario	26.2	7.4	5.1	4.4	2.5	1.4	1.1	1.1	0.9	0.6	0.2	0.8
Canada	19.3	4.7	4.1	3.0	2.1	1.2	1.1	0.9	0.6	0.5	0.3	0.5

Note: The Employment Equity Act defines visible minorities as 'persons, other than Aboriginal peoples, who are non-Caucasian in race or non-white in colour';
(1) Includes 'East Indian,' 'Pakistani,' 'Sri Lankan,' etc.; (2) Includes 'Vietnamese,' 'Cambodian,' 'Malaysian,' 'Laotian,' etc.; (3) Includes 'Iranian,' 'Afghan,' etc.; (4) Includes respondents who reported more than one visible minority group by checking two or more mark-in circles, e.g., 'Black' and 'South Asian.'
Source: Statistics Canada. 2013. 2011 National Household Survey. Statistics Canada Catalogue no. 99-004-XWE. Ottawa. Released September 11, 2013.

PROFILES / Greater Sudbury, Ontario

Aboriginal Population

Area	Aboriginal Identity[1]	First Nations (North American Indian) Single Identity[2]	Métis Single Identity	Inuk (Inuit) Single Identity	Multiple Aboriginal Identities[3]	Aboriginal Identities Not Included Elsewhere
Number						
Total						
Greater Sudbury	12,960	6,045	6,455	40	90	330
Ontario	301,430	201,100	86,020	3,355	2,910	8,040
Canada	1,400,685	851,560	451,795	59,440	11,415	26,475
Males						
Greater Sudbury	6,265	2,910	3,100	0	50	185
Ontario	145,020	96,620	41,755	1,475	1,420	3,750
Canada	682,190	411,785	223,335	29,495	5,525	12,055
Females						
Greater Sudbury	6,700	3,135	3,355	25	40	140
Ontario	156,410	104,485	44,260	1,880	1,490	4,295
Canada	718,500	439,775	228,460	29,950	5,890	14,420
Percent of Population						
Total						
Greater Sudbury	8.2	3.8	4.1	0.0	0.1	0.2
Ontario	2.4	1.6	0.7	0.0	0.0	0.1
Canada	4.3	2.6	1.4	0.2	0.0	0.1
Males						
Greater Sudbury	8.1	3.8	4.0	0.0	0.1	0.2
Ontario	2.3	1.6	0.7	0.0	0.0	0.1
Canada	4.2	2.5	1.4	0.2	0.0	0.1
Females						
Greater Sudbury	8.3	3.9	4.2	0.0	0.0	0.2
Ontario	2.4	1.6	0.7	0.0	0.0	0.1
Canada	4.3	2.6	1.4	0.2	0.0	0.1

Note: (1) Includes persons who reported being an Aboriginal person, that is, First Nations (North American Indian), Métis or Inuk (Inuit) and/or those who reported Registered or Treaty Indian status, that is registered under the Indian Act of Canada, and/or those who reported membership in a First Nation or Indian band. Aboriginal peoples of Canada are defined in the Constitution Act, 1982, section 35-2 as including the Indian, Inuit and Métis peoples of Canada; (2) Users should be aware that the estimates associated with this variable are more affected than most by the incomplete enumeration of certain Indian reserves and Indian settlements in the National Household Survey (NHS); (3) Includes persons who reported being any two or all three of the following: First Nations (North American Indian), Métis or Inuk (Inuit).
Source: Statistics Canada. 2013. 2011 National Household Survey. Statistics Canada Catalogue no. 99-004-XWE. Ottawa. Released September 11, 2013.

Ethnic Origin

Area	North American Aboriginal	Other North American	European	Caribbean	Latin, Central and South American	African	Asian	Oceania
Number								
Total								
Greater Sudbury	17,280	67,620	124,495	535	625	1,030	3,425	175
Ontario	441,395	3,059,480	8,231,410	396,485	271,545	331,460	2,604,595	19,410
Canada	1,836,035	11,070,455	20,157,965	627,590	544,375	766,735	5,011,225	74,875
Males								
Greater Sudbury	8,285	32,605	60,650	310	305	535	1,910	85
Ontario	210,490	1,507,105	4,019,885	181,805	130,035	160,940	1,265,540	9,855
Canada	885,675	5,462,685	9,913,150	291,640	264,635	387,360	2,435,540	37,490
Females								
Greater Sudbury	9,000	35,015	63,850	220	315	490	1,520	95
Ontario	230,905	1,552,380	4,211,525	214,675	141,510	170,515	1,339,050	9,555
Canada	950,360	5,607,770	10,244,820	335,945	279,740	379,380	2,575,680	37,385
Percent of Population								
Total								
Greater Sudbury	11.0	42.9	78.9	0.3	0.4	0.7	2.2	0.1
Ontario	3.5	24.2	65.1	3.1	2.1	2.6	20.6	0.2
Canada	5.6	33.7	61.4	1.9	1.7	2.3	15.3	0.2
Males								
Greater Sudbury	10.7	42.2	78.6	0.4	0.4	0.7	2.5	0.1
Ontario	3.4	24.4	65.0	2.9	2.1	2.6	20.5	0.2
Canada	5.5	33.8	61.3	1.8	1.6	2.4	15.1	0.2
Females								
Greater Sudbury	11.2	43.5	79.2	0.3	0.4	0.6	1.9	0.1
Ontario	3.6	24.0	65.1	3.3	2.2	2.6	20.7	0.1
Canada	5.7	33.6	61.4	2.0	1.7	2.3	15.4	0.2

Note: The sum of the ethnic groups in this table is greater than the total population estimate because a person may report more than one ethnic origin in the NHS.
Source: Statistics Canada. 2013. 2011 National Household Survey. Statistics Canada Catalogue no. 99-004-XWE. Ottawa. Released September 11, 2013.

Religion

Area	Buddhist	Christian	Hindu	Jewish	Muslim	Sikh	Traditional (Aboriginal) Spirituality	Other Religions	No Religious Affiliation
				Number Total					
Greater Sudbury	295	127,090	340	120	650	75	300	405	28,490
Ontario	163,750	8,167,295	366,720	195,540	581,950	179,765	15,905	53,080	2,927,790
Canada	366,830	22,102,745	497,965	329,495	1,053,945	454,965	64,935	130,835	7,850,605
				Males					
Greater Sudbury	195	60,120	185	75	375	45	190	200	15,805
Ontario	75,355	3,839,925	183,580	95,795	293,925	90,515	7,600	23,555	1,571,195
Canada	168,465	10,497,775	250,435	161,265	540,555	229,435	31,805	57,745	4,225,645
				Females					
Greater Sudbury	100	66,970	155	45	270	25	115	205	12,685
Ontario	88,395	4,327,365	183,140	99,740	288,025	89,250	8,310	29,525	1,356,600
Canada	198,365	11,604,975	247,525	168,235	513,395	225,530	33,135	73,090	3,624,965
				Percent of Population Total					
Greater Sudbury	0.2	80.6	0.2	0.1	0.4	0.0	0.2	0.3	18.1
Ontario	1.3	64.6	2.9	1.5	4.6	1.4	0.1	0.4	23.1
Canada	1.1	67.3	1.5	1.0	3.2	1.4	0.2	0.4	23.9
				Males					
Greater Sudbury	0.3	77.9	0.2	0.1	0.5	0.1	0.2	0.3	20.5
Ontario	1.2	62.1	3.0	1.5	4.8	1.5	0.1	0.4	25.4
Canada	1.0	64.9	1.5	1.0	3.3	1.4	0.2	0.4	26.1
				Females					
Greater Sudbury	0.1	83.1	0.2	0.1	0.3	0.0	0.1	0.3	15.7
Ontario	1.4	66.9	2.8	1.5	4.5	1.4	0.1	0.5	21.0
Canada	1.2	69.5	1.5	1.0	3.1	1.4	0.2	0.4	21.7

Note: Religion refers to the person's self-identification as having a connection or affiliation with any religious denomination, group, body, sect, cult or other religiously defined community or system of belief. Religion is not limited to formal membership in a religious organization or group. Persons without a religious connection or affiliation can self-identify as atheist, agnostic or humanist, or can provide another applicable response.
Source: Statistics Canada. 2013. 2011 National Household Survey. Statistics Canada Catalogue no. 99-004-XWE. Ottawa. Released September 11, 2013.

Religion—Christian Denominations

Area	Anglican	Baptist	Catholic	Christian Orthodox	Lutheran	Pentecostal	Presbyterian	United Church	Other Christian
				Number Total					
Greater Sudbury	6,800	2,080	92,495	925	3,040	1,890	1,525	9,785	8,545
Ontario	774,560	244,650	3,976,610	297,710	163,460	213,945	319,585	952,465	1,224,300
Canada	1,631,845	635,840	12,810,705	550,690	478,185	478,705	472,385	2,007,610	3,036,780
				Males					
Greater Sudbury	3,265	1,055	44,245	490	1,405	810	735	4,420	3,690
Ontario	355,175	112,285	1,895,940	145,825	75,225	94,955	148,535	435,255	576,730
Canada	752,945	293,905	6,167,290	270,205	221,525	217,850	218,955	912,545	1,442,550
				Females					
Greater Sudbury	3,530	1,025	48,245	440	1,635	1,075	795	5,365	4,855
Ontario	419,390	132,370	2,080,665	151,885	88,230	118,990	171,050	517,210	647,570
Canada	878,900	341,940	6,643,415	280,485	256,660	260,850	253,430	1,095,065	1,594,230
				Percent of Population Total					
Greater Sudbury	4.3	1.3	58.6	0.6	1.9	1.2	1.0	6.2	5.4
Ontario	6.1	1.9	31.4	2.4	1.3	1.7	2.5	7.5	9.7
Canada	5.0	1.9	39.0	1.7	1.5	1.5	1.4	6.1	9.2
				Males					
Greater Sudbury	4.2	1.4	57.3	0.6	1.8	1.0	1.0	5.7	4.8
Ontario	5.7	1.8	30.7	2.4	1.2	1.5	2.4	7.0	9.3
Canada	4.7	1.8	38.2	1.7	1.4	1.3	1.4	5.6	8.9
				Females					
Greater Sudbury	4.4	1.3	59.9	0.5	2.0	1.3	1.0	6.7	6.0
Ontario	6.5	2.0	32.2	2.3	1.4	1.8	2.6	8.0	10.0
Canada	5.3	2.0	39.8	1.7	1.5	1.6	1.5	6.6	9.6

Note: Religion refers to the person's self-identification as having a connection or affiliation with any religious denomination, group, body, sect, cult or other religiously defined community or system of belief. Religion is not limited to formal membership in a religious organization or group. Persons without a religious connection or affiliation can self-identify as atheist, agnostic or humanist, or can provide another applicable response.
Source: Statistics Canada. 2013. 2011 National Household Survey. Statistics Canada Catalogue no. 99-004-XWE. Ottawa. Released September 11, 2013.

Immigrant Status and Period of Immigration

Area	Non-Immigrants[1]	Immigrants All	Before 1971	1971 to 1980	1981 to 1990	1991 to 2000	2001 to 2005	2006 to 2011	Non-Permanent Residents[3]
				Number					
				Total					
Greater Sudbury	147,385	9,775	5,645	1,320	675	905	565	665	605
Ontario	8,906,000	3,611,365	723,030	464,380	538,285	866,220	518,405	501,060	134,425
Canada	25,720,175	6,775,765	1,261,055	870,775	949,890	1,539,050	992,070	1,162,915	356,385
				Males					
Greater Sudbury	72,145	4,700	2,795	610	315	435	225	320	340
Ontario	4,410,240	1,706,385	341,820	217,990	258,095	408,270	245,850	234,360	64,825
Canada	12,753,235	3,231,370	605,430	416,670	454,570	724,905	474,545	555,245	178,515
				Females					
Greater Sudbury	75,240	5,070	2,855	710	355	465	340	345	265
Ontario	4,495,765	1,904,985	381,210	246,390	280,190	457,950	272,550	266,695	69,600
Canada	12,966,935	3,544,400	655,625	454,105	495,325	814,145	517,530	607,670	177,870
				Percent of Population					
				Total					
Greater Sudbury	93.4	6.2	3.6	0.8	0.4	0.6	0.4	0.4	0.4
Ontario	70.4	28.5	5.7	3.7	4.3	6.8	4.1	4.0	1.1
Canada	78.3	20.6	3.8	2.7	2.9	4.7	3.0	3.5	1.1
				Males					
Greater Sudbury	93.5	6.1	3.6	0.8	0.4	0.6	0.3	0.4	0.4
Ontario	71.3	27.6	5.5	3.5	4.2	6.6	4.0	3.8	1.0
Canada	78.9	20.0	3.7	2.6	2.8	4.5	2.9	3.4	1.1
				Females					
Greater Sudbury	93.4	6.3	3.5	0.9	0.4	0.6	0.4	0.4	0.3
Ontario	69.5	29.4	5.9	3.8	4.3	7.1	4.2	4.1	1.1
Canada	77.7	21.2	3.9	2.7	3.0	4.9	3.1	3.6	1.1

Note: (1) Non-immigrant refers to a person who is a Canadian citizen by birth; (2) Immigrant refers to a person who is or has ever been a landed immigrant/permanent resident. This person has been granted the right to live in Canada permanently by immigration authorities. Some immigrants have resided in Canada for a number of years, while others have arrived recently. Some immigrants are Canadian citizens, while others are not. Most immigrants are born outside Canada, but a small number are born in Canada. In the 2011 National Household Survey, 'Immigrants' includes immigrants who landed in Canada prior to May 10, 2011; (3) Non-permanent resident refers to a person from another country who has a work or study permit, or who is a refugee claimant, and any non-Canadian-born family member living in Canada with them.
Source: Statistics Canada. 2013. 2011 National Household Survey. Statistics Canada Catalogue no. 99-004-XWE. Ottawa. Released September 11, 2013.

Mother Tongue

Area	English	French	Non-official Language	English & French	English & Non-official Language	French & Non-official Language	English, French & Non-official Language
			Number				
			Total				
Greater Sudbury	102,320	42,805	10,290	2,500	630	105	45
Ontario	8,677,040	493,300	3,264,435	46,605	219,425	13,645	7,615
Canada	18,858,980	7,054,975	6,567,680	144,685	396,330	74,430	24,095
			Males				
Greater Sudbury	50,925	20,290	4,895	1,185	305	50	25
Ontario	4,276,970	232,785	1,562,190	21,805	106,790	6,285	3,495
Canada	9,345,225	3,452,380	3,157,785	69,975	192,000	36,535	11,965
			Females				
Greater Sudbury	51,400	22,515	5,395	1,315	325	55	20
Ontario	4,400,065	260,510	1,702,240	24,795	112,635	7,365	4,115
Canada	9,513,750	3,602,590	3,409,895	74,710	204,330	37,890	12,130
			Percent of Population				
			Total				
Greater Sudbury	64.5	27.0	6.5	1.6	0.4	0.1	0.0
Ontario	68.2	3.9	25.7	0.4	1.7	0.1	0.1
Canada	56.9	21.3	19.8	0.4	1.2	0.2	0.1
			Males				
Greater Sudbury	65.6	26.1	6.3	1.5	0.4	0.1	0.0
Ontario	68.9	3.7	25.2	0.4	1.7	0.1	0.1
Canada	57.5	21.2	19.4	0.4	1.2	0.2	0.1
			Females				
Greater Sudbury	63.4	27.8	6.7	1.6	0.4	0.1	0.0
Ontario	67.6	4.0	26.1	0.4	1.7	0.1	0.1
Canada	56.4	21.4	20.2	0.4	1.2	0.2	0.1

Note: Figures cover total population excluding institutional residents.
Source: Statistics Canada. 2012. Census Profile. 2011 Census. Statistics Canada Catalogue no. 98-316-XWE. Ottawa. Released October 24 2012.
http://www12.statcan.gc.ca/census-recensement/2011/dp-pd/prof/index.cfm?Lang=E

Language Spoken Most Often at Home

Area	English	French	Non-official Language	English & French	English & Non-official Language	French & Non-official Language	English, French & Non-official Language
			Number				
			Total				
Greater Sudbury	128,305	23,500	3,230	2,385	1,195	45	50
Ontario	10,044,810	284,115	1,827,870	37,955	509,105	6,370	11,845
Canada	21,457,075	6,827,865	3,673,865	131,205	875,135	109,700	46,330
			Males				
Greater Sudbury	63,660	10,840	1,470	1,100	560	20	20
Ontario	4,930,610	133,495	872,860	17,250	248,050	2,855	5,225
Canada	10,585,620	3,348,235	1,767,310	63,475	425,370	53,010	22,845
			Females				
Greater Sudbury	64,645	12,660	1,755	1,285	640	20	30
Ontario	5,114,200	150,620	955,010	20,705	261,055	3,520	6,620
Canada	10,871,455	3,479,625	1,906,555	67,730	449,765	56,690	23,485
			Percent of Population				
			Total				
Greater Sudbury	80.8	14.8	2.0	1.5	0.8	0.0	0.0
Ontario	79.0	2.2	14.4	0.3	4.0	0.1	0.1
Canada	64.8	20.6	11.1	0.4	2.6	0.3	0.1
			Males				
Greater Sudbury	82.0	14.0	1.9	1.4	0.7	0.0	0.0
Ontario	79.4	2.1	14.1	0.3	4.0	0.0	0.1
Canada	65.1	20.6	10.9	0.4	2.6	0.3	0.1
			Females				
Greater Sudbury	79.8	15.6	2.2	1.6	0.8	0.0	0.0
Ontario	78.5	2.3	14.7	0.3	4.0	0.1	0.1
Canada	64.5	20.6	11.3	0.4	2.7	0.3	0.1

Note: Figures cover total population excluding institutional residents.
Source: Statistics Canada. 2012. Census Profile. 2011 Census. Statistics Canada Catalogue no. 98-316-XWE. Ottawa. Released October 24 2012.
http://www12.statcan.gc.ca/census-recensement/2011/dp-pd/prof/index.cfm?Lang=E

Knowledge of Official Languages

Area	English Only	French Only	English & French	Neither English nor French
		Number		
		Total		
Greater Sudbury	94,925	1,665	61,770	345
Ontario	10,984,360	42,980	1,395,805	298,920
Canada	22,564,665	4,165,015	5,795,570	595,920
		Males		
Greater Sudbury	48,005	720	28,835	120
Ontario	5,445,050	18,805	627,725	118,765
Canada	11,222,185	1,925,340	2,876,560	241,790
		Females		
Greater Sudbury	46,915	950	32,940	225
Ontario	5,539,310	24,175	768,085	180,155
Canada	11,342,485	2,239,680	2,919,005	354,135
		Percent of Population		
		Total		
Greater Sudbury	59.8	1.0	38.9	0.2
Ontario	86.3	0.3	11.0	2.3
Canada	68.1	12.6	17.5	1.8
		Males		
Greater Sudbury	61.8	0.9	37.1	0.2
Ontario	87.7	0.3	10.1	1.9
Canada	69.0	11.8	17.7	1.5
		Females		
Greater Sudbury	57.9	1.2	40.7	0.3
Ontario	85.1	0.4	11.8	2.8
Canada	67.3	13.3	17.3	2.1

Note: Figures cover total population excluding institutional residents.
Source: Statistics Canada. 2012. Census Profile. 2011 Census. Statistics Canada Catalogue no. 98-316-XWE. Ottawa. Released October 24 2012.
http://www12.statcan.gc.ca/census-recensement/2011/dp-pd/prof/index.cfm?Lang=E

Guelph, Ontario

Background

The City of Guelph is located in southwestern Ontario, approximately 28 kilometres east of Waterloo and 100 kilometres west of downtown Toronto. It is called "The Royal City" in tribute of its namesake, King George the IV, from the Guelph lineage.

Founded in 1827, Guelph is considered one of Canada's first planned towns. The area was the headquarters of "Canada Company," a British development firm responsible for attracting settlers to the region. The town was designed to resemble a European city centre with a central town square, narrow side streets and broad main streets. The late 19th-century stone bridges spanning across the city's Speed River are now considered national historical sites.

Guelph is situated in one of the fastest growing economic regions in Canada. In addition to a diverse economic base that includes advanced manufacturing, life sciences and area-based research in agri-business, food safety and alternative energies, Guelph is recognized as a leader in Ontario's agricultural biotechnology sector. The University of Guelph research facility specializes in agricultural sciences. Guelph's Ontario Veterinary College is the oldest school of its kind in the Western hemisphere (est. 1862).

In 2012, the City of Guelph, along with fellow member cities of the Ontario Clean Technology Alliance, announced support for a $60-million consortium for developing new water technologies and facilities in North America.

Special city attractions include the Guelph Civic Museum, a former 1854 convent, and McCrae House (birthplace of "In Flanders Fields" poet, John McCrae). Guelph's "Fab 5" Festivals are the annual Contemporary Dance Festival, Hillside Festival, Jazz Festival, Festival of Moving Media and the Eden Mills Writers Festival.

Guelph has summer highs of plus 24.57 degrees Celsius, winter lows of minus 10.03 degrees Celsius, and an average rainfall just over 771 mm per year.

Rankings

- Guelph ranked #6 on the Canadian Learning Index (CLI) in 2010. The CLI measures learning conditions in more than 4,500 communities across Canada. Statistical indicators show how Canadians learn at school, in the home, at work or within the community. Guelph's #6 ranking was shared with Edmonton and Halifax with a score of 83. The national CLI average score was 75. *Canadian Council of Learning, Composite Learning Index (CLI), "Canada's score on annual learning index stalls," May 20th, 2010*
- Guelph ranked #1 as Canada's most caring community. Almost 70% of Guelph residents (over the age of 15) volunteered their time in 2004. Thirty-seven Canadian cities were evaluated based on their local volunteer rates. Kingston (ON) ranked #2 and Fredericton (NB), #3. *The Canadian Council on Learning with files from Statistics Canada: Canada Survey of Giving, Volunteering and Participation 2004*

PROFILES / Guelph, Ontario

Population Growth and Density

Area	Population in 2001	Population in 2006	Population in 2011	Population Change 2001–2006	Population Change 2006–2011	Land Area (sq. km)	Population Density per sq. km
Guelph	106,170	114,943	121,688	8.3	5.9	87.20	1,395.4
Ontario	11,410,046	12,160,282	12,851,821	6.6	5.7	908,607.67	14.1
Canada	30,007,094	31,612,897	33,476,688	5.4	5.9	8,965,121.42	3.7

Source: Statistics Canada. 2012. Census Profile. 2011 Census. Statistics Canada Catalogue no. 98-316-XWE. Ottawa. Released October 24 2012. http://www12.statcan.gc.ca/census-recensement/2011/dp-pd/prof/index.cfm?Lang=E;
Statistics Canada 2007. 2006 Community Profiles. 2006 Census. Statistics Canada Catalogue no. 92-591-XWE. Ottawa. Released March 13 2007.
http://www12.statcan.ca/census-recensement/2006/dp-pd/prof/92-591/index.cfm?Lang=E

Gender

Area	Males	Females
Number		
Guelph	59,000	62,690
Ontario	6,263,140	6,588,685
Canada	16,414,225	17,062,460
Percent of Population		
Guelph	48.5	51.5
Ontario	48.7	51.3
Canada	49.0	51.0

Source: Statistics Canada. 2012. Census Profile. 2011 Census. Statistics Canada Catalogue no. 98-316-XWE. Ottawa. Released October 24 2012.
http://www12.statcan.gc.ca/census-recensement/2011/dp-pd/prof/index.cfm?Lang=E

Marital Status

Area	Married[1]	Living Common-law	Single[2]	Separated	Divorced	Widowed
Number						
Total						
Guelph	48,760	9,135	28,115	3,060	5,955	5,125
Ontario	5,367,400	791,210	2,985,020	319,805	593,730	613,880
Canada	12,941,960	3,142,525	7,816,045	698,240	1,686,035	1,584,530
Males						
Guelph	24,300	4,540	14,840	1,250	2,165	930
Ontario	2,681,320	397,620	1,583,760	133,790	231,160	117,980
Canada	6,470,300	1,575,495	4,206,320	299,655	680,415	310,940
Females						
Guelph	24,460	4,595	13,270	1,810	3,790	4,190
Ontario	2,686,075	393,590	1,401,260	186,015	362,570	495,905
Canada	6,471,660	1,567,035	3,609,730	398,585	1,005,620	1,273,590
Percent of Population						
Total						
Guelph	48.7	9.1	28.1	3.1	5.9	5.1
Ontario	50.3	7.4	28.0	3.0	5.6	5.8
Canada	46.4	11.3	28.0	2.5	6.0	5.7
Males						
Guelph	50.6	9.5	30.9	2.6	4.5	1.9
Ontario	52.1	7.7	30.8	2.6	4.5	2.3
Canada	47.8	11.6	31.1	2.2	5.0	2.3
Females						
Guelph	46.9	8.8	25.5	3.5	7.3	8.0
Ontario	48.6	7.1	25.4	3.4	6.6	9.0
Canada	45.2	10.9	25.2	2.8	7.0	8.9

Note: (1) and not separated, (2) never legally married
Source: Statistics Canada. 2012. Census Profile. 2011 Census. Statistics Canada Catalogue no. 98-316-XWE. Ottawa. Released October 24 2012.
http://www12.statcan.gc.ca/census-recensement/2011/dp-pd/prof/index.cfm?Lang=E

Age Characteristics: 0 to 49 Years

Area	0 to 4 Years	5 to 9 Years	10 to 14 Years	15 to 19 Years	20 to 24 Years	25 to 29 Years	30 to 34 Years	35 to 39 Years	40 to 44 Years	45 to 49 Years
					Number					
					Total					
Guelph	7,395	7,050	7,100	7,990	9,290	9,040	8,475	8,500	8,780	9,545
Ontario	704,260	712,755	763,755	863,635	852,910	815,120	800,365	844,335	924,075	1,055,880
Canada	1,877,095	1,809,895	1,920,355	2,178,135	2,187,450	2,169,590	2,162,905	2,173,930	2,324,875	2,675,130
					Males					
Guelph	3,765	3,600	3,605	4,115	4,485	4,440	4,190	4,135	4,310	4,755
Ontario	360,590	365,290	391,630	443,680	432,490	400,045	383,340	405,845	447,920	517,510
Canada	961,150	925,965	983,995	1,115,845	1,108,775	1,077,275	1,058,810	1,064,200	1,141,720	1,318,715
					Females					
Guelph	3,625	3,445	3,500	3,880	4,810	4,600	4,275	4,365	4,470	4,790
Ontario	343,670	347,465	372,125	419,950	420,415	415,075	417,030	438,485	476,155	538,370
Canada	915,945	883,935	936,360	1,062,295	1,078,670	1,092,315	1,104,095	1,109,735	1,183,155	1,356,420
					Percent of Population					
					Total					
Guelph	6.1	5.8	5.8	6.6	7.6	7.4	7.0	7.0	7.2	7.8
Ontario	5.5	5.5	5.9	6.7	6.6	6.3	6.2	6.6	7.2	8.2
Canada	5.6	5.4	5.7	6.5	6.5	6.5	6.5	6.5	6.9	8.0
					Males					
Guelph	6.4	6.1	6.1	7.0	7.6	7.5	7.1	7.0	7.3	8.1
Ontario	5.8	5.8	6.3	7.1	6.9	6.4	6.1	6.5	7.2	8.3
Canada	5.9	5.6	6.0	6.8	6.8	6.6	6.5	6.5	7.0	8.0
					Females					
Guelph	5.8	5.5	5.6	6.2	7.7	7.3	6.8	7.0	7.1	7.6
Ontario	5.2	5.3	5.6	6.4	6.4	6.3	6.3	6.7	7.2	8.2
Canada	5.4	5.2	5.5	6.2	6.3	6.4	6.5	6.5	6.9	7.9

Source: Statistics Canada. 2012. Census Profile. 2011 Census. Statistics Canada Catalogue no. 98-316-XWE. Ottawa. Released October 24 2012.
http://www12.statcan.gc.ca/census-recensement/2011/dp-pd/prof/index.cfm?Lang=E

Age Characteristics: 50 Years and Over, and Median Age

Area	50 to 54 Years	55 to 59 Years	60 to 64 Years	65 to 69 Years	70 to 74 Years	75 to 79 Years	80 to 84 Years	85 Years and Over	Median Age
				Number					
				Total					
Guelph	8,885	7,500	6,300	4,555	3,485	3,020	2,640	2,150	37.7
Ontario	1,006,140	864,620	765,655	563,485	440,780	356,150	271,510	246,400	40.4
Canada	2,658,965	2,340,635	2,052,670	1,521,715	1,153,065	922,700	702,070	645,515	40.6
				Males					
Guelph	4,320	3,540	2,950	2,125	1,525	1,325	1,080	730	36.6
Ontario	492,560	418,755	370,370	270,875	206,350	161,345	113,620	80,925	39.4
Canada	1,309,030	1,147,300	1,002,690	738,010	543,435	417,945	291,085	208,300	39.6
				Females					
Guelph	4,565	3,955	3,350	2,435	1,960	1,690	1,555	1,420	38.7
Ontario	513,580	445,865	395,275	292,610	234,435	194,805	157,890	165,475	41.3
Canada	1,349,940	1,193,335	1,049,985	783,705	609,630	504,755	410,985	437,215	41.5
				Percent of Population					
				Total					
Guelph	7.3	6.2	5.2	3.7	2.9	2.5	2.2	1.8	—
Ontario	7.8	6.7	6.0	4.4	3.4	2.8	2.1	1.9	—
Canada	7.9	7.0	6.1	4.5	3.4	2.8	2.1	1.9	—
				Males					
Guelph	7.3	6.0	5.0	3.6	2.6	2.2	1.8	1.2	—
Ontario	7.9	6.7	5.9	4.3	3.3	2.6	1.8	1.3	—
Canada	8.0	7.0	6.1	4.5	3.3	2.5	1.8	1.3	—
				Females					
Guelph	7.3	6.3	5.3	3.9	3.1	2.7	2.5	2.3	—
Ontario	7.8	6.8	6.0	4.4	3.6	3.0	2.4	2.5	—
Canada	7.9	7.0	6.2	4.6	3.6	3.0	2.4	2.6	—

Source: Statistics Canada. 2012. Census Profile. 2011 Census. Statistics Canada Catalogue no. 98-316-XWE. Ottawa. Released October 24 2012.
http://www12.statcan.gc.ca/census-recensement/2011/dp-pd/prof/index.cfm?Lang=E

PROFILES / Guelph, Ontario

Private Households by Household Size

Area	1 Person	2 Persons	3 Persons	4 Persons	5 Persons	6 or More Persons	Average Number of Persons in Private Households
				Households			
Guelph	12,750	15,725	7,985	7,705	2,700	1,245	2.5
Ontario	1,230,975	1,584,415	803,030	783,925	310,860	174,305	2.6
Canada	3,673,310	4,544,820	2,081,900	1,903,300	724,405	392,885	2.5
				Percent of Households			
Guelph	26.5	32.7	16.6	16.0	5.6	2.6	–
Ontario	25.2	32.4	16.4	16.0	6.4	3.6	–
Canada	27.6	34.1	15.6	14.3	5.4	2.9	–

Source: Statistics Canada. 2012. Census Profile. 2011 Census. Statistics Canada Catalogue no. 98-316-XWE. Ottawa. Released October 24 2012.
http://www12.statcan.gc.ca/census-recensement/2011/dp-pd/prof/index.cfm?Lang=E

Dwelling Type

Area	Single-detached House	Semi-detached House	Row House	Apartment: Building with Five or More Storeys	Apartment: Building with Fewer Than Five Storeys	Duplex Apartment	Movable Dwelling	Other Single-attached House
				Number				
Guelph	26,305	2,230	5,970	5,160	5,760	2,640	0	55
Ontario	2,718,880	279,470	415,225	789,970	498,160	160,460	15,800	9,540
Canada	7,329,150	646,245	791,600	1,234,770	2,397,550	704,485	183,510	33,310
				Percent of Dwellings				
Guelph	54.7	4.6	12.4	10.7	12.0	5.5	0.0	0.1
Ontario	55.6	5.7	8.5	16.2	10.2	3.3	0.3	0.2
Canada	55.0	4.9	5.9	9.3	18.0	5.3	1.4	0.3

Source: Statistics Canada. 2012. Census Profile. 2011 Census. Statistics Canada Catalogue no. 98-316-XWE. Ottawa. Released October 24 2012.
http://www12.statcan.gc.ca/census-recensement/2011/dp-pd/prof/index.cfm?Lang=E

Shelter Costs

	Owned Dwellings					Rented Dwellings		
Area	Number	Median Value[1] ($)	Average Value[1] ($)	Median Monthly Costs[2] ($)	Average Monthly Costs[2] ($)	Number	Median Monthly Costs[3] ($)	Average Monthly Costs[3] ($)
Guelph	33,585	299,689	324,426	1,264	1,278	14,525	859	888
Ontario	3,446,650	300,862	367,428	1,163	1,284	1,385,535	892	926
Canada	9,013,410	280,552	345,182	978	1,141	4,060,385	784	848

Note: All figures cover non-farm, non-reserve private dwellings; (1) Refers to the dollar amount expected by the owner if the dwelling were to be sold; (2) Includes all shelter expenses paid by households that own their dwellings, such as the mortgage payment and the costs of electricity, heat, water and other municipal services, property taxes and condominium fees; (3) Includes all shelter expenses paid by households that rent their dwellings, such as the monthly rent and the costs of electricity, heat and municipal services.
Source: Statistics Canada. 2013. 2011 National Household Survey. Statistics Canada Catalogue no. 99-004-XWE. Ottawa. Released September 11, 2013.

Occupied Private Dwellings by Period of Construction

Area	1960 or Before	1961 to 1980	1981 to 1990	1991 to 2000	2001 to 2005	2006 to 2011
			Number			
Guelph	10,975	13,085	7,340	7,405	5,345	3,965
Ontario	1,330,235	1,420,570	763,430	609,310	414,795	348,310
Canada	3,273,105	4,152,715	2,112,110	1,707,880	1,031,020	1,042,430
			Percent of Dwellings			
Guelph	22.8	27.2	15.3	15.4	11.1	8.2
Ontario	27.2	29.1	15.6	12.5	8.5	7.1
Canada	24.6	31.2	15.9	12.8	7.7	7.8

Note: Figures cover non-farm, non-reserve private dwellings and includes data up to May 10, 2011.
Source: Statistics Canada. 2013. 2011 National Household Survey. Statistics Canada Catalogue no. 99-004-XWE. Ottawa. Released September 11, 2013.

Educational Attainment

Area	No Certificate, Diploma or Degree	High School Diploma or Equivalent[1]	Apprenticeship or Trades Certificate or Diploma[2]	College, CÉGEP or Other Non-University Certificate or Diploma	University Certificate or Diploma Below the Bachelor Level[3]	Bachelor's Degree	University Certificate, Diploma or Degree Above Bachelor Level[4]
				Number			
				Total			
Guelph	17,165	26,695	6,795	18,685	3,520	15,685	10,515
Ontario	1,954,520	2,801,805	771,140	2,070,875	427,150	1,515,075	933,100
Canada	5,485,400	6,968,935	2,950,685	4,970,020	1,200,130	3,634,425	2,049,930
				Males			
Guelph	8,685	12,805	4,450	7,870	1,720	7,005	5,050
Ontario	957,040	1,337,055	520,390	894,235	193,355	692,345	470,290
Canada	2,742,875	3,305,415	1,928,970	2,118,430	513,235	1,643,080	1,043,350
				Females			
Guelph	8,485	13,890	2,350	10,810	1,795	8,680	5,460
Ontario	997,475	1,464,755	250,750	1,176,640	233,790	822,730	462,805
Canada	2,742,520	3,663,515	1,021,715	2,851,595	686,890	1,991,345	1,006,585
				Percent of Population			
				Total			
Guelph	17.3	26.9	6.9	18.9	3.6	15.8	10.6
Ontario	18.7	26.8	7.4	19.8	4.1	14.5	8.9
Canada	20.1	25.6	10.8	18.2	4.4	13.3	7.5
				Males			
Guelph	18.2	26.9	9.3	16.5	3.6	14.7	10.6
Ontario	18.9	26.4	10.3	17.7	3.8	13.7	9.3
Canada	20.6	24.9	14.5	15.9	3.9	12.4	7.8
				Females			
Guelph	16.5	27.0	4.6	21.0	3.5	16.9	10.6
Ontario	18.4	27.1	4.6	21.8	4.3	15.2	8.6
Canada	19.6	26.2	7.3	20.4	4.9	14.3	7.2

Note: Figures cover total population aged 15 years and over by highest certificate, diploma or degree; (1) Includes persons who have graduated from a secondary school or equivalent. It excludes persons with a postsecondary certificate, diploma or degree; (2) Includes Registered Apprenticeship certificates (including Certificate of Qualification, Journeyperson's designation) and other trades certificates or diplomas such as pre-employment or vocational certificates and diplomas from brief trade programs completed at community colleges, institutes of technology, vocational centres, and similar institutions; (3) Comparisons with other data sources suggest that the category 'University certificate or diploma below the bachelor's level' was over-reported in the NHS. This category likely includes some responses that are actually college certificates or diplomas, bachelor's degrees or other types of education (e.g., university transfer programs, bachelor's programs completed in other countries, incomplete bachelor's programs, non-university professional designations). We recommend users interpret the results for the 'University certificate or diploma below the bachelor's level' category with caution; (4) 'University certificate or diploma above bachelor level' includes the categories: 'Degree in medicine, dentistry, veterinary medicine or optometry,' 'Master's degree' and 'Earned doctorate.'
Source: Statistics Canada. 2013. 2011 National Household Survey. Statistics Canada Catalogue no. 99-004-XWE. Ottawa. Released September 11, 2013.

Household Income Distribution

Area	Less than $10,000	$10,000 to $19,999	$20,000 to $29,999	$30,000 to $39,999	$40,000 to $49,999	$50,000 to $59,999	$60,000 to $79,999	$80,000 to $99,999	$100,000 to $124,999	$125,000 to $149,999	$150,000 and Over
						Households					
Guelph	1,975	3,565	3,780	3,930	4,225	3,640	6,755	5,865	5,675	3,270	5,420
Ontario	201,780	354,530	405,725	425,410	425,720	398,705	680,850	552,660	497,970	331,460	611,840
Canada	626,705	1,141,945	1,193,925	1,271,675	1,206,800	1,102,120	1,865,280	1,458,240	1,260,770	802,555	1,389,240
						Percent of Households					
Guelph	4.1	7.4	7.9	8.2	8.8	7.6	14.0	12.2	11.8	6.8	11.3
Ontario	4.1	7.3	8.3	8.7	8.7	8.2	13.9	11.3	10.2	6.8	12.5
Canada	4.7	8.6	9.0	9.5	9.1	8.3	14.0	10.9	9.5	6.0	10.4

Note: Household income is the sum of the total incomes of all members of that household. Total income refers to monetary receipts from certain sources, before income taxes and deductions, during calendar year 2010.
Source: Statistics Canada. 2013. 2011 National Household Survey. Statistics Canada Catalogue no. 99-004-XWE. Ottawa. Released September 11, 2013.

Median and Average Household and Economic Family Income

Area	Median Household Income ($)	Average Household Income ($)	Median After-tax Household Income ($)	Average After-tax Household Income ($)	Median Economic Family Income ($)	Average Economic Family Income ($)	Median After-tax Economic Family Income ($)	Average After-tax Economic Family Income ($)
Guelph	68,570	83,047	60,271	69,581	85,993	99,587	74,662	82,993
Ontario	66,358	85,772	58,717	71,523	80,987	100,152	71,128	83,322
Canada	61,072	79,102	54,089	66,149	76,511	94,125	67,044	78,517

Note: Figures cover household and economic familiy income in 2010. A household is defined as a person or a group of persons (other than foreign residents) who occupy the same private dwelling and do not have a usual place of residence elsewhere in Canada. Every person is a member of one and only one household. An economic family is defined as a group of two or more persons who live in the same dwelling and are related to each other by blood, marriage, common-law, adoption or a foster relationship. A couple may be of opposite or same sex.
Source: Statistics Canada. 2013. 2011 National Household Survey. Statistics Canada Catalogue no. 99-004-XWE. Ottawa. Released September 11, 2013.

Individual Income Distribution

Area	Less than $10,000	$10,000 to $19,999	$20,000 to $29,999	$30,000 to $39,999	$40,000 to $49,999	$50,000 to $59,999	$60,000 to $79,999	$80,000 to $99,999	$100,000 to $124,999	$125,000 and Over
Number										
Total										
Guelph	15,615	15,465	12,575	10,750	11,245	8,145	9,795	5,690	2,720	2,680
Ontario	1,780,355	1,748,060	1,361,710	1,136,730	980,790	746,360	964,280	574,710	293,865	330,285
Canada	4,492,040	4,835,710	3,670,020	3,180,360	2,603,520	1,921,650	2,437,440	1,302,045	693,580	782,135
Males										
Guelph	6,550	5,725	5,115	4,595	5,640	4,540	5,770	3,475	2,050	2,055
Ontario	781,095	669,815	580,990	535,255	491,125	407,005	569,205	341,160	201,125	244,500
Canada	1,936,365	1,864,880	1,588,260	1,522,190	1,333,510	1,079,780	1,473,145	823,720	492,905	599,905
Females										
Guelph	9,065	9,740	7,455	6,155	5,605	3,605	4,025	2,220	670	630
Ontario	999,265	1,078,245	780,720	601,475	489,665	339,360	395,075	233,550	92,740	85,790
Canada	2,555,675	2,970,825	2,081,760	1,658,170	1,270,010	841,870	964,300	478,330	200,680	182,230
Percent of Population										
Total										
Guelph	16.5	16.3	13.3	11.4	11.9	8.6	10.3	6.0	2.9	2.8
Ontario	18.0	17.6	13.7	11.5	9.9	7.5	9.7	5.8	3.0	3.3
Canada	17.3	18.7	14.2	12.3	10.0	7.4	9.4	5.0	2.7	3.0
Males										
Guelph	14.4	12.6	11.2	10.1	12.4	10.0	12.7	7.6	4.5	4.5
Ontario	16.2	13.9	12.1	11.1	10.2	8.4	11.8	7.1	4.2	5.1
Canada	15.2	14.7	12.5	12.0	10.5	8.5	11.6	6.5	3.9	4.7
Females										
Guelph	18.4	19.8	15.2	12.5	11.4	7.3	8.2	4.5	1.4	1.3
Ontario	19.6	21.2	15.3	11.8	9.6	6.7	7.8	4.6	1.8	1.7
Canada	19.4	22.5	15.8	12.6	9.6	6.4	7.3	3.6	1.5	1.4

Note: Figures cover individuals aged 15 years and over with income. Income refers to monetary receipts from certain sources, before income taxes and deductions, during calendar year 2010.
Source: Statistics Canada. 2013. 2011 National Household Survey. Statistics Canada Catalogue no. 99-004-XWE. Ottawa. Released September 11, 2013.

Labour Force Status

Area	In the Labour Force — All	Employed	Unemployed	Not in the Labour Force
Number				
Total				
Guelph	69,085	64,280	4,800	29,975
Ontario	6,864,990	6,297,005	567,985	3,608,685
Canada	17,990,080	16,595,035	1,395,045	9,269,445
Males				
Guelph	35,345	32,975	2,370	12,250
Ontario	3,542,030	3,249,165	292,865	1,522,690
Canada	9,388,570	8,634,310	754,255	3,906,785
Females				
Guelph	33,735	31,305	2,435	17,725
Ontario	3,322,955	3,047,840	275,120	2,085,990
Canada	8,601,515	7,960,725	640,790	5,362,660
Percent of Labour Force				
Total				
Guelph	69.7	64.9	6.9	30.3
Ontario	65.5	60.1	8.3	34.5
Canada	66.0	60.9	7.8	34.0
Males				
Guelph	74.3	69.3	6.7	25.7
Ontario	69.9	64.2	8.3	30.1
Canada	70.6	64.9	8.0	29.4
Females				
Guelph	65.5	60.8	7.2	34.4
Ontario	61.4	56.3	8.3	38.6
Canada	61.6	57.0	7.4	38.4

Note: Figures are based on total population 15 years and over
Source: Statistics Canada. 2013. 2011 National Household Survey. Statistics Canada Catalogue no. 99-004-XWE. Ottawa. Released September 11, 2013.

Labour Force by Industry (NAICS Codes 11–52)

Area	Agriculture, forestry, fishing & hunting	Mining, quarrying, & oil & gas extraction	Utilities	Construction	Manufacturing	Wholesale Trade	Retail Trade	Transportation & warehousing	Information & cultural industries	Finance & insurance
					Number					
					Total					
Guelph	480	185	320	3,090	13,760	3,160	6,635	2,455	815	2,585
Ontario	101,280	29,985	57,035	417,900	697,565	305,030	751,200	307,405	178,720	364,415
Canada	437,650	261,050	149,940	1,215,380	1,619,295	733,445	2,031,665	827,780	420,830	767,960
					Males					
Guelph	215	180	230	2,630	9,595	1,935	3,090	1,680	370	1,050
Ontario	66,485	25,650	42,685	369,300	493,305	197,770	344,480	225,245	98,835	153,125
Canada	307,370	211,690	110,765	1,068,710	1,167,680	494,545	933,850	617,305	235,875	296,995
					Females					
Guelph	260	0	90	455	4,165	1,225	3,540	775	440	1,530
Ontario	34,800	4,340	14,350	48,595	204,260	107,260	406,720	82,160	79,885	211,290
Canada	130,285	49,360	39,175	146,670	451,615	238,900	1,097,820	210,475	184,955	470,960
					Percent of Labour Force					
					Total					
Guelph	0.7	0.3	0.5	4.6	20.3	4.7	9.8	3.6	1.2	3.8
Ontario	1.5	0.4	0.9	6.3	10.4	4.6	11.2	4.6	2.7	5.5
Canada	2.5	1.5	0.9	6.9	9.2	4.2	11.6	4.7	2.4	4.4
					Males					
Guelph	0.6	0.5	0.7	7.6	27.6	5.6	8.9	4.8	1.1	3.0
Ontario	1.9	0.7	1.2	10.7	14.3	5.7	10.0	6.5	2.9	4.4
Canada	3.3	2.3	1.2	11.6	12.7	5.4	10.2	6.7	2.6	3.2
					Females					
Guelph	0.8	0.0	0.3	1.4	12.6	3.7	10.7	2.3	1.3	4.6
Ontario	1.1	0.1	0.4	1.5	6.3	3.3	12.6	2.5	2.5	6.5
Canada	1.6	0.6	0.5	1.7	5.4	2.8	13.1	2.5	2.2	5.6

Note: Figures are based on total experienced labour force 15 years and over. Experienced labour force refers to persons who, during the week of Sunday, May 1 to Saturday, May 7, 2011, were employed and the unemployed who had last worked for pay or in self-employment in either 2010 or 2011.
Source: Statistics Canada. 2013. 2011 National Household Survey. Statistics Canada Catalogue no. 99-004-XWE. Ottawa. Released September 11, 2013.

Labour Force by Industry (NAICS Codes 53–91)

Area	Real estate & rental & leasing	Profess., scientific & tech. services	Mgmt of companies & enterprises	Admin. & support, waste mgmt & remed. services	Educational services	Health care & social assistance	Arts, entertain. & recreation	Accomm. & food services	Other services (except public admin.)	Public admin.
					Number					
					Total					
Guelph	945	4,600	70	2,495	8,180	6,300	1,220	4,305	2,700	3,410
Ontario	133,980	511,020	6,525	309,630	499,690	692,130	144,065	417,675	296,340	458,665
Canada	321,895	1,240,850	17,460	728,330	1,301,435	1,949,650	363,405	1,130,750	807,800	1,261,050
					Males					
Guelph	510	2,400	65	1,355	2,975	975	590	1,795	1,220	1,865
Ontario	72,835	281,420	3,540	172,475	162,765	120,165	75,035	177,240	133,795	236,655
Canada	179,090	688,625	9,380	411,250	424,915	349,430	188,270	469,990	372,940	652,510
					Females					
Guelph	435	2,200	10	1,145	5,200	5,320	630	2,510	1,485	1,550
Ontario	61,145	229,600	2,990	137,155	336,925	571,965	69,030	240,430	162,550	222,015
Canada	142,805	552,225	8,075	317,085	876,515	1,600,220	175,135	660,760	434,865	608,535
					Percent of Labour Force					
					Total					
Guelph	1.4	6.8	0.1	3.7	12.1	9.3	1.8	6.4	4.0	5.0
Ontario	2.0	7.6	0.1	4.6	7.5	10.4	2.2	6.3	4.4	6.9
Canada	1.8	7.1	0.1	4.1	7.4	11.1	2.1	6.4	4.6	7.2
					Males					
Guelph	1.5	6.9	0.2	3.9	8.6	2.8	1.7	5.2	3.5	5.4
Ontario	2.1	8.2	0.1	5.0	4.7	3.5	2.2	5.1	3.9	6.9
Canada	1.9	7.5	0.1	4.5	4.6	3.8	2.0	5.1	4.1	7.1
					Females					
Guelph	1.3	6.7	0.0	3.5	15.8	16.1	1.9	7.6	4.5	4.7
Ontario	1.9	7.1	0.1	4.2	10.4	17.7	2.1	7.4	5.0	6.9
Canada	1.7	6.6	0.1	3.8	10.4	19.1	2.1	7.9	5.2	7.2

Note: Figures are based on total experienced labour force 15 years and over. Experienced labour force refers to persons who, during the week of Sunday, May 1 to Saturday, May 7, 2011, were employed and the unemployed who had last worked for pay or in self-employment in either 2010 or 2011.
Source: Statistics Canada. 2013. 2011 National Household Survey. Statistics Canada Catalogue no. 99-004-XWE. Ottawa. Released September 11, 2013.

PROFILES / Guelph, Ontario

Occupation

Area	Mgmt	Business, Finance & Admin.	Natural/ Applied Sciences & Related	Health	Education, Law & Social, Community & Government Services	Art, Culture, Recreation & Sport	Sales & Service	Trades, Transport & Equip. Operators & Related	Natural Resources, Agri. & Related Production	Mfg & Utilities
Number									
Total									
Guelph	7,285	10,050	4,800	3,480	9,140	1,645	14,735	7,905	880	7,785
Ontario	770,580	1,138,330	494,500	392,695	801,465	206,420	1,550,260	868,515	106,810	350,685
Canada	1,963,600	2,902,045	1,237,775	1,107,200	2,064,675	503,415	4,068,170	2,537,775	397,930	805,040
Males									
Guelph	4,575	2,875	3,720	660	3,135	680	6,210	7,175	640	5,050
Ontario	474,655	352,505	384,345	78,330	264,570	96,055	673,880	812,280	82,610	233,565
Canada	1,229,460	854,190	966,355	217,520	676,550	232,535	1,745,705	2,385,615	318,945	564,300
Females									
Guelph	2,710	7,175	1,075	2,820	6,010	965	8,520	730	240	2,730
Ontario	295,920	785,825	110,150	314,370	536,895	110,370	876,380	56,230	24,200	117,115
Canada	734,140	2,047,855	271,415	889,675	1,388,130	270,875	2,322,465	152,165	78,980	240,740
Percent of Labour Force									
Total									
Guelph	10.8	14.8	7.1	5.1	13.5	2.4	21.8	11.7	1.3	11.5
Ontario	11.5	17.0	7.4	5.9	12.0	3.1	23.2	13.0	1.6	5.2
Canada	11.2	16.5	7.0	6.3	11.7	2.9	23.1	14.4	2.3	4.6
Males									
Guelph	13.2	8.3	10.7	1.9	9.0	2.0	17.9	20.7	1.8	14.5
Ontario	13.7	10.2	11.1	2.3	7.7	2.8	19.5	23.5	2.4	6.8
Canada	13.4	9.3	10.5	2.4	7.4	2.5	19.0	26.0	3.5	6.1
Females									
Guelph	8.2	21.8	3.3	8.6	18.2	2.9	25.8	2.2	0.7	8.3
Ontario	9.2	24.3	3.4	9.7	16.6	3.4	27.2	1.7	0.7	3.6
Canada	8.7	24.4	3.2	10.6	16.5	3.2	27.7	1.8	0.9	2.9

Note: Figures are based on total experienced labour force 15 years and over
Source: Statistics Canada. 2013. 2011 National Household Survey. Statistics Canada Catalogue no. 99-004-XWE. Ottawa. Released September 11, 2013.

Place of Work Status

Area	Worked at Home	Worked Outside Canada	No Fixed Workplace Address	Worked at Usual Place
Number				
Total				
Guelph	3,515	310	5,420	55,035
Ontario	423,790	31,390	670,835	5,170,980
Canada	1,142,640	66,460	1,868,245	13,517,690
Males				
Guelph	1,685	245	3,845	27,200
Ontario	216,900	21,150	486,560	2,524,555
Canada	582,150	47,355	1,400,485	6,604,325
Females				
Guelph	1,830	65	1,575	27,835
Ontario	206,895	10,240	184,275	2,646,420
Canada	560,490	19,100	467,760	6,913,370
Percent of Labour Force				
Total				
Guelph	5.5	0.5	8.4	85.6
Ontario	6.7	0.5	10.7	82.1
Canada	6.9	0.4	11.3	81.5
Males				
Guelph	5.1	0.7	11.7	82.5
Ontario	6.7	0.7	15.0	77.7
Canada	6.7	0.5	16.2	76.5
Females				
Guelph	5.8	0.2	5.0	88.9
Ontario	6.8	0.3	6.0	86.8
Canada	7.0	0.2	5.9	86.8

Note: Figures are based on total employed labour force 15 years and over.
Source: Statistics Canada. 2013. 2011 National Household Survey. Statistics Canada Catalogue no. 99-004-XWE. Ottawa. Released September 11, 2013.

Mode of Transportation to Work

Area	Car; Truck; Van; as Driver	Car; Truck; Van; as Passenger	Public Transit	Walked	Bicycled	All Other Modes
			Number			
			Total			
Guelph	46,965	4,430	4,110	3,305	1,060	585
Ontario	4,235,315	357,110	818,270	299,095	69,885	62,145
Canada	11,393,140	867,050	1,851,525	880,815	201,780	191,625
			Males			
Guelph	24,750	1,935	1,960	1,385	680	335
Ontario	2,316,680	143,410	340,995	131,765	47,635	30,635
Canada	6,238,835	349,530	788,290	387,580	135,840	104,725
			Females			
Guelph	22,215	2,495	2,150	1,915	380	250
Ontario	1,918,640	213,700	477,275	167,325	22,250	31,515
Canada	5,154,305	517,520	1,063,235	493,230	65,940	86,900
			Percent of Labour Force			
			Total			
Guelph	77.7	7.3	6.8	5.5	1.8	1.0
Ontario	72.5	6.1	14.0	5.1	1.2	1.1
Canada	74.0	5.6	12.0	5.7	1.3	1.2
			Males			
Guelph	79.7	6.2	6.3	4.5	2.2	1.1
Ontario	76.9	4.8	11.3	4.4	1.6	1.0
Canada	77.9	4.4	9.8	4.8	1.7	1.3
			Females			
Guelph	75.5	8.5	7.3	6.5	1.3	0.9
Ontario	67.8	7.5	16.9	5.9	0.8	1.1
Canada	69.8	7.0	14.4	6.7	0.9	1.2

Note: Figures are based on total employed labour force 15 years and over.
Source: Statistics Canada. 2013. 2011 National Household Survey. Statistics Canada Catalogue no. 99-004-XWE. Ottawa. Released September 11, 2013.

Visible Minority Population Characteristics

Area	Total Minority	South Asian[1]	Chinese	Black	Filipino	Latin American	Arab	SE Asian[2]	West Asian[3]	Korean	Japanese	Multiple[4]
					Number							
					Total							
Guelph	18,920	4,970	3,350	1,695	1,960	1,150	640	2,890	975	280	145	655
Ontario	3,279,565	965,990	629,140	539,205	275,380	172,560	151,645	137,875	122,530	78,290	29,085	96,735
Canada	6,264,750	1,567,400	1,324,750	945,665	619,310	381,280	380,620	312,075	206,840	161,130	87,270	171,935
					Males							
Guelph	9,305	2,345	1,595	890	915	565	365	1,535	470	100	75	330
Ontario	1,582,480	484,355	301,575	251,295	116,825	83,205	79,620	67,645	62,515	38,045	13,345	46,765
Canada	3,043,010	790,755	632,325	453,005	268,885	186,355	203,485	154,035	105,620	77,165	38,270	83,335
					Females							
Guelph	9,615	2,625	1,760	800	1,045	590	270	1,360	505	180	70	330
Ontario	1,697,085	481,635	327,570	287,915	158,555	89,360	72,025	70,230	60,010	40,250	15,740	49,970
Canada	3,221,745	776,650	692,420	492,660	350,425	194,925	177,140	158,045	101,220	83,965	48,990	88,600
					Percent of Population							
					Total							
Guelph	15.7	4.1	2.8	1.4	1.6	1.0	0.5	2.4	0.8	0.2	0.1	0.5
Ontario	25.9	7.6	5.0	4.3	2.2	1.4	1.2	1.1	1.0	0.6	0.2	0.8
Canada	19.1	4.8	4.0	2.9	1.9	1.2	1.2	0.9	0.6	0.5	0.3	0.5
					Males							
Guelph	15.9	4.0	2.7	1.5	1.6	1.0	0.6	2.6	0.8	0.2	0.1	0.6
Ontario	25.6	7.8	4.9	4.1	1.9	1.3	1.3	1.1	1.0	0.6	0.2	0.8
Canada	18.8	4.9	3.9	2.8	1.7	1.2	1.3	1.0	0.7	0.5	0.2	0.5
					Females							
Guelph	15.5	4.2	2.8	1.3	1.7	1.0	0.4	2.2	0.8	0.3	0.1	0.5
Ontario	26.2	7.4	5.1	4.4	2.5	1.4	1.1	1.1	0.9	0.6	0.2	0.8
Canada	19.3	4.7	4.1	3.0	2.1	1.2	1.1	0.9	0.6	0.5	0.3	0.5

Note: The Employment Equity Act defines visible minorities as 'persons, other than Aboriginal peoples, who are non-Caucasian in race or non-white in colour'; (1) Includes 'East Indian,' 'Pakistani,' 'Sri Lankan,' etc.; (2) Includes 'Vietnamese,' 'Cambodian,' 'Malaysian,' 'Laotian,' etc.; (3) Includes 'Iranian,' 'Afghan,' etc.; (4) Includes respondents who reported more than one visible minority group by checking two or more mark-in circles, e.g., 'Black' and 'South Asian.'
Source: Statistics Canada. 2013. 2011 National Household Survey. Statistics Canada Catalogue no. 99-004-XWE. Ottawa. Released September 11, 2013.

PROFILES / Guelph, Ontario

Aboriginal Population

Area	Aboriginal Identity[1]	First Nations (North American Indian) Single Identity[2]	Métis Single Identity	Inuk (Inuit) Single Identity	Multiple Aboriginal Identities[3]	Aboriginal Identities Not Included Elsewhere
			Number			
			Total			
Guelph	1,950	1,165	710	0	0	45
Ontario	301,430	201,100	86,020	3,355	2,910	8,040
Canada	1,400,685	851,560	451,795	59,440	11,415	26,475
			Males			
Guelph	815	550	215	0	0	25
Ontario	145,020	96,620	41,755	1,475	1,420	3,750
Canada	682,190	411,785	223,335	29,495	5,525	12,055
			Females			
Guelph	1,135	615	490	0	0	15
Ontario	156,410	104,485	44,260	1,880	1,490	4,295
Canada	718,500	439,775	228,460	29,950	5,890	14,420
			Percent of Population			
			Total			
Guelph	1.6	1.0	0.6	0.0	0.0	0.0
Ontario	2.4	1.6	0.7	0.0	0.0	0.1
Canada	4.3	2.6	1.4	0.2	0.0	0.1
			Males			
Guelph	1.4	0.9	0.4	0.0	0.0	0.0
Ontario	2.3	1.6	0.7	0.0	0.0	0.1
Canada	4.2	2.5	1.4	0.2	0.0	0.1
			Females			
Guelph	1.8	1.0	0.8	0.0	0.0	0.0
Ontario	2.4	1.6	0.7	0.0	0.0	0.1
Canada	4.3	2.6	1.4	0.2	0.0	0.1

Note: (1) Includes persons who reported being an Aboriginal person, that is, First Nations (North American Indian), Métis or Inuk (Inuit) and/or those who reported Registered or Treaty Indian status, that is registered under the Indian Act of Canada, and/or those who reported membership in a First Nation or Indian band. Aboriginal peoples of Canada are defined in the Constitution Act, 1982, section 35-2 as including the Indian, Inuit and Métis peoples of Canada; (2) Users should be aware that the estimates associated with this variable are more affected than most by the incomplete enumeration of certain Indian reserves and Indian settlements in the National Household Survey (NHS); (3) Includes persons who reported being any two or all three of the following: First Nations (North American Indian), Métis or Inuk (Inuit).
Source: Statistics Canada. 2013. 2011 National Household Survey. Statistics Canada Catalogue no. 99-004-XWE. Ottawa. Released September 11, 2013.

Ethnic Origin

Area	North American Aboriginal	Other North American	European	Caribbean	Latin, Central and South American	African	Asian	Oceania
				Number				
				Total				
Guelph	3,390	32,070	90,405	1,360	1,760	1,610	16,480	385
Ontario	441,395	3,059,480	8,231,410	396,485	271,545	331,460	2,604,595	19,410
Canada	1,836,035	11,070,455	20,157,965	627,590	544,375	766,735	5,011,225	74,875
				Males				
Guelph	1,505	16,155	43,240	720	875	835	7,970	185
Ontario	210,490	1,507,105	4,019,885	181,805	130,035	160,940	1,265,540	9,855
Canada	885,675	5,462,685	9,913,150	291,640	264,635	387,360	2,435,540	37,490
				Females				
Guelph	1,890	15,910	47,160	635	880	775	8,515	205
Ontario	230,905	1,552,380	4,211,525	214,675	141,510	170,515	1,339,050	9,555
Canada	950,360	5,607,770	10,244,820	335,945	279,740	379,380	2,575,680	37,385
				Percent of Population				
				Total				
Guelph	2.8	26.6	75.0	1.1	1.5	1.3	13.7	0.3
Ontario	3.5	24.2	65.1	3.1	2.1	2.6	20.6	0.2
Canada	5.6	33.7	61.4	1.9	1.7	2.3	15.3	0.2
				Males				
Guelph	2.6	27.6	73.8	1.2	1.5	1.4	13.6	0.3
Ontario	3.4	24.4	65.0	2.9	2.1	2.6	20.5	0.2
Canada	5.5	33.8	61.3	1.8	1.6	2.4	15.1	0.2
				Females				
Guelph	3.1	25.7	76.2	1.0	1.4	1.3	13.7	0.3
Ontario	3.6	24.0	65.1	3.3	2.2	2.6	20.7	0.1
Canada	5.7	33.6	61.4	2.0	1.7	2.3	15.4	0.2

Note: The sum of the ethnic groups in this table is greater than the total population estimate because a person may report more than one ethnic origin in the NHS.
Source: Statistics Canada. 2013. 2011 National Household Survey. Statistics Canada Catalogue no. 99-004-XWE. Ottawa. Released September 11, 2013.

Religion

Area	Buddhist	Christian	Hindu	Jewish	Muslim	Sikh	Traditional (Aboriginal) Spirituality	Other Religions	No Religious Affiliation
				Number Total					
Guelph	2,265	74,495	1,800	490	3,185	1,195	15	600	36,500
Ontario	163,750	8,167,295	366,720	195,540	581,950	179,765	15,905	53,080	2,927,790
Canada	366,830	22,102,745	497,965	329,495	1,053,945	454,965	64,935	130,835	7,850,605
				Males					
Guelph	1,080	34,070	800	280	1,690	535	0	240	19,930
Ontario	75,355	3,839,925	183,580	95,795	293,925	90,515	7,600	23,555	1,571,195
Canada	168,465	10,497,775	250,435	161,265	540,555	229,435	31,805	57,745	4,225,645
				Females					
Guelph	1,190	40,425	1,000	210	1,495	660	15	360	16,575
Ontario	88,395	4,327,365	183,140	99,740	288,025	89,250	8,310	29,525	1,356,600
Canada	198,365	11,604,975	247,525	168,235	513,395	225,530	33,135	73,090	3,624,965
				Percent of Population Total					
Guelph	1.9	61.8	1.5	0.4	2.6	1.0	0.0	0.5	30.3
Ontario	1.3	64.6	2.9	1.5	4.6	1.4	0.1	0.4	23.1
Canada	1.1	67.3	1.5	1.0	3.2	1.4	0.2	0.4	23.9
				Males					
Guelph	1.8	58.1	1.4	0.5	2.9	0.9	0.0	0.4	34.0
Ontario	1.2	62.1	3.0	1.5	4.8	1.5	0.1	0.4	25.4
Canada	1.0	64.9	1.5	1.0	3.3	1.4	0.2	0.4	26.1
				Females					
Guelph	1.9	65.3	1.6	0.3	2.4	1.1	0.0	0.6	26.8
Ontario	1.4	66.9	2.8	1.5	4.5	1.4	0.1	0.5	21.0
Canada	1.2	69.5	1.5	1.0	3.1	1.4	0.2	0.4	21.7

Note: Religion refers to the person's self-identification as having a connection or affiliation with any religious denomination, group, body, sect, cult or other religiously defined community or system of belief. Religion is not limited to formal membership in a religious organization or group. Persons without a religious connection or affiliation can self-identify as atheist, agnostic or humanist, or can provide another applicable response.
Source: Statistics Canada. 2013. 2011 National Household Survey. Statistics Canada Catalogue no. 99-004-XWE. Ottawa. Released September 11, 2013.

Religion—Christian Denominations

Area	Anglican	Baptist	Catholic	Christian Orthodox	Lutheran	Pentecostal	Presbyterian	United Church	Other Christian
				Number Total					
Guelph	8,110	2,140	34,580	1,365	1,320	935	5,145	9,320	11,580
Ontario	774,560	244,650	3,976,610	297,710	163,460	213,945	319,585	952,465	1,224,300
Canada	1,631,845	635,840	12,810,705	550,690	478,185	478,705	472,385	2,007,610	3,036,780
				Males					
Guelph	3,645	1,030	16,015	665	535	375	2,365	3,905	5,535
Ontario	355,175	112,285	1,895,940	145,825	75,225	94,955	148,535	435,255	576,730
Canada	752,945	293,905	6,167,290	270,205	221,525	217,850	218,955	912,545	1,442,550
				Females					
Guelph	4,460	1,110	18,570	700	785	565	2,785	5,415	6,045
Ontario	419,390	132,370	2,080,665	151,885	88,230	118,990	171,050	517,210	647,570
Canada	878,900	341,940	6,643,415	280,485	256,660	260,850	253,430	1,095,065	1,594,230
				Percent of Population Total					
Guelph	6.7	1.8	28.7	1.1	1.1	0.8	4.3	7.7	9.6
Ontario	6.1	1.9	31.4	2.4	1.3	1.7	2.5	7.5	9.7
Canada	5.0	1.9	39.0	1.7	1.5	1.5	1.4	6.1	9.2
				Males					
Guelph	6.2	1.8	27.3	1.1	0.9	0.6	4.0	6.7	9.4
Ontario	5.7	1.8	30.7	2.4	1.2	1.5	2.4	7.0	9.3
Canada	4.7	1.8	38.2	1.7	1.4	1.3	1.4	5.6	8.9
				Females					
Guelph	7.2	1.8	30.0	1.1	1.3	0.9	4.5	8.7	9.8
Ontario	6.5	2.0	32.2	2.3	1.4	1.8	2.6	8.0	10.0
Canada	5.3	2.0	39.8	1.7	1.5	1.6	1.5	6.6	9.6

Note: Religion refers to the person's self-identification as having a connection or affiliation with any religious denomination, group, body, sect, cult or other religiously defined community or system of belief. Religion is not limited to formal membership in a religious organization or group. Persons without a religious connection or affiliation can self-identify as atheist, agnostic or humanist, or can provide another applicable response.
Source: Statistics Canada. 2013. 2011 National Household Survey. Statistics Canada Catalogue no. 99-004-XWE. Ottawa. Released September 11, 2013.

PROFILES / Guelph, Ontario

Immigrant Status and Period of Immigration

Area	Non-Immigrants[1]	Immigrants All	Before 1971	1971 to 1980	1981 to 1990	1991 to 2000	2001 to 2005	2006 to 2011	Non-Permanent Residents[3]
				Number					
				Total					
Guelph	94,885	24,885	6,505	2,825	3,695	5,375	3,530	2,965	785
Ontario	8,906,000	3,611,365	723,030	464,380	538,285	866,220	518,405	501,060	134,425
Canada	25,720,175	6,775,765	1,261,055	870,775	949,890	1,539,050	992,070	1,162,915	356,385
				Males					
Guelph	46,365	11,820	2,985	1,315	1,990	2,615	1,600	1,315	440
Ontario	4,410,240	1,706,385	341,820	217,990	258,095	408,270	245,850	234,360	64,825
Canada	12,753,235	3,231,370	605,430	416,670	454,570	724,905	474,545	555,245	178,515
				Females					
Guelph	48,520	13,060	3,520	1,510	1,700	2,760	1,930	1,640	345
Ontario	4,495,765	1,904,985	381,210	246,390	280,190	457,950	272,550	266,695	69,600
Canada	12,966,935	3,544,400	655,625	454,105	495,325	814,145	517,530	607,670	177,870
				Percent of Population					
				Total					
Guelph	78.7	20.6	5.4	2.3	3.1	4.5	2.9	2.5	0.7
Ontario	70.4	28.5	5.7	3.7	4.3	6.8	4.1	4.0	1.1
Canada	78.3	20.6	3.8	2.7	2.9	4.7	3.0	3.5	1.1
				Males					
Guelph	79.1	20.2	5.1	2.2	3.4	4.5	2.7	2.2	0.8
Ontario	71.3	27.6	5.5	3.5	4.2	6.6	4.0	3.8	1.0
Canada	78.9	20.0	3.7	2.6	2.8	4.5	2.9	3.4	1.1
				Females					
Guelph	78.3	21.1	5.7	2.4	2.7	4.5	3.1	2.6	0.6
Ontario	69.5	29.4	5.9	3.8	4.3	7.1	4.2	4.1	1.1
Canada	77.7	21.2	3.9	2.7	3.0	4.9	3.1	3.6	1.1

Note: (1) Non-immigrant refers to a person who is a Canadian citizen by birth; (2) Immigrant refers to a person who is or has ever been a landed immigrant/permanent resident. This person has been granted the right to live in Canada permanently by immigration authorities. Some immigrants have resided in Canada for a number of years, while others have arrived recently. Some immigrants are Canadian citizens, while others are not. Most immigrants are born outside Canada, but a small number are born in Canada. In the 2011 National Household Survey, 'Immigrants' includes immigrants who landed in Canada prior to May 10, 2011; (3) Non-permanent resident refers to a person from another country who has a work or study permit, or who is a refugee claimant, and any non-Canadian-born family member living in Canada with them.
Source: Statistics Canada. 2013. 2011 National Household Survey. Statistics Canada Catalogue no. 99-004-XWE. Ottawa. Released September 11, 2013.

Mother Tongue

Area	English	French	Non-official Language	English & French	English & Non-official Language	French & Non-official Language	English, French & Non-official Language
			Number				
			Total				
Guelph	95,845	1,605	21,890	280	1,395	55	15
Ontario	8,677,040	493,300	3,264,435	46,605	219,425	13,645	7,615
Canada	18,858,980	7,054,975	6,567,680	144,685	396,330	74,430	24,095
			Males				
Guelph	46,635	720	10,560	120	695	20	5
Ontario	4,276,970	232,785	1,562,190	21,805	106,790	6,285	3,495
Canada	9,345,225	3,452,380	3,157,785	69,975	192,000	36,535	11,965
			Females				
Guelph	49,215	890	11,330	155	700	35	10
Ontario	4,400,065	260,510	1,702,240	24,795	112,635	7,365	4,115
Canada	9,513,750	3,602,590	3,409,895	74,710	204,330	37,890	12,130
			Percent of Population				
			Total				
Guelph	79.2	1.3	18.1	0.2	1.2	0.0	0.0
Ontario	68.2	3.9	25.7	0.4	1.7	0.1	0.1
Canada	56.9	21.3	19.8	0.4	1.2	0.2	0.1
			Males				
Guelph	79.4	1.2	18.0	0.2	1.2	0.0	0.0
Ontario	68.9	3.7	25.2	0.4	1.7	0.1	0.1
Canada	57.5	21.2	19.4	0.4	1.2	0.2	0.1
			Females				
Guelph	79.0	1.4	18.2	0.2	1.1	0.1	0.0
Ontario	67.6	4.0	26.1	0.4	1.7	0.1	0.1
Canada	56.4	21.4	20.2	0.4	1.2	0.2	0.1

Note: Figures cover total population excluding institutional residents.
Source: Statistics Canada. 2012. Census Profile. 2011 Census. Statistics Canada Catalogue no. 98-316-XWE. Ottawa. Released October 24 2012.
http://www12.statcan.gc.ca/census-recensement/2011/dp-pd/prof/index.cfm?Lang=E

Language Spoken Most Often at Home

Area	English	French	Non-official Language	English & French	English & Non-official Language	French & Non-official Language	English, French & Non-official Language
			Number				
			Total				
Guelph	105,850	500	11,460	125	3,100	15	35
Ontario	10,044,810	284,115	1,827,870	37,955	509,105	6,370	11,845
Canada	21,457,075	6,827,865	3,673,865	131,205	875,135	109,700	46,330
			Males				
Guelph	51,370	200	5,585	55	1,520	5	10
Ontario	4,930,610	133,495	872,860	17,250	248,050	2,855	5,225
Canada	10,585,620	3,348,235	1,767,310	63,475	425,370	53,010	22,845
			Females				
Guelph	54,480	300	5,875	65	1,580	5	25
Ontario	5,114,200	150,620	955,010	20,705	261,055	3,520	6,620
Canada	10,871,455	3,479,625	1,906,555	67,730	449,765	56,690	23,485
			Percent of Population				
			Total				
Guelph	87.4	0.4	9.5	0.1	2.6	0.0	0.0
Ontario	79.0	2.2	14.4	0.3	4.0	0.1	0.1
Canada	64.8	20.6	11.1	0.4	2.6	0.3	0.1
			Males				
Guelph	87.4	0.3	9.5	0.1	2.6	0.0	0.0
Ontario	79.4	2.1	14.1	0.3	4.0	0.0	0.1
Canada	65.1	20.6	10.9	0.4	2.6	0.3	0.1
			Females				
Guelph	87.4	0.5	9.4	0.1	2.5	0.0	0.0
Ontario	78.5	2.3	14.7	0.3	4.0	0.1	0.1
Canada	64.5	20.6	11.3	0.4	2.7	0.3	0.1

Note: Figures cover total population excluding institutional residents.
Source: Statistics Canada. 2012. Census Profile. 2011 Census. Statistics Canada Catalogue no. 98-316-XWE. Ottawa. Released October 24 2012.
http://www12.statcan.gc.ca/census-recensement/2011/dp-pd/prof/index.cfm?Lang=E

Knowledge of Official Languages

Area	English Only	French Only	English & French	Neither English nor French
		Number		
		Total		
Guelph	109,280	50	10,355	1,395
Ontario	10,984,360	42,980	1,395,805	298,920
Canada	22,564,665	4,165,015	5,795,570	595,920
		Males		
Guelph	53,860	20	4,345	530
Ontario	5,445,050	18,805	627,725	118,765
Canada	11,222,185	1,925,340	2,876,560	241,790
		Females		
Guelph	55,425	35	6,010	865
Ontario	5,539,310	24,175	768,085	180,155
Canada	11,342,485	2,239,680	2,919,005	354,135
		Percent of Population		
		Total		
Guelph	90.3	0.0	8.6	1.2
Ontario	86.3	0.3	11.0	2.3
Canada	68.1	12.6	17.5	1.8
		Males		
Guelph	91.7	0.0	7.4	0.9
Ontario	87.7	0.3	10.1	1.9
Canada	69.0	11.8	17.7	1.5
		Females		
Guelph	88.9	0.1	9.6	1.4
Ontario	85.1	0.4	11.8	2.8
Canada	67.3	13.3	17.3	2.1

Note: Figures cover total population excluding institutional residents.
Source: Statistics Canada. 2012. Census Profile. 2011 Census. Statistics Canada Catalogue no. 98-316-XWE. Ottawa. Released October 24 2012.
http://www12.statcan.gc.ca/census-recensement/2011/dp-pd/prof/index.cfm?Lang=E

Halifax, Nova Scotia

Background

Halifax is located on the east coast of Nova Scotia. The city faces the North Atlantic Ocean and is the largest municipality in the Atlantic Provinces as well as the provincial capital. Halifax is a seaport city and is situated around the second largest natural harbour in the world.

In 1749, the Town of Halifax was founded by the British government. Halifax acted as Nova Scotia's capital from 1841 until 1996, when the city amalgamated with 196 neighbouring communities to form Halifax Regional Municipality (HRM).

Halifax Port is the centre of the city's pedestrian-friendly downtown. The neighbouring communities that make up the HRM are all accessible by short bus rides. For example, the city's bridges, the MacKay and Macdonald, lead to Dartmouth, a community with 23 lakes. Halifax is also linked to surrounding areas by the oldest salt-water ferry service in North America (est. 1752).

In recent years, Halifax has attracted significant investment: modernization of the Halifax Shipyard ($549 million); King's Wharf Waterfront development ($500 million); and Dalhousie University capital ($304 million). In 2010, the major employers in the region were healthcare, the government (including the Department of National Defence) and education. Almost 70% of Halifax's working-age population has trade, college or university qualifications.

The city is renowned for its arts and culture, particularly the nightly music performed at over 450 local bars, pubs and taverns. Other highlights include Neptune Theatre, the annual Atlantic Film Festival, Symphony Nova Scotia and the Maritime Museum of the Atlantic. Every year Halifax hosts the Atlantic Jazz Festival and Fringe (theatre) Festival.

Halifax has summer highs of plus 21.77 degrees Celsius, winter lows of minus 7.27 degrees Celsius, and an average rainfall just over 1356 mm per year.

Rankings

- Halifax was ranked #4 out of 190 Canadian cities in *Money Sense Magazine's* "Top 35 Places to Live in 2012" rankings. The previous year, Halifax ranked #21 overall. The city was awarded high marks in the categories of weather, home affordability, culture, employment, clean air and walk/bike commute. Halifax ranked #9 for its accessibility to doctors. *Money Sense Magazine, "Canada's Best Places to Live 2012," March 20, 2012*
- *Maclean's Magazine* ranked Halifax as #28 out of 100 cities for most crimes committed (#1 had the most crime). The annual National Crime Ratings survey uses Statistics Canada 2010 Crime Severity Index (CSI) rates. The rates were calculated per 100,000 people for six crimes: homicide, sexual assault, aggravated assault, vehicle theft, robbery and breaking and entering. *Maclean's Magazine, "National Crime Ratings: Canada's Most Dangerous Cities," December 15, 2011*
- Halifax's School of Business Administration at Dalhousie University and the Sobey School of Business at Saint Mary's University both ranked in the top 10 MBA programs in Canada (8th and 9th respectively). The 2012 Annual Knight Schools Survey ranked 35 Canadian MBA schools. The Schulich School of Business at York University in Toronto ranked #1. *Corporate Knights, 2012 Annual Knight Schools Survey, released September 11, 2012*

PROFILES / Halifax, Nova Scotia

Population Growth and Density

Area	Population in 2001	Population in 2006	Population in 2011	Population Change 2001–2006	Population Change 2006–2011	Land Area (sq. km)	Population Density per sq. km
Halifax	359,111	372,679	390,096	3.8	4.7	5,490.28	71.1
Nova Scotia	908,007	913,462	921,727	0.6	0.9	52,939.44	17.4
Canada	30,007,094	31,612,897	33,476,688	5.4	5.9	8,965,121.42	3.7

Source: Statistics Canada. 2012. Census Profile. 2011 Census. Statistics Canada Catalogue no. 98-316-XWE. Ottawa. Released October 24 2012.
http://www12.statcan.gc.ca/census-recensement/2011/dp-pd/prof/index.cfm?Lang=E;
Statistics Canada 2007. 2006 Community Profiles. 2006 Census. Statistics Canada Catalogue no. 92-591-XWE. Ottawa. Released March 13 2007.
http://www12.statcan.ca/census-recensement/2006/dp-pd/prof/92-591/index.cfm?Lang=E

Gender

Area	Males	Females
	Number	
Halifax	188,585	201,505
Nova Scotia	445,585	476,140
Canada	16,414,225	17,062,460
	Percent of Population	
Halifax	48.3	51.7
Nova Scotia	48.3	51.7
Canada	49.0	51.0

Source: Statistics Canada. 2012. Census Profile. 2011 Census. Statistics Canada Catalogue no. 98-316-XWE. Ottawa. Released October 24 2012.
http://www12.statcan.gc.ca/census-recensement/2011/dp-pd/prof/index.cfm?Lang=E

Marital Status

Area	Married[1]	Living Common-law	Single[2]	Separated	Divorced	Widowed
			Number			
			Total			
Halifax	151,740	33,895	99,205	9,355	19,480	16,815
Nova Scotia	376,020	77,075	209,180	23,545	46,065	51,625
Canada	12,941,960	3,142,525	7,816,045	698,240	1,686,035	1,584,530
			Males			
Halifax	75,860	16,950	50,815	3,970	7,200	3,235
Nova Scotia	187,865	38,440	109,775	10,105	18,690	9,940
Canada	6,470,300	1,575,495	4,206,320	299,655	680,415	310,940
			Females			
Halifax	75,880	16,945	48,390	5,385	12,280	13,575
Nova Scotia	188,155	38,635	99,405	13,445	27,375	41,690
Canada	6,471,660	1,567,035	3,609,730	398,585	1,005,620	1,273,590
			Percent of Population			
			Total			
Halifax	45.9	10.3	30.0	2.8	5.9	5.1
Nova Scotia	48.0	9.8	26.7	3.0	5.9	6.6
Canada	46.4	11.3	28.0	2.5	6.0	5.7
			Males			
Halifax	48.0	10.7	32.2	2.5	4.6	2.0
Nova Scotia	50.1	10.3	29.3	2.7	5.0	2.7
Canada	47.8	11.6	31.1	2.2	5.0	2.3
			Females			
Halifax	44.0	9.8	28.1	3.1	7.1	7.9
Nova Scotia	46.0	9.5	24.3	3.3	6.7	10.2
Canada	45.2	10.9	25.2	2.8	7.0	8.9

Note: (1) and not separated, (2) never legally married
Source: Statistics Canada. 2012. Census Profile. 2011 Census. Statistics Canada Catalogue no. 98-316-XWE. Ottawa. Released October 24 2012.
http://www12.statcan.gc.ca/census-recensement/2011/dp-pd/prof/index.cfm?Lang=E

Age Characteristics: 0 to 49 Years

Area	0 to 4 Years	5 to 9 Years	10 to 14 Years	15 to 19 Years	20 to 24 Years	25 to 29 Years	30 to 34 Years	35 to 39 Years	40 to 44 Years	45 to 49 Years
					Number					
					Total					
Halifax	19,965	19,155	20,485	23,870	31,230	28,400	25,925	26,490	27,810	33,100
Nova Scotia	43,985	44,425	49,810	57,440	59,620	51,920	51,545	56,380	62,115	76,275
Canada	1,877,095	1,809,895	1,920,355	2,178,135	2,187,450	2,169,590	2,162,905	2,173,930	2,324,875	2,675,130
					Males					
Halifax	10,265	9,780	10,520	12,045	15,630	13,985	12,485	12,745	13,260	16,170
Nova Scotia	22,565	22,660	25,555	29,235	30,055	25,405	24,470	26,835	29,895	37,010
Canada	961,150	925,965	983,995	1,115,845	1,108,775	1,077,275	1,058,810	1,064,200	1,141,720	1,318,715
					Females					
Halifax	9,705	9,380	9,965	11,825	15,600	14,415	13,440	13,745	14,550	16,925
Nova Scotia	21,415	21,765	24,260	28,205	29,560	26,515	27,070	29,545	32,220	39,265
Canada	915,945	883,935	936,360	1,062,295	1,078,670	1,092,315	1,104,095	1,109,735	1,183,155	1,356,420
					Percent of Population					
					Total					
Halifax	5.1	4.9	5.3	6.1	8.0	7.3	6.6	6.8	7.1	8.5
Nova Scotia	4.8	4.8	5.4	6.2	6.5	5.6	5.6	6.1	6.7	8.3
Canada	5.6	5.4	5.7	6.5	6.5	6.5	6.5	6.5	6.9	8.0
					Males					
Halifax	5.4	5.2	5.6	6.4	8.3	7.4	6.6	6.8	7.0	8.6
Nova Scotia	5.1	5.1	5.7	6.6	6.7	5.7	5.5	6.0	6.7	8.3
Canada	5.9	5.6	6.0	6.8	6.8	6.6	6.5	6.5	7.0	8.0
					Females					
Halifax	4.8	4.7	4.9	5.9	7.7	7.2	6.7	6.8	7.2	8.4
Nova Scotia	4.5	4.6	5.1	5.9	6.2	5.6	5.7	6.2	6.8	8.2
Canada	5.4	5.2	5.5	6.2	6.3	6.4	6.5	6.5	6.9	7.9

Source: Statistics Canada. 2012. Census Profile. 2011 Census. Statistics Canada Catalogue no. 98-316-XWE. Ottawa. Released October 24 2012.
http://www12.statcan.gc.ca/census-recensement/2011/dp-pd/prof/index.cfm?Lang=E

Age Characteristics: 50 Years and Over, and Median Age

Area	50 to 54 Years	55 to 59 Years	60 to 64 Years	65 to 69 Years	70 to 74 Years	75 to 79 Years	80 to 84 Years	85 Years and Over	Median Age
					Number				
					Total				
Halifax	31,555	27,185	23,895	16,785	11,840	9,125	6,620	6,650	39.9
Nova Scotia	77,465	70,960	66,425	48,920	36,395	27,655	20,015	20,385	43.7
Canada	2,658,965	2,340,635	2,052,670	1,521,715	1,153,065	922,700	702,070	645,515	40.6
					Males				
Halifax	15,265	12,875	11,425	8,025	5,470	4,050	2,620	1,980	38.8
Nova Scotia	37,465	34,200	32,310	23,840	17,300	12,460	8,040	6,285	42.7
Canada	1,309,030	1,147,300	1,002,690	738,010	543,435	417,945	291,085	208,300	39.6
					Females				
Halifax	16,290	14,310	12,470	8,760	6,370	5,070	4,005	4,675	40.9
Nova Scotia	39,995	36,760	34,115	25,075	19,095	15,195	11,975	14,105	44.6
Canada	1,349,940	1,193,335	1,049,985	783,705	609,630	504,755	410,985	437,215	41.5
					Percent of Population				
					Total				
Halifax	8.1	7.0	6.1	4.3	3.0	2.3	1.7	1.7	—
Nova Scotia	8.4	7.7	7.2	5.3	3.9	3.0	2.2	2.2	—
Canada	7.9	7.0	6.1	4.5	3.4	2.8	2.1	1.9	—
					Males				
Halifax	8.1	6.8	6.1	4.3	2.9	2.1	1.4	1.0	—
Nova Scotia	8.4	7.7	7.3	5.4	3.9	2.8	1.8	1.4	—
Canada	8.0	7.0	6.1	4.5	3.3	2.5	1.8	1.3	—
					Females				
Halifax	8.1	7.1	6.2	4.3	3.2	2.5	2.0	2.3	—
Nova Scotia	8.4	7.7	7.2	5.3	4.0	3.2	2.5	3.0	—
Canada	7.9	7.0	6.2	4.6	3.6	3.0	2.4	2.6	—

Source: Statistics Canada. 2012. Census Profile. 2011 Census. Statistics Canada Catalogue no. 98-316-XWE. Ottawa. Released October 24 2012.
http://www12.statcan.gc.ca/census-recensement/2011/dp-pd/prof/index.cfm?Lang=E

PROFILES / Halifax, Nova Scotia

Private Households by Household Size

Area	1 Person	2 Persons	3 Persons	4 Persons	5 Persons	6 or More Persons	Average Number of Persons in Private Households
Households							
Halifax	47,140	60,235	26,980	21,220	6,830	2,625	2.3
Nova Scotia	108,795	149,105	62,005	47,900	15,995	6,480	2.3
Canada	3,673,310	4,544,820	2,081,900	1,903,300	724,405	392,885	2.5
Percent of Households							
Halifax	28.6	36.5	16.3	12.9	4.1	1.6	–
Nova Scotia	27.9	38.2	15.9	12.3	4.1	1.7	–
Canada	27.6	34.1	15.6	14.3	5.4	2.9	–

Source: Statistics Canada. 2012. Census Profile. 2011 Census. Statistics Canada Catalogue no. 98-316-XWE. Ottawa. Released October 24 2012.
http://www12.statcan.gc.ca/census-recensement/2011/dp-pd/prof/index.cfm?Lang=E

Dwelling Type

Area	Single-detached House	Semi-detached House	Row House	Apartment: Building with Five or More Storeys	Apartment: Building with Fewer Than Five Storeys	Duplex Apartment	Movable Dwelling	Other Single-attached House
Number								
Halifax	84,265	11,290	6,165	17,605	35,330	6,200	3,915	260
Nova Scotia	260,435	19,450	9,180	17,880	56,485	11,970	14,175	710
Canada	7,329,150	646,245	791,600	1,234,770	2,397,550	704,485	183,510	33,310
Percent of Dwellings								
Halifax	51.1	6.8	3.7	10.7	21.4	3.8	2.4	0.2
Nova Scotia	66.7	5.0	2.4	4.6	14.5	3.1	3.6	0.2
Canada	55.0	4.9	5.9	9.3	18.0	5.3	1.4	0.3

Source: Statistics Canada. 2012. Census Profile. 2011 Census. Statistics Canada Catalogue no. 98-316-XWE. Ottawa. Released October 24 2012.
http://www12.statcan.gc.ca/census-recensement/2011/dp-pd/prof/index.cfm?Lang=E

Shelter Costs

	Owned Dwellings					Rented Dwellings		
Area	Number	Median Value[1] ($)	Average Value[1] ($)	Median Monthly Costs[2] ($)	Average Monthly Costs[2] ($)	Number	Median Monthly Costs[3] ($)	Average Monthly Costs[3] ($)
Halifax	103,620	240,409	268,612	1,068	1,134	61,375	819	873
Nova Scotia	273,435	174,743	201,991	722	876	111,430	727	771
Canada	9,013,410	280,552	345,182	978	1,141	4,060,385	784	848

Note: All figures cover non-farm, non-reserve private dwellings; (1) Refers to the dollar amount expected by the owner if the dwelling were to be sold; (2) Includes all shelter expenses paid by households that own their dwellings, such as the mortgage payment and the costs of electricity, heat, water and other municipal services, property taxes and condominium fees; (3) Includes all shelter expenses paid by households that rent their dwellings, such as the monthly rent and the costs of electricity, heat and municipal services.
Source: Statistics Canada. 2013. 2011 National Household Survey. Statistics Canada Catalogue no. 99-004-XWE. Ottawa. Released September 11, 2013.

Occupied Private Dwellings by Period of Construction

Area	1960 or Before	1961 to 1980	1981 to 1990	1991 to 2000	2001 to 2005	2006 to 2011
Number						
Halifax	37,050	49,350	28,800	24,160	14,145	11,545
Nova Scotia	119,040	112,455	63,170	48,725	24,515	22,370
Canada	3,273,105	4,152,715	2,112,110	1,707,880	1,031,020	1,042,430
Percent of Dwellings						
Halifax	22.4	29.9	17.4	14.6	8.6	7.0
Nova Scotia	30.5	28.8	16.2	12.5	6.3	5.7
Canada	24.6	31.2	15.9	12.8	7.7	7.8

Note: Figures cover non-farm, non-reserve private dwellings and includes data up to May 10, 2011.
Source: Statistics Canada. 2013. 2011 National Household Survey. Statistics Canada Catalogue no. 99-004-XWE. Ottawa. Released September 11, 2013.

Educational Attainment

Area	No Certificate, Diploma or Degree	High School Diploma or Equivalent[1]	Apprenticeship or Trades Certificate or Diploma[2]	College, CÉGEP or Other Non-University Certificate or Diploma	University Certificate or Diploma Below the Bachelor Level[3]	Bachelor's Degree	University Certificate, Diploma or Degree Above Bachelor Level[4]
				Number			
				Total			
Halifax	52,050	78,340	31,935	61,540	13,355	57,175	30,450
Nova Scotia	171,510	183,310	90,315	148,700	28,825	93,710	51,685
Canada	5,485,400	6,968,935	2,950,685	4,970,020	1,200,130	3,634,425	2,049,930
				Males			
Halifax	25,885	38,170	20,485	25,830	5,740	25,340	14,165
Nova Scotia	87,625	87,115	58,595	59,380	11,480	40,425	24,020
Canada	2,742,875	3,305,415	1,928,970	2,118,430	513,235	1,643,080	1,043,350
				Females			
Halifax	26,160	40,170	11,455	35,715	7,615	31,835	16,285
Nova Scotia	83,885	96,195	31,725	89,325	17,340	53,290	27,660
Canada	2,742,520	3,663,515	1,021,715	2,851,595	686,890	1,991,345	1,006,585
				Percent of Population			
				Total			
Halifax	16.0	24.1	9.8	18.9	4.1	17.6	9.4
Nova Scotia	22.3	23.9	11.8	19.4	3.8	12.2	6.7
Canada	20.1	25.6	10.8	18.2	4.4	13.3	7.5
				Males			
Halifax	16.6	24.5	13.2	16.6	3.7	16.3	9.1
Nova Scotia	23.8	23.6	15.9	16.1	3.1	11.0	6.5
Canada	20.6	24.9	14.5	15.9	3.9	12.4	7.8
				Females			
Halifax	15.5	23.7	6.8	21.1	4.5	18.8	9.6
Nova Scotia	21.0	24.1	7.9	22.4	4.3	13.3	6.9
Canada	19.6	26.2	7.3	20.4	4.9	14.3	7.2

Note: Figures cover total population aged 15 years and over by highest certificate, diploma or degree; (1) Includes persons who have graduated from a secondary school or equivalent. It excludes persons with a postsecondary certificate, diploma or degree; (2) Includes Registered Apprenticeship certificates (including Certificate of Qualification, Journeyperson's designation) and other trades certificates or diplomas such as pre-employment or vocational certificates and diplomas from brief trade programs completed at community colleges, institutes of technology, vocational centres, and similar institutions; (3) Comparisons with other data sources suggest that the category 'University certificate or diploma below the bachelor's level' was over-reported in the NHS. This category likely includes some responses that are actually college certificates or diplomas, bachelor's degrees or other types of education (e.g., university transfer programs, bachelor's programs completed in other countries, incomplete bachelor's programs, non-university professional designations). We recommend users interpret the results for the 'University certificate or diploma below the bachelor's level' category with caution; (4) 'University certificate or diploma above bachelor level' includes the categories: 'Degree in medicine, dentistry, veterinary medicine or optometry,' 'Master's degree' and 'Earned doctorate.'
Source: Statistics Canada. 2013. 2011 National Household Survey. Statistics Canada Catalogue no. 99-004-XWE. Ottawa. Released September 11, 2013.

Household Income Distribution

Area	Less than $10,000	$10,000 to $19,999	$20,000 to $29,999	$30,000 to $39,999	$40,000 to $49,999	$50,000 to $59,999	$60,000 to $79,999	$80,000 to $99,999	$100,000 to $124,999	$125,000 to $149,999	$150,000 and Over
					Households						
Halifax	9,870	12,060	13,945	15,805	14,985	13,050	23,700	19,040	16,290	10,685	15,600
Nova Scotia	22,240	37,825	41,650	42,015	38,570	33,335	56,565	41,240	32,920	19,180	24,740
Canada	626,705	1,141,945	1,193,925	1,271,675	1,206,800	1,102,120	1,865,280	1,458,240	1,260,770	802,555	1,389,240
					Percent of Households						
Halifax	6.0	7.3	8.4	9.6	9.1	7.9	14.4	11.5	9.9	6.5	9.5
Nova Scotia	5.7	9.7	10.7	10.8	9.9	8.5	14.5	10.6	8.4	4.9	6.3
Canada	4.7	8.6	9.0	9.5	9.1	8.3	14.0	10.9	9.5	6.0	10.4

Note: Household income is the sum of the total incomes of all members of that household. Total income refers to monetary receipts from certain sources, before income taxes and deductions, during calendar year 2010.
Source: Statistics Canada. 2013. 2011 National Household Survey. Statistics Canada Catalogue no. 99-004-XWE. Ottawa. Released September 11, 2013.

Median and Average Household and Economic Family Income

Area	Median Household Income ($)	Average Household Income ($)	Median After-tax Household Income ($)	Average After-tax Household Income ($)	Median Economic Family Income ($)	Average Economic Family Income ($)	Median After-tax Economic Family Income ($)	Average After-tax Economic Family Income ($)
Halifax	62,069	76,210	53,399	62,545	80,097	92,829	67,939	75,818
Nova Scotia	53,606	66,590	47,495	55,883	68,102	79,838	59,371	66,745
Canada	61,072	79,102	54,089	66,149	76,511	94,125	67,044	78,517

Note: Figures cover household and economic familiy income in 2010. A household is defined as a person or a group of persons (other than foreign residents) who occupy the same private dwelling and do not have a usual place of residence elsewhere in Canada. Every person is a member of one and only one household. An economic family is defined as a group of two or more persons who live in the same dwelling and are related to each other by blood, marriage, common-law, adoption or a foster relationship. A couple may be of opposite or same sex.
Source: Statistics Canada. 2013. 2011 National Household Survey. Statistics Canada Catalogue no. 99-004-XWE. Ottawa. Released September 11, 2013.

PROFILES / Halifax, Nova Scotia

Individual Income Distribution

Area	Less than $10,000	$10,000 to $19,999	$20,000 to $29,999	$30,000 to $39,999	$40,000 to $49,999	$50,000 to $59,999	$60,000 to $79,999	$80,000 to $99,999	$100,000 to $124,999	$125,000 and Over
Number										
Total										
Halifax	52,630	52,495	41,695	39,935	32,865	24,650	34,850	16,285	7,475	7,990
Nova Scotia	132,125	145,930	113,665	97,630	72,510	51,495	66,320	27,960	12,470	12,425
Canada	4,492,040	4,835,710	3,670,020	3,180,360	2,603,520	1,921,650	2,437,440	1,302,045	693,580	782,135
Males										
Halifax	22,550	18,895	17,380	17,205	16,515	13,610	20,945	10,670	5,395	6,225
Nova Scotia	52,685	54,040	49,790	46,925	40,480	31,050	40,725	18,625	8,965	9,860
Canada	1,936,365	1,864,880	1,588,260	1,522,190	1,333,510	1,079,780	1,473,145	823,720	492,905	599,905
Females										
Halifax	30,080	33,600	24,320	22,730	16,350	11,040	13,905	5,620	2,085	1,765
Nova Scotia	79,440	91,890	63,870	50,705	32,030	20,450	25,595	9,340	3,505	2,565
Canada	2,555,675	2,970,825	2,081,760	1,658,170	1,270,010	841,870	964,300	478,330	200,680	182,230
Percent of Population										
Total										
Halifax	16.9	16.9	13.4	12.8	10.6	7.9	11.2	5.2	2.4	2.6
Nova Scotia	18.0	19.9	15.5	13.3	9.9	7.0	9.1	3.8	1.7	1.7
Canada	17.3	18.7	14.2	12.3	10.0	7.4	9.4	5.0	2.7	3.0
Males										
Halifax	15.1	12.6	11.6	11.5	11.1	9.1	14.0	7.1	3.6	4.2
Nova Scotia	14.9	15.3	14.1	13.3	11.5	8.8	11.5	5.3	2.5	2.8
Canada	15.2	14.7	12.5	12.0	10.5	8.5	11.6	6.5	3.9	4.7
Females										
Halifax	18.6	20.8	15.1	14.1	10.1	6.8	8.6	3.5	1.3	1.1
Nova Scotia	20.9	24.2	16.8	13.4	8.4	5.4	6.7	2.5	0.9	0.7
Canada	19.4	22.5	15.8	12.6	9.6	6.4	7.3	3.6	1.5	1.4

Note: Figures cover individuals aged 15 years and over with income. Income refers to monetary receipts from certain sources, before income taxes and deductions, during calendar year 2010.
Source: Statistics Canada. 2013. 2011 National Household Survey. Statistics Canada Catalogue no. 99-004-XWE. Ottawa. Released September 11, 2013.

Labour Force Status

Area	In the Labour Force - All	In the Labour Force - Employed	In the Labour Force - Unemployed	Not in the Labour Force
Number				
Total				
Halifax	224,510	208,285	16,230	100,335
Nova Scotia	484,585	435,895	48,690	283,475
Canada	17,990,080	16,595,035	1,395,045	9,269,445
Males				
Halifax	113,915	105,285	8,630	41,690
Nova Scotia	247,725	220,810	26,910	120,910
Canada	9,388,570	8,634,310	754,255	3,906,785
Females				
Halifax	110,595	103,000	7,595	58,640
Nova Scotia	236,860	215,085	21,775	162,560
Canada	8,601,515	7,960,725	640,790	5,362,660
Percent of Labour Force				
Total				
Halifax	69.1	64.1	7.2	30.9
Nova Scotia	63.1	56.8	10.0	36.9
Canada	66.0	60.9	7.8	34.0
Males				
Halifax	73.2	67.7	7.6	26.8
Nova Scotia	67.2	59.9	10.9	32.8
Canada	70.6	64.9	8.0	29.4
Females				
Halifax	65.3	60.9	6.9	34.6
Nova Scotia	59.3	53.8	9.2	40.7
Canada	61.6	57.0	7.4	38.4

Note: Figures are based on total population 15 years and over
Source: Statistics Canada. 2013. 2011 National Household Survey. Statistics Canada Catalogue no. 99-004-XWE. Ottawa. Released September 11, 2013.

Labour Force by Industry (NAICS Codes 11–52)

Area	Agriculture, forestry, fishing & hunting	Mining, quarrying, & oil & gas extraction	Utilities	Construction	Manufacturing	Wholesale Trade	Retail Trade	Transportation & warehousing	Information & cultural industries	Finance & insurance
					Number Total					
Halifax	1,105	1,035	1,330	13,215	10,285	8,110	26,150	9,620	6,455	10,235
Nova Scotia	18,340	3,670	2,955	32,245	33,875	15,380	60,900	19,425	9,885	15,735
Canada	437,650	261,050	149,940	1,215,380	1,619,295	733,445	2,031,665	827,780	420,830	767,960
					Males					
Halifax	895	830	890	11,560	7,620	5,985	11,595	7,565	3,580	3,810
Nova Scotia	14,740	3,265	2,250	28,835	25,055	11,235	26,185	15,340	5,515	5,375
Canada	307,370	211,690	110,765	1,068,710	1,167,680	494,545	933,850	617,305	235,875	296,995
					Females					
Halifax	210	205	440	1,650	2,660	2,125	14,560	2,060	2,870	6,425
Nova Scotia	3,595	405	700	3,405	8,830	4,145	34,720	4,080	4,375	10,355
Canada	130,285	49,360	39,175	146,670	451,615	238,900	1,097,820	210,475	184,955	470,960
					Percent of Labour Force Total					
Halifax	0.5	0.5	0.6	6.0	4.6	3.7	11.8	4.3	2.9	4.6
Nova Scotia	3.9	0.8	0.6	6.8	7.1	3.2	12.8	4.1	2.1	3.3
Canada	2.5	1.5	0.9	6.9	9.2	4.2	11.6	4.7	2.4	4.4
					Males					
Halifax	0.8	0.7	0.8	10.3	6.8	5.3	10.3	6.7	3.2	3.4
Nova Scotia	6.1	1.3	0.9	11.9	10.3	4.6	10.8	6.3	2.3	2.2
Canada	3.3	2.3	1.2	11.6	12.7	5.4	10.2	6.7	2.6	3.2
					Females					
Halifax	0.2	0.2	0.4	1.5	2.4	2.0	13.4	1.9	2.6	5.9
Nova Scotia	1.6	0.2	0.3	1.5	3.8	1.8	15.0	1.8	1.9	4.5
Canada	1.6	0.6	0.5	1.7	5.4	2.8	13.1	2.5	2.2	5.6

Note: Figures are based on total experienced labour force 15 years and over. Experienced labour force refers to persons who, during the week of Sunday, May 1 to Saturday, May 7, 2011, were employed and the unemployed who had last worked for pay or in self-employment in either 2010 or 2011.
Source: Statistics Canada. 2013. 2011 National Household Survey. Statistics Canada Catalogue no. 99-004-XWE. Ottawa. Released September 11, 2013.

Labour Force by Industry (NAICS Codes 53–91)

Area	Real estate & rental & leasing	Profess., scientific & tech. services	Mgmt of companies & enterprises	Admin. & support, waste mgmt & remed. services	Educational services	Health care & social assistance	Arts, entertain. & recreation	Accomm. & food services	Other services (except public admin.)	Public admin.
					Number Total					
Halifax	4,265	15,495	140	11,725	18,365	26,415	4,545	15,165	9,160	28,390
Nova Scotia	7,025	23,905	330	23,775	38,895	59,670	9,635	31,710	20,230	47,075
Canada	321,895	1,240,850	17,460	728,330	1,301,435	1,949,650	363,405	1,130,750	807,800	1,261,050
					Males					
Halifax	2,345	8,655	80	6,415	5,905	5,110	2,125	6,335	3,955	17,080
Nova Scotia	4,005	12,800	165	12,395	12,430	10,090	4,675	11,160	9,650	27,600
Canada	179,090	688,625	9,380	411,250	424,915	349,430	188,270	469,990	372,940	652,510
					Females					
Halifax	1,915	6,845	60	5,315	12,455	21,300	2,420	8,825	5,200	11,315
Nova Scotia	3,010	11,105	170	11,385	26,470	49,575	4,965	20,550	10,575	19,475
Canada	142,805	552,225	8,075	317,085	876,515	1,600,220	175,135	660,760	434,865	608,535
					Percent of Labour Force Total					
Halifax	1.9	7.0	0.1	5.3	8.3	11.9	2.1	6.9	4.1	12.8
Nova Scotia	1.5	5.0	0.1	5.0	8.2	12.6	2.0	6.7	4.3	9.9
Canada	1.8	7.1	0.1	4.1	7.4	11.1	2.1	6.4	4.6	7.2
					Males					
Halifax	2.1	7.7	0.1	5.7	5.3	4.5	1.9	5.6	3.5	15.2
Nova Scotia	1.6	5.3	0.1	5.1	5.1	4.2	1.9	4.6	4.0	11.4
Canada	1.9	7.5	0.1	4.5	4.6	3.8	2.0	5.1	4.1	7.1
					Females					
Halifax	1.8	6.3	0.1	4.9	11.4	19.6	2.2	8.1	4.8	10.4
Nova Scotia	1.3	4.8	0.1	4.9	11.4	21.4	2.1	8.9	4.6	8.4
Canada	1.7	6.6	0.1	3.8	10.4	19.1	2.1	7.9	5.2	7.2

Note: Figures are based on total experienced labour force 15 years and over. Experienced labour force refers to persons who, during the week of Sunday, May 1 to Saturday, May 7, 2011, were employed and the unemployed who had last worked for pay or in self-employment in either 2010 or 2011.
Source: Statistics Canada. 2013. 2011 National Household Survey. Statistics Canada Catalogue no. 99-004-XWE. Ottawa. Released September 11, 2013.

Occupation

Area	Mgmt	Business, Finance & Admin.	Natural/ Applied Sciences & Related	Health	Education, Law & Social, Community & Government Services	Art, Culture, Recreation & Sport	Sales & Service	Trades, Transport & Equip. Operators & Related	Natural Resources, Agri. & Related Production	Mfg & Utilities
					Number Total					
Halifax	24,455	38,140	17,365	16,010	31,265	6,605	55,310	25,980	2,185	3,885
Nova Scotia	48,000	70,355	28,280	33,580	61,450	11,305	116,265	69,025	18,265	18,130
Canada	1,963,600	2,902,045	1,237,775	1,107,200	2,064,675	503,415	4,068,170	2,537,775	397,930	805,040
					Males					
Halifax	14,660	11,215	14,245	3,280	12,310	3,160	23,910	24,860	1,805	2,890
Nova Scotia	28,825	18,490	23,065	6,080	21,520	5,085	45,190	65,975	15,385	13,150
Canada	1,229,460	854,190	966,355	217,520	676,550	232,535	1,745,705	2,385,615	318,945	564,300
					Females					
Halifax	9,795	26,920	3,120	12,725	18,950	3,445	31,400	1,120	380	995
Nova Scotia	19,175	51,870	5,210	27,500	39,930	6,225	71,075	3,050	2,875	4,980
Canada	734,140	2,047,855	271,415	889,675	1,388,130	270,875	2,322,465	152,165	78,980	240,740
					Percent of Labour Force Total					
Halifax	11.1	17.2	7.9	7.2	14.1	3.0	25.0	11.7	1.0	1.8
Nova Scotia	10.1	14.8	6.0	7.1	12.9	2.4	24.5	14.5	3.8	3.8
Canada	11.2	16.5	7.0	6.3	11.7	2.9	23.1	14.4	2.3	4.6
					Males					
Halifax	13.0	10.0	12.7	2.9	11.0	2.8	21.3	22.1	1.6	2.6
Nova Scotia	11.9	7.6	9.5	2.5	8.9	2.1	18.6	27.2	6.3	5.4
Canada	13.4	9.3	10.5	2.4	7.4	2.5	19.0	26.0	3.5	6.1
					Females					
Halifax	9.0	24.7	2.9	11.7	17.4	3.2	28.8	1.0	0.3	0.9
Nova Scotia	8.3	22.4	2.2	11.9	17.2	2.7	30.7	1.3	1.2	2.1
Canada	8.7	24.4	3.2	10.6	16.5	3.2	27.7	1.8	0.9	2.9

Note: Figures are based on total experienced labour force 15 years and over
Source: Statistics Canada. 2013. 2011 National Household Survey. Statistics Canada Catalogue no. 99-004-XWE. Ottawa. Released September 11, 2013.

Place of Work Status

Area	Worked at Home	Worked Outside Canada	No Fixed Workplace Address	Worked at Usual Place
		Number Total		
Halifax	11,615	785	21,980	173,905
Nova Scotia	25,900	1,425	53,305	355,265
Canada	1,142,640	66,460	1,868,245	13,517,690
		Males		
Halifax	5,765	640	16,505	82,380
Nova Scotia	12,790	1,175	41,130	165,715
Canada	582,150	47,355	1,400,485	6,604,325
		Females		
Halifax	5,855	150	5,480	91,520
Nova Scotia	13,110	250	12,170	189,545
Canada	560,490	19,100	467,760	6,913,370
		Percent of Labour Force Total		
Halifax	5.6	0.4	10.6	83.5
Nova Scotia	5.9	0.3	12.2	81.5
Canada	6.9	0.4	11.3	81.5
		Males		
Halifax	5.5	0.6	15.7	78.2
Nova Scotia	5.8	0.5	18.6	75.0
Canada	6.7	0.5	16.2	76.5
		Females		
Halifax	5.7	0.1	5.3	88.9
Nova Scotia	6.1	0.1	5.7	88.1
Canada	7.0	0.2	5.9	86.8

Note: Figures are based on total employed labour force 15 years and over.
Source: Statistics Canada. 2013. 2011 National Household Survey. Statistics Canada Catalogue no. 99-004-XWE. Ottawa. Released September 11, 2013.

Mode of Transportation to Work

Area	Car; Truck; Van; as Driver	Car; Truck; Van; as Passenger	Public Transit	Walked	Bicycled	All Other Modes
			Number			
			Total			
Halifax	134,475	15,490	24,435	16,705	2,210	2,575
Nova Scotia	313,295	32,195	27,015	27,935	2,755	5,380
Canada	11,393,140	867,050	1,851,525	880,815	201,780	191,625
			Males			
Halifax	72,690	5,195	10,270	7,880	1,485	1,370
Nova Scotia	163,650	13,275	11,790	13,100	1,905	3,125
Canada	6,238,835	349,530	788,290	387,580	135,840	104,725
			Females			
Halifax	61,780	10,295	14,160	8,820	725	1,205
Nova Scotia	149,640	18,915	15,225	14,835	850	2,250
Canada	5,154,305	517,520	1,063,235	493,230	65,940	86,900
			Percent of Labour Force			
			Total			
Halifax	68.6	7.9	12.5	8.5	1.1	1.3
Nova Scotia	76.7	7.9	6.6	6.8	0.7	1.3
Canada	74.0	5.6	12.0	5.7	1.3	1.2
			Males			
Halifax	73.5	5.3	10.4	8.0	1.5	1.4
Nova Scotia	79.1	6.4	5.7	6.3	0.9	1.5
Canada	77.9	4.4	9.8	4.8	1.7	1.3
			Females			
Halifax	63.7	10.6	14.6	9.1	0.7	1.2
Nova Scotia	74.2	9.4	7.5	7.4	0.4	1.1
Canada	69.8	7.0	14.4	6.7	0.9	1.2

Note: Figures are based on total employed labour force 15 years and over.
Source: Statistics Canada. 2013. 2011 National Household Survey. Statistics Canada Catalogue no. 99-004-XWE. Ottawa. Released September 11, 2013.

Visible Minority Population Characteristics

Area	Total Minority	South Asian[1]	Chinese	Black	Filipino	Latin American	Arab	SE Asian[2]	West Asian[3]	Korean	Japanese	Multiple[4]
						Number						
						Total						
Halifax	35,040	3,995	4,620	13,780	1,320	1,025	5,525	900	1,205	845	290	1,090
Nova Scotia	47,270	4,965	6,050	20,790	1,890	1,360	6,290	1,155	1,365	960	445	1,290
Canada	6,264,750	1,567,400	1,324,750	945,665	619,310	381,280	380,620	312,075	206,840	161,130	87,270	171,935
						Males						
Halifax	17,860	2,140	2,410	6,805	560	515	3,255	430	645	345	110	450
Nova Scotia	23,975	2,585	3,035	10,545	815	645	3,810	520	680	375	150	555
Canada	3,043,010	790,755	632,325	453,005	268,885	186,355	203,485	154,035	105,620	77,165	38,270	83,335
						Females						
Halifax	17,185	1,855	2,210	6,970	760	510	2,270	470	565	500	180	640
Nova Scotia	23,295	2,375	3,015	10,245	1,070	720	2,480	640	685	580	295	735
Canada	3,221,745	776,650	692,420	492,660	350,425	194,925	177,140	158,045	101,220	83,965	48,990	88,600
						Percent of Population						
						Total						
Halifax	9.1	1.0	1.2	3.6	0.3	0.3	1.4	0.2	0.3	0.2	0.1	0.3
Nova Scotia	5.2	0.5	0.7	2.3	0.2	0.2	0.7	0.1	0.2	0.1	0.0	0.1
Canada	19.1	4.8	4.0	2.9	1.9	1.2	1.2	0.9	0.6	0.5	0.3	0.5
						Males						
Halifax	9.6	1.1	1.3	3.7	0.3	0.3	1.7	0.2	0.3	0.2	0.1	0.2
Nova Scotia	5.5	0.6	0.7	2.4	0.2	0.1	0.9	0.1	0.2	0.1	0.0	0.1
Canada	18.8	4.9	3.9	2.8	1.7	1.2	1.3	1.0	0.7	0.5	0.2	0.5
						Females						
Halifax	8.7	0.9	1.1	3.5	0.4	0.3	1.1	0.2	0.3	0.3	0.1	0.3
Nova Scotia	5.0	0.5	0.6	2.2	0.2	0.2	0.5	0.1	0.1	0.1	0.1	0.2
Canada	19.3	4.7	4.1	3.0	2.1	1.2	1.1	0.9	0.6	0.5	0.3	0.5

Note: The Employment Equity Act defines visible minorities as 'persons, other than Aboriginal peoples, who are non-Caucasian in race or non-white in colour'; (1) Includes 'East Indian,' 'Pakistani,' 'Sri Lankan,' etc.; (2) Includes 'Vietnamese,' 'Cambodian,' 'Malaysian,' 'Laotian,' etc.; (3) Includes 'Iranian,' 'Afghan,' etc.; (4) Includes respondents who reported more than one visible minority group by checking two or more mark-in circles, e.g., 'Black' and 'South Asian.'
Source: Statistics Canada. 2013. 2011 National Household Survey. Statistics Canada Catalogue no. 99-004-XWE. Ottawa. Released September 11, 2013.

PROFILES / Halifax, Nova Scotia

Aboriginal Population

Area	Aboriginal Identity[1]	First Nations (North American Indian) Single Identity[2]	Métis Single Identity	Inuk (Inuit) Single Identity	Multiple Aboriginal Identities[3]	Aboriginal Identities Not Included Elsewhere
			Number			
			Total			
Halifax	9,585	5,765	3,095	265	60	400
Nova Scotia	33,850	21,895	10,050	695	225	980
Canada	1,400,685	851,560	451,795	59,440	11,415	26,475
			Males			
Halifax	4,480	2,610	1,565	125	30	150
Nova Scotia	16,440	10,405	5,210	270	120	440
Canada	682,190	411,785	223,335	29,495	5,525	12,055
			Females			
Halifax	5,110	3,160	1,530	140	30	245
Nova Scotia	17,405	11,495	4,840	430	105	545
Canada	718,500	439,775	228,460	29,950	5,890	14,420
			Percent of Population			
			Total			
Halifax	2.5	1.5	0.8	0.1	0.0	0.1
Nova Scotia	3.7	2.4	1.1	0.1	0.0	0.1
Canada	4.3	2.6	1.4	0.2	0.0	0.1
			Males			
Halifax	2.4	1.4	0.8	0.1	0.0	0.1
Nova Scotia	3.7	2.4	1.2	0.1	0.0	0.1
Canada	4.2	2.5	1.4	0.2	0.0	0.1
			Females			
Halifax	2.6	1.6	0.8	0.1	0.0	0.1
Nova Scotia	3.7	2.5	1.0	0.1	0.0	0.1
Canada	4.3	2.6	1.4	0.2	0.0	0.1

Note: (1) Includes persons who reported being an Aboriginal person, that is, First Nations (North American Indian), Métis or Inuk (Inuit) and/or those who reported Registered or Treaty Indian status, that is registered under the Indian Act of Canada, and/or those who reported membership in a First Nation or Indian band. Aboriginal peoples of Canada are defined in the Constitution Act, 1982, section 35-2 as including the Indian, Inuit and Métis peoples of Canada; (2) Users should be aware that the estimates associated with this variable are more affected than most by the incomplete enumeration of certain Indian reserves and Indian settlements in the National Household Survey (NHS); (3) Includes persons who reported being any two or all three of the following: First Nations (North American Indian), Métis or Inuk (Inuit).
Source: Statistics Canada. 2013. 2011 National Household Survey. Statistics Canada Catalogue no. 99-004-XWE. Ottawa. Released September 11, 2013.

Ethnic Origin

Area	North American Aboriginal	Other North American	European	Caribbean	Latin, Central and South American	African	Asian	Oceania
				Number				
				Total				
Halifax	17,665	151,025	277,675	2,695	1,755	10,240	24,015	370
Nova Scotia	52,930	376,285	659,350	4,215	2,380	15,110	31,875	685
Canada	1,836,035	11,070,455	20,157,965	627,590	544,375	766,735	5,011,225	74,875
				Males				
Halifax	8,145	72,940	132,530	1,355	855	5,330	12,505	225
Nova Scotia	24,960	182,160	317,245	2,145	1,145	7,780	16,275	440
Canada	885,675	5,462,685	9,913,150	291,640	264,635	387,360	2,435,540	37,490
				Females				
Halifax	9,520	78,085	145,145	1,340	900	4,915	11,510	145
Nova Scotia	27,965	194,125	342,105	2,065	1,225	7,335	15,600	245
Canada	950,360	5,607,770	10,244,820	335,945	279,740	379,380	2,575,680	37,385
				Percent of Population				
				Total				
Halifax	4.6	39.3	72.2	0.7	0.5	2.7	6.2	0.1
Nova Scotia	5.8	41.5	72.8	0.5	0.3	1.7	3.5	0.1
Canada	5.6	33.7	61.4	1.9	1.7	2.3	15.3	0.2
				Males				
Halifax	4.4	39.2	71.2	0.7	0.5	2.9	6.7	0.1
Nova Scotia	5.7	41.4	72.2	0.5	0.3	1.8	3.7	0.1
Canada	5.5	33.8	61.3	1.8	1.6	2.4	15.1	0.2
				Females				
Halifax	4.8	39.4	73.2	0.7	0.5	2.5	5.8	0.1
Nova Scotia	6.0	41.6	73.3	0.4	0.3	1.6	3.3	0.1
Canada	5.7	33.6	61.4	2.0	1.7	2.3	15.4	0.2

Note: The sum of the ethnic groups in this table is greater than the total population estimate because a person may report more than one ethnic origin in the NHS.
Source: Statistics Canada. 2013. 2011 National Household Survey. Statistics Canada Catalogue no. 99-004-XWE. Ottawa. Released September 11, 2013.

Religion

Area	Buddhist	Christian	Hindu	Jewish	Muslim	Sikh	Traditional (Aboriginal) Spirituality	Other Religions	No Religious Affiliation
				Number Total					
Halifax	1,590	274,780	1,540	1,340	7,535	350	45	1,515	95,630
Nova Scotia	2,205	690,460	1,850	1,805	8,505	390	570	2,720	197,665
Canada	366,830	22,102,745	497,965	329,495	1,053,945	454,965	64,935	130,835	7,850,605
				Males					
Halifax	825	127,320	800	630	4,205	180	15	620	51,575
Nova Scotia	1,025	323,005	925	875	4,835	200	295	1,090	107,320
Canada	168,465	10,497,775	250,435	161,265	540,555	229,435	31,805	57,745	4,225,645
				Females					
Halifax	765	147,460	740	715	3,330	170	30	895	44,055
Nova Scotia	1,180	367,460	925	930	3,670	185	275	1,630	90,345
Canada	198,365	11,604,975	247,525	168,235	513,395	225,530	33,135	73,090	3,624,965
				Percent of Population Total					
Halifax	0.4	71.5	0.4	0.3	2.0	0.1	0.0	0.4	24.9
Nova Scotia	0.2	76.2	0.2	0.2	0.9	0.0	0.1	0.3	21.8
Canada	1.1	67.3	1.5	1.0	3.2	1.4	0.2	0.4	23.9
				Males					
Halifax	0.4	68.4	0.4	0.3	2.3	0.1	0.0	0.3	27.7
Nova Scotia	0.2	73.5	0.2	0.2	1.1	0.0	0.1	0.2	24.4
Canada	1.0	64.9	1.5	1.0	3.3	1.4	0.2	0.4	26.1
				Females					
Halifax	0.4	74.4	0.4	0.4	1.7	0.1	0.0	0.5	22.2
Nova Scotia	0.3	78.8	0.2	0.2	0.8	0.0	0.1	0.3	19.4
Canada	1.2	69.5	1.5	1.0	3.1	1.4	0.2	0.4	21.7

Note: Religion refers to the person's self-identification as having a connection or affiliation with any religious denomination, group, body, sect, cult or other religiously defined community or system of belief. Religion is not limited to formal membership in a religious organization or group. Persons without a religious connection or affiliation can self-identify as atheist, agnostic or humanist, or can provide another applicable response.
Source: Statistics Canada. 2013. 2011 National Household Survey. Statistics Canada Catalogue no. 99-004-XWE. Ottawa. Released September 11, 2013.

Religion—Christian Denominations

Area	Anglican	Baptist	Catholic	Christian Orthodox	Lutheran	Pentecostal	Presbyterian	United Church	Other Christian
				Number Total					
Halifax	50,470	22,625	121,300	2,645	2,800	3,830	5,300	42,340	23,470
Nova Scotia	100,120	80,815	298,270	3,370	9,485	9,595	23,555	109,700	55,555
Canada	1,631,845	635,840	12,810,705	550,690	478,185	478,705	472,385	2,007,610	3,036,780
				Males					
Halifax	23,930	10,125	56,360	1,470	1,405	1,665	2,535	18,895	10,935
Nova Scotia	47,375	37,000	141,230	1,920	4,680	4,095	11,085	49,470	26,155
Canada	752,945	293,905	6,167,290	270,205	221,525	217,850	218,955	912,545	1,442,550
				Females					
Halifax	26,540	12,505	64,935	1,170	1,400	2,160	2,765	23,445	12,535
Nova Scotia	52,740	43,815	157,040	1,450	4,810	5,500	12,465	60,235	29,405
Canada	878,900	341,940	6,643,415	280,485	256,660	260,850	253,430	1,095,065	1,594,230
				Percent of Population Total					
Halifax	13.1	5.9	31.6	0.7	0.7	1.0	1.4	11.0	6.1
Nova Scotia	11.0	8.9	32.9	0.4	1.0	1.1	2.6	12.1	6.1
Canada	5.0	1.9	39.0	1.7	1.5	1.5	1.4	6.1	9.2
				Males					
Halifax	12.9	5.4	30.3	0.8	0.8	0.9	1.4	10.1	5.9
Nova Scotia	10.8	8.4	32.1	0.4	1.1	0.9	2.5	11.3	6.0
Canada	4.7	1.8	38.2	1.7	1.4	1.3	1.4	5.6	8.9
				Females					
Halifax	13.4	6.3	32.8	0.6	0.7	1.1	1.4	11.8	6.3
Nova Scotia	11.3	9.4	33.7	0.3	1.0	1.2	2.7	12.9	6.3
Canada	5.3	2.0	39.8	1.7	1.5	1.6	1.5	6.6	9.6

Note: Religion refers to the person's self-identification as having a connection or affiliation with any religious denomination, group, body, sect, cult or other religiously defined community or system of belief. Religion is not limited to formal membership in a religious organization or group. Persons without a religious connection or affiliation can self-identify as atheist, agnostic or humanist, or can provide another applicable response.
Source: Statistics Canada. 2013. 2011 National Household Survey. Statistics Canada Catalogue no. 99-004-XWE. Ottawa. Released September 11, 2013.

PROFILES / Halifax, Nova Scotia

Immigrant Status and Period of Immigration

Area	Non-Immigrants[1]	Immigrants All	Before 1971	1971 to 1980	1981 to 1990	1991 to 2000	2001 to 2005	2006 to 2011	Non-Permanent Residents[3]
Number									
Total									
Halifax	348,350	31,245	6,765	4,340	3,345	4,950	3,550	8,305	4,735
Nova Scotia	851,035	48,275	12,895	7,690	4,910	6,600	5,320	10,860	6,865
Canada	25,720,175	6,775,765	1,261,055	870,775	949,890	1,539,050	992,070	1,162,915	356,385
Males									
Halifax	167,545	15,980	3,330	2,185	1,730	2,525	1,770	4,430	2,650
Nova Scotia	411,880	23,850	6,255	3,655	2,435	3,215	2,590	5,705	3,840
Canada	12,753,235	3,231,370	605,430	416,670	454,570	724,905	474,545	555,245	178,515
Females									
Halifax	180,805	15,270	3,430	2,160	1,610	2,420	1,780	3,865	2,085
Nova Scotia	439,155	24,425	6,640	4,035	2,480	3,385	2,730	5,150	3,030
Canada	12,966,935	3,544,400	655,625	454,105	495,325	814,145	517,530	607,670	177,870
Percent of Population									
Total									
Halifax	90.6	8.1	1.8	1.1	0.9	1.3	0.9	2.2	1.2
Nova Scotia	93.9	5.3	1.4	0.8	0.5	0.7	0.6	1.2	0.8
Canada	78.3	20.6	3.8	2.7	2.9	4.7	3.0	3.5	1.1
Males									
Halifax	90.0	8.6	1.8	1.2	0.9	1.4	1.0	2.4	1.4
Nova Scotia	93.7	5.4	1.4	0.8	0.6	0.7	0.6	1.3	0.9
Canada	78.9	20.0	3.7	2.6	2.8	4.5	2.9	3.4	1.1
Females									
Halifax	91.2	7.7	1.7	1.1	0.8	1.2	0.9	2.0	1.1
Nova Scotia	94.1	5.2	1.4	0.9	0.5	0.7	0.6	1.1	0.6
Canada	77.7	21.2	3.9	2.7	3.0	4.9	3.1	3.6	1.1

Note: (1) Non-immigrant refers to a person who is a Canadian citizen by birth; (2) Immigrant refers to a person who is or has ever been a landed immigrant/permanent resident. This person has been granted the right to live in Canada permanently by immigration authorities. Some immigrants have resided in Canada for a number of years, while others have arrived recently. Some immigrants are Canadian citizens, while others are not. Most immigrants are born outside Canada, but a small number are born in Canada. In the 2011 National Household Survey, 'Immigrants' includes immigrants who landed in Canada prior to May 10, 2011; (3) Non-permanent resident refers to a person from another country who has a work or study permit, or who is a refugee claimant, and any non-Canadian-born family member living in Canada with them.
Source: Statistics Canada. 2013. 2011 National Household Survey. Statistics Canada Catalogue no. 99-004-XWE. Ottawa. Released September 11, 2013.

Mother Tongue

Area	English	French	Non-official Language	English & French	English & Non-official Language	French & Non-official Language	English, French & Non-official Language
Number							
Total							
Halifax	348,515	10,155	23,855	1,465	1,895	215	105
Nova Scotia	836,085	31,105	37,090	3,035	2,855	315	130
Canada	18,858,980	7,054,975	6,567,680	144,685	396,330	74,430	24,095
Males							
Halifax	167,925	5,015	12,305	680	940	110	60
Nova Scotia	404,330	15,005	18,825	1,400	1,385	170	75
Canada	9,345,225	3,452,380	3,157,785	69,975	192,000	36,535	11,965
Females							
Halifax	180,590	5,145	11,550	785	955	100	45
Nova Scotia	431,760	16,100	18,260	1,635	1,470	150	55
Canada	9,513,750	3,602,590	3,409,895	74,710	204,330	37,890	12,130
Percent of Population							
Total							
Halifax	90.2	2.6	6.2	0.4	0.5	0.1	0.0
Nova Scotia	91.8	3.4	4.1	0.3	0.3	0.0	0.0
Canada	56.9	21.3	19.8	0.4	1.2	0.2	0.1
Males							
Halifax	89.8	2.7	6.6	0.4	0.5	0.1	0.0
Nova Scotia	91.6	3.4	4.3	0.3	0.3	0.0	0.0
Canada	57.5	21.2	19.4	0.4	1.2	0.2	0.1
Females							
Halifax	90.7	2.6	5.8	0.4	0.5	0.1	0.0
Nova Scotia	92.0	3.4	3.9	0.3	0.3	0.0	0.0
Canada	56.4	21.4	20.2	0.4	1.2	0.2	0.1

Note: Figures cover total population excluding institutional residents.
Source: Statistics Canada. 2012. Census Profile. 2011 Census. Statistics Canada Catalogue no. 98-316-XWE. Ottawa. Released October 24 2012.
http://www12.statcan.gc.ca/census-recensement/2011/dp-pd/prof/index.cfm?Lang=E

Language Spoken Most Often at Home

Area	English	French	Non-official Language	English & French	English & Non-official Language	French & Non-official Language	English, French & Non-official Language
			Number				
			Total				
Halifax	365,300	3,660	12,305	830	3,880	90	140
Nova Scotia	868,765	15,935	18,510	1,815	5,295	115	180
Canada	21,457,075	6,827,865	3,673,865	131,205	875,135	109,700	46,330
			Males				
Halifax	176,335	1,810	6,380	405	1,990	45	70
Nova Scotia	420,340	7,625	9,570	860	2,640	60	85
Canada	10,585,620	3,348,235	1,767,310	63,475	425,370	53,010	22,845
			Females				
Halifax	188,960	1,850	5,920	425	1,890	45	70
Nova Scotia	448,425	8,315	8,940	950	2,655	60	90
Canada	10,871,455	3,479,625	1,906,555	67,730	449,765	56,690	23,485
			Percent of Population				
			Total				
Halifax	94.6	0.9	3.2	0.2	1.0	0.0	0.0
Nova Scotia	95.4	1.7	2.0	0.2	0.6	0.0	0.0
Canada	64.8	20.6	11.1	0.4	2.6	0.3	0.1
			Males				
Halifax	94.3	1.0	3.4	0.2	1.1	0.0	0.0
Nova Scotia	95.3	1.7	2.2	0.2	0.6	0.0	0.0
Canada	65.1	20.6	10.9	0.4	2.6	0.3	0.1
			Females				
Halifax	94.9	0.9	3.0	0.2	0.9	0.0	0.0
Nova Scotia	95.5	1.8	1.9	0.2	0.6	0.0	0.0
Canada	64.5	20.6	11.3	0.4	2.7	0.3	0.1

Note: Figures cover total population excluding institutional residents.
Source: Statistics Canada. 2012. Census Profile. 2011 Census. Statistics Canada Catalogue no. 98-316-XWE. Ottawa. Released October 24 2012.
http://www12.statcan.gc.ca/census-recensement/2011/dp-pd/prof/index.cfm?Lang=E

Knowledge of Official Languages

Area	English Only	French Only	English & French	Neither English nor French
		Number		
		Total		
Halifax	338,245	380	46,385	1,190
Nova Scotia	814,670	875	93,435	1,635
Canada	22,564,665	4,165,015	5,795,570	595,920
		Males		
Halifax	165,935	165	20,410	520
Nova Scotia	398,830	385	41,245	735
Canada	11,222,185	1,925,340	2,876,560	241,790
		Females		
Halifax	172,305	215	25,970	670
Nova Scotia	415,845	490	52,185	900
Canada	11,342,485	2,239,680	2,919,005	354,135
		Percent of Population		
		Total		
Halifax	87.6	0.1	12.0	0.3
Nova Scotia	89.5	0.1	10.3	0.2
Canada	68.1	12.6	17.5	1.8
		Males		
Halifax	88.7	0.1	10.9	0.3
Nova Scotia	90.4	0.1	9.3	0.2
Canada	69.0	11.8	17.7	1.5
		Females		
Halifax	86.5	0.1	13.0	0.3
Nova Scotia	88.6	0.1	11.1	0.2
Canada	67.3	13.3	17.3	2.1

Note: Figures cover total population excluding institutional residents.
Source: Statistics Canada. 2012. Census Profile. 2011 Census. Statistics Canada Catalogue no. 98-316-XWE. Ottawa. Released October 24 2012.
http://www12.statcan.gc.ca/census-recensement/2011/dp-pd/prof/index.cfm?Lang=E

Hamilton, Ontario

Background

Hamilton is a port city located at the western end of the Golden Horseshoe in southern Ontario. The city is situated on the western shores of Lake Ontario and offers easy access to highways, rail lines, Hamilton port, three international airports and the U.S. border. The Greater Toronto Area (GTA) is less than an hour east of Hamilton.

Hamilton was first settled by the Iroquois Confederacy of Five (later Six) Nations. After the War of 1812, settlers arrived and Hamilton incorporated in 1846. The city was situated near the limestone in the Niagara Escarpment, the coal from Appalachia and the iron ore in the Canadian Shield. The two World Wars spiked the demand for Hamilton's production of steel, arms, munitions and textiles.

Hamilton has a variety of nicknames that relate to its history as a major Canadian industrial centre and the site of Canada's two principal steel-producing companies: Dofasco (now ArcelorMittal) and Stelco (now U.S. Steel). The City of Hamilton has been called Ambitious City, Steeltown, the Hammer, Hammertown and the Lunchbucket City. However, heavy industry is no longer Hamilton's largest employer. Today, health care, education, government, services and technology sectors are Hamilton's emerging industries.

Recently Hamilton launched its "Setting Sail" strategy for the redevelopment of the city waterfront. As new commercial operations, condo developments, hotels and cultural spaces are unveiled, Hamilton hopes to rebrand itself as The Bay City.

In 2012, Hamilton hosted special events such as the 8th Annual Food and Drink Fest, the 2nd Annual Hispanic Heritage Week and the "Hamilton Makes Steel" exhibit presented by the Hamilton Museum of Steam and Technology.

Hamilton has summer highs of plus 25.03 degrees Celsius, winter lows of minus 8.33 degrees Celsius, and an average rainfall just over 764 mm per year.

Rankings

- In fDi's North American Cities of the Future 2009/10 survey, Hamilton was ranked #3 in North America in the large cities (populations between 500,000 and 1 million) category for its quality of life. Nearly 400 North American cities were ranked in six categories: economic potential, human resources, cost effectiveness, quality of life, infrastructure and friendliness. *Foreign Direct Investment (fDi), "North American Cities of the Future 2009/10 survey," April 21st, 2009*
- Hamilton was ranked #8 out of 27 Canadian cities for sustainable transportation initiatives in the 2008 GreenApple SMART Transportation Ranking Report. Cities are ranked on 17 indicators in four policy categories: air quality, public policy, transport policy and technology adoption. Hamilton's award-winning policies included trip reduction programs, promotion of sustainable transportation options, use of hybrid vehicles and an anti-idling campaign. Victoria, Vancouver and Ottawa-Gatineau were the Top 3 respectively. *Appleton Charitable Foundation, GreenApple Canada 2008: SMART Transportation Ranking Report," released November 13, 2008*
- Hamilton was selected as having some of the best pollution prevention policies in Canada. The 2008 Canadian Council of Ministers of the Environment (CCME) Pollution Prevention Awards recognized Hamilton in the Greenhouse Gases Reduction category. Additional winners were Airdrie (AB), Markham (ON) and Toronto (ON). *Canadian Council of Ministers of the Environment (CCME) Pollution Prevention (P2) Award: Hamilton Renewable Power Inc. (HRP Inc.), announced June 11, 2008*

PROFILES / Hamilton, Ontario

Population Growth and Density

Area	Population in 2001	Population in 2006	Population in 2011	Population Change 2001–2006	Population Change 2006–2011	Land Area (sq. km)	Population Density per sq. km
Hamilton	490,268	504,559	519,949	0.0	3.1	1,117.23	465.4
Ontario	11,410,046	12,160,282	12,851,821	6.6	5.7	908,607.67	14.1
Canada	30,007,094	31,612,897	33,476,688	5.4	5.9	8,965,121.42	3.7

Source: Statistics Canada. 2012. Census Profile. 2011 Census. Statistics Canada Catalogue no. 98-316-XWE. Ottawa. Released October 24 2012. http://www12.statcan.gc.ca/census-recensement/2011/dp-pd/prof/index.cfm?Lang=E;
Statistics Canada 2007. 2006 Community Profiles. 2006 Census. Statistics Canada Catalogue no. 92-591-XWE. Ottawa. Released March 13 2007. http://www12.statcan.ca/census-recensement/2006/dp-pd/prof/92-591/index.cfm?Lang=E

Gender

Area	Males	Females
Number		
Hamilton	253,775	266,175
Ontario	6,263,140	6,588,685
Canada	16,414,225	17,062,460
Percent of Population		
Hamilton	48.8	51.2
Ontario	48.7	51.3
Canada	49.0	51.0

Source: Statistics Canada. 2012. Census Profile. 2011 Census. Statistics Canada Catalogue no. 98-316-XWE. Ottawa. Released October 24 2012. http://www12.statcan.gc.ca/census-recensement/2011/dp-pd/prof/index.cfm?Lang=E

Marital Status

Area	Married[1]	Living Common-law	Single[2]	Separated	Divorced	Widowed
Number						
Total						
Hamilton	205,725	32,600	125,895	14,380	27,285	28,350
Ontario	5,367,400	791,210	2,985,020	319,805	593,730	613,880
Canada	12,941,960	3,142,525	7,816,045	698,240	1,686,035	1,584,530
Males						
Hamilton	102,750	16,270	68,010	6,150	10,890	5,540
Ontario	2,681,320	397,620	1,583,760	133,790	231,160	117,980
Canada	6,470,300	1,575,495	4,206,320	299,655	680,415	310,940
Females						
Hamilton	102,975	16,330	57,885	8,225	16,400	22,800
Ontario	2,686,075	393,590	1,401,260	186,015	362,570	495,905
Canada	6,471,660	1,567,035	3,609,730	398,585	1,005,620	1,273,590
Percent of Population						
Total						
Hamilton	47.4	7.5	29.0	3.3	6.3	6.5
Ontario	50.3	7.4	28.0	3.0	5.6	5.8
Canada	46.4	11.3	28.0	2.5	6.0	5.7
Males						
Hamilton	49.0	7.8	32.4	2.9	5.2	2.6
Ontario	52.1	7.7	30.8	2.6	4.5	2.3
Canada	47.8	11.6	31.1	2.2	5.0	2.3
Females						
Hamilton	45.8	7.3	25.8	3.7	7.3	10.2
Ontario	48.6	7.1	25.4	3.4	6.6	9.0
Canada	45.2	10.9	25.2	2.8	7.0	8.9

Note: (1) and not separated, (2) never legally married
Source: Statistics Canada. 2012. Census Profile. 2011 Census. Statistics Canada Catalogue no. 98-316-XWE. Ottawa. Released October 24 2012. http://www12.statcan.gc.ca/census-recensement/2011/dp-pd/prof/index.cfm?Lang=E

Age Characteristics: 0 to 49 Years

Area	0 to 4 Years	5 to 9 Years	10 to 14 Years	15 to 19 Years	20 to 24 Years	25 to 29 Years	30 to 34 Years	35 to 39 Years	40 to 44 Years	45 to 49 Years
					Number					
					Total					
Hamilton	27,430	27,995	30,290	36,200	36,375	33,195	30,905	31,370	35,610	41,890
Ontario	704,260	712,755	763,755	863,635	852,910	815,120	800,365	844,335	924,075	1,055,880
Canada	1,877,095	1,809,895	1,920,355	2,178,135	2,187,450	2,169,590	2,162,905	2,173,930	2,324,875	2,675,130
					Males					
Hamilton	14,115	14,370	15,685	18,690	18,515	16,460	14,960	15,165	17,435	20,665
Ontario	360,590	365,290	391,630	443,680	432,490	400,045	383,340	405,845	447,920	517,510
Canada	961,150	925,965	983,995	1,115,845	1,108,775	1,077,275	1,058,810	1,064,200	1,141,720	1,318,715
					Females					
Hamilton	13,320	13,630	14,610	17,515	17,855	16,735	15,940	16,200	18,175	21,225
Ontario	343,670	347,465	372,125	419,950	420,415	415,075	417,030	438,485	476,155	538,370
Canada	915,945	883,935	936,360	1,062,295	1,078,670	1,092,315	1,104,095	1,109,735	1,183,155	1,356,420
					Percent of Population					
					Total					
Hamilton	5.3	5.4	5.8	7.0	7.0	6.4	5.9	6.0	6.8	8.1
Ontario	5.5	5.5	5.9	6.7	6.6	6.3	6.2	6.6	7.2	8.2
Canada	5.6	5.4	5.7	6.5	6.5	6.5	6.5	6.5	6.9	8.0
					Males					
Hamilton	5.6	5.7	6.2	7.4	7.3	6.5	5.9	6.0	6.9	8.1
Ontario	5.8	5.8	6.3	7.1	6.9	6.4	6.1	6.5	7.2	8.3
Canada	5.9	5.6	6.0	6.8	6.8	6.6	6.5	6.5	7.0	8.0
					Females					
Hamilton	5.0	5.1	5.5	6.6	6.7	6.3	6.0	6.1	6.8	8.0
Ontario	5.2	5.3	5.6	6.4	6.4	6.3	6.3	6.7	7.2	8.2
Canada	5.4	5.2	5.5	6.2	6.3	6.4	6.5	6.5	6.9	7.9

Source: Statistics Canada. 2012. Census Profile. 2011 Census. Statistics Canada Catalogue no. 98-316-XWE. Ottawa. Released October 24 2012.
http://www12.statcan.gc.ca/census-recensement/2011/dp-pd/prof/index.cfm?Lang=E

Age Characteristics: 50 Years and Over, and Median Age

Area	50 to 54 Years	55 to 59 Years	60 to 64 Years	65 to 69 Years	70 to 74 Years	75 to 79 Years	80 to 84 Years	85 Years and Over	Median Age
					Number				
					Total				
Hamilton	40,875	35,430	30,810	22,930	18,455	15,675	12,635	11,880	40.9
Ontario	1,006,140	864,620	765,655	563,485	440,780	356,150	271,510	246,400	40.4
Canada	2,658,965	2,340,635	2,052,670	1,521,715	1,153,065	922,700	702,070	645,515	40.6
					Males				
Hamilton	20,200	17,120	14,840	10,995	8,645	6,860	5,140	3,925	39.7
Ontario	492,560	418,755	370,370	270,875	206,350	161,345	113,620	80,925	39.4
Canada	1,309,030	1,147,300	1,002,690	738,010	543,435	417,945	291,085	208,300	39.6
					Females				
Hamilton	20,680	18,305	15,970	11,935	9,805	8,815	7,495	7,955	42.0
Ontario	513,580	445,865	395,275	292,610	234,435	194,805	157,890	165,475	41.3
Canada	1,349,940	1,193,335	1,049,985	783,705	609,630	504,755	410,985	437,215	41.5
					Percent of Population				
					Total				
Hamilton	7.9	6.8	5.9	4.4	3.5	3.0	2.4	2.3	—
Ontario	7.8	6.7	6.0	4.4	3.4	2.8	2.1	1.9	—
Canada	7.9	7.0	6.1	4.5	3.4	2.8	2.1	1.9	—
					Males				
Hamilton	8.0	6.7	5.8	4.3	3.4	2.7	2.0	1.5	—
Ontario	7.9	6.7	5.9	4.3	3.3	2.6	1.8	1.3	—
Canada	8.0	7.0	6.1	4.5	3.3	2.5	1.8	1.3	—
					Females				
Hamilton	7.8	6.9	6.0	4.5	3.7	3.3	2.8	3.0	—
Ontario	7.8	6.8	6.0	4.4	3.6	3.0	2.4	2.5	—
Canada	7.9	7.0	6.2	4.6	3.6	3.0	2.4	2.6	—

Source: Statistics Canada. 2012. Census Profile. 2011 Census. Statistics Canada Catalogue no. 98-316-XWE. Ottawa. Released October 24 2012.
http://www12.statcan.gc.ca/census-recensement/2011/dp-pd/prof/index.cfm?Lang=E

PROFILES / Hamilton, Ontario

Private Households by Household Size

Area	1 Person	2 Persons	3 Persons	4 Persons	5 Persons	6 or More Persons	Average Number of Persons in Private Households
			Households				
Hamilton	56,930	65,185	32,465	30,865	12,035	6,325	2.5
Ontario	1,230,975	1,584,415	803,030	783,925	310,860	174,305	2.6
Canada	3,673,310	4,544,820	2,081,900	1,903,300	724,405	392,885	2.5
			Percent of Households				
Hamilton	27.9	32.0	15.9	15.1	5.9	3.1	–
Ontario	25.2	32.4	16.4	16.0	6.4	3.6	–
Canada	27.6	34.1	15.6	14.3	5.4	2.9	–

Source: Statistics Canada. 2012. Census Profile. 2011 Census. Statistics Canada Catalogue no. 98-316-XWE. Ottawa. Released October 24 2012.
http://www12.statcan.gc.ca/census-recensement/2011/dp-pd/prof/index.cfm?Lang=E

Dwelling Type

Area	Single-detached House	Semi-detached House	Row House	Apartment: Building with Five or More Storeys	Apartment: Building with Fewer Than Five Storeys	Duplex Apartment	Movable Dwelling	Other Single-attached House
				Number				
Hamilton	118,105	6,330	21,440	33,145	17,660	6,325	370	440
Ontario	2,718,880	279,470	415,225	789,970	498,160	160,460	15,800	9,540
Canada	7,329,150	646,245	791,600	1,234,770	2,397,550	704,485	183,510	33,310
				Percent of Dwellings				
Hamilton	58.0	3.1	10.5	16.3	8.7	3.1	0.2	0.2
Ontario	55.6	5.7	8.5	16.2	10.2	3.3	0.3	0.2
Canada	55.0	4.9	5.9	9.3	18.0	5.3	1.4	0.3

Source: Statistics Canada. 2012. Census Profile. 2011 Census. Statistics Canada Catalogue no. 98-316-XWE. Ottawa. Released October 24 2012.
http://www12.statcan.gc.ca/census-recensement/2011/dp-pd/prof/index.cfm?Lang=E

Shelter Costs

	Owned Dwellings					Rented Dwellings		
Area	Number	Median Value[1] ($)	Average Value[1] ($)	Median Monthly Costs[2] ($)	Average Monthly Costs[2] ($)	Number	Median Monthly Costs[3] ($)	Average Monthly Costs[3] ($)
Hamilton	138,770	275,620	308,307	1,089	1,197	64,425	750	770
Ontario	3,446,650	300,862	367,428	1,163	1,284	1,385,535	892	926
Canada	9,013,410	280,552	345,182	978	1,141	4,060,385	784	848

Note: All figures cover non-farm, non-reserve private dwellings; (1) Refers to the dollar amount expected by the owner if the dwelling were to be sold; (2) Includes all shelter expenses paid by households that own their dwellings, such as the mortgage payment and the costs of electricity, heat, water and other municipal services, property taxes and condominium fees; (3) Includes all shelter expenses paid by households that rent their dwellings, such as the monthly rent and the costs of electricity, heat and municipal services.
Source: Statistics Canada. 2013. 2011 National Household Survey. Statistics Canada Catalogue no. 99-004-XWE. Ottawa. Released September 11, 2013.

Occupied Private Dwellings by Period of Construction

Area	1960 or Before	1961 to 1980	1981 to 1990	1991 to 2000	2001 to 2005	2006 to 2011
			Number			
Hamilton	78,360	59,660	25,675	19,895	10,285	9,935
Ontario	1,330,235	1,420,570	763,430	609,310	414,795	348,310
Canada	3,273,105	4,152,715	2,112,110	1,707,880	1,031,020	1,042,430
			Percent of Dwellings			
Hamilton	38.4	29.3	12.6	9.8	5.0	4.9
Ontario	27.2	29.1	15.6	12.5	8.5	7.1
Canada	24.6	31.2	15.9	12.8	7.7	7.8

Note: Figures cover non-farm, non-reserve private dwellings and includes data up to May 10, 2011.
Source: Statistics Canada. 2013. 2011 National Household Survey. Statistics Canada Catalogue no. 99-004-XWE. Ottawa. Released September 11, 2013.

PROFILES / Hamilton, Ontario

Educational Attainment

Area	No Certificate, Diploma or Degree	High School Diploma or Equivalent[1]	Apprenticeship or Trades Certificate or Diploma[2]	College, CÉGEP or Other Non-University Certificate or Diploma	University Certificate or Diploma Below the Bachelor Level[3]	Bachelor's Degree	University Certificate, Diploma or Degree Above Bachelor Level[4]
				Number			
				Total			
Hamilton	92,385	115,720	36,255	88,785	14,690	45,595	30,625
Ontario	1,954,520	2,801,805	771,140	2,070,875	427,150	1,515,075	933,100
Canada	5,485,400	6,968,935	2,950,685	4,970,020	1,200,130	3,634,425	2,049,930
				Males			
Hamilton	44,225	56,790	24,410	37,900	6,645	20,165	15,065
Ontario	957,040	1,337,055	520,390	894,235	193,355	692,345	470,290
Canada	2,742,875	3,305,415	1,928,970	2,118,430	513,235	1,643,080	1,043,350
				Females			
Hamilton	48,155	58,925	11,845	50,885	8,040	25,430	15,560
Ontario	997,475	1,464,755	250,750	1,176,640	233,790	822,730	462,805
Canada	2,742,520	3,663,515	1,021,715	2,851,595	686,890	1,991,345	1,006,585
				Percent of Population			
				Total			
Hamilton	21.8	27.3	8.5	20.9	3.5	10.8	7.2
Ontario	18.7	26.8	7.4	19.8	4.1	14.5	8.9
Canada	20.1	25.6	10.8	18.2	4.4	13.3	7.5
				Males			
Hamilton	21.6	27.7	11.9	18.5	3.2	9.8	7.3
Ontario	18.9	26.4	10.3	17.7	3.8	13.7	9.3
Canada	20.6	24.9	14.5	15.9	3.9	12.4	7.8
				Females			
Hamilton	22.0	26.9	5.4	23.3	3.7	11.6	7.1
Ontario	18.4	27.1	4.6	21.8	4.3	15.2	8.6
Canada	19.6	26.2	7.3	20.4	4.9	14.3	7.2

Note: Figures cover total population aged 15 years and over by highest certificate, diploma or degree; (1) Includes persons who have graduated from a secondary school or equivalent. It excludes persons with a postsecondary certificate, diploma or degree; (2) Includes Registered Apprenticeship certificates (including Certificate of Qualification, Journeyperson's designation) and other trades certificates or diplomas such as pre-employment or vocational certificates and diplomas from brief trade programs completed at community colleges, institutes of technology, vocational centres, and similar institutions; (3) Comparisons with other data sources suggest that the category 'University certificate or diploma below the bachelor's level' was over-reported in the NHS. This category likely includes some responses that are actually college certificates or diplomas, bachelor's degrees or other types of education (e.g., university transfer programs, bachelor's programs completed in other countries, incomplete bachelor's programs, non-university professional designations). We recommend users interpret the results for the 'University certificate or diploma below the bachelor's level' category with caution; (4) 'University certificate or diploma above bachelor level' includes the categories: 'Degree in medicine, dentistry, veterinary medicine or optometry,' 'Master's degree' and 'Earned doctorate.'
Source: Statistics Canada. 2013. 2011 National Household Survey. Statistics Canada Catalogue no. 99-004-XWE. Ottawa. Released September 11, 2013.

Household Income Distribution

Area	Less than $10,000	$10,000 to $19,999	$20,000 to $29,999	$30,000 to $39,999	$40,000 to $49,999	$50,000 to $59,999	$60,000 to $79,999	$80,000 to $99,999	$100,000 to $124,999	$125,000 to $149,999	$150,000 and Over
						Households					
Hamilton	8,745	18,680	19,685	19,115	18,845	16,380	27,605	22,790	19,125	12,560	20,285
Ontario	201,780	354,530	405,725	425,410	425,720	398,705	680,850	552,660	497,970	331,460	611,840
Canada	626,705	1,141,945	1,193,925	1,271,675	1,206,800	1,102,120	1,865,280	1,458,240	1,260,770	802,555	1,389,240
						Percent of Households					
Hamilton	4.3	9.2	9.7	9.4	9.2	8.0	13.5	11.2	9.4	6.2	10.0
Ontario	4.1	7.3	8.3	8.7	8.7	8.2	13.9	11.3	10.2	6.8	12.5
Canada	4.7	8.6	9.0	9.5	9.1	8.3	14.0	10.9	9.5	6.0	10.4

Note: Household income is the sum of the total incomes of all members of that household. Total income refers to monetary receipts from certain sources, before income taxes and deductions, during calendar year 2010.
Source: Statistics Canada. 2013. 2011 National Household Survey. Statistics Canada Catalogue no. 99-004-XWE. Ottawa. Released September 11, 2013.

Median and Average Household and Economic Family Income

Area	Median Household Income ($)	Average Household Income ($)	Median After-tax Household Income ($)	Average After-tax Household Income ($)	Median Economic Family Income ($)	Average Economic Family Income ($)	Median After-tax Economic Family Income ($)	Average After-tax Economic Family Income ($)
Hamilton	60,259	76,742	53,974	65,113	77,497	92,240	68,421	77,967
Ontario	66,358	85,772	58,717	71,523	80,987	100,152	71,128	83,322
Canada	61,072	79,102	54,089	66,149	76,511	94,125	67,044	78,517

Note: Figures cover household and economic familiy income in 2010. A household is defined as a person or a group of persons (other than foreign residents) who occupy the same private dwelling and do not have a usual place of residence elsewhere in Canada. Every person is a member of one and only one household. An economic family is defined as a group of two or more persons who live in the same dwelling and are related to each other by blood, marriage, common-law, adoption or a foster relationship. A couple may be of opposite or same sex.
Source: Statistics Canada. 2013. 2011 National Household Survey. Statistics Canada Catalogue no. 99-004-XWE. Ottawa. Released September 11, 2013.

Individual Income Distribution

Area	Less than $10,000	$10,000 to $19,999	$20,000 to $29,999	$30,000 to $39,999	$40,000 to $49,999	$50,000 to $59,999	$60,000 to $79,999	$80,000 to $99,999	$100,000 to $124,999	$125,000 and Over
					Number					
					Total					
Hamilton	70,525	74,150	59,430	48,140	41,055	30,020	37,755	21,585	9,170	9,580
Ontario	1,780,355	1,748,060	1,361,710	1,136,730	980,790	746,360	964,280	574,710	293,865	330,285
Canada	4,492,040	4,835,710	3,670,020	3,180,360	2,603,520	1,921,650	2,437,440	1,302,045	693,580	782,135
					Males					
Hamilton	31,490	28,670	24,940	22,050	20,655	17,000	23,820	12,795	6,455	7,385
Ontario	781,095	669,815	580,990	535,255	491,125	407,005	569,205	341,160	201,125	244,500
Canada	1,936,365	1,864,880	1,588,260	1,522,190	1,333,510	1,079,780	1,473,145	823,720	492,905	599,905
					Females					
Hamilton	39,025	45,485	34,490	26,090	20,400	13,025	13,935	8,795	2,710	2,195
Ontario	999,265	1,078,245	780,720	601,475	489,665	339,360	395,075	233,550	92,740	85,790
Canada	2,555,675	2,970,825	2,081,760	1,658,170	1,270,010	841,870	964,300	478,330	200,680	182,230
					Percent of Population					
					Total					
Hamilton	17.6	18.5	14.8	12.0	10.2	7.5	9.4	5.4	2.3	2.4
Ontario	18.0	17.6	13.7	11.5	9.9	7.5	9.7	5.8	3.0	3.3
Canada	17.3	18.7	14.2	12.3	10.0	7.4	9.4	5.0	2.7	3.0
					Males					
Hamilton	16.1	14.7	12.8	11.3	10.6	8.7	12.2	6.6	3.3	3.8
Ontario	16.2	13.9	12.1	11.1	10.2	8.4	11.8	7.1	4.2	5.1
Canada	15.2	14.7	12.5	12.0	10.5	8.5	11.6	6.5	3.9	4.7
					Females					
Hamilton	18.9	22.1	16.7	12.7	9.9	6.3	6.8	4.3	1.3	1.1
Ontario	19.6	21.2	15.3	11.8	9.6	6.7	7.8	4.6	1.8	1.7
Canada	19.4	22.5	15.8	12.6	9.6	6.4	7.3	3.6	1.5	1.4

Note: Figures cover individuals aged 15 years and over with income. Income refers to monetary receipts from certain sources, before income taxes and deductions, during calendar year 2010.
Source: Statistics Canada. 2013. 2011 National Household Survey. Statistics Canada Catalogue no. 99-004-XWE. Ottawa. Released September 11, 2013.

Labour Force Status

Area	In the Labour Force - All	Employed	Unemployed	Not in the Labour Force
		Number		
		Total		
Hamilton	266,200	243,075	23,120	157,860
Ontario	6,864,990	6,297,005	567,985	3,608,685
Canada	17,990,080	16,595,035	1,395,045	9,269,445
		Males		
Hamilton	137,550	124,960	12,595	67,660
Ontario	3,542,030	3,249,165	292,865	1,522,690
Canada	9,388,570	8,634,310	754,255	3,906,785
		Females		
Hamilton	128,645	118,120	10,525	90,195
Ontario	3,322,955	3,047,840	275,120	2,085,990
Canada	8,601,515	7,960,725	640,790	5,362,660
		Percent of Labour Force		
		Total		
Hamilton	62.8	57.3	8.7	37.2
Ontario	65.5	60.1	8.3	34.5
Canada	66.0	60.9	7.8	34.0
		Males		
Hamilton	67.0	60.9	9.2	33.0
Ontario	69.9	64.2	8.3	30.1
Canada	70.6	64.9	8.0	29.4
		Females		
Hamilton	58.8	54.0	8.2	41.2
Ontario	61.4	56.3	8.3	38.6
Canada	61.6	57.0	7.4	38.4

Note: Figures are based on total population 15 years and over
Source: Statistics Canada. 2013. 2011 National Household Survey. Statistics Canada Catalogue no. 99-004-XWE. Ottawa. Released September 11, 2013.

PROFILES / Hamilton, Ontario

Labour Force by Industry (NAICS Codes 11–52)

Area	Agriculture, forestry, fishing & hunting	Mining, quarrying, & oil & gas extraction	Utilities	Construction	Manufacturing	Wholesale Trade	Retail Trade	Transportation & warehousing	Information & cultural industries	Finance & insurance
					Number					
					Total					
Hamilton	2,900	315	1,630	17,405	31,610	11,615	30,315	11,230	4,980	10,815
Ontario	101,280	29,985	57,035	417,900	697,565	305,030	751,200	307,405	178,720	364,415
Canada	437,650	261,050	149,940	1,215,380	1,619,295	733,445	2,031,665	827,780	420,830	767,960
					Males					
Hamilton	1,640	250	1,300	15,450	24,400	8,350	13,015	8,350	2,740	3,855
Ontario	66,485	25,650	42,685	369,300	493,305	197,770	344,480	225,245	98,835	153,125
Canada	307,370	211,690	110,765	1,068,710	1,167,680	494,545	933,850	617,305	235,875	296,995
					Females					
Hamilton	1,265	65	330	1,960	7,205	3,265	17,300	2,885	2,240	6,960
Ontario	34,800	4,340	14,350	48,595	204,260	107,260	406,720	82,160	79,885	211,290
Canada	130,285	49,360	39,175	146,670	451,615	238,900	1,097,820	210,475	184,955	470,960
					Percent of Labour Force					
					Total					
Hamilton	1.1	0.1	0.6	6.7	12.2	4.5	11.7	4.3	1.9	4.2
Ontario	1.5	0.4	0.9	6.3	10.4	4.6	11.2	4.6	2.7	5.5
Canada	2.5	1.5	0.9	6.9	9.2	4.2	11.6	4.7	2.4	4.4
					Males					
Hamilton	1.2	0.2	1.0	11.5	18.2	6.2	9.7	6.2	2.0	2.9
Ontario	1.9	0.7	1.2	10.7	14.3	5.7	10.0	6.5	2.9	4.4
Canada	3.3	2.3	1.2	11.6	12.7	5.4	10.2	6.7	2.6	3.2
					Females					
Hamilton	1.0	0.1	0.3	1.6	5.8	2.6	13.8	2.3	1.8	5.6
Ontario	1.1	0.1	0.4	1.5	6.3	3.3	12.6	2.5	2.5	6.5
Canada	1.6	0.6	0.5	1.7	5.4	2.8	13.1	2.5	2.2	5.6

Note: Figures are based on total experienced labour force 15 years and over. Experienced labour force refers to persons who, during the week of Sunday, May 1 to Saturday, May 7, 2011, were employed and the unemployed who had last worked for pay or in self-employment in either 2010 or 2011.
Source: Statistics Canada. 2013. 2011 National Household Survey. Statistics Canada Catalogue no. 99-004-XWE. Ottawa. Released September 11, 2013.

Labour Force by Industry (NAICS Codes 53–91)

Area	Real estate & rental & leasing	Profess., scientific & tech. services	Mgmt of companies & enterprises	Admin. & support, waste mgmt & remed. services	Educational services	Health care & social assistance	Arts, entertain. & recreation	Accomm. & food services	Other services (except public admin.)	Public admin.
					Number					
					Total					
Hamilton	4,735	14,635	255	12,820	24,160	33,635	4,440	15,760	12,355	13,270
Ontario	133,980	511,020	6,525	309,630	499,690	692,130	144,065	417,675	296,340	458,665
Canada	321,895	1,240,850	17,460	728,330	1,301,435	1,949,650	363,405	1,130,750	807,800	1,261,050
					Males					
Hamilton	2,535	7,825	130	7,835	8,010	6,020	2,430	6,480	6,000	7,170
Ontario	72,835	281,420	3,540	172,475	162,765	120,165	75,035	177,240	133,795	236,655
Canada	179,090	688,625	9,380	411,250	424,915	349,430	188,270	469,990	372,940	652,510
					Females					
Hamilton	2,200	6,810	125	4,990	16,150	27,620	2,005	9,285	6,350	6,095
Ontario	61,145	229,600	2,990	137,155	336,925	571,965	69,030	240,430	162,550	222,015
Canada	142,805	552,225	8,075	317,085	876,515	1,600,220	175,135	660,760	434,865	608,535
					Percent of Labour Force					
					Total					
Hamilton	1.8	5.7	0.1	5.0	9.3	13.0	1.7	6.1	4.8	5.1
Ontario	2.0	7.6	0.1	4.6	7.5	10.4	2.2	6.3	4.4	6.9
Canada	1.8	7.1	0.1	4.1	7.4	11.1	2.1	6.4	4.6	7.2
					Males					
Hamilton	1.9	5.8	0.1	5.9	6.0	4.5	1.8	4.8	4.5	5.4
Ontario	2.1	8.2	0.1	5.0	4.7	3.5	2.2	5.1	3.9	6.9
Canada	1.9	7.5	0.1	4.5	4.6	3.8	2.0	5.1	4.1	7.1
					Females					
Hamilton	1.8	5.4	0.1	4.0	12.9	22.1	1.6	7.4	5.1	4.9
Ontario	1.9	7.1	0.1	4.2	10.4	17.7	2.1	7.4	5.0	6.9
Canada	1.7	6.6	0.1	3.8	10.4	19.1	2.1	7.9	5.2	7.2

Note: Figures are based on total experienced labour force 15 years and over. Experienced labour force refers to persons who, during the week of Sunday, May 1 to Saturday, May 7, 2011, were employed and the unemployed who had last worked for pay or in self-employment in either 2010 or 2011.
Source: Statistics Canada. 2013. 2011 National Household Survey. Statistics Canada Catalogue no. 99-004-XWE. Ottawa. Released September 11, 2013.

PROFILES / Hamilton, Ontario

Occupation

Area	Mgmt	Business, Finance & Admin.	Natural/ Applied Sciences & Related	Health	Education, Law & Social, Community & Government Services	Art, Culture, Recreation & Sport	Sales & Service	Trades, Transport & Equip. Operators & Related	Natural Resources, Agri. & Related Production	Mfg & Utilities
\multicolumn{11}{c	}{Number — Total}
Hamilton	25,455	39,350	14,675	19,565	33,110	6,695	62,850	38,260	4,090	14,835
Ontario	770,580	1,138,330	494,500	392,695	801,465	206,420	1,550,260	868,515	106,810	350,685
Canada	1,963,600	2,902,045	1,237,775	1,107,200	2,064,675	503,415	4,068,170	2,537,775	397,930	805,040
\multicolumn{11}{c	}{Males}
Hamilton	15,605	11,220	11,775	4,020	11,075	3,180	26,655	36,025	2,960	11,280
Ontario	474,655	352,505	384,345	78,330	264,570	96,055	673,880	812,280	82,610	233,565
Canada	1,229,460	854,190	966,355	217,520	676,550	232,535	1,745,705	2,385,615	318,945	564,300
\multicolumn{11}{c	}{Females}
Hamilton	9,850	28,130	2,905	15,545	22,035	3,515	36,195	2,230	1,125	3,555
Ontario	295,920	785,825	110,150	314,370	536,895	110,370	876,380	56,230	24,200	117,115
Canada	734,140	2,047,855	271,415	889,675	1,388,130	270,875	2,322,465	152,165	78,980	240,740
\multicolumn{11}{c	}{Percent of Labour Force — Total}
Hamilton	9.8	15.2	5.7	7.6	12.8	2.6	24.3	14.8	1.6	5.7
Ontario	11.5	17.0	7.4	5.9	12.0	3.1	23.2	13.0	1.6	5.2
Canada	11.2	16.5	7.0	6.3	11.7	2.9	23.1	14.4	2.3	4.6
\multicolumn{11}{c	}{Males}
Hamilton	11.7	8.4	8.8	3.0	8.3	2.4	19.9	26.9	2.2	8.4
Ontario	13.7	10.2	11.1	2.3	7.7	2.8	19.5	23.5	2.4	6.8
Canada	13.4	9.3	10.5	2.4	7.4	2.5	19.0	26.0	3.5	6.1
\multicolumn{11}{c	}{Females}
Hamilton	7.9	22.5	2.3	12.4	17.6	2.8	28.9	1.8	0.9	2.8
Ontario	9.2	24.3	3.4	9.7	16.6	3.4	27.2	1.7	0.7	3.6
Canada	8.7	24.4	3.2	10.6	16.5	3.2	27.7	1.8	0.9	2.9

Note: Figures are based on total experienced labour force 15 years and over
Source: Statistics Canada. 2013. 2011 National Household Survey. Statistics Canada Catalogue no. 99-004-XWE. Ottawa. Released September 11, 2013.

Place of Work Status

Area	Worked at Home	Worked Outside Canada	No Fixed Workplace Address	Worked at Usual Place
\multicolumn{5}{c	}{Number — Total}
Hamilton	14,045	845	26,345	201,850
Ontario	423,790	31,390	670,835	5,170,980
Canada	1,142,640	66,460	1,868,245	13,517,690
\multicolumn{5}{c	}{Males}
Hamilton	7,430	660	19,135	97,735
Ontario	216,900	21,150	486,560	2,524,555
Canada	582,150	47,355	1,400,485	6,604,325
\multicolumn{5}{c	}{Females}
Hamilton	6,615	185	7,210	104,110
Ontario	206,895	10,240	184,275	2,646,420
Canada	560,490	19,100	467,760	6,913,370
\multicolumn{5}{c	}{Percent of Labour Force — Total}
Hamilton	5.8	0.3	10.8	83.0
Ontario	6.7	0.5	10.7	82.1
Canada	6.9	0.4	11.3	81.5
\multicolumn{5}{c	}{Males}
Hamilton	5.9	0.5	15.3	78.2
Ontario	6.7	0.7	15.0	77.7
Canada	6.7	0.5	16.2	76.5
\multicolumn{5}{c	}{Females}
Hamilton	5.6	0.2	6.1	88.1
Ontario	6.8	0.3	6.0	86.8
Canada	7.0	0.2	5.9	86.8

Note: Figures are based on total employed labour force 15 years and over.
Source: Statistics Canada. 2013. 2011 National Household Survey. Statistics Canada Catalogue no. 99-004-XWE. Ottawa. Released September 11, 2013.

Mode of Transportation to Work

Area	Car; Truck; Van; as Driver	Car; Truck; Van; as Passenger	Public Transit	Walked	Bicycled	All Other Modes
			Number			
			Total			
Hamilton	174,405	16,075	22,480	11,230	1,810	2,190
Ontario	4,235,315	357,110	818,270	299,095	69,885	62,145
Canada	11,393,140	867,050	1,851,525	880,815	201,780	191,625
			Males			
Hamilton	93,455	7,140	9,095	4,685	1,350	1,150
Ontario	2,316,680	143,410	340,995	131,765	47,635	30,635
Canada	6,238,835	349,530	788,290	387,580	135,840	104,725
			Females			
Hamilton	80,955	8,935	13,380	6,555	455	1,045
Ontario	1,918,640	213,700	477,275	167,325	22,250	31,515
Canada	5,154,305	517,520	1,063,235	493,230	65,940	86,900
			Percent of Labour Force			
			Total			
Hamilton	76.4	7.0	9.9	4.9	0.8	1.0
Ontario	72.5	6.1	14.0	5.1	1.2	1.1
Canada	74.0	5.6	12.0	5.7	1.3	1.2
			Males			
Hamilton	80.0	6.1	7.8	4.0	1.2	1.0
Ontario	76.9	4.8	11.3	4.4	1.6	1.0
Canada	77.9	4.4	9.8	4.8	1.7	1.3
			Females			
Hamilton	72.7	8.0	12.0	5.9	0.4	0.9
Ontario	67.8	7.5	16.9	5.9	0.8	1.1
Canada	69.8	7.0	14.4	6.7	0.9	1.2

Note: Figures are based on total employed labour force 15 years and over.
Source: Statistics Canada. 2013. 2011 National Household Survey. Statistics Canada Catalogue no. 99-004-XWE. Ottawa. Released September 11, 2013.

Visible Minority Population Characteristics

Area	Total Minority	South Asian[1]	Chinese	Black	Filipino	Latin American	Arab	SE Asian[2]	West Asian[3]	Korean	Japanese	Multiple[4]
					Number							
					Total							
Hamilton	79,970	17,240	8,505	16,110	7,170	7,335	7,075	5,875	4,260	1,970	860	2,180
Ontario	3,279,565	965,990	629,140	539,205	275,380	172,560	151,645	137,875	122,530	78,290	29,085	96,735
Canada	6,264,750	1,567,400	1,324,750	945,665	619,310	381,280	380,620	312,075	206,840	161,130	87,270	171,935
					Males							
Hamilton	39,480	8,800	4,235	8,190	3,180	3,230	3,705	2,890	2,095	950	465	1,020
Ontario	1,582,480	484,355	301,575	251,295	116,825	83,205	79,620	67,645	62,515	38,045	13,345	46,765
Canada	3,043,010	790,755	632,325	453,005	268,885	186,355	203,485	154,035	105,620	77,165	38,270	83,335
					Females							
Hamilton	40,490	8,440	4,270	7,920	3,995	4,110	3,370	2,985	2,170	1,025	390	1,160
Ontario	1,697,085	481,635	327,570	287,915	158,555	89,360	72,025	70,230	60,010	40,250	15,740	49,970
Canada	3,221,745	776,650	692,420	492,660	350,425	194,925	177,140	158,045	101,220	83,965	48,990	88,600
					Percent of Population							
					Total							
Hamilton	15.7	3.4	1.7	3.2	1.4	1.4	1.4	1.2	0.8	0.4	0.2	0.4
Ontario	25.9	7.6	5.0	4.3	2.2	1.4	1.2	1.1	1.0	0.6	0.2	0.8
Canada	19.1	4.8	4.0	2.9	1.9	1.2	1.2	0.9	0.6	0.5	0.3	0.5
					Males							
Hamilton	15.8	3.5	1.7	3.3	1.3	1.3	1.5	1.2	0.8	0.4	0.2	0.4
Ontario	25.6	7.8	4.9	4.1	1.9	1.3	1.3	1.1	1.0	0.6	0.2	0.8
Canada	18.8	4.9	3.9	2.8	1.7	1.2	1.3	1.0	0.7	0.5	0.2	0.5
					Females							
Hamilton	15.6	3.2	1.6	3.0	1.5	1.6	1.3	1.1	0.8	0.4	0.2	0.4
Ontario	26.2	7.4	5.1	4.4	2.5	1.4	1.1	1.1	0.9	0.6	0.2	0.8
Canada	19.3	4.7	4.1	3.0	2.1	1.2	1.1	0.9	0.6	0.5	0.3	0.5

Note: The Employment Equity Act defines visible minorities as 'persons, other than Aboriginal peoples, who are non-Caucasian in race or non-white in colour'; (1) Includes 'East Indian,' 'Pakistani,' 'Sri Lankan,' etc.; (2) Includes 'Vietnamese,' 'Cambodian,' 'Malaysian,' 'Laotian,' etc.; (3) Includes 'Iranian,' 'Afghan,' etc.; (4) Includes respondents who reported more than one visible minority group by checking two or more mark-in circles, e.g., 'Black' and 'South Asian.'
Source: Statistics Canada. 2013. 2011 National Household Survey. Statistics Canada Catalogue no. 99-004-XWE. Ottawa. Released September 11, 2013.

PROFILES / Hamilton, Ontario

Aboriginal Population

Area	Aboriginal Identity[1]	First Nations (North American Indian) Single Identity[2]	Métis Single Identity	Inuk (Inuit) Single Identity	Multiple Aboriginal Identities[3]	Aboriginal Identities Not Included Elsewhere
			Number			
			Total			
Hamilton	10,320	7,960	1,780	50	230	310
Ontario	301,430	201,100	86,020	3,355	2,910	8,040
Canada	1,400,685	851,560	451,795	59,440	11,415	26,475
			Males			
Hamilton	4,775	3,720	760	0	140	115
Ontario	145,020	96,620	41,755	1,475	1,420	3,750
Canada	682,190	411,785	223,335	29,495	5,525	12,055
			Females			
Hamilton	5,545	4,240	1,015	10	90	190
Ontario	156,410	104,485	44,260	1,880	1,490	4,295
Canada	718,500	439,775	228,460	29,950	5,890	14,420
			Percent of Population			
			Total			
Hamilton	2.0	1.6	0.3	0.0	0.0	0.1
Ontario	2.4	1.6	0.7	0.0	0.0	0.1
Canada	4.3	2.6	1.4	0.2	0.0	0.1
			Males			
Hamilton	1.9	1.5	0.3	0.0	0.1	0.0
Ontario	2.3	1.6	0.7	0.0	0.0	0.1
Canada	4.2	2.5	1.4	0.2	0.0	0.1
			Females			
Hamilton	2.1	1.6	0.4	0.0	0.0	0.1
Ontario	2.4	1.6	0.7	0.0	0.0	0.1
Canada	4.3	2.6	1.4	0.2	0.0	0.1

Note: (1) Includes persons who reported being an Aboriginal person, that is, First Nations (North American Indian), Métis or Inuk (Inuit) and/or those who reported Registered or Treaty Indian status, that is registered under the Indian Act of Canada, and/or those who reported membership in a First Nation or Indian band. Aboriginal peoples of Canada are defined in the Constitution Act, 1982, section 35-2 as including the Indian, Inuit and Métis peoples of Canada; (2) Users should be aware that the estimates associated with this variable are more affected than most by the incomplete enumeration of certain Indian reserves and Indian settlements in the National Household Survey (NHS); (3) Includes persons who reported being any two or all three of the following: First Nations (North American Indian), Métis or Inuk (Inuit).
Source: Statistics Canada. 2013. 2011 National Household Survey. Statistics Canada Catalogue no. 99-004-XWE. Ottawa. Released September 11, 2013.

Ethnic Origin

Area	North American Aboriginal	Other North American	European	Caribbean	Latin, Central and South American	African	Asian	Oceania
				Number				
				Total				
Hamilton	15,840	127,025	384,730	10,540	9,605	10,930	58,575	725
Ontario	441,395	3,059,480	8,231,410	396,485	271,545	331,460	2,604,595	19,410
Canada	1,836,035	11,070,455	20,157,965	627,590	544,375	766,735	5,011,225	74,875
				Males				
Hamilton	7,520	62,790	187,820	5,215	4,355	5,365	29,140	420
Ontario	210,490	1,507,105	4,019,885	181,805	130,035	160,940	1,265,540	9,855
Canada	885,675	5,462,685	9,913,150	291,640	264,635	387,360	2,435,540	37,490
				Females				
Hamilton	8,320	64,240	196,910	5,330	5,250	5,565	29,435	310
Ontario	230,905	1,552,380	4,211,525	214,675	141,510	170,515	1,339,050	9,555
Canada	950,360	5,607,770	10,244,820	335,945	279,740	379,380	2,575,680	37,385
				Percent of Population				
				Total				
Hamilton	3.1	24.9	75.5	2.1	1.9	2.1	11.5	0.1
Ontario	3.5	24.2	65.1	3.1	2.1	2.6	20.6	0.2
Canada	5.6	33.7	61.4	1.9	1.7	2.3	15.3	0.2
				Males				
Hamilton	3.0	25.1	75.2	2.1	1.7	2.1	11.7	0.2
Ontario	3.4	24.4	65.0	2.9	2.1	2.6	20.5	0.2
Canada	5.5	33.8	61.3	1.8	1.6	2.4	15.1	0.2
				Females				
Hamilton	3.2	24.7	75.8	2.1	2.0	2.1	11.3	0.1
Ontario	3.6	24.0	65.1	3.3	2.2	2.6	20.7	0.1
Canada	5.7	33.6	61.4	2.0	1.7	2.3	15.4	0.2

Note: The sum of the ethnic groups in this table is greater than the total population estimate because a person may report more than one ethnic origin in the NHS.
Source: Statistics Canada. 2013. 2011 National Household Survey. Statistics Canada Catalogue no. 99-004-XWE. Ottawa. Released September 11, 2013.

Religion

Area	Buddhist	Christian	Hindu	Jewish	Muslim	Sikh	Traditional (Aboriginal) Spirituality	Other Religions	No Religious Affiliation
				Number Total					
Hamilton	4,635	344,625	3,910	3,335	19,025	4,260	450	2,705	126,700
Ontario	163,750	8,167,295	366,720	195,540	581,950	179,765	15,905	53,080	2,927,790
Canada	366,830	22,102,745	497,965	329,495	1,053,945	454,965	64,935	130,835	7,850,605
				Males					
Hamilton	2,140	161,670	1,970	1,710	9,905	2,175	130	1,240	68,845
Ontario	75,355	3,839,925	183,580	95,795	293,925	90,515	7,600	23,555	1,571,195
Canada	168,465	10,497,775	250,435	161,265	540,555	229,435	31,805	57,745	4,225,645
				Females					
Hamilton	2,495	182,955	1,940	1,620	9,120	2,090	315	1,460	57,845
Ontario	88,395	4,327,365	183,140	99,740	288,025	89,250	8,310	29,525	1,356,600
Canada	198,365	11,604,975	247,525	168,235	513,395	225,530	33,135	73,090	3,624,965
				Percent of Population Total					
Hamilton	0.9	67.6	0.8	0.7	3.7	0.8	0.1	0.5	24.9
Ontario	1.3	64.6	2.9	1.5	4.6	1.4	0.1	0.4	23.1
Canada	1.1	67.3	1.5	1.0	3.2	1.4	0.2	0.4	23.9
				Males					
Hamilton	0.9	64.7	0.8	0.7	4.0	0.9	0.1	0.5	27.6
Ontario	1.2	62.1	3.0	1.5	4.8	1.5	0.1	0.4	25.4
Canada	1.0	64.9	1.5	1.0	3.3	1.4	0.2	0.4	26.1
				Females					
Hamilton	1.0	70.4	0.7	0.6	3.5	0.8	0.1	0.6	22.3
Ontario	1.4	66.9	2.8	1.5	4.5	1.4	0.1	0.5	21.0
Canada	1.2	69.5	1.5	1.0	3.1	1.4	0.2	0.4	21.7

Note: Religion refers to the person's self-identification as having a connection or affiliation with any religious denomination, group, body, sect, cult or other religiously defined community or system of belief. Religion is not limited to formal membership in a religious organization or group. Persons without a religious connection or affiliation can self-identify as atheist, agnostic or humanist, or can provide another applicable response.
Source: Statistics Canada. 2013. 2011 National Household Survey. Statistics Canada Catalogue no. 99-004-XWE. Ottawa. Released September 11, 2013.

Religion—Christian Denominations

Area	Anglican	Baptist	Catholic	Christian Orthodox	Lutheran	Pentecostal	Presbyterian	United Church	Other Christian
				Number Total					
Hamilton	32,720	10,175	174,760	14,880	4,905	8,180	15,855	33,275	49,870
Ontario	774,560	244,650	3,976,610	297,710	163,460	213,945	319,585	952,465	1,224,300
Canada	1,631,845	635,840	12,810,705	550,690	478,185	478,705	472,385	2,007,610	3,036,780
				Males					
Hamilton	14,885	4,550	83,415	7,520	2,040	3,530	7,230	14,595	23,905
Ontario	355,175	112,285	1,895,940	145,825	75,225	94,955	148,535	435,255	576,730
Canada	752,945	293,905	6,167,290	270,205	221,525	217,850	218,955	912,545	1,442,550
				Females					
Hamilton	17,840	5,620	91,345	7,360	2,865	4,655	8,620	18,680	25,965
Ontario	419,390	132,370	2,080,665	151,885	88,230	118,990	171,050	517,210	647,570
Canada	878,900	341,940	6,643,415	280,485	256,660	260,850	253,430	1,095,065	1,594,230
				Percent of Population Total					
Hamilton	6.4	2.0	34.3	2.9	1.0	1.6	3.1	6.5	9.8
Ontario	6.1	1.9	31.4	2.4	1.3	1.7	2.5	7.5	9.7
Canada	5.0	1.9	39.0	1.7	1.5	1.5	1.4	6.1	9.2
				Males					
Hamilton	6.0	1.8	33.4	3.0	0.8	1.4	2.9	5.8	9.6
Ontario	5.7	1.8	30.7	2.4	1.2	1.5	2.4	7.0	9.3
Canada	4.7	1.8	38.2	1.7	1.4	1.3	1.4	5.6	8.9
				Females					
Hamilton	6.9	2.2	35.2	2.8	1.1	1.8	3.3	7.2	10.0
Ontario	6.5	2.0	32.2	2.3	1.4	1.8	2.6	8.0	10.0
Canada	5.3	2.0	39.8	1.7	1.5	1.6	1.5	6.6	9.6

Note: Religion refers to the person's self-identification as having a connection or affiliation with any religious denomination, group, body, sect, cult or other religiously defined community or system of belief. Religion is not limited to formal membership in a religious organization or group. Persons without a religious connection or affiliation can self-identify as atheist, agnostic or humanist, or can provide another applicable response.
Source: Statistics Canada. 2013. 2011 National Household Survey. Statistics Canada Catalogue no. 99-004-XWE. Ottawa. Released September 11, 2013.

PROFILES / Hamilton, Ontario

Immigrant Status and Period of Immigration

Area	Non-Immigrants[1]	Immigrants All	Before 1971	1971 to 1980	1981 to 1990	1991 to 2000	2001 to 2005	2006 to 2011	Non-Permanent Residents[3]
				Number					
				Total					
Hamilton	380,090	125,010	38,860	16,090	17,810	24,505	12,925	14,820	4,530
Ontario	8,906,000	3,611,365	723,030	464,380	538,285	866,220	518,405	501,060	134,425
Canada	25,720,175	6,775,765	1,261,055	870,775	949,890	1,539,050	992,070	1,162,915	356,385
				Males					
Hamilton	187,435	60,015	18,280	8,160	8,580	11,970	5,920	7,100	2,360
Ontario	4,410,240	1,706,385	341,820	217,990	258,095	408,270	245,850	234,360	64,825
Canada	12,753,235	3,231,370	605,430	416,670	454,570	724,905	474,545	555,245	178,515
				Females					
Hamilton	192,660	65,000	20,580	7,930	9,230	12,530	7,010	7,720	2,170
Ontario	4,495,765	1,904,985	381,210	246,390	280,190	457,950	272,550	266,695	69,600
Canada	12,966,935	3,544,400	655,625	454,105	495,325	814,145	517,530	607,670	177,870
				Percent of Population					
				Total					
Hamilton	74.6	24.5	7.6	3.2	3.5	4.8	2.5	2.9	0.9
Ontario	70.4	28.5	5.7	3.7	4.3	6.8	4.1	4.0	1.1
Canada	78.3	20.6	3.8	2.7	2.9	4.7	3.0	3.5	1.1
				Males					
Hamilton	75.0	24.0	7.3	3.3	3.4	4.8	2.4	2.8	0.9
Ontario	71.3	27.6	5.5	3.5	4.2	6.6	4.0	3.8	1.0
Canada	78.9	20.0	3.7	2.6	2.8	4.5	2.9	3.4	1.1
				Females					
Hamilton	74.1	25.0	7.9	3.1	3.6	4.8	2.7	3.0	0.8
Ontario	69.5	29.4	5.9	3.8	4.3	7.1	4.2	4.1	1.1
Canada	77.7	21.2	3.9	2.7	3.0	4.9	3.1	3.6	1.1

Note: (1) Non-immigrant refers to a person who is a Canadian citizen by birth; (2) Immigrant refers to a person who is or has ever been a landed immigrant/permanent resident. This person has been granted the right to live in Canada permanently by immigration authorities. Some immigrants have resided in Canada for a number of years, while others have arrived recently. Some immigrants are Canadian citizens, while others are not. Most immigrants are born outside Canada, but a small number are born in Canada. In the 2011 National Household Survey, 'Immigrants' includes immigrants who landed in Canada prior to May 10, 2011; (3) Non-permanent resident refers to a person from another country who has a work or study permit, or who is a refugee claimant, and any non-Canadian-born family member living in Canada with them.
Source: Statistics Canada. 2013. 2011 National Household Survey. Statistics Canada Catalogue no. 99-004-XWE. Ottawa. Released September 11, 2013.

Mother Tongue

Area	English	French	Non-official Language	English & French	English & Non-official Language	French & Non-official Language	English, French & Non-official Language
			Number				
			Total				
Hamilton	378,590	6,765	118,420	1,055	7,545	625	175
Ontario	8,677,040	493,300	3,264,435	46,605	219,425	13,645	7,615
Canada	18,858,980	7,054,975	6,567,680	144,685	396,330	74,430	24,095
			Males				
Hamilton	186,285	3,120	56,945	490	3,725	310	85
Ontario	4,276,970	232,785	1,562,190	21,805	106,790	6,285	3,495
Canada	9,345,225	3,452,380	3,157,785	69,975	192,000	36,535	11,965
			Females				
Hamilton	192,300	3,640	61,475	565	3,820	315	95
Ontario	4,400,065	260,510	1,702,240	24,795	112,635	7,365	4,115
Canada	9,513,750	3,602,590	3,409,895	74,710	204,330	37,890	12,130
			Percent of Population				
			Total				
Hamilton	73.8	1.3	23.1	0.2	1.5	0.1	0.0
Ontario	68.2	3.9	25.7	0.4	1.7	0.1	0.1
Canada	56.9	21.3	19.8	0.4	1.2	0.2	0.1
			Males				
Hamilton	74.2	1.2	22.7	0.2	1.5	0.1	0.0
Ontario	68.9	3.7	25.2	0.4	1.7	0.1	0.1
Canada	57.5	21.2	19.4	0.4	1.2	0.2	0.1
			Females				
Hamilton	73.3	1.4	23.4	0.2	1.5	0.1	0.0
Ontario	67.6	4.0	26.1	0.4	1.7	0.1	0.1
Canada	56.4	21.4	20.2	0.4	1.2	0.2	0.1

Note: Figures cover total population excluding institutional residents.
Source: Statistics Canada. 2012. Census Profile. 2011 Census. Statistics Canada Catalogue no. 98-316-XWE. Ottawa. Released October 24 2012.
http://www12.statcan.gc.ca/census-recensement/2011/dp-pd/prof/index.cfm?Lang=E

Language Spoken Most Often at Home

Area	English	French	Non-official Language	English & French	English & Non-official Language	French & Non-official Language	English, French & Non-official Language
\multicolumn{8}{c}{Number}							
\multicolumn{8}{c}{Total}							
Hamilton	431,670	2,245	60,180	635	17,830	295	315
Ontario	10,044,810	284,115	1,827,870	37,955	509,105	6,370	11,845
Canada	21,457,075	6,827,865	3,673,865	131,205	875,135	109,700	46,330
\multicolumn{8}{c}{Males}							
Hamilton	211,815	1,005	28,845	320	8,675	145	140
Ontario	4,930,610	133,495	872,860	17,250	248,050	2,855	5,225
Canada	10,585,620	3,348,235	1,767,310	63,475	425,370	53,010	22,845
\multicolumn{8}{c}{Females}							
Hamilton	219,850	1,240	31,335	315	9,155	150	170
Ontario	5,114,200	150,620	955,010	20,705	261,055	3,520	6,620
Canada	10,871,455	3,479,625	1,906,555	67,730	449,765	56,690	23,485
\multicolumn{8}{c}{Percent of Population}							
\multicolumn{8}{c}{Total}							
Hamilton	84.1	0.4	11.7	0.1	3.5	0.1	0.1
Ontario	79.0	2.2	14.4	0.3	4.0	0.1	0.1
Canada	64.8	20.6	11.1	0.4	2.6	0.3	0.1
\multicolumn{8}{c}{Males}							
Hamilton	84.4	0.4	11.5	0.1	3.5	0.1	0.1
Ontario	79.4	2.1	14.1	0.3	4.0	0.0	0.1
Canada	65.1	20.6	10.9	0.4	2.6	0.3	0.1
\multicolumn{8}{c}{Females}							
Hamilton	83.8	0.5	12.0	0.1	3.5	0.1	0.1
Ontario	78.5	2.3	14.7	0.3	4.0	0.1	0.1
Canada	64.5	20.6	11.3	0.4	2.7	0.3	0.1

Note: Figures cover total population excluding institutional residents.
Source: Statistics Canada. 2012. Census Profile. 2011 Census. Statistics Canada Catalogue no. 98-316-XWE. Ottawa. Released October 24 2012.
http://www12.statcan.gc.ca/census-recensement/2011/dp-pd/prof/index.cfm?Lang=E

Knowledge of Official Languages

Area	English Only	French Only	English & French	Neither English nor French
\multicolumn{5}{c}{Number}				
\multicolumn{5}{c}{Total}				
Hamilton	475,350	360	28,495	8,960
Ontario	10,984,360	42,980	1,395,805	298,920
Canada	22,564,665	4,165,015	5,795,570	595,920
\multicolumn{5}{c}{Males}				
Hamilton	234,900	170	12,350	3,540
Ontario	5,445,050	18,805	627,725	118,765
Canada	11,222,185	1,925,340	2,876,560	241,790
\multicolumn{5}{c}{Females}				
Hamilton	240,455	195	16,145	5,425
Ontario	5,539,310	24,175	768,085	180,155
Canada	11,342,485	2,239,680	2,919,005	354,135
\multicolumn{5}{c}{Percent of Population}				
\multicolumn{5}{c}{Total}				
Hamilton	92.6	0.1	5.6	1.7
Ontario	86.3	0.3	11.0	2.3
Canada	68.1	12.6	17.5	1.8
\multicolumn{5}{c}{Males}				
Hamilton	93.6	0.1	4.9	1.4
Ontario	87.7	0.3	10.1	1.9
Canada	69.0	11.8	17.7	1.5
\multicolumn{5}{c}{Females}				
Hamilton	91.7	0.1	6.2	2.1
Ontario	85.1	0.4	11.8	2.8
Canada	67.3	13.3	17.3	2.1

Note: Figures cover total population excluding institutional residents.
Source: Statistics Canada. 2012. Census Profile. 2011 Census. Statistics Canada Catalogue no. 98-316-XWE. Ottawa. Released October 24 2012.
http://www12.statcan.gc.ca/census-recensement/2011/dp-pd/prof/index.cfm?Lang=E

Kelowna, British Columbia

Background

Kelowna is located on Okanagan Lake in the Okanagan Valley of British Columbia's southern interior. Kelowna is the largest city in the valley, with a population of 117,312 (2011). The city's name is Interior Salish and means "grizzly bear." Kelowna is surrounded by some of the best fruit-and-vegetable growing land in the world.

The nomadic tribes of the Okanagan Valley populated the Kelowna region prior to the late 1880s. The Federal Indian Act (1876) moved First Nations people out of Kelowna and into three nearby reserves. When Kelowna was incorporated in 1905, the town was a farming community with a population of 600 people. Kelowna's orchard boom began in the 1900s as irrigation systems were built throughout the region's semi-arid hillsides.

Today, Kelowna's downtown Cultural District is the former site of the Okanagan Fruit Packing industry. The city's library, four museums, community theatre, art gallery and centre for the arts are located in the award-winning district. Every year the city's cultural sector generates $143 million into the local economy.

Recently the city launched a community strategy, "Kelowna 2030: Greening Our Future," to promote sustainable transportation, increase affordable housing and protect sensitive ecosystems. In 2011, the City of Kelowna finished its $6.9-million expansion to Kelowna Y and also increased the availability of affordable housing with a $10-million supportive housing project.

The city's international airport is currently undergoing a multi-million expansion that will feature geothermal and thermal massing to reduce the airport's energy footprint.

In a recent national survey, 90% of Kelowna residents reported, "My city is a great place to live."

Kelowna has summer highs of plus 26.27 degrees Celsius, winter lows of minus 6.43 degrees Celsius, and an average rainfall just over 298 mm per year.

Rankings

- *Global News* ranked Kelowna as having one of the most satisfied municipal populations in Canada. Kelowna residents consistently rated municipal leadership and issues positively. Close to 6,900 Canadians were interviewed from the following areas: Metro Vancouver, Kelowna Area, Calgary, Edmonton, Regina, Saskatoon, Winnipeg, Toronto, Montreal, Halifax, Nova Scotia outside Halifax, New Brunswick and the rest of Canada. Across Canada, the top city issues were infrastructure and healthcare (tied for #1), the economy, and high taxes. *Global News/Ipsos Reid, "Canada Pulse 2011 survey," August 26 to September 1st, 2011*
- The Federation of Canadian Municipalities (FCM) ranked the City of Kelowna as one of Canada's most sustainable cities in 2009. The city has received the Distinguished Budget Presentation award every year since the annual award nominations were established in 2000. Criteria for Budget award: ability of budget to serve as a policy document, financial plan, operations guide and communications device. In 2010, Kelowna ranked #1 as an FCM Sustainable Community for Residential Development. FCM nominations are open to all municipal governments across Canada. *Federation of Canadian Municipalities, Sustainable Communities Awards, 2009-2010*

PROFILES / Kelowna, British Columbia

Population Growth and Density

Area	Population in 2001	Population in 2006	Population in 2011	Population Change 2001–2006	Population Change 2006–2011	Land Area (sq. km)	Population Density per sq. km
Kelowna	96,288	107,035	117,312	10.8	9.6	211.82	553.8
British Columbia	3,907,738	4,113,487	4,400,057	5.3	7.0	922,509.29	4.8
Canada	30,007,094	31,612,897	33,476,688	5.4	5.9	8,965,121.42	3.7

Source: Statistics Canada. 2012. Census Profile. 2011 Census. Statistics Canada Catalogue no. 98-316-XWE. Ottawa. Released October 24 2012.
http://www12.statcan.gc.ca/census-recensement/2011/dp-pd/prof/index.cfm?Lang=E;
Statistics Canada 2007. 2006 Community Profiles. 2006 Census. Statistics Canada Catalogue no. 92-591-XWE. Ottawa. Released March 13 2007.
http://www12.statcan.ca/census-recensement/2006/dp-pd/prof/92-591/index.cfm?Lang=E

Gender

Area	Males	Females
Number		
Kelowna	56,280	61,030
British Columbia	2,156,600	2,243,455
Canada	16,414,225	17,062,460
Percent of Population		
Kelowna	48.0	52.0
British Columbia	49.0	51.0
Canada	49.0	51.0

Source: Statistics Canada. 2012. Census Profile. 2011 Census. Statistics Canada Catalogue no. 98-316-XWE. Ottawa. Released October 24 2012.
http://www12.statcan.gc.ca/census-recensement/2011/dp-pd/prof/index.cfm?Lang=E

Marital Status

Area	Married[1]	Living Common-law	Single[2]	Separated	Divorced	Widowed
Number — Total						
Kelowna	47,600	9,055	26,110	3,035	7,850	6,800
British Columbia	1,832,605	321,965	1,014,270	102,040	246,515	205,300
Canada	12,941,960	3,142,525	7,816,045	698,240	1,686,035	1,584,530
Males						
Kelowna	23,760	4,555	14,065	1,250	2,890	1,260
British Columbia	913,430	161,530	550,830	43,570	98,130	41,550
Canada	6,470,300	1,575,495	4,206,320	299,655	680,415	310,940
Females						
Kelowna	23,840	4,500	12,050	1,790	4,955	5,540
British Columbia	919,175	160,435	463,435	58,470	148,385	163,750
Canada	6,471,660	1,567,035	3,609,730	398,585	1,005,620	1,273,590
Percent of Population — Total						
Kelowna	47.4	9.0	26.0	3.0	7.8	6.8
British Columbia	49.2	8.6	27.2	2.7	6.6	5.5
Canada	46.4	11.3	28.0	2.5	6.0	5.7
Males						
Kelowna	49.7	9.5	29.4	2.6	6.0	2.6
British Columbia	50.5	8.9	30.4	2.4	5.4	2.3
Canada	47.8	11.6	31.1	2.2	5.0	2.3
Females						
Kelowna	45.3	8.5	22.9	3.4	9.4	10.5
British Columbia	48.0	8.4	24.2	3.1	7.8	8.6
Canada	45.2	10.9	25.2	2.8	7.0	8.9

Note: (1) and not separated, (2) never legally married
Source: Statistics Canada. 2012. Census Profile. 2011 Census. Statistics Canada Catalogue no. 98-316-XWE. Ottawa. Released October 24 2012.
http://www12.statcan.gc.ca/census-recensement/2011/dp-pd/prof/index.cfm?Lang=E

Age Characteristics: 0 to 49 Years

Area	0 to 4 Years	5 to 9 Years	10 to 14 Years	15 to 19 Years	20 to 24 Years	25 to 29 Years	30 to 34 Years	35 to 39 Years	40 to 44 Years	45 to 49 Years
					Number					
					Total					
Kelowna	5,340	5,450	6,070	7,090	8,585	8,090	6,730	6,705	7,510	8,895
British Columbia	219,665	218,915	238,780	275,165	279,825	288,780	275,985	280,870	313,765	350,600
Canada	1,877,095	1,809,895	1,920,355	2,178,135	2,187,450	2,169,590	2,162,905	2,173,930	2,324,875	2,675,130
					Males					
Kelowna	2,685	2,735	3,090	3,615	4,335	4,105	3,335	3,305	3,675	4,180
British Columbia	112,885	112,200	122,465	141,670	142,290	143,475	135,220	135,455	151,430	170,580
Canada	961,150	925,965	983,995	1,115,845	1,108,775	1,077,275	1,058,810	1,064,200	1,141,720	1,318,715
					Females					
Kelowna	2,655	2,715	2,985	3,475	4,255	3,980	3,390	3,400	3,835	4,715
British Columbia	106,775	106,715	116,315	133,500	137,535	145,305	140,755	145,415	162,335	180,020
Canada	915,945	883,935	936,360	1,062,295	1,078,670	1,092,315	1,104,095	1,109,735	1,183,155	1,356,420
					Percent of Population					
					Total					
Kelowna	4.6	4.6	5.2	6.0	7.3	6.9	5.7	5.7	6.4	7.6
British Columbia	5.0	5.0	5.4	6.3	6.4	6.6	6.3	6.4	7.1	8.0
Canada	5.6	5.4	5.7	6.5	6.5	6.5	6.5	6.5	6.9	8.0
					Males					
Kelowna	4.8	4.9	5.5	6.4	7.7	7.3	5.9	5.9	6.5	7.4
British Columbia	5.2	5.2	5.7	6.6	6.6	6.7	6.3	6.3	7.0	7.9
Canada	5.9	5.6	6.0	6.8	6.8	6.6	6.5	6.5	7.0	8.0
					Females					
Kelowna	4.4	4.4	4.9	5.7	7.0	6.5	5.6	5.6	6.3	7.7
British Columbia	4.8	4.8	5.2	6.0	6.1	6.5	6.3	6.5	7.2	8.0
Canada	5.4	5.2	5.5	6.2	6.3	6.4	6.5	6.5	6.9	7.9

Source: Statistics Canada. 2012. Census Profile. 2011 Census. Statistics Canada Catalogue no. 98-316-XWE. Ottawa. Released October 24 2012.
http://www12.statcan.gc.ca/census-recensement/2011/dp-pd/prof/index.cfm?Lang=E

Age Characteristics: 50 Years and Over, and Median Age

Area	50 to 54 Years	55 to 59 Years	60 to 64 Years	65 to 69 Years	70 to 74 Years	75 to 79 Years	80 to 84 Years	85 Years and Over	Median Age
				Number					
				Total					
Kelowna	9,015	8,055	7,365	5,635	4,975	4,365	3,690	3,750	43.0
British Columbia	354,610	323,335	291,040	210,900	160,715	127,480	96,945	92,675	41.9
Canada	2,658,965	2,340,635	2,052,670	1,521,715	1,153,065	922,700	702,070	645,515	40.6
				Males					
Kelowna	4,240	3,705	3,555	2,635	2,270	1,985	1,550	1,290	41.3
British Columbia	172,060	157,455	142,645	103,785	77,350	60,720	42,745	32,150	41.1
Canada	1,309,030	1,147,300	1,002,690	738,010	543,435	417,945	291,085	208,300	39.6
				Females					
Kelowna	4,775	4,350	3,810	3,005	2,710	2,380	2,145	2,455	44.8
British Columbia	182,550	165,880	148,395	107,115	83,360	66,760	54,200	60,520	42.7
Canada	1,349,940	1,193,335	1,049,985	783,705	609,630	504,755	410,985	437,215	41.5
				Percent of Population					
				Total					
Kelowna	7.7	6.9	6.3	4.8	4.2	3.7	3.1	3.2	–
British Columbia	8.1	7.3	6.6	4.8	3.7	2.9	2.2	2.1	–
Canada	7.9	7.0	6.1	4.5	3.4	2.8	2.1	1.9	–
				Males					
Kelowna	7.5	6.6	6.3	4.7	4.0	3.5	2.8	2.3	–
British Columbia	8.0	7.3	6.6	4.8	3.6	2.8	2.0	1.5	–
Canada	8.0	7.0	6.1	4.5	3.3	2.5	1.8	1.3	–
				Females					
Kelowna	7.8	7.1	6.2	4.9	4.4	3.9	3.5	4.0	–
British Columbia	8.1	7.4	6.6	4.8	3.7	3.0	2.4	2.7	–
Canada	7.9	7.0	6.2	4.6	3.6	3.0	2.4	2.6	–

Source: Statistics Canada. 2012. Census Profile. 2011 Census. Statistics Canada Catalogue no. 98-316-XWE. Ottawa. Released October 24 2012.
http://www12.statcan.gc.ca/census-recensement/2011/dp-pd/prof/index.cfm?Lang=E

PROFILES / Kelowna, British Columbia

Private Households by Household Size

Area	1 Person	2 Persons	3 Persons	4 Persons	5 Persons	6 or More Persons	Average Number of Persons in Private Households
			Households				
Kelowna	14,625	19,065	6,795	5,985	2,185	1,010	2.3
British Columbia	498,925	613,270	264,135	237,725	91,600	58,985	2.5
Canada	3,673,310	4,544,820	2,081,900	1,903,300	724,405	392,885	2.5
			Percent of Households				
Kelowna	29.4	38.4	13.7	12.0	4.4	2.0	–
British Columbia	28.3	34.8	15.0	13.5	5.2	3.3	–
Canada	27.6	34.1	15.6	14.3	5.4	2.9	–

Source: Statistics Canada. 2012. Census Profile. 2011 Census. Statistics Canada Catalogue no. 98-316-XWE. Ottawa. Released October 24 2012.
http://www12.statcan.gc.ca/census-recensement/2011/dp-pd/prof/index.cfm?Lang=E

Dwelling Type

Area	Single-detached House	Semi-detached House	Row House	Apartment: Building with Five or More Storeys	Apartment: Building with Fewer Than Five Storeys	Duplex Apartment	Movable Dwelling	Other Single-attached House
				Number				
Kelowna	24,860	2,465	3,410	1,155	12,875	4,020	795	85
British Columbia	842,120	52,825	130,365	143,970	361,150	184,355	46,960	2,885
Canada	7,329,150	646,245	791,600	1,234,770	2,397,550	704,485	183,510	33,310
				Percent of Dwellings				
Kelowna	50.1	5.0	6.9	2.3	25.9	8.1	1.6	0.2
British Columbia	47.7	3.0	7.4	8.2	20.5	10.4	2.7	0.2
Canada	55.0	4.9	5.9	9.3	18.0	5.3	1.4	0.3

Source: Statistics Canada. 2012. Census Profile. 2011 Census. Statistics Canada Catalogue no. 98-316-XWE. Ottawa. Released October 24 2012.
http://www12.statcan.gc.ca/census-recensement/2011/dp-pd/prof/index.cfm?Lang=E

Shelter Costs

		Owned Dwellings				Rented Dwellings		
Area	Number	Median Value[1] ($)	Average Value[1] ($)	Median Monthly Costs[2] ($)	Average Monthly Costs[2] ($)	Number	Median Monthly Costs[3] ($)	Average Monthly Costs[3] ($)
Kelowna	35,310	415,710	467,313	1,064	1,207	14,095	1,001	1,098
British Columbia	1,202,000	448,835	543,635	1,023	1,228	519,855	903	989
Canada	9,013,410	280,552	345,182	978	1,141	4,060,385	784	848

Note: All figures cover non-farm, non-reserve private dwellings; (1) Refers to the dollar amount expected by the owner if the dwelling were to be sold; (2) Includes all shelter expenses paid by households that own their dwellings, such as the mortgage payment and the costs of electricity, heat, water and other municipal services, property taxes and condominium fees; (3) Includes all shelter expenses paid by households that rent their dwellings, such as the monthly rent and the costs of electricity, heat and municipal services.
Source: Statistics Canada. 2013. 2011 National Household Survey. Statistics Canada Catalogue no. 99-004-XWE. Ottawa. Released September 11, 2013.

Occupied Private Dwellings by Period of Construction

Area	1960 or Before	1961 to 1980	1981 to 1990	1991 to 2000	2001 to 2005	2006 to 2011
			Number			
Kelowna	3,695	15,710	8,810	10,050	5,530	5,875
British Columbia	282,675	551,655	308,450	329,780	133,235	158,845
Canada	3,273,105	4,152,715	2,112,110	1,707,880	1,031,020	1,042,430
			Percent of Dwellings			
Kelowna	7.4	31.6	17.7	20.2	11.1	11.8
British Columbia	16.0	31.3	17.5	18.7	7.6	9.0
Canada	24.6	31.2	15.9	12.8	7.7	7.8

Note: Figures cover non-farm, non-reserve private dwellings and includes data up to May 10, 2011.
Source: Statistics Canada. 2013. 2011 National Household Survey. Statistics Canada Catalogue no. 99-004-XWE. Ottawa. Released September 11, 2013.

Educational Attainment

Area	No Certificate, Diploma or Degree	High School Diploma or Equivalent[1]	Apprenticeship or Trades Certificate or Diploma[2]	College, CÉGEP or Other Non-University Certificate or Diploma	University Certificate or Diploma Below the Bachelor Level[3]	Bachelor's Degree	University Certificate, Diploma or Degree Above Bachelor Level[4]
			Number				
			Total				
Kelowna	15,415	27,500	12,965	20,430	4,780	10,570	6,215
British Columbia	607,655	1,009,400	387,455	628,115	208,245	511,240	294,725
Canada	5,485,400	6,968,935	2,950,685	4,970,020	1,200,130	3,634,425	2,049,930
			Males				
Kelowna	7,470	12,780	8,495	8,215	1,825	4,570	3,370
British Columbia	305,040	475,670	262,245	260,580	86,995	235,620	149,300
Canada	2,742,875	3,305,415	1,928,970	2,118,430	513,235	1,643,080	1,043,350
			Females				
Kelowna	7,950	14,725	4,470	12,210	2,955	6,000	2,845
British Columbia	302,620	533,735	125,210	367,535	121,250	275,625	145,425
Canada	2,742,520	3,663,515	1,021,715	2,851,595	686,890	1,991,345	1,006,585
			Percent of Population				
			Total				
Kelowna	15.8	28.1	13.2	20.9	4.9	10.8	6.4
British Columbia	16.7	27.7	10.6	17.2	5.7	14.0	8.1
Canada	20.1	25.6	10.8	18.2	4.4	13.3	7.5
			Males				
Kelowna	16.0	27.4	18.2	17.6	3.9	9.8	7.2
British Columbia	17.2	26.8	14.8	14.7	4.9	13.3	8.4
Canada	20.6	24.9	14.5	15.9	3.9	12.4	7.8
			Females				
Kelowna	15.5	28.8	8.7	23.9	5.8	11.7	5.6
British Columbia	16.2	28.5	6.7	19.6	6.5	14.7	7.8
Canada	19.6	26.2	7.3	20.4	4.9	14.3	7.2

Note: Figures cover total population aged 15 years and over by highest certificate, diploma or degree; (1) Includes persons who have graduated from a secondary school or equivalent. It excludes persons with a postsecondary certificate, diploma or degree; (2) Includes Registered Apprenticeship certificates (including Certificate of Qualification, Journeyperson's designation) and other trades certificates or diplomas such as pre-employment or vocational certificates and diplomas from brief trade programs completed at community colleges, institutes of technology, vocational centres, and similar institutions; (3) Comparisons with other data sources suggest that the category 'University certificate or diploma below the bachelor's level' was over-reported in the NHS. This category likely includes some responses that are actually college certificates or diplomas, bachelor's degrees or other types of education (e.g., university transfer programs, bachelor's programs completed in other countries, incomplete bachelor's programs, non-university professional designations). We recommend users interpret the results for the 'University certificate or diploma below the bachelor's level' category with caution; (4) 'University certificate or diploma above bachelor level' includes the categories: 'Degree in medicine, dentistry, veterinary medicine or optometry,' 'Master's degree' and 'Earned doctorate.'
Source: Statistics Canada. 2013. 2011 National Household Survey. Statistics Canada Catalogue no. 99-004-XWE. Ottawa. Released September 11, 2013.

Household Income Distribution

Area	Less than $10,000	$10,000 to $19,999	$20,000 to $29,999	$30,000 to $39,999	$40,000 to $49,999	$50,000 to $59,999	$60,000 to $79,999	$80,000 to $99,999	$100,000 to $124,999	$125,000 to $149,999	$150,000 and Over
					Households						
Kelowna	1,770	4,570	4,990	5,505	4,685	4,135	6,855	5,410	4,795	2,760	4,195
British Columbia	96,465	156,565	157,605	167,220	158,400	140,340	246,720	193,180	167,415	106,325	174,385
Canada	626,705	1,141,945	1,193,925	1,271,675	1,206,800	1,102,120	1,865,280	1,458,240	1,260,770	802,555	1,389,240
					Percent of Households						
Kelowna	3.6	9.2	10.0	11.1	9.4	8.3	13.8	10.9	9.7	5.6	8.4
British Columbia	5.5	8.9	8.9	9.5	9.0	8.0	14.0	10.9	9.5	6.0	9.9
Canada	4.7	8.6	9.0	9.5	9.1	8.3	14.0	10.9	9.5	6.0	10.4

Note: Household income is the sum of the total incomes of all members of that household. Total income refers to monetary receipts from certain sources, before income taxes and deductions, during calendar year 2010.
Source: Statistics Canada. 2013. 2011 National Household Survey. Statistics Canada Catalogue no. 99-004-XWE. Ottawa. Released September 11, 2013.

Median and Average Household and Economic Family Income

Area	Median Household Income ($)	Average Household Income ($)	Median After-tax Household Income ($)	Average After-tax Household Income ($)	Median Economic Family Income ($)	Average Economic Family Income ($)	Median After-tax Economic Family Income ($)	Average After-tax Economic Family Income ($)
Kelowna	57,948	74,975	52,258	64,723	74,697	90,084	66,389	77,452
British Columbia	60,333	77,378	54,379	66,264	75,797	91,967	67,915	78,580
Canada	61,072	79,102	54,089	66,149	76,511	94,125	67,044	78,517

Note: Figures cover household and economic familiy income in 2010. A household is defined as a person or a group of persons (other than foreign residents) who occupy the same private dwelling and do not have a usual place of residence elsewhere in Canada. Every person is a member of one and only one household. An economic family is defined as a group of two or more persons who live in the same dwelling and are related to each other by blood, marriage, common-law, adoption or a foster relationship. A couple may be of opposite or same sex.
Source: Statistics Canada. 2013. 2011 National Household Survey. Statistics Canada Catalogue no. 99-004-XWE. Ottawa. Released September 11, 2013.

PROFILES / Kelowna, British Columbia

Individual Income Distribution

Area	Less than $10,000	$10,000 to $19,999	$20,000 to $29,999	$30,000 to $39,999	$40,000 to $49,999	$50,000 to $59,999	$60,000 to $79,999	$80,000 to $99,999	$100,000 to $124,999	$125,000 and Over
					Number					
					Total					
Kelowna	14,475	18,610	14,255	12,495	9,805	7,250	8,585	4,200	2,160	2,450
British Columbia	645,915	666,060	470,255	404,860	338,595	253,215	330,590	169,190	89,520	96,055
Canada	4,492,040	4,835,710	3,670,020	3,180,360	2,603,520	1,921,650	2,437,440	1,302,045	693,580	782,135
					Males					
Kelowna	6,210	6,805	5,755	5,685	4,930	4,235	5,305	2,680	1,535	1,855
British Columbia	275,815	263,170	201,000	186,285	167,400	143,765	206,400	112,525	65,050	74,260
Canada	1,936,365	1,864,880	1,588,260	1,522,190	1,333,510	1,079,780	1,473,145	823,720	492,905	599,905
					Females					
Kelowna	8,260	11,800	8,505	6,815	4,880	3,010	3,280	1,525	620	590
British Columbia	370,100	402,880	269,255	218,575	171,190	109,445	124,195	56,670	24,470	21,795
Canada	2,555,675	2,970,825	2,081,760	1,658,170	1,270,010	841,870	964,300	478,330	200,680	182,230
					Percent of Population					
					Total					
Kelowna	15.4	19.7	15.1	13.3	10.4	7.7	9.1	4.5	2.3	2.6
British Columbia	18.6	19.2	13.6	11.7	9.8	7.3	9.5	4.9	2.6	2.8
Canada	17.3	18.7	14.2	12.3	10.0	7.4	9.4	5.0	2.7	3.0
					Males					
Kelowna	13.8	15.1	12.8	12.6	11.0	9.4	11.8	6.0	3.4	4.1
British Columbia	16.3	15.5	11.9	11.0	9.9	8.5	12.2	6.6	3.8	4.4
Canada	15.2	14.7	12.5	12.0	10.5	8.5	11.6	6.5	3.9	4.7
					Females					
Kelowna	16.8	23.9	17.3	13.8	9.9	6.1	6.7	3.1	1.3	1.2
British Columbia	20.9	22.8	15.2	12.4	9.7	6.2	7.0	3.2	1.4	1.2
Canada	19.4	22.5	15.8	12.6	9.6	6.4	7.3	3.6	1.5	1.4

Note: Figures cover individuals aged 15 years and over with income. Income refers to monetary receipts from certain sources, before income taxes and deductions, during calendar year 2010.
Source: Statistics Canada. 2013. 2011 National Household Survey. Statistics Canada Catalogue no. 99-004-XWE. Ottawa. Released September 11, 2013.

Labour Force Status

Area	In the Labour Force - All	Employed	Unemployed	Not in the Labour Force
		Number		
		Total		
Kelowna	63,570	58,440	5,125	34,305
British Columbia	2,354,245	2,171,465	182,775	1,292,595
Canada	17,990,080	16,595,035	1,395,045	9,269,445
		Males		
Kelowna	32,490	29,810	2,680	14,240
British Columbia	1,223,375	1,124,590	98,785	552,070
Canada	9,388,570	8,634,310	754,255	3,906,785
		Females		
Kelowna	31,080	28,630	2,445	20,060
British Columbia	1,130,870	1,046,875	83,990	740,530
Canada	8,601,515	7,960,725	640,790	5,362,660
		Percent of Labour Force		
		Total		
Kelowna	65.0	59.7	8.1	35.1
British Columbia	64.6	59.5	7.8	35.4
Canada	66.0	60.9	7.8	34.0
		Males		
Kelowna	69.5	63.8	8.2	30.5
British Columbia	68.9	63.3	8.1	31.1
Canada	70.6	64.9	8.0	29.4
		Females		
Kelowna	60.8	56.0	7.9	39.2
British Columbia	60.4	55.9	7.4	39.6
Canada	61.6	57.0	7.4	38.4

Note: Figures are based on total population 15 years and over
Source: Statistics Canada. 2013. 2011 National Household Survey. Statistics Canada Catalogue no. 99-004-XWE. Ottawa. Released September 11, 2013.

Labour Force by Industry (NAICS Codes 11–52)

Area	Agriculture, forestry, fishing & hunting	Mining, quarrying, & oil & gas extraction	Utilities	Construction	Manufacturing	Wholesale Trade	Retail Trade	Transportation & warehousing	Information & cultural industries	Finance & insurance
					Number					
					Total					
Kelowna	1,010	465	390	6,585	3,085	2,245	8,470	2,130	1,540	2,325
British Columbia	61,210	25,450	13,215	181,510	148,810	90,560	266,265	118,675	62,235	91,790
Canada	437,650	261,050	149,940	1,215,380	1,619,295	733,445	2,031,665	827,780	420,830	767,960
					Males					
Kelowna	720	430	335	5,710	2,125	1,485	3,815	1,475	870	830
British Columbia	40,810	21,175	9,650	159,605	108,480	61,730	121,750	89,155	37,250	35,375
Canada	307,370	211,690	110,765	1,068,710	1,167,680	494,545	933,850	617,305	235,875	296,995
					Females					
Kelowna	295	35	55	875	965	760	4,660	660	670	1,490
British Columbia	20,405	4,275	3,560	21,910	40,335	28,820	144,515	29,520	24,980	56,415
Canada	130,285	49,360	39,175	146,670	451,615	238,900	1,097,820	210,475	184,955	470,960
					Percent of Labour Force					
					Total					
Kelowna	1.6	0.7	0.6	10.6	5.0	3.6	13.6	3.4	2.5	3.7
British Columbia	2.7	1.1	0.6	7.9	6.5	3.9	11.6	5.1	2.7	4.0
Canada	2.5	1.5	0.9	6.9	9.2	4.2	11.6	4.7	2.4	4.4
					Males					
Kelowna	2.3	1.3	1.0	17.9	6.6	4.6	11.9	4.6	2.7	2.6
British Columbia	3.4	1.8	0.8	13.3	9.0	5.1	10.1	7.4	3.1	2.9
Canada	3.3	2.3	1.2	11.6	12.7	5.4	10.2	6.7	2.6	3.2
					Females					
Kelowna	1.0	0.1	0.2	2.9	3.2	2.5	15.4	2.2	2.2	4.9
British Columbia	1.8	0.4	0.3	2.0	3.6	2.6	13.1	2.7	2.3	5.1
Canada	1.6	0.6	0.5	1.7	5.4	2.8	13.1	2.5	2.2	5.6

Note: Figures are based on total experienced labour force 15 years and over. Experienced labour force refers to persons who, during the week of Sunday, May 1 to Saturday, May 7, 2011, were employed and the unemployed who had last worked for pay or in self-employment in either 2010 or 2011.
Source: Statistics Canada. 2013. 2011 National Household Survey. Statistics Canada Catalogue no. 99-004-XWE. Ottawa. Released September 11, 2013.

Labour Force by Industry (NAICS Codes 53–91)

Area	Real estate & rental & leasing	Profess., scientific & tech. services	Mgmt of companies & enterprises	Admin. & support, waste mgmt & remed. services	Educational services	Health care & social assistance	Arts, entertain. & recreation	Accomm. & food services	Other services (except public admin.)	Public admin.
					Number					
					Total					
Kelowna	1,815	4,355	35	2,860	4,150	8,130	1,740	4,695	3,390	2,900
British Columbia	54,840	179,355	2,440	98,890	167,875	249,030	56,915	179,625	112,745	143,875
Canada	321,895	1,240,850	17,460	728,330	1,301,435	1,949,650	363,405	1,130,750	807,800	1,261,050
					Males					
Kelowna	1,080	2,205	30	1,795	1,440	1,880	945	1,965	1,430	1,400
British Columbia	29,790	98,760	1,320	55,745	55,635	47,020	29,750	73,570	49,130	74,040
Canada	179,090	688,625	9,380	411,250	424,915	349,430	188,270	469,990	372,940	652,510
					Females					
Kelowna	735	2,145	0	1,060	2,710	6,245	790	2,730	1,960	1,495
British Columbia	25,055	80,590	1,120	43,145	112,235	202,010	27,175	106,055	63,615	69,840
Canada	142,805	552,225	8,075	317,085	876,515	1,600,220	175,135	660,760	434,865	608,535
					Percent of Labour Force					
					Total					
Kelowna	2.9	7.0	0.1	4.6	6.7	13.0	2.8	7.5	5.4	4.7
British Columbia	2.4	7.8	0.1	4.3	7.3	10.8	2.5	7.8	4.9	6.2
Canada	1.8	7.1	0.1	4.1	7.4	11.1	2.1	6.4	4.6	7.2
					Males					
Kelowna	3.4	6.9	0.1	5.6	4.5	5.9	3.0	6.1	4.5	4.4
British Columbia	2.5	8.2	0.1	4.6	4.6	3.9	2.5	6.1	4.1	6.2
Canada	1.9	7.5	0.1	4.5	4.6	3.8	2.0	5.1	4.1	7.1
					Females					
Kelowna	2.4	7.1	0.0	3.5	8.9	20.6	2.6	9.0	6.5	4.9
British Columbia	2.3	7.3	0.1	3.9	10.2	18.3	2.5	9.6	5.8	6.3
Canada	1.7	6.6	0.1	3.8	10.4	19.1	2.1	7.9	5.2	7.2

Note: Figures are based on total experienced labour force 15 years and over. Experienced labour force refers to persons who, during the week of Sunday, May 1 to Saturday, May 7, 2011, were employed and the unemployed who had last worked for pay or in self-employment in either 2010 or 2011.
Source: Statistics Canada. 2013. 2011 National Household Survey. Statistics Canada Catalogue no. 99-004-XWE. Ottawa. Released September 11, 2013.

PROFILES / Kelowna, British Columbia

Occupation

Area	Mgmt	Business, Finance & Admin.	Natural/ Applied Sciences & Related	Health	Education, Law & Social, Community & Government Services	Art, Culture, Recreation & Sport	Sales & Service	Trades, Transport & Equip. Operators & Related	Natural Resources, Agri. & Related Production	Mfg & Utilities
Number										
Total										
Kelowna	6,935	9,890	3,860	4,750	6,450	1,905	15,965	9,200	1,740	1,620
British Columbia	263,685	368,980	154,055	147,620	265,910	78,565	554,345	337,140	60,295	74,720
Canada	1,963,600	2,902,045	1,237,775	1,107,200	2,064,675	503,415	4,068,170	2,537,775	397,930	805,040
Males										
Kelowna	4,470	2,315	3,155	1,245	2,100	970	6,625	8,615	1,415	1,055
British Columbia	162,365	104,285	122,570	32,490	89,645	38,300	233,065	317,385	45,155	54,470
Canada	1,229,460	854,190	966,355	217,520	676,550	232,535	1,745,705	2,385,615	318,945	564,300
Females										
Kelowna	2,465	7,570	705	3,500	4,345	930	9,335	585	325	565
British Columbia	101,320	264,690	31,480	115,125	176,265	40,270	321,285	19,755	15,135	20,250
Canada	734,140	2,047,855	271,415	889,675	1,388,130	270,875	2,322,465	152,165	78,980	240,740
Percent of Labour Force										
Total										
Kelowna	11.1	15.9	6.2	7.6	10.4	3.1	25.6	14.8	2.8	2.6
British Columbia	11.4	16.0	6.7	6.4	11.5	3.4	24.0	14.6	2.6	3.2
Canada	11.2	16.5	7.0	6.3	11.7	2.9	23.1	14.4	2.3	4.6
Males										
Kelowna	14.0	7.2	9.9	3.9	6.6	3.0	20.7	26.9	4.4	3.3
British Columbia	13.5	8.7	10.2	2.7	7.5	3.2	19.4	26.5	3.8	4.5
Canada	13.4	9.3	10.5	2.4	7.4	2.5	19.0	26.0	3.5	6.1
Females										
Kelowna	8.1	25.0	2.3	11.5	14.3	3.1	30.8	1.9	1.1	1.9
British Columbia	9.2	23.9	2.8	10.4	15.9	3.6	29.1	1.8	1.4	1.8
Canada	8.7	24.4	3.2	10.6	16.5	3.2	27.7	1.8	0.9	2.9

Note: Figures are based on total experienced labour force 15 years and over
Source: Statistics Canada. 2013. 2011 National Household Survey. Statistics Canada Catalogue no. 99-004-XWE. Ottawa. Released September 11, 2013.

Place of Work Status

Area	Worked at Home	Worked Outside Canada	No Fixed Workplace Address	Worked at Usual Place
Number				
Total				
Kelowna	4,530	235	8,210	45,465
British Columbia	174,000	12,480	304,465	1,680,525
Canada	1,142,640	66,460	1,868,245	13,517,690
Males				
Kelowna	2,205	195	6,270	21,135
British Columbia	84,015	9,210	225,840	805,525
Canada	582,150	47,355	1,400,485	6,604,325
Females				
Kelowna	2,325	40	1,935	24,330
British Columbia	89,990	3,270	78,620	875,000
Canada	560,490	19,100	467,760	6,913,370
Percent of Labour Force				
Total				
Kelowna	7.8	0.4	14.0	77.8
British Columbia	8.0	0.6	14.0	77.4
Canada	6.9	0.4	11.3	81.5
Males				
Kelowna	7.4	0.7	21.0	70.9
British Columbia	7.5	0.8	20.1	71.6
Canada	6.7	0.5	16.2	76.5
Females				
Kelowna	8.1	0.1	6.8	85.0
British Columbia	8.6	0.3	7.5	83.6
Canada	7.0	0.2	5.9	86.8

Note: Figures are based on total employed labour force 15 years and over.
Source: Statistics Canada. 2013. 2011 National Household Survey. Statistics Canada Catalogue no. 99-004-XWE. Ottawa. Released September 11, 2013.

Mode of Transportation to Work

Area	Car; Truck; Van; as Driver	Car; Truck; Van; as Passenger	Public Transit	Walked	Bicycled	All Other Modes
			Number			
			Total			
Kelowna	42,650	2,890	2,170	3,020	1,900	1,035
British Columbia	1,415,745	110,695	250,450	132,205	42,260	33,635
Canada	11,393,140	867,050	1,851,525	880,815	201,780	191,625
			Males			
Kelowna	22,270	1,455	905	1,000	1,150	620
British Columbia	773,160	47,425	107,645	57,000	26,595	19,535
Canada	6,238,835	349,530	788,290	387,580	135,840	104,725
			Females			
Kelowna	20,385	1,435	1,270	2,025	745	415
British Columbia	642,580	63,270	142,810	75,205	15,665	14,100
Canada	5,154,305	517,520	1,063,235	493,230	65,940	86,900
			Percent of Labour Force			
			Total			
Kelowna	79.5	5.4	4.0	5.6	3.5	1.9
British Columbia	71.3	5.6	12.6	6.7	2.1	1.7
Canada	74.0	5.6	12.0	5.7	1.3	1.2
			Males			
Kelowna	81.3	5.3	3.3	3.6	4.2	2.3
British Columbia	75.0	4.6	10.4	5.5	2.6	1.9
Canada	77.9	4.4	9.8	4.8	1.7	1.3
			Females			
Kelowna	77.6	5.5	4.8	7.7	2.8	1.6
British Columbia	67.4	6.6	15.0	7.9	1.6	1.5
Canada	69.8	7.0	14.4	6.7	0.9	1.2

Note: Figures are based on total employed labour force 15 years and over.
Source: Statistics Canada. 2013. 2011 National Household Survey. Statistics Canada Catalogue no. 99-004-XWE. Ottawa. Released September 11, 2013.

Visible Minority Population Characteristics

Area	Total Minority	South Asian[1]	Chinese	Black	Filipino	Latin American	Arab	SE Asian[2]	West Asian[3]	Korean	Japanese	Multiple[4]
						Number						
						Total						
Kelowna	8,750	2,630	1,480	685	870	525	195	325	125	440	1,060	215
British Columbia	1,180,870	313,440	438,140	33,260	126,040	35,465	14,090	51,970	38,960	53,770	38,120	31,160
Canada	6,264,750	1,567,400	1,324,750	945,665	619,310	381,280	380,620	312,075	206,840	161,130	87,270	171,935
						Males						
Kelowna	4,175	1,310	745	340	325	275	95	185	50	235	435	100
British Columbia	565,965	157,135	208,175	17,365	53,715	16,985	8,010	25,055	19,420	25,325	16,295	15,255
Canada	3,043,010	790,755	632,325	453,005	268,885	186,355	203,485	154,035	105,620	77,165	38,270	83,335
						Females						
Kelowna	4,575	1,320	740	345	545	255	100	140	80	205	630	120
British Columbia	614,905	156,300	229,960	15,895	72,320	18,480	6,080	26,920	19,540	28,440	21,820	15,905
Canada	3,221,745	776,650	692,420	492,660	350,425	194,925	177,140	158,045	101,220	83,965	48,990	88,600
						Percent of Population						
						Total						
Kelowna	7.6	2.3	1.3	0.6	0.8	0.5	0.2	0.3	0.1	0.4	0.9	0.2
British Columbia	27.3	7.2	10.1	0.8	2.9	0.8	0.3	1.2	0.9	1.2	0.9	0.7
Canada	19.1	4.8	4.0	2.9	1.9	1.2	1.2	0.9	0.6	0.5	0.3	0.5
						Males						
Kelowna	7.5	2.4	1.3	0.6	0.6	0.5	0.2	0.3	0.1	0.4	0.8	0.2
British Columbia	26.6	7.4	9.8	0.8	2.5	0.8	0.4	1.2	0.9	1.2	0.8	0.7
Canada	18.8	4.9	3.9	2.8	1.7	1.2	1.3	1.0	0.7	0.5	0.2	0.5
						Females						
Kelowna	7.7	2.2	1.2	0.6	0.9	0.4	0.2	0.2	0.1	0.3	1.1	0.2
British Columbia	28.0	7.1	10.5	0.7	3.3	0.8	0.3	1.2	0.9	1.3	1.0	0.7
Canada	19.3	4.7	4.1	3.0	2.1	1.2	1.1	0.9	0.6	0.5	0.3	0.5

Note: The Employment Equity Act defines visible minorities as 'persons, other than Aboriginal peoples, who are non-Caucasian in race or non-white in colour'; (1) Includes 'East Indian,' 'Pakistani,' 'Sri Lankan,' etc.; (2) Includes 'Vietnamese,' 'Cambodian,' 'Malaysian,' 'Laotian,' etc.; (3) Includes 'Iranian,' 'Afghan,' etc.; (4) Includes respondents who reported more than one visible minority group by checking two or more mark-in circles, e.g., 'Black' and 'South Asian.'
Source: Statistics Canada. 2013. 2011 National Household Survey. Statistics Canada Catalogue no. 99-004-XWE. Ottawa. Released September 11, 2013.

PROFILES / Kelowna, British Columbia

Aboriginal Population

Area	Aboriginal Identity[1]	First Nations (North American Indian) Single Identity[2]	Métis Single Identity	Inuk (Inuit) Single Identity	Multiple Aboriginal Identities[3]	Aboriginal Identities Not Included Elsewhere
Number						
Total						
Kelowna	5,145	2,420	2,595	30	45	55
British Columbia	232,290	155,020	69,475	1,570	2,480	3,745
Canada	1,400,685	851,560	451,795	59,440	11,415	26,475
Males						
Kelowna	2,485	1,115	1,325	0	15	30
British Columbia	113,080	75,400	33,940	820	1,190	1,735
Canada	682,190	411,785	223,335	29,495	5,525	12,055
Females						
Kelowna	2,665	1,305	1,270	25	30	20
British Columbia	119,215	79,620	35,540	750	1,290	2,015
Canada	718,500	439,775	228,460	29,950	5,890	14,420
Percent of Population						
Total						
Kelowna	4.5	2.1	2.3	0.0	0.0	0.0
British Columbia	5.4	3.6	1.6	0.0	0.1	0.1
Canada	4.3	2.6	1.4	0.2	0.0	0.1
Males						
Kelowna	4.5	2.0	2.4	0.0	0.0	0.1
British Columbia	5.3	3.5	1.6	0.0	0.1	0.1
Canada	4.2	2.5	1.4	0.2	0.0	0.1
Females						
Kelowna	4.5	2.2	2.1	0.0	0.1	0.0
British Columbia	5.4	3.6	1.6	0.0	0.1	0.1
Canada	4.3	2.6	1.4	0.2	0.0	0.1

Note: (1) Includes persons who reported being an Aboriginal person, that is, First Nations (North American Indian), Métis or Inuk (Inuit) and/or those who reported Registered or Treaty Indian status, that is registered under the Indian Act of Canada, and/or those who reported membership in a First Nation or Indian band. Aboriginal peoples of Canada are defined in the Constitution Act, 1982, section 35-2 as including the Indian, Inuit and Métis peoples of Canada; (2) Users should be aware that the estimates associated with this variable are more affected than most by the incomplete enumeration of certain Indian reserves and Indian settlements in the National Household Survey (NHS); (3) Includes persons who reported being any two or all three of the following: First Nations (North American Indian), Métis or Inuk (Inuit).
Source: Statistics Canada. 2013. 2011 National Household Survey. Statistics Canada Catalogue no. 99-004-XWE. Ottawa. Released September 11, 2013.

Ethnic Origin

Area	North American Aboriginal	Other North American	European	Caribbean	Latin, Central and South American	African	Asian	Oceania
Number								
Total								
Kelowna	6,325	29,200	95,555	605	975	855	8,140	470
British Columbia	267,085	884,490	2,812,935	20,035	52,725	47,185	1,122,445	35,770
Canada	1,836,035	11,070,455	20,157,965	627,590	544,375	766,735	5,011,225	74,875
Males								
Kelowna	2,925	14,050	46,090	305	470	330	3,790	260
British Columbia	128,880	440,920	1,387,940	10,225	25,605	23,575	535,825	17,425
Canada	885,675	5,462,685	9,913,150	291,640	264,635	387,360	2,435,540	37,490
Females								
Kelowna	3,395	15,145	49,455	300	495	525	4,350	215
British Columbia	138,205	443,570	1,424,990	9,810	27,120	23,610	586,620	18,340
Canada	950,360	5,607,770	10,244,820	335,945	279,740	379,380	2,575,680	37,385
Percent of Population								
Total								
Kelowna	5.5	25.5	83.4	0.5	0.9	0.7	7.1	0.4
British Columbia	6.2	20.5	65.0	0.5	1.2	1.1	26.0	0.8
Canada	5.6	33.7	61.4	1.9	1.7	2.3	15.3	0.2
Males								
Kelowna	5.3	25.4	83.3	0.6	0.8	0.6	6.9	0.5
British Columbia	6.1	20.7	65.3	0.5	1.2	1.1	25.2	0.8
Canada	5.5	33.8	61.3	1.8	1.6	2.4	15.1	0.2
Females								
Kelowna	5.7	25.6	83.5	0.5	0.8	0.9	7.3	0.4
British Columbia	6.3	20.2	64.8	0.4	1.2	1.1	26.7	0.8
Canada	5.7	33.6	61.4	2.0	1.7	2.3	15.4	0.2

Note: The sum of the ethnic groups in this table is greater than the total population estimate because a person may report more than one ethnic origin in the NHS.
Source: Statistics Canada. 2013. 2011 National Household Survey. Statistics Canada Catalogue no. 99-004-XWE. Ottawa. Released September 11, 2013.

Religion

Area	Buddhist	Christian	Hindu	Jewish	Muslim	Sikh	Traditional (Aboriginal) Spirituality	Other Religions	No Religious Affiliation
					Number Total				
Kelowna	570	62,410	455	215	480	1,525	70	960	47,885
British Columbia	90,620	1,930,415	45,795	23,130	79,310	201,110	10,295	35,500	1,908,285
Canada	366,830	22,102,745	497,965	329,495	1,053,945	454,965	64,935	130,835	7,850,605
					Males				
Kelowna	250	28,090	195	115	235	820	40	375	25,210
British Columbia	40,175	883,680	22,945	11,255	39,780	100,610	5,085	14,680	1,007,420
Canada	168,465	10,497,775	250,435	161,265	540,555	229,435	31,805	57,745	4,225,645
					Females				
Kelowna	320	34,325	265	100	240	700	30	590	22,680
British Columbia	50,440	1,046,735	22,845	11,880	39,530	100,500	5,210	20,820	900,865
Canada	198,365	11,604,975	247,525	168,235	513,395	225,530	33,135	73,090	3,624,965
					Percent of Population Total				
Kelowna	0.5	54.5	0.4	0.2	0.4	1.3	0.1	0.8	41.8
British Columbia	2.1	44.6	1.1	0.5	1.8	4.7	0.2	0.8	44.1
Canada	1.1	67.3	1.5	1.0	3.2	1.4	0.2	0.4	23.9
					Males				
Kelowna	0.5	50.8	0.4	0.2	0.4	1.5	0.1	0.7	45.6
British Columbia	1.9	41.6	1.1	0.5	1.9	4.7	0.2	0.7	47.4
Canada	1.0	64.9	1.5	1.0	3.3	1.4	0.2	0.4	26.1
					Females				
Kelowna	0.5	57.9	0.4	0.2	0.4	1.2	0.1	1.0	38.3
British Columbia	2.3	47.6	1.0	0.5	1.8	4.6	0.2	0.9	41.0
Canada	1.2	69.5	1.5	1.0	3.1	1.4	0.2	0.4	21.7

Note: Religion refers to the person's self-identification as having a connection or affiliation with any religious denomination, group, body, sect, cult or other religiously defined community or system of belief. Religion is not limited to formal membership in a religious organization or group. Persons without a religious connection or affiliation can self-identify as atheist, agnostic or humanist, or can provide another applicable response.
Source: Statistics Canada. 2013. 2011 National Household Survey. Statistics Canada Catalogue no. 99-004-XWE. Ottawa. Released September 11, 2013.

Religion—Christian Denominations

Area	Anglican	Baptist	Catholic	Christian Orthodox	Lutheran	Pentecostal	Presbyterian	United Church	Other Christian
					Number Total				
Kelowna	5,715	4,165	18,300	880	3,615	2,180	840	8,080	18,630
British Columbia	213,975	91,575	650,360	39,845	71,470	58,300	44,635	222,230	538,030
Canada	1,631,845	635,840	12,810,705	550,690	478,185	478,705	472,385	2,007,610	3,036,780
					Males				
Kelowna	2,725	1,885	8,290	460	1,655	1,040	360	3,065	8,610
British Columbia	94,330	41,565	303,300	19,475	32,205	26,590	19,925	94,020	252,270
Canada	752,945	293,905	6,167,290	270,205	221,525	217,850	218,955	912,545	1,442,550
					Females				
Kelowna	2,990	2,285	10,010	425	1,960	1,145	480	5,015	10,025
British Columbia	119,645	50,010	347,060	20,375	39,270	31,710	24,710	128,210	285,770
Canada	878,900	341,940	6,643,415	280,485	256,660	260,850	253,430	1,095,065	1,594,230
					Percent of Population Total				
Kelowna	5.0	3.6	16.0	0.8	3.2	1.9	0.7	7.1	16.3
British Columbia	4.9	2.1	15.0	0.9	1.7	1.3	1.0	5.1	12.4
Canada	5.0	1.9	39.0	1.7	1.5	1.5	1.4	6.1	9.2
					Males				
Kelowna	4.9	3.4	15.0	0.8	3.0	1.9	0.7	5.5	15.6
British Columbia	4.4	2.0	14.3	0.9	1.5	1.3	0.9	4.4	11.9
Canada	4.7	1.8	38.2	1.7	1.4	1.3	1.4	5.6	8.9
					Females				
Kelowna	5.0	3.9	16.9	0.7	3.3	1.9	0.8	8.5	16.9
British Columbia	5.4	2.3	15.8	0.9	1.8	1.4	1.1	5.8	13.0
Canada	5.3	2.0	39.8	1.7	1.5	1.6	1.5	6.6	9.6

Note: Religion refers to the person's self-identification as having a connection or affiliation with any religious denomination, group, body, sect, cult or other religiously defined community or system of belief. Religion is not limited to formal membership in a religious organization or group. Persons without a religious connection or affiliation can self-identify as atheist, agnostic or humanist, or can provide another applicable response.
Source: Statistics Canada. 2013. 2011 National Household Survey. Statistics Canada Catalogue no. 99-004-XWE. Ottawa. Released September 11, 2013.

PROFILES / Kelowna, British Columbia

Immigrant Status and Period of Immigration

Area	Non-Immigrants[1]	Immigrants All	Before 1971	1971 to 1980	1981 to 1990	1991 to 2000	2001 to 2005	2006 to 2011	Non-Permanent Residents[3]
Number									
Total									
Kelowna	97,660	15,970	5,965	2,080	1,510	2,835	1,320	2,265	940
British Columbia	3,067,590	1,191,875	223,215	161,335	156,445	305,655	160,100	185,115	64,995
Canada	25,720,175	6,775,765	1,261,055	870,775	949,890	1,539,050	992,070	1,162,915	356,385
Males									
Kelowna	47,265	7,675	2,905	980	710	1,350	545	1,180	385
British Columbia	1,533,255	561,490	109,510	76,865	72,625	140,985	74,395	87,110	30,880
Canada	12,753,235	3,231,370	605,430	416,670	454,570	724,905	474,545	555,245	178,515
Females									
Kelowna	50,395	8,300	3,055	1,095	800	1,485	775	1,090	550
British Columbia	1,534,330	630,385	113,710	84,470	83,820	164,675	85,710	98,005	34,115
Canada	12,966,935	3,544,400	655,625	454,105	495,325	814,145	517,530	607,670	177,870
Percent of Population									
Total									
Kelowna	85.2	13.9	5.2	1.8	1.3	2.5	1.2	2.0	0.8
British Columbia	70.9	27.6	5.2	3.7	3.6	7.1	3.7	4.3	1.5
Canada	78.3	20.6	3.8	2.7	2.9	4.7	3.0	3.5	1.1
Males									
Kelowna	85.4	13.9	5.3	1.8	1.3	2.4	1.0	2.1	0.7
British Columbia	72.1	26.4	5.2	3.6	3.4	6.6	3.5	4.1	1.5
Canada	78.9	20.0	3.7	2.6	2.8	4.5	2.9	3.4	1.1
Females									
Kelowna	85.1	14.0	5.2	1.8	1.4	2.5	1.3	1.8	0.9
British Columbia	69.8	28.7	5.2	3.8	3.8	7.5	3.9	4.5	1.6
Canada	77.7	21.2	3.9	2.7	3.0	4.9	3.1	3.6	1.1

Note: (1) Non-immigrant refers to a person who is a Canadian citizen by birth; (2) Immigrant refers to a person who is or has ever been a landed immigrant/permanent resident. This person has been granted the right to live in Canada permanently by immigration authorities. Some immigrants have resided in Canada for a number of years, while others have arrived recently. Some immigrants are Canadian citizens, while others are not. Most immigrants are born outside Canada, but a small number are born in Canada. In the 2011 National Household Survey, 'Immigrants' includes immigrants who landed in Canada prior to May 10, 2011; (3) Non-permanent resident refers to a person from another country who has a work or study permit, or who is a refugee claimant, and any non-Canadian-born family member living in Canada with them.
Source: Statistics Canada. 2013. 2011 National Household Survey. Statistics Canada Catalogue no. 99-004-XWE. Ottawa. Released September 11, 2013.

Mother Tongue

Area	English	French	Non-official Language	English & French	English & Non-official Language	French & Non-official Language	English, French & Non-official Language
Number							
Total							
Kelowna	98,145	1,930	14,215	280	925	60	25
British Columbia	3,062,435	57,275	1,154,215	8,600	68,800	3,345	1,530
Canada	18,858,980	7,054,975	6,567,680	144,685	396,330	74,430	24,095
Males							
Kelowna	47,595	890	6,495	110	395	30	15
British Columbia	1,526,350	28,315	543,395	4,065	32,875	1,520	725
Canada	9,345,225	3,452,380	3,157,785	69,975	192,000	36,535	11,965
Females							
Kelowna	50,550	1,045	7,715	170	520	30	15
British Columbia	1,536,085	28,965	610,825	4,535	35,925	1,830	805
Canada	9,513,750	3,602,590	3,409,895	74,710	204,330	37,890	12,130
Percent of Population							
Total							
Kelowna	84.9	1.7	12.3	0.2	0.8	0.1	0.0
British Columbia	70.3	1.3	26.5	0.2	1.6	0.1	0.0
Canada	56.9	21.3	19.8	0.4	1.2	0.2	0.1
Males							
Kelowna	85.7	1.6	11.7	0.2	0.7	0.1	0.0
British Columbia	71.4	1.3	25.4	0.2	1.5	0.1	0.0
Canada	57.5	21.2	19.4	0.4	1.2	0.2	0.1
Females							
Kelowna	84.2	1.7	12.8	0.3	0.9	0.0	0.0
British Columbia	69.2	1.3	27.5	0.2	1.6	0.1	0.0
Canada	56.4	21.4	20.2	0.4	1.2	0.2	0.1

Note: Figures cover total population excluding institutional residents.
Source: Statistics Canada. 2012. Census Profile. 2011 Census. Statistics Canada Catalogue no. 98-316-XWE. Ottawa. Released October 24 2012.
http://www12.statcan.gc.ca/census-recensement/2011/dp-pd/prof/index.cfm?Lang=E

Language Spoken Most Often at Home

Area	English	French	Non-official Language	English & French	English & Non-official Language	French & Non-official Language	English, French & Non-official Language
			Number				
			Total				
Kelowna	108,770	470	4,465	135	1,695	10	30
British Columbia	3,506,595	16,685	670,100	4,700	155,065	930	2,130
Canada	21,457,075	6,827,865	3,673,865	131,205	875,135	109,700	46,330
			Males				
Kelowna	52,335	205	2,120	70	785	0	15
British Columbia	1,733,775	8,015	317,670	2,240	74,155	435	940
Canada	10,585,620	3,348,235	1,767,310	63,475	425,370	53,010	22,845
			Females				
Kelowna	56,435	270	2,345	65	905	10	15
British Columbia	1,772,820	8,665	352,430	2,460	80,905	495	1,185
Canada	10,871,455	3,479,625	1,906,555	67,730	449,765	56,690	23,485
			Percent of Population				
			Total				
Kelowna	94.1	0.4	3.9	0.1	1.5	0.0	0.0
British Columbia	80.5	0.4	15.4	0.1	3.6	0.0	0.0
Canada	64.8	20.6	11.1	0.4	2.6	0.3	0.1
			Males				
Kelowna	94.2	0.4	3.8	0.1	1.4	0.0	0.0
British Columbia	81.1	0.4	14.9	0.1	3.5	0.0	0.0
Canada	65.1	20.6	10.9	0.4	2.6	0.3	0.1
			Females				
Kelowna	94.0	0.4	3.9	0.1	1.5	0.0	0.0
British Columbia	79.9	0.4	15.9	0.1	3.6	0.0	0.1
Canada	64.5	20.6	11.3	0.4	2.7	0.3	0.1

Note: Figures cover total population excluding institutional residents.
Source: Statistics Canada. 2012. Census Profile. 2011 Census. Statistics Canada Catalogue no. 98-316-XWE. Ottawa. Released October 24 2012.
http://www12.statcan.gc.ca/census-recensement/2011/dp-pd/prof/index.cfm?Lang=E

Knowledge of Official Languages

Area	English Only	French Only	English & French	Neither English nor French
		Number		
		Total		
Kelowna	107,180	50	7,790	545
British Columbia	3,912,950	2,045	296,645	144,555
Canada	22,564,665	4,165,015	5,795,570	595,920
		Males		
Kelowna	51,815	20	3,475	220
British Columbia	1,943,760	950	132,940	59,590
Canada	11,222,185	1,925,340	2,876,560	241,790
		Females		
Kelowna	55,370	30	4,320	325
British Columbia	1,969,190	1,095	163,705	84,965
Canada	11,342,485	2,239,680	2,919,005	354,135
		Percent of Population		
		Total		
Kelowna	92.7	0.0	6.7	0.5
British Columbia	89.8	0.0	6.8	3.3
Canada	68.1	12.6	17.5	1.8
		Males		
Kelowna	93.3	0.0	6.3	0.4
British Columbia	90.9	0.0	6.2	2.8
Canada	69.0	11.8	17.7	1.5
		Females		
Kelowna	92.2	0.0	7.2	0.5
British Columbia	88.7	0.0	7.4	3.8
Canada	67.3	13.3	17.3	2.1

Note: Figures cover total population excluding institutional residents.
Source: Statistics Canada. 2012. Census Profile. 2011 Census. Statistics Canada Catalogue no. 98-316-XWE. Ottawa. Released October 24 2012.
http://www12.statcan.gc.ca/census-recensement/2011/dp-pd/prof/index.cfm?Lang=E

Kingston, Ontario

Background

Kingston is located in eastern Ontario, midway between Toronto and Montréal. The city is situated where the St. Lawrence River flows out of Lake Ontario. The city is approximately two hours away from major cities such as Toronto, Ottawa, Montréal and Syracuse, New York. The U.S. border crossing at 1000 Islands, one of the least congested crossings between the two countries, is 30 minutes from Kingston.

Kingston was originally a First Nations settlement, later an important European trading post and then the first capital of the Province of Canada, from 1841 to 1844. Kingston remained the county seat of Frontenac County until 1998.

The city's historic downtown is a mixture of 19th century neighbourhoods, limestone architecture and the scenic Cataraqui River waterfront. Kingston is the gateway to the Gananoque 1000 Islands on the St. Lawrence River and the Rideau Canal, a UNESCO World Heritage site. Rideau Canal cruises regularly depart from Kingston and pass along 202 kilometres of lakes, rivers and locks to Ottawa, Canada's current capital city.

The City of Kingston's knowledge-based economy is expanding rapidly. Queen's University is an emerging biotechnology cluster responsible for more than 40 start-up companies in the region. Kingston's research and development in fuel cell and hydrogen alternative energy technologies is considered some of the most advanced in Canada. Additional sector strengths include manufacturing, logistics and distribution, and information technology. The Royal Military College of Canada is also located in Kingston.

Kingston hosts a regular roster of events such as Music in the Park, Movies in the Square, First Capital celebrations, Buskers Festival, the 1000 Islands Poker Run, the Canadian Olympic Regatta Kingston (CORK), the Wolfe Island Music Festival and the Limestone City Blues Festival.

Kingston has summer highs of plus 23.40 degrees Celsius, winter lows of minus 10.67 degrees Celsius, and an average rainfall just over 794 mm per year.

Rankings

- *Money Sense Magazine* ranked Kingston #3 of Canada's "Best Cities to Live 2012." Out of 190 Canadian cities, the City of Kingston ranked #1 as "Best Place to Retire." Ottawa (ON) was the best city in which to live and Burlington (ON) placed second. *Money Sense Magazine, "Canada's Best Places to Live 2012," March 20, 2012*
- The City of Kingston's Queen's University ranked #4 out of 49 universities across Canada. The *Maclean's Magazine* annual university rankings use 14 numerical indicators to evaluate quality of students, faculty, libraries and finances. In 2011, Queen's was outranked by Montréal's McGill University (#1), University of Toronto (#2), and University of British Columbia (#3). *Maclean's, "2011 University Rankings," October 26th, 2011*

PROFILES / Kingston, Ontario

Population Growth and Density

Area	Population in 2001	Population in 2006	Population in 2011	Population Change 2001–2006	Population Change 2006–2011	Land Area (sq. km)	Population Density per sq. km
Kingston	114,195	117,207	123,363	2.6	5.3	451.17	273.4
Ontario	11,410,046	12,160,282	12,851,821	6.6	5.7	908,607.67	14.1
Canada	30,007,094	31,612,897	33,476,688	5.4	5.9	8,965,121.42	3.7

Source: Statistics Canada. 2012. Census Profile. 2011 Census. Statistics Canada Catalogue no. 98-316-XWE. Ottawa. Released October 24 2012.
http://www12.statcan.gc.ca/census-recensement/2011/dp-pd/prof/index.cfm?Lang=E;
Statistics Canada 2007. 2006 Community Profiles. 2006 Census. Statistics Canada Catalogue no. 92-591-XWE. Ottawa. Released March 13 2007.
http://www12.statcan.ca/census-recensement/2006/dp-pd/prof/92-591/index.cfm?Lang=E

Gender

Area	Males	Females
Number		
Kingston	59,905	63,455
Ontario	6,263,140	6,588,685
Canada	16,414,225	17,062,460
Percent of Population		
Kingston	48.6	51.4
Ontario	48.7	51.3
Canada	49.0	51.0

Source: Statistics Canada. 2012. Census Profile. 2011 Census. Statistics Canada Catalogue no. 98-316-XWE. Ottawa. Released October 24 2012.
http://www12.statcan.gc.ca/census-recensement/2011/dp-pd/prof/index.cfm?Lang=E

Marital Status

Area	Married[1]	Living Common-law	Single[2]	Separated	Divorced	Widowed
Number						
Total						
Kingston	45,825	10,560	31,925	3,480	6,895	6,580
Ontario	5,367,400	791,210	2,985,020	319,805	593,730	613,880
Canada	12,941,960	3,142,525	7,816,045	698,240	1,686,035	1,584,530
Males						
Kingston	22,940	5,260	17,195	1,430	2,535	1,260
Ontario	2,681,320	397,620	1,583,760	133,790	231,160	117,980
Canada	6,470,300	1,575,495	4,206,320	299,655	680,415	310,940
Females						
Kingston	22,880	5,300	14,730	2,055	4,360	5,315
Ontario	2,686,075	393,590	1,401,260	186,015	362,570	495,905
Canada	6,471,660	1,567,035	3,609,730	398,585	1,005,620	1,273,590
Percent of Population						
Total						
Kingston	43.5	10.0	30.3	3.3	6.6	6.3
Ontario	50.3	7.4	28.0	3.0	5.6	5.8
Canada	46.4	11.3	28.0	2.5	6.0	5.7
Males						
Kingston	45.3	10.4	34.0	2.8	5.0	2.5
Ontario	52.1	7.7	30.8	2.6	4.5	2.3
Canada	47.8	11.6	31.1	2.2	5.0	2.3
Females						
Kingston	41.9	9.7	27.0	3.8	8.0	9.7
Ontario	48.6	7.1	25.4	3.4	6.6	9.0
Canada	45.2	10.9	25.2	2.8	7.0	8.9

Note: (1) and not separated, (2) never legally married
Source: Statistics Canada. 2012. Census Profile. 2011 Census. Statistics Canada Catalogue no. 98-316-XWE. Ottawa. Released October 24 2012.
http://www12.statcan.gc.ca/census-recensement/2011/dp-pd/prof/index.cfm?Lang=E

Age Characteristics: 0 to 49 Years

Area	0 to 4 Years	5 to 9 Years	10 to 14 Years	15 to 19 Years	20 to 24 Years	25 to 29 Years	30 to 34 Years	35 to 39 Years	40 to 44 Years	45 to 49 Years
					Number					
					Total					
Kingston	6,165	5,825	6,105	8,125	10,915	9,165	7,825	7,025	7,855	9,510
Ontario	704,260	712,755	763,755	863,635	852,910	815,120	800,365	844,335	924,075	1,055,880
Canada	1,877,095	1,809,895	1,920,355	2,178,135	2,187,450	2,169,590	2,162,905	2,173,930	2,324,875	2,675,130
					Males					
Kingston	3,085	3,030	3,165	4,090	5,645	4,600	3,970	3,550	3,900	4,660
Ontario	360,590	365,290	391,630	443,680	432,490	400,045	383,340	405,845	447,920	517,510
Canada	961,150	925,965	983,995	1,115,845	1,108,775	1,077,275	1,058,810	1,064,200	1,141,720	1,318,715
					Females					
Kingston	3,085	2,800	2,940	4,035	5,270	4,570	3,850	3,475	3,950	4,845
Ontario	343,670	347,465	372,125	419,950	420,415	415,075	417,030	438,485	476,155	538,370
Canada	915,945	883,935	936,360	1,062,295	1,078,670	1,092,315	1,104,095	1,109,735	1,183,155	1,356,420
					Percent of Population					
					Total					
Kingston	5.0	4.7	4.9	6.6	8.8	7.4	6.3	5.7	6.4	7.7
Ontario	5.5	5.5	5.9	6.7	6.6	6.3	6.2	6.6	7.2	8.2
Canada	5.6	5.4	5.7	6.5	6.5	6.5	6.5	6.5	6.9	8.0
					Males					
Kingston	5.1	5.1	5.3	6.8	9.4	7.7	6.6	5.9	6.5	7.8
Ontario	5.8	5.8	6.3	7.1	6.9	6.4	6.1	6.5	7.2	8.3
Canada	5.9	5.6	6.0	6.8	6.8	6.6	6.5	6.5	7.0	8.0
					Females					
Kingston	4.9	4.4	4.6	6.4	8.3	7.2	6.1	5.5	6.2	7.6
Ontario	5.2	5.3	5.6	6.4	6.4	6.3	6.3	6.7	7.2	8.2
Canada	5.4	5.2	5.5	6.2	6.3	6.4	6.5	6.5	6.9	7.9

Source: Statistics Canada. 2012. Census Profile. 2011 Census. Statistics Canada Catalogue no. 98-316-XWE. Ottawa. Released October 24 2012.
http://www12.statcan.gc.ca/census-recensement/2011/dp-pd/prof/index.cfm?Lang=E

Age Characteristics: 50 Years and Over, and Median Age

Area	50 to 54 Years	55 to 59 Years	60 to 64 Years	65 to 69 Years	70 to 74 Years	75 to 79 Years	80 to 84 Years	85 Years and Over	Median Age
					Number				
					Total				
Kingston	9,030	8,100	7,365	5,725	4,535	4,015	3,080	2,980	40.3
Ontario	1,006,140	864,620	765,655	563,485	440,780	356,150	271,510	246,400	40.4
Canada	2,658,965	2,340,635	2,052,670	1,521,715	1,153,065	922,700	702,070	645,515	40.6
					Males				
Kingston	4,235	3,845	3,420	2,655	2,085	1,740	1,265	950	38.3
Ontario	492,560	418,755	370,370	270,875	206,350	161,345	113,620	80,925	39.4
Canada	1,309,030	1,147,300	1,002,690	738,010	543,435	417,945	291,085	208,300	39.6
					Females				
Kingston	4,795	4,255	3,950	3,070	2,455	2,280	1,815	2,025	42.1
Ontario	513,580	445,865	395,275	292,610	234,435	194,805	157,890	165,475	41.3
Canada	1,349,940	1,193,335	1,049,985	783,705	609,630	504,755	410,985	437,215	41.5
					Percent of Population				
					Total				
Kingston	7.3	6.6	6.0	4.6	3.7	3.3	2.5	2.4	–
Ontario	7.8	6.7	6.0	4.4	3.4	2.8	2.1	1.9	–
Canada	7.9	7.0	6.1	4.5	3.4	2.8	2.1	1.9	–
					Males				
Kingston	7.1	6.4	5.7	4.4	3.5	2.9	2.1	1.6	–
Ontario	7.9	6.7	5.9	4.3	3.3	2.6	1.8	1.3	–
Canada	8.0	7.0	6.1	4.5	3.3	2.5	1.8	1.3	–
					Females				
Kingston	7.6	6.7	6.2	4.8	3.9	3.6	2.9	3.2	–
Ontario	7.8	6.8	6.0	4.4	3.6	3.0	2.4	2.5	–
Canada	7.9	7.0	6.2	4.6	3.6	3.0	2.4	2.6	–

Source: Statistics Canada. 2012. Census Profile. 2011 Census. Statistics Canada Catalogue no. 98-316-XWE. Ottawa. Released October 24 2012.
http://www12.statcan.gc.ca/census-recensement/2011/dp-pd/prof/index.cfm?Lang=E

PROFILES / Kingston, Ontario

Private Households by Household Size

Area	1 Person	2 Persons	3 Persons	4 Persons	5 Persons	6 or More Persons	Average Number of Persons in Private Households
			Households				
Kingston	16,490	18,850	7,705	6,390	2,155	825	2.3
Ontario	1,230,975	1,584,415	803,030	783,925	310,860	174,305	2.6
Canada	3,673,310	4,544,820	2,081,900	1,903,300	724,405	392,885	2.5
			Percent of Households				
Kingston	31.5	36.0	14.7	12.2	4.1	1.6	–
Ontario	25.2	32.4	16.4	16.0	6.4	3.6	–
Canada	27.6	34.1	15.6	14.3	5.4	2.9	–

Source: Statistics Canada. 2012. Census Profile. 2011 Census. Statistics Canada Catalogue no. 98-316-XWE. Ottawa. Released October 24 2012.
http://www12.statcan.gc.ca/census-recensement/2011/dp-pd/prof/index.cfm?Lang=E

Dwelling Type

Area	Single-detached House	Semi-detached House	Row House	Apartment: Building with Five or More Storeys	Apartment: Building with Fewer Than Five Storeys	Duplex Apartment	Movable Dwelling	Other Single-attached House
				Number				
Kingston	25,970	4,135	3,485	7,895	8,740	1,885	175	130
Ontario	2,718,880	279,470	415,225	789,970	498,160	160,460	15,800	9,540
Canada	7,329,150	646,245	791,600	1,234,770	2,397,550	704,485	183,510	33,310
				Percent of Dwellings				
Kingston	49.6	7.9	6.6	15.1	16.7	3.6	0.3	0.2
Ontario	55.6	5.7	8.5	16.2	10.2	3.3	0.3	0.2
Canada	55.0	4.9	5.9	9.3	18.0	5.3	1.4	0.3

Source: Statistics Canada. 2012. Census Profile. 2011 Census. Statistics Canada Catalogue no. 98-316-XWE. Ottawa. Released October 24 2012.
http://www12.statcan.gc.ca/census-recensement/2011/dp-pd/prof/index.cfm?Lang=E

Shelter Costs

	Owned Dwellings				Rented Dwellings		
Area	Number	Median Value[1] ($)	Average Value[1] ($)	Median Monthly Costs[2] ($)	Average Monthly Costs[2] ($)	Number	Median Monthly Costs[3] ($)	Average Monthly Costs[3] ($)
Kingston	32,170	264,340	301,488	1,066	1,154	20,105	849	899
Ontario	3,446,650	300,862	367,428	1,163	1,284	1,385,535	892	926
Canada	9,013,410	280,552	345,182	978	1,141	4,060,385	784	848

Note: All figures cover non-farm, non-reserve private dwellings; (1) Refers to the dollar amount expected by the owner if the dwelling were to be sold; (2) Includes all shelter expenses paid by households that own their dwellings, such as the mortgage payment and the costs of electricity, heat, water and other municipal services, property taxes and condominium fees; (3) Includes all shelter expenses paid by households that rent their dwellings, such as the monthly rent and the costs of electricity, heat and municipal services.
Source: Statistics Canada. 2013. 2011 National Household Survey. Statistics Canada Catalogue no. 99-004-XWE. Ottawa. Released September 11, 2013.

Occupied Private Dwellings by Period of Construction

Area	1960 or Before	1961 to 1980	1981 to 1990	1991 to 2000	2001 to 2005	2006 to 2011
			Number			
Kingston	13,630	16,320	9,660	6,105	3,135	3,565
Ontario	1,330,235	1,420,570	763,430	609,310	414,795	348,310
Canada	3,273,105	4,152,715	2,112,110	1,707,880	1,031,020	1,042,430
			Percent of Dwellings			
Kingston	26.0	31.1	18.4	11.6	6.0	6.8
Ontario	27.2	29.1	15.6	12.5	8.5	7.1
Canada	24.6	31.2	15.9	12.8	7.7	7.8

Note: Figures cover non-farm, non-reserve private dwellings and includes data up to May 10, 2011.
Source: Statistics Canada. 2013. 2011 National Household Survey. Statistics Canada Catalogue no. 99-004-XWE. Ottawa. Released September 11, 2013.

Educational Attainment

Area	No Certificate, Diploma or Degree	High School Diploma or Equivalent[1]	Apprenticeship or Trades Certificate or Diploma[2]	College, CÉGEP or Other Non-University Certificate or Diploma	University Certificate or Diploma Below the Bachelor Level[3]	Bachelor's Degree	University Certificate, Diploma or Degree Above Bachelor Level[4]
Number							
Total							
Kingston	15,320	27,025	7,655	22,000	2,820	13,605	12,400
Ontario	1,954,520	2,801,805	771,140	2,070,875	427,150	1,515,075	933,100
Canada	5,485,400	6,968,935	2,950,685	4,970,020	1,200,130	3,634,425	2,049,930
Males							
Kingston	7,265	12,975	5,080	8,815	1,120	5,730	6,675
Ontario	957,040	1,337,055	520,390	894,235	193,355	692,345	470,290
Canada	2,742,875	3,305,415	1,928,970	2,118,430	513,235	1,643,080	1,043,350
Females							
Kingston	8,060	14,045	2,575	13,185	1,700	7,875	5,720
Ontario	997,475	1,464,755	250,750	1,176,640	233,790	822,730	462,805
Canada	2,742,520	3,663,515	1,021,715	2,851,595	686,890	1,991,345	1,006,585
Percent of Population							
Total							
Kingston	15.2	26.8	7.6	21.8	2.8	13.5	12.3
Ontario	18.7	26.8	7.4	19.8	4.1	14.5	8.9
Canada	20.1	25.6	10.8	18.2	4.4	13.3	7.5
Males							
Kingston	15.2	27.2	10.7	18.5	2.3	12.0	14.0
Ontario	18.9	26.4	10.3	17.7	3.8	13.7	9.3
Canada	20.6	24.9	14.5	15.9	3.9	12.4	7.8
Females							
Kingston	15.2	26.4	4.8	24.8	3.2	14.8	10.8
Ontario	18.4	27.1	4.6	21.8	4.3	15.2	8.6
Canada	19.6	26.2	7.3	20.4	4.9	14.3	7.2

Note: Figures cover total population aged 15 years and over by highest certificate, diploma or degree; (1) Includes persons who have graduated from a secondary school or equivalent. It excludes persons with a postsecondary certificate, diploma or degree; (2) Includes Registered Apprenticeship certificates (including Certificate of Qualification, Journeyperson's designation) and other trades certificates or diplomas such as pre-employment or vocational certificates and diplomas from brief trade programs completed at community colleges, institutes of technology, vocational centres, and similar institutions; (3) Comparisons with other data sources suggest that the category 'University certificate or diploma below the bachelor's level' was over-reported in the NHS. This category likely includes some responses that are actually college certificates or diplomas, bachelor's degrees or other types of education (e.g., university transfer programs, bachelor's programs completed in other countries, incomplete bachelor's programs, non-university professional designations). We recommend users interpret the results for the 'University certificate or diploma below the bachelor's level' category with caution; (4) 'University certificate or diploma above bachelor level' includes the categories: 'Degree in medicine, dentistry, veterinary medicine or optometry,' 'Master's degree' and 'Earned doctorate.'
Source: Statistics Canada. 2013. 2011 National Household Survey. Statistics Canada Catalogue no. 99-004-XWE. Ottawa. Released September 11, 2013.

Household Income Distribution

Area	Less than $10,000	$10,000 to $19,999	$20,000 to $29,999	$30,000 to $39,999	$40,000 to $49,999	$50,000 to $59,999	$60,000 to $79,999	$80,000 to $99,999	$100,000 to $124,999	$125,000 to $149,999	$150,000 and Over
Households												
Kingston	2,185	4,830	5,195	5,010	4,615	4,400	7,245	5,815	4,500	3,560	5,040
Ontario	201,780	354,530	405,725	425,410	425,720	398,705	680,850	552,660	497,970	331,460	611,840
Canada	626,705	1,141,945	1,193,925	1,271,675	1,206,800	1,102,120	1,865,280	1,458,240	1,260,770	802,555	1,389,240
Percent of Households												
Kingston	4.2	9.2	9.9	9.6	8.8	8.4	13.8	11.1	8.6	6.8	9.6
Ontario	4.1	7.3	8.3	8.7	8.7	8.2	13.9	11.3	10.2	6.8	12.5
Canada	4.7	8.6	9.0	9.5	9.1	8.3	14.0	10.9	9.5	6.0	10.4

Note: Household income is the sum of the total incomes of all members of that household. Total income refers to monetary receipts from certain sources, before income taxes and deductions, during calendar year 2010.
Source: Statistics Canada. 2013. 2011 National Household Survey. Statistics Canada Catalogue no. 99-004-XWE. Ottawa. Released September 11, 2013.

Median and Average Household and Economic Family Income

Area	Median Household Income ($)	Average Household Income ($)	Median After-tax Household Income ($)	Average After-tax Household Income ($)	Median Economic Family Income ($)	Average Economic Family Income ($)	Median After-tax Economic Family Income ($)	Average After-tax Economic Family Income ($)
Kingston	59,935	76,020	53,331	64,074	79,562	95,059	70,192	79,622
Ontario	66,358	85,772	58,717	71,523	80,987	100,152	71,128	83,322
Canada	61,072	79,102	54,089	66,149	76,511	94,125	67,044	78,517

Note: Figures cover household and economic familiy income in 2010. A household is defined as a person or a group of persons (other than foreign residents) who occupy the same private dwelling and do not have a usual place of residence elsewhere in Canada. Every person is a member of one and only one household. An economic family is defined as a group of two or more persons who live in the same dwelling and are related to each other by blood, marriage, common-law, adoption or a foster relationship. A couple may be of opposite or same sex.
Source: Statistics Canada. 2013. 2011 National Household Survey. Statistics Canada Catalogue no. 99-004-XWE. Ottawa. Released September 11, 2013.

PROFILES / Kingston, Ontario

Individual Income Distribution

Area	Less than $10,000	$10,000 to $19,999	$20,000 to $29,999	$30,000 to $39,999	$40,000 to $49,999	$50,000 to $59,999	$60,000 to $79,999	$80,000 to $99,999	$100,000 to $124,999	$125,000 and Over
					Number Total					
Kingston	15,805	17,220	13,840	11,240	10,475	7,625	9,620	5,345	2,985	2,900
Ontario	1,780,355	1,748,060	1,361,710	1,136,730	980,790	746,360	964,280	574,710	293,865	330,285
Canada	4,492,040	4,835,710	3,670,020	3,180,360	2,603,520	1,921,650	2,437,440	1,302,045	693,580	782,135
					Males					
Kingston	7,065	6,475	5,765	4,945	5,210	4,050	5,390	3,080	1,995	2,100
Ontario	781,095	669,815	580,990	535,255	491,125	407,005	569,205	341,160	201,125	244,500
Canada	1,936,365	1,864,880	1,588,260	1,522,190	1,333,510	1,079,780	1,473,145	823,720	492,905	599,905
					Females					
Kingston	8,740	10,750	8,070	6,295	5,265	3,575	4,230	2,270	995	800
Ontario	999,265	1,078,245	780,720	601,475	489,665	339,360	395,075	233,550	92,740	85,790
Canada	2,555,675	2,970,825	2,081,760	1,658,170	1,270,010	841,870	964,300	478,330	200,680	182,230
					Percent of Population Total					
Kingston	16.3	17.7	14.3	11.6	10.8	7.9	9.9	5.5	3.1	3.0
Ontario	18.0	17.6	13.7	11.5	9.9	7.5	9.7	5.8	3.0	3.3
Canada	17.3	18.7	14.2	12.3	10.0	7.4	9.4	5.0	2.7	3.0
					Males					
Kingston	15.3	14.1	12.5	10.7	11.3	8.8	11.7	6.7	4.3	4.6
Ontario	16.2	13.9	12.1	11.1	10.2	8.4	11.8	7.1	4.2	5.1
Canada	15.2	14.7	12.5	12.0	10.5	8.5	11.6	6.5	3.9	4.7
					Females					
Kingston	17.1	21.1	15.8	12.3	10.3	7.0	8.3	4.5	2.0	1.6
Ontario	19.6	21.2	15.3	11.8	9.6	6.7	7.8	4.6	1.8	1.7
Canada	19.4	22.5	15.8	12.6	9.6	6.4	7.3	3.6	1.5	1.4

Note: Figures cover individuals aged 15 years and over with income. Income refers to monetary receipts from certain sources, before income taxes and deductions, during calendar year 2010.
Source: Statistics Canada. 2013. 2011 National Household Survey. Statistics Canada Catalogue no. 99-004-XWE. Ottawa. Released September 11, 2013.

Labour Force Status

Area	In the Labour Force - All	In the Labour Force - Employed	In the Labour Force - Unemployed	Not in the Labour Force
		Number Total		
Kingston	64,935	59,470	5,465	35,895
Ontario	6,864,990	6,297,005	567,985	3,608,685
Canada	17,990,080	16,595,035	1,395,045	9,269,445
		Males		
Kingston	32,185	29,655	2,530	15,480
Ontario	3,542,030	3,249,165	292,865	1,522,690
Canada	9,388,570	8,634,310	754,255	3,906,785
		Females		
Kingston	32,745	29,815	2,935	20,410
Ontario	3,322,955	3,047,840	275,120	2,085,990
Canada	8,601,515	7,960,725	640,790	5,362,660
		Percent of Labour Force Total		
Kingston	64.4	59.0	8.4	35.6
Ontario	65.5	60.1	8.3	34.5
Canada	66.0	60.9	7.8	34.0
		Males		
Kingston	67.5	62.2	7.9	32.5
Ontario	69.9	64.2	8.3	30.1
Canada	70.6	64.9	8.0	29.4
		Females		
Kingston	61.6	56.1	9.0	38.4
Ontario	61.4	56.3	8.3	38.6
Canada	61.6	57.0	7.4	38.4

Note: Figures are based on total population 15 years and over
Source: Statistics Canada. 2013. 2011 National Household Survey. Statistics Canada Catalogue no. 99-004-XWE. Ottawa. Released September 11, 2013.

Labour Force by Industry (NAICS Codes 11–52)

Area	Agriculture, forestry, fishing & hunting	Mining, quarrying, & oil & gas extraction	Utilities	Construction	Manufacturing	Wholesale Trade	Retail Trade	Transportation & warehousing	Information & cultural industries	Finance & insurance
Number										
Total										
Kingston	235	55	285	3,345	2,595	1,290	7,105	1,685	1,050	1,970
Ontario	101,280	29,985	57,035	417,900	697,565	305,030	751,200	307,405	178,720	364,415
Canada	437,650	261,050	149,940	1,215,380	1,619,295	733,445	2,031,665	827,780	420,830	767,960
Males										
Kingston	175	40	250	3,055	2,060	960	3,405	1,280	390	650
Ontario	66,485	25,650	42,685	369,300	493,305	197,770	344,480	225,245	98,835	153,125
Canada	307,370	211,690	110,765	1,068,710	1,167,680	494,545	933,850	617,305	235,875	296,995
Females										
Kingston	60	0	35	295	530	330	3,700	405	660	1,320
Ontario	34,800	4,340	14,350	48,595	204,260	107,260	406,720	82,160	79,885	211,290
Canada	130,285	49,360	39,175	146,670	451,615	238,900	1,097,820	210,475	184,955	470,960
Percent of Labour Force										
Total										
Kingston	0.4	0.1	0.4	5.3	4.1	2.0	11.2	2.6	1.6	3.1
Ontario	1.5	0.4	0.9	6.3	10.4	4.6	11.2	4.6	2.7	5.5
Canada	2.5	1.5	0.9	6.9	9.2	4.2	11.6	4.7	2.4	4.4
Males										
Kingston	0.6	0.1	0.8	9.6	6.5	3.0	10.7	4.0	1.2	2.0
Ontario	1.9	0.7	1.2	10.7	14.3	5.7	10.0	6.5	2.9	4.4
Canada	3.3	2.3	1.2	11.6	12.7	5.4	10.2	6.7	2.6	3.2
Females										
Kingston	0.2	0.0	0.1	0.9	1.7	1.0	11.6	1.3	2.1	4.1
Ontario	1.1	0.1	0.4	1.5	6.3	3.3	12.6	2.5	2.5	6.5
Canada	1.6	0.6	0.5	1.7	5.4	2.8	13.1	2.5	2.2	5.6

Note: Figures are based on total experienced labour force 15 years and over. Experienced labour force refers to persons who, during the week of Sunday, May 1 to Saturday, May 7, 2011, were employed and the unemployed who had last worked for pay or in self-employment in either 2010 or 2011.
Source: Statistics Canada. 2013. 2011 National Household Survey. Statistics Canada Catalogue no. 99-004-XWE. Ottawa. Released September 11, 2013.

Labour Force by Industry (NAICS Codes 53–91)

Area	Real estate & rental & leasing	Profess., scientific & tech. services	Mgmt of companies & enterprises	Admin. & support, waste mgmt & remed. services	Educational services	Health care & social assistance	Arts, entertain. & recreation	Accomm. & food services	Other services (except public admin.)	Public admin.
Number										
Total										
Kingston	1,185	2,960	50	2,880	10,020	9,085	1,270	5,965	2,250	8,405
Ontario	133,980	511,020	6,525	309,630	499,690	692,130	144,065	417,675	296,340	458,665
Canada	321,895	1,240,850	17,460	728,330	1,301,435	1,949,650	363,405	1,130,750	807,800	1,261,050
Males										
Kingston	695	1,585	25	1,635	4,160	2,040	690	2,525	955	5,135
Ontario	72,835	281,420	3,540	172,475	162,765	120,165	75,035	177,240	133,795	236,655
Canada	179,090	688,625	9,380	411,250	424,915	349,430	188,270	469,990	372,940	652,510
Females										
Kingston	490	1,375	20	1,245	5,855	7,040	580	3,435	1,295	3,275
Ontario	61,145	229,600	2,990	137,155	336,925	571,965	69,030	240,430	162,550	222,015
Canada	142,805	552,225	8,075	317,085	876,515	1,600,220	175,135	660,760	434,865	608,535
Percent of Labour Force										
Total										
Kingston	1.9	4.6	0.1	4.5	15.7	14.3	2.0	9.4	3.5	13.2
Ontario	2.0	7.6	0.1	4.6	7.5	10.4	2.2	6.3	4.4	6.9
Canada	1.8	7.1	0.1	4.1	7.4	11.1	2.1	6.4	4.6	7.2
Males										
Kingston	2.2	5.0	0.1	5.2	13.1	6.4	2.2	8.0	3.0	16.2
Ontario	2.1	8.2	0.1	5.0	4.7	3.5	2.2	5.1	3.9	6.9
Canada	1.9	7.5	0.1	4.5	4.6	3.8	2.0	5.1	4.1	7.1
Females										
Kingston	1.5	4.3	0.1	3.9	18.3	22.0	1.8	10.7	4.1	10.2
Ontario	1.9	7.1	0.1	4.2	10.4	17.7	2.1	7.4	5.0	6.9
Canada	1.7	6.6	0.1	3.8	10.4	19.1	2.1	7.9	5.2	7.2

Note: Figures are based on total experienced labour force 15 years and over. Experienced labour force refers to persons who, during the week of Sunday, May 1 to Saturday, May 7, 2011, were employed and the unemployed who had last worked for pay or in self-employment in either 2010 or 2011.
Source: Statistics Canada. 2013. 2011 National Household Survey. Statistics Canada Catalogue no. 99-004-XWE. Ottawa. Released September 11, 2013.

Occupation

Area	Mgmt	Business, Finance & Admin.	Natural/ Applied Sciences & Related	Health	Education, Law & Social, Community & Government Services	Art, Culture, Recreation & Sport	Sales & Service	Trades, Transport & Equip. Operators & Related	Natural Resources, Agri. & Related Production	Mfg & Utilities
					Number					
					Total					
Kingston	6,435	9,160	3,700	5,535	12,740	2,065	16,340	6,090	605	1,015
Ontario	770,580	1,138,330	494,500	392,695	801,465	206,420	1,550,260	868,515	106,810	350,685
Canada	1,963,600	2,902,045	1,237,775	1,107,200	2,064,675	503,415	4,068,170	2,537,775	397,930	805,040
					Males					
Kingston	3,955	2,505	2,870	1,345	5,800	830	7,240	5,775	525	875
Ontario	474,655	352,505	384,345	78,330	264,570	96,055	673,880	812,280	82,610	233,565
Canada	1,229,460	854,190	966,355	217,520	676,550	232,535	1,745,705	2,385,615	318,945	564,300
					Females					
Kingston	2,480	6,650	835	4,185	6,940	1,235	9,095	315	80	145
Ontario	295,920	785,825	110,150	314,370	536,895	110,370	876,380	56,230	24,200	117,115
Canada	734,140	2,047,855	271,415	889,675	1,388,130	270,875	2,322,465	152,165	78,980	240,740
					Percent of Labour Force					
					Total					
Kingston	10.1	14.4	5.8	8.7	20.0	3.2	25.7	9.6	0.9	1.6
Ontario	11.5	17.0	7.4	5.9	12.0	3.1	23.2	13.0	1.6	5.2
Canada	11.2	16.5	7.0	6.3	11.7	2.9	23.1	14.4	2.3	4.6
					Males					
Kingston	12.5	7.9	9.0	4.2	18.3	2.6	22.8	18.2	1.7	2.8
Ontario	13.7	10.2	11.1	2.3	7.7	2.8	19.5	23.5	2.4	6.8
Canada	13.4	9.3	10.5	2.4	7.4	2.5	19.0	26.0	3.5	6.1
					Females					
Kingston	7.8	20.8	2.6	13.1	21.7	3.9	28.5	1.0	0.3	0.5
Ontario	9.2	24.3	3.4	9.7	16.6	3.4	27.2	1.7	0.7	3.6
Canada	8.7	24.4	3.2	10.6	16.5	3.2	27.7	1.8	0.9	2.9

Note: Figures are based on total experienced labour force 15 years and over.
Source: Statistics Canada. 2013. 2011 National Household Survey. Statistics Canada Catalogue no. 99-004-XWE. Ottawa. Released September 11, 2013.

Place of Work Status

Area	Worked at Home	Worked Outside Canada	No Fixed Workplace Address	Worked at Usual Place
		Number		
		Total		
Kingston	3,130	270	5,440	50,635
Ontario	423,790	31,390	670,835	5,170,980
Canada	1,142,640	66,460	1,868,245	13,517,690
		Males		
Kingston	1,485	195	3,855	24,120
Ontario	216,900	21,150	486,560	2,524,555
Canada	582,150	47,355	1,400,485	6,604,325
		Females		
Kingston	1,645	75	1,585	26,515
Ontario	206,895	10,240	184,275	2,646,420
Canada	560,490	19,100	467,760	6,913,370
		Percent of Labour Force		
		Total		
Kingston	5.3	0.5	9.1	85.1
Ontario	6.7	0.5	10.7	82.1
Canada	6.9	0.4	11.3	81.5
		Males		
Kingston	5.0	0.7	13.0	81.3
Ontario	6.7	0.7	15.0	77.7
Canada	6.7	0.5	16.2	76.5
		Females		
Kingston	5.5	0.3	5.3	88.9
Ontario	6.8	0.3	6.0	86.8
Canada	7.0	0.2	5.9	86.8

Note: Figures are based on total employed labour force 15 years and over.
Source: Statistics Canada. 2013. 2011 National Household Survey. Statistics Canada Catalogue no. 99-004-XWE. Ottawa. Released September 11, 2013.

Mode of Transportation to Work

Area	Car; Truck; Van; as Driver	Car; Truck; Van; as Passenger	Public Transit	Walked	Bicycled	All Other Modes
Number						
Total						
Kingston	40,075	4,530	3,450	5,875	1,500	640
Ontario	4,235,315	357,110	818,270	299,095	69,885	62,145
Canada	11,393,140	867,050	1,851,525	880,815	201,780	191,625
Males						
Kingston	20,600	1,705	1,345	2,910	1,070	355
Ontario	2,316,680	143,410	340,995	131,765	47,635	30,635
Canada	6,238,835	349,530	788,290	387,580	135,840	104,725
Females						
Kingston	19,480	2,825	2,105	2,965	430	290
Ontario	1,918,640	213,700	477,275	167,325	22,250	31,515
Canada	5,154,305	517,520	1,063,235	493,230	65,940	86,900
Percent of Labour Force						
Total						
Kingston	71.5	8.1	6.2	10.5	2.7	1.1
Ontario	72.5	6.1	14.0	5.1	1.2	1.1
Canada	74.0	5.6	12.0	5.7	1.3	1.2
Males						
Kingston	73.6	6.1	4.8	10.4	3.8	1.3
Ontario	76.9	4.8	11.3	4.4	1.6	1.0
Canada	77.9	4.4	9.8	4.8	1.7	1.3
Females						
Kingston	69.3	10.1	7.5	10.6	1.5	1.0
Ontario	67.8	7.5	16.9	5.9	0.8	1.1
Canada	69.8	7.0	14.4	6.7	0.9	1.2

Note: Figures are based on total employed labour force 15 years and over.
Source: Statistics Canada. 2013. 2011 National Household Survey. Statistics Canada Catalogue no. 99-004-XWE. Ottawa. Released September 11, 2013.

Visible Minority Population Characteristics

Area	Total Minority	South Asian[1]	Chinese	Black	Filipino	Latin American	Arab	SE Asian[2]	West Asian[3]	Korean	Japanese	Multiple[4]
Number												
Total												
Kingston	8,785	1,995	1,885	1,105	695	805	660	340	405	430	190	175
Ontario	3,279,565	965,990	629,140	539,205	275,380	172,560	151,645	137,875	122,530	78,290	29,085	96,735
Canada	6,264,750	1,567,400	1,324,750	945,665	619,310	381,280	380,620	312,075	206,840	161,130	87,270	171,935
Males												
Kingston	4,190	1,045	900	490	300	340	360	160	215	200	60	90
Ontario	1,582,480	484,355	301,575	251,295	116,825	83,205	79,620	67,645	62,515	38,045	13,345	46,765
Canada	3,043,010	790,755	632,325	453,005	268,885	186,355	203,485	154,035	105,620	77,165	38,270	83,335
Females												
Kingston	4,595	940	985	610	400	460	295	185	190	230	135	85
Ontario	1,697,085	481,635	327,570	287,915	158,555	89,360	72,025	70,230	60,010	40,250	15,740	49,970
Canada	3,221,745	776,650	692,420	492,660	350,425	194,925	177,140	158,045	101,220	83,965	48,990	88,600
Percent of Population												
Total												
Kingston	7.4	1.7	1.6	0.9	0.6	0.7	0.6	0.3	0.3	0.4	0.2	0.1
Ontario	25.9	7.6	5.0	4.3	2.2	1.4	1.2	1.1	1.0	0.6	0.2	0.8
Canada	19.1	4.8	4.0	2.9	1.9	1.2	1.2	0.9	0.6	0.5	0.3	0.5
Males												
Kingston	7.4	1.8	1.6	0.9	0.5	0.6	0.6	0.3	0.4	0.4	0.1	0.2
Ontario	25.6	7.8	4.9	4.1	1.9	1.3	1.3	1.1	1.0	0.6	0.2	0.8
Canada	18.8	4.9	3.9	2.8	1.7	1.2	1.3	1.0	0.7	0.5	0.2	0.5
Females												
Kingston	7.4	1.5	1.6	1.0	0.6	0.7	0.5	0.3	0.3	0.4	0.2	0.1
Ontario	26.2	7.4	5.1	4.4	2.5	1.4	1.1	1.1	0.9	0.6	0.2	0.8
Canada	19.3	4.7	4.1	3.0	2.1	1.2	1.1	0.9	0.6	0.5	0.3	0.5

Note: The Employment Equity Act defines visible minorities as 'persons, other than Aboriginal peoples, who are non-Caucasian in race or non-white in colour';
(1) Includes 'East Indian,' 'Pakistani,' 'Sri Lankan,' etc.; (2) Includes 'Vietnamese,' 'Cambodian,' 'Malaysian,' 'Laotian,' etc.; (3) Includes 'Iranian,' 'Afghan,' etc.; (4) Includes respondents who reported more than one visible minority group by checking two or more mark-in circles, e.g., 'Black' and 'South Asian.'
Source: Statistics Canada. 2013. 2011 National Household Survey. Statistics Canada Catalogue no. 99-004-XWE. Ottawa. Released September 11, 2013.

PROFILES / Kingston, Ontario

Aboriginal Population

Area	Aboriginal Identity[1]	First Nations (North American Indian) Single Identity[2]	Métis Single Identity	Inuk (Inuit) Single Identity	Multiple Aboriginal Identities[3]	Aboriginal Identities Not Included Elsewhere
Number						
Total						
Kingston	3,485	2,350	945	60	15	115
Ontario	301,430	201,100	86,020	3,355	2,910	8,040
Canada	1,400,685	851,560	451,795	59,440	11,415	26,475
Males						
Kingston	1,805	1,280	430	0	0	60
Ontario	145,020	96,620	41,755	1,475	1,420	3,750
Canada	682,190	411,785	223,335	29,495	5,525	12,055
Females						
Kingston	1,680	1,070	520	30	0	55
Ontario	156,410	104,485	44,260	1,880	1,490	4,295
Canada	718,500	439,775	228,460	29,950	5,890	14,420
Percent of Population						
Total						
Kingston	2.9	2.0	0.8	0.1	0.0	0.1
Ontario	2.4	1.6	0.7	0.0	0.0	0.1
Canada	4.3	2.6	1.4	0.2	0.0	0.1
Males						
Kingston	3.2	2.2	0.8	0.0	0.0	0.1
Ontario	2.3	1.6	0.7	0.0	0.0	0.1
Canada	4.2	2.5	1.4	0.2	0.0	0.1
Females						
Kingston	2.7	1.7	0.8	0.0	0.0	0.1
Ontario	2.4	1.6	0.7	0.0	0.0	0.1
Canada	4.3	2.6	1.4	0.2	0.0	0.1

Note: (1) Includes persons who reported being an Aboriginal person, that is, First Nations (North American Indian), Métis or Inuk (Inuit) and/or those who reported Registered or Treaty Indian status, that is registered under the Indian Act of Canada, and/or those who reported membership in a First Nation or Indian band. Aboriginal peoples of Canada are defined in the Constitution Act, 1982, section 35-2 as including the Indian, Inuit and Métis peoples of Canada; (2) Users should be aware that the estimates associated with this variable are more affected than most by the incomplete enumeration of certain Indian reserves and Indian settlements in the National Household Survey (NHS); (3) Includes persons who reported being any two or all three of the following: First Nations (North American Indian), Métis or Inuk (Inuit).
Source: Statistics Canada. 2013. 2011 National Household Survey. Statistics Canada Catalogue no. 99-004-XWE. Ottawa. Released September 11, 2013.

Ethnic Origin

Area	North American Aboriginal	Other North American	European	Caribbean	Latin, Central and South American	African	Asian	Oceania
Number								
Total								
Kingston	5,785	40,810	93,475	1,000	1,150	1,130	7,640	225
Ontario	441,395	3,059,480	8,231,410	396,485	271,545	331,460	2,604,595	19,410
Canada	1,836,035	11,070,455	20,157,965	627,590	544,375	766,735	5,011,225	74,875
Males								
Kingston	2,880	19,565	44,615	455	515	530	3,820	115
Ontario	210,490	1,507,105	4,019,885	181,805	130,035	160,940	1,265,540	9,855
Canada	885,675	5,462,685	9,913,150	291,640	264,635	387,360	2,435,540	37,490
Females								
Kingston	2,905	21,250	48,855	540	635	600	3,820	110
Ontario	230,905	1,552,380	4,211,525	214,675	141,510	170,515	1,339,050	9,555
Canada	950,360	5,607,770	10,244,820	335,945	279,740	379,380	2,575,680	37,385
Percent of Population								
Total								
Kingston	4.9	34.3	78.6	0.8	1.0	1.0	6.4	0.2
Ontario	3.5	24.2	65.1	3.1	2.1	2.6	20.6	0.2
Canada	5.6	33.7	61.4	1.9	1.7	2.3	15.3	0.2
Males								
Kingston	5.1	34.3	78.3	0.8	0.9	0.9	6.7	0.2
Ontario	3.4	24.4	65.0	2.9	2.1	2.6	20.5	0.2
Canada	5.5	33.8	61.3	1.8	1.6	2.4	15.1	0.2
Females								
Kingston	4.7	34.3	78.9	0.9	1.0	1.0	6.2	0.2
Ontario	3.6	24.0	65.1	3.3	2.2	2.6	20.7	0.1
Canada	5.7	33.6	61.4	2.0	1.7	2.3	15.4	0.2

Note: The sum of the ethnic groups in this table is greater than the total population estimate because a person may report more than one ethnic origin in the NHS.
Source: Statistics Canada. 2013. 2011 National Household Survey. Statistics Canada Catalogue no. 99-004-XWE. Ottawa. Released September 11, 2013.

Religion

Area	Buddhist	Christian	Hindu	Jewish	Muslim	Sikh	Traditional (Aboriginal) Spirituality	Other Religions	No Religious Affiliation
				Number Total					
Kingston	375	78,880	520	785	1,735	125	70	1,000	35,435
Ontario	163,750	8,167,295	366,720	195,540	581,950	179,765	15,905	53,080	2,927,790
Canada	366,830	22,102,745	497,965	329,495	1,053,945	454,965	64,935	130,835	7,850,605
				Males					
Kingston	195	35,620	300	360	955	50	45	405	19,080
Ontario	75,355	3,839,925	183,580	95,795	293,925	90,515	7,600	23,555	1,571,195
Canada	168,465	10,497,775	250,435	161,265	540,555	229,435	31,805	57,745	4,225,645
				Females					
Kingston	185	43,250	225	420	780	80	30	595	16,350
Ontario	88,395	4,327,365	183,140	99,740	288,025	89,250	8,310	29,525	1,356,600
Canada	198,365	11,604,975	247,525	168,235	513,395	225,530	33,135	73,090	3,624,965
				Percent of Population Total					
Kingston	0.3	66.3	0.4	0.7	1.5	0.1	0.1	0.8	29.8
Ontario	1.3	64.6	2.9	1.5	4.6	1.4	0.1	0.4	23.1
Canada	1.1	67.3	1.5	1.0	3.2	1.4	0.2	0.4	23.9
				Males					
Kingston	0.3	62.5	0.5	0.6	1.7	0.1	0.1	0.7	33.5
Ontario	1.2	62.1	3.0	1.5	4.8	1.5	0.1	0.4	25.4
Canada	1.0	64.9	1.5	1.0	3.3	1.4	0.2	0.4	26.1
				Females					
Kingston	0.3	69.8	0.4	0.7	1.3	0.1	0.0	1.0	26.4
Ontario	1.4	66.9	2.8	1.5	4.5	1.4	0.1	0.5	21.0
Canada	1.2	69.5	1.5	1.0	3.1	1.4	0.2	0.4	21.7

Note: Religion refers to the person's self-identification as having a connection or affiliation with any religious denomination, group, body, sect, cult or other religiously defined community or system of belief. Religion is not limited to formal membership in a religious organization or group. Persons without a religious connection or affiliation can self-identify as atheist, agnostic or humanist, or can provide another applicable response.
Source: Statistics Canada. 2013. 2011 National Household Survey. Statistics Canada Catalogue no. 99-004-XWE. Ottawa. Released September 11, 2013.

Religion—Christian Denominations

Area	Anglican	Baptist	Catholic	Christian Orthodox	Lutheran	Pentecostal	Presbyterian	United Church	Other Christian
				Number Total					
Kingston	12,430	1,310	33,410	1,065	870	1,930	2,375	15,520	9,955
Ontario	774,560	244,650	3,976,610	297,710	163,460	213,945	319,585	952,465	1,224,300
Canada	1,631,845	635,840	12,810,705	550,690	478,185	478,705	472,385	2,007,610	3,036,780
				Males					
Kingston	5,175	555	15,725	490	370	785	1,040	6,890	4,590
Ontario	355,175	112,285	1,895,940	145,825	75,225	94,955	148,535	435,255	576,730
Canada	752,945	293,905	6,167,290	270,205	221,525	217,850	218,955	912,545	1,442,550
				Females					
Kingston	7,255	760	17,685	570	495	1,150	1,340	8,630	5,365
Ontario	419,390	132,370	2,080,665	151,885	88,230	118,990	171,050	517,210	647,570
Canada	878,900	341,940	6,643,415	280,485	256,660	260,850	253,430	1,095,065	1,594,230
				Percent of Population Total					
Kingston	10.5	1.1	28.1	0.9	0.7	1.6	2.0	13.0	8.4
Ontario	6.1	1.9	31.4	2.4	1.3	1.7	2.5	7.5	9.7
Canada	5.0	1.9	39.0	1.7	1.5	1.5	1.4	6.1	9.2
				Males					
Kingston	9.1	1.0	27.6	0.9	0.6	1.4	1.8	12.1	8.1
Ontario	5.7	1.8	30.7	2.4	1.2	1.5	2.4	7.0	9.3
Canada	4.7	1.8	38.2	1.7	1.4	1.3	1.4	5.6	8.9
				Females					
Kingston	11.7	1.2	28.6	0.9	0.8	1.9	2.2	13.9	8.7
Ontario	6.5	2.0	32.2	2.3	1.4	1.8	2.6	8.0	10.0
Canada	5.3	2.0	39.8	1.7	1.5	1.6	1.5	6.6	9.6

Note: Religion refers to the person's self-identification as having a connection or affiliation with any religious denomination, group, body, sect, cult or other religiously defined community or system of belief. Religion is not limited to formal membership in a religious organization or group. Persons without a religious connection or affiliation can self-identify as atheist, agnostic or humanist, or can provide another applicable response.
Source: Statistics Canada. 2013. 2011 National Household Survey. Statistics Canada Catalogue no. 99-004-XWE. Ottawa. Released September 11, 2013.

PROFILES / Kingston, Ontario

Immigrant Status and Period of Immigration

Area	Non-Immigrants[1]	Immigrants All	Before 1971	1971 to 1980	1981 to 1990	1991 to 2000	2001 to 2005	2006 to 2011	Non-Permanent Residents[3]
				Number Total					
Kingston	102,365	15,445	5,915	2,135	1,980	2,090	1,650	1,685	1,120
Ontario	8,906,000	3,611,365	723,030	464,380	538,285	866,220	518,405	501,060	134,425
Canada	25,720,175	6,775,765	1,261,055	870,775	949,890	1,539,050	992,070	1,162,915	356,385
				Males					
Kingston	49,140	7,230	2,655	980	930	1,060	810	795	635
Ontario	4,410,240	1,706,385	341,820	217,990	258,095	408,270	245,850	234,360	64,825
Canada	12,753,235	3,231,370	605,430	416,670	454,570	724,905	474,545	555,245	178,515
				Females					
Kingston	53,225	8,215	3,255	1,155	1,050	1,035	835	890	485
Ontario	4,495,765	1,904,985	381,210	246,390	280,190	457,950	272,550	266,695	69,600
Canada	12,966,935	3,544,400	655,625	454,105	495,325	814,145	517,530	607,670	177,870
				Percent of Population Total					
Kingston	86.1	13.0	5.0	1.8	1.7	1.8	1.4	1.4	0.9
Ontario	70.4	28.5	5.7	3.7	4.3	6.8	4.1	4.0	1.1
Canada	78.3	20.6	3.8	2.7	2.9	4.7	3.0	3.5	1.1
				Males					
Kingston	86.2	12.7	4.7	1.7	1.6	1.9	1.4	1.4	1.1
Ontario	71.3	27.6	5.5	3.5	4.2	6.6	4.0	3.8	1.0
Canada	78.9	20.0	3.7	2.6	2.8	4.5	2.9	3.4	1.1
				Females					
Kingston	86.0	13.3	5.3	1.9	1.7	1.7	1.3	1.4	0.8
Ontario	69.5	29.4	5.9	3.8	4.3	7.1	4.2	4.1	1.1
Canada	77.7	21.2	3.9	2.7	3.0	4.9	3.1	3.6	1.1

Note: (1) Non-immigrant refers to a person who is a Canadian citizen by birth; (2) Immigrant refers to a person who is or has ever been a landed immigrant/permanent resident. This person has been granted the right to live in Canada permanently by immigration authorities. Some immigrants have resided in Canada for a number of years, while others have arrived recently. Some immigrants are Canadian citizens, while others are not. Most immigrants are born outside Canada, but a small number are born in Canada. In the 2011 National Household Survey, 'Immigrants' includes immigrants who landed in Canada prior to May 10, 2011; (3) Non-permanent resident refers to a person from another country who has a work or study permit, or who is a refugee claimant, and any non-Canadian-born family member living in Canada with them.
Source: Statistics Canada. 2013. 2011 National Household Survey. Statistics Canada Catalogue no. 99-004-XWE. Ottawa. Released September 11, 2013.

Mother Tongue

Area	English	French	Non-official Language	English & French	English & Non-official Language	French & Non-official Language	English, French & Non-official Language
			Number Total				
Kingston	102,845	4,315	11,750	485	790	85	50
Ontario	8,677,040	493,300	3,264,435	46,605	219,425	13,645	7,615
Canada	18,858,980	7,054,975	6,567,680	144,685	396,330	74,430	24,095
			Males				
Kingston	49,485	2,155	5,610	215	345	40	30
Ontario	4,276,970	232,785	1,562,190	21,805	106,790	6,285	3,495
Canada	9,345,225	3,452,380	3,157,785	69,975	192,000	36,535	11,965
			Females				
Kingston	53,365	2,165	6,140	270	435	50	20
Ontario	4,400,065	260,510	1,702,240	24,795	112,635	7,365	4,115
Canada	9,513,750	3,602,590	3,409,895	74,710	204,330	37,890	12,130
			Percent of Population Total				
Kingston	85.5	3.6	9.8	0.4	0.7	0.1	0.0
Ontario	68.2	3.9	25.7	0.4	1.7	0.1	0.1
Canada	56.9	21.3	19.8	0.4	1.2	0.2	0.1
			Males				
Kingston	85.5	3.7	9.7	0.4	0.6	0.1	0.1
Ontario	68.9	3.7	25.2	0.4	1.7	0.1	0.1
Canada	57.5	21.2	19.4	0.4	1.2	0.2	0.1
			Females				
Kingston	85.5	3.5	9.8	0.4	0.7	0.1	0.0
Ontario	67.6	4.0	26.1	0.4	1.7	0.1	0.1
Canada	56.4	21.4	20.2	0.4	1.2	0.2	0.1

Note: Figures cover total population excluding institutional residents.
Source: Statistics Canada. 2012. Census Profile. 2011 Census. Statistics Canada Catalogue no. 98-316-XWE. Ottawa. Released October 24 2012.
http://www12.statcan.gc.ca/census-recensement/2011/dp-pd/prof/index.cfm?Lang=E

Language Spoken Most Often at Home

Area	English	French	Non-official Language	English & French	English & Non-official Language	French & Non-official Language	English, French & Non-official Language
Number							
Total							
Kingston	111,415	2,160	4,705	360	1,565	30	85
Ontario	10,044,810	284,115	1,827,870	37,955	509,105	6,370	11,845
Canada	21,457,075	6,827,865	3,673,865	131,205	875,135	109,700	46,330
Males							
Kingston	53,545	1,105	2,240	160	780	15	25
Ontario	4,930,610	133,495	872,860	17,250	248,050	2,855	5,225
Canada	10,585,620	3,348,235	1,767,310	63,475	425,370	53,010	22,845
Females							
Kingston	57,865	1,055	2,465	205	790	15	55
Ontario	5,114,200	150,620	955,010	20,705	261,055	3,520	6,620
Canada	10,871,455	3,479,625	1,906,555	67,730	449,765	56,690	23,485
Percent of Population							
Total							
Kingston	92.6	1.8	3.9	0.3	1.3	0.0	0.1
Ontario	79.0	2.2	14.4	0.3	4.0	0.1	0.1
Canada	64.8	20.6	11.1	0.4	2.6	0.3	0.1
Males							
Kingston	92.5	1.9	3.9	0.3	1.3	0.0	0.0
Ontario	79.4	2.1	14.1	0.3	4.0	0.0	0.1
Canada	65.1	20.6	10.9	0.4	2.6	0.3	0.1
Females							
Kingston	92.7	1.7	3.9	0.3	1.3	0.0	0.1
Ontario	78.5	2.3	14.7	0.3	4.0	0.1	0.1
Canada	64.5	20.6	11.3	0.4	2.7	0.3	0.1

Note: Figures cover total population excluding institutional residents.
Source: Statistics Canada. 2012. Census Profile. 2011 Census. Statistics Canada Catalogue no. 98-316-XWE. Ottawa. Released October 24 2012.
http://www12.statcan.gc.ca/census-recensement/2011/dp-pd/prof/index.cfm?Lang=E

Knowledge of Official Languages

Area	English Only	French Only	English & French	Neither English nor French
Number				
Total				
Kingston	103,460	290	16,010	555
Ontario	10,984,360	42,980	1,395,805	298,920
Canada	22,564,665	4,165,015	5,795,570	595,920
Males				
Kingston	50,020	140	7,495	220
Ontario	5,445,050	18,805	627,725	118,765
Canada	11,222,185	1,925,340	2,876,560	241,790
Females				
Kingston	53,440	155	8,515	340
Ontario	5,539,310	24,175	768,085	180,155
Canada	11,342,485	2,239,680	2,919,005	354,135
Percent of Population				
Total				
Kingston	86.0	0.2	13.3	0.5
Ontario	86.3	0.3	11.0	2.3
Canada	68.1	12.6	17.5	1.8
Males				
Kingston	86.4	0.2	13.0	0.4
Ontario	87.7	0.3	10.1	1.9
Canada	69.0	11.8	17.7	1.5
Females				
Kingston	85.6	0.2	13.6	0.5
Ontario	85.1	0.4	11.8	2.8
Canada	67.3	13.3	17.3	2.1

Note: Figures cover total population excluding institutional residents.
Source: Statistics Canada. 2012. Census Profile. 2011 Census. Statistics Canada Catalogue no. 98-316-XWE. Ottawa. Released October 24 2012.
http://www12.statcan.gc.ca/census-recensement/2011/dp-pd/prof/index.cfm?Lang=E

Kitchener, Ontario

Background

Kitchener is located in Southern Ontario, approximately 100 kilometres west of Toronto. The metropolitan area is surrounded by the cities of Cambridge to the south and Waterloo to the north. The City of Kitchener is often called "Kitchener–Waterloo" despite the areas having separate municipal governments. Kitchener is the largest municipality in the Waterloo Region as well as the seat of the municipal region.

Kitchener was shaped by German Mennonite farming families from Pennsylvania who immigrated to the region in the early 1800s. In 1816, the settlement was designated the Township of Waterloo and renamed Berlin in 1833. When "Busy Berlin" began its industrialization in the 19th century, the city was considered Canada's "German capital" and the only Canadian city with a non-British, non-French majority. Berlin changed its name to the City of Kitchener during World War I in 1916. The city's post-war economy was manufacturing of bricks, rubber, tires, textiles and leather goods.

Today, Kitchener has four heritage conservation districts that preserve the architecture of the post-World War II era, the former village of Doon (est. 1914), Victorian architecture and historic civic buildings.

In recent years, Kitchener has been investing in key industries such as life sciences, biotechnology and digital media. The University of Waterloo and Wilfred Laurier University are opening downtown Kitchener campuses and McMaster University recently opened a satellite of its medical school. Kitchener's downtown is undergoing a revitalization that includes high-density development as well as the conversion of a former tannery plant into Google Canada's head office.

Since 1969, Kitchener has hosted the largest Bavarian festival in North America, the Kitchener–Waterloo Oktoberfest. Other festivities include Hockey Town, KW Multicultural Festival and the Festival of Neighbourhoods.

Kitchener has summer highs of plus 24.67 degrees Celsius, winter lows of minus 9.67 degrees Celsius, and an average rainfall just over 765 mm per year.

Rankings

- Kitchener was ranked #75 out of 190 Canadian cities in *Money Sense Magazine's* annual "Best Places to Live" list. The 2012 survey ranked Kitchener #66 for "Best Place for Finding a Job" and #78 for "Best Place to Raise Kids." *Money Sense Magazine, "Canada's Best Places to Live 2012," March 20, 2012*
- Kitchener was ranked #1 for best overall project in Canada in 2011. The Canadian Urban Institute's annual Brownie Awards recognizes leadership, innovation and environmental sustainability in the redevelopment of brownfields across Canada. Kitchener's Tannery District outranked finalists from Vancouver, Toronto and Uxbridge (ON). *Canadian Urban Institute's Annual Brownie Awards, 2011 Winner, Category 4: Excellence in Project Scale at the Building Scale," October 4th, 2011*
- The Tourism Industry Association of Canada (TIAC) ranked Kitchener as one of the finalists in the 2012 Canadian Tourism Awards. Criteria: success, leadership, innovation, superior tourism experiences. Kitchener ranked as 1 of 4 finalists competing for the Via Rail Canada Community Service Award. Other cities included Cambridge/Waterloo, Toronto and Winnipeg. *Tourism Industry Association of Canada (TIAC), "Finalists for the 2012 Canadian Tourism Awards, Oct 4th, 2012" (Winners to be announced November 20, 2012)*

PROFILES / Kitchener, Ontario

Population Growth and Density

Area	Population in 2001	Population in 2006	Population in 2011	Population Change 2001–2006	Population Change 2006–2011	Land Area (sq. km)	Population Density per sq. km
Kitchener	190,399	204,668	219,153	7.5	7.1	136.79	1,602.1
Ontario	11,410,046	12,160,282	12,851,821	6.6	5.7	908,607.67	14.1
Canada	30,007,094	31,612,897	33,476,688	5.4	5.9	8,965,121.42	3.7

Source: Statistics Canada. 2012. Census Profile. 2011 Census. Statistics Canada Catalogue no. 98-316-XWE. Ottawa. Released October 24 2012.
http://www12.statcan.gc.ca/census-recensement/2011/dp-pd/prof/index.cfm?Lang=E;
Statistics Canada 2007. 2006 Community Profiles. 2006 Census. Statistics Canada Catalogue no. 92-591-XWE. Ottawa. Released March 13 2007.
http://www12.statcan.ca/census-recensement/2006/dp-pd/prof/92-591/index.cfm?Lang=E

Gender

Area	Males	Females
Number		
Kitchener	107,735	111,420
Ontario	6,263,140	6,588,685
Canada	16,414,225	17,062,460
Percent of Population		
Kitchener	49.2	50.8
Ontario	48.7	51.3
Canada	49.0	51.0

Source: Statistics Canada. 2012. Census Profile. 2011 Census. Statistics Canada Catalogue no. 98-316-XWE. Ottawa. Released October 24 2012.
http://www12.statcan.gc.ca/census-recensement/2011/dp-pd/prof/index.cfm?Lang=E

Marital Status

Area	Married[1]	Living Common-law	Single[2]	Separated	Divorced	Widowed
Number — Total						
Kitchener	87,105	16,060	50,960	6,045	11,020	9,310
Ontario	5,367,400	791,210	2,985,020	319,805	593,730	613,880
Canada	12,941,960	3,142,525	7,816,045	698,240	1,686,035	1,584,530
Males						
Kitchener	43,550	8,005	27,810	2,465	4,325	1,815
Ontario	2,681,320	397,620	1,583,760	133,790	231,160	117,980
Canada	6,470,300	1,575,495	4,206,320	299,655	680,415	310,940
Females						
Kitchener	43,555	8,055	23,155	3,580	6,695	7,495
Ontario	2,686,075	393,590	1,401,260	186,015	362,570	495,905
Canada	6,471,660	1,567,035	3,609,730	398,585	1,005,620	1,273,590
Percent of Population — Total						
Kitchener	48.3	8.9	28.2	3.3	6.1	5.2
Ontario	50.3	7.4	28.0	3.0	5.6	5.8
Canada	46.4	11.3	28.0	2.5	6.0	5.7
Males						
Kitchener	49.5	9.1	31.6	2.8	4.9	2.1
Ontario	52.1	7.7	30.8	2.6	4.5	2.3
Canada	47.8	11.6	31.1	2.2	5.0	2.3
Females						
Kitchener	47.1	8.7	25.0	3.9	7.2	8.1
Ontario	48.6	7.1	25.4	3.4	6.6	9.0
Canada	45.2	10.9	25.2	2.8	7.0	8.9

Note: (1) and not separated, (2) never legally married
Source: Statistics Canada. 2012. Census Profile. 2011 Census. Statistics Canada Catalogue no. 98-316-XWE. Ottawa. Released October 24 2012.
http://www12.statcan.gc.ca/census-recensement/2011/dp-pd/prof/index.cfm?Lang=E

Age Characteristics: 0 to 49 Years

Area	0 to 4 Years	5 to 9 Years	10 to 14 Years	15 to 19 Years	20 to 24 Years	25 to 29 Years	30 to 34 Years	35 to 39 Years	40 to 44 Years	45 to 49 Years
					Number					
					Total					
Kitchener	13,705	12,320	12,620	14,025	15,955	17,620	16,395	15,500	15,850	17,245
Ontario	704,260	712,755	763,755	863,635	852,910	815,120	800,365	844,335	924,075	1,055,880
Canada	1,877,095	1,809,895	1,920,355	2,178,135	2,187,450	2,169,590	2,162,905	2,173,930	2,324,875	2,675,130
					Males					
Kitchener	7,010	6,270	6,485	7,205	7,980	8,720	8,230	7,745	7,935	8,535
Ontario	360,590	365,290	391,630	443,680	432,490	400,045	383,340	405,845	447,920	517,510
Canada	961,150	925,965	983,995	1,115,845	1,108,775	1,077,275	1,058,810	1,064,200	1,141,720	1,318,715
					Females					
Kitchener	6,700	6,055	6,135	6,820	7,970	8,900	8,160	7,750	7,915	8,705
Ontario	343,670	347,465	372,125	419,950	420,415	415,075	417,030	438,485	476,155	538,370
Canada	915,945	883,935	936,360	1,062,295	1,078,670	1,092,315	1,104,095	1,109,735	1,183,155	1,356,420
					Percent of Population					
					Total					
Kitchener	6.3	5.6	5.8	6.4	7.3	8.0	7.5	7.1	7.2	7.9
Ontario	5.5	5.5	5.9	6.7	6.6	6.3	6.2	6.6	7.2	8.2
Canada	5.6	5.4	5.7	6.5	6.5	6.5	6.5	6.5	6.9	8.0
					Males					
Kitchener	6.5	5.8	6.0	6.7	7.4	8.1	7.6	7.2	7.4	7.9
Ontario	5.8	5.8	6.3	7.1	6.9	6.4	6.1	6.5	7.2	8.3
Canada	5.9	5.6	6.0	6.8	6.8	6.6	6.5	6.5	7.0	8.0
					Females					
Kitchener	6.0	5.4	5.5	6.1	7.2	8.0	7.3	7.0	7.1	7.8
Ontario	5.2	5.3	5.6	6.4	6.4	6.3	6.3	6.7	7.2	8.2
Canada	5.4	5.2	5.5	6.2	6.3	6.4	6.5	6.5	6.9	7.9

Source: Statistics Canada. 2012. Census Profile. 2011 Census. Statistics Canada Catalogue no. 98-316-XWE. Ottawa. Released October 24 2012.
http://www12.statcan.gc.ca/census-recensement/2011/dp-pd/prof/index.cfm?Lang=E

Age Characteristics: 50 Years and Over, and Median Age

Area	50 to 54 Years	55 to 59 Years	60 to 64 Years	65 to 69 Years	70 to 74 Years	75 to 79 Years	80 to 84 Years	85 Years and Over	Median Age
				Number					
				Total					
Kitchener	16,065	13,655	11,330	8,115	6,260	4,985	3,980	3,525	37.2
Ontario	1,006,140	864,620	765,655	563,485	440,780	356,150	271,510	246,400	40.4
Canada	2,658,965	2,340,635	2,052,670	1,521,715	1,153,065	922,700	702,070	645,515	40.6
				Males					
Kitchener	7,900	6,570	5,485	3,795	2,955	2,190	1,595	1,135	36.3
Ontario	492,560	418,755	370,370	270,875	206,350	161,345	113,620	80,925	39.4
Canada	1,309,030	1,147,300	1,002,690	738,010	543,435	417,945	291,085	208,300	39.6
				Females					
Kitchener	8,160	7,090	5,845	4,325	3,305	2,800	2,390	2,390	38.1
Ontario	513,580	445,865	395,275	292,610	234,435	194,805	157,890	165,475	41.3
Canada	1,349,940	1,193,335	1,049,985	783,705	609,630	504,755	410,985	437,215	41.5
				Percent of Population					
				Total					
Kitchener	7.3	6.2	5.2	3.7	2.9	2.3	1.8	1.6	–
Ontario	7.8	6.7	6.0	4.4	3.4	2.8	2.1	1.9	–
Canada	7.9	7.0	6.1	4.5	3.4	2.8	2.1	1.9	–
				Males					
Kitchener	7.3	6.1	5.1	3.5	2.7	2.0	1.5	1.1	–
Ontario	7.9	6.7	5.9	4.3	3.3	2.6	1.8	1.3	–
Canada	8.0	7.0	6.1	4.5	3.3	2.5	1.8	1.3	–
				Females					
Kitchener	7.3	6.4	5.2	3.9	3.0	2.5	2.1	2.1	–
Ontario	7.8	6.8	6.0	4.4	3.6	3.0	2.4	2.5	–
Canada	7.9	7.0	6.2	4.6	3.6	3.0	2.4	2.6	–

Source: Statistics Canada. 2012. Census Profile. 2011 Census. Statistics Canada Catalogue no. 98-316-XWE. Ottawa. Released October 24 2012.
http://www12.statcan.gc.ca/census-recensement/2011/dp-pd/prof/index.cfm?Lang=E

PROFILES / Kitchener, Ontario

Private Households by Household Size

Area	1 Person	2 Persons	3 Persons	4 Persons	5 Persons	6 or More Persons	Average Number of Persons in Private Households
			Households				
Kitchener	22,970	28,550	14,525	13,095	4,800	2,430	2.5
Ontario	1,230,975	1,584,415	803,030	783,925	310,860	174,305	2.6
Canada	3,673,310	4,544,820	2,081,900	1,903,300	724,405	392,885	2.5
			Percent of Households				
Kitchener	26.6	33.1	16.8	15.2	5.6	2.8	—
Ontario	25.2	32.4	16.4	16.0	6.4	3.6	—
Canada	27.6	34.1	15.6	14.3	5.4	2.9	—

Source: Statistics Canada. 2012. Census Profile. 2011 Census. Statistics Canada Catalogue no. 98-316-XWE. Ottawa. Released October 24 2012.
http://www12.statcan.gc.ca/census-recensement/2011/dp-pd/prof/index.cfm?Lang=E

Dwelling Type

Area	Single-detached House	Semi-detached House	Row House	Apartment: Building with Five or More Storeys	Apartment: Building with Fewer Than Five Storeys	Duplex Apartment	Movable Dwelling	Other Single-attached House
				Number				
Kitchener	43,105	5,425	9,745	12,240	13,160	2,620	20	70
Ontario	2,718,880	279,470	415,225	789,970	498,160	160,460	15,800	9,540
Canada	7,329,150	646,245	791,600	1,234,770	2,397,550	704,485	183,510	33,310
				Percent of Dwellings				
Kitchener	49.9	6.3	11.3	14.2	15.2	3.0	0.0	0.1
Ontario	55.6	5.7	8.5	16.2	10.2	3.3	0.3	0.2
Canada	55.0	4.9	5.9	9.3	18.0	5.3	1.4	0.3

Source: Statistics Canada. 2012. Census Profile. 2011 Census. Statistics Canada Catalogue no. 98-316-XWE. Ottawa. Released October 24 2012.
http://www12.statcan.gc.ca/census-recensement/2011/dp-pd/prof/index.cfm?Lang=E

Shelter Costs

		Owned Dwellings					Rented Dwellings	
Area	Number	Median Value[1] ($)	Average Value[1] ($)	Median Monthly Costs[2] ($)	Average Monthly Costs[2] ($)	Number	Median Monthly Costs[3] ($)	Average Monthly Costs[3] ($)
Kitchener	56,120	274,740	299,641	1,250	1,241	30,250	832	854
Ontario	3,446,650	300,862	367,428	1,163	1,284	1,385,535	892	926
Canada	9,013,410	280,552	345,182	978	1,141	4,060,385	784	848

Note: All figures cover non-farm, non-reserve private dwellings; (1) Refers to the dollar amount expected by the owner if the dwelling were to be sold; (2) Includes all shelter expenses paid by households that own their dwellings, such as the mortgage payment and the costs of electricity, heat, water and other municipal services, property taxes and condominium fees; (3) Includes all shelter expenses paid by households that rent their dwellings, such as the monthly rent and the costs of electricity, heat and municipal services.
Source: Statistics Canada. 2013. 2011 National Household Survey. Statistics Canada Catalogue no. 99-004-XWE. Ottawa. Released September 11, 2013.

Occupied Private Dwellings by Period of Construction

Area	1960 or Before	1961 to 1980	1981 to 1990	1991 to 2000	2001 to 2005	2006 to 2011
			Number			
Kitchener	19,515	29,165	13,300	9,350	8,065	6,970
Ontario	1,330,235	1,420,570	763,430	609,310	414,795	348,310
Canada	3,273,105	4,152,715	2,112,110	1,707,880	1,031,020	1,042,430
			Percent of Dwellings			
Kitchener	22.6	33.8	15.4	10.8	9.3	8.1
Ontario	27.2	29.1	15.6	12.5	8.5	7.1
Canada	24.6	31.2	15.9	12.8	7.7	7.8

Note: Figures cover non-farm, non-reserve private dwellings and includes data up to May 10, 2011.
Source: Statistics Canada. 2013. 2011 National Household Survey. Statistics Canada Catalogue no. 99-004-XWE. Ottawa. Released September 11, 2013.

Educational Attainment

Area	No Certificate, Diploma or Degree	High School Diploma or Equivalent[1]	Apprenticeship or Trades Certificate or Diploma[2]	College, CEGEP or Other Non-University Certificate or Diploma	University Certificate or Diploma Below the Bachelor Level[3]	Bachelor's Degree	University Certificate, Diploma or Degree Above Bachelor Level[4]
			Number				
			Total				
Kitchener	35,620	50,455	13,465	37,530	5,395	22,160	12,645
Ontario	1,954,520	2,801,805	771,140	2,070,875	427,150	1,515,075	933,100
Canada	5,485,400	6,968,935	2,950,685	4,970,020	1,200,130	3,634,425	2,049,930
			Males				
Kitchener	17,370	24,550	8,990	16,595	2,555	10,465	6,280
Ontario	957,040	1,337,055	520,390	894,235	193,355	692,345	470,290
Canada	2,742,875	3,305,415	1,928,970	2,118,430	513,235	1,643,080	1,043,350
			Females				
Kitchener	18,255	25,910	4,470	20,940	2,840	11,695	6,360
Ontario	997,475	1,464,755	250,750	1,176,640	233,790	822,730	462,805
Canada	2,742,520	3,663,515	1,021,715	2,851,595	686,890	1,991,345	1,006,585
			Percent of Population				
			Total				
Kitchener	20.1	28.5	7.6	21.2	3.0	12.5	7.1
Ontario	18.7	26.8	7.4	19.8	4.1	14.5	8.9
Canada	20.1	25.6	10.8	18.2	4.4	13.3	7.5
			Males				
Kitchener	20.0	28.3	10.4	19.1	2.9	12.1	7.2
Ontario	18.9	26.4	10.3	17.7	3.8	13.7	9.3
Canada	20.6	24.9	14.5	15.9	3.9	12.4	7.8
			Females				
Kitchener	20.2	28.6	4.9	23.1	3.1	12.9	7.0
Ontario	18.4	27.1	4.6	21.8	4.3	15.2	8.6
Canada	19.6	26.2	7.3	20.4	4.9	14.3	7.2

Note: Figures cover total population aged 15 years and over by highest certificate, diploma or degree; (1) Includes persons who have graduated from a secondary school or equivalent. It excludes persons with a postsecondary certificate, diploma or degree; (2) Includes Registered Apprenticeship certificates (including Certificate of Qualification, Journeyperson's designation) and other trades certificates or diplomas such as pre-employment or vocational certificates and diplomas from brief trade programs completed at community colleges, institutes of technology, vocational centres, and similar institutions; (3) Comparisons with other data sources suggest that the category 'University certificate or diploma below the bachelor's level' was over-reported in the NHS. This category likely includes some responses that are actually college certificates or diplomas, bachelor's degrees or other types of education (e.g., university transfer programs, bachelor's programs completed in other countries, incomplete bachelor's programs, non-university professional designations). We recommend users interpret the results for the 'University certificate or diploma below the bachelor's level' category with caution; (4) 'University certificate or diploma above bachelor level' includes the categories: 'Degree in medicine, dentistry, veterinary medicine or optometry,' 'Master's degree' and 'Earned doctorate.'
Source: Statistics Canada. 2013. 2011 National Household Survey. Statistics Canada Catalogue no. 99-004-XWE. Ottawa. Released September 11, 2013.

Household Income Distribution

Area	Less than $10,000	$10,000 to $19,999	$20,000 to $29,999	$30,000 to $39,999	$40,000 to $49,999	$50,000 to $59,999	$60,000 to $79,999	$80,000 to $99,999	$100,000 to $124,999	$125,000 to $149,999	$150,000 and Over
					Households						
Kitchener	3,240	6,245	7,425	7,835	7,990	7,760	13,255	10,635	9,180	5,470	7,345
Ontario	201,780	354,530	405,725	425,410	425,720	398,705	680,850	552,660	497,970	331,460	611,840
Canada	626,705	1,141,945	1,193,925	1,271,675	1,206,800	1,102,120	1,865,280	1,458,240	1,260,770	802,555	1,389,240
					Percent of Households						
Kitchener	3.8	7.2	8.6	9.1	9.3	9.0	15.3	12.3	10.6	6.3	8.5
Ontario	4.1	7.3	8.3	8.7	8.7	8.2	13.9	11.3	10.2	6.8	12.5
Canada	4.7	8.6	9.0	9.5	9.1	8.3	14.0	10.9	9.5	6.0	10.4

Note: Household income is the sum of the total incomes of all members of that household. Total income refers to monetary receipts from certain sources, before income taxes and deductions, during calendar year 2010.
Source: Statistics Canada. 2013. 2011 National Household Survey. Statistics Canada Catalogue no. 99-004-XWE. Ottawa. Released September 11, 2013.

Median and Average Household and Economic Family Income

Area	Median Household Income ($)	Average Household Income ($)	Median After-tax Household Income ($)	Average After-tax Household Income ($)	Median Economic Family Income ($)	Average Economic Family Income ($)	Median After-tax Economic Family Income ($)	Average After-tax Economic Family Income ($)
Kitchener	63,709	76,770	56,554	65,371	77,690	90,106	68,369	76,621
Ontario	66,358	85,772	58,717	71,523	80,987	100,152	71,128	83,322
Canada	61,072	79,102	54,089	66,149	76,511	94,125	67,044	78,517

Note: Figures cover household and economic familiy income in 2010. A household is defined as a person or a group of persons (other than foreign residents) who occupy the same private dwelling and do not have a usual place of residence elsewhere in Canada. Every person is a member of one and only one household. An economic family is defined as a group of two or more persons who live in the same dwelling and are related to each other by blood, marriage, common-law, adoption or a foster relationship. A couple may be of opposite or same sex.
Source: Statistics Canada. 2013. 2011 National Household Survey. Statistics Canada Catalogue no. 99-004-XWE. Ottawa. Released September 11, 2013.

PROFILES / Kitchener, Ontario

Individual Income Distribution

Area	Less than $10,000	$10,000 to $19,999	$20,000 to $29,999	$30,000 to $39,999	$40,000 to $49,999	$50,000 to $59,999	$60,000 to $79,999	$80,000 to $99,999	$100,000 to $124,999	$125,000 and Over
					Number Total					
Kitchener	26,855	29,040	24,685	22,650	19,185	13,820	16,690	8,660	3,850	3,295
Ontario	1,780,355	1,748,060	1,361,710	1,136,730	980,790	746,360	964,280	574,710	293,865	330,285
Canada	4,492,040	4,835,710	3,670,020	3,180,360	2,603,520	1,921,650	2,437,440	1,302,045	693,580	782,135
					Males					
Kitchener	11,450	10,830	10,765	10,595	9,690	8,070	10,865	5,480	2,680	2,475
Ontario	781,095	669,815	580,990	535,255	491,125	407,005	569,205	341,160	201,125	244,500
Canada	1,936,365	1,864,880	1,588,260	1,522,190	1,333,510	1,079,780	1,473,145	823,720	492,905	599,905
					Females					
Kitchener	15,400	18,210	13,920	12,050	9,500	5,750	5,825	3,180	1,170	820
Ontario	999,265	1,078,245	780,720	601,475	489,665	339,360	395,075	233,550	92,740	85,790
Canada	2,555,675	2,970,825	2,081,760	1,658,170	1,270,010	841,870	964,300	478,330	200,680	182,230
				Percent of Population Total						
Kitchener	15.9	17.2	14.6	13.4	11.4	8.2	9.9	5.1	2.3	2.0
Ontario	18.0	17.6	13.7	11.5	9.9	7.5	9.7	5.8	3.0	3.3
Canada	17.3	18.7	14.2	12.3	10.0	7.4	9.4	5.0	2.7	3.0
					Males					
Kitchener	13.8	13.1	13.0	12.8	11.7	9.7	13.1	6.6	3.2	3.0
Ontario	16.2	13.9	12.1	11.1	10.2	8.4	11.8	7.1	4.2	5.1
Canada	15.2	14.7	12.5	12.0	10.5	8.5	11.6	6.5	3.9	4.7
					Females					
Kitchener	17.9	21.2	16.2	14.0	11.1	6.7	6.8	3.7	1.4	1.0
Ontario	19.6	21.2	15.3	11.8	9.6	6.7	7.8	4.6	1.8	1.7
Canada	19.4	22.5	15.8	12.6	9.6	6.4	7.3	3.6	1.5	1.4

Note: Figures cover individuals aged 15 years and over with income. Income refers to monetary receipts from certain sources, before income taxes and deductions, during calendar year 2010.
Source: Statistics Canada. 2013. 2011 National Household Survey. Statistics Canada Catalogue no. 99-004-XWE. Ottawa. Released September 11, 2013.

Labour Force Status

Area	In the Labour Force All	Employed	Unemployed	Not in the Labour Force
		Number Total		
Kitchener	123,580	114,800	8,785	53,685
Ontario	6,864,990	6,297,005	567,985	3,608,685
Canada	17,990,080	16,595,035	1,395,045	9,269,445
		Males		
Kitchener	64,330	59,800	4,530	22,475
Ontario	3,542,030	3,249,165	292,865	1,522,690
Canada	9,388,570	8,634,310	754,255	3,906,785
		Females		
Kitchener	59,250	54,995	4,255	31,215
Ontario	3,322,955	3,047,840	275,120	2,085,990
Canada	8,601,515	7,960,725	640,790	5,362,660
	Percent of Labour Force Total			
Kitchener	69.7	64.8	7.1	30.3
Ontario	65.5	60.1	8.3	34.5
Canada	66.0	60.9	7.8	34.0
		Males		
Kitchener	74.1	68.9	7.0	25.9
Ontario	69.9	64.2	8.3	30.1
Canada	70.6	64.9	8.0	29.4
		Females		
Kitchener	65.5	60.8	7.2	34.5
Ontario	61.4	56.3	8.3	38.6
Canada	61.6	57.0	7.4	38.4

Note: Figures are based on total population 15 years and over
Source: Statistics Canada. 2013. 2011 National Household Survey. Statistics Canada Catalogue no. 99-004-XWE. Ottawa. Released September 11, 2013.

Labour Force by Industry (NAICS Codes 11–52)

Area	Agriculture, forestry, fishing & hunting	Mining, quarrying, & oil & gas extraction	Utilities	Construction	Manufacturing	Wholesale Trade	Retail Trade	Transportation & warehousing	Information & cultural industries	Finance & insurance
Number										
Total										
Kitchener	515	95	455	7,675	23,030	5,310	13,540	5,650	2,860	7,660
Ontario	101,280	29,985	57,035	417,900	697,565	305,030	751,200	307,405	178,720	364,415
Canada	437,650	261,050	149,940	1,215,380	1,619,295	733,445	2,031,665	827,780	420,830	767,960
Males										
Kitchener	270	90	335	6,995	16,240	3,690	6,130	4,395	1,350	2,385
Ontario	66,485	25,650	42,685	369,300	493,305	197,770	344,480	225,245	98,835	153,125
Canada	307,370	211,690	110,765	1,068,710	1,167,680	494,545	933,850	617,305	235,875	296,995
Females										
Kitchener	250	0	120	680	6,790	1,620	7,410	1,260	1,515	5,275
Ontario	34,800	4,340	14,350	48,595	204,260	107,260	406,720	82,160	79,885	211,290
Canada	130,285	49,360	39,175	146,670	451,615	238,900	1,097,820	210,475	184,955	470,960
Percent of Labour Force										
Total										
Kitchener	0.4	0.1	0.4	6.4	19.1	4.4	11.2	4.7	2.4	6.3
Ontario	1.5	0.4	0.9	6.3	10.4	4.6	11.2	4.6	2.7	5.5
Canada	2.5	1.5	0.9	6.9	9.2	4.2	11.6	4.7	2.4	4.4
Males										
Kitchener	0.4	0.1	0.5	11.1	25.8	5.9	9.7	7.0	2.1	3.8
Ontario	1.9	0.7	1.2	10.7	14.3	5.7	10.0	6.5	2.9	4.4
Canada	3.3	2.3	1.2	11.6	12.7	5.4	10.2	6.7	2.6	3.2
Females										
Kitchener	0.4	0.0	0.2	1.2	11.8	2.8	12.8	2.2	2.6	9.1
Ontario	1.1	0.1	0.4	1.5	6.3	3.3	12.6	2.5	2.5	6.5
Canada	1.6	0.6	0.5	1.7	5.4	2.8	13.1	2.5	2.2	5.6

Note: Figures are based on total experienced labour force 15 years and over. Experienced labour force refers to persons who, during the week of Sunday, May 1 to Saturday, May 7, 2011, were employed and the unemployed who had last worked for pay or in self-employment in either 2010 or 2011.
Source: Statistics Canada. 2013. 2011 National Household Survey. Statistics Canada Catalogue no. 99-004-XWE. Ottawa. Released September 11, 2013.

Labour Force by Industry (NAICS Codes 53–91)

Area	Real estate & rental & leasing	Profess., scientific & tech. services	Mgmt of companies & enterprises	Admin. & support, waste mgmt & remed. services	Educational services	Health care & social assistance	Arts, entertain. & recreation	Accomm. & food services	Other services (except public admin.)	Public admin.
Number										
Total										
Kitchener	2,115	7,515	65	5,550	9,255	11,175	1,625	7,505	4,465	4,685
Ontario	133,980	511,020	6,525	309,630	499,690	692,130	144,065	417,675	296,340	458,665
Canada	321,895	1,240,850	17,460	728,330	1,301,435	1,949,650	363,405	1,130,750	807,800	1,261,050
Males										
Kitchener	985	4,220	50	2,960	3,205	1,525	830	3,010	2,100	2,245
Ontario	72,835	281,420	3,540	172,475	162,765	120,165	75,035	177,240	133,795	236,655
Canada	179,090	688,625	9,380	411,250	424,915	349,430	188,270	469,990	372,940	652,510
Females										
Kitchener	1,135	3,295	20	2,580	6,055	9,650	795	4,500	2,370	2,435
Ontario	61,145	229,600	2,990	137,155	336,925	571,965	69,030	240,430	162,550	222,015
Canada	142,805	552,225	8,075	317,085	876,515	1,600,220	175,135	660,760	434,865	608,535
Percent of Labour Force										
Total										
Kitchener	1.8	6.2	0.1	4.6	7.7	9.3	1.3	6.2	3.7	3.9
Ontario	2.0	7.6	0.1	4.6	7.5	10.4	2.2	6.3	4.4	6.9
Canada	1.8	7.1	0.1	4.1	7.4	11.1	2.1	6.4	4.6	7.2
Males										
Kitchener	1.6	6.7	0.1	4.7	5.1	2.4	1.3	4.8	3.3	3.6
Ontario	2.1	8.2	0.1	5.0	4.7	3.5	2.2	5.1	3.9	6.9
Canada	1.9	7.5	0.1	4.5	4.6	3.8	2.0	5.1	4.1	7.1
Females										
Kitchener	2.0	5.7	0.0	4.5	10.5	16.7	1.4	7.8	4.1	4.2
Ontario	1.9	7.1	0.1	4.2	10.4	17.7	2.1	7.4	5.0	6.9
Canada	1.7	6.6	0.1	3.8	10.4	19.1	2.1	7.9	5.2	7.2

Note: Figures are based on total experienced labour force 15 years and over. Experienced labour force refers to persons who, during the week of Sunday, May 1 to Saturday, May 7, 2011, were employed and the unemployed who had last worked for pay or in self-employment in either 2010 or 2011.
Source: Statistics Canada. 2013. 2011 National Household Survey. Statistics Canada Catalogue no. 99-004-XWE. Ottawa. Released September 11, 2013.

PROFILES / Kitchener, Ontario

Occupation

Area	Mgmt	Business, Finance & Admin.	Natural/ Applied Sciences & Related	Health	Education, Law & Social, Community & Government Services	Art, Culture, Recreation & Sport	Sales & Service	Trades, Transport & Equip. Operators & Related	Natural Resources, Agri. & Related Production	Mfg & Utilities
					Number					
					Total					
Kitchener	11,455	19,220	10,320	6,370	12,405	2,845	28,100	17,355	1,095	11,585
Ontario	770,580	1,138,330	494,500	392,695	801,465	206,420	1,550,260	868,515	106,810	350,685
Canada	1,963,600	2,902,045	1,237,775	1,107,200	2,064,675	503,415	4,068,170	2,537,775	397,930	805,040
					Males					
Kitchener	6,800	5,840	8,150	1,025	3,725	1,290	11,480	16,355	860	7,465
Ontario	474,655	352,505	384,345	78,330	264,570	96,055	673,880	812,280	82,610	233,565
Canada	1,229,460	854,190	966,355	217,520	676,550	232,535	1,745,705	2,385,615	318,945	564,300
					Females					
Kitchener	4,655	13,380	2,165	5,345	8,675	1,555	16,620	1,000	240	4,120
Ontario	295,920	785,825	110,150	314,370	536,895	110,370	876,380	56,230	24,200	117,115
Canada	734,140	2,047,855	271,415	889,675	1,388,130	270,875	2,322,465	152,165	78,980	240,740
					Percent of Labour Force					
					Total					
Kitchener	9.5	15.9	8.5	5.3	10.3	2.4	23.3	14.4	0.9	9.6
Ontario	11.5	17.0	7.4	5.9	12.0	3.1	23.2	13.0	1.6	5.2
Canada	11.2	16.5	7.0	6.3	11.7	2.9	23.1	14.4	2.3	4.6
					Males					
Kitchener	10.8	9.3	12.9	1.6	5.9	2.0	18.2	26.0	1.4	11.9
Ontario	13.7	10.2	11.1	2.3	7.7	2.8	19.5	23.5	2.4	6.8
Canada	13.4	9.3	10.5	2.4	7.4	2.5	19.0	26.0	3.5	6.1
					Females					
Kitchener	8.1	23.2	3.7	9.3	15.0	2.7	28.8	1.7	0.4	7.1
Ontario	9.2	24.3	3.4	9.7	16.6	3.4	27.2	1.7	0.7	3.6
Canada	8.7	24.4	3.2	10.6	16.5	3.2	27.7	1.8	0.9	2.9

Note: Figures are based on total experienced labour force 15 years and over
Source: Statistics Canada. 2013. 2011 National Household Survey. Statistics Canada Catalogue no. 99-004-XWE. Ottawa. Released September 11, 2013.

Place of Work Status

Area	Worked at Home	Worked Outside Canada	No Fixed Workplace Address	Worked at Usual Place
		Number		
		Total		
Kitchener	5,020	470	10,670	98,635
Ontario	423,790	31,390	670,835	5,170,980
Canada	1,142,640	66,460	1,868,245	13,517,690
		Males		
Kitchener	2,480	305	7,600	49,415
Ontario	216,900	21,150	486,560	2,524,555
Canada	582,150	47,355	1,400,485	6,604,325
		Females		
Kitchener	2,545	165	3,065	49,215
Ontario	206,895	10,240	184,275	2,646,420
Canada	560,490	19,100	467,760	6,913,370
		Percent of Labour Force		
		Total		
Kitchener	4.4	0.4	9.3	85.9
Ontario	6.7	0.5	10.7	82.1
Canada	6.9	0.4	11.3	81.5
		Males		
Kitchener	4.1	0.5	12.7	82.6
Ontario	6.7	0.7	15.0	77.7
Canada	6.7	0.5	16.2	76.5
		Females		
Kitchener	4.6	0.3	5.6	89.5
Ontario	6.8	0.3	6.0	86.8
Canada	7.0	0.2	5.9	86.8

Note: Figures are based on total employed labour force 15 years and over.
Source: Statistics Canada. 2013. 2011 National Household Survey. Statistics Canada Catalogue no. 99-004-XWE. Ottawa. Released September 11, 2013.

Mode of Transportation to Work

Area	Car; Truck; Van; as Driver	Car; Truck; Van; as Passenger	Public Transit	Walked	Bicycled	All Other Modes
			Number			
			Total			
Kitchener	88,360	7,155	7,165	4,665	980	980
Ontario	4,235,315	357,110	818,270	299,095	69,885	62,145
Canada	11,393,140	867,050	1,851,525	880,815	201,780	191,625
			Males			
Kitchener	47,275	3,000	3,390	2,055	760	540
Ontario	2,316,680	143,410	340,995	131,765	47,635	30,635
Canada	6,238,835	349,530	788,290	387,580	135,840	104,725
			Females			
Kitchener	41,085	4,155	3,775	2,610	215	440
Ontario	1,918,640	213,700	477,275	167,325	22,250	31,515
Canada	5,154,305	517,520	1,063,235	493,230	65,940	86,900
			Percent of Labour Force			
			Total			
Kitchener	80.8	6.5	6.6	4.3	0.9	0.9
Ontario	72.5	6.1	14.0	5.1	1.2	1.1
Canada	74.0	5.6	12.0	5.7	1.3	1.2
			Males			
Kitchener	82.9	5.3	5.9	3.6	1.3	0.9
Ontario	76.9	4.8	11.3	4.4	1.6	1.0
Canada	77.9	4.4	9.8	4.8	1.7	1.3
			Females			
Kitchener	78.6	7.9	7.2	5.0	0.4	0.8
Ontario	67.8	7.5	16.9	5.9	0.8	1.1
Canada	69.8	7.0	14.4	6.7	0.9	1.2

Note: Figures are based on total employed labour force 15 years and over.
Source: Statistics Canada. 2013. 2011 National Household Survey. Statistics Canada Catalogue no. 99-004-XWE. Ottawa. Released September 11, 2013.

Visible Minority Population Characteristics

Area	Total Minority	South Asian[1]	Chinese	Black	Filipino	Latin American	Arab	SE Asian[2]	West Asian[3]	Korean	Japanese	Multiple[4]
						Number						
						Total						
Kitchener	39,720	8,960	3,975	6,635	1,375	5,735	2,520	5,005	2,550	560	310	1,290
Ontario	3,279,565	965,990	629,140	539,205	275,380	172,560	151,645	137,875	122,530	78,290	29,085	96,735
Canada	6,264,750	1,567,400	1,324,750	945,665	619,310	381,280	380,620	312,075	206,840	161,130	87,270	171,935
						Males						
Kitchener	19,720	4,275	1,975	3,455	645	2,775	1,375	2,520	1,225	245	130	675
Ontario	1,582,480	484,355	301,575	251,295	116,825	83,205	79,620	67,645	62,515	38,045	13,345	46,765
Canada	3,043,010	790,755	632,325	453,005	268,885	186,355	203,485	154,035	105,620	77,165	38,270	83,335
						Females						
Kitchener	20,000	4,685	2,005	3,175	725	2,960	1,140	2,485	1,325	315	175	615
Ontario	1,697,085	481,635	327,570	287,915	158,555	89,360	72,025	70,230	60,010	40,250	15,740	49,970
Canada	3,221,745	776,650	692,420	492,660	350,425	194,925	177,140	158,045	101,220	83,965	48,990	88,600
						Percent of Population						
						Total						
Kitchener	18.4	4.1	1.8	3.1	0.6	2.7	1.2	2.3	1.2	0.3	0.1	0.6
Ontario	25.9	7.6	5.0	4.3	2.2	1.4	1.2	1.1	1.0	0.6	0.2	0.8
Canada	19.1	4.8	4.0	2.9	1.9	1.2	1.2	0.9	0.6	0.5	0.3	0.5
						Males						
Kitchener	18.5	4.0	1.8	3.2	0.6	2.6	1.3	2.4	1.1	0.2	0.1	0.6
Ontario	25.6	7.8	4.9	4.1	1.9	1.3	1.3	1.1	1.0	0.6	0.2	0.8
Canada	18.8	4.9	3.9	2.8	1.7	1.2	1.3	1.0	0.7	0.5	0.2	0.5
						Females						
Kitchener	18.3	4.3	1.8	2.9	0.7	2.7	1.0	2.3	1.2	0.3	0.2	0.6
Ontario	26.2	7.4	5.1	4.4	2.5	1.4	1.1	1.1	0.9	0.6	0.2	0.8
Canada	19.3	4.7	4.1	3.0	2.1	1.2	1.1	0.9	0.6	0.5	0.3	0.5

Note: The Employment Equity Act defines visible minorities as 'persons, other than Aboriginal peoples, who are non-Caucasian in race or non-white in colour';
(1) Includes 'East Indian,' 'Pakistani,' 'Sri Lankan,' etc.; (2) Includes 'Vietnamese,' 'Cambodian,' 'Malaysian,' 'Laotian,' etc.; (3) Includes 'Iranian,' 'Afghan,' etc.; (4) Includes respondents who reported more than one visible minority group by checking two or more mark-in circles, e.g., 'Black' and 'South Asian.'
Source: Statistics Canada. 2013. 2011 National Household Survey. Statistics Canada Catalogue no. 99-004-XWE. Ottawa. Released September 11, 2013.

PROFILES / Kitchener, Ontario

Aboriginal Population

Area	Aboriginal Identity[1]	First Nations (North American Indian) Single Identity[2]	Métis Single Identity	Inuk (Inuit) Single Identity	Multiple Aboriginal Identities[3]	Aboriginal Identities Not Included Elsewhere
			Number			
			Total			
Kitchener	3,155	1,985	1,010	30	50	80
Ontario	301,430	201,100	86,020	3,355	2,910	8,040
Canada	1,400,685	851,560	451,795	59,440	11,415	26,475
			Males			
Kitchener	1,565	1,015	475	15	25	30
Ontario	145,020	96,620	41,755	1,475	1,420	3,750
Canada	682,190	411,785	223,335	29,495	5,525	12,055
			Females			
Kitchener	1,590	970	530	0	30	45
Ontario	156,410	104,485	44,260	1,880	1,490	4,295
Canada	718,500	439,775	228,460	29,950	5,890	14,420
			Percent of Population			
			Total			
Kitchener	1.5	0.9	0.5	0.0	0.0	0.0
Ontario	2.4	1.6	0.7	0.0	0.0	0.1
Canada	4.3	2.6	1.4	0.2	0.0	0.1
			Males			
Kitchener	1.5	1.0	0.4	0.0	0.0	0.0
Ontario	2.3	1.6	0.7	0.0	0.0	0.1
Canada	4.2	2.5	1.4	0.2	0.0	0.1
			Females			
Kitchener	1.5	0.9	0.5	0.0	0.0	0.0
Ontario	2.4	1.6	0.7	0.0	0.0	0.1
Canada	4.3	2.6	1.4	0.2	0.0	0.1

Note: (1) Includes persons who reported being an Aboriginal person, that is, First Nations (North American Indian), Métis or Inuk (Inuit) and/or those who reported Registered or Treaty Indian status, that is registered under the Indian Act of Canada, and/or those who reported membership in a First Nation or Indian band. Aboriginal peoples of Canada are defined in the Constitution Act, 1982, section 35-2 as including the Indian, Inuit and Métis peoples of Canada; (2) Users should be aware that the estimates associated with this variable are more affected than most by the incomplete enumeration of certain Indian reserves and Indian settlements in the National Household Survey (NHS); (3) Includes persons who reported being any two or all three of the following: First Nations (North American Indian), Métis or Inuk (Inuit).
Source: Statistics Canada. 2013. 2011 National Household Survey. Statistics Canada Catalogue no. 99-004-XWE. Ottawa. Released September 11, 2013.

Ethnic Origin

Area	North American Aboriginal	Other North American	European	Caribbean	Latin, Central and South American	African	Asian	Oceania
				Number				
				Total				
Kitchener	6,415	52,095	155,860	3,340	7,005	5,375	28,320	210
Ontario	441,395	3,059,480	8,231,410	396,485	271,545	331,460	2,604,595	19,410
Canada	1,836,035	11,070,455	20,157,965	627,590	544,375	766,735	5,011,225	74,875
				Males				
Kitchener	3,065	25,795	76,890	1,680	3,580	2,850	13,920	105
Ontario	210,490	1,507,105	4,019,885	181,805	130,035	160,940	1,265,540	9,855
Canada	885,675	5,462,685	9,913,150	291,640	264,635	387,360	2,435,540	37,490
				Females				
Kitchener	3,350	26,305	78,970	1,660	3,415	2,530	14,400	100
Ontario	230,905	1,552,380	4,211,525	214,675	141,510	170,515	1,339,050	9,555
Canada	950,360	5,607,770	10,244,820	335,945	279,740	379,380	2,575,680	37,385
				Percent of Population				
				Total				
Kitchener	3.0	24.1	72.2	1.5	3.2	2.5	13.1	0.1
Ontario	3.5	24.2	65.1	3.1	2.1	2.6	20.6	0.2
Canada	5.6	33.7	61.4	1.9	1.7	2.3	15.3	0.2
				Males				
Kitchener	2.9	24.1	72.0	1.6	3.4	2.7	13.0	0.1
Ontario	3.4	24.4	65.0	2.9	2.1	2.6	20.5	0.2
Canada	5.5	33.8	61.3	1.8	1.6	2.4	15.1	0.2
				Females				
Kitchener	3.1	24.1	72.4	1.5	3.1	2.3	13.2	0.1
Ontario	3.6	24.0	65.1	3.3	2.2	2.6	20.7	0.1
Canada	5.7	33.6	61.4	2.0	1.7	2.3	15.4	0.2

Note: The sum of the ethnic groups in this table is greater than the total population estimate because a person may report more than one ethnic origin in the NHS.
Source: Statistics Canada. 2013. 2011 National Household Survey. Statistics Canada Catalogue no. 99-004-XWE. Ottawa. Released September 11, 2013.

Religion

Area	Buddhist	Christian	Hindu	Jewish	Muslim	Sikh	Traditional (Aboriginal) Spirituality	Other Religions	No Religious Affiliation
\multicolumn{10}{c|}{Number}									
\multicolumn{10}{c|}{Total}									
Kitchener	3,070	142,360	2,580	620	10,590	1,360	85	1,160	54,125
Ontario	163,750	8,167,295	366,720	195,540	581,950	179,765	15,905	53,080	2,927,790
Canada	366,830	22,102,745	497,965	329,495	1,053,945	454,965	64,935	130,835	7,850,605
\multicolumn{10}{c|}{Males}									
Kitchener	1,545	67,570	1,315	330	5,175	680	40	540	29,630
Ontario	75,355	3,839,925	183,580	95,795	293,925	90,515	7,600	23,555	1,571,195
Canada	168,465	10,497,775	250,435	161,265	540,555	229,435	31,805	57,745	4,225,645
\multicolumn{10}{c|}{Females}									
Kitchener	1,525	74,795	1,265	290	5,415	680	45	625	24,490
Ontario	88,395	4,327,365	183,140	99,740	288,025	89,250	8,310	29,525	1,356,600
Canada	198,365	11,604,975	247,525	168,235	513,395	225,530	33,135	73,090	3,624,965
\multicolumn{10}{c|}{Percent of Population}									
\multicolumn{10}{c|}{Total}									
Kitchener	1.4	65.9	1.2	0.3	4.9	0.6	0.0	0.5	25.1
Ontario	1.3	64.6	2.9	1.5	4.6	1.4	0.1	0.4	23.1
Canada	1.1	67.3	1.5	1.0	3.2	1.4	0.2	0.4	23.9
\multicolumn{10}{c|}{Males}									
Kitchener	1.4	63.3	1.2	0.3	4.8	0.6	0.0	0.5	27.7
Ontario	1.2	62.1	3.0	1.5	4.8	1.5	0.1	0.4	25.4
Canada	1.0	64.9	1.5	1.0	3.3	1.4	0.2	0.4	26.1
\multicolumn{10}{c|}{Females}									
Kitchener	1.4	68.5	1.2	0.3	5.0	0.6	0.0	0.6	22.4
Ontario	1.4	66.9	2.8	1.5	4.5	1.4	0.1	0.5	21.0
Canada	1.2	69.5	1.5	1.0	3.1	1.4	0.2	0.4	21.7

Note: Religion refers to the person's self-identification as having a connection or affiliation with any religious denomination, group, body, sect, cult or other religiously defined community or system of belief. Religion is not limited to formal membership in a religious organization or group. Persons without a religious connection or affiliation can self-identify as atheist, agnostic or humanist, or can provide another applicable response.
Source: Statistics Canada. 2013. 2011 National Household Survey. Statistics Canada Catalogue no. 99-004-XWE. Ottawa. Released September 11, 2013.

Religion—Christian Denominations

Area	Anglican	Baptist	Catholic	Christian Orthodox	Lutheran	Pentecostal	Presbyterian	United Church	Other Christian
\multicolumn{10}{c|}{Number}									
\multicolumn{10}{c|}{Total}									
Kitchener	8,465	5,155	61,970	9,215	11,375	5,050	6,280	10,520	24,330
Ontario	774,560	244,650	3,976,610	297,710	163,460	213,945	319,585	952,465	1,224,300
Canada	1,631,845	635,840	12,810,705	550,690	478,185	478,705	472,385	2,007,610	3,036,780
\multicolumn{10}{c|}{Males}									
Kitchener	3,820	2,365	29,695	4,585	5,380	2,360	2,920	4,520	11,905
Ontario	355,175	112,285	1,895,940	145,825	75,225	94,955	148,535	435,255	576,730
Canada	752,945	293,905	6,167,290	270,205	221,525	217,850	218,955	912,545	1,442,550
\multicolumn{10}{c|}{Females}									
Kitchener	4,645	2,795	32,275	4,625	5,990	2,685	3,350	6,000	12,425
Ontario	419,390	132,370	2,080,665	151,885	88,230	118,990	171,050	517,210	647,570
Canada	878,900	341,940	6,643,415	280,485	256,660	260,850	253,430	1,095,065	1,594,230
\multicolumn{10}{c|}{Percent of Population}									
\multicolumn{10}{c|}{Total}									
Kitchener	3.9	2.4	28.7	4.3	5.3	2.3	2.9	4.9	11.3
Ontario	6.1	1.9	31.4	2.4	1.3	1.7	2.5	7.5	9.7
Canada	5.0	1.9	39.0	1.7	1.5	1.5	1.4	6.1	9.2
\multicolumn{10}{c|}{Males}									
Kitchener	3.6	2.2	27.8	4.3	5.0	2.2	2.7	4.2	11.1
Ontario	5.7	1.8	30.7	2.4	1.2	1.5	2.4	7.0	9.3
Canada	4.7	1.8	38.2	1.7	1.4	1.3	1.4	5.6	8.9
\multicolumn{10}{c|}{Females}									
Kitchener	4.3	2.6	29.6	4.2	5.5	2.5	3.1	5.5	11.4
Ontario	6.5	2.0	32.2	2.3	1.4	1.8	2.6	8.0	10.0
Canada	5.3	2.0	39.8	1.7	1.5	1.6	1.5	6.6	9.6

Note: Religion refers to the person's self-identification as having a connection or affiliation with any religious denomination, group, body, sect, cult or other religiously defined community or system of belief. Religion is not limited to formal membership in a religious organization or group. Persons without a religious connection or affiliation can self-identify as atheist, agnostic or humanist, or can provide another applicable response.
Source: Statistics Canada. 2013. 2011 National Household Survey. Statistics Canada Catalogue no. 99-004-XWE. Ottawa. Released September 11, 2013.

Immigrant Status and Period of Immigration

Area	Non-Immigrants[1]	Immigrants All	Before 1971	1971 to 1980	1981 to 1990	1991 to 2000	2001 to 2005	2006 to 2011	Non-Permanent Residents[3]
				Number Total					
Kitchener	157,710	56,430	10,900	6,635	8,520	13,715	7,860	8,805	1,805
Ontario	8,906,000	3,611,365	723,030	464,380	538,285	866,220	518,405	501,060	134,425
Canada	25,720,175	6,775,765	1,261,055	870,775	949,890	1,539,050	992,070	1,162,915	356,385
				Males					
Kitchener	78,490	27,380	5,090	3,240	4,380	6,555	3,890	4,225	945
Ontario	4,410,240	1,706,385	341,820	217,990	258,095	408,270	245,850	234,360	64,825
Canada	12,753,235	3,231,370	605,430	416,670	454,570	724,905	474,545	555,245	178,515
				Females					
Kitchener	79,220	29,045	5,805	3,390	4,145	7,160	3,965	4,585	865
Ontario	4,495,765	1,904,985	381,210	246,390	280,190	457,950	272,550	266,695	69,600
Canada	12,966,935	3,544,400	655,625	454,105	495,325	814,145	517,530	607,670	177,870
				Percent of Population Total					
Kitchener	73.0	26.1	5.0	3.1	3.9	6.4	3.6	4.1	0.8
Ontario	70.4	28.5	5.7	3.7	4.3	6.8	4.1	4.0	1.1
Canada	78.3	20.6	3.8	2.7	2.9	4.7	3.0	3.5	1.1
				Males					
Kitchener	73.5	25.6	4.8	3.0	4.1	6.1	3.6	4.0	0.9
Ontario	71.3	27.6	5.5	3.5	4.2	6.6	4.0	3.8	1.0
Canada	78.9	20.0	3.7	2.6	2.8	4.5	2.9	3.4	1.1
				Females					
Kitchener	72.6	26.6	5.3	3.1	3.8	6.6	3.6	4.2	0.8
Ontario	69.5	29.4	5.9	3.8	4.3	7.1	4.2	4.1	1.1
Canada	77.7	21.2	3.9	2.7	3.0	4.9	3.1	3.6	1.1

Note: (1) Non-immigrant refers to a person who is a Canadian citizen by birth; (2) Immigrant refers to a person who is or has ever been a landed immigrant/permanent resident. This person has been granted the right to live in Canada permanently by immigration authorities. Some immigrants have resided in Canada for a number of years, while others have arrived recently. Some immigrants are Canadian citizens, while others are not. Most immigrants are born outside Canada, but a small number are born in Canada. In the 2011 National Household Survey, 'Immigrants' includes immigrants who landed in Canada prior to May 10, 2011; (3) Non-permanent resident refers to a person from another country who has a work or study permit, or who is a refugee claimant, and any non-Canadian-born family member living in Canada with them.
Source: Statistics Canada. 2013. 2011 National Household Survey. Statistics Canada Catalogue no. 99-004-XWE. Ottawa. Released September 11, 2013.

Mother Tongue

Area	English	French	Non-official Language	English & French	English & Non-official Language	French & Non-official Language	English, French & Non-official Language
			Number Total				
Kitchener	154,125	2,860	55,620	455	3,110	110	80
Ontario	8,677,040	493,300	3,264,435	46,605	219,425	13,645	7,615
Canada	18,858,980	7,054,975	6,567,680	144,685	396,330	74,430	24,095
			Males				
Kitchener	76,450	1,320	27,095	220	1,555	50	35
Ontario	4,276,970	232,785	1,562,190	21,805	106,790	6,285	3,495
Canada	9,345,225	3,452,380	3,157,785	69,975	192,000	36,535	11,965
			Females				
Kitchener	77,675	1,540	28,525	240	1,555	60	45
Ontario	4,400,065	260,510	1,702,240	24,795	112,635	7,365	4,115
Canada	9,513,750	3,602,590	3,409,895	74,710	204,330	37,890	12,130
			Percent of Population Total				
Kitchener	71.2	1.3	25.7	0.2	1.4	0.1	0.0
Ontario	68.2	3.9	25.7	0.4	1.7	0.1	0.1
Canada	56.9	21.3	19.8	0.4	1.2	0.2	0.1
			Males				
Kitchener	71.6	1.2	25.4	0.2	1.5	0.0	0.0
Ontario	68.9	3.7	25.2	0.4	1.7	0.1	0.1
Canada	57.5	21.2	19.4	0.4	1.2	0.2	0.1
			Females				
Kitchener	70.8	1.4	26.0	0.2	1.4	0.1	0.0
Ontario	67.6	4.0	26.1	0.4	1.7	0.1	0.1
Canada	56.4	21.4	20.2	0.4	1.2	0.2	0.1

Note: Figures cover total population excluding institutional residents.
Source: Statistics Canada. 2012. Census Profile. 2011 Census. Statistics Canada Catalogue no. 98-316-XWE. Ottawa. Released October 24 2012.
http://www12.statcan.gc.ca/census-recensement/2011/dp-pd/prof/index.cfm?Lang=E

Language Spoken Most Often at Home

Area	English	French	Non-official Language	English & French	English & Non-official Language	French & Non-official Language	English, French & Non-official Language
			Number				
			Total				
Kitchener	175,985	795	30,570	265	8,565	40	150
Ontario	10,044,810	284,115	1,827,870	37,955	509,105	6,370	11,845
Canada	21,457,075	6,827,865	3,673,865	131,205	875,135	109,700	46,330
			Males				
Kitchener	87,070	355	14,875	120	4,210	10	75
Ontario	4,930,610	133,495	872,860	17,250	248,050	2,855	5,225
Canada	10,585,620	3,348,235	1,767,310	63,475	425,370	53,010	22,845
			Females				
Kitchener	88,910	440	15,690	140	4,355	25	80
Ontario	5,114,200	150,620	955,010	20,705	261,055	3,520	6,620
Canada	10,871,455	3,479,625	1,906,555	67,730	449,765	56,690	23,485
			Percent of Population				
			Total				
Kitchener	81.3	0.4	14.1	0.1	4.0	0.0	0.1
Ontario	79.0	2.2	14.4	0.3	4.0	0.1	0.1
Canada	64.8	20.6	11.1	0.4	2.6	0.3	0.1
			Males				
Kitchener	81.6	0.3	13.9	0.1	3.9	0.0	0.1
Ontario	79.4	2.1	14.1	0.3	4.0	0.0	0.1
Canada	65.1	20.6	10.9	0.4	2.6	0.3	0.1
			Females				
Kitchener	81.1	0.4	14.3	0.1	4.0	0.0	0.1
Ontario	78.5	2.3	14.7	0.3	4.0	0.1	0.1
Canada	64.5	20.6	11.3	0.4	2.7	0.3	0.1

Note: Figures cover total population excluding institutional residents.
Source: Statistics Canada. 2012. Census Profile. 2011 Census. Statistics Canada Catalogue no. 98-316-XWE. Ottawa. Released October 24 2012.
http://www12.statcan.gc.ca/census-recensement/2011/dp-pd/prof/index.cfm?Lang=E

Knowledge of Official Languages

Area	English Only	French Only	English & French	Neither English nor French
		Number		
		Total		
Kitchener	198,930	110	13,505	3,820
Ontario	10,984,360	42,980	1,395,805	298,920
Canada	22,564,665	4,165,015	5,795,570	595,920
		Males		
Kitchener	99,320	40	5,880	1,475
Ontario	5,445,050	18,805	627,725	118,765
Canada	11,222,185	1,925,340	2,876,560	241,790
		Females		
Kitchener	99,610	65	7,620	2,345
Ontario	5,539,310	24,175	768,085	180,155
Canada	11,342,485	2,239,680	2,919,005	354,135
		Percent of Population		
		Total		
Kitchener	91.9	0.1	6.2	1.8
Ontario	86.3	0.3	11.0	2.3
Canada	68.1	12.6	17.5	1.8
		Males		
Kitchener	93.1	0.0	5.5	1.4
Ontario	87.7	0.3	10.1	1.9
Canada	69.0	11.8	17.7	1.5
		Females		
Kitchener	90.9	0.1	7.0	2.1
Ontario	85.1	0.4	11.8	2.8
Canada	67.3	13.3	17.3	2.1

Note: Figures cover total population excluding institutional residents.
Source: Statistics Canada. 2012. Census Profile. 2011 Census. Statistics Canada Catalogue no. 98-316-XWE. Ottawa. Released October 24 2012.
http://www12.statcan.gc.ca/census-recensement/2011/dp-pd/prof/index.cfm?Lang=E

Langley, British Columbia

Background

Langley is located in Fraser Valley in the Lower Mainland of British Columbia. The City of Langley spreads out across 10 square kilometres and is the eastern portion of the Metro Vancouver area. Langley is divided into two municipalities: the City of Langley, constituting the downtown core (est. 1955); and the Township of Langley, approximately 320 square kilometres of surrounding area.

Fort Langley was built on the south bank of the Fraser River in an area first inhabited by the Kwantlen First Nation. With the onset of the Fraser River Gold Rush in 1858, the Fort Langley trading post was transformed into a Crown Colony of British Columbia, but prosperity faded as the 19th century closed. With the building of the TransCanada Highway in the 1960s, commercial investment such as high-tech companies, warehouses and wineries rejuvenated Langley's growth and prosperity.

Today Langley has become one of Metro Vancouver's regional city centres. Langley is made up of six residential neighbourhoods, a natural wetland, more than 120 hectares (300 acres) of parkland, high-density residential development and a pedestrian-friendly downtown core.

In 2009, the city launched plans to revitalize downtown by adding more multi-family residences, residential/commercial buildings and cultural centres. As land prices have continued to increase in Vancouver and adjacent communities, Langley has experienced significant commercial and residential growth because of its lower real estate prices, suburban neighbourhoods, central location and skilled labour force.

Culinary tourism is an increasingly popular sector in Langley; Domaine de Chaberton is the oldest and largest winery in the Fraser Valley. Langley's lush vineyards are attributed to the area's microclimate, where rainfall is 30% less than in nearby Vancouver.

Langley has summer highs of plus 21.57 degrees Celsius, winter lows of plus 0.23 degree Celsius, and an average rainfall just over 1418 mm per year.

Rankings

- Langley Township grew faster in 2011 than did the Metro Vancouver area or Canada. The 2011 Census reported Langley Township increased by 11.2% between 2006 and 2011. Metro Vancouver grew by 9.3% and the national average was 5.9% for the same period. Langley City also grew but less dramatically; the city population increased by 6.2%. *Statistics Canada, 2012: Focus on Geography Series, 2011 Census with files from Langley Times, February 8th, 2012*
- In 2011, the City of Langley (pop: 27,118) was ranked #9 overall on the Crime Severity Index, which looked at 239 police services in communities over 10,000 people. The Township of Langley (pop.: 107,061) was ranked #66 overall. North Battleford, Saskatchewan, was ranked #1. *Statistics Canada, Canadian Centre for Justice Statistics, Uniform Crime Reporting Survey, July 24, 2012*

PROFILES / Langley, British Columbia

Population Growth and Density

Area	Population in 2001	Population in 2006	Population in 2011	Population Change 2001–2006	Population Change 2006–2011	Land Area (sq. km)	Population Density per sq. km
Langley	86,896	93,726	104,177	7.9	11.2	308.03	338.2
British Columbia	3,907,738	4,113,487	4,400,057	5.3	7.0	922,509.29	4.8
Canada	30,007,094	31,612,897	33,476,688	5.4	5.9	8,965,121.42	3.7

Source: Statistics Canada. 2012. Census Profile. 2011 Census. Statistics Canada Catalogue no. 98-316-XWE. Ottawa. Released October 24 2012.
http://www12.statcan.gc.ca/census-recensement/2011/dp-pd/prof/index.cfm?Lang=E;
Statistics Canada 2007. 2006 Community Profiles. 2006 Census. Statistics Canada Catalogue no. 92-591-XWE. Ottawa. Released March 13 2007.
http://www12.statcan.ca/census-recensement/2006/dp-pd/prof/92-591/index.cfm?Lang=E

Gender

Area	Males	Females
Number		
Langley	51,050	53,130
British Columbia	2,156,600	2,243,455
Canada	16,414,225	17,062,460
Percent of Population		
Langley	49.0	51.0
British Columbia	49.0	51.0
Canada	49.0	51.0

Source: Statistics Canada. 2012. Census Profile. 2011 Census. Statistics Canada Catalogue no. 98-316-XWE. Ottawa. Released October 24 2012.
http://www12.statcan.gc.ca/census-recensement/2011/dp-pd/prof/index.cfm?Lang=E

Marital Status

Area	Married[1]	Living Common-law	Single[2]	Separated	Divorced	Widowed
Number — Total						
Langley	46,555	6,255	20,860	2,085	4,835	4,235
British Columbia	1,832,605	321,965	1,014,270	102,040	246,515	205,300
Canada	12,941,960	3,142,525	7,816,045	698,240	1,686,035	1,584,530
Males						
Langley	23,220	3,130	11,190	840	1,880	890
British Columbia	913,430	161,530	550,830	43,570	98,130	41,550
Canada	6,470,300	1,575,495	4,206,320	299,655	680,415	310,940
Females						
Langley	23,335	3,130	9,670	1,240	2,960	3,345
British Columbia	919,175	160,435	463,435	58,470	148,385	163,750
Canada	6,471,660	1,567,035	3,609,730	398,585	1,005,620	1,273,590
Percent of Population — Total						
Langley	54.9	7.4	24.6	2.5	5.7	5.0
British Columbia	49.2	8.6	27.2	2.7	6.6	5.5
Canada	46.4	11.3	28.0	2.5	6.0	5.7
Males						
Langley	56.4	7.6	27.2	2.0	4.6	2.2
British Columbia	50.5	8.9	30.4	2.4	5.4	2.3
Canada	47.8	11.6	31.1	2.2	5.0	2.3
Females						
Langley	53.4	7.2	22.1	2.8	6.8	7.7
British Columbia	48.0	8.4	24.2	3.1	7.8	8.6
Canada	45.2	10.9	25.2	2.8	7.0	8.9

Note: (1) and not separated, (2) never legally married
Source: Statistics Canada. 2012. Census Profile. 2011 Census. Statistics Canada Catalogue no. 98-316-XWE. Ottawa. Released October 24 2012.
http://www12.statcan.gc.ca/census-recensement/2011/dp-pd/prof/index.cfm?Lang=E

Age Characteristics: 0 to 49 Years

Area	0 to 4 Years	5 to 9 Years	10 to 14 Years	15 to 19 Years	20 to 24 Years	25 to 29 Years	30 to 34 Years	35 to 39 Years	40 to 44 Years	45 to 49 Years
					Number					
					Total					
Langley	5,915	6,455	6,975	7,830	6,220	5,555	5,815	6,760	7,900	8,690
British Columbia	219,665	218,915	238,780	275,165	279,825	288,780	275,985	280,870	313,765	350,600
Canada	1,877,095	1,809,895	1,920,355	2,178,135	2,187,450	2,169,590	2,162,905	2,173,930	2,324,875	2,675,130
					Males					
Langley	3,000	3,270	3,630	3,975	3,185	2,740	2,780	3,250	3,755	4,220
British Columbia	112,885	112,200	122,465	141,670	142,290	143,475	135,220	135,455	151,430	170,580
Canada	961,150	925,965	983,995	1,115,845	1,108,775	1,077,275	1,058,810	1,064,200	1,141,720	1,318,715
					Females					
Langley	2,915	3,190	3,345	3,860	3,035	2,815	3,035	3,505	4,140	4,465
British Columbia	106,775	106,715	116,315	133,500	137,535	145,305	140,755	145,415	162,335	180,020
Canada	915,945	883,935	936,360	1,062,295	1,078,670	1,092,315	1,104,095	1,109,735	1,183,155	1,356,420
					Percent of Population					
					Total					
Langley	5.7	6.2	6.7	7.5	6.0	5.3	5.6	6.5	7.6	8.3
British Columbia	5.0	5.0	5.4	6.3	6.4	6.6	6.3	6.4	7.1	8.0
Canada	5.6	5.4	5.7	6.5	6.5	6.5	6.5	6.5	6.9	8.0
					Males					
Langley	5.9	6.4	7.1	7.8	6.2	5.4	5.4	6.4	7.4	8.3
British Columbia	5.2	5.2	5.7	6.6	6.6	6.7	6.3	6.3	7.0	7.9
Canada	5.9	5.6	6.0	6.8	6.8	6.6	6.5	6.5	7.0	8.0
					Females					
Langley	5.5	6.0	6.3	7.3	5.7	5.3	5.7	6.6	7.8	8.4
British Columbia	4.8	4.8	5.2	6.0	6.1	6.5	6.3	6.5	7.2	8.0
Canada	5.4	5.2	5.5	6.2	6.3	6.4	6.5	6.5	6.9	7.9

Source: Statistics Canada. 2012. Census Profile. 2011 Census. Statistics Canada Catalogue no. 98-316-XWE. Ottawa. Released October 24 2012.
http://www12.statcan.gc.ca/census-recensement/2011/dp-pd/prof/index.cfm?Lang=E

Age Characteristics: 50 Years and Over, and Median Age

Area	50 to 54 Years	55 to 59 Years	60 to 64 Years	65 to 69 Years	70 to 74 Years	75 to 79 Years	80 to 84 Years	85 Years and Over	Median Age
				Number					
				Total					
Langley	8,480	7,370	6,325	4,620	3,155	2,445	1,890	1,770	40.3
British Columbia	354,610	323,335	291,040	210,900	160,715	127,480	96,945	92,675	41.9
Canada	2,658,965	2,340,635	2,052,670	1,521,715	1,153,065	922,700	702,070	645,515	40.6
				Males					
Langley	4,160	3,630	3,095	2,260	1,530	1,160	785	610	39.5
British Columbia	172,060	157,455	142,645	103,785	77,350	60,720	42,745	32,150	41.1
Canada	1,309,030	1,147,300	1,002,690	738,010	543,435	417,945	291,085	208,300	39.6
				Females					
Langley	4,320	3,740	3,230	2,365	1,625	1,280	1,105	1,160	41.0
British Columbia	182,550	165,880	148,395	107,115	83,360	66,760	54,200	60,520	42.7
Canada	1,349,940	1,193,335	1,049,985	783,705	609,630	504,755	410,985	437,215	41.5
				Percent of Population					
				Total					
Langley	8.1	7.1	6.1	4.4	3.0	2.3	1.8	1.7	—
British Columbia	8.1	7.3	6.6	4.8	3.7	2.9	2.2	2.1	—
Canada	7.9	7.0	6.1	4.5	3.4	2.8	2.1	1.9	—
				Males					
Langley	8.1	7.1	6.1	4.4	3.0	2.3	1.5	1.2	—
British Columbia	8.0	7.3	6.6	4.8	3.6	2.8	2.0	1.5	—
Canada	8.0	7.0	6.1	4.5	3.3	2.5	1.8	1.3	—
				Females					
Langley	8.1	7.0	6.1	4.5	3.1	2.4	2.1	2.2	—
British Columbia	8.1	7.4	6.6	4.8	3.7	3.0	2.4	2.7	—
Canada	7.9	7.0	6.2	4.6	3.6	3.0	2.4	2.6	—

Source: Statistics Canada. 2012. Census Profile. 2011 Census. Statistics Canada Catalogue no. 98-316-XWE. Ottawa. Released October 24 2012.
http://www12.statcan.gc.ca/census-recensement/2011/dp-pd/prof/index.cfm?Lang=E

PROFILES / Langley, British Columbia

Private Households by Household Size

Area	1 Person	2 Persons	3 Persons	4 Persons	5 Persons	6 or More Persons	Average Number of Persons in Private Households
			Households				
Langley	7,360	12,305	6,220	6,995	2,705	1,645	2.8
British Columbia	498,925	613,270	264,135	237,725	91,600	58,985	2.5
Canada	3,673,310	4,544,820	2,081,900	1,903,300	724,405	392,885	2.5
			Percent of Households				
Langley	19.8	33.0	16.7	18.8	7.3	4.4	–
British Columbia	28.3	34.8	15.0	13.5	5.2	3.3	–
Canada	27.6	34.1	15.6	14.3	5.4	2.9	–

Source: Statistics Canada. 2012. Census Profile. 2011 Census. Statistics Canada Catalogue no. 98-316-XWE. Ottawa. Released October 24 2012.
http://www12.statcan.gc.ca/census-recensement/2011/dp-pd/prof/index.cfm?Lang=E

Dwelling Type

Area	Single-detached House	Semi-detached House	Row House	Apartment: Building with Five or More Storeys	Apartment: Building with Fewer Than Five Storeys	Duplex Apartment	Movable Dwelling	Other Single-attached House
				Number				
Langley	21,940	980	5,260	0	2,915	4,155	1,890	95
British Columbia	842,120	52,825	130,365	143,970	361,150	184,355	46,960	2,885
Canada	7,329,150	646,245	791,600	1,234,770	2,397,550	704,485	183,510	33,310
				Percent of Dwellings				
Langley	58.9	2.6	14.1	0.0	7.8	11.2	5.1	0.3
British Columbia	47.7	3.0	7.4	8.2	20.5	10.4	2.7	0.2
Canada	55.0	4.9	5.9	9.3	18.0	5.3	1.4	0.3

Source: Statistics Canada. 2012. Census Profile. 2011 Census. Statistics Canada Catalogue no. 98-316-XWE. Ottawa. Released October 24 2012.
http://www12.statcan.gc.ca/census-recensement/2011/dp-pd/prof/index.cfm?Lang=E

Shelter Costs

	Owned Dwellings					Rented Dwellings		
Area	Number	Median Value[1] ($)	Average Value[1] ($)	Median Monthly Costs[2] ($)	Average Monthly Costs[2] ($)	Number	Median Monthly Costs[3] ($)	Average Monthly Costs[3] ($)
Langley	30,780	501,361	548,062	1,381	1,432	5,630	1,001	1,106
British Columbia	1,202,000	448,835	543,635	1,023	1,228	519,855	903	989
Canada	9,013,410	280,552	345,182	978	1,141	4,060,385	784	848

Note: All figures cover non-farm, non-reserve private dwellings; (1) Refers to the dollar amount expected by the owner if the dwelling were to be sold; (2) Includes all shelter expenses paid by households that own their dwellings, such as the mortgage payment and the costs of electricity, heat, water and other municipal services, property taxes and condominium fees; (3) Includes all shelter expenses paid by households that rent their dwellings, such as the monthly rent and the costs of electricity, heat and municipal services.
Source: Statistics Canada. 2013. 2011 National Household Survey. Statistics Canada Catalogue no. 99-004-XWE. Ottawa. Released September 11, 2013.

Occupied Private Dwellings by Period of Construction

Area	1960 or Before	1961 to 1980	1981 to 1990	1991 to 2000	2001 to 2005	2006 to 2011
			Number			
Langley	2,105	9,635	7,995	9,055	3,890	4,570
British Columbia	282,675	551,655	308,450	329,780	133,235	158,845
Canada	3,273,105	4,152,715	2,112,110	1,707,880	1,031,020	1,042,430
			Percent of Dwellings			
Langley	5.7	25.9	21.5	24.3	10.4	12.3
British Columbia	16.0	31.3	17.5	18.7	7.6	9.0
Canada	24.6	31.2	15.9	12.8	7.7	7.8

Note: Figures cover non-farm, non-reserve private dwellings and includes data up to May 10, 2011.
Source: Statistics Canada. 2013. 2011 National Household Survey. Statistics Canada Catalogue no. 99-004-XWE. Ottawa. Released September 11, 2013.

PROFILES / Langley, British Columbia

Educational Attainment

Area	No Certificate, Diploma or Degree	High School Diploma or Equivalent[1]	Apprenticeship or Trades Certificate or Diploma[2]	College, CÉGEP or Other Non-University Certificate or Diploma	University Certificate or Diploma Below the Bachelor Level[3]	Bachelor's Degree	University Certificate, Diploma or Degree Above Bachelor Level[4]
			Number Total				
Langley	13,075	26,030	10,515	15,375	4,970	8,865	4,960
British Columbia	607,655	1,009,400	387,455	628,115	208,245	511,240	294,725
Canada	5,485,400	6,968,935	2,950,685	4,970,020	1,200,130	3,634,425	2,049,930
			Males				
Langley	6,985	11,650	7,565	6,335	2,000	3,865	2,380
British Columbia	305,040	475,670	262,245	260,580	86,995	235,620	149,300
Canada	2,742,875	3,305,415	1,928,970	2,118,430	513,235	1,643,080	1,043,350
			Females				
Langley	6,095	14,380	2,950	9,040	2,975	4,995	2,575
British Columbia	302,620	533,735	125,210	367,535	121,250	275,625	145,425
Canada	2,742,520	3,663,515	1,021,715	2,851,595	686,890	1,991,345	1,006,585
			Percent of Population Total				
Langley	15.6	31.1	12.5	18.3	5.9	10.6	5.9
British Columbia	16.7	27.7	10.6	17.2	5.7	14.0	8.1
Canada	20.1	25.6	10.8	18.2	4.4	13.3	7.5
			Males				
Langley	17.1	28.6	18.6	15.5	4.9	9.5	5.8
British Columbia	17.2	26.8	14.8	14.7	4.9	13.3	8.4
Canada	20.6	24.9	14.5	15.9	3.9	12.4	7.8
			Females				
Langley	14.2	33.4	6.9	21.0	6.9	11.6	6.0
British Columbia	16.2	28.5	6.7	19.6	6.5	14.7	7.8
Canada	19.6	26.2	7.3	20.4	4.9	14.3	7.2

Note: Figures cover total population aged 15 years and over by highest certificate, diploma or degree; (1) Includes persons who have graduated from a secondary school or equivalent. It excludes persons with a postsecondary certificate, diploma or degree; (2) Includes Registered Apprenticeship certificates (including Certificate of Qualification, Journeyperson's designation) and other trades certificates or diplomas such as pre-employment or vocational certificates and diplomas from brief trade programs completed at community colleges, institutes of technology, vocational centres, and similar institutions; (3) Comparisons with other data sources suggest that the category 'University certificate or diploma below the bachelor's level' was over-reported in the NHS. This category likely includes some responses that are actually college certificates or diplomas, bachelor's degrees or other types of education (e.g., university transfer programs, bachelor's programs completed in other countries, incomplete bachelor's programs, non-university professional designations). We recommend users interpret the results for the 'University certificate or diploma below the bachelor's level' category with caution; (4) 'University certificate or diploma above bachelor level' includes the categories: 'Degree in medicine, dentistry, veterinary medicine or optometry,' 'Master's degree' and 'Earned doctorate.'
Source: Statistics Canada. 2013. 2011 National Household Survey. Statistics Canada Catalogue no. 99-004-XWE. Ottawa. Released September 11, 2013.

Household Income Distribution

Area	Less than $10,000	$10,000 to $19,999	$20,000 to $29,999	$30,000 to $39,999	$40,000 to $49,999	$50,000 to $59,999	$60,000 to $79,999	$80,000 to $99,999	$100,000 to $124,999	$125,000 to $149,999	$150,000 and Over
						Households					
Langley	1,400	2,070	2,175	3,055	2,680	2,790	5,385	4,385	4,790	3,355	5,165
British Columbia	96,465	156,565	157,605	167,220	158,400	140,340	246,720	193,180	167,415	106,325	174,385
Canada	626,705	1,141,945	1,193,925	1,271,675	1,206,800	1,102,120	1,865,280	1,458,240	1,260,770	802,555	1,389,240
						Percent of Households					
Langley	3.8	5.6	5.8	8.2	7.2	7.5	14.5	11.8	12.9	9.0	13.9
British Columbia	5.5	8.9	8.9	9.5	9.0	8.0	14.0	10.9	9.5	6.0	9.9
Canada	4.7	8.6	9.0	9.5	9.1	8.3	14.0	10.9	9.5	6.0	10.4

Note: Household income is the sum of the total incomes of all members of that household. Total income refers to monetary receipts from certain sources, before income taxes and deductions, during calendar year 2010.
Source: Statistics Canada. 2013. 2011 National Household Survey. Statistics Canada Catalogue no. 99-004-XWE. Ottawa. Released September 11, 2013.

Median and Average Household and Economic Family Income

Area	Median Household Income ($)	Average Household Income ($)	Median After-tax Household Income ($)	Average After-tax Household Income ($)	Median Economic Family Income ($)	Average Economic Family Income ($)	Median After-tax Economic Family Income ($)	Average After-tax Economic Family Income ($)
Langley	76,847	91,875	68,007	78,175	88,986	101,897	77,864	86,675
British Columbia	60,333	77,378	54,379	66,264	75,797	91,967	67,915	78,580
Canada	61,072	79,102	54,089	66,149	76,511	94,125	67,044	78,517

Note: Figures cover household and economic familiy income in 2010. A household is defined as a person or a group of persons (other than foreign residents) who occupy the same private dwelling and do not have a usual place of residence elsewhere in Canada. Every person is a member of one and only one household. An economic family is defined as a group of two or more persons who live in the same dwelling and are related to each other by blood, marriage, common-law, adoption or a foster relationship. A couple may be of opposite or same sex.
Source: Statistics Canada. 2013. 2011 National Household Survey. Statistics Canada Catalogue no. 99-004-XWE. Ottawa. Released September 11, 2013.

PROFILES / Langley, British Columbia

Individual Income Distribution

Area	Less than $10,000	$10,000 to $19,999	$20,000 to $29,999	$30,000 to $39,999	$40,000 to $49,999	$50,000 to $59,999	$60,000 to $79,999	$80,000 to $99,999	$100,000 to $124,999	$125,000 and Over
Number											
Total											
Langley	13,605	12,950	9,760	9,295	8,350	6,625	9,140	4,505	2,725	2,510
British Columbia	645,915	666,060	470,255	404,860	338,595	253,215	330,590	169,190	89,520	96,055
Canada	4,492,040	4,835,710	3,670,020	3,180,360	2,603,520	1,921,650	2,437,440	1,302,045	693,580	782,135
Males											
Langley	5,285	4,595	4,155	3,940	3,835	3,740	5,995	3,130	2,025	2,040
British Columbia	275,815	263,170	201,000	186,285	167,400	143,765	206,400	112,525	65,050	74,260
Canada	1,936,365	1,864,880	1,588,260	1,522,190	1,333,510	1,079,780	1,473,145	823,720	492,905	599,905
Females											
Langley	8,320	8,355	5,600	5,360	4,510	2,890	3,150	1,375	700	470
British Columbia	370,100	402,880	269,255	218,575	171,190	109,445	124,195	56,670	24,470	21,795
Canada	2,555,675	2,970,825	2,081,760	1,658,170	1,270,010	841,870	964,300	478,330	200,680	182,230
Percent of Population											
Total											
Langley	17.1	16.3	12.3	11.7	10.5	8.3	11.5	5.7	3.4	3.2
British Columbia	18.6	19.2	13.6	11.7	9.8	7.3	9.5	4.9	2.6	2.8
Canada	17.3	18.7	14.2	12.3	10.0	7.4	9.4	5.0	2.7	3.0
Males											
Langley	13.6	11.9	10.7	10.2	9.9	9.7	15.5	8.1	5.2	5.3
British Columbia	16.3	15.5	11.9	11.0	9.9	8.5	12.2	6.6	3.8	4.4
Canada	15.2	14.7	12.5	12.0	10.5	8.5	11.6	6.5	3.9	4.7
Females											
Langley	20.4	20.5	13.8	13.2	11.1	7.1	7.7	3.4	1.7	1.2
British Columbia	20.9	22.8	15.2	12.4	9.7	6.2	7.0	3.2	1.4	1.2
Canada	19.4	22.5	15.8	12.6	9.6	6.4	7.3	3.6	1.5	1.4

Note: Figures cover individuals aged 15 years and over with income. Income refers to monetary receipts from certain sources, before income taxes and deductions, during calendar year 2010.
Source: Statistics Canada. 2013. 2011 National Household Survey. Statistics Canada Catalogue no. 99-004-XWE. Ottawa. Released September 11, 2013.

Labour Force Status

Area	In the Labour Force - All	In the Labour Force - Employed	In the Labour Force - Unemployed	Not in the Labour Force
Number				
Total				
Langley	58,535	54,975	3,565	25,255
British Columbia	2,354,245	2,171,465	182,775	1,292,595
Canada	17,990,080	16,595,035	1,395,045	9,269,445
Males				
Langley	30,685	28,850	1,830	10,095
British Columbia	1,223,375	1,124,590	98,785	552,070
Canada	9,388,570	8,634,310	754,255	3,906,785
Females				
Langley	27,850	26,125	1,730	15,160
British Columbia	1,130,870	1,046,875	83,990	740,530
Canada	8,601,515	7,960,725	640,790	5,362,660
Percent of Labour Force				
Total				
Langley	69.9	65.6	6.1	30.1
British Columbia	64.6	59.5	7.8	35.4
Canada	66.0	60.9	7.8	34.0
Males				
Langley	75.2	70.7	6.0	24.8
British Columbia	68.9	63.3	8.1	31.1
Canada	70.6	64.9	8.0	29.4
Females				
Langley	64.7	60.7	6.2	35.2
British Columbia	60.4	55.9	7.4	39.6
Canada	61.6	57.0	7.4	38.4

Note: Figures are based on total population 15 years and over
Source: Statistics Canada. 2013. 2011 National Household Survey. Statistics Canada Catalogue no. 99-004-XWE. Ottawa. Released September 11, 2013.

Labour Force by Industry (NAICS Codes 11–52)

Area	Agriculture, forestry, fishing & hunting	Mining, quarrying, & oil & gas extraction	Utilities	Construction	Manufacturing	Wholesale Trade	Retail Trade	Transportation & warehousing	Information & cultural industries	Finance & insurance
					Number					
					Total					
Langley	1,950	180	340	5,990	4,570	3,735	6,700	3,370	1,140	2,095
British Columbia	61,210	25,450	13,215	181,510	148,810	90,560	266,265	118,675	62,235	91,790
Canada	437,650	261,050	149,940	1,215,380	1,619,295	733,445	2,031,665	827,780	420,830	767,960
					Males					
Langley	1,110	150	270	5,170	3,360	2,480	2,930	2,480	675	750
British Columbia	40,810	21,175	9,650	159,605	108,480	61,730	121,750	89,155	37,250	35,375
Canada	307,370	211,690	110,765	1,068,710	1,167,680	494,545	933,850	617,305	235,875	296,995
					Females					
Langley	840	25	70	815	1,210	1,255	3,770	895	470	1,345
British Columbia	20,405	4,275	3,560	21,910	40,335	28,820	144,515	29,520	24,980	56,415
Canada	130,285	49,360	39,175	146,670	451,615	238,900	1,097,820	210,475	184,955	470,960
					Percent of Labour Force					
					Total					
Langley	3.4	0.3	0.6	10.4	8.0	6.5	11.7	5.9	2.0	3.6
British Columbia	2.7	1.1	0.6	7.9	6.5	3.9	11.6	5.1	2.7	4.0
Canada	2.5	1.5	0.9	6.9	9.2	4.2	11.6	4.7	2.4	4.4
					Males					
Langley	3.7	0.5	0.9	17.2	11.2	8.2	9.7	8.2	2.2	2.5
British Columbia	3.4	1.8	0.8	13.3	9.0	5.1	10.1	7.4	3.1	2.9
Canada	3.3	2.3	1.2	11.6	12.7	5.4	10.2	6.7	2.6	3.2
					Females					
Langley	3.1	0.1	0.3	3.0	4.4	4.6	13.8	3.3	1.7	4.9
British Columbia	1.8	0.4	0.3	2.0	3.6	2.6	13.1	2.7	2.3	5.1
Canada	1.6	0.6	0.5	1.7	5.4	2.8	13.1	2.5	2.2	5.6

Note: Figures are based on total experienced labour force 15 years and over. Experienced labour force refers to persons who, during the week of Sunday, May 1 to Saturday, May 7, 2011, were employed and the unemployed who had last worked for pay or in self-employment in either 2010 or 2011.
Source: Statistics Canada. 2013. 2011 National Household Survey. Statistics Canada Catalogue no. 99-004-XWE. Ottawa. Released September 11, 2013.

Labour Force by Industry (NAICS Codes 53–91)

Area	Real estate & rental & leasing	Profess., scientific & tech. services	Mgmt of companies & enterprises	Admin. & support, waste mgmt & remed. services	Educational services	Health care & social assistance	Arts, entertain. & recreation	Accomm. & food services	Other services (except public admin.)	Public admin.
					Number					
					Total					
Langley	1,285	3,055	50	2,030	4,170	5,350	1,130	3,775	2,870	3,685
British Columbia	54,840	179,355	2,440	98,890	167,875	249,030	56,915	179,625	112,745	143,875
Canada	321,895	1,240,850	17,460	728,330	1,301,435	1,949,650	363,405	1,130,750	807,800	1,261,050
					Males					
Langley	695	1,455	25	1,225	1,270	690	550	1,480	1,395	1,965
British Columbia	29,790	98,760	1,320	55,745	55,635	47,020	29,750	73,570	49,130	74,040
Canada	179,090	688,625	9,380	411,250	424,915	349,430	188,270	469,990	372,940	652,510
					Females					
Langley	590	1,595	30	800	2,900	4,670	585	2,290	1,480	1,725
British Columbia	25,055	80,590	1,120	43,145	112,235	202,010	27,175	106,055	63,615	69,840
Canada	142,805	552,225	8,075	317,085	876,515	1,600,220	175,135	660,760	434,865	608,535
					Percent of Labour Force					
					Total					
Langley	2.2	5.3	0.1	3.5	7.3	9.3	2.0	6.6	5.0	6.4
British Columbia	2.4	7.8	0.1	4.3	7.3	10.8	2.5	7.8	4.9	6.2
Canada	1.8	7.1	0.1	4.1	7.4	11.1	2.1	6.4	4.6	7.2
					Males					
Langley	2.3	4.8	0.1	4.1	4.2	2.3	1.8	4.9	4.6	6.5
British Columbia	2.5	8.2	0.1	4.6	4.6	3.9	2.5	6.1	4.1	6.2
Canada	1.9	7.5	0.1	4.5	4.6	3.8	2.0	5.1	4.1	7.1
					Females					
Langley	2.2	5.8	0.1	2.9	10.6	17.1	2.1	8.4	5.4	6.3
British Columbia	2.3	7.3	0.1	3.9	10.2	18.3	2.5	9.6	5.8	6.3
Canada	1.7	6.6	0.1	3.8	10.4	19.1	2.1	7.9	5.2	7.2

Note: Figures are based on total experienced labour force 15 years and over. Experienced labour force refers to persons who, during the week of Sunday, May 1 to Saturday, May 7, 2011, were employed and the unemployed who had last worked for pay or in self-employment in either 2010 or 2011.
Source: Statistics Canada. 2013. 2011 National Household Survey. Statistics Canada Catalogue no. 99-004-XWE. Ottawa. Released September 11, 2013.

PROFILES / Langley, British Columbia

Occupation

Area	Mgmt	Business, Finance & Admin.	Natural/ Applied Sciences & Related	Health	Education, Law & Social, Community & Government Services	Art, Culture, Recreation & Sport	Sales & Service	Trades, Transport & Equip. Operators & Related	Natural Resources, Agri. & Related Production	Mfg & Utilities
\multicolumn{11}{c}{Number}										
\multicolumn{11}{c}{Total}										
Langley	7,790	9,900	2,995	3,165	6,565	1,350	12,075	10,405	1,530	1,695
British Columbia	263,685	368,980	154,055	147,620	265,910	78,565	554,345	337,140	60,295	74,720
Canada	1,963,600	2,902,045	1,237,775	1,107,200	2,064,675	503,415	4,068,170	2,537,775	397,930	805,040
\multicolumn{11}{c}{Males}										
Langley	5,110	2,230	2,450	520	2,345	580	4,905	9,725	940	1,315
British Columbia	162,365	104,285	122,570	32,490	89,645	38,300	233,065	317,385	45,155	54,470
Canada	1,229,460	854,190	966,355	217,520	676,550	232,535	1,745,705	2,385,615	318,945	564,300
\multicolumn{11}{c}{Females}										
Langley	2,685	7,670	550	2,645	4,215	770	7,170	680	585	380
British Columbia	101,320	264,690	31,480	115,125	176,265	40,270	321,285	19,755	15,135	20,250
Canada	734,140	2,047,855	271,415	889,675	1,388,130	270,875	2,322,465	152,165	78,980	240,740
\multicolumn{11}{c}{Percent of Labour Force}										
\multicolumn{11}{c}{Total}										
Langley	13.6	17.2	5.2	5.5	11.4	2.3	21.0	18.1	2.7	2.9
British Columbia	11.4	16.0	6.7	6.4	11.5	3.4	24.0	14.6	2.6	3.2
Canada	11.2	16.5	7.0	6.3	11.7	2.9	23.1	14.4	2.3	4.6
\multicolumn{11}{c}{Males}										
Langley	17.0	7.4	8.1	1.7	7.8	1.9	16.3	32.3	3.1	4.4
British Columbia	13.5	8.7	10.2	2.7	7.5	3.2	19.4	26.5	3.8	4.5
Canada	13.4	9.3	10.5	2.4	7.4	2.5	19.0	26.0	3.5	6.1
\multicolumn{11}{c}{Females}										
Langley	9.8	28.0	2.0	9.7	15.4	2.8	26.2	2.5	2.1	1.4
British Columbia	9.2	23.9	2.8	10.4	15.9	3.6	29.1	1.8	1.4	1.8
Canada	8.7	24.4	3.2	10.6	16.5	3.2	27.7	1.8	0.9	2.9

Note: Figures are based on total experienced labour force 15 years and over
Source: Statistics Canada. 2013. 2011 National Household Survey. Statistics Canada Catalogue no. 99-004-XWE. Ottawa. Released September 11, 2013.

Place of Work Status

Area	Worked at Home	Worked Outside Canada	No Fixed Workplace Address	Worked at Usual Place
\multicolumn{5}{c}{Number}				
\multicolumn{5}{c}{Total}				
Langley	5,145	225	8,025	41,570
British Columbia	174,000	12,480	304,465	1,680,525
Canada	1,142,640	66,460	1,868,245	13,517,690
\multicolumn{5}{c}{Males}				
Langley	2,415	155	6,220	20,060
British Columbia	84,015	9,210	225,840	805,525
Canada	582,150	47,355	1,400,485	6,604,325
\multicolumn{5}{c}{Females}				
Langley	2,730	75	1,810	21,510
British Columbia	89,990	3,270	78,620	875,000
Canada	560,490	19,100	467,760	6,913,370
\multicolumn{5}{c}{Percent of Labour Force}				
\multicolumn{5}{c}{Total}				
Langley	9.4	0.4	14.6	75.6
British Columbia	8.0	0.6	14.0	77.4
Canada	6.9	0.4	11.3	81.5
\multicolumn{5}{c}{Males}				
Langley	8.4	0.5	21.6	69.5
British Columbia	7.5	0.8	20.1	71.6
Canada	6.7	0.5	16.2	76.5
\multicolumn{5}{c}{Females}				
Langley	10.4	0.3	6.9	82.3
British Columbia	8.6	0.3	7.5	83.6
Canada	7.0	0.2	5.9	86.8

Note: Figures are based on total employed labour force 15 years and over.
Source: Statistics Canada. 2013. 2011 National Household Survey. Statistics Canada Catalogue no. 99-004-XWE. Ottawa. Released September 11, 2013.

Mode of Transportation to Work

Area	Car; Truck; Van; as Driver	Car; Truck; Van; as Passenger	Public Transit	Walked	Bicycled	All Other Modes
			Number			
			Total			
Langley	42,705	2,605	1,740	1,635	245	665
British Columbia	1,415,745	110,695	250,450	132,205	42,260	33,635
Canada	11,393,140	867,050	1,851,525	880,815	201,780	191,625
			Males			
Langley	22,945	1,255	840	745	195	300
British Columbia	773,160	47,425	107,645	57,000	26,595	19,535
Canada	6,238,835	349,530	788,290	387,580	135,840	104,725
			Females			
Langley	19,760	1,355	900	885	50	370
British Columbia	642,580	63,270	142,810	75,205	15,665	14,100
Canada	5,154,305	517,520	1,063,235	493,230	65,940	86,900
			Percent of Labour Force			
			Total			
Langley	86.1	5.3	3.5	3.3	0.5	1.3
British Columbia	71.3	5.6	12.6	6.7	2.1	1.7
Canada	74.0	5.6	12.0	5.7	1.3	1.2
			Males			
Langley	87.3	4.8	3.2	2.8	0.7	1.1
British Columbia	75.0	4.6	10.4	5.5	2.6	1.9
Canada	77.9	4.4	9.8	4.8	1.7	1.3
			Females			
Langley	84.7	5.8	3.9	3.8	0.2	1.6
British Columbia	67.4	6.6	15.0	7.9	1.6	1.5
Canada	69.8	7.0	14.4	6.7	0.9	1.2

Note: Figures are based on total employed labour force 15 years and over.
Source: Statistics Canada. 2013. 2011 National Household Survey. Statistics Canada Catalogue no. 99-004-XWE. Ottawa. Released September 11, 2013.

Visible Minority Population Characteristics

Area	Total Minority	South Asian[1]	Chinese	Black	Filipino	Latin American	Arab	SE Asian[2]	West Asian[3]	Korean	Japanese	Multiple[4]
					Number							
					Total							
Langley	13,805	2,765	3,055	470	1,340	650	225	1,115	185	2,705	710	530
British Columbia	1,180,870	313,440	438,140	33,260	126,040	35,465	14,090	51,970	38,960	53,770	38,120	31,160
Canada	6,264,750	1,567,400	1,324,750	945,665	619,310	381,280	380,620	312,075	206,840	161,130	87,270	171,935
					Males							
Langley	6,835	1,425	1,580	300	610	315	90	530	105	1,265	330	250
British Columbia	565,965	157,135	208,175	17,365	53,715	16,985	8,010	25,055	19,420	25,325	16,295	15,255
Canada	3,043,010	790,755	632,325	453,005	268,885	186,355	203,485	154,035	105,620	77,165	38,270	83,335
					Females							
Langley	6,970	1,340	1,470	170	730	335	135	585	80	1,440	380	275
British Columbia	614,905	156,300	229,960	15,895	72,320	18,480	6,080	26,920	19,540	28,440	21,820	15,905
Canada	3,221,745	776,650	692,420	492,660	350,425	194,925	177,140	158,045	101,220	83,965	48,990	88,600
					Percent of Population							
					Total							
Langley	13.4	2.7	3.0	0.5	1.3	0.6	0.2	1.1	0.2	2.6	0.7	0.5
British Columbia	27.3	7.2	10.1	0.8	2.9	0.8	0.3	1.2	0.9	1.2	0.9	0.7
Canada	19.1	4.8	4.0	2.9	1.9	1.2	1.2	0.9	0.6	0.5	0.3	0.5
					Males							
Langley	13.5	2.8	3.1	0.6	1.2	0.6	0.2	1.0	0.2	2.5	0.7	0.5
British Columbia	26.6	7.4	9.8	0.8	2.5	0.8	0.4	1.2	0.9	1.2	0.8	0.7
Canada	18.8	4.9	3.9	2.8	1.7	1.2	1.3	1.0	0.7	0.5	0.2	0.5
					Females							
Langley	13.3	2.6	2.8	0.3	1.4	0.6	0.3	1.1	0.2	2.7	0.7	0.5
British Columbia	28.0	7.1	10.5	0.7	3.3	0.8	0.3	1.2	0.9	1.3	1.0	0.7
Canada	19.3	4.7	4.1	3.0	2.1	1.2	1.1	0.9	0.6	0.5	0.3	0.5

Note: The Employment Equity Act defines visible minorities as 'persons, other than Aboriginal peoples, who are non-Caucasian in race or non-white in colour'; (1) Includes 'East Indian,' 'Pakistani,' 'Sri Lankan,' etc.; (2) Includes 'Vietnamese,' 'Cambodian,' 'Malaysian,' 'Laotian,' etc.; (3) Includes 'Iranian,' 'Afghan,' etc.; (4) Includes respondents who reported more than one visible minority group by checking two or more mark-in circles, e.g., 'Black' and 'South Asian.'
Source: Statistics Canada. 2013. 2011 National Household Survey. Statistics Canada Catalogue no. 99-004-XWE. Ottawa. Released September 11, 2013.

PROFILES / Langley, British Columbia

Aboriginal Population

Area	Aboriginal Identity[1]	First Nations (North American Indian) Single Identity[2]	Métis Single Identity	Inuk (Inuit) Single Identity	Multiple Aboriginal Identities[3]	Aboriginal Identities Not Included Elsewhere
			Number			
			Total			
Langley	3,490	1,625	1,790	0	50	25
British Columbia	232,290	155,020	69,475	1,570	2,480	3,745
Canada	1,400,685	851,560	451,795	59,440	11,415	26,475
			Males			
Langley	1,665	760	870	0	0	0
British Columbia	113,080	75,400	33,940	820	1,190	1,735
Canada	682,190	411,785	223,335	29,495	5,525	12,055
			Females			
Langley	1,825	865	920	0	20	0
British Columbia	119,215	79,620	35,540	750	1,290	2,015
Canada	718,500	439,775	228,460	29,950	5,890	14,420
			Percent of Population			
			Total			
Langley	3.4	1.6	1.7	0.0	0.0	0.0
British Columbia	5.4	3.6	1.6	0.0	0.1	0.1
Canada	4.3	2.6	1.4	0.2	0.0	0.1
			Males			
Langley	3.3	1.5	1.7	0.0	0.0	0.0
British Columbia	5.3	3.5	1.6	0.0	0.1	0.1
Canada	4.2	2.5	1.4	0.2	0.0	0.1
			Females			
Langley	3.5	1.6	1.8	0.0	0.0	0.0
British Columbia	5.4	3.6	1.6	0.0	0.1	0.1
Canada	4.3	2.6	1.4	0.2	0.0	0.1

Note: (1) Includes persons who reported being an Aboriginal person, that is, First Nations (North American Indian), Métis or Inuk (Inuit) and/or those who reported Registered or Treaty Indian status, that is registered under the Indian Act of Canada, and/or those who reported membership in a First Nation or Indian band. Aboriginal peoples of Canada are defined in the Constitution Act, 1982, section 35-2 as including the Indian, Inuit and Métis peoples of Canada; (2) Users should be aware that the estimates associated with this variable are more affected than most by the incomplete enumeration of certain Indian reserves and Indian settlements in the National Household Survey (NHS); (3) Includes persons who reported being any two or all three of the following: First Nations (North American Indian), Métis or Inuk (Inuit).
Source: Statistics Canada. 2013. 2011 National Household Survey. Statistics Canada Catalogue no. 99-004-XWE. Ottawa. Released September 11, 2013.

Ethnic Origin

Area	North American Aboriginal	Other North American	European	Caribbean	Latin, Central and South American	African	Asian	Oceania
				Number				
				Total				
Langley	4,410	26,850	80,105	395	1,060	1,080	13,480	760
British Columbia	267,085	884,490	2,812,935	20,035	52,725	47,185	1,122,445	35,770
Canada	1,836,035	11,070,455	20,157,965	627,590	544,375	766,735	5,011,225	74,875
				Males				
Langley	1,990	13,175	39,240	230	470	530	6,535	400
British Columbia	128,880	440,920	1,387,940	10,225	25,605	23,575	535,825	17,425
Canada	885,675	5,462,685	9,913,150	291,640	264,635	387,360	2,435,540	37,490
				Females				
Langley	2,420	13,670	40,865	165	585	550	6,945	365
British Columbia	138,205	443,570	1,424,990	9,810	27,120	23,610	586,620	18,340
Canada	950,360	5,607,770	10,244,820	335,945	279,740	379,380	2,575,680	37,385
				Percent of Population				
				Total				
Langley	4.3	26.0	77.7	0.4	1.0	1.0	13.1	0.7
British Columbia	6.2	20.5	65.0	0.5	1.2	1.1	26.0	0.8
Canada	5.6	33.7	61.4	1.9	1.7	2.3	15.3	0.2
				Males				
Langley	3.9	26.0	77.4	0.5	0.9	1.0	12.9	0.8
British Columbia	6.1	20.7	65.3	0.5	1.2	1.1	25.2	0.8
Canada	5.5	33.8	61.3	1.8	1.6	2.4	15.1	0.2
				Females				
Langley	4.6	26.0	77.9	0.3	1.1	1.0	13.2	0.7
British Columbia	6.3	20.2	64.8	0.4	1.2	1.1	26.7	0.8
Canada	5.7	33.6	61.4	2.0	1.7	2.3	15.4	0.2

Note: The sum of the ethnic groups in this table is greater than the total population estimate because a person may report more than one ethnic origin in the NHS.
Source: Statistics Canada. 2013. 2011 National Household Survey. Statistics Canada Catalogue no. 99-004-XWE. Ottawa. Released September 11, 2013.

Religion

Area	Buddhist	Christian	Hindu	Jewish	Muslim	Sikh	Traditional (Aboriginal) Spirituality	Other Religions	No Religious Affiliation
				Number Total					
Langley	1,445	54,550	215	170	575	1,965	0	530	43,680
British Columbia	90,620	1,930,415	45,795	23,130	79,310	201,110	10,295	35,500	1,908,285
Canada	366,830	22,102,745	497,965	329,495	1,053,945	454,965	64,935	130,835	7,850,605
				Males					
Langley	720	25,120	120	85	285	975	0	175	23,180
British Columbia	40,175	883,680	22,945	11,255	39,780	100,610	5,085	14,680	1,007,420
Canada	168,465	10,497,775	250,435	161,265	540,555	229,435	31,805	57,745	4,225,645
				Females					
Langley	730	29,430	95	80	290	990	0	355	20,495
British Columbia	50,440	1,046,735	22,845	11,880	39,530	100,500	5,210	20,820	900,865
Canada	198,365	11,604,975	247,525	168,235	513,395	225,530	33,135	73,090	3,624,965
				Percent of Population Total					
Langley	1.4	52.9	0.2	0.2	0.6	1.9	0.0	0.5	42.3
British Columbia	2.1	44.6	1.1	0.5	1.8	4.7	0.2	0.8	44.1
Canada	1.1	67.3	1.5	1.0	3.2	1.4	0.2	0.4	23.9
				Males					
Langley	1.4	49.6	0.2	0.2	0.6	1.9	0.0	0.3	45.8
British Columbia	1.9	41.6	1.1	0.5	1.9	4.7	0.2	0.7	47.4
Canada	1.0	64.9	1.5	1.0	3.3	1.4	0.2	0.4	26.1
				Females					
Langley	1.4	56.1	0.2	0.2	0.6	1.9	0.0	0.7	39.1
British Columbia	2.3	47.6	1.0	0.5	1.8	4.6	0.2	0.9	41.0
Canada	1.2	69.5	1.5	1.0	3.1	1.4	0.2	0.4	21.7

Note: Religion refers to the person's self-identification as having a connection or affiliation with any religious denomination, group, body, sect, cult or other religiously defined community or system of belief. Religion is not limited to formal membership in a religious organization or group. Persons without a religious connection or affiliation can self-identify as atheist, agnostic or humanist, or can provide another applicable response.
Source: Statistics Canada. 2013. 2011 National Household Survey. Statistics Canada Catalogue no. 99-004-XWE. Ottawa. Released September 11, 2013.

Religion—Christian Denominations

Area	Anglican	Baptist	Catholic	Christian Orthodox	Lutheran	Pentecostal	Presbyterian	United Church	Other Christian
				Number Total					
Langley	5,055	2,420	13,515	795	2,220	2,760	1,300	6,115	20,370
British Columbia	213,975	91,575	650,360	39,845	71,470	58,300	44,635	222,230	538,030
Canada	1,631,845	635,840	12,810,705	550,690	478,185	478,705	472,385	2,007,610	3,036,780
				Males					
Langley	2,215	1,110	6,490	415	990	1,275	515	2,595	9,520
British Columbia	94,330	41,565	303,300	19,475	32,205	26,590	19,925	94,020	252,270
Canada	752,945	293,905	6,167,290	270,205	221,525	217,850	218,955	912,545	1,442,550
				Females					
Langley	2,840	1,305	7,025	380	1,230	1,490	790	3,525	10,850
British Columbia	119,645	50,010	347,060	20,375	39,270	31,710	24,710	128,210	285,770
Canada	878,900	341,940	6,643,415	280,485	256,660	260,850	253,430	1,095,065	1,594,230
				Percent of Population Total					
Langley	4.9	2.3	13.1	0.8	2.2	2.7	1.3	5.9	19.7
British Columbia	4.9	2.1	15.0	0.9	1.7	1.3	1.0	5.1	12.4
Canada	5.0	1.9	39.0	1.7	1.5	1.5	1.4	6.1	9.2
				Males					
Langley	4.4	2.2	12.8	0.8	2.0	2.5	1.0	5.1	18.8
British Columbia	4.4	2.0	14.3	0.9	1.5	1.3	0.9	4.4	11.9
Canada	4.7	1.8	38.2	1.7	1.4	1.3	1.4	5.6	8.9
				Females					
Langley	5.4	2.5	13.4	0.7	2.3	2.8	1.5	6.7	20.7
British Columbia	5.4	2.3	15.8	0.9	1.8	1.4	1.1	5.8	13.0
Canada	5.3	2.0	39.8	1.7	1.5	1.6	1.5	6.6	9.6

Note: Religion refers to the person's self-identification as having a connection or affiliation with any religious denomination, group, body, sect, cult or other religiously defined community or system of belief. Religion is not limited to formal membership in a religious organization or group. Persons without a religious connection or affiliation can self-identify as atheist, agnostic or humanist, or can provide another applicable response.
Source: Statistics Canada. 2013. 2011 National Household Survey. Statistics Canada Catalogue no. 99-004-XWE. Ottawa. Released September 11, 2013.

PROFILES / Langley, British Columbia

Immigrant Status and Period of Immigration

Area	Non-Immigrants[1]	Immigrants All	Before 1971	1971 to 1980	1981 to 1990	1991 to 2000	2001 to 2005	2006 to 2011	Non-Permanent Residents[3]
Number									
Total									
Langley	83,705	18,520	5,000	2,715	1,875	4,180	2,560	2,180	920
British Columbia	3,067,590	1,191,875	223,215	161,335	156,445	305,655	160,100	185,115	64,995
Canada	25,720,175	6,775,765	1,261,055	870,775	949,890	1,539,050	992,070	1,162,915	356,385
Males									
Langley	41,135	9,110	2,540	1,330	920	2,000	1,290	1,040	410
British Columbia	1,533,255	561,490	109,510	76,865	72,625	140,985	74,395	87,110	30,880
Canada	12,753,235	3,231,370	605,430	416,670	454,570	724,905	474,545	555,245	178,515
Females									
Langley	42,570	9,405	2,465	1,390	960	2,185	1,270	1,140	510
British Columbia	1,534,330	630,385	113,710	84,470	83,820	164,675	85,710	98,005	34,115
Canada	12,966,935	3,544,400	655,625	454,105	495,325	814,145	517,530	607,670	177,870
Percent of Population									
Total									
Langley	81.2	18.0	4.8	2.6	1.8	4.1	2.5	2.1	0.9
British Columbia	70.9	27.6	5.2	3.7	3.6	7.1	3.7	4.3	1.5
Canada	78.3	20.6	3.8	2.7	2.9	4.7	3.0	3.5	1.1
Males									
Langley	81.2	18.0	5.0	2.6	1.8	3.9	2.5	2.1	0.8
British Columbia	72.1	26.4	5.2	3.6	3.4	6.6	3.5	4.1	1.5
Canada	78.9	20.0	3.7	2.6	2.8	4.5	2.9	3.4	1.1
Females									
Langley	81.1	17.9	4.7	2.6	1.8	4.2	2.4	2.2	1.0
British Columbia	69.8	28.7	5.2	3.8	3.8	7.5	3.9	4.5	1.6
Canada	77.7	21.2	3.9	2.7	3.0	4.9	3.1	3.6	1.1

Note: (1) Non-immigrant refers to a person who is a Canadian citizen by birth; (2) Immigrant refers to a person who is or has ever been a landed immigrant/permanent resident. This person has been granted the right to live in Canada permanently by immigration authorities. Some immigrants have resided in Canada for a number of years, while others have arrived recently. Some immigrants are Canadian citizens, while others are not. Most immigrants are born outside Canada, but a small number are born in Canada. In the 2011 National Household Survey, 'Immigrants' includes immigrants who landed in Canada prior to May 10, 2011; (3) Non-permanent resident refers to a person from another country who has a work or study permit, or who is a refugee claimant, and any non-Canadian-born family member living in Canada with them.
Source: Statistics Canada. 2013. 2011 National Household Survey. Statistics Canada Catalogue no. 99-004-XWE. Ottawa. Released September 11, 2013.

Mother Tongue

Area	English	French	Non-official Language	English & French	English & Non-official Language	French & Non-official Language	English, French & Non-official Language
Number							
Total							
Langley	85,820	1,025	15,390	135	935	65	15
British Columbia	3,062,435	57,275	1,154,215	8,600	68,800	3,345	1,530
Canada	18,858,980	7,054,975	6,567,680	144,685	396,330	74,430	24,095
Males							
Langley	42,320	500	7,365	60	440	30	10
British Columbia	1,526,350	28,315	543,395	4,065	32,875	1,520	725
Canada	9,345,225	3,452,380	3,157,785	69,975	192,000	36,535	11,965
Females							
Langley	43,505	520	8,025	70	495	30	10
British Columbia	1,536,085	28,965	610,825	4,535	35,925	1,830	805
Canada	9,513,750	3,602,590	3,409,895	74,710	204,330	37,890	12,130
Percent of Population							
Total							
Langley	83.0	1.0	14.9	0.1	0.9	0.1	0.0
British Columbia	70.3	1.3	26.5	0.2	1.6	0.1	0.0
Canada	56.9	21.3	19.8	0.4	1.2	0.2	0.1
Males							
Langley	83.4	1.0	14.5	0.1	0.9	0.1	0.0
British Columbia	71.4	1.3	25.4	0.2	1.5	0.1	0.0
Canada	57.5	21.2	19.4	0.4	1.2	0.2	0.1
Females							
Langley	82.6	1.0	15.2	0.1	0.9	0.1	0.0
British Columbia	69.2	1.3	27.5	0.2	1.6	0.1	0.0
Canada	56.4	21.4	20.2	0.4	1.2	0.2	0.1

Note: Figures cover total population excluding institutional residents.
Source: Statistics Canada. 2012. Census Profile. 2011 Census. Statistics Canada Catalogue no. 98-316-XWE. Ottawa. Released October 24 2012.
http://www12.statcan.gc.ca/census-recensement/2011/dp-pd/prof/index.cfm?Lang=E

Language Spoken Most Often at Home

Area	English	French	Non-official Language	English & French	English & Non-official Language	French & Non-official Language	English, French & Non-official Language
			Number				
			Total				
Langley	94,230	205	7,090	70	1,750	10	25
British Columbia	3,506,595	16,685	670,100	4,700	155,065	930	2,130
Canada	21,457,075	6,827,865	3,673,865	131,205	875,135	109,700	46,330
			Males				
Langley	46,320	95	3,420	30	840	5	15
British Columbia	1,733,775	8,015	317,670	2,240	74,155	435	940
Canada	10,585,620	3,348,235	1,767,310	63,475	425,370	53,010	22,845
			Females				
Langley	47,910	110	3,670	35	915	5	10
British Columbia	1,772,820	8,665	352,430	2,460	80,905	495	1,185
Canada	10,871,455	3,479,625	1,906,555	67,730	449,765	56,690	23,485
			Percent of Population				
			Total				
Langley	91.1	0.2	6.9	0.1	1.7	0.0	0.0
British Columbia	80.5	0.4	15.4	0.1	3.6	0.0	0.0
Canada	64.8	20.6	11.1	0.4	2.6	0.3	0.1
			Males				
Langley	91.3	0.2	6.7	0.1	1.7	0.0	0.0
British Columbia	81.1	0.4	14.9	0.1	3.5	0.0	0.0
Canada	65.1	20.6	10.9	0.4	2.6	0.3	0.1
			Females				
Langley	91.0	0.2	7.0	0.1	1.7	0.0	0.0
British Columbia	79.9	0.4	15.9	0.1	3.6	0.0	0.1
Canada	64.5	20.6	11.3	0.4	2.7	0.3	0.1

Note: Figures cover total population excluding institutional residents.
Source: Statistics Canada. 2012. Census Profile. 2011 Census. Statistics Canada Catalogue no. 98-316-XWE. Ottawa. Released October 24 2012.
http://www12.statcan.gc.ca/census-recensement/2011/dp-pd/prof/index.cfm?Lang=E

Knowledge of Official Languages

Area	English Only	French Only	English & French	Neither English nor French
		Number		
		Total		
Langley	96,395	20	5,760	1,200
British Columbia	3,912,950	2,045	296,645	144,555
Canada	22,564,665	4,165,015	5,795,570	595,920
		Males		
Langley	47,740	10	2,470	515
British Columbia	1,943,760	950	132,940	59,590
Canada	11,222,185	1,925,340	2,876,560	241,790
		Females		
Langley	48,660	10	3,290	685
British Columbia	1,969,190	1,095	163,705	84,965
Canada	11,342,485	2,239,680	2,919,005	354,135
		Percent of Population		
		Total		
Langley	93.2	0.0	5.6	1.2
British Columbia	89.8	0.0	6.8	3.3
Canada	68.1	12.6	17.5	1.8
		Males		
Langley	94.1	0.0	4.9	1.0
British Columbia	90.9	0.0	6.2	2.8
Canada	69.0	11.8	17.7	1.5
		Females		
Langley	92.4	0.0	6.2	1.3
British Columbia	88.7	0.0	7.4	3.8
Canada	67.3	13.3	17.3	2.1

Note: Figures cover total population excluding institutional residents.
Source: Statistics Canada. 2012. Census Profile. 2011 Census. Statistics Canada Catalogue no. 98-316-XWE. Ottawa. Released October 24 2012.
http://www12.statcan.gc.ca/census-recensement/2011/dp-pd/prof/index.cfm?Lang=E

Laval, Québec

Background

Laval is located in southwestern Québec and occupies the Island of Jesus (Ile Jésus). The city is approximately 20 kilometres north of Montréal, across the Des Prairies River. Situated halfway between Montréal and the Laurentian Mountains, the municipality has the particular distinction of being its own region, city and island. Laval is one of the 17 administrative regions of Québec.

The Laval area was originally inhabited by the Kanien'kehake (Mohawk Nation). French Jesuits were granted a seigneury of the island and founded a mission in 1636. The island was named "Jesus Island" because the rural settlement was owned by the Jesuits. In 1675, the seigneury was passed to the first bishop of Québec, François de Montmorency-Laval, and the island was renamed in the bishop's honour. In 1975, the government of Québec amalgamated the island's 12 villages and towns into a single city. Today, approximately 20% of Laval residents were born outside of Canada, particularly from the French Caribbean, North Africa, the Middle East and Europe.

Laval remains mostly rural, with about 30% of the island being currently used as farmland, but it is still one of Québec's largest cities. Manufacturing is a key sector while biotechnology and information sciences are emerging economies. The city is intersected by major roads and railway lines and acts as a transfer point between Montréal and the province's northern regions.

Laval's Centre d'information sur l'eau (C.I.EAU) is the only interactive centre in Québec dedicated to the evolution of drinking water around the world. Summertime cruises around the Rivière-des-Mille-Îles are popular and often include giant turtle sightings. Laval's Cosmodôme is a recreational-educational complex about space sciences; in 2012, the newly revamped Cosmodôme opened a $10.5-million virtual-reality space exhibit.

Laval has summer highs of plus 24.87 degrees Celsius, winter lows of minus 12.67 degrees Celsius, and an average rainfall just over 763 mm per year.

Rankings

- Laval was ranked as one of Canada's safest cities in terms of cybercrime. The city ranked #4 out of 50 cities. Cybercrime indicators included web attacks, malware infections and spam originating from city. The major cities of Québec dominated the "Top 10 Least Risky" rankings with seven out of the 10 top spots. *Symantec, "Do you live in one of Canada's 'riskiest' online cities?" posted February 22nd, 2012*
- Forum Research identified Laval as having one of the highest percentages of residents who were satisfied with the delivery of their municipal services. The study polled Canada's 30 most populated towns and cities and Laval ranked #6. When polled about municipal services, 34% of residents expressed "very satisfied" responses. *Forum Research, Nationwide Municipal Issues Poll, released May 2012*
- The 2011 Census identified Laval's population growth as significantly higher than the national average. Laval (Ville) had a percentage change of 8.9% between 2006 and 2011. In the same time period, Canada's average population grew by 5.9%. *Statistics Canada, Focus on Geography Series, 2011 Census. October 24, 2012*

PROFILES / Laval, Québec

Population Growth and Density

Area	Population in 2001	Population in 2006	Population in 2011	Population Change 2001–2006	Population Change 2006–2011	Land Area (sq. km)	Population Density per sq. km
Laval	343,005	368,709	401,553	7.5	8.9	247.09	1,625.1
Québec	7,237,479	7,546,131	7,903,001	4.3	4.7	1,356,547.02	5.8
Canada	30,007,094	31,612,897	33,476,688	5.4	5.9	8,965,121.42	3.7

Source: Statistics Canada. 2012. Census Profile. 2011 Census. Statistics Canada Catalogue no. 98-316-XWE. Ottawa. Released October 24 2012.
http://www12.statcan.gc.ca/census-recensement/2011/dp-pd/prof/index.cfm?Lang=E;
Statistics Canada 2007. 2006 Community Profiles. 2006 Census. Statistics Canada Catalogue no. 92-591-XWE. Ottawa. Released March 13 2007.
http://www12.statcan.ca/census-recensement/2006/dp-pd/prof/92-591/index.cfm?Lang=E

Gender

Area	Males	Females
	Number	
Laval	194,885	206,665
Québec	3,875,860	4,027,140
Canada	16,414,225	17,062,460
	Percent of Population	
Laval	48.5	51.5
Québec	49.0	51.0
Canada	49.0	51.0

Source: Statistics Canada. 2012. Census Profile. 2011 Census. Statistics Canada Catalogue no. 98-316-XWE. Ottawa. Released October 24 2012.
http://www12.statcan.gc.ca/census-recensement/2011/dp-pd/prof/index.cfm?Lang=E

Marital Status

Area	Married[1]	Living Common-law	Single[2]	Separated	Divorced	Widowed
			Number			
			Total			
Laval	142,455	49,725	93,875	5,230	21,740	19,220
Québec	2,353,770	1,391,550	1,942,090	105,195	463,830	387,945
Canada	12,941,960	3,142,525	7,816,045	698,240	1,686,035	1,584,530
			Males			
Laval	71,330	24,885	49,695	2,145	7,885	3,645
Québec	1,177,720	697,695	1,045,540	46,465	188,265	77,430
Canada	6,470,300	1,575,495	4,206,320	299,655	680,415	310,940
			Females			
Laval	71,125	24,840	44,180	3,090	13,850	15,580
Québec	1,176,050	693,850	896,545	58,720	275,565	310,515
Canada	6,471,660	1,567,035	3,609,730	398,585	1,005,620	1,273,590
			Percent of Population			
			Total			
Laval	42.9	15.0	28.3	1.6	6.5	5.8
Québec	35.4	20.9	29.2	1.6	7.0	5.8
Canada	46.4	11.3	28.0	2.5	6.0	5.7
			Males			
Laval	44.7	15.6	31.1	1.3	4.9	2.3
Québec	36.4	21.6	32.3	1.4	5.8	2.4
Canada	47.8	11.6	31.1	2.2	5.0	2.3
			Females			
Laval	41.2	14.4	25.6	1.8	8.0	9.0
Québec	34.5	20.3	26.3	1.7	8.1	9.1
Canada	45.2	10.9	25.2	2.8	7.0	8.9

Note: (1) and not separated, (2) never legally married
Source: Statistics Canada. 2012. Census Profile. 2011 Census. Statistics Canada Catalogue no. 98-316-XWE. Ottawa. Released October 24 2012.
http://www12.statcan.gc.ca/census-recensement/2011/dp-pd/prof/index.cfm?Lang=E

PROFILES / Laval, Québec

Age Characteristics: 0 to 49 Years

Area	0 to 4 Years	5 to 9 Years	10 to 14 Years	15 to 19 Years	20 to 24 Years	25 to 29 Years	30 to 34 Years	35 to 39 Years	40 to 44 Years	45 to 49 Years
					Number Total					
Laval	23,125	22,450	23,730	27,580	24,950	22,195	24,565	26,800	29,890	33,350
Québec	440,840	399,575	418,205	491,980	489,185	490,665	531,445	498,225	520,805	623,575
Canada	1,877,095	1,809,895	1,920,355	2,178,135	2,187,450	2,169,590	2,162,905	2,173,930	2,324,875	2,675,130
					Males					
Laval	11,810	11,395	12,100	13,965	12,530	11,050	11,745	12,930	14,660	16,530
Québec	225,525	203,675	213,540	249,960	246,850	245,695	264,980	249,610	261,120	311,320
Canada	961,150	925,965	983,995	1,115,845	1,108,775	1,077,275	1,058,810	1,064,200	1,141,720	1,318,715
					Females					
Laval	11,320	11,055	11,630	13,615	12,415	11,150	12,820	13,875	15,230	16,825
Québec	215,320	195,900	204,665	242,020	242,340	244,970	266,460	248,615	259,690	312,250
Canada	915,945	883,935	936,360	1,062,295	1,078,670	1,092,315	1,104,095	1,109,735	1,183,155	1,356,420
					Percent of Population Total					
Laval	5.8	5.6	5.9	6.9	6.2	5.5	6.1	6.7	7.4	8.3
Québec	5.6	5.1	5.3	6.2	6.2	6.2	6.7	6.3	6.6	7.9
Canada	5.6	5.4	5.7	6.5	6.5	6.5	6.5	6.5	6.9	8.0
					Males					
Laval	6.1	5.8	6.2	7.2	6.4	5.7	6.0	6.6	7.5	8.5
Québec	5.8	5.3	5.5	6.4	6.4	6.3	6.8	6.4	6.7	8.0
Canada	5.9	5.6	6.0	6.8	6.8	6.6	6.5	6.5	7.0	8.0
					Females					
Laval	5.5	5.3	5.6	6.6	6.0	5.4	6.2	6.7	7.4	8.1
Québec	5.3	4.9	5.1	6.0	6.0	6.1	6.6	6.2	6.4	7.8
Canada	5.4	5.2	5.5	6.2	6.3	6.4	6.5	6.5	6.9	7.9

Source: Statistics Canada. 2012. Census Profile. 2011 Census. Statistics Canada Catalogue no. 98-316-XWE. Ottawa. Released October 24 2012.
http://www12.statcan.gc.ca/census-recensement/2011/dp-pd/prof/index.cfm?Lang=E

Age Characteristics: 50 Years and Over, and Median Age

Area	50 to 54 Years	55 to 59 Years	60 to 64 Years	65 to 69 Years	70 to 74 Years	75 to 79 Years	80 to 84 Years	85 Years and Over	Median Age
				Number Total					
Laval	32,370	26,140	21,820	18,050	14,765	13,000	9,585	7,185	40.9
Québec	648,695	579,280	512,830	403,210	291,755	232,355	176,420	153,945	41.9
Canada	2,658,965	2,340,635	2,052,670	1,521,715	1,153,065	922,700	702,070	645,515	40.6
				Males					
Laval	16,090	12,555	10,575	8,385	6,750	5,740	3,830	2,265	40.0
Québec	320,695	285,295	250,675	194,305	135,830	101,675	69,170	45,945	40.7
Canada	1,309,030	1,147,300	1,002,690	738,010	543,435	417,945	291,085	208,300	39.6
				Females					
Laval	16,280	13,590	11,240	9,670	8,020	7,260	5,755	4,915	41.8
Québec	327,995	293,990	262,155	208,905	155,925	130,680	107,250	108,005	43.0
Canada	1,349,940	1,193,335	1,049,985	783,705	609,630	504,755	410,985	437,215	41.5
				Percent of Population Total					
Laval	8.1	6.5	5.4	4.5	3.7	3.2	2.4	1.8	—
Québec	8.2	7.3	6.5	5.1	3.7	2.9	2.2	1.9	—
Canada	7.9	7.0	6.1	4.5	3.4	2.8	2.1	1.9	—
				Males					
Laval	8.3	6.4	5.4	4.3	3.5	2.9	2.0	1.2	—
Québec	8.3	7.4	6.5	5.0	3.5	2.6	1.8	1.2	—
Canada	8.0	7.0	6.1	4.5	3.3	2.5	1.8	1.3	—
				Females					
Laval	7.9	6.6	5.4	4.7	3.9	3.5	2.8	2.4	—
Québec	8.1	7.3	6.5	5.2	3.9	3.2	2.7	2.7	—
Canada	7.9	7.0	6.2	4.6	3.6	3.0	2.4	2.6	—

Source: Statistics Canada. 2012. Census Profile. 2011 Census. Statistics Canada Catalogue no. 98-316-XWE. Ottawa. Released October 24 2012.
http://www12.statcan.gc.ca/census-recensement/2011/dp-pd/prof/index.cfm?Lang=E

PROFILES / Laval, Québec

Private Households by Household Size

Area	1 Person	2 Persons	3 Persons	4 Persons	5 Persons	6 or More Persons	Average Number of Persons in Private Households
			Households				
Laval	39,930	49,790	25,405	25,840	9,365	4,125	2.5
Québec	1,094,410	1,181,240	496,140	421,080	142,555	59,920	2.3
Canada	3,673,310	4,544,820	2,081,900	1,903,300	724,405	392,885	2.5
			Percent of Households				
Laval	25.9	32.2	16.4	16.7	6.1	2.7	–
Québec	32.2	34.8	14.6	12.4	4.2	1.8	–
Canada	27.6	34.1	15.6	14.3	5.4	2.9	–

Source: Statistics Canada. 2012. Census Profile. 2011 Census. Statistics Canada Catalogue no. 98-316-XWE. Ottawa. Released October 24 2012.
http://www12.statcan.gc.ca/census-recensement/2011/dp-pd/prof/index.cfm?Lang=E

Dwelling Type

Area	Single-detached House	Semi-detached House	Row House	Apartment: Building with Five or More Storeys	Apartment: Building with Fewer Than Five Storeys	Duplex Apartment	Movable Dwelling	Other Single-attached House
				Number				
Laval	74,510	14,690	4,405	9,470	46,335	4,670	50	325
Québec	1,560,405	171,435	86,040	171,115	1,103,845	263,860	22,995	15,645
Canada	7,329,150	646,245	791,600	1,234,770	2,397,550	704,485	183,510	33,310
				Percent of Dwellings				
Laval	48.2	9.5	2.9	6.1	30.0	3.0	0.0	0.2
Québec	46.0	5.0	2.5	5.0	32.5	7.8	0.7	0.5
Canada	55.0	4.9	5.9	9.3	18.0	5.3	1.4	0.3

Source: Statistics Canada. 2012. Census Profile. 2011 Census. Statistics Canada Catalogue no. 98-316-XWE. Ottawa. Released October 24 2012.
http://www12.statcan.gc.ca/census-recensement/2011/dp-pd/prof/index.cfm?Lang=E

Shelter Costs

		Owned Dwellings				Rented Dwellings		
Area	Number	Median Value[1] ($)	Average Value[1] ($)	Median Monthly Costs[2] ($)	Average Monthly Costs[2] ($)	Number	Median Monthly Costs[3] ($)	Average Monthly Costs[3] ($)
Laval	107,015	259,801	291,954	1,036	1,064	47,370	703	748
Québec	2,056,665	214,537	249,427	841	936	1,308,465	643	685
Canada	9,013,410	280,552	345,182	978	1,141	4,060,385	784	848

Note: All figures cover non-farm, non-reserve private dwellings; (1) Refers to the dollar amount expected by the owner if the dwelling were to be sold; (2) Includes all shelter expenses paid by households that own their dwellings, such as the mortgage payment and the costs of electricity, heat, water and other municipal services, property taxes and condominium fees; (3) Includes all shelter expenses paid by households that rent their dwellings, such as the monthly rent and the costs of electricity, heat and municipal services.
Source: Statistics Canada. 2013. 2011 National Household Survey. Statistics Canada Catalogue no. 99-004-XWE. Ottawa. Released September 11, 2013.

Occupied Private Dwellings by Period of Construction

Area	1960 or Before	1961 to 1980	1981 to 1990	1991 to 2000	2001 to 2005	2006 to 2011
			Number			
Laval	24,370	56,165	29,590	20,305	12,170	11,860
Québec	946,900	1,115,455	533,790	353,355	206,035	239,685
Canada	3,273,105	4,152,715	2,112,110	1,707,880	1,031,020	1,042,430
			Percent of Dwellings			
Laval	15.8	36.4	19.2	13.1	7.9	7.7
Québec	27.9	32.9	15.7	10.4	6.1	7.1
Canada	24.6	31.2	15.9	12.8	7.7	7.8

Note: Figures cover non-farm, non-reserve private dwellings and includes data up to May 10, 2011.
Source: Statistics Canada. 2013. 2011 National Household Survey. Statistics Canada Catalogue no. 99-004-XWE. Ottawa. Released September 11, 2013.

PROFILES / Laval, Québec

Educational Attainment

Area	No Certificate, Diploma or Degree	High School Diploma or Equivalent[1]	Apprenticeship or Trades Certificate or Diploma[2]	College, CÉGEP or Other Non-University Certificate or Diploma	University Certificate or Diploma Below the Bachelor Level[3]	Bachelor's Degree	University Certificate, Diploma or Degree Above Bachelor Level[4]
				Number			
				Total			
Laval	66,315	75,795	45,135	55,280	19,280	41,595	20,065
Québec	1,436,025	1,404,755	1,049,470	1,075,855	305,330	766,100	437,050
Canada	5,485,400	6,968,935	2,950,685	4,970,020	1,200,130	3,634,425	2,049,930
				Males			
Laval	32,470	35,140	26,090	24,400	8,200	18,885	10,865
Québec	714,090	650,660	635,435	472,360	126,565	343,535	227,990
Canada	2,742,875	3,305,415	1,928,970	2,118,430	513,235	1,643,080	1,043,350
				Females			
Laval	33,845	40,655	19,045	30,880	11,085	22,710	9,200
Québec	721,930	754,095	414,035	603,495	178,765	422,565	209,065
Canada	2,742,520	3,663,515	1,021,715	2,851,595	686,890	1,991,345	1,006,585
				Percent of Population			
				Total			
Laval	20.5	23.4	14.0	17.1	6.0	12.9	6.2
Québec	22.2	21.7	16.2	16.6	4.7	11.8	6.8
Canada	20.1	25.6	10.8	18.2	4.4	13.3	7.5
				Males			
Laval	20.8	22.5	16.7	15.6	5.3	12.1	7.0
Québec	22.5	20.5	20.0	14.9	4.0	10.8	7.2
Canada	20.6	24.9	14.5	15.9	3.9	12.4	7.8
				Females			
Laval	20.2	24.3	11.4	18.4	6.6	13.6	5.5
Québec	21.9	22.8	12.5	18.3	5.4	12.8	6.3
Canada	19.6	26.2	7.3	20.4	4.9	14.3	7.2

Note: Figures cover total population aged 15 years and over by highest certificate, diploma or degree; (1) Includes persons who have graduated from a secondary school or equivalent. It excludes persons with a postsecondary certificate, diploma or degree; (2) Includes Registered Apprenticeship certificates (including Certificate of Qualification, Journeyperson's designation) and other trades certificates or diplomas such as pre-employment or vocational certificates and diplomas from brief trade programs completed at community colleges, institutes of technology, vocational centres, and similar institutions; (3) Comparisons with other data sources suggest that the category 'University certificate or diploma below the bachelor's level' was over-reported in the NHS. This category likely includes some responses that are actually college certificates or diplomas, bachelor's degrees or other types of education (e.g., university transfer programs, bachelor's programs completed in other countries, incomplete bachelor's programs, non-university professional designations). We recommend users interpret the results for the 'University certificate or diploma below the bachelor's level' category with caution; (4) 'University certificate or diploma above bachelor level' includes the categories: 'Degree in medicine, dentistry, veterinary medicine or optometry,' 'Master's degree' and 'Earned doctorate.'
Source: Statistics Canada. 2013. 2011 National Household Survey. Statistics Canada Catalogue no. 99-004-XWE. Ottawa. Released September 11, 2013.

Household Income Distribution

Area	Less than $10,000	$10,000 to $19,999	$20,000 to $29,999	$30,000 to $39,999	$40,000 to $49,999	$50,000 to $59,999	$60,000 to $79,999	$80,000 to $99,999	$100,000 to $124,999	$125,000 to $149,999	$150,000 and Over
						Households					
Laval	5,790	12,250	13,130	15,425	15,040	14,225	23,620	18,440	15,090	9,105	12,345
Québec	179,790	377,210	353,470	382,000	343,730	302,595	483,085	344,435	267,995	148,950	211,965
Canada	626,705	1,141,945	1,193,925	1,271,675	1,206,800	1,102,120	1,865,280	1,458,240	1,260,770	802,555	1,389,240
						Percent of Households					
Laval	3.7	7.9	8.5	10.0	9.7	9.2	15.3	11.9	9.8	5.9	8.0
Québec	5.3	11.1	10.4	11.3	10.1	8.9	14.2	10.1	7.9	4.4	6.2
Canada	4.7	8.6	9.0	9.5	9.1	8.3	14.0	10.9	9.5	6.0	10.4

Note: Household income is the sum of the total incomes of all members of that household. Total income refers to monetary receipts from certain sources, before income taxes and deductions, during calendar year 2010.
Source: Statistics Canada. 2013. 2011 National Household Survey. Statistics Canada Catalogue no. 99-004-XWE. Ottawa. Released September 11, 2013.

Median and Average Household and Economic Family Income

Area	Median Household Income ($)	Average Household Income ($)	Median After-tax Household Income ($)	Average After-tax Household Income ($)	Median Economic Family Income ($)	Average Economic Family Income ($)	Median After-tax Economic Family Income ($)	Average After-tax Economic Family Income ($)
Laval	60,952	73,999	53,382	61,432	75,020	86,790	64,699	72,018
Québec	51,842	66,205	45,968	55,121	68,344	82,045	59,560	68,091
Canada	61,072	79,102	54,089	66,149	76,511	94,125	67,044	78,517

Note: Figures cover household and economic familiy income in 2010. A household is defined as a person or a group of persons (other than foreign residents) who occupy the same private dwelling and do not have a usual place of residence elsewhere in Canada. Every person is a member of one and only one household. An economic family is defined as a group of two or more persons who live in the same dwelling and are related to each other by blood, marriage, common-law, adoption or a foster relationship. A couple may be of opposite or same sex.
Source: Statistics Canada. 2013. 2011 National Household Survey. Statistics Canada Catalogue no. 99-004-XWE. Ottawa. Released September 11, 2013.

PROFILES / Laval, Québec

Individual Income Distribution

Area	Less than $10,000	$10,000 to $19,999	$20,000 to $29,999	$30,000 to $39,999	$40,000 to $49,999	$50,000 to $59,999	$60,000 to $79,999	$80,000 to $99,999	$100,000 to $124,999	$125,000 and Over
					Number					
					Total					
Laval	48,890	60,720	44,370	42,515	33,535	23,875	28,405	11,695	6,095	6,250
Québec	1,005,600	1,309,515	941,630	866,290	653,400	449,185	515,815	211,070	109,975	120,915
Canada	4,492,040	4,835,710	3,670,020	3,180,360	2,603,520	1,921,650	2,437,440	1,302,045	693,580	782,135
					Males					
Laval	21,595	23,250	20,515	19,945	16,530	13,230	16,460	7,865	4,465	4,765
Québec	441,455	516,150	427,295	432,625	345,950	256,700	313,880	143,785	80,000	91,475
Canada	1,936,365	1,864,880	1,588,260	1,522,190	1,333,510	1,079,780	1,473,145	823,720	492,905	599,905
					Females					
Laval	27,295	37,475	23,860	22,565	17,005	10,640	11,940	3,825	1,635	1,485
Québec	564,150	793,365	514,335	433,670	307,455	192,485	201,935	67,275	29,980	29,440
Canada	2,555,675	2,970,825	2,081,760	1,658,170	1,270,010	841,870	964,300	478,330	200,680	182,230
				Percent of Population						
					Total					
Laval	16.0	19.8	14.5	13.9	10.9	7.8	9.3	3.8	2.0	2.0
Québec	16.3	21.2	15.2	14.0	10.6	7.3	8.3	3.4	1.8	2.0
Canada	17.3	18.7	14.2	12.3	10.0	7.4	9.4	5.0	2.7	3.0
					Males					
Laval	14.5	15.6	13.8	13.4	11.1	8.9	11.1	5.3	3.0	3.2
Québec	14.5	16.9	14.0	14.2	11.3	8.4	10.3	4.7	2.6	3.0
Canada	15.2	14.7	12.5	12.0	10.5	8.5	11.6	6.5	3.9	4.7
					Females					
Laval	17.3	23.8	15.1	14.3	10.8	6.7	7.6	2.4	1.0	0.9
Québec	18.0	25.3	16.4	13.8	9.8	6.1	6.4	2.1	1.0	0.9
Canada	19.4	22.5	15.8	12.6	9.6	6.4	7.3	3.6	1.5	1.4

Note: Figures cover individuals aged 15 years and over with income. Income refers to monetary receipts from certain sources, before income taxes and deductions, during calendar year 2010.
Source: Statistics Canada. 2013. 2011 National Household Survey. Statistics Canada Catalogue no. 99-004-XWE. Ottawa. Released September 11, 2013.

Labour Force Status

| | In the Labour Force | | | Not in the |
Area	All	Employed	Unemployed	Labour Force
		Number		
		Total		
Laval	215,155	200,535	14,620	108,315
Québec	4,183,445	3,880,425	303,020	2,291,145
Canada	17,990,080	16,595,035	1,395,045	9,269,445
		Males		
Laval	110,565	102,655	7,905	45,475
Québec	2,188,555	2,014,810	173,745	982,080
Canada	9,388,570	8,634,310	754,255	3,906,785
		Females		
Laval	104,590	97,880	6,710	62,835
Québec	1,994,885	1,865,610	129,275	1,309,065
Canada	8,601,515	7,960,725	640,790	5,362,660
	Percent of Labour Force			
		Total		
Laval	66.5	62.0	6.8	33.5
Québec	64.6	59.9	7.2	35.4
Canada	66.0	60.9	7.8	34.0
		Males		
Laval	70.9	65.8	7.1	29.1
Québec	69.0	63.5	7.9	31.0
Canada	70.6	64.9	8.0	29.4
		Females		
Laval	62.5	58.5	6.4	37.5
Québec	60.4	56.5	6.5	39.6
Canada	61.6	57.0	7.4	38.4

Note: Figures are based on total population 15 years and over
Source: Statistics Canada. 2013. 2011 National Household Survey. Statistics Canada Catalogue no. 99-004-XWE. Ottawa. Released September 11, 2013.

Labour Force by Industry (NAICS Codes 11–52)

Area	Agriculture, forestry, fishing & hunting	Mining, quarrying, & oil & gas extraction	Utilities	Construction	Manufacturing	Wholesale Trade	Retail Trade	Transportation & warehousing	Information & cultural industries	Finance & insurance
					Number					
					Total					
Laval	645	195	1,470	11,745	23,115	13,145	29,030	11,380	6,055	10,555
Québec	84,470	20,770	33,815	241,780	476,390	169,825	501,380	181,295	98,340	159,230
Canada	437,650	261,050	149,940	1,215,380	1,619,295	733,445	2,031,665	827,780	420,830	767,960
					Males					
Laval	435	130	890	9,865	15,775	7,545	13,860	8,570	3,405	3,730
Québec	61,540	18,035	24,560	213,605	343,345	113,545	234,725	137,745	56,455	56,930
Canada	307,370	211,690	110,765	1,068,710	1,167,680	494,545	933,850	617,305	235,875	296,995
					Females					
Laval	205	60	580	1,880	7,345	5,595	15,175	2,810	2,650	6,825
Québec	22,925	2,730	9,255	28,170	133,045	56,280	266,650	43,550	41,885	102,295
Canada	130,285	49,360	39,175	146,670	451,615	238,900	1,097,820	210,475	184,955	470,960
					Percent of Labour Force					
					Total					
Laval	0.3	0.1	0.7	5.6	11.0	6.3	13.8	5.4	2.9	5.0
Québec	2.1	0.5	0.8	5.9	11.7	4.2	12.3	4.4	2.4	3.9
Canada	2.5	1.5	0.9	6.9	9.2	4.2	11.6	4.7	2.4	4.4
					Males					
Laval	0.4	0.1	0.8	9.1	14.6	7.0	12.9	7.9	3.2	3.5
Québec	2.9	0.8	1.1	10.0	16.1	5.3	11.0	6.4	2.6	2.7
Canada	3.3	2.3	1.2	11.6	12.7	5.4	10.2	6.7	2.6	3.2
					Females					
Laval	0.2	0.1	0.6	1.8	7.2	5.5	14.9	2.8	2.6	6.7
Québec	1.2	0.1	0.5	1.4	6.8	2.9	13.7	2.2	2.2	5.3
Canada	1.6	0.6	0.5	1.7	5.4	2.8	13.1	2.5	2.2	5.6

Note: Figures are based on total experienced labour force 15 years and over. Experienced labour force refers to persons who, during the week of Sunday, May 1 to Saturday, May 7, 2011, were employed and the unemployed who had last worked for pay or in self-employment in either 2010 or 2011.
Source: Statistics Canada. 2013. 2011 National Household Survey. Statistics Canada Catalogue no. 99-004-XWE. Ottawa. Released September 11, 2013.

Labour Force by Industry (NAICS Codes 53–91)

Area	Real estate & rental & leasing	Profess., scientific & tech. services	Mgmt of companies & enterprises	Admin. & support, waste mgmt & remed. services	Educational services	Health care & social assistance	Arts, entertain. & recreation	Accomm. & food services	Other services (except public admin.)	Public admin.
					Number					
					Total					
Laval	3,635	17,285	185	9,230	13,305	23,545	3,415	12,925	8,485	10,355
Québec	61,365	282,115	3,965	156,130	301,425	496,125	78,795	253,145	189,290	295,480
Canada	321,895	1,240,850	17,460	728,330	1,301,435	1,949,650	363,405	1,130,750	807,800	1,261,050
					Males					
Laval	2,295	9,545	85	5,495	3,910	4,450	1,785	6,875	4,085	5,115
Québec	35,940	158,920	2,250	92,530	99,565	97,255	41,535	112,650	88,710	147,645
Canada	179,090	688,625	9,380	411,250	424,915	349,430	188,270	469,990	372,940	652,510
					Females					
Laval	1,340	7,735	105	3,730	9,395	19,090	1,625	6,055	4,400	5,240
Québec	25,425	123,205	1,715	63,605	201,860	398,870	37,260	140,495	100,585	147,835
Canada	142,805	552,225	8,075	317,085	876,515	1,600,220	175,135	660,760	434,865	608,535
					Percent of Labour Force					
					Total					
Laval	1.7	8.2	0.1	4.4	6.3	11.2	1.6	6.2	4.0	4.9
Québec	1.5	6.9	0.1	3.8	7.4	12.1	1.9	6.2	4.6	7.2
Canada	1.8	7.1	0.1	4.1	7.4	11.1	2.1	6.4	4.6	7.2
					Males					
Laval	2.1	8.8	0.1	5.1	3.6	4.1	1.7	6.4	3.8	4.7
Québec	1.7	7.4	0.1	4.3	4.7	4.5	1.9	5.3	4.2	6.9
Canada	1.9	7.5	0.1	4.5	4.6	3.8	2.0	5.1	4.1	7.1
					Females					
Laval	1.3	7.6	0.1	3.7	9.2	18.7	1.6	5.9	4.3	5.1
Québec	1.3	6.3	0.1	3.3	10.4	20.5	1.9	7.2	5.2	7.6
Canada	1.7	6.6	0.1	3.8	10.4	19.1	2.1	7.9	5.2	7.2

Note: Figures are based on total experienced labour force 15 years and over. Experienced labour force refers to persons who, during the week of Sunday, May 1 to Saturday, May 7, 2011, were employed and the unemployed who had last worked for pay or in self-employment in either 2010 or 2011.
Source: Statistics Canada. 2013. 2011 National Household Survey. Statistics Canada Catalogue no. 99-004-XWE. Ottawa. Released September 11, 2013.

Occupation

Area	Mgmt	Business, Finance & Admin.	Natural/ Applied Sciences & Related	Health	Education, Law & Social, Community & Government Services	Art, Culture, Recreation & Sport	Sales & Service	Trades, Transport & Equip. Operators & Related	Natural Resources, Agri. & Related Production	Mfg & Utilities
					Number					
					Total					
Laval	23,240	40,885	17,330	12,865	20,370	5,550	54,570	25,490	885	8,515
Québec	411,425	687,715	287,015	268,610	479,505	123,665	969,740	573,075	65,625	218,740
Canada	1,963,600	2,902,045	1,237,775	1,107,200	2,064,675	503,415	4,068,170	2,537,775	397,930	805,040
					Males					
Laval	14,760	12,490	13,580	2,390	5,730	2,525	25,650	24,160	785	5,785
Québec	261,620	207,545	221,430	53,480	148,715	58,150	436,370	542,055	53,640	154,485
Canada	1,229,460	854,190	966,355	217,520	676,550	232,535	1,745,705	2,385,615	318,945	564,300
					Females					
Laval	8,475	28,395	3,745	10,475	14,640	3,030	28,920	1,335	100	2,725
Québec	149,800	480,170	65,585	215,130	330,795	65,520	533,370	31,025	11,995	64,250
Canada	734,140	2,047,855	271,415	889,675	1,388,130	270,875	2,322,465	152,165	78,980	240,740
					Percent of Labour Force					
					Total					
Laval	11.1	19.5	8.3	6.1	9.7	2.6	26.0	12.2	0.4	4.1
Québec	10.1	16.8	7.0	6.6	11.7	3.0	23.7	14.0	1.6	5.4
Canada	11.2	16.5	7.0	6.3	11.7	2.9	23.1	14.4	2.3	4.6
					Males					
Laval	13.7	11.6	12.6	2.2	5.3	2.3	23.8	22.4	0.7	5.4
Québec	12.2	9.7	10.4	2.5	7.0	2.7	20.4	25.4	2.5	7.2
Canada	13.4	9.3	10.5	2.4	7.4	2.5	19.0	26.0	3.5	6.1
					Females					
Laval	8.3	27.9	3.7	10.3	14.4	3.0	28.4	1.3	0.1	2.7
Québec	7.7	24.7	3.4	11.0	17.0	3.4	27.4	1.6	0.6	3.3
Canada	8.7	24.4	3.2	10.6	16.5	3.2	27.7	1.8	0.9	2.9

Note: Figures are based on total experienced labour force 15 years and over
Source: Statistics Canada. 2013. 2011 National Household Survey. Statistics Canada Catalogue no. 99-004-XWE. Ottawa. Released September 11, 2013.

Place of Work Status

Area	Worked at Home	Worked Outside Canada	No Fixed Workplace Address	Worked at Usual Place
		Number		
		Total		
Laval	10,615	335	17,110	172,470
Québec	237,625	9,705	331,525	3,301,560
Canada	1,142,640	66,460	1,868,245	13,517,690
		Males		
Laval	5,780	260	12,645	83,975
Québec	122,060	7,055	249,535	1,636,165
Canada	582,150	47,355	1,400,485	6,604,325
		Females		
Laval	4,835	80	4,470	88,500
Québec	115,565	2,650	81,995	1,665,395
Canada	560,490	19,100	467,760	6,913,370
		Percent of Labour Force		
		Total		
Laval	5.3	0.2	8.5	86.0
Québec	6.1	0.3	8.5	85.1
Canada	6.9	0.4	11.3	81.5
		Males		
Laval	5.6	0.3	12.3	81.8
Québec	6.1	0.4	12.4	81.2
Canada	6.7	0.5	16.2	76.5
		Females		
Laval	4.9	0.1	4.6	90.4
Québec	6.2	0.1	4.4	89.3
Canada	7.0	0.2	5.9	86.8

Note: Figures are based on total employed labour force 15 years and over.
Source: Statistics Canada. 2013. 2011 National Household Survey. Statistics Canada Catalogue no. 99-004-XWE. Ottawa. Released September 11, 2013.

Mode of Transportation to Work

Area	Car; Truck; Van; as Driver	Car; Truck; Van; as Passenger	Public Transit	Walked	Bicycled	All Other Modes
			Number			
			Total			
Laval	145,450	6,725	30,540	4,480	955	1,435
Québec	2,713,295	136,490	484,600	215,210	48,870	34,620
Canada	11,393,140	867,050	1,851,525	880,815	201,780	191,625
			Males			
Laval	79,540	2,140	11,910	1,745	620	675
Québec	1,484,305	50,905	203,035	95,100	33,065	19,285
Canada	6,238,835	349,530	788,290	387,580	135,840	104,725
			Females			
Laval	65,910	4,585	18,630	2,740	335	760
Québec	1,228,995	85,585	281,565	120,110	15,800	15,335
Canada	5,154,305	517,520	1,063,235	493,230	65,940	86,900
			Percent of Labour Force			
			Total			
Laval	76.7	3.5	16.1	2.4	0.5	0.8
Québec	74.7	3.8	13.3	5.9	1.3	1.0
Canada	74.0	5.6	12.0	5.7	1.3	1.2
			Males			
Laval	82.3	2.2	12.3	1.8	0.6	0.7
Québec	78.7	2.7	10.8	5.0	1.8	1.0
Canada	77.9	4.4	9.8	4.8	1.7	1.3
			Females			
Laval	70.9	4.9	20.0	2.9	0.4	0.8
Québec	70.3	4.9	16.1	6.9	0.9	0.9
Canada	69.8	7.0	14.4	6.7	0.9	1.2

Note: Figures are based on total employed labour force 15 years and over.
Source: Statistics Canada. 2013. 2011 National Household Survey. Statistics Canada Catalogue no. 99-004-XWE. Ottawa. Released September 11, 2013.

Visible Minority Population Characteristics

Area	Total Minority	South Asian[1]	Chinese	Black	Filipino	Latin American	Arab	SE Asian[2]	West Asian[3]	Korean	Japanese	Multiple[4]
						Number						
						Total						
Laval	81,215	6,650	3,195	24,225	785	9,855	23,295	7,780	3,195	215	95	1,370
Québec	850,235	83,320	82,845	243,625	31,495	116,380	166,260	65,855	23,445	6,665	4,025	17,420
Canada	6,264,750	1,567,400	1,324,750	945,665	619,310	381,280	380,620	312,075	206,840	161,130	87,270	171,935
						Males						
Laval	39,985	3,490	1,370	11,695	315	4,790	11,840	3,770	1,665	115	35	630
Québec	418,545	43,410	37,295	116,605	12,435	56,940	89,505	32,940	12,070	3,135	1,565	8,315
Canada	3,043,010	790,755	632,325	453,005	268,885	186,355	203,485	154,035	105,620	77,165	38,270	83,335
						Females						
Laval	41,225	3,155	1,825	12,530	475	5,065	11,455	4,015	1,520	100	60	740
Québec	431,695	39,915	45,550	127,020	19,055	59,440	76,750	32,920	11,380	3,530	2,465	9,105
Canada	3,221,745	776,650	692,420	492,660	350,425	194,925	177,140	158,045	101,220	83,965	48,990	88,600
						Percent of Population						
						Total						
Laval	20.7	1.7	0.8	6.2	0.2	2.5	5.9	2.0	0.8	0.1	0.0	0.3
Québec	11.0	1.1	1.1	3.2	0.4	1.5	2.2	0.9	0.3	0.1	0.1	0.2
Canada	19.1	4.8	4.0	2.9	1.9	1.2	1.2	0.9	0.6	0.5	0.3	0.5
						Males						
Laval	20.9	1.8	0.7	6.1	0.2	2.5	6.2	2.0	0.9	0.1	0.0	0.3
Québec	11.0	1.1	1.0	3.1	0.3	1.5	2.3	0.9	0.3	0.1	0.0	0.2
Canada	18.8	4.9	3.9	2.8	1.7	1.2	1.3	1.0	0.7	0.5	0.2	0.5
						Females						
Laval	20.5	1.6	0.9	6.2	0.2	2.5	5.7	2.0	0.8	0.0	0.0	0.4
Québec	11.0	1.0	1.2	3.2	0.5	1.5	2.0	0.8	0.3	0.1	0.1	0.2
Canada	19.3	4.7	4.1	3.0	2.1	1.2	1.1	0.9	0.6	0.5	0.3	0.5

Note: The Employment Equity Act defines visible minorities as 'persons, other than Aboriginal peoples, who are non-Caucasian in race or non-white in colour';
(1) Includes 'East Indian,' 'Pakistani,' 'Sri Lankan,' etc.; (2) Includes 'Vietnamese,' 'Cambodian,' 'Malaysian,' 'Laotian,' etc.; (3) Includes 'Iranian,' 'Afghan,' etc.; (4) Includes respondents who reported more than one visible minority group by checking two or more mark-in circles, e.g., 'Black' and 'South Asian.'
Source: Statistics Canada. 2013. 2011 National Household Survey. Statistics Canada Catalogue no. 99-004-XWE. Ottawa. Released September 11, 2013.

PROFILES / Laval, Québec

Aboriginal Population

Area	Aboriginal Identity[1]	First Nations (North American Indian) Single Identity[2]	Métis Single Identity	Inuk (Inuit) Single Identity	Multiple Aboriginal Identities[3]	Aboriginal Identities Not Included Elsewhere
Number						
Total						
Laval	2,330	1,265	815	60	55	140
Québec	141,915	82,425	40,960	12,570	1,545	4,415
Canada	1,400,685	851,560	451,795	59,440	11,415	26,475
Males						
Laval	1,085	585	415	20	25	30
Québec	70,205	40,105	21,300	6,265	720	1,815
Canada	682,190	411,785	223,335	29,495	5,525	12,055
Females						
Laval	1,250	675	400	40	25	105
Québec	71,710	42,315	19,660	6,305	830	2,600
Canada	718,500	439,775	228,460	29,950	5,890	14,420
Percent of Population						
Total						
Laval	0.6	0.3	0.2	0.0	0.0	0.0
Québec	1.8	1.1	0.5	0.2	0.0	0.1
Canada	4.3	2.6	1.4	0.2	0.0	0.1
Males						
Laval	0.6	0.3	0.2	0.0	0.0	0.0
Québec	1.8	1.1	0.6	0.2	0.0	0.0
Canada	4.2	2.5	1.4	0.2	0.0	0.1
Females						
Laval	0.6	0.3	0.2	0.0	0.0	0.1
Québec	1.8	1.1	0.5	0.2	0.0	0.1
Canada	4.3	2.6	1.4	0.2	0.0	0.1

Note: (1) Includes persons who reported being an Aboriginal person, that is, First Nations (North American Indian), Métis or Inuk (Inuit) and/or those who reported Registered or Treaty Indian status, that is registered under the Indian Act of Canada, and/or those who reported membership in a First Nation or Indian band. Aboriginal peoples of Canada are defined in the Constitution Act, 1982, section 35-2 as including the Indian, Inuit and Métis peoples of Canada; (2) Users should be aware that the estimates associated with this variable are more affected than most by the incomplete enumeration of certain Indian reserves and Indian settlements in the National Household Survey (NHS); (3) Includes persons who reported being any two or all three of the following: First Nations (North American Indian), Métis or Inuk (Inuit).
Source: Statistics Canada. 2013. 2011 National Household Survey. Statistics Canada Catalogue no. 99-004-XWE. Ottawa. Released September 11, 2013.

Ethnic Origin

Area	North American Aboriginal	Other North American	European	Caribbean	Latin, Central and South American	African	Asian	Oceania
Number								
Total								
Laval	7,455	170,055	181,225	20,335	11,645	23,835	56,285	100
Québec	307,445	4,776,875	3,390,330	167,590	137,255	260,785	488,905	2,305
Canada	1,836,035	11,070,455	20,157,965	627,590	544,375	766,735	5,011,225	74,875
Males								
Laval	3,335	81,430	89,360	9,615	5,790	11,810	28,090	45
Québec	146,725	2,345,180	1,678,310	77,665	67,195	135,740	241,515	1,135
Canada	885,675	5,462,685	9,913,150	291,640	264,635	387,360	2,435,540	37,490
Females								
Laval	4,120	88,625	91,865	10,720	5,855	12,025	28,200	60
Québec	160,725	2,431,700	1,712,015	89,925	70,065	125,040	247,390	1,175
Canada	950,360	5,607,770	10,244,820	335,945	279,740	379,380	2,575,680	37,385
Percent of Population								
Total								
Laval	1.9	43.3	46.1	5.2	3.0	6.1	14.3	0.0
Québec	4.0	61.8	43.8	2.2	1.8	3.4	6.3	0.0
Canada	5.6	33.7	61.4	1.9	1.7	2.3	15.3	0.2
Males								
Laval	1.7	42.6	46.7	5.0	3.0	6.2	14.7	0.0
Québec	3.8	61.5	44.0	2.0	1.8	3.6	6.3	0.0
Canada	5.5	33.8	61.3	1.8	1.6	2.4	15.1	0.2
Females								
Laval	2.0	44.0	45.6	5.3	2.9	6.0	14.0	0.0
Québec	4.1	62.1	43.7	2.3	1.8	3.2	6.3	0.0
Canada	5.7	33.6	61.4	2.0	1.7	2.3	15.4	0.2

Note: The sum of the ethnic groups in this table is greater than the total population estimate because a person may report more than one ethnic origin in the NHS.
Source: Statistics Canada. 2013. 2011 National Household Survey. Statistics Canada Catalogue no. 99-004-XWE. Ottawa. Released September 11, 2013.

Religion

Area	Buddhist	Christian	Hindu	Jewish	Muslim	Sikh	Traditional (Aboriginal) Spirituality	Other Religions	No Religious Affiliation
				Number Total					
Laval	5,625	316,010	2,425	2,915	25,740	1,015	0	490	38,500
Québec	52,390	6,356,880	33,540	85,100	243,430	9,275	2,025	12,340	937,545
Canada	366,830	22,102,745	497,965	329,495	1,053,945	454,965	64,935	130,835	7,850,605
				Males					
Laval	2,645	151,770	1,195	1,475	12,820	550	0	265	20,505
Québec	24,630	3,079,855	17,055	41,455	128,815	5,090	925	6,155	510,055
Canada	168,465	10,497,775	250,435	161,265	540,555	229,435	31,805	57,745	4,225,645
				Females					
Laval	2,985	164,235	1,235	1,440	12,920	465	0	225	17,995
Québec	27,760	3,277,020	16,480	43,645	114,615	4,185	1,100	6,175	427,485
Canada	198,365	11,604,975	247,525	168,235	513,395	225,530	33,135	73,090	3,624,965
				Percent of Population Total					
Laval	1.4	80.5	0.6	0.7	6.6	0.3	0.0	0.1	9.8
Québec	0.7	82.2	0.4	1.1	3.1	0.1	0.0	0.2	12.1
Canada	1.1	67.3	1.5	1.0	3.2	1.4	0.2	0.4	23.9
				Males					
Laval	1.4	79.4	0.6	0.8	6.7	0.3	0.0	0.1	10.7
Québec	0.6	80.8	0.4	1.1	3.4	0.1	0.0	0.2	13.4
Canada	1.0	64.9	1.5	1.0	3.3	1.4	0.2	0.4	26.1
				Females					
Laval	1.5	81.5	0.6	0.7	6.4	0.2	0.0	0.1	8.9
Québec	0.7	83.6	0.4	1.1	2.9	0.1	0.0	0.2	10.9
Canada	1.2	69.5	1.5	1.0	3.1	1.4	0.2	0.4	21.7

Note: Religion refers to the person's self-identification as having a connection or affiliation with any religious denomination, group, body, sect, cult or other religiously defined community or system of belief. Religion is not limited to formal membership in a religious organization or group. Persons without a religious connection or affiliation can self-identify as atheist, agnostic or humanist, or can provide another applicable response.
Source: Statistics Canada. 2013. 2011 National Household Survey. Statistics Canada Catalogue no. 99-004-XWE. Ottawa. Released September 11, 2013.

Religion—Christian Denominations

Area	Anglican	Baptist	Catholic	Christian Orthodox	Lutheran	Pentecostal	Presbyterian	United Church	Other Christian
				Number Total					
Laval	915	3,095	256,200	31,990	425	2,685	345	480	19,865
Québec	73,550	36,615	5,775,740	129,780	7,200	41,070	11,440	32,930	248,560
Canada	1,631,845	635,840	12,810,705	550,690	478,185	478,705	472,385	2,007,610	3,036,780
				Males					
Laval	470	1,365	122,430	15,930	165	1,290	180	245	9,700
Québec	34,815	16,585	2,802,920	63,960	3,425	18,640	5,265	14,945	119,305
Canada	752,945	293,905	6,167,290	270,205	221,525	217,850	218,955	912,545	1,442,550
				Females					
Laval	445	1,735	133,770	16,060	265	1,400	165	235	10,170
Québec	38,735	20,030	2,972,820	65,820	3,770	22,430	6,175	17,985	129,260
Canada	878,900	341,940	6,643,415	280,485	256,660	260,850	253,430	1,095,065	1,594,230
				Percent of Population Total					
Laval	0.2	0.8	65.2	8.1	0.1	0.7	0.1	0.1	5.1
Québec	1.0	0.5	74.7	1.7	0.1	0.5	0.1	0.4	3.2
Canada	5.0	1.9	39.0	1.7	1.5	1.5	1.4	6.1	9.2
				Males					
Laval	0.2	0.7	64.0	8.3	0.1	0.7	0.1	0.1	5.1
Québec	0.9	0.4	73.5	1.7	0.1	0.5	0.1	0.4	3.1
Canada	4.7	1.8	38.2	1.7	1.4	1.3	1.4	5.6	8.9
				Females					
Laval	0.2	0.9	66.4	8.0	0.1	0.7	0.1	0.1	5.0
Québec	1.0	0.5	75.9	1.7	0.1	0.6	0.2	0.5	3.3
Canada	5.3	2.0	39.8	1.7	1.5	1.6	1.5	6.6	9.6

Note: Religion refers to the person's self-identification as having a connection or affiliation with any religious denomination, group, body, sect, cult or other religiously defined community or system of belief. Religion is not limited to formal membership in a religious organization or group. Persons without a religious connection or affiliation can self-identify as atheist, agnostic or humanist, or can provide another applicable response.
Source: Statistics Canada. 2013. 2011 National Household Survey. Statistics Canada Catalogue no. 99-004-XWE. Ottawa. Released September 11, 2013.

PROFILES / Laval, Québec

Immigrant Status and Period of Immigration

Area	Non-Immigrants[1]	Immigrants All	Before 1971	1971 to 1980	1981 to 1990	1991 to 2000	2001 to 2005	2006 to 2011	Non-Permanent Residents[3]
Number									
Total									
Laval	293,990	96,645	15,355	14,265	16,970	21,320	15,460	13,275	2,095
Québec	6,690,530	974,895	151,825	115,640	130,680	195,925	157,425	223,400	67,095
Canada	25,720,175	6,775,765	1,261,055	870,775	949,890	1,539,050	992,070	1,162,915	356,385
Males									
Laval	142,715	47,515	7,845	7,135	8,295	10,570	7,410	6,265	990
Québec	3,301,435	477,240	75,255	57,410	64,080	94,110	76,780	109,605	35,370
Canada	12,753,235	3,231,370	605,430	416,670	454,570	724,905	474,545	555,245	178,515
Females									
Laval	151,270	49,125	7,510	7,125	8,675	10,755	8,045	7,015	1,105
Québec	3,389,095	497,655	76,565	58,235	66,600	101,810	80,645	113,795	31,725
Canada	12,966,935	3,544,400	655,625	454,105	495,325	814,145	517,530	607,670	177,870
Percent of Population									
Total									
Laval	74.9	24.6	3.9	3.6	4.3	5.4	3.9	3.4	0.5
Québec	86.5	12.6	2.0	1.5	1.7	2.5	2.0	2.9	0.9
Canada	78.3	20.6	3.8	2.7	2.9	4.7	3.0	3.5	1.1
Males									
Laval	74.6	24.8	4.1	3.7	4.3	5.5	3.9	3.3	0.5
Québec	86.6	12.5	2.0	1.5	1.7	2.5	2.0	2.9	0.9
Canada	78.9	20.0	3.7	2.6	2.8	4.5	2.9	3.4	1.1
Females									
Laval	75.1	24.4	3.7	3.5	4.3	5.3	4.0	3.5	0.5
Québec	86.5	12.7	2.0	1.5	1.7	2.6	2.1	2.9	0.8
Canada	77.7	21.2	3.9	2.7	3.0	4.9	3.1	3.6	1.1

Note: (1) Non-immigrant refers to a person who is a Canadian citizen by birth; (2) Immigrant refers to a person who is or has ever been a landed immigrant/permanent resident. This person has been granted the right to live in Canada permanently by immigration authorities. Some immigrants have resided in Canada for a number of years, while others have arrived recently. Some immigrants are Canadian citizens, while others are not. Most immigrants are born outside Canada, but a small number are born in Canada. In the 2011 National Household Survey, 'Immigrants' includes immigrants who landed in Canada prior to May 10, 2011; (3) Non-permanent resident refers to a person from another country who has a work or study permit, or who is a refugee claimant, and any non-Canadian-born family member living in Canada with them.
Source: Statistics Canada. 2013. 2011 National Household Survey. Statistics Canada Catalogue no. 99-004-XWE. Ottawa. Released September 11, 2013.

Mother Tongue

Area	English	French	Non-official Language	English & French	English & Non-official Language	French & Non-official Language	English, French & Non-official Language
Number							
Total							
Laval	27,680	241,615	113,160	3,775	2,740	6,550	2,045
Québec	599,225	6,102,210	961,700	64,800	23,435	51,640	12,950
Canada	18,858,980	7,054,975	6,567,680	144,685	396,330	74,430	24,095
Males							
Laval	14,235	115,405	55,780	1,865	1,375	3,240	1,060
Québec	297,875	2,994,300	472,635	32,390	11,455	25,810	6,790
Canada	9,345,225	3,452,380	3,157,785	69,975	192,000	36,535	11,965
Females							
Laval	13,450	126,215	57,385	1,915	1,365	3,315	985
Québec	301,355	3,107,910	489,060	32,405	11,975	25,825	6,155
Canada	9,513,750	3,602,590	3,409,895	74,710	204,330	37,890	12,130
Percent of Population							
Total							
Laval	7.0	60.8	28.5	0.9	0.7	1.6	0.5
Québec	7.7	78.1	12.3	0.8	0.3	0.7	0.2
Canada	56.9	21.3	19.8	0.4	1.2	0.2	0.1
Males							
Laval	7.4	59.8	28.9	1.0	0.7	1.7	0.5
Québec	7.8	78.0	12.3	0.8	0.3	0.7	0.2
Canada	57.5	21.2	19.4	0.4	1.2	0.2	0.1
Females							
Laval	6.6	61.7	28.0	0.9	0.7	1.6	0.5
Québec	7.6	78.2	12.3	0.8	0.3	0.6	0.2
Canada	56.4	21.4	20.2	0.4	1.2	0.2	0.1

Note: Figures cover total population excluding institutional residents.
Source: Statistics Canada. 2012. Census Profile. 2011 Census. Statistics Canada Catalogue no. 98-316-XWE. Ottawa. Released October 24 2012.
http://www12.statcan.gc.ca/census-recensement/2011/dp-pd/prof/index.cfm?Lang=E

Language Spoken Most Often at Home

Area	English	French	Non-official Language	English & French	English & Non-official Language	French & Non-official Language	English, French & Non-official Language
			Number				
			Total				
Laval	51,335	259,090	59,055	5,380	5,175	13,040	4,490
Québec	767,415	6,249,080	554,400	71,555	43,765	100,110	29,625
Canada	21,457,075	6,827,865	3,673,865	131,205	875,135	109,700	46,330
			Males				
Laval	26,025	124,415	28,670	2,680	2,590	6,290	2,280
Québec	379,915	3,071,635	268,640	35,860	21,305	48,590	15,315
Canada	10,585,620	3,348,235	1,767,310	63,475	425,370	53,010	22,845
			Females				
Laval	25,310	134,675	30,380	2,700	2,590	6,750	2,210
Québec	387,500	3,177,450	285,760	35,695	22,460	51,525	14,310
Canada	10,871,455	3,479,625	1,906,555	67,730	449,765	56,690	23,485
			Percent of Population				
			Total				
Laval	12.9	65.2	14.9	1.4	1.3	3.3	1.1
Québec	9.8	80.0	7.1	0.9	0.6	1.3	0.4
Canada	64.8	20.6	11.1	0.4	2.6	0.3	0.1
			Males				
Laval	13.5	64.5	14.9	1.4	1.3	3.3	1.2
Québec	9.9	80.0	7.0	0.9	0.6	1.3	0.4
Canada	65.1	20.6	10.9	0.4	2.6	0.3	0.1
			Females				
Laval	12.4	65.8	14.8	1.3	1.3	3.3	1.1
Québec	9.7	79.9	7.2	0.9	0.6	1.3	0.4
Canada	64.5	20.6	11.3	0.4	2.7	0.3	0.1

Note: Figures cover total population excluding institutional residents.
Source: Statistics Canada. 2012. Census Profile. 2011 Census. Statistics Canada Catalogue no. 98-316-XWE. Ottawa. Released October 24 2012.
http://www12.statcan.gc.ca/census-recensement/2011/dp-pd/prof/index.cfm?Lang=E

Knowledge of Official Languages

Area	English Only	French Only	English & French	Neither English nor French
		Number		
		Total		
Laval	19,905	145,655	224,625	7,380
Québec	363,860	4,047,175	3,328,725	76,190
Canada	22,564,665	4,165,015	5,795,570	595,920
		Males		
Laval	10,195	63,555	116,400	2,800
Québec	180,175	1,871,500	1,758,410	31,175
Canada	11,222,185	1,925,340	2,876,560	241,790
		Females		
Laval	9,715	82,105	108,225	4,580
Québec	183,690	2,175,675	1,570,310	45,015
Canada	11,342,485	2,239,680	2,919,005	354,135
		Percent of Population		
		Total		
Laval	5.0	36.6	56.5	1.9
Québec	4.7	51.8	42.6	1.0
Canada	68.1	12.6	17.5	1.8
		Males		
Laval	5.3	32.9	60.3	1.5
Québec	4.7	48.7	45.8	0.8
Canada	69.0	11.8	17.7	1.5
		Females		
Laval	4.7	40.1	52.9	2.2
Québec	4.6	54.7	39.5	1.1
Canada	67.3	13.3	17.3	2.1

Note: Figures cover total population excluding institutional residents.
Source: Statistics Canada. 2012. Census Profile. 2011 Census. Statistics Canada Catalogue no. 98-316-XWE. Ottawa. Released October 24 2012.
http://www12.statcan.gc.ca/census-recensement/2011/dp-pd/prof/index.cfm?Lang=E

London, Ontario

Background

London is located in southwestern Ontario along the Québec City–Windsor Corridor, Canada's most densely populated region. The City of London is within a 200-kilometre radius of major cities like Toronto, Windsor, Detroit and Buffalo, New York. Known as the "Forest City," London is home to 4.5 million trees.

In 1826, London was founded as the government seat for London District, a region covering the majority of central Western Ontario. The Rebellions of 1837 encouraged the British to build a garrison in the region. Between 1838 and 1869, British troops grew London's population and economy. By 1840, London was incorporated as a town. The prosperity from road building, tanneries and the railway built through town heralded a boom in building and land speculation. London was incorporated as a city in 1855.

Both London's downtown core and residential suburbs pay homage to the city's past through the preservation of key historical buildings and heritage streets. The city manages more than 200 parks, ranging from urban parks like 140-hectare Springbank Park, to residential green spaces as well as urban woodlands, meadows and ponds.

London's Western University has been a leader in wind engineering since 1965. In partnership with the City of London, Western will open the world's first Wind Engineering, Energy and Environment (WindEEE) Dome research facility. The city's major industry sectors are renewable technology, manufacturing, life sciences and information technology.

In 2012, London launched its Cultural Prosperity Plan to foster city-wide collaboration between community leaders and cultural organizations in developing the cultural and economic prosperity of the city.

London has summer highs of plus 25.10 degrees Celsius, winter lows of minus 8.77 degrees Celsius, and an average rainfall just over 817 mm per year.

Rankings

- The *Next Cities Report* ranked London #9 out of 27 Canadian cities in terms of the best "hot spots" for young professionals. Next Generation Consulting, a U.S. firm specializing in the 20- to 40-year-old demographic, used seven lifestyle indexes to measure city work/life balance: vitality, earning, learning, social capital, lifestyle cost, after hours and around town. The Top 3 Canadian cities for young professionals were Victoria, Ottawa and Vancouver. *Next Cities, "The Top Canadian Hot Spots for Young, Talented Workers: 2009-2010 Canada Version," released July 28th, 2009*
- London was ranked as one of the most active cities in Canada. Households in London were #8 in terms of spending money on sports and recreation. Almost 50% of London households were rated as active Canadians investing in healthy leisure. In 2006, the biggest sports-and-recreation household spenders lived in Calgary (58.5%), Ottawa-Hull (58.3%) and Victoria (56.7%). *Canadian Council on Learning with files from Statistics Canada, special tabulation, unpublished data, Survey of Household Spending, 2006*

PROFILES / London, Ontario

Population Growth and Density

Area	Population in 2001	Population in 2006	Population in 2011	Population Change 2001–2006	Population Change 2006–2011	Land Area (sq. km)	Population Density per sq. km
London	336,539	352,395	366,151	4.7	3.9	420.57	870.6
Ontario	11,410,046	12,160,282	12,851,821	6.6	5.7	908,607.67	14.1
Canada	30,007,094	31,612,897	33,476,688	5.4	5.9	8,965,121.42	3.7

Source: Statistics Canada. 2012. Census Profile. 2011 Census. Statistics Canada Catalogue no. 98-316-XWE. Ottawa. Released October 24 2012.
http://www12.statcan.gc.ca/census-recensement/2011/dp-pd/prof/index.cfm?Lang=E;
Statistics Canada 2007. 2006 Community Profiles. 2006 Census. Statistics Canada Catalogue no. 92-591-XWE. Ottawa. Released March 13 2007.
http://www12.statcan.ca/census-recensement/2006/dp-pd/prof/92-591/index.cfm?Lang=E

Gender

Area	Males	Females
	Number	
London	176,495	189,655
Ontario	6,263,140	6,588,685
Canada	16,414,225	17,062,460
	Percent of Population	
London	48.2	51.8
Ontario	48.7	51.3
Canada	49.0	51.0

Source: Statistics Canada. 2012. Census Profile. 2011 Census. Statistics Canada
Catalogue no. 98-316-XWE. Ottawa. Released October 24 2012.
http://www12.statcan.gc.ca/census-recensement/2011/dp-pd/prof/index.cfm?Lang=E

Marital Status

Area	Married[1]	Living Common-law	Single[2]	Separated	Divorced	Widowed
			Number			
			Total			
London	140,055	26,485	91,660	10,620	20,180	17,775
Ontario	5,367,400	791,210	2,985,020	319,805	593,730	613,880
Canada	12,941,960	3,142,525	7,816,045	698,240	1,686,035	1,584,530
			Males			
London	69,880	13,240	47,845	4,395	7,445	3,355
Ontario	2,681,320	397,620	1,583,760	133,790	231,160	117,980
Canada	6,470,300	1,575,495	4,206,320	299,655	680,415	310,940
			Females			
London	70,175	13,250	43,815	6,230	12,740	14,420
Ontario	2,686,075	393,590	1,401,260	186,015	362,570	495,905
Canada	6,471,660	1,567,035	3,609,730	398,585	1,005,620	1,273,590
			Percent of Population			
			Total			
London	45.7	8.6	29.9	3.5	6.6	5.8
Ontario	50.3	7.4	28.0	3.0	5.6	5.8
Canada	46.4	11.3	28.0	2.5	6.0	5.7
			Males			
London	47.8	9.1	32.7	3.0	5.1	2.3
Ontario	52.1	7.7	30.8	2.6	4.5	2.3
Canada	47.8	11.6	31.1	2.2	5.0	2.3
			Females			
London	43.7	8.2	27.3	3.9	7.9	9.0
Ontario	48.6	7.1	25.4	3.4	6.6	9.0
Canada	45.2	10.9	25.2	2.8	7.0	8.9

Note: (1) and not separated, (2) never legally married
Source: Statistics Canada. 2012. Census Profile. 2011 Census. Statistics Canada Catalogue no. 98-316-XWE. Ottawa. Released October 24 2012.
http://www12.statcan.gc.ca/census-recensement/2011/dp-pd/prof/index.cfm?Lang=E

Age Characteristics: 0 to 49 Years

Area	0 to 4 Years	5 to 9 Years	10 to 14 Years	15 to 19 Years	20 to 24 Years	25 to 29 Years	30 to 34 Years	35 to 39 Years	40 to 44 Years	45 to 49 Years
Number										
Total										
London	19,990	19,010	20,365	24,715	28,920	26,990	23,835	22,530	24,240	28,490
Ontario	704,260	712,755	763,755	863,635	852,910	815,120	800,365	844,335	924,075	1,055,880
Canada	1,877,095	1,809,895	1,920,355	2,178,135	2,187,450	2,169,590	2,162,905	2,173,930	2,324,875	2,675,130
Males										
London	10,290	9,665	10,380	12,675	14,225	13,180	11,735	11,070	11,875	13,715
Ontario	360,590	365,290	391,630	443,680	432,490	400,045	383,340	405,845	447,920	517,510
Canada	961,150	925,965	983,995	1,115,845	1,108,775	1,077,275	1,058,810	1,064,200	1,141,720	1,318,715
Females										
London	9,705	9,345	9,985	12,040	14,695	13,810	12,095	11,460	12,365	14,780
Ontario	343,670	347,465	372,125	419,950	420,415	415,075	417,030	438,485	476,155	538,370
Canada	915,945	883,935	936,360	1,062,295	1,078,670	1,092,315	1,104,095	1,109,735	1,183,155	1,356,420
Percent of Population										
Total										
London	5.5	5.2	5.6	6.7	7.9	7.4	6.5	6.2	6.6	7.8
Ontario	5.5	5.5	5.9	6.7	6.6	6.3	6.2	6.6	7.2	8.2
Canada	5.6	5.4	5.7	6.5	6.5	6.5	6.5	6.5	6.9	8.0
Males										
London	5.8	5.5	5.9	7.2	8.1	7.5	6.6	6.3	6.7	7.8
Ontario	5.8	5.8	6.3	7.1	6.9	6.4	6.1	6.5	7.2	8.3
Canada	5.9	5.6	6.0	6.8	6.8	6.6	6.5	6.5	7.0	8.0
Females										
London	5.1	4.9	5.3	6.3	7.7	7.3	6.4	6.0	6.5	7.8
Ontario	5.2	5.3	5.6	6.4	6.4	6.3	6.3	6.7	7.2	8.2
Canada	5.4	5.2	5.5	6.2	6.3	6.4	6.5	6.5	6.9	7.9

Source: Statistics Canada. 2012. Census Profile. 2011 Census. Statistics Canada Catalogue no. 98-316-XWE. Ottawa. Released October 24 2012.
http://www12.statcan.gc.ca/census-recensement/2011/dp-pd/prof/index.cfm?Lang=E

Age Characteristics: 50 Years and Over, and Median Age

Area	50 to 54 Years	55 to 59 Years	60 to 64 Years	65 to 69 Years	70 to 74 Years	75 to 79 Years	80 to 84 Years	85 Years and Over	Median Age
Number									
Total									
London	27,835	24,270	21,250	15,540	11,955	10,070	8,030	8,110	39.3
Ontario	1,006,140	864,620	765,655	563,485	440,780	356,150	271,510	246,400	40.4
Canada	2,658,965	2,340,635	2,052,670	1,521,715	1,153,065	922,700	702,070	645,515	40.6
Males									
London	13,280	11,440	10,080	7,240	5,450	4,360	3,245	2,580	37.7
Ontario	492,560	418,755	370,370	270,875	206,350	161,345	113,620	80,925	39.4
Canada	1,309,030	1,147,300	1,002,690	738,010	543,435	417,945	291,085	208,300	39.6
Females									
London	14,555	12,825	11,170	8,295	6,510	5,710	4,785	5,530	40.7
Ontario	513,580	445,865	395,275	292,610	234,435	194,805	157,890	165,475	41.3
Canada	1,349,940	1,193,335	1,049,985	783,705	609,630	504,755	410,985	437,215	41.5
Percent of Population									
Total									
London	7.6	6.6	5.8	4.2	3.3	2.8	2.2	2.2	–
Ontario	7.8	6.7	6.0	4.4	3.4	2.8	2.1	1.9	–
Canada	7.9	7.0	6.1	4.5	3.4	2.8	2.1	1.9	–
Males									
London	7.5	6.5	5.7	4.1	3.1	2.5	1.8	1.5	–
Ontario	7.9	6.7	5.9	4.3	3.3	2.6	1.8	1.3	–
Canada	8.0	7.0	6.1	4.5	3.3	2.5	1.8	1.3	–
Females									
London	7.7	6.8	5.9	4.4	3.4	3.0	2.5	2.9	–
Ontario	7.8	6.8	6.0	4.4	3.6	3.0	2.4	2.5	–
Canada	7.9	7.0	6.2	4.6	3.6	3.0	2.4	2.6	–

Source: Statistics Canada. 2012. Census Profile. 2011 Census. Statistics Canada Catalogue no. 98-316-XWE. Ottawa. Released October 24 2012.
http://www12.statcan.gc.ca/census-recensement/2011/dp-pd/prof/index.cfm?Lang=E

PROFILES / London, Ontario

Private Households by Household Size

Area	1 Person	2 Persons	3 Persons	4 Persons	5 Persons	6 or More Persons	Average Number of Persons in Private Households
			Households				
London	47,515	51,955	23,115	20,300	7,420	3,320	2.3
Ontario	1,230,975	1,584,415	803,030	783,925	310,860	174,305	2.6
Canada	3,673,310	4,544,820	2,081,900	1,903,300	724,405	392,885	2.5
			Percent of Households				
London	30.9	33.8	15.0	13.2	4.8	2.2	–
Ontario	25.2	32.4	16.4	16.0	6.4	3.6	–
Canada	27.6	34.1	15.6	14.3	5.4	2.9	–

Source: Statistics Canada. 2012. Census Profile. 2011 Census. Statistics Canada Catalogue no. 98-316-XWE. Ottawa. Released October 24 2012.
http://www12.statcan.gc.ca/census-recensement/2011/dp-pd/prof/index.cfm?Lang=E

Dwelling Type

Area	Single-detached House	Semi-detached House	Row House	Apartment: Building with Five or More Storeys	Apartment: Building with Fewer Than Five Storeys	Duplex Apartment	Movable Dwelling	Other Single-attached House
				Number				
London	77,865	5,860	19,085	30,935	15,615	3,965	160	155
Ontario	2,718,880	279,470	415,225	789,970	498,160	160,460	15,800	9,540
Canada	7,329,150	646,245	791,600	1,234,770	2,397,550	704,485	183,510	33,310
				Percent of Dwellings				
London	50.7	3.8	12.4	20.1	10.2	2.6	0.1	0.1
Ontario	55.6	5.7	8.5	16.2	10.2	3.3	0.3	0.2
Canada	55.0	4.9	5.9	9.3	18.0	5.3	1.4	0.3

Source: Statistics Canada. 2012. Census Profile. 2011 Census. Statistics Canada Catalogue no. 98-316-XWE. Ottawa. Released October 24 2012.
http://www12.statcan.gc.ca/census-recensement/2011/dp-pd/prof/index.cfm?Lang=E

Shelter Costs

		Owned Dwellings				Rented Dwellings		
Area	Number	Median Value[1] ($)	Average Value[1] ($)	Median Monthly Costs[2] ($)	Average Monthly Costs[2] ($)	Number	Median Monthly Costs[3] ($)	Average Monthly Costs[3] ($)
London	96,665	229,634	256,613	1,045	1,119	56,900	782	822
Ontario	3,446,650	300,862	367,428	1,163	1,284	1,385,535	892	926
Canada	9,013,410	280,552	345,182	978	1,141	4,060,385	784	848

Note: All figures cover non-farm, non-reserve private dwellings; (1) Refers to the dollar amount expected by the owner if the dwelling were to be sold; (2) Includes all shelter expenses paid by households that own their dwellings, such as the mortgage payment and the costs of electricity, heat, water and other municipal services, property taxes and condominium fees; (3) Includes all shelter expenses paid by households that rent their dwellings, such as the monthly rent and the costs of electricity, heat and municipal services.
Source: Statistics Canada. 2013. 2011 National Household Survey. Statistics Canada Catalogue no. 99-004-XWE. Ottawa. Released September 11, 2013.

Occupied Private Dwellings by Period of Construction

Area	1960 or Before	1961 to 1980	1981 to 1990	1991 to 2000	2001 to 2005	2006 to 2011
			Number			
London	40,725	50,505	25,965	17,120	9,340	9,970
Ontario	1,330,235	1,420,570	763,430	609,310	414,795	348,310
Canada	3,273,105	4,152,715	2,112,110	1,707,880	1,031,020	1,042,430
			Percent of Dwellings			
London	26.5	32.9	16.9	11.1	6.1	6.5
Ontario	27.2	29.1	15.6	12.5	8.5	7.1
Canada	24.6	31.2	15.9	12.8	7.7	7.8

Note: Figures cover non-farm, non-reserve private dwellings and includes data up to May 10, 2011.
Source: Statistics Canada. 2013. 2011 National Household Survey. Statistics Canada Catalogue no. 99-004-XWE. Ottawa. Released September 11, 2013.

PROFILES / London, Ontario

Educational Attainment

Area	No Certificate, Diploma or Degree	High School Diploma or Equivalent[1]	Apprenticeship or Trades Certificate or Diploma[2]	College, CÉGEP or Other Non-University Certificate or Diploma	University Certificate or Diploma Below the Bachelor Level[3]	Bachelor's Degree	University Certificate, Diploma or Degree Above Bachelor Level[4]
				Number			
				Total			
London	51,205	83,450	20,825	66,980	10,735	39,985	28,255
Ontario	1,954,520	2,801,805	771,140	2,070,875	427,150	1,515,075	933,100
Canada	5,485,400	6,968,935	2,950,685	4,970,020	1,200,130	3,634,425	2,049,930
				Males			
London	24,960	40,040	13,595	28,765	4,660	17,670	14,365
Ontario	957,040	1,337,055	520,390	894,235	193,355	692,345	470,290
Canada	2,742,875	3,305,415	1,928,970	2,118,430	513,235	1,643,080	1,043,350
				Females			
London	26,240	43,405	7,225	38,215	6,075	22,315	13,890
Ontario	997,475	1,464,755	250,750	1,176,640	233,790	822,730	462,805
Canada	2,742,520	3,663,515	1,021,715	2,851,595	686,890	1,991,345	1,006,585
				Percent of Population			
				Total			
London	17.0	27.7	6.9	22.2	3.6	13.3	9.4
Ontario	18.7	26.8	7.4	19.8	4.1	14.5	8.9
Canada	20.1	25.6	10.8	18.2	4.4	13.3	7.5
				Males			
London	17.3	27.8	9.4	20.0	3.2	12.3	10.0
Ontario	18.9	26.4	10.3	17.7	3.8	13.7	9.3
Canada	20.6	24.9	14.5	15.9	3.9	12.4	7.8
				Females			
London	16.7	27.6	4.6	24.3	3.9	14.2	8.8
Ontario	18.4	27.1	4.6	21.8	4.3	15.2	8.6
Canada	19.6	26.2	7.3	20.4	4.9	14.3	7.2

Note: Figures cover total population aged 15 years and over by highest certificate, diploma or degree; (1) Includes persons who have graduated from a secondary school or equivalent. It excludes persons with a postsecondary certificate, diploma or degree; (2) Includes Registered Apprenticeship certificates (including Certificate of Qualification, Journeyperson's designation) and other trades certificates or diplomas such as pre-employment or vocational certificates and diplomas from brief trade programs completed at community colleges, institutes of technology, vocational centres, and similar institutions; (3) Comparisons with other data sources suggest that the category 'University certificate or diploma below the bachelor's level' was over-reported in the NHS. This category likely includes some responses that are actually college certificates or diplomas, bachelor's degrees or other types of education (e.g., university transfer programs, bachelor's programs completed in other countries, incomplete bachelor's programs, non-university professional designations). We recommend users interpret the results for the 'University certificate or diploma below the bachelor's level' category with caution; (4) 'University certificate or diploma above bachelor level' includes the categories: 'Degree in medicine, dentistry, veterinary medicine or optometry,' 'Master's degree' and 'Earned doctorate.'
Source: Statistics Canada. 2013. 2011 National Household Survey. Statistics Canada Catalogue no. 99-004-XWE. Ottawa. Released September 11, 2013.

Household Income Distribution

Area	Less than $10,000	$10,000 to $19,999	$20,000 to $29,999	$30,000 to $39,999	$40,000 to $49,999	$50,000 to $59,999	$60,000 to $79,999	$80,000 to $99,999	$100,000 to $124,999	$125,000 to $149,999	$150,000 and Over
						Households					
London	8,175	13,525	15,630	15,545	15,525	12,965	20,825	16,300	13,550	8,320	13,285
Ontario	201,780	354,530	405,725	425,410	425,720	398,705	680,850	552,660	497,970	331,460	611,840
Canada	626,705	1,141,945	1,193,925	1,271,675	1,206,800	1,102,120	1,865,280	1,458,240	1,260,770	802,555	1,389,240
						Percent of Households					
London	5.3	8.8	10.2	10.1	10.1	8.4	13.6	10.6	8.8	5.4	8.6
Ontario	4.1	7.3	8.3	8.7	8.7	8.2	13.9	11.3	10.2	6.8	12.5
Canada	4.7	8.6	9.0	9.5	9.1	8.3	14.0	10.9	9.5	6.0	10.4

Note: Household income is the sum of the total incomes of all members of that household. Total income refers to monetary receipts from certain sources, before income taxes and deductions, during calendar year 2010.
Source: Statistics Canada. 2013. 2011 National Household Survey. Statistics Canada Catalogue no. 99-004-XWE. Ottawa. Released September 11, 2013.

Median and Average Household and Economic Family Income

Area	Median Household Income ($)	Average Household Income ($)	Median After-tax Household Income ($)	Average After-tax Household Income ($)	Median Economic Family Income ($)	Average Economic Family Income ($)	Median After-tax Economic Family Income ($)	Average After-tax Economic Family Income ($)
London	56,241	73,107	50,678	61,980	74,448	89,591	65,851	75,703
Ontario	66,358	85,772	58,717	71,523	80,987	100,152	71,128	83,322
Canada	61,072	79,102	54,089	66,149	76,511	94,125	67,044	78,517

Note: Figures cover household and economic familiy income in 2010. A household is defined as a person or a group of persons (other than foreign residents) who occupy the same private dwelling and do not have a usual place of residence elsewhere in Canada. Every person is a member of one and only one household. An economic family is defined as a group of two or more persons who live in the same dwelling and are related to each other by blood, marriage, common-law, adoption or a foster relationship. A couple may be of opposite or same sex.
Source: Statistics Canada. 2013. 2011 National Household Survey. Statistics Canada Catalogue no. 99-004-XWE. Ottawa. Released September 11, 2013.

Individual Income Distribution

Area	Less than $10,000	$10,000 to $19,999	$20,000 to $29,999	$30,000 to $39,999	$40,000 to $49,999	$50,000 to $59,999	$60,000 to $79,999	$80,000 to $99,999	$100,000 to $124,999	$125,000 and Over
					Number Total					
London	51,265	51,460	42,455	34,400	29,795	21,085	26,460	15,240	7,445	6,695
Ontario	1,780,355	1,748,060	1,361,710	1,136,730	980,790	746,360	964,280	574,710	293,865	330,285
Canada	4,492,040	4,835,710	3,670,020	3,180,360	2,603,520	1,921,650	2,437,440	1,302,045	693,580	782,135
					Males					
London	23,185	20,445	18,210	15,335	14,815	11,080	15,065	8,895	4,975	5,045
Ontario	781,095	669,815	580,990	535,255	491,125	407,005	569,205	341,160	201,125	244,500
Canada	1,936,365	1,864,880	1,588,260	1,522,190	1,333,510	1,079,780	1,473,145	823,720	492,905	599,905
					Females					
London	28,080	31,010	24,250	19,070	14,980	10,010	11,395	6,345	2,465	1,650
Ontario	999,265	1,078,245	780,720	601,475	489,665	339,360	395,075	233,550	92,740	85,790
Canada	2,555,675	2,970,825	2,081,760	1,658,170	1,270,010	841,870	964,300	478,330	200,680	182,230
					Percent of Population Total					
London	17.9	18.0	14.8	12.0	10.4	7.4	9.2	5.3	2.6	2.3
Ontario	18.0	17.6	13.7	11.5	9.9	7.5	9.7	5.8	3.0	3.3
Canada	17.3	18.7	14.2	12.3	10.0	7.4	9.4	5.0	2.7	3.0
					Males					
London	16.9	14.9	13.3	11.2	10.8	8.1	11.0	6.5	3.6	3.7
Ontario	16.2	13.9	12.1	11.1	10.2	8.4	11.8	7.1	4.2	5.1
Canada	15.2	14.7	12.5	12.0	10.5	8.5	11.6	6.5	3.9	4.7
					Females					
London	18.8	20.8	16.2	12.8	10.0	6.7	7.6	4.3	1.7	1.1
Ontario	19.6	21.2	15.3	11.8	9.6	6.7	7.8	4.6	1.8	1.7
Canada	19.4	22.5	15.8	12.6	9.6	6.4	7.3	3.6	1.5	1.4

Note: Figures cover individuals aged 15 years and over with income. Income refers to monetary receipts from certain sources, before income taxes and deductions, during calendar year 2010.
Source: Statistics Canada. 2013. 2011 National Household Survey. Statistics Canada Catalogue no. 99-004-XWE. Ottawa. Released September 11, 2013.

Labour Force Status

Area	In the Labour Force All	Employed	Unemployed	Not in the Labour Force
		Number Total		
London	196,370	178,675	17,690	105,060
Ontario	6,864,990	6,297,005	567,985	3,608,685
Canada	17,990,080	16,595,035	1,395,045	9,269,445
		Males		
London	99,600	90,230	9,375	44,460
Ontario	3,542,030	3,249,165	292,865	1,522,690
Canada	9,388,570	8,634,310	754,255	3,906,785
		Females		
London	96,770	88,450	8,320	60,600
Ontario	3,322,955	3,047,840	275,120	2,085,990
Canada	8,601,515	7,960,725	640,790	5,362,660
		Percent of Labour Force Total		
London	65.1	59.3	9.0	34.9
Ontario	65.5	60.1	8.3	34.5
Canada	66.0	60.9	7.8	34.0
		Males		
London	69.1	62.6	9.4	30.9
Ontario	69.9	64.2	8.3	30.1
Canada	70.6	64.9	8.0	29.4
		Females		
London	61.5	56.2	8.6	38.5
Ontario	61.4	56.3	8.3	38.6
Canada	61.6	57.0	7.4	38.4

Note: Figures are based on total population 15 years and over
Source: Statistics Canada. 2013. 2011 National Household Survey. Statistics Canada Catalogue no. 99-004-XWE. Ottawa. Released September 11, 2013.

Labour Force by Industry (NAICS Codes 11–52)

Area	Agriculture, forestry, fishing & hunting	Mining, quarrying, & oil & gas extraction	Utilities	Construction	Manufacturing	Wholesale Trade	Retail Trade	Transportation & warehousing	Information & cultural industries	Finance & insurance
					Number Total					
London	800	195	865	10,235	20,030	6,410	22,205	8,305	3,880	11,355
Ontario	101,280	29,985	57,035	417,900	697,565	305,030	751,200	307,405	178,720	364,415
Canada	437,650	261,050	149,940	1,215,380	1,619,295	733,445	2,031,665	827,780	420,830	767,960
					Males					
London	480	150	670	9,145	14,810	4,605	10,165	6,385	1,940	4,390
Ontario	66,485	25,650	42,685	369,300	493,305	197,770	344,480	225,245	98,835	153,125
Canada	307,370	211,690	110,765	1,068,710	1,167,680	494,545	933,850	617,305	235,875	296,995
					Females					
London	320	45	195	1,090	5,215	1,805	12,040	1,915	1,940	6,965
Ontario	34,800	4,340	14,350	48,595	204,260	107,260	406,720	82,160	79,885	211,290
Canada	130,285	49,360	39,175	146,670	451,615	238,900	1,097,820	210,475	184,955	470,960
					Percent of Labour Force Total					
London	0.4	0.1	0.5	5.4	10.5	3.4	11.7	4.4	2.0	6.0
Ontario	1.5	0.4	0.9	6.3	10.4	4.6	11.2	4.6	2.7	5.5
Canada	2.5	1.5	0.9	6.9	9.2	4.2	11.6	4.7	2.4	4.4
					Males					
London	0.5	0.2	0.7	9.5	15.3	4.8	10.5	6.6	2.0	4.5
Ontario	1.9	0.7	1.2	10.7	14.3	5.7	10.0	6.5	2.9	4.4
Canada	3.3	2.3	1.2	11.6	12.7	5.4	10.2	6.7	2.6	3.2
					Females					
London	0.3	0.0	0.2	1.2	5.6	1.9	12.8	2.0	2.1	7.4
Ontario	1.1	0.1	0.4	1.5	6.3	3.3	12.6	2.5	2.5	6.5
Canada	1.6	0.6	0.5	1.7	5.4	2.8	13.1	2.5	2.2	5.6

Note: Figures are based on total experienced labour force 15 years and over. Experienced labour force refers to persons who, during the week of Sunday, May 1 to Saturday, May 7, 2011, were employed and the unemployed who had last worked for pay or in self-employment in either 2010 or 2011.
Source: Statistics Canada. 2013. 2011 National Household Survey. Statistics Canada Catalogue no. 99-004-XWE. Ottawa. Released September 11, 2013.

Labour Force by Industry (NAICS Codes 53–91)

Area	Real estate & rental & leasing	Profess., scientific & tech. services	Mgmt of companies & enterprises	Admin. & support, waste mgmt & remed. services	Educational services	Health care & social assistance	Arts, entertain. & recreation	Accomm. & food services	Other services (except public admin.)	Public admin.
					Number Total					
London	3,835	11,935	85	10,250	18,735	26,330	4,420	14,380	7,730	8,505
Ontario	133,980	511,020	6,525	309,630	499,690	692,130	144,065	417,675	296,340	458,665
Canada	321,895	1,240,850	17,460	728,330	1,301,435	1,949,650	363,405	1,130,750	807,800	1,261,050
					Males					
London	2,220	6,645	50	5,545	7,280	5,310	2,320	6,255	3,505	4,640
Ontario	72,835	281,420	3,540	172,475	162,765	120,165	75,035	177,240	133,795	236,655
Canada	179,090	688,625	9,380	411,250	424,915	349,430	188,270	469,990	372,940	652,510
					Females					
London	1,615	5,290	35	4,700	11,450	21,020	2,095	8,130	4,220	3,870
Ontario	61,145	229,600	2,990	137,155	336,925	571,965	69,030	240,430	162,550	222,015
Canada	142,805	552,225	8,075	317,085	876,515	1,600,220	175,135	660,760	434,865	608,535
					Percent of Labour Force Total					
London	2.0	6.3	0.0	5.4	9.8	13.8	2.3	7.5	4.1	4.5
Ontario	2.0	7.6	0.1	4.6	7.5	10.4	2.2	6.3	4.4	6.9
Canada	1.8	7.1	0.1	4.1	7.4	11.1	2.1	6.4	4.6	7.2
					Males					
London	2.3	6.9	0.1	5.7	7.5	5.5	2.4	6.5	3.6	4.8
Ontario	2.1	8.2	0.1	5.0	4.7	3.5	2.2	5.1	3.9	6.9
Canada	1.9	7.5	0.1	4.5	4.6	3.8	2.0	5.1	4.1	7.1
					Females					
London	1.7	5.6	0.0	5.0	12.2	22.4	2.2	8.7	4.5	4.1
Ontario	1.9	7.1	0.1	4.2	10.4	17.7	2.1	7.4	5.0	6.9
Canada	1.7	6.6	0.1	3.8	10.4	19.1	2.1	7.9	5.2	7.2

Note: Figures are based on total experienced labour force 15 years and over. Experienced labour force refers to persons who, during the week of Sunday, May 1 to Saturday, May 7, 2011, were employed and the unemployed who had last worked for pay or in self-employment in either 2010 or 2011.
Source: Statistics Canada. 2013. 2011 National Household Survey. Statistics Canada Catalogue no. 99-004-XWE. Ottawa. Released September 11, 2013.

Occupation

Area	Mgmt	Business, Finance & Admin.	Natural/ Applied Sciences & Related	Health	Education, Law & Social, Community & Government Services	Art, Culture, Recreation & Sport	Sales & Service	Trades, Transport & Equip. Operators & Related	Natural Resources, Agri. & Related Production	Mfg & Utilities
					Number					
					Total					
London	17,675	30,220	11,390	14,660	25,850	5,060	50,505	23,000	1,845	10,265
Ontario	770,580	1,138,330	494,500	392,695	801,465	206,420	1,550,260	868,515	106,810	350,685
Canada	1,963,600	2,902,045	1,237,775	1,107,200	2,064,675	503,415	4,068,170	2,537,775	397,930	805,040
					Males					
London	10,740	8,940	8,990	3,370	9,180	2,335	22,195	21,725	1,550	7,495
Ontario	474,655	352,505	384,345	78,330	264,570	96,055	673,880	812,280	82,610	233,565
Canada	1,229,460	854,190	966,355	217,520	676,550	232,535	1,745,705	2,385,615	318,945	564,300
					Females					
London	6,935	21,275	2,405	11,290	16,670	2,730	28,305	1,270	295	2,765
Ontario	295,920	785,825	110,150	314,370	536,895	110,370	876,380	56,230	24,200	117,115
Canada	734,140	2,047,855	271,415	889,675	1,388,130	270,875	2,322,465	152,165	78,980	240,740
					Percent of Labour Force					
					Total					
London	9.3	15.9	6.0	7.7	13.6	2.7	26.5	12.1	1.0	5.4
Ontario	11.5	17.0	7.4	5.9	12.0	3.1	23.2	13.0	1.6	5.2
Canada	11.2	16.5	7.0	6.3	11.7	2.9	23.1	14.4	2.3	4.6
					Males					
London	11.1	9.3	9.3	3.5	9.5	2.4	23.0	22.5	1.6	7.8
Ontario	13.7	10.2	11.1	2.3	7.7	2.8	19.5	23.5	2.4	6.8
Canada	13.4	9.3	10.5	2.4	7.4	2.5	19.0	26.0	3.5	6.1
					Females					
London	7.4	22.6	2.6	12.0	17.7	2.9	30.1	1.4	0.3	2.9
Ontario	9.2	24.3	3.4	9.7	16.6	3.4	27.2	1.7	0.7	3.6
Canada	8.7	24.4	3.2	10.6	16.5	3.2	27.7	1.8	0.9	2.9

Note: Figures are based on total experienced labour force 15 years and over
Source: Statistics Canada. 2013. 2011 National Household Survey. Statistics Canada Catalogue no. 99-004-XWE. Ottawa. Released September 11, 2013.

Place of Work Status

Area	Worked at Home	Worked Outside Canada	No Fixed Workplace Address	Worked at Usual Place
		Number		
		Total		
London	10,515	595	17,150	150,415
Ontario	423,790	31,390	670,835	5,170,980
Canada	1,142,640	66,460	1,868,245	13,517,690
		Males		
London	5,545	465	12,380	71,835
Ontario	216,900	21,150	486,560	2,524,555
Canada	582,150	47,355	1,400,485	6,604,325
		Females		
London	4,975	125	4,770	78,580
Ontario	206,895	10,240	184,275	2,646,420
Canada	560,490	19,100	467,760	6,913,370
		Percent of Labour Force		
		Total		
London	5.9	0.3	9.6	84.2
Ontario	6.7	0.5	10.7	82.1
Canada	6.9	0.4	11.3	81.5
		Males		
London	6.1	0.5	13.7	79.6
Ontario	6.7	0.7	15.0	77.7
Canada	6.7	0.5	16.2	76.5
		Females		
London	5.6	0.1	5.4	88.8
Ontario	6.8	0.3	6.0	86.8
Canada	7.0	0.2	5.9	86.8

Note: Figures are based on total employed labour force 15 years and over.
Source: Statistics Canada. 2013. 2011 National Household Survey. Statistics Canada Catalogue no. 99-004-XWE. Ottawa. Released September 11, 2013.

Mode of Transportation to Work

Area	Car; Truck; Van; as Driver	Car; Truck; Van; as Passenger	Public Transit	Walked	Bicycled	All Other Modes
			Number			
			Total			
London	127,330	11,665	14,520	9,790	2,810	1,445
Ontario	4,235,315	357,110	818,270	299,095	69,885	62,145
Canada	11,393,140	867,050	1,851,525	880,815	201,780	191,625
			Males			
London	66,270	4,975	5,920	4,385	2,010	655
Ontario	2,316,680	143,410	340,995	131,765	47,635	30,635
Canada	6,238,835	349,530	788,290	387,580	135,840	104,725
			Females			
London	61,070	6,685	8,600	5,410	800	790
Ontario	1,918,640	213,700	477,275	167,325	22,250	31,515
Canada	5,154,305	517,520	1,063,235	493,230	65,940	86,900
			Percent of Labour Force			
			Total			
London	76.0	7.0	8.7	5.8	1.7	0.9
Ontario	72.5	6.1	14.0	5.1	1.2	1.1
Canada	74.0	5.6	12.0	5.7	1.3	1.2
			Males			
London	78.7	5.9	7.0	5.2	2.4	0.8
Ontario	76.9	4.8	11.3	4.4	1.6	1.0
Canada	77.9	4.4	9.8	4.8	1.7	1.3
			Females			
London	73.3	8.0	10.3	6.5	1.0	0.9
Ontario	67.8	7.5	16.9	5.9	0.8	1.1
Canada	69.8	7.0	14.4	6.7	0.9	1.2

Note: Figures are based on total employed labour force 15 years and over.
Source: Statistics Canada. 2013. 2011 National Household Survey. Statistics Canada Catalogue no. 99-004-XWE. Ottawa. Released September 11, 2013.

Visible Minority Population Characteristics

Area	Total Minority	South Asian[1]	Chinese	Black	Filipino	Latin American	Arab	SE Asian[2]	West Asian[3]	Korean	Japanese	Multiple[4]
					Number							
					Total							
London	57,965	8,010	7,140	8,760	2,270	9,640	9,320	3,750	2,955	2,990	495	1,870
Ontario	3,279,565	965,990	629,140	539,205	275,380	172,560	151,645	137,875	122,530	78,290	29,085	96,735
Canada	6,264,750	1,567,400	1,324,750	945,665	619,310	381,280	380,620	312,075	206,840	161,130	87,270	171,935
					Males							
London	29,015	3,945	3,345	4,590	915	5,080	4,690	1,905	1,585	1,515	225	835
Ontario	1,582,480	484,355	301,575	251,295	116,825	83,205	79,620	67,645	62,515	38,045	13,345	46,765
Canada	3,043,010	790,755	632,325	453,005	268,885	186,355	203,485	154,035	105,620	77,165	38,270	83,335
					Females							
London	28,950	4,065	3,795	4,175	1,350	4,555	4,630	1,845	1,370	1,475	270	1,035
Ontario	1,697,085	481,635	327,570	287,915	158,555	89,360	72,025	70,230	60,010	40,250	15,740	49,970
Canada	3,221,745	776,650	692,420	492,660	350,425	194,925	177,140	158,045	101,220	83,965	48,990	88,600
					Percent of Population							
					Total							
London	16.1	2.2	2.0	2.4	0.6	2.7	2.6	1.0	0.8	0.8	0.1	0.5
Ontario	25.9	7.6	5.0	4.3	2.2	1.4	1.2	1.1	1.0	0.6	0.2	0.8
Canada	19.1	4.8	4.0	2.9	1.9	1.2	1.2	0.9	0.6	0.5	0.3	0.5
					Males							
London	16.6	2.3	1.9	2.6	0.5	2.9	2.7	1.1	0.9	0.9	0.1	0.5
Ontario	25.6	7.8	4.9	4.1	1.9	1.3	1.3	1.1	1.0	0.6	0.2	0.8
Canada	18.8	4.9	3.9	2.8	1.7	1.2	1.3	1.0	0.7	0.5	0.2	0.5
					Females							
London	15.6	2.2	2.0	2.2	0.7	2.5	2.5	1.0	0.7	0.8	0.1	0.6
Ontario	26.2	7.4	5.1	4.4	2.5	1.4	1.1	1.1	0.9	0.6	0.2	0.8
Canada	19.3	4.7	4.1	3.0	2.1	1.2	1.1	0.9	0.6	0.5	0.3	0.5

Note: The Employment Equity Act defines visible minorities as 'persons, other than Aboriginal peoples, who are non-Caucasian in race or non-white in colour';
(1) Includes 'East Indian,' 'Pakistani,' 'Sri Lankan,' etc.; (2) Includes 'Vietnamese,' 'Cambodian,' 'Malaysian,' 'Laotian,' etc.; (3) Includes 'Iranian,' 'Afghan,' etc.; (4) Includes respondents who reported more than one visible minority group by checking two or more mark-in circles, e.g., 'Black' and 'South Asian.'
Source: Statistics Canada. 2013. 2011 National Household Survey. Statistics Canada Catalogue no. 99-004-XWE. Ottawa. Released September 11, 2013.

PROFILES / London, Ontario

Aboriginal Population

Area	Aboriginal Identity[1]	First Nations (North American Indian) Single Identity[2]	Métis Single Identity	Inuk (Inuit) Single Identity	Multiple Aboriginal Identities[3]	Aboriginal Identities Not Included Elsewhere
			Number			
			Total			
London	6,845	5,030	1,445	35	95	230
Ontario	301,430	201,100	86,020	3,355	2,910	8,040
Canada	1,400,685	851,560	451,795	59,440	11,415	26,475
			Males			
London	3,280	2,370	695	0	80	130
Ontario	145,020	96,620	41,755	1,475	1,420	3,750
Canada	682,190	411,785	223,335	29,495	5,525	12,055
			Females			
London	3,560	2,670	755	20	20	105
Ontario	156,410	104,485	44,260	1,880	1,490	4,295
Canada	718,500	439,775	228,460	29,950	5,890	14,420
			Percent of Population			
			Total			
London	1.9	1.4	0.4	0.0	0.0	0.1
Ontario	2.4	1.6	0.7	0.0	0.0	0.1
Canada	4.3	2.6	1.4	0.2	0.0	0.1
			Males			
London	1.9	1.4	0.4	0.0	0.0	0.1
Ontario	2.3	1.6	0.7	0.0	0.0	0.1
Canada	4.2	2.5	1.4	0.2	0.0	0.1
			Females			
London	1.9	1.4	0.4	0.0	0.0	0.1
Ontario	2.4	1.6	0.7	0.0	0.0	0.1
Canada	4.3	2.6	1.4	0.2	0.0	0.1

Note: (1) Includes persons who reported being an Aboriginal person, that is, First Nations (North American Indian), Métis or Inuk (Inuit) and/or those who reported Registered or Treaty Indian status, that is registered under the Indian Act of Canada, and/or those who reported membership in a First Nation or Indian band. Aboriginal peoples of Canada are defined in the Constitution Act, 1982, section 35-2 as including the Indian, Inuit and Métis peoples of Canada; (2) Users should be aware that the estimates associated with this variable are more affected than most by the incomplete enumeration of certain Indian reserves and Indian settlements in the National Household Survey (NHS); (3) Includes persons who reported being any two or all three of the following: First Nations (North American Indian), Métis or Inuk (Inuit).
Source: Statistics Canada. 2013. 2011 National Household Survey. Statistics Canada Catalogue no. 99-004-XWE. Ottawa. Released September 11, 2013.

Ethnic Origin

Area	North American Aboriginal	Other North American	European	Caribbean	Latin, Central and South American	African	Asian	Oceania
				Number				
				Total				
London	10,620	97,230	265,000	5,195	10,800	7,325	41,585	610
Ontario	441,395	3,059,480	8,231,410	396,485	271,545	331,460	2,604,595	19,410
Canada	1,836,035	11,070,455	20,157,965	627,590	544,375	766,735	5,011,225	74,875
				Males				
London	5,090	46,895	127,585	2,665	5,545	3,745	20,225	275
Ontario	210,490	1,507,105	4,019,885	181,805	130,035	160,940	1,265,540	9,855
Canada	885,675	5,462,685	9,913,150	291,640	264,635	387,360	2,435,540	37,490
				Females				
London	5,530	50,335	137,420	2,535	5,250	3,590	21,360	340
Ontario	230,905	1,552,380	4,211,525	214,675	141,510	170,515	1,339,050	9,555
Canada	950,360	5,607,770	10,244,820	335,945	279,740	379,380	2,575,680	37,385
				Percent of Population				
				Total				
London	2.9	27.0	73.5	1.4	3.0	2.0	11.5	0.2
Ontario	3.5	24.2	65.1	3.1	2.1	2.6	20.6	0.2
Canada	5.6	33.7	61.4	1.9	1.7	2.3	15.3	0.2
				Males				
London	2.9	26.8	73.0	1.5	3.2	2.1	11.6	0.2
Ontario	3.4	24.4	65.0	2.9	2.1	2.6	20.5	0.2
Canada	5.5	33.8	61.3	1.8	1.6	2.4	15.1	0.2
				Females				
London	3.0	27.1	73.9	1.4	2.8	1.9	11.5	0.2
Ontario	3.6	24.0	65.1	3.3	2.2	2.6	20.7	0.1
Canada	5.7	33.6	61.4	2.0	1.7	2.3	15.4	0.2

Note: The sum of the ethnic groups in this table is greater than the total population estimate because a person may report more than one ethnic origin in the NHS.
Source: Statistics Canada. 2013. 2011 National Household Survey. Statistics Canada Catalogue no. 99-004-XWE. Ottawa. Released September 11, 2013.

Religion

Area	Buddhist	Christian	Hindu	Jewish	Muslim	Sikh	Traditional (Aboriginal) Spirituality	Other Religions	No Religious Affiliation
				Number Total					
London	2,760	226,615	2,790	1,715	15,780	715	280	2,080	107,975
Ontario	163,750	8,167,295	366,720	195,540	581,950	179,765	15,905	53,080	2,927,790
Canada	366,830	22,102,745	497,965	329,495	1,053,945	454,965	64,935	130,835	7,850,605
				Males					
London	1,310	104,125	1,315	815	7,980	345	170	940	57,800
Ontario	75,355	3,839,925	183,580	95,795	293,925	90,515	7,600	23,555	1,571,195
Canada	168,465	10,497,775	250,435	161,265	540,555	229,435	31,805	57,745	4,225,645
				Females					
London	1,455	122,490	1,470	900	7,805	370	115	1,140	50,175
Ontario	88,395	4,327,365	183,140	99,740	288,025	89,250	8,310	29,525	1,356,600
Canada	198,365	11,604,975	247,525	168,235	513,395	225,530	33,135	73,090	3,624,965
				Percent of Population Total					
London	0.8	62.8	0.8	0.5	4.4	0.2	0.1	0.6	29.9
Ontario	1.3	64.6	2.9	1.5	4.6	1.4	0.1	0.4	23.1
Canada	1.1	67.3	1.5	1.0	3.2	1.4	0.2	0.4	23.9
				Males					
London	0.7	59.6	0.8	0.5	4.6	0.2	0.1	0.5	33.1
Ontario	1.2	62.1	3.0	1.5	4.8	1.5	0.1	0.4	25.4
Canada	1.0	64.9	1.5	1.0	3.3	1.4	0.2	0.4	26.1
				Females					
London	0.8	65.9	0.8	0.5	4.2	0.2	0.1	0.6	27.0
Ontario	1.4	66.9	2.8	1.5	4.5	1.4	0.1	0.5	21.0
Canada	1.2	69.5	1.5	1.0	3.1	1.4	0.2	0.4	21.7

Note: Religion refers to the person's self-identification as having a connection or affiliation with any religious denomination, group, body, sect, cult or other religiously defined community or system of belief. Religion is not limited to formal membership in a religious organization or group. Persons without a religious connection or affiliation can self-identify as atheist, agnostic or humanist, or can provide another applicable response.
Source: Statistics Canada. 2013. 2011 National Household Survey. Statistics Canada Catalogue no. 99-004-XWE. Ottawa. Released September 11, 2013.

Religion—Christian Denominations

Area	Anglican	Baptist	Catholic	Christian Orthodox	Lutheran	Pentecostal	Presbyterian	United Church	Other Christian
				Number Total					
London	27,490	9,540	97,285	6,535	4,420	4,350	10,140	34,185	32,665
Ontario	774,560	244,650	3,976,610	297,710	163,460	213,945	319,585	952,465	1,224,300
Canada	1,631,845	635,840	12,810,705	550,690	478,185	478,705	472,385	2,007,610	3,036,780
				Males					
London	12,095	4,390	45,390	3,295	1,970	1,980	4,535	15,075	15,395
Ontario	355,175	112,285	1,895,940	145,825	75,225	94,955	148,535	435,255	576,730
Canada	752,945	293,905	6,167,290	270,205	221,525	217,850	218,955	912,545	1,442,550
				Females					
London	15,395	5,150	51,895	3,245	2,455	2,370	5,600	19,105	17,270
Ontario	419,390	132,370	2,080,665	151,885	88,230	118,990	171,050	517,210	647,570
Canada	878,900	341,940	6,643,415	280,485	256,660	260,850	253,430	1,095,065	1,594,230
				Percent of Population Total					
London	7.6	2.6	27.0	1.8	1.2	1.2	2.8	9.5	9.1
Ontario	6.1	1.9	31.4	2.4	1.3	1.7	2.5	7.5	9.7
Canada	5.0	1.9	39.0	1.7	1.5	1.5	1.4	6.1	9.2
				Males					
London	6.9	2.5	26.0	1.9	1.1	1.1	2.6	8.6	8.8
Ontario	5.7	1.8	30.7	2.4	1.2	1.5	2.4	7.0	9.3
Canada	4.7	1.8	38.2	1.7	1.4	1.3	1.4	5.6	8.9
				Females					
London	8.3	2.8	27.9	1.7	1.3	1.3	3.0	10.3	9.3
Ontario	6.5	2.0	32.2	2.3	1.4	1.8	2.6	8.0	10.0
Canada	5.3	2.0	39.8	1.7	1.5	1.6	1.5	6.6	9.6

Note: Religion refers to the person's self-identification as having a connection or affiliation with any religious denomination, group, body, sect, cult or other religiously defined community or system of belief. Religion is not limited to formal membership in a religious organization or group. Persons without a religious connection or affiliation can self-identify as atheist, agnostic or humanist, or can provide another applicable response.
Source: Statistics Canada. 2013. 2011 National Household Survey. Statistics Canada Catalogue no. 99-004-XWE. Ottawa. Released September 11, 2013.

PROFILES / London, Ontario

Immigrant Status and Period of Immigration

Area	Non-Immigrants[1]	Immigrants All	Before 1971	1971 to 1980	1981 to 1990	1991 to 2000	2001 to 2005	2006 to 2011	Non-Permanent Residents[3]
Number									
Total									
London	279,580	76,585	20,020	9,025	12,580	13,750	9,805	11,410	4,555
Ontario	8,906,000	3,611,365	723,030	464,380	538,285	866,220	518,405	501,060	134,425
Canada	25,720,175	6,775,765	1,261,055	870,775	949,890	1,539,050	992,070	1,162,915	356,385
Males									
London	135,875	36,580	9,230	4,125	6,285	6,605	4,765	5,570	2,335
Ontario	4,410,240	1,706,385	341,820	217,990	258,095	408,270	245,850	234,360	64,825
Canada	12,753,235	3,231,370	605,430	416,670	454,570	724,905	474,545	555,245	178,515
Females									
London	143,700	40,000	10,790	4,905	6,290	7,140	5,040	5,840	2,220
Ontario	4,495,765	1,904,985	381,210	246,390	280,190	457,950	272,550	266,695	69,600
Canada	12,966,935	3,544,400	655,625	454,105	495,325	814,145	517,530	607,670	177,870
Percent of Population									
Total									
London	77.5	21.2	5.6	2.5	3.5	3.8	2.7	3.2	1.3
Ontario	70.4	28.5	5.7	3.7	4.3	6.8	4.1	4.0	1.1
Canada	78.3	20.6	3.8	2.7	2.9	4.7	3.0	3.5	1.1
Males									
London	77.7	20.9	5.3	2.4	3.6	3.8	2.7	3.2	1.3
Ontario	71.3	27.6	5.5	3.5	4.2	6.6	4.0	3.8	1.0
Canada	78.9	20.0	3.7	2.6	2.8	4.5	2.9	3.4	1.1
Females									
London	77.3	21.5	5.8	2.6	3.4	3.8	2.7	3.1	1.2
Ontario	69.5	29.4	5.9	3.8	4.3	7.1	4.2	4.1	1.1
Canada	77.7	21.2	3.9	2.7	3.0	4.9	3.1	3.6	1.1

Note: (1) Non-immigrant refers to a person who is a Canadian citizen by birth; (2) Immigrant refers to a person who is or has ever been a landed immigrant/permanent resident. This person has been granted the right to live in Canada permanently by immigration authorities. Some immigrants have resided in Canada for a number of years, while others have arrived recently. Some immigrants are Canadian citizens, while others are not. Most immigrants are born outside Canada, but a small number are born in Canada. In the 2011 National Household Survey, 'Immigrants' includes immigrants who landed in Canada prior to May 10, 2011; (3) Non-permanent resident refers to a person from another country who has a work or study permit, or who is a refugee claimant, and any non-Canadian-born family member living in Canada with them.
Source: Statistics Canada. 2013. 2011 National Household Survey. Statistics Canada Catalogue no. 99-004-XWE. Ottawa. Released September 11, 2013.

Mother Tongue

Area	English	French	Non-official Language	English & French	English & Non-official Language	French & Non-official Language	English, French & Non-official Language
Number							
Total							
London	281,995	4,780	69,650	870	4,480	305	180
Ontario	8,677,040	493,300	3,264,435	46,605	219,425	13,645	7,615
Canada	18,858,980	7,054,975	6,567,680	144,685	396,330	74,430	24,095
Males							
London	136,650	2,110	33,395	380	2,215	140	85
Ontario	4,276,970	232,785	1,562,190	21,805	106,790	6,285	3,495
Canada	9,345,225	3,452,380	3,157,785	69,975	192,000	36,535	11,965
Females							
London	145,340	2,670	36,260	485	2,265	170	100
Ontario	4,400,065	260,510	1,702,240	24,795	112,635	7,365	4,115
Canada	9,513,750	3,602,590	3,409,895	74,710	204,330	37,890	12,130
Percent of Population							
Total							
London	77.8	1.3	19.2	0.2	1.2	0.1	0.0
Ontario	68.2	3.9	25.7	0.4	1.7	0.1	0.1
Canada	56.9	21.3	19.8	0.4	1.2	0.2	0.1
Males							
London	78.1	1.2	19.1	0.2	1.3	0.1	0.0
Ontario	68.9	3.7	25.2	0.4	1.7	0.1	0.1
Canada	57.5	21.2	19.4	0.4	1.2	0.2	0.1
Females							
London	77.6	1.4	19.4	0.3	1.2	0.1	0.1
Ontario	67.6	4.0	26.1	0.4	1.7	0.1	0.1
Canada	56.4	21.4	20.2	0.4	1.2	0.2	0.1

Note: Figures cover total population excluding institutional residents.
Source: Statistics Canada. 2012. Census Profile. 2011 Census. Statistics Canada Catalogue no. 98-316-XWE. Ottawa. Released October 24 2012.
http://www12.statcan.gc.ca/census-recensement/2011/dp-pd/prof/index.cfm?Lang=E

Language Spoken Most Often at Home

Area	English	French	Non-official Language	English & French	English & Non-official Language	French & Non-official Language	English, French & Non-official Language
			Number				
			Total				
London	314,010	1,460	35,190	495	10,775	85	245
Ontario	10,044,810	284,115	1,827,870	37,955	509,105	6,370	11,845
Canada	21,457,075	6,827,865	3,673,865	131,205	875,135	109,700	46,330
			Males				
London	151,850	675	16,830	220	5,245	40	100
Ontario	4,930,610	133,495	872,860	17,250	248,050	2,855	5,225
Canada	10,585,620	3,348,235	1,767,310	63,475	425,370	53,010	22,845
			Females				
London	162,160	785	18,360	275	5,530	40	145
Ontario	5,114,200	150,620	955,010	20,705	261,055	3,520	6,620
Canada	10,871,455	3,479,625	1,906,555	67,730	449,765	56,690	23,485
			Percent of Population				
			Total				
London	86.7	0.4	9.7	0.1	3.0	0.0	0.1
Ontario	79.0	2.2	14.4	0.3	4.0	0.1	0.1
Canada	64.8	20.6	11.1	0.4	2.6	0.3	0.1
			Males				
London	86.8	0.4	9.6	0.1	3.0	0.0	0.1
Ontario	79.4	2.1	14.1	0.3	4.0	0.0	0.1
Canada	65.1	20.6	10.9	0.4	2.6	0.3	0.1
			Females				
London	86.6	0.4	9.8	0.1	3.0	0.0	0.1
Ontario	78.5	2.3	14.7	0.3	4.0	0.1	0.1
Canada	64.5	20.6	11.3	0.4	2.7	0.3	0.1

Note: Figures cover total population excluding institutional residents.
Source: Statistics Canada. 2012. Census Profile. 2011 Census. Statistics Canada Catalogue no. 98-316-XWE. Ottawa. Released October 24 2012.
http://www12.statcan.gc.ca/census-recensement/2011/dp-pd/prof/index.cfm?Lang=E

Knowledge of Official Languages

Area	English Only	French Only	English & French	Neither English nor French
		Number		
		Total		
London	331,035	235	26,360	4,640
Ontario	10,984,360	42,980	1,395,805	298,920
Canada	22,564,665	4,165,015	5,795,570	595,920
		Males		
London	161,845	120	11,240	1,765
Ontario	5,445,050	18,805	627,725	118,765
Canada	11,222,185	1,925,340	2,876,560	241,790
		Females		
London	169,190	115	15,120	2,875
Ontario	5,539,310	24,175	768,085	180,155
Canada	11,342,485	2,239,680	2,919,005	354,135
		Percent of Population		
		Total		
London	91.4	0.1	7.3	1.3
Ontario	86.3	0.3	11.0	2.3
Canada	68.1	12.6	17.5	1.8
		Males		
London	92.5	0.1	6.4	1.0
Ontario	87.7	0.3	10.1	1.9
Canada	69.0	11.8	17.7	1.5
		Females		
London	90.3	0.1	8.1	1.5
Ontario	85.1	0.4	11.8	2.8
Canada	67.3	13.3	17.3	2.1

Note: Figures cover total population excluding institutional residents.
Source: Statistics Canada. 2012. Census Profile. 2011 Census. Statistics Canada Catalogue no. 98-316-XWE. Ottawa. Released October 24 2012.
http://www12.statcan.gc.ca/census-recensement/2011/dp-pd/prof/index.cfm?Lang=E

Longueuil, Québec

Background

Longueuil is located on the southern shore of the St. Lawrence River in the Montérégie Region of Québec, directly across from Montréal. Longueuil is Montréal's most populous suburb and is connected to the city by four bridges. Ferries also connect the two cities, travelling seven kilometres in 20 minutes across the St. Lawrence.

In 1657, a prominent Ville-Marie (Montréal) merchant was awarded a tract of land along the south side of the St. Lawrence River. Charles Le Moyne de Longueuil et de Châteauguay named the area in honour of his mother's village in France. Longueuil was a municipality under the rural parish of Saint-Antoine in 1845 and was later incorporated as a distinct municipality. It became a town in 1874 and was incorporated as a city in 1920. The City of Longueuil was formed in 2002 as an amalgamation of eight former municipalities, including the former city of Longueuil.

The four bridges connecting Longueuil to Montréal are the Victoria (1859), Jacques-Cartier (1930), and Champlain (1962) bridges and the Louis-Hippolyte-Lafontaine tunnel-bridge (1967). The city's Regional Park offers year-round hiking trails and day camps. The fragile marsh section of the park features observation areas overlooking hundreds of species of birds. Almost 100 kilometres of bike lanes intersect the city, including approximately eight kilometres of trail bordering the St. Lawrence River. Cyclists can cross over to the island of Montréal National Park and the Îles-de-Boucherville by ferry.

Plein Sud is a contemporary art and activity centre showcasing regional, national and international works of art. The Marie-Rose Centre is a highlight of Longueuil's religious tourism; founded in 1843, the centre was one of Canada's first all-women congregations.

Longueuil's close proximity to Montréal allows the city to enjoy over 40 annual festivals that attract two million visitors to the region every year. Longueuil's own celebrations include the International Percussion Festival and Festival Métiers & Traditions de Longueuil, a celebration of 19th-century country life.

Longueuil has summer highs of plus 24.87 degrees Celsius, winter lows of minus 12.67 degrees Celsius, and an average rainfall just over 763 mm per year.

Rankings

- Longueuil ranked #5 of Canada's best-run cities. *Maclean's Magazine* ranked 31 cities based on city efficiency and the effectiveness of services such as road and park maintenance, garbage collection and fire control. The top 4 cities were Burnaby, Saskatoon, Surrey and Vancouver. *Maclean's Magazine,* "Canada's best and worst run cities," July 16, 2009
- Forum Research identified Longueuil as a city whose residents were "very satisfied" with the delivery of municipal services. The study polled Canada's 30 most populated towns and cities; Longueuil ranked #8 overall. Thirty per cent of polled residents expressed above-average satisfaction. *Forum Research, Nationwide Municipal Issues Poll, released May 2012*

PROFILES / Longueuil, Québec

Population Growth and Density

Area	Population in 2001	Population in 2006	Population in 2011	Population Change 2001–2006	Population Change 2006–2011	Land Area (sq. km)	Population Density per sq. km
Longueuil	225,761	229,330	231,409	1.6	0.9	115.59	2,002.0
Québec	7,237,479	7,546,131	7,903,001	4.3	4.7	1,356,547.02	5.8
Canada	30,007,094	31,612,897	33,476,688	5.4	5.9	8,965,121.42	3.7

Source: Statistics Canada. 2012. Census Profile. 2011 Census. Statistics Canada Catalogue no. 98-316-XWE. Ottawa. Released October 24 2012.
http://www12.statcan.gc.ca/census-recensement/2011/dp-pd/prof/index.cfm?Lang=E;
Statistics Canada 2007. 2006 Community Profiles. 2006 Census. Statistics Canada Catalogue no. 92-591-XWE. Ottawa. Released March 13 2007.
http://www12.statcan.ca/census-recensement/2006/dp-pd/prof/92-591/index.cfm?Lang=E

Gender

Area	Males	Females
	Number	
Longueuil	111,995	119,415
Québec	3,875,860	4,027,140
Canada	16,414,225	17,062,460
	Percent of Population	
Longueuil	48.4	51.6
Québec	49.0	51.0
Canada	49.0	51.0

Source: Statistics Canada. 2012. Census Profile. 2011 Census. Statistics Canada Catalogue no. 98-316-XWE. Ottawa. Released October 24 2012.
http://www12.statcan.gc.ca/census-recensement/2011/dp-pd/prof/index.cfm?Lang=E

Marital Status

Area	Married[1]	Living Common-law	Single[2]	Separated	Divorced	Widowed
			Number			
			Total			
Longueuil	65,095	38,900	62,210	3,540	16,250	10,915
Québec	2,353,770	1,391,550	1,942,090	105,195	463,830	387,945
Canada	12,941,960	3,142,525	7,816,045	698,240	1,686,035	1,584,530
			Males			
Longueuil	32,550	19,495	32,985	1,515	5,855	2,140
Québec	1,177,720	697,695	1,045,540	46,465	188,265	77,430
Canada	6,470,300	1,575,495	4,206,320	299,655	680,415	310,940
			Females			
Longueuil	32,545	19,415	29,230	2,020	10,395	8,780
Québec	1,176,050	693,850	896,545	58,720	275,565	310,515
Canada	6,471,660	1,567,035	3,609,730	398,585	1,005,620	1,273,590
			Percent of Population			
			Total			
Longueuil	33.1	19.8	31.6	1.8	8.3	5.5
Québec	35.4	20.9	29.2	1.6	7.0	5.8
Canada	46.4	11.3	28.0	2.5	6.0	5.7
			Males			
Longueuil	34.4	20.6	34.9	1.6	6.2	2.3
Québec	36.4	21.6	32.3	1.4	5.8	2.4
Canada	47.8	11.6	31.1	2.2	5.0	2.3
			Females			
Longueuil	31.8	19.0	28.6	2.0	10.2	8.6
Québec	34.5	20.3	26.3	1.7	8.1	9.1
Canada	45.2	10.9	25.2	2.8	7.0	8.9

Note: (1) and not separated, (2) never legally married
Source: Statistics Canada. 2012. Census Profile. 2011 Census. Statistics Canada Catalogue no. 98-316-XWE. Ottawa. Released October 24 2012.
http://www12.statcan.gc.ca/census-recensement/2011/dp-pd/prof/index.cfm?Lang=E

PROFILES / Longueuil, Québec

Age Characteristics: 0 to 49 Years

Area	0 to 4 Years	5 to 9 Years	10 to 14 Years	15 to 19 Years	20 to 24 Years	25 to 29 Years	30 to 34 Years	35 to 39 Years	40 to 44 Years	45 to 49 Years
Number										
Total										
Longueuil	12,090	10,725	11,680	14,965	15,785	15,165	15,250	14,350	14,885	18,530
Québec	440,840	399,575	418,205	491,980	489,185	490,665	531,445	498,225	520,805	623,575
Canada	1,877,095	1,809,895	1,920,355	2,178,135	2,187,450	2,169,590	2,162,905	2,173,930	2,324,875	2,675,130
Males										
Longueuil	6,160	5,410	5,885	7,520	7,945	7,625	7,700	7,180	7,360	9,185
Québec	225,525	203,675	213,540	249,960	246,850	245,695	264,980	249,610	261,120	311,320
Canada	961,150	925,965	983,995	1,115,845	1,108,775	1,077,275	1,058,810	1,064,200	1,141,720	1,318,715
Females										
Longueuil	5,930	5,315	5,795	7,445	7,840	7,545	7,545	7,165	7,530	9,345
Québec	215,320	195,900	204,665	242,020	242,340	244,970	266,460	248,615	259,690	312,250
Canada	915,945	883,935	936,360	1,062,295	1,078,670	1,092,315	1,104,095	1,109,735	1,183,155	1,356,420
Percent of Population										
Total										
Longueuil	5.2	4.6	5.0	6.5	6.8	6.6	6.6	6.2	6.4	8.0
Québec	5.6	5.1	5.3	6.2	6.2	6.2	6.7	6.3	6.6	7.9
Canada	5.6	5.4	5.7	6.5	6.5	6.5	6.5	6.5	6.9	8.0
Males										
Longueuil	5.5	4.8	5.3	6.7	7.1	6.8	6.9	6.4	6.6	8.2
Québec	5.8	5.3	5.5	6.4	6.4	6.3	6.8	6.4	6.7	8.0
Canada	5.9	5.6	6.0	6.8	6.8	6.6	6.5	6.5	7.0	8.0
Females										
Longueuil	5.0	4.5	4.9	6.2	6.6	6.3	6.3	6.0	6.3	7.8
Québec	5.3	4.9	5.1	6.0	6.0	6.1	6.6	6.2	6.4	7.8
Canada	5.4	5.2	5.5	6.2	6.3	6.4	6.5	6.5	6.9	7.9

Source: Statistics Canada. 2012. Census Profile. 2011 Census. Statistics Canada Catalogue no. 98-316-XWE. Ottawa. Released October 24 2012.
http://www12.statcan.gc.ca/census-recensement/2011/dp-pd/prof/index.cfm?Lang=E

Age Characteristics: 50 Years and Over, and Median Age

Area	50 to 54 Years	55 to 59 Years	60 to 64 Years	65 to 69 Years	70 to 74 Years	75 to 79 Years	80 to 84 Years	85 Years and Over	Median Age
Number									
Total									
Longueuil	19,970	17,365	15,230	12,200	8,600	6,490	4,495	3,635	41.9
Québec	648,695	579,280	512,830	403,210	291,755	232,355	176,420	153,945	41.9
Canada	2,658,965	2,340,635	2,052,670	1,521,715	1,153,065	922,700	702,070	645,515	40.6
Males									
Longueuil	9,595	8,395	6,950	5,650	3,865	2,795	1,805	960	40.4
Québec	320,695	285,295	250,675	194,305	135,830	101,675	69,170	45,945	40.7
Canada	1,309,030	1,147,300	1,002,690	738,010	543,435	417,945	291,085	208,300	39.6
Females									
Longueuil	10,370	8,965	8,280	6,545	4,730	3,700	2,690	2,675	43.5
Québec	327,995	293,990	262,155	208,905	155,925	130,680	107,250	108,005	43.0
Canada	1,349,940	1,193,335	1,049,985	783,705	609,630	504,755	410,985	437,215	41.5
Percent of Population									
Total									
Longueuil	8.6	7.5	6.6	5.3	3.7	2.8	1.9	1.6	–
Québec	8.2	7.3	6.5	5.1	3.7	2.9	2.2	1.9	–
Canada	7.9	7.0	6.1	4.5	3.4	2.8	2.1	1.9	–
Males									
Longueuil	8.6	7.5	6.2	5.0	3.5	2.5	1.6	0.9	–
Québec	8.3	7.4	6.5	5.0	3.5	2.6	1.8	1.2	–
Canada	8.0	7.0	6.1	4.5	3.3	2.5	1.8	1.3	–
Females									
Longueuil	8.7	7.5	6.9	5.5	4.0	3.1	2.3	2.2	–
Québec	8.1	7.3	6.5	5.2	3.9	3.2	2.7	2.7	–
Canada	7.9	7.0	6.2	4.6	3.6	3.0	2.4	2.6	–

Source: Statistics Canada. 2012. Census Profile. 2011 Census. Statistics Canada Catalogue no. 98-316-XWE. Ottawa. Released October 24 2012.
http://www12.statcan.gc.ca/census-recensement/2011/dp-pd/prof/index.cfm?Lang=E

PROFILES / Longueuil, Québec

Private Households by Household Size

Area	1 Person	2 Persons	3 Persons	4 Persons	5 Persons	6 or More Persons	Average Number of Persons in Private Households
				Households			
Longueuil	34,380	34,890	15,490	11,655	3,970	1,680	2.2
Québec	1,094,410	1,181,240	496,140	421,080	142,555	59,920	2.3
Canada	3,673,310	4,544,820	2,081,900	1,903,300	724,405	392,885	2.5
				Percent of Households			
Longueuil	33.7	34.2	15.2	11.4	3.9	1.6	–
Québec	32.2	34.8	14.6	12.4	4.2	1.8	–
Canada	27.6	34.1	15.6	14.3	5.4	2.9	–

Source: Statistics Canada. 2012. Census Profile. 2011 Census. Statistics Canada Catalogue no. 98-316-XWE. Ottawa. Released October 24 2012.
http://www12.statcan.gc.ca/census-recensement/2011/dp-pd/prof/index.cfm?Lang=E

Dwelling Type

Area	Single-detached House	Semi-detached House	Row House	Apartment: Building with Five or More Storeys	Apartment: Building with Fewer Than Five Storeys	Duplex Apartment	Movable Dwelling	Other Single-attached House
				Number				
Longueuil	34,515	5,225	3,210	4,835	47,850	5,665	380	390
Québec	1,560,405	171,435	86,040	171,115	1,103,845	263,860	22,995	15,645
Canada	7,329,150	646,245	791,600	1,234,770	2,397,550	704,485	183,510	33,310
				Percent of Dwellings				
Longueuil	33.8	5.1	3.1	4.7	46.9	5.6	0.4	0.4
Québec	46.0	5.0	2.5	5.0	32.5	7.8	0.7	0.5
Canada	55.0	4.9	5.9	9.3	18.0	5.3	1.4	0.3

Source: Statistics Canada. 2012. Census Profile. 2011 Census. Statistics Canada Catalogue no. 98-316-XWE. Ottawa. Released October 24 2012.
http://www12.statcan.gc.ca/census-recensement/2011/dp-pd/prof/index.cfm?Lang=E

Shelter Costs

	Owned Dwellings					Rented Dwellings		
Area	Number	Median Value[1] ($)	Average Value[1] ($)	Median Monthly Costs[2] ($)	Average Monthly Costs[2] ($)	Number	Median Monthly Costs[3] ($)	Average Monthly Costs[3] ($)
Longueuil	54,640	249,984	258,520	911	966	47,415	667	697
Québec	2,056,665	214,537	249,427	841	936	1,308,465	643	685
Canada	9,013,410	280,552	345,182	978	1,141	4,060,385	784	848

Note: All figures cover non-farm, non-reserve private dwellings; (1) Refers to the dollar amount expected by the owner if the dwelling were to be sold; (2) Includes all shelter expenses paid by households that own their dwellings, such as the mortgage payment and the costs of electricity, heat, water and other municipal services, property taxes and condominium fees; (3) Includes all shelter expenses paid by households that rent their dwellings, such as the monthly rent and the costs of electricity, heat and municipal services.
Source: Statistics Canada. 2013. 2011 National Household Survey. Statistics Canada Catalogue no. 99-004-XWE. Ottawa. Released September 11, 2013.

Occupied Private Dwellings by Period of Construction

Area	1960 or Before	1961 to 1980	1981 to 1990	1991 to 2000	2001 to 2005	2006 to 2011
			Number			
Longueuil	19,295	45,960	19,030	8,915	3,720	5,140
Québec	946,900	1,115,455	533,790	353,355	206,035	239,685
Canada	3,273,105	4,152,715	2,112,110	1,707,880	1,031,020	1,042,430
			Percent of Dwellings			
Longueuil	18.9	45.0	18.6	8.7	3.6	5.0
Québec	27.9	32.9	15.7	10.4	6.1	7.1
Canada	24.6	31.2	15.9	12.8	7.7	7.8

Note: Figures cover non-farm, non-reserve private dwellings and includes data up to May 10, 2011.
Source: Statistics Canada. 2013. 2011 National Household Survey. Statistics Canada Catalogue no. 99-004-XWE. Ottawa. Released September 11, 2013.

Educational Attainment

Area	No Certificate, Diploma or Degree	High School Diploma or Equivalent[1]	Apprenticeship or Trades Certificate or Diploma[2]	College, CÉGEP or Other Non-University Certificate or Diploma	University Certificate or Diploma Below the Bachelor Level[3]	Bachelor's Degree	University Certificate, Diploma or Degree Above Bachelor Level[4]
				Number			
				Total			
Longueuil	43,805	43,645	30,680	31,100	10,855	21,650	11,780
Québec	1,436,025	1,404,755	1,049,470	1,075,855	305,330	766,100	437,050
Canada	5,485,400	6,968,935	2,950,685	4,970,020	1,200,130	3,634,425	2,049,930
				Males			
Longueuil	21,040	19,900	18,145	13,795	4,385	9,930	6,230
Québec	714,090	650,660	635,435	472,360	126,565	343,535	227,990
Canada	2,742,875	3,305,415	1,928,970	2,118,430	513,235	1,643,080	1,043,350
				Females			
Longueuil	22,770	23,740	12,535	17,300	6,470	11,715	5,540
Québec	721,930	754,095	414,035	603,495	178,765	422,565	209,065
Canada	2,742,520	3,663,515	1,021,715	2,851,595	686,890	1,991,345	1,006,585
				Percent of Population			
				Total			
Longueuil	22.6	22.6	15.9	16.1	5.6	11.2	6.1
Québec	22.2	21.7	16.2	16.6	4.7	11.8	6.8
Canada	20.1	25.6	10.8	18.2	4.4	13.3	7.5
				Males			
Longueuil	22.5	21.3	19.4	14.8	4.7	10.6	6.7
Québec	22.5	20.5	20.0	14.9	4.0	10.8	7.2
Canada	20.6	24.9	14.5	15.9	3.9	12.4	7.8
				Females			
Longueuil	22.8	23.7	12.5	17.3	6.5	11.7	5.5
Québec	21.9	22.8	12.5	18.3	5.4	12.8	6.3
Canada	19.6	26.2	7.3	20.4	4.9	14.3	7.2

Note: Figures cover total population aged 15 years and over by highest certificate, diploma or degree; (1) Includes persons who have graduated from a secondary school or equivalent. It excludes persons with a postsecondary certificate, diploma or degree; (2) Includes Registered Apprenticeship certificates (including Certificate of Qualification, Journeyperson's designation) and other trades certificates or diplomas such as pre-employment or vocational certificates and diplomas from brief trade programs completed at community colleges, institutes of technology, vocational centres, and similar institutions; (3) Comparisons with other data sources suggest that the category 'University certificate or diploma below the bachelor's level' was over-reported in the NHS. This category likely includes some responses that are actually college certificates or diplomas, bachelor's degrees or other types of education (e.g., university transfer programs, bachelor's programs completed in other countries, incomplete bachelor's programs, non-university professional designations). We recommend users interpret the results for the 'University certificate or diploma below the bachelor's level' category with caution; (4) 'University certificate or diploma above bachelor level' includes the categories: 'Degree in medicine, dentistry, veterinary medicine or optometry,' 'Master's degree' and 'Earned doctorate.'
Source: Statistics Canada. 2013. 2011 National Household Survey. Statistics Canada Catalogue no. 99-004-XWE. Ottawa. Released September 11, 2013.

Household Income Distribution

Area	Less than $10,000	$10,000 to $19,999	$20,000 to $29,999	$30,000 to $39,999	$40,000 to $49,999	$50,000 to $59,999	$60,000 to $79,999	$80,000 to $99,999	$100,000 to $124,999	$125,000 to $149,999	$150,000 and Over
					Households						
Longueuil	5,695	11,375	10,645	11,765	10,065	9,870	14,800	10,090	7,760	4,130	5,875
Québec	179,790	377,210	353,470	382,000	343,730	302,595	483,085	344,435	267,995	148,950	211,965
Canada	626,705	1,141,945	1,193,925	1,271,675	1,206,800	1,102,120	1,865,280	1,458,240	1,260,770	802,555	1,389,240
					Percent of Households						
Longueuil	5.6	11.1	10.4	11.5	9.9	9.7	14.5	9.9	7.6	4.0	5.8
Québec	5.3	11.1	10.4	11.3	10.1	8.9	14.2	10.1	7.9	4.4	6.2
Canada	4.7	8.6	9.0	9.5	9.1	8.3	14.0	10.9	9.5	6.0	10.4

Note: Household income is the sum of the total incomes of all members of that household. Total income refers to monetary receipts from certain sources, before income taxes and deductions, during calendar year 2010.
Source: Statistics Canada. 2013. 2011 National Household Survey. Statistics Canada Catalogue no. 99-004-XWE. Ottawa. Released September 11, 2013.

Median and Average Household and Economic Family Income

Area	Median Household Income ($)	Average Household Income ($)	Median After-tax Household Income ($)	Average After-tax Household Income ($)	Median Economic Family Income ($)	Average Economic Family Income ($)	Median After-tax Economic Family Income ($)	Average After-tax Economic Family Income ($)
Longueuil	51,336	63,686	45,322	53,259	68,020	79,517	59,226	66,271
Québec	51,842	66,205	45,968	55,121	68,344	82,045	59,560	68,091
Canada	61,072	79,102	54,089	66,149	76,511	94,125	67,044	78,517

Note: Figures cover household and economic familiy income in 2010. A household is defined as a person or a group of persons (other than foreign residents) who occupy the same private dwelling and do not have a usual place of residence elsewhere in Canada. Every person is a member of one and only one household. An economic family is defined as a group of two or more persons who live in the same dwelling and are related to each other by blood, marriage, common-law, adoption or a foster relationship. A couple may be of opposite or same sex.
Source: Statistics Canada. 2013. 2011 National Household Survey. Statistics Canada Catalogue no. 99-004-XWE. Ottawa. Released September 11, 2013.

Individual Income Distribution

Area	Less than $10,000	$10,000 to $19,999	$20,000 to $29,999	$30,000 to $39,999	$40,000 to $49,999	$50,000 to $59,999	$60,000 to $79,999	$80,000 to $99,999	$100,000 to $124,999	$125,000 and Over
					Number					
					Total					
Longueuil	30,375	38,095	28,175	26,760	20,000	13,805	14,955	6,375	3,045	2,880
Québec	1,005,600	1,309,515	941,630	866,290	653,400	449,185	515,815	211,070	109,975	120,915
Canada	4,492,040	4,835,710	3,670,020	3,180,360	2,603,520	1,921,650	2,437,440	1,302,045	693,580	782,135
					Males					
Longueuil	13,590	14,295	12,480	13,630	10,050	7,660	9,220	4,085	2,195	2,280
Québec	441,455	516,150	427,295	432,625	345,950	256,700	313,880	143,785	80,000	91,475
Canada	1,936,365	1,864,880	1,588,260	1,522,190	1,333,510	1,079,780	1,473,145	823,720	492,905	599,905
					Females					
Longueuil	16,780	23,800	15,700	13,130	9,950	6,145	5,735	2,290	850	595
Québec	564,150	793,365	514,335	433,670	307,455	192,485	201,935	67,275	29,980	29,440
Canada	2,555,675	2,970,825	2,081,760	1,658,170	1,270,010	841,870	964,300	478,330	200,680	182,230
					Percent of Population					
					Total					
Longueuil	16.5	20.7	15.3	14.5	10.8	7.5	8.1	3.5	1.7	1.6
Québec	16.3	21.2	15.2	14.0	10.6	7.3	8.3	3.4	1.8	2.0
Canada	17.3	18.7	14.2	12.3	10.0	7.4	9.4	5.0	2.7	3.0
					Males					
Longueuil	15.2	16.0	13.9	15.2	11.2	8.6	10.3	4.6	2.5	2.5
Québec	14.5	16.9	14.0	14.2	11.3	8.4	10.3	4.7	2.6	3.0
Canada	15.2	14.7	12.5	12.0	10.5	8.5	11.6	6.5	3.9	4.7
					Females					
Longueuil	17.7	25.1	16.5	13.8	10.5	6.5	6.0	2.4	0.9	0.6
Québec	18.0	25.3	16.4	13.8	9.8	6.1	6.4	2.1	1.0	0.9
Canada	19.4	22.5	15.8	12.6	9.6	6.4	7.3	3.6	1.5	1.4

Note: Figures cover individuals aged 15 years and over with income. Income refers to monetary receipts from certain sources, before income taxes and deductions, during calendar year 2010.
Source: Statistics Canada. 2013. 2011 National Household Survey. Statistics Canada Catalogue no. 99-004-XWE. Ottawa. Released September 11, 2013.

Labour Force Status

Area	In the Labour Force - All	In the Labour Force - Employed	In the Labour Force - Unemployed	Not in the Labour Force
	Number			
	Total			
Longueuil	124,985	115,665	9,320	68,515
Québec	4,183,445	3,880,425	303,020	2,291,145
Canada	17,990,080	16,595,035	1,395,045	9,269,445
	Males			
Longueuil	64,910	59,615	5,295	28,515
Québec	2,188,555	2,014,810	173,745	982,080
Canada	9,388,570	8,634,310	754,255	3,906,785
	Females			
Longueuil	60,075	56,045	4,025	40,000
Québec	1,994,885	1,865,610	129,275	1,309,065
Canada	8,601,515	7,960,725	640,790	5,362,660
	Percent of Labour Force			
	Total			
Longueuil	64.6	59.8	7.5	35.4
Québec	64.6	59.9	7.2	35.4
Canada	66.0	60.9	7.8	34.0
	Males			
Longueuil	69.5	63.8	8.2	30.5
Québec	69.0	63.5	7.9	31.0
Canada	70.6	64.9	8.0	29.4
	Females			
Longueuil	60.0	56.0	6.7	40.0
Québec	60.4	56.5	6.5	39.6
Canada	61.6	57.0	7.4	38.4

Note: Figures are based on total population 15 years and over
Source: Statistics Canada. 2013. 2011 National Household Survey. Statistics Canada Catalogue no. 99-004-XWE. Ottawa. Released September 11, 2013.

Labour Force by Industry (NAICS Codes 11–52)

Area	Agriculture, forestry, fishing & hunting	Mining, quarrying, & oil & gas extraction	Utilities	Construction	Manufacturing	Wholesale Trade	Retail Trade	Transportation & warehousing	Information & cultural industries	Finance & insurance
					Number Total					
Longueuil	265	130	1,420	6,125	13,040	5,000	16,785	6,430	4,540	5,975
Québec	84,470	20,770	33,815	241,780	476,390	169,825	501,380	181,295	98,340	159,230
Canada	437,650	261,050	149,940	1,215,380	1,619,295	733,445	2,031,665	827,780	420,830	767,960
					Males					
Longueuil	185	85	995	5,435	9,375	3,420	8,035	4,870	2,640	2,045
Québec	61,540	18,035	24,560	213,605	343,345	113,545	234,725	137,745	56,455	56,930
Canada	307,370	211,690	110,765	1,068,710	1,167,680	494,545	933,850	617,305	235,875	296,995
					Females					
Longueuil	85	45	430	690	3,665	1,580	8,755	1,560	1,905	3,930
Québec	22,925	2,730	9,255	28,170	133,045	56,280	266,650	43,550	41,885	102,295
Canada	130,285	49,360	39,175	146,670	451,615	238,900	1,097,820	210,475	184,955	470,960
					Percent of Labour Force Total					
Longueuil	0.2	0.1	1.2	5.0	10.7	4.1	13.8	5.3	3.7	4.9
Québec	2.1	0.5	0.8	5.9	11.7	4.2	12.3	4.4	2.4	3.9
Canada	2.5	1.5	0.9	6.9	9.2	4.2	11.6	4.7	2.4	4.4
					Males					
Longueuil	0.3	0.1	1.6	8.6	14.9	5.4	12.8	7.7	4.2	3.2
Québec	2.9	0.8	1.1	10.0	16.1	5.3	11.0	6.4	2.6	2.7
Canada	3.3	2.3	1.2	11.6	12.7	5.4	10.2	6.7	2.6	3.2
					Females					
Longueuil	0.1	0.1	0.7	1.2	6.3	2.7	15.0	2.7	3.3	6.7
Québec	1.2	0.1	0.5	1.4	6.8	2.9	13.7	2.2	2.2	5.3
Canada	1.6	0.6	0.5	1.7	5.4	2.8	13.1	2.5	2.2	5.6

Note: Figures are based on total experienced labour force 15 years and over. Experienced labour force refers to persons who, during the week of Sunday, May 1 to Saturday, May 7, 2011, were employed and the unemployed who had last worked for pay or in self-employment in either 2010 or 2011.
Source: Statistics Canada. 2013. 2011 National Household Survey. Statistics Canada Catalogue no. 99-004-XWE. Ottawa. Released September 11, 2013.

Labour Force by Industry (NAICS Codes 53–91)

Area	Real estate & rental & leasing	Profess., scientific & tech. services	Mgmt of companies & enterprises	Admin. & support, waste mgmt & remed. services	Educational services	Health care & social assistance	Arts, entertain. & recreation	Accomm. & food services	Other services (except public admin.)	Public admin.
					Number Total					
Longueuil	1,975	9,615	140	5,675	8,150	14,495	2,240	7,030	4,970	7,520
Québec	61,365	282,115	3,965	156,130	301,425	496,125	78,795	253,145	189,290	295,480
Canada	321,895	1,240,850	17,460	728,330	1,301,435	1,949,650	363,405	1,130,750	807,800	1,261,050
					Males					
Longueuil	1,230	5,535	50	3,395	2,705	2,750	1,115	3,230	2,155	3,770
Québec	35,940	158,920	2,250	92,530	99,565	97,255	41,535	112,650	88,710	147,645
Canada	179,090	688,625	9,380	411,250	424,915	349,430	188,270	469,990	372,940	652,510
					Females					
Longueuil	740	4,080	90	2,280	5,445	11,750	1,130	3,805	2,810	3,750
Québec	25,425	123,205	1,715	63,605	201,860	398,870	37,260	140,495	100,585	147,835
Canada	142,805	552,225	8,075	317,085	876,515	1,600,220	175,135	660,760	434,865	608,535
					Percent of Labour Force Total					
Longueuil	1.6	7.9	0.1	4.7	6.7	11.9	1.8	5.8	4.1	6.2
Québec	1.5	6.9	0.1	3.8	7.4	12.1	1.9	6.2	4.6	7.2
Canada	1.8	7.1	0.1	4.1	7.4	11.1	2.1	6.4	4.6	7.2
					Males					
Longueuil	2.0	8.8	0.1	5.4	4.3	4.4	1.8	5.1	3.4	6.0
Québec	1.7	7.4	0.1	4.3	4.7	4.5	1.9	5.3	4.2	6.9
Canada	1.9	7.5	0.1	4.5	4.6	3.8	2.0	5.1	4.1	7.1
					Females					
Longueuil	1.3	7.0	0.2	3.9	9.3	20.1	1.9	6.5	4.8	6.4
Québec	1.3	6.3	0.1	3.3	10.4	20.5	1.9	7.2	5.2	7.6
Canada	1.7	6.6	0.1	3.8	10.4	19.1	2.1	7.9	5.2	7.2

Note: Figures are based on total experienced labour force 15 years and over. Experienced labour force refers to persons who, during the week of Sunday, May 1 to Saturday, May 7, 2011, were employed and the unemployed who had last worked for pay or in self-employment in either 2010 or 2011.
Source: Statistics Canada. 2013. 2011 National Household Survey. Statistics Canada Catalogue no. 99-004-XWE. Ottawa. Released September 11, 2013.

PROFILES / Longueuil, Québec

Occupation

Area	Mgmt	Business, Finance & Admin.	Natural/ Applied Sciences & Related	Health	Education, Law & Social, Community & Government Services	Art, Culture, Recreation & Sport	Sales & Service	Trades, Transport & Equip. Operators & Related	Natural Resources, Agri. & Related Production	Mfg & Utilities
					Number					
					Total					
Longueuil	10,310	23,960	9,455	7,490	12,270	3,670	31,320	16,670	795	5,590
Québec	411,425	687,715	287,015	268,610	479,505	123,665	969,740	573,075	65,625	218,740
Canada	1,963,600	2,902,045	1,237,775	1,107,200	2,064,675	503,415	4,068,170	2,537,775	397,930	805,040
					Males					
Longueuil	5,970	7,940	7,435	1,315	3,705	1,865	14,645	15,595	755	3,790
Québec	261,620	207,545	221,430	53,480	148,715	58,150	436,370	542,055	53,640	154,485
Canada	1,229,460	854,190	966,355	217,520	676,550	232,535	1,745,705	2,385,615	318,945	564,300
					Females					
Longueuil	4,340	16,020	2,020	6,180	8,565	1,810	16,670	1,075	40	1,795
Québec	149,800	480,170	65,585	215,130	330,795	65,520	533,370	31,025	11,995	64,250
Canada	734,140	2,047,855	271,415	889,675	1,388,130	270,875	2,322,465	152,165	78,980	240,740
					Percent of Labour Force					
					Total					
Longueuil	8.5	19.7	7.8	6.2	10.1	3.0	25.8	13.7	0.7	4.6
Québec	10.1	16.8	7.0	6.6	11.7	3.0	23.7	14.0	1.6	5.4
Canada	11.2	16.5	7.0	6.3	11.7	2.9	23.1	14.4	2.3	4.6
					Males					
Longueuil	9.5	12.6	11.8	2.1	5.9	3.0	23.2	24.7	1.2	6.0
Québec	12.2	9.7	10.4	2.5	7.0	2.7	20.4	25.4	2.5	7.2
Canada	13.4	9.3	10.5	2.4	7.4	2.5	19.0	26.0	3.5	6.1
					Females					
Longueuil	7.4	27.4	3.5	10.6	14.6	3.1	28.5	1.8	0.1	3.1
Québec	7.7	24.7	3.4	11.0	17.0	3.4	27.4	1.6	0.6	3.3
Canada	8.7	24.4	3.2	10.6	16.5	3.2	27.7	1.8	0.9	2.9

Note: Figures are based on total experienced labour force 15 years and over.
Source: Statistics Canada. 2013. 2011 National Household Survey. Statistics Canada Catalogue no. 99-004-XWE. Ottawa. Released September 11, 2013.

Place of Work Status

Area	Worked at Home	Worked Outside Canada	No Fixed Workplace Address	Worked at Usual Place
		Number		
		Total		
Longueuil	4,760	215	9,925	100,755
Québec	237,625	9,705	331,525	3,301,560
Canada	1,142,640	66,460	1,868,245	13,517,690
		Males		
Longueuil	2,515	170	7,330	49,605
Québec	122,060	7,055	249,535	1,636,165
Canada	582,150	47,355	1,400,485	6,604,325
		Females		
Longueuil	2,250	45	2,595	51,155
Québec	115,565	2,650	81,995	1,665,395
Canada	560,490	19,100	467,760	6,913,370
		Percent of Labour Force		
		Total		
Longueuil	4.1	0.2	8.6	87.1
Québec	6.1	0.3	8.5	85.1
Canada	6.9	0.4	11.3	81.5
		Males		
Longueuil	4.2	0.3	12.3	83.2
Québec	6.1	0.4	12.4	81.2
Canada	6.7	0.5	16.2	76.5
		Females		
Longueuil	4.0	0.1	4.6	91.3
Québec	6.2	0.1	4.4	89.3
Canada	7.0	0.2	5.9	86.8

Note: Figures are based on total employed labour force 15 years and over.
Source: Statistics Canada. 2013. 2011 National Household Survey. Statistics Canada Catalogue no. 99-004-XWE. Ottawa. Released September 11, 2013.

Mode of Transportation to Work

Area	Car; Truck; Van; as Driver	Car; Truck; Van; as Passenger	Public Transit	Walked	Bicycled	All Other Modes
			Number			
			Total			
Longueuil	75,475	3,670	24,550	4,545	1,435	1,010
Québec	2,713,295	136,490	484,600	215,210	48,870	34,620
Canada	11,393,140	867,050	1,851,525	880,815	201,780	191,625
			Males			
Longueuil	42,260	1,305	10,065	1,835	1,075	390
Québec	1,484,305	50,905	203,035	95,100	33,065	19,285
Canada	6,238,835	349,530	788,290	387,580	135,840	104,725
			Females			
Longueuil	33,215	2,365	14,480	2,710	360	625
Québec	1,228,995	85,585	281,565	120,110	15,800	15,335
Canada	5,154,305	517,520	1,063,235	493,230	65,940	86,900
			Percent of Labour Force			
			Total			
Longueuil	68.2	3.3	22.2	4.1	1.3	0.9
Québec	74.7	3.8	13.3	5.9	1.3	1.0
Canada	74.0	5.6	12.0	5.7	1.3	1.2
			Males			
Longueuil	74.2	2.3	17.7	3.2	1.9	0.7
Québec	78.7	2.7	10.8	5.0	1.8	1.0
Canada	77.9	4.4	9.8	4.8	1.7	1.3
			Females			
Longueuil	61.8	4.4	26.9	5.0	0.7	1.2
Québec	70.3	4.9	16.1	6.9	0.9	0.9
Canada	69.8	7.0	14.4	6.7	0.9	1.2

Note: Figures are based on total employed labour force 15 years and over.
Source: Statistics Canada. 2013. 2011 National Household Survey. Statistics Canada Catalogue no. 99-004-XWE. Ottawa. Released September 11, 2013.

Visible Minority Population Characteristics

Area	Total Minority	South Asian[1]	Chinese	Black	Filipino	Latin American	Arab	SE Asian[2]	West Asian[3]	Korean	Japanese	Multiple[4]
						Number						
						Total						
Longueuil	32,380	2,085	2,870	10,500	480	5,810	5,290	2,605	1,275	195	170	560
Québec	850,235	83,320	82,845	243,625	31,495	116,380	166,260	65,855	23,445	6,665	4,025	17,420
Canada	6,264,750	1,567,400	1,324,750	945,665	619,310	381,280	380,620	312,075	206,840	161,130	87,270	171,935
						Males						
Longueuil	16,000	1,095	1,335	4,865	180	2,960	2,920	1,335	605	95	50	255
Québec	418,545	43,410	37,295	116,605	12,435	56,940	89,505	32,940	12,070	3,135	1,565	8,315
Canada	3,043,010	790,755	632,325	453,005	268,885	186,355	203,485	154,035	105,620	77,165	38,270	83,335
						Females						
Longueuil	16,385	990	1,530	5,635	305	2,855	2,365	1,265	670	100	125	300
Québec	431,695	39,915	45,550	127,020	19,055	59,440	76,750	32,920	11,380	3,530	2,465	9,105
Canada	3,221,745	776,650	692,420	492,660	350,425	194,925	177,140	158,045	101,220	83,965	48,990	88,600
						Percent of Population						
						Total						
Longueuil	14.2	0.9	1.3	4.6	0.2	2.5	2.3	1.1	0.6	0.1	0.1	0.2
Québec	11.0	1.1	1.1	3.2	0.4	1.5	2.2	0.9	0.3	0.1	0.1	0.2
Canada	19.1	4.8	4.0	2.9	1.9	1.2	1.2	0.9	0.6	0.5	0.3	0.5
						Males						
Longueuil	14.4	1.0	1.2	4.4	0.2	2.7	2.6	1.2	0.5	0.1	0.0	0.2
Québec	11.0	1.1	1.0	3.1	0.3	1.5	2.3	0.9	0.3	0.1	0.0	0.2
Canada	18.8	4.9	3.9	2.8	1.7	1.2	1.3	1.0	0.7	0.5	0.2	0.5
						Females						
Longueuil	14.0	0.8	1.3	4.8	0.3	2.4	2.0	1.1	0.6	0.1	0.1	0.3
Québec	11.0	1.0	1.2	3.2	0.5	1.5	2.0	0.8	0.3	0.1	0.1	0.2
Canada	19.3	4.7	4.1	3.0	2.1	1.2	1.1	0.9	0.6	0.5	0.3	0.5

Note: The Employment Equity Act defines visible minorities as 'persons, other than Aboriginal peoples, who are non-Caucasian in race or non-white in colour';
(1) Includes 'East Indian,' 'Pakistani,' 'Sri Lankan,' etc.; (2) Includes 'Vietnamese,' 'Cambodian,' 'Malaysian,' 'Laotian,' etc.; (3) Includes 'Iranian,' 'Afghan,' etc.; (4) Includes respondents who reported more than one visible minority group by checking two or more mark-in circles, e.g., 'Black' and 'South Asian.'
Source: Statistics Canada. 2013. 2011 National Household Survey. Statistics Canada Catalogue no. 99-004-XWE. Ottawa. Released September 11, 2013.

PROFILES / Longueuil, Québec

Aboriginal Population

Area	Aboriginal Identity[1]	First Nations (North American Indian) Single Identity[2]	Métis Single Identity	Inuk (Inuit) Single Identity	Multiple Aboriginal Identities[3]	Aboriginal Identities Not Included Elsewhere
			Number			
			Total			
Longueuil	2,230	1,330	645	50	25	180
Québec	141,915	82,425	40,960	12,570	1,545	4,415
Canada	1,400,685	851,560	451,795	59,440	11,415	26,475
			Males			
Longueuil	1,030	615	290	25	10	90
Québec	70,205	40,105	21,300	6,265	720	1,815
Canada	682,190	411,785	223,335	29,495	5,525	12,055
			Females			
Longueuil	1,200	715	355	25	20	85
Québec	71,710	42,315	19,660	6,305	830	2,600
Canada	718,500	439,775	228,460	29,950	5,890	14,420
			Percent of Population			
			Total			
Longueuil	1.0	0.6	0.3	0.0	0.0	0.1
Québec	1.8	1.1	0.5	0.2	0.0	0.1
Canada	4.3	2.6	1.4	0.2	0.0	0.1
			Males			
Longueuil	0.9	0.6	0.3	0.0	0.0	0.1
Québec	1.8	1.1	0.6	0.2	0.0	0.0
Canada	4.2	2.5	1.4	0.2	0.0	0.1
			Females			
Longueuil	1.0	0.6	0.3	0.0	0.0	0.1
Québec	1.8	1.1	0.5	0.2	0.0	0.1
Canada	4.3	2.6	1.4	0.2	0.0	0.1

Note: (1) Includes persons who reported being an Aboriginal person, that is, First Nations (North American Indian), Métis or Inuk (Inuit) and/or those who reported Registered or Treaty Indian status, that is registered under the Indian Act of Canada, and/or those who reported membership in a First Nation or Indian band. Aboriginal peoples of Canada are defined in the Constitution Act, 1982, section 35-2 as including the Indian, Inuit and Métis peoples of Canada; (2) Users should be aware that the estimates associated with this variable are more affected than most by the incomplete enumeration of certain Indian reserves and Indian settlements in the National Household Survey (NHS); (3) Includes persons who reported being any two or all three of the following: First Nations (North American Indian), Métis or Inuk (Inuit).
Source: Statistics Canada. 2013. 2011 National Household Survey. Statistics Canada Catalogue no. 99-004-XWE. Ottawa. Released September 11, 2013.

Ethnic Origin

Area	North American Aboriginal	Other North American	European	Caribbean	Latin, Central and South American	African	Asian	Oceania
				Number				
				Total				
Longueuil	8,135	134,355	103,505	6,895	6,945	11,035	13,970	75
Québec	307,445	4,776,875	3,390,330	167,590	137,255	260,785	488,905	2,305
Canada	1,836,035	11,070,455	20,157,965	627,590	544,375	766,735	5,011,225	74,875
				Males				
Longueuil	3,985	64,695	50,065	3,260	3,430	5,660	6,920	35
Québec	146,725	2,345,180	1,678,310	77,665	67,195	135,740	241,515	1,135
Canada	885,675	5,462,685	9,913,150	291,640	264,635	387,360	2,435,540	37,490
				Females				
Longueuil	4,155	69,665	53,440	3,640	3,510	5,370	7,050	35
Québec	160,725	2,431,700	1,712,015	89,925	70,065	125,040	247,390	1,175
Canada	950,360	5,607,770	10,244,820	335,945	279,740	379,380	2,575,680	37,385
				Percent of Population				
				Total				
Longueuil	3.6	58.9	45.4	3.0	3.0	4.8	6.1	0.0
Québec	4.0	61.8	43.8	2.2	1.8	3.4	6.3	0.0
Canada	5.6	33.7	61.4	1.9	1.7	2.3	15.3	0.2
				Males				
Longueuil	3.6	58.4	45.2	2.9	3.1	5.1	6.2	0.0
Québec	3.8	61.5	44.0	2.0	1.8	3.6	6.3	0.0
Canada	5.5	33.8	61.3	1.8	1.6	2.4	15.1	0.2
				Females				
Longueuil	3.5	59.5	45.6	3.1	3.0	4.6	6.0	0.0
Québec	4.1	62.1	43.7	2.3	1.8	3.2	6.3	0.0
Canada	5.7	33.6	61.4	2.0	1.7	2.3	15.4	0.2

Note: The sum of the ethnic groups in this table is greater than the total population estimate because a person may report more than one ethnic origin in the NHS.
Source: Statistics Canada. 2013. 2011 National Household Survey. Statistics Canada Catalogue no. 99-004-XWE. Ottawa. Released September 11, 2013.

Religion

Area	Buddhist	Christian	Hindu	Jewish	Muslim	Sikh	Traditional (Aboriginal) Spirituality	Other Religions	No Religious Affiliation
				Number Total					
Longueuil	1,955	181,230	545	185	9,565	65	0	415	34,000
Québec	52,390	6,356,880	33,540	85,100	243,430	9,275	2,025	12,340	937,545
Canada	366,830	22,102,745	497,965	329,495	1,053,945	454,965	64,935	130,835	7,850,605
				Males					
Longueuil	920	85,870	310	110	4,945	55	0	185	18,450
Québec	24,630	3,079,855	17,055	41,455	128,815	5,090	925	6,155	510,055
Canada	168,465	10,497,775	250,435	161,265	540,555	229,435	31,805	57,745	4,225,645
				Females					
Longueuil	1,035	95,365	240	75	4,625	0	0	230	15,550
Québec	27,760	3,277,020	16,480	43,645	114,615	4,185	1,100	6,175	427,485
Canada	198,365	11,604,975	247,525	168,235	513,395	225,530	33,135	73,090	3,624,965
				Percent of Population Total					
Longueuil	0.9	79.5	0.2	0.1	4.2	0.0	0.0	0.2	14.9
Québec	0.7	82.2	0.4	1.1	3.1	0.1	0.0	0.2	12.1
Canada	1.1	67.3	1.5	1.0	3.2	1.4	0.2	0.4	23.9
				Males					
Longueuil	0.8	77.5	0.3	0.1	4.5	0.0	0.0	0.2	16.6
Québec	0.6	80.8	0.4	1.1	3.4	0.1	0.0	0.2	13.4
Canada	1.0	64.9	1.5	1.0	3.3	1.4	0.2	0.4	26.1
				Females					
Longueuil	0.9	81.4	0.2	0.1	3.9	0.0	0.0	0.2	13.3
Québec	0.7	83.6	0.4	1.1	2.9	0.1	0.0	0.2	10.9
Canada	1.2	69.5	1.5	1.0	3.1	1.4	0.2	0.4	21.7

Note: Religion refers to the person's self-identification as having a connection or affiliation with any religious denomination, group, body, sect, cult or other religiously defined community or system of belief. Religion is not limited to formal membership in a religious organization or group. Persons without a religious connection or affiliation can self-identify as atheist, agnostic or humanist, or can provide another applicable response.
Source: Statistics Canada. 2013. 2011 National Household Survey. Statistics Canada Catalogue no. 99-004-XWE. Ottawa. Released September 11, 2013.

Religion—Christian Denominations

Area	Anglican	Baptist	Catholic	Christian Orthodox	Lutheran	Pentecostal	Presbyterian	United Church	Other Christian
				Number Total					
Longueuil	1,595	1,145	163,200	3,545	155	1,905	280	775	8,635
Québec	73,550	36,615	5,775,740	129,780	7,200	41,070	11,440	32,930	248,560
Canada	1,631,845	635,840	12,810,705	550,690	478,185	478,705	472,385	2,007,610	3,036,780
				Males					
Longueuil	670	575	77,540	1,685	65	860	135	345	3,995
Québec	34,815	16,585	2,802,920	63,960	3,425	18,640	5,265	14,945	119,305
Canada	752,945	293,905	6,167,290	270,205	221,525	217,850	218,955	912,545	1,442,550
				Females					
Longueuil	925	570	85,660	1,860	85	1,045	145	430	4,640
Québec	38,735	20,030	2,972,820	65,820	3,770	22,430	6,175	17,985	129,260
Canada	878,900	341,940	6,643,415	280,485	256,660	260,850	253,430	1,095,065	1,594,230
				Percent of Population Total					
Longueuil	0.7	0.5	71.6	1.6	0.1	0.8	0.1	0.3	3.8
Québec	1.0	0.5	74.7	1.7	0.1	0.5	0.1	0.4	3.2
Canada	5.0	1.9	39.0	1.7	1.5	1.5	1.4	6.1	9.2
				Males					
Longueuil	0.6	0.5	70.0	1.5	0.1	0.8	0.1	0.3	3.6
Québec	0.9	0.4	73.5	1.7	0.1	0.5	0.1	0.4	3.1
Canada	4.7	1.8	38.2	1.7	1.4	1.3	1.4	5.6	8.9
				Females					
Longueuil	0.8	0.5	73.1	1.6	0.1	0.9	0.1	0.4	4.0
Québec	1.0	0.5	75.9	1.7	0.1	0.6	0.2	0.5	3.3
Canada	5.3	2.0	39.8	1.7	1.5	1.6	1.5	6.6	9.6

Note: Religion refers to the person's self-identification as having a connection or affiliation with any religious denomination, group, body, sect, cult or other religiously defined community or system of belief. Religion is not limited to formal membership in a religious organization or group. Persons without a religious connection or affiliation can self-identify as atheist, agnostic or humanist, or can provide another applicable response.
Source: Statistics Canada. 2013. 2011 National Household Survey. Statistics Canada Catalogue no. 99-004-XWE. Ottawa. Released September 11, 2013.

PROFILES / Longueuil, Québec

Immigrant Status and Period of Immigration

Area	Non-Immigrants[1]	Immigrants All	Before 1971	1971 to 1980	1981 to 1990	1991 to 2000	2001 to 2005	2006 to 2011	Non-Permanent Residents[3]
Number									
Total									
Longueuil	192,885	33,500	3,650	4,555	4,135	5,585	6,665	8,905	1,580
Québec	6,690,530	974,895	151,825	115,640	130,680	195,925	157,425	223,400	67,095
Canada	25,720,175	6,775,765	1,261,055	870,775	949,890	1,539,050	992,070	1,162,915	356,385
Males									
Longueuil	93,470	16,570	1,845	2,300	1,895	2,655	3,400	4,470	795
Québec	3,301,435	477,240	75,255	57,410	64,080	94,110	76,780	109,605	35,370
Canada	12,753,235	3,231,370	605,430	416,670	454,570	724,905	474,545	555,245	178,515
Females									
Longueuil	99,415	16,930	1,805	2,260	2,240	2,930	3,260	4,435	785
Québec	3,389,095	497,655	76,565	58,235	66,600	101,810	80,645	113,795	31,725
Canada	12,966,935	3,544,400	655,625	454,105	495,325	814,145	517,530	607,670	177,870
Percent of Population									
Total									
Longueuil	84.6	14.7	1.6	2.0	1.8	2.4	2.9	3.9	0.7
Québec	86.5	12.6	2.0	1.5	1.7	2.5	2.0	2.9	0.9
Canada	78.3	20.6	3.8	2.7	2.9	4.7	3.0	3.5	1.1
Males									
Longueuil	84.3	15.0	1.7	2.1	1.7	2.4	3.1	4.0	0.7
Québec	86.6	12.5	2.0	1.5	1.7	2.5	2.0	2.9	0.9
Canada	78.9	20.0	3.7	2.6	2.8	4.5	2.9	3.4	1.1
Females									
Longueuil	84.9	14.5	1.5	1.9	1.9	2.5	2.8	3.8	0.7
Québec	86.5	12.7	2.0	1.5	1.7	2.6	2.1	2.9	0.8
Canada	77.7	21.2	3.9	2.7	3.0	4.9	3.1	3.6	1.1

Note: (1) Non-immigrant refers to a person who is a Canadian citizen by birth; (2) Immigrant refers to a person who is or has ever been a landed immigrant/permanent resident. This person has been granted the right to live in Canada permanently by immigration authorities. Some immigrants have resided in Canada for a number of years, while others have arrived recently. Some immigrants are Canadian citizens, while others are not. Most immigrants are born outside Canada, but a small number are born in Canada. In the 2011 National Household Survey, 'Immigrants' includes immigrants who landed in Canada prior to May 10, 2011; (3) Non-permanent resident refers to a person from another country who has a work or study permit, or who is a refugee claimant, and any non-Canadian-born family member living in Canada with them.
Source: Statistics Canada. 2013. 2011 National Household Survey. Statistics Canada Catalogue no. 99-004-XWE. Ottawa. Released September 11, 2013.

Mother Tongue

Area	English	French	Non-official Language	English & French	English & Non-official Language	French & Non-official Language	English, French & Non-official Language
Number							
Total							
Longueuil	14,155	181,800	28,115	2,460	390	2,305	330
Québec	599,225	6,102,210	961,700	64,800	23,435	51,640	12,950
Canada	18,858,980	7,054,975	6,567,680	144,685	396,330	74,430	24,095
Males							
Longueuil	6,965	87,680	13,860	1,220	200	1,155	180
Québec	297,875	2,994,300	472,635	32,390	11,455	25,810	6,790
Canada	9,345,225	3,452,380	3,157,785	69,975	192,000	36,535	11,965
Females							
Longueuil	7,190	94,120	14,250	1,235	190	1,150	155
Québec	301,355	3,107,910	489,060	32,405	11,975	25,825	6,155
Canada	9,513,750	3,602,590	3,409,895	74,710	204,330	37,890	12,130
Percent of Population							
Total							
Longueuil	6.2	79.2	12.2	1.1	0.2	1.0	0.1
Québec	7.7	78.1	12.3	0.8	0.3	0.7	0.2
Canada	56.9	21.3	19.8	0.4	1.2	0.2	0.1
Males							
Longueuil	6.3	78.8	12.5	1.1	0.2	1.0	0.2
Québec	7.8	78.0	12.3	0.8	0.3	0.7	0.2
Canada	57.5	21.2	19.4	0.4	1.2	0.2	0.1
Females							
Longueuil	6.1	79.6	12.0	1.0	0.2	1.0	0.1
Québec	7.6	78.2	12.3	0.8	0.3	0.6	0.2
Canada	56.4	21.4	20.2	0.4	1.2	0.2	0.1

Note: Figures cover total population excluding institutional residents.
Source: Statistics Canada. 2012. Census Profile. 2011 Census. Statistics Canada Catalogue no. 98-316-XWE. Ottawa. Released October 24 2012.
http://www12.statcan.gc.ca/census-recensement/2011/dp-pd/prof/index.cfm?Lang=E

Language Spoken Most Often at Home

Area	English	French	Non-official Language	English & French	English & Non-official Language	French & Non-official Language	English, French & Non-official Language
			Number				
			Total				
Longueuil	16,530	188,520	15,730	2,590	715	4,650	810
Québec	767,415	6,249,080	554,400	71,555	43,765	100,110	29,625
Canada	21,457,075	6,827,865	3,673,865	131,205	875,135	109,700	46,330
			Males				
Longueuil	8,110	91,230	7,545	1,300	370	2,285	420
Québec	379,915	3,071,635	268,640	35,860	21,305	48,590	15,315
Canada	10,585,620	3,348,235	1,767,310	63,475	425,370	53,010	22,845
			Females				
Longueuil	8,415	97,295	8,185	1,295	340	2,360	390
Québec	387,500	3,177,450	285,760	35,695	22,460	51,525	14,310
Canada	10,871,455	3,479,625	1,906,555	67,730	449,765	56,690	23,485
			Percent of Population				
			Total				
Longueuil	7.2	82.1	6.9	1.1	0.3	2.0	0.4
Québec	9.8	80.0	7.1	0.9	0.6	1.3	0.4
Canada	64.8	20.6	11.1	0.4	2.6	0.3	0.1
			Males				
Longueuil	7.3	82.0	6.8	1.2	0.3	2.1	0.4
Québec	9.9	80.0	7.0	0.9	0.6	1.3	0.4
Canada	65.1	20.6	10.9	0.4	2.6	0.3	0.1
			Females				
Longueuil	7.1	82.3	6.9	1.1	0.3	2.0	0.3
Québec	9.7	79.9	7.2	0.9	0.6	1.3	0.4
Canada	64.5	20.6	11.3	0.4	2.7	0.3	0.1

Note: Figures cover total population excluding institutional residents.
Source: Statistics Canada. 2012. Census Profile. 2011 Census. Statistics Canada Catalogue no. 98-316-XWE. Ottawa. Released October 24 2012.
http://www12.statcan.gc.ca/census-recensement/2011/dp-pd/prof/index.cfm?Lang=E

Knowledge of Official Languages

Area	English Only	French Only	English & French	Neither English nor French
		Number		
		Total		
Longueuil	6,435	109,935	111,205	1,980
Québec	363,860	4,047,175	3,328,725	76,190
Canada	22,564,665	4,165,015	5,795,570	595,920
		Males		
Longueuil	3,150	48,570	58,785	755
Québec	180,175	1,871,500	1,758,410	31,175
Canada	11,222,185	1,925,340	2,876,560	241,790
		Females		
Longueuil	3,280	61,365	52,420	1,220
Québec	183,690	2,175,675	1,570,310	45,015
Canada	11,342,485	2,239,680	2,919,005	354,135
		Percent of Population		
		Total		
Longueuil	2.8	47.9	48.4	0.9
Québec	4.7	51.8	42.6	1.0
Canada	68.1	12.6	17.5	1.8
		Males		
Longueuil	2.8	43.7	52.8	0.7
Québec	4.7	48.7	45.8	0.8
Canada	69.0	11.8	17.7	1.5
		Females		
Longueuil	2.8	51.9	44.3	1.0
Québec	4.6	54.7	39.5	1.1
Canada	67.3	13.3	17.3	2.1

Note: Figures cover total population excluding institutional residents.
Source: Statistics Canada. 2012. Census Profile. 2011 Census. Statistics Canada Catalogue no. 98-316-XWE. Ottawa. Released October 24 2012.
http://www12.statcan.gc.ca/census-recensement/2011/dp-pd/prof/index.cfm?Lang=E

Lévis, Québec

Background

Lévis is located on the south shore of the St. Lawrence River in eastern Québec, directly across from Québec City, the province's capital. Lévis' close proximity to Québec City (a 10-minute ferry ride of 1 kilometre) offers panoramic views of Old Québec's Château Frontenac and Cape Diamond.

Lévis was originally settled by Europeans in the early 17th century. Between 1865 and 1872, three British forts were built in Lévis to protect Québec City from American invasion. Today, the city's "Fort No. 1" is a National Historic Site of Canada. North America's first naval shipyard, the A.C. Davie Shipyard (1829), is located in Lévis and a variety of guided tours are offered through historic "Old Lévis" as well as neighbouring "Old Québec" across the river. The Maison Alphonse-Desjardins, another popular historical site dating from 1883, is a museum recreating the first credit union established in Canada, and before that the home of the Desjardins and their 10 children.

Fruit picking, sugar shacks and cheese making are at the centre of Lévis' renowned agri-tourism. The area's vineyards and cider makers are complemented by local farms offering tours and educational programs. Throughout the year, artists invite the public into their studios and workshops to admire local painting, sculpture, pottery and woodwork. Centre d'art de Lévis, Galerie d'Art des Deux-Ponts and Galerie Louise-Carrier are larger galleries featuring exhibitions of visual arts and crafts by Lévis artists. Sports and outdoor recreational activities such as canoeing, horseback riding, snowmobiling, skiing and dog sledding are popular activities for residents and visitors.

In 2012, the city hosted the Eastern Canadian Artistic Gymnastics and Trampoline Championships. In preparation for Canada's 150th birthday in 2017, Canadian Heritage granted the City of Lévis close to $8,000 through its "Building Communities through Arts and Heritage" program. Every year Lévis hosts community-minded events and festivals such as the Lévis Rodeo, Hot Air Balloon Festival, Festival Jazz etcetera Lévis, Operation Pumpkin and the Lévis Christmas Market.

Lévis has summer highs of plus 23.53 degrees Celsius, winter lows of minus 15.67 degrees Celsius, and an average rainfall just over 923 mm per year.

Rankings
- Lévis was ranked #21 out of 190 Canadian cities in *Money Sense Magazine's* "Top 35 Places to Live in 2012" rankings. The city's highest marks were awarded in the categories of weather, walk/bike to work percentage and discretionary income. *Money Sense Magazine, "Canada's Best Places to Live 2012," March 20, 2012*
- *Canadian Business Magazine* ranked Lévis as one of the best Canadian cities to do business: #2 out of the magazine's top 40 cities. Criteria: annual operating costs, cost of living index, building permit average growth (%), unemployment variance from 5.5%, and crime rate per 100,000 people. Sherbrooke ranked #1 and Québec City #3. *Canadian Business Magazine, "Best Places to do Business in Canada," 2008*
- Lévis ranked as Canada's safest city for online activity. Cybercrime includes web attacks, malware infections and city-generated spam. Fifty cities across Canada were ranked and the major cities of Québec dominated the "Top 10 Least Risky" rankings with seven out of the 10 spots. *Symantec, "Do you live in one of Canada's 'riskiest' online cities?", posted February 22nd, 2012*

PROFILES / Lévis, Québec

Population Growth and Density

Area	Population in 2001	Population in 2006	Population in 2011	Population Change 2001–2006	Population Change 2006–2011	Land Area (sq. km)	Population Density per sq. km
Lévis	121,999	130,006	138,769	6.6	6.7	449.31	308.8
Québec	7,237,479	7,546,131	7,903,001	4.3	4.7	1,356,547.02	5.8
Canada	30,007,094	31,612,897	33,476,688	5.4	5.9	8,965,121.42	3.7

Source: Statistics Canada. 2012. Census Profile. 2011 Census. Statistics Canada Catalogue no. 98-316-XWE. Ottawa. Released October 24 2012. http://www12.statcan.gc.ca/census-recensement/2011/dp-pd/prof/index.cfm?Lang=E;
Statistics Canada 2007. 2006 Community Profiles. 2006 Census. Statistics Canada Catalogue no. 92-591-XWE. Ottawa. Released March 13 2007. http://www12.statcan.ca/census-recensement/2006/dp-pd/prof/92-591/index.cfm?Lang=E

Gender

Area	Males	Females
Number		
Lévis	67,705	71,065
Québec	3,875,860	4,027,140
Canada	16,414,225	17,062,460
Percent of Population		
Lévis	48.8	51.2
Québec	49.0	51.0
Canada	49.0	51.0

Source: Statistics Canada. 2012. Census Profile. 2011 Census. Statistics Canada Catalogue no. 98-316-XWE. Ottawa. Released October 24 2012.
http://www12.statcan.gc.ca/census-recensement/2011/dp-pd/prof/index.cfm?Lang=E

Marital Status

Area	Married[1]	Living Common-law	Single[2]	Separated	Divorced	Widowed
Number						
Total						
Lévis	38,605	31,905	30,730	1,400	6,910	5,490
Québec	2,353,770	1,391,550	1,942,090	105,195	463,830	387,945
Canada	12,941,960	3,142,525	7,816,045	698,240	1,686,035	1,584,530
Males						
Lévis	19,300	15,985	16,005	610	2,680	1,030
Québec	1,177,720	697,695	1,045,540	46,465	188,265	77,430
Canada	6,470,300	1,575,495	4,206,320	299,655	680,415	310,940
Females						
Lévis	19,315	15,925	14,725	790	4,230	4,465
Québec	1,176,050	693,850	896,545	58,720	275,565	310,515
Canada	6,471,660	1,567,035	3,609,730	398,585	1,005,620	1,273,590
Percent of Population						
Total						
Lévis	33.6	27.7	26.7	1.2	6.0	4.8
Québec	35.4	20.9	29.2	1.6	7.0	5.8
Canada	46.4	11.3	28.0	2.5	6.0	5.7
Males						
Lévis	34.7	28.7	28.8	1.1	4.8	1.9
Québec	36.4	21.6	32.3	1.4	5.8	2.4
Canada	47.8	11.6	31.1	2.2	5.0	2.3
Females						
Lévis	32.5	26.8	24.8	1.3	7.1	7.5
Québec	34.5	20.3	26.3	1.7	8.1	9.1
Canada	45.2	10.9	25.2	2.8	7.0	8.9

Note: (1) and not separated, (2) never legally married
Source: Statistics Canada. 2012. Census Profile. 2011 Census. Statistics Canada Catalogue no. 98-316-XWE. Ottawa. Released October 24 2012.
http://www12.statcan.gc.ca/census-recensement/2011/dp-pd/prof/index.cfm?Lang=E

Age Characteristics: 0 to 49 Years

Area	0 to 4 Years	5 to 9 Years	10 to 14 Years	15 to 19 Years	20 to 24 Years	25 to 29 Years	30 to 34 Years	35 to 39 Years	40 to 44 Years	45 to 49 Years
					Number					
					Total					
Lévis	8,380	7,580	7,760	8,995	8,200	8,220	9,815	9,190	9,145	10,880
Québec	440,840	399,575	418,205	491,980	489,185	490,665	531,445	498,225	520,805	623,575
Canada	1,877,095	1,809,895	1,920,355	2,178,135	2,187,450	2,169,590	2,162,905	2,173,930	2,324,875	2,675,130
					Males					
Lévis	4,295	3,840	3,970	4,525	4,070	4,160	4,880	4,510	4,595	5,285
Québec	225,525	203,675	213,540	249,960	246,850	245,695	264,980	249,610	261,120	311,320
Canada	961,150	925,965	983,995	1,115,845	1,108,775	1,077,275	1,058,810	1,064,200	1,141,720	1,318,715
					Females					
Lévis	4,090	3,740	3,795	4,465	4,130	4,060	4,935	4,680	4,550	5,600
Québec	215,320	195,900	204,665	242,020	242,340	244,970	266,460	248,615	259,690	312,250
Canada	915,945	883,935	936,360	1,062,295	1,078,670	1,092,315	1,104,095	1,109,735	1,183,155	1,356,420
					Percent of Population					
					Total					
Lévis	6.0	5.5	5.6	6.5	5.9	5.9	7.1	6.6	6.6	7.8
Québec	5.6	5.1	5.3	6.2	6.2	6.2	6.7	6.3	6.6	7.9
Canada	5.6	5.4	5.7	6.5	6.5	6.5	6.5	6.5	6.9	8.0
					Males					
Lévis	6.3	5.7	5.9	6.7	6.0	6.1	7.2	6.7	6.8	7.8
Québec	5.8	5.3	5.5	6.4	6.4	6.3	6.8	6.4	6.7	8.0
Canada	5.9	5.6	6.0	6.8	6.8	6.6	6.5	6.5	7.0	8.0
					Females					
Lévis	5.8	5.3	5.3	6.3	5.8	5.7	6.9	6.6	6.4	7.9
Québec	5.3	4.9	5.1	6.0	6.0	6.1	6.6	6.2	6.4	7.8
Canada	5.4	5.2	5.5	6.2	6.3	6.4	6.5	6.5	6.9	7.9

Source: Statistics Canada. 2012. Census Profile. 2011 Census. Statistics Canada Catalogue no. 98-316-XWE. Ottawa. Released October 24 2012.
http://www12.statcan.gc.ca/census-recensement/2011/dp-pd/prof/index.cfm?Lang=E

Age Characteristics: 50 Years and Over, and Median Age

Area	50 to 54 Years	55 to 59 Years	60 to 64 Years	65 to 69 Years	70 to 74 Years	75 to 79 Years	80 to 84 Years	85 Years and Over	Median Age
				Number					
				Total					
Lévis	11,440	10,630	9,670	7,025	4,255	3,065	2,275	2,240	40.7
Québec	648,695	579,280	512,830	403,210	291,755	232,355	176,420	153,945	41.9
Canada	2,658,965	2,340,635	2,052,670	1,521,715	1,153,065	922,700	702,070	645,515	40.6
				Males					
Lévis	5,470	5,135	4,730	3,385	1,995	1,360	875	635	39.6
Québec	320,695	285,295	250,675	194,305	135,830	101,675	69,170	45,945	40.7
Canada	1,309,030	1,147,300	1,002,690	738,010	543,435	417,945	291,085	208,300	39.6
				Females					
Lévis	5,970	5,495	4,940	3,640	2,260	1,710	1,395	1,610	41.8
Québec	327,995	293,990	262,155	208,905	155,925	130,680	107,250	108,005	43.0
Canada	1,349,940	1,193,335	1,049,985	783,705	609,630	504,755	410,985	437,215	41.5
				Percent of Population					
				Total					
Lévis	8.2	7.7	7.0	5.1	3.1	2.2	1.6	1.6	—
Québec	8.2	7.3	6.5	5.1	3.7	2.9	2.2	1.9	—
Canada	7.9	7.0	6.1	4.5	3.4	2.8	2.1	1.9	—
				Males					
Lévis	8.1	7.6	7.0	5.0	2.9	2.0	1.3	0.9	—
Québec	8.3	7.4	6.5	5.0	3.5	2.6	1.8	1.2	—
Canada	8.0	7.0	6.1	4.5	3.3	2.5	1.8	1.3	—
				Females					
Lévis	8.4	7.7	7.0	5.1	3.2	2.4	2.0	2.3	—
Québec	8.1	7.3	6.5	5.2	3.9	3.2	2.7	2.7	—
Canada	7.9	7.0	6.2	4.6	3.6	3.0	2.4	2.6	—

Source: Statistics Canada. 2012. Census Profile. 2011 Census. Statistics Canada Catalogue no. 98-316-XWE. Ottawa. Released October 24 2012.
http://www12.statcan.gc.ca/census-recensement/2011/dp-pd/prof/index.cfm?Lang=E

PROFILES / Lévis, Québec

Private Households by Household Size

Area	1 Person	2 Persons	3 Persons	4 Persons	5 Persons	6 or More Persons	Average Number of Persons in Private Households
			Households				
Lévis	15,890	21,420	8,795	8,540	2,440	685	2.4
Québec	1,094,410	1,181,240	496,140	421,080	142,555	59,920	2.3
Canada	3,673,310	4,544,820	2,081,900	1,903,300	724,405	392,885	2.5
			Percent of Households				
Lévis	27.5	37.1	15.2	14.8	4.2	1.2	–
Québec	32.2	34.8	14.6	12.4	4.2	1.8	–
Canada	27.6	34.1	15.6	14.3	5.4	2.9	–

Source: Statistics Canada. 2012. Census Profile. 2011 Census. Statistics Canada Catalogue no. 98-316-XWE. Ottawa. Released October 24 2012.
http://www12.statcan.gc.ca/census-recensement/2011/dp-pd/prof/index.cfm?Lang=E

Dwelling Type

Area	Single-detached House	Semi-detached House	Row House	Apartment: Building with Five or More Storeys	Apartment: Building with Fewer Than Five Storeys	Duplex Apartment	Movable Dwelling	Other Single-attached House
				Number				
Lévis	31,820	3,940	1,295	695	15,915	3,340	615	145
Québec	1,560,405	171,435	86,040	171,115	1,103,845	263,860	22,995	15,645
Canada	7,329,150	646,245	791,600	1,234,770	2,397,550	704,485	183,510	33,310
				Percent of Dwellings				
Lévis	55.1	6.8	2.2	1.2	27.6	5.8	1.1	0.3
Québec	46.0	5.0	2.5	5.0	32.5	7.8	0.7	0.5
Canada	55.0	4.9	5.9	9.3	18.0	5.3	1.4	0.3

Source: Statistics Canada. 2012. Census Profile. 2011 Census. Statistics Canada Catalogue no. 98-316-XWE. Ottawa. Released October 24 2012.
http://www12.statcan.gc.ca/census-recensement/2011/dp-pd/prof/index.cfm?Lang=E

Shelter Costs

	Owned Dwellings				Rented Dwellings		
Area	Number	Median Value[1] ($)	Average Value[1] ($)	Median Monthly Costs[2] ($)	Average Monthly Costs[2] ($)	Number	Median Monthly Costs[3] ($)	Average Monthly Costs[3] ($)
Lévis	40,325	224,586	242,781	860	897	17,340	655	676
Québec	2,056,665	214,537	249,427	841	936	1,308,465	643	685
Canada	9,013,410	280,552	345,182	978	1,141	4,060,385	784	848

Note: All figures cover non-farm, non-reserve private dwellings; (1) Refers to the dollar amount expected by the owner if the dwelling were to be sold; (2) Includes all shelter expenses paid by households that own their dwellings, such as the mortgage payment and the costs of electricity, heat, water and other municipal services, property taxes and condominium fees; (3) Includes all shelter expenses paid by households that rent their dwellings, such as the monthly rent and the costs of electricity, heat and municipal services.
Source: Statistics Canada. 2013. 2011 National Household Survey. Statistics Canada Catalogue no. 99-004-XWE. Ottawa. Released September 11, 2013.

Occupied Private Dwellings by Period of Construction

Area	1960 or Before	1961 to 1980	1981 to 1990	1991 to 2000	2001 to 2005	2006 to 2011
			Number			
Lévis	9,445	17,400	11,460	8,860	5,225	5,370
Québec	946,900	1,115,455	533,790	353,355	206,035	239,685
Canada	3,273,105	4,152,715	2,112,110	1,707,880	1,031,020	1,042,430
			Percent of Dwellings			
Lévis	16.4	30.1	19.8	15.3	9.0	9.3
Québec	27.9	32.9	15.7	10.4	6.1	7.1
Canada	24.6	31.2	15.9	12.8	7.7	7.8

Note: Figures cover non-farm, non-reserve private dwellings and includes data up to May 10, 2011.
Source: Statistics Canada. 2013. 2011 National Household Survey. Statistics Canada Catalogue no. 99-004-XWE. Ottawa. Released September 11, 2013.

Educational Attainment

Area	No Certificate, Diploma or Degree	High School Diploma or Equivalent[1]	Apprenticeship or Trades Certificate or Diploma[2]	College, CÉGEP or Other Non-University Certificate or Diploma	University Certificate or Diploma Below the Bachelor Level[3]	Bachelor's Degree	University Certificate, Diploma or Degree Above Bachelor Level[4]
			Number				
			Total				
Lévis	16,935	23,220	20,045	23,615	5,650	15,605	7,020
Québec	1,436,025	1,404,755	1,049,470	1,075,855	305,330	766,100	437,050
Canada	5,485,400	6,968,935	2,950,685	4,970,020	1,200,130	3,634,425	2,049,930
			Males				
Lévis	8,435	10,700	12,115	10,485	2,325	7,180	3,485
Québec	714,090	650,660	635,435	472,360	126,565	343,535	227,990
Canada	2,742,875	3,305,415	1,928,970	2,118,430	513,235	1,643,080	1,043,350
			Females				
Lévis	8,495	12,520	7,925	13,130	3,325	8,430	3,540
Québec	721,930	754,095	414,035	603,495	178,765	422,565	209,065
Canada	2,742,520	3,663,515	1,021,715	2,851,595	686,890	1,991,345	1,006,585
			Percent of Population				
			Total				
Lévis	15.1	20.7	17.9	21.1	5.0	13.9	6.3
Québec	22.2	21.7	16.2	16.6	4.7	11.8	6.8
Canada	20.1	25.6	10.8	18.2	4.4	13.3	7.5
			Males				
Lévis	15.4	19.6	22.1	19.2	4.2	13.1	6.4
Québec	22.5	20.5	20.0	14.9	4.0	10.8	7.2
Canada	20.6	24.9	14.5	15.9	3.9	12.4	7.8
			Females				
Lévis	14.8	21.8	13.8	22.9	5.8	14.7	6.2
Québec	21.9	22.8	12.5	18.3	5.4	12.8	6.3
Canada	19.6	26.2	7.3	20.4	4.9	14.3	7.2

Note: Figures cover total population aged 15 years and over by highest certificate, diploma or degree; (1) Includes persons who have graduated from a secondary school or equivalent. It excludes persons with a postsecondary certificate, diploma or degree; (2) Includes Registered Apprenticeship certificates (including Certificate of Qualification, Journeyperson's designation) and other trades certificates or diplomas such as pre-employment or vocational certificates and diplomas from brief trade programs completed at community colleges, institutes of technology, vocational centres, and similar institutions; (3) Comparisons with other data sources suggest that the category 'University certificate or diploma below the bachelor's level' was over-reported in the NHS. This category likely includes some responses that are actually college certificates or diplomas, bachelor's degrees or other types of education (e.g., university transfer programs, bachelor's programs completed in other countries, incomplete bachelor's programs, non-university professional designations). We recommend users interpret the results for the 'University certificate or diploma below the bachelor's level' category with caution; (4) 'University certificate or diploma above bachelor level' includes the categories: 'Degree in medicine, dentistry, veterinary medicine or optometry,' 'Master's degree' and 'Earned doctorate.'
Source: Statistics Canada. 2013. 2011 National Household Survey. Statistics Canada Catalogue no. 99-004-XWE. Ottawa. Released September 11, 2013.

Household Income Distribution

Area	Less than $10,000	$10,000 to $19,999	$20,000 to $29,999	$30,000 to $39,999	$40,000 to $49,999	$50,000 to $59,999	$60,000 to $79,999	$80,000 to $99,999	$100,000 to $124,999	$125,000 to $149,999	$150,000 and Over
					Households						
Lévis	1,620	4,020	4,430	5,635	5,465	5,315	9,380	7,560	6,400	3,655	4,285
Québec	179,790	377,210	353,470	382,000	343,730	302,595	483,085	344,435	267,995	148,950	211,965
Canada	626,705	1,141,945	1,193,925	1,271,675	1,206,800	1,102,120	1,865,280	1,458,240	1,260,770	802,555	1,389,240
					Percent of Households						
Lévis	2.8	7.0	7.7	9.8	9.5	9.2	16.2	13.1	11.1	6.3	7.4
Québec	5.3	11.1	10.4	11.3	10.1	8.9	14.2	10.1	7.9	4.4	6.2
Canada	4.7	8.6	9.0	9.5	9.1	8.3	14.0	10.9	9.5	6.0	10.4

Note: Household income is the sum of the total incomes of all members of that household. Total income refers to monetary receipts from certain sources, before income taxes and deductions, during calendar year 2010.
Source: Statistics Canada. 2013. 2011 National Household Survey. Statistics Canada Catalogue no. 99-004-XWE. Ottawa. Released September 11, 2013.

Median and Average Household and Economic Family Income

Area	Median Household Income ($)	Average Household Income ($)	Median After-tax Household Income ($)	Average After-tax Household Income ($)	Median Economic Family Income ($)	Average Economic Family Income ($)	Median After-tax Economic Family Income ($)	Average After-tax Economic Family Income ($)
Lévis	65,055	75,789	55,915	62,903	81,038	90,978	68,803	75,350
Québec	51,842	66,205	45,968	55,121	68,344	82,045	59,560	68,091
Canada	61,072	79,102	54,089	66,149	76,511	94,125	67,044	78,517

Note: Figures cover household and economic familiy income in 2010. A household is defined as a person or a group of persons (other than foreign residents) who occupy the same private dwelling and do not have a usual place of residence elsewhere in Canada. Every person is a member of one and only one household. An economic family is defined as a group of two or more persons who live in the same dwelling and are related to each other by blood, marriage, common-law, adoption or a foster relationship. A couple may be of opposite or same sex.
Source: Statistics Canada. 2013. 2011 National Household Survey. Statistics Canada Catalogue no. 99-004-XWE. Ottawa. Released September 11, 2013.

Individual Income Distribution

Area	Less than $10,000	$10,000 to $19,999	$20,000 to $29,999	$30,000 to $39,999	$40,000 to $49,999	$50,000 to $59,999	$60,000 to $79,999	$80,000 to $99,999	$100,000 to $124,999	$125,000 and Over
					Number					
					Total					
Lévis	13,805	17,770	14,605	16,960	14,600	10,260	11,900	4,240	2,330	2,065
Québec	1,005,600	1,309,515	941,630	866,290	653,400	449,185	515,815	211,070	109,975	120,915
Canada	4,492,040	4,835,710	3,670,020	3,180,360	2,603,520	1,921,650	2,437,440	1,302,045	693,580	782,135
					Males					
Lévis	5,775	6,585	6,320	7,720	7,460	5,730	7,235	3,015	1,775	1,675
Québec	441,455	516,150	427,295	432,625	345,950	256,700	313,880	143,785	80,000	91,475
Canada	1,936,365	1,864,880	1,588,260	1,522,190	1,333,510	1,079,780	1,473,145	823,720	492,905	599,905
					Females					
Lévis	8,030	11,190	8,280	9,240	7,140	4,525	4,660	1,225	550	395
Québec	564,150	793,365	514,335	433,670	307,455	192,485	201,935	67,275	29,980	29,440
Canada	2,555,675	2,970,825	2,081,760	1,658,170	1,270,010	841,870	964,300	478,330	200,680	182,230
					Percent of Population					
					Total					
Lévis	12.7	16.4	13.5	15.6	13.5	9.5	11.0	3.9	2.1	1.9
Québec	16.3	21.2	15.2	14.0	10.6	7.3	8.3	3.4	1.8	2.0
Canada	17.3	18.7	14.2	12.3	10.0	7.4	9.4	5.0	2.7	3.0
					Males					
Lévis	10.8	12.4	11.9	14.5	14.0	10.8	13.6	5.7	3.3	3.1
Québec	14.5	16.9	14.0	14.2	11.3	8.4	10.3	4.7	2.6	3.0
Canada	15.2	14.7	12.5	12.0	10.5	8.5	11.6	6.5	3.9	4.7
					Females					
Lévis	14.5	20.3	15.0	16.7	12.9	8.2	8.4	2.2	1.0	0.7
Québec	18.0	25.3	16.4	13.8	9.8	6.1	6.4	2.1	1.0	0.9
Canada	19.4	22.5	15.8	12.6	9.6	6.4	7.3	3.6	1.5	1.4

Note: Figures cover individuals aged 15 years and over with income. Income refers to monetary receipts from certain sources, before income taxes and deductions, during calendar year 2010.
Source: Statistics Canada. 2013. 2011 National Household Survey. Statistics Canada Catalogue no. 99-004-XWE. Ottawa. Released September 11, 2013.

Labour Force Status

Area	In the Labour Force - All	In the Labour Force - Employed	In the Labour Force - Unemployed	Not in the Labour Force
		Number		
		Total		
Lévis	79,980	76,760	3,220	32,115
Québec	4,183,445	3,880,425	303,020	2,291,145
Canada	17,990,080	16,595,035	1,395,045	9,269,445
		Males		
Lévis	40,960	39,025	1,935	13,765
Québec	2,188,555	2,014,810	173,745	982,080
Canada	9,388,570	8,634,310	754,255	3,906,785
		Females		
Lévis	39,020	37,740	1,285	18,345
Québec	1,994,885	1,865,610	129,275	1,309,065
Canada	8,601,515	7,960,725	640,790	5,362,660
		Percent of Labour Force		
		Total		
Lévis	71.4	68.5	4.0	28.7
Québec	64.6	59.9	7.2	35.4
Canada	66.0	60.9	7.8	34.0
		Males		
Lévis	74.8	71.3	4.7	25.2
Québec	69.0	63.5	7.9	31.0
Canada	70.6	64.9	8.0	29.4
		Females		
Lévis	68.0	65.8	3.3	32.0
Québec	60.4	56.5	6.5	39.6
Canada	61.6	57.0	7.4	38.4

Note: Figures are based on total population 15 years and over
Source: Statistics Canada. 2013. 2011 National Household Survey. Statistics Canada Catalogue no. 99-004-XWE. Ottawa. Released September 11, 2013.

Labour Force by Industry (NAICS Codes 11–52)

Area	Agriculture, forestry, fishing & hunting	Mining, quarrying, & oil & gas extraction	Utilities	Construction	Manufacturing	Wholesale Trade	Retail Trade	Transportation & warehousing	Information & cultural industries	Finance & insurance
					Number					
					Total					
Lévis	655	90	335	4,670	8,740	3,440	9,345	3,040	905	6,245
Québec	84,470	20,770	33,815	241,780	476,390	169,825	501,380	181,295	98,340	159,230
Canada	437,650	261,050	149,940	1,215,380	1,619,295	733,445	2,031,665	827,780	420,830	767,960
					Males					
Lévis	455	85	290	4,175	6,480	2,565	4,345	2,545	530	2,230
Québec	61,540	18,035	24,560	213,605	343,345	113,545	234,725	137,745	56,455	56,930
Canada	307,370	211,690	110,765	1,068,710	1,167,680	494,545	933,850	617,305	235,875	296,995
					Females					
Lévis	195	0	45	495	2,255	870	4,995	495	375	4,010
Québec	22,925	2,730	9,255	28,170	133,045	56,280	266,650	43,550	41,885	102,295
Canada	130,285	49,360	39,175	146,670	451,615	238,900	1,097,820	210,475	184,955	470,960
					Percent of Labour Force					
					Total					
Lévis	0.8	0.1	0.4	5.9	11.0	4.3	11.8	3.8	1.1	7.9
Québec	2.1	0.5	0.8	5.9	11.7	4.2	12.3	4.4	2.4	3.9
Canada	2.5	1.5	0.9	6.9	9.2	4.2	11.6	4.7	2.4	4.4
					Males					
Lévis	1.1	0.2	0.7	10.3	16.0	6.3	10.7	6.3	1.3	5.5
Québec	2.9	0.8	1.1	10.0	16.1	5.3	11.0	6.4	2.6	2.7
Canada	3.3	2.3	1.2	11.6	12.7	5.4	10.2	6.7	2.6	3.2
					Females					
Lévis	0.5	0.0	0.1	1.3	5.8	2.3	12.9	1.3	1.0	10.4
Québec	1.2	0.1	0.5	1.4	6.8	2.9	13.7	2.2	2.2	5.3
Canada	1.6	0.6	0.5	1.7	5.4	2.8	13.1	2.5	2.2	5.6

Note: Figures are based on total experienced labour force 15 years and over. Experienced labour force refers to persons who, during the week of Sunday, May 1 to Saturday, May 7, 2011, were employed and the unemployed who had last worked for pay or in self-employment in either 2010 or 2011.
Source: Statistics Canada. 2013. 2011 National Household Survey. Statistics Canada Catalogue no. 99-004-XWE. Ottawa. Released September 11, 2013.

Labour Force by Industry (NAICS Codes 53–91)

Area	Real estate & rental & leasing	Profess., scientific & tech. services	Mgmt of companies & enterprises	Admin. & support, waste mgmt & remed. services	Educational services	Health care & social assistance	Arts, entertain. & recreation	Accomm. & food services	Other services (except public admin.)	Public admin.
					Number					
					Total					
Lévis	1,125	5,135	70	2,520	5,870	10,810	965	4,510	3,180	7,545
Québec	61,365	282,115	3,965	156,130	301,425	496,125	78,795	253,145	189,290	295,480
Canada	321,895	1,240,850	17,460	728,330	1,301,435	1,949,650	363,405	1,130,750	807,800	1,261,050
					Males					
Lévis	585	2,985	25	1,510	1,800	1,925	425	2,110	1,650	3,840
Québec	35,940	158,920	2,250	92,530	99,565	97,255	41,535	112,650	88,710	147,645
Canada	179,090	688,625	9,380	411,250	424,915	349,430	188,270	469,990	372,940	652,510
					Females					
Lévis	535	2,155	50	1,010	4,075	8,880	540	2,400	1,530	3,710
Québec	25,425	123,205	1,715	63,605	201,860	398,870	37,260	140,495	100,585	147,835
Canada	142,805	552,225	8,075	317,085	876,515	1,600,220	175,135	660,760	434,865	608,535
					Percent of Labour Force					
					Total					
Lévis	1.4	6.5	0.1	3.2	7.4	13.6	1.2	5.7	4.0	9.5
Québec	1.5	6.9	0.1	3.8	7.4	12.1	1.9	6.2	4.6	7.2
Canada	1.8	7.1	0.1	4.1	7.4	11.1	2.1	6.4	4.6	7.2
					Males					
Lévis	1.4	7.4	0.1	3.7	4.4	4.7	1.0	5.2	4.1	9.5
Québec	1.7	7.4	0.1	4.3	4.7	4.5	1.9	5.3	4.2	6.9
Canada	1.9	7.5	0.1	4.5	4.6	3.8	2.0	5.1	4.1	7.1
					Females					
Lévis	1.4	5.6	0.1	2.6	10.5	23.0	1.4	6.2	4.0	9.6
Québec	1.3	6.3	0.1	3.3	10.4	20.5	1.9	7.2	5.2	7.6
Canada	1.7	6.6	0.1	3.8	10.4	19.1	2.1	7.9	5.2	7.2

Note: Figures are based on total experienced labour force 15 years and over. Experienced labour force refers to persons who, during the week of Sunday, May 1 to Saturday, May 7, 2011, were employed and the unemployed who had last worked for pay or in self-employment in either 2010 or 2011.
Source: Statistics Canada. 2013. 2011 National Household Survey. Statistics Canada Catalogue no. 99-004-XWE. Ottawa. Released September 11, 2013.

PROFILES / Lévis, Québec

Occupation

Area	Mgmt	Business, Finance & Admin.	Natural/ Applied Sciences & Related	Health	Education, Law & Social, Community & Government Services	Art, Culture, Recreation & Sport	Sales & Service	Trades, Transport & Equip. Operators & Related	Natural Resources, Agri. & Related Production	Mfg & Utilities
Number - Total										
Lévis	7,450	14,725	6,840	6,100	9,660	1,790	18,315	10,090	590	3,640
Québec	411,425	687,715	287,015	268,610	479,505	123,665	969,740	573,075	65,625	218,740
Canada	1,963,600	2,902,045	1,237,775	1,107,200	2,064,675	503,415	4,068,170	2,537,775	397,930	805,040
Males										
Lévis	4,810	4,560	5,185	980	2,930	715	8,490	9,720	455	2,715
Québec	261,620	207,545	221,430	53,480	148,715	58,150	436,370	542,055	53,640	154,485
Canada	1,229,460	854,190	966,355	217,520	676,550	232,535	1,745,705	2,385,615	318,945	564,300
Females										
Lévis	2,640	10,165	1,655	5,120	6,730	1,080	9,825	375	140	930
Québec	149,800	480,170	65,585	215,130	330,795	65,520	533,370	31,025	11,995	64,250
Canada	734,140	2,047,855	271,415	889,675	1,388,130	270,875	2,322,465	152,165	78,980	240,740
Percent of Labour Force - Total										
Lévis	9.4	18.6	8.6	7.7	12.2	2.3	23.1	12.7	0.7	4.6
Québec	10.1	16.8	7.0	6.6	11.7	3.0	23.7	14.0	1.6	5.4
Canada	11.2	16.5	7.0	6.3	11.7	2.9	23.1	14.4	2.3	4.6
Males										
Lévis	11.9	11.2	12.8	2.4	7.2	1.8	20.9	24.0	1.1	6.7
Québec	12.2	9.7	10.4	2.5	7.0	2.7	20.4	25.4	2.5	7.2
Canada	13.4	9.3	10.5	2.4	7.4	2.5	19.0	26.0	3.5	6.1
Females										
Lévis	6.8	26.3	4.3	13.3	17.4	2.8	25.4	1.0	0.4	2.4
Québec	7.7	24.7	3.4	11.0	17.0	3.4	27.4	1.6	0.6	3.3
Canada	8.7	24.4	3.2	10.6	16.5	3.2	27.7	1.8	0.9	2.9

Note: Figures are based on total experienced labour force 15 years and over
Source: Statistics Canada. 2013. 2011 National Household Survey. Statistics Canada Catalogue no. 99-004-XWE. Ottawa. Released September 11, 2013.

Place of Work Status

Area	Worked at Home	Worked Outside Canada	No Fixed Workplace Address	Worked at Usual Place
Number - Total				
Lévis	3,830	70	5,900	66,970
Québec	237,625	9,705	331,525	3,301,560
Canada	1,142,640	66,460	1,868,245	13,517,690
Males				
Lévis	1,895	45	4,570	32,510
Québec	122,060	7,055	249,535	1,636,165
Canada	582,150	47,355	1,400,485	6,604,325
Females				
Lévis	1,930	20	1,325	34,455
Québec	115,565	2,650	81,995	1,665,395
Canada	560,490	19,100	467,760	6,913,370
Percent of Labour Force - Total				
Lévis	5.0	0.1	7.7	87.2
Québec	6.1	0.3	8.5	85.1
Canada	6.9	0.4	11.3	81.5
Males				
Lévis	4.9	0.1	11.7	83.3
Québec	6.1	0.4	12.4	81.2
Canada	6.7	0.5	16.2	76.5
Females				
Lévis	5.1	0.1	3.5	91.3
Québec	6.2	0.1	4.4	89.3
Canada	7.0	0.2	5.9	86.8

Note: Figures are based on total employed labour force 15 years and over.
Source: Statistics Canada. 2013. 2011 National Household Survey. Statistics Canada Catalogue no. 99-004-XWE. Ottawa. Released September 11, 2013.

Mode of Transportation to Work

Area	Car; Truck; Van; as Driver	Car; Truck; Van; as Passenger	Public Transit	Walked	Bicycled	All Other Modes
			Number			
			Total			
Lévis	62,235	2,785	3,965	2,765	455	665
Québec	2,713,295	136,490	484,600	215,210	48,870	34,620
Canada	11,393,140	867,050	1,851,525	880,815	201,780	191,625
			Males			
Lévis	32,680	1,135	1,420	1,125	365	360
Québec	1,484,305	50,905	203,035	95,100	33,065	19,285
Canada	6,238,835	349,530	788,290	387,580	135,840	104,725
			Females			
Lévis	29,560	1,650	2,545	1,635	90	305
Québec	1,228,995	85,585	281,565	120,110	15,800	15,335
Canada	5,154,305	517,520	1,063,235	493,230	65,940	86,900
			Percent of Labour Force			
			Total			
Lévis	85.4	3.8	5.4	3.8	0.6	0.9
Québec	74.7	3.8	13.3	5.9	1.3	1.0
Canada	74.0	5.6	12.0	5.7	1.3	1.2
			Males			
Lévis	88.1	3.1	3.8	3.0	1.0	1.0
Québec	78.7	2.7	10.8	5.0	1.8	1.0
Canada	77.9	4.4	9.8	4.8	1.7	1.3
			Females			
Lévis	82.6	4.6	7.1	4.6	0.3	0.9
Québec	70.3	4.9	16.1	6.9	0.9	0.9
Canada	69.8	7.0	14.4	6.7	0.9	1.2

Note: Figures are based on total employed labour force 15 years and over.
Source: Statistics Canada. 2013. 2011 National Household Survey. Statistics Canada Catalogue no. 99-004-XWE. Ottawa. Released September 11, 2013.

Visible Minority Population Characteristics

Area	Total Minority	South Asian[1]	Chinese	Black	Filipino	Latin American	Arab	SE Asian[2]	West Asian[3]	Korean	Japanese	Multiple[4]
						Number						
						Total						
Lévis	1,935	30	370	500	20	340	240	270	0	20	30	80
Québec	850,235	83,320	82,845	243,625	31,495	116,380	166,260	65,855	23,445	6,665	4,025	17,420
Canada	6,264,750	1,567,400	1,324,750	945,665	619,310	381,280	380,620	312,075	206,840	161,130	87,270	171,935
						Males						
Lévis	915	10	75	255	0	150	185	140	0	0	0	45
Québec	418,545	43,410	37,295	116,605	12,435	56,940	89,505	32,940	12,070	3,135	1,565	8,315
Canada	3,043,010	790,755	632,325	453,005	268,885	186,355	203,485	154,035	105,620	77,165	38,270	83,335
						Females						
Lévis	1,015	20	295	250	15	185	60	130	0	0	0	35
Québec	431,695	39,915	45,550	127,020	19,055	59,440	76,750	32,920	11,380	3,530	2,465	9,105
Canada	3,221,745	776,650	692,420	492,660	350,425	194,925	177,140	158,045	101,220	83,965	48,990	88,600
						Percent of Population						
						Total						
Lévis	1.4	0.0	0.3	0.4	0.0	0.3	0.2	0.2	0.0	0.0	0.0	0.1
Québec	11.0	1.1	1.1	3.2	0.4	1.5	2.2	0.9	0.3	0.1	0.1	0.2
Canada	19.1	4.8	4.0	2.9	1.9	1.2	1.2	0.9	0.6	0.5	0.3	0.5
						Males						
Lévis	1.4	0.0	0.1	0.4	0.0	0.2	0.3	0.2	0.0	0.0	0.0	0.1
Québec	11.0	1.1	1.0	3.1	0.3	1.5	2.3	0.9	0.3	0.1	0.0	0.2
Canada	18.8	4.9	3.9	2.8	1.7	1.2	1.3	1.0	0.7	0.5	0.2	0.5
						Females						
Lévis	1.5	0.0	0.4	0.4	0.0	0.3	0.1	0.2	0.0	0.0	0.0	0.1
Québec	11.0	1.0	1.2	3.2	0.5	1.5	2.0	0.8	0.3	0.1	0.1	0.2
Canada	19.3	4.7	4.1	3.0	2.1	1.2	1.1	0.9	0.6	0.5	0.3	0.5

Note: The Employment Equity Act defines visible minorities as 'persons, other than Aboriginal peoples, who are non-Caucasian in race or non-white in colour';
(1) Includes 'East Indian,' 'Pakistani,' 'Sri Lankan,' etc.; (2) Includes 'Vietnamese,' 'Cambodian,' 'Malaysian,' 'Laotian,' etc.; (3) Includes 'Iranian,' 'Afghan,' etc.; (4) Includes respondents who reported more than one visible minority group by checking two or more mark-in circles, e.g., 'Black' and 'South Asian.'
Source: Statistics Canada. 2013. 2011 National Household Survey. Statistics Canada Catalogue no. 99-004-XWE. Ottawa. Released September 11, 2013.

PROFILES / Lévis, Québec

Aboriginal Population

Area	Aboriginal Identity[1]	First Nations (North American Indian) Single Identity[2]	Métis Single Identity	Inuk (Inuit) Single Identity	Multiple Aboriginal Identities[3]	Aboriginal Identities Not Included Elsewhere
Number						
Total						
Lévis	745	340	315	0	30	55
Québec	141,915	82,425	40,960	12,570	1,545	4,415
Canada	1,400,685	851,560	451,795	59,440	11,415	26,475
Males						
Lévis	380	140	210	0	0	20
Québec	70,205	40,105	21,300	6,265	720	1,815
Canada	682,190	411,785	223,335	29,495	5,525	12,055
Females						
Lévis	370	200	110	0	25	30
Québec	71,710	42,315	19,660	6,305	830	2,600
Canada	718,500	439,775	228,460	29,950	5,890	14,420
Percent of Population						
Total						
Lévis	0.5	0.3	0.2	0.0	0.0	0.0
Québec	1.8	1.1	0.5	0.2	0.0	0.1
Canada	4.3	2.6	1.4	0.2	0.0	0.1
Males						
Lévis	0.6	0.2	0.3	0.0	0.0	0.0
Québec	1.8	1.1	0.6	0.2	0.0	0.0
Canada	4.2	2.5	1.4	0.2	0.0	0.1
Females						
Lévis	0.5	0.3	0.2	0.0	0.0	0.0
Québec	1.8	1.1	0.5	0.2	0.0	0.1
Canada	4.3	2.6	1.4	0.2	0.0	0.1

Note: (1) Includes persons who reported being an Aboriginal person, that is, First Nations (North American Indian), Métis or Inuk (Inuit) and/or those who reported Registered or Treaty Indian status, that is registered under the Indian Act of Canada, and/or those who reported membership in a First Nation or Indian band. Aboriginal peoples of Canada are defined in the Constitution Act, 1982, section 35-2 as including the Indian, Inuit and Métis peoples of Canada; (2) Users should be aware that the estimates associated with this variable are more affected than most by the incomplete enumeration of certain Indian reserves and Indian settlements in the National Household Survey (NHS); (3) Includes persons who reported being any two or all three of the following: First Nations (North American Indian), Métis or Inuk (Inuit).
Source: Statistics Canada. 2013. 2011 National Household Survey. Statistics Canada Catalogue no. 99-004-XWE. Ottawa. Released September 11, 2013.

Ethnic Origin

Area	North American Aboriginal	Other North American	European	Caribbean	Latin, Central and South American	African	Asian	Oceania
Number								
Total								
Lévis	3,130	101,920	56,290	200	555	760	1,240	0
Québec	307,445	4,776,875	3,390,330	167,590	137,255	260,785	488,905	2,305
Canada	1,836,035	11,070,455	20,157,965	627,590	544,375	766,735	5,011,225	74,875
Males								
Lévis	1,470	50,030	28,040	110	250	450	455	0
Québec	146,725	2,345,180	1,678,310	77,665	67,195	135,740	241,515	1,135
Canada	885,675	5,462,685	9,913,150	291,640	264,635	387,360	2,435,540	37,490
Females								
Lévis	1,660	51,885	28,250	90	300	310	780	0
Québec	160,725	2,431,700	1,712,015	89,925	70,065	125,040	247,390	1,175
Canada	950,360	5,607,770	10,244,820	335,945	279,740	379,380	2,575,680	37,385
Percent of Population								
Total								
Lévis	2.3	75.0	41.4	0.1	0.4	0.6	0.9	0.0
Québec	4.0	61.8	43.8	2.2	1.8	3.4	6.3	0.0
Canada	5.6	33.7	61.4	1.9	1.7	2.3	15.3	0.2
Males								
Lévis	2.2	74.8	41.9	0.2	0.4	0.7	0.7	0.0
Québec	3.8	61.5	44.0	2.0	1.8	3.6	6.3	0.0
Canada	5.5	33.8	61.3	1.8	1.6	2.4	15.1	0.2
Females								
Lévis	2.4	75.2	41.0	0.1	0.4	0.4	1.1	0.0
Québec	4.1	62.1	43.7	2.3	1.8	3.2	6.3	0.0
Canada	5.7	33.6	61.4	2.0	1.7	2.3	15.4	0.2

Note: The sum of the ethnic groups in this table is greater than the total population estimate because a person may report more than one ethnic origin in the NHS.
Source: Statistics Canada. 2013. 2011 National Household Survey. Statistics Canada Catalogue no. 99-004-XWE. Ottawa. Released September 11, 2013.

Religion

Area	Buddhist	Christian	Hindu	Jewish	Muslim	Sikh	Traditional (Aboriginal) Spirituality	Other Religions	No Religious Affiliation
				Number Total					
Lévis	260	122,425	0	25	420	0	0	120	12,585
Québec	52,390	6,356,880	33,540	85,100	243,430	9,275	2,025	12,340	937,545
Canada	366,830	22,102,745	497,965	329,495	1,053,945	454,965	64,935	130,835	7,850,605
				Males					
Lévis	105	59,195	0	20	275	0	0	45	7,215
Québec	24,630	3,079,855	17,055	41,455	128,815	5,090	925	6,155	510,055
Canada	168,465	10,497,775	250,435	161,265	540,555	229,435	31,805	57,745	4,225,645
				Females					
Lévis	150	63,230	0	0	145	0	0	75	5,375
Québec	27,760	3,277,020	16,480	43,645	114,615	4,185	1,100	6,175	427,485
Canada	198,365	11,604,975	247,525	168,235	513,395	225,530	33,135	73,090	3,624,965
				Percent of Population Total					
Lévis	0.2	90.1	0.0	0.0	0.3	0.0	0.0	0.1	9.3
Québec	0.7	82.2	0.4	1.1	3.1	0.1	0.0	0.2	12.1
Canada	1.1	67.3	1.5	1.0	3.2	1.4	0.2	0.4	23.9
				Males					
Lévis	0.2	88.5	0.0	0.0	0.4	0.0	0.0	0.1	10.8
Québec	0.6	80.8	0.4	1.1	3.4	0.1	0.0	0.2	13.4
Canada	1.0	64.9	1.5	1.0	3.3	1.4	0.2	0.4	26.1
				Females					
Lévis	0.2	91.7	0.0	0.0	0.2	0.0	0.0	0.1	7.8
Québec	0.7	83.6	0.4	1.1	2.9	0.1	0.0	0.2	10.9
Canada	1.2	69.5	1.5	1.0	3.1	1.4	0.2	0.4	21.7

Note: Religion refers to the person's self-identification as having a connection or affiliation with any religious denomination, group, body, sect, cult or other religiously defined community or system of belief. Religion is not limited to formal membership in a religious organization or group. Persons without a religious connection or affiliation can self-identify as atheist, agnostic or humanist, or can provide another applicable response.
Source: Statistics Canada. 2013. 2011 National Household Survey. Statistics Canada Catalogue no. 99-004-XWE. Ottawa. Released September 11, 2013.

Religion—Christian Denominations

Area	Anglican	Baptist	Catholic	Christian Orthodox	Lutheran	Pentecostal	Presbyterian	United Church	Other Christian
				Number Total					
Lévis	135	115	119,675	75	30	215	45	25	2,105
Québec	73,550	36,615	5,775,740	129,780	7,200	41,070	11,440	32,930	248,560
Canada	1,631,845	635,840	12,810,705	550,690	478,185	478,705	472,385	2,007,610	3,036,780
				Males					
Lévis	55	50	57,895	45	10	100	20	0	1,020
Québec	34,815	16,585	2,802,920	63,960	3,425	18,640	5,265	14,945	119,305
Canada	752,945	293,905	6,167,290	270,205	221,525	217,850	218,955	912,545	1,442,550
				Females					
Lévis	80	70	61,780	40	20	120	25	0	1,085
Québec	38,735	20,030	2,972,820	65,820	3,770	22,430	6,175	17,985	129,260
Canada	878,900	341,940	6,643,415	280,485	256,660	260,850	253,430	1,095,065	1,594,230
				Percent of Population Total					
Lévis	0.1	0.1	88.1	0.1	0.0	0.2	0.0	0.0	1.5
Québec	1.0	0.5	74.7	1.7	0.1	0.5	0.1	0.4	3.2
Canada	5.0	1.9	39.0	1.7	1.5	1.5	1.4	6.1	9.2
				Males					
Lévis	0.1	0.1	86.6	0.1	0.0	0.1	0.0	0.0	1.5
Québec	0.9	0.4	73.5	1.7	0.1	0.5	0.1	0.4	3.1
Canada	4.7	1.8	38.2	1.7	1.4	1.3	1.4	5.6	8.9
				Females					
Lévis	0.1	0.1	89.6	0.1	0.0	0.2	0.0	0.0	1.6
Québec	1.0	0.5	75.9	1.7	0.1	0.6	0.2	0.5	3.3
Canada	5.3	2.0	39.8	1.7	1.5	1.6	1.5	6.6	9.6

Note: Religion refers to the person's self-identification as having a connection or affiliation with any religious denomination, group, body, sect, cult or other religiously defined community or system of belief. Religion is not limited to formal membership in a religious organization or group. Persons without a religious connection or affiliation can self-identify as atheist, agnostic or humanist, or can provide another applicable response.
Source: Statistics Canada. 2013. 2011 National Household Survey. Statistics Canada Catalogue no. 99-004-XWE. Ottawa. Released September 11, 2013.

PROFILES / Lévis, Québec

Immigrant Status and Period of Immigration

Area	Non-Immigrants[1]	Immigrants All	Before 1971	1971 to 1980	1981 to 1990	1991 to 2000	2001 to 2005	2006 to 2011	Non-Permanent Residents[3]
Number									
Total									
Lévis	132,735	2,970	380	315	340	680	550	700	135
Québec	6,690,530	974,895	151,825	115,640	130,680	195,925	157,425	223,400	67,095
Canada	25,720,175	6,775,765	1,261,055	870,775	949,890	1,539,050	992,070	1,162,915	356,385
Males									
Lévis	65,230	1,560	255	155	185	305	295	365	70
Québec	3,301,435	477,240	75,255	57,410	64,080	94,110	76,780	109,605	35,370
Canada	12,753,235	3,231,370	605,430	416,670	454,570	724,905	474,545	555,245	178,515
Females									
Lévis	67,505	1,415	125	165	160	370	255	330	60
Québec	3,389,095	497,655	76,565	58,235	66,600	101,810	80,645	113,795	31,725
Canada	12,966,935	3,544,400	655,625	454,105	495,325	814,145	517,530	607,670	177,870
Percent of Population									
Total									
Lévis	97.7	2.2	0.3	0.2	0.3	0.5	0.4	0.5	0.1
Québec	86.5	12.6	2.0	1.5	1.7	2.5	2.0	2.9	0.9
Canada	78.3	20.6	3.8	2.7	2.9	4.7	3.0	3.5	1.1
Males									
Lévis	97.6	2.3	0.4	0.2	0.3	0.5	0.4	0.5	0.1
Québec	86.6	12.5	2.0	1.5	1.7	2.5	2.0	2.9	0.9
Canada	78.9	20.0	3.7	2.6	2.8	4.5	2.9	3.4	1.1
Females									
Lévis	97.9	2.1	0.2	0.2	0.2	0.5	0.4	0.5	0.1
Québec	86.5	12.7	2.0	1.5	1.7	2.6	2.1	2.9	0.8
Canada	77.7	21.2	3.9	2.7	3.0	4.9	3.1	3.6	1.1

Note: (1) Non-immigrant refers to a person who is a Canadian citizen by birth; (2) Immigrant refers to a person who is or has ever been a landed immigrant/permanent resident. This person has been granted the right to live in Canada permanently by immigration authorities. Some immigrants have resided in Canada for a number of years, while others have arrived recently. Some immigrants are Canadian citizens, while others are not. Most immigrants are born outside Canada, but a small number are born in Canada. In the 2011 National Household Survey, 'Immigrants' includes immigrants who landed in Canada prior to May 10, 2011; (3) Non-permanent resident refers to a person from another country who has a work or study permit, or who is a refugee claimant, and any non-Canadian-born family member living in Canada with them.
Source: Statistics Canada. 2013. 2011 National Household Survey. Statistics Canada Catalogue no. 99-004-XWE. Ottawa. Released September 11, 2013.

Mother Tongue

Area	English	French	Non-official Language	English & French	English & Non-official Language	French & Non-official Language	English, French & Non-official Language
Number							
Total							
Lévis	1,350	133,905	1,285	460	15	160	30
Québec	599,225	6,102,210	961,700	64,800	23,435	51,640	12,950
Canada	18,858,980	7,054,975	6,567,680	144,685	396,330	74,430	24,095
Males							
Lévis	680	65,545	645	250	5	95	15
Québec	297,875	2,994,300	472,635	32,390	11,455	25,810	6,790
Canada	9,345,225	3,452,380	3,157,785	69,975	192,000	36,535	11,965
Females							
Lévis	665	68,350	640	210	10	65	15
Québec	301,355	3,107,910	489,060	32,405	11,975	25,825	6,155
Canada	9,513,750	3,602,590	3,409,895	74,710	204,330	37,890	12,130
Percent of Population							
Total							
Lévis	1.0	97.6	0.9	0.3	0.0	0.1	0.0
Québec	7.7	78.1	12.3	0.8	0.3	0.7	0.2
Canada	56.9	21.3	19.8	0.4	1.2	0.2	0.1
Males							
Lévis	1.0	97.5	1.0	0.4	0.0	0.1	0.0
Québec	7.8	78.0	12.3	0.8	0.3	0.7	0.2
Canada	57.5	21.2	19.4	0.4	1.2	0.2	0.1
Females							
Lévis	1.0	97.7	0.9	0.3	0.0	0.1	0.0
Québec	7.6	78.2	12.3	0.8	0.3	0.6	0.2
Canada	56.4	21.4	20.2	0.4	1.2	0.2	0.1

Note: Figures cover total population excluding institutional residents.
Source: Statistics Canada. 2012. Census Profile. 2011 Census. Statistics Canada Catalogue no. 98-316-XWE. Ottawa. Released October 24 2012.
http://www12.statcan.gc.ca/census-recensement/2011/dp-pd/prof/index.cfm?Lang=E

Language Spoken Most Often at Home

Area	English	French	Non-official Language	English & French	English & Non-official Language	French & Non-official Language	English, French & Non-official Language
			Number				
			Total				
Lévis	880	135,075	515	385	15	275	55
Québec	767,415	6,249,080	554,400	71,555	43,765	100,110	29,625
Canada	21,457,075	6,827,865	3,673,865	131,205	875,135	109,700	46,330
			Males				
Lévis	415	66,200	255	200	5	135	25
Québec	379,915	3,071,635	268,640	35,860	21,305	48,590	15,315
Canada	10,585,620	3,348,235	1,767,310	63,475	425,370	53,010	22,845
			Females				
Lévis	455	68,880	260	185	10	140	30
Québec	387,500	3,177,450	285,760	35,695	22,460	51,525	14,310
Canada	10,871,455	3,479,625	1,906,555	67,730	449,765	56,690	23,485
			Percent of Population				
			Total				
Lévis	0.6	98.5	0.4	0.3	0.0	0.2	0.0
Québec	9.8	80.0	7.1	0.9	0.6	1.3	0.4
Canada	64.8	20.6	11.1	0.4	2.6	0.3	0.1
			Males				
Lévis	0.6	98.5	0.4	0.3	0.0	0.2	0.0
Québec	9.9	80.0	7.0	0.9	0.6	1.3	0.4
Canada	65.1	20.6	10.9	0.4	2.6	0.3	0.1
			Females				
Lévis	0.7	98.5	0.4	0.3	0.0	0.2	0.0
Québec	9.7	79.9	7.2	0.9	0.6	1.3	0.4
Canada	64.5	20.6	11.3	0.4	2.7	0.3	0.1

Note: Figures cover total population excluding institutional residents.
Source: Statistics Canada. 2012. Census Profile. 2011 Census. Statistics Canada Catalogue no. 98-316-XWE. Ottawa. Released October 24 2012.
http://www12.statcan.gc.ca/census-recensement/2011/dp-pd/prof/index.cfm?Lang=E

Knowledge of Official Languages

Area	English Only	French Only	English & French	Neither English nor French
		Number		
		Total		
Lévis	135	92,895	44,120	45
Québec	363,860	4,047,175	3,328,725	76,190
Canada	22,564,665	4,165,015	5,795,570	595,920
		Males		
Lévis	70	42,510	24,640	25
Québec	180,175	1,871,500	1,758,410	31,175
Canada	11,222,185	1,925,340	2,876,560	241,790
		Females		
Lévis	65	50,390	19,485	20
Québec	183,690	2,175,675	1,570,310	45,015
Canada	11,342,485	2,239,680	2,919,005	354,135
		Percent of Population		
		Total		
Lévis	0.1	67.7	32.2	0.0
Québec	4.7	51.8	42.6	1.0
Canada	68.1	12.6	17.5	1.8
		Males		
Lévis	0.1	63.2	36.6	0.0
Québec	4.7	48.7	45.8	0.8
Canada	69.0	11.8	17.7	1.5
		Females		
Lévis	0.1	72.0	27.9	0.0
Québec	4.6	54.7	39.5	1.1
Canada	67.3	13.3	17.3	2.1

Note: Figures cover total population excluding institutional residents.
Source: Statistics Canada. 2012. Census Profile. 2011 Census. Statistics Canada Catalogue no. 98-316-XWE. Ottawa. Released October 24 2012.
http://www12.statcan.gc.ca/census-recensement/2011/dp-pd/prof/index.cfm?Lang=E

Markham, Ontario

Background

Markham is located within the centre of the Greater Toronto Area (GTA) in the Regional Municipality of York, Ontario. The City of Markham is considered "Canada's High-Technology Capital." There are close to 900 high-technology and life sciences companies in Markham. The city is one of Ontario's fastest-growing municipalities.

The township of Markham was originally surveyed in 1793 and 1794. The majority of settlers were Pennsylvania-Germans who harnessed the Rouge River's power and built saw, grist and wool mills along the riverbanks. The settlement was incorporated as a village in 1873 and a modern town in 1971.

Today, more than 400 corporate offices are located in Markham. Global organizations with Canadian headquarters include IBM Canada, American Express, GE Digital Energy, and Johnson & Johnson. Key industry clusters are information and communications technology (ICT), advanced manufacturing, life sciences and healthcare technologies. Other key sectors include financial and insurance services and clean technology.

The recent "Markham 2020" economic strategy focused on converging the city's knowledge-based industries, particularly technology and life sciences sectors. In 2012, General Electric (GE) opened its $40-million Grid IQ Global Innovation Centre in Markham.

Over 60% of Markham's population identify as visible minorities. Throughout the year, festivals and special events celebrate cultures from around the world. The city's arts and culture programs are hosted by Markham Museum, Markham Theatre, Varley Art Gallery and the public library. Popular community-minded events include the Markham Village Music Festival, Ribfest and Music Festival, Beer Festival, and Jazz Festival.

Markham has summer highs of plus 25.2 degrees Celsius, winter lows of minus 9.13 degrees Celsius, and an average rainfall just over 735 mm per year.

Rankings

- *Canadian Family Magazine* ranked Markham as one of Canada's top family-friendly cities. Markham was ranked #7 out of 40 Canadian cities and towns with populations of 100,000 or more. Criteria: child-injury hospitalization rates; general and family health practitioners; life expectancy; student literacy; numeracy and problem-solving skills; high-school dropout rates and post-secondary achievement; childcare funding levels; child and youth services; diversity; unemployment rate; median income; housing affordability; crime rate; air quality; fitness and recreational sports centres; cultural institutions; bars and restaurants; theatre companies; and performing arts centres. *Canadian Family, "Top 10 Family-Friendly Canadian Cities," 2006*
- Markham ranked #1 in The Branham Group "Top 25 ICT Multinational Companies Operating in Canada" category, referring to the city's IBM Canada headquarters. In the tech consultancy's "Top 250 Canadian ICT Companies," 16 Markham-based tech companies were listed. Criteria: Revenues in 2011. *Branham300—Canada's Top Tech Companies, "Top 25 ICT Multinational Companies operating in Canada" and "Top 250 Canadian ICT Companies," April/May 2012*
- The City of Markham ranked a B grade when compared to 26 Canadian census metropolitan areas (CMAs) for its ability to attract skilled workers and mobile populations. Categories: economy, health, society, housing, environment, innovation and education. Markham's B rating was shared with Edmonton (AB), Guelph (ON), Victoria (BC), Vaughan (ON), Kingston (ON), Toronto (ON), Oakville (ON), London (ON), Halifax (NS), Lévis (QC), Regina (SK), Québec City (QC) and Burlington (ON). *Conference Board of Canada, "City Magnets: Benchmarking the Attractiveness of Canada's CMAs," December 2007*

PROFILES / Markham, Ontario

Population Growth and Density

Area	Population in 2001	Population in 2006	Population in 2011	Population Change 2001–2006	Population Change 2006–2011	Land Area (sq. km)	Population Density per sq. km
Markham	208,615	261,573	301,709	25.4	15.3	212.58	1,419.3
Ontario	11,410,046	12,160,282	12,851,821	6.6	5.7	908,607.67	14.1
Canada	30,007,094	31,612,897	33,476,688	5.4	5.9	8,965,121.42	3.7

Source: Statistics Canada. 2012. Census Profile. 2011 Census. Statistics Canada Catalogue no. 98-316-XWE. Ottawa. Released October 24 2012.
http://www12.statcan.gc.ca/census-recensement/2011/dp-pd/prof/index.cfm?Lang=E;
Statistics Canada 2007. 2006 Community Profiles. 2006 Census. Statistics Canada Catalogue no. 92-591-XWE. Ottawa. Released March 13 2007.
http://www12.statcan.ca/census-recensement/2006/dp-pd/prof/92-591/index.cfm?Lang=E

Gender

Area	Males	Females
Number		
Markham	147,285	154,425
Ontario	6,263,140	6,588,685
Canada	16,414,225	17,062,460
Percent of Population		
Markham	48.8	51.2
Ontario	48.7	51.3
Canada	49.0	51.0

Source: Statistics Canada. 2012. Census Profile. 2011 Census. Statistics Canada
Catalogue no. 98-316-XWE. Ottawa. Released October 24 2012.
http://www12.statcan.gc.ca/census-recensement/2011/dp-pd/prof/index.cfm?Lang=E

Marital Status

Area	Married[1]	Living Common-law	Single[2]	Separated	Divorced	Widowed
Number — Total						
Markham	148,920	6,535	68,560	4,475	9,535	11,170
Ontario	5,367,400	791,210	2,985,020	319,805	593,730	613,880
Canada	12,941,960	3,142,525	7,816,045	698,240	1,686,035	1,584,530
Males						
Markham	74,120	3,270	36,070	1,665	3,170	1,910
Ontario	2,681,320	397,620	1,583,760	133,790	231,160	117,980
Canada	6,470,300	1,575,495	4,206,320	299,655	680,415	310,940
Females						
Markham	74,800	3,265	32,490	2,815	6,360	9,255
Ontario	2,686,075	393,590	1,401,260	186,015	362,570	495,905
Canada	6,471,660	1,567,035	3,609,730	398,585	1,005,620	1,273,590
Percent of Population — Total						
Markham	59.8	2.6	27.5	1.8	3.8	4.5
Ontario	50.3	7.4	28.0	3.0	5.6	5.8
Canada	46.4	11.3	28.0	2.5	6.0	5.7
Males						
Markham	61.7	2.7	30.0	1.4	2.6	1.6
Ontario	52.1	7.7	30.8	2.6	4.5	2.3
Canada	47.8	11.6	31.1	2.2	5.0	2.3
Females						
Markham	58.0	2.5	25.2	2.2	4.9	7.2
Ontario	48.6	7.1	25.4	3.4	6.6	9.0
Canada	45.2	10.9	25.2	2.8	7.0	8.9

Note: (1) and not separated, (2) never legally married
Source: Statistics Canada. 2012. Census Profile. 2011 Census. Statistics Canada Catalogue no. 98-316-XWE. Ottawa. Released October 24 2012.
http://www12.statcan.gc.ca/census-recensement/2011/dp-pd/prof/index.cfm?Lang=E

Age Characteristics: 0 to 49 Years

Area	0 to 4 Years	5 to 9 Years	10 to 14 Years	15 to 19 Years	20 to 24 Years	25 to 29 Years	30 to 34 Years	35 to 39 Years	40 to 44 Years	45 to 49 Years
					Number					
					Total					
Markham	16,430	17,315	18,775	21,280	20,590	19,235	17,890	21,030	23,105	25,180
Ontario	704,260	712,755	763,755	863,635	852,910	815,120	800,365	844,335	924,075	1,055,880
Canada	1,877,095	1,809,895	1,920,355	2,178,135	2,187,450	2,169,590	2,162,905	2,173,930	2,324,875	2,675,130
					Males					
Markham	8,455	8,950	9,685	11,095	10,730	9,665	8,330	9,710	10,675	11,970
Ontario	360,590	365,290	391,630	443,680	432,490	400,045	383,340	405,845	447,920	517,510
Canada	961,150	925,965	983,995	1,115,845	1,108,775	1,077,275	1,058,810	1,064,200	1,141,720	1,318,715
					Females					
Markham	7,980	8,365	9,090	10,185	9,865	9,570	9,560	11,320	12,435	13,210
Ontario	343,670	347,465	372,125	419,950	420,415	415,075	417,030	438,485	476,155	538,370
Canada	915,945	883,935	936,360	1,062,295	1,078,670	1,092,315	1,104,095	1,109,735	1,183,155	1,356,420
					Percent of Population					
					Total					
Markham	5.4	5.7	6.2	7.1	6.8	6.4	5.9	7.0	7.7	8.3
Ontario	5.5	5.5	5.9	6.7	6.6	6.3	6.2	6.6	7.2	8.2
Canada	5.6	5.4	5.7	6.5	6.5	6.5	6.5	6.5	6.9	8.0
					Males					
Markham	5.7	6.1	6.6	7.5	7.3	6.6	5.7	6.6	7.2	8.1
Ontario	5.8	5.8	6.3	7.1	6.9	6.4	6.1	6.5	7.2	8.3
Canada	5.9	5.6	6.0	6.8	6.8	6.6	6.5	6.5	7.0	8.0
					Females					
Markham	5.2	5.4	5.9	6.6	6.4	6.2	6.2	7.3	8.1	8.6
Ontario	5.2	5.3	5.6	6.4	6.4	6.3	6.3	6.7	7.2	8.2
Canada	5.4	5.2	5.5	6.2	6.3	6.4	6.5	6.5	6.9	7.9

Source: Statistics Canada. 2012. Census Profile. 2011 Census. Statistics Canada Catalogue no. 98-316-XWE. Ottawa. Released October 24 2012.
http://www12.statcan.gc.ca/census-recensement/2011/dp-pd/prof/index.cfm?Lang=E

Age Characteristics: 50 Years and Over, and Median Age

Area	50 to 54 Years	55 to 59 Years	60 to 64 Years	65 to 69 Years	70 to 74 Years	75 to 79 Years	80 to 84 Years	85 Years and Over	Median Age
					Number				
					Total				
Markham	23,645	21,610	18,600	12,395	9,225	6,820	4,740	3,835	39.6
Ontario	1,006,140	864,620	765,655	563,485	440,780	356,150	271,510	246,400	40.4
Canada	2,658,965	2,340,635	2,052,670	1,521,715	1,153,065	922,700	702,070	645,515	40.6
					Males				
Markham	11,365	10,425	9,120	6,030	4,500	3,215	2,000	1,370	38.6
Ontario	492,560	418,755	370,370	270,875	206,350	161,345	113,620	80,925	39.4
Canada	1,309,030	1,147,300	1,002,690	738,010	543,435	417,945	291,085	208,300	39.6
					Females				
Markham	12,285	11,185	9,480	6,365	4,730	3,600	2,745	2,465	40.5
Ontario	513,580	445,865	395,275	292,610	234,435	194,805	157,890	165,475	41.3
Canada	1,349,940	1,193,335	1,049,985	783,705	609,630	504,755	410,985	437,215	41.5
					Percent of Population				
					Total				
Markham	7.8	7.2	6.2	4.1	3.1	2.3	1.6	1.3	–
Ontario	7.8	6.7	6.0	4.4	3.4	2.8	2.1	1.9	–
Canada	7.9	7.0	6.1	4.5	3.4	2.8	2.1	1.9	–
					Males				
Markham	7.7	7.1	6.2	4.1	3.1	2.2	1.4	0.9	–
Ontario	7.9	6.7	5.9	4.3	3.3	2.6	1.8	1.3	–
Canada	8.0	7.0	6.1	4.5	3.3	2.5	1.8	1.3	–
					Females				
Markham	8.0	7.2	6.1	4.1	3.1	2.3	1.8	1.6	–
Ontario	7.8	6.8	6.0	4.4	3.6	3.0	2.4	2.5	–
Canada	7.9	7.0	6.2	4.6	3.6	3.0	2.4	2.6	–

Source: Statistics Canada. 2012. Census Profile. 2011 Census. Statistics Canada Catalogue no. 98-316-XWE. Ottawa. Released October 24 2012.
http://www12.statcan.gc.ca/census-recensement/2011/dp-pd/prof/index.cfm?Lang=E

PROFILES / Markham, Ontario

Private Households by Household Size

Area	1 Person	2 Persons	3 Persons	4 Persons	5 Persons	6 or More Persons	Average Number of Persons in Private Households
			Households				
Markham	10,225	21,285	19,340	22,425	9,845	7,420	3.3
Ontario	1,230,975	1,584,415	803,030	783,925	310,860	174,305	2.6
Canada	3,673,310	4,544,820	2,081,900	1,903,300	724,405	392,885	2.5
			Percent of Households				
Markham	11.3	23.5	21.4	24.8	10.9	8.2	–
Ontario	25.2	32.4	16.4	16.0	6.4	3.6	–
Canada	27.6	34.1	15.6	14.3	5.4	2.9	–

Source: Statistics Canada. 2012. Census Profile. 2011 Census. Statistics Canada Catalogue no. 98-316-XWE. Ottawa. Released October 24 2012.
http://www12.statcan.gc.ca/census-recensement/2011/dp-pd/prof/index.cfm?Lang=E

Dwelling Type

Area	Single-detached House	Semi-detached House	Row House	Apartment: Building with Five or More Storeys	Apartment: Building with Fewer Than Five Storeys	Duplex Apartment	Movable Dwelling	Other Single-attached House
				Number				
Markham	58,045	5,090	10,935	9,225	1,695	5,530	5	10
Ontario	2,718,880	279,470	415,225	789,970	498,160	160,460	15,800	9,540
Canada	7,329,150	646,245	791,600	1,234,770	2,397,550	704,485	183,510	33,310
				Percent of Dwellings				
Markham	64.1	5.6	12.1	10.2	1.9	6.1	0.0	0.0
Ontario	55.6	5.7	8.5	16.2	10.2	3.3	0.3	0.2
Canada	55.0	4.9	5.9	9.3	18.0	5.3	1.4	0.3

Source: Statistics Canada. 2012. Census Profile. 2011 Census. Statistics Canada Catalogue no. 98-316-XWE. Ottawa. Released October 24 2012.
http://www12.statcan.gc.ca/census-recensement/2011/dp-pd/prof/index.cfm?Lang=E

Shelter Costs

		Owned Dwellings				Rented Dwellings		
Area	Number	Median Value[1] ($)	Average Value[1] ($)	Median Monthly Costs[2] ($)	Average Monthly Costs[2] ($)	Number	Median Monthly Costs[3] ($)	Average Monthly Costs[3] ($)
Markham	80,660	500,741	547,560	1,460	1,521	9,855	1,179	1,191
Ontario	3,446,650	300,862	367,428	1,163	1,284	1,385,535	892	926
Canada	9,013,410	280,552	345,182	978	1,141	4,060,385	784	848

Note: All figures cover non-farm, non-reserve private dwellings; (1) Refers to the dollar amount expected by the owner if the dwelling were to be sold; (2) Includes all shelter expenses paid by households that own their dwellings, such as the mortgage payment and the costs of electricity, heat, water and other municipal services, property taxes and condominium fees; (3) Includes all shelter expenses paid by households that rent their dwellings, such as the monthly rent and the costs of electricity, heat and municipal services.
Source: Statistics Canada. 2013. 2011 National Household Survey. Statistics Canada Catalogue no. 99-004-XWE. Ottawa. Released September 11, 2013.

Occupied Private Dwellings by Period of Construction

Area	1960 or Before	1961 to 1980	1981 to 1990	1991 to 2000	2001 to 2005	2006 to 2011
			Number			
Markham	2,665	17,850	22,245	16,780	17,635	13,360
Ontario	1,330,235	1,420,570	763,430	609,310	414,795	348,310
Canada	3,273,105	4,152,715	2,112,110	1,707,880	1,031,020	1,042,430
			Percent of Dwellings			
Markham	2.9	19.7	24.6	18.5	19.5	14.8
Ontario	27.2	29.1	15.6	12.5	8.5	7.1
Canada	24.6	31.2	15.9	12.8	7.7	7.8

Note: Figures cover non-farm, non-reserve private dwellings and includes data up to May 10, 2011.
Source: Statistics Canada. 2013. 2011 National Household Survey. Statistics Canada Catalogue no. 99-004-XWE. Ottawa. Released September 11, 2013.

PROFILES / Markham, Ontario

Educational Attainment

Area	No Certificate, Diploma or Degree	High School Diploma or Equivalent[1]	Apprenticeship or Trades Certificate or Diploma[2]	College, CÉGEP or Other Non-University Certificate or Diploma	University Certificate or Diploma Below the Bachelor Level[3]	Bachelor's Degree	University Certificate, Diploma or Degree Above Bachelor Level[4]
				Number			
				Total			
Markham	40,615	61,235	10,385	36,775	16,520	53,795	28,300
Ontario	1,954,520	2,801,805	771,140	2,070,875	427,150	1,515,075	933,100
Canada	5,485,400	6,968,935	2,950,685	4,970,020	1,200,130	3,634,425	2,049,930
				Males			
Markham	18,580	29,010	6,400	16,475	7,980	26,245	15,110
Ontario	957,040	1,337,055	520,390	894,235	193,355	692,345	470,290
Canada	2,742,875	3,305,415	1,928,970	2,118,430	513,235	1,643,080	1,043,350
				Females			
Markham	22,035	32,225	3,985	20,305	8,535	27,550	13,195
Ontario	997,475	1,464,755	250,750	1,176,640	233,790	822,730	462,805
Canada	2,742,520	3,663,515	1,021,715	2,851,595	686,890	1,991,345	1,006,585
				Percent of Population			
				Total			
Markham	16.4	24.7	4.2	14.9	6.7	21.7	11.4
Ontario	18.7	26.8	7.4	19.8	4.1	14.5	8.9
Canada	20.1	25.6	10.8	18.2	4.4	13.3	7.5
				Males			
Markham	15.5	24.2	5.3	13.8	6.7	21.9	12.6
Ontario	18.9	26.4	10.3	17.7	3.8	13.7	9.3
Canada	20.6	24.9	14.5	15.9	3.9	12.4	7.8
				Females			
Markham	17.2	25.2	3.1	15.9	6.7	21.6	10.3
Ontario	18.4	27.1	4.6	21.8	4.3	15.2	8.6
Canada	19.6	26.2	7.3	20.4	4.9	14.3	7.2

Note: Figures cover total population aged 15 years and over by highest certificate, diploma or degree; (1) Includes persons who have graduated from a secondary school or equivalent. It excludes persons with a postsecondary certificate, diploma or degree; (2) Includes Registered Apprenticeship certificates (including Certificate of Qualification, Journeyperson's designation) and other trades certificates or diplomas such as pre-employment or vocational certificates and diplomas from brief trade programs completed at community colleges, institutes of technology, vocational centres, and similar institutions; (3) Comparisons with other data sources suggest that the category 'University certificate or diploma below the bachelor's level' was over-reported in the NHS. This category likely includes some responses that are actually college certificates or diplomas, bachelor's degrees or other types of education (e.g., university transfer programs, bachelor's programs completed in other countries, incomplete bachelor's programs, non-university professional designations). We recommend users interpret the results for the 'University certificate or diploma below the bachelor's level' category with caution; (4) 'University certificate or diploma above bachelor level' includes the categories: 'Degree in medicine, dentistry, veterinary medicine or optometry,' 'Master's degree' and 'Earned doctorate.'
Source: Statistics Canada. 2013. 2011 National Household Survey. Statistics Canada Catalogue no. 99-004-XWE. Ottawa. Released September 11, 2013.

Household Income Distribution

Area	Less than $10,000	$10,000 to $19,999	$20,000 to $29,999	$30,000 to $39,999	$40,000 to $49,999	$50,000 to $59,999	$60,000 to $79,999	$80,000 to $99,999	$100,000 to $124,999	$125,000 to $149,999	$150,000 and Over
						Households					
Markham	3,240	4,100	4,885	6,320	5,970	5,970	11,550	10,800	10,510	8,205	18,975
Ontario	201,780	354,530	405,725	425,410	425,720	398,705	680,850	552,660	497,970	331,460	611,840
Canada	626,705	1,141,945	1,193,925	1,271,675	1,206,800	1,102,120	1,865,280	1,458,240	1,260,770	802,555	1,389,240
						Percent of Households					
Markham	3.6	4.5	5.4	7.0	6.6	6.6	12.8	11.9	11.6	9.1	21.0
Ontario	4.1	7.3	8.3	8.7	8.7	8.2	13.9	11.3	10.2	6.8	12.5
Canada	4.7	8.6	9.0	9.5	9.1	8.3	14.0	10.9	9.5	6.0	10.4

Note: Household income is the sum of the total incomes of all members of that household. Total income refers to monetary receipts from certain sources, before income taxes and deductions, during calendar year 2010.
Source: Statistics Canada. 2013. 2011 National Household Survey. Statistics Canada Catalogue no. 99-004-XWE. Ottawa. Released September 11, 2013.

Median and Average Household and Economic Family Income

Area	Median Household Income ($)	Average Household Income ($)	Median After-tax Household Income ($)	Average After-tax Household Income ($)	Median Economic Family Income ($)	Average Economic Family Income ($)	Median After-tax Economic Family Income ($)	Average After-tax Economic Family Income ($)
Markham	86,022	108,520	75,135	89,708	92,173	114,304	80,483	94,406
Ontario	66,358	85,772	58,717	71,523	80,987	100,152	71,128	83,322
Canada	61,072	79,102	54,089	66,149	76,511	94,125	67,044	78,517

Note: Figures cover household and economic familiy income in 2010. A household is defined as a person or a group of persons (other than foreign residents) who occupy the same private dwelling and do not have a usual place of residence elsewhere in Canada. Every person is a member of one and only one household. An economic family is defined as a group of two or more persons who live in the same dwelling and are related to each other by blood, marriage, common-law, adoption or a foster relationship. A couple may be of opposite or same sex.
Source: Statistics Canada. 2013. 2011 National Household Survey. Statistics Canada Catalogue no. 99-004-XWE. Ottawa. Released September 11, 2013.

Individual Income Distribution

Area	Less than $10,000	$10,000 to $19,999	$20,000 to $29,999	$30,000 to $39,999	$40,000 to $49,999	$50,000 to $59,999	$60,000 to $79,999	$80,000 to $99,999	$100,000 to $124,999	$125,000 and Over
					Number					
					Total					
Markham	52,300	42,125	27,045	22,840	18,385	14,925	20,980	14,145	7,985	9,830
Ontario	1,780,355	1,748,060	1,361,710	1,136,730	980,790	746,360	964,280	574,710	293,865	330,285
Canada	4,492,040	4,835,710	3,670,020	3,180,360	2,603,520	1,921,650	2,437,440	1,302,045	693,580	782,135
					Males					
Markham	23,870	17,670	12,410	10,485	8,465	7,370	11,255	8,195	5,265	7,240
Ontario	781,095	669,815	580,990	535,255	491,125	407,005	569,205	341,160	201,125	244,500
Canada	1,936,365	1,864,880	1,588,260	1,522,190	1,333,510	1,079,780	1,473,145	823,720	492,905	599,905
					Females					
Markham	28,435	24,465	14,640	12,350	9,925	7,560	9,725	5,960	2,715	2,595
Ontario	999,265	1,078,245	780,720	601,475	489,665	339,360	395,075	233,550	92,740	85,790
Canada	2,555,675	2,970,825	2,081,760	1,658,170	1,270,010	841,870	964,300	478,330	200,680	182,230
					Percent of Population					
					Total					
Markham	22.7	18.3	11.7	9.9	8.0	6.5	9.1	6.1	3.5	4.3
Ontario	18.0	17.6	13.7	11.5	9.9	7.5	9.7	5.8	3.0	3.3
Canada	17.3	18.7	14.2	12.3	10.0	7.4	9.4	5.0	2.7	3.0
					Males					
Markham	21.3	15.7	11.1	9.3	7.5	6.6	10.0	7.3	4.7	6.5
Ontario	16.2	13.9	12.1	11.1	10.2	8.4	11.8	7.1	4.2	5.1
Canada	15.2	14.7	12.5	12.0	10.5	8.5	11.6	6.5	3.9	4.7
					Females					
Markham	24.0	20.7	12.4	10.4	8.4	6.4	8.2	5.0	2.3	2.2
Ontario	19.6	21.2	15.3	11.8	9.6	6.7	7.8	4.6	1.8	1.7
Canada	19.4	22.5	15.8	12.6	9.6	6.4	7.3	3.6	1.5	1.4

Note: Figures cover individuals aged 15 years and over with income. Income refers to monetary receipts from certain sources, before income taxes and deductions, during calendar year 2010.
Source: Statistics Canada. 2013. 2011 National Household Survey. Statistics Canada Catalogue no. 99-004-XWE. Ottawa. Released September 11, 2013.

Labour Force Status

| | In the Labour Force ||| Not in the |
Area	All	Employed	Unemployed	Labour Force
		Number		
		Total		
Markham	160,225	147,315	12,910	87,395
Ontario	6,864,990	6,297,005	567,985	3,608,685
Canada	17,990,080	16,595,035	1,395,045	9,269,445
		Males		
Markham	83,685	77,130	6,550	36,110
Ontario	3,542,030	3,249,165	292,865	1,522,690
Canada	9,388,570	8,634,310	754,255	3,906,785
		Females		
Markham	76,535	70,180	6,355	51,285
Ontario	3,322,955	3,047,840	275,120	2,085,990
Canada	8,601,515	7,960,725	640,790	5,362,660
		Percent of Labour Force		
		Total		
Markham	64.7	59.5	8.1	35.3
Ontario	65.5	60.1	8.3	34.5
Canada	66.0	60.9	7.8	34.0
		Males		
Markham	69.9	64.4	7.8	30.1
Ontario	69.9	64.2	8.3	30.1
Canada	70.6	64.9	8.0	29.4
		Females		
Markham	59.9	54.9	8.3	40.1
Ontario	61.4	56.3	8.3	38.6
Canada	61.6	57.0	7.4	38.4

Note: Figures are based on total population 15 years and over
Source: Statistics Canada. 2013. 2011 National Household Survey. Statistics Canada Catalogue no. 99-004-XWE. Ottawa. Released September 11, 2013.

Labour Force by Industry (NAICS Codes 11–52)

Area	Agriculture, forestry, fishing & hunting	Mining, quarrying, & oil & gas extraction	Utilities	Construction	Manufacturing	Wholesale Trade	Retail Trade	Transportation & warehousing	Information & cultural industries	Finance & insurance
					Number					
					Total					
Markham	300	155	1,125	5,610	15,345	12,025	16,515	4,835	5,855	15,980
Ontario	101,280	29,985	57,035	417,900	697,565	305,030	751,200	307,405	178,720	364,415
Canada	437,650	261,050	149,940	1,215,380	1,619,295	733,445	2,031,665	827,780	420,830	767,960
					Males					
Markham	185	105	775	4,640	9,525	7,165	8,355	3,785	3,290	7,770
Ontario	66,485	25,650	42,685	369,300	493,305	197,770	344,480	225,245	98,835	153,125
Canada	307,370	211,690	110,765	1,068,710	1,167,680	494,545	933,850	617,305	235,875	296,995
					Females					
Markham	120	50	345	965	5,820	4,860	8,165	1,055	2,560	8,205
Ontario	34,800	4,340	14,350	48,595	204,260	107,260	406,720	82,160	79,885	211,290
Canada	130,285	49,360	39,175	146,670	451,615	238,900	1,097,820	210,475	184,955	470,960
					Percent of Labour Force					
					Total					
Markham	0.2	0.1	0.7	3.6	9.9	7.7	10.6	3.1	3.8	10.3
Ontario	1.5	0.4	0.9	6.3	10.4	4.6	11.2	4.6	2.7	5.5
Canada	2.5	1.5	0.9	6.9	9.2	4.2	11.6	4.7	2.4	4.4
					Males					
Markham	0.2	0.1	1.0	5.7	11.7	8.8	10.3	4.7	4.0	9.6
Ontario	1.9	0.7	1.2	10.7	14.3	5.7	10.0	6.5	2.9	4.4
Canada	3.3	2.3	1.2	11.6	12.7	5.4	10.2	6.7	2.6	3.2
					Females					
Markham	0.2	0.1	0.5	1.3	7.8	6.5	11.0	1.4	3.4	11.0
Ontario	1.1	0.1	0.4	1.5	6.3	3.3	12.6	2.5	2.5	6.5
Canada	1.6	0.6	0.5	1.7	5.4	2.8	13.1	2.5	2.2	5.6

Note: Figures are based on total experienced labour force 15 years and over. Experienced labour force refers to persons who, during the week of Sunday, May 1 to Saturday, May 7, 2011, were employed and the unemployed who had last worked for pay or in self-employment in either 2010 or 2011.
Source: Statistics Canada. 2013. 2011 National Household Survey. Statistics Canada Catalogue no. 99-004-XWE. Ottawa. Released September 11, 2013.

Labour Force by Industry (NAICS Codes 53–91)

Area	Real estate & rental & leasing	Profess., scientific & tech. services	Mgmt of companies & enterprises	Admin. & support, waste mgmt & remed. services	Educational services	Health care & social assistance	Arts, entertain. & recreation	Accomm. & food services	Other services (except public admin.)	Public admin.
					Number					
					Total					
Markham	4,190	18,600	295	6,830	10,375	12,875	2,120	10,170	6,330	6,040
Ontario	133,980	511,020	6,525	309,630	499,690	692,130	144,065	417,675	296,340	458,665
Canada	321,895	1,240,850	17,460	728,330	1,301,435	1,949,650	363,405	1,130,750	807,800	1,261,050
					Males					
Markham	2,255	10,780	145	3,820	3,185	2,790	1,070	5,685	2,735	3,225
Ontario	72,835	281,420	3,540	172,475	162,765	120,165	75,035	177,240	133,795	236,655
Canada	179,090	688,625	9,380	411,250	424,915	349,430	188,270	469,990	372,940	652,510
					Females					
Markham	1,935	7,820	150	3,015	7,185	10,085	1,050	4,490	3,600	2,820
Ontario	61,145	229,600	2,990	137,155	336,925	571,965	69,030	240,430	162,550	222,015
Canada	142,805	552,225	8,075	317,085	876,515	1,600,220	175,135	660,760	434,865	608,535
					Percent of Labour Force					
					Total					
Markham	2.7	12.0	0.2	4.4	6.7	8.3	1.4	6.5	4.1	3.9
Ontario	2.0	7.6	0.1	4.6	7.5	10.4	2.2	6.3	4.4	6.9
Canada	1.8	7.1	0.1	4.1	7.4	11.1	2.1	6.4	4.6	7.2
					Males					
Markham	2.8	13.3	0.2	4.7	3.9	3.4	1.3	7.0	3.4	4.0
Ontario	2.1	8.2	0.1	5.0	4.7	3.5	2.2	5.1	3.9	6.9
Canada	1.9	7.5	0.1	4.5	4.6	3.8	2.0	5.1	4.1	7.1
					Females					
Markham	2.6	10.5	0.2	4.1	9.7	13.6	1.4	6.0	4.8	3.8
Ontario	1.9	7.1	0.1	4.2	10.4	17.7	2.1	7.4	5.0	6.9
Canada	1.7	6.6	0.1	3.8	10.4	19.1	2.1	7.9	5.2	7.2

Note: Figures are based on total experienced labour force 15 years and over. Experienced labour force refers to persons who, during the week of Sunday, May 1 to Saturday, May 7, 2011, were employed and the unemployed who had last worked for pay or in self-employment in either 2010 or 2011.
Source: Statistics Canada. 2013. 2011 National Household Survey. Statistics Canada Catalogue no. 99-004-XWE. Ottawa. Released September 11, 2013.

Occupation

Area	Mgmt	Business, Finance & Admin.	Natural/ Applied Sciences & Related	Health	Education, Law & Social, Community & Government Services	Art, Culture, Recreation & Sport	Sales & Service	Trades, Transport & Equip. Operators & Related	Natural Resources, Agri. & Related Production	Mfg & Utilities
					Number					
					Total					
Markham	20,340	33,035	19,100	7,900	15,270	4,565	36,225	10,460	985	7,700
Ontario	770,580	1,138,330	494,500	392,695	801,465	206,420	1,550,260	868,515	106,810	350,685
Canada	1,963,600	2,902,045	1,237,775	1,107,200	2,064,675	503,415	4,068,170	2,537,775	397,930	805,040
					Males					
Markham	12,890	11,480	14,660	2,150	4,700	2,180	18,685	9,610	870	4,070
Ontario	474,655	352,505	384,345	78,330	264,570	96,055	673,880	812,280	82,610	233,565
Canada	1,229,460	854,190	966,355	217,520	676,550	232,535	1,745,705	2,385,615	318,945	564,300
					Females					
Markham	7,450	21,555	4,440	5,750	10,575	2,385	17,540	855	120	3,625
Ontario	295,920	785,825	110,150	314,370	536,895	110,370	876,380	56,230	24,200	117,115
Canada	734,140	2,047,855	271,415	889,675	1,388,130	270,875	2,322,465	152,165	78,980	240,740
					Percent of Labour Force					
					Total					
Markham	13.1	21.2	12.3	5.1	9.8	2.9	23.3	6.7	0.6	4.9
Ontario	11.5	17.0	7.4	5.9	12.0	3.1	23.2	13.0	1.6	5.2
Canada	11.2	16.5	7.0	6.3	11.7	2.9	23.1	14.4	2.3	4.6
					Males					
Markham	15.9	14.1	18.0	2.6	5.8	2.7	23.0	11.8	1.1	5.0
Ontario	13.7	10.2	11.1	2.3	7.7	2.8	19.5	23.5	2.4	6.8
Canada	13.4	9.3	10.5	2.4	7.4	2.5	19.0	26.0	3.5	6.1
					Females					
Markham	10.0	29.0	6.0	7.7	14.2	3.2	23.6	1.2	0.2	4.9
Ontario	9.2	24.3	3.4	9.7	16.6	3.4	27.2	1.7	0.7	3.6
Canada	8.7	24.4	3.2	10.6	16.5	3.2	27.7	1.8	0.9	2.9

Note: Figures are based on total experienced labour force 15 years and over
Source: Statistics Canada. 2013. 2011 National Household Survey. Statistics Canada Catalogue no. 99-004-XWE. Ottawa. Released September 11, 2013.

Place of Work Status

Area	Worked at Home	Worked Outside Canada	No Fixed Workplace Address	Worked at Usual Place
		Number		
		Total		
Markham	10,800	1,215	14,510	120,785
Ontario	423,790	31,390	670,835	5,170,980
Canada	1,142,640	66,460	1,868,245	13,517,690
		Males		
Markham	5,325	865	9,850	61,095
Ontario	216,900	21,150	486,560	2,524,555
Canada	582,150	47,355	1,400,485	6,604,325
		Females		
Markham	5,480	345	4,660	59,695
Ontario	206,895	10,240	184,275	2,646,420
Canada	560,490	19,100	467,760	6,913,370
		Percent of Labour Force		
		Total		
Markham	7.3	0.8	9.8	82.0
Ontario	6.7	0.5	10.7	82.1
Canada	6.9	0.4	11.3	81.5
		Males		
Markham	6.9	1.1	12.8	79.2
Ontario	6.7	0.7	15.0	77.7
Canada	6.7	0.5	16.2	76.5
		Females		
Markham	7.8	0.5	6.6	85.1
Ontario	6.8	0.3	6.0	86.8
Canada	7.0	0.2	5.9	86.8

Note: Figures are based on total employed labour force 15 years and over.
Source: Statistics Canada. 2013. 2011 National Household Survey. Statistics Canada Catalogue no. 99-004-XWE. Ottawa. Released September 11, 2013.

Mode of Transportation to Work

Area	Car; Truck; Van; as Driver	Car; Truck; Van; as Passenger	Public Transit	Walked	Bicycled	All Other Modes
			Number			
			Total			
Markham	100,100	9,640	21,495	2,425	345	1,295
Ontario	4,235,315	357,110	818,270	299,095	69,885	62,145
Canada	11,393,140	867,050	1,851,525	880,815	201,780	191,625
			Males			
Markham	56,920	2,760	9,565	905	245	550
Ontario	2,316,680	143,410	340,995	131,765	47,635	30,635
Canada	6,238,835	349,530	788,290	387,580	135,840	104,725
			Females			
Markham	43,185	6,880	11,925	1,520	105	745
Ontario	1,918,640	213,700	477,275	167,325	22,250	31,515
Canada	5,154,305	517,520	1,063,235	493,230	65,940	86,900
			Percent of Labour Force			
			Total			
Markham	74.0	7.1	15.9	1.8	0.3	1.0
Ontario	72.5	6.1	14.0	5.1	1.2	1.1
Canada	74.0	5.6	12.0	5.7	1.3	1.2
			Males			
Markham	80.2	3.9	13.5	1.3	0.3	0.8
Ontario	76.9	4.8	11.3	4.4	1.6	1.0
Canada	77.9	4.4	9.8	4.8	1.7	1.3
			Females			
Markham	67.1	10.7	18.5	2.4	0.2	1.2
Ontario	67.8	7.5	16.9	5.9	0.8	1.1
Canada	69.8	7.0	14.4	6.7	0.9	1.2

Note: Figures are based on total employed labour force 15 years and over.
Source: Statistics Canada. 2013. 2011 National Household Survey. Statistics Canada Catalogue no. 99-004-XWE. Ottawa. Released September 11, 2013.

Visible Minority Population Characteristics

Area	Total Minority	South Asian[1]	Chinese	Black	Filipino	Latin American	Arab	SE Asian[2]	West Asian[3]	Korean	Japanese	Multiple[4]
						Number						
						Total						
Markham	217,095	57,375	114,950	9,715	9,020	1,600	3,400	2,750	6,185	3,160	1,145	5,805
Ontario	3,279,565	965,990	629,140	539,205	275,380	172,560	151,645	137,875	122,530	78,290	29,085	96,735
Canada	6,264,750	1,567,400	1,324,750	945,665	619,310	381,280	380,620	312,075	206,840	161,130	87,270	171,935
						Males						
Markham	105,910	28,760	55,960	4,535	3,835	795	1,725	1,350	3,115	1,530	615	2,710
Ontario	1,582,480	484,355	301,575	251,295	116,825	83,205	79,620	67,645	62,515	38,045	13,345	46,765
Canada	3,043,010	790,755	632,325	453,005	268,885	186,355	203,485	154,035	105,620	77,165	38,270	83,335
						Females						
Markham	111,185	28,615	58,985	5,180	5,185	810	1,670	1,395	3,065	1,630	530	3,095
Ontario	1,697,085	481,635	327,570	287,915	158,555	89,360	72,025	70,230	60,010	40,250	15,740	49,970
Canada	3,221,745	776,650	692,420	492,660	350,425	194,925	177,140	158,045	101,220	83,965	48,990	88,600
						Percent of Population						
						Total						
Markham	72.3	19.1	38.3	3.2	3.0	0.5	1.1	0.9	2.1	1.1	0.4	1.9
Ontario	25.9	7.6	5.0	4.3	2.2	1.4	1.2	1.1	1.0	0.6	0.2	0.8
Canada	19.1	4.8	4.0	2.9	1.9	1.2	1.2	0.9	0.6	0.5	0.3	0.5
						Males						
Markham	72.2	19.6	38.1	3.1	2.6	0.5	1.2	0.9	2.1	1.0	0.4	1.8
Ontario	25.6	7.8	4.9	4.1	1.9	1.3	1.3	1.1	1.0	0.6	0.2	0.8
Canada	18.8	4.9	3.9	2.8	1.7	1.2	1.3	1.0	0.7	0.5	0.2	0.5
						Females						
Markham	72.5	18.7	38.5	3.4	3.4	0.5	1.1	0.9	2.0	1.1	0.3	2.0
Ontario	26.2	7.4	5.1	4.4	2.5	1.4	1.1	1.1	0.9	0.6	0.2	0.8
Canada	19.3	4.7	4.1	3.0	2.1	1.2	1.1	0.9	0.6	0.5	0.3	0.5

Note: The Employment Equity Act defines visible minorities as 'persons, other than Aboriginal peoples, who are non-Caucasian in race or non-white in colour';
(1) Includes 'East Indian,' 'Pakistani,' 'Sri Lankan,' etc.; (2) Includes 'Vietnamese,' 'Cambodian,' 'Malaysian,' 'Laotian,' etc.; (3) Includes 'Iranian,' 'Afghan,' etc.; (4) Includes respondents who reported more than one visible minority group by checking two or more mark-in circles, e.g., 'Black' and 'South Asian.'
Source: Statistics Canada. 2013. 2011 National Household Survey. Statistics Canada Catalogue no. 99-004-XWE. Ottawa. Released September 11, 2013.

PROFILES / Markham, Ontario

Aboriginal Population

Area	Aboriginal Identity[1]	First Nations (North American Indian) Single Identity[2]	Métis Single Identity	Inuk (Inuit) Single Identity	Multiple Aboriginal Identities[3]	Aboriginal Identities Not Included Elsewhere
Number						
Total						
Markham	485	255	180	0	30	30
Ontario	301,430	201,100	86,020	3,355	2,910	8,040
Canada	1,400,685	851,560	451,795	59,440	11,415	26,475
Males						
Markham	260	170	65	0	0	20
Ontario	145,020	96,620	41,755	1,475	1,420	3,750
Canada	682,190	411,785	223,335	29,495	5,525	12,055
Females						
Markham	230	90	115	0	20	0
Ontario	156,410	104,485	44,260	1,880	1,490	4,295
Canada	718,500	439,775	228,460	29,950	5,890	14,420
Percent of Population						
Total						
Markham	0.2	0.1	0.1	0.0	0.0	0.0
Ontario	2.4	1.6	0.7	0.0	0.0	0.1
Canada	4.3	2.6	1.4	0.2	0.0	0.1
Males						
Markham	0.2	0.1	0.0	0.0	0.0	0.0
Ontario	2.3	1.6	0.7	0.0	0.0	0.1
Canada	4.2	2.5	1.4	0.2	0.0	0.1
Females						
Markham	0.1	0.1	0.1	0.0	0.0	0.0
Ontario	2.4	1.6	0.7	0.0	0.0	0.1
Canada	4.3	2.6	1.4	0.2	0.0	0.1

Note: (1) Includes persons who reported being an Aboriginal person, that is, First Nations (North American Indian), Métis or Inuk (Inuit) and/or those who reported Registered or Treaty Indian status, that is registered under the Indian Act of Canada, and/or those who reported membership in a First Nation or Indian band. Aboriginal peoples of Canada are defined in the Constitution Act, 1982, section 35-2 as including the Indian, Inuit and Métis peoples of Canada; (2) Users should be aware that the estimates associated with this variable are more affected than most by the incomplete enumeration of certain Indian reserves and Indian settlements in the National Household Survey (NHS); (3) Includes persons who reported being any two or all three of the following: First Nations (North American Indian), Métis or Inuk (Inuit).
Source: Statistics Canada. 2013. 2011 National Household Survey. Statistics Canada Catalogue no. 99-004-XWE. Ottawa. Released September 11, 2013.

Ethnic Origin

Area	North American Aboriginal	Other North American	European	Caribbean	Latin, Central and South American	African	Asian	Oceania
Number								
Total								
Markham	1,035	25,350	82,225	10,695	4,700	6,595	204,940	205
Ontario	441,395	3,059,480	8,231,410	396,485	271,545	331,460	2,604,595	19,410
Canada	1,836,035	11,070,455	20,157,965	627,590	544,375	766,735	5,011,225	74,875
Males								
Markham	445	12,745	40,305	4,935	2,140	3,365	99,915	105
Ontario	210,490	1,507,105	4,019,885	181,805	130,035	160,940	1,265,540	9,855
Canada	885,675	5,462,685	9,913,150	291,640	264,635	387,360	2,435,540	37,490
Females								
Markham	590	12,600	41,920	5,755	2,560	3,235	105,025	100
Ontario	230,905	1,552,380	4,211,525	214,675	141,510	170,515	1,339,050	9,555
Canada	950,360	5,607,770	10,244,820	335,945	279,740	379,380	2,575,680	37,385
Percent of Population								
Total								
Markham	0.3	8.4	27.4	3.6	1.6	2.2	68.3	0.1
Ontario	3.5	24.2	65.1	3.1	2.1	2.6	20.6	0.2
Canada	5.6	33.7	61.4	1.9	1.7	2.3	15.3	0.2
Males								
Markham	0.3	8.7	27.5	3.4	1.5	2.3	68.1	0.1
Ontario	3.4	24.4	65.0	2.9	2.1	2.6	20.5	0.2
Canada	5.5	33.8	61.3	1.8	1.6	2.4	15.1	0.2
Females								
Markham	0.4	8.2	27.3	3.8	1.7	2.1	68.5	0.1
Ontario	3.6	24.0	65.1	3.3	2.2	2.6	20.7	0.1
Canada	5.7	33.6	61.4	2.0	1.7	2.3	15.4	0.2

Note: The sum of the ethnic groups in this table is greater than the total population estimate because a person may report more than one ethnic origin in the NHS.
Source: Statistics Canada. 2013. 2011 National Household Survey. Statistics Canada Catalogue no. 99-004-XWE. Ottawa. Released September 11, 2013.

Religion

Area	Buddhist	Christian	Hindu	Jewish	Muslim	Sikh	Traditional (Aboriginal) Spirituality	Other Religions	No Religious Affiliation
				Number Total					
Markham	13,280	132,230	29,540	7,330	22,415	4,335	20	1,290	89,695
Ontario	163,750	8,167,295	366,720	195,540	581,950	179,765	15,905	53,080	2,927,790
Canada	366,830	22,102,745	497,965	329,495	1,053,945	454,965	64,935	130,835	7,850,605
				Males					
Markham	5,895	62,090	14,860	3,520	11,165	2,240	15	620	46,380
Ontario	75,355	3,839,925	183,580	95,795	293,925	90,515	7,600	23,555	1,571,195
Canada	168,465	10,497,775	250,435	161,265	540,555	229,435	31,805	57,745	4,225,645
				Females					
Markham	7,385	70,135	14,680	3,815	11,255	2,095	0	665	43,315
Ontario	88,395	4,327,365	183,140	99,740	288,025	89,250	8,310	29,525	1,356,600
Canada	198,365	11,604,975	247,525	168,235	513,395	225,530	33,135	73,090	3,624,965
				Percent of Population Total					
Markham	4.4	44.1	9.8	2.4	7.5	1.4	0.0	0.4	29.9
Ontario	1.3	64.6	2.9	1.5	4.6	1.4	0.1	0.4	23.1
Canada	1.1	67.3	1.5	1.0	3.2	1.4	0.2	0.4	23.9
				Males					
Markham	4.0	42.3	10.1	2.4	7.6	1.5	0.0	0.4	31.6
Ontario	1.2	62.1	3.0	1.5	4.8	1.5	0.1	0.4	25.4
Canada	1.0	64.9	1.5	1.0	3.3	1.4	0.2	0.4	26.1
				Females					
Markham	4.8	45.7	9.6	2.5	7.3	1.4	0.0	0.4	28.2
Ontario	1.4	66.9	2.8	1.5	4.5	1.4	0.1	0.5	21.0
Canada	1.2	69.5	1.5	1.0	3.1	1.4	0.2	0.4	21.7

Note: Religion refers to the person's self-identification as having a connection or affiliation with any religious denomination, group, body, sect, cult or other religiously defined community or system of belief. Religion is not limited to formal membership in a religious organization or group. Persons without a religious connection or affiliation can self-identify as atheist, agnostic or humanist, or can provide another applicable response.
Source: Statistics Canada. 2013. 2011 National Household Survey. Statistics Canada Catalogue no. 99-004-XWE. Ottawa. Released September 11, 2013.

Religion—Christian Denominations

Area	Anglican	Baptist	Catholic	Christian Orthodox	Lutheran	Pentecostal	Presbyterian	United Church	Other Christian
				Number Total					
Markham	8,865	6,460	63,025	11,780	1,375	3,450	4,260	7,310	25,710
Ontario	774,560	244,650	3,976,610	297,710	163,460	213,945	319,585	952,465	1,224,300
Canada	1,631,845	635,840	12,810,705	550,690	478,185	478,705	472,385	2,007,610	3,036,780
				Males					
Markham	4,090	2,910	29,880	5,915	610	1,690	1,880	3,305	11,820
Ontario	355,175	112,285	1,895,940	145,825	75,225	94,955	148,535	435,255	576,730
Canada	752,945	293,905	6,167,290	270,205	221,525	217,850	218,955	912,545	1,442,550
				Females					
Markham	4,775	3,550	33,150	5,865	765	1,760	2,380	4,005	13,890
Ontario	419,390	132,370	2,080,665	151,885	88,230	118,990	171,050	517,210	647,570
Canada	878,900	341,940	6,643,415	280,485	256,660	260,850	253,430	1,095,065	1,594,230
				Percent of Population Total					
Markham	3.0	2.2	21.0	3.9	0.5	1.1	1.4	2.4	8.6
Ontario	6.1	1.9	31.4	2.4	1.3	1.7	2.5	7.5	9.7
Canada	5.0	1.9	39.0	1.7	1.5	1.5	1.4	6.1	9.2
				Males					
Markham	2.8	2.0	20.4	4.0	0.4	1.2	1.3	2.3	8.1
Ontario	5.7	1.8	30.7	2.4	1.2	1.5	2.4	7.0	9.3
Canada	4.7	1.8	38.2	1.7	1.4	1.3	1.4	5.6	8.9
				Females					
Markham	3.1	2.3	21.6	3.8	0.5	1.1	1.6	2.6	9.1
Ontario	6.5	2.0	32.2	2.3	1.4	1.8	2.6	8.0	10.0
Canada	5.3	2.0	39.8	1.7	1.5	1.6	1.5	6.6	9.6

Note: Religion refers to the person's self-identification as having a connection or affiliation with any religious denomination, group, body, sect, cult or other religiously defined community or system of belief. Religion is not limited to formal membership in a religious organization or group. Persons without a religious connection or affiliation can self-identify as atheist, agnostic or humanist, or can provide another applicable response.
Source: Statistics Canada. 2013. 2011 National Household Survey. Statistics Canada Catalogue no. 99-004-XWE. Ottawa. Released September 11, 2013.

PROFILES / Markham, Ontario

Immigrant Status and Period of Immigration

Area	Non-Immigrants[1]	Immigrants All	Before 1971	1971 to 1980	1981 to 1990	1991 to 2000	2001 to 2005	2006 to 2011	Non-Permanent Residents[3]
				Number					
				Total					
Markham	122,335	173,895	14,830	22,025	33,380	60,215	25,060	18,380	3,910
Ontario	8,906,000	3,611,365	723,030	464,380	538,285	866,220	518,405	501,060	134,425
Canada	25,720,175	6,775,765	1,261,055	870,775	949,890	1,539,050	992,070	1,162,915	356,385
				Males					
Markham	62,160	82,860	7,420	10,595	16,025	28,515	11,800	8,510	1,775
Ontario	4,410,240	1,706,385	341,820	217,990	258,095	408,270	245,850	234,360	64,825
Canada	12,753,235	3,231,370	605,430	416,670	454,570	724,905	474,545	555,245	178,515
				Females					
Markham	60,180	91,035	7,410	11,430	17,360	31,700	13,260	9,865	2,140
Ontario	4,495,765	1,904,985	381,210	246,390	280,190	457,950	272,550	266,695	69,600
Canada	12,966,935	3,544,400	655,625	454,105	495,325	814,145	517,530	607,670	177,870
				Percent of Population					
				Total					
Markham	40.8	57.9	4.9	7.3	11.1	20.1	8.3	6.1	1.3
Ontario	70.4	28.5	5.7	3.7	4.3	6.8	4.1	4.0	1.1
Canada	78.3	20.6	3.8	2.7	2.9	4.7	3.0	3.5	1.1
				Males					
Markham	42.3	56.4	5.1	7.2	10.9	19.4	8.0	5.8	1.2
Ontario	71.3	27.6	5.5	3.5	4.2	6.6	4.0	3.8	1.0
Canada	78.9	20.0	3.7	2.6	2.8	4.5	2.9	3.4	1.1
				Females					
Markham	39.2	59.4	4.8	7.5	11.3	20.7	8.6	6.4	1.4
Ontario	69.5	29.4	5.9	3.8	4.3	7.1	4.2	4.1	1.1
Canada	77.7	21.2	3.9	2.7	3.0	4.9	3.1	3.6	1.1

Note: (1) Non-immigrant refers to a person who is a Canadian citizen by birth; (2) Immigrant refers to a person who is or has ever been a landed immigrant/permanent resident. This person has been granted the right to live in Canada permanently by immigration authorities. Some immigrants have resided in Canada for a number of years, while others have arrived recently. Some immigrants are Canadian citizens, while others are not. Most immigrants are born outside Canada, but a small number are born in Canada. In the 2011 National Household Survey, 'Immigrants' includes immigrants who landed in Canada prior to May 10, 2011; (3) Non-permanent resident refers to a person from another country who has a work or study permit, or who is a refugee claimant, and any non-Canadian-born family member living in Canada with them.
Source: Statistics Canada. 2013. 2011 National Household Survey. Statistics Canada Catalogue no. 99-004-XWE. Ottawa. Released September 11, 2013.

Mother Tongue

Area	English	French	Non-official Language	English & French	English & Non-official Language	French & Non-official Language	English, French & Non-official Language
			Number				
			Total				
Markham	115,750	2,035	171,875	525	9,980	255	260
Ontario	8,677,040	493,300	3,264,435	46,605	219,425	13,645	7,615
Canada	18,858,980	7,054,975	6,567,680	144,685	396,330	74,430	24,095
			Males				
Markham	58,175	955	82,505	230	4,865	120	115
Ontario	4,276,970	232,785	1,562,190	21,805	106,790	6,285	3,495
Canada	9,345,225	3,452,380	3,157,785	69,975	192,000	36,535	11,965
			Females				
Markham	57,570	1,075	89,370	290	5,115	140	140
Ontario	4,400,065	260,510	1,702,240	24,795	112,635	7,365	4,115
Canada	9,513,750	3,602,590	3,409,895	74,710	204,330	37,890	12,130
			Percent of Population				
			Total				
Markham	38.5	0.7	57.2	0.2	3.3	0.1	0.1
Ontario	68.2	3.9	25.7	0.4	1.7	0.1	0.1
Canada	56.9	21.3	19.8	0.4	1.2	0.2	0.1
			Males				
Markham	39.6	0.6	56.1	0.2	3.3	0.1	0.1
Ontario	68.9	3.7	25.2	0.4	1.7	0.1	0.1
Canada	57.5	21.2	19.4	0.4	1.2	0.2	0.1
			Females				
Markham	37.5	0.7	58.1	0.2	3.3	0.1	0.1
Ontario	67.6	4.0	26.1	0.4	1.7	0.1	0.1
Canada	56.4	21.4	20.2	0.4	1.2	0.2	0.1

Note: Figures cover total population excluding institutional residents.
Source: Statistics Canada. 2012. Census Profile. 2011 Census. Statistics Canada Catalogue no. 98-316-XWE. Ottawa. Released October 24 2012.
http://www12.statcan.gc.ca/census-recensement/2011/dp-pd/prof/index.cfm?Lang=E

Language Spoken Most Often at Home

Area	English	French	Non-official Language	English & French	English & Non-official Language	French & Non-official Language	English, French & Non-official Language
			Number				
			Total				
Markham	156,850	920	116,295	435	25,715	75	385
Ontario	10,044,810	284,115	1,827,870	37,955	509,105	6,370	11,845
Canada	21,457,075	6,827,865	3,673,865	131,205	875,135	109,700	46,330
			Males				
Markham	77,755	420	55,735	220	12,665	25	155
Ontario	4,930,610	133,495	872,860	17,250	248,050	2,855	5,225
Canada	10,585,620	3,348,235	1,767,310	63,475	425,370	53,010	22,845
			Females				
Markham	79,090	500	60,565	215	13,055	45	230
Ontario	5,114,200	150,620	955,010	20,705	261,055	3,520	6,620
Canada	10,871,455	3,479,625	1,906,555	67,730	449,765	56,690	23,485
			Percent of Population				
			Total				
Markham	52.2	0.3	38.7	0.1	8.6	0.0	0.1
Ontario	79.0	2.2	14.4	0.3	4.0	0.1	0.1
Canada	64.8	20.6	11.1	0.4	2.6	0.3	0.1
			Males				
Markham	52.9	0.3	37.9	0.1	8.6	0.0	0.1
Ontario	79.4	2.1	14.1	0.3	4.0	0.0	0.1
Canada	65.1	20.6	10.9	0.4	2.6	0.3	0.1
			Females				
Markham	51.5	0.3	39.4	0.1	8.5	0.0	0.1
Ontario	78.5	2.3	14.7	0.3	4.0	0.1	0.1
Canada	64.5	20.6	11.3	0.4	2.7	0.3	0.1

Note: Figures cover total population excluding institutional residents.
Source: Statistics Canada. 2012. Census Profile. 2011 Census. Statistics Canada Catalogue no. 98-316-XWE. Ottawa. Released October 24 2012.
http://www12.statcan.gc.ca/census-recensement/2011/dp-pd/prof/index.cfm?Lang=E

Knowledge of Official Languages

Area	English Only	French Only	English & French	Neither English nor French
		Number		
		Total		
Markham	257,730	175	17,760	25,015
Ontario	10,984,360	42,980	1,395,805	298,920
Canada	22,564,665	4,165,015	5,795,570	595,920
		Males		
Markham	128,700	75	7,795	10,405
Ontario	5,445,050	18,805	627,725	118,765
Canada	11,222,185	1,925,340	2,876,560	241,790
		Females		
Markham	129,030	105	9,970	14,610
Ontario	5,539,310	24,175	768,085	180,155
Canada	11,342,485	2,239,680	2,919,005	354,135
		Percent of Population		
		Total		
Markham	85.7	0.1	5.9	8.3
Ontario	86.3	0.3	11.0	2.3
Canada	68.1	12.6	17.5	1.8
		Males		
Markham	87.6	0.1	5.3	7.1
Ontario	87.7	0.3	10.1	1.9
Canada	69.0	11.8	17.7	1.5
		Females		
Markham	83.9	0.1	6.5	9.5
Ontario	85.1	0.4	11.8	2.8
Canada	67.3	13.3	17.3	2.1

Note: Figures cover total population excluding institutional residents.
Source: Statistics Canada. 2012. Census Profile. 2011 Census. Statistics Canada Catalogue no. 98-316-XWE. Ottawa. Released October 24 2012.
http://www12.statcan.gc.ca/census-recensement/2011/dp-pd/prof/index.cfm?Lang=E

Mississauga, Ontario

Background

Mississauga is located in the western part of the Greater Toronto Area (GTA) along the shores of Lake Ontario. The city is 90 minutes from the U.S. border and within a one-day drive from North America's largest cities. Branded as "Canada's Gateway," Mississauga is the site of the GTA's Pearson International, Canada's largest airport.

Throughout the 19th and 20th centuries, farming villages and larger towns comprised the Mississauga region. In the early 1960s, two of the largest communities, Port Credit and Streetsville, were incorporated as two towns while the remaining area was incorporated in 1968. In 1974, the towns of Mississauga, Port Credit, Streetsville, and portions of the townships of Toronto Gore and Trafalgar became the City of Mississauga.

The City of Mississauga has more than 480 parks and 23 major trail systems, including a 780-kilometre waterfront trail from Niagara-on-the-Lake to the Québec border. Due to the city's central location, 10 universities and 11 colleges are within commuting distance. The University of Toronto has a campus in Mississauga, as does the Sheridan Institute of Technology and Advanced Learning.

With almost 55,000 registered businesses, Mississauga is one of Canada's leading corporate capitals. Over 60 "Fortune 500" Canadian companies are based in the city as well as dozens of "Fortune Global 500" Canadian headquarters. Leading industry clusters include life sciences, aerospace, automotive, information and communications technologies, and financial services.

Popular heritage attractions like the Museums of Mississauga, which includes Bradley Museum (1830s), Benares Historic House (early 20th century) and the recently refurbished Leslie Log House (1826), preserve the city's 200-year-old history. The city also operates a local history resource centre and funds non-profit heritage research, advocacy and interpretation.

Mississauga has summer highs of plus 25.37 degrees Celsius, winter lows of minus 8.97 degrees Celsius, and an average rainfall just over 684 mm per year.

Rankings

- *fDi Magazine* ranked Mississauga in the Top 5 American Cities of the Future. Mississauga was ranked #4 out of 405 cities across North and South America. It was evaluated in the "Large Cities of the Future" category and recognized for economic potential and infrastructure. Toronto ranked #4 overall in the "Major Cities of the Future" category behind New York, Chicago and Houston. *fDi Intelligence, "American Cities of the Future, 2011/12," released April 8, 2011*
- *Corporate Knights Magazine* ranked Mississauga the second most sustainable mid-sized municipality in Canada. Assessment categories: ecological integrity; economic security; governance and empowerment; infrastructure and built environment; and social well-being. Mississauga ranked highest in water quality and waste diversion. The city's worst ranking was in its allocation of green space. The most sustainable mid-size municipality was Vancouver. *Corporate Knights Magazine, "The 2011 Most Sustainable Cities in Canada," February 9th, 2011*
- *Site Selection Magazine* identified Mississauga as one of "Canada's Best Locations" for industrial development. The annual report ranked the city's Economic Development Office as one of the "Top 10 Economic Development Groups in Canada." Criteria (all per capita): number of new facilities and expansions; projects; project capital investment; project job creation; 100+ job projects. *Site Selection, "Canada's Best Locations: Industrial Development," September 2010*

PROFILES / Mississauga, Ontario

Population Growth and Density

Area	Population in 2001	Population in 2006	Population in 2011	Population Change 2001–2006	Population Change 2006–2011	Land Area (sq. km)	Population Density per sq. km
Mississauga	612,925	668,599	713,443	9.1	6.7	292.40	2,439.9
Ontario	11,410,046	12,160,282	12,851,821	6.6	5.7	908,607.67	14.1
Canada	30,007,094	31,612,897	33,476,688	5.4	5.9	8,965,121.42	3.7

Source: Statistics Canada. 2012. Census Profile. 2011 Census. Statistics Canada Catalogue no. 98-316-XWE. Ottawa. Released October 24 2012.
http://www12.statcan.gc.ca/census-recensement/2011/dp-pd/prof/index.cfm?Lang=E;
Statistics Canada 2007. 2006 Community Profiles. 2006 Census. Statistics Canada Catalogue no. 92-591-XWE. Ottawa. Released March 13 2007.
http://www12.statcan.ca/census-recensement/2006/dp-pd/prof/92-591/index.cfm?Lang=E

Gender

Area	Males	Females
Number		
Mississauga	348,860	364,585
Ontario	6,263,140	6,588,685
Canada	16,414,225	17,062,460
Percent of Population		
Mississauga	48.9	51.1
Ontario	48.7	51.3
Canada	49.0	51.0

Source: Statistics Canada. 2012. Census Profile. 2011 Census. Statistics Canada Catalogue no. 98-316-XWE. Ottawa. Released October 24 2012.
http://www12.statcan.gc.ca/census-recensement/2011/dp-pd/prof/index.cfm?Lang=E

Marital Status

Area	Married[1]	Living Common-law	Single[2]	Separated	Divorced	Widowed
Number — Total						
Mississauga	318,325	24,335	172,445	14,940	27,475	27,165
Ontario	5,367,400	791,210	2,985,020	319,805	593,730	613,880
Canada	12,941,960	3,142,525	7,816,045	698,240	1,686,035	1,584,530
Males						
Mississauga	158,825	12,195	91,130	5,750	9,695	4,915
Ontario	2,681,320	397,620	1,583,760	133,790	231,160	117,980
Canada	6,470,300	1,575,495	4,206,320	299,655	680,415	310,940
Females						
Mississauga	159,495	12,140	81,320	9,190	17,770	22,250
Ontario	2,686,075	393,590	1,401,260	186,015	362,570	495,905
Canada	6,471,660	1,567,035	3,609,730	398,585	1,005,620	1,273,590
Percent of Population — Total						
Mississauga	54.4	4.2	29.5	2.6	4.7	4.6
Ontario	50.3	7.4	28.0	3.0	5.6	5.8
Canada	46.4	11.3	28.0	2.5	6.0	5.7
Males						
Mississauga	56.2	4.3	32.3	2.0	3.4	1.7
Ontario	52.1	7.7	30.8	2.6	4.5	2.3
Canada	47.8	11.6	31.1	2.2	5.0	2.3
Females						
Mississauga	52.8	4.0	26.9	3.0	5.9	7.4
Ontario	48.6	7.1	25.4	3.4	6.6	9.0
Canada	45.2	10.9	25.2	2.8	7.0	8.9

Note: (1) and not separated, (2) never legally married
Source: Statistics Canada. 2012. Census Profile. 2011 Census. Statistics Canada Catalogue no. 98-316-XWE. Ottawa. Released October 24 2012.
http://www12.statcan.gc.ca/census-recensement/2011/dp-pd/prof/index.cfm?Lang=E

Age Characteristics: 0 to 49 Years

Area	0 to 4 Years	5 to 9 Years	10 to 14 Years	15 to 19 Years	20 to 24 Years	25 to 29 Years	30 to 34 Years	35 to 39 Years	40 to 44 Years	45 to 49 Years
					Number					
					Total					
Mississauga	39,170	42,375	47,220	53,805	50,510	45,900	44,110	48,575	55,805	62,760
Ontario	704,260	712,755	763,755	863,635	852,910	815,120	800,365	844,335	924,075	1,055,880
Canada	1,877,095	1,809,895	1,920,355	2,178,135	2,187,450	2,169,590	2,162,905	2,173,930	2,324,875	2,675,130
					Males					
Mississauga	20,105	21,890	24,355	27,975	25,925	22,585	20,495	22,465	26,445	30,520
Ontario	360,590	365,290	391,630	443,680	432,490	400,045	383,340	405,845	447,920	517,510
Canada	961,150	925,965	983,995	1,115,845	1,108,775	1,077,275	1,058,810	1,064,200	1,141,720	1,318,715
					Females					
Mississauga	19,065	20,490	22,865	25,830	24,585	23,315	23,610	26,105	29,350	32,240
Ontario	343,670	347,465	372,125	419,950	420,415	415,075	417,030	438,485	476,155	538,370
Canada	915,945	883,935	936,360	1,062,295	1,078,670	1,092,315	1,104,095	1,109,735	1,183,155	1,356,420
					Percent of Population					
					Total					
Mississauga	5.5	5.9	6.6	7.5	7.1	6.4	6.2	6.8	7.8	8.8
Ontario	5.5	5.5	5.9	6.7	6.6	6.3	6.2	6.6	7.2	8.2
Canada	5.6	5.4	5.7	6.5	6.5	6.5	6.5	6.5	6.9	8.0
					Males					
Mississauga	5.8	6.3	7.0	8.0	7.4	6.5	5.9	6.4	7.6	8.7
Ontario	5.8	5.8	6.3	7.1	6.9	6.4	6.1	6.5	7.2	8.3
Canada	5.9	5.6	6.0	6.8	6.8	6.6	6.5	6.5	7.0	8.0
					Females					
Mississauga	5.2	5.6	6.3	7.1	6.7	6.4	6.5	7.2	8.1	8.8
Ontario	5.2	5.3	5.6	6.4	6.4	6.3	6.3	6.7	7.2	8.2
Canada	5.4	5.2	5.5	6.2	6.3	6.4	6.5	6.5	6.9	7.9

Source: Statistics Canada. 2012. Census Profile. 2011 Census. Statistics Canada Catalogue no. 98-316-XWE. Ottawa. Released October 24 2012.
http://www12.statcan.gc.ca/census-recensement/2011/dp-pd/prof/index.cfm?Lang=E

Age Characteristics: 50 Years and Over, and Median Age

Area	50 to 54 Years	55 to 59 Years	60 to 64 Years	65 to 69 Years	70 to 74 Years	75 to 79 Years	80 to 84 Years	85 Years and Over	Median Age
				Number					
				Total					
Mississauga	57,570	46,315	37,860	26,495	20,240	15,290	10,585	8,855	38.5
Ontario	1,006,140	864,620	765,655	563,485	440,780	356,150	271,510	246,400	40.4
Canada	2,658,965	2,340,635	2,052,670	1,521,715	1,153,065	922,700	702,070	645,515	40.6
				Males					
Mississauga	28,170	22,750	18,345	12,795	9,590	6,970	4,550	2,925	37.6
Ontario	492,560	418,755	370,370	270,875	206,350	161,345	113,620	80,925	39.4
Canada	1,309,030	1,147,300	1,002,690	738,010	543,435	417,945	291,085	208,300	39.6
				Females					
Mississauga	29,405	23,560	19,510	13,705	10,645	8,320	6,040	5,935	39.3
Ontario	513,580	445,865	395,275	292,610	234,435	194,805	157,890	165,475	41.3
Canada	1,349,940	1,193,335	1,049,985	783,705	609,630	504,755	410,985	437,215	41.5
				Percent of Population					
				Total					
Mississauga	8.1	6.5	5.3	3.7	2.8	2.1	1.5	1.2	–
Ontario	7.8	6.7	6.0	4.4	3.4	2.8	2.1	1.9	–
Canada	7.9	7.0	6.1	4.5	3.4	2.8	2.1	1.9	–
				Males					
Mississauga	8.1	6.5	5.3	3.7	2.7	2.0	1.3	0.8	–
Ontario	7.9	6.7	5.9	4.3	3.3	2.6	1.8	1.3	–
Canada	8.0	7.0	6.1	4.5	3.3	2.5	1.8	1.3	–
				Females					
Mississauga	8.1	6.5	5.4	3.8	2.9	2.3	1.7	1.6	–
Ontario	7.8	6.8	6.0	4.4	3.6	3.0	2.4	2.5	–
Canada	7.9	7.0	6.2	4.6	3.6	3.0	2.4	2.6	–

Source: Statistics Canada. 2012. Census Profile. 2011 Census. Statistics Canada Catalogue no. 98-316-XWE. Ottawa. Released October 24 2012.
http://www12.statcan.gc.ca/census-recensement/2011/dp-pd/prof/index.cfm?Lang=E

PROFILES / Mississauga, Ontario

Private Households by Household Size

Area	1 Person	2 Persons	3 Persons	4 Persons	5 Persons	6 or More Persons	Average Number of Persons in Private Households
			Households				
Mississauga	41,625	59,990	45,775	50,575	22,145	14,475	3.0
Ontario	1,230,975	1,584,415	803,030	783,925	310,860	174,305	2.6
Canada	3,673,310	4,544,820	2,081,900	1,903,300	724,405	392,885	2.5
			Percent of Households				
Mississauga	17.7	25.6	19.5	21.6	9.4	6.2	–
Ontario	25.2	32.4	16.4	16.0	6.4	3.6	–
Canada	27.6	34.1	15.6	14.3	5.4	2.9	–

Source: Statistics Canada. 2012. Census Profile. 2011 Census. Statistics Canada Catalogue no. 98-316-XWE. Ottawa. Released October 24 2012. http://www12.statcan.gc.ca/census-recensement/2011/dp-pd/prof/index.cfm?Lang=E

Dwelling Type

Area	Single-detached House	Semi-detached House	Row House	Apartment: Building with Five or More Storeys	Apartment: Building with Fewer Than Five Storeys	Duplex Apartment	Movable Dwelling	Other Single-attached House
				Number				
Mississauga	91,690	26,460	33,100	58,820	16,595	7,535	290	80
Ontario	2,718,880	279,470	415,225	789,970	498,160	160,460	15,800	9,540
Canada	7,329,150	646,245	791,600	1,234,770	2,397,550	704,485	183,510	33,310
				Percent of Dwellings				
Mississauga	39.1	11.3	14.1	25.1	7.1	3.2	0.1	0.0
Ontario	55.6	5.7	8.5	16.2	10.2	3.3	0.3	0.2
Canada	55.0	4.9	5.9	9.3	18.0	5.3	1.4	0.3

Source: Statistics Canada. 2012. Census Profile. 2011 Census. Statistics Canada Catalogue no. 98-316-XWE. Ottawa. Released October 24 2012. http://www12.statcan.gc.ca/census-recensement/2011/dp-pd/prof/index.cfm?Lang=E

Shelter Costs

	Owned Dwellings				Rented Dwellings		
Area	Number	Median Value[1] ($)	Average Value[1] ($)	Median Monthly Costs[2] ($)	Average Monthly Costs[2] ($)	Number	Median Monthly Costs[3] ($)	Average Monthly Costs[3] ($)
Mississauga	175,705	401,175	455,942	1,519	1,509	58,875	1,062	1,080
Ontario	3,446,650	300,862	367,428	1,163	1,284	1,385,535	892	926
Canada	9,013,410	280,552	345,182	978	1,141	4,060,385	784	848

Note: All figures cover non-farm, non-reserve private dwellings; (1) Refers to the dollar amount expected by the owner if the dwelling were to be sold; (2) Includes all shelter expenses paid by households that own their dwellings, such as the mortgage payment and the costs of electricity, heat, water and other municipal services, property taxes and condominium fees; (3) Includes all shelter expenses paid by households that rent their dwellings, such as the monthly rent and the costs of electricity, heat and municipal services.
Source: Statistics Canada. 2013. 2011 National Household Survey. Statistics Canada Catalogue no. 99-004-XWE. Ottawa. Released September 11, 2013.

Occupied Private Dwellings by Period of Construction

Area	1960 or Before	1961 to 1980	1981 to 1990	1991 to 2000	2001 to 2005	2006 to 2011
			Number			
Mississauga	16,690	75,310	55,060	46,305	25,750	15,465
Ontario	1,330,235	1,420,570	763,430	609,310	414,795	348,310
Canada	3,273,105	4,152,715	2,112,110	1,707,880	1,031,020	1,042,430
			Percent of Dwellings			
Mississauga	7.1	32.1	23.5	19.7	11.0	6.6
Ontario	27.2	29.1	15.6	12.5	8.5	7.1
Canada	24.6	31.2	15.9	12.8	7.7	7.8

Note: Figures cover non-farm, non-reserve private dwellings and includes data up to May 10, 2011.
Source: Statistics Canada. 2013. 2011 National Household Survey. Statistics Canada Catalogue no. 99-004-XWE. Ottawa. Released September 11, 2013.

PROFILES / Mississauga, Ontario

Educational Attainment

Area	No Certificate, Diploma or Degree	High School Diploma or Equivalent[1]	Apprenticeship or Trades Certificate or Diploma[2]	College, CÉGEP or Other Non-University Certificate or Diploma	University Certificate or Diploma Below the Bachelor Level[3]	Bachelor's Degree	University Certificate, Diploma or Degree Above Bachelor Level[4]
				Number			
				Total			
Mississauga	88,175	147,340	32,300	101,720	37,735	105,480	67,245
Ontario	1,954,520	2,801,805	771,140	2,070,875	427,150	1,515,075	933,100
Canada	5,485,400	6,968,935	2,950,685	4,970,020	1,200,130	3,634,425	2,049,930
				Males			
Mississauga	41,880	70,380	20,655	45,730	17,825	49,865	34,860
Ontario	957,040	1,337,055	520,390	894,235	193,355	692,345	470,290
Canada	2,742,875	3,305,415	1,928,970	2,118,430	513,235	1,643,080	1,043,350
				Females			
Mississauga	46,300	76,960	11,645	55,985	19,910	55,615	32,390
Ontario	997,475	1,464,755	250,750	1,176,640	233,790	822,730	462,805
Canada	2,742,520	3,663,515	1,021,715	2,851,595	686,890	1,991,345	1,006,585
				Percent of Population			
				Total			
Mississauga	15.2	25.4	5.6	17.5	6.5	18.2	11.6
Ontario	18.7	26.8	7.4	19.8	4.1	14.5	8.9
Canada	20.1	25.6	10.8	18.2	4.4	13.3	7.5
				Males			
Mississauga	14.9	25.0	7.3	16.3	6.3	17.7	12.4
Ontario	18.9	26.4	10.3	17.7	3.8	13.7	9.3
Canada	20.6	24.9	14.5	15.9	3.9	12.4	7.8
				Females			
Mississauga	15.5	25.8	3.9	18.7	6.7	18.6	10.8
Ontario	18.4	27.1	4.6	21.8	4.3	15.2	8.6
Canada	19.6	26.2	7.3	20.4	4.9	14.3	7.2

Note: Figures cover total population aged 15 years and over by highest certificate, diploma or degree; (1) Includes persons who have graduated from a secondary school or equivalent. It excludes persons with a postsecondary certificate, diploma or degree; (2) Includes Registered Apprenticeship certificates (including Certificate of Qualification, Journeyperson's designation) and other trades certificates or diplomas such as pre-employment or vocational certificates and diplomas from brief trade programs completed at community colleges, institutes of technology, vocational centres, and similar institutions; (3) Comparisons with other data sources suggest that the category 'University certificate or diploma below the bachelor's level' was over-reported in the NHS. This category likely includes some responses that are actually college certificates or diplomas, bachelor's degrees or other types of education (e.g., university transfer programs, bachelor's programs completed in other countries, incomplete bachelor's programs, non-university professional designations). We recommend users interpret the results for the 'University certificate or diploma below the bachelor's level' category with caution; (4) 'University certificate or diploma above bachelor level' includes the categories: 'Degree in medicine, dentistry, veterinary medicine or optometry,' 'Master's degree' and 'Earned doctorate.'
Source: Statistics Canada. 2013. 2011 National Household Survey. Statistics Canada Catalogue no. 99-004-XWE. Ottawa. Released September 11, 2013.

Household Income Distribution

Area	Less than $10,000	$10,000 to $19,999	$20,000 to $29,999	$30,000 to $39,999	$40,000 to $49,999	$50,000 to $59,999	$60,000 to $79,999	$80,000 to $99,999	$100,000 to $124,999	$125,000 to $149,999	$150,000 and Over
						Households					
Mississauga	9,410	11,720	15,280	17,065	18,475	19,315	32,495	28,090	26,740	18,770	37,215
Ontario	201,780	354,530	405,725	425,410	425,720	398,705	680,850	552,660	497,970	331,460	611,840
Canada	626,705	1,141,945	1,193,925	1,271,675	1,206,800	1,102,120	1,865,280	1,458,240	1,260,770	802,555	1,389,240
						Percent of Households					
Mississauga	4.0	5.0	6.5	7.3	7.9	8.2	13.9	12.0	11.4	8.0	15.9
Ontario	4.1	7.3	8.3	8.7	8.7	8.2	13.9	11.3	10.2	6.8	12.5
Canada	4.7	8.6	9.0	9.5	9.1	8.3	14.0	10.9	9.5	6.0	10.4

Note: Household income is the sum of the total incomes of all members of that household. Total income refers to monetary receipts from certain sources, before income taxes and deductions, during calendar year 2010.
Source: Statistics Canada. 2013. 2011 National Household Survey. Statistics Canada Catalogue no. 99-004-XWE. Ottawa. Released September 11, 2013.

Median and Average Household and Economic Family Income

Area	Median Household Income ($)	Average Household Income ($)	Median After-tax Household Income ($)	Average After-tax Household Income ($)	Median Economic Family Income ($)	Average Economic Family Income ($)	Median After-tax Economic Family Income ($)	Average After-tax Economic Family Income ($)
Mississauga	75,556	95,052	66,464	79,229	85,829	104,278	75,141	86,951
Ontario	66,358	85,772	58,717	71,523	80,987	100,152	71,128	83,322
Canada	61,072	79,102	54,089	66,149	76,511	94,125	67,044	78,517

Note: Figures cover household and economic familiy income in 2010. A household is defined as a person or a group of persons (other than foreign residents) who occupy the same private dwelling and do not have a usual place of residence elsewhere in Canada. Every person is a member of one and only one household. An economic family is defined as a group of two or more persons who live in the same dwelling and are related to each other by blood, marriage, common-law, adoption or a foster relationship. A couple may be of opposite or same sex.
Source: Statistics Canada. 2013. 2011 National Household Survey. Statistics Canada Catalogue no. 99-004-XWE. Ottawa. Released September 11, 2013.

PROFILES / Mississauga, Ontario

Individual Income Distribution

Area	Less than $10,000	$10,000 to $19,999	$20,000 to $29,999	$30,000 to $39,999	$40,000 to $49,999	$50,000 to $59,999	$60,000 to $79,999	$80,000 to $99,999	$100,000 to $124,999	$125,000 and Over
					Number					
					Total					
Mississauga	111,395	91,640	67,855	58,955	53,015	41,060	50,640	31,245	15,890	18,005
Ontario	1,780,355	1,748,060	1,361,710	1,136,730	980,790	746,360	964,280	574,710	293,865	330,285
Canada	4,492,040	4,835,710	3,670,020	3,180,360	2,603,520	1,921,650	2,437,440	1,302,045	693,580	782,135
					Males					
Mississauga	48,865	37,320	29,825	28,330	25,875	20,890	29,730	18,570	10,635	13,385
Ontario	781,095	669,815	580,990	535,255	491,125	407,005	569,205	341,160	201,125	244,500
Canada	1,936,365	1,864,880	1,588,260	1,522,190	1,333,510	1,079,780	1,473,145	823,720	492,905	599,905
					Females					
Mississauga	62,530	54,320	38,020	30,625	27,150	20,170	20,915	12,680	5,250	4,620
Ontario	999,265	1,078,245	780,720	601,475	489,665	339,360	395,075	233,550	92,740	85,790
Canada	2,555,675	2,970,825	2,081,760	1,658,170	1,270,010	841,870	964,300	478,330	200,680	182,230
					Percent of Population					
					Total					
Mississauga	20.6	17.0	12.6	10.9	9.8	7.6	9.4	5.8	2.9	3.3
Ontario	18.0	17.6	13.7	11.5	9.9	7.5	9.7	5.8	3.0	3.3
Canada	17.3	18.7	14.2	12.3	10.0	7.4	9.4	5.0	2.7	3.0
					Males					
Mississauga	18.5	14.2	11.3	10.8	9.8	7.9	11.3	7.0	4.0	5.1
Ontario	16.2	13.9	12.1	11.1	10.2	8.4	11.8	7.1	4.2	5.1
Canada	15.2	14.7	12.5	12.0	10.5	8.5	11.6	6.5	3.9	4.7
					Females					
Mississauga	22.6	19.7	13.8	11.1	9.8	7.3	7.6	4.6	1.9	1.7
Ontario	19.6	21.2	15.3	11.8	9.6	6.7	7.8	4.6	1.8	1.7
Canada	19.4	22.5	15.8	12.6	9.6	6.4	7.3	3.6	1.5	1.4

Note: Figures cover individuals aged 15 years and over with income. Income refers to monetary receipts from certain sources, before income taxes and deductions, during calendar year 2010.
Source: Statistics Canada. 2013. 2011 National Household Survey. Statistics Canada Catalogue no. 99-004-XWE. Ottawa. Released September 11, 2013.

Labour Force Status

Area	In the Labour Force - All	In the Labour Force - Employed	In the Labour Force - Unemployed	Not in the Labour Force
	Number			
	Total			
Mississauga	395,805	361,315	34,490	184,190
Ontario	6,864,990	6,297,005	567,985	3,608,685
Canada	17,990,080	16,595,035	1,395,045	9,269,445
	Males			
Mississauga	206,050	189,240	16,805	75,145
Ontario	3,542,030	3,249,165	292,865	1,522,690
Canada	9,388,570	8,634,310	754,255	3,906,785
	Females			
Mississauga	189,755	172,065	17,685	109,045
Ontario	3,322,955	3,047,840	275,120	2,085,990
Canada	8,601,515	7,960,725	640,790	5,362,660
	Percent of Labour Force			
	Total			
Mississauga	68.2	62.3	8.7	31.8
Ontario	65.5	60.1	8.3	34.5
Canada	66.0	60.9	7.8	34.0
	Males			
Mississauga	73.3	67.3	8.2	26.7
Ontario	69.9	64.2	8.3	30.1
Canada	70.6	64.9	8.0	29.4
	Females			
Mississauga	63.5	57.6	9.3	36.5
Ontario	61.4	56.3	8.3	38.6
Canada	61.6	57.0	7.4	38.4

Note: Figures are based on total population 15 years and over
Source: Statistics Canada. 2013. 2011 National Household Survey. Statistics Canada Catalogue no. 99-004-XWE. Ottawa. Released September 11, 2013.

Labour Force by Industry (NAICS Codes 11–52)

Area	Agriculture, forestry, fishing & hunting	Mining, quarrying, & oil & gas extraction	Utilities	Construction	Manufacturing	Wholesale Trade	Retail Trade	Transportation & warehousing	Information & cultural industries	Finance & insurance
					Number					
					Total					
Mississauga	1,010	670	2,070	20,575	44,595	27,155	44,170	26,380	11,340	29,430
Ontario	101,280	29,985	57,035	417,900	697,565	305,030	751,200	307,405	178,720	364,415
Canada	437,650	261,050	149,940	1,215,380	1,619,295	733,445	2,031,665	827,780	420,830	767,960
					Males					
Mississauga	635	415	1,520	17,955	29,765	16,275	20,425	18,240	6,685	12,675
Ontario	66,485	25,650	42,685	369,300	493,305	197,770	344,480	225,245	98,835	153,125
Canada	307,370	211,690	110,765	1,068,710	1,167,680	494,545	933,850	617,305	235,875	296,995
					Females					
Mississauga	375	255	550	2,615	14,825	10,885	23,745	8,140	4,660	16,755
Ontario	34,800	4,340	14,350	48,595	204,260	107,260	406,720	82,160	79,885	211,290
Canada	130,285	49,360	39,175	146,670	451,615	238,900	1,097,820	210,475	184,955	470,960
					Percent of Labour Force					
					Total					
Mississauga	0.3	0.2	0.5	5.4	11.6	7.1	11.5	6.9	3.0	7.7
Ontario	1.5	0.4	0.9	6.3	10.4	4.6	11.2	4.6	2.7	5.5
Canada	2.5	1.5	0.9	6.9	9.2	4.2	11.6	4.7	2.4	4.4
					Males					
Mississauga	0.3	0.2	0.8	9.0	14.8	8.1	10.2	9.1	3.3	6.3
Ontario	1.9	0.7	1.2	10.7	14.3	5.7	10.0	6.5	2.9	4.4
Canada	3.3	2.3	1.2	11.6	12.7	5.4	10.2	6.7	2.6	3.2
					Females					
Mississauga	0.2	0.1	0.3	1.4	8.1	6.0	13.0	4.5	2.6	9.2
Ontario	1.1	0.1	0.4	1.5	6.3	3.3	12.6	2.5	2.5	6.5
Canada	1.6	0.6	0.5	1.7	5.4	2.8	13.1	2.5	2.2	5.6

Note: Figures are based on total experienced labour force 15 years and over. Experienced labour force refers to persons who, during the week of Sunday, May 1 to Saturday, May 7, 2011, were employed and the unemployed who had last worked for pay or in self-employment in either 2010 or 2011.
Source: Statistics Canada. 2013. 2011 National Household Survey. Statistics Canada Catalogue no. 99-004-XWE. Ottawa. Released September 11, 2013.

Labour Force by Industry (NAICS Codes 53–91)

Area	Real estate & rental & leasing	Profess., scientific & tech. services	Mgmt of companies & enterprises	Admin. & support, waste mgmt & remed. services	Educational services	Health care & social assistance	Arts, entertain. & recreation	Accomm. & food services	Other services (except public admin.)	Public admin.
					Number					
					Total					
Mississauga	8,980	36,670	485	20,460	22,565	29,800	5,385	21,145	15,240	15,050
Ontario	133,980	511,020	6,525	309,630	499,690	692,130	144,065	417,675	296,340	458,665
Canada	321,895	1,240,850	17,460	728,330	1,301,435	1,949,650	363,405	1,130,750	807,800	1,261,050
					Males					
Mississauga	4,970	21,410	240	10,830	6,810	4,945	3,000	9,175	7,270	7,280
Ontario	72,835	281,420	3,540	172,475	162,765	120,165	75,035	177,240	133,795	236,655
Canada	179,090	688,625	9,380	411,250	424,915	349,430	188,270	469,990	372,940	652,510
					Females					
Mississauga	4,010	15,265	240	9,630	15,760	24,850	2,390	11,965	7,970	7,765
Ontario	61,145	229,600	2,990	137,155	336,925	571,965	69,030	240,430	162,550	222,015
Canada	142,805	552,225	8,075	317,085	876,515	1,600,220	175,135	660,760	434,865	608,535
					Percent of Labour Force					
					Total					
Mississauga	2.3	9.6	0.1	5.3	5.9	7.8	1.4	5.5	4.0	3.9
Ontario	2.0	7.6	0.1	4.6	7.5	10.4	2.2	6.3	4.4	6.9
Canada	1.8	7.1	0.1	4.1	7.4	11.1	2.1	6.4	4.6	7.2
					Males					
Mississauga	2.5	10.7	0.1	5.4	3.4	2.5	1.5	4.6	3.6	3.6
Ontario	2.1	8.2	0.1	5.0	4.7	3.5	2.2	5.1	3.9	6.9
Canada	1.9	7.5	0.1	4.5	4.6	3.8	2.0	5.1	4.1	7.1
					Females					
Mississauga	2.2	8.4	0.1	5.3	8.6	13.6	1.3	6.6	4.4	4.3
Ontario	1.9	7.1	0.1	4.2	10.4	17.7	2.1	7.4	5.0	6.9
Canada	1.7	6.6	0.1	3.8	10.4	19.1	2.1	7.9	5.2	7.2

Note: Figures are based on total experienced labour force 15 years and over. Experienced labour force refers to persons who, during the week of Sunday, May 1 to Saturday, May 7, 2011, were employed and the unemployed who had last worked for pay or in self-employment in either 2010 or 2011.
Source: Statistics Canada. 2013. 2011 National Household Survey. Statistics Canada Catalogue no. 99-004-XWE. Ottawa. Released September 11, 2013.

PROFILES / Mississauga, Ontario

Occupation

Area	Mgmt	Business, Finance & Admin.	Natural/ Applied Sciences & Related	Health	Education, Law & Social, Community & Government Services	Art, Culture, Recreation & Sport	Sales & Service	Trades, Transport & Equip. Operators & Related	Natural Resources, Agri. & Related Production	Mfg & Utilities
Number										
Total										
Mississauga	44,925	78,495	37,750	18,030	33,605	9,200	91,625	45,120	2,840	21,570
Ontario	770,580	1,138,330	494,500	392,695	801,465	206,420	1,550,260	868,515	106,810	350,685
Canada	1,963,600	2,902,045	1,237,775	1,107,200	2,064,675	503,415	4,068,170	2,537,775	397,930	805,040
Males										
Mississauga	28,245	27,115	29,240	3,655	9,650	4,460	40,960	41,915	2,325	12,965
Ontario	474,655	352,505	384,345	78,330	264,570	96,055	673,880	812,280	82,610	233,565
Canada	1,229,460	854,190	966,355	217,520	676,550	232,535	1,745,705	2,385,615	318,945	564,300
Females										
Mississauga	16,680	51,385	8,510	14,380	23,955	4,745	50,665	3,210	515	8,605
Ontario	295,920	785,825	110,150	314,370	536,895	110,370	876,380	56,230	24,200	117,115
Canada	734,140	2,047,855	271,415	889,675	1,388,130	270,875	2,322,465	152,165	78,980	240,740
Percent of Labour Force										
Total										
Mississauga	11.7	20.5	9.9	4.7	8.8	2.4	23.9	11.8	0.7	5.6
Ontario	11.5	17.0	7.4	5.9	12.0	3.1	23.2	13.0	1.6	5.2
Canada	11.2	16.5	7.0	6.3	11.7	2.9	23.1	14.4	2.3	4.6
Males										
Mississauga	14.1	13.5	14.6	1.8	4.8	2.2	20.4	20.9	1.2	6.5
Ontario	13.7	10.2	11.1	2.3	7.7	2.8	19.5	23.5	2.4	6.8
Canada	13.4	9.3	10.5	2.4	7.4	2.5	19.0	26.0	3.5	6.1
Females										
Mississauga	9.1	28.1	4.7	7.9	13.1	2.6	27.7	1.8	0.3	4.7
Ontario	9.2	24.3	3.4	9.7	16.6	3.4	27.2	1.7	0.7	3.6
Canada	8.7	24.4	3.2	10.6	16.5	3.2	27.7	1.8	0.9	2.9

Note: Figures are based on total experienced labour force 15 years and over.
Source: Statistics Canada. 2013. 2011 National Household Survey. Statistics Canada Catalogue no. 99-004-XWE. Ottawa. Released September 11, 2013.

Place of Work Status

Area	Worked at Home	Worked Outside Canada	No Fixed Workplace Address	Worked at Usual Place
Number				
Total				
Mississauga	20,060	1,835	37,290	302,125
Ontario	423,790	31,390	670,835	5,170,980
Canada	1,142,640	66,460	1,868,245	13,517,690
Males				
Mississauga	10,790	1,400	26,495	150,560
Ontario	216,900	21,150	486,560	2,524,555
Canada	582,150	47,355	1,400,485	6,604,325
Females				
Mississauga	9,270	435	10,795	151,570
Ontario	206,895	10,240	184,275	2,646,420
Canada	560,490	19,100	467,760	6,913,370
Percent of Labour Force				
Total				
Mississauga	5.6	0.5	10.3	83.6
Ontario	6.7	0.5	10.7	82.1
Canada	6.9	0.4	11.3	81.5
Males				
Mississauga	5.7	0.7	14.0	79.6
Ontario	6.7	0.7	15.0	77.7
Canada	6.7	0.5	16.2	76.5
Females				
Mississauga	5.4	0.3	6.3	88.1
Ontario	6.8	0.3	6.0	86.8
Canada	7.0	0.2	5.9	86.8

Note: Figures are based on total employed labour force 15 years and over.
Source: Statistics Canada. 2013. 2011 National Household Survey. Statistics Canada Catalogue no. 99-004-XWE. Ottawa. Released September 11, 2013.

Mode of Transportation to Work

Area	Car; Truck; Van; as Driver	Car; Truck; Van; as Passenger	Public Transit	Walked	Bicycled	All Other Modes
			Number			
			Total			
Mississauga	252,330	20,095	53,985	7,815	1,410	3,785
Ontario	4,235,315	357,110	818,270	299,095	69,885	62,145
Canada	11,393,140	867,050	1,851,525	880,815	201,780	191,625
			Males			
Mississauga	143,030	6,905	21,375	2,855	1,170	1,715
Ontario	2,316,680	143,410	340,995	131,765	47,635	30,635
Canada	6,238,835	349,530	788,290	387,580	135,840	104,725
			Females			
Mississauga	109,295	13,190	32,610	4,960	235	2,070
Ontario	1,918,640	213,700	477,275	167,325	22,250	31,515
Canada	5,154,305	517,520	1,063,235	493,230	65,940	86,900
			Percent of Labour Force			
			Total			
Mississauga	74.3	5.9	15.9	2.3	0.4	1.1
Ontario	72.5	6.1	14.0	5.1	1.2	1.1
Canada	74.0	5.6	12.0	5.7	1.3	1.2
			Males			
Mississauga	80.8	3.9	12.1	1.6	0.7	1.0
Ontario	76.9	4.8	11.3	4.4	1.6	1.0
Canada	77.9	4.4	9.8	4.8	1.7	1.3
			Females			
Mississauga	67.3	8.1	20.1	3.1	0.1	1.3
Ontario	67.8	7.5	16.9	5.9	0.8	1.1
Canada	69.8	7.0	14.4	6.7	0.9	1.2

Note: Figures are based on total employed labour force 15 years and over.
Source: Statistics Canada. 2013. 2011 National Household Survey. Statistics Canada Catalogue no. 99-004-XWE. Ottawa. Released September 11, 2013.

Visible Minority Population Characteristics

Area	Total Minority	South Asian[1]	Chinese	Black	Filipino	Latin American	Arab	SE Asian[2]	West Asian[3]	Korean	Japanese	Multiple[4]
						Number						
						Total						
Mississauga	380,870	154,210	50,120	44,775	39,800	15,360	24,870	15,750	7,955	6,300	2,095	10,435
Ontario	3,279,565	965,990	629,140	539,205	275,380	172,560	151,645	137,875	122,530	78,290	29,085	96,735
Canada	6,264,750	1,567,400	1,324,750	945,665	619,310	381,280	380,620	312,075	206,840	161,130	87,270	171,935
						Males						
Mississauga	185,355	77,020	24,220	20,420	18,010	7,330	13,065	7,930	4,200	3,100	955	4,950
Ontario	1,582,480	484,355	301,575	251,295	116,825	83,205	79,620	67,645	62,515	38,045	13,345	46,765
Canada	3,043,010	790,755	632,325	453,005	268,885	186,355	203,485	154,035	105,620	77,165	38,270	83,335
						Females						
Mississauga	195,515	77,195	25,895	24,355	21,790	8,030	11,800	7,815	3,755	3,195	1,150	5,490
Ontario	1,697,085	481,635	327,570	287,915	158,555	89,360	72,025	70,230	60,010	40,250	15,740	49,970
Canada	3,221,745	776,650	692,420	492,660	350,425	194,925	177,140	158,045	101,220	83,965	48,990	88,600
						Percent of Population						
						Total						
Mississauga	53.7	21.8	7.1	6.3	5.6	2.2	3.5	2.2	1.1	0.9	0.3	1.5
Ontario	25.9	7.6	5.0	4.3	2.2	1.4	1.2	1.1	1.0	0.6	0.2	0.8
Canada	19.1	4.8	4.0	2.9	1.9	1.2	1.2	0.9	0.6	0.5	0.3	0.5
						Males						
Mississauga	53.4	22.2	7.0	5.9	5.2	2.1	3.8	2.3	1.2	0.9	0.3	1.4
Ontario	25.6	7.8	4.9	4.1	1.9	1.3	1.3	1.1	1.0	0.6	0.2	0.8
Canada	18.8	4.9	3.9	2.8	1.7	1.2	1.3	1.0	0.7	0.5	0.2	0.5
						Females						
Mississauga	54.1	21.4	7.2	6.7	6.0	2.2	3.3	2.2	1.0	0.9	0.3	1.5
Ontario	26.2	7.4	5.1	4.4	2.5	1.4	1.1	1.1	0.9	0.6	0.2	0.8
Canada	19.3	4.7	4.1	3.0	2.1	1.2	1.1	0.9	0.6	0.5	0.3	0.5

Note: The Employment Equity Act defines visible minorities as 'persons, other than Aboriginal peoples, who are non-Caucasian in race or non-white in colour';
(1) Includes 'East Indian,' 'Pakistani,' 'Sri Lankan,' etc.; (2) Includes 'Vietnamese,' 'Cambodian,' 'Malaysian,' 'Laotian,' etc.; (3) Includes 'Iranian,' 'Afghan,' etc.; (4) Includes respondents who reported more than one visible minority group by checking two or more mark-in circles, e.g., 'Black' and 'South Asian.'
Source: Statistics Canada. 2013. 2011 National Household Survey. Statistics Canada Catalogue no. 99-004-XWE. Ottawa. Released September 11, 2013.

PROFILES / Mississauga, Ontario

Aboriginal Population

Area	Aboriginal Identity[1]	First Nations (North American Indian) Single Identity[2]	Métis Single Identity	Inuk (Inuit) Single Identity	Multiple Aboriginal Identities[3]	Aboriginal Identities Not Included Elsewhere
Number						
Total						
Mississauga	3,200	1,890	955	55	95	205
Ontario	301,430	201,100	86,020	3,355	2,910	8,040
Canada	1,400,685	851,560	451,795	59,440	11,415	26,475
Males						
Mississauga	1,660	945	505	25	50	135
Ontario	145,020	96,620	41,755	1,475	1,420	3,750
Canada	682,190	411,785	223,335	29,495	5,525	12,055
Females						
Mississauga	1,535	945	450	30	45	65
Ontario	156,410	104,485	44,260	1,880	1,490	4,295
Canada	718,500	439,775	228,460	29,950	5,890	14,420
Percent of Population						
Total						
Mississauga	0.5	0.3	0.1	0.0	0.0	0.0
Ontario	2.4	1.6	0.7	0.0	0.0	0.1
Canada	4.3	2.6	1.4	0.2	0.0	0.1
Males						
Mississauga	0.5	0.3	0.1	0.0	0.0	0.0
Ontario	2.3	1.6	0.7	0.0	0.0	0.1
Canada	4.2	2.5	1.4	0.2	0.0	0.1
Females						
Mississauga	0.4	0.3	0.1	0.0	0.0	0.0
Ontario	2.4	1.6	0.7	0.0	0.0	0.1
Canada	4.3	2.6	1.4	0.2	0.0	0.1

Note: (1) Includes persons who reported being an Aboriginal person, that is, First Nations (North American Indian), Métis or Inuk (Inuit) and/or those who reported Registered or Treaty Indian status, that is registered under the Indian Act of Canada, and/or those who reported membership in a First Nation or Indian band. Aboriginal peoples of Canada are defined in the Constitution Act, 1982, section 35-2 as including the Indian, Inuit and Métis peoples of Canada; (2) Users should be aware that the estimates associated with this variable are more affected than most by the incomplete enumeration of certain Indian reserves and Indian settlements in the National Household Survey (NHS); (3) Includes persons who reported being any two or all three of the following: First Nations (North American Indian), Métis or Inuk (Inuit).
Source: Statistics Canada. 2013. 2011 National Household Survey. Statistics Canada Catalogue no. 99-004-XWE. Ottawa. Released September 11, 2013.

Ethnic Origin

Area	North American Aboriginal	Other North American	European	Caribbean	Latin, Central and South American	African	Asian	Oceania
Number								
Total								
Mississauga	5,835	83,250	322,380	38,820	23,380	28,960	310,935	925
Ontario	441,395	3,059,480	8,231,410	396,485	271,545	331,460	2,604,595	19,410
Canada	1,836,035	11,070,455	20,157,965	627,590	544,375	766,735	5,011,225	74,875
Males								
Mississauga	2,710	41,155	158,195	17,410	10,995	14,265	152,850	555
Ontario	210,490	1,507,105	4,019,885	181,805	130,035	160,940	1,265,540	9,855
Canada	885,675	5,462,685	9,913,150	291,640	264,635	387,360	2,435,540	37,490
Females								
Mississauga	3,130	42,095	164,190	21,410	12,385	14,690	158,085	365
Ontario	230,905	1,552,380	4,211,525	214,675	141,510	170,515	1,339,050	9,555
Canada	950,360	5,607,770	10,244,820	335,945	279,740	379,380	2,575,680	37,385
Percent of Population								
Total								
Mississauga	0.8	11.7	45.5	5.5	3.3	4.1	43.9	0.1
Ontario	3.5	24.2	65.1	3.1	2.1	2.6	20.6	0.2
Canada	5.6	33.7	61.4	1.9	1.7	2.3	15.3	0.2
Males								
Mississauga	0.8	11.8	45.5	5.0	3.2	4.1	44.0	0.2
Ontario	3.4	24.4	65.0	2.9	2.1	2.6	20.5	0.2
Canada	5.5	33.8	61.3	1.8	1.6	2.4	15.1	0.2
Females								
Mississauga	0.9	11.6	45.4	5.9	3.4	4.1	43.7	0.1
Ontario	3.6	24.0	65.1	3.3	2.2	2.6	20.7	0.1
Canada	5.7	33.6	61.4	2.0	1.7	2.3	15.4	0.2

Note: The sum of the ethnic groups in this table is greater than the total population estimate because a person may report more than one ethnic origin in the NHS.
Source: Statistics Canada. 2013. 2011 National Household Survey. Statistics Canada Catalogue no. 99-004-XWE. Ottawa. Released September 11, 2013.

Religion

Area	Buddhist	Christian	Hindu	Jewish	Muslim	Sikh	Traditional (Aboriginal) Spirituality	Other Religions	No Religious Affiliation
				Number					
				Total					
Mississauga	15,615	424,715	49,325	1,830	84,325	23,995	65	3,185	105,660
Ontario	163,750	8,167,295	366,720	195,540	581,950	179,765	15,905	53,080	2,927,790
Canada	366,830	22,102,745	497,965	329,495	1,053,945	454,965	64,935	130,835	7,850,605
				Males					
Mississauga	7,445	200,575	24,390	955	43,205	12,190	30	1,555	56,985
Ontario	75,355	3,839,925	183,580	95,795	293,925	90,515	7,600	23,555	1,571,195
Canada	168,465	10,497,775	250,435	161,265	540,555	229,435	31,805	57,745	4,225,645
				Females					
Mississauga	8,170	224,145	24,940	875	41,120	11,810	35	1,630	48,675
Ontario	88,395	4,327,365	183,140	99,740	288,025	89,250	8,310	29,525	1,356,600
Canada	198,365	11,604,975	247,525	168,235	513,395	225,530	33,135	73,090	3,624,965
				Percent of Population					
				Total					
Mississauga	2.2	59.9	7.0	0.3	11.9	3.4	0.0	0.4	14.9
Ontario	1.3	64.6	2.9	1.5	4.6	1.4	0.1	0.4	23.1
Canada	1.1	67.3	1.5	1.0	3.2	1.4	0.2	0.4	23.9
				Males					
Mississauga	2.1	57.7	7.0	0.3	12.4	3.5	0.0	0.4	16.4
Ontario	1.2	62.1	3.0	1.5	4.8	1.5	0.1	0.4	25.4
Canada	1.0	64.9	1.5	1.0	3.3	1.4	0.2	0.4	26.1
				Females					
Mississauga	2.3	62.0	6.9	0.2	11.4	3.3	0.0	0.5	13.5
Ontario	1.4	66.9	2.8	1.5	4.5	1.4	0.1	0.5	21.0
Canada	1.2	69.5	1.5	1.0	3.1	1.4	0.2	0.4	21.7

Note: Religion refers to the person's self-identification as having a connection or affiliation with any religious denomination, group, body, sect, cult or other religiously defined community or system of belief. Religion is not limited to formal membership in a religious organization or group. Persons without a religious connection or affiliation can self-identify as atheist, agnostic or humanist, or can provide another applicable response.
Source: Statistics Canada. 2013. 2011 National Household Survey. Statistics Canada Catalogue no. 99-004-XWE. Ottawa. Released September 11, 2013.

Religion—Christian Denominations

Area	Anglican	Baptist	Catholic	Christian Orthodox	Lutheran	Pentecostal	Presbyterian	United Church	Other Christian
				Number					
				Total					
Mississauga	24,810	9,915	261,355	25,370	4,140	11,980	11,050	21,255	54,830
Ontario	774,560	244,650	3,976,610	297,710	163,460	213,945	319,585	952,465	1,224,300
Canada	1,631,845	635,840	12,810,705	550,690	478,185	478,705	472,385	2,007,610	3,036,780
				Males					
Mississauga	11,575	4,495	125,170	12,550	1,820	5,050	5,185	9,655	25,080
Ontario	355,175	112,285	1,895,940	145,825	75,225	94,955	148,535	435,255	576,730
Canada	752,945	293,905	6,167,290	270,205	221,525	217,850	218,955	912,545	1,442,550
				Females					
Mississauga	13,240	5,420	136,180	12,820	2,325	6,930	5,865	11,610	29,750
Ontario	419,390	132,370	2,080,665	151,885	88,230	118,990	171,050	517,210	647,570
Canada	878,900	341,940	6,643,415	280,485	256,660	260,850	253,430	1,095,065	1,594,230
				Percent of Population					
				Total					
Mississauga	3.5	1.4	36.9	3.6	0.6	1.7	1.6	3.0	7.7
Ontario	6.1	1.9	31.4	2.4	1.3	1.7	2.5	7.5	9.7
Canada	5.0	1.9	39.0	1.7	1.5	1.5	1.4	6.1	9.2
				Males					
Mississauga	3.3	1.3	36.0	3.6	0.5	1.5	1.5	2.8	7.2
Ontario	5.7	1.8	30.7	2.4	1.2	1.5	2.4	7.0	9.3
Canada	4.7	1.8	38.2	1.7	1.4	1.3	1.4	5.6	8.9
				Females					
Mississauga	3.7	1.5	37.7	3.5	0.6	1.9	1.6	3.2	8.2
Ontario	6.5	2.0	32.2	2.3	1.4	1.8	2.6	8.0	10.0
Canada	5.3	2.0	39.8	1.7	1.5	1.6	1.5	6.6	9.6

Note: Religion refers to the person's self-identification as having a connection or affiliation with any religious denomination, group, body, sect, cult or other religiously defined community or system of belief. Religion is not limited to formal membership in a religious organization or group. Persons without a religious connection or affiliation can self-identify as atheist, agnostic or humanist, or can provide another applicable response.
Source: Statistics Canada. 2013. 2011 National Household Survey. Statistics Canada Catalogue no. 99-004-XWE. Ottawa. Released September 11, 2013.

PROFILES / Mississauga, Ontario

Immigrant Status and Period of Immigration

Area	Non-Immigrants[1]	Immigrants All	Before 1971	1971 to 1980	1981 to 1990	1991 to 2000	2001 to 2005	2006 to 2011	Non-Permanent Residents[3]
Number									
Total									
Mississauga	325,880	374,575	43,255	44,625	55,945	100,680	70,280	59,795	8,275
Ontario	8,906,000	3,611,365	723,030	464,380	538,285	866,220	518,405	501,060	134,425
Canada	25,720,175	6,775,765	1,261,055	870,775	949,890	1,539,050	992,070	1,162,915	356,385
Males									
Mississauga	164,130	179,275	20,800	20,970	26,855	48,210	34,115	28,330	3,925
Ontario	4,410,240	1,706,385	341,820	217,990	258,095	408,270	245,850	234,360	64,825
Canada	12,753,235	3,231,370	605,430	416,670	454,570	724,905	474,545	555,245	178,515
Females									
Mississauga	161,750	195,295	22,450	23,655	29,095	52,470	36,165	31,465	4,350
Ontario	4,495,765	1,904,985	381,210	246,390	280,190	457,950	272,550	266,695	69,600
Canada	12,966,935	3,544,400	655,625	454,105	495,325	814,145	517,530	607,670	177,870
Percent of Population									
Total									
Mississauga	46.0	52.9	6.1	6.3	7.9	14.2	9.9	8.4	1.2
Ontario	70.4	28.5	5.7	3.7	4.3	6.8	4.1	4.0	1.1
Canada	78.3	20.6	3.8	2.7	2.9	4.7	3.0	3.5	1.1
Males									
Mississauga	47.3	51.6	6.0	6.0	7.7	13.9	9.8	8.2	1.1
Ontario	71.3	27.6	5.5	3.5	4.2	6.6	4.0	3.8	1.0
Canada	78.9	20.0	3.7	2.6	2.8	4.5	2.9	3.4	1.1
Females									
Mississauga	44.8	54.0	6.2	6.5	8.1	14.5	10.0	8.7	1.2
Ontario	69.5	29.4	5.9	3.8	4.3	7.1	4.2	4.1	1.1
Canada	77.7	21.2	3.9	2.7	3.0	4.9	3.1	3.6	1.1

Note: (1) Non-immigrant refers to a person who is a Canadian citizen by birth; (2) Immigrant refers to a person who is or has ever been a landed immigrant/permanent resident. This person has been granted the right to live in Canada permanently by immigration authorities. Some immigrants have resided in Canada for a number of years, while others have arrived recently. Some immigrants are Canadian citizens, while others are not. Most immigrants are born outside Canada, but a small number are born in Canada. In the 2011 National Household Survey, 'Immigrants' includes immigrants who landed in Canada prior to May 10, 2011; (3) Non-permanent resident refers to a person from another country who has a work or study permit, or who is a refugee claimant, and any non-Canadian-born family member living in Canada with them.
Source: Statistics Canada. 2013. 2011 National Household Survey. Statistics Canada Catalogue no. 99-004-XWE. Ottawa. Released September 11, 2013.

Mother Tongue

Area	English	French	Non-official Language	English & French	English & Non-official Language	French & Non-official Language	English, French & Non-official Language
Number							
Total							
Mississauga	338,280	7,400	334,060	1,585	27,335	975	845
Ontario	8,677,040	493,300	3,264,435	46,605	219,425	13,645	7,615
Canada	18,858,980	7,054,975	6,567,680	144,685	396,330	74,430	24,095
Males							
Mississauga	167,990	3,275	161,610	750	13,435	455	410
Ontario	4,276,970	232,785	1,562,190	21,805	106,790	6,285	3,495
Canada	9,345,225	3,452,380	3,157,785	69,975	192,000	36,535	11,965
Females							
Mississauga	170,290	4,125	172,445	835	13,900	520	440
Ontario	4,400,065	260,510	1,702,240	24,795	112,635	7,365	4,115
Canada	9,513,750	3,602,590	3,409,895	74,710	204,330	37,890	12,130
Percent of Population							
Total							
Mississauga	47.6	1.0	47.0	0.2	3.8	0.1	0.1
Ontario	68.2	3.9	25.7	0.4	1.7	0.1	0.1
Canada	56.9	21.3	19.8	0.4	1.2	0.2	0.1
Males							
Mississauga	48.3	0.9	46.5	0.2	3.9	0.1	0.1
Ontario	68.9	3.7	25.2	0.4	1.7	0.1	0.1
Canada	57.5	21.2	19.4	0.4	1.2	0.2	0.1
Females							
Mississauga	47.0	1.1	47.6	0.2	3.8	0.1	0.1
Ontario	67.6	4.0	26.1	0.4	1.7	0.1	0.1
Canada	56.4	21.4	20.2	0.4	1.2	0.2	0.1

Note: Figures cover total population excluding institutional residents.
Source: Statistics Canada. 2012. Census Profile. 2011 Census. Statistics Canada Catalogue no. 98-316-XWE. Ottawa. Released October 24 2012.
http://www12.statcan.gc.ca/census-recensement/2011/dp-pd/prof/index.cfm?Lang=E

Language Spoken Most Often at Home

Area	English	French	Non-official Language	English & French	English & Non-official Language	French & Non-official Language	English, French & Non-official Language
			Number				
			Total				
Mississauga	446,305	3,520	191,080	1,365	66,560	370	1,275
Ontario	10,044,810	284,115	1,827,870	37,955	509,105	6,370	11,845
Canada	21,457,075	6,827,865	3,673,865	131,205	875,135	109,700	46,330
			Males				
Mississauga	219,725	1,655	92,240	580	32,980	175	555
Ontario	4,930,610	133,495	872,860	17,250	248,050	2,855	5,225
Canada	10,585,620	3,348,235	1,767,310	63,475	425,370	53,010	22,845
			Females				
Mississauga	226,575	1,860	98,840	785	33,580	195	720
Ontario	5,114,200	150,620	955,010	20,705	261,055	3,520	6,620
Canada	10,871,455	3,479,625	1,906,555	67,730	449,765	56,690	23,485
			Percent of Population				
			Total				
Mississauga	62.8	0.5	26.9	0.2	9.4	0.1	0.2
Ontario	79.0	2.2	14.4	0.3	4.0	0.1	0.1
Canada	64.8	20.6	11.1	0.4	2.6	0.3	0.1
			Males				
Mississauga	63.2	0.5	26.5	0.2	9.5	0.1	0.2
Ontario	79.4	2.1	14.1	0.3	4.0	0.0	0.1
Canada	65.1	20.6	10.9	0.4	2.6	0.3	0.1
			Females				
Mississauga	62.5	0.5	27.3	0.2	9.3	0.1	0.2
Ontario	78.5	2.3	14.7	0.3	4.0	0.1	0.1
Canada	64.5	20.6	11.3	0.4	2.7	0.3	0.1

Note: Figures cover total population excluding institutional residents.
Source: Statistics Canada. 2012. Census Profile. 2011 Census. Statistics Canada Catalogue no. 98-316-XWE. Ottawa. Released October 24 2012.
http://www12.statcan.gc.ca/census-recensement/2011/dp-pd/prof/index.cfm?Lang=E

Knowledge of Official Languages

Area	English Only	French Only	English & French	Neither English nor French
		Number		
		Total		
Mississauga	635,660	575	49,125	25,115
Ontario	10,984,360	42,980	1,395,805	298,920
Canada	22,564,665	4,165,015	5,795,570	595,920
		Males		
Mississauga	317,230	240	21,040	9,415
Ontario	5,445,050	18,805	627,725	118,765
Canada	11,222,185	1,925,340	2,876,560	241,790
		Females		
Mississauga	318,425	335	28,090	15,700
Ontario	5,539,310	24,175	768,085	180,155
Canada	11,342,485	2,239,680	2,919,005	354,135
		Percent of Population		
		Total		
Mississauga	89.5	0.1	6.9	3.5
Ontario	86.3	0.3	11.0	2.3
Canada	68.1	12.6	17.5	1.8
		Males		
Mississauga	91.2	0.1	6.0	2.7
Ontario	87.7	0.3	10.1	1.9
Canada	69.0	11.8	17.7	1.5
		Females		
Mississauga	87.8	0.1	7.7	4.3
Ontario	85.1	0.4	11.8	2.8
Canada	67.3	13.3	17.3	2.1

Note: Figures cover total population excluding institutional residents.
Source: Statistics Canada. 2012. Census Profile. 2011 Census. Statistics Canada Catalogue no. 98-316-XWE. Ottawa. Released October 24 2012.
http://www12.statcan.gc.ca/census-recensement/2011/dp-pd/prof/index.cfm?Lang=E

Montréal, Québec

Background

The City of Montréal is situated in southwestern Québec. Located at the confluence of the St. Lawrence and Ottawa Rivers, Montréal is surrounded by water and has suburbs across the river in all directions.

In 1535, Jacques Cartier arrived in the Iroquois village of Hochelaga (present-day Montréal), which stood at the base of a 234-metre mountain which Cartier named "Mont-Royal." Samuel de Champlain, the founder of New France, established a trading post in the area in 1609. From 1841 until 1849, Montréal was the capital of Upper Canada (Ontario) and Lower Canada (Québec).

Today, the Montréal census metropolitan area (CMA) is the second largest in Canada and consists of over 80 cities and towns. The City of Montréal represents 45% of the CMA population. The city's most prominent geographical feature is Mont-Royal, the highest point on the island and the area's most famous park. Montréal is home to 11 institutions of higher learning, including globally recognized universities such as McGill, Concordia, Université de Montréal and Université de Québec à Montréal.

The city has one of the world's leading life science industries with investment in university research and regular generation of science patents. Canada's largest concentration of biotech research and development is based in Montréal. Also one of three world hubs for aerospace, Montréal is home to more than 20 leaders in the aerospace industry, including the United Nations' International Civil Aviation Organization and Concordia University's Institute for Aerospace Design and Innovation. Other key clusters include information and communications technologies, manufacturing and agri-food. Montréal is one of the world's busiest inland ports and is a key transfer point for trans-Atlantic cargo.

Every year the city hosts more than 40 events that attract two million visitors to the region. The city's international film and jazz festivals are renowned around the world. Montréal is considered "Canada's Cultural Capital" and was named a UNESCO City of Design in 2007.

Montréal has summer highs of plus 24.87 degrees Celsius, winter lows of minus 12.67 degrees Celsius, and an average rainfall just over 763 mm per year.

Rankings

- The Leger Marketing survey for the Association of Canadian Studies ranked Montréal #1 in terms of best city for livability and quality of life. Just over 1,500 Canadians from eight cities were asked to rank their city as excellent, good or poor. Indices: cost of living, job opportunities, a place to raise children, recreational and outdoor activities, the climate, cultural activities, opportunities to meet people and make friends, and shopping. Montréal ranked #1 in shopping (67.4% excellent), cultural activities (63.6%), recreation (63.5%) and opportunities to meet people (51.2%). *Association for Canadian Studies, "Vancouver may be nicest, but when it comes to cost of living, it's Québec City and Montréal that take the top spots," July 8, 2011*
- U-Haul International identified Montréal in Canada's Top 25 destination cities. The annual national migration trend report ranks destinations for movers travelling more than 80 kilometres and included all Canadian cities, regardless of size. Montréal ranked #5. The top four destination cities were Toronto (ON), Calgary (AB), Vancouver (BC) and Edmonton (AB), respectively. *U-Haul International Inc., "The 2011 Top 25 Canadian Destination Cities," March 23rd, 2011*

PROFILES / Montréal, Québec

Population Growth and Density

Area	Population in 2001	Population in 2006	Population in 2011	Population Change 2001–2006	Population Change 2006–2011	Land Area (sq. km)	Population Density per sq. km
Montréal	1,583,590	1,620,693	1,649,519	2.3	1.8	365.13	4,517.6
Québec	7,237,479	7,546,131	7,903,001	4.3	4.7	1,356,547.02	5.8
Canada	30,007,094	31,612,897	33,476,688	5.4	5.9	8,965,121.42	3.7

Source: Statistics Canada. 2012. Census Profile. 2011 Census. Statistics Canada Catalogue no. 98-316-XWE. Ottawa. Released October 24 2012.
http://www12.statcan.gc.ca/census-recensement/2011/dp-pd/prof/index.cfm?Lang=E;
Statistics Canada 2007. 2006 Community Profiles. 2006 Census. Statistics Canada Catalogue no. 92-591-XWE. Ottawa. Released March 13 2007.
http://www12.statcan.ca/census-recensement/2006/dp-pd/prof/92-591/index.cfm?Lang=E

Gender

Area	Males	Females
Number		
Montréal	799,880	849,635
Québec	3,875,860	4,027,140
Canada	16,414,225	17,062,460
Percent of Population		
Montréal	48.5	51.5
Québec	49.0	51.0
Canada	49.0	51.0

Source: Statistics Canada. 2012. Census Profile. 2011 Census. Statistics Canada Catalogue no. 98-316-XWE. Ottawa. Released October 24 2012.
http://www12.statcan.gc.ca/census-recensement/2011/dp-pd/prof/index.cfm?Lang=E

Marital Status

Area	Married[1]	Living Common-law	Single[2]	Separated	Divorced	Widowed
Number – Total						
Montréal	471,770	192,985	511,190	30,890	112,565	82,150
Québec	2,353,770	1,391,550	1,942,090	105,195	463,830	387,945
Canada	12,941,960	3,142,525	7,816,045	698,240	1,686,035	1,584,530
Males						
Montréal	236,510	98,450	269,060	12,860	42,215	14,770
Québec	1,177,720	697,695	1,045,540	46,465	188,265	77,430
Canada	6,470,300	1,575,495	4,206,320	299,655	680,415	310,940
Females						
Montréal	235,260	94,535	242,130	18,035	70,350	67,380
Québec	1,176,050	693,850	896,545	58,720	275,565	310,515
Canada	6,471,660	1,567,035	3,609,730	398,585	1,005,620	1,273,590
Percent of Population – Total						
Montréal	33.7	13.8	36.5	2.2	8.0	5.9
Québec	35.4	20.9	29.2	1.6	7.0	5.8
Canada	46.4	11.3	28.0	2.5	6.0	5.7
Males						
Montréal	35.1	14.6	39.9	1.9	6.3	2.2
Québec	36.4	21.6	32.3	1.4	5.8	2.4
Canada	47.8	11.6	31.1	2.2	5.0	2.3
Females						
Montréal	32.3	13.0	33.3	2.5	9.7	9.3
Québec	34.5	20.3	26.3	1.7	8.1	9.1
Canada	45.2	10.9	25.2	2.8	7.0	8.9

Note: (1) and not separated, (2) never legally married
Source: Statistics Canada. 2012. Census Profile. 2011 Census. Statistics Canada Catalogue no. 98-316-XWE. Ottawa. Released October 24 2012.
http://www12.statcan.gc.ca/census-recensement/2011/dp-pd/prof/index.cfm?Lang=E

Age Characteristics: 0 to 49 Years

Area	0 to 4 Years	5 to 9 Years	10 to 14 Years	15 to 19 Years	20 to 24 Years	25 to 29 Years	30 to 34 Years	35 to 39 Years	40 to 44 Years	45 to 49 Years
Number										
Total										
Montréal	95,345	77,280	75,350	87,070	119,725	139,605	140,290	121,790	115,805	118,695
Québec	440,840	399,575	418,205	491,980	489,185	490,665	531,445	498,225	520,805	623,575
Canada	1,877,095	1,809,895	1,920,355	2,178,135	2,187,450	2,169,590	2,162,905	2,173,930	2,324,875	2,675,130
Males										
Montréal	48,560	39,080	38,390	43,620	58,330	68,300	70,065	62,290	60,020	61,170
Québec	225,525	203,675	213,540	249,960	246,850	245,695	264,980	249,610	261,120	311,320
Canada	961,150	925,965	983,995	1,115,845	1,108,775	1,077,275	1,058,810	1,064,200	1,141,720	1,318,715
Females										
Montréal	46,790	38,205	36,960	43,450	61,395	71,305	70,220	59,495	55,785	57,525
Québec	215,320	195,900	204,665	242,020	242,340	244,970	266,460	248,615	259,690	312,250
Canada	915,945	883,935	936,360	1,062,295	1,078,670	1,092,315	1,104,095	1,109,735	1,183,155	1,356,420
Percent of Population										
Total										
Montréal	5.8	4.7	4.6	5.3	7.3	8.5	8.5	7.4	7.0	7.2
Québec	5.6	5.1	5.3	6.2	6.2	6.2	6.7	6.3	6.6	7.9
Canada	5.6	5.4	5.7	6.5	6.5	6.5	6.5	6.5	6.9	8.0
Males										
Montréal	6.1	4.9	4.8	5.5	7.3	8.5	8.8	7.8	7.5	7.6
Québec	5.8	5.3	5.5	6.4	6.4	6.3	6.8	6.4	6.7	8.0
Canada	5.9	5.6	6.0	6.8	6.8	6.6	6.5	6.5	7.0	8.0
Females										
Montréal	5.5	4.5	4.4	5.1	7.2	8.4	8.3	7.0	6.6	6.8
Québec	5.3	4.9	5.1	6.0	6.0	6.1	6.6	6.2	6.4	7.8
Canada	5.4	5.2	5.5	6.2	6.3	6.4	6.5	6.5	6.9	7.9

Source: Statistics Canada. 2012. Census Profile. 2011 Census. Statistics Canada Catalogue no. 98-316-XWE. Ottawa. Released October 24 2012.
http://www12.statcan.gc.ca/census-recensement/2011/dp-pd/prof/index.cfm?Lang=E

Age Characteristics: 50 Years and Over, and Median Age

Area	50 to 54 Years	55 to 59 Years	60 to 64 Years	65 to 69 Years	70 to 74 Years	75 to 79 Years	80 to 84 Years	85 Years and Over	Median Age
Number									
Total									
Montréal	116,465	102,585	88,990	67,930	56,235	49,905	40,380	36,085	38.6
Québec	648,695	579,280	512,830	403,210	291,755	232,355	176,420	153,945	41.9
Canada	2,658,965	2,340,635	2,052,670	1,521,715	1,153,065	922,700	702,070	645,515	40.6
Males									
Montréal	57,860	49,520	41,960	30,720	24,230	20,645	14,930	10,190	37.6
Québec	320,695	285,295	250,675	194,305	135,830	101,675	69,170	45,945	40.7
Canada	1,309,030	1,147,300	1,002,690	738,010	543,435	417,945	291,085	208,300	39.6
Females									
Montréal	58,600	53,065	47,030	37,215	32,000	29,265	25,450	25,890	39.7
Québec	327,995	293,990	262,155	208,905	155,925	130,680	107,250	108,005	43.0
Canada	1,349,940	1,193,335	1,049,985	783,705	609,630	504,755	410,985	437,215	41.5
Percent of Population									
Total									
Montréal	7.1	6.2	5.4	4.1	3.4	3.0	2.4	2.2	–
Québec	8.2	7.3	6.5	5.1	3.7	2.9	2.2	1.9	–
Canada	7.9	7.0	6.1	4.5	3.4	2.8	2.1	1.9	–
Males									
Montréal	7.2	6.2	5.2	3.8	3.0	2.6	1.9	1.3	–
Québec	8.3	7.4	6.5	5.0	3.5	2.6	1.8	1.2	–
Canada	8.0	7.0	6.1	4.5	3.3	2.5	1.8	1.3	–
Females									
Montréal	6.9	6.2	5.5	4.4	3.8	3.4	3.0	3.0	–
Québec	8.1	7.3	6.5	5.2	3.9	3.2	2.7	2.7	–
Canada	7.9	7.0	6.2	4.6	3.6	3.0	2.4	2.6	–

Source: Statistics Canada. 2012. Census Profile. 2011 Census. Statistics Canada Catalogue no. 98-316-XWE. Ottawa. Released October 24 2012.
http://www12.statcan.gc.ca/census-recensement/2011/dp-pd/prof/index.cfm?Lang=E

PROFILES / Montréal, Québec

Private Households by Household Size

Area	1 Person	2 Persons	3 Persons	4 Persons	5 Persons	6 or More Persons	Average Number of Persons in Private Households
			Households				
Montréal	309,220	230,245	102,630	76,260	27,910	13,685	2.1
Québec	1,094,410	1,181,240	496,140	421,080	142,555	59,920	2.3
Canada	3,673,310	4,544,820	2,081,900	1,903,300	724,405	392,885	2.5
			Percent of Households				
Montréal	40.7	30.3	13.5	10.0	3.7	1.8	–
Québec	32.2	34.8	14.6	12.4	4.2	1.8	–
Canada	27.6	34.1	15.6	14.3	5.4	2.9	–

Source: Statistics Canada. 2012. Census Profile. 2011 Census. Statistics Canada Catalogue no. 98-316-XWE. Ottawa. Released October 24 2012.
http://www12.statcan.gc.ca/census-recensement/2011/dp-pd/prof/index.cfm?Lang=E

Dwelling Type

Area	Single-detached House	Semi-detached House	Row House	Apartment: Building with Five or More Storeys	Apartment: Building with Fewer Than Five Storeys	Duplex Apartment	Movable Dwelling	Other Single-attached House
				Number				
Montréal	56,815	25,070	24,795	97,650	442,540	109,155	445	3,485
Québec	1,560,405	171,435	86,040	171,115	1,103,845	263,860	22,995	15,645
Canada	7,329,150	646,245	791,600	1,234,770	2,397,550	704,485	183,510	33,310
				Percent of Dwellings				
Montréal	7.5	3.3	3.3	12.8	58.2	14.4	0.1	0.5
Québec	46.0	5.0	2.5	5.0	32.5	7.8	0.7	0.5
Canada	55.0	4.9	5.9	9.3	18.0	5.3	1.4	0.3

Source: Statistics Canada. 2012. Census Profile. 2011 Census. Statistics Canada Catalogue no. 98-316-XWE. Ottawa. Released October 24 2012.
http://www12.statcan.gc.ca/census-recensement/2011/dp-pd/prof/index.cfm?Lang=E

Shelter Costs

		Owned Dwellings					Rented Dwellings		
Area	Number	Median Value[1] ($)	Average Value[1] ($)	Median Monthly Costs[2] ($)	Average Monthly Costs[2] ($)	Number	Median Monthly Costs[3] ($)	Average Monthly Costs[3] ($)
Montréal	272,180	338,139	373,475	1,041	1,161	487,770	684	732
Québec	2,056,665	214,537	249,427	841	936	1,308,465	643	685
Canada	9,013,410	280,552	345,182	978	1,141	4,060,385	784	848

Note: All figures cover non-farm, non-reserve private dwellings; (1) Refers to the dollar amount expected by the owner if the dwelling were to be sold; (2) Includes all shelter expenses paid by households that own their dwellings, such as the mortgage payment and the costs of electricity, heat, water and other municipal services, property taxes and condominium fees; (3) Includes all shelter expenses paid by households that rent their dwellings, such as the monthly rent and the costs of electricity, heat and municipal services.
Source: Statistics Canada. 2013. 2011 National Household Survey. Statistics Canada Catalogue no. 99-004-XWE. Ottawa. Released September 11, 2013.

Occupied Private Dwellings by Period of Construction

Area	1960 or Before	1961 to 1980	1981 to 1990	1991 to 2000	2001 to 2005	2006 to 2011
			Number			
Montréal	325,285	248,955	87,705	41,200	26,405	30,395
Québec	946,900	1,115,455	533,790	353,355	206,035	239,685
Canada	3,273,105	4,152,715	2,112,110	1,707,880	1,031,020	1,042,430
			Percent of Dwellings			
Montréal	42.8	32.8	11.5	5.4	3.5	4.0
Québec	27.9	32.9	15.7	10.4	6.1	7.1
Canada	24.6	31.2	15.9	12.8	7.7	7.8

Note: Figures cover non-farm, non-reserve private dwellings and includes data up to May 10, 2011.
Source: Statistics Canada. 2013. 2011 National Household Survey. Statistics Canada Catalogue no. 99-004-XWE. Ottawa. Released September 11, 2013.

Educational Attainment

Area	No Certificate, Diploma or Degree	High School Diploma or Equivalent[1]	Apprenticeship or Trades Certificate or Diploma[2]	College, CÉGEP or Other Non-University Certificate or Diploma	University Certificate or Diploma Below the Bachelor Level[3]	Bachelor's Degree	University Certificate, Diploma or Degree Above Bachelor Level[4]
				Number			
				Total			
Montréal	273,365	283,135	140,785	206,890	77,685	225,400	157,550
Québec	1,436,025	1,404,755	1,049,470	1,075,855	305,330	766,100	437,050
Canada	5,485,400	6,968,935	2,950,685	4,970,020	1,200,130	3,634,425	2,049,930
				Males			
Montréal	125,800	137,440	78,190	95,750	34,560	106,525	81,645
Québec	714,090	650,660	635,435	472,360	126,565	343,535	227,990
Canada	2,742,875	3,305,415	1,928,970	2,118,430	513,235	1,643,080	1,043,350
				Females			
Montréal	147,560	145,700	62,595	111,140	43,125	118,875	75,905
Québec	721,930	754,095	414,035	603,495	178,765	422,565	209,065
Canada	2,742,520	3,663,515	1,021,715	2,851,595	686,890	1,991,345	1,006,585
				Percent of Population			
				Total			
Montréal	20.0	20.7	10.3	15.2	5.7	16.5	11.5
Québec	22.2	21.7	16.2	16.6	4.7	11.8	6.8
Canada	20.1	25.6	10.8	18.2	4.4	13.3	7.5
				Males			
Montréal	19.1	20.8	11.8	14.5	5.2	16.1	12.4
Québec	22.5	20.5	20.0	14.9	4.0	10.8	7.2
Canada	20.6	24.9	14.5	15.9	3.9	12.4	7.8
				Females			
Montréal	20.9	20.7	8.9	15.8	6.1	16.9	10.8
Québec	21.9	22.8	12.5	18.3	5.4	12.8	6.3
Canada	19.6	26.2	7.3	20.4	4.9	14.3	7.2

Note: Figures cover total population aged 15 years and over by highest certificate, diploma or degree; (1) Includes persons who have graduated from a secondary school or equivalent. It excludes persons with a postsecondary certificate, diploma or degree; (2) Includes Registered Apprenticeship certificates (including Certificate of Qualification, Journeyperson's designation) and other trades certificates or diplomas such as pre-employment or vocational certificates and diplomas from brief trade programs completed at community colleges, institutes of technology, vocational centres, and similar institutions; (3) Comparisons with other data sources suggest that the category 'University certificate or diploma below the bachelor's level' was over-reported in the NHS. This category likely includes some responses that are actually college certificates or diplomas, bachelor's degrees or other types of education (e.g., university transfer programs, bachelor's programs completed in other countries, incomplete bachelor's programs, non-university professional designations). We recommend users interpret the results for the 'University certificate or diploma below the bachelor's level' category with caution; (4) 'University certificate or diploma above bachelor level' includes the categories: 'Degree in medicine, dentistry, veterinary medicine or optometry,' 'Master's degree' and 'Earned doctorate.'
Source: Statistics Canada. 2013. 2011 National Household Survey. Statistics Canada Catalogue no. 99-004-XWE. Ottawa. Released September 11, 2013.

Household Income Distribution

Area	Less than $10,000	$10,000 to $19,999	$20,000 to $29,999	$30,000 to $39,999	$40,000 to $49,999	$50,000 to $59,999	$60,000 to $79,999	$80,000 to $99,999	$100,000 to $124,999	$125,000 to $149,999	$150,000 and Over
						Households					
Montréal	67,490	107,980	93,770	92,125	81,160	64,440	90,510	56,430	42,070	24,080	39,885
Québec	179,790	377,210	353,470	382,000	343,730	302,595	483,085	344,435	267,995	148,950	211,965
Canada	626,705	1,141,945	1,193,925	1,271,675	1,206,800	1,102,120	1,865,280	1,458,240	1,260,770	802,555	1,389,240
						Percent of Households					
Montréal	8.9	14.2	12.3	12.1	10.7	8.5	11.9	7.4	5.5	3.2	5.2
Québec	5.3	11.1	10.4	11.3	10.1	8.9	14.2	10.1	7.9	4.4	6.2
Canada	4.7	8.6	9.0	9.5	9.1	8.3	14.0	10.9	9.5	6.0	10.4

Note: Household income is the sum of the total incomes of all members of that household. Total income refers to monetary receipts from certain sources, before income taxes and deductions, during calendar year 2010.
Source: Statistics Canada. 2013. 2011 National Household Survey. Statistics Canada Catalogue no. 99-004-XWE. Ottawa. Released September 11, 2013.

Median and Average Household and Economic Family Income

Area	Median Household Income ($)	Average Household Income ($)	Median After-tax Household Income ($)	Average After-tax Household Income ($)	Median Economic Family Income ($)	Average Economic Family Income ($)	Median After-tax Economic Family Income ($)	Average After-tax Economic Family Income ($)
Montréal	42,052	57,717	38,177	48,223	57,270	75,368	51,940	62,843
Québec	51,842	66,205	45,968	55,121	68,344	82,045	59,560	68,091
Canada	61,072	79,102	54,089	66,149	76,511	94,125	67,044	78,517

Note: Figures cover household and economic familiy income in 2010. A household is defined as a person or a group of persons (other than foreign residents) who occupy the same private dwelling and do not have a usual place of residence elsewhere in Canada. Every person is a member of one and only one household. An economic family is defined as a group of two or more persons who live in the same dwelling and are related to each other by blood, marriage, common-law, adoption or a foster relationship. A couple may be of opposite or same sex.
Source: Statistics Canada. 2013. 2011 National Household Survey. Statistics Canada Catalogue no. 99-004-XWE. Ottawa. Released September 11, 2013.

PROFILES / Montréal, Québec

Individual Income Distribution

Area	Less than $10,000	$10,000 to $19,999	$20,000 to $29,999	$30,000 to $39,999	$40,000 to $49,999	$50,000 to $59,999	$60,000 to $79,999	$80,000 to $99,999	$100,000 to $124,999	$125,000 and Over
Number										
Total										
Montréal	259,725	301,720	200,690	164,405	115,705	77,840	88,495	38,325	21,735	26,780
Québec	1,005,600	1,309,515	941,630	866,290	653,400	449,185	515,815	211,070	109,975	120,915
Canada	4,492,040	4,835,710	3,670,020	3,180,360	2,603,520	1,921,650	2,437,440	1,302,045	693,580	782,135
Males										
Montréal	127,295	125,690	92,930	80,775	56,375	40,955	48,755	23,250	14,165	18,900
Québec	441,455	516,150	427,295	432,625	345,950	256,700	313,880	143,785	80,000	91,475
Canada	1,936,365	1,864,880	1,588,260	1,522,190	1,333,510	1,079,780	1,473,145	823,720	492,905	599,905
Females										
Montréal	132,430	176,025	107,760	83,630	59,330	36,885	39,745	15,075	7,570	7,875
Québec	564,150	793,365	514,335	433,670	307,455	192,485	201,935	67,275	29,980	29,440
Canada	2,555,675	2,970,825	2,081,760	1,658,170	1,270,010	841,870	964,300	478,330	200,680	182,230
Percent of Population										
Total										
Montréal	20.0	23.3	15.5	12.7	8.9	6.0	6.8	3.0	1.7	2.1
Québec	16.3	21.2	15.2	14.0	10.6	7.3	8.3	3.4	1.8	2.0
Canada	17.3	18.7	14.2	12.3	10.0	7.4	9.4	5.0	2.7	3.0
Males										
Montréal	20.2	20.0	14.8	12.8	9.0	6.5	7.8	3.7	2.3	3.0
Québec	14.5	16.9	14.0	14.2	11.3	8.4	10.3	4.7	2.6	3.0
Canada	15.2	14.7	12.5	12.0	10.5	8.5	11.6	6.5	3.9	4.7
Females										
Montréal	19.9	26.4	16.2	12.6	8.9	5.5	6.0	2.3	1.1	1.2
Québec	18.0	25.3	16.4	13.8	9.8	6.1	6.4	2.1	1.0	0.9
Canada	19.4	22.5	15.8	12.6	9.6	6.4	7.3	3.6	1.5	1.4

Note: Figures cover individuals aged 15 years and over with income. Income refers to monetary receipts from certain sources, before income taxes and deductions, during calendar year 2010.
Source: Statistics Canada. 2013. 2011 National Household Survey. Statistics Canada Catalogue no. 99-004-XWE. Ottawa. Released September 11, 2013.

Labour Force Status

Area	In the Labour Force - All	In the Labour Force - Employed	In the Labour Force - Unemployed	Not in the Labour Force
Number				
Total				
Montréal	862,810	776,535	86,270	502,000
Québec	4,183,445	3,880,425	303,020	2,291,145
Canada	17,990,080	16,595,035	1,395,045	9,269,445
Males				
Montréal	448,780	401,855	46,925	211,130
Québec	2,188,555	2,014,810	173,745	982,080
Canada	9,388,570	8,634,310	754,255	3,906,785
Females				
Montréal	414,025	374,685	39,345	290,870
Québec	1,994,885	1,865,610	129,275	1,309,065
Canada	8,601,515	7,960,725	640,790	5,362,660
Percent of Labour Force				
Total				
Montréal	63.2	56.9	10.0	36.8
Québec	64.6	59.9	7.2	35.4
Canada	66.0	60.9	7.8	34.0
Males				
Montréal	68.0	60.9	10.5	32.0
Québec	69.0	63.5	7.9	31.0
Canada	70.6	64.9	8.0	29.4
Females				
Montréal	58.7	53.2	9.5	41.3
Québec	60.4	56.5	6.5	39.6
Canada	61.6	57.0	7.4	38.4

Note: Figures are based on total population 15 years and over
Source: Statistics Canada. 2013. 2011 National Household Survey. Statistics Canada Catalogue no. 99-004-XWE. Ottawa. Released September 11, 2013.

Labour Force by Industry (NAICS Codes 11–52)

Area	Agriculture, forestry, fishing & hunting	Mining, quarrying, & oil & gas extraction	Utilities	Construction	Manufacturing	Wholesale Trade	Retail Trade	Transportation & warehousing	Information & cultural industries	Finance & insurance
					Number					
					Total					
Montréal	1,980	660	4,930	26,745	78,250	39,195	90,690	35,295	36,970	39,275
Québec	84,470	20,770	33,815	241,780	476,390	169,825	501,380	181,295	98,340	159,230
Canada	437,650	261,050	149,940	1,215,380	1,619,295	733,445	2,031,665	827,780	420,830	767,960
					Males					
Montréal	1,330	460	2,950	23,420	52,545	24,260	43,990	26,725	21,450	16,790
Québec	61,540	18,035	24,560	213,605	343,345	113,545	234,725	137,745	56,455	56,930
Canada	307,370	211,690	110,765	1,068,710	1,167,680	494,545	933,850	617,305	235,875	296,995
					Females					
Montréal	650	200	1,980	3,330	25,700	14,935	46,700	8,570	15,525	22,485
Québec	22,925	2,730	9,255	28,170	133,045	56,280	266,650	43,550	41,885	102,295
Canada	130,285	49,360	39,175	146,670	451,615	238,900	1,097,820	210,475	184,955	470,960
					Percent of Labour Force					
					Total					
Montréal	0.2	0.1	0.6	3.2	9.5	4.7	11.0	4.3	4.5	4.8
Québec	2.1	0.5	0.8	5.9	11.7	4.2	12.3	4.4	2.4	3.9
Canada	2.5	1.5	0.9	6.9	9.2	4.2	11.6	4.7	2.4	4.4
					Males					
Montréal	0.3	0.1	0.7	5.5	12.2	5.7	10.3	6.2	5.0	3.9
Québec	2.9	0.8	1.1	10.0	16.1	5.3	11.0	6.4	2.6	2.7
Canada	3.3	2.3	1.2	11.6	12.7	5.4	10.2	6.7	2.6	3.2
					Females					
Montréal	0.2	0.1	0.5	0.8	6.5	3.8	11.8	2.2	3.9	5.7
Québec	1.2	0.1	0.5	1.4	6.8	2.9	13.7	2.2	2.2	5.3
Canada	1.6	0.6	0.5	1.7	5.4	2.8	13.1	2.5	2.2	5.6

Note: Figures are based on total experienced labour force 15 years and over. Experienced labour force refers to persons who, during the week of Sunday, May 1 to Saturday, May 7, 2011, were employed and the unemployed who had last worked for pay or in self-employment in either 2010 or 2011.
Source: Statistics Canada. 2013. 2011 National Household Survey. Statistics Canada Catalogue no. 99-004-XWE. Ottawa. Released September 11, 2013.

Labour Force by Industry (NAICS Codes 53–91)

Area	Real estate & rental & leasing	Profess., scientific & tech. services	Mgmt of companies & enterprises	Admin. & support, waste mgmt & remed. services	Educational services	Health care & social assistance	Arts, entertain. & recreation	Accomm. & food services	Other services (except public admin.)	Public admin.
					Number					
					Total					
Montréal	15,510	83,590	930	42,325	71,050	101,065	21,195	58,640	38,095	39,175
Québec	61,365	282,115	3,965	156,130	301,425	496,125	78,795	253,145	189,290	295,480
Canada	321,895	1,240,850	17,460	728,330	1,301,435	1,949,650	363,405	1,130,750	807,800	1,261,050
					Males					
Montréal	9,145	48,735	495	24,825	27,625	24,315	11,335	32,845	16,570	19,175
Québec	35,940	158,920	2,250	92,530	99,565	97,255	41,535	112,650	88,710	147,645
Canada	179,090	688,625	9,380	411,250	424,915	349,430	188,270	469,990	372,940	652,510
					Females					
Montréal	6,355	34,850	435	17,505	43,420	76,750	9,860	25,800	21,525	20,000
Québec	25,425	123,205	1,715	63,605	201,860	398,870	37,260	140,495	100,585	147,835
Canada	142,805	552,225	8,075	317,085	876,515	1,600,220	175,135	660,760	434,865	608,535
					Percent of Labour Force					
					Total					
Montréal	1.9	10.1	0.1	5.1	8.6	12.2	2.6	7.1	4.6	4.7
Québec	1.5	6.9	0.1	3.8	7.4	12.1	1.9	6.2	4.6	7.2
Canada	1.8	7.1	0.1	4.1	7.4	11.1	2.1	6.4	4.6	7.2
					Males					
Montréal	2.1	11.4	0.1	5.8	6.4	5.7	2.6	7.7	3.9	4.5
Québec	1.7	7.4	0.1	4.3	4.7	4.5	1.9	5.3	4.2	6.9
Canada	1.9	7.5	0.1	4.5	4.6	3.8	2.0	5.1	4.1	7.1
					Females					
Montréal	1.6	8.8	0.1	4.4	10.9	19.4	2.5	6.5	5.4	5.0
Québec	1.3	6.3	0.1	3.3	10.4	20.5	1.9	7.2	5.2	7.6
Canada	1.7	6.6	0.1	3.8	10.4	19.1	2.1	7.9	5.2	7.2

Note: Figures are based on total experienced labour force 15 years and over. Experienced labour force refers to persons who, during the week of Sunday, May 1 to Saturday, May 7, 2011, were employed and the unemployed who had last worked for pay or in self-employment in either 2010 or 2011.
Source: Statistics Canada. 2013. 2011 National Household Survey. Statistics Canada Catalogue no. 99-004-XWE. Ottawa. Released September 11, 2013.

Occupation

Area	Mgmt	Business, Finance & Admin.	Natural/ Applied Sciences & Related	Health	Education, Law & Social, Community & Government Services	Art, Culture, Recreation & Sport	Sales & Service	Trades, Transport & Equip. Operators & Related	Natural Resources, Agri. & Related Production	Mfg & Utilities
					Number					
					Total					
Montréal	79,555	148,485	70,655	53,750	106,520	45,220	210,115	71,925	3,820	35,515
Québec	411,425	687,715	287,015	268,610	479,505	123,665	969,740	573,075	65,625	218,740
Canada	1,963,600	2,902,045	1,237,775	1,107,200	2,064,675	503,415	4,068,170	2,537,775	397,930	805,040
					Males					
Montréal	48,845	53,660	54,740	13,805	35,440	22,925	106,845	67,220	3,165	22,340
Québec	261,620	207,545	221,430	53,480	148,715	58,150	436,370	542,055	53,640	154,485
Canada	1,229,460	854,190	966,355	217,520	676,550	232,535	1,745,705	2,385,615	318,945	564,300
					Females					
Montréal	30,710	94,825	15,920	39,945	71,075	22,290	103,275	4,705	650	13,175
Québec	149,800	480,170	65,585	215,130	330,795	65,520	533,370	31,025	11,995	64,250
Canada	734,140	2,047,855	271,415	889,675	1,388,130	270,875	2,322,465	152,165	78,980	240,740
					Percent of Labour Force					
					Total					
Montréal	9.6	18.0	8.6	6.5	12.9	5.5	25.5	8.7	0.5	4.3
Québec	10.1	16.8	7.0	6.6	11.7	3.0	23.7	14.0	1.6	5.4
Canada	11.2	16.5	7.0	6.3	11.7	2.9	23.1	14.4	2.3	4.6
					Males					
Montréal	11.4	12.5	12.8	3.2	8.3	5.3	24.9	15.7	0.7	5.2
Québec	12.2	9.7	10.4	2.5	7.0	2.7	20.4	25.4	2.5	7.2
Canada	13.4	9.3	10.5	2.4	7.4	2.5	19.0	26.0	3.5	6.1
					Females					
Montréal	7.7	23.9	4.0	10.1	17.9	5.6	26.0	1.2	0.2	3.3
Québec	7.7	24.7	3.4	11.0	17.0	3.4	27.4	1.6	0.6	3.3
Canada	8.7	24.4	3.2	10.6	16.5	3.2	27.7	1.8	0.9	2.9

Note: Figures are based on total experienced labour force 15 years and over
Source: Statistics Canada. 2013. 2011 National Household Survey. Statistics Canada Catalogue no. 99-004-XWE. Ottawa. Released September 11, 2013.

Place of Work Status

Area	Worked at Home	Worked Outside Canada	No Fixed Workplace Address	Worked at Usual Place
		Number		
		Total		
Montréal	45,940	3,140	62,735	664,715
Québec	237,625	9,705	331,525	3,301,560
Canada	1,142,640	66,460	1,868,245	13,517,690
		Males		
Montréal	24,685	1,960	44,300	330,905
Québec	122,060	7,055	249,535	1,636,165
Canada	582,150	47,355	1,400,485	6,604,325
		Females		
Montréal	21,255	1,185	18,435	333,810
Québec	115,565	2,650	81,995	1,665,395
Canada	560,490	19,100	467,760	6,913,370
		Percent of Labour Force		
		Total		
Montréal	5.9	0.4	8.1	85.6
Québec	6.1	0.3	8.5	85.1
Canada	6.9	0.4	11.3	81.5
		Males		
Montréal	6.1	0.5	11.0	82.3
Québec	6.1	0.4	12.4	81.2
Canada	6.7	0.5	16.2	76.5
		Females		
Montréal	5.7	0.3	4.9	89.1
Québec	6.2	0.1	4.4	89.3
Canada	7.0	0.2	5.9	86.8

Note: Figures are based on total employed labour force 15 years and over.
Source: Statistics Canada. 2013. 2011 National Household Survey. Statistics Canada Catalogue no. 99-004-XWE. Ottawa. Released September 11, 2013.

Mode of Transportation to Work

Area	Car; Truck; Van; as Driver	Car; Truck; Van; as Passenger	Public Transit	Walked	Bicycled	All Other Modes
			Number			
			Total			
Montréal	350,780	21,260	263,875	61,870	22,935	6,740
Québec	2,713,295	136,490	484,600	215,210	48,870	34,620
Canada	11,393,140	867,050	1,851,525	880,815	201,780	191,625
			Males			
Montréal	210,375	6,935	112,225	27,805	14,120	3,750
Québec	1,484,305	50,905	203,035	95,100	33,065	19,285
Canada	6,238,835	349,530	788,290	387,580	135,840	104,725
			Females			
Montréal	140,400	14,325	151,650	34,070	8,815	2,985
Québec	1,228,995	85,585	281,565	120,110	15,800	15,335
Canada	5,154,305	517,520	1,063,235	493,230	65,940	86,900
			Percent of Labour Force			
			Total			
Montréal	48.2	2.9	36.3	8.5	3.2	0.9
Québec	74.7	3.8	13.3	5.9	1.3	1.0
Canada	74.0	5.6	12.0	5.7	1.3	1.2
			Males			
Montréal	56.1	1.8	29.9	7.4	3.8	1.0
Québec	78.7	2.7	10.8	5.0	1.8	1.0
Canada	77.9	4.4	9.8	4.8	1.7	1.3
			Females			
Montréal	39.9	4.1	43.1	9.7	2.5	0.8
Québec	70.3	4.9	16.1	6.9	0.9	0.9
Canada	69.8	7.0	14.4	6.7	0.9	1.2

Note: Figures are based on total employed labour force 15 years and over.
Source: Statistics Canada. 2013. 2011 National Household Survey. Statistics Canada Catalogue no. 99-004-XWE. Ottawa. Released September 11, 2013.

Visible Minority Population Characteristics

Area	Total Minority	South Asian[1]	Chinese	Black	Filipino	Latin American	Arab	SE Asian[2]	West Asian[3]	Korean	Japanese	Multiple[4]
						Number						
						Total						
Montréal	510,665	53,515	46,845	147,100	21,750	67,160	102,625	39,570	12,155	3,330	2,020	10,150
Québec	850,235	83,320	82,845	243,625	31,495	116,380	166,260	65,855	23,445	6,665	4,025	17,420
Canada	6,264,750	1,567,400	1,324,750	945,665	619,310	381,280	380,620	312,075	206,840	161,130	87,270	171,935
						Males						
Montréal	252,130	28,005	22,035	69,680	8,415	33,025	55,650	19,860	6,230	1,540	670	4,890
Québec	418,545	43,410	37,295	116,605	12,435	56,940	89,505	32,940	12,070	3,135	1,565	8,315
Canada	3,043,010	790,755	632,325	453,005	268,885	186,355	203,485	154,035	105,620	77,165	38,270	83,335
						Females						
Montréal	258,530	25,510	24,810	77,420	13,340	34,135	46,975	19,710	5,925	1,790	1,355	5,265
Québec	431,695	39,915	45,550	127,020	19,055	59,440	76,750	32,920	11,380	3,530	2,465	9,105
Canada	3,221,745	776,650	692,420	492,660	350,425	194,925	177,140	158,045	101,220	83,965	48,990	88,600
						Percent of Population						
						Total						
Montréal	31.7	3.3	2.9	9.1	1.3	4.2	6.4	2.5	0.8	0.2	0.1	0.6
Québec	11.0	1.1	1.1	3.2	0.4	1.5	2.2	0.9	0.3	0.1	0.1	0.2
Canada	19.1	4.8	4.0	2.9	1.9	1.2	1.2	0.9	0.6	0.5	0.3	0.5
						Males						
Montréal	32.0	3.6	2.8	8.9	1.1	4.2	7.1	2.5	0.8	0.2	0.1	0.6
Québec	11.0	1.1	1.0	3.1	0.3	1.5	2.3	0.9	0.3	0.1	0.0	0.2
Canada	18.8	4.9	3.9	2.8	1.7	1.2	1.3	1.0	0.7	0.5	0.2	0.5
						Females						
Montréal	31.3	3.1	3.0	9.4	1.6	4.1	5.7	2.4	0.7	0.2	0.2	0.6
Québec	11.0	1.0	1.2	3.2	0.5	1.5	2.0	0.8	0.3	0.1	0.1	0.2
Canada	19.3	4.7	4.1	3.0	2.1	1.2	1.1	0.9	0.6	0.5	0.3	0.5

Note: The Employment Equity Act defines visible minorities as 'persons, other than Aboriginal peoples, who are non-Caucasian in race or non-white in colour';
(1) Includes 'East Indian,' 'Pakistani,' 'Sri Lankan,' etc.; (2) Includes 'Vietnamese,' 'Cambodian,' 'Malaysian,' 'Laotian,' etc.; (3) Includes 'Iranian,' 'Afghan,' etc.; (4) Includes respondents who reported more than one visible minority group by checking two or more mark-in circles, e.g., 'Black' and 'South Asian.'
Source: Statistics Canada. 2013. 2011 National Household Survey. Statistics Canada Catalogue no. 99-004-XWE. Ottawa. Released September 11, 2013.

Aboriginal Population

Area	Aboriginal Identity[1]	First Nations (North American Indian) Single Identity[2]	Métis Single Identity	Inuk (Inuit) Single Identity	Multiple Aboriginal Identities[3]	Aboriginal Identities Not Included Elsewhere
			Number			
			Total			
Montréal	9,510	5,080	3,250	360	220	595
Québec	141,915	82,425	40,960	12,570	1,545	4,415
Canada	1,400,685	851,560	451,795	59,440	11,415	26,475
			Males			
Montréal	4,480	2,340	1,585	190	75	300
Québec	70,205	40,105	21,300	6,265	720	1,815
Canada	682,190	411,785	223,335	29,495	5,525	12,055
			Females			
Montréal	5,030	2,740	1,670	175	150	300
Québec	71,710	42,315	19,660	6,305	830	2,600
Canada	718,500	439,775	228,460	29,950	5,890	14,420
			Percent of Population			
			Total			
Montréal	0.6	0.3	0.2	0.0	0.0	0.0
Québec	1.8	1.1	0.5	0.2	0.0	0.1
Canada	4.3	2.6	1.4	0.2	0.0	0.1
			Males			
Montréal	0.6	0.3	0.2	0.0	0.0	0.0
Québec	1.8	1.1	0.6	0.2	0.0	0.0
Canada	4.2	2.5	1.4	0.2	0.0	0.1
			Females			
Montréal	0.6	0.3	0.2	0.0	0.0	0.0
Québec	1.8	1.1	0.5	0.2	0.0	0.1
Canada	4.3	2.6	1.4	0.2	0.0	0.1

Note: (1) Includes persons who reported being an Aboriginal person, that is, First Nations (North American Indian), Métis or Inuk (Inuit) and/or those who reported Registered or Treaty Indian status, that is registered under the Indian Act of Canada, and/or those who reported membership in a First Nation or Indian band. Aboriginal peoples of Canada are defined in the Constitution Act, 1982, section 35-2 as including the Indian, Inuit and Métis peoples of Canada; (2) Users should be aware that the estimates associated with this variable are more affected than most by the incomplete enumeration of certain Indian reserves and Indian settlements in the National Household Survey (NHS); (3) Includes persons who reported being any two or all three of the following: First Nations (North American Indian), Métis or Inuk (Inuit).
Source: Statistics Canada. 2013. 2011 National Household Survey. Statistics Canada Catalogue no. 99-004-XWE. Ottawa. Released September 11, 2013.

Ethnic Origin

Area	North American Aboriginal	Other North American	European	Caribbean	Latin, Central and South American	African	Asian	Oceania
				Number				
				Total				
Montréal	36,270	547,640	751,645	101,295	73,655	152,880	275,710	915
Québec	307,445	4,776,875	3,390,330	167,590	137,255	260,785	488,905	2,305
Canada	1,836,035	11,070,455	20,157,965	627,590	544,375	766,735	5,011,225	74,875
				Males				
Montréal	16,010	260,160	366,805	46,265	36,060	79,815	137,040	425
Québec	146,725	2,345,180	1,678,310	77,665	67,195	135,740	241,515	1,135
Canada	885,675	5,462,685	9,913,150	291,640	264,635	387,360	2,435,540	37,490
				Females				
Montréal	20,260	287,475	384,840	55,030	37,595	73,060	138,665	495
Québec	160,725	2,431,700	1,712,015	89,925	70,065	125,040	247,390	1,175
Canada	950,360	5,607,770	10,244,820	335,945	279,740	379,380	2,575,680	37,385
				Percent of Population				
				Total				
Montréal	2.2	34.0	46.6	6.3	4.6	9.5	17.1	0.1
Québec	4.0	61.8	43.8	2.2	1.8	3.4	6.3	0.0
Canada	5.6	33.7	61.4	1.9	1.7	2.3	15.3	0.2
				Males				
Montréal	2.0	33.1	46.6	5.9	4.6	10.1	17.4	0.1
Québec	3.8	61.5	44.0	2.0	1.8	3.6	6.3	0.0
Canada	5.5	33.8	61.3	1.8	1.6	2.4	15.1	0.2
				Females				
Montréal	2.5	34.8	46.6	6.7	4.6	8.8	16.8	0.1
Québec	4.1	62.1	43.7	2.3	1.8	3.2	6.3	0.0
Canada	5.7	33.6	61.4	2.0	1.7	2.3	15.4	0.2

Note: The sum of the ethnic groups in this table is greater than the total population estimate because a person may report more than one ethnic origin in the NHS.
Source: Statistics Canada. 2013. 2011 National Household Survey. Statistics Canada Catalogue no. 99-004-XWE. Ottawa. Released September 11, 2013.

Religion

Area	Buddhist	Christian	Hindu	Jewish	Muslim	Sikh	Traditional (Aboriginal) Spirituality	Other Religions	No Religious Affiliation
				Number Total					
Montréal	32,205	1,061,605	22,580	35,785	154,540	5,415	105	4,195	296,215
Québec	52,390	6,356,880	33,540	85,100	243,430	9,275	2,025	12,340	937,545
Canada	366,830	22,102,745	497,965	329,495	1,053,945	454,965	64,935	130,835	7,850,605
				Males					
Montréal	15,175	494,940	11,505	17,550	82,235	3,090	35	2,110	160,105
Québec	24,630	3,079,855	17,055	41,455	128,815	5,090	925	6,155	510,055
Canada	168,465	10,497,775	250,435	161,265	540,555	229,435	31,805	57,745	4,225,645
				Females					
Montréal	17,030	566,660	11,080	18,235	72,310	2,330	65	2,090	136,110
Québec	27,760	3,277,020	16,480	43,645	114,615	4,185	1,100	6,175	427,485
Canada	198,365	11,604,975	247,525	168,235	513,395	225,530	33,135	73,090	3,624,965
				Percent of Population Total					
Montréal	2.0	65.8	1.4	2.2	9.6	0.3	0.0	0.3	18.4
Québec	0.7	82.2	0.4	1.1	3.1	0.1	0.0	0.2	12.1
Canada	1.1	67.3	1.5	1.0	3.2	1.4	0.2	0.4	23.9
				Males					
Montréal	1.9	62.9	1.5	2.2	10.5	0.4	0.0	0.3	20.4
Québec	0.6	80.8	0.4	1.1	3.4	0.1	0.0	0.2	13.4
Canada	1.0	64.9	1.5	1.0	3.3	1.4	0.2	0.4	26.1
				Females					
Montréal	2.1	68.6	1.3	2.2	8.8	0.3	0.0	0.3	16.5
Québec	0.7	83.6	0.4	1.1	2.9	0.1	0.0	0.2	10.9
Canada	1.2	69.5	1.5	1.0	3.1	1.4	0.2	0.4	21.7

Note: Religion refers to the person's self-identification as having a connection or affiliation with any religious denomination, group, body, sect, cult or other religiously defined community or system of belief. Religion is not limited to formal membership in a religious organization or group. Persons without a religious connection or affiliation can self-identify as atheist, agnostic or humanist, or can provide another applicable response.
Source: Statistics Canada. 2013. 2011 National Household Survey. Statistics Canada Catalogue no. 99-004-XWE. Ottawa. Released September 11, 2013.

Religion—Christian Denominations

Area	Anglican	Baptist	Catholic	Christian Orthodox	Lutheran	Pentecostal	Presbyterian	United Church	Other Christian
				Number Total					
Montréal	14,120	13,335	852,200	59,395	2,255	15,665	3,650	6,255	94,725
Québec	73,550	36,615	5,775,740	129,780	7,200	41,070	11,440	32,930	248,560
Canada	1,631,845	635,840	12,810,705	550,690	478,185	478,705	472,385	2,007,610	3,036,780
				Males					
Montréal	6,315	5,825	397,215	28,815	1,140	6,680	1,595	2,665	44,695
Québec	34,815	16,585	2,802,920	63,960	3,425	18,640	5,265	14,945	119,305
Canada	752,945	293,905	6,167,290	270,205	221,525	217,850	218,955	912,545	1,442,550
				Females					
Montréal	7,805	7,510	454,990	30,580	1,115	8,980	2,055	3,590	50,035
Québec	38,735	20,030	2,972,820	65,820	3,770	22,430	6,175	17,985	129,260
Canada	878,900	341,940	6,643,415	280,485	256,660	260,850	253,430	1,095,065	1,594,230
				Percent of Population Total					
Montréal	0.9	0.8	52.8	3.7	0.1	1.0	0.2	0.4	5.9
Québec	1.0	0.5	74.7	1.7	0.1	0.5	0.1	0.4	3.2
Canada	5.0	1.9	39.0	1.7	1.5	1.5	1.4	6.1	9.2
				Males					
Montréal	0.8	0.7	50.5	3.7	0.1	0.8	0.2	0.3	5.7
Québec	0.9	0.4	73.5	1.7	0.1	0.5	0.1	0.4	3.1
Canada	4.7	1.8	38.2	1.7	1.4	1.3	1.4	5.6	8.9
				Females					
Montréal	0.9	0.9	55.1	3.7	0.1	1.1	0.2	0.4	6.1
Québec	1.0	0.5	75.9	1.7	0.1	0.6	0.2	0.5	3.3
Canada	5.3	2.0	39.8	1.7	1.5	1.6	1.5	6.6	9.6

Note: Religion refers to the person's self-identification as having a connection or affiliation with any religious denomination, group, body, sect, cult or other religiously defined community or system of belief. Religion is not limited to formal membership in a religious organization or group. Persons without a religious connection or affiliation can self-identify as atheist, agnostic or humanist, or can provide another applicable response.
Source: Statistics Canada. 2013. 2011 National Household Survey. Statistics Canada Catalogue no. 99-004-XWE. Ottawa. Released September 11, 2013.

PROFILES / Montréal, Québec

Immigrant Status and Period of Immigration

Area	Non-Immigrants[1]	Immigrants All	Before 1971	1971 to 1980	1981 to 1990	1991 to 2000	2001 to 2005	2006 to 2011	Non-Permanent Residents[3]
				Number					
				Total					
Montréal	1,025,370	538,280	79,795	55,145	70,420	108,555	83,050	141,315	48,990
Québec	6,690,530	974,895	151,825	115,640	130,680	195,925	157,425	223,400	67,095
Canada	25,720,175	6,775,765	1,261,055	870,775	949,890	1,539,050	992,070	1,162,915	356,385
				Males					
Montréal	498,290	262,280	38,055	26,705	34,445	52,165	40,930	69,985	26,165
Québec	3,301,435	477,240	75,255	57,410	64,080	94,110	76,780	109,605	35,370
Canada	12,753,235	3,231,370	605,430	416,670	454,570	724,905	474,545	555,245	178,515
				Females					
Montréal	527,080	276,005	41,735	28,445	35,975	56,385	42,120	71,330	22,825
Québec	3,389,095	497,655	76,565	58,235	66,600	101,810	80,645	113,795	31,725
Canada	12,966,935	3,544,400	655,625	454,105	495,325	814,145	517,530	607,670	177,870
				Percent of Population					
				Total					
Montréal	63.6	33.4	4.9	3.4	4.4	6.7	5.1	8.8	3.0
Québec	86.5	12.6	2.0	1.5	1.7	2.5	2.0	2.9	0.9
Canada	78.3	20.6	3.8	2.7	2.9	4.7	3.0	3.5	1.1
				Males					
Montréal	63.3	33.3	4.8	3.4	4.4	6.6	5.2	8.9	3.3
Québec	86.6	12.5	2.0	1.5	1.7	2.5	2.0	2.9	0.9
Canada	78.9	20.0	3.7	2.6	2.8	4.5	2.9	3.4	1.1
				Females					
Montréal	63.8	33.4	5.1	3.4	4.4	6.8	5.1	8.6	2.8
Québec	86.5	12.7	2.0	1.5	1.7	2.6	2.1	2.9	0.8
Canada	77.7	21.2	3.9	2.7	3.0	4.9	3.1	3.6	1.1

Note: (1) Non-immigrant refers to a person who is a Canadian citizen by birth; (2) Immigrant refers to a person who is or has ever been a landed immigrant/permanent resident. This person has been granted the right to live in Canada permanently by immigration authorities. Some immigrants have resided in Canada for a number of years, while others have arrived recently. Some immigrants are Canadian citizens, while others are not. Most immigrants are born outside Canada, but a small number are born in Canada. In the 2011 National Household Survey, 'Immigrants' includes immigrants who landed in Canada prior to May 10, 2011; (3) Non-permanent resident refers to a person from another country who has a work or study permit, or who is a refugee claimant, and any non-Canadian-born family member living in Canada with them.
Source: Statistics Canada. 2013. 2011 National Household Survey. Statistics Canada Catalogue no. 99-004-XWE. Ottawa. Released September 11, 2013.

Mother Tongue

Area	English	French	Non-official Language	English & French	English & Non-official Language	French & Non-official Language	English, French & Non-official Language
			Number				
			Total				
Montréal	206,210	818,970	536,560	17,430	13,155	29,085	6,535
Québec	599,225	6,102,210	961,700	64,800	23,435	51,640	12,950
Canada	18,858,980	7,054,975	6,567,680	144,685	396,330	74,430	24,095
			Males				
Montréal	102,495	393,470	262,135	8,715	6,390	14,415	3,430
Québec	297,875	2,994,300	472,635	32,390	11,455	25,810	6,790
Canada	9,345,225	3,452,380	3,157,785	69,975	192,000	36,535	11,965
			Females				
Montréal	103,710	425,500	274,430	8,715	6,765	14,665	3,105
Québec	301,355	3,107,910	489,060	32,405	11,975	25,825	6,155
Canada	9,513,750	3,602,590	3,409,895	74,710	204,330	37,890	12,130
			Percent of Population				
			Total				
Montréal	12.7	50.3	33.0	1.1	0.8	1.8	0.4
Québec	7.7	78.1	12.3	0.8	0.3	0.7	0.2
Canada	56.9	21.3	19.8	0.4	1.2	0.2	0.1
			Males				
Montréal	13.0	49.7	33.1	1.1	0.8	1.8	0.4
Québec	7.8	78.0	12.3	0.8	0.3	0.7	0.2
Canada	57.5	21.2	19.4	0.4	1.2	0.2	0.1
			Females				
Montréal	12.4	50.8	32.8	1.0	0.8	1.8	0.4
Québec	7.6	78.2	12.3	0.8	0.3	0.6	0.2
Canada	56.4	21.4	20.2	0.4	1.2	0.2	0.1

Note: Figures cover total population excluding institutional residents.
Source: Statistics Canada. 2012. Census Profile. 2011 Census. Statistics Canada Catalogue no. 98-316-XWE. Ottawa. Released October 24 2012.
http://www12.statcan.gc.ca/census-recensement/2011/dp-pd/prof/index.cfm?Lang=E

Language Spoken Most Often at Home

Area	English	French	Non-official Language	English & French	English & Non-official Language	French & Non-official Language	English, French & Non-official Language
			Number				
			Total				
Montréal	298,955	886,075	319,960	22,835	26,025	58,005	16,095
Québec	767,415	6,249,080	554,400	71,555	43,765	100,110	29,625
Canada	21,457,075	6,827,865	3,673,865	131,205	875,135	109,700	46,330
			Males				
Montréal	147,925	428,505	153,640	11,720	12,645	28,145	8,470
Québec	379,915	3,071,635	268,640	35,860	21,305	48,590	15,315
Canada	10,585,620	3,348,235	1,767,310	63,475	425,370	53,010	22,845
			Females				
Montréal	151,030	457,575	166,315	11,115	13,380	29,860	7,625
Québec	387,500	3,177,450	285,760	35,695	22,460	51,525	14,310
Canada	10,871,455	3,479,625	1,906,555	67,730	449,765	56,690	23,485
			Percent of Population				
			Total				
Montréal	18.4	54.4	19.7	1.4	1.6	3.6	1.0
Québec	9.8	80.0	7.1	0.9	0.6	1.3	0.4
Canada	64.8	20.6	11.1	0.4	2.6	0.3	0.1
			Males				
Montréal	18.7	54.2	19.4	1.5	1.6	3.6	1.1
Québec	9.9	80.0	7.0	0.9	0.6	1.3	0.4
Canada	65.1	20.6	10.9	0.4	2.6	0.3	0.1
			Females				
Montréal	18.0	54.7	19.9	1.3	1.6	3.6	0.9
Québec	9.7	79.9	7.2	0.9	0.6	1.3	0.4
Canada	64.5	20.6	11.3	0.4	2.7	0.3	0.1

Note: Figures cover total population excluding institutional residents.
Source: Statistics Canada. 2012. Census Profile. 2011 Census. Statistics Canada Catalogue no. 98-316-XWE. Ottawa. Released October 24 2012.
http://www12.statcan.gc.ca/census-recensement/2011/dp-pd/prof/index.cfm?Lang=E

Knowledge of Official Languages

Area	English Only	French Only	English & French	Neither English nor French
		Number		
		Total		
Montréal	167,775	506,670	908,090	45,420
Québec	363,860	4,047,175	3,328,725	76,190
Canada	22,564,665	4,165,015	5,795,570	595,920
		Males		
Montréal	83,580	222,725	467,060	17,690
Québec	180,175	1,871,500	1,758,410	31,175
Canada	11,222,185	1,925,340	2,876,560	241,790
		Females		
Montréal	84,190	283,945	441,030	27,730
Québec	183,690	2,175,675	1,570,310	45,015
Canada	11,342,485	2,239,680	2,919,005	354,135
		Percent of Population		
		Total		
Montréal	10.3	31.1	55.8	2.8
Québec	4.7	51.8	42.6	1.0
Canada	68.1	12.6	17.5	1.8
		Males		
Montréal	10.6	28.2	59.0	2.2
Québec	4.7	48.7	45.8	0.8
Canada	69.0	11.8	17.7	1.5
		Females		
Montréal	10.1	33.9	52.7	3.3
Québec	4.6	54.7	39.5	1.1
Canada	67.3	13.3	17.3	2.1

Note: Figures cover total population excluding institutional residents.
Source: Statistics Canada. 2012. Census Profile. 2011 Census. Statistics Canada Catalogue no. 98-316-XWE. Ottawa. Released October 24 2012.
http://www12.statcan.gc.ca/census-recensement/2011/dp-pd/prof/index.cfm?Lang=E

Oakville, Ontario

Background

Oakville is on the shores of Lake Ontario and is a part of the Greater Toronto Area (GTA) in Ontario. The city's extensive shoreline includes two harbours: Bronte Harbour on Bronte Creek and Oakville Harbour on Sixteen Mile. The three major rivers emptying into Lake Ontario—Credit River, Sixteen Mile Creek and Twelve Mile Creek (now called Bronte Creek)—were pivotal to Oakville's success as a shipbuilding and grist-and-sawmill hub in the 19th century. In the 1820s, well developed areas such as Kingston were not offering a lot of transport by water to the Atlantic. To solve the problem, the first schooner was built and launched from Oakville Harbour in 1828, heralding the beginning of Oakville's vibrant shipbuilding industry.

Oakville honours its nautical past through various historical societies and museums, landmark preservation efforts such as the Oakville lighthouse (1837) and refurbished heritage homes. Today residents and visitors can visit Oakville Museum at Erchless Estate, the four-acre home and gardens of Oakville's founding family of shipbuilders, the Chisholms.

Every August, Oakville hosts one of the leading jazz festivals in the Greater Toronto Area. Since 1992 the Downtown Oakville Jazz Festival has welcomed tens of thousands of music lovers to the city's three-day outdoor event. Oakville's central location plays a role in the popularity of its vibrant arts and culture community. Toronto is less than 40 kilometres away and Niagara Falls and the U.S. border only an hour's drive away.

Oakville has average summer highs of plus 24.77 degrees Celsius, winter lows of minus 7.93 degrees Celsius, and an average rainfall just over 725 mm per year.

Rankings

- Oakville is one of Canada's wealthiest communities with a median family income of $101,675. In 2011, Canada's wealthiest big city was Vancouver with a household net worth of approximately $612,000, followed by Toronto ($542,000) and Calgary ($541,000). *Statistics Canada, Oakville, Ontario: 2006 Census Community Profiles, released March 13, 2007 with files from Environics Analytics, WealthScapes 2012*
- Oakville was identified as one of Canada's most generous gift givers. Between 2007 and 2009, 31% of Oakville residents gave charitable gifts on their tax returns compared to 25% of Ontarians and 24% of Canadians. The size of gifts was also larger: approximately $360 each year was donated by Oakville residents compared to $310 by Ontario residents and $250 across Canada. *Statistics Canada, Income Statistics Division, 2009-2007, Financial Data and Charitable Donations*
- Oakville has one of the lowest crime rates in Canada, tying with two other cities (Burlington and Halton Hills) for third place. The criteria used to rank the cities were violent crime rate, total crimes per 100,000 people and crime severity rate for 2010. In the overall competition, the city was ranked #17 out of 190 cities for "Best City to Live." *Money Sense, Best Places to Live, March 20, 2012*
- Sixty-one percent (61%) of Oakville residents aged 15 years or older have a certificate, diploma or degree from a university or college, which is 10% higher than the provincial average. *Statistics Canada, Oakville, Ontario: 2006 Census Community Profiles, released March 13, 2007*
- Oakville was selected as having the best weather in Canada by *Money Sense Magazine*. The 2011 study evaluated the weather patterns of 180 Canadian cities based on amount of precipitation, wet days and days below 0 degrees Celsius. Oakville receives 808 millimetres of precipitation annually and has a low average of 117 precipitation days. The city experiences an average of 143 days below freezing every year. *Money Sense, Best Cities by Category: Best Weather, March 16, 2011*

PROFILES / Oakville, Ontario

Population Growth and Density

Area	Population in 2001	Population in 2006	Population in 2011	Population Change 2001–2006	Population Change 2006–2011	Land Area (sq. km)	Population Density per sq. km
Oakville	144,738	165,613	182,520	14.4	10.2	138.88	1,314.2
Ontario	11,410,046	12,160,282	12,851,821	6.6	5.7	908,607.67	14.1
Canada	30,007,094	31,612,897	33,476,688	5.4	5.9	8,965,121.42	3.7

Source: Statistics Canada. 2012. Census Profile. 2011 Census. Statistics Canada Catalogue no. 98-316-XWE. Ottawa. Released October 24 2012. http://www12.statcan.gc.ca/census-recensement/2011/dp-pd/prof/index.cfm?Lang=E;
Statistics Canada 2007. 2006 Community Profiles. 2006 Census. Statistics Canada Catalogue no. 92-591-XWE. Ottawa. Released March 13 2007. http://www12.statcan.ca/census-recensement/2006/dp-pd/prof/92-591/index.cfm?Lang=E

Gender

Area	Males	Females
Number		
Oakville	88,190	94,330
Ontario	6,263,140	6,588,685
Canada	16,414,225	17,062,460
Percent of Population		
Oakville	48.3	51.7
Ontario	48.7	51.3
Canada	49.0	51.0

Source: Statistics Canada. 2012. Census Profile. 2011 Census. Statistics Canada Catalogue no. 98-316-XWE. Ottawa. Released October 24 2012.
http://www12.statcan.gc.ca/census-recensement/2011/dp-pd/prof/index.cfm?Lang=E

Marital Status

Area	Married[1]	Living Common-law	Single[2]	Separated	Divorced	Widowed
Number						
Total						
Oakville	84,930	6,590	38,360	3,465	6,505	6,980
Ontario	5,367,400	791,210	2,985,020	319,805	593,730	613,880
Canada	12,941,960	3,142,525	7,816,045	698,240	1,686,035	1,584,530
Males						
Oakville	42,305	3,295	19,720	1,355	2,110	1,295
Ontario	2,681,320	397,620	1,583,760	133,790	231,160	117,980
Canada	6,470,300	1,575,495	4,206,320	299,655	680,415	310,940
Females						
Oakville	42,620	3,290	18,640	2,110	4,390	5,690
Ontario	2,686,075	393,590	1,401,260	186,015	362,570	495,905
Canada	6,471,660	1,567,035	3,609,730	398,585	1,005,620	1,273,590
Percent of Population						
Total						
Oakville	57.8	4.5	26.1	2.4	4.4	4.8
Ontario	50.3	7.4	28.0	3.0	5.6	5.8
Canada	46.4	11.3	28.0	2.5	6.0	5.7
Males						
Oakville	60.4	4.7	28.1	1.9	3.0	1.8
Ontario	52.1	7.7	30.8	2.6	4.5	2.3
Canada	47.8	11.6	31.1	2.2	5.0	2.3
Females						
Oakville	55.5	4.3	24.3	2.7	5.7	7.4
Ontario	48.6	7.1	25.4	3.4	6.6	9.0
Canada	45.2	10.9	25.2	2.8	7.0	8.9

Note: (1) and not separated, (2) never legally married
Source: Statistics Canada. 2012. Census Profile. 2011 Census. Statistics Canada Catalogue no. 98-316-XWE. Ottawa. Released October 24 2012.
http://www12.statcan.gc.ca/census-recensement/2011/dp-pd/prof/index.cfm?Lang=E

Age Characteristics: 0 to 49 Years

Area	0 to 4 Years	5 to 9 Years	10 to 14 Years	15 to 19 Years	20 to 24 Years	25 to 29 Years	30 to 34 Years	35 to 39 Years	40 to 44 Years	45 to 49 Years
					Number					
					Total					
Oakville	10,330	12,405	12,960	14,090	11,530	7,950	8,705	12,830	15,700	16,565
Ontario	704,260	712,755	763,755	863,635	852,910	815,120	800,365	844,335	924,075	1,055,880
Canada	1,877,095	1,809,895	1,920,355	2,178,135	2,187,450	2,169,590	2,162,905	2,173,930	2,324,875	2,675,130
					Males					
Oakville	5,160	6,340	6,615	7,215	5,850	3,890	3,905	5,880	7,345	8,035
Ontario	360,590	365,290	391,630	443,680	432,490	400,045	383,340	405,845	447,920	517,510
Canada	961,150	925,965	983,995	1,115,845	1,108,775	1,077,275	1,058,810	1,064,200	1,141,720	1,318,715
					Females					
Oakville	5,170	6,070	6,345	6,870	5,675	4,060	4,800	6,950	8,350	8,530
Ontario	343,670	347,465	372,125	419,950	420,415	415,075	417,030	438,485	476,155	538,370
Canada	915,945	883,935	936,360	1,062,295	1,078,670	1,092,315	1,104,095	1,109,735	1,183,155	1,356,420
					Percent of Population					
					Total					
Oakville	5.7	6.8	7.1	7.7	6.3	4.4	4.8	7.0	8.6	9.1
Ontario	5.5	5.5	5.9	6.7	6.6	6.3	6.2	6.6	7.2	8.2
Canada	5.6	5.4	5.7	6.5	6.5	6.5	6.5	6.5	6.9	8.0
					Males					
Oakville	5.9	7.2	7.5	8.2	6.6	4.4	4.4	6.7	8.3	9.1
Ontario	5.8	5.8	6.3	7.1	6.9	6.4	6.1	6.5	7.2	8.3
Canada	5.9	5.6	6.0	6.8	6.8	6.6	6.5	6.5	7.0	8.0
					Females					
Oakville	5.5	6.4	6.7	7.3	6.0	4.3	5.1	7.4	8.9	9.0
Ontario	5.2	5.3	5.6	6.4	6.4	6.3	6.3	6.7	7.2	8.2
Canada	5.4	5.2	5.5	6.2	6.3	6.4	6.5	6.5	6.9	7.9

Source: Statistics Canada. 2012. Census Profile. 2011 Census. Statistics Canada Catalogue no. 98-316-XWE. Ottawa. Released October 24 2012.
http://www12.statcan.gc.ca/census-recensement/2011/dp-pd/prof/index.cfm?Lang=E

Age Characteristics: 50 Years and Over, and Median Age

Area	50 to 54 Years	55 to 59 Years	60 to 64 Years	65 to 69 Years	70 to 74 Years	75 to 79 Years	80 to 84 Years	85 Years and Over	Median Age
				Number					
				Total					
Oakville	15,140	11,445	9,410	7,080	5,515	4,520	3,350	3,010	40.2
Ontario	1,006,140	864,620	765,655	563,485	440,780	356,150	271,510	246,400	40.4
Canada	2,658,965	2,340,635	2,052,670	1,521,715	1,153,065	922,700	702,070	645,515	40.6
				Males					
Oakville	7,380	5,625	4,485	3,380	2,590	2,025	1,435	1,040	39.5
Ontario	492,560	418,755	370,370	270,875	206,350	161,345	113,620	80,925	39.4
Canada	1,309,030	1,147,300	1,002,690	738,010	543,435	417,945	291,085	208,300	39.6
				Females					
Oakville	7,760	5,825	4,925	3,700	2,925	2,490	1,915	1,975	40.7
Ontario	513,580	445,865	395,275	292,610	234,435	194,805	157,890	165,475	41.3
Canada	1,349,940	1,193,335	1,049,985	783,705	609,630	504,755	410,985	437,215	41.5
				Percent of Population					
				Total					
Oakville	8.3	6.3	5.2	3.9	3.0	2.5	1.8	1.6	–
Ontario	7.8	6.7	6.0	4.4	3.4	2.8	2.1	1.9	–
Canada	7.9	7.0	6.1	4.5	3.4	2.8	2.1	1.9	–
				Males					
Oakville	8.4	6.4	5.1	3.8	2.9	2.3	1.6	1.2	–
Ontario	7.9	6.7	5.9	4.3	3.3	2.6	1.8	1.3	–
Canada	8.0	7.0	6.1	4.5	3.3	2.5	1.8	1.3	–
				Females					
Oakville	8.2	6.2	5.2	3.9	3.1	2.6	2.0	2.1	–
Ontario	7.8	6.8	6.0	4.4	3.6	3.0	2.4	2.5	–
Canada	7.9	7.0	6.2	4.6	3.6	3.0	2.4	2.6	–

Source: Statistics Canada. 2012. Census Profile. 2011 Census. Statistics Canada Catalogue no. 98-316-XWE. Ottawa. Released October 24 2012.
http://www12.statcan.gc.ca/census-recensement/2011/dp-pd/prof/index.cfm?Lang=E

PROFILES / Oakville, Ontario

Private Households by Household Size

Area	1 Person	2 Persons	3 Persons	4 Persons	5 Persons	6 or More Persons	Average Number of Persons in Private Households
Households							
Oakville	10,885	18,070	11,170	14,625	5,525	2,135	2.9
Ontario	1,230,975	1,584,415	803,030	783,925	310,860	174,305	2.6
Canada	3,673,310	4,544,820	2,081,900	1,903,300	724,405	392,885	2.5
Percent of Households							
Oakville	17.4	29.0	17.9	23.4	8.9	3.4	–
Ontario	25.2	32.4	16.4	16.0	6.4	3.6	–
Canada	27.6	34.1	15.6	14.3	5.4	2.9	–

Source: Statistics Canada. 2012. Census Profile. 2011 Census. Statistics Canada Catalogue no. 98-316-XWE. Ottawa. Released October 24 2012.
http://www12.statcan.gc.ca/census-recensement/2011/dp-pd/prof/index.cfm?Lang=E

Dwelling Type

Area	Single-detached House	Semi-detached House	Row House	Apartment: Building with Five or More Storeys	Apartment: Building with Fewer Than Five Storeys	Duplex Apartment	Movable Dwelling	Other Single-attached House
Number								
Oakville	39,455	2,570	9,720	7,175	2,535	890	0	60
Ontario	2,718,880	279,470	415,225	789,970	498,160	160,460	15,800	9,540
Canada	7,329,150	646,245	791,600	1,234,770	2,397,550	704,485	183,510	33,310
Percent of Dwellings								
Oakville	63.2	4.1	15.6	11.5	4.1	1.4	0.0	0.1
Ontario	55.6	5.7	8.5	16.2	10.2	3.3	0.3	0.2
Canada	55.0	4.9	5.9	9.3	18.0	5.3	1.4	0.3

Source: Statistics Canada. 2012. Census Profile. 2011 Census. Statistics Canada Catalogue no. 98-316-XWE. Ottawa. Released October 24 2012.
http://www12.statcan.gc.ca/census-recensement/2011/dp-pd/prof/index.cfm?Lang=E

Shelter Costs

	Owned Dwellings				Rented Dwellings		
Area	Number	Median Value[1] ($)	Average Value[1] ($)	Median Monthly Costs[2] ($)	Average Monthly Costs[2] ($)	Number	Median Monthly Costs[3] ($)	Average Monthly Costs[3] ($)
Oakville	52,315	510,886	598,576	1,577	1,683	10,095	1,149	1,212
Ontario	3,446,650	300,862	367,428	1,163	1,284	1,385,535	892	926
Canada	9,013,410	280,552	345,182	978	1,141	4,060,385	784	848

Note: All figures cover non-farm, non-reserve private dwellings; (1) Refers to the dollar amount expected by the owner if the dwelling were to be sold; (2) Includes all shelter expenses paid by households that own their dwellings, such as the mortgage payment and the costs of electricity, heat, water and other municipal services, property taxes and condominium fees; (3) Includes all shelter expenses paid by households that rent their dwellings, such as the monthly rent and the costs of electricity, heat and municipal services.
Source: Statistics Canada. 2013. 2011 National Household Survey. Statistics Canada Catalogue no. 99-004-XWE. Ottawa. Released September 11, 2013.

Occupied Private Dwellings by Period of Construction

Area	1960 or Before	1961 to 1980	1981 to 1990	1991 to 2000	2001 to 2005	2006 to 2011
Number						
Oakville	7,440	14,320	14,420	10,845	9,285	6,105
Ontario	1,330,235	1,420,570	763,430	609,310	414,795	348,310
Canada	3,273,105	4,152,715	2,112,110	1,707,880	1,031,020	1,042,430
Percent of Dwellings						
Oakville	11.9	22.9	23.1	17.4	14.9	9.8
Ontario	27.2	29.1	15.6	12.5	8.5	7.1
Canada	24.6	31.2	15.9	12.8	7.7	7.8

Note: Figures cover non-farm, non-reserve private dwellings and includes data up to May 10, 2011.
Source: Statistics Canada. 2013. 2011 National Household Survey. Statistics Canada Catalogue no. 99-004-XWE. Ottawa. Released September 11, 2013.

Educational Attainment

Area	No Certificate, Diploma or Degree	High School Diploma or Equivalent[1]	Apprenticeship or Trades Certificate or Diploma[2]	College, CÉGEP or Other Non-University Certificate or Diploma	University Certificate or Diploma Below the Bachelor Level[3]	Bachelor's Degree	University Certificate, Diploma or Degree Above Bachelor Level[4]
Number							
Total							
Oakville	17,465	32,335	6,485	27,300	7,970	33,155	19,820
Ontario	1,954,520	2,801,805	771,140	2,070,875	427,150	1,515,075	933,100
Canada	5,485,400	6,968,935	2,950,685	4,970,020	1,200,130	3,634,425	2,049,930
Males							
Oakville	8,435	14,800	4,155	11,765	3,640	15,800	10,900
Ontario	957,040	1,337,055	520,390	894,235	193,355	692,345	470,290
Canada	2,742,875	3,305,415	1,928,970	2,118,430	513,235	1,643,080	1,043,350
Females							
Oakville	9,025	17,535	2,330	15,530	4,330	17,355	8,920
Ontario	997,475	1,464,755	250,750	1,176,640	233,790	822,730	462,805
Canada	2,742,520	3,663,515	1,021,715	2,851,595	686,890	1,991,345	1,006,585
Percent of Population							
Total							
Oakville	12.1	22.4	4.5	18.9	5.5	22.9	13.7
Ontario	18.7	26.8	7.4	19.8	4.1	14.5	8.9
Canada	20.1	25.6	10.8	18.2	4.4	13.3	7.5
Males							
Oakville	12.1	21.3	6.0	16.9	5.2	22.7	15.7
Ontario	18.9	26.4	10.3	17.7	3.8	13.7	9.3
Canada	20.6	24.9	14.5	15.9	3.9	12.4	7.8
Females							
Oakville	12.0	23.4	3.1	20.7	5.8	23.1	11.9
Ontario	18.4	27.1	4.6	21.8	4.3	15.2	8.6
Canada	19.6	26.2	7.3	20.4	4.9	14.3	7.2

Note: Figures cover total population aged 15 years and over by highest certificate, diploma or degree; (1) Includes persons who have graduated from a secondary school or equivalent. It excludes persons with a postsecondary certificate, diploma or degree; (2) Includes Registered Apprenticeship certificates (including Certificate of Qualification, Journeyperson's designation) and other trades certificates or diplomas such as pre-employment or vocational certificates and diplomas from brief trade programs completed at community colleges, institutes of technology, vocational centres, and similar institutions; (3) Comparisons with other data sources suggest that the category 'University certificate or diploma below the bachelor's level' was over-reported in the NHS. This category likely includes some responses that are actually college certificates or diplomas, bachelor's degrees or other types of education (e.g., university transfer programs, bachelor's programs completed in other countries, incomplete bachelor's programs, non-university professional designations). We recommend users interpret the results for the 'University certificate or diploma below the bachelor's level' category with caution; (4) 'University certificate or diploma above bachelor level' includes the categories: 'Degree in medicine, dentistry, veterinary medicine or optometry,' 'Master's degree' and 'Earned doctorate.'
Source: Statistics Canada. 2013. 2011 National Household Survey. Statistics Canada Catalogue no. 99-004-XWE. Ottawa. Released September 11, 2013.

Household Income Distribution

Area	Less than $10,000	$10,000 to $19,999	$20,000 to $29,999	$30,000 to $39,999	$40,000 to $49,999	$50,000 to $59,999	$60,000 to $79,999	$80,000 to $99,999	$100,000 to $124,999	$125,000 to $149,999	$150,000 and Over
Households											
Oakville	1,700	2,580	2,835	3,240	3,570	3,395	6,825	6,570	6,685	5,855	19,160
Ontario	201,780	354,530	405,725	425,410	425,720	398,705	680,850	552,660	497,970	331,460	611,840
Canada	626,705	1,141,945	1,193,925	1,271,675	1,206,800	1,102,120	1,865,280	1,458,240	1,260,770	802,555	1,389,240
Percent of Households											
Oakville	2.7	4.1	4.5	5.2	5.7	5.4	10.9	10.5	10.7	9.4	30.7
Ontario	4.1	7.3	8.3	8.7	8.7	8.2	13.9	11.3	10.2	6.8	12.5
Canada	4.7	8.6	9.0	9.5	9.1	8.3	14.0	10.9	9.5	6.0	10.4

Note: Household income is the sum of the total incomes of all members of that household. Total income refers to monetary receipts from certain sources, before income taxes and deductions, during calendar year 2010.
Source: Statistics Canada. 2013. 2011 National Household Survey. Statistics Canada Catalogue no. 99-004-XWE. Ottawa. Released September 11, 2013.

Median and Average Household and Economic Family Income

Area	Median Household Income ($)	Average Household Income ($)	Median After-tax Household Income ($)	Average After-tax Household Income ($)	Median Economic Family Income ($)	Average Economic Family Income ($)	Median After-tax Economic Family Income ($)	Average After-tax Economic Family Income ($)
Oakville	101,713	142,490	85,743	108,880	118,671	160,442	98,950	122,028
Ontario	66,358	85,772	58,717	71,523	80,987	100,152	71,128	83,322
Canada	61,072	79,102	54,089	66,149	76,511	94,125	67,044	78,517

Note: Figures cover household and economic familiy income in 2010. A household is defined as a person or a group of persons (other than foreign residents) who occupy the same private dwelling and do not have a usual place of residence elsewhere in Canada. Every person is a member of one and only one household. An economic family is defined as a group of two or more persons who live in the same dwelling and are related to each other by blood, marriage, common-law, adoption or a foster relationship. A couple may be of opposite or same sex.
Source: Statistics Canada. 2013. 2011 National Household Survey. Statistics Canada Catalogue no. 99-004-XWE. Ottawa. Released September 11, 2013.

Individual Income Distribution

Area	Less than $10,000	$10,000 to $19,999	$20,000 to $29,999	$30,000 to $39,999	$40,000 to $49,999	$50,000 to $59,999	$60,000 to $79,999	$80,000 to $99,999	$100,000 to $124,999	$125,000 and Over
					Number					
					Total					
Oakville	25,520	18,275	13,355	12,060	10,685	9,445	14,445	11,240	7,600	14,285
Ontario	1,780,355	1,748,060	1,361,710	1,136,730	980,790	746,360	964,280	574,710	293,865	330,285
Canada	4,492,040	4,835,710	3,670,020	3,180,360	2,603,520	1,921,650	2,437,440	1,302,045	693,580	782,135
					Males					
Oakville	10,715	6,715	5,045	5,430	4,630	4,345	7,290	6,200	5,120	10,910
Ontario	781,095	669,815	580,990	535,255	491,125	407,005	569,205	341,160	201,125	244,500
Canada	1,936,365	1,864,880	1,588,260	1,522,190	1,333,510	1,079,780	1,473,145	823,720	492,905	599,905
					Females					
Oakville	14,810	11,555	8,315	6,630	6,055	5,105	7,160	5,040	2,485	3,375
Ontario	999,265	1,078,245	780,720	601,475	489,665	339,360	395,075	233,550	92,740	85,790
Canada	2,555,675	2,970,825	2,081,760	1,658,170	1,270,010	841,870	964,300	478,330	200,680	182,230
					Percent of Population					
					Total					
Oakville	18.6	13.3	9.8	8.8	7.8	6.9	10.5	8.2	5.6	10.4
Ontario	18.0	17.6	13.7	11.5	9.9	7.5	9.7	5.8	3.0	3.3
Canada	17.3	18.7	14.2	12.3	10.0	7.4	9.4	5.0	2.7	3.0
					Males					
Oakville	16.1	10.1	7.6	8.2	7.0	6.5	11.0	9.3	7.7	16.4
Ontario	16.2	13.9	12.1	11.1	10.2	8.4	11.8	7.1	4.2	5.1
Canada	15.2	14.7	12.5	12.0	10.5	8.5	11.6	6.5	3.9	4.7
					Females					
Oakville	21.0	16.4	11.8	9.4	8.6	7.2	10.2	7.1	3.5	4.8
Ontario	19.6	21.2	15.3	11.8	9.6	6.7	7.8	4.6	1.8	1.7
Canada	19.4	22.5	15.8	12.6	9.6	6.4	7.3	3.6	1.5	1.4

Note: Figures cover individuals aged 15 years and over with income. Income refers to monetary receipts from certain sources, before income taxes and deductions, during calendar year 2010.
Source: Statistics Canada. 2013. 2011 National Household Survey. Statistics Canada Catalogue no. 99-004-XWE. Ottawa. Released September 11, 2013.

Labour Force Status

Area	In the Labour Force - All	Employed	Unemployed	Not in the Labour Force
		Number		
		Total		
Oakville	100,565	93,490	7,075	43,965
Ontario	6,864,990	6,297,005	567,985	3,608,685
Canada	17,990,080	16,595,035	1,395,045	9,269,445
		Males		
Oakville	52,255	48,840	3,415	17,250
Ontario	3,542,030	3,249,165	292,865	1,522,690
Canada	9,388,570	8,634,310	754,255	3,906,785
		Females		
Oakville	48,310	44,650	3,660	26,715
Ontario	3,322,955	3,047,840	275,120	2,085,990
Canada	8,601,515	7,960,725	640,790	5,362,660
		Percent of Labour Force		
		Total		
Oakville	69.6	64.7	7.0	30.4
Ontario	65.5	60.1	8.3	34.5
Canada	66.0	60.9	7.8	34.0
		Males		
Oakville	75.2	70.3	6.5	24.8
Ontario	69.9	64.2	8.3	30.1
Canada	70.6	64.9	8.0	29.4
		Females		
Oakville	64.4	59.5	7.6	35.6
Ontario	61.4	56.3	8.3	38.6
Canada	61.6	57.0	7.4	38.4

Note: Figures are based on total population 15 years and over
Source: Statistics Canada. 2013. 2011 National Household Survey. Statistics Canada Catalogue no. 99-004-XWE. Ottawa. Released September 11, 2013.

PROFILES / Oakville, Ontario

Labour Force by Industry (NAICS Codes 11–52)

Area	Agriculture, forestry, fishing & hunting	Mining, quarrying, & oil & gas extraction	Utilities	Construction	Manufacturing	Wholesale Trade	Retail Trade	Transportation & warehousing	Information & cultural industries	Finance & insurance
					Number					
					Total					
Oakville	225	280	815	4,355	8,620	6,560	10,620	3,775	2,895	9,960
Ontario	101,280	29,985	57,035	417,900	697,565	305,030	751,200	307,405	178,720	364,415
Canada	437,650	261,050	149,940	1,215,380	1,619,295	733,445	2,031,665	827,780	420,830	767,960
					Males					
Oakville	65	240	565	3,635	5,965	3,935	5,070	2,480	1,825	5,400
Ontario	66,485	25,650	42,685	369,300	493,305	197,770	344,480	225,245	98,835	153,125
Canada	307,370	211,690	110,765	1,068,710	1,167,680	494,545	933,850	617,305	235,875	296,995
					Females					
Oakville	155	35	250	725	2,655	2,630	5,550	1,290	1,075	4,555
Ontario	34,800	4,340	14,350	48,595	204,260	107,260	406,720	82,160	79,885	211,290
Canada	130,285	49,360	39,175	146,670	451,615	238,900	1,097,820	210,475	184,955	470,960
					Percent of Labour Force					
					Total					
Oakville	0.2	0.3	0.8	4.4	8.7	6.7	10.8	3.8	2.9	10.1
Ontario	1.5	0.4	0.9	6.3	10.4	4.6	11.2	4.6	2.7	5.5
Canada	2.5	1.5	0.9	6.9	9.2	4.2	11.6	4.7	2.4	4.4
					Males					
Oakville	0.1	0.5	1.1	7.1	11.6	7.7	9.9	4.8	3.6	10.5
Ontario	1.9	0.7	1.2	10.7	14.3	5.7	10.0	6.5	2.9	4.4
Canada	3.3	2.3	1.2	11.6	12.7	5.4	10.2	6.7	2.6	3.2
					Females					
Oakville	0.3	0.1	0.5	1.5	5.6	5.6	11.7	2.7	2.3	9.6
Ontario	1.1	0.1	0.4	1.5	6.3	3.3	12.6	2.5	2.5	6.5
Canada	1.6	0.6	0.5	1.7	5.4	2.8	13.1	2.5	2.2	5.6

Note: Figures are based on total experienced labour force 15 years and over. Experienced labour force refers to persons who, during the week of Sunday, May 1 to Saturday, May 7, 2011, were employed and the unemployed who had last worked for pay or in self-employment in either 2010 or 2011.
Source: Statistics Canada. 2013. 2011 National Household Survey. Statistics Canada Catalogue no. 99-004-XWE. Ottawa. Released September 11, 2013.

Labour Force by Industry (NAICS Codes 53–91)

Area	Real estate & rental & leasing	Profess., scientific & tech. services	Mgmt of companies & enterprises	Admin. & support, waste mgmt & remed. services	Educational services	Health care & social assistance	Arts, entertain. & recreation	Accomm. & food services	Other services (except public admin.)	Public admin.
					Number					
					Total					
Oakville	2,715	12,035	255	3,635	7,110	8,205	2,005	5,595	4,215	4,770
Ontario	133,980	511,020	6,525	309,630	499,690	692,130	144,065	417,675	296,340	458,665
Canada	321,895	1,240,850	17,460	728,330	1,301,435	1,949,650	363,405	1,130,750	807,800	1,261,050
					Males					
Oakville	1,470	6,725	150	2,120	2,205	1,615	1,150	2,605	1,660	2,450
Ontario	72,835	281,420	3,540	172,475	162,765	120,165	75,035	177,240	133,795	236,655
Canada	179,090	688,625	9,380	411,250	424,915	349,430	188,270	469,990	372,940	652,510
					Females					
Oakville	1,245	5,305	105	1,515	4,905	6,585	855	2,990	2,555	2,325
Ontario	61,145	229,600	2,990	137,155	336,925	571,965	69,030	240,430	162,550	222,015
Canada	142,805	552,225	8,075	317,085	876,515	1,600,220	175,135	660,760	434,865	608,535
					Percent of Labour Force					
					Total					
Oakville	2.8	12.2	0.3	3.7	7.2	8.3	2.0	5.7	4.3	4.8
Ontario	2.0	7.6	0.1	4.6	7.5	10.4	2.2	6.3	4.4	6.9
Canada	1.8	7.1	0.1	4.1	7.4	11.1	2.1	6.4	4.6	7.2
					Males					
Oakville	2.9	13.1	0.3	4.1	4.3	3.1	2.2	5.1	3.2	4.8
Ontario	2.1	8.2	0.1	5.0	4.7	3.5	2.2	5.1	3.9	6.9
Canada	1.9	7.5	0.1	4.5	4.6	3.8	2.0	5.1	4.1	7.1
					Females					
Oakville	2.6	11.2	0.2	3.2	10.4	13.9	1.8	6.3	5.4	4.9
Ontario	1.9	7.1	0.1	4.2	10.4	17.7	2.1	7.4	5.0	6.9
Canada	1.7	6.6	0.1	3.8	10.4	19.1	2.1	7.9	5.2	7.2

Note: Figures are based on total experienced labour force 15 years and over. Experienced labour force refers to persons who, during the week of Sunday, May 1 to Saturday, May 7, 2011, were employed and the unemployed who had last worked for pay or in self-employment in either 2010 or 2011.
Source: Statistics Canada. 2013. 2011 National Household Survey. Statistics Canada Catalogue no. 99-004-XWE. Ottawa. Released September 11, 2013.

Occupation

Area	Mgmt	Business, Finance & Admin.	Natural/ Applied Sciences & Related	Health	Education, Law & Social, Community & Government Services	Art, Culture, Recreation & Sport	Sales & Service	Trades, Transport & Equip. Operators & Related	Natural Resources, Agri. & Related Production	Mfg & Utilities
					Number					
					Total					
Oakville	18,475	19,250	8,935	4,845	11,635	3,450	21,920	6,740	995	2,400
Ontario	770,580	1,138,330	494,500	392,695	801,465	206,420	1,550,260	868,515	106,810	350,685
Canada	1,963,600	2,902,045	1,237,775	1,107,200	2,064,675	503,415	4,068,170	2,537,775	397,930	805,040
					Males					
Oakville	12,010	6,935	6,805	1,225	3,650	1,595	10,370	6,370	750	1,620
Ontario	474,655	352,505	384,345	78,330	264,570	96,055	673,880	812,280	82,610	233,565
Canada	1,229,460	854,190	966,355	217,520	676,550	232,535	1,745,705	2,385,615	318,945	564,300
					Females					
Oakville	6,465	12,310	2,130	3,625	7,985	1,855	11,555	370	240	775
Ontario	295,920	785,825	110,150	314,370	536,895	110,370	876,380	56,230	24,200	117,115
Canada	734,140	2,047,855	271,415	889,675	1,388,130	270,875	2,322,465	152,165	78,980	240,740
					Percent of Labour Force					
					Total					
Oakville	18.7	19.5	9.1	4.9	11.8	3.5	22.2	6.8	1.0	2.4
Ontario	11.5	17.0	7.4	5.9	12.0	3.1	23.2	13.0	1.6	5.2
Canada	11.2	16.5	7.0	6.3	11.7	2.9	23.1	14.4	2.3	4.6
					Males					
Oakville	23.4	13.5	13.3	2.4	7.1	3.1	20.2	12.4	1.5	3.2
Ontario	13.7	10.2	11.1	2.3	7.7	2.8	19.5	23.5	2.4	6.8
Canada	13.4	9.3	10.5	2.4	7.4	2.5	19.0	26.0	3.5	6.1
					Females					
Oakville	13.7	26.0	4.5	7.7	16.9	3.9	24.4	0.8	0.5	1.6
Ontario	9.2	24.3	3.4	9.7	16.6	3.4	27.2	1.7	0.7	3.6
Canada	8.7	24.4	3.2	10.6	16.5	3.2	27.7	1.8	0.9	2.9

Note: Figures are based on total experienced labour force 15 years and over
Source: Statistics Canada. 2013. 2011 National Household Survey. Statistics Canada Catalogue no. 99-004-XWE. Ottawa. Released September 11, 2013.

Place of Work Status

Area	Worked at Home	Worked Outside Canada	No Fixed Workplace Address	Worked at Usual Place
		Number		
		Total		
Oakville	8,320	465	8,030	76,665
Ontario	423,790	31,390	670,835	5,170,980
Canada	1,142,640	66,460	1,868,245	13,517,690
		Males		
Oakville	4,005	345	5,490	39,000
Ontario	216,900	21,150	486,560	2,524,555
Canada	582,150	47,355	1,400,485	6,604,325
		Females		
Oakville	4,320	125	2,545	37,670
Ontario	206,895	10,240	184,275	2,646,420
Canada	560,490	19,100	467,760	6,913,370
		Percent of Labour Force		
		Total		
Oakville	8.9	0.5	8.6	82.0
Ontario	6.7	0.5	10.7	82.1
Canada	6.9	0.4	11.3	81.5
		Males		
Oakville	8.2	0.7	11.2	79.9
Ontario	6.7	0.7	15.0	77.7
Canada	6.7	0.5	16.2	76.5
		Females		
Oakville	9.7	0.3	5.7	84.4
Ontario	6.8	0.3	6.0	86.8
Canada	7.0	0.2	5.9	86.8

Note: Figures are based on total employed labour force 15 years and over.
Source: Statistics Canada. 2013. 2011 National Household Survey. Statistics Canada Catalogue no. 99-004-XWE. Ottawa. Released September 11, 2013.

Mode of Transportation to Work

Area	Car; Truck; Van; as Driver	Car; Truck; Van; as Passenger	Public Transit	Walked	Bicycled	All Other Modes
			Number			
			Total			
Oakville	63,845	4,725	12,095	2,650	440	945
Ontario	4,235,315	357,110	818,270	299,095	69,885	62,145
Canada	11,393,140	867,050	1,851,525	880,815	201,780	191,625
			Males			
Oakville	34,720	1,715	6,130	1,140	350	425
Ontario	2,316,680	143,410	340,995	131,765	47,635	30,635
Canada	6,238,835	349,530	788,290	387,580	135,840	104,725
			Females			
Oakville	29,125	3,005	5,965	1,510	90	515
Ontario	1,918,640	213,700	477,275	167,325	22,250	31,515
Canada	5,154,305	517,520	1,063,235	493,230	65,940	86,900
			Percent of Labour Force			
			Total			
Oakville	75.4	5.6	14.3	3.1	0.5	1.1
Ontario	72.5	6.1	14.0	5.1	1.2	1.1
Canada	74.0	5.6	12.0	5.7	1.3	1.2
			Males			
Oakville	78.0	3.9	13.8	2.6	0.8	1.0
Ontario	76.9	4.8	11.3	4.4	1.6	1.0
Canada	77.9	4.4	9.8	4.8	1.7	1.3
			Females			
Oakville	72.4	7.5	14.8	3.8	0.2	1.3
Ontario	67.8	7.5	16.9	5.9	0.8	1.1
Canada	69.8	7.0	14.4	6.7	0.9	1.2

Note: Figures are based on total employed labour force 15 years and over.
Source: Statistics Canada. 2013. 2011 National Household Survey. Statistics Canada Catalogue no. 99-004-XWE. Ottawa. Released September 11, 2013.

Visible Minority Population Characteristics

Area	Total Minority	South Asian[1]	Chinese	Black	Filipino	Latin American	Arab	SE Asian[2]	West Asian[3]	Korean	Japanese	Multiple[4]
						Number						
						Total						
Oakville	41,100	12,935	6,240	4,820	3,380	2,640	2,830	1,550	1,310	2,490	770	1,440
Ontario	3,279,565	965,990	629,140	539,205	275,380	172,560	151,645	137,875	122,530	78,290	29,085	96,735
Canada	6,264,750	1,567,400	1,324,750	945,665	619,310	381,280	380,620	312,075	206,840	161,130	87,270	171,935
						Males						
Oakville	19,255	6,290	2,900	2,225	1,355	1,150	1,375	695	660	1,290	325	675
Ontario	1,582,480	484,355	301,575	251,295	116,825	83,205	79,620	67,645	62,515	38,045	13,345	46,765
Canada	3,043,010	790,755	632,325	453,005	268,885	186,355	203,485	154,035	105,620	77,165	38,270	83,335
						Females						
Oakville	21,845	6,635	3,340	2,595	2,025	1,490	1,455	860	645	1,195	440	765
Ontario	1,697,085	481,635	327,570	287,915	158,555	89,360	72,025	70,230	60,010	40,250	15,740	49,970
Canada	3,221,745	776,650	692,420	492,660	350,425	194,925	177,140	158,045	101,220	83,965	48,990	88,600
						Percent of Population						
						Total						
Oakville	22.8	7.2	3.5	2.7	1.9	1.5	1.6	0.9	0.7	1.4	0.4	0.8
Ontario	25.9	7.6	5.0	4.3	2.2	1.4	1.2	1.1	1.0	0.6	0.2	0.8
Canada	19.1	4.8	4.0	2.9	1.9	1.2	1.2	0.9	0.6	0.5	0.3	0.5
						Males						
Oakville	22.0	7.2	3.3	2.5	1.5	1.3	1.6	0.8	0.8	1.5	0.4	0.8
Ontario	25.6	7.8	4.9	4.1	1.9	1.3	1.3	1.1	1.0	0.6	0.2	0.8
Canada	18.8	4.9	3.9	2.8	1.7	1.2	1.3	1.0	0.7	0.5	0.2	0.5
						Females						
Oakville	23.5	7.1	3.6	2.8	2.2	1.6	1.6	0.9	0.7	1.3	0.5	0.8
Ontario	26.2	7.4	5.1	4.4	2.5	1.4	1.1	1.1	0.9	0.6	0.2	0.8
Canada	19.3	4.7	4.1	3.0	2.1	1.2	1.1	0.9	0.6	0.5	0.3	0.5

Note: The Employment Equity Act defines visible minorities as 'persons, other than Aboriginal peoples, who are non-Caucasian in race or non-white in colour'; (1) Includes 'East Indian,' 'Pakistani,' 'Sri Lankan,' etc.; (2) Includes 'Vietnamese,' 'Cambodian,' 'Malaysian,' 'Laotian,' etc.; (3) Includes 'Iranian,' 'Afghan,' etc.; (4) Includes respondents who reported more than one visible minority group by checking two or more mark-in circles, e.g., 'Black' and 'South Asian.'
Source: Statistics Canada. 2013. 2011 National Household Survey. Statistics Canada Catalogue no. 99-004-XWE. Ottawa. Released September 11, 2013.

PROFILES / Oakville, Ontario

Aboriginal Population

Area	Aboriginal Identity[1]	First Nations (North American Indian) Single Identity[2]	Métis Single Identity	Inuk (Inuit) Single Identity	Multiple Aboriginal Identities[3]	Aboriginal Identities Not Included Elsewhere
Number						
Total						
Oakville	1,160	755	370	0	0	25
Ontario	301,430	201,100	86,020	3,355	2,910	8,040
Canada	1,400,685	851,560	451,795	59,440	11,415	26,475
Males						
Oakville	560	380	165	0	0	0
Ontario	145,020	96,620	41,755	1,475	1,420	3,750
Canada	682,190	411,785	223,335	29,495	5,525	12,055
Females						
Oakville	595	365	200	0	0	15
Ontario	156,410	104,485	44,260	1,880	1,490	4,295
Canada	718,500	439,775	228,460	29,950	5,890	14,420
Percent of Population						
Total						
Oakville	0.6	0.4	0.2	0.0	0.0	0.0
Ontario	2.4	1.6	0.7	0.0	0.0	0.1
Canada	4.3	2.6	1.4	0.2	0.0	0.1
Males						
Oakville	0.6	0.4	0.2	0.0	0.0	0.0
Ontario	2.3	1.6	0.7	0.0	0.0	0.1
Canada	4.2	2.5	1.4	0.2	0.0	0.1
Females						
Oakville	0.6	0.4	0.2	0.0	0.0	0.0
Ontario	2.4	1.6	0.7	0.0	0.0	0.1
Canada	4.3	2.6	1.4	0.2	0.0	0.1

Note: (1) Includes persons who reported being an Aboriginal person, that is, First Nations (North American Indian), Métis or Inuk (Inuit) and/or those who reported Registered or Treaty Indian status, that is registered under the Indian Act of Canada, and/or those who reported membership in a First Nation or Indian band. Aboriginal peoples of Canada are defined in the Constitution Act, 1982, section 35-2 as including the Indian, Inuit and Métis peoples of Canada; (2) Users should be aware that the estimates associated with this variable are more affected than most by the incomplete enumeration of certain Indian reserves and Indian settlements in the National Household Survey (NHS); (3) Includes persons who reported being any two or all three of the following: First Nations (North American Indian), Métis or Inuk (Inuit).
Source: Statistics Canada. 2013. 2011 National Household Survey. Statistics Canada Catalogue no. 99-004-XWE. Ottawa. Released September 11, 2013.

Ethnic Origin

Area	North American Aboriginal	Other North American	European	Caribbean	Latin, Central and South American	African	Asian	Oceania
Number								
Total								
Oakville	2,525	35,990	131,385	4,630	4,275	4,815	34,435	550
Ontario	441,395	3,059,480	8,231,410	396,485	271,545	331,460	2,604,595	19,410
Canada	1,836,035	11,070,455	20,157,965	627,590	544,375	766,735	5,011,225	74,875
Males								
Oakville	1,250	17,635	64,125	2,055	1,920	2,280	16,315	290
Ontario	210,490	1,507,105	4,019,885	181,805	130,035	160,940	1,265,540	9,855
Canada	885,675	5,462,685	9,913,150	291,640	264,635	387,360	2,435,540	37,490
Females								
Oakville	1,265	18,355	67,255	2,580	2,355	2,535	18,120	255
Ontario	230,905	1,552,380	4,211,525	214,675	141,510	170,515	1,339,050	9,555
Canada	950,360	5,607,770	10,244,820	335,945	279,740	379,380	2,575,680	37,385
Percent of Population								
Total								
Oakville	1.4	19.9	72.8	2.6	2.4	2.7	19.1	0.3
Ontario	3.5	24.2	65.1	3.1	2.1	2.6	20.6	0.2
Canada	5.6	33.7	61.4	1.9	1.7	2.3	15.3	0.2
Males								
Oakville	1.4	20.2	73.3	2.3	2.2	2.6	18.6	0.3
Ontario	3.4	24.4	65.0	2.9	2.1	2.6	20.5	0.2
Canada	5.5	33.8	61.3	1.8	1.6	2.4	15.1	0.2
Females								
Oakville	1.4	19.8	72.4	2.8	2.5	2.7	19.5	0.3
Ontario	3.6	24.0	65.1	3.3	2.2	2.6	20.7	0.1
Canada	5.7	33.6	61.4	2.0	1.7	2.3	15.4	0.2

Note: The sum of the ethnic groups in this table is greater than the total population estimate because a person may report more than one ethnic origin in the NHS.
Source: Statistics Canada. 2013. 2011 National Household Survey. Statistics Canada Catalogue no. 99-004-XWE. Ottawa. Released September 11, 2013.

Religion

Area	Buddhist	Christian	Hindu	Jewish	Muslim	Sikh	Traditional (Aboriginal) Spirituality	Other Religions	No Religious Affiliation
				Number					
				Total					
Oakville	1,415	126,570	3,700	910	7,180	2,610	0	820	37,210
Ontario	163,750	8,167,295	366,720	195,540	581,950	179,765	15,905	53,080	2,927,790
Canada	366,830	22,102,745	497,965	329,495	1,053,945	454,965	64,935	130,835	7,850,605
				Males					
Oakville	600	59,570	1,840	415	3,600	1,220	0	295	19,950
Ontario	75,355	3,839,925	183,580	95,795	293,925	90,515	7,600	23,555	1,571,195
Canada	168,465	10,497,775	250,435	161,265	540,555	229,435	31,805	57,745	4,225,645
				Females					
Oakville	810	67,000	1,865	490	3,580	1,390	0	520	17,265
Ontario	88,395	4,327,365	183,140	99,740	288,025	89,250	8,310	29,525	1,356,600
Canada	198,365	11,604,975	247,525	168,235	513,395	225,530	33,135	73,090	3,624,965
				Percent of Population					
				Total					
Oakville	0.8	70.1	2.1	0.5	4.0	1.4	0.0	0.5	20.6
Ontario	1.3	64.6	2.9	1.5	4.6	1.4	0.1	0.4	23.1
Canada	1.1	67.3	1.5	1.0	3.2	1.4	0.2	0.4	23.9
				Males					
Oakville	0.7	68.1	2.1	0.5	4.1	1.4	0.0	0.3	22.8
Ontario	1.2	62.1	3.0	1.5	4.8	1.5	0.1	0.4	25.4
Canada	1.0	64.9	1.5	1.0	3.3	1.4	0.2	0.4	26.1
				Females					
Oakville	0.9	72.1	2.0	0.5	3.9	1.5	0.0	0.6	18.6
Ontario	1.4	66.9	2.8	1.5	4.5	1.4	0.1	0.5	21.0
Canada	1.2	69.5	1.5	1.0	3.1	1.4	0.2	0.4	21.7

Note: Religion refers to the person's self-identification as having a connection or affiliation with any religious denomination, group, body, sect, cult or other religiously defined community or system of belief. Religion is not limited to formal membership in a religious organization or group. Persons without a religious connection or affiliation can self-identify as atheist, agnostic or humanist, or can provide another applicable response.
Source: Statistics Canada. 2013. 2011 National Household Survey. Statistics Canada Catalogue no. 99-004-XWE. Ottawa. Released September 11, 2013.

Religion—Christian Denominations

Area	Anglican	Baptist	Catholic	Christian Orthodox	Lutheran	Pentecostal	Presbyterian	United Church	Other Christian
				Number					
				Total					
Oakville	13,690	2,960	68,415	6,400	2,075	2,015	4,965	13,195	12,850
Ontario	774,560	244,650	3,976,610	297,710	163,460	213,945	319,585	952,465	1,224,300
Canada	1,631,845	635,840	12,810,705	550,690	478,185	478,705	472,385	2,007,610	3,036,780
				Males					
Oakville	6,375	1,400	32,465	3,250	960	930	2,310	6,050	5,835
Ontario	355,175	112,285	1,895,940	145,825	75,225	94,955	148,535	435,255	576,730
Canada	752,945	293,905	6,167,290	270,205	221,525	217,850	218,955	912,545	1,442,550
				Females					
Oakville	7,310	1,560	35,950	3,150	1,115	1,085	2,660	7,155	7,020
Ontario	419,390	132,370	2,080,665	151,885	88,230	118,990	171,050	517,210	647,570
Canada	878,900	341,940	6,643,415	280,485	256,660	260,850	253,430	1,095,065	1,594,230
				Percent of Population					
				Total					
Oakville	7.6	1.6	37.9	3.5	1.2	1.1	2.8	7.3	7.1
Ontario	6.1	1.9	31.4	2.4	1.3	1.7	2.5	7.5	9.7
Canada	5.0	1.9	39.0	1.7	1.5	1.5	1.4	6.1	9.2
				Males					
Oakville	7.3	1.6	37.1	3.7	1.1	1.1	2.6	6.9	6.7
Ontario	5.7	1.8	30.7	2.4	1.2	1.5	2.4	7.0	9.3
Canada	4.7	1.8	38.2	1.7	1.4	1.3	1.4	5.6	8.9
				Females					
Oakville	7.9	1.7	38.7	3.4	1.2	1.2	2.9	7.7	7.6
Ontario	6.5	2.0	32.2	2.3	1.4	1.8	2.6	8.0	10.0
Canada	5.3	2.0	39.8	1.7	1.5	1.6	1.5	6.6	9.6

Note: Religion refers to the person's self-identification as having a connection or affiliation with any religious denomination, group, body, sect, cult or other religiously defined community or system of belief. Religion is not limited to formal membership in a religious organization or group. Persons without a religious connection or affiliation can self-identify as atheist, agnostic or humanist, or can provide another applicable response.
Source: Statistics Canada. 2013. 2011 National Household Survey. Statistics Canada Catalogue no. 99-004-XWE. Ottawa. Released September 11, 2013.

PROFILES / Oakville, Ontario

Immigrant Status and Period of Immigration

Area	Non-Immigrants[1]	Immigrants All	Before 1971	1971 to 1980	1981 to 1990	1991 to 2000	2001 to 2005	2006 to 2011	Non-Permanent Residents[3]
Number — Total									
Oakville	120,355	57,815	12,460	8,690	8,295	12,130	8,945	7,300	2,260
Ontario	8,906,000	3,611,365	723,030	464,380	538,285	866,220	518,405	501,060	134,425
Canada	25,720,175	6,775,765	1,261,055	870,775	949,890	1,539,050	992,070	1,162,915	356,385
Males									
Oakville	59,350	27,220	5,820	4,040	4,015	5,680	4,260	3,405	935
Ontario	4,410,240	1,706,385	341,820	217,990	258,095	408,270	245,850	234,360	64,825
Canada	12,753,235	3,231,370	605,430	416,670	454,570	724,905	474,545	555,245	178,515
Females									
Oakville	61,005	30,595	6,635	4,655	4,285	6,450	4,685	3,890	1,320
Ontario	4,495,765	1,904,985	381,210	246,390	280,190	457,950	272,550	266,695	69,600
Canada	12,966,935	3,544,400	655,625	454,105	495,325	814,145	517,530	607,670	177,870
Percent of Population — Total									
Oakville	66.7	32.0	6.9	4.8	4.6	6.7	5.0	4.0	1.3
Ontario	70.4	28.5	5.7	3.7	4.3	6.8	4.1	4.0	1.1
Canada	78.3	20.6	3.8	2.7	2.9	4.7	3.0	3.5	1.1
Males									
Oakville	67.8	31.1	6.7	4.6	4.6	6.5	4.9	3.9	1.1
Ontario	71.3	27.6	5.5	3.5	4.2	6.6	4.0	3.8	1.0
Canada	78.9	20.0	3.7	2.6	2.8	4.5	2.9	3.4	1.1
Females									
Oakville	65.7	32.9	7.1	5.0	4.6	6.9	5.0	4.2	1.4
Ontario	69.5	29.4	5.9	3.8	4.3	7.1	4.2	4.1	1.1
Canada	77.7	21.2	3.9	2.7	3.0	4.9	3.1	3.6	1.1

Note: (1) Non-immigrant refers to a person who is a Canadian citizen by birth; (2) Immigrant refers to a person who is or has ever been a landed immigrant/permanent resident. This person has been granted the right to live in Canada permanently by immigration authorities. Some immigrants have resided in Canada for a number of years, while others have arrived recently. Some immigrants are Canadian citizens, while others are not. Most immigrants are born outside Canada, but a small number are born in Canada. In the 2011 National Household Survey, 'Immigrants' includes immigrants who landed in Canada prior to May 10, 2011; (3) Non-permanent resident refers to a person from another country who has a work or study permit, or who is a refugee claimant, and any non-Canadian-born family member living in Canada with them.
Source: Statistics Canada. 2013. 2011 National Household Survey. Statistics Canada Catalogue no. 99-004-XWE. Ottawa. Released September 11, 2013.

Mother Tongue

Area	English	French	Non-official Language	English & French	English & Non-official Language	French & Non-official Language	English, French & Non-official Language
Number — Total							
Oakville	126,220	3,280	47,935	515	3,210	155	145
Ontario	8,677,040	493,300	3,264,435	46,605	219,425	13,645	7,615
Canada	18,858,980	7,054,975	6,567,680	144,685	396,330	74,430	24,095
Males							
Oakville	61,880	1,410	22,615	235	1,530	80	60
Ontario	4,276,970	232,785	1,562,190	21,805	106,790	6,285	3,495
Canada	9,345,225	3,452,380	3,157,785	69,975	192,000	36,535	11,965
Females							
Oakville	64,340	1,865	25,320	275	1,680	80	80
Ontario	4,400,065	260,510	1,702,240	24,795	112,635	7,365	4,115
Canada	9,513,750	3,602,590	3,409,895	74,710	204,330	37,890	12,130
Percent of Population — Total							
Oakville	69.6	1.8	26.4	0.3	1.8	0.1	0.1
Ontario	68.2	3.9	25.7	0.4	1.7	0.1	0.1
Canada	56.9	21.3	19.8	0.4	1.2	0.2	0.1
Males							
Oakville	70.5	1.6	25.8	0.3	1.7	0.1	0.1
Ontario	68.9	3.7	25.2	0.4	1.7	0.1	0.1
Canada	57.5	21.2	19.4	0.4	1.2	0.2	0.1
Females							
Oakville	68.7	2.0	27.0	0.3	1.8	0.1	0.1
Ontario	67.6	4.0	26.1	0.4	1.7	0.1	0.1
Canada	56.4	21.4	20.2	0.4	1.2	0.2	0.1

Note: Figures cover total population excluding institutional residents.
Source: Statistics Canada. 2012. Census Profile. 2011 Census. Statistics Canada Catalogue no. 98-316-XWE. Ottawa. Released October 24 2012.
http://www12.statcan.gc.ca/census-recensement/2011/dp-pd/prof/index.cfm?Lang=E

Language Spoken Most Often at Home

Area	English	French	Non-official Language	English & French	English & Non-official Language	French & Non-official Language	English, French & Non-official Language
			Number				
			Total				
Oakville	150,715	1,355	21,785	355	7,020	40	185
Ontario	10,044,810	284,115	1,827,870	37,955	509,105	6,370	11,845
Canada	21,457,075	6,827,865	3,673,865	131,205	875,135	109,700	46,330
			Males				
Oakville	73,235	600	10,355	165	3,360	20	80
Ontario	4,930,610	133,495	872,860	17,250	248,050	2,855	5,225
Canada	10,585,620	3,348,235	1,767,310	63,475	425,370	53,010	22,845
			Females				
Oakville	77,480	755	11,430	190	3,655	20	105
Ontario	5,114,200	150,620	955,010	20,705	261,055	3,520	6,620
Canada	10,871,455	3,479,625	1,906,555	67,730	449,765	56,690	23,485
			Percent of Population				
			Total				
Oakville	83.1	0.7	12.0	0.2	3.9	0.0	0.1
Ontario	79.0	2.2	14.4	0.3	4.0	0.1	0.1
Canada	64.8	20.6	11.1	0.4	2.6	0.3	0.1
			Males				
Oakville	83.4	0.7	11.8	0.2	3.8	0.0	0.1
Ontario	79.4	2.1	14.1	0.3	4.0	0.0	0.1
Canada	65.1	20.6	10.9	0.4	2.6	0.3	0.1
			Females				
Oakville	82.7	0.8	12.2	0.2	3.9	0.0	0.1
Ontario	78.5	2.3	14.7	0.3	4.0	0.1	0.1
Canada	64.5	20.6	11.3	0.4	2.7	0.3	0.1

Note: Figures cover total population excluding institutional residents.
Source: Statistics Canada. 2012. Census Profile. 2011 Census. Statistics Canada Catalogue no. 98-316-XWE. Ottawa. Released October 24 2012.
http://www12.statcan.gc.ca/census-recensement/2011/dp-pd/prof/index.cfm?Lang=E

Knowledge of Official Languages

Area	English Only	French Only	English & French	Neither English nor French
		Number		
		Total		
Oakville	158,545	145	20,410	2,360
Ontario	10,984,360	42,980	1,395,805	298,920
Canada	22,564,665	4,165,015	5,795,570	595,920
		Males		
Oakville	78,055	60	8,840	865
Ontario	5,445,050	18,805	627,725	118,765
Canada	11,222,185	1,925,340	2,876,560	241,790
		Females		
Oakville	80,485	80	11,570	1,500
Ontario	5,539,310	24,175	768,085	180,155
Canada	11,342,485	2,239,680	2,919,005	354,135
		Percent of Population		
		Total		
Oakville	87.4	0.1	11.2	1.3
Ontario	86.3	0.3	11.0	2.3
Canada	68.1	12.6	17.5	1.8
		Males		
Oakville	88.9	0.1	10.1	1.0
Ontario	87.7	0.3	10.1	1.9
Canada	69.0	11.8	17.7	1.5
		Females		
Oakville	86.0	0.1	12.4	1.6
Ontario	85.1	0.4	11.8	2.8
Canada	67.3	13.3	17.3	2.1

Note: Figures cover total population excluding institutional residents.
Source: Statistics Canada. 2012. Census Profile. 2011 Census. Statistics Canada Catalogue no. 98-316-XWE. Ottawa. Released October 24 2012.
http://www12.statcan.gc.ca/census-recensement/2011/dp-pd/prof/index.cfm?Lang=E

Oshawa, Ontario

Background

Oshawa is located on the northern shore of Lake Ontario in Durham Region. The City of Oshawa is considered the eastern gateway to the Toronto Greater Area (GTA) because of its location along the northern Golden Horseshoe, the most densely populated region of Southern Ontario. In 2011, Oshawa reclaimed its "Automotive Capital of Canada" title.

A French trading post was established at the mouth of Oshawa Creek in 1750. The pioneer settlement grew as Empire Loyalists from the U.S. migrated to the area in the 1800s. In 1924, Oshawa was granted city status.

The City of Oshawa is Canada's first and largest automotive manufacturing centre. The Canadian headquarters of General Motors of Canada was founded in Oshawa in 1876 and remains the city's major employer. The city is located less than 70 kilometres from Toronto and is serviced by multi-lane expressways, a municipal airport, a deep-sea port, two national railways and a full-service transit system that includes commuter trains and buses.

The city's University of Ontario Institute of Technology (UOIT) is one of Canada's newest post-secondary institutions. UOIT opened in 2003 and is the only Canadian university offering degree programs in automotive engineering and nuclear engineering. Along with automotive production and research, additional key sectors include advanced manufacturing, energy, and health services and research.

In 2012, GM Canada announced an investment of $850-million in research and development at its plants in Oshawa. The Automotive Centre of Excellence (ACE) recently opened one of the largest wind tunnels in the world, producing winds up to 240 kilometres per hour and temperatures from minus 40 to plus 60 degrees Celsius. The cost of the facility, located at UOIT, is estimated at $100 million.

Oshawa has summer highs of plus 23.63 degrees Celsius, winter lows of minus 7.60 degrees Celsius, and an average rainfall just over 759 mm per year.

Rankings

- *Money Sense Magazine* ranked Oshawa #22 out of 190 Canadian cities for "Best Place to Live 2012." The city's best overall ratings were in weather (#9), low crime (#18) and transit (#36). Oshawa's biggest downside was accessibility to doctors (#175). *Money Sense, "Canada's Best Places to Live," March 20, 2012*
- The Share the Road Cycling Coalition identified Oshawa as an emerging cycle-friendly city. The city received a bronze ranking as part of the Bicycle Friendly Communities Program, an initiative of the Washington-based League of American Bicyclists. Categories: engineering; education; encouragement; enforcement; and evaluation and planning. Ontario municipalities London and Blue Mountains also received bronze rankings and Hamilton received silver. *Share the Road Cycling Coalition (SRCC), "Announces Bicycle Friendly Communities Awards at Association of Municipalities of Ontario Annual Conference," August 23rd, 2011*
- Oshawa ranked in Canada's Top 10 Caring Communities. The city ranked #8 out of 37 Canadian cities for the percentage of residents (over the age of 15) doing volunteer work. Almost 55% of Oshawa residents volunteered in 2004. The top 3 cities were Guelph (ON), Kingston (ON) and Fredericton (NB). *The Canadian Council on Learning with files from Statistics Canada: Canada Survey of Giving, Volunteering and Participation 2004*

PROFILES / Oshawa, Ontario

Population Growth and Density

Area	Population in 2001	Population in 2006	Population in 2011	Population Change 2001–2006	Population Change 2006–2011	Land Area (sq. km)	Population Density per sq. km
Oshawa	139,051	141,590	149,607	1.8	5.7	145.68	1,027.0
Ontario	11,410,046	12,160,282	12,851,821	6.6	5.7	908,607.67	14.1
Canada	30,007,094	31,612,897	33,476,688	5.4	5.9	8,965,121.42	3.7

Source: Statistics Canada. 2012. Census Profile. 2011 Census. Statistics Canada Catalogue no. 98-316-XWE. Ottawa. Released October 24 2012.
http://www12.statcan.gc.ca/census-recensement/2011/dp-pd/prof/index.cfm?Lang=E;
Statistics Canada 2007. 2006 Community Profiles. 2006 Census. Statistics Canada Catalogue no. 92-591-XWE. Ottawa. Released March 13 2007.
http://www12.statcan.ca/census-recensement/2006/dp-pd/prof/92-591/index.cfm?Lang=E

Gender

Area	Males	Females
	Number	
Oshawa	72,705	76,900
Ontario	6,263,140	6,588,685
Canada	16,414,225	17,062,460
	Percent of Population	
Oshawa	48.6	51.4
Ontario	48.7	51.3
Canada	49.0	51.0

Source: Statistics Canada. 2012. Census Profile. 2011 Census. Statistics Canada Catalogue no. 98-316-XWE. Ottawa. Released October 24 2012.
http://www12.statcan.gc.ca/census-recensement/2011/dp-pd/prof/index.cfm?Lang=E

Marital Status

Area	Married[1]	Living Common-law	Single[2]	Separated	Divorced	Widowed
			Number			
			Total			
Oshawa	55,140	12,750	35,335	4,940	8,860	7,675
Ontario	5,367,400	791,210	2,985,020	319,805	593,730	613,880
Canada	12,941,960	3,142,525	7,816,045	698,240	1,686,035	1,584,530
			Males			
Oshawa	27,540	6,345	19,115	1,975	3,620	1,530
Ontario	2,681,320	397,620	1,583,760	133,790	231,160	117,980
Canada	6,470,300	1,575,495	4,206,320	299,655	680,415	310,940
			Females			
Oshawa	27,595	6,400	16,220	2,965	5,240	6,145
Ontario	2,686,075	393,590	1,401,260	186,015	362,570	495,905
Canada	6,471,660	1,567,035	3,609,730	398,585	1,005,620	1,273,590
			Percent of Population			
			Total			
Oshawa	44.2	10.2	28.3	4.0	7.1	6.2
Ontario	50.3	7.4	28.0	3.0	5.6	5.8
Canada	46.4	11.3	28.0	2.5	6.0	5.7
			Males			
Oshawa	45.8	10.6	31.8	3.3	6.0	2.5
Ontario	52.1	7.7	30.8	2.6	4.5	2.3
Canada	47.8	11.6	31.1	2.2	5.0	2.3
			Females			
Oshawa	42.7	9.9	25.1	4.6	8.1	9.5
Ontario	48.6	7.1	25.4	3.4	6.6	9.0
Canada	45.2	10.9	25.2	2.8	7.0	8.9

Note: (1) and not separated, (2) never legally married
Source: Statistics Canada. 2012. Census Profile. 2011 Census. Statistics Canada Catalogue no. 98-316-XWE. Ottawa. Released October 24 2012.
http://www12.statcan.gc.ca/census-recensement/2011/dp-pd/prof/index.cfm?Lang=E

PROFILES / Oshawa, Ontario

Age Characteristics: 0 to 49 Years

Area	0 to 4 Years	5 to 9 Years	10 to 14 Years	15 to 19 Years	20 to 24 Years	25 to 29 Years	30 to 34 Years	35 to 39 Years	40 to 44 Years	45 to 49 Years
					Number					
					Total					
Oshawa	8,355	7,995	8,565	10,155	10,160	9,610	9,385	9,495	10,120	12,775
Ontario	704,260	712,755	763,755	863,635	852,910	815,120	800,365	844,335	924,075	1,055,880
Canada	1,877,095	1,809,895	1,920,355	2,178,135	2,187,450	2,169,590	2,162,905	2,173,930	2,324,875	2,675,130
					Males					
Oshawa	4,210	4,090	4,275	5,140	5,235	4,785	4,570	4,645	4,950	6,240
Ontario	360,590	365,290	391,630	443,680	432,490	400,045	383,340	405,845	447,920	517,510
Canada	961,150	925,965	983,995	1,115,845	1,108,775	1,077,275	1,058,810	1,064,200	1,141,720	1,318,715
					Females					
Oshawa	4,140	3,905	4,290	5,015	4,925	4,820	4,805	4,855	5,170	6,540
Ontario	343,670	347,465	372,125	419,950	420,415	415,075	417,030	438,485	476,155	538,370
Canada	915,945	883,935	936,360	1,062,295	1,078,670	1,092,315	1,104,095	1,109,735	1,183,155	1,356,420
					Percent of Population					
					Total					
Oshawa	5.6	5.3	5.7	6.8	6.8	6.4	6.3	6.3	6.8	8.5
Ontario	5.5	5.5	5.9	6.7	6.6	6.3	6.2	6.6	7.2	8.2
Canada	5.6	5.4	5.7	6.5	6.5	6.5	6.5	6.5	6.9	8.0
					Males					
Oshawa	5.8	5.6	5.9	7.1	7.2	6.6	6.3	6.4	6.8	8.6
Ontario	5.8	5.8	6.3	7.1	6.9	6.4	6.1	6.5	7.2	8.3
Canada	5.9	5.6	6.0	6.8	6.8	6.6	6.5	6.5	7.0	8.0
					Females					
Oshawa	5.4	5.1	5.6	6.5	6.4	6.3	6.2	6.3	6.7	8.5
Ontario	5.2	5.3	5.6	6.4	6.4	6.3	6.3	6.7	7.2	8.2
Canada	5.4	5.2	5.5	6.2	6.3	6.4	6.5	6.5	6.9	7.9

Source: Statistics Canada. 2012. Census Profile. 2011 Census. Statistics Canada Catalogue no. 98-316-XWE. Ottawa. Released October 24 2012.
http://www12.statcan.gc.ca/census-recensement/2011/dp-pd/prof/index.cfm?Lang=E

Age Characteristics: 50 Years and Over, and Median Age

Area	50 to 54 Years	55 to 59 Years	60 to 64 Years	65 to 69 Years	70 to 74 Years	75 to 79 Years	80 to 84 Years	85 Years and Over	Median Age
					Number				
					Total				
Oshawa	12,235	10,105	8,780	6,445	5,050	4,220	3,250	2,920	40.6
Ontario	1,006,140	864,620	765,655	563,485	440,780	356,150	271,510	246,400	40.4
Canada	2,658,965	2,340,635	2,052,670	1,521,715	1,153,065	922,700	702,070	645,515	40.6
					Males				
Oshawa	6,080	4,870	4,180	3,025	2,315	1,850	1,300	940	39.4
Ontario	492,560	418,755	370,370	270,875	206,350	161,345	113,620	80,925	39.4
Canada	1,309,030	1,147,300	1,002,690	738,010	543,435	417,945	291,085	208,300	39.6
					Females				
Oshawa	6,155	5,230	4,600	3,420	2,735	2,365	1,945	1,975	41.7
Ontario	513,580	445,865	395,275	292,610	234,435	194,805	157,890	165,475	41.3
Canada	1,349,940	1,193,335	1,049,985	783,705	609,630	504,755	410,985	437,215	41.5
					Percent of Population				
					Total				
Oshawa	8.2	6.8	5.9	4.3	3.4	2.8	2.2	2.0	—
Ontario	7.8	6.7	6.0	4.4	3.4	2.8	2.1	1.9	—
Canada	7.9	7.0	6.1	4.5	3.4	2.8	2.1	1.9	—
					Males				
Oshawa	8.4	6.7	5.7	4.2	3.2	2.5	1.8	1.3	—
Ontario	7.9	6.7	5.9	4.3	3.3	2.6	1.8	1.3	—
Canada	8.0	7.0	6.1	4.5	3.3	2.5	1.8	1.3	—
					Females				
Oshawa	8.0	6.8	6.0	4.4	3.6	3.1	2.5	2.6	—
Ontario	7.8	6.8	6.0	4.4	3.6	3.0	2.4	2.5	—
Canada	7.9	7.0	6.2	4.6	3.6	3.0	2.4	2.6	—

Source: Statistics Canada. 2012. Census Profile. 2011 Census. Statistics Canada Catalogue no. 98-316-XWE. Ottawa. Released October 24 2012.
http://www12.statcan.gc.ca/census-recensement/2011/dp-pd/prof/index.cfm?Lang=E

PROFILES / Oshawa, Ontario

Private Households by Household Size

Area	1 Person	2 Persons	3 Persons	4 Persons	5 Persons	6 or More Persons	Average Number of Persons in Private Households
			Households				
Oshawa	14,845	19,885	10,410	8,710	3,365	1,585	2.5
Ontario	1,230,975	1,584,415	803,030	783,925	310,860	174,305	2.6
Canada	3,673,310	4,544,820	2,081,900	1,903,300	724,405	392,885	2.5
			Percent of Households				
Oshawa	25.2	33.8	17.7	14.8	5.7	2.7	–
Ontario	25.2	32.4	16.4	16.0	6.4	3.6	–
Canada	27.6	34.1	15.6	14.3	5.4	2.9	–

Source: Statistics Canada. 2012. Census Profile. 2011 Census. Statistics Canada Catalogue no. 98-316-XWE. Ottawa. Released October 24 2012.
http://www12.statcan.gc.ca/census-recensement/2011/dp-pd/prof/index.cfm?Lang=E

Dwelling Type

Area	Single-detached House	Semi-detached House	Row House	Apartment: Building with Five or More Storeys	Apartment: Building with Fewer Than Five Storeys	Duplex Apartment	Movable Dwelling	Other Single-attached House
				Number				
Oshawa	32,845	5,255	5,220	6,660	5,725	2,970	5	120
Ontario	2,718,880	279,470	415,225	789,970	498,160	160,460	15,800	9,540
Canada	7,329,150	646,245	791,600	1,234,770	2,397,550	704,485	183,510	33,310
				Percent of Dwellings				
Oshawa	55.9	8.9	8.9	11.3	9.7	5.1	0.0	0.2
Ontario	55.6	5.7	8.5	16.2	10.2	3.3	0.3	0.2
Canada	55.0	4.9	5.9	9.3	18.0	5.3	1.4	0.3

Source: Statistics Canada. 2012. Census Profile. 2011 Census. Statistics Canada Catalogue no. 98-316-XWE. Ottawa. Released October 24 2012.
http://www12.statcan.gc.ca/census-recensement/2011/dp-pd/prof/index.cfm?Lang=E

Shelter Costs

	Owned Dwellings					Rented Dwellings		
Area	Number	Median Value[1] ($)	Average Value[1] ($)	Median Monthly Costs[2] ($)	Average Monthly Costs[2] ($)	Number	Median Monthly Costs[3] ($)	Average Monthly Costs[3] ($)
Oshawa	41,350	240,415	267,269	1,267	1,269	17,425	871	862
Ontario	3,446,650	300,862	367,428	1,163	1,284	1,385,535	892	926
Canada	9,013,410	280,552	345,182	978	1,141	4,060,385	784	848

Note: All figures cover non-farm, non-reserve private dwellings; (1) Refers to the dollar amount expected by the owner if the dwelling were to be sold; (2) Includes all shelter expenses paid by households that own their dwellings, such as the mortgage payment and the costs of electricity, heat, water and other municipal services, property taxes and condominium fees; (3) Includes all shelter expenses paid by households that rent their dwellings, such as the monthly rent and the costs of electricity, heat and municipal services.
Source: Statistics Canada. 2013. 2011 National Household Survey. Statistics Canada Catalogue no. 99-004-XWE. Ottawa. Released September 11, 2013.

Occupied Private Dwellings by Period of Construction

Area	1960 or Before	1961 to 1980	1981 to 1990	1991 to 2000	2001 to 2005	2006 to 2011
			Number			
Oshawa	15,735	22,350	8,145	5,280	3,720	3,560
Ontario	1,330,235	1,420,570	763,430	609,310	414,795	348,310
Canada	3,273,105	4,152,715	2,112,110	1,707,880	1,031,020	1,042,430
			Percent of Dwellings			
Oshawa	26.8	38.0	13.9	9.0	6.3	6.1
Ontario	27.2	29.1	15.6	12.5	8.5	7.1
Canada	24.6	31.2	15.9	12.8	7.7	7.8

Note: Figures cover non-farm, non-reserve private dwellings and includes data up to May 10, 2011.
Source: Statistics Canada. 2013. 2011 National Household Survey. Statistics Canada Catalogue no. 99-004-XWE. Ottawa. Released September 11, 2013.

Educational Attainment

Area	No Certificate, Diploma or Degree	High School Diploma or Equivalent[1]	Apprenticeship or Trades Certificate or Diploma[2]	College, CÉGEP or Other Non-University Certificate or Diploma	University Certificate or Diploma Below the Bachelor Level[3]	Bachelor's Degree	University Certificate, Diploma or Degree Above Bachelor Level[4]
				Number			
				Total			
Oshawa	26,925	38,370	10,780	29,380	3,325	9,585	4,550
Ontario	1,954,520	2,801,805	771,140	2,070,875	427,150	1,515,075	933,100
Canada	5,485,400	6,968,935	2,950,685	4,970,020	1,200,130	3,634,425	2,049,930
				Males			
Oshawa	13,470	18,620	7,460	12,205	1,290	4,205	2,170
Ontario	957,040	1,337,055	520,390	894,235	193,355	692,345	470,290
Canada	2,742,875	3,305,415	1,928,970	2,118,430	513,235	1,643,080	1,043,350
				Females			
Oshawa	13,455	19,750	3,320	17,180	2,030	5,375	2,385
Ontario	997,475	1,464,755	250,750	1,176,640	233,790	822,730	462,805
Canada	2,742,520	3,663,515	1,021,715	2,851,595	686,890	1,991,345	1,006,585
				Percent of Population			
				Total			
Oshawa	21.9	31.2	8.8	23.9	2.7	7.8	3.7
Ontario	18.7	26.8	7.4	19.8	4.1	14.5	8.9
Canada	20.1	25.6	10.8	18.2	4.4	13.3	7.5
				Males			
Oshawa	22.7	31.3	12.6	20.5	2.2	7.1	3.7
Ontario	18.9	26.4	10.3	17.7	3.8	13.7	9.3
Canada	20.6	24.9	14.5	15.9	3.9	12.4	7.8
				Females			
Oshawa	21.2	31.1	5.2	27.1	3.2	8.5	3.8
Ontario	18.4	27.1	4.6	21.8	4.3	15.2	8.6
Canada	19.6	26.2	7.3	20.4	4.9	14.3	7.2

Note: Figures cover total population aged 15 years and over by highest certificate, diploma or degree; (1) Includes persons who have graduated from a secondary school or equivalent. It excludes persons with a postsecondary certificate, diploma or degree; (2) Includes Registered Apprenticeship certificates (including Certificate of Qualification, Journeyperson's designation) and other trades certificates or diplomas such as pre-employment or vocational certificates and diplomas from brief trade programs completed at community colleges, institutes of technology, vocational centres, and similar institutions; (3) Comparisons with other data sources suggest that the category 'University certificate or diploma below the bachelor's level' was over-reported in the NHS. This category likely includes some responses that are actually college certificates or diplomas, bachelor's degrees or other types of education (e.g., university transfer programs, bachelor's programs completed in other countries, incomplete bachelor's programs, non-university professional designations). We recommend users interpret the results for the 'University certificate or diploma below the bachelor's level' category with caution; (4) 'University certificate or diploma above bachelor level' includes the categories: 'Degree in medicine, dentistry, veterinary medicine or optometry,' 'Master's degree' and 'Earned doctorate.'
Source: Statistics Canada. 2013. 2011 National Household Survey. Statistics Canada Catalogue no. 99-004-XWE. Ottawa. Released September 11, 2013.

Household Income Distribution

Area	Less than $10,000	$10,000 to $19,999	$20,000 to $29,999	$30,000 to $39,999	$40,000 to $49,999	$50,000 to $59,999	$60,000 to $79,999	$80,000 to $99,999	$100,000 to $124,999	$125,000 to $149,999	$150,000 and Over
					Households						
Oshawa	2,365	4,270	5,530	4,865	5,750	5,030	8,615	7,160	5,885	3,820	5,510
Ontario	201,780	354,530	405,725	425,410	425,720	398,705	680,850	552,660	497,970	331,460	611,840
Canada	626,705	1,141,945	1,193,925	1,271,675	1,206,800	1,102,120	1,865,280	1,458,240	1,260,770	802,555	1,389,240
					Percent of Households						
Oshawa	4.0	7.3	9.4	8.3	9.8	8.6	14.7	12.2	10.0	6.5	9.4
Ontario	4.1	7.3	8.3	8.7	8.7	8.2	13.9	11.3	10.2	6.8	12.5
Canada	4.7	8.6	9.0	9.5	9.1	8.3	14.0	10.9	9.5	6.0	10.4

Note: Household income is the sum of the total incomes of all members of that household. Total income refers to monetary receipts from certain sources, before income taxes and deductions, during calendar year 2010.
Source: Statistics Canada. 2013. 2011 National Household Survey. Statistics Canada Catalogue no. 99-004-XWE. Ottawa. Released September 11, 2013.

Median and Average Household and Economic Family Income

Area	Median Household Income ($)	Average Household Income ($)	Median After-tax Household Income ($)	Average After-tax Household Income ($)	Median Economic Family Income ($)	Average Economic Family Income ($)	Median After-tax Economic Family Income ($)	Average After-tax Economic Family Income ($)
Oshawa	63,136	75,833	55,977	64,744	76,992	87,701	67,559	74,785
Ontario	66,358	85,772	58,717	71,523	80,987	100,152	71,128	83,322
Canada	61,072	79,102	54,089	66,149	76,511	94,125	67,044	78,517

Note: Figures cover household and economic familiy income in 2010. A household is defined as a person or a group of persons (other than foreign residents) who occupy the same private dwelling and do not have a usual place of residence elsewhere in Canada. Every person is a member of one and only one household. An economic family is defined as a group of two or more persons who live in the same dwelling and are related to each other by blood, marriage, common-law, adoption or a foster relationship. A couple may be of opposite or same sex.
Source: Statistics Canada. 2013. 2011 National Household Survey. Statistics Canada Catalogue no. 99-004-XWE. Ottawa. Released September 11, 2013.

PROFILES / Oshawa, Ontario

Individual Income Distribution

Area	Less than $10,000	$10,000 to $19,999	$20,000 to $29,999	$30,000 to $39,999	$40,000 to $49,999	$50,000 to $59,999	$60,000 to $79,999	$80,000 to $99,999	$100,000 to $124,999	$125,000 and Over
Number										
Total										
Oshawa	20,110	20,050	15,615	14,910	12,670	9,365	11,135	6,525	3,255	2,135
Ontario	1,780,355	1,748,060	1,361,710	1,136,730	980,790	746,360	964,280	574,710	293,865	330,285
Canada	4,492,040	4,835,710	3,670,020	3,180,360	2,603,520	1,921,650	2,437,440	1,302,045	693,580	782,135
Males										
Oshawa	8,960	7,295	6,290	7,390	6,255	5,160	6,610	4,115	2,405	1,705
Ontario	781,095	669,815	580,990	535,255	491,125	407,005	569,205	341,160	201,125	244,500
Canada	1,936,365	1,864,880	1,588,260	1,522,190	1,333,510	1,079,780	1,473,145	823,720	492,905	599,905
Females										
Oshawa	11,150	12,750	9,320	7,525	6,420	4,205	4,525	2,410	850	430
Ontario	999,265	1,078,245	780,720	601,475	489,665	339,360	395,075	233,550	92,740	85,790
Canada	2,555,675	2,970,825	2,081,760	1,658,170	1,270,010	841,870	964,300	478,330	200,680	182,230
Percent of Population										
Total										
Oshawa	17.4	17.3	13.5	12.9	10.9	8.1	9.6	5.6	2.8	1.8
Ontario	18.0	17.6	13.7	11.5	9.9	7.5	9.7	5.8	3.0	3.3
Canada	17.3	18.7	14.2	12.3	10.0	7.4	9.4	5.0	2.7	3.0
Males										
Oshawa	15.9	13.0	11.2	13.2	11.1	9.2	11.8	7.3	4.3	3.0
Ontario	16.2	13.9	12.1	11.1	10.2	8.4	11.8	7.1	4.2	5.1
Canada	15.2	14.7	12.5	12.0	10.5	8.5	11.6	6.5	3.9	4.7
Females										
Oshawa	18.7	21.4	15.6	12.6	10.8	7.1	7.6	4.0	1.4	0.7
Ontario	19.6	21.2	15.3	11.8	9.6	6.7	7.8	4.6	1.8	1.7
Canada	19.4	22.5	15.8	12.6	9.6	6.4	7.3	3.6	1.5	1.4

Note: Figures cover individuals aged 15 years and over with income. Income refers to monetary receipts from certain sources, before income taxes and deductions, during calendar year 2010.
Source: Statistics Canada. 2013. 2011 National Household Survey. Statistics Canada Catalogue no. 99-004-XWE. Ottawa. Released September 11, 2013.

Labour Force Status

Area	In the Labour Force — All	Employed	Unemployed	Not in the Labour Force
Number				
Total				
Oshawa	78,385	69,945	8,435	44,550
Ontario	6,864,990	6,297,005	567,985	3,608,685
Canada	17,990,080	16,595,035	1,395,045	9,269,445
Males				
Oshawa	40,085	35,510	4,575	19,340
Ontario	3,542,030	3,249,165	292,865	1,522,690
Canada	9,388,570	8,634,310	754,255	3,906,785
Females				
Oshawa	38,295	34,440	3,860	25,200
Ontario	3,322,955	3,047,840	275,120	2,085,990
Canada	8,601,515	7,960,725	640,790	5,362,660
Percent of Labour Force				
Total				
Oshawa	63.8	56.9	10.8	36.2
Ontario	65.5	60.1	8.3	34.5
Canada	66.0	60.9	7.8	34.0
Males				
Oshawa	67.4	59.8	11.4	32.5
Ontario	69.9	64.2	8.3	30.1
Canada	70.6	64.9	8.0	29.4
Females				
Oshawa	60.3	54.2	10.1	39.7
Ontario	61.4	56.3	8.3	38.6
Canada	61.6	57.0	7.4	38.4

Note: Figures are based on total population 15 years and over
Source: Statistics Canada. 2013. 2011 National Household Survey. Statistics Canada Catalogue no. 99-004-XWE. Ottawa. Released September 11, 2013.

Labour Force by Industry (NAICS Codes 11–52)

Area	Agriculture, forestry, fishing & hunting	Mining, quarrying, & oil & gas extraction	Utilities	Construction	Manufacturing	Wholesale Trade	Retail Trade	Transportation & warehousing	Information & cultural industries	Finance & insurance
					Number					
					Total					
Oshawa	335	65	1,780	5,430	7,885	3,405	9,695	3,900	1,910	2,965
Ontario	101,280	29,985	57,035	417,900	697,565	305,030	751,200	307,405	178,720	364,415
Canada	437,650	261,050	149,940	1,215,380	1,619,295	733,445	2,031,665	827,780	420,830	767,960
					Males					
Oshawa	205	55	1,315	4,855	5,875	2,425	4,180	3,140	1,050	1,070
Ontario	66,485	25,650	42,685	369,300	493,305	197,770	344,480	225,245	98,835	153,125
Canada	307,370	211,690	110,765	1,068,710	1,167,680	494,545	933,850	617,305	235,875	296,995
					Females					
Oshawa	130	0	470	575	2,010	975	5,515	765	865	1,895
Ontario	34,800	4,340	14,350	48,595	204,260	107,260	406,720	82,160	79,885	211,290
Canada	130,285	49,360	39,175	146,670	451,615	238,900	1,097,820	210,475	184,955	470,960
					Percent of Labour Force					
					Total					
Oshawa	0.4	0.1	2.4	7.2	10.5	4.5	12.9	5.2	2.5	3.9
Ontario	1.5	0.4	0.9	6.3	10.4	4.6	11.2	4.6	2.7	5.5
Canada	2.5	1.5	0.9	6.9	9.2	4.2	11.6	4.7	2.4	4.4
					Males					
Oshawa	0.5	0.1	3.4	12.5	15.2	6.3	10.8	8.1	2.7	2.8
Ontario	1.9	0.7	1.2	10.7	14.3	5.7	10.0	6.5	2.9	4.4
Canada	3.3	2.3	1.2	11.6	12.7	5.4	10.2	6.7	2.6	3.2
					Females					
Oshawa	0.4	0.0	1.3	1.6	5.5	2.7	15.0	2.1	2.4	5.2
Ontario	1.1	0.1	0.4	1.5	6.3	3.3	12.6	2.5	2.5	6.5
Canada	1.6	0.6	0.5	1.7	5.4	2.8	13.1	2.5	2.2	5.6

Note: Figures are based on total experienced labour force 15 years and over. Experienced labour force refers to persons who, during the week of Sunday, May 1 to Saturday, May 7, 2011, were employed and the unemployed who had last worked for pay or in self-employment in either 2010 or 2011.
Source: Statistics Canada. 2013. 2011 National Household Survey. Statistics Canada Catalogue no. 99-004-XWE. Ottawa. Released September 11, 2013.

Labour Force by Industry (NAICS Codes 53–91)

Area	Real estate & rental & leasing	Profess., scientific & tech. services	Mgmt of companies & enterprises	Admin. & support, waste mgmt & remed. services	Educational services	Health care & social assistance	Arts, entertain. & recreation	Accomm. & food services	Other services (except public admin.)	Public admin.
					Number					
					Total					
Oshawa	1,355	3,525	70	4,340	5,595	8,830	1,500	4,750	3,260	4,805
Ontario	133,980	511,020	6,525	309,630	499,690	692,130	144,065	417,675	296,340	458,665
Canada	321,895	1,240,850	17,460	728,330	1,301,435	1,949,650	363,405	1,130,750	807,800	1,261,050
					Males					
Oshawa	840	1,690	45	2,315	2,040	1,165	725	1,755	1,585	2,375
Ontario	72,835	281,420	3,540	172,475	162,765	120,165	75,035	177,240	133,795	236,655
Canada	179,090	688,625	9,380	411,250	424,915	349,430	188,270	469,990	372,940	652,510
					Females					
Oshawa	515	1,835	0	2,030	3,560	7,670	780	2,990	1,670	2,430
Ontario	61,145	229,600	2,990	137,155	336,925	571,965	69,030	240,430	162,550	222,015
Canada	142,805	552,225	8,075	317,085	876,515	1,600,220	175,135	660,760	434,865	608,535
					Percent of Labour Force					
					Total					
Oshawa	1.8	4.7	0.1	5.8	7.4	11.7	2.0	6.3	4.3	6.4
Ontario	2.0	7.6	0.1	4.6	7.5	10.4	2.2	6.3	4.4	6.9
Canada	1.8	7.1	0.1	4.1	7.4	11.1	2.1	6.4	4.6	7.2
					Males					
Oshawa	2.2	4.4	0.1	6.0	5.3	3.0	1.9	4.5	4.1	6.1
Ontario	2.1	8.2	0.1	5.0	4.7	3.5	2.2	5.1	3.9	6.9
Canada	1.9	7.5	0.1	4.5	4.6	3.8	2.0	5.1	4.1	7.1
					Females					
Oshawa	1.4	5.0	0.0	5.5	9.7	20.9	2.1	8.1	4.5	6.6
Ontario	1.9	7.1	0.1	4.2	10.4	17.7	2.1	7.4	5.0	6.9
Canada	1.7	6.6	0.1	3.8	10.4	19.1	2.1	7.9	5.2	7.2

Note: Figures are based on total experienced labour force 15 years and over. Experienced labour force refers to persons who, during the week of Sunday, May 1 to Saturday, May 7, 2011, were employed and the unemployed who had last worked for pay or in self-employment in either 2010 or 2011.
Source: Statistics Canada. 2013. 2011 National Household Survey. Statistics Canada Catalogue no. 99-004-XWE. Ottawa. Released September 11, 2013.

Occupation

Area	Mgmt	Business, Finance & Admin.	Natural/Applied Sciences & Related	Health	Education, Law & Social, Community & Government Services	Art, Culture, Recreation & Sport	Sales & Service	Trades, Transport & Equip. Operators & Related	Natural Resources, Agri. & Related Production	Mfg & Utilities
					Number					
					Total					
Oshawa	7,120	11,820	3,775	4,530	8,585	1,690	19,685	12,780	960	4,460
Ontario	770,580	1,138,330	494,500	392,695	801,465	206,420	1,550,260	868,515	106,810	350,685
Canada	1,963,600	2,902,045	1,237,775	1,107,200	2,064,675	503,415	4,068,170	2,537,775	397,930	805,040
					Males					
Oshawa	4,055	3,595	2,990	655	2,620	780	7,895	12,020	785	3,310
Ontario	474,655	352,505	384,345	78,330	264,570	96,055	673,880	812,280	82,610	233,565
Canada	1,229,460	854,190	966,355	217,520	676,550	232,535	1,745,705	2,385,615	318,945	564,300
					Females					
Oshawa	3,065	8,230	785	3,870	5,970	915	11,790	760	170	1,150
Ontario	295,920	785,825	110,150	314,370	536,895	110,370	876,380	56,230	24,200	117,115
Canada	734,140	2,047,855	271,415	889,675	1,388,130	270,875	2,322,465	152,165	78,980	240,740
					Percent of Labour Force					
					Total					
Oshawa	9.4	15.7	5.0	6.0	11.4	2.2	26.1	16.9	1.3	5.9
Ontario	11.5	17.0	7.4	5.9	12.0	3.1	23.2	13.0	1.6	5.2
Canada	11.2	16.5	7.0	6.3	11.7	2.9	23.1	14.4	2.3	4.6
					Males					
Oshawa	10.5	9.3	7.7	1.7	6.8	2.0	20.4	31.1	2.0	8.6
Ontario	13.7	10.2	11.1	2.3	7.7	2.8	19.5	23.5	2.4	6.8
Canada	13.4	9.3	10.5	2.4	7.4	2.5	19.0	26.0	3.5	6.1
					Females					
Oshawa	8.4	22.4	2.1	10.5	16.3	2.5	32.1	2.1	0.5	3.1
Ontario	9.2	24.3	3.4	9.7	16.6	3.4	27.2	1.7	0.7	3.6
Canada	8.7	24.4	3.2	10.6	16.5	3.2	27.7	1.8	0.9	2.9

Note: Figures are based on total experienced labour force 15 years and over
Source: Statistics Canada. 2013. 2011 National Household Survey. Statistics Canada Catalogue no. 99-004-XWE. Ottawa. Released September 11, 2013.

Place of Work Status

Area	Worked at Home	Worked Outside Canada	No Fixed Workplace Address	Worked at Usual Place
		Number		
		Total		
Oshawa	2,995	135	8,095	58,720
Ontario	423,790	31,390	670,835	5,170,980
Canada	1,142,640	66,460	1,868,245	13,517,690
		Males		
Oshawa	1,425	95	5,875	28,115
Ontario	216,900	21,150	486,560	2,524,555
Canada	582,150	47,355	1,400,485	6,604,325
		Females		
Oshawa	1,580	35	2,220	30,605
Ontario	206,895	10,240	184,275	2,646,420
Canada	560,490	19,100	467,760	6,913,370
		Percent of Labour Force		
		Total		
Oshawa	4.3	0.2	11.6	84.0
Ontario	6.7	0.5	10.7	82.1
Canada	6.9	0.4	11.3	81.5
		Males		
Oshawa	4.0	0.3	16.5	79.2
Ontario	6.7	0.7	15.0	77.7
Canada	6.7	0.5	16.2	76.5
		Females		
Oshawa	4.6	0.1	6.4	88.9
Ontario	6.8	0.3	6.0	86.8
Canada	7.0	0.2	5.9	86.8

Note: Figures are based on total employed labour force 15 years and over.
Source: Statistics Canada. 2013. 2011 National Household Survey. Statistics Canada Catalogue no. 99-004-XWE. Ottawa. Released September 11, 2013.

Mode of Transportation to Work

Area	Car; Truck; Van; as Driver	Car; Truck; Van; as Passenger	Public Transit	Walked	Bicycled	All Other Modes
			Number			
			Total			
Oshawa	52,985	4,525	5,440	2,750	320	790
Ontario	4,235,315	357,110	818,270	299,095	69,885	62,145
Canada	11,393,140	867,050	1,851,525	880,815	201,780	191,625
			Males			
Oshawa	28,170	2,130	2,185	1,030	200	280
Ontario	2,316,680	143,410	340,995	131,765	47,635	30,635
Canada	6,238,835	349,530	788,290	387,580	135,840	104,725
			Females			
Oshawa	24,815	2,395	3,260	1,730	120	510
Ontario	1,918,640	213,700	477,275	167,325	22,250	31,515
Canada	5,154,305	517,520	1,063,235	493,230	65,940	86,900
			Percent of Labour Force			
			Total			
Oshawa	79.3	6.8	8.1	4.1	0.5	1.2
Ontario	72.5	6.1	14.0	5.1	1.2	1.1
Canada	74.0	5.6	12.0	5.7	1.3	1.2
			Males			
Oshawa	82.9	6.3	6.4	3.0	0.6	0.8
Ontario	76.9	4.8	11.3	4.4	1.6	1.0
Canada	77.9	4.4	9.8	4.8	1.7	1.3
			Females			
Oshawa	75.6	7.3	9.9	5.3	0.4	1.6
Ontario	67.8	7.5	16.9	5.9	0.8	1.1
Canada	69.8	7.0	14.4	6.7	0.9	1.2

Note: Figures are based on total employed labour force 15 years and over.
Source: Statistics Canada. 2013. 2011 National Household Survey. Statistics Canada Catalogue no. 99-004-XWE. Ottawa. Released September 11, 2013.

Visible Minority Population Characteristics

Area	Total Minority	South Asian[1]	Chinese	Black	Filipino	Latin American	Arab	SE Asian[2]	West Asian[3]	Korean	Japanese	Multiple[4]
						Number						
						Total						
Oshawa	13,795	2,790	1,340	4,675	1,290	1,060	340	445	400	210	115	610
Ontario	3,279,565	965,990	629,140	539,205	275,380	172,560	151,645	137,875	122,530	78,290	29,085	96,735
Canada	6,264,750	1,567,400	1,324,750	945,665	619,310	381,280	380,620	312,075	206,840	161,130	87,270	171,935
						Males						
Oshawa	6,965	1,455	695	2,310	550	560	170	200	180	105	70	340
Ontario	1,582,480	484,355	301,575	251,295	116,825	83,205	79,620	67,645	62,515	38,045	13,345	46,765
Canada	3,043,010	790,755	632,325	453,005	268,885	186,355	203,485	154,035	105,620	77,165	38,270	83,335
						Females						
Oshawa	6,835	1,335	640	2,360	740	500	165	250	220	110	50	270
Ontario	1,697,085	481,635	327,570	287,915	158,555	89,360	72,025	70,230	60,010	40,250	15,740	49,970
Canada	3,221,745	776,650	692,420	492,660	350,425	194,925	177,140	158,045	101,220	83,965	48,990	88,600
						Percent of Population						
						Total						
Oshawa	9.3	1.9	0.9	3.2	0.9	0.7	0.2	0.3	0.3	0.1	0.1	0.4
Ontario	25.9	7.6	5.0	4.3	2.2	1.4	1.2	1.1	1.0	0.6	0.2	0.8
Canada	19.1	4.8	4.0	2.9	1.9	1.2	1.2	0.9	0.6	0.5	0.3	0.5
						Males						
Oshawa	9.7	2.0	1.0	3.2	0.8	0.8	0.2	0.3	0.2	0.1	0.1	0.5
Ontario	25.6	7.8	4.9	4.1	1.9	1.3	1.3	1.1	1.0	0.6	0.2	0.8
Canada	18.8	4.9	3.9	2.8	1.7	1.2	1.3	1.0	0.7	0.5	0.2	0.5
						Females						
Oshawa	9.0	1.8	0.8	3.1	1.0	0.7	0.2	0.3	0.3	0.1	0.1	0.4
Ontario	26.2	7.4	5.1	4.4	2.5	1.4	1.1	1.1	0.9	0.6	0.2	0.8
Canada	19.3	4.7	4.1	3.0	2.1	1.2	1.1	0.9	0.6	0.5	0.3	0.5

Note: The Employment Equity Act defines visible minorities as 'persons, other than Aboriginal peoples, who are non-Caucasian in race or non-white in colour';
(1) Includes 'East Indian,' 'Pakistani,' 'Sri Lankan,' etc.; (2) Includes 'Vietnamese,' 'Cambodian,' 'Malaysian,' 'Laotian,' etc.; (3) Includes 'Iranian,' 'Afghan,' etc.; (4) Includes respondents who reported more than one visible minority group by checking two or more mark-in circles, e.g., 'Black' and 'South Asian.'
Source: Statistics Canada. 2013. 2011 National Household Survey. Statistics Canada Catalogue no. 99-004-XWE. Ottawa. Released September 11, 2013.

PROFILES / Oshawa, Ontario

Aboriginal Population

Area	Aboriginal Identity[1]	First Nations (North American Indian) Single Identity[2]	Métis Single Identity	Inuk (Inuit) Single Identity	Multiple Aboriginal Identities[3]	Aboriginal Identities Not Included Elsewhere
			Number			
			Total			
Oshawa	2,940	1,655	1,135	20	30	100
Ontario	301,430	201,100	86,020	3,355	2,910	8,040
Canada	1,400,685	851,560	451,795	59,440	11,415	26,475
			Males			
Oshawa	1,550	885	615	0	10	25
Ontario	145,020	96,620	41,755	1,475	1,420	3,750
Canada	682,190	411,785	223,335	29,495	5,525	12,055
			Females			
Oshawa	1,395	770	520	0	20	70
Ontario	156,410	104,485	44,260	1,880	1,490	4,295
Canada	718,500	439,775	228,460	29,950	5,890	14,420
			Percent of Population			
			Total			
Oshawa	2.0	1.1	0.8	0.0	0.0	0.1
Ontario	2.4	1.6	0.7	0.0	0.0	0.1
Canada	4.3	2.6	1.4	0.2	0.0	0.1
			Males			
Oshawa	2.2	1.2	0.9	0.0	0.0	0.0
Ontario	2.3	1.6	0.7	0.0	0.0	0.1
Canada	4.2	2.5	1.4	0.2	0.0	0.1
			Females			
Oshawa	1.8	1.0	0.7	0.0	0.0	0.1
Ontario	2.4	1.6	0.7	0.0	0.0	0.1
Canada	4.3	2.6	1.4	0.2	0.0	0.1

Note: (1) Includes persons who reported being an Aboriginal person, that is, First Nations (North American Indian), Métis or Inuk (Inuit) and/or those who reported Registered or Treaty Indian status, that is registered under the Indian Act of Canada, and/or those who reported membership in a First Nation or Indian band. Aboriginal peoples of Canada are defined in the Constitution Act, 1982, section 35-2 as including the Indian, Inuit and Métis peoples of Canada; (2) Users should be aware that the estimates associated with this variable are more affected than most by the incomplete enumeration of certain Indian reserves and Indian settlements in the National Household Survey (NHS); (3) Includes persons who reported being any two or all three of the following: First Nations (North American Indian), Métis or Inuk (Inuit).
Source: Statistics Canada. 2013. 2011 National Household Survey. Statistics Canada Catalogue no. 99-004-XWE. Ottawa. Released September 11, 2013.

Ethnic Origin

Area	North American Aboriginal	Other North American	European	Caribbean	Latin, Central and South American	African	Asian	Oceania
				Number				
				Total				
Oshawa	5,760	50,340	113,110	4,320	1,920	1,930	8,080	260
Ontario	441,395	3,059,480	8,231,410	396,485	271,545	331,460	2,604,595	19,410
Canada	1,836,035	11,070,455	20,157,965	627,590	544,375	766,735	5,011,225	74,875
				Males				
Oshawa	2,805	24,705	54,315	2,215	1,025	1,000	3,985	145
Ontario	210,490	1,507,105	4,019,885	181,805	130,035	160,940	1,265,540	9,855
Canada	885,675	5,462,685	9,913,150	291,640	264,635	387,360	2,435,540	37,490
				Females				
Oshawa	2,955	25,635	58,790	2,110	900	935	4,095	115
Ontario	230,905	1,552,380	4,211,525	214,675	141,510	170,515	1,339,050	9,555
Canada	950,360	5,607,770	10,244,820	335,945	279,740	379,380	2,575,680	37,385
				Percent of Population				
				Total				
Oshawa	3.9	34.1	76.6	2.9	1.3	1.3	5.5	0.2
Ontario	3.5	24.2	65.1	3.1	2.1	2.6	20.6	0.2
Canada	5.6	33.7	61.4	1.9	1.7	2.3	15.3	0.2
				Males				
Oshawa	3.9	34.3	75.4	3.1	1.4	1.4	5.5	0.2
Ontario	3.4	24.4	65.0	2.9	2.1	2.6	20.5	0.2
Canada	5.5	33.8	61.3	1.8	1.6	2.4	15.1	0.2
				Females				
Oshawa	3.9	33.9	77.7	2.8	1.2	1.2	5.4	0.2
Ontario	3.6	24.0	65.1	3.3	2.2	2.6	20.7	0.1
Canada	5.7	33.6	61.4	2.0	1.7	2.3	15.4	0.2

Note: The sum of the ethnic groups in this table is greater than the total population estimate because a person may report more than one ethnic origin in the NHS.
Source: Statistics Canada. 2013. 2011 National Household Survey. Statistics Canada Catalogue no. 99-004-XWE. Ottawa. Released September 11, 2013.

Religion

Area	Buddhist	Christian	Hindu	Jewish	Muslim	Sikh	Traditional (Aboriginal) Spirituality	Other Religions	No Religious Affiliation
					Number				
					Total				
Oshawa	625	100,785	710	440	1,895	195	35	535	42,460
Ontario	163,750	8,167,295	366,720	195,540	581,950	179,765	15,905	53,080	2,927,790
Canada	366,830	22,102,745	497,965	329,495	1,053,945	454,965	64,935	130,835	7,850,605
					Males				
Oshawa	295	46,755	400	230	955	110	0	185	23,100
Ontario	75,355	3,839,925	183,580	95,795	293,925	90,515	7,600	23,555	1,571,195
Canada	168,465	10,497,775	250,435	161,265	540,555	229,435	31,805	57,745	4,225,645
					Females				
Oshawa	330	54,025	310	210	940	85	10	345	19,360
Ontario	88,395	4,327,365	183,140	99,740	288,025	89,250	8,310	29,525	1,356,600
Canada	198,365	11,604,975	247,525	168,235	513,395	225,530	33,135	73,090	3,624,965
					Percent of Population				
					Total				
Oshawa	0.4	68.2	0.5	0.3	1.3	0.1	0.0	0.4	28.8
Ontario	1.3	64.6	2.9	1.5	4.6	1.4	0.1	0.4	23.1
Canada	1.1	67.3	1.5	1.0	3.2	1.4	0.2	0.4	23.9
					Males				
Oshawa	0.4	64.9	0.6	0.3	1.3	0.2	0.0	0.3	32.1
Ontario	1.2	62.1	3.0	1.5	4.8	1.5	0.1	0.4	25.4
Canada	1.0	64.9	1.5	1.0	3.3	1.4	0.2	0.4	26.1
					Females				
Oshawa	0.4	71.4	0.4	0.3	1.2	0.1	0.0	0.5	25.6
Ontario	1.4	66.9	2.8	1.5	4.5	1.4	0.1	0.5	21.0
Canada	1.2	69.5	1.5	1.0	3.1	1.4	0.2	0.4	21.7

Note: Religion refers to the person's self-identification as having a connection or affiliation with any religious denomination, group, body, sect, cult or other religiously defined community or system of belief. Religion is not limited to formal membership in a religious organization or group. Persons without a religious connection or affiliation can self-identify as atheist, agnostic or humanist, or can provide another applicable response.
Source: Statistics Canada. 2013. 2011 National Household Survey. Statistics Canada Catalogue no. 99-004-XWE. Ottawa. Released September 11, 2013.

Religion—Christian Denominations

Area	Anglican	Baptist	Catholic	Christian Orthodox	Lutheran	Pentecostal	Presbyterian	United Church	Other Christian
					Number				
					Total				
Oshawa	11,220	3,845	43,375	1,915	1,085	3,995	3,610	16,620	15,110
Ontario	774,560	244,650	3,976,610	297,710	163,460	213,945	319,585	952,465	1,224,300
Canada	1,631,845	635,840	12,810,705	550,690	478,185	478,705	472,385	2,007,610	3,036,780
					Males				
Oshawa	4,930	1,610	20,635	970	520	1,800	1,695	7,425	7,165
Ontario	355,175	112,285	1,895,940	145,825	75,225	94,955	148,535	435,255	576,730
Canada	752,945	293,905	6,167,290	270,205	221,525	217,850	218,955	912,545	1,442,550
					Females				
Oshawa	6,295	2,235	22,740	945	565	2,190	1,915	9,190	7,945
Ontario	419,390	132,370	2,080,665	151,885	88,230	118,990	171,050	517,210	647,570
Canada	878,900	341,940	6,643,415	280,485	256,660	260,850	253,430	1,095,065	1,594,230
					Percent of Population				
					Total				
Oshawa	7.6	2.6	29.4	1.3	0.7	2.7	2.4	11.3	10.2
Ontario	6.1	1.9	31.4	2.4	1.3	1.7	2.5	7.5	9.7
Canada	5.0	1.9	39.0	1.7	1.5	1.5	1.4	6.1	9.2
					Males				
Oshawa	6.8	2.2	28.6	1.3	0.7	2.5	2.4	10.3	9.9
Ontario	5.7	1.8	30.7	2.4	1.2	1.5	2.4	7.0	9.3
Canada	4.7	1.8	38.2	1.7	1.4	1.3	1.4	5.6	8.9
					Females				
Oshawa	8.3	3.0	30.1	1.2	0.7	2.9	2.5	12.2	10.5
Ontario	6.5	2.0	32.2	2.3	1.4	1.8	2.6	8.0	10.0
Canada	5.3	2.0	39.8	1.7	1.5	1.6	1.5	6.6	9.6

Note: Religion refers to the person's self-identification as having a connection or affiliation with any religious denomination, group, body, sect, cult or other religiously defined community or system of belief. Religion is not limited to formal membership in a religious organization or group. Persons without a religious connection or affiliation can self-identify as atheist, agnostic or humanist, or can provide another applicable response.
Source: Statistics Canada. 2013. 2011 National Household Survey. Statistics Canada Catalogue no. 99-004-XWE. Ottawa. Released September 11, 2013.

PROFILES / Oshawa, Ontario

Immigrant Status and Period of Immigration

Area	Non-Immigrants[1]	Immigrants All	Before 1971	1971 to 1980	1981 to 1990	1991 to 2000	2001 to 2005	2006 to 2011	Non-Permanent Residents[3]
				Number					
				Total					
Oshawa	125,595	21,620	8,340	3,865	3,015	3,175	1,700	1,525	460
Ontario	8,906,000	3,611,365	723,030	464,380	538,285	866,220	518,405	501,060	134,425
Canada	25,720,175	6,775,765	1,261,055	870,775	949,890	1,539,050	992,070	1,162,915	356,385
				Males					
Oshawa	61,330	10,450	4,005	1,880	1,565	1,530	785	685	280
Ontario	4,410,240	1,706,385	341,820	217,990	258,095	408,270	245,850	234,360	64,825
Canada	12,753,235	3,231,370	605,430	416,670	454,570	724,905	474,545	555,245	178,515
				Females					
Oshawa	64,270	11,175	4,335	1,980	1,460	1,650	920	840	185
Ontario	4,495,765	1,904,985	381,210	246,390	280,190	457,950	272,550	266,695	69,600
Canada	12,966,935	3,544,400	655,625	454,105	495,325	814,145	517,530	607,670	177,870
				Percent of Population					
				Total					
Oshawa	85.0	14.6	5.6	2.6	2.0	2.1	1.2	1.0	0.3
Ontario	70.4	28.5	5.7	3.7	4.3	6.8	4.1	4.0	1.1
Canada	78.3	20.6	3.8	2.7	2.9	4.7	3.0	3.5	1.1
				Males					
Oshawa	85.1	14.5	5.6	2.6	2.2	2.1	1.1	1.0	0.4
Ontario	71.3	27.6	5.5	3.5	4.2	6.6	4.0	3.8	1.0
Canada	78.9	20.0	3.7	2.6	2.8	4.5	2.9	3.4	1.1
				Females					
Oshawa	85.0	14.8	5.7	2.6	1.9	2.2	1.2	1.1	0.2
Ontario	69.5	29.4	5.9	3.8	4.3	7.1	4.2	4.1	1.1
Canada	77.7	21.2	3.9	2.7	3.0	4.9	3.1	3.6	1.1

Note: (1) Non-immigrant refers to a person who is a Canadian citizen by birth; (2) Immigrant refers to a person who is or has ever been a landed immigrant/permanent resident. This person has been granted the right to live in Canada permanently by immigration authorities. Some immigrants have resided in Canada for a number of years, while others have arrived recently. Some immigrants are Canadian citizens, while others are not. Most immigrants are born outside Canada, but a small number are born in Canada. In the 2011 National Household Survey, 'Immigrants' includes immigrants who landed in Canada prior to May 10, 2011; (3) Non-permanent resident refers to a person from another country who has a work or study permit, or who is a refugee claimant, and any non-Canadian-born family member living in Canada with them.
Source: Statistics Canada. 2013. 2011 National Household Survey. Statistics Canada Catalogue no. 99-004-XWE. Ottawa. Released September 11, 2013.

Mother Tongue

Area	English	French	Non-official Language	English & French	English & Non-official Language	French & Non-official Language	English, French & Non-official Language
			Number				
			Total				
Oshawa	128,555	3,205	14,825	430	1,120	75	20
Ontario	8,677,040	493,300	3,264,435	46,605	219,425	13,645	7,615
Canada	18,858,980	7,054,975	6,567,680	144,685	396,330	74,430	24,095
			Males				
Oshawa	62,860	1,530	7,070	200	545	40	10
Ontario	4,276,970	232,785	1,562,190	21,805	106,790	6,285	3,495
Canada	9,345,225	3,452,380	3,157,785	69,975	192,000	36,535	11,965
			Females				
Oshawa	65,695	1,670	7,755	225	575	35	10
Ontario	4,400,065	260,510	1,702,240	24,795	112,635	7,365	4,115
Canada	9,513,750	3,602,590	3,409,895	74,710	204,330	37,890	12,130
			Percent of Population				
			Total				
Oshawa	86.7	2.2	10.0	0.3	0.8	0.1	0.0
Ontario	68.2	3.9	25.7	0.4	1.7	0.1	0.1
Canada	56.9	21.3	19.8	0.4	1.2	0.2	0.1
			Males				
Oshawa	87.0	2.1	9.8	0.3	0.8	0.1	0.0
Ontario	68.9	3.7	25.2	0.4	1.7	0.1	0.1
Canada	57.5	21.2	19.4	0.4	1.2	0.2	0.1
			Females				
Oshawa	86.5	2.2	10.2	0.3	0.8	0.0	0.0
Ontario	67.6	4.0	26.1	0.4	1.7	0.1	0.1
Canada	56.4	21.4	20.2	0.4	1.2	0.2	0.1

Note: Figures cover total population excluding institutional residents.
Source: Statistics Canada. 2012. Census Profile. 2011 Census. Statistics Canada Catalogue no. 98-316-XWE. Ottawa. Released October 24 2012.
http://www12.statcan.gc.ca/census-recensement/2011/dp-pd/prof/index.cfm?Lang=E

Language Spoken Most Often at Home

Area	English	French	Non-official Language	English & French	English & Non-official Language	French & Non-official Language	English, French & Non-official Language
			Number				
			Total				
Oshawa	138,680	1,200	5,790	315	2,180	15	55
Ontario	10,044,810	284,115	1,827,870	37,955	509,105	6,370	11,845
Canada	21,457,075	6,827,865	3,673,865	131,205	875,135	109,700	46,330
			Males				
Oshawa	67,775	580	2,705	140	1,040	5	15
Ontario	4,930,610	133,495	872,860	17,250	248,050	2,855	5,225
Canada	10,585,620	3,348,235	1,767,310	63,475	425,370	53,010	22,845
			Females				
Oshawa	70,910	625	3,085	170	1,135	10	40
Ontario	5,114,200	150,620	955,010	20,705	261,055	3,520	6,620
Canada	10,871,455	3,479,625	1,906,555	67,730	449,765	56,690	23,485
			Percent of Population				
			Total				
Oshawa	93.6	0.8	3.9	0.2	1.5	0.0	0.0
Ontario	79.0	2.2	14.4	0.3	4.0	0.1	0.1
Canada	64.8	20.6	11.1	0.4	2.6	0.3	0.1
			Males				
Oshawa	93.8	0.8	3.7	0.2	1.4	0.0	0.0
Ontario	79.4	2.1	14.1	0.3	4.0	0.0	0.1
Canada	65.1	20.6	10.9	0.4	2.6	0.3	0.1
			Females				
Oshawa	93.3	0.8	4.1	0.2	1.5	0.0	0.1
Ontario	78.5	2.3	14.7	0.3	4.0	0.1	0.1
Canada	64.5	20.6	11.3	0.4	2.7	0.3	0.1

Note: Figures cover total population excluding institutional residents.
Source: Statistics Canada. 2012. Census Profile. 2011 Census. Statistics Canada Catalogue no. 98-316-XWE. Ottawa. Released October 24 2012.
http://www12.statcan.gc.ca/census-recensement/2011/dp-pd/prof/index.cfm?Lang=E

Knowledge of Official Languages

Area	English Only	French Only	English & French	Neither English nor French
		Number		
		Total		
Oshawa	137,930	155	9,435	710
Ontario	10,984,360	42,980	1,395,805	298,920
Canada	22,564,665	4,165,015	5,795,570	595,920
		Males		
Oshawa	67,775	75	4,140	265
Ontario	5,445,050	18,805	627,725	118,765
Canada	11,222,185	1,925,340	2,876,560	241,790
		Females		
Oshawa	70,155	75	5,300	440
Ontario	5,539,310	24,175	768,085	180,155
Canada	11,342,485	2,239,680	2,919,005	354,135
		Percent of Population		
		Total		
Oshawa	93.0	0.1	6.4	0.5
Ontario	86.3	0.3	11.0	2.3
Canada	68.1	12.6	17.5	1.8
		Males		
Oshawa	93.8	0.1	5.7	0.4
Ontario	87.7	0.3	10.1	1.9
Canada	69.0	11.8	17.7	1.5
		Females		
Oshawa	92.3	0.1	7.0	0.6
Ontario	85.1	0.4	11.8	2.8
Canada	67.3	13.3	17.3	2.1

Note: Figures cover total population excluding institutional residents.
Source: Statistics Canada. 2012. Census Profile. 2011 Census. Statistics Canada Catalogue no. 98-316-XWE. Ottawa. Released October 24 2012.
http://www12.statcan.gc.ca/census-recensement/2011/dp-pd/prof/index.cfm?Lang=E

Ottawa, Ontario

Background

Ottawa is situated on the south bank of the Ottawa River in southeastern Ontario. The city is Canada's capital city and borders Gatineau, Québec, on the north bank of the Ottawa River. Together, the two areas form the National Capital Region (NCR).

When Lower Canada and Upper Canada joined in 1841, a seat of government was required for the new Province of Canada. In 1857, Ottawa was named the permanent capital. Ottawa was a lumber town less developed than Toronto, Kingston, Montréal and Québec City, but it was the farthest from the American border and hence the safest.

The Rideau Canal system that winds through downtown offers bike and walking paths and the worlds longest skateway (7.8 kilometres) in winter. The city's Parliament Buildings are the seat of Canada's national government and host year-round festivities, including the nation's largest Canada Day celebrations. The Gatineau Hills in the city's woodland and lakeland district feature some of Canada's most spectacular fall foliage.

The City of Ottawa has one of the most educated labour forces in Canada and is only second to Silicon Valley in terms of science and engineering employment. It is a global technology centre as well as a top research-and-development hub. Nearly half a million residents speak English and French fluently. Over 100,000 of the city's population are employed by government.

Ottawa attractions include the Canada Aviation and Space Museum, Canadian Museum of Nature, Canada Science and Technology Museum, Canadian War Museum, and the National Gallery of Canada. The Université d'Ottawa and Carleton University are the city's two major post-secondary institutions.

Popular events include the Canadian Tulip Festival, the changing of the guard on Parliament Hill, the International Jazz Festival, the Rideau Canal Festival and Winterlude.

Ottawa has summer highs of plus 25.07 degrees Celsius, winter lows of minus 12.77 degrees Celsius, and an average rainfall just over 733 mm per year.

Rankings

- *Money Sense Magazine* ranked Ottawa the "Best City to Live in Canada 2012." Ottawa ranked #1 out of 190 cities and towns. Criteria: walk/bike to work ratio, affordable housing, household income, discretionary income, new cars, population growth, low crime, doctors per 1,000 residents, weather, jobless rate and culture. Ottawa's highest individual ranking was in culture (#7); the city has the highest concentration of museums in Canada. *Money Sense, "Canada's Best Places to Live," March 20, 2012*
- Ottawa ranked as one of the "Most Sustainable Major Cities in Canada." The city ranked #3 in terms of: ecological integrity; economic security; governance and empowerment; infrastructure and built environment; and social well-being. Cities with populations of 700,000 or more were categorized as major urban centres. Toronto (#1) and Edmonton (#2) were the top two centres. *Corporate Knights Magazine, "The 2011 Most Sustainable Cities in Canada," February 9, 2011*
- The Conference Board of Canada gave Ottawa an A for its business competitiveness. Fifty cities were ranked. Criteria included: economy, health, environment, housing and innovation, society, and education. Other top-ranked cities were Waterloo (ON), Calgary (AB), Vancouver (BC), St. John's (NL) and Richmond Hill (ON). *Conference Board of Canada, "City Magnets: Benchmarking the Attractiveness of Canada's CMAs," December 2007*
- *Maclean's Magazine* ranked Ottawa #4 out of more than 4,500 communities across Canada in terms of lifelong learning opportunities. Canada's Top 4 "Smartest Cities" were Victoria (BC), Saskatoon (SK), Calgary (AB) and Ottawa. Criteria: learning to know; learning to do; learning to live. *Maclean's Magazine, "Canada's Smartest Cities: 2010 Rankings," May 20, 2010 based on the Canadian Council on Learning's 2010 Composite Learning Index*

PROFILES / Ottawa, Ontario

Population Growth and Density

Area	Population in 2001	Population in 2006	Population in 2011	Population Change 2001–2006	Population Change 2006–2011	Land Area (sq. km)	Population Density per sq. km
Ottawa	774,072	812,129	883,391	4.9	8.8	2,790.22	316.6
Ontario	11,410,046	12,160,282	12,851,821	6.6	5.7	908,607.67	14.1
Canada	30,007,094	31,612,897	33,476,688	5.4	5.9	8,965,121.42	3.7

Source: Statistics Canada. 2012. Census Profile. 2011 Census. Statistics Canada Catalogue no. 98-316-XWE. Ottawa. Released October 24 2012.
http://www12.statcan.gc.ca/census-recensement/2011/dp-pd/prof/index.cfm?Lang=E;
Statistics Canada 2007. 2006 Community Profiles. 2006 Census. Statistics Canada Catalogue no. 92-591-XWE. Ottawa. Released March 13 2007.
http://www12.statcan.ca/census-recensement/2006/dp-pd/prof/92-591/index.cfm?Lang=E

Gender

Area	Males	Females
Number		
Ottawa	428,455	454,935
Ontario	6,263,140	6,588,685
Canada	16,414,225	17,062,460
Percent of Population		
Ottawa	48.5	51.5
Ontario	48.7	51.3
Canada	49.0	51.0

Source: Statistics Canada. 2012. Census Profile. 2011 Census. Statistics Canada Catalogue no. 98-316-XWE. Ottawa. Released October 24 2012.
http://www12.statcan.gc.ca/census-recensement/2011/dp-pd/prof/index.cfm?Lang=E

Marital Status

Area	Married[1]	Living Common-law	Single[2]	Separated	Divorced	Widowed
Number — Total						
Ottawa	348,520	62,595	224,340	20,630	42,710	36,030
Ontario	5,367,400	791,210	2,985,020	319,805	593,730	613,880
Canada	12,941,960	3,142,525	7,816,045	698,240	1,686,035	1,584,530
Males						
Ottawa	173,900	31,570	117,055	8,385	15,540	6,730
Ontario	2,681,320	397,620	1,583,760	133,790	231,160	117,980
Canada	6,470,300	1,575,495	4,206,320	299,655	680,415	310,940
Females						
Ottawa	174,625	31,020	107,290	12,240	27,170	29,300
Ontario	2,686,075	393,590	1,401,260	186,015	362,570	495,905
Canada	6,471,660	1,567,035	3,609,730	398,585	1,005,620	1,273,590
Percent of Population — Total						
Ottawa	47.4	8.5	30.5	2.8	5.8	4.9
Ontario	50.3	7.4	28.0	3.0	5.6	5.8
Canada	46.4	11.3	28.0	2.5	6.0	5.7
Males						
Ottawa	49.2	8.9	33.1	2.4	4.4	1.9
Ontario	52.1	7.7	30.8	2.6	4.5	2.3
Canada	47.8	11.6	31.1	2.2	5.0	2.3
Females						
Ottawa	45.8	8.1	28.1	3.2	7.1	7.7
Ontario	48.6	7.1	25.4	3.4	6.6	9.0
Canada	45.2	10.9	25.2	2.8	7.0	8.9

Note: (1) and not separated, (2) never legally married
Source: Statistics Canada. 2012. Census Profile. 2011 Census. Statistics Canada Catalogue no. 98-316-XWE. Ottawa. Released October 24 2012.
http://www12.statcan.gc.ca/census-recensement/2011/dp-pd/prof/index.cfm?Lang=E

Age Characteristics: 0 to 49 Years

Area	0 to 4 Years	5 to 9 Years	10 to 14 Years	15 to 19 Years	20 to 24 Years	25 to 29 Years	30 to 34 Years	35 to 39 Years	40 to 44 Years	45 to 49 Years
\multicolumn{11}{c}{Number}
\multicolumn{11}{c}{Total}
Ottawa	49,140	48,765	50,665	58,305	65,960	61,230	57,745	60,360	64,285	73,190
Ontario	704,260	712,755	763,755	863,635	852,910	815,120	800,365	844,335	924,075	1,055,880
Canada	1,877,095	1,809,895	1,920,355	2,178,135	2,187,450	2,169,590	2,162,905	2,173,930	2,324,875	2,675,130
\multicolumn{11}{c}{Males}
Ottawa	24,925	24,660	25,690	29,675	33,100	30,185	27,675	28,765	31,215	35,935
Ontario	360,590	365,290	391,630	443,680	432,490	400,045	383,340	405,845	447,920	517,510
Canada	961,150	925,965	983,995	1,115,845	1,108,775	1,077,275	1,058,810	1,064,200	1,141,720	1,318,715
\multicolumn{11}{c}{Females}
Ottawa	24,215	24,100	24,975	28,630	32,865	31,045	30,065	31,600	33,065	37,255
Ontario	343,670	347,465	372,125	419,950	420,415	415,075	417,030	438,485	476,155	538,370
Canada	915,945	883,935	936,360	1,062,295	1,078,670	1,092,315	1,104,095	1,109,735	1,183,155	1,356,420
\multicolumn{11}{c}{Percent of Population}
\multicolumn{11}{c}{Total}
Ottawa	5.6	5.5	5.7	6.6	7.5	6.9	6.5	6.8	7.3	8.3
Ontario	5.5	5.5	5.9	6.7	6.6	6.3	6.2	6.6	7.2	8.2
Canada	5.6	5.4	5.7	6.5	6.5	6.5	6.5	6.5	6.9	8.0
\multicolumn{11}{c}{Males}
Ottawa	5.8	5.8	6.0	6.9	7.7	7.0	6.5	6.7	7.3	8.4
Ontario	5.8	5.8	6.3	7.1	6.9	6.4	6.1	6.5	7.2	8.3
Canada	5.9	5.6	6.0	6.8	6.8	6.6	6.5	6.5	7.0	8.0
\multicolumn{11}{c}{Females}
Ottawa	5.3	5.3	5.5	6.3	7.2	6.8	6.6	6.9	7.3	8.2
Ontario	5.2	5.3	5.6	6.4	6.4	6.3	6.3	6.7	7.2	8.2
Canada	5.4	5.2	5.5	6.2	6.3	6.4	6.5	6.5	6.9	7.9

Source: Statistics Canada. 2012. Census Profile. 2011 Census. Statistics Canada Catalogue no. 98-316-XWE. Ottawa. Released October 24 2012.
http://www12.statcan.gc.ca/census-recensement/2011/dp-pd/prof/index.cfm?Lang=E

Age Characteristics: 50 Years and Over, and Median Age

Area	50 to 54 Years	55 to 59 Years	60 to 64 Years	65 to 69 Years	70 to 74 Years	75 to 79 Years	80 to 84 Years	85 Years and Over	Median Age
\multicolumn{10}{c}{Number}
\multicolumn{10}{c}{Total}
Ottawa	69,010	57,735	50,410	35,865	26,810	21,275	16,305	16,335	39.2
Ontario	1,006,140	864,620	765,655	563,485	440,780	356,150	271,510	246,400	40.4
Canada	2,658,965	2,340,635	2,052,670	1,521,715	1,153,065	922,700	702,070	645,515	40.6
\multicolumn{10}{c}{Males}
Ottawa	33,595	28,030	24,385	16,935	12,360	9,545	6,600	5,185	38.2
Ontario	492,560	418,755	370,370	270,875	206,350	161,345	113,620	80,925	39.4
Canada	1,309,030	1,147,300	1,002,690	738,010	543,435	417,945	291,085	208,300	39.6
\multicolumn{10}{c}{Females}
Ottawa	35,415	29,705	26,025	18,925	14,445	11,725	9,710	11,150	40.0
Ontario	513,580	445,865	395,275	292,610	234,435	194,805	157,890	165,475	41.3
Canada	1,349,940	1,193,335	1,049,985	783,705	609,630	504,755	410,985	437,215	41.5
\multicolumn{10}{c}{Percent of Population}
\multicolumn{10}{c}{Total}
Ottawa	7.8	6.5	5.7	4.1	3.0	2.4	1.8	1.8	–
Ontario	7.8	6.7	6.0	4.4	3.4	2.8	2.1	1.9	–
Canada	7.9	7.0	6.1	4.5	3.4	2.8	2.1	1.9	–
\multicolumn{10}{c}{Males}
Ottawa	7.8	6.5	5.7	4.0	2.9	2.2	1.5	1.2	–
Ontario	7.9	6.7	5.9	4.3	3.3	2.6	1.8	1.3	–
Canada	8.0	7.0	6.1	4.5	3.3	2.5	1.8	1.3	–
\multicolumn{10}{c}{Females}
Ottawa	7.8	6.5	5.7	4.2	3.2	2.6	2.1	2.5	–
Ontario	7.8	6.8	6.0	4.4	3.6	3.0	2.4	2.5	–
Canada	7.9	7.0	6.2	4.6	3.6	3.0	2.4	2.6	–

Source: Statistics Canada. 2012. Census Profile. 2011 Census. Statistics Canada Catalogue no. 98-316-XWE. Ottawa. Released October 24 2012.
http://www12.statcan.gc.ca/census-recensement/2011/dp-pd/prof/index.cfm?Lang=E

Private Households by Household Size

Area	1 Person	2 Persons	3 Persons	4 Persons	5 Persons	6 or More Persons	Average Number of Persons in Private Households
			Households				
Ottawa	99,905	116,385	55,635	52,880	19,185	9,250	2.5
Ontario	1,230,975	1,584,415	803,030	783,925	310,860	174,305	2.6
Canada	3,673,310	4,544,820	2,081,900	1,903,300	724,405	392,885	2.5
			Percent of Households				
Ottawa	28.3	32.9	15.7	15.0	5.4	2.6	–
Ontario	25.2	32.4	16.4	16.0	6.4	3.6	–
Canada	27.6	34.1	15.6	14.3	5.4	2.9	–

Source: Statistics Canada. 2012. Census Profile. 2011 Census. Statistics Canada Catalogue no. 98-316-XWE. Ottawa. Released October 24 2012.
http://www12.statcan.gc.ca/census-recensement/2011/dp-pd/prof/index.cfm?Lang=E

Dwelling Type

Area	Single-detached House	Semi-detached House	Row House	Apartment: Building with Five or More Storeys	Apartment: Building with Fewer Than Five Storeys	Duplex Apartment	Movable Dwelling	Other Single-attached House
				Number				
Ottawa	151,495	19,305	72,540	65,495	36,190	6,850	935	440
Ontario	2,718,880	279,470	415,225	789,970	498,160	160,460	15,800	9,540
Canada	7,329,150	646,245	791,600	1,234,770	2,397,550	704,485	183,510	33,310
				Percent of Dwellings				
Ottawa	42.9	5.5	20.5	18.5	10.2	1.9	0.3	0.1
Ontario	55.6	5.7	8.5	16.2	10.2	3.3	0.3	0.2
Canada	55.0	4.9	5.9	9.3	18.0	5.3	1.4	0.3

Source: Statistics Canada. 2012. Census Profile. 2011 Census. Statistics Canada Catalogue no. 98-316-XWE. Ottawa. Released October 24 2012.
http://www12.statcan.gc.ca/census-recensement/2011/dp-pd/prof/index.cfm?Lang=E

Shelter Costs

		Owned Dwellings				Rented Dwellings		
Area	Number	Median Value[1] ($)	Average Value[1] ($)	Median Monthly Costs[2] ($)	Average Monthly Costs[2] ($)	Number	Median Monthly Costs[3] ($)	Average Monthly Costs[3] ($)
Ottawa	236,820	349,151	387,862	1,307	1,361	115,620	953	983
Ontario	3,446,650	300,862	367,428	1,163	1,284	1,385,535	892	926
Canada	9,013,410	280,552	345,182	978	1,141	4,060,385	784	848

Note: All figures cover non-farm, non-reserve private dwellings; (1) Refers to the dollar amount expected by the owner if the dwelling were to be sold; (2) Includes all shelter expenses paid by households that own their dwellings, such as the mortgage payment and the costs of electricity, heat, water and other municipal services, property taxes and condominium fees; (3) Includes all shelter expenses paid by households that rent their dwellings, such as the monthly rent and the costs of electricity, heat and municipal services.
Source: Statistics Canada. 2013. 2011 National Household Survey. Statistics Canada Catalogue no. 99-004-XWE. Ottawa. Released September 11, 2013.

Occupied Private Dwellings by Period of Construction

Area	1960 or Before	1961 to 1980	1981 to 1990	1991 to 2000	2001 to 2005	2006 to 2011
			Number			
Ottawa	69,470	114,260	66,270	43,200	29,935	30,105
Ontario	1,330,235	1,420,570	763,430	609,310	414,795	348,310
Canada	3,273,105	4,152,715	2,112,110	1,707,880	1,031,020	1,042,430
			Percent of Dwellings			
Ottawa	19.7	32.3	18.8	12.2	8.5	8.5
Ontario	27.2	29.1	15.6	12.5	8.5	7.1
Canada	24.6	31.2	15.9	12.8	7.7	7.8

Note: Figures cover non-farm, non-reserve private dwellings and includes data up to May 10, 2011.
Source: Statistics Canada. 2013. 2011 National Household Survey. Statistics Canada Catalogue no. 99-004-XWE. Ottawa. Released September 11, 2013.

PROFILES / Ottawa, Ontario

Educational Attainment

Area	No Certificate, Diploma or Degree	High School Diploma or Equivalent[1]	Apprenticeship or Trades Certificate or Diploma[2]	College, CÉGEP or Other Non-University Certificate or Diploma	University Certificate or Diploma Below the Bachelor Level[3]	Bachelor's Degree	University Certificate, Diploma or Degree Above Bachelor Level[4]
				Number			
				Total			
Ottawa	92,930	168,390	37,285	136,840	28,935	149,465	105,105
Ontario	1,954,520	2,801,805	771,140	2,070,875	427,150	1,515,075	933,100
Canada	5,485,400	6,968,935	2,950,685	4,970,020	1,200,130	3,634,425	2,049,930
				Males			
Ottawa	45,410	79,490	22,315	61,995	12,810	69,420	55,320
Ontario	957,040	1,337,055	520,390	894,235	193,355	692,345	470,290
Canada	2,742,875	3,305,415	1,928,970	2,118,430	513,235	1,643,080	1,043,350
				Females			
Ottawa	47,515	88,895	14,965	74,845	16,125	80,045	49,790
Ontario	997,475	1,464,755	250,750	1,176,640	233,790	822,730	462,805
Canada	2,742,520	3,663,515	1,021,715	2,851,595	686,890	1,991,345	1,006,585
				Percent of Population			
				Total			
Ottawa	12.9	23.4	5.2	19.0	4.0	20.8	14.6
Ontario	18.7	26.8	7.4	19.8	4.1	14.5	8.9
Canada	20.1	25.6	10.8	18.2	4.4	13.3	7.5
				Males			
Ottawa	13.1	22.9	6.4	17.9	3.7	20.0	16.0
Ontario	18.9	26.4	10.3	17.7	3.8	13.7	9.3
Canada	20.6	24.9	14.5	15.9	3.9	12.4	7.8
				Females			
Ottawa	12.8	23.9	4.0	20.1	4.3	21.5	13.4
Ontario	18.4	27.1	4.6	21.8	4.3	15.2	8.6
Canada	19.6	26.2	7.3	20.4	4.9	14.3	7.2

Note: Figures cover total population aged 15 years and over by highest certificate, diploma or degree; (1) Includes persons who have graduated from a secondary school or equivalent. It excludes persons with a postsecondary certificate, diploma or degree; (2) Includes Registered Apprenticeship certificates (including Certificate of Qualification, Journeyperson's designation) and other trades certificates or diplomas such as pre-employment or vocational certificates and diplomas from brief trade programs completed at community colleges, institutes of technology, vocational centres, and similar institutions; (3) Comparisons with other data sources suggest that the category 'University certificate or diploma below the bachelor's level' was over-reported in the NHS. This category likely includes some responses that are actually college certificates or diplomas, bachelor's degrees or other types of education (e.g., university transfer programs, bachelor's programs completed in other countries, incomplete bachelor's programs, non-university professional designations). We recommend users interpret the results for the 'University certificate or diploma below the bachelor's level' category with caution; (4) 'University certificate or diploma above bachelor level' includes the categories: 'Degree in medicine, dentistry, veterinary medicine or optometry,' 'Master's degree' and 'Earned doctorate.'
Source: Statistics Canada. 2013. 2011 National Household Survey. Statistics Canada Catalogue no. 99-004-XWE. Ottawa. Released September 11, 2013.

Household Income Distribution

Area	Less than $10,000	$10,000 to $19,999	$20,000 to $29,999	$30,000 to $39,999	$40,000 to $49,999	$50,000 to $59,999	$60,000 to $79,999	$80,000 to $99,999	$100,000 to $124,999	$125,000 to $149,999	$150,000 and Over
						Households					
Ottawa	12,765	22,040	20,830	23,000	25,030	26,170	47,625	41,660	41,695	29,735	62,690
Ontario	201,780	354,530	405,725	425,410	425,720	398,705	680,850	552,660	497,970	331,460	611,840
Canada	626,705	1,141,945	1,193,925	1,271,675	1,206,800	1,102,120	1,865,280	1,458,240	1,260,770	802,555	1,389,240
						Percent of Households					
Ottawa	3.6	6.2	5.9	6.5	7.1	7.4	13.5	11.8	11.8	8.4	17.7
Ontario	4.1	7.3	8.3	8.7	8.7	8.2	13.9	11.3	10.2	6.8	12.5
Canada	4.7	8.6	9.0	9.5	9.1	8.3	14.0	10.9	9.5	6.0	10.4

Note: Household income is the sum of the total incomes of all members of that household. Total income refers to monetary receipts from certain sources, before income taxes and deductions, during calendar year 2010.
Source: Statistics Canada. 2013. 2011 National Household Survey. Statistics Canada Catalogue no. 99-004-XWE. Ottawa. Released September 11, 2013.

Median and Average Household and Economic Family Income

Area	Median Household Income ($)	Average Household Income ($)	Median After-tax Household Income ($)	Average After-tax Household Income ($)	Median Economic Family Income ($)	Average Economic Family Income ($)	Median After-tax Economic Family Income ($)	Average After-tax Economic Family Income ($)
Ottawa	79,634	96,815	68,160	79,356	101,134	116,630	85,635	95,260
Ontario	66,358	85,772	58,717	71,523	80,987	100,152	71,128	83,322
Canada	61,072	79,102	54,089	66,149	76,511	94,125	67,044	78,517

Note: Figures cover household and economic familiy income in 2010. A household is defined as a person or a group of persons (other than foreign residents) who occupy the same private dwelling and do not have a usual place of residence elsewhere in Canada. Every person is a member of one and only one household. An economic family is defined as a group of two or more persons who live in the same dwelling and are related to each other by blood, marriage, common-law, adoption or a foster relationship. A couple may be of opposite or same sex.
Source: Statistics Canada. 2013. 2011 National Household Survey. Statistics Canada Catalogue no. 99-004-XWE. Ottawa. Released September 11, 2013.

PROFILES / Ottawa, Ontario

Individual Income Distribution

Area	Less than $10,000	$10,000 to $19,999	$20,000 to $29,999	$30,000 to $39,999	$40,000 to $49,999	$50,000 to $59,999	$60,000 to $79,999	$80,000 to $99,999	$100,000 to $124,999	$125,000 and Over
					Number					
					Total					
Ottawa	108,650	100,715	71,575	65,005	64,040	60,490	86,925	59,990	34,820	34,170
Ontario	1,780,355	1,748,060	1,361,710	1,136,730	980,790	746,360	964,280	574,710	293,865	330,285
Canada	4,492,040	4,835,710	3,670,020	3,180,360	2,603,520	1,921,650	2,437,440	1,302,045	693,580	782,135
					Males					
Ottawa	48,525	39,835	29,580	28,505	29,010	28,655	45,570	33,605	23,710	25,285
Ontario	781,095	669,815	580,990	535,255	491,125	407,005	569,205	341,160	201,125	244,500
Canada	1,936,365	1,864,880	1,588,260	1,522,190	1,333,510	1,079,780	1,473,145	823,720	492,905	599,905
					Females					
Ottawa	60,130	60,875	42,000	36,505	35,030	31,835	41,355	26,385	11,110	8,890
Ontario	999,265	1,078,245	780,720	601,475	489,665	339,360	395,075	233,550	92,740	85,790
Canada	2,555,675	2,970,825	2,081,760	1,658,170	1,270,010	841,870	964,300	478,330	200,680	182,230
					Percent of Population					
					Total					
Ottawa	15.8	14.7	10.4	9.5	9.3	8.8	12.7	8.7	5.1	5.0
Ontario	18.0	17.6	13.7	11.5	9.9	7.5	9.7	5.8	3.0	3.3
Canada	17.3	18.7	14.2	12.3	10.0	7.4	9.4	5.0	2.7	3.0
					Males					
Ottawa	14.6	12.0	8.9	8.6	8.7	8.6	13.7	10.1	7.1	7.6
Ontario	16.2	13.9	12.1	11.1	10.2	8.4	11.8	7.1	4.2	5.1
Canada	15.2	14.7	12.5	12.0	10.5	8.5	11.6	6.5	3.9	4.7
					Females					
Ottawa	17.0	17.2	11.9	10.3	9.9	9.0	11.7	7.5	3.1	2.5
Ontario	19.6	21.2	15.3	11.8	9.6	6.7	7.8	4.6	1.8	1.7
Canada	19.4	22.5	15.8	12.6	9.6	6.4	7.3	3.6	1.5	1.4

Note: Figures cover individuals aged 15 years and over with income. Income refers to monetary receipts from certain sources, before income taxes and deductions, during calendar year 2010.
Source: Statistics Canada. 2013. 2011 National Household Survey. Statistics Canada Catalogue no. 99-004-XWE. Ottawa. Released September 11, 2013.

Labour Force Status

Area	In the Labour Force - All	In the Labour Force - Employed	In the Labour Force - Unemployed	Not in the Labour Force
		Number		
		Total		
Ottawa	498,370	463,625	34,745	220,590
Ontario	6,864,990	6,297,005	567,985	3,608,685
Canada	17,990,080	16,595,035	1,395,045	9,269,445
		Males		
Ottawa	253,485	235,350	18,130	93,285
Ontario	3,542,030	3,249,165	292,865	1,522,690
Canada	9,388,570	8,634,310	754,255	3,906,785
		Females		
Ottawa	244,885	228,275	16,615	127,305
Ontario	3,322,955	3,047,840	275,120	2,085,990
Canada	8,601,515	7,960,725	640,790	5,362,660
		Percent of Labour Force		
		Total		
Ottawa	69.3	64.5	7.0	30.7
Ontario	65.5	60.1	8.3	34.5
Canada	66.0	60.9	7.8	34.0
		Males		
Ottawa	73.1	67.9	7.2	26.9
Ontario	69.9	64.2	8.3	30.1
Canada	70.6	64.9	8.0	29.4
		Females		
Ottawa	65.8	61.3	6.8	34.2
Ontario	61.4	56.3	8.3	38.6
Canada	61.6	57.0	7.4	38.4

Note: Figures are based on total population 15 years and over
Source: Statistics Canada. 2013. 2011 National Household Survey. Statistics Canada Catalogue no. 99-004-XWE. Ottawa. Released September 11, 2013.

Labour Force by Industry (NAICS Codes 11–52)

Area	Agriculture, forestry, fishing & hunting	Mining, quarrying, & oil & gas extraction	Utilities	Construction	Manufacturing	Wholesale Trade	Retail Trade	Transportation & warehousing	Information & cultural industries	Finance & insurance
					Number					
					Total					
Ottawa	2,305	400	1,560	21,165	17,320	13,160	48,670	14,375	13,775	16,865
Ontario	101,280	29,985	57,035	417,900	697,565	305,030	751,200	307,405	178,720	364,415
Canada	437,650	261,050	149,940	1,215,380	1,619,295	733,445	2,031,665	827,780	420,830	767,960
					Males					
Ottawa	1,540	305	1,175	18,580	12,420	9,560	24,105	10,580	8,225	7,475
Ontario	66,485	25,650	42,685	369,300	493,305	197,770	344,480	225,245	98,835	153,125
Canada	307,370	211,690	110,765	1,068,710	1,167,680	494,545	933,850	617,305	235,875	296,995
					Females					
Ottawa	760	95	385	2,590	4,900	3,605	24,565	3,790	5,545	9,385
Ontario	34,800	4,340	14,350	48,595	204,260	107,260	406,720	82,160	79,885	211,290
Canada	130,285	49,360	39,175	146,670	451,615	238,900	1,097,820	210,475	184,955	470,960
					Percent of Labour Force					
					Total					
Ottawa	0.5	0.1	0.3	4.3	3.5	2.7	10.0	2.9	2.8	3.5
Ontario	1.5	0.4	0.9	6.3	10.4	4.6	11.2	4.6	2.7	5.5
Canada	2.5	1.5	0.9	6.9	9.2	4.2	11.6	4.7	2.4	4.4
					Males					
Ottawa	0.6	0.1	0.5	7.5	5.0	3.9	9.7	4.3	3.3	3.0
Ontario	1.9	0.7	1.2	10.7	14.3	5.7	10.0	6.5	2.9	4.4
Canada	3.3	2.3	1.2	11.6	12.7	5.4	10.2	6.7	2.6	3.2
					Females					
Ottawa	0.3	0.0	0.2	1.1	2.0	1.5	10.2	1.6	2.3	3.9
Ontario	1.1	0.1	0.4	1.5	6.3	3.3	12.6	2.5	2.5	6.5
Canada	1.6	0.6	0.5	1.7	5.4	2.8	13.1	2.5	2.2	5.6

Note: Figures are based on total experienced labour force 15 years and over. Experienced labour force refers to persons who, during the week of Sunday, May 1 to Saturday, May 7, 2011, were employed and the unemployed who had last worked for pay or in self-employment in either 2010 or 2011.
Source: Statistics Canada. 2013. 2011 National Household Survey. Statistics Canada Catalogue no. 99-004-XWE. Ottawa. Released September 11, 2013.

Labour Force by Industry (NAICS Codes 53–91)

Area	Real estate & rental & leasing	Profess., scientific & tech. services	Mgmt of companies & enterprises	Admin. & support, waste mgmt & remed. services	Educational services	Health care & social assistance	Arts, entertain. & recreation	Accomm. & food services	Other services (except public admin.)	Public admin.
					Number					
					Total					
Ottawa	8,530	48,470	250	18,720	36,860	49,860	8,710	30,380	22,770	113,970
Ontario	133,980	511,020	6,525	309,630	499,690	692,130	144,065	417,675	296,340	458,665
Canada	321,895	1,240,850	17,460	728,330	1,301,435	1,949,650	363,405	1,130,750	807,800	1,261,050
					Males					
Ottawa	5,030	29,665	170	11,520	12,640	10,200	4,470	15,220	8,965	56,395
Ontario	72,835	281,420	3,540	172,475	162,765	120,165	75,035	177,240	133,795	236,655
Canada	179,090	688,625	9,380	411,250	424,915	349,430	188,270	469,990	372,940	652,510
					Females					
Ottawa	3,505	18,810	80	7,205	24,215	39,660	4,240	15,160	13,805	57,575
Ontario	61,145	229,600	2,990	137,155	336,925	571,965	69,030	240,430	162,550	222,015
Canada	142,805	552,225	8,075	317,085	876,515	1,600,220	175,135	660,760	434,865	608,535
					Percent of Labour Force					
					Total					
Ottawa	1.7	9.9	0.1	3.8	7.6	10.2	1.8	6.2	4.7	23.3
Ontario	2.0	7.6	0.1	4.6	7.5	10.4	2.2	6.3	4.4	6.9
Canada	1.8	7.1	0.1	4.1	7.4	11.1	2.1	6.4	4.6	7.2
					Males					
Ottawa	2.0	12.0	0.1	4.6	5.1	4.1	1.8	6.1	3.6	22.7
Ontario	2.1	8.2	0.1	5.0	4.7	3.5	2.2	5.1	3.9	6.9
Canada	1.9	7.5	0.1	4.5	4.6	3.8	2.0	5.1	4.1	7.1
					Females					
Ottawa	1.5	7.8	0.0	3.0	10.1	16.5	1.8	6.3	5.8	24.0
Ontario	1.9	7.1	0.1	4.2	10.4	17.7	2.1	7.4	5.0	6.9
Canada	1.7	6.6	0.1	3.8	10.4	19.1	2.1	7.9	5.2	7.2

Note: Figures are based on total experienced labour force 15 years and over. Experienced labour force refers to persons who, during the week of Sunday, May 1 to Saturday, May 7, 2011, were employed and the unemployed who had last worked for pay or in self-employment in either 2010 or 2011.
Source: Statistics Canada. 2013. 2011 National Household Survey. Statistics Canada Catalogue no. 99-004-XWE. Ottawa. Released September 11, 2013.

Occupation

Area	Mgmt	Business, Finance & Admin.	Natural/ Applied Sciences & Related	Health	Education, Law & Social, Community & Government Services	Art, Culture, Recreation & Sport	Sales & Service	Trades, Transport & Equip. Operators & Related	Natural Resources, Agri. & Related Production	Mfg & Utilities
					Number					
					Total					
Ottawa	61,200	94,835	62,020	28,820	76,930	18,195	101,610	34,895	3,990	5,620
Ontario	770,580	1,138,330	494,500	392,695	801,465	206,420	1,550,260	868,515	106,810	350,685
Canada	1,963,600	2,902,045	1,237,775	1,107,200	2,064,675	503,415	4,068,170	2,537,775	397,930	805,040
					Males					
Ottawa	36,775	31,885	46,575	6,860	28,585	7,800	49,740	32,755	3,205	4,050
Ontario	474,655	352,505	384,345	78,330	264,570	96,055	673,880	812,280	82,610	233,565
Canada	1,229,460	854,190	966,355	217,520	676,550	232,535	1,745,705	2,385,615	318,945	564,300
					Females					
Ottawa	24,430	62,950	15,440	21,960	48,345	10,395	51,870	2,140	780	1,575
Ontario	295,920	785,825	110,150	314,370	536,895	110,370	876,380	56,230	24,200	117,115
Canada	734,140	2,047,855	271,415	889,675	1,388,130	270,875	2,322,465	152,165	78,980	240,740
					Percent of Labour Force					
					Total					
Ottawa	12.5	19.4	12.7	5.9	15.8	3.7	20.8	7.1	0.8	1.2
Ontario	11.5	17.0	7.4	5.9	12.0	3.1	23.2	13.0	1.6	5.2
Canada	11.2	16.5	7.0	6.3	11.7	2.9	23.1	14.4	2.3	4.6
					Males					
Ottawa	14.8	12.8	18.8	2.8	11.5	3.1	20.0	13.2	1.3	1.6
Ontario	13.7	10.2	11.1	2.3	7.7	2.8	19.5	23.5	2.4	6.8
Canada	13.4	9.3	10.5	2.4	7.4	2.5	19.0	26.0	3.5	6.1
					Females					
Ottawa	10.2	26.2	6.4	9.2	20.2	4.3	21.6	0.9	0.3	0.7
Ontario	9.2	24.3	3.4	9.7	16.6	3.4	27.2	1.7	0.7	3.6
Canada	8.7	24.4	3.2	10.6	16.5	3.2	27.7	1.8	0.9	2.9

Note: Figures are based on total experienced labour force 15 years and over
Source: Statistics Canada. 2013. 2011 National Household Survey. Statistics Canada Catalogue no. 99-004-XWE. Ottawa. Released September 11, 2013.

Place of Work Status

Area	Worked at Home	Worked Outside Canada	No Fixed Workplace Address	Worked at Usual Place
		Number		
		Total		
Ottawa	29,625	2,025	37,810	394,165
Ontario	423,790	31,390	670,835	5,170,980
Canada	1,142,640	66,460	1,868,245	13,517,690
		Males		
Ottawa	14,765	1,365	26,720	192,510
Ontario	216,900	21,150	486,560	2,524,555
Canada	582,150	47,355	1,400,485	6,604,325
		Females		
Ottawa	14,860	660	11,085	201,665
Ontario	206,895	10,240	184,275	2,646,420
Canada	560,490	19,100	467,760	6,913,370
		Percent of Labour Force		
		Total		
Ottawa	6.4	0.4	8.2	85.0
Ontario	6.7	0.5	10.7	82.1
Canada	6.9	0.4	11.3	81.5
		Males		
Ottawa	6.3	0.6	11.4	81.8
Ontario	6.7	0.7	15.0	77.7
Canada	6.7	0.5	16.2	76.5
		Females		
Ottawa	6.5	0.3	4.9	88.3
Ontario	6.8	0.3	6.0	86.8
Canada	7.0	0.2	5.9	86.8

Note: Figures are based on total employed labour force 15 years and over.
Source: Statistics Canada. 2013. 2011 National Household Survey. Statistics Canada Catalogue no. 99-004-XWE. Ottawa. Released September 11, 2013.

Mode of Transportation to Work

Area	Car; Truck; Van; as Driver	Car; Truck; Van; as Passenger	Public Transit	Walked	Bicycled	All Other Modes
			Number			
			Total			
Ottawa	260,660	27,570	97,125	31,345	10,800	4,470
Ontario	4,235,315	357,110	818,270	299,095	69,885	62,145
Canada	11,393,140	867,050	1,851,525	880,815	201,780	191,625
			Males			
Ottawa	143,455	8,510	43,175	14,950	7,070	2,065
Ontario	2,316,680	143,410	340,995	131,765	47,635	30,635
Canada	6,238,835	349,530	788,290	387,580	135,840	104,725
			Females			
Ottawa	117,205	19,055	53,955	16,395	3,725	2,405
Ontario	1,918,640	213,700	477,275	167,325	22,250	31,515
Canada	5,154,305	517,520	1,063,235	493,230	65,940	86,900
			Percent of Labour Force			
			Total			
Ottawa	60.3	6.4	22.5	7.3	2.5	1.0
Ontario	72.5	6.1	14.0	5.1	1.2	1.1
Canada	74.0	5.6	12.0	5.7	1.3	1.2
			Males			
Ottawa	65.4	3.9	19.7	6.8	3.2	0.9
Ontario	76.9	4.8	11.3	4.4	1.6	1.0
Canada	77.9	4.4	9.8	4.8	1.7	1.3
			Females			
Ottawa	55.1	9.0	25.4	7.7	1.8	1.1
Ontario	67.8	7.5	16.9	5.9	0.8	1.1
Canada	69.8	7.0	14.4	6.7	0.9	1.2

Note: Figures are based on total employed labour force 15 years and over.
Source: Statistics Canada. 2013. 2011 National Household Survey. Statistics Canada Catalogue no. 99-004-XWE. Ottawa. Released September 11, 2013.

Visible Minority Population Characteristics

Area	Total Minority	South Asian[1]	Chinese	Black	Filipino	Latin American	Arab	SE Asian[2]	West Asian[3]	Korean	Japanese	Multiple[4]
						Number						
						Total						
Ottawa	205,155	33,805	34,855	49,650	10,530	10,255	32,340	13,650	7,590	2,250	2,005	6,100
Ontario	3,279,565	965,990	629,140	539,205	275,380	172,560	151,645	137,875	122,530	78,290	29,085	96,735
Canada	6,264,750	1,567,400	1,324,750	945,665	619,310	381,280	380,620	312,075	206,840	161,130	87,270	171,935
						Males						
Ottawa	98,360	17,070	16,395	22,765	4,040	4,875	16,815	6,490	3,940	1,135	875	2,950
Ontario	1,582,480	484,355	301,575	251,295	116,825	83,205	79,620	67,645	62,515	38,045	13,345	46,765
Canada	3,043,010	790,755	632,325	453,005	268,885	186,355	203,485	154,035	105,620	77,165	38,270	83,335
						Females						
Ottawa	106,795	16,730	18,460	26,880	6,490	5,375	15,530	7,155	3,645	1,110	1,135	3,150
Ontario	1,697,085	481,635	327,570	287,915	158,555	89,360	72,025	70,230	60,010	40,250	15,740	49,970
Canada	3,221,745	776,650	692,420	492,660	350,425	194,925	177,140	158,045	101,220	83,965	48,990	88,600
						Percent of Population						
						Total						
Ottawa	23.7	3.9	4.0	5.7	1.2	1.2	3.7	1.6	0.9	0.3	0.2	0.7
Ontario	25.9	7.6	5.0	4.3	2.2	1.4	1.2	1.1	1.0	0.6	0.2	0.8
Canada	19.1	4.8	4.0	2.9	1.9	1.2	1.2	0.9	0.6	0.5	0.3	0.5
						Males						
Ottawa	23.3	4.1	3.9	5.4	1.0	1.2	4.0	1.5	0.9	0.3	0.2	0.7
Ontario	25.6	7.8	4.9	4.1	1.9	1.3	1.3	1.1	1.0	0.6	0.2	0.8
Canada	18.8	4.9	3.9	2.8	1.7	1.2	1.3	1.0	0.7	0.5	0.2	0.5
						Females						
Ottawa	24.0	3.8	4.1	6.0	1.5	1.2	3.5	1.6	0.8	0.2	0.3	0.7
Ontario	26.2	7.4	5.1	4.4	2.5	1.4	1.1	1.1	0.9	0.6	0.2	0.8
Canada	19.3	4.7	4.1	3.0	2.1	1.2	1.1	0.9	0.6	0.5	0.3	0.5

Note: The Employment Equity Act defines visible minorities as 'persons, other than Aboriginal peoples, who are non-Caucasian in race or non-white in colour';
(1) Includes 'East Indian,' 'Pakistani,' 'Sri Lankan,' etc.; (2) Includes 'Vietnamese,' 'Cambodian,' 'Malaysian,' 'Laotian,' etc.; (3) Includes 'Iranian,' 'Afghan,' etc.; (4) Includes respondents who reported more than one visible minority group by checking two or more mark-in circles, e.g., 'Black' and 'South Asian.'
Source: Statistics Canada. 2013. 2011 National Household Survey. Statistics Canada Catalogue no. 99-004-XWE. Ottawa. Released September 11, 2013.

PROFILES / Ottawa, Ontario

Aboriginal Population

Area	Aboriginal Identity[1]	First Nations (North American Indian) Single Identity[2]	Métis Single Identity	Inuk (Inuit) Single Identity	Multiple Aboriginal Identities[3]	Aboriginal Identities Not Included Elsewhere
Number						
Total						
Ottawa	18,180	10,310	6,405	705	175	585
Ontario	301,430	201,100	86,020	3,355	2,910	8,040
Canada	1,400,685	851,560	451,795	59,440	11,415	26,475
Males						
Ottawa	8,425	4,745	3,080	270	70	265
Ontario	145,020	96,620	41,755	1,475	1,420	3,750
Canada	682,190	411,785	223,335	29,495	5,525	12,055
Females						
Ottawa	9,750	5,565	3,325	440	110	315
Ontario	156,410	104,485	44,260	1,880	1,490	4,295
Canada	718,500	439,775	228,460	29,950	5,890	14,420
Percent of Population						
Total						
Ottawa	2.1	1.2	0.7	0.1	0.0	0.1
Ontario	2.4	1.6	0.7	0.0	0.0	0.1
Canada	4.3	2.6	1.4	0.2	0.0	0.1
Males						
Ottawa	2.0	1.1	0.7	0.1	0.0	0.1
Ontario	2.3	1.6	0.7	0.0	0.0	0.1
Canada	4.2	2.5	1.4	0.2	0.0	0.1
Females						
Ottawa	2.2	1.2	0.7	0.1	0.0	0.1
Ontario	2.4	1.6	0.7	0.0	0.0	0.1
Canada	4.3	2.6	1.4	0.2	0.0	0.1

Note: (1) Includes persons who reported being an Aboriginal person, that is, First Nations (North American Indian), Métis or Inuk (Inuit) and/or those who reported Registered or Treaty Indian status, that is registered under the Indian Act of Canada, and/or those who reported membership in a First Nation or Indian band. Aboriginal peoples of Canada are defined in the Constitution Act, 1982, section 35-2 as including the Indian, Inuit and Métis peoples of Canada; (2) Users should be aware that the estimates associated with this variable are more affected than most by the incomplete enumeration of certain Indian reserves and Indian settlements in the National Household Survey (NHS); (3) Includes persons who reported being any two or all three of the following: First Nations (North American Indian), Métis or Inuk (Inuit).
Source: Statistics Canada. 2013. 2011 National Household Survey. Statistics Canada Catalogue no. 99-004-XWE. Ottawa. Released September 11, 2013.

Ethnic Origin

Area	North American Aboriginal	Other North American	European	Caribbean	Latin, Central and South American	African	Asian	Oceania
Number								
Total								
Ottawa	35,155	248,810	580,415	22,285	14,940	43,980	156,040	1,660
Ontario	441,395	3,059,480	8,231,410	396,485	271,545	331,460	2,604,595	19,410
Canada	1,836,035	11,070,455	20,157,965	627,590	544,375	766,735	5,011,225	74,875
Males								
Ottawa	16,665	120,800	282,530	10,035	6,915	20,780	75,660	850
Ontario	210,490	1,507,105	4,019,885	181,805	130,035	160,940	1,265,540	9,855
Canada	885,675	5,462,685	9,913,150	291,640	264,635	387,360	2,435,540	37,490
Females								
Ottawa	18,495	128,010	297,885	12,255	8,020	23,200	80,385	815
Ontario	230,905	1,552,380	4,211,525	214,675	141,510	170,515	1,339,050	9,555
Canada	950,360	5,607,770	10,244,820	335,945	279,740	379,380	2,575,680	37,385
Percent of Population								
Total								
Ottawa	4.1	28.7	66.9	2.6	1.7	5.1	18.0	0.2
Ontario	3.5	24.2	65.1	3.1	2.1	2.6	20.6	0.2
Canada	5.6	33.7	61.4	1.9	1.7	2.3	15.3	0.2
Males								
Ottawa	4.0	28.7	67.1	2.4	1.6	4.9	18.0	0.2
Ontario	3.4	24.4	65.0	2.9	2.1	2.6	20.5	0.2
Canada	5.5	33.8	61.3	1.8	1.6	2.4	15.1	0.2
Females								
Ottawa	4.1	28.7	66.8	2.7	1.8	5.2	18.0	0.2
Ontario	3.6	24.0	65.1	3.3	2.2	2.6	20.7	0.1
Canada	5.7	33.6	61.4	2.0	1.7	2.3	15.4	0.2

Note: The sum of the ethnic groups in this table is greater than the total population estimate because a person may report more than one ethnic origin in the NHS.
Source: Statistics Canada. 2013. 2011 National Household Survey. Statistics Canada Catalogue no. 99-004-XWE. Ottawa. Released September 11, 2013.

Religion

Area	Buddhist	Christian	Hindu	Jewish	Muslim	Sikh	Traditional (Aboriginal) Spirituality	Other Religions	No Religious Affiliation
				Number Total					
Ottawa	11,705	567,485	11,965	10,615	58,415	3,410	310	5,255	197,930
Ontario	163,750	8,167,295	366,720	195,540	581,950	179,765	15,905	53,080	2,927,790
Canada	366,830	22,102,745	497,965	329,495	1,053,945	454,965	64,935	130,835	7,850,605
				Males					
Ottawa	5,370	263,940	6,165	5,400	29,460	1,855	125	2,235	106,770
Ontario	75,355	3,839,925	183,580	95,795	293,925	90,515	7,600	23,555	1,571,195
Canada	168,465	10,497,775	250,435	161,265	540,555	229,435	31,805	57,745	4,225,645
				Females					
Ottawa	6,330	303,545	5,805	5,210	28,955	1,555	190	3,025	91,160
Ontario	88,395	4,327,365	183,140	99,740	288,025	89,250	8,310	29,525	1,356,600
Canada	198,365	11,604,975	247,525	168,235	513,395	225,530	33,135	73,090	3,624,965
				Percent of Population Total					
Ottawa	1.3	65.4	1.4	1.2	6.7	0.4	0.0	0.6	22.8
Ontario	1.3	64.6	2.9	1.5	4.6	1.4	0.1	0.4	23.1
Canada	1.1	67.3	1.5	1.0	3.2	1.4	0.2	0.4	23.9
				Males					
Ottawa	1.3	62.6	1.5	1.3	7.0	0.4	0.0	0.5	25.3
Ontario	1.2	62.1	3.0	1.5	4.8	1.5	0.1	0.4	25.4
Canada	1.0	64.9	1.5	1.0	3.3	1.4	0.2	0.4	26.1
				Females					
Ottawa	1.4	68.1	1.3	1.2	6.5	0.3	0.0	0.7	20.4
Ontario	1.4	66.9	2.8	1.5	4.5	1.4	0.1	0.5	21.0
Canada	1.2	69.5	1.5	1.0	3.1	1.4	0.2	0.4	21.7

Note: Religion refers to the person's self-identification as having a connection or affiliation with any religious denomination, group, body, sect, cult or other religiously defined community or system of belief. Religion is not limited to formal membership in a religious organization or group. Persons without a religious connection or affiliation can self-identify as atheist, agnostic or humanist, or can provide another applicable response.
Source: Statistics Canada. 2013. 2011 National Household Survey. Statistics Canada Catalogue no. 99-004-XWE. Ottawa. Released September 11, 2013.

Religion—Christian Denominations

Area	Anglican	Baptist	Catholic	Christian Orthodox	Lutheran	Pentecostal	Presbyterian	United Church	Other Christian
				Number Total					
Ottawa	55,955	10,295	333,625	17,475	9,025	9,785	12,950	53,690	64,680
Ontario	774,560	244,650	3,976,610	297,710	163,460	213,945	319,585	952,465	1,224,300
Canada	1,631,845	635,840	12,810,705	550,690	478,185	478,705	472,385	2,007,610	3,036,780
				Males					
Ottawa	25,715	4,630	156,510	7,940	4,200	4,235	6,250	24,500	29,960
Ontario	355,175	112,285	1,895,940	145,825	75,225	94,955	148,535	435,255	576,730
Canada	752,945	293,905	6,167,290	270,205	221,525	217,850	218,955	912,545	1,442,550
				Females					
Ottawa	30,240	5,665	177,115	9,535	4,825	5,550	6,695	29,200	34,725
Ontario	419,390	132,370	2,080,665	151,885	88,230	118,990	171,050	517,210	647,570
Canada	878,900	341,940	6,643,415	280,485	256,660	260,850	253,430	1,095,065	1,594,230
				Percent of Population Total					
Ottawa	6.5	1.2	38.5	2.0	1.0	1.1	1.5	6.2	7.5
Ontario	6.1	1.9	31.4	2.4	1.3	1.7	2.5	7.5	9.7
Canada	5.0	1.9	39.0	1.7	1.5	1.5	1.4	6.1	9.2
				Males					
Ottawa	6.1	1.1	37.1	1.9	1.0	1.0	1.5	5.8	7.1
Ontario	5.7	1.8	30.7	2.4	1.2	1.5	2.4	7.0	9.3
Canada	4.7	1.8	38.2	1.7	1.4	1.3	1.4	5.6	8.9
				Females					
Ottawa	6.8	1.3	39.7	2.1	1.1	1.2	1.5	6.6	7.8
Ontario	6.5	2.0	32.2	2.3	1.4	1.8	2.6	8.0	10.0
Canada	5.3	2.0	39.8	1.7	1.5	1.6	1.5	6.6	9.6

Note: Religion refers to the person's self-identification as having a connection or affiliation with any religious denomination, group, body, sect, cult or other religiously defined community or system of belief. Religion is not limited to formal membership in a religious organization or group. Persons without a religious connection or affiliation can self-identify as atheist, agnostic or humanist, or can provide another applicable response.
Source: Statistics Canada. 2013. 2011 National Household Survey. Statistics Canada Catalogue no. 99-004-XWE. Ottawa. Released September 11, 2013.

PROFILES / Ottawa, Ontario

Immigrant Status and Period of Immigration

Area	Non-Immigrants[1]	Immigrants All	Before 1971	1971 to 1980	1981 to 1990	1991 to 2000	2001 to 2005	2006 to 2011	Non-Permanent Residents[3]
Number — Total									
Ottawa	653,135	202,605	35,145	23,350	31,895	53,015	26,720	32,485	11,340
Ontario	8,906,000	3,611,365	723,030	464,380	538,285	866,220	518,405	501,060	134,425
Canada	25,720,175	6,775,765	1,261,055	870,775	949,890	1,539,050	992,070	1,162,915	356,385
Males									
Ottawa	321,055	94,710	16,950	11,295	15,150	24,670	11,670	14,975	5,550
Ontario	4,410,240	1,706,385	341,820	217,990	258,095	408,270	245,850	234,360	64,825
Canada	12,753,235	3,231,370	605,430	416,670	454,570	724,905	474,545	555,245	178,515
Females									
Ottawa	332,085	107,895	18,190	12,050	16,745	28,350	15,050	17,515	5,790
Ontario	4,495,765	1,904,985	381,210	246,390	280,190	457,950	272,550	266,695	69,600
Canada	12,966,935	3,544,400	655,625	454,105	495,325	814,145	517,530	607,670	177,870
Percent of Population — Total									
Ottawa	75.3	23.4	4.1	2.7	3.7	6.1	3.1	3.7	1.3
Ontario	70.4	28.5	5.7	3.7	4.3	6.8	4.1	4.0	1.1
Canada	78.3	20.6	3.8	2.7	2.9	4.7	3.0	3.5	1.1
Males									
Ottawa	76.2	22.5	4.0	2.7	3.6	5.9	2.8	3.6	1.3
Ontario	71.3	27.6	5.5	3.5	4.2	6.6	4.0	3.8	1.0
Canada	78.9	20.0	3.7	2.6	2.8	4.5	2.9	3.4	1.1
Females									
Ottawa	74.5	24.2	4.1	2.7	3.8	6.4	3.4	3.9	1.3
Ontario	69.5	29.4	5.9	3.8	4.3	7.1	4.2	4.1	1.1
Canada	77.7	21.2	3.9	2.7	3.0	4.9	3.1	3.6	1.1

Note: (1) Non-immigrant refers to a person who is a Canadian citizen by birth; (2) Immigrant refers to a person who is or has ever been a landed immigrant/permanent resident. This person has been granted the right to live in Canada permanently by immigration authorities. Some immigrants have resided in Canada for a number of years, while others have arrived recently. Some immigrants are Canadian citizens, while others are not. Most immigrants are born outside Canada, but a small number are born in Canada. In the 2011 National Household Survey, 'Immigrants' includes immigrants who landed in Canada prior to May 10, 2011; (3) Non-permanent resident refers to a person from another country who has a work or study permit, or who is a refugee claimant, and any non-Canadian-born family member living in Canada with them.
Source: Statistics Canada. 2013. 2011 National Household Survey. Statistics Canada Catalogue no. 99-004-XWE. Ottawa. Released September 11, 2013.

Mother Tongue

Area	English	French	Non-official Language	English & French	English & Non-official Language	French & Non-official Language	English, French & Non-official Language
Number — Total							
Ottawa	544,045	123,925	178,120	10,755	11,090	2,950	1,565
Ontario	8,677,040	493,300	3,264,435	46,605	219,425	13,645	7,615
Canada	18,858,980	7,054,975	6,567,680	144,685	396,330	74,430	24,095
Males							
Ottawa	270,365	56,845	84,250	5,085	5,430	1,330	695
Ontario	4,276,970	232,785	1,562,190	21,805	106,790	6,285	3,495
Canada	9,345,225	3,452,380	3,157,785	69,975	192,000	36,535	11,965
Females							
Ottawa	273,680	67,075	93,875	5,665	5,660	1,620	870
Ontario	4,400,065	260,510	1,702,240	24,795	112,635	7,365	4,115
Canada	9,513,750	3,602,590	3,409,895	74,710	204,330	37,890	12,130
Percent of Population — Total							
Ottawa	62.4	14.2	20.4	1.2	1.3	0.3	0.2
Ontario	68.2	3.9	25.7	0.4	1.7	0.1	0.1
Canada	56.9	21.3	19.8	0.4	1.2	0.2	0.1
Males							
Ottawa	63.8	13.4	19.9	1.2	1.3	0.3	0.2
Ontario	68.9	3.7	25.2	0.4	1.7	0.1	0.1
Canada	57.5	21.2	19.4	0.4	1.2	0.2	0.1
Females							
Ottawa	61.0	15.0	20.9	1.3	1.3	0.4	0.2
Ontario	67.6	4.0	26.1	0.4	1.7	0.1	0.1
Canada	56.4	21.4	20.2	0.4	1.2	0.2	0.1

Note: Figures cover total population excluding institutional residents.
Source: Statistics Canada. 2012. Census Profile. 2011 Census. Statistics Canada Catalogue no. 98-316-XWE. Ottawa. Released October 24 2012.
http://www12.statcan.gc.ca/census-recensement/2011/dp-pd/prof/index.cfm?Lang=E

Language Spoken Most Often at Home

Area	English	French	Non-official Language	English & French	English & Non-official Language	French & Non-official Language	English, French & Non-official Language
			Number				
			Total				
Ottawa	652,455	86,035	91,990	10,775	25,800	2,405	2,985
Ontario	10,044,810	284,115	1,827,870	37,955	509,105	6,370	11,845
Canada	21,457,075	6,827,865	3,673,865	131,205	875,135	109,700	46,330
			Males				
Ottawa	321,710	38,940	43,445	4,930	12,580	1,025	1,370
Ontario	4,930,610	133,495	872,860	17,250	248,050	2,855	5,225
Canada	10,585,620	3,348,235	1,767,310	63,475	425,370	53,010	22,845
			Females				
Ottawa	330,745	47,095	48,545	5,845	13,220	1,375	1,620
Ontario	5,114,200	150,620	955,010	20,705	261,055	3,520	6,620
Canada	10,871,455	3,479,625	1,906,555	67,730	449,765	56,690	23,485
			Percent of Population				
			Total				
Ottawa	74.8	9.9	10.5	1.2	3.0	0.3	0.3
Ontario	79.0	2.2	14.4	0.3	4.0	0.1	0.1
Canada	64.8	20.6	11.1	0.4	2.6	0.3	0.1
			Males				
Ottawa	75.9	9.2	10.2	1.2	3.0	0.2	0.3
Ontario	79.4	2.1	14.1	0.3	4.0	0.0	0.1
Canada	65.1	20.6	10.9	0.4	2.6	0.3	0.1
			Females				
Ottawa	73.8	10.5	10.8	1.3	2.9	0.3	0.4
Ontario	78.5	2.3	14.7	0.3	4.0	0.1	0.1
Canada	64.5	20.6	11.3	0.4	2.7	0.3	0.1

Note: Figures cover total population excluding institutional residents.
Source: Statistics Canada. 2012. Census Profile. 2011 Census. Statistics Canada Catalogue no. 98-316-XWE. Ottawa. Released October 24 2012.
http://www12.statcan.gc.ca/census-recensement/2011/dp-pd/prof/index.cfm?Lang=E

Knowledge of Official Languages

Area	English Only	French Only	English & French	Neither English nor French
		Number		
		Total		
Ottawa	522,980	12,915	324,690	11,860
Ontario	10,984,360	42,980	1,395,805	298,920
Canada	22,564,665	4,165,015	5,795,570	595,920
		Males		
Ottawa	264,790	5,245	149,495	4,470
Ontario	5,445,050	18,805	627,725	118,765
Canada	11,222,185	1,925,340	2,876,560	241,790
		Females		
Ottawa	258,195	7,675	175,195	7,390
Ontario	5,539,310	24,175	768,085	180,155
Canada	11,342,485	2,239,680	2,919,005	354,135
		Percent of Population		
		Total		
Ottawa	59.9	1.5	37.2	1.4
Ontario	86.3	0.3	11.0	2.3
Canada	68.1	12.6	17.5	1.8
		Males		
Ottawa	62.5	1.2	35.3	1.1
Ontario	87.7	0.3	10.1	1.9
Canada	69.0	11.8	17.7	1.5
		Females		
Ottawa	57.6	1.7	39.1	1.6
Ontario	85.1	0.4	11.8	2.8
Canada	67.3	13.3	17.3	2.1

Note: Figures cover total population excluding institutional residents.
Source: Statistics Canada. 2012. Census Profile. 2011 Census. Statistics Canada Catalogue no. 98-316-XWE. Ottawa. Released October 24 2012.
http://www12.statcan.gc.ca/census-recensement/2011/dp-pd/prof/index.cfm?Lang=E

Québec, Québec

Background

Québec City, Québec, is a seaport located on the north shore of the St. Lawrence where the river meets with the Rivière Saint-Charles. The fortified city is situated 98 metres above a narrow one-kilometre stretch of the St. Lawrence. Québec City, which is the province's capital, was once called the "Gibraltar of North America" because of its fortified, strategic position. Québec is a derivative of the Algonquin word *kebek* meaning "narrowing of the river."

Samuel de Champlain established a fur-trading post in the region in 1608. At the base of Cape Diamond and within the settlement's fortifications, French religious, political and commercial institutions thrived. New France became a subject of the British Crown when Québec City fell to the English in 1759.

Today, Québec City is one of the oldest cities in North America and the only fortified city north of Mexico. Québec City's historic Old Town was declared a UNESCO World Heritage Site in 1985. The city showcases more than 400 years of history and is considered the cradle of French civilization in North America. The Plains of Abraham (Battlefields Park) is branded as where Canada was born; it was the site of clashes between French and British soldiers between 1759 and 1760. The city's towering Fairmont Le Château Frontenac is a National Historic Site and the first of the grand railway hotels built in the late 19th and early 20th centuries.

The majority of employment is concentrated in public administration, defence, commerce, transport and tourism. Approximately 10% of jobs are in manufacturing products such as pulp and paper, processed food, metal/wood products and chemicals.

The largest winter carnival in the world has been held in Québec City since 1894. The Québec Winter Carnival happens every February, runs for 17 days and generates more than $31 million per winter season.

Québec City has summer highs of plus 23.53 degrees Celsius, winter lows of minus 15.67 degrees Celsius, and an average rainfall just over 923 mm per year.

Rankings

- *Travel + Leisure Magazine* ranked Québec City #2 among Canadian destinations and one of the Top 10 North American destinations for tourists. Criteria in 2012: sights; culture and the arts; restaurants and food; people; shopping; and value. Two of the city's hotels, Auberge St-Antoine and the Fairmont Le Château, ranked #1 and #4 in the Top City Hotel (Canada) category. Vancouver ranked #1 among Canadian destinations. *Travel + Leisure, "World's Best Awards: Top 10 Cities, U.S. and Canada," July 6, 2012*
- Québec City was identified as having the most National Historic Sites of any city in Canada. Parks Canada administers six of the city's 30 sites, including Artillery Park, Fortification of Québec and Maillou House. The Historic District of Old Québec is one of 15 World Heritage Sites in Canada. *"The Historic District of Old-Québec," www.pc.gc.ca, accessed Nov. 8, 2012.*
- Québec City was cited as one of Canada's "Weather Winners" by Environment Canada. Out of 100 major Canadian cities, Québec City ranked #1 for greatest average snow depth in January (57.84 cm). The category was dominated by cities in the province of Québec; of the Top 10, six were in Québec. *Environment Canada, Canadian Cities are Weather Winners!, May 29, 2012*

PROFILES / Québec, Québec

Population Growth and Density

Area	Population in 2001	Population in 2006	Population in 2011	Population Change 2001–2006	Population Change 2006–2011	Land Area (sq. km)	Population Density per sq. km
Québec	476,330	491,142	516,622	3.1	5.2	454.10	1,137.7
Québec	7,237,479	7,546,131	7,903,001	4.3	4.7	1,356,547.02	5.8
Canada	30,007,094	31,612,897	33,476,688	5.4	5.9	8,965,121.42	3.7

Source: Statistics Canada. 2012. Census Profile. 2011 Census. Statistics Canada Catalogue no. 98-316-XWE. Ottawa. Released October 24 2012.
http://www12.statcan.gc.ca/census-recensement/2011/dp-pd/prof/index.cfm?Lang=E;
Statistics Canada 2007. 2006 Community Profiles. 2006 Census. Statistics Canada Catalogue no. 92-591-XWE. Ottawa. Released March 13 2007.
http://www12.statcan.ca/census-recensement/2006/dp-pd/prof/92-591/index.cfm?Lang=E

Gender

Area	Males	Females
Number		
Québec	248,620	268,005
Québec	3,875,860	4,027,140
Canada	16,414,225	17,062,460
Percent of Population		
Québec	48.1	51.9
Québec	49.0	51.0
Canada	49.0	51.0

Source: Statistics Canada. 2012. Census Profile. 2011 Census. Statistics Canada
Catalogue no. 98-316-XWE. Ottawa. Released October 24 2012.
http://www12.statcan.gc.ca/census-recensement/2011/dp-pd/prof/index.cfm?Lang=E

Marital Status

Area	Married[1]	Living Common-law	Single[2]	Separated	Divorced	Widowed
Number						
Total						
Québec	131,990	106,930	142,865	6,930	32,875	27,480
Québec	2,353,770	1,391,550	1,942,090	105,195	463,830	387,945
Canada	12,941,960	3,142,525	7,816,045	698,240	1,686,035	1,584,530
Males						
Québec	65,985	53,715	74,240	2,955	12,295	5,090
Québec	1,177,720	697,695	1,045,540	46,465	188,265	77,430
Canada	6,470,300	1,575,495	4,206,320	299,655	680,415	310,940
Females						
Québec	66,000	53,215	68,620	3,980	20,585	22,395
Québec	1,176,050	693,850	896,545	58,720	275,565	310,515
Canada	6,471,660	1,567,035	3,609,730	398,585	1,005,620	1,273,590
Percent of Population						
Total						
Québec	29.4	23.8	31.8	1.5	7.3	6.1
Québec	35.4	20.9	29.2	1.6	7.0	5.8
Canada	46.4	11.3	28.0	2.5	6.0	5.7
Males						
Québec	30.8	25.1	34.6	1.4	5.7	2.4
Québec	36.4	21.6	32.3	1.4	5.8	2.4
Canada	47.8	11.6	31.1	2.2	5.0	2.3
Females						
Québec	28.1	22.7	29.2	1.7	8.8	9.5
Québec	34.5	20.3	26.3	1.7	8.1	9.1
Canada	45.2	10.9	25.2	2.8	7.0	8.9

Note: (1) and not separated, (2) never legally married
Source: Statistics Canada. 2012. Census Profile. 2011 Census. Statistics Canada Catalogue no. 98-316-XWE. Ottawa. Released October 24 2012.
http://www12.statcan.gc.ca/census-recensement/2011/dp-pd/prof/index.cfm?Lang=E

PROFILES / Québec, Québec

Age Characteristics: 0 to 49 Years

Area	0 to 4 Years	5 to 9 Years	10 to 14 Years	15 to 19 Years	20 to 24 Years	25 to 29 Years	30 to 34 Years	35 to 39 Years	40 to 44 Years	45 to 49 Years
					Number					
					Total					
Québec	24,565	20,900	22,090	28,365	37,200	38,200	36,310	29,805	30,165	37,935
Québec	440,840	399,575	418,205	491,980	489,185	490,665	531,445	498,225	520,805	623,575
Canada	1,877,095	1,809,895	1,920,355	2,178,135	2,187,450	2,169,590	2,162,905	2,173,930	2,324,875	2,675,130
					Males					
Québec	12,425	10,615	11,305	14,210	18,260	19,735	18,715	15,440	15,145	18,820
Québec	225,525	203,675	213,540	249,960	246,850	245,695	264,980	249,610	261,120	311,320
Canada	961,150	925,965	983,995	1,115,845	1,108,775	1,077,275	1,058,810	1,064,200	1,141,720	1,318,715
					Females					
Québec	12,140	10,280	10,785	14,155	18,935	18,465	17,600	14,365	15,020	19,110
Québec	215,320	195,900	204,665	242,020	242,340	244,970	266,460	248,615	259,690	312,250
Canada	915,945	883,935	936,360	1,062,295	1,078,670	1,092,315	1,104,095	1,109,735	1,183,155	1,356,420
					Percent of Population					
					Total					
Québec	4.8	4.0	4.3	5.5	7.2	7.4	7.0	5.8	5.8	7.3
Québec	5.6	5.1	5.3	6.2	6.2	6.2	6.7	6.3	6.6	7.9
Canada	5.6	5.4	5.7	6.5	6.5	6.5	6.5	6.5	6.9	8.0
					Males					
Québec	5.0	4.3	4.5	5.7	7.3	7.9	7.5	6.2	6.1	7.6
Québec	5.8	5.3	5.5	6.4	6.4	6.3	6.8	6.4	6.7	8.0
Canada	5.9	5.6	6.0	6.8	6.8	6.6	6.5	6.5	7.0	8.0
					Females					
Québec	4.5	3.8	4.0	5.3	7.1	6.9	6.6	5.4	5.6	7.1
Québec	5.3	4.9	5.1	6.0	6.0	6.1	6.6	6.2	6.4	7.8
Canada	5.4	5.2	5.5	6.2	6.3	6.4	6.5	6.5	6.9	7.9

Source: Statistics Canada. 2012. Census Profile. 2011 Census. Statistics Canada Catalogue no. 98-316-XWE. Ottawa. Released October 24 2012.
http://www12.statcan.gc.ca/census-recensement/2011/dp-pd/prof/index.cfm?Lang=E

Age Characteristics: 50 Years and Over, and Median Age

Area	50 to 54 Years	55 to 59 Years	60 to 64 Years	65 to 69 Years	70 to 74 Years	75 to 79 Years	80 to 84 Years	85 Years and Over	Median Age
					Number				
					Total				
Québec	41,805	39,425	35,875	29,255	21,120	17,415	13,555	12,645	43.5
Québec	648,695	579,280	512,830	403,210	291,755	232,355	176,420	153,945	41.9
Canada	2,658,965	2,340,635	2,052,670	1,521,715	1,153,065	922,700	702,070	645,515	40.6
					Males				
Québec	20,300	18,680	16,855	13,445	9,290	7,120	4,880	3,375	41.2
Québec	320,695	285,295	250,675	194,305	135,830	101,675	69,170	45,945	40.7
Canada	1,309,030	1,147,300	1,002,690	738,010	543,435	417,945	291,085	208,300	39.6
					Females				
Québec	21,505	20,745	19,025	15,805	11,835	10,285	8,675	9,265	45.7
Québec	327,995	293,990	262,155	208,905	155,925	130,680	107,250	108,005	43.0
Canada	1,349,940	1,193,335	1,049,985	783,705	609,630	504,755	410,985	437,215	41.5
					Percent of Population				
					Total				
Québec	8.1	7.6	6.9	5.7	4.1	3.4	2.6	2.4	–
Québec	8.2	7.3	6.5	5.1	3.7	2.9	2.2	1.9	–
Canada	7.9	7.0	6.1	4.5	3.4	2.8	2.1	1.9	–
					Males				
Québec	8.2	7.5	6.8	5.4	3.7	2.9	2.0	1.4	–
Québec	8.3	7.4	6.5	5.0	3.5	2.6	1.8	1.2	–
Canada	8.0	7.0	6.1	4.5	3.3	2.5	1.8	1.3	–
					Females				
Québec	8.0	7.7	7.1	5.9	4.4	3.8	3.2	3.5	–
Québec	8.1	7.3	6.5	5.2	3.9	3.2	2.7	2.7	–
Canada	7.9	7.0	6.2	4.6	3.6	3.0	2.4	2.6	–

Source: Statistics Canada. 2012. Census Profile. 2011 Census. Statistics Canada Catalogue no. 98-316-XWE. Ottawa. Released October 24 2012.
http://www12.statcan.gc.ca/census-recensement/2011/dp-pd/prof/index.cfm?Lang=E

PROFILES / Québec, Québec

Private Households by Household Size

Area	1 Person	2 Persons	3 Persons	4 Persons	5 Persons	6 or More Persons	Average Number of Persons in Private Households
Households							
Québec	94,685	87,800	30,920	23,310	6,455	2,190	2.0
Québec	1,094,410	1,181,240	496,140	421,080	142,555	59,920	2.3
Canada	3,673,310	4,544,820	2,081,900	1,903,300	724,405	392,885	2.5
Percent of Households							
Québec	38.6	35.8	12.6	9.5	2.6	0.9	–
Québec	32.2	34.8	14.6	12.4	4.2	1.8	–
Canada	27.6	34.1	15.6	14.3	5.4	2.9	–

Source: Statistics Canada. 2012. Census Profile. 2011 Census. Statistics Canada Catalogue no. 98-316-XWE. Ottawa. Released October 24 2012.
http://www12.statcan.gc.ca/census-recensement/2011/dp-pd/prof/index.cfm?Lang=E

Dwelling Type

Area	Single-detached House	Semi-detached House	Row House	Apartment: Building with Five or More Storeys	Apartment: Building with Fewer Than Five Storeys	Duplex Apartment	Movable Dwelling	Other Single-attached House
Number								
Québec	78,560	12,430	6,030	19,885	108,555	17,335	1,255	1,315
Québec	1,560,405	171,435	86,040	171,115	1,103,845	263,860	22,995	15,645
Canada	7,329,150	646,245	791,600	1,234,770	2,397,550	704,485	183,510	33,310
Percent of Dwellings								
Québec	32.0	5.1	2.5	8.1	44.2	7.1	0.5	0.5
Québec	46.0	5.0	2.5	5.0	32.5	7.8	0.7	0.5
Canada	55.0	4.9	5.9	9.3	18.0	5.3	1.4	0.3

Source: Statistics Canada. 2012. Census Profile. 2011 Census. Statistics Canada Catalogue no. 98-316-XWE. Ottawa. Released October 24 2012.
http://www12.statcan.gc.ca/census-recensement/2011/dp-pd/prof/index.cfm?Lang=E

Shelter Costs

	Owned Dwellings				Rented Dwellings		
Area	Number	Median Value[1] ($)	Average Value[1] ($)	Median Monthly Costs[2] ($)	Average Monthly Costs[2] ($)	Number	Median Monthly Costs[3] ($)	Average Monthly Costs[3] ($)
Québec	129,815	229,482	250,313	874	933	115,500	655	704
Québec	2,056,665	214,537	249,427	841	936	1,308,465	643	685
Canada	9,013,410	280,552	345,182	978	1,141	4,060,385	784	848

Note: All figures cover non-farm, non-reserve private dwellings; (1) Refers to the dollar amount expected by the owner if the dwelling were to be sold; (2) Includes all shelter expenses paid by households that own their dwellings, such as the mortgage payment and the costs of electricity, heat, water and other municipal services, property taxes and condominium fees; (3) Includes all shelter expenses paid by households that rent their dwellings, such as the monthly rent and the costs of electricity, heat and municipal services.
Source: Statistics Canada. 2013. 2011 National Household Survey. Statistics Canada Catalogue no. 99-004-XWE. Ottawa. Released September 11, 2013.

Occupied Private Dwellings by Period of Construction

Area	1960 or Before	1961 to 1980	1981 to 1990	1991 to 2000	2001 to 2005	2006 to 2011
Number						
Québec	61,800	84,950	41,515	26,515	13,605	16,975
Québec	946,900	1,115,455	533,790	353,355	206,035	239,685
Canada	3,273,105	4,152,715	2,112,110	1,707,880	1,031,020	1,042,430
Percent of Dwellings						
Québec	25.2	34.6	16.9	10.8	5.5	6.9
Québec	27.9	32.9	15.7	10.4	6.1	7.1
Canada	24.6	31.2	15.9	12.8	7.7	7.8

Note: Figures cover non-farm, non-reserve private dwellings and includes data up to May 10, 2011.
Source: Statistics Canada. 2013. 2011 National Household Survey. Statistics Canada Catalogue no. 99-004-XWE. Ottawa. Released September 11, 2013.

PROFILES / Québec, Québec

Educational Attainment

Area	No Certificate, Diploma or Degree	High School Diploma or Equivalent[1]	Apprenticeship or Trades Certificate or Diploma[2]	College, CÉGEP or Other Non-University Certificate or Diploma	University Certificate or Diploma Below the Bachelor Level[3]	Bachelor's Degree	University Certificate, Diploma or Degree Above Bachelor Level[4]
Number							
Total							
Québec	67,865	93,195	66,710	85,295	21,410	61,815	38,740
Québec	1,436,025	1,404,755	1,049,470	1,075,855	305,330	766,100	437,050
Canada	5,485,400	6,968,935	2,950,685	4,970,020	1,200,130	3,634,425	2,049,930
Males							
Québec	31,035	41,760	41,095	37,450	8,375	28,775	20,840
Québec	714,090	650,660	635,435	472,360	126,565	343,535	227,990
Canada	2,742,875	3,305,415	1,928,970	2,118,430	513,235	1,643,080	1,043,350
Females							
Québec	36,825	51,440	25,615	47,845	13,030	33,035	17,895
Québec	721,930	754,095	414,035	603,495	178,765	422,565	209,065
Canada	2,742,520	3,663,515	1,021,715	2,851,595	686,890	1,991,345	1,006,585
Percent of Population							
Total							
Québec	15.6	21.4	15.3	19.6	4.9	14.2	8.9
Québec	22.2	21.7	16.2	16.6	4.7	11.8	6.8
Canada	20.1	25.6	10.8	18.2	4.4	13.3	7.5
Males							
Québec	14.8	19.9	19.6	17.9	4.0	13.7	10.0
Québec	22.5	20.5	20.0	14.9	4.0	10.8	7.2
Canada	20.6	24.9	14.5	15.9	3.9	12.4	7.8
Females							
Québec	16.3	22.8	11.3	21.2	5.8	14.6	7.9
Québec	21.9	22.8	12.5	18.3	5.4	12.8	6.3
Canada	19.6	26.2	7.3	20.4	4.9	14.3	7.2

Note: Figures cover total population aged 15 years and over by highest certificate, diploma or degree; (1) Includes persons who have graduated from a secondary school or equivalent. It excludes persons with a postsecondary certificate, diploma or degree; (2) Includes Registered Apprenticeship certificates (including Certificate of Qualification, Journeyperson's designation) and other trades certificates or diplomas such as pre-employment or vocational certificates and diplomas from brief trade programs completed at community colleges, institutes of technology, vocational centres, and similar institutions; (3) Comparisons with other data sources suggest that the category 'University certificate or diploma below the bachelor's level' was over-reported in the NHS. This category likely includes some responses that are actually college certificates or diplomas, bachelor's degrees or other types of education (e.g., university transfer programs, bachelor's programs completed in other countries, incomplete bachelor's programs, non-university professional designations). We recommend users interpret the results for the 'University certificate or diploma below the bachelor's level' category with caution; (4) 'University certificate or diploma above bachelor level' includes the categories: 'Degree in medicine, dentistry, veterinary medicine or optometry,' 'Master's degree' and 'Earned doctorate.'
Source: Statistics Canada. 2013. 2011 National Household Survey. Statistics Canada Catalogue no. 99-004-XWE. Ottawa. Released September 11, 2013.

Household Income Distribution

Area	Less than $10,000	$10,000 to $19,999	$20,000 to $29,999	$30,000 to $39,999	$40,000 to $49,999	$50,000 to $59,999	$60,000 to $79,999	$80,000 to $99,999	$100,000 to $124,999	$125,000 to $149,999	$150,000 and Over
Households											
Québec	11,645	27,010	25,000	29,265	25,490	22,165	35,295	25,605	19,345	10,770	13,770
Québec	179,790	377,210	353,470	382,000	343,730	302,595	483,085	344,435	267,995	148,950	211,965
Canada	626,705	1,141,945	1,193,925	1,271,675	1,206,800	1,102,120	1,865,280	1,458,240	1,260,770	802,555	1,389,240
Percent of Households											
Québec	4.7	11.0	10.2	11.9	10.4	9.0	14.4	10.4	7.9	4.4	5.6
Québec	5.3	11.1	10.4	11.3	10.1	8.9	14.2	10.1	7.9	4.4	6.2
Canada	4.7	8.6	9.0	9.5	9.1	8.3	14.0	10.9	9.5	6.0	10.4

Note: Household income is the sum of the total incomes of all members of that household. Total income refers to monetary receipts from certain sources, before income taxes and deductions, during calendar year 2010.
Source: Statistics Canada. 2013. 2011 National Household Survey. Statistics Canada Catalogue no. 99-004-XWE. Ottawa. Released September 11, 2013.

Median and Average Household and Economic Family Income

Area	Median Household Income ($)	Average Household Income ($)	Median After-tax Household Income ($)	Average After-tax Household Income ($)	Median Economic Family Income ($)	Average Economic Family Income ($)	Median After-tax Economic Family Income ($)	Average After-tax Economic Family Income ($)
Québec	51,775	65,153	45,119	54,069	73,477	85,696	63,183	70,593
Québec	51,842	66,205	45,968	55,121	68,344	82,045	59,560	68,091
Canada	61,072	79,102	54,089	66,149	76,511	94,125	67,044	78,517

Note: Figures cover household and economic familiy income in 2010. A household is defined as a person or a group of persons (other than foreign residents) who occupy the same private dwelling and do not have a usual place of residence elsewhere in Canada. Every person is a member of one and only one household. An economic family is defined as a group of two or more persons who live in the same dwelling and are related to each other by blood, marriage, common-law, adoption or a foster relationship. A couple may be of opposite or same sex.
Source: Statistics Canada. 2013. 2011 National Household Survey. Statistics Canada Catalogue no. 99-004-XWE. Ottawa. Released September 11, 2013.

Individual Income Distribution

Area	Less than $10,000	$10,000 to $19,999	$20,000 to $29,999	$30,000 to $39,999	$40,000 to $49,999	$50,000 to $59,999	$60,000 to $79,999	$80,000 to $99,999	$100,000 to $124,999	$125,000 and Over
					Number					
					Total					
Québec	57,945	82,225	62,155	64,085	51,170	35,010	39,515	14,880	7,065	7,660
Québec	1,005,600	1,309,515	941,630	866,290	653,400	449,185	515,815	211,070	109,975	120,915
Canada	4,492,040	4,835,710	3,670,020	3,180,360	2,603,520	1,921,650	2,437,440	1,302,045	693,580	782,135
					Males					
Québec	25,195	31,595	26,490	30,595	25,150	19,475	24,585	9,950	5,040	5,875
Québec	441,455	516,150	427,295	432,625	345,950	256,700	313,880	143,785	80,000	91,475
Canada	1,936,365	1,864,880	1,588,260	1,522,190	1,333,510	1,079,780	1,473,145	823,720	492,905	599,905
					Females					
Québec	32,750	50,630	35,665	33,490	26,020	15,535	14,930	4,935	2,025	1,785
Québec	564,150	793,365	514,335	433,670	307,455	192,485	201,935	67,275	29,980	29,440
Canada	2,555,675	2,970,825	2,081,760	1,658,170	1,270,010	841,870	964,300	478,330	200,680	182,230
					Percent of Population					
					Total					
Québec	13.7	19.5	14.7	15.2	12.1	8.3	9.4	3.5	1.7	1.8
Québec	16.3	21.2	15.2	14.0	10.6	7.3	8.3	3.4	1.8	2.0
Canada	17.3	18.7	14.2	12.3	10.0	7.4	9.4	5.0	2.7	3.0
					Males					
Québec	12.4	15.5	13.0	15.0	12.3	9.5	12.1	4.9	2.5	2.9
Québec	14.5	16.9	14.0	14.2	11.3	8.4	10.3	4.7	2.6	3.0
Canada	15.2	14.7	12.5	12.0	10.5	8.5	11.6	6.5	3.9	4.7
					Females					
Québec	15.0	23.2	16.4	15.4	11.9	7.1	6.9	2.3	0.9	0.8
Québec	18.0	25.3	16.4	13.8	9.8	6.1	6.4	2.1	1.0	0.9
Canada	19.4	22.5	15.8	12.6	9.6	6.4	7.3	3.6	1.5	1.4

Note: Figures cover individuals aged 15 years and over with income. Income refers to monetary receipts from certain sources, before income taxes and deductions, during calendar year 2010.
Source: Statistics Canada. 2013. 2011 National Household Survey. Statistics Canada Catalogue no. 99-004-XWE. Ottawa. Released September 11, 2013.

Labour Force Status

Area	All	Employed	Unemployed	Not in the Labour Force
		Number		
		Total		
Québec	283,980	270,505	13,470	151,050
Québec	4,183,445	3,880,425	303,020	2,291,145
Canada	17,990,080	16,595,035	1,395,045	9,269,445
		Males		
Québec	146,380	138,775	7,610	62,955
Québec	2,188,555	2,014,810	173,745	982,080
Canada	9,388,570	8,634,310	754,255	3,906,785
		Females		
Québec	137,600	131,735	5,860	88,090
Québec	1,994,885	1,865,610	129,275	1,309,065
Canada	8,601,515	7,960,725	640,790	5,362,660
		Percent of Labour Force		
		Total		
Québec	65.3	62.2	4.7	34.7
Québec	64.6	59.9	7.2	35.4
Canada	66.0	60.9	7.8	34.0
		Males		
Québec	69.9	66.3	5.2	30.1
Québec	69.0	63.5	7.9	31.0
Canada	70.6	64.9	8.0	29.4
		Females		
Québec	61.0	58.4	4.3	39.0
Québec	60.4	56.5	6.5	39.6
Canada	61.6	57.0	7.4	38.4

Note: Figures are based on total population 15 years and over
Source: Statistics Canada. 2013. 2011 National Household Survey. Statistics Canada Catalogue no. 99-004-XWE. Ottawa. Released September 11, 2013.

Labour Force by Industry (NAICS Codes 11–52)

Area	Agriculture, forestry, fishing & hunting	Mining, quarrying, & oil & gas extraction	Utilities	Construction	Manufacturing	Wholesale Trade	Retail Trade	Transportation & warehousing	Information & cultural industries	Finance & insurance
					Number					
					Total					
Québec	815	330	1,685	12,935	17,145	8,535	36,160	10,065	5,520	11,640
Québec	84,470	20,770	33,815	241,780	476,390	169,825	501,380	181,295	98,340	159,230
Canada	437,650	261,050	149,940	1,215,380	1,619,295	733,445	2,031,665	827,780	420,830	767,960
					Males					
Québec	475	260	1,230	11,540	12,395	6,150	17,685	8,090	3,510	4,125
Québec	61,540	18,035	24,560	213,605	343,345	113,545	234,725	137,745	56,455	56,930
Canada	307,370	211,690	110,765	1,068,710	1,167,680	494,545	933,850	617,305	235,875	296,995
					Females					
Québec	340	70	460	1,385	4,750	2,385	18,480	1,975	2,005	7,520
Québec	22,925	2,730	9,255	28,170	133,045	56,280	266,650	43,550	41,885	102,295
Canada	130,285	49,360	39,175	146,670	451,615	238,900	1,097,820	210,475	184,955	470,960
					Percent of Labour Force					
					Total					
Québec	0.3	0.1	0.6	4.6	6.1	3.1	12.9	3.6	2.0	4.2
Québec	2.1	0.5	0.8	5.9	11.7	4.2	12.3	4.4	2.4	3.9
Canada	2.5	1.5	0.9	6.9	9.2	4.2	11.6	4.7	2.4	4.4
					Males					
Québec	0.3	0.2	0.9	8.0	8.6	4.3	12.3	5.6	2.4	2.9
Québec	2.9	0.8	1.1	10.0	16.1	5.3	11.0	6.4	2.6	2.7
Canada	3.3	2.3	1.2	11.6	12.7	5.4	10.2	6.7	2.6	3.2
					Females					
Québec	0.3	0.1	0.3	1.0	3.5	1.8	13.6	1.5	1.5	5.6
Québec	1.2	0.1	0.5	1.4	6.8	2.9	13.7	2.2	2.2	5.3
Canada	1.6	0.6	0.5	1.7	5.4	2.8	13.1	2.5	2.2	5.6

Note: Figures are based on total experienced labour force 15 years and over. Experienced labour force refers to persons who, during the week of Sunday, May 1 to Saturday, May 7, 2011, were employed and the unemployed who had last worked for pay or in self-employment in either 2010 or 2011.
Source: Statistics Canada. 2013. 2011 National Household Survey. Statistics Canada Catalogue no. 99-004-XWE. Ottawa. Released September 11, 2013.

Labour Force by Industry (NAICS Codes 53–91)

Area	Real estate & rental & leasing	Profess., scientific & tech. services	Mgmt of companies & enterprises	Admin. & support, waste mgmt & remed. services	Educational services	Health care & social assistance	Arts, entertain. & recreation	Accomm. & food services	Other services (except public admin.)	Public admin.
					Number					
					Total					
Québec	4,340	21,715	115	10,915	21,130	37,130	5,170	21,520	12,660	40,305
Québec	61,365	282,115	3,965	156,130	301,425	496,125	78,795	253,145	189,290	295,480
Canada	321,895	1,240,850	17,460	728,330	1,301,435	1,949,650	363,405	1,130,750	807,800	1,261,050
					Males					
Québec	2,610	13,015	70	6,725	7,910	8,945	2,690	10,855	5,785	20,270
Québec	35,940	158,920	2,250	92,530	99,565	97,255	41,535	112,650	88,710	147,645
Canada	179,090	688,625	9,380	411,250	424,915	349,430	188,270	469,990	372,940	652,510
					Females					
Québec	1,725	8,700	50	4,185	13,225	28,180	2,480	10,670	6,875	20,040
Québec	25,425	123,205	1,715	63,605	201,860	398,870	37,260	140,495	100,585	147,835
Canada	142,805	552,225	8,075	317,085	876,515	1,600,220	175,135	660,760	434,865	608,535
					Percent of Labour Force					
					Total					
Québec	1.6	7.8	0.0	3.9	7.6	13.3	1.8	7.7	4.5	14.4
Québec	1.5	6.9	0.1	3.8	7.4	12.1	1.9	6.2	4.6	7.2
Canada	1.8	7.1	0.1	4.1	7.4	11.1	2.1	6.4	4.6	7.2
					Males					
Québec	1.8	9.0	0.0	4.7	5.5	6.2	1.9	7.5	4.0	14.0
Québec	1.7	7.4	0.1	4.3	4.7	4.5	1.9	5.3	4.2	6.9
Canada	1.9	7.5	0.1	4.5	4.6	3.8	2.0	5.1	4.1	7.1
					Females					
Québec	1.3	6.4	0.0	3.1	9.8	20.8	1.8	7.9	5.1	14.8
Québec	1.3	6.3	0.1	3.3	10.4	20.5	1.9	7.2	5.2	7.6
Canada	1.7	6.6	0.1	3.8	10.4	19.1	2.1	7.9	5.2	7.2

Note: Figures are based on total experienced labour force 15 years and over. Experienced labour force refers to persons who, during the week of Sunday, May 1 to Saturday, May 7, 2011, were employed and the unemployed who had last worked for pay or in self-employment in either 2010 or 2011.
Source: Statistics Canada. 2013. 2011 National Household Survey. Statistics Canada Catalogue no. 99-004-XWE. Ottawa. Released September 11, 2013.

Occupation

Area	Mgmt	Business, Finance & Admin.	Natural/ Applied Sciences & Related	Health	Education, Law & Social, Community & Government Services	Art, Culture, Recreation & Sport	Sales & Service	Trades, Transport & Equip. Operators & Related	Natural Resources, Agri. & Related Production	Mfg & Utilities
\multicolumn{11}{c}{Number — Total}
Québec	23,280	51,980	26,020	21,510	36,880	9,445	72,610	29,685	1,520	6,910
Québec	411,425	687,715	287,015	268,610	479,505	123,665	969,740	573,075	65,625	218,740
Canada	1,963,600	2,902,045	1,237,775	1,107,200	2,064,675	503,415	4,068,170	2,537,775	397,930	805,040
\multicolumn{11}{c}{Males}
Québec	14,675	16,320	19,445	4,955	14,595	4,700	34,895	28,365	1,325	5,070
Québec	261,620	207,545	221,430	53,480	148,715	58,150	436,370	542,055	53,640	154,485
Canada	1,229,460	854,190	966,355	217,520	676,550	232,535	1,745,705	2,385,615	318,945	564,300
\multicolumn{11}{c}{Females}
Québec	8,605	35,660	6,575	16,555	22,290	4,740	37,715	1,315	195	1,845
Québec	149,800	480,170	65,585	215,130	330,795	65,520	533,370	31,025	11,995	64,250
Canada	734,140	2,047,855	271,415	889,675	1,388,130	270,875	2,322,465	152,165	78,980	240,740
\multicolumn{11}{c}{Percent of Labour Force — Total}
Québec	8.3	18.6	9.3	7.7	13.2	3.4	25.9	10.6	0.5	2.5
Québec	10.1	16.8	7.0	6.6	11.7	3.0	23.7	14.0	1.6	5.4
Canada	11.2	16.5	7.0	6.3	11.7	2.9	23.1	14.4	2.3	4.6
\multicolumn{11}{c}{Males}
Québec	10.2	11.3	13.5	3.4	10.1	3.3	24.2	19.7	0.9	3.5
Québec	12.2	9.7	10.4	2.5	7.0	2.7	20.4	25.4	2.5	7.2
Canada	13.4	9.3	10.5	2.4	7.4	2.5	19.0	26.0	3.5	6.1
\multicolumn{11}{c}{Females}
Québec	6.4	26.3	4.9	12.2	16.5	3.5	27.8	1.0	0.1	1.4
Québec	7.7	24.7	3.4	11.0	17.0	3.4	27.4	1.6	0.6	3.3
Canada	8.7	24.4	3.2	10.6	16.5	3.2	27.7	1.8	0.9	2.9

Note: Figures are based on total experienced labour force 15 years and over
Source: Statistics Canada. 2013. 2011 National Household Survey. Statistics Canada Catalogue no. 99-004-XWE. Ottawa. Released September 11, 2013.

Place of Work Status

Area	Worked at Home	Worked Outside Canada	No Fixed Workplace Address	Worked at Usual Place
\multicolumn{5}{c}{Number — Total}
Québec	11,765	625	20,495	237,620
Québec	237,625	9,705	331,525	3,301,560
Canada	1,142,640	66,460	1,868,245	13,517,690
\multicolumn{5}{c}{Males}
Québec	5,590	480	15,205	117,490
Québec	122,060	7,055	249,535	1,636,165
Canada	582,150	47,355	1,400,485	6,604,325
\multicolumn{5}{c}{Females}
Québec	6,175	145	5,285	120,130
Québec	115,565	2,650	81,995	1,665,395
Canada	560,490	19,100	467,760	6,913,370
\multicolumn{5}{c}{Percent of Labour Force — Total}
Québec	4.3	0.2	7.6	87.8
Québec	6.1	0.3	8.5	85.1
Canada	6.9	0.4	11.3	81.5
\multicolumn{5}{c}{Males}
Québec	4.0	0.3	11.0	84.7
Québec	6.1	0.4	12.4	81.2
Canada	6.7	0.5	16.2	76.5
\multicolumn{5}{c}{Females}
Québec	4.7	0.1	4.0	91.2
Québec	6.2	0.1	4.4	89.3
Canada	7.0	0.2	5.9	86.8

Note: Figures are based on total employed labour force 15 years and over.
Source: Statistics Canada. 2013. 2011 National Household Survey. Statistics Canada Catalogue no. 99-004-XWE. Ottawa. Released September 11, 2013.

Mode of Transportation to Work

Area	Car; Truck; Van; as Driver	Car; Truck; Van; as Passenger	Public Transit	Walked	Bicycled	All Other Modes
			Number			
			Total			
Québec	183,525	10,690	37,875	19,985	4,160	1,880
Québec	2,713,295	136,490	484,600	215,210	48,870	34,620
Canada	11,393,140	867,050	1,851,525	880,815	201,780	191,625
			Males			
Québec	100,315	3,415	15,200	9,645	3,080	1,040
Québec	1,484,305	50,905	203,035	95,100	33,065	19,285
Canada	6,238,835	349,530	788,290	387,580	135,840	104,725
			Females			
Québec	83,210	7,270	22,675	10,340	1,080	845
Québec	1,228,995	85,585	281,565	120,110	15,800	15,335
Canada	5,154,305	517,520	1,063,235	493,230	65,940	86,900
			Percent of Labour Force			
			Total			
Québec	71.1	4.1	14.7	7.7	1.6	0.7
Québec	74.7	3.8	13.3	5.9	1.3	1.0
Canada	74.0	5.6	12.0	5.7	1.3	1.2
			Males			
Québec	75.6	2.6	11.5	7.3	2.3	0.8
Québec	78.7	2.7	10.8	5.0	1.8	1.0
Canada	77.9	4.4	9.8	4.8	1.7	1.3
			Females			
Québec	66.3	5.8	18.1	8.2	0.9	0.7
Québec	70.3	4.9	16.1	6.9	0.9	0.9
Canada	69.8	7.0	14.4	6.7	0.9	1.2

Note: Figures are based on total employed labour force 15 years and over.
Source: Statistics Canada. 2013. 2011 National Household Survey. Statistics Canada Catalogue no. 99-004-XWE. Ottawa. Released September 11, 2013.

Visible Minority Population Characteristics

Area	Total Minority	South Asian[1]	Chinese	Black	Filipino	Latin American	Arab	SE Asian[2]	West Asian[3]	Korean	Japanese	Multiple[4]
						Number						
						Total						
Québec	20,245	855	1,710	5,760	95	5,085	3,785	1,760	260	165	205	315
Québec	850,235	83,320	82,845	243,625	31,495	116,380	166,260	65,855	23,445	6,665	4,025	17,420
Canada	6,264,750	1,567,400	1,324,750	945,665	619,310	381,280	380,620	312,075	206,840	161,130	87,270	171,935
						Males						
Québec	10,185	455	560	2,980	35	2,500	2,150	865	115	105	100	170
Québec	418,545	43,410	37,295	116,605	12,435	56,940	89,505	32,940	12,070	3,135	1,565	8,315
Canada	3,043,010	790,755	632,325	453,005	268,885	186,355	203,485	154,035	105,620	77,165	38,270	83,335
						Females						
Québec	10,060	400	1,150	2,780	60	2,585	1,635	895	145	60	105	150
Québec	431,695	39,915	45,550	127,020	19,055	59,440	76,750	32,920	11,380	3,530	2,465	9,105
Canada	3,221,745	776,650	692,420	492,660	350,425	194,925	177,140	158,045	101,220	83,965	48,990	88,600
						Percent of Population						
						Total						
Québec	4.0	0.2	0.3	1.1	0.0	1.0	0.8	0.4	0.1	0.0	0.0	0.1
Québec	11.0	1.1	1.1	3.2	0.4	1.5	2.2	0.9	0.3	0.1	0.1	0.2
Canada	19.1	4.8	4.0	2.9	1.9	1.2	1.2	0.9	0.6	0.5	0.3	0.5
						Males						
Québec	4.2	0.2	0.2	1.2	0.0	1.0	0.9	0.4	0.0	0.0	0.0	0.1
Québec	11.0	1.1	1.0	3.1	0.3	1.5	2.3	0.9	0.3	0.1	0.0	0.2
Canada	18.8	4.9	3.9	2.8	1.7	1.2	1.3	1.0	0.7	0.5	0.2	0.5
						Females						
Québec	3.9	0.2	0.4	1.1	0.0	1.0	0.6	0.3	0.1	0.0	0.0	0.1
Québec	11.0	1.0	1.2	3.2	0.5	1.5	2.0	0.8	0.3	0.1	0.1	0.2
Canada	19.3	4.7	4.1	3.0	2.1	1.2	1.1	0.9	0.6	0.5	0.3	0.5

Note: The Employment Equity Act defines visible minorities as 'persons, other than Aboriginal peoples, who are non-Caucasian in race or non-white in colour';
(1) Includes 'East Indian,' 'Pakistani,' 'Sri Lankan,' etc.; (2) Includes 'Vietnamese,' 'Cambodian,' 'Malaysian,' 'Laotian,' etc.; (3) Includes 'Iranian,' 'Afghan,' etc.; (4) Includes respondents who reported more than one visible minority group by checking two or more mark-in circles, e.g., 'Black' and 'South Asian.'
Source: Statistics Canada. 2013. 2011 National Household Survey. Statistics Canada Catalogue no. 99-004-XWE. Ottawa. Released September 11, 2013.

PROFILES / Québec, Québec

Aboriginal Population

Area	Aboriginal Identity[1]	First Nations (North American Indian) Single Identity[2]	Métis Single Identity	Inuk (Inuit) Single Identity	Multiple Aboriginal Identities[3]	Aboriginal Identities Not Included Elsewhere
Number						
Total						
Québec	4,635	2,425	1,765	100	95	245
Québec	141,915	82,425	40,960	12,570	1,545	4,415
Canada	1,400,685	851,560	451,795	59,440	11,415	26,475
Males						
Québec	2,000	970	895	30	30	75
Québec	70,205	40,105	21,300	6,265	720	1,815
Canada	682,190	411,785	223,335	29,495	5,525	12,055
Females						
Québec	2,630	1,460	870	70	65	165
Québec	71,710	42,315	19,660	6,305	830	2,600
Canada	718,500	439,775	228,460	29,950	5,890	14,420
Percent of Population						
Total						
Québec	0.9	0.5	0.4	0.0	0.0	0.0
Québec	1.8	1.1	0.5	0.2	0.0	0.1
Canada	4.3	2.6	1.4	0.2	0.0	0.1
Males						
Québec	0.8	0.4	0.4	0.0	0.0	0.0
Québec	1.8	1.1	0.6	0.2	0.0	0.0
Canada	4.2	2.5	1.4	0.2	0.0	0.1
Females						
Québec	1.0	0.6	0.3	0.0	0.0	0.1
Québec	1.8	1.1	0.5	0.2	0.0	0.1
Canada	4.3	2.6	1.4	0.2	0.0	0.1

Note: (1) Includes persons who reported being an Aboriginal person, that is, First Nations (North American Indian), Métis or Inuk (Inuit) and/or those who reported Registered or Treaty Indian status, that is registered under the Indian Act of Canada, and/or those who reported membership in a First Nation or Indian band. Aboriginal peoples of Canada are defined in the Constitution Act, 1982, section 35-2 as including the Indian, Inuit and Métis peoples of Canada; (2) Users should be aware that the estimates associated with this variable are more affected than most by the incomplete enumeration of certain Indian reserves and Indian settlements in the National Household Survey (NHS); (3) Includes persons who reported being any two or all three of the following: First Nations (North American Indian), Métis or Inuk (Inuit).
Source: Statistics Canada. 2013. 2011 National Household Survey. Statistics Canada Catalogue no. 99-004-XWE. Ottawa. Released September 11, 2013.

Ethnic Origin

Area	North American Aboriginal	Other North American	European	Caribbean	Latin, Central and South American	African	Asian	Oceania
Number								
Total								
Québec	14,300	361,740	218,310	1,790	6,050	8,945	8,640	125
Québec	307,445	4,776,875	3,390,330	167,590	137,255	260,785	488,905	2,305
Canada	1,836,035	11,070,455	20,157,965	627,590	544,375	766,735	5,011,225	74,875
Males								
Québec	6,470	173,400	107,760	865	2,925	4,880	4,205	75
Québec	146,725	2,345,180	1,678,310	77,665	67,195	135,740	241,515	1,135
Canada	885,675	5,462,685	9,913,150	291,640	264,635	387,360	2,435,540	37,490
Females								
Québec	7,830	188,340	110,555	920	3,125	4,060	4,430	50
Québec	160,725	2,431,700	1,712,015	89,925	70,065	125,040	247,390	1,175
Canada	950,360	5,607,770	10,244,820	335,945	279,740	379,380	2,575,680	37,385
Percent of Population								
Total								
Québec	2.8	72.0	43.4	0.4	1.2	1.8	1.7	0.0
Québec	4.0	61.8	43.8	2.2	1.8	3.4	6.3	0.0
Canada	5.6	33.7	61.4	1.9	1.7	2.3	15.3	0.2
Males								
Québec	2.7	71.2	44.2	0.4	1.2	2.0	1.7	0.0
Québec	3.8	61.5	44.0	2.0	1.8	3.6	6.3	0.0
Canada	5.5	33.8	61.3	1.8	1.6	2.4	15.1	0.2
Females								
Québec	3.0	72.7	42.7	0.4	1.2	1.6	1.7	0.0
Québec	4.1	62.1	43.7	2.3	1.8	3.2	6.3	0.0
Canada	5.7	33.6	61.4	2.0	1.7	2.3	15.4	0.2

Note: The sum of the ethnic groups in this table is greater than the total population estimate because a person may report more than one ethnic origin in the NHS.
Source: Statistics Canada. 2013. 2011 National Household Survey. Statistics Canada Catalogue no. 99-004-XWE. Ottawa. Released September 11, 2013.

Religion

Area	Buddhist	Christian	Hindu	Jewish	Muslim	Sikh	Traditional (Aboriginal) Spirituality	Other Religions	No Religious Affiliation
				Number Total					
Québec	1,325	428,380	360	140	6,125	0	20	800	65,450
Québec	52,390	6,356,880	33,540	85,100	243,430	9,275	2,025	12,340	937,545
Canada	366,830	22,102,745	497,965	329,495	1,053,945	454,965	64,935	130,835	7,850,605
				Males					
Québec	650	202,470	185	85	3,320	0	0	430	36,480
Québec	24,630	3,079,855	17,055	41,455	128,815	5,090	925	6,155	510,055
Canada	168,465	10,497,775	250,435	161,265	540,555	229,435	31,805	57,745	4,225,645
				Females					
Québec	670	225,910	175	55	2,805	0	0	370	28,970
Québec	27,760	3,277,020	16,480	43,645	114,615	4,185	1,100	6,175	427,485
Canada	198,365	11,604,975	247,525	168,235	513,395	225,530	33,135	73,090	3,624,965
				Percent of Population Total					
Québec	0.3	85.2	0.1	0.0	1.2	0.0	0.0	0.2	13.0
Québec	0.7	82.2	0.4	1.1	3.1	0.1	0.0	0.2	12.1
Canada	1.1	67.3	1.5	1.0	3.2	1.4	0.2	0.4	23.9
				Males					
Québec	0.3	83.1	0.1	0.0	1.4	0.0	0.0	0.2	15.0
Québec	0.6	80.8	0.4	1.1	3.4	0.1	0.0	0.2	13.4
Canada	1.0	64.9	1.5	1.0	3.3	1.4	0.2	0.4	26.1
				Females					
Québec	0.3	87.2	0.1	0.0	1.1	0.0	0.0	0.1	11.2
Québec	0.7	83.6	0.4	1.1	2.9	0.1	0.0	0.2	10.9
Canada	1.2	69.5	1.5	1.0	3.1	1.4	0.2	0.4	21.7

Note: Religion refers to the person's self-identification as having a connection or affiliation with any religious denomination, group, body, sect, cult or other religiously defined community or system of belief. Religion is not limited to formal membership in a religious organization or group. Persons without a religious connection or affiliation can self-identify as atheist, agnostic or humanist, or can provide another applicable response.
Source: Statistics Canada. 2013. 2011 National Household Survey. Statistics Canada Catalogue no. 99-004-XWE. Ottawa. Released September 11, 2013.

Religion—Christian Denominations

Area	Anglican	Baptist	Catholic	Christian Orthodox	Lutheran	Pentecostal	Presbyterian	United Church	Other Christian
				Number Total					
Québec	545	880	415,025	1,360	160	1,360	165	270	8,620
Québec	73,550	36,615	5,775,740	129,780	7,200	41,070	11,440	32,930	248,560
Canada	1,631,845	635,840	12,810,705	550,690	478,185	478,705	472,385	2,007,610	3,036,780
				Males					
Québec	260	395	195,790	685	70	695	75	140	4,365
Québec	34,815	16,585	2,802,920	63,960	3,425	18,640	5,265	14,945	119,305
Canada	752,945	293,905	6,167,290	270,205	221,525	217,850	218,955	912,545	1,442,550
				Females					
Québec	285	480	219,230	675	90	670	90	135	4,250
Québec	38,735	20,030	2,972,820	65,820	3,770	22,430	6,175	17,985	129,260
Canada	878,900	341,940	6,643,415	280,485	256,660	260,850	253,430	1,095,065	1,594,230
				Percent of Population Total					
Québec	0.1	0.2	82.6	0.3	0.0	0.3	0.0	0.1	1.7
Québec	1.0	0.5	74.7	1.7	0.1	0.5	0.1	0.4	3.2
Canada	5.0	1.9	39.0	1.7	1.5	1.5	1.4	6.1	9.2
				Males					
Québec	0.1	0.2	80.4	0.3	0.0	0.3	0.0	0.1	1.8
Québec	0.9	0.4	73.5	1.7	0.1	0.5	0.1	0.4	3.1
Canada	4.7	1.8	38.2	1.7	1.4	1.3	1.4	5.6	8.9
				Females					
Québec	0.1	0.2	84.7	0.3	0.0	0.3	0.0	0.1	1.6
Québec	1.0	0.5	75.9	1.7	0.1	0.6	0.2	0.5	3.3
Canada	5.3	2.0	39.8	1.7	1.5	1.6	1.5	6.6	9.6

Note: Religion refers to the person's self-identification as having a connection or affiliation with any religious denomination, group, body, sect, cult or other religiously defined community or system of belief. Religion is not limited to formal membership in a religious organization or group. Persons without a religious connection or affiliation can self-identify as atheist, agnostic or humanist, or can provide another applicable response.
Source: Statistics Canada. 2013. 2011 National Household Survey. Statistics Canada Catalogue no. 99-004-XWE. Ottawa. Released September 11, 2013.

PROFILES / Québec, Québec

Immigrant Status and Period of Immigration

Area	Non-Immigrants[1]	Immigrants All	Before 1971	1971 to 1980	1981 to 1990	1991 to 2000	2001 to 2005	2006 to 2011	Non-Permanent Residents[3]
Number									
Total									
Québec	472,700	27,230	2,610	2,005	2,915	4,590	5,740	9,375	2,665
Québec	6,690,530	974,895	151,825	115,640	130,680	195,925	157,425	223,400	67,095
Canada	25,720,175	6,775,765	1,261,055	870,775	949,890	1,539,050	992,070	1,162,915	356,385
Males									
Québec	228,395	13,830	1,510	1,260	1,500	2,205	2,870	4,480	1,410
Québec	3,301,435	477,240	75,255	57,410	64,080	94,110	76,780	109,605	35,370
Canada	12,753,235	3,231,370	605,430	416,670	454,570	724,905	474,545	555,245	178,515
Females									
Québec	244,310	13,400	1,095	740	1,415	2,385	2,870	4,890	1,250
Québec	3,389,095	497,655	76,565	58,235	66,600	101,810	80,645	113,795	31,725
Canada	12,966,935	3,544,400	655,625	454,105	495,325	814,145	517,530	607,670	177,870
Percent of Population									
Total									
Québec	94.1	5.4	0.5	0.4	0.6	0.9	1.1	1.9	0.5
Québec	86.5	12.6	2.0	1.5	1.7	2.5	2.0	2.9	0.9
Canada	78.3	20.6	3.8	2.7	2.9	4.7	3.0	3.5	1.1
Males									
Québec	93.7	5.7	0.6	0.5	0.6	0.9	1.2	1.8	0.6
Québec	86.6	12.5	2.0	1.5	1.7	2.5	2.0	2.9	0.9
Canada	78.9	20.0	3.7	2.6	2.8	4.5	2.9	3.4	1.1
Females									
Québec	94.3	5.2	0.4	0.3	0.5	0.9	1.1	1.9	0.5
Québec	86.5	12.7	2.0	1.5	1.7	2.6	2.1	2.9	0.8
Canada	77.7	21.2	3.9	2.7	3.0	4.9	3.1	3.6	1.1

Note: (1) Non-immigrant refers to a person who is a Canadian citizen by birth; (2) Immigrant refers to a person who is or has ever been a landed immigrant/permanent resident. This person has been granted the right to live in Canada permanently by immigration authorities. Some immigrants have resided in Canada for a number of years, while others have arrived recently. Some immigrants are Canadian citizens, while others are not. Most immigrants are born outside Canada, but a small number are born in Canada. In the 2011 National Household Survey, 'Immigrants' includes immigrants who landed in Canada prior to May 10, 2011; (3) Non-permanent resident refers to a person from another country who has a work or study permit, or who is a refugee claimant, and any non-Canadian-born family member living in Canada with them.
Source: Statistics Canada. 2013. 2011 National Household Survey. Statistics Canada Catalogue no. 99-004-XWE. Ottawa. Released September 11, 2013.

Mother Tongue

Area	English	French	Non-official Language	English & French	English & Non-official Language	French & Non-official Language	English, French & Non-official Language
Number							
Total							
Québec	7,370	478,395	19,790	2,315	175	1,705	165
Québec	599,225	6,102,210	961,700	64,800	23,435	51,640	12,950
Canada	18,858,980	7,054,975	6,567,680	144,685	396,330	74,430	24,095
Males							
Québec	3,855	229,785	10,010	1,195	90	895	90
Québec	297,875	2,994,300	472,635	32,390	11,455	25,810	6,790
Canada	9,345,225	3,452,380	3,157,785	69,975	192,000	36,535	11,965
Females							
Québec	3,510	248,610	9,780	1,115	85	810	70
Québec	301,355	3,107,910	489,060	32,405	11,975	25,825	6,155
Canada	9,513,750	3,602,590	3,409,895	74,710	204,330	37,890	12,130
Percent of Population							
Total							
Québec	1.4	93.8	3.9	0.5	0.0	0.3	0.0
Québec	7.7	78.1	12.3	0.8	0.3	0.7	0.2
Canada	56.9	21.3	19.8	0.4	1.2	0.2	0.1
Males							
Québec	1.6	93.4	4.1	0.5	0.0	0.4	0.0
Québec	7.8	78.0	12.3	0.8	0.3	0.7	0.2
Canada	57.5	21.2	19.4	0.4	1.2	0.2	0.1
Females							
Québec	1.3	94.2	3.7	0.4	0.0	0.3	0.0
Québec	7.6	78.2	12.3	0.8	0.3	0.6	0.2
Canada	56.4	21.4	20.2	0.4	1.2	0.2	0.1

Note: Figures cover total population excluding institutional residents.
Source: Statistics Canada. 2012. Census Profile. 2011 Census. Statistics Canada Catalogue no. 98-316-XWE. Ottawa. Released October 24 2012.
http://www12.statcan.gc.ca/census-recensement/2011/dp-pd/prof/index.cfm?Lang=E

Language Spoken Most Often at Home

Area	English	French	Non-official Language	English & French	English & Non-official Language	French & Non-official Language	English, French & Non-official Language
			Number				
			Total				
Québec	5,165	488,430	10,540	2,000	155	3,260	370
Québec	767,415	6,249,080	554,400	71,555	43,765	100,110	29,625
Canada	21,457,075	6,827,865	3,673,865	131,205	875,135	109,700	46,330
			Males				
Québec	2,625	235,225	5,155	1,040	75	1,600	200
Québec	379,915	3,071,635	268,640	35,860	21,305	48,590	15,315
Canada	10,585,620	3,348,235	1,767,310	63,475	425,370	53,010	22,845
			Females				
Québec	2,540	253,205	5,390	955	80	1,660	170
Québec	387,500	3,177,450	285,760	35,695	22,460	51,525	14,310
Canada	10,871,455	3,479,625	1,906,555	67,730	449,765	56,690	23,485
			Percent of Population				
			Total				
Québec	1.0	95.8	2.1	0.4	0.0	0.6	0.1
Québec	9.8	80.0	7.1	0.9	0.6	1.3	0.4
Canada	64.8	20.6	11.1	0.4	2.6	0.3	0.1
			Males				
Québec	1.1	95.7	2.1	0.4	0.0	0.7	0.1
Québec	9.9	80.0	7.0	0.9	0.6	1.3	0.4
Canada	65.1	20.6	10.9	0.4	2.6	0.3	0.1
			Females				
Québec	1.0	95.9	2.0	0.4	0.0	0.6	0.1
Québec	9.7	79.9	7.2	0.9	0.6	1.3	0.4
Canada	64.5	20.6	11.3	0.4	2.7	0.3	0.1

Note: Figures cover total population excluding institutional residents.
Source: Statistics Canada. 2012. Census Profile. 2011 Census. Statistics Canada Catalogue no. 98-316-XWE. Ottawa. Released October 24 2012.
http://www12.statcan.gc.ca/census-recensement/2011/dp-pd/prof/index.cfm?Lang=E

Knowledge of Official Languages

Area	English Only	French Only	English & French	Neither English nor French
		Number		
		Total		
Québec	1,130	316,635	190,630	1,520
Québec	363,860	4,047,175	3,328,725	76,190
Canada	22,564,665	4,165,015	5,795,570	595,920
		Males		
Québec	615	139,735	104,900	670
Québec	180,175	1,871,500	1,758,410	31,175
Canada	11,222,185	1,925,340	2,876,560	241,790
		Females		
Québec	520	176,900	85,730	850
Québec	183,690	2,175,675	1,570,310	45,015
Canada	11,342,485	2,239,680	2,919,005	354,135
		Percent of Population		
		Total		
Québec	0.2	62.1	37.4	0.3
Québec	4.7	51.8	42.6	1.0
Canada	68.1	12.6	17.5	1.8
		Males		
Québec	0.3	56.8	42.7	0.3
Québec	4.7	48.7	45.8	0.8
Canada	69.0	11.8	17.7	1.5
		Females		
Québec	0.2	67.0	32.5	0.3
Québec	4.6	54.7	39.5	1.1
Canada	67.3	13.3	17.3	2.1

Note: Figures cover total population excluding institutional residents.
Source: Statistics Canada. 2012. Census Profile. 2011 Census. Statistics Canada Catalogue no. 98-316-XWE. Ottawa. Released October 24 2012.
http://www12.statcan.gc.ca/census-recensement/2011/dp-pd/prof/index.cfm?Lang=E

Regina, Saskatchewan

Background

Regina is located in southern Saskatchewan, a province producing more than half of the wheat grown in Canada, and is situated in the treeless southern plains. It is the second largest city in the province and the centre of the world's largest breadbasket. Called the "Queen City" after Queen Victoria Regina, "I ♥ R" or "I Love Regina" is the city's official slogan.

Massive herds of buffalo once roamed the plains surrounding present-day Regina. The Cree hunted in the area and built spiritual offerings in the form of buffalo bones piled up to two metres (six feet) high and 12 metres (40 feet) in diameter. The first settlement was called *Oskana ka-asateki*, "the bones that are piled together." Regina was settled in 1882 and incorporated as a city in 1903. It was named the provincial capital in 1906.

Today Regina is home to an urban forest of over 350,000 hand-planted trees. The city is one of Canada's leading economies with an annual gross domestic product (GDP) averaging 3% between 2007 and 2012. The city is the site of a global transportation hub since it is located on both Canada and U.S. major rail lines. Major industries stem from the Regina Research Park, the Petroleum Technology Research Centre, the Titanium Pilot Project and the Greenhouse Gas Technology Centre. Other sector strengths include industrial manufacturing, logistics, agri-business and natural resource development.

Some of the city's best known highlights are the Saskatchewan Legislative Building, the RCMP Heritage Centre, the Saskatchewan Science Centre, the MacKenzie Art Gallery and the Saskatchewan Sports and Hall of Fame Museum. Popular festivals include the Regina Folk Festival, Festi-Ale, Canadian Western Agri-bition and the Mosaic Festival of Trees.

Regina has summer highs of plus 24.73 degrees Celsius, winter lows of minus 19.07 degrees Celsius, and an average rainfall just over 304 mm per year.

Rankings

- Regina ranked #3 of Canada's 103 best entrepreneurial cities. Cities were placed according to 14 indicators in three main categories: Presence (scale and growth, industrial diversity), Perspective (optimism and growth plans), and Policy (local government and business taxation and regulation). Five Saskatchewan cities were in the top 10, including Saskatoon (SK) (#2). Grand Prairie (AB) ranked #1 overall. *Canadian Federation of Independent Business (CFIB), "Communities in Boom: Canada's Top Entrepreneurial Cities Report," October 2012*
- Regina ranked in the Top 10 of Canada's smartest cities. The annual Composite Learning Index ranked the city #5 out of more than 4,500 communities across Canada. The study measured traditional literacy, work-related skill, community involvement and personal learning. *Maclean's Magazine, "Canada's Smartest Cities: 2010 Rankings," May 20, 2010 with files from the 2010 Composite Learning Index*

PROFILES / Regina, Saskatchewan

Population Growth and Density

Area	Population in 2001	Population in 2006	Population in 2011	Population Change 2001–2006	Population Change 2006–2011	Land Area (sq. km)	Population Density per sq. km
Regina	178,225	179,282	193,100	0.6	7.7	145.45	1,327.6
Saskatchewan	978,933	968,157	1,033,381	-1.1	6.7	588,239.21	1.8
Canada	30,007,094	31,612,897	33,476,688	5.4	5.9	8,965,121.42	3.7

Source: Statistics Canada. 2012. Census Profile. 2011 Census. Statistics Canada Catalogue no. 98-316-XWE. Ottawa. Released October 24 2012. http://www12.statcan.gc.ca/census-recensement/2011/dp-pd/prof/index.cfm?Lang=E;
Statistics Canada 2007. 2006 Community Profiles. 2006 Census. Statistics Canada Catalogue no. 92-591-XWE. Ottawa. Released March 13 2007. http://www12.statcan.ca/census-recensement/2006/dp-pd/prof/92-591/index.cfm?Lang=E

Gender

Area	Males	Females
Number		
Regina	94,025	99,075
Saskatchewan	511,555	521,825
Canada	16,414,225	17,062,460
Percent of Population		
Regina	48.7	51.3
Saskatchewan	49.5	50.5
Canada	49.0	51.0

Source: Statistics Canada. 2012. Census Profile. 2011 Census. Statistics Canada Catalogue no. 98-316-XWE. Ottawa. Released October 24 2012. http://www12.statcan.gc.ca/census-recensement/2011/dp-pd/prof/index.cfm?Lang=E

Marital Status

Area	Married[1]	Living Common-law	Single[2]	Separated	Divorced	Widowed
Number — Total						
Regina	73,790	13,350	49,190	3,605	10,270	9,355
Saskatchewan	416,355	71,630	232,160	18,210	43,665	53,500
Canada	12,941,960	3,142,525	7,816,045	698,240	1,686,035	1,584,530
Males						
Regina	37,010	6,670	26,035	1,480	4,015	1,705
Saskatchewan	208,700	35,785	128,325	8,220	19,500	10,015
Canada	6,470,300	1,575,495	4,206,320	299,655	680,415	310,940
Females						
Regina	36,785	6,675	23,155	2,125	6,260	7,650
Saskatchewan	207,655	35,845	103,835	9,990	24,170	43,490
Canada	6,471,660	1,567,035	3,609,730	398,585	1,005,620	1,273,590
Percent of Population — Total						
Regina	46.2	8.4	30.8	2.3	6.4	5.9
Saskatchewan	49.8	8.6	27.8	2.2	5.2	6.4
Canada	46.4	11.3	28.0	2.5	6.0	5.7
Males						
Regina	48.1	8.7	33.9	1.9	5.2	2.2
Saskatchewan	50.8	8.7	31.3	2.0	4.7	2.4
Canada	47.8	11.6	31.1	2.2	5.0	2.3
Females						
Regina	44.5	8.1	28.0	2.6	7.6	9.3
Saskatchewan	48.9	8.4	24.4	2.4	5.7	10.2
Canada	45.2	10.9	25.2	2.8	7.0	8.9

Note: (1) and not separated, (2) never legally married
Source: Statistics Canada. 2012. Census Profile. 2011 Census. Statistics Canada Catalogue no. 98-316-XWE. Ottawa. Released October 24 2012. http://www12.statcan.gc.ca/census-recensement/2011/dp-pd/prof/index.cfm?Lang=E

Age Characteristics: 0 to 49 Years

Area	0 to 4 Years	5 to 9 Years	10 to 14 Years	15 to 19 Years	20 to 24 Years	25 to 29 Years	30 to 34 Years	35 to 39 Years	40 to 44 Years	45 to 49 Years
					Number					
					Total					
Regina	12,125	10,635	10,780	12,545	15,340	15,595	14,100	12,520	11,915	14,495
Saskatchewan	68,760	63,350	65,750	71,760	72,610	70,395	65,340	61,150	61,475	74,630
Canada	1,877,095	1,809,895	1,920,355	2,178,135	2,187,450	2,169,590	2,162,905	2,173,930	2,324,875	2,675,130
					Males					
Regina	6,235	5,420	5,465	6,365	7,635	7,945	6,990	6,210	5,935	6,990
Saskatchewan	35,070	32,480	33,465	36,870	37,135	35,510	32,750	30,265	30,550	36,820
Canada	961,150	925,965	983,995	1,115,845	1,108,775	1,077,275	1,058,810	1,064,200	1,141,720	1,318,715
					Females					
Regina	5,885	5,215	5,320	6,175	7,705	7,650	7,110	6,315	5,975	7,505
Saskatchewan	33,690	30,865	32,285	34,885	35,470	34,885	32,590	30,880	30,920	37,810
Canada	915,945	883,935	936,360	1,062,295	1,078,670	1,092,315	1,104,095	1,109,735	1,183,155	1,356,420
					Percent of Population					
					Total					
Regina	6.3	5.5	5.6	6.5	7.9	8.1	7.3	6.5	6.2	7.5
Saskatchewan	6.7	6.1	6.4	6.9	7.0	6.8	6.3	5.9	5.9	7.2
Canada	5.6	5.4	5.7	6.5	6.5	6.5	6.5	6.5	6.9	8.0
					Males					
Regina	6.6	5.8	5.8	6.8	8.1	8.4	7.4	6.6	6.3	7.4
Saskatchewan	6.9	6.3	6.5	7.2	7.3	6.9	6.4	5.9	6.0	7.2
Canada	5.9	5.6	6.0	6.8	6.8	6.6	6.5	6.5	7.0	8.0
					Females					
Regina	5.9	5.3	5.4	6.2	7.8	7.7	7.2	6.4	6.0	7.6
Saskatchewan	6.5	5.9	6.2	6.7	6.8	6.7	6.2	5.9	5.9	7.2
Canada	5.4	5.2	5.5	6.2	6.3	6.4	6.5	6.5	6.9	7.9

Source: Statistics Canada. 2012. Census Profile. 2011 Census. Statistics Canada Catalogue no. 98-316-XWE. Ottawa. Released October 24 2012.
http://www12.statcan.gc.ca/census-recensement/2011/dp-pd/prof/index.cfm?Lang=E

Age Characteristics: 50 Years and Over, and Median Age

Area	50 to 54 Years	55 to 59 Years	60 to 64 Years	65 to 69 Years	70 to 74 Years	75 to 79 Years	80 to 84 Years	85 Years and Over	Median Age
				Number					
				Total					
Regina	14,470	12,640	10,075	6,930	5,725	4,990	4,025	4,195	37.1
Saskatchewan	77,480	70,050	56,945	41,500	33,820	28,950	23,955	25,475	38.2
Canada	2,658,965	2,340,635	2,052,670	1,521,715	1,153,065	922,700	702,070	645,515	40.6
				Males					
Regina	7,105	6,125	4,840	3,230	2,550	2,095	1,645	1,250	35.7
Saskatchewan	38,855	35,185	28,305	20,445	16,050	13,200	10,165	8,435	37.0
Canada	1,309,030	1,147,300	1,002,690	738,010	543,435	417,945	291,085	208,300	39.6
				Females					
Regina	7,365	6,520	5,235	3,700	3,175	2,900	2,385	2,945	38.5
Saskatchewan	38,625	34,865	28,645	21,055	17,770	15,750	13,795	17,035	39.2
Canada	1,349,940	1,193,335	1,049,985	783,705	609,630	504,755	410,985	437,215	41.5
				Percent of Population					
				Total					
Regina	7.5	6.5	5.2	3.6	3.0	2.6	2.1	2.2	–
Saskatchewan	7.5	6.8	5.5	4.0	3.3	2.8	2.3	2.5	–
Canada	7.9	7.0	6.1	4.5	3.4	2.8	2.1	1.9	–
				Males					
Regina	7.6	6.5	5.1	3.4	2.7	2.2	1.7	1.3	–
Saskatchewan	7.6	6.9	5.5	4.0	3.1	2.6	2.0	1.6	–
Canada	8.0	7.0	6.1	4.5	3.3	2.5	1.8	1.3	–
				Females					
Regina	7.4	6.6	5.3	3.7	3.2	2.9	2.4	3.0	–
Saskatchewan	7.4	6.7	5.5	4.0	3.4	3.0	2.6	3.3	–
Canada	7.9	7.0	6.2	4.6	3.6	3.0	2.4	2.6	–

Source: Statistics Canada. 2012. Census Profile. 2011 Census. Statistics Canada Catalogue no. 98-316-XWE. Ottawa. Released October 24 2012.
http://www12.statcan.gc.ca/census-recensement/2011/dp-pd/prof/index.cfm?Lang=E

PROFILES / Regina, Saskatchewan

Private Households by Household Size

Area	1 Person	2 Persons	3 Persons	4 Persons	5 Persons	6 or More Persons	Average Number of Persons in Private Households
			Households				
Regina	23,795	27,130	12,180	10,695	3,805	2,000	2.4
Saskatchewan	114,385	146,850	57,410	53,070	23,455	14,470	2.5
Canada	3,673,310	4,544,820	2,081,900	1,903,300	724,405	392,885	2.5
			Percent of Households				
Regina	29.9	34.1	15.3	13.4	4.8	2.5	–
Saskatchewan	27.9	35.8	14.0	13.0	5.7	3.5	–
Canada	27.6	34.1	15.6	14.3	5.4	2.9	–

Source: Statistics Canada. 2012. Census Profile. 2011 Census. Statistics Canada Catalogue no. 98-316-XWE. Ottawa. Released October 24 2012.
http://www12.statcan.gc.ca/census-recensement/2011/dp-pd/prof/index.cfm?Lang=E

Dwelling Type

Area	Single-detached House	Semi-detached House	Row House	Apartment: Building with Five or More Storeys	Apartment: Building with Fewer Than Five Storeys	Duplex Apartment	Movable Dwelling	Other Single-attached House
				Number				
Regina	53,625	1,970	4,355	3,805	14,595	1,095	135	30
Saskatchewan	303,250	11,945	14,370	10,830	52,655	7,090	8,805	700
Canada	7,329,150	646,245	791,600	1,234,770	2,397,550	704,485	183,510	33,310
				Percent of Dwellings				
Regina	67.4	2.5	5.5	4.8	18.3	1.4	0.2	0.0
Saskatchewan	74.0	2.9	3.5	2.6	12.9	1.7	2.1	0.2
Canada	55.0	4.9	5.9	9.3	18.0	5.3	1.4	0.3

Source: Statistics Canada. 2012. Census Profile. 2011 Census. Statistics Canada Catalogue no. 98-316-XWE. Ottawa. Released October 24 2012.
http://www12.statcan.gc.ca/census-recensement/2011/dp-pd/prof/index.cfm?Lang=E

Shelter Costs

	Owned Dwellings				Rented Dwellings		
Area	Number	Median Value[1] ($)	Average Value[1] ($)	Median Monthly Costs[2] ($)	Average Monthly Costs[2] ($)	Number	Median Monthly Costs[3] ($)	Average Monthly Costs[3] ($)
Regina	55,120	299,748	318,333	967	1,077	24,490	882	930
Saskatchewan	273,345	250,347	267,006	751	943	99,410	793	837
Canada	9,013,410	280,552	345,182	978	1,141	4,060,385	784	848

Note: All figures cover non-farm, non-reserve private dwellings; (1) Refers to the dollar amount expected by the owner if the dwelling were to be sold; (2) Includes all shelter expenses paid by households that own their dwellings, such as the mortgage payment and the costs of electricity, heat, water and other municipal services, property taxes and condominium fees; (3) Includes all shelter expenses paid by households that rent their dwellings, such as the monthly rent and the costs of electricity, heat and municipal services.
Source: Statistics Canada. 2013. 2011 National Household Survey. Statistics Canada Catalogue no. 99-004-XWE. Ottawa. Released September 11, 2013.

Occupied Private Dwellings by Period of Construction

Area	1960 or Before	1961 to 1980	1981 to 1990	1991 to 2000	2001 to 2005	2006 to 2011
			Number			
Regina	20,990	32,695	12,585	4,830	3,665	4,855
Saskatchewan	108,390	154,185	68,215	32,570	18,505	27,705
Canada	3,273,105	4,152,715	2,112,110	1,707,880	1,031,020	1,042,430
			Percent of Dwellings			
Regina	26.4	41.1	15.8	6.1	4.6	6.1
Saskatchewan	26.5	37.6	16.7	8.0	4.5	6.8
Canada	24.6	31.2	15.9	12.8	7.7	7.8

Note: Figures cover non-farm, non-reserve private dwellings and includes data up to May 10, 2011.
Source: Statistics Canada. 2013. 2011 National Household Survey. Statistics Canada Catalogue no. 99-004-XWE. Ottawa. Released September 11, 2013.

Educational Attainment

Area	No Certificate, Diploma or Degree	High School Diploma or Equivalent[1]	Apprenticeship or Trades Certificate or Diploma[2]	College, CÉGEP or Other Non-University Certificate or Diploma	University Certificate or Diploma Below the Bachelor Level[3]	Bachelor's Degree	University Certificate, Diploma or Degree Above Bachelor Level[4]
			Number				
			Total				
Regina	28,850	46,905	15,400	23,605	7,380	25,090	8,965
Saskatchewan	200,430	228,755	98,820	127,295	32,780	90,720	33,705
Canada	5,485,400	6,968,935	2,950,685	4,970,020	1,200,130	3,634,425	2,049,930
			Males				
Regina	14,515	22,500	10,465	9,000	2,975	11,525	4,690
Saskatchewan	106,880	115,075	65,090	44,805	12,735	38,930	17,445
Canada	2,742,875	3,305,415	1,928,970	2,118,430	513,235	1,643,080	1,043,350
			Females				
Regina	14,335	24,410	4,935	14,605	4,410	13,560	4,275
Saskatchewan	93,550	113,680	33,730	82,490	20,040	51,785	16,260
Canada	2,742,520	3,663,515	1,021,715	2,851,595	686,890	1,991,345	1,006,585
			Percent of Population				
			Total				
Regina	18.5	30.0	9.9	15.1	4.7	16.1	5.7
Saskatchewan	24.7	28.2	12.2	15.7	4.0	11.2	4.1
Canada	20.1	25.6	10.8	18.2	4.4	13.3	7.5
			Males				
Regina	19.2	29.7	13.8	11.9	3.9	15.2	6.2
Saskatchewan	26.7	28.7	16.2	11.2	3.2	9.7	4.4
Canada	20.6	24.9	14.5	15.9	3.9	12.4	7.8
			Females				
Regina	17.8	30.3	6.1	18.1	5.5	16.8	5.3
Saskatchewan	22.7	27.6	8.2	20.0	4.9	12.6	4.0
Canada	19.6	26.2	7.3	20.4	4.9	14.3	7.2

Note: Figures cover total population aged 15 years and over by highest certificate, diploma or degree; (1) Includes persons who have graduated from a secondary school or equivalent. It excludes persons with a postsecondary certificate, diploma or degree; (2) Includes Registered Apprenticeship certificates (including Certificate of Qualification, Journeyperson's designation) and other trades certificates or diplomas such as pre-employment or vocational certificates and diplomas from brief trade programs completed at community colleges, institutes of technology, vocational centres, and similar institutions; (3) Comparisons with other data sources suggest that the category 'University certificate or diploma below the bachelor's level' was over-reported in the NHS. This category likely includes some responses that are actually college certificates or diplomas, bachelor's degrees or other types of education (e.g., university transfer programs, bachelor's programs completed in other countries, incomplete bachelor's programs, non-university professional designations). We recommend users interpret the results for the 'University certificate or diploma below the bachelor's level' category with caution; (4) 'University certificate or diploma above bachelor level' includes the categories: 'Degree in medicine, dentistry, veterinary medicine or optometry,' 'Master's degree' and 'Earned doctorate.'
Source: Statistics Canada. 2013. 2011 National Household Survey. Statistics Canada Catalogue no. 99-004-XWE. Ottawa. Released September 11, 2013.

Household Income Distribution

Area	Less than $10,000	$10,000 to $19,999	$20,000 to $29,999	$30,000 to $39,999	$40,000 to $49,999	$50,000 to $59,999	$60,000 to $79,999	$80,000 to $99,999	$100,000 to $124,999	$125,000 to $149,999	$150,000 and Over
					Households						
Regina	3,180	5,540	6,010	6,985	6,440	6,345	11,160	8,855	8,475	6,105	10,515
Saskatchewan	17,365	37,195	36,770	38,910	36,000	33,020	57,220	44,980	40,505	26,620	40,990
Canada	626,705	1,141,945	1,193,925	1,271,675	1,206,800	1,102,120	1,865,280	1,458,240	1,260,770	802,555	1,389,240
					Percent of Households						
Regina	4.0	7.0	7.5	8.8	8.1	8.0	14.0	11.1	10.6	7.7	13.2
Saskatchewan	4.2	9.1	9.0	9.5	8.8	8.1	14.0	11.0	9.9	6.5	10.0
Canada	4.7	8.6	9.0	9.5	9.1	8.3	14.0	10.9	9.5	6.0	10.4

Note: Household income is the sum of the total incomes of all members of that household. Total income refers to monetary receipts from certain sources, before income taxes and deductions, during calendar year 2010.
Source: Statistics Canada. 2013. 2011 National Household Survey. Statistics Canada Catalogue no. 99-004-XWE. Ottawa. Released September 11, 2013.

Median and Average Household and Economic Family Income

Area	Median Household Income ($)	Average Household Income ($)	Median After-tax Household Income ($)	Average After-tax Household Income ($)	Median Economic Family Income ($)	Average Economic Family Income ($)	Median After-tax Economic Family Income ($)	Average After-tax Economic Family Income ($)
Regina	69,192	86,246	59,727	71,413	89,172	105,089	76,549	86,671
Saskatchewan	61,703	77,317	54,628	65,050	77,448	91,877	68,046	77,161
Canada	61,072	79,102	54,089	66,149	76,511	94,125	67,044	78,517

Note: Figures cover household and economic familiy income in 2010. A household is defined as a person or a group of persons (other than foreign residents) who occupy the same private dwelling and do not have a usual place of residence elsewhere in Canada. Every person is a member of one and only one household. An economic family is defined as a group of two or more persons who live in the same dwelling and are related to each other by blood, marriage, common-law, adoption or a foster relationship. A couple may be of opposite or same sex.
Source: Statistics Canada. 2013. 2011 National Household Survey. Statistics Canada Catalogue no. 99-004-XWE. Ottawa. Released September 11, 2013.

Individual Income Distribution

Area	Less than $10,000	$10,000 to $19,999	$20,000 to $29,999	$30,000 to $39,999	$40,000 to $49,999	$50,000 to $59,999	$60,000 to $79,999	$80,000 to $99,999	$100,000 to $124,999	$125,000 and Over
					Number Total					
Regina	20,775	21,865	19,785	19,775	16,610	13,110	18,495	9,720	5,055	5,055
Saskatchewan	125,400	138,190	108,765	100,155	81,730	58,995	77,820	40,360	23,430	21,345
Canada	4,492,040	4,835,710	3,670,020	3,180,360	2,603,520	1,921,650	2,437,440	1,302,045	693,580	782,135
					Males					
Regina	9,200	7,875	8,390	9,200	7,805	6,770	10,780	5,740	3,505	3,740
Saskatchewan	55,995	51,705	45,025	46,150	42,655	33,030	48,665	26,490	17,835	17,185
Canada	1,936,365	1,864,880	1,588,260	1,522,190	1,333,510	1,079,780	1,473,145	823,720	492,905	599,905
					Females					
Regina	11,565	13,985	11,390	10,580	8,810	6,340	7,710	3,980	1,550	1,320
Saskatchewan	69,405	86,485	63,745	54,010	39,075	25,965	29,155	13,865	5,595	4,165
Canada	2,555,675	2,970,825	2,081,760	1,658,170	1,270,010	841,870	964,300	478,330	200,680	182,230
					Percent of Population Total					
Regina	13.8	14.6	13.2	13.2	11.1	8.7	12.3	6.5	3.4	3.4
Saskatchewan	16.2	17.8	14.0	12.9	10.5	7.6	10.0	5.2	3.0	2.7
Canada	17.3	18.7	14.2	12.3	10.0	7.4	9.4	5.0	2.7	3.0
					Males					
Regina	12.6	10.8	11.5	12.6	10.7	9.3	14.8	7.9	4.8	5.1
Saskatchewan	14.6	13.4	11.7	12.0	11.1	8.6	12.6	6.9	4.6	4.5
Canada	15.2	14.7	12.5	12.0	10.5	8.5	11.6	6.5	3.9	4.7
					Females					
Regina	15.0	18.1	14.7	13.7	11.4	8.2	10.0	5.2	2.0	1.7
Saskatchewan	17.7	22.1	16.3	13.8	10.0	6.6	7.4	3.5	1.4	1.1
Canada	19.4	22.5	15.8	12.6	9.6	6.4	7.3	3.6	1.5	1.4

Note: Figures cover individuals aged 15 years and over with income. Income refers to monetary receipts from certain sources, before income taxes and deductions, during calendar year 2010.
Source: Statistics Canada. 2013. 2011 National Household Survey. Statistics Canada Catalogue no. 99-004-XWE. Ottawa. Released September 11, 2013.

Labour Force Status

Area	In the Labour Force – All	Employed	Unemployed	Not in the Labour Force
		Number Total		
Regina	113,055	107,390	5,670	43,140
Saskatchewan	562,310	529,100	33,210	250,190
Canada	17,990,080	16,595,035	1,395,045	9,269,445
		Males		
Regina	58,510	55,740	2,775	17,155
Saskatchewan	300,420	282,565	17,850	100,545
Canada	9,388,570	8,634,310	754,255	3,906,785
		Females		
Regina	54,545	51,650	2,890	25,990
Saskatchewan	261,885	246,530	15,355	149,650
Canada	8,601,515	7,960,725	640,790	5,362,660
		Percent of Labour Force Total		
Regina	72.4	68.8	5.0	27.6
Saskatchewan	69.2	65.1	5.9	30.8
Canada	66.0	60.9	7.8	34.0
		Males		
Regina	77.3	73.7	4.7	22.7
Saskatchewan	74.9	70.5	5.9	25.1
Canada	70.6	64.9	8.0	29.4
		Females		
Regina	67.7	64.1	5.3	32.3
Saskatchewan	63.6	59.9	5.9	36.4
Canada	61.6	57.0	7.4	38.4

Note: Figures are based on total population 15 years and over
Source: Statistics Canada. 2013. 2011 National Household Survey. Statistics Canada Catalogue no. 99-004-XWE. Ottawa. Released September 11, 2013.

Labour Force by Industry (NAICS Codes 11–52)

Area	Agriculture, forestry, fishing & hunting	Mining, quarrying, & oil & gas extraction	Utilities	Construction	Manufacturing	Wholesale Trade	Retail Trade	Transportation & warehousing	Information & cultural industries	Finance & insurance
Number										
Total										
Regina	935	980	1,685	8,515	5,365	4,870	13,015	4,840	4,085	7,355
Saskatchewan	51,360	22,985	5,330	42,975	26,460	21,135	60,940	25,390	10,900	21,120
Canada	437,650	261,050	149,940	1,215,380	1,619,295	733,445	2,031,665	827,780	420,830	767,960
Males										
Regina	680	825	1,040	7,665	4,410	3,650	6,480	3,820	2,315	2,765
Saskatchewan	37,210	19,940	3,810	38,140	21,000	15,950	28,545	19,460	5,390	6,425
Canada	307,370	211,690	110,765	1,068,710	1,167,680	494,545	933,850	617,305	235,875	296,995
Females										
Regina	255	155	645	850	950	1,225	6,535	1,020	1,770	4,590
Saskatchewan	14,150	3,045	1,520	4,830	5,460	5,185	32,395	5,930	5,510	14,695
Canada	130,285	49,360	39,175	146,670	451,615	238,900	1,097,820	210,475	184,955	470,960
Percent of Labour Force										
Total										
Regina	0.8	0.9	1.5	7.6	4.8	4.4	11.7	4.3	3.7	6.6
Saskatchewan	9.3	4.1	1.0	7.7	4.8	3.8	11.0	4.6	2.0	3.8
Canada	2.5	1.5	0.9	6.9	9.2	4.2	11.6	4.7	2.4	4.4
Males										
Regina	1.2	1.4	1.8	13.2	7.6	6.3	11.2	6.6	4.0	4.8
Saskatchewan	12.5	6.7	1.3	12.9	7.1	5.4	9.6	6.6	1.8	2.2
Canada	3.3	2.3	1.2	11.6	12.7	5.4	10.2	6.7	2.6	3.2
Females										
Regina	0.5	0.3	1.2	1.6	1.8	2.3	12.1	1.9	3.3	8.5
Saskatchewan	5.5	1.2	0.6	1.9	2.1	2.0	12.6	2.3	2.1	5.7
Canada	1.6	0.6	0.5	1.7	5.4	2.8	13.1	2.5	2.2	5.6

Note: Figures are based on total experienced labour force 15 years and over. Experienced labour force refers to persons who, during the week of Sunday, May 1 to Saturday, May 7, 2011, were employed and the unemployed who had last worked for pay or in self-employment in either 2010 or 2011.
Source: Statistics Canada. 2013. 2011 National Household Survey. Statistics Canada Catalogue no. 99-004-XWE. Ottawa. Released September 11, 2013.

Labour Force by Industry (NAICS Codes 53–91)

Area	Real estate & rental & leasing	Profess., scientific & tech. services	Mgmt of companies & enterprises	Admin. & support, waste mgmt & remed. services	Educational services	Health care & social assistance	Arts, entertain. & recreation	Accomm. & food services	Other services (except public admin.)	Public admin.
Number										
Total										
Regina	1,840	5,955	105	3,525	7,655	13,520	2,275	7,480	5,635	12,075
Saskatchewan	7,445	23,520	575	13,425	43,995	65,450	9,825	34,085	25,445	42,335
Canada	321,895	1,240,850	17,460	728,330	1,301,435	1,949,650	363,405	1,130,750	807,800	1,261,050
Males										
Regina	1,165	3,455	40	1,985	2,575	2,405	1,155	2,955	2,640	5,845
Saskatchewan	4,140	12,180	240	7,390	14,600	9,635	5,035	12,620	12,695	22,310
Canada	179,090	688,625	9,380	411,250	424,915	349,430	188,270	469,990	372,940	652,510
Females										
Regina	670	2,495	60	1,540	5,080	11,110	1,115	4,525	2,990	6,230
Saskatchewan	3,305	11,345	330	6,035	29,400	55,815	4,795	21,460	12,750	20,025
Canada	142,805	552,225	8,075	317,085	876,515	1,600,220	175,135	660,760	434,865	608,535
Percent of Labour Force										
Total										
Regina	1.6	5.3	0.1	3.2	6.9	12.1	2.0	6.7	5.0	10.8
Saskatchewan	1.3	4.2	0.1	2.4	7.9	11.8	1.8	6.1	4.6	7.6
Canada	1.8	7.1	0.1	4.1	7.4	11.1	2.1	6.4	4.6	7.2
Males										
Regina	2.0	6.0	0.1	3.4	4.4	4.2	2.0	5.1	4.6	10.1
Saskatchewan	1.4	4.1	0.1	2.5	4.9	3.2	1.7	4.3	4.3	7.5
Canada	1.9	7.5	0.1	4.5	4.6	3.8	2.0	5.1	4.1	7.1
Females										
Regina	1.2	4.6	0.1	2.9	9.4	20.6	2.1	8.4	5.6	11.6
Saskatchewan	1.3	4.4	0.1	2.3	11.4	21.6	1.9	8.3	4.9	7.8
Canada	1.7	6.6	0.1	3.8	10.4	19.1	2.1	7.9	5.2	7.2

Note: Figures are based on total experienced labour force 15 years and over. Experienced labour force refers to persons who, during the week of Sunday, May 1 to Saturday, May 7, 2011, were employed and the unemployed who had last worked for pay or in self-employment in either 2010 or 2011.
Source: Statistics Canada. 2013. 2011 National Household Survey. Statistics Canada Catalogue no. 99-004-XWE. Ottawa. Released September 11, 2013.

PROFILES / Regina, Saskatchewan

Occupation

Area	Mgmt	Business, Finance & Admin.	Natural/ Applied Sciences & Related	Health	Education, Law & Social, Community & Government Services	Art, Culture, Recreation & Sport	Sales & Service	Trades, Transport & Equip. Operators & Related	Natural Resources, Agri. & Related Production	Mfg & Utilities
Number										
Total										
Regina	11,655	21,530	7,805	7,565	13,420	2,640	26,225	17,175	1,215	2,475
Saskatchewan	81,235	80,645	26,280	38,800	62,310	10,000	118,755	94,870	26,390	15,445
Canada	1,963,600	2,902,045	1,237,775	1,107,200	2,064,675	503,415	4,068,170	2,537,775	397,930	805,040
Males										
Regina	6,725	6,485	6,160	1,465	4,805	1,275	11,665	16,110	1,050	2,155
Saskatchewan	54,370	20,530	20,525	6,145	20,645	3,950	47,770	89,055	20,960	12,760
Canada	1,229,460	854,190	966,355	217,520	676,550	232,535	1,745,705	2,385,615	318,945	564,300
Females										
Regina	4,930	15,045	1,645	6,100	8,615	1,365	14,555	1,065	165	320
Saskatchewan	26,860	60,110	5,750	32,660	41,665	6,045	70,980	5,810	5,430	2,685
Canada	734,140	2,047,855	271,415	889,675	1,388,130	270,875	2,322,465	152,165	78,980	240,740
Percent of Labour Force										
Total										
Regina	10.4	19.3	7.0	6.8	12.0	2.4	23.5	15.4	1.1	2.2
Saskatchewan	14.6	14.5	4.7	7.0	11.2	1.8	21.4	17.1	4.8	2.8
Canada	11.2	16.5	7.0	6.3	11.7	2.9	23.1	14.4	2.3	4.6
Males										
Regina	11.6	11.2	10.6	2.5	8.3	2.2	20.2	27.8	1.8	3.7
Saskatchewan	18.3	6.9	6.9	2.1	7.0	1.3	16.1	30.0	7.1	4.3
Canada	13.4	9.3	10.5	2.4	7.4	2.5	19.0	26.0	3.5	6.1
Females										
Regina	9.2	28.0	3.1	11.3	16.0	2.5	27.0	2.0	0.3	0.6
Saskatchewan	10.4	23.3	2.2	12.7	16.1	2.3	27.5	2.3	2.1	1.0
Canada	8.7	24.4	3.2	10.6	16.5	3.2	27.7	1.8	0.9	2.9

Note: Figures are based on total experienced labour force 15 years and over
Source: Statistics Canada. 2013. 2011 National Household Survey. Statistics Canada Catalogue no. 99-004-XWE. Ottawa. Released September 11, 2013.

Place of Work Status

Area	Worked at Home	Worked Outside Canada	No Fixed Workplace Address	Worked at Usual Place
Number				
Total				
Regina	4,010	125	10,870	92,385
Saskatchewan	59,365	655	64,710	404,365
Canada	1,142,640	66,460	1,868,245	13,517,690
Males				
Regina	1,795	75	8,825	45,045
Saskatchewan	35,590	455	52,585	193,940
Canada	582,150	47,355	1,400,485	6,604,325
Females				
Regina	2,215	55	2,045	47,335
Saskatchewan	23,770	200	12,130	210,430
Canada	560,490	19,100	467,760	6,913,370
Percent of Labour Force				
Total				
Regina	3.7	0.1	10.1	86.0
Saskatchewan	11.2	0.1	12.2	76.4
Canada	6.9	0.4	11.3	81.5
Males				
Regina	3.2	0.1	15.8	80.8
Saskatchewan	12.6	0.2	18.6	68.6
Canada	6.7	0.5	16.2	76.5
Females				
Regina	4.3	0.1	4.0	91.6
Saskatchewan	9.6	0.1	4.9	85.4
Canada	7.0	0.2	5.9	86.8

Note: Figures are based on total employed labour force 15 years and over.
Source: Statistics Canada. 2013. 2011 National Household Survey. Statistics Canada Catalogue no. 99-004-XWE. Ottawa. Released September 11, 2013.

Mode of Transportation to Work

Area	Car; Truck; Van; as Driver	Car; Truck; Van; as Passenger	Public Transit	Walked	Bicycled	All Other Modes
			Number			
			Total			
Regina	83,865	7,000	5,305	5,000	1,305	780
Saskatchewan	382,000	28,715	12,990	31,480	5,705	8,185
Canada	11,393,140	867,050	1,851,525	880,815	201,780	191,625
			Males			
Regina	45,705	2,275	2,130	2,370	1,005	385
Saskatchewan	206,540	12,025	5,475	13,285	3,970	5,235
Canada	6,238,835	349,530	788,290	387,580	135,840	104,725
			Females			
Regina	38,160	4,725	3,170	2,630	305	390
Saskatchewan	175,460	16,695	7,515	18,200	1,735	2,950
Canada	5,154,305	517,520	1,063,235	493,230	65,940	86,900
			Percent of Labour Force			
			Total			
Regina	81.2	6.8	5.1	4.8	1.3	0.8
Saskatchewan	81.4	6.1	2.8	6.7	1.2	1.7
Canada	74.0	5.6	12.0	5.7	1.3	1.2
			Males			
Regina	84.8	4.2	4.0	4.4	1.9	0.7
Saskatchewan	83.8	4.9	2.2	5.4	1.6	2.1
Canada	77.9	4.4	9.8	4.8	1.7	1.3
			Females			
Regina	77.3	9.6	6.4	5.3	0.6	0.8
Saskatchewan	78.8	7.5	3.4	8.2	0.8	1.3
Canada	69.8	7.0	14.4	6.7	0.9	1.2

Note: Figures are based on total employed labour force 15 years and over.
Source: Statistics Canada. 2013. 2011 National Household Survey. Statistics Canada Catalogue no. 99-004-XWE. Ottawa. Released September 11, 2013.

Visible Minority Population Characteristics

Area	Total Minority	South Asian[1]	Chinese	Black	Filipino	Latin American	Arab	SE Asian[2]	West Asian[3]	Korean	Japanese	Multiple[4]
						Number						
						Total						
Regina	21,765	4,885	3,645	3,065	4,135	1,270	590	2,500	470	395	145	530
Saskatchewan	63,275	12,325	11,300	7,255	16,025	3,250	2,095	4,910	1,600	1,270	720	1,775
Canada	6,264,750	1,567,400	1,324,750	945,665	619,310	381,280	380,620	312,075	206,840	161,130	87,270	171,935
						Males						
Regina	11,115	2,625	1,715	1,605	2,015	600	270	1,380	255	220	60	305
Saskatchewan	32,460	6,605	5,535	3,935	7,970	1,610	1,075	2,615	850	675	320	910
Canada	3,043,010	790,755	632,325	453,005	268,885	186,355	203,485	154,035	105,620	77,165	38,270	83,335
						Females						
Regina	10,655	2,265	1,925	1,455	2,120	670	320	1,120	220	180	80	225
Saskatchewan	30,815	5,715	5,760	3,320	8,055	1,635	1,025	2,300	745	595	400	860
Canada	3,221,745	776,650	692,420	492,660	350,425	194,925	177,140	158,045	101,220	83,965	48,990	88,600
						Percent of Population						
						Total						
Regina	11.5	2.6	1.9	1.6	2.2	0.7	0.3	1.3	0.2	0.2	0.1	0.3
Saskatchewan	6.3	1.2	1.1	0.7	1.6	0.3	0.2	0.5	0.2	0.1	0.1	0.2
Canada	19.1	4.8	4.0	2.9	1.9	1.2	1.2	0.9	0.6	0.5	0.3	0.5
						Males						
Regina	12.0	2.8	1.8	1.7	2.2	0.6	0.3	1.5	0.3	0.2	0.1	0.3
Saskatchewan	6.5	1.3	1.1	0.8	1.6	0.3	0.2	0.5	0.2	0.1	0.1	0.2
Canada	18.8	4.9	3.9	2.8	1.7	1.2	1.3	1.0	0.7	0.5	0.2	0.5
						Females						
Regina	11.0	2.3	2.0	1.5	2.2	0.7	0.3	1.2	0.2	0.2	0.1	0.2
Saskatchewan	6.1	1.1	1.1	0.7	1.6	0.3	0.2	0.5	0.1	0.1	0.1	0.2
Canada	19.3	4.7	4.1	3.0	2.1	1.2	1.1	0.9	0.6	0.5	0.3	0.5

Note: The Employment Equity Act defines visible minorities as 'persons, other than Aboriginal peoples, who are non-Caucasian in race or non-white in colour';
(1) Includes 'East Indian,' 'Pakistani,' 'Sri Lankan,' etc.; (2) Includes 'Vietnamese,' 'Cambodian,' 'Malaysian,' 'Laotian,' etc.; (3) Includes 'Iranian,' 'Afghan,' etc.; (4) Includes respondents who reported more than one visible minority group by checking two or more mark-in circles, e.g., 'Black' and 'South Asian.'
Source: Statistics Canada. 2013. 2011 National Household Survey. Statistics Canada Catalogue no. 99-004-XWE. Ottawa. Released September 11, 2013.

PROFILES / Regina, Saskatchewan

Aboriginal Population

Area	Aboriginal Identity[1]	First Nations (North American Indian) Single Identity[2]	Métis Single Identity	Inuk (Inuit) Single Identity	Multiple Aboriginal Identities[3]	Aboriginal Identities Not Included Elsewhere
Number						
Total						
Regina	18,750	10,955	7,410	0	220	135
Saskatchewan	157,740	103,205	52,450	290	675	1,120
Canada	1,400,685	851,560	451,795	59,440	11,415	26,475
Males						
Regina	8,675	5,055	3,500	0	60	50
Saskatchewan	75,845	50,170	24,780	145	250	500
Canada	682,190	411,785	223,335	29,495	5,525	12,055
Females						
Regina	10,070	5,905	3,910	0	165	90
Saskatchewan	81,895	53,040	27,670	145	420	620
Canada	718,500	439,775	228,460	29,950	5,890	14,420
Percent of Population						
Total						
Regina	9.9	5.8	3.9	0.0	0.1	0.1
Saskatchewan	15.6	10.2	5.2	0.0	0.1	0.1
Canada	4.3	2.6	1.4	0.2	0.0	0.1
Males						
Regina	9.4	5.5	3.8	0.0	0.1	0.1
Saskatchewan	15.1	10.0	4.9	0.0	0.0	0.1
Canada	4.2	2.5	1.4	0.2	0.0	0.1
Females						
Regina	10.4	6.1	4.0	0.0	0.2	0.1
Saskatchewan	16.1	10.4	5.5	0.0	0.1	0.1
Canada	4.3	2.6	1.4	0.2	0.0	0.1

Note: (1) Includes persons who reported being an Aboriginal person, that is, First Nations (North American Indian), Métis or Inuk (Inuit) and/or those who reported Registered or Treaty Indian status, that is registered under the Indian Act of Canada, and/or those who reported membership in a First Nation or Indian band. Aboriginal peoples of Canada are defined in the Constitution Act, 1982, section 35-2 as including the Indian, Inuit and Métis peoples of Canada; (2) Users should be aware that the estimates associated with this variable are more affected than most by the incomplete enumeration of certain Indian reserves and Indian settlements in the National Household Survey (NHS); (3) Includes persons who reported being any two or all three of the following: First Nations (North American Indian), Métis or Inuk (Inuit).
Source: Statistics Canada. 2013. 2011 National Household Survey. Statistics Canada Catalogue no. 99-004-XWE. Ottawa. Released September 11, 2013.

Ethnic Origin

Area	North American Aboriginal	Other North American	European	Caribbean	Latin, Central and South American	African	Asian	Oceania
Number								
Total								
Regina	19,355	36,965	146,100	1,290	1,480	2,830	17,735	225
Saskatchewan	161,245	201,245	765,170	2,710	4,990	8,060	55,100	1,350
Canada	1,836,035	11,070,455	20,157,965	627,590	544,375	766,735	5,011,225	74,875
Males								
Regina	9,120	18,315	71,025	695	740	1,530	8,960	130
Saskatchewan	78,215	100,980	378,270	1,485	2,510	4,355	28,140	750
Canada	885,675	5,462,685	9,913,150	291,640	264,635	387,360	2,435,540	37,490
Females								
Regina	10,240	18,650	75,075	595	740	1,305	8,780	100
Saskatchewan	83,030	100,260	386,900	1,220	2,480	3,710	26,955	595
Canada	950,360	5,607,770	10,244,820	335,945	279,740	379,380	2,575,680	37,385
Percent of Population								
Total								
Regina	10.2	19.5	77.0	0.7	0.8	1.5	9.3	0.1
Saskatchewan	16.0	19.9	75.9	0.3	0.5	0.8	5.5	0.1
Canada	5.6	33.7	61.4	1.9	1.7	2.3	15.3	0.2
Males								
Regina	9.8	19.8	76.6	0.7	0.8	1.7	9.7	0.1
Saskatchewan	15.6	20.1	75.5	0.3	0.5	0.9	5.6	0.1
Canada	5.5	33.8	61.3	1.8	1.6	2.4	15.1	0.2
Females								
Regina	10.6	19.2	77.4	0.6	0.8	1.3	9.0	0.1
Saskatchewan	16.4	19.8	76.2	0.2	0.5	0.7	5.3	0.1
Canada	5.7	33.6	61.4	2.0	1.7	2.3	15.4	0.2

Note: The sum of the ethnic groups in this table is greater than the total population estimate because a person may report more than one ethnic origin in the NHS.
Source: Statistics Canada. 2013. 2011 National Household Survey. Statistics Canada Catalogue no. 99-004-XWE. Ottawa. Released September 11, 2013.

PROFILES / Regina, Saskatchewan

Religion

Area	Buddhist	Christian	Hindu	Jewish	Muslim	Sikh	Traditional (Aboriginal) Spirituality	Other Religions	No Religious Affiliation
Number									
Total									
Regina	1,655	128,755	1,545	335	3,545	925	885	675	51,420
Saskatchewan	4,265	726,920	3,570	940	10,040	1,650	12,240	2,810	246,305
Canada	366,830	22,102,745	497,965	329,495	1,053,945	454,965	64,935	130,835	7,850,605
Males									
Regina	790	59,865	880	190	1,805	490	460	325	27,890
Saskatchewan	2,060	347,455	1,985	535	5,150	935	6,195	1,295	135,535
Canada	168,465	10,497,775	250,435	161,265	540,555	229,435	31,805	57,745	4,225,645
Females									
Regina	870	68,890	665	140	1,740	435	420	345	23,535
Saskatchewan	2,205	379,465	1,580	410	4,890	715	6,045	1,525	110,775
Canada	198,365	11,604,975	247,525	168,235	513,395	225,530	33,135	73,090	3,624,965
Percent of Population									
Total									
Regina	0.9	67.9	0.8	0.2	1.9	0.5	0.5	0.4	27.1
Saskatchewan	0.4	72.1	0.4	0.1	1.0	0.2	1.2	0.3	24.4
Canada	1.1	67.3	1.5	1.0	3.2	1.4	0.2	0.4	23.9
Males									
Regina	0.9	64.6	0.9	0.2	1.9	0.5	0.5	0.4	30.1
Saskatchewan	0.4	69.3	0.4	0.1	1.0	0.2	1.2	0.3	27.0
Canada	1.0	64.9	1.5	1.0	3.3	1.4	0.2	0.4	26.1
Females									
Regina	0.9	71.0	0.7	0.1	1.8	0.4	0.4	0.4	24.3
Saskatchewan	0.4	74.8	0.3	0.1	1.0	0.1	1.2	0.3	21.8
Canada	1.2	69.5	1.5	1.0	3.1	1.4	0.2	0.4	21.7

Note: Religion refers to the person's self-identification as having a connection or affiliation with any religious denomination, group, body, sect, cult or other religiously defined community or system of belief. Religion is not limited to formal membership in a religious organization or group. Persons without a religious connection or affiliation can self-identify as atheist, agnostic or humanist, or can provide another applicable response.
Source: Statistics Canada. 2013. 2011 National Household Survey. Statistics Canada Catalogue no. 99-004-XWE. Ottawa. Released September 11, 2013.

Religion—Christian Denominations

Area	Anglican	Baptist	Catholic	Christian Orthodox	Lutheran	Pentecostal	Presbyterian	United Church	Other Christian
Number									
Total									
Regina	6,575	3,670	57,765	2,840	13,680	2,345	1,435	21,520	18,925
Saskatchewan	54,645	16,270	297,860	12,140	63,765	16,215	7,990	134,835	123,195
Canada	1,631,845	635,840	12,810,705	550,690	478,185	478,705	472,385	2,007,610	3,036,780
Males									
Regina	3,025	1,750	27,525	1,375	5,885	1,035	640	9,240	9,390
Saskatchewan	25,810	7,780	145,055	5,795	29,435	7,555	3,765	61,825	60,430
Canada	752,945	293,905	6,167,290	270,205	221,525	217,850	218,955	912,545	1,442,550
Females									
Regina	3,550	1,915	30,245	1,470	7,790	1,310	795	12,275	9,540
Saskatchewan	28,840	8,495	152,805	6,340	34,325	8,665	4,225	73,010	62,765
Canada	878,900	341,940	6,643,415	280,485	256,660	260,850	253,430	1,095,065	1,594,230
Percent of Population									
Total									
Regina	3.5	1.9	30.4	1.5	7.2	1.2	0.8	11.3	10.0
Saskatchewan	5.4	1.6	29.5	1.2	6.3	1.6	0.8	13.4	12.2
Canada	5.0	1.9	39.0	1.7	1.5	1.5	1.4	6.1	9.2
Males									
Regina	3.3	1.9	29.7	1.5	6.3	1.1	0.7	10.0	10.1
Saskatchewan	5.2	1.6	28.9	1.2	5.9	1.5	0.8	12.3	12.1
Canada	4.7	1.8	38.2	1.7	1.4	1.3	1.4	5.6	8.9
Females									
Regina	3.7	2.0	31.2	1.5	8.0	1.3	0.8	12.6	9.8
Saskatchewan	5.7	1.7	30.1	1.2	6.8	1.7	0.8	14.4	12.4
Canada	5.3	2.0	39.8	1.7	1.5	1.6	1.5	6.6	9.6

Note: Religion refers to the person's self-identification as having a connection or affiliation with any religious denomination, group, body, sect, cult or other religiously defined community or system of belief. Religion is not limited to formal membership in a religious organization or group. Persons without a religious connection or affiliation can self-identify as atheist, agnostic or humanist, or can provide another applicable response.
Source: Statistics Canada. 2013. 2011 National Household Survey. Statistics Canada Catalogue no. 99-004-XWE. Ottawa. Released September 11, 2013.

PROFILES / Regina, Saskatchewan

Immigrant Status and Period of Immigration

Area	Non-Immigrants[1]	Immigrants All	Before 1971	1971 to 1980	1981 to 1990	1991 to 2000	2001 to 2005	2006 to 2011	Non-Permanent Residents[3]
				Number					
				Total					
Regina	166,325	21,180	3,765	1,945	2,070	2,915	2,470	8,015	2,240
Saskatchewan	931,710	68,780	12,720	6,300	6,020	8,855	7,955	26,920	8,270
Canada	25,720,175	6,775,765	1,261,055	870,775	949,890	1,539,050	992,070	1,162,915	356,385
				Males					
Regina	80,835	10,410	1,805	1,005	1,000	1,320	1,280	4,000	1,460
Saskatchewan	462,535	33,780	5,935	3,230	2,880	4,345	3,905	13,500	4,830
Canada	12,753,235	3,231,370	605,430	416,670	454,570	724,905	474,545	555,245	178,515
				Females					
Regina	85,490	10,770	1,960	940	1,070	1,595	1,190	4,015	780
Saskatchewan	469,175	34,995	6,790	3,065	3,145	4,515	4,050	13,425	3,445
Canada	12,966,935	3,544,400	655,625	454,105	495,325	814,145	517,530	607,670	177,870
				Percent of Population					
				Total					
Regina	87.7	11.2	2.0	1.0	1.1	1.5	1.3	4.2	1.2
Saskatchewan	92.4	6.8	1.3	0.6	0.6	0.9	0.8	2.7	0.8
Canada	78.3	20.6	3.8	2.7	2.9	4.7	3.0	3.5	1.1
				Males					
Regina	87.2	11.2	1.9	1.1	1.1	1.4	1.4	4.3	1.6
Saskatchewan	92.3	6.7	1.2	0.6	0.6	0.9	0.8	2.7	1.0
Canada	78.9	20.0	3.7	2.6	2.8	4.5	2.9	3.4	1.1
				Females					
Regina	88.1	11.1	2.0	1.0	1.1	1.6	1.2	4.1	0.8
Saskatchewan	92.4	6.9	1.3	0.6	0.6	0.9	0.8	2.6	0.7
Canada	77.7	21.2	3.9	2.7	3.0	4.9	3.1	3.6	1.1

Note: (1) Non-immigrant refers to a person who is a Canadian citizen by birth; (2) Immigrant refers to a person who is or has ever been a landed immigrant/permanent resident. This person has been granted the right to live in Canada permanently by immigration authorities. Some immigrants have resided in Canada for a number of years, while others have arrived recently. Some immigrants are Canadian citizens, while others are not. Most immigrants are born outside Canada, but a small number are born in Canada. In the 2011 National Household Survey, 'Immigrants' includes immigrants who landed in Canada prior to May 10, 2011; (3) Non-permanent resident refers to a person from another country who has a work or study permit, or who is a refugee claimant, and any non-Canadian-born family member living in Canada with them.
Source: Statistics Canada. 2013. 2011 National Household Survey. Statistics Canada Catalogue no. 99-004-XWE. Ottawa. Released September 11, 2013.

Mother Tongue

Area	English	French	Non-official Language	English & French	English & Non-official Language	French & Non-official Language	English, French & Non-official Language
			Number				
			Total				
Regina	162,475	2,355	23,500	360	2,015	105	55
Saskatchewan	860,500	16,280	129,035	1,730	9,850	750	175
Canada	18,858,980	7,054,975	6,567,680	144,685	396,330	74,430	24,095
			Males				
Regina	79,230	1,080	11,635	175	990	50	25
Saskatchewan	428,115	7,760	63,245	805	4,720	360	75
Canada	9,345,225	3,452,380	3,157,785	69,975	192,000	36,535	11,965
			Females				
Regina	83,245	1,275	11,865	185	1,025	55	30
Saskatchewan	432,385	8,525	65,785	920	5,125	390	95
Canada	9,513,750	3,602,590	3,409,895	74,710	204,330	37,890	12,130
			Percent of Population				
			Total				
Regina	85.1	1.2	12.3	0.2	1.1	0.1	0.0
Saskatchewan	84.5	1.6	12.7	0.2	1.0	0.1	0.0
Canada	56.9	21.3	19.8	0.4	1.2	0.2	0.1
			Males				
Regina	85.0	1.2	12.5	0.2	1.1	0.1	0.0
Saskatchewan	84.8	1.5	12.5	0.2	0.9	0.1	0.0
Canada	57.5	21.2	19.4	0.4	1.2	0.2	0.1
			Females				
Regina	85.2	1.3	12.1	0.2	1.0	0.1	0.0
Saskatchewan	84.2	1.7	12.8	0.2	1.0	0.1	0.0
Canada	56.4	21.4	20.2	0.4	1.2	0.2	0.1

Note: Figures cover total population excluding institutional residents.
Source: Statistics Canada. 2012. Census Profile. 2011 Census. Statistics Canada Catalogue no. 98-316-XWE. Ottawa. Released October 24 2012.
http://www12.statcan.gc.ca/census-recensement/2011/dp-pd/prof/index.cfm?Lang=E

Language Spoken Most Often at Home

Area	English	French	Non-official Language	English & French	English & Non-official Language	French & Non-official Language	English, French & Non-official Language
			Number				
			Total				
Regina	174,745	840	11,015	175	3,985	35	70
Saskatchewan	938,170	4,295	59,240	855	15,360	205	185
Canada	21,457,075	6,827,865	3,673,865	131,205	875,135	109,700	46,330
			Males				
Regina	85,080	390	5,600	85	1,985	20	20
Saskatchewan	465,005	1,990	30,005	400	7,500	110	75
Canada	10,585,620	3,348,235	1,767,310	63,475	425,370	53,010	22,845
			Females				
Regina	89,665	455	5,410	95	2,005	15	45
Saskatchewan	473,170	2,305	29,230	460	7,860	95	110
Canada	10,871,455	3,479,625	1,906,555	67,730	449,765	56,690	23,485
			Percent of Population				
			Total				
Regina	91.6	0.4	5.8	0.1	2.1	0.0	0.0
Saskatchewan	92.1	0.4	5.8	0.1	1.5	0.0	0.0
Canada	64.8	20.6	11.1	0.4	2.6	0.3	0.1
			Males				
Regina	91.3	0.4	6.0	0.1	2.1	0.0	0.0
Saskatchewan	92.1	0.4	5.9	0.1	1.5	0.0	0.0
Canada	65.1	20.6	10.9	0.4	2.6	0.3	0.1
			Females				
Regina	91.8	0.5	5.5	0.1	2.1	0.0	0.0
Saskatchewan	92.2	0.4	5.7	0.1	1.5	0.0	0.0
Canada	64.5	20.6	11.3	0.4	2.7	0.3	0.1

Note: Figures cover total population excluding institutional residents.
Source: Statistics Canada. 2012. Census Profile. 2011 Census. Statistics Canada Catalogue no. 98-316-XWE. Ottawa. Released October 24 2012.
http://www12.statcan.gc.ca/census-recensement/2011/dp-pd/prof/index.cfm?Lang=E

Knowledge of Official Languages

Area	English Only	French Only	English & French	Neither English nor French
		Number		
		Total		
Regina	178,140	140	11,145	1,445
Saskatchewan	965,920	430	46,570	5,395
Canada	22,564,665	4,165,015	5,795,570	595,920
		Males		
Regina	87,530	60	4,950	645
Saskatchewan	481,535	195	20,855	2,505
Canada	11,222,185	1,925,340	2,876,560	241,790
		Females		
Regina	90,605	80	6,195	795
Saskatchewan	484,390	235	25,715	2,885
Canada	11,342,485	2,239,680	2,919,005	354,135
		Percent of Population		
		Total		
Regina	93.3	0.1	5.8	0.8
Saskatchewan	94.9	0.0	4.6	0.5
Canada	68.1	12.6	17.5	1.8
		Males		
Regina	93.9	0.1	5.3	0.7
Saskatchewan	95.3	0.0	4.1	0.5
Canada	69.0	11.8	17.7	1.5
		Females		
Regina	92.8	0.1	6.3	0.8
Saskatchewan	94.4	0.0	5.0	0.6
Canada	67.3	13.3	17.3	2.1

Note: Figures cover total population excluding institutional residents.
Source: Statistics Canada. 2012. Census Profile. 2011 Census. Statistics Canada Catalogue no. 98-316-XWE. Ottawa. Released October 24 2012.
http://www12.statcan.gc.ca/census-recensement/2011/dp-pd/prof/index.cfm?Lang=E

Richmond, British Columbia

Background

Richmond is a coastal city that is a part of Metro Vancouver, British Columbia. The city is located on the Pacific Coast and is surrounded by the Coast Mountain range and comprised of a series of islands at the mouth of the Fraser River, including Sea Island, most of Lulu Island and 15 smaller islands. Richmond is 20 minutes from downtown Vancouver and 25 minutes from the U.S. border.

The Coast Salish First Nations were the first to come to the Richmond islands to fish and collect berries. European settlers arrived in the 1860s and dairy farming and berry growing (cranberries and blueberries) thrived. Soon, fishermen, canneries and boat builders, as well as Chinese contract workers who built the province's railway, were attracted to the region. The municipality was incorporated in 1879 and designated a city in 1990.

Today Richmond is one of the fastest-growing and ethnically diverse cities in Canada. The majority of Richmond's population growth has come from Asian immigration, particularly since the 1990s. In 2011, more than 60% of Richmond residents were of Chinese or South Asian ancestry.

Vancouver International Airport, Canada's second busiest airport and one of the most important airports on the west coast of North America, is in Richmond. The city was also a venue city for the 2010 Winter Olympic Games.

The city's economy is made up of tourism, light manufacturing, airport services and aviation, fishing and agriculture. Cranberries are the dominant crop and account for approximately 33% of the province's cranberry acreage. In recent years, Richmond has emerged as a leading centre for high-tech industries. The city is the largest commercial fishing hub in Canada and the largest producer of salmon worldwide.

Richmond has summer highs of plus 22.87 degrees Celsius, winter lows of plus 0.47 degree Celsius, and an average rainfall just over 1239 mm per year.

Rankings

- The Public Health Agency of Canada and the Canadian Institute for Health Information ranked the City of Richmond Canada's healthiest, fittest city. In 2011, 5.3% of the population was obese compared to the nationwide average of approximately 25%. The ranking is attributed to the city's mild climate, long-time fitness lifestyle and availability of clean air and green space. Richmond is also renowned for having the longest life expectancy in Canada. Residents live an average of 83.4 years while the national average is 81.2. *Canadian Population Health Initiative of the Canadian Institute for Health Informationand the Public Health Agency of Canada, "Obesity in Canada," June 20th, 2011 with files from The Richmond Review, "A tale of the tape: How waistlines differ in Richmond, Va. and Richmond, B.C.," May 9th, 2012*
- The Canadian Broadcasting Corporation (CBC) identified Richmond's No. 5 Road, known as the "Highway to Heaven," as one of 52 finalists in the 2007 Seven Wonders of Canada contest. The road features multiple churches, temples and other places of worship. The area was selected to represent Canada's religious, racial and cultural inclusiveness. *CBC, "Seven Wonders of Canada" with files from Discover Richmond.ca, Awards 2007*

PROFILES / Richmond, British Columbia

Population Growth and Density

Area	Population in 2001	Population in 2006	Population in 2011	Population Change 2001–2006	Population Change 2006–2011	Land Area (sq. km)	Population Density per sq. km
Richmond	164,345	174,461	190,473	6.2	9.2	129.27	1,473.5
British Columbia	3,907,738	4,113,487	4,400,057	5.3	7.0	922,509.29	4.8
Canada	30,007,094	31,612,897	33,476,688	5.4	5.9	8,965,121.42	3.7

Source: Statistics Canada. 2012. Census Profile. 2011 Census. Statistics Canada Catalogue no. 98-316-XWE. Ottawa. Released October 24 2012.
http://www12.statcan.gc.ca/census-recensement/2011/dp-pd/prof/index.cfm?Lang=E;
Statistics Canada 2007. 2006 Community Profiles. 2006 Census. Statistics Canada Catalogue no. 92-591-XWE. Ottawa. Released March 13 2007.
http://www12.statcan.ca/census-recensement/2006/dp-pd/prof/92-591/index.cfm?Lang=E

Gender

Area	Males	Females
Number		
Richmond	91,240	99,230
British Columbia	2,156,600	2,243,455
Canada	16,414,225	17,062,460
Percent of Population		
Richmond	47.9	52.1
British Columbia	49.0	51.0
Canada	49.0	51.0

Source: Statistics Canada. 2012. Census Profile. 2011 Census. Statistics Canada Catalogue no. 98-316-XWE. Ottawa. Released October 24 2012.
http://www12.statcan.gc.ca/census-recensement/2011/dp-pd/prof/index.cfm?Lang=E

Marital Status

Area	Married[1]	Living Common-law	Single[2]	Separated	Divorced	Widowed
Number						
Total						
Richmond	90,625	6,420	46,305	3,285	8,855	7,625
British Columbia	1,832,605	321,965	1,014,270	102,040	246,515	205,300
Canada	12,941,960	3,142,525	7,816,045	698,240	1,686,035	1,584,530
Males						
Richmond	44,720	3,190	23,945	1,195	2,855	1,355
British Columbia	913,430	161,530	550,830	43,570	98,130	41,550
Canada	6,470,300	1,575,495	4,206,320	299,655	680,415	310,940
Females						
Richmond	45,905	3,235	22,360	2,090	6,000	6,270
British Columbia	919,175	160,435	463,435	58,470	148,385	163,750
Canada	6,471,660	1,567,035	3,609,730	398,585	1,005,620	1,273,590
Percent of Population						
Total						
Richmond	55.6	3.9	28.4	2.0	5.4	4.7
British Columbia	49.2	8.6	27.2	2.7	6.6	5.5
Canada	46.4	11.3	28.0	2.5	6.0	5.7
Males						
Richmond	57.9	4.1	31.0	1.5	3.7	1.8
British Columbia	50.5	8.9	30.4	2.4	5.4	2.3
Canada	47.8	11.6	31.1	2.2	5.0	2.3
Females						
Richmond	53.5	3.8	26.0	2.4	7.0	7.3
British Columbia	48.0	8.4	24.2	3.1	7.8	8.6
Canada	45.2	10.9	25.2	2.8	7.0	8.9

Note: (1) and not separated, (2) never legally married
Source: Statistics Canada. 2012. Census Profile. 2011 Census. Statistics Canada Catalogue no. 98-316-XWE. Ottawa. Released October 24 2012.
http://www12.statcan.gc.ca/census-recensement/2011/dp-pd/prof/index.cfm?Lang=E

Age Characteristics: 0 to 49 Years

Area	0 to 4 Years	5 to 9 Years	10 to 14 Years	15 to 19 Years	20 to 24 Years	25 to 29 Years	30 to 34 Years	35 to 39 Years	40 to 44 Years	45 to 49 Years
					Number					
					Total					
Richmond	8,395	8,855	10,110	12,535	13,680	12,740	11,160	11,720	14,510	16,640
British Columbia	219,665	218,915	238,780	275,165	279,825	288,780	275,985	280,870	313,765	350,600
Canada	1,877,095	1,809,895	1,920,355	2,178,135	2,187,450	2,169,590	2,162,905	2,173,930	2,324,875	2,675,130
					Males					
Richmond	4,270	4,595	5,115	6,520	7,100	6,315	5,390	5,195	6,425	7,650
British Columbia	112,885	112,200	122,465	141,670	142,290	143,475	135,220	135,455	151,430	170,580
Canada	961,150	925,965	983,995	1,115,845	1,108,775	1,077,275	1,058,810	1,064,200	1,141,720	1,318,715
					Females					
Richmond	4,125	4,255	4,995	6,015	6,580	6,430	5,765	6,525	8,085	8,985
British Columbia	106,775	106,715	116,315	133,500	137,535	145,305	140,755	145,415	162,335	180,020
Canada	915,945	883,935	936,360	1,062,295	1,078,670	1,092,315	1,104,095	1,109,735	1,183,155	1,356,420
					Percent of Population					
					Total					
Richmond	4.4	4.6	5.3	6.6	7.2	6.7	5.9	6.2	7.6	8.7
British Columbia	5.0	5.0	5.4	6.3	6.4	6.6	6.3	6.4	7.1	8.0
Canada	5.6	5.4	5.7	6.5	6.5	6.5	6.5	6.5	6.9	8.0
					Males					
Richmond	4.7	5.0	5.6	7.1	7.8	6.9	5.9	5.7	7.0	8.4
British Columbia	5.2	5.2	5.7	6.6	6.6	6.7	6.3	6.3	7.0	7.9
Canada	5.9	5.6	6.0	6.8	6.8	6.6	6.5	6.5	7.0	8.0
					Females					
Richmond	4.2	4.3	5.0	6.1	6.6	6.5	5.8	6.6	8.1	9.1
British Columbia	4.8	4.8	5.2	6.0	6.1	6.5	6.3	6.5	7.2	8.0
Canada	5.4	5.2	5.5	6.2	6.3	6.4	6.5	6.5	6.9	7.9

Source: Statistics Canada. 2012. Census Profile. 2011 Census. Statistics Canada Catalogue no. 98-316-XWE. Ottawa. Released October 24 2012.
http://www12.statcan.gc.ca/census-recensement/2011/dp-pd/prof/index.cfm?Lang=E

Age Characteristics: 50 Years and Over, and Median Age

Area	50 to 54 Years	55 to 59 Years	60 to 64 Years	65 to 69 Years	70 to 74 Years	75 to 79 Years	80 to 84 Years	85 Years and Over	Median Age
				Number					
				Total					
Richmond	16,490	14,910	12,720	8,010	6,195	5,030	3,595	3,175	42.1
British Columbia	354,610	323,335	291,040	210,900	160,715	127,480	96,945	92,675	41.9
Canada	2,658,965	2,340,635	2,052,670	1,521,715	1,153,065	922,700	702,070	645,515	40.6
				Males					
Richmond	7,620	7,085	6,155	3,820	2,910	2,370	1,565	1,130	40.9
British Columbia	172,060	157,455	142,645	103,785	77,350	60,720	42,745	32,150	41.1
Canada	1,309,030	1,147,300	1,002,690	738,010	543,435	417,945	291,085	208,300	39.6
				Females					
Richmond	8,865	7,820	6,565	4,190	3,285	2,665	2,030	2,050	43.0
British Columbia	182,550	165,880	148,395	107,115	83,360	66,760	54,200	60,520	42.7
Canada	1,349,940	1,193,335	1,049,985	783,705	609,630	504,755	410,985	437,215	41.5
				Percent of Population					
				Total					
Richmond	8.7	7.8	6.7	4.2	3.3	2.6	1.9	1.7	—
British Columbia	8.1	7.3	6.6	4.8	3.7	2.9	2.2	2.1	—
Canada	7.9	7.0	6.1	4.5	3.4	2.8	2.1	1.9	—
				Males					
Richmond	8.4	7.8	6.7	4.2	3.2	2.6	1.7	1.2	—
British Columbia	8.0	7.3	6.6	4.8	3.6	2.8	2.0	1.5	—
Canada	8.0	7.0	6.1	4.5	3.3	2.5	1.8	1.3	—
				Females					
Richmond	8.9	7.9	6.6	4.2	3.3	2.7	2.0	2.1	—
British Columbia	8.1	7.4	6.6	4.8	3.7	3.0	2.4	2.7	—
Canada	7.9	7.0	6.2	4.6	3.6	3.0	2.4	2.6	—

Source: Statistics Canada. 2012. Census Profile. 2011 Census. Statistics Canada Catalogue no. 98-316-XWE. Ottawa. Released October 24 2012.
http://www12.statcan.gc.ca/census-recensement/2011/dp-pd/prof/index.cfm?Lang=E

PROFILES / Richmond, British Columbia

Private Households by Household Size

Area	1 Person	2 Persons	3 Persons	4 Persons	5 Persons	6 or More Persons	Average Number of Persons in Private Households
				Households			
Richmond	14,175	19,830	13,920	12,145	4,625	3,275	2.8
British Columbia	498,925	613,270	264,135	237,725	91,600	58,985	2.5
Canada	3,673,310	4,544,820	2,081,900	1,903,300	724,405	392,885	2.5
				Percent of Households			
Richmond	20.9	29.2	20.5	17.9	6.8	4.8	–
British Columbia	28.3	34.8	15.0	13.5	5.2	3.3	–
Canada	27.6	34.1	15.6	14.3	5.4	2.9	–

Source: Statistics Canada. 2012. Census Profile. 2011 Census. Statistics Canada Catalogue no. 98-316-XWE. Ottawa. Released October 24 2012.
http://www12.statcan.gc.ca/census-recensement/2011/dp-pd/prof/index.cfm?Lang=E

Dwelling Type

Area	Single-detached House	Semi-detached House	Row House	Apartment: Building with Five or More Storeys	Apartment: Building with Fewer Than Five Storeys	Duplex Apartment	Movable Dwelling	Other Single-attached House
				Number				
Richmond	25,320	1,695	13,445	6,950	16,210	4,090	250	20
British Columbia	842,120	52,825	130,365	143,970	361,150	184,355	46,960	2,885
Canada	7,329,150	646,245	791,600	1,234,770	2,397,550	704,485	183,510	33,310
				Percent of Dwellings				
Richmond	37.2	2.5	19.8	10.2	23.8	6.0	0.4	0.0
British Columbia	47.7	3.0	7.4	8.2	20.5	10.4	2.7	0.2
Canada	55.0	4.9	5.9	9.3	18.0	5.3	1.4	0.3

Source: Statistics Canada. 2012. Census Profile. 2011 Census. Statistics Canada Catalogue no. 98-316-XWE. Ottawa. Released October 24 2012.
http://www12.statcan.gc.ca/census-recensement/2011/dp-pd/prof/index.cfm?Lang=E

Shelter Costs

	Owned Dwellings				Rented Dwellings		
Area	Number	Median Value[1] ($)	Average Value[1] ($)	Median Monthly Costs[2] ($)	Average Monthly Costs[2] ($)	Number	Median Monthly Costs[3] ($)	Average Monthly Costs[3] ($)
Richmond	52,305	601,945	696,406	1,047	1,286	15,545	1,101	1,142
British Columbia	1,202,000	448,835	543,635	1,023	1,228	519,855	903	989
Canada	9,013,410	280,552	345,182	978	1,141	4,060,385	784	848

Note: All figures cover non-farm, non-reserve private dwellings; (1) Refers to the dollar amount expected by the owner if the dwelling were to be sold; (2) Includes all shelter expenses paid by households that own their dwellings, such as the mortgage payment and the costs of electricity, heat, water and other municipal services, property taxes and condominium fees; (3) Includes all shelter expenses paid by households that rent their dwellings, such as the monthly rent and the costs of electricity, heat and municipal services.
Source: Statistics Canada. 2013. 2011 National Household Survey. Statistics Canada Catalogue no. 99-004-XWE. Ottawa. Released September 11, 2013.

Occupied Private Dwellings by Period of Construction

Area	1960 or Before	1961 to 1980	1981 to 1990	1991 to 2000	2001 to 2005	2006 to 2011
			Number			
Richmond	3,455	20,685	14,200	15,015	6,335	8,280
British Columbia	282,675	551,655	308,450	329,780	133,235	158,845
Canada	3,273,105	4,152,715	2,112,110	1,707,880	1,031,020	1,042,430
			Percent of Dwellings			
Richmond	5.1	30.4	20.9	22.1	9.3	12.2
British Columbia	16.0	31.3	17.5	18.7	7.6	9.0
Canada	24.6	31.2	15.9	12.8	7.7	7.8

Note: Figures cover non-farm, non-reserve private dwellings and includes data up to May 10, 2011.
Source: Statistics Canada. 2013. 2011 National Household Survey. Statistics Canada Catalogue no. 99-004-XWE. Ottawa. Released September 11, 2013.

PROFILES / Richmond, British Columbia

Educational Attainment

Area	No Certificate, Diploma or Degree	High School Diploma or Equivalent[1]	Apprenticeship or Trades Certificate or Diploma[2]	College, CÉGEP or Other Non-University Certificate or Diploma	University Certificate or Diploma Below the Bachelor Level[3]	Bachelor's Degree	University Certificate, Diploma or Degree Above Bachelor Level[4]
			Number				
			Total				
Richmond	22,995	45,185	9,650	23,315	12,610	33,190	15,100
British Columbia	607,655	1,009,400	387,455	628,115	208,245	511,240	294,725
Canada	5,485,400	6,968,935	2,950,685	4,970,020	1,200,130	3,634,425	2,049,930
			Males				
Richmond	10,510	20,730	6,025	10,285	5,505	15,715	8,110
British Columbia	305,040	475,670	262,245	260,580	86,995	235,620	149,300
Canada	2,742,875	3,305,415	1,928,970	2,118,430	513,235	1,643,080	1,043,350
			Females				
Richmond	12,485	24,455	3,625	13,030	7,105	17,475	6,995
British Columbia	302,620	533,735	125,210	367,535	121,250	275,625	145,425
Canada	2,742,520	3,663,515	1,021,715	2,851,595	686,890	1,991,345	1,006,585
			Percent of Population				
			Total				
Richmond	14.2	27.9	6.0	14.4	7.8	20.5	9.3
British Columbia	16.7	27.7	10.6	17.2	5.7	14.0	8.1
Canada	20.1	25.6	10.8	18.2	4.4	13.3	7.5
			Males				
Richmond	13.7	27.0	7.8	13.4	7.2	20.4	10.5
British Columbia	17.2	26.8	14.8	14.7	4.9	13.3	8.4
Canada	20.6	24.9	14.5	15.9	3.9	12.4	7.8
			Females				
Richmond	14.7	28.7	4.3	15.3	8.3	20.5	8.2
British Columbia	16.2	28.5	6.7	19.6	6.5	14.7	7.8
Canada	19.6	26.2	7.3	20.4	4.9	14.3	7.2

Note: Figures cover total population aged 15 years and over by highest certificate, diploma or degree; (1) Includes persons who have graduated from a secondary school or equivalent. It excludes persons with a postsecondary certificate, diploma or degree; (2) Includes Registered Apprenticeship certificates (including Certificate of Qualification, Journeyperson's designation) and other trades certificates or diplomas such as pre-employment or vocational certificates and diplomas from brief trade programs completed at community colleges, institutes of technology, vocational centres, and similar institutions; (3) Comparisons with other data sources suggest that the category 'University certificate or diploma below the bachelor's level' was over-reported in the NHS. This category likely includes some responses that are actually college certificates or diplomas, bachelor's degrees or other types of education (e.g., university transfer programs, bachelor's programs completed in other countries, incomplete bachelor's programs, non-university professional designations). We recommend users interpret the results for the 'University certificate or diploma below the bachelor's level' category with caution; (4) 'University certificate or diploma above bachelor level' includes the categories: 'Degree in medicine, dentistry, veterinary medicine or optometry,' 'Master's degree' and 'Earned doctorate.'
Source: Statistics Canada. 2013. 2011 National Household Survey. Statistics Canada Catalogue no. 99-004-XWE. Ottawa. Released September 11, 2013.

Household Income Distribution

Area	Less than $10,000	$10,000 to $19,999	$20,000 to $29,999	$30,000 to $39,999	$40,000 to $49,999	$50,000 to $59,999	$60,000 to $79,999	$80,000 to $99,999	$100,000 to $124,999	$125,000 to $149,999	$150,000 and Over
						Households					
Richmond	4,920	5,350	6,265	6,270	5,535	5,400	9,440	7,270	6,250	4,020	7,250
British Columbia	96,465	156,565	157,605	167,220	158,400	140,340	246,720	193,180	167,415	106,325	174,385
Canada	626,705	1,141,945	1,193,925	1,271,675	1,206,800	1,102,120	1,865,280	1,458,240	1,260,770	802,555	1,389,240
						Percent of Households					
Richmond	7.2	7.9	9.2	9.2	8.1	7.9	13.9	10.7	9.2	5.9	10.7
British Columbia	5.5	8.9	8.9	9.5	9.0	8.0	14.0	10.9	9.5	6.0	9.9
Canada	4.7	8.6	9.0	9.5	9.1	8.3	14.0	10.9	9.5	6.0	10.4

Note: Household income is the sum of the total incomes of all members of that household. Total income refers to monetary receipts from certain sources, before income taxes and deductions, during calendar year 2010.
Source: Statistics Canada. 2013. 2011 National Household Survey. Statistics Canada Catalogue no. 99-004-XWE. Ottawa. Released September 11, 2013.

Median and Average Household and Economic Family Income

Area	Median Household Income ($)	Average Household Income ($)	Median After-tax Household Income ($)	Average After-tax Household Income ($)	Median Economic Family Income ($)	Average Economic Family Income ($)	Median After-tax Economic Family Income ($)	Average After-tax Economic Family Income ($)
Richmond	60,479	77,782	54,597	67,352	69,553	86,843	63,307	75,285
British Columbia	60,333	77,378	54,379	66,264	75,797	91,967	67,915	78,580
Canada	61,072	79,102	54,089	66,149	76,511	94,125	67,044	78,517

Note: Figures cover household and economic familiy income in 2010. A household is defined as a person or a group of persons (other than foreign residents) who occupy the same private dwelling and do not have a usual place of residence elsewhere in Canada. Every person is a member of one and only one household. An economic family is defined as a group of two or more persons who live in the same dwelling and are related to each other by blood, marriage, common-law, adoption or a foster relationship. A couple may be of opposite or same sex.
Source: Statistics Canada. 2013. 2011 National Household Survey. Statistics Canada Catalogue no. 99-004-XWE. Ottawa. Released September 11, 2013.

Individual Income Distribution

Area	Less than $10,000	$10,000 to $19,999	$20,000 to $29,999	$30,000 to $39,999	$40,000 to $49,999	$50,000 to $59,999	$60,000 to $79,999	$80,000 to $99,999	$100,000 to $124,999	$125,000 and Over
Number										
Total										
Richmond	37,765	30,055	18,665	16,025	13,450	9,725	12,580	5,920	3,405	3,455
British Columbia	645,915	666,060	470,255	404,860	338,595	253,215	330,590	169,190	89,520	96,055
Canada	4,492,040	4,835,710	3,670,020	3,180,360	2,603,520	1,921,650	2,437,440	1,302,045	693,580	782,135
Males										
Richmond	16,955	12,155	8,155	7,375	6,330	5,190	7,525	3,750	2,295	2,635
British Columbia	275,815	263,170	201,000	186,285	167,400	143,765	206,400	112,525	65,050	74,260
Canada	1,936,365	1,864,880	1,588,260	1,522,190	1,333,510	1,079,780	1,473,145	823,720	492,905	599,905
Females										
Richmond	20,820	17,900	10,505	8,645	7,115	4,540	5,055	2,165	1,105	820
British Columbia	370,100	402,880	269,255	218,575	171,190	109,445	124,195	56,670	24,470	21,795
Canada	2,555,675	2,970,825	2,081,760	1,658,170	1,270,010	841,870	964,300	478,330	200,680	182,230
Percent of Population										
Total										
Richmond	25.0	19.9	12.4	10.6	8.9	6.4	8.3	3.9	2.3	2.3
British Columbia	18.6	19.2	13.6	11.7	9.8	7.3	9.5	4.9	2.6	2.8
Canada	17.3	18.7	14.2	12.3	10.0	7.4	9.4	5.0	2.7	3.0
Males										
Richmond	23.4	16.8	11.3	10.2	8.7	7.2	10.4	5.2	3.2	3.6
British Columbia	16.3	15.5	11.9	11.0	9.9	8.5	12.2	6.6	3.8	4.4
Canada	15.2	14.7	12.5	12.0	10.5	8.5	11.6	6.5	3.9	4.7
Females										
Richmond	26.5	22.8	13.4	11.0	9.0	5.8	6.4	2.8	1.4	1.0
British Columbia	20.9	22.8	15.2	12.4	9.7	6.2	7.0	3.2	1.4	1.2
Canada	19.4	22.5	15.8	12.6	9.6	6.4	7.3	3.6	1.5	1.4

Note: Figures cover individuals aged 15 years and over with income. Income refers to monetary receipts from certain sources, before income taxes and deductions, during calendar year 2010.
Source: Statistics Canada. 2013. 2011 National Household Survey. Statistics Canada Catalogue no. 99-004-XWE. Ottawa. Released September 11, 2013.

Labour Force Status

Area	In the Labour Force — All	Employed	Unemployed	Not in the Labour Force
Number				
Total				
Richmond	99,910	92,850	7,065	62,130
British Columbia	2,354,245	2,171,465	182,775	1,292,595
Canada	17,990,080	16,595,035	1,395,045	9,269,445
Males				
Richmond	51,195	47,615	3,585	25,680
British Columbia	1,223,375	1,124,590	98,785	552,070
Canada	9,388,570	8,634,310	754,255	3,906,785
Females				
Richmond	48,715	45,235	3,475	36,450
British Columbia	1,130,870	1,046,875	83,990	740,530
Canada	8,601,515	7,960,725	640,790	5,362,660
Percent of Labour Force				
Total				
Richmond	61.7	57.3	7.1	38.3
British Columbia	64.6	59.5	7.8	35.4
Canada	66.0	60.9	7.8	34.0
Males				
Richmond	66.6	61.9	7.0	33.4
British Columbia	68.9	63.3	8.1	31.1
Canada	70.6	64.9	8.0	29.4
Females				
Richmond	57.2	53.1	7.1	42.8
British Columbia	60.4	55.9	7.4	39.6
Canada	61.6	57.0	7.4	38.4

Note: Figures are based on total population 15 years and over
Source: Statistics Canada. 2013. 2011 National Household Survey. Statistics Canada Catalogue no. 99-004-XWE. Ottawa. Released September 11, 2013.

Labour Force by Industry (NAICS Codes 11–52)

Area	Agriculture, forestry, fishing & hunting	Mining, quarrying, & oil & gas extraction	Utilities	Construction	Manufacturing	Wholesale Trade	Retail Trade	Transportation & warehousing	Information & cultural industries	Finance & insurance
					Number					
					Total					
Richmond	680	290	455	4,080	6,340	5,830	12,315	6,820	3,110	6,870
British Columbia	61,210	25,450	13,215	181,510	148,810	90,560	266,265	118,675	62,235	91,790
Canada	437,650	261,050	149,940	1,215,380	1,619,295	733,445	2,031,665	827,780	420,830	767,960
					Males					
Richmond	460	185	325	3,435	3,925	3,750	5,910	4,475	1,960	2,955
British Columbia	40,810	21,175	9,650	159,605	108,480	61,730	121,750	89,155	37,250	35,375
Canada	307,370	211,690	110,765	1,068,710	1,167,680	494,545	933,850	617,305	235,875	296,995
					Females					
Richmond	225	105	130	650	2,420	2,080	6,405	2,345	1,150	3,915
British Columbia	20,405	4,275	3,560	21,910	40,335	28,820	144,515	29,520	24,980	56,415
Canada	130,285	49,360	39,175	146,670	451,615	238,900	1,097,820	210,475	184,955	470,960
					Percent of Labour Force					
					Total					
Richmond	0.7	0.3	0.5	4.2	6.5	6.0	12.7	7.0	3.2	7.1
British Columbia	2.7	1.1	0.6	7.9	6.5	3.9	11.6	5.1	2.7	4.0
Canada	2.5	1.5	0.9	6.9	9.2	4.2	11.6	4.7	2.4	4.4
					Males					
Richmond	0.9	0.4	0.7	6.9	7.9	7.5	11.9	9.0	3.9	5.9
British Columbia	3.4	1.8	0.8	13.3	9.0	5.1	10.1	7.4	3.1	2.9
Canada	3.3	2.3	1.2	11.6	12.7	5.4	10.2	6.7	2.6	3.2
					Females					
Richmond	0.5	0.2	0.3	1.4	5.1	4.4	13.5	5.0	2.4	8.3
British Columbia	1.8	0.4	0.3	2.0	3.6	2.6	13.1	2.7	2.3	5.1
Canada	1.6	0.6	0.5	1.7	5.4	2.8	13.1	2.5	2.2	5.6

Note: Figures are based on total experienced labour force 15 years and over. Experienced labour force refers to persons who, during the week of Sunday, May 1 to Saturday, May 7, 2011, were employed and the unemployed who had last worked for pay or in self-employment in either 2010 or 2011.
Source: Statistics Canada. 2013. 2011 National Household Survey. Statistics Canada Catalogue no. 99-004-XWE. Ottawa. Released September 11, 2013.

Labour Force by Industry (NAICS Codes 53–91)

Area	Real estate & rental & leasing	Profess., scientific & tech. services	Mgmt of companies & enterprises	Admin. & support, waste mgmt & remed. services	Educational services	Health care & social assistance	Arts, entertain. & recreation	Accomm. & food services	Other services (except public admin.)	Public admin.
					Number					
					Total					
Richmond	2,930	9,230	180	4,630	5,910	7,895	1,980	8,950	4,420	4,245
British Columbia	54,840	179,355	2,440	98,890	167,875	249,030	56,915	179,625	112,745	143,875
Canada	321,895	1,240,850	17,460	728,330	1,301,435	1,949,650	363,405	1,130,750	807,800	1,261,050
					Males					
Richmond	1,655	5,300	65	2,405	2,140	1,550	1,075	4,025	1,840	2,390
British Columbia	29,790	98,760	1,320	55,745	55,635	47,020	29,750	73,570	49,130	74,040
Canada	179,090	688,625	9,380	411,250	424,915	349,430	188,270	469,990	372,940	652,510
					Females					
Richmond	1,275	3,935	110	2,225	3,770	6,345	905	4,930	2,575	1,855
British Columbia	25,055	80,590	1,120	43,145	112,235	202,010	27,175	106,055	63,615	69,840
Canada	142,805	552,225	8,075	317,085	876,515	1,600,220	175,135	660,760	434,865	608,535
					Percent of Labour Force					
					Total					
Richmond	3.0	9.5	0.2	4.8	6.1	8.1	2.0	9.2	4.5	4.4
British Columbia	2.4	7.8	0.1	4.3	7.3	10.8	2.5	7.8	4.9	6.2
Canada	1.8	7.1	0.1	4.1	7.4	11.1	2.1	6.4	4.6	7.2
					Males					
Richmond	3.3	10.6	0.1	4.8	4.3	3.1	2.2	8.1	3.7	4.8
British Columbia	2.5	8.2	0.1	4.6	4.6	3.9	2.5	6.1	4.1	6.2
Canada	1.9	7.5	0.1	4.5	4.6	3.8	2.0	5.1	4.1	7.1
					Females					
Richmond	2.7	8.3	0.2	4.7	8.0	13.4	1.9	10.4	5.4	3.9
British Columbia	2.3	7.3	0.1	3.9	10.2	18.3	2.5	9.6	5.8	6.3
Canada	1.7	6.6	0.1	3.8	10.4	19.1	2.1	7.9	5.2	7.2

Note: Figures are based on total experienced labour force 15 years and over. Experienced labour force refers to persons who, during the week of Sunday, May 1 to Saturday, May 7, 2011, were employed and the unemployed who had last worked for pay or in self-employment in either 2010 or 2011.
Source: Statistics Canada. 2013. 2011 National Household Survey. Statistics Canada Catalogue no. 99-004-XWE. Ottawa. Released September 11, 2013.

Occupation

Area	Mgmt	Business, Finance & Admin.	Natural/ Applied Sciences & Related	Health	Education, Law & Social, Community & Government Services	Art, Culture, Recreation & Sport	Sales & Service	Trades, Transport & Equip. Operators & Related	Natural Resources, Agri. & Related Production	Mfg & Utilities
				Number						
				Total						
Richmond	12,090	19,400	7,980	5,070	9,000	3,020	27,845	8,920	960	2,870
British Columbia	263,685	368,980	154,055	147,620	265,910	78,565	554,345	337,140	60,295	74,720
Canada	1,963,600	2,902,045	1,237,775	1,107,200	2,064,675	503,415	4,068,170	2,537,775	397,930	805,040
				Males						
Richmond	7,475	6,645	6,395	1,265	3,140	1,495	12,650	8,330	740	1,695
British Columbia	162,365	104,285	122,570	32,490	89,645	38,300	233,065	317,385	45,155	54,470
Canada	1,229,460	854,190	966,355	217,520	676,550	232,535	1,745,705	2,385,615	318,945	564,300
				Females						
Richmond	4,620	12,750	1,585	3,810	5,860	1,525	15,190	590	215	1,180
British Columbia	101,320	264,690	31,480	115,125	176,265	40,270	321,285	19,755	15,135	20,250
Canada	734,140	2,047,855	271,415	889,675	1,388,130	270,875	2,322,465	152,165	78,980	240,740
				Percent of Labour Force						
				Total						
Richmond	12.4	20.0	8.2	5.2	9.3	3.1	28.7	9.2	1.0	3.0
British Columbia	11.4	16.0	6.7	6.4	11.5	3.4	24.0	14.6	2.6	3.2
Canada	11.2	16.5	7.0	6.3	11.7	2.9	23.1	14.4	2.3	4.6
				Males						
Richmond	15.0	13.3	12.8	2.5	6.3	3.0	25.4	16.7	1.5	3.4
British Columbia	13.5	8.7	10.2	2.7	7.5	3.2	19.4	26.5	3.8	4.5
Canada	13.4	9.3	10.5	2.4	7.4	2.5	19.0	26.0	3.5	6.1
				Females						
Richmond	9.8	26.9	3.3	8.0	12.4	3.2	32.1	1.2	0.5	2.5
British Columbia	9.2	23.9	2.8	10.4	15.9	3.6	29.1	1.8	1.4	1.8
Canada	8.7	24.4	3.2	10.6	16.5	3.2	27.7	1.8	0.9	2.9

Note: Figures are based on total experienced labour force 15 years and over
Source: Statistics Canada. 2013. 2011 National Household Survey. Statistics Canada Catalogue no. 99-004-XWE. Ottawa. Released September 11, 2013.

Place of Work Status

Area	Worked at Home	Worked Outside Canada	No Fixed Workplace Address	Worked at Usual Place
		Number		
		Total		
Richmond	7,365	1,595	9,615	74,275
British Columbia	174,000	12,480	304,465	1,680,525
Canada	1,142,640	66,460	1,868,245	13,517,690
		Males		
Richmond	3,675	1,185	6,650	36,100
British Columbia	84,015	9,210	225,840	805,525
Canada	582,150	47,355	1,400,485	6,604,325
		Females		
Richmond	3,690	410	2,965	38,175
British Columbia	89,990	3,270	78,620	875,000
Canada	560,490	19,100	467,760	6,913,370
		Percent of Labour Force		
		Total		
Richmond	7.9	1.7	10.4	80.0
British Columbia	8.0	0.6	14.0	77.4
Canada	6.9	0.4	11.3	81.5
		Males		
Richmond	7.7	2.5	14.0	75.8
British Columbia	7.5	0.8	20.1	71.6
Canada	6.7	0.5	16.2	76.5
		Females		
Richmond	8.2	0.9	6.6	84.4
British Columbia	8.6	0.3	7.5	83.6
Canada	7.0	0.2	5.9	86.8

Note: Figures are based on total employed labour force 15 years and over.
Source: Statistics Canada. 2013. 2011 National Household Survey. Statistics Canada Catalogue no. 99-004-XWE. Ottawa. Released September 11, 2013.

PROFILES / Richmond, British Columbia

Mode of Transportation to Work

Area	Car; Truck; Van; as Driver	Car; Truck; Van; as Passenger	Public Transit	Walked	Bicycled	All Other Modes
			Number			
			Total			
Richmond	58,520	5,270	15,125	2,930	1,055	995
British Columbia	1,415,745	110,695	250,450	132,205	42,260	33,635
Canada	11,393,140	867,050	1,851,525	880,815	201,780	191,625
			Males			
Richmond	32,845	1,590	5,845	1,280	625	575
British Columbia	773,160	47,425	107,645	57,000	26,595	19,535
Canada	6,238,835	349,530	788,290	387,580	135,840	104,725
			Females			
Richmond	25,680	3,680	9,275	1,655	430	425
British Columbia	642,580	63,270	142,810	75,205	15,665	14,100
Canada	5,154,305	517,520	1,063,235	493,230	65,940	86,900
			Percent of Labour Force			
			Total			
Richmond	69.8	6.3	18.0	3.5	1.3	1.2
British Columbia	71.3	5.6	12.6	6.7	2.1	1.7
Canada	74.0	5.6	12.0	5.7	1.3	1.2
			Males			
Richmond	76.8	3.7	13.7	3.0	1.5	1.3
British Columbia	75.0	4.6	10.4	5.5	2.6	1.9
Canada	77.9	4.4	9.8	4.8	1.7	1.3
			Females			
Richmond	62.4	8.9	22.5	4.0	1.0	1.0
British Columbia	67.4	6.6	15.0	7.9	1.6	1.5
Canada	69.8	7.0	14.4	6.7	0.9	1.2

Note: Figures are based on total employed labour force 15 years and over.
Source: Statistics Canada. 2013. 2011 National Household Survey. Statistics Canada Catalogue no. 99-004-XWE. Ottawa. Released September 11, 2013.

Visible Minority Population Characteristics

Area	Total Minority	South Asian[1]	Chinese	Black	Filipino	Latin American	Arab	SE Asian[2]	West Asian[3]	Korean	Japanese	Multiple[4]
						Number						
						Total						
Richmond	133,320	14,515	89,045	1,245	12,670	1,680	950	2,150	1,255	1,370	3,765	4,305
British Columbia	1,180,870	313,440	438,140	33,260	126,040	35,465	14,090	51,970	38,960	53,770	38,120	31,160
Canada	6,264,750	1,567,400	1,324,750	945,665	619,310	381,280	380,620	312,075	206,840	161,130	87,270	171,935
						Males						
Richmond	63,195	7,340	42,125	605	5,505	715	520	1,015	575	635	1,775	2,200
British Columbia	565,965	157,135	208,175	17,365	53,715	16,985	8,010	25,055	19,420	25,325	16,295	15,255
Canada	3,043,010	790,755	632,325	453,005	268,885	186,355	203,485	154,035	105,620	77,165	38,270	83,335
						Females						
Richmond	70,130	7,175	46,915	640	7,160	970	430	1,130	685	735	1,990	2,105
British Columbia	614,905	156,300	229,960	15,895	72,320	18,480	6,080	26,920	19,540	28,440	21,820	15,905
Canada	3,221,745	776,650	692,420	492,660	350,425	194,925	177,140	158,045	101,220	83,965	48,990	88,600
						Percent of Population						
						Total						
Richmond	70.4	7.7	47.0	0.7	6.7	0.9	0.5	1.1	0.7	0.7	2.0	2.3
British Columbia	27.3	7.2	10.1	0.8	2.9	0.8	0.3	1.2	0.9	1.2	0.9	0.7
Canada	19.1	4.8	4.0	2.9	1.9	1.2	1.2	0.9	0.6	0.5	0.3	0.5
						Males						
Richmond	69.4	8.1	46.3	0.7	6.0	0.8	0.6	1.1	0.6	0.7	2.0	2.4
British Columbia	26.6	7.4	9.8	0.8	2.5	0.8	0.4	1.2	0.9	1.2	0.8	0.7
Canada	18.8	4.9	3.9	2.8	1.7	1.2	1.3	1.0	0.7	0.5	0.2	0.5
						Females						
Richmond	71.3	7.3	47.7	0.7	7.3	1.0	0.4	1.1	0.7	0.7	2.0	2.1
British Columbia	28.0	7.1	10.5	0.7	3.3	0.8	0.3	1.2	0.9	1.3	1.0	0.7
Canada	19.3	4.7	4.1	3.0	2.1	1.2	1.1	0.9	0.6	0.5	0.3	0.5

Note: The Employment Equity Act defines visible minorities as 'persons, other than Aboriginal peoples, who are non-Caucasian in race or non-white in colour';
(1) Includes 'East Indian,' 'Pakistani,' 'Sri Lankan,' etc.; (2) Includes 'Vietnamese,' 'Cambodian,' 'Malaysian,' 'Laotian,' etc.; (3) Includes 'Iranian,' 'Afghan,' etc.; (4) Includes respondents who reported more than one visible minority group by checking two or more mark-in circles, e.g., 'Black' and 'South Asian.'
Source: Statistics Canada. 2013. 2011 National Household Survey. Statistics Canada Catalogue no. 99-004-XWE. Ottawa. Released September 11, 2013.

PROFILES / Richmond, British Columbia

Aboriginal Population

Area	Aboriginal Identity[1]	First Nations (North American Indian) Single Identity[2]	Métis Single Identity	Inuk (Inuit) Single Identity	Multiple Aboriginal Identities[3]	Aboriginal Identities Not Included Elsewhere
Number						
Total						
Richmond	1,935	1,280	580	20	0	50
British Columbia	232,290	155,020	69,475	1,570	2,480	3,745
Canada	1,400,685	851,560	451,795	59,440	11,415	26,475
Males						
Richmond	905	590	270	0	0	0
British Columbia	113,080	75,400	33,940	820	1,190	1,735
Canada	682,190	411,785	223,335	29,495	5,525	12,055
Females						
Richmond	1,025	695	305	0	0	20
British Columbia	119,215	79,620	35,540	750	1,290	2,015
Canada	718,500	439,775	228,460	29,950	5,890	14,420
Percent of Population						
Total						
Richmond	1.0	0.7	0.3	0.0	0.0	0.0
British Columbia	5.4	3.6	1.6	0.0	0.1	0.1
Canada	4.3	2.6	1.4	0.2	0.0	0.1
Males						
Richmond	1.0	0.6	0.3	0.0	0.0	0.0
British Columbia	5.3	3.5	1.6	0.0	0.1	0.1
Canada	4.2	2.5	1.4	0.2	0.0	0.1
Females						
Richmond	1.0	0.7	0.3	0.0	0.0	0.0
British Columbia	5.4	3.6	1.6	0.0	0.1	0.1
Canada	4.3	2.6	1.4	0.2	0.0	0.1

Note: (1) Includes persons who reported being an Aboriginal person, that is, First Nations (North American Indian), Métis or Inuk (Inuit) and/or those who reported Registered or Treaty Indian status, that is registered under the Indian Act of Canada, and/or those who reported membership in a First Nation or Indian band. Aboriginal peoples of Canada are defined in the Constitution Act, 1982, section 35-2 as including the Indian, Inuit and Métis peoples of Canada; (2) Users should be aware that the estimates associated with this variable are more affected than most by the incomplete enumeration of certain Indian reserves and Indian settlements in the National Household Survey (NHS); (3) Includes persons who reported being any two or all three of the following: First Nations (North American Indian), Métis or Inuk (Inuit).
Source: Statistics Canada. 2013. 2011 National Household Survey. Statistics Canada Catalogue no. 99-004-XWE. Ottawa. Released September 11, 2013.

Ethnic Origin

Area	North American Aboriginal	Other North American	European	Caribbean	Latin, Central and South American	African	Asian	Oceania
Number								
Total								
Richmond	2,590	16,100	58,165	760	2,265	1,885	130,135	1,115
British Columbia	267,085	884,490	2,812,935	20,035	52,725	47,185	1,122,445	35,770
Canada	1,836,035	11,070,455	20,157,965	627,590	544,375	766,735	5,011,225	74,875
Males								
Richmond	1,185	8,195	28,850	390	1,075	925	61,695	500
British Columbia	128,880	440,920	1,387,940	10,225	25,605	23,575	535,825	17,425
Canada	885,675	5,462,685	9,913,150	291,640	264,635	387,360	2,435,540	37,490
Females								
Richmond	1,405	7,900	29,315	370	1,190	960	68,445	620
British Columbia	138,205	443,570	1,424,990	9,810	27,120	23,610	586,620	18,340
Canada	950,360	5,607,770	10,244,820	335,945	279,740	379,380	2,575,680	37,385
Percent of Population								
Total								
Richmond	1.4	8.5	30.7	0.4	1.2	1.0	68.7	0.6
British Columbia	6.2	20.5	65.0	0.5	1.2	1.1	26.0	0.8
Canada	5.6	33.7	61.4	1.9	1.7	2.3	15.3	0.2
Males								
Richmond	1.3	9.0	31.7	0.4	1.2	1.0	67.8	0.5
British Columbia	6.1	20.7	65.3	0.5	1.2	1.1	25.2	0.8
Canada	5.5	33.8	61.3	1.8	1.6	2.4	15.1	0.2
Females								
Richmond	1.4	8.0	29.8	0.4	1.2	1.0	69.6	0.6
British Columbia	6.3	20.2	64.8	0.4	1.2	1.1	26.7	0.8
Canada	5.7	33.6	61.4	2.0	1.7	2.3	15.4	0.2

Note: The sum of the ethnic groups in this table is greater than the total population estimate because a person may report more than one ethnic origin in the NHS.
Source: Statistics Canada. 2013. 2011 National Household Survey. Statistics Canada Catalogue no. 99-004-XWE. Ottawa. Released September 11, 2013.

Religion

Area	Buddhist	Christian	Hindu	Jewish	Muslim	Sikh	Traditional (Aboriginal) Spirituality	Other Religions	No Religious Affiliation
					Number				
					Total				
Richmond	12,330	71,030	2,675	2,885	5,530	7,155	35	860	86,805
British Columbia	90,620	1,930,415	45,795	23,130	79,310	201,110	10,295	35,500	1,908,285
Canada	366,830	22,102,745	497,965	329,495	1,053,945	454,965	64,935	130,835	7,850,605
					Males				
Richmond	5,415	31,975	1,280	1,520	2,860	3,640	0	375	43,925
British Columbia	40,175	883,680	22,945	11,255	39,780	100,610	5,085	14,680	1,007,420
Canada	168,465	10,497,775	250,435	161,265	540,555	229,435	31,805	57,745	4,225,645
					Females				
Richmond	6,915	39,050	1,390	1,365	2,675	3,515	0	485	42,875
British Columbia	50,440	1,046,735	22,845	11,880	39,530	100,500	5,210	20,820	900,865
Canada	198,365	11,604,975	247,525	168,235	513,395	225,530	33,135	73,090	3,624,965
				Percent of Population					
					Total				
Richmond	6.5	37.5	1.4	1.5	2.9	3.8	0.0	0.5	45.9
British Columbia	2.1	44.6	1.1	0.5	1.8	4.7	0.2	0.8	44.1
Canada	1.1	67.3	1.5	1.0	3.2	1.4	0.2	0.4	23.9
					Males				
Richmond	5.9	35.1	1.4	1.7	3.1	4.0	0.0	0.4	48.3
British Columbia	1.9	41.6	1.1	0.5	1.9	4.7	0.2	0.7	47.4
Canada	1.0	64.9	1.5	1.0	3.3	1.4	0.2	0.4	26.1
					Females				
Richmond	7.0	39.7	1.4	1.4	2.7	3.6	0.0	0.5	43.6
British Columbia	2.3	47.6	1.0	0.5	1.8	4.6	0.2	0.9	41.0
Canada	1.2	69.5	1.5	1.0	3.1	1.4	0.2	0.4	21.7

Note: Religion refers to the person's self-identification as having a connection or affiliation with any religious denomination, group, body, sect, cult or other religiously defined community or system of belief. Religion is not limited to formal membership in a religious organization or group. Persons without a religious connection or affiliation can self-identify as atheist, agnostic or humanist, or can provide another applicable response.
Source: Statistics Canada. 2013. 2011 National Household Survey. Statistics Canada Catalogue no. 99-004-XWE. Ottawa. Released September 11, 2013.

Religion—Christian Denominations

Area	Anglican	Baptist	Catholic	Christian Orthodox	Lutheran	Pentecostal	Presbyterian	United Church	Other Christian
					Number				
					Total				
Richmond	4,995	3,670	29,960	2,450	1,525	1,410	1,095	4,920	21,000
British Columbia	213,975	91,575	650,360	39,845	71,470	58,300	44,635	222,230	538,030
Canada	1,631,845	635,840	12,810,705	550,690	478,185	478,705	472,385	2,007,610	3,036,780
					Males				
Richmond	2,175	1,580	13,560	1,175	720	625	500	2,155	9,500
British Columbia	94,330	41,565	303,300	19,475	32,205	26,590	19,925	94,020	252,270
Canada	752,945	293,905	6,167,290	270,205	221,525	217,850	218,955	912,545	1,442,550
					Females				
Richmond	2,820	2,100	16,400	1,270	815	785	595	2,765	11,500
British Columbia	119,645	50,010	347,060	20,375	39,270	31,710	24,710	128,210	285,770
Canada	878,900	341,940	6,643,415	280,485	256,660	260,850	253,430	1,095,065	1,594,230
				Percent of Population					
					Total				
Richmond	2.6	1.9	15.8	1.3	0.8	0.7	0.6	2.6	11.1
British Columbia	4.9	2.1	15.0	0.9	1.7	1.3	1.0	5.1	12.4
Canada	5.0	1.9	39.0	1.7	1.5	1.5	1.4	6.1	9.2
					Males				
Richmond	2.4	1.7	14.9	1.3	0.8	0.7	0.5	2.4	10.4
British Columbia	4.4	2.0	14.3	0.9	1.5	1.3	0.9	4.4	11.9
Canada	4.7	1.8	38.2	1.7	1.4	1.3	1.4	5.6	8.9
					Females				
Richmond	2.9	2.1	16.7	1.3	0.8	0.8	0.6	2.8	11.7
British Columbia	5.4	2.3	15.8	0.9	1.8	1.4	1.1	5.8	13.0
Canada	5.3	2.0	39.8	1.7	1.5	1.6	1.5	6.6	9.6

Note: Religion refers to the person's self-identification as having a connection or affiliation with any religious denomination, group, body, sect, cult or other religiously defined community or system of belief. Religion is not limited to formal membership in a religious organization or group. Persons without a religious connection or affiliation can self-identify as atheist, agnostic or humanist, or can provide another applicable response.
Source: Statistics Canada. 2013. 2011 National Household Survey. Statistics Canada Catalogue no. 99-004-XWE. Ottawa. Released September 11, 2013.

Immigrant Status and Period of Immigration

Area	Non-Immigrants[1]	Immigrants All	Before 1971	1971 to 1980	1981 to 1990	1991 to 2000	2001 to 2005	2006 to 2011	Non-Permanent Residents[3]
				Number					
				Total					
Richmond	72,480	112,875	8,335	10,890	15,365	41,955	17,650	18,685	3,955
British Columbia	3,067,590	1,191,875	223,215	161,335	156,445	305,655	160,100	185,115	64,995
Canada	25,720,175	6,775,765	1,261,055	870,775	949,890	1,539,050	992,070	1,162,915	356,385
				Males					
Richmond	36,425	52,675	4,135	5,250	7,140	19,500	8,085	8,555	1,915
British Columbia	1,533,255	561,490	109,510	76,865	72,625	140,985	74,395	87,110	30,880
Canada	12,753,235	3,231,370	605,430	416,670	454,570	724,905	474,545	555,245	178,515
				Females					
Richmond	36,055	60,205	4,195	5,640	8,230	22,455	9,565	10,130	2,035
British Columbia	1,534,330	630,385	113,710	84,470	83,820	164,675	85,710	98,005	34,115
Canada	12,966,935	3,544,400	655,625	454,105	495,325	814,145	517,530	607,670	177,870
				Percent of Population					
				Total					
Richmond	38.3	59.6	4.4	5.8	8.1	22.2	9.3	9.9	2.1
British Columbia	70.9	27.6	5.2	3.7	3.6	7.1	3.7	4.3	1.5
Canada	78.3	20.6	3.8	2.7	2.9	4.7	3.0	3.5	1.1
				Males					
Richmond	40.0	57.9	4.5	5.8	7.8	21.4	8.9	9.4	2.1
British Columbia	72.1	26.4	5.2	3.6	3.4	6.6	3.5	4.1	1.5
Canada	78.9	20.0	3.7	2.6	2.8	4.5	2.9	3.4	1.1
				Females					
Richmond	36.7	61.2	4.3	5.7	8.4	22.8	9.7	10.3	2.1
British Columbia	69.8	28.7	5.2	3.8	3.8	7.5	3.9	4.5	1.6
Canada	77.7	21.2	3.9	2.7	3.0	4.9	3.1	3.6	1.1

Note: (1) Non-immigrant refers to a person who is a Canadian citizen by birth; (2) Immigrant refers to a person who is or has ever been a landed immigrant/permanent resident. This person has been granted the right to live in Canada permanently by immigration authorities. Some immigrants have resided in Canada for a number of years, while others have arrived recently. Some immigrants are Canadian citizens, while others are not. Most immigrants are born outside Canada, but a small number are born in Canada. In the 2011 National Household Survey, 'Immigrants' includes immigrants who landed in Canada prior to May 10, 2011; (3) Non-permanent resident refers to a person from another country who has a work or study permit, or who is a refugee claimant, and any non-Canadian-born family member living in Canada with them.
Source: Statistics Canada. 2013. 2011 National Household Survey. Statistics Canada Catalogue no. 99-004-XWE. Ottawa. Released September 11, 2013.

Mother Tongue

Area	English	French	Non-official Language	English & French	English & Non-official Language	French & Non-official Language	English, French & Non-official Language
			Number				
			Total				
Richmond	69,460	1,115	112,895	220	5,760	160	135
British Columbia	3,062,435	57,275	1,154,215	8,600	68,800	3,345	1,530
Canada	18,858,980	7,054,975	6,567,680	144,685	396,330	74,430	24,095
			Males				
Richmond	34,995	540	52,475	110	2,720	75	60
British Columbia	1,526,350	28,315	543,395	4,065	32,875	1,520	725
Canada	9,345,225	3,452,380	3,157,785	69,975	192,000	36,535	11,965
			Females				
Richmond	34,465	570	60,415	115	3,035	90	70
British Columbia	1,536,085	28,965	610,825	4,535	35,925	1,830	805
Canada	9,513,750	3,602,590	3,409,895	74,710	204,330	37,890	12,130
			Percent of Population				
			Total				
Richmond	36.6	0.6	59.5	0.1	3.0	0.1	0.1
British Columbia	70.3	1.3	26.5	0.2	1.6	0.1	0.0
Canada	56.9	21.3	19.8	0.4	1.2	0.2	0.1
			Males				
Richmond	38.5	0.6	57.7	0.1	3.0	0.1	0.1
British Columbia	71.4	1.3	25.4	0.2	1.5	0.1	0.0
Canada	57.5	21.2	19.4	0.4	1.2	0.2	0.1
			Females				
Richmond	34.9	0.6	61.2	0.1	3.1	0.1	0.1
British Columbia	69.2	1.3	27.5	0.2	1.6	0.1	0.0
Canada	56.4	21.4	20.2	0.4	1.2	0.2	0.1

Note: Figures cover total population excluding institutional residents.
Source: Statistics Canada. 2012. Census Profile. 2011 Census. Statistics Canada Catalogue no. 98-316-XWE. Ottawa. Released October 24 2012.
http://www12.statcan.gc.ca/census-recensement/2011/dp-pd/prof/index.cfm?Lang=E

Language Spoken Most Often at Home

Area	English	French	Non-official Language	English & French	English & Non-official Language	French & Non-official Language	English, French & Non-official Language
Number							
Total							
Richmond	93,715	370	80,545	185	14,675	80	170
British Columbia	3,506,595	16,685	670,100	4,700	155,065	930	2,130
Canada	21,457,075	6,827,865	3,673,865	131,205	875,135	109,700	46,330
Males							
Richmond	46,125	180	37,475	85	6,995	30	75
British Columbia	1,733,775	8,015	317,670	2,240	74,155	435	940
Canada	10,585,620	3,348,235	1,767,310	63,475	425,370	53,010	22,845
Females							
Richmond	47,590	195	43,075	95	7,680	45	90
British Columbia	1,772,820	8,665	352,430	2,460	80,905	495	1,185
Canada	10,871,455	3,479,625	1,906,555	67,730	449,765	56,690	23,485
Percent of Population							
Total							
Richmond	49.4	0.2	42.5	0.1	7.7	0.0	0.1
British Columbia	80.5	0.4	15.4	0.1	3.6	0.0	0.0
Canada	64.8	20.6	11.1	0.4	2.6	0.3	0.1
Males							
Richmond	50.7	0.2	41.2	0.1	7.7	0.0	0.1
British Columbia	81.1	0.4	14.9	0.1	3.5	0.0	0.0
Canada	65.1	20.6	10.9	0.4	2.6	0.3	0.1
Females							
Richmond	48.2	0.2	43.6	0.1	7.8	0.0	0.1
British Columbia	79.9	0.4	15.9	0.1	3.6	0.0	0.1
Canada	64.5	20.6	11.3	0.4	2.7	0.3	0.1

Note: Figures cover total population excluding institutional residents.
Source: Statistics Canada. 2012. Census Profile. 2011 Census. Statistics Canada Catalogue no. 98-316-XWE. Ottawa. Released October 24 2012.
http://www12.statcan.gc.ca/census-recensement/2011/dp-pd/prof/index.cfm?Lang=E

Knowledge of Official Languages

Area	English Only	French Only	English & French	Neither English nor French
Number				
Total				
Richmond	160,045	75	9,875	19,745
British Columbia	3,912,950	2,045	296,645	144,555
Canada	22,564,665	4,165,015	5,795,570	595,920
Males				
Richmond	78,305	35	4,380	8,255
British Columbia	1,943,760	950	132,940	59,590
Canada	11,222,185	1,925,340	2,876,560	241,790
Females				
Richmond	81,740	40	5,495	11,485
British Columbia	1,969,190	1,095	163,705	84,965
Canada	11,342,485	2,239,680	2,919,005	354,135
Percent of Population				
Total				
Richmond	84.3	0.0	5.2	10.4
British Columbia	89.8	0.0	6.8	3.3
Canada	68.1	12.6	17.5	1.8
Males				
Richmond	86.1	0.0	4.8	9.1
British Columbia	90.9	0.0	6.2	2.8
Canada	69.0	11.8	17.7	1.5
Females				
Richmond	82.8	0.0	5.6	11.6
British Columbia	88.7	0.0	7.4	3.8
Canada	67.3	13.3	17.3	2.1

Note: Figures cover total population excluding institutional residents.
Source: Statistics Canada. 2012. Census Profile. 2011 Census. Statistics Canada Catalogue no. 98-316-XWE. Ottawa. Released October 24 2012.
http://www12.statcan.gc.ca/census-recensement/2011/dp-pd/prof/index.cfm?Lang=E

Richmond Hill, Ontario

Background

Richmond Hill is located in the central portion of York Region in southern Ontario. The Town of Richmond Hill is part of the northern Greater Toronto Area (GTA) and is situated halfway between Toronto and Lake Simcoe. The town's unofficial motto is "A little north, a little nicer."

The Town of Richmond began as a farming settlement spread across two nearby townships, Vaughn and Markham. Richmond Hill was incorporated as a village in 1872. By the early 20th century, Richmond Hill was the "Rose Capital of Canada" because of the region's large greenhouse operations. Following the post-war population boom, Richmond Hill acquired town status in 1957. The town's population is expected to reach 200,000 by 2021.

Recreational and sporting facilities, nature trails and over 150 green spaces like Phyllis Rawlinson Park, Sunset Beach Park and Mill Pond Park are popular attractions. There are several local golf courses as well as world-class courses nearby such as Angus Glen Golf Club and Glen Abbey Golf Club. Canada's largest optical telescope is located at the David Dunlap Observatory. The 23-tonne telescope was used to discover evidence of a black hole in 1972.

Over 5,000 organizations are based in Richmond Hill. Key industry clusters are information and communications technology (ICT), advanced manufacturing, life sciences and healthcare technologies, financial and insurance services, clean technology, and building and construction. In 2012, Volvo Cars of Canada Corporation announced the building of a new headquarters facility in Richmond Hill. Automotive companies BMW, Suzuki and Mazda are also headquartered in the community. Every year Richmond Hill competes in the "International Communities in Bloom" competition to showcase the town's gardens, parks and open spaces. The Richmond Hill Public Library offers various heritage programs, including the largest repository of local genealogical data in York Region. Arts in the community are represented through non-profit groups such as the Richmond Hill Group of Artists (RHGA), the Burr House Spinners, and the Weavers and Hill Potters' Guild.

Richmond Hill has summer highs of plus 25.2 degrees Celsius, winter lows of minus 9.13 degrees Celsius, and an average rainfall just over 735 mm per year.

Rankings

- The Conference Board of Canada ranked Richmond Hill as one of the best cities for attracting skilled and mobile workers. The city received an A grading by the Conference Board of Canada. Criteria included economy, health, environment, housing and innovation, society and education. Other top-ranked cities were St. John's (NL), Ottawa (ON), Waterloo (ON), Calgary (AB) and Vancouver (BC). *Conference Board of Canada, "City Magnets: Benchmarking the Attractiveness of Canada's CMAs," December 2007*
- The *Recycling Council of Ontario* recognized Richmond Hill in 2011 with the Waste Management Award for its partnership with Toronto Recycling Inc. in the collection and recycling of electronic waste materials. Richmond Hill had diverted 37,000 tonnes of waste from its landfills. *Richmond Hill, "Richmond Hill Wins Waste Management Award," October, 2011.*

PROFILES / Richmond Hill, Ontario

Population Growth and Density

Area	Population in 2001	Population in 2006	Population in 2011	Population Change 2001–2006	Population Change 2006–2011	Land Area (sq. km)	Population Density per sq. km
Richmond Hill	132,030	162,704	185,541	23.2	14.0	100.95	1,838.0
Ontario	11,410,046	12,160,282	12,851,821	6.6	5.7	908,607.67	14.1
Canada	30,007,094	31,612,897	33,476,688	5.4	5.9	8,965,121.42	3.7

Source: Statistics Canada. 2012. Census Profile. 2011 Census. Statistics Canada Catalogue no. 98-316-XWE. Ottawa. Released October 24 2012.
http://www12.statcan.gc.ca/census-recensement/2011/dp-pd/prof/index.cfm?Lang=E;
Statistics Canada 2007. 2006 Community Profiles. 2006 Census. Statistics Canada Catalogue no. 92-591-XWE. Ottawa. Released March 13 2007.
http://www12.statcan.ca/census-recensement/2006/dp-pd/prof/92-591/index.cfm?Lang=E

Gender

Area	Males	Females
Number		
Richmond Hill	90,365	95,180
Ontario	6,263,140	6,588,685
Canada	16,414,225	17,062,460
Percent of Population		
Richmond Hill	48.7	51.3
Ontario	48.7	51.3
Canada	49.0	51.0

Source: Statistics Canada. 2012. Census Profile. 2011 Census. Statistics Canada Catalogue no. 98-316-XWE. Ottawa. Released October 24 2012.
http://www12.statcan.gc.ca/census-recensement/2011/dp-pd/prof/index.cfm?Lang=E

Marital Status

Area	Married[1]	Living Common-law	Single[2]	Separated	Divorced	Widowed
Number						
Total						
Richmond Hill	89,455	4,465	41,915	3,040	6,360	6,660
Ontario	5,367,400	791,210	2,985,020	319,805	593,730	613,880
Canada	12,941,960	3,142,525	7,816,045	698,240	1,686,035	1,584,530
Males						
Richmond Hill	44,470	2,230	21,955	1,085	1,990	1,075
Ontario	2,681,320	397,620	1,583,760	133,790	231,160	117,980
Canada	6,470,300	1,575,495	4,206,320	299,655	680,415	310,940
Females						
Richmond Hill	44,990	2,235	19,965	1,955	4,370	5,580
Ontario	2,686,075	393,590	1,401,260	186,015	362,570	495,905
Canada	6,471,660	1,567,035	3,609,730	398,585	1,005,620	1,273,590
Percent of Population						
Total						
Richmond Hill	58.9	2.9	27.6	2.0	4.2	4.4
Ontario	50.3	7.4	28.0	3.0	5.6	5.8
Canada	46.4	11.3	28.0	2.5	6.0	5.7
Males						
Richmond Hill	61.1	3.1	30.2	1.5	2.7	1.5
Ontario	52.1	7.7	30.8	2.6	4.5	2.3
Canada	47.8	11.6	31.1	2.2	5.0	2.3
Females						
Richmond Hill	56.9	2.8	25.2	2.5	5.5	7.1
Ontario	48.6	7.1	25.4	3.4	6.6	9.0
Canada	45.2	10.9	25.2	2.8	7.0	8.9

Note: (1) and not separated, (2) never legally married
Source: Statistics Canada. 2012. Census Profile. 2011 Census. Statistics Canada Catalogue no. 98-316-XWE. Ottawa. Released October 24 2012.
http://www12.statcan.gc.ca/census-recensement/2011/dp-pd/prof/index.cfm?Lang=E

PROFILES / Richmond Hill, Ontario

Age Characteristics: 0 to 49 Years

Area	0 to 4 Years	5 to 9 Years	10 to 14 Years	15 to 19 Years	20 to 24 Years	25 to 29 Years	30 to 34 Years	35 to 39 Years	40 to 44 Years	45 to 49 Years
Number										
Total										
Richmond Hill	9,800	11,650	12,190	13,560	12,355	10,185	10,025	13,480	16,590	17,320
Ontario	704,260	712,755	763,755	863,635	852,910	815,120	800,365	844,335	924,075	1,055,880
Canada	1,877,095	1,809,895	1,920,355	2,178,135	2,187,450	2,169,590	2,162,905	2,173,930	2,324,875	2,675,130
Males										
Richmond Hill	5,035	6,130	6,395	7,000	6,435	5,120	4,505	6,070	7,675	8,405
Ontario	360,590	365,290	391,630	443,680	432,490	400,045	383,340	405,845	447,920	517,510
Canada	961,150	925,965	983,995	1,115,845	1,108,775	1,077,275	1,058,810	1,064,200	1,141,720	1,318,715
Females										
Richmond Hill	4,765	5,520	5,795	6,555	5,920	5,065	5,520	7,415	8,915	8,915
Ontario	343,670	347,465	372,125	419,950	420,415	415,075	417,030	438,485	476,155	538,370
Canada	915,945	883,935	936,360	1,062,295	1,078,670	1,092,315	1,104,095	1,109,735	1,183,155	1,356,420
Percent of Population										
Total										
Richmond Hill	5.3	6.3	6.6	7.3	6.7	5.5	5.4	7.3	8.9	9.3
Ontario	5.5	5.5	5.9	6.7	6.6	6.3	6.2	6.6	7.2	8.2
Canada	5.6	5.4	5.7	6.5	6.5	6.5	6.5	6.5	6.9	8.0
Males										
Richmond Hill	5.6	6.8	7.1	7.7	7.1	5.7	5.0	6.7	8.5	9.3
Ontario	5.8	5.8	6.3	7.1	6.9	6.4	6.1	6.5	7.2	8.3
Canada	5.9	5.6	6.0	6.8	6.8	6.6	6.5	6.5	7.0	8.0
Females										
Richmond Hill	5.0	5.8	6.1	6.9	6.2	5.3	5.8	7.8	9.4	9.4
Ontario	5.2	5.3	5.6	6.4	6.4	6.3	6.3	6.7	7.2	8.2
Canada	5.4	5.2	5.5	6.2	6.3	6.4	6.4	6.5	6.9	7.9

Source: Statistics Canada. 2012. Census Profile. 2011 Census. Statistics Canada Catalogue no. 98-316-XWE. Ottawa. Released October 24 2012.
http://www12.statcan.gc.ca/census-recensement/2011/dp-pd/prof/index.cfm?Lang=E

Age Characteristics: 50 Years and Over, and Median Age

Area	50 to 54 Years	55 to 59 Years	60 to 64 Years	65 to 69 Years	70 to 74 Years	75 to 79 Years	80 to 84 Years	85 Years and Over	Median Age
Number									
Total									
Richmond Hill	15,380	11,920	10,140	6,510	5,280	4,030	2,800	2,330	39.8
Ontario	1,006,140	864,620	765,655	563,485	440,780	356,150	271,510	246,400	40.4
Canada	2,658,965	2,340,635	2,052,670	1,521,715	1,153,065	922,700	702,070	645,515	40.6
Males									
Richmond Hill	7,425	5,805	4,935	3,100	2,510	1,880	1,190	745	38.8
Ontario	492,560	418,755	370,370	270,875	206,350	161,345	113,620	80,925	39.4
Canada	1,309,030	1,147,300	1,002,690	738,010	543,435	417,945	291,085	208,300	39.6
Females									
Richmond Hill	7,955	6,115	5,205	3,410	2,770	2,150	1,610	1,585	40.6
Ontario	513,580	445,865	395,275	292,610	234,435	194,805	157,890	165,475	41.3
Canada	1,349,940	1,193,335	1,049,985	783,705	609,630	504,755	410,985	437,215	41.5
Percent of Population									
Total									
Richmond Hill	8.3	6.4	5.5	3.5	2.8	2.2	1.5	1.3	–
Ontario	7.8	6.7	6.0	4.4	3.4	2.8	2.1	1.9	–
Canada	7.9	7.0	6.1	4.5	3.4	2.8	2.1	1.9	–
Males									
Richmond Hill	8.2	6.4	5.5	3.4	2.8	2.1	1.3	0.8	–
Ontario	7.9	6.7	5.9	4.3	3.3	2.6	1.8	1.3	–
Canada	8.0	7.0	6.1	4.5	3.3	2.5	1.8	1.3	–
Females									
Richmond Hill	8.4	6.4	5.5	3.6	2.9	2.3	1.7	1.7	–
Ontario	7.8	6.8	6.0	4.4	3.6	3.0	2.4	2.5	–
Canada	7.9	7.0	6.2	4.6	3.6	3.0	2.4	2.6	–

Source: Statistics Canada. 2012. Census Profile. 2011 Census. Statistics Canada Catalogue no. 98-316-XWE. Ottawa. Released October 24 2012.
http://www12.statcan.gc.ca/census-recensement/2011/dp-pd/prof/index.cfm?Lang=E

PROFILES / Richmond Hill, Ontario

Private Households by Household Size

Area	1 Person	2 Persons	3 Persons	4 Persons	5 Persons	6 or More Persons	Average Number of Persons in Private Households
Households							
Richmond Hill	8,115	13,820	12,785	14,730	5,840	3,355	3.1
Ontario	1,230,975	1,584,415	803,030	783,925	310,860	174,305	2.6
Canada	3,673,310	4,544,820	2,081,900	1,903,300	724,405	392,885	2.5
Percent of Households							
Richmond Hill	13.8	23.6	21.8	25.1	10.0	5.7	—
Ontario	25.2	32.4	16.4	16.0	6.4	3.6	—
Canada	27.6	34.1	15.6	14.3	5.4	2.9	—

Source: Statistics Canada. 2012. Census Profile. 2011 Census. Statistics Canada Catalogue no. 98-316-XWE. Ottawa. Released October 24 2012.
http://www12.statcan.gc.ca/census-recensement/2011/dp-pd/prof/index.cfm?Lang=E

Dwelling Type

Area	Single-detached House	Semi-detached House	Row House	Apartment: Building with Five or More Storeys	Apartment: Building with Fewer Than Five Storeys	Duplex Apartment	Movable Dwelling	Other Single-attached House
Number								
Richmond Hill	36,435	2,400	8,460	8,100	1,355	1,840	5	55
Ontario	2,718,880	279,470	415,225	789,970	498,160	160,460	15,800	9,540
Canada	7,329,150	646,245	791,600	1,234,770	2,397,550	704,485	183,510	33,310
Percent of Dwellings								
Richmond Hill	62.1	4.1	14.4	13.8	2.3	3.1	0.0	0.1
Ontario	55.6	5.7	8.5	16.2	10.2	3.3	0.3	0.2
Canada	55.0	4.9	5.9	9.3	18.0	5.3	1.4	0.3

Source: Statistics Canada. 2012. Census Profile. 2011 Census. Statistics Canada Catalogue no. 98-316-XWE. Ottawa. Released October 24 2012.
http://www12.statcan.gc.ca/census-recensement/2011/dp-pd/prof/index.cfm?Lang=E

Shelter Costs

	Owned Dwellings				Rented Dwellings		
Area	Number	Median Value[1] ($)	Average Value[1] ($)	Median Monthly Costs[2] ($)	Average Monthly Costs[2] ($)	Number	Median Monthly Costs[3] ($)	Average Monthly Costs[3] ($)
Richmond Hill	50,340	550,573	587,427	1,660	1,672	8,310	1,116	1,129
Ontario	3,446,650	300,862	367,428	1,163	1,284	1,385,535	892	926
Canada	9,013,410	280,552	345,182	978	1,141	4,060,385	784	848

Note: All figures cover non-farm, non-reserve private dwellings; (1) Refers to the dollar amount expected by the owner if the dwelling were to be sold; (2) Includes all shelter expenses paid by households that own their dwellings, such as the mortgage payment and the costs of electricity, heat, water and other municipal services, property taxes and condominium fees; (3) Includes all shelter expenses paid by households that rent their dwellings, such as the monthly rent and the costs of electricity, heat and municipal services.
Source: Statistics Canada. 2013. 2011 National Household Survey. Statistics Canada Catalogue no. 99-004-XWE. Ottawa. Released September 11, 2013.

Occupied Private Dwellings by Period of Construction

Area	1960 or Before	1961 to 1980	1981 to 1990	1991 to 2000	2001 to 2005	2006 to 2011
Number						
Richmond Hill	4,390	6,615	12,975	15,610	11,970	7,085
Ontario	1,330,235	1,420,570	763,430	609,310	414,795	348,310
Canada	3,273,105	4,152,715	2,112,110	1,707,880	1,031,020	1,042,430
Percent of Dwellings						
Richmond Hill	7.5	11.3	22.1	26.6	20.4	12.1
Ontario	27.2	29.1	15.6	12.5	8.5	7.1
Canada	24.6	31.2	15.9	12.8	7.7	7.8

Note: Figures cover non-farm, non-reserve private dwellings and includes data up to May 10, 2011.
Source: Statistics Canada. 2013. 2011 National Household Survey. Statistics Canada Catalogue no. 99-004-XWE. Ottawa. Released September 11, 2013.

Educational Attainment

Area	No Certificate, Diploma or Degree	High School Diploma or Equivalent[1]	Apprenticeship or Trades Certificate or Diploma[2]	College, CÉGEP or Other Non-University Certificate or Diploma	University Certificate or Diploma Below the Bachelor Level[3]	Bachelor's Degree	University Certificate, Diploma or Degree Above Bachelor Level[4]
				Number			
				Total			
Richmond Hill	20,175	33,185	7,315	23,375	9,265	35,785	21,635
Ontario	1,954,520	2,801,805	771,140	2,070,875	427,150	1,515,075	933,100
Canada	5,485,400	6,968,935	2,950,685	4,970,020	1,200,130	3,634,425	2,049,930
				Males			
Richmond Hill	9,340	15,000	4,560	10,270	4,100	17,125	12,140
Ontario	957,040	1,337,055	520,390	894,235	193,355	692,345	470,290
Canada	2,742,875	3,305,415	1,928,970	2,118,430	513,235	1,643,080	1,043,350
				Females			
Richmond Hill	10,830	18,190	2,755	13,105	5,165	18,660	9,495
Ontario	997,475	1,464,755	250,750	1,176,640	233,790	822,730	462,805
Canada	2,742,520	3,663,515	1,021,715	2,851,595	686,890	1,991,345	1,006,585
				Percent of Population			
				Total			
Richmond Hill	13.4	22.0	4.9	15.5	6.1	23.7	14.4
Ontario	18.7	26.8	7.4	19.8	4.1	14.5	8.9
Canada	20.1	25.6	10.8	18.2	4.4	13.3	7.5
				Males			
Richmond Hill	12.9	20.7	6.3	14.2	5.7	23.6	16.7
Ontario	18.9	26.4	10.3	17.7	3.8	13.7	9.3
Canada	20.6	24.9	14.5	15.9	3.9	12.4	7.8
				Females			
Richmond Hill	13.8	23.3	3.5	16.8	6.6	23.9	12.1
Ontario	18.4	27.1	4.6	21.8	4.3	15.2	8.6
Canada	19.6	26.2	7.3	20.4	4.9	14.3	7.2

Note: Figures cover total population aged 15 years and over by highest certificate, diploma or degree; (1) Includes persons who have graduated from a secondary school or equivalent. It excludes persons with a postsecondary certificate, diploma or degree; (2) Includes Registered Apprenticeship certificates (including Certificate of Qualification, Journeyperson's designation) and other trades certificates or diplomas such as pre-employment or vocational certificates and diplomas from brief trade programs completed at community colleges, institutes of technology, vocational centres, and similar institutions; (3) Comparisons with other data sources suggest that the category 'University certificate or diploma below the bachelor's level' was over-reported in the NHS. This category likely includes some responses that are actually college certificates or diplomas, bachelor's degrees or other types of education (e.g., university transfer programs, bachelor's programs completed in other countries, incomplete bachelor's programs, non-university professional designations). We recommend users interpret the results for the 'University certificate or diploma below the bachelor's level' category with caution; (4) 'University certificate or diploma above bachelor level' includes the categories: 'Degree in medicine, dentistry, veterinary medicine or optometry,' 'Master's degree' and 'Earned doctorate.'
Source: Statistics Canada. 2013. 2011 National Household Survey. Statistics Canada Catalogue no. 99-004-XWE. Ottawa. Released September 11, 2013.

Household Income Distribution

Area	Less than $10,000	$10,000 to $19,999	$20,000 to $29,999	$30,000 to $39,999	$40,000 to $49,999	$50,000 to $59,999	$60,000 to $79,999	$80,000 to $99,999	$100,000 to $124,999	$125,000 to $149,999	$150,000 and Over
						Households					
Richmond Hill	2,165	2,930	3,740	3,665	3,590	3,555	6,980	6,470	6,870	5,435	13,255
Ontario	201,780	354,530	405,725	425,410	425,720	398,705	680,850	552,660	497,970	331,460	611,840
Canada	626,705	1,141,945	1,193,925	1,271,675	1,206,800	1,102,120	1,865,280	1,458,240	1,260,770	802,555	1,389,240
						Percent of Households					
Richmond Hill	3.7	5.0	6.4	6.2	6.1	6.1	11.9	11.0	11.7	9.3	22.6
Ontario	4.1	7.3	8.3	8.7	8.7	8.2	13.9	11.3	10.2	6.8	12.5
Canada	4.7	8.6	9.0	9.5	9.1	8.3	14.0	10.9	9.5	6.0	10.4

Note: Household income is the sum of the total incomes of all members of that household. Total income refers to monetary receipts from certain sources, before income taxes and deductions, during calendar year 2010.
Source: Statistics Canada. 2013. 2011 National Household Survey. Statistics Canada Catalogue no. 99-004-XWE. Ottawa. Released September 11, 2013.

Median and Average Household and Economic Family Income

Area	Median Household Income ($)	Average Household Income ($)	Median After-tax Household Income ($)	Average After-tax Household Income ($)	Median Economic Family Income ($)	Average Economic Family Income ($)	Median After-tax Economic Family Income ($)	Average After-tax Economic Family Income ($)
Richmond Hill	87,388	108,979	75,464	89,440	98,073	117,876	84,537	96,675
Ontario	66,358	85,772	58,717	71,523	80,987	100,152	71,128	83,322
Canada	61,072	79,102	54,089	66,149	76,511	94,125	67,044	78,517

Note: Figures cover household and economic familiy income in 2010. A household is defined as a person or a group of persons (other than foreign residents) who occupy the same private dwelling and do not have a usual place of residence elsewhere in Canada. Every person is a member of one and only one household. An economic family is defined as a group of two or more persons who live in the same dwelling and are related to each other by blood, marriage, common-law, adoption or a foster relationship. A couple may be of opposite or same sex.
Source: Statistics Canada. 2013. 2011 National Household Survey. Statistics Canada Catalogue no. 99-004-XWE. Ottawa. Released September 11, 2013.

PROFILES / Richmond Hill, Ontario

Individual Income Distribution

Area	Less than $10,000	$10,000 to $19,999	$20,000 to $29,999	$30,000 to $39,999	$40,000 to $49,999	$50,000 to $59,999	$60,000 to $79,999	$80,000 to $99,999	$100,000 to $124,999	$125,000 and Over
					Number Total					
Richmond Hill	29,680	24,035	15,875	12,690	11,350	10,045	14,550	10,030	5,305	7,175
Ontario	1,780,355	1,748,060	1,361,710	1,136,730	980,790	746,360	964,280	574,710	293,865	330,285
Canada	4,492,040	4,835,710	3,670,020	3,180,360	2,603,520	1,921,650	2,437,440	1,302,045	693,580	782,135
					Males					
Richmond Hill	13,490	9,245	6,850	5,755	5,020	4,915	7,935	5,655	3,640	5,540
Ontario	781,095	669,815	580,990	535,255	491,125	407,005	569,205	341,160	201,125	244,500
Canada	1,936,365	1,864,880	1,588,260	1,522,190	1,333,510	1,079,780	1,473,145	823,720	492,905	599,905
					Females					
Richmond Hill	16,185	14,790	9,020	6,935	6,335	5,130	6,615	4,385	1,660	1,630
Ontario	999,265	1,078,245	780,720	601,475	489,665	339,360	395,075	233,550	92,740	85,790
Canada	2,555,675	2,970,825	2,081,760	1,658,170	1,270,010	841,870	964,300	478,330	200,680	182,230
					Percent of Population Total					
Richmond Hill	21.1	17.1	11.3	9.0	8.1	7.1	10.3	7.1	3.8	5.1
Ontario	18.0	17.6	13.7	11.5	9.9	7.5	9.7	5.8	3.0	3.3
Canada	17.3	18.7	14.2	12.3	10.0	7.4	9.4	5.0	2.7	3.0
					Males					
Richmond Hill	19.8	13.6	10.1	8.5	7.4	7.2	11.7	8.3	5.4	8.1
Ontario	16.2	13.9	12.1	11.1	10.2	8.4	11.8	7.1	4.2	5.1
Canada	15.2	14.7	12.5	12.0	10.5	8.5	11.6	6.5	3.9	4.7
					Females					
Richmond Hill	22.3	20.3	12.4	9.5	8.7	7.1	9.1	6.0	2.3	2.2
Ontario	19.6	21.2	15.3	11.8	9.6	6.7	7.8	4.6	1.8	1.7
Canada	19.4	22.5	15.8	12.6	9.6	6.4	7.3	3.6	1.5	1.4

Note: Figures cover individuals aged 15 years and over with income. Income refers to monetary receipts from certain sources, before income taxes and deductions, during calendar year 2010.
Source: Statistics Canada. 2013. 2011 National Household Survey. Statistics Canada Catalogue no. 99-004-XWE. Ottawa. Released September 11, 2013.

Labour Force Status

Area	In the Labour Force – All	Employed	Unemployed	Not in the Labour Force
	Number Total			
Richmond Hill	102,085	95,055	7,030	48,655
Ontario	6,864,990	6,297,005	567,985	3,608,685
Canada	17,990,080	16,595,035	1,395,045	9,269,445
	Males			
Richmond Hill	52,825	49,325	3,500	19,710
Ontario	3,542,030	3,249,165	292,865	1,522,690
Canada	9,388,570	8,634,310	754,255	3,906,785
	Females			
Richmond Hill	49,260	45,735	3,530	28,945
Ontario	3,322,955	3,047,840	275,120	2,085,990
Canada	8,601,515	7,960,725	640,790	5,362,660
	Percent of Labour Force Total			
Richmond Hill	67.7	63.1	6.9	32.3
Ontario	65.5	60.1	8.3	34.5
Canada	66.0	60.9	7.8	34.0
	Males			
Richmond Hill	72.8	68.0	6.6	27.2
Ontario	69.9	64.2	8.3	30.1
Canada	70.6	64.9	8.0	29.4
	Females			
Richmond Hill	63.0	58.5	7.2	37.0
Ontario	61.4	56.3	8.3	38.6
Canada	61.6	57.0	7.4	38.4

Note: Figures are based on total population 15 years and over
Source: Statistics Canada. 2013. 2011 National Household Survey. Statistics Canada Catalogue no. 99-004-XWE. Ottawa. Released September 11, 2013.

Labour Force by Industry (NAICS Codes 11–52)

Area	Agriculture, forestry, fishing & hunting	Mining, quarrying, & oil & gas extraction	Utilities	Construction	Manufacturing	Wholesale Trade	Retail Trade	Transportation & warehousing	Information & cultural industries	Finance & insurance
					Number					
					Total					
Richmond Hill	125	155	705	5,525	8,050	6,735	11,685	2,940	3,695	9,705
Ontario	101,280	29,985	57,035	417,900	697,565	305,030	751,200	307,405	178,720	364,415
Canada	437,650	261,050	149,940	1,215,380	1,619,295	733,445	2,031,665	827,780	420,830	767,960
					Males					
Richmond Hill	85	130	440	4,695	5,290	4,030	5,655	2,150	2,005	4,570
Ontario	66,485	25,650	42,685	369,300	493,305	197,770	344,480	225,245	98,835	153,125
Canada	307,370	211,690	110,765	1,068,710	1,167,680	494,545	933,850	617,305	235,875	296,995
					Females					
Richmond Hill	40	30	270	830	2,765	2,700	6,030	785	1,690	5,135
Ontario	34,800	4,340	14,350	48,595	204,260	107,260	406,720	82,160	79,885	211,290
Canada	130,285	49,360	39,175	146,670	451,615	238,900	1,097,820	210,475	184,955	470,960
					Percent of Labour Force					
					Total					
Richmond Hill	0.1	0.2	0.7	5.5	8.1	6.8	11.7	3.0	3.7	9.7
Ontario	1.5	0.4	0.9	6.3	10.4	4.6	11.2	4.6	2.7	5.5
Canada	2.5	1.5	0.9	6.9	9.2	4.2	11.6	4.7	2.4	4.4
					Males					
Richmond Hill	0.2	0.3	0.9	9.1	10.3	7.8	11.0	4.2	3.9	8.9
Ontario	1.9	0.7	1.2	10.7	14.3	5.7	10.0	6.5	2.9	4.4
Canada	3.3	2.3	1.2	11.6	12.7	5.4	10.2	6.7	2.6	3.2
					Females					
Richmond Hill	0.1	0.1	0.6	1.7	5.8	5.6	12.5	1.6	3.5	10.7
Ontario	1.1	0.1	0.4	1.5	6.3	3.3	12.6	2.5	2.5	6.5
Canada	1.6	0.6	0.5	1.7	5.4	2.8	13.1	2.5	2.2	5.6

Note: Figures are based on total experienced labour force 15 years and over. Experienced labour force refers to persons who, during the week of Sunday, May 1 to Saturday, May 7, 2011, were employed and the unemployed who had last worked for pay or in self-employment in either 2010 or 2011.
Source: Statistics Canada. 2013. 2011 National Household Survey. Statistics Canada Catalogue no. 99-004-XWE. Ottawa. Released September 11, 2013.

Labour Force by Industry (NAICS Codes 53–91)

Area	Real estate & rental & leasing	Profess., scientific & tech. services	Mgmt of companies & enterprises	Admin. & support, waste mgmt & remed. services	Educational services	Health care & social assistance	Arts, entertain. & recreation	Accomm. & food services	Other services (except public admin.)	Public admin.
					Number					
					Total					
Richmond Hill	3,160	13,225	160	3,285	7,785	8,135	1,655	4,675	4,220	3,985
Ontario	133,980	511,020	6,525	309,630	499,690	692,130	144,065	417,675	296,340	458,665
Canada	321,895	1,240,850	17,460	728,330	1,301,435	1,949,650	363,405	1,130,750	807,800	1,261,050
					Males					
Richmond Hill	1,610	7,580	110	1,925	2,410	1,850	985	2,345	1,770	1,930
Ontario	72,835	281,420	3,540	172,475	162,765	120,165	75,035	177,240	133,795	236,655
Canada	179,090	688,625	9,380	411,250	424,915	349,430	188,270	469,990	372,940	652,510
					Females					
Richmond Hill	1,545	5,645	50	1,360	5,375	6,285	670	2,330	2,445	2,060
Ontario	61,145	229,600	2,990	137,155	336,925	571,965	69,030	240,430	162,550	222,015
Canada	142,805	552,225	8,075	317,085	876,515	1,600,220	175,135	660,760	434,865	608,535
					Percent of Labour Force					
					Total					
Richmond Hill	3.2	13.3	0.2	3.3	7.8	8.2	1.7	4.7	4.2	4.0
Ontario	2.0	7.6	0.1	4.6	7.5	10.4	2.2	6.3	4.4	6.9
Canada	1.8	7.1	0.1	4.1	7.4	11.1	2.1	6.4	4.6	7.2
					Males					
Richmond Hill	3.1	14.7	0.2	3.7	4.7	3.6	1.9	4.5	3.4	3.7
Ontario	2.1	8.2	0.1	5.0	4.7	3.5	2.2	5.1	3.9	6.9
Canada	1.9	7.5	0.1	4.5	4.6	3.8	2.0	5.1	4.1	7.1
					Females					
Richmond Hill	3.2	11.7	0.1	2.8	11.2	13.1	1.4	4.8	5.1	4.3
Ontario	1.9	7.1	0.1	4.2	10.4	17.7	2.1	7.4	5.0	6.9
Canada	1.7	6.6	0.1	3.8	10.4	19.1	2.1	7.9	5.2	7.2

Note: Figures are based on total experienced labour force 15 years and over. Experienced labour force refers to persons who, during the week of Sunday, May 1 to Saturday, May 7, 2011, were employed and the unemployed who had last worked for pay or in self-employment in either 2010 or 2011.
Source: Statistics Canada. 2013. 2011 National Household Survey. Statistics Canada Catalogue no. 99-004-XWE. Ottawa. Released September 11, 2013.

PROFILES / Richmond Hill, Ontario

Occupation

Area	Mgmt	Business, Finance & Admin.	Natural/ Applied Sciences & Related	Health	Education, Law & Social, Community & Government Services	Art, Culture, Recreation & Sport	Sales & Service	Trades, Transport & Equip. Operators & Related	Natural Resources, Agri. & Related Production	Mfg & Utilities
					Number					
					Total					
Richmond Hill	14,880	20,050	13,560	5,350	11,025	3,305	20,905	7,410	620	2,495
Ontario	770,580	1,138,330	494,500	392,695	801,465	206,420	1,550,260	868,515	106,810	350,685
Canada	1,963,600	2,902,045	1,237,775	1,107,200	2,064,675	503,415	4,068,170	2,537,775	397,930	805,040
					Males					
Richmond Hill	9,530	6,550	9,765	1,845	3,330	1,515	9,885	7,030	505	1,585
Ontario	474,655	352,505	384,345	78,330	264,570	96,055	673,880	812,280	82,610	233,565
Canada	1,229,460	854,190	966,355	217,520	676,550	232,535	1,745,705	2,385,615	318,945	564,300
					Females					
Richmond Hill	5,345	13,495	3,795	3,500	7,695	1,790	11,020	385	120	905
Ontario	295,920	785,825	110,150	314,370	536,895	110,370	876,380	56,230	24,200	117,115
Canada	734,140	2,047,855	271,415	889,675	1,388,130	270,875	2,322,465	152,165	78,980	240,740
					Percent of Labour Force					
					Total					
Richmond Hill	14.9	20.1	13.6	5.4	11.1	3.3	21.0	7.4	0.6	2.5
Ontario	11.5	17.0	7.4	5.9	12.0	3.1	23.2	13.0	1.6	5.2
Canada	11.2	16.5	7.0	6.3	11.7	2.9	23.1	14.4	2.3	4.6
					Males					
Richmond Hill	18.5	12.7	18.9	3.6	6.5	2.9	19.2	13.6	1.0	3.1
Ontario	13.7	10.2	11.1	2.3	7.7	2.8	19.5	23.5	2.4	6.8
Canada	13.4	9.3	10.5	2.4	7.4	2.5	19.0	26.0	3.5	6.1
					Females					
Richmond Hill	11.1	28.1	7.9	7.3	16.0	3.7	22.9	0.8	0.2	1.9
Ontario	9.2	24.3	3.4	9.7	16.6	3.4	27.2	1.7	0.7	3.6
Canada	8.7	24.4	3.2	10.6	16.5	3.2	27.7	1.8	0.9	2.9

Note: Figures are based on total experienced labour force 15 years and over
Source: Statistics Canada. 2013. 2011 National Household Survey. Statistics Canada Catalogue no. 99-004-XWE. Ottawa. Released September 11, 2013.

Place of Work Status

Area	Worked at Home	Worked Outside Canada	No Fixed Workplace Address	Worked at Usual Place
		Number		
		Total		
Richmond Hill	8,545	840	10,185	75,490
Ontario	423,790	31,390	670,835	5,170,980
Canada	1,142,640	66,460	1,868,245	13,517,690
		Males		
Richmond Hill	4,260	625	7,075	37,365
Ontario	216,900	21,150	486,560	2,524,555
Canada	582,150	47,355	1,400,485	6,604,325
		Females		
Richmond Hill	4,280	215	3,110	38,130
Ontario	206,895	10,240	184,275	2,646,420
Canada	560,490	19,100	467,760	6,913,370
		Percent of Labour Force		
		Total		
Richmond Hill	9.0	0.9	10.7	79.4
Ontario	6.7	0.5	10.7	82.1
Canada	6.9	0.4	11.3	81.5
		Males		
Richmond Hill	8.6	1.3	14.3	75.8
Ontario	6.7	0.7	15.0	77.7
Canada	6.7	0.5	16.2	76.5
		Females		
Richmond Hill	9.4	0.5	6.8	83.4
Ontario	6.8	0.3	6.0	86.8
Canada	7.0	0.2	5.9	86.8

Note: Figures are based on total employed labour force 15 years and over.
Source: Statistics Canada. 2013. 2011 National Household Survey. Statistics Canada Catalogue no. 99-004-XWE. Ottawa. Released September 11, 2013.

Mode of Transportation to Work

Area	Car; Truck; Van; as Driver	Car; Truck; Van; as Passenger	Public Transit	Walked	Bicycled	All Other Modes
			Number			
			Total			
Richmond Hill	65,565	4,860	12,255	1,755	285	955
Ontario	4,235,315	357,110	818,270	299,095	69,885	62,145
Canada	11,393,140	867,050	1,851,525	880,815	201,780	191,625
			Males			
Richmond Hill	36,085	1,625	5,425	670	205	430
Ontario	2,316,680	143,410	340,995	131,765	47,635	30,635
Canada	6,238,835	349,530	788,290	387,580	135,840	104,725
			Females			
Richmond Hill	29,475	3,235	6,835	1,085	80	520
Ontario	1,918,640	213,700	477,275	167,325	22,250	31,515
Canada	5,154,305	517,520	1,063,235	493,230	65,940	86,900
			Percent of Labour Force			
			Total			
Richmond Hill	76.5	5.7	14.3	2.0	0.3	1.1
Ontario	72.5	6.1	14.0	5.1	1.2	1.1
Canada	74.0	5.6	12.0	5.7	1.3	1.2
			Males			
Richmond Hill	81.2	3.7	12.2	1.5	0.5	1.0
Ontario	76.9	4.8	11.3	4.4	1.6	1.0
Canada	77.9	4.4	9.8	4.8	1.7	1.3
			Females			
Richmond Hill	71.5	7.8	16.6	2.6	0.2	1.3
Ontario	67.8	7.5	16.9	5.9	0.8	1.1
Canada	69.8	7.0	14.4	6.7	0.9	1.2

Note: Figures are based on total employed labour force 15 years and over.
Source: Statistics Canada. 2013. 2011 National Household Survey. Statistics Canada Catalogue no. 99-004-XWE. Ottawa. Released September 11, 2013.

Visible Minority Population Characteristics

Area	Total Minority	South Asian[1]	Chinese	Black	Filipino	Latin American	Arab	SE Asian[2]	West Asian[3]	Korean	Japanese	Multiple[4]
						Number						
						Total						
Richmond Hill	97,465	15,015	43,530	3,720	4,050	1,730	3,045	1,410	15,890	5,045	970	2,345
Ontario	3,279,565	965,990	629,140	539,205	275,380	172,560	151,645	137,875	122,530	78,290	29,085	96,735
Canada	6,264,750	1,567,400	1,324,750	945,665	619,310	381,280	380,620	312,075	206,840	161,130	87,270	171,935
						Males						
Richmond Hill	47,090	7,450	21,235	1,730	1,685	795	1,490	555	7,825	2,410	450	1,090
Ontario	1,582,480	484,355	301,575	251,295	116,825	83,205	79,620	67,645	62,515	38,045	13,345	46,765
Canada	3,043,010	790,755	632,325	453,005	268,885	186,355	203,485	154,035	105,620	77,165	38,270	83,335
						Females						
Richmond Hill	50,365	7,560	22,300	1,990	2,365	930	1,555	855	8,065	2,635	525	1,255
Ontario	1,697,085	481,635	327,570	287,915	158,555	89,360	72,025	70,230	60,010	40,250	15,740	49,970
Canada	3,221,745	776,650	692,420	492,660	350,425	194,925	177,140	158,045	101,220	83,965	48,990	88,600
						Percent of Population						
						Total						
Richmond Hill	52.9	8.1	23.6	2.0	2.2	0.9	1.7	0.8	8.6	2.7	0.5	1.3
Ontario	25.9	7.6	5.0	4.3	2.2	1.4	1.2	1.1	1.0	0.6	0.2	0.8
Canada	19.1	4.8	4.0	2.9	1.9	1.2	1.2	0.9	0.6	0.5	0.3	0.5
						Males						
Richmond Hill	52.3	8.3	23.6	1.9	1.9	0.9	1.7	0.6	8.7	2.7	0.5	1.2
Ontario	25.6	7.8	4.9	4.1	1.9	1.3	1.3	1.1	1.0	0.6	0.2	0.8
Canada	18.8	4.9	3.9	2.8	1.7	1.2	1.3	1.0	0.7	0.5	0.2	0.5
						Females						
Richmond Hill	53.4	8.0	23.6	2.1	2.5	1.0	1.6	0.9	8.5	2.8	0.6	1.3
Ontario	26.2	7.4	5.1	4.4	2.5	1.4	1.1	1.1	0.9	0.6	0.2	0.8
Canada	19.3	4.7	4.1	3.0	2.1	1.2	1.1	0.9	0.6	0.5	0.3	0.5

Note: The Employment Equity Act defines visible minorities as 'persons, other than Aboriginal peoples, who are non-Caucasian in race or non-white in colour'; (1) Includes 'East Indian,' 'Pakistani,' 'Sri Lankan,' etc.; (2) Includes 'Vietnamese,' 'Cambodian,' 'Malaysian,' 'Laotian,' etc.; (3) Includes 'Iranian,' 'Afghan,' etc.; (4) Includes respondents who reported more than one visible minority group by checking two or more mark-in circles, e.g., 'Black' and 'South Asian.'
Source: Statistics Canada. 2013. 2011 National Household Survey. Statistics Canada Catalogue no. 99-004-XWE. Ottawa. Released September 11, 2013.

PROFILES / Richmond Hill, Ontario

Aboriginal Population

Area	Aboriginal Identity[1]	First Nations (North American Indian) Single Identity[2]	Métis Single Identity	Inuk (Inuit) Single Identity	Multiple Aboriginal Identities[3]	Aboriginal Identities Not Included Elsewhere
			Number			
			Total			
Richmond Hill	395	265	65	0	0	45
Ontario	301,430	201,100	86,020	3,355	2,910	8,040
Canada	1,400,685	851,560	451,795	59,440	11,415	26,475
			Males			
Richmond Hill	170	125	25	0	0	15
Ontario	145,020	96,620	41,755	1,475	1,420	3,750
Canada	682,190	411,785	223,335	29,495	5,525	12,055
			Females			
Richmond Hill	225	145	40	0	0	30
Ontario	156,410	104,485	44,260	1,880	1,490	4,295
Canada	718,500	439,775	228,460	29,950	5,890	14,420
			Percent of Population			
			Total			
Richmond Hill	0.2	0.1	0.0	0.0	0.0	0.0
Ontario	2.4	1.6	0.7	0.0	0.0	0.1
Canada	4.3	2.6	1.4	0.2	0.0	0.1
			Males			
Richmond Hill	0.2	0.1	0.0	0.0	0.0	0.0
Ontario	2.3	1.6	0.7	0.0	0.0	0.1
Canada	4.2	2.5	1.4	0.2	0.0	0.1
			Females			
Richmond Hill	0.2	0.2	0.0	0.0	0.0	0.0
Ontario	2.4	1.6	0.7	0.0	0.0	0.1
Canada	4.3	2.6	1.4	0.2	0.0	0.1

Note: (1) Includes persons who reported being an Aboriginal person, that is, First Nations (North American Indian), Métis or Inuk (Inuit) and/or those who reported Registered or Treaty Indian status, that is registered under the Indian Act of Canada, and/or those who reported membership in a First Nation or Indian band. Aboriginal peoples of Canada are defined in the Constitution Act, 1982, section 35-2 as including the Indian, Inuit and Métis peoples of Canada; (2) Users should be aware that the estimates associated with this variable are more affected than most by the incomplete enumeration of certain Indian reserves and Indian settlements in the National Household Survey (NHS); (3) Includes persons who reported being any two or all three of the following: First Nations (North American Indian), Métis or Inuk (Inuit).
Source: Statistics Canada. 2013. 2011 National Household Survey. Statistics Canada Catalogue no. 99-004-XWE. Ottawa. Released September 11, 2013.

Ethnic Origin

Area	North American Aboriginal	Other North American	European	Caribbean	Latin, Central and South American	African	Asian	Oceania
			Number					
			Total					
Richmond Hill	1,140	16,900	82,520	3,410	2,745	4,915	95,980	170
Ontario	441,395	3,059,480	8,231,410	396,485	271,545	331,460	2,604,595	19,410
Canada	1,836,035	11,070,455	20,157,965	627,590	544,375	766,735	5,011,225	74,875
			Males					
Richmond Hill	470	8,260	40,280	1,585	1,250	2,370	46,695	90
Ontario	210,490	1,507,105	4,019,885	181,805	130,035	160,940	1,265,540	9,855
Canada	885,675	5,462,685	9,913,150	291,640	264,635	387,360	2,435,540	37,490
			Females					
Richmond Hill	670	8,640	42,235	1,820	1,490	2,550	49,285	80
Ontario	230,905	1,552,380	4,211,525	214,675	141,510	170,515	1,339,050	9,555
Canada	950,360	5,607,770	10,244,820	335,945	279,740	379,380	2,575,680	37,385
			Percent of Population					
			Total					
Richmond Hill	0.6	9.2	44.8	1.8	1.5	2.7	52.1	0.1
Ontario	3.5	24.2	65.1	3.1	2.1	2.6	20.6	0.2
Canada	5.6	33.7	61.4	1.9	1.7	2.3	15.3	0.2
			Males					
Richmond Hill	0.5	9.2	44.7	1.8	1.4	2.6	51.9	0.1
Ontario	3.4	24.4	65.0	2.9	2.1	2.6	20.5	0.2
Canada	5.5	33.8	61.3	1.8	1.6	2.4	15.1	0.2
			Females					
Richmond Hill	0.7	9.2	44.8	1.9	1.6	2.7	52.2	0.1
Ontario	3.6	24.0	65.1	3.3	2.2	2.6	20.7	0.1
Canada	5.7	33.6	61.4	2.0	1.7	2.3	15.4	0.2

Note: The sum of the ethnic groups in this table is greater than the total population estimate because a person may report more than one ethnic origin in the NHS.
Source: Statistics Canada. 2013. 2011 National Household Survey. Statistics Canada Catalogue no. 99-004-XWE. Ottawa. Released September 11, 2013.

Religion

Area	Buddhist	Christian	Hindu	Jewish	Muslim	Sikh	Traditional (Aboriginal) Spirituality	Other Religions	No Religious Affiliation
				Number					
				Total					
Richmond Hill	5,125	92,195	4,390	10,125	21,245	910	0	1,695	48,690
Ontario	163,750	8,167,295	366,720	195,540	581,950	179,765	15,905	53,080	2,927,790
Canada	366,830	22,102,745	497,965	329,495	1,053,945	454,965	64,935	130,835	7,850,605
				Males					
Richmond Hill	2,360	43,315	2,250	5,010	10,325	510	0	800	25,455
Ontario	75,355	3,839,925	183,580	95,795	293,925	90,515	7,600	23,555	1,571,195
Canada	168,465	10,497,775	250,435	161,265	540,555	229,435	31,805	57,745	4,225,645
				Females					
Richmond Hill	2,760	48,875	2,140	5,115	10,920	400	0	895	23,240
Ontario	88,395	4,327,365	183,140	99,740	288,025	89,250	8,310	29,525	1,356,600
Canada	198,365	11,604,975	247,525	168,235	513,395	225,530	33,135	73,090	3,624,965
				Percent of Population					
				Total					
Richmond Hill	2.8	50.0	2.4	5.5	11.5	0.5	0.0	0.9	26.4
Ontario	1.3	64.6	2.9	1.5	4.6	1.4	0.1	0.4	23.1
Canada	1.1	67.3	1.5	1.0	3.2	1.4	0.2	0.4	23.9
				Males					
Richmond Hill	2.6	48.1	2.5	5.6	11.5	0.6	0.0	0.9	28.3
Ontario	1.2	62.1	3.0	1.5	4.8	1.5	0.1	0.4	25.4
Canada	1.0	64.9	1.5	1.0	3.3	1.4	0.2	0.4	26.1
				Females					
Richmond Hill	2.9	51.8	2.3	5.4	11.6	0.4	0.0	0.9	24.6
Ontario	1.4	66.9	2.8	1.5	4.5	1.4	0.1	0.5	21.0
Canada	1.2	69.5	1.5	1.0	3.1	1.4	0.2	0.4	21.7

Note: Religion refers to the person's self-identification as having a connection or affiliation with any religious denomination, group, body, sect, cult or other religiously defined community or system of belief. Religion is not limited to formal membership in a religious organization or group. Persons without a religious connection or affiliation can self-identify as atheist, agnostic or humanist, or can provide another applicable response.
Source: Statistics Canada. 2013. 2011 National Household Survey. Statistics Canada Catalogue no. 99-004-XWE. Ottawa. Released September 11, 2013.

Religion—Christian Denominations

Area	Anglican	Baptist	Catholic	Christian Orthodox	Lutheran	Pentecostal	Presbyterian	United Church	Other Christian
				Number					
				Total					
Richmond Hill	4,865	2,520	47,040	12,145	1,090	1,185	3,145	4,220	15,985
Ontario	774,560	244,650	3,976,610	297,710	163,460	213,945	319,585	952,465	1,224,300
Canada	1,631,845	635,840	12,810,705	550,690	478,185	478,705	472,385	2,007,610	3,036,780
				Males					
Richmond Hill	2,330	1,055	22,255	5,835	580	570	1,460	1,900	7,325
Ontario	355,175	112,285	1,895,940	145,825	75,225	94,955	148,535	435,255	576,730
Canada	752,945	293,905	6,167,290	270,205	221,525	217,850	218,955	912,545	1,442,550
				Females					
Richmond Hill	2,535	1,465	24,780	6,310	510	615	1,680	2,325	8,655
Ontario	419,390	132,370	2,080,665	151,885	88,230	118,990	171,050	517,210	647,570
Canada	878,900	341,940	6,643,415	280,485	256,660	260,850	253,430	1,095,065	1,594,230
				Percent of Population					
				Total					
Richmond Hill	2.6	1.4	25.5	6.6	0.6	0.6	1.7	2.3	8.7
Ontario	6.1	1.9	31.4	2.4	1.3	1.7	2.5	7.5	9.7
Canada	5.0	1.9	39.0	1.7	1.5	1.5	1.4	6.1	9.2
				Males					
Richmond Hill	2.6	1.2	24.7	6.5	0.6	0.6	1.6	2.1	8.1
Ontario	5.7	1.8	30.7	2.4	1.2	1.5	2.4	7.0	9.3
Canada	4.7	1.8	38.2	1.7	1.4	1.3	1.4	5.6	8.9
				Females					
Richmond Hill	2.7	1.6	26.3	6.7	0.5	0.7	1.8	2.5	9.2
Ontario	6.5	2.0	32.2	2.3	1.4	1.8	2.6	8.0	10.0
Canada	5.3	2.0	39.8	1.7	1.5	1.6	1.5	6.6	9.6

Note: Religion refers to the person's self-identification as having a connection or affiliation with any religious denomination, group, body, sect, cult or other religiously defined community or system of belief. Religion is not limited to formal membership in a religious organization or group. Persons without a religious connection or affiliation can self-identify as atheist, agnostic or humanist, or can provide another applicable response.
Source: Statistics Canada. 2013. 2011 National Household Survey. Statistics Canada Catalogue no. 99-004-XWE. Ottawa. Released September 11, 2013.

PROFILES / Richmond Hill, Ontario

Immigrant Status and Period of Immigration

Area	Non-Immigrants[1]	Immigrants All	Before 1971	1971 to 1980	1981 to 1990	1991 to 2000	2001 to 2005	2006 to 2011	Non-Permanent Residents[3]
Number – Total									
Richmond Hill	81,530	101,170	11,140	10,630	15,825	34,375	16,450	12,750	1,665
Ontario	8,906,000	3,611,365	723,030	464,380	538,285	866,220	518,405	501,060	134,425
Canada	25,720,175	6,775,765	1,261,055	870,775	949,890	1,539,050	992,070	1,162,915	356,385
Males									
Richmond Hill	41,395	47,975	5,455	5,140	7,410	16,320	7,865	5,790	650
Ontario	4,410,240	1,706,385	341,820	217,990	258,095	408,270	245,850	234,360	64,825
Canada	12,753,235	3,231,370	605,430	416,670	454,570	724,905	474,545	555,245	178,515
Females									
Richmond Hill	40,135	53,200	5,685	5,495	8,415	18,050	8,585	6,960	1,020
Ontario	4,495,765	1,904,985	381,210	246,390	280,190	457,950	272,550	266,695	69,600
Canada	12,966,935	3,544,400	655,625	454,105	495,325	814,145	517,530	607,670	177,870
Percent of Population – Total									
Richmond Hill	44.2	54.9	6.0	5.8	8.6	18.6	8.9	6.9	0.9
Ontario	70.4	28.5	5.7	3.7	4.3	6.8	4.1	4.0	1.1
Canada	78.3	20.6	3.8	2.7	2.9	4.7	3.0	3.5	1.1
Males									
Richmond Hill	46.0	53.3	6.1	5.7	8.2	18.1	8.7	6.4	0.7
Ontario	71.3	27.6	5.5	3.5	4.2	6.6	4.0	3.8	1.0
Canada	78.9	20.0	3.7	2.6	2.8	4.5	2.9	3.4	1.1
Females									
Richmond Hill	42.5	56.4	6.0	5.8	8.9	19.1	9.1	7.4	1.1
Ontario	69.5	29.4	5.9	3.8	4.3	7.1	4.2	4.1	1.1
Canada	77.7	21.2	3.9	2.7	3.0	4.9	3.1	3.6	1.1

Note: (1) Non-immigrant refers to a person who is a Canadian citizen by birth; (2) Immigrant refers to a person who is or has ever been a landed immigrant/permanent resident. This person has been granted the right to live in Canada permanently by immigration authorities. Some immigrants have resided in Canada for a number of years, while others have arrived recently. Some immigrants are Canadian citizens, while others are not. Most immigrants are born outside Canada, but a small number are born in Canada. In the 2011 National Household Survey, 'Immigrants' includes immigrants who landed in Canada prior to May 10, 2011; (3) Non-permanent resident refers to a person from another country who has a work or study permit, or who is a refugee claimant, and any non-Canadian-born family member living in Canada with them.
Source: Statistics Canada. 2013. 2011 National Household Survey. Statistics Canada Catalogue no. 99-004-XWE. Ottawa. Released September 11, 2013.

Mother Tongue

Area	English	French	Non-official Language	English & French	English & Non-official Language	French & Non-official Language	English, French & Non-official Language
Number – Total							
Richmond Hill	75,125	1,335	101,945	360	5,240	255	205
Ontario	8,677,040	493,300	3,264,435	46,605	219,425	13,645	7,615
Canada	18,858,980	7,054,975	6,567,680	144,685	396,330	74,430	24,095
Males							
Richmond Hill	37,895	575	48,655	170	2,570	120	85
Ontario	4,276,970	232,785	1,562,190	21,805	106,790	6,285	3,495
Canada	9,345,225	3,452,380	3,157,785	69,975	192,000	36,535	11,965
Females							
Richmond Hill	37,230	760	53,285	190	2,670	135	115
Ontario	4,400,065	260,510	1,702,240	24,795	112,635	7,365	4,115
Canada	9,513,750	3,602,590	3,409,895	74,710	204,330	37,890	12,130
Percent of Population – Total							
Richmond Hill	40.7	0.7	55.3	0.2	2.8	0.1	0.1
Ontario	68.2	3.9	25.7	0.4	1.7	0.1	0.1
Canada	56.9	21.3	19.8	0.4	1.2	0.2	0.1
Males							
Richmond Hill	42.1	0.6	54.0	0.2	2.9	0.1	0.1
Ontario	68.9	3.7	25.2	0.4	1.7	0.1	0.1
Canada	57.5	21.2	19.4	0.4	1.2	0.2	0.1
Females							
Richmond Hill	39.4	0.8	56.5	0.2	2.8	0.1	0.1
Ontario	67.6	4.0	26.1	0.4	1.7	0.1	0.1
Canada	56.4	21.4	20.2	0.4	1.2	0.2	0.1

Note: Figures cover total population excluding institutional residents.
Source: Statistics Canada. 2012. Census Profile. 2011 Census. Statistics Canada Catalogue no. 98-316-XWE. Ottawa. Released October 24 2012.
http://www12.statcan.gc.ca/census-recensement/2011/dp-pd/prof/index.cfm?Lang=E

Language Spoken Most Often at Home

Area	English	French	Non-official Language	English & French	English & Non-official Language	French & Non-official Language	English, French & Non-official Language
			Number				
			Total				
Richmond Hill	106,250	580	63,200	295	13,770	65	295
Ontario	10,044,810	284,115	1,827,870	37,955	509,105	6,370	11,845
Canada	21,457,075	6,827,865	3,673,865	131,205	875,135	109,700	46,330
			Males				
Richmond Hill	52,755	260	30,115	130	6,665	35	110
Ontario	4,930,610	133,495	872,860	17,250	248,050	2,855	5,225
Canada	10,585,620	3,348,235	1,767,310	63,475	425,370	53,010	22,845
			Females				
Richmond Hill	53,495	325	33,085	165	7,105	25	185
Ontario	5,114,200	150,620	955,010	20,705	261,055	3,520	6,620
Canada	10,871,455	3,479,625	1,906,555	67,730	449,765	56,690	23,485
			Percent of Population				
			Total				
Richmond Hill	57.6	0.3	34.3	0.2	7.5	0.0	0.2
Ontario	79.0	2.2	14.4	0.3	4.0	0.1	0.1
Canada	64.8	20.6	11.1	0.4	2.6	0.3	0.1
			Males				
Richmond Hill	58.6	0.3	33.4	0.1	7.4	0.0	0.1
Ontario	79.4	2.1	14.1	0.3	4.0	0.0	0.1
Canada	65.1	20.6	10.9	0.4	2.6	0.3	0.1
			Females				
Richmond Hill	56.7	0.3	35.1	0.2	7.5	0.0	0.2
Ontario	78.5	2.3	14.7	0.3	4.0	0.1	0.1
Canada	64.5	20.6	11.3	0.4	2.7	0.3	0.1

Note: Figures cover total population excluding institutional residents.
Source: Statistics Canada. 2012. Census Profile. 2011 Census. Statistics Canada Catalogue no. 98-316-XWE. Ottawa. Released October 24 2012.
http://www12.statcan.gc.ca/census-recensement/2011/dp-pd/prof/index.cfm?Lang=E

Knowledge of Official Languages

Area	English Only	French Only	English & French	Neither English nor French
		Number		
		Total		
Richmond Hill	160,835	150	14,125	9,350
Ontario	10,984,360	42,980	1,395,805	298,920
Canada	22,564,665	4,165,015	5,795,570	595,920
		Males		
Richmond Hill	80,370	60	6,050	3,590
Ontario	5,445,050	18,805	627,725	118,765
Canada	11,222,185	1,925,340	2,876,560	241,790
		Females		
Richmond Hill	80,470	85	8,070	5,760
Ontario	5,539,310	24,175	768,085	180,155
Canada	11,342,485	2,239,680	2,919,005	354,135
		Percent of Population		
		Total		
Richmond Hill	87.2	0.1	7.7	5.1
Ontario	86.3	0.3	11.0	2.3
Canada	68.1	12.6	17.5	1.8
		Males		
Richmond Hill	89.2	0.1	6.7	4.0
Ontario	87.7	0.3	10.1	1.9
Canada	69.0	11.8	17.7	1.5
		Females		
Richmond Hill	85.3	0.1	8.6	6.1
Ontario	85.1	0.4	11.8	2.8
Canada	67.3	13.3	17.3	2.1

Note: Figures cover total population excluding institutional residents.
Source: Statistics Canada. 2012. Census Profile. 2011 Census. Statistics Canada Catalogue no. 98-316-XWE. Ottawa. Released October 24 2012.
http://www12.statcan.gc.ca/census-recensement/2011/dp-pd/prof/index.cfm?Lang=E

Saanich, British Columbia

Background

Saanich is located on the southern tip of Vancouver Island, British Columbia. The District of Saanich is the largest of the four municipalities in Victoria, the province's capital city, which is situated immediately north of Saanich. The district is accessible by transit, ferry or airport (in Victoria).

The forested lands of the Saanich Peninsula were transformed into fields by the settlers of the late 1800s and early 1900s. The peninsula is one of the oldest agricultural settlements in BC. The area's farms and dairy herds serviced Victoria's growing population. Saanich was also renowned for its crops of fruit and flowers—resources still cultivated today.

Saanich is a major residential area in the Capital Regional District. The area's important agricultural base is protected through the Urban Containment Boundary (UCB) concept, which controls residential growth in order to protect rural/agricultural lands. Approximately 52% of Saanich is considered rural land and almost 20% has been assessed as Agricultural Land Reserve area. Saanich's urban planning policy revolves around building "centres" and "villages" that accommodate future growth and follow green building practices.

The area's long-time rural/urban connections are supported through various Saanich Council strategies that improve food security and promote local food productions in both rural and urban areas. Approximately 380 properties in Saanich have been designated as having farm status.

Saanich residents are encouraged to participate in initiatives such as community gardens, community kitchens, urban backyard agriculture and home delivery of local organic produce. Recently, an animal bylaw was amended in Saanich, allowing residents to keep chickens in their backyards.

The University of Victoria, Royal Roads University (RRU) and Camosun College are all within close proximity to Saanich and draw record numbers of international students to the Greater Victoria area. The majority of international students attending RRU, for example, are from Saudi Arabia, Palestine, Israel, Russia, China and India.

Saanich has summer highs of plus 20.90 degrees Celsius, winter lows of plus 1.73 degree Celsius, and an average rainfall just over 879 mm per year.

Rankings

- The Canadian Community Newspaper Association ranked the local Saanich newspaper as one of the best in Canada. The 2012 nominations for *Saanich News* were Best Environmental Writing and Best National Editorial. Both nominations were in the highest circulation class of 10,000 and over. More than 340 newspapers across Canada submitted a total of 2,494 entries. *Canadian Community Newspaper Association (CCNA) Winners 2012, April 26th, 2012 with files from the Saanich News, "Your newspaper is among Canada's best," March 27, 2012*
- Statistics Canada showed the District municipality of Saanich as having a growth rate of 1.4% from 2006 to 2011. In 2011, the national average growth rate was 5.9%. *Statistics Canada. 2012. Focus on Geography Series, 2011 Census, September 19th, 2012*
- In 2011, Saanich was ranked as one of Canada's safest cities. Saanich ranked #203 out of 239 communities over 10,000 people, with #1 being the city with the most severe crime. North Saanich ranked in the top 10% of safe cities in Canada with a ranking of #223. *Statistics Canada, Canadian Centre for Justice Statistics, Uniform Crime Reporting Survey, July 24, 2012*

PROFILES / Saanich, British Columbia

Population Growth and Density

Area	Population in 2001	Population in 2006	Population in 2011	Population Change 2001–2006	Population Change 2006–2011	Land Area (sq. km)	Population Density per sq. km
Saanich	103,654	108,265	109,752	4.4	1.4	103.78	1,057.6
British Columbia	3,907,738	4,113,487	4,400,057	5.3	7.0	922,509.29	4.8
Canada	30,007,094	31,612,897	33,476,688	5.4	5.9	8,965,121.42	3.7

Source: Statistics Canada. 2012. Census Profile. 2011 Census. Statistics Canada Catalogue no. 98-316-XWE. Ottawa. Released October 24 2012. http://www12.statcan.gc.ca/census-recensement/2011/dp-pd/prof/index.cfm?Lang=E;
Statistics Canada 2007. 2006 Community Profiles. 2006 Census. Statistics Canada Catalogue no. 92-591-XWE. Ottawa. Released March 13 2007. http://www12.statcan.ca/census-recensement/2006/dp-pd/prof/92-591/index.cfm?Lang=E

Gender

Area	Males	Females
Number		
Saanich	52,940	56,815
British Columbia	2,156,600	2,243,455
Canada	16,414,225	17,062,460
Percent of Population		
Saanich	48.2	51.8
British Columbia	49.0	51.0
Canada	49.0	51.0

Source: Statistics Canada. 2012. Census Profile. 2011 Census. Statistics Canada Catalogue no. 98-316-XWE. Ottawa. Released October 24 2012.
http://www12.statcan.gc.ca/census-recensement/2011/dp-pd/prof/index.cfm?Lang=E

Marital Status

Area	Married[1]	Living Common-law	Single[2]	Separated	Divorced	Widowed
Number						
Total						
Saanich	46,675	7,455	26,145	2,230	6,520	5,690
British Columbia	1,832,605	321,965	1,014,270	102,040	246,515	205,300
Canada	12,941,960	3,142,525	7,816,045	698,240	1,686,035	1,584,530
Males						
Saanich	23,290	3,705	13,905	900	2,235	1,140
British Columbia	913,430	161,530	550,830	43,570	98,130	41,550
Canada	6,470,300	1,575,495	4,206,320	299,655	680,415	310,940
Females						
Saanich	23,385	3,745	12,245	1,325	4,285	4,550
British Columbia	919,175	160,435	463,435	58,470	148,385	163,750
Canada	6,471,660	1,567,035	3,609,730	398,585	1,005,620	1,273,590
Percent of Population						
Total						
Saanich	49.3	7.9	27.6	2.4	6.9	6.0
British Columbia	49.2	8.6	27.2	2.7	6.6	5.5
Canada	46.4	11.3	28.0	2.5	6.0	5.7
Males						
Saanich	51.5	8.2	30.8	2.0	4.9	2.5
British Columbia	50.5	8.9	30.4	2.4	5.4	2.3
Canada	47.8	11.6	31.1	2.2	5.0	2.3
Females						
Saanich	47.2	7.6	24.7	2.7	8.7	9.2
British Columbia	48.0	8.4	24.2	3.1	7.8	8.6
Canada	45.2	10.9	25.2	2.8	7.0	8.9

Note: (1) and not separated, (2) never legally married
Source: Statistics Canada. 2012. Census Profile. 2011 Census. Statistics Canada Catalogue no. 98-316-XWE. Ottawa. Released October 24 2012.
http://www12.statcan.gc.ca/census-recensement/2011/dp-pd/prof/index.cfm?Lang=E

Age Characteristics: 0 to 49 Years

Area	0 to 4 Years	5 to 9 Years	10 to 14 Years	15 to 19 Years	20 to 24 Years	25 to 29 Years	30 to 34 Years	35 to 39 Years	40 to 44 Years	45 to 49 Years
					Number					
					Total					
Saanich	4,560	4,925	5,565	7,220	8,370	6,630	5,760	6,190	7,040	8,325
British Columbia	219,665	218,915	238,780	275,165	279,825	288,780	275,985	280,870	313,765	350,600
Canada	1,877,095	1,809,895	1,920,355	2,178,135	2,187,450	2,169,590	2,162,905	2,173,930	2,324,875	2,675,130
					Males					
Saanich	2,375	2,560	2,830	3,735	4,220	3,420	2,825	2,970	3,350	3,905
British Columbia	112,885	112,200	122,465	141,670	142,290	143,475	135,220	135,455	151,430	170,580
Canada	961,150	925,965	983,995	1,115,845	1,108,775	1,077,275	1,058,810	1,064,200	1,141,720	1,318,715
					Females					
Saanich	2,180	2,365	2,730	3,480	4,145	3,215	2,935	3,220	3,690	4,420
British Columbia	106,775	106,715	116,315	133,500	137,535	145,305	140,755	145,415	162,335	180,020
Canada	915,945	883,935	936,360	1,062,295	1,078,670	1,092,315	1,104,095	1,109,735	1,183,155	1,356,420
					Percent of Population					
					Total					
Saanich	4.2	4.5	5.1	6.6	7.6	6.0	5.2	5.6	6.4	7.6
British Columbia	5.0	5.0	5.4	6.3	6.4	6.6	6.3	6.4	7.1	8.0
Canada	5.6	5.4	5.7	6.5	6.5	6.5	6.5	6.5	6.9	8.0
					Males					
Saanich	4.5	4.8	5.3	7.1	8.0	6.5	5.3	5.6	6.3	7.4
British Columbia	5.2	5.2	5.7	6.6	6.6	6.7	6.3	6.3	7.0	7.9
Canada	5.9	5.6	6.0	6.8	6.8	6.6	6.5	6.5	7.0	8.0
					Females					
Saanich	3.8	4.2	4.8	6.1	7.3	5.7	5.2	5.7	6.5	7.8
British Columbia	4.8	4.8	5.2	6.0	6.1	6.5	6.3	6.5	7.2	8.0
Canada	5.4	5.2	5.5	6.2	6.3	6.4	6.5	6.5	6.9	7.9

Source: Statistics Canada. 2012. Census Profile. 2011 Census. Statistics Canada Catalogue no. 98-316-XWE. Ottawa. Released October 24 2012.
http://www12.statcan.gc.ca/census-recensement/2011/dp-pd/prof/index.cfm?Lang=E

Age Characteristics: 50 Years and Over, and Median Age

Area	50 to 54 Years	55 to 59 Years	60 to 64 Years	65 to 69 Years	70 to 74 Years	75 to 79 Years	80 to 84 Years	85 Years and Over	Median Age
					Number				
					Total				
Saanich	8,845	8,535	7,745	5,585	4,240	3,795	3,100	3,330	44.0
British Columbia	354,610	323,335	291,040	210,900	160,715	127,480	96,945	92,675	41.9
Canada	2,658,965	2,340,635	2,052,670	1,521,715	1,153,065	922,700	702,070	645,515	40.6
					Males				
Saanich	4,050	4,010	3,670	2,670	1,990	1,720	1,340	1,290	42.2
British Columbia	172,060	157,455	142,645	103,785	77,350	60,720	42,745	32,150	41.1
Canada	1,309,030	1,147,300	1,002,690	738,010	543,435	417,945	291,085	208,300	39.6
					Females				
Saanich	4,795	4,525	4,075	2,920	2,250	2,070	1,760	2,035	45.6
British Columbia	182,550	165,880	148,395	107,115	83,360	66,760	54,200	60,520	42.7
Canada	1,349,940	1,193,335	1,049,985	783,705	609,630	504,755	410,985	437,215	41.5
					Percent of Population				
					Total				
Saanich	8.1	7.8	7.1	5.1	3.9	3.5	2.8	3.0	–
British Columbia	8.1	7.3	6.6	4.8	3.7	2.9	2.2	2.1	–
Canada	7.9	7.0	6.1	4.5	3.4	2.8	2.1	1.9	–
					Males				
Saanich	7.7	7.6	6.9	5.0	3.8	3.2	2.5	2.4	–
British Columbia	8.0	7.3	6.6	4.8	3.6	2.8	2.0	1.5	–
Canada	8.0	7.0	6.1	4.5	3.3	2.5	1.8	1.3	–
					Females				
Saanich	8.4	8.0	7.2	5.1	4.0	3.6	3.1	3.6	–
British Columbia	8.1	7.4	6.6	4.8	3.7	3.0	2.4	2.7	–
Canada	7.9	7.0	6.2	4.6	3.6	3.0	2.4	2.6	–

Source: Statistics Canada. 2012. Census Profile. 2011 Census. Statistics Canada Catalogue no. 98-316-XWE. Ottawa. Released October 24 2012.
http://www12.statcan.gc.ca/census-recensement/2011/dp-pd/prof/index.cfm?Lang=E

PROFILES / Saanich, British Columbia

Private Households by Household Size

Area	1 Person	2 Persons	3 Persons	4 Persons	5 Persons	6 or More Persons	Average Number of Persons in Private Households
			Households				
Saanich	12,435	16,880	7,075	5,990	2,065	955	2.4
British Columbia	498,925	613,270	264,135	237,725	91,600	58,985	2.5
Canada	3,673,310	4,544,820	2,081,900	1,903,300	724,405	392,885	2.5
			Percent of Households				
Saanich	27.4	37.2	15.6	13.2	4.5	2.1	–
British Columbia	28.3	34.8	15.0	13.5	5.2	3.3	–
Canada	27.6	34.1	15.6	14.3	5.4	2.9	–

Source: Statistics Canada. 2012. Census Profile. 2011 Census. Statistics Canada Catalogue no. 98-316-XWE. Ottawa. Released October 24 2012.
http://www12.statcan.gc.ca/census-recensement/2011/dp-pd/prof/index.cfm?Lang=E

Dwelling Type

Area	Single-detached House	Semi-detached House	Row House	Apartment: Building with Five or More Storeys	Apartment: Building with Fewer Than Five Storeys	Duplex Apartment	Movable Dwelling	Other Single-attached House
				Number				
Saanich	22,815	1,190	3,395	380	8,350	9,170	20	65
British Columbia	842,120	52,825	130,365	143,970	361,150	184,355	46,960	2,885
Canada	7,329,150	646,245	791,600	1,234,770	2,397,550	704,485	183,510	33,310
				Percent of Dwellings				
Saanich	50.3	2.6	7.5	0.8	18.4	20.2	0.0	0.1
British Columbia	47.7	3.0	7.4	8.2	20.5	10.4	2.7	0.2
Canada	55.0	4.9	5.9	9.3	18.0	5.3	1.4	0.3

Source: Statistics Canada. 2012. Census Profile. 2011 Census. Statistics Canada Catalogue no. 98-316-XWE. Ottawa. Released October 24 2012.
http://www12.statcan.gc.ca/census-recensement/2011/dp-pd/prof/index.cfm?Lang=E

Shelter Costs

		Owned Dwellings					Rented Dwellings		
Area	Number	Median Value[1] ($)	Average Value[1] ($)	Median Monthly Costs[2] ($)	Average Monthly Costs[2] ($)	Number	Median Monthly Costs[3] ($)	Average Monthly Costs[3] ($)
Saanich	33,095	598,306	615,348	935	1,247	12,145	948	1,025
British Columbia	1,202,000	448,835	543,635	1,023	1,228	519,855	903	989
Canada	9,013,410	280,552	345,182	978	1,141	4,060,385	784	848

Note: All figures cover non-farm, non-reserve private dwellings; (1) Refers to the dollar amount expected by the owner if the dwelling were to be sold; (2) Includes all shelter expenses paid by households that own their dwellings, such as the mortgage payment and the costs of electricity, heat, water and other municipal services, property taxes and condominium fees; (3) Includes all shelter expenses paid by households that rent their dwellings, such as the monthly rent and the costs of electricity, heat and municipal services.
Source: Statistics Canada. 2013. 2011 National Household Survey. Statistics Canada Catalogue no. 99-004-XWE. Ottawa. Released September 11, 2013.

Occupied Private Dwellings by Period of Construction

Area	1960 or Before	1961 to 1980	1981 to 1990	1991 to 2000	2001 to 2005	2006 to 2011
			Number			
Saanich	12,530	14,895	8,820	5,770	1,880	1,495
British Columbia	282,675	551,655	308,450	329,780	133,235	158,845
Canada	3,273,105	4,152,715	2,112,110	1,707,880	1,031,020	1,042,430
			Percent of Dwellings			
Saanich	27.6	32.8	19.4	12.7	4.1	3.3
British Columbia	16.0	31.3	17.5	18.7	7.6	9.0
Canada	24.6	31.2	15.9	12.8	7.7	7.8

Note: Figures cover non-farm, non-reserve private dwellings and includes data up to May 10, 2011.
Source: Statistics Canada. 2013. 2011 National Household Survey. Statistics Canada Catalogue no. 99-004-XWE. Ottawa. Released September 11, 2013.

Educational Attainment

Area	No Certificate, Diploma or Degree	High School Diploma or Equivalent[1]	Apprenticeship or Trades Certificate or Diploma[2]	College, CEGEP or Other Non-University Certificate or Diploma	University Certificate or Diploma Below the Bachelor Level[3]	Bachelor's Degree	University Certificate, Diploma or Degree Above Bachelor Level[4]
				Number			
				Total			
Saanich	12,110	24,620	8,300	15,755	4,895	16,450	10,745
British Columbia	607,655	1,009,400	387,455	628,115	208,245	511,240	294,725
Canada	5,485,400	6,968,935	2,950,685	4,970,020	1,200,130	3,634,425	2,049,930
				Males			
Saanich	5,865	11,585	5,385	6,460	2,060	7,225	5,780
British Columbia	305,040	475,670	262,245	260,580	86,995	235,620	149,300
Canada	2,742,875	3,305,415	1,928,970	2,118,430	513,235	1,643,080	1,043,350
				Females			
Saanich	6,245	13,035	2,910	9,295	2,840	9,230	4,960
British Columbia	302,620	533,735	125,210	367,535	121,250	275,625	145,425
Canada	2,742,520	3,663,515	1,021,715	2,851,595	686,890	1,991,345	1,006,585
				Percent of Population			
				Total			
Saanich	13.0	26.5	8.9	17.0	5.3	17.7	11.6
British Columbia	16.7	27.7	10.6	17.2	5.7	14.0	8.1
Canada	20.1	25.6	10.8	18.2	4.4	13.3	7.5
				Males			
Saanich	13.2	26.1	12.1	14.6	4.6	16.3	13.0
British Columbia	17.2	26.8	14.8	14.7	4.9	13.3	8.4
Canada	20.6	24.9	14.5	15.9	3.9	12.4	7.8
				Females			
Saanich	12.9	26.9	6.0	19.2	5.9	19.0	10.2
British Columbia	16.2	28.5	6.7	19.6	6.5	14.7	7.8
Canada	19.6	26.2	7.3	20.4	4.9	14.3	7.2

Note: Figures cover total population aged 15 years and over by highest certificate, diploma or degree; (1) Includes persons who have graduated from a secondary school or equivalent. It excludes persons with a postsecondary certificate, diploma or degree; (2) Includes Registered Apprenticeship certificates (including Certificate of Qualification, Journeyperson's designation) and other trades certificates or diplomas such as pre-employment or vocational certificates and diplomas from brief trade programs completed at community colleges, institutes of technology, vocational centres, and similar institutions; (3) Comparisons with other data sources suggest that the category 'University certificate or diploma below the bachelor's level' was over-reported in the NHS. This category likely includes some responses that are actually college certificates or diplomas, bachelor's degrees or other types of education (e.g., university transfer programs, bachelor's programs completed in other countries, incomplete bachelor's programs, non-university professional designations). We recommend users interpret the results for the 'University certificate or diploma below the bachelor's level' category with caution; (4) 'University certificate or diploma above bachelor level' includes the categories: 'Degree in medicine, dentistry, veterinary medicine or optometry,' 'Master's degree' and 'Earned doctorate.'
Source: Statistics Canada. 2013. 2011 National Household Survey. Statistics Canada Catalogue no. 99-004-XWE. Ottawa. Released September 11, 2013.

Household Income Distribution

Area	Less than $10,000	$10,000 to $19,999	$20,000 to $29,999	$30,000 to $39,999	$40,000 to $49,999	$50,000 to $59,999	$60,000 to $79,999	$80,000 to $99,999	$100,000 to $124,999	$125,000 to $149,999	$150,000 and Over
						Households					
Saanich	1,805	3,205	3,330	3,765	4,100	3,640	6,585	5,415	4,870	3,290	5,385
British Columbia	96,465	156,565	157,605	167,220	158,400	140,340	246,720	193,180	167,415	106,325	174,385
Canada	626,705	1,141,945	1,193,925	1,271,675	1,206,800	1,102,120	1,865,280	1,458,240	1,260,770	802,555	1,389,240
						Percent of Households					
Saanich	4.0	7.1	7.3	8.3	9.0	8.0	14.5	11.9	10.7	7.2	11.9
British Columbia	5.5	8.9	8.9	9.5	9.0	8.0	14.0	10.9	9.5	6.0	9.9
Canada	4.7	8.6	9.0	9.5	9.1	8.3	14.0	10.9	9.5	6.0	10.4

Note: Household income is the sum of the total incomes of all members of that household. Total income refers to monetary receipts from certain sources, before income taxes and deductions, during calendar year 2010.
Source: Statistics Canada. 2013. 2011 National Household Survey. Statistics Canada Catalogue no. 99-004-XWE. Ottawa. Released September 11, 2013.

Median and Average Household and Economic Family Income

Area	Median Household Income ($)	Average Household Income ($)	Median After-tax Household Income ($)	Average After-tax Household Income ($)	Median Economic Family Income ($)	Average Economic Family Income ($)	Median After-tax Economic Family Income ($)	Average After-tax Economic Family Income ($)
Saanich	68,393	83,345	60,876	71,457	85,402	98,428	75,622	84,246
British Columbia	60,333	77,378	54,379	66,264	75,797	91,967	67,915	78,580
Canada	61,072	79,102	54,089	66,149	76,511	94,125	67,044	78,517

Note: Figures cover household and economic familiy income in 2010. A household is defined as a person or a group of persons (other than foreign residents) who occupy the same private dwelling and do not have a usual place of residence elsewhere in Canada. Every person is a member of one and only one household. An economic family is defined as a group of two or more persons who live in the same dwelling and are related to each other by blood, marriage, common-law, adoption or a foster relationship. A couple may be of opposite or same sex.
Source: Statistics Canada. 2013. 2011 National Household Survey. Statistics Canada Catalogue no. 99-004-XWE. Ottawa. Released September 11, 2013.

PROFILES / Saanich, British Columbia

Individual Income Distribution

Area	Less than $10,000	$10,000 to $19,999	$20,000 to $29,999	$30,000 to $39,999	$40,000 to $49,999	$50,000 to $59,999	$60,000 to $79,999	$80,000 to $99,999	$100,000 to $124,999	$125,000 and Over
					Number					
					Total					
Saanich	14,470	14,605	10,940	10,915	9,835	7,605	10,570	4,835	2,780	2,530
British Columbia	645,915	666,060	470,255	404,860	338,595	253,215	330,590	169,190	89,520	96,055
Canada	4,492,040	4,835,710	3,670,020	3,180,360	2,603,520	1,921,650	2,437,440	1,302,045	693,580	782,135
					Males					
Saanich	6,110	5,815	4,325	4,845	4,495	4,065	6,105	2,900	1,925	1,920
British Columbia	275,815	263,170	201,000	186,285	167,400	143,765	206,400	112,525	65,050	74,260
Canada	1,936,365	1,864,880	1,588,260	1,522,190	1,333,510	1,079,780	1,473,145	823,720	492,905	599,905
					Females					
Saanich	8,360	8,785	6,615	6,065	5,345	3,540	4,465	1,935	855	615
British Columbia	370,100	402,880	269,255	218,575	171,190	109,445	124,195	56,670	24,470	21,795
Canada	2,555,675	2,970,825	2,081,760	1,658,170	1,270,010	841,870	964,300	478,330	200,680	182,230
					Percent of Population					
					Total					
Saanich	16.2	16.4	12.3	12.3	11.0	8.5	11.9	5.4	3.1	2.8
British Columbia	18.6	19.2	13.6	11.7	9.8	7.3	9.5	4.9	2.6	2.8
Canada	17.3	18.7	14.2	12.3	10.0	7.4	9.4	5.0	2.7	3.0
					Males					
Saanich	14.4	13.7	10.2	11.4	10.6	9.6	14.4	6.8	4.5	4.5
British Columbia	16.3	15.5	11.9	11.0	9.9	8.5	12.2	6.6	3.8	4.4
Canada	15.2	14.7	12.5	12.0	10.5	8.5	11.6	6.5	3.9	4.7
					Females					
Saanich	17.9	18.9	14.2	13.0	11.5	7.6	9.6	4.2	1.8	1.3
British Columbia	20.9	22.8	15.2	12.4	9.7	6.2	7.0	3.2	1.4	1.2
Canada	19.4	22.5	15.8	12.6	9.6	6.4	7.3	3.6	1.5	1.4

Note: Figures cover individuals aged 15 years and over with income. Income refers to monetary receipts from certain sources, before income taxes and deductions, during calendar year 2010.
Source: Statistics Canada. 2013. 2011 National Household Survey. Statistics Canada Catalogue no. 99-004-XWE. Ottawa. Released September 11, 2013.

Labour Force Status

Area	In the Labour Force All	Employed	Unemployed	Not in the Labour Force
		Number		
		Total		
Saanich	59,860	56,470	3,390	33,025
British Columbia	2,354,245	2,171,465	182,775	1,292,595
Canada	17,990,080	16,595,035	1,395,045	9,269,445
		Males		
Saanich	30,100	28,355	1,745	14,265
British Columbia	1,223,375	1,124,590	98,785	552,070
Canada	9,388,570	8,634,310	754,255	3,906,785
		Females		
Saanich	29,760	28,120	1,645	18,755
British Columbia	1,130,870	1,046,875	83,990	740,530
Canada	8,601,515	7,960,725	640,790	5,362,660
		Percent of Labour Force		
		Total		
Saanich	64.4	60.8	5.7	35.6
British Columbia	64.6	59.5	7.8	35.4
Canada	66.0	60.9	7.8	34.0
		Males		
Saanich	67.8	63.9	5.8	32.2
British Columbia	68.9	63.3	8.1	31.1
Canada	70.6	64.9	8.0	29.4
		Females		
Saanich	61.3	58.0	5.5	38.7
British Columbia	60.4	55.9	7.4	39.6
Canada	61.6	57.0	7.4	38.4

Note: Figures are based on total population 15 years and over
Source: Statistics Canada. 2013. 2011 National Household Survey. Statistics Canada Catalogue no. 99-004-XWE. Ottawa. Released September 11, 2013.

Labour Force by Industry (NAICS Codes 11–52)

Area	Agriculture, forestry, fishing & hunting	Mining, quarrying, & oil & gas extraction	Utilities	Construction	Manufacturing	Wholesale Trade	Retail Trade	Transportation & warehousing	Information & cultural industries	Finance & insurance
					Number					
					Total					
Saanich	485	80	205	3,990	1,855	1,680	6,935	1,900	1,045	1,835
British Columbia	61,210	25,450	13,215	181,510	148,810	90,560	266,265	118,675	62,235	91,790
Canada	437,650	261,050	149,940	1,215,380	1,619,295	733,445	2,031,665	827,780	420,830	767,960
					Males					
Saanich	240	80	185	3,650	1,320	1,320	3,435	1,385	605	740
British Columbia	40,810	21,175	9,650	159,605	108,480	61,730	121,750	89,155	37,250	35,375
Canada	307,370	211,690	110,765	1,068,710	1,167,680	494,545	933,850	617,305	235,875	296,995
					Females					
Saanich	245	0	15	345	535	355	3,500	515	445	1,095
British Columbia	20,405	4,275	3,560	21,910	40,335	28,820	144,515	29,520	24,980	56,415
Canada	130,285	49,360	39,175	146,670	451,615	238,900	1,097,820	210,475	184,955	470,960
					Percent of Labour Force					
					Total					
Saanich	0.8	0.1	0.3	6.7	3.1	2.8	11.7	3.2	1.8	3.1
British Columbia	2.7	1.1	0.6	7.9	6.5	3.9	11.6	5.1	2.7	4.0
Canada	2.5	1.5	0.9	6.9	9.2	4.2	11.6	4.7	2.4	4.4
					Males					
Saanich	0.8	0.3	0.6	12.3	4.4	4.4	11.5	4.6	2.0	2.5
British Columbia	3.4	1.8	0.8	13.3	9.0	5.1	10.1	7.4	3.1	2.9
Canada	3.3	2.3	1.2	11.6	12.7	5.4	10.2	6.7	2.6	3.2
					Females					
Saanich	0.8	0.0	0.1	1.2	1.8	1.2	11.9	1.8	1.5	3.7
British Columbia	1.8	0.4	0.3	2.0	3.6	2.6	13.1	2.7	2.3	5.1
Canada	1.6	0.6	0.5	1.7	5.4	2.8	13.1	2.5	2.2	5.6

Note: Figures are based on total experienced labour force 15 years and over. Experienced labour force refers to persons who, during the week of Sunday, May 1 to Saturday, May 7, 2011, were employed and the unemployed who had last worked for pay or in self-employment in either 2010 or 2011.
Source: Statistics Canada. 2013. 2011 National Household Survey. Statistics Canada Catalogue no. 99-004-XWE. Ottawa. Released September 11, 2013.

Labour Force by Industry (NAICS Codes 53–91)

Area	Real estate & rental & leasing	Profess., scientific & tech. services	Mgmt of companies & enterprises	Admin. & support, waste mgmt & remed. services	Educational services	Health care & social assistance	Arts, entertain. & recreation	Accomm. & food services	Other services (except public admin.)	Public admin.
					Number					
					Total					
Saanich	1,220	5,085	45	2,295	5,580	8,140	1,410	4,815	2,520	7,990
British Columbia	54,840	179,355	2,440	98,890	167,875	249,030	56,915	179,625	112,745	143,875
Canada	321,895	1,240,850	17,460	728,330	1,301,435	1,949,650	363,405	1,130,750	807,800	1,261,050
					Males					
Saanich	675	2,940	0	1,435	2,005	1,770	690	2,390	1,010	3,895
British Columbia	29,790	98,760	1,320	55,745	55,635	47,020	29,750	73,570	49,130	74,040
Canada	179,090	688,625	9,380	411,250	424,915	349,430	188,270	469,990	372,940	652,510
					Females					
Saanich	540	2,140	20	865	3,575	6,370	720	2,420	1,510	4,100
British Columbia	25,055	80,590	1,120	43,145	112,235	202,010	27,175	106,055	63,615	69,840
Canada	142,805	552,225	8,075	317,085	876,515	1,600,220	175,135	660,760	434,865	608,535
					Percent of Labour Force					
					Total					
Saanich	2.1	8.6	0.1	3.9	9.4	13.8	2.4	8.1	4.3	13.5
British Columbia	2.4	7.8	0.1	4.3	7.3	10.8	2.5	7.8	4.9	6.2
Canada	1.8	7.1	0.1	4.1	7.4	11.1	2.1	6.4	4.6	7.2
					Males					
Saanich	2.3	9.9	0.0	4.8	6.7	5.9	2.3	8.0	3.4	13.1
British Columbia	2.5	8.2	0.1	4.6	4.6	3.9	2.5	6.1	4.1	6.2
Canada	1.9	7.5	0.1	4.5	4.6	3.8	2.0	5.1	4.1	7.1
					Females					
Saanich	1.8	7.3	0.1	2.9	12.2	21.7	2.5	8.3	5.1	14.0
British Columbia	2.3	7.3	0.1	3.9	10.2	18.3	2.5	9.6	5.8	6.3
Canada	1.7	6.6	0.1	3.8	10.4	19.1	2.1	7.9	5.2	7.2

Note: Figures are based on total experienced labour force 15 years and over. Experienced labour force refers to persons who, during the week of Sunday, May 1 to Saturday, May 7, 2011, were employed and the unemployed who had last worked for pay or in self-employment in either 2010 or 2011.
Source: Statistics Canada. 2013. 2011 National Household Survey. Statistics Canada Catalogue no. 99-004-XWE. Ottawa. Released September 11, 2013.

PROFILES / Saanich, British Columbia

Occupation

Area	Mgmt	Business, Finance & Admin.	Natural/ Applied Sciences & Related	Health	Education, Law & Social, Community & Government Services	Art, Culture, Recreation & Sport	Sales & Service	Trades, Transport & Equip. Operators & Related	Natural Resources, Agri. & Related Production	Mfg & Utilities
Number										
Total										
Saanich	6,695	10,020	4,880	4,595	8,525	1,950	14,290	6,245	1,030	880
British Columbia	263,685	368,980	154,055	147,620	265,910	78,565	554,345	337,140	60,295	74,720
Canada	1,963,600	2,902,045	1,237,775	1,107,200	2,064,675	503,415	4,068,170	2,537,775	397,930	805,040
Males										
Saanich	4,035	2,825	3,785	1,020	3,095	855	6,805	5,925	805	640
British Columbia	162,365	104,285	122,570	32,490	89,645	38,300	233,065	317,385	45,155	54,470
Canada	1,229,460	854,190	966,355	217,520	676,550	232,535	1,745,705	2,385,615	318,945	564,300
Females										
Saanich	2,665	7,195	1,095	3,575	5,435	1,095	7,490	315	225	240
British Columbia	101,320	264,690	31,480	115,125	176,265	40,270	321,285	19,755	15,135	20,250
Canada	734,140	2,047,855	271,415	889,675	1,388,130	270,875	2,322,465	152,165	78,980	240,740
Percent of Labour Force										
Total										
Saanich	11.3	17.0	8.3	7.8	14.4	3.3	24.2	10.6	1.7	1.5
British Columbia	11.4	16.0	6.7	6.4	11.5	3.4	24.0	14.6	2.6	3.2
Canada	11.2	16.5	7.0	6.3	11.7	2.9	23.1	14.4	2.3	4.6
Males										
Saanich	13.5	9.5	12.7	3.4	10.4	2.9	22.8	19.9	2.7	2.1
British Columbia	13.5	8.7	10.2	2.7	7.5	3.2	19.4	26.5	3.8	4.5
Canada	13.4	9.3	10.5	2.4	7.4	2.5	19.0	26.0	3.5	6.1
Females										
Saanich	9.1	24.5	3.7	12.2	18.5	3.7	25.5	1.1	0.8	0.8
British Columbia	9.2	23.9	2.8	10.4	15.9	3.6	29.1	1.8	1.4	1.8
Canada	8.7	24.4	3.2	10.6	16.5	3.2	27.7	1.8	0.9	2.9

Note: Figures are based on total experienced labour force 15 years and over
Source: Statistics Canada. 2013. 2011 National Household Survey. Statistics Canada Catalogue no. 99-004-XWE. Ottawa. Released September 11, 2013.

Place of Work Status

Area	Worked at Home	Worked Outside Canada	No Fixed Workplace Address	Worked at Usual Place
Number				
Total				
Saanich	4,160	215	6,635	45,460
British Columbia	174,000	12,480	304,465	1,680,525
Canada	1,142,640	66,460	1,868,245	13,517,690
Males				
Saanich	2,225	145	4,835	21,145
British Columbia	84,015	9,210	225,840	805,525
Canada	582,150	47,355	1,400,485	6,604,325
Females				
Saanich	1,935	70	1,800	24,315
British Columbia	89,990	3,270	78,620	875,000
Canada	560,490	19,100	467,760	6,913,370
Percent of Labour Force				
Total				
Saanich	7.4	0.4	11.7	80.5
British Columbia	8.0	0.6	14.0	77.4
Canada	6.9	0.4	11.3	81.5
Males				
Saanich	7.8	0.5	17.1	74.6
British Columbia	7.5	0.8	20.1	71.6
Canada	6.7	0.5	16.2	76.5
Females				
Saanich	6.9	0.2	6.4	86.5
British Columbia	8.6	0.3	7.5	83.6
Canada	7.0	0.2	5.9	86.8

Note: Figures are based on total employed labour force 15 years and over.
Source: Statistics Canada. 2013. 2011 National Household Survey. Statistics Canada Catalogue no. 99-004-XWE. Ottawa. Released September 11, 2013.

Mode of Transportation to Work

Area	Car; Truck; Van; as Driver	Car; Truck; Van; as Passenger	Public Transit	Walked	Bicycled	All Other Modes
			Number			
			Total			
Saanich	35,925	2,755	6,455	3,035	2,790	1,135
British Columbia	1,415,745	110,695	250,450	132,205	42,260	33,635
Canada	11,393,140	867,050	1,851,525	880,815	201,780	191,625
			Males			
Saanich	18,510	1,025	2,765	1,230	1,840	605
British Columbia	773,160	47,425	107,645	57,000	26,595	19,535
Canada	6,238,835	349,530	788,290	387,580	135,840	104,725
			Females			
Saanich	17,415	1,730	3,690	1,810	945	525
British Columbia	642,580	63,270	142,810	75,205	15,665	14,100
Canada	5,154,305	517,520	1,063,235	493,230	65,940	86,900
			Percent of Labour Force			
			Total			
Saanich	69.0	5.3	12.4	5.8	5.4	2.2
British Columbia	71.3	5.6	12.6	6.7	2.1	1.7
Canada	74.0	5.6	12.0	5.7	1.3	1.2
			Males			
Saanich	71.2	3.9	10.6	4.7	7.1	2.3
British Columbia	75.0	4.6	10.4	5.5	2.6	1.9
Canada	77.9	4.4	9.8	4.8	1.7	1.3
			Females			
Saanich	66.7	6.6	14.1	6.9	3.6	2.0
British Columbia	67.4	6.6	15.0	7.9	1.6	1.5
Canada	69.8	7.0	14.4	6.7	0.9	1.2

Note: Figures are based on total employed labour force 15 years and over.
Source: Statistics Canada. 2013. 2011 National Household Survey. Statistics Canada Catalogue no. 99-004-XWE. Ottawa. Released September 11, 2013.

Visible Minority Population Characteristics

Area	Total Minority	South Asian[1]	Chinese	Black	Filipino	Latin American	Arab	SE Asian[2]	West Asian[3]	Korean	Japanese	Multiple[4]
						Number						
						Total						
Saanich	19,420	4,125	7,795	1,200	1,815	760	415	820	310	685	820	450
British Columbia	1,180,870	313,440	438,140	33,260	126,040	35,465	14,090	51,970	38,960	53,770	38,120	31,160
Canada	6,264,750	1,567,400	1,324,750	945,665	619,310	381,280	380,620	312,075	206,840	161,130	87,270	171,935
						Males						
Saanich	9,235	2,040	3,845	665	690	350	205	345	150	295	300	245
British Columbia	565,965	157,135	208,175	17,365	53,715	16,985	8,010	25,055	19,420	25,325	16,295	15,255
Canada	3,043,010	790,755	632,325	453,005	268,885	186,355	203,485	154,035	105,620	77,165	38,270	83,335
						Females						
Saanich	10,185	2,085	3,950	530	1,125	410	210	475	160	390	520	205
British Columbia	614,905	156,300	229,960	15,895	72,320	18,480	6,080	26,920	19,540	28,440	21,820	15,905
Canada	3,221,745	776,650	692,420	492,660	350,425	194,925	177,140	158,045	101,220	83,965	48,990	88,600
						Percent of Population						
						Total						
Saanich	18.0	3.8	7.2	1.1	1.7	0.7	0.4	0.8	0.3	0.6	0.8	0.4
British Columbia	27.3	7.2	10.1	0.8	2.9	0.8	0.3	1.2	0.9	1.2	0.9	0.7
Canada	19.1	4.8	4.0	2.9	1.9	1.2	1.2	0.9	0.6	0.5	0.3	0.5
						Males						
Saanich	17.7	3.9	7.4	1.3	1.3	0.7	0.4	0.7	0.3	0.6	0.6	0.5
British Columbia	26.6	7.4	9.8	0.8	2.5	0.8	0.4	1.2	0.9	1.2	0.8	0.7
Canada	18.8	4.9	3.9	2.8	1.7	1.2	1.3	1.0	0.7	0.5	0.2	0.5
						Females						
Saanich	18.3	3.8	7.1	1.0	2.0	0.7	0.4	0.9	0.3	0.7	0.9	0.4
British Columbia	28.0	7.1	10.5	0.7	3.3	0.8	0.3	1.2	0.9	1.3	1.0	0.7
Canada	19.3	4.7	4.1	3.0	2.1	1.2	1.1	0.9	0.6	0.5	0.3	0.5

Note: The Employment Equity Act defines visible minorities as 'persons, other than Aboriginal peoples, who are non-Caucasian in race or non-white in colour'; (1) Includes 'East Indian,' 'Pakistani,' 'Sri Lankan,' etc.; (2) Includes 'Vietnamese,' 'Cambodian,' 'Malaysian,' 'Laotian,' etc.; (3) Includes 'Iranian,' 'Afghan,' etc.; (4) Includes respondents who reported more than one visible minority group by checking two or more mark-in circles, e.g., 'Black' and 'South Asian.'
Source: Statistics Canada. 2013. 2011 National Household Survey. Statistics Canada Catalogue no. 99-004-XWE. Ottawa. Released September 11, 2013.

PROFILES / Saanich, British Columbia

Aboriginal Population

Area	Aboriginal Identity[1]	First Nations (North American Indian) Single Identity[2]	Métis Single Identity	Inuk (Inuit) Single Identity	Multiple Aboriginal Identities[3]	Aboriginal Identities Not Included Elsewhere
			Number			
			Total			
Saanich	2,930	1,610	1,200	25	50	50
British Columbia	232,290	155,020	69,475	1,570	2,480	3,745
Canada	1,400,685	851,560	451,795	59,440	11,415	26,475
			Males			
Saanich	1,505	780	665	0	30	20
British Columbia	113,080	75,400	33,940	820	1,190	1,735
Canada	682,190	411,785	223,335	29,495	5,525	12,055
			Females			
Saanich	1,430	830	535	0	15	35
British Columbia	119,215	79,620	35,540	750	1,290	2,015
Canada	718,500	439,775	228,460	29,950	5,890	14,420
			Percent of Population			
			Total			
Saanich	2.7	1.5	1.1	0.0	0.0	0.0
British Columbia	5.4	3.6	1.6	0.0	0.1	0.1
Canada	4.3	2.6	1.4	0.2	0.0	0.1
			Males			
Saanich	2.9	1.5	1.3	0.0	0.1	0.0
British Columbia	5.3	3.5	1.6	0.0	0.1	0.1
Canada	4.2	2.5	1.4	0.2	0.0	0.1
			Females			
Saanich	2.6	1.5	1.0	0.0	0.0	0.1
British Columbia	5.4	3.6	1.6	0.0	0.1	0.1
Canada	4.3	2.6	1.4	0.2	0.0	0.1

Note: (1) Includes persons who reported being an Aboriginal person, that is, First Nations (North American Indian), Métis or Inuk (Inuit) and/or those who reported Registered or Treaty Indian status, that is registered under the Indian Act of Canada, and/or those who reported membership in a First Nation or Indian band. Aboriginal peoples of Canada are defined in the Constitution Act, 1982, section 35-2 as including the Indian, Inuit and Métis peoples of Canada; (2) Users should be aware that the estimates associated with this variable are more affected than most by the incomplete enumeration of certain Indian reserves and Indian settlements in the National Household Survey (NHS); (3) Includes persons who reported being any two or all three of the following: First Nations (North American Indian), Métis or Inuk (Inuit).
Source: Statistics Canada. 2013. 2011 National Household Survey. Statistics Canada Catalogue no. 99-004-XWE. Ottawa. Released September 11, 2013.

Ethnic Origin

Area	North American Aboriginal	Other North American	European	Caribbean	Latin, Central and South American	African	Asian	Oceania
				Number				
				Total				
Saanich	4,275	25,325	82,640	780	1,325	1,550	17,965	680
British Columbia	267,085	884,490	2,812,935	20,035	52,725	47,185	1,122,445	35,770
Canada	1,836,035	11,070,455	20,157,965	627,590	544,375	766,735	5,011,225	74,875
				Males				
Saanich	2,160	12,210	40,035	400	615	790	8,640	375
British Columbia	128,880	440,920	1,387,940	10,225	25,605	23,575	535,825	17,425
Canada	885,675	5,462,685	9,913,150	291,640	264,635	387,360	2,435,540	37,490
				Females				
Saanich	2,120	13,120	42,605	380	710	755	9,330	300
British Columbia	138,205	443,570	1,424,990	9,810	27,120	23,610	586,620	18,340
Canada	950,360	5,607,770	10,244,820	335,945	279,740	379,380	2,575,680	37,385
				Percent of Population				
				Total				
Saanich	4.0	23.5	76.6	0.7	1.2	1.4	16.7	0.6
British Columbia	6.2	20.5	65.0	0.5	1.2	1.1	26.0	0.8
Canada	5.6	33.7	61.4	1.9	1.7	2.3	15.3	0.2
				Males				
Saanich	4.1	23.4	76.6	0.8	1.2	1.5	16.5	0.7
British Columbia	6.1	20.7	65.3	0.5	1.2	1.1	25.2	0.8
Canada	5.5	33.8	61.3	1.8	1.6	2.4	15.1	0.2
				Females				
Saanich	3.8	23.6	76.7	0.7	1.3	1.4	16.8	0.5
British Columbia	6.3	20.2	64.8	0.4	1.2	1.1	26.7	0.8
Canada	5.7	33.6	61.4	2.0	1.7	2.3	15.4	0.2

Note: The sum of the ethnic groups in this table is greater than the total population estimate because a person may report more than one ethnic origin in the NHS.
Source: Statistics Canada. 2013. 2011 National Household Survey. Statistics Canada Catalogue no. 99-004-XWE. Ottawa. Released September 11, 2013.

Religion

Area	Buddhist	Christian	Hindu	Jewish	Muslim	Sikh	Traditional (Aboriginal) Spirituality	Other Religions	No Religious Affiliation
				Number					
				Total					
Saanich	1,555	48,640	650	555	1,120	2,380	25	1,105	51,825
British Columbia	90,620	1,930,415	45,795	23,130	79,310	201,110	10,295	35,500	1,908,285
Canada	366,830	22,102,745	497,965	329,495	1,053,945	454,965	64,935	130,835	7,850,605
				Males					
Saanich	705	21,650	360	225	565	1,150	0	385	27,235
British Columbia	40,175	883,680	22,945	11,255	39,780	100,610	5,085	14,680	1,007,420
Canada	168,465	10,497,775	250,435	161,265	540,555	229,435	31,805	57,745	4,225,645
				Females					
Saanich	850	26,990	290	330	555	1,235	20	720	24,585
British Columbia	50,440	1,046,735	22,845	11,880	39,530	100,500	5,210	20,820	900,865
Canada	198,365	11,604,975	247,525	168,235	513,395	225,530	33,135	73,090	3,624,965
				Percent of Population					
				Total					
Saanich	1.4	45.1	0.6	0.5	1.0	2.2	0.0	1.0	48.0
British Columbia	2.1	44.6	1.1	0.5	1.8	4.7	0.2	0.8	44.1
Canada	1.1	67.3	1.5	1.0	3.2	1.4	0.2	0.4	23.9
				Males					
Saanich	1.3	41.4	0.7	0.4	1.1	2.2	0.0	0.7	52.1
British Columbia	1.9	41.6	1.1	0.5	1.9	4.7	0.2	0.7	47.4
Canada	1.0	64.9	1.5	1.0	3.3	1.4	0.2	0.4	26.1
				Females					
Saanich	1.5	48.6	0.5	0.6	1.0	2.2	0.0	1.3	44.2
British Columbia	2.3	47.6	1.0	0.5	1.8	4.6	0.2	0.9	41.0
Canada	1.2	69.5	1.5	1.0	3.1	1.4	0.2	0.4	21.7

Note: Religion refers to the person's self-identification as having a connection or affiliation with any religious denomination, group, body, sect, cult or other religiously defined community or system of belief. Religion is not limited to formal membership in a religious organization or group. Persons without a religious connection or affiliation can self-identify as atheist, agnostic or humanist, or can provide another applicable response.
Source: Statistics Canada. 2013. 2011 National Household Survey. Statistics Canada Catalogue no. 99-004-XWE. Ottawa. Released September 11, 2013.

Religion—Christian Denominations

Area	Anglican	Baptist	Catholic	Christian Orthodox	Lutheran	Pentecostal	Presbyterian	United Church	Other Christian
				Number					
				Total					
Saanich	9,155	2,745	14,290	635	1,475	1,360	1,395	6,965	10,635
British Columbia	213,975	91,575	650,360	39,845	71,470	58,300	44,635	222,230	538,030
Canada	1,631,845	635,840	12,810,705	550,690	478,185	478,705	472,385	2,007,610	3,036,780
				Males					
Saanich	4,260	1,185	6,545	325	540	540	580	2,875	4,805
British Columbia	94,330	41,565	303,300	19,475	32,205	26,590	19,925	94,020	252,270
Canada	752,945	293,905	6,167,290	270,205	221,525	217,850	218,955	912,545	1,442,550
				Females					
Saanich	4,895	1,550	7,745	310	940	820	815	4,085	5,835
British Columbia	119,645	50,010	347,060	20,375	39,270	31,710	24,710	128,210	285,770
Canada	878,900	341,940	6,643,415	280,485	256,660	260,850	253,430	1,095,065	1,594,230
				Percent of Population					
				Total					
Saanich	8.5	2.5	13.2	0.6	1.4	1.3	1.3	6.5	9.9
British Columbia	4.9	2.1	15.0	0.9	1.7	1.3	1.0	5.1	12.4
Canada	5.0	1.9	39.0	1.7	1.5	1.5	1.4	6.1	9.2
				Males					
Saanich	8.1	2.3	12.5	0.6	1.0	1.0	1.1	5.5	9.2
British Columbia	4.4	2.0	14.3	0.9	1.5	1.3	0.9	4.4	11.9
Canada	4.7	1.8	38.2	1.7	1.4	1.3	1.4	5.6	8.9
				Females					
Saanich	8.8	2.8	13.9	0.6	1.7	1.5	1.5	7.3	10.5
British Columbia	5.4	2.3	15.8	0.9	1.8	1.4	1.1	5.8	13.0
Canada	5.3	2.0	39.8	1.7	1.5	1.6	1.5	6.6	9.6

Note: Religion refers to the person's self-identification as having a connection or affiliation with any religious denomination, group, body, sect, cult or other religiously defined community or system of belief. Religion is not limited to formal membership in a religious organization or group. Persons without a religious connection or affiliation can self-identify as atheist, agnostic or humanist, or can provide another applicable response.
Source: Statistics Canada. 2013. 2011 National Household Survey. Statistics Canada Catalogue no. 99-004-XWE. Ottawa. Released September 11, 2013.

Immigrant Status and Period of Immigration

Area	Non-Immigrants[1]	Immigrants All	Before 1971	1971 to 1980	1981 to 1990	1991 to 2000	2001 to 2005	2006 to 2011	Non-Permanent Residents[3]
Number									
Total									
Saanich	82,795	23,535	7,405	4,075	2,935	4,420	2,065	2,630	1,525
British Columbia	3,067,590	1,191,875	223,215	161,335	156,445	305,655	160,100	185,115	64,995
Canada	25,720,175	6,775,765	1,261,055	870,775	949,890	1,539,050	992,070	1,162,915	356,385
Males									
Saanich	40,775	10,905	3,590	1,980	1,310	1,945	885	1,195	595
British Columbia	1,533,255	561,490	109,510	76,865	72,625	140,985	74,395	87,110	30,880
Canada	12,753,235	3,231,370	605,430	416,670	454,570	724,905	474,545	555,245	178,515
Females									
Saanich	42,020	12,630	3,815	2,090	1,625	2,480	1,180	1,440	935
British Columbia	1,534,330	630,385	113,710	84,470	83,820	164,675	85,710	98,005	34,115
Canada	12,966,935	3,544,400	655,625	454,105	495,325	814,145	517,530	607,670	177,870
Percent of Population									
Total									
Saanich	76.8	21.8	6.9	3.8	2.7	4.1	1.9	2.4	1.4
British Columbia	70.9	27.6	5.2	3.7	3.6	7.1	3.7	4.3	1.5
Canada	78.3	20.6	3.8	2.7	2.9	4.7	3.0	3.5	1.1
Males									
Saanich	78.0	20.9	6.9	3.8	2.5	3.7	1.7	2.3	1.1
British Columbia	72.1	26.4	5.2	3.6	3.4	6.6	3.5	4.1	1.5
Canada	78.9	20.0	3.7	2.6	2.8	4.5	2.9	3.4	1.1
Females									
Saanich	75.6	22.7	6.9	3.8	2.9	4.5	2.1	2.6	1.7
British Columbia	69.8	28.7	5.2	3.8	3.8	7.5	3.9	4.5	1.6
Canada	77.7	21.2	3.9	2.7	3.0	4.9	3.1	3.6	1.1

Note: (1) Non-immigrant refers to a person who is a Canadian citizen by birth; (2) Immigrant refers to a person who is or has ever been a landed immigrant/permanent resident. This person has been granted the right to live in Canada permanently by immigration authorities. Some immigrants have resided in Canada for a number of years, while others have arrived recently. Some immigrants are Canadian citizens, while others are not. Most immigrants are born outside Canada, but a small number are born in Canada. In the 2011 National Household Survey, 'Immigrants' includes immigrants who landed in Canada prior to May 10, 2011; (3) Non-permanent resident refers to a person from another country who has a work or study permit, or who is a refugee claimant, and any non-Canadian-born family member living in Canada with them.
Source: Statistics Canada. 2013. 2011 National Household Survey. Statistics Canada Catalogue no. 99-004-XWE. Ottawa. Released September 11, 2013.

Mother Tongue

Area	English	French	Non-official Language	English & French	English & Non-official Language	French & Non-official Language	English, French & Non-official Language
Number							
Total							
Saanich	86,590	1,360	19,285	245	1,260	60	35
British Columbia	3,062,435	57,275	1,154,215	8,600	68,800	3,345	1,530
Canada	18,858,980	7,054,975	6,567,680	144,685	396,330	74,430	24,095
Males							
Saanich	42,265	650	8,780	110	605	25	20
British Columbia	1,526,350	28,315	543,395	4,065	32,875	1,520	725
Canada	9,345,225	3,452,380	3,157,785	69,975	192,000	36,535	11,965
Females							
Saanich	44,320	705	10,510	140	660	35	20
British Columbia	1,536,085	28,965	610,825	4,535	35,925	1,830	805
Canada	9,513,750	3,602,590	3,409,895	74,710	204,330	37,890	12,130
Percent of Population							
Total							
Saanich	79.6	1.2	17.7	0.2	1.2	0.1	0.0
British Columbia	70.3	1.3	26.5	0.2	1.6	0.1	0.0
Canada	56.9	21.3	19.8	0.4	1.2	0.2	0.1
Males							
Saanich	80.6	1.2	16.7	0.2	1.2	0.0	0.0
British Columbia	71.4	1.3	25.4	0.2	1.5	0.1	0.0
Canada	57.5	21.2	19.4	0.4	1.2	0.2	0.1
Females							
Saanich	78.6	1.3	18.6	0.2	1.2	0.1	0.0
British Columbia	69.2	1.3	27.5	0.2	1.6	0.1	0.0
Canada	56.4	21.4	20.2	0.4	1.2	0.2	0.1

Note: Figures cover total population excluding institutional residents.
Source: Statistics Canada. 2012. Census Profile. 2011 Census. Statistics Canada Catalogue no. 98-316-XWE. Ottawa. Released October 24 2012.
http://www12.statcan.gc.ca/census-recensement/2011/dp-pd/prof/index.cfm?Lang=E

Language Spoken Most Often at Home

Area	English	French	Non-official Language	English & French	English & Non-official Language	French & Non-official Language	English, French & Non-official Language
			Number				
			Total				
Saanich	96,615	375	9,185	145	2,470	20	30
British Columbia	3,506,595	16,685	670,100	4,700	155,065	930	2,130
Canada	21,457,075	6,827,865	3,673,865	131,205	875,135	109,700	46,330
			Males				
Saanich	46,810	175	4,225	55	1,170	10	10
British Columbia	1,733,775	8,015	317,670	2,240	74,155	435	940
Canada	10,585,620	3,348,235	1,767,310	63,475	425,370	53,010	22,845
			Females				
Saanich	49,810	200	4,955	90	1,300	10	25
British Columbia	1,772,820	8,665	352,430	2,460	80,905	495	1,185
Canada	10,871,455	3,479,625	1,906,555	67,730	449,765	56,690	23,485
			Percent of Population				
			Total				
Saanich	88.8	0.3	8.4	0.1	2.3	0.0	0.0
British Columbia	80.5	0.4	15.4	0.1	3.6	0.0	0.0
Canada	64.8	20.6	11.1	0.4	2.6	0.3	0.1
			Males				
Saanich	89.2	0.3	8.1	0.1	2.2	0.0	0.0
British Columbia	81.1	0.4	14.9	0.1	3.5	0.0	0.0
Canada	65.1	20.6	10.9	0.4	2.6	0.3	0.1
			Females				
Saanich	88.3	0.4	8.8	0.2	2.3	0.0	0.0
British Columbia	79.9	0.4	15.9	0.1	3.6	0.0	0.1
Canada	64.5	20.6	11.3	0.4	2.7	0.3	0.1

Note: Figures cover total population excluding institutional residents.
Source: Statistics Canada. 2012. Census Profile. 2011 Census. Statistics Canada Catalogue no. 98-316-XWE. Ottawa. Released October 24 2012.
http://www12.statcan.gc.ca/census-recensement/2011/dp-pd/prof/index.cfm?Lang=E

Knowledge of Official Languages

Area	English Only	French Only	English & French	Neither English nor French
		Number		
		Total		
Saanich	97,850	25	9,390	1,570
British Columbia	3,912,950	2,045	296,645	144,555
Canada	22,564,665	4,165,015	5,795,570	595,920
		Males		
Saanich	47,645	10	4,160	635
British Columbia	1,943,760	950	132,940	59,590
Canada	11,222,185	1,925,340	2,876,560	241,790
		Females		
Saanich	50,205	15	5,230	940
British Columbia	1,969,190	1,095	163,705	84,965
Canada	11,342,485	2,239,680	2,919,005	354,135
		Percent of Population		
		Total		
Saanich	89.9	0.0	8.6	1.4
British Columbia	89.8	0.0	6.8	3.3
Canada	68.1	12.6	17.5	1.8
		Males		
Saanich	90.8	0.0	7.9	1.2
British Columbia	90.9	0.0	6.2	2.8
Canada	69.0	11.8	17.7	1.5
		Females		
Saanich	89.0	0.0	9.3	1.7
British Columbia	88.7	0.0	7.4	3.8
Canada	67.3	13.3	17.3	2.1

Note: Figures cover total population excluding institutional residents.
Source: Statistics Canada. 2012. Census Profile. 2011 Census. Statistics Canada Catalogue no. 98-316-XWE. Ottawa. Released October 24 2012.
http://www12.statcan.gc.ca/census-recensement/2011/dp-pd/prof/index.cfm?Lang=E

Saguenay, Québec

Background

Saguenay is located in the central region of Québec, 200 kilometres north of Québec City, the province's capital. Saguenay's surrounding landscape is so vast and desolate that the area is often referred to as "le royaume" (the Kingdom). Ninety percent of the region is forest. The area's fjord (a long, narrow inlet created by glaciers) is one of the world's longest, measuring nearly 100 kilometres.

A former fur trading centre, Saguenay can be reached by air from Montréal and Québec City. The city and region are also accessible by water. Prior to its amalgamation in 2002, Saguenay was seven distinct municipalities; it is currently divided into three districts: Chicoutimi, Jonquière and La Baie.

Large metallurgy, forestry, and pulp and paper industries are well established in the region. Almost half of the province's aluminum production is generated by Saguenay and timber harvesting yields 20% of Québec's total forest biomass. More than 250 companies harvest an average of 15 million kilograms of Saguenay blueberries every year. The region is home to various research centres, including the Centre for Research on the Boreal Forest at the University of Québec in Chicoutimi and the National Research Council's Aluminum Technology Centre.

Other leading industries in Saguenay are tourism and eco-tourism. National parks such as Parc national du Fjord-du-Saguenay attract visitors year-round to kilometres of hiking and backcountry skiing trails. The fjord in Parc national du Fjord-du-Saguenay is one of the area's most popular tourist attractions. In 2012, the park rebuilt a 60-metre suspension footbridge over Rivière Sainte-Marguerite that had been washed out by an ice jam.

Saguenay has summer highs of plus 22.23 degrees Celsius, winter lows of minus 17.27 degrees Celsius, and an average rainfall just over 700 mm per year.

Rankings

- *Canadian Business Magazine* ranked Saguenay one of the best Canadian cities to do business. The city ranked #6 out of the magazine's top 40 cities. Criteria: annual operating costs, cost of living index, building permit average growth (%), unemployment variance from 5.5%, and crime rate per 100,000 people. Québec cities dominated the top three spots on the list. *Canadian Business Magazine, "Best Places to do Business in Canada," 2008*
- The City of Saguenay ranked #31 out of 37 Canadian cities in terms of volunteerism practised by residents over 15 years of age. Almost 38% of Saguenay residents volunteered their time over 12 months. The top three cities for annual volunteer turnout were Guelph (ON), Kingston (ON) and Fredericton (NB). *The Canadian Council on Learning with files from Statistics Canada: Canada Survey of Giving, Volunteering and Participation 2004*

PROFILES / Saguenay, Québec

Population Growth and Density

Area	Population in 2001	Population in 2006	Population in 2011	Population Change 2001–2006	Population Change 2006–2011	Land Area (sq. km)	Population Density per sq. km
Saguenay	147,133	143,692	144,746	-2.3	0.7	1,126.48	128.5
Québec	7,237,479	7,546,131	7,903,001	4.3	4.7	1,356,547.02	5.8
Canada	30,007,094	31,612,897	33,476,688	5.4	5.9	8,965,121.42	3.7

Source: Statistics Canada. 2012. Census Profile. 2011 Census. Statistics Canada Catalogue no. 98-316-XWE. Ottawa. Released October 24 2012.
http://www12.statcan.gc.ca/census-recensement/2011/dp-pd/prof/index.cfm?Lang=E;
Statistics Canada 2007. 2006 Community Profiles. 2006 Census. Statistics Canada Catalogue no. 92-591-XWE. Ottawa. Released March 13 2007.
http://www12.statcan.ca/census-recensement/2006/dp-pd/prof/92-591/index.cfm?Lang=E

Gender

Area	Males	Females
Number		
Saguenay	71,125	73,620
Québec	3,875,860	4,027,140
Canada	16,414,225	17,062,460
Percent of Population		
Saguenay	49.1	50.9
Québec	49.0	51.0
Canada	49.0	51.0

Source: Statistics Canada. 2012. Census Profile. 2011 Census. Statistics Canada
Catalogue no. 98-316-XWE. Ottawa. Released October 24 2012.
http://www12.statcan.gc.ca/census-recensement/2011/dp-pd/prof/index.cfm?Lang=E

Marital Status

Area	Married[1]	Living Common-law	Single[2]	Separated	Divorced	Widowed
Number						
Total						
Saguenay	44,405	29,070	32,480	1,630	8,380	8,430
Québec	2,353,770	1,391,550	1,942,090	105,195	463,830	387,945
Canada	12,941,960	3,142,525	7,816,045	698,240	1,686,035	1,584,530
Males						
Saguenay	22,170	14,520	18,005	745	3,550	1,735
Québec	1,177,720	697,695	1,045,540	46,465	188,265	77,430
Canada	6,470,300	1,575,495	4,206,320	299,655	680,415	310,940
Females						
Saguenay	22,235	14,550	14,475	885	4,830	6,695
Québec	1,176,050	693,850	896,545	58,720	275,565	310,515
Canada	6,471,660	1,567,035	3,609,730	398,585	1,005,620	1,273,590
Percent of Population						
Total						
Saguenay	35.7	23.4	26.1	1.3	6.7	6.8
Québec	35.4	20.9	29.2	1.6	7.0	5.8
Canada	46.4	11.3	28.0	2.5	6.0	5.7
Males						
Saguenay	36.5	23.9	29.7	1.2	5.8	2.9
Québec	36.4	21.6	32.3	1.4	5.8	2.4
Canada	47.8	11.6	31.1	2.2	5.0	2.3
Females						
Saguenay	34.9	22.9	22.7	1.4	7.6	10.5
Québec	34.5	20.3	26.3	1.7	8.1	9.1
Canada	45.2	10.9	25.2	2.8	7.0	8.9

Note: (1) and not separated, (2) never legally married
Source: Statistics Canada. 2012. Census Profile. 2011 Census. Statistics Canada Catalogue no. 98-316-XWE. Ottawa. Released October 24 2012.
http://www12.statcan.gc.ca/census-recensement/2011/dp-pd/prof/index.cfm?Lang=E

Age Characteristics: 0 to 49 Years

Area	0 to 4 Years	5 to 9 Years	10 to 14 Years	15 to 19 Years	20 to 24 Years	25 to 29 Years	30 to 34 Years	35 to 39 Years	40 to 44 Years	45 to 49 Years
					Number					
					Total					
Saguenay	6,985	6,445	6,920	8,895	8,965	8,580	8,955	7,750	7,735	11,350
Québec	440,840	399,575	418,205	491,980	489,185	490,665	531,445	498,225	520,805	623,575
Canada	1,877,095	1,809,895	1,920,355	2,178,135	2,187,450	2,169,590	2,162,905	2,173,930	2,324,875	2,675,130
					Males					
Saguenay	3,585	3,250	3,565	4,465	4,645	4,495	4,700	3,955	3,825	5,590
Québec	225,525	203,675	213,540	249,960	246,850	245,695	264,980	249,610	261,120	311,320
Canada	961,150	925,965	983,995	1,115,845	1,108,775	1,077,275	1,058,810	1,064,200	1,141,720	1,318,715
					Females					
Saguenay	3,400	3,190	3,360	4,430	4,315	4,085	4,260	3,795	3,915	5,770
Québec	215,320	195,900	204,665	242,020	242,340	244,970	266,460	248,615	259,690	312,250
Canada	915,945	883,935	936,360	1,062,295	1,078,670	1,092,315	1,104,095	1,109,735	1,183,155	1,356,420
					Percent of Population					
					Total					
Saguenay	4.8	4.5	4.8	6.1	6.2	5.9	6.2	5.4	5.3	7.8
Québec	5.6	5.1	5.3	6.2	6.2	6.2	6.7	6.3	6.6	7.9
Canada	5.6	5.4	5.7	6.5	6.5	6.5	6.5	6.5	6.9	8.0
					Males					
Saguenay	5.0	4.6	5.0	6.3	6.5	6.3	6.6	5.6	5.4	7.9
Québec	5.8	5.3	5.5	6.4	6.4	6.3	6.8	6.4	6.7	8.0
Canada	5.9	5.6	6.0	6.8	6.8	6.6	6.5	6.5	7.0	8.0
					Females					
Saguenay	4.6	4.3	4.6	6.0	5.9	5.5	5.8	5.2	5.3	7.8
Québec	5.3	4.9	5.1	6.0	6.0	6.1	6.6	6.2	6.4	7.8
Canada	5.4	5.2	5.5	6.2	6.3	6.4	6.5	6.5	6.9	7.9

Source: Statistics Canada. 2012. Census Profile. 2011 Census. Statistics Canada Catalogue no. 98-316-XWE. Ottawa. Released October 24 2012.
http://www12.statcan.gc.ca/census-recensement/2011/dp-pd/prof/index.cfm?Lang=E

Age Characteristics: 50 Years and Over, and Median Age

Area	50 to 54 Years	55 to 59 Years	60 to 64 Years	65 to 69 Years	70 to 74 Years	75 to 79 Years	80 to 84 Years	85 Years and Over	Median Age
				Number					
				Total					
Saguenay	13,605	12,365	10,465	8,200	5,920	4,915	3,725	2,980	45.6
Québec	648,695	579,280	512,830	403,210	291,755	232,355	176,420	153,945	41.9
Canada	2,658,965	2,340,635	2,052,670	1,521,715	1,153,065	922,700	702,070	645,515	40.6
				Males					
Saguenay	6,715	6,220	5,220	3,920	2,685	2,050	1,385	865	43.9
Québec	320,695	285,295	250,675	194,305	135,830	101,675	69,170	45,945	40.7
Canada	1,309,030	1,147,300	1,002,690	738,010	543,435	417,945	291,085	208,300	39.6
				Females					
Saguenay	6,890	6,140	5,240	4,280	3,235	2,865	2,340	2,115	46.9
Québec	327,995	293,990	262,155	208,905	155,925	130,680	107,250	108,005	43.0
Canada	1,349,940	1,193,335	1,049,985	783,705	609,630	504,755	410,985	437,215	41.5
				Percent of Population					
				Total					
Saguenay	9.4	8.5	7.2	5.7	4.1	3.4	2.6	2.1	–
Québec	8.2	7.3	6.5	5.1	3.7	2.9	2.2	1.9	–
Canada	7.9	7.0	6.1	4.5	3.4	2.8	2.1	1.9	–
				Males					
Saguenay	9.4	8.7	7.3	5.5	3.8	2.9	1.9	1.2	–
Québec	8.3	7.4	6.5	5.0	3.5	2.6	1.8	1.2	–
Canada	8.0	7.0	6.1	4.5	3.3	2.5	1.8	1.3	–
				Females					
Saguenay	9.4	8.3	7.1	5.8	4.4	3.9	3.2	2.9	–
Québec	8.1	7.3	6.5	5.2	3.9	3.2	2.7	2.7	–
Canada	7.9	7.0	6.2	4.6	3.6	3.0	2.4	2.6	–

Source: Statistics Canada. 2012. Census Profile. 2011 Census. Statistics Canada Catalogue no. 98-316-XWE. Ottawa. Released October 24 2012.
http://www12.statcan.gc.ca/census-recensement/2011/dp-pd/prof/index.cfm?Lang=E

PROFILES / Saguenay, Québec

Private Households by Household Size

Area	1 Person	2 Persons	3 Persons	4 Persons	5 Persons	6 or More Persons	Average Number of Persons in Private Households
			Households				
Saguenay	20,425	24,400	9,235	7,320	2,170	675	2.2
Québec	1,094,410	1,181,240	496,140	421,080	142,555	59,920	2.3
Canada	3,673,310	4,544,820	2,081,900	1,903,300	724,405	392,885	2.5
			Percent of Households				
Saguenay	31.8	38.0	14.4	11.4	3.4	1.1	–
Québec	32.2	34.8	14.6	12.4	4.2	1.8	–
Canada	27.6	34.1	15.6	14.3	5.4	2.9	–

Source: Statistics Canada. 2012. Census Profile. 2011 Census. Statistics Canada Catalogue no. 98-316-XWE. Ottawa. Released October 24 2012.
http://www12.statcan.gc.ca/census-recensement/2011/dp-pd/prof/index.cfm?Lang=E

Dwelling Type

Area	Single-detached House	Semi-detached House	Row House	Apartment: Building with Five or More Storeys	Apartment: Building with Fewer Than Five Storeys	Duplex Apartment	Movable Dwelling	Other Single-attached House
				Number				
Saguenay	30,695	4,410	1,485	1,000	16,865	9,125	440	205
Québec	1,560,405	171,435	86,040	171,115	1,103,845	263,860	22,995	15,645
Canada	7,329,150	646,245	791,600	1,234,770	2,397,550	704,485	183,510	33,310
				Percent of Dwellings				
Saguenay	47.8	6.9	2.3	1.6	26.3	14.2	0.7	0.3
Québec	46.0	5.0	2.5	5.0	32.5	7.8	0.7	0.5
Canada	55.0	4.9	5.9	9.3	18.0	5.3	1.4	0.3

Source: Statistics Canada. 2012. Census Profile. 2011 Census. Statistics Canada Catalogue no. 98-316-XWE. Ottawa. Released October 24 2012.
http://www12.statcan.gc.ca/census-recensement/2011/dp-pd/prof/index.cfm?Lang=E

Shelter Costs

	Owned Dwellings				Rented Dwellings		
Area	Number	Median Value[1] ($)	Average Value[1] ($)	Median Monthly Costs[2] ($)	Average Monthly Costs[2] ($)	Number	Median Monthly Costs[3] ($)	Average Monthly Costs[3] ($)
Saguenay	39,840	174,395	183,162	797	824	24,240	534	579
Québec	2,056,665	214,537	249,427	841	936	1,308,465	643	685
Canada	9,013,410	280,552	345,182	978	1,141	4,060,385	784	848

Note: All figures cover non-farm, non-reserve private dwellings; (1) Refers to the dollar amount expected by the owner if the dwelling were to be sold; (2) Includes all shelter expenses paid by households that own their dwellings, such as the mortgage payment and the costs of electricity, heat, water and other municipal services, property taxes and condominium fees; (3) Includes all shelter expenses paid by households that rent their dwellings, such as the monthly rent and the costs of electricity, heat and municipal services.
Source: Statistics Canada. 2013. 2011 National Household Survey. Statistics Canada Catalogue no. 99-004-XWE. Ottawa. Released September 11, 2013.

Occupied Private Dwellings by Period of Construction

Area	1960 or Before	1961 to 1980	1981 to 1990	1991 to 2000	2001 to 2005	2006 to 2011
			Number			
Saguenay	19,045	22,990	10,880	6,330	1,975	3,005
Québec	946,900	1,115,455	533,790	353,355	206,035	239,685
Canada	3,273,105	4,152,715	2,112,110	1,707,880	1,031,020	1,042,430
			Percent of Dwellings			
Saguenay	29.7	35.8	16.9	9.9	3.1	4.7
Québec	27.9	32.9	15.7	10.4	6.1	7.1
Canada	24.6	31.2	15.9	12.8	7.7	7.8

Note: Figures cover non-farm, non-reserve private dwellings and includes data up to May 10, 2011.
Source: Statistics Canada. 2013. 2011 National Household Survey. Statistics Canada Catalogue no. 99-004-XWE. Ottawa. Released September 11, 2013.

PROFILES / Saguenay, Québec

Educational Attainment

Area	No Certificate, Diploma or Degree	High School Diploma or Equivalent[1]	Apprenticeship or Trades Certificate or Diploma[2]	College, CÉGEP or Other Non-University Certificate or Diploma	University Certificate or Diploma Below the Bachelor Level[3]	Bachelor's Degree	University Certificate, Diploma or Degree Above Bachelor Level[4]
				Number			
				Total			
Saguenay	23,760	22,800	27,810	23,805	5,330	12,220	5,215
Québec	1,436,025	1,404,755	1,049,470	1,075,855	305,330	766,100	437,050
Canada	5,485,400	6,968,935	2,950,685	4,970,020	1,200,130	3,634,425	2,049,930
				Males			
Saguenay	10,330	10,395	16,935	11,240	2,160	5,665	2,840
Québec	714,090	650,660	635,435	472,360	126,565	343,535	227,990
Canada	2,742,875	3,305,415	1,928,970	2,118,430	513,235	1,643,080	1,043,350
				Females			
Saguenay	13,435	12,405	10,875	12,570	3,175	6,560	2,375
Québec	721,930	754,095	414,035	603,495	178,765	422,565	209,065
Canada	2,742,520	3,663,515	1,021,715	2,851,595	686,890	1,991,345	1,006,585
				Percent of Population			
				Total			
Saguenay	19.6	18.9	23.0	19.7	4.4	10.1	4.3
Québec	22.2	21.7	16.2	16.6	4.7	11.8	6.8
Canada	20.1	25.6	10.8	18.2	4.4	13.3	7.5
				Males			
Saguenay	17.3	17.5	28.4	18.9	3.6	9.5	4.8
Québec	22.5	20.5	20.0	14.9	4.0	10.8	7.2
Canada	20.6	24.9	14.5	15.9	3.9	12.4	7.8
				Females			
Saguenay	21.9	20.2	17.7	20.5	5.2	10.7	3.9
Québec	21.9	22.8	12.5	18.3	5.4	12.8	6.3
Canada	19.6	26.2	7.3	20.4	4.9	14.3	7.2

Note: Figures cover total population aged 15 years and over by highest certificate, diploma or degree; (1) Includes persons who have graduated from a secondary school or equivalent. It excludes persons with a postsecondary certificate, diploma or degree; (2) Includes Registered Apprenticeship certificates (including Certificate of Qualification, Journeyperson's designation) and other trades certificates or diplomas such as pre-employment or vocational certificates and diplomas from brief trade programs completed at community colleges, institutes of technology, vocational centres, and similar institutions; (3) Comparisons with other data sources suggest that the category 'University certificate or diploma below the bachelor's level' was over-reported in the NHS. This category likely includes some responses that are actually college certificates or diplomas, bachelor's degrees or other types of education (e.g., university transfer programs, bachelor's programs completed in other countries, incomplete bachelor's programs, non-university professional designations). We recommend users interpret the results for the 'University certificate or diploma below the bachelor's level' category with caution; (4) 'University certificate or diploma above bachelor level' includes the categories: 'Degree in medicine, dentistry, veterinary medicine or optometry,' 'Master's degree' and 'Earned doctorate.'
Source: Statistics Canada. 2013. 2011 National Household Survey. Statistics Canada Catalogue no. 99-004-XWE. Ottawa. Released September 11, 2013.

Household Income Distribution

Area	Less than $10,000	$10,000 to $19,999	$20,000 to $29,999	$30,000 to $39,999	$40,000 to $49,999	$50,000 to $59,999	$60,000 to $79,999	$80,000 to $99,999	$100,000 to $124,999	$125,000 to $149,999	$150,000 and Over
						Households					
Saguenay	3,155	7,525	6,500	7,055	6,220	6,180	9,030	7,055	5,025	3,000	3,470
Québec	179,790	377,210	353,470	382,000	343,730	302,595	483,085	344,435	267,995	148,950	211,965
Canada	626,705	1,141,945	1,193,925	1,271,675	1,206,800	1,102,120	1,865,280	1,458,240	1,260,770	802,555	1,389,240
						Percent of Households					
Saguenay	4.9	11.7	10.1	11.0	9.7	9.6	14.1	11.0	7.8	4.7	5.4
Québec	5.3	11.1	10.4	11.3	10.1	8.9	14.2	10.1	7.9	4.4	6.2
Canada	4.7	8.6	9.0	9.5	9.1	8.3	14.0	10.9	9.5	6.0	10.4

Note: Household income is the sum of the total incomes of all members of that household. Total income refers to monetary receipts from certain sources, before income taxes and deductions, during calendar year 2010.
Source: Statistics Canada. 2013. 2011 National Household Survey. Statistics Canada Catalogue no. 99-004-XWE. Ottawa. Released September 11, 2013.

Median and Average Household and Economic Family Income

Area	Median Household Income ($)	Average Household Income ($)	Median After-tax Household Income ($)	Average After-tax Household Income ($)	Median Economic Family Income ($)	Average Economic Family Income ($)	Median After-tax Economic Family Income ($)	Average After-tax Economic Family Income ($)
Saguenay	52,534	64,083	46,416	53,555	68,662	79,200	59,515	65,948
Québec	51,842	66,205	45,968	55,121	68,344	82,045	59,560	68,091
Canada	61,072	79,102	54,089	66,149	76,511	94,125	67,044	78,517

Note: Figures cover household and economic familiy income in 2010. A household is defined as a person or a group of persons (other than foreign residents) who occupy the same private dwelling and do not have a usual place of residence elsewhere in Canada. Every person is a member of one and only one household. An economic family is defined as a group of two or more persons who live in the same dwelling and are related to each other by blood, marriage, common-law, adoption or a foster relationship. A couple may be of opposite or same sex.
Source: Statistics Canada. 2013. 2011 National Household Survey. Statistics Canada Catalogue no. 99-004-XWE. Ottawa. Released September 11, 2013.

MAJOR CANADIAN CITIES: COMPARED AND RANKED

Individual Income Distribution

Area	Less than $10,000	$10,000 to $19,999	$20,000 to $29,999	$30,000 to $39,999	$40,000 to $49,999	$50,000 to $59,999	$60,000 to $79,999	$80,000 to $99,999	$100,000 to $124,999	$125,000 and Over
					Number Total					
Saguenay	18,950	24,780	16,375	16,640	11,815	8,605	9,325	4,675	2,320	1,900
Québec	1,005,600	1,309,515	941,630	866,290	653,400	449,185	515,815	211,070	109,975	120,915
Canada	4,492,040	4,835,710	3,670,020	3,180,360	2,603,520	1,921,650	2,437,440	1,302,045	693,580	782,135
					Males					
Saguenay	7,310	8,110	7,065	8,885	7,180	5,615	6,110	3,925	1,975	1,595
Québec	441,455	516,150	427,295	432,625	345,950	256,700	313,880	143,785	80,000	91,475
Canada	1,936,365	1,864,880	1,588,260	1,522,190	1,333,510	1,079,780	1,473,145	823,720	492,905	599,905
					Females					
Saguenay	11,645	16,675	9,315	7,755	4,640	2,990	3,215	750	345	305
Québec	564,150	793,365	514,335	433,670	307,455	192,485	201,935	67,275	29,980	29,440
Canada	2,555,675	2,970,825	2,081,760	1,658,170	1,270,010	841,870	964,300	478,330	200,680	182,230
					Percent of Population Total					
Saguenay	16.4	21.5	14.2	14.4	10.2	7.5	8.1	4.1	2.0	1.6
Québec	16.3	21.2	15.2	14.0	10.6	7.3	8.3	3.4	1.8	2.0
Canada	17.3	18.7	14.2	12.3	10.0	7.4	9.4	5.0	2.7	3.0
					Males					
Saguenay	12.7	14.0	12.2	15.4	12.4	9.7	10.6	6.8	3.4	2.8
Québec	14.5	16.9	14.0	14.2	11.3	8.4	10.3	4.7	2.6	3.0
Canada	15.2	14.7	12.5	12.0	10.5	8.5	11.6	6.5	3.9	4.7
					Females					
Saguenay	20.2	28.9	16.2	13.5	8.1	5.2	5.6	1.3	0.6	0.5
Québec	18.0	25.3	16.4	13.8	9.8	6.1	6.4	2.1	1.0	0.9
Canada	19.4	22.5	15.8	12.6	9.6	6.4	7.3	3.6	1.5	1.4

Note: Figures cover individuals aged 15 years and over with income. Income refers to monetary receipts from certain sources, before income taxes and deductions, during calendar year 2010.
Source: Statistics Canada. 2013. 2011 National Household Survey. Statistics Canada Catalogue no. 99-004-XWE. Ottawa. Released September 11, 2013.

Labour Force Status

Area	All (In the Labour Force)	Employed	Unemployed	Not in the Labour Force
		Number Total		
Saguenay	73,730	68,760	4,970	47,210
Québec	4,183,445	3,880,425	303,020	2,291,145
Canada	17,990,080	16,595,035	1,395,045	9,269,445
		Males		
Saguenay	40,155	37,130	3,030	19,395
Québec	2,188,555	2,014,810	173,745	982,080
Canada	9,388,570	8,634,310	754,255	3,906,785
		Females		
Saguenay	33,575	31,630	1,945	27,810
Québec	1,994,885	1,865,610	129,275	1,309,065
Canada	8,601,515	7,960,725	640,790	5,362,660
		Percent of Labour Force Total		
Saguenay	61.0	56.9	6.7	39.0
Québec	64.6	59.9	7.2	35.4
Canada	66.0	60.9	7.8	34.0
		Males		
Saguenay	67.4	62.4	7.5	32.6
Québec	69.0	63.5	7.9	31.0
Canada	70.6	64.9	8.0	29.4
		Females		
Saguenay	54.7	51.5	5.8	45.3
Québec	60.4	56.5	6.5	39.6
Canada	61.6	57.0	7.4	38.4

Note: Figures are based on total population 15 years and over
Source: Statistics Canada. 2013. 2011 National Household Survey. Statistics Canada Catalogue no. 99-004-XWE. Ottawa. Released September 11, 2013.

Labour Force by Industry (NAICS Codes 11–52)

Area	Agriculture, forestry, fishing & hunting	Mining, quarrying, & oil & gas extraction	Utilities	Construction	Manufacturing	Wholesale Trade	Retail Trade	Transportation & warehousing	Information & cultural industries	Finance & insurance
					Number Total					
Saguenay	835	660	885	4,765	8,230	2,155	10,165	2,445	1,080	1,840
Québec	84,470	20,770	33,815	241,780	476,390	169,825	501,380	181,295	98,340	159,230
Canada	437,650	261,050	149,940	1,215,380	1,619,295	733,445	2,031,665	827,780	420,830	767,960
					Males					
Saguenay	690	595	740	4,290	6,980	1,610	4,525	2,120	625	630
Québec	61,540	18,035	24,560	213,605	343,345	113,545	234,725	137,745	56,455	56,930
Canada	307,370	211,690	110,765	1,068,710	1,167,680	494,545	933,850	617,305	235,875	296,995
					Females					
Saguenay	140	65	150	475	1,250	550	5,645	320	460	1,210
Québec	22,925	2,730	9,255	28,170	133,045	56,280	266,650	43,550	41,885	102,295
Canada	130,285	49,360	39,175	146,670	451,615	238,900	1,097,820	210,475	184,955	470,960
					Percent of Labour Force Total					
Saguenay	1.2	0.9	1.2	6.6	11.4	3.0	14.1	3.4	1.5	2.5
Québec	2.1	0.5	0.8	5.9	11.7	4.2	12.3	4.4	2.4	3.9
Canada	2.5	1.5	0.9	6.9	9.2	4.2	11.6	4.7	2.4	4.4
					Males					
Saguenay	1.8	1.5	1.9	10.9	17.7	4.1	11.5	5.4	1.6	1.6
Québec	2.9	0.8	1.1	10.0	16.1	5.3	11.0	6.4	2.6	2.7
Canada	3.3	2.3	1.2	11.6	12.7	5.4	10.2	6.7	2.6	3.2
					Females					
Saguenay	0.4	0.2	0.5	1.4	3.8	1.7	17.2	1.0	1.4	3.7
Québec	1.2	0.1	0.5	1.4	6.8	2.9	13.7	2.2	2.2	5.3
Canada	1.6	0.6	0.5	1.7	5.4	2.8	13.1	2.5	2.2	5.6

Note: Figures are based on total experienced labour force 15 years and over. Experienced labour force refers to persons who, during the week of Sunday, May 1 to Saturday, May 7, 2011, were employed and the unemployed who had last worked for pay or in self-employment in either 2010 or 2011.
Source: Statistics Canada. 2013. 2011 National Household Survey. Statistics Canada Catalogue no. 99-004-XWE. Ottawa. Released September 11, 2013.

Labour Force by Industry (NAICS Codes 53–91)

Area	Real estate & rental & leasing	Profess., scientific & tech. services	Mgmt of companies & enterprises	Admin. & support, waste mgmt & remed. services	Educational services	Health care & social assistance	Arts, entertain. & recreation	Accomm. & food services	Other services (except public admin.)	Public admin.
					Number Total					
Saguenay	900	4,170	40	2,565	6,190	9,630	850	4,960	3,795	6,025
Québec	61,365	282,115	3,965	156,130	301,425	496,125	78,795	253,145	189,290	295,480
Canada	321,895	1,240,850	17,460	728,330	1,301,435	1,949,650	363,405	1,130,750	807,800	1,261,050
					Males					
Saguenay	515	2,540	20	1,680	2,135	1,915	425	1,970	1,900	3,465
Québec	35,940	158,920	2,250	92,530	99,565	97,255	41,535	112,650	88,710	147,645
Canada	179,090	688,625	9,380	411,250	424,915	349,430	188,270	469,990	372,940	652,510
					Females					
Saguenay	385	1,625	20	885	4,055	7,715	425	2,990	1,890	2,560
Québec	25,425	123,205	1,715	63,605	201,860	398,870	37,260	140,495	100,585	147,835
Canada	142,805	552,225	8,075	317,085	876,515	1,600,220	175,135	660,760	434,865	608,535
					Percent of Labour Force Total					
Saguenay	1.2	5.8	0.1	3.6	8.6	13.3	1.2	6.9	5.3	8.3
Québec	1.5	6.9	0.1	3.8	7.4	12.1	1.9	6.2	4.6	7.2
Canada	1.8	7.1	0.1	4.1	7.4	11.1	2.1	6.4	4.6	7.2
					Males					
Saguenay	1.3	6.5	0.1	4.3	5.4	4.9	1.1	5.0	4.8	8.8
Québec	1.7	7.4	0.1	4.3	4.7	4.5	1.9	5.3	4.2	6.9
Canada	1.9	7.5	0.1	4.5	4.6	3.8	2.0	5.1	4.1	7.1
					Females					
Saguenay	1.2	5.0	0.1	2.7	12.4	23.5	1.3	9.1	5.8	7.8
Québec	1.3	6.3	0.1	3.3	10.4	20.5	1.9	7.2	5.2	7.6
Canada	1.7	6.6	0.1	3.8	10.4	19.1	2.1	7.9	5.2	7.2

Note: Figures are based on total experienced labour force 15 years and over. Experienced labour force refers to persons who, during the week of Sunday, May 1 to Saturday, May 7, 2011, were employed and the unemployed who had last worked for pay or in self-employment in either 2010 or 2011.
Source: Statistics Canada. 2013. 2011 National Household Survey. Statistics Canada Catalogue no. 99-004-XWE. Ottawa. Released September 11, 2013.

Occupation

Area	Mgmt	Business, Finance & Admin.	Natural/ Applied Sciences & Related	Health	Education, Law & Social, Community & Government Services	Art, Culture, Recreation & Sport	Sales & Service	Trades, Transport & Equip. Operators & Related	Natural Resources, Agri. & Related Production	Mfg & Utilities
					Number					
					Total					
Saguenay	5,845	10,920	5,150	4,880	9,715	1,335	18,305	12,010	705	3,330
Québec	411,425	687,715	287,015	268,610	479,505	123,665	969,740	573,075	65,625	218,740
Canada	1,963,600	2,902,045	1,237,775	1,107,200	2,064,675	503,415	4,068,170	2,537,775	397,930	805,040
					Males					
Saguenay	3,680	3,350	4,355	930	3,220	635	8,005	11,610	660	2,920
Québec	261,620	207,545	221,430	53,480	148,715	58,150	436,370	542,055	53,640	154,485
Canada	1,229,460	854,190	966,355	217,520	676,550	232,535	1,745,705	2,385,615	318,945	564,300
					Females					
Saguenay	2,165	7,570	795	3,945	6,495	700	10,300	395	35	410
Québec	149,800	480,170	65,585	215,130	330,795	65,520	533,370	31,025	11,995	64,250
Canada	734,140	2,047,855	271,415	889,675	1,388,130	270,875	2,322,465	152,165	78,980	240,740
					Percent of Labour Force					
					Total					
Saguenay	8.1	15.1	7.1	6.8	13.5	1.8	25.4	16.6	1.0	4.6
Québec	10.1	16.8	7.0	6.6	11.7	3.0	23.7	14.0	1.6	5.4
Canada	11.2	16.5	7.0	6.3	11.7	2.9	23.1	14.4	2.3	4.6
					Males					
Saguenay	9.3	8.5	11.1	2.4	8.2	1.6	20.3	29.5	1.7	7.4
Québec	12.2	9.7	10.4	2.5	7.0	2.7	20.4	25.4	2.5	7.2
Canada	13.4	9.3	10.5	2.4	7.4	2.5	19.0	26.0	3.5	6.1
					Females					
Saguenay	6.6	23.1	2.4	12.0	19.8	2.1	31.4	1.2	0.1	1.2
Québec	7.7	24.7	3.4	11.0	17.0	3.4	27.4	1.6	0.6	3.3
Canada	8.7	24.4	3.2	10.6	16.5	3.2	27.7	1.8	0.9	2.9

Note: Figures are based on total experienced labour force 15 years and over
Source: Statistics Canada. 2013. 2011 National Household Survey. Statistics Canada Catalogue no. 99-004-XWE. Ottawa. Released September 11, 2013.

Place of Work Status

Area	Worked at Home	Worked Outside Canada	No Fixed Workplace Address	Worked at Usual Place
		Number		
		Total		
Saguenay	2,240	125	5,410	60,985
Québec	237,625	9,705	331,525	3,301,560
Canada	1,142,640	66,460	1,868,245	13,517,690
		Males		
Saguenay	1,040	110	4,015	31,955
Québec	122,060	7,055	249,535	1,636,165
Canada	582,150	47,355	1,400,485	6,604,325
		Females		
Saguenay	1,200	0	1,390	29,025
Québec	115,565	2,650	81,995	1,665,395
Canada	560,490	19,100	467,760	6,913,370
		Percent of Labour Force		
		Total		
Saguenay	3.3	0.2	7.9	88.7
Québec	6.1	0.3	8.5	85.1
Canada	6.9	0.4	11.3	81.5
		Males		
Saguenay	2.8	0.3	10.8	86.1
Québec	6.1	0.4	12.4	81.2
Canada	6.7	0.5	16.2	76.5
		Females		
Saguenay	3.8	0.0	4.4	91.7
Québec	6.2	0.1	4.4	89.3
Canada	7.0	0.2	5.9	86.8

Note: Figures are based on total employed labour force 15 years and over.
Source: Statistics Canada. 2013. 2011 National Household Survey. Statistics Canada Catalogue no. 99-004-XWE. Ottawa. Released September 11, 2013.

Mode of Transportation to Work

Area	Car; Truck; Van; as Driver	Car; Truck; Van; as Passenger	Public Transit	Walked	Bicycled	All Other Modes
			Number			
			Total			
Saguenay	58,400	2,345	1,640	2,835	315	855
Québec	2,713,295	136,490	484,600	215,210	48,870	34,620
Canada	11,393,140	867,050	1,851,525	880,815	201,780	191,625
			Males			
Saguenay	32,085	1,005	680	1,385	280	540
Québec	1,484,305	50,905	203,035	95,100	33,065	19,285
Canada	6,238,835	349,530	788,290	387,580	135,840	104,725
			Females			
Saguenay	26,315	1,340	960	1,445	30	320
Québec	1,228,995	85,585	281,565	120,110	15,800	15,335
Canada	5,154,305	517,520	1,063,235	493,230	65,940	86,900
			Percent of Labour Force			
			Total			
Saguenay	88.0	3.5	2.5	4.3	0.5	1.3
Québec	74.7	3.8	13.3	5.9	1.3	1.0
Canada	74.0	5.6	12.0	5.7	1.3	1.2
			Males			
Saguenay	89.2	2.8	1.9	3.8	0.8	1.5
Québec	78.7	2.7	10.8	5.0	1.8	1.0
Canada	77.9	4.4	9.8	4.8	1.7	1.3
			Females			
Saguenay	86.5	4.4	3.2	4.8	0.1	1.1
Québec	70.3	4.9	16.1	6.9	0.9	0.9
Canada	69.8	7.0	14.4	6.7	0.9	1.2

Note: Figures are based on total employed labour force 15 years and over.
Source: Statistics Canada. 2013. 2011 National Household Survey. Statistics Canada Catalogue no. 99-004-XWE. Ottawa. Released September 11, 2013.

Visible Minority Population Characteristics

Area	Total Minority	South Asian[1]	Chinese	Black	Filipino	Latin American	Arab	SE Asian[2]	West Asian[3]	Korean	Japanese	Multiple[4]
					Number							
					Total							
Saguenay	1,260	35	240	385	40	190	230	40	0	20	0	30
Québec	850,235	83,320	82,845	243,625	31,495	116,380	166,260	65,855	23,445	6,665	4,025	17,420
Canada	6,264,750	1,567,400	1,324,750	945,665	619,310	381,280	380,620	312,075	206,840	161,130	87,270	171,935
					Males							
Saguenay	605	30	40	200	0	115	140	25	0	0	0	0
Québec	418,545	43,410	37,295	116,605	12,435	56,940	89,505	32,940	12,070	3,135	1,565	8,315
Canada	3,043,010	790,755	632,325	453,005	268,885	186,355	203,485	154,035	105,620	77,165	38,270	83,335
					Females							
Saguenay	655	0	195	180	35	70	90	15	0	0	0	0
Québec	431,695	39,915	45,550	127,020	19,055	59,440	76,750	32,920	11,380	3,530	2,465	9,105
Canada	3,221,745	776,650	692,420	492,660	350,425	194,925	177,140	158,045	101,220	83,965	48,990	88,600
					Percent of Population							
					Total							
Saguenay	0.9	0.0	0.2	0.3	0.0	0.1	0.2	0.0	0.0	0.0	0.0	0.0
Québec	11.0	1.1	1.1	3.2	0.4	1.5	2.2	0.9	0.3	0.1	0.1	0.2
Canada	19.1	4.8	4.0	2.9	1.9	1.2	1.2	0.9	0.6	0.5	0.3	0.5
					Males							
Saguenay	0.9	0.0	0.1	0.3	0.0	0.2	0.2	0.0	0.0	0.0	0.0	0.0
Québec	11.0	1.1	1.0	3.1	0.3	1.5	2.3	0.9	0.3	0.1	0.0	0.2
Canada	18.8	4.9	3.9	2.8	1.7	1.2	1.3	1.0	0.7	0.5	0.2	0.5
					Females							
Saguenay	0.9	0.0	0.3	0.3	0.0	0.1	0.1	0.0	0.0	0.0	0.0	0.0
Québec	11.0	1.0	1.2	3.2	0.5	1.5	2.0	0.8	0.3	0.1	0.1	0.2
Canada	19.3	4.7	4.1	3.0	2.1	1.2	1.1	0.9	0.6	0.5	0.3	0.5

Note: The Employment Equity Act defines visible minorities as 'persons, other than Aboriginal peoples, who are non-Caucasian in race or non-white in colour';
(1) Includes 'East Indian,' 'Pakistani,' 'Sri Lankan,' etc.; (2) Includes 'Vietnamese,' 'Cambodian,' 'Malaysian,' 'Laotian,' etc.; (3) Includes 'Iranian,' 'Afghan,' etc.; (4) Includes respondents who reported more than one visible minority group by checking two or more mark-in circles, e.g., 'Black' and 'South Asian.'
Source: Statistics Canada. 2013. 2011 National Household Survey. Statistics Canada Catalogue no. 99-004-XWE. Ottawa. Released September 11, 2013.

PROFILES / Saguenay, Québec

Aboriginal Population

Area	Aboriginal Identity[1]	First Nations (North American Indian) Single Identity[2]	Métis Single Identity	Inuk (Inuit) Single Identity	Multiple Aboriginal Identities[3]	Aboriginal Identities Not Included Elsewhere
Number						
Total						
Saguenay	3,550	1,120	2,240	25	45	115
Québec	141,915	82,425	40,960	12,570	1,545	4,415
Canada	1,400,685	851,560	451,795	59,440	11,415	26,475
Males						
Saguenay	1,875	515	1,280	0	25	50
Québec	70,205	40,105	21,300	6,265	720	1,815
Canada	682,190	411,785	223,335	29,495	5,525	12,055
Females						
Saguenay	1,675	605	960	0	20	70
Québec	71,710	42,315	19,660	6,305	830	2,600
Canada	718,500	439,775	228,460	29,950	5,890	14,420
Percent of Population						
Total						
Saguenay	2.5	0.8	1.6	0.0	0.0	0.1
Québec	1.8	1.1	0.5	0.2	0.0	0.1
Canada	4.3	2.6	1.4	0.2	0.0	0.1
Males						
Saguenay	2.7	0.7	1.8	0.0	0.0	0.1
Québec	1.8	1.1	0.6	0.2	0.0	0.0
Canada	4.2	2.5	1.4	0.2	0.0	0.1
Females						
Saguenay	2.3	0.8	1.3	0.0	0.0	0.1
Québec	1.8	1.1	0.5	0.2	0.0	0.1
Canada	4.3	2.6	1.4	0.2	0.0	0.1

Note: (1) Includes persons who reported being an Aboriginal person, that is, First Nations (North American Indian), Métis or Inuk (Inuit) and/or those who reported Registered or Treaty Indian status, that is registered under the Indian Act of Canada, and/or those who reported membership in a First Nation or Indian band. Aboriginal peoples of Canada are defined in the Constitution Act, 1982, section 35-2 as including the Indian, Inuit and Métis peoples of Canada; (2) Users should be aware that the estimates associated with this variable are more affected than most by the incomplete enumeration of certain Indian reserves and Indian settlements in the National Household Survey (NHS); (3) Includes persons who reported being any two or all three of the following: First Nations (North American Indian), Métis or Inuk (Inuit).
Source: Statistics Canada. 2013. 2011 National Household Survey. Statistics Canada Catalogue no. 99-004-XWE. Ottawa. Released September 11, 2013.

Ethnic Origin

Area	North American Aboriginal	Other North American	European	Caribbean	Latin, Central and South American	African	Asian	Oceania
Number								
Total								
Saguenay	5,755	114,615	51,415	180	210	505	725	35
Québec	307,445	4,776,875	3,390,330	167,590	137,255	260,785	488,905	2,305
Canada	1,836,035	11,070,455	20,157,965	627,590	544,375	766,735	5,011,225	74,875
Males								
Saguenay	2,970	56,365	25,725	100	135	280	330	20
Québec	146,725	2,345,180	1,678,310	77,665	67,195	135,740	241,515	1,135
Canada	885,675	5,462,685	9,913,150	291,640	264,635	387,360	2,435,540	37,490
Females								
Saguenay	2,780	58,255	25,695	75	80	225	400	10
Québec	160,725	2,431,700	1,712,015	89,925	70,065	125,040	247,390	1,175
Canada	950,360	5,607,770	10,244,820	335,945	279,740	379,380	2,575,680	37,385
Percent of Population								
Total								
Saguenay	4.1	81.1	36.4	0.1	0.1	0.4	0.5	0.0
Québec	4.0	61.8	43.8	2.2	1.8	3.4	6.3	0.0
Canada	5.6	33.7	61.4	1.9	1.7	2.3	15.3	0.2
Males								
Saguenay	4.2	80.6	36.8	0.1	0.2	0.4	0.5	0.0
Québec	3.8	61.5	44.0	2.0	1.8	3.6	6.3	0.0
Canada	5.5	33.8	61.3	1.8	1.6	2.4	15.1	0.2
Females								
Saguenay	3.9	81.6	36.0	0.1	0.1	0.3	0.6	0.0
Québec	4.1	62.1	43.7	2.3	1.8	3.2	6.3	0.0
Canada	5.7	33.6	61.4	2.0	1.7	2.3	15.4	0.2

Note: The sum of the ethnic groups in this table is greater than the total population estimate because a person may report more than one ethnic origin in the NHS.
Source: Statistics Canada. 2013. 2011 National Household Survey. Statistics Canada Catalogue no. 99-004-XWE. Ottawa. Released September 11, 2013.

Religion

Area	Buddhist	Christian	Hindu	Jewish	Muslim	Sikh	Traditional (Aboriginal) Spirituality	Other Religions	No Religious Affiliation
					Number Total				
Saguenay	60	132,335	0	0	335	0	0	150	8,420
Québec	52,390	6,356,880	33,540	85,100	243,430	9,275	2,025	12,340	937,545
Canada	366,830	22,102,745	497,965	329,495	1,053,945	454,965	64,935	130,835	7,850,605
					Males				
Saguenay	40	64,580	0	0	160	0	0	75	5,045
Québec	24,630	3,079,855	17,055	41,455	128,815	5,090	925	6,155	510,055
Canada	168,465	10,497,775	250,435	161,265	540,555	229,435	31,805	57,745	4,225,645
					Females				
Saguenay	20	67,755	0	0	180	0	0	70	3,375
Québec	27,760	3,277,020	16,480	43,645	114,615	4,185	1,100	6,175	427,485
Canada	198,365	11,604,975	247,525	168,235	513,395	225,530	33,135	73,090	3,624,965
					Percent of Population Total				
Saguenay	0.0	93.6	0.0	0.0	0.2	0.0	0.0	0.1	6.0
Québec	0.7	82.2	0.4	1.1	3.1	0.1	0.0	0.2	12.1
Canada	1.1	67.3	1.5	1.0	3.2	1.4	0.2	0.4	23.9
					Males				
Saguenay	0.1	92.4	0.0	0.0	0.2	0.0	0.0	0.1	7.2
Québec	0.6	80.8	0.4	1.1	3.4	0.1	0.0	0.2	13.4
Canada	1.0	64.9	1.5	1.0	3.3	1.4	0.2	0.4	26.1
					Females				
Saguenay	0.0	94.9	0.0	0.0	0.3	0.0	0.0	0.1	4.7
Québec	0.7	83.6	0.4	1.1	2.9	0.1	0.0	0.2	10.9
Canada	1.2	69.5	1.5	1.0	3.1	1.4	0.2	0.4	21.7

Note: Religion refers to the person's self-identification as having a connection or affiliation with any religious denomination, group, body, sect, cult or other religiously defined community or system of belief. Religion is not limited to formal membership in a religious organization or group. Persons without a religious connection or affiliation can self-identify as atheist, agnostic or humanist, or can provide another applicable response.
Source: Statistics Canada. 2013. 2011 National Household Survey. Statistics Canada Catalogue no. 99-004-XWE. Ottawa. Released September 11, 2013.

Religion—Christian Denominations

Area	Anglican	Baptist	Catholic	Christian Orthodox	Lutheran	Pentecostal	Presbyterian	United Church	Other Christian
					Number Total				
Saguenay	75	370	129,345	25	25	85	30	40	2,325
Québec	73,550	36,615	5,775,740	129,780	7,200	41,070	11,440	32,930	248,560
Canada	1,631,845	635,840	12,810,705	550,690	478,185	478,705	472,385	2,007,610	3,036,780
					Males				
Saguenay	60	195	63,090	15	0	30	25	20	1,140
Québec	34,815	16,585	2,802,920	63,960	3,425	18,640	5,265	14,945	119,305
Canada	752,945	293,905	6,167,290	270,205	221,525	217,850	218,955	912,545	1,442,550
					Females				
Saguenay	20	175	66,260	15	15	55	0	20	1,190
Québec	38,735	20,030	2,972,820	65,820	3,770	22,430	6,175	17,985	129,260
Canada	878,900	341,940	6,643,415	280,485	256,660	260,850	253,430	1,095,065	1,594,230
					Percent of Population Total				
Saguenay	0.1	0.3	91.5	0.0	0.0	0.1	0.0	0.0	1.6
Québec	1.0	0.5	74.7	1.7	0.1	0.5	0.1	0.4	3.2
Canada	5.0	1.9	39.0	1.7	1.5	1.5	1.4	6.1	9.2
					Males				
Saguenay	0.1	0.3	90.2	0.0	0.0	0.0	0.0	0.0	1.6
Québec	0.9	0.4	73.5	1.7	0.1	0.5	0.1	0.4	3.1
Canada	4.7	1.8	38.2	1.7	1.4	1.3	1.4	5.6	8.9
					Females				
Saguenay	0.0	0.2	92.8	0.0	0.0	0.1	0.0	0.0	1.7
Québec	1.0	0.5	75.9	1.7	0.1	0.6	0.2	0.5	3.3
Canada	5.3	2.0	39.8	1.7	1.5	1.6	1.5	6.6	9.6

Note: Religion refers to the person's self-identification as having a connection or affiliation with any religious denomination, group, body, sect, cult or other religiously defined community or system of belief. Religion is not limited to formal membership in a religious organization or group. Persons without a religious connection or affiliation can self-identify as atheist, agnostic or humanist, or can provide another applicable response.
Source: Statistics Canada. 2013. 2011 National Household Survey. Statistics Canada Catalogue no. 99-004-XWE. Ottawa. Released September 11, 2013.

PROFILES / Saguenay, Québec

Immigrant Status and Period of Immigration

Area	Non-Immigrants[1]	Immigrants All	Before 1971	1971 to 1980	1981 to 1990	1991 to 2000	2001 to 2005	2006 to 2011	Non-Permanent Residents[3]
Number									
Total									
Saguenay	139,500	1,620	105	125	200	320	365	505	205
Québec	6,690,530	974,895	151,825	115,640	130,680	195,925	157,425	223,400	67,095
Canada	25,720,175	6,775,765	1,261,055	870,775	949,890	1,539,050	992,070	1,162,915	356,385
Males									
Saguenay	68,955	825	60	75	110	135	180	260	140
Québec	3,301,435	477,240	75,255	57,410	64,080	94,110	76,780	109,605	35,370
Canada	12,753,235	3,231,370	605,430	416,670	454,570	724,905	474,545	555,245	178,515
Females									
Saguenay	70,545	800	40	45	95	185	190	250	65
Québec	3,389,095	497,655	76,565	58,235	66,600	101,810	80,645	113,795	31,725
Canada	12,966,935	3,544,400	655,625	454,105	495,325	814,145	517,530	607,670	177,870
Percent of Population									
Total									
Saguenay	98.7	1.1	0.1	0.1	0.1	0.2	0.3	0.4	0.1
Québec	86.5	12.6	2.0	1.5	1.7	2.5	2.0	2.9	0.9
Canada	78.3	20.6	3.8	2.7	2.9	4.7	3.0	3.5	1.1
Males									
Saguenay	98.6	1.2	0.1	0.1	0.2	0.2	0.3	0.4	0.2
Québec	86.6	12.5	2.0	1.5	1.7	2.5	2.0	2.9	0.9
Canada	78.9	20.0	3.7	2.6	2.8	4.5	2.9	3.4	1.1
Females									
Saguenay	98.8	1.1	0.1	0.1	0.1	0.3	0.3	0.4	0.1
Québec	86.5	12.7	2.0	1.5	1.7	2.6	2.1	2.9	0.8
Canada	77.7	21.2	3.9	2.7	3.0	4.9	3.1	3.6	1.1

Note: (1) Non-immigrant refers to a person who is a Canadian citizen by birth; (2) Immigrant refers to a person who is or has ever been a landed immigrant/permanent resident. This person has been granted the right to live in Canada permanently by immigration authorities. Some immigrants have resided in Canada for a number of years, while others have arrived recently. Some immigrants are Canadian citizens, while others are not. Most immigrants are born outside Canada, but a small number are born in Canada. In the 2011 National Household Survey, 'Immigrants' includes immigrants who landed in Canada prior to May 10, 2011; (3) Non-permanent resident refers to a person from another country who has a work or study permit, or who is a refugee claimant, and any non-Canadian-born family member living in Canada with them.
Source: Statistics Canada. 2013. 2011 National Household Survey. Statistics Canada Catalogue no. 99-004-XWE. Ottawa. Released September 11, 2013.

Mother Tongue

Area	English	French	Non-official Language	English & French	English & Non-official Language	French & Non-official Language	English, French & Non-official Language
Number							
Total							
Saguenay	1,185	140,915	975	350	25	95	10
Québec	599,225	6,102,210	961,700	64,800	23,435	51,640	12,950
Canada	18,858,980	7,054,975	6,567,680	144,685	396,330	74,430	24,095
Males							
Saguenay	625	69,260	500	195	10	45	5
Québec	297,875	2,994,300	472,635	32,390	11,455	25,810	6,790
Canada	9,345,225	3,452,380	3,157,785	69,975	192,000	36,535	11,965
Females							
Saguenay	560	71,650	475	160	20	50	5
Québec	301,355	3,107,910	489,060	32,405	11,975	25,825	6,155
Canada	9,513,750	3,602,590	3,409,895	74,710	204,330	37,890	12,130
Percent of Population							
Total							
Saguenay	0.8	98.2	0.7	0.2	0.0	0.1	0.0
Québec	7.7	78.1	12.3	0.8	0.3	0.7	0.2
Canada	56.9	21.3	19.8	0.4	1.2	0.2	0.1
Males							
Saguenay	0.9	98.0	0.7	0.3	0.0	0.1	0.0
Québec	7.8	78.0	12.3	0.8	0.3	0.7	0.2
Canada	57.5	21.2	19.4	0.4	1.2	0.2	0.1
Females							
Saguenay	0.8	98.3	0.7	0.2	0.0	0.1	0.0
Québec	7.6	78.2	12.3	0.8	0.3	0.6	0.2
Canada	56.4	21.4	20.2	0.4	1.2	0.2	0.1

Note: Figures cover total population excluding institutional residents.
Source: Statistics Canada. 2012. Census Profile. 2011 Census. Statistics Canada Catalogue no. 98-316-XWE. Ottawa. Released October 24 2012.
http://www12.statcan.gc.ca/census-recensement/2011/dp-pd/prof/index.cfm?Lang=E

Language Spoken Most Often at Home

Area	English	French	Non-official Language	English & French	English & Non-official Language	French & Non-official Language	English, French & Non-official Language
			Number				
			Total				
Saguenay	765	141,880	405	300	10	180	30
Québec	767,415	6,249,080	554,400	71,555	43,765	100,110	29,625
Canada	21,457,075	6,827,865	3,673,865	131,205	875,135	109,700	46,330
			Males				
Saguenay	400	69,775	190	170	5	90	15
Québec	379,915	3,071,635	268,640	35,860	21,305	48,590	15,315
Canada	10,585,620	3,348,235	1,767,310	63,475	425,370	53,010	22,845
			Females				
Saguenay	360	72,100	210	130	5	90	15
Québec	387,500	3,177,450	285,760	35,695	22,460	51,525	14,310
Canada	10,871,455	3,479,625	1,906,555	67,730	449,765	56,690	23,485
			Percent of Population				
			Total				
Saguenay	0.5	98.8	0.3	0.2	0.0	0.1	0.0
Québec	9.8	80.0	7.1	0.9	0.6	1.3	0.4
Canada	64.8	20.6	11.1	0.4	2.6	0.3	0.1
			Males				
Saguenay	0.6	98.8	0.3	0.2	0.0	0.1	0.0
Québec	9.9	80.0	7.0	0.9	0.6	1.3	0.4
Canada	65.1	20.6	10.9	0.4	2.6	0.3	0.1
			Females				
Saguenay	0.5	98.9	0.3	0.2	0.0	0.1	0.0
Québec	9.7	79.9	7.2	0.9	0.6	1.3	0.4
Canada	64.5	20.6	11.3	0.4	2.7	0.3	0.1

Note: Figures cover total population excluding institutional residents.
Source: Statistics Canada. 2012. Census Profile. 2011 Census. Statistics Canada Catalogue no. 98-316-XWE. Ottawa. Released October 24 2012.
http://www12.statcan.gc.ca/census-recensement/2011/dp-pd/prof/index.cfm?Lang=E

Knowledge of Official Languages

Area	English Only	French Only	English & French	Neither English nor French
		Number		
		Total		
Saguenay	150	114,120	29,240	45
Québec	363,860	4,047,175	3,328,725	76,190
Canada	22,564,665	4,165,015	5,795,570	595,920
		Males		
Saguenay	75	52,830	17,715	20
Québec	180,175	1,871,500	1,758,410	31,175
Canada	11,222,185	1,925,340	2,876,560	241,790
		Females		
Saguenay	75	61,290	11,530	25
Québec	183,690	2,175,675	1,570,310	45,015
Canada	11,342,485	2,239,680	2,919,005	354,135
		Percent of Population		
		Total		
Saguenay	0.1	79.5	20.4	0.0
Québec	4.7	51.8	42.6	1.0
Canada	68.1	12.6	17.5	1.8
		Males		
Saguenay	0.1	74.8	25.1	0.0
Québec	4.7	48.7	45.8	0.8
Canada	69.0	11.8	17.7	1.5
		Females		
Saguenay	0.1	84.1	15.8	0.0
Québec	4.6	54.7	39.5	1.1
Canada	67.3	13.3	17.3	2.1

Note: Figures cover total population excluding institutional residents.
Source: Statistics Canada. 2012. Census Profile. 2011 Census. Statistics Canada Catalogue no. 98-316-XWE. Ottawa. Released October 24 2012.
http://www12.statcan.gc.ca/census-recensement/2011/dp-pd/prof/index.cfm?Lang=E

Saskatoon, Saskatchewan

Background

Saskatoon is situated on the banks of the South Saskatchewan River. Located in central Saskatchewan, the city is named the "City of Bridges" in recognition of its seven bridge crossings within city limits. Saskatchewan's largest and youngest city (the average resident is under 35), Saskatoon is also the provincial capital and one of Canada's fastest growing cities.

Although the area surrounding Saskatoon has been inhabited for over 6,000 years, the city was not officially incorporated until 1906. The city's name is Cree, from the area's first Aboriginal inhabitants, and refers to a local indigenous berry. Tourists regularly go home with Saskatoon berry pies, jams and sweets.

The University of Saskatchewan is located in Saskatoon and is the only university in Canada with five health science colleges and a teaching hospital on one campus. Some of the experiments aboard NASA's space shuttle *Discovery* in 1990 were a result of research conducted at the University of Saskatchewan. Today, Saskatoon is home to the national synchrotron research facility and Canada's largest scientific project in history, *The Canadian Light Source Synchrotron* project, a giant particle accelerator.

Saskatoon has hosted a variety of notable events such as the 2007 Juno Awards, the IIHF World Junior Hockey Championships (2010, 1991) and the 2012 Canadian Country Music Awards. In 2011, Saskatoon's Broadway Avenue was named one of the "Great Streets in Canada" by the Canadian Institute of Planners.

Saskatoon has average summer highs of plus 24.07 degrees Celsius, winter lows of minus 19.27 degrees Celsius, and an average rainfall just over 252 mm per year.

Rankings

- Saskatoon ranked as one of the four Canadian cities with the highest rates of population growth. Since 2006, Saskatoon has grown at 11.4%. The other top cities, all from Western Canada, are Calgary, 12.6%; Edmonton, 12.1%; and Kelowna, 10.8%. *The Globe and Mail, "How Canada's Cities are Changing," February 8, 2012*
- In 2011, Statistics Canada released population estimates concluding that Saskatoon and its surrounding areas were the fastest growing and youngest populations in Canada. The population of Saskatoon exceeded 265,000 people, indicating a 3% increase from the previous year and 30,000 new Saskatoon residents since 2005. High birth rates among the First Nations population and young families immigrating from overseas were factors contributing to Saskatoon being the youngest of Canada's metropolitan areas, with half of the city's population under the age of 35.4. *Saskatoon Regional Economic Development Authority, February 11, 2011*
- A research study by the Canadian Council on Learning, an organization that measures lifelong community learning, leisure pursuits and cultural engagement, showed that more than half (52%) of all households in Saskatoon spent money on sports and recreation in 2006. The highest percentage of sports-and-recreation household spenders lived in the following three cities: Calgary, 58.5%; Ottawa-Hull, 58.3%; and Victoria, 56.7%. *Canadian Council on Learning with files from Statistics Canada, special tabulation, unpublished data, Survey of Household Spending, 2006*
- Saskatoon was ranked as one of the best rental markets in Canada for Canadians wanting to make money by renting out real estate. Based on 2011 Canada Mortgage and Housing Corporation data, *Canadian Real Estate Magazine* attributed the 5.5% rental increase in 2011 to resource-sector growth and multiple universities. Despite Saskatoon's stable vacancy rate of 2.6%, the city's rents for houses and three-bedroom apartments rose 10.9%. *Canadian Real Estate Magazine, "Canada's Top 50 Rental Markets," March 16th, 2012*

PROFILES / Saskatoon, Saskatchewan

Population Growth and Density

Area	Population in 2001	Population in 2006	Population in 2011	Population Change 2001–2006	Population Change 2006–2011	Land Area (sq. km)	Population Density per sq. km
Saskatoon	196,861	202,408	222,189	2.8	9.8	209.56	1,060.3
Saskatchewan	978,933	968,157	1,033,381	-1.1	6.7	588,239.21	1.8
Canada	30,007,094	31,612,897	33,476,688	5.4	5.9	8,965,121.42	3.7

Source: Statistics Canada. 2012. Census Profile. 2011 Census. Statistics Canada Catalogue no. 98-316-XWE. Ottawa. Released October 24 2012.
http://www12.statcan.gc.ca/census-recensement/2011/dp-pd/prof/index.cfm?Lang=E;
Statistics Canada 2007. 2006 Community Profiles. 2006 Census. Statistics Canada Catalogue no. 92-591-XWE. Ottawa. Released March 13 2007.
http://www12.statcan.ca/census-recensement/2006/dp-pd/prof/92-591/index.cfm?Lang=E

Gender

Area	Males	Females
Number		
Saskatoon	108,640	113,550
Saskatchewan	511,555	521,825
Canada	16,414,225	17,062,460
Percent of Population		
Saskatoon	48.9	51.1
Saskatchewan	49.5	50.5
Canada	49.0	51.0

Source: Statistics Canada. 2012. Census Profile. 2011 Census. Statistics Canada Catalogue no. 98-316-XWE. Ottawa. Released October 24 2012.
http://www12.statcan.gc.ca/census-recensement/2011/dp-pd/prof/index.cfm?Lang=E

Marital Status

Area	Married[1]	Living Common-law	Single[2]	Separated	Divorced	Widowed
Number						
Total						
Saskatoon	83,585	14,900	60,560	4,125	11,140	10,070
Saskatchewan	416,355	71,630	232,160	18,210	43,665	53,500
Canada	12,941,960	3,142,525	7,816,045	698,240	1,686,035	1,584,530
Males						
Saskatoon	41,865	7,460	32,135	1,760	4,390	1,650
Saskatchewan	208,700	35,785	128,325	8,220	19,500	10,015
Canada	6,470,300	1,575,495	4,206,320	299,655	680,415	310,940
Females						
Saskatoon	41,720	7,440	28,420	2,365	6,755	8,420
Saskatchewan	207,655	35,845	103,835	9,990	24,170	43,490
Canada	6,471,660	1,567,035	3,609,730	398,585	1,005,620	1,273,590
Percent of Population						
Total						
Saskatoon	45.3	8.1	32.8	2.2	6.0	5.5
Saskatchewan	49.8	8.6	27.8	2.2	5.2	6.4
Canada	46.4	11.3	28.0	2.5	6.0	5.7
Males						
Saskatoon	46.9	8.4	36.0	2.0	4.9	1.8
Saskatchewan	50.8	8.7	31.3	2.0	4.7	2.4
Canada	47.8	11.6	31.1	2.2	5.0	2.3
Females						
Saskatoon	43.9	7.8	29.9	2.5	7.1	8.9
Saskatchewan	48.9	8.4	24.4	2.4	5.7	10.2
Canada	45.2	10.9	25.2	2.8	7.0	8.9

Note: (1) and not separated, (2) never legally married
Source: Statistics Canada. 2012. Census Profile. 2011 Census. Statistics Canada Catalogue no. 98-316-XWE. Ottawa. Released October 24 2012.
http://www12.statcan.gc.ca/census-recensement/2011/dp-pd/prof/index.cfm?Lang=E

Age Characteristics: 0 to 49 Years

Area	0 to 4 Years	5 to 9 Years	10 to 14 Years	15 to 19 Years	20 to 24 Years	25 to 29 Years	30 to 34 Years	35 to 39 Years	40 to 44 Years	45 to 49 Years
					Number Total					
Saskatoon	13,525	12,035	12,245	14,840	21,130	19,525	16,105	13,990	13,695	16,015
Saskatchewan	68,760	63,350	65,750	71,760	72,610	70,395	65,340	61,150	61,475	74,630
Canada	1,877,095	1,809,895	1,920,355	2,178,135	2,187,450	2,169,590	2,162,905	2,173,930	2,324,875	2,675,130
					Males					
Saskatoon	6,935	6,165	6,280	7,470	10,560	9,850	8,180	6,955	6,890	7,925
Saskatchewan	35,070	32,480	33,465	36,870	37,135	35,510	32,750	30,265	30,550	36,820
Canada	961,150	925,965	983,995	1,115,845	1,108,775	1,077,275	1,058,810	1,064,200	1,141,720	1,318,715
					Females					
Saskatoon	6,590	5,865	5,965	7,365	10,570	9,680	7,930	7,040	6,805	8,090
Saskatchewan	33,690	30,865	32,285	34,885	35,470	34,885	32,590	30,880	30,920	37,810
Canada	915,945	883,935	936,360	1,062,295	1,078,670	1,092,315	1,104,095	1,109,735	1,183,155	1,356,420
					Percent of Population Total					
Saskatoon	6.1	5.4	5.5	6.7	9.5	8.8	7.2	6.3	6.2	7.2
Saskatchewan	6.7	6.1	6.4	6.9	7.0	6.8	6.3	5.9	5.9	7.2
Canada	5.6	5.4	5.7	6.5	6.5	6.5	6.5	6.5	6.9	8.0
					Males					
Saskatoon	6.4	5.7	5.8	6.9	9.7	9.1	7.5	6.4	6.3	7.3
Saskatchewan	6.9	6.3	6.5	7.2	7.3	6.9	6.4	5.9	6.0	7.2
Canada	5.9	5.6	6.0	6.8	6.8	6.6	6.5	6.5	7.0	8.0
					Females					
Saskatoon	5.8	5.2	5.3	6.5	9.3	8.5	7.0	6.2	6.0	7.1
Saskatchewan	6.5	5.9	6.2	6.7	6.8	6.7	6.2	5.9	5.9	7.2
Canada	5.4	5.2	5.5	6.2	6.3	6.4	6.5	6.5	6.9	7.9

Source: Statistics Canada. 2012. Census Profile. 2011 Census. Statistics Canada Catalogue no. 98-316-XWE. Ottawa. Released October 24 2012.
http://www12.statcan.gc.ca/census-recensement/2011/dp-pd/prof/index.cfm?Lang=E

Age Characteristics: 50 Years and Over, and Median Age

Area	50 to 54 Years	55 to 59 Years	60 to 64 Years	65 to 69 Years	70 to 74 Years	75 to 79 Years	80 to 84 Years	85 Years and Over	Median Age
				Number Total					
Saskatoon	16,045	13,910	10,730	7,315	6,175	5,545	4,465	4,900	35.6
Saskatchewan	77,480	70,050	56,945	41,500	33,820	28,950	23,955	25,475	38.2
Canada	2,658,965	2,340,635	2,052,670	1,521,715	1,153,065	922,700	702,070	645,515	40.6
				Males					
Saskatoon	7,850	6,745	5,150	3,435	2,695	2,400	1,695	1,460	34.2
Saskatchewan	38,855	35,185	28,305	20,445	16,050	13,200	10,165	8,435	37.0
Canada	1,309,030	1,147,300	1,002,690	738,010	543,435	417,945	291,085	208,300	39.6
				Females					
Saskatoon	8,195	7,165	5,580	3,880	3,485	3,150	2,775	3,435	37.0
Saskatchewan	38,625	34,865	28,645	21,055	17,770	15,750	13,795	17,035	39.2
Canada	1,349,940	1,193,335	1,049,985	783,705	609,630	504,755	410,985	437,215	41.5
				Percent of Population Total					
Saskatoon	7.2	6.3	4.8	3.3	2.8	2.5	2.0	2.2	—
Saskatchewan	7.5	6.8	5.5	4.0	3.3	2.8	2.3	2.5	—
Canada	7.9	7.0	6.1	4.5	3.4	2.8	2.1	1.9	—
				Males					
Saskatoon	7.2	6.2	4.7	3.2	2.5	2.2	1.6	1.3	—
Saskatchewan	7.6	6.9	5.5	4.0	3.1	2.6	2.0	1.6	—
Canada	8.0	7.0	6.1	4.5	3.3	2.5	1.8	1.3	—
				Females					
Saskatoon	7.2	6.3	4.9	3.4	3.1	2.8	2.4	3.0	—
Saskatchewan	7.4	6.7	5.5	4.0	3.4	3.0	2.6	3.3	—
Canada	7.9	7.0	6.2	4.6	3.6	3.0	2.4	2.6	—

Source: Statistics Canada. 2012. Census Profile. 2011 Census. Statistics Canada Catalogue no. 98-316-XWE. Ottawa. Released October 24 2012.
http://www12.statcan.gc.ca/census-recensement/2011/dp-pd/prof/index.cfm?Lang=E

PROFILES / Saskatoon, Saskatchewan

Private Households by Household Size

Area	1 Person	2 Persons	3 Persons	4 Persons	5 Persons	6 or More Persons	Average Number of Persons in Private Households
			Households				
Saskatoon	26,835	31,065	13,830	12,075	4,740	2,390	2.4
Saskatchewan	114,385	146,850	57,410	53,070	23,455	14,470	2.5
Canada	3,673,310	4,544,820	2,081,900	1,903,300	724,405	392,885	2.5
			Percent of Households				
Saskatoon	29.5	34.2	15.2	13.3	5.2	2.6	–
Saskatchewan	27.9	35.8	14.0	13.0	5.7	3.5	–
Canada	27.6	34.1	15.6	14.3	5.4	2.9	–

Source: Statistics Canada. 2012. Census Profile. 2011 Census. Statistics Canada Catalogue no. 98-316-XWE. Ottawa. Released October 24 2012.
http://www12.statcan.gc.ca/census-recensement/2011/dp-pd/prof/index.cfm?Lang=E

Dwelling Type

Area	Single-detached House	Semi-detached House	Row House	Apartment: Building with Five or More Storeys	Apartment: Building with Fewer Than Five Storeys	Duplex Apartment	Movable Dwelling	Other Single-attached House
				Number				
Saskatoon	51,940	3,840	4,660	5,000	20,880	4,185	380	50
Saskatchewan	303,250	11,945	14,370	10,830	52,655	7,090	8,805	700
Canada	7,329,150	646,245	791,600	1,234,770	2,397,550	704,485	183,510	33,310
				Percent of Dwellings				
Saskatoon	57.1	4.2	5.1	5.5	23.0	4.6	0.4	0.1
Saskatchewan	74.0	2.9	3.5	2.6	12.9	1.7	2.1	0.2
Canada	55.0	4.9	5.9	9.3	18.0	5.3	1.4	0.3

Source: Statistics Canada. 2012. Census Profile. 2011 Census. Statistics Canada Catalogue no. 98-316-XWE. Ottawa. Released October 24 2012.
http://www12.statcan.gc.ca/census-recensement/2011/dp-pd/prof/index.cfm?Lang=E

Shelter Costs

		Owned Dwellings					Rented Dwellings	
Area	Number	Median Value[1] ($)	Average Value[1] ($)	Median Monthly Costs[2] ($)	Average Monthly Costs[2] ($)	Number	Median Monthly Costs[3] ($)	Average Monthly Costs[3] ($)
Saskatoon	60,255	318,012	337,971	1,034	1,133	30,685	913	961
Saskatchewan	273,345	250,347	267,006	751	943	99,410	793	837
Canada	9,013,410	280,552	345,182	978	1,141	4,060,385	784	848

Note: All figures cover non-farm, non-reserve private dwellings; (1) Refers to the dollar amount expected by the owner if the dwelling were to be sold; (2) Includes all shelter expenses paid by households that own their dwellings, such as the mortgage payment and the costs of electricity, heat, water and other municipal services, property taxes and condominium fees; (3) Includes all shelter expenses paid by households that rent their dwellings, such as the monthly rent and the costs of electricity, heat and municipal services.
Source: Statistics Canada. 2013. 2011 National Household Survey. Statistics Canada Catalogue no. 99-004-XWE. Ottawa. Released September 11, 2013.

Occupied Private Dwellings by Period of Construction

Area	1960 or Before	1961 to 1980	1981 to 1990	1991 to 2000	2001 to 2005	2006 to 2011
			Number			
Saskatoon	19,365	33,475	18,005	7,825	5,365	6,900
Saskatchewan	108,390	154,185	68,215	32,570	18,505	27,705
Canada	3,273,105	4,152,715	2,112,110	1,707,880	1,031,020	1,042,430
			Percent of Dwellings			
Saskatoon	21.3	36.8	19.8	8.6	5.9	7.6
Saskatchewan	26.5	37.6	16.7	8.0	4.5	6.8
Canada	24.6	31.2	15.9	12.8	7.7	7.8

Note: Figures cover non-farm, non-reserve private dwellings and includes data up to May 10, 2011.
Source: Statistics Canada. 2013. 2011 National Household Survey. Statistics Canada Catalogue no. 99-004-XWE. Ottawa. Released September 11, 2013.

Educational Attainment

Area	No Certificate, Diploma or Degree	High School Diploma or Equivalent[1]	Apprenticeship or Trades Certificate or Diploma[2]	College, CÉGEP or Other Non-University Certificate or Diploma	University Certificate or Diploma Below the Bachelor Level[3]	Bachelor's Degree	University Certificate, Diploma or Degree Above Bachelor Level[4]
Number							
Total							
Saskatoon	31,005	49,405	19,040	29,600	7,725	29,905	13,970
Saskatchewan	200,430	228,755	98,820	127,295	32,780	90,720	33,705
Canada	5,485,400	6,968,935	2,950,685	4,970,020	1,200,130	3,634,425	2,049,930
Males							
Saskatoon	15,855	25,330	12,125	10,510	3,090	13,420	7,430
Saskatchewan	106,880	115,075	65,090	44,805	12,735	38,930	17,445
Canada	2,742,875	3,305,415	1,928,970	2,118,430	513,235	1,643,080	1,043,350
Females							
Saskatoon	15,155	24,070	6,910	19,090	4,635	16,485	6,540
Saskatchewan	93,550	113,680	33,730	82,490	20,040	51,785	16,260
Canada	2,742,520	3,663,515	1,021,715	2,851,595	686,890	1,991,345	1,006,585
Percent of Population							
Total							
Saskatoon	17.2	27.3	10.5	16.4	4.3	16.6	7.7
Saskatchewan	24.7	28.2	12.2	15.7	4.0	11.2	4.1
Canada	20.1	25.6	10.8	18.2	4.4	13.3	7.5
Males							
Saskatoon	18.1	28.9	13.8	12.0	3.5	15.3	8.5
Saskatchewan	26.7	28.7	16.2	11.2	3.2	9.7	4.4
Canada	20.6	24.9	14.5	15.9	3.9	12.4	7.8
Females							
Saskatoon	16.3	25.9	7.4	20.6	5.0	17.7	7.0
Saskatchewan	22.7	27.6	8.2	20.0	4.9	12.6	4.0
Canada	19.6	26.2	7.3	20.4	4.9	14.3	7.2

Note: Figures cover total population aged 15 years and over by highest certificate, diploma or degree; (1) Includes persons who have graduated from a secondary school or equivalent. It excludes persons with a postsecondary certificate, diploma or degree; (2) Includes Registered Apprenticeship certificates (including Certificate of Qualification, Journeyperson's designation) and other trades certificates or diplomas such as pre-employment or vocational certificates and diplomas from brief trade programs completed at community colleges, institutes of technology, vocational centres, and similar institutions; (3) Comparisons with other data sources suggest that the category 'University certificate or diploma below the bachelor's level' was over-reported in the NHS. This category likely includes some responses that are actually college certificates or diplomas, bachelor's degrees or other types of education (e.g., university transfer programs, bachelor's programs completed in other countries, incomplete bachelor's programs, non-university professional designations). We recommend users interpret the results for the 'University certificate or diploma below the bachelor's level' category with caution; (4) 'University certificate or diploma above bachelor level' includes the categories: 'Degree in medicine, dentistry, veterinary medicine or optometry,' 'Master's degree' and 'Earned doctorate.'
Source: Statistics Canada. 2013. 2011 National Household Survey. Statistics Canada Catalogue no. 99-004-XWE. Ottawa. Released September 11, 2013.

Household Income Distribution

Area	Less than $10,000	$10,000 to $19,999	$20,000 to $29,999	$30,000 to $39,999	$40,000 to $49,999	$50,000 to $59,999	$60,000 to $79,999	$80,000 to $99,999	$100,000 to $124,999	$125,000 to $149,999	$150,000 and Over
Households											
Saskatoon	3,780	7,405	7,825	7,580	7,765	7,335	12,670	10,515	9,815	5,615	10,630
Saskatchewan	17,365	37,195	36,770	38,910	36,000	33,020	57,220	44,980	40,505	26,620	40,990
Canada	626,705	1,141,945	1,193,925	1,271,675	1,206,800	1,102,120	1,865,280	1,458,240	1,260,770	802,555	1,389,240
Percent of Households											
Saskatoon	4.2	8.1	8.6	8.3	8.5	8.1	13.9	11.6	10.8	6.2	11.7
Saskatchewan	4.2	9.1	9.0	9.5	8.8	8.1	14.0	11.0	9.9	6.5	10.0
Canada	4.7	8.6	9.0	9.5	9.1	8.3	14.0	10.9	9.5	6.0	10.4

Note: Household income is the sum of the total incomes of all members of that household. Total income refers to monetary receipts from certain sources, before income taxes and deductions, during calendar year 2010.
Source: Statistics Canada. 2013. 2011 National Household Survey. Statistics Canada Catalogue no. 99-004-XWE. Ottawa. Released September 11, 2013.

Median and Average Household and Economic Family Income

Area	Median Household Income ($)	Average Household Income ($)	Median After-tax Household Income ($)	Average After-tax Household Income ($)	Median Economic Family Income ($)	Average Economic Family Income ($)	Median After-tax Economic Family Income ($)	Average After-tax Economic Family Income ($)
Saskatoon	65,524	82,543	57,007	68,656	83,774	99,883	72,678	82,820
Saskatchewan	61,703	77,317	54,628	65,050	77,448	91,877	68,046	77,161
Canada	61,072	79,102	54,089	66,149	76,511	94,125	67,044	78,517

Note: Figures cover household and economic familiy income in 2010. A household is defined as a person or a group of persons (other than foreign residents) who occupy the same private dwelling and do not have a usual place of residence elsewhere in Canada. Every person is a member of one and only one household. An economic family is defined as a group of two or more persons who live in the same dwelling and are related to each other by blood, marriage, common-law, adoption or a foster relationship. A couple may be of opposite or same sex.
Source: Statistics Canada. 2013. 2011 National Household Survey. Statistics Canada Catalogue no. 99-004-XWE. Ottawa. Released September 11, 2013.

PROFILES / Saskatoon, Saskatchewan

Individual Income Distribution

Area	Less than $10,000	$10,000 to $19,999	$20,000 to $29,999	$30,000 to $39,999	$40,000 to $49,999	$50,000 to $59,999	$60,000 to $79,999	$80,000 to $99,999	$100,000 to $124,999	$125,000 and Over
Number – Total										
Saskatoon	25,440	28,975	23,570	22,595	18,650	14,650	18,035	9,415	5,540	5,695
Saskatchewan	125,400	138,190	108,765	100,155	81,730	58,995	77,820	40,360	23,430	21,345
Canada	4,492,040	4,835,710	3,670,020	3,180,360	2,603,520	1,921,650	2,437,440	1,302,045	693,580	782,135
Males										
Saskatoon	10,935	10,865	9,400	9,780	9,640	7,730	11,125	5,930	4,055	4,495
Saskatchewan	55,995	51,705	45,025	46,150	42,655	33,030	48,665	26,490	17,835	17,185
Canada	1,936,365	1,864,880	1,588,260	1,522,190	1,333,510	1,079,780	1,473,145	823,720	492,905	599,905
Females										
Saskatoon	14,500	18,110	14,175	12,820	9,010	6,920	6,915	3,490	1,480	1,200
Saskatchewan	69,405	86,485	63,745	54,010	39,075	25,965	29,155	13,865	5,595	4,165
Canada	2,555,675	2,970,825	2,081,760	1,658,170	1,270,010	841,870	964,300	478,330	200,680	182,230
Percent of Population – Total										
Saskatoon	14.7	16.8	13.7	13.1	10.8	8.5	10.5	5.5	3.2	3.3
Saskatchewan	16.2	17.8	14.0	12.9	10.5	7.6	10.0	5.2	3.0	2.7
Canada	17.3	18.7	14.2	12.3	10.0	7.4	9.4	5.0	2.7	3.0
Males										
Saskatoon	13.0	12.9	11.2	11.7	11.5	9.2	13.3	7.1	4.8	5.4
Saskatchewan	14.6	13.4	11.7	12.0	11.1	8.6	12.6	6.9	4.6	4.5
Canada	15.2	14.7	12.5	12.0	10.5	8.5	11.6	6.5	3.9	4.7
Females										
Saskatoon	16.4	20.4	16.0	14.5	10.2	7.8	7.8	3.9	1.7	1.4
Saskatchewan	17.7	22.1	16.3	13.8	10.0	6.6	7.4	3.5	1.4	1.1
Canada	19.4	22.5	15.8	12.6	9.6	6.4	7.3	3.6	1.5	1.4

Note: Figures cover individuals aged 15 years and over with income. Income refers to monetary receipts from certain sources, before income taxes and deductions, during calendar year 2010.
Source: Statistics Canada. 2013. 2011 National Household Survey. Statistics Canada Catalogue no. 99-004-XWE. Ottawa. Released September 11, 2013.

Labour Force Status

Area	In the Labour Force – All	Employed	Unemployed	Not in the Labour Force
Number – Total				
Saskatoon	129,225	121,830	7,395	51,425
Saskatchewan	562,310	529,100	33,210	250,190
Canada	17,990,080	16,595,035	1,395,045	9,269,445
Males				
Saskatoon	67,390	63,860	3,530	20,365
Saskatchewan	300,420	282,565	17,850	100,545
Canada	9,388,570	8,634,310	754,255	3,906,785
Females				
Saskatoon	61,840	57,970	3,865	31,055
Saskatchewan	261,885	246,530	15,355	149,650
Canada	8,601,515	7,960,725	640,790	5,362,660
Percent of Labour Force – Total				
Saskatoon	71.5	67.4	5.7	28.5
Saskatchewan	69.2	65.1	5.9	30.8
Canada	66.0	60.9	7.8	34.0
Males				
Saskatoon	76.8	72.8	5.2	23.2
Saskatchewan	74.9	70.5	5.9	25.1
Canada	70.6	64.9	8.0	29.4
Females				
Saskatoon	66.6	62.4	6.3	33.4
Saskatchewan	63.6	59.9	5.9	36.4
Canada	61.6	57.0	7.4	38.4

Note: Figures are based on total population 15 years and over
Source: Statistics Canada. 2013. 2011 National Household Survey. Statistics Canada Catalogue no. 99-004-XWE. Ottawa. Released September 11, 2013.

Labour Force by Industry (NAICS Codes 11–52)

Area	Agriculture, forestry, fishing & hunting	Mining, quarrying, & oil & gas extraction	Utilities	Construction	Manufacturing	Wholesale Trade	Retail Trade	Transportation & warehousing	Information & cultural industries	Finance & insurance
					Number					
					Total					
Saskatoon	1,550	3,710	530	10,425	8,310	5,520	14,805	5,320	2,685	3,950
Saskatchewan	51,360	22,985	5,330	42,975	26,460	21,135	60,940	25,390	10,900	21,120
Canada	437,650	261,050	149,940	1,215,380	1,619,295	733,445	2,031,665	827,780	420,830	767,960
					Males					
Saskatoon	965	3,040	385	9,250	6,465	4,260	6,980	4,000	1,320	1,300
Saskatchewan	37,210	19,940	3,810	38,140	21,000	15,950	28,545	19,460	5,390	6,425
Canada	307,370	211,690	110,765	1,068,710	1,167,680	494,545	933,850	617,305	235,875	296,995
					Females					
Saskatoon	590	675	145	1,170	1,845	1,255	7,825	1,315	1,365	2,650
Saskatchewan	14,150	3,045	1,520	4,830	5,460	5,185	32,395	5,930	5,510	14,695
Canada	130,285	49,360	39,175	146,670	451,615	238,900	1,097,820	210,475	184,955	470,960
				Percent of Labour Force						
					Total					
Saskatoon	1.2	2.9	0.4	8.2	6.5	4.3	11.6	4.2	2.1	3.1
Saskatchewan	9.3	4.1	1.0	7.7	4.8	3.8	11.0	4.6	2.0	3.8
Canada	2.5	1.5	0.9	6.9	9.2	4.2	11.6	4.7	2.4	4.4
					Males					
Saskatoon	1.4	4.6	0.6	13.8	9.7	6.4	10.4	6.0	2.0	1.9
Saskatchewan	12.5	6.7	1.3	12.9	7.1	5.4	9.6	6.6	1.8	2.2
Canada	3.3	2.3	1.2	11.6	12.7	5.4	10.2	6.7	2.6	3.2
					Females					
Saskatoon	1.0	1.1	0.2	1.9	3.0	2.1	12.8	2.2	2.2	4.3
Saskatchewan	5.5	1.2	0.6	1.9	2.1	2.0	12.6	2.3	2.1	5.7
Canada	1.6	0.6	0.5	1.7	5.4	2.8	13.1	2.5	2.2	5.6

Note: Figures are based on total experienced labour force 15 years and over. Experienced labour force refers to persons who, during the week of Sunday, May 1 to Saturday, May 7, 2011, were employed and the unemployed who had last worked for pay or in self-employment in either 2010 or 2011.
Source: Statistics Canada. 2013. 2011 National Household Survey. Statistics Canada Catalogue no. 99-004-XWE. Ottawa. Released September 11, 2013.

Labour Force by Industry (NAICS Codes 53–91)

Area	Real estate & rental & leasing	Profess., scientific & tech. services	Mgmt of companies & enterprises	Admin. & support, waste mgmt & remed. services	Educational services	Health care & social assistance	Arts, entertain. & recreation	Accomm. & food services	Other services (except public admin.)	Public admin.
					Number					
					Total					
Saskatoon	2,320	8,690	160	3,670	13,700	15,610	2,150	10,205	6,490	7,945
Saskatchewan	7,445	23,520	575	13,425	43,995	65,450	9,825	34,085	25,445	42,335
Canada	321,895	1,240,850	17,460	728,330	1,301,435	1,949,650	363,405	1,130,750	807,800	1,261,050
					Males					
Saskatoon	1,260	4,670	50	2,010	5,665	2,675	1,225	4,325	2,775	4,180
Saskatchewan	4,140	12,180	240	7,390	14,600	9,635	5,035	12,620	12,695	22,310
Canada	179,090	688,625	9,380	411,250	424,915	349,430	188,270	469,990	372,940	652,510
					Females					
Saskatoon	1,060	4,015	105	1,660	8,035	12,940	920	5,880	3,715	3,765
Saskatchewan	3,305	11,345	330	6,035	29,400	55,815	4,795	21,460	12,750	20,025
Canada	142,805	552,225	8,075	317,085	876,515	1,600,220	175,135	660,760	434,865	608,535
				Percent of Labour Force						
					Total					
Saskatoon	1.8	6.8	0.1	2.9	10.7	12.2	1.7	8.0	5.1	6.2
Saskatchewan	1.3	4.2	0.1	2.4	7.9	11.8	1.8	6.1	4.6	7.6
Canada	1.8	7.1	0.1	4.1	7.4	11.1	2.1	6.4	4.6	7.2
					Males					
Saskatoon	1.9	7.0	0.1	3.0	8.5	4.0	1.8	6.5	4.2	6.3
Saskatchewan	1.4	4.1	0.1	2.5	4.9	3.2	1.7	4.3	4.3	7.5
Canada	1.9	7.5	0.1	4.5	4.6	3.8	2.0	5.1	4.1	7.1
					Females					
Saskatoon	1.7	6.6	0.2	2.7	13.2	21.2	1.5	9.6	6.1	6.2
Saskatchewan	1.3	4.4	0.1	2.3	11.4	21.6	1.9	8.3	4.9	7.8
Canada	1.7	6.6	0.1	3.8	10.4	19.1	2.1	7.9	5.2	7.2

Note: Figures are based on total experienced labour force 15 years and over. Experienced labour force refers to persons who, during the week of Sunday, May 1 to Saturday, May 7, 2011, were employed and the unemployed who had last worked for pay or in self-employment in either 2010 or 2011.
Source: Statistics Canada. 2013. 2011 National Household Survey. Statistics Canada Catalogue no. 99-004-XWE. Ottawa. Released September 11, 2013.

PROFILES / Saskatoon, Saskatchewan

Occupation

Area	Mgmt	Business, Finance & Admin.	Natural/ Applied Sciences & Related	Health	Education, Law & Social, Community & Government Services	Art, Culture, Recreation & Sport	Sales & Service	Trades, Transport & Equip. Operators & Related	Natural Resources, Agri. & Related Production	Mfg & Utilities
				Number						
				Total						
Saskatoon	12,660	19,945	8,665	10,350	16,240	2,980	30,805	19,740	2,265	4,095
Saskatchewan	81,235	80,645	26,280	38,800	62,310	10,000	118,755	94,870	26,390	15,445
Canada	1,963,600	2,902,045	1,237,775	1,107,200	2,064,675	503,415	4,068,170	2,537,775	397,930	805,040
				Males						
Saskatoon	7,965	5,620	6,630	2,065	6,075	1,370	13,600	18,575	1,810	3,095
Saskatchewan	54,370	20,530	20,525	6,145	20,645	3,950	47,770	89,055	20,960	12,760
Canada	1,229,460	854,190	966,355	217,520	676,550	232,535	1,745,705	2,385,615	318,945	564,300
				Females						
Saskatoon	4,695	14,325	2,035	8,280	10,165	1,610	17,205	1,165	460	995
Saskatchewan	26,860	60,110	5,750	32,660	41,665	6,045	70,980	5,810	5,430	2,685
Canada	734,140	2,047,855	271,415	889,675	1,388,130	270,875	2,322,465	152,165	78,980	240,740
				Percent of Labour Force						
				Total						
Saskatoon	9.9	15.6	6.8	8.1	12.7	2.3	24.1	15.5	1.8	3.2
Saskatchewan	14.6	14.5	4.7	7.0	11.2	1.8	21.4	17.1	4.8	2.8
Canada	11.2	16.5	7.0	6.3	11.7	2.9	23.1	14.4	2.3	4.6
				Males						
Saskatoon	11.9	8.4	9.9	3.1	9.1	2.1	20.4	27.8	2.7	4.6
Saskatchewan	18.3	6.9	6.9	2.1	7.0	1.3	16.1	30.0	7.1	4.3
Canada	13.4	9.3	10.5	2.4	7.4	2.5	19.0	26.0	3.5	6.1
				Females						
Saskatoon	7.7	23.5	3.3	13.6	16.7	2.6	28.2	1.9	0.8	1.6
Saskatchewan	10.4	23.3	2.2	12.7	16.1	2.3	27.5	2.3	2.1	1.0
Canada	8.7	24.4	3.2	10.6	16.5	3.2	27.7	1.8	0.9	2.9

Note: Figures are based on total experienced labour force 15 years and over
Source: Statistics Canada. 2013. 2011 National Household Survey. Statistics Canada Catalogue no. 99-004-XWE. Ottawa. Released September 11, 2013.

Place of Work Status

Area	Worked at Home	Worked Outside Canada	No Fixed Workplace Address	Worked at Usual Place
		Number		
		Total		
Saskatoon	4,990	220	14,490	102,130
Saskatchewan	59,365	655	64,710	404,365
Canada	1,142,640	66,460	1,868,245	13,517,690
		Males		
Saskatoon	2,410	145	11,150	50,150
Saskatchewan	35,590	455	52,585	193,940
Canada	582,150	47,355	1,400,485	6,604,325
		Females		
Saskatoon	2,575	80	3,340	51,975
Saskatchewan	23,770	200	12,130	210,430
Canada	560,490	19,100	467,760	6,913,370
		Percent of Labour Force		
		Total		
Saskatoon	4.1	0.2	11.9	83.8
Saskatchewan	11.2	0.1	12.2	76.4
Canada	6.9	0.4	11.3	81.5
		Males		
Saskatoon	3.8	0.2	17.5	78.5
Saskatchewan	12.6	0.2	18.6	68.6
Canada	6.7	0.5	16.2	76.5
		Females		
Saskatoon	4.4	0.1	5.8	89.7
Saskatchewan	9.6	0.1	4.9	85.4
Canada	7.0	0.2	5.9	86.8

Note: Figures are based on total employed labour force 15 years and over.
Source: Statistics Canada. 2013. 2011 National Household Survey. Statistics Canada Catalogue no. 99-004-XWE. Ottawa. Released September 11, 2013.

Mode of Transportation to Work

Area	Car; Truck; Van; as Driver	Car; Truck; Van; as Passenger	Public Transit	Walked	Bicycled	All Other Modes
			Number			
			Total			
Saskatoon	92,665	7,055	5,915	6,160	2,600	2,225
Saskatchewan	382,000	28,715	12,990	31,480	5,705	8,185
Canada	11,393,140	867,050	1,851,525	880,815	201,780	191,625
			Males			
Saskatoon	50,235	2,830	2,400	2,630	1,700	1,510
Saskatchewan	206,540	12,025	5,475	13,285	3,970	5,235
Canada	6,238,835	349,530	788,290	387,580	135,840	104,725
			Females			
Saskatoon	42,430	4,225	3,515	3,535	905	710
Saskatchewan	175,460	16,695	7,515	18,200	1,735	2,950
Canada	5,154,305	517,520	1,063,235	493,230	65,940	86,900
			Percent of Labour Force			
			Total			
Saskatoon	79.5	6.0	5.1	5.3	2.2	1.9
Saskatchewan	81.4	6.1	2.8	6.7	1.2	1.7
Canada	74.0	5.6	12.0	5.7	1.3	1.2
			Males			
Saskatoon	81.9	4.6	3.9	4.3	2.8	2.5
Saskatchewan	83.8	4.9	2.2	5.4	1.6	2.1
Canada	77.9	4.4	9.8	4.8	1.7	1.3
			Females			
Saskatoon	76.7	7.6	6.4	6.4	1.6	1.3
Saskatchewan	78.8	7.5	3.4	8.2	0.8	1.3
Canada	69.8	7.0	14.4	6.7	0.9	1.2

Note: Figures are based on total employed labour force 15 years and over.
Source: Statistics Canada. 2013. 2011 National Household Survey. Statistics Canada Catalogue no. 99-004-XWE. Ottawa. Released September 11, 2013.

Visible Minority Population Characteristics

Area	Total Minority	South Asian[1]	Chinese	Black	Filipino	Latin American	Arab	SE Asian[2]	West Asian[3]	Korean	Japanese	Multiple[4]
						Number						
						Total						
Saskatoon	28,025	5,925	5,330	2,480	6,830	1,235	1,410	1,725	1,080	385	280	910
Saskatchewan	63,275	12,325	11,300	7,255	16,025	3,250	2,095	4,910	1,600	1,270	720	1,775
Canada	6,264,750	1,567,400	1,324,750	945,665	619,310	381,280	380,620	312,075	206,840	161,130	87,270	171,935
						Males						
Saskatoon	14,325	3,130	2,545	1,335	3,490	665	755	905	575	200	135	415
Saskatchewan	32,460	6,605	5,535	3,935	7,970	1,610	1,075	2,615	850	675	320	910
Canada	3,043,010	790,755	632,325	453,005	268,885	186,355	203,485	154,035	105,620	77,165	38,270	83,335
						Females						
Saskatoon	13,700	2,800	2,775	1,145	3,345	570	655	820	495	190	145	500
Saskatchewan	30,815	5,715	5,760	3,320	8,055	1,635	1,025	2,300	745	595	400	860
Canada	3,221,745	776,650	692,420	492,660	350,425	194,925	177,140	158,045	101,220	83,965	48,990	88,600
						Percent of Population						
						Total						
Saskatoon	12.8	2.7	2.4	1.1	3.1	0.6	0.6	0.8	0.5	0.2	0.1	0.4
Saskatchewan	6.3	1.2	1.1	0.7	1.6	0.3	0.2	0.5	0.2	0.1	0.1	0.2
Canada	19.1	4.8	4.0	2.9	1.9	1.2	1.2	0.9	0.6	0.5	0.3	0.5
						Males						
Saskatoon	13.4	2.9	2.4	1.2	3.3	0.6	0.7	0.8	0.5	0.2	0.1	0.4
Saskatchewan	6.5	1.3	1.1	0.8	1.6	0.3	0.2	0.5	0.2	0.1	0.1	0.2
Canada	18.8	4.9	3.9	2.8	1.7	1.2	1.3	1.0	0.7	0.5	0.2	0.5
						Females						
Saskatoon	12.3	2.5	2.5	1.0	3.0	0.5	0.6	0.7	0.4	0.2	0.1	0.5
Saskatchewan	6.1	1.1	1.1	0.7	1.6	0.3	0.2	0.5	0.1	0.1	0.1	0.2
Canada	19.3	4.7	4.1	3.0	2.1	1.2	1.1	0.9	0.6	0.5	0.3	0.5

Note: The Employment Equity Act defines visible minorities as 'persons, other than Aboriginal peoples, who are non-Caucasian in race or non-white in colour';
(1) Includes 'East Indian,' 'Pakistani,' 'Sri Lankan,' etc.; (2) Includes 'Vietnamese,' 'Cambodian,' 'Malaysian,' 'Laotian,' etc.; (3) Includes 'Iranian,' 'Afghan,' etc.; (4) Includes respondents who reported more than one visible minority group by checking two or more mark-in circles, e.g., 'Black' and 'South Asian.'
Source: Statistics Canada. 2013. 2011 National Household Survey. Statistics Canada Catalogue no. 99-004-XWE. Ottawa. Released September 11, 2013.

PROFILES / Saskatoon, Saskatchewan

Aboriginal Population

Area	Aboriginal Identity[1]	First Nations (North American Indian) Single Identity[2]	Métis Single Identity	Inuk (Inuit) Single Identity	Multiple Aboriginal Identities[3]	Aboriginal Identities Not Included Elsewhere
			Number Total			
Saskatoon	21,335	10,680	10,095	75	145	345
Saskatchewan	157,740	103,205	52,450	290	675	1,120
Canada	1,400,685	851,560	451,795	59,440	11,415	26,475
			Males			
Saskatoon	9,760	4,735	4,755	40	80	150
Saskatchewan	75,845	50,170	24,780	145	250	500
Canada	682,190	411,785	223,335	29,495	5,525	12,055
			Females			
Saskatoon	11,575	5,945	5,340	30	60	195
Saskatchewan	81,895	53,040	27,670	145	420	620
Canada	718,500	439,775	228,460	29,950	5,890	14,420
			Percent of Population Total			
Saskatoon	9.8	4.9	4.6	0.0	0.1	0.2
Saskatchewan	15.6	10.2	5.2	0.0	0.1	0.1
Canada	4.3	2.6	1.4	0.2	0.0	0.1
			Males			
Saskatoon	9.1	4.4	4.4	0.0	0.1	0.1
Saskatchewan	15.1	10.0	4.9	0.0	0.0	0.1
Canada	4.2	2.5	1.4	0.2	0.0	0.1
			Females			
Saskatoon	10.4	5.4	4.8	0.0	0.1	0.2
Saskatchewan	16.1	10.4	5.5	0.0	0.1	0.1
Canada	4.3	2.6	1.4	0.2	0.0	0.1

Note: (1) Includes persons who reported being an Aboriginal person, that is, First Nations (North American Indian), Métis or Inuk (Inuit) and/or those who reported Registered or Treaty Indian status, that is registered under the Indian Act of Canada, and/or those who reported membership in a First Nation or Indian band. Aboriginal peoples of Canada are defined in the Constitution Act, 1982, section 35-2 as including the Indian, Inuit and Métis peoples of Canada; (2) Users should be aware that the estimates associated with this variable are more affected than most by the incomplete enumeration of certain Indian reserves and Indian settlements in the National Household Survey (NHS); (3) Includes persons who reported being any two or all three of the following: First Nations (North American Indian), Métis or Inuk (Inuit).
Source: Statistics Canada. 2013. 2011 National Household Survey. Statistics Canada Catalogue no. 99-004-XWE. Ottawa. Released September 11, 2013.

Ethnic Origin

Area	North American Aboriginal	Other North American	European	Caribbean	Latin, Central and South American	African	Asian	Oceania
				Number Total				
Saskatoon	22,360	41,605	168,375	705	1,825	2,945	24,760	420
Saskatchewan	161,245	201,245	765,170	2,710	4,990	8,060	55,100	1,350
Canada	1,836,035	11,070,455	20,157,965	627,590	544,375	766,735	5,011,225	74,875
				Males				
Saskatoon	10,600	20,580	82,110	390	895	1,560	12,575	200
Saskatchewan	78,215	100,980	378,270	1,485	2,510	4,355	28,140	750
Canada	885,675	5,462,685	9,913,150	291,640	264,635	387,360	2,435,540	37,490
				Females				
Saskatoon	11,760	21,025	86,265	310	930	1,385	12,185	220
Saskatchewan	83,030	100,260	386,900	1,220	2,480	3,710	26,955	595
Canada	950,360	5,607,770	10,244,820	335,945	279,740	379,380	2,575,680	37,385
				Percent of Population Total				
Saskatoon	10.2	19.1	77.1	0.3	0.8	1.3	11.3	0.2
Saskatchewan	16.0	19.9	75.9	0.3	0.5	0.8	5.5	0.1
Canada	5.6	33.7	61.4	1.9	1.7	2.3	15.3	0.2
				Males				
Saskatoon	9.9	19.2	76.6	0.4	0.8	1.5	11.7	0.2
Saskatchewan	15.6	20.1	75.5	0.3	0.5	0.9	5.6	0.1
Canada	5.5	33.8	61.3	1.8	1.6	2.4	15.1	0.2
				Females				
Saskatoon	10.6	18.9	77.6	0.3	0.8	1.2	11.0	0.2
Saskatchewan	16.4	19.8	76.2	0.2	0.5	0.7	5.3	0.1
Canada	5.7	33.6	61.4	2.0	1.7	2.3	15.4	0.2

Note: The sum of the ethnic groups in this table is greater than the total population estimate because a person may report more than one ethnic origin in the NHS.
Source: Statistics Canada. 2013. 2011 National Household Survey. Statistics Canada Catalogue no. 99-004-XWE. Ottawa. Released September 11, 2013.

Religion

Area	Buddhist	Christian	Hindu	Jewish	Muslim	Sikh	Traditional (Aboriginal) Spirituality	Other Religions	No Religious Affiliation
				Number Total					
Saskatoon	1,670	144,200	1,575	420	5,655	580	1,080	850	62,285
Saskatchewan	4,265	726,920	3,570	940	10,040	1,650	12,240	2,810	246,305
Canada	366,830	22,102,745	497,965	329,495	1,053,945	454,965	64,935	130,835	7,850,605
				Males					
Saskatoon	820	66,865	810	225	2,930	360	435	445	34,330
Saskatchewan	2,060	347,455	1,985	535	5,150	935	6,195	1,295	135,535
Canada	168,465	10,497,775	250,435	161,265	540,555	229,435	31,805	57,745	4,225,645
				Females					
Saskatoon	855	77,335	770	190	2,725	220	645	410	27,950
Saskatchewan	2,205	379,465	1,580	410	4,890	715	6,045	1,525	110,775
Canada	198,365	11,604,975	247,525	168,235	513,395	225,530	33,135	73,090	3,624,965
				Percent of Population Total					
Saskatoon	0.8	66.0	0.7	0.2	2.6	0.3	0.5	0.4	28.5
Saskatchewan	0.4	72.1	0.4	0.1	1.0	0.2	1.2	0.3	24.4
Canada	1.1	67.3	1.5	1.0	3.2	1.4	0.2	0.4	23.9
				Males					
Saskatoon	0.8	62.4	0.8	0.2	2.7	0.3	0.4	0.4	32.0
Saskatchewan	0.4	69.3	0.4	0.1	1.0	0.2	1.2	0.3	27.0
Canada	1.0	64.9	1.5	1.0	3.3	1.4	0.2	0.4	26.1
				Females					
Saskatoon	0.8	69.6	0.7	0.2	2.5	0.2	0.6	0.4	25.2
Saskatchewan	0.4	74.8	0.3	0.1	1.0	0.1	1.2	0.3	21.8
Canada	1.2	69.5	1.5	1.0	3.1	1.4	0.2	0.4	21.7

Note: Religion refers to the person's self-identification as having a connection or affiliation with any religious denomination, group, body, sect, cult or other religiously defined community or system of belief. Religion is not limited to formal membership in a religious organization or group. Persons without a religious connection or affiliation can self-identify as atheist, agnostic or humanist, or can provide another applicable response.
Source: Statistics Canada. 2013. 2011 National Household Survey. Statistics Canada Catalogue no. 99-004-XWE. Ottawa. Released September 11, 2013.

Religion—Christian Denominations

Area	Anglican	Baptist	Catholic	Christian Orthodox	Lutheran	Pentecostal	Presbyterian	United Church	Other Christian
				Number Total					
Saskatoon	8,300	3,495	62,190	3,120	9,185	3,130	1,585	23,715	29,475
Saskatchewan	54,645	16,270	297,860	12,140	63,765	16,215	7,990	134,835	123,195
Canada	1,631,845	635,840	12,810,705	550,690	478,185	478,705	472,385	2,007,610	3,036,780
				Males					
Saskatoon	3,640	1,585	29,535	1,330	4,280	1,435	690	10,380	13,990
Saskatchewan	25,810	7,780	145,055	5,795	29,435	7,555	3,765	61,825	60,430
Canada	752,945	293,905	6,167,290	270,205	221,525	217,850	218,955	912,545	1,442,550
				Females					
Saskatoon	4,665	1,910	32,650	1,795	4,905	1,705	895	13,335	15,485
Saskatchewan	28,840	8,495	152,805	6,340	34,325	8,665	4,225	73,010	62,765
Canada	878,900	341,940	6,643,415	280,485	256,660	260,850	253,430	1,095,065	1,594,230
				Percent of Population Total					
Saskatoon	3.8	1.6	28.5	1.4	4.2	1.4	0.7	10.9	13.5
Saskatchewan	5.4	1.6	29.5	1.2	6.3	1.6	0.8	13.4	12.2
Canada	5.0	1.9	39.0	1.7	1.5	1.5	1.4	6.1	9.2
				Males					
Saskatoon	3.4	1.5	27.5	1.2	4.0	1.3	0.6	9.7	13.0
Saskatchewan	5.2	1.6	28.9	1.2	5.9	1.5	0.8	12.3	12.1
Canada	4.7	1.8	38.2	1.7	1.4	1.3	1.4	5.6	8.9
				Females					
Saskatoon	4.2	1.7	29.4	1.6	4.4	1.5	0.8	12.0	13.9
Saskatchewan	5.7	1.7	30.1	1.2	6.8	1.7	0.8	14.4	12.4
Canada	5.3	2.0	39.8	1.7	1.5	1.6	1.5	6.6	9.6

Note: Religion refers to the person's self-identification as having a connection or affiliation with any religious denomination, group, body, sect, cult or other religiously defined community or system of belief. Religion is not limited to formal membership in a religious organization or group. Persons without a religious connection or affiliation can self-identify as atheist, agnostic or humanist, or can provide another applicable response.
Source: Statistics Canada. 2013. 2011 National Household Survey. Statistics Canada Catalogue no. 99-004-XWE. Ottawa. Released September 11, 2013.

PROFILES / Saskatoon, Saskatchewan

Immigrant Status and Period of Immigration

Area	Non-Immigrants[1]	Immigrants All	Before 1971	1971 to 1980	1981 to 1990	1991 to 2000	2001 to 2005	2006 to 2011	Non-Permanent Residents[3]
Number									
Total									
Saskatoon	188,815	26,050	3,520	2,045	2,195	3,590	3,505	11,190	3,455
Saskatchewan	931,710	68,780	12,720	6,300	6,020	8,855	7,955	26,920	8,270
Canada	25,720,175	6,775,765	1,261,055	870,775	949,890	1,539,050	992,070	1,162,915	356,385
Males									
Saskatoon	92,135	13,110	1,665	1,025	1,165	1,765	1,820	5,670	1,975
Saskatchewan	462,535	33,780	5,935	3,230	2,880	4,345	3,905	13,500	4,830
Canada	12,753,235	3,231,370	605,430	416,670	454,570	724,905	474,545	555,245	178,515
Females									
Saskatoon	96,690	12,935	1,850	1,025	1,035	1,825	1,685	5,515	1,480
Saskatchewan	469,175	34,995	6,790	3,065	3,145	4,515	4,050	13,425	3,445
Canada	12,966,935	3,544,400	655,625	454,105	495,325	814,145	517,530	607,670	177,870
Percent of Population									
Total									
Saskatoon	86.5	11.9	1.6	0.9	1.0	1.6	1.6	5.1	1.6
Saskatchewan	92.4	6.8	1.3	0.6	0.6	0.9	0.8	2.7	0.8
Canada	78.3	20.6	3.8	2.7	2.9	4.7	3.0	3.5	1.1
Males									
Saskatoon	85.9	12.2	1.6	1.0	1.1	1.6	1.7	5.3	1.8
Saskatchewan	92.3	6.7	1.2	0.6	0.6	0.9	0.8	2.7	1.0
Canada	78.9	20.0	3.7	2.6	2.8	4.5	2.9	3.4	1.1
Females									
Saskatoon	87.0	11.6	1.7	0.9	0.9	1.6	1.5	5.0	1.3
Saskatchewan	92.4	6.9	1.3	0.6	0.6	0.9	0.8	2.6	0.7
Canada	77.7	21.2	3.9	2.7	3.0	4.9	3.1	3.6	1.1

Note: (1) Non-immigrant refers to a person who is a Canadian citizen by birth; (2) Immigrant refers to a person who is or has ever been a landed immigrant/permanent resident. This person has been granted the right to live in Canada permanently by immigration authorities. Some immigrants have resided in Canada for a number of years, while others have arrived recently. Some immigrants are Canadian citizens, while others are not. Most immigrants are born outside Canada, but a small number are born in Canada. In the 2011 National Household Survey, 'Immigrants' includes immigrants who landed in Canada prior to May 10, 2011; (3) Non-permanent resident refers to a person from another country who has a work or study permit, or who is a refugee claimant, and any non-Canadian-born family member living in Canada with them.
Source: Statistics Canada. 2013. 2011 National Household Survey. Statistics Canada Catalogue no. 99-004-XWE. Ottawa. Released September 11, 2013.

Mother Tongue

Area	English	French	Non-official Language	English & French	English & Non-official Language	French & Non-official Language	English, French & Non-official Language
Number							
Total							
Saskatoon	178,470	3,240	33,410	465	2,720	300	60
Saskatchewan	860,500	16,280	129,035	1,730	9,850	750	175
Canada	18,858,980	7,054,975	6,567,680	144,685	396,330	74,430	24,095
Males							
Saskatoon	87,795	1,480	16,270	225	1,275	150	30
Saskatchewan	428,115	7,760	63,245	805	4,720	360	75
Canada	9,345,225	3,452,380	3,157,785	69,975	192,000	36,535	11,965
Females							
Saskatoon	90,675	1,760	17,135	245	1,445	150	30
Saskatchewan	432,385	8,525	65,785	920	5,125	390	95
Canada	9,513,750	3,602,590	3,409,895	74,710	204,330	37,890	12,130
Percent of Population							
Total							
Saskatoon	81.6	1.5	15.3	0.2	1.2	0.1	0.0
Saskatchewan	84.5	1.6	12.7	0.2	1.0	0.1	0.0
Canada	56.9	21.3	19.8	0.4	1.2	0.2	0.1
Males							
Saskatoon	81.9	1.4	15.2	0.2	1.2	0.1	0.0
Saskatchewan	84.8	1.5	12.5	0.2	0.9	0.1	0.0
Canada	57.5	21.2	19.4	0.4	1.2	0.2	0.1
Females							
Saskatoon	81.4	1.6	15.4	0.2	1.3	0.1	0.0
Saskatchewan	84.2	1.7	12.8	0.2	1.0	0.1	0.0
Canada	56.4	21.4	20.2	0.4	1.2	0.2	0.1

Note: Figures cover total population excluding institutional residents.
Source: Statistics Canada. 2012. Census Profile. 2011 Census. Statistics Canada Catalogue no. 98-316-XWE. Ottawa. Released October 24 2012.
http://www12.statcan.gc.ca/census-recensement/2011/dp-pd/prof/index.cfm?Lang=E

Language Spoken Most Often at Home

Area	English	French	Non-official Language	English & French	English & Non-official Language	French & Non-official Language	English, French & Non-official Language
			Number				
			Total				
Saskatoon	196,180	860	15,905	245	5,290	110	75
Saskatchewan	938,170	4,295	59,240	855	15,360	205	185
Canada	21,457,075	6,827,865	3,673,865	131,205	875,135	109,700	46,330
			Males				
Saskatoon	95,920	400	8,125	115	2,575	55	30
Saskatchewan	465,005	1,990	30,005	400	7,500	110	75
Canada	10,585,620	3,348,235	1,767,310	63,475	425,370	53,010	22,845
			Females				
Saskatoon	100,260	465	7,780	135	2,715	50	45
Saskatchewan	473,170	2,305	29,230	460	7,860	95	110
Canada	10,871,455	3,479,625	1,906,555	67,730	449,765	56,690	23,485
			Percent of Population				
			Total				
Saskatoon	89.7	0.4	7.3	0.1	2.4	0.1	0.0
Saskatchewan	92.1	0.4	5.8	0.1	1.5	0.0	0.0
Canada	64.8	20.6	11.1	0.4	2.6	0.3	0.1
			Males				
Saskatoon	89.5	0.4	7.6	0.1	2.4	0.1	0.0
Saskatchewan	92.1	0.4	5.9	0.1	1.5	0.0	0.0
Canada	65.1	20.6	10.9	0.4	2.6	0.3	0.1
			Females				
Saskatoon	90.0	0.4	7.0	0.1	2.4	0.0	0.0
Saskatchewan	92.2	0.4	5.7	0.1	1.5	0.0	0.0
Canada	64.5	20.6	11.3	0.4	2.7	0.3	0.1

Note: Figures cover total population excluding institutional residents.
Source: Statistics Canada. 2012. Census Profile. 2011 Census. Statistics Canada Catalogue no. 98-316-XWE. Ottawa. Released October 24 2012.
http://www12.statcan.gc.ca/census-recensement/2011/dp-pd/prof/index.cfm?Lang=E

Knowledge of Official Languages

Area	English Only	French Only	English & French	Neither English nor French
		Number		
		Total		
Saskatoon	202,610	105	13,930	2,020
Saskatchewan	965,920	430	46,570	5,395
Canada	22,564,665	4,165,015	5,795,570	595,920
		Males		
Saskatoon	100,085	45	6,175	915
Saskatchewan	481,535	195	20,855	2,505
Canada	11,222,185	1,925,340	2,876,560	241,790
		Females		
Saskatoon	102,525	60	7,755	1,105
Saskatchewan	484,390	235	25,715	2,885
Canada	11,342,485	2,239,680	2,919,005	354,135
		Percent of Population		
		Total		
Saskatoon	92.7	0.0	6.4	0.9
Saskatchewan	94.9	0.0	4.6	0.5
Canada	68.1	12.6	17.5	1.8
		Males		
Saskatoon	93.3	0.0	5.8	0.9
Saskatchewan	95.3	0.0	4.1	0.5
Canada	69.0	11.8	17.7	1.5
		Females		
Saskatoon	92.0	0.1	7.0	1.0
Saskatchewan	94.4	0.0	5.0	0.6
Canada	67.3	13.3	17.3	2.1

Note: Figures cover total population excluding institutional residents.
Source: Statistics Canada. 2012. Census Profile. 2011 Census. Statistics Canada Catalogue no. 98-316-XWE. Ottawa. Released October 24 2012.
http://www12.statcan.gc.ca/census-recensement/2011/dp-pd/prof/index.cfm?Lang=E

Sherbrooke, Québec

Background

Sherbrooke is located in the Eastern Township region of Québec and is the only major city in the Eastern Region. The city is situated at the confluence of the Magog and Saint-François rivers and at the crossroads of major highways with Montréal 148 kilometres to the west and Québec City 235 kilometres to the northeast.

Sherbrooke was originally a fur-trading post. The area was settled by Loyalist farmers in the early 19th century who gradually converted the area into a grist-milling centre. In 1818, the village was named after the Governor General of Canada, Sir John Coape Sherbrooke.

A portion of Québec's almost 5,000 kilometre trail system, *La Route Verte* (in English, the "Green Route" or the "Greenway") is accessible in Sherbrooke. The city's marshland park features boardwalk-style trails with interpretive displays, guided tours and picnic areas. Municipal greenhouses growing annuals, perennials, cacti and fruits and vegetables are open to the public. Just outside city limits, Parc National de Frontenac and Lake Saint-François offer all-season activities such as hiking, canoeing, snowshoeing and cross-country skiing.

Sherbrooke has two bilingual universities: the University of Sherbrooke and Bishop's University. Nearly 50 research centres are based in the region as well as two science and research parks and four industrial zones. The city's economy is a blend of science and technology and manufacturing industries. Specific key sectors include life sciences, information and communication technologies, micro-nano technologies, advanced manufacturing and environmental technologies.

Popular attractions include the Museum of Science and Nature and the Sherbrooke Historical Interpretation Centre. The city hosts annual community-minded festivities such as the Fête du Lac des Nations (fireworks festival) and the Traditions of the World Festival. Sherbrooke is the host of the 2013 Canada Summer Games.

Sherbrooke has summer highs of plus 23.37 degrees Celsius, winter lows of minus 16.07 degrees Celsius, and an average rainfall just over 873 mm per year.

Rankings

- Sherbrooke ranked the best place to do business out of 40 Canadian cities. *Canadian Business Magazine* used the following criteria: annual operating costs, cost of living index, building permit average growth (%), unemployment variance from 5.5%, and crime rate per 100,000 people. Lévis (QC) and Québec City ranked #2 and #3 respectively. *Canadian Business Magazine, "Best Places to do Business in Canada," 2008*
- Sherbrooke moved up two spots from the previous year in the reputation category of the *Maclean's 2011 University Rankings*. Forty-nine Canadian universities were divided into three categories based on levels of research funding, offerings and range of graduate programs. The University of Sherbrooke was ranked #14 overall out of 15 universities in the "medical doctoral" category. Indicators: quality of students, faculty, libraries, reputation and finances. *Maclean's Magazine, "2011 University Rankings," October 26th, 2011*
- Sherbrooke ranked #4 out of Canada's 30 largest towns and cities for citizens' satisfaction with delivery of municipal services. The Forum Research poll defined services as the maintenance of parks and community centres, garbage collection, fire services, police services, libraries, road maintenance, snow removal and public transportation. When polled about municipal services, 38% of Sherbrooke residents expressed "very satisfied" responses. Québec City ranked #1 with 52% of respondents expressing a high level of satisfaction. *Forum Research, Nationwide Municipal Issues Poll, released May 2012*

PROFILES / Sherbrooke, Québec

Population Growth and Density

Area	Population in 2001	Population in 2006	Population in 2011	Population Change 2001–2006	Population Change 2006–2011	Land Area (sq. km)	Population Density per sq. km
Sherbrooke	138,785	147,427	154,601	6.2	4.9	353.49	437.4
Québec	7,237,479	7,546,131	7,903,001	4.3	4.7	1,356,547.02	5.8
Canada	30,007,094	31,612,897	33,476,688	5.4	5.9	8,965,121.42	3.7

Source: Statistics Canada. 2012. Census Profile. 2011 Census. Statistics Canada Catalogue no. 98-316-XWE. Ottawa. Released October 24 2012.
http://www12.statcan.gc.ca/census-recensement/2011/dp-pd/prof/index.cfm?Lang=E;
Statistics Canada 2007. 2006 Community Profiles. 2006 Census. Statistics Canada Catalogue no. 92-591-XWE. Ottawa. Released March 13 2007.
http://www12.statcan.ca/census-recensement/2006/dp-pd/prof/92-591/index.cfm?Lang=E

Gender

Area	Males	Females
	Number	
Sherbrooke	74,765	79,835
Québec	3,875,860	4,027,140
Canada	16,414,225	17,062,460
	Percent of Population	
Sherbrooke	48.4	51.6
Québec	49.0	51.0
Canada	49.0	51.0

Source: Statistics Canada. 2012. Census Profile. 2011 Census. Statistics Canada Catalogue no. 98-316-XWE. Ottawa. Released October 24 2012.
http://www12.statcan.gc.ca/census-recensement/2011/dp-pd/prof/index.cfm?Lang=E

Marital Status

Area	Married[1]	Living Common-law	Single[2]	Separated	Divorced	Widowed
			Number			
			Total			
Sherbrooke	39,345	30,280	40,600	1,760	10,720	7,650
Québec	2,353,770	1,391,550	1,942,090	105,195	463,830	387,945
Canada	12,941,960	3,142,525	7,816,045	698,240	1,686,035	1,584,530
			Males			
Sherbrooke	19,645	15,110	21,205	750	4,105	1,420
Québec	1,177,720	697,695	1,045,540	46,465	188,265	77,430
Canada	6,470,300	1,575,495	4,206,320	299,655	680,415	310,940
			Females			
Sherbrooke	19,695	15,165	19,395	1,015	6,615	6,225
Québec	1,176,050	693,850	896,545	58,720	275,565	310,515
Canada	6,471,660	1,567,035	3,609,730	398,585	1,005,620	1,273,590
			Percent of Population			
			Total			
Sherbrooke	30.2	23.2	31.1	1.4	8.2	5.9
Québec	35.4	20.9	29.2	1.6	7.0	5.8
Canada	46.4	11.3	28.0	2.5	6.0	5.7
			Males			
Sherbrooke	31.6	24.3	34.1	1.2	6.6	2.3
Québec	36.4	21.6	32.3	1.4	5.8	2.4
Canada	47.8	11.6	31.1	2.2	5.0	2.3
			Females			
Sherbrooke	28.9	22.3	28.5	1.5	9.7	9.1
Québec	34.5	20.3	26.3	1.7	8.1	9.1
Canada	45.2	10.9	25.2	2.8	7.0	8.9

Note: (1) and not separated, (2) never legally married
Source: Statistics Canada. 2012. Census Profile. 2011 Census. Statistics Canada Catalogue no. 98-316-XWE. Ottawa. Released October 24 2012.
http://www12.statcan.gc.ca/census-recensement/2011/dp-pd/prof/index.cfm?Lang=E

PROFILES / Sherbrooke, Québec

Age Characteristics: 0 to 49 Years

Area	0 to 4 Years	5 to 9 Years	10 to 14 Years	15 to 19 Years	20 to 24 Years	25 to 29 Years	30 to 34 Years	35 to 39 Years	40 to 44 Years	45 to 49 Years
					Number					
					Total					
Sherbrooke	8,370	7,655	8,220	9,820	12,470	11,115	10,330	8,975	9,220	11,025
Québec	440,840	399,575	418,205	491,980	489,185	490,665	531,445	498,225	520,805	623,575
Canada	1,877,095	1,809,895	1,920,355	2,178,135	2,187,450	2,169,590	2,162,905	2,173,930	2,324,875	2,675,130
					Males					
Sherbrooke	4,245	3,945	4,340	4,915	6,280	5,725	5,200	4,435	4,640	5,430
Québec	225,525	203,675	213,540	249,960	246,850	245,695	264,980	249,610	261,120	311,320
Canada	961,150	925,965	983,995	1,115,845	1,108,775	1,077,275	1,058,810	1,064,200	1,141,720	1,318,715
					Females					
Sherbrooke	4,125	3,710	3,885	4,900	6,190	5,385	5,125	4,540	4,580	5,590
Québec	215,320	195,900	204,665	242,020	242,340	244,970	266,460	248,615	259,690	312,250
Canada	915,945	883,935	936,360	1,062,295	1,078,670	1,092,315	1,104,095	1,109,735	1,183,155	1,356,420
					Percent of Population					
					Total					
Sherbrooke	5.4	5.0	5.3	6.4	8.1	7.2	6.7	5.8	6.0	7.1
Québec	5.6	5.1	5.3	6.2	6.2	6.2	6.7	6.3	6.6	7.9
Canada	5.6	5.4	5.7	6.5	6.5	6.5	6.5	6.5	6.9	8.0
					Males					
Sherbrooke	5.7	5.3	5.8	6.6	8.4	7.7	7.0	5.9	6.2	7.3
Québec	5.8	5.3	5.5	6.4	6.4	6.3	6.8	6.4	6.7	8.0
Canada	5.9	5.6	6.0	6.8	6.8	6.6	6.5	6.5	7.0	8.0
					Females					
Sherbrooke	5.2	4.6	4.9	6.1	7.8	6.7	6.4	5.7	5.7	7.0
Québec	5.3	4.9	5.1	6.0	6.0	6.1	6.6	6.2	6.4	7.8
Canada	5.4	5.2	5.5	6.2	6.3	6.4	6.5	6.5	6.9	7.9

Source: Statistics Canada. 2012. Census Profile. 2011 Census. Statistics Canada Catalogue no. 98-316-XWE. Ottawa. Released October 24 2012.
http://www12.statcan.gc.ca/census-recensement/2011/dp-pd/prof/index.cfm?Lang=E

Age Characteristics: 50 Years and Over, and Median Age

Area	50 to 54 Years	55 to 59 Years	60 to 64 Years	65 to 69 Years	70 to 74 Years	75 to 79 Years	80 to 84 Years	85 Years and Over	Median Age
				Number					
				Total					
Sherbrooke	11,555	10,880	9,785	7,790	5,445	4,570	3,600	3,785	40.2
Québec	648,695	579,280	512,830	403,210	291,755	232,355	176,420	153,945	41.9
Canada	2,658,965	2,340,635	2,052,670	1,521,715	1,153,065	922,700	702,070	645,515	40.6
				Males					
Sherbrooke	5,530	5,160	4,630	3,665	2,435	1,865	1,270	1,045	38.0
Québec	320,695	285,295	250,675	194,305	135,830	101,675	69,170	45,945	40.7
Canada	1,309,030	1,147,300	1,002,690	738,010	543,435	417,945	291,085	208,300	39.6
				Females					
Sherbrooke	6,025	5,715	5,155	4,125	3,005	2,705	2,325	2,735	42.3
Québec	327,995	293,990	262,155	208,905	155,925	130,680	107,250	108,005	43.0
Canada	1,349,940	1,193,335	1,049,985	783,705	609,630	504,755	410,985	437,215	41.5
				Percent of Population					
				Total					
Sherbrooke	7.5	7.0	6.3	5.0	3.5	3.0	2.3	2.4	—
Québec	8.2	7.3	6.5	5.1	3.7	2.9	2.2	1.9	—
Canada	7.9	7.0	6.1	4.5	3.4	2.8	2.1	1.9	—
				Males					
Sherbrooke	7.4	6.9	6.2	4.9	3.3	2.5	1.7	1.4	—
Québec	8.3	7.4	6.5	5.0	3.5	2.6	1.8	1.2	—
Canada	8.0	7.0	6.1	4.5	3.3	2.5	1.8	1.3	—
				Females					
Sherbrooke	7.5	7.2	6.5	5.2	3.8	3.4	2.9	3.4	—
Québec	8.1	7.3	6.5	5.2	3.9	3.2	2.7	2.7	—
Canada	7.9	7.0	6.2	4.6	3.6	3.0	2.4	2.6	—

Source: Statistics Canada. 2012. Census Profile. 2011 Census. Statistics Canada Catalogue no. 98-316-XWE. Ottawa. Released October 24 2012.
http://www12.statcan.gc.ca/census-recensement/2011/dp-pd/prof/index.cfm?Lang=E

PROFILES / Sherbrooke, Québec

Private Households by Household Size

Area	1 Person	2 Persons	3 Persons	4 Persons	5 Persons	6 or More Persons	Average Number of Persons in Private Households
			Households				
Sherbrooke	26,355	24,555	8,820	7,370	2,495	980	2.1
Québec	1,094,410	1,181,240	496,140	421,080	142,555	59,920	2.3
Canada	3,673,310	4,544,820	2,081,900	1,903,300	724,405	392,885	2.5
			Percent of Households				
Sherbrooke	37.3	34.8	12.5	10.4	3.5	1.4	—
Québec	32.2	34.8	14.6	12.4	4.2	1.8	—
Canada	27.6	34.1	15.6	14.3	5.4	2.9	—

Source: Statistics Canada. 2012. Census Profile. 2011 Census. Statistics Canada Catalogue no. 98-316-XWE. Ottawa. Released October 24 2012.
http://www12.statcan.gc.ca/census-recensement/2011/dp-pd/prof/index.cfm?Lang=E

Dwelling Type

Area	Single-detached House	Semi-detached House	Row House	Apartment: Building with Five or More Storeys	Apartment: Building with Fewer Than Five Storeys	Duplex Apartment	Movable Dwelling	Other Single-attached House
				Number				
Sherbrooke	27,375	2,930	1,580	2,120	31,650	4,280	405	230
Québec	1,560,405	171,435	86,040	171,115	1,103,845	263,860	22,995	15,645
Canada	7,329,150	646,245	791,600	1,234,770	2,397,550	704,485	183,510	33,310
				Percent of Dwellings				
Sherbrooke	38.8	4.2	2.2	3.0	44.8	6.1	0.6	0.3
Québec	46.0	5.0	2.5	5.0	32.5	7.8	0.7	0.5
Canada	55.0	4.9	5.9	9.3	18.0	5.3	1.4	0.3

Source: Statistics Canada. 2012. Census Profile. 2011 Census. Statistics Canada Catalogue no. 98-316-XWE. Ottawa. Released October 24 2012.
http://www12.statcan.gc.ca/census-recensement/2011/dp-pd/prof/index.cfm?Lang=E

Shelter Costs

	Owned Dwellings					Rented Dwellings		
Area	Number	Median Value[1] ($)	Average Value[1] ($)	Median Monthly Costs[2] ($)	Average Monthly Costs[2] ($)	Number	Median Monthly Costs[3] ($)	Average Monthly Costs[3] ($)
Sherbrooke	35,570	189,838	212,463	880	903	34,955	582	626
Québec	2,056,665	214,537	249,427	841	936	1,308,465	643	685
Canada	9,013,410	280,552	345,182	978	1,141	4,060,385	784	848

Note: All figures cover non-farm, non-reserve private dwellings; (1) Refers to the dollar amount expected by the owner if the dwelling were to be sold; (2) Includes all shelter expenses paid by households that own their dwellings, such as the mortgage payment and the costs of electricity, heat, water and other municipal services, property taxes and condominium fees; (3) Includes all shelter expenses paid by households that rent their dwellings, such as the monthly rent and the costs of electricity, heat and municipal services.
Source: Statistics Canada. 2013. 2011 National Household Survey. Statistics Canada Catalogue no. 99-004-XWE. Ottawa. Released September 11, 2013.

Occupied Private Dwellings by Period of Construction

Area	1960 or Before	1961 to 1980	1981 to 1990	1991 to 2000	2001 to 2005	2006 to 2011
			Number			
Sherbrooke	16,220	22,360	12,270	9,135	4,640	5,945
Québec	946,900	1,115,455	533,790	353,355	206,035	239,685
Canada	3,273,105	4,152,715	2,112,110	1,707,880	1,031,020	1,042,430
			Percent of Dwellings			
Sherbrooke	23.0	31.7	17.4	12.9	6.6	8.4
Québec	27.9	32.9	15.7	10.4	6.1	7.1
Canada	24.6	31.2	15.9	12.8	7.7	7.8

Note: Figures cover non-farm, non-reserve private dwellings and includes data up to May 10, 2011.
Source: Statistics Canada. 2013. 2011 National Household Survey. Statistics Canada Catalogue no. 99-004-XWE. Ottawa. Released September 11, 2013.

Educational Attainment

Area	No Certificate, Diploma or Degree	High School Diploma or Equivalent[1]	Apprenticeship or Trades Certificate or Diploma[2]	College, CÉGEP or Other Non-University Certificate or Diploma	University Certificate or Diploma Below the Bachelor Level[3]	Bachelor's Degree	University Certificate, Diploma or Degree Above Bachelor Level[4]
			Number Total				
Sherbrooke	25,275	26,295	21,305	22,640	5,325	14,920	10,295
Québec	1,436,025	1,404,755	1,049,470	1,075,855	305,330	766,100	437,050
Canada	5,485,400	6,968,935	2,950,685	4,970,020	1,200,130	3,634,425	2,049,930
			Males				
Sherbrooke	12,560	12,340	12,490	9,530	2,095	6,365	5,380
Québec	714,090	650,660	635,435	472,360	126,565	343,535	227,990
Canada	2,742,875	3,305,415	1,928,970	2,118,430	513,235	1,643,080	1,043,350
			Females				
Sherbrooke	12,715	13,955	8,820	13,105	3,235	8,555	4,910
Québec	721,930	754,095	414,035	603,495	178,765	422,565	209,065
Canada	2,742,520	3,663,515	1,021,715	2,851,595	686,890	1,991,345	1,006,585
			Percent of Population Total				
Sherbrooke	20.1	20.9	16.9	18.0	4.2	11.8	8.2
Québec	22.2	21.7	16.2	16.6	4.7	11.8	6.8
Canada	20.1	25.6	10.8	18.2	4.4	13.3	7.5
			Males				
Sherbrooke	20.7	20.3	20.6	15.7	3.4	10.5	8.9
Québec	22.5	20.5	20.0	14.9	4.0	10.8	7.2
Canada	20.6	24.9	14.5	15.9	3.9	12.4	7.8
			Females				
Sherbrooke	19.5	21.4	13.5	20.1	5.0	13.1	7.5
Québec	21.9	22.8	12.5	18.3	5.4	12.8	6.3
Canada	19.6	26.2	7.3	20.4	4.9	14.3	7.2

Note: Figures cover total population aged 15 years and over by highest certificate, diploma or degree; (1) Includes persons who have graduated from a secondary school or equivalent. It excludes persons with a postsecondary certificate, diploma or degree; (2) Includes Registered Apprenticeship certificates (including Certificate of Qualification, Journeyperson's designation) and other trades certificates or diplomas such as pre-employment or vocational certificates and diplomas from brief trade programs completed at community colleges, institutes of technology, vocational centres, and similar institutions; (3) Comparisons with other data sources suggest that the category 'University certificate or diploma below the bachelor's level' was over-reported in the NHS. This category likely includes some responses that are actually college certificates or diplomas, bachelor's degrees or other types of education (e.g., university transfer programs, bachelor's programs completed in other countries, incomplete bachelor's programs, non-university professional designations). We recommend users interpret the results for the 'University certificate or diploma below the bachelor's level' category with caution; (4) 'University certificate or diploma above bachelor level' includes the categories: 'Degree in medicine, dentistry, veterinary medicine or optometry,' 'Master's degree' and 'Earned doctorate.'
Source: Statistics Canada. 2013. 2011 National Household Survey. Statistics Canada Catalogue no. 99-004-XWE. Ottawa. Released September 11, 2013.

Household Income Distribution

Area	Less than $10,000	$10,000 to $19,999	$20,000 to $29,999	$30,000 to $39,999	$40,000 to $49,999	$50,000 to $59,999	$60,000 to $79,999	$80,000 to $99,999	$100,000 to $124,999	$125,000 to $149,999	$150,000 and Over
					Households						
Sherbrooke	4,030	10,250	8,945	8,390	7,235	5,785	9,475	6,490	4,550	2,465	2,955
Québec	179,790	377,210	353,470	382,000	343,730	302,595	483,085	344,435	267,995	148,950	211,965
Canada	626,705	1,141,945	1,193,925	1,271,675	1,206,800	1,102,120	1,865,280	1,458,240	1,260,770	802,555	1,389,240
					Percent of Households						
Sherbrooke	5.7	14.5	12.7	11.9	10.3	8.2	13.4	9.2	6.4	3.5	4.2
Québec	5.3	11.1	10.4	11.3	10.1	8.9	14.2	10.1	7.9	4.4	6.2
Canada	4.7	8.6	9.0	9.5	9.1	8.3	14.0	10.9	9.5	6.0	10.4

Note: Household income is the sum of the total incomes of all members of that household. Total income refers to monetary receipts from certain sources, before income taxes and deductions, during calendar year 2010.
Source: Statistics Canada. 2013. 2011 National Household Survey. Statistics Canada Catalogue no. 99-004-XWE. Ottawa. Released September 11, 2013.

Median and Average Household and Economic Family Income

Area	Median Household Income ($)	Average Household Income ($)	Median After-tax Household Income ($)	Average After-tax Household Income ($)	Median Economic Family Income ($)	Average Economic Family Income ($)	Median After-tax Economic Family Income ($)	Average After-tax Economic Family Income ($)
Sherbrooke	44,551	57,859	40,249	48,970	64,558	75,508	56,587	63,559
Québec	51,842	66,205	45,968	55,121	68,344	82,045	59,560	68,091
Canada	61,072	79,102	54,089	66,149	76,511	94,125	67,044	78,517

Note: Figures cover household and economic family income in 2010. A household is defined as a person or a group of persons (other than foreign residents) who occupy the same private dwelling and do not have a usual place of residence elsewhere in Canada. Every person is a member of one and only one household. An economic family is defined as a group of two or more persons who live in the same dwelling and are related to each other by blood, marriage, common-law, adoption or a foster relationship. A couple may be of opposite or same sex.
Source: Statistics Canada. 2013. 2011 National Household Survey. Statistics Canada Catalogue no. 99-004-XWE. Ottawa. Released September 11, 2013.

Individual Income Distribution

Area	Less than $10,000	$10,000 to $19,999	$20,000 to $29,999	$30,000 to $39,999	$40,000 to $49,999	$50,000 to $59,999	$60,000 to $79,999	$80,000 to $99,999	$100,000 to $124,999	$125,000 and Over
					Number Total					
Sherbrooke	19,515	27,250	19,515	17,085	13,365	8,650	9,050	3,305	1,470	1,640
Québec	1,005,600	1,309,515	941,630	866,290	653,400	449,185	515,815	211,070	109,975	120,915
Canada	4,492,040	4,835,710	3,670,020	3,180,360	2,603,520	1,921,650	2,437,440	1,302,045	693,580	782,135
					Males					
Sherbrooke	9,125	10,755	8,690	7,910	6,975	5,110	5,290	2,225	1,085	1,175
Québec	441,455	516,150	427,295	432,625	345,950	256,700	313,880	143,785	80,000	91,475
Canada	1,936,365	1,864,880	1,588,260	1,522,190	1,333,510	1,079,780	1,473,145	823,720	492,905	599,905
					Females					
Sherbrooke	10,390	16,490	10,825	9,175	6,380	3,545	3,760	1,080	385	470
Québec	564,150	793,365	514,335	433,670	307,455	192,485	201,935	67,275	29,980	29,440
Canada	2,555,675	2,970,825	2,081,760	1,658,170	1,270,010	841,870	964,300	478,330	200,680	182,230
					Percent of Population Total					
Sherbrooke	16.1	22.5	16.1	14.1	11.1	7.2	7.5	2.7	1.2	1.4
Québec	16.3	21.2	15.2	14.0	10.6	7.3	8.3	3.4	1.8	2.0
Canada	17.3	18.7	14.2	12.3	10.0	7.4	9.4	5.0	2.7	3.0
					Males					
Sherbrooke	15.6	18.4	14.9	13.6	12.0	8.8	9.1	3.8	1.9	2.0
Québec	14.5	16.9	14.0	14.2	11.3	8.4	10.3	4.7	2.6	3.0
Canada	15.2	14.7	12.5	12.0	10.5	8.5	11.6	6.5	3.9	4.7
					Females					
Sherbrooke	16.6	26.4	17.3	14.7	10.2	5.7	6.0	1.7	0.6	0.8
Québec	18.0	25.3	16.4	13.8	9.8	6.1	6.4	2.1	1.0	0.9
Canada	19.4	22.5	15.8	12.6	9.6	6.4	7.3	3.6	1.5	1.4

Note: Figures cover individuals aged 15 years and over with income. Income refers to monetary receipts from certain sources, before income taxes and deductions, during calendar year 2010.
Source: Statistics Canada. 2013. 2011 National Household Survey. Statistics Canada Catalogue no. 99-004-XWE. Ottawa. Released September 11, 2013.

Labour Force Status

Area	In the Labour Force All	Employed	Unemployed	Not in the Labour Force
		Number Total		
Sherbrooke	79,020	73,880	5,145	47,035
Québec	4,183,445	3,880,425	303,020	2,291,145
Canada	17,990,080	16,595,035	1,395,045	9,269,445
		Males		
Sherbrooke	40,095	37,210	2,885	20,660
Québec	2,188,555	2,014,810	173,745	982,080
Canada	9,388,570	8,634,310	754,255	3,906,785
		Females		
Sherbrooke	38,920	36,670	2,255	26,375
Québec	1,994,885	1,865,610	129,275	1,309,065
Canada	8,601,515	7,960,725	640,790	5,362,660
		Percent of Labour Force Total		
Sherbrooke	62.7	58.6	6.5	37.3
Québec	64.6	59.9	7.2	35.4
Canada	66.0	60.9	7.8	34.0
		Males		
Sherbrooke	66.0	61.2	7.2	34.0
Québec	69.0	63.5	7.9	31.0
Canada	70.6	64.9	8.0	29.4
		Females		
Sherbrooke	59.6	56.2	5.8	40.4
Québec	60.4	56.5	6.5	39.6
Canada	61.6	57.0	7.4	38.4

Note: Figures are based on total population 15 years and over
Source: Statistics Canada. 2013. 2011 National Household Survey. Statistics Canada Catalogue no. 99-004-XWE. Ottawa. Released September 11, 2013.

Labour Force by Industry (NAICS Codes 11–52)

Area	Agriculture, forestry, fishing & hunting	Mining, quarrying, & oil & gas extraction	Utilities	Construction	Manufacturing	Wholesale Trade	Retail Trade	Transportation & warehousing	Information & cultural industries	Finance & insurance
					Number Total					
Sherbrooke	470	135	345	4,265	9,090	1,870	9,900	2,180	1,145	2,460
Québec	84,470	20,770	33,815	241,780	476,390	169,825	501,380	181,295	98,340	159,230
Canada	437,650	261,050	149,940	1,215,380	1,619,295	733,445	2,031,665	827,780	420,830	767,960
					Males					
Sherbrooke	370	120	285	3,860	6,895	1,415	4,480	1,770	605	860
Québec	61,540	18,035	24,560	213,605	343,345	113,545	234,725	137,745	56,455	56,930
Canada	307,370	211,690	110,765	1,068,710	1,167,680	494,545	933,850	617,305	235,875	296,995
					Females					
Sherbrooke	100	0	60	410	2,200	455	5,420	410	545	1,590
Québec	22,925	2,730	9,255	28,170	133,045	56,280	266,650	43,550	41,885	102,295
Canada	130,285	49,360	39,175	146,670	451,615	238,900	1,097,820	210,475	184,955	470,960
					Percent of Labour Force Total					
Sherbrooke	0.6	0.2	0.4	5.5	11.8	2.4	12.8	2.8	1.5	3.2
Québec	2.1	0.5	0.8	5.9	11.7	4.2	12.3	4.4	2.4	3.9
Canada	2.5	1.5	0.9	6.9	9.2	4.2	11.6	4.7	2.4	4.4
					Males					
Sherbrooke	0.9	0.3	0.7	9.9	17.6	3.6	11.4	4.5	1.5	2.2
Québec	2.9	0.8	1.1	10.0	16.1	5.3	11.0	6.4	2.6	2.7
Canada	3.3	2.3	1.2	11.6	12.7	5.4	10.2	6.7	2.6	3.2
					Females					
Sherbrooke	0.3	0.0	0.2	1.1	5.8	1.2	14.2	1.1	1.4	4.2
Québec	1.2	0.1	0.5	1.4	6.8	2.9	13.7	2.2	2.2	5.3
Canada	1.6	0.6	0.5	1.7	5.4	2.8	13.1	2.5	2.2	5.6

Note: Figures are based on total experienced labour force 15 years and over. Experienced labour force refers to persons who, during the week of Sunday, May 1 to Saturday, May 7, 2011, were employed and the unemployed who had last worked for pay or in self-employment in either 2010 or 2011.
Source: Statistics Canada. 2013. 2011 National Household Survey. Statistics Canada Catalogue no. 99-004-XWE. Ottawa. Released September 11, 2013.

Labour Force by Industry (NAICS Codes 53–91)

Area	Real estate & rental & leasing	Profess., scientific & tech. services	Mgmt of companies & enterprises	Admin. & support, waste mgmt & remed. services	Educational services	Health care & social assistance	Arts, entertain. & recreation	Accomm. & food services	Other services (except public admin.)	Public admin.
					Number Total					
Sherbrooke	990	4,985	75	3,220	9,200	12,825	955	5,215	3,545	4,420
Québec	61,365	282,115	3,965	156,130	301,425	496,125	78,795	253,145	189,290	295,480
Canada	321,895	1,240,850	17,460	728,330	1,301,435	1,949,650	363,405	1,130,750	807,800	1,261,050
					Males					
Sherbrooke	565	3,030	50	1,785	3,575	2,745	490	2,360	1,670	2,220
Québec	35,940	158,920	2,250	92,530	99,565	97,255	41,535	112,650	88,710	147,645
Canada	179,090	688,625	9,380	411,250	424,915	349,430	188,270	469,990	372,940	652,510
					Females					
Sherbrooke	425	1,955	30	1,435	5,625	10,075	460	2,855	1,875	2,195
Québec	25,425	123,205	1,715	63,605	201,860	398,870	37,260	140,495	100,585	147,835
Canada	142,805	552,225	8,075	317,085	876,515	1,600,220	175,135	660,760	434,865	608,535
					Percent of Labour Force Total					
Sherbrooke	1.3	6.5	0.1	4.2	11.9	16.6	1.2	6.7	4.6	5.7
Québec	1.5	6.9	0.1	3.8	7.4	12.1	1.9	6.2	4.6	7.2
Canada	1.8	7.1	0.1	4.1	7.4	11.1	2.1	6.4	4.6	7.2
					Males					
Sherbrooke	1.4	7.7	0.1	4.6	9.1	7.0	1.3	6.0	4.3	5.7
Québec	1.7	7.4	0.1	4.3	4.7	4.5	1.9	5.3	4.2	6.9
Canada	1.9	7.5	0.1	4.5	4.6	3.8	2.0	5.1	4.1	7.1
					Females					
Sherbrooke	1.1	5.1	0.1	3.8	14.8	26.4	1.2	7.5	4.9	5.8
Québec	1.3	6.3	0.1	3.3	10.4	20.5	1.9	7.2	5.2	7.6
Canada	1.7	6.6	0.1	3.8	10.4	19.1	2.1	7.9	5.2	7.2

Note: Figures are based on total experienced labour force 15 years and over. Experienced labour force refers to persons who, during the week of Sunday, May 1 to Saturday, May 7, 2011, were employed and the unemployed who had last worked for pay or in self-employment in either 2010 or 2011.
Source: Statistics Canada. 2013. 2011 National Household Survey. Statistics Canada Catalogue no. 99-004-XWE. Ottawa. Released September 11, 2013.

PROFILES / Sherbrooke, Québec

Occupation

Area	Mgmt	Business, Finance & Admin.	Natural/ Applied Sciences & Related	Health	Education, Law & Social, Community & Government Services	Art, Culture, Recreation & Sport	Sales & Service	Trades, Transport & Equip. Operators & Related	Natural Resources, Agri. & Related Production	Mfg & Utilities
Number										
Total										
Sherbrooke	6,255	11,670	5,295	7,295	11,365	1,900	19,105	9,645	760	3,985
Québec	411,425	687,715	287,015	268,610	479,505	123,665	969,740	573,075	65,625	218,740
Canada	1,963,600	2,902,045	1,237,775	1,107,200	2,064,675	503,415	4,068,170	2,537,775	397,930	805,040
Males										
Sherbrooke	4,090	3,475	4,165	1,555	3,870	850	8,340	9,190	680	2,930
Québec	261,620	207,545	221,430	53,480	148,715	58,150	436,370	542,055	53,640	154,485
Canada	1,229,460	854,190	966,355	217,520	676,550	232,535	1,745,705	2,385,615	318,945	564,300
Females										
Sherbrooke	2,165	8,200	1,125	5,745	7,495	1,055	10,770	455	80	1,055
Québec	149,800	480,170	65,585	215,130	330,795	65,520	533,370	31,025	11,995	64,250
Canada	734,140	2,047,855	271,415	889,675	1,388,130	270,875	2,322,465	152,165	78,980	240,740
Percent of Labour Force										
Total										
Sherbrooke	8.1	15.1	6.9	9.4	14.7	2.5	24.7	12.5	1.0	5.2
Québec	10.1	16.8	7.0	6.6	11.7	3.0	23.7	14.0	1.6	5.4
Canada	11.2	16.5	7.0	6.3	11.7	2.9	23.1	14.4	2.3	4.6
Males										
Sherbrooke	10.4	8.9	10.6	4.0	9.9	2.2	21.3	23.5	1.7	7.5
Québec	12.2	9.7	10.4	2.5	7.0	2.7	20.4	25.4	2.5	7.2
Canada	13.4	9.3	10.5	2.4	7.4	2.5	19.0	26.0	3.5	6.1
Females										
Sherbrooke	5.7	21.5	3.0	15.1	19.7	2.8	28.2	1.2	0.2	2.8
Québec	7.7	24.7	3.4	11.0	17.0	3.4	27.4	1.6	0.6	3.3
Canada	8.7	24.4	3.2	10.6	16.5	3.2	27.7	1.8	0.9	2.9

Note: Figures are based on total experienced labour force 15 years and over
Source: Statistics Canada. 2013. 2011 National Household Survey. Statistics Canada Catalogue no. 99-004-XWE. Ottawa. Released September 11, 2013.

Place of Work Status

Area	Worked at Home	Worked Outside Canada	No Fixed Workplace Address	Worked at Usual Place
Number				
Total				
Sherbrooke	3,570	180	4,950	65,180
Québec	237,625	9,705	331,525	3,301,560
Canada	1,142,640	66,460	1,868,245	13,517,690
Males				
Sherbrooke	1,765	150	3,510	31,790
Québec	122,060	7,055	249,535	1,636,165
Canada	582,150	47,355	1,400,485	6,604,325
Females				
Sherbrooke	1,805	30	1,440	33,395
Québec	115,565	2,650	81,995	1,665,395
Canada	560,490	19,100	467,760	6,913,370
Percent of Labour Force				
Total				
Sherbrooke	4.8	0.2	6.7	88.2
Québec	6.1	0.3	8.5	85.1
Canada	6.9	0.4	11.3	81.5
Males				
Sherbrooke	4.7	0.4	9.4	85.4
Québec	6.1	0.4	12.4	81.2
Canada	6.7	0.5	16.2	76.5
Females				
Sherbrooke	4.9	0.1	3.9	91.1
Québec	6.2	0.1	4.4	89.3
Canada	7.0	0.2	5.9	86.8

Note: Figures are based on total employed labour force 15 years and over.
Source: Statistics Canada. 2013. 2011 National Household Survey. Statistics Canada Catalogue no. 99-004-XWE. Ottawa. Released September 11, 2013.

Mode of Transportation to Work

Area	Car; Truck; Van; as Driver	Car; Truck; Van; as Passenger	Public Transit	Walked	Bicycled	All Other Modes
			Number			
			Total			
Sherbrooke	57,535	2,845	3,630	4,875	595	650
Québec	2,713,295	136,490	484,600	215,210	48,870	34,620
Canada	11,393,140	867,050	1,851,525	880,815	201,780	191,625
			Males			
Sherbrooke	29,905	1,130	1,355	2,205	405	300
Québec	1,484,305	50,905	203,035	95,100	33,065	19,285
Canada	6,238,835	349,530	788,290	387,580	135,840	104,725
			Females			
Sherbrooke	27,635	1,710	2,280	2,670	190	355
Québec	1,228,995	85,585	281,565	120,110	15,800	15,335
Canada	5,154,305	517,520	1,063,235	493,230	65,940	86,900
			Percent of Labour Force			
			Total			
Sherbrooke	82.0	4.1	5.2	7.0	0.8	0.9
Québec	74.7	3.8	13.3	5.9	1.3	1.0
Canada	74.0	5.6	12.0	5.7	1.3	1.2
			Males			
Sherbrooke	84.7	3.2	3.8	6.2	1.1	0.8
Québec	78.7	2.7	10.8	5.0	1.8	1.0
Canada	77.9	4.4	9.8	4.8	1.7	1.3
			Females			
Sherbrooke	79.3	4.9	6.5	7.7	0.5	1.0
Québec	70.3	4.9	16.1	6.9	0.9	0.9
Canada	69.8	7.0	14.4	6.7	0.9	1.2

Note: Figures are based on total employed labour force 15 years and over.
Source: Statistics Canada. 2013. 2011 National Household Survey. Statistics Canada Catalogue no. 99-004-XWE. Ottawa. Released September 11, 2013.

Visible Minority Population Characteristics

Area	Total Minority	South Asian[1]	Chinese	Black	Filipino	Latin American	Arab	SE Asian[2]	West Asian[3]	Korean	Japanese	Multiple[4]
					Number							
					Total							
Sherbrooke	8,215	455	405	2,530	35	2,110	1,375	570	450	70	0	165
Québec	850,235	83,320	82,845	243,625	31,495	116,380	166,260	65,855	23,445	6,665	4,025	17,420
Canada	6,264,750	1,567,400	1,324,750	945,665	619,310	381,280	380,620	312,075	206,840	161,130	87,270	171,935
					Males							
Sherbrooke	4,325	250	155	1,315	0	1,130	755	310	235	50	0	85
Québec	418,545	43,410	37,295	116,605	12,435	56,940	89,505	32,940	12,070	3,135	1,565	8,315
Canada	3,043,010	790,755	632,325	453,005	268,885	186,355	203,485	154,035	105,620	77,165	38,270	83,335
					Females							
Sherbrooke	3,890	205	245	1,215	15	980	620	260	215	20	0	85
Québec	431,695	39,915	45,550	127,020	19,055	59,440	76,750	32,920	11,380	3,530	2,465	9,105
Canada	3,221,745	776,650	692,420	492,660	350,425	194,925	177,140	158,045	101,220	83,965	48,990	88,600
					Percent of Population							
					Total							
Sherbrooke	5.5	0.3	0.3	1.7	0.0	1.4	0.9	0.4	0.3	0.0	0.0	0.1
Québec	11.0	1.1	1.1	3.2	0.4	1.5	2.2	0.9	0.3	0.1	0.1	0.2
Canada	19.1	4.8	4.0	2.9	1.9	1.2	1.2	0.9	0.6	0.5	0.3	0.5
					Males							
Sherbrooke	5.9	0.3	0.2	1.8	0.0	1.5	1.0	0.4	0.3	0.1	0.0	0.1
Québec	11.0	1.1	1.0	3.1	0.3	1.5	2.3	0.9	0.3	0.1	0.0	0.2
Canada	18.8	4.9	3.9	2.8	1.7	1.2	1.3	1.0	0.7	0.5	0.2	0.5
					Females							
Sherbrooke	5.1	0.3	0.3	1.6	0.0	1.3	0.8	0.3	0.3	0.0	0.0	0.1
Québec	11.0	1.0	1.2	3.2	0.5	1.5	2.0	0.8	0.3	0.1	0.1	0.2
Canada	19.3	4.7	4.1	3.0	2.1	1.2	1.1	0.9	0.6	0.5	0.3	0.5

Note: The Employment Equity Act defines visible minorities as 'persons, other than Aboriginal peoples, who are non-Caucasian in race or non-white in colour';
(1) Includes 'East Indian,' 'Pakistani,' 'Sri Lankan,' etc.; (2) Includes 'Vietnamese,' 'Cambodian,' 'Malaysian,' 'Laotian,' etc.; (3) Includes 'Iranian,' 'Afghan,' etc.; (4) Includes respondents who reported more than one visible minority group by checking two or more mark-in circles, e.g., 'Black' and 'South Asian.'
Source: Statistics Canada. 2013. 2011 National Household Survey. Statistics Canada Catalogue no. 99-004-XWE. Ottawa. Released September 11, 2013.

Aboriginal Population

Area	Aboriginal Identity[1]	First Nations (North American Indian) Single Identity[2]	Métis Single Identity	Inuk (Inuit) Single Identity	Multiple Aboriginal Identities[3]	Aboriginal Identities Not Included Elsewhere
Number						
Total						
Sherbrooke	1,345	770	480	0	25	65
Québec	141,915	82,425	40,960	12,570	1,545	4,415
Canada	1,400,685	851,560	451,795	59,440	11,415	26,475
Males						
Sherbrooke	700	405	250	0	15	25
Québec	70,205	40,105	21,300	6,265	720	1,815
Canada	682,190	411,785	223,335	29,495	5,525	12,055
Females						
Sherbrooke	645	360	230	0	0	40
Québec	71,710	42,315	19,660	6,305	830	2,600
Canada	718,500	439,775	228,460	29,950	5,890	14,420
Percent of Population						
Total						
Sherbrooke	0.9	0.5	0.3	0.0	0.0	0.0
Québec	1.8	1.1	0.5	0.2	0.0	0.1
Canada	4.3	2.6	1.4	0.2	0.0	0.1
Males						
Sherbrooke	1.0	0.6	0.3	0.0	0.0	0.0
Québec	1.8	1.1	0.6	0.2	0.0	0.0
Canada	4.2	2.5	1.4	0.2	0.0	0.1
Females						
Sherbrooke	0.8	0.5	0.3	0.0	0.0	0.1
Québec	1.8	1.1	0.5	0.2	0.0	0.1
Canada	4.3	2.6	1.4	0.2	0.0	0.1

Note: (1) Includes persons who reported being an Aboriginal person, that is, First Nations (North American Indian), Métis or Inuk (Inuit) and/or those who reported Registered or Treaty Indian status, that is registered under the Indian Act of Canada, and/or those who reported membership in a First Nation or Indian band. Aboriginal peoples of Canada are defined in the Constitution Act, 1982, section 35-2 as including the Indian, Inuit and Métis peoples of Canada; (2) Users should be aware that the estimates associated with this variable are more affected than most by the incomplete enumeration of certain Indian reserves and Indian settlements in the National Household Survey (NHS); (3) Includes persons who reported being any two or all three of the following: First Nations (North American Indian), Métis or Inuk (Inuit).
Source: Statistics Canada. 2013. 2011 National Household Survey. Statistics Canada Catalogue no. 99-004-XWE. Ottawa. Released September 11, 2013.

Ethnic Origin

Area	North American Aboriginal	Other North American	European	Caribbean	Latin, Central and South American	African	Asian	Oceania
Number								
Total								
Sherbrooke	5,925	106,095	64,405	690	2,580	3,535	3,325	15
Québec	307,445	4,776,875	3,390,330	167,590	137,255	260,785	488,905	2,305
Canada	1,836,035	11,070,455	20,157,965	627,590	544,375	766,735	5,011,225	74,875
Males								
Sherbrooke	2,800	51,535	31,205	370	1,435	1,900	1,725	0
Québec	146,725	2,345,180	1,678,310	77,665	67,195	135,740	241,515	1,135
Canada	885,675	5,462,685	9,913,150	291,640	264,635	387,360	2,435,540	37,490
Females								
Sherbrooke	3,125	54,560	33,200	315	1,140	1,630	1,590	0
Québec	160,725	2,431,700	1,712,015	89,925	70,065	125,040	247,390	1,175
Canada	950,360	5,607,770	10,244,820	335,945	279,740	379,380	2,575,680	37,385
Percent of Population								
Total								
Sherbrooke	3.9	70.6	42.9	0.5	1.7	2.4	2.2	0.0
Québec	4.0	61.8	43.8	2.2	1.8	3.4	6.3	0.0
Canada	5.6	33.7	61.4	1.9	1.7	2.3	15.3	0.2
Males								
Sherbrooke	3.8	70.3	42.6	0.5	2.0	2.6	2.4	0.0
Québec	3.8	61.5	44.0	2.0	1.8	3.6	6.3	0.0
Canada	5.5	33.8	61.3	1.8	1.6	2.4	15.1	0.2
Females								
Sherbrooke	4.1	70.9	43.1	0.4	1.5	2.1	2.1	0.0
Québec	4.1	62.1	43.7	2.3	1.8	3.2	6.3	0.0
Canada	5.7	33.6	61.4	2.0	1.7	2.3	15.4	0.2

Note: The sum of the ethnic groups in this table is greater than the total population estimate because a person may report more than one ethnic origin in the NHS.
Source: Statistics Canada. 2013. 2011 National Household Survey. Statistics Canada Catalogue no. 99-004-XWE. Ottawa. Released September 11, 2013.

Religion

Area	Buddhist	Christian	Hindu	Jewish	Muslim	Sikh	Traditional (Aboriginal) Spirituality	Other Religions	No Religious Affiliation
				Number Total					
Sherbrooke	260	126,220	295	85	2,515	0	10	195	20,670
Québec	52,390	6,356,880	33,540	85,100	243,430	9,275	2,025	12,340	937,545
Canada	366,830	22,102,745	497,965	329,495	1,053,945	454,965	64,935	130,835	7,850,605
				Males					
Sherbrooke	115	60,210	150	35	1,410	0	0	100	11,245
Québec	24,630	3,079,855	17,055	41,455	128,815	5,090	925	6,155	510,055
Canada	168,465	10,497,775	250,435	161,265	540,555	229,435	31,805	57,745	4,225,645
				Females					
Sherbrooke	145	66,010	145	50	1,100	0	10	95	9,430
Québec	27,760	3,277,020	16,480	43,645	114,615	4,185	1,100	6,175	427,485
Canada	198,365	11,604,975	247,525	168,235	513,395	225,530	33,135	73,090	3,624,965
				Percent of Population Total					
Sherbrooke	0.2	84.0	0.2	0.1	1.7	0.0	0.0	0.1	13.8
Québec	0.7	82.2	0.4	1.1	3.1	0.1	0.0	0.2	12.1
Canada	1.1	67.3	1.5	1.0	3.2	1.4	0.2	0.4	23.9
				Males					
Sherbrooke	0.2	82.2	0.2	0.0	1.9	0.0	0.0	0.1	15.3
Québec	0.6	80.8	0.4	1.1	3.4	0.1	0.0	0.2	13.4
Canada	1.0	64.9	1.5	1.0	3.3	1.4	0.2	0.4	26.1
				Females					
Sherbrooke	0.2	85.7	0.2	0.1	1.4	0.0	0.0	0.1	12.2
Québec	0.7	83.6	0.4	1.1	2.9	0.1	0.0	0.2	10.9
Canada	1.2	69.5	1.5	1.0	3.1	1.4	0.2	0.4	21.7

Note: Religion refers to the person's self-identification as having a connection or affiliation with any religious denomination, group, body, sect, cult or other religiously defined community or system of belief. Religion is not limited to formal membership in a religious organization or group. Persons without a religious connection or affiliation can self-identify as atheist, agnostic or humanist, or can provide another applicable response.
Source: Statistics Canada. 2013. 2011 National Household Survey. Statistics Canada Catalogue no. 99-004-XWE. Ottawa. Released September 11, 2013.

Religion—Christian Denominations

Area	Anglican	Baptist	Catholic	Christian Orthodox	Lutheran	Pentecostal	Presbyterian	United Church	Other Christian
				Number Total					
Sherbrooke	930	915	117,745	930	35	280	195	715	4,465
Québec	73,550	36,615	5,775,740	129,780	7,200	41,070	11,440	32,930	248,560
Canada	1,631,845	635,840	12,810,705	550,690	478,185	478,705	472,385	2,007,610	3,036,780
				Males					
Sherbrooke	385	425	56,140	490	25	100	115	325	2,205
Québec	34,815	16,585	2,802,920	63,960	3,425	18,640	5,265	14,945	119,305
Canada	752,945	293,905	6,167,290	270,205	221,525	217,850	218,955	912,545	1,442,550
				Females					
Sherbrooke	545	490	61,605	440	0	180	85	395	2,260
Québec	38,735	20,030	2,972,820	65,820	3,770	22,430	6,175	17,985	129,260
Canada	878,900	341,940	6,643,415	280,485	256,660	260,850	253,430	1,095,065	1,594,230
				Percent of Population Total					
Sherbrooke	0.6	0.6	78.4	0.6	0.0	0.2	0.1	0.5	3.0
Québec	1.0	0.5	74.7	1.7	0.1	0.5	0.1	0.4	3.2
Canada	5.0	1.9	39.0	1.7	1.5	1.5	1.4	6.1	9.2
				Males					
Sherbrooke	0.5	0.6	76.6	0.7	0.0	0.1	0.2	0.4	3.0
Québec	0.9	0.4	73.5	1.7	0.1	0.5	0.1	0.4	3.1
Canada	4.7	1.8	38.2	1.7	1.4	1.3	1.4	5.6	8.9
				Females					
Sherbrooke	0.7	0.6	80.0	0.6	0.0	0.2	0.1	0.5	2.9
Québec	1.0	0.5	75.9	1.7	0.1	0.6	0.2	0.5	3.3
Canada	5.3	2.0	39.8	1.7	1.5	1.6	1.5	6.6	9.6

Note: Religion refers to the person's self-identification as having a connection or affiliation with any religious denomination, group, body, sect, cult or other religiously defined community or system of belief. Religion is not limited to formal membership in a religious organization or group. Persons without a religious connection or affiliation can self-identify as atheist, agnostic or humanist, or can provide another applicable response.
Source: Statistics Canada. 2013. 2011 National Household Survey. Statistics Canada Catalogue no. 99-004-XWE. Ottawa. Released September 11, 2013.

PROFILES / Sherbrooke, Québec

Immigrant Status and Period of Immigration

Area	Non-Immigrants[1]	Immigrants All	Before 1971	1971 to 1980	1981 to 1990	1991 to 2000	2001 to 2005	2006 to 2011	Non-Permanent Residents[3]
Number — Total									
Sherbrooke	138,625	10,645	805	800	790	2,115	2,270	3,875	985
Québec	6,690,530	974,895	151,825	115,640	130,680	195,925	157,425	223,400	67,095
Canada	25,720,175	6,775,765	1,261,055	870,775	949,890	1,539,050	992,070	1,162,915	356,385
Males									
Sherbrooke	67,160	5,580	375	435	405	1,120	1,195	2,045	530
Québec	3,301,435	477,240	75,255	57,410	64,080	94,110	76,780	109,605	35,370
Canada	12,753,235	3,231,370	605,430	416,670	454,570	724,905	474,545	555,245	178,515
Females									
Sherbrooke	71,470	5,070	425	365	390	990	1,075	1,825	455
Québec	3,389,095	497,655	76,565	58,235	66,600	101,810	80,645	113,795	31,725
Canada	12,966,935	3,544,400	655,625	454,105	495,325	814,145	517,530	607,670	177,870
Percent of Population — Total									
Sherbrooke	92.3	7.1	0.5	0.5	0.5	1.4	1.5	2.6	0.7
Québec	86.5	12.6	2.0	1.5	1.7	2.5	2.0	2.9	0.9
Canada	78.3	20.6	3.8	2.7	2.9	4.7	3.0	3.5	1.1
Males									
Sherbrooke	91.7	7.6	0.5	0.6	0.6	1.5	1.6	2.8	0.7
Québec	86.6	12.5	2.0	1.5	1.7	2.5	2.0	2.9	0.9
Canada	78.9	20.0	3.7	2.6	2.8	4.5	2.9	3.4	1.1
Females									
Sherbrooke	92.8	6.6	0.6	0.5	0.5	1.3	1.4	2.4	0.6
Québec	86.5	12.7	2.0	1.5	1.7	2.6	2.1	2.9	0.8
Canada	77.7	21.2	3.9	2.7	3.0	4.9	3.1	3.6	1.1

Note: (1) Non-immigrant refers to a person who is a Canadian citizen by birth; (2) Immigrant refers to a person who is or has ever been a landed immigrant/permanent resident. This person has been granted the right to live in Canada permanently by immigration authorities. Some immigrants have resided in Canada for a number of years, while others have arrived recently. Some immigrants are Canadian citizens, while others are not. Most immigrants are born outside Canada, but a small number are born in Canada. In the 2011 National Household Survey, 'Immigrants' includes immigrants who landed in Canada prior to May 10, 2011; (3) Non-permanent resident refers to a person from another country who has a work or study permit, or who is a refugee claimant, and any non-Canadian-born family member living in Canada with them.
Source: Statistics Canada. 2013. 2011 National Household Survey. Statistics Canada Catalogue no. 99-004-XWE. Ottawa. Released September 11, 2013.

Mother Tongue

Area	English	French	Non-official Language	English & French	English & Non-official Language	French & Non-official Language	English, French & Non-official Language
Number — Total							
Sherbrooke	6,235	135,790	8,580	1,125	95	555	70
Québec	599,225	6,102,210	961,700	64,800	23,435	51,640	12,950
Canada	18,858,980	7,054,975	6,567,680	144,685	396,330	74,430	24,095
Males							
Sherbrooke	2,995	65,720	4,340	545	60	290	40
Québec	297,875	2,994,300	472,635	32,390	11,455	25,810	6,790
Canada	9,345,225	3,452,380	3,157,785	69,975	192,000	36,535	11,965
Females							
Sherbrooke	3,245	70,065	4,240	585	40	260	25
Québec	301,355	3,107,910	489,060	32,405	11,975	25,825	6,155
Canada	9,513,750	3,602,590	3,409,895	74,710	204,330	37,890	12,130
Percent of Population — Total							
Sherbrooke	4.1	89.1	5.6	0.7	0.1	0.4	0.0
Québec	7.7	78.1	12.3	0.8	0.3	0.7	0.2
Canada	56.9	21.3	19.8	0.4	1.2	0.2	0.1
Males							
Sherbrooke	4.0	88.8	5.9	0.7	0.1	0.4	0.1
Québec	7.8	78.0	12.3	0.8	0.3	0.7	0.2
Canada	57.5	21.2	19.4	0.4	1.2	0.2	0.1
Females							
Sherbrooke	4.1	89.3	5.4	0.7	0.1	0.3	0.0
Québec	7.6	78.2	12.3	0.8	0.3	0.6	0.2
Canada	56.4	21.4	20.2	0.4	1.2	0.2	0.1

Note: Figures cover total population excluding institutional residents.
Source: Statistics Canada. 2012. Census Profile. 2011 Census. Statistics Canada Catalogue no. 98-316-XWE. Ottawa. Released October 24 2012.
http://www12.statcan.gc.ca/census-recensement/2011/dp-pd/prof/index.cfm?Lang=E

Language Spoken Most Often at Home

Area	English	French	Non-official Language	English & French	English & Non-official Language	French & Non-official Language	English, French & Non-official Language
			Number				
			Total				
Sherbrooke	5,845	138,530	5,480	1,095	125	1,210	150
Québec	767,415	6,249,080	554,400	71,555	43,765	100,110	29,625
Canada	21,457,075	6,827,865	3,673,865	131,205	875,135	109,700	46,330
			Males				
Sherbrooke	2,805	67,185	2,740	525	65	590	85
Québec	379,915	3,071,635	268,640	35,860	21,305	48,590	15,315
Canada	10,585,620	3,348,235	1,767,310	63,475	425,370	53,010	22,845
			Females				
Sherbrooke	3,045	71,350	2,745	570	65	620	65
Québec	387,500	3,177,450	285,760	35,695	22,460	51,525	14,310
Canada	10,871,455	3,479,625	1,906,555	67,730	449,765	56,690	23,485
			Percent of Population				
			Total				
Sherbrooke	3.8	90.9	3.6	0.7	0.1	0.8	0.1
Québec	9.8	80.0	7.1	0.9	0.6	1.3	0.4
Canada	64.8	20.6	11.1	0.4	2.6	0.3	0.1
			Males				
Sherbrooke	3.8	90.8	3.7	0.7	0.1	0.8	0.1
Québec	9.9	80.0	7.0	0.9	0.6	1.3	0.4
Canada	65.1	20.6	10.9	0.4	2.6	0.3	0.1
			Females				
Sherbrooke	3.9	90.9	3.5	0.7	0.1	0.8	0.1
Québec	9.7	79.9	7.2	0.9	0.6	1.3	0.4
Canada	64.5	20.6	11.3	0.4	2.7	0.3	0.1

Note: Figures cover total population excluding institutional residents.
Source: Statistics Canada. 2012. Census Profile. 2011 Census. Statistics Canada Catalogue no. 98-316-XWE. Ottawa. Released October 24 2012.
http://www12.statcan.gc.ca/census-recensement/2011/dp-pd/prof/index.cfm?Lang=E

Knowledge of Official Languages

Area	English Only	French Only	English & French	Neither English nor French
		Number		
		Total		
Sherbrooke	2,020	85,820	63,810	795
Québec	363,860	4,047,175	3,328,725	76,190
Canada	22,564,665	4,165,015	5,795,570	595,920
		Males		
Sherbrooke	920	38,525	34,230	315
Québec	180,175	1,871,500	1,758,410	31,175
Canada	11,222,185	1,925,340	2,876,560	241,790
		Females		
Sherbrooke	1,100	47,295	29,585	485
Québec	183,690	2,175,675	1,570,310	45,015
Canada	11,342,485	2,239,680	2,919,005	354,135
		Percent of Population		
		Total		
Sherbrooke	1.3	56.3	41.9	0.5
Québec	4.7	51.8	42.6	1.0
Canada	68.1	12.6	17.5	1.8
		Males		
Sherbrooke	1.2	52.1	46.3	0.4
Québec	4.7	48.7	45.8	0.8
Canada	69.0	11.8	17.7	1.5
		Females		
Sherbrooke	1.4	60.3	37.7	0.6
Québec	4.6	54.7	39.5	1.1
Canada	67.3	13.3	17.3	2.1

Note: Figures cover total population excluding institutional residents.
Source: Statistics Canada. 2012. Census Profile. 2011 Census. Statistics Canada Catalogue no. 98-316-XWE. Ottawa. Released October 24 2012.
http://www12.statcan.gc.ca/census-recensement/2011/dp-pd/prof/index.cfm?Lang=E

St. Catharines, Ontario

Background

St. Catharines is located in the Niagara Region in southern Ontario. The city is just over 50 kilometres south of Toronto and less than 20 kilometres from the Niagara River U.S. boundary. The city's official nickname is "The Garden City" because of the municipality's 1,000 acres of public parks, gardens and trails. St. Catharines is the northern entrance of the Welland Canal that connects Lake Ontario and Lake Erie. The eight-lock canal is ranked as one of the most outstanding engineering projects of the 20th century.

St. Catharines was originally a farming community settled by United Empire Loyalists in the late 18th century. The city's original canals were built between 1824 and 1829 and made St. Catharines the most important industrial centre in the Niagara region.

A signature feature of the city is Lock 3 and the site of St. Catharines Museum and Welland Canals Centre. The centre's elevated observation deck allows visitors to watch large lakers and ocean vessels from around the world pass through the lock as they navigate the St. Lawrence Seaway System. The outdoor Discovery Park shows the resources and engineering involved in building the locks.

Key industries include manufacturing, automotive, tourism and agri-business. Green energy is an emerging sector; Rankin Renewable Power and PlanET Biogas are headquartered in the city. Arts and knowledge-based economies are also on the rise. In 2009, Silicon Knights, the world's largest independent game developer, partnered with the city, Brock University and other stakeholders to create nGen, the Niagara Interactive Media Generator.

In recent years more than $1.6 billion worth of economic activity has occurred in the city. Examples include the Brock University International Service Building ($10 million), the Downtown Performing Arts Centre ($54 million) and the Carlisle Street Parking Garage ($30 million).

St. Catharines has summer highs of plus 25.77 degrees Celsius, winter lows of minus 6.53 degrees Celsius, and an average rainfall just over 745 mm per year.

Rankings

- St. Catharines ranked in the Top 20 of Canada's smartest cities. The annual Composite Learning Index ranked the city #18 out of more than 4,500 communities across Canada. The study measured traditional literacy, work-related skill, community involvement and personal learning. *Maclean's Magazine, "Canada's Smartest Cities: 2010 Rankings," May 20, 2010 with files from the 2010 Composite Learning Index*
- The Canadian Council of Learning ranked St. Catharines #17 out of 37 Canadian cities in terms of volunteerism practised by residents over 15 years of age. Just over 47% of St. Catharines' population volunteered their time over the course of a 12-month period. The top 3 cities for annual volunteer turnout were Guelph (ON), Kingston (ON) and Fredericton (NB). *The Canadian Council on Learning with files from Statistics Canada: Canada Survey of Giving, Volunteering and Participation 2004*
- The 2011 Census calculated that the population of St. Catharines–Niagara census metropolitan area (CMA) had a percentage change of only 0.5% between 2006 and 2011. The change was significantly lower than the national population growth of 5.9% for the same time period. Between 2006 and 2011, the average growth among all CMAs was 7.4%. *Statistics Canada, Focus on Geography Series, 2011 Census, October 24, 2012*

PROFILES / St. Catharines, Ontario

Population Growth and Density

Area	Population in 2001	Population in 2006	Population in 2011	Population Change 2001–2006	Population Change 2006–2011	Land Area (sq. km)	Population Density per sq. km
St. Catharines	129,170	131,989	131,400	2.2	-0.4	96.11	1,367.2
Ontario	11,410,046	12,160,282	12,851,821	6.6	5.7	908,607.67	14.1
Canada	30,007,094	31,612,897	33,476,688	5.4	5.9	8,965,121.42	3.7

Source: Statistics Canada. 2012. Census Profile. 2011 Census. Statistics Canada Catalogue no. 98-316-XWE. Ottawa. Released October 24 2012.
http://www12.statcan.gc.ca/census-recensement/2011/dp-pd/prof/index.cfm?Lang=E;
Statistics Canada 2007. 2006 Community Profiles. 2006 Census. Statistics Canada Catalogue no. 92-591-XWE. Ottawa. Released March 13 2007.
http://www12.statcan.ca/census-recensement/2006/dp-pd/prof/92-591/index.cfm?Lang=E

Gender

Area	Males	Females
Number		
St. Catharines	62,675	68,730
Ontario	6,263,140	6,588,685
Canada	16,414,225	17,062,460
Percent of Population		
St. Catharines	47.7	52.3
Ontario	48.7	51.3
Canada	49.0	51.0

Source: Statistics Canada. 2012. Census Profile. 2011 Census. Statistics Canada Catalogue no. 98-316-XWE. Ottawa. Released October 24 2012.
http://www12.statcan.gc.ca/census-recensement/2011/dp-pd/prof/index.cfm?Lang=E

Marital Status

Area	Married[1]	Living Common-law	Single[2]	Separated	Divorced	Widowed
Number — Total						
St. Catharines	51,660	8,970	30,585	4,315	7,680	8,645
Ontario	5,367,400	791,210	2,985,020	319,805	593,730	613,880
Canada	12,941,960	3,142,525	7,816,045	698,240	1,686,035	1,584,530
Males						
St. Catharines	25,795	4,465	16,120	1,770	2,920	1,635
Ontario	2,681,320	397,620	1,583,760	133,790	231,160	117,980
Canada	6,470,300	1,575,495	4,206,320	299,655	680,415	310,940
Females						
St. Catharines	25,870	4,500	14,470	2,545	4,765	7,010
Ontario	2,686,075	393,590	1,401,260	186,015	362,570	495,905
Canada	6,471,660	1,567,035	3,609,730	398,585	1,005,620	1,273,590
Percent of Population — Total						
St. Catharines	46.2	8.0	27.3	3.9	6.9	7.7
Ontario	50.3	7.4	28.0	3.0	5.6	5.8
Canada	46.4	11.3	28.0	2.5	6.0	5.7
Males						
St. Catharines	48.9	8.5	30.6	3.4	5.5	3.1
Ontario	52.1	7.7	30.8	2.6	4.5	2.3
Canada	47.8	11.6	31.1	2.2	5.0	2.3
Females						
St. Catharines	43.7	7.6	24.5	4.3	8.1	11.8
Ontario	48.6	7.1	25.4	3.4	6.6	9.0
Canada	45.2	10.9	25.2	2.8	7.0	8.9

Note: (1) and not separated, (2) never legally married
Source: Statistics Canada. 2012. Census Profile. 2011 Census. Statistics Canada Catalogue no. 98-316-XWE. Ottawa. Released October 24 2012.
http://www12.statcan.gc.ca/census-recensement/2011/dp-pd/prof/index.cfm?Lang=E

Age Characteristics: 0 to 49 Years

Area	0 to 4 Years	5 to 9 Years	10 to 14 Years	15 to 19 Years	20 to 24 Years	25 to 29 Years	30 to 34 Years	35 to 39 Years	40 to 44 Years	45 to 49 Years
Number										
Total										
St. Catharines	6,295	6,225	7,025	8,550	9,300	8,095	7,150	7,315	8,230	10,055
Ontario	704,260	712,755	763,755	863,635	852,910	815,120	800,365	844,335	924,075	1,055,880
Canada	1,877,095	1,809,895	1,920,355	2,178,135	2,187,450	2,169,590	2,162,905	2,173,930	2,324,875	2,675,130
Males										
St. Catharines	3,215	3,170	3,590	4,300	4,630	4,015	3,490	3,510	3,960	4,780
Ontario	360,590	365,290	391,630	443,680	432,490	400,045	383,340	405,845	447,920	517,510
Canada	961,150	925,965	983,995	1,115,845	1,108,775	1,077,275	1,058,810	1,064,200	1,141,720	1,318,715
Females										
St. Catharines	3,080	3,055	3,435	4,245	4,675	4,080	3,665	3,800	4,270	5,280
Ontario	343,670	347,465	372,125	419,950	420,415	415,075	417,030	438,485	476,155	538,370
Canada	915,945	883,935	936,360	1,062,295	1,078,670	1,092,315	1,104,095	1,109,735	1,183,155	1,356,420
Percent of Population										
Total										
St. Catharines	4.8	4.7	5.3	6.5	7.1	6.2	5.4	5.6	6.3	7.7
Ontario	5.5	5.5	5.9	6.7	6.6	6.3	6.2	6.6	7.2	8.2
Canada	5.6	5.4	5.7	6.5	6.5	6.5	6.5	6.5	6.9	8.0
Males										
St. Catharines	5.1	5.1	5.7	6.9	7.4	6.4	5.6	5.6	6.3	7.6
Ontario	5.8	5.8	6.3	7.1	6.9	6.4	6.1	6.5	7.2	8.3
Canada	5.9	5.6	6.0	6.8	6.8	6.6	6.5	6.5	7.0	8.0
Females										
St. Catharines	4.5	4.4	5.0	6.2	6.8	5.9	5.3	5.5	6.2	7.7
Ontario	5.2	5.3	5.6	6.4	6.4	6.3	6.3	6.7	7.2	8.2
Canada	5.4	5.2	5.5	6.2	6.3	6.4	6.5	6.5	6.9	7.9

Source: Statistics Canada. 2012. Census Profile. 2011 Census. Statistics Canada Catalogue no. 98-316-XWE. Ottawa. Released October 24 2012.
http://www12.statcan.gc.ca/census-recensement/2011/dp-pd/prof/index.cfm?Lang=E

Age Characteristics: 50 Years and Over, and Median Age

Area	50 to 54 Years	55 to 59 Years	60 to 64 Years	65 to 69 Years	70 to 74 Years	75 to 79 Years	80 to 84 Years	85 Years and Over	Median Age
Number									
Total									
St. Catharines	9,830	9,135	8,800	7,005	5,570	4,875	4,060	3,890	43.5
Ontario	1,006,140	864,620	765,655	563,485	440,780	356,150	271,510	246,400	40.4
Canada	2,658,965	2,340,635	2,052,670	1,521,715	1,153,065	922,700	702,070	645,515	40.6
Males									
St. Catharines	4,705	4,305	4,145	3,290	2,565	2,095	1,675	1,245	41.8
Ontario	492,560	418,755	370,370	270,875	206,350	161,345	113,620	80,925	39.4
Canada	1,309,030	1,147,300	1,002,690	738,010	543,435	417,945	291,085	208,300	39.6
Females									
St. Catharines	5,125	4,830	4,650	3,715	3,005	2,780	2,390	2,645	45.1
Ontario	513,580	445,865	395,275	292,610	234,435	194,805	157,890	165,475	41.3
Canada	1,349,940	1,193,335	1,049,985	783,705	609,630	504,755	410,985	437,215	41.5
Percent of Population									
Total									
St. Catharines	7.5	7.0	6.7	5.3	4.2	3.7	3.1	3.0	–
Ontario	7.8	6.7	6.0	4.4	3.4	2.8	2.1	1.9	–
Canada	7.9	7.0	6.1	4.5	3.4	2.8	2.1	1.9	–
Males									
St. Catharines	7.5	6.9	6.6	5.2	4.1	3.3	2.7	2.0	–
Ontario	7.9	6.7	5.9	4.3	3.3	2.6	1.8	1.3	–
Canada	8.0	7.0	6.1	4.5	3.3	2.5	1.8	1.3	–
Females									
St. Catharines	7.5	7.0	6.8	5.4	4.4	4.0	3.5	3.8	–
Ontario	7.8	6.8	6.0	4.4	3.6	3.0	2.4	2.5	–
Canada	7.9	7.0	6.2	4.6	3.6	3.0	2.4	2.6	–

Source: Statistics Canada. 2012. Census Profile. 2011 Census. Statistics Canada Catalogue no. 98-316-XWE. Ottawa. Released October 24 2012.
http://www12.statcan.gc.ca/census-recensement/2011/dp-pd/prof/index.cfm?Lang=E

PROFILES / St. Catharines, Ontario

Private Households by Household Size

Area	1 Person	2 Persons	3 Persons	4 Persons	5 Persons	6 or More Persons	Average Number of Persons in Private Households
Households							
St. Catharines	16,880	19,655	8,265	6,945	2,575	1,100	2.3
Ontario	1,230,975	1,584,415	803,030	783,925	310,860	174,305	2.6
Canada	3,673,310	4,544,820	2,081,900	1,903,300	724,405	392,885	2.5
Percent of Households							
St. Catharines	30.5	35.5	14.9	12.5	4.6	2.0	–
Ontario	25.2	32.4	16.4	16.0	6.4	3.6	–
Canada	27.6	34.1	15.6	14.3	5.4	2.9	–

Source: Statistics Canada. 2012. Census Profile. 2011 Census. Statistics Canada Catalogue no. 98-316-XWE. Ottawa. Released October 24 2012.
http://www12.statcan.gc.ca/census-recensement/2011/dp-pd/prof/index.cfm?Lang=E

Dwelling Type

Area	Single-detached House	Semi-detached House	Row House	Apartment: Building with Five or More Storeys	Apartment: Building with Fewer Than Five Storeys	Duplex Apartment	Movable Dwelling	Other Single-attached House
Number								
St. Catharines	32,235	3,230	4,400	5,795	7,340	2,140	90	190
Ontario	2,718,880	279,470	415,225	789,970	498,160	160,460	15,800	9,540
Canada	7,329,150	646,245	791,600	1,234,770	2,397,550	704,485	183,510	33,310
Percent of Dwellings								
St. Catharines	58.2	5.8	7.9	10.5	13.2	3.9	0.2	0.3
Ontario	55.6	5.7	8.5	16.2	10.2	3.3	0.3	0.2
Canada	55.0	4.9	5.9	9.3	18.0	5.3	1.4	0.3

Source: Statistics Canada. 2012. Census Profile. 2011 Census. Statistics Canada Catalogue no. 98-316-XWE. Ottawa. Released October 24 2012.
http://www12.statcan.gc.ca/census-recensement/2011/dp-pd/prof/index.cfm?Lang=E

Shelter Costs

	Owned Dwellings					Rented Dwellings		
Area	Number	Median Value[1] ($)	Average Value[1] ($)	Median Monthly Costs[2] ($)	Average Monthly Costs[2] ($)	Number	Median Monthly Costs[3] ($)	Average Monthly Costs[3] ($)
St. Catharines	38,220	218,613	240,536	942	1,058	17,130	772	785
Ontario	3,446,650	300,862	367,428	1,163	1,284	1,385,535	892	926
Canada	9,013,410	280,552	345,182	978	1,141	4,060,385	784	848

Note: All figures cover non-farm, non-reserve private dwellings; (1) Refers to the dollar amount expected by the owner if the dwelling were to be sold; (2) Includes all shelter expenses paid by households that own their dwellings, such as the mortgage payment and the costs of electricity, heat, water and other municipal services, property taxes and condominium fees; (3) Includes all shelter expenses paid by households that rent their dwellings, such as the monthly rent and the costs of electricity, heat and municipal services.
Source: Statistics Canada. 2013. 2011 National Household Survey. Statistics Canada Catalogue no. 99-004-XWE. Ottawa. Released September 11, 2013.

Occupied Private Dwellings by Period of Construction

Area	1960 or Before	1961 to 1980	1981 to 1990	1991 to 2000	2001 to 2005	2006 to 2011
Number						
St. Catharines	20,540	21,100	6,600	4,430	1,680	1,070
Ontario	1,330,235	1,420,570	763,430	609,310	414,795	348,310
Canada	3,273,105	4,152,715	2,112,110	1,707,880	1,031,020	1,042,430
Percent of Dwellings						
St. Catharines	37.1	38.1	11.9	8.0	3.0	1.9
Ontario	27.2	29.1	15.6	12.5	8.5	7.1
Canada	24.6	31.2	15.9	12.8	7.7	7.8

Note: Figures cover non-farm, non-reserve private dwellings and includes data up to May 10, 2011.
Source: Statistics Canada. 2013. 2011 National Household Survey. Statistics Canada Catalogue no. 99-004-XWE. Ottawa. Released September 11, 2013.

Educational Attainment

Area	No Certificate, Diploma or Degree	High School Diploma or Equivalent[1]	Apprenticeship or Trades Certificate or Diploma[2]	College, CÉGEP or Other Non-University Certificate or Diploma	University Certificate or Diploma Below the Bachelor Level[3]	Bachelor's Degree	University Certificate, Diploma or Degree Above Bachelor Level[4]
			Number				
			Total				
St. Catharines	22,480	32,340	9,700	23,205	3,455	11,125	7,185
Ontario	1,954,520	2,801,805	771,140	2,070,875	427,150	1,515,075	933,100
Canada	5,485,400	6,968,935	2,950,685	4,970,020	1,200,130	3,634,425	2,049,930
			Males				
St. Catharines	10,615	14,880	6,445	9,835	1,495	5,160	3,445
Ontario	957,040	1,337,055	520,390	894,235	193,355	692,345	470,290
Canada	2,742,875	3,305,415	1,928,970	2,118,430	513,235	1,643,080	1,043,350
			Females				
St. Catharines	11,865	17,460	3,255	13,370	1,955	5,965	3,745
Ontario	997,475	1,464,755	250,750	1,176,640	233,790	822,730	462,805
Canada	2,742,520	3,663,515	1,021,715	2,851,595	686,890	1,991,345	1,006,585
			Percent of Population				
			Total				
St. Catharines	20.5	29.5	8.9	21.2	3.2	10.2	6.6
Ontario	18.7	26.8	7.4	19.8	4.1	14.5	8.9
Canada	20.1	25.6	10.8	18.2	4.4	13.3	7.5
			Males				
St. Catharines	20.5	28.7	12.4	19.0	2.9	9.9	6.6
Ontario	18.9	26.4	10.3	17.7	3.8	13.7	9.3
Canada	20.6	24.9	14.5	15.9	3.9	12.4	7.8
			Females				
St. Catharines	20.6	30.3	5.6	23.2	3.4	10.4	6.5
Ontario	18.4	27.1	4.6	21.8	4.3	15.2	8.6
Canada	19.6	26.2	7.3	20.4	4.9	14.3	7.2

Note: Figures cover total population aged 15 years and over by highest certificate, diploma or degree; (1) Includes persons who have graduated from a secondary school or equivalent. It excludes persons with a postsecondary certificate, diploma or degree; (2) Includes Registered Apprenticeship certificates (including Certificate of Qualification, Journeyperson's designation) and other trades certificates or diplomas such as pre-employment or vocational certificates and diplomas from brief trade programs completed at community colleges, institutes of technology, vocational centres, and similar institutions; (3) Comparisons with other data sources suggest that the category 'University certificate or diploma below the bachelor's level' was over-reported in the NHS. This category likely includes some responses that are actually college certificates or diplomas, bachelor's degrees or other types of education (e.g., university transfer programs, bachelor's programs completed in other countries, incomplete bachelor's programs, non-university professional designations). We recommend users interpret the results for the 'University certificate or diploma below the bachelor's level' category with caution; (4) 'University certificate or diploma above bachelor level' includes the categories: 'Degree in medicine, dentistry, veterinary medicine or optometry,' 'Master's degree' and 'Earned doctorate.'
Source: Statistics Canada. 2013. 2011 National Household Survey. Statistics Canada Catalogue no. 99-004-XWE. Ottawa. Released September 11, 2013.

Household Income Distribution

Area	Less than $10,000	$10,000 to $19,999	$20,000 to $29,999	$30,000 to $39,999	$40,000 to $49,999	$50,000 to $59,999	$60,000 to $79,999	$80,000 to $99,999	$100,000 to $124,999	$125,000 to $149,999	$150,000 and Over
					Households						
St. Catharines	1,990	4,820	6,020	6,410	6,130	4,885	8,275	5,585	4,500	2,715	4,075
Ontario	201,780	354,530	405,725	425,410	425,720	398,705	680,850	552,660	497,970	331,460	611,840
Canada	626,705	1,141,945	1,193,925	1,271,675	1,206,800	1,102,120	1,865,280	1,458,240	1,260,770	802,555	1,389,240
					Percent of Households						
St. Catharines	3.6	8.7	10.9	11.6	11.1	8.8	14.9	10.1	8.1	4.9	7.4
Ontario	4.1	7.3	8.3	8.7	8.7	8.2	13.9	11.3	10.2	6.8	12.5
Canada	4.7	8.6	9.0	9.5	9.1	8.3	14.0	10.9	9.5	6.0	10.4

Note: Household income is the sum of the total incomes of all members of that household. Total income refers to monetary receipts from certain sources, before income taxes and deductions, during calendar year 2010.
Source: Statistics Canada. 2013. 2011 National Household Survey. Statistics Canada Catalogue no. 99-004-XWE. Ottawa. Released September 11, 2013.

Median and Average Household and Economic Family Income

Area	Median Household Income ($)	Average Household Income ($)	Median After-tax Household Income ($)	Average After-tax Household Income ($)	Median Economic Family Income ($)	Average Economic Family Income ($)	Median After-tax Economic Family Income ($)	Average After-tax Economic Family Income ($)
St. Catharines	54,409	68,482	49,358	59,067	69,658	83,112	62,771	71,450
Ontario	66,358	85,772	58,717	71,523	80,987	100,152	71,128	83,322
Canada	61,072	79,102	54,089	66,149	76,511	94,125	67,044	78,517

Note: Figures cover household and economic familiy income in 2010. A household is defined as a person or a group of persons (other than foreign residents) who occupy the same private dwelling and do not have a usual place of residence elsewhere in Canada. Every person is a member of one and only one household. An economic family is defined as a group of two or more persons who live in the same dwelling and are related to each other by blood, marriage, common-law, adoption or a foster relationship. A couple may be of opposite or same sex.
Source: Statistics Canada. 2013. 2011 National Household Survey. Statistics Canada Catalogue no. 99-004-XWE. Ottawa. Released September 11, 2013.

Individual Income Distribution

Area	Less than $10,000	$10,000 to $19,999	$20,000 to $29,999	$30,000 to $39,999	$40,000 to $49,999	$50,000 to $59,999	$60,000 to $79,999	$80,000 to $99,999	$100,000 to $124,999	$125,000 and Over
Number — Total										
St. Catharines	16,900	21,535	17,340	13,520	11,465	7,110	8,260	4,575	2,300	1,955
Ontario	1,780,355	1,748,060	1,361,710	1,136,730	980,790	746,360	964,280	574,710	293,865	330,285
Canada	4,492,040	4,835,710	3,670,020	3,180,360	2,603,520	1,921,650	2,437,440	1,302,045	693,580	782,135
Males										
St. Catharines	7,385	7,460	6,790	6,445	6,095	4,365	5,170	2,840	1,775	1,585
Ontario	781,095	669,815	580,990	535,255	491,125	407,005	569,205	341,160	201,125	244,500
Canada	1,936,365	1,864,880	1,588,260	1,522,190	1,333,510	1,079,780	1,473,145	823,720	492,905	599,905
Females										
St. Catharines	9,515	14,080	10,555	7,075	5,365	2,745	3,095	1,740	520	370
Ontario	999,265	1,078,245	780,720	601,475	489,665	339,360	395,075	233,550	92,740	85,790
Canada	2,555,675	2,970,825	2,081,760	1,658,170	1,270,010	841,870	964,300	478,330	200,680	182,230
Percent of Population — Total										
St. Catharines	16.1	20.5	16.5	12.9	10.9	6.8	7.9	4.4	2.2	1.9
Ontario	18.0	17.6	13.7	11.5	9.9	7.5	9.7	5.8	3.0	3.3
Canada	17.3	18.7	14.2	12.3	10.0	7.4	9.4	5.0	2.7	3.0
Males										
St. Catharines	14.8	14.9	13.6	12.9	12.2	8.7	10.4	5.7	3.6	3.2
Ontario	16.2	13.9	12.1	11.1	10.2	8.4	11.8	7.1	4.2	5.1
Canada	15.2	14.7	12.5	12.0	10.5	8.5	11.6	6.5	3.9	4.7
Females										
St. Catharines	17.3	25.6	19.2	12.8	9.7	5.0	5.6	3.2	0.9	0.7
Ontario	19.6	21.2	15.3	11.8	9.6	6.7	7.8	4.6	1.8	1.7
Canada	19.4	22.5	15.8	12.6	9.6	6.4	7.3	3.6	1.5	1.4

Note: Figures cover individuals aged 15 years and over with income. Income refers to monetary receipts from certain sources, before income taxes and deductions, during calendar year 2010.
Source: Statistics Canada. 2013. 2011 National Household Survey. Statistics Canada Catalogue no. 99-004-XWE. Ottawa. Released September 11, 2013.

Labour Force Status

Area	In the Labour Force — All	Employed	Unemployed	Not in the Labour Force
Number — Total				
St. Catharines	67,540	61,000	6,540	41,960
Ontario	6,864,990	6,297,005	567,985	3,608,685
Canada	17,990,080	16,595,035	1,395,045	9,269,445
Males				
St. Catharines	34,220	30,655	3,565	17,660
Ontario	3,542,030	3,249,165	292,865	1,522,690
Canada	9,388,570	8,634,310	754,255	3,906,785
Females				
St. Catharines	33,325	30,345	2,980	24,300
Ontario	3,322,955	3,047,840	275,120	2,085,990
Canada	8,601,515	7,960,725	640,790	5,362,660
Percent of Labour Force — Total				
St. Catharines	61.7	55.7	9.7	38.3
Ontario	65.5	60.1	8.3	34.5
Canada	66.0	60.9	7.8	34.0
Males				
St. Catharines	66.0	59.1	10.4	34.0
Ontario	69.9	64.2	8.3	30.1
Canada	70.6	64.9	8.0	29.4
Females				
St. Catharines	57.8	52.7	8.9	42.2
Ontario	61.4	56.3	8.3	38.6
Canada	61.6	57.0	7.4	38.4

Note: Figures are based on total population 15 years and over
Source: Statistics Canada. 2013. 2011 National Household Survey. Statistics Canada Catalogue no. 99-004-XWE. Ottawa. Released September 11, 2013.

Labour Force by Industry (NAICS Codes 11–52)

Area	Agriculture, forestry, fishing & hunting	Mining, quarrying, & oil & gas extraction	Utilities	Construction	Manufacturing	Wholesale Trade	Retail Trade	Transportation & warehousing	Information & cultural industries	Finance & insurance
					Number					
					Total					
St. Catharines	1,615	50	365	3,890	6,465	2,530	9,240	2,410	1,195	2,205
Ontario	101,280	29,985	57,035	417,900	697,565	305,030	751,200	307,405	178,720	364,415
Canada	437,650	261,050	149,940	1,215,380	1,619,295	733,445	2,031,665	827,780	420,830	767,960
					Males					
St. Catharines	885	40	260	3,375	4,830	1,725	4,170	1,830	650	920
Ontario	66,485	25,650	42,685	369,300	493,305	197,770	344,480	225,245	98,835	153,125
Canada	307,370	211,690	110,765	1,068,710	1,167,680	494,545	933,850	617,305	235,875	296,995
					Females					
St. Catharines	730	0	105	520	1,640	805	5,070	585	545	1,280
Ontario	34,800	4,340	14,350	48,595	204,260	107,260	406,720	82,160	79,885	211,290
Canada	130,285	49,360	39,175	146,670	451,615	238,900	1,097,820	210,475	184,955	470,960
					Percent of Labour Force					
					Total					
St. Catharines	2.5	0.1	0.6	5.9	9.9	3.9	14.1	3.7	1.8	3.4
Ontario	1.5	0.4	0.9	6.3	10.4	4.6	11.2	4.6	2.7	5.5
Canada	2.5	1.5	0.9	6.9	9.2	4.2	11.6	4.7	2.4	4.4
					Males					
St. Catharines	2.7	0.1	0.8	10.2	14.6	5.2	12.6	5.5	2.0	2.8
Ontario	1.9	0.7	1.2	10.7	14.3	5.7	10.0	6.5	2.9	4.4
Canada	3.3	2.3	1.2	11.6	12.7	5.4	10.2	6.7	2.6	3.2
					Females					
St. Catharines	2.3	0.0	0.3	1.6	5.1	2.5	15.7	1.8	1.7	4.0
Ontario	1.1	0.1	0.4	1.5	6.3	3.3	12.6	2.5	2.5	6.5
Canada	1.6	0.6	0.5	1.7	5.4	2.8	13.1	2.5	2.2	5.6

Note: Figures are based on total experienced labour force 15 years and over. Experienced labour force refers to persons who, during the week of Sunday, May 1 to Saturday, May 7, 2011, were employed and the unemployed who had last worked for pay or in self-employment in either 2010 or 2011.
Source: Statistics Canada. 2013. 2011 National Household Survey. Statistics Canada Catalogue no. 99-004-XWE. Ottawa. Released September 11, 2013.

Labour Force by Industry (NAICS Codes 53–91)

Area	Real estate & rental & leasing	Profess., scientific & tech. services	Mgmt of companies & enterprises	Admin. & support, waste mgmt & remed. services	Educational services	Health care & social assistance	Arts, entertain. & recreation	Accomm. & food services	Other services (except public admin.)	Public admin.
					Number					
					Total					
St. Catharines	1,245	2,970	75	3,790	5,555	7,095	1,940	6,160	2,995	3,600
Ontario	133,980	511,020	6,525	309,630	499,690	692,130	144,065	417,675	296,340	458,665
Canada	321,895	1,240,850	17,460	728,330	1,301,435	1,949,650	363,405	1,130,750	807,800	1,261,050
					Males					
St. Catharines	630	1,475	20	2,120	1,995	1,095	1,050	2,745	1,430	1,900
Ontario	72,835	281,420	3,540	172,475	162,765	120,165	75,035	177,240	133,795	236,655
Canada	179,090	688,625	9,380	411,250	424,915	349,430	188,270	469,990	372,940	652,510
					Females					
St. Catharines	615	1,495	0	1,670	3,565	6,005	895	3,410	1,565	1,700
Ontario	61,145	229,600	2,990	137,155	336,925	571,965	69,030	240,430	162,550	222,015
Canada	142,805	552,225	8,075	317,085	876,515	1,600,220	175,135	660,760	434,865	608,535
					Percent of Labour Force					
					Total					
St. Catharines	1.9	4.5	0.1	5.8	8.5	10.8	3.0	9.4	4.6	5.5
Ontario	2.0	7.6	0.1	4.6	7.5	10.4	2.2	6.3	4.4	6.9
Canada	1.8	7.1	0.1	4.1	7.4	11.1	2.1	6.4	4.6	7.2
					Males					
St. Catharines	1.9	4.5	0.1	6.4	6.0	3.3	3.2	8.3	4.3	5.7
Ontario	2.1	8.2	0.1	5.0	4.7	3.5	2.2	5.1	3.9	6.9
Canada	1.9	7.5	0.1	4.5	4.6	3.8	2.0	5.1	4.1	7.1
					Females					
St. Catharines	1.9	4.6	0.0	5.2	11.0	18.6	2.8	10.6	4.9	5.3
Ontario	1.9	7.1	0.1	4.2	10.4	17.7	2.1	7.4	5.0	6.9
Canada	1.7	6.6	0.1	3.8	10.4	19.1	2.1	7.9	5.2	7.2

Note: Figures are based on total experienced labour force 15 years and over. Experienced labour force refers to persons who, during the week of Sunday, May 1 to Saturday, May 7, 2011, were employed and the unemployed who had last worked for pay or in self-employment in either 2010 or 2011.
Source: Statistics Canada. 2013. 2011 National Household Survey. Statistics Canada Catalogue no. 99-004-XWE. Ottawa. Released September 11, 2013.

PROFILES / St. Catharines, Ontario

Occupation

Area	Mgmt	Business, Finance & Admin.	Natural/ Applied Sciences & Related	Health	Education, Law & Social, Community & Government Services	Art, Culture, Recreation & Sport	Sales & Service	Trades, Transport & Equip. Operators & Related	Natural Resources, Agri. & Related Production	Mfg & Utilities
					Number					
					Total					
St. Catharines	6,265	9,955	3,150	3,900	7,460	1,900	19,745	8,380	1,600	3,055
Ontario	770,580	1,138,330	494,500	392,695	801,465	206,420	1,550,260	868,515	106,810	350,685
Canada	1,963,600	2,902,045	1,237,775	1,107,200	2,064,675	503,415	4,068,170	2,537,775	397,930	805,040
					Males					
St. Catharines	3,745	3,040	2,520	615	2,645	845	8,385	7,950	1,075	2,315
Ontario	474,655	352,505	384,345	78,330	264,570	96,055	673,880	812,280	82,610	233,565
Canada	1,229,460	854,190	966,355	217,520	676,550	232,535	1,745,705	2,385,615	318,945	564,300
					Females					
St. Catharines	2,525	6,915	630	3,285	4,815	1,055	11,355	420	525	745
Ontario	295,920	785,825	110,150	314,370	536,895	110,370	876,380	56,230	24,200	117,115
Canada	734,140	2,047,855	271,415	889,675	1,388,130	270,875	2,322,465	152,165	78,980	240,740
					Percent of Labour Force					
					Total					
St. Catharines	9.6	15.2	4.8	6.0	11.4	2.9	30.2	12.8	2.4	4.7
Ontario	11.5	17.0	7.4	5.9	12.0	3.1	23.2	13.0	1.6	5.2
Canada	11.2	16.5	7.0	6.3	11.7	2.9	23.1	14.4	2.3	4.6
					Males					
St. Catharines	11.3	9.2	7.6	1.9	8.0	2.5	25.3	24.0	3.2	7.0
Ontario	13.7	10.2	11.1	2.3	7.7	2.8	19.5	23.5	2.4	6.8
Canada	13.4	9.3	10.5	2.4	7.4	2.5	19.0	26.0	3.5	6.1
					Females					
St. Catharines	7.8	21.4	2.0	10.2	14.9	3.3	35.2	1.3	1.6	2.3
Ontario	9.2	24.3	3.4	9.7	16.6	3.4	27.2	1.7	0.7	3.6
Canada	8.7	24.4	3.2	10.6	16.5	3.2	27.7	1.8	0.9	2.9

Note: Figures are based on total experienced labour force 15 years and over.
Source: Statistics Canada. 2013. 2011 National Household Survey. Statistics Canada Catalogue no. 99-004-XWE. Ottawa. Released September 11, 2013.

Place of Work Status

Area	Worked at Home	Worked Outside Canada	No Fixed Workplace Address	Worked at Usual Place
		Number		
		Total		
St. Catharines	3,330	205	5,970	51,495
Ontario	423,790	31,390	670,835	5,170,980
Canada	1,142,640	66,460	1,868,245	13,517,690
		Males		
St. Catharines	1,630	130	4,370	24,520
Ontario	216,900	21,150	486,560	2,524,555
Canada	582,150	47,355	1,400,485	6,604,325
		Females		
St. Catharines	1,700	75	1,595	26,975
Ontario	206,895	10,240	184,275	2,646,420
Canada	560,490	19,100	467,760	6,913,370
		Percent of Labour Force		
		Total		
St. Catharines	5.5	0.3	9.8	84.4
Ontario	6.7	0.5	10.7	82.1
Canada	6.9	0.4	11.3	81.5
		Males		
St. Catharines	5.3	0.4	14.3	80.0
Ontario	6.7	0.7	15.0	77.7
Canada	6.7	0.5	16.2	76.5
		Females		
St. Catharines	5.6	0.2	5.3	88.9
Ontario	6.8	0.3	6.0	86.8
Canada	7.0	0.2	5.9	86.8

Note: Figures are based on total employed labour force 15 years and over.
Source: Statistics Canada. 2013. 2011 National Household Survey. Statistics Canada Catalogue no. 99-004-XWE. Ottawa. Released September 11, 2013.

Mode of Transportation to Work

Area	Car; Truck; Van; as Driver	Car; Truck; Van; as Passenger	Public Transit	Walked	Bicycled	All Other Modes
			Number			
			Total			
St. Catharines	45,755	4,520	2,695	3,280	780	435
Ontario	4,235,315	357,110	818,270	299,095	69,885	62,145
Canada	11,393,140	867,050	1,851,525	880,815	201,780	191,625
			Males			
St. Catharines	23,330	2,275	880	1,640	525	245
Ontario	2,316,680	143,410	340,995	131,765	47,635	30,635
Canada	6,238,835	349,530	788,290	387,580	135,840	104,725
			Females			
St. Catharines	22,420	2,245	1,815	1,640	255	190
Ontario	1,918,640	213,700	477,275	167,325	22,250	31,515
Canada	5,154,305	517,520	1,063,235	493,230	65,940	86,900
			Percent of Labour Force			
			Total			
St. Catharines	79.6	7.9	4.7	5.7	1.4	0.8
Ontario	72.5	6.1	14.0	5.1	1.2	1.1
Canada	74.0	5.6	12.0	5.7	1.3	1.2
			Males			
St. Catharines	80.7	7.9	3.0	5.7	1.8	0.8
Ontario	76.9	4.8	11.3	4.4	1.6	1.0
Canada	77.9	4.4	9.8	4.8	1.7	1.3
			Females			
St. Catharines	78.5	7.9	6.4	5.7	0.9	0.7
Ontario	67.8	7.5	16.9	5.9	0.8	1.1
Canada	69.8	7.0	14.4	6.7	0.9	1.2

Note: Figures are based on total employed labour force 15 years and over.
Source: Statistics Canada. 2013. 2011 National Household Survey. Statistics Canada Catalogue no. 99-004-XWE. Ottawa. Released September 11, 2013.

Visible Minority Population Characteristics

Area	Total Minority	South Asian[1]	Chinese	Black	Filipino	Latin American	Arab	SE Asian[2]	West Asian[3]	Korean	Japanese	Multiple[4]
						Number						
						Total						
St. Catharines	12,690	1,430	1,905	2,675	1,045	1,920	1,220	630	410	360	300	430
Ontario	3,279,565	965,990	629,140	539,205	275,380	172,560	151,645	137,875	122,530	78,290	29,085	96,735
Canada	6,264,750	1,567,400	1,324,750	945,665	619,310	381,280	380,620	312,075	206,840	161,130	87,270	171,935
						Males						
St. Catharines	6,525	730	895	1,505	435	1,045	645	325	220	195	165	230
Ontario	1,582,480	484,355	301,575	251,295	116,825	83,205	79,620	67,645	62,515	38,045	13,345	46,765
Canada	3,043,010	790,755	632,325	453,005	268,885	186,355	203,485	154,035	105,620	77,165	38,270	83,335
						Females						
St. Catharines	6,160	700	1,010	1,170	610	880	575	310	185	165	135	200
Ontario	1,697,085	481,635	327,570	287,915	158,555	89,360	72,025	70,230	60,010	40,250	15,740	49,970
Canada	3,221,745	776,650	692,420	492,660	350,425	194,925	177,140	158,045	101,220	83,965	48,990	88,600
						Percent of Population						
						Total						
St. Catharines	9.9	1.1	1.5	2.1	0.8	1.5	0.9	0.5	0.3	0.3	0.2	0.3
Ontario	25.9	7.6	5.0	4.3	2.2	1.4	1.2	1.1	1.0	0.6	0.2	0.8
Canada	19.1	4.8	4.0	2.9	1.9	1.2	1.2	0.9	0.6	0.5	0.3	0.5
						Males						
St. Catharines	10.6	1.2	1.5	2.4	0.7	1.7	1.0	0.5	0.4	0.3	0.3	0.4
Ontario	25.6	7.8	4.9	4.1	1.9	1.3	1.3	1.1	1.0	0.6	0.2	0.8
Canada	18.8	4.9	3.9	2.8	1.7	1.2	1.3	1.0	0.7	0.5	0.2	0.5
						Females						
St. Catharines	9.2	1.0	1.5	1.7	0.9	1.3	0.9	0.5	0.3	0.2	0.2	0.3
Ontario	26.2	7.4	5.1	4.4	2.5	1.4	1.1	1.1	0.9	0.6	0.2	0.8
Canada	19.3	4.7	4.1	3.0	2.1	1.2	1.1	0.9	0.6	0.5	0.3	0.5

Note: The Employment Equity Act defines visible minorities as 'persons, other than Aboriginal peoples, who are non-Caucasian in race or non-white in colour';
(1) Includes 'East Indian,' 'Pakistani,' 'Sri Lankan,' etc.; (2) Includes 'Vietnamese,' 'Cambodian,' 'Malaysian,' 'Laotian,' etc.; (3) Includes 'Iranian,' 'Afghan,' etc.; (4) Includes respondents who reported more than one visible minority group by checking two or more mark-in circles, e.g., 'Black' and 'South Asian.'
Source: Statistics Canada. 2013. 2011 National Household Survey. Statistics Canada Catalogue no. 99-004-XWE. Ottawa. Released September 11, 2013.

PROFILES / St. Catharines, Ontario

Aboriginal Population

Area	Aboriginal Identity[1]	First Nations (North American Indian) Single Identity[2]	Métis Single Identity	Inuk (Inuit) Single Identity	Multiple Aboriginal Identities[3]	Aboriginal Identities Not Included Elsewhere
			Number			
			Total			
St. Catharines	2,425	1,515	740	75	0	85
Ontario	301,430	201,100	86,020	3,355	2,910	8,040
Canada	1,400,685	851,560	451,795	59,440	11,415	26,475
			Males			
St. Catharines	1,015	740	225	0	0	35
Ontario	145,020	96,620	41,755	1,475	1,420	3,750
Canada	682,190	411,785	223,335	29,495	5,525	12,055
			Females			
St. Catharines	1,405	780	510	75	0	45
Ontario	156,410	104,485	44,260	1,880	1,490	4,295
Canada	718,500	439,775	228,460	29,950	5,890	14,420
			Percent of Population			
			Total			
St. Catharines	1.9	1.2	0.6	0.1	0.0	0.1
Ontario	2.4	1.6	0.7	0.0	0.0	0.1
Canada	4.3	2.6	1.4	0.2	0.0	0.1
			Males			
St. Catharines	1.7	1.2	0.4	0.0	0.0	0.1
Ontario	2.3	1.6	0.7	0.0	0.0	0.1
Canada	4.2	2.5	1.4	0.2	0.0	0.1
			Females			
St. Catharines	2.1	1.2	0.8	0.1	0.0	0.1
Ontario	2.4	1.6	0.7	0.0	0.0	0.1
Canada	4.3	2.6	1.4	0.2	0.0	0.1

Note: (1) Includes persons who reported being an Aboriginal person, that is, First Nations (North American Indian), Métis or Inuk (Inuit) and/or those who reported Registered or Treaty Indian status, that is registered under the Indian Act of Canada, and/or those who reported membership in a First Nation or Indian band. Aboriginal peoples of Canada are defined in the Constitution Act, 1982, section 35-2 as including the Indian, Inuit and Métis peoples of Canada; (2) Users should be aware that the estimates associated with this variable are more affected than most by the incomplete enumeration of certain Indian reserves and Indian settlements in the National Household Survey (NHS); (3) Includes persons who reported being any two or all three of the following: First Nations (North American Indian), Métis or Inuk (Inuit).
Source: Statistics Canada. 2013. 2011 National Household Survey. Statistics Canada Catalogue no. 99-004-XWE. Ottawa. Released September 11, 2013.

Ethnic Origin

Area	North American Aboriginal	Other North American	European	Caribbean	Latin, Central and South American	African	Asian	Oceania
			Number					
			Total					
St. Catharines	4,835	34,405	103,590	1,950	2,390	2,465	8,530	240
Ontario	441,395	3,059,480	8,231,410	396,485	271,545	331,460	2,604,595	19,410
Canada	1,836,035	11,070,455	20,157,965	627,590	544,375	766,735	5,011,225	74,875
			Males					
St. Catharines	2,100	16,655	48,960	1,155	1,205	1,200	4,195	100
Ontario	210,490	1,507,105	4,019,885	181,805	130,035	160,940	1,265,540	9,855
Canada	885,675	5,462,685	9,913,150	291,640	264,635	387,360	2,435,540	37,490
			Females					
St. Catharines	2,730	17,745	54,620	795	1,185	1,270	4,330	145
Ontario	230,905	1,552,380	4,211,525	214,675	141,510	170,515	1,339,050	9,555
Canada	950,360	5,607,770	10,244,820	335,945	279,740	379,380	2,575,680	37,385
			Percent of Population					
			Total					
St. Catharines	3.8	26.7	80.4	1.5	1.9	1.9	6.6	0.2
Ontario	3.5	24.2	65.1	3.1	2.1	2.6	20.6	0.2
Canada	5.6	33.7	61.4	1.9	1.7	2.3	15.3	0.2
			Males					
St. Catharines	3.4	27.1	79.7	1.9	2.0	2.0	6.8	0.2
Ontario	3.4	24.4	65.0	2.9	2.1	2.6	20.5	0.2
Canada	5.5	33.8	61.3	1.8	1.6	2.4	15.1	0.2
			Females					
St. Catharines	4.1	26.4	81.2	1.2	1.8	1.9	6.4	0.2
Ontario	3.6	24.0	65.1	3.3	2.2	2.6	20.7	0.1
Canada	5.7	33.6	61.4	2.0	1.7	2.3	15.4	0.2

Note: The sum of the ethnic groups in this table is greater than the total population estimate because a person may report more than one ethnic origin in the NHS.
Source: Statistics Canada. 2013. 2011 National Household Survey. Statistics Canada Catalogue no. 99-004-XWE. Ottawa. Released September 11, 2013.

Religion

Area	Buddhist	Christian	Hindu	Jewish	Muslim	Sikh	Traditional (Aboriginal) Spirituality	Other Religions	No Religious Affiliation
Number									
Total									
St. Catharines	750	92,410	370	480	2,630	35	60	485	31,550
Ontario	163,750	8,167,295	366,720	195,540	581,950	179,765	15,905	53,080	2,927,790
Canada	366,830	22,102,745	497,965	329,495	1,053,945	454,965	64,935	130,835	7,850,605
Males									
St. Catharines	335	42,340	165	300	1,365	20	0	205	16,695
Ontario	75,355	3,839,925	183,580	95,795	293,925	90,515	7,600	23,555	1,571,195
Canada	168,465	10,497,775	250,435	161,265	540,555	229,435	31,805	57,745	4,225,645
Females									
St. Catharines	415	50,075	210	175	1,255	20	20	280	14,855
Ontario	88,395	4,327,365	183,140	99,740	288,025	89,250	8,310	29,525	1,356,600
Canada	198,365	11,604,975	247,525	168,235	513,395	225,530	33,135	73,090	3,624,965
Percent of Population									
Total									
St. Catharines	0.6	71.8	0.3	0.4	2.0	0.0	0.0	0.4	24.5
Ontario	1.3	64.6	2.9	1.5	4.6	1.4	0.1	0.4	23.1
Canada	1.1	67.3	1.5	1.0	3.2	1.4	0.2	0.4	23.9
Males									
St. Catharines	0.5	68.9	0.3	0.5	2.2	0.0	0.0	0.3	27.2
Ontario	1.2	62.1	3.0	1.5	4.8	1.5	0.1	0.4	25.4
Canada	1.0	64.9	1.5	1.0	3.3	1.4	0.2	0.4	26.1
Females									
St. Catharines	0.6	74.4	0.3	0.3	1.9	0.0	0.0	0.4	22.1
Ontario	1.4	66.9	2.8	1.5	4.5	1.4	0.1	0.5	21.0
Canada	1.2	69.5	1.5	1.0	3.1	1.4	0.2	0.4	21.7

Note: Religion refers to the person's self-identification as having a connection or affiliation with any religious denomination, group, body, sect, cult or other religiously defined community or system of belief. Religion is not limited to formal membership in a religious organization or group. Persons without a religious connection or affiliation can self-identify as atheist, agnostic or humanist, or can provide another applicable response.
Source: Statistics Canada. 2013. 2011 National Household Survey. Statistics Canada Catalogue no. 99-004-XWE. Ottawa. Released September 11, 2013.

Religion—Christian Denominations

Area	Anglican	Baptist	Catholic	Christian Orthodox	Lutheran	Pentecostal	Presbyterian	United Church	Other Christian
Number									
Total									
St. Catharines	12,265	2,265	41,090	1,750	1,835	2,285	4,680	9,725	16,505
Ontario	774,560	244,650	3,976,610	297,710	163,460	213,945	319,585	952,465	1,224,300
Canada	1,631,845	635,840	12,810,705	550,690	478,185	478,705	472,385	2,007,610	3,036,780
Males									
St. Catharines	5,420	995	19,215	910	870	1,055	2,005	4,150	7,715
Ontario	355,175	112,285	1,895,940	145,825	75,225	94,955	148,535	435,255	576,730
Canada	752,945	293,905	6,167,290	270,205	221,525	217,850	218,955	912,545	1,442,550
Females									
St. Catharines	6,845	1,275	21,870	845	970	1,230	2,675	5,580	8,790
Ontario	419,390	132,370	2,080,665	151,885	88,230	118,990	171,050	517,210	647,570
Canada	878,900	341,940	6,643,415	280,485	256,660	260,850	253,430	1,095,065	1,594,230
Percent of Population									
Total									
St. Catharines	9.5	1.8	31.9	1.4	1.4	1.8	3.6	7.6	12.8
Ontario	6.1	1.9	31.4	2.4	1.3	1.7	2.5	7.5	9.7
Canada	5.0	1.9	39.0	1.7	1.5	1.5	1.4	6.1	9.2
Males									
St. Catharines	8.8	1.6	31.3	1.5	1.4	1.7	3.3	6.8	12.6
Ontario	5.7	1.8	30.7	2.4	1.2	1.5	2.4	7.0	9.3
Canada	4.7	1.8	38.2	1.7	1.4	1.3	1.4	5.6	8.9
Females									
St. Catharines	10.2	1.9	32.5	1.3	1.4	1.8	4.0	8.3	13.1
Ontario	6.5	2.0	32.2	2.3	1.4	1.8	2.6	8.0	10.0
Canada	5.3	2.0	39.8	1.7	1.5	1.6	1.5	6.6	9.6

Note: Religion refers to the person's self-identification as having a connection or affiliation with any religious denomination, group, body, sect, cult or other religiously defined community or system of belief. Religion is not limited to formal membership in a religious organization or group. Persons without a religious connection or affiliation can self-identify as atheist, agnostic or humanist, or can provide another applicable response.
Source: Statistics Canada. 2013. 2011 National Household Survey. Statistics Canada Catalogue no. 99-004-XWE. Ottawa. Released September 11, 2013.

PROFILES / St. Catharines, Ontario

Immigrant Status and Period of Immigration

Area	Non-Immigrants[1]	Immigrants All	Before 1971	1971 to 1980	1981 to 1990	1991 to 2000	2001 to 2005	2006 to 2011	Non-Permanent Residents[3]
				Number					
				Total					
St. Catharines	102,505	25,030	9,845	4,105	2,890	3,420	2,230	2,545	1,230
Ontario	8,906,000	3,611,365	723,030	464,380	538,285	866,220	518,405	501,060	134,425
Canada	25,720,175	6,775,765	1,261,055	870,775	949,890	1,539,050	992,070	1,162,915	356,385
				Males					
St. Catharines	49,390	11,430	4,305	1,865	1,420	1,545	1,155	1,140	640
Ontario	4,410,240	1,706,385	341,820	217,990	258,095	408,270	245,850	234,360	64,825
Canada	12,753,235	3,231,370	605,430	416,670	454,570	724,905	474,545	555,245	178,515
				Females					
St. Catharines	53,120	13,600	5,540	2,240	1,475	1,875	1,075	1,400	590
Ontario	4,495,765	1,904,985	381,210	246,390	280,190	457,950	272,550	266,695	69,600
Canada	12,966,935	3,544,400	655,625	454,105	495,325	814,145	517,530	607,670	177,870
				Percent of Population					
				Total					
St. Catharines	79.6	19.4	7.6	3.2	2.2	2.7	1.7	2.0	1.0
Ontario	70.4	28.5	5.7	3.7	4.3	6.8	4.1	4.0	1.1
Canada	78.3	20.6	3.8	2.7	2.9	4.7	3.0	3.5	1.1
				Males					
St. Catharines	80.4	18.6	7.0	3.0	2.3	2.5	1.9	1.9	1.0
Ontario	71.3	27.6	5.5	3.5	4.2	6.6	4.0	3.8	1.0
Canada	78.9	20.0	3.7	2.6	2.8	4.5	2.9	3.4	1.1
				Females					
St. Catharines	78.9	20.2	8.2	3.3	2.2	2.8	1.6	2.1	0.9
Ontario	69.5	29.4	5.9	3.8	4.3	7.1	4.2	4.1	1.1
Canada	77.7	21.2	3.9	2.7	3.0	4.9	3.1	3.6	1.1

Note: (1) Non-immigrant refers to a person who is a Canadian citizen by birth; (2) Immigrant refers to a person who is or has ever been a landed immigrant/permanent resident. This person has been granted the right to live in Canada permanently by immigration authorities. Some immigrants have resided in Canada for a number of years, while others have arrived recently. Some immigrants are Canadian citizens, while others are not. Most immigrants are born outside Canada, but a small number are born in Canada. In the 2011 National Household Survey, 'Immigrants' includes immigrants who landed in Canada prior to May 10, 2011; (3) Non-permanent resident refers to a person from another country who has a work or study permit, or who is a refugee claimant, and any non-Canadian-born family member living in Canada with them.
Source: Statistics Canada. 2013. 2011 National Household Survey. Statistics Canada Catalogue no. 99-004-XWE. Ottawa. Released September 11, 2013.

Mother Tongue

Area	English	French	Non-official Language	English & French	English & Non-official Language	French & Non-official Language	English, French & Non-official Language
			Number				
			Total				
St. Catharines	103,640	2,890	20,755	400	1,310	70	40
Ontario	8,677,040	493,300	3,264,435	46,605	219,425	13,645	7,615
Canada	18,858,980	7,054,975	6,567,680	144,685	396,330	74,430	24,095
			Males				
St. Catharines	50,055	1,320	9,675	190	610	25	20
Ontario	4,276,970	232,785	1,562,190	21,805	106,790	6,285	3,495
Canada	9,345,225	3,452,380	3,157,785	69,975	192,000	36,535	11,965
			Females				
St. Catharines	53,590	1,570	11,085	210	705	40	20
Ontario	4,400,065	260,510	1,702,240	24,795	112,635	7,365	4,115
Canada	9,513,750	3,602,590	3,409,895	74,710	204,330	37,890	12,130
			Percent of Population				
			Total				
St. Catharines	80.3	2.2	16.1	0.3	1.0	0.1	0.0
Ontario	68.2	3.9	25.7	0.4	1.7	0.1	0.1
Canada	56.9	21.3	19.8	0.4	1.2	0.2	0.1
			Males				
St. Catharines	80.9	2.1	15.6	0.3	1.0	0.0	0.0
Ontario	68.9	3.7	25.2	0.4	1.7	0.1	0.1
Canada	57.5	21.2	19.4	0.4	1.2	0.2	0.1
			Females				
St. Catharines	79.7	2.3	16.5	0.3	1.0	0.1	0.0
Ontario	67.6	4.0	26.1	0.4	1.7	0.1	0.1
Canada	56.4	21.4	20.2	0.4	1.2	0.2	0.1

Note: Figures cover total population excluding institutional residents.
Source: Statistics Canada. 2012. Census Profile. 2011 Census. Statistics Canada Catalogue no. 98-316-XWE. Ottawa. Released October 24 2012.
http://www12.statcan.gc.ca/census-recensement/2011/dp-pd/prof/index.cfm?Lang=E

Language Spoken Most Often at Home

Area	English	French	Non-official Language	English & French	English & Non-official Language	French & Non-official Language	English, French & Non-official Language
			Number				
			Total				
St. Catharines	116,525	890	8,625	260	2,715	25	65
Ontario	10,044,810	284,115	1,827,870	37,955	509,105	6,370	11,845
Canada	21,457,075	6,827,865	3,673,865	131,205	875,135	109,700	46,330
			Males				
St. Catharines	56,080	400	4,010	105	1,260	10	25
Ontario	4,930,610	133,495	872,860	17,250	248,050	2,855	5,225
Canada	10,585,620	3,348,235	1,767,310	63,475	425,370	53,010	22,845
			Females				
St. Catharines	60,450	495	4,615	155	1,460	15	40
Ontario	5,114,200	150,620	955,010	20,705	261,055	3,520	6,620
Canada	10,871,455	3,479,625	1,906,555	67,730	449,765	56,690	23,485
			Percent of Population				
			Total				
St. Catharines	90.3	0.7	6.7	0.2	2.1	0.0	0.1
Ontario	79.0	2.2	14.4	0.3	4.0	0.1	0.1
Canada	64.8	20.6	11.1	0.4	2.6	0.3	0.1
			Males				
St. Catharines	90.6	0.6	6.5	0.2	2.0	0.0	0.0
Ontario	79.4	2.1	14.1	0.3	4.0	0.0	0.1
Canada	65.1	20.6	10.9	0.4	2.6	0.3	0.1
			Females				
St. Catharines	89.9	0.7	6.9	0.2	2.2	0.0	0.1
Ontario	78.5	2.3	14.7	0.3	4.0	0.1	0.1
Canada	64.5	20.6	11.3	0.4	2.7	0.3	0.1

Note: Figures cover total population excluding institutional residents.
Source: Statistics Canada. 2012. Census Profile. 2011 Census. Statistics Canada Catalogue no. 98-316-XWE. Ottawa. Released October 24 2012.
http://www12.statcan.gc.ca/census-recensement/2011/dp-pd/prof/index.cfm?Lang=E

Knowledge of Official Languages

Area	English Only	French Only	English & French	Neither English nor French
		Number		
		Total		
St. Catharines	119,230	115	8,820	945
Ontario	10,984,360	42,980	1,395,805	298,920
Canada	22,564,665	4,165,015	5,795,570	595,920
		Males		
St. Catharines	57,705	50	3,775	360
Ontario	5,445,050	18,805	627,725	118,765
Canada	11,222,185	1,925,340	2,876,560	241,790
		Females		
St. Catharines	61,530	60	5,045	585
Ontario	5,539,310	24,175	768,085	180,155
Canada	11,342,485	2,239,680	2,919,005	354,135
		Percent of Population		
		Total		
St. Catharines	92.3	0.1	6.8	0.7
Ontario	86.3	0.3	11.0	2.3
Canada	68.1	12.6	17.5	1.8
		Males		
St. Catharines	93.2	0.1	6.1	0.6
Ontario	87.7	0.3	10.1	1.9
Canada	69.0	11.8	17.7	1.5
		Females		
St. Catharines	91.5	0.1	7.5	0.9
Ontario	85.1	0.4	11.8	2.8
Canada	67.3	13.3	17.3	2.1

Note: Figures cover total population excluding institutional residents.
Source: Statistics Canada. 2012. Census Profile. 2011 Census. Statistics Canada Catalogue no. 98-316-XWE. Ottawa. Released October 24 2012.
http://www12.statcan.gc.ca/census-recensement/2011/dp-pd/prof/index.cfm?Lang=E

St. John's, Newfoundland and Labrador

Background

St. John's is located on the island of Newfoundland, on the eastern tip of the Avalon Peninsula. The city is the provincial capital of Newfoundland and Labrador as well as the largest municipality. Access from the mainland is by ferry, car, air or cruise ship.

The oldest English-founded city (est. 1497) and most easterly port in North America, St. John's has been shaped by First Nations, Vikings, European explorers, soldiers and pirates for more than 500 years. It was incorporated as a city in 1921.

St. John's is renowned for its hilly downtown harbour, picturesque side streets, brightly coloured row houses and surrounding hills. Two National Historic Sites are situated in St. John's: Signal Hill was the site of the first transatlantic wireless signal (1901) and Cape Spear, the oldest surviving lighthouse in Newfoundland.

Minke, humpback and blue whales can be seen from the city in summer and massive icebergs float offshore in spring. A nearby bird sanctuary attracts migrating seabirds and other marine life.

The City of St. John's is an emerging global energy capital because of the nearby oil fields in Grand Banks and the offshore energy potential of the Atlantic Margin reservoirs. Other key industries include ocean technology; fishery and marine biotechnology; marine tourism; education and training; research and development; infrastructure; and culture.

The City of St. John's claims to have the highest concentration of musicians, artists, writers, dancers and craftspeople per capita in Canada. It is known as the "City of Legends" because of its deep appreciation of folklore and storytelling.

St. John's has summer highs of plus 18.70 degrees Celsius, winter lows of minus 7.80 degrees Celsius, and an average rainfall just over 1191 mm per year.

Rankings

- St. John's was ranked as one of the top places to do business in Canada by KPMG, a global firm specializing in audit, tax and advisory services. The City of St. John's was ranked #4 out of 16 Canadian cities. The report evaluated three key areas: corporate income tax, other corporate taxes (e.g., sales tax, property tax) and statutory labour costs. The study's total tax index ranked St. John's #4 out of 113 global cities, with an index of 45.4. *KPMG, "Competitive Alternatives: Special Report: Focus on Tax," released September 25, 2012*
- In 2012, St. John's ranked #5 of Canada's best cities for real estate investors, moving up from #9 in 2011. Favourable factors included an offshore oil sector, a growing economy and an emerging metal mining sector. Average house prices in St. John's were still an affordable $270,000 in 2012. *Money Sense, "Where to Buy Now," May 29, 2012*
- The City of St. John's was ranked as having the most wet days (215) and the most days with a temperature below freezing (174) in Canada. Oakville, Ontario, was ranked #1 for best weather in Canada with only 118 wet days. *Money Sense, "No Where to Go But Up: Worst Weather in Canada," March 20, 2012*

PROFILES / St. John's, Newfoundland and Labrador

Population Growth and Density

Area	Population in 2001	Population in 2006	Population in 2011	Population Change 2001–2006	Population Change 2006–2011	Land Area (sq. km)	Population Density per sq. km
St. John's	99,182	100,646	106,172	1.5	5.5	446.06	238.0
N.L.	512,930	505,469	514,536	-1.5	1.8	370,510.76	1.4
Canada	30,007,094	31,612,897	33,476,688	5.4	5.9	8,965,121.42	3.7

Source: Statistics Canada. 2012. Census Profile. 2011 Census. Statistics Canada Catalogue no. 98-316-XWE. Ottawa. Released October 24 2012. http://www12.statcan.gc.ca/census-recensement/2011/dp-pd/prof/index.cfm?Lang=E;
Statistics Canada 2007. 2006 Community Profiles. 2006 Census. Statistics Canada Catalogue no. 92-591-XWE. Ottawa. Released March 13 2007. http://www12.statcan.ca/census-recensement/2006/dp-pd/prof/92-591/index.cfm?Lang=E

Gender

Area	Males	Females
	Number	
St. John's	50,505	55,670
N.L.	250,570	263,970
Canada	16,414,225	17,062,460
	Percent of Population	
St. John's	47.6	52.4
N.L.	48.7	51.3
Canada	49.0	51.0

Source: Statistics Canada. 2012. Census Profile. 2011 Census. Statistics Canada Catalogue no. 98-316-XWE. Ottawa. Released October 24 2012.
http://www12.statcan.gc.ca/census-recensement/2011/dp-pd/prof/index.cfm?Lang=E

Marital Status

Area	Married[1]	Living Common-law	Single[2]	Separated	Divorced	Widowed
			Number			
			Total			
St. John's	38,130	8,790	31,030	2,235	5,725	5,555
N.L.	231,745	41,295	107,375	8,705	19,855	28,935
Canada	12,941,960	3,142,525	7,816,045	698,240	1,686,035	1,584,530
			Males			
St. John's	19,070	4,390	15,625	840	2,095	965
N.L.	115,840	20,605	56,945	3,755	8,545	5,620
Canada	6,470,300	1,575,495	4,206,320	299,655	680,415	310,940
			Females			
St. John's	19,060	4,395	15,405	1,390	3,635	4,585
N.L.	115,905	20,690	50,425	4,950	11,315	23,315
Canada	6,471,660	1,567,035	3,609,730	398,585	1,005,620	1,273,590
			Percent of Population			
			Total			
St. John's	41.7	9.6	33.9	2.4	6.3	6.1
N.L.	52.9	9.4	24.5	2.0	4.5	6.6
Canada	46.4	11.3	28.0	2.5	6.0	5.7
			Males			
St. John's	44.4	10.2	36.3	2.0	4.9	2.2
N.L.	54.8	9.8	26.9	1.8	4.0	2.7
Canada	47.8	11.6	31.1	2.2	5.0	2.3
			Females			
St. John's	39.3	9.1	31.8	2.9	7.5	9.5
N.L.	51.1	9.1	22.3	2.2	5.0	10.3
Canada	45.2	10.9	25.2	2.8	7.0	8.9

Note: (1) and not separated, (2) never legally married
Source: Statistics Canada. 2012. Census Profile. 2011 Census. Statistics Canada Catalogue no. 98-316-XWE. Ottawa. Released October 24 2012.
http://www12.statcan.gc.ca/census-recensement/2011/dp-pd/prof/index.cfm?Lang=E

Age Characteristics: 0 to 49 Years

Area	0 to 4 Years	5 to 9 Years	10 to 14 Years	15 to 19 Years	20 to 24 Years	25 to 29 Years	30 to 34 Years	35 to 39 Years	40 to 44 Years	45 to 49 Years
					Number					
					Total					
St. John's	5,000	4,735	4,965	6,055	9,785	8,830	7,200	6,710	7,055	8,110
N.L.	24,495	25,105	27,035	29,590	30,050	28,305	29,275	33,375	38,015	42,225
Canada	1,877,095	1,809,895	1,920,355	2,178,135	2,187,450	2,169,590	2,162,905	2,173,930	2,324,875	2,675,130
					Males					
St. John's	2,505	2,455	2,555	3,040	4,835	4,415	3,505	3,245	3,310	3,785
N.L.	12,620	12,845	13,795	15,175	15,075	13,605	13,840	15,895	18,385	20,545
Canada	961,150	925,965	983,995	1,115,845	1,108,775	1,077,275	1,058,810	1,064,200	1,141,720	1,318,715
					Females					
St. John's	2,500	2,285	2,410	3,015	4,950	4,410	3,690	3,465	3,740	4,325
N.L.	11,875	12,260	13,235	14,410	14,975	14,705	15,435	17,480	19,630	21,680
Canada	915,945	883,935	936,360	1,062,295	1,078,670	1,092,315	1,104,095	1,109,735	1,183,155	1,356,420
					Percent of Population					
					Total					
St. John's	4.7	4.5	4.7	5.7	9.2	8.3	6.8	6.3	6.6	7.6
N.L.	4.8	4.9	5.3	5.8	5.8	5.5	5.7	6.5	7.4	8.2
Canada	5.6	5.4	5.7	6.5	6.5	6.5	6.5	6.5	6.9	8.0
					Males					
St. John's	5.0	4.9	5.1	6.0	9.6	8.7	6.9	6.4	6.6	7.5
N.L.	5.0	5.1	5.5	6.1	6.0	5.4	5.5	6.3	7.3	8.2
Canada	5.9	5.6	6.0	6.8	6.8	6.6	6.5	6.5	7.0	8.0
					Females					
St. John's	4.5	4.1	4.3	5.4	8.9	7.9	6.6	6.2	6.7	7.8
N.L.	4.5	4.6	5.0	5.5	5.7	5.6	5.8	6.6	7.4	8.2
Canada	5.4	5.2	5.5	6.2	6.2	6.4	6.5	6.5	6.9	7.9

Source: Statistics Canada. 2012. Census Profile. 2011 Census. Statistics Canada Catalogue no. 98-316-XWE. Ottawa. Released October 24 2012.
http://www12.statcan.gc.ca/census-recensement/2011/dp-pd/prof/index.cfm?Lang=E

Age Characteristics: 50 Years and Over, and Median Age

Area	50 to 54 Years	55 to 59 Years	60 to 64 Years	65 to 69 Years	70 to 74 Years	75 to 79 Years	80 to 84 Years	85 Years and Over	Median Age
				Number					
				Total					
St. John's	8,045	7,500	6,595	5,070	3,630	2,735	2,130	2,025	39.9
N.L.	43,185	42,645	39,135	28,740	20,115	14,620	10,075	8,560	44.0
Canada	2,658,965	2,340,635	2,052,670	1,521,715	1,153,065	922,700	702,070	645,515	40.6
				Males					
St. John's	3,790	3,535	3,115	2,325	1,650	1,095	755	580	38.0
N.L.	21,075	20,950	19,235	14,100	9,775	6,750	4,110	2,800	43.4
Canada	1,309,030	1,147,300	1,002,690	738,010	543,435	417,945	291,085	208,300	39.6
				Females					
St. John's	4,255	3,960	3,480	2,740	1,975	1,640	1,375	1,445	41.5
N.L.	22,110	21,695	19,895	14,645	10,340	7,875	5,965	5,755	44.5
Canada	1,349,940	1,193,335	1,049,985	783,705	609,630	504,755	410,985	437,215	41.5
				Percent of Population					
				Total					
St. John's	7.6	7.1	6.2	4.8	3.4	2.6	2.0	1.9	—
N.L.	8.4	8.3	7.6	5.6	3.9	2.8	2.0	1.7	—
Canada	7.9	7.0	6.1	4.5	3.4	2.8	2.1	1.9	—
				Males					
St. John's	7.5	7.0	6.2	4.6	3.3	2.2	1.5	1.1	—
N.L.	8.4	8.4	7.7	5.6	3.9	2.7	1.6	1.1	—
Canada	8.0	7.0	6.1	4.5	3.3	2.5	1.8	1.3	—
				Females					
St. John's	7.6	7.1	6.3	4.9	3.5	2.9	2.5	2.6	—
N.L.	8.4	8.2	7.5	5.5	3.9	3.0	2.3	2.2	—
Canada	7.9	7.0	6.2	4.6	3.6	3.0	2.4	2.6	—

Source: Statistics Canada. 2012. Census Profile. 2011 Census. Statistics Canada Catalogue no. 98-316-XWE. Ottawa. Released October 24 2012.
http://www12.statcan.gc.ca/census-recensement/2011/dp-pd/prof/index.cfm?Lang=E

PROFILES / St. John's, Newfoundland and Labrador

Private Households by Household Size

Area	1 Person	2 Persons	3 Persons	4 Persons	5 Persons	6 or More Persons	Average Number of Persons in Private Households
Households							
St. John's	13,080	16,110	7,830	5,715	1,705	585	2.3
N.L.	46,325	82,260	39,400	29,880	8,200	2,765	2.4
Canada	3,673,310	4,544,820	2,081,900	1,903,300	724,405	392,885	2.5
Percent of Households							
St. John's	29.1	35.8	17.4	12.7	3.8	1.3	–
N.L.	22.2	39.4	18.9	14.3	3.9	1.3	–
Canada	27.6	34.1	15.6	14.3	5.4	2.9	–

Source: Statistics Canada. 2012. Census Profile. 2011 Census. Statistics Canada Catalogue no. 98-316-XWE. Ottawa. Released October 24 2012.
http://www12.statcan.gc.ca/census-recensement/2011/dp-pd/prof/index.cfm?Lang=E

Dwelling Type

Area	Single-detached House	Semi-detached House	Row House	Apartment: Building with Five or More Storeys	Apartment: Building with Fewer Than Five Storeys	Duplex Apartment	Movable Dwelling	Other Single-attached House
Number								
St. John's	20,120	2,915	5,170	510	5,810	10,270	100	125
N.L.	155,295	8,330	10,050	710	11,370	21,305	1,360	415
Canada	7,329,150	646,245	791,600	1,234,770	2,397,550	704,485	183,510	33,310
Percent of Dwellings								
St. John's	44.7	6.5	11.5	1.1	12.9	22.8	0.2	0.3
N.L.	74.4	4.0	4.8	0.3	5.4	10.2	0.7	0.2
Canada	55.0	4.9	5.9	9.3	18.0	5.3	1.4	0.3

Source: Statistics Canada. 2012. Census Profile. 2011 Census. Statistics Canada Catalogue no. 98-316-XWE. Ottawa. Released October 24 2012.
http://www12.statcan.gc.ca/census-recensement/2011/dp-pd/prof/index.cfm?Lang=E

Shelter Costs

	Owned Dwellings				Rented Dwellings		
Area	Number	Median Value[1] ($)	Average Value[1] ($)	Median Monthly Costs[2] ($)	Average Monthly Costs[2] ($)	Number	Median Monthly Costs[3] ($)	Average Monthly Costs[3] ($)
St. John's	27,860	259,615	285,730	994	1,095	17,160	734	752
N.L.	161,410	174,405	191,315	575	779	46,460	663	682
Canada	9,013,410	280,552	345,182	978	1,141	4,060,385	784	848

Note: All figures cover non-farm, non-reserve private dwellings; (1) Refers to the dollar amount expected by the owner if the dwelling were to be sold; (2) Includes all shelter expenses paid by households that own their dwellings, such as the mortgage payment and the costs of electricity, heat, water and other municipal services, property taxes and condominium fees; (3) Includes all shelter expenses paid by households that rent their dwellings, such as the monthly rent and the costs of electricity, heat and municipal services.
Source: Statistics Canada. 2013. 2011 National Household Survey. Statistics Canada Catalogue no. 99-004-XWE. Ottawa. Released September 11, 2013.

Occupied Private Dwellings by Period of Construction

Area	1960 or Before	1961 to 1980	1981 to 1990	1991 to 2000	2001 to 2005	2006 to 2011
Number						
St. John's	11,380	15,165	6,755	4,545	3,265	3,925
N.L.	45,560	73,085	36,835	24,930	12,675	15,750
Canada	3,273,105	4,152,715	2,112,110	1,707,880	1,031,020	1,042,430
Percent of Dwellings						
St. John's	25.3	33.7	15.0	10.1	7.2	8.7
N.L.	21.8	35.0	17.6	11.9	6.1	7.5
Canada	24.6	31.2	15.9	12.8	7.7	7.8

Note: Figures cover non-farm, non-reserve private dwellings and includes data up to May 10, 2011.
Source: Statistics Canada. 2013. 2011 National Household Survey. Statistics Canada Catalogue no. 99-004-XWE. Ottawa. Released September 11, 2013.

Educational Attainment

Area	No Certificate, Diploma or Degree	High School Diploma or Equivalent[1]	Apprenticeship or Trades Certificate or Diploma[2]	College, CÉGEP or Other Non-University Certificate or Diploma	University Certificate or Diploma Below the Bachelor Level[3]	Bachelor's Degree	University Certificate, Diploma or Degree Above Bachelor Level[4]
Number							
Total							
St. John's	14,885	21,840	8,155	17,305	3,700	14,475	9,075
N.L.	120,640	100,215	56,010	84,130	12,850	37,280	19,925
Canada	5,485,400	6,968,935	2,950,685	4,970,020	1,200,130	3,634,425	2,049,930
Males							
St. John's	7,110	10,510	4,890	7,020	1,655	6,270	4,545
N.L.	59,050	45,930	36,870	36,150	5,350	15,490	9,665
Canada	2,742,875	3,305,415	1,928,970	2,118,430	513,235	1,643,080	1,043,350
Females							
St. John's	7,775	11,325	3,265	10,285	2,045	8,205	4,525
N.L.	61,590	54,285	19,135	47,985	7,495	21,795	10,255
Canada	2,742,520	3,663,515	1,021,715	2,851,595	686,890	1,991,345	1,006,585
Percent of Population							
Total							
St. John's	16.6	24.4	9.1	19.4	4.1	16.2	10.1
N.L.	28.0	23.2	13.0	19.5	3.0	8.6	4.6
Canada	20.1	25.6	10.8	18.2	4.4	13.3	7.5
Males							
St. John's	16.9	25.0	11.6	16.7	3.9	14.9	10.8
N.L.	28.3	22.0	17.7	17.3	2.6	7.4	4.6
Canada	20.6	24.9	14.5	15.9	3.9	12.4	7.8
Females							
St. John's	16.4	23.9	6.9	21.7	4.3	17.3	9.5
N.L.	27.7	24.4	8.6	21.6	3.4	9.8	4.6
Canada	19.6	26.2	7.3	20.4	4.9	14.3	7.2

Note: Figures cover total population aged 15 years and over by highest certificate, diploma or degree; (1) Includes persons who have graduated from a secondary school or equivalent. It excludes persons with a postsecondary certificate, diploma or degree; (2) Includes Registered Apprenticeship certificates (including Certificate of Qualification, Journeyperson's designation) and other trades certificates or diplomas such as pre-employment or vocational certificates and diplomas from brief trade programs completed at community colleges, institutes of technology, vocational centres, and similar institutions; (3) Comparisons with other data sources suggest that the category 'University certificate or diploma below the bachelor's level' was over-reported in the NHS. This category likely includes some responses that are actually college certificates or diplomas, bachelor's degrees or other types of education (e.g., university transfer programs, bachelor's programs completed in other countries, incomplete bachelor's programs, non-university professional designations). We recommend users interpret the results for the 'University certificate or diploma below the bachelor's level' category with caution; (4) 'University certificate or diploma above bachelor level' includes the categories: 'Degree in medicine, dentistry, veterinary medicine or optometry,' 'Master's degree' and 'Earned doctorate.'
Source: Statistics Canada. 2013. 2011 National Household Survey. Statistics Canada Catalogue no. 99-004-XWE. Ottawa. Released September 11, 2013.

Household Income Distribution

Area	Less than $10,000	$10,000 to $19,999	$20,000 to $29,999	$30,000 to $39,999	$40,000 to $49,999	$50,000 to $59,999	$60,000 to $79,999	$80,000 to $99,999	$100,000 to $124,999	$125,000 to $149,999	$150,000 and Over
Households											
St. John's	2,490	4,620	4,550	3,940	3,770	3,120	5,920	4,520	4,245	2,645	5,210
N.L.	8,690	22,015	24,005	22,410	19,505	17,555	28,460	20,415	18,250	11,400	16,140
Canada	626,705	1,141,945	1,193,925	1,271,675	1,206,800	1,102,120	1,865,280	1,458,240	1,260,770	802,555	1,389,240
Percent of Households											
St. John's	5.5	10.3	10.1	8.7	8.4	6.9	13.1	10.0	9.4	5.9	11.6
N.L.	4.2	10.5	11.5	10.7	9.3	8.4	13.6	9.8	8.7	5.5	7.7
Canada	4.7	8.6	9.0	9.5	9.1	8.3	14.0	10.9	9.5	6.0	10.4

Note: Household income is the sum of the total incomes of all members of that household. Total income refers to monetary receipts from certain sources, before income taxes and deductions, during calendar year 2010.
Source: Statistics Canada. 2013. 2011 National Household Survey. Statistics Canada Catalogue no. 99-004-XWE. Ottawa. Released September 11, 2013.

Median and Average Household and Economic Family Income

Area	Median Household Income ($)	Average Household Income ($)	Median After-tax Household Income ($)	Average After-tax Household Income ($)	Median Economic Family Income ($)	Average Economic Family Income ($)	Median After-tax Economic Family Income ($)	Average After-tax Economic Family Income ($)
St. John's	59,978	77,600	52,259	64,149	79,054	95,887	68,156	78,725
N.L.	54,156	68,979	48,735	58,454	64,890	79,409	57,658	67,081
Canada	61,072	79,102	54,089	66,149	76,511	94,125	67,044	78,517

Note: Figures cover household and economic familiy income in 2010. A household is defined as a person or a group of persons (other than foreign residents) who occupy the same private dwelling and do not have a usual place of residence elsewhere in Canada. Every person is a member of one and only one household. An economic family is defined as a group of two or more persons who live in the same dwelling and are related to each other by blood, marriage, common-law, adoption or a foster relationship. A couple may be of opposite or same sex.
Source: Statistics Canada. 2013. 2011 National Household Survey. Statistics Canada Catalogue no. 99-004-XWE. Ottawa. Released September 11, 2013.

PROFILES / St. John's, Newfoundland and Labrador

Individual Income Distribution

Area	Less than $10,000	$10,000 to $19,999	$20,000 to $29,999	$30,000 to $39,999	$40,000 to $49,999	$50,000 to $59,999	$60,000 to $79,999	$80,000 to $99,999	$100,000 to $124,999	$125,000 and Over
Number										
Total										
St. John's	14,300	16,225	13,040	10,780	7,990	5,795	8,095	4,560	2,265	2,935
N.L.	66,920	98,430	69,050	52,045	35,090	24,045	30,905	17,070	8,570	8,420
Canada	4,492,040	4,835,710	3,670,020	3,180,360	2,603,520	1,921,650	2,437,440	1,302,045	693,580	782,135
Males										
St. John's	6,415	5,850	5,395	4,815	3,975	3,030	4,390	2,460	1,585	2,365
N.L.	25,600	36,840	31,410	28,275	20,025	14,615	18,255	11,035	6,820	7,220
Canada	1,936,365	1,864,880	1,588,260	1,522,190	1,333,510	1,079,780	1,473,145	823,720	492,905	599,905
Females										
St. John's	7,890	10,375	7,645	5,965	4,015	2,760	3,700	2,100	680	565
N.L.	41,315	61,585	37,635	23,770	15,065	9,430	12,645	6,035	1,750	1,200
Canada	2,555,675	2,970,825	2,081,760	1,658,170	1,270,010	841,870	964,300	478,330	200,680	182,230
Percent of Population										
Total										
St. John's	16.6	18.9	15.2	12.5	9.3	6.7	9.4	5.3	2.6	3.4
N.L.	16.3	24.0	16.8	12.7	8.5	5.9	7.5	4.2	2.1	2.1
Canada	17.3	18.7	14.2	12.3	10.0	7.4	9.4	5.0	2.7	3.0
Males										
St. John's	15.9	14.5	13.4	12.0	9.9	7.5	10.9	6.1	3.9	5.9
N.L.	12.8	18.4	15.7	14.1	10.0	7.3	9.1	5.5	3.4	3.6
Canada	15.2	14.7	12.5	12.0	10.5	8.5	11.6	6.5	3.9	4.7
Females										
St. John's	17.3	22.7	16.7	13.1	8.8	6.0	8.1	4.6	1.5	1.2
N.L.	19.6	29.3	17.9	11.3	7.2	4.5	6.0	2.9	0.8	0.6
Canada	19.4	22.5	15.8	12.6	9.6	6.4	7.3	3.6	1.5	1.4

Note: Figures cover individuals aged 15 years and over with income. Income refers to monetary receipts from certain sources, before income taxes and deductions, during calendar year 2010.
Source: Statistics Canada. 2013. 2011 National Household Survey. Statistics Canada Catalogue no. 99-004-XWE. Ottawa. Released September 11, 2013.

Labour Force Status

Area	In the Labour Force - All	In the Labour Force - Employed	In the Labour Force - Unemployed	Not in the Labour Force
Number				
Total				
St. John's	56,615	52,085	4,535	32,810
N.L.	255,890	218,630	37,265	175,160
Canada	17,990,080	16,595,035	1,395,045	9,269,445
Males				
St. John's	28,375	25,990	2,380	13,630
N.L.	133,200	111,175	22,025	75,305
Canada	9,388,570	8,634,310	754,255	3,906,785
Females				
St. John's	28,240	26,090	2,155	19,185
N.L.	122,690	107,455	15,235	99,855
Canada	8,601,515	7,960,725	640,790	5,362,660
Percent of Labour Force				
Total				
St. John's	63.3	58.2	8.0	36.7
N.L.	59.4	50.7	14.6	40.6
Canada	66.0	60.9	7.8	34.0
Males				
St. John's	67.6	61.9	8.4	32.4
N.L.	63.9	53.3	16.5	36.1
Canada	70.6	64.9	8.0	29.4
Females				
St. John's	59.5	55.0	7.6	40.5
N.L.	55.1	48.3	12.4	44.9
Canada	61.6	57.0	7.4	38.4

Note: Figures are based on total population 15 years and over
Source: Statistics Canada. 2013. 2011 National Household Survey. Statistics Canada Catalogue no. 99-004-XWE. Ottawa. Released September 11, 2013.

Labour Force by Industry (NAICS Codes 11–52)

Area	Agriculture, forestry, fishing & hunting	Mining, quarrying, & oil & gas extraction	Utilities	Construction	Manufacturing	Wholesale Trade	Retail Trade	Transportation & warehousing	Information & cultural industries	Finance & insurance
					Number					
					Total					
St. John's	225	1,320	395	3,025	2,130	1,435	6,990	1,730	1,615	1,415
N.L.	9,700	8,515	2,455	22,055	17,515	6,245	32,000	12,165	4,095	5,275
Canada	437,650	261,050	149,940	1,215,380	1,619,295	733,445	2,031,665	827,780	420,830	767,960
					Males					
St. John's	155	1,160	295	2,735	1,695	1,065	3,110	1,385	800	505
N.L.	7,335	7,300	1,915	20,000	11,955	4,770	13,605	9,385	2,115	1,560
Canada	307,370	211,690	110,765	1,068,710	1,167,680	494,545	933,850	617,305	235,875	296,995
					Females					
St. John's	70	155	105	285	430	370	3,885	345	815	910
N.L.	2,365	1,215	540	2,055	5,560	1,480	18,395	2,785	1,980	3,720
Canada	130,285	49,360	39,175	146,670	451,615	238,900	1,097,820	210,475	184,955	470,960
					Percent of Labour Force					
					Total					
St. John's	0.4	2.4	0.7	5.4	3.8	2.6	12.6	3.1	2.9	2.5
N.L.	3.9	3.4	1.0	8.8	7.0	2.5	12.8	4.9	1.6	2.1
Canada	2.5	1.5	0.9	6.9	9.2	4.2	11.6	4.7	2.4	4.4
					Males					
St. John's	0.6	4.2	1.1	9.9	6.1	3.8	11.2	5.0	2.9	1.8
N.L.	5.6	5.6	1.5	15.3	9.2	3.7	10.4	7.2	1.6	1.2
Canada	3.3	2.3	1.2	11.6	12.7	5.4	10.2	6.7	2.6	3.2
					Females					
St. John's	0.3	0.6	0.4	1.0	1.5	1.3	14.0	1.2	2.9	3.3
N.L.	2.0	1.0	0.4	1.7	4.6	1.2	15.3	2.3	1.6	3.1
Canada	1.6	0.6	0.5	1.7	5.4	2.8	13.1	2.5	2.2	5.6

Note: Figures are based on total experienced labour force 15 years and over. Experienced labour force refers to persons who, during the week of Sunday, May 1 to Saturday, May 7, 2011, were employed and the unemployed who had last worked for pay or in self-employment in either 2010 or 2011.
Source: Statistics Canada. 2013. 2011 National Household Survey. Statistics Canada Catalogue no. 99-004-XWE. Ottawa. Released September 11, 2013.

Labour Force by Industry (NAICS Codes 53–91)

Area	Real estate & rental & leasing	Profess., scientific & tech. services	Mgmt of companies & enterprises	Admin. & support, waste mgmt & remed. services	Educational services	Health care & social assistance	Arts, entertain. & recreation	Accomm. & food services	Other services (except public admin.)	Public admin.
					Number					
					Total					
St. John's	875	3,620	30	2,610	5,450	8,010	1,045	4,175	2,655	6,825
N.L.	2,860	9,785	205	8,655	18,100	35,300	3,245	15,640	11,775	25,200
Canada	321,895	1,240,850	17,460	728,330	1,301,435	1,949,650	363,405	1,130,750	807,800	1,261,050
					Males					
St. John's	565	2,290	0	1,460	2,110	1,800	590	1,820	980	3,210
N.L.	1,655	5,760	120	5,095	6,995	6,045	1,820	4,990	4,795	13,410
Canada	179,090	688,625	9,380	411,250	424,915	349,430	188,270	469,990	372,940	652,510
					Females					
St. John's	310	1,330	20	1,150	3,335	6,215	455	2,355	1,680	3,620
N.L.	1,205	4,025	80	3,560	11,100	29,260	1,430	10,650	6,980	11,790
Canada	142,805	552,225	8,075	317,085	876,515	1,600,220	175,135	660,760	434,865	608,535
					Percent of Labour Force					
					Total					
St. John's	1.6	6.5	0.1	4.7	9.8	14.4	1.9	7.5	4.8	12.3
N.L.	1.1	3.9	0.1	3.5	7.2	14.1	1.3	6.2	4.7	10.0
Canada	1.8	7.1	0.1	4.1	7.4	11.1	2.1	6.4	4.6	7.2
					Males					
St. John's	2.0	8.3	0.0	5.3	7.6	6.5	2.1	6.6	3.5	11.6
N.L.	1.3	4.4	0.1	3.9	5.4	4.6	1.4	3.8	3.7	10.3
Canada	1.9	7.5	0.1	4.5	4.6	3.8	2.0	5.1	4.1	7.1
					Females					
St. John's	1.1	4.8	0.1	4.1	12.0	22.3	1.6	8.5	6.0	13.0
N.L.	1.0	3.3	0.1	3.0	9.2	24.3	1.2	8.9	5.8	9.8
Canada	1.7	6.6	0.1	3.8	10.4	19.1	2.1	7.9	5.2	7.2

Note: Figures are based on total experienced labour force 15 years and over. Experienced labour force refers to persons who, during the week of Sunday, May 1 to Saturday, May 7, 2011, were employed and the unemployed who had last worked for pay or in self-employment in either 2010 or 2011.
Source: Statistics Canada. 2013. 2011 National Household Survey. Statistics Canada Catalogue no. 99-004-XWE. Ottawa. Released September 11, 2013.

PROFILES / St. John's, Newfoundland and Labrador

Occupation

Area	Mgmt	Business, Finance & Admin.	Natural/ Applied Sciences & Related	Health	Education, Law & Social, Community & Government Services	Art, Culture, Recreation & Sport	Sales & Service	Trades, Transport & Equip. Operators & Related	Natural Resources, Agri. & Related Production	Mfg & Utilities
Number										
Total										
St. John's	5,885	9,245	4,915	4,740	8,430	1,740	13,735	5,170	575	1,135
N.L.	20,445	33,225	16,545	18,145	32,915	4,200	55,760	45,975	12,135	11,440
Canada	1,963,600	2,902,045	1,237,775	1,107,200	2,064,675	503,415	4,068,170	2,537,775	397,930	805,040
Males										
St. John's	3,370	2,585	4,040	1,025	3,165	990	6,175	5,005	500	885
N.L.	11,740	8,285	13,450	3,225	10,015	1,990	20,685	43,835	10,205	7,185
Canada	1,229,460	854,190	966,355	217,520	676,550	232,535	1,745,705	2,385,615	318,945	564,300
Females										
St. John's	2,520	6,660	880	3,720	5,260	750	7,565	165	70	245
N.L.	8,710	24,945	3,090	14,920	22,895	2,210	35,075	2,140	1,930	4,250
Canada	734,140	2,047,855	271,415	889,675	1,388,130	270,875	2,322,465	152,165	78,980	240,740
Percent of Labour Force										
Total										
St. John's	10.6	16.6	8.8	8.5	15.2	3.1	24.7	9.3	1.0	2.0
N.L.	8.2	13.2	6.6	7.2	13.1	1.7	22.2	18.3	4.8	4.6
Canada	11.2	16.5	7.0	6.3	11.7	2.9	23.1	14.4	2.3	4.6
Males										
St. John's	12.1	9.3	14.6	3.7	11.4	3.6	22.3	18.0	1.8	3.2
N.L.	9.0	6.3	10.3	2.5	7.7	1.5	15.8	33.6	7.8	5.5
Canada	13.4	9.3	10.5	2.4	7.4	2.5	19.0	26.0	3.5	6.1
Females										
St. John's	9.1	23.9	3.2	13.4	18.9	2.7	27.2	0.6	0.3	0.9
N.L.	7.2	20.8	2.6	12.4	19.1	1.8	29.2	1.8	1.6	3.5
Canada	8.7	24.4	3.2	10.6	16.5	3.2	27.7	1.8	0.9	2.9

Note: Figures are based on total experienced labour force 15 years and over.
Source: Statistics Canada. 2013. 2011 National Household Survey. Statistics Canada Catalogue no. 99-004-XWE. Ottawa. Released September 11, 2013.

Place of Work Status

Area	Worked at Home	Worked Outside Canada	No Fixed Workplace Address	Worked at Usual Place
Number				
Total				
St. John's	1,795	275	4,600	45,410
N.L.	9,155	1,050	27,930	180,490
Canada	1,142,640	66,460	1,868,245	13,517,690
Males				
St. John's	850	265	3,285	21,595
N.L.	4,180	975	21,975	84,040
Canada	582,150	47,355	1,400,485	6,604,325
Females				
St. John's	945	0	1,315	23,820
N.L.	4,980	75	5,950	96,445
Canada	560,490	19,100	467,760	6,913,370
Percent of Labour Force				
Total				
St. John's	3.4	0.5	8.8	87.2
N.L.	4.2	0.5	12.8	82.6
Canada	6.9	0.4	11.3	81.5
Males				
St. John's	3.3	1.0	12.6	83.1
N.L.	3.8	0.9	19.8	75.6
Canada	6.7	0.5	16.2	76.5
Females				
St. John's	3.6	0.0	5.0	91.3
N.L.	4.6	0.1	5.5	89.8
Canada	7.0	0.2	5.9	86.8

Note: Figures are based on total employed labour force 15 years and over.
Source: Statistics Canada. 2013. 2011 National Household Survey. Statistics Canada Catalogue no. 99-004-XWE. Ottawa. Released September 11, 2013.

Mode of Transportation to Work

Area	Car; Truck; Van; as Driver	Car; Truck; Van; as Passenger	Public Transit	Walked	Bicycled	All Other Modes
			Number			
			Total			
St. John's	36,930	5,145	2,455	4,350	170	965
N.L.	165,340	18,645	4,855	12,980	395	6,210
Canada	11,393,140	867,050	1,851,525	880,815	201,780	191,625
			Males			
St. John's	19,180	2,055	1,025	1,860	130	630
N.L.	84,875	7,705	2,855	5,655	260	4,680
Canada	6,238,835	349,530	788,290	387,580	135,840	104,725
			Females			
St. John's	17,745	3,090	1,430	2,490	35	335
N.L.	80,465	10,945	2,000	7,320	135	1,535
Canada	5,154,305	517,520	1,063,235	493,230	65,940	86,900
			Percent of Labour Force			
			Total			
St. John's	73.8	10.3	4.9	8.7	0.3	1.9
N.L.	79.3	8.9	2.3	6.2	0.2	3.0
Canada	74.0	5.6	12.0	5.7	1.3	1.2
			Males			
St. John's	77.1	8.3	4.1	7.5	0.5	2.5
N.L.	80.1	7.3	2.7	5.3	0.2	4.4
Canada	77.9	4.4	9.8	4.8	1.7	1.3
			Females			
St. John's	70.6	12.3	5.7	9.9	0.1	1.3
N.L.	78.6	10.7	2.0	7.1	0.1	1.5
Canada	69.8	7.0	14.4	6.7	0.9	1.2

Note: Figures are based on total employed labour force 15 years and over.
Source: Statistics Canada. 2013. 2011 National Household Survey. Statistics Canada Catalogue no. 99-004-XWE. Ottawa. Released September 11, 2013.

Visible Minority Population Characteristics

Area	Total Minority	South Asian[1]	Chinese	Black	Filipino	Latin American	Arab	SE Asian[2]	West Asian[3]	Korean	Japanese	Multiple[4]
						Number						
						Total						
St. John's	4,205	1,195	990	930	110	130	195	200	140	60	50	140
N.L.	6,930	1,855	1,645	1,455	350	185	370	320	155	80	60	250
Canada	6,264,750	1,567,400	1,324,750	945,665	619,310	381,280	380,620	312,075	206,840	161,130	87,270	171,935
						Males						
St. John's	2,365	690	500	560	45	75	105	155	80	25	35	70
N.L.	3,745	1,050	830	835	140	110	205	215	85	35	40	120
Canada	3,043,010	790,755	632,325	453,005	268,885	186,355	203,485	154,035	105,620	77,165	38,270	83,335
						Females						
St. John's	1,835	500	490	375	65	55	85	45	60	30	15	75
N.L.	3,185	810	810	620	210	70	170	105	70	45	15	130
Canada	3,221,745	776,650	692,420	492,660	350,425	194,925	177,140	158,045	101,220	83,965	48,990	88,600
						Percent of Population						
						Total						
St. John's	4.0	1.2	1.0	0.9	0.1	0.1	0.2	0.2	0.1	0.1	0.0	0.1
N.L.	1.4	0.4	0.3	0.3	0.1	0.0	0.1	0.1	0.0	0.0	0.0	0.0
Canada	19.1	4.8	4.0	2.9	1.9	1.2	1.2	0.9	0.6	0.5	0.3	0.5
						Males						
St. John's	4.8	1.4	1.0	1.1	0.1	0.2	0.2	0.3	0.2	0.1	0.1	0.1
N.L.	1.5	0.4	0.3	0.3	0.1	0.0	0.1	0.1	0.0	0.0	0.0	0.0
Canada	18.8	4.9	3.9	2.8	1.7	1.2	1.3	1.0	0.7	0.5	0.2	0.5
						Females						
St. John's	3.4	0.9	0.9	0.7	0.1	0.1	0.2	0.1	0.1	0.1	0.0	0.1
N.L.	1.2	0.3	0.3	0.2	0.1	0.0	0.1	0.0	0.0	0.0	0.0	0.1
Canada	19.3	4.7	4.1	3.0	2.1	1.2	1.1	0.9	0.6	0.5	0.3	0.5

Note: The Employment Equity Act defines visible minorities as 'persons, other than Aboriginal peoples, who are non-Caucasian in race or non-white in colour';
(1) Includes 'East Indian,' 'Pakistani,' 'Sri Lankan,' etc.; (2) Includes 'Vietnamese,' 'Cambodian,' 'Malaysian,' 'Laotian,' etc.; (3) Includes 'Iranian,' 'Afghan,' etc.; (4) Includes respondents who reported more than one visible minority group by checking two or more mark-in circles, e.g., 'Black' and 'South Asian.'
Source: Statistics Canada. 2013. 2011 National Household Survey. Statistics Canada Catalogue no. 99-004-XWE. Ottawa. Released September 11, 2013.

PROFILES / St. John's, Newfoundland and Labrador

Aboriginal Population

Area	Aboriginal Identity[1]	First Nations (North American Indian) Single Identity[2]	Métis Single Identity	Inuk (Inuit) Single Identity	Multiple Aboriginal Identities[3]	Aboriginal Identities Not Included Elsewhere
			Number			
			Total			
St. John's	2,705	1,210	780	455	0	240
N.L.	35,800	19,315	7,660	6,265	260	2,300
Canada	1,400,685	851,560	451,795	59,440	11,415	26,475
			Males			
St. John's	1,305	550	350	255	0	155
N.L.	17,835	9,485	3,975	3,165	130	1,080
Canada	682,190	411,785	223,335	29,495	5,525	12,055
			Females			
St. John's	1,395	665	435	205	0	85
N.L.	17,965	9,830	3,690	3,095	130	1,225
Canada	718,500	439,775	228,460	29,950	5,890	14,420
			Percent of Population			
			Total			
St. John's	2.6	1.2	0.8	0.4	0.0	0.2
N.L.	7.1	3.8	1.5	1.2	0.1	0.5
Canada	4.3	2.6	1.4	0.2	0.0	0.1
			Males			
St. John's	2.6	1.1	0.7	0.5	0.0	0.3
N.L.	7.2	3.8	1.6	1.3	0.1	0.4
Canada	4.2	2.5	1.4	0.2	0.0	0.1
			Females			
St. John's	2.6	1.2	0.8	0.4	0.0	0.2
N.L.	6.9	3.8	1.4	1.2	0.1	0.5
Canada	4.3	2.6	1.4	0.2	0.0	0.1

Note: (1) Includes persons who reported being an Aboriginal person, that is, First Nations (North American Indian), Métis or Inuk (Inuit) and/or those who reported Registered or Treaty Indian status, that is registered under the Indian Act of Canada, and/or those who reported membership in a First Nation or Indian band. Aboriginal peoples of Canada are defined in the Constitution Act, 1982, section 35-2 as including the Indian, Inuit and Métis peoples of Canada; (2) Users should be aware that the estimates associated with this variable are more affected than most by the incomplete enumeration of certain Indian reserves and Indian settlements in the National Household Survey (NHS); (3) Includes persons who reported being any two or all three of the following: First Nations (North American Indian), Métis or Inuk (Inuit).
Source: Statistics Canada. 2013. 2011 National Household Survey. Statistics Canada Catalogue no. 99-004-XWE. Ottawa. Released September 11, 2013.

Ethnic Origin

Area	North American Aboriginal	Other North American	European	Caribbean	Latin, Central and South American	African	Asian	Oceania
			Number					
			Total					
St. John's	4,305	44,565	70,345	515	300	755	3,630	75
N.L.	43,395	253,260	304,655	750	500	1,445	6,310	135
Canada	1,836,035	11,070,455	20,157,965	627,590	544,375	766,735	5,011,225	74,875
			Males					
St. John's	1,870	21,120	33,395	290	180	435	1,965	30
N.L.	21,355	123,900	148,055	420	260	770	3,285	45
Canada	885,675	5,462,685	9,913,150	291,640	264,635	387,360	2,435,540	37,490
			Females					
St. John's	2,435	23,440	36,955	230	120	315	1,665	45
N.L.	22,035	129,355	156,600	335	240	675	3,035	90
Canada	950,360	5,607,770	10,244,820	335,945	279,740	379,380	2,575,680	37,385
			Percent of Population					
			Total					
St. John's	4.1	42.9	67.7	0.5	0.3	0.7	3.5	0.1
N.L.	8.6	49.9	60.1	0.1	0.1	0.3	1.2	0.0
Canada	5.6	33.7	61.4	1.9	1.7	2.3	15.3	0.2
			Males					
St. John's	3.8	42.7	67.5	0.6	0.4	0.9	4.0	0.1
N.L.	8.6	50.0	59.7	0.2	0.1	0.3	1.3	0.0
Canada	5.5	33.8	61.3	1.8	1.6	2.4	15.1	0.2
			Females					
St. John's	4.5	43.1	67.9	0.4	0.2	0.6	3.1	0.1
N.L.	8.5	49.9	60.4	0.1	0.1	0.3	1.2	0.0
Canada	5.7	33.6	61.4	2.0	1.7	2.3	15.4	0.2

Note: The sum of the ethnic groups in this table is greater than the total population estimate because a person may report more than one ethnic origin in the NHS.
Source: Statistics Canada. 2013. 2011 National Household Survey. Statistics Canada Catalogue no. 99-004-XWE. Ottawa. Released September 11, 2013.

Religion

Area	Buddhist	Christian	Hindu	Jewish	Muslim	Sikh	Traditional (Aboriginal) Spirituality	Other Religions	No Religious Affiliation
Number									
Total									
St. John's	240	90,225	505	110	960	85	0	270	11,505
N.L.	400	472,720	635	175	1,200	100	30	685	31,330
Canada	366,830	22,102,745	497,965	329,495	1,053,945	454,965	64,935	130,835	7,850,605
Males									
St. John's	150	41,820	265	50	570	60	0	160	6,415
N.L.	230	228,825	325	95	710	65	15	335	17,350
Canada	168,465	10,497,775	250,435	161,265	540,555	229,435	31,805	57,745	4,225,645
Females									
St. John's	90	48,410	240	60	390	25	0	110	5,090
N.L.	165	243,895	310	80	490	35	10	350	13,975
Canada	198,365	11,604,975	247,525	168,235	513,395	225,530	33,135	73,090	3,624,965
Percent of Population									
Total									
St. John's	0.2	86.8	0.5	0.1	0.9	0.1	0.0	0.3	11.1
N.L.	0.1	93.2	0.1	0.0	0.2	0.0	0.0	0.1	6.2
Canada	1.1	67.3	1.5	1.0	3.2	1.4	0.2	0.4	23.9
Males									
St. John's	0.3	84.5	0.5	0.1	1.2	0.1	0.0	0.3	13.0
N.L.	0.1	92.3	0.1	0.0	0.3	0.0	0.0	0.1	7.0
Canada	1.0	64.9	1.5	1.0	3.3	1.4	0.2	0.4	26.1
Females									
St. John's	0.2	89.0	0.4	0.1	0.7	0.0	0.0	0.2	9.4
N.L.	0.1	94.1	0.1	0.0	0.2	0.0	0.0	0.1	5.4
Canada	1.2	69.5	1.5	1.0	3.1	1.4	0.2	0.4	21.7

Note: Religion refers to the person's self-identification as having a connection or affiliation with any religious denomination, group, body, sect, cult or other religiously defined community or system of belief. Religion is not limited to formal membership in a religious organization or group. Persons without a religious connection or affiliation can self-identify as atheist, agnostic or humanist, or can provide another applicable response.
Source: Statistics Canada. 2013. 2011 National Household Survey. Statistics Canada Catalogue no. 99-004-XWE. Ottawa. Released September 11, 2013.

Religion—Christian Denominations

Area	Anglican	Baptist	Catholic	Christian Orthodox	Lutheran	Pentecostal	Presbyterian	United Church	Other Christian
Number									
Total									
St. John's	16,745	385	50,370	130	140	2,390	1,010	13,345	5,715
N.L.	127,255	1,230	181,590	265	430	33,195	1,750	78,380	48,630
Canada	1,631,845	635,840	12,810,705	550,690	478,185	478,705	472,385	2,007,610	3,036,780
Males									
St. John's	7,540	185	23,335	85	40	1,075	470	6,190	2,905
N.L.	61,330	630	87,305	155	245	15,945	800	38,330	24,080
Canada	752,945	293,905	6,167,290	270,205	221,525	217,850	218,955	912,545	1,442,550
Females									
St. John's	9,205	205	27,035	45	100	1,315	545	7,150	2,815
N.L.	65,920	600	94,285	105	185	17,245	950	40,045	24,545
Canada	878,900	341,940	6,643,415	280,485	256,660	260,850	253,430	1,095,065	1,594,230
Percent of Population									
Total									
St. John's	16.1	0.4	48.5	0.1	0.1	2.3	1.0	12.8	5.5
N.L.	25.1	0.2	35.8	0.1	0.1	6.5	0.3	15.5	9.6
Canada	5.0	1.9	39.0	1.7	1.5	1.5	1.4	6.1	9.2
Males									
St. John's	15.2	0.4	47.1	0.2	0.1	2.2	0.9	12.5	5.9
N.L.	24.7	0.3	35.2	0.1	0.1	6.4	0.3	15.5	9.7
Canada	4.7	1.8	38.2	1.7	1.4	1.3	1.4	5.6	8.9
Females									
St. John's	16.9	0.4	49.7	0.1	0.2	2.4	1.0	13.1	5.2
N.L.	25.4	0.2	36.4	0.0	0.1	6.7	0.4	15.4	9.5
Canada	5.3	2.0	39.8	1.7	1.5	1.6	1.5	6.6	9.6

Note: Religion refers to the person's self-identification as having a connection or affiliation with any religious denomination, group, body, sect, cult or other religiously defined community or system of belief. Religion is not limited to formal membership in a religious organization or group. Persons without a religious connection or affiliation can self-identify as atheist, agnostic or humanist, or can provide another applicable response.
Source: Statistics Canada. 2013. 2011 National Household Survey. Statistics Canada Catalogue no. 99-004-XWE. Ottawa. Released September 11, 2013.

PROFILES / St. John's, Newfoundland and Labrador

Immigrant Status and Period of Immigration

Area	Non-Immigrants[1]	Immigrants All	Before 1971	1971 to 1980	1981 to 1990	1991 to 2000	2001 to 2005	2006 to 2011	Non-Permanent Residents[3]
Number – Total									
St. John's	98,150	4,505	855	660	445	730	460	1,350	1,250
N.L.	496,400	9,160	2,190	1,520	1,095	1,300	845	2,220	1,705
Canada	25,720,175	6,775,765	1,261,055	870,775	949,890	1,539,050	992,070	1,162,915	356,385
Males									
St. John's	46,330	2,345	360	355	275	370	255	725	815
N.L.	242,175	4,720	1,140	735	635	630	430	1,140	1,065
Canada	12,753,235	3,231,370	605,430	416,670	454,570	724,905	474,545	555,245	178,515
Females									
St. John's	51,815	2,160	495	310	170	355	200	625	435
N.L.	254,230	4,445	1,045	780	455	670	410	1,075	640
Canada	12,966,935	3,544,400	655,625	454,105	495,325	814,145	517,530	607,670	177,870
Percent of Population – Total									
St. John's	94.5	4.3	0.8	0.6	0.4	0.7	0.4	1.3	1.2
N.L.	97.9	1.8	0.4	0.3	0.2	0.3	0.2	0.4	0.3
Canada	78.3	20.6	3.8	2.7	2.9	4.7	3.0	3.5	1.1
Males									
St. John's	93.6	4.7	0.7	0.7	0.6	0.7	0.5	1.5	1.6
N.L.	97.7	1.9	0.5	0.3	0.3	0.3	0.2	0.5	0.4
Canada	78.9	20.0	3.7	2.6	2.8	4.5	2.9	3.4	1.1
Females									
St. John's	95.2	4.0	0.9	0.6	0.3	0.7	0.4	1.1	0.8
N.L.	98.0	1.7	0.4	0.3	0.2	0.3	0.2	0.4	0.2
Canada	77.7	21.2	3.9	2.7	3.0	4.9	3.1	3.6	1.1

Note: (1) Non-immigrant refers to a person who is a Canadian citizen by birth; (2) Immigrant refers to a person who is or has ever been a landed immigrant/permanent resident. This person has been granted the right to live in Canada permanently by immigration authorities. Some immigrants have resided in Canada for a number of years, while others have arrived recently. Some immigrants are Canadian citizens, while others are not. Most immigrants are born outside Canada, but a small number are born in Canada. In the 2011 National Household Survey, 'Immigrants' includes immigrants who landed in Canada prior to May 10, 2011; (3) Non-permanent resident refers to a person from another country who has a work or study permit, or who is a refugee claimant, and any non-Canadian-born family member living in Canada with them.
Source: Statistics Canada. 2013. 2011 National Household Survey. Statistics Canada Catalogue no. 99-004-XWE. Ottawa. Released September 11, 2013.

Mother Tongue

Area	English	French	Non-official Language	English & French	English & Non-official Language	French & Non-official Language	English, French & Non-official Language
Number – Total							
St. John's	99,745	500	3,960	155	305	25	20
N.L.	497,565	2,480	8,790	465	585	45	25
Canada	18,858,980	7,054,975	6,567,680	144,685	396,330	74,430	24,095
Males							
St. John's	47,315	250	2,100	65	165	15	5
N.L.	242,450	1,250	4,585	215	295	20	10
Canada	9,345,225	3,452,380	3,157,785	69,975	192,000	36,535	11,965
Females							
St. John's	52,430	250	1,860	90	145	15	5
N.L.	255,110	1,235	4,205	255	285	20	10
Canada	9,513,750	3,602,590	3,409,895	74,710	204,330	37,890	12,130
Percent of Population – Total							
St. John's	95.3	0.5	3.8	0.1	0.3	0.0	0.0
N.L.	97.6	0.5	1.7	0.1	0.1	0.0	0.0
Canada	56.9	21.3	19.8	0.4	1.2	0.2	0.1
Males							
St. John's	94.8	0.5	4.2	0.1	0.3	0.0	0.0
N.L.	97.4	0.5	1.8	0.1	0.1	0.0	0.0
Canada	57.5	21.2	19.4	0.4	1.2	0.2	0.1
Females							
St. John's	95.7	0.5	3.4	0.2	0.3	0.0	0.0
N.L.	97.7	0.5	1.6	0.1	0.1	0.0	0.0
Canada	56.4	21.4	20.2	0.4	1.2	0.2	0.1

Note: Figures cover total population excluding institutional residents.
Source: Statistics Canada. 2012. Census Profile. 2011 Census. Statistics Canada Catalogue no. 98-316-XWE. Ottawa. Released October 24 2012.
http://www12.statcan.gc.ca/census-recensement/2011/dp-pd/prof/index.cfm?Lang=E

Language Spoken Most Often at Home

Area	English	French	Non-official Language	English & French	English & Non-official Language	French & Non-official Language	English, French & Non-official Language
			Number				
			Total				
St. John's	101,680	225	2,105	90	585	5	25
N.L.	502,475	1,140	5,000	240	1,035	10	40
Canada	21,457,075	6,827,865	3,673,865	131,205	875,135	109,700	46,330
			Males				
St. John's	48,365	95	1,105	35	300	5	10
N.L.	245,050	550	2,570	100	530	0	20
Canada	10,585,620	3,348,235	1,767,310	63,475	425,370	53,010	22,845
			Females				
St. John's	53,315	135	1,000	50	285	5	10
N.L.	257,425	590	2,435	145	500	10	20
Canada	10,871,455	3,479,625	1,906,555	67,730	449,765	56,690	23,485
			Percent of Population				
			Total				
St. John's	97.1	0.2	2.0	0.1	0.6	0.0	0.0
N.L.	98.5	0.2	1.0	0.0	0.2	0.0	0.0
Canada	64.8	20.6	11.1	0.4	2.6	0.3	0.1
			Males				
St. John's	96.9	0.2	2.2	0.1	0.6	0.0	0.0
N.L.	98.5	0.2	1.0	0.0	0.2	0.0	0.0
Canada	65.1	20.6	10.9	0.4	2.6	0.3	0.1
			Females				
St. John's	97.3	0.2	1.8	0.1	0.5	0.0	0.0
N.L.	98.6	0.2	0.9	0.1	0.2	0.0	0.0
Canada	64.5	20.6	11.3	0.4	2.7	0.3	0.1

Note: Figures cover total population excluding institutional residents.
Source: Statistics Canada. 2012. Census Profile. 2011 Census. Statistics Canada Catalogue no. 98-316-XWE. Ottawa. Released October 24 2012.
http://www12.statcan.gc.ca/census-recensement/2011/dp-pd/prof/index.cfm?Lang=E

Knowledge of Official Languages

Area	English Only	French Only	English & French	Neither English nor French
		Number		
		Total		
St. John's	95,580	30	8,830	275
N.L.	485,745	135	23,455	630
Canada	22,564,665	4,165,015	5,795,570	595,920
		Males		
St. John's	46,185	15	3,585	130
N.L.	239,010	65	9,445	305
Canada	11,222,185	1,925,340	2,876,560	241,790
		Females		
St. John's	49,395	20	5,245	145
N.L.	246,735	65	14,005	320
Canada	11,342,485	2,239,680	2,919,005	354,135
		Percent of Population		
		Total		
St. John's	91.3	0.0	8.4	0.3
N.L.	95.3	0.0	4.6	0.1
Canada	68.1	12.6	17.5	1.8
		Males		
St. John's	92.5	0.0	7.2	0.3
N.L.	96.1	0.0	3.8	0.1
Canada	69.0	11.8	17.7	1.5
		Females		
St. John's	90.1	0.0	9.6	0.3
N.L.	94.5	0.0	5.4	0.1
Canada	67.3	13.3	17.3	2.1

Note: Figures cover total population excluding institutional residents.
Source: Statistics Canada. 2012. Census Profile. 2011 Census. Statistics Canada Catalogue no. 98-316-XWE. Ottawa. Released October 24 2012.
http://www12.statcan.gc.ca/census-recensement/2011/dp-pd/prof/index.cfm?Lang=E

Surrey, British Columbia

Background

Part of Metro Vancouver and the second largest city in British Columbia, Surrey is located on the Canada–U.S. border, 40 minutes southeast of Vancouver. It is known as the "City of Parks," with over 2,400 hectares (6,000 acres) of parkland and green spaces.

The Semiahmoo and Kwantlen First Nations were the first inhabitants of the area. When Surrey was incorporated in 1879, the region was populated by European explorers, settlers, road-builders and loggers. Surrey officially became a city in 1993.

Surrey's title as part of the "Gateway to the Pacific" is defined by the city's access to two international airports, two U.S. border crossings, national and provincial highways, railways and a deep-sea port. The city is closely linked to Vancouver and surrounding communities through a light rail system.

Surrey's economy is built on the clean energy, manufacturing, farming, health and education industries. A large part of what is considered "industrial" land in Surrey is vacant or has non-industrial purposes. More than 35% of Surrey land is actively farmed. In 2012, the City of Surrey announced plans to build North America's largest organic biofuel facility. Surrey was named the "Community of the Year" by the province's Clean Energy Association in recognition of the municipality's ongoing sustainability and energy conservation efforts.

Surrey's educational facilities are Simon Fraser University's Surrey campus, Kwantlen Polytechnic University and the Surrey School District, the largest school district in the province. More than 70 languages are spoken in Surrey, particularly Punjabi, Hindi and Tagalog (Filipino).

Throughout the year, the City of Surrey hosts five major festivals: Canada Day, Fusion Festival, Winter Fest, Party for the Planet and the Children's Festival.

Surrey has summer highs of plus 22.07 degrees Celsius, winter lows of plus 0.67 degree Celsius, and an average rainfall just over 1358 mm per year.

Rankings

- In 2012, the City of Surrey was ranked as one of Canada's best cities in terms of sustainable development and clean capitalism. The 2013 Clean50 award selects nominees based on environmental leadership, creativity, courage and delivery of results. Surrey was recognized for its *ENERGYShift* program: promoting sustainable land use and development; reduction of solid waste; encouragement of walking, cycling and transit; development of sustainable buildings; and the creation of sustainable energy infrastructure. Approximately 500 entries from across Canada were submitted to the award's 16 categories.
- The editors of *Canada's Top 100 Employers* ranked the City of Surrey as one of Canada's "Top Employers for Young People." Criteria: efforts to attract and retain young people; partnerships with post-secondary institutions; opportunities for work and internships/co-op work-study programs; mentorship and training programs; career management programs; and youth engagement initiatives. The 2012 competition also recognized Surrey as a national leader in assisting post-secondary students to transition from school to the workplace. One-third of Surrey's population is under the age of 19. *Canada's Top 100 Employers, "City of Surrey: Top Employers for Young People," September 24, 2012*
- *Business Review Canada* ranked the City of Surrey in the Top 5 for real estate investment cities in Canada. Criteria included market stability, housing prices and future growth potential. Surrey's strategic location for local, national and international business was praised. Other top cities were Barrie (ON), Maple Ridge (BC), Pitt Meadows (BC) and Red Deer (AB). *Business Review Canada, "Canada's Top Cities for Real Estate Investment," August 8, 2012*

PROFILES / Surrey, British Columbia

Population Growth and Density

Area	Population in 2001	Population in 2006	Population in 2011	Population Change 2001–2006	Population Change 2006–2011	Land Area (sq. km)	Population Density per sq. km
Surrey	347,820	394,976	468,251	13.6	18.6	316.41	1,479.9
British Columbia	3,907,738	4,113,487	4,400,057	5.3	7.0	922,509.29	4.8
Canada	30,007,094	31,612,897	33,476,688	5.4	5.9	8,965,121.42	3.7

Source: Statistics Canada. 2012. Census Profile. 2011 Census. Statistics Canada Catalogue no. 98-316-XWE. Ottawa. Released October 24 2012.
http://www12.statcan.gc.ca/census-recensement/2011/dp-pd/prof/index.cfm?Lang=E;
Statistics Canada 2007. 2006 Community Profiles. 2006 Census. Statistics Canada Catalogue no. 92-591-XWE. Ottawa. Released March 13 2007.
http://www12.statcan.ca/census-recensement/2006/dp-pd/prof/92-591/index.cfm?Lang=E

Gender

Area	Males	Females
Number		
Surrey	231,570	236,680
British Columbia	2,156,600	2,243,455
Canada	16,414,225	17,062,460
Percent of Population		
Surrey	49.5	50.5
British Columbia	49.0	51.0
Canada	49.0	51.0

Source: Statistics Canada. 2012. Census Profile. 2011 Census. Statistics Canada Catalogue no. 98-316-XWE. Ottawa. Released October 24 2012.
http://www12.statcan.gc.ca/census-recensement/2011/dp-pd/prof/index.cfm?Lang=E

Marital Status

Area	Married[1]	Living Common-law	Single[2]	Separated	Divorced	Widowed
Number — Total						
Surrey	210,295	20,825	100,530	9,690	19,430	18,730
British Columbia	1,832,605	321,965	1,014,270	102,040	246,515	205,300
Canada	12,941,960	3,142,525	7,816,045	698,240	1,686,035	1,584,530
Males						
Surrey	104,895	10,405	54,915	4,065	7,770	3,640
British Columbia	913,430	161,530	550,830	43,570	98,130	41,550
Canada	6,470,300	1,575,495	4,206,320	299,655	680,415	310,940
Females						
Surrey	105,400	10,425	45,615	5,630	11,665	15,090
British Columbia	919,175	160,435	463,435	58,470	148,385	163,750
Canada	6,471,660	1,567,035	3,609,730	398,585	1,005,620	1,273,590
Percent of Population — Total						
Surrey	55.4	5.5	26.5	2.6	5.1	4.9
British Columbia	49.2	8.6	27.2	2.7	6.6	5.5
Canada	46.4	11.3	28.0	2.5	6.0	5.7
Males						
Surrey	56.5	5.6	29.6	2.2	4.2	2.0
British Columbia	50.5	8.9	30.4	2.4	5.4	2.3
Canada	47.8	11.6	31.1	2.2	5.0	2.3
Females						
Surrey	54.4	5.4	23.5	2.9	6.0	7.8
British Columbia	48.0	8.4	24.2	3.1	7.8	8.6
Canada	45.2	10.9	25.2	2.8	7.0	8.9

Note: (1) and not separated, (2) never legally married
Source: Statistics Canada. 2012. Census Profile. 2011 Census. Statistics Canada Catalogue no. 98-316-XWE. Ottawa. Released October 24 2012.
http://www12.statcan.gc.ca/census-recensement/2011/dp-pd/prof/index.cfm?Lang=E

Age Characteristics: 0 to 49 Years

Area	0 to 4 Years	5 to 9 Years	10 to 14 Years	15 to 19 Years	20 to 24 Years	25 to 29 Years	30 to 34 Years	35 to 39 Years	40 to 44 Years	45 to 49 Years
					Number Total					
Surrey	29,160	28,800	30,785	33,130	31,085	32,275	32,150	32,900	35,030	36,530
British Columbia	219,665	218,915	238,780	275,165	279,825	288,780	275,985	280,870	313,765	350,600
Canada	1,877,095	1,809,895	1,920,355	2,178,135	2,187,450	2,169,590	2,162,905	2,173,930	2,324,875	2,675,130
					Males					
Surrey	15,115	14,820	15,955	17,230	15,750	15,835	15,405	15,650	17,090	18,250
British Columbia	112,885	112,200	122,465	141,670	142,290	143,475	135,220	135,455	151,430	170,580
Canada	961,150	925,965	983,995	1,115,845	1,108,775	1,077,275	1,058,810	1,064,200	1,141,720	1,318,715
					Females					
Surrey	14,050	13,980	14,830	15,905	15,335	16,435	16,745	17,250	17,940	18,285
British Columbia	106,775	106,715	116,315	133,500	137,535	145,305	140,755	145,415	162,335	180,020
Canada	915,945	883,935	936,360	1,062,295	1,078,670	1,092,315	1,104,095	1,109,735	1,183,155	1,356,420
					Percent of Population Total					
Surrey	6.2	6.2	6.6	7.1	6.6	6.9	6.9	7.0	7.5	7.8
British Columbia	5.0	5.0	5.4	6.3	6.4	6.6	6.3	6.4	7.1	8.0
Canada	5.6	5.4	5.7	6.5	6.5	6.5	6.5	6.5	6.9	8.0
					Males					
Surrey	6.5	6.4	6.9	7.4	6.8	6.8	6.7	6.8	7.4	7.9
British Columbia	5.2	5.2	5.7	6.6	6.6	6.7	6.3	6.3	7.0	7.9
Canada	5.9	5.6	6.0	6.8	6.8	6.6	6.5	6.5	7.0	8.0
					Females					
Surrey	5.9	5.9	6.3	6.7	6.5	6.9	7.1	7.3	7.6	7.7
British Columbia	4.8	4.8	5.2	6.0	6.1	6.5	6.3	6.5	7.2	8.0
Canada	5.4	5.2	5.5	6.2	6.3	6.4	6.5	6.5	6.9	7.9

Source: Statistics Canada. 2012. Census Profile. 2011 Census. Statistics Canada Catalogue no. 98-316-XWE. Ottawa. Released October 24 2012.
http://www12.statcan.gc.ca/census-recensement/2011/dp-pd/prof/index.cfm?Lang=E

Age Characteristics: 50 Years and Over, and Median Age

Area	50 to 54 Years	55 to 59 Years	60 to 64 Years	65 to 69 Years	70 to 74 Years	75 to 79 Years	80 to 84 Years	85 Years and Over	Median Age
				Number Total					
Surrey	34,340	29,825	25,670	18,530	13,585	10,180	7,400	6,875	37.5
British Columbia	354,610	323,335	291,040	210,900	160,715	127,480	96,945	92,675	41.9
Canada	2,658,965	2,340,635	2,052,670	1,521,715	1,153,065	922,700	702,070	645,515	40.6
				Males					
Surrey	17,055	14,770	12,570	9,095	6,560	4,750	3,235	2,430	36.8
British Columbia	172,060	157,455	142,645	103,785	77,350	60,720	42,745	32,150	41.1
Canada	1,309,030	1,147,300	1,002,690	738,010	543,435	417,945	291,085	208,300	39.6
				Females					
Surrey	17,285	15,050	13,100	9,435	7,025	5,425	4,165	4,445	38.2
British Columbia	182,550	165,880	148,395	107,115	83,360	66,760	54,200	60,520	42.7
Canada	1,349,940	1,193,335	1,049,985	783,705	609,630	504,755	410,985	437,215	41.5
				Percent of Population Total					
Surrey	7.3	6.4	5.5	4.0	2.9	2.2	1.6	1.5	–
British Columbia	8.1	7.3	6.6	4.8	3.7	2.9	2.2	2.1	–
Canada	7.9	7.0	6.1	4.5	3.4	2.8	2.1	1.9	–
				Males					
Surrey	7.4	6.4	5.4	3.9	2.8	2.1	1.4	1.0	–
British Columbia	8.0	7.3	6.6	4.8	3.6	2.8	2.0	1.5	–
Canada	8.0	7.0	6.1	4.5	3.3	2.5	1.8	1.3	–
				Females					
Surrey	7.3	6.4	5.5	4.0	3.0	2.3	1.8	1.9	–
British Columbia	8.1	7.4	6.6	4.8	3.7	3.0	2.4	2.7	–
Canada	7.9	7.0	6.2	4.6	3.0	3.0	2.4	2.6	–

Source: Statistics Canada. 2012. Census Profile. 2011 Census. Statistics Canada Catalogue no. 98-316-XWE. Ottawa. Released October 24 2012.
http://www12.statcan.gc.ca/census-recensement/2011/dp-pd/prof/index.cfm?Lang=E

PROFILES / Surrey, British Columbia

Private Households by Household Size

Area	1 Person	2 Persons	3 Persons	4 Persons	5 Persons	6 or More Persons	Average Number of Persons in Private Households
			Households				
Surrey	30,145	42,950	25,100	27,760	13,625	13,275	3.0
British Columbia	498,925	613,270	264,135	237,725	91,600	58,985	2.5
Canada	3,673,310	4,544,820	2,081,900	1,903,300	724,405	392,885	2.5
			Percent of Households				
Surrey	19.7	28.1	16.4	18.2	8.9	8.7	–
British Columbia	28.3	34.8	15.0	13.5	5.2	3.3	–
Canada	27.6	34.1	15.6	14.3	5.4	2.9	–

Source: Statistics Canada. 2012. Census Profile. 2011 Census. Statistics Canada Catalogue no. 98-316-XWE. Ottawa. Released October 24 2012.
http://www12.statcan.gc.ca/census-recensement/2011/dp-pd/prof/index.cfm?Lang=E

Dwelling Type

Area	Single-detached House	Semi-detached House	Row House	Apartment: Building with Five or More Storeys	Apartment: Building with Fewer Than Five Storeys	Duplex Apartment	Movable Dwelling	Other Single-attached House
				Number				
Surrey	64,515	3,345	20,900	3,800	31,345	27,410	1,440	100
British Columbia	842,120	52,825	130,365	143,970	361,150	184,355	46,960	2,885
Canada	7,329,150	646,245	791,600	1,234,770	2,397,550	704,485	183,510	33,310
				Percent of Dwellings				
Surrey	42.2	2.2	13.7	2.5	20.5	17.9	0.9	0.1
British Columbia	47.7	3.0	7.4	8.2	20.5	10.4	2.7	0.2
Canada	55.0	4.9	5.9	9.3	18.0	5.3	1.4	0.3

Source: Statistics Canada. 2012. Census Profile. 2011 Census. Statistics Canada Catalogue no. 98-316-XWE. Ottawa. Released October 24 2012.
http://www12.statcan.gc.ca/census-recensement/2011/dp-pd/prof/index.cfm?Lang=E

Shelter Costs

	Owned Dwellings					Rented Dwellings		
Area	Number	Median Value[1] ($)	Average Value[1] ($)	Median Monthly Costs[2] ($)	Average Monthly Costs[2] ($)	Number	Median Monthly Costs[3] ($)	Average Monthly Costs[3] ($)
Surrey	111,470	500,746	544,819	1,391	1,422	41,160	794	895
British Columbia	1,202,000	448,835	543,635	1,023	1,228	519,855	903	989
Canada	9,013,410	280,552	345,182	978	1,141	4,060,385	784	848

Note: All figures cover non-farm, non-reserve private dwellings. (1) Refers to the dollar amount expected by the owner if the dwelling were to be sold; (2) Includes all shelter expenses paid by households that own their dwellings, such as the mortgage payment and the costs of electricity, heat, water and other municipal services, property taxes and condominium fees; (3) Includes all shelter expenses paid by households that rent their dwellings, such as the monthly rent and the costs of electricity, heat and municipal services.
Source: Statistics Canada. 2013. 2011 National Household Survey. Statistics Canada Catalogue no. 99-004-XWE. Ottawa. Released September 11, 2013.

Occupied Private Dwellings by Period of Construction

Area	1960 or Before	1961 to 1980	1981 to 1990	1991 to 2000	2001 to 2005	2006 to 2011
			Number			
Surrey	9,175	29,605	35,810	38,305	19,225	20,735
British Columbia	282,675	551,655	308,450	329,780	133,235	158,845
Canada	3,273,105	4,152,715	2,112,110	1,707,880	1,031,020	1,042,430
			Percent of Dwellings			
Surrey	6.0	19.4	23.4	25.1	12.6	13.6
British Columbia	16.0	31.3	17.5	18.7	7.6	9.0
Canada	24.6	31.2	15.9	12.8	7.7	7.8

Note: Figures cover non-farm, non-reserve private dwellings and includes data up to May 10, 2011.
Source: Statistics Canada. 2013. 2011 National Household Survey. Statistics Canada Catalogue no. 99-004-XWE. Ottawa. Released September 11, 2013.

Educational Attainment

Area	No Certificate, Diploma or Degree	High School Diploma or Equivalent[1]	Apprenticeship or Trades Certificate or Diploma[2]	College, CÉGEP or Other Non-University Certificate or Diploma	University Certificate or Diploma Below the Bachelor Level[3]	Bachelor's Degree	University Certificate, Diploma or Degree Above Bachelor Level[4]
			Number				
			Total				
Surrey	71,425	116,155	31,805	58,505	25,590	44,750	26,085
British Columbia	607,655	1,009,400	387,455	628,115	208,245	511,240	294,725
Canada	5,485,400	6,968,935	2,950,685	4,970,020	1,200,130	3,634,425	2,049,930
			Males				
Surrey	34,810	56,765	21,340	24,910	11,430	21,095	13,240
British Columbia	305,040	475,670	262,245	260,580	86,995	235,620	149,300
Canada	2,742,875	3,305,415	1,928,970	2,118,430	513,235	1,643,080	1,043,350
			Females				
Surrey	36,620	59,390	10,460	33,590	14,155	23,665	12,840
British Columbia	302,620	533,735	125,210	367,535	121,250	275,625	145,425
Canada	2,742,520	3,663,515	1,021,715	2,851,595	686,890	1,991,345	1,006,585
			Percent of Population				
			Total				
Surrey	19.1	31.0	8.5	15.6	6.8	12.0	7.0
British Columbia	16.7	27.7	10.6	17.2	5.7	14.0	8.1
Canada	20.1	25.6	10.8	18.2	4.4	13.3	7.5
			Males				
Surrey	19.0	30.9	11.6	13.6	6.2	11.5	7.2
British Columbia	17.2	26.8	14.8	14.7	4.9	13.3	8.4
Canada	20.6	24.9	14.5	15.9	3.9	12.4	7.8
			Females				
Surrey	19.2	31.1	5.5	17.6	7.4	12.4	6.7
British Columbia	16.2	28.5	6.7	19.6	6.5	14.7	7.8
Canada	19.6	26.2	7.3	20.4	4.9	14.3	7.2

Note: Figures cover total population aged 15 years and over by highest certificate, diploma or degree; (1) Includes persons who have graduated from a secondary school or equivalent. It excludes persons with a postsecondary certificate, diploma or degree; (2) Includes Registered Apprenticeship certificates (including Certificate of Qualification, Journeyperson's designation) and other trades certificates or diplomas such as pre-employment or vocational certificates and diplomas from brief trade programs completed at community colleges, institutes of technology, vocational centres, and similar institutions; (3) Comparisons with other data sources suggest that the category 'University certificate or diploma below the bachelor's level' was over-reported in the NHS. This category likely includes some responses that are actually college certificates or diplomas, bachelor's degrees or other types of education (e.g., university transfer programs, bachelor's programs completed in other countries, incomplete bachelor's programs, non-university professional designations). We recommend users interpret the results for the 'University certificate or diploma below the bachelor's level' category with caution; (4) 'University certificate or diploma above bachelor level' includes the categories: 'Degree in medicine, dentistry, veterinary medicine or optometry,' 'Master's degree' and 'Earned doctorate.'
Source: Statistics Canada. 2013. 2011 National Household Survey. Statistics Canada Catalogue no. 99-004-XWE. Ottawa. Released September 11, 2013.

Household Income Distribution

Area	Less than $10,000	$10,000 to $19,999	$20,000 to $29,999	$30,000 to $39,999	$40,000 to $49,999	$50,000 to $59,999	$60,000 to $79,999	$80,000 to $99,999	$100,000 to $124,999	$125,000 to $149,999	$150,000 and Over
					Households						
Surrey	7,360	10,320	11,495	12,920	13,030	12,185	22,375	18,165	16,085	10,995	17,910
British Columbia	96,465	156,565	157,605	167,220	158,400	140,340	246,720	193,180	167,415	106,325	174,385
Canada	626,705	1,141,945	1,193,925	1,271,675	1,206,800	1,102,120	1,865,280	1,458,240	1,260,770	802,555	1,389,240
					Percent of Households						
Surrey	4.8	6.8	7.5	8.5	8.5	8.0	14.6	11.9	10.5	7.2	11.7
British Columbia	5.5	8.9	8.9	9.5	9.0	8.0	14.0	10.9	9.5	6.0	9.9
Canada	4.7	8.6	9.0	9.5	9.1	8.3	14.0	10.9	9.5	6.0	10.4

Note: Household income is the sum of the total incomes of all members of that household. Total income refers to monetary receipts from certain sources, before income taxes and deductions, during calendar year 2010.
Source: Statistics Canada. 2013. 2011 National Household Survey. Statistics Canada Catalogue no. 99-004-XWE. Ottawa. Released September 11, 2013.

Median and Average Household and Economic Family Income

Area	Median Household Income ($)	Average Household Income ($)	Median After-tax Household Income ($)	Average After-tax Household Income ($)	Median Economic Family Income ($)	Average Economic Family Income ($)	Median After-tax Economic Family Income ($)	Average After-tax Economic Family Income ($)
Surrey	67,702	82,789	61,023	71,603	78,283	92,446	69,935	79,873
British Columbia	60,333	77,378	54,379	66,264	75,797	91,967	67,915	78,580
Canada	61,072	79,102	54,089	66,149	76,511	94,125	67,044	78,517

Note: Figures cover household and economic familiy income in 2010. A household is defined as a person or a group of persons (other than foreign residents) who occupy the same private dwelling and do not have a usual place of residence elsewhere in Canada. Every person is a member of one and only one household. An economic family is defined as a group of two or more persons who live in the same dwelling and are related to each other by blood, marriage, common-law, adoption or a foster relationship. A couple may be of opposite or same sex.
Source: Statistics Canada. 2013. 2011 National Household Survey. Statistics Canada Catalogue no. 99-004-XWE. Ottawa. Released September 11, 2013.

PROFILES / Surrey, British Columbia

Individual Income Distribution

Area	Less than $10,000	$10,000 to $19,999	$20,000 to $29,999	$30,000 to $39,999	$40,000 to $49,999	$50,000 to $59,999	$60,000 to $79,999	$80,000 to $99,999	$100,000 to $124,999	$125,000 and Over
					Number					
					Total					
Surrey	71,030	69,110	48,115	40,910	34,685	24,840	30,570	14,360	7,665	7,865
British Columbia	645,915	666,060	470,255	404,860	338,595	253,215	330,590	169,190	89,520	96,055
Canada	4,492,040	4,835,710	3,670,020	3,180,360	2,603,520	1,921,650	2,437,440	1,302,045	693,580	782,135
					Males					
Surrey	30,170	27,710	21,395	19,260	17,005	14,900	19,985	9,940	5,625	6,415
British Columbia	275,815	263,170	201,000	186,285	167,400	143,765	206,400	112,525	65,050	74,260
Canada	1,936,365	1,864,880	1,588,260	1,522,190	1,333,510	1,079,780	1,473,145	823,720	492,905	599,905
					Females					
Surrey	40,850	41,410	26,715	21,650	17,685	9,945	10,585	4,420	2,035	1,445
British Columbia	370,100	402,880	269,255	218,575	171,190	109,445	124,195	56,670	24,470	21,795
Canada	2,555,675	2,970,825	2,081,760	1,658,170	1,270,010	841,870	964,300	478,330	200,680	182,230
					Percent of Population					
					Total					
Surrey	20.3	19.8	13.8	11.7	9.9	7.1	8.8	4.1	2.2	2.3
British Columbia	18.6	19.2	13.6	11.7	9.8	7.3	9.5	4.9	2.6	2.8
Canada	17.3	18.7	14.2	12.3	10.0	7.4	9.4	5.0	2.7	3.0
					Males					
Surrey	17.5	16.1	12.4	11.2	9.9	8.6	11.6	5.8	3.3	3.7
British Columbia	16.3	15.5	11.9	11.0	9.9	8.5	12.2	6.6	3.8	4.4
Canada	15.2	14.7	12.5	12.0	10.5	8.5	11.6	6.5	3.9	4.7
					Females					
Surrey	23.1	23.4	15.1	12.2	10.0	5.6	6.0	2.5	1.2	0.8
British Columbia	20.9	22.8	15.2	12.4	9.7	6.2	7.0	3.2	1.4	1.2
Canada	19.4	22.5	15.8	12.6	9.6	6.4	7.3	3.6	1.5	1.4

Note: Figures cover individuals aged 15 years and over with income. Income refers to monetary receipts from certain sources, before income taxes and deductions, during calendar year 2010.
Source: Statistics Canada. 2013. 2011 National Household Survey. Statistics Canada Catalogue no. 99-004-XWE. Ottawa. Released September 11, 2013.

Labour Force Status

Area	In the Labour Force - All	Employed	Unemployed	Not in the Labour Force
		Number		
		Total		
Surrey	245,645	226,155	19,490	128,670
British Columbia	2,354,245	2,171,465	182,775	1,292,595
Canada	17,990,080	16,595,035	1,395,045	9,269,445
		Males		
Surrey	130,535	120,895	9,645	53,050
British Columbia	1,223,375	1,124,590	98,785	552,070
Canada	9,388,570	8,634,310	754,255	3,906,785
		Females		
Surrey	115,105	105,260	9,850	75,620
British Columbia	1,130,870	1,046,875	83,990	740,530
Canada	8,601,515	7,960,725	640,790	5,362,660
		Percent of Labour Force		
		Total		
Surrey	65.6	60.4	7.9	34.4
British Columbia	64.6	59.5	7.8	35.4
Canada	66.0	60.9	7.8	34.0
		Males		
Surrey	71.1	65.9	7.4	28.9
British Columbia	68.9	63.3	8.1	31.1
Canada	70.6	64.9	8.0	29.4
		Females		
Surrey	60.4	55.2	8.6	39.6
British Columbia	60.4	55.9	7.4	39.6
Canada	61.6	57.0	7.4	38.4

Note: Figures are based on total population 15 years and over
Source: Statistics Canada. 2013. 2011 National Household Survey. Statistics Canada Catalogue no. 99-004-XWE. Ottawa. Released September 11, 2013.

Labour Force by Industry (NAICS Codes 11–52)

Area	Agriculture, forestry, fishing & hunting	Mining, quarrying, & oil & gas extraction	Utilities	Construction	Manufacturing	Wholesale Trade	Retail Trade	Transportation & warehousing	Information & cultural industries	Finance & insurance
					Number					
					Total					
Surrey	5,240	565	1,190	21,680	22,260	12,290	28,050	19,950	5,065	9,550
British Columbia	61,210	25,450	13,215	181,510	148,810	90,560	266,265	118,675	62,235	91,790
Canada	437,650	261,050	149,940	1,215,380	1,619,295	733,445	2,031,665	827,780	420,830	767,960
					Males					
Surrey	2,380	420	790	19,210	15,610	8,465	13,275	15,730	3,170	3,745
British Columbia	40,810	21,175	9,650	159,605	108,480	61,730	121,750	89,155	37,250	35,375
Canada	307,370	211,690	110,765	1,068,710	1,167,680	494,545	933,850	617,305	235,875	296,995
					Females					
Surrey	2,860	150	395	2,470	6,650	3,825	14,775	4,220	1,895	5,805
British Columbia	20,405	4,275	3,560	21,910	40,335	28,820	144,515	29,520	24,980	56,415
Canada	130,285	49,360	39,175	146,670	451,615	238,900	1,097,820	210,475	184,955	470,960
					Percent of Labour Force					
					Total					
Surrey	2.2	0.2	0.5	9.1	9.3	5.1	11.7	8.3	2.1	4.0
British Columbia	2.7	1.1	0.6	7.9	6.5	3.9	11.6	5.1	2.7	4.0
Canada	2.5	1.5	0.9	6.9	9.2	4.2	11.6	4.7	2.4	4.4
					Males					
Surrey	1.9	0.3	0.6	15.0	12.2	6.6	10.4	12.3	2.5	2.9
British Columbia	3.4	1.8	0.8	13.3	9.0	5.1	10.1	7.4	3.1	2.9
Canada	3.3	2.3	1.2	11.6	12.7	5.4	10.2	6.7	2.6	3.2
					Females					
Surrey	2.6	0.1	0.4	2.2	6.0	3.4	13.2	3.8	1.7	5.2
British Columbia	1.8	0.4	0.3	2.0	3.6	2.6	13.1	2.7	2.3	5.1
Canada	1.6	0.6	0.5	1.7	5.4	2.8	13.1	2.5	2.2	5.6

Note: Figures are based on total experienced labour force 15 years and over. Experienced labour force refers to persons who, during the week of Sunday, May 1 to Saturday, May 7, 2011, were employed and the unemployed who had last worked for pay or in self-employment in either 2010 or 2011.
Source: Statistics Canada. 2013. 2011 National Household Survey. Statistics Canada Catalogue no. 99-004-XWE. Ottawa. Released September 11, 2013.

Labour Force by Industry (NAICS Codes 53–91)

Area	Real estate & rental & leasing	Profess., scientific & tech. services	Mgmt of companies & enterprises	Admin. & support, waste mgmt & remed. services	Educational services	Health care & social assistance	Arts, entertain. & recreation	Accomm. & food services	Other services (except public admin.)	Public admin.
					Number					
					Total					
Surrey	4,895	14,535	240	12,275	13,860	23,500	4,265	16,130	12,295	11,615
British Columbia	54,840	179,355	2,440	98,890	167,875	249,030	56,915	179,625	112,745	143,875
Canada	321,895	1,240,850	17,460	728,330	1,301,435	1,949,650	363,405	1,130,750	807,800	1,261,050
					Males					
Surrey	2,715	7,945	160	7,175	4,100	3,860	2,180	5,590	5,640	5,665
British Columbia	29,790	98,760	1,320	55,745	55,635	47,020	29,750	73,570	49,130	74,040
Canada	179,090	688,625	9,380	411,250	424,915	349,430	188,270	469,990	372,940	652,510
					Females					
Surrey	2,180	6,595	75	5,100	9,765	19,645	2,090	10,535	6,655	5,950
British Columbia	25,055	80,590	1,120	43,145	112,235	202,010	27,175	106,055	63,615	69,840
Canada	142,805	552,225	8,075	317,085	876,515	1,600,220	175,135	660,760	434,865	608,535
					Percent of Labour Force					
					Total					
Surrey	2.0	6.1	0.1	5.1	5.8	9.8	1.8	6.7	5.1	4.9
British Columbia	2.4	7.8	0.1	4.3	7.3	10.8	2.5	7.8	4.9	6.2
Canada	1.8	7.1	0.1	4.1	7.4	11.1	2.1	6.4	4.6	7.2
					Males					
Surrey	2.1	6.2	0.1	5.6	3.2	3.0	1.7	4.4	4.4	4.4
British Columbia	2.5	8.2	0.1	4.6	4.6	3.9	2.5	6.1	4.1	6.2
Canada	1.9	7.5	0.1	4.5	4.6	3.8	2.0	5.1	4.1	7.1
					Females					
Surrey	2.0	5.9	0.1	4.6	8.7	17.6	1.9	9.4	6.0	5.3
British Columbia	2.3	7.3	0.1	3.9	10.2	18.3	2.5	9.6	5.8	6.3
Canada	1.7	6.6	0.1	3.8	10.4	19.1	2.1	7.9	5.2	7.2

Note: Figures are based on total experienced labour force 15 years and over. Experienced labour force refers to persons who, during the week of Sunday, May 1 to Saturday, May 7, 2011, were employed and the unemployed who had last worked for pay or in self-employment in either 2010 or 2011.
Source: Statistics Canada. 2013. 2011 National Household Survey. Statistics Canada Catalogue no. 99-004-XWE. Ottawa. Released September 11, 2013.

PROFILES / Surrey, British Columbia

Occupation

Area	Mgmt	Business, Finance & Admin.	Natural/ Applied Sciences & Related	Health	Education, Law & Social, Community & Government Services	Art, Culture, Recreation & Sport	Sales & Service	Trades, Transport & Equip. Operators & Related	Natural Resources, Agri. & Related Production	Mfg & Utilities
Number										
Total										
Surrey	25,055	38,430	12,560	14,390	22,500	5,145	59,595	44,130	5,610	12,060
British Columbia	263,685	368,980	154,055	147,620	265,910	78,565	554,345	337,140	60,295	74,720
Canada	1,963,600	2,902,045	1,237,775	1,107,200	2,064,675	503,415	4,068,170	2,537,775	397,930	805,040
Males										
Surrey	16,075	11,900	10,320	2,520	7,190	2,430	25,135	41,520	3,070	7,660
British Columbia	162,365	104,285	122,570	32,490	89,645	38,300	233,065	317,385	45,155	54,470
Canada	1,229,460	854,190	966,355	217,520	676,550	232,535	1,745,705	2,385,615	318,945	564,300
Females										
Surrey	8,985	26,530	2,235	11,875	15,310	2,715	34,455	2,605	2,535	4,400
British Columbia	101,320	264,690	31,480	115,125	176,265	40,270	321,285	19,755	15,135	20,250
Canada	734,140	2,047,855	271,415	889,675	1,388,130	270,875	2,322,465	152,165	78,980	240,740
Percent of Labour Force										
Total										
Surrey	10.5	16.0	5.2	6.0	9.4	2.1	24.9	18.4	2.3	5.0
British Columbia	11.4	16.0	6.7	6.4	11.5	3.4	24.0	14.6	2.6	3.2
Canada	11.2	16.5	7.0	6.3	11.7	2.9	23.1	14.4	2.3	4.6
Males										
Surrey	12.6	9.3	8.1	2.0	5.6	1.9	19.7	32.5	2.4	6.0
British Columbia	13.5	8.7	10.2	2.7	7.5	3.2	19.4	26.5	3.8	4.5
Canada	13.4	9.3	10.5	2.4	7.4	2.5	19.0	26.0	3.5	6.1
Females										
Surrey	8.0	23.8	2.0	10.6	13.7	2.4	30.9	2.3	2.3	3.9
British Columbia	9.2	23.9	2.8	10.4	15.9	3.6	29.1	1.8	1.4	1.8
Canada	8.7	24.4	3.2	10.6	16.5	3.2	27.7	1.8	0.9	2.9

Note: Figures are based on total experienced labour force 15 years and over
Source: Statistics Canada. 2013. 2011 National Household Survey. Statistics Canada Catalogue no. 99-004-XWE. Ottawa. Released September 11, 2013.

Place of Work Status

Area	Worked at Home	Worked Outside Canada	No Fixed Workplace Address	Worked at Usual Place
Number				
Total				
Surrey	13,230	1,205	37,970	173,755
British Columbia	174,000	12,480	304,465	1,680,525
Canada	1,142,640	66,460	1,868,245	13,517,690
Males				
Surrey	6,305	915	28,565	85,100
British Columbia	84,015	9,210	225,840	805,525
Canada	582,150	47,355	1,400,485	6,604,325
Females				
Surrey	6,920	290	9,400	88,650
British Columbia	89,990	3,270	78,620	875,000
Canada	560,490	19,100	467,760	6,913,370
Percent of Labour Force				
Total				
Surrey	5.9	0.5	16.8	76.8
British Columbia	8.0	0.6	14.0	77.4
Canada	6.9	0.4	11.3	81.5
Males				
Surrey	5.2	0.8	23.6	70.4
British Columbia	7.5	0.8	20.1	71.6
Canada	6.7	0.5	16.2	76.5
Females				
Surrey	6.6	0.3	8.9	84.2
British Columbia	8.6	0.3	7.5	83.6
Canada	7.0	0.2	5.9	86.8

Note: Figures are based on total employed labour force 15 years and over.
Source: Statistics Canada. 2013. 2011 National Household Survey. Statistics Canada Catalogue no. 99-004-XWE. Ottawa. Released September 11, 2013.

Mode of Transportation to Work

Area	Car; Truck; Van; as Driver	Car; Truck; Van; as Passenger	Public Transit	Walked	Bicycled	All Other Modes
			Number			
			Total			
Surrey	162,090	13,985	27,040	5,465	730	2,410
British Columbia	1,415,745	110,695	250,450	132,205	42,260	33,635
Canada	11,393,140	867,050	1,851,525	880,815	201,780	191,625
			Males			
Surrey	91,810	6,210	11,930	1,875	585	1,260
British Columbia	773,160	47,425	107,645	57,000	26,595	19,535
Canada	6,238,835	349,530	788,290	387,580	135,840	104,725
			Females			
Surrey	70,280	7,775	15,110	3,590	145	1,150
British Columbia	642,580	63,270	142,810	75,205	15,665	14,100
Canada	5,154,305	517,520	1,063,235	493,230	65,940	86,900
			Percent of Labour Force			
			Total			
Surrey	76.6	6.6	12.8	2.6	0.3	1.1
British Columbia	71.3	5.6	12.6	6.7	2.1	1.7
Canada	74.0	5.6	12.0	5.7	1.3	1.2
			Males			
Surrey	80.8	5.5	10.5	1.6	0.5	1.1
British Columbia	75.0	4.6	10.4	5.5	2.6	1.9
Canada	77.9	4.4	9.8	4.8	1.7	1.3
			Females			
Surrey	71.7	7.9	15.4	3.7	0.1	1.2
British Columbia	67.4	6.6	15.0	7.9	1.6	1.5
Canada	69.8	7.0	14.4	6.7	0.9	1.2

Note: Figures are based on total employed labour force 15 years and over.
Source: Statistics Canada. 2013. 2011 National Household Survey. Statistics Canada Catalogue no. 99-004-XWE. Ottawa. Released September 11, 2013.

Visible Minority Population Characteristics

Area	Total Minority	South Asian[1]	Chinese	Black	Filipino	Latin American	Arab	SE Asian[2]	West Asian[3]	Korean	Japanese	Multiple[4]
					Number							
					Total							
Surrey	243,760	142,445	28,480	6,150	26,480	5,340	3,265	13,080	2,350	8,385	2,405	4,295
British Columbia	1,180,870	313,440	438,140	33,260	126,040	35,465	14,090	51,970	38,960	53,770	38,120	31,160
Canada	6,264,750	1,567,400	1,324,750	945,665	619,310	381,280	380,620	312,075	206,840	161,130	87,270	171,935
					Males							
Surrey	120,795	71,615	13,715	3,090	12,260	2,755	1,740	6,425	1,285	4,220	1,100	2,080
British Columbia	565,965	157,135	208,175	17,365	53,715	16,985	8,010	25,055	19,420	25,325	16,295	15,255
Canada	3,043,010	790,755	632,325	453,005	268,885	186,355	203,485	154,035	105,620	77,165	38,270	83,335
					Females							
Surrey	122,965	70,830	14,765	3,060	14,215	2,580	1,525	6,655	1,065	4,170	1,305	2,210
British Columbia	614,905	156,300	229,960	15,895	72,320	18,480	6,080	26,920	19,540	28,440	21,820	15,905
Canada	3,221,745	776,650	692,420	492,660	350,425	194,925	177,140	158,045	101,220	83,965	48,990	88,600
					Percent of Population							
					Total							
Surrey	52.6	30.7	6.1	1.3	5.7	1.2	0.7	2.8	0.5	1.8	0.5	0.9
British Columbia	27.3	7.2	10.1	0.8	2.9	0.8	0.3	1.2	0.9	1.2	0.9	0.7
Canada	19.1	4.8	4.0	2.9	1.9	1.2	1.2	0.9	0.6	0.5	0.3	0.5
					Males							
Surrey	52.6	31.2	6.0	1.3	5.3	1.2	0.8	2.8	0.6	1.8	0.5	0.9
British Columbia	26.6	7.4	9.8	0.8	2.5	0.8	0.4	1.2	0.9	1.2	0.8	0.7
Canada	18.8	4.9	3.9	2.8	1.7	1.2	1.3	1.0	0.7	0.5	0.2	0.5
					Females							
Surrey	52.7	30.3	6.3	1.3	6.1	1.1	0.7	2.8	0.5	1.8	0.6	0.9
British Columbia	28.0	7.1	10.5	0.7	3.3	0.8	0.3	1.2	0.9	1.3	1.0	0.7
Canada	19.3	4.7	4.1	3.0	2.1	1.2	1.1	0.9	0.6	0.5	0.3	0.5

Note: The Employment Equity Act defines visible minorities as 'persons, other than Aboriginal peoples, who are non-Caucasian in race or non-white in colour';
(1) Includes 'East Indian,' 'Pakistani,' 'Sri Lankan,' etc.; (2) Includes 'Vietnamese,' 'Cambodian,' 'Malaysian,' 'Laotian,' etc.; (3) Includes 'Iranian,' 'Afghan,' etc.; (4) Includes respondents who reported more than one visible minority group by checking two or more mark-in circles, e.g., 'Black' and 'South Asian.'
Source: Statistics Canada. 2013. 2011 National Household Survey. Statistics Canada Catalogue no. 99-004-XWE. Ottawa. Released September 11, 2013.

PROFILES / Surrey, British Columbia

Aboriginal Population

Area	Aboriginal Identity[1]	First Nations (North American Indian) Single Identity[2]	Métis Single Identity	Inuk (Inuit) Single Identity	Multiple Aboriginal Identities[3]	Aboriginal Identities Not Included Elsewhere
			Number			
			Total			
Surrey	10,955	6,135	4,225	175	265	155
British Columbia	232,290	155,020	69,475	1,570	2,480	3,745
Canada	1,400,685	851,560	451,795	59,440	11,415	26,475
			Males			
Surrey	5,195	2,980	1,935	110	95	80
British Columbia	113,080	75,400	33,940	820	1,190	1,735
Canada	682,190	411,785	223,335	29,495	5,525	12,055
			Females			
Surrey	5,760	3,150	2,290	65	170	75
British Columbia	119,215	79,620	35,540	750	1,290	2,015
Canada	718,500	439,775	228,460	29,950	5,890	14,420
			Percent of Population			
			Total			
Surrey	2.4	1.3	0.9	0.0	0.1	0.0
British Columbia	5.4	3.6	1.6	0.0	0.1	0.1
Canada	4.3	2.6	1.4	0.2	0.0	0.1
			Males			
Surrey	2.3	1.3	0.8	0.0	0.0	0.0
British Columbia	5.3	3.5	1.6	0.0	0.1	0.1
Canada	4.2	2.5	1.4	0.2	0.0	0.1
			Females			
Surrey	2.5	1.3	1.0	0.0	0.1	0.0
British Columbia	5.4	3.6	1.6	0.0	0.1	0.1
Canada	4.3	2.6	1.4	0.2	0.0	0.1

Note: (1) Includes persons who reported being an Aboriginal person, that is, First Nations (North American Indian), Métis or Inuk (Inuit) and/or those who reported Registered or Treaty Indian status, that is registered under the Indian Act of Canada, and/or those who reported membership in a First Nation or Indian band. Aboriginal peoples of Canada are defined in the Constitution Act, 1982, section 35-2 as including the Indian, Inuit and Métis peoples of Canada; (2) Users should be aware that the estimates associated with this variable are more affected than most by the incomplete enumeration of certain Indian reserves and Indian settlements in the National Household Survey (NHS); (3) Includes persons who reported being any two or all three of the following: First Nations (North American Indian), Métis or Inuk (Inuit).
Source: Statistics Canada. 2013. 2011 National Household Survey. Statistics Canada Catalogue no. 99-004-XWE. Ottawa. Released September 11, 2013.

Ethnic Origin

Area	North American Aboriginal	Other North American	European	Caribbean	Latin, Central and South American	African	Asian	Oceania
			Number					
			Total					
Surrey	13,305	73,645	198,105	2,770	6,925	7,440	225,540	9,005
British Columbia	267,085	884,490	2,812,935	20,035	52,725	47,185	1,122,445	35,770
Canada	1,836,035	11,070,455	20,157,965	627,590	544,375	766,735	5,011,225	74,875
			Males					
Surrey	6,160	37,180	97,930	1,365	3,615	3,515	111,340	4,425
British Columbia	128,880	440,920	1,387,940	10,225	25,605	23,575	535,825	17,425
Canada	885,675	5,462,685	9,913,150	291,640	264,635	387,360	2,435,540	37,490
			Females					
Surrey	7,145	36,465	100,175	1,405	3,310	3,925	114,205	4,580
British Columbia	138,205	443,570	1,424,990	9,810	27,120	23,610	586,620	18,340
Canada	950,360	5,607,770	10,244,820	335,945	279,740	379,380	2,575,680	37,385
			Percent of Population					
			Total					
Surrey	2.9	15.9	42.8	0.6	1.5	1.6	48.7	1.9
British Columbia	6.2	20.5	65.0	0.5	1.2	1.1	26.0	0.8
Canada	5.6	33.7	61.4	1.9	1.7	2.3	15.3	0.2
			Males					
Surrey	2.7	16.2	42.6	0.6	1.6	1.5	48.4	1.9
British Columbia	6.1	20.7	65.3	0.5	1.2	1.1	25.2	0.8
Canada	5.5	33.8	61.3	1.8	1.6	2.4	15.1	0.2
			Females					
Surrey	3.1	15.6	42.9	0.6	1.4	1.7	48.9	2.0
British Columbia	6.3	20.2	64.8	0.4	1.2	1.1	26.7	0.8
Canada	5.7	33.6	61.4	2.0	1.7	2.3	15.4	0.2

Note: The sum of the ethnic groups in this table is greater than the total population estimate because a person may report more than one ethnic origin in the NHS.
Source: Statistics Canada. 2013. 2011 National Household Survey. Statistics Canada Catalogue no. 99-004-XWE. Ottawa. Released September 11, 2013.

Religion

Area	Buddhist	Christian	Hindu	Jewish	Muslim	Sikh	Traditional (Aboriginal) Spirituality	Other Religions	No Religious Affiliation
Number									
Total									
Surrey	10,520	177,020	16,790	1,105	18,345	104,720	180	2,015	132,635
British Columbia	90,620	1,930,415	45,795	23,130	79,310	201,110	10,295	35,500	1,908,285
Canada	366,830	22,102,745	497,965	329,495	1,053,945	454,965	64,935	130,835	7,850,605
Males									
Surrey	4,915	82,645	8,470	565	9,200	52,380	90	835	70,710
British Columbia	40,175	883,680	22,945	11,255	39,780	100,610	5,085	14,680	1,007,420
Canada	168,465	10,497,775	250,435	161,265	540,555	229,435	31,805	57,745	4,225,645
Females									
Surrey	5,610	94,380	8,325	540	9,145	52,345	85	1,180	61,925
British Columbia	50,440	1,046,735	22,845	11,880	39,530	100,500	5,210	20,820	900,865
Canada	198,365	11,604,975	247,525	168,235	513,395	225,530	33,135	73,090	3,624,965
Percent of Population									
Total									
Surrey	2.3	38.2	3.6	0.2	4.0	22.6	0.0	0.4	28.6
British Columbia	2.1	44.6	1.1	0.5	1.8	4.7	0.2	0.8	44.1
Canada	1.1	67.3	1.5	1.0	3.2	1.4	0.2	0.4	23.9
Males									
Surrey	2.1	36.0	3.7	0.2	4.0	22.8	0.0	0.4	30.8
British Columbia	1.9	41.6	1.1	0.5	1.9	4.7	0.2	0.7	47.4
Canada	1.0	64.9	1.5	1.0	3.3	1.4	0.2	0.4	26.1
Females									
Surrey	2.4	40.4	3.6	0.2	3.9	22.4	0.0	0.5	26.5
British Columbia	2.3	47.6	1.0	0.5	1.8	4.6	0.2	0.9	41.0
Canada	1.2	69.5	1.5	1.0	3.1	1.4	0.2	0.4	21.7

Note: Religion refers to the person's self-identification as having a connection or affiliation with any religious denomination, group, body, sect, cult or other religiously defined community or system of belief. Religion is not limited to formal membership in a religious organization or group. Persons without a religious connection or affiliation can self-identify as atheist, agnostic or humanist, or can provide another applicable response.
Source: Statistics Canada. 2013. 2011 National Household Survey. Statistics Canada Catalogue no. 99-004-XWE. Ottawa. Released September 11, 2013.

Religion—Christian Denominations

Area	Anglican	Baptist	Catholic	Christian Orthodox	Lutheran	Pentecostal	Presbyterian	United Church	Other Christian
Number									
Total									
Surrey	13,140	8,665	64,185	3,600	5,965	7,400	4,100	15,150	54,820
British Columbia	213,975	91,575	650,360	39,845	71,470	58,300	44,635	222,230	538,030
Canada	1,631,845	635,840	12,810,705	550,690	478,185	478,705	472,385	2,007,610	3,036,780
Males									
Surrey	5,895	3,960	30,200	1,695	2,680	3,570	1,885	6,520	26,245
British Columbia	94,330	41,565	303,300	19,475	32,205	26,590	19,925	94,020	252,270
Canada	752,945	293,905	6,167,290	270,205	221,525	217,850	218,955	912,545	1,442,550
Females									
Surrey	7,250	4,705	33,990	1,905	3,280	3,830	2,215	8,635	28,575
British Columbia	119,645	50,010	347,060	20,375	39,270	31,710	24,710	128,210	285,770
Canada	878,900	341,940	6,643,415	280,485	256,660	260,850	253,430	1,095,065	1,594,230
Percent of Population									
Total									
Surrey	2.8	1.9	13.9	0.8	1.3	1.6	0.9	3.3	11.8
British Columbia	4.9	2.1	15.0	0.9	1.7	1.3	1.0	5.1	12.4
Canada	5.0	1.9	39.0	1.7	1.5	1.5	1.4	6.1	9.2
Males									
Surrey	2.6	1.7	13.1	0.7	1.2	1.6	0.8	2.8	11.4
British Columbia	4.4	2.0	14.3	0.9	1.5	1.3	0.9	4.4	11.9
Canada	4.7	1.8	38.2	1.7	1.4	1.3	1.4	5.6	8.9
Females									
Surrey	3.1	2.0	14.6	0.8	1.4	1.6	0.9	3.7	12.2
British Columbia	5.4	2.3	15.8	0.9	1.8	1.4	1.1	5.8	13.0
Canada	5.3	2.0	39.8	1.7	1.5	1.4	1.5	6.6	9.6

Note: Religion refers to the person's self-identification as having a connection or affiliation with any religious denomination, group, body, sect, cult or other religiously defined community or system of belief. Religion is not limited to formal membership in a religious organization or group. Persons without a religious connection or affiliation can self-identify as atheist, agnostic or humanist, or can provide another applicable response.
Source: Statistics Canada. 2013. 2011 National Household Survey. Statistics Canada Catalogue no. 99-004-XWE. Ottawa. Released September 11, 2013.

PROFILES / Surrey, British Columbia

Immigrant Status and Period of Immigration

Area	Non-Immigrants[1]	Immigrants All	Before 1971	1971 to 1980	1981 to 1990	1991 to 2000	2001 to 2005	2006 to 2011	Non-Permanent Residents[3]
				Number Total					
Surrey	270,735	187,845	17,760	21,595	25,655	55,865	32,085	34,880	4,760
British Columbia	3,067,590	1,191,875	223,215	161,335	156,445	305,655	160,100	185,115	64,995
Canada	25,720,175	6,775,765	1,261,055	870,775	949,890	1,539,050	992,070	1,162,915	356,385
				Males					
Surrey	137,085	90,490	9,070	10,390	12,400	26,505	15,265	16,860	2,235
British Columbia	1,533,255	561,490	109,510	76,865	72,625	140,985	74,395	87,110	30,880
Canada	12,753,235	3,231,370	605,430	416,670	454,570	724,905	474,545	555,245	178,515
				Females					
Surrey	133,655	97,350	8,690	11,200	13,260	29,355	16,825	18,015	2,525
British Columbia	1,534,330	630,385	113,710	84,470	83,820	164,675	85,710	98,005	34,115
Canada	12,966,935	3,544,400	655,625	454,105	495,325	814,145	517,530	607,670	177,870
				Percent of Population Total					
Surrey	58.4	40.5	3.8	4.7	5.5	12.1	6.9	7.5	1.0
British Columbia	70.9	27.6	5.2	3.7	3.6	7.1	3.7	4.3	1.5
Canada	78.3	20.6	3.8	2.7	2.9	4.7	3.0	3.5	1.1
				Males					
Surrey	59.7	39.4	3.9	4.5	5.4	11.5	6.6	7.3	1.0
British Columbia	72.1	26.4	5.2	3.6	3.4	6.6	3.5	4.1	1.5
Canada	78.9	20.0	3.7	2.6	2.8	4.5	2.9	3.4	1.1
				Females					
Surrey	57.2	41.7	3.7	4.8	5.7	12.6	7.2	7.7	1.1
British Columbia	69.8	28.7	5.2	3.8	3.8	7.5	3.9	4.5	1.6
Canada	77.7	21.2	3.9	2.7	3.0	4.9	3.1	3.6	1.1

Note: (1) Non-immigrant refers to a person who is a Canadian citizen by birth; (2) Immigrant refers to a person who is or has ever been a landed immigrant/permanent resident. This person has been granted the right to live in Canada permanently by immigration authorities. Some immigrants have resided in Canada for a number of years, while others have arrived recently. Some immigrants are Canadian citizens, while others are not. Most immigrants are born outside Canada, but a small number are born in Canada. In the 2011 National Household Survey, 'Immigrants' includes immigrants who landed in Canada prior to May 10, 2011; (3) Non-permanent resident refers to a person from another country who has a work or study permit, or who is a refugee claimant, and any non-Canadian-born family member living in Canada with them.
Source: Statistics Canada. 2013. 2011 National Household Survey. Statistics Canada Catalogue no. 99-004-XWE. Ottawa. Released September 11, 2013.

Mother Tongue

Area	English	French	Non-official Language	English & French	English & Non-official Language	French & Non-official Language	English, French & Non-official Language
			Number Total				
Surrey	240,485	3,475	205,815	635	14,055	350	190
British Columbia	3,062,435	57,275	1,154,215	8,600	68,800	3,345	1,530
Canada	18,858,980	7,054,975	6,567,680	144,685	396,330	74,430	24,095
			Males				
Surrey	120,785	1,710	100,120	295	6,915	165	100
British Columbia	1,526,350	28,315	543,395	4,065	32,875	1,520	725
Canada	9,345,225	3,452,380	3,157,785	69,975	192,000	36,535	11,965
			Females				
Surrey	119,705	1,760	105,695	340	7,140	190	85
British Columbia	1,536,085	28,965	610,825	4,535	35,925	1,830	805
Canada	9,513,750	3,602,590	3,409,895	74,710	204,330	37,890	12,130
			Percent of Population Total				
Surrey	51.7	0.7	44.3	0.1	3.0	0.1	0.0
British Columbia	70.3	1.3	26.5	0.2	1.6	0.1	0.0
Canada	56.9	21.3	19.8	0.4	1.2	0.2	0.1
			Males				
Surrey	52.5	0.7	43.5	0.1	3.0	0.1	0.0
British Columbia	71.4	1.3	25.4	0.2	1.5	0.1	0.0
Canada	57.5	21.2	19.4	0.4	1.2	0.2	0.1
			Females				
Surrey	51.0	0.7	45.0	0.1	3.0	0.1	0.0
British Columbia	69.2	1.3	27.5	0.2	1.6	0.1	0.0
Canada	56.4	21.4	20.2	0.4	1.2	0.2	0.1

Note: Figures cover total population excluding institutional residents.
Source: Statistics Canada. 2012. Census Profile. 2011 Census. Statistics Canada Catalogue no. 98-316-XWE. Ottawa. Released October 24 2012.
http://www12.statcan.gc.ca/census-recensement/2011/dp-pd/prof/index.cfm?Lang=E

Language Spoken Most Often at Home

Area	English	French	Non-official Language	English & French	English & Non-official Language	French & Non-official Language	English, French & Non-official Language
			Number				
			Total				
Surrey	291,155	1,050	137,380	400	34,500	135	385
British Columbia	3,506,595	16,685	670,100	4,700	155,065	930	2,130
Canada	21,457,075	6,827,865	3,673,865	131,205	875,135	109,700	46,330
			Males				
Surrey	144,725	505	67,275	170	17,170	70	170
British Columbia	1,733,775	8,015	317,670	2,240	74,155	435	940
Canada	10,585,620	3,348,235	1,767,310	63,475	425,370	53,010	22,845
			Females				
Surrey	146,430	540	70,100	235	17,325	65	220
British Columbia	1,772,820	8,665	352,430	2,460	80,905	495	1,185
Canada	10,871,455	3,479,625	1,906,555	67,730	449,765	56,690	23,485
			Percent of Population				
			Total				
Surrey	62.6	0.2	29.5	0.1	7.4	0.0	0.1
British Columbia	80.5	0.4	15.4	0.1	3.6	0.0	0.0
Canada	64.8	20.6	11.1	0.4	2.6	0.3	0.1
			Males				
Surrey	62.9	0.2	29.2	0.1	7.5	0.0	0.1
British Columbia	81.1	0.4	14.9	0.1	3.5	0.0	0.0
Canada	65.1	20.6	10.9	0.4	2.6	0.3	0.1
			Females				
Surrey	62.3	0.2	29.8	0.1	7.4	0.0	0.1
British Columbia	79.9	0.4	15.9	0.1	3.6	0.0	0.1
Canada	64.5	20.6	11.3	0.4	2.7	0.3	0.1

Note: Figures cover total population excluding institutional residents.
Source: Statistics Canada. 2012. Census Profile. 2011 Census. Statistics Canada Catalogue no. 98-316-XWE. Ottawa. Released October 24 2012.
http://www12.statcan.gc.ca/census-recensement/2011/dp-pd/prof/index.cfm?Lang=E

Knowledge of Official Languages

Area	English Only	French Only	English & French	Neither English nor French
		Number		
		Total		
Surrey	413,830	225	21,305	29,650
British Columbia	3,912,950	2,045	296,645	144,555
Canada	22,564,665	4,165,015	5,795,570	595,920
		Males		
Surrey	208,255	100	9,540	12,195
British Columbia	1,943,760	950	132,940	59,590
Canada	11,222,185	1,925,340	2,876,560	241,790
		Females		
Surrey	205,575	125	11,770	17,450
British Columbia	1,969,190	1,095	163,705	84,965
Canada	11,342,485	2,239,680	2,919,005	354,135
		Percent of Population		
		Total		
Surrey	89.0	0.0	4.6	6.4
British Columbia	89.8	0.0	6.8	3.3
Canada	68.1	12.6	17.5	1.8
		Males		
Surrey	90.5	0.0	4.1	5.3
British Columbia	90.9	0.0	6.2	2.8
Canada	69.0	11.8	17.7	1.5
		Females		
Surrey	87.5	0.1	5.0	7.4
British Columbia	88.7	0.0	7.4	3.8
Canada	67.3	13.3	17.3	2.1

Note: Figures cover total population excluding institutional residents.
Source: Statistics Canada. 2012. Census Profile. 2011 Census. Statistics Canada Catalogue no. 98-316-XWE. Ottawa. Released October 24 2012.
http://www12.statcan.gc.ca/census-recensement/2011/dp-pd/prof/index.cfm?Lang=E

Terrebonne, Québec

Background

Terrebonne is located approximately 12 kilometres northeast of the island of Montréal in western Québec. The off-island city is situated along the northern shores of Rivière des Mille-Îles and Rivière des Prairies. The City of Terrebonne is considered the gateway to the southern Lanaudière region and one of the most distinguished heritage districts in Québec.

One of the province's oldest cities, Terrbonne dates back to the original seigneury granted in 1673. The area was incorporated into a city twice: in 1860 and again in 1985 with the merger of a nearby parish municipality. Terrebonne's founding districts—Terrebonne, Lachenaie and La Plaine in greater Terrebonne—were amalgamated into the City of Terrebonne in 2001.

The city is renowned for its 18th- and 19th-century seigneurial buildings and offers guided tours at the majority of its cultural sites. Vieux-Terrebonne (Old Terrebonne) is the city's historical quarter and features the Île-des-Moulins (Mill Island) historical site, a collection of 19th-century buildings that are considered Québec's second most important restoration site (after Québec City's Place Royale). The Théâtre du Vieux-Terrebonne showcases French shows and performances by provincial and international artists.

A network of pedestrian paths intersects the city, including the 41-kilometre Trans-Terrebonne trail. Terrebonne has more than 90 parks and green spaces as well as some of Québec's best golf courses. A skiing and sliding centre is popular in the winter as are the city's various ski resorts.

Popular outdoor activities include Carnaval Glisse et Glace de Terrebonne, the Fête des Voyageurs and the Christmas parade, Marché de Noël de Terrebonne.

Terrebonne has summer highs of plus 24.87 degrees Celsius, winter lows of minus 12.67 degrees Celsius, and an average rainfall just over 763 mm per year.

Rankings
- Terrebonne ranked #72 out of 190 Canadian cities in *Money Sense Magazine's* "Best Places to Live 2012" rankings. The 2012 survey listed Terrebonne #68 for "Best Place for Finding a Job," and #24 for "Best Place to Raise Kids." Ottawa ranked #1 overall as the Best Place to Live in Canada. *Money Sense Magazine, "Canada's Best Places to Live 2012," March 20, 2012*
- Terrebonne was cited as one of Canada's "Weather Winners" by Environment Canada. Weather data was collected from 100 major Canadian cities over a 30-year period. In the four major seasonal categories, Terrebonne ranked #25 in hottest summer; #38 in warmest fall/autumn; #50 in coldest winter; and #49 for sunniest spring. *Environment Canada, Canadian Cities are Weather Winners!, May 29, 2012*

PROFILES / Terrebonne, Québec

Population Growth and Density

Area	Population in 2001	Population in 2006	Population in 2011	Population Change 2001–2006	Population Change 2006–2011	Land Area (sq. km)	Population Density per sq. km
Terrebonne	80,536	94,703	106,322	17.6	12.3	154.74	687.1
Québec	7,237,479	7,546,131	7,903,001	4.3	4.7	1,356,547.02	5.8
Canada	30,007,094	31,612,897	33,476,688	5.4	5.9	8,965,121.42	3.7

Source: Statistics Canada. 2012. Census Profile. 2011 Census. Statistics Canada Catalogue no. 98-316-XWE. Ottawa. Released October 24 2012.
http://www12.statcan.gc.ca/census-recensement/2011/dp-pd/prof/index.cfm?Lang=E;
Statistics Canada 2007. 2006 Community Profiles. 2006 Census. Statistics Canada Catalogue no. 92-591-XWE. Ottawa. Released March 13 2007.
http://www12.statcan.ca/census-recensement/2006/dp-pd/prof/92-591/index.cfm?Lang=E

Gender

Area	Males	Females
Number		
Terrebonne	52,835	53,490
Québec	3,875,860	4,027,140
Canada	16,414,225	17,062,460
Percent of Population		
Terrebonne	49.7	50.3
Québec	49.0	51.0
Canada	49.0	51.0

Source: Statistics Canada. 2012. Census Profile. 2011 Census. Statistics Canada Catalogue no. 98-316-XWE. Ottawa. Released October 24 2012.
http://www12.statcan.gc.ca/census-recensement/2011/dp-pd/prof/index.cfm?Lang=E

Marital Status

Area	Married[1]	Living Common-law	Single[2]	Separated	Divorced	Widowed
Number						
Total						
Terrebonne	29,545	23,640	22,975	1,165	4,855	2,985
Québec	2,353,770	1,391,550	1,942,090	105,195	463,830	387,945
Canada	12,941,960	3,142,525	7,816,045	698,240	1,686,035	1,584,530
Males						
Terrebonne	14,765	11,780	12,365	490	1,855	680
Québec	1,177,720	697,695	1,045,540	46,465	188,265	77,430
Canada	6,470,300	1,575,495	4,206,320	299,655	680,415	310,940
Females						
Terrebonne	14,780	11,855	10,615	675	3,000	2,310
Québec	1,176,050	693,850	896,545	58,720	275,565	310,515
Canada	6,471,660	1,567,035	3,609,730	398,585	1,005,620	1,273,590
Percent of Population						
Total						
Terrebonne	34.7	27.8	27.0	1.4	5.7	3.5
Québec	35.4	20.9	29.2	1.6	7.0	5.8
Canada	46.4	11.3	28.0	2.5	6.0	5.7
Males						
Terrebonne	35.2	28.1	29.5	1.2	4.4	1.6
Québec	36.4	21.6	32.3	1.4	5.8	2.4
Canada	47.8	11.6	31.1	2.2	5.0	2.3
Females						
Terrebonne	34.2	27.4	24.6	1.6	6.9	5.3
Québec	34.5	20.3	26.3	1.7	8.1	9.1
Canada	45.2	10.9	25.2	2.8	7.0	8.9

Note: (1) and not separated, (2) never legally married
Source: Statistics Canada. 2012. Census Profile. 2011 Census. Statistics Canada Catalogue no. 98-316-XWE. Ottawa. Released October 24 2012.
http://www12.statcan.gc.ca/census-recensement/2011/dp-pd/prof/index.cfm?Lang=E

Age Characteristics: 0 to 49 Years

Area	0 to 4 Years	5 to 9 Years	10 to 14 Years	15 to 19 Years	20 to 24 Years	25 to 29 Years	30 to 34 Years	35 to 39 Years	40 to 44 Years	45 to 49 Years
					Number					
					Total					
Terrebonne	7,515	6,670	6,975	8,270	6,495	5,860	7,840	8,140	8,110	9,420
Québec	440,840	399,575	418,205	491,980	489,185	490,665	531,445	498,225	520,805	623,575
Canada	1,877,095	1,809,895	1,920,355	2,178,135	2,187,450	2,169,590	2,162,905	2,173,930	2,324,875	2,675,130
					Males					
Terrebonne	3,860	3,405	3,630	4,265	3,290	2,895	3,750	3,965	4,020	4,640
Québec	225,525	203,675	213,540	249,960	246,850	245,695	264,980	249,610	261,120	311,320
Canada	961,150	925,965	983,995	1,115,845	1,108,775	1,077,275	1,058,810	1,064,200	1,141,720	1,318,715
					Females					
Terrebonne	3,660	3,260	3,345	4,005	3,205	2,960	4,095	4,175	4,090	4,775
Québec	215,320	195,900	204,665	242,020	242,340	244,970	266,460	248,615	259,690	312,250
Canada	915,945	883,935	936,360	1,062,295	1,078,670	1,092,315	1,104,095	1,109,735	1,183,155	1,356,420
					Percent of Population					
					Total					
Terrebonne	7.1	6.3	6.6	7.8	6.1	5.5	7.4	7.7	7.6	8.9
Québec	5.6	5.1	5.3	6.2	6.2	6.2	6.7	6.3	6.6	7.9
Canada	5.6	5.4	5.7	6.5	6.5	6.5	6.5	6.5	6.9	8.0
					Males					
Terrebonne	7.3	6.4	6.9	8.1	6.2	5.5	7.1	7.5	7.6	8.8
Québec	5.8	5.3	5.5	6.4	6.4	6.3	6.8	6.4	6.7	8.0
Canada	5.9	5.6	6.0	6.8	6.8	6.6	6.5	6.5	7.0	8.0
					Females					
Terrebonne	6.8	6.1	6.3	7.5	6.0	5.5	7.7	7.8	7.6	8.9
Québec	5.3	4.9	5.1	6.0	6.0	6.1	6.6	6.2	6.4	7.8
Canada	5.4	5.2	5.5	6.2	6.3	6.4	6.5	6.5	6.9	7.9

Source: Statistics Canada. 2012. Census Profile. 2011 Census. Statistics Canada Catalogue no. 98-316-XWE. Ottawa. Released October 24 2012.
http://www12.statcan.gc.ca/census-recensement/2011/dp-pd/prof/index.cfm?Lang=E

Age Characteristics: 50 Years and Over, and Median Age

Area	50 to 54 Years	55 to 59 Years	60 to 64 Years	65 to 69 Years	70 to 74 Years	75 to 79 Years	80 to 84 Years	85 Years and Over	Median Age
					Number				
					Total				
Terrebonne	8,880	6,785	5,470	4,190	2,500	1,660	920	640	37.1
Québec	648,695	579,280	512,830	403,210	291,755	232,355	176,420	153,945	41.9
Canada	2,658,965	2,340,635	2,052,670	1,521,715	1,153,065	922,700	702,070	645,515	40.6
					Males				
Terrebonne	4,405	3,395	2,715	2,065	1,160	790	400	190	36.6
Québec	320,695	285,295	250,675	194,305	135,830	101,675	69,170	45,945	40.7
Canada	1,309,030	1,147,300	1,002,690	738,010	543,435	417,945	291,085	208,300	39.6
					Females				
Terrebonne	4,470	3,395	2,745	2,125	1,340	870	525	450	37.5
Québec	327,995	293,990	262,155	208,905	155,925	130,680	107,250	108,005	43.0
Canada	1,349,940	1,193,335	1,049,985	783,705	609,630	504,755	410,985	437,215	41.5
					Percent of Population				
					Total				
Terrebonne	8.4	6.4	5.1	3.9	2.4	1.6	0.9	0.6	—
Québec	8.2	7.3	6.5	5.1	3.7	2.9	2.2	1.9	—
Canada	7.9	7.0	6.1	4.5	3.4	2.8	2.1	1.9	—
					Males				
Terrebonne	8.3	6.4	5.1	3.9	2.2	1.5	0.8	0.4	—
Québec	8.3	7.4	6.5	5.0	3.5	2.6	1.8	1.2	—
Canada	8.0	7.0	6.1	4.5	3.3	2.5	1.8	1.3	—
					Females				
Terrebonne	8.4	6.3	5.1	4.0	2.5	1.6	1.0	0.8	—
Québec	8.1	7.3	6.5	5.2	3.9	3.2	2.7	2.7	—
Canada	7.9	7.0	6.2	4.6	3.6	3.0	2.4	2.6	—

Source: Statistics Canada. 2012. Census Profile. 2011 Census. Statistics Canada Catalogue no. 98-316-XWE. Ottawa. Released October 24 2012.
http://www12.statcan.gc.ca/census-recensement/2011/dp-pd/prof/index.cfm?Lang=E

PROFILES / Terrebonne, Québec

Private Households by Household Size

Area	1 Person	2 Persons	3 Persons	4 Persons	5 Persons	6 or More Persons	Average Number of Persons in Private Households
			Households				
Terrebonne	7,560	13,220	7,615	7,595	2,415	985	2.7
Québec	1,094,410	1,181,240	496,140	421,080	142,555	59,920	2.3
Canada	3,673,310	4,544,820	2,081,900	1,903,300	724,405	392,885	2.5
			Percent of Households				
Terrebonne	19.2	33.6	19.3	19.3	6.1	2.5	–
Québec	32.2	34.8	14.6	12.4	4.2	1.8	–
Canada	27.6	34.1	15.6	14.3	5.4	2.9	–

Source: Statistics Canada. 2012. Census Profile. 2011 Census. Statistics Canada Catalogue no. 98-316-XWE. Ottawa. Released October 24 2012.
http://www12.statcan.gc.ca/census-recensement/2011/dp-pd/prof/index.cfm?Lang=E

Dwelling Type

Area	Single-detached House	Semi-detached House	Row House	Apartment: Building with Five or More Storeys	Apartment: Building with Fewer Than Five Storeys	Duplex Apartment	Movable Dwelling	Other Single-attached House
				Number				
Terrebonne	26,645	2,595	295	55	7,280	2,090	380	55
Québec	1,560,405	171,435	86,040	171,115	1,103,845	263,860	22,995	15,645
Canada	7,329,150	646,245	791,600	1,234,770	2,397,550	704,485	183,510	33,310
				Percent of Dwellings				
Terrebonne	67.6	6.6	0.7	0.1	18.5	5.3	1.0	0.1
Québec	46.0	5.0	2.5	5.0	32.5	7.8	0.7	0.5
Canada	55.0	4.9	5.9	9.3	18.0	5.3	1.4	0.3

Source: Statistics Canada. 2012. Census Profile. 2011 Census. Statistics Canada Catalogue no. 98-316-XWE. Ottawa. Released October 24 2012.
http://www12.statcan.gc.ca/census-recensement/2011/dp-pd/prof/index.cfm?Lang=E

Shelter Costs

		Owned Dwellings				Rented Dwellings		
Area	Number	Median Value[1] ($)	Average Value[1] ($)	Median Monthly Costs[2] ($)	Average Monthly Costs[2] ($)	Number	Median Monthly Costs[3] ($)	Average Monthly Costs[3] ($)
Terrebonne	31,660	239,623	249,317	1,109	1,105	7,705	726	735
Québec	2,056,665	214,537	249,427	841	936	1,308,465	643	685
Canada	9,013,410	280,552	345,182	978	1,141	4,060,385	784	848

Note: All figures cover non-farm, non-reserve private dwellings; (1) Refers to the dollar amount expected by the owner if the dwelling were to be sold; (2) Includes all shelter expenses paid by households that own their dwellings, such as the mortgage payment and the costs of electricity, heat, water and other municipal services, property taxes and condominium fees; (3) Includes all shelter expenses paid by households that rent their dwellings, such as the monthly rent and the costs of electricity, heat and municipal services.
Source: Statistics Canada. 2013. 2011 National Household Survey. Statistics Canada Catalogue no. 99-004-XWE. Ottawa. Released September 11, 2013.

Occupied Private Dwellings by Period of Construction

Area	1960 or Before	1961 to 1980	1981 to 1990	1991 to 2000	2001 to 2005	2006 to 2011
			Number			
Terrebonne	2,070	9,705	9,865	6,745	6,110	4,905
Québec	946,900	1,115,455	533,790	353,355	206,035	239,685
Canada	3,273,105	4,152,715	2,112,110	1,707,880	1,031,020	1,042,430
			Percent of Dwellings			
Terrebonne	5.3	24.6	25.0	17.1	15.5	12.5
Québec	27.9	32.9	15.7	10.4	6.1	7.1
Canada	24.6	31.2	15.9	12.8	7.7	7.8

Note: Figures cover non-farm, non-reserve private dwellings and includes data up to May 10, 2011.
Source: Statistics Canada. 2013. 2011 National Household Survey. Statistics Canada Catalogue no. 99-004-XWE. Ottawa. Released September 11, 2013.

Educational Attainment

Area	No Certificate, Diploma or Degree	High School Diploma or Equivalent[1]	Apprenticeship or Trades Certificate or Diploma[2]	College, CÉGEP or Other Non-University Certificate or Diploma	University Certificate or Diploma Below the Bachelor Level[3]	Bachelor's Degree	University Certificate, Diploma or Degree Above Bachelor Level[4]
			Number				
			Total				
Terrebonne	18,850	20,320	17,605	14,425	3,735	7,155	2,360
Québec	1,436,025	1,404,755	1,049,470	1,075,855	305,330	766,100	437,050
Canada	5,485,400	6,968,935	2,950,685	4,970,020	1,200,130	3,634,425	2,049,930
			Males				
Terrebonne	9,710	9,290	10,575	6,445	1,620	2,800	1,235
Québec	714,090	650,660	635,435	472,360	126,565	343,535	227,990
Canada	2,742,875	3,305,415	1,928,970	2,118,430	513,235	1,643,080	1,043,350
			Females				
Terrebonne	9,140	11,025	7,030	7,980	2,115	4,355	1,130
Québec	721,930	754,095	414,035	603,495	178,765	422,565	209,065
Canada	2,742,520	3,663,515	1,021,715	2,851,595	686,890	1,991,345	1,006,585
			Percent of Population				
			Total				
Terrebonne	22.3	24.1	20.8	17.1	4.4	8.5	2.8
Québec	22.2	21.7	16.2	16.6	4.7	11.8	6.8
Canada	20.1	25.6	10.8	18.2	4.4	13.3	7.5
			Males				
Terrebonne	23.3	22.3	25.4	15.5	3.9	6.7	3.0
Québec	22.5	20.5	20.0	14.9	4.0	10.8	7.2
Canada	20.6	24.9	14.5	15.9	3.9	12.4	7.8
			Females				
Terrebonne	21.4	25.8	16.4	18.7	4.9	10.2	2.6
Québec	21.9	22.8	12.5	18.3	5.4	12.8	6.3
Canada	19.6	26.2	7.3	20.4	4.9	14.3	7.2

Note: Figures cover total population aged 15 years and over by highest certificate, diploma or degree; (1) Includes persons who have graduated from a secondary school or equivalent. It excludes persons with a postsecondary certificate, diploma or degree; (2) Includes Registered Apprenticeship certificates (including Certificate of Qualification, Journeyperson's designation) and other trades certificates or diplomas such as pre-employment or vocational certificates and diplomas from brief trade programs completed at community colleges, institutes of technology, vocational centres, and similar institutions; (3) Comparisons with other data sources suggest that the category 'University certificate or diploma below the bachelor's level' was over-reported in the NHS. This category likely includes some responses that are actually college certificates or diplomas, bachelor's degrees or other types of education (e.g., university transfer programs, bachelor's programs completed in other countries, incomplete bachelor's programs, non-university professional designations). We recommend users interpret the results for the 'University certificate or diploma below the bachelor's level' category with caution; (4) 'University certificate or diploma above bachelor level' includes the categories: 'Degree in medicine, dentistry, veterinary medicine or optometry,' 'Master's degree' and 'Earned doctorate.'
Source: Statistics Canada. 2013. 2011 National Household Survey. Statistics Canada Catalogue no. 99-004-XWE. Ottawa. Released September 11, 2013.

Household Income Distribution

Area	Less than $10,000	$10,000 to $19,999	$20,000 to $29,999	$30,000 to $39,999	$40,000 to $49,999	$50,000 to $59,999	$60,000 to $79,999	$80,000 to $99,999	$100,000 to $124,999	$125,000 to $149,999	$150,000 and Over
					Households						
Terrebonne	1,190	2,320	2,495	3,545	3,785	3,280	6,690	5,580	4,820	2,640	3,050
Québec	179,790	377,210	353,470	382,000	343,730	302,595	483,085	344,435	267,995	148,950	211,965
Canada	626,705	1,141,945	1,193,925	1,271,675	1,206,800	1,102,120	1,865,280	1,458,240	1,260,770	802,555	1,389,240
					Percent of Households						
Terrebonne	3.0	5.9	6.3	9.0	9.6	8.3	17.0	14.2	12.2	6.7	7.7
Québec	5.3	11.1	10.4	11.3	10.1	8.9	14.2	10.1	7.9	4.4	6.2
Canada	4.7	8.6	9.0	9.5	9.1	8.3	14.0	10.9	9.5	6.0	10.4

Note: Household income is the sum of the total incomes of all members of that household. Total income refers to monetary receipts from certain sources, before income taxes and deductions, during calendar year 2010.
Source: Statistics Canada. 2013. 2011 National Household Survey. Statistics Canada Catalogue no. 99-004-XWE. Ottawa. Released September 11, 2013.

Median and Average Household and Economic Family Income

Area	Median Household Income ($)	Average Household Income ($)	Median After-tax Household Income ($)	Average After-tax Household Income ($)	Median Economic Family Income ($)	Average Economic Family Income ($)	Median After-tax Economic Family Income ($)	Average After-tax Economic Family Income ($)
Terrebonne	68,841	77,896	59,042	64,749	78,770	86,911	67,224	72,249
Québec	51,842	66,205	45,968	55,121	68,344	82,045	59,560	68,091
Canada	61,072	79,102	54,089	66,149	76,511	94,125	67,044	78,517

Note: Figures cover household and economic familiy income in 2010. A household is defined as a person or a group of persons (other than foreign residents) who occupy the same private dwelling and do not have a usual place of residence elsewhere in Canada. Every person is a member of one and only one household. An economic family is defined as a group of two or more persons who live in the same dwelling and are related to each other by blood, marriage, common-law, adoption or a foster relationship. A couple may be of opposite or same sex.
Source: Statistics Canada. 2013. 2011 National Household Survey. Statistics Canada Catalogue no. 99-004-XWE. Ottawa. Released September 11, 2013.

PROFILES / Terrebonne, Québec

Individual Income Distribution

Area	Less than $10,000	$10,000 to $19,999	$20,000 to $29,999	$30,000 to $39,999	$40,000 to $49,999	$50,000 to $59,999	$60,000 to $79,999	$80,000 to $99,999	$100,000 to $124,999	$125,000 and Over
					Number					
					Total					
Terrebonne	11,460	13,875	11,290	11,775	9,335	7,250	8,640	3,390	1,495	1,260
Québec	1,005,600	1,309,515	941,630	866,290	653,400	449,185	515,815	211,070	109,975	120,915
Canada	4,492,040	4,835,710	3,670,020	3,180,360	2,603,520	1,921,650	2,437,440	1,302,045	693,580	782,135
					Males					
Terrebonne	4,645	4,970	4,805	5,480	4,830	4,255	5,960	2,465	1,170	1,020
Québec	441,455	516,150	427,295	432,625	345,950	256,700	313,880	143,785	80,000	91,475
Canada	1,936,365	1,864,880	1,588,260	1,522,190	1,333,510	1,079,780	1,473,145	823,720	492,905	599,905
					Females					
Terrebonne	6,815	8,910	6,485	6,295	4,505	3,000	2,675	925	320	240
Québec	564,150	793,365	514,335	433,670	307,455	192,485	201,935	67,275	29,980	29,440
Canada	2,555,675	2,970,825	2,081,760	1,658,170	1,270,010	841,870	964,300	478,330	200,680	182,230
					Percent of Population					
					Total					
Terrebonne	14.4	17.4	14.2	14.8	11.7	9.1	10.8	4.2	1.9	1.6
Québec	16.3	21.2	15.2	14.0	10.6	7.3	8.3	3.4	1.8	2.0
Canada	17.3	18.7	14.2	12.3	10.0	7.4	9.4	5.0	2.7	3.0
					Males					
Terrebonne	11.7	12.6	12.1	13.8	12.2	10.7	15.1	6.2	3.0	2.6
Québec	14.5	16.9	14.0	14.2	11.3	8.4	10.3	4.7	2.6	3.0
Canada	15.2	14.7	12.5	12.0	10.5	8.5	11.6	6.5	3.9	4.7
					Females					
Terrebonne	17.0	22.2	16.1	15.7	11.2	7.5	6.7	2.3	0.8	0.6
Québec	18.0	25.3	16.4	13.8	9.8	6.1	6.4	2.1	1.0	0.9
Canada	19.4	22.5	15.8	12.6	9.6	6.4	7.3	3.6	1.5	1.4

Note: Figures cover individuals aged 15 years and over with income. Income refers to monetary receipts from certain sources, before income taxes and deductions, during calendar year 2010.
Source: Statistics Canada. 2013. 2011 National Household Survey. Statistics Canada Catalogue no. 99-004-XWE. Ottawa. Released September 11, 2013.

Labour Force Status

Area	In the Labour Force - All	Employed	Unemployed	Not in the Labour Force
		Number		
		Total		
Terrebonne	61,610	58,415	3,200	22,835
Québec	4,183,445	3,880,425	303,020	2,291,145
Canada	17,990,080	16,595,035	1,395,045	9,269,445
		Males		
Terrebonne	31,840	30,175	1,665	9,840
Québec	2,188,555	2,014,810	173,745	982,080
Canada	9,388,570	8,634,310	754,255	3,906,785
		Females		
Terrebonne	29,775	28,240	1,540	12,995
Québec	1,994,885	1,865,610	129,275	1,309,065
Canada	8,601,515	7,960,725	640,790	5,362,660
		Percent of Labour Force		
		Total		
Terrebonne	73.0	69.2	5.2	27.0
Québec	64.6	59.9	7.2	35.4
Canada	66.0	60.9	7.8	34.0
		Males		
Terrebonne	76.4	72.4	5.2	23.6
Québec	69.0	63.5	7.9	31.0
Canada	70.6	64.9	8.0	29.4
		Females		
Terrebonne	69.6	66.0	5.2	30.4
Québec	60.4	56.5	6.5	39.6
Canada	61.6	57.0	7.4	38.4

Note: Figures are based on total population 15 years and over
Source: Statistics Canada. 2013. 2011 National Household Survey. Statistics Canada Catalogue no. 99-004-XWE. Ottawa. Released September 11, 2013.

Labour Force by Industry (NAICS Codes 11–52)

Area	Agriculture, forestry, fishing & hunting	Mining, quarrying, & oil & gas extraction	Utilities	Construction	Manufacturing	Wholesale Trade	Retail Trade	Transportation & warehousing	Information & cultural industries	Finance & insurance
					Number Total					
Terrebonne	195	45	550	5,730	7,745	3,220	8,515	3,100	1,460	2,310
Québec	84,470	20,770	33,815	241,780	476,390	169,825	501,380	181,295	98,340	159,230
Canada	437,650	261,050	149,940	1,215,380	1,619,295	733,445	2,031,665	827,780	420,830	767,960
					Males					
Terrebonne	130	40	375	5,010	5,145	2,235	3,945	2,305	820	745
Québec	61,540	18,035	24,560	213,605	343,345	113,545	234,725	137,745	56,455	56,930
Canada	307,370	211,690	110,765	1,068,710	1,167,680	494,545	933,850	617,305	235,875	296,995
					Females					
Terrebonne	60	0	170	715	2,600	980	4,570	800	645	1,565
Québec	22,925	2,730	9,255	28,170	133,045	56,280	266,650	43,550	41,885	102,295
Canada	130,285	49,360	39,175	146,670	451,615	238,900	1,097,820	210,475	184,955	470,960
					Percent of Labour Force Total					
Terrebonne	0.3	0.1	0.9	9.5	12.8	5.3	14.1	5.1	2.4	3.8
Québec	2.1	0.5	0.8	5.9	11.7	4.2	12.3	4.4	2.4	3.9
Canada	2.5	1.5	0.9	6.9	9.2	4.2	11.6	4.7	2.4	4.4
					Males					
Terrebonne	0.4	0.1	1.2	16.0	16.4	7.1	12.6	7.4	2.6	2.4
Québec	2.9	0.8	1.1	10.0	16.1	5.3	11.0	6.4	2.6	2.7
Canada	3.3	2.3	1.2	11.6	12.7	5.4	10.2	6.7	2.6	3.2
					Females					
Terrebonne	0.2	0.0	0.6	2.4	8.9	3.4	15.6	2.7	2.2	5.4
Québec	1.2	0.1	0.5	1.4	6.8	2.9	13.7	2.2	2.2	5.3
Canada	1.6	0.6	0.5	1.7	5.4	2.8	13.1	2.5	2.2	5.6

Note: Figures are based on total experienced labour force 15 years and over. Experienced labour force refers to persons who, during the week of Sunday, May 1 to Saturday, May 7, 2011, were employed and the unemployed who had last worked for pay or in self-employment in either 2010 or 2011.
Source: Statistics Canada. 2013. 2011 National Household Survey. Statistics Canada Catalogue no. 99-004-XWE. Ottawa. Released September 11, 2013.

Labour Force by Industry (NAICS Codes 53–91)

Area	Real estate & rental & leasing	Profess., scientific & tech. services	Mgmt of companies & enterprises	Admin. & support, waste mgmt & remed. services	Educational services	Health care & social assistance	Arts, entertain. & recreation	Accomm. & food services	Other services (except public admin.)	Public admin.
					Number Total					
Terrebonne	1,030	3,165	60	2,290	3,800	7,360	960	3,010	2,570	3,460
Québec	61,365	282,115	3,965	156,130	301,425	496,125	78,795	253,145	189,290	295,480
Canada	321,895	1,240,850	17,460	728,330	1,301,435	1,949,650	363,405	1,130,750	807,800	1,261,050
					Males					
Terrebonne	555	1,655	30	1,310	1,080	1,105	565	1,155	1,265	1,885
Québec	35,940	158,920	2,250	92,530	99,565	97,255	41,535	112,650	88,710	147,645
Canada	179,090	688,625	9,380	411,250	424,915	349,430	188,270	469,990	372,940	652,510
					Females					
Terrebonne	480	1,510	30	975	2,715	6,260	395	1,855	1,305	1,580
Québec	25,425	123,205	1,715	63,605	201,860	398,870	37,260	140,495	100,585	147,835
Canada	142,805	552,225	8,075	317,085	876,515	1,600,220	175,135	660,760	434,865	608,535
					Percent of Labour Force Total					
Terrebonne	1.7	5.2	0.1	3.8	6.3	12.1	1.6	5.0	4.2	5.7
Québec	1.5	6.9	0.1	3.8	7.4	12.1	1.9	6.2	4.6	7.2
Canada	1.8	7.1	0.1	4.1	7.4	11.1	2.1	6.4	4.6	7.2
					Males					
Terrebonne	1.8	5.3	0.1	4.2	3.4	3.5	1.8	3.7	4.0	6.0
Québec	1.7	7.4	0.1	4.3	4.7	4.5	1.9	5.3	4.2	6.9
Canada	1.9	7.5	0.1	4.5	4.6	3.8	2.0	5.1	4.1	7.1
					Females					
Terrebonne	1.6	5.2	0.1	3.3	9.3	21.4	1.4	6.3	4.5	5.4
Québec	1.3	6.3	0.1	3.3	10.4	20.5	1.9	7.2	5.2	7.6
Canada	1.7	6.6	0.1	3.8	10.4	19.1	2.1	7.9	5.2	7.2

Note: Figures are based on total experienced labour force 15 years and over. Experienced labour force refers to persons who, during the week of Sunday, May 1 to Saturday, May 7, 2011, were employed and the unemployed who had last worked for pay or in self-employment in either 2010 or 2011.
Source: Statistics Canada. 2013. 2011 National Household Survey. Statistics Canada Catalogue no. 99-004-XWE. Ottawa. Released September 11, 2013.

PROFILES / Terrebonne, Québec

Occupation

Area	Mgmt	Business, Finance & Admin.	Natural/ Applied Sciences & Related	Health	Education, Law & Social, Community & Government Services	Art, Culture, Recreation & Sport	Sales & Service	Trades, Transport & Equip. Operators & Related	Natural Resources, Agri. & Related Production	Mfg & Utilities
					Number					
					Total					
Terrebonne	6,365	10,450	3,215	3,845	6,590	1,220	13,970	11,095	485	3,345
Québec	411,425	687,715	287,015	268,610	479,505	123,665	969,740	573,075	65,625	218,740
Canada	1,963,600	2,902,045	1,237,775	1,107,200	2,064,675	503,415	4,068,170	2,537,775	397,930	805,040
					Males					
Terrebonne	4,260	2,840	2,540	505	1,915	485	5,950	10,355	395	2,115
Québec	261,620	207,545	221,430	53,480	148,715	58,150	436,370	542,055	53,640	154,485
Canada	1,229,460	854,190	966,355	217,520	676,550	232,535	1,745,705	2,385,615	318,945	564,300
					Females					
Terrebonne	2,105	7,610	675	3,345	4,675	740	8,020	735	85	1,230
Québec	149,800	480,170	65,585	215,130	330,795	65,520	533,370	31,025	11,995	64,250
Canada	734,140	2,047,855	271,415	889,675	1,388,130	270,875	2,322,465	152,165	78,980	240,740
					Percent of Labour Force					
					Total					
Terrebonne	10.5	17.2	5.3	6.3	10.9	2.0	23.1	18.3	0.8	5.5
Québec	10.1	16.8	7.0	6.6	11.7	3.0	23.7	14.0	1.6	5.4
Canada	11.2	16.5	7.0	6.3	11.7	2.9	23.1	14.4	2.3	4.6
					Males					
Terrebonne	13.6	9.1	8.1	1.6	6.1	1.5	19.0	33.0	1.3	6.7
Québec	12.2	9.7	10.4	2.5	7.0	2.7	20.4	25.4	2.5	7.2
Canada	13.4	9.3	10.5	2.4	7.4	2.5	19.0	26.0	3.5	6.1
					Females					
Terrebonne	7.2	26.0	2.3	11.4	16.0	2.5	27.4	2.5	0.3	4.2
Québec	7.7	24.7	3.4	11.0	17.0	3.4	27.4	1.6	0.6	3.3
Canada	8.7	24.4	3.2	10.6	16.5	3.2	27.7	1.8	0.9	2.9

Note: Figures are based on total experienced labour force 15 years and over
Source: Statistics Canada. 2013. 2011 National Household Survey. Statistics Canada Catalogue no. 99-004-XWE. Ottawa. Released September 11, 2013.

Place of Work Status

Area	Worked at Home	Worked Outside Canada	No Fixed Workplace Address	Worked at Usual Place
		Number		
		Total		
Terrebonne	2,905	45	6,110	49,350
Québec	237,625	9,705	331,525	3,301,560
Canada	1,142,640	66,460	1,868,245	13,517,690
		Males		
Terrebonne	1,360	30	4,720	24,065
Québec	122,060	7,055	249,535	1,636,165
Canada	582,150	47,355	1,400,485	6,604,325
		Females		
Terrebonne	1,550	0	1,395	25,285
Québec	115,565	2,650	81,995	1,665,395
Canada	560,490	19,100	467,760	6,913,370
		Percent of Labour Force		
		Total		
Terrebonne	5.0	0.1	10.5	84.5
Québec	6.1	0.3	8.5	85.1
Canada	6.9	0.4	11.3	81.5
		Males		
Terrebonne	4.5	0.1	15.6	79.8
Québec	6.1	0.4	12.4	81.2
Canada	6.7	0.5	16.2	76.5
		Females		
Terrebonne	5.5	0.0	4.9	89.6
Québec	6.2	0.1	4.4	89.3
Canada	7.0	0.2	5.9	86.8

Note: Figures are based on total employed labour force 15 years and over.
Source: Statistics Canada. 2013. 2011 National Household Survey. Statistics Canada Catalogue no. 99-004-XWE. Ottawa. Released September 11, 2013.

Mode of Transportation to Work

Area	Car; Truck; Van; as Driver	Car; Truck; Van; as Passenger	Public Transit	Walked	Bicycled	All Other Modes
			Number			
			Total			
Terrebonne	48,955	1,755	2,960	1,110	280	405
Québec	2,713,295	136,490	484,600	215,210	48,870	34,620
Canada	11,393,140	867,050	1,851,525	880,815	201,780	191,625
			Males			
Terrebonne	26,050	675	1,150	450	225	230
Québec	1,484,305	50,905	203,035	95,100	33,065	19,285
Canada	6,238,835	349,530	788,290	387,580	135,840	104,725
			Females			
Terrebonne	22,905	1,080	1,810	655	55	175
Québec	1,228,995	85,585	281,565	120,110	15,800	15,335
Canada	5,154,305	517,520	1,063,235	493,230	65,940	86,900
			Percent of Labour Force			
			Total			
Terrebonne	88.3	3.2	5.3	2.0	0.5	0.7
Québec	74.7	3.8	13.3	5.9	1.3	1.0
Canada	74.0	5.6	12.0	5.7	1.3	1.2
			Males			
Terrebonne	90.5	2.3	4.0	1.6	0.8	0.8
Québec	78.7	2.7	10.8	5.0	1.8	1.0
Canada	77.9	4.4	9.8	4.8	1.7	1.3
			Females			
Terrebonne	85.9	4.0	6.8	2.5	0.2	0.7
Québec	70.3	4.9	16.1	6.9	0.9	0.9
Canada	69.8	7.0	14.4	6.7	0.9	1.2

Note: Figures are based on total employed labour force 15 years and over.
Source: Statistics Canada. 2013. 2011 National Household Survey. Statistics Canada Catalogue no. 99-004-XWE. Ottawa. Released September 11, 2013.

Visible Minority Population Characteristics

Area	Total Minority	South Asian[1]	Chinese	Black	Filipino	Latin American	Arab	SE Asian[2]	West Asian[3]	Korean	Japanese	Multiple[4]
					Number							
					Total							
Terrebonne	7,990	105	205	4,710	30	1,340	1,130	230	65	25	0	80
Québec	850,235	83,320	82,845	243,625	31,495	116,380	166,260	65,855	23,445	6,665	4,025	17,420
Canada	6,264,750	1,567,400	1,324,750	945,665	619,310	381,280	380,620	312,075	206,840	161,130	87,270	171,935
					Males							
Terrebonne	3,665	45	70	2,160	0	605	540	100	60	0	0	30
Québec	418,545	43,410	37,295	116,605	12,435	56,940	89,505	32,940	12,070	3,135	1,565	8,315
Canada	3,043,010	790,755	632,325	453,005	268,885	186,355	203,485	154,035	105,620	77,165	38,270	83,335
					Females							
Terrebonne	4,330	60	135	2,545	20	730	585	130	0	20	0	55
Québec	431,695	39,915	45,550	127,020	19,055	59,440	76,750	32,920	11,380	3,530	2,465	9,105
Canada	3,221,745	776,650	692,420	492,660	350,425	194,925	177,140	158,045	101,220	83,965	48,990	88,600
					Percent of Population							
					Total							
Terrebonne	7.6	0.1	0.2	4.5	0.0	1.3	1.1	0.2	0.1	0.0	0.0	0.1
Québec	11.0	1.1	1.1	3.2	0.4	1.5	2.2	0.9	0.3	0.1	0.1	0.2
Canada	19.1	4.8	4.0	2.9	1.9	1.2	1.2	0.9	0.6	0.5	0.3	0.5
					Males							
Terrebonne	7.0	0.1	0.1	4.1	0.0	1.2	1.0	0.2	0.1	0.0	0.0	0.1
Québec	11.0	1.1	1.0	3.1	0.3	1.5	2.3	0.9	0.3	0.1	0.0	0.2
Canada	18.8	4.9	3.9	2.8	1.7	1.2	1.3	1.0	0.7	0.5	0.2	0.5
					Females							
Terrebonne	8.2	0.1	0.3	4.8	0.0	1.4	1.1	0.2	0.0	0.0	0.0	0.1
Québec	11.0	1.0	1.2	3.2	0.5	1.5	2.0	0.8	0.3	0.1	0.1	0.2
Canada	19.3	4.7	4.1	3.0	2.1	1.2	1.1	0.9	0.6	0.5	0.3	0.5

Note: The Employment Equity Act defines visible minorities as 'persons, other than Aboriginal peoples, who are non-Caucasian in race or non-white in colour';
(1) Includes 'East Indian,' 'Pakistani,' 'Sri Lankan,' etc.; (2) Includes 'Vietnamese,' 'Cambodian,' 'Malaysian,' 'Laotian,' etc.; (3) Includes 'Iranian,' 'Afghan,' etc.; (4) Includes respondents who reported more than one visible minority group by checking two or more mark-in circles, e.g., 'Black' and 'South Asian.'
Source: Statistics Canada. 2013. 2011 National Household Survey. Statistics Canada Catalogue no. 99-004-XWE. Ottawa. Released September 11, 2013.

Aboriginal Population

Area	Aboriginal Identity[1]	First Nations (North American Indian) Single Identity[2]	Métis Single Identity	Inuk (Inuit) Single Identity	Multiple Aboriginal Identities[3]	Aboriginal Identities Not Included Elsewhere
			Number			
			Total			
Terrebonne	740	555	130	0	0	45
Québec	141,915	82,425	40,960	12,570	1,545	4,415
Canada	1,400,685	851,560	451,795	59,440	11,415	26,475
			Males			
Terrebonne	350	260	65	0	0	15
Québec	70,205	40,105	21,300	6,265	720	1,815
Canada	682,190	411,785	223,335	29,495	5,525	12,055
			Females			
Terrebonne	385	295	65	0	0	25
Québec	71,710	42,315	19,660	6,305	830	2,600
Canada	718,500	439,775	228,460	29,950	5,890	14,420
			Percent of Population			
			Total			
Terrebonne	0.7	0.5	0.1	0.0	0.0	0.0
Québec	1.8	1.1	0.5	0.2	0.0	0.1
Canada	4.3	2.6	1.4	0.2	0.0	0.1
			Males			
Terrebonne	0.7	0.5	0.1	0.0	0.0	0.0
Québec	1.8	1.1	0.6	0.2	0.0	0.0
Canada	4.2	2.5	1.4	0.2	0.0	0.1
			Females			
Terrebonne	0.7	0.6	0.1	0.0	0.0	0.0
Québec	1.8	1.1	0.5	0.2	0.0	0.1
Canada	4.3	2.6	1.4	0.2	0.0	0.1

Note: (1) Includes persons who reported being an Aboriginal person, that is, First Nations (North American Indian), Métis or Inuk (Inuit) and/or those who reported Registered or Treaty Indian status, that is registered under the Indian Act of Canada, and/or those who reported membership in a First Nation or Indian band. Aboriginal peoples of Canada are defined in the Constitution Act, 1982, section 35-2 as including the Indian, Inuit and Métis peoples of Canada; (2) Users should be aware that the estimates associated with this variable are more affected than most by the incomplete enumeration of certain Indian reserves and Indian settlements in the National Household Survey (NHS); (3) Includes persons who reported being any two or all three of the following: First Nations (North American Indian), Métis or Inuk (Inuit).
Source: Statistics Canada. 2013. 2011 National Household Survey. Statistics Canada Catalogue no. 99-004-XWE. Ottawa. Released September 11, 2013.

Ethnic Origin

Area	North American Aboriginal	Other North American	European	Caribbean	Latin, Central and South American	African	Asian	Oceania
			Number					
			Total					
Terrebonne	3,385	76,395	40,345	4,115	1,595	2,180	1,705	0
Québec	307,445	4,776,875	3,390,330	167,590	137,255	260,785	488,905	2,305
Canada	1,836,035	11,070,455	20,157,965	627,590	544,375	766,735	5,011,225	74,875
			Males					
Terrebonne	1,515	37,765	20,325	1,815	725	1,090	900	0
Québec	146,725	2,345,180	1,678,310	77,665	67,195	135,740	241,515	1,135
Canada	885,675	5,462,685	9,913,150	291,640	264,635	387,360	2,435,540	37,490
			Females					
Terrebonne	1,870	38,625	20,020	2,300	870	1,085	805	0
Québec	160,725	2,431,700	1,712,015	89,925	70,065	125,040	247,390	1,175
Canada	950,360	5,607,770	10,244,820	335,945	279,740	379,380	2,575,680	37,385
			Percent of Population					
			Total					
Terrebonne	3.2	72.3	38.2	3.9	1.5	2.1	1.6	0.0
Québec	4.0	61.8	43.8	2.2	1.8	3.4	6.3	0.0
Canada	5.6	33.7	61.4	1.9	1.7	2.3	15.3	0.2
			Males					
Terrebonne	2.9	71.8	38.6	3.5	1.4	2.1	1.7	0.0
Québec	3.8	61.5	44.0	2.0	1.8	3.6	6.3	0.0
Canada	5.5	33.8	61.3	1.8	1.6	2.4	15.1	0.2
			Females					
Terrebonne	3.5	72.8	37.8	4.3	1.6	2.0	1.5	0.0
Québec	4.1	62.1	43.7	2.3	1.8	3.2	6.3	0.0
Canada	5.7	33.6	61.4	2.0	1.7	2.3	15.4	0.2

Note: The sum of the ethnic groups in this table is greater than the total population estimate because a person may report more than one ethnic origin in the NHS.
Source: Statistics Canada. 2013. 2011 National Household Survey. Statistics Canada Catalogue no. 99-004-XWE. Ottawa. Released September 11, 2013.

Religion

Area	Buddhist	Christian	Hindu	Jewish	Muslim	Sikh	Traditional (Aboriginal) Spirituality	Other Religions	No Religious Affiliation
				Number Total					
Terrebonne	105	92,085	0	50	1,580	0	0	30	11,740
Québec	52,390	6,356,880	33,540	85,100	243,430	9,275	2,025	12,340	937,545
Canada	366,830	22,102,745	497,965	329,495	1,053,945	454,965	64,935	130,835	7,850,605
				Males					
Terrebonne	50	45,220	0	35	850	0	0	10	6,420
Québec	24,630	3,079,855	17,055	41,455	128,815	5,090	925	6,155	510,055
Canada	168,465	10,497,775	250,435	161,265	540,555	229,435	31,805	57,745	4,225,645
				Females					
Terrebonne	60	46,865	0	20	735	0	0	20	5,315
Québec	27,760	3,277,020	16,480	43,645	114,615	4,185	1,100	6,175	427,485
Canada	198,365	11,604,975	247,525	168,235	513,395	225,530	33,135	73,090	3,624,965
				Percent of Population Total					
Terrebonne	0.1	87.2	0.0	0.0	1.5	0.0	0.0	0.0	11.1
Québec	0.7	82.2	0.4	1.1	3.1	0.1	0.0	0.2	12.1
Canada	1.1	67.3	1.5	1.0	3.2	1.4	0.2	0.4	23.9
				Males					
Terrebonne	0.1	86.0	0.0	0.1	1.6	0.0	0.0	0.0	12.2
Québec	0.6	80.8	0.4	1.1	3.4	0.1	0.0	0.2	13.4
Canada	1.0	64.9	1.5	1.0	3.3	1.4	0.2	0.4	26.1
				Females					
Terrebonne	0.1	88.4	0.0	0.0	1.4	0.0	0.0	0.0	10.0
Québec	0.7	83.6	0.4	1.1	2.9	0.1	0.0	0.2	10.9
Canada	1.2	69.5	1.5	1.0	3.1	1.4	0.2	0.4	21.7

Note: Religion refers to the person's self-identification as having a connection or affiliation with any religious denomination, group, body, sect, cult or other religiously defined community or system of belief. Religion is not limited to formal membership in a religious organization or group. Persons without a religious connection or affiliation can self-identify as atheist, agnostic or humanist, or can provide another applicable response.
Source: Statistics Canada. 2013. 2011 National Household Survey. Statistics Canada Catalogue no. 99-004-XWE. Ottawa. Released September 11, 2013.

Religion—Christian Denominations

Area	Anglican	Baptist	Catholic	Christian Orthodox	Lutheran	Pentecostal	Presbyterian	United Church	Other Christian
				Number Total					
Terrebonne	135	665	86,825	400	0	455	10	70	3,510
Québec	73,550	36,615	5,775,740	129,780	7,200	41,070	11,440	32,930	248,560
Canada	1,631,845	635,840	12,810,705	550,690	478,185	478,705	472,385	2,007,610	3,036,780
				Males					
Terrebonne	40	275	42,790	200	0	210	0	30	1,650
Québec	34,815	16,585	2,802,920	63,960	3,425	18,640	5,265	14,945	119,305
Canada	752,945	293,905	6,167,290	270,205	221,525	217,850	218,955	912,545	1,442,550
				Females					
Terrebonne	90	390	44,035	200	0	240	0	40	1,855
Québec	38,735	20,030	2,972,820	65,820	3,770	22,430	6,175	17,985	129,260
Canada	878,900	341,940	6,643,415	280,485	256,660	260,850	253,430	1,095,065	1,594,230
				Percent of Population Total					
Terrebonne	0.1	0.6	82.2	0.4	0.0	0.4	0.0	0.1	3.3
Québec	1.0	0.5	74.7	1.7	0.1	0.5	0.1	0.4	3.2
Canada	5.0	1.9	39.0	1.7	1.5	1.5	1.4	6.1	9.2
				Males					
Terrebonne	0.1	0.5	81.4	0.4	0.0	0.4	0.0	0.1	3.1
Québec	0.9	0.4	73.5	1.7	0.1	0.5	0.1	0.4	3.1
Canada	4.7	1.8	38.2	1.7	1.4	1.3	1.4	5.6	8.9
				Females					
Terrebonne	0.2	0.7	83.1	0.4	0.0	0.5	0.0	0.1	3.5
Québec	1.0	0.5	75.9	1.7	0.1	0.6	0.2	0.5	3.3
Canada	5.3	2.0	39.8	1.7	1.5	1.6	1.5	6.6	9.6

Note: Religion refers to the person's self-identification as having a connection or affiliation with any religious denomination, group, body, sect, cult or other religiously defined community or system of belief. Religion is not limited to formal membership in a religious organization or group. Persons without a religious connection or affiliation can self-identify as atheist, agnostic or humanist, or can provide another applicable response.
Source: Statistics Canada. 2013. 2011 National Household Survey. Statistics Canada Catalogue no. 99-004-XWE. Ottawa. Released September 11, 2013.

PROFILES / Terrebonne, Québec

Immigrant Status and Period of Immigration

Area	Non-Immigrants[1]	Immigrants All	Before 1971	1971 to 1980	1981 to 1990	1991 to 2000	2001 to 2005	2006 to 2011	Non-Permanent Residents[3]
Number									
Total									
Terrebonne	98,655	6,835	845	1,090	1,135	1,380	1,470	915	115
Québec	6,690,530	974,895	151,825	115,640	130,680	195,925	157,425	223,400	67,095
Canada	25,720,175	6,775,765	1,261,055	870,775	949,890	1,539,050	992,070	1,162,915	356,385
Males									
Terrebonne	49,165	3,370	495	520	580	625	705	445	55
Québec	3,301,435	477,240	75,255	57,410	64,080	94,110	76,780	109,605	35,370
Canada	12,753,235	3,231,370	605,430	416,670	454,570	724,905	474,545	555,245	178,515
Females									
Terrebonne	49,495	3,465	355	565	550	760	765	470	60
Québec	3,389,095	497,655	76,565	58,235	66,600	101,810	80,645	113,795	31,725
Canada	12,966,935	3,544,400	655,625	454,105	495,325	814,145	517,530	607,670	177,870
Percent of Population									
Total									
Terrebonne	93.4	6.5	0.8	1.0	1.1	1.3	1.4	0.9	0.1
Québec	86.5	12.6	2.0	1.5	1.7	2.5	2.0	2.9	0.9
Canada	78.3	20.6	3.8	2.7	2.9	4.7	3.0	3.5	1.1
Males									
Terrebonne	93.5	6.4	0.9	1.0	1.1	1.2	1.3	0.8	0.1
Québec	86.6	12.5	2.0	1.5	1.7	2.5	2.0	2.9	0.9
Canada	78.9	20.0	3.7	2.6	2.8	4.5	2.9	3.4	1.1
Females									
Terrebonne	93.4	6.5	0.7	1.1	1.0	1.4	1.4	0.9	0.1
Québec	86.5	12.7	2.0	1.5	1.7	2.6	2.1	2.9	0.8
Canada	77.7	21.2	3.9	2.7	3.0	4.9	3.1	3.6	1.1

Note: (1) Non-immigrant refers to a person who is a Canadian citizen by birth; (2) Immigrant refers to a person who is or has ever been a landed immigrant/permanent resident. This person has been granted the right to live in Canada permanently by immigration authorities. Some immigrants have resided in Canada for a number of years, while others have arrived recently. Some immigrants are Canadian citizens, while others are not. Most immigrants are born outside Canada, but a small number are born in Canada. In the 2011 National Household Survey, 'Immigrants' includes immigrants who landed in Canada prior to May 10, 2011; (3) Non-permanent resident refers to a person from another country who has a work or study permit, or who is a refugee claimant, and any non-Canadian-born family member living in Canada with them.
Source: Statistics Canada. 2013. 2011 National Household Survey. Statistics Canada Catalogue no. 99-004-XWE. Ottawa. Released September 11, 2013.

Mother Tongue

Area	English	French	Non-official Language	English & French	English & Non-official Language	French & Non-official Language	English, French & Non-official Language
Number							
Total							
Terrebonne	2,190	95,940	6,310	685	110	630	95
Québec	599,225	6,102,210	961,700	64,800	23,435	51,640	12,950
Canada	18,858,980	7,054,975	6,567,680	144,685	396,330	74,430	24,095
Males							
Terrebonne	1,130	47,590	3,205	350	60	320	50
Québec	297,875	2,994,300	472,635	32,390	11,455	25,810	6,790
Canada	9,345,225	3,452,380	3,157,785	69,975	192,000	36,535	11,965
Females							
Terrebonne	1,070	48,350	3,110	340	45	310	45
Québec	301,355	3,107,910	489,060	32,405	11,975	25,825	6,155
Canada	9,513,750	3,602,590	3,409,895	74,710	204,330	37,890	12,130
Percent of Population							
Total							
Terrebonne	2.1	90.5	6.0	0.6	0.1	0.6	0.1
Québec	7.7	78.1	12.3	0.8	0.3	0.7	0.2
Canada	56.9	21.3	19.8	0.4	1.2	0.2	0.1
Males							
Terrebonne	2.1	90.3	6.1	0.7	0.1	0.6	0.1
Québec	7.8	78.0	12.3	0.8	0.3	0.7	0.2
Canada	57.5	21.2	19.4	0.4	1.2	0.2	0.1
Females							
Terrebonne	2.0	90.8	5.8	0.6	0.1	0.6	0.1
Québec	7.6	78.2	12.3	0.8	0.3	0.6	0.2
Canada	56.4	21.4	20.2	0.4	1.2	0.2	0.1

Note: Figures cover total population excluding institutional residents.
Source: Statistics Canada. 2012. Census Profile. 2011 Census. Statistics Canada Catalogue no. 98-316-XWE. Ottawa. Released October 24 2012.
http://www12.statcan.gc.ca/census-recensement/2011/dp-pd/prof/index.cfm?Lang=E

Language Spoken Most Often at Home

Area	English	French	Non-official Language	English & French	English & Non-official Language	French & Non-official Language	English, French & Non-official Language
			Number				
			Total				
Terrebonne	2,480	98,920	2,260	760	90	1,230	230
Québec	767,415	6,249,080	554,400	71,555	43,765	100,110	29,625
Canada	21,457,075	6,827,865	3,673,865	131,205	875,135	109,700	46,330
			Males				
Terrebonne	1,245	49,205	1,065	395	50	615	120
Québec	379,915	3,071,635	268,640	35,860	21,305	48,590	15,315
Canada	10,585,620	3,348,235	1,767,310	63,475	425,370	53,010	22,845
			Females				
Terrebonne	1,230	49,715	1,190	365	45	615	110
Québec	387,500	3,177,450	285,760	35,695	22,460	51,525	14,310
Canada	10,871,455	3,479,625	1,906,555	67,730	449,765	56,690	23,485
			Percent of Population				
			Total				
Terrebonne	2.3	93.4	2.1	0.7	0.1	1.2	0.2
Québec	9.8	80.0	7.1	0.9	0.6	1.3	0.4
Canada	64.8	20.6	11.1	0.4	2.6	0.3	0.1
			Males				
Terrebonne	2.4	93.4	2.0	0.7	0.1	1.2	0.2
Québec	9.9	80.0	7.0	0.9	0.6	1.3	0.4
Canada	65.1	20.6	10.9	0.4	2.6	0.3	0.1
			Females				
Terrebonne	2.3	93.3	2.2	0.7	0.1	1.2	0.2
Québec	9.7	79.9	7.2	0.9	0.6	1.3	0.4
Canada	64.5	20.6	11.3	0.4	2.7	0.3	0.1

Note: Figures cover total population excluding institutional residents.
Source: Statistics Canada. 2012. Census Profile. 2011 Census. Statistics Canada Catalogue no. 98-316-XWE. Ottawa. Released October 24 2012.
http://www12.statcan.gc.ca/census-recensement/2011/dp-pd/prof/index.cfm?Lang=E

Knowledge of Official Languages

Area	English Only	French Only	English & French	Neither English nor French
		Number		
		Total		
Terrebonne	455	62,925	42,330	255
Québec	363,860	4,047,175	3,328,725	76,190
Canada	22,564,665	4,165,015	5,795,570	595,920
		Males		
Terrebonne	230	29,390	22,990	90
Québec	180,175	1,871,500	1,758,410	31,175
Canada	11,222,185	1,925,340	2,876,560	241,790
		Females		
Terrebonne	220	33,535	19,350	160
Québec	183,690	2,175,675	1,570,310	45,015
Canada	11,342,485	2,239,680	2,919,005	354,135
		Percent of Population		
		Total		
Terrebonne	0.4	59.4	39.9	0.2
Québec	4.7	51.8	42.6	1.0
Canada	68.1	12.6	17.5	1.8
		Males		
Terrebonne	0.4	55.8	43.6	0.2
Québec	4.7	48.7	45.8	0.8
Canada	69.0	11.8	17.7	1.5
		Females		
Terrebonne	0.4	63.0	36.3	0.3
Québec	4.6	54.7	39.5	1.1
Canada	67.3	13.3	17.3	2.1

Note: Figures cover total population excluding institutional residents.
Source: Statistics Canada. 2012. Census Profile. 2011 Census. Statistics Canada Catalogue no. 98-316-XWE. Ottawa. Released October 24 2012.
http://www12.statcan.gc.ca/census-recensement/2011/dp-pd/prof/index.cfm?Lang=E

Thunder Bay, Ontario

Background

Thunder Bay is located on the northwestern shore of Lake Superior, the largest freshwater lake in Ontario and the world. The area's history can be traced back 11,000 years. Ancient spear points, axe heads and copper fish hooks are regularly discovered throughout the region. By the time of European contact in the 17th century, the Ojibwa were well established throughout the Thunder Bay area. In 1678, a French trading post was established at the junction of Lake Superior and the Kaministiquia River but it was overtaken by the Northwest Company in 1803. By 1815, the Fort William trading post was a powerful gathering of fur traders made up of voyageurs, English aristocrats and First Nations peoples.

Today, Fort William Historical Park is one of the best preserved trading posts in the country and a National Historic Site of Canada. The Sibley Peninsula, which surrounds the bay, when seen from the city of Thunder Bay, resembles a giant sleeping person and is called "the Sleeping Giant."

Thunder Bay was once two cities, Port Arthur and Fort William, but amalgamated in 1970. The city's economy has since shifted away from its pulp-and-paper industry. New growth is coming to the region through the development of the city's two major educational institutions: Lakehead University and Confederation College. In 2005, Lakehead partnered with Sudbury's Laurentian University to open the Northern Ontario School of Medicine: the first medical school in Canada hosted by two universities.

Thunder Bay has average summer highs of plus 22.63 degrees Celsius, winter lows of minus 18.83 degrees Celsius, and an average rainfall just over 559 mm per year.

Rankings

- Of Canada's 33 CMAs (census metropolitan area with a total population of 100,000 or more), only Thunder Bay (-1.1%) and Windsor (-1.3%) experienced population declines between 2006 and 2011. *Statistics Canada, Census of Population, 1851 to 2011*
- Thunder Bay was awarded Play Works' "Youth Friendly Community Recognition Program" award in 2006. Play Works is made up of sports and recreation, fitness, civic engagement, arts and culture, and rural youth organizations. The award criteria: offering continuous access to "play" such as sport, recreation, drama, dance, music, arts, service leadership and/or volunteerism for youth between the ages of 13 and 19. *Play Works: The Partnership for Active and Engaged Youth, Youth Friendly Communities, 2006*
- The Department of Canadian Heritage named Thunder Bay a "Cultural Capital of Canada" in recognition of the city's excellence in the field of arts and culture and cultural diversity. *Department of Canadian Heritage, Cultural Capitals of Canada national award program, 2003*
- The *Toronto Star* newspaper ranked 849 national historic sites and listed Thunder Bay's Fort William Historical Park in the Top 10 most impressive. Others among the top 10 sites included Ottawa's Rideau Canal and Port-Royal in Annapolis Royal, Nova Scotia. *Toronto Star, "Top 10 Historic Sites," March 29, 2003*
- Thunder Bay was selected as one of Canada's "Weather Winners" by Environment Canada. A climatologist analysed 30 years of weather data for Canada's 100 largest cities. Thunder Bay ranked #9 in the "Sunniest Winter" category and #28 for "Most Sunny Days Year-Round" with 305 sunny days per year. *Environment Canada, Canadian Cities are Weather Winners!, May 29, 2012*

Population Growth and Density

Area	Population in 2001	Population in 2006	Population in 2011	Population Change 2001–2006	Population Change 2006–2011	Land Area (sq. km)	Population Density per sq. km
Thunder Bay	109,016	109,160	108,359	0.1	-0.7	328.24	330.1
Ontario	11,410,046	12,160,282	12,851,821	6.6	5.7	908,607.67	14.1
Canada	30,007,094	31,612,897	33,476,688	5.4	5.9	8,965,121.42	3.7

Source: Statistics Canada. 2012. Census Profile. 2011 Census. Statistics Canada Catalogue no. 98-316-XWE. Ottawa. Released October 24 2012.
http://www12.statcan.gc.ca/census-recensement/2011/dp-pd/prof/index.cfm?Lang=E;
Statistics Canada 2007. 2006 Community Profiles. 2006 Census. Statistics Canada Catalogue no. 92-591-XWE. Ottawa. Released March 13 2007.
http://www12.statcan.ca/census-recensement/2006/dp-pd/prof/92-591/index.cfm?Lang=E

Gender

Area	Males	Females
	Number	
Thunder Bay	52,475	55,885
Ontario	6,263,140	6,588,685
Canada	16,414,225	17,062,460
	Percent of Population	
Thunder Bay	48.4	51.6
Ontario	48.7	51.3
Canada	49.0	51.0

Source: Statistics Canada. 2012. Census Profile. 2011 Census. Statistics Canada Catalogue no. 98-316-XWE. Ottawa. Released October 24 2012.
http://www12.statcan.gc.ca/census-recensement/2011/dp-pd/prof/index.cfm?Lang=E

Marital Status

Area	Married[1]	Living Common-law	Single[2]	Separated	Divorced	Widowed
			Number			
			Total			
Thunder Bay	41,205	8,400	26,345	3,430	5,810	7,180
Ontario	5,367,400	791,210	2,985,020	319,805	593,730	613,880
Canada	12,941,960	3,142,525	7,816,045	698,240	1,686,035	1,584,530
			Males			
Thunder Bay	20,575	4,180	14,330	1,470	2,470	1,375
Ontario	2,681,320	397,620	1,583,760	133,790	231,160	117,980
Canada	6,470,300	1,575,495	4,206,320	299,655	680,415	310,940
			Females			
Thunder Bay	20,635	4,220	12,015	1,955	3,335	5,800
Ontario	2,686,075	393,590	1,401,260	186,015	362,570	495,905
Canada	6,471,660	1,567,035	3,609,730	398,585	1,005,620	1,273,590
			Percent of Population			
			Total			
Thunder Bay	44.6	9.1	28.5	3.7	6.3	7.8
Ontario	50.3	7.4	28.0	3.0	5.6	5.8
Canada	46.4	11.3	28.0	2.5	6.0	5.7
			Males			
Thunder Bay	46.3	9.4	32.3	3.3	5.6	3.1
Ontario	52.1	7.7	30.8	2.6	4.5	2.3
Canada	47.8	11.6	31.1	2.2	5.0	2.3
			Females			
Thunder Bay	43.0	8.8	25.0	4.1	7.0	12.1
Ontario	48.6	7.1	25.4	3.4	6.6	9.0
Canada	45.2	10.9	25.2	2.8	7.0	8.9

Note: (1) and not separated, (2) never legally married
Source: Statistics Canada. 2012. Census Profile. 2011 Census. Statistics Canada Catalogue no. 98-316-XWE. Ottawa. Released October 24 2012.
http://www12.statcan.gc.ca/census-recensement/2011/dp-pd/prof/index.cfm?Lang=E

Age Characteristics: 0 to 49 Years

Area	0 to 4 Years	5 to 9 Years	10 to 14 Years	15 to 19 Years	20 to 24 Years	25 to 29 Years	30 to 34 Years	35 to 39 Years	40 to 44 Years	45 to 49 Years
					Number					
					Total					
Thunder Bay	5,110	5,130	5,745	6,910	7,345	6,640	6,125	6,455	7,095	8,310
Ontario	704,260	712,755	763,755	863,635	852,910	815,120	800,365	844,335	924,075	1,055,880
Canada	1,877,095	1,809,895	1,920,355	2,178,135	2,187,450	2,169,590	2,162,905	2,173,930	2,324,875	2,675,130
					Males					
Thunder Bay	2,555	2,605	2,915	3,495	3,660	3,320	3,010	3,125	3,480	4,075
Ontario	360,590	365,290	391,630	443,680	432,490	400,045	383,340	405,845	447,920	517,510
Canada	961,150	925,965	983,995	1,115,845	1,108,775	1,077,275	1,058,810	1,064,200	1,141,720	1,318,715
					Females					
Thunder Bay	2,555	2,530	2,835	3,410	3,690	3,325	3,115	3,330	3,615	4,235
Ontario	343,670	347,465	372,125	419,950	420,415	415,075	417,030	438,485	476,155	538,370
Canada	915,945	883,935	936,360	1,062,295	1,078,670	1,092,315	1,104,095	1,109,735	1,183,155	1,356,420
					Percent of Population					
					Total					
Thunder Bay	4.7	4.7	5.3	6.4	6.8	6.1	5.7	6.0	6.5	7.7
Ontario	5.5	5.5	5.9	6.7	6.6	6.3	6.2	6.6	7.2	8.2
Canada	5.6	5.4	5.7	6.5	6.5	6.5	6.5	6.5	6.9	8.0
					Males					
Thunder Bay	4.9	5.0	5.6	6.7	7.0	6.3	5.7	6.0	6.6	7.8
Ontario	5.8	5.8	6.3	7.1	6.9	6.4	6.1	6.5	7.2	8.3
Canada	5.9	5.6	6.0	6.8	6.8	6.6	6.5	6.5	7.0	8.0
					Females					
Thunder Bay	4.6	4.5	5.1	6.1	6.6	5.9	5.6	6.0	6.5	7.6
Ontario	5.2	5.3	5.6	6.4	6.4	6.3	6.3	6.7	7.2	8.2
Canada	5.4	5.2	5.5	6.2	6.3	6.4	6.5	6.5	6.9	7.9

Source: Statistics Canada. 2012. Census Profile. 2011 Census. Statistics Canada Catalogue no. 98-316-XWE. Ottawa. Released October 24 2012.
http://www12.statcan.gc.ca/census-recensement/2011/dp-pd/prof/index.cfm?Lang=E

Age Characteristics: 50 Years and Over, and Median Age

Area	50 to 54 Years	55 to 59 Years	60 to 64 Years	65 to 69 Years	70 to 74 Years	75 to 79 Years	80 to 84 Years	85 Years and Over	Median Age
				Number					
				Total					
Thunder Bay	9,015	8,145	7,260	5,165	4,265	3,565	3,000	3,080	43.3
Ontario	1,006,140	864,620	765,655	563,485	440,780	356,150	271,510	246,400	40.4
Canada	2,658,965	2,340,635	2,052,670	1,521,715	1,153,065	922,700	702,070	645,515	40.6
				Males					
Thunder Bay	4,400	4,010	3,590	2,500	1,990	1,595	1,225	945	42.2
Ontario	492,560	418,755	370,370	270,875	206,350	161,345	113,620	80,925	39.4
Canada	1,309,030	1,147,300	1,002,690	738,010	543,435	417,945	291,085	208,300	39.6
				Females					
Thunder Bay	4,615	4,130	3,675	2,665	2,270	1,970	1,775	2,130	44.4
Ontario	513,580	445,865	395,275	292,610	234,435	194,805	157,890	165,475	41.3
Canada	1,349,940	1,193,335	1,049,985	783,705	609,630	504,755	410,985	437,215	41.5
				Percent of Population					
				Total					
Thunder Bay	8.3	7.5	6.7	4.8	3.9	3.3	2.8	2.8	–
Ontario	7.8	6.7	6.0	4.4	3.4	2.8	2.1	1.9	–
Canada	7.9	7.0	6.1	4.5	3.4	2.8	2.1	1.9	–
				Males					
Thunder Bay	8.4	7.6	6.8	4.8	3.8	3.0	2.3	1.8	–
Ontario	7.9	6.7	5.9	4.3	3.3	2.6	1.8	1.3	–
Canada	8.0	7.0	6.1	4.5	3.3	2.5	1.8	1.3	–
				Females					
Thunder Bay	8.3	7.4	6.6	4.8	4.1	3.5	3.2	3.8	–
Ontario	7.8	6.8	6.0	4.4	3.6	3.0	2.4	2.5	–
Canada	7.9	7.0	6.2	4.6	3.6	3.0	2.4	2.6	–

Source: Statistics Canada. 2012. Census Profile. 2011 Census. Statistics Canada Catalogue no. 98-316-XWE. Ottawa. Released October 24 2012.
http://www12.statcan.gc.ca/census-recensement/2011/dp-pd/prof/index.cfm?Lang=E

PROFILES / Thunder Bay, Ontario

Private Households by Household Size

Area	1 Person	2 Persons	3 Persons	4 Persons	5 Persons	6 or More Persons	Average Number of Persons in Private Households
			Households				
Thunder Bay	15,415	16,210	6,910	5,745	1,920	750	2.3
Ontario	1,230,975	1,584,415	803,030	783,925	310,860	174,305	2.6
Canada	3,673,310	4,544,820	2,081,900	1,903,300	724,405	392,885	2.5
			Percent of Households				
Thunder Bay	32.8	34.5	14.7	12.2	4.1	1.6	—
Ontario	25.2	32.4	16.4	16.0	6.4	3.6	—
Canada	27.6	34.1	15.6	14.3	5.4	2.9	—

Source: Statistics Canada. 2012. Census Profile. 2011 Census. Statistics Canada Catalogue no. 98-316-XWE. Ottawa. Released October 24 2012.
http://www12.statcan.gc.ca/census-recensement/2011/dp-pd/prof/index.cfm?Lang=E

Dwelling Type

Area	Single-detached House	Semi-detached House	Row House	Apartment: Building with Five or More Storeys	Apartment: Building with Fewer Than Five Storeys	Duplex Apartment	Movable Dwelling	Other Single-attached House
				Number				
Thunder Bay	31,090	2,045	1,305	2,550	7,360	2,270	200	125
Ontario	2,718,880	279,470	415,225	789,970	498,160	160,460	15,800	9,540
Canada	7,329,150	646,245	791,600	1,234,770	2,397,550	704,485	183,510	33,310
				Percent of Dwellings				
Thunder Bay	66.2	4.4	2.8	5.4	15.7	4.8	0.4	0.3
Ontario	55.6	5.7	8.5	16.2	10.2	3.3	0.3	0.2
Canada	55.0	4.9	5.9	9.3	18.0	5.3	1.4	0.3

Source: Statistics Canada. 2012. Census Profile. 2011 Census. Statistics Canada Catalogue no. 98-316-XWE. Ottawa. Released October 24 2012.
http://www12.statcan.gc.ca/census-recensement/2011/dp-pd/prof/index.cfm?Lang=E

Shelter Costs

	Owned Dwellings					Rented Dwellings		
Area	Number	Median Value[1] ($)	Average Value[1] ($)	Median Monthly Costs[2] ($)	Average Monthly Costs[2] ($)	Number	Median Monthly Costs[3] ($)	Average Monthly Costs[3] ($)
Thunder Bay	32,695	159,997	179,768	719	886	14,245	698	701
Ontario	3,446,650	300,862	367,428	1,163	1,284	1,385,535	892	926
Canada	9,013,410	280,552	345,182	978	1,141	4,060,385	784	848

Note: All figures cover non-farm, non-reserve private dwellings; (1) Refers to the dollar amount expected by the owner if the dwelling were to be sold; (2) Includes all shelter expenses paid by households that own their dwellings, such as the mortgage payment and the costs of electricity, heat, water and other municipal services, property taxes and condominium fees; (3) Includes all shelter expenses paid by households that rent their dwellings, such as the monthly rent and the costs of electricity, heat and municipal services.
Source: Statistics Canada. 2013. 2011 National Household Survey. Statistics Canada Catalogue no. 99-004-XWE. Ottawa. Released September 11, 2013.

Occupied Private Dwellings by Period of Construction

Area	1960 or Before	1961 to 1980	1981 to 1990	1991 to 2000	2001 to 2005	2006 to 2011
			Number			
Thunder Bay	20,150	15,665	5,390	3,580	1,165	1,000
Ontario	1,330,235	1,420,570	763,430	609,310	414,795	348,310
Canada	3,273,105	4,152,715	2,112,110	1,707,880	1,031,020	1,042,430
			Percent of Dwellings			
Thunder Bay	42.9	33.4	11.5	7.6	2.5	2.1
Ontario	27.2	29.1	15.6	12.5	8.5	7.1
Canada	24.6	31.2	15.9	12.8	7.7	7.8

Note: Figures cover non-farm, non-reserve private dwellings and includes data up to May 10, 2011.
Source: Statistics Canada. 2013. 2011 National Household Survey. Statistics Canada Catalogue no. 99-004-XWE. Ottawa. Released September 11, 2013.

Educational Attainment

Area	No Certificate, Diploma or Degree	High School Diploma or Equivalent[1]	Apprenticeship or Trades Certificate or Diploma[2]	College, CÉGEP or Other Non-University Certificate or Diploma	University Certificate or Diploma Below the Bachelor Level[3]	Bachelor's Degree	University Certificate, Diploma or Degree Above Bachelor Level[4]
\multicolumn{8}{c}{Number}
\multicolumn{8}{c}{Total}
Thunder Bay	19,585	22,670	9,335	20,160	2,350	9,835	5,930
Ontario	1,954,520	2,801,805	771,140	2,070,875	427,150	1,515,075	933,100
Canada	5,485,400	6,968,935	2,950,685	4,970,020	1,200,130	3,634,425	2,049,930
\multicolumn{8}{c}{Males}
Thunder Bay	9,260	11,010	6,895	8,075	1,075	4,155	2,915
Ontario	957,040	1,337,055	520,390	894,235	193,355	692,345	470,290
Canada	2,742,875	3,305,415	1,928,970	2,118,430	513,235	1,643,080	1,043,350
\multicolumn{8}{c}{Females}
Thunder Bay	10,330	11,655	2,445	12,080	1,275	5,675	3,010
Ontario	997,475	1,464,755	250,750	1,176,640	233,790	822,730	462,805
Canada	2,742,520	3,663,515	1,021,715	2,851,595	686,890	1,991,345	1,006,585
\multicolumn{8}{c}{Percent of Population}
\multicolumn{8}{c}{Total}
Thunder Bay	21.8	25.2	10.4	22.4	2.6	10.9	6.6
Ontario	18.7	26.8	7.4	19.8	4.1	14.5	8.9
Canada	20.1	25.6	10.8	18.2	4.4	13.3	7.5
\multicolumn{8}{c}{Males}
Thunder Bay	21.3	25.4	15.9	18.6	2.5	9.6	6.7
Ontario	18.9	26.4	10.3	17.7	3.8	13.7	9.3
Canada	20.6	24.9	14.5	15.9	3.9	12.4	7.8
\multicolumn{8}{c}{Females}
Thunder Bay	22.2	25.1	5.3	26.0	2.7	12.2	6.5
Ontario	18.4	27.1	4.6	21.8	4.3	15.2	8.6
Canada	19.6	26.2	7.3	20.4	4.9	14.3	7.2

Note: Figures cover total population aged 15 years and over by highest certificate, diploma or degree; (1) Includes persons who have graduated from a secondary school or equivalent. It excludes persons with a postsecondary certificate, diploma or degree; (2) Includes Registered Apprenticeship certificates (including Certificate of Qualification, Journeyperson's designation) and other trades certificates or diplomas such as pre-employment or vocational certificates and diplomas from brief trade programs completed at community colleges, institutes of technology, vocational centres, and similar institutions; (3) Comparisons with other data sources suggest that the category 'University certificate or diploma below the bachelor's level' was over-reported in the NHS. This category likely includes some responses that are actually college certificates or diplomas, bachelor's degrees or other types of education (e.g., university transfer programs, bachelor's programs completed in other countries, incomplete bachelor's programs, non-university professional designations). We recommend users interpret the results for the 'University certificate or diploma below the bachelor's level' category with caution; (4) 'University certificate or diploma above bachelor level' includes the categories: 'Degree in medicine, dentistry, veterinary medicine or optometry,' 'Master's degree' and 'Earned doctorate.'
Source: Statistics Canada. 2013. 2011 National Household Survey. Statistics Canada Catalogue no. 99-004-XWE. Ottawa. Released September 11, 2013.

Household Income Distribution

Area	Less than $10,000	$10,000 to $19,999	$20,000 to $29,999	$30,000 to $39,999	$40,000 to $49,999	$50,000 to $59,999	$60,000 to $79,999	$80,000 to $99,999	$100,000 to $124,999	$125,000 to $149,999	$150,000 and Over
\multicolumn{12}{c}{Households}
Thunder Bay	1,890	4,595	5,010	4,445	4,330	4,160	6,765	4,995	4,590	2,455	3,700
Ontario	201,780	354,530	405,725	425,410	425,720	398,705	680,850	552,660	497,970	331,460	611,840
Canada	626,705	1,141,945	1,193,925	1,271,675	1,206,800	1,102,120	1,865,280	1,458,240	1,260,770	802,555	1,389,240
\multicolumn{12}{c}{Percent of Households}
Thunder Bay	4.0	9.8	10.7	9.5	9.2	8.9	14.4	10.6	9.8	5.2	7.9
Ontario	4.1	7.3	8.3	8.7	8.7	8.2	13.9	11.3	10.2	6.8	12.5
Canada	4.7	8.6	9.0	9.5	9.1	8.3	14.0	10.9	9.5	6.0	10.4

Note: Household income is the sum of the total incomes of all members of that household. Total income refers to monetary receipts from certain sources, before income taxes and deductions, during calendar year 2010.
Source: Statistics Canada. 2013. 2011 National Household Survey. Statistics Canada Catalogue no. 99-004-XWE. Ottawa. Released September 11, 2013.

Median and Average Household and Economic Family Income

Area	Median Household Income ($)	Average Household Income ($)	Median After-tax Household Income ($)	Average After-tax Household Income ($)	Median Economic Family Income ($)	Average Economic Family Income ($)	Median After-tax Economic Family Income ($)	Average After-tax Economic Family Income ($)
Thunder Bay	57,646	71,142	51,514	60,894	76,861	88,672	67,862	75,550
Ontario	66,358	85,772	58,717	71,523	80,987	100,152	71,128	83,322
Canada	61,072	79,102	54,089	66,149	76,511	94,125	67,044	78,517

Note: Figures cover household and economic familiy income in 2010. A household is defined as a person or a group of persons (other than foreign residents) who occupy the same private dwelling and do not have a usual place of residence elsewhere in Canada. Every person is a member of one and only one household. An economic family is defined as a group of two or more persons who live in the same dwelling and are related to each other by blood, marriage, common-law, adoption or a foster relationship. A couple may be of opposite or same sex.
Source: Statistics Canada. 2013. 2011 National Household Survey. Statistics Canada Catalogue no. 99-004-XWE. Ottawa. Released September 11, 2013.

PROFILES / Thunder Bay, Ontario

Individual Income Distribution

Area	Less than $10,000	$10,000 to $19,999	$20,000 to $29,999	$30,000 to $39,999	$40,000 to $49,999	$50,000 to $59,999	$60,000 to $79,999	$80,000 to $99,999	$100,000 to $124,999	$125,000 and Over
Number										
Total										
Thunder Bay	12,605	16,010	13,075	11,190	9,560	7,065	8,335	4,735	1,920	1,600
Ontario	1,780,355	1,748,060	1,361,710	1,136,730	980,790	746,360	964,280	574,710	293,865	330,285
Canada	4,492,040	4,835,710	3,670,020	3,180,360	2,603,520	1,921,650	2,437,440	1,302,045	693,580	782,135
Males										
Thunder Bay	5,745	5,730	5,255	5,145	4,985	4,165	5,220	2,785	1,405	1,255
Ontario	781,095	669,815	580,990	535,255	491,125	407,005	569,205	341,160	201,125	244,500
Canada	1,936,365	1,864,880	1,588,260	1,522,190	1,333,510	1,079,780	1,473,145	823,720	492,905	599,905
Females										
Thunder Bay	6,860	10,280	7,815	6,040	4,570	2,900	3,115	1,955	510	345
Ontario	999,265	1,078,245	780,720	601,475	489,665	339,360	395,075	233,550	92,740	85,790
Canada	2,555,675	2,970,825	2,081,760	1,658,170	1,270,010	841,870	964,300	478,330	200,680	182,230
Percent of Population										
Total										
Thunder Bay	14.6	18.6	15.2	13.0	11.1	8.2	9.7	5.5	2.2	1.9
Ontario	18.0	17.6	13.7	11.5	9.9	7.5	9.7	5.8	3.0	3.3
Canada	17.3	18.7	14.2	12.3	10.0	7.4	9.4	5.0	2.7	3.0
Males										
Thunder Bay	13.8	13.7	12.6	12.3	12.0	10.0	12.5	6.7	3.4	3.0
Ontario	16.2	13.9	12.1	11.1	10.2	8.4	11.8	7.1	4.2	5.1
Canada	15.2	14.7	12.5	12.0	10.5	8.5	11.6	6.5	3.9	4.7
Females										
Thunder Bay	15.5	23.2	17.6	13.6	10.3	6.5	7.0	4.4	1.1	0.8
Ontario	19.6	21.2	15.3	11.8	9.6	6.7	7.8	4.6	1.8	1.7
Canada	19.4	22.5	15.8	12.6	9.6	6.4	7.3	3.6	1.5	1.4

Note: Figures cover individuals aged 15 years and over with income. Income refers to monetary receipts from certain sources, before income taxes and deductions, during calendar year 2010.
Source: Statistics Canada. 2013. 2011 National Household Survey. Statistics Canada Catalogue no. 99-004-XWE. Ottawa. Released September 11, 2013.

Labour Force Status

Area	In the Labour Force — All	In the Labour Force — Employed	In the Labour Force — Unemployed	Not in the Labour Force
Number				
Total				
Thunder Bay	55,115	50,685	4,430	34,755
Ontario	6,864,990	6,297,005	567,985	3,608,685
Canada	17,990,080	16,595,035	1,395,045	9,269,445
Males				
Thunder Bay	27,900	25,405	2,490	15,485
Ontario	3,542,030	3,249,165	292,865	1,522,690
Canada	9,388,570	8,634,310	754,255	3,906,785
Females				
Thunder Bay	27,215	25,280	1,935	19,265
Ontario	3,322,955	3,047,840	275,120	2,085,990
Canada	8,601,515	7,960,725	640,790	5,362,660
Percent of Labour Force				
Total				
Thunder Bay	61.3	56.4	8.0	38.7
Ontario	65.5	60.1	8.3	34.5
Canada	66.0	60.9	7.8	34.0
Males				
Thunder Bay	64.3	58.6	8.9	35.7
Ontario	69.9	64.2	8.3	30.1
Canada	70.6	64.9	8.0	29.4
Females				
Thunder Bay	58.6	54.4	7.1	41.4
Ontario	61.4	56.3	8.3	38.6
Canada	61.6	57.0	7.4	38.4

Note: Figures are based on total population 15 years and over
Source: Statistics Canada. 2013. 2011 National Household Survey. Statistics Canada Catalogue no. 99-004-XWE. Ottawa. Released September 11, 2013.

Labour Force by Industry (NAICS Codes 11–52)

Area	Agriculture, forestry, fishing & hunting	Mining, quarrying, & oil & gas extraction	Utilities	Construction	Manufacturing	Wholesale Trade	Retail Trade	Transportation & warehousing	Information & cultural industries	Finance & insurance
					Number					
					Total					
Thunder Bay	530	715	595	3,410	2,650	1,450	6,760	2,605	1,050	1,575
Ontario	101,280	29,985	57,035	417,900	697,565	305,030	751,200	307,405	178,720	364,415
Canada	437,650	261,050	149,940	1,215,380	1,619,295	733,445	2,031,665	827,780	420,830	767,960
					Males					
Thunder Bay	415	525	530	3,060	2,170	1,125	3,130	2,160	615	470
Ontario	66,485	25,650	42,685	369,300	493,305	197,770	344,480	225,245	98,835	153,125
Canada	307,370	211,690	110,765	1,068,710	1,167,680	494,545	933,850	617,305	235,875	296,995
					Females					
Thunder Bay	110	185	65	350	480	330	3,630	445	435	1,100
Ontario	34,800	4,340	14,350	48,595	204,260	107,260	406,720	82,160	79,885	211,290
Canada	130,285	49,360	39,175	146,670	451,615	238,900	1,097,820	210,475	184,955	470,960
					Percent of Labour Force					
					Total					
Thunder Bay	1.0	1.3	1.1	6.3	4.9	2.7	12.5	4.8	1.9	2.9
Ontario	1.5	0.4	0.9	6.3	10.4	4.6	11.2	4.6	2.7	5.5
Canada	2.5	1.5	0.9	6.9	9.2	4.2	11.6	4.7	2.4	4.4
					Males					
Thunder Bay	1.5	1.9	2.0	11.3	8.0	4.2	11.6	8.0	2.3	1.7
Ontario	1.9	0.7	1.2	10.7	14.3	5.7	10.0	6.5	2.9	4.4
Canada	3.3	2.3	1.2	11.6	12.7	5.4	10.2	6.7	2.6	3.2
					Females					
Thunder Bay	0.4	0.7	0.2	1.3	1.8	1.2	13.5	1.7	1.6	4.1
Ontario	1.1	0.1	0.4	1.5	6.3	3.3	12.6	2.5	2.5	6.5
Canada	1.6	0.6	0.5	1.7	5.4	2.8	13.1	2.5	2.2	5.6

Note: Figures are based on total experienced labour force 15 years and over. Experienced labour force refers to persons who, during the week of Sunday, May 1 to Saturday, May 7, 2011, were employed and the unemployed who had last worked for pay or in self-employment in either 2010 or 2011.
Source: Statistics Canada. 2013. 2011 National Household Survey. Statistics Canada Catalogue no. 99-004-XWE. Ottawa. Released September 11, 2013.

Labour Force by Industry (NAICS Codes 53–91)

Area	Real estate & rental & leasing	Profess., scientific & tech. services	Mgmt of companies & enterprises	Admin. & support, waste mgmt & remed. services	Educational services	Health care & social assistance	Arts, entertain. & recreation	Accomm. & food services	Other services (except public admin.)	Public admin.
					Number					
					Total					
Thunder Bay	890	2,870	10	1,705	5,145	8,565	1,220	4,335	2,570	5,220
Ontario	133,980	511,020	6,525	309,630	499,690	692,130	144,065	417,675	296,340	458,665
Canada	321,895	1,240,850	17,460	728,330	1,301,435	1,949,650	363,405	1,130,750	807,800	1,261,050
					Males					
Thunder Bay	490	1,575	0	940	1,860	1,550	750	1,655	1,470	2,585
Ontario	72,835	281,420	3,540	172,475	162,765	120,165	75,035	177,240	133,795	236,655
Canada	179,090	688,625	9,380	411,250	424,915	349,430	188,270	469,990	372,940	652,510
					Females					
Thunder Bay	400	1,295	0	765	3,280	7,020	475	2,680	1,100	2,640
Ontario	61,145	229,600	2,990	137,155	336,925	571,965	69,030	240,430	162,550	222,015
Canada	142,805	552,225	8,075	317,085	876,515	1,600,220	175,135	660,760	434,865	608,535
					Percent of Labour Force					
					Total					
Thunder Bay	1.7	5.3	0.0	3.2	9.5	15.9	2.3	8.0	4.8	9.7
Ontario	2.0	7.6	0.1	4.6	7.5	10.4	2.2	6.3	4.4	6.9
Canada	1.8	7.1	0.1	4.1	7.4	11.1	2.1	6.4	4.6	7.2
					Males					
Thunder Bay	1.8	5.8	0.0	3.5	6.9	5.7	2.8	6.1	5.4	9.5
Ontario	2.1	8.2	0.1	5.0	4.7	3.5	2.2	5.1	3.9	6.9
Canada	1.9	7.5	0.1	4.5	4.6	3.8	2.0	5.1	4.1	7.1
					Females					
Thunder Bay	1.5	4.8	0.0	2.9	12.2	26.2	1.8	10.0	4.1	9.9
Ontario	1.9	7.1	0.1	4.2	10.4	17.7	2.1	7.4	5.0	6.9
Canada	1.7	6.6	0.1	3.8	10.4	19.1	2.1	7.9	5.2	7.2

Note: Figures are based on total experienced labour force 15 years and over. Experienced labour force refers to persons who, during the week of Sunday, May 1 to Saturday, May 7, 2011, were employed and the unemployed who had last worked for pay or in self-employment in either 2010 or 2011.
Source: Statistics Canada. 2013. 2011 National Household Survey. Statistics Canada Catalogue no. 99-004-XWE. Ottawa. Released September 11, 2013.

Occupation

Area	Mgmt	Business, Finance & Admin.	Natural/ Applied Sciences & Related	Health	Education, Law & Social, Community & Government Services	Art, Culture, Recreation & Sport	Sales & Service	Trades, Transport & Equip. Operators & Related	Natural Resources, Agri. & Related Production	Mfg & Utilities
					Number					
					Total					
Thunder Bay	4,315	8,115	3,395	4,425	8,190	1,005	13,900	8,335	950	1,265
Ontario	770,580	1,138,330	494,500	392,695	801,465	206,420	1,550,260	868,515	106,810	350,685
Canada	1,963,600	2,902,045	1,237,775	1,107,200	2,064,675	503,415	4,068,170	2,537,775	397,930	805,040
					Males					
Thunder Bay	2,370	2,010	2,805	755	2,925	395	5,810	8,020	880	1,125
Ontario	474,655	352,505	384,345	78,330	264,570	96,055	673,880	812,280	82,610	233,565
Canada	1,229,460	854,190	966,355	217,520	676,550	232,535	1,745,705	2,385,615	318,945	564,300
					Females					
Thunder Bay	1,950	6,105	590	3,670	5,265	610	8,085	315	75	135
Ontario	295,920	785,825	110,150	314,370	536,895	110,370	876,380	56,230	24,200	117,115
Canada	734,140	2,047,855	271,415	889,675	1,388,130	270,875	2,322,465	152,165	78,980	240,740
					Percent of Labour Force					
					Total					
Thunder Bay	8.0	15.1	6.3	8.2	15.2	1.9	25.8	15.5	1.8	2.3
Ontario	11.5	17.0	7.4	5.9	12.0	3.1	23.2	13.0	1.6	5.2
Canada	11.2	16.5	7.0	6.3	11.7	2.9	23.1	14.4	2.3	4.6
					Males					
Thunder Bay	8.7	7.4	10.4	2.8	10.8	1.5	21.4	29.6	3.2	4.2
Ontario	13.7	10.2	11.1	2.3	7.7	2.8	19.5	23.5	2.4	6.8
Canada	13.4	9.3	10.5	2.4	7.4	2.5	19.0	26.0	3.5	6.1
					Females					
Thunder Bay	7.3	22.8	2.2	13.7	19.6	2.3	30.2	1.2	0.3	0.5
Ontario	9.2	24.3	3.4	9.7	16.6	3.4	27.2	1.7	0.7	3.6
Canada	8.7	24.4	3.2	10.6	16.5	3.2	27.7	1.8	0.9	2.9

Note: Figures are based on total experienced labour force 15 years and over
Source: Statistics Canada. 2013. 2011 National Household Survey. Statistics Canada Catalogue no. 99-004-XWE. Ottawa. Released September 11, 2013.

Place of Work Status

Area	Worked at Home	Worked Outside Canada	No Fixed Workplace Address	Worked at Usual Place
		Number		
		Total		
Thunder Bay	1,525	95	5,735	43,325
Ontario	423,790	31,390	670,835	5,170,980
Canada	1,142,640	66,460	1,868,245	13,517,690
		Males		
Thunder Bay	685	80	4,210	20,435
Ontario	216,900	21,150	486,560	2,524,555
Canada	582,150	47,355	1,400,485	6,604,325
		Females		
Thunder Bay	845	20	1,525	22,895
Ontario	206,895	10,240	184,275	2,646,420
Canada	560,490	19,100	467,760	6,913,370
		Percent of Labour Force		
		Total		
Thunder Bay	3.0	0.2	11.3	85.5
Ontario	6.7	0.5	10.7	82.1
Canada	6.9	0.4	11.3	81.5
		Males		
Thunder Bay	2.7	0.3	16.6	80.4
Ontario	6.7	0.7	15.0	77.7
Canada	6.7	0.5	16.2	76.5
		Females		
Thunder Bay	3.3	0.1	6.0	90.6
Ontario	6.8	0.3	6.0	86.8
Canada	7.0	0.2	5.9	86.8

Note: Figures are based on total employed labour force 15 years and over.
Source: Statistics Canada. 2013. 2011 National Household Survey. Statistics Canada Catalogue no. 99-004-XWE. Ottawa. Released September 11, 2013.

PROFILES / Thunder Bay, Ontario

Mode of Transportation to Work

Area	Car; Truck; Van; as Driver	Car; Truck; Van; as Passenger	Public Transit	Walked	Bicycled	All Other Modes
			Number			
			Total			
Thunder Bay	39,845	3,150	1,930	2,580	705	850
Ontario	4,235,315	357,110	818,270	299,095	69,885	62,145
Canada	11,393,140	867,050	1,851,525	880,815	201,780	191,625
			Males			
Thunder Bay	20,185	1,215	740	1,440	590	470
Ontario	2,316,680	143,410	340,995	131,765	47,635	30,635
Canada	6,238,835	349,530	788,290	387,580	135,840	104,725
			Females			
Thunder Bay	19,660	1,930	1,190	1,135	115	380
Ontario	1,918,640	213,700	477,275	167,325	22,250	31,515
Canada	5,154,305	517,520	1,063,235	493,230	65,940	86,900
			Percent of Labour Force			
			Total			
Thunder Bay	81.2	6.4	3.9	5.3	1.4	1.7
Ontario	72.5	6.1	14.0	5.1	1.2	1.1
Canada	74.0	5.6	12.0	5.7	1.3	1.2
			Males			
Thunder Bay	81.9	4.9	3.0	5.8	2.4	1.9
Ontario	76.9	4.8	11.3	4.4	1.6	1.0
Canada	77.9	4.4	9.8	4.8	1.7	1.3
			Females			
Thunder Bay	80.5	7.9	4.9	4.6	0.5	1.6
Ontario	67.8	7.5	16.9	5.9	0.8	1.1
Canada	69.8	7.0	14.4	6.7	0.9	1.2

Note: Figures are based on total employed labour force 15 years and over.
Source: Statistics Canada. 2013. 2011 National Household Survey. Statistics Canada Catalogue no. 99-004-XWE. Ottawa. Released September 11, 2013.

Visible Minority Population Characteristics

Area	Total Minority	South Asian[1]	Chinese	Black	Filipino	Latin American	Arab	SE Asian[2]	West Asian[3]	Korean	Japanese	Multiple[4]
					Number							
					Total							
Thunder Bay	3,565	575	715	485	440	205	115	330	55	15	290	220
Ontario	3,279,565	965,990	629,140	539,205	275,380	172,560	151,645	137,875	122,530	78,290	29,085	96,735
Canada	6,264,750	1,567,400	1,324,750	945,665	619,310	381,280	380,620	312,075	206,840	161,130	87,270	171,935
					Males							
Thunder Bay	1,930	325	400	235	200	105	65	150	40	0	195	115
Ontario	1,582,480	484,355	301,575	251,295	116,825	83,205	79,620	67,645	62,515	38,045	13,345	46,765
Canada	3,043,010	790,755	632,325	453,005	268,885	186,355	203,485	154,035	105,620	77,165	38,270	83,335
					Females							
Thunder Bay	1,635	245	320	255	240	100	50	180	0	0	90	100
Ontario	1,697,085	481,635	327,570	287,915	158,555	89,360	72,025	70,230	60,010	40,250	15,740	49,970
Canada	3,221,745	776,650	692,420	492,660	350,425	194,925	177,140	158,045	101,220	83,965	48,990	88,600
					Percent of Population							
					Total							
Thunder Bay	3.4	0.5	0.7	0.5	0.4	0.2	0.1	0.3	0.1	0.0	0.3	0.2
Ontario	25.9	7.6	5.0	4.3	2.2	1.4	1.2	1.1	1.0	0.6	0.2	0.8
Canada	19.1	4.8	4.0	2.9	1.9	1.2	1.2	0.9	0.6	0.5	0.3	0.5
					Males							
Thunder Bay	3.7	0.6	0.8	0.5	0.4	0.2	0.1	0.3	0.1	0.0	0.4	0.2
Ontario	25.6	7.8	4.9	4.1	1.9	1.3	1.3	1.1	1.0	0.6	0.2	0.8
Canada	18.8	4.9	3.9	2.8	1.7	1.2	1.3	1.0	0.7	0.5	0.2	0.5
					Females							
Thunder Bay	3.0	0.5	0.6	0.5	0.4	0.2	0.1	0.3	0.0	0.0	0.2	0.2
Ontario	26.2	7.4	5.1	4.4	2.5	1.4	1.1	1.1	0.9	0.6	0.2	0.8
Canada	19.3	4.7	4.1	3.0	2.1	1.2	1.1	0.9	0.6	0.5	0.3	0.5

Note: The Employment Equity Act defines visible minorities as 'persons, other than Aboriginal peoples, who are non-Caucasian in race or non-white in colour';
(1) Includes 'East Indian,' 'Pakistani,' 'Sri Lankan,' etc.; (2) Includes 'Vietnamese,' 'Cambodian,' 'Malaysian,' 'Laotian,' etc.; (3) Includes 'Iranian,' 'Afghan,' etc.; (4) Includes respondents who reported more than one visible minority group by checking two or more mark-in circles, e.g., 'Black' and 'South Asian.'
Source: Statistics Canada. 2013. 2011 National Household Survey. Statistics Canada Catalogue no. 99-004-XWE. Ottawa. Released September 11, 2013.

Aboriginal Population

Area	Aboriginal Identity[1]	First Nations (North American Indian) Single Identity[2]	Métis Single Identity	Inuk (Inuit) Single Identity	Multiple Aboriginal Identities[3]	Aboriginal Identities Not Included Elsewhere
Number						
Total						
Thunder Bay	10,085	7,755	2,115	10	100	100
Ontario	301,430	201,100	86,020	3,355	2,910	8,040
Canada	1,400,685	851,560	451,795	59,440	11,415	26,475
Males						
Thunder Bay	4,680	3,605	1,000	0	40	30
Ontario	145,020	96,620	41,755	1,475	1,420	3,750
Canada	682,190	411,785	223,335	29,495	5,525	12,055
Females						
Thunder Bay	5,410	4,155	1,115	0	60	75
Ontario	156,410	104,485	44,260	1,880	1,490	4,295
Canada	718,500	439,775	228,460	29,950	5,890	14,420
Percent of Population						
Total						
Thunder Bay	9.5	7.3	2.0	0.0	0.1	0.1
Ontario	2.4	1.6	0.7	0.0	0.0	0.1
Canada	4.3	2.6	1.4	0.2	0.0	0.1
Males						
Thunder Bay	9.1	7.0	1.9	0.0	0.1	0.1
Ontario	2.3	1.6	0.7	0.0	0.0	0.1
Canada	4.2	2.5	1.4	0.2	0.0	0.1
Females						
Thunder Bay	10.0	7.6	2.1	0.0	0.1	0.1
Ontario	2.4	1.6	0.7	0.0	0.0	0.1
Canada	4.3	2.6	1.4	0.2	0.0	0.1

Note: (1) Includes persons who reported being an Aboriginal person, that is, First Nations (North American Indian), Métis or Inuk (Inuit) and/or those who reported Registered or Treaty Indian status, that is registered under the Indian Act of Canada, and/or those who reported membership in a First Nation or Indian band. Aboriginal peoples of Canada are defined in the Constitution Act, 1982, section 35-2 as including the Indian, Inuit and Métis peoples of Canada; (2) Users should be aware that the estimates associated with this variable are more affected than most by the incomplete enumeration of certain Indian reserves and Indian settlements in the National Household Survey (NHS); (3) Includes persons who reported being any two or all three of the following: First Nations (North American Indian), Métis or Inuk (Inuit).
Source: Statistics Canada. 2013. 2011 National Household Survey. Statistics Canada Catalogue no. 99-004-XWE. Ottawa. Released September 11, 2013.

Ethnic Origin

Area	North American Aboriginal	Other North American	European	Caribbean	Latin, Central and South American	African	Asian	Oceania
Number								
Total								
Thunder Bay	10,345	25,305	90,015	350	490	475	3,105	95
Ontario	441,395	3,059,480	8,231,410	396,485	271,545	331,460	2,604,595	19,410
Canada	1,836,035	11,070,455	20,157,965	627,590	544,375	766,735	5,011,225	74,875
Males								
Thunder Bay	4,680	12,485	43,625	170	240	265	1,770	50
Ontario	210,490	1,507,105	4,019,885	181,805	130,035	160,940	1,265,540	9,855
Canada	885,675	5,462,685	9,913,150	291,640	264,635	387,360	2,435,540	37,490
Females								
Thunder Bay	5,660	12,815	46,385	175	250	210	1,335	45
Ontario	230,905	1,552,380	4,211,525	214,675	141,510	170,515	1,339,050	9,555
Canada	950,360	5,607,770	10,244,820	335,945	279,740	379,380	2,575,680	37,385
Percent of Population								
Total								
Thunder Bay	9.8	23.9	85.0	0.3	0.5	0.4	2.9	0.1
Ontario	3.5	24.2	65.1	3.1	2.1	2.6	20.6	0.2
Canada	5.6	33.7	61.4	1.9	1.7	2.3	15.3	0.2
Males								
Thunder Bay	9.1	24.2	84.5	0.3	0.5	0.5	3.4	0.1
Ontario	3.4	24.4	65.0	2.9	2.1	2.6	20.5	0.2
Canada	5.5	33.8	61.3	1.8	1.6	2.4	15.1	0.2
Females								
Thunder Bay	10.4	23.6	85.4	0.3	0.5	0.4	2.5	0.1
Ontario	3.6	24.0	65.1	3.3	2.2	2.6	20.7	0.1
Canada	5.7	33.6	61.4	2.0	1.7	2.3	15.4	0.2

Note: The sum of the ethnic groups in this table is greater than the total population estimate because a person may report more than one ethnic origin in the NHS.
Source: Statistics Canada. 2013. 2011 National Household Survey. Statistics Canada Catalogue no. 99-004-XWE. Ottawa. Released September 11, 2013.

Religion

Area	Buddhist	Christian	Hindu	Jewish	Muslim	Sikh	Traditional (Aboriginal) Spirituality	Other Religions	No Religious Affiliation
Number									
Total									
Thunder Bay	210	76,245	125	135	345	60	535	350	27,950
Ontario	163,750	8,167,295	366,720	195,540	581,950	179,765	15,905	53,080	2,927,790
Canada	366,830	22,102,745	497,965	329,495	1,053,945	454,965	64,935	130,835	7,850,605
Males									
Thunder Bay	80	35,490	65	80	205	30	195	155	15,320
Ontario	75,355	3,839,925	183,580	95,795	293,925	90,515	7,600	23,555	1,571,195
Canada	168,465	10,497,775	250,435	161,265	540,555	229,435	31,805	57,745	4,225,645
Females									
Thunder Bay	130	40,750	55	55	140	30	340	195	12,630
Ontario	88,395	4,327,365	183,140	99,740	288,025	89,250	8,310	29,525	1,356,600
Canada	198,365	11,604,975	247,525	168,235	513,395	225,530	33,135	73,090	3,624,965
Percent of Population									
Total									
Thunder Bay	0.2	72.0	0.1	0.1	0.3	0.1	0.5	0.3	26.4
Ontario	1.3	64.6	2.9	1.5	4.6	1.4	0.1	0.4	23.1
Canada	1.1	67.3	1.5	1.0	3.2	1.4	0.2	0.4	23.9
Males									
Thunder Bay	0.2	68.8	0.1	0.2	0.4	0.1	0.4	0.3	29.7
Ontario	1.2	62.1	3.0	1.5	4.8	1.5	0.1	0.4	25.4
Canada	1.0	64.9	1.5	1.0	3.3	1.4	0.2	0.4	26.1
Females									
Thunder Bay	0.2	75.0	0.1	0.1	0.3	0.1	0.6	0.4	23.2
Ontario	1.4	66.9	2.8	1.5	4.5	1.4	0.1	0.5	21.0
Canada	1.2	69.5	1.5	1.0	3.1	1.4	0.2	0.4	21.7

Note: Religion refers to the person's self-identification as having a connection or affiliation with any religious denomination, group, body, sect, cult or other religiously defined community or system of belief. Religion is not limited to formal membership in a religious organization or group. Persons without a religious connection or affiliation can self-identify as atheist, agnostic or humanist, or can provide another applicable response.
Source: Statistics Canada. 2013. 2011 National Household Survey. Statistics Canada Catalogue no. 99-004-XWE. Ottawa. Released September 11, 2013.

Religion—Christian Denominations

Area	Anglican	Baptist	Catholic	Christian Orthodox	Lutheran	Pentecostal	Presbyterian	United Church	Other Christian
Number									
Total									
Thunder Bay	7,850	1,870	39,850	995	5,895	655	3,015	8,780	7,330
Ontario	774,560	244,650	3,976,610	297,710	163,460	213,945	319,585	952,465	1,224,300
Canada	1,631,845	635,840	12,810,705	550,690	478,185	478,705	472,385	2,007,610	3,036,780
Males									
Thunder Bay	3,610	815	18,930	530	2,655	305	1,365	3,860	3,425
Ontario	355,175	112,285	1,895,940	145,825	75,225	94,955	148,535	435,255	576,730
Canada	752,945	293,905	6,167,290	270,205	221,525	217,850	218,955	912,545	1,442,550
Females									
Thunder Bay	4,235	1,060	20,920	465	3,235	350	1,655	4,915	3,905
Ontario	419,390	132,370	2,080,665	151,885	88,230	118,990	171,050	517,210	647,570
Canada	878,900	341,940	6,643,415	280,485	256,660	260,850	253,430	1,095,065	1,594,230
Percent of Population									
Total									
Thunder Bay	7.4	1.8	37.6	0.9	5.6	0.6	2.8	8.3	6.9
Ontario	6.1	1.9	31.4	2.4	1.3	1.7	2.5	7.5	9.7
Canada	5.0	1.9	39.0	1.7	1.5	1.5	1.4	6.1	9.2
Males									
Thunder Bay	7.0	1.6	36.7	1.0	5.1	0.6	2.6	7.5	6.6
Ontario	5.7	1.8	30.7	2.4	1.2	1.5	2.4	7.0	9.3
Canada	4.7	1.8	38.2	1.7	1.4	1.3	1.4	5.6	8.9
Females									
Thunder Bay	7.8	2.0	38.5	0.9	6.0	0.6	3.0	9.0	7.2
Ontario	6.5	2.0	32.2	2.3	1.4	1.8	2.6	8.0	10.0
Canada	5.3	2.0	39.8	1.7	1.5	1.6	1.5	6.6	9.6

Note: Religion refers to the person's self-identification as having a connection or affiliation with any religious denomination, group, body, sect, cult or other religiously defined community or system of belief. Religion is not limited to formal membership in a religious organization or group. Persons without a religious connection or affiliation can self-identify as atheist, agnostic or humanist, or can provide another applicable response.
Source: Statistics Canada. 2013. 2011 National Household Survey. Statistics Canada Catalogue no. 99-004-XWE. Ottawa. Released September 11, 2013.

Immigrant Status and Period of Immigration

Area	Non-Immigrants[1]	Immigrants All	Before 1971	1971 to 1980	1981 to 1990	1991 to 2000	2001 to 2005	2006 to 2011	Non-Permanent Residents[3]
				Number					
				Total					
Thunder Bay	95,510	10,185	5,860	1,360	850	700	610	805	260
Ontario	8,906,000	3,611,365	723,030	464,380	538,285	866,220	518,405	501,060	134,425
Canada	25,720,175	6,775,765	1,261,055	870,775	949,890	1,539,050	992,070	1,162,915	356,385
				Males					
Thunder Bay	46,745	4,755	2,670	650	420	350	280	380	115
Ontario	4,410,240	1,706,385	341,820	217,990	258,095	408,270	245,850	234,360	64,825
Canada	12,753,235	3,231,370	605,430	416,670	454,570	724,905	474,545	555,245	178,515
				Females					
Thunder Bay	48,760	5,430	3,190	710	425	355	325	430	135
Ontario	4,495,765	1,904,985	381,210	246,390	280,190	457,950	272,550	266,695	69,600
Canada	12,966,935	3,544,400	655,625	454,105	495,325	814,145	517,530	607,670	177,870
				Percent of Population					
				Total					
Thunder Bay	90.1	9.6	5.5	1.3	0.8	0.7	0.6	0.8	0.2
Ontario	70.4	28.5	5.7	3.7	4.3	6.8	4.1	4.0	1.1
Canada	78.3	20.6	3.8	2.7	2.9	4.7	3.0	3.5	1.1
				Males					
Thunder Bay	90.6	9.2	5.2	1.3	0.8	0.7	0.5	0.7	0.2
Ontario	71.3	27.6	5.5	3.5	4.2	6.6	4.0	3.8	1.0
Canada	78.9	20.0	3.7	2.6	2.8	4.5	2.9	3.4	1.1
				Females					
Thunder Bay	89.8	10.0	5.9	1.3	0.8	0.7	0.6	0.8	0.2
Ontario	69.5	29.4	5.9	3.8	4.3	7.1	4.2	4.1	1.1
Canada	77.7	21.2	3.9	2.7	3.0	4.9	3.1	3.6	1.1

Note: (1) Non-immigrant refers to a person who is a Canadian citizen by birth; (2) Immigrant refers to a person who is or has ever been a landed immigrant/permanent resident. This person has been granted the right to live in Canada permanently by immigration authorities. Some immigrants have resided in Canada for a number of years, while others have arrived recently. Some immigrants are Canadian citizens, while others are not. Most immigrants are born outside Canada, but a small number are born in Canada. In the 2011 National Household Survey, 'Immigrants' includes immigrants who landed in Canada prior to May 10, 2011; (3) Non-permanent resident refers to a person from another country who has a work or study permit, or who is a refugee claimant, and any non-Canadian-born family member living in Canada with them.
Source: Statistics Canada. 2013. 2011 National Household Survey. Statistics Canada Catalogue no. 99-004-XWE. Ottawa. Released September 11, 2013.

Mother Tongue

Area	English	French	Non-official Language	English & French	English & Non-official Language	French & Non-official Language	English, French & Non-official Language
			Number				
			Total				
Thunder Bay	90,145	2,515	12,710	305	950	65	15
Ontario	8,677,040	493,300	3,264,435	46,605	219,425	13,645	7,615
Canada	18,858,980	7,054,975	6,567,680	144,685	396,330	74,430	24,095
			Males				
Thunder Bay	44,095	1,220	5,880	135	425	25	10
Ontario	4,276,970	232,785	1,562,190	21,805	106,790	6,285	3,495
Canada	9,345,225	3,452,380	3,157,785	69,975	192,000	36,535	11,965
			Females				
Thunder Bay	46,050	1,295	6,825	165	525	35	5
Ontario	4,400,065	260,510	1,702,240	24,795	112,635	7,365	4,115
Canada	9,513,750	3,602,590	3,409,895	74,710	204,330	37,890	12,130
			Percent of Population				
			Total				
Thunder Bay	84.5	2.4	11.9	0.3	0.9	0.1	0.0
Ontario	68.2	3.9	25.7	0.4	1.7	0.1	0.1
Canada	56.9	21.3	19.8	0.4	1.2	0.2	0.1
			Males				
Thunder Bay	85.1	2.4	11.4	0.3	0.8	0.0	0.0
Ontario	68.9	3.7	25.2	0.4	1.7	0.1	0.1
Canada	57.5	21.2	19.4	0.4	1.2	0.2	0.1
			Females				
Thunder Bay	83.9	2.4	12.4	0.3	1.0	0.1	0.0
Ontario	67.6	4.0	26.1	0.4	1.7	0.1	0.1
Canada	56.4	21.4	20.2	0.4	1.2	0.2	0.1

Note: Figures cover total population excluding institutional residents.
Source: Statistics Canada. 2012. Census Profile. 2011 Census. Statistics Canada Catalogue no. 98-316-XWE. Ottawa. Released October 24 2012.
http://www12.statcan.gc.ca/census-recensement/2011/dp-pd/prof/index.cfm?Lang=E

PROFILES / Thunder Bay, Ontario

Language Spoken Most Often at Home

Area	English	French	Non-official Language	English & French	English & Non-official Language	French & Non-official Language	English, French & Non-official Language
\multicolumn{8}{c}{Number}
\multicolumn{8}{c}{Total}
Thunder Bay	100,545	770	3,680	200	1,465	10	25
Ontario	10,044,810	284,115	1,827,870	37,955	509,105	6,370	11,845
Canada	21,457,075	6,827,865	3,673,865	131,205	875,135	109,700	46,330
\multicolumn{8}{c}{Males}
Thunder Bay	48,970	365	1,655	95	695	5	15
Ontario	4,930,610	133,495	872,860	17,250	248,050	2,855	5,225
Canada	10,585,620	3,348,235	1,767,310	63,475	425,370	53,010	22,845
\multicolumn{8}{c}{Females}
Thunder Bay	51,580	410	2,020	110	770	5	15
Ontario	5,114,200	150,620	955,010	20,705	261,055	3,520	6,620
Canada	10,871,455	3,479,625	1,906,555	67,730	449,765	56,690	23,485
\multicolumn{8}{c}{Percent of Population}
\multicolumn{8}{c}{Total}
Thunder Bay	94.2	0.7	3.4	0.2	1.4	0.0	0.0
Ontario	79.0	2.2	14.4	0.3	4.0	0.1	0.1
Canada	64.8	20.6	11.1	0.4	2.6	0.3	0.1
\multicolumn{8}{c}{Males}
Thunder Bay	94.6	0.7	3.2	0.2	1.3	0.0	0.0
Ontario	79.4	2.1	14.1	0.3	4.0	0.0	0.1
Canada	65.1	20.6	10.9	0.4	2.6	0.3	0.1
\multicolumn{8}{c}{Females}
Thunder Bay	93.9	0.7	3.7	0.2	1.4	0.0	0.0
Ontario	78.5	2.3	14.7	0.3	4.0	0.1	0.1
Canada	64.5	20.6	11.3	0.4	2.7	0.3	0.1

Note: Figures cover total population excluding institutional residents.
Source: Statistics Canada. 2012. Census Profile. 2011 Census. Statistics Canada Catalogue no. 98-316-XWE. Ottawa. Released October 24 2012.
http://www12.statcan.gc.ca/census-recensement/2011/dp-pd/prof/index.cfm?Lang=E

Knowledge of Official Languages

Area	English Only	French Only	English & French	Neither English nor French
\multicolumn{5}{c}{Number}
\multicolumn{5}{c}{Total}
Thunder Bay	98,005	120	8,025	540
Ontario	10,984,360	42,980	1,395,805	298,920
Canada	22,564,665	4,165,015	5,795,570	595,920
\multicolumn{5}{c}{Males}
Thunder Bay	47,990	65	3,540	195
Ontario	5,445,050	18,805	627,725	118,765
Canada	11,222,185	1,925,340	2,876,560	241,790
\multicolumn{5}{c}{Females}
Thunder Bay	50,020	55	4,490	340
Ontario	5,539,310	24,175	768,085	180,155
Canada	11,342,485	2,239,680	2,919,005	354,135
\multicolumn{5}{c}{Percent of Population}
\multicolumn{5}{c}{Total}
Thunder Bay	91.9	0.1	7.5	0.5
Ontario	86.3	0.3	11.0	2.3
Canada	68.1	12.6	17.5	1.8
\multicolumn{5}{c}{Males}
Thunder Bay	92.7	0.1	6.8	0.4
Ontario	87.7	0.3	10.1	1.9
Canada	69.0	11.8	17.7	1.5
\multicolumn{5}{c}{Females}
Thunder Bay	91.1	0.1	8.2	0.6
Ontario	85.1	0.4	11.8	2.8
Canada	67.3	13.3	17.3	2.1

Note: Figures cover total population excluding institutional residents.
Source: Statistics Canada. 2012. Census Profile. 2011 Census. Statistics Canada Catalogue no. 98-316-XWE. Ottawa. Released October 24 2012.
http://www12.statcan.gc.ca/census-recensement/2011/dp-pd/prof/index.cfm?Lang=E

MAJOR CANADIAN CITIES: COMPARED AND RANKED

Toronto, Ontario

Background

Toronto is located in south-central Ontario, on the tip of Lake Ontario. The city is considered the anchor city of the "Golden Horseshoe" region, which is home to half of Ontario's population. Toronto's Queen's Park is the seat of government of Ontario.

Founded by the first lieutenant governor of Upper Canada, John Graves Simcoe, in 1793, Fort York is the birthplace of urban Toronto because of its pivotal role in the War of 1812 and importance as a government capital.

In 1997, six municipalities (North York, East York, York, Etobicoke, Scarborough and the former city of Toronto) amalgamated to become the current City of Toronto. Today, more than 2.6 million people live in the City of Toronto and 5.5 million Canadians live in the Greater Toronto Area (GTA). The city has five Chinatowns, two Little Italys, a Greektown, a Little India and a Koreatown. Over 140 languages and dialects are spoken in Toronto and almost half of the city's inhabitants identify their primary language as something other than English or French. The United Nations ranks Toronto as the most ethnically diverse city in the world.

Toronto is called "Hollywood North" by the film industry, which supports 28,000 jobs and generates $1.5 billion for the economy every year. The city's most famous landmark, and the world's tallest tower at 553 metres, is the CN Tower. Toronto is home to 125 museums and public archives, over 50 ballet and dance companies, six opera companies, and two symphony orchestras. World-renowned architects such as Frank Gehry and Daniel Libeskind have shaped Toronto's recent architectural renaissance with major expansions at the Art Gallery of Ontario and the Royal Ontario Museum.

Toronto has average summer highs of plus 25.07 degrees Celsius, winter lows of minus 5.77 degrees Celsius, and an average rainfall just over 709 mm per year.

Rankings

- Toronto ranked #10 in the "Innovation Cities Top 100 Index(tm)" in 2011. Cities worldwide were rated on ability to generate product, process, service and other innovation types across an urban economy. There were 331 cities in the study. *Innovation Cities Indexes 2011 Launch, October 18th, 2011*
- *Economist Intelligence Unit* ranked Toronto #4 in the world for liveability in 2010 and 2011. The annual survey rates 140 cities worldwide. Cities are rated across five categories: stability, health care, culture and environment, education, and infrastructure. *Economist Intelligence Unit, The Economist, 2010-11*
- *Corporate Knights Magazine* ranked Toronto the most sustainable large city in Canada in 2010 and 2011. There were five assessment categories: ecological integrity, economic security, governance and empowerment, infrastructure and built environment, and social well-being. *Corporate Knights Magazine, February 10, 2011*
- *Reader's Digest* ranked 36 of the world's cities for politeness and Toronto ranked #3 overall. Criteria: holding open of doors; being thanked by store sales assistants; strangers stopping to assist with collection of dropped sheets of papers. The two most polite cities in the world were New York and Zurich, Switzerland. *Reader's Digest, "How Polite Are We?"May 2012*
- *Canadian Business* ranked Canada's real-estate markets based solely on raw house prices. Toronto was ranked #17 of the most expensive places to live in Canada, with homes averaging at $474,300 in price. *Canadian Business, "Canada's most expensive real estate markets," March 26, 2012*
- People for the Ethical Treatment of Animals (PETA) ranked Toronto #3 of the "Best Vegetarian-Friendly Cities in Canada." The city's CN Tower was praised for offering a full-vegetarian menu in its revolving restaurant. PETA also ranked Toronto as one of the best veggie-burger capitals of the world. *PETA, Best Vegetarian-Friendly Cities in Canada, 2006*

PROFILES / Toronto, Ontario

Population Growth and Density

Area	Population in 2001	Population in 2006	Population in 2011	Population Change 2001–2006	Population Change 2006–2011	Land Area (sq. km)	Population Density per sq. km
Toronto	2,481,494	2,503,281	2,615,060	0.9	4.5	630.21	4,149.5
Ontario	11,410,046	12,160,282	12,851,821	6.6	5.7	908,607.67	14.1
Canada	30,007,094	31,612,897	33,476,688	5.4	5.9	8,965,121.42	3.7

Source: Statistics Canada. 2012. Census Profile. 2011 Census. Statistics Canada Catalogue no. 98-316-XWE. Ottawa. Released October 24 2012.
http://www12.statcan.gc.ca/census-recensement/2011/dp-pd/prof/index.cfm?Lang=E;
Statistics Canada 2007. 2006 Community Profiles. 2006 Census. Statistics Canada Catalogue no. 92-591-XWE. Ottawa. Released March 13 2007.
http://www12.statcan.ca/census-recensement/2006/dp-pd/prof/92-591/index.cfm?Lang=E

Gender

Area	Males	Females
Number		
Toronto	1,255,585	1,359,475
Ontario	6,263,140	6,588,685
Canada	16,414,225	17,062,460
Percent of Population		
Toronto	48.0	52.0
Ontario	48.7	51.3
Canada	49.0	51.0

Source: Statistics Canada. 2012. Census Profile. 2011 Census. Statistics Canada Catalogue no. 98-316-XWE. Ottawa. Released October 24 2012.
http://www12.statcan.gc.ca/census-recensement/2011/dp-pd/prof/index.cfm?Lang=E

Marital Status

Area	Married[1]	Living Common-law	Single[2]	Separated	Divorced	Widowed
Number						
Total						
Toronto	991,700	140,080	746,190	69,600	140,240	126,385
Ontario	5,367,400	791,210	2,985,020	319,805	593,730	613,880
Canada	12,941,960	3,142,525	7,816,045	698,240	1,686,035	1,584,530
Males						
Toronto	494,850	72,300	380,905	27,915	51,850	22,510
Ontario	2,681,320	397,620	1,583,760	133,790	231,160	117,980
Canada	6,470,300	1,575,495	4,206,320	299,655	680,415	310,940
Females						
Toronto	496,850	67,780	365,285	41,685	88,390	103,875
Ontario	2,686,075	393,590	1,401,260	186,015	362,570	495,905
Canada	6,471,660	1,567,035	3,609,730	398,585	1,005,620	1,273,590
Percent of Population						
Total						
Toronto	44.8	6.3	33.7	3.1	6.3	5.7
Ontario	50.3	7.4	28.0	3.0	5.6	5.8
Canada	46.4	11.3	28.0	2.5	6.0	5.7
Males						
Toronto	47.1	6.9	36.3	2.7	4.9	2.1
Ontario	52.1	7.7	30.8	2.6	4.5	2.3
Canada	47.8	11.6	31.1	2.2	5.0	2.3
Females						
Toronto	42.7	5.8	31.4	3.6	7.6	8.9
Ontario	48.6	7.1	25.4	3.4	6.6	9.0
Canada	45.2	10.9	25.2	2.8	7.0	8.9

Note: (1) and not separated, (2) never legally married
Source: Statistics Canada. 2012. Census Profile. 2011 Census. Statistics Canada Catalogue no. 98-316-XWE. Ottawa. Released October 24 2012.
http://www12.statcan.gc.ca/census-recensement/2011/dp-pd/prof/index.cfm?Lang=E

Age Characteristics: 0 to 49 Years

Area	0 to 4 Years	5 to 9 Years	10 to 14 Years	15 to 19 Years	20 to 24 Years	25 to 29 Years	30 to 34 Years	35 to 39 Years	40 to 44 Years	45 to 49 Years
					Number Total					
Toronto	140,510	128,060	132,290	150,045	183,470	211,850	201,165	190,405	197,400	207,625
Ontario	704,260	712,755	763,755	863,635	852,910	815,120	800,365	844,335	924,075	1,055,880
Canada	1,877,095	1,809,895	1,920,355	2,178,135	2,187,450	2,169,590	2,162,905	2,173,930	2,324,875	2,675,130
					Males					
Toronto	72,085	65,400	67,765	76,850	90,730	101,285	95,730	91,285	95,550	101,815
Ontario	360,590	365,290	391,630	443,680	432,490	400,045	383,340	405,845	447,920	517,510
Canada	961,150	925,965	983,995	1,115,845	1,108,775	1,077,275	1,058,810	1,064,200	1,141,720	1,318,715
					Females					
Toronto	68,425	62,665	64,525	73,195	92,735	110,565	105,435	99,120	101,855	105,810
Ontario	343,670	347,465	372,125	419,950	420,415	415,075	417,030	438,485	476,155	538,370
Canada	915,945	883,935	936,360	1,062,295	1,078,670	1,092,315	1,104,095	1,109,735	1,183,155	1,356,420
					Percent of Population Total					
Toronto	5.4	4.9	5.1	5.7	7.0	8.1	7.7	7.3	7.5	7.9
Ontario	5.5	5.5	5.9	6.7	6.6	6.3	6.2	6.6	7.2	8.2
Canada	5.6	5.4	5.7	6.5	6.5	6.5	6.5	6.5	6.9	8.0
					Males					
Toronto	5.7	5.2	5.4	6.1	7.2	8.1	7.6	7.3	7.6	8.1
Ontario	5.8	5.8	6.3	7.1	6.9	6.4	6.1	6.5	7.2	8.3
Canada	5.9	5.6	6.0	6.8	6.8	6.6	6.5	6.5	7.0	8.0
					Females					
Toronto	5.0	4.6	4.7	5.4	6.8	8.1	7.8	7.3	7.5	7.8
Ontario	5.2	5.3	5.6	6.4	6.4	6.3	6.3	6.7	7.2	8.2
Canada	5.4	5.2	5.5	6.2	6.3	6.4	6.5	6.5	6.9	7.9

Source: Statistics Canada. 2012. Census Profile. 2011 Census. Statistics Canada Catalogue no. 98-316-XWE. Ottawa. Released October 24 2012.
http://www12.statcan.gc.ca/census-recensement/2011/dp-pd/prof/index.cfm?Lang=E

Age Characteristics: 50 Years and Over, and Median Age

Area	50 to 54 Years	55 to 59 Years	60 to 64 Years	65 to 69 Years	70 to 74 Years	75 to 79 Years	80 to 84 Years	85 Years and Over	Median Age
					Number Total				
Toronto	191,290	162,535	140,960	102,445	86,185	74,215	59,630	54,965	39.2
Ontario	1,006,140	864,620	765,655	563,485	440,780	356,150	271,510	246,400	40.4
Canada	2,658,965	2,340,635	2,052,670	1,521,715	1,153,065	922,700	702,070	645,515	40.6
					Males				
Toronto	92,855	76,950	66,220	47,275	38,060	32,455	24,515	18,755	38.2
Ontario	492,560	418,755	370,370	270,875	206,350	161,345	113,620	80,925	39.4
Canada	1,309,030	1,147,300	1,002,690	738,010	543,435	417,945	291,085	208,300	39.6
					Females				
Toronto	98,440	85,585	74,740	55,175	48,130	41,755	35,115	36,210	40.1
Ontario	513,580	445,865	395,275	292,610	234,435	194,805	157,890	165,475	41.3
Canada	1,349,940	1,193,335	1,049,985	783,705	609,630	504,755	410,985	437,215	41.5
					Percent of Population Total				
Toronto	7.3	6.2	5.4	3.9	3.3	2.8	2.3	2.1	–
Ontario	7.8	6.7	6.0	4.4	3.4	2.8	2.1	1.9	–
Canada	7.9	7.0	6.1	4.5	3.4	2.8	2.1	1.9	–
					Males				
Toronto	7.4	6.1	5.3	3.8	3.0	2.6	2.0	1.5	–
Ontario	7.9	6.7	5.9	4.3	3.3	2.6	1.8	1.3	–
Canada	8.0	7.0	6.1	4.5	3.3	2.5	1.8	1.3	–
					Females				
Toronto	7.2	6.3	5.5	4.1	3.5	3.1	2.6	2.7	–
Ontario	7.8	6.8	6.0	4.4	3.6	3.0	2.4	2.5	–
Canada	7.9	7.0	6.2	4.6	3.6	3.0	2.4	2.6	–

Source: Statistics Canada. 2012. Census Profile. 2011 Census. Statistics Canada Catalogue no. 98-316-XWE. Ottawa. Released October 24 2012.
http://www12.statcan.gc.ca/census-recensement/2011/dp-pd/prof/index.cfm?Lang=E

PROFILES / Toronto, Ontario

Private Households by Household Size

Area	1 Person	2 Persons	3 Persons	4 Persons	5 Persons	6 or More Persons	Average Number of Persons in Private Households
Households							
Toronto	331,180	307,845	168,750	142,760	59,005	38,340	2.5
Ontario	1,230,975	1,584,415	803,030	783,925	310,860	174,305	2.6
Canada	3,673,310	4,544,820	2,081,900	1,903,300	724,405	392,885	2.5
Percent of Households							
Toronto	31.6	29.4	16.1	13.6	5.6	3.7	–
Ontario	25.2	32.4	16.4	16.0	6.4	3.6	–
Canada	27.6	34.1	15.6	14.3	5.4	2.9	–

Source: Statistics Canada. 2012. Census Profile. 2011 Census. Statistics Canada Catalogue no. 98-316-XWE. Ottawa. Released October 24 2012.
http://www12.statcan.gc.ca/census-recensement/2011/dp-pd/prof/index.cfm?Lang=E

Dwelling Type

Area	Single-detached House	Semi-detached House	Row House	Apartment: Building with Five or More Storeys	Apartment: Building with Fewer Than Five Storeys	Duplex Apartment	Movable Dwelling	Other Single-attached House
Number								
Toronto	275,015	72,400	60,295	429,225	163,895	44,740	110	2,195
Ontario	2,718,880	279,470	415,225	789,970	498,160	160,460	15,800	9,540
Canada	7,329,150	646,245	791,600	1,234,770	2,397,550	704,485	183,510	33,310
Percent of Dwellings								
Toronto	26.2	6.9	5.8	41.0	15.6	4.3	0.0	0.2
Ontario	55.6	5.7	8.5	16.2	10.2	3.3	0.3	0.2
Canada	55.0	4.9	5.9	9.3	18.0	5.3	1.4	0.3

Source: Statistics Canada. 2012. Census Profile. 2011 Census. Statistics Canada Catalogue no. 98-316-XWE. Ottawa. Released October 24 2012.
http://www12.statcan.gc.ca/census-recensement/2011/dp-pd/prof/index.cfm?Lang=E

Shelter Costs

	Owned Dwellings					Rented Dwellings		
Area	Number	Median Value[1] ($)	Average Value[1] ($)	Median Monthly Costs[2] ($)	Average Monthly Costs[2] ($)	Number	Median Monthly Costs[3] ($)	Average Monthly Costs[3] ($)
Toronto	571,785	401,400	517,309	1,304	1,443	476,085	1,001	1,026
Ontario	3,446,650	300,862	367,428	1,163	1,284	1,385,535	892	926
Canada	9,013,410	280,552	345,182	978	1,141	4,060,385	784	848

Note: All figures cover non-farm, non-reserve private dwellings; (1) Refers to the dollar amount expected by the owner if the dwelling were to be sold; (2) Includes all shelter expenses paid by households that own their dwellings, such as the mortgage payment and the costs of electricity, heat, water and other municipal services, property taxes and condominium fees; (3) Includes all shelter expenses paid by households that rent their dwellings, such as the monthly rent and the costs of electricity, heat and municipal services.
Source: Statistics Canada. 2013. 2011 National Household Survey. Statistics Canada Catalogue no. 99-004-XWE. Ottawa. Released September 11, 2013.

Occupied Private Dwellings by Period of Construction

Area	1960 or Before	1961 to 1980	1981 to 1990	1991 to 2000	2001 to 2005	2006 to 2011
Number						
Toronto	377,575	344,160	122,915	77,925	61,570	63,730
Ontario	1,330,235	1,420,570	763,430	609,310	414,795	348,310
Canada	3,273,105	4,152,715	2,112,110	1,707,880	1,031,020	1,042,430
Percent of Dwellings						
Toronto	36.0	32.8	11.7	7.4	5.9	6.1
Ontario	27.2	29.1	15.6	12.5	8.5	7.1
Canada	24.6	31.2	15.9	12.8	7.7	7.8

Note: Figures cover non-farm, non-reserve private dwellings and includes data up to May 10, 2011.
Source: Statistics Canada. 2013. 2011 National Household Survey. Statistics Canada Catalogue no. 99-004-XWE. Ottawa. Released September 11, 2013.

PROFILES / Toronto, Ontario

Educational Attainment

Area	No Certificate, Diploma or Degree	High School Diploma or Equivalent[1]	Apprenticeship or Trades Certificate or Diploma[2]	College, CÉGEP or Other Non-University Certificate or Diploma	University Certificate or Diploma Below the Bachelor Level[3]	Bachelor's Degree	University Certificate, Diploma or Degree Above Bachelor Level[4]
			Number Total				
Toronto	380,965	523,320	111,450	330,080	113,640	436,755	279,625
Ontario	1,954,520	2,801,805	771,140	2,070,875	427,150	1,515,075	933,100
Canada	5,485,400	6,968,935	2,950,685	4,970,020	1,200,130	3,634,425	2,049,930
			Males				
Toronto	176,285	250,335	68,500	143,770	49,965	204,265	140,870
Ontario	957,040	1,337,055	520,390	894,235	193,355	692,345	470,290
Canada	2,742,875	3,305,415	1,928,970	2,118,430	513,235	1,643,080	1,043,350
			Females				
Toronto	204,685	272,985	42,950	186,310	63,670	232,490	138,755
Ontario	997,475	1,464,755	250,750	1,176,640	233,790	822,730	462,805
Canada	2,742,520	3,663,515	1,021,715	2,851,595	686,890	1,991,345	1,006,585
			Percent of Population Total				
Toronto	17.5	24.1	5.1	15.2	5.2	20.1	12.9
Ontario	18.7	26.8	7.4	19.8	4.1	14.5	8.9
Canada	20.1	25.6	10.8	18.2	4.4	13.3	7.5
			Males				
Toronto	17.0	24.2	6.6	13.9	4.8	19.8	13.6
Ontario	18.9	26.4	10.3	17.7	3.8	13.7	9.3
Canada	20.6	24.9	14.5	15.9	3.9	12.4	7.8
			Females				
Toronto	17.9	23.9	3.8	16.3	5.6	20.4	12.2
Ontario	18.4	27.1	4.6	21.8	4.3	15.2	8.6
Canada	19.6	26.2	7.3	20.4	4.9	14.3	7.2

Note: Figures cover total population aged 15 years and over by highest certificate, diploma or degree; (1) Includes persons who have graduated from a secondary school or equivalent. It excludes persons with a postsecondary certificate, diploma or degree; (2) Includes Registered Apprenticeship certificates (including Certificate of Qualification, Journeyperson's designation) and other trades certificates or diplomas such as pre-employment or vocational certificates and diplomas from brief trade programs completed at community colleges, institutes of technology, vocational centres, and similar institutions; (3) Comparisons with other data sources suggest that the category 'University certificate or diploma below the bachelor's level' was over-reported in the NHS. This category likely includes some responses that are actually college certificates or diplomas, bachelor's degrees or other types of education (e.g., university transfer programs, bachelor's programs completed in other countries, incomplete bachelor's programs, non-university professional designations). We recommend users interpret the results for the 'University certificate or diploma below the bachelor's level' category with caution; (4) 'University certificate or diploma above bachelor level' includes the categories: 'Degree in medicine, dentistry, veterinary medicine or optometry,' 'Master's degree' and 'Earned doctorate.'
Source: Statistics Canada. 2013. 2011 National Household Survey. Statistics Canada Catalogue no. 99-004-XWE. Ottawa. Released September 11, 2013.

Household Income Distribution

Area	Less than $10,000	$10,000 to $19,999	$20,000 to $29,999	$30,000 to $39,999	$40,000 to $49,999	$50,000 to $59,999	$60,000 to $79,999	$80,000 to $99,999	$100,000 to $124,999	$125,000 to $149,999	$150,000 and Over
					Households						
Toronto	64,350	95,340	99,650	97,935	95,330	84,030	135,840	101,985	84,855	56,140	132,425
Ontario	201,780	354,530	405,725	425,410	425,720	398,705	680,850	552,660	497,970	331,460	611,840
Canada	626,705	1,141,945	1,193,925	1,271,675	1,206,800	1,102,120	1,865,280	1,458,240	1,260,770	802,555	1,389,240
					Percent of Households						
Toronto	6.1	9.1	9.5	9.3	9.1	8.0	13.0	9.7	8.1	5.4	12.6
Ontario	4.1	7.3	8.3	8.7	8.7	8.2	13.9	11.3	10.2	6.8	12.5
Canada	4.7	8.6	9.0	9.5	9.1	8.3	14.0	10.9	9.5	6.0	10.4

Note: Household income is the sum of the total incomes of all members of that household. Total income refers to monetary receipts from certain sources, before income taxes and deductions, during calendar year 2010.
Source: Statistics Canada. 2013. 2011 National Household Survey. Statistics Canada Catalogue no. 99-004-XWE. Ottawa. Released September 11, 2013.

Median and Average Household and Economic Family Income

Area	Median Household Income ($)	Average Household Income ($)	Median After-tax Household Income ($)	Average After-tax Household Income ($)	Median Economic Family Income ($)	Average Economic Family Income ($)	Median After-tax Economic Family Income ($)	Average After-tax Economic Family Income ($)
Toronto	58,381	87,038	52,149	70,945	72,890	105,526	65,335	85,701
Ontario	66,358	85,772	58,717	71,523	80,987	100,152	71,128	83,322
Canada	61,072	79,102	54,089	66,149	76,511	94,125	67,044	78,517

Note: Figures cover household and economic familiy income in 2010. A household is defined as a person or a group of persons (other than foreign residents) who occupy the same private dwelling and do not have a usual place of residence elsewhere in Canada. Every person is a member of one and only one household. An economic family is defined as a group of two or more persons who live in the same dwelling and are related to each other by blood, marriage, common-law, adoption or a foster relationship. A couple may be of opposite or same sex.
Source: Statistics Canada. 2013. 2011 National Household Survey. Statistics Canada Catalogue no. 99-004-XWE. Ottawa. Released September 11, 2013.

PROFILES / Toronto, Ontario

Individual Income Distribution

Area	Less than $10,000	$10,000 to $19,999	$20,000 to $29,999	$30,000 to $39,999	$40,000 to $49,999	$50,000 to $59,999	$60,000 to $79,999	$80,000 to $99,999	$100,000 to $124,999	$125,000 and Over
					Number Total					
Toronto	405,445	395,005	285,550	218,580	180,965	134,430	175,655	102,985	58,850	91,295
Ontario	1,780,355	1,748,060	1,361,710	1,136,730	980,790	746,360	964,280	574,710	293,865	330,285
Canada	4,492,040	4,835,710	3,670,020	3,180,360	2,603,520	1,921,650	2,437,440	1,302,045	693,580	782,135
					Males					
Toronto	185,620	161,670	126,200	104,260	88,830	68,685	92,790	55,330	34,310	61,225
Ontario	781,095	669,815	580,990	535,255	491,125	407,005	569,205	341,160	201,125	244,500
Canada	1,936,365	1,864,880	1,588,260	1,522,190	1,333,510	1,079,780	1,473,145	823,720	492,905	599,905
					Females					
Toronto	219,830	233,340	159,355	114,325	92,135	65,745	82,865	47,655	24,540	30,075
Ontario	999,265	1,078,245	780,720	601,475	489,665	339,360	395,075	233,550	92,740	85,790
Canada	2,555,675	2,970,825	2,081,760	1,658,170	1,270,010	841,870	964,300	478,330	200,680	182,230
					Percent of Population Total					
Toronto	19.8	19.3	13.9	10.7	8.8	6.6	8.6	5.0	2.9	4.5
Ontario	18.0	17.6	13.7	11.5	9.9	7.5	9.7	5.8	3.0	3.3
Canada	17.3	18.7	14.2	12.3	10.0	7.4	9.4	5.0	2.7	3.0
					Males					
Toronto	19.0	16.5	12.9	10.7	9.1	7.0	9.5	5.7	3.5	6.3
Ontario	16.2	13.9	12.1	11.1	10.2	8.4	11.8	7.1	4.2	5.1
Canada	15.2	14.7	12.5	12.0	10.5	8.5	11.6	6.5	3.9	4.7
					Females					
Toronto	20.5	21.8	14.9	10.7	8.6	6.1	7.7	4.5	2.3	2.8
Ontario	19.6	21.2	15.3	11.8	9.6	6.7	7.8	4.6	1.8	1.7
Canada	19.4	22.5	15.8	12.6	9.6	6.4	7.3	3.6	1.5	1.4

Note: Figures cover individuals aged 15 years and over with income. Income refers to monetary receipts from certain sources, before income taxes and deductions, during calendar year 2010.
Source: Statistics Canada. 2013. 2011 National Household Survey. Statistics Canada Catalogue no. 99-004-XWE. Ottawa. Released September 11, 2013.

Labour Force Status

Area	All	Employed	Unemployed	Not in the Labour Force
		Number Total		
Toronto	1,399,985	1,269,150	130,835	775,845
Ontario	6,864,990	6,297,005	567,985	3,608,685
Canada	17,990,080	16,595,035	1,395,045	9,269,445
		Males		
Toronto	714,745	650,740	64,005	319,245
Ontario	3,542,030	3,249,165	292,865	1,522,690
Canada	9,388,570	8,634,310	754,255	3,906,785
		Females		
Toronto	685,240	618,410	66,830	456,600
Ontario	3,322,955	3,047,840	275,120	2,085,990
Canada	8,601,515	7,960,725	640,790	5,362,660
		Percent of Labour Force Total		
Toronto	64.3	58.3	9.3	35.7
Ontario	65.5	60.1	8.3	34.5
Canada	66.0	60.9	7.8	34.0
		Males		
Toronto	69.1	62.9	9.0	30.9
Ontario	69.9	64.2	8.3	30.1
Canada	70.6	64.9	8.0	29.4
		Females		
Toronto	60.0	54.2	9.8	40.0
Ontario	61.4	56.3	8.3	38.6
Canada	61.6	57.0	7.4	38.4

Note: Figures are based on total population 15 years and over
Source: Statistics Canada. 2013. 2011 National Household Survey. Statistics Canada Catalogue no. 99-004-XWE. Ottawa. Released September 11, 2013.

Labour Force by Industry (NAICS Codes 11–52)

Area	Agriculture, forestry, fishing & hunting	Mining, quarrying, & oil & gas extraction	Utilities	Construction	Manufacturing	Wholesale Trade	Retail Trade	Transportation & warehousing	Information & cultural industries	Finance & insurance
					Number					
					Total					
Toronto	1,935	2,360	7,260	64,910	109,465	57,710	133,240	51,345	62,860	112,415
Ontario	101,280	29,985	57,035	417,900	697,565	305,030	751,200	307,405	178,720	364,415
Canada	437,650	261,050	149,940	1,215,380	1,619,295	733,445	2,031,665	827,780	420,830	767,960
					Males					
Toronto	1,135	1,505	4,760	58,380	73,185	35,580	62,555	38,650	35,260	53,730
Ontario	66,485	25,650	42,685	369,300	493,305	197,770	344,480	225,245	98,835	153,125
Canada	307,370	211,690	110,765	1,068,710	1,167,680	494,545	933,850	617,305	235,875	296,995
					Females					
Toronto	800	850	2,505	6,535	36,285	22,135	70,680	12,695	27,600	58,685
Ontario	34,800	4,340	14,350	48,595	204,260	107,260	406,720	82,160	79,885	211,290
Canada	130,285	49,360	39,175	146,670	451,615	238,900	1,097,820	210,475	184,955	470,960
					Percent of Labour Force					
					Total					
Toronto	0.1	0.2	0.5	4.8	8.1	4.3	9.9	3.8	4.7	8.3
Ontario	1.5	0.4	0.9	6.3	10.4	4.6	11.2	4.6	2.7	5.5
Canada	2.5	1.5	0.9	6.9	9.2	4.2	11.6	4.7	2.4	4.4
					Males					
Toronto	0.2	0.2	0.7	8.4	10.6	5.1	9.1	5.6	5.1	7.8
Ontario	1.9	0.7	1.2	10.7	14.3	5.7	10.0	6.5	2.9	4.4
Canada	3.3	2.3	1.2	11.6	12.7	5.4	10.2	6.7	2.6	3.2
					Females					
Toronto	0.1	0.1	0.4	1.0	5.5	3.4	10.7	1.9	4.2	8.9
Ontario	1.1	0.1	0.4	1.5	6.3	3.3	12.6	2.5	2.5	6.5
Canada	1.6	0.6	0.5	1.7	5.4	2.8	13.1	2.5	2.2	5.6

Note: Figures are based on total experienced labour force 15 years and over. Experienced labour force refers to persons who, during the week of Sunday, May 1 to Saturday, May 7, 2011, were employed and the unemployed who had last worked for pay or in self-employment in either 2010 or 2011.
Source: Statistics Canada. 2013. 2011 National Household Survey. Statistics Canada Catalogue no. 99-004-XWE. Ottawa. Released September 11, 2013.

Labour Force by Industry (NAICS Codes 53–91)

Area	Real estate & rental & leasing	Profess., scientific & tech. services	Mgmt of companies & enterprises	Admin. & support, waste mgmt & remed. services	Educational services	Health care & social assistance	Arts, entertain. & recreation	Accomm. & food services	Other services (except public admin.)	Public admin.
					Number					
					Total					
Toronto	35,215	155,435	1,975	72,625	100,865	131,520	32,250	88,295	67,375	60,140
Ontario	133,980	511,020	6,525	309,630	499,690	692,130	144,065	417,675	296,340	458,665
Canada	321,895	1,240,850	17,460	728,330	1,301,435	1,949,650	363,405	1,130,750	807,800	1,261,050
					Males					
Toronto	19,590	86,300	950	38,445	37,230	29,315	16,685	43,225	26,300	28,185
Ontario	72,835	281,420	3,540	172,475	162,765	120,165	75,035	177,240	133,795	236,655
Canada	179,090	688,625	9,380	411,250	424,915	349,430	188,270	469,990	372,940	652,510
					Females					
Toronto	15,625	69,135	1,020	34,175	63,640	102,200	15,560	45,070	41,075	31,960
Ontario	61,145	229,600	2,990	137,155	336,925	571,965	69,030	240,430	162,550	222,015
Canada	142,805	552,225	8,075	317,085	876,515	1,600,220	175,135	660,760	434,865	608,535
					Percent of Labour Force					
					Total					
Toronto	2.6	11.5	0.1	5.4	7.5	9.7	2.4	6.5	5.0	4.5
Ontario	2.0	7.6	0.1	4.6	7.5	10.4	2.2	6.3	4.4	6.9
Canada	1.8	7.1	0.1	4.1	7.4	11.1	2.1	6.4	4.6	7.2
					Males					
Toronto	2.8	12.5	0.1	5.6	5.4	4.2	2.4	6.3	3.8	4.1
Ontario	2.1	8.2	0.1	5.0	4.7	3.5	2.2	5.1	3.9	6.9
Canada	1.9	7.5	0.1	4.5	4.6	3.8	2.0	5.1	4.1	7.1
					Females					
Toronto	2.4	10.5	0.2	5.2	9.7	15.5	2.4	6.8	6.2	4.9
Ontario	1.9	7.1	0.1	4.2	10.4	17.7	2.1	7.4	5.0	6.9
Canada	1.7	6.6	0.1	3.8	10.4	19.1	2.1	7.9	5.2	7.2

Note: Figures are based on total experienced labour force 15 years and over. Experienced labour force refers to persons who, during the week of Sunday, May 1 to Saturday, May 7, 2011, were employed and the unemployed who had last worked for pay or in self-employment in either 2010 or 2011.
Source: Statistics Canada. 2013. 2011 National Household Survey. Statistics Canada Catalogue no. 99-004-XWE. Ottawa. Released September 11, 2013.

Occupation

Area	Mgmt	Business, Finance & Admin.	Natural/ Applied Sciences & Related	Health	Education, Law & Social, Community & Government Services	Art, Culture, Recreation & Sport	Sales & Service	Trades, Transport & Equip. Operators & Related	Natural Resources, Agri. & Related Production	Mfg & Utilities
					Number Total					
Toronto	153,440	256,410	111,835	72,980	174,850	72,110	315,905	121,260	7,235	63,165
Ontario	770,580	1,138,330	494,500	392,695	801,465	206,420	1,550,260	868,515	106,810	350,685
Canada	1,963,600	2,902,045	1,237,775	1,107,200	2,064,675	503,415	4,068,170	2,537,775	397,930	805,040
					Males					
Toronto	90,465	93,030	86,035	18,990	58,640	37,100	149,760	113,555	6,140	37,260
Ontario	474,655	352,505	384,345	78,330	264,570	96,055	673,880	812,280	82,610	233,565
Canada	1,229,460	854,190	966,355	217,520	676,550	232,535	1,745,705	2,385,615	318,945	564,300
					Females					
Toronto	62,980	163,380	25,795	53,990	116,210	35,010	166,150	7,710	1,095	25,905
Ontario	295,920	785,825	110,150	314,370	536,895	110,370	876,380	56,230	24,200	117,115
Canada	734,140	2,047,855	271,415	889,675	1,388,130	270,875	2,322,465	152,165	78,980	240,740
					Percent of Labour Force Total					
Toronto	11.4	19.0	8.3	5.4	13.0	5.3	23.4	9.0	0.5	4.7
Ontario	11.5	17.0	7.4	5.9	12.0	3.1	23.2	13.0	1.6	5.2
Canada	11.2	16.5	7.0	6.3	11.7	2.9	23.1	14.4	2.3	4.6
					Males					
Toronto	13.1	13.5	12.5	2.7	8.5	5.4	21.7	16.4	0.9	5.4
Ontario	13.7	10.2	11.1	2.3	7.7	2.8	19.5	23.5	2.4	6.8
Canada	13.4	9.3	10.5	2.4	7.4	2.5	19.0	26.0	3.5	6.1
					Females					
Toronto	9.6	24.8	3.9	8.2	17.7	5.3	25.2	1.2	0.2	3.9
Ontario	9.2	24.3	3.4	9.7	16.6	3.4	27.2	1.7	0.7	3.6
Canada	8.7	24.4	3.2	10.6	16.5	3.2	27.7	1.8	0.9	2.9

Note: Figures are based on total experienced labour force 15 years and over
Source: Statistics Canada. 2013. 2011 National Household Survey. Statistics Canada Catalogue no. 99-004-XWE. Ottawa. Released September 11, 2013.

Place of Work Status

Area	Worked at Home	Worked Outside Canada	No Fixed Workplace Address	Worked at Usual Place
		Number Total		
Toronto	87,795	6,745	140,480	1,034,130
Ontario	423,790	31,390	670,835	5,170,980
Canada	1,142,640	66,460	1,868,245	13,517,690
		Males		
Toronto	44,715	4,365	97,480	504,180
Ontario	216,900	21,150	486,560	2,524,555
Canada	582,150	47,355	1,400,485	6,604,325
		Females		
Toronto	43,080	2,380	43,005	529,945
Ontario	206,895	10,240	184,275	2,646,420
Canada	560,490	19,100	467,760	6,913,370
		Percent of Labour Force Total		
Toronto	6.9	0.5	11.1	81.5
Ontario	6.7	0.5	10.7	82.1
Canada	6.9	0.4	11.3	81.5
		Males		
Toronto	6.9	0.7	15.0	77.5
Ontario	6.7	0.7	15.0	77.7
Canada	6.7	0.5	16.2	76.5
		Females		
Toronto	7.0	0.4	7.0	85.7
Ontario	6.8	0.3	6.0	86.8
Canada	7.0	0.2	5.9	86.8

Note: Figures are based on total employed labour force 15 years and over.
Source: Statistics Canada. 2013. 2011 National Household Survey. Statistics Canada Catalogue no. 99-004-XWE. Ottawa. Released September 11, 2013.

Mode of Transportation to Work

Area	Car; Truck; Van; as Driver	Car; Truck; Van; as Passenger	Public Transit	Walked	Bicycled	All Other Modes
			Number			
			Total			
Toronto	567,555	53,380	429,275	85,475	25,350	13,585
Ontario	4,235,315	357,110	818,270	299,095	69,885	62,145
Canada	11,393,140	867,050	1,851,525	880,815	201,780	191,625
			Males			
Toronto	345,885	19,495	176,285	38,040	15,740	6,210
Ontario	2,316,680	143,410	340,995	131,765	47,635	30,635
Canada	6,238,835	349,530	788,290	387,580	135,840	104,725
			Females			
Toronto	221,675	33,880	252,985	47,435	9,605	7,375
Ontario	1,918,640	213,700	477,275	167,325	22,250	31,515
Canada	5,154,305	517,520	1,063,235	493,230	65,940	86,900
			Percent of Labour Force			
			Total			
Toronto	48.3	4.5	36.5	7.3	2.2	1.2
Ontario	72.5	6.1	14.0	5.1	1.2	1.1
Canada	74.0	5.6	12.0	5.7	1.3	1.2
			Males			
Toronto	57.5	3.2	29.3	6.3	2.6	1.0
Ontario	76.9	4.8	11.3	4.4	1.6	1.0
Canada	77.9	4.4	9.8	4.8	1.7	1.3
			Females			
Toronto	38.7	5.9	44.2	8.3	1.7	1.3
Ontario	67.8	7.5	16.9	5.9	0.8	1.1
Canada	69.8	7.0	14.4	6.7	0.9	1.2

Note: Figures are based on total employed labour force 15 years and over.
Source: Statistics Canada. 2013. 2011 National Household Survey. Statistics Canada Catalogue no. 99-004-XWE. Ottawa. Released September 11, 2013.

Visible Minority Population Characteristics

Area	Total Minority	South Asian[1]	Chinese	Black	Filipino	Latin American	Arab	SE Asian[2]	West Asian[3]	Korean	Japanese	Multiple[4]
						Number						
						Total						
Toronto	1,264,395	317,100	278,390	218,160	132,445	71,205	28,920	46,825	50,235	37,225	12,315	37,920
Ontario	3,279,565	965,990	629,140	539,205	275,380	172,560	151,645	137,875	122,530	78,290	29,085	96,735
Canada	6,264,750	1,567,400	1,324,750	945,665	619,310	381,280	380,620	312,075	206,840	161,130	87,270	171,935
						Males						
Toronto	598,925	158,835	132,140	97,825	55,315	34,135	15,605	22,920	25,720	17,730	5,450	18,130
Ontario	1,582,480	484,355	301,575	251,295	116,825	83,205	79,620	67,645	62,515	38,045	13,345	46,765
Canada	3,043,010	790,755	632,325	453,005	268,885	186,355	203,485	154,035	105,620	77,165	38,270	83,335
						Females						
Toronto	665,465	158,260	146,250	120,335	77,130	37,065	13,310	23,910	24,515	19,490	6,865	19,785
Ontario	1,697,085	481,635	327,570	287,915	158,555	89,360	72,025	70,230	60,010	40,250	15,740	49,970
Canada	3,221,745	776,650	692,420	492,660	350,425	194,925	177,140	158,045	101,220	83,965	48,990	88,600
						Percent of Population						
						Total						
Toronto	49.1	12.3	10.8	8.5	5.1	2.8	1.1	1.8	2.0	1.4	0.5	1.5
Ontario	25.9	7.6	5.0	4.3	2.2	1.4	1.2	1.1	1.0	0.6	0.2	0.8
Canada	19.1	4.8	4.0	2.9	1.9	1.2	1.2	0.9	0.6	0.5	0.3	0.5
						Males						
Toronto	48.3	12.8	10.7	7.9	4.5	2.8	1.3	1.8	2.1	1.4	0.4	1.5
Ontario	25.6	7.8	4.9	4.1	1.9	1.3	1.3	1.1	1.0	0.6	0.2	0.8
Canada	18.8	4.9	3.9	2.8	1.7	1.2	1.3	1.0	0.7	0.5	0.2	0.5
						Females						
Toronto	49.8	11.8	10.9	9.0	5.8	2.8	1.0	1.8	1.8	1.5	0.5	1.5
Ontario	26.2	7.4	5.1	4.4	2.5	1.4	1.1	1.1	0.9	0.6	0.2	0.8
Canada	19.3	4.7	4.1	3.0	2.1	1.2	1.1	0.9	0.6	0.5	0.3	0.5

Note: The Employment Equity Act defines visible minorities as 'persons, other than Aboriginal peoples, who are non-Caucasian in race or non-white in colour';
(1) Includes 'East Indian,' 'Pakistani,' 'Sri Lankan,' etc.; (2) Includes 'Vietnamese,' 'Cambodian,' 'Malaysian,' 'Laotian,' etc.; (3) Includes 'Iranian,' 'Afghan,' etc.; (4) Includes respondents who reported more than one visible minority group by checking two or more mark-in circles, e.g., 'Black' and 'South Asian.'
Source: Statistics Canada. 2013. 2011 National Household Survey. Statistics Canada Catalogue no. 99-004-XWE. Ottawa. Released September 11, 2013.

PROFILES / Toronto, Ontario

Aboriginal Population

Area	Aboriginal Identity[1]	First Nations (North American Indian) Single Identity[2]	Métis Single Identity	Inuk (Inuit) Single Identity	Multiple Aboriginal Identities[3]	Aboriginal Identities Not Included Elsewhere
			Number			
			Total			
Toronto	19,265	12,990	4,875	305	180	920
Ontario	301,430	201,100	86,020	3,355	2,910	8,040
Canada	1,400,685	851,560	451,795	59,440	11,415	26,475
			Males			
Toronto	8,980	6,060	2,250	165	80	430
Ontario	145,020	96,620	41,755	1,475	1,420	3,750
Canada	682,190	411,785	223,335	29,495	5,525	12,055
			Females			
Toronto	10,290	6,925	2,625	140	95	495
Ontario	156,410	104,485	44,260	1,880	1,490	4,295
Canada	718,500	439,775	228,460	29,950	5,890	14,420
			Percent of Population			
			Total			
Toronto	0.7	0.5	0.2	0.0	0.0	0.0
Ontario	2.4	1.6	0.7	0.0	0.0	0.1
Canada	4.3	2.6	1.4	0.2	0.0	0.1
			Males			
Toronto	0.7	0.5	0.2	0.0	0.0	0.0
Ontario	2.3	1.6	0.7	0.0	0.0	0.1
Canada	4.2	2.5	1.4	0.2	0.0	0.1
			Females			
Toronto	0.8	0.5	0.2	0.0	0.0	0.0
Ontario	2.4	1.6	0.7	0.0	0.0	0.1
Canada	4.3	2.6	1.4	0.2	0.0	0.1

Note: (1) Includes persons who reported being an Aboriginal person, that is, First Nations (North American Indian), Métis or Inuk (Inuit) and/or those who reported Registered or Treaty Indian status, that is registered under the Indian Act of Canada, and/or those who reported membership in a First Nation or Indian band. Aboriginal peoples of Canada are defined in the Constitution Act, 1982, section 35-2 as including the Indian, Inuit and Métis peoples of Canada; (2) Users should be aware that the estimates associated with this variable are more affected than most by the incomplete enumeration of certain Indian reserves and Indian settlements in the National Household Survey (NHS); (3) Includes persons who reported being any two or all three of the following: First Nations (North American Indian), Métis or Inuk (Inuit).
Source: Statistics Canada. 2013. 2011 National Household Survey. Statistics Canada Catalogue no. 99-004-XWE. Ottawa. Released September 11, 2013.

Ethnic Origin

Area	North American Aboriginal	Other North American	European	Caribbean	Latin, Central and South American	African	Asian	Oceania
				Number				
				Total				
Toronto	31,390	313,895	1,288,430	148,755	103,360	126,025	981,770	5,125
Ontario	441,395	3,059,480	8,231,410	396,485	271,545	331,460	2,604,595	19,410
Canada	1,836,035	11,070,455	20,157,965	627,590	544,375	766,735	5,011,225	74,875
				Males				
Toronto	14,860	155,080	623,940	65,410	48,940	59,970	470,315	2,525
Ontario	210,490	1,507,105	4,019,885	181,805	130,035	160,940	1,265,540	9,855
Canada	885,675	5,462,685	9,913,150	291,640	264,635	387,360	2,435,540	37,490
				Females				
Toronto	16,530	158,815	664,490	83,345	54,420	66,060	511,445	2,595
Ontario	230,905	1,552,380	4,211,525	214,675	141,510	170,515	1,339,050	9,555
Canada	950,360	5,607,770	10,244,820	335,945	279,740	379,380	2,575,680	37,385
				Percent of Population				
				Total				
Toronto	1.2	12.2	50.0	5.8	4.0	4.9	38.1	0.2
Ontario	3.5	24.2	65.1	3.1	2.1	2.6	20.6	0.2
Canada	5.6	33.7	61.4	1.9	1.7	2.3	15.3	0.2
				Males				
Toronto	1.2	12.5	50.3	5.3	3.9	4.8	38.0	0.2
Ontario	3.4	24.4	65.0	2.9	2.1	2.6	20.5	0.2
Canada	5.5	33.8	61.3	1.8	1.6	2.4	15.1	0.2
				Females				
Toronto	1.2	11.9	49.7	6.2	4.1	4.9	38.3	0.2
Ontario	3.6	24.0	65.1	3.3	2.2	2.6	20.7	0.1
Canada	5.7	33.6	61.4	2.0	1.7	2.3	15.4	0.2

Note: The sum of the ethnic groups in this table is greater than the total population estimate because a person may report more than one ethnic origin in the NHS.
Source: Statistics Canada. 2013. 2011 National Household Survey. Statistics Canada Catalogue no. 99-004-XWE. Ottawa. Released September 11, 2013.

Religion

Area	Buddhist	Christian	Hindu	Jewish	Muslim	Sikh	Traditional (Aboriginal) Spirituality	Other Religions	No Religious Affiliation
				Number Total					
Toronto	68,885	1,394,210	145,035	98,690	212,345	20,405	850	12,950	622,655
Ontario	163,750	8,167,295	366,720	195,540	581,950	179,765	15,905	53,080	2,927,790
Canada	366,830	22,102,745	497,965	329,495	1,053,945	454,965	64,935	130,835	7,850,605
				Males					
Toronto	30,910	637,595	72,750	47,925	106,425	10,185	400	5,945	327,085
Ontario	75,355	3,839,925	183,580	95,795	293,925	90,515	7,600	23,555	1,571,195
Canada	168,465	10,497,775	250,435	161,265	540,555	229,435	31,805	57,745	4,225,645
				Females					
Toronto	37,975	756,610	72,285	50,765	105,920	10,220	450	7,005	295,570
Ontario	88,395	4,327,365	183,140	99,740	288,025	89,250	8,310	29,525	1,356,600
Canada	198,365	11,604,975	247,525	168,235	513,395	225,530	33,135	73,090	3,624,965
				Percent of Population Total					
Toronto	2.7	54.1	5.6	3.8	8.2	0.8	0.0	0.5	24.2
Ontario	1.3	64.6	2.9	1.5	4.6	1.4	0.1	0.4	23.1
Canada	1.1	67.3	1.5	1.0	3.2	1.4	0.2	0.4	23.9
				Males					
Toronto	2.5	51.5	5.9	3.9	8.6	0.8	0.0	0.5	26.4
Ontario	1.2	62.1	3.0	1.5	4.8	1.5	0.1	0.4	25.4
Canada	1.0	64.9	1.5	1.0	3.3	1.4	0.2	0.4	26.1
				Females					
Toronto	2.8	56.6	5.4	3.8	7.9	0.8	0.0	0.5	22.1
Ontario	1.4	66.9	2.8	1.5	4.5	1.4	0.1	0.5	21.0
Canada	1.2	69.5	1.5	1.0	3.1	1.4	0.2	0.4	21.7

Note: Religion refers to the person's self-identification as having a connection or affiliation with any religious denomination, group, body, sect, cult or other religiously defined community or system of belief. Religion is not limited to formal membership in a religious organization or group. Persons without a religious connection or affiliation can self-identify as atheist, agnostic or humanist, or can provide another applicable response.
Source: Statistics Canada. 2013. 2011 National Household Survey. Statistics Canada Catalogue no. 99-004-XWE. Ottawa. Released September 11, 2013.

Religion—Christian Denominations

Area	Anglican	Baptist	Catholic	Christian Orthodox	Lutheran	Pentecostal	Presbyterian	United Church	Other Christian
				Number Total					
Toronto	99,655	35,310	725,565	111,430	15,645	41,330	38,140	77,070	250,065
Ontario	774,560	244,650	3,976,610	297,710	163,460	213,945	319,585	952,465	1,224,300
Canada	1,631,845	635,840	12,810,705	550,690	478,185	478,705	472,385	2,007,610	3,036,780
				Males					
Toronto	44,835	15,325	335,060	53,890	6,980	16,915	17,505	33,285	113,795
Ontario	355,175	112,285	1,895,940	145,825	75,225	94,955	148,535	435,255	576,730
Canada	752,945	293,905	6,167,290	270,205	221,525	217,850	218,955	912,545	1,442,550
				Females					
Toronto	54,815	19,980	390,500	57,535	8,660	24,415	20,635	43,785	136,270
Ontario	419,390	132,370	2,080,665	151,885	88,230	118,990	171,050	517,210	647,570
Canada	878,900	341,940	6,643,415	280,485	256,660	260,850	253,430	1,095,065	1,594,230
				Percent of Population Total					
Toronto	3.9	1.4	28.2	4.3	0.6	1.6	1.5	3.0	9.7
Ontario	6.1	1.9	31.4	2.4	1.3	1.7	2.5	7.5	9.7
Canada	5.0	1.9	39.0	1.7	1.5	1.5	1.4	6.1	9.2
				Males					
Toronto	3.6	1.2	27.0	4.3	0.6	1.4	1.4	2.7	9.2
Ontario	5.7	1.8	30.7	2.4	1.2	1.5	2.4	7.0	9.3
Canada	4.7	1.8	38.2	1.7	1.4	1.3	1.4	5.6	8.9
				Females					
Toronto	4.1	1.5	29.2	4.3	0.6	1.8	1.5	3.3	10.2
Ontario	6.5	2.0	32.2	2.3	1.4	1.8	2.6	8.0	10.0
Canada	5.3	2.0	39.8	1.7	1.5	1.6	1.5	6.6	9.6

Note: Religion refers to the person's self-identification as having a connection or affiliation with any religious denomination, group, body, sect, cult or other religiously defined community or system of belief. Religion is not limited to formal membership in a religious organization or group. Persons without a religious connection or affiliation can self-identify as atheist, agnostic or humanist, or can provide another applicable response.
Source: Statistics Canada. 2013. 2011 National Household Survey. Statistics Canada Catalogue no. 99-004-XWE. Ottawa. Released September 11, 2013.

PROFILES / Toronto, Ontario

Immigrant Status and Period of Immigration

Area	Non-Immigrants[1]	Immigrants All	Before 1971	1971 to 1980	1981 to 1990	1991 to 2000	2001 to 2005	2006 to 2011	Non-Permanent Residents[3]
Number									
Total									
Toronto	1,258,870	1,252,215	190,000	150,585	185,680	314,470	194,955	216,525	64,945
Ontario	8,906,000	3,611,365	723,030	464,380	538,285	866,220	518,405	501,060	134,425
Canada	25,720,175	6,775,765	1,261,055	870,775	949,890	1,539,050	992,070	1,162,915	356,385
Males									
Toronto	627,405	580,795	86,745	68,700	87,080	144,865	91,890	101,515	31,025
Ontario	4,410,240	1,706,385	341,820	217,990	258,095	408,270	245,850	234,360	64,825
Canada	12,753,235	3,231,370	605,430	416,670	454,570	724,905	474,545	555,245	178,515
Females									
Toronto	631,460	671,420	103,255	81,880	98,605	169,610	103,065	115,010	33,915
Ontario	4,495,765	1,904,985	381,210	246,390	280,190	457,950	272,550	266,695	69,600
Canada	12,966,935	3,544,400	655,625	454,105	495,325	814,145	517,530	607,670	177,870
Percent of Population									
Total									
Toronto	48.9	48.6	7.4	5.8	7.2	12.2	7.6	8.4	2.5
Ontario	70.4	28.5	5.7	3.7	4.3	6.8	4.1	4.0	1.1
Canada	78.3	20.6	3.8	2.7	2.9	4.7	3.0	3.5	1.1
Males									
Toronto	50.6	46.9	7.0	5.5	7.0	11.7	7.4	8.2	2.5
Ontario	71.3	27.6	5.5	3.5	4.2	6.6	4.0	3.8	1.0
Canada	78.9	20.0	3.7	2.6	2.8	4.5	2.9	3.4	1.1
Females									
Toronto	47.2	50.2	7.7	6.1	7.4	12.7	7.7	8.6	2.5
Ontario	69.5	29.4	5.9	3.8	4.3	7.1	4.2	4.1	1.1
Canada	77.7	21.2	3.9	2.7	3.0	4.9	3.1	3.6	1.1

Note: (1) Non-immigrant refers to a person who is a Canadian citizen by birth; (2) Immigrant refers to a person who is or has ever been a landed immigrant/permanent resident. This person has been granted the right to live in Canada permanently by immigration authorities. Some immigrants have resided in Canada for a number of years, while others have arrived recently. Some immigrants are Canadian citizens, while others are not. Most immigrants are born outside Canada, but a small number are born in Canada. In the 2011 National Household Survey, 'Immigrants' includes immigrants who landed in Canada prior to May 10, 2011; (3) Non-permanent resident refers to a person from another country who has a work or study permit, or who is a refugee claimant, and any non-Canadian-born family member living in Canada with them.
Source: Statistics Canada. 2013. 2011 National Household Survey. Statistics Canada Catalogue no. 99-004-XWE. Ottawa. Released September 11, 2013.

Mother Tongue

Area	English	French	Non-official Language	English & French	English & Non-official Language	French & Non-official Language	English, French & Non-official Language
Number							
Total							
Toronto	1,317,025	32,665	1,154,245	6,345	73,000	3,715	2,090
Ontario	8,677,040	493,300	3,264,435	46,605	219,425	13,645	7,615
Canada	18,858,980	7,054,975	6,567,680	144,685	396,330	74,430	24,095
Males							
Toronto	645,720	15,305	542,440	2,985	34,965	1,715	995
Ontario	4,276,970	232,785	1,562,190	21,805	106,790	6,285	3,495
Canada	9,345,225	3,452,380	3,157,785	69,975	192,000	36,535	11,965
Females							
Toronto	671,305	17,365	611,800	3,365	38,035	2,000	1,090
Ontario	4,400,065	260,510	1,702,240	24,795	112,635	7,365	4,115
Canada	9,513,750	3,602,590	3,409,895	74,710	204,330	37,890	12,130
Percent of Population							
Total							
Toronto	50.9	1.3	44.6	0.2	2.8	0.1	0.1
Ontario	68.2	3.9	25.7	0.4	1.7	0.1	0.1
Canada	56.9	21.3	19.8	0.4	1.2	0.2	0.1
Males							
Toronto	51.9	1.2	43.6	0.2	2.8	0.1	0.1
Ontario	68.9	3.7	25.2	0.4	1.7	0.1	0.1
Canada	57.5	21.2	19.4	0.4	1.2	0.2	0.1
Females							
Toronto	49.9	1.3	45.5	0.3	2.8	0.1	0.1
Ontario	67.6	4.0	26.1	0.4	1.7	0.1	0.1
Canada	56.4	21.4	20.2	0.4	1.2	0.2	0.1

Note: Figures cover total population excluding institutional residents.
Source: Statistics Canada. 2012. Census Profile. 2011 Census. Statistics Canada Catalogue no. 98-316-XWE. Ottawa. Released October 24 2012.
http://www12.statcan.gc.ca/census-recensement/2011/dp-pd/prof/index.cfm?Lang=E

Language Spoken Most Often at Home

Area	English	French	Non-official Language	English & French	English & Non-official Language	French & Non-official Language	English, French & Non-official Language
			Number				
			Total				
Toronto	1,657,835	15,575	733,125	4,940	173,030	1,580	3,010
Ontario	10,044,810	284,115	1,827,870	37,955	509,105	6,370	11,845
Canada	21,457,075	6,827,865	3,673,865	131,205	875,135	109,700	46,330
			Males				
Toronto	804,725	7,340	344,995	2,290	82,735	690	1,350
Ontario	4,930,610	133,495	872,860	17,250	248,050	2,855	5,225
Canada	10,585,620	3,348,235	1,767,310	63,475	425,370	53,010	22,845
			Females				
Toronto	853,105	8,240	388,135	2,645	90,295	885	1,660
Ontario	5,114,200	150,620	955,010	20,705	261,055	3,520	6,620
Canada	10,871,455	3,479,625	1,906,555	67,730	449,765	56,690	23,485
			Percent of Population				
			Total				
Toronto	64.0	0.6	28.3	0.2	6.7	0.1	0.1
Ontario	79.0	2.2	14.4	0.3	4.0	0.1	0.1
Canada	64.8	20.6	11.1	0.4	2.6	0.3	0.1
			Males				
Toronto	64.7	0.6	27.7	0.2	6.7	0.1	0.1
Ontario	79.4	2.1	14.1	0.3	4.0	0.0	0.1
Canada	65.1	20.6	10.9	0.4	2.6	0.3	0.1
			Females				
Toronto	63.4	0.6	28.9	0.2	6.7	0.1	0.1
Ontario	78.5	2.3	14.7	0.3	4.0	0.1	0.1
Canada	64.5	20.6	11.3	0.4	2.7	0.3	0.1

Note: Figures cover total population excluding institutional residents.
Source: Statistics Canada. 2012. Census Profile. 2011 Census. Statistics Canada Catalogue no. 98-316-XWE. Ottawa. Released October 24 2012.
http://www12.statcan.gc.ca/census-recensement/2011/dp-pd/prof/index.cfm?Lang=E

Knowledge of Official Languages

Area	English Only	French Only	English & French	Neither English nor French
		Number		
		Total		
Toronto	2,222,700	2,975	227,375	136,035
Ontario	10,984,360	42,980	1,395,805	298,920
Canada	22,564,665	4,165,015	5,795,570	595,920
		Males		
Toronto	1,087,900	1,270	100,570	54,390
Ontario	5,445,050	18,805	627,725	118,765
Canada	11,222,185	1,925,340	2,876,560	241,790
		Females		
Toronto	1,134,795	1,710	126,805	81,650
Ontario	5,539,310	24,175	768,085	180,155
Canada	11,342,485	2,239,680	2,919,005	354,135
		Percent of Population		
		Total		
Toronto	85.8	0.1	8.8	5.3
Ontario	86.3	0.3	11.0	2.3
Canada	68.1	12.6	17.5	1.8
		Males		
Toronto	87.4	0.1	8.1	4.4
Ontario	87.7	0.3	10.1	1.9
Canada	69.0	11.8	17.7	1.5
		Females		
Toronto	84.4	0.1	9.4	6.1
Ontario	85.1	0.4	11.8	2.8
Canada	67.3	13.3	17.3	2.1

Note: Figures cover total population excluding institutional residents.
Source: Statistics Canada. 2012. Census Profile. 2011 Census. Statistics Canada Catalogue no. 98-316-XWE. Ottawa. Released October 24 2012.
http://www12.statcan.gc.ca/census-recensement/2011/dp-pd/prof/index.cfm?Lang=E

Trois-Rivières, Québec

Background

Trois-Rivières is located on the north shore of the St. Lawrence River in Québec. The city is part of the Québec City–Windsor Corridor, the most densely populated and industrialized region in Canada. Trois-Rivières is approximately halfway between Montréal and Québec City, the province's capital. The city's name is French for "three rivers."

Trois-Rivières is Canada's oldest industrial city and was the second permanent settlement in New France. Originally set up as a permanent fur trading post in 1634, Trois-Rivières became an iron ore producer in 1734. A railway was built in 1879 to accommodate the city's booming lumber industry. By the 1920s, Trois-Rivières was the pulp-and-paper capital of the world. The city's natural resource sectors shifted in the 1960s and tourism, culture and education became primary industries. Throughout the 1980s and 1990s, Trois-Rivières was the unemployment capital of Canada.

Since the city's celebration of its 375th anniversary in 2009, Trois-Rivières' boom-and-bust cycles have ended. The city's award-winning downtown (Vieux-Trois-Rivières) is a blend of cafés, restaurants, art galleries and museums. The University of Québec's Trois-Rivières campus enrols more than 11,000 students. Every year, the city hosts events and festivities such as the International Poetry Festival, the Encore International Dance Festival and *Le FestiVoix de Trois-Rivières*, a music festival.

Today Trois-Rivières is a city with multi-million-dollar real estate developments and a thriving wind energy manufacturing industry. In 2012, the city announced investment of nearly $3 million in the channelling of Pointe-du-Lac wastewater to Trois-Rivières' main sewer system. Marmen is based in Trois-Rivières and is one of North America's top manufacturers of wind towers. The company employs nearly 1,000 residents at its five plants in Trois-Rivières and Matane.

Trois-Rivières has summer highs of plus 24.27 degrees Celsius, winter lows of minus 15.27 degrees Celsius, and an average rainfall just over 858 mm per year.

Rankings
- The International Downtown Association ranked Trois-Rivières' historic downtown core one of the best in the world. The 600-member association rated cities worldwide on criteria such as innovation, replication, representation, sustainability and outcome. *International Downtown Association (Washington, DC), "Downtown Achievement Award," 2005*
- Trois-Rivières received a Canadian Heritage designation in 2009 and was recognized as the year's Cultural Capital of Canada for cities with populations of 125,000 residents or more. The city's 375th anniversary celebration project, "Trois-Rivières, City of History and Culture, 1634-2009," received special mention for promoting cultural identity and economic development within the municipality. *Department of Canadian Heritage, Cultural Capitals of Canada national award program, 2009*
- Trois-Rivières was selected as one of Canada's "Weather Winners" by Environment Canada. Out of 100 major Canadian cities, Trois-Rivières ranked #14 for highest average snow depth in January (39.58 cm) and #15 for most deep snow cover days of 10 cm or more (118 days). Québec City was ranked #1 for highest average snow depth (57.84 cm) and Yellowknife (NWT) had most deep snow cover days (165 days). *Environment Canada, Canadian Cities are Weather Winners!, May 29, 2012*

PROFILES / Trois-Rivières, Québec

Population Growth and Density

Area	Population in 2001	Population in 2006	Population in 2011	Population Change 2001–2006	Population Change 2006–2011	Land Area (sq. km)	Population Density per sq. km
Trois-Rivières	122,395	126,293	131,338	3.2	4.0	288.90	454.6
Québec	7,237,479	7,546,131	7,903,001	4.3	4.7	1,356,547.02	5.8
Canada	30,007,094	31,612,897	33,476,688	5.4	5.9	8,965,121.42	3.7

Source: Statistics Canada. 2012. Census Profile. 2011 Census. Statistics Canada Catalogue no. 98-316-XWE. Ottawa. Released October 24 2012.
http://www12.statcan.gc.ca/census-recensement/2011/dp-pd/prof/index.cfm?Lang=E;
Statistics Canada 2007. 2006 Community Profiles. 2006 Census. Statistics Canada Catalogue no. 92-591-XWE. Ottawa. Released March 13 2007.
http://www12.statcan.ca/census-recensement/2006/dp-pd/prof/92-591/index.cfm?Lang=E

Gender

Area	Males	Females
Number		
Trois-Rivières	63,205	68,135
Québec	3,875,860	4,027,140
Canada	16,414,225	17,062,460
Percent of Population		
Trois-Rivières	48.1	51.9
Québec	49.0	51.0
Canada	49.0	51.0

Source: Statistics Canada. 2012. Census Profile. 2011 Census. Statistics Canada Catalogue no. 98-316-XWE. Ottawa. Released October 24 2012.
http://www12.statcan.gc.ca/census-recensement/2011/dp-pd/prof/index.cfm?Lang=E

Marital Status

Area	Married[1]	Living Common-law	Single[2]	Separated	Divorced	Widowed
Number — Total						
Trois-Rivières	34,800	25,880	34,120	1,615	9,540	7,925
Québec	2,353,770	1,391,550	1,942,090	105,195	463,830	387,945
Canada	12,941,960	3,142,525	7,816,045	698,240	1,686,035	1,584,530
Males						
Trois-Rivières	17,410	12,930	17,845	685	3,835	1,520
Québec	1,177,720	697,695	1,045,540	46,465	188,265	77,430
Canada	6,470,300	1,575,495	4,206,320	299,655	680,415	310,940
Females						
Trois-Rivières	17,390	12,950	16,270	925	5,705	6,395
Québec	1,176,050	693,850	896,545	58,720	275,565	310,515
Canada	6,471,660	1,567,035	3,609,730	398,585	1,005,620	1,273,590
Percent of Population — Total						
Trois-Rivières	30.6	22.7	30.0	1.4	8.4	7.0
Québec	35.4	20.9	29.2	1.6	7.0	5.8
Canada	46.4	11.3	28.0	2.5	6.0	5.7
Males						
Trois-Rivières	32.1	23.8	32.9	1.3	7.1	2.8
Québec	36.4	21.6	32.3	1.4	5.8	2.4
Canada	47.8	11.6	31.1	2.2	5.0	2.3
Females						
Trois-Rivières	29.2	21.7	27.3	1.6	9.6	10.7
Québec	34.5	20.3	26.3	1.7	8.1	9.1
Canada	45.2	10.9	25.2	2.8	7.0	8.9

Note: (1) and not separated, (2) never legally married
Source: Statistics Canada. 2012. Census Profile. 2011 Census. Statistics Canada Catalogue no. 98-316-XWE. Ottawa. Released October 24 2012.
http://www12.statcan.gc.ca/census-recensement/2011/dp-pd/prof/index.cfm?Lang=E

Age Characteristics: 0 to 49 Years

Area	0 to 4 Years	5 to 9 Years	10 to 14 Years	15 to 19 Years	20 to 24 Years	25 to 29 Years	30 to 34 Years	35 to 39 Years	40 to 44 Years	45 to 49 Years
					Number					
					Total					
Trois-Rivières	5,975	5,465	6,035	8,020	8,740	7,970	7,750	6,640	7,475	10,095
Québec	440,840	399,575	418,205	491,980	489,185	490,665	531,445	498,225	520,805	623,575
Canada	1,877,095	1,809,895	1,920,355	2,178,135	2,187,450	2,169,590	2,162,905	2,173,930	2,324,875	2,675,130
					Males					
Trois-Rivières	3,085	2,825	3,055	3,980	4,375	4,095	3,990	3,360	3,685	4,920
Québec	225,525	203,675	213,540	249,960	246,850	245,695	264,980	249,610	261,120	311,320
Canada	961,150	925,965	983,995	1,115,845	1,108,775	1,077,275	1,058,810	1,064,200	1,141,720	1,318,715
					Females					
Trois-Rivières	2,890	2,635	2,980	4,040	4,370	3,880	3,760	3,285	3,795	5,175
Québec	215,320	195,900	204,665	242,020	242,340	244,970	266,460	248,615	259,690	312,250
Canada	915,945	883,935	936,360	1,062,295	1,078,670	1,092,315	1,104,095	1,109,735	1,183,155	1,356,420
					Percent of Population					
					Total					
Trois-Rivières	4.5	4.2	4.6	6.1	6.7	6.1	5.9	5.1	5.7	7.7
Québec	5.6	5.1	5.3	6.2	6.2	6.2	6.7	6.3	6.6	7.9
Canada	5.6	5.4	5.7	6.5	6.5	6.5	6.5	6.5	6.9	8.0
					Males					
Trois-Rivières	4.9	4.5	4.8	6.3	6.9	6.5	6.3	5.3	5.8	7.8
Québec	5.8	5.3	5.5	6.4	6.4	6.3	6.8	6.4	6.7	8.0
Canada	5.9	5.6	6.0	6.8	6.8	6.6	6.5	6.5	7.0	8.0
					Females					
Trois-Rivières	4.2	3.9	4.4	5.9	6.4	5.7	5.5	4.8	5.6	7.6
Québec	5.3	4.9	5.1	6.0	6.0	6.1	6.6	6.2	6.4	7.8
Canada	5.4	5.2	5.5	6.2	6.3	6.4	6.5	6.5	6.9	7.9

Source: Statistics Canada. 2012. Census Profile. 2011 Census. Statistics Canada Catalogue no. 98-316-XWE. Ottawa. Released October 24 2012.
http://www12.statcan.gc.ca/census-recensement/2011/dp-pd/prof/index.cfm?Lang=E

Age Characteristics: 50 Years and Over, and Median Age

Area	50 to 54 Years	55 to 59 Years	60 to 64 Years	65 to 69 Years	70 to 74 Years	75 to 79 Years	80 to 84 Years	85 Years and Over	Median Age
				Number					
				Total					
Trois-Rivières	11,170	10,515	9,515	7,985	5,860	4,830	3,870	3,425	45.9
Québec	648,695	579,280	512,830	403,210	291,755	232,355	176,420	153,945	41.9
Canada	2,658,965	2,340,635	2,052,670	1,521,715	1,153,065	922,700	702,070	645,515	40.6
				Males					
Trois-Rivières	5,425	5,095	4,590	3,705	2,640	2,020	1,440	915	43.9
Québec	320,695	285,295	250,675	194,305	135,830	101,675	69,170	45,945	40.7
Canada	1,309,030	1,147,300	1,002,690	738,010	543,435	417,945	291,085	208,300	39.6
				Females					
Trois-Rivières	5,750	5,420	4,925	4,275	3,215	2,805	2,425	2,510	47.5
Québec	327,995	293,990	262,155	208,905	155,925	130,680	107,250	108,005	43.0
Canada	1,349,940	1,193,335	1,049,985	783,705	609,630	504,755	410,985	437,215	41.5
				Percent of Population					
				Total					
Trois-Rivières	8.5	8.0	7.2	6.1	4.5	3.7	2.9	2.6	–
Québec	8.2	7.3	6.5	5.1	3.7	2.9	2.2	1.9	–
Canada	7.9	7.0	6.1	4.5	3.4	2.8	2.1	1.9	–
				Males					
Trois-Rivières	8.6	8.1	7.3	5.9	4.2	3.2	2.3	1.4	–
Québec	8.3	7.4	6.5	5.0	3.5	2.6	1.8	1.2	–
Canada	8.0	7.0	6.1	4.5	3.3	2.5	1.8	1.3	–
				Females					
Trois-Rivières	8.4	8.0	7.2	6.3	4.7	4.1	3.6	3.7	–
Québec	8.1	7.3	6.5	5.2	3.9	3.2	2.7	2.7	–
Canada	7.9	7.0	6.2	4.6	3.6	3.0	2.4	2.6	–

Source: Statistics Canada. 2012. Census Profile. 2011 Census. Statistics Canada Catalogue no. 98-316-XWE. Ottawa. Released October 24 2012.
http://www12.statcan.gc.ca/census-recensement/2011/dp-pd/prof/index.cfm?Lang=E

PROFILES / Trois-Rivières, Québec

Private Households by Household Size

Area	1 Person	2 Persons	3 Persons	4 Persons	5 Persons	6 or More Persons	Average Number of Persons in Private Households
				Households			
Trois-Rivières	23,125	22,260	7,710	6,050	1,690	555	2.1
Québec	1,094,410	1,181,240	496,140	421,080	142,555	59,920	2.3
Canada	3,673,310	4,544,820	2,081,900	1,903,300	724,405	392,885	2.5
				Percent of Households			
Trois-Rivières	37.7	36.3	12.6	9.9	2.8	0.9	–
Québec	32.2	34.8	14.6	12.4	4.2	1.8	–
Canada	27.6	34.1	15.6	14.3	5.4	2.9	–

Source: Statistics Canada. 2012. Census Profile. 2011 Census. Statistics Canada Catalogue no. 98-316-XWE. Ottawa. Released October 24 2012.
http://www12.statcan.gc.ca/census-recensement/2011/dp-pd/prof/index.cfm?Lang=E

Dwelling Type

Area	Single-detached House	Semi-detached House	Row House	Apartment: Building with Five or More Storeys	Apartment: Building with Fewer Than Five Storeys	Duplex Apartment	Movable Dwelling	Other Single-attached House
				Number				
Trois-Rivières	26,320	3,885	1,510	1,320	22,855	5,020	200	275
Québec	1,560,405	171,435	86,040	171,115	1,103,845	263,860	22,995	15,645
Canada	7,329,150	646,245	791,600	1,234,770	2,397,550	704,485	183,510	33,310
				Percent of Dwellings				
Trois-Rivières	42.9	6.3	2.5	2.2	37.2	8.2	0.3	0.4
Québec	46.0	5.0	2.5	5.0	32.5	7.8	0.7	0.5
Canada	55.0	4.9	5.9	9.3	18.0	5.3	1.4	0.3

Source: Statistics Canada. 2012. Census Profile. 2011 Census. Statistics Canada Catalogue no. 98-316-XWE. Ottawa. Released October 24 2012.
http://www12.statcan.gc.ca/census-recensement/2011/dp-pd/prof/index.cfm?Lang=E

Shelter Costs

	Owned Dwellings					Rented Dwellings		
Area	Number	Median Value[1] ($)	Average Value[1] ($)	Median Monthly Costs[2] ($)	Average Monthly Costs[2] ($)	Number	Median Monthly Costs[3] ($)	Average Monthly Costs[3] ($)
Trois-Rivières	34,010	150,221	165,879	709	798	27,345	533	584
Québec	2,056,665	214,537	249,427	841	936	1,308,465	643	685
Canada	9,013,410	280,552	345,182	978	1,141	4,060,385	784	848

Note: All figures cover non-farm, non-reserve private dwellings; (1) Refers to the dollar amount expected by the owner if the dwelling were to be sold; (2) Includes all shelter expenses paid by households that own their dwellings, such as the mortgage payment and the costs of electricity, heat, water and other municipal services, property taxes and condominium fees; (3) Includes all shelter expenses paid by households that rent their dwellings, such as the monthly rent and the costs of electricity, heat and municipal services.
Source: Statistics Canada. 2013. 2011 National Household Survey. Statistics Canada Catalogue no. 99-004-XWE. Ottawa. Released September 11, 2013.

Occupied Private Dwellings by Period of Construction

Area	1960 or Before	1961 to 1980	1981 to 1990	1991 to 2000	2001 to 2005	2006 to 2011
			Number			
Trois-Rivières	16,350	20,450	10,450	6,975	2,925	4,235
Québec	946,900	1,115,455	533,790	353,355	206,035	239,685
Canada	3,273,105	4,152,715	2,112,110	1,707,880	1,031,020	1,042,430
			Percent of Dwellings			
Trois-Rivières	26.6	33.3	17.0	11.4	4.8	6.9
Québec	27.9	32.9	15.7	10.4	6.1	7.1
Canada	24.6	31.2	15.9	12.8	7.7	7.8

Note: Figures cover non-farm, non-reserve private dwellings and includes data up to May 10, 2011.
Source: Statistics Canada. 2013. 2011 National Household Survey. Statistics Canada Catalogue no. 99-004-XWE. Ottawa. Released September 11, 2013.

Educational Attainment

Area	No Certificate, Diploma or Degree	High School Diploma or Equivalent[1]	Apprenticeship or Trades Certificate or Diploma[2]	College, CÉGEP or Other Non-University Certificate or Diploma	University Certificate or Diploma Below the Bachelor Level[3]	Bachelor's Degree	University Certificate, Diploma or Degree Above Bachelor Level[4]
				Number			
				Total			
Trois-Rivières	22,435	24,495	19,465	20,630	5,275	11,650	5,675
Québec	1,436,025	1,404,755	1,049,470	1,075,855	305,330	766,100	437,050
Canada	5,485,400	6,968,935	2,950,685	4,970,020	1,200,130	3,634,425	2,049,930
				Males			
Trois-Rivières	9,975	11,170	12,270	9,065	2,105	5,120	3,095
Québec	714,090	650,660	635,435	472,360	126,565	343,535	227,990
Canada	2,742,875	3,305,415	1,928,970	2,118,430	513,235	1,643,080	1,043,350
				Females			
Trois-Rivières	12,460	13,320	7,200	11,565	3,165	6,530	2,575
Québec	721,930	754,095	414,035	603,495	178,765	422,565	209,065
Canada	2,742,520	3,663,515	1,021,715	2,851,595	686,890	1,991,345	1,006,585
				Percent of Population			
				Total			
Trois-Rivières	20.5	22.3	17.8	18.8	4.8	10.6	5.2
Québec	22.2	21.7	16.2	16.6	4.7	11.8	6.8
Canada	20.1	25.6	10.8	18.2	4.4	13.3	7.5
				Males			
Trois-Rivières	18.9	21.2	23.2	17.2	4.0	9.7	5.9
Québec	22.5	20.5	20.0	14.9	4.0	10.8	7.2
Canada	20.6	24.9	14.5	15.9	3.9	12.4	7.8
				Females			
Trois-Rivières	21.9	23.4	12.7	20.4	5.6	11.5	4.5
Québec	21.9	22.8	12.5	18.3	5.4	12.8	6.3
Canada	19.6	26.2	7.3	20.4	4.9	14.3	7.2

Note: Figures cover total population aged 15 years and over by highest certificate, diploma or degree; (1) Includes persons who have graduated from a secondary school or equivalent. It excludes persons with a postsecondary certificate, diploma or degree; (2) Includes Registered Apprenticeship certificates (including Certificate of Qualification, Journeyperson's designation) and other trades certificates or diplomas such as pre-employment or vocational certificates and diplomas from brief trade programs completed at community colleges, institutes of technology, vocational centres, and similar institutions; (3) Comparisons with other data sources suggest that the category 'University certificate or diploma below the bachelor's level' was over-reported in the NHS. This category likely includes some responses that are actually college certificates or diplomas, bachelor's degrees or other types of education (e.g., university transfer programs, bachelor's programs completed in other countries, incomplete bachelor's programs, non-university professional designations). We recommend users interpret the results for the 'University certificate or diploma below the bachelor's level' category with caution; (4) 'University certificate or diploma above bachelor level' includes the categories: 'Degree in medicine, dentistry, veterinary medicine or optometry,' 'Master's degree' and 'Earned doctorate.'
Source: Statistics Canada. 2013. 2011 National Household Survey. Statistics Canada Catalogue no. 99-004-XWE. Ottawa. Released September 11, 2013.

Household Income Distribution

Area	Less than $10,000	$10,000 to $19,999	$20,000 to $29,999	$30,000 to $39,999	$40,000 to $49,999	$50,000 to $59,999	$60,000 to $79,999	$80,000 to $99,999	$100,000 to $124,999	$125,000 to $149,999	$150,000 and Over
					Households						
Trois-Rivières	3,720	9,275	7,185	7,385	6,415	5,405	8,130	5,025	3,975	2,285	2,580
Québec	179,790	377,210	353,470	382,000	343,730	302,595	483,085	344,435	267,995	148,950	211,965
Canada	626,705	1,141,945	1,193,925	1,271,675	1,206,800	1,102,120	1,865,280	1,458,240	1,260,770	802,555	1,389,240
					Percent of Households						
Trois-Rivières	6.1	15.1	11.7	12.0	10.4	8.8	13.2	8.2	6.5	3.7	4.2
Québec	5.3	11.1	10.4	11.3	10.1	8.9	14.2	10.1	7.9	4.4	6.2
Canada	4.7	8.6	9.0	9.5	9.1	8.3	14.0	10.9	9.5	6.0	10.4

Note: Household income is the sum of the total incomes of all members of that household. Total income refers to monetary receipts from certain sources, before income taxes and deductions, during calendar year 2010.
Source: Statistics Canada. 2013. 2011 National Household Survey. Statistics Canada Catalogue no. 99-004-XWE. Ottawa. Released September 11, 2013.

Median and Average Household and Economic Family Income

Area	Median Household Income ($)	Average Household Income ($)	Median After-tax Household Income ($)	Average After-tax Household Income ($)	Median Economic Family Income ($)	Average Economic Family Income ($)	Median After-tax Economic Family Income ($)	Average After-tax Economic Family Income ($)
Trois-Rivières	44,976	57,133	40,499	48,285	62,962	74,758	55,248	62,809
Québec	51,842	66,205	45,968	55,121	68,344	82,045	59,560	68,091
Canada	61,072	79,102	54,089	66,149	76,511	94,125	67,044	78,517

Note: Figures cover household and economic familiy income in 2010. A household is defined as a person or a group of persons (other than foreign residents) who occupy the same private dwelling and do not have a usual place of residence elsewhere in Canada. Every person is a member of one and only one household. An economic family is defined as a group of two or more persons who live in the same dwelling and are related to each other by blood, marriage, common-law, adoption or a foster relationship. A couple may be of opposite or same sex.
Source: Statistics Canada. 2013. 2011 National Household Survey. Statistics Canada Catalogue no. 99-004-XWE. Ottawa. Released September 11, 2013.

PROFILES / Trois-Rivières, Québec

Individual Income Distribution

Area	Less than $10,000	$10,000 to $19,999	$20,000 to $29,999	$30,000 to $39,999	$40,000 to $49,999	$50,000 to $59,999	$60,000 to $79,999	$80,000 to $99,999	$100,000 to $124,999	$125,000 and Over
Number — Total										
Trois-Rivières	17,105	25,615	16,815	14,690	10,380	6,715	7,680	3,160	1,560	1,515
Québec	1,005,600	1,309,515	941,630	866,290	653,400	449,185	515,815	211,070	109,975	120,915
Canada	4,492,040	4,835,710	3,670,020	3,180,360	2,603,520	1,921,650	2,437,440	1,302,045	693,580	782,135
Males										
Trois-Rivières	6,970	9,415	7,885	7,440	5,650	3,950	4,895	2,410	1,235	1,265
Québec	441,455	516,150	427,295	432,625	345,950	256,700	313,880	143,785	80,000	91,475
Canada	1,936,365	1,864,880	1,588,260	1,522,190	1,333,510	1,079,780	1,473,145	823,720	492,905	599,905
Females										
Trois-Rivières	10,130	16,200	8,930	7,250	4,730	2,770	2,785	745	320	250
Québec	564,150	793,365	514,335	433,670	307,455	192,485	201,935	67,275	29,980	29,440
Canada	2,555,675	2,970,825	2,081,760	1,658,170	1,270,010	841,870	964,300	478,330	200,680	182,230
Percent of Population — Total										
Trois-Rivières	16.3	24.3	16.0	14.0	9.9	6.4	7.3	3.0	1.5	1.4
Québec	16.3	21.2	15.2	14.0	10.6	7.3	8.3	3.4	1.8	2.0
Canada	17.3	18.7	14.2	12.3	10.0	7.4	9.4	5.0	2.7	3.0
Males										
Trois-Rivières	13.6	18.4	15.4	14.6	11.1	7.7	9.6	4.7	2.4	2.5
Québec	14.5	16.9	14.0	14.2	11.3	8.4	10.3	4.7	2.6	3.0
Canada	15.2	14.7	12.5	12.0	10.5	8.5	11.6	6.5	3.9	4.7
Females										
Trois-Rivières	18.7	29.9	16.5	13.4	8.7	5.1	5.1	1.4	0.6	0.5
Québec	18.0	25.3	16.4	13.8	9.8	6.1	6.4	2.1	1.0	0.9
Canada	19.4	22.5	15.8	12.6	9.6	6.4	7.3	3.6	1.5	1.4

Note: Figures cover individuals aged 15 years and over with income. Income refers to monetary receipts from certain sources, before income taxes and deductions, during calendar year 2010.
Source: Statistics Canada. 2013. 2011 National Household Survey. Statistics Canada Catalogue no. 99-004-XWE. Ottawa. Released September 11, 2013.

Labour Force Status

Area	In the Labour Force — All	Employed	Unemployed	Not in the Labour Force
Number — Total				
Trois-Rivières	65,945	60,765	5,175	43,680
Québec	4,183,445	3,880,425	303,020	2,291,145
Canada	17,990,080	16,595,035	1,395,045	9,269,445
Males				
Trois-Rivières	34,085	30,925	3,160	18,715
Québec	2,188,555	2,014,810	173,745	982,080
Canada	9,388,570	8,634,310	754,255	3,906,785
Females				
Trois-Rivières	31,860	29,840	2,020	24,970
Québec	1,994,885	1,865,610	129,275	1,309,065
Canada	8,601,515	7,960,725	640,790	5,362,660
Percent of Labour Force — Total				
Trois-Rivières	60.2	55.4	7.8	39.8
Québec	64.6	59.9	7.2	35.4
Canada	66.0	60.9	7.8	34.0
Males				
Trois-Rivières	64.6	58.6	9.3	35.4
Québec	69.0	63.5	7.9	31.0
Canada	70.6	64.9	8.0	29.4
Females				
Trois-Rivières	56.1	52.5	6.3	43.9
Québec	60.4	56.5	6.5	39.6
Canada	61.6	57.0	7.4	38.4

Note: Figures are based on total population 15 years and over
Source: Statistics Canada. 2013. 2011 National Household Survey. Statistics Canada Catalogue no. 99-004-XWE. Ottawa. Released September 11, 2013.

Labour Force by Industry (NAICS Codes 11–52)

Area	Agriculture, forestry, fishing & hunting	Mining, quarrying, & oil & gas extraction	Utilities	Construction	Manufacturing	Wholesale Trade	Retail Trade	Transportation & warehousing	Information & cultural industries	Finance & insurance
					Number					
					Total					
Trois-Rivières	360	115	1,235	3,435	7,385	2,130	8,870	2,375	1,500	1,705
Québec	84,470	20,770	33,815	241,780	476,390	169,825	501,380	181,295	98,340	159,230
Canada	437,650	261,050	149,940	1,215,380	1,619,295	733,445	2,031,665	827,780	420,830	767,960
					Males					
Trois-Rivières	245	110	1,015	3,055	6,010	1,590	3,765	1,990	750	600
Québec	61,540	18,035	24,560	213,605	343,345	113,545	234,725	137,745	56,455	56,930
Canada	307,370	211,690	110,765	1,068,710	1,167,680	494,545	933,850	617,305	235,875	296,995
					Females					
Trois-Rivières	115	0	220	385	1,380	540	5,105	385	750	1,100
Québec	22,925	2,730	9,255	28,170	133,045	56,280	266,650	43,550	41,885	102,295
Canada	130,285	49,360	39,175	146,670	451,615	238,900	1,097,820	210,475	184,955	470,960
					Percent of Labour Force					
					Total					
Trois-Rivières	0.6	0.2	1.9	5.4	11.5	3.3	13.8	3.7	2.3	2.7
Québec	2.1	0.5	0.8	5.9	11.7	4.2	12.3	4.4	2.4	3.9
Canada	2.5	1.5	0.9	6.9	9.2	4.2	11.6	4.7	2.4	4.4
					Males					
Trois-Rivières	0.7	0.3	3.1	9.2	18.1	4.8	11.4	6.0	2.3	1.8
Québec	2.9	0.8	1.1	10.0	16.1	5.3	11.0	6.4	2.6	2.7
Canada	3.3	2.3	1.2	11.6	12.7	5.4	10.2	6.7	2.6	3.2
					Females					
Trois-Rivières	0.4	0.0	0.7	1.2	4.5	1.7	16.5	1.2	2.4	3.5
Québec	1.2	0.1	0.5	1.4	6.8	2.9	13.7	2.2	2.2	5.3
Canada	1.6	0.6	0.5	1.7	5.4	2.8	13.1	2.5	2.2	5.6

Note: Figures are based on total experienced labour force 15 years and over. Experienced labour force refers to persons who, during the week of Sunday, May 1 to Saturday, May 7, 2011, were employed and the unemployed who had last worked for pay or in self-employment in either 2010 or 2011.
Source: Statistics Canada. 2013. 2011 National Household Survey. Statistics Canada Catalogue no. 99-004-XWE. Ottawa. Released September 11, 2013.

Labour Force by Industry (NAICS Codes 53–91)

Area	Real estate & rental & leasing	Profess., scientific & tech. services	Mgmt of companies & enterprises	Admin. & support, waste mgmt & remed. services	Educational services	Health care & social assistance	Arts, entertain. & recreation	Accomm. & food services	Other services (except public admin.)	Public admin.
					Number					
					Total					
Trois-Rivières	840	3,175	35	2,690	5,690	9,610	1,110	4,660	3,075	4,170
Québec	61,365	282,115	3,965	156,130	301,425	496,125	78,795	253,145	189,290	295,480
Canada	321,895	1,240,850	17,460	728,330	1,301,435	1,949,650	363,405	1,130,750	807,800	1,261,050
					Males					
Trois-Rivières	460	1,865	30	1,705	2,050	2,100	535	2,040	1,270	1,970
Québec	35,940	158,920	2,250	92,530	99,565	97,255	41,535	112,650	88,710	147,645
Canada	179,090	688,625	9,380	411,250	424,915	349,430	188,270	469,990	372,940	652,510
					Females					
Trois-Rivières	380	1,305	0	985	3,640	7,510	580	2,625	1,800	2,195
Québec	25,425	123,205	1,715	63,605	201,860	398,870	37,260	140,495	100,585	147,835
Canada	142,805	552,225	8,075	317,085	876,515	1,600,220	175,135	660,760	434,865	608,535
					Percent of Labour Force					
					Total					
Trois-Rivières	1.3	4.9	0.1	4.2	8.9	15.0	1.7	7.3	4.8	6.5
Québec	1.5	6.9	0.1	3.8	7.4	12.1	1.9	6.2	4.6	7.2
Canada	1.8	7.1	0.1	4.1	7.4	11.1	2.1	6.4	4.6	7.2
					Males					
Trois-Rivières	1.4	5.6	0.1	5.1	6.2	6.3	1.6	6.2	3.8	5.9
Québec	1.7	7.4	0.1	4.3	4.7	4.5	1.9	5.3	4.2	6.9
Canada	1.9	7.5	0.1	4.5	4.6	3.8	2.0	5.1	4.1	7.1
					Females					
Trois-Rivières	1.2	4.2	0.0	3.2	11.7	24.2	1.9	8.5	5.8	7.1
Québec	1.3	6.3	0.1	3.3	10.4	20.5	1.9	7.2	5.2	7.6
Canada	1.7	6.6	0.1	3.8	10.4	19.1	2.1	7.9	5.2	7.2

Note: Figures are based on total experienced labour force 15 years and over. Experienced labour force refers to persons who, during the week of Sunday, May 1 to Saturday, May 7, 2011, were employed and the unemployed who had last worked for pay or in self-employment in either 2010 or 2011.
Source: Statistics Canada. 2013. 2011 National Household Survey. Statistics Canada Catalogue no. 99-004-XWE. Ottawa. Released September 11, 2013.

PROFILES / Trois-Rivières, Québec

Occupation

Area	Mgmt	Business, Finance & Admin.	Natural/ Applied Sciences & Related	Health	Education, Law & Social, Community & Government Services	Art, Culture, Recreation & Sport	Sales & Service	Trades, Transport & Equip. Operators & Related	Natural Resources, Agri. & Related Production	Mfg & Utilities
Number										
Total										
Trois-Rivières	5,330	9,565	3,960	5,175	8,665	1,590	16,725	9,345	445	3,350
Québec	411,425	687,715	287,015	268,610	479,505	123,665	969,740	573,075	65,625	218,740
Canada	1,963,600	2,902,045	1,237,775	1,107,200	2,064,675	503,415	4,068,170	2,537,775	397,930	805,040
Males										
Trois-Rivières	3,315	2,830	3,185	1,030	2,980	705	7,060	8,970	370	2,705
Québec	261,620	207,545	221,430	53,480	148,715	58,150	436,370	542,055	53,640	154,485
Canada	1,229,460	854,190	966,355	217,520	676,550	232,535	1,745,705	2,385,615	318,945	564,300
Females										
Trois-Rivières	2,020	6,740	775	4,140	5,685	880	9,670	380	75	645
Québec	149,800	480,170	65,585	215,130	330,795	65,520	533,370	31,025	11,995	64,250
Canada	734,140	2,047,855	271,415	889,675	1,388,130	270,875	2,322,465	152,165	78,980	240,740
Percent of Labour Force										
Total										
Trois-Rivières	8.3	14.9	6.2	8.1	13.5	2.5	26.1	14.6	0.7	5.2
Québec	10.1	16.8	7.0	6.6	11.7	3.0	23.7	14.0	1.6	5.4
Canada	11.2	16.5	7.0	6.3	11.7	2.9	23.1	14.4	2.3	4.6
Males										
Trois-Rivières	10.0	8.5	9.6	3.1	9.0	2.1	21.3	27.1	1.1	8.2
Québec	12.2	9.7	10.4	2.5	7.0	2.7	20.4	25.4	2.5	7.2
Canada	13.4	9.3	10.5	2.4	7.4	2.5	19.0	26.0	3.5	6.1
Females										
Trois-Rivières	6.5	21.7	2.5	13.4	18.3	2.8	31.2	1.2	0.2	2.1
Québec	7.7	24.7	3.4	11.0	17.0	3.4	27.4	1.6	0.6	3.3
Canada	8.7	24.4	3.2	10.6	16.5	3.2	27.7	1.8	0.9	2.9

Note: Figures are based on total experienced labour force 15 years and over
Source: Statistics Canada. 2013. 2011 National Household Survey. Statistics Canada Catalogue no. 99-004-XWE. Ottawa. Released September 11, 2013.

Place of Work Status

Area	Worked at Home	Worked Outside Canada	No Fixed Workplace Address	Worked at Usual Place
Number				
Total				
Trois-Rivières	2,680	170	4,745	53,165
Québec	237,625	9,705	331,525	3,301,560
Canada	1,142,640	66,460	1,868,245	13,517,690
Males				
Trois-Rivières	1,305	130	3,560	25,935
Québec	122,060	7,055	249,535	1,636,165
Canada	582,150	47,355	1,400,485	6,604,325
Females				
Trois-Rivières	1,375	40	1,190	27,230
Québec	115,565	2,650	81,995	1,665,395
Canada	560,490	19,100	467,760	6,913,370
Percent of Labour Force				
Total				
Trois-Rivières	4.4	0.3	7.8	87.5
Québec	6.1	0.3	8.5	85.1
Canada	6.9	0.4	11.3	81.5
Males				
Trois-Rivières	4.2	0.4	11.5	83.9
Québec	6.1	0.4	12.4	81.2
Canada	6.7	0.5	16.2	76.5
Females				
Trois-Rivières	4.6	0.1	4.0	91.3
Québec	6.2	0.1	4.4	89.3
Canada	7.0	0.2	5.9	86.8

Note: Figures are based on total employed labour force 15 years and over.
Source: Statistics Canada. 2013. 2011 National Household Survey. Statistics Canada Catalogue no. 99-004-XWE. Ottawa. Released September 11, 2013.

Mode of Transportation to Work

Area	Car; Truck; Van; as Driver	Car; Truck; Van; as Passenger	Public Transit	Walked	Bicycled	All Other Modes
			Number			
			Total			
Trois-Rivières	50,350	2,045	1,465	3,015	600	440
Québec	2,713,295	136,490	484,600	215,210	48,870	34,620
Canada	11,393,140	867,050	1,851,525	880,815	201,780	191,625
			Males			
Trois-Rivières	25,885	1,020	535	1,345	450	265
Québec	1,484,305	50,905	203,035	95,100	33,065	19,285
Canada	6,238,835	349,530	788,290	387,580	135,840	104,725
			Females			
Trois-Rivières	24,470	1,025	935	1,670	150	175
Québec	1,228,995	85,585	281,565	120,110	15,800	15,335
Canada	5,154,305	517,520	1,063,235	493,230	65,940	86,900
			Percent of Labour Force			
			Total			
Trois-Rivières	86.9	3.5	2.5	5.2	1.0	0.8
Québec	74.7	3.8	13.3	5.9	1.3	1.0
Canada	74.0	5.6	12.0	5.7	1.3	1.2
			Males			
Trois-Rivières	87.8	3.5	1.8	4.6	1.5	0.9
Québec	78.7	2.7	10.8	5.0	1.8	1.0
Canada	77.9	4.4	9.8	4.8	1.7	1.3
			Females			
Trois-Rivières	86.1	3.6	3.3	5.9	0.5	0.6
Québec	70.3	4.9	16.1	6.9	0.9	0.9
Canada	69.8	7.0	14.4	6.7	0.9	1.2

Note: Figures are based on total employed labour force 15 years and over.
Source: Statistics Canada. 2013. 2011 National Household Survey. Statistics Canada Catalogue no. 99-004-XWE. Ottawa. Released September 11, 2013.

Visible Minority Population Characteristics

Area	Total Minority	South Asian[1]	Chinese	Black	Filipino	Latin American	Arab	SE Asian[2]	West Asian[3]	Korean	Japanese	Multiple[4]
					Number							
					Total							
Trois-Rivières	3,230	40	235	1,175	80	820	630	100	0	0	65	35
Québec	850,235	83,320	82,845	243,625	31,495	116,380	166,260	65,855	23,445	6,665	4,025	17,420
Canada	6,264,750	1,567,400	1,324,750	945,665	619,310	381,280	380,620	312,075	206,840	161,130	87,270	171,935
					Males							
Trois-Rivières	1,645	0	70	630	60	395	340	50	0	0	40	25
Québec	418,545	43,410	37,295	116,605	12,435	56,940	89,505	32,940	12,070	3,135	1,565	8,315
Canada	3,043,010	790,755	632,325	453,005	268,885	186,355	203,485	154,035	105,620	77,165	38,270	83,335
					Females							
Trois-Rivières	1,585	25	170	545	25	420	290	50	0	0	25	0
Québec	431,695	39,915	45,550	127,020	19,055	59,440	76,750	32,920	11,380	3,530	2,465	9,105
Canada	3,221,745	776,650	692,420	492,660	350,425	194,925	177,140	158,045	101,220	83,965	48,990	88,600
					Percent of Population							
					Total							
Trois-Rivières	2.5	0.0	0.2	0.9	0.1	0.6	0.5	0.1	0.0	0.0	0.1	0.0
Québec	11.0	1.1	1.1	3.2	0.4	1.5	2.2	0.9	0.3	0.1	0.1	0.2
Canada	19.1	4.8	4.0	2.9	1.9	1.2	1.2	0.9	0.6	0.5	0.3	0.5
					Males							
Trois-Rivières	2.7	0.0	0.1	1.0	0.1	0.6	0.6	0.1	0.0	0.0	0.1	0.0
Québec	11.0	1.1	1.0	3.1	0.3	1.5	2.3	0.9	0.3	0.1	0.0	0.2
Canada	18.8	4.9	3.9	2.8	1.7	1.2	1.3	1.0	0.7	0.5	0.2	0.5
					Females							
Trois-Rivières	2.4	0.0	0.3	0.8	0.0	0.6	0.4	0.1	0.0	0.0	0.0	0.0
Québec	11.0	1.0	1.2	3.2	0.5	1.5	2.0	0.8	0.3	0.1	0.1	0.2
Canada	19.3	4.7	4.1	3.0	2.1	1.2	1.1	0.9	0.6	0.5	0.3	0.5

Note: The Employment Equity Act defines visible minorities as 'persons, other than Aboriginal peoples, who are non-Caucasian in race or non-white in colour';
(1) Includes 'East Indian,' 'Pakistani,' 'Sri Lankan,' etc.; (2) Includes 'Vietnamese,' 'Cambodian,' 'Malaysian,' 'Laotian,' etc.; (3) Includes 'Iranian,' 'Afghan,' etc.; (4) Includes respondents who reported more than one visible minority group by checking two or more mark-in circles, e.g., 'Black' and 'South Asian.'
Source: Statistics Canada. 2013. 2011 National Household Survey. Statistics Canada Catalogue no. 99-004-XWE. Ottawa. Released September 11, 2013.

PROFILES / Trois-Rivières, Québec

Aboriginal Population

Area	Aboriginal Identity[1]	First Nations (North American Indian) Single Identity[2]	Métis Single Identity	Inuk (Inuit) Single Identity	Multiple Aboriginal Identities[3]	Aboriginal Identities Not Included Elsewhere
Number						
Total						
Trois-Rivières	1,430	805	560	0	0	40
Québec	141,915	82,425	40,960	12,570	1,545	4,415
Canada	1,400,685	851,560	451,795	59,440	11,415	26,475
Males						
Trois-Rivières	705	360	305	0	0	15
Québec	70,205	40,105	21,300	6,265	720	1,815
Canada	682,190	411,785	223,335	29,495	5,525	12,055
Females						
Trois-Rivières	725	440	255	0	0	25
Québec	71,710	42,315	19,660	6,305	830	2,600
Canada	718,500	439,775	228,460	29,950	5,890	14,420
Percent of Population						
Total						
Trois-Rivières	1.1	0.6	0.4	0.0	0.0	0.0
Québec	1.8	1.1	0.5	0.2	0.0	0.1
Canada	4.3	2.6	1.4	0.2	0.0	0.1
Males						
Trois-Rivières	1.1	0.6	0.5	0.0	0.0	0.0
Québec	1.8	1.1	0.6	0.2	0.0	0.0
Canada	4.2	2.5	1.4	0.2	0.0	0.1
Females						
Trois-Rivières	1.1	0.7	0.4	0.0	0.0	0.0
Québec	1.8	1.1	0.5	0.2	0.0	0.1
Canada	4.3	2.6	1.4	0.2	0.0	0.1

Note: (1) Includes persons who reported being an Aboriginal person, that is, First Nations (North American Indian), Métis or Inuk (Inuit) and/or those who reported Registered or Treaty Indian status, that is registered under the Indian Act of Canada, and/or those who reported membership in a First Nation or Indian band. Aboriginal peoples of Canada are defined in the Constitution Act, 1982, section 35-2 as including the Indian, Inuit and Métis peoples of Canada; (2) Users should be aware that the estimates associated with this variable are more affected than most by the incomplete enumeration of certain Indian reserves and Indian settlements in the National Household Survey (NHS); (3) Includes persons who reported being any two or all three of the following: First Nations (North American Indian), Métis or Inuk (Inuit).
Source: Statistics Canada. 2013. 2011 National Household Survey. Statistics Canada Catalogue no. 99-004-XWE. Ottawa. Released September 11, 2013.

Ethnic Origin

Area	North American Aboriginal	Other North American	European	Caribbean	Latin, Central and South American	African	Asian	Oceania
Number								
Total								
Trois-Rivières	3,625	96,595	51,115	425	945	1,545	1,160	0
Québec	307,445	4,776,875	3,390,330	167,590	137,255	260,785	488,905	2,305
Canada	1,836,035	11,070,455	20,157,965	627,590	544,375	766,735	5,011,225	74,875
Males								
Trois-Rivières	1,715	46,635	24,870	175	420	845	560	0
Québec	146,725	2,345,180	1,678,310	77,665	67,195	135,740	241,515	1,135
Canada	885,675	5,462,685	9,913,150	291,640	264,635	387,360	2,435,540	37,490
Females								
Trois-Rivières	1,910	49,955	26,245	250	530	700	600	0
Québec	160,725	2,431,700	1,712,015	89,925	70,065	125,040	247,390	1,175
Canada	950,360	5,607,770	10,244,820	335,945	279,740	379,380	2,575,680	37,385
Percent of Population								
Total								
Trois-Rivières	2.9	76.1	40.3	0.3	0.7	1.2	0.9	0.0
Québec	4.0	61.8	43.8	2.2	1.8	3.4	6.3	0.0
Canada	5.6	33.7	61.4	1.9	1.7	2.3	15.3	0.2
Males								
Trois-Rivières	2.8	75.8	40.4	0.3	0.7	1.4	0.9	0.0
Québec	3.8	61.5	44.0	2.0	1.8	3.6	6.3	0.0
Canada	5.5	33.8	61.3	1.8	1.6	2.4	15.1	0.2
Females								
Trois-Rivières	2.9	76.3	40.1	0.4	0.8	1.1	0.9	0.0
Québec	4.1	62.1	43.7	2.3	1.8	3.2	6.3	0.0
Canada	5.7	33.6	61.4	2.0	1.7	2.3	15.4	0.2

Note: The sum of the ethnic groups in this table is greater than the total population estimate because a person may report more than one ethnic origin in the NHS.
Source: Statistics Canada. 2013. 2011 National Household Survey. Statistics Canada Catalogue no. 99-004-XWE. Ottawa. Released September 11, 2013.

PROFILES / Trois-Rivières, Québec

Religion

Area	Buddhist	Christian	Hindu	Jewish	Muslim	Sikh	Traditional (Aboriginal) Spirituality	Other Religions	No Religious Affiliation
Number									
Total									
Trois-Rivières	165	114,210	0	15	910	0	0	80	11,585
Québec	52,390	6,356,880	33,540	85,100	243,430	9,275	2,025	12,340	937,545
Canada	366,830	22,102,745	497,965	329,495	1,053,945	454,965	64,935	130,835	7,850,605
Males									
Trois-Rivières	95	54,435	0	0	495	0	0	40	6,450
Québec	24,630	3,079,855	17,055	41,455	128,815	5,090	925	6,155	510,055
Canada	168,465	10,497,775	250,435	161,265	540,555	229,435	31,805	57,745	4,225,645
Females									
Trois-Rivières	70	59,775	0	0	415	0	0	45	5,140
Québec	27,760	3,277,020	16,480	43,645	114,615	4,185	1,100	6,175	427,485
Canada	198,365	11,604,975	247,525	168,235	513,395	225,530	33,135	73,090	3,624,965
Percent of Population									
Total									
Trois-Rivières	0.1	89.9	0.0	0.0	0.7	0.0	0.0	0.1	9.1
Québec	0.7	82.2	0.4	1.1	3.1	0.1	0.0	0.2	12.1
Canada	1.1	67.3	1.5	1.0	3.2	1.4	0.2	0.4	23.9
Males									
Trois-Rivières	0.2	88.5	0.0	0.0	0.8	0.0	0.0	0.1	10.5
Québec	0.6	80.8	0.4	1.1	3.4	0.1	0.0	0.2	13.4
Canada	1.0	64.9	1.5	1.0	3.3	1.4	0.2	0.4	26.1
Females									
Trois-Rivières	0.1	91.3	0.0	0.0	0.6	0.0	0.0	0.1	7.9
Québec	0.7	83.6	0.4	1.1	2.9	0.1	0.0	0.2	10.9
Canada	1.2	69.5	1.5	1.0	3.1	1.4	0.2	0.4	21.7

Note: Religion refers to the person's self-identification as having a connection or affiliation with any religious denomination, group, body, sect, cult or other religiously defined community or system of belief. Religion is not limited to formal membership in a religious organization or group. Persons without a religious connection or affiliation can self-identify as atheist, agnostic or humanist, or can provide another applicable response.
Source: Statistics Canada. 2013. 2011 National Household Survey. Statistics Canada Catalogue no. 99-004-XWE. Ottawa. Released September 11, 2013.

Religion—Christian Denominations

Area	Anglican	Baptist	Catholic	Christian Orthodox	Lutheran	Pentecostal	Presbyterian	United Church	Other Christian
Number									
Total									
Trois-Rivières	60	430	110,855	190	35	310	0	45	2,275
Québec	73,550	36,615	5,775,740	129,780	7,200	41,070	11,440	32,930	248,560
Canada	1,631,845	635,840	12,810,705	550,690	478,185	478,705	472,385	2,007,610	3,036,780
Males									
Trois-Rivières	45	180	52,815	110	15	160	0	30	1,065
Québec	34,815	16,585	2,802,920	63,960	3,425	18,640	5,265	14,945	119,305
Canada	752,945	293,905	6,167,290	270,205	221,525	217,850	218,955	912,545	1,442,550
Females									
Trois-Rivières	10	250	58,040	75	20	145	0	0	1,210
Québec	38,735	20,030	2,972,820	65,820	3,770	22,430	6,175	17,985	129,260
Canada	878,900	341,940	6,643,415	280,485	256,660	260,850	253,430	1,095,065	1,594,230
Percent of Population									
Total									
Trois-Rivières	0.0	0.3	87.3	0.1	0.0	0.2	0.0	0.0	1.8
Québec	1.0	0.5	74.7	1.7	0.1	0.5	0.1	0.4	3.2
Canada	5.0	1.9	39.0	1.7	1.5	1.5	1.4	6.1	9.2
Males									
Trois-Rivières	0.1	0.3	85.8	0.2	0.0	0.3	0.0	0.0	1.7
Québec	0.9	0.4	73.5	1.7	0.1	0.5	0.1	0.4	3.1
Canada	4.7	1.8	38.2	1.7	1.4	1.3	1.4	5.6	8.9
Females									
Trois-Rivières	0.0	0.4	88.7	0.1	0.0	0.2	0.0	0.0	1.8
Québec	1.0	0.5	75.9	1.7	0.1	0.6	0.2	0.5	3.3
Canada	5.3	2.0	39.8	1.7	1.5	1.6	1.5	6.6	9.6

Note: Religion refers to the person's self-identification as having a connection or affiliation with any religious denomination, group, body, sect, cult or other religiously defined community or system of belief. Religion is not limited to formal membership in a religious organization or group. Persons without a religious connection or affiliation can self-identify as atheist, agnostic or humanist, or can provide another applicable response.
Source: Statistics Canada. 2013. 2011 National Household Survey. Statistics Canada Catalogue no. 99-004-XWE. Ottawa. Released September 11, 2013.

PROFILES / Trois-Rivières, Québec

Immigrant Status and Period of Immigration

Area	Non-Immigrants[1]	Immigrants All	Before 1971	1971 to 1980	1981 to 1990	1991 to 2000	2001 to 2005	2006 to 2011	Non-Permanent Residents[3]
Number									
Total									
Trois-Rivières	122,850	3,645	340	280	230	480	860	1,450	485
Québec	6,690,530	974,895	151,825	115,640	130,680	195,925	157,425	223,400	67,095
Canada	25,720,175	6,775,765	1,261,055	870,775	949,890	1,539,050	992,070	1,162,915	356,385
Males									
Trois-Rivières	59,510	1,690	170	130	110	200	430	655	320
Québec	3,301,435	477,240	75,255	57,410	64,080	94,110	76,780	109,605	35,370
Canada	12,753,235	3,231,370	605,430	416,670	454,570	724,905	474,545	555,245	178,515
Females									
Trois-Rivières	63,335	1,950	175	150	120	285	425	795	165
Québec	3,389,095	497,655	76,565	58,235	66,600	101,810	80,645	113,795	31,725
Canada	12,966,935	3,544,400	655,625	454,105	495,325	814,145	517,530	607,670	177,870
Percent of Population									
Total									
Trois-Rivières	96.7	2.9	0.3	0.2	0.2	0.4	0.7	1.1	0.4
Québec	86.5	12.6	2.0	1.5	1.7	2.5	2.0	2.9	0.9
Canada	78.3	20.6	3.8	2.7	2.9	4.7	3.0	3.5	1.1
Males									
Trois-Rivières	96.7	2.7	0.3	0.2	0.2	0.3	0.7	1.1	0.5
Québec	86.6	12.5	2.0	1.5	1.7	2.5	2.0	2.9	0.9
Canada	78.9	20.0	3.7	2.6	2.8	4.5	2.9	3.4	1.1
Females									
Trois-Rivières	96.8	3.0	0.3	0.2	0.2	0.4	0.6	1.2	0.3
Québec	86.5	12.7	2.0	1.5	1.7	2.6	2.1	2.9	0.8
Canada	77.7	21.2	3.9	2.7	3.0	4.9	3.1	3.6	1.1

Note: (1) Non-immigrant refers to a person who is a Canadian citizen by birth; (2) Immigrant refers to a person who is or has ever been a landed immigrant/permanent resident. This person has been granted the right to live in Canada permanently by immigration authorities. Some immigrants have resided in Canada for a number of years, while others have arrived recently. Some immigrants are Canadian citizens, while others are not. Most immigrants are born outside Canada, but a small number are born in Canada. In the 2011 National Household Survey, 'Immigrants' includes immigrants who landed in Canada prior to May 10, 2011; (3) Non-permanent resident refers to a person from another country who has a work or study permit, or who is a refugee claimant, and any non-Canadian-born family member living in Canada with them.
Source: Statistics Canada. 2013. 2011 National Household Survey. Statistics Canada Catalogue no. 99-004-XWE. Ottawa. Released September 11, 2013.

Mother Tongue

Area	English	French	Non-official Language	English & French	English & Non-official Language	French & Non-official Language	English, French & Non-official Language
Number							
Total							
Trois-Rivières	1,480	124,970	2,485	520	15	225	20
Québec	599,225	6,102,210	961,700	64,800	23,435	51,640	12,950
Canada	18,858,980	7,054,975	6,567,680	144,685	396,330	74,430	24,095
Males							
Trois-Rivières	730	60,115	1,280	250	10	130	15
Québec	297,875	2,994,300	472,635	32,390	11,455	25,810	6,790
Canada	9,345,225	3,452,380	3,157,785	69,975	192,000	36,535	11,965
Females							
Trois-Rivières	745	64,855	1,205	270	10	95	5
Québec	301,355	3,107,910	489,060	32,405	11,975	25,825	6,155
Canada	9,513,750	3,602,590	3,409,895	74,710	204,330	37,890	12,130
Percent of Population							
Total							
Trois-Rivières	1.1	96.3	1.9	0.4	0.0	0.2	0.0
Québec	7.7	78.1	12.3	0.8	0.3	0.7	0.2
Canada	56.9	21.3	19.8	0.4	1.2	0.2	0.1
Males							
Trois-Rivières	1.2	96.1	2.0	0.4	0.0	0.2	0.0
Québec	7.8	78.0	12.3	0.8	0.3	0.7	0.2
Canada	57.5	21.2	19.4	0.4	1.2	0.2	0.1
Females							
Trois-Rivières	1.1	96.5	1.8	0.4	0.0	0.1	0.0
Québec	7.6	78.2	12.3	0.8	0.3	0.6	0.2
Canada	56.4	21.4	20.2	0.4	1.2	0.2	0.1

Note: Figures cover total population excluding institutional residents.
Source: Statistics Canada. 2012. Census Profile. 2011 Census. Statistics Canada Catalogue no. 98-316-XWE. Ottawa. Released October 24 2012.
http://www12.statcan.gc.ca/census-recensement/2011/dp-pd/prof/index.cfm?Lang=E

Language Spoken Most Often at Home

Area	English	French	Non-official Language	English & French	English & Non-official Language	French & Non-official Language	English, French & Non-official Language
			Number				
			Total				
Trois-Rivières	900	126,585	1,225	440	35	480	50
Québec	767,415	6,249,080	554,400	71,555	43,765	100,110	29,625
Canada	21,457,075	6,827,865	3,673,865	131,205	875,135	109,700	46,330
			Males				
Trois-Rivières	425	60,965	625	230	20	235	30
Québec	379,915	3,071,635	268,640	35,860	21,305	48,590	15,315
Canada	10,585,620	3,348,235	1,767,310	63,475	425,370	53,010	22,845
			Females				
Trois-Rivières	475	65,625	595	205	15	250	15
Québec	387,500	3,177,450	285,760	35,695	22,460	51,525	14,310
Canada	10,871,455	3,479,625	1,906,555	67,730	449,765	56,690	23,485
			Percent of Population				
			Total				
Trois-Rivières	0.7	97.6	0.9	0.3	0.0	0.4	0.0
Québec	9.8	80.0	7.1	0.9	0.6	1.3	0.4
Canada	64.8	20.6	11.1	0.4	2.6	0.3	0.1
			Males				
Trois-Rivières	0.7	97.5	1.0	0.4	0.0	0.4	0.0
Québec	9.9	80.0	7.0	0.9	0.6	1.3	0.4
Canada	65.1	20.6	10.9	0.4	2.6	0.3	0.1
			Females				
Trois-Rivières	0.7	97.7	0.9	0.3	0.0	0.4	0.0
Québec	9.7	79.9	7.2	0.9	0.6	1.3	0.4
Canada	64.5	20.6	11.3	0.4	2.7	0.3	0.1

Note: Figures cover total population excluding institutional residents.
Source: Statistics Canada. 2012. Census Profile. 2011 Census. Statistics Canada Catalogue no. 98-316-XWE. Ottawa. Released October 24 2012.
http://www12.statcan.gc.ca/census-recensement/2011/dp-pd/prof/index.cfm?Lang=E

Knowledge of Official Languages

Area	English Only	French Only	English & French	Neither English nor French
		Number		
		Total		
Trois-Rivières	175	91,465	37,875	200
Québec	363,860	4,047,175	3,328,725	76,190
Canada	22,564,665	4,165,015	5,795,570	595,920
		Males		
Trois-Rivières	105	41,010	21,325	85
Québec	180,175	1,871,500	1,758,410	31,175
Canada	11,222,185	1,925,340	2,876,560	241,790
		Females		
Trois-Rivières	70	50,455	16,545	115
Québec	183,690	2,175,675	1,570,310	45,015
Canada	11,342,485	2,239,680	2,919,005	354,135
		Percent of Population		
		Total		
Trois-Rivières	0.1	70.5	29.2	0.2
Québec	4.7	51.8	42.6	1.0
Canada	68.1	12.6	17.5	1.8
		Males		
Trois-Rivières	0.2	65.6	34.1	0.1
Québec	4.7	48.7	45.8	0.8
Canada	69.0	11.8	17.7	1.5
		Females		
Trois-Rivières	0.1	75.1	24.6	0.2
Québec	4.6	54.7	39.5	1.1
Canada	67.3	13.3	17.3	2.1

Note: Figures cover total population excluding institutional residents.
Source: Statistics Canada. 2012. Census Profile. 2011 Census. Statistics Canada Catalogue no. 98-316-XWE. Ottawa. Released October 24 2012.
http://www12.statcan.gc.ca/census-recensement/2011/dp-pd/prof/index.cfm?Lang=E

Vancouver, British Columbia

Background

Vancouver is a coastal port city located on the mainland of British Columbia. It is situated on the western half of the Burrard Peninsula. The Greater Area of Vancouver is home to more than half of BC's population.

Vancouver was founded on the territory of three Coast Salish Nations. The city was built by immigrants and made prosperous through international trade. Over the past 125 years, five cultures have significantly shaped the city's growth: Japanese, Chinese, First Nations, Indian and Italian.

Vancouver is renowned for its quality of life and ranks highly in worldwide "livability" ratings. In 2009, Vancouver announced its goal to be the Greenest City in the World. The green economy in Vancouver is growing twice as fast as the region's traditional sectors like shipping, forestry, mining, software development, biotechnology and film. Vancouver was host city of the XXI Olympic Winter Games in 2010.

Of the 603,502 people living in Vancouver in 2011, almost half of the population spoke English as their first language while 25.3% spoke Chinese. After English and Chinese, the most common languages spoken were Punjabi, German, Italian, French, Tagalog (Filipino) and Spanish. Vancouver's annual Cultural Harmony Awards recognize local residents and organizations that promote cultural acceptance and positive relationships between people of different backgrounds.

Canada's largest dragon boat event, an autumn Apple Festival, the Powell Street (Japanese) Festival and the Chinese New Year Parade are annual festivities. Whistler Resort, the Canadian Rockies and Vancouver Island are all easily accessible tourist destinations. Vancouver is also the home port for Alaska cruises.

Vancouver has average summer highs of plus 20.93 degrees Celsius, winter lows of plus 0.93 degree Celsius, and an average rainfall just over 1154 mm per year.

Rankings

- Vancouver was ranked the world's most livable city from 2002 to 2011. The annual survey by the *Economist Intelligence Unit* evaluates cities' stability, health care, culture and environment, education and infrastructure. When Vancouver ranked #1 in 2011, the city scored 98%. Vancouver ranked #3 overall in 2012. *Economist Intelligence Unit, "Liveability and Overview 2012," released August 14, 2012 with files from 2002 to 2011*
- Vancouver and North Vancouver were identified as the two best cities for Canadian culture. The municipalities ranked #1 and #2 out of 190 Canadian cities. Victoria, BC's capital city, ranked #3. Criteria: the percentage of people employed in arts, culture, recreation and sports. *Money Sense Magazine, "Canada's Best Places to Live 2012," March 20, 2012*
- Vancouver was ranked in the Top 4 by Environment Canada in six national climate categories: #1 for Fewest Freezing Days (46 days); #2 for Warmest Year-Round (plus 10.8 degrees Celsius); #3 for Fewest Snow Days (11 days); #3 for Lowest Snowfall (48 cm); #4 for Warmest Spring (9.43 degrees Celsius); and #4 for Mildest Winter (an average of 6.77 degrees Celsius). *Environment Canada, Canadian Cities are Weather Winners!, May 29, 2012*

PROFILES / Vancouver, British Columbia

Population Growth and Density

Area	Population in 2001	Population in 2006	Population in 2011	Population Change 2001–2006	Population Change 2006–2011	Land Area (sq. km)	Population Density per sq. km
Vancouver	545,671	578,041	603,502	5.9	4.4	114.97	5,249.1
British Columbia	3,907,738	4,113,487	4,400,057	5.3	7.0	922,509.29	4.8
Canada	30,007,094	31,612,897	33,476,688	5.4	5.9	8,965,121.42	3.7

Source: Statistics Canada. 2012. Census Profile. 2011 Census. Statistics Canada Catalogue no. 98-316-XWE. Ottawa. Released October 24 2012. http://www12.statcan.gc.ca/census-recensement/2011/dp-pd/prof/index.cfm?Lang=E;
Statistics Canada 2007. 2006 Community Profiles. 2006 Census. Statistics Canada Catalogue no. 92-591-XWE. Ottawa. Released March 13 2007. http://www12.statcan.ca/census-recensement/2006/dp-pd/prof/92-591/index.cfm?Lang=E

Gender

Area	Males	Females
Number		
Vancouver	295,095	308,400
British Columbia	2,156,600	2,243,455
Canada	16,414,225	17,062,460
Percent of Population		
Vancouver	48.9	51.1
British Columbia	49.0	51.0
Canada	49.0	51.0

Source: Statistics Canada. 2012. Census Profile. 2011 Census. Statistics Canada Catalogue no. 98-316-XWE. Ottawa. Released October 24 2012.
http://www12.statcan.gc.ca/census-recensement/2011/dp-pd/prof/index.cfm?Lang=E

Marital Status

Area	Married[1]	Living Common-law	Single[2]	Separated	Divorced	Widowed
Number						
Total						
Vancouver	216,815	47,285	194,270	12,850	35,825	25,110
British Columbia	1,832,605	321,965	1,014,270	102,040	246,515	205,300
Canada	12,941,960	3,142,525	7,816,045	698,240	1,686,035	1,584,530
Males						
Vancouver	107,845	24,395	102,030	5,445	14,020	4,570
British Columbia	913,430	161,530	550,830	43,570	98,130	41,550
Canada	6,470,300	1,575,495	4,206,320	299,655	680,415	310,940
Females						
Vancouver	108,965	22,890	92,240	7,400	21,800	20,545
British Columbia	919,175	160,435	463,435	58,470	148,385	163,750
Canada	6,471,660	1,567,035	3,609,730	398,585	1,005,620	1,273,590
Percent of Population						
Total						
Vancouver	40.7	8.9	36.5	2.4	6.7	4.7
British Columbia	49.2	8.6	27.2	2.7	6.6	5.5
Canada	46.4	11.3	28.0	2.5	6.0	5.7
Males						
Vancouver	41.8	9.4	39.5	2.1	5.4	1.8
British Columbia	50.5	8.9	30.4	2.4	5.4	2.3
Canada	47.8	11.6	31.1	2.2	5.0	2.3
Females						
Vancouver	39.8	8.4	33.7	2.7	8.0	7.5
British Columbia	48.0	8.4	24.2	3.1	7.8	8.6
Canada	45.2	10.9	25.2	2.8	7.0	8.9

Note: (1) and not separated, (2) never legally married
Source: Statistics Canada. 2012. Census Profile. 2011 Census. Statistics Canada Catalogue no. 98-316-XWE. Ottawa. Released October 24 2012.
http://www12.statcan.gc.ca/census-recensement/2011/dp-pd/prof/index.cfm?Lang=E

PROFILES / Vancouver, British Columbia

Age Characteristics: 0 to 49 Years

Area	0 to 4 Years	5 to 9 Years	10 to 14 Years	15 to 19 Years	20 to 24 Years	25 to 29 Years	30 to 34 Years	35 to 39 Years	40 to 44 Years	45 to 49 Years
					Number					
					Total					
Vancouver	24,770	22,400	24,175	29,095	44,285	59,465	53,335	47,230	48,640	49,195
British Columbia	219,665	218,915	238,780	275,165	279,825	288,780	275,985	280,870	313,765	350,600
Canada	1,877,095	1,809,895	1,920,355	2,178,135	2,187,450	2,169,590	2,162,905	2,173,930	2,324,875	2,675,130
					Males					
Vancouver	12,725	11,625	12,435	14,950	21,710	28,810	26,355	23,055	23,950	24,730
British Columbia	112,885	112,200	122,465	141,670	142,290	143,475	135,220	135,455	151,430	170,580
Canada	961,150	925,965	983,995	1,115,845	1,108,775	1,077,275	1,058,810	1,064,200	1,141,720	1,318,715
					Females					
Vancouver	12,050	10,775	11,740	14,150	22,570	30,655	26,980	24,175	24,690	24,460
British Columbia	106,775	106,715	116,315	133,500	137,535	145,305	140,755	145,415	162,335	180,020
Canada	915,945	883,935	936,360	1,062,295	1,078,670	1,092,315	1,104,095	1,109,735	1,183,155	1,356,420
					Percent of Population					
					Total					
Vancouver	4.1	3.7	4.0	4.8	7.3	9.9	8.8	7.8	8.1	8.2
British Columbia	5.0	5.0	5.4	6.3	6.4	6.6	6.3	6.4	7.1	8.0
Canada	5.6	5.4	5.7	6.5	6.5	6.5	6.5	6.5	6.9	8.0
					Males					
Vancouver	4.3	3.9	4.2	5.1	7.4	9.8	8.9	7.8	8.1	8.4
British Columbia	5.2	5.2	5.7	6.6	6.6	6.7	6.3	6.3	7.0	7.9
Canada	5.9	5.6	6.0	6.8	6.8	6.6	6.5	6.5	7.0	8.0
					Females					
Vancouver	3.9	3.5	3.8	4.6	7.3	9.9	8.7	7.8	8.0	7.9
British Columbia	4.8	4.8	5.2	6.0	6.1	6.5	6.3	6.5	7.2	8.0
Canada	5.4	5.2	5.5	6.2	6.3	6.4	6.5	6.5	6.9	7.9

Source: Statistics Canada. 2012. Census Profile. 2011 Census. Statistics Canada Catalogue no. 98-316-XWE. Ottawa. Released October 24 2012.
http://www12.statcan.gc.ca/census-recensement/2011/dp-pd/prof/index.cfm?Lang=E

Age Characteristics: 50 Years and Over, and Median Age

Area	50 to 54 Years	55 to 59 Years	60 to 64 Years	65 to 69 Years	70 to 74 Years	75 to 79 Years	80 to 84 Years	85 Years and Over	Median Age
					Number				
					Total				
Vancouver	44,105	39,500	35,365	22,845	18,800	15,870	12,305	12,110	39.7
British Columbia	354,610	323,335	291,040	210,900	160,715	127,480	96,945	92,675	41.9
Canada	2,658,965	2,340,635	2,052,670	1,521,715	1,153,065	922,700	702,070	645,515	40.6
					Males				
Vancouver	21,435	19,315	17,370	11,110	8,720	7,425	5,410	3,955	39.1
British Columbia	172,060	157,455	142,645	103,785	77,350	60,720	42,745	32,150	41.1
Canada	1,309,030	1,147,300	1,002,690	738,010	543,435	417,945	291,085	208,300	39.6
					Females				
Vancouver	22,670	20,185	17,995	11,735	10,080	8,440	6,895	8,155	40.2
British Columbia	182,550	165,880	148,395	107,115	83,360	66,760	54,200	60,520	42.7
Canada	1,349,940	1,193,335	1,049,985	783,705	609,630	504,755	410,985	437,215	41.5
					Percent of Population				
					Total				
Vancouver	7.3	6.5	5.9	3.8	3.1	2.6	2.0	2.0	—
British Columbia	8.1	7.3	6.6	4.8	3.7	2.9	2.2	2.1	—
Canada	7.9	7.0	6.1	4.5	3.4	2.8	2.1	1.9	—
					Males				
Vancouver	7.3	6.5	5.9	3.8	3.0	2.5	1.8	1.3	—
British Columbia	8.0	7.3	6.6	4.8	3.6	2.8	2.0	1.5	—
Canada	8.0	7.0	6.1	4.5	3.3	2.5	1.8	1.3	—
					Females				
Vancouver	7.4	6.5	5.8	3.8	3.3	2.7	2.2	2.6	—
British Columbia	8.1	7.4	6.6	4.8	3.7	3.0	2.4	2.7	—
Canada	7.9	7.0	6.2	4.6	3.6	3.0	2.4	2.6	—

Source: Statistics Canada. 2012. Census Profile. 2011 Census. Statistics Canada Catalogue no. 98-316-XWE. Ottawa. Released October 24 2012.
http://www12.statcan.gc.ca/census-recensement/2011/dp-pd/prof/index.cfm?Lang=E

PROFILES / Vancouver, British Columbia

Private Households by Household Size

Area	1 Person	2 Persons	3 Persons	4 Persons	5 Persons	6 or More Persons	Average Number of Persons in Private Households
			Households				
Vancouver	101,205	81,465	34,770	28,070	10,985	8,070	2.2
British Columbia	498,925	613,270	264,135	237,725	91,600	58,985	2.5
Canada	3,673,310	4,544,820	2,081,900	1,903,300	724,405	392,885	2.5
			Percent of Households				
Vancouver	38.3	30.8	13.1	10.6	4.2	3.1	–
British Columbia	28.3	34.8	15.0	13.5	5.2	3.3	–
Canada	27.6	34.1	15.6	14.3	5.4	2.9	–

Source: Statistics Canada. 2012. Census Profile. 2011 Census. Statistics Canada Catalogue no. 98-316-XWE. Ottawa. Released October 24 2012.
http://www12.statcan.gc.ca/census-recensement/2011/dp-pd/prof/index.cfm?Lang=E

Dwelling Type

Area	Single-detached House	Semi-detached House	Row House	Apartment: Building with Five or More Storeys	Apartment: Building with Fewer Than Five Storeys	Duplex Apartment	Movable Dwelling	Other Single-attached House
				Number				
Vancouver	47,530	4,000	9,040	70,270	87,430	45,845	65	390
British Columbia	842,120	52,825	130,365	143,970	361,150	184,355	46,960	2,885
Canada	7,329,150	646,245	791,600	1,234,770	2,397,550	704,485	183,510	33,310
				Percent of Dwellings				
Vancouver	18.0	1.5	3.4	26.6	33.0	17.3	0.0	0.1
British Columbia	47.7	3.0	7.4	8.2	20.5	10.4	2.7	0.2
Canada	55.0	4.9	5.9	9.3	18.0	5.3	1.4	0.3

Source: Statistics Canada. 2012. Census Profile. 2011 Census. Statistics Canada Catalogue no. 98-316-XWE. Ottawa. Released October 24 2012.
http://www12.statcan.gc.ca/census-recensement/2011/dp-pd/prof/index.cfm?Lang=E

Shelter Costs

	Owned Dwellings					Rented Dwellings		
Area	Number	Median Value[1] ($)	Average Value[1] ($)	Median Monthly Costs[2] ($)	Average Monthly Costs[2] ($)	Number	Median Monthly Costs[3] ($)	Average Monthly Costs[3] ($)
Vancouver	128,430	752,016	929,049	1,119	1,462	136,135	1,004	1,089
British Columbia	1,202,000	448,835	543,635	1,023	1,228	519,855	903	989
Canada	9,013,410	280,552	345,182	978	1,141	4,060,385	784	848

Note: All figures cover non-farm, non-reserve private dwellings; (1) Refers to the dollar amount expected by the owner if the dwelling were to be sold; (2) Includes all shelter expenses paid by households that own their dwellings, such as the mortgage payment and the costs of electricity, heat, water and other municipal services, property taxes and condominium fees; (3) Includes all shelter expenses paid by households that rent their dwellings, such as the monthly rent and the costs of electricity, heat and municipal services.
Source: Statistics Canada. 2013. 2011 National Household Survey. Statistics Canada Catalogue no. 99-004-XWE. Ottawa. Released September 11, 2013.

Occupied Private Dwellings by Period of Construction

Area	1960 or Before	1961 to 1980	1981 to 1990	1991 to 2000	2001 to 2005	2006 to 2011
			Number			
Vancouver	73,615	68,460	37,795	43,275	21,085	20,340
British Columbia	282,675	551,655	308,450	329,780	133,235	158,845
Canada	3,273,105	4,152,715	2,112,110	1,707,880	1,031,020	1,042,430
			Percent of Dwellings			
Vancouver	27.8	25.9	14.3	16.4	8.0	7.7
British Columbia	16.0	31.3	17.5	18.7	7.6	9.0
Canada	24.6	31.2	15.9	12.8	7.7	7.8

Note: Figures cover non-farm, non-reserve private dwellings and includes data up to May 10, 2011.
Source: Statistics Canada. 2013. 2011 National Household Survey. Statistics Canada Catalogue no. 99-004-XWE. Ottawa. Released September 11, 2013.

Educational Attainment

Area	No Certificate, Diploma or Degree	High School Diploma or Equivalent[1]	Apprenticeship or Trades Certificate or Diploma[2]	College, CÉGEP or Other Non-University Certificate or Diploma	University Certificate or Diploma Below the Bachelor Level[3]	Bachelor's Degree	University Certificate, Diploma or Degree Above Bachelor Level[4]
				Number Total			
Vancouver	72,105	118,345	31,730	75,970	31,640	119,565	69,615
British Columbia	607,655	1,009,400	387,455	628,115	208,245	511,240	294,725
Canada	5,485,400	6,968,935	2,950,685	4,970,020	1,200,130	3,634,425	2,049,930
				Males			
Vancouver	33,640	58,175	19,630	34,385	14,330	57,140	34,005
British Columbia	305,040	475,670	262,245	260,580	86,995	235,620	149,300
Canada	2,742,875	3,305,415	1,928,970	2,118,430	513,235	1,643,080	1,043,350
				Females			
Vancouver	38,470	60,170	12,095	41,585	17,310	62,425	35,610
British Columbia	302,620	533,735	125,210	367,535	121,250	275,625	145,425
Canada	2,742,520	3,663,515	1,021,715	2,851,595	686,890	1,991,345	1,006,585
				Percent of Population Total			
Vancouver	13.9	22.8	6.1	14.6	6.1	23.0	13.4
British Columbia	16.7	27.7	10.6	17.2	5.7	14.0	8.1
Canada	20.1	25.6	10.8	18.2	4.4	13.3	7.5
				Males			
Vancouver	13.4	23.1	7.8	13.7	5.7	22.7	13.5
British Columbia	17.2	26.8	14.8	14.7	4.9	13.3	8.4
Canada	20.6	24.9	14.5	15.9	3.9	12.4	7.8
				Females			
Vancouver	14.4	22.5	4.5	15.5	6.5	23.3	13.3
British Columbia	16.2	28.5	6.7	19.6	6.5	14.7	7.8
Canada	19.6	26.2	7.3	20.4	4.9	14.3	7.2

Note: Figures cover total population aged 15 years and over by highest certificate, diploma or degree; (1) Includes persons who have graduated from a secondary school or equivalent. It excludes persons with a postsecondary certificate, diploma or degree; (2) Includes Registered Apprenticeship certificates (including Certificate of Qualification, Journeyperson's designation) and other trades certificates or diplomas such as pre-employment or vocational certificates and diplomas from brief trade programs completed at community colleges, institutes of technology, vocational centres, and similar institutions; (3) Comparisons with other data sources suggest that the category 'University certificate or diploma below the bachelor's level' was over-reported in the NHS. This category likely includes some responses that are actually college certificates or diplomas, bachelor's degrees or other types of education (e.g., university transfer programs, bachelor's programs completed in other countries, incomplete bachelor's programs, non-university professional designations). We recommend users interpret the results for the 'University certificate or diploma below the bachelor's level' category with caution; (4) 'University certificate or diploma above bachelor level' includes the categories: 'Degree in medicine, dentistry, veterinary medicine or optometry,' 'Master's degree' and 'Earned doctorate.'
Source: Statistics Canada. 2013. 2011 National Household Survey. Statistics Canada Catalogue no. 99-004-XWE. Ottawa. Released September 11, 2013.

Household Income Distribution

Area	Less than $10,000	$10,000 to $19,999	$20,000 to $29,999	$30,000 to $39,999	$40,000 to $49,999	$50,000 to $59,999	$60,000 to $79,999	$80,000 to $99,999	$100,000 to $124,999	$125,000 to $149,999	$150,000 and Over
					Households						
Vancouver	20,970	28,800	23,885	23,065	23,490	19,445	33,690	25,370	21,650	13,935	30,270
British Columbia	96,465	156,565	157,605	167,220	158,400	140,340	246,720	193,180	167,415	106,325	174,385
Canada	626,705	1,141,945	1,193,925	1,271,675	1,206,800	1,102,120	1,865,280	1,458,240	1,260,770	802,555	1,389,240
					Percent of Households						
Vancouver	7.9	10.9	9.0	8.7	8.9	7.3	12.7	9.6	8.2	5.3	11.4
British Columbia	5.5	8.9	8.9	9.5	9.0	8.0	14.0	10.9	9.5	6.0	9.9
Canada	4.7	8.6	9.0	9.5	9.1	8.3	14.0	10.9	9.5	6.0	10.4

Note: Household income is the sum of the total incomes of all members of that household. Total income refers to monetary receipts from certain sources, before income taxes and deductions, during calendar year 2010.
Source: Statistics Canada. 2013. 2011 National Household Survey. Statistics Canada Catalogue no. 99-004-XWE. Ottawa. Released September 11, 2013.

Median and Average Household and Economic Family Income

Area	Median Household Income ($)	Average Household Income ($)	Median After-tax Household Income ($)	Average After-tax Household Income ($)	Median Economic Family Income ($)	Average Economic Family Income ($)	Median After-tax Economic Family Income ($)	Average After-tax Economic Family Income ($)
Vancouver	56,113	80,460	50,116	67,295	77,515	104,278	69,271	86,865
British Columbia	60,333	77,378	54,379	66,264	75,797	91,967	67,915	78,580
Canada	61,072	79,102	54,089	66,149	76,511	94,125	67,044	78,517

Note: Figures cover household and economic familiy income in 2010. A household is defined as a person or a group of persons (other than foreign residents) who occupy the same private dwelling and do not have a usual place of residence elsewhere in Canada. Every person is a member of one and only one household. An economic family is defined as a group of two or more persons who live in the same dwelling and are related to each other by blood, marriage, common-law, adoption or a foster relationship. A couple may be of opposite or same sex.
Source: Statistics Canada. 2013. 2011 National Household Survey. Statistics Canada Catalogue no. 99-004-XWE. Ottawa. Released September 11, 2013.

PROFILES / Vancouver, British Columbia

Individual Income Distribution

Area	Less than $10,000	$10,000 to $19,999	$20,000 to $29,999	$30,000 to $39,999	$40,000 to $49,999	$50,000 to $59,999	$60,000 to $79,999	$80,000 to $99,999	$100,000 to $124,999	$125,000 and Over
Number — Total										
Vancouver	97,860	99,625	60,870	51,345	46,645	33,460	44,475	24,605	14,645	20,860
British Columbia	645,915	666,060	470,255	404,860	338,595	253,215	330,590	169,190	89,520	96,055
Canada	4,492,040	4,835,710	3,670,020	3,180,360	2,603,520	1,921,650	2,437,440	1,302,045	693,580	782,135
Males										
Vancouver	44,945	42,470	28,065	24,395	21,970	17,480	23,540	14,030	9,100	14,730
British Columbia	275,815	263,170	201,000	186,285	167,400	143,765	206,400	112,525	65,050	74,260
Canada	1,936,365	1,864,880	1,588,260	1,522,190	1,333,510	1,079,780	1,473,145	823,720	492,905	599,905
Females										
Vancouver	52,915	57,160	32,805	26,955	24,675	15,980	20,935	10,570	5,555	6,125
British Columbia	370,100	402,880	269,255	218,575	171,190	109,445	124,195	56,670	24,470	21,795
Canada	2,555,675	2,970,825	2,081,760	1,658,170	1,270,010	841,870	964,300	478,330	200,680	182,230
Percent of Population — Total										
Vancouver	19.8	20.2	12.3	10.4	9.4	6.8	9.0	5.0	3.0	4.2
British Columbia	18.6	19.2	13.6	11.7	9.8	7.3	9.5	4.9	2.6	2.8
Canada	17.3	18.7	14.2	12.3	10.0	7.4	9.4	5.0	2.7	3.0
Males										
Vancouver	18.7	17.6	11.7	10.1	9.1	7.3	9.8	5.8	3.8	6.1
British Columbia	16.3	15.5	11.9	11.0	9.9	8.5	12.2	6.6	3.8	4.4
Canada	15.2	14.7	12.5	12.0	10.5	8.5	11.6	6.5	3.9	4.7
Females										
Vancouver	20.9	22.5	12.9	10.6	9.7	6.3	8.3	4.2	2.2	2.4
British Columbia	20.9	22.8	15.2	12.4	9.7	6.2	7.0	3.2	1.4	1.2
Canada	19.4	22.5	15.8	12.6	9.6	6.4	7.3	3.6	1.5	1.4

Note: Figures cover individuals aged 15 years and over with income. Income refers to monetary receipts from certain sources, before income taxes and deductions, during calendar year 2010.
Source: Statistics Canada. 2013. 2011 National Household Survey. Statistics Canada Catalogue no. 99-004-XWE. Ottawa. Released September 11, 2013.

Labour Force Status

Area	In the Labour Force - All	Employed	Unemployed	Not in the Labour Force
Number — Total				
Vancouver	349,145	324,475	24,670	169,830
British Columbia	2,354,245	2,171,465	182,775	1,292,595
Canada	17,990,080	16,595,035	1,395,045	9,269,445
Males				
Vancouver	178,875	166,015	12,850	72,435
British Columbia	1,223,375	1,124,590	98,785	552,070
Canada	9,388,570	8,634,310	754,255	3,906,785
Females				
Vancouver	170,270	158,460	11,820	97,390
British Columbia	1,130,870	1,046,875	83,990	740,530
Canada	8,601,515	7,960,725	640,790	5,362,660
Percent of Labour Force — Total				
Vancouver	67.3	62.5	7.1	32.7
British Columbia	64.6	59.5	7.8	35.4
Canada	66.0	60.9	7.8	34.0
Males				
Vancouver	71.2	66.1	7.2	28.8
British Columbia	68.9	63.3	8.1	31.1
Canada	70.6	64.9	8.0	29.4
Females				
Vancouver	63.6	59.2	6.9	36.4
British Columbia	60.4	55.9	7.4	39.6
Canada	61.6	57.0	7.4	38.4

Note: Figures are based on total population 15 years and over
Source: Statistics Canada. 2013. 2011 National Household Survey. Statistics Canada Catalogue no. 99-004-XWE. Ottawa. Released September 11, 2013.

Labour Force by Industry (NAICS Codes 11–52)

Area	Agriculture, forestry, fishing & hunting	Mining, quarrying, & oil & gas extraction	Utilities	Construction	Manufacturing	Wholesale Trade	Retail Trade	Transportation & warehousing	Information & cultural industries	Finance & insurance
					Number					
					Total					
Vancouver	1,435	1,900	1,640	15,500	17,515	12,880	31,220	13,085	16,640	17,850
British Columbia	61,210	25,450	13,215	181,510	148,810	90,560	266,265	118,675	62,235	91,790
Canada	437,650	261,050	149,940	1,215,380	1,619,295	733,445	2,031,665	827,780	420,830	767,960
					Males					
Vancouver	800	1,185	1,055	13,635	11,185	8,070	14,930	9,345	10,685	8,225
British Columbia	40,810	21,175	9,650	159,605	108,480	61,730	121,750	89,155	37,250	35,375
Canada	307,370	211,690	110,765	1,068,710	1,167,680	494,545	933,850	617,305	235,875	296,995
					Females					
Vancouver	635	715	580	1,860	6,335	4,815	16,290	3,745	5,960	9,625
British Columbia	20,405	4,275	3,560	21,910	40,335	28,820	144,515	29,520	24,980	56,415
Canada	130,285	49,360	39,175	146,670	451,615	238,900	1,097,820	210,475	184,955	470,960
					Percent of Labour Force					
					Total					
Vancouver	0.4	0.6	0.5	4.5	5.1	3.8	9.1	3.8	4.9	5.2
British Columbia	2.7	1.1	0.6	7.9	6.5	3.9	11.6	5.1	2.7	4.0
Canada	2.5	1.5	0.9	6.9	9.2	4.2	11.6	4.7	2.4	4.4
					Males					
Vancouver	0.5	0.7	0.6	7.8	6.4	4.6	8.5	5.3	6.1	4.7
British Columbia	3.4	1.8	0.8	13.3	9.0	5.1	10.1	7.4	3.1	2.9
Canada	3.3	2.3	1.2	11.6	12.7	5.4	10.2	6.7	2.6	3.2
					Females					
Vancouver	0.4	0.4	0.3	1.1	3.8	2.9	9.8	2.2	3.6	5.8
British Columbia	1.8	0.4	0.3	2.0	3.6	2.6	13.1	2.7	2.3	5.1
Canada	1.6	0.6	0.5	1.7	5.4	2.8	13.1	2.5	2.2	5.6

Note: Figures are based on total experienced labour force 15 years and over. Experienced labour force refers to persons who, during the week of Sunday, May 1 to Saturday, May 7, 2011, were employed and the unemployed who had last worked for pay or in self-employment in either 2010 or 2011.
Source: Statistics Canada. 2013. 2011 National Household Survey. Statistics Canada Catalogue no. 99-004-XWE. Ottawa. Released September 11, 2013.

Labour Force by Industry (NAICS Codes 53–91)

Area	Real estate & rental & leasing	Profess., scientific & tech. services	Mgmt of companies & enterprises	Admin. & support, waste mgmt & remed. services	Educational services	Health care & social assistance	Arts, entertain. & recreation	Accomm. & food services	Other services (except public admin.)	Public admin.
					Number					
					Total					
Vancouver	10,265	43,855	570	15,425	29,615	36,510	11,135	34,015	16,975	14,060
British Columbia	54,840	179,355	2,440	98,890	167,875	249,030	56,915	179,625	112,745	143,875
Canada	321,895	1,240,850	17,460	728,330	1,301,435	1,949,650	363,405	1,130,750	807,800	1,261,050
					Males					
Vancouver	5,940	25,695	320	8,585	11,470	9,165	5,795	16,475	6,375	6,525
British Columbia	29,790	98,760	1,320	55,745	55,635	47,020	29,750	73,570	49,130	74,040
Canada	179,090	688,625	9,380	411,250	424,915	349,430	188,270	469,990	372,940	652,510
					Females					
Vancouver	4,330	18,155	260	6,840	18,145	27,345	5,340	17,540	10,600	7,530
British Columbia	25,055	80,590	1,120	43,145	112,235	202,010	27,175	106,055	63,615	69,840
Canada	142,805	552,225	8,075	317,085	876,515	1,600,220	175,135	660,760	434,865	608,535
					Percent of Labour Force					
					Total					
Vancouver	3.0	12.8	0.2	4.5	8.7	10.7	3.3	9.9	5.0	4.1
British Columbia	2.4	7.8	0.1	4.3	7.3	10.8	2.5	7.8	4.9	6.2
Canada	1.8	7.1	0.1	4.1	7.4	11.1	2.1	6.4	4.6	7.2
					Males					
Vancouver	3.4	14.6	0.2	4.9	6.5	5.2	3.3	9.4	3.6	3.7
British Columbia	2.5	8.2	0.1	4.6	4.6	3.9	2.5	6.1	4.1	6.2
Canada	1.9	7.5	0.1	4.5	4.6	3.8	2.0	5.1	4.1	7.1
					Females					
Vancouver	2.6	10.9	0.2	4.1	10.9	16.4	3.2	10.5	6.4	4.5
British Columbia	2.3	7.3	0.1	3.9	10.2	18.3	2.5	9.6	5.8	6.3
Canada	1.7	6.6	0.1	3.8	10.4	19.1	2.1	7.9	5.2	7.2

Note: Figures are based on total experienced labour force 15 years and over. Experienced labour force refers to persons who, during the week of Sunday, May 1 to Saturday, May 7, 2011, were employed and the unemployed who had last worked for pay or in self-employment in either 2010 or 2011.
Source: Statistics Canada. 2013. 2011 National Household Survey. Statistics Canada Catalogue no. 99-004-XWE. Ottawa. Released September 11, 2013.

PROFILES / Vancouver, British Columbia

Occupation

Area	Mgmt	Business, Finance & Admin.	Natural/ Applied Sciences & Related	Health	Education, Law & Social, Community & Government Services	Art, Culture, Recreation & Sport	Sales & Service	Trades, Transport & Equip. Operators & Related	Natural Resources, Agri. & Related Production	Mfg & Utilities
Number — Total										
Vancouver	39,775	59,225	29,835	22,845	44,580	22,620	85,295	25,890	3,015	9,005
British Columbia	263,685	368,980	154,055	147,620	265,910	78,565	554,345	337,140	60,295	74,720
Canada	1,963,600	2,902,045	1,237,775	1,107,200	2,064,675	503,415	4,068,170	2,537,775	397,930	805,040
Males										
Vancouver	23,730	21,485	23,270	6,715	16,135	12,305	40,285	24,145	2,250	5,130
British Columbia	162,365	104,285	122,570	32,490	89,645	38,300	233,065	317,385	45,155	54,470
Canada	1,229,460	854,190	966,355	217,520	676,550	232,535	1,745,705	2,385,615	318,945	564,300
Females										
Vancouver	16,045	37,745	6,565	16,135	28,445	10,315	45,015	1,750	765	3,870
British Columbia	101,320	264,690	31,480	115,125	176,265	40,270	321,285	19,755	15,135	20,250
Canada	734,140	2,047,855	271,415	889,675	1,388,130	270,875	2,322,465	152,165	78,980	240,740
Percent of Labour Force — Total										
Vancouver	11.6	17.3	8.7	6.7	13.0	6.6	24.9	7.6	0.9	2.6
British Columbia	11.4	16.0	6.7	6.4	11.5	3.4	24.0	14.6	2.6	3.2
Canada	11.2	16.5	7.0	6.3	11.7	2.9	23.1	14.4	2.3	4.6
Males										
Vancouver	13.5	12.2	13.3	3.8	9.2	7.0	23.0	13.8	1.3	2.9
British Columbia	13.5	8.7	10.2	2.7	7.5	3.2	19.4	26.5	3.8	4.5
Canada	13.4	9.3	10.5	2.4	7.4	2.5	19.0	26.0	3.5	6.1
Females										
Vancouver	9.6	22.6	3.9	9.7	17.1	6.2	27.0	1.1	0.5	2.3
British Columbia	9.2	23.9	2.8	10.4	15.9	3.6	29.1	1.8	1.4	1.8
Canada	8.7	24.4	3.2	10.6	16.5	3.2	27.7	1.8	0.9	2.9

Note: Figures are based on total experienced labour force 15 years and over
Source: Statistics Canada. 2013. 2011 National Household Survey. Statistics Canada Catalogue no. 99-004-XWE. Ottawa. Released September 11, 2013.

Place of Work Status

Area	Worked at Home	Worked Outside Canada	No Fixed Workplace Address	Worked at Usual Place
Number — Total				
Vancouver	26,785	2,905	37,580	257,210
British Columbia	174,000	12,480	304,465	1,680,525
Canada	1,142,640	66,460	1,868,245	13,517,690
Males				
Vancouver	13,420	2,050	25,320	125,230
British Columbia	84,015	9,210	225,840	805,525
Canada	582,150	47,355	1,400,485	6,604,325
Females				
Vancouver	13,370	855	12,260	131,980
British Columbia	89,990	3,270	78,620	875,000
Canada	560,490	19,100	467,760	6,913,370
Percent of Labour Force — Total				
Vancouver	8.3	0.9	11.6	79.3
British Columbia	8.0	0.6	14.0	77.4
Canada	6.9	0.4	11.3	81.5
Males				
Vancouver	8.1	1.2	15.3	75.4
British Columbia	7.5	0.8	20.1	71.6
Canada	6.7	0.5	16.2	76.5
Females				
Vancouver	8.4	0.5	7.7	83.3
British Columbia	8.6	0.3	7.5	83.6
Canada	7.0	0.2	5.9	86.8

Note: Figures are based on total employed labour force 15 years and over.
Source: Statistics Canada. 2013. 2011 National Household Survey. Statistics Canada Catalogue no. 99-004-XWE. Ottawa. Released September 11, 2013.

Mode of Transportation to Work

Area	Car; Truck; Van; as Driver	Car; Truck; Van; as Passenger	Public Transit	Walked	Bicycled	All Other Modes
			Number			
			Total			
Vancouver	141,435	10,685	88,290	36,960	12,855	4,570
British Columbia	1,415,745	110,695	250,450	132,205	42,260	33,635
Canada	11,393,140	867,050	1,851,525	880,815	201,780	191,625
			Males			
Vancouver	82,105	3,370	37,610	17,170	7,795	2,495
British Columbia	773,160	47,425	107,645	57,000	26,595	19,535
Canada	6,238,835	349,530	788,290	387,580	135,840	104,725
			Females			
Vancouver	59,325	7,315	50,680	19,785	5,065	2,070
British Columbia	642,580	63,270	142,810	75,205	15,665	14,100
Canada	5,154,305	517,520	1,063,235	493,230	65,940	86,900
			Percent of Labour Force			
			Total			
Vancouver	48.0	3.6	30.0	12.5	4.4	1.6
British Columbia	71.3	5.6	12.6	6.7	2.1	1.7
Canada	74.0	5.6	12.0	5.7	1.3	1.2
			Males			
Vancouver	54.5	2.2	25.0	11.4	5.2	1.7
British Columbia	75.0	4.6	10.4	5.5	2.6	1.9
Canada	77.9	4.4	9.8	4.8	1.7	1.3
			Females			
Vancouver	41.1	5.1	35.1	13.7	3.5	1.4
British Columbia	67.4	6.6	15.0	7.9	1.6	1.5
Canada	69.8	7.0	14.4	6.7	0.9	1.2

Note: Figures are based on total employed labour force 15 years and over.
Source: Statistics Canada. 2013. 2011 National Household Survey. Statistics Canada Catalogue no. 99-004-XWE. Ottawa. Released September 11, 2013.

Visible Minority Population Characteristics

Area	Total Minority	South Asian[1]	Chinese	Black	Filipino	Latin American	Arab	SE Asian[2]	West Asian[3]	Korean	Japanese	Multiple[4]
						Number						
						Total						
Vancouver	305,615	35,140	163,230	5,720	35,490	9,595	2,975	17,870	6,885	8,780	10,080	8,680
British Columbia	1,180,870	313,440	438,140	33,260	126,040	35,465	14,090	51,970	38,960	53,770	38,120	31,160
Canada	6,264,750	1,567,400	1,324,750	945,665	619,310	381,280	380,620	312,075	206,840	161,130	87,270	171,935
						Males						
Vancouver	143,525	17,715	76,990	3,120	14,695	4,640	1,950	8,400	3,620	3,775	3,855	4,185
British Columbia	565,965	157,135	208,175	17,365	53,715	16,985	8,010	25,055	19,420	25,325	16,295	15,255
Canada	3,043,010	790,755	632,325	453,005	268,885	186,355	203,485	154,035	105,620	77,165	38,270	83,335
						Females						
Vancouver	162,090	17,425	86,235	2,600	20,800	4,955	1,030	9,470	3,265	5,000	6,230	4,495
British Columbia	614,905	156,300	229,960	15,895	72,320	18,480	6,080	26,920	19,540	28,440	21,820	15,905
Canada	3,221,745	776,650	692,420	492,660	350,425	194,925	177,140	158,045	101,220	83,965	48,990	88,600
						Percent of Population						
						Total						
Vancouver	51.8	6.0	27.7	1.0	6.0	1.6	0.5	3.0	1.2	1.5	1.7	1.5
British Columbia	27.3	7.2	10.1	0.8	2.9	0.8	0.3	1.2	0.9	1.2	0.9	0.7
Canada	19.1	4.8	4.0	2.9	1.9	1.2	1.2	0.9	0.6	0.5	0.3	0.5
						Males						
Vancouver	49.8	6.1	26.7	1.1	5.1	1.6	0.7	2.9	1.3	1.3	1.3	1.5
British Columbia	26.6	7.4	9.8	0.8	2.5	0.8	0.4	1.2	0.9	1.2	0.8	0.7
Canada	18.8	4.9	3.9	2.8	1.7	1.2	1.3	1.0	0.7	0.5	0.2	0.5
						Females						
Vancouver	53.7	5.8	28.6	0.9	6.9	1.6	0.3	3.1	1.1	1.7	2.1	1.5
British Columbia	28.0	7.1	10.5	0.7	3.3	0.8	0.3	1.2	0.9	1.3	1.0	0.7
Canada	19.3	4.7	4.1	3.0	2.1	1.2	1.1	0.9	0.6	0.5	0.3	0.5

Note: The Employment Equity Act defines visible minorities as 'persons, other than Aboriginal peoples, who are non-Caucasian in race or non-white in colour';
(1) Includes 'East Indian,' 'Pakistani,' 'Sri Lankan,' etc.; (2) Includes 'Vietnamese,' 'Cambodian,' 'Malaysian,' 'Laotian,' etc.; (3) Includes 'Iranian,' 'Afghan,' etc.; (4) Includes respondents who reported more than one visible minority group by checking two or more mark-in circles, e.g., 'Black' and 'South Asian.'
Source: Statistics Canada. 2013. 2011 National Household Survey. Statistics Canada Catalogue no. 99-004-XWE. Ottawa. Released September 11, 2013.

PROFILES / Vancouver, British Columbia

Aboriginal Population

Area	Aboriginal Identity[1]	First Nations (North American Indian) Single Identity[2]	Métis Single Identity	Inuk (Inuit) Single Identity	Multiple Aboriginal Identities[3]	Aboriginal Identities Not Included Elsewhere
Number						
Total						
Vancouver	11,945	7,865	3,595	70	100	305
British Columbia	232,290	155,020	69,475	1,570	2,480	3,745
Canada	1,400,685	851,560	451,795	59,440	11,415	26,475
Males						
Vancouver	5,785	3,665	1,840	30	45	200
British Columbia	113,080	75,400	33,940	820	1,190	1,735
Canada	682,190	411,785	223,335	29,495	5,525	12,055
Females						
Vancouver	6,165	4,200	1,755	40	60	105
British Columbia	119,215	79,620	35,540	750	1,290	2,015
Canada	718,500	439,775	228,460	29,950	5,890	14,420
Percent of Population						
Total						
Vancouver	2.0	1.3	0.6	0.0	0.0	0.1
British Columbia	5.4	3.6	1.6	0.0	0.1	0.1
Canada	4.3	2.6	1.4	0.2	0.0	0.1
Males						
Vancouver	2.0	1.3	0.6	0.0	0.0	0.1
British Columbia	5.3	3.5	1.6	0.0	0.1	0.1
Canada	4.2	2.5	1.4	0.2	0.0	0.1
Females						
Vancouver	2.0	1.4	0.6	0.0	0.0	0.0
British Columbia	5.4	3.6	1.6	0.0	0.1	0.1
Canada	4.3	2.6	1.4	0.2	0.0	0.1

Note: (1) Includes persons who reported being an Aboriginal person, that is, First Nations (North American Indian), Métis or Inuk (Inuit) and/or those who reported Registered or Treaty Indian status, that is registered under the Indian Act of Canada, and/or those who reported membership in a First Nation or Indian band. Aboriginal peoples of Canada are defined in the Constitution Act, 1982, section 35-2 as including the Indian, Inuit and Métis peoples of Canada; (2) Users should be aware that the estimates associated with this variable are more affected than most by the incomplete enumeration of certain Indian reserves and Indian settlements in the National Household Survey (NHS); (3) Includes persons who reported being any two or all three of the following: First Nations (North American Indian), Métis or Inuk (Inuit).
Source: Statistics Canada. 2013. 2011 National Household Survey. Statistics Canada Catalogue no. 99-004-XWE. Ottawa. Released September 11, 2013.

Ethnic Origin

Area	North American Aboriginal	Other North American	European	Caribbean	Latin, Central and South American	African	Asian	Oceania
Number								
Total								
Vancouver	14,675	73,550	277,835	3,420	11,900	8,025	292,445	5,040
British Columbia	267,085	884,490	2,812,935	20,035	52,725	47,185	1,122,445	35,770
Canada	1,836,035	11,070,455	20,157,965	627,590	544,375	766,735	5,011,225	74,875
Males								
Vancouver	7,080	37,535	139,600	1,960	5,930	4,070	136,690	2,485
British Columbia	128,880	440,920	1,387,940	10,225	25,605	23,575	535,825	17,425
Canada	885,675	5,462,685	9,913,150	291,640	264,635	387,360	2,435,540	37,490
Females								
Vancouver	7,590	36,010	138,235	1,460	5,980	3,955	155,755	2,555
British Columbia	138,205	443,570	1,424,990	9,810	27,120	23,610	586,620	18,340
Canada	950,360	5,607,770	10,244,820	335,945	279,740	379,380	2,575,680	37,385
Percent of Population								
Total								
Vancouver	2.5	12.5	47.1	0.6	2.0	1.4	49.5	0.9
British Columbia	6.2	20.5	65.0	0.5	1.2	1.1	26.0	0.8
Canada	5.6	33.7	61.4	1.9	1.7	2.3	15.3	0.2
Males								
Vancouver	2.5	13.0	48.4	0.7	2.1	1.4	47.4	0.9
British Columbia	6.1	20.7	65.3	0.5	1.2	1.1	25.2	0.8
Canada	5.5	33.8	61.3	1.8	1.6	2.4	15.1	0.2
Females								
Vancouver	2.5	11.9	45.8	0.5	2.0	1.3	51.6	0.8
British Columbia	6.3	20.2	64.8	0.4	1.2	1.1	26.7	0.8
Canada	5.7	33.6	61.4	2.0	1.7	2.3	15.4	0.2

Note: The sum of the ethnic groups in this table is greater than the total population estimate because a person may report more than one ethnic origin in the NHS.
Source: Statistics Canada. 2013. 2011 National Household Survey. Statistics Canada Catalogue no. 99-004-XWE. Ottawa. Released September 11, 2013.

Religion

Area	Buddhist	Christian	Hindu	Jewish	Muslim	Sikh	Traditional (Aboriginal) Spirituality	Other Religions	No Religious Affiliation
				Number Total					
Vancouver	33,450	213,855	8,220	10,350	13,255	16,815	545	5,275	288,435
British Columbia	90,620	1,930,415	45,795	23,130	79,310	201,110	10,295	35,500	1,908,285
Canada	366,830	22,102,745	497,965	329,495	1,053,945	454,965	64,935	130,835	7,850,605
				Males					
Vancouver	14,505	96,175	4,260	4,995	6,865	8,575	285	2,340	150,235
British Columbia	40,175	883,680	22,945	11,255	39,780	100,610	5,085	14,680	1,007,420
Canada	168,465	10,497,775	250,435	161,265	540,555	229,435	31,805	57,745	4,225,645
				Females					
Vancouver	18,950	117,680	3,960	5,355	6,395	8,235	265	2,930	138,205
British Columbia	50,440	1,046,735	22,845	11,880	39,530	100,500	5,210	20,820	900,865
Canada	198,365	11,604,975	247,525	168,235	513,395	225,530	33,135	73,090	3,624,965
				Percent of Population Total					
Vancouver	5.7	36.2	1.4	1.8	2.2	2.8	0.1	0.9	48.9
British Columbia	2.1	44.6	1.1	0.5	1.8	4.7	0.2	0.8	44.1
Canada	1.1	67.3	1.5	1.0	3.2	1.4	0.2	0.4	23.9
				Males					
Vancouver	5.0	33.4	1.5	1.7	2.4	3.0	0.1	0.8	52.1
British Columbia	1.9	41.6	1.1	0.5	1.9	4.7	0.2	0.7	47.4
Canada	1.0	64.9	1.5	1.0	3.3	1.4	0.2	0.4	26.1
				Females					
Vancouver	6.3	39.0	1.3	1.8	2.1	2.7	0.1	1.0	45.8
British Columbia	2.3	47.6	1.0	0.5	1.8	4.6	0.2	0.9	41.0
Canada	1.2	69.5	1.5	1.0	3.1	1.4	0.2	0.4	21.7

Note: Religion refers to the person's self-identification as having a connection or affiliation with any religious denomination, group, body, sect, cult or other religiously defined community or system of belief. Religion is not limited to formal membership in a religious organization or group. Persons without a religious connection or affiliation can self-identify as atheist, agnostic or humanist, or can provide another applicable response.
Source: Statistics Canada. 2013. 2011 National Household Survey. Statistics Canada Catalogue no. 99-004-XWE. Ottawa. Released September 11, 2013.

Religion—Christian Denominations

Area	Anglican	Baptist	Catholic	Christian Orthodox	Lutheran	Pentecostal	Presbyterian	United Church	Other Christian
				Number Total					
Vancouver	18,250	8,620	101,520	8,545	4,500	3,235	4,050	15,065	50,075
British Columbia	213,975	91,575	650,360	39,845	71,470	58,300	44,635	222,230	538,030
Canada	1,631,845	635,840	12,810,705	550,690	478,185	478,705	472,385	2,007,610	3,036,780
				Males					
Vancouver	8,165	3,815	46,465	4,100	2,170	1,350	1,815	6,235	22,050
British Columbia	94,330	41,565	303,300	19,475	32,205	26,590	19,925	94,020	252,270
Canada	752,945	293,905	6,167,290	270,205	221,525	217,850	218,955	912,545	1,442,550
				Females					
Vancouver	10,090	4,800	55,055	4,440	2,330	1,885	2,230	8,830	28,020
British Columbia	119,645	50,010	347,060	20,375	39,270	31,710	24,710	128,210	285,770
Canada	878,900	341,940	6,643,415	280,485	256,660	260,850	253,430	1,095,065	1,594,230
				Percent of Population Total					
Vancouver	3.1	1.5	17.2	1.4	0.8	0.5	0.7	2.6	8.5
British Columbia	4.9	2.1	15.0	0.9	1.7	1.3	1.0	5.1	12.4
Canada	5.0	1.9	39.0	1.7	1.5	1.5	1.4	6.1	9.2
				Males					
Vancouver	2.8	1.3	16.1	1.4	0.8	0.5	0.6	2.2	7.7
British Columbia	4.4	2.0	14.3	0.9	1.5	1.3	0.9	4.4	11.9
Canada	4.7	1.8	38.2	1.7	1.4	1.3	1.4	5.6	8.9
				Females					
Vancouver	3.3	1.6	18.2	1.5	0.8	0.6	0.7	2.9	9.3
British Columbia	5.4	2.3	15.8	0.9	1.8	1.4	1.1	5.8	13.0
Canada	5.3	2.0	39.8	1.7	1.5	1.6	1.5	6.6	9.6

Note: Religion refers to the person's self-identification as having a connection or affiliation with any religious denomination, group, body, sect, cult or other religiously defined community or system of belief. Religion is not limited to formal membership in a religious organization or group. Persons without a religious connection or affiliation can self-identify as atheist, agnostic or humanist, or can provide another applicable response.
Source: Statistics Canada. 2013. 2011 National Household Survey. Statistics Canada Catalogue no. 99-004-XWE. Ottawa. Released September 11, 2013.

PROFILES / Vancouver, British Columbia

Immigrant Status and Period of Immigration

Area	Non-Immigrants[1]	Immigrants All	Before 1971	1971 to 1980	1981 to 1990	1991 to 2000	2001 to 2005	2006 to 2011	Non-Permanent Residents[3]
				Number					
				Total					
Vancouver	308,495	258,750	33,350	37,665	41,970	70,790	32,750	42,230	22,965
British Columbia	3,067,590	1,191,875	223,215	161,335	156,445	305,655	160,100	185,115	64,995
Canada	25,720,175	6,775,765	1,261,055	870,775	949,890	1,539,050	992,070	1,162,915	356,385
				Males					
Vancouver	157,435	119,670	16,275	17,885	18,905	31,630	15,045	19,925	11,125
British Columbia	1,533,255	561,490	109,510	76,865	72,625	140,985	74,395	87,110	30,880
Canada	12,753,235	3,231,370	605,430	416,670	454,570	724,905	474,545	555,245	178,515
				Females					
Vancouver	151,060	139,080	17,075	19,775	23,065	39,165	17,705	22,300	11,840
British Columbia	1,534,330	630,385	113,710	84,470	83,820	164,675	85,710	98,005	34,115
Canada	12,966,935	3,544,400	655,625	454,105	495,325	814,145	517,530	607,670	177,870
				Percent of Population					
				Total					
Vancouver	52.3	43.8	5.7	6.4	7.1	12.0	5.5	7.2	3.9
British Columbia	70.9	27.6	5.2	3.7	3.6	7.1	3.7	4.3	1.5
Canada	78.3	20.6	3.8	2.7	2.9	4.7	3.0	3.5	1.1
				Males					
Vancouver	54.6	41.5	5.6	6.2	6.6	11.0	5.2	6.9	3.9
British Columbia	72.1	26.4	5.2	3.6	3.4	6.6	3.5	4.1	1.5
Canada	78.9	20.0	3.7	2.6	2.8	4.5	2.9	3.4	1.1
				Females					
Vancouver	50.0	46.1	5.7	6.5	7.6	13.0	5.9	7.4	3.9
British Columbia	69.8	28.7	5.2	3.8	3.8	7.5	3.9	4.5	1.6
Canada	77.7	21.2	3.9	2.7	3.0	4.9	3.1	3.6	1.1

Note: (1) Non-immigrant refers to a person who is a Canadian citizen by birth; (2) Immigrant refers to a person who is or has ever been a landed immigrant/permanent resident. This person has been granted the right to live in Canada permanently by immigration authorities. Some immigrants have resided in Canada for a number of years, while others have arrived recently. Some immigrants are Canadian citizens, while others are not. Most immigrants are born outside Canada, but a small number are born in Canada. In the 2011 National Household Survey, 'Immigrants' includes immigrants who landed in Canada prior to May 10, 2011; (3) Non-permanent resident refers to a person from another country who has a work or study permit, or who is a refugee claimant, and any non-Canadian-born family member living in Canada with them.
Source: Statistics Canada. 2013. 2011 National Household Survey. Statistics Canada Catalogue no. 99-004-XWE. Ottawa. Released September 11, 2013.

Mother Tongue

Area	English	French	Non-official Language	English & French	English & Non-official Language	French & Non-official Language	English, French & Non-official Language
			Number				
			Total				
Vancouver	299,290	8,905	270,490	1,500	14,425	755	355
British Columbia	3,062,435	57,275	1,154,215	8,600	68,800	3,345	1,530
Canada	18,858,980	7,054,975	6,567,680	144,685	396,330	74,430	24,095
			Males				
Vancouver	154,040	4,575	124,825	760	6,800	345	170
British Columbia	1,526,350	28,315	543,395	4,065	32,875	1,520	725
Canada	9,345,225	3,452,380	3,157,785	69,975	192,000	36,535	11,965
			Females				
Vancouver	145,250	4,330	145,670	745	7,625	410	185
British Columbia	1,536,085	28,965	610,825	4,535	35,925	1,830	805
Canada	9,513,750	3,602,590	3,409,895	74,710	204,330	37,890	12,130
			Percent of Population				
			Total				
Vancouver	50.2	1.5	45.4	0.3	2.4	0.1	0.1
British Columbia	70.3	1.3	26.5	0.2	1.6	0.1	0.0
Canada	56.9	21.3	19.8	0.4	1.2	0.2	0.1
			Males				
Vancouver	52.8	1.6	42.8	0.3	2.3	0.1	0.1
British Columbia	71.4	1.3	25.4	0.2	1.5	0.1	0.0
Canada	57.5	21.2	19.4	0.4	1.2	0.2	0.1
			Females				
Vancouver	47.7	1.4	47.9	0.2	2.5	0.1	0.1
British Columbia	69.2	1.3	27.5	0.2	1.6	0.1	0.0
Canada	56.4	21.4	20.2	0.4	1.2	0.2	0.1

Note: Figures cover total population excluding institutional residents.
Source: Statistics Canada. 2012. Census Profile. 2011 Census. Statistics Canada Catalogue no. 98-316-XWE. Ottawa. Released October 24 2012.
http://www12.statcan.gc.ca/census-recensement/2011/dp-pd/prof/index.cfm?Lang=E

Language Spoken Most Often at Home

Area	English	French	Non-official Language	English & French	English & Non-official Language	French & Non-official Language	English, French & Non-official Language
			Number				
			Total				
Vancouver	387,300	3,560	169,485	885	33,780	255	450
British Columbia	3,506,595	16,685	670,100	4,700	155,065	930	2,130
Canada	21,457,075	6,827,865	3,673,865	131,205	875,135	109,700	46,330
			Males				
Vancouver	194,815	1,735	78,360	475	15,805	125	195
British Columbia	1,733,775	8,015	317,670	2,240	74,155	435	940
Canada	10,585,620	3,348,235	1,767,310	63,475	425,370	53,010	22,845
			Females				
Vancouver	192,485	1,825	91,130	415	17,975	130	260
British Columbia	1,772,820	8,665	352,430	2,460	80,905	495	1,185
Canada	10,871,455	3,479,625	1,906,555	67,730	449,765	56,690	23,485
			Percent of Population				
			Total				
Vancouver	65.0	0.6	28.5	0.1	5.7	0.0	0.1
British Columbia	80.5	0.4	15.4	0.1	3.6	0.0	0.0
Canada	64.8	20.6	11.1	0.4	2.6	0.3	0.1
			Males				
Vancouver	66.8	0.6	26.9	0.2	5.4	0.0	0.1
British Columbia	81.1	0.4	14.9	0.1	3.5	0.0	0.0
Canada	65.1	20.6	10.9	0.4	2.6	0.3	0.1
			Females				
Vancouver	63.3	0.6	30.0	0.1	5.9	0.0	0.1
British Columbia	79.9	0.4	15.9	0.1	3.6	0.0	0.1
Canada	64.5	20.6	11.3	0.4	2.7	0.3	0.1

Note: Figures cover total population excluding institutional residents.
Source: Statistics Canada. 2012. Census Profile. 2011 Census. Statistics Canada Catalogue no. 98-316-XWE. Ottawa. Released October 24 2012.
http://www12.statcan.gc.ca/census-recensement/2011/dp-pd/prof/index.cfm?Lang=E

Knowledge of Official Languages

Area	English Only	French Only	English & French	Neither English nor French
		Number		
		Total		
Vancouver	490,430	430	58,905	45,960
British Columbia	3,912,950	2,045	296,645	144,555
Canada	22,564,665	4,165,015	5,795,570	595,920
		Males		
Vancouver	245,600	205	26,855	18,835
British Columbia	1,943,760	950	132,940	59,590
Canada	11,222,185	1,925,340	2,876,560	241,790
		Females		
Vancouver	244,825	225	32,045	27,120
British Columbia	1,969,190	1,095	163,705	84,965
Canada	11,342,485	2,239,680	2,919,005	354,135
		Percent of Population		
		Total		
Vancouver	82.3	0.1	9.9	7.7
British Columbia	89.8	0.0	6.8	3.3
Canada	68.1	12.6	17.5	1.8
		Males		
Vancouver	84.3	0.1	9.2	6.5
British Columbia	90.9	0.0	6.2	2.8
Canada	69.0	11.8	17.7	1.5
		Females		
Vancouver	80.5	0.1	10.5	8.9
British Columbia	88.7	0.0	7.4	3.8
Canada	67.3	13.3	17.3	2.1

Note: Figures cover total population excluding institutional residents.
Source: Statistics Canada. 2012. Census Profile. 2011 Census. Statistics Canada Catalogue no. 98-316-XWE. Ottawa. Released October 24 2012.
http://www12.statcan.gc.ca/census-recensement/2011/dp-pd/prof/index.cfm?Lang=E

Vaughan, Ontario

Background

Vaughan is located 30 kilometres north of downtown Toronto, Ontario, and is a part of the Greater Toronto Area (GTA). Vaughan is one of Canada's fastest-growing municipalities and has nearly doubled in population since the city was incorporated in 1991.

When British North America was divided into Upper and Lower Canada in 1791, pioneers were encouraged to populate sparsely settled areas. Settlers arrived in the township of Vaughan by 1800 and the original settlement of 19 men, 5 women and 30 children grew into a community of 4,300 people by the year 1840. The pioneer township changed little until after World War II when significant immigration began developing Vaughan's commercial and industrial economy.

The region's pioneer past is evident in the four historic villages within the City of Vaughan: Woodbridge, Maple, Kleinburg-Nashville and Thornhill. Every year the four villages host events such as the Woodbridge Fair, Kleinburg's Binder Twine Festival and Maplefest. The McMichael Canadian Art Collection in Kleinburg features close to 6,000 artworks by Tom Thomson and the Group of Seven, First Nations, Inuit and other Canadian artists.

Canada's largest amusement park, Canada's Wonderland, is one of Vaughan's most popular attractions as is Vaughan Mills, one of the GTA's largest shopping malls. Vaughan is also home to the Ontario Soccer Association (OSA), the largest sports organization in Canada, and the Canadian Soccer Hall of Fame and Museum.

In September 2012, the City of Vaughan launched a business development trade mission with the Province of Milan in Italy. Vaughan has long-time international partnerships with the Italian cities of Sora, Lanciano and Delia. Approximately 40% of Vaughan residents identify themselves as Italian Canadian.

Vaughan has average summer highs of plus 25.47 degrees Celsius, winter lows of minus 9.4 degrees Celsius, and an average rainfall just over 693 mm per year.

Rankings

- Vaughan was ranked #102 out of 190 Canadian cities in the "Best Places to Live" listings. *Money Sense Magazine* evaluated each city using 22 different criteria and point systems such as affordable housing, population growth, air quality and walk/bike to work ratios. *Money Sense, Canada's Best Places to Live, March 20, 2012*
- *Canadian Business* ranked Canada's 10 most expensive real-estate markets based on raw house prices. Vaughn was ranked #9 with an average house price of $562,600. The Top 10 list was dominated by cities in Ontario and British Columbia. *Canadian Business, "Canada's most expensive real estate markets," March 26, 2012*

PROFILES / Vaughan, Ontario

Population Growth and Density

Area	Population in 2001	Population in 2006	Population in 2011	Population Change 2001–2006	Population Change 2006–2011	Land Area (sq. km)	Population Density per sq. km
Vaughan	182,022	238,866	288,301	31.2	20.7	273.52	1,054.0
Ontario	11,410,046	12,160,282	12,851,821	6.6	5.7	908,607.67	14.1
Canada	30,007,094	31,612,897	33,476,688	5.4	5.9	8,965,121.42	3.7

Source: Statistics Canada. 2012. Census Profile. 2011 Census. Statistics Canada Catalogue no. 98-316-XWE. Ottawa. Released October 24 2012. http://www12.statcan.gc.ca/census-recensement/2011/dp-pd/prof/index.cfm?Lang=E;
Statistics Canada 2007. 2006 Community Profiles. 2006 Census. Statistics Canada Catalogue no. 92-591-XWE. Ottawa. Released March 13 2007. http://www12.statcan.ca/census-recensement/2006/dp-pd/prof/92-591/index.cfm?Lang=E

Gender

Area	Males	Females
	Number	
Vaughan	140,910	147,390
Ontario	6,263,140	6,588,685
Canada	16,414,225	17,062,460
	Percent of Population	
Vaughan	48.9	51.1
Ontario	48.7	51.3
Canada	49.0	51.0

Source: Statistics Canada. 2012. Census Profile. 2011 Census. Statistics Canada Catalogue no. 98-316-XWE. Ottawa. Released October 24 2012. http://www12.statcan.gc.ca/census-recensement/2011/dp-pd/prof/index.cfm?Lang=E

Marital Status

Area	Married[1]	Living Common-law	Single[2]	Separated	Divorced	Widowed
			Number			
			Total			
Vaughan	139,570	5,895	61,825	4,310	7,780	10,465
Ontario	5,367,400	791,210	2,985,020	319,805	593,730	613,880
Canada	12,941,960	3,142,525	7,816,045	698,240	1,686,035	1,584,530
			Males			
Vaughan	69,505	2,950	32,450	1,580	2,710	1,825
Ontario	2,681,320	397,620	1,583,760	133,790	231,160	117,980
Canada	6,470,300	1,575,495	4,206,320	299,655	680,415	310,940
			Females			
Vaughan	70,060	2,945	29,375	2,730	5,070	8,635
Ontario	2,686,075	393,590	1,401,260	186,015	362,570	495,905
Canada	6,471,660	1,567,035	3,609,730	398,585	1,005,620	1,273,590
			Percent of Population			
			Total			
Vaughan	60.7	2.6	26.9	1.9	3.4	4.6
Ontario	50.3	7.4	28.0	3.0	5.6	5.8
Canada	46.4	11.3	28.0	2.5	6.0	5.7
			Males			
Vaughan	62.6	2.7	29.2	1.4	2.4	1.6
Ontario	52.1	7.7	30.8	2.6	4.5	2.3
Canada	47.8	11.6	31.1	2.2	5.0	2.3
			Females			
Vaughan	59.0	2.5	24.7	2.3	4.3	7.3
Ontario	48.6	7.1	25.4	3.4	6.6	9.0
Canada	45.2	10.9	25.2	2.8	7.0	8.9

Note: (1) and not separated, (2) never legally married
Source: Statistics Canada. 2012. Census Profile. 2011 Census. Statistics Canada Catalogue no. 98-316-XWE. Ottawa. Released October 24 2012. http://www12.statcan.gc.ca/census-recensement/2011/dp-pd/prof/index.cfm?Lang=E

Age Characteristics: 0 to 49 Years

Area	0 to 4 Years	5 to 9 Years	10 to 14 Years	15 to 19 Years	20 to 24 Years	25 to 29 Years	30 to 34 Years	35 to 39 Years	40 to 44 Years	45 to 49 Years
					Number					
					Total					
Vaughan	18,050	20,095	20,315	20,685	18,865	16,470	17,680	21,925	24,600	24,415
Ontario	704,260	712,755	763,755	863,635	852,910	815,120	800,365	844,335	924,075	1,055,880
Canada	1,877,095	1,809,895	1,920,355	2,178,135	2,187,450	2,169,590	2,162,905	2,173,930	2,324,875	2,675,130
					Males					
Vaughan	9,225	10,250	10,410	10,705	9,515	8,115	8,105	10,185	11,815	11,925
Ontario	360,590	365,290	391,630	443,680	432,490	400,045	383,340	405,845	447,920	517,510
Canada	961,150	925,965	983,995	1,115,845	1,108,775	1,077,275	1,058,810	1,064,200	1,141,720	1,318,715
					Females					
Vaughan	8,825	9,845	9,900	9,985	9,350	8,350	9,575	11,745	12,790	12,490
Ontario	343,670	347,465	372,125	419,950	420,415	415,075	417,030	438,485	476,155	538,370
Canada	915,945	883,935	936,360	1,062,295	1,078,670	1,092,315	1,104,095	1,109,735	1,183,155	1,356,420
					Percent of Population					
					Total					
Vaughan	6.3	7.0	7.0	7.2	6.5	5.7	6.1	7.6	8.5	8.5
Ontario	5.5	5.5	5.9	6.7	6.6	6.3	6.2	6.6	7.2	8.2
Canada	5.6	5.4	5.7	6.5	6.5	6.5	6.5	6.5	6.9	8.0
					Males					
Vaughan	6.5	7.3	7.4	7.6	6.8	5.8	5.8	7.2	8.4	8.5
Ontario	5.8	5.8	6.3	7.1	6.9	6.4	6.1	6.5	7.2	8.3
Canada	5.9	5.6	6.0	6.8	6.8	6.6	6.5	6.5	7.0	8.0
					Females					
Vaughan	6.0	6.7	6.7	6.8	6.3	5.7	6.5	8.0	8.7	8.5
Ontario	5.2	5.3	5.6	6.4	6.4	6.3	6.3	6.7	7.2	8.2
Canada	5.4	5.2	5.5	6.2	6.3	6.4	6.5	6.5	6.9	7.9

Source: Statistics Canada. 2012. Census Profile. 2011 Census. Statistics Canada Catalogue no. 98-316-XWE. Ottawa. Released October 24 2012.
http://www12.statcan.gc.ca/census-recensement/2011/dp-pd/prof/index.cfm?Lang=E

Age Characteristics: 50 Years and Over, and Median Age

Area	50 to 54 Years	55 to 59 Years	60 to 64 Years	65 to 69 Years	70 to 74 Years	75 to 79 Years	80 to 84 Years	85 Years and Over	Median Age
				Number					
				Total					
Vaughan	21,480	16,665	14,870	9,685	8,585	6,320	4,110	3,490	37.9
Ontario	1,006,140	864,620	765,655	563,485	440,780	356,150	271,510	246,400	40.4
Canada	2,658,965	2,340,635	2,052,670	1,521,715	1,153,065	922,700	702,070	645,515	40.6
				Males					
Vaughan	10,365	7,970	7,240	4,770	4,155	3,055	1,825	1,280	37.2
Ontario	492,560	418,755	370,370	270,875	206,350	161,345	113,620	80,925	39.4
Canada	1,309,030	1,147,300	1,002,690	738,010	543,435	417,945	291,085	208,300	39.6
				Females					
Vaughan	11,115	8,700	7,630	4,915	4,430	3,265	2,285	2,205	38.5
Ontario	513,580	445,865	395,275	292,610	234,435	194,805	157,890	165,475	41.3
Canada	1,349,940	1,193,335	1,049,985	783,705	609,630	504,755	410,985	437,215	41.5
				Percent of Population					
				Total					
Vaughan	7.5	5.8	5.2	3.4	3.0	2.2	1.4	1.2	—
Ontario	7.8	6.7	6.0	4.4	3.4	2.8	2.1	1.9	—
Canada	7.9	7.0	6.1	4.5	3.4	2.8	2.1	1.9	—
				Males					
Vaughan	7.4	5.7	5.1	3.4	2.9	2.2	1.3	0.9	—
Ontario	7.9	6.7	5.9	4.3	3.3	2.6	1.8	1.3	—
Canada	8.0	7.0	6.1	4.5	3.3	2.5	1.8	1.3	—
				Females					
Vaughan	7.5	5.9	5.2	3.3	3.0	2.2	1.6	1.5	—
Ontario	7.8	6.8	6.0	4.4	3.6	3.0	2.4	2.5	—
Canada	7.9	7.0	6.2	4.6	3.6	3.0	2.4	2.6	—

Source: Statistics Canada. 2012. Census Profile. 2011 Census. Statistics Canada Catalogue no. 98-316-XWE. Ottawa. Released October 24 2012.
http://www12.statcan.gc.ca/census-recensement/2011/dp-pd/prof/index.cfm?Lang=E

PROFILES / Vaughan, Ontario

Private Households by Household Size

Area	1 Person	2 Persons	3 Persons	4 Persons	5 Persons	6 or More Persons	Average Number of Persons in Private Households
				Households			
Vaughan	9,160	19,935	17,160	23,400	10,395	6,025	3.3
Ontario	1,230,975	1,584,415	803,030	783,925	310,860	174,305	2.6
Canada	3,673,310	4,544,820	2,081,900	1,903,300	724,405	392,885	2.5
				Percent of Households			
Vaughan	10.6	23.2	19.9	27.2	12.1	7.0	–
Ontario	25.2	32.4	16.4	16.0	6.4	3.6	–
Canada	27.6	34.1	15.6	14.3	5.4	2.9	–

Source: Statistics Canada. 2012. Census Profile. 2011 Census. Statistics Canada Catalogue no. 98-316-XWE. Ottawa. Released October 24 2012.
http://www12.statcan.gc.ca/census-recensement/2011/dp-pd/prof/index.cfm?Lang=E

Dwelling Type

Area	Single-detached House	Semi-detached House	Row House	Apartment: Building with Five or More Storeys	Apartment: Building with Fewer Than Five Storeys	Duplex Apartment	Movable Dwelling	Other Single-attached House
				Number				
Vaughan	58,205	7,200	9,305	6,940	1,330	3,070	5	10
Ontario	2,718,880	279,470	415,225	789,970	498,160	160,460	15,800	9,540
Canada	7,329,150	646,245	791,600	1,234,770	2,397,550	704,485	183,510	33,310
				Percent of Dwellings				
Vaughan	67.6	8.4	10.8	8.1	1.5	3.6	0.0	0.0
Ontario	55.6	5.7	8.5	16.2	10.2	3.3	0.3	0.2
Canada	55.0	4.9	5.9	9.3	18.0	5.3	1.4	0.3

Source: Statistics Canada. 2012. Census Profile. 2011 Census. Statistics Canada Catalogue no. 98-316-XWE. Ottawa. Released October 24 2012.
http://www12.statcan.gc.ca/census-recensement/2011/dp-pd/prof/index.cfm?Lang=E

Shelter Costs

	Owned Dwellings					Rented Dwellings		
Area	Number	Median Value[1] ($)	Average Value[1] ($)	Median Monthly Costs[2] ($)	Average Monthly Costs[2] ($)	Number	Median Monthly Costs[3] ($)	Average Monthly Costs[3] ($)
Vaughan	79,370	527,560	582,380	1,629	1,636	6,670	1,324	1,283
Ontario	3,446,650	300,862	367,428	1,163	1,284	1,385,535	892	926
Canada	9,013,410	280,552	345,182	978	1,141	4,060,385	784	848

Note: All figures cover non-farm, non-reserve private dwellings; (1) Refers to the dollar amount expected by the owner if the dwelling were to be sold; (2) Includes all shelter expenses paid by households that own their dwellings, such as the mortgage payment and the costs of electricity, heat, water and other municipal services, property taxes and condominium fees; (3) Includes all shelter expenses paid by households that rent their dwellings, such as the monthly rent and the costs of electricity, heat and municipal services.
Source: Statistics Canada. 2013. 2011 National Household Survey. Statistics Canada Catalogue no. 99-004-XWE. Ottawa. Released September 11, 2013.

Occupied Private Dwellings by Period of Construction

Area	1960 or Before	1961 to 1980	1981 to 1990	1991 to 2000	2001 to 2005	2006 to 2011
			Number			
Vaughan	1,600	6,055	21,535	22,530	18,485	15,855
Ontario	1,330,235	1,420,570	763,430	609,310	414,795	348,310
Canada	3,273,105	4,152,715	2,112,110	1,707,880	1,031,020	1,042,430
			Percent of Dwellings			
Vaughan	1.9	7.0	25.0	26.2	21.5	18.4
Ontario	27.2	29.1	15.6	12.5	8.5	7.1
Canada	24.6	31.2	15.9	12.8	7.7	7.8

Note: Figures cover non-farm, non-reserve private dwellings and includes data up to May 10, 2011.
Source: Statistics Canada. 2013. 2011 National Household Survey. Statistics Canada Catalogue no. 99-004-XWE. Ottawa. Released September 11, 2013.

Educational Attainment

Area	No Certificate, Diploma or Degree	High School Diploma or Equivalent[1]	Apprenticeship or Trades Certificate or Diploma[2]	College, CÉGEP or Other Non-University Certificate or Diploma	University Certificate or Diploma Below the Bachelor Level[3]	Bachelor's Degree	University Certificate, Diploma or Degree Above Bachelor Level[4]
				Number			
				Total			
Vaughan	43,090	54,630	13,875	38,395	12,795	39,805	25,140
Ontario	1,954,520	2,801,805	771,140	2,070,875	427,150	1,515,075	933,100
Canada	5,485,400	6,968,935	2,950,685	4,970,020	1,200,130	3,634,425	2,049,930
				Males			
Vaughan	20,700	26,225	9,170	17,225	6,040	18,435	12,575
Ontario	957,040	1,337,055	520,390	894,235	193,355	692,345	470,290
Canada	2,742,875	3,305,415	1,928,970	2,118,430	513,235	1,643,080	1,043,350
				Females			
Vaughan	22,395	28,400	4,705	21,170	6,750	21,365	12,560
Ontario	997,475	1,464,755	250,750	1,176,640	233,790	822,730	462,805
Canada	2,742,520	3,663,515	1,021,715	2,851,595	686,890	1,991,345	1,006,585
				Percent of Population			
				Total			
Vaughan	18.9	24.0	6.1	16.9	5.6	17.5	11.0
Ontario	18.7	26.8	7.4	19.8	4.1	14.5	8.9
Canada	20.1	25.6	10.8	18.2	4.4	13.3	7.5
				Males			
Vaughan	18.8	23.8	8.3	15.6	5.5	16.7	11.4
Ontario	18.9	26.4	10.3	17.7	3.8	13.7	9.3
Canada	20.6	24.9	14.5	15.9	3.9	12.4	7.8
				Females			
Vaughan	19.1	24.2	4.0	18.0	5.8	18.2	10.7
Ontario	18.4	27.1	4.6	21.8	4.3	15.2	8.6
Canada	19.6	26.2	7.3	20.4	4.9	14.3	7.2

Note: Figures cover total population aged 15 years and over by highest certificate, diploma or degree; (1) Includes persons who have graduated from a secondary school or equivalent. It excludes persons with a postsecondary certificate, diploma or degree; (2) Includes Registered Apprenticeship certificates (including Certificate of Qualification, Journeyperson's designation) and other trades certificates or diplomas such as pre-employment or vocational certificates and diplomas from brief trade programs completed at community colleges, institutes of technology, vocational centres, and similar institutions; (3) Comparisons with other data sources suggest that the category 'University certificate or diploma below the bachelor's level' was over-reported in the NHS. This category likely includes some responses that are actually college certificates or diplomas, bachelor's degrees or other types of education (e.g., university transfer programs, bachelor's programs completed in other countries, incomplete bachelor's programs, non-university professional designations). We recommend users interpret the results for the 'University certificate or diploma below the bachelor's level' category with caution; (4) 'University certificate or diploma above bachelor level' includes the categories: 'Degree in medicine, dentistry, veterinary medicine or optometry,' 'Master's degree' and 'Earned doctorate.'
Source: Statistics Canada. 2013. 2011 National Household Survey. Statistics Canada Catalogue no. 99-004-XWE. Ottawa. Released September 11, 2013.

Household Income Distribution

Area	Less than $10,000	$10,000 to $19,999	$20,000 to $29,999	$30,000 to $39,999	$40,000 to $49,999	$50,000 to $59,999	$60,000 to $79,999	$80,000 to $99,999	$100,000 to $124,999	$125,000 to $149,999	$150,000 and Over
						Households					
Vaughan	2,410	3,380	4,230	4,595	5,340	5,705	10,465	10,155	11,705	8,755	19,325
Ontario	201,780	354,530	405,725	425,410	425,720	398,705	680,850	552,660	497,970	331,460	611,840
Canada	626,705	1,141,945	1,193,925	1,271,675	1,206,800	1,102,120	1,865,280	1,458,240	1,260,770	802,555	1,389,240
						Percent of Households					
Vaughan	2.8	3.9	4.9	5.3	6.2	6.6	12.2	11.8	13.6	10.2	22.5
Ontario	4.1	7.3	8.3	8.7	8.7	8.2	13.9	11.3	10.2	6.8	12.5
Canada	4.7	8.6	9.0	9.5	9.1	8.3	14.0	10.9	9.5	6.0	10.4

Note: Household income is the sum of the total incomes of all members of that household. Total income refers to monetary receipts from certain sources, before income taxes and deductions, during calendar year 2010.
Source: Statistics Canada. 2013. 2011 National Household Survey. Statistics Canada Catalogue no. 99-004-XWE. Ottawa. Released September 11, 2013.

Median and Average Household and Economic Family Income

Area	Median Household Income ($)	Average Household Income ($)	Median After-tax Household Income ($)	Average After-tax Household Income ($)	Median Economic Family Income ($)	Average Economic Family Income ($)	Median After-tax Economic Family Income ($)	Average After-tax Economic Family Income ($)
Vaughan	93,816	113,988	81,112	93,867	100,256	120,275	86,659	99,086
Ontario	66,358	85,772	58,717	71,523	80,987	100,152	71,128	83,322
Canada	61,072	79,102	54,089	66,149	76,511	94,125	67,044	78,517

Note: Figures cover household and economic familiy income in 2010. A household is defined as a person or a group of persons (other than foreign residents) who occupy the same private dwelling and do not have a usual place of residence elsewhere in Canada. Every person is a member of one and only one household. An economic family is defined as a group of two or more persons who live in the same dwelling and are related to each other by blood, marriage, common-law, adoption or a foster relationship. A couple may be of opposite or same sex.
Source: Statistics Canada. 2013. 2011 National Household Survey. Statistics Canada Catalogue no. 99-004-XWE. Ottawa. Released September 11, 2013.

PROFILES / Vaughan, Ontario

Individual Income Distribution

Area	Less than $10,000	$10,000 to $19,999	$20,000 to $29,999	$30,000 to $39,999	$40,000 to $49,999	$50,000 to $59,999	$60,000 to $79,999	$80,000 to $99,999	$100,000 to $124,999	$125,000 and Over
Number										
Total										
Vaughan	40,745	35,135	26,145	22,055	19,785	15,615	23,480	13,970	7,920	9,295
Ontario	1,780,355	1,748,060	1,361,710	1,136,730	980,790	746,360	964,280	574,710	293,865	330,285
Canada	4,492,040	4,835,710	3,670,020	3,180,360	2,603,520	1,921,650	2,437,440	1,302,045	693,580	782,135
Males										
Vaughan	17,910	13,260	11,385	10,290	9,210	7,890	13,650	8,205	5,400	7,015
Ontario	781,095	669,815	580,990	535,255	491,125	407,005	569,205	341,160	201,125	244,500
Canada	1,936,365	1,864,880	1,588,260	1,522,190	1,333,510	1,079,780	1,473,145	823,720	492,905	599,905
Females										
Vaughan	22,830	21,875	14,760	11,775	10,575	7,720	9,830	5,765	2,515	2,285
Ontario	999,265	1,078,245	780,720	601,475	489,665	339,360	395,075	233,550	92,740	85,790
Canada	2,555,675	2,970,825	2,081,760	1,658,170	1,270,010	841,870	964,300	478,330	200,680	182,230
Percent of Population										
Total										
Vaughan	19.0	16.4	12.2	10.3	9.2	7.3	11.0	6.5	3.7	4.3
Ontario	18.0	17.6	13.7	11.5	9.9	7.5	9.7	5.8	3.0	3.3
Canada	17.3	18.7	14.2	12.3	10.0	7.4	9.4	5.0	2.7	3.0
Males										
Vaughan	17.2	12.7	10.9	9.9	8.8	7.6	13.1	7.9	5.2	6.7
Ontario	16.2	13.9	12.1	11.1	10.2	8.4	11.8	7.1	4.2	5.1
Canada	15.2	14.7	12.5	12.0	10.5	8.5	11.6	6.5	3.9	4.7
Females										
Vaughan	20.8	19.9	13.4	10.7	9.6	7.0	8.9	5.2	2.3	2.1
Ontario	19.6	21.2	15.3	11.8	9.6	6.7	7.8	4.6	1.8	1.7
Canada	19.4	22.5	15.8	12.6	9.6	6.4	7.3	3.6	1.5	1.4

Note: Figures cover individuals aged 15 years and over with income. Income refers to monetary receipts from certain sources, before income taxes and deductions, during calendar year 2010.
Source: Statistics Canada. 2013. 2011 National Household Survey. Statistics Canada Catalogue no. 99-004-XWE. Ottawa. Released September 11, 2013.

Labour Force Status

Area	In the Labour Force - All	In the Labour Force - Employed	In the Labour Force - Unemployed	Not in the Labour Force
Number				
Total				
Vaughan	158,990	148,410	10,580	68,735
Ontario	6,864,990	6,297,005	567,985	3,608,685
Canada	17,990,080	16,595,035	1,395,045	9,269,445
Males				
Vaughan	82,250	77,185	5,065	28,135
Ontario	3,542,030	3,249,165	292,865	1,522,690
Canada	9,388,570	8,634,310	754,255	3,906,785
Females				
Vaughan	76,735	71,225	5,515	40,605
Ontario	3,322,955	3,047,840	275,120	2,085,990
Canada	8,601,515	7,960,725	640,790	5,362,660
Percent of Labour Force				
Total				
Vaughan	69.8	65.2	6.7	30.2
Ontario	65.5	60.1	8.3	34.5
Canada	66.0	60.9	7.8	34.0
Males				
Vaughan	74.5	69.9	6.2	25.5
Ontario	69.9	64.2	8.3	30.1
Canada	70.6	64.9	8.0	29.4
Females				
Vaughan	65.4	60.7	7.2	34.6
Ontario	61.4	56.3	8.3	38.6
Canada	61.6	57.0	7.4	38.4

Note: Figures are based on total population 15 years and over
Source: Statistics Canada. 2013. 2011 National Household Survey. Statistics Canada Catalogue no. 99-004-XWE. Ottawa. Released September 11, 2013.

Labour Force by Industry (NAICS Codes 11–52)

Area	Agriculture, forestry, fishing & hunting	Mining, quarrying, & oil & gas extraction	Utilities	Construction	Manufacturing	Wholesale Trade	Retail Trade	Transportation & warehousing	Information & cultural industries	Finance & insurance
					Number Total					
Vaughan	340	85	720	14,040	18,475	9,415	18,705	6,695	4,610	11,085
Ontario	101,280	29,985	57,035	417,900	697,565	305,030	751,200	307,405	178,720	364,415
Canada	437,650	261,050	149,940	1,215,380	1,619,295	733,445	2,031,665	827,780	420,830	767,960
					Males					
Vaughan	205	40	470	11,635	12,060	5,675	8,510	4,985	2,580	4,765
Ontario	66,485	25,650	42,685	369,300	493,305	197,770	344,480	225,245	98,835	153,125
Canada	307,370	211,690	110,765	1,068,710	1,167,680	494,545	933,850	617,305	235,875	296,995
					Females					
Vaughan	135	40	255	2,410	6,410	3,740	10,190	1,710	2,030	6,315
Ontario	34,800	4,340	14,350	48,595	204,260	107,260	406,720	82,160	79,885	211,290
Canada	130,285	49,360	39,175	146,670	451,615	238,900	1,097,820	210,475	184,955	470,960
					Percent of Labour Force Total					
Vaughan	0.2	0.1	0.5	9.0	11.9	6.0	12.0	4.3	3.0	7.1
Ontario	1.5	0.4	0.9	6.3	10.4	4.6	11.2	4.6	2.7	5.5
Canada	2.5	1.5	0.9	6.9	9.2	4.2	11.6	4.7	2.4	4.4
					Males					
Vaughan	0.3	0.0	0.6	14.4	14.9	7.0	10.5	6.2	3.2	5.9
Ontario	1.9	0.7	1.2	10.7	14.3	5.7	10.0	6.5	2.9	4.4
Canada	3.3	2.3	1.2	11.6	12.7	5.4	10.2	6.7	2.6	3.2
					Females					
Vaughan	0.2	0.1	0.3	3.2	8.5	5.0	13.6	2.3	2.7	8.4
Ontario	1.1	0.1	0.4	1.5	6.3	3.3	12.6	2.5	2.5	6.5
Canada	1.6	0.6	0.5	1.7	5.4	2.8	13.1	2.5	2.2	5.6

Note: Figures are based on total experienced labour force 15 years and over. Experienced labour force refers to persons who, during the week of Sunday, May 1 to Saturday, May 7, 2011, were employed and the unemployed who had last worked for pay or in self-employment in either 2010 or 2011.
Source: Statistics Canada. 2013. 2011 National Household Survey. Statistics Canada Catalogue no. 99-004-XWE. Ottawa. Released September 11, 2013.

Labour Force by Industry (NAICS Codes 53–91)

Area	Real estate & rental & leasing	Profess., scientific & tech. services	Mgmt of companies & enterprises	Admin. & support, waste mgmt & remed. services	Educational services	Health care & social assistance	Arts, entertain. & recreation	Accomm. & food services	Other services (except public admin.)	Public admin.
					Number Total					
Vaughan	3,990	15,105	190	5,040	12,030	12,810	2,355	6,260	7,840	5,890
Ontario	133,980	511,020	6,525	309,630	499,690	692,130	144,065	417,675	296,340	458,665
Canada	321,895	1,240,850	17,460	728,330	1,301,435	1,949,650	363,405	1,130,750	807,800	1,261,050
					Males					
Vaughan	2,100	8,265	105	2,910	3,115	2,680	1,295	3,025	3,370	2,890
Ontario	72,835	281,420	3,540	172,475	162,765	120,165	75,035	177,240	133,795	236,655
Canada	179,090	688,625	9,380	411,250	424,915	349,430	188,270	469,990	372,940	652,510
					Females					
Vaughan	1,890	6,845	80	2,135	8,915	10,130	1,065	3,230	4,470	3,000
Ontario	61,145	229,600	2,990	137,155	336,925	571,965	69,030	240,430	162,550	222,015
Canada	142,805	552,225	8,075	317,085	876,515	1,600,220	175,135	660,760	434,865	608,535
					Percent of Labour Force Total					
Vaughan	2.6	9.7	0.1	3.2	7.7	8.2	1.5	4.0	5.0	3.8
Ontario	2.0	7.6	0.1	4.6	7.5	10.4	2.2	6.3	4.4	6.9
Canada	1.8	7.1	0.1	4.1	7.4	11.1	2.1	6.4	4.6	7.2
					Males					
Vaughan	2.6	10.2	0.1	3.6	3.9	3.3	1.6	3.7	4.2	3.6
Ontario	2.1	8.2	0.1	5.0	4.7	3.5	2.2	5.1	3.9	6.9
Canada	1.9	7.5	0.1	4.5	4.6	3.8	2.0	5.1	4.1	7.1
					Females					
Vaughan	2.5	9.1	0.1	2.8	11.9	13.5	1.4	4.3	6.0	4.0
Ontario	1.9	7.1	0.1	4.2	10.4	17.7	2.1	7.4	5.0	6.9
Canada	1.7	6.6	0.1	3.8	10.4	19.1	2.1	7.9	5.2	7.2

Note: Figures are based on total experienced labour force 15 years and over. Experienced labour force refers to persons who, during the week of Sunday, May 1 to Saturday, May 7, 2011, were employed and the unemployed who had last worked for pay or in self-employment in either 2010 or 2011.
Source: Statistics Canada. 2013. 2011 National Household Survey. Statistics Canada Catalogue no. 99-004-XWE. Ottawa. Released September 11, 2013.

PROFILES / Vaughan, Ontario

Occupation

Area	Mgmt	Business, Finance & Admin.	Natural/ Applied Sciences & Related	Health	Education, Law & Social, Community & Government Services	Art, Culture, Recreation & Sport	Sales & Service	Trades, Transport & Equip. Operators & Related	Natural Resources, Agri. & Related Production	Mfg & Utilities
Number										
Total										
Vaughan	21,280	31,705	13,205	7,340	17,545	4,205	33,380	19,060	1,010	6,940
Ontario	770,580	1,138,330	494,500	392,695	801,465	206,420	1,550,260	868,515	106,810	350,685
Canada	1,963,600	2,902,045	1,237,775	1,107,200	2,064,675	503,415	4,068,170	2,537,775	397,930	805,040
Males										
Vaughan	13,930	9,640	10,020	2,035	4,590	1,865	15,425	18,160	910	4,090
Ontario	474,655	352,505	384,345	78,330	264,570	96,055	673,880	812,280	82,610	233,565
Canada	1,229,460	854,190	966,355	217,520	676,550	232,535	1,745,705	2,385,615	318,945	564,300
Females										
Vaughan	7,345	22,070	3,185	5,305	12,955	2,345	17,960	900	95	2,850
Ontario	295,920	785,825	110,150	314,370	536,895	110,370	876,380	56,230	24,200	117,115
Canada	734,140	2,047,855	271,415	889,675	1,388,130	270,875	2,322,465	152,165	78,980	240,740
Percent of Labour Force										
Total										
Vaughan	13.7	20.4	8.5	4.7	11.3	2.7	21.4	12.2	0.6	4.5
Ontario	11.5	17.0	7.4	5.9	12.0	3.1	23.2	13.0	1.6	5.2
Canada	11.2	16.5	7.0	6.3	11.7	2.9	23.1	14.4	2.3	4.6
Males										
Vaughan	17.3	11.9	12.4	2.5	5.7	2.3	19.1	22.5	1.1	5.1
Ontario	13.7	10.2	11.1	2.3	7.7	2.8	19.5	23.5	2.4	6.8
Canada	13.4	9.3	10.5	2.4	7.4	2.5	19.0	26.0	3.5	6.1
Females										
Vaughan	9.8	29.4	4.2	7.1	17.3	3.1	23.9	1.2	0.1	3.8
Ontario	9.2	24.3	3.4	9.7	16.6	3.4	27.2	1.7	0.7	3.6
Canada	8.7	24.4	3.2	10.6	16.5	3.2	27.7	1.8	0.9	2.9

Note: Figures are based on total experienced labour force 15 years and over
Source: Statistics Canada. 2013. 2011 National Household Survey. Statistics Canada Catalogue no. 99-004-XWE. Ottawa. Released September 11, 2013.

Place of Work Status

Area	Worked at Home	Worked Outside Canada	No Fixed Workplace Address	Worked at Usual Place
Number				
Total				
Vaughan	9,540	475	17,365	121,030
Ontario	423,790	31,390	670,835	5,170,980
Canada	1,142,640	66,460	1,868,245	13,517,690
Males				
Vaughan	4,505	330	12,780	59,570
Ontario	216,900	21,150	486,560	2,524,555
Canada	582,150	47,355	1,400,485	6,604,325
Females				
Vaughan	5,035	140	4,585	61,465
Ontario	206,895	10,240	184,275	2,646,420
Canada	560,490	19,100	467,760	6,913,370
Percent of Labour Force				
Total				
Vaughan	6.4	0.3	11.7	81.6
Ontario	6.7	0.5	10.7	82.1
Canada	6.9	0.4	11.3	81.5
Males				
Vaughan	5.8	0.4	16.6	77.2
Ontario	6.7	0.7	15.0	77.7
Canada	6.7	0.5	16.2	76.5
Females				
Vaughan	7.1	0.2	6.4	86.3
Ontario	6.8	0.3	6.0	86.8
Canada	7.0	0.2	5.9	86.8

Note: Figures are based on total employed labour force 15 years and over.
Source: Statistics Canada. 2013. 2011 National Household Survey. Statistics Canada Catalogue no. 99-004-XWE. Ottawa. Released September 11, 2013.

Mode of Transportation to Work

Area	Car; Truck; Van; as Driver	Car; Truck; Van; as Passenger	Public Transit	Walked	Bicycled	All Other Modes
			Number			
			Total			
Vaughan	111,860	7,540	15,595	2,115	250	1,040
Ontario	4,235,315	357,110	818,270	299,095	69,885	62,145
Canada	11,393,140	867,050	1,851,525	880,815	201,780	191,625
			Males			
Vaughan	62,195	2,570	6,205	840	205	320
Ontario	2,316,680	143,410	340,995	131,765	47,635	30,635
Canada	6,238,835	349,530	788,290	387,580	135,840	104,725
			Females			
Vaughan	49,660	4,970	9,385	1,275	45	720
Ontario	1,918,640	213,700	477,275	167,325	22,250	31,515
Canada	5,154,305	517,520	1,063,235	493,230	65,940	86,900
			Percent of Labour Force			
			Total			
Vaughan	80.8	5.4	11.3	1.5	0.2	0.8
Ontario	72.5	6.1	14.0	5.1	1.2	1.1
Canada	74.0	5.6	12.0	5.7	1.3	1.2
			Males			
Vaughan	86.0	3.6	8.6	1.2	0.3	0.4
Ontario	76.9	4.8	11.3	4.4	1.6	1.0
Canada	77.9	4.4	9.8	4.8	1.7	1.3
			Females			
Vaughan	75.2	7.5	14.2	1.9	0.1	1.1
Ontario	67.8	7.5	16.9	5.9	0.8	1.1
Canada	69.8	7.0	14.4	6.7	0.9	1.2

Note: Figures are based on total employed labour force 15 years and over.
Source: Statistics Canada. 2013. 2011 National Household Survey. Statistics Canada Catalogue no. 99-004-XWE. Ottawa. Released September 11, 2013.

Visible Minority Population Characteristics

Area	Total Minority	South Asian[1]	Chinese	Black	Filipino	Latin American	Arab	SE Asian[2]	West Asian[3]	Korean	Japanese	Multiple[4]
						Number						
						Total						
Vaughan	89,975	27,725	13,475	7,765	8,585	6,055	2,785	7,735	6,215	4,300	260	2,865
Ontario	3,279,565	965,990	629,140	539,205	275,380	172,560	151,645	137,875	122,530	78,290	29,085	96,735
Canada	6,264,750	1,567,400	1,324,750	945,665	619,310	381,280	380,620	312,075	206,840	161,130	87,270	171,935
						Males						
Vaughan	43,355	13,970	6,565	3,725	3,435	2,925	1,405	3,565	3,260	2,125	125	1,295
Ontario	1,582,480	484,355	301,575	251,295	116,825	83,205	79,620	67,645	62,515	38,045	13,345	46,765
Canada	3,043,010	790,755	632,325	453,005	268,885	186,355	203,485	154,035	105,620	77,165	38,270	83,335
						Females						
Vaughan	46,620	13,755	6,910	4,040	5,150	3,135	1,380	4,160	2,960	2,185	140	1,570
Ontario	1,697,085	481,635	327,570	287,915	158,555	89,360	72,025	70,230	60,010	40,250	15,740	49,970
Canada	3,221,745	776,650	692,420	492,660	350,425	194,925	177,140	158,045	101,220	83,965	48,990	88,600
						Percent of Population						
						Total						
Vaughan	31.4	9.7	4.7	2.7	3.0	2.1	1.0	2.7	2.2	1.5	0.1	1.0
Ontario	25.9	7.6	5.0	4.3	2.2	1.4	1.2	1.1	1.0	0.6	0.2	0.8
Canada	19.1	4.8	4.0	2.9	1.9	1.2	1.2	0.9	0.6	0.5	0.3	0.5
						Males						
Vaughan	30.9	10.0	4.7	2.7	2.5	2.1	1.0	2.5	2.3	1.5	0.1	0.9
Ontario	25.6	7.8	4.9	4.1	1.9	1.3	1.3	1.1	1.0	0.6	0.2	0.8
Canada	18.8	4.9	3.9	2.8	1.7	1.2	1.3	1.0	0.7	0.5	0.2	0.5
						Females						
Vaughan	31.9	9.4	4.7	2.8	3.5	2.1	0.9	2.8	2.0	1.5	0.1	1.1
Ontario	26.2	7.4	5.1	4.4	2.5	1.4	1.1	1.1	0.9	0.6	0.2	0.8
Canada	19.3	4.7	4.1	3.0	2.1	1.2	1.1	0.9	0.6	0.5	0.3	0.5

Note: The Employment Equity Act defines visible minorities as 'persons, other than Aboriginal peoples, who are non-Caucasian in race or non-white in colour';
(1) Includes 'East Indian,' 'Pakistani,' 'Sri Lankan,' etc.; (2) Includes 'Vietnamese,' 'Cambodian,' 'Malaysian,' 'Laotian,' etc.; (3) Includes 'Iranian,' 'Afghan,' etc.; (4) Includes respondents who reported more than one visible minority group by checking two or more mark-in circles, e.g., 'Black' and 'South Asian.'
Source: Statistics Canada. 2013. 2011 National Household Survey. Statistics Canada Catalogue no. 99-004-XWE. Ottawa. Released September 11, 2013.

PROFILES / Vaughan, Ontario

Aboriginal Population

Area	Aboriginal Identity[1]	First Nations (North American Indian) Single Identity[2]	Métis Single Identity	Inuk (Inuit) Single Identity	Multiple Aboriginal Identities[3]	Aboriginal Identities Not Included Elsewhere
Number						
Total						
Vaughan	555	330	125	15	0	75
Ontario	301,430	201,100	86,020	3,355	2,910	8,040
Canada	1,400,685	851,560	451,795	59,440	11,415	26,475
Males						
Vaughan	235	160	40	0	0	35
Ontario	145,020	96,620	41,755	1,475	1,420	3,750
Canada	682,190	411,785	223,335	29,495	5,525	12,055
Females						
Vaughan	320	175	90	0	0	40
Ontario	156,410	104,485	44,260	1,880	1,490	4,295
Canada	718,500	439,775	228,460	29,950	5,890	14,420
Percent of Population						
Total						
Vaughan	0.2	0.1	0.0	0.0	0.0	0.0
Ontario	2.4	1.6	0.7	0.0	0.0	0.1
Canada	4.3	2.6	1.4	0.2	0.0	0.1
Males						
Vaughan	0.2	0.1	0.0	0.0	0.0	0.0
Ontario	2.3	1.6	0.7	0.0	0.0	0.1
Canada	4.2	2.5	1.4	0.2	0.0	0.1
Females						
Vaughan	0.2	0.1	0.1	0.0	0.0	0.0
Ontario	2.4	1.6	0.7	0.0	0.0	0.1
Canada	4.3	2.6	1.4	0.2	0.0	0.1

Note: (1) Includes persons who reported being an Aboriginal person, that is, First Nations (North American Indian), Métis or Inuk (Inuit) and/or those who reported Registered or Treaty Indian status, that is registered under the Indian Act of Canada, and/or those who reported membership in a First Nation or Indian band. Aboriginal peoples of Canada are defined in the Constitution Act, 1982, section 35-2 as including the Indian, Inuit and Métis peoples of Canada; (2) Users should be aware that the estimates associated with this variable are more affected than most by the incomplete enumeration of certain Indian reserves and Indian settlements in the National Household Survey (NHS); (3) Includes persons who reported being any two or all three of the following: First Nations (North American Indian), Métis or Inuk (Inuit).
Source: Statistics Canada. 2013. 2011 National Household Survey. Statistics Canada Catalogue no. 99-004-XWE. Ottawa. Released September 11, 2013.

Ethnic Origin

Area	North American Aboriginal	Other North American	European	Caribbean	Latin, Central and South American	African	Asian	Oceania
Number								
Total								
Vaughan	735	23,490	190,750	6,230	9,035	6,985	81,900	190
Ontario	441,395	3,059,480	8,231,410	396,485	271,545	331,460	2,604,595	19,410
Canada	1,836,035	11,070,455	20,157,965	627,590	544,375	766,735	5,011,225	74,875
Males								
Vaughan	260	11,980	93,935	2,860	4,340	3,440	39,600	90
Ontario	210,490	1,507,105	4,019,885	181,805	130,035	160,940	1,265,540	9,855
Canada	885,675	5,462,685	9,913,150	291,640	264,635	387,360	2,435,540	37,490
Females								
Vaughan	470	11,510	96,810	3,370	4,700	3,545	42,305	100
Ontario	230,905	1,552,380	4,211,525	214,675	141,510	170,515	1,339,050	9,555
Canada	950,360	5,607,770	10,244,820	335,945	279,740	379,380	2,575,680	37,385
Percent of Population								
Total								
Vaughan	0.3	8.2	66.6	2.2	3.2	2.4	28.6	0.1
Ontario	3.5	24.2	65.1	3.1	2.1	2.6	20.6	0.2
Canada	5.6	33.7	61.4	1.9	1.7	2.3	15.3	0.2
Males								
Vaughan	0.2	8.5	67.0	2.0	3.1	2.5	28.2	0.1
Ontario	3.4	24.4	65.0	2.9	2.1	2.6	20.5	0.2
Canada	5.5	33.8	61.3	1.8	1.6	2.4	15.1	0.2
Females								
Vaughan	0.3	7.9	66.3	2.3	3.2	2.4	29.0	0.1
Ontario	3.6	24.0	65.1	3.3	2.2	2.6	20.7	0.1
Canada	5.7	33.6	61.4	2.0	1.7	2.3	15.4	0.2

Note: The sum of the ethnic groups in this table is greater than the total population estimate because a person may report more than one ethnic origin in the NHS.
Source: Statistics Canada. 2013. 2011 National Household Survey. Statistics Canada Catalogue no. 99-004-XWE. Ottawa. Released September 11, 2013.

Religion

Area	Buddhist	Christian	Hindu	Jewish	Muslim	Sikh	Traditional (Aboriginal) Spirituality	Other Religions	No Religious Affiliation
				Number Total					
Vaughan	7,215	173,565	12,880	43,760	14,080	5,030	25	1,010	28,735
Ontario	163,750	8,167,295	366,720	195,540	581,950	179,765	15,905	53,080	2,927,790
Canada	366,830	22,102,745	497,965	329,495	1,053,945	454,965	64,935	130,835	7,850,605
				Males					
Vaughan	3,335	83,600	6,525	21,405	7,080	2,500	10	565	15,165
Ontario	75,355	3,839,925	183,580	95,795	293,925	90,515	7,600	23,555	1,571,195
Canada	168,465	10,497,775	250,435	161,265	540,555	229,435	31,805	57,745	4,225,645
				Females					
Vaughan	3,880	89,965	6,355	22,355	7,000	2,540	10	445	13,570
Ontario	88,395	4,327,365	183,140	99,740	288,025	89,250	8,310	29,525	1,356,600
Canada	198,365	11,604,975	247,525	168,235	513,395	225,530	33,135	73,090	3,624,965
				Percent of Population Total					
Vaughan	2.5	60.6	4.5	15.3	4.9	1.8	0.0	0.4	10.0
Ontario	1.3	64.6	2.9	1.5	4.6	1.4	0.1	0.4	23.1
Canada	1.1	67.3	1.5	1.0	3.2	1.4	0.2	0.4	23.9
				Males					
Vaughan	2.4	59.6	4.7	15.3	5.1	1.8	0.0	0.4	10.8
Ontario	1.2	62.1	3.0	1.5	4.8	1.5	0.1	0.4	25.4
Canada	1.0	64.9	1.5	1.0	3.3	1.4	0.2	0.4	26.1
				Females					
Vaughan	2.7	61.6	4.3	15.3	4.8	1.7	0.0	0.3	9.3
Ontario	1.4	66.9	2.8	1.5	4.5	1.4	0.1	0.5	21.0
Canada	1.2	69.5	1.5	1.0	3.1	1.4	0.2	0.4	21.7

Note: Religion refers to the person's self-identification as having a connection or affiliation with any religious denomination, group, body, sect, cult or other religiously defined community or system of belief. Religion is not limited to formal membership in a religious organization or group. Persons without a religious connection or affiliation can self-identify as atheist, agnostic or humanist, or can provide another applicable response.
Source: Statistics Canada. 2013. 2011 National Household Survey. Statistics Canada Catalogue no. 99-004-XWE. Ottawa. Released September 11, 2013.

Religion—Christian Denominations

Area	Anglican	Baptist	Catholic	Christian Orthodox	Lutheran	Pentecostal	Presbyterian	United Church	Other Christian
				Number Total					
Vaughan	2,290	1,555	132,345	14,080	530	3,105	2,535	2,065	15,050
Ontario	774,560	244,650	3,976,610	297,710	163,460	213,945	319,585	952,465	1,224,300
Canada	1,631,845	635,840	12,810,705	550,690	478,185	478,705	472,385	2,007,610	3,036,780
				Males					
Vaughan	1,045	710	64,440	6,765	230	1,470	1,180	980	6,770
Ontario	355,175	112,285	1,895,940	145,825	75,225	94,955	148,535	435,255	576,730
Canada	752,945	293,905	6,167,290	270,205	221,525	217,850	218,955	912,545	1,442,550
				Females					
Vaughan	1,250	845	67,900	7,315	300	1,635	1,360	1,090	8,280
Ontario	419,390	132,370	2,080,665	151,885	88,230	118,990	171,050	517,210	647,570
Canada	878,900	341,940	6,643,415	280,485	256,660	260,850	253,430	1,095,065	1,594,230
				Percent of Population Total					
Vaughan	0.8	0.5	46.2	4.9	0.2	1.1	0.9	0.7	5.3
Ontario	6.1	1.9	31.4	2.4	1.3	1.7	2.5	7.5	9.7
Canada	5.0	1.9	39.0	1.7	1.5	1.5	1.4	6.1	9.2
				Males					
Vaughan	0.7	0.5	46.0	4.8	0.2	1.0	0.8	0.7	4.8
Ontario	5.7	1.8	30.7	2.4	1.2	1.5	2.4	7.0	9.3
Canada	4.7	1.8	38.2	1.7	1.4	1.3	1.4	5.6	8.9
				Females					
Vaughan	0.9	0.6	46.5	5.0	0.2	1.1	0.9	0.7	5.7
Ontario	6.5	2.0	32.2	2.3	1.4	1.8	2.6	8.0	10.0
Canada	5.3	2.0	39.8	1.7	1.5	1.6	1.5	6.6	9.6

Note: Religion refers to the person's self-identification as having a connection or affiliation with any religious denomination, group, body, sect, cult or other religiously defined community or system of belief. Religion is not limited to formal membership in a religious organization or group. Persons without a religious connection or affiliation can self-identify as atheist, agnostic or humanist, or can provide another applicable response.
Source: Statistics Canada. 2013. 2011 National Household Survey. Statistics Canada Catalogue no. 99-004-XWE. Ottawa. Released September 11, 2013.

PROFILES / Vaughan, Ontario

Immigrant Status and Period of Immigration

Area	Non-Immigrants[1]	Immigrants All	Before 1971	1971 to 1980	1981 to 1990	1991 to 2000	2001 to 2005	2006 to 2011	Non-Permanent Residents[3]
Number – Total									
Vaughan	150,375	132,970	30,575	16,905	20,630	34,820	18,095	11,940	2,965
Ontario	8,906,000	3,611,365	723,030	464,380	538,285	866,220	518,405	501,060	134,425
Canada	25,720,175	6,775,765	1,261,055	870,775	949,890	1,539,050	992,070	1,162,915	356,385
Males									
Vaughan	75,450	63,710	14,720	8,315	10,315	16,430	8,550	5,385	1,030
Ontario	4,410,240	1,706,385	341,820	217,990	258,095	408,270	245,850	234,360	64,825
Canada	12,753,235	3,231,370	605,430	416,670	454,570	724,905	474,545	555,245	178,515
Females									
Vaughan	74,925	69,255	15,855	8,590	10,315	18,400	9,545	6,555	1,935
Ontario	4,495,765	1,904,985	381,210	246,390	280,190	457,950	272,550	266,695	69,600
Canada	12,966,935	3,544,400	655,625	454,105	495,325	814,145	517,530	607,670	177,870
Percent of Population – Total									
Vaughan	52.5	46.4	10.7	5.9	7.2	12.2	6.3	4.2	1.0
Ontario	70.4	28.5	5.7	3.7	4.3	6.8	4.1	4.0	1.1
Canada	78.3	20.6	3.8	2.7	2.9	4.7	3.0	3.5	1.1
Males									
Vaughan	53.8	45.4	10.5	5.9	7.4	11.7	6.1	3.8	0.7
Ontario	71.3	27.6	5.5	3.5	4.2	6.6	4.0	3.8	1.0
Canada	78.9	20.0	3.7	2.6	2.8	4.5	2.9	3.4	1.1
Females									
Vaughan	51.3	47.4	10.9	5.9	7.1	12.6	6.5	4.5	1.3
Ontario	69.5	29.4	5.9	3.8	4.3	7.1	4.2	4.1	1.1
Canada	77.7	21.2	3.9	2.7	3.0	4.9	3.1	3.6	1.1

Note: (1) Non-immigrant refers to a person who is a Canadian citizen by birth; (2) Immigrant refers to a person who is or has ever been a landed immigrant/permanent resident. This person has been granted the right to live in Canada permanently by immigration authorities. Some immigrants have resided in Canada for a number of years, while others have arrived recently. Some immigrants are Canadian citizens, while others are not. Most immigrants are born outside Canada, but a small number are born in Canada. In the 2011 National Household Survey, 'Immigrants' includes immigrants who landed in Canada prior to May 10, 2011; (3) Non-permanent resident refers to a person from another country who has a work or study permit, or who is a refugee claimant, and any non-Canadian-born family member living in Canada with them.
Source: Statistics Canada. 2013. 2011 National Household Survey. Statistics Canada Catalogue no. 99-004-XWE. Ottawa. Released September 11, 2013.

Mother Tongue

Area	English	French	Non-official Language	English & French	English & Non-official Language	French & Non-official Language	English, French & Non-official Language
Number – Total							
Vaughan	131,770	1,795	143,250	395	9,115	415	210
Ontario	8,677,040	493,300	3,264,435	46,605	219,425	13,645	7,615
Canada	18,858,980	7,054,975	6,567,680	144,685	396,330	74,430	24,095
Males							
Vaughan	66,225	820	68,580	190	4,380	180	80
Ontario	4,276,970	232,785	1,562,190	21,805	106,790	6,285	3,495
Canada	9,345,225	3,452,380	3,157,785	69,975	192,000	36,535	11,965
Females							
Vaughan	65,535	975	74,670	200	4,740	230	125
Ontario	4,400,065	260,510	1,702,240	24,795	112,635	7,365	4,115
Canada	9,513,750	3,602,590	3,409,895	74,710	204,330	37,890	12,130
Percent of Population – Total							
Vaughan	45.9	0.6	49.9	0.1	3.2	0.1	0.1
Ontario	68.2	3.9	25.7	0.4	1.7	0.1	0.1
Canada	56.9	21.3	19.8	0.4	1.2	0.2	0.1
Males							
Vaughan	47.1	0.6	48.8	0.1	3.1	0.1	0.1
Ontario	68.9	3.7	25.2	0.4	1.7	0.1	0.1
Canada	57.5	21.2	19.4	0.4	1.2	0.2	0.1
Females							
Vaughan	44.7	0.7	51.0	0.1	3.2	0.2	0.1
Ontario	67.6	4.0	26.1	0.4	1.7	0.1	0.1
Canada	56.4	21.4	20.2	0.4	1.2	0.2	0.1

Note: Figures cover total population excluding institutional residents.
Source: Statistics Canada. 2012. Census Profile. 2011 Census. Statistics Canada Catalogue no. 98-316-XWE. Ottawa. Released October 24 2012.
http://www12.statcan.gc.ca/census-recensement/2011/dp-pd/prof/index.cfm?Lang=E

Language Spoken Most Often at Home

Area	English	French	Non-official Language	English & French	English & Non-official Language	French & Non-official Language	English, French & Non-official Language
			Number				
			Total				
Vaughan	188,745	670	74,890	375	21,840	95	330
Ontario	10,044,810	284,115	1,827,870	37,955	509,105	6,370	11,845
Canada	21,457,075	6,827,865	3,673,865	131,205	875,135	109,700	46,330
			Males				
Vaughan	93,485	295	35,675	160	10,665	35	135
Ontario	4,930,610	133,495	872,860	17,250	248,050	2,855	5,225
Canada	10,585,620	3,348,235	1,767,310	63,475	425,370	53,010	22,845
			Females				
Vaughan	95,260	375	39,210	210	11,170	55	195
Ontario	5,114,200	150,620	955,010	20,705	261,055	3,520	6,620
Canada	10,871,455	3,479,625	1,906,555	67,730	449,765	56,690	23,485
			Percent of Population				
			Total				
Vaughan	65.8	0.2	26.1	0.1	7.6	0.0	0.1
Ontario	79.0	2.2	14.4	0.3	4.0	0.1	0.1
Canada	64.8	20.6	11.1	0.4	2.6	0.3	0.1
			Males				
Vaughan	66.6	0.2	25.4	0.1	7.6	0.0	0.1
Ontario	79.4	2.1	14.1	0.3	4.0	0.0	0.1
Canada	65.1	20.6	10.9	0.4	2.6	0.3	0.1
			Females				
Vaughan	65.0	0.3	26.8	0.1	7.6	0.0	0.1
Ontario	78.5	2.3	14.7	0.3	4.0	0.1	0.1
Canada	64.5	20.6	11.3	0.4	2.7	0.3	0.1

Note: Figures cover total population excluding institutional residents.
Source: Statistics Canada. 2012. Census Profile. 2011 Census. Statistics Canada Catalogue no. 98-316-XWE. Ottawa. Released October 24 2012.
http://www12.statcan.gc.ca/census-recensement/2011/dp-pd/prof/index.cfm?Lang=E

Knowledge of Official Languages

Area	English Only	French Only	English & French	Neither English nor French
		Number		
		Total		
Vaughan	258,300	175	16,950	11,520
Ontario	10,984,360	42,980	1,395,805	298,920
Canada	22,564,665	4,165,015	5,795,570	595,920
		Males		
Vaughan	128,930	70	7,090	4,370
Ontario	5,445,050	18,805	627,725	118,765
Canada	11,222,185	1,925,340	2,876,560	241,790
		Females		
Vaughan	129,370	110	9,860	7,155
Ontario	5,539,310	24,175	768,085	180,155
Canada	11,342,485	2,239,680	2,919,005	354,135
		Percent of Population		
		Total		
Vaughan	90.0	0.1	5.9	4.0
Ontario	86.3	0.3	11.0	2.3
Canada	68.1	12.6	17.5	1.8
		Males		
Vaughan	91.8	0.0	5.0	3.1
Ontario	87.7	0.3	10.1	1.9
Canada	69.0	11.8	17.7	1.5
		Females		
Vaughan	88.3	0.1	6.7	4.9
Ontario	85.1	0.4	11.8	2.8
Canada	67.3	13.3	17.3	2.1

Note: Figures cover total population excluding institutional residents.
Source: Statistics Canada. 2012. Census Profile. 2011 Census. Statistics Canada Catalogue no. 98-316-XWE. Ottawa. Released October 24 2012.
http://www12.statcan.gc.ca/census-recensement/2011/dp-pd/prof/index.cfm?Lang=E

Whitby, Ontario

Background
Whitby is a town located 48 kilometres east of Toronto in the Durham Region of Ontario. The town has a population of 122,022 people (census 2011) and is within a day's drive of two-thirds of the Canadian market. The town is close to all major 400 series highways.

The land surrounding Whitby was originally patented in the 1790s as a way of generating settlement in Upper Canada. Settlement was slow and Whitby did not start to develop until 1836. When Whitby was granted a County government seat in 1852, the town's fortunes boomed. The town was incorporated in 1855 and a thriving harbour and railway soon followed. By 1871, Whitby had grown into an important financial and manufacturing centre.

Today, Whitby homes more than 470 businesses in its two historic downtowns: Downtown Whitby ("the heart of the town") and Downtown Brooklin. The town's award-winning marina overlooks Lake Ontario, and the Iroquois Park Sports Centre is the largest municipally owned and operated sports and recreation complex in Canada.

Festivals such as the Brooklin Harvest Festival, County Town Carnival and Harbour Day happen throughout the year. Art exhibitions and displays are offered at the Station Gallery, and theatrical performances happen at the Whitby Courthouse Theatre. The Whitby Brass Band, a volunteer community band, will celebrate 150 years of music in 2013.

Whitby has average summer highs of plus 23.87 degrees Celsius, winter lows of minus 10.13 degrees Celsius, and an average rainfall just over 815 mm per year.

Rankings
- Whitby was ranked #16 out of 190 Canadian cities for "Best Places to Live." *Money Sense Magazine* evaluated each city using 22 different criteria and point systems such as affordable housing, population growth, air quality and walk/bike to work ratios. *Money Sense, Canada's Best Places to Live, March 20, 2012*
- Port Whitby is ranked in the top 5% of eco-rated facilities in Ontario. Port Whitby has won the Eco-Friendly Award three times: 2003, 2006 and 2009. Environmental audit criteria: best practices; water quality and habitat preservation; hazardous substance handling and reduction; water conservation; energy efficiency; and waste reduction. *Ontario Marine Operators Association Clean Marine Program with files from GreenLeaf Environmental Communications, Inc., 2003 to 2011*

PROFILES / Whitby, Ontario

Population Growth and Density

Area	Population in 2001	Population in 2006	Population in 2011	Population Change 2001–2006	Population Change 2006–2011	Land Area (sq. km)	Population Density per sq. km
Whitby	87,413	111,184	122,022	27.2	9.7	146.53	832.7
Ontario	11,410,046	12,160,282	12,851,821	6.6	5.7	908,607.67	14.1
Canada	30,007,094	31,612,897	33,476,688	5.4	5.9	8,965,121.42	3.7

Source: Statistics Canada. 2012. Census Profile. 2011 Census. Statistics Canada Catalogue no. 98-316-XWE. Ottawa. Released October 24 2012. http://www12.statcan.gc.ca/census-recensement/2011/dp-pd/prof/index.cfm?Lang=E;
Statistics Canada 2007. 2006 Community Profiles. 2006 Census. Statistics Canada Catalogue no. 92-591-XWE. Ottawa. Released March 13 2007. http://www12.statcan.ca/census-recensement/2006/dp-pd/prof/92-591/index.cfm?Lang=E

Gender

Area	Males	Females
	Number	
Whitby	59,415	62,610
Ontario	6,263,140	6,588,685
Canada	16,414,225	17,062,460
	Percent of Population	
Whitby	48.7	51.3
Ontario	48.7	51.3
Canada	49.0	51.0

Source: Statistics Canada. 2012. Census Profile. 2011 Census. Statistics Canada Catalogue no. 98-316-XWE. Ottawa. Released October 24 2012. http://www12.statcan.gc.ca/census-recensement/2011/dp-pd/prof/index.cfm?Lang=E

Marital Status

Area	Married[1]	Living Common-law	Single[2]	Separated	Divorced	Widowed
			Number			
			Total			
Whitby	52,515	6,545	25,800	2,885	4,695	4,245
Ontario	5,367,400	791,210	2,985,020	319,805	593,730	613,880
Canada	12,941,960	3,142,525	7,816,045	698,240	1,686,035	1,584,530
			Males			
Whitby	26,205	3,275	13,455	1,130	1,575	800
Ontario	2,681,320	397,620	1,583,760	133,790	231,160	117,980
Canada	6,470,300	1,575,495	4,206,320	299,655	680,415	310,940
			Females			
Whitby	26,310	3,275	12,345	1,750	3,120	3,445
Ontario	2,686,075	393,590	1,401,260	186,015	362,570	495,905
Canada	6,471,660	1,567,035	3,609,730	398,585	1,005,620	1,273,590
			Percent of Population			
			Total			
Whitby	54.3	6.8	26.7	3.0	4.9	4.4
Ontario	50.3	7.4	28.0	3.0	5.6	5.8
Canada	46.4	11.3	28.0	2.5	6.0	5.7
			Males			
Whitby	56.4	7.1	29.0	2.4	3.4	1.7
Ontario	52.1	7.7	30.8	2.6	4.5	2.3
Canada	47.8	11.6	31.1	2.2	5.0	2.3
			Females			
Whitby	52.4	6.5	24.6	3.5	6.2	6.9
Ontario	48.6	7.1	25.4	3.4	6.6	9.0
Canada	45.2	10.9	25.2	2.8	7.0	8.9

Note: (1) and not separated, (2) never legally married
Source: Statistics Canada. 2012. Census Profile. 2011 Census. Statistics Canada Catalogue no. 98-316-XWE. Ottawa. Released October 24 2012. http://www12.statcan.gc.ca/census-recensement/2011/dp-pd/prof/index.cfm?Lang=E

Age Characteristics: 0 to 49 Years

Area	0 to 4 Years	5 to 9 Years	10 to 14 Years	15 to 19 Years	20 to 24 Years	25 to 29 Years	30 to 34 Years	35 to 39 Years	40 to 44 Years	45 to 49 Years
					Number Total					
Whitby	7,770	8,610	8,965	9,695	7,560	6,315	7,380	9,250	10,085	11,115
Ontario	704,260	712,755	763,755	863,635	852,910	815,120	800,365	844,335	924,075	1,055,880
Canada	1,877,095	1,809,895	1,920,355	2,178,135	2,187,450	2,169,590	2,162,905	2,173,930	2,324,875	2,675,130
					Males					
Whitby	3,965	4,440	4,570	5,010	3,830	3,125	3,405	4,315	4,785	5,480
Ontario	360,590	365,290	391,630	443,680	432,490	400,045	383,340	405,845	447,920	517,510
Canada	961,150	925,965	983,995	1,115,845	1,108,775	1,077,275	1,058,810	1,064,200	1,141,720	1,318,715
					Females					
Whitby	3,805	4,170	4,400	4,690	3,730	3,195	3,975	4,930	5,295	5,640
Ontario	343,670	347,465	372,125	419,950	420,415	415,075	417,030	438,485	476,155	538,370
Canada	915,945	883,935	936,360	1,062,295	1,078,670	1,092,315	1,104,095	1,109,735	1,183,155	1,356,420
					Percent of Population Total					
Whitby	6.4	7.1	7.3	7.9	6.2	5.2	6.0	7.6	8.3	9.1
Ontario	5.5	5.5	5.9	6.7	6.6	6.3	6.2	6.6	7.2	8.2
Canada	5.6	5.4	5.7	6.5	6.5	6.5	6.5	6.5	6.9	8.0
					Males					
Whitby	6.7	7.5	7.7	8.4	6.4	5.3	5.7	7.3	8.1	9.2
Ontario	5.8	5.8	6.3	7.1	6.9	6.4	6.1	6.5	7.2	8.3
Canada	5.9	5.6	6.0	6.8	6.8	6.6	6.5	6.5	7.0	8.0
					Females					
Whitby	6.1	6.7	7.0	7.5	6.0	5.1	6.3	7.9	8.5	9.0
Ontario	5.2	5.3	5.6	6.4	6.4	6.3	6.3	6.7	7.2	8.2
Canada	5.4	5.2	5.5	6.2	6.4	6.4	6.5	6.5	6.9	7.9

Source: Statistics Canada. 2012. Census Profile. 2011 Census. Statistics Canada Catalogue no. 98-316-XWE. Ottawa. Released October 24 2012.
http://www12.statcan.gc.ca/census-recensement/2011/dp-pd/prof/index.cfm?Lang=E

Age Characteristics: 50 Years and Over, and Median Age

Area	50 to 54 Years	55 to 59 Years	60 to 64 Years	65 to 69 Years	70 to 74 Years	75 to 79 Years	80 to 84 Years	85 Years and Over	Median Age
				Number Total					
Whitby	9,440	7,270	5,975	3,960	2,845	2,380	1,840	1,560	37.6
Ontario	1,006,140	864,620	765,655	563,485	440,780	356,150	271,510	246,400	40.4
Canada	2,658,965	2,340,635	2,052,670	1,521,715	1,153,065	922,700	702,070	645,515	40.6
				Males					
Whitby	4,635	3,525	2,855	1,910	1,325	1,040	710	490	36.7
Ontario	492,560	418,755	370,370	270,875	206,350	161,345	113,620	80,925	39.4
Canada	1,309,030	1,147,300	1,002,690	738,010	543,435	417,945	291,085	208,300	39.6
				Females					
Whitby	4,800	3,745	3,115	2,055	1,520	1,340	1,130	1,075	38.4
Ontario	513,580	445,865	395,275	292,610	234,435	194,805	157,890	165,475	41.3
Canada	1,349,940	1,193,335	1,049,985	783,705	609,630	504,755	410,985	437,215	41.5
				Percent of Population Total					
Whitby	7.7	6.0	4.9	3.2	2.3	2.0	1.5	1.3	—
Ontario	7.8	6.7	6.0	4.4	3.4	2.8	2.1	1.9	—
Canada	7.9	7.0	6.1	4.5	3.4	2.8	2.1	1.9	—
				Males					
Whitby	7.8	5.9	4.8	3.2	2.2	1.8	1.2	0.8	—
Ontario	7.9	6.7	5.9	4.3	3.3	2.6	1.8	1.3	—
Canada	8.0	7.0	6.1	4.5	3.3	2.5	1.8	1.3	—
				Females					
Whitby	7.7	6.0	5.0	3.3	2.4	2.1	1.8	1.7	—
Ontario	7.8	6.8	6.0	4.4	3.6	3.0	2.4	2.5	—
Canada	7.9	7.0	6.2	4.6	3.6	3.0	2.4	2.6	—

Source: Statistics Canada. 2012. Census Profile. 2011 Census. Statistics Canada Catalogue no. 98-316-XWE. Ottawa. Released October 24 2012.
http://www12.statcan.gc.ca/census-recensement/2011/dp-pd/prof/index.cfm?Lang=E

PROFILES / Whitby, Ontario

Private Households by Household Size

Area	1 Person	2 Persons	3 Persons	4 Persons	5 Persons	6 or More Persons	Average Number of Persons in Private Households
			Households				
Whitby	6,775	11,540	7,865	9,615	3,655	1,575	2.9
Ontario	1,230,975	1,584,415	803,030	783,925	310,860	174,305	2.6
Canada	3,673,310	4,544,820	2,081,900	1,903,300	724,405	392,885	2.5
			Percent of Households				
Whitby	16.5	28.1	19.2	23.4	8.9	3.8	–
Ontario	25.2	32.4	16.4	16.0	6.4	3.6	–
Canada	27.6	34.1	15.6	14.3	5.4	2.9	–

Source: Statistics Canada. 2012. Census Profile. 2011 Census. Statistics Canada Catalogue no. 98-316-XWE. Ottawa. Released October 24 2012.
http://www12.statcan.gc.ca/census-recensement/2011/dp-pd/prof/index.cfm?Lang=E

Dwelling Type

Area	Single-detached House	Semi-detached House	Row House	Apartment: Building with Five or More Storeys	Apartment: Building with Fewer Than Five Storeys	Duplex Apartment	Movable Dwelling	Other Single-attached House
				Number				
Whitby	29,255	1,305	4,855	2,675	2,125	725	50	25
Ontario	2,718,880	279,470	415,225	789,970	498,160	160,460	15,800	9,540
Canada	7,329,150	646,245	791,600	1,234,770	2,397,550	704,485	183,510	33,310
				Percent of Dwellings				
Whitby	71.3	3.2	11.8	6.5	5.2	1.8	0.1	0.1
Ontario	55.6	5.7	8.5	16.2	10.2	3.3	0.3	0.2
Canada	55.0	4.9	5.9	9.3	18.0	5.3	1.4	0.3

Source: Statistics Canada. 2012. Census Profile. 2011 Census. Statistics Canada Catalogue no. 98-316-XWE. Ottawa. Released October 24 2012.
http://www12.statcan.gc.ca/census-recensement/2011/dp-pd/prof/index.cfm?Lang=E

Shelter Costs

	Owned Dwellings					Rented Dwellings		
Area	Number	Median Value[1] ($)	Average Value[1] ($)	Median Monthly Costs[2] ($)	Average Monthly Costs[2] ($)	Number	Median Monthly Costs[3] ($)	Average Monthly Costs[3] ($)
Whitby	35,010	341,505	358,478	1,595	1,545	5,935	974	1,048
Ontario	3,446,650	300,862	367,428	1,163	1,284	1,385,535	892	926
Canada	9,013,410	280,552	345,182	978	1,141	4,060,385	784	848

Note: All figures cover non-farm, non-reserve private dwellings. (1) Refers to the dollar amount expected by the owner if the dwelling were to be sold; (2) Includes all shelter expenses paid by households that own their dwellings, such as the mortgage payment and the costs of electricity, heat, water and other municipal services, property taxes and condominium fees; (3) Includes all shelter expenses paid by households that rent their dwellings, such as the monthly rent and the costs of electricity, heat and municipal services.
Source: Statistics Canada. 2013. 2011 National Household Survey. Statistics Canada Catalogue no. 99-004-XWE. Ottawa. Released September 11, 2013.

Occupied Private Dwellings by Period of Construction

Area	1960 or Before	1961 to 1980	1981 to 1990	1991 to 2000	2001 to 2005	2006 to 2011
			Number			
Whitby	3,725	7,330	8,405	8,515	8,720	4,330
Ontario	1,330,235	1,420,570	763,430	609,310	414,795	348,310
Canada	3,273,105	4,152,715	2,112,110	1,707,880	1,031,020	1,042,430
			Percent of Dwellings			
Whitby	9.1	17.9	20.5	20.8	21.3	10.6
Ontario	27.2	29.1	15.6	12.5	8.5	7.1
Canada	24.6	31.2	15.9	12.8	7.7	7.8

Note: Figures cover non-farm, non-reserve private dwellings and includes data up to May 10, 2011.
Source: Statistics Canada. 2013. 2011 National Household Survey. Statistics Canada Catalogue no. 99-004-XWE. Ottawa. Released September 11, 2013.

Educational Attainment

Area	No Certificate, Diploma or Degree	High School Diploma or Equivalent[1]	Apprenticeship or Trades Certificate or Diploma[2]	College, CÉGEP or Other Non-University Certificate or Diploma	University Certificate or Diploma Below the Bachelor Level[3]	Bachelor's Degree	University Certificate, Diploma or Degree Above Bachelor Level[4]
			Number				
			Total				
Whitby	13,670	26,110	5,695	24,060	3,650	14,645	7,190
Ontario	1,954,520	2,801,805	771,140	2,070,875	427,150	1,515,075	933,100
Canada	5,485,400	6,968,935	2,950,685	4,970,020	1,200,130	3,634,425	2,049,930
			Males				
Whitby	6,805	12,685	3,980	10,890	1,760	6,375	3,360
Ontario	957,040	1,337,055	520,390	894,235	193,355	692,345	470,290
Canada	2,742,875	3,305,415	1,928,970	2,118,430	513,235	1,643,080	1,043,350
			Females				
Whitby	6,865	13,425	1,715	13,165	1,895	8,275	3,825
Ontario	997,475	1,464,755	250,750	1,176,640	233,790	822,730	462,805
Canada	2,742,520	3,663,515	1,021,715	2,851,595	686,890	1,991,345	1,006,585
			Percent of Population				
			Total				
Whitby	14.4	27.5	6.0	25.3	3.8	15.4	7.6
Ontario	18.7	26.8	7.4	19.8	4.1	14.5	8.9
Canada	20.1	25.6	10.8	18.2	4.4	13.3	7.5
			Males				
Whitby	14.8	27.7	8.7	23.7	3.8	13.9	7.3
Ontario	18.9	26.4	10.3	17.7	3.8	13.7	9.3
Canada	20.6	24.9	14.5	15.9	3.9	12.4	7.8
			Females				
Whitby	14.0	27.3	3.5	26.8	3.9	16.8	7.8
Ontario	18.4	27.1	4.6	21.8	4.3	15.2	8.6
Canada	19.6	26.2	7.3	20.4	4.9	14.3	7.2

Note: Figures cover total population aged 15 years and over by highest certificate, diploma or degree; (1) Includes persons who have graduated from a secondary school or equivalent. It excludes persons with a postsecondary certificate, diploma or degree; (2) Includes Registered Apprenticeship certificates (including Certificate of Qualification, Journeyperson's designation) and other trades certificates or diplomas such as pre-employment or vocational certificates and diplomas from brief trade programs completed at community colleges, institutes of technology, vocational centres, and similar institutions; (3) Comparisons with other data sources suggest that the category 'University certificate or diploma below the bachelor's level' was over-reported in the NHS. This category likely includes some responses that are actually college certificates or diplomas, bachelor's degrees or other types of education (e.g., university transfer programs, bachelor's programs completed in other countries, incomplete bachelor's programs, non-university professional designations). We recommend users interpret the results for the 'University certificate or diploma below the bachelor's level' category with caution; (4) 'University certificate or diploma above bachelor level' includes the categories: 'Degree in medicine, dentistry, veterinary medicine or optometry,' 'Master's degree' and 'Earned doctorate.'
Source: Statistics Canada. 2013. 2011 National Household Survey. Statistics Canada Catalogue no. 99-004-XWE. Ottawa. Released September 11, 2013.

Household Income Distribution

Area	Less than $10,000	$10,000 to $19,999	$20,000 to $29,999	$30,000 to $39,999	$40,000 to $49,999	$50,000 to $59,999	$60,000 to $79,999	$80,000 to $99,999	$100,000 to $124,999	$125,000 to $149,999	$150,000 and Over
					Households						
Whitby	970	1,785	1,820	2,270	2,460	2,675	4,880	4,985	5,710	4,315	9,155
Ontario	201,780	354,530	405,725	425,410	425,720	398,705	680,850	552,660	497,970	331,460	611,840
Canada	626,705	1,141,945	1,193,925	1,271,675	1,206,800	1,102,120	1,865,280	1,458,240	1,260,770	802,555	1,389,240
					Percent of Households						
Whitby	2.4	4.4	4.4	5.5	6.0	6.5	11.9	12.2	13.9	10.5	22.3
Ontario	4.1	7.3	8.3	8.7	8.7	8.2	13.9	11.3	10.2	6.8	12.5
Canada	4.7	8.6	9.0	9.5	9.1	8.3	14.0	10.9	9.5	6.0	10.4

Note: Household income is the sum of the total incomes of all members of that household. Total income refers to monetary receipts from certain sources, before income taxes and deductions, during calendar year 2010.
Source: Statistics Canada. 2013. 2011 National Household Survey. Statistics Canada Catalogue no. 99-004-XWE. Ottawa. Released September 11, 2013.

Median and Average Household and Economic Family Income

Area	Median Household Income ($)	Average Household Income ($)	Median After-tax Household Income ($)	Average After-tax Household Income ($)	Median Economic Family Income ($)	Average Economic Family Income ($)	Median After-tax Economic Family Income ($)	Average After-tax Economic Family Income ($)
Whitby	94,685	109,030	79,956	88,795	105,019	120,396	88,802	97,852
Ontario	66,358	85,772	58,717	71,523	80,987	100,152	71,128	83,322
Canada	61,072	79,102	54,089	66,149	76,511	94,125	67,044	78,517

Note: Figures cover household and economic familiy income in 2010. A household is defined as a person or a group of persons (other than foreign residents) who occupy the same private dwelling and do not have a usual place of residence elsewhere in Canada. Every person is a member of one and only one household. An economic family is defined as a group of two or more persons who live in the same dwelling and are related to each other by blood, marriage, common-law, adoption or a foster relationship. A couple may be of opposite or same sex.
Source: Statistics Canada. 2013. 2011 National Household Survey. Statistics Canada Catalogue no. 99-004-XWE. Ottawa. Released September 11, 2013.

Individual Income Distribution

Area	Less than $10,000	$10,000 to $19,999	$20,000 to $29,999	$30,000 to $39,999	$40,000 to $49,999	$50,000 to $59,999	$60,000 to $79,999	$80,000 to $99,999	$100,000 to $124,999	$125,000 and Over
					Number Total					
Whitby	15,780	12,325	9,175	8,930	7,620	7,210	11,030	8,250	4,830	4,455
Ontario	1,780,355	1,748,060	1,361,710	1,136,730	980,790	746,360	964,280	574,710	293,865	330,285
Canada	4,492,040	4,835,710	3,670,020	3,180,360	2,603,520	1,921,650	2,437,440	1,302,045	693,580	782,135
					Males					
Whitby	6,720	4,385	3,710	3,810	3,495	3,485	6,100	4,945	3,295	3,525
Ontario	781,095	669,815	580,990	535,255	491,125	407,005	569,205	341,160	201,125	244,500
Canada	1,936,365	1,864,880	1,588,260	1,522,190	1,333,510	1,079,780	1,473,145	823,720	492,905	599,905
					Females					
Whitby	9,065	7,940	5,465	5,120	4,120	3,725	4,925	3,305	1,535	935
Ontario	999,265	1,078,245	780,720	601,475	489,665	339,360	395,075	233,550	92,740	85,790
Canada	2,555,675	2,970,825	2,081,760	1,658,170	1,270,010	841,870	964,300	478,330	200,680	182,230
					Percent of Population Total					
Whitby	17.6	13.8	10.2	10.0	8.5	8.0	12.3	9.2	5.4	5.0
Ontario	18.0	17.6	13.7	11.5	9.9	7.5	9.7	5.8	3.0	3.3
Canada	17.3	18.7	14.2	12.3	10.0	7.4	9.4	5.0	2.7	3.0
					Males					
Whitby	15.5	10.1	8.5	8.8	8.0	8.0	14.0	11.4	7.6	8.1
Ontario	16.2	13.9	12.1	11.1	10.2	8.4	11.8	7.1	4.2	5.1
Canada	15.2	14.7	12.5	12.0	10.5	8.5	11.6	6.5	3.9	4.7
					Females					
Whitby	19.6	17.2	11.8	11.1	8.9	8.1	10.7	7.2	3.3	2.0
Ontario	19.6	21.2	15.3	11.8	9.6	6.7	7.8	4.6	1.8	1.7
Canada	19.4	22.5	15.8	12.6	9.6	6.4	7.3	3.6	1.5	1.4

Note: Figures cover individuals aged 15 years and over with income. Income refers to monetary receipts from certain sources, before income taxes and deductions, during calendar year 2010.
Source: Statistics Canada. 2013. 2011 National Household Survey. Statistics Canada Catalogue no. 99-004-XWE. Ottawa. Released September 11, 2013.

Labour Force Status

Area	In the Labour Force - All	In the Labour Force - Employed	In the Labour Force - Unemployed	Not in the Labour Force
	Number Total			
Whitby	68,575	63,540	5,030	26,450
Ontario	6,864,990	6,297,005	567,985	3,608,685
Canada	17,990,080	16,595,035	1,395,045	9,269,445
	Males			
Whitby	34,895	32,320	2,570	10,965
Ontario	3,542,030	3,249,165	292,865	1,522,690
Canada	9,388,570	8,634,310	754,255	3,906,785
	Females			
Whitby	33,685	31,225	2,455	15,485
Ontario	3,322,955	3,047,840	275,120	2,085,990
Canada	8,601,515	7,960,725	640,790	5,362,660
	Percent of Labour Force Total			
Whitby	72.2	66.9	7.3	27.8
Ontario	65.5	60.1	8.3	34.5
Canada	66.0	60.9	7.8	34.0
	Males			
Whitby	76.1	70.5	7.4	23.9
Ontario	69.9	64.2	8.3	30.1
Canada	70.6	64.9	8.0	29.4
	Females			
Whitby	68.5	63.5	7.3	31.5
Ontario	61.4	56.3	8.3	38.6
Canada	61.6	57.0	7.4	38.4

Note: Figures are based on total population 15 years and over
Source: Statistics Canada. 2013. 2011 National Household Survey. Statistics Canada Catalogue no. 99-004-XWE. Ottawa. Released September 11, 2013.

Labour Force by Industry (NAICS Codes 11–52)

Area	Agriculture, forestry, fishing & hunting	Mining, quarrying, & oil & gas extraction	Utilities	Construction	Manufacturing	Wholesale Trade	Retail Trade	Transportation & warehousing	Information & cultural industries	Finance & insurance
					Number Total					
Whitby	265	85	2,230	3,815	5,460	3,510	7,760	2,620	2,535	4,885
Ontario	101,280	29,985	57,035	417,900	697,565	305,030	751,200	307,405	178,720	364,415
Canada	437,650	261,050	149,940	1,215,380	1,619,295	733,445	2,031,665	827,780	420,830	767,960
					Males					
Whitby	130	50	1,630	3,355	3,925	2,210	3,720	1,990	1,465	2,070
Ontario	66,485	25,650	42,685	369,300	493,305	197,770	344,480	225,245	98,835	153,125
Canada	307,370	211,690	110,765	1,068,710	1,167,680	494,545	933,850	617,305	235,875	296,995
					Females					
Whitby	135	35	605	455	1,530	1,300	4,035	630	1,075	2,815
Ontario	34,800	4,340	14,350	48,595	204,260	107,260	406,720	82,160	79,885	211,290
Canada	130,285	49,360	39,175	146,670	451,615	238,900	1,097,820	210,475	184,955	470,960
					Percent of Labour Force Total					
Whitby	0.4	0.1	3.3	5.7	8.2	5.2	11.6	3.9	3.8	7.3
Ontario	1.5	0.4	0.9	6.3	10.4	4.6	11.2	4.6	2.7	5.5
Canada	2.5	1.5	0.9	6.9	9.2	4.2	11.6	4.7	2.4	4.4
					Males					
Whitby	0.4	0.1	4.8	9.8	11.5	6.5	10.9	5.8	4.3	6.1
Ontario	1.9	0.7	1.2	10.7	14.3	5.7	10.0	6.5	2.9	4.4
Canada	3.3	2.3	1.2	11.6	12.7	5.4	10.2	6.7	2.6	3.2
					Females					
Whitby	0.4	0.1	1.8	1.4	4.7	4.0	12.3	1.9	3.3	8.6
Ontario	1.1	0.1	0.4	1.5	6.3	3.3	12.6	2.5	2.5	6.5
Canada	1.6	0.6	0.5	1.7	5.4	2.8	13.1	2.5	2.2	5.6

Note: Figures are based on total experienced labour force 15 years and over. Experienced labour force refers to persons who, during the week of Sunday, May 1 to Saturday, May 7, 2011, were employed and the unemployed who had last worked for pay or in self-employment in either 2010 or 2011.
Source: Statistics Canada. 2013. 2011 National Household Survey. Statistics Canada Catalogue no. 99-004-XWE. Ottawa. Released September 11, 2013.

Labour Force by Industry (NAICS Codes 53–91)

Area	Real estate & rental & leasing	Profess., scientific & tech. services	Mgmt of companies & enterprises	Admin. & support, waste mgmt & remed. services	Educational services	Health care & social assistance	Arts, entertain. & recreation	Accomm. & food services	Other services (except public admin.)	Public admin.
					Number Total					
Whitby	1,565	5,360	35	2,750	5,855	6,255	1,390	3,330	2,475	4,765
Ontario	133,980	511,020	6,525	309,630	499,690	692,130	144,065	417,675	296,340	458,665
Canada	321,895	1,240,850	17,460	728,330	1,301,435	1,949,650	363,405	1,130,750	807,800	1,261,050
					Males					
Whitby	720	2,830	15	1,525	1,575	945	730	1,475	1,110	2,595
Ontario	72,835	281,420	3,540	172,475	162,765	120,165	75,035	177,240	133,795	236,655
Canada	179,090	688,625	9,380	411,250	424,915	349,430	188,270	469,990	372,940	652,510
					Females					
Whitby	845	2,530	15	1,225	4,285	5,305	665	1,855	1,370	2,165
Ontario	61,145	229,600	2,990	137,155	336,925	571,965	69,030	240,430	162,550	222,015
Canada	142,805	552,225	8,075	317,085	876,515	1,600,220	175,135	660,760	434,865	608,535
					Percent of Labour Force Total					
Whitby	2.3	8.0	0.1	4.1	8.7	9.3	2.1	5.0	3.7	7.1
Ontario	2.0	7.6	0.1	4.6	7.5	10.4	2.2	6.3	4.4	6.9
Canada	1.8	7.1	0.1	4.1	7.4	11.1	2.1	6.4	4.6	7.2
					Males					
Whitby	2.1	8.3	0.0	4.5	4.6	2.8	2.1	4.3	3.3	7.6
Ontario	2.1	8.2	0.1	5.0	4.7	3.5	2.2	5.1	3.9	6.9
Canada	1.9	7.5	0.1	4.5	4.6	3.8	2.0	5.1	4.1	7.1
					Females					
Whitby	2.6	7.7	0.0	3.7	13.0	16.1	2.0	5.6	4.2	6.6
Ontario	1.9	7.1	0.1	4.2	10.4	17.7	2.1	7.4	5.0	6.9
Canada	1.7	6.6	0.1	3.8	10.4	19.1	2.1	7.9	5.2	7.2

Note: Figures are based on total experienced labour force 15 years and over. Experienced labour force refers to persons who, during the week of Sunday, May 1 to Saturday, May 7, 2011, were employed and the unemployed who had last worked for pay or in self-employment in either 2010 or 2011.
Source: Statistics Canada. 2013. 2011 National Household Survey. Statistics Canada Catalogue no. 99-004-XWE. Ottawa. Released September 11, 2013.

Occupation

Area	Mgmt	Business, Finance & Admin.	Natural/ Applied Sciences & Related	Health	Education, Law & Social, Community & Government Services	Art, Culture, Recreation & Sport	Sales & Service	Trades, Transport & Equip. Operators & Related	Natural Resources, Agri. & Related Production	Mfg & Utilities
					Number					
					Total					
Whitby	9,735	12,370	5,155	3,280	9,525	1,985	14,815	7,025	780	2,275
Ontario	770,580	1,138,330	494,500	392,695	801,465	206,420	1,550,260	868,515	106,810	350,685
Canada	1,963,600	2,902,045	1,237,775	1,107,200	2,064,675	503,415	4,068,170	2,537,775	397,930	805,040
					Males					
Whitby	5,860	3,750	4,075	550	3,255	850	6,690	6,645	640	1,775
Ontario	474,655	352,505	384,345	78,330	264,570	96,055	673,880	812,280	82,610	233,565
Canada	1,229,460	854,190	966,355	217,520	676,550	232,535	1,745,705	2,385,615	318,945	564,300
					Females					
Whitby	3,875	8,620	1,085	2,730	6,275	1,140	8,120	380	145	500
Ontario	295,920	785,825	110,150	314,370	536,895	110,370	876,380	56,230	24,200	117,115
Canada	734,140	2,047,855	271,415	889,675	1,388,130	270,875	2,322,465	152,165	78,980	240,740
					Percent of Labour Force					
					Total					
Whitby	14.5	18.5	7.7	4.9	14.2	3.0	22.1	10.5	1.2	3.4
Ontario	11.5	17.0	7.4	5.9	12.0	3.1	23.2	13.0	1.6	5.2
Canada	11.2	16.5	7.0	6.3	11.7	2.9	23.1	14.4	2.3	4.6
					Males					
Whitby	17.2	11.0	12.0	1.6	9.6	2.5	19.6	19.5	1.9	5.2
Ontario	13.7	10.2	11.1	2.3	7.7	2.8	19.5	23.5	2.4	6.8
Canada	13.4	9.3	10.5	2.4	7.4	2.5	19.0	26.0	3.5	6.1
					Females					
Whitby	11.8	26.2	3.3	8.3	19.1	3.5	24.7	1.2	0.4	1.5
Ontario	9.2	24.3	3.4	9.7	16.6	3.4	27.2	1.7	0.7	3.6
Canada	8.7	24.4	3.2	10.6	16.5	3.2	27.7	1.8	0.9	2.9

Note: Figures are based on total experienced labour force 15 years and over
Source: Statistics Canada. 2013. 2011 National Household Survey. Statistics Canada Catalogue no. 99-004-XWE. Ottawa. Released September 11, 2013.

Place of Work Status

Area	Worked at Home	Worked Outside Canada	No Fixed Workplace Address	Worked at Usual Place
		Number		
		Total		
Whitby	4,565	130	6,360	52,490
Ontario	423,790	31,390	670,835	5,170,980
Canada	1,142,640	66,460	1,868,245	13,517,690
		Males		
Whitby	2,025	90	4,730	25,480
Ontario	216,900	21,150	486,560	2,524,555
Canada	582,150	47,355	1,400,485	6,604,325
		Females		
Whitby	2,540	45	1,630	27,010
Ontario	206,895	10,240	184,275	2,646,420
Canada	560,490	19,100	467,760	6,913,370
	Percent of Labour Force			
		Total		
Whitby	7.2	0.2	10.0	82.6
Ontario	6.7	0.5	10.7	82.1
Canada	6.9	0.4	11.3	81.5
		Males		
Whitby	6.3	0.3	14.6	78.8
Ontario	6.7	0.7	15.0	77.7
Canada	6.7	0.5	16.2	76.5
		Females		
Whitby	8.1	0.1	5.2	86.5
Ontario	6.8	0.3	6.0	86.8
Canada	7.0	0.2	5.9	86.8

Note: Figures are based on total employed labour force 15 years and over.
Source: Statistics Canada. 2013. 2011 National Household Survey. Statistics Canada Catalogue no. 99-004-XWE. Ottawa. Released September 11, 2013.

PROFILES / Whitby, Ontario

Mode of Transportation to Work

Area	Car; Truck; Van; as Driver	Car; Truck; Van; as Passenger	Public Transit	Walked	Bicycled	All Other Modes
			Number			
			Total			
Whitby	46,770	3,135	6,695	1,415	240	590
Ontario	4,235,315	357,110	818,270	299,095	69,885	62,145
Canada	11,393,140	867,050	1,851,525	880,815	201,780	191,625
			Males			
Whitby	25,185	1,275	2,855	540	135	215
Ontario	2,316,680	143,410	340,995	131,765	47,635	30,635
Canada	6,238,835	349,530	788,290	387,580	135,840	104,725
			Females			
Whitby	21,585	1,865	3,840	875	105	375
Ontario	1,918,640	213,700	477,275	167,325	22,250	31,515
Canada	5,154,305	517,520	1,063,235	493,230	65,940	86,900
			Percent of Labour Force			
			Total			
Whitby	79.5	5.3	11.4	2.4	0.4	1.0
Ontario	72.5	6.1	14.0	5.1	1.2	1.1
Canada	74.0	5.6	12.0	5.7	1.3	1.2
			Males			
Whitby	83.4	4.2	9.5	1.8	0.4	0.7
Ontario	76.9	4.8	11.3	4.4	1.6	1.0
Canada	77.9	4.4	9.8	4.8	1.7	1.3
			Females			
Whitby	75.4	6.5	13.4	3.1	0.4	1.3
Ontario	67.8	7.5	16.9	5.9	0.8	1.1
Canada	69.8	7.0	14.4	6.7	0.9	1.2

Note: Figures are based on total employed labour force 15 years and over.
Source: Statistics Canada. 2013. 2011 National Household Survey. Statistics Canada Catalogue no. 99-004-XWE. Ottawa. Released September 11, 2013.

Visible Minority Population Characteristics

Area	Total Minority	South Asian[1]	Chinese	Black	Filipino	Latin American	Arab	SE Asian[2]	West Asian[3]	Korean	Japanese	Multiple[4]
						Number						
						Total						
Whitby	23,125	5,700	2,290	7,440	2,255	995	755	340	630	410	275	1,180
Ontario	3,279,565	965,990	629,140	539,205	275,380	172,560	151,645	137,875	122,530	78,290	29,085	96,735
Canada	6,264,750	1,567,400	1,324,750	945,665	619,310	381,280	380,620	312,075	206,840	161,130	87,270	171,935
						Males						
Whitby	11,025	2,655	1,100	3,715	920	430	380	165	280	260	125	635
Ontario	1,582,480	484,355	301,575	251,295	116,825	83,205	79,620	67,645	62,515	38,045	13,345	46,765
Canada	3,043,010	790,755	632,325	453,005	268,885	186,355	203,485	154,035	105,620	77,165	38,270	83,335
						Females						
Whitby	12,095	3,045	1,195	3,730	1,335	565	380	175	350	150	150	545
Ontario	1,697,085	481,635	327,570	287,915	158,555	89,360	72,025	70,230	60,010	40,250	15,740	49,970
Canada	3,221,745	776,650	692,420	492,660	350,425	194,925	177,140	158,045	101,220	83,965	48,990	88,600
						Percent of Population						
						Total						
Whitby	19.2	4.7	1.9	6.2	1.9	0.8	0.6	0.3	0.5	0.3	0.2	1.0
Ontario	25.9	7.6	5.0	4.3	2.2	1.4	1.2	1.1	1.0	0.6	0.2	0.8
Canada	19.1	4.8	4.0	2.9	1.9	1.2	1.2	0.9	0.6	0.5	0.3	0.5
						Males						
Whitby	18.7	4.5	1.9	6.3	1.6	0.7	0.6	0.3	0.5	0.4	0.2	1.1
Ontario	25.6	7.8	4.9	4.1	1.9	1.3	1.3	1.1	1.0	0.6	0.2	0.8
Canada	18.8	4.9	3.9	2.8	1.7	1.2	1.3	1.0	0.7	0.5	0.2	0.5
						Females						
Whitby	19.7	5.0	1.9	6.1	2.2	0.9	0.6	0.3	0.6	0.2	0.2	0.9
Ontario	26.2	7.4	5.1	4.4	2.5	1.4	1.1	1.1	0.9	0.6	0.2	0.8
Canada	19.3	4.7	4.1	3.0	2.1	1.2	1.1	0.9	0.6	0.5	0.3	0.5

Note: The Employment Equity Act defines visible minorities as 'persons, other than Aboriginal peoples, who are non-Caucasian in race or non-white in colour';
(1) Includes 'East Indian,' 'Pakistani,' 'Sri Lankan,' etc.; (2) Includes 'Vietnamese,' 'Cambodian,' 'Malaysian,' 'Laotian,' etc.; (3) Includes 'Iranian,' 'Afghan,' etc.; (4) Includes respondents who reported more than one visible minority group by checking two or more mark-in circles, e.g., 'Black' and 'South Asian.'
Source: Statistics Canada. 2013. 2011 National Household Survey. Statistics Canada Catalogue no. 99-004-XWE. Ottawa. Released September 11, 2013.

PROFILES / Whitby, Ontario

Aboriginal Population

Area	Aboriginal Identity[1]	First Nations (North American Indian) Single Identity[2]	Métis Single Identity	Inuk (Inuit) Single Identity	Multiple Aboriginal Identities[3]	Aboriginal Identities Not Included Elsewhere
Number						
Total						
Whitby	1,485	900	455	100	0	30
Ontario	301,430	201,100	86,020	3,355	2,910	8,040
Canada	1,400,685	851,560	451,795	59,440	11,415	26,475
Males						
Whitby	680	385	245	40	0	0
Ontario	145,020	96,620	41,755	1,475	1,420	3,750
Canada	682,190	411,785	223,335	29,495	5,525	12,055
Females						
Whitby	800	520	205	60	0	20
Ontario	156,410	104,485	44,260	1,880	1,490	4,295
Canada	718,500	439,775	228,460	29,950	5,890	14,420
Percent of Population						
Total						
Whitby	1.2	0.7	0.4	0.1	0.0	0.0
Ontario	2.4	1.6	0.7	0.0	0.0	0.1
Canada	4.3	2.6	1.4	0.2	0.0	0.1
Males						
Whitby	1.2	0.7	0.4	0.1	0.0	0.0
Ontario	2.3	1.6	0.7	0.0	0.0	0.1
Canada	4.2	2.5	1.4	0.2	0.0	0.1
Females						
Whitby	1.3	0.8	0.3	0.1	0.0	0.0
Ontario	2.4	1.6	0.7	0.0	0.0	0.1
Canada	4.3	2.6	1.4	0.2	0.0	0.1

Note: (1) Includes persons who reported being an Aboriginal person, that is, First Nations (North American Indian), Métis or Inuk (Inuit) and/or those who reported Registered or Treaty Indian status, that is registered under the Indian Act of Canada, and/or those who reported membership in a First Nation or Indian band. Aboriginal peoples of Canada are defined in the Constitution Act, 1982, section 35-2 as including the Indian, Inuit and Métis peoples of Canada; (2) Users should be aware that the estimates associated with this variable are more affected than most by the incomplete enumeration of certain Indian reserves and Indian settlements in the National Household Survey (NHS); (3) Includes persons who reported being any two or all three of the following: First Nations (North American Indian), Métis or Inuk (Inuit).
Source: Statistics Canada. 2013. 2011 National Household Survey. Statistics Canada Catalogue no. 99-004-XWE. Ottawa. Released September 11, 2013.

Ethnic Origin

Area	North American Aboriginal	Other North American	European	Caribbean	Latin, Central and South American	African	Asian	Oceania
Number								
Total								
Whitby	2,810	35,495	88,960	7,055	2,575	3,050	14,995	220
Ontario	441,395	3,059,480	8,231,410	396,485	271,545	331,460	2,604,595	19,410
Canada	1,836,035	11,070,455	20,157,965	627,590	544,375	766,735	5,011,225	74,875
Males								
Whitby	1,295	17,770	43,730	3,390	1,255	1,555	7,105	120
Ontario	210,490	1,507,105	4,019,885	181,805	130,035	160,940	1,265,540	9,855
Canada	885,675	5,462,685	9,913,150	291,640	264,635	387,360	2,435,540	37,490
Females								
Whitby	1,505	17,730	45,230	3,670	1,315	1,500	7,885	105
Ontario	230,905	1,552,380	4,211,525	214,675	141,510	170,515	1,339,050	9,555
Canada	950,360	5,607,770	10,244,820	335,945	279,740	379,380	2,575,680	37,385
Percent of Population								
Total								
Whitby	2.3	29.5	74.0	5.9	2.1	2.5	12.5	0.2
Ontario	3.5	24.2	65.1	3.1	2.1	2.6	20.6	0.2
Canada	5.6	33.7	61.4	1.9	1.7	2.3	15.3	0.2
Males								
Whitby	2.2	30.2	74.3	5.8	2.1	2.6	12.1	0.2
Ontario	3.4	24.4	65.0	2.9	2.1	2.6	20.5	0.2
Canada	5.5	33.8	61.3	1.8	1.6	2.4	15.1	0.2
Females								
Whitby	2.4	28.9	73.6	6.0	2.1	2.4	12.8	0.2
Ontario	3.6	24.0	65.1	3.3	2.2	2.6	20.7	0.1
Canada	5.7	33.6	61.4	2.0	1.7	2.3	15.4	0.2

Note: The sum of the ethnic groups in this table is greater than the total population estimate because a person may report more than one ethnic origin in the NHS.
Source: Statistics Canada. 2013. 2011 National Household Survey. Statistics Canada Catalogue no. 99-004-XWE. Ottawa. Released September 11, 2013.

Religion

Area	Buddhist	Christian	Hindu	Jewish	Muslim	Sikh	Traditional (Aboriginal) Spirituality	Other Religions	No Religious Affiliation
					Number Total				
Whitby	505	85,125	1,905	445	3,485	245	25	340	28,225
Ontario	163,750	8,167,295	366,720	195,540	581,950	179,765	15,905	53,080	2,927,790
Canada	366,830	22,102,745	497,965	329,495	1,053,945	454,965	64,935	130,835	7,850,605
					Males				
Whitby	250	40,305	950	275	1,745	110	0	100	15,095
Ontario	75,355	3,839,925	183,580	95,795	293,925	90,515	7,600	23,555	1,571,195
Canada	168,465	10,497,775	250,435	161,265	540,555	229,435	31,805	57,745	4,225,645
					Females				
Whitby	250	44,815	955	165	1,735	135	0	235	13,130
Ontario	88,395	4,327,365	183,140	99,740	288,025	89,250	8,310	29,525	1,356,600
Canada	198,365	11,604,975	247,525	168,235	513,395	225,530	33,135	73,090	3,624,965
				Percent of Population Total					
Whitby	0.4	70.8	1.6	0.4	2.9	0.2	0.0	0.3	23.5
Ontario	1.3	64.6	2.9	1.5	4.6	1.4	0.1	0.4	23.1
Canada	1.1	67.3	1.5	1.0	3.2	1.4	0.2	0.4	23.9
					Males				
Whitby	0.4	68.5	1.6	0.5	3.0	0.2	0.0	0.2	25.6
Ontario	1.2	62.1	3.0	1.5	4.8	1.5	0.1	0.4	25.4
Canada	1.0	64.9	1.5	1.0	3.3	1.4	0.2	0.4	26.1
					Females				
Whitby	0.4	72.9	1.6	0.3	2.8	0.2	0.0	0.4	21.4
Ontario	1.4	66.9	2.8	1.5	4.5	1.4	0.1	0.5	21.0
Canada	1.2	69.5	1.5	1.0	3.1	1.4	0.2	0.4	21.7

Note: Religion refers to the person's self-identification as having a connection or affiliation with any religious denomination, group, body, sect, cult or other religiously defined community or system of belief. Religion is not limited to formal membership in a religious organization or group. Persons without a religious connection or affiliation can self-identify as atheist, agnostic or humanist, or can provide another applicable response.
Source: Statistics Canada. 2013. 2011 National Household Survey. Statistics Canada Catalogue no. 99-004-XWE. Ottawa. Released September 11, 2013.

Religion—Christian Denominations

Area	Anglican	Baptist	Catholic	Christian Orthodox	Lutheran	Pentecostal	Presbyterian	United Church	Other Christian
					Number Total				
Whitby	10,080	2,540	39,050	2,960	920	3,175	3,100	11,600	11,700
Ontario	774,560	244,650	3,976,610	297,710	163,460	213,945	319,585	952,465	1,224,300
Canada	1,631,845	635,840	12,810,705	550,690	478,185	478,705	472,385	2,007,610	3,036,780
					Males				
Whitby	4,670	1,130	18,905	1,345	425	1,455	1,445	5,120	5,810
Ontario	355,175	112,285	1,895,940	145,825	75,225	94,955	148,535	435,255	576,730
Canada	752,945	293,905	6,167,290	270,205	221,525	217,850	218,955	912,545	1,442,550
					Females				
Whitby	5,405	1,410	20,145	1,615	495	1,720	1,655	6,475	5,895
Ontario	419,390	132,370	2,080,665	151,885	88,230	118,990	171,050	517,210	647,570
Canada	878,900	341,940	6,643,415	280,485	256,660	260,850	253,430	1,095,065	1,594,230
				Percent of Population Total					
Whitby	8.4	2.1	32.5	2.5	0.8	2.6	2.6	9.6	9.7
Ontario	6.1	1.9	31.4	2.4	1.3	1.7	2.5	7.5	9.7
Canada	5.0	1.9	39.0	1.7	1.5	1.5	1.4	6.1	9.2
					Males				
Whitby	7.9	1.9	32.1	2.3	0.7	2.5	2.5	8.7	9.9
Ontario	5.7	1.8	30.7	2.4	1.2	1.5	2.4	7.0	9.3
Canada	4.7	1.8	38.2	1.7	1.4	1.3	1.4	5.6	8.9
					Females				
Whitby	8.8	2.3	32.8	2.6	0.8	2.8	2.7	10.5	9.6
Ontario	6.5	2.0	32.2	2.3	1.4	1.8	2.6	8.0	10.0
Canada	5.3	2.0	39.8	1.7	1.5	1.6	1.5	6.6	9.6

Note: Religion refers to the person's self-identification as having a connection or affiliation with any religious denomination, group, body, sect, cult or other religiously defined community or system of belief. Religion is not limited to formal membership in a religious organization or group. Persons without a religious connection or affiliation can self-identify as atheist, agnostic or humanist, or can provide another applicable response.
Source: Statistics Canada. 2013. 2011 National Household Survey. Statistics Canada Catalogue no. 99-004-XWE. Ottawa. Released September 11, 2013.

PROFILES / Whitby, Ontario

Immigrant Status and Period of Immigration

Area	Non-Immigrants[1]	Immigrants All	Before 1971	1971 to 1980	1981 to 1990	1991 to 2000	2001 to 2005	2006 to 2011	Non-Permanent Residents[3]
Number									
Total									
Whitby	94,640	25,160	6,835	4,535	4,130	4,915	2,640	2,105	485
Ontario	8,906,000	3,611,365	723,030	464,380	538,285	866,220	518,405	501,060	134,425
Canada	25,720,175	6,775,765	1,261,055	870,775	949,890	1,539,050	992,070	1,162,915	356,385
Males									
Whitby	46,605	12,030	3,465	2,110	1,895	2,235	1,265	1,060	220
Ontario	4,410,240	1,706,385	341,820	217,990	258,095	408,270	245,850	234,360	64,825
Canada	12,753,235	3,231,370	605,430	416,670	454,570	724,905	474,545	555,245	178,515
Females									
Whitby	48,040	13,130	3,370	2,425	2,235	2,680	1,380	1,040	265
Ontario	4,495,765	1,904,985	381,210	246,390	280,190	457,950	272,550	266,695	69,600
Canada	12,966,935	3,544,400	655,625	454,105	495,325	814,145	517,530	607,670	177,870
Percent of Population									
Total									
Whitby	78.7	20.9	5.7	3.8	3.4	4.1	2.2	1.7	0.4
Ontario	70.4	28.5	5.7	3.7	4.3	6.8	4.1	4.0	1.1
Canada	78.3	20.6	3.8	2.7	2.9	4.7	3.0	3.5	1.1
Males									
Whitby	79.2	20.4	5.9	3.6	3.2	3.8	2.1	1.8	0.4
Ontario	71.3	27.6	5.5	3.5	4.2	6.6	4.0	3.8	1.0
Canada	78.9	20.0	3.7	2.6	2.8	4.5	2.9	3.4	1.1
Females									
Whitby	78.2	21.4	5.5	3.9	3.6	4.4	2.2	1.7	0.4
Ontario	69.5	29.4	5.9	3.8	4.3	7.1	4.2	4.1	1.1
Canada	77.7	21.2	3.9	2.7	3.0	4.9	3.1	3.6	1.1

Note: (1) Non-immigrant refers to a person who is a Canadian citizen by birth; (2) Immigrant refers to a person who is or has ever been a landed immigrant/permanent resident. This person has been granted the right to live in Canada permanently by immigration authorities. Some immigrants have resided in Canada for a number of years, while others have arrived recently. Some immigrants are Canadian citizens, while others are not. Most immigrants are born outside Canada, but a small number are born in Canada. In the 2011 National Household Survey, 'Immigrants' includes immigrants who landed in Canada prior to May 10, 2011; (3) Non-permanent resident refers to a person from another country who has a work or study permit, or who is a refugee claimant, and any non-Canadian-born family member living in Canada with them.
Source: Statistics Canada. 2013. 2011 National Household Survey. Statistics Canada Catalogue no. 99-004-XWE. Ottawa. Released September 11, 2013.

Mother Tongue

Area	English	French	Non-official Language	English & French	English & Non-official Language	French & Non-official Language	English, French & Non-official Language
Number							
Total							
Whitby	101,320	2,050	15,885	310	1,305	100	60
Ontario	8,677,040	493,300	3,264,435	46,605	219,425	13,645	7,615
Canada	18,858,980	7,054,975	6,567,680	144,685	396,330	74,430	24,095
Males							
Whitby	49,670	950	7,535	140	620	45	35
Ontario	4,276,970	232,785	1,562,190	21,805	106,790	6,285	3,495
Canada	9,345,225	3,452,380	3,157,785	69,975	192,000	36,535	11,965
Females							
Whitby	51,645	1,110	8,350	175	685	50	30
Ontario	4,400,065	260,510	1,702,240	24,795	112,635	7,365	4,115
Canada	9,513,750	3,602,590	3,409,895	74,710	204,330	37,890	12,130
Percent of Population							
Total							
Whitby	83.7	1.7	13.1	0.3	1.1	0.1	0.0
Ontario	68.2	3.9	25.7	0.4	1.7	0.1	0.1
Canada	56.9	21.3	19.8	0.4	1.2	0.2	0.1
Males							
Whitby	84.2	1.6	12.8	0.2	1.1	0.1	0.1
Ontario	68.9	3.7	25.2	0.4	1.7	0.1	0.1
Canada	57.5	21.2	19.4	0.4	1.2	0.2	0.1
Females							
Whitby	83.2	1.8	13.5	0.3	1.1	0.1	0.0
Ontario	67.6	4.0	26.1	0.4	1.7	0.1	0.1
Canada	56.4	21.4	20.2	0.4	1.2	0.2	0.1

Note: Figures cover total population excluding institutional residents.
Source: Statistics Canada. 2012. Census Profile. 2011 Census. Statistics Canada Catalogue no. 98-316-XWE. Ottawa. Released October 24 2012.
http://www12.statcan.gc.ca/census-recensement/2011/dp-pd/prof/index.cfm?Lang=E

Language Spoken Most Often at Home

Area	English	French	Non-official Language	English & French	English & Non-official Language	French & Non-official Language	English, French & Non-official Language
			Number				
			Total				
Whitby	111,240	845	6,080	245	2,510	20	80
Ontario	10,044,810	284,115	1,827,870	37,955	509,105	6,370	11,845
Canada	21,457,075	6,827,865	3,673,865	131,205	875,135	109,700	46,330
			Males				
Whitby	54,425	385	2,835	105	1,190	5	35
Ontario	4,930,610	133,495	872,860	17,250	248,050	2,855	5,225
Canada	10,585,620	3,348,235	1,767,310	63,475	425,370	53,010	22,845
			Females				
Whitby	56,825	460	3,245	140	1,320	15	45
Ontario	5,114,200	150,620	955,010	20,705	261,055	3,520	6,620
Canada	10,871,455	3,479,625	1,906,555	67,730	449,765	56,690	23,485
			Percent of Population				
			Total				
Whitby	91.9	0.7	5.0	0.2	2.1	0.0	0.1
Ontario	79.0	2.2	14.4	0.3	4.0	0.1	0.1
Canada	64.8	20.6	11.1	0.4	2.6	0.3	0.1
			Males				
Whitby	92.3	0.7	4.8	0.2	2.0	0.0	0.1
Ontario	79.4	2.1	14.1	0.3	4.0	0.0	0.1
Canada	65.1	20.6	10.9	0.4	2.6	0.3	0.1
			Females				
Whitby	91.6	0.7	5.2	0.2	2.1	0.0	0.1
Ontario	78.5	2.3	14.7	0.3	4.0	0.1	0.1
Canada	64.5	20.6	11.3	0.4	2.7	0.3	0.1

Note: Figures cover total population excluding institutional residents.
Source: Statistics Canada. 2012. Census Profile. 2011 Census. Statistics Canada Catalogue no. 98-316-XWE. Ottawa. Released October 24 2012.
http://www12.statcan.gc.ca/census-recensement/2011/dp-pd/prof/index.cfm?Lang=E

Knowledge of Official Languages

Area	English Only	French Only	English & French	Neither English nor French
		Number		
		Total		
Whitby	110,970	65	9,280	710
Ontario	10,984,360	42,980	1,395,805	298,920
Canada	22,564,665	4,165,015	5,795,570	595,920
		Males		
Whitby	54,825	25	3,890	245
Ontario	5,445,050	18,805	627,725	118,765
Canada	11,222,185	1,925,340	2,876,560	241,790
		Females		
Whitby	56,150	35	5,395	465
Ontario	5,539,310	24,175	768,085	180,155
Canada	11,342,485	2,239,680	2,919,005	354,135
		Percent of Population		
		Total		
Whitby	91.7	0.1	7.7	0.6
Ontario	86.3	0.3	11.0	2.3
Canada	68.1	12.6	17.5	1.8
		Males		
Whitby	93.0	0.0	6.6	0.4
Ontario	87.7	0.3	10.1	1.9
Canada	69.0	11.8	17.7	1.5
		Females		
Whitby	90.5	0.1	8.7	0.7
Ontario	85.1	0.4	11.8	2.8
Canada	67.3	13.3	17.3	2.1

Note: Figures cover total population excluding institutional residents.
Source: Statistics Canada. 2012. Census Profile. 2011 Census. Statistics Canada Catalogue no. 98-316-XWE. Ottawa. Released October 24 2012.
http://www12.statcan.gc.ca/census-recensement/2011/dp-pd/prof/index.cfm?Lang=E

Windsor, Ontario

Background

Windsor is located in southern Ontario at the western end of the Québec City–Windsor Corridor (QWC), Canada's most urbanized and industrialized area. Windsor is the southernmost city in Canada and the site of the busiest Canada-U.S. commercial border crossing. Approximately 27,000 to 29,000 vehicles pass through the underwater Detroit–Windsor Tunnel on a daily basis.

Windsor played a crucial role in the War of 1812. Major-General Isaac Brock and Aboriginal leader Tecumseh crossed the Detroit River August 16, 1812, with 330 civilians, 400 militia and 600 Aboriginals. Their strategy was to capture Fort Detroit. Within hours of their attack, Fort Detroit surrendered and Upper Canada seized 96,561 square kilometres of Michigan Territory.

On August 25, 2012, the City of Windsor hosted an all-day festival commemorating the War of 1812 and celebrating 200 years of peace.

Windsor is the birthplace of the automotive industry in Canada. Ford Motor Company of Canada was founded in Windsor in 1904. The first 100% Canadian-made Ford automobile was built in Windsor in 1913. The recent downturn in the Canadian auto industry has deeply impacted the city. In 2011, Windsor was one of the few major Canadian cities with a declining population.

Windsor has 215 parks and more than 2,800 acres of green space. The riverfront's Odette Sculpture Park is considered one of the world's most outstanding outdoor sculpture gardens.

Windsor has average summer highs of plus 26.63 degrees Celsius, winter lows of minus 6.63 degrees Celsius, and an average rainfall just over 805 mm per year.

Rankings

- Windsor ranked as one of two CMAs (census metropolitan area with a total population of 100,000 or more), of 33 in Canada, that underwent population decline between 2006 and 2011 (-1.3%). Thunder Bay (-1.1%) was the other. *Statistics Canada, Census of Population, 1851 to 2011*
- Windsor was selected as one of Canada's "Weather Winners" by Environment Canada. Out of 100 major Canadian cities, Windsor ranked #1 for warmest autumn with the highest average daily temperature during the months of September, October and November. The city was ranked #3 in the hottest summer category with an average temperature of 26.63 Celsius. *Environment Canada, Canadian Cities are Weather Winners!, May 29, 2012*

PROFILES / Windsor, Ontario

Population Growth and Density

Area	Population in 2001	Population in 2006	Population in 2011	Population Change 2001–2006	Population Change 2006–2011	Land Area (sq. km)	Population Density per sq. km
Windsor	209,218	216,473	210,891	3.5	-2.6	146.32	1,441.3
Ontario	11,410,046	12,160,282	12,851,821	6.6	5.7	908,607.67	14.1
Canada	30,007,094	31,612,897	33,476,688	5.4	5.9	8,965,121.42	3.7

Source: Statistics Canada. 2012. Census Profile. 2011 Census. Statistics Canada Catalogue no. 98-316-XWE. Ottawa. Released October 24 2012. http://www12.statcan.gc.ca/census-recensement/2011/dp-pd/prof/index.cfm?Lang=E;
Statistics Canada 2007. 2006 Community Profiles. 2006 Census. Statistics Canada Catalogue no. 92-591-XWE. Ottawa. Released March 13 2007.
http://www12.statcan.ca/census-recensement/2006/dp-pd/prof/92-591/index.cfm?Lang=E

Gender

Area	Males	Females
Number		
Windsor	102,365	108,530
Ontario	6,263,140	6,588,685
Canada	16,414,225	17,062,460
Percent of Population		
Windsor	48.5	51.5
Ontario	48.7	51.3
Canada	49.0	51.0

Source: Statistics Canada. 2012. Census Profile. 2011 Census. Statistics Canada Catalogue no. 98-316-XWE. Ottawa. Released October 24 2012.
http://www12.statcan.gc.ca/census-recensement/2011/dp-pd/prof/index.cfm?Lang=E

Marital Status

Area	Married[1]	Living Common-law	Single[2]	Separated	Divorced	Widowed
Number — Total						
Windsor	78,520	11,965	52,700	6,205	13,300	11,930
Ontario	5,367,400	791,210	2,985,020	319,805	593,730	613,880
Canada	12,941,960	3,142,525	7,816,045	698,240	1,686,035	1,584,530
Males						
Windsor	39,205	6,020	28,230	2,600	5,345	2,335
Ontario	2,681,320	397,620	1,583,760	133,790	231,160	117,980
Canada	6,470,300	1,575,495	4,206,320	299,655	680,415	310,940
Females						
Windsor	39,315	5,950	24,470	3,610	7,960	9,595
Ontario	2,686,075	393,590	1,401,260	186,015	362,570	495,905
Canada	6,471,660	1,567,035	3,609,730	398,585	1,005,620	1,273,590
Percent of Population — Total						
Windsor	45.0	6.9	30.2	3.6	7.6	6.8
Ontario	50.3	7.4	28.0	3.0	5.6	5.8
Canada	46.4	11.3	28.0	2.5	6.0	5.7
Males						
Windsor	46.8	7.2	33.7	3.1	6.4	2.8
Ontario	52.1	7.7	30.8	2.6	4.5	2.3
Canada	47.8	11.6	31.1	2.2	5.0	2.3
Females						
Windsor	43.3	6.5	26.9	4.0	8.8	10.6
Ontario	48.6	7.1	25.4	3.4	6.6	9.0
Canada	45.2	10.9	25.2	2.8	7.0	8.9

Note: (1) and not separated, (2) never legally married
Source: Statistics Canada. 2012. Census Profile. 2011 Census. Statistics Canada Catalogue no. 98-316-XWE. Ottawa. Released October 24 2012.
http://www12.statcan.gc.ca/census-recensement/2011/dp-pd/prof/index.cfm?Lang=E

Age Characteristics: 0 to 49 Years

Area	0 to 4 Years	5 to 9 Years	10 to 14 Years	15 to 19 Years	20 to 24 Years	25 to 29 Years	30 to 34 Years	35 to 39 Years	40 to 44 Years	45 to 49 Years
					Number					
					Total					
Windsor	11,855	11,975	12,440	13,885	14,625	13,325	13,035	13,870	14,810	16,155
Ontario	704,260	712,755	763,755	863,635	852,910	815,120	800,365	844,335	924,075	1,055,880
Canada	1,877,095	1,809,895	1,920,355	2,178,135	2,187,450	2,169,590	2,162,905	2,173,930	2,324,875	2,675,130
					Males					
Windsor	6,085	6,150	6,400	7,105	7,405	6,310	6,190	6,640	7,340	8,065
Ontario	360,590	365,290	391,630	443,680	432,490	400,045	383,340	405,845	447,920	517,510
Canada	961,150	925,965	983,995	1,115,845	1,108,775	1,077,275	1,058,810	1,064,200	1,141,720	1,318,715
					Females					
Windsor	5,770	5,825	6,045	6,785	7,220	7,020	6,845	7,230	7,475	8,090
Ontario	343,670	347,465	372,125	419,950	420,415	415,075	417,030	438,485	476,155	538,370
Canada	915,945	883,935	936,360	1,062,295	1,078,670	1,092,315	1,104,095	1,109,735	1,183,155	1,356,420
					Percent of Population					
					Total					
Windsor	5.6	5.7	5.9	6.6	6.9	6.3	6.2	6.6	7.0	7.7
Ontario	5.5	5.5	5.9	6.7	6.6	6.3	6.2	6.6	7.2	8.2
Canada	5.6	5.4	5.7	6.5	6.5	6.5	6.5	6.5	6.9	8.0
					Males					
Windsor	5.9	6.0	6.3	6.9	7.2	6.2	6.0	6.5	7.2	7.9
Ontario	5.8	5.8	6.3	7.1	6.9	6.4	6.1	6.5	7.2	8.3
Canada	5.9	5.6	6.0	6.8	6.8	6.6	6.5	6.5	7.0	8.0
					Females					
Windsor	5.3	5.4	5.6	6.3	6.7	6.5	6.3	6.7	6.9	7.5
Ontario	5.2	5.3	5.6	6.4	6.4	6.3	6.3	6.7	7.2	8.2
Canada	5.4	5.2	5.5	6.2	6.3	6.4	6.5	6.5	6.9	7.9

Source: Statistics Canada. 2012. Census Profile. 2011 Census. Statistics Canada Catalogue no. 98-316-XWE. Ottawa. Released October 24 2012.
http://www12.statcan.gc.ca/census-recensement/2011/dp-pd/prof/index.cfm?Lang=E

Age Characteristics: 50 Years and Over, and Median Age

Area	50 to 54 Years	55 to 59 Years	60 to 64 Years	65 to 69 Years	70 to 74 Years	75 to 79 Years	80 to 84 Years	85 Years and Over	Median Age
				Number					
				Total					
Windsor	15,640	13,680	12,410	9,270	7,710	6,365	5,140	4,700	40.1
Ontario	1,006,140	864,620	765,655	563,485	440,780	356,150	271,510	246,400	40.4
Canada	2,658,965	2,340,635	2,052,670	1,521,715	1,153,065	922,700	702,070	645,515	40.6
				Males					
Windsor	7,790	6,660	5,925	4,410	3,490	2,800	2,075	1,515	39.2
Ontario	492,560	418,755	370,370	270,875	206,350	161,345	113,620	80,925	39.4
Canada	1,309,030	1,147,300	1,002,690	738,010	543,435	417,945	291,085	208,300	39.6
				Females					
Windsor	7,850	7,020	6,480	4,855	4,220	3,570	3,060	3,180	41.0
Ontario	513,580	445,865	395,275	292,610	234,435	194,805	157,890	165,475	41.3
Canada	1,349,940	1,193,335	1,049,985	783,705	609,630	504,755	410,985	437,215	41.5
				Percent of Population					
				Total					
Windsor	7.4	6.5	5.9	4.4	3.7	3.0	2.4	2.2	–
Ontario	7.8	6.7	6.0	4.4	3.4	2.8	2.1	1.9	–
Canada	7.9	7.0	6.1	4.5	3.4	2.8	2.1	1.9	–
				Males					
Windsor	7.6	6.5	5.8	4.3	3.4	2.7	2.0	1.5	–
Ontario	7.9	6.7	5.9	4.3	3.3	2.6	1.8	1.3	–
Canada	8.0	7.0	6.1	4.5	3.3	2.5	1.8	1.3	–
				Females					
Windsor	7.2	6.5	6.0	4.5	3.9	3.3	2.8	2.9	–
Ontario	7.8	6.8	6.0	4.4	3.6	3.0	2.4	2.5	–
Canada	7.9	7.0	6.2	4.6	3.6	3.0	2.4	2.6	–

Source: Statistics Canada. 2012. Census Profile. 2011 Census. Statistics Canada Catalogue no. 98-316-XWE. Ottawa. Released October 24 2012.
http://www12.statcan.gc.ca/census-recensement/2011/dp-pd/prof/index.cfm?Lang=E

PROFILES / Windsor, Ontario

Private Households by Household Size

Area	1 Person	2 Persons	3 Persons	4 Persons	5 Persons	6 or More Persons	Average Number of Persons in Private Households
			Households				
Windsor	28,510	27,675	13,360	11,250	4,465	2,570	2.4
Ontario	1,230,975	1,584,415	803,030	783,925	310,860	174,305	2.6
Canada	3,673,310	4,544,820	2,081,900	1,903,300	724,405	392,885	2.5
			Percent of Households				
Windsor	32.5	31.5	15.2	12.8	5.1	2.9	–
Ontario	25.2	32.4	16.4	16.0	6.4	3.6	–
Canada	27.6	34.1	15.6	14.3	5.4	2.9	–

Source: Statistics Canada. 2012. Census Profile. 2011 Census. Statistics Canada Catalogue no. 98-316-XWE. Ottawa. Released October 24 2012.
http://www12.statcan.gc.ca/census-recensement/2011/dp-pd/prof/index.cfm?Lang=E

Dwelling Type

Area	Single-detached House	Semi-detached House	Row House	Apartment: Building with Five or More Storeys	Apartment: Building with Fewer Than Five Storeys	Duplex Apartment	Movable Dwelling	Other Single-attached House
				Number				
Windsor	54,615	3,945	5,420	11,525	8,920	3,260	15	140
Ontario	2,718,880	279,470	415,225	789,970	498,160	160,460	15,800	9,540
Canada	7,329,150	646,245	791,600	1,234,770	2,397,550	704,485	183,510	33,310
				Percent of Dwellings				
Windsor	62.2	4.5	6.2	13.1	10.2	3.7	0.0	0.2
Ontario	55.6	5.7	8.5	16.2	10.2	3.3	0.3	0.2
Canada	55.0	4.9	5.9	9.3	18.0	5.3	1.4	0.3

Source: Statistics Canada. 2012. Census Profile. 2011 Census. Statistics Canada Catalogue no. 98-316-XWE. Ottawa. Released October 24 2012.
http://www12.statcan.gc.ca/census-recensement/2011/dp-pd/prof/index.cfm?Lang=E

Shelter Costs

	Owned Dwellings					Rented Dwellings		
Area	Number	Median Value[1] ($)	Average Value[1] ($)	Median Monthly Costs[2] ($)	Average Monthly Costs[2] ($)	Number	Median Monthly Costs[3] ($)	Average Monthly Costs[3] ($)
Windsor	57,215	151,473	169,799	851	959	30,620	692	695
Ontario	3,446,650	300,862	367,428	1,163	1,284	1,385,535	892	926
Canada	9,013,410	280,552	345,182	978	1,141	4,060,385	784	848

Note: All figures cover non-farm, non-reserve private dwellings; (1) Refers to the dollar amount expected by the owner if the dwelling were to be sold; (2) Includes all shelter expenses paid by households that own their dwellings, such as the mortgage payment and the costs of electricity, heat, water and other municipal services, property taxes and condominium fees; (3) Includes all shelter expenses paid by households that rent their dwellings, such as the monthly rent and the costs of electricity, heat and municipal services.
Source: Statistics Canada. 2013. 2011 National Household Survey. Statistics Canada Catalogue no. 99-004-XWE. Ottawa. Released September 11, 2013.

Occupied Private Dwellings by Period of Construction

Area	1960 or Before	1961 to 1980	1981 to 1990	1991 to 2000	2001 to 2005	2006 to 2011
			Number			
Windsor	38,415	24,695	6,450	10,240	5,905	2,125
Ontario	1,330,235	1,420,570	763,430	609,310	414,795	348,310
Canada	3,273,105	4,152,715	2,112,110	1,707,880	1,031,020	1,042,430
			Percent of Dwellings			
Windsor	43.7	28.1	7.3	11.7	6.7	2.4
Ontario	27.2	29.1	15.6	12.5	8.5	7.1
Canada	24.6	31.2	15.9	12.8	7.7	7.8

Note: Figures cover non-farm, non-reserve private dwellings and includes data up to May 10, 2011.
Source: Statistics Canada. 2013. 2011 National Household Survey. Statistics Canada Catalogue no. 99-004-XWE. Ottawa. Released September 11, 2013.

PROFILES / Windsor, Ontario

Educational Attainment

Area	No Certificate, Diploma or Degree	High School Diploma or Equivalent[1]	Apprenticeship or Trades Certificate or Diploma[2]	College, CÉGEP or Other Non-University Certificate or Diploma	University Certificate or Diploma Below the Bachelor Level[3]	Bachelor's Degree	University Certificate, Diploma or Degree Above Bachelor Level[4]
				Number			
				Total			
Windsor	33,615	53,145	12,605	33,175	6,105	19,380	13,735
Ontario	1,954,520	2,801,805	771,140	2,070,875	427,150	1,515,075	933,100
Canada	5,485,400	6,968,935	2,950,685	4,970,020	1,200,130	3,634,425	2,049,930
				Males			
Windsor	15,505	25,280	8,210	14,535	2,870	8,770	7,340
Ontario	957,040	1,337,055	520,390	894,235	193,355	692,345	470,290
Canada	2,742,875	3,305,415	1,928,970	2,118,430	513,235	1,643,080	1,043,350
				Females			
Windsor	18,115	27,865	4,395	18,645	3,235	10,610	6,395
Ontario	997,475	1,464,755	250,750	1,176,640	233,790	822,730	462,805
Canada	2,742,520	3,663,515	1,021,715	2,851,595	686,890	1,991,345	1,006,585
				Percent of Population			
				Total			
Windsor	19.6	30.9	7.3	19.3	3.6	11.3	8.0
Ontario	18.7	26.8	7.4	19.8	4.1	14.5	8.9
Canada	20.1	25.6	10.8	18.2	4.4	13.3	7.5
				Males			
Windsor	18.8	30.6	10.0	17.6	3.5	10.6	8.9
Ontario	18.9	26.4	10.3	17.7	3.8	13.7	9.3
Canada	20.6	24.9	14.5	15.9	3.9	12.4	7.8
				Females			
Windsor	20.3	31.2	4.9	20.9	3.6	11.9	7.2
Ontario	18.4	27.1	4.6	21.8	4.3	15.2	8.6
Canada	19.6	26.2	7.3	20.4	4.9	14.3	7.2

Note: Figures cover total population aged 15 years and over by highest certificate, diploma or degree; (1) Includes persons who have graduated from a secondary school or equivalent. It excludes persons with a postsecondary certificate, diploma or degree; (2) Includes Registered Apprenticeship certificates (including Certificate of Qualification, Journeyperson's designation) and other trades certificates or diplomas such as pre-employment or vocational certificates and diplomas from brief trade programs completed at community colleges, institutes of technology, vocational centres, and similar institutions; (3) Comparisons with other data sources suggest that the category 'University certificate or diploma below the bachelor's level' was over-reported in the NHS. This category likely includes some responses that are actually college certificates or diplomas, bachelor's degrees or other types of education (e.g., university transfer programs, bachelor's programs completed in other countries, incomplete bachelor's programs, non-university professional designations). We recommend users interpret the results for the 'University certificate or diploma below the bachelor's level' category with caution; (4) 'University certificate or diploma above bachelor level' includes the categories: 'Degree in medicine, dentistry, veterinary medicine or optometry,' 'Master's degree' and 'Earned doctorate.'
Source: Statistics Canada. 2013. 2011 National Household Survey. Statistics Canada Catalogue no. 99-004-XWE. Ottawa. Released September 11, 2013.

Household Income Distribution

Area	Less than $10,000	$10,000 to $19,999	$20,000 to $29,999	$30,000 to $39,999	$40,000 to $49,999	$50,000 to $59,999	$60,000 to $79,999	$80,000 to $99,999	$100,000 to $124,999	$125,000 to $149,999	$150,000 and Over
						Households					
Windsor	5,995	10,100	10,130	9,660	8,900	7,640	11,200	8,895	6,510	4,080	4,715
Ontario	201,780	354,530	405,725	425,410	425,720	398,705	680,850	552,660	497,970	331,460	611,840
Canada	626,705	1,141,945	1,193,925	1,271,675	1,206,800	1,102,120	1,865,280	1,458,240	1,260,770	802,555	1,389,240
						Percent of Households					
Windsor	6.8	11.5	11.5	11.0	10.1	8.7	12.8	10.1	7.4	4.6	5.4
Ontario	4.1	7.3	8.3	8.7	8.7	8.2	13.9	11.3	10.2	6.8	12.5
Canada	4.7	8.6	9.0	9.5	9.1	8.3	14.0	10.9	9.5	6.0	10.4

Note: Household income is the sum of the total incomes of all members of that household. Total income refers to monetary receipts from certain sources, before income taxes and deductions, during calendar year 2010.
Source: Statistics Canada. 2013. 2011 National Household Survey. Statistics Canada Catalogue no. 99-004-XWE. Ottawa. Released September 11, 2013.

Median and Average Household and Economic Family Income

Area	Median Household Income ($)	Average Household Income ($)	Median After-tax Household Income ($)	Average After-tax Household Income ($)	Median Economic Family Income ($)	Average Economic Family Income ($)	Median After-tax Economic Family Income ($)	Average After-tax Economic Family Income ($)
Windsor	49,113	62,175	45,009	54,283	63,418	76,143	57,568	66,406
Ontario	66,358	85,772	58,717	71,523	80,987	100,152	71,128	83,322
Canada	61,072	79,102	54,089	66,149	76,511	94,125	67,044	78,517

Note: Figures cover household and economic familiy income in 2010. A household is defined as a person or a group of persons (other than foreign residents) who occupy the same private dwelling and do not have a usual place of residence elsewhere in Canada. Every person is a member of one and only one household. An economic family is defined as a group of two or more persons who live in the same dwelling and are related to each other by blood, marriage, common-law, adoption or a foster relationship. A couple may be of opposite or same sex.
Source: Statistics Canada. 2013. 2011 National Household Survey. Statistics Canada Catalogue no. 99-004-XWE. Ottawa. Released September 11, 2013.

PROFILES / Windsor, Ontario

Individual Income Distribution

Area	Less than $10,000	$10,000 to $19,999	$20,000 to $29,999	$30,000 to $39,999	$40,000 to $49,999	$50,000 to $59,999	$60,000 to $79,999	$80,000 to $99,999	$100,000 to $124,999	$125,000 and Over
					Number Total					
Windsor	33,270	32,570	23,685	19,465	15,685	10,500	13,600	7,305	2,405	2,090
Ontario	1,780,355	1,748,060	1,361,710	1,136,730	980,790	746,360	964,280	574,710	293,865	330,285
Canada	4,492,040	4,835,710	3,670,020	3,180,360	2,603,520	1,921,650	2,437,440	1,302,045	693,580	782,135
					Males					
Windsor	15,630	11,800	9,830	8,920	8,575	5,975	8,830	4,665	1,890	1,670
Ontario	781,095	669,815	580,990	535,255	491,125	407,005	569,205	341,160	201,125	244,500
Canada	1,936,365	1,864,880	1,588,260	1,522,190	1,333,510	1,079,780	1,473,145	823,720	492,905	599,905
					Females					
Windsor	17,645	20,775	13,860	10,540	7,110	4,530	4,770	2,645	520	420
Ontario	999,265	1,078,245	780,720	601,475	489,665	339,360	395,075	233,550	92,740	85,790
Canada	2,555,675	2,970,825	2,081,760	1,658,170	1,270,010	841,870	964,300	478,330	200,680	182,230
					Percent of Population Total					
Windsor	20.7	20.3	14.7	12.1	9.8	6.5	8.5	4.5	1.5	1.3
Ontario	18.0	17.6	13.7	11.5	9.9	7.5	9.7	5.8	3.0	3.3
Canada	17.3	18.7	14.2	12.3	10.0	7.4	9.4	5.0	2.7	3.0
					Males					
Windsor	20.1	15.2	12.6	11.5	11.0	7.7	11.4	6.0	2.4	2.1
Ontario	16.2	13.9	12.1	11.1	10.2	8.4	11.8	7.1	4.2	5.1
Canada	15.2	14.7	12.5	12.0	10.5	8.5	11.6	6.5	3.9	4.7
					Females					
Windsor	21.3	25.1	16.7	12.7	8.6	5.5	5.8	3.2	0.6	0.5
Ontario	19.6	21.2	15.3	11.8	9.6	6.7	7.8	4.6	1.8	1.7
Canada	19.4	22.5	15.8	12.6	9.6	6.4	7.3	3.6	1.5	1.4

Note: Figures cover individuals aged 15 years and over with income. Income refers to monetary receipts from certain sources, before income taxes and deductions, during calendar year 2010.
Source: Statistics Canada. 2013. 2011 National Household Survey. Statistics Canada Catalogue no. 99-004-XWE. Ottawa. Released September 11, 2013.

Labour Force Status

Area	In the Labour Force All	Employed	Unemployed	Not in the Labour Force
		Number Total		
Windsor	97,290	85,445	11,850	74,475
Ontario	6,864,990	6,297,005	567,985	3,608,685
Canada	17,990,080	16,595,035	1,395,045	9,269,445
		Males		
Windsor	50,485	43,875	6,610	32,020
Ontario	3,542,030	3,249,165	292,865	1,522,690
Canada	9,388,570	8,634,310	754,255	3,906,785
		Females		
Windsor	46,805	41,570	5,235	42,455
Ontario	3,322,955	3,047,840	275,120	2,085,990
Canada	8,601,515	7,960,725	640,790	5,362,660
		Percent of Labour Force Total		
Windsor	56.6	49.7	12.2	43.4
Ontario	65.5	60.1	8.3	34.5
Canada	66.0	60.9	7.8	34.0
		Males		
Windsor	61.2	53.2	13.1	38.8
Ontario	69.9	64.2	8.3	30.1
Canada	70.6	64.9	8.0	29.4
		Females		
Windsor	52.4	46.6	11.2	47.6
Ontario	61.4	56.3	8.3	38.6
Canada	61.6	57.0	7.4	38.4

Note: Figures are based on total population 15 years and over
Source: Statistics Canada. 2013. 2011 National Household Survey. Statistics Canada Catalogue no. 99-004-XWE. Ottawa. Released September 11, 2013.

Labour Force by Industry (NAICS Codes 11–52)

Area	Agriculture, forestry, fishing & hunting	Mining, quarrying, & oil & gas extraction	Utilities	Construction	Manufacturing	Wholesale Trade	Retail Trade	Transportation & warehousing	Information & cultural industries	Finance & insurance
					Number					
					Total					
Windsor	930	125	315	4,780	16,145	2,545	10,810	4,120	1,190	2,725
Ontario	101,280	29,985	57,035	417,900	697,565	305,030	751,200	307,405	178,720	364,415
Canada	437,650	261,050	149,940	1,215,380	1,619,295	733,445	2,031,665	827,780	420,830	767,960
					Males					
Windsor	455	110	245	4,290	12,145	1,745	4,500	2,930	705	1,075
Ontario	66,485	25,650	42,685	369,300	493,305	197,770	344,480	225,245	98,835	153,125
Canada	307,370	211,690	110,765	1,068,710	1,167,680	494,545	933,850	617,305	235,875	296,995
					Females					
Windsor	480	0	70	500	4,000	805	6,310	1,195	485	1,650
Ontario	34,800	4,340	14,350	48,595	204,260	107,260	406,720	82,160	79,885	211,290
Canada	130,285	49,360	39,175	146,670	451,615	238,900	1,097,820	210,475	184,955	470,960
					Percent of Labour Force					
					Total					
Windsor	1.0	0.1	0.3	5.2	17.5	2.8	11.7	4.5	1.3	2.9
Ontario	1.5	0.4	0.9	6.3	10.4	4.6	11.2	4.6	2.7	5.5
Canada	2.5	1.5	0.9	6.9	9.2	4.2	11.6	4.7	2.4	4.4
					Males					
Windsor	0.9	0.2	0.5	8.9	25.3	3.6	9.4	6.1	1.5	2.2
Ontario	1.9	0.7	1.2	10.7	14.3	5.7	10.0	6.5	2.9	4.4
Canada	3.3	2.3	1.2	11.6	12.7	5.4	10.2	6.7	2.6	3.2
					Females					
Windsor	1.1	0.0	0.2	1.1	9.0	1.8	14.2	2.7	1.1	3.7
Ontario	1.1	0.1	0.4	1.5	6.3	3.3	12.6	2.5	2.5	6.5
Canada	1.6	0.6	0.5	1.7	5.4	2.8	13.1	2.5	2.2	5.6

Note: Figures are based on total experienced labour force 15 years and over. Experienced labour force refers to persons who, during the week of Sunday, May 1 to Saturday, May 7, 2011, were employed and the unemployed who had last worked for pay or in self-employment in either 2010 or 2011.
Source: Statistics Canada. 2013. 2011 National Household Survey. Statistics Canada Catalogue no. 99-004-XWE. Ottawa. Released September 11, 2013.

Labour Force by Industry (NAICS Codes 53–91)

Area	Real estate & rental & leasing	Profess., scientific & tech. services	Mgmt of companies & enterprises	Admin. & support, waste mgmt & remed. services	Educational services	Health care & social assistance	Arts, entertain. & recreation	Accomm. & food services	Other services (except public admin.)	Public admin.
					Number					
					Total					
Windsor	1,305	4,535	100	4,715	7,925	11,125	3,995	7,070	4,080	3,845
Ontario	133,980	511,020	6,525	309,630	499,690	692,130	144,065	417,675	296,340	458,665
Canada	321,895	1,240,850	17,460	728,330	1,301,435	1,949,650	363,405	1,130,750	807,800	1,261,050
					Males					
Windsor	765	2,575	50	2,700	2,850	1,985	2,070	2,940	1,880	1,940
Ontario	72,835	281,420	3,540	172,475	162,765	120,165	75,035	177,240	133,795	236,655
Canada	179,090	688,625	9,380	411,250	424,915	349,430	188,270	469,990	372,940	652,510
					Females					
Windsor	540	1,965	50	2,020	5,075	9,135	1,925	4,130	2,205	1,910
Ontario	61,145	229,600	2,990	137,155	336,925	571,965	69,030	240,430	162,550	222,015
Canada	142,805	552,225	8,075	317,085	876,515	1,600,220	175,135	660,760	434,865	608,535
					Percent of Labour Force					
					Total					
Windsor	1.4	4.9	0.1	5.1	8.6	12.0	4.3	7.7	4.4	4.2
Ontario	2.0	7.6	0.1	4.6	7.5	10.4	2.2	6.3	4.4	6.9
Canada	1.8	7.1	0.1	4.1	7.4	11.1	2.1	6.4	4.6	7.2
					Males					
Windsor	1.6	5.4	0.1	5.6	5.9	4.1	4.3	6.1	3.9	4.0
Ontario	2.1	8.2	0.1	5.0	4.7	3.5	2.2	5.1	3.9	6.9
Canada	1.9	7.5	0.1	4.5	4.6	3.8	2.0	5.1	4.1	7.1
					Females					
Windsor	1.2	4.4	0.1	4.5	11.4	20.6	4.3	9.3	5.0	4.3
Ontario	1.9	7.1	0.1	4.2	10.4	17.7	2.1	7.4	5.0	6.9
Canada	1.7	6.6	0.1	3.8	10.4	19.1	2.1	7.9	5.2	7.2

Note: Figures are based on total experienced labour force 15 years and over. Experienced labour force refers to persons who, during the week of Sunday, May 1 to Saturday, May 7, 2011, were employed and the unemployed who had last worked for pay or in self-employment in either 2010 or 2011.
Source: Statistics Canada. 2013. 2011 National Household Survey. Statistics Canada Catalogue no. 99-004-XWE. Ottawa. Released September 11, 2013.

PROFILES / Windsor, Ontario

Occupation

Area	Mgmt	Business, Finance & Admin.	Natural/ Applied Sciences & Related	Health	Education, Law & Social, Community & Government Services	Art, Culture, Recreation & Sport	Sales & Service	Trades, Transport & Equip. Operators & Related	Natural Resources, Agri. & Related Production	Mfg & Utilities
					Number					
					Total					
Windsor	6,850	11,865	6,205	6,900	10,395	1,955	25,620	12,705	1,405	8,510
Ontario	770,580	1,138,330	494,500	392,695	801,465	206,420	1,550,260	868,515	106,810	350,685
Canada	1,963,600	2,902,045	1,237,775	1,107,200	2,064,675	503,415	4,068,170	2,537,775	397,930	805,040
					Males					
Windsor	3,965	3,520	5,140	1,380	3,615	860	10,815	12,040	925	5,700
Ontario	474,655	352,505	384,345	78,330	264,570	96,055	673,880	812,280	82,610	233,565
Canada	1,229,460	854,190	966,355	217,520	676,550	232,535	1,745,705	2,385,615	318,945	564,300
					Females					
Windsor	2,885	8,345	1,065	5,520	6,780	1,100	14,805	665	480	2,805
Ontario	295,920	785,825	110,150	314,370	536,895	110,370	876,380	56,230	24,200	117,115
Canada	734,140	2,047,855	271,415	889,675	1,388,130	270,875	2,322,465	152,165	78,980	240,740
					Percent of Labour Force					
					Total					
Windsor	7.4	12.8	6.7	7.5	11.2	2.1	27.7	13.7	1.5	9.2
Ontario	11.5	17.0	7.4	5.9	12.0	3.1	23.2	13.0	1.6	5.2
Canada	11.2	16.5	7.0	6.3	11.7	2.9	23.1	14.4	2.3	4.6
					Males					
Windsor	8.3	7.3	10.7	2.9	7.5	1.8	22.6	25.1	1.9	11.9
Ontario	13.7	10.2	11.1	2.3	7.7	2.8	19.5	23.5	2.4	6.8
Canada	13.4	9.3	10.5	2.4	7.4	2.5	19.0	26.0	3.5	6.1
					Females					
Windsor	6.5	18.8	2.4	12.4	15.3	2.5	33.3	1.5	1.1	6.3
Ontario	9.2	24.3	3.4	9.7	16.6	3.4	27.2	1.7	0.7	3.6
Canada	8.7	24.4	3.2	10.6	16.5	3.2	27.7	1.8	0.9	2.9

Note: Figures are based on total experienced labour force 15 years and over
Source: Statistics Canada. 2013. 2011 National Household Survey. Statistics Canada Catalogue no. 99-004-XWE. Ottawa. Released September 11, 2013.

Place of Work Status

Area	Worked at Home	Worked Outside Canada	No Fixed Workplace Address	Worked at Usual Place
		Number		
		Total		
Windsor	2,965	3,695	7,490	71,295
Ontario	423,790	31,390	670,835	5,170,980
Canada	1,142,640	66,460	1,868,245	13,517,690
		Males		
Windsor	1,435	2,285	5,045	35,110
Ontario	216,900	21,150	486,560	2,524,555
Canada	582,150	47,355	1,400,485	6,604,325
		Females		
Windsor	1,530	1,410	2,440	36,190
Ontario	206,895	10,240	184,275	2,646,420
Canada	560,490	19,100	467,760	6,913,370
		Percent of Labour Force		
		Total		
Windsor	3.5	4.3	8.8	83.4
Ontario	6.7	0.5	10.7	82.1
Canada	6.9	0.4	11.3	81.5
		Males		
Windsor	3.3	5.2	11.5	80.0
Ontario	6.7	0.7	15.0	77.7
Canada	6.7	0.5	16.2	76.5
		Females		
Windsor	3.7	3.4	5.9	87.1
Ontario	6.8	0.3	6.0	86.8
Canada	7.0	0.2	5.9	86.8

Note: Figures are based on total employed labour force 15 years and over.
Source: Statistics Canada. 2013. 2011 National Household Survey. Statistics Canada Catalogue no. 99-004-XWE. Ottawa. Released September 11, 2013.

Mode of Transportation to Work

Area	Car; Truck; Van; as Driver	Car; Truck; Van; as Passenger	Public Transit	Walked	Bicycled	All Other Modes
			Number			
			Total			
Windsor	64,670	5,015	3,545	3,735	1,095	730
Ontario	4,235,315	357,110	818,270	299,095	69,885	62,145
Canada	11,393,140	867,050	1,851,525	880,815	201,780	191,625
			Males			
Windsor	33,840	2,030	1,325	1,750	860	360
Ontario	2,316,680	143,410	340,995	131,765	47,635	30,635
Canada	6,238,835	349,530	788,290	387,580	135,840	104,725
			Females			
Windsor	30,825	2,990	2,215	1,990	240	375
Ontario	1,918,640	213,700	477,275	167,325	22,250	31,515
Canada	5,154,305	517,520	1,063,235	493,230	65,940	86,900
			Percent of Labour Force			
			Total			
Windsor	82.1	6.4	4.5	4.7	1.4	0.9
Ontario	72.5	6.1	14.0	5.1	1.2	1.1
Canada	74.0	5.6	12.0	5.7	1.3	1.2
			Males			
Windsor	84.3	5.1	3.3	4.4	2.1	0.9
Ontario	76.9	4.8	11.3	4.4	1.6	1.0
Canada	77.9	4.4	9.8	4.8	1.7	1.3
			Females			
Windsor	79.8	7.7	5.7	5.2	0.6	1.0
Ontario	67.8	7.5	16.9	5.9	0.8	1.1
Canada	69.8	7.0	14.4	6.7	0.9	1.2

Note: Figures are based on total employed labour force 15 years and over.
Source: Statistics Canada. 2013. 2011 National Household Survey. Statistics Canada Catalogue no. 99-004-XWE. Ottawa. Released September 11, 2013.

Visible Minority Population Characteristics

Area	Total Minority	South Asian[1]	Chinese	Black	Filipino	Latin American	Arab	SE Asian[2]	West Asian[3]	Korean	Japanese	Multiple[4]
						Number						
						Total						
Windsor	47,675	8,020	6,245	9,480	3,180	2,255	11,510	3,190	1,580	285	80	1,090
Ontario	3,279,565	965,990	629,140	539,205	275,380	172,560	151,645	137,875	122,530	78,290	29,085	96,735
Canada	6,264,750	1,567,400	1,324,750	945,665	619,310	381,280	380,620	312,075	206,840	161,130	87,270	171,935
						Males						
Windsor	23,620	4,170	3,150	4,295	1,405	1,150	5,955	1,615	815	160	25	475
Ontario	1,582,480	484,355	301,575	251,295	116,825	83,205	79,620	67,645	62,515	38,045	13,345	46,765
Canada	3,043,010	790,755	632,325	453,005	268,885	186,355	203,485	154,035	105,620	77,165	38,270	83,335
						Females						
Windsor	24,055	3,850	3,085	5,185	1,775	1,105	5,560	1,575	765	125	55	615
Ontario	1,697,085	481,635	327,570	287,915	158,555	89,360	72,025	70,230	60,010	40,250	15,740	49,970
Canada	3,221,745	776,650	692,420	492,660	350,425	194,925	177,140	158,045	101,220	83,965	48,990	88,600
						Percent of Population						
						Total						
Windsor	22.9	3.9	3.0	4.6	1.5	1.1	5.5	1.5	0.8	0.1	0.0	0.5
Ontario	25.9	7.6	5.0	4.3	2.2	1.4	1.2	1.1	1.0	0.6	0.2	0.8
Canada	19.1	4.8	4.0	2.9	1.9	1.2	1.2	0.9	0.6	0.5	0.3	0.5
						Males						
Windsor	23.3	4.1	3.1	4.2	1.4	1.1	5.9	1.6	0.8	0.2	0.0	0.5
Ontario	25.6	7.8	4.9	4.1	1.9	1.3	1.3	1.1	1.0	0.6	0.2	0.8
Canada	18.8	4.9	3.9	2.8	1.7	1.2	1.3	1.0	0.7	0.5	0.2	0.5
						Females						
Windsor	22.5	3.6	2.9	4.9	1.7	1.0	5.2	1.5	0.7	0.1	0.1	0.6
Ontario	26.2	7.4	5.1	4.4	2.5	1.4	1.1	1.1	0.9	0.6	0.2	0.8
Canada	19.3	4.7	4.1	3.0	2.1	1.2	1.1	0.9	0.6	0.5	0.3	0.5

Note: The Employment Equity Act defines visible minorities as 'persons, other than Aboriginal peoples, who are non-Caucasian in race or non-white in colour';
(1) Includes 'East Indian,' 'Pakistani,' 'Sri Lankan,' etc.; (2) Includes 'Vietnamese,' 'Cambodian,' 'Malaysian,' 'Laotian,' etc.; (3) Includes 'Iranian,' 'Afghan,' etc.; (4) Includes respondents who reported more than one visible minority group by checking two or more mark-in circles, e.g., 'Black' and 'South Asian.'
Source: Statistics Canada. 2013. 2011 National Household Survey. Statistics Canada Catalogue no. 99-004-XWE. Ottawa. Released September 11, 2013.

PROFILES / Windsor, Ontario

Aboriginal Population

Area	Aboriginal Identity[1]	First Nations (North American Indian) Single Identity[2]	Métis Single Identity	Inuk (Inuit) Single Identity	Multiple Aboriginal Identities[3]	Aboriginal Identities Not Included Elsewhere
Number						
Total						
Windsor	4,735	2,625	1,780	15	150	165
Ontario	301,430	201,100	86,020	3,355	2,910	8,040
Canada	1,400,685	851,560	451,795	59,440	11,415	26,475
Males						
Windsor	2,235	1,145	910	0	80	95
Ontario	145,020	96,620	41,755	1,475	1,420	3,750
Canada	682,190	411,785	223,335	29,495	5,525	12,055
Females						
Windsor	2,500	1,485	870	0	75	70
Ontario	156,410	104,485	44,260	1,880	1,490	4,295
Canada	718,500	439,775	228,460	29,950	5,890	14,420
Percent of Population						
Total						
Windsor	2.3	1.3	0.9	0.0	0.1	0.1
Ontario	2.4	1.6	0.7	0.0	0.0	0.1
Canada	4.3	2.6	1.4	0.2	0.0	0.1
Males						
Windsor	2.2	1.1	0.9	0.0	0.1	0.1
Ontario	2.3	1.6	0.7	0.0	0.0	0.1
Canada	4.2	2.5	1.4	0.2	0.0	0.1
Females						
Windsor	2.3	1.4	0.8	0.0	0.1	0.1
Ontario	2.4	1.6	0.7	0.0	0.0	0.1
Canada	4.3	2.6	1.4	0.2	0.0	0.1

Note: (1) Includes persons who reported being an Aboriginal person, that is, First Nations (North American Indian), Métis or Inuk (Inuit) and/or those who reported Registered or Treaty Indian status, that is registered under the Indian Act of Canada, and/or those who reported membership in a First Nation or Indian band. Aboriginal peoples of Canada are defined in the Constitution Act, 1982, section 35-2 as including the Indian, Inuit and Métis peoples of Canada; (2) Users should be aware that the estimates associated with this variable are more affected than most by the incomplete enumeration of certain Indian reserves and Indian settlements in the National Household Survey (NHS); (3) Includes persons who reported being any two or all three of the following: First Nations (North American Indian), Métis or Inuk (Inuit).
Source: Statistics Canada. 2013. 2011 National Household Survey. Statistics Canada Catalogue no. 99-004-XWE. Ottawa. Released September 11, 2013.

Ethnic Origin

Area	North American Aboriginal	Other North American	European	Caribbean	Latin, Central and South American	African	Asian	Oceania
Number								
Total								
Windsor	8,235	50,960	139,940	2,675	2,545	7,590	40,565	160
Ontario	441,395	3,059,480	8,231,410	396,485	271,545	331,460	2,604,595	19,410
Canada	1,836,035	11,070,455	20,157,965	627,590	544,375	766,735	5,011,225	74,875
Males								
Windsor	4,005	24,260	67,500	1,235	1,305	3,575	20,345	115
Ontario	210,490	1,507,105	4,019,885	181,805	130,035	160,940	1,265,540	9,855
Canada	885,675	5,462,685	9,913,150	291,640	264,635	387,360	2,435,540	37,490
Females								
Windsor	4,225	26,700	72,440	1,440	1,245	4,015	20,225	50
Ontario	230,905	1,552,380	4,211,525	214,675	141,510	170,515	1,339,050	9,555
Canada	950,360	5,607,770	10,244,820	335,945	279,740	379,380	2,575,680	37,385
Percent of Population								
Total								
Windsor	4.0	24.5	67.3	1.3	1.2	3.6	19.5	0.1
Ontario	3.5	24.2	65.1	3.1	2.1	2.6	20.6	0.2
Canada	5.6	33.7	61.4	1.9	1.7	2.3	15.3	0.2
Males								
Windsor	4.0	24.0	66.7	1.2	1.3	3.5	20.1	0.1
Ontario	3.4	24.4	65.0	2.9	2.1	2.6	20.5	0.2
Canada	5.5	33.8	61.3	1.8	1.6	2.4	15.1	0.2
Females								
Windsor	4.0	25.0	67.8	1.3	1.2	3.8	18.9	0.0
Ontario	3.6	24.0	65.1	3.3	2.2	2.6	20.7	0.1
Canada	5.7	33.6	61.4	2.0	1.7	2.3	15.4	0.2

Note: The sum of the ethnic groups in this table is greater than the total population estimate because a person may report more than one ethnic origin in the NHS.
Source: Statistics Canada. 2013. 2011 National Household Survey. Statistics Canada Catalogue no. 99-004-XWE. Ottawa. Released September 11, 2013.

Religion

Area	Buddhist	Christian	Hindu	Jewish	Muslim	Sikh	Traditional (Aboriginal) Spirituality	Other Religions	No Religious Affiliation
				Number					
				Total					
Windsor	2,390	143,945	2,510	925	14,305	1,500	60	785	41,605
Ontario	163,750	8,167,295	366,720	195,540	581,950	179,765	15,905	53,080	2,927,790
Canada	366,830	22,102,745	497,965	329,495	1,053,945	454,965	64,935	130,835	7,850,605
				Males					
Windsor	1,255	67,425	1,335	445	7,295	765	20	430	22,290
Ontario	75,355	3,839,925	183,580	95,795	293,925	90,515	7,600	23,555	1,571,195
Canada	168,465	10,497,775	250,435	161,265	540,555	229,435	31,805	57,745	4,225,645
				Females					
Windsor	1,135	76,520	1,175	480	7,010	730	40	355	19,315
Ontario	88,395	4,327,365	183,140	99,740	288,025	89,250	8,310	29,525	1,356,600
Canada	198,365	11,604,975	247,525	168,235	513,395	225,530	33,135	73,090	3,624,965
				Percent of Population					
				Total					
Windsor	1.1	69.2	1.2	0.4	6.9	0.7	0.0	0.4	20.0
Ontario	1.3	64.6	2.9	1.5	4.6	1.4	0.1	0.4	23.1
Canada	1.1	67.3	1.5	1.0	3.2	1.4	0.2	0.4	23.9
				Males					
Windsor	1.2	66.6	1.3	0.4	7.2	0.8	0.0	0.4	22.0
Ontario	1.2	62.1	3.0	1.5	4.8	1.5	0.1	0.4	25.4
Canada	1.0	64.9	1.5	1.0	3.3	1.4	0.2	0.4	26.1
				Females					
Windsor	1.1	71.7	1.1	0.4	6.6	0.7	0.0	0.3	18.1
Ontario	1.4	66.9	2.8	1.5	4.5	1.4	0.1	0.5	21.0
Canada	1.2	69.5	1.5	1.0	3.1	1.4	0.2	0.4	21.7

Note: Religion refers to the person's self-identification as having a connection or affiliation with any religious denomination, group, body, sect, cult or other religiously defined community or system of belief. Religion is not limited to formal membership in a religious organization or group. Persons without a religious connection or affiliation can self-identify as atheist, agnostic or humanist, or can provide another applicable response.
Source: Statistics Canada. 2013. 2011 National Household Survey. Statistics Canada Catalogue no. 99-004-XWE. Ottawa. Released September 11, 2013.

Religion—Christian Denominations

Area	Anglican	Baptist	Catholic	Christian Orthodox	Lutheran	Pentecostal	Presbyterian	United Church	Other Christian
				Number					
				Total					
Windsor	10,715	4,255	87,020	8,480	1,955	3,295	3,165	7,295	17,760
Ontario	774,560	244,650	3,976,610	297,710	163,460	213,945	319,585	952,465	1,224,300
Canada	1,631,845	635,840	12,810,705	550,690	478,185	478,705	472,385	2,007,610	3,036,780
				Males					
Windsor	4,730	1,995	41,100	4,250	860	1,485	1,470	3,350	8,180
Ontario	355,175	112,285	1,895,940	145,825	75,225	94,955	148,535	435,255	576,730
Canada	752,945	293,905	6,167,290	270,205	221,525	217,850	218,955	912,545	1,442,550
				Females					
Windsor	5,980	2,260	45,920	4,230	1,095	1,805	1,690	3,945	9,585
Ontario	419,390	132,370	2,080,665	151,885	88,230	118,990	171,050	517,210	647,570
Canada	878,900	341,940	6,643,415	280,485	256,660	260,850	253,430	1,095,065	1,594,230
				Percent of Population					
				Total					
Windsor	5.2	2.0	41.8	4.1	0.9	1.6	1.5	3.5	8.5
Ontario	6.1	1.9	31.4	2.4	1.3	1.7	2.5	7.5	9.7
Canada	5.0	1.9	39.0	1.7	1.5	1.5	1.4	6.1	9.2
				Males					
Windsor	4.7	2.0	40.6	4.2	0.8	1.5	1.5	3.3	8.1
Ontario	5.7	1.8	30.7	2.4	1.2	1.5	2.4	7.0	9.3
Canada	4.7	1.8	38.2	1.7	1.4	1.3	1.4	5.6	8.9
				Females					
Windsor	5.6	2.1	43.0	4.0	1.0	1.7	1.6	3.7	9.0
Ontario	6.5	2.0	32.2	2.3	1.4	1.8	2.6	8.0	10.0
Canada	5.3	2.0	39.8	1.7	1.5	1.6	1.5	6.1	9.6

Note: Religion refers to the person's self-identification as having a connection or affiliation with any religious denomination, group, body, sect, cult or other religiously defined community or system of belief. Religion is not limited to formal membership in a religious organization or group. Persons without a religious connection or affiliation can self-identify as atheist, agnostic or humanist, or can provide another applicable response.
Source: Statistics Canada. 2013. 2011 National Household Survey. Statistics Canada Catalogue no. 99-004-XWE. Ottawa. Released September 11, 2013.

Immigrant Status and Period of Immigration

Area	Non-Immigrants[1]	Immigrants All	Before 1971	1971 to 1980	1981 to 1990	1991 to 2000	2001 to 2005	2006 to 2011	Non-Permanent Residents[3]
				Number					
				Total					
Windsor	148,860	56,355	12,475	5,990	6,815	15,070	7,550	8,450	2,795
Ontario	8,906,000	3,611,365	723,030	464,380	538,285	866,220	518,405	501,060	134,425
Canada	25,720,175	6,775,765	1,261,055	870,775	949,890	1,539,050	992,070	1,162,915	356,385
				Males					
Windsor	72,995	26,650	5,660	2,845	3,450	7,180	3,670	3,845	1,610
Ontario	4,410,240	1,706,385	341,820	217,990	258,095	408,270	245,850	234,360	64,825
Canada	12,753,235	3,231,370	605,430	416,670	454,570	724,905	474,545	555,245	178,515
				Females					
Windsor	75,870	29,705	6,815	3,145	3,365	7,895	3,885	4,605	1,190
Ontario	4,495,765	1,904,985	381,210	246,390	280,190	457,950	272,550	266,695	69,600
Canada	12,966,935	3,544,400	655,625	454,105	495,325	814,145	517,530	607,670	177,870
				Percent of Population					
				Total					
Windsor	71.6	27.1	6.0	2.9	3.3	7.2	3.6	4.1	1.3
Ontario	70.4	28.5	5.7	3.7	4.3	6.8	4.1	4.0	1.1
Canada	78.3	20.6	3.8	2.7	2.9	4.7	3.0	3.5	1.1
				Males					
Windsor	72.1	26.3	5.6	2.8	3.4	7.1	3.6	3.8	1.6
Ontario	71.3	27.6	5.5	3.5	4.2	6.6	4.0	3.8	1.0
Canada	78.9	20.0	3.7	2.6	2.8	4.5	2.9	3.4	1.1
				Females					
Windsor	71.1	27.8	6.4	2.9	3.2	7.4	3.6	4.3	1.1
Ontario	69.5	29.4	5.9	3.8	4.3	7.1	4.2	4.1	1.1
Canada	77.7	21.2	3.9	2.7	3.0	4.9	3.1	3.6	1.1

Note: (1) Non-immigrant refers to a person who is a Canadian citizen by birth; (2) Immigrant refers to a person who is or has ever been a landed immigrant/permanent resident. This person has been granted the right to live in Canada permanently by immigration authorities. Some immigrants have resided in Canada for a number of years, while others have arrived recently. Some immigrants are Canadian citizens, while others are not. Most immigrants are born outside Canada, but a small number are born in Canada. In the 2011 National Household Survey, 'Immigrants' includes immigrants who landed in Canada prior to May 10, 2011; (3) Non-permanent resident refers to a person from another country who has a work or study permit, or who is a refugee claimant, and any non-Canadian-born family member living in Canada with them.
Source: Statistics Canada. 2013. 2011 National Household Survey. Statistics Canada Catalogue no. 99-004-XWE. Ottawa. Released September 11, 2013.

Mother Tongue

Area	English	French	Non-official Language	English & French	English & Non-official Language	French & Non-official Language	English, French & Non-official Language
			Number				
			Total				
Windsor	142,795	5,405	55,320	865	3,940	310	185
Ontario	8,677,040	493,300	3,264,435	46,605	219,425	13,645	7,615
Canada	18,858,980	7,054,975	6,567,680	144,685	396,330	74,430	24,095
			Males				
Windsor	69,685	2,455	26,835	400	1,915	140	85
Ontario	4,276,970	232,785	1,562,190	21,805	106,790	6,285	3,495
Canada	9,345,225	3,452,380	3,157,785	69,975	192,000	36,535	11,965
			Females				
Windsor	73,115	2,945	28,485	465	2,020	170	100
Ontario	4,400,065	260,510	1,702,240	24,795	112,635	7,365	4,115
Canada	9,513,750	3,602,590	3,409,895	74,710	204,330	37,890	12,130
			Percent of Population				
			Total				
Windsor	68.4	2.6	26.5	0.4	1.9	0.1	0.1
Ontario	68.2	3.9	25.7	0.4	1.7	0.1	0.1
Canada	56.9	21.3	19.8	0.4	1.2	0.2	0.1
			Males				
Windsor	68.6	2.4	26.4	0.4	1.9	0.1	0.1
Ontario	68.9	3.7	25.2	0.4	1.7	0.1	0.1
Canada	57.5	21.2	19.4	0.4	1.2	0.2	0.1
			Females				
Windsor	68.1	2.7	26.5	0.4	1.9	0.2	0.1
Ontario	67.6	4.0	26.1	0.4	1.7	0.1	0.1
Canada	56.4	21.4	20.2	0.4	1.2	0.2	0.1

Note: Figures cover total population excluding institutional residents.
Source: Statistics Canada. 2012. Census Profile. 2011 Census. Statistics Canada Catalogue no. 98-316-XWE. Ottawa. Released October 24 2012.
http://www12.statcan.gc.ca/census-recensement/2011/dp-pd/prof/index.cfm?Lang=E

Language Spoken Most Often at Home

Area	English	French	Non-official Language	English & French	English & Non-official Language	French & Non-official Language	English, French & Non-official Language
			Number				
			Total				
Windsor	166,280	1,640	30,840	450	9,215	105	295
Ontario	10,044,810	284,115	1,827,870	37,955	509,105	6,370	11,845
Canada	21,457,075	6,827,865	3,673,865	131,205	875,135	109,700	46,330
			Males				
Windsor	81,140	740	14,680	205	4,570	60	130
Ontario	4,930,610	133,495	872,860	17,250	248,050	2,855	5,225
Canada	10,585,620	3,348,235	1,767,310	63,475	425,370	53,010	22,845
			Females				
Windsor	85,140	895	16,155	245	4,650	45	160
Ontario	5,114,200	150,620	955,010	20,705	261,055	3,520	6,620
Canada	10,871,455	3,479,625	1,906,555	67,730	449,765	56,690	23,485
			Percent of Population				
			Total				
Windsor	79.6	0.8	14.8	0.2	4.4	0.1	0.1
Ontario	79.0	2.2	14.4	0.3	4.0	0.1	0.1
Canada	64.8	20.6	11.1	0.4	2.6	0.3	0.1
			Males				
Windsor	79.9	0.7	14.5	0.2	4.5	0.1	0.1
Ontario	79.4	2.1	14.1	0.3	4.0	0.0	0.1
Canada	65.1	20.6	10.9	0.4	2.6	0.3	0.1
			Females				
Windsor	79.3	0.8	15.1	0.2	4.3	0.0	0.1
Ontario	78.5	2.3	14.7	0.3	4.0	0.1	0.1
Canada	64.5	20.6	11.3	0.4	2.7	0.3	0.1

Note: Figures cover total population excluding institutional residents.
Source: Statistics Canada. 2012. Census Profile. 2011 Census. Statistics Canada Catalogue no. 98-316-XWE. Ottawa. Released October 24 2012.
http://www12.statcan.gc.ca/census-recensement/2011/dp-pd/prof/index.cfm?Lang=E

Knowledge of Official Languages

Area	English Only	French Only	English & French	Neither English nor French
		Number		
		Total		
Windsor	186,940	310	17,435	4,140
Ontario	10,984,360	42,980	1,395,805	298,920
Canada	22,564,665	4,165,015	5,795,570	595,920
		Males		
Windsor	92,085	140	7,800	1,500
Ontario	5,445,050	18,805	627,725	118,765
Canada	11,222,185	1,925,340	2,876,560	241,790
		Females		
Windsor	94,850	170	9,635	2,640
Ontario	5,539,310	24,175	768,085	180,155
Canada	11,342,485	2,239,680	2,919,005	354,135
		Percent of Population		
		Total		
Windsor	89.5	0.1	8.3	2.0
Ontario	86.3	0.3	11.0	2.3
Canada	68.1	12.6	17.5	1.8
		Males		
Windsor	90.7	0.1	7.7	1.5
Ontario	87.7	0.3	10.1	1.9
Canada	69.0	11.8	17.7	1.5
		Females		
Windsor	88.4	0.2	9.0	2.5
Ontario	85.1	0.4	11.8	2.8
Canada	67.3	13.3	17.3	2.1

Note: Figures cover total population excluding institutional residents.
Source: Statistics Canada. 2012. Census Profile. 2011 Census. Statistics Canada Catalogue no. 98-316-XWE. Ottawa. Released October 24 2012.
http://www12.statcan.gc.ca/census-recensement/2011/dp-pd/prof/index.cfm?Lang=E

Winnipeg, Manitoba

Background

Winnipeg is located in southern Manitoba and is the geographic centre of North America. The word Winnipeg means "muddy water" in Cree and refers to the junction of the Red River and the Assiniboine River. Called "The Forks," this junction has been a gathering place for more than 6,000 years. Winnipeg's fur-trading history dates back to the early 18th century, when it was the headquarters of the Hudson's Bay Company for western Canada.

Winnipeg is a significant grain centre in North America and is the financial, commercial, wholesale and manufacturing grain hub of the West. The Royal Canadian Mint is located in Winnipeg and the province's best known symbol, a 13.5-foot bronze statue called the Golden Boy, is poised atop the dome of the Legislative Building. The Golden Boy (officially named Eternal Youth) faces north in tribute of the province's rich natural resources.

Winnipeg's weather is a defining characteristic of the city. The 1997 spring flood of the Red River is considered "the flood of the century" and one of Canada's worst natural disasters. By the time the flood reached downtown Winnipeg, the river's crest was 12 metres above winter levels, and forced some 28,000 Manitoba residents to be evacuated. Canadians jokingly call Winnipeg "Winterpeg" because of the city's long, cold winters characterized by powerful Arctic winds and some of Canada's coldest temperatures. The city's *Festival du Voyageur* is the largest winter festival in western Canada.

Winnipeg has average summer highs of plus 24.7 degrees Celsius, winter lows of minus 20.2 degrees Celsius, and an average rainfall just over 415 mm per year.

Rankings

- Statistics Canada noted that Winnipeg's crime severity rate had fallen 13% and the province's crime by 8% from 2009 to 2010. The city showed a violent crime severity index of 163.9 (per 100,000 people) in 2010. *Statistics Canada, Violent Crime Severity Index 2010*
- Winnipeg's more than 1,100 restaurants offer residents the largest selection of cuisine anywhere in Canada. According to the Government of Manitoba, the mid-sized, culturally diverse city (2011 population: 730,018) has the most restaurants per capita of any city in Canada or the United States. *Immigrate to Manitoba, Government of Manitoba Immigration website*
- Winnipeg was ranked #3 out of 36 cities in *Money Sense Magazine's* ranking of Canada's best places to buy real estate. Based on statistics and assigned letter grades tracked by Canada Mortgage and Housing Corporation, Winnipeg showed an average home price of $250,000, an average annual household income of $81,897 and an above-average affordability rating. The ranking concludes that a little more than three years of household income can purchase a home in Winnipeg. *Money Sense, Where to Buy Now, May 25, 2012*
- Winnipeg was selected as one of Canada's "Weather Winners" by Environment Canada. A climatologist analysed 30 years of weather data for Canada's 100 largest cities. Winnipeg ranked #2 for "Sunniest Spring" and #2 for "Sunniest Winter." Criteria: the greatest number of hours of sunshine in March, April and May; the greatest number of hours of sunshine in December, January and February. *Environment Canada, Canadian Cities are Weather Winners!, May 29, 2012*

PROFILES / Winnipeg, Manitoba

Population Growth and Density

Area	Population in 2001	Population in 2006	Population in 2011	Population Change 2001–2006	Population Change 2006–2011	Land Area (sq. km)	Population Density per sq. km
Winnipeg	619,544	633,451	663,617	2.2	4.8	464.08	1,430.0
Manitoba	1,119,583	1,148,401	1,208,268	2.6	5.2	552,329.52	2.2
Canada	30,007,094	31,612,897	33,476,688	5.4	5.9	8,965,121.42	3.7

Source: Statistics Canada. 2012. Census Profile. 2011 Census. Statistics Canada Catalogue no. 98-316-XWE. Ottawa. Released October 24 2012. http://www12.statcan.gc.ca/census-recensement/2011/dp-pd/prof/index.cfm?Lang=E;
Statistics Canada 2007. 2006 Community Profiles. 2006 Census. Statistics Canada Catalogue no. 92-591-XWE. Ottawa. Released March 13 2007. http://www12.statcan.ca/census-recensement/2006/dp-pd/prof/92-591/index.cfm?Lang=E

Gender

Area	Males	Females
	Number	
Winnipeg	322,195	341,425
Manitoba	594,550	613,715
Canada	16,414,225	17,062,460
	Percent of Population	
Winnipeg	48.6	51.4
Manitoba	49.2	50.8
Canada	49.0	51.0

Source: Statistics Canada. 2012. Census Profile. 2011 Census. Statistics Canada Catalogue no. 98-316-XWE. Ottawa. Released October 24 2012. http://www12.statcan.gc.ca/census-recensement/2011/dp-pd/prof/index.cfm?Lang=E

Marital Status

Area	Married[1]	Living Common-law	Single[2]	Separated	Divorced	Widowed
			Number			
			Total			
Winnipeg	253,130	43,185	171,185	14,655	35,260	34,340
Manitoba	480,140	78,370	282,465	23,620	52,215	60,300
Canada	12,941,960	3,142,525	7,816,045	698,240	1,686,035	1,584,530
			Males			
Winnipeg	126,455	21,560	90,430	6,230	13,795	6,345
Manitoba	240,170	39,125	152,410	10,530	22,000	11,700
Canada	6,470,300	1,575,495	4,206,320	299,655	680,415	310,940
			Females			
Winnipeg	126,675	21,625	80,755	8,425	21,475	28,000
Manitoba	239,970	39,245	130,050	13,090	30,215	48,610
Canada	6,471,660	1,567,035	3,609,730	398,585	1,005,620	1,273,590
			Percent of Population			
			Total			
Winnipeg	45.9	7.8	31.0	2.7	6.4	6.2
Manitoba	49.1	8.0	28.9	2.4	5.3	6.2
Canada	46.4	11.3	28.0	2.5	6.0	5.7
			Males			
Winnipeg	47.8	8.1	34.1	2.4	5.2	2.4
Manitoba	50.5	8.2	32.0	2.2	4.6	2.5
Canada	47.8	11.6	31.1	2.2	5.0	2.3
			Females			
Winnipeg	44.1	7.5	28.1	2.9	7.5	9.8
Manitoba	47.9	7.8	25.9	2.6	6.0	9.7
Canada	45.2	10.9	25.2	2.8	7.0	8.9

Note: (1) and not separated, (2) never legally married
Source: Statistics Canada. 2012. Census Profile. 2011 Census. Statistics Canada Catalogue no. 98-316-XWE. Ottawa. Released October 24 2012. http://www12.statcan.gc.ca/census-recensement/2011/dp-pd/prof/index.cfm?Lang=E

Age Characteristics: 0 to 49 Years

Area	0 to 4 Years	5 to 9 Years	10 to 14 Years	15 to 19 Years	20 to 24 Years	25 to 29 Years	30 to 34 Years	35 to 39 Years	40 to 44 Years	45 to 49 Years
					Number					
					Total					
Winnipeg	36,860	35,925	39,075	44,320	48,470	47,490	44,885	43,555	44,175	50,700
Manitoba	77,185	74,620	79,355	86,215	82,925	78,185	75,260	75,575	77,770	90,090
Canada	1,877,095	1,809,895	1,920,355	2,178,135	2,187,450	2,169,590	2,162,905	2,173,930	2,324,875	2,675,130
					Males					
Winnipeg	18,645	18,455	20,275	22,585	24,265	23,505	22,035	21,480	21,775	25,015
Manitoba	39,280	38,380	40,965	44,180	41,935	38,900	36,995	37,475	38,455	44,695
Canada	961,150	925,965	983,995	1,115,845	1,108,775	1,077,275	1,058,810	1,064,200	1,141,720	1,318,715
					Females					
Winnipeg	18,210	17,470	18,795	21,735	24,205	23,990	22,850	22,075	22,400	25,680
Manitoba	37,905	36,240	38,395	42,035	40,990	39,285	38,265	38,095	39,320	45,395
Canada	915,945	883,935	936,360	1,062,295	1,078,670	1,092,315	1,104,095	1,109,735	1,183,155	1,356,420
					Percent of Population					
					Total					
Winnipeg	5.6	5.4	5.9	6.7	7.3	7.2	6.8	6.6	6.7	7.6
Manitoba	6.4	6.2	6.6	7.1	6.9	6.5	6.2	6.3	6.4	7.5
Canada	5.6	5.4	5.7	6.5	6.5	6.5	6.5	6.5	6.9	8.0
					Males					
Winnipeg	5.8	5.7	6.3	7.0	7.5	7.3	6.8	6.7	6.8	7.8
Manitoba	6.6	6.5	6.9	7.4	7.1	6.5	6.2	6.3	6.5	7.5
Canada	5.9	5.6	6.0	6.8	6.8	6.6	6.5	6.5	7.0	8.0
					Females					
Winnipeg	5.3	5.1	5.5	6.4	7.1	7.0	6.7	6.5	6.6	7.5
Manitoba	6.2	5.9	6.3	6.8	6.7	6.4	6.2	6.2	6.4	7.4
Canada	5.4	5.2	5.5	6.2	6.3	6.4	6.5	6.5	6.9	7.9

Source: Statistics Canada. 2012. Census Profile. 2011 Census. Statistics Canada Catalogue no. 98-316-XWE. Ottawa. Released October 24 2012.
http://www12.statcan.gc.ca/census-recensement/2011/dp-pd/prof/index.cfm?Lang=E

Age Characteristics: 50 Years and Over, and Median Age

Area	50 to 54 Years	55 to 59 Years	60 to 64 Years	65 to 69 Years	70 to 74 Years	75 to 79 Years	80 to 84 Years	85 Years and Over	Median Age
					Number				
					Total				
Winnipeg	50,015	44,460	38,140	26,880	20,460	17,870	14,880	15,455	39.0
Manitoba	89,970	79,770	68,895	50,240	38,425	31,575	25,545	26,665	38.4
Canada	2,658,965	2,340,635	2,052,670	1,521,715	1,153,065	922,700	702,070	645,515	40.6
					Males				
Winnipeg	24,735	21,530	18,190	12,640	9,180	7,680	5,665	4,535	37.6
Manitoba	44,940	39,350	33,730	24,400	18,035	14,100	10,400	8,345	37.2
Canada	1,309,030	1,147,300	1,002,690	738,010	543,435	417,945	291,085	208,300	39.6
					Females				
Winnipeg	25,280	22,935	19,950	14,240	11,275	10,195	9,215	10,920	40.3
Manitoba	45,025	40,420	35,170	25,840	20,390	17,475	15,145	18,320	39.4
Canada	1,349,940	1,193,335	1,049,985	783,705	609,630	504,755	410,985	437,215	41.5
					Percent of Population				
					Total				
Winnipeg	7.5	6.7	5.7	4.1	3.1	2.7	2.2	2.3	—
Manitoba	7.4	6.6	5.7	4.2	3.2	2.6	2.1	2.2	—
Canada	7.9	7.0	6.1	4.5	3.4	2.8	2.1	1.9	—
					Males				
Winnipeg	7.7	6.7	5.6	3.9	2.8	2.4	1.8	1.4	—
Manitoba	7.6	6.6	5.7	4.1	3.0	2.4	1.7	1.4	—
Canada	8.0	7.0	6.1	4.5	3.3	2.5	1.8	1.3	—
					Females				
Winnipeg	7.4	6.7	5.8	4.2	3.3	3.0	2.7	3.2	—
Manitoba	7.3	6.6	5.7	4.2	3.3	2.8	2.5	3.0	—
Canada	7.9	7.0	6.2	4.6	3.6	3.0	2.4	2.6	—

Source: Statistics Canada. 2012. Census Profile. 2011 Census. Statistics Canada Catalogue no. 98-316-XWE. Ottawa. Released October 24 2012.
http://www12.statcan.gc.ca/census-recensement/2011/dp-pd/prof/index.cfm?Lang=E

PROFILES / Winnipeg, Manitoba

Private Households by Household Size

Area	1 Person	2 Persons	3 Persons	4 Persons	5 Persons	6 or More Persons	Average Number of Persons in Private Households
			Households				
Winnipeg	83,515	85,495	40,425	36,690	14,295	8,320	2.4
Manitoba	131,475	155,355	67,745	64,575	27,885	19,105	2.5
Canada	3,673,310	4,544,820	2,081,900	1,903,300	724,405	392,885	2.5
			Percent of Households				
Winnipeg	31.1	31.8	15.0	13.7	5.3	3.1	—
Manitoba	28.2	33.3	14.5	13.9	6.0	4.1	—
Canada	27.6	34.1	15.6	14.3	5.4	2.9	—

Source: Statistics Canada. 2012. Census Profile. 2011 Census. Statistics Canada Catalogue no. 98-316-XWE. Ottawa. Released October 24 2012.
http://www12.statcan.gc.ca/census-recensement/2011/dp-pd/prof/index.cfm?Lang=E

Dwelling Type

Area	Single-detached House	Semi-detached House	Row House	Apartment: Building with Five or More Storeys	Apartment: Building with Fewer Than Five Storeys	Duplex Apartment	Movable Dwelling	Other Single-attached House
				Number				
Winnipeg	162,175	10,300	8,845	35,350	46,480	4,675	630	300
Manitoba	322,800	14,445	14,435	37,670	61,410	6,110	8,545	730
Canada	7,329,150	646,245	791,600	1,234,770	2,397,550	704,485	183,510	33,310
				Percent of Dwellings				
Winnipeg	60.3	3.8	3.3	13.2	17.3	1.7	0.2	0.1
Manitoba	69.2	3.1	3.1	8.1	13.2	1.3	1.8	0.2
Canada	55.0	4.9	5.9	9.3	18.0	5.3	1.4	0.3

Source: Statistics Canada. 2012. Census Profile. 2011 Census. Statistics Canada Catalogue no. 98-316-XWE. Ottawa. Released October 24 2012.
http://www12.statcan.gc.ca/census-recensement/2011/dp-pd/prof/index.cfm?Lang=E

Shelter Costs

	Owned Dwellings					Rented Dwellings		
Area	Number	Median Value[1] ($)	Average Value[1] ($)	Median Monthly Costs[2] ($)	Average Monthly Costs[2] ($)	Number	Median Monthly Costs[3] ($)	Average Monthly Costs[3] ($)
Winnipeg	177,590	240,168	257,574	882	976	91,180	723	749
Manitoba	314,425	219,915	238,861	780	901	125,655	689	716
Canada	9,013,410	280,552	345,182	978	1,141	4,060,385	784	848

Note: All figures cover non-farm, non-reserve private dwellings; (1) Refers to the dollar amount expected by the owner if the dwelling were to be sold; (2) Includes all shelter expenses paid by households that own their dwellings, such as the mortgage payment and the costs of electricity, heat, water and other municipal services, property taxes and condominium fees; (3) Includes all shelter expenses paid by households that rent their dwellings, such as the monthly rent and the costs of electricity, heat and municipal services.
Source: Statistics Canada. 2013. 2011 National Household Survey. Statistics Canada Catalogue no. 99-004-XWE. Ottawa. Released September 11, 2013.

Occupied Private Dwellings by Period of Construction

Area	1960 or Before	1961 to 1980	1981 to 1990	1991 to 2000	2001 to 2005	2006 to 2011
			Number			
Winnipeg	100,395	92,955	38,435	16,165	8,720	12,125
Manitoba	149,310	157,420	69,440	40,705	21,620	27,310
Canada	3,273,105	4,152,715	2,112,110	1,707,880	1,031,020	1,042,430
			Percent of Dwellings			
Winnipeg	37.4	34.6	14.3	6.0	3.2	4.5
Manitoba	32.1	33.8	14.9	8.7	4.6	5.9
Canada	24.6	31.2	15.9	12.8	7.7	7.8

Note: Figures cover non-farm, non-reserve private dwellings and includes data up to May 10, 2011.
Source: Statistics Canada. 2013. 2011 National Household Survey. Statistics Canada Catalogue no. 99-004-XWE. Ottawa. Released September 11, 2013.

Educational Attainment

Area	No Certificate, Diploma or Degree	High School Diploma or Equivalent[1]	Apprenticeship or Trades Certificate or Diploma[2]	College, CÉGEP or Other Non-University Certificate or Diploma	University Certificate or Diploma Below the Bachelor Level[3]	Bachelor's Degree	University Certificate, Diploma or Degree Above Bachelor Level[4]
			Number				
			Total				
Winnipeg	106,795	153,960	44,710	86,025	24,505	80,745	41,700
Manitoba	237,615	262,500	89,285	150,445	38,600	113,345	55,150
Canada	5,485,400	6,968,935	2,950,685	4,970,020	1,200,130	3,634,425	2,049,930
			Males				
Winnipeg	52,835	73,670	28,000	37,135	10,525	35,995	21,385
Manitoba	123,235	126,430	56,815	62,255	16,780	49,385	28,225
Canada	2,742,875	3,305,415	1,928,970	2,118,430	513,235	1,643,080	1,043,350
			Females				
Winnipeg	53,960	80,285	16,710	48,895	13,985	44,745	20,315
Manitoba	114,380	136,070	32,470	88,195	21,820	63,960	26,925
Canada	2,742,520	3,663,515	1,021,715	2,851,595	686,890	1,991,345	1,006,585
			Percent of Population				
			Total				
Winnipeg	19.8	28.6	8.3	16.0	4.6	15.0	7.7
Manitoba	25.1	27.7	9.4	15.9	4.1	12.0	5.8
Canada	20.1	25.6	10.8	18.2	4.4	13.3	7.5
			Males				
Winnipeg	20.4	28.4	10.8	14.3	4.1	13.9	8.2
Manitoba	26.6	27.3	12.3	13.4	3.6	10.7	6.1
Canada	20.6	24.9	14.5	15.9	3.9	12.4	7.8
			Females				
Winnipeg	19.3	28.8	6.0	17.5	5.0	16.0	7.3
Manitoba	23.6	28.1	6.7	18.2	4.5	13.2	5.6
Canada	19.6	26.2	7.3	20.4	4.9	14.3	7.2

Note: Figures cover total population aged 15 years and over by highest certificate, diploma or degree; (1) Includes persons who have graduated from a secondary school or equivalent. It excludes persons with a postsecondary certificate, diploma or degree; (2) Includes Registered Apprenticeship certificates (including Certificate of Qualification, Journeyperson's designation) and other trades certificates or diplomas such as pre-employment or vocational certificates and diplomas from brief trade programs completed at community colleges, institutes of technology, vocational centres, and similar institutions; (3) Comparisons with other data sources suggest that the category 'University certificate or diploma below the bachelor's level' was over-reported in the NHS. This category likely includes some responses that are actually college certificates or diplomas, bachelor's degrees or other types of education (e.g., university transfer programs, bachelor's programs completed in other countries, incomplete bachelor's programs, non-university professional designations). We recommend users interpret the results for the 'University certificate or diploma below the bachelor's level' category with caution; (4) 'University certificate or diploma above bachelor level' includes the categories: 'Degree in medicine, dentistry, veterinary medicine or optometry,' 'Master's degree' and 'Earned doctorate.'
Source: Statistics Canada. 2013. 2011 National Household Survey. Statistics Canada Catalogue no. 99-004-XWE. Ottawa. Released September 11, 2013.

Household Income Distribution

Area	Less than $10,000	$10,000 to $19,999	$20,000 to $29,999	$30,000 to $39,999	$40,000 to $49,999	$50,000 to $59,999	$60,000 to $79,999	$80,000 to $99,999	$100,000 to $124,999	$125,000 to $149,999	$150,000 and Over
					Households						
Winnipeg	14,440	22,305	25,140	27,435	26,540	23,040	39,315	29,110	24,695	15,160	21,605
Manitoba	24,960	41,375	44,110	47,695	45,370	39,855	68,350	51,095	42,305	25,505	35,175
Canada	626,705	1,141,945	1,193,925	1,271,675	1,206,800	1,102,120	1,865,280	1,458,240	1,260,770	802,555	1,389,240
					Percent of Households						
Winnipeg	5.4	8.3	9.4	10.2	9.9	8.6	14.6	10.8	9.2	5.6	8.0
Manitoba	5.4	8.9	9.5	10.2	9.7	8.6	14.7	11.0	9.1	5.5	7.6
Canada	4.7	8.6	9.0	9.5	9.1	8.3	14.0	10.9	9.5	6.0	10.4

Note: Household income is the sum of the total incomes of all members of that household. Total income refers to monetary receipts from certain sources, before income taxes and deductions, during calendar year 2010.
Source: Statistics Canada. 2013. 2011 National Household Survey. Statistics Canada Catalogue no. 99-004-XWE. Ottawa. Released September 11, 2013.

Median and Average Household and Economic Family Income

Area	Median Household Income ($)	Average Household Income ($)	Median After-tax Household Income ($)	Average After-tax Household Income ($)	Median Economic Family Income ($)	Average Economic Family Income ($)	Median After-tax Economic Family Income ($)	Average After-tax Economic Family Income ($)
Winnipeg	57,925	72,612	50,537	60,386	75,395	88,899	64,970	73,680
Manitoba	57,299	70,984	50,392	59,381	72,404	84,761	62,819	70,695
Canada	61,072	79,102	54,089	66,149	76,511	94,125	67,044	78,517

Note: Figures cover household and economic familiy income in 2010. A household is defined as a person or a group of persons (other than foreign residents) who occupy the same private dwelling and do not have a usual place of residence elsewhere in Canada. Every person is a member of one and only one household. An economic family is defined as a group of two or more persons who live in the same dwelling and are related to each other by blood, marriage, common-law, adoption or a foster relationship. A couple may be of opposite or same sex.
Source: Statistics Canada. 2013. 2011 National Household Survey. Statistics Canada Catalogue no. 99-004-XWE. Ottawa. Released September 11, 2013.

PROFILES / Winnipeg, Manitoba

Individual Income Distribution

Area	Less than $10,000	$10,000 to $19,999	$20,000 to $29,999	$30,000 to $39,999	$40,000 to $49,999	$50,000 to $59,999	$60,000 to $79,999	$80,000 to $99,999	$100,000 to $124,999	$125,000 and Over
					Number					
					Total					
Winnipeg	86,025	88,705	78,260	70,800	56,820	40,205	48,940	21,090	9,905	10,725
Manitoba	162,905	164,195	135,385	123,090	95,695	66,930	82,785	36,310	16,840	16,900
Canada	4,492,040	4,835,710	3,670,020	3,180,360	2,603,520	1,921,650	2,437,440	1,302,045	693,580	782,135
					Males					
Winnipeg	37,985	33,630	32,000	33,610	29,100	23,660	28,575	13,305	6,695	8,100
Manitoba	72,275	61,560	56,925	59,635	51,335	40,975	50,390	23,460	11,970	12,975
Canada	1,936,365	1,864,880	1,588,260	1,522,190	1,333,510	1,079,780	1,473,145	823,720	492,905	599,905
					Females					
Winnipeg	48,045	55,070	46,255	37,190	27,720	16,540	20,365	7,790	3,210	2,620
Manitoba	90,630	102,635	78,460	63,450	44,365	25,960	32,395	12,850	4,875	3,925
Canada	2,555,675	2,970,825	2,081,760	1,658,170	1,270,010	841,870	964,300	478,330	200,680	182,230
					Percent of Population					
					Total					
Winnipeg	16.8	17.3	15.3	13.8	11.1	7.9	9.6	4.1	1.9	2.1
Manitoba	18.1	18.2	15.0	13.7	10.6	7.4	9.2	4.0	1.9	1.9
Canada	17.3	18.7	14.2	12.3	10.0	7.4	9.4	5.0	2.7	3.0
					Males					
Winnipeg	15.4	13.6	13.0	13.6	11.8	9.6	11.6	5.4	2.7	3.3
Manitoba	16.4	13.9	12.9	13.5	11.6	9.3	11.4	5.3	2.7	2.9
Canada	15.2	14.7	12.5	12.0	10.5	8.5	11.6	6.5	3.9	4.7
					Females					
Winnipeg	18.1	20.8	17.5	14.0	10.5	6.2	7.7	2.9	1.2	1.0
Manitoba	19.7	22.3	17.1	13.8	9.7	5.6	7.0	2.8	1.1	0.9
Canada	19.4	22.5	15.8	12.6	9.6	6.4	7.3	3.6	1.5	1.4

Note: Figures cover individuals aged 15 years and over with income. Income refers to monetary receipts from certain sources, before income taxes and deductions, during calendar year 2010.
Source: Statistics Canada. 2013. 2011 National Household Survey. Statistics Canada Catalogue no. 99-004-XWE. Ottawa. Released September 11, 2013.

Labour Force Status

Area	In the Labour Force - All	In the Labour Force - Employed	In the Labour Force - Unemployed	Not in the Labour Force
		Number		
		Total		
Winnipeg	367,555	345,805	21,750	170,885
Manitoba	636,835	597,290	39,550	310,105
Canada	17,990,080	16,595,035	1,395,045	9,269,445
		Males		
Winnipeg	188,935	177,650	11,285	70,610
Manitoba	334,160	312,870	21,295	128,960
Canada	9,388,570	8,634,310	754,255	3,906,785
		Females		
Winnipeg	178,620	168,155	10,465	100,270
Manitoba	302,675	284,425	18,255	181,145
Canada	8,601,515	7,960,725	640,790	5,362,660
		Percent of Labour Force		
		Total		
Winnipeg	68.3	64.2	5.9	31.7
Manitoba	67.3	63.1	6.2	32.7
Canada	66.0	60.9	7.8	34.0
		Males		
Winnipeg	72.8	68.4	6.0	27.2
Manitoba	72.2	67.6	6.4	27.8
Canada	70.6	64.9	8.0	29.4
		Females		
Winnipeg	64.0	60.3	5.9	36.0
Manitoba	62.6	58.8	6.0	37.4
Canada	61.6	57.0	7.4	38.4

Note: Figures are based on total population 15 years and over
Source: Statistics Canada. 2013. 2011 National Household Survey. Statistics Canada Catalogue no. 99-004-XWE. Ottawa. Released September 11, 2013.

Labour Force by Industry (NAICS Codes 11–52)

Area	Agriculture, forestry, fishing & hunting	Mining, quarrying, & oil & gas extraction	Utilities	Construction	Manufacturing	Wholesale Trade	Retail Trade	Transportation & warehousing	Information & cultural industries	Finance & insurance
					Number Total					
Winnipeg	1,915	475	4,320	20,570	33,310	14,110	40,920	18,935	8,155	17,865
Manitoba	27,385	5,325	8,040	41,385	55,295	21,555	68,720	33,355	11,485	26,045
Canada	437,650	261,050	149,940	1,215,380	1,619,295	733,445	2,031,665	827,780	420,830	767,960
					Males					
Winnipeg	1,145	395	3,085	18,475	25,060	9,970	19,525	14,900	4,505	6,690
Manitoba	20,095	4,850	6,165	36,980	42,010	15,480	32,305	26,295	6,085	8,990
Canada	307,370	211,690	110,765	1,068,710	1,167,680	494,545	933,850	617,305	235,875	296,995
					Females					
Winnipeg	765	85	1,235	2,095	8,245	4,145	21,400	4,035	3,645	11,175
Manitoba	7,290	480	1,875	4,410	13,280	6,080	36,415	7,060	5,400	17,055
Canada	130,285	49,360	39,175	146,670	451,615	238,900	1,097,820	210,475	184,955	470,960
					Percent of Labour Force Total					
Winnipeg	0.5	0.1	1.2	5.7	9.2	3.9	11.3	5.2	2.3	4.9
Manitoba	4.4	0.9	1.3	6.6	8.8	3.4	11.0	5.3	1.8	4.2
Canada	2.5	1.5	0.9	6.9	9.2	4.2	11.6	4.7	2.4	4.4
					Males					
Winnipeg	0.6	0.2	1.7	9.9	13.5	5.4	10.5	8.0	2.4	3.6
Manitoba	6.1	1.5	1.9	11.2	12.8	4.7	9.8	8.0	1.8	2.7
Canada	3.3	2.3	1.2	11.6	12.7	5.4	10.2	6.7	2.6	3.2
					Females					
Winnipeg	0.4	0.0	0.7	1.2	4.7	2.4	12.2	2.3	2.1	6.4
Manitoba	2.5	0.2	0.6	1.5	4.5	2.0	12.3	2.4	1.8	5.7
Canada	1.6	0.6	0.5	1.7	5.4	2.8	13.1	2.5	2.2	5.6

Note: Figures are based on total experienced labour force 15 years and over. Experienced labour force refers to persons who, during the week of Sunday, May 1 to Saturday, May 7, 2011, were employed and the unemployed who had last worked for pay or in self-employment in either 2010 or 2011.
Source: Statistics Canada. 2013. 2011 National Household Survey. Statistics Canada Catalogue no. 99-004-XWE. Ottawa. Released September 11, 2013.

Labour Force by Industry (NAICS Codes 53–91)

Area	Real estate & rental & leasing	Profess., scientific & tech. services	Mgmt of companies & enterprises	Admin. & support, waste mgmt & remed. services	Educational services	Health care & social assistance	Arts, entertain. & recreation	Accomm. & food services	Other services (except public admin.)	Public admin.
					Number Total					
Winnipeg	5,670	19,220	375	14,905	29,885	49,610	8,470	26,340	16,285	30,235
Manitoba	8,105	26,880	505	21,285	52,525	83,700	12,495	40,490	27,535	53,690
Canada	321,895	1,240,850	17,460	728,330	1,301,435	1,949,650	363,405	1,130,750	807,800	1,261,050
					Males					
Winnipeg	3,355	10,835	240	8,615	10,235	10,650	4,465	11,330	7,675	14,970
Manitoba	4,560	14,770	325	12,475	16,905	16,100	6,475	16,070	13,795	28,260
Canada	179,090	688,625	9,380	411,250	424,915	349,430	188,270	469,990	372,940	652,510
					Females					
Winnipeg	2,310	8,390	140	6,290	19,655	38,965	4,010	15,010	8,615	15,265
Manitoba	3,545	12,110	185	8,805	35,615	67,600	6,020	24,415	13,735	25,435
Canada	142,805	552,225	8,075	317,085	876,515	1,600,220	175,135	660,760	434,865	608,535
					Percent of Labour Force Total					
Winnipeg	1.6	5.3	0.1	4.1	8.3	13.7	2.3	7.3	4.5	8.4
Manitoba	1.3	4.3	0.1	3.4	8.4	13.4	2.0	6.5	4.4	8.6
Canada	1.8	7.1	0.1	4.1	7.4	11.1	2.1	6.4	4.6	7.2
					Males					
Winnipeg	1.8	5.8	0.1	4.6	5.5	5.7	2.4	6.1	4.1	8.0
Manitoba	1.4	4.5	0.1	3.8	5.1	4.9	2.0	4.9	4.2	8.6
Canada	1.9	7.5	0.1	4.5	4.6	3.8	2.0	5.1	4.1	7.1
					Females					
Winnipeg	1.3	4.8	0.1	3.6	11.2	22.2	2.3	8.6	4.9	8.7
Manitoba	1.2	4.1	0.1	3.0	12.0	22.8	2.0	8.2	4.6	8.6
Canada	1.7	6.6	0.1	3.8	10.4	19.1	2.1	7.9	5.2	7.2

Note: Figures are based on total experienced labour force 15 years and over. Experienced labour force refers to persons who, during the week of Sunday, May 1 to Saturday, May 7, 2011, were employed and the unemployed who had last worked for pay or in self-employment in either 2010 or 2011.
Source: Statistics Canada. 2013. 2011 National Household Survey. Statistics Canada Catalogue no. 99-004-XWE. Ottawa. Released September 11, 2013.

Occupation

Area	Mgmt	Business, Finance & Admin.	Natural/ Applied Sciences & Related	Health	Education, Law & Social, Community & Government Services	Art, Culture, Recreation & Sport	Sales & Service	Trades, Transport & Equip. Operators & Related	Natural Resources, Agri. & Related Production	Mfg & Utilities
					Number					
					Total					
Winnipeg	33,075	63,220	23,570	27,950	48,050	9,800	88,715	46,750	3,410	17,045
Manitoba	69,775	97,840	33,630	46,560	82,195	13,470	140,965	95,085	17,380	28,895
Canada	1,963,600	2,902,045	1,237,775	1,107,200	2,064,675	503,415	4,068,170	2,537,775	397,930	805,040
					Males					
Winnipeg	19,905	19,945	18,605	6,470	16,750	4,715	40,040	44,470	2,790	12,420
Manitoba	45,005	28,285	26,800	9,570	27,695	5,995	59,645	90,405	13,985	21,600
Canada	1,229,460	854,190	966,355	217,520	676,550	232,535	1,745,705	2,385,615	318,945	564,300
					Females					
Winnipeg	13,170	43,270	4,960	21,480	31,300	5,085	48,675	2,280	620	4,630
Manitoba	24,770	69,560	6,835	36,985	54,500	7,475	81,320	4,680	3,395	7,290
Canada	734,140	2,047,855	271,415	889,675	1,388,130	270,875	2,322,465	152,165	78,980	240,740
					Percent of Labour Force					
					Total					
Winnipeg	9.1	17.5	6.5	7.7	13.3	2.7	24.5	12.9	0.9	4.7
Manitoba	11.1	15.6	5.4	7.4	13.1	2.2	22.5	15.2	2.8	4.6
Canada	11.2	16.5	7.0	6.3	11.7	2.9	23.1	14.4	2.3	4.6
					Males					
Winnipeg	10.7	10.7	10.0	3.5	9.0	2.5	21.5	23.9	1.5	6.7
Manitoba	13.7	8.6	8.1	2.9	8.4	1.8	18.1	27.5	4.3	6.6
Canada	13.4	9.3	10.5	2.4	7.4	2.5	19.0	26.0	3.5	6.1
					Females					
Winnipeg	7.5	24.7	2.8	12.2	17.8	2.9	27.7	1.3	0.4	2.6
Manitoba	8.3	23.4	2.3	12.5	18.4	2.5	27.4	1.6	1.1	2.5
Canada	8.7	24.4	3.2	10.6	16.5	3.2	27.7	1.8	0.9	2.9

Note: Figures are based on total experienced labour force 15 years and over
Source: Statistics Canada. 2013. 2011 National Household Survey. Statistics Canada Catalogue no. 99-004-XWE. Ottawa. Released September 11, 2013.

Place of Work Status

Area	Worked at Home	Worked Outside Canada	No Fixed Workplace Address	Worked at Usual Place
		Number		
		Total		
Winnipeg	13,185	835	34,430	297,360
Manitoba	40,475	1,500	66,110	489,200
Canada	1,142,640	66,460	1,868,245	13,517,690
		Males		
Winnipeg	6,390	485	25,545	145,230
Manitoba	22,740	985	50,710	238,425
Canada	582,150	47,355	1,400,485	6,604,325
		Females		
Winnipeg	6,800	350	8,880	152,125
Manitoba	17,735	515	15,400	250,770
Canada	560,490	19,100	467,760	6,913,370
		Percent of Labour Force		
		Total		
Winnipeg	3.8	0.2	10.0	86.0
Manitoba	6.8	0.3	11.1	81.9
Canada	6.9	0.4	11.3	81.5
		Males		
Winnipeg	3.6	0.3	14.4	81.8
Manitoba	7.3	0.3	16.2	76.2
Canada	6.7	0.5	16.2	76.5
		Females		
Winnipeg	4.0	0.2	5.3	90.5
Manitoba	6.2	0.2	5.4	88.2
Canada	7.0	0.2	5.9	86.8

Note: Figures are based on total employed labour force 15 years and over.
Source: Statistics Canada. 2013. 2011 National Household Survey. Statistics Canada Catalogue no. 99-004-XWE. Ottawa. Released September 11, 2013.

Mode of Transportation to Work

Area	Car; Truck; Van; as Driver	Car; Truck; Van; as Passenger	Public Transit	Walked	Bicycled	All Other Modes
			Number			
			Total			
Winnipeg	229,155	24,380	48,530	18,095	7,075	4,550
Manitoba	409,350	40,080	51,015	37,530	9,615	7,725
Canada	11,393,140	867,050	1,851,525	880,815	201,780	191,625
			Males			
Winnipeg	128,400	7,860	19,795	7,855	4,970	1,905
Manitoba	226,570	15,160	20,925	16,105	6,715	3,660
Canada	6,238,835	349,530	788,290	387,580	135,840	104,725
			Females			
Winnipeg	100,760	16,520	28,735	10,240	2,105	2,650
Manitoba	182,780	24,915	30,085	21,430	2,895	4,065
Canada	5,154,305	517,520	1,063,235	493,230	65,940	86,900
			Percent of Labour Force			
			Total			
Winnipeg	69.1	7.3	14.6	5.5	2.1	1.4
Manitoba	73.7	7.2	9.2	6.8	1.7	1.4
Canada	74.0	5.6	12.0	5.7	1.3	1.2
			Males			
Winnipeg	75.2	4.6	11.6	4.6	2.9	1.1
Manitoba	78.4	5.2	7.2	5.6	2.3	1.3
Canada	77.9	4.4	9.8	4.8	1.7	1.3
			Females			
Winnipeg	62.6	10.3	17.8	6.4	1.3	1.6
Manitoba	68.7	9.4	11.3	8.1	1.1	1.5
Canada	69.8	7.0	14.4	6.7	0.9	1.2

Note: Figures are based on total employed labour force 15 years and over.
Source: Statistics Canada. 2013. 2011 National Household Survey. Statistics Canada Catalogue no. 99-004-XWE. Ottawa. Released September 11, 2013.

Visible Minority Population Characteristics

Area	Total Minority	South Asian[1]	Chinese	Black	Filipino	Latin American	Arab	SE Asian[2]	West Asian[3]	Korean	Japanese	Multiple[4]
						Number						
						Total						
Winnipeg	139,190	22,940	14,975	17,410	56,400	6,475	2,670	6,990	1,970	2,690	1,400	3,770
Manitoba	153,625	25,265	17,025	19,610	59,220	9,140	3,235	7,565	2,040	3,045	1,745	3,975
Canada	6,264,750	1,567,400	1,324,750	945,665	619,310	381,280	380,620	312,075	206,840	161,130	87,270	171,935
						Males						
Winnipeg	68,710	11,500	7,415	8,900	27,015	3,475	1,415	3,575	975	1,170	605	1,850
Manitoba	76,350	12,695	8,505	10,095	28,415	4,920	1,730	3,915	1,025	1,365	765	1,980
Canada	3,043,010	790,755	632,325	453,005	268,885	186,355	203,485	154,035	105,620	77,165	38,270	83,335
						Females						
Winnipeg	70,480	11,445	7,560	8,510	29,385	3,000	1,255	3,415	995	1,520	790	1,920
Manitoba	77,280	12,575	8,515	9,515	30,805	4,220	1,510	3,650	1,015	1,680	980	1,995
Canada	3,221,745	776,650	692,420	492,660	350,425	194,925	177,140	158,045	101,220	83,965	48,990	88,600
						Percent of Population						
						Total						
Winnipeg	21.4	3.5	2.3	2.7	8.7	1.0	0.4	1.1	0.3	0.4	0.2	0.6
Manitoba	13.1	2.2	1.4	1.7	5.0	0.8	0.3	0.6	0.2	0.3	0.1	0.3
Canada	19.1	4.8	4.0	2.9	1.9	1.2	1.2	0.9	0.6	0.5	0.3	0.5
						Males						
Winnipeg	21.7	3.6	2.3	2.8	8.5	1.1	0.4	1.1	0.3	0.4	0.2	0.6
Manitoba	13.2	2.2	1.5	1.7	4.9	0.8	0.3	0.7	0.2	0.2	0.1	0.3
Canada	18.8	4.9	3.9	2.8	1.7	1.2	1.3	1.0	0.7	0.5	0.2	0.5
						Females						
Winnipeg	21.1	3.4	2.3	2.6	8.8	0.9	0.4	1.0	0.3	0.5	0.2	0.6
Manitoba	13.0	2.1	1.4	1.6	5.2	0.7	0.3	0.6	0.2	0.3	0.2	0.3
Canada	19.3	4.7	4.1	3.0	2.1	1.2	1.1	0.9	0.6	0.5	0.3	0.5

Note: The Employment Equity Act defines visible minorities as 'persons, other than Aboriginal peoples, who are non-Caucasian in race or non-white in colour';
(1) Includes 'East Indian,' 'Pakistani,' 'Sri Lankan,' etc.; (2) Includes 'Vietnamese,' 'Cambodian,' 'Malaysian,' 'Laotian,' etc.; (3) Includes 'Iranian,' 'Afghan,' etc.; (4) Includes respondents who reported more than one visible minority group by checking two or more mark-in circles, e.g., 'Black' and 'South Asian.'
Source: Statistics Canada. 2013. 2011 National Household Survey. Statistics Canada Catalogue no. 99-004-XWE. Ottawa. Released September 11, 2013.

PROFILES / Winnipeg, Manitoba

Aboriginal Population

Area	Aboriginal Identity[1]	First Nations (North American Indian) Single Identity[2]	Métis Single Identity	Inuk (Inuit) Single Identity	Multiple Aboriginal Identities[3]	Aboriginal Identities Not Included Elsewhere
			Number			
			Total			
Winnipeg	72,335	29,485	41,235	340	745	530
Manitoba	195,895	114,225	78,830	580	1,200	1,055
Canada	1,400,685	851,560	451,795	59,440	11,415	26,475
			Males			
Winnipeg	34,355	13,310	20,300	120	380	245
Manitoba	95,605	55,025	39,260	180	615	525
Canada	682,190	411,785	223,335	29,495	5,525	12,055
			Females			
Winnipeg	37,980	16,180	20,935	220	365	280
Manitoba	100,290	59,205	39,570	400	585	530
Canada	718,500	439,775	228,460	29,950	5,890	14,420
			Percent of Population			
			Total			
Winnipeg	11.1	4.5	6.3	0.1	0.1	0.1
Manitoba	16.7	9.7	6.7	0.0	0.1	0.1
Canada	4.3	2.6	1.4	0.2	0.0	0.1
			Males			
Winnipeg	10.8	4.2	6.4	0.0	0.1	0.1
Manitoba	16.5	9.5	6.8	0.0	0.1	0.1
Canada	4.2	2.5	1.4	0.2	0.0	0.1
			Females			
Winnipeg	11.4	4.9	6.3	0.1	0.1	0.1
Manitoba	16.9	10.0	6.7	0.1	0.1	0.1
Canada	4.3	2.6	1.4	0.2	0.0	0.1

Note: (1) Includes persons who reported being an Aboriginal person, that is, First Nations (North American Indian), Métis or Inuk (Inuit) and/or those who reported Registered or Treaty Indian status, that is registered under the Indian Act of Canada, and/or those who reported membership in a First Nation or Indian band. Aboriginal peoples of Canada are defined in the Constitution Act, 1982, section 35-2 as including the Indian, Inuit and Métis peoples of Canada; (2) Users should be aware that the estimates associated with this variable are more affected than most by the incomplete enumeration of certain Indian reserves and Indian settlements in the National Household Survey (NHS); (3) Includes persons who reported being any two or all three of the following: First Nations (North American Indian), Métis or Inuk (Inuit).
Source: Statistics Canada. 2013. 2011 National Household Survey. Statistics Canada Catalogue no. 99-004-XWE. Ottawa. Released September 11, 2013.

Ethnic Origin

Area	North American Aboriginal	Other North American	European	Caribbean	Latin, Central and South American	African	Asian	Oceania
				Number				
				Total				
Winnipeg	76,055	113,485	458,075	7,565	9,455	15,765	116,260	790
Manitoba	199,940	224,100	841,985	8,605	17,845	18,015	126,600	1,285
Canada	1,836,035	11,070,455	20,157,965	627,590	544,375	766,735	5,011,225	74,875
				Males				
Winnipeg	36,010	55,485	221,980	3,770	4,855	8,200	56,660	425
Manitoba	97,615	110,695	414,405	4,345	9,190	9,385	61,960	710
Canada	885,675	5,462,685	9,913,150	291,640	264,635	387,360	2,435,540	37,490
				Females				
Winnipeg	40,040	58,000	236,100	3,795	4,600	7,565	59,595	365
Manitoba	102,325	113,405	427,580	4,260	8,655	8,630	64,640	570
Canada	950,360	5,607,770	10,244,820	335,945	279,740	379,380	2,575,680	37,385
				Percent of Population				
				Total				
Winnipeg	11.7	17.5	70.5	1.2	1.5	2.4	17.9	0.1
Manitoba	17.0	19.1	71.7	0.7	1.5	1.5	10.8	0.1
Canada	5.6	33.7	61.4	1.9	1.7	2.3	15.3	0.2
				Males				
Winnipeg	11.4	17.5	70.1	1.2	1.5	2.6	17.9	0.1
Manitoba	16.8	19.1	71.5	0.7	1.6	1.6	10.7	0.1
Canada	5.5	33.8	61.3	1.8	1.6	2.4	15.1	0.2
				Females				
Winnipeg	12.0	17.4	70.8	1.1	1.4	2.3	17.9	0.1
Manitoba	17.2	19.1	71.9	0.7	1.5	1.5	10.9	0.1
Canada	5.7	33.6	61.4	2.0	1.7	2.3	15.4	0.2

Note: The sum of the ethnic groups in this table is greater than the total population estimate because a person may report more than one ethnic origin in the NHS.
Source: Statistics Canada. 2013. 2011 National Household Survey. Statistics Canada Catalogue no. 99-004-XWE. Ottawa. Released September 11, 2013.

Religion

Area	Buddhist	Christian	Hindu	Jewish	Muslim	Sikh	Traditional (Aboriginal) Spirituality	Other Religions	No Religious Affiliation
				Number					
				Total					
Winnipeg	6,260	414,270	6,795	10,535	11,230	9,800	1,775	2,835	186,510
Manitoba	6,770	803,640	7,720	11,110	12,405	10,200	7,155	4,245	311,105
Canada	366,830	22,102,745	497,965	329,495	1,053,945	454,965	64,935	130,835	7,850,605
				Males					
Winnipeg	3,010	192,570	3,385	5,170	5,715	4,910	695	1,215	99,995
Manitoba	3,280	382,310	3,875	5,460	6,340	5,115	3,415	1,840	168,335
Canada	168,465	10,497,775	250,435	161,265	540,555	229,435	31,805	57,745	4,225,645
				Females					
Winnipeg	3,250	221,695	3,405	5,365	5,520	4,890	1,080	1,620	86,510
Manitoba	3,490	421,335	3,850	5,650	6,065	5,080	3,740	2,405	142,765
Canada	198,365	11,604,975	247,525	168,235	513,395	225,530	33,135	73,090	3,624,965
				Percent of Population					
				Total					
Winnipeg	1.0	63.7	1.0	1.6	1.7	1.5	0.3	0.4	28.7
Manitoba	0.6	68.4	0.7	0.9	1.1	0.9	0.6	0.4	26.5
Canada	1.1	67.3	1.5	1.0	3.2	1.4	0.2	0.4	23.9
				Males					
Winnipeg	1.0	60.8	1.1	1.6	1.8	1.6	0.2	0.4	31.6
Manitoba	0.6	65.9	0.7	0.9	1.1	0.9	0.6	0.3	29.0
Canada	1.0	64.9	1.5	1.0	3.3	1.4	0.2	0.4	26.1
				Females					
Winnipeg	1.0	66.5	1.0	1.6	1.7	1.5	0.3	0.5	26.0
Manitoba	0.6	70.9	0.6	1.0	1.0	0.9	0.6	0.4	24.0
Canada	1.2	69.5	1.5	1.0	3.1	1.4	0.2	0.4	21.7

Note: Religion refers to the person's self-identification as having a connection or affiliation with any religious denomination, group, body, sect, cult or other religiously defined community or system of belief. Religion is not limited to formal membership in a religious organization or group. Persons without a religious connection or affiliation can self-identify as atheist, agnostic or humanist, or can provide another applicable response.
Source: Statistics Canada. 2013. 2011 National Household Survey. Statistics Canada Catalogue no. 99-004-XWE. Ottawa. Released September 11, 2013.

Religion—Christian Denominations

Area	Anglican	Baptist	Catholic	Christian Orthodox	Lutheran	Pentecostal	Presbyterian	United Church	Other Christian
				Number					
				Total					
Winnipeg	29,620	10,230	193,030	9,895	20,610	9,970	4,435	52,955	83,520
Manitoba	67,040	19,815	309,455	14,665	40,915	22,665	9,760	130,220	189,110
Canada	1,631,845	635,840	12,810,705	550,690	478,185	478,705	472,385	2,007,610	3,036,780
				Males					
Winnipeg	13,280	4,780	91,915	4,690	9,345	4,515	2,010	22,815	39,215
Manitoba	30,975	9,655	150,275	7,080	19,225	10,755	4,455	59,080	90,815
Canada	752,945	293,905	6,167,290	270,205	221,525	217,850	218,955	912,545	1,442,550
				Females					
Winnipeg	16,345	5,450	101,120	5,205	11,260	5,455	2,430	30,135	44,300
Manitoba	36,070	10,160	159,175	7,585	21,685	11,910	5,305	71,140	98,295
Canada	878,900	341,940	6,643,415	280,485	256,660	260,850	253,430	1,095,065	1,594,230
				Percent of Population					
				Total					
Winnipeg	4.6	1.6	29.7	1.5	3.2	1.5	0.7	8.1	12.8
Manitoba	5.7	1.7	26.4	1.2	3.5	1.9	0.8	11.1	16.1
Canada	5.0	1.9	39.0	1.7	1.5	1.5	1.4	6.1	9.2
				Males					
Winnipeg	4.2	1.5	29.0	1.5	3.0	1.4	0.6	7.2	12.4
Manitoba	5.3	1.7	25.9	1.2	3.3	1.9	0.8	10.2	15.7
Canada	4.7	1.8	38.2	1.7	1.4	1.3	1.4	5.6	8.9
				Females					
Winnipeg	4.9	1.6	30.3	1.6	3.4	1.6	0.7	9.0	13.3
Manitoba	6.1	1.7	26.8	1.3	3.6	2.0	0.9	12.0	16.5
Canada	5.3	2.0	39.8	1.7	1.5	1.6	1.5	6.6	9.6

Note: Religion refers to the person's self-identification as having a connection or affiliation with any religious denomination, group, body, sect, cult or other religiously defined community or system of belief. Religion is not limited to formal membership in a religious organization or group. Persons without a religious connection or affiliation can self-identify as atheist, agnostic or humanist, or can provide another applicable response.
Source: Statistics Canada. 2013. 2011 National Household Survey. Statistics Canada Catalogue no. 99-004-XWE. Ottawa. Released September 11, 2013.

PROFILES / Winnipeg, Manitoba

Immigrant Status and Period of Immigration

Area	Non-Immigrants[1]	Immigrants All	Before 1971	1971 to 1980	1981 to 1990	1991 to 2000	2001 to 2005	2006 to 2011	Non-Permanent Residents[3]
Number									
Total									
Winnipeg	501,410	142,230	24,200	18,790	17,315	19,735	17,420	44,780	6,355
Manitoba	981,200	184,505	32,675	22,995	21,950	25,010	24,220	57,655	8,635
Canada	25,720,175	6,775,765	1,261,055	870,775	949,890	1,539,050	992,070	1,162,915	356,385
Males									
Winnipeg	244,360	68,980	11,235	9,275	8,350	9,400	8,535	22,185	3,320
Manitoba	485,355	90,010	15,435	11,390	10,700	12,000	11,860	28,615	4,610
Canada	12,753,235	3,231,370	605,430	416,670	454,570	724,905	474,545	555,245	178,515
Females									
Winnipeg	257,045	73,250	12,965	9,515	8,965	10,335	8,885	22,595	3,040
Manitoba	495,850	94,495	17,245	11,600	11,245	13,005	12,360	29,045	4,030
Canada	12,966,935	3,544,400	655,625	454,105	495,325	814,145	517,530	607,670	177,870
Percent of Population									
Total									
Winnipeg	77.1	21.9	3.7	2.9	2.7	3.0	2.7	6.9	1.0
Manitoba	83.6	15.7	2.8	2.0	1.9	2.1	2.1	4.9	0.7
Canada	78.3	20.6	3.8	2.7	2.9	4.7	3.0	3.5	1.1
Males									
Winnipeg	77.2	21.8	3.5	2.9	2.6	3.0	2.7	7.0	1.0
Manitoba	83.7	15.5	2.7	2.0	1.8	2.1	2.0	4.9	0.8
Canada	78.9	20.0	3.7	2.6	2.8	4.5	2.9	3.4	1.1
Females									
Winnipeg	77.1	22.0	3.9	2.9	2.7	3.1	2.7	6.8	0.9
Manitoba	83.4	15.9	2.9	2.0	1.9	2.2	2.1	4.9	0.7
Canada	77.7	21.2	3.9	2.7	3.0	4.9	3.1	3.6	1.1

Note: (1) Non-immigrant refers to a person who is a Canadian citizen by birth; (2) Immigrant refers to a person who is or has ever been a landed immigrant/permanent resident. This person has been granted the right to live in Canada permanently by immigration authorities. Some immigrants have resided in Canada for a number of years, while others have arrived recently. Some immigrants are Canadian citizens, while others are not. Most immigrants are born outside Canada, but a small number are born in Canada. In the 2011 National Household Survey, 'Immigrants' includes immigrants who landed in Canada prior to May 10, 2011; (3) Non-permanent resident refers to a person from another country who has a work or study permit, or who is a refugee claimant, and any non-Canadian-born family member living in Canada with them.
Source: Statistics Canada. 2013. 2011 National Household Survey. Statistics Canada Catalogue no. 99-004-XWE. Ottawa. Released September 11, 2013.

Mother Tongue

Area	English	French	Non-official Language	English & French	English & Non-official Language	French & Non-official Language	English, French & Non-official Language
Number							
Total							
Winnipeg	468,305	23,455	146,340	2,565	13,730	925	280
Manitoba	869,990	42,090	256,500	3,795	18,940	1,425	365
Canada	18,858,980	7,054,975	6,567,680	144,685	396,330	74,430	24,095
Males							
Winnipeg	230,515	10,710	69,440	1,220	6,530	445	120
Manitoba	432,080	20,140	124,185	1,790	9,030	710	160
Canada	9,345,225	3,452,380	3,157,785	69,975	192,000	36,535	11,965
Females							
Winnipeg	237,790	12,745	76,895	1,345	7,200	480	160
Manitoba	437,905	21,945	132,315	2,005	9,910	710	205
Canada	9,513,750	3,602,590	3,409,895	74,710	204,330	37,890	12,130
Percent of Population							
Total							
Winnipeg	71.4	3.6	22.3	0.4	2.1	0.1	0.0
Manitoba	72.9	3.5	21.5	0.3	1.6	0.1	0.0
Canada	56.9	21.3	19.8	0.4	1.2	0.2	0.1
Males							
Winnipeg	72.3	3.4	21.8	0.4	2.0	0.1	0.0
Manitoba	73.5	3.4	21.1	0.3	1.5	0.1	0.0
Canada	57.5	21.2	19.4	0.4	1.2	0.2	0.1
Females							
Winnipeg	70.6	3.8	22.8	0.4	2.1	0.1	0.0
Manitoba	72.4	3.6	21.9	0.3	1.6	0.1	0.0
Canada	56.4	21.4	20.2	0.4	1.2	0.2	0.1

Note: Figures cover total population excluding institutional residents.
Source: Statistics Canada. 2012. Census Profile. 2011 Census. Statistics Canada Catalogue no. 98-316-XWE. Ottawa. Released October 24 2012.
http://www12.statcan.gc.ca/census-recensement/2011/dp-pd/prof/index.cfm?Lang=E

Language Spoken Most Often at Home

Area	English	French	Non-official Language	English & French	English & Non-official Language	French & Non-official Language	English, French & Non-official Language
			Number				
			Total				
Winnipeg	543,440	9,700	70,060	1,640	29,880	460	415
Manitoba	1,007,325	17,950	125,280	2,485	38,935	635	485
Canada	21,457,075	6,827,865	3,673,865	131,205	875,135	109,700	46,330
			Males				
Winnipeg	265,310	4,185	33,820	740	14,485	225	215
Manitoba	497,620	8,180	61,670	1,140	18,940	295	255
Canada	10,585,620	3,348,235	1,767,310	63,475	425,370	53,010	22,845
			Females				
Winnipeg	278,130	5,515	36,240	905	15,400	235	195
Manitoba	509,710	9,775	63,615	1,345	19,990	335	230
Canada	10,871,455	3,479,625	1,906,555	67,730	449,765	56,690	23,485
			Percent of Population				
			Total				
Winnipeg	82.9	1.5	10.7	0.3	4.6	0.1	0.1
Manitoba	84.4	1.5	10.5	0.2	3.3	0.1	0.0
Canada	64.8	20.6	11.1	0.4	2.6	0.3	0.1
			Males				
Winnipeg	83.2	1.3	10.6	0.2	4.5	0.1	0.1
Manitoba	84.6	1.4	10.5	0.2	3.2	0.1	0.0
Canada	65.1	20.6	10.9	0.4	2.6	0.3	0.1
			Females				
Winnipeg	82.6	1.6	10.8	0.3	4.6	0.1	0.1
Manitoba	84.3	1.6	10.5	0.2	3.3	0.1	0.0
Canada	64.5	20.6	11.3	0.4	2.7	0.3	0.1

Note: Figures cover total population excluding institutional residents.
Source: Statistics Canada. 2012. Census Profile. 2011 Census. Statistics Canada Catalogue no. 98-316-XWE. Ottawa. Released October 24 2012.
http://www12.statcan.gc.ca/census-recensement/2011/dp-pd/prof/index.cfm?Lang=E

Knowledge of Official Languages

Area	English Only	French Only	English & French	Neither English nor French
		Number		
		Total		
Winnipeg	578,905	930	67,280	8,485
Manitoba	1,074,335	1,490	103,140	14,135
Canada	22,564,665	4,165,015	5,795,570	595,920
		Males		
Winnipeg	285,135	410	29,920	3,510
Manitoba	534,555	670	46,720	6,150
Canada	11,222,185	1,925,340	2,876,560	241,790
		Females		
Winnipeg	293,775	520	37,360	4,970
Manitoba	539,775	820	56,420	7,980
Canada	11,342,485	2,239,680	2,919,005	354,135
		Percent of Population		
		Total		
Winnipeg	88.3	0.1	10.3	1.3
Manitoba	90.0	0.1	8.6	1.2
Canada	68.1	12.6	17.5	1.8
		Males		
Winnipeg	89.4	0.1	9.4	1.1
Manitoba	90.9	0.1	7.9	1.0
Canada	69.0	11.8	17.7	1.5
		Females		
Winnipeg	87.3	0.2	11.1	1.5
Manitoba	89.2	0.1	9.3	1.3
Canada	67.3	13.3	17.3	2.1

Note: Figures cover total population excluding institutional residents.
Source: Statistics Canada. 2012. Census Profile. 2011 Census. Statistics Canada Catalogue no. 98-316-XWE. Ottawa. Released October 24 2012.
http://www12.statcan.gc.ca/census-recensement/2011/dp-pd/prof/index.cfm?Lang=E

Ranking Tables

Cities Ranked by Population, Population Growth, and Population Density

Population in 2011

Rank	City	Number
1	Toronto, ON	2,615,060
2	Montréal, QC	1,649,519
3	Calgary, AB	1,096,833
4	Ottawa, ON	883,391
5	Edmonton, AB	812,201
6	Mississauga, ON	713,443
7	Winnipeg, MB	663,617
8	Vancouver, BC	603,502
9	Brampton, ON	523,911
10	Hamilton, ON	519,949
11	Québec, QC	516,622
12	Surrey, BC	468,251
13	Laval, QC	401,553
14	Halifax, NS	390,096
15	London, ON	366,151
16	Markham, ON	301,709
17	Vaughan, ON	288,301
18	Gatineau, QC	265,349
19	Longueuil, QC	231,409
20	Burnaby, BC	223,218
21	Saskatoon, SK	222,189
22	Kitchener, ON	219,153
23	Windsor, ON	210,891
24	Regina, SK	193,100
25	Richmond, BC	190,473
26	Richmond Hill, ON	185,541
27	Oakville, ON	182,520
28	Burlington, ON	175,779
29	Greater Sudbury, ON	160,274
30	Sherbrooke, QC	154,601
31	Oshawa, ON	149,607
32	Saguenay, QC	144,746
33	Lévis, QC	138,769
34	Barrie, ON	135,711
35	Abbotsford, BC	133,497
36	St. Catharines, ON	131,400
37	Trois-Rivières, QC	131,338
38	Cambridge, ON	126,748
39	Coquitlam, BC	126,456
40	Kingston, ON	123,363
41	Whitby, ON	122,022
42	Guelph, ON	121,688
43	Kelowna, BC	117,312
44	Saanich, BC	109,752
45	Ajax, ON	109,600
46	Thunder Bay, ON	108,359
47	Terrebonne, QC	106,322
48	St. John's, NL	106,172
49	Langley, BC	104,177
50	Chatham-Kent, ON	103,671
–	Canada	33,476,688

Population Growth 2006–2011

Rank	City	Number
1	Ajax, ON	21.6%
2	Brampton, ON	20.8%
3	Vaughan, ON	20.7%
4	Surrey, BC	18.6%
5	Markham, ON	15.3%
6	Richmond Hill, ON	14.0%
7	Terrebonne, QC	12.3%
8	Edmonton, AB	11.2%
8	Langley, BC	11.2%
10	Calgary, AB	10.9%
11	Coquitlam, BC	10.4%
12	Oakville, ON	10.2%
13	Burnaby, BC	10.1%
14	Saskatoon, SK	9.8%
15	Whitby, ON	9.7%
16	Gatineau, QC	9.6%
16	Kelowna, BC	9.6%
18	Richmond, BC	9.2%
19	Laval, QC	8.9%
20	Ottawa, ON	8.8%
21	Regina, SK	7.7%
22	Abbotsford, BC	7.4%
23	Kitchener, ON	7.1%
24	Burlington, ON	6.9%
25	Lévis, QC	6.7%
25	Mississauga, ON	6.7%
27	Guelph, ON	5.9%
28	Barrie, ON	5.7%
28	Oshawa, ON	5.7%
30	St. John's, NL	5.5%
31	Cambridge, ON	5.3%
31	Kingston, ON	5.3%
33	Québec, QC	5.2%
34	Sherbrooke, QC	4.9%
35	Winnipeg, MB	4.8%
36	Halifax, NS	4.7%
37	Toronto, ON	4.5%
38	Vancouver, BC	4.4%
39	Trois-Rivières, QC	4.0%
40	London, ON	3.9%
41	Hamilton, ON	3.1%
42	Montréal, QC	1.8%
43	Greater Sudbury, ON	1.5%
44	Saanich, BC	1.4%
45	Longueuil, QC	0.9%
46	Saguenay, QC	0.7%
47	St. Catharines, ON	-0.4%
48	Thunder Bay, ON	-0.7%
49	Windsor, ON	-2.6%
50	Chatham-Kent, ON	-4.2%
–	Canada	5.9%

Population Density per sq. km

Rank	City	Number
1	Vancouver, BC	5,249.1
2	Montréal, QC	4,517.6
3	Toronto, ON	4,149.5
4	Burnaby, BC	2,463.5
5	Mississauga, ON	2,439.9
6	Longueuil, QC	2,002.0
7	Brampton, ON	1,967.1
8	Richmond Hill, ON	1,838.0
9	Barrie, ON	1,753.6
10	Ajax, ON	1,634.2
11	Laval, QC	1,625.1
12	Kitchener, ON	1,602.1
13	Surrey, BC	1,479.9
14	Richmond, BC	1,473.5
15	Windsor, ON	1,441.3
16	Winnipeg, MB	1,430.0
17	Markham, ON	1,419.3
18	Guelph, ON	1,395.4
19	St. Catharines, ON	1,367.2
20	Calgary, AB	1,329.0
21	Regina, SK	1,327.6
22	Oakville, ON	1,314.2
23	Edmonton, AB	1,186.8
24	Québec, QC	1,137.7
25	Cambridge, ON	1,121.7
26	Saskatoon, SK	1,060.3
27	Saanich, BC	1,057.6
28	Vaughan, ON	1,054.0
29	Coquitlam, BC	1,034.0
30	Oshawa, ON	1,027.0
31	Burlington, ON	946.8
32	London, ON	870.6
33	Whitby, ON	832.7
34	Gatineau, QC	773.7
35	Terrebonne, QC	687.1
36	Kelowna, BC	553.8
37	Hamilton, ON	465.4
38	Trois-Rivières, QC	454.6
39	Sherbrooke, QC	437.4
40	Abbotsford, BC	355.5
41	Langley, BC	338.2
42	Thunder Bay, ON	330.1
43	Ottawa, ON	316.6
44	Lévis, QC	308.8
45	Kingston, ON	273.4
46	St. John's, NL	238.0
47	Saguenay, QC	128.5
48	Halifax, NS	71.1
49	Greater Sudbury, ON	49.7
50	Chatham-Kent, ON	42.2
–	Canada	3.7

Source: Statistics Canada. 2012. Census Profile. 2011 Census. Statistics Canada Catalogue no. 98-316-XWE. Ottawa. Released October 24 2012.
http://www12.statcan.gc.ca/census-recensement/2011/dp-pd/prof/index.cfm?Lang=E

Cities Ranked by Median Age

Total

Rank	City	Years
1	Trois-Rivières, QC	45.9
2	Saguenay, QC	45.6
3	Saanich, BC	44.0
4	Chatham-Kent, ON	43.9
5	Québec, QC	43.5
5	St. Catharines, ON	43.5
7	Thunder Bay, ON	43.3
8	Kelowna, BC	43.0
9	Greater Sudbury, ON	42.3
10	Richmond, BC	42.1
11	Longueuil, QC	41.9
12	Burlington, ON	41.8
13	Hamilton, ON	40.9
13	Laval, QC	40.9
15	Lévis, QC	40.7
16	Oshawa, ON	40.6
17	Coquitlam, BC	40.3
17	Kingston, ON	40.3
17	Langley, BC	40.3
20	Oakville, ON	40.2
20	Sherbrooke, QC	40.2
22	Windsor, ON	40.1
23	Halifax, NS	39.9
23	St. John's, NL	39.9
25	Burnaby, BC	39.8
25	Richmond Hill, ON	39.8
27	Vancouver, BC	39.7
28	Markham, ON	39.6
29	London, ON	39.3
30	Ottawa, ON	39.2
30	Toronto, ON	39.2
32	Winnipeg, MB	39.0
33	Montréal, QC	38.6
34	Mississauga, ON	38.5
35	Gatineau, QC	38.4
36	Cambridge, ON	38.0
37	Abbotsford, BC	37.9
37	Vaughan, ON	37.9
39	Guelph, ON	37.7
40	Whitby, ON	37.6
41	Surrey, BC	37.5
42	Barrie, ON	37.2
42	Kitchener, ON	37.2
44	Regina, SK	37.1
44	Terrebonne, QC	37.1
46	Calgary, AB	36.4
47	Ajax, ON	36.2
48	Edmonton, AB	36.0
49	Saskatoon, SK	35.6
50	Brampton, ON	34.7
–	Canada	40.6

Male

Rank	City	Years
1	Saguenay, QC	43.9
1	Trois-Rivières, QC	43.9
3	Chatham-Kent, ON	42.6
4	Saanich, BC	42.2
4	Thunder Bay, ON	42.2
6	St. Catharines, ON	41.8
7	Kelowna, BC	41.3
8	Québec, QC	41.2
9	Greater Sudbury, ON	41.1
10	Richmond, BC	40.9
11	Burlington, ON	40.5
12	Longueuil, QC	40.4
13	Laval, QC	40.0
14	Hamilton, ON	39.7
15	Lévis, QC	39.6
16	Langley, BC	39.5
16	Oakville, ON	39.5
18	Oshawa, ON	39.4
19	Coquitlam, BC	39.3
20	Windsor, ON	39.2
21	Vancouver, BC	39.1
22	Halifax, NS	38.8
22	Richmond Hill, ON	38.8
24	Burnaby, BC	38.6
24	Markham, ON	38.6
26	Kingston, ON	38.3
27	Ottawa, ON	38.2
27	Toronto, ON	38.2
29	Sherbrooke, QC	38.0
29	St. John's, NL	38.0
31	London, ON	37.7
32	Mississauga, ON	37.6
32	Montréal, QC	37.6
32	Winnipeg, MB	37.6
35	Cambridge, ON	37.3
35	Gatineau, QC	37.3
37	Vaughan, ON	37.2
38	Surrey, BC	36.8
39	Abbotsford, BC	36.7
39	Whitby, ON	36.7
41	Guelph, ON	36.6
41	Terrebonne, QC	36.6
43	Kitchener, ON	36.3
44	Barrie, ON	36.0
45	Calgary, AB	35.9
46	Regina, SK	35.7
47	Ajax, ON	35.3
47	Edmonton, AB	35.3
49	Saskatoon, SK	34.2
50	Brampton, ON	34.1
–	Canada	39.6

Female

Rank	City	Years
1	Trois-Rivières, QC	47.5
2	Saguenay, QC	46.9
3	Québec, QC	45.7
4	Saanich, BC	45.6
5	Chatham-Kent, ON	45.1
5	St. Catharines, ON	45.1
7	Kelowna, BC	44.8
8	Thunder Bay, ON	44.4
9	Greater Sudbury, ON	43.5
9	Longueuil, QC	43.5
11	Burlington, ON	43.0
11	Richmond, BC	43.0
13	Sherbrooke, QC	42.3
14	Kingston, ON	42.1
15	Hamilton, ON	42.0
16	Laval, QC	41.8
16	Lévis, QC	41.8
18	Oshawa, ON	41.7
19	St. John's, NL	41.5
20	Coquitlam, BC	41.2
21	Langley, BC	41.0
21	Windsor, ON	41.0
23	Halifax, NS	40.9
24	Burnaby, BC	40.8
25	London, ON	40.7
25	Oakville, ON	40.7
27	Richmond Hill, ON	40.6
28	Markham, ON	40.5
29	Winnipeg, MB	40.3
30	Vancouver, BC	40.2
31	Toronto, ON	40.1
32	Ottawa, ON	40.0
33	Montréal, QC	39.7
34	Gatineau, QC	39.4
35	Mississauga, ON	39.3
36	Abbotsford, BC	38.9
37	Cambridge, ON	38.7
37	Guelph, ON	38.7
39	Regina, SK	38.5
39	Vaughan, ON	38.5
41	Whitby, ON	38.4
42	Barrie, ON	38.3
43	Surrey, BC	38.2
44	Kitchener, ON	38.1
45	Terrebonne, QC	37.5
46	Saskatoon, SK	37.0
47	Ajax, ON	36.9
47	Edmonton, AB	36.9
49	Calgary, AB	36.8
50	Brampton, ON	35.3
–	Canada	41.5

Source: Statistics Canada. 2012. Census Profile. 2011 Census. Statistics Canada Catalogue no. 98-316-XWE. Ottawa. Released October 24 2012. http://www12.statcan.gc.ca/census-recensement/2011/dp-pd/prof/index.cfm?Lang=E

Cities Ranked by Household Size: 1 Person

	Households			Percent of Households	
Rank	City	Number	Rank	City	Percent
1	Toronto, ON	331,180	1	Montréal, QC	40.7%
2	Montréal, QC	309,220	2	Québec, QC	38.6%
3	Calgary, AB	110,005	3	Vancouver, BC	38.3%
4	Vancouver, BC	101,205	4	Trois-Rivières, QC	37.7%
5	Ottawa, ON	99,905	5	Sherbrooke, QC	37.3%
6	Edmonton, AB	94,910	6	Longueuil, QC	33.7%
7	Québec, QC	94,685	7	Thunder Bay, ON	32.8%
8	Winnipeg, MB	83,515	8	Windsor, ON	32.5%
9	Hamilton, ON	56,930	9	Saguenay, QC	31.8%
10	London, ON	47,515	10	Toronto, ON	31.6%
11	Halifax, NS	47,140	11	Kingston, ON	31.5%
12	Mississauga, ON	41,625	12	Winnipeg, MB	31.1%
13	Laval, QC	39,930	13	Gatineau, QC	30.9%
14	Gatineau, QC	34,830	13	London, ON	30.9%
15	Longueuil, QC	34,380	15	St. Catharines, ON	30.5%
16	Surrey, BC	30,145	16	Regina, SK	29.9%
17	Windsor, ON	28,510	17	Saskatoon, SK	29.5%
18	Saskatoon, SK	26,835	18	Kelowna, BC	29.4%
19	Sherbrooke, QC	26,355	19	Edmonton, AB	29.2%
20	Regina, SK	23,795	20	St. John's, NL	29.1%
21	Burnaby, BC	23,650	21	Halifax, NS	28.6%
22	Trois-Rivières, QC	23,125	22	Greater Sudbury, ON	28.4%
23	Kitchener, ON	22,970	23	Ottawa, ON	28.3%
24	Saguenay, QC	20,425	24	Chatham-Kent, ON	28.0%
25	Greater Sudbury, ON	19,165	25	Hamilton, ON	27.9%
26	Brampton, ON	18,050	26	Lévis, QC	27.5%
27	Burlington, ON	16,940	27	Saanich, BC	27.4%
28	St. Catharines, ON	16,880	28	Burnaby, BC	27.2%
29	Kingston, ON	16,490	29	Kitchener, ON	26.6%
30	Lévis, QC	15,890	30	Guelph, ON	26.5%
31	Thunder Bay, ON	15,415	31	Calgary, AB	26.0%
32	Oshawa, ON	14,845	32	Laval, QC	25.9%
33	Kelowna, BC	14,625	33	Oshawa, ON	25.2%
34	Richmond, BC	14,175	34	Burlington, ON	24.6%
35	St. John's, NL	13,080	35	Abbotsford, BC	23.6%
36	Guelph, ON	12,750	36	Barrie, ON	21.9%
37	Saanich, BC	12,435	37	Cambridge, ON	21.6%
38	Chatham-Kent, ON	12,010	38	Coquitlam, BC	21.4%
39	Barrie, ON	10,960	39	Richmond, BC	20.9%
40	Abbotsford, BC	10,950	40	Langley, BC	19.8%
41	Oakville, ON	10,885	41	Surrey, BC	19.7%
42	Markham, ON	10,225	42	Terrebonne, QC	19.2%
43	Cambridge, ON	10,040	43	Mississauga, ON	17.7%
44	Coquitlam, BC	9,750	44	Oakville, ON	17.4%
45	Vaughan, ON	9,160	45	Whitby, ON	16.5%
46	Richmond Hill, ON	8,115	46	Ajax, ON	14.4%
47	Terrebonne, QC	7,560	47	Richmond Hill, ON	13.8%
48	Langley, BC	7,360	48	Brampton, ON	12.1%
49	Whitby, ON	6,775	49	Markham, ON	11.3%
50	Ajax, ON	5,055	50	Vaughan, ON	10.6%
–	Canada	3,673,310	–	Canada	27.6%

Source: Statistics Canada. 2012. Census Profile. 2011 Census. Statistics Canada Catalogue no. 98-316-XWE. Ottawa. Released October 24 2012.
http://www12.statcan.gc.ca/census-recensement/2011/dp-pd/prof/index.cfm?Lang=E

Cities Ranked by Household Size: 2 Persons

	Households			Percent of Households	
Rank	City	Number	Rank	City	Percent
1	Toronto, ON	307,845	1	Kelowna, BC	38.4%
2	Montréal, QC	230,245	2	Saguenay, QC	38.0%
3	Calgary, AB	136,260	3	Chatham-Kent, ON	37.7%
4	Ottawa, ON	116,385	4	Saanich, BC	37.2%
5	Edmonton, AB	105,815	5	Lévis, QC	37.1%
6	Québec, QC	87,800	6	Greater Sudbury, ON	36.5%
7	Winnipeg, MB	85,495	6	Halifax, NS	36.5%
8	Vancouver, BC	81,465	8	Trois-Rivières, QC	36.3%
9	Hamilton, ON	65,185	9	Kingston, ON	36.0%
10	Halifax, NS	60,235	10	Québec, QC	35.8%
11	Mississauga, ON	59,990	10	St. John's, NL	35.8%
12	London, ON	51,955	12	St. Catharines, ON	35.5%
13	Laval, QC	49,790	13	Sherbrooke, QC	34.8%
14	Surrey, BC	42,950	14	Thunder Bay, ON	34.5%
15	Gatineau, QC	37,905	15	Burlington, ON	34.3%
16	Longueuil, QC	34,890	16	Longueuil, QC	34.2%
17	Brampton, ON	31,520	16	Saskatoon, SK	34.2%
18	Saskatoon, SK	31,065	18	Regina, SK	34.1%
19	Kitchener, ON	28,550	19	London, ON	33.8%
20	Windsor, ON	27,675	19	Oshawa, ON	33.8%
21	Regina, SK	27,130	21	Gatineau, QC	33.6%
22	Burnaby, BC	26,860	21	Terrebonne, QC	33.6%
23	Greater Sudbury, ON	24,685	23	Kitchener, ON	33.1%
24	Sherbrooke, QC	24,555	24	Langley, BC	33.0%
25	Saguenay, QC	24,400	25	Ottawa, ON	32.9%
26	Burlington, ON	23,610	26	Guelph, ON	32.7%
27	Trois-Rivières, QC	22,260	27	Edmonton, AB	32.6%
28	Lévis, QC	21,420	28	Calgary, AB	32.2%
29	Markham, ON	21,285	28	Laval, QC	32.2%
30	Vaughan, ON	19,935	30	Barrie, ON	32.0%
31	Oshawa, ON	19,885	30	Hamilton, ON	32.0%
32	Richmond, BC	19,830	32	Winnipeg, MB	31.8%
33	St. Catharines, ON	19,655	33	Cambridge, ON	31.7%
34	Kelowna, BC	19,065	34	Abbotsford, BC	31.6%
35	Kingston, ON	18,850	35	Windsor, ON	31.5%
36	Oakville, ON	18,070	36	Burnaby, BC	30.9%
37	Saanich, BC	16,880	37	Vancouver, BC	30.8%
38	Thunder Bay, ON	16,210	38	Montréal, QC	30.3%
39	Chatham-Kent, ON	16,155	39	Coquitlam, BC	29.4%
40	St. John's, NL	16,110	39	Toronto, ON	29.4%
41	Barrie, ON	15,975	41	Richmond, BC	29.2%
42	Guelph, ON	15,725	42	Oakville, ON	29.0%
43	Cambridge, ON	14,730	43	Surrey, BC	28.1%
44	Abbotsford, BC	14,660	43	Whitby, ON	28.1%
45	Richmond Hill, ON	13,820	45	Mississauga, ON	25.6%
46	Coquitlam, BC	13,400	46	Ajax, ON	25.2%
47	Terrebonne, QC	13,220	47	Richmond Hill, ON	23.6%
48	Langley, BC	12,305	48	Markham, ON	23.5%
49	Whitby, ON	11,540	49	Vaughan, ON	23.2%
50	Ajax, ON	8,815	50	Brampton, ON	21.1%
–	Canada	4,544,820	–	Canada	34.1%

Source: Statistics Canada. 2012. Census Profile. 2011 Census. Statistics Canada Catalogue no. 98-316-XWE. Ottawa. Released October 24 2012.
http://www12.statcan.gc.ca/census-recensement/2011/dp-pd/prof/index.cfm?Lang=E

Cities Ranked by Household Size: 3 Persons

Households

Rank	City	Number
1	Toronto, ON	168,750
2	Montréal, QC	102,630
3	Calgary, AB	70,975
4	Ottawa, ON	55,635
5	Edmonton, AB	51,940
6	Mississauga, ON	45,775
7	Winnipeg, MB	40,425
8	Vancouver, BC	34,770
9	Hamilton, ON	32,465
10	Québec, QC	30,920
11	Brampton, ON	27,825
12	Halifax, NS	26,980
13	Laval, QC	25,405
14	Surrey, BC	25,100
15	London, ON	23,115
16	Markham, ON	19,340
17	Gatineau, QC	18,445
18	Vaughan, ON	17,160
19	Burnaby, BC	15,580
20	Longueuil, QC	15,490
21	Kitchener, ON	14,525
22	Richmond, BC	13,920
23	Saskatoon, SK	13,830
24	Windsor, ON	13,360
25	Richmond Hill, ON	12,785
26	Regina, SK	12,180
27	Oakville, ON	11,170
28	Burlington, ON	11,025
29	Greater Sudbury, ON	10,735
30	Oshawa, ON	10,410
31	Saguenay, QC	9,235
32	Barrie, ON	8,925
33	Sherbrooke, QC	8,820
34	Lévis, QC	8,795
35	Coquitlam, BC	8,610
36	Cambridge, ON	8,400
37	St. Catharines, ON	8,265
38	Guelph, ON	7,985
39	Whitby, ON	7,865
40	St. John's, NL	7,830
41	Trois-Rivières, QC	7,710
42	Kingston, ON	7,705
43	Terrebonne, QC	7,615
44	Ajax, ON	7,125
45	Saanich, BC	7,075
46	Thunder Bay, ON	6,910
47	Kelowna, BC	6,795
48	Abbotsford, BC	6,635
49	Langley, BC	6,220
50	Chatham-Kent, ON	6,180
–	Canada	2,081,900

Percent of Households

Rank	City	Percent
1	Richmond Hill, ON	21.8%
2	Markham, ON	21.4%
3	Richmond, BC	20.5%
4	Ajax, ON	20.3%
5	Vaughan, ON	19.9%
6	Mississauga, ON	19.5%
7	Terrebonne, QC	19.3%
8	Whitby, ON	19.2%
9	Coquitlam, BC	18.9%
10	Brampton, ON	18.6%
11	Cambridge, ON	18.1%
12	Barrie, ON	17.9%
12	Burnaby, BC	17.9%
12	Oakville, ON	17.9%
15	Oshawa, ON	17.7%
16	St. John's, NL	17.4%
17	Calgary, AB	16.8%
17	Kitchener, ON	16.8%
19	Langley, BC	16.7%
20	Guelph, ON	16.6%
21	Gatineau, QC	16.4%
21	Laval, QC	16.4%
21	Surrey, BC	16.4%
24	Halifax, NS	16.3%
25	Toronto, ON	16.1%
26	Burlington, ON	16.0%
26	Edmonton, AB	16.0%
28	Greater Sudbury, ON	15.9%
28	Hamilton, ON	15.9%
30	Ottawa, ON	15.7%
31	Saanich, BC	15.6%
32	Regina, SK	15.3%
33	Longueuil, QC	15.2%
33	Lévis, QC	15.2%
33	Saskatoon, SK	15.2%
33	Windsor, ON	15.2%
37	London, ON	15.0%
37	Winnipeg, MB	15.0%
39	St. Catharines, ON	14.9%
40	Kingston, ON	14.7%
40	Thunder Bay, ON	14.7%
42	Chatham-Kent, ON	14.4%
42	Saguenay, QC	14.4%
44	Abbotsford, BC	14.3%
45	Kelowna, BC	13.7%
46	Montréal, QC	13.5%
47	Vancouver, BC	13.1%
48	Québec, QC	12.6%
48	Trois-Rivières, QC	12.6%
50	Sherbrooke, QC	12.5%
–	Canada	15.6%

Source: Statistics Canada. 2012. Census Profile. 2011 Census. Statistics Canada Catalogue no. 98-316-XWE. Ottawa. Released October 24 2012.
http://www12.statcan.gc.ca/census-recensement/2011/dp-pd/prof/index.cfm?Lang=E

Cities Ranked by Household Size: 4 Persons

Households

Rank	City	Number
1	Toronto, ON	142,760
2	Montréal, QC	76,260
3	Calgary, AB	66,935
4	Ottawa, ON	52,880
5	Mississauga, ON	50,575
6	Edmonton, AB	43,960
7	Winnipeg, MB	36,690
8	Brampton, ON	35,720
9	Hamilton, ON	30,865
10	Vancouver, BC	28,070
11	Surrey, BC	27,760
12	Laval, QC	25,840
13	Vaughan, ON	23,400
14	Québec, QC	23,310
15	Markham, ON	22,425
16	Halifax, NS	21,220
17	London, ON	20,300
18	Gatineau, QC	14,885
19	Richmond Hill, ON	14,730
20	Oakville, ON	14,625
21	Kitchener, ON	13,095
22	Burnaby, BC	12,930
23	Richmond, BC	12,145
24	Saskatoon, SK	12,075
25	Burlington, ON	11,825
26	Longueuil, QC	11,655
27	Windsor, ON	11,250
28	Regina, SK	10,695
29	Whitby, ON	9,615
30	Greater Sudbury, ON	9,310
31	Coquitlam, BC	9,075
32	Barrie, ON	9,025
33	Oshawa, ON	8,710
34	Lévis, QC	8,540
35	Cambridge, ON	8,460
36	Ajax, ON	8,305
37	Guelph, ON	7,705
38	Terrebonne, QC	7,595
39	Sherbrooke, QC	7,370
40	Saguenay, QC	7,320
41	Langley, BC	6,995
42	Abbotsford, BC	6,990
43	St. Catharines, ON	6,945
44	Kingston, ON	6,390
45	Trois-Rivières, QC	6,050
46	Saanich, BC	5,990
47	Kelowna, BC	5,985
48	Thunder Bay, ON	5,745
49	St. John's, NL	5,715
50	Chatham-Kent, ON	5,460
–	Canada	1,903,300

Percent of Households

Rank	City	Percent
1	Vaughan, ON	27.2%
2	Richmond Hill, ON	25.1%
3	Markham, ON	24.8%
4	Brampton, ON	23.9%
5	Ajax, ON	23.7%
6	Oakville, ON	23.4%
6	Whitby, ON	23.4%
8	Mississauga, ON	21.6%
9	Coquitlam, BC	19.9%
10	Terrebonne, QC	19.3%
11	Langley, BC	18.8%
12	Cambridge, ON	18.2%
12	Surrey, BC	18.2%
14	Barrie, ON	18.1%
15	Richmond, BC	17.9%
16	Burlington, ON	17.2%
17	Laval, QC	16.7%
18	Guelph, ON	16.0%
19	Calgary, AB	15.8%
20	Kitchener, ON	15.2%
21	Hamilton, ON	15.1%
22	Abbotsford, BC	15.0%
22	Ottawa, ON	15.0%
24	Burnaby, BC	14.9%
25	Lévis, QC	14.8%
25	Oshawa, ON	14.8%
27	Greater Sudbury, ON	13.8%
28	Winnipeg, MB	13.7%
29	Toronto, ON	13.6%
30	Edmonton, AB	13.5%
31	Regina, SK	13.4%
32	Saskatoon, SK	13.3%
33	Gatineau, QC	13.2%
33	London, ON	13.2%
33	Saanich, BC	13.2%
36	Halifax, NS	12.9%
37	Windsor, ON	12.8%
38	Chatham-Kent, ON	12.7%
38	St. John's, NL	12.7%
40	St. Catharines, ON	12.5%
41	Kingston, ON	12.2%
41	Thunder Bay, ON	12.2%
43	Kelowna, BC	12.0%
44	Longueuil, QC	11.4%
44	Saguenay, QC	11.4%
46	Vancouver, BC	10.6%
47	Sherbrooke, QC	10.4%
48	Montréal, QC	10.0%
49	Trois-Rivières, QC	9.9%
50	Québec, QC	9.5%
–	Canada	14.3%

Source: Statistics Canada. 2012. Census Profile. 2011 Census. Statistics Canada Catalogue no. 98-316-XWE. Ottawa. Released October 24 2012.
http://www12.statcan.gc.ca/census-recensement/2011/dp-pd/prof/index.cfm?Lang=E

Cities Ranked by Household Size: 5 Persons

Households

Rank	City	Number
1	Toronto, ON	59,005
2	Montréal, QC	27,910
3	Calgary, AB	25,145
4	Mississauga, ON	22,145
5	Ottawa, ON	19,185
6	Brampton, ON	18,590
7	Edmonton, AB	17,635
8	Winnipeg, MB	14,295
9	Surrey, BC	13,625
10	Hamilton, ON	12,035
11	Vancouver, BC	10,985
12	Vaughan, ON	10,395
13	Markham, ON	9,845
14	Laval, QC	9,365
15	London, ON	7,420
16	Halifax, NS	6,830
17	Québec, QC	6,455
18	Richmond Hill, ON	5,840
19	Oakville, ON	5,525
20	Gatineau, QC	4,825
21	Kitchener, ON	4,800
22	Saskatoon, SK	4,740
23	Burnaby, BC	4,710
24	Richmond, BC	4,625
25	Windsor, ON	4,465
26	Longueuil, QC	3,970
27	Burlington, ON	3,880
28	Regina, SK	3,805
29	Abbotsford, BC	3,720
30	Ajax, ON	3,660
31	Whitby, ON	3,655
32	Barrie, ON	3,530
33	Oshawa, ON	3,365
34	Cambridge, ON	3,265
35	Coquitlam, BC	3,065
36	Greater Sudbury, ON	2,775
37	Langley, BC	2,705
38	Guelph, ON	2,700
39	St. Catharines, ON	2,575
40	Sherbrooke, QC	2,495
41	Lévis, QC	2,440
42	Terrebonne, QC	2,415
43	Kelowna, BC	2,185
44	Saguenay, QC	2,170
45	Kingston, ON	2,155
46	Saanich, BC	2,065
47	Chatham-Kent, ON	1,980
48	Thunder Bay, ON	1,920
49	St. John's, NL	1,705
50	Trois-Rivières, QC	1,690
–	Canada	724,405

Percent of Households

Rank	City	Percent
1	Brampton, ON	12.5%
2	Vaughan, ON	12.1%
3	Markham, ON	10.9%
4	Ajax, ON	10.4%
5	Richmond Hill, ON	10.0%
6	Mississauga, ON	9.4%
7	Oakville, ON	8.9%
7	Surrey, BC	8.9%
7	Whitby, ON	8.9%
10	Abbotsford, BC	8.0%
11	Langley, BC	7.3%
12	Barrie, ON	7.1%
13	Cambridge, ON	7.0%
14	Richmond, BC	6.8%
15	Coquitlam, BC	6.7%
16	Laval, QC	6.1%
16	Terrebonne, QC	6.1%
18	Calgary, AB	5.9%
18	Hamilton, ON	5.9%
20	Oshawa, ON	5.7%
21	Burlington, ON	5.6%
21	Guelph, ON	5.6%
21	Kitchener, ON	5.6%
21	Toronto, ON	5.6%
25	Burnaby, BC	5.4%
25	Edmonton, AB	5.4%
25	Ottawa, ON	5.4%
28	Winnipeg, MB	5.3%
29	Saskatoon, SK	5.2%
30	Windsor, ON	5.1%
31	London, ON	4.8%
31	Regina, SK	4.8%
33	Chatham-Kent, ON	4.6%
33	St. Catharines, ON	4.6%
35	Saanich, BC	4.5%
36	Kelowna, BC	4.4%
37	Gatineau, QC	4.3%
38	Lévis, QC	4.2%
38	Vancouver, BC	4.2%
40	Greater Sudbury, ON	4.1%
40	Halifax, NS	4.1%
40	Kingston, ON	4.1%
40	Thunder Bay, ON	4.1%
44	Longueuil, QC	3.9%
45	St. John's, NL	3.8%
46	Montréal, QC	3.7%
47	Sherbrooke, QC	3.5%
48	Saguenay, QC	3.4%
49	Trois-Rivières, QC	2.8%
50	Québec, QC	2.6%
–	Canada	5.4%

Source: Statistics Canada. 2012. Census Profile. 2011 Census. Statistics Canada Catalogue no. 98-316-XWE. Ottawa. Released October 24 2012.
http://www12.statcan.gc.ca/census-recensement/2011/dp-pd/prof/index.cfm?Lang=E

Cities Ranked by Household Size: 6 or More Persons

	Households				Percent of Households	
Rank	City	Number		Rank	City	Percent
1	Toronto, ON	38,340		1	Brampton, ON	11.8%
2	Brampton, ON	17,570		2	Surrey, BC	8.7%
3	Mississauga, ON	14,475		3	Markham, ON	8.2%
4	Calgary, AB	14,100		4	Abbotsford, BC	7.5%
5	Montréal, QC	13,685		5	Vaughan, ON	7.0%
6	Surrey, BC	13,275		6	Mississauga, ON	6.2%
7	Edmonton, AB	10,495		7	Ajax, ON	5.9%
8	Ottawa, ON	9,250		8	Richmond Hill, ON	5.7%
9	Winnipeg, MB	8,320		9	Richmond, BC	4.8%
10	Vancouver, BC	8,070		10	Langley, BC	4.4%
11	Markham, ON	7,420		11	Whitby, ON	3.8%
12	Hamilton, ON	6,325		12	Toronto, ON	3.7%
13	Vaughan, ON	6,025		13	Burnaby, BC	3.6%
14	Laval, QC	4,125		13	Coquitlam, BC	3.6%
15	Abbotsford, BC	3,495		15	Cambridge, ON	3.4%
16	Richmond Hill, ON	3,355		15	Oakville, ON	3.4%
17	London, ON	3,320		17	Calgary, AB	3.3%
18	Richmond, BC	3,275		18	Edmonton, AB	3.2%
19	Burnaby, BC	3,110		19	Barrie, ON	3.1%
20	Halifax, NS	2,625		19	Hamilton, ON	3.1%
21	Windsor, ON	2,570		19	Vancouver, BC	3.1%
22	Kitchener, ON	2,430		19	Winnipeg, MB	3.1%
23	Saskatoon, SK	2,390		23	Windsor, ON	2.9%
24	Québec, QC	2,190		24	Kitchener, ON	2.8%
25	Oakville, ON	2,135		25	Laval, QC	2.7%
26	Ajax, ON	2,075		25	Oshawa, ON	2.7%
27	Regina, SK	2,000		27	Guelph, ON	2.6%
28	Gatineau, QC	1,870		27	Ottawa, ON	2.6%
29	Longueuil, QC	1,680		27	Saskatoon, SK	2.6%
30	Coquitlam, BC	1,655		30	Chatham-Kent, ON	2.5%
31	Langley, BC	1,645		30	Regina, SK	2.5%
32	Oshawa, ON	1,585		30	Terrebonne, QC	2.5%
33	Whitby, ON	1,575		33	Burlington, ON	2.2%
34	Cambridge, ON	1,570		33	London, ON	2.2%
35	Barrie, ON	1,525		35	Saanich, BC	2.1%
36	Burlington, ON	1,500		36	Kelowna, BC	2.0%
37	Guelph, ON	1,245		36	St. Catharines, ON	2.0%
38	St. Catharines, ON	1,100		38	Montréal, QC	1.8%
39	Chatham-Kent, ON	1,060		39	Gatineau, QC	1.7%
40	Kelowna, BC	1,010		40	Halifax, NS	1.6%
41	Terrebonne, QC	985		40	Kingston, ON	1.6%
42	Sherbrooke, QC	980		40	Longueuil, QC	1.6%
43	Saanich, BC	955		40	Thunder Bay, ON	1.6%
44	Greater Sudbury, ON	930		44	Greater Sudbury, ON	1.4%
45	Kingston, ON	825		44	Sherbrooke, QC	1.4%
46	Thunder Bay, ON	750		46	St. John's, NL	1.3%
47	Lévis, QC	685		47	Lévis, QC	1.2%
48	Saguenay, QC	675		48	Saguenay, QC	1.1%
49	St. John's, NL	585		49	Québec, QC	0.9%
50	Trois-Rivières, QC	555		49	Trois-Rivières, QC	0.9%
–	Canada	392,885		–	Canada	2.9%

Source: Statistics Canada. 2012. Census Profile. 2011 Census. Statistics Canada Catalogue no. 98-316-XWE. Ottawa. Released October 24 2012.
http://www12.statcan.gc.ca/census-recensement/2011/dp-pd/prof/index.cfm?Lang=E

Cities Ranked by Average Number of Persons in Private Households

Rank	City	Average Number
1	Brampton, ON	3.5
2	Markham, ON	3.3
2	Vaughan, ON	3.3
4	Ajax, ON	3.1
4	Richmond Hill, ON	3.1
6	Mississauga, ON	3.0
6	Surrey, BC	3.0
8	Oakville, ON	2.9
8	Whitby, ON	2.9
10	Abbotsford, BC	2.8
10	Langley, BC	2.8
10	Richmond, BC	2.8
13	Barrie, ON	2.7
13	Cambridge, ON	2.7
13	Coquitlam, BC	2.7
13	Terrebonne, QC	2.7
17	Calgary, AB	2.6
18	Burlington, ON	2.5
18	Burnaby, BC	2.5
18	Edmonton, AB	2.5
18	Guelph, ON	2.5
18	Hamilton, ON	2.5
18	Kitchener, ON	2.5
18	Laval, QC	2.5
18	Oshawa, ON	2.5
18	Ottawa, ON	2.5
18	Toronto, ON	2.5
28	Chatham-Kent, ON	2.4
28	Lévis, QC	2.4
28	Regina, SK	2.4
28	Saanich, BC	2.4
28	Saskatoon, SK	2.4
28	Windsor, ON	2.4
28	Winnipeg, MB	2.4
35	Gatineau, QC	2.3
35	Greater Sudbury, ON	2.3
35	Halifax, NS	2.3
35	Kelowna, BC	2.3
35	Kingston, ON	2.3
35	London, ON	2.3
35	St. Catharines, ON	2.3
35	St. John's, NL	2.3
35	Thunder Bay, ON	2.3
44	Longueuil, QC	2.2
44	Saguenay, QC	2.2
44	Vancouver, BC	2.2
47	Montréal, QC	2.1
47	Sherbrooke, QC	2.1
47	Trois-Rivières, QC	2.1
50	Québec, QC	2.0
–	Canada	2.5

Source: Statistics Canada. 2012. Census Profile. 2011 Census. Statistics Canada Catalogue no. 98-316-XWE. Ottawa. Released October 24 2012.
http://www12.statcan.gc.ca/census-recensement/2011/dp-pd/prof/index.cfm?Lang=E

Cities Ranked by Shelter Costs

Median Value of Owned Dwellings[1]

Rank	City	Dollars
1	Vancouver, BC	$752,016
2	Richmond, BC	$601,945
3	Burnaby, BC	$600,941
4	Coquitlam, BC	$599,465
5	Saanich, BC	$598,306
6	Richmond Hill, ON	$550,573
7	Vaughan, ON	$527,560
8	Oakville, ON	$510,886
9	Langley, BC	$501,361
10	Surrey, BC	$500,746
11	Markham, ON	$500,741
12	Kelowna, BC	$415,710
13	Toronto, ON	$401,400
14	Mississauga, ON	$401,175
15	Calgary, AB	$400,697
16	Burlington, ON	$399,402
17	Abbotsford, BC	$393,600
18	Brampton, ON	$359,741
19	Edmonton, AB	$349,154
20	Ottawa, ON	$349,151
21	Whitby, ON	$341,505
22	Montréal, QC	$338,139
23	Ajax, ON	$333,633
24	Saskatoon, SK	$318,012
25	Regina, SK	$299,748
26	Guelph, ON	$299,689
27	Barrie, ON	$276,279
28	Hamilton, ON	$275,620
29	Kitchener, ON	$274,740
30	Cambridge, ON	$269,837
31	Kingston, ON	$264,340
32	Laval, QC	$259,801
33	St. John's, NL	$259,615
34	Longueuil, QC	$249,984
35	Oshawa, ON	$240,415
36	Halifax, NS	$240,409
37	Winnipeg, MB	$240,168
38	Terrebonne, QC	$239,623
39	London, ON	$229,634
40	Québec, QC	$229,482
41	Greater Sudbury, ON	$225,236
42	Lévis, QC	$224,586
43	Gatineau, QC	$219,283
44	St. Catharines, ON	$218,613
45	Sherbrooke, QC	$189,838
46	Saguenay, QC	$174,395
47	Thunder Bay, ON	$159,997
48	Windsor, ON	$151,473
49	Trois-Rivières, QC	$150,221
50	Chatham-Kent, ON	$149,775
–	Canada	$280,552

Median Monthly Costs of Owned Dwellings[2]

Rank	City	Dollars
1	Brampton, ON	$1,666
2	Richmond Hill, ON	$1,660
3	Ajax, ON	$1,650
4	Vaughan, ON	$1,629
5	Whitby, ON	$1,595
6	Oakville, ON	$1,577
7	Mississauga, ON	$1,519
8	Markham, ON	$1,460
9	Barrie, ON	$1,413
10	Surrey, BC	$1,391
11	Langley, BC	$1,381
12	Calgary, AB	$1,366
13	Burlington, ON	$1,328
14	Coquitlam, BC	$1,310
15	Ottawa, ON	$1,307
16	Toronto, ON	$1,304
17	Cambridge, ON	$1,284
18	Oshawa, ON	$1,267
19	Guelph, ON	$1,264
20	Kitchener, ON	$1,250
21	Edmonton, AB	$1,222
22	Abbotsford, BC	$1,204
23	Vancouver, BC	$1,119
24	Terrebonne, QC	$1,109
25	Hamilton, ON	$1,089
26	Gatineau, QC	$1,070
27	Halifax, NS	$1,068
28	Kingston, ON	$1,066
29	Kelowna, BC	$1,064
30	Richmond, BC	$1,047
31	London, ON	$1,045
32	Montréal, QC	$1,041
33	Laval, QC	$1,036
34	Saskatoon, SK	$1,034
35	Burnaby, BC	$1,030
36	Greater Sudbury, ON	$1,002
37	St. John's, NL	$994
38	Regina, SK	$967
39	St. Catharines, ON	$942
40	Saanich, BC	$935
41	Longueuil, QC	$911
42	Winnipeg, MB	$882
43	Sherbrooke, QC	$880
44	Québec, QC	$874
45	Lévis, QC	$860
46	Windsor, ON	$851
47	Saguenay, QC	$797
48	Chatham-Kent, ON	$738
49	Thunder Bay, ON	$719
50	Trois-Rivières, QC	$709
–	Canada	$978

Median Monthly Costs of Rented Dwellings[3]

Rank	City	Dollars
1	Vaughan, ON	$1,324
2	Markham, ON	$1,179
3	Oakville, ON	$1,149
4	Richmond Hill, ON	$1,116
5	Richmond, BC	$1,101
6	Calgary, AB	$1,093
7	Mississauga, ON	$1,062
8	Burlington, ON	$1,056
9	Ajax, ON	$1,050
10	Brampton, ON	$1,022
11	Vancouver, BC	$1,004
12	Edmonton, AB	$1,003
13	Barrie, ON	$1,001
13	Kelowna, BC	$1,001
13	Langley, BC	$1,001
13	Toronto, ON	$1,001
17	Whitby, ON	$974
18	Burnaby, BC	$966
19	Ottawa, ON	$953
20	Coquitlam, BC	$949
21	Saanich, BC	$948
22	Saskatoon, SK	$913
23	Regina, SK	$882
24	Oshawa, ON	$871
25	Guelph, ON	$859
26	Kingston, ON	$849
27	Kitchener, ON	$832
28	Halifax, NS	$819
29	Cambridge, ON	$805
30	Abbotsford, BC	$801
31	Surrey, BC	$794
32	London, ON	$782
33	St. Catharines, ON	$772
34	Greater Sudbury, ON	$750
34	Hamilton, ON	$750
36	St. John's, NL	$734
37	Gatineau, QC	$733
38	Terrebonne, QC	$726
39	Winnipeg, MB	$723
40	Laval, QC	$703
41	Thunder Bay, ON	$698
42	Windsor, ON	$692
43	Montréal, QC	$684
44	Longueuil, QC	$667
45	Lévis, QC	$655
45	Québec, QC	$655
47	Chatham-Kent, ON	$654
48	Sherbrooke, QC	$582
49	Saguenay, QC	$534
50	Trois-Rivières, QC	$533
–	Canada	$784

Note: All figures cover non-farm, non-reserve private dwellings; (1) Refers to the dollar amount expected by the owner if the dwelling were to be sold; (2) Includes all shelter expenses paid by households that own their dwellings, such as the mortgage payment and the costs of electricity, heat, water and other municipal services, property taxes and condominium fees; (3) Includes all shelter expenses paid by households that rent their dwellings, such as the monthly rent and the costs of electricity, heat and municipal services.
Source: Statistics Canada. 2013. 2011 National Household Survey. Statistics Canada Catalogue no. 99-004-XWE. Ottawa. Released September 11, 2013.

Cities Ranked by Highest Level of Education: High School Diploma
By Number

Total

Rank	City	Number
1	Toronto, ON	523,320
2	Montréal, QC	283,135
3	Calgary, AB	218,615
4	Edmonton, AB	172,970
5	Ottawa, ON	168,390
6	Winnipeg, MB	153,960
7	Mississauga, ON	147,340
8	Brampton, ON	118,630
9	Vancouver, BC	118,345
10	Surrey, BC	116,155
11	Hamilton, ON	115,720
12	Québec, QC	93,195
13	London, ON	83,450
14	Halifax, NS	78,340
15	Laval, QC	75,795
16	Markham, ON	61,235
17	Vaughan, ON	54,630
18	Windsor, ON	53,145
19	Kitchener, ON	50,455
20	Saskatoon, SK	49,405
21	Burnaby, BC	47,740
22	Gatineau, QC	47,370
23	Regina, SK	46,905
24	Richmond, BC	45,185
25	Longueuil, QC	43,645
26	Oshawa, ON	38,370
27	Burlington, ON	37,775
28	Richmond Hill, ON	33,185
29	Abbotsford, BC	32,865
30	Greater Sudbury, ON	32,555
31	St. Catharines, ON	32,340
32	Oakville, ON	32,335
33	Barrie, ON	32,115
34	Cambridge, ON	30,810
35	Coquitlam, BC	28,560
36	Kelowna, BC	27,500
37	Kingston, ON	27,025
38	Guelph, ON	26,695
39	Sherbrooke, QC	26,295
40	Whitby, ON	26,110
41	Langley, BC	26,030
42	Chatham-Kent, ON	25,990
43	Ajax, ON	25,245
44	Saanich, BC	24,620
45	Trois-Rivières, QC	24,495
46	Lévis, QC	23,220
47	Saguenay, QC	22,800
48	Thunder Bay, ON	22,670
49	St. John's, NL	21,840
50	Terrebonne, QC	20,320
–	Canada	6,968,935

Male

Rank	City	Number
1	Toronto, ON	250,335
2	Montréal, QC	137,440
3	Calgary, AB	105,985
4	Edmonton, AB	83,415
5	Ottawa, ON	79,490
6	Winnipeg, MB	73,670
7	Mississauga, ON	70,380
8	Brampton, ON	58,495
9	Vancouver, BC	58,175
10	Hamilton, ON	56,790
11	Surrey, BC	56,765
12	Québec, QC	41,760
13	London, ON	40,040
14	Halifax, NS	38,170
15	Laval, QC	35,140
16	Markham, ON	29,010
17	Vaughan, ON	26,225
18	Saskatoon, SK	25,330
19	Windsor, ON	25,280
20	Kitchener, ON	24,550
21	Burnaby, BC	22,665
22	Regina, SK	22,500
23	Gatineau, QC	21,680
24	Richmond, BC	20,730
25	Longueuil, QC	19,900
26	Oshawa, ON	18,620
27	Burlington, ON	17,245
28	Abbotsford, BC	15,925
29	Barrie, ON	15,480
30	Greater Sudbury, ON	15,255
31	Richmond Hill, ON	15,000
32	Cambridge, ON	14,965
33	St. Catharines, ON	14,880
34	Oakville, ON	14,800
35	Coquitlam, BC	13,365
36	Kingston, ON	12,975
37	Guelph, ON	12,805
38	Kelowna, BC	12,780
39	Whitby, ON	12,685
40	Chatham-Kent, ON	12,615
41	Sherbrooke, QC	12,340
42	Ajax, ON	12,175
43	Langley, BC	11,650
44	Saanich, BC	11,585
45	Trois-Rivières, QC	11,170
46	Thunder Bay, ON	11,010
47	Lévis, QC	10,700
48	St. John's, NL	10,510
49	Saguenay, QC	10,395
50	Terrebonne, QC	9,290
–	Canada	3,305,415

Female

Rank	City	Number
1	Toronto, ON	272,985
2	Montréal, QC	145,700
3	Calgary, AB	112,630
4	Edmonton, AB	89,550
5	Ottawa, ON	88,895
6	Winnipeg, MB	80,285
7	Mississauga, ON	76,960
8	Vancouver, BC	60,170
9	Brampton, ON	60,135
10	Surrey, BC	59,390
11	Hamilton, ON	58,925
12	Québec, QC	51,440
13	London, ON	43,405
14	Laval, QC	40,655
15	Halifax, NS	40,170
16	Markham, ON	32,225
17	Vaughan, ON	28,400
18	Windsor, ON	27,865
19	Kitchener, ON	25,910
20	Gatineau, QC	25,695
21	Burnaby, BC	25,070
22	Richmond, BC	24,455
23	Regina, SK	24,410
24	Saskatoon, SK	24,070
25	Longueuil, QC	23,740
26	Burlington, ON	20,530
27	Oshawa, ON	19,750
28	Richmond Hill, ON	18,190
29	Oakville, ON	17,535
30	St. Catharines, ON	17,460
31	Greater Sudbury, ON	17,295
32	Abbotsford, BC	16,940
33	Barrie, ON	16,635
34	Cambridge, ON	15,850
35	Coquitlam, BC	15,200
36	Kelowna, BC	14,725
37	Langley, BC	14,380
38	Kingston, ON	14,045
39	Sherbrooke, QC	13,955
40	Guelph, ON	13,890
41	Whitby, ON	13,425
42	Chatham-Kent, ON	13,375
43	Trois-Rivières, QC	13,320
44	Ajax, ON	13,070
45	Saanich, BC	13,035
46	Lévis, QC	12,520
47	Saguenay, QC	12,405
48	Thunder Bay, ON	11,655
49	St. John's, NL	11,325
50	Terrebonne, QC	11,025
–	Canada	3,663,515

Note: Figures cover total population aged 15 years and over by highest certificate, diploma or degree; "High School Diploma" includes persons who have graduated from a secondary school or equivalent. It excludes persons with a postsecondary certificate, diploma or degree.
Source: Statistics Canada. 2013. 2011 National Household Survey. Statistics Canada Catalogue no. 99-004-XWE. Ottawa. Released September 11, 2013.

Cities Ranked by Highest Level of Education: High School Diploma

By Percent

Total

Rank	City	Percent
1	Oshawa, ON	31.2%
2	Abbotsford, BC	31.1%
2	Langley, BC	31.1%
4	Surrey, BC	31.0%
5	Chatham-Kent, ON	30.9%
5	Windsor, ON	30.9%
7	Cambridge, ON	30.6%
8	Barrie, ON	30.0%
8	Regina, SK	30.0%
10	St. Catharines, ON	29.5%
11	Ajax, ON	29.2%
11	Brampton, ON	29.2%
13	Winnipeg, MB	28.6%
14	Kitchener, ON	28.5%
15	Kelowna, BC	28.1%
16	Richmond, BC	27.9%
17	London, ON	27.7%
18	Whitby, ON	27.5%
19	Coquitlam, BC	27.4%
20	Hamilton, ON	27.3%
20	Saskatoon, SK	27.3%
22	Guelph, ON	26.9%
23	Kingston, ON	26.8%
24	Saanich, BC	26.5%
25	Burlington, ON	26.3%
26	Edmonton, AB	26.2%
27	Mississauga, ON	25.4%
28	Burnaby, BC	25.2%
28	Thunder Bay, ON	25.2%
30	Calgary, AB	24.7%
30	Markham, ON	24.7%
32	Greater Sudbury, ON	24.6%
33	St. John's, NL	24.4%
34	Halifax, NS	24.1%
34	Terrebonne, QC	24.1%
34	Toronto, ON	24.1%
37	Vaughan, ON	24.0%
38	Laval, QC	23.4%
38	Ottawa, ON	23.4%
40	Vancouver, BC	22.8%
41	Longueuil, QC	22.6%
42	Oakville, ON	22.4%
43	Trois-Rivières, QC	22.3%
44	Gatineau, QC	22.0%
44	Richmond Hill, ON	22.0%
46	Québec, QC	21.4%
47	Sherbrooke, QC	20.9%
48	Lévis, QC	20.7%
48	Montréal, QC	20.7%
50	Saguenay, QC	18.9%
–	Canada	25.6%

Male

Rank	City	Percent
1	Oshawa, ON	31.3%
2	Abbotsford, BC	30.9%
2	Chatham-Kent, ON	30.9%
2	Surrey, BC	30.9%
5	Windsor, ON	30.6%
6	Cambridge, ON	30.4%
7	Barrie, ON	30.1%
8	Regina, SK	29.7%
9	Ajax, ON	29.5%
9	Brampton, ON	29.5%
11	Saskatoon, SK	28.9%
12	St. Catharines, ON	28.7%
13	Langley, BC	28.6%
14	Winnipeg, MB	28.4%
15	Kitchener, ON	28.3%
16	London, ON	27.8%
17	Hamilton, ON	27.7%
17	Whitby, ON	27.7%
19	Kelowna, BC	27.4%
20	Kingston, ON	27.2%
21	Richmond, BC	27.0%
22	Guelph, ON	26.9%
23	Coquitlam, BC	26.3%
24	Saanich, BC	26.1%
25	Edmonton, AB	25.4%
25	Thunder Bay, ON	25.4%
27	Burlington, ON	25.2%
28	Mississauga, ON	25.0%
28	St. John's, NL	25.0%
30	Burnaby, BC	24.6%
31	Halifax, NS	24.5%
32	Markham, ON	24.2%
32	Toronto, ON	24.2%
34	Calgary, AB	24.0%
35	Vaughan, ON	23.8%
36	Greater Sudbury, ON	23.7%
37	Vancouver, BC	23.1%
38	Ottawa, ON	22.9%
39	Laval, QC	22.5%
40	Terrebonne, QC	22.3%
41	Longueuil, QC	21.3%
41	Oakville, ON	21.3%
43	Trois-Rivières, QC	21.2%
44	Gatineau, QC	20.9%
45	Montréal, QC	20.8%
46	Richmond Hill, ON	20.7%
47	Sherbrooke, QC	20.3%
48	Québec, QC	19.9%
49	Lévis, QC	19.6%
50	Saguenay, QC	17.5%
–	Canada	24.9%

Female

Rank	City	Percent
1	Langley, BC	33.4%
2	Abbotsford, BC	31.3%
3	Windsor, ON	31.2%
4	Oshawa, ON	31.1%
4	Surrey, BC	31.1%
6	Chatham-Kent, ON	30.9%
7	Cambridge, ON	30.8%
8	Regina, SK	30.3%
8	St. Catharines, ON	30.3%
10	Barrie, ON	30.0%
11	Ajax, ON	28.9%
12	Brampton, ON	28.8%
12	Kelowna, BC	28.8%
12	Winnipeg, MB	28.8%
15	Richmond, BC	28.7%
16	Kitchener, ON	28.6%
17	Coquitlam, BC	28.4%
18	London, ON	27.6%
19	Burlington, ON	27.3%
19	Whitby, ON	27.3%
21	Guelph, ON	27.0%
22	Edmonton, AB	26.9%
22	Hamilton, ON	26.9%
22	Saanich, BC	26.9%
25	Kingston, ON	26.4%
26	Saskatoon, SK	25.9%
27	Burnaby, BC	25.8%
27	Mississauga, ON	25.8%
27	Terrebonne, QC	25.8%
30	Greater Sudbury, ON	25.4%
31	Calgary, AB	25.3%
32	Markham, ON	25.2%
33	Thunder Bay, ON	25.1%
34	Laval, QC	24.3%
35	Vaughan, ON	24.2%
36	Ottawa, ON	23.9%
36	St. John's, NL	23.9%
36	Toronto, ON	23.9%
39	Halifax, NS	23.7%
39	Longueuil, QC	23.7%
41	Oakville, ON	23.4%
41	Trois-Rivières, QC	23.4%
43	Richmond Hill, ON	23.3%
44	Gatineau, QC	22.9%
45	Québec, QC	22.8%
46	Vancouver, BC	22.5%
47	Lévis, QC	21.8%
48	Sherbrooke, QC	21.4%
49	Montréal, QC	20.7%
50	Saguenay, QC	20.2%
–	Canada	26.2%

Note: Figures cover total population aged 15 years and over by highest certificate, diploma or degree; "High School Diploma" includes persons who have graduated from a secondary school or equivalent. It excludes persons with a postsecondary certificate, diploma or degree.
Source: Statistics Canada. 2013. 2011 National Household Survey. Statistics Canada Catalogue no. 99-004-XWE. Ottawa. Released September 11, 2013.

Cities Ranked by Highest Level of Education: Bachelor's Degree

By Number

Total

Rank	City	Number
1	Toronto, ON	436,755
2	Montréal, QC	225,400
3	Calgary, AB	180,675
4	Ottawa, ON	149,465
5	Vancouver, BC	119,565
6	Edmonton, AB	105,925
7	Mississauga, ON	105,480
8	Winnipeg, MB	80,745
9	Québec, QC	61,815
10	Halifax, NS	57,175
11	Markham, ON	53,795
12	Brampton, ON	50,370
13	Hamilton, ON	45,595
14	Surrey, BC	44,750
15	Laval, QC	41,595
16	London, ON	39,985
17	Vaughan, ON	39,805
18	Burnaby, BC	37,320
19	Richmond Hill, ON	35,785
20	Richmond, BC	33,190
21	Oakville, ON	33,155
22	Gatineau, QC	30,325
23	Saskatoon, SK	29,905
24	Burlington, ON	25,500
25	Regina, SK	25,090
26	Kitchener, ON	22,160
27	Longueuil, QC	21,650
28	Windsor, ON	19,380
29	Coquitlam, BC	17,920
30	Saanich, BC	16,450
31	Guelph, ON	15,685
32	Lévis, QC	15,605
33	Sherbrooke, QC	14,920
34	Whitby, ON	14,645
35	St. John's, NL	14,475
36	Kingston, ON	13,605
37	Greater Sudbury, ON	13,210
38	Ajax, ON	12,300
39	Saguenay, QC	12,220
40	Trois-Rivières, QC	11,650
41	St. Catharines, ON	11,125
42	Kelowna, BC	10,570
43	Barrie, ON	10,355
44	Thunder Bay, ON	9,835
45	Oshawa, ON	9,585
46	Abbotsford, BC	8,870
47	Langley, BC	8,865
48	Cambridge, ON	8,850
49	Terrebonne, QC	7,155
50	Chatham-Kent, ON	5,610
–	Canada	3,634,425

Male

Rank	City	Number
1	Toronto, ON	204,265
2	Montréal, QC	106,525
3	Calgary, AB	87,580
4	Ottawa, ON	69,420
5	Vancouver, BC	57,140
6	Mississauga, ON	49,865
7	Edmonton, AB	48,300
8	Winnipeg, MB	35,995
9	Québec, QC	28,775
10	Markham, ON	26,245
11	Halifax, NS	25,340
12	Brampton, ON	23,810
13	Surrey, BC	21,095
14	Hamilton, ON	20,165
15	Laval, QC	18,885
16	Vaughan, ON	18,435
17	Burnaby, BC	18,155
18	London, ON	17,670
19	Richmond Hill, ON	17,125
20	Oakville, ON	15,800
21	Richmond, BC	15,715
22	Saskatoon, SK	13,420
23	Gatineau, QC	12,735
24	Burlington, ON	12,190
25	Regina, SK	11,525
26	Kitchener, ON	10,465
27	Longueuil, QC	9,930
28	Windsor, ON	8,770
29	Coquitlam, BC	8,625
30	Saanich, BC	7,225
31	Lévis, QC	7,180
32	Guelph, ON	7,005
33	Whitby, ON	6,375
34	Sherbrooke, QC	6,365
35	St. John's, NL	6,270
36	Kingston, ON	5,730
37	Saguenay, QC	5,665
38	Greater Sudbury, ON	5,635
39	St. Catharines, ON	5,160
40	Ajax, ON	5,140
41	Trois-Rivières, QC	5,120
42	Kelowna, BC	4,570
43	Barrie, ON	4,425
44	Oshawa, ON	4,205
45	Thunder Bay, ON	4,155
46	Cambridge, ON	4,055
47	Abbotsford, BC	3,880
48	Langley, BC	3,865
49	Terrebonne, QC	2,800
50	Chatham-Kent, ON	2,480
–	Canada	1,643,080

Female

Rank	City	Number
1	Toronto, ON	232,490
2	Montréal, QC	118,875
3	Calgary, AB	93,095
4	Ottawa, ON	80,045
5	Vancouver, BC	62,425
6	Edmonton, AB	57,625
7	Mississauga, ON	55,615
8	Winnipeg, MB	44,745
9	Québec, QC	33,035
10	Halifax, NS	31,835
11	Markham, ON	27,550
12	Brampton, ON	26,550
13	Hamilton, ON	25,430
14	Surrey, BC	23,665
15	Laval, QC	22,710
16	London, ON	22,315
17	Vaughan, ON	21,365
18	Burnaby, BC	19,170
19	Richmond Hill, ON	18,660
20	Gatineau, QC	17,590
21	Richmond, BC	17,475
22	Oakville, ON	17,355
23	Saskatoon, SK	16,485
24	Regina, SK	13,560
25	Burlington, ON	13,305
26	Longueuil, QC	11,715
27	Kitchener, ON	11,695
28	Windsor, ON	10,610
29	Coquitlam, BC	9,290
30	Saanich, BC	9,230
31	Guelph, ON	8,680
32	Sherbrooke, QC	8,555
33	Lévis, QC	8,430
34	Whitby, ON	8,275
35	St. John's, NL	8,205
36	Kingston, ON	7,875
37	Greater Sudbury, ON	7,580
38	Ajax, ON	7,165
39	Saguenay, QC	6,560
40	Trois-Rivières, QC	6,530
41	Kelowna, BC	6,000
42	St. Catharines, ON	5,965
43	Barrie, ON	5,935
44	Thunder Bay, ON	5,675
45	Oshawa, ON	5,375
46	Langley, BC	4,995
47	Abbotsford, BC	4,990
48	Cambridge, ON	4,795
49	Terrebonne, QC	4,355
50	Chatham-Kent, ON	3,135
–	Canada	1,991,345

Note: Figures cover total population aged 15 years and over by highest certificate, diploma or degree.
Source: Statistics Canada. 2013. 2011 National Household Survey. Statistics Canada Catalogue no. 99-004-XWE. Ottawa. Released September 11, 2013.

Cities Ranked by Highest Level of Education: Bachelor's Degree

By Percent

Total

Rank	City	Percent
1	Richmond Hill, ON	23.7%
2	Vancouver, BC	23.0%
3	Oakville, ON	22.9%
4	Markham, ON	21.7%
5	Ottawa, ON	20.8%
6	Richmond, BC	20.5%
7	Calgary, AB	20.4%
8	Toronto, ON	20.1%
9	Burnaby, BC	19.7%
10	Mississauga, ON	18.2%
11	Burlington, ON	17.8%
12	Saanich, BC	17.7%
13	Halifax, NS	17.6%
14	Vaughan, ON	17.5%
15	Coquitlam, BC	17.2%
16	Saskatoon, SK	16.6%
17	Montréal, QC	16.5%
18	St. John's, NL	16.2%
19	Regina, SK	16.1%
20	Edmonton, AB	16.0%
21	Guelph, ON	15.8%
22	Whitby, ON	15.4%
23	Winnipeg, MB	15.0%
24	Ajax, ON	14.2%
24	Québec, QC	14.2%
26	Gatineau, QC	14.1%
27	Lévis, QC	13.9%
28	Kingston, ON	13.5%
29	London, ON	13.3%
30	Laval, QC	12.9%
31	Kitchener, ON	12.5%
32	Brampton, ON	12.4%
33	Surrey, BC	12.0%
34	Sherbrooke, QC	11.8%
35	Windsor, ON	11.3%
36	Longueuil, QC	11.2%
37	Thunder Bay, ON	10.9%
38	Hamilton, ON	10.8%
38	Kelowna, BC	10.8%
40	Langley, BC	10.6%
40	Trois-Rivières, QC	10.6%
42	St. Catharines, ON	10.2%
43	Saguenay, QC	10.1%
44	Greater Sudbury, ON	10.0%
45	Barrie, ON	9.7%
46	Cambridge, ON	8.8%
47	Terrebonne, QC	8.5%
48	Abbotsford, BC	8.4%
49	Oshawa, ON	7.8%
50	Chatham-Kent, ON	6.7%
–	Canada	13.3%

Male

Rank	City	Percent
1	Richmond Hill, ON	23.6%
2	Oakville, ON	22.7%
2	Vancouver, BC	22.7%
4	Markham, ON	21.9%
5	Richmond, BC	20.4%
6	Ottawa, ON	20.0%
7	Calgary, AB	19.9%
8	Toronto, ON	19.8%
9	Burnaby, BC	19.7%
10	Burlington, ON	17.8%
11	Mississauga, ON	17.7%
12	Coquitlam, BC	17.0%
13	Vaughan, ON	16.7%
14	Halifax, NS	16.3%
14	Saanich, BC	16.3%
16	Montréal, QC	16.1%
17	Saskatoon, SK	15.3%
18	Regina, SK	15.2%
19	St. John's, NL	14.9%
20	Edmonton, AB	14.7%
20	Guelph, ON	14.7%
22	Whitby, ON	13.9%
22	Winnipeg, MB	13.9%
24	Québec, QC	13.7%
25	Lévis, QC	13.1%
26	Ajax, ON	12.5%
27	Gatineau, QC	12.3%
27	London, ON	12.3%
29	Kitchener, ON	12.1%
29	Laval, QC	12.1%
31	Brampton, ON	12.0%
31	Kingston, ON	12.0%
33	Surrey, BC	11.5%
34	Longueuil, QC	10.6%
34	Windsor, ON	10.6%
36	Sherbrooke, QC	10.5%
37	St. Catharines, ON	9.9%
38	Hamilton, ON	9.8%
38	Kelowna, BC	9.8%
40	Trois-Rivières, QC	9.7%
41	Thunder Bay, ON	9.6%
42	Langley, BC	9.5%
42	Saguenay, QC	9.5%
44	Greater Sudbury, ON	8.8%
45	Barrie, ON	8.6%
46	Cambridge, ON	8.2%
47	Abbotsford, BC	7.5%
48	Oshawa, ON	7.1%
49	Terrebonne, QC	6.7%
50	Chatham-Kent, ON	6.1%
–	Canada	12.4%

Female

Rank	City	Percent
1	Richmond Hill, ON	23.9%
2	Vancouver, BC	23.3%
3	Oakville, ON	23.1%
4	Markham, ON	21.6%
5	Ottawa, ON	21.5%
6	Calgary, AB	20.9%
7	Richmond, BC	20.5%
8	Toronto, ON	20.4%
9	Burnaby, BC	19.7%
10	Saanich, BC	19.0%
11	Halifax, NS	18.8%
12	Mississauga, ON	18.6%
13	Vaughan, ON	18.2%
14	Burlington, ON	17.7%
14	Saskatoon, SK	17.7%
16	Coquitlam, BC	17.3%
16	Edmonton, AB	17.3%
16	St. John's, NL	17.3%
19	Guelph, ON	16.9%
19	Montréal, QC	16.9%
21	Regina, SK	16.8%
21	Whitby, ON	16.8%
23	Winnipeg, MB	16.0%
24	Ajax, ON	15.8%
25	Gatineau, QC	15.7%
26	Kingston, ON	14.8%
27	Lévis, QC	14.7%
28	Québec, QC	14.6%
29	London, ON	14.2%
30	Laval, QC	13.6%
31	Sherbrooke, QC	13.1%
32	Kitchener, ON	12.9%
33	Brampton, ON	12.7%
34	Surrey, BC	12.4%
35	Thunder Bay, ON	12.2%
36	Windsor, ON	11.9%
37	Kelowna, BC	11.7%
37	Longueuil, QC	11.7%
39	Hamilton, ON	11.6%
39	Langley, BC	11.6%
41	Trois-Rivières, QC	11.5%
42	Greater Sudbury, ON	11.1%
43	Barrie, ON	10.7%
43	Saguenay, QC	10.7%
45	St. Catharines, ON	10.4%
46	Terrebonne, QC	10.2%
47	Cambridge, ON	9.3%
48	Abbotsford, BC	9.2%
49	Oshawa, ON	8.5%
50	Chatham-Kent, ON	7.2%
–	Canada	14.3%

Note: Figures cover total population aged 15 years and over by highest certificate, diploma or degree.
Source: Statistics Canada. 2013. 2011 National Household Survey. Statistics Canada Catalogue no. 99-004-XWE. Ottawa. Released September 11, 2013.

Cities Ranked by Highest Level of Education: University Certificate or Diploma above Bachelor Level
By Number

Total

Rank	City	Number
1	Toronto, ON	279,625
2	Montréal, QC	157,550
3	Ottawa, ON	105,105
4	Calgary, AB	82,025
5	Vancouver, BC	69,615
6	Mississauga, ON	67,245
7	Edmonton, AB	55,205
8	Winnipeg, MB	41,700
9	Québec, QC	38,740
10	Brampton, ON	31,605
11	Hamilton, ON	30,625
12	Halifax, NS	30,450
13	Markham, ON	28,300
14	London, ON	28,255
15	Surrey, BC	26,085
16	Vaughan, ON	25,140
17	Richmond Hill, ON	21,635
18	Laval, QC	20,065
19	Oakville, ON	19,820
20	Gatineau, QC	18,970
21	Burnaby, BC	18,880
22	Richmond, BC	15,100
23	Saskatoon, SK	13,970
24	Burlington, ON	13,760
25	Windsor, ON	13,735
26	Kitchener, ON	12,645
27	Kingston, ON	12,400
28	Longueuil, QC	11,780
29	Saanich, BC	10,745
30	Guelph, ON	10,515
31	Sherbrooke, QC	10,295
32	Coquitlam, BC	9,910
33	St. John's, NL	9,075
34	Regina, SK	8,965
35	Greater Sudbury, ON	7,555
36	Whitby, ON	7,190
37	St. Catharines, ON	7,185
38	Lévis, QC	7,020
39	Abbotsford, BC	6,295
40	Kelowna, BC	6,215
41	Thunder Bay, ON	5,930
42	Ajax, ON	5,770
43	Trois-Rivières, QC	5,675
44	Barrie, ON	5,450
45	Saguenay, QC	5,215
46	Langley, BC	4,960
47	Cambridge, ON	4,720
48	Oshawa, ON	4,550
49	Chatham-Kent, ON	2,750
50	Terrebonne, QC	2,360
–	Canada	2,049,930

Male

Rank	City	Number
1	Toronto, ON	140,870
2	Montréal, QC	81,645
3	Ottawa, ON	55,320
4	Calgary, AB	43,175
5	Mississauga, ON	34,860
6	Vancouver, BC	34,005
7	Edmonton, AB	29,150
8	Winnipeg, MB	21,385
9	Québec, QC	20,840
10	Brampton, ON	15,260
11	Markham, ON	15,110
12	Hamilton, ON	15,065
13	London, ON	14,365
14	Halifax, NS	14,165
15	Surrey, BC	13,240
16	Vaughan, ON	12,575
17	Richmond Hill, ON	12,140
18	Oakville, ON	10,900
19	Laval, QC	10,865
20	Gatineau, QC	9,900
21	Burnaby, BC	9,645
22	Richmond, BC	8,110
23	Saskatoon, SK	7,430
24	Windsor, ON	7,340
25	Burlington, ON	6,900
26	Kingston, ON	6,675
27	Kitchener, ON	6,280
28	Longueuil, QC	6,230
29	Saanich, BC	5,780
30	Sherbrooke, QC	5,380
31	Guelph, ON	5,050
32	Coquitlam, BC	4,990
33	Regina, SK	4,690
34	St. John's, NL	4,545
35	Lévis, QC	3,485
36	St. Catharines, ON	3,445
37	Abbotsford, BC	3,420
37	Greater Sudbury, ON	3,420
39	Kelowna, BC	3,370
40	Whitby, ON	3,360
41	Trois-Rivières, QC	3,095
42	Ajax, ON	2,925
43	Thunder Bay, ON	2,915
44	Saguenay, QC	2,840
45	Langley, BC	2,380
46	Barrie, ON	2,325
47	Cambridge, ON	2,275
48	Oshawa, ON	2,170
49	Chatham-Kent, ON	1,240
50	Terrebonne, QC	1,235
–	Canada	1,043,350

Female

Rank	City	Number
1	Toronto, ON	138,755
2	Montréal, QC	75,905
3	Ottawa, ON	49,790
4	Calgary, AB	38,845
5	Vancouver, BC	35,610
6	Mississauga, ON	32,390
7	Edmonton, AB	26,060
8	Winnipeg, MB	20,315
9	Québec, QC	17,895
10	Brampton, ON	16,345
11	Halifax, NS	16,285
12	Hamilton, ON	15,560
13	London, ON	13,890
14	Markham, ON	13,195
15	Surrey, BC	12,840
16	Vaughan, ON	12,560
17	Richmond Hill, ON	9,495
18	Burnaby, BC	9,230
19	Laval, QC	9,200
20	Gatineau, QC	9,070
21	Oakville, ON	8,920
22	Richmond, BC	6,995
23	Burlington, ON	6,860
24	Saskatoon, SK	6,540
25	Windsor, ON	6,395
26	Kitchener, ON	6,360
27	Kingston, ON	5,720
28	Longueuil, QC	5,540
29	Guelph, ON	5,460
30	Saanich, BC	4,960
31	Coquitlam, BC	4,920
32	Sherbrooke, QC	4,910
33	St. John's, NL	4,525
34	Regina, SK	4,275
35	Greater Sudbury, ON	4,130
36	Whitby, ON	3,825
37	St. Catharines, ON	3,745
38	Lévis, QC	3,540
39	Barrie, ON	3,125
40	Thunder Bay, ON	3,010
41	Abbotsford, BC	2,870
42	Ajax, ON	2,845
42	Kelowna, BC	2,845
44	Langley, BC	2,575
44	Trois-Rivières, QC	2,575
46	Cambridge, ON	2,445
47	Oshawa, ON	2,385
48	Saguenay, QC	2,375
49	Chatham-Kent, ON	1,510
50	Terrebonne, QC	1,130
–	Canada	1,006,585

Note: Figures cover total population aged 15 years and over by highest certificate, diploma or degree; "University certificate or diploma above bachelor level" includes the following categories: Degree in medicine, dentistry, veterinary medicine or optometry; Master's degree; and Earned doctorate.
Source: Statistics Canada. 2013. 2011 National Household Survey. Statistics Canada Catalogue no. 99-004-XWE. Ottawa. Released September 11, 2013.

Cities Ranked by Highest Level of Education: University Certificate or Diploma above Bachelor Level

By Percent

Total

Rank	City	Percent
1	Ottawa, ON	14.6%
2	Richmond Hill, ON	14.4%
3	Oakville, ON	13.7%
4	Vancouver, BC	13.4%
5	Toronto, ON	12.9%
6	Kingston, ON	12.3%
7	Mississauga, ON	11.6%
7	Saanich, BC	11.6%
9	Montréal, QC	11.5%
10	Markham, ON	11.4%
11	Vaughan, ON	11.0%
12	Guelph, ON	10.6%
13	St. John's, NL	10.1%
14	Burnaby, BC	10.0%
15	Burlington, ON	9.6%
16	Coquitlam, BC	9.5%
17	Halifax, NS	9.4%
17	London, ON	9.4%
19	Calgary, AB	9.3%
19	Richmond, BC	9.3%
21	Québec, QC	8.9%
22	Gatineau, QC	8.8%
23	Edmonton, AB	8.4%
24	Sherbrooke, QC	8.2%
25	Windsor, ON	8.0%
26	Brampton, ON	7.8%
27	Saskatoon, SK	7.7%
27	Winnipeg, MB	7.7%
29	Whitby, ON	7.6%
30	Hamilton, ON	7.2%
31	Kitchener, ON	7.1%
32	Surrey, BC	7.0%
33	Ajax, ON	6.7%
34	St. Catharines, ON	6.6%
34	Thunder Bay, ON	6.6%
36	Kelowna, BC	6.4%
37	Lévis, QC	6.3%
38	Laval, QC	6.2%
39	Longueuil, QC	6.1%
40	Abbotsford, BC	6.0%
41	Langley, BC	5.9%
42	Greater Sudbury, ON	5.7%
42	Regina, SK	5.7%
44	Trois-Rivières, QC	5.2%
45	Barrie, ON	5.1%
46	Cambridge, ON	4.7%
47	Saguenay, QC	4.3%
48	Oshawa, ON	3.7%
49	Chatham-Kent, ON	3.3%
50	Terrebonne, QC	2.8%
–	Canada	7.5%

Male

Rank	City	Percent
1	Richmond Hill, ON	16.7%
2	Ottawa, ON	16.0%
3	Oakville, ON	15.7%
4	Kingston, ON	14.0%
5	Toronto, ON	13.6%
6	Vancouver, BC	13.5%
7	Saanich, BC	13.0%
8	Markham, ON	12.6%
9	Mississauga, ON	12.4%
9	Montréal, QC	12.4%
11	Vaughan, ON	11.4%
12	St. John's, NL	10.8%
13	Guelph, ON	10.6%
14	Burnaby, BC	10.5%
14	Richmond, BC	10.5%
16	Burlington, ON	10.1%
17	London, ON	10.0%
17	Québec, QC	10.0%
19	Calgary, AB	9.8%
19	Coquitlam, BC	9.8%
21	Gatineau, QC	9.6%
22	Halifax, NS	9.1%
23	Edmonton, AB	8.9%
23	Sherbrooke, QC	8.9%
23	Windsor, ON	8.9%
26	Saskatoon, SK	8.5%
27	Winnipeg, MB	8.2%
28	Brampton, ON	7.7%
29	Hamilton, ON	7.3%
29	Whitby, ON	7.3%
31	Kelowna, BC	7.2%
31	Kitchener, ON	7.2%
31	Surrey, BC	7.2%
34	Ajax, ON	7.1%
35	Laval, QC	7.0%
36	Longueuil, QC	6.7%
36	Thunder Bay, ON	6.7%
38	Abbotsford, BC	6.6%
38	St. Catharines, ON	6.6%
40	Lévis, QC	6.4%
41	Regina, SK	6.2%
42	Trois-Rivières, QC	5.9%
43	Langley, BC	5.8%
44	Greater Sudbury, ON	5.3%
45	Saguenay, QC	4.8%
46	Cambridge, ON	4.6%
47	Barrie, ON	4.5%
48	Oshawa, ON	3.7%
49	Chatham-Kent, ON	3.0%
49	Terrebonne, QC	3.0%
–	Canada	7.8%

Female

Rank	City	Percent
1	Ottawa, ON	13.4%
2	Vancouver, BC	13.3%
3	Toronto, ON	12.2%
4	Richmond Hill, ON	12.1%
5	Oakville, ON	11.9%
6	Kingston, ON	10.8%
6	Mississauga, ON	10.8%
6	Montréal, QC	10.8%
9	Vaughan, ON	10.7%
10	Guelph, ON	10.6%
11	Markham, ON	10.3%
12	Saanich, BC	10.2%
13	Halifax, NS	9.6%
14	Burnaby, BC	9.5%
14	St. John's, NL	9.5%
16	Coquitlam, BC	9.2%
17	Burlington, ON	9.1%
18	London, ON	8.8%
19	Calgary, AB	8.7%
20	Richmond, BC	8.2%
21	Gatineau, QC	8.1%
22	Québec, QC	7.9%
23	Brampton, ON	7.8%
23	Edmonton, AB	7.8%
23	Whitby, ON	7.8%
26	Sherbrooke, QC	7.5%
27	Winnipeg, MB	7.3%
28	Windsor, ON	7.2%
29	Hamilton, ON	7.1%
30	Kitchener, ON	7.0%
30	Saskatoon, SK	7.0%
32	Surrey, BC	6.7%
33	St. Catharines, ON	6.5%
33	Thunder Bay, ON	6.5%
35	Ajax, ON	6.3%
36	Lévis, QC	6.2%
37	Greater Sudbury, ON	6.1%
38	Langley, BC	6.0%
39	Barrie, ON	5.6%
39	Kelowna, BC	5.6%
41	Laval, QC	5.5%
41	Longueuil, QC	5.5%
43	Abbotsford, BC	5.3%
43	Regina, SK	5.3%
45	Cambridge, ON	4.8%
46	Trois-Rivières, QC	4.5%
47	Saguenay, QC	3.9%
48	Oshawa, ON	3.8%
49	Chatham-Kent, ON	3.5%
50	Terrebonne, QC	2.6%
–	Canada	7.2%

Note: Figures cover total population aged 15 years and over by highest certificate, diploma or degree; "University certificate or diploma above bachelor level" includes the following categories: Degree in medicine, dentistry, veterinary medicine or optometry; Master's degree; and Earned doctorate.
Source: Statistics Canada. 2013. 2011 National Household Survey. Statistics Canada Catalogue no. 99-004-XWE. Ottawa. Released September 11, 2013.

Cities Ranked by Median Economic Family Income

Median Economic Family Income

Rank	City	Dollars
1	Oakville, ON	$118,671
2	Whitby, ON	$105,019
3	Ottawa, ON	$101,134
4	Vaughan, ON	$100,256
5	Burlington, ON	$98,995
6	Richmond Hill, ON	$98,073
7	Calgary, AB	$97,790
8	Ajax, ON	$96,573
9	Markham, ON	$92,173
10	Edmonton, AB	$89,252
11	Regina, SK	$89,172
12	Langley, BC	$88,986
13	Guelph, ON	$85,993
14	Mississauga, ON	$85,829
15	Saanich, BC	$85,402
16	Saskatoon, SK	$83,774
17	Brampton, ON	$82,935
18	Gatineau, QC	$82,580
19	Coquitlam, BC	$82,067
20	Cambridge, ON	$81,184
21	Lévis, QC	$81,038
22	Barrie, ON	$80,247
23	Halifax, NS	$80,097
24	Greater Sudbury, ON	$80,084
25	Kingston, ON	$79,562
26	St. John's, NL	$79,054
27	Terrebonne, QC	$78,770
28	Surrey, BC	$78,283
29	Kitchener, ON	$77,690
30	Vancouver, BC	$77,515
31	Hamilton, ON	$77,497
32	Oshawa, ON	$76,992
33	Thunder Bay, ON	$76,861
34	Abbotsford, BC	$75,807
35	Winnipeg, MB	$75,395
36	Laval, QC	$75,020
37	Kelowna, BC	$74,697
38	London, ON	$74,448
39	Québec, QC	$73,477
40	Toronto, ON	$72,890
41	Burnaby, BC	$71,511
42	St. Catharines, ON	$69,658
43	Richmond, BC	$69,553
44	Saguenay, QC	$68,662
45	Longueuil, QC	$68,020
46	Chatham-Kent, ON	$64,670
47	Sherbrooke, QC	$64,558
48	Windsor, ON	$63,418
49	Trois-Rivières, QC	$62,962
50	Montréal, QC	$57,270
–	Canada	$76,511

Median After-tax Economic Family Income

Rank	City	Dollars
1	Oakville, ON	$98,950
2	Whitby, ON	$88,802
3	Vaughan, ON	$86,659
4	Ottawa, ON	$85,635
5	Richmond Hill, ON	$84,537
6	Burlington, ON	$84,225
7	Calgary, AB	$83,669
8	Ajax, ON	$82,904
9	Markham, ON	$80,483
10	Langley, BC	$77,864
11	Edmonton, AB	$77,447
12	Regina, SK	$76,549
13	Saanich, BC	$75,622
14	Mississauga, ON	$75,141
15	Guelph, ON	$74,662
16	Brampton, ON	$73,450
17	Coquitlam, BC	$73,064
18	Saskatoon, SK	$72,678
19	Cambridge, ON	$71,130
20	Kingston, ON	$70,192
21	Greater Sudbury, ON	$69,972
22	Surrey, BC	$69,935
23	Barrie, ON	$69,539
24	Vancouver, BC	$69,271
25	Gatineau, QC	$69,226
26	Lévis, QC	$68,803
27	Hamilton, ON	$68,421
28	Kitchener, ON	$68,369
29	St. John's, NL	$68,156
30	Abbotsford, BC	$68,020
31	Halifax, NS	$67,939
32	Thunder Bay, ON	$67,862
33	Oshawa, ON	$67,559
34	Terrebonne, QC	$67,224
35	Kelowna, BC	$66,389
36	London, ON	$65,851
37	Toronto, ON	$65,335
38	Winnipeg, MB	$64,970
39	Laval, QC	$64,699
40	Burnaby, BC	$64,587
41	Richmond, BC	$63,307
42	Québec, QC	$63,183
43	St. Catharines, ON	$62,771
44	Saguenay, QC	$59,515
45	Longueuil, QC	$59,226
46	Chatham-Kent, ON	$58,692
47	Windsor, ON	$57,568
48	Sherbrooke, QC	$56,587
49	Trois-Rivières, QC	$55,248
50	Montréal, QC	$51,940
–	Canada	$67,044

Note: Figures cover economic familiy income in 2010. An economic family is defined as a group of two or more persons who live in the same dwelling and are related to each other by blood, marriage, common-law, adoption or a foster relationship. A couple may be of opposite or same sex.
Source: Statistics Canada. 2013. 2011 National Household Survey. Statistics Canada Catalogue no. 99-004-XWE. Ottawa. Released September 11, 2013.

Cities Ranked by Occupation: Management
By Number

Total

Rank	City	Number
1	Toronto, ON	153,440
2	Montréal, QC	79,555
3	Calgary, AB	72,585
4	Ottawa, ON	61,200
5	Edmonton, AB	46,670
6	Mississauga, ON	44,925
7	Vancouver, BC	39,775
8	Winnipeg, MB	33,075
9	Hamilton, ON	25,455
10	Surrey, BC	25,055
11	Halifax, NS	24,455
12	Brampton, ON	23,540
13	Québec, QC	23,280
14	Laval, QC	23,240
15	Vaughan, ON	21,280
16	Markham, ON	20,340
17	Oakville, ON	18,475
18	London, ON	17,675
19	Burlington, ON	14,965
20	Richmond Hill, ON	14,880
21	Gatineau, QC	14,390
22	Saskatoon, SK	12,660
23	Burnaby, BC	12,495
24	Richmond, BC	12,090
25	Regina, SK	11,655
26	Kitchener, ON	11,455
27	Longueuil, QC	10,310
28	Whitby, ON	9,735
29	Coquitlam, BC	8,245
30	Barrie, ON	8,145
31	Ajax, ON	7,890
32	Langley, BC	7,790
33	Lévis, QC	7,450
34	Cambridge, ON	7,285
34	Guelph, ON	7,285
36	Oshawa, ON	7,120
37	Kelowna, BC	6,935
38	Abbotsford, BC	6,875
38	Greater Sudbury, ON	6,875
40	Windsor, ON	6,850
41	Saanich, BC	6,695
42	Kingston, ON	6,435
43	Terrebonne, QC	6,365
44	St. Catharines, ON	6,265
45	Sherbrooke, QC	6,255
46	St. John's, NL	5,885
47	Saguenay, QC	5,845
48	Chatham-Kent, ON	5,785
49	Trois-Rivières, QC	5,330
50	Thunder Bay, ON	4,315
–	Canada	1,963,600

Male

Rank	City	Number
1	Toronto, ON	90,465
2	Montréal, QC	48,845
3	Calgary, AB	46,650
4	Ottawa, ON	36,775
5	Edmonton, AB	28,535
6	Mississauga, ON	28,245
7	Vancouver, BC	23,730
8	Winnipeg, MB	19,905
9	Surrey, BC	16,075
10	Hamilton, ON	15,605
11	Laval, QC	14,760
12	Québec, QC	14,675
13	Halifax, NS	14,660
14	Brampton, ON	14,345
15	Vaughan, ON	13,930
16	Markham, ON	12,890
17	Oakville, ON	12,010
18	London, ON	10,740
19	Burlington, ON	9,880
20	Richmond Hill, ON	9,530
21	Gatineau, QC	8,445
22	Saskatoon, SK	7,965
23	Burnaby, BC	7,885
24	Richmond, BC	7,475
25	Kitchener, ON	6,800
26	Regina, SK	6,725
27	Longueuil, QC	5,970
28	Whitby, ON	5,860
29	Coquitlam, BC	5,265
30	Barrie, ON	5,205
31	Langley, BC	5,110
32	Ajax, ON	4,810
32	Lévis, QC	4,810
34	Abbotsford, BC	4,740
35	Guelph, ON	4,575
36	Cambridge, ON	4,480
37	Kelowna, BC	4,470
38	Terrebonne, QC	4,260
39	Sherbrooke, QC	4,090
40	Oshawa, ON	4,055
41	Saanich, BC	4,035
42	Windsor, ON	3,965
43	Kingston, ON	3,955
44	Greater Sudbury, ON	3,880
45	Chatham-Kent, ON	3,850
46	St. Catharines, ON	3,745
47	Saguenay, QC	3,680
48	St. John's, NL	3,370
49	Trois-Rivières, QC	3,315
50	Thunder Bay, ON	2,370
–	Canada	1,229,460

Female

Rank	City	Number
1	Toronto, ON	62,980
2	Montréal, QC	30,710
3	Calgary, AB	25,935
4	Ottawa, ON	24,430
5	Edmonton, AB	18,135
6	Mississauga, ON	16,680
7	Vancouver, BC	16,045
8	Winnipeg, MB	13,170
9	Hamilton, ON	9,850
10	Halifax, NS	9,795
11	Brampton, ON	9,190
12	Surrey, BC	8,985
13	Québec, QC	8,605
14	Laval, QC	8,475
15	Markham, ON	7,450
16	Vaughan, ON	7,345
17	London, ON	6,935
18	Oakville, ON	6,465
19	Gatineau, QC	5,945
20	Richmond Hill, ON	5,345
21	Burlington, ON	5,085
22	Regina, SK	4,930
23	Saskatoon, SK	4,695
24	Kitchener, ON	4,655
25	Richmond, BC	4,620
26	Burnaby, BC	4,605
27	Longueuil, QC	4,340
28	Whitby, ON	3,875
29	Ajax, ON	3,075
30	Oshawa, ON	3,065
31	Greater Sudbury, ON	2,995
32	Coquitlam, BC	2,980
33	Barrie, ON	2,940
34	Windsor, ON	2,885
35	Cambridge, ON	2,805
36	Guelph, ON	2,710
37	Langley, BC	2,685
38	Saanich, BC	2,665
39	Lévis, QC	2,640
40	St. Catharines, ON	2,525
41	St. John's, NL	2,520
42	Kingston, ON	2,480
43	Kelowna, BC	2,465
44	Saguenay, QC	2,165
44	Sherbrooke, QC	2,165
46	Abbotsford, BC	2,130
47	Terrebonne, QC	2,105
48	Trois-Rivières, QC	2,020
49	Thunder Bay, ON	1,950
50	Chatham-Kent, ON	1,930
–	Canada	734,140

Note: Figures are based on total experienced labour force 15 years and over
Source: Statistics Canada. 2013. 2011 National Household Survey. Statistics Canada Catalogue no. 99-004-XWE. Ottawa. Released September 11, 2013.

Cities Ranked by Occupation: Management
By Percent

Total

Rank	City	Percent
1	Oakville, ON	18.7%
2	Burlington, ON	15.4%
3	Richmond Hill, ON	14.9%
4	Whitby, ON	14.5%
5	Vaughan, ON	13.7%
6	Langley, BC	13.6%
7	Markham, ON	13.1%
8	Ajax, ON	12.9%
9	Ottawa, ON	12.5%
10	Richmond, BC	12.4%
11	Coquitlam, BC	12.1%
12	Chatham-Kent, ON	11.7%
12	Mississauga, ON	11.7%
14	Vancouver, BC	11.6%
15	Toronto, ON	11.4%
16	Saanich, BC	11.3%
17	Barrie, ON	11.2%
17	Calgary, AB	11.2%
19	Halifax, NS	11.1%
19	Kelowna, BC	11.1%
19	Laval, QC	11.1%
22	Guelph, ON	10.8%
23	Cambridge, ON	10.7%
24	Burnaby, BC	10.6%
24	St. John's, NL	10.6%
26	Surrey, BC	10.5%
26	Terrebonne, QC	10.5%
28	Regina, SK	10.4%
29	Kingston, ON	10.1%
30	Abbotsford, BC	10.0%
31	Edmonton, AB	9.9%
31	Saskatoon, SK	9.9%
33	Hamilton, ON	9.8%
34	Gatineau, QC	9.7%
35	Montréal, QC	9.6%
35	St. Catharines, ON	9.6%
37	Kitchener, ON	9.5%
38	Lévis, QC	9.4%
38	Oshawa, ON	9.4%
40	London, ON	9.3%
41	Winnipeg, MB	9.1%
42	Brampton, ON	8.7%
43	Longueuil, QC	8.5%
44	Greater Sudbury, ON	8.4%
45	Québec, QC	8.3%
45	Trois-Rivières, QC	8.3%
47	Saguenay, QC	8.1%
47	Sherbrooke, QC	8.1%
49	Thunder Bay, ON	8.0%
50	Windsor, ON	7.4%
–	Canada	11.2%

Male

Rank	City	Percent
1	Oakville, ON	23.4%
2	Burlington, ON	19.8%
3	Richmond Hill, ON	18.5%
4	Vaughan, ON	17.3%
5	Whitby, ON	17.2%
6	Langley, BC	17.0%
7	Ajax, ON	15.9%
7	Markham, ON	15.9%
9	Chatham-Kent, ON	15.0%
9	Richmond, BC	15.0%
11	Ottawa, ON	14.8%
12	Coquitlam, BC	14.7%
13	Mississauga, ON	14.1%
14	Barrie, ON	14.0%
14	Kelowna, BC	14.0%
16	Laval, QC	13.7%
17	Terrebonne, QC	13.6%
18	Saanich, BC	13.5%
18	Vancouver, BC	13.5%
20	Calgary, AB	13.4%
21	Guelph, ON	13.2%
22	Toronto, ON	13.1%
23	Halifax, NS	13.0%
24	Abbotsford, BC	12.9%
24	Burnaby, BC	12.9%
26	Surrey, BC	12.6%
27	Cambridge, ON	12.5%
27	Kingston, ON	12.5%
29	St. John's, NL	12.1%
30	Lévis, QC	11.9%
30	Saskatoon, SK	11.9%
32	Hamilton, ON	11.7%
33	Regina, SK	11.6%
34	Montréal, QC	11.4%
35	Edmonton, AB	11.3%
35	Gatineau, QC	11.3%
35	St. Catharines, ON	11.3%
38	London, ON	11.1%
39	Kitchener, ON	10.8%
40	Winnipeg, MB	10.7%
41	Oshawa, ON	10.5%
42	Sherbrooke, QC	10.4%
43	Québec, QC	10.2%
44	Brampton, ON	10.0%
44	Trois-Rivières, QC	10.0%
46	Longueuil, QC	9.5%
47	Greater Sudbury, ON	9.3%
47	Saguenay, QC	9.3%
49	Thunder Bay, ON	8.7%
50	Windsor, ON	8.3%
–	Canada	13.4%

Female

Rank	City	Percent
1	Oakville, ON	13.7%
2	Whitby, ON	11.8%
3	Richmond Hill, ON	11.1%
4	Burlington, ON	10.8%
5	Ottawa, ON	10.2%
6	Ajax, ON	10.0%
6	Markham, ON	10.0%
8	Langley, BC	9.8%
8	Richmond, BC	9.8%
8	Vaughan, ON	9.8%
11	Toronto, ON	9.6%
11	Vancouver, BC	9.6%
13	Coquitlam, BC	9.2%
13	Regina, SK	9.2%
15	Mississauga, ON	9.1%
15	Saanich, BC	9.1%
15	St. John's, NL	9.1%
18	Halifax, NS	9.0%
19	Calgary, AB	8.7%
20	Cambridge, ON	8.6%
21	Oshawa, ON	8.4%
22	Barrie, ON	8.3%
22	Laval, QC	8.3%
24	Burnaby, BC	8.2%
24	Chatham-Kent, ON	8.2%
24	Edmonton, AB	8.2%
24	Guelph, ON	8.2%
28	Gatineau, QC	8.1%
28	Kelowna, BC	8.1%
28	Kitchener, ON	8.1%
31	Surrey, BC	8.0%
32	Hamilton, ON	7.9%
33	Kingston, ON	7.8%
33	St. Catharines, ON	7.8%
35	Montréal, QC	7.7%
35	Saskatoon, SK	7.7%
37	Greater Sudbury, ON	7.5%
37	Winnipeg, MB	7.5%
39	London, ON	7.4%
39	Longueuil, QC	7.4%
41	Thunder Bay, ON	7.3%
42	Brampton, ON	7.2%
42	Terrebonne, QC	7.2%
44	Lévis, QC	6.8%
45	Abbotsford, BC	6.6%
45	Saguenay, QC	6.6%
47	Trois-Rivières, QC	6.5%
47	Windsor, ON	6.5%
49	Québec, QC	6.4%
50	Sherbrooke, QC	5.7%
–	Canada	8.7%

Note: Figures are based on total experienced labour force 15 years and over
Source: Statistics Canada. 2013. 2011 National Household Survey. Statistics Canada Catalogue no. 99-004-XWE. Ottawa. Released September 11, 2013.

Cities Ranked by Occupation: Business, Finance & Administration
By Number

Total

Rank	City	Number
1	Toronto, ON	256,410
2	Montréal, QC	148,485
3	Calgary, AB	122,555
4	Ottawa, ON	94,835
5	Edmonton, AB	80,795
6	Mississauga, ON	78,495
7	Winnipeg, MB	63,220
8	Vancouver, BC	59,225
9	Québec, QC	51,980
10	Brampton, ON	51,505
11	Laval, QC	40,885
12	Hamilton, ON	39,350
13	Surrey, BC	38,430
14	Halifax, NS	38,140
15	Gatineau, QC	34,585
16	Markham, ON	33,035
17	Vaughan, ON	31,705
18	London, ON	30,220
19	Longueuil, QC	23,960
20	Burnaby, BC	22,120
21	Regina, SK	21,530
22	Richmond Hill, ON	20,050
23	Saskatoon, SK	19,945
24	Richmond, BC	19,400
25	Oakville, ON	19,250
26	Kitchener, ON	19,220
27	Burlington, ON	17,700
28	Lévis, QC	14,725
29	Greater Sudbury, ON	13,900
30	Ajax, ON	12,965
31	Coquitlam, BC	12,695
32	Whitby, ON	12,370
33	Windsor, ON	11,865
34	Oshawa, ON	11,820
35	Sherbrooke, QC	11,670
36	Saguenay, QC	10,920
37	Cambridge, ON	10,530
38	Terrebonne, QC	10,450
39	Barrie, ON	10,280
40	Guelph, ON	10,050
41	Saanich, BC	10,020
42	St. Catharines, ON	9,955
43	Langley, BC	9,900
44	Kelowna, BC	9,890
45	Abbotsford, BC	9,790
46	Trois-Rivières, QC	9,565
47	St. John's, NL	9,245
48	Kingston, ON	9,160
49	Thunder Bay, ON	8,115
50	Chatham-Kent, ON	6,225
–	Canada	2,902,045

Male

Rank	City	Number
1	Toronto, ON	93,030
2	Montréal, QC	53,660
3	Calgary, AB	38,045
4	Ottawa, ON	31,885
5	Mississauga, ON	27,115
6	Edmonton, AB	24,545
7	Vancouver, BC	21,485
8	Winnipeg, MB	19,945
9	Brampton, ON	17,370
10	Québec, QC	16,320
11	Laval, QC	12,490
12	Surrey, BC	11,900
13	Markham, ON	11,480
14	Hamilton, ON	11,220
15	Halifax, NS	11,215
16	Gatineau, QC	10,320
17	Vaughan, ON	9,640
18	London, ON	8,940
19	Longueuil, QC	7,940
20	Burnaby, BC	7,030
21	Oakville, ON	6,935
22	Richmond, BC	6,645
23	Richmond Hill, ON	6,550
24	Regina, SK	6,485
25	Kitchener, ON	5,840
26	Burlington, ON	5,805
27	Saskatoon, SK	5,620
28	Lévis, QC	4,560
29	Coquitlam, BC	3,870
30	Whitby, ON	3,750
31	Ajax, ON	3,650
32	Oshawa, ON	3,595
33	Windsor, ON	3,520
34	Greater Sudbury, ON	3,475
34	Sherbrooke, QC	3,475
36	Saguenay, QC	3,350
37	St. Catharines, ON	3,040
38	Cambridge, ON	3,030
39	Barrie, ON	2,925
40	Guelph, ON	2,875
41	Terrebonne, QC	2,840
42	Trois-Rivières, QC	2,830
43	Saanich, BC	2,825
44	St. John's, NL	2,585
45	Kingston, ON	2,505
46	Abbotsford, BC	2,405
47	Kelowna, BC	2,315
48	Langley, BC	2,230
49	Thunder Bay, ON	2,010
50	Chatham-Kent, ON	1,420
–	Canada	854,190

Female

Rank	City	Number
1	Toronto, ON	163,380
2	Montréal, QC	94,825
3	Calgary, AB	84,510
4	Ottawa, ON	62,950
5	Edmonton, AB	56,250
6	Mississauga, ON	51,385
7	Winnipeg, MB	43,270
8	Vancouver, BC	37,745
9	Québec, QC	35,660
10	Brampton, ON	34,140
11	Laval, QC	28,395
12	Hamilton, ON	28,130
13	Halifax, NS	26,920
14	Surrey, BC	26,530
15	Gatineau, QC	24,265
16	Vaughan, ON	22,070
17	Markham, ON	21,555
18	London, ON	21,275
19	Longueuil, QC	16,020
20	Burnaby, BC	15,095
21	Regina, SK	15,045
22	Saskatoon, SK	14,325
23	Richmond Hill, ON	13,495
24	Kitchener, ON	13,380
25	Richmond, BC	12,750
26	Oakville, ON	12,310
27	Burlington, ON	11,895
28	Greater Sudbury, ON	10,420
29	Lévis, QC	10,165
30	Ajax, ON	9,310
31	Coquitlam, BC	8,825
32	Whitby, ON	8,620
33	Windsor, ON	8,345
34	Oshawa, ON	8,230
35	Sherbrooke, QC	8,200
36	Langley, BC	7,670
37	Terrebonne, QC	7,610
38	Kelowna, BC	7,570
38	Saguenay, QC	7,570
40	Cambridge, ON	7,505
41	Abbotsford, BC	7,385
42	Barrie, ON	7,355
43	Saanich, BC	7,195
44	Guelph, ON	7,175
45	St. Catharines, ON	6,915
46	Trois-Rivières, QC	6,740
47	St. John's, NL	6,660
48	Kingston, ON	6,650
49	Thunder Bay, ON	6,105
50	Chatham-Kent, ON	4,805
–	Canada	2,047,855

Note: Figures are based on total experienced labour force 15 years and over
Source: Statistics Canada. 2013. 2011 National Household Survey. Statistics Canada Catalogue no. 99-004-XWE. Ottawa. Released September 11, 2013.

Cities Ranked by Occupation: Business, Finance & Administration
By Percent

Total

Rank	City	Percent
1	Gatineau, QC	23.3%
2	Ajax, ON	21.3%
3	Markham, ON	21.2%
4	Mississauga, ON	20.5%
5	Vaughan, ON	20.4%
6	Richmond Hill, ON	20.1%
7	Richmond, BC	20.0%
8	Longueuil, QC	19.7%
9	Laval, QC	19.5%
9	Oakville, ON	19.5%
11	Ottawa, ON	19.4%
12	Regina, SK	19.3%
13	Brampton, ON	19.0%
13	Calgary, AB	19.0%
13	Toronto, ON	19.0%
16	Burnaby, BC	18.9%
17	Coquitlam, BC	18.6%
17	Lévis, QC	18.6%
17	Québec, QC	18.6%
20	Whitby, ON	18.5%
21	Burlington, ON	18.2%
22	Montréal, QC	18.0%
23	Winnipeg, MB	17.5%
24	Vancouver, BC	17.3%
25	Halifax, NS	17.2%
25	Langley, BC	17.2%
25	Terrebonne, QC	17.2%
28	Edmonton, AB	17.1%
29	Greater Sudbury, ON	17.0%
29	Saanich, BC	17.0%
31	St. John's, NL	16.6%
32	Surrey, BC	16.0%
33	Kelowna, BC	15.9%
33	Kitchener, ON	15.9%
33	London, ON	15.9%
36	Oshawa, ON	15.7%
37	Saskatoon, SK	15.6%
38	Cambridge, ON	15.4%
39	Hamilton, ON	15.2%
39	St. Catharines, ON	15.2%
41	Saguenay, QC	15.1%
41	Sherbrooke, QC	15.1%
41	Thunder Bay, ON	15.1%
44	Trois-Rivières, QC	14.9%
45	Guelph, ON	14.8%
46	Kingston, ON	14.4%
47	Abbotsford, BC	14.2%
47	Barrie, ON	14.2%
49	Windsor, ON	12.8%
50	Chatham-Kent, ON	12.6%
–	Canada	16.5%

Male

Rank	City	Percent
1	Markham, ON	14.1%
2	Gatineau, QC	13.8%
3	Mississauga, ON	13.5%
3	Oakville, ON	13.5%
3	Toronto, ON	13.5%
6	Richmond, BC	13.3%
7	Ottawa, ON	12.8%
8	Richmond Hill, ON	12.7%
9	Longueuil, QC	12.6%
10	Montréal, QC	12.5%
11	Vancouver, BC	12.2%
12	Ajax, ON	12.1%
12	Brampton, ON	12.1%
14	Vaughan, ON	11.9%
15	Burlington, ON	11.6%
15	Laval, QC	11.6%
17	Burnaby, BC	11.5%
18	Québec, QC	11.3%
19	Lévis, QC	11.2%
19	Regina, SK	11.2%
21	Calgary, AB	11.0%
21	Whitby, ON	11.0%
23	Coquitlam, BC	10.8%
24	Winnipeg, MB	10.7%
25	Halifax, NS	10.0%
26	Edmonton, AB	9.7%
27	Saanich, BC	9.5%
28	Kitchener, ON	9.3%
28	London, ON	9.3%
28	Oshawa, ON	9.3%
28	St. John's, NL	9.3%
28	Surrey, BC	9.3%
33	St. Catharines, ON	9.2%
34	Terrebonne, QC	9.1%
35	Sherbrooke, QC	8.9%
36	Cambridge, ON	8.5%
36	Saguenay, QC	8.5%
36	Trois-Rivières, QC	8.5%
39	Hamilton, ON	8.4%
39	Saskatoon, SK	8.4%
41	Greater Sudbury, ON	8.3%
41	Guelph, ON	8.3%
43	Kingston, ON	7.9%
44	Barrie, ON	7.8%
45	Langley, BC	7.4%
45	Thunder Bay, ON	7.4%
47	Windsor, ON	7.3%
48	Kelowna, BC	7.2%
49	Abbotsford, BC	6.6%
50	Chatham-Kent, ON	5.5%
–	Canada	9.3%

Female

Rank	City	Percent
1	Gatineau, QC	33.2%
2	Ajax, ON	30.3%
3	Vaughan, ON	29.4%
4	Markham, ON	29.0%
5	Calgary, AB	28.2%
6	Mississauga, ON	28.1%
6	Richmond Hill, ON	28.1%
8	Langley, BC	28.0%
8	Regina, SK	28.0%
10	Laval, QC	27.9%
11	Longueuil, QC	27.4%
12	Coquitlam, BC	27.3%
13	Burnaby, BC	26.9%
13	Richmond, BC	26.9%
15	Brampton, ON	26.8%
16	Lévis, QC	26.3%
16	Québec, QC	26.3%
18	Ottawa, ON	26.2%
18	Whitby, ON	26.2%
20	Greater Sudbury, ON	26.1%
21	Oakville, ON	26.0%
21	Terrebonne, QC	26.0%
23	Edmonton, AB	25.4%
24	Burlington, ON	25.2%
25	Kelowna, BC	25.0%
26	Toronto, ON	24.8%
27	Halifax, NS	24.7%
27	Winnipeg, MB	24.7%
29	Saanich, BC	24.5%
30	Montréal, QC	23.9%
30	St. John's, NL	23.9%
32	Surrey, BC	23.8%
33	Saskatoon, SK	23.5%
34	Kitchener, ON	23.2%
35	Cambridge, ON	23.1%
35	Saguenay, QC	23.1%
37	Abbotsford, BC	22.9%
38	Thunder Bay, ON	22.8%
39	London, ON	22.6%
39	Vancouver, BC	22.6%
41	Hamilton, ON	22.5%
42	Oshawa, ON	22.4%
43	Guelph, ON	21.8%
44	Trois-Rivières, QC	21.7%
45	Sherbrooke, QC	21.5%
46	St. Catharines, ON	21.4%
47	Barrie, ON	20.8%
47	Kingston, ON	20.8%
49	Chatham-Kent, ON	20.4%
50	Windsor, ON	18.8%
–	Canada	24.4%

Note: Figures are based on total experienced labour force 15 years and over
Source: Statistics Canada. 2013. 2011 National Household Survey. Statistics Canada Catalogue no. 99-004-XWE. Ottawa. Released September 11, 2013.

Cities Ranked by Occupation: Natural/Applied Sciences & Related
By Number

	Total			Male			Female	
Rank	City	Number	Rank	City	Number	Rank	City	Number
1	Toronto, ON	111,835	1	Toronto, ON	86,035	1	Toronto, ON	25,795
2	Calgary, AB	77,990	2	Calgary, AB	60,295	2	Calgary, AB	17,690
3	Montréal, QC	70,655	3	Montréal, QC	54,740	3	Montréal, QC	15,920
4	Ottawa, ON	62,020	4	Ottawa, ON	46,575	4	Ottawa, ON	15,440
5	Edmonton, AB	38,230	5	Edmonton, AB	29,660	5	Edmonton, AB	8,565
6	Mississauga, ON	37,750	6	Mississauga, ON	29,240	6	Mississauga, ON	8,510
7	Vancouver, BC	29,835	7	Vancouver, BC	23,270	7	Québec, QC	6,575
8	Québec, QC	26,020	8	Québec, QC	19,445	8	Vancouver, BC	6,565
9	Winnipeg, MB	23,570	9	Winnipeg, MB	18,605	9	Winnipeg, MB	4,960
10	Markham, ON	19,100	10	Markham, ON	14,660	10	Markham, ON	4,440
11	Brampton, ON	18,140	11	Brampton, ON	14,380	11	Richmond Hill, ON	3,795
12	Halifax, NS	17,365	12	Halifax, NS	14,245	12	Brampton, ON	3,760
13	Laval, QC	17,330	13	Laval, QC	13,580	13	Laval, QC	3,745
14	Hamilton, ON	14,675	14	Hamilton, ON	11,775	14	Vaughan, ON	3,185
15	Richmond Hill, ON	13,560	15	Surrey, BC	10,320	15	Halifax, NS	3,120
16	Vaughan, ON	13,205	16	Vaughan, ON	10,020	16	Hamilton, ON	2,905
17	Burnaby, BC	12,630	17	Burnaby, BC	9,840	17	Burnaby, BC	2,790
18	Surrey, BC	12,560	18	Richmond Hill, ON	9,765	18	Gatineau, QC	2,695
19	Gatineau, QC	11,735	19	Gatineau, QC	9,030	19	London, ON	2,405
20	London, ON	11,390	20	London, ON	8,990	20	Surrey, BC	2,235
21	Kitchener, ON	10,320	21	Kitchener, ON	8,150	21	Kitchener, ON	2,165
22	Longueuil, QC	9,455	22	Longueuil, QC	7,435	22	Oakville, ON	2,130
23	Oakville, ON	8,935	23	Oakville, ON	6,805	23	Saskatoon, SK	2,035
24	Saskatoon, SK	8,665	24	Saskatoon, SK	6,630	24	Longueuil, QC	2,020
25	Richmond, BC	7,980	25	Richmond, BC	6,395	25	Burlington, ON	1,680
26	Burlington, ON	7,810	26	Regina, SK	6,160	26	Lévis, QC	1,655
27	Regina, SK	7,805	27	Burlington, ON	6,125	27	Regina, SK	1,645
28	Lévis, QC	6,840	28	Lévis, QC	5,185	28	Richmond, BC	1,585
29	Windsor, ON	6,205	29	Windsor, ON	5,140	29	Coquitlam, BC	1,225
30	Coquitlam, BC	5,875	30	Coquitlam, BC	4,645	30	Ajax, ON	1,180
31	Sherbrooke, QC	5,295	31	Saguenay, QC	4,355	31	Sherbrooke, QC	1,125
32	Whitby, ON	5,155	32	Sherbrooke, QC	4,165	32	Saanich, BC	1,095
33	Saguenay, QC	5,150	33	Whitby, ON	4,075	33	Whitby, ON	1,085
34	Ajax, ON	5,050	34	St. John's, NL	4,040	34	Guelph, ON	1,075
35	St. John's, NL	4,915	35	Greater Sudbury, ON	3,900	35	Windsor, ON	1,065
36	Saanich, BC	4,880	36	Ajax, ON	3,875	36	Cambridge, ON	940
37	Guelph, ON	4,800	37	Saanich, BC	3,785	37	St. John's, NL	880
38	Greater Sudbury, ON	4,750	38	Guelph, ON	3,720	38	Greater Sudbury, ON	850
39	Cambridge, ON	4,155	39	Barrie, ON	3,275	39	Kingston, ON	835
40	Trois-Rivières, QC	3,960	40	Cambridge, ON	3,215	40	Saguenay, QC	795
41	Kelowna, BC	3,860	41	Trois-Rivières, QC	3,185	41	Oshawa, ON	785
42	Barrie, ON	3,845	42	Kelowna, BC	3,155	42	Trois-Rivières, QC	775
43	Oshawa, ON	3,775	43	Oshawa, ON	2,990	43	Kelowna, BC	705
44	Kingston, ON	3,700	44	Kingston, ON	2,870	44	Terrebonne, QC	675
45	Thunder Bay, ON	3,395	45	Thunder Bay, ON	2,805	45	St. Catharines, ON	630
46	Terrebonne, QC	3,215	46	Terrebonne, QC	2,540	46	Thunder Bay, ON	590
47	St. Catharines, ON	3,150	47	St. Catharines, ON	2,520	47	Barrie, ON	570
48	Langley, BC	2,995	48	Langley, BC	2,450	48	Langley, BC	550
49	Abbotsford, BC	2,790	49	Abbotsford, BC	2,340	49	Abbotsford, BC	445
50	Chatham-Kent, ON	1,915	50	Chatham-Kent, ON	1,625	50	Chatham-Kent, ON	290
–	Canada	1,237,775	–	Canada	966,355	–	Canada	271,415

Note: Figures are based on total experienced labour force 15 years and over
Source: Statistics Canada. 2013. 2011 National Household Survey. Statistics Canada Catalogue no. 99-004-XWE. Ottawa. Released September 11, 2013.

Cities Ranked by Occupation: Natural/Applied Sciences & Related
By Percent

Total

Rank	City	Percent
1	Richmond Hill, ON	13.6%
2	Ottawa, ON	12.7%
3	Markham, ON	12.3%
4	Calgary, AB	12.1%
5	Burnaby, BC	10.8%
6	Mississauga, ON	9.9%
7	Québec, QC	9.3%
8	Oakville, ON	9.1%
9	St. John's, NL	8.8%
10	Vancouver, BC	8.7%
11	Coquitlam, BC	8.6%
11	Lévis, QC	8.6%
11	Montréal, QC	8.6%
14	Kitchener, ON	8.5%
14	Vaughan, ON	8.5%
16	Ajax, ON	8.3%
16	Laval, QC	8.3%
16	Saanich, BC	8.3%
16	Toronto, ON	8.3%
20	Richmond, BC	8.2%
21	Edmonton, AB	8.1%
22	Burlington, ON	8.0%
23	Gatineau, QC	7.9%
23	Halifax, NS	7.9%
25	Longueuil, QC	7.8%
26	Whitby, ON	7.7%
27	Guelph, ON	7.1%
27	Saguenay, QC	7.1%
29	Regina, SK	7.0%
30	Sherbrooke, QC	6.9%
31	Saskatoon, SK	6.8%
32	Brampton, ON	6.7%
32	Windsor, ON	6.7%
34	Winnipeg, MB	6.5%
35	Thunder Bay, ON	6.3%
36	Kelowna, BC	6.2%
36	Trois-Rivières, QC	6.2%
38	Cambridge, ON	6.1%
39	London, ON	6.0%
40	Greater Sudbury, ON	5.8%
40	Kingston, ON	5.8%
42	Hamilton, ON	5.7%
43	Barrie, ON	5.3%
43	Terrebonne, QC	5.3%
45	Langley, BC	5.2%
45	Surrey, BC	5.2%
47	Oshawa, ON	5.0%
48	St. Catharines, ON	4.8%
49	Abbotsford, BC	4.0%
50	Chatham-Kent, ON	3.9%
–	Canada	7.0%

Male

Rank	City	Percent
1	Richmond Hill, ON	18.9%
2	Ottawa, ON	18.8%
3	Markham, ON	18.0%
4	Calgary, AB	17.4%
5	Burnaby, BC	16.1%
6	Mississauga, ON	14.6%
6	St. John's, NL	14.6%
8	Québec, QC	13.5%
9	Oakville, ON	13.3%
9	Vancouver, BC	13.3%
11	Coquitlam, BC	13.0%
12	Kitchener, ON	12.9%
13	Ajax, ON	12.8%
13	Lévis, QC	12.8%
13	Montréal, QC	12.8%
13	Richmond, BC	12.8%
17	Halifax, NS	12.7%
17	Saanich, BC	12.7%
19	Laval, QC	12.6%
20	Toronto, ON	12.5%
21	Vaughan, ON	12.4%
22	Burlington, ON	12.3%
23	Gatineau, QC	12.0%
23	Whitby, ON	12.0%
25	Edmonton, AB	11.8%
25	Longueuil, QC	11.8%
27	Saguenay, QC	11.1%
28	Guelph, ON	10.7%
28	Windsor, ON	10.7%
30	Regina, SK	10.6%
30	Sherbrooke, QC	10.6%
32	Thunder Bay, ON	10.4%
33	Brampton, ON	10.0%
33	Winnipeg, MB	10.0%
35	Kelowna, BC	9.9%
35	Saskatoon, SK	9.9%
37	Trois-Rivières, QC	9.6%
38	Greater Sudbury, ON	9.3%
38	London, ON	9.3%
40	Cambridge, ON	9.0%
40	Kingston, ON	9.0%
42	Barrie, ON	8.8%
42	Hamilton, ON	8.8%
44	Langley, BC	8.1%
44	Surrey, BC	8.1%
44	Terrebonne, QC	8.1%
47	Oshawa, ON	7.7%
48	St. Catharines, ON	7.6%
49	Abbotsford, BC	6.4%
50	Chatham-Kent, ON	6.3%
–	Canada	10.5%

Female

Rank	City	Percent
1	Richmond Hill, ON	7.9%
2	Ottawa, ON	6.4%
3	Markham, ON	6.0%
4	Calgary, AB	5.9%
5	Burnaby, BC	5.0%
6	Québec, QC	4.9%
7	Mississauga, ON	4.7%
8	Oakville, ON	4.5%
9	Lévis, QC	4.3%
10	Vaughan, ON	4.2%
11	Montréal, QC	4.0%
12	Edmonton, AB	3.9%
12	Toronto, ON	3.9%
12	Vancouver, BC	3.9%
15	Ajax, ON	3.8%
15	Coquitlam, BC	3.8%
17	Gatineau, QC	3.7%
17	Kitchener, ON	3.7%
17	Laval, QC	3.7%
17	Saanich, BC	3.7%
21	Burlington, ON	3.6%
22	Longueuil, QC	3.5%
23	Guelph, ON	3.3%
23	Richmond, BC	3.3%
23	Saskatoon, SK	3.3%
23	Whitby, ON	3.3%
27	St. John's, NL	3.2%
28	Regina, SK	3.1%
29	Sherbrooke, QC	3.0%
30	Brampton, ON	2.9%
30	Cambridge, ON	2.9%
30	Halifax, NS	2.9%
33	Winnipeg, MB	2.8%
34	Kingston, ON	2.6%
34	London, ON	2.6%
36	Trois-Rivières, QC	2.5%
37	Saguenay, QC	2.4%
37	Windsor, ON	2.4%
39	Hamilton, ON	2.3%
39	Kelowna, BC	2.3%
39	Terrebonne, QC	2.3%
42	Thunder Bay, ON	2.2%
43	Greater Sudbury, ON	2.1%
43	Oshawa, ON	2.1%
45	Langley, BC	2.0%
45	St. Catharines, ON	2.0%
45	Surrey, BC	2.0%
48	Barrie, ON	1.6%
49	Abbotsford, BC	1.4%
50	Chatham-Kent, ON	1.2%
–	Canada	3.2%

Note: Figures are based on total experienced labour force 15 years and over
Source: Statistics Canada. 2013. 2011 National Household Survey. Statistics Canada Catalogue no. 99-004-XWE. Ottawa. Released September 11, 2013.

Cities Ranked by Occupation: Health
By Number

Total

Rank	City	Number
1	Toronto, ON	72,980
2	Montréal, QC	53,750
3	Calgary, AB	36,665
4	Edmonton, AB	33,870
5	Ottawa, ON	28,820
6	Winnipeg, MB	27,950
7	Vancouver, BC	22,845
8	Québec, QC	21,510
9	Hamilton, ON	19,565
10	Mississauga, ON	18,030
11	Halifax, NS	16,010
12	London, ON	14,660
13	Surrey, BC	14,390
14	Laval, QC	12,865
15	Brampton, ON	11,415
16	Saskatoon, SK	10,350
17	Gatineau, QC	8,320
18	Markham, ON	7,900
19	Regina, SK	7,565
20	Longueuil, QC	7,490
21	Vaughan, ON	7,340
22	Sherbrooke, QC	7,295
23	Burnaby, BC	7,235
24	Windsor, ON	6,900
25	Kitchener, ON	6,370
26	Lévis, QC	6,100
27	Greater Sudbury, ON	6,070
28	Kingston, ON	5,535
29	Burlington, ON	5,520
30	Richmond Hill, ON	5,350
31	Trois-Rivières, QC	5,175
32	Richmond, BC	5,070
33	Saguenay, QC	4,880
34	Oakville, ON	4,845
35	Kelowna, BC	4,750
36	St. John's, NL	4,740
37	Barrie, ON	4,645
38	Saanich, BC	4,595
39	Oshawa, ON	4,530
40	Thunder Bay, ON	4,425
41	Coquitlam, BC	4,085
42	Abbotsford, BC	4,030
43	St. Catharines, ON	3,900
44	Terrebonne, QC	3,845
45	Ajax, ON	3,630
46	Chatham-Kent, ON	3,520
47	Guelph, ON	3,480
48	Whitby, ON	3,280
49	Langley, BC	3,165
50	Cambridge, ON	3,015
–	Canada	1,107,200

Male

Rank	City	Number
1	Toronto, ON	18,990
2	Montréal, QC	13,805
3	Edmonton, AB	7,200
4	Calgary, AB	7,060
5	Ottawa, ON	6,860
6	Vancouver, BC	6,715
7	Winnipeg, MB	6,470
8	Québec, QC	4,955
9	Hamilton, ON	4,020
10	Mississauga, ON	3,655
11	London, ON	3,370
12	Halifax, NS	3,280
13	Surrey, BC	2,520
14	Laval, QC	2,390
15	Markham, ON	2,150
16	Saskatoon, SK	2,065
17	Vaughan, ON	2,035
18	Richmond Hill, ON	1,845
19	Gatineau, QC	1,755
20	Brampton, ON	1,725
21	Burnaby, BC	1,620
22	Sherbrooke, QC	1,555
23	Regina, SK	1,465
24	Windsor, ON	1,380
25	Kingston, ON	1,345
26	Longueuil, QC	1,315
27	Richmond, BC	1,265
28	Kelowna, BC	1,245
29	Oakville, ON	1,225
30	Greater Sudbury, ON	1,135
31	Trois-Rivières, QC	1,030
32	Kitchener, ON	1,025
32	St. John's, NL	1,025
34	Saanich, BC	1,020
35	Burlington, ON	1,005
36	Lévis, QC	980
37	Coquitlam, BC	950
38	Saguenay, QC	930
39	Abbotsford, BC	920
40	Thunder Bay, ON	755
41	Guelph, ON	660
42	Oshawa, ON	655
43	Ajax, ON	650
44	Barrie, ON	635
45	St. Catharines, ON	615
46	Whitby, ON	550
47	Langley, BC	520
48	Terrebonne, QC	505
49	Chatham-Kent, ON	485
50	Cambridge, ON	380
–	Canada	217,520

Female

Rank	City	Number
1	Toronto, ON	53,990
2	Montréal, QC	39,945
3	Calgary, AB	29,605
4	Edmonton, AB	26,675
5	Ottawa, ON	21,960
6	Winnipeg, MB	21,480
7	Québec, QC	16,555
8	Vancouver, BC	16,135
9	Hamilton, ON	15,545
10	Mississauga, ON	14,380
11	Halifax, NS	12,725
12	Surrey, BC	11,875
13	London, ON	11,290
14	Laval, QC	10,475
15	Brampton, ON	9,685
16	Saskatoon, SK	8,280
17	Gatineau, QC	6,570
18	Longueuil, QC	6,180
19	Regina, SK	6,100
20	Markham, ON	5,750
21	Sherbrooke, QC	5,745
22	Burnaby, BC	5,615
23	Windsor, ON	5,520
24	Kitchener, ON	5,345
25	Vaughan, ON	5,305
26	Lévis, QC	5,120
27	Greater Sudbury, ON	4,935
28	Burlington, ON	4,515
29	Kingston, ON	4,185
30	Trois-Rivières, QC	4,140
31	Barrie, ON	4,010
32	Saguenay, QC	3,945
33	Oshawa, ON	3,870
34	Richmond, BC	3,810
35	St. John's, NL	3,720
36	Thunder Bay, ON	3,670
37	Oakville, ON	3,625
38	Saanich, BC	3,575
39	Kelowna, BC	3,500
39	Richmond Hill, ON	3,500
41	Terrebonne, QC	3,345
42	St. Catharines, ON	3,285
43	Coquitlam, BC	3,135
44	Abbotsford, BC	3,110
45	Chatham-Kent, ON	3,030
46	Ajax, ON	2,980
47	Guelph, ON	2,820
48	Whitby, ON	2,730
49	Langley, BC	2,645
50	Cambridge, ON	2,635
–	Canada	889,675

Note: Figures are based on total experienced labour force 15 years and over
Source: Statistics Canada. 2013. 2011 National Household Survey. Statistics Canada Catalogue no. 99-004-XWE. Ottawa. Released September 11, 2013.

Cities Ranked by Occupation: Health
By Percent

	Total			Male			Female	
Rank	City	Percent	Rank	City	Percent	Rank	City	Percent
1	Sherbrooke, QC	9.4%	1	Kingston, ON	4.2%	1	Sherbrooke, QC	15.1%
2	Kingston, ON	8.7%	2	Sherbrooke, QC	4.0%	2	Thunder Bay, ON	13.7%
3	St. John's, NL	8.5%	3	Kelowna, BC	3.9%	3	Saskatoon, SK	13.6%
4	Thunder Bay, ON	8.2%	4	Vancouver, BC	3.8%	4	St. John's, NL	13.4%
5	Saskatoon, SK	8.1%	5	St. John's, NL	3.7%	4	Trois-Rivières, QC	13.4%
5	Trois-Rivières, QC	8.1%	6	Richmond Hill, ON	3.6%	6	Lévis, QC	13.3%
7	Saanich, BC	7.8%	7	London, ON	3.5%	7	Kingston, ON	13.1%
8	London, ON	7.7%	7	Winnipeg, MB	3.5%	8	Chatham-Kent, ON	12.8%
8	Lévis, QC	7.7%	9	Québec, QC	3.4%	9	Greater Sudbury, ON	12.4%
8	Québec, QC	7.7%	9	Saanich, BC	3.4%	9	Hamilton, ON	12.4%
8	Winnipeg, MB	7.7%	11	Montréal, QC	3.2%	9	Windsor, ON	12.4%
12	Hamilton, ON	7.6%	12	Saskatoon, SK	3.1%	12	Québec, QC	12.2%
12	Kelowna, BC	7.6%	12	Trois-Rivières, QC	3.1%	12	Saanich, BC	12.2%
14	Windsor, ON	7.5%	14	Hamilton, ON	3.0%	12	Winnipeg, MB	12.2%
15	Greater Sudbury, ON	7.4%	15	Edmonton, AB	2.9%	15	Edmonton, AB	12.1%
16	Edmonton, AB	7.2%	15	Halifax, NS	2.9%	16	London, ON	12.0%
16	Halifax, NS	7.2%	15	Windsor, ON	2.9%	16	Saguenay, QC	12.0%
18	Chatham-Kent, ON	7.1%	18	Ottawa, ON	2.8%	18	Halifax, NS	11.7%
19	Regina, SK	6.8%	18	Thunder Bay, ON	2.8%	19	Kelowna, BC	11.5%
19	Saguenay, QC	6.8%	20	Coquitlam, BC	2.7%	20	Barrie, ON	11.4%
21	Vancouver, BC	6.7%	20	Greater Sudbury, ON	2.7%	20	Terrebonne, QC	11.4%
22	Montréal, QC	6.5%	20	Toronto, ON	2.7%	22	Regina, SK	11.3%
23	Barrie, ON	6.4%	23	Burnaby, BC	2.6%	23	Longueuil, QC	10.6%
24	Terrebonne, QC	6.3%	23	Markham, ON	2.6%	23	Surrey, BC	10.6%
25	Burnaby, BC	6.2%	25	Abbotsford, BC	2.5%	25	Oshawa, ON	10.5%
25	Longueuil, QC	6.2%	25	Regina, SK	2.5%	26	Laval, QC	10.3%
27	Laval, QC	6.1%	25	Richmond, BC	2.5%	27	St. Catharines, ON	10.2%
28	Ajax, ON	6.0%	25	Vaughan, ON	2.5%	28	Montréal, QC	10.1%
28	Coquitlam, BC	6.0%	29	Lévis, QC	2.4%	29	Burnaby, BC	10.0%
28	Oshawa, ON	6.0%	29	Oakville, ON	2.4%	30	Calgary, AB	9.9%
28	St. Catharines, ON	6.0%	29	Saguenay, QC	2.4%	31	Ajax, ON	9.7%
28	Surrey, BC	6.0%	32	Gatineau, QC	2.3%	31	Coquitlam, BC	9.7%
33	Ottawa, ON	5.9%	33	Laval, QC	2.2%	31	Langley, BC	9.7%
34	Abbotsford, BC	5.8%	34	Ajax, ON	2.1%	31	Vancouver, BC	9.7%
35	Burlington, ON	5.7%	34	Longueuil, QC	2.1%	35	Abbotsford, BC	9.6%
35	Calgary, AB	5.7%	36	Burlington, ON	2.0%	35	Burlington, ON	9.6%
37	Gatineau, QC	5.6%	36	Calgary, AB	2.0%	37	Kitchener, ON	9.3%
38	Langley, BC	5.5%	36	Surrey, BC	2.0%	38	Ottawa, ON	9.2%
39	Richmond Hill, ON	5.4%	39	Chatham-Kent, ON	1.9%	39	Gatineau, QC	9.0%
39	Toronto, ON	5.4%	39	Guelph, ON	1.9%	40	Guelph, ON	8.6%
41	Kitchener, ON	5.3%	39	St. Catharines, ON	1.9%	41	Whitby, ON	8.3%
42	Richmond, BC	5.2%	42	Mississauga, ON	1.8%	42	Toronto, ON	8.2%
43	Guelph, ON	5.1%	43	Barrie, ON	1.7%	43	Cambridge, ON	8.1%
43	Markham, ON	5.1%	43	Langley, BC	1.7%	44	Richmond, BC	8.0%
45	Oakville, ON	4.9%	43	Oshawa, ON	1.7%	45	Mississauga, ON	7.9%
45	Whitby, ON	4.9%	46	Kitchener, ON	1.6%	46	Markham, ON	7.7%
47	Mississauga, ON	4.7%	46	Terrebonne, QC	1.6%	46	Oakville, ON	7.7%
47	Vaughan, ON	4.7%	46	Whitby, ON	1.6%	48	Brampton, ON	7.6%
49	Cambridge, ON	4.4%	49	Brampton, ON	1.2%	49	Richmond Hill, ON	7.3%
50	Brampton, ON	4.2%	50	Cambridge, ON	1.1%	50	Vaughan, ON	7.1%
–	Canada	6.3%	–	Canada	2.4%	–	Canada	10.6%

Note: Figures are based on total experienced labour force 15 years and over
Source: Statistics Canada. 2013. 2011 National Household Survey. Statistics Canada Catalogue no. 99-004-XWE. Ottawa. Released September 11, 2013.

Cities Ranked by Occupation: Education, Law & Social, Community & Government Services
By Number

Total

Rank	City	Number
1	Toronto, ON	174,850
2	Montréal, QC	106,520
3	Ottawa, ON	76,930
4	Calgary, AB	63,930
5	Edmonton, AB	53,090
6	Winnipeg, MB	48,050
7	Vancouver, BC	44,580
8	Québec, QC	36,880
9	Mississauga, ON	33,605
10	Hamilton, ON	33,110
11	Halifax, NS	31,265
12	London, ON	25,850
13	Surrey, BC	22,500
14	Gatineau, QC	21,700
15	Brampton, ON	21,425
16	Laval, QC	20,370
17	Vaughan, ON	17,545
18	Saskatoon, SK	16,240
19	Markham, ON	15,270
20	Regina, SK	13,420
21	Kingston, ON	12,740
22	Kitchener, ON	12,405
23	Longueuil, QC	12,270
24	Burnaby, BC	12,220
25	Burlington, ON	11,880
26	Oakville, ON	11,635
27	Sherbrooke, QC	11,365
28	Richmond Hill, ON	11,025
29	Windsor, ON	10,395
30	Greater Sudbury, ON	10,320
31	Saguenay, QC	9,715
32	Lévis, QC	9,660
33	Whitby, ON	9,525
34	Guelph, ON	9,140
35	Barrie, ON	9,045
36	Richmond, BC	9,000
37	Trois-Rivières, QC	8,665
38	Oshawa, ON	8,585
39	Saanich, BC	8,525
40	St. John's, NL	8,430
41	Thunder Bay, ON	8,190
42	Abbotsford, BC	7,530
43	St. Catharines, ON	7,460
44	Coquitlam, BC	7,235
45	Terrebonne, QC	6,590
46	Langley, BC	6,565
47	Kelowna, BC	6,450
48	Ajax, ON	6,270
49	Cambridge, ON	6,215
50	Chatham-Kent, ON	4,910
–	Canada	2,064,675

Male

Rank	City	Number
1	Toronto, ON	58,640
2	Montréal, QC	35,440
3	Ottawa, ON	28,585
4	Calgary, AB	20,815
5	Edmonton, AB	20,220
6	Winnipeg, MB	16,750
7	Vancouver, BC	16,135
8	Québec, QC	14,595
9	Halifax, NS	12,310
10	Hamilton, ON	11,075
11	Mississauga, ON	9,650
12	London, ON	9,180
13	Gatineau, QC	8,065
14	Surrey, BC	7,190
15	Saskatoon, SK	6,075
16	Kingston, ON	5,800
17	Laval, QC	5,730
18	Brampton, ON	5,725
19	Regina, SK	4,805
20	Markham, ON	4,700
21	Vaughan, ON	4,590
22	Burnaby, BC	4,230
23	Sherbrooke, QC	3,870
24	Kitchener, ON	3,725
25	Burlington, ON	3,720
26	Longueuil, QC	3,705
27	Oakville, ON	3,650
28	Windsor, ON	3,615
29	Richmond Hill, ON	3,330
30	Whitby, ON	3,255
31	Saguenay, QC	3,220
32	St. John's, NL	3,165
33	Greater Sudbury, ON	3,155
34	Richmond, BC	3,140
35	Guelph, ON	3,135
36	Saanich, BC	3,095
37	Barrie, ON	3,000
38	Trois-Rivières, QC	2,980
39	Lévis, QC	2,930
40	Thunder Bay, ON	2,925
41	Abbotsford, BC	2,710
42	St. Catharines, ON	2,645
43	Oshawa, ON	2,620
44	Langley, BC	2,345
45	Coquitlam, BC	2,305
46	Kelowna, BC	2,100
47	Terrebonne, QC	1,915
48	Ajax, ON	1,810
49	Cambridge, ON	1,715
50	Chatham-Kent, ON	1,415
–	Canada	676,550

Female

Rank	City	Number
1	Toronto, ON	116,210
2	Montréal, QC	71,075
3	Ottawa, ON	48,345
4	Calgary, AB	43,115
5	Edmonton, AB	32,865
6	Winnipeg, MB	31,300
7	Vancouver, BC	28,445
8	Mississauga, ON	23,955
9	Québec, QC	22,290
10	Hamilton, ON	22,035
11	Halifax, NS	18,950
12	London, ON	16,670
13	Brampton, ON	15,700
14	Surrey, BC	15,310
15	Laval, QC	14,640
16	Gatineau, QC	13,640
17	Vaughan, ON	12,955
18	Markham, ON	10,575
19	Saskatoon, SK	10,165
20	Kitchener, ON	8,675
21	Regina, SK	8,615
22	Longueuil, QC	8,565
23	Burlington, ON	8,160
24	Burnaby, BC	7,985
24	Oakville, ON	7,985
26	Richmond Hill, ON	7,695
27	Sherbrooke, QC	7,495
28	Greater Sudbury, ON	7,160
29	Kingston, ON	6,940
30	Windsor, ON	6,780
31	Lévis, QC	6,730
32	Saguenay, QC	6,495
33	Whitby, ON	6,275
34	Barrie, ON	6,040
35	Guelph, ON	6,010
36	Oshawa, ON	5,970
37	Richmond, BC	5,860
38	Trois-Rivières, QC	5,685
39	Saanich, BC	5,435
40	Thunder Bay, ON	5,265
41	St. John's, NL	5,260
42	Coquitlam, BC	4,930
43	Abbotsford, BC	4,815
43	St. Catharines, ON	4,815
45	Terrebonne, QC	4,675
46	Cambridge, ON	4,500
47	Ajax, ON	4,465
48	Kelowna, BC	4,345
49	Langley, BC	4,215
50	Chatham-Kent, ON	3,495
–	Canada	1,388,130

Note: Figures are based on total experienced labour force 15 years and over
Source: Statistics Canada. 2013. 2011 National Household Survey. Statistics Canada Catalogue no. 99-004-XWE. Ottawa. Released September 11, 2013.

Cities Ranked by Occupation: Education, Law & Social, Community & Government Services
By Percent

Total

Rank	City	Percent
1	Kingston, ON	20.0%
2	Ottawa, ON	15.8%
3	St. John's, NL	15.2%
3	Thunder Bay, ON	15.2%
5	Sherbrooke, QC	14.7%
6	Gatineau, QC	14.6%
7	Saanich, BC	14.4%
8	Whitby, ON	14.2%
9	Halifax, NS	14.1%
10	London, ON	13.6%
11	Guelph, ON	13.5%
11	Saguenay, QC	13.5%
11	Trois-Rivières, QC	13.5%
14	Winnipeg, MB	13.3%
15	Québec, QC	13.2%
16	Toronto, ON	13.0%
16	Vancouver, BC	13.0%
18	Montréal, QC	12.9%
19	Hamilton, ON	12.8%
20	Saskatoon, SK	12.7%
21	Greater Sudbury, ON	12.6%
22	Barrie, ON	12.5%
23	Burlington, ON	12.2%
23	Lévis, QC	12.2%
25	Regina, SK	12.0%
26	Oakville, ON	11.8%
27	Langley, BC	11.4%
27	Oshawa, ON	11.4%
27	St. Catharines, ON	11.4%
30	Vaughan, ON	11.3%
31	Edmonton, AB	11.2%
31	Windsor, ON	11.2%
33	Richmond Hill, ON	11.1%
34	Abbotsford, BC	10.9%
34	Terrebonne, QC	10.9%
36	Coquitlam, BC	10.6%
37	Burnaby, BC	10.4%
37	Kelowna, BC	10.4%
39	Ajax, ON	10.3%
39	Kitchener, ON	10.3%
41	Longueuil, QC	10.1%
42	Chatham-Kent, ON	10.0%
43	Calgary, AB	9.9%
44	Markham, ON	9.8%
45	Laval, QC	9.7%
46	Surrey, BC	9.4%
47	Richmond, BC	9.3%
48	Cambridge, ON	9.1%
49	Mississauga, ON	8.8%
50	Brampton, ON	7.9%
–	Canada	11.7%

Male

Rank	City	Percent
1	Kingston, ON	18.3%
2	Ottawa, ON	11.5%
3	St. John's, NL	11.4%
4	Halifax, NS	11.0%
5	Thunder Bay, ON	10.8%
6	Gatineau, QC	10.7%
7	Saanich, BC	10.4%
8	Québec, QC	10.1%
9	Sherbrooke, QC	9.9%
10	Whitby, ON	9.6%
11	London, ON	9.5%
12	Vancouver, BC	9.2%
13	Saskatoon, SK	9.1%
14	Guelph, ON	9.0%
14	Trois-Rivières, QC	9.0%
14	Winnipeg, MB	9.0%
17	Toronto, ON	8.5%
18	Hamilton, ON	8.3%
18	Montréal, QC	8.3%
18	Regina, SK	8.3%
21	Saguenay, QC	8.2%
22	Barrie, ON	8.0%
22	Edmonton, AB	8.0%
22	St. Catharines, ON	8.0%
25	Langley, BC	7.8%
26	Burlington, ON	7.5%
26	Greater Sudbury, ON	7.5%
26	Windsor, ON	7.5%
29	Abbotsford, BC	7.4%
30	Lévis, QC	7.2%
31	Oakville, ON	7.1%
32	Burnaby, BC	6.9%
33	Oshawa, ON	6.8%
34	Kelowna, BC	6.6%
35	Coquitlam, BC	6.5%
35	Richmond Hill, ON	6.5%
37	Richmond, BC	6.3%
38	Terrebonne, QC	6.1%
39	Ajax, ON	6.0%
39	Calgary, AB	6.0%
41	Kitchener, ON	5.9%
41	Longueuil, QC	5.9%
43	Markham, ON	5.8%
44	Vaughan, ON	5.7%
45	Surrey, BC	5.6%
46	Chatham-Kent, ON	5.5%
47	Laval, QC	5.3%
48	Cambridge, ON	4.8%
48	Mississauga, ON	4.8%
50	Brampton, ON	4.0%
–	Canada	7.4%

Female

Rank	City	Percent
1	Kingston, ON	21.7%
2	Ottawa, ON	20.2%
3	Saguenay, QC	19.8%
4	Sherbrooke, QC	19.7%
5	Thunder Bay, ON	19.6%
6	Whitby, ON	19.1%
7	St. John's, NL	18.9%
8	Gatineau, QC	18.6%
9	Saanich, BC	18.5%
10	Trois-Rivières, QC	18.3%
11	Guelph, ON	18.2%
12	Greater Sudbury, ON	17.9%
12	Montréal, QC	17.9%
14	Winnipeg, MB	17.8%
15	London, ON	17.7%
15	Toronto, ON	17.7%
17	Hamilton, ON	17.6%
18	Halifax, NS	17.4%
18	Lévis, QC	17.4%
20	Burlington, ON	17.3%
20	Vaughan, ON	17.3%
22	Barrie, ON	17.1%
22	Vancouver, BC	17.1%
24	Oakville, ON	16.9%
25	Saskatoon, SK	16.7%
26	Québec, QC	16.5%
27	Oshawa, ON	16.3%
28	Regina, SK	16.0%
28	Richmond Hill, ON	16.0%
28	Terrebonne, QC	16.0%
31	Langley, BC	15.4%
32	Windsor, ON	15.3%
33	Coquitlam, BC	15.2%
34	Kitchener, ON	15.0%
35	Abbotsford, BC	14.9%
35	Edmonton, AB	14.9%
35	St. Catharines, ON	14.9%
38	Chatham-Kent, ON	14.8%
39	Longueuil, QC	14.6%
40	Ajax, ON	14.5%
41	Calgary, AB	14.4%
41	Laval, QC	14.4%
43	Kelowna, BC	14.3%
44	Burnaby, BC	14.2%
44	Markham, ON	14.2%
46	Cambridge, ON	13.8%
47	Surrey, BC	13.7%
48	Mississauga, ON	13.1%
49	Richmond, BC	12.4%
50	Brampton, ON	12.3%
–	Canada	16.5%

Note: Figures are based on total experienced labour force 15 years and over
Source: Statistics Canada. 2013. 2011 National Household Survey. Statistics Canada Catalogue no. 99-004-XWE. Ottawa. Released September 11, 2013.

Cities Ranked by Occupation: Art, Culture, Recreation & Sport
By Number

Total

Rank	City	Number
1	Toronto, ON	72,110
2	Montréal, QC	45,220
3	Vancouver, BC	22,620
4	Ottawa, ON	18,195
5	Calgary, AB	16,400
6	Edmonton, AB	12,180
7	Winnipeg, MB	9,800
8	Québec, QC	9,445
9	Mississauga, ON	9,200
10	Hamilton, ON	6,695
11	Halifax, NS	6,605
12	Laval, QC	5,550
13	Surrey, BC	5,145
14	Gatineau, QC	5,060
14	London, ON	5,060
16	Markham, ON	4,565
17	Brampton, ON	4,425
18	Vaughan, ON	4,205
19	Burnaby, BC	4,000
20	Longueuil, QC	3,670
21	Oakville, ON	3,450
22	Richmond Hill, ON	3,305
23	Richmond, BC	3,020
24	Saskatoon, SK	2,980
25	Kitchener, ON	2,845
26	Burlington, ON	2,725
27	Regina, SK	2,640
28	Barrie, ON	2,210
29	Kingston, ON	2,065
30	Coquitlam, BC	2,060
31	Whitby, ON	1,985
32	Windsor, ON	1,955
33	Saanich, BC	1,950
34	Kelowna, BC	1,905
35	Sherbrooke, QC	1,900
35	St. Catharines, ON	1,900
37	Lévis, QC	1,790
38	St. John's, NL	1,740
39	Oshawa, ON	1,690
40	Guelph, ON	1,645
41	Greater Sudbury, ON	1,630
42	Ajax, ON	1,615
43	Abbotsford, BC	1,605
44	Trois-Rivières, QC	1,590
45	Langley, BC	1,350
46	Saguenay, QC	1,335
47	Cambridge, ON	1,325
48	Terrebonne, QC	1,220
49	Thunder Bay, ON	1,005
50	Chatham-Kent, ON	735
–	Canada	503,415

Male

Rank	City	Number
1	Toronto, ON	37,100
2	Montréal, QC	22,925
3	Vancouver, BC	12,305
4	Ottawa, ON	7,800
5	Calgary, AB	7,215
6	Edmonton, AB	5,410
7	Winnipeg, MB	4,715
8	Québec, QC	4,700
9	Mississauga, ON	4,460
10	Hamilton, ON	3,180
11	Halifax, NS	3,160
12	Laval, QC	2,525
13	Surrey, BC	2,430
14	Gatineau, QC	2,350
15	London, ON	2,335
16	Burnaby, BC	2,255
17	Markham, ON	2,180
18	Brampton, ON	2,140
19	Longueuil, QC	1,865
19	Vaughan, ON	1,865
21	Oakville, ON	1,595
22	Richmond Hill, ON	1,515
23	Richmond, BC	1,495
24	Saskatoon, SK	1,370
25	Kitchener, ON	1,290
26	Regina, SK	1,275
27	Burlington, ON	1,260
28	Barrie, ON	1,025
29	St. John's, NL	990
30	Kelowna, BC	970
31	Coquitlam, BC	945
32	Windsor, ON	860
33	Saanich, BC	855
34	Sherbrooke, QC	850
34	Whitby, ON	850
36	St. Catharines, ON	845
37	Kingston, ON	830
38	Oshawa, ON	780
39	Greater Sudbury, ON	775
40	Lévis, QC	715
41	Ajax, ON	710
42	Trois-Rivières, QC	705
43	Guelph, ON	680
44	Abbotsford, BC	645
45	Saguenay, QC	635
46	Cambridge, ON	590
47	Langley, BC	580
48	Terrebonne, QC	485
49	Thunder Bay, ON	395
50	Chatham-Kent, ON	335
–	Canada	232,535

Female

Rank	City	Number
1	Toronto, ON	35,010
2	Montréal, QC	22,290
3	Ottawa, ON	10,395
4	Vancouver, BC	10,315
5	Calgary, AB	9,185
6	Edmonton, AB	6,770
7	Winnipeg, MB	5,085
8	Mississauga, ON	4,745
9	Québec, QC	4,740
10	Hamilton, ON	3,515
11	Halifax, NS	3,445
12	Laval, QC	3,030
13	London, ON	2,730
14	Surrey, BC	2,715
15	Gatineau, QC	2,710
16	Markham, ON	2,385
17	Vaughan, ON	2,345
18	Brampton, ON	2,280
19	Oakville, ON	1,855
20	Longueuil, QC	1,810
21	Richmond Hill, ON	1,790
22	Burnaby, BC	1,745
23	Saskatoon, SK	1,610
24	Kitchener, ON	1,555
25	Richmond, BC	1,525
26	Burlington, ON	1,460
27	Regina, SK	1,365
28	Kingston, ON	1,235
29	Barrie, ON	1,185
30	Whitby, ON	1,140
31	Coquitlam, BC	1,120
32	Windsor, ON	1,100
33	Saanich, BC	1,095
34	Lévis, QC	1,080
35	Sherbrooke, QC	1,055
35	St. Catharines, ON	1,055
37	Guelph, ON	965
38	Abbotsford, BC	960
39	Kelowna, BC	930
40	Oshawa, ON	915
41	Ajax, ON	905
42	Trois-Rivières, QC	880
43	Greater Sudbury, ON	860
44	Langley, BC	770
45	St. John's, NL	750
46	Terrebonne, QC	740
47	Cambridge, ON	735
48	Saguenay, QC	700
49	Thunder Bay, ON	610
50	Chatham-Kent, ON	405
–	Canada	270,875

Note: Figures are based on total experienced labour force 15 years and over
Source: Statistics Canada. 2013. 2011 National Household Survey. Statistics Canada Catalogue no. 99-004-XWE. Ottawa. Released September 11, 2013.

Cities Ranked by Occupation: Art, Culture, Recreation & Sport
By Percent

Total

Rank	City	Percent
1	Vancouver, BC	6.6%
2	Montréal, QC	5.5%
3	Toronto, ON	5.3%
4	Ottawa, ON	3.7%
5	Oakville, ON	3.5%
6	Burnaby, BC	3.4%
6	Gatineau, QC	3.4%
6	Québec, QC	3.4%
9	Richmond Hill, ON	3.3%
9	Saanich, BC	3.3%
11	Kingston, ON	3.2%
12	Kelowna, BC	3.1%
12	Richmond, BC	3.1%
12	St. John's, NL	3.1%
15	Barrie, ON	3.0%
15	Coquitlam, BC	3.0%
15	Halifax, NS	3.0%
15	Longueuil, QC	3.0%
15	Whitby, ON	3.0%
20	Markham, ON	2.9%
20	St. Catharines, ON	2.9%
22	Burlington, ON	2.8%
23	London, ON	2.7%
23	Vaughan, ON	2.7%
23	Winnipeg, MB	2.7%
26	Ajax, ON	2.6%
26	Edmonton, AB	2.6%
26	Hamilton, ON	2.6%
26	Laval, QC	2.6%
30	Calgary, AB	2.5%
30	Sherbrooke, QC	2.5%
30	Trois-Rivières, QC	2.5%
33	Guelph, ON	2.4%
33	Kitchener, ON	2.4%
33	Mississauga, ON	2.4%
33	Regina, SK	2.4%
37	Abbotsford, BC	2.3%
37	Langley, BC	2.3%
37	Lévis, QC	2.3%
37	Saskatoon, SK	2.3%
41	Oshawa, ON	2.2%
42	Surrey, BC	2.1%
42	Windsor, ON	2.1%
44	Greater Sudbury, ON	2.0%
44	Terrebonne, QC	2.0%
46	Cambridge, ON	1.9%
46	Thunder Bay, ON	1.9%
48	Saguenay, QC	1.8%
49	Brampton, ON	1.6%
50	Chatham-Kent, ON	1.5%
–	Canada	2.9%

Male

Rank	City	Percent
1	Vancouver, BC	7.0%
2	Toronto, ON	5.4%
3	Montréal, QC	5.3%
4	Burnaby, BC	3.7%
5	St. John's, NL	3.6%
6	Québec, QC	3.3%
7	Gatineau, QC	3.1%
7	Oakville, ON	3.1%
7	Ottawa, ON	3.1%
10	Kelowna, BC	3.0%
10	Longueuil, QC	3.0%
10	Richmond, BC	3.0%
13	Richmond Hill, ON	2.9%
13	Saanich, BC	2.9%
15	Halifax, NS	2.8%
16	Barrie, ON	2.7%
16	Markham, ON	2.7%
18	Coquitlam, BC	2.6%
18	Kingston, ON	2.6%
20	Burlington, ON	2.5%
20	St. Catharines, ON	2.5%
20	Whitby, ON	2.5%
20	Winnipeg, MB	2.5%
24	Hamilton, ON	2.4%
24	London, ON	2.4%
26	Ajax, ON	2.3%
26	Laval, QC	2.3%
26	Vaughan, ON	2.3%
29	Mississauga, ON	2.2%
29	Regina, SK	2.2%
29	Sherbrooke, QC	2.2%
32	Calgary, AB	2.1%
32	Edmonton, AB	2.1%
32	Saskatoon, SK	2.1%
32	Trois-Rivières, QC	2.1%
36	Guelph, ON	2.0%
36	Kitchener, ON	2.0%
36	Oshawa, ON	2.0%
39	Langley, BC	1.9%
39	Surrey, BC	1.9%
41	Abbotsford, BC	1.8%
41	Greater Sudbury, ON	1.8%
41	Lévis, QC	1.8%
41	Windsor, ON	1.8%
45	Cambridge, ON	1.6%
45	Saguenay, QC	1.6%
47	Brampton, ON	1.5%
47	Terrebonne, QC	1.5%
47	Thunder Bay, ON	1.5%
50	Chatham-Kent, ON	1.3%
–	Canada	2.5%

Female

Rank	City	Percent
1	Vancouver, BC	6.2%
2	Montréal, QC	5.6%
3	Toronto, ON	5.3%
4	Ottawa, ON	4.3%
5	Kingston, ON	3.9%
5	Oakville, ON	3.9%
7	Gatineau, QC	3.7%
7	Richmond Hill, ON	3.7%
7	Saanich, BC	3.7%
10	Coquitlam, BC	3.5%
10	Québec, QC	3.5%
10	Whitby, ON	3.5%
13	Barrie, ON	3.4%
14	St. Catharines, ON	3.3%
15	Halifax, NS	3.2%
15	Markham, ON	3.2%
15	Richmond, BC	3.2%
18	Burlington, ON	3.1%
18	Burnaby, BC	3.1%
18	Calgary, AB	3.1%
18	Edmonton, AB	3.1%
18	Kelowna, BC	3.1%
18	Longueuil, QC	3.1%
18	Vaughan, ON	3.1%
25	Abbotsford, BC	3.0%
25	Laval, QC	3.0%
27	Ajax, ON	2.9%
27	Guelph, ON	2.9%
27	London, ON	2.9%
27	Winnipeg, MB	2.9%
31	Hamilton, ON	2.8%
31	Langley, BC	2.8%
31	Lévis, QC	2.8%
31	Sherbrooke, QC	2.8%
31	Trois-Rivières, QC	2.8%
36	Kitchener, ON	2.7%
36	St. John's, NL	2.7%
38	Mississauga, ON	2.6%
38	Saskatoon, SK	2.6%
40	Oshawa, ON	2.5%
40	Regina, SK	2.5%
40	Terrebonne, QC	2.5%
40	Windsor, ON	2.5%
44	Surrey, BC	2.4%
45	Cambridge, ON	2.3%
45	Thunder Bay, ON	2.3%
47	Greater Sudbury, ON	2.2%
48	Saguenay, QC	2.1%
49	Brampton, ON	1.8%
50	Chatham-Kent, ON	1.7%
–	Canada	3.2%

Note: Figures are based on total experienced labour force 15 years and over
Source: Statistics Canada. 2013. 2011 National Household Survey. Statistics Canada Catalogue no. 99-004-XWE. Ottawa. Released September 11, 2013.

Cities Ranked by Occupation: Sales & Service
By Number

Total

Rank	City	Number
1	Toronto, ON	315,905
2	Montréal, QC	210,115
3	Calgary, AB	143,640
4	Edmonton, AB	108,655
5	Ottawa, ON	101,610
6	Mississauga, ON	91,625
7	Winnipeg, MB	88,715
8	Vancouver, BC	85,295
9	Québec, QC	72,610
10	Hamilton, ON	62,850
11	Brampton, ON	61,540
12	Surrey, BC	59,595
13	Halifax, NS	55,310
14	Laval, QC	54,570
15	London, ON	50,505
16	Markham, ON	36,225
17	Gatineau, QC	33,855
18	Vaughan, ON	33,380
19	Longueuil, QC	31,320
20	Saskatoon, SK	30,805
21	Burnaby, BC	30,155
22	Kitchener, ON	28,100
23	Richmond, BC	27,845
24	Regina, SK	26,225
25	Windsor, ON	25,620
26	Burlington, ON	23,105
27	Oakville, ON	21,920
28	Richmond Hill, ON	20,905
29	St. Catharines, ON	19,745
30	Oshawa, ON	19,685
31	Greater Sudbury, ON	19,420
32	Barrie, ON	19,105
32	Sherbrooke, QC	19,105
34	Lévis, QC	18,315
35	Saguenay, QC	18,305
36	Trois-Rivières, QC	16,725
37	Kingston, ON	16,340
38	Coquitlam, BC	16,300
39	Cambridge, ON	16,005
40	Kelowna, BC	15,965
41	Abbotsford, BC	15,275
42	Whitby, ON	14,815
43	Guelph, ON	14,735
44	Saanich, BC	14,290
45	Terrebonne, QC	13,970
46	Thunder Bay, ON	13,900
47	St. John's, NL	13,735
48	Ajax, ON	13,685
49	Chatham-Kent, ON	12,095
50	Langley, BC	12,075
–	Canada	4,068,170

Male

Rank	City	Number
1	Toronto, ON	149,760
2	Montréal, QC	106,845
3	Calgary, AB	64,825
4	Ottawa, ON	49,740
5	Edmonton, AB	46,655
6	Mississauga, ON	40,960
7	Vancouver, BC	40,285
8	Winnipeg, MB	40,040
9	Québec, QC	34,895
10	Hamilton, ON	26,655
11	Brampton, ON	25,820
12	Laval, QC	25,650
13	Surrey, BC	25,135
14	Halifax, NS	23,910
15	London, ON	22,195
16	Markham, ON	18,685
17	Gatineau, QC	17,625
18	Vaughan, ON	15,425
19	Longueuil, QC	14,645
20	Burnaby, BC	13,850
21	Saskatoon, SK	13,600
22	Richmond, BC	12,650
23	Regina, SK	11,665
24	Kitchener, ON	11,480
25	Windsor, ON	10,815
26	Burlington, ON	10,380
27	Oakville, ON	10,370
28	Richmond Hill, ON	9,885
29	Lévis, QC	8,490
30	St. Catharines, ON	8,385
31	Sherbrooke, QC	8,340
32	Saguenay, QC	8,005
33	Oshawa, ON	7,895
34	Greater Sudbury, ON	7,850
35	Barrie, ON	7,770
36	Kingston, ON	7,240
37	Coquitlam, BC	7,160
38	Trois-Rivières, QC	7,060
39	Saanich, BC	6,805
40	Whitby, ON	6,690
41	Kelowna, BC	6,625
42	Guelph, ON	6,210
43	Cambridge, ON	6,205
44	Ajax, ON	6,185
45	St. John's, NL	6,175
46	Terrebonne, QC	5,950
47	Abbotsford, BC	5,830
48	Thunder Bay, ON	5,810
49	Langley, BC	4,905
50	Chatham-Kent, ON	4,555
–	Canada	1,745,705

Female

Rank	City	Number
1	Toronto, ON	166,150
2	Montréal, QC	103,275
3	Calgary, AB	78,815
4	Edmonton, AB	61,995
5	Ottawa, ON	51,870
6	Mississauga, ON	50,665
7	Winnipeg, MB	48,675
8	Vancouver, BC	45,015
9	Québec, QC	37,715
10	Hamilton, ON	36,195
11	Brampton, ON	35,725
12	Surrey, BC	34,455
13	Halifax, NS	31,400
14	Laval, QC	28,920
15	London, ON	28,305
16	Vaughan, ON	17,960
17	Markham, ON	17,540
18	Saskatoon, SK	17,205
19	Longueuil, QC	16,670
20	Kitchener, ON	16,620
21	Burnaby, BC	16,300
22	Gatineau, QC	16,230
23	Richmond, BC	15,190
24	Windsor, ON	14,805
25	Regina, SK	14,555
26	Burlington, ON	12,720
27	Oshawa, ON	11,790
28	Greater Sudbury, ON	11,570
29	Oakville, ON	11,555
30	St. Catharines, ON	11,355
31	Barrie, ON	11,335
32	Richmond Hill, ON	11,020
33	Sherbrooke, QC	10,770
34	Saguenay, QC	10,300
35	Lévis, QC	9,825
36	Cambridge, ON	9,805
37	Trois-Rivières, QC	9,670
38	Abbotsford, BC	9,450
39	Kelowna, BC	9,335
40	Coquitlam, BC	9,135
41	Kingston, ON	9,095
42	Guelph, ON	8,520
43	Whitby, ON	8,120
44	Thunder Bay, ON	8,085
45	Terrebonne, QC	8,020
46	St. John's, NL	7,565
47	Chatham-Kent, ON	7,540
48	Ajax, ON	7,505
49	Saanich, BC	7,490
50	Langley, BC	7,170
–	Canada	2,322,465

Note: Figures are based on total experienced labour force 15 years and over
Source: Statistics Canada. 2013. 2011 National Household Survey. Statistics Canada Catalogue no. 99-004-XWE. Ottawa. Released September 11, 2013.

Cities Ranked by Occupation: Sales & Service
By Percent

Total

Rank	City	Percent
1	St. Catharines, ON	30.2%
2	Richmond, BC	28.7%
3	Windsor, ON	27.7%
4	London, ON	26.5%
5	Barrie, ON	26.3%
6	Oshawa, ON	26.1%
6	Trois-Rivières, QC	26.1%
8	Laval, QC	26.0%
9	Québec, QC	25.9%
10	Longueuil, QC	25.8%
10	Thunder Bay, ON	25.8%
12	Burnaby, BC	25.7%
12	Kingston, ON	25.7%
14	Kelowna, BC	25.6%
15	Montréal, QC	25.5%
16	Saguenay, QC	25.4%
17	Halifax, NS	25.0%
18	Surrey, BC	24.9%
18	Vancouver, BC	24.9%
20	Sherbrooke, QC	24.7%
20	St. John's, NL	24.7%
22	Chatham-Kent, ON	24.5%
22	Winnipeg, MB	24.5%
24	Hamilton, ON	24.3%
25	Saanich, BC	24.2%
26	Saskatoon, SK	24.1%
27	Coquitlam, BC	23.9%
27	Mississauga, ON	23.9%
29	Burlington, ON	23.8%
30	Greater Sudbury, ON	23.7%
31	Regina, SK	23.5%
32	Cambridge, ON	23.4%
32	Toronto, ON	23.4%
34	Kitchener, ON	23.3%
34	Markham, ON	23.3%
36	Lévis, QC	23.1%
36	Terrebonne, QC	23.1%
38	Edmonton, AB	23.0%
39	Gatineau, QC	22.8%
40	Brampton, ON	22.7%
41	Ajax, ON	22.5%
42	Abbotsford, BC	22.2%
42	Calgary, AB	22.2%
42	Oakville, ON	22.2%
45	Whitby, ON	22.1%
46	Guelph, ON	21.8%
47	Vaughan, ON	21.4%
48	Langley, BC	21.0%
48	Richmond Hill, ON	21.0%
50	Ottawa, ON	20.8%
–	Canada	23.1%

Male

Rank	City	Percent
1	Richmond, BC	25.4%
2	St. Catharines, ON	25.3%
3	Montréal, QC	24.9%
4	Québec, QC	24.2%
5	Laval, QC	23.8%
6	Gatineau, QC	23.5%
7	Longueuil, QC	23.2%
8	London, ON	23.0%
8	Markham, ON	23.0%
8	Vancouver, BC	23.0%
11	Kingston, ON	22.8%
11	Saanich, BC	22.8%
13	Burnaby, BC	22.6%
13	Windsor, ON	22.6%
15	St. John's, NL	22.3%
16	Toronto, ON	21.7%
17	Winnipeg, MB	21.5%
18	Thunder Bay, ON	21.4%
19	Halifax, NS	21.3%
19	Sherbrooke, QC	21.3%
19	Trois-Rivières, QC	21.3%
22	Lévis, QC	20.9%
23	Barrie, ON	20.8%
23	Burlington, ON	20.8%
25	Kelowna, BC	20.7%
26	Ajax, ON	20.5%
27	Mississauga, ON	20.4%
27	Oshawa, ON	20.4%
27	Saskatoon, SK	20.4%
30	Saguenay, QC	20.3%
31	Oakville, ON	20.2%
31	Regina, SK	20.2%
33	Coquitlam, BC	20.0%
33	Ottawa, ON	20.0%
35	Hamilton, ON	19.9%
36	Surrey, BC	19.7%
37	Whitby, ON	19.6%
38	Richmond Hill, ON	19.2%
39	Vaughan, ON	19.1%
40	Terrebonne, QC	19.0%
41	Calgary, AB	18.7%
41	Greater Sudbury, ON	18.7%
43	Edmonton, AB	18.5%
44	Kitchener, ON	18.2%
45	Brampton, ON	17.9%
45	Guelph, ON	17.9%
47	Chatham-Kent, ON	17.7%
48	Cambridge, ON	17.3%
49	Langley, BC	16.3%
50	Abbotsford, BC	15.9%
–	Canada	19.0%

Female

Rank	City	Percent
1	St. Catharines, ON	35.2%
2	Windsor, ON	33.3%
3	Barrie, ON	32.1%
3	Oshawa, ON	32.1%
3	Richmond, BC	32.1%
6	Chatham-Kent, ON	31.9%
7	Saguenay, QC	31.4%
8	Trois-Rivières, QC	31.2%
9	Surrey, BC	30.9%
10	Kelowna, BC	30.8%
11	Thunder Bay, ON	30.2%
12	Cambridge, ON	30.1%
12	London, ON	30.1%
14	Abbotsford, BC	29.3%
15	Burnaby, BC	29.1%
16	Greater Sudbury, ON	29.0%
17	Hamilton, ON	28.9%
18	Halifax, NS	28.8%
18	Kitchener, ON	28.8%
20	Kingston, ON	28.5%
20	Longueuil, QC	28.5%
22	Laval, QC	28.4%
23	Coquitlam, BC	28.2%
23	Saskatoon, SK	28.2%
23	Sherbrooke, QC	28.2%
26	Brampton, ON	28.0%
26	Edmonton, AB	28.0%
28	Québec, QC	27.8%
29	Mississauga, ON	27.7%
29	Winnipeg, MB	27.7%
31	Terrebonne, QC	27.4%
32	St. John's, NL	27.2%
33	Burlington, ON	27.0%
33	Regina, SK	27.0%
33	Vancouver, BC	27.0%
36	Calgary, AB	26.3%
37	Langley, BC	26.2%
38	Montréal, QC	26.0%
39	Guelph, ON	25.8%
40	Saanich, BC	25.5%
41	Lévis, QC	25.4%
42	Toronto, ON	25.2%
43	Whitby, ON	24.7%
44	Ajax, ON	24.4%
44	Oakville, ON	24.4%
46	Vaughan, ON	23.9%
47	Markham, ON	23.6%
48	Richmond Hill, ON	22.9%
49	Gatineau, QC	22.2%
50	Ottawa, ON	21.6%
–	Canada	27.7%

Note: Figures are based on total experienced labour force 15 years and over
Source: Statistics Canada. 2013. 2011 National Household Survey. Statistics Canada Catalogue no. 99-004-XWE. Ottawa. Released September 11, 2013.

Cities Ranked by Occupation: Trades, Transport & Equipment Operators & Related
By Number

Total

Rank	City	Number
1	Toronto, ON	121,260
2	Calgary, AB	88,890
3	Edmonton, AB	79,900
4	Montréal, QC	71,925
5	Brampton, ON	50,210
6	Winnipeg, MB	46,750
7	Mississauga, ON	45,120
8	Surrey, BC	44,130
9	Hamilton, ON	38,260
10	Ottawa, ON	34,895
11	Québec, QC	29,685
12	Halifax, NS	25,980
13	Vancouver, BC	25,890
14	Laval, QC	25,490
15	London, ON	23,000
16	Saskatoon, SK	19,740
17	Vaughan, ON	19,060
18	Kitchener, ON	17,355
19	Regina, SK	17,175
20	Longueuil, QC	16,670
21	Gatineau, QC	15,670
22	Greater Sudbury, ON	13,485
23	Abbotsford, BC	13,020
24	Oshawa, ON	12,780
25	Windsor, ON	12,705
26	Burnaby, BC	12,400
27	Saguenay, QC	12,010
28	Cambridge, ON	11,760
29	Terrebonne, QC	11,095
30	Markham, ON	10,460
31	Barrie, ON	10,440
32	Langley, BC	10,405
33	Lévis, QC	10,090
34	Sherbrooke, QC	9,645
35	Trois-Rivières, QC	9,345
36	Burlington, ON	9,280
37	Kelowna, BC	9,200
38	Coquitlam, BC	9,135
39	Chatham-Kent, ON	8,920
39	Richmond, BC	8,920
41	St. Catharines, ON	8,380
42	Thunder Bay, ON	8,335
43	Guelph, ON	7,905
44	Richmond Hill, ON	7,410
45	Whitby, ON	7,025
46	Ajax, ON	6,750
47	Oakville, ON	6,740
48	Saanich, BC	6,245
49	Kingston, ON	6,090
50	St. John's, NL	5,170
–	Canada	2,537,775

Male

Rank	City	Number
1	Toronto, ON	113,555
2	Calgary, AB	83,255
3	Edmonton, AB	74,260
4	Montréal, QC	67,220
5	Brampton, ON	46,300
6	Winnipeg, MB	44,470
7	Mississauga, ON	41,915
8	Surrey, BC	41,520
9	Hamilton, ON	36,025
10	Ottawa, ON	32,755
11	Québec, QC	28,365
12	Halifax, NS	24,860
13	Laval, QC	24,160
14	Vancouver, BC	24,145
15	London, ON	21,725
16	Saskatoon, SK	18,575
17	Vaughan, ON	18,160
18	Kitchener, ON	16,355
19	Regina, SK	16,110
20	Longueuil, QC	15,595
21	Gatineau, QC	14,995
22	Greater Sudbury, ON	12,745
23	Abbotsford, BC	12,405
24	Windsor, ON	12,040
25	Oshawa, ON	12,020
26	Burnaby, BC	11,855
27	Saguenay, QC	11,610
28	Cambridge, ON	10,980
29	Terrebonne, QC	10,355
30	Barrie, ON	9,775
31	Langley, BC	9,725
32	Lévis, QC	9,720
33	Markham, ON	9,610
34	Sherbrooke, QC	9,190
35	Trois-Rivières, QC	8,970
36	Coquitlam, BC	8,760
37	Burlington, ON	8,630
38	Kelowna, BC	8,615
39	Richmond, BC	8,330
40	Chatham-Kent, ON	8,310
41	Thunder Bay, ON	8,020
42	St. Catharines, ON	7,950
43	Guelph, ON	7,175
44	Richmond Hill, ON	7,030
45	Whitby, ON	6,645
46	Oakville, ON	6,370
47	Ajax, ON	6,285
48	Saanich, BC	5,925
49	Kingston, ON	5,775
50	St. John's, NL	5,005
–	Canada	2,385,615

Female

Rank	City	Number
1	Toronto, ON	7,710
2	Calgary, AB	5,635
2	Edmonton, AB	5,635
4	Montréal, QC	4,705
5	Brampton, ON	3,905
6	Mississauga, ON	3,210
7	Surrey, BC	2,605
8	Winnipeg, MB	2,280
9	Hamilton, ON	2,230
10	Ottawa, ON	2,140
11	Vancouver, BC	1,750
12	Laval, QC	1,335
13	Québec, QC	1,315
14	London, ON	1,270
15	Saskatoon, SK	1,165
16	Halifax, NS	1,120
17	Longueuil, QC	1,075
18	Regina, SK	1,065
19	Kitchener, ON	1,000
20	Vaughan, ON	900
21	Markham, ON	855
22	Cambridge, ON	780
23	Oshawa, ON	760
24	Greater Sudbury, ON	740
25	Terrebonne, QC	735
26	Guelph, ON	730
27	Langley, BC	680
28	Gatineau, QC	675
29	Barrie, ON	665
29	Windsor, ON	665
31	Burlington, ON	650
32	Abbotsford, BC	610
32	Chatham-Kent, ON	610
34	Richmond, BC	590
35	Kelowna, BC	585
36	Burnaby, BC	545
37	Ajax, ON	465
38	Sherbrooke, QC	455
39	St. Catharines, ON	420
40	Saguenay, QC	395
41	Richmond Hill, ON	385
42	Trois-Rivières, QC	380
42	Whitby, ON	380
44	Coquitlam, BC	375
44	Lévis, QC	375
46	Oakville, ON	370
47	Kingston, ON	315
47	Saanich, BC	315
47	Thunder Bay, ON	315
50	St. John's, NL	165
–	Canada	152,165

Note: Figures are based on total experienced labour force 15 years and over
Source: Statistics Canada. 2013. 2011 National Household Survey. Statistics Canada Catalogue no. 99-004-XWE. Ottawa. Released September 11, 2013.

Cities Ranked by Occupation: Trades, Transport & Equipment Operators & Related
By Percent

Total

Rank	City	Percent
1	Abbotsford, BC	18.9%
2	Brampton, ON	18.5%
3	Surrey, BC	18.4%
4	Terrebonne, QC	18.3%
5	Chatham-Kent, ON	18.1%
5	Langley, BC	18.1%
7	Cambridge, ON	17.2%
8	Edmonton, AB	16.9%
8	Oshawa, ON	16.9%
10	Saguenay, QC	16.6%
11	Greater Sudbury, ON	16.5%
12	Saskatoon, SK	15.5%
12	Thunder Bay, ON	15.5%
14	Regina, SK	15.4%
15	Hamilton, ON	14.8%
15	Kelowna, BC	14.8%
17	Trois-Rivières, QC	14.6%
18	Barrie, ON	14.4%
18	Kitchener, ON	14.4%
20	Calgary, AB	13.8%
21	Longueuil, QC	13.7%
21	Windsor, ON	13.7%
23	Coquitlam, BC	13.4%
24	Winnipeg, MB	12.9%
25	St. Catharines, ON	12.8%
26	Lévis, QC	12.7%
27	Sherbrooke, QC	12.5%
28	Laval, QC	12.2%
28	Vaughan, ON	12.2%
30	London, ON	12.1%
31	Mississauga, ON	11.8%
32	Guelph, ON	11.7%
32	Halifax, NS	11.7%
34	Ajax, ON	11.1%
35	Burnaby, BC	10.6%
35	Gatineau, QC	10.6%
35	Québec, QC	10.6%
35	Saanich, BC	10.6%
39	Whitby, ON	10.5%
40	Burlington, ON	9.6%
40	Kingston, ON	9.6%
42	St. John's, NL	9.3%
43	Richmond, BC	9.2%
44	Toronto, ON	9.0%
45	Montréal, QC	8.7%
46	Vancouver, BC	7.6%
47	Richmond Hill, ON	7.4%
48	Ottawa, ON	7.1%
49	Oakville, ON	6.8%
50	Markham, ON	6.7%
–	Canada	14.4%

Male

Rank	City	Percent
1	Abbotsford, BC	33.8%
2	Terrebonne, QC	33.0%
3	Surrey, BC	32.5%
4	Chatham-Kent, ON	32.4%
5	Langley, BC	32.3%
6	Brampton, ON	32.2%
7	Oshawa, ON	31.1%
8	Cambridge, ON	30.7%
9	Greater Sudbury, ON	30.4%
10	Thunder Bay, ON	29.6%
11	Edmonton, AB	29.5%
11	Saguenay, QC	29.5%
13	Regina, SK	27.8%
13	Saskatoon, SK	27.8%
15	Trois-Rivières, QC	27.1%
16	Hamilton, ON	26.9%
16	Kelowna, BC	26.9%
18	Barrie, ON	26.2%
19	Kitchener, ON	26.0%
20	Windsor, ON	25.1%
21	Longueuil, QC	24.7%
22	Coquitlam, BC	24.5%
23	Calgary, AB	24.0%
23	Lévis, QC	24.0%
23	St. Catharines, ON	24.0%
26	Winnipeg, MB	23.9%
27	Sherbrooke, QC	23.5%
28	London, ON	22.5%
28	Vaughan, ON	22.5%
30	Laval, QC	22.4%
31	Halifax, NS	22.1%
32	Mississauga, ON	20.9%
33	Ajax, ON	20.8%
34	Guelph, ON	20.7%
35	Gatineau, QC	20.0%
36	Saanich, BC	19.9%
37	Québec, QC	19.7%
38	Whitby, ON	19.5%
39	Burnaby, BC	19.4%
40	Kingston, ON	18.2%
41	St. John's, NL	18.0%
42	Burlington, ON	17.3%
43	Richmond, BC	16.7%
44	Toronto, ON	16.4%
45	Montréal, QC	15.7%
46	Vancouver, BC	13.8%
47	Richmond Hill, ON	13.6%
48	Ottawa, ON	13.2%
49	Oakville, ON	12.4%
50	Markham, ON	11.8%
–	Canada	26.0%

Female

Rank	City	Percent
1	Brampton, ON	3.1%
2	Chatham-Kent, ON	2.6%
3	Edmonton, AB	2.5%
3	Langley, BC	2.5%
3	Terrebonne, QC	2.5%
6	Cambridge, ON	2.4%
7	Surrey, BC	2.3%
8	Guelph, ON	2.2%
9	Oshawa, ON	2.1%
10	Regina, SK	2.0%
11	Abbotsford, BC	1.9%
11	Barrie, ON	1.9%
11	Calgary, AB	1.9%
11	Greater Sudbury, ON	1.9%
11	Kelowna, BC	1.9%
11	Saskatoon, SK	1.9%
17	Hamilton, ON	1.8%
17	Longueuil, QC	1.8%
17	Mississauga, ON	1.8%
20	Kitchener, ON	1.7%
21	Ajax, ON	1.5%
21	Windsor, ON	1.5%
23	Burlington, ON	1.4%
23	London, ON	1.4%
25	Laval, QC	1.3%
25	St. Catharines, ON	1.3%
25	Winnipeg, MB	1.3%
28	Coquitlam, BC	1.2%
28	Markham, ON	1.2%
28	Montréal, QC	1.2%
28	Richmond, BC	1.2%
28	Saguenay, QC	1.2%
28	Sherbrooke, QC	1.2%
28	Thunder Bay, ON	1.2%
28	Toronto, ON	1.2%
28	Trois-Rivières, QC	1.2%
28	Vaughan, ON	1.2%
28	Whitby, ON	1.2%
39	Saanich, BC	1.1%
39	Vancouver, BC	1.1%
41	Burnaby, BC	1.0%
41	Halifax, NS	1.0%
41	Kingston, ON	1.0%
41	Lévis, QC	1.0%
41	Québec, QC	1.0%
46	Gatineau, QC	0.9%
46	Ottawa, ON	0.9%
48	Oakville, ON	0.8%
48	Richmond Hill, ON	0.8%
50	St. John's, NL	0.6%
–	Canada	1.8%

Note: Figures are based on total experienced labour force 15 years and over
Source: Statistics Canada. 2013. 2011 National Household Survey. Statistics Canada Catalogue no. 99-004-XWE. Ottawa. Released September 11, 2013.

Cities Ranked by Occupation: Natural Resources, Agriculture & Related Production

By Number

Total

Rank	City	Number
1	Calgary, AB	8,720
2	Toronto, ON	7,235
3	Edmonton, AB	6,710
4	Surrey, BC	5,610
5	Abbotsford, BC	4,560
6	Hamilton, ON	4,090
7	Ottawa, ON	3,990
8	Montréal, QC	3,820
9	Greater Sudbury, ON	3,800
10	Winnipeg, MB	3,410
11	Vancouver, BC	3,015
12	Mississauga, ON	2,840
13	Saskatoon, SK	2,265
14	Halifax, NS	2,185
15	Brampton, ON	2,035
16	London, ON	1,845
17	Chatham-Kent, ON	1,840
18	Kelowna, BC	1,740
19	St. Catharines, ON	1,600
20	Langley, BC	1,530
21	Québec, QC	1,520
22	Windsor, ON	1,405
23	Regina, SK	1,215
24	Kitchener, ON	1,095
25	Saanich, BC	1,030
26	Vaughan, ON	1,010
27	Burlington, ON	995
27	Oakville, ON	995
29	Markham, ON	985
30	Cambridge, ON	975
31	Gatineau, QC	970
32	Oshawa, ON	960
32	Richmond, BC	960
34	Thunder Bay, ON	950
35	Burnaby, BC	900
36	Laval, QC	885
37	Guelph, ON	880
38	Longueuil, QC	795
39	Whitby, ON	780
40	Sherbrooke, QC	760
41	Barrie, ON	735
42	Saguenay, QC	705
43	Ajax, ON	625
44	Richmond Hill, ON	620
45	Kingston, ON	605
46	Lévis, QC	590
47	St. John's, NL	575
48	Coquitlam, BC	520
49	Terrebonne, QC	485
50	Trois-Rivières, QC	445
–	Canada	397,930

Male

Rank	City	Number
1	Calgary, AB	7,275
2	Toronto, ON	6,140
3	Edmonton, AB	5,870
4	Greater Sudbury, ON	3,565
5	Ottawa, ON	3,205
6	Montréal, QC	3,165
7	Surrey, BC	3,070
8	Hamilton, ON	2,960
9	Winnipeg, MB	2,790
10	Mississauga, ON	2,325
11	Vancouver, BC	2,250
12	Abbotsford, BC	2,205
13	Saskatoon, SK	1,810
14	Halifax, NS	1,805
15	Brampton, ON	1,690
16	London, ON	1,550
17	Kelowna, BC	1,415
18	Québec, QC	1,325
19	Chatham-Kent, ON	1,285
20	St. Catharines, ON	1,075
21	Regina, SK	1,050
22	Langley, BC	940
23	Windsor, ON	925
24	Vaughan, ON	910
25	Thunder Bay, ON	880
26	Markham, ON	870
27	Gatineau, QC	865
28	Kitchener, ON	860
29	Burlington, ON	805
29	Saanich, BC	805
31	Laval, QC	785
31	Oshawa, ON	785
33	Longueuil, QC	755
34	Oakville, ON	750
35	Richmond, BC	740
36	Burnaby, BC	735
37	Cambridge, ON	705
38	Sherbrooke, QC	680
39	Saguenay, QC	660
40	Guelph, ON	640
40	Whitby, ON	640
42	Ajax, ON	535
42	Barrie, ON	535
44	Kingston, ON	525
45	Richmond Hill, ON	505
46	St. John's, NL	500
47	Lévis, QC	455
48	Coquitlam, BC	450
49	Terrebonne, QC	395
50	Trois-Rivières, QC	370
–	Canada	318,945

Female

Rank	City	Number
1	Surrey, BC	2,535
2	Abbotsford, BC	2,360
3	Calgary, AB	1,445
4	Hamilton, ON	1,125
5	Toronto, ON	1,095
6	Edmonton, AB	840
7	Ottawa, ON	780
8	Vancouver, BC	765
9	Montréal, QC	650
10	Winnipeg, MB	620
11	Langley, BC	585
12	Chatham-Kent, ON	555
13	St. Catharines, ON	525
14	Mississauga, ON	515
15	Windsor, ON	480
16	Saskatoon, SK	460
17	Halifax, NS	380
18	Brampton, ON	345
19	Kelowna, BC	325
20	London, ON	295
21	Cambridge, ON	270
22	Guelph, ON	240
22	Kitchener, ON	240
22	Oakville, ON	240
25	Greater Sudbury, ON	235
26	Saanich, BC	225
27	Richmond, BC	215
28	Barrie, ON	200
29	Québec, QC	195
30	Burlington, ON	190
31	Oshawa, ON	170
32	Regina, SK	165
33	Burnaby, BC	160
34	Whitby, ON	145
35	Lévis, QC	140
36	Markham, ON	120
36	Richmond Hill, ON	120
38	Gatineau, QC	105
39	Laval, QC	100
40	Vaughan, ON	95
41	Ajax, ON	85
41	Terrebonne, QC	85
43	Kingston, ON	80
43	Sherbrooke, QC	80
45	Coquitlam, BC	75
45	Thunder Bay, ON	75
45	Trois-Rivières, QC	75
48	St. John's, NL	70
49	Longueuil, QC	40
50	Saguenay, QC	35
–	Canada	78,980

Note: Figures are based on total experienced labour force 15 years and over
Source: Statistics Canada. 2013. 2011 National Household Survey. Statistics Canada Catalogue no. 99-004-XWE. Ottawa. Released September 11, 2013.

Cities Ranked by Occupation: Natural Resources, Agriculture & Related Production
By Percent

Total

Rank	City	Percent
1	Abbotsford, BC	6.6%
2	Greater Sudbury, ON	4.6%
3	Chatham-Kent, ON	3.7%
4	Kelowna, BC	2.8%
5	Langley, BC	2.7%
6	St. Catharines, ON	2.4%
7	Surrey, BC	2.3%
8	Saskatoon, SK	1.8%
8	Thunder Bay, ON	1.8%
10	Saanich, BC	1.7%
11	Hamilton, ON	1.6%
12	Windsor, ON	1.5%
13	Cambridge, ON	1.4%
13	Edmonton, AB	1.4%
15	Calgary, AB	1.3%
15	Guelph, ON	1.3%
15	Oshawa, ON	1.3%
18	Whitby, ON	1.2%
19	Regina, SK	1.1%
20	Ajax, ON	1.0%
20	Barrie, ON	1.0%
20	Burlington, ON	1.0%
20	Halifax, NS	1.0%
20	London, ON	1.0%
20	Oakville, ON	1.0%
20	Richmond, BC	1.0%
20	Saguenay, QC	1.0%
20	Sherbrooke, QC	1.0%
20	St. John's, NL	1.0%
30	Kingston, ON	0.9%
30	Kitchener, ON	0.9%
30	Vancouver, BC	0.9%
30	Winnipeg, MB	0.9%
34	Burnaby, BC	0.8%
34	Coquitlam, BC	0.8%
34	Ottawa, ON	0.8%
34	Terrebonne, QC	0.8%
38	Brampton, ON	0.7%
38	Gatineau, QC	0.7%
38	Longueuil, QC	0.7%
38	Lévis, QC	0.7%
38	Mississauga, ON	0.7%
38	Trois-Rivières, QC	0.7%
44	Markham, ON	0.6%
44	Richmond Hill, ON	0.6%
44	Vaughan, ON	0.6%
47	Montréal, QC	0.5%
47	Québec, QC	0.5%
47	Toronto, ON	0.5%
50	Laval, QC	0.4%
–	Canada	2.3%

Male

Rank	City	Percent
1	Greater Sudbury, ON	8.5%
2	Abbotsford, BC	6.0%
3	Chatham-Kent, ON	5.0%
4	Kelowna, BC	4.4%
5	St. Catharines, ON	3.2%
5	Thunder Bay, ON	3.2%
7	Langley, BC	3.1%
8	Saanich, BC	2.7%
8	Saskatoon, SK	2.7%
10	Surrey, BC	2.4%
11	Edmonton, AB	2.3%
12	Hamilton, ON	2.2%
13	Calgary, AB	2.1%
14	Cambridge, ON	2.0%
14	Oshawa, ON	2.0%
16	Whitby, ON	1.9%
16	Windsor, ON	1.9%
18	Ajax, ON	1.8%
18	Guelph, ON	1.8%
18	Regina, SK	1.8%
18	St. John's, NL	1.8%
22	Kingston, ON	1.7%
22	Saguenay, QC	1.7%
22	Sherbrooke, QC	1.7%
25	Burlington, ON	1.6%
25	Halifax, NS	1.6%
25	London, ON	1.6%
28	Oakville, ON	1.5%
28	Richmond, BC	1.5%
28	Winnipeg, MB	1.5%
31	Barrie, ON	1.4%
31	Kitchener, ON	1.4%
33	Coquitlam, BC	1.3%
33	Ottawa, ON	1.3%
33	Terrebonne, QC	1.3%
33	Vancouver, BC	1.3%
37	Brampton, ON	1.2%
37	Burnaby, BC	1.2%
37	Gatineau, QC	1.2%
37	Longueuil, QC	1.2%
37	Mississauga, ON	1.2%
42	Lévis, QC	1.1%
42	Markham, ON	1.1%
42	Trois-Rivières, QC	1.1%
42	Vaughan, ON	1.1%
46	Richmond Hill, ON	1.0%
47	Québec, QC	0.9%
47	Toronto, ON	0.9%
49	Laval, QC	0.7%
49	Montréal, QC	0.7%
–	Canada	3.5%

Female

Rank	City	Percent
1	Abbotsford, BC	7.3%
2	Chatham-Kent, ON	2.4%
3	Surrey, BC	2.3%
4	Langley, BC	2.1%
5	St. Catharines, ON	1.6%
6	Kelowna, BC	1.1%
6	Windsor, ON	1.1%
8	Hamilton, ON	0.9%
9	Cambridge, ON	0.8%
9	Saanich, BC	0.8%
9	Saskatoon, SK	0.8%
12	Guelph, ON	0.7%
13	Barrie, ON	0.6%
13	Greater Sudbury, ON	0.6%
15	Calgary, AB	0.5%
15	Oakville, ON	0.5%
15	Oshawa, ON	0.5%
15	Richmond, BC	0.5%
15	Vancouver, BC	0.5%
20	Burlington, ON	0.4%
20	Edmonton, AB	0.4%
20	Kitchener, ON	0.4%
20	Lévis, QC	0.4%
20	Whitby, ON	0.4%
20	Winnipeg, MB	0.4%
26	Ajax, ON	0.3%
26	Brampton, ON	0.3%
26	Burnaby, BC	0.3%
26	Halifax, NS	0.3%
26	Kingston, ON	0.3%
26	London, ON	0.3%
26	Mississauga, ON	0.3%
26	Ottawa, ON	0.3%
26	Regina, SK	0.3%
26	St. John's, NL	0.3%
26	Terrebonne, QC	0.3%
26	Thunder Bay, ON	0.3%
38	Coquitlam, BC	0.2%
38	Markham, ON	0.2%
38	Montréal, QC	0.2%
38	Richmond Hill, ON	0.2%
38	Sherbrooke, QC	0.2%
38	Toronto, ON	0.2%
38	Trois-Rivières, QC	0.2%
45	Gatineau, QC	0.1%
45	Laval, QC	0.1%
45	Longueuil, QC	0.1%
45	Québec, QC	0.1%
45	Saguenay, QC	0.1%
45	Vaughan, ON	0.1%
–	Canada	0.9%

Note: Figures are based on total experienced labour force 15 years and over
Source: Statistics Canada. 2013. 2011 National Household Survey. Statistics Canada Catalogue no. 99-004-XWE. Ottawa. Released September 11, 2013.

Cities Ranked by Occupation: Manufacturing & Utilities
By Number

Total

Rank	City	Number
1	Toronto, ON	63,165
2	Montréal, QC	35,515
3	Brampton, ON	27,215
4	Mississauga, ON	21,570
5	Winnipeg, MB	17,045
6	Calgary, AB	15,090
7	Hamilton, ON	14,835
8	Edmonton, AB	13,100
9	Surrey, BC	12,060
10	Kitchener, ON	11,585
11	London, ON	10,265
12	Vancouver, BC	9,005
13	Laval, QC	8,515
14	Windsor, ON	8,510
15	Guelph, ON	7,785
16	Markham, ON	7,700
17	Cambridge, ON	7,065
18	Vaughan, ON	6,940
19	Québec, QC	6,910
20	Ottawa, ON	5,620
21	Longueuil, QC	5,590
22	Oshawa, ON	4,460
23	Barrie, ON	4,195
24	Saskatoon, SK	4,095
25	Sherbrooke, QC	3,985
26	Halifax, NS	3,885
27	Lévis, QC	3,640
28	Abbotsford, BC	3,450
29	Trois-Rivières, QC	3,350
30	Terrebonne, QC	3,345
31	Chatham-Kent, ON	3,330
31	Saguenay, QC	3,330
33	Burnaby, BC	3,180
34	Burlington, ON	3,125
35	St. Catharines, ON	3,055
36	Richmond, BC	2,870
37	Richmond Hill, ON	2,495
38	Regina, SK	2,475
39	Ajax, ON	2,470
40	Oakville, ON	2,400
41	Whitby, ON	2,275
42	Coquitlam, BC	1,955
43	Gatineau, QC	1,930
44	Langley, BC	1,695
45	Greater Sudbury, ON	1,625
46	Kelowna, BC	1,620
47	Thunder Bay, ON	1,265
48	St. John's, NL	1,135
49	Kingston, ON	1,015
50	Saanich, BC	880
–	Canada	805,040

Male

Rank	City	Number
1	Toronto, ON	37,260
2	Montréal, QC	22,340
3	Brampton, ON	14,440
4	Mississauga, ON	12,965
5	Winnipeg, MB	12,420
6	Calgary, AB	11,455
7	Hamilton, ON	11,280
8	Edmonton, AB	9,745
9	Surrey, BC	7,660
10	London, ON	7,495
11	Kitchener, ON	7,465
12	Laval, QC	5,785
13	Windsor, ON	5,700
14	Vancouver, BC	5,130
15	Québec, QC	5,070
16	Guelph, ON	5,050
17	Cambridge, ON	4,480
18	Vaughan, ON	4,090
19	Markham, ON	4,070
20	Ottawa, ON	4,050
21	Longueuil, QC	3,790
22	Oshawa, ON	3,310
23	Barrie, ON	3,170
24	Saskatoon, SK	3,095
25	Sherbrooke, QC	2,930
26	Saguenay, QC	2,920
27	Halifax, NS	2,890
28	Lévis, QC	2,715
29	Trois-Rivières, QC	2,705
30	Abbotsford, BC	2,475
31	Chatham-Kent, ON	2,390
32	St. Catharines, ON	2,315
33	Burlington, ON	2,295
34	Regina, SK	2,155
35	Terrebonne, QC	2,115
36	Burnaby, BC	1,945
37	Whitby, ON	1,775
38	Ajax, ON	1,735
39	Richmond, BC	1,695
40	Oakville, ON	1,620
41	Gatineau, QC	1,590
42	Richmond Hill, ON	1,585
43	Greater Sudbury, ON	1,450
44	Coquitlam, BC	1,380
45	Langley, BC	1,315
46	Thunder Bay, ON	1,125
47	Kelowna, BC	1,055
48	St. John's, NL	885
49	Kingston, ON	875
50	Saanich, BC	640
–	Canada	564,300

Female

Rank	City	Number
1	Toronto, ON	25,905
2	Montréal, QC	13,175
3	Brampton, ON	12,780
4	Mississauga, ON	8,605
5	Winnipeg, MB	4,630
6	Surrey, BC	4,400
7	Kitchener, ON	4,120
8	Vancouver, BC	3,870
9	Calgary, AB	3,640
10	Markham, ON	3,625
11	Hamilton, ON	3,555
12	Edmonton, AB	3,355
13	Vaughan, ON	2,850
14	Windsor, ON	2,805
15	London, ON	2,765
16	Guelph, ON	2,730
17	Laval, QC	2,725
18	Cambridge, ON	2,585
19	Québec, QC	1,845
20	Longueuil, QC	1,795
21	Ottawa, ON	1,575
22	Burnaby, BC	1,235
23	Terrebonne, QC	1,230
24	Richmond, BC	1,180
25	Oshawa, ON	1,150
26	Sherbrooke, QC	1,055
27	Barrie, ON	1,025
28	Halifax, NS	995
28	Saskatoon, SK	995
30	Abbotsford, BC	975
31	Chatham-Kent, ON	940
32	Lévis, QC	930
33	Richmond Hill, ON	905
34	Burlington, ON	835
35	Oakville, ON	775
36	St. Catharines, ON	745
37	Ajax, ON	730
38	Trois-Rivières, QC	645
39	Coquitlam, BC	575
40	Kelowna, BC	565
41	Whitby, ON	500
42	Saguenay, QC	410
43	Langley, BC	380
44	Gatineau, QC	340
45	Regina, SK	320
46	St. John's, NL	245
47	Saanich, BC	240
48	Greater Sudbury, ON	180
49	Kingston, ON	145
50	Thunder Bay, ON	135
–	Canada	240,740

Note: Figures are based on total experienced labour force 15 years and over
Source: Statistics Canada. 2013. 2011 National Household Survey. Statistics Canada Catalogue no. 99-004-XWE. Ottawa. Released September 11, 2013.

Cities Ranked by Occupation: Manufacturing & Utilities
By Percent

Total

Rank	City	Percent
1	Guelph, ON	11.5%
2	Cambridge, ON	10.3%
3	Brampton, ON	10.0%
4	Kitchener, ON	9.6%
5	Windsor, ON	9.2%
6	Chatham-Kent, ON	6.8%
7	Oshawa, ON	5.9%
8	Barrie, ON	5.8%
9	Hamilton, ON	5.7%
10	Mississauga, ON	5.6%
11	Terrebonne, QC	5.5%
12	London, ON	5.4%
13	Sherbrooke, QC	5.2%
13	Trois-Rivières, QC	5.2%
15	Abbotsford, BC	5.0%
15	Surrey, BC	5.0%
17	Markham, ON	4.9%
18	St. Catharines, ON	4.7%
18	Toronto, ON	4.7%
18	Winnipeg, MB	4.7%
21	Longueuil, QC	4.6%
21	Lévis, QC	4.6%
21	Saguenay, QC	4.6%
24	Vaughan, ON	4.5%
25	Montréal, QC	4.3%
26	Ajax, ON	4.1%
26	Laval, QC	4.1%
28	Whitby, ON	3.4%
29	Burlington, ON	3.2%
29	Saskatoon, SK	3.2%
31	Richmond, BC	3.0%
32	Coquitlam, BC	2.9%
32	Langley, BC	2.9%
34	Edmonton, AB	2.8%
35	Burnaby, BC	2.7%
36	Kelowna, BC	2.6%
36	Vancouver, BC	2.6%
38	Québec, QC	2.5%
38	Richmond Hill, ON	2.5%
40	Oakville, ON	2.4%
41	Calgary, AB	2.3%
41	Thunder Bay, ON	2.3%
43	Regina, SK	2.2%
44	Greater Sudbury, ON	2.0%
44	St. John's, NL	2.0%
46	Halifax, NS	1.8%
47	Kingston, ON	1.6%
48	Saanich, BC	1.5%
49	Gatineau, QC	1.3%
50	Ottawa, ON	1.2%
–	Canada	4.6%

Male

Rank	City	Percent
1	Guelph, ON	14.5%
2	Cambridge, ON	12.5%
3	Kitchener, ON	11.9%
3	Windsor, ON	11.9%
5	Brampton, ON	10.0%
6	Chatham-Kent, ON	9.3%
7	Oshawa, ON	8.6%
8	Barrie, ON	8.5%
9	Hamilton, ON	8.4%
10	Trois-Rivières, QC	8.2%
11	London, ON	7.8%
12	Sherbrooke, QC	7.5%
13	Saguenay, QC	7.4%
14	St. Catharines, ON	7.0%
15	Abbotsford, BC	6.7%
15	Lévis, QC	6.7%
15	Terrebonne, QC	6.7%
15	Winnipeg, MB	6.7%
19	Mississauga, ON	6.5%
20	Longueuil, QC	6.0%
20	Surrey, BC	6.0%
22	Ajax, ON	5.7%
23	Laval, QC	5.4%
23	Toronto, ON	5.4%
25	Montréal, QC	5.2%
25	Whitby, ON	5.2%
27	Vaughan, ON	5.1%
28	Markham, ON	5.0%
29	Burlington, ON	4.6%
29	Saskatoon, SK	4.6%
31	Langley, BC	4.4%
32	Thunder Bay, ON	4.2%
33	Coquitlam, BC	3.9%
33	Edmonton, AB	3.9%
35	Regina, SK	3.7%
36	Greater Sudbury, ON	3.5%
36	Québec, QC	3.5%
38	Richmond, BC	3.4%
39	Calgary, AB	3.3%
39	Kelowna, BC	3.3%
41	Burnaby, BC	3.2%
41	Oakville, ON	3.2%
41	St. John's, NL	3.2%
44	Richmond Hill, ON	3.1%
45	Vancouver, BC	2.9%
46	Kingston, ON	2.8%
47	Halifax, NS	2.6%
48	Gatineau, QC	2.1%
48	Saanich, BC	2.1%
50	Ottawa, ON	1.6%
–	Canada	6.1%

Female

Rank	City	Percent
1	Brampton, ON	10.0%
2	Guelph, ON	8.3%
3	Cambridge, ON	7.9%
4	Kitchener, ON	7.1%
5	Windsor, ON	6.3%
6	Markham, ON	4.9%
7	Mississauga, ON	4.7%
8	Terrebonne, QC	4.2%
9	Chatham-Kent, ON	4.0%
10	Surrey, BC	3.9%
10	Toronto, ON	3.9%
12	Vaughan, ON	3.8%
13	Montréal, QC	3.3%
14	Longueuil, QC	3.1%
14	Oshawa, ON	3.1%
16	Abbotsford, BC	3.0%
17	Barrie, ON	2.9%
17	London, ON	2.9%
19	Hamilton, ON	2.8%
19	Sherbrooke, QC	2.8%
21	Laval, QC	2.7%
22	Winnipeg, MB	2.6%
23	Richmond, BC	2.5%
24	Ajax, ON	2.4%
24	Lévis, QC	2.4%
26	St. Catharines, ON	2.3%
26	Vancouver, BC	2.3%
28	Burnaby, BC	2.2%
29	Trois-Rivières, QC	2.1%
30	Kelowna, BC	1.9%
30	Richmond Hill, ON	1.9%
32	Burlington, ON	1.8%
32	Coquitlam, BC	1.8%
34	Oakville, ON	1.6%
34	Saskatoon, SK	1.6%
36	Edmonton, AB	1.5%
36	Whitby, ON	1.5%
38	Langley, BC	1.4%
38	Québec, QC	1.4%
40	Calgary, AB	1.2%
40	Saguenay, QC	1.2%
42	Halifax, NS	0.9%
42	St. John's, NL	0.9%
44	Saanich, BC	0.8%
45	Ottawa, ON	0.7%
46	Regina, SK	0.6%
47	Gatineau, QC	0.5%
47	Greater Sudbury, ON	0.5%
47	Kingston, ON	0.5%
47	Thunder Bay, ON	0.5%
–	Canada	2.9%

Note: Figures are based on total experienced labour force 15 years and over
Source: Statistics Canada. 2013. 2011 National Household Survey. Statistics Canada Catalogue no. 99-004-XWE. Ottawa. Released September 11, 2013.

Cities Ranked by Mode of Transportation to Work: Car, Truck or Van, as Driver

By Number

Total

Rank	City	Number
1	Toronto, ON	567,555
2	Calgary, AB	403,475
3	Montréal, QC	350,780
4	Edmonton, AB	310,675
5	Ottawa, ON	260,660
6	Mississauga, ON	252,330
7	Winnipeg, MB	229,155
8	Brampton, ON	192,050
9	Québec, QC	183,525
10	Hamilton, ON	174,405
11	Surrey, BC	162,090
12	Laval, QC	145,450
13	Vancouver, BC	141,435
14	Halifax, NS	134,475
15	London, ON	127,330
16	Vaughan, ON	111,860
17	Markham, ON	100,100
18	Gatineau, QC	93,800
19	Saskatoon, SK	92,665
20	Kitchener, ON	88,360
21	Regina, SK	83,865
22	Longueuil, QC	75,475
23	Burlington, ON	68,900
24	Richmond Hill, ON	65,565
25	Windsor, ON	64,670
26	Oakville, ON	63,845
27	Burnaby, BC	63,525
28	Lévis, QC	62,235
29	Greater Sudbury, ON	60,090
30	Richmond, BC	58,520
31	Saguenay, QC	58,400
32	Sherbrooke, QC	57,535
33	Oshawa, ON	52,985
34	Barrie, ON	51,540
35	Cambridge, ON	51,105
36	Trois-Rivières, QC	50,350
37	Abbotsford, BC	50,215
38	Terrebonne, QC	48,955
39	Guelph, ON	46,965
40	Whitby, ON	46,770
41	St. Catharines, ON	45,755
42	Coquitlam, BC	43,285
43	Langley, BC	42,705
44	Kelowna, BC	42,650
45	Ajax, ON	40,440
46	Kingston, ON	40,075
47	Thunder Bay, ON	39,845
48	St. John's, NL	36,930
49	Chatham-Kent, ON	36,310
50	Saanich, BC	35,925
–	Canada	11,393,140

Male

Rank	City	Number
1	Toronto, ON	345,885
2	Calgary, AB	231,765
3	Montréal, QC	210,375
4	Edmonton, AB	177,860
5	Ottawa, ON	143,455
6	Mississauga, ON	143,030
7	Winnipeg, MB	128,400
8	Brampton, ON	109,630
9	Québec, QC	100,315
10	Hamilton, ON	93,455
11	Surrey, BC	91,810
12	Vancouver, BC	82,105
13	Laval, QC	79,540
14	Halifax, NS	72,690
15	London, ON	66,270
16	Vaughan, ON	62,195
17	Markham, ON	56,920
18	Gatineau, QC	50,750
19	Saskatoon, SK	50,235
20	Kitchener, ON	47,275
21	Regina, SK	45,705
22	Longueuil, QC	42,260
23	Burnaby, BC	37,085
24	Burlington, ON	36,270
25	Richmond Hill, ON	36,085
26	Oakville, ON	34,720
27	Windsor, ON	33,840
28	Richmond, BC	32,845
29	Lévis, QC	32,680
30	Saguenay, QC	32,085
31	Greater Sudbury, ON	31,615
32	Sherbrooke, QC	29,905
33	Oshawa, ON	28,170
34	Barrie, ON	27,575
35	Abbotsford, BC	27,560
36	Cambridge, ON	27,405
37	Terrebonne, QC	26,050
38	Trois-Rivières, QC	25,885
39	Whitby, ON	25,185
40	Guelph, ON	24,750
41	Coquitlam, BC	24,440
42	St. Catharines, ON	23,330
43	Langley, BC	22,945
44	Kelowna, BC	22,270
45	Ajax, ON	22,065
46	Kingston, ON	20,600
47	Thunder Bay, ON	20,185
48	St. John's, NL	19,180
49	Chatham-Kent, ON	18,540
50	Saanich, BC	18,510
–	Canada	6,238,835

Female

Rank	City	Number
1	Toronto, ON	221,675
2	Calgary, AB	171,705
3	Montréal, QC	140,400
4	Edmonton, AB	132,810
5	Ottawa, ON	117,205
6	Mississauga, ON	109,295
7	Winnipeg, MB	100,760
8	Québec, QC	83,210
9	Brampton, ON	82,420
10	Hamilton, ON	80,955
11	Surrey, BC	70,280
12	Laval, QC	65,910
13	Halifax, NS	61,780
14	London, ON	61,070
15	Vancouver, BC	59,325
16	Vaughan, ON	49,660
17	Markham, ON	43,185
18	Gatineau, QC	43,050
19	Saskatoon, SK	42,430
20	Kitchener, ON	41,085
21	Regina, SK	38,160
22	Longueuil, QC	33,215
23	Burlington, ON	32,625
24	Windsor, ON	30,825
25	Lévis, QC	29,560
26	Richmond Hill, ON	29,475
27	Oakville, ON	29,125
28	Greater Sudbury, ON	28,470
29	Sherbrooke, QC	27,635
30	Burnaby, BC	26,435
31	Saguenay, QC	26,315
32	Richmond, BC	25,680
33	Oshawa, ON	24,815
34	Trois-Rivières, QC	24,470
35	Barrie, ON	23,960
36	Cambridge, ON	23,700
37	Terrebonne, QC	22,905
38	Abbotsford, BC	22,655
39	St. Catharines, ON	22,420
40	Guelph, ON	22,215
41	Whitby, ON	21,585
42	Kelowna, BC	20,385
43	Langley, BC	19,760
44	Thunder Bay, ON	19,660
45	Kingston, ON	19,480
46	Coquitlam, BC	18,835
47	Ajax, ON	18,380
48	Chatham-Kent, ON	17,770
49	St. John's, NL	17,745
50	Saanich, BC	17,415
–	Canada	5,154,305

Note: Figures are based on total employed labour force 15 years and over.
Source: Statistics Canada. 2013. 2011 National Household Survey. Statistics Canada Catalogue no. 99-004-XWE. Ottawa. Released September 11, 2013.

Cities Ranked by Mode of Transportation to Work: Car, Truck or Van, as Driver
By Percent

Total

Rank	City	Percent
1	Terrebonne, QC	88.3%
2	Saguenay, QC	88.0%
3	Trois-Rivières, QC	86.9%
4	Chatham-Kent, ON	86.8%
5	Langley, BC	86.1%
6	Lévis, QC	85.4%
7	Abbotsford, BC	84.8%
8	Cambridge, ON	83.7%
9	Windsor, ON	82.1%
10	Sherbrooke, QC	82.0%
11	Regina, SK	81.2%
11	Thunder Bay, ON	81.2%
13	Kitchener, ON	80.8%
13	Vaughan, ON	80.8%
15	Greater Sudbury, ON	80.7%
16	Barrie, ON	80.5%
17	Burlington, ON	80.1%
18	St. Catharines, ON	79.6%
19	Kelowna, BC	79.5%
19	Saskatoon, SK	79.5%
19	Whitby, ON	79.5%
22	Oshawa, ON	79.3%
23	Brampton, ON	78.7%
24	Guelph, ON	77.7%
25	Laval, QC	76.7%
26	Surrey, BC	76.6%
27	Richmond Hill, ON	76.5%
28	Hamilton, ON	76.4%
29	London, ON	76.0%
30	Oakville, ON	75.4%
31	Mississauga, ON	74.3%
32	Ajax, ON	74.0%
32	Markham, ON	74.0%
34	St. John's, NL	73.8%
35	Coquitlam, BC	72.6%
36	Edmonton, AB	72.2%
37	Kingston, ON	71.5%
38	Québec, QC	71.1%
39	Richmond, BC	69.8%
40	Calgary, AB	69.7%
41	Winnipeg, MB	69.1%
42	Saanich, BC	69.0%
43	Gatineau, QC	68.6%
43	Halifax, NS	68.6%
45	Longueuil, QC	68.2%
46	Burnaby, BC	61.1%
47	Ottawa, ON	60.3%
48	Toronto, ON	48.3%
49	Montréal, QC	48.2%
50	Vancouver, BC	48.0%
–	Canada	74.0%

Male

Rank	City	Percent
1	Terrebonne, QC	90.5%
2	Saguenay, QC	89.2%
3	Lévis, QC	88.1%
4	Trois-Rivières, QC	87.8%
5	Chatham-Kent, ON	87.5%
6	Langley, BC	87.3%
7	Abbotsford, BC	86.8%
8	Vaughan, ON	86.0%
9	Cambridge, ON	85.5%
10	Regina, SK	84.8%
11	Sherbrooke, QC	84.7%
12	Brampton, ON	84.4%
13	Windsor, ON	84.3%
14	Whitby, ON	83.4%
15	Barrie, ON	83.1%
16	Kitchener, ON	82.9%
16	Oshawa, ON	82.9%
18	Greater Sudbury, ON	82.8%
19	Burlington, ON	82.4%
20	Laval, QC	82.3%
21	Saskatoon, SK	81.9%
21	Thunder Bay, ON	81.9%
23	Kelowna, BC	81.3%
24	Richmond Hill, ON	81.2%
25	Ajax, ON	81.0%
26	Mississauga, ON	80.8%
26	Surrey, BC	80.8%
28	St. Catharines, ON	80.7%
29	Markham, ON	80.2%
30	Hamilton, ON	80.0%
31	Guelph, ON	79.7%
32	London, ON	78.7%
33	Oakville, ON	78.0%
34	Coquitlam, BC	77.9%
35	Edmonton, AB	77.2%
36	St. John's, NL	77.1%
37	Richmond, BC	76.8%
38	Québec, QC	75.6%
39	Winnipeg, MB	75.2%
40	Calgary, AB	74.2%
40	Longueuil, QC	74.2%
42	Gatineau, QC	73.7%
43	Kingston, ON	73.6%
44	Halifax, NS	73.5%
45	Saanich, BC	71.2%
46	Burnaby, BC	68.8%
47	Ottawa, ON	65.4%
48	Toronto, ON	57.5%
49	Montréal, QC	56.1%
50	Vancouver, BC	54.5%
–	Canada	77.9%

Female

Rank	City	Percent
1	Saguenay, QC	86.5%
2	Trois-Rivières, QC	86.1%
3	Chatham-Kent, ON	86.0%
4	Terrebonne, QC	85.9%
5	Langley, BC	84.7%
6	Lévis, QC	82.6%
7	Abbotsford, BC	82.4%
8	Cambridge, ON	81.8%
9	Thunder Bay, ON	80.5%
10	Windsor, ON	79.8%
11	Sherbrooke, QC	79.3%
12	Kitchener, ON	78.6%
13	St. Catharines, ON	78.5%
14	Greater Sudbury, ON	78.4%
15	Barrie, ON	77.7%
16	Burlington, ON	77.6%
16	Kelowna, BC	77.6%
18	Regina, SK	77.3%
19	Saskatoon, SK	76.7%
20	Oshawa, ON	75.6%
21	Guelph, ON	75.5%
22	Whitby, ON	75.4%
23	Vaughan, ON	75.2%
24	London, ON	73.3%
25	Hamilton, ON	72.7%
26	Oakville, ON	72.4%
27	Brampton, ON	72.2%
28	Surrey, BC	71.7%
29	Richmond Hill, ON	71.5%
30	Laval, QC	70.9%
31	St. John's, NL	70.6%
32	Kingston, ON	69.3%
33	Mississauga, ON	67.3%
34	Markham, ON	67.1%
35	Ajax, ON	67.0%
36	Saanich, BC	66.7%
37	Coquitlam, BC	66.6%
38	Edmonton, AB	66.5%
39	Québec, QC	66.3%
40	Calgary, AB	64.4%
41	Halifax, NS	63.7%
42	Gatineau, QC	63.5%
43	Winnipeg, MB	62.6%
44	Richmond, BC	62.4%
45	Longueuil, QC	61.8%
46	Ottawa, ON	55.1%
47	Burnaby, BC	52.9%
48	Vancouver, BC	41.1%
49	Montréal, QC	39.9%
50	Toronto, ON	38.7%
–	Canada	69.8%

Note: Figures are based on total employed labour force 15 years and over.
Source: Statistics Canada. 2013. 2011 National Household Survey. Statistics Canada Catalogue no. 99-004-XWE. Ottawa. Released September 11, 2013.

Cities Ranked by Mode of Transportation to Work: Public Transit
By Number

Total

Rank	City	Number
1	Toronto, ON	429,275
2	Montréal, QC	263,875
3	Calgary, AB	99,445
4	Ottawa, ON	97,125
5	Vancouver, BC	88,290
6	Edmonton, AB	63,670
7	Mississauga, ON	53,985
8	Winnipeg, MB	48,530
9	Québec, QC	37,875
10	Laval, QC	30,540
11	Burnaby, BC	29,240
12	Brampton, ON	28,765
13	Surrey, BC	27,040
14	Longueuil, QC	24,550
15	Halifax, NS	24,435
16	Gatineau, QC	23,720
17	Hamilton, ON	22,480
18	Markham, ON	21,495
19	Vaughan, ON	15,595
20	Richmond, BC	15,125
21	London, ON	14,520
22	Richmond Hill, ON	12,255
23	Oakville, ON	12,095
24	Coquitlam, BC	10,215
25	Ajax, ON	8,710
26	Burlington, ON	7,560
27	Kitchener, ON	7,165
28	Whitby, ON	6,695
29	Saanich, BC	6,455
30	Saskatoon, SK	5,915
31	Oshawa, ON	5,440
32	Regina, SK	5,305
33	Guelph, ON	4,110
34	Lévis, QC	3,965
35	Sherbrooke, QC	3,630
36	Barrie, ON	3,600
37	Windsor, ON	3,545
38	Kingston, ON	3,450
39	Greater Sudbury, ON	3,370
40	Terrebonne, QC	2,960
41	Cambridge, ON	2,730
42	St. Catharines, ON	2,695
43	St. John's, NL	2,455
44	Kelowna, BC	2,170
45	Thunder Bay, ON	1,930
46	Langley, BC	1,740
47	Saguenay, QC	1,640
48	Trois-Rivières, QC	1,465
49	Abbotsford, BC	1,135
50	Chatham-Kent, ON	545
–	Canada	1,851,525

Male

Rank	City	Number
1	Toronto, ON	176,285
2	Montréal, QC	112,225
3	Calgary, AB	46,755
4	Ottawa, ON	43,175
5	Vancouver, BC	37,610
6	Edmonton, AB	26,400
7	Mississauga, ON	21,375
8	Winnipeg, MB	19,795
9	Québec, QC	15,200
10	Burnaby, BC	12,440
11	Surrey, BC	11,930
12	Laval, QC	11,910
13	Brampton, ON	11,785
14	Halifax, NS	10,270
15	Longueuil, QC	10,065
16	Gatineau, QC	10,030
17	Markham, ON	9,565
18	Hamilton, ON	9,095
19	Vaughan, ON	6,205
20	Oakville, ON	6,130
21	London, ON	5,920
22	Richmond, BC	5,845
23	Richmond Hill, ON	5,425
24	Coquitlam, BC	4,465
25	Burlington, ON	3,560
26	Kitchener, ON	3,390
27	Ajax, ON	3,095
28	Whitby, ON	2,855
29	Saanich, BC	2,765
30	Saskatoon, SK	2,400
31	Oshawa, ON	2,185
32	Regina, SK	2,130
33	Guelph, ON	1,960
34	Barrie, ON	1,420
34	Lévis, QC	1,420
36	Sherbrooke, QC	1,355
37	Kingston, ON	1,345
38	Windsor, ON	1,325
39	Greater Sudbury, ON	1,305
40	Terrebonne, QC	1,150
41	Cambridge, ON	1,115
42	St. John's, NL	1,025
43	Kelowna, BC	905
44	St. Catharines, ON	880
45	Langley, BC	840
46	Thunder Bay, ON	740
47	Saguenay, QC	680
48	Abbotsford, BC	540
49	Trois-Rivières, QC	535
50	Chatham-Kent, ON	240
–	Canada	788,290

Female

Rank	City	Number
1	Toronto, ON	252,985
2	Montréal, QC	151,650
3	Ottawa, ON	53,955
4	Calgary, AB	52,695
5	Vancouver, BC	50,680
6	Edmonton, AB	37,265
7	Mississauga, ON	32,610
8	Winnipeg, MB	28,735
9	Québec, QC	22,675
10	Laval, QC	18,630
11	Brampton, ON	16,985
12	Burnaby, BC	16,800
13	Surrey, BC	15,110
14	Longueuil, QC	14,480
15	Halifax, NS	14,160
16	Gatineau, QC	13,690
17	Hamilton, ON	13,380
18	Markham, ON	11,925
19	Vaughan, ON	9,385
20	Richmond, BC	9,275
21	London, ON	8,600
22	Richmond Hill, ON	6,835
23	Oakville, ON	5,965
24	Coquitlam, BC	5,745
25	Ajax, ON	5,615
26	Burlington, ON	4,000
27	Whitby, ON	3,840
28	Kitchener, ON	3,775
29	Saanich, BC	3,690
30	Saskatoon, SK	3,515
31	Oshawa, ON	3,260
32	Regina, SK	3,170
33	Lévis, QC	2,545
34	Sherbrooke, QC	2,280
35	Windsor, ON	2,215
36	Barrie, ON	2,180
37	Guelph, ON	2,150
38	Kingston, ON	2,105
39	Greater Sudbury, ON	2,060
40	St. Catharines, ON	1,815
41	Terrebonne, QC	1,810
42	Cambridge, ON	1,615
43	St. John's, NL	1,430
44	Kelowna, BC	1,270
45	Thunder Bay, ON	1,190
46	Saguenay, QC	960
47	Trois-Rivières, QC	935
48	Langley, BC	900
49	Abbotsford, BC	600
50	Chatham-Kent, ON	310
–	Canada	1,063,235

Note: Figures are based on total employed labour force 15 years and over.
Source: Statistics Canada. 2013. 2011 National Household Survey. Statistics Canada Catalogue no. 99-004-XWE. Ottawa. Released September 11, 2013.

Cities Ranked by Mode of Transportation to Work: Public Transit

By Percent

Total

Rank	City	Percent
1	Toronto, ON	36.5%
2	Montréal, QC	36.3%
3	Vancouver, BC	30.0%
4	Burnaby, BC	28.1%
5	Ottawa, ON	22.5%
6	Longueuil, QC	22.2%
7	Richmond, BC	18.0%
8	Gatineau, QC	17.3%
9	Calgary, AB	17.2%
10	Coquitlam, BC	17.1%
11	Laval, QC	16.1%
12	Ajax, ON	15.9%
12	Markham, ON	15.9%
12	Mississauga, ON	15.9%
15	Edmonton, AB	14.8%
16	Québec, QC	14.7%
17	Winnipeg, MB	14.6%
18	Oakville, ON	14.3%
18	Richmond Hill, ON	14.3%
20	Surrey, BC	12.8%
21	Halifax, NS	12.5%
22	Saanich, BC	12.4%
23	Brampton, ON	11.8%
24	Whitby, ON	11.4%
25	Vaughan, ON	11.3%
26	Hamilton, ON	9.9%
27	Burlington, ON	8.8%
28	London, ON	8.7%
29	Oshawa, ON	8.1%
30	Guelph, ON	6.8%
31	Kitchener, ON	6.6%
32	Kingston, ON	6.2%
33	Barrie, ON	5.6%
34	Lévis, QC	5.4%
35	Terrebonne, QC	5.3%
36	Sherbrooke, QC	5.2%
37	Regina, SK	5.1%
37	Saskatoon, SK	5.1%
39	St. John's, NL	4.9%
40	St. Catharines, ON	4.7%
41	Cambridge, ON	4.5%
41	Greater Sudbury, ON	4.5%
41	Windsor, ON	4.5%
44	Kelowna, BC	4.0%
45	Thunder Bay, ON	3.9%
46	Langley, BC	3.5%
47	Saguenay, QC	2.5%
47	Trois-Rivières, QC	2.5%
49	Abbotsford, BC	1.9%
50	Chatham-Kent, ON	1.3%
–	Canada	12.0%

Male

Rank	City	Percent
1	Montréal, QC	29.9%
2	Toronto, ON	29.3%
3	Vancouver, BC	25.0%
4	Burnaby, BC	23.1%
5	Ottawa, ON	19.7%
6	Longueuil, QC	17.7%
7	Calgary, AB	15.0%
8	Gatineau, QC	14.6%
9	Coquitlam, BC	14.2%
10	Oakville, ON	13.8%
11	Richmond, BC	13.7%
12	Markham, ON	13.5%
13	Laval, QC	12.3%
14	Richmond Hill, ON	12.2%
15	Mississauga, ON	12.1%
16	Winnipeg, MB	11.6%
17	Edmonton, AB	11.5%
17	Québec, QC	11.5%
19	Ajax, ON	11.4%
20	Saanich, BC	10.6%
21	Surrey, BC	10.5%
22	Halifax, NS	10.4%
23	Whitby, ON	9.5%
24	Brampton, ON	9.1%
25	Vaughan, ON	8.6%
26	Burlington, ON	8.1%
27	Hamilton, ON	7.8%
28	London, ON	7.0%
29	Oshawa, ON	6.4%
30	Guelph, ON	6.3%
31	Kitchener, ON	5.9%
32	Kingston, ON	4.8%
33	Barrie, ON	4.3%
34	St. John's, NL	4.1%
35	Regina, SK	4.0%
35	Terrebonne, QC	4.0%
37	Saskatoon, SK	3.9%
38	Lévis, QC	3.8%
38	Sherbrooke, QC	3.8%
40	Cambridge, ON	3.5%
41	Greater Sudbury, ON	3.4%
42	Kelowna, BC	3.3%
42	Windsor, ON	3.3%
44	Langley, BC	3.2%
45	St. Catharines, ON	3.0%
45	Thunder Bay, ON	3.0%
47	Saguenay, QC	1.9%
48	Trois-Rivières, QC	1.8%
49	Abbotsford, BC	1.7%
50	Chatham-Kent, ON	1.1%
–	Canada	9.8%

Female

Rank	City	Percent
1	Toronto, ON	44.2%
2	Montréal, QC	43.1%
3	Vancouver, BC	35.1%
4	Burnaby, BC	33.6%
5	Longueuil, QC	26.9%
6	Ottawa, ON	25.4%
7	Richmond, BC	22.5%
8	Ajax, ON	20.5%
9	Coquitlam, BC	20.3%
10	Gatineau, QC	20.2%
11	Mississauga, ON	20.1%
12	Laval, QC	20.0%
13	Calgary, AB	19.8%
14	Edmonton, AB	18.7%
15	Markham, ON	18.5%
16	Québec, QC	18.1%
17	Winnipeg, MB	17.8%
18	Richmond Hill, ON	16.6%
19	Surrey, BC	15.4%
20	Brampton, ON	14.9%
21	Oakville, ON	14.8%
22	Halifax, NS	14.6%
23	Vaughan, ON	14.2%
24	Saanich, BC	14.1%
25	Whitby, ON	13.4%
26	Hamilton, ON	12.0%
27	London, ON	10.3%
28	Oshawa, ON	9.9%
29	Burlington, ON	9.5%
30	Kingston, ON	7.5%
31	Guelph, ON	7.3%
32	Kitchener, ON	7.2%
33	Barrie, ON	7.1%
33	Lévis, QC	7.1%
35	Terrebonne, QC	6.8%
36	Sherbrooke, QC	6.5%
37	Regina, SK	6.4%
37	Saskatoon, SK	6.4%
37	St. Catharines, ON	6.4%
40	Greater Sudbury, ON	5.7%
40	St. John's, NL	5.7%
40	Windsor, ON	5.7%
43	Cambridge, ON	5.6%
44	Thunder Bay, ON	4.9%
45	Kelowna, BC	4.8%
46	Langley, BC	3.9%
47	Trois-Rivières, QC	3.3%
48	Saguenay, QC	3.2%
49	Abbotsford, BC	2.2%
50	Chatham-Kent, ON	1.5%
–	Canada	14.4%

Note: Figures are based on total employed labour force 15 years and over.
Source: Statistics Canada. 2013. 2011 National Household Survey. Statistics Canada Catalogue no. 99-004-XWE. Ottawa. Released September 11, 2013.

Cities Ranked by Mode of Transportation to Work: Walked

By Number

Total

Rank	City	Number
1	Toronto, ON	85,475
2	Montréal, QC	61,870
3	Vancouver, BC	36,960
4	Ottawa, ON	31,345
5	Calgary, AB	29,260
6	Québec, QC	19,985
7	Edmonton, AB	19,825
8	Winnipeg, MB	18,095
9	Halifax, NS	16,705
10	Hamilton, ON	11,230
11	London, ON	9,790
12	Mississauga, ON	7,815
13	Gatineau, QC	6,165
14	Saskatoon, SK	6,160
15	Kingston, ON	5,875
16	Surrey, BC	5,465
17	Regina, SK	5,000
18	Sherbrooke, QC	4,875
19	Kitchener, ON	4,665
20	Longueuil, QC	4,545
21	Burnaby, BC	4,490
22	Laval, QC	4,480
23	St. John's, NL	4,350
24	Brampton, ON	4,015
25	Greater Sudbury, ON	3,950
26	Windsor, ON	3,735
27	Guelph, ON	3,305
28	St. Catharines, ON	3,280
29	Burlington, ON	3,165
30	Saanich, BC	3,035
31	Kelowna, BC	3,020
32	Trois-Rivières, QC	3,015
33	Richmond, BC	2,930
34	Saguenay, QC	2,835
35	Lévis, QC	2,765
36	Oshawa, ON	2,750
37	Barrie, ON	2,745
38	Oakville, ON	2,650
39	Thunder Bay, ON	2,580
40	Markham, ON	2,425
41	Vaughan, ON	2,115
42	Coquitlam, BC	2,075
43	Chatham-Kent, ON	2,030
44	Cambridge, ON	1,945
45	Richmond Hill, ON	1,755
46	Langley, BC	1,635
47	Abbotsford, BC	1,605
48	Whitby, ON	1,415
49	Ajax, ON	1,335
50	Terrebonne, QC	1,110
–	Canada	880,815

Male

Rank	City	Number
1	Toronto, ON	38,040
2	Montréal, QC	27,805
3	Vancouver, BC	17,170
4	Ottawa, ON	14,950
5	Calgary, AB	13,730
6	Québec, QC	9,645
7	Edmonton, AB	8,750
8	Halifax, NS	7,880
9	Winnipeg, MB	7,855
10	Hamilton, ON	4,685
11	London, ON	4,385
12	Kingston, ON	2,910
13	Mississauga, ON	2,855
14	Gatineau, QC	2,825
15	Saskatoon, SK	2,630
16	Regina, SK	2,370
17	Sherbrooke, QC	2,205
18	Kitchener, ON	2,055
19	Surrey, BC	1,875
20	St. John's, NL	1,860
21	Longueuil, QC	1,835
22	Burnaby, BC	1,800
23	Greater Sudbury, ON	1,785
24	Windsor, ON	1,750
25	Laval, QC	1,745
26	St. Catharines, ON	1,640
27	Thunder Bay, ON	1,440
28	Guelph, ON	1,385
28	Saguenay, QC	1,385
30	Brampton, ON	1,380
31	Trois-Rivières, QC	1,345
32	Richmond, BC	1,280
33	Saanich, BC	1,230
34	Barrie, ON	1,215
35	Oakville, ON	1,140
36	Burlington, ON	1,130
37	Lévis, QC	1,125
38	Oshawa, ON	1,030
39	Kelowna, BC	1,000
40	Markham, ON	905
41	Cambridge, ON	890
42	Vaughan, ON	840
43	Coquitlam, BC	815
44	Chatham-Kent, ON	785
45	Langley, BC	745
46	Abbotsford, BC	695
47	Richmond Hill, ON	670
48	Ajax, ON	540
48	Whitby, ON	540
50	Terrebonne, QC	450
–	Canada	387,580

Female

Rank	City	Number
1	Toronto, ON	47,435
2	Montréal, QC	34,070
3	Vancouver, BC	19,785
4	Ottawa, ON	16,395
5	Calgary, AB	15,530
6	Edmonton, AB	11,070
7	Québec, QC	10,340
8	Winnipeg, MB	10,240
9	Halifax, NS	8,820
10	Hamilton, ON	6,555
11	London, ON	5,410
12	Mississauga, ON	4,960
13	Surrey, BC	3,590
14	Saskatoon, SK	3,535
15	Gatineau, QC	3,340
16	Kingston, ON	2,965
17	Laval, QC	2,740
18	Longueuil, QC	2,710
19	Burnaby, BC	2,690
20	Sherbrooke, QC	2,670
21	Brampton, ON	2,630
21	Regina, SK	2,630
23	Kitchener, ON	2,610
24	St. John's, NL	2,490
25	Greater Sudbury, ON	2,165
26	Burlington, ON	2,035
27	Kelowna, BC	2,025
28	Windsor, ON	1,990
29	Guelph, ON	1,915
30	Saanich, BC	1,810
31	Oshawa, ON	1,730
32	Trois-Rivières, QC	1,670
33	Richmond, BC	1,655
34	St. Catharines, ON	1,640
35	Lévis, QC	1,635
36	Barrie, ON	1,530
37	Markham, ON	1,520
38	Oakville, ON	1,510
39	Saguenay, QC	1,445
40	Vaughan, ON	1,275
41	Coquitlam, BC	1,260
42	Chatham-Kent, ON	1,245
43	Thunder Bay, ON	1,135
44	Richmond Hill, ON	1,085
45	Cambridge, ON	1,050
46	Abbotsford, BC	910
47	Langley, BC	885
48	Whitby, ON	875
49	Ajax, ON	800
50	Terrebonne, QC	655
–	Canada	493,230

Note: Figures are based on total employed labour force 15 years and over.
Source: Statistics Canada. 2013. 2011 National Household Survey. Statistics Canada Catalogue no. 99-004-XWE. Ottawa. Released September 11, 2013.

Cities Ranked by Mode of Transportation to Work: Walked
By Percent

Total

Rank	City	Percent
1	Vancouver, BC	12.5%
2	Kingston, ON	10.5%
3	St. John's, NL	8.7%
4	Halifax, NS	8.5%
4	Montréal, QC	8.5%
6	Québec, QC	7.7%
7	Ottawa, ON	7.3%
7	Toronto, ON	7.3%
9	Sherbrooke, QC	7.0%
10	London, ON	5.8%
10	Saanich, BC	5.8%
12	St. Catharines, ON	5.7%
13	Kelowna, BC	5.6%
14	Guelph, ON	5.5%
14	Winnipeg, MB	5.5%
16	Greater Sudbury, ON	5.3%
16	Saskatoon, SK	5.3%
16	Thunder Bay, ON	5.3%
19	Trois-Rivières, QC	5.2%
20	Calgary, AB	5.1%
21	Chatham-Kent, ON	4.9%
21	Hamilton, ON	4.9%
23	Regina, SK	4.8%
24	Windsor, ON	4.7%
25	Edmonton, AB	4.6%
26	Gatineau, QC	4.5%
27	Barrie, ON	4.3%
27	Burnaby, BC	4.3%
27	Kitchener, ON	4.3%
27	Saguenay, QC	4.3%
31	Longueuil, QC	4.1%
31	Oshawa, ON	4.1%
33	Lévis, QC	3.8%
34	Burlington, ON	3.7%
35	Coquitlam, BC	3.5%
35	Richmond, BC	3.5%
37	Langley, BC	3.3%
38	Cambridge, ON	3.2%
39	Oakville, ON	3.1%
40	Abbotsford, BC	2.7%
41	Surrey, BC	2.6%
42	Ajax, ON	2.4%
42	Laval, QC	2.4%
42	Whitby, ON	2.4%
45	Mississauga, ON	2.3%
46	Richmond Hill, ON	2.0%
46	Terrebonne, QC	2.0%
48	Markham, ON	1.8%
49	Brampton, ON	1.6%
50	Vaughan, ON	1.5%
–	Canada	5.7%

Male

Rank	City	Percent
1	Vancouver, BC	11.4%
2	Kingston, ON	10.4%
3	Halifax, NS	8.0%
4	St. John's, NL	7.5%
5	Montréal, QC	7.4%
6	Québec, QC	7.3%
7	Ottawa, ON	6.8%
8	Toronto, ON	6.3%
9	Sherbrooke, QC	6.2%
10	Thunder Bay, ON	5.8%
11	St. Catharines, ON	5.7%
12	London, ON	5.2%
13	Greater Sudbury, ON	4.7%
13	Saanich, BC	4.7%
15	Trois-Rivières, QC	4.6%
15	Winnipeg, MB	4.6%
17	Guelph, ON	4.5%
18	Calgary, AB	4.4%
18	Regina, SK	4.4%
18	Windsor, ON	4.4%
21	Saskatoon, SK	4.3%
22	Gatineau, QC	4.1%
23	Hamilton, ON	4.0%
24	Edmonton, AB	3.8%
24	Saguenay, QC	3.8%
26	Barrie, ON	3.7%
26	Chatham-Kent, ON	3.7%
28	Kelowna, BC	3.6%
28	Kitchener, ON	3.6%
30	Burnaby, BC	3.3%
31	Longueuil, QC	3.2%
32	Lévis, QC	3.0%
32	Oshawa, ON	3.0%
32	Richmond, BC	3.0%
35	Cambridge, ON	2.8%
35	Langley, BC	2.8%
37	Burlington, ON	2.6%
37	Coquitlam, BC	2.6%
37	Oakville, ON	2.6%
40	Abbotsford, BC	2.2%
41	Ajax, ON	2.0%
42	Laval, QC	1.8%
42	Whitby, ON	1.8%
44	Mississauga, ON	1.6%
44	Surrey, BC	1.6%
44	Terrebonne, QC	1.6%
47	Richmond Hill, ON	1.5%
48	Markham, ON	1.3%
49	Vaughan, ON	1.2%
50	Brampton, ON	1.1%
–	Canada	4.8%

Female

Rank	City	Percent
1	Vancouver, BC	13.7%
2	Kingston, ON	10.6%
3	St. John's, NL	9.9%
4	Montréal, QC	9.7%
5	Halifax, NS	9.1%
6	Toronto, ON	8.3%
7	Québec, QC	8.2%
8	Kelowna, BC	7.7%
8	Ottawa, ON	7.7%
8	Sherbrooke, QC	7.7%
11	Saanich, BC	6.9%
12	Guelph, ON	6.5%
12	London, ON	6.5%
14	Saskatoon, SK	6.4%
14	Winnipeg, MB	6.4%
16	Chatham-Kent, ON	6.0%
16	Greater Sudbury, ON	6.0%
18	Hamilton, ON	5.9%
18	Trois-Rivières, QC	5.9%
20	Calgary, AB	5.8%
21	St. Catharines, ON	5.7%
22	Edmonton, AB	5.5%
23	Burnaby, BC	5.4%
24	Oshawa, ON	5.3%
24	Regina, SK	5.3%
26	Windsor, ON	5.2%
27	Barrie, ON	5.0%
27	Kitchener, ON	5.0%
27	Longueuil, QC	5.0%
30	Gatineau, QC	4.9%
31	Burlington, ON	4.8%
31	Saguenay, QC	4.8%
33	Lévis, QC	4.6%
33	Thunder Bay, ON	4.6%
35	Coquitlam, BC	4.5%
36	Richmond, BC	4.0%
37	Langley, BC	3.8%
37	Oakville, ON	3.8%
39	Surrey, BC	3.7%
40	Cambridge, ON	3.6%
41	Abbotsford, BC	3.3%
42	Mississauga, ON	3.1%
42	Whitby, ON	3.1%
44	Ajax, ON	2.9%
44	Laval, QC	2.9%
46	Richmond Hill, ON	2.6%
47	Terrebonne, QC	2.5%
48	Markham, ON	2.4%
49	Brampton, ON	2.3%
50	Vaughan, ON	1.9%
–	Canada	6.7%

Note: Figures are based on total employed labour force 15 years and over.
Source: Statistics Canada. 2013. 2011 National Household Survey. Statistics Canada Catalogue no. 99-004-XWE. Ottawa. Released September 11, 2013.

Cities Ranked by Visible Minority Population: Total Minority
By Number

Total

Rank	City	Number
1	Toronto, ON	1,264,395
2	Montréal, QC	510,665
3	Mississauga, ON	380,870
4	Brampton, ON	346,230
5	Calgary, AB	325,390
6	Vancouver, BC	305,615
7	Surrey, BC	243,760
8	Edmonton, AB	238,755
9	Markham, ON	217,095
10	Ottawa, ON	205,155
11	Winnipeg, MB	139,190
12	Richmond, BC	133,320
13	Burnaby, BC	130,945
14	Richmond Hill, ON	97,465
15	Vaughan, ON	89,975
16	Laval, QC	81,215
17	Hamilton, ON	79,970
18	London, ON	57,965
19	Coquitlam, BC	54,750
20	Ajax, ON	49,995
21	Windsor, ON	47,675
22	Oakville, ON	41,100
23	Kitchener, ON	39,720
24	Abbotsford, BC	38,700
25	Halifax, NS	35,040
26	Longueuil, QC	32,380
27	Saskatoon, SK	28,025
28	Gatineau, QC	26,930
29	Whitby, ON	23,125
30	Regina, SK	21,765
31	Burlington, ON	20,785
32	Québec, QC	20,245
33	Saanich, BC	19,420
34	Guelph, ON	18,920
35	Cambridge, ON	15,775
36	Langley, BC	13,805
37	Oshawa, ON	13,795
38	St. Catharines, ON	12,690
39	Barrie, ON	10,095
40	Kingston, ON	8,785
41	Kelowna, BC	8,750
42	Sherbrooke, QC	8,215
43	Terrebonne, QC	7,990
44	St. John's, NL	4,205
45	Greater Sudbury, ON	4,200
46	Chatham-Kent, ON	4,010
47	Thunder Bay, ON	3,565
48	Trois-Rivières, QC	3,230
49	Lévis, QC	1,935
50	Saguenay, QC	1,260
–	Canada	6,264,750

Male

Rank	City	Number
1	Toronto, ON	598,925
2	Montréal, QC	252,130
3	Mississauga, ON	185,355
4	Brampton, ON	170,860
5	Calgary, AB	161,190
6	Vancouver, BC	143,525
7	Surrey, BC	120,795
8	Edmonton, AB	118,865
9	Markham, ON	105,910
10	Ottawa, ON	98,360
11	Winnipeg, MB	68,710
12	Richmond, BC	63,195
13	Burnaby, BC	62,590
14	Richmond Hill, ON	47,090
15	Vaughan, ON	43,355
16	Laval, QC	39,985
17	Hamilton, ON	39,480
18	London, ON	29,015
19	Coquitlam, BC	26,460
20	Ajax, ON	23,850
21	Windsor, ON	23,620
22	Kitchener, ON	19,720
23	Abbotsford, BC	19,330
24	Oakville, ON	19,255
25	Halifax, NS	17,860
26	Longueuil, QC	16,000
27	Saskatoon, SK	14,325
28	Gatineau, QC	13,225
29	Regina, SK	11,115
30	Whitby, ON	11,025
31	Québec, QC	10,185
32	Burlington, ON	10,110
33	Guelph, ON	9,305
34	Saanich, BC	9,235
35	Cambridge, ON	7,800
36	Oshawa, ON	6,965
37	Langley, BC	6,835
38	St. Catharines, ON	6,525
39	Barrie, ON	5,090
40	Sherbrooke, QC	4,325
41	Kingston, ON	4,190
42	Kelowna, BC	4,175
43	Terrebonne, QC	3,665
44	St. John's, NL	2,365
45	Greater Sudbury, ON	2,255
46	Chatham-Kent, ON	2,040
47	Thunder Bay, ON	1,930
48	Trois-Rivières, QC	1,645
49	Lévis, QC	915
50	Saguenay, QC	605
–	Canada	3,043,010

Female

Rank	City	Number
1	Toronto, ON	665,465
2	Montréal, QC	258,530
3	Mississauga, ON	195,515
4	Brampton, ON	175,380
5	Calgary, AB	164,195
6	Vancouver, BC	162,090
7	Surrey, BC	122,965
8	Edmonton, AB	119,890
9	Markham, ON	111,185
10	Ottawa, ON	106,795
11	Winnipeg, MB	70,480
12	Richmond, BC	70,130
13	Burnaby, BC	68,355
14	Richmond Hill, ON	50,365
15	Vaughan, ON	46,620
16	Laval, QC	41,225
17	Hamilton, ON	40,490
18	London, ON	28,950
19	Coquitlam, BC	28,285
20	Ajax, ON	26,145
21	Windsor, ON	24,055
22	Oakville, ON	21,845
23	Kitchener, ON	20,000
24	Abbotsford, BC	19,370
25	Halifax, NS	17,185
26	Longueuil, QC	16,385
27	Gatineau, QC	13,705
28	Saskatoon, SK	13,700
29	Whitby, ON	12,095
30	Burlington, ON	10,675
31	Regina, SK	10,655
32	Saanich, BC	10,185
33	Québec, QC	10,060
34	Guelph, ON	9,615
35	Cambridge, ON	7,975
36	Langley, BC	6,970
37	Oshawa, ON	6,835
38	St. Catharines, ON	6,160
39	Barrie, ON	5,005
40	Kingston, ON	4,595
41	Kelowna, BC	4,575
42	Terrebonne, QC	4,330
43	Sherbrooke, QC	3,890
44	Chatham-Kent, ON	1,975
45	Greater Sudbury, ON	1,945
46	St. John's, NL	1,835
47	Thunder Bay, ON	1,635
48	Trois-Rivières, QC	1,585
49	Lévis, QC	1,015
50	Saguenay, QC	655
–	Canada	3,221,745

Note: The Employment Equity Act defines visible minorities as 'persons, other than Aboriginal peoples, who are non-Caucasian in race or non-white in colour.'
Source: Statistics Canada. 2013. 2011 National Household Survey. Statistics Canada Catalogue no. 99-004-XWE. Ottawa. Released September 11, 2013.

Cities Ranked by Visible Minority Population: Total Minority
By Percent

Total

Rank	City	Percent
1	Markham, ON	72.3%
2	Richmond, BC	70.4%
3	Brampton, ON	66.4%
4	Burnaby, BC	59.5%
5	Mississauga, ON	53.7%
6	Richmond Hill, ON	52.9%
7	Surrey, BC	52.6%
8	Vancouver, BC	51.8%
9	Toronto, ON	49.1%
10	Ajax, ON	45.8%
11	Coquitlam, BC	43.8%
12	Montréal, QC	31.7%
13	Vaughan, ON	31.4%
14	Calgary, AB	30.1%
15	Edmonton, AB	30.0%
16	Abbotsford, BC	29.6%
17	Ottawa, ON	23.7%
18	Windsor, ON	22.9%
19	Oakville, ON	22.8%
20	Winnipeg, MB	21.4%
21	Laval, QC	20.7%
22	Whitby, ON	19.2%
23	Kitchener, ON	18.4%
24	Saanich, BC	18.0%
25	London, ON	16.1%
26	Guelph, ON	15.7%
26	Hamilton, ON	15.7%
28	Longueuil, QC	14.2%
29	Langley, BC	13.4%
30	Saskatoon, SK	12.8%
31	Cambridge, ON	12.6%
32	Burlington, ON	12.0%
33	Regina, SK	11.5%
34	Gatineau, QC	10.3%
35	St. Catharines, ON	9.9%
36	Oshawa, ON	9.3%
37	Halifax, NS	9.1%
38	Barrie, ON	7.6%
38	Kelowna, BC	7.6%
38	Terrebonne, QC	7.6%
41	Kingston, ON	7.4%
42	Sherbrooke, QC	5.5%
43	Québec, QC	4.0%
43	St. John's, NL	4.0%
45	Chatham-Kent, ON	3.9%
46	Thunder Bay, ON	3.4%
47	Greater Sudbury, ON	2.7%
48	Trois-Rivières, QC	2.5%
49	Lévis, QC	1.4%
50	Saguenay, QC	0.9%
–	Canada	19.1%

Male

Rank	City	Percent
1	Markham, ON	72.2%
2	Richmond, BC	69.4%
3	Brampton, ON	66.4%
4	Burnaby, BC	57.9%
5	Mississauga, ON	53.4%
6	Surrey, BC	52.6%
7	Richmond Hill, ON	52.3%
8	Vancouver, BC	49.8%
9	Toronto, ON	48.3%
10	Ajax, ON	45.2%
11	Coquitlam, BC	43.0%
12	Montréal, QC	32.0%
13	Vaughan, ON	30.9%
14	Abbotsford, BC	29.9%
14	Edmonton, AB	29.9%
16	Calgary, AB	29.8%
17	Ottawa, ON	23.3%
17	Windsor, ON	23.3%
19	Oakville, ON	22.0%
20	Winnipeg, MB	21.7%
21	Laval, QC	20.9%
22	Whitby, ON	18.7%
23	Kitchener, ON	18.5%
24	Saanich, BC	17.7%
25	London, ON	16.6%
26	Guelph, ON	15.9%
27	Hamilton, ON	15.8%
28	Longueuil, QC	14.4%
29	Langley, BC	13.5%
30	Saskatoon, SK	13.4%
31	Cambridge, ON	12.7%
32	Burlington, ON	12.1%
33	Regina, SK	12.0%
34	St. Catharines, ON	10.6%
35	Gatineau, QC	10.4%
36	Oshawa, ON	9.7%
37	Halifax, NS	9.6%
38	Barrie, ON	7.9%
39	Kelowna, BC	7.5%
40	Kingston, ON	7.4%
41	Terrebonne, QC	7.0%
42	Sherbrooke, QC	5.9%
43	St. John's, NL	4.8%
44	Québec, QC	4.2%
45	Chatham-Kent, ON	4.1%
46	Thunder Bay, ON	3.7%
47	Greater Sudbury, ON	2.9%
48	Trois-Rivières, QC	2.7%
49	Lévis, QC	1.4%
50	Saguenay, QC	0.9%
–	Canada	18.8%

Female

Rank	City	Percent
1	Markham, ON	72.5%
2	Richmond, BC	71.3%
3	Brampton, ON	66.5%
4	Burnaby, BC	60.9%
5	Mississauga, ON	54.1%
6	Vancouver, BC	53.7%
7	Richmond Hill, ON	53.4%
8	Surrey, BC	52.7%
9	Toronto, ON	49.8%
10	Ajax, ON	46.3%
11	Coquitlam, BC	44.6%
12	Vaughan, ON	31.9%
13	Montréal, QC	31.3%
14	Calgary, AB	30.3%
15	Edmonton, AB	30.1%
16	Abbotsford, BC	29.2%
17	Ottawa, ON	24.0%
18	Oakville, ON	23.5%
19	Windsor, ON	22.5%
20	Winnipeg, MB	21.1%
21	Laval, QC	20.5%
22	Whitby, ON	19.7%
23	Kitchener, ON	18.3%
23	Saanich, BC	18.3%
25	Hamilton, ON	15.6%
25	London, ON	15.6%
27	Guelph, ON	15.5%
28	Longueuil, QC	14.0%
29	Langley, BC	13.3%
30	Cambridge, ON	12.6%
31	Saskatoon, SK	12.3%
32	Burlington, ON	11.9%
33	Regina, SK	11.0%
34	Gatineau, QC	10.2%
35	St. Catharines, ON	9.2%
36	Oshawa, ON	9.0%
37	Halifax, NS	8.7%
38	Terrebonne, QC	8.2%
39	Kelowna, BC	7.7%
40	Kingston, ON	7.4%
41	Barrie, ON	7.3%
42	Sherbrooke, QC	5.1%
43	Québec, QC	3.9%
44	Chatham-Kent, ON	3.8%
45	St. John's, NL	3.4%
46	Thunder Bay, ON	3.0%
47	Greater Sudbury, ON	2.4%
47	Trois-Rivières, QC	2.4%
49	Lévis, QC	1.5%
50	Saguenay, QC	0.9%
–	Canada	19.3%

Note: The Employment Equity Act defines visible minorities as 'persons, other than Aboriginal peoples, who are non-Caucasian in race or non-white in colour.'
Source: Statistics Canada. 2013. 2011 National Household Survey. Statistics Canada Catalogue no. 99-004-XWE. Ottawa. Released September 11, 2013.

Cities Ranked by Visible Minority Population: South Asian
By Number

Total

Rank	City	Number
1	Toronto, ON	317,100
2	Brampton, ON	200,220
3	Mississauga, ON	154,210
4	Surrey, BC	142,445
5	Calgary, AB	81,180
6	Edmonton, AB	57,500
7	Markham, ON	57,375
8	Montréal, QC	53,515
9	Vancouver, BC	35,140
10	Ottawa, ON	33,805
11	Abbotsford, BC	29,725
12	Vaughan, ON	27,725
13	Winnipeg, MB	22,940
14	Burnaby, BC	17,480
15	Hamilton, ON	17,240
16	Ajax, ON	15,025
17	Richmond Hill, ON	15,015
18	Richmond, BC	14,515
19	Oakville, ON	12,935
20	Kitchener, ON	8,960
21	Windsor, ON	8,020
22	London, ON	8,010
23	Laval, QC	6,650
24	Cambridge, ON	6,520
25	Burlington, ON	6,325
26	Saskatoon, SK	5,925
27	Whitby, ON	5,700
28	Coquitlam, BC	5,245
29	Guelph, ON	4,970
30	Regina, SK	4,885
31	Saanich, BC	4,125
32	Halifax, NS	3,995
33	Oshawa, ON	2,790
34	Langley, BC	2,765
35	Kelowna, BC	2,630
36	Longueuil, QC	2,085
37	Kingston, ON	1,995
38	Barrie, ON	1,760
39	St. Catharines, ON	1,430
40	St. John's, NL	1,195
41	Québec, QC	855
42	Gatineau, QC	795
43	Greater Sudbury, ON	630
44	Thunder Bay, ON	575
45	Chatham-Kent, ON	485
46	Sherbrooke, QC	455
47	Terrebonne, QC	105
48	Trois-Rivières, QC	40
49	Saguenay, QC	35
50	Lévis, QC	30
–	Canada	1,567,400

Male

Rank	City	Number
1	Toronto, ON	158,835
2	Brampton, ON	100,775
3	Mississauga, ON	77,020
4	Surrey, BC	71,615
5	Calgary, AB	41,835
6	Edmonton, AB	29,630
7	Markham, ON	28,760
8	Montréal, QC	28,005
9	Vancouver, BC	17,715
10	Ottawa, ON	17,070
11	Abbotsford, BC	14,845
12	Vaughan, ON	13,970
13	Winnipeg, MB	11,500
14	Burnaby, BC	8,850
15	Hamilton, ON	8,800
16	Richmond Hill, ON	7,450
17	Ajax, ON	7,400
18	Richmond, BC	7,340
19	Oakville, ON	6,290
20	Kitchener, ON	4,275
21	Windsor, ON	4,170
22	London, ON	3,945
23	Laval, QC	3,490
24	Cambridge, ON	3,320
25	Burlington, ON	3,150
26	Saskatoon, SK	3,130
27	Whitby, ON	2,655
28	Regina, SK	2,625
29	Coquitlam, BC	2,565
30	Guelph, ON	2,345
31	Halifax, NS	2,140
32	Saanich, BC	2,040
33	Oshawa, ON	1,455
34	Langley, BC	1,425
35	Kelowna, BC	1,310
36	Longueuil, QC	1,095
37	Kingston, ON	1,045
38	Barrie, ON	970
39	St. Catharines, ON	730
40	St. John's, NL	690
41	Québec, QC	455
42	Gatineau, QC	380
43	Greater Sudbury, ON	355
44	Thunder Bay, ON	325
45	Chatham-Kent, ON	250
45	Sherbrooke, QC	250
47	Terrebonne, QC	45
48	Saguenay, QC	30
49	Lévis, QC	10
50	Trois-Rivières, QC	0
–	Canada	790,755

Female

Rank	City	Number
1	Toronto, ON	158,260
2	Brampton, ON	99,445
3	Mississauga, ON	77,195
4	Surrey, BC	70,830
5	Calgary, AB	39,345
6	Markham, ON	28,615
7	Edmonton, AB	27,870
8	Montréal, QC	25,510
9	Vancouver, BC	17,425
10	Ottawa, ON	16,730
11	Abbotsford, BC	14,880
12	Vaughan, ON	13,755
13	Winnipeg, MB	11,445
14	Burnaby, BC	8,630
15	Hamilton, ON	8,440
16	Ajax, ON	7,625
17	Richmond Hill, ON	7,560
18	Richmond, BC	7,175
19	Oakville, ON	6,635
20	Kitchener, ON	4,685
21	London, ON	4,065
22	Windsor, ON	3,850
23	Cambridge, ON	3,200
24	Burlington, ON	3,180
25	Laval, QC	3,155
26	Whitby, ON	3,045
27	Saskatoon, SK	2,800
28	Coquitlam, BC	2,685
29	Guelph, ON	2,625
30	Regina, SK	2,265
31	Saanich, BC	2,085
32	Halifax, NS	1,855
33	Langley, BC	1,340
34	Oshawa, ON	1,335
35	Kelowna, BC	1,320
36	Longueuil, QC	990
37	Kingston, ON	940
38	Barrie, ON	785
39	St. Catharines, ON	700
40	St. John's, NL	500
41	Gatineau, QC	415
42	Québec, QC	400
43	Greater Sudbury, ON	275
44	Thunder Bay, ON	245
45	Chatham-Kent, ON	235
46	Sherbrooke, QC	205
47	Terrebonne, QC	60
48	Trois-Rivières, QC	25
49	Lévis, QC	20
50	Saguenay, QC	0
–	Canada	776,650

Note: The Employment Equity Act defines visible minorities as 'persons, other than Aboriginal peoples, who are non-Caucasian in race or non-white in colour'; South Asian includes 'East Indian,' 'Pakistani,' 'Sri Lankan,' etc.
Source: Statistics Canada. 2013. 2011 National Household Survey. Statistics Canada Catalogue no. 99-004-XWE. Ottawa. Released September 11, 2013.

Cities Ranked by Visible Minority Population: South Asian

By Percent

Total

Rank	City	Percent
1	Brampton, ON	38.4%
2	Surrey, BC	30.7%
3	Abbotsford, BC	22.7%
4	Mississauga, ON	21.8%
5	Markham, ON	19.1%
6	Ajax, ON	13.8%
7	Toronto, ON	12.3%
8	Vaughan, ON	9.7%
9	Richmond Hill, ON	8.1%
10	Burnaby, BC	7.9%
11	Richmond, BC	7.7%
12	Calgary, AB	7.5%
13	Edmonton, AB	7.2%
13	Oakville, ON	7.2%
15	Vancouver, BC	6.0%
16	Cambridge, ON	5.2%
17	Whitby, ON	4.7%
18	Coquitlam, BC	4.2%
19	Guelph, ON	4.1%
19	Kitchener, ON	4.1%
21	Ottawa, ON	3.9%
21	Windsor, ON	3.9%
23	Saanich, BC	3.8%
24	Burlington, ON	3.6%
25	Winnipeg, MB	3.5%
26	Hamilton, ON	3.4%
27	Montréal, QC	3.3%
28	Langley, BC	2.7%
28	Saskatoon, SK	2.7%
30	Regina, SK	2.6%
31	Kelowna, BC	2.3%
32	London, ON	2.2%
33	Oshawa, ON	1.9%
34	Kingston, ON	1.7%
34	Laval, QC	1.7%
36	Barrie, ON	1.3%
37	St. John's, NL	1.2%
38	St. Catharines, ON	1.1%
39	Halifax, NS	1.0%
40	Longueuil, QC	0.9%
41	Chatham-Kent, ON	0.5%
41	Thunder Bay, ON	0.5%
43	Greater Sudbury, ON	0.4%
44	Gatineau, QC	0.3%
44	Sherbrooke, QC	0.3%
46	Québec, QC	0.2%
47	Terrebonne, QC	0.1%
48	Lévis, QC	0.0%
48	Saguenay, QC	0.0%
48	Trois-Rivières, QC	0.0%
–	Canada	4.8%

Male

Rank	City	Percent
1	Brampton, ON	39.1%
2	Surrey, BC	31.2%
3	Abbotsford, BC	23.0%
4	Mississauga, ON	22.2%
5	Markham, ON	19.6%
6	Ajax, ON	14.0%
7	Toronto, ON	12.8%
8	Vaughan, ON	10.0%
9	Richmond Hill, ON	8.3%
10	Burnaby, BC	8.2%
11	Richmond, BC	8.1%
12	Calgary, AB	7.7%
13	Edmonton, AB	7.5%
14	Oakville, ON	7.2%
15	Vancouver, BC	6.1%
16	Cambridge, ON	5.4%
17	Whitby, ON	4.5%
18	Coquitlam, BC	4.2%
19	Ottawa, ON	4.1%
19	Windsor, ON	4.1%
21	Guelph, ON	4.0%
21	Kitchener, ON	4.0%
23	Saanich, BC	3.9%
24	Burlington, ON	3.8%
25	Montréal, QC	3.6%
25	Winnipeg, MB	3.6%
27	Hamilton, ON	3.5%
28	Saskatoon, SK	2.9%
29	Langley, BC	2.8%
29	Regina, SK	2.8%
31	Kelowna, BC	2.4%
32	London, ON	2.3%
33	Oshawa, ON	2.0%
34	Kingston, ON	1.8%
34	Laval, QC	1.8%
36	Barrie, ON	1.5%
37	St. John's, NL	1.4%
38	St. Catharines, ON	1.2%
39	Halifax, NS	1.1%
40	Longueuil, QC	1.0%
41	Thunder Bay, ON	0.6%
42	Chatham-Kent, ON	0.5%
42	Greater Sudbury, ON	0.5%
44	Gatineau, QC	0.3%
44	Sherbrooke, QC	0.3%
46	Québec, QC	0.2%
47	Terrebonne, QC	0.1%
48	Lévis, QC	0.0%
48	Saguenay, QC	0.0%
48	Trois-Rivières, QC	0.0%
–	Canada	4.9%

Female

Rank	City	Percent
1	Brampton, ON	37.7%
2	Surrey, BC	30.3%
3	Abbotsford, BC	22.4%
4	Mississauga, ON	21.4%
5	Markham, ON	18.7%
6	Ajax, ON	13.5%
7	Toronto, ON	11.8%
8	Vaughan, ON	9.4%
9	Richmond Hill, ON	8.0%
10	Burnaby, BC	7.7%
11	Calgary, AB	7.3%
11	Richmond, BC	7.3%
13	Oakville, ON	7.1%
14	Edmonton, AB	7.0%
15	Vancouver, BC	5.8%
16	Cambridge, ON	5.0%
16	Whitby, ON	5.0%
18	Kitchener, ON	4.3%
19	Coquitlam, BC	4.2%
19	Guelph, ON	4.2%
21	Ottawa, ON	3.8%
21	Saanich, BC	3.8%
23	Windsor, ON	3.6%
24	Burlington, ON	3.5%
25	Winnipeg, MB	3.4%
26	Hamilton, ON	3.2%
27	Montréal, QC	3.1%
28	Langley, BC	2.6%
29	Saskatoon, SK	2.5%
30	Regina, SK	2.3%
31	Kelowna, BC	2.2%
31	London, ON	2.2%
33	Oshawa, ON	1.8%
34	Laval, QC	1.6%
35	Kingston, ON	1.5%
36	Barrie, ON	1.1%
37	St. Catharines, ON	1.0%
38	Halifax, NS	0.9%
38	St. John's, NL	0.9%
40	Longueuil, QC	0.8%
41	Chatham-Kent, ON	0.5%
41	Thunder Bay, ON	0.5%
43	Gatineau, QC	0.3%
43	Greater Sudbury, ON	0.3%
43	Sherbrooke, QC	0.3%
46	Québec, QC	0.2%
47	Terrebonne, QC	0.1%
48	Lévis, QC	0.0%
48	Saguenay, QC	0.0%
48	Trois-Rivières, QC	0.0%
–	Canada	4.7%

Note: The Employment Equity Act defines visible minorities as 'persons, other than Aboriginal peoples, who are non-Caucasian in race or non-white in colour'; South Asian includes 'East Indian,' 'Pakistani,' 'Sri Lankan,' etc.

Source: Statistics Canada. 2013. 2011 National Household Survey. Statistics Canada Catalogue no. 99-004-XWE. Ottawa. Released September 11, 2013.

Cities Ranked by Visible Minority Population: Chinese
By Number

Total

Rank	City	Number
1	Toronto, ON	278,390
2	Vancouver, BC	163,230
3	Markham, ON	114,950
4	Richmond, BC	89,045
5	Calgary, AB	74,070
6	Burnaby, BC	67,780
7	Mississauga, ON	50,120
8	Edmonton, AB	49,660
9	Montréal, QC	46,845
10	Richmond Hill, ON	43,530
11	Ottawa, ON	34,855
12	Surrey, BC	28,480
13	Coquitlam, BC	21,575
14	Winnipeg, MB	14,975
15	Vaughan, ON	13,475
16	Hamilton, ON	8,505
17	Brampton, ON	8,035
18	Saanich, BC	7,795
19	London, ON	7,140
20	Windsor, ON	6,245
21	Oakville, ON	6,240
22	Saskatoon, SK	5,330
23	Halifax, NS	4,620
24	Kitchener, ON	3,975
25	Regina, SK	3,645
26	Guelph, ON	3,350
27	Laval, QC	3,195
28	Langley, BC	3,055
29	Longueuil, QC	2,870
30	Burlington, ON	2,845
31	Ajax, ON	2,555
32	Whitby, ON	2,290
33	Gatineau, QC	2,030
34	St. Catharines, ON	1,905
35	Kingston, ON	1,885
36	Abbotsford, BC	1,805
37	Québec, QC	1,710
38	Kelowna, BC	1,480
39	Oshawa, ON	1,340
40	Cambridge, ON	1,135
41	St. John's, NL	990
42	Barrie, ON	975
43	Greater Sudbury, ON	795
44	Thunder Bay, ON	715
45	Sherbrooke, QC	405
46	Lévis, QC	370
47	Saguenay, QC	240
48	Trois-Rivières, QC	235
49	Chatham-Kent, ON	215
50	Terrebonne, QC	205
–	Canada	1,324,750

Male

Rank	City	Number
1	Toronto, ON	132,140
2	Vancouver, BC	76,990
3	Markham, ON	55,960
4	Richmond, BC	42,125
5	Calgary, AB	35,805
6	Burnaby, BC	32,375
7	Mississauga, ON	24,220
8	Edmonton, AB	24,190
9	Montréal, QC	22,035
10	Richmond Hill, ON	21,235
11	Ottawa, ON	16,395
12	Surrey, BC	13,715
13	Coquitlam, BC	10,460
14	Winnipeg, MB	7,415
15	Vaughan, ON	6,565
16	Hamilton, ON	4,235
17	Brampton, ON	3,980
18	Saanich, BC	3,845
19	London, ON	3,345
20	Windsor, ON	3,150
21	Oakville, ON	2,900
22	Saskatoon, SK	2,545
23	Halifax, NS	2,410
24	Kitchener, ON	1,975
25	Regina, SK	1,715
26	Guelph, ON	1,595
27	Langley, BC	1,580
28	Laval, QC	1,370
29	Burlington, ON	1,350
30	Longueuil, QC	1,335
31	Ajax, ON	1,205
32	Whitby, ON	1,100
33	Kingston, ON	900
34	St. Catharines, ON	895
35	Abbotsford, BC	890
36	Gatineau, QC	880
37	Kelowna, BC	745
38	Oshawa, ON	695
39	Québec, QC	560
40	Cambridge, ON	520
41	St. John's, NL	500
42	Barrie, ON	455
42	Greater Sudbury, ON	455
44	Thunder Bay, ON	400
45	Sherbrooke, QC	155
46	Chatham-Kent, ON	85
47	Lévis, QC	75
48	Terrebonne, QC	70
48	Trois-Rivières, QC	70
50	Saguenay, QC	40
–	Canada	632,325

Female

Rank	City	Number
1	Toronto, ON	146,250
2	Vancouver, BC	86,235
3	Markham, ON	58,985
4	Richmond, BC	46,915
5	Calgary, AB	38,265
6	Burnaby, BC	35,400
7	Mississauga, ON	25,895
8	Edmonton, AB	25,470
9	Montréal, QC	24,810
10	Richmond Hill, ON	22,300
11	Ottawa, ON	18,460
12	Surrey, BC	14,765
13	Coquitlam, BC	11,120
14	Winnipeg, MB	7,560
15	Vaughan, ON	6,910
16	Hamilton, ON	4,270
17	Brampton, ON	4,055
18	Saanich, BC	3,950
19	London, ON	3,795
20	Oakville, ON	3,340
21	Windsor, ON	3,085
22	Saskatoon, SK	2,775
23	Halifax, NS	2,210
24	Kitchener, ON	2,005
25	Regina, SK	1,925
26	Laval, QC	1,825
27	Guelph, ON	1,760
28	Longueuil, QC	1,530
29	Burlington, ON	1,500
30	Langley, BC	1,470
31	Ajax, ON	1,350
32	Whitby, ON	1,195
33	Gatineau, QC	1,150
33	Québec, QC	1,150
35	St. Catharines, ON	1,010
36	Kingston, ON	985
37	Abbotsford, BC	915
38	Kelowna, BC	740
39	Oshawa, ON	640
40	Cambridge, ON	615
41	Barrie, ON	520
42	St. John's, NL	490
43	Greater Sudbury, ON	345
44	Thunder Bay, ON	320
45	Lévis, QC	295
46	Sherbrooke, QC	245
47	Saguenay, QC	195
48	Trois-Rivières, QC	170
49	Chatham-Kent, ON	135
49	Terrebonne, QC	135
–	Canada	692,420

Note: The Employment Equity Act defines visible minorities as 'persons, other than Aboriginal peoples, who are non-Caucasian in race or non-white in colour.'
Source: Statistics Canada. 2013. 2011 National Household Survey. Statistics Canada Catalogue no. 99-004-XWE. Ottawa. Released September 11, 2013.

Cities Ranked by Visible Minority Population: Chinese
By Percent

Total

Rank	City	Percent
1	Richmond, BC	47.0%
2	Markham, ON	38.3%
3	Burnaby, BC	30.8%
4	Vancouver, BC	27.7%
5	Richmond Hill, ON	23.6%
6	Coquitlam, BC	17.3%
7	Toronto, ON	10.8%
8	Saanich, BC	7.2%
9	Mississauga, ON	7.1%
10	Calgary, AB	6.8%
11	Edmonton, AB	6.2%
12	Surrey, BC	6.1%
13	Vaughan, ON	4.7%
14	Ottawa, ON	4.0%
15	Oakville, ON	3.5%
16	Langley, BC	3.0%
16	Windsor, ON	3.0%
18	Montréal, QC	2.9%
19	Guelph, ON	2.8%
20	Saskatoon, SK	2.4%
21	Ajax, ON	2.3%
21	Winnipeg, MB	2.3%
23	London, ON	2.0%
24	Regina, SK	1.9%
24	Whitby, ON	1.9%
26	Kitchener, ON	1.8%
27	Hamilton, ON	1.7%
28	Burlington, ON	1.6%
28	Kingston, ON	1.6%
30	Brampton, ON	1.5%
30	St. Catharines, ON	1.5%
32	Abbotsford, BC	1.4%
33	Kelowna, BC	1.3%
33	Longueuil, QC	1.3%
35	Halifax, NS	1.2%
36	St. John's, NL	1.0%
37	Cambridge, ON	0.9%
37	Oshawa, ON	0.9%
39	Gatineau, QC	0.8%
39	Laval, QC	0.8%
41	Barrie, ON	0.7%
41	Thunder Bay, ON	0.7%
43	Greater Sudbury, ON	0.5%
44	Lévis, QC	0.3%
44	Québec, QC	0.3%
44	Sherbrooke, QC	0.3%
47	Chatham-Kent, ON	0.2%
47	Saguenay, QC	0.2%
47	Terrebonne, QC	0.2%
47	Trois-Rivières, QC	0.2%
–	Canada	4.0%

Male

Rank	City	Percent
1	Richmond, BC	46.3%
2	Markham, ON	38.1%
3	Burnaby, BC	30.0%
4	Vancouver, BC	26.7%
5	Richmond Hill, ON	23.6%
6	Coquitlam, BC	17.0%
7	Toronto, ON	10.7%
8	Saanich, BC	7.4%
9	Mississauga, ON	7.0%
10	Calgary, AB	6.6%
11	Edmonton, AB	6.1%
12	Surrey, BC	6.0%
13	Vaughan, ON	4.7%
14	Ottawa, ON	3.9%
15	Oakville, ON	3.3%
16	Langley, BC	3.1%
16	Windsor, ON	3.1%
18	Montréal, QC	2.8%
19	Guelph, ON	2.7%
20	Saskatoon, SK	2.4%
21	Ajax, ON	2.3%
21	Winnipeg, MB	2.3%
23	London, ON	1.9%
23	Whitby, ON	1.9%
25	Kitchener, ON	1.8%
25	Regina, SK	1.8%
27	Hamilton, ON	1.7%
28	Burlington, ON	1.6%
28	Kingston, ON	1.6%
30	Brampton, ON	1.5%
30	St. Catharines, ON	1.5%
32	Abbotsford, BC	1.4%
33	Halifax, NS	1.3%
33	Kelowna, BC	1.3%
35	Longueuil, QC	1.2%
36	Oshawa, ON	1.0%
36	St. John's, NL	1.0%
38	Cambridge, ON	0.8%
38	Thunder Bay, ON	0.8%
40	Barrie, ON	0.7%
40	Gatineau, QC	0.7%
40	Laval, QC	0.7%
43	Greater Sudbury, ON	0.6%
44	Chatham-Kent, ON	0.2%
44	Québec, QC	0.2%
44	Sherbrooke, QC	0.2%
47	Lévis, QC	0.1%
47	Saguenay, QC	0.1%
47	Terrebonne, QC	0.1%
47	Trois-Rivières, QC	0.1%
–	Canada	3.9%

Female

Rank	City	Percent
1	Richmond, BC	47.7%
2	Markham, ON	38.5%
3	Burnaby, BC	31.6%
4	Vancouver, BC	28.6%
5	Richmond Hill, ON	23.6%
6	Coquitlam, BC	17.5%
7	Toronto, ON	10.9%
8	Mississauga, ON	7.2%
9	Calgary, AB	7.1%
9	Saanich, BC	7.1%
11	Edmonton, AB	6.4%
12	Surrey, BC	6.3%
13	Vaughan, ON	4.7%
14	Ottawa, ON	4.1%
15	Oakville, ON	3.6%
16	Montréal, QC	3.0%
17	Windsor, ON	2.9%
18	Guelph, ON	2.8%
18	Langley, BC	2.8%
20	Saskatoon, SK	2.5%
21	Ajax, ON	2.4%
22	Winnipeg, MB	2.3%
23	London, ON	2.0%
23	Regina, SK	2.0%
25	Whitby, ON	1.9%
26	Kitchener, ON	1.8%
27	Burlington, ON	1.7%
28	Hamilton, ON	1.6%
28	Kingston, ON	1.6%
30	Brampton, ON	1.5%
30	St. Catharines, ON	1.5%
32	Abbotsford, BC	1.4%
33	Longueuil, QC	1.3%
34	Kelowna, BC	1.2%
35	Halifax, NS	1.1%
36	Cambridge, ON	1.0%
37	Gatineau, QC	0.9%
37	Laval, QC	0.9%
37	St. John's, NL	0.9%
40	Barrie, ON	0.8%
40	Oshawa, ON	0.8%
42	Thunder Bay, ON	0.6%
43	Greater Sudbury, ON	0.4%
43	Lévis, QC	0.4%
43	Québec, QC	0.4%
46	Chatham-Kent, ON	0.3%
46	Saguenay, QC	0.3%
46	Sherbrooke, QC	0.3%
46	Terrebonne, QC	0.3%
46	Trois-Rivières, QC	0.3%
–	Canada	4.1%

Note: The Employment Equity Act defines visible minorities as 'persons, other than Aboriginal peoples, who are non-Caucasian in race or non-white in colour.'
Source: Statistics Canada. 2013. 2011 National Household Survey. Statistics Canada Catalogue no. 99-004-XWE. Ottawa. Released September 11, 2013.

Cities Ranked by Visible Minority Population: Black
By Number

Total

Rank	City	Number
1	Toronto, ON	218,160
2	Montréal, QC	147,100
3	Brampton, ON	70,290
4	Ottawa, ON	49,650
5	Mississauga, ON	44,775
6	Calgary, AB	31,870
7	Edmonton, AB	30,355
8	Laval, QC	24,225
9	Ajax, ON	17,510
10	Winnipeg, MB	17,410
11	Hamilton, ON	16,110
12	Halifax, NS	13,780
13	Longueuil, QC	10,500
14	Gatineau, QC	10,165
15	Markham, ON	9,715
16	Windsor, ON	9,480
17	London, ON	8,760
18	Vaughan, ON	7,765
19	Whitby, ON	7,440
20	Kitchener, ON	6,635
21	Surrey, BC	6,150
22	Québec, QC	5,760
23	Vancouver, BC	5,720
24	Oakville, ON	4,820
25	Terrebonne, QC	4,710
26	Oshawa, ON	4,675
27	Richmond Hill, ON	3,720
28	Burnaby, BC	3,445
29	Regina, SK	3,065
30	Burlington, ON	2,830
31	St. Catharines, ON	2,675
32	Sherbrooke, QC	2,530
33	Barrie, ON	2,525
34	Saskatoon, SK	2,480
35	Cambridge, ON	2,320
36	Chatham-Kent, ON	1,890
37	Guelph, ON	1,695
38	Coquitlam, BC	1,265
39	Richmond, BC	1,245
40	Saanich, BC	1,200
41	Trois-Rivières, QC	1,175
42	Abbotsford, BC	1,120
43	Kingston, ON	1,105
44	Greater Sudbury, ON	935
45	St. John's, NL	930
46	Kelowna, BC	685
47	Lévis, QC	500
48	Thunder Bay, ON	485
49	Langley, BC	470
50	Saguenay, QC	385
–	Canada	945,665

Male

Rank	City	Number
1	Toronto, ON	97,825
2	Montréal, QC	69,680
3	Brampton, ON	33,005
4	Ottawa, ON	22,765
5	Mississauga, ON	20,420
6	Calgary, AB	16,710
7	Edmonton, AB	15,600
8	Laval, QC	11,695
9	Winnipeg, MB	8,900
10	Ajax, ON	8,390
11	Hamilton, ON	8,190
12	Halifax, NS	6,805
13	Longueuil, QC	4,865
14	Gatineau, QC	4,730
15	London, ON	4,590
16	Markham, ON	4,535
17	Windsor, ON	4,295
18	Vaughan, ON	3,725
19	Whitby, ON	3,715
20	Kitchener, ON	3,455
21	Vancouver, BC	3,120
22	Surrey, BC	3,090
23	Québec, QC	2,980
24	Oshawa, ON	2,310
25	Oakville, ON	2,225
26	Terrebonne, QC	2,160
27	Richmond Hill, ON	1,730
28	Burnaby, BC	1,705
29	Regina, SK	1,605
30	St. Catharines, ON	1,505
31	Barrie, ON	1,430
32	Burlington, ON	1,340
33	Saskatoon, SK	1,335
34	Sherbrooke, QC	1,315
35	Cambridge, ON	1,170
36	Chatham-Kent, ON	995
37	Guelph, ON	890
38	Saanich, BC	665
39	Coquitlam, BC	660
40	Abbotsford, BC	645
41	Trois-Rivières, QC	630
42	Richmond, BC	605
43	St. John's, NL	560
44	Greater Sudbury, ON	520
45	Kingston, ON	490
46	Kelowna, BC	340
47	Langley, BC	300
48	Lévis, QC	255
49	Thunder Bay, ON	235
50	Saguenay, QC	200
–	Canada	453,005

Female

Rank	City	Number
1	Toronto, ON	120,335
2	Montréal, QC	77,420
3	Brampton, ON	37,285
4	Ottawa, ON	26,880
5	Mississauga, ON	24,355
6	Calgary, AB	15,155
7	Edmonton, AB	14,755
8	Laval, QC	12,530
9	Ajax, ON	9,115
10	Winnipeg, MB	8,510
11	Hamilton, ON	7,920
12	Halifax, NS	6,970
13	Longueuil, QC	5,635
14	Gatineau, QC	5,435
15	Windsor, ON	5,185
16	Markham, ON	5,180
17	London, ON	4,175
18	Vaughan, ON	4,040
19	Whitby, ON	3,730
20	Kitchener, ON	3,175
21	Surrey, BC	3,060
22	Québec, QC	2,780
23	Vancouver, BC	2,600
24	Oakville, ON	2,595
25	Terrebonne, QC	2,545
26	Oshawa, ON	2,360
27	Richmond Hill, ON	1,990
28	Burnaby, BC	1,740
29	Burlington, ON	1,485
30	Regina, SK	1,455
31	Sherbrooke, QC	1,215
32	St. Catharines, ON	1,170
33	Cambridge, ON	1,155
34	Saskatoon, SK	1,145
35	Barrie, ON	1,095
36	Chatham-Kent, ON	890
37	Guelph, ON	800
38	Richmond, BC	640
39	Kingston, ON	610
40	Coquitlam, BC	600
41	Trois-Rivières, QC	545
42	Saanich, BC	530
43	Abbotsford, BC	470
44	Greater Sudbury, ON	410
45	St. John's, NL	375
46	Kelowna, BC	345
47	Thunder Bay, ON	255
48	Lévis, QC	250
49	Saguenay, QC	180
50	Langley, BC	170
–	Canada	492,660

Note: The Employment Equity Act defines visible minorities as 'persons, other than Aboriginal peoples, who are non-Caucasian in race or non-white in colour.'
Source: Statistics Canada. 2013. 2011 National Household Survey. Statistics Canada Catalogue no. 99-004-XWE. Ottawa. Released September 11, 2013.

Cities Ranked by Visible Minority Population: Black
By Percent

Total

Rank	City	Percent
1	Ajax, ON	16.0%
2	Brampton, ON	13.5%
3	Montréal, QC	9.1%
4	Toronto, ON	8.5%
5	Mississauga, ON	6.3%
6	Laval, QC	6.2%
6	Whitby, ON	6.2%
8	Ottawa, ON	5.7%
9	Longueuil, QC	4.6%
9	Windsor, ON	4.6%
11	Terrebonne, QC	4.5%
12	Gatineau, QC	3.9%
13	Edmonton, AB	3.8%
14	Halifax, NS	3.6%
15	Hamilton, ON	3.2%
15	Markham, ON	3.2%
15	Oshawa, ON	3.2%
18	Kitchener, ON	3.1%
19	Calgary, AB	2.9%
20	Oakville, ON	2.7%
20	Vaughan, ON	2.7%
20	Winnipeg, MB	2.7%
23	London, ON	2.4%
24	St. Catharines, ON	2.1%
25	Richmond Hill, ON	2.0%
26	Barrie, ON	1.9%
26	Cambridge, ON	1.9%
26	Chatham-Kent, ON	1.9%
29	Sherbrooke, QC	1.7%
30	Burlington, ON	1.6%
30	Burnaby, BC	1.6%
30	Regina, SK	1.6%
33	Guelph, ON	1.4%
34	Surrey, BC	1.3%
35	Québec, QC	1.1%
35	Saanich, BC	1.1%
35	Saskatoon, SK	1.1%
38	Coquitlam, BC	1.0%
38	Vancouver, BC	1.0%
40	Abbotsford, BC	0.9%
40	Kingston, ON	0.9%
40	St. John's, NL	0.9%
40	Trois-Rivières, QC	0.9%
44	Richmond, BC	0.7%
45	Greater Sudbury, ON	0.6%
45	Kelowna, BC	0.6%
47	Langley, BC	0.5%
47	Thunder Bay, ON	0.5%
49	Lévis, QC	0.4%
50	Saguenay, QC	0.3%
–	Canada	2.9%

Male

Rank	City	Percent
1	Ajax, ON	15.9%
2	Brampton, ON	12.8%
3	Montréal, QC	8.9%
4	Toronto, ON	7.9%
5	Whitby, ON	6.3%
6	Laval, QC	6.1%
7	Mississauga, ON	5.9%
8	Ottawa, ON	5.4%
9	Longueuil, QC	4.4%
10	Windsor, ON	4.2%
11	Terrebonne, QC	4.1%
12	Edmonton, AB	3.9%
13	Gatineau, QC	3.7%
13	Halifax, NS	3.7%
15	Hamilton, ON	3.3%
16	Kitchener, ON	3.2%
16	Oshawa, ON	3.2%
18	Calgary, AB	3.1%
18	Markham, ON	3.1%
20	Winnipeg, MB	2.8%
21	Vaughan, ON	2.7%
22	London, ON	2.6%
23	Oakville, ON	2.5%
24	St. Catharines, ON	2.4%
25	Barrie, ON	2.2%
26	Chatham-Kent, ON	2.0%
27	Cambridge, ON	1.9%
27	Richmond Hill, ON	1.9%
29	Sherbrooke, QC	1.8%
30	Regina, SK	1.7%
31	Burlington, ON	1.6%
31	Burnaby, BC	1.6%
33	Guelph, ON	1.5%
34	Saanich, BC	1.3%
34	Surrey, BC	1.3%
36	Québec, QC	1.2%
36	Saskatoon, SK	1.2%
38	Coquitlam, BC	1.1%
38	St. John's, NL	1.1%
38	Vancouver, BC	1.1%
41	Abbotsford, BC	1.0%
41	Trois-Rivières, QC	1.0%
43	Kingston, ON	0.9%
44	Greater Sudbury, ON	0.7%
44	Richmond, BC	0.7%
46	Kelowna, BC	0.6%
46	Langley, BC	0.6%
48	Thunder Bay, ON	0.5%
49	Lévis, QC	0.4%
50	Saguenay, QC	0.3%
–	Canada	2.8%

Female

Rank	City	Percent
1	Ajax, ON	16.2%
2	Brampton, ON	14.1%
3	Montréal, QC	9.4%
4	Toronto, ON	9.0%
5	Mississauga, ON	6.7%
6	Laval, QC	6.2%
7	Whitby, ON	6.1%
8	Ottawa, ON	6.0%
9	Windsor, ON	4.9%
10	Longueuil, QC	4.8%
10	Terrebonne, QC	4.8%
12	Gatineau, QC	4.0%
13	Edmonton, AB	3.7%
14	Halifax, NS	3.5%
15	Markham, ON	3.4%
16	Oshawa, ON	3.1%
17	Hamilton, ON	3.0%
18	Kitchener, ON	2.9%
19	Calgary, AB	2.8%
19	Oakville, ON	2.8%
19	Vaughan, ON	2.8%
22	Winnipeg, MB	2.6%
23	London, ON	2.2%
24	Richmond Hill, ON	2.1%
25	Cambridge, ON	1.8%
26	Burlington, ON	1.7%
26	Chatham-Kent, ON	1.7%
26	St. Catharines, ON	1.7%
29	Barrie, ON	1.6%
29	Burnaby, BC	1.6%
29	Sherbrooke, QC	1.6%
32	Regina, SK	1.5%
33	Guelph, ON	1.3%
33	Surrey, BC	1.3%
35	Québec, QC	1.1%
36	Kingston, ON	1.0%
36	Saanich, BC	1.0%
36	Saskatoon, SK	1.0%
39	Coquitlam, BC	0.9%
39	Vancouver, BC	0.9%
41	Trois-Rivières, QC	0.8%
42	Abbotsford, BC	0.7%
42	Richmond, BC	0.7%
42	St. John's, NL	0.7%
45	Kelowna, BC	0.6%
46	Greater Sudbury, ON	0.5%
46	Thunder Bay, ON	0.5%
48	Lévis, QC	0.4%
49	Langley, BC	0.3%
49	Saguenay, QC	0.3%
–	Canada	3.0%

Note: The Employment Equity Act defines visible minorities as 'persons, other than Aboriginal peoples, who are non-Caucasian in race or non-white in colour.'
Source: Statistics Canada. 2013. 2011 National Household Survey. Statistics Canada Catalogue no. 99-004-XWE. Ottawa. Released September 11, 2013.

Cities Ranked by Visible Minority Population: Filipino
By Number

Total

Rank	City	Number
1	Toronto, ON	132,445
2	Winnipeg, MB	56,400
3	Calgary, AB	47,350
4	Mississauga, ON	39,800
5	Edmonton, AB	36,565
6	Vancouver, BC	35,490
7	Surrey, BC	26,480
8	Montréal, QC	21,750
9	Brampton, ON	17,905
10	Burnaby, BC	12,905
11	Richmond, BC	12,670
12	Ottawa, ON	10,530
13	Markham, ON	9,020
14	Vaughan, ON	8,585
15	Hamilton, ON	7,170
16	Saskatoon, SK	6,830
17	Coquitlam, BC	4,865
18	Ajax, ON	4,820
19	Regina, SK	4,135
20	Richmond Hill, ON	4,050
21	Oakville, ON	3,380
22	Windsor, ON	3,180
23	London, ON	2,270
24	Whitby, ON	2,255
25	Guelph, ON	1,960
26	Saanich, BC	1,815
27	Burlington, ON	1,600
28	Kitchener, ON	1,375
29	Langley, BC	1,340
30	Halifax, NS	1,320
31	Oshawa, ON	1,290
32	St. Catharines, ON	1,045
33	Abbotsford, BC	895
34	Kelowna, BC	870
35	Cambridge, ON	830
36	Barrie, ON	815
37	Laval, QC	785
38	Kingston, ON	695
39	Longueuil, QC	480
40	Thunder Bay, ON	440
41	Gatineau, QC	420
42	Chatham-Kent, ON	220
43	Greater Sudbury, ON	195
44	St. John's, NL	110
45	Québec, QC	95
46	Trois-Rivières, QC	80
47	Saguenay, QC	40
48	Sherbrooke, QC	35
49	Terrebonne, QC	30
50	Lévis, QC	20
–	Canada	619,310

Male

Rank	City	Number
1	Toronto, ON	55,315
2	Winnipeg, MB	27,015
3	Calgary, AB	21,100
4	Mississauga, ON	18,010
5	Edmonton, AB	16,695
6	Vancouver, BC	14,695
7	Surrey, BC	12,260
8	Brampton, ON	8,490
9	Montréal, QC	8,415
10	Richmond, BC	5,505
11	Burnaby, BC	5,490
12	Ottawa, ON	4,040
13	Markham, ON	3,835
14	Saskatoon, SK	3,490
15	Vaughan, ON	3,435
16	Hamilton, ON	3,180
17	Ajax, ON	2,115
18	Coquitlam, BC	2,075
19	Regina, SK	2,015
20	Richmond Hill, ON	1,685
21	Windsor, ON	1,405
22	Oakville, ON	1,355
23	Whitby, ON	920
24	Guelph, ON	915
24	London, ON	915
26	Burlington, ON	700
27	Saanich, BC	690
28	Kitchener, ON	645
29	Langley, BC	610
30	Halifax, NS	560
31	Oshawa, ON	550
32	St. Catharines, ON	435
33	Abbotsford, BC	425
34	Cambridge, ON	345
35	Kelowna, BC	325
36	Laval, QC	315
37	Barrie, ON	305
38	Kingston, ON	300
39	Thunder Bay, ON	200
40	Gatineau, QC	180
40	Longueuil, QC	180
42	Greater Sudbury, ON	90
43	Chatham-Kent, ON	65
44	Trois-Rivières, QC	60
45	St. John's, NL	45
46	Québec, QC	35
47	Lévis, QC	0
47	Saguenay, QC	0
47	Sherbrooke, QC	0
47	Terrebonne, QC	0
–	Canada	268,885

Female

Rank	City	Number
1	Toronto, ON	77,130
2	Winnipeg, MB	29,385
3	Calgary, AB	26,245
4	Mississauga, ON	21,790
5	Vancouver, BC	20,800
6	Edmonton, AB	19,865
7	Surrey, BC	14,215
8	Montréal, QC	13,340
9	Brampton, ON	9,415
10	Burnaby, BC	7,415
11	Richmond, BC	7,160
12	Ottawa, ON	6,490
13	Markham, ON	5,185
14	Vaughan, ON	5,150
15	Hamilton, ON	3,995
16	Saskatoon, SK	3,345
17	Coquitlam, BC	2,790
18	Ajax, ON	2,710
19	Richmond Hill, ON	2,365
20	Regina, SK	2,120
21	Oakville, ON	2,025
22	Windsor, ON	1,775
23	London, ON	1,350
24	Whitby, ON	1,335
25	Saanich, BC	1,125
26	Guelph, ON	1,045
27	Burlington, ON	900
28	Halifax, NS	760
29	Oshawa, ON	740
30	Langley, BC	730
31	Kitchener, ON	725
32	St. Catharines, ON	610
33	Kelowna, BC	545
34	Barrie, ON	510
35	Cambridge, ON	490
36	Laval, QC	475
37	Abbotsford, BC	470
38	Kingston, ON	400
39	Longueuil, QC	305
40	Thunder Bay, ON	240
41	Gatineau, QC	230
42	Chatham-Kent, ON	150
43	Greater Sudbury, ON	105
44	St. John's, NL	65
45	Québec, QC	60
46	Saguenay, QC	35
47	Trois-Rivières, QC	25
48	Terrebonne, QC	20
49	Lévis, QC	15
49	Sherbrooke, QC	15
–	Canada	350,425

Note: The Employment Equity Act defines visible minorities as 'persons, other than Aboriginal peoples, who are non-Caucasian in race or non-white in colour.'
Source: Statistics Canada. 2013. 2011 National Household Survey. Statistics Canada Catalogue no. 99-004-XWE. Ottawa. Released September 11, 2013.

Cities Ranked by Visible Minority Population: Filipino
By Percent

Total

Rank	City	Percent
1	Winnipeg, MB	8.7%
2	Richmond, BC	6.7%
3	Vancouver, BC	6.0%
4	Burnaby, BC	5.9%
5	Surrey, BC	5.7%
6	Mississauga, ON	5.6%
7	Toronto, ON	5.1%
8	Edmonton, AB	4.6%
9	Ajax, ON	4.4%
9	Calgary, AB	4.4%
11	Coquitlam, BC	3.9%
12	Brampton, ON	3.4%
13	Saskatoon, SK	3.1%
14	Markham, ON	3.0%
14	Vaughan, ON	3.0%
16	Regina, SK	2.2%
16	Richmond Hill, ON	2.2%
18	Oakville, ON	1.9%
18	Whitby, ON	1.9%
20	Saanich, BC	1.7%
21	Guelph, ON	1.6%
22	Windsor, ON	1.5%
23	Hamilton, ON	1.4%
24	Langley, BC	1.3%
24	Montréal, QC	1.3%
26	Ottawa, ON	1.2%
27	Burlington, ON	0.9%
27	Oshawa, ON	0.9%
29	Kelowna, BC	0.8%
29	St. Catharines, ON	0.8%
31	Abbotsford, BC	0.7%
31	Cambridge, ON	0.7%
33	Barrie, ON	0.6%
33	Kingston, ON	0.6%
33	Kitchener, ON	0.6%
33	London, ON	0.6%
37	Thunder Bay, ON	0.4%
38	Halifax, NS	0.3%
39	Chatham-Kent, ON	0.2%
39	Gatineau, QC	0.2%
39	Laval, QC	0.2%
39	Longueuil, QC	0.2%
43	Greater Sudbury, ON	0.1%
43	St. John's, NL	0.1%
43	Trois-Rivières, QC	0.1%
46	Lévis, QC	0.0%
46	Québec, QC	0.0%
46	Saguenay, QC	0.0%
46	Sherbrooke, QC	0.0%
46	Terrebonne, QC	0.0%
–	Canada	1.9%

Male

Rank	City	Percent
1	Winnipeg, MB	8.5%
2	Richmond, BC	6.0%
3	Surrey, BC	5.3%
4	Mississauga, ON	5.2%
5	Burnaby, BC	5.1%
5	Vancouver, BC	5.1%
7	Toronto, ON	4.5%
8	Edmonton, AB	4.2%
9	Ajax, ON	4.0%
10	Calgary, AB	3.9%
11	Coquitlam, BC	3.4%
12	Brampton, ON	3.3%
12	Saskatoon, SK	3.3%
14	Markham, ON	2.6%
15	Vaughan, ON	2.5%
16	Regina, SK	2.2%
17	Richmond Hill, ON	1.9%
18	Guelph, ON	1.6%
18	Whitby, ON	1.6%
20	Oakville, ON	1.5%
21	Windsor, ON	1.4%
22	Hamilton, ON	1.3%
22	Saanich, BC	1.3%
24	Langley, BC	1.2%
25	Montréal, QC	1.1%
26	Ottawa, ON	1.0%
27	Burlington, ON	0.8%
27	Oshawa, ON	0.8%
29	Abbotsford, BC	0.7%
29	St. Catharines, ON	0.7%
31	Cambridge, ON	0.6%
31	Kelowna, BC	0.6%
31	Kitchener, ON	0.6%
34	Barrie, ON	0.5%
34	Kingston, ON	0.5%
34	London, ON	0.5%
37	Thunder Bay, ON	0.4%
38	Halifax, NS	0.3%
39	Laval, QC	0.2%
39	Longueuil, QC	0.2%
41	Chatham-Kent, ON	0.1%
41	Gatineau, QC	0.1%
41	Greater Sudbury, ON	0.1%
41	St. John's, NL	0.1%
41	Trois-Rivières, QC	0.1%
46	Lévis, QC	0.0%
46	Québec, QC	0.0%
46	Saguenay, QC	0.0%
46	Sherbrooke, QC	0.0%
46	Terrebonne, QC	0.0%
–	Canada	1.7%

Female

Rank	City	Percent
1	Winnipeg, MB	8.8%
2	Richmond, BC	7.3%
3	Vancouver, BC	6.9%
4	Burnaby, BC	6.6%
5	Surrey, BC	6.1%
6	Mississauga, ON	6.0%
7	Toronto, ON	5.8%
8	Edmonton, AB	5.0%
9	Ajax, ON	4.8%
9	Calgary, AB	4.8%
11	Coquitlam, BC	4.4%
12	Brampton, ON	3.6%
13	Vaughan, ON	3.5%
14	Markham, ON	3.4%
15	Saskatoon, SK	3.0%
16	Richmond Hill, ON	2.5%
17	Oakville, ON	2.2%
17	Regina, SK	2.2%
17	Whitby, ON	2.2%
20	Saanich, BC	2.0%
21	Guelph, ON	1.7%
21	Windsor, ON	1.7%
23	Montréal, QC	1.6%
24	Hamilton, ON	1.5%
24	Ottawa, ON	1.5%
26	Langley, BC	1.4%
27	Burlington, ON	1.0%
27	Oshawa, ON	1.0%
29	Kelowna, BC	0.9%
29	St. Catharines, ON	0.9%
31	Cambridge, ON	0.8%
32	Abbotsford, BC	0.7%
32	Barrie, ON	0.7%
32	Kitchener, ON	0.7%
32	London, ON	0.7%
36	Kingston, ON	0.6%
37	Halifax, NS	0.4%
37	Thunder Bay, ON	0.4%
39	Chatham-Kent, ON	0.3%
39	Longueuil, QC	0.3%
41	Gatineau, QC	0.2%
41	Laval, QC	0.2%
43	Greater Sudbury, ON	0.1%
43	St. John's, NL	0.1%
45	Lévis, QC	0.0%
45	Québec, QC	0.0%
45	Saguenay, QC	0.0%
45	Sherbrooke, QC	0.0%
45	Terrebonne, QC	0.0%
45	Trois-Rivières, QC	0.0%
–	Canada	2.1%

Note: The Employment Equity Act defines visible minorities as 'persons, other than Aboriginal peoples, who are non-Caucasian in race or non-white in colour.'
Source: Statistics Canada. 2013. 2011 National Household Survey. Statistics Canada Catalogue no. 99-004-XWE. Ottawa. Released September 11, 2013.

Cities Ranked by Visible Minority Population: Latin American
By Number

Total

Rank	City	Number
1	Toronto, ON	71,205
2	Montréal, QC	67,160
3	Calgary, AB	19,870
4	Mississauga, ON	15,360
5	Edmonton, AB	13,330
6	Brampton, ON	11,405
7	Ottawa, ON	10,255
8	Laval, QC	9,855
9	London, ON	9,640
10	Vancouver, BC	9,595
11	Hamilton, ON	7,335
12	Winnipeg, MB	6,475
13	Vaughan, ON	6,055
14	Longueuil, QC	5,810
15	Kitchener, ON	5,735
16	Surrey, BC	5,340
17	Québec, QC	5,085
18	Gatineau, QC	3,855
19	Burnaby, BC	3,765
20	Oakville, ON	2,640
21	Windsor, ON	2,255
22	Sherbrooke, QC	2,110
23	St. Catharines, ON	1,920
24	Coquitlam, BC	1,895
25	Richmond Hill, ON	1,730
26	Richmond, BC	1,680
27	Burlington, ON	1,660
28	Markham, ON	1,600
29	Terrebonne, QC	1,340
30	Regina, SK	1,270
31	Cambridge, ON	1,265
32	Saskatoon, SK	1,235
33	Guelph, ON	1,150
34	Barrie, ON	1,105
35	Ajax, ON	1,065
36	Oshawa, ON	1,060
37	Halifax, NS	1,025
38	Whitby, ON	995
39	Trois-Rivières, QC	820
40	Kingston, ON	805
41	Saanich, BC	760
42	Abbotsford, BC	755
43	Langley, BC	650
44	Kelowna, BC	525
45	Chatham-Kent, ON	350
46	Lévis, QC	340
47	Greater Sudbury, ON	290
48	Thunder Bay, ON	205
49	Saguenay, QC	190
50	St. John's, NL	130
–	Canada	381,280

Male

Rank	City	Number
1	Toronto, ON	34,135
2	Montréal, QC	33,025
3	Calgary, AB	10,445
4	Mississauga, ON	7,330
5	Edmonton, AB	6,680
6	Brampton, ON	5,735
7	London, ON	5,080
8	Ottawa, ON	4,875
9	Laval, QC	4,790
10	Vancouver, BC	4,640
11	Winnipeg, MB	3,475
12	Hamilton, ON	3,230
13	Longueuil, QC	2,960
14	Vaughan, ON	2,925
15	Kitchener, ON	2,775
16	Surrey, BC	2,755
17	Québec, QC	2,500
18	Gatineau, QC	1,875
19	Burnaby, BC	1,780
20	Oakville, ON	1,150
20	Windsor, ON	1,150
22	Sherbrooke, QC	1,130
23	St. Catharines, ON	1,045
24	Coquitlam, BC	850
25	Markham, ON	795
25	Richmond Hill, ON	795
27	Burlington, ON	735
28	Richmond, BC	715
29	Saskatoon, SK	665
30	Cambridge, ON	655
31	Terrebonne, QC	605
32	Regina, SK	600
33	Guelph, ON	565
34	Oshawa, ON	560
35	Halifax, NS	515
36	Ajax, ON	440
37	Whitby, ON	430
38	Barrie, ON	425
39	Trois-Rivières, QC	395
40	Abbotsford, BC	360
41	Saanich, BC	350
42	Kingston, ON	340
43	Langley, BC	315
44	Kelowna, BC	275
45	Chatham-Kent, ON	185
46	Lévis, QC	150
47	Greater Sudbury, ON	120
48	Saguenay, QC	115
49	Thunder Bay, ON	105
50	St. John's, NL	75
–	Canada	186,355

Female

Rank	City	Number
1	Toronto, ON	37,065
2	Montréal, QC	34,135
3	Calgary, AB	9,420
4	Mississauga, ON	8,030
5	Edmonton, AB	6,645
6	Brampton, ON	5,670
7	Ottawa, ON	5,375
8	Laval, QC	5,065
9	Vancouver, BC	4,955
10	London, ON	4,555
11	Hamilton, ON	4,110
12	Vaughan, ON	3,135
13	Winnipeg, MB	3,000
14	Kitchener, ON	2,960
15	Longueuil, QC	2,855
16	Québec, QC	2,585
17	Surrey, BC	2,580
18	Burnaby, BC	1,980
18	Gatineau, QC	1,980
20	Oakville, ON	1,490
21	Windsor, ON	1,105
22	Coquitlam, BC	1,040
23	Sherbrooke, QC	980
24	Richmond, BC	970
25	Burlington, ON	930
25	Richmond Hill, ON	930
27	St. Catharines, ON	880
28	Markham, ON	810
29	Terrebonne, QC	730
30	Barrie, ON	680
31	Regina, SK	670
32	Ajax, ON	625
33	Cambridge, ON	610
34	Guelph, ON	590
35	Saskatoon, SK	570
36	Whitby, ON	565
37	Halifax, NS	510
38	Oshawa, ON	500
39	Kingston, ON	460
40	Trois-Rivières, QC	420
41	Saanich, BC	410
42	Abbotsford, BC	400
43	Langley, BC	335
44	Kelowna, BC	255
45	Lévis, QC	185
46	Chatham-Kent, ON	170
46	Greater Sudbury, ON	170
48	Thunder Bay, ON	100
49	Saguenay, QC	70
50	St. John's, NL	55
–	Canada	194,925

Note: The Employment Equity Act defines visible minorities as 'persons, other than Aboriginal peoples, who are non-Caucasian in race or non-white in colour.'
Source: Statistics Canada. 2013. 2011 National Household Survey. Statistics Canada Catalogue no. 99-004-XWE. Ottawa. Released September 11, 2013.

Cities Ranked by Visible Minority Population: Latin American
By Percent

Total

Rank	City	Percent
1	Montréal, QC	4.2%
2	Toronto, ON	2.8%
3	Kitchener, ON	2.7%
3	London, ON	2.7%
5	Laval, QC	2.5%
5	Longueuil, QC	2.5%
7	Brampton, ON	2.2%
7	Mississauga, ON	2.2%
9	Vaughan, ON	2.1%
10	Calgary, AB	1.8%
11	Burnaby, BC	1.7%
11	Edmonton, AB	1.7%
13	Vancouver, BC	1.6%
14	Coquitlam, BC	1.5%
14	Gatineau, QC	1.5%
14	Oakville, ON	1.5%
14	St. Catharines, ON	1.5%
18	Hamilton, ON	1.4%
18	Sherbrooke, QC	1.4%
20	Terrebonne, QC	1.3%
21	Ottawa, ON	1.2%
21	Surrey, BC	1.2%
23	Windsor, ON	1.1%
24	Ajax, ON	1.0%
24	Burlington, ON	1.0%
24	Cambridge, ON	1.0%
24	Guelph, ON	1.0%
24	Québec, QC	1.0%
24	Winnipeg, MB	1.0%
30	Richmond, BC	0.9%
30	Richmond Hill, ON	0.9%
32	Barrie, ON	0.8%
32	Whitby, ON	0.8%
34	Kingston, ON	0.7%
34	Oshawa, ON	0.7%
34	Regina, SK	0.7%
34	Saanich, BC	0.7%
38	Abbotsford, BC	0.6%
38	Langley, BC	0.6%
38	Saskatoon, SK	0.6%
38	Trois-Rivières, QC	0.6%
42	Kelowna, BC	0.5%
42	Markham, ON	0.5%
44	Chatham-Kent, ON	0.3%
44	Halifax, NS	0.3%
44	Lévis, QC	0.3%
47	Greater Sudbury, ON	0.2%
47	Thunder Bay, ON	0.2%
49	Saguenay, QC	0.1%
49	St. John's, NL	0.1%
–	Canada	1.2%

Male

Rank	City	Percent
1	Montréal, QC	4.2%
2	London, ON	2.9%
3	Toronto, ON	2.8%
4	Longueuil, QC	2.7%
5	Kitchener, ON	2.6%
6	Laval, QC	2.5%
7	Brampton, ON	2.2%
8	Mississauga, ON	2.1%
8	Vaughan, ON	2.1%
10	Calgary, AB	1.9%
11	Edmonton, AB	1.7%
11	St. Catharines, ON	1.7%
13	Burnaby, BC	1.6%
13	Vancouver, BC	1.6%
15	Gatineau, QC	1.5%
15	Sherbrooke, QC	1.5%
17	Coquitlam, BC	1.4%
18	Hamilton, ON	1.3%
18	Oakville, ON	1.3%
20	Ottawa, ON	1.2%
20	Surrey, BC	1.2%
20	Terrebonne, QC	1.2%
23	Cambridge, ON	1.1%
23	Windsor, ON	1.1%
23	Winnipeg, MB	1.1%
26	Guelph, ON	1.0%
26	Québec, QC	1.0%
28	Burlington, ON	0.9%
28	Richmond Hill, ON	0.9%
30	Ajax, ON	0.8%
30	Oshawa, ON	0.8%
30	Richmond, BC	0.8%
33	Barrie, ON	0.7%
33	Saanich, BC	0.7%
33	Whitby, ON	0.7%
36	Abbotsford, BC	0.6%
36	Kingston, ON	0.6%
36	Langley, BC	0.6%
36	Regina, SK	0.6%
36	Saskatoon, SK	0.6%
36	Trois-Rivières, QC	0.6%
42	Kelowna, BC	0.5%
42	Markham, ON	0.5%
44	Chatham-Kent, ON	0.4%
45	Halifax, NS	0.3%
46	Greater Sudbury, ON	0.2%
46	Lévis, QC	0.2%
46	Saguenay, QC	0.2%
46	St. John's, NL	0.2%
46	Thunder Bay, ON	0.2%
–	Canada	1.2%

Female

Rank	City	Percent
1	Montréal, QC	4.1%
2	Toronto, ON	2.8%
3	Kitchener, ON	2.7%
4	Laval, QC	2.5%
4	London, ON	2.5%
6	Longueuil, QC	2.4%
7	Mississauga, ON	2.2%
8	Brampton, ON	2.1%
8	Vaughan, ON	2.1%
10	Burnaby, BC	1.8%
11	Calgary, AB	1.7%
11	Edmonton, AB	1.7%
13	Coquitlam, BC	1.6%
13	Hamilton, ON	1.6%
13	Oakville, ON	1.6%
13	Vancouver, BC	1.6%
17	Gatineau, QC	1.5%
18	Terrebonne, QC	1.4%
19	Sherbrooke, QC	1.3%
19	St. Catharines, ON	1.3%
21	Ottawa, ON	1.2%
22	Ajax, ON	1.1%
22	Surrey, BC	1.1%
24	Barrie, ON	1.0%
24	Burlington, ON	1.0%
24	Cambridge, ON	1.0%
24	Guelph, ON	1.0%
24	Québec, QC	1.0%
24	Richmond, BC	1.0%
24	Richmond Hill, ON	1.0%
24	Windsor, ON	1.0%
32	Whitby, ON	0.9%
32	Winnipeg, MB	0.9%
34	Kingston, ON	0.7%
34	Oshawa, ON	0.7%
34	Regina, SK	0.7%
34	Saanich, BC	0.7%
38	Abbotsford, BC	0.6%
38	Langley, BC	0.6%
38	Trois-Rivières, QC	0.6%
41	Markham, ON	0.5%
41	Saskatoon, SK	0.5%
43	Kelowna, BC	0.4%
44	Chatham-Kent, ON	0.3%
44	Halifax, NS	0.3%
44	Lévis, QC	0.3%
47	Greater Sudbury, ON	0.2%
47	Thunder Bay, ON	0.2%
49	Saguenay, QC	0.1%
49	St. John's, NL	0.1%
–	Canada	1.2%

Note: The Employment Equity Act defines visible minorities as 'persons, other than Aboriginal peoples, who are non-Caucasian in race or non-white in colour.'
Source: Statistics Canada. 2013. 2011 National Household Survey. Statistics Canada Catalogue no. 99-004-XWE. Ottawa. Released September 11, 2013.

Cities Ranked by Visible Minority Population: Arab
By Number

Total

Rank	City	Number
1	Montréal, QC	102,625
2	Ottawa, ON	32,340
3	Toronto, ON	28,920
4	Mississauga, ON	24,870
5	Laval, QC	23,295
6	Calgary, AB	16,745
7	Edmonton, AB	13,800
8	Windsor, ON	11,510
9	London, ON	9,320
10	Hamilton, ON	7,075
11	Gatineau, QC	6,455
12	Halifax, NS	5,525
13	Longueuil, QC	5,290
14	Brampton, ON	4,125
15	Québec, QC	3,785
16	Markham, ON	3,400
17	Surrey, BC	3,265
18	Richmond Hill, ON	3,045
19	Vancouver, BC	2,975
20	Oakville, ON	2,830
21	Vaughan, ON	2,785
22	Winnipeg, MB	2,670
23	Kitchener, ON	2,520
24	Burlington, ON	1,600
25	Burnaby, BC	1,535
26	Saskatoon, SK	1,410
27	Sherbrooke, QC	1,375
28	St. Catharines, ON	1,220
29	Ajax, ON	1,165
30	Terrebonne, QC	1,130
31	Coquitlam, BC	995
32	Richmond, BC	950
33	Whitby, ON	755
34	Cambridge, ON	700
35	Kingston, ON	660
36	Guelph, ON	640
37	Trois-Rivières, QC	630
38	Regina, SK	590
39	Greater Sudbury, ON	455
40	Saanich, BC	415
41	Oshawa, ON	340
42	Barrie, ON	325
43	Abbotsford, BC	250
44	Lévis, QC	240
45	Saguenay, QC	230
46	Langley, BC	225
47	Kelowna, BC	195
47	St. John's, NL	195
49	Thunder Bay, ON	115
50	Chatham-Kent, ON	35
–	Canada	380,620

Male

Rank	City	Number
1	Montréal, QC	55,650
2	Ottawa, ON	16,815
3	Toronto, ON	15,605
4	Mississauga, ON	13,065
5	Laval, QC	11,840
6	Calgary, AB	8,615
7	Edmonton, AB	7,440
8	Windsor, ON	5,955
9	London, ON	4,690
10	Hamilton, ON	3,705
11	Gatineau, QC	3,575
12	Halifax, NS	3,255
13	Longueuil, QC	2,920
14	Brampton, ON	2,165
15	Québec, QC	2,150
16	Vancouver, BC	1,950
17	Surrey, BC	1,740
18	Markham, ON	1,725
19	Richmond Hill, ON	1,490
20	Winnipeg, MB	1,415
21	Vaughan, ON	1,405
22	Kitchener, ON	1,375
22	Oakville, ON	1,375
24	Burnaby, BC	895
25	Burlington, ON	870
26	Saskatoon, SK	755
26	Sherbrooke, QC	755
28	Ajax, ON	665
29	St. Catharines, ON	645
30	Terrebonne, QC	540
31	Coquitlam, BC	530
32	Richmond, BC	520
33	Whitby, ON	380
34	Cambridge, ON	365
34	Guelph, ON	365
36	Kingston, ON	360
37	Trois-Rivières, QC	340
38	Regina, SK	270
39	Greater Sudbury, ON	245
40	Saanich, BC	205
41	Barrie, ON	200
42	Lévis, QC	185
43	Oshawa, ON	170
44	Saguenay, QC	140
45	Abbotsford, BC	135
46	St. John's, NL	105
47	Kelowna, BC	95
48	Langley, BC	90
49	Thunder Bay, ON	65
50	Chatham-Kent, ON	25
–	Canada	203,485

Female

Rank	City	Number
1	Montréal, QC	46,975
2	Ottawa, ON	15,530
3	Toronto, ON	13,310
4	Mississauga, ON	11,800
5	Laval, QC	11,455
6	Calgary, AB	8,125
7	Edmonton, AB	6,365
8	Windsor, ON	5,560
9	London, ON	4,630
10	Hamilton, ON	3,370
11	Gatineau, QC	2,885
12	Longueuil, QC	2,365
13	Halifax, NS	2,270
14	Brampton, ON	1,960
15	Markham, ON	1,670
16	Québec, QC	1,635
17	Richmond Hill, ON	1,555
18	Surrey, BC	1,525
19	Oakville, ON	1,455
20	Vaughan, ON	1,380
21	Winnipeg, MB	1,255
22	Kitchener, ON	1,140
23	Vancouver, BC	1,030
24	Burlington, ON	730
25	Saskatoon, SK	655
26	Burnaby, BC	640
27	Sherbrooke, QC	620
28	Terrebonne, QC	585
29	St. Catharines, ON	575
30	Ajax, ON	500
31	Coquitlam, BC	465
32	Richmond, BC	430
33	Whitby, ON	380
34	Cambridge, ON	335
35	Regina, SK	320
36	Kingston, ON	295
37	Trois-Rivières, QC	290
38	Guelph, ON	270
39	Greater Sudbury, ON	210
39	Saanich, BC	210
41	Oshawa, ON	165
42	Langley, BC	135
43	Barrie, ON	120
44	Abbotsford, BC	115
45	Kelowna, BC	100
46	Saguenay, QC	90
47	St. John's, NL	85
48	Lévis, QC	60
49	Thunder Bay, ON	50
50	Chatham-Kent, ON	0
–	Canada	177,140

Note: The Employment Equity Act defines visible minorities as 'persons, other than Aboriginal peoples, who are non-Caucasian in race or non-white in colour.'
Source: Statistics Canada. 2013. 2011 National Household Survey. Statistics Canada Catalogue no. 99-004-XWE. Ottawa. Released September 11, 2013.

Cities Ranked by Visible Minority Population: Arab
By Percent

Total

Rank	City	Percent
1	Montréal, QC	6.4%
2	Laval, QC	5.9%
3	Windsor, ON	5.5%
4	Ottawa, ON	3.7%
5	Mississauga, ON	3.5%
6	London, ON	2.6%
7	Gatineau, QC	2.5%
8	Longueuil, QC	2.3%
9	Edmonton, AB	1.7%
9	Richmond Hill, ON	1.7%
11	Oakville, ON	1.6%
12	Calgary, AB	1.5%
13	Halifax, NS	1.4%
13	Hamilton, ON	1.4%
15	Kitchener, ON	1.2%
16	Ajax, ON	1.1%
16	Markham, ON	1.1%
16	Terrebonne, QC	1.1%
16	Toronto, ON	1.1%
20	Vaughan, ON	1.0%
21	Burlington, ON	0.9%
21	Sherbrooke, QC	0.9%
21	St. Catharines, ON	0.9%
24	Brampton, ON	0.8%
24	Coquitlam, BC	0.8%
24	Québec, QC	0.8%
27	Burnaby, BC	0.7%
27	Surrey, BC	0.7%
29	Cambridge, ON	0.6%
29	Kingston, ON	0.6%
29	Saskatoon, SK	0.6%
29	Whitby, ON	0.6%
33	Guelph, ON	0.5%
33	Richmond, BC	0.5%
33	Trois-Rivières, QC	0.5%
33	Vancouver, BC	0.5%
37	Saanich, BC	0.4%
37	Winnipeg, MB	0.4%
39	Greater Sudbury, ON	0.3%
39	Regina, SK	0.3%
41	Abbotsford, BC	0.2%
41	Barrie, ON	0.2%
41	Kelowna, BC	0.2%
41	Langley, BC	0.2%
41	Lévis, QC	0.2%
41	Oshawa, ON	0.2%
41	Saguenay, QC	0.2%
41	St. John's, NL	0.2%
49	Thunder Bay, ON	0.1%
50	Chatham-Kent, ON	0.0%
–	Canada	1.2%

Male

Rank	City	Percent
1	Montréal, QC	7.1%
2	Laval, QC	6.2%
3	Windsor, ON	5.9%
4	Ottawa, ON	4.0%
5	Mississauga, ON	3.8%
6	Gatineau, QC	2.8%
7	London, ON	2.7%
8	Longueuil, QC	2.6%
9	Edmonton, AB	1.9%
10	Halifax, NS	1.7%
10	Richmond Hill, ON	1.7%
12	Calgary, AB	1.6%
12	Oakville, ON	1.6%
14	Hamilton, ON	1.5%
15	Ajax, ON	1.3%
15	Kitchener, ON	1.3%
15	Toronto, ON	1.3%
18	Markham, ON	1.2%
19	Burlington, ON	1.0%
19	Sherbrooke, QC	1.0%
19	St. Catharines, ON	1.0%
19	Terrebonne, QC	1.0%
19	Vaughan, ON	1.0%
24	Coquitlam, BC	0.9%
24	Québec, QC	0.9%
26	Brampton, ON	0.8%
26	Burnaby, BC	0.8%
26	Surrey, BC	0.8%
29	Saskatoon, SK	0.7%
29	Vancouver, BC	0.7%
31	Cambridge, ON	0.6%
31	Guelph, ON	0.6%
31	Kingston, ON	0.6%
31	Richmond, BC	0.6%
31	Trois-Rivières, QC	0.6%
31	Whitby, ON	0.6%
37	Saanich, BC	0.4%
37	Winnipeg, MB	0.4%
39	Barrie, ON	0.3%
39	Greater Sudbury, ON	0.3%
39	Lévis, QC	0.3%
39	Regina, SK	0.3%
43	Abbotsford, BC	0.2%
43	Kelowna, BC	0.2%
43	Langley, BC	0.2%
43	Oshawa, ON	0.2%
43	Saguenay, QC	0.2%
43	St. John's, NL	0.2%
49	Chatham-Kent, ON	0.1%
49	Thunder Bay, ON	0.1%
–	Canada	1.3%

Female

Rank	City	Percent
1	Laval, QC	5.7%
1	Montréal, QC	5.7%
3	Windsor, ON	5.2%
4	Ottawa, ON	3.5%
5	Mississauga, ON	3.3%
6	London, ON	2.5%
7	Gatineau, QC	2.1%
8	Longueuil, QC	2.0%
9	Edmonton, AB	1.6%
9	Oakville, ON	1.6%
9	Richmond Hill, ON	1.6%
12	Calgary, AB	1.5%
13	Hamilton, ON	1.3%
14	Halifax, NS	1.1%
14	Markham, ON	1.1%
14	Terrebonne, QC	1.1%
17	Kitchener, ON	1.0%
17	Toronto, ON	1.0%
19	Ajax, ON	0.9%
19	St. Catharines, ON	0.9%
19	Vaughan, ON	0.9%
22	Burlington, ON	0.8%
22	Sherbrooke, QC	0.8%
24	Brampton, ON	0.7%
24	Coquitlam, BC	0.7%
24	Surrey, BC	0.7%
27	Burnaby, BC	0.6%
27	Québec, QC	0.6%
27	Saskatoon, SK	0.6%
27	Whitby, ON	0.6%
31	Cambridge, ON	0.5%
31	Kingston, ON	0.5%
33	Guelph, ON	0.4%
33	Richmond, BC	0.4%
33	Saanich, BC	0.4%
33	Trois-Rivières, QC	0.4%
33	Winnipeg, MB	0.4%
38	Greater Sudbury, ON	0.3%
38	Langley, BC	0.3%
38	Regina, SK	0.3%
38	Vancouver, BC	0.3%
42	Abbotsford, BC	0.2%
42	Barrie, ON	0.2%
42	Kelowna, BC	0.2%
42	Oshawa, ON	0.2%
42	St. John's, NL	0.2%
47	Lévis, QC	0.1%
47	Saguenay, QC	0.1%
47	Thunder Bay, ON	0.1%
50	Chatham-Kent, ON	0.0%
–	Canada	1.1%

Note: The Employment Equity Act defines visible minorities as 'persons, other than Aboriginal peoples, who are non-Caucasian in race or non-white in colour.'
Source: Statistics Canada. 2013. 2011 National Household Survey. Statistics Canada Catalogue no. 99-004-XWE. Ottawa. Released September 11, 2013.

Cities Ranked by Visible Minority Population: Southeast Asian

By Number

Total

Rank	City	Number
1	Toronto, ON	46,825
2	Montréal, QC	39,570
3	Calgary, AB	20,530
4	Vancouver, BC	17,870
5	Mississauga, ON	15,750
6	Edmonton, AB	15,480
7	Ottawa, ON	13,650
8	Surrey, BC	13,080
9	Brampton, ON	8,630
10	Laval, QC	7,780
11	Vaughan, ON	7,735
12	Winnipeg, MB	6,990
13	Hamilton, ON	5,875
14	Kitchener, ON	5,005
15	Burnaby, BC	3,945
16	London, ON	3,750
17	Windsor, ON	3,190
18	Guelph, ON	2,890
19	Markham, ON	2,750
20	Longueuil, QC	2,605
21	Regina, SK	2,500
22	Richmond, BC	2,150
23	Québec, QC	1,760
24	Saskatoon, SK	1,725
25	Coquitlam, BC	1,550
25	Oakville, ON	1,550
27	Richmond Hill, ON	1,410
28	Gatineau, QC	1,305
29	Cambridge, ON	1,300
30	Langley, BC	1,115
31	Abbotsford, BC	1,110
32	Halifax, NS	900
33	Saanich, BC	820
34	Burlington, ON	670
35	Ajax, ON	645
36	Barrie, ON	640
37	St. Catharines, ON	630
38	Sherbrooke, QC	570
39	Oshawa, ON	445
40	Kingston, ON	340
40	Whitby, ON	340
42	Thunder Bay, ON	330
43	Greater Sudbury, ON	325
43	Kelowna, BC	325
45	Lévis, QC	270
46	Chatham-Kent, ON	265
47	Terrebonne, QC	230
48	St. John's, NL	200
49	Trois-Rivières, QC	100
50	Saguenay, QC	40
–	Canada	312,075

Male

Rank	City	Number
1	Toronto, ON	22,920
2	Montréal, QC	19,860
3	Calgary, AB	10,095
4	Vancouver, BC	8,400
5	Mississauga, ON	7,930
6	Edmonton, AB	7,820
7	Ottawa, ON	6,490
8	Surrey, BC	6,425
9	Brampton, ON	4,240
10	Laval, QC	3,770
11	Winnipeg, MB	3,575
12	Vaughan, ON	3,565
13	Hamilton, ON	2,890
14	Kitchener, ON	2,520
15	London, ON	1,905
16	Burnaby, BC	1,900
17	Windsor, ON	1,615
18	Guelph, ON	1,535
19	Regina, SK	1,380
20	Markham, ON	1,350
21	Longueuil, QC	1,335
22	Richmond, BC	1,015
23	Saskatoon, SK	905
24	Québec, QC	865
25	Coquitlam, BC	770
26	Oakville, ON	695
27	Gatineau, QC	680
28	Cambridge, ON	660
29	Richmond Hill, ON	555
30	Abbotsford, BC	530
30	Langley, BC	530
32	Halifax, NS	430
33	Burlington, ON	370
34	Saanich, BC	345
35	Barrie, ON	340
36	St. Catharines, ON	325
37	Sherbrooke, QC	310
38	Ajax, ON	255
39	Oshawa, ON	200
40	Kelowna, BC	185
41	Greater Sudbury, ON	170
42	Whitby, ON	165
43	Kingston, ON	160
44	St. John's, NL	155
45	Thunder Bay, ON	150
46	Lévis, QC	140
47	Chatham-Kent, ON	125
48	Terrebonne, QC	100
49	Trois-Rivières, QC	50
50	Saguenay, QC	25
–	Canada	154,035

Female

Rank	City	Number
1	Toronto, ON	23,910
2	Montréal, QC	19,710
3	Calgary, AB	10,435
4	Vancouver, BC	9,470
5	Mississauga, ON	7,815
6	Edmonton, AB	7,665
7	Ottawa, ON	7,155
8	Surrey, BC	6,655
9	Brampton, ON	4,390
10	Vaughan, ON	4,160
11	Laval, QC	4,015
12	Winnipeg, MB	3,415
13	Hamilton, ON	2,985
14	Kitchener, ON	2,485
15	Burnaby, BC	2,050
16	London, ON	1,845
17	Windsor, ON	1,575
18	Markham, ON	1,395
19	Guelph, ON	1,360
20	Longueuil, QC	1,265
21	Richmond, BC	1,130
22	Regina, SK	1,120
23	Québec, QC	895
24	Oakville, ON	860
25	Richmond Hill, ON	855
26	Saskatoon, SK	820
27	Coquitlam, BC	780
28	Cambridge, ON	640
29	Gatineau, QC	625
30	Langley, BC	585
31	Abbotsford, BC	580
32	Saanich, BC	475
33	Halifax, NS	470
34	Ajax, ON	390
35	St. Catharines, ON	310
36	Barrie, ON	305
37	Burlington, ON	295
38	Sherbrooke, QC	260
39	Oshawa, ON	250
40	Kingston, ON	185
41	Thunder Bay, ON	180
42	Whitby, ON	175
43	Greater Sudbury, ON	150
44	Chatham-Kent, ON	140
44	Kelowna, BC	140
46	Lévis, QC	130
46	Terrebonne, QC	130
48	Trois-Rivières, QC	50
49	St. John's, NL	45
50	Saguenay, QC	15
–	Canada	158,045

Note: The Employment Equity Act defines visible minorities as 'persons, other than Aboriginal peoples, who are non-Caucasian in race or non-white in colour'; Southeast Asian includes 'Vietnamese,' 'Cambodian,' 'Malaysian,' 'Laotian,' etc.
Source: Statistics Canada. 2013. 2011 National Household Survey. Statistics Canada Catalogue no. 99-004-XWE. Ottawa. Released September 11, 2013.

Cities Ranked by Visible Minority Population: Southeast Asian
By Percent

Total

Rank	City	Percent
1	Vancouver, BC	3.0%
2	Surrey, BC	2.8%
3	Vaughan, ON	2.7%
4	Montréal, QC	2.5%
5	Guelph, ON	2.4%
6	Kitchener, ON	2.3%
7	Mississauga, ON	2.2%
8	Laval, QC	2.0%
9	Calgary, AB	1.9%
9	Edmonton, AB	1.9%
11	Burnaby, BC	1.8%
11	Toronto, ON	1.8%
13	Brampton, ON	1.7%
14	Ottawa, ON	1.6%
15	Windsor, ON	1.5%
16	Regina, SK	1.3%
17	Coquitlam, BC	1.2%
17	Hamilton, ON	1.2%
19	Langley, BC	1.1%
19	Longueuil, QC	1.1%
19	Richmond, BC	1.1%
19	Winnipeg, MB	1.1%
23	Cambridge, ON	1.0%
23	London, ON	1.0%
25	Markham, ON	0.9%
25	Oakville, ON	0.9%
27	Abbotsford, BC	0.8%
27	Richmond Hill, ON	0.8%
27	Saanich, BC	0.8%
27	Saskatoon, SK	0.8%
31	Ajax, ON	0.6%
32	Barrie, ON	0.5%
32	Gatineau, QC	0.5%
32	St. Catharines, ON	0.5%
35	Burlington, ON	0.4%
35	Québec, QC	0.4%
35	Sherbrooke, QC	0.4%
38	Chatham-Kent, ON	0.3%
38	Kelowna, BC	0.3%
38	Kingston, ON	0.3%
38	Oshawa, ON	0.3%
38	Thunder Bay, ON	0.3%
38	Whitby, ON	0.3%
44	Greater Sudbury, ON	0.2%
44	Halifax, NS	0.2%
44	Lévis, QC	0.2%
44	St. John's, NL	0.2%
44	Terrebonne, QC	0.2%
49	Trois-Rivières, QC	0.1%
50	Saguenay, QC	0.0%
–	Canada	0.9%

Male

Rank	City	Percent
1	Vancouver, BC	2.9%
2	Surrey, BC	2.8%
3	Guelph, ON	2.6%
4	Montréal, QC	2.5%
4	Vaughan, ON	2.5%
6	Kitchener, ON	2.4%
7	Mississauga, ON	2.3%
8	Edmonton, AB	2.0%
8	Laval, QC	2.0%
10	Calgary, AB	1.9%
11	Burnaby, BC	1.8%
11	Toronto, ON	1.8%
13	Brampton, ON	1.6%
13	Windsor, ON	1.6%
15	Ottawa, ON	1.5%
15	Regina, SK	1.5%
17	Coquitlam, BC	1.3%
18	Hamilton, ON	1.2%
18	Longueuil, QC	1.2%
20	Cambridge, ON	1.1%
20	London, ON	1.1%
20	Richmond, BC	1.1%
20	Winnipeg, MB	1.1%
24	Langley, BC	1.0%
25	Markham, ON	0.9%
26	Abbotsford, BC	0.8%
26	Oakville, ON	0.8%
26	Saskatoon, SK	0.8%
29	Saanich, BC	0.7%
30	Richmond Hill, ON	0.6%
31	Ajax, ON	0.5%
31	Barrie, ON	0.5%
31	Gatineau, QC	0.5%
31	St. Catharines, ON	0.5%
35	Burlington, ON	0.4%
35	Québec, QC	0.4%
35	Sherbrooke, QC	0.4%
38	Chatham-Kent, ON	0.3%
38	Kelowna, BC	0.3%
38	Kingston, ON	0.3%
38	Oshawa, ON	0.3%
38	St. John's, NL	0.3%
38	Thunder Bay, ON	0.3%
38	Whitby, ON	0.3%
45	Greater Sudbury, ON	0.2%
45	Halifax, NS	0.2%
45	Lévis, QC	0.2%
45	Terrebonne, QC	0.2%
49	Trois-Rivières, QC	0.1%
50	Saguenay, QC	0.0%
–	Canada	1.0%

Female

Rank	City	Percent
1	Vancouver, BC	3.1%
2	Surrey, BC	2.8%
2	Vaughan, ON	2.8%
4	Montréal, QC	2.4%
5	Kitchener, ON	2.3%
6	Guelph, ON	2.2%
6	Mississauga, ON	2.2%
8	Laval, QC	2.0%
9	Calgary, AB	1.9%
9	Edmonton, AB	1.9%
11	Burnaby, BC	1.8%
11	Toronto, ON	1.8%
13	Brampton, ON	1.7%
14	Ottawa, ON	1.6%
15	Windsor, ON	1.5%
16	Coquitlam, BC	1.2%
16	Regina, SK	1.2%
18	Hamilton, ON	1.1%
18	Langley, BC	1.1%
18	Longueuil, QC	1.1%
18	Richmond, BC	1.1%
22	Cambridge, ON	1.0%
22	London, ON	1.0%
22	Winnipeg, MB	1.0%
25	Abbotsford, BC	0.9%
25	Markham, ON	0.9%
25	Oakville, ON	0.9%
25	Richmond Hill, ON	0.9%
25	Saanich, BC	0.9%
30	Ajax, ON	0.7%
30	Saskatoon, SK	0.7%
32	Gatineau, QC	0.5%
32	St. Catharines, ON	0.5%
34	Barrie, ON	0.4%
35	Burlington, ON	0.3%
35	Chatham-Kent, ON	0.3%
35	Kingston, ON	0.3%
35	Oshawa, ON	0.3%
35	Québec, QC	0.3%
35	Sherbrooke, QC	0.3%
35	Thunder Bay, ON	0.3%
35	Whitby, ON	0.3%
43	Greater Sudbury, ON	0.2%
43	Halifax, NS	0.2%
43	Kelowna, BC	0.2%
43	Lévis, QC	0.2%
43	Terrebonne, QC	0.2%
48	St. John's, NL	0.1%
48	Trois-Rivières, QC	0.1%
50	Saguenay, QC	0.0%
–	Canada	0.9%

Note: The Employment Equity Act defines visible minorities as 'persons, other than Aboriginal peoples, who are non-Caucasian in race or non-white in colour'; Southeast Asian includes 'Vietnamese,' 'Cambodian,' 'Malaysian,' 'Laotian,' etc.
Source: Statistics Canada. 2013. 2011 National Household Survey. Statistics Canada Catalogue no. 99-004-XWE. Ottawa. Released September 11, 2013.

Cities Ranked by Visible Minority Population: West Asian

By Number

Total

Rank	City	Number
1	Toronto, ON	50,235
2	Richmond Hill, ON	15,890
3	Montréal, QC	12,155
4	Calgary, AB	8,470
5	Mississauga, ON	7,955
6	Ottawa, ON	7,590
7	Vancouver, BC	6,885
8	Edmonton, AB	6,610
9	Coquitlam, BC	6,380
10	Vaughan, ON	6,215
11	Markham, ON	6,185
12	Burnaby, BC	4,440
13	Hamilton, ON	4,260
14	Brampton, ON	3,485
15	Laval, QC	3,195
16	London, ON	2,955
17	Kitchener, ON	2,550
18	Surrey, BC	2,350
19	Winnipeg, MB	1,970
20	Ajax, ON	1,770
21	Windsor, ON	1,580
22	Oakville, ON	1,310
23	Longueuil, QC	1,275
24	Richmond, BC	1,255
25	Halifax, NS	1,205
26	Saskatoon, SK	1,080
27	Guelph, ON	975
28	Burlington, ON	785
29	Whitby, ON	630
30	Gatineau, QC	590
31	Regina, SK	470
32	Sherbrooke, QC	450
33	St. Catharines, ON	410
34	Kingston, ON	405
35	Oshawa, ON	400
36	Cambridge, ON	390
37	Saanich, BC	310
38	Québec, QC	260
39	Langley, BC	185
40	St. John's, NL	140
41	Abbotsford, BC	130
42	Barrie, ON	125
42	Kelowna, BC	125
44	Greater Sudbury, ON	90
45	Chatham-Kent, ON	80
46	Terrebonne, QC	65
47	Thunder Bay, ON	55
48	Lévis, QC	0
48	Saguenay, QC	0
48	Trois-Rivières, QC	0
–	Canada	206,840

Male

Rank	City	Number
1	Toronto, ON	25,720
2	Richmond Hill, ON	7,825
3	Montréal, QC	6,230
4	Calgary, AB	4,565
5	Mississauga, ON	4,200
6	Ottawa, ON	3,940
7	Vancouver, BC	3,620
8	Edmonton, AB	3,490
9	Vaughan, ON	3,260
10	Coquitlam, BC	3,160
11	Markham, ON	3,115
12	Burnaby, BC	2,160
13	Hamilton, ON	2,095
14	Brampton, ON	1,735
15	Laval, QC	1,665
16	London, ON	1,585
17	Surrey, BC	1,285
18	Kitchener, ON	1,225
19	Winnipeg, MB	975
20	Ajax, ON	900
21	Windsor, ON	815
22	Oakville, ON	660
23	Halifax, NS	645
24	Longueuil, QC	605
25	Richmond, BC	575
25	Saskatoon, SK	575
27	Guelph, ON	470
28	Burlington, ON	405
29	Gatineau, QC	310
30	Whitby, ON	280
31	Regina, SK	255
32	Sherbrooke, QC	235
33	St. Catharines, ON	220
34	Kingston, ON	215
35	Cambridge, ON	180
35	Oshawa, ON	180
37	Saanich, BC	150
38	Québec, QC	115
39	Langley, BC	105
40	St. John's, NL	80
41	Barrie, ON	70
42	Abbotsford, BC	60
42	Terrebonne, QC	60
44	Greater Sudbury, ON	55
45	Kelowna, BC	50
46	Thunder Bay, ON	40
47	Chatham-Kent, ON	20
48	Lévis, QC	0
48	Saguenay, QC	0
48	Trois-Rivières, QC	0
–	Canada	105,620

Female

Rank	City	Number
1	Toronto, ON	24,515
2	Richmond Hill, ON	8,065
3	Montréal, QC	5,925
4	Calgary, AB	3,905
5	Mississauga, ON	3,755
6	Ottawa, ON	3,645
7	Vancouver, BC	3,265
8	Coquitlam, BC	3,220
9	Edmonton, AB	3,115
10	Markham, ON	3,065
11	Vaughan, ON	2,960
12	Burnaby, BC	2,280
13	Hamilton, ON	2,170
14	Brampton, ON	1,755
15	Laval, QC	1,520
16	London, ON	1,370
17	Kitchener, ON	1,325
18	Surrey, BC	1,065
19	Winnipeg, MB	995
20	Ajax, ON	870
21	Windsor, ON	765
22	Richmond, BC	685
23	Longueuil, QC	670
24	Oakville, ON	645
25	Halifax, NS	565
26	Guelph, ON	505
27	Saskatoon, SK	495
28	Burlington, ON	390
29	Whitby, ON	350
30	Gatineau, QC	280
31	Oshawa, ON	220
31	Regina, SK	220
33	Sherbrooke, QC	215
34	Cambridge, ON	205
35	Kingston, ON	190
36	St. Catharines, ON	185
37	Saanich, BC	160
38	Québec, QC	145
39	Kelowna, BC	80
39	Langley, BC	80
41	Abbotsford, BC	65
42	Chatham-Kent, ON	60
42	St. John's, NL	60
44	Barrie, ON	50
45	Greater Sudbury, ON	30
46	Lévis, QC	0
46	Saguenay, QC	0
46	Terrebonne, QC	0
46	Thunder Bay, ON	0
46	Trois-Rivières, QC	0
–	Canada	101,220

Note: The Employment Equity Act defines visible minorities as 'persons, other than Aboriginal peoples, who are non-Caucasian in race or non-white in colour'; West Asian includes 'Iranian,' 'Afghan,' etc.
Source: Statistics Canada. 2013. 2011 National Household Survey. Statistics Canada Catalogue no. 99-004-XWE. Ottawa. Released September 11, 2013.

Cities Ranked by Visible Minority Population: West Asian
By Percent

Total

Rank	City	Percent
1	Richmond Hill, ON	8.6%
2	Coquitlam, BC	5.1%
3	Vaughan, ON	2.2%
4	Markham, ON	2.1%
5	Burnaby, BC	2.0%
5	Toronto, ON	2.0%
7	Ajax, ON	1.6%
8	Kitchener, ON	1.2%
8	Vancouver, BC	1.2%
10	Mississauga, ON	1.1%
11	Ottawa, ON	0.9%
12	Calgary, AB	0.8%
12	Edmonton, AB	0.8%
12	Guelph, ON	0.8%
12	Hamilton, ON	0.8%
12	Laval, QC	0.8%
12	London, ON	0.8%
12	Montréal, QC	0.8%
12	Windsor, ON	0.8%
20	Brampton, ON	0.7%
20	Oakville, ON	0.7%
20	Richmond, BC	0.7%
23	Longueuil, QC	0.6%
24	Burlington, ON	0.5%
24	Saskatoon, SK	0.5%
24	Surrey, BC	0.5%
24	Whitby, ON	0.5%
28	Cambridge, ON	0.3%
28	Halifax, NS	0.3%
28	Kingston, ON	0.3%
28	Oshawa, ON	0.3%
28	Saanich, BC	0.3%
28	Sherbrooke, QC	0.3%
28	St. Catharines, ON	0.3%
28	Winnipeg, MB	0.3%
36	Gatineau, QC	0.2%
36	Langley, BC	0.2%
36	Regina, SK	0.2%
39	Abbotsford, BC	0.1%
39	Barrie, ON	0.1%
39	Chatham-Kent, ON	0.1%
39	Greater Sudbury, ON	0.1%
39	Kelowna, BC	0.1%
39	Québec, QC	0.1%
39	St. John's, NL	0.1%
39	Terrebonne, QC	0.1%
39	Thunder Bay, ON	0.1%
48	Lévis, QC	0.0%
48	Saguenay, QC	0.0%
48	Trois-Rivières, QC	0.0%
–	Canada	0.6%

Male

Rank	City	Percent
1	Richmond Hill, ON	8.7%
2	Coquitlam, BC	5.1%
3	Vaughan, ON	2.3%
4	Markham, ON	2.1%
4	Toronto, ON	2.1%
6	Burnaby, BC	2.0%
7	Ajax, ON	1.7%
8	Vancouver, BC	1.3%
9	Mississauga, ON	1.2%
10	Kitchener, ON	1.1%
11	Edmonton, AB	0.9%
11	Laval, QC	0.9%
11	London, ON	0.9%
11	Ottawa, ON	0.9%
15	Calgary, AB	0.8%
15	Guelph, ON	0.8%
15	Hamilton, ON	0.8%
15	Montréal, QC	0.8%
15	Oakville, ON	0.8%
15	Windsor, ON	0.8%
21	Brampton, ON	0.7%
22	Richmond, BC	0.6%
22	Surrey, BC	0.6%
24	Burlington, ON	0.5%
24	Longueuil, QC	0.5%
24	Saskatoon, SK	0.5%
24	Whitby, ON	0.5%
28	Kingston, ON	0.4%
28	St. Catharines, ON	0.4%
30	Cambridge, ON	0.3%
30	Halifax, NS	0.3%
30	Regina, SK	0.3%
30	Saanich, BC	0.3%
30	Sherbrooke, QC	0.3%
30	Winnipeg, MB	0.3%
36	Gatineau, QC	0.2%
36	Langley, BC	0.2%
36	Oshawa, ON	0.2%
36	St. John's, NL	0.2%
40	Abbotsford, BC	0.1%
40	Barrie, ON	0.1%
40	Greater Sudbury, ON	0.1%
40	Kelowna, BC	0.1%
40	Terrebonne, QC	0.1%
40	Thunder Bay, ON	0.1%
46	Chatham-Kent, ON	0.0%
46	Lévis, QC	0.0%
46	Québec, QC	0.0%
46	Saguenay, QC	0.0%
46	Trois-Rivières, QC	0.0%
–	Canada	0.7%

Female

Rank	City	Percent
1	Richmond Hill, ON	8.5%
2	Coquitlam, BC	5.1%
3	Burnaby, BC	2.0%
3	Markham, ON	2.0%
3	Vaughan, ON	2.0%
6	Toronto, ON	1.8%
7	Ajax, ON	1.5%
8	Kitchener, ON	1.2%
9	Vancouver, BC	1.1%
10	Mississauga, ON	1.0%
11	Edmonton, AB	0.8%
11	Guelph, ON	0.8%
11	Hamilton, ON	0.8%
11	Laval, QC	0.8%
11	Ottawa, ON	0.8%
16	Brampton, ON	0.7%
16	Calgary, AB	0.7%
16	London, ON	0.7%
16	Montréal, QC	0.7%
16	Oakville, ON	0.7%
16	Richmond, BC	0.7%
16	Windsor, ON	0.7%
23	Longueuil, QC	0.6%
23	Whitby, ON	0.6%
25	Surrey, BC	0.5%
26	Burlington, ON	0.4%
26	Saskatoon, SK	0.4%
28	Cambridge, ON	0.3%
28	Halifax, NS	0.3%
28	Kingston, ON	0.3%
28	Oshawa, ON	0.3%
28	Saanich, BC	0.3%
28	Sherbrooke, QC	0.3%
28	St. Catharines, ON	0.3%
28	Winnipeg, MB	0.3%
36	Gatineau, QC	0.2%
36	Langley, BC	0.2%
36	Regina, SK	0.2%
39	Abbotsford, BC	0.1%
39	Barrie, ON	0.1%
39	Chatham-Kent, ON	0.1%
39	Kelowna, BC	0.1%
39	Québec, QC	0.1%
39	St. John's, NL	0.1%
45	Greater Sudbury, ON	0.0%
45	Lévis, QC	0.0%
45	Saguenay, QC	0.0%
45	Terrebonne, QC	0.0%
45	Thunder Bay, ON	0.0%
45	Trois-Rivières, QC	0.0%
–	Canada	0.6%

Note: The Employment Equity Act defines visible minorities as 'persons, other than Aboriginal peoples, who are non-Caucasian in race or non-white in colour'; West Asian includes 'Iranian,' 'Afghan,' etc.
Source: Statistics Canada. 2013. 2011 National Household Survey. Statistics Canada Catalogue no. 99-004-XWE. Ottawa. Released September 11, 2013.

Cities Ranked by Visible Minority Population: Korean

By Number

Total

Rank	City	Number
1	Toronto, ON	37,225
2	Vancouver, BC	8,780
3	Surrey, BC	8,385
4	Calgary, AB	8,160
5	Coquitlam, BC	7,830
6	Burnaby, BC	7,645
7	Mississauga, ON	6,300
8	Richmond Hill, ON	5,045
9	Edmonton, AB	4,565
10	Vaughan, ON	4,300
11	Montréal, QC	3,330
12	Markham, ON	3,160
13	London, ON	2,990
14	Langley, BC	2,705
15	Winnipeg, MB	2,690
16	Oakville, ON	2,490
17	Ottawa, ON	2,250
18	Hamilton, ON	1,970
19	Abbotsford, BC	1,470
20	Richmond, BC	1,370
21	Burlington, ON	895
22	Halifax, NS	845
23	Saanich, BC	685
24	Kitchener, ON	560
25	Barrie, ON	535
26	Brampton, ON	525
27	Kelowna, BC	440
28	Kingston, ON	430
29	Whitby, ON	410
30	Regina, SK	395
31	Saskatoon, SK	385
32	St. Catharines, ON	360
33	Windsor, ON	285
34	Guelph, ON	280
35	Gatineau, QC	220
36	Laval, QC	215
37	Oshawa, ON	210
38	Ajax, ON	205
38	Chatham-Kent, ON	205
40	Longueuil, QC	195
41	Cambridge, ON	175
41	Greater Sudbury, ON	175
43	Québec, QC	165
44	Sherbrooke, QC	70
45	St. John's, NL	60
46	Terrebonne, QC	25
47	Lévis, QC	20
47	Saguenay, QC	20
49	Thunder Bay, ON	15
50	Trois-Rivières, QC	0
–	Canada	161,130

Male

Rank	City	Number
1	Toronto, ON	17,730
2	Surrey, BC	4,220
3	Calgary, AB	3,960
4	Vancouver, BC	3,775
5	Coquitlam, BC	3,770
6	Burnaby, BC	3,730
7	Mississauga, ON	3,100
8	Richmond Hill, ON	2,410
9	Vaughan, ON	2,125
10	Edmonton, AB	2,040
11	Montréal, QC	1,540
12	Markham, ON	1,530
13	London, ON	1,515
14	Oakville, ON	1,290
15	Langley, BC	1,265
16	Winnipeg, MB	1,170
17	Ottawa, ON	1,135
18	Hamilton, ON	950
19	Abbotsford, BC	675
20	Richmond, BC	635
21	Burlington, ON	430
22	Halifax, NS	345
23	Saanich, BC	295
24	Whitby, ON	260
25	Barrie, ON	255
26	Kitchener, ON	245
27	Kelowna, BC	235
28	Brampton, ON	220
28	Regina, SK	220
30	Kingston, ON	200
30	Saskatoon, SK	200
32	St. Catharines, ON	195
33	Windsor, ON	160
34	Chatham-Kent, ON	125
35	Cambridge, ON	115
35	Laval, QC	115
37	Oshawa, ON	105
37	Québec, QC	105
39	Guelph, ON	100
40	Ajax, ON	95
40	Longueuil, QC	95
42	Gatineau, QC	85
43	Greater Sudbury, ON	80
44	Sherbrooke, QC	50
45	St. John's, NL	25
46	Lévis, QC	0
46	Saguenay, QC	0
46	Terrebonne, QC	0
46	Thunder Bay, ON	0
46	Trois-Rivières, QC	0
–	Canada	77,165

Female

Rank	City	Number
1	Toronto, ON	19,490
2	Vancouver, BC	5,000
3	Calgary, AB	4,200
4	Surrey, BC	4,170
5	Coquitlam, BC	4,060
6	Burnaby, BC	3,915
7	Mississauga, ON	3,195
8	Richmond Hill, ON	2,635
9	Edmonton, AB	2,525
10	Vaughan, ON	2,185
11	Montréal, QC	1,790
12	Markham, ON	1,630
13	Winnipeg, MB	1,520
14	London, ON	1,475
15	Langley, BC	1,440
16	Oakville, ON	1,195
17	Ottawa, ON	1,110
18	Hamilton, ON	1,025
19	Abbotsford, BC	795
20	Richmond, BC	735
21	Halifax, NS	500
22	Burlington, ON	460
23	Saanich, BC	390
24	Kitchener, ON	315
25	Brampton, ON	310
26	Barrie, ON	285
27	Kingston, ON	230
28	Kelowna, BC	205
29	Saskatoon, SK	190
30	Guelph, ON	180
30	Regina, SK	180
32	St. Catharines, ON	165
33	Whitby, ON	150
34	Gatineau, QC	130
35	Windsor, ON	125
36	Ajax, ON	110
36	Oshawa, ON	110
38	Greater Sudbury, ON	100
38	Laval, QC	100
38	Longueuil, QC	100
41	Chatham-Kent, ON	80
42	Cambridge, ON	60
42	Québec, QC	60
44	St. John's, NL	30
45	Sherbrooke, QC	20
45	Terrebonne, QC	20
47	Lévis, QC	0
47	Saguenay, QC	0
47	Thunder Bay, ON	0
47	Trois-Rivières, QC	0
–	Canada	83,965

Note: The Employment Equity Act defines visible minorities as 'persons, other than Aboriginal peoples, who are non-Caucasian in race or non-white in colour.'
Source: Statistics Canada. 2013. 2011 National Household Survey. Statistics Canada Catalogue no. 99-004-XWE. Ottawa. Released September 11, 2013.

Cities Ranked by Visible Minority Population: Korean
By Percent

Total

Rank	City	Percent
1	Coquitlam, BC	6.3%
2	Burnaby, BC	3.5%
3	Richmond Hill, ON	2.7%
4	Langley, BC	2.6%
5	Surrey, BC	1.8%
6	Vancouver, BC	1.5%
6	Vaughan, ON	1.5%
8	Oakville, ON	1.4%
8	Toronto, ON	1.4%
10	Abbotsford, BC	1.1%
10	Markham, ON	1.1%
12	Mississauga, ON	0.9%
13	Calgary, AB	0.8%
13	London, ON	0.8%
15	Richmond, BC	0.7%
16	Edmonton, AB	0.6%
16	Saanich, BC	0.6%
18	Burlington, ON	0.5%
19	Barrie, ON	0.4%
19	Hamilton, ON	0.4%
19	Kelowna, BC	0.4%
19	Kingston, ON	0.4%
19	Winnipeg, MB	0.4%
24	Kitchener, ON	0.3%
24	Ottawa, ON	0.3%
24	St. Catharines, ON	0.3%
24	Whitby, ON	0.3%
28	Ajax, ON	0.2%
28	Chatham-Kent, ON	0.2%
28	Guelph, ON	0.2%
28	Halifax, NS	0.2%
28	Montréal, QC	0.2%
28	Regina, SK	0.2%
28	Saskatoon, SK	0.2%
35	Brampton, ON	0.1%
35	Cambridge, ON	0.1%
35	Gatineau, QC	0.1%
35	Greater Sudbury, ON	0.1%
35	Laval, QC	0.1%
35	Longueuil, QC	0.1%
35	Oshawa, ON	0.1%
35	St. John's, NL	0.1%
35	Windsor, ON	0.1%
44	Lévis, QC	0.0%
44	Québec, QC	0.0%
44	Saguenay, QC	0.0%
44	Sherbrooke, QC	0.0%
44	Terrebonne, QC	0.0%
44	Thunder Bay, ON	0.0%
44	Trois-Rivières, QC	0.0%
–	Canada	0.5%

Male

Rank	City	Percent
1	Coquitlam, BC	6.1%
2	Burnaby, BC	3.5%
3	Richmond Hill, ON	2.7%
4	Langley, BC	2.5%
5	Surrey, BC	1.8%
6	Oakville, ON	1.5%
6	Vaughan, ON	1.5%
8	Toronto, ON	1.4%
9	Vancouver, BC	1.3%
10	Abbotsford, BC	1.0%
10	Markham, ON	1.0%
12	London, ON	0.9%
12	Mississauga, ON	0.9%
14	Calgary, AB	0.7%
14	Richmond, BC	0.7%
16	Saanich, BC	0.6%
17	Burlington, ON	0.5%
17	Edmonton, AB	0.5%
19	Barrie, ON	0.4%
19	Hamilton, ON	0.4%
19	Kelowna, BC	0.4%
19	Kingston, ON	0.4%
19	Whitby, ON	0.4%
19	Winnipeg, MB	0.4%
25	Chatham-Kent, ON	0.3%
25	Ottawa, ON	0.3%
25	St. Catharines, ON	0.3%
28	Ajax, ON	0.2%
28	Cambridge, ON	0.2%
28	Guelph, ON	0.2%
28	Halifax, NS	0.2%
28	Kitchener, ON	0.2%
28	Montréal, QC	0.2%
28	Regina, SK	0.2%
28	Saskatoon, SK	0.2%
28	Windsor, ON	0.2%
37	Brampton, ON	0.1%
37	Gatineau, QC	0.1%
37	Greater Sudbury, ON	0.1%
37	Laval, QC	0.1%
37	Longueuil, QC	0.1%
37	Oshawa, ON	0.1%
37	Sherbrooke, QC	0.1%
37	St. John's, NL	0.1%
45	Lévis, QC	0.0%
45	Québec, QC	0.0%
45	Saguenay, QC	0.0%
45	Terrebonne, QC	0.0%
45	Thunder Bay, ON	0.0%
45	Trois-Rivières, QC	0.0%
–	Canada	0.5%

Female

Rank	City	Percent
1	Coquitlam, BC	6.4%
2	Burnaby, BC	3.5%
3	Richmond Hill, ON	2.8%
4	Langley, BC	2.7%
5	Surrey, BC	1.8%
6	Vancouver, BC	1.7%
7	Toronto, ON	1.5%
7	Vaughan, ON	1.5%
9	Oakville, ON	1.3%
10	Abbotsford, BC	1.2%
11	Markham, ON	1.1%
12	Mississauga, ON	0.9%
13	Calgary, AB	0.8%
13	London, ON	0.8%
15	Richmond, BC	0.7%
15	Saanich, BC	0.7%
17	Edmonton, AB	0.6%
18	Burlington, ON	0.5%
18	Winnipeg, MB	0.5%
20	Barrie, ON	0.4%
20	Hamilton, ON	0.4%
20	Kingston, ON	0.4%
23	Guelph, ON	0.3%
23	Halifax, NS	0.3%
23	Kelowna, BC	0.3%
23	Kitchener, ON	0.3%
27	Ajax, ON	0.2%
27	Chatham-Kent, ON	0.2%
27	Montréal, QC	0.2%
27	Ottawa, ON	0.2%
27	Regina, SK	0.2%
27	Saskatoon, SK	0.2%
27	St. Catharines, ON	0.2%
27	Whitby, ON	0.2%
35	Brampton, ON	0.1%
35	Cambridge, ON	0.1%
35	Gatineau, QC	0.1%
35	Greater Sudbury, ON	0.1%
35	Longueuil, QC	0.1%
35	Oshawa, ON	0.1%
35	St. John's, NL	0.1%
35	Windsor, ON	0.1%
43	Laval, QC	0.0%
43	Lévis, QC	0.0%
43	Québec, QC	0.0%
43	Saguenay, QC	0.0%
43	Sherbrooke, QC	0.0%
43	Terrebonne, QC	0.0%
43	Thunder Bay, ON	0.0%
43	Trois-Rivières, QC	0.0%
–	Canada	0.5%

Note: The Employment Equity Act defines visible minorities as 'persons, other than Aboriginal peoples, who are non-Caucasian in race or non-white in colour.'
Source: Statistics Canada. 2013. 2011 National Household Survey. Statistics Canada Catalogue no. 99-004-XWE. Ottawa. Released September 11, 2013.

Cities Ranked by Visible Minority Population: Japanese
By Number

Total

Rank	City	Number
1	Toronto, ON	12,315
2	Vancouver, BC	10,080
3	Calgary, AB	5,160
4	Burnaby, BC	3,780
5	Richmond, BC	3,765
6	Surrey, BC	2,405
7	Mississauga, ON	2,095
8	Edmonton, AB	2,080
9	Montréal, QC	2,020
10	Ottawa, ON	2,005
11	Winnipeg, MB	1,400
12	Coquitlam, BC	1,310
13	Markham, ON	1,145
14	Kelowna, BC	1,060
15	Richmond Hill, ON	970
16	Hamilton, ON	860
17	Saanich, BC	820
18	Oakville, ON	770
19	Langley, BC	710
20	Brampton, ON	675
21	Abbotsford, BC	510
22	London, ON	495
23	Burlington, ON	435
24	Kitchener, ON	310
25	Ajax, ON	305
26	St. Catharines, ON	300
27	Halifax, NS	290
27	Thunder Bay, ON	290
29	Barrie, ON	280
29	Saskatoon, SK	280
31	Whitby, ON	275
32	Vaughan, ON	260
33	Gatineau, QC	250
34	Cambridge, ON	245
35	Québec, QC	205
36	Kingston, ON	190
37	Longueuil, QC	170
38	Guelph, ON	145
38	Regina, SK	145
40	Chatham-Kent, ON	140
41	Oshawa, ON	115
42	Laval, QC	95
43	Windsor, ON	80
44	Trois-Rivières, QC	65
45	St. John's, NL	50
46	Lévis, QC	30
47	Greater Sudbury, ON	25
48	Saguenay, QC	0
48	Sherbrooke, QC	0
48	Terrebonne, QC	0
–	Canada	87,270

Male

Rank	City	Number
1	Toronto, ON	5,450
2	Vancouver, BC	3,855
3	Calgary, AB	2,230
4	Richmond, BC	1,775
5	Burnaby, BC	1,745
6	Surrey, BC	1,100
7	Mississauga, ON	955
8	Ottawa, ON	875
9	Edmonton, AB	845
10	Coquitlam, BC	670
10	Montréal, QC	670
12	Markham, ON	615
13	Winnipeg, MB	605
14	Hamilton, ON	465
15	Richmond Hill, ON	450
16	Kelowna, BC	435
17	Brampton, ON	425
18	Langley, BC	330
19	Oakville, ON	325
20	Saanich, BC	300
21	London, ON	225
22	Abbotsford, BC	215
22	Burlington, ON	215
24	Thunder Bay, ON	195
25	St. Catharines, ON	165
26	Gatineau, QC	150
27	Barrie, ON	135
27	Saskatoon, SK	135
29	Kitchener, ON	130
30	Vaughan, ON	125
30	Whitby, ON	125
32	Ajax, ON	120
33	Halifax, NS	110
34	Québec, QC	100
35	Cambridge, ON	85
36	Chatham-Kent, ON	80
37	Guelph, ON	75
38	Oshawa, ON	70
39	Kingston, ON	60
39	Regina, SK	60
41	Longueuil, QC	50
42	Trois-Rivières, QC	40
43	Laval, QC	35
43	St. John's, NL	35
45	Windsor, ON	25
46	Greater Sudbury, ON	0
46	Lévis, QC	0
46	Saguenay, QC	0
46	Sherbrooke, QC	0
46	Terrebonne, QC	0
–	Canada	38,270

Female

Rank	City	Number
1	Toronto, ON	6,865
2	Vancouver, BC	6,230
3	Calgary, AB	2,925
4	Burnaby, BC	2,035
5	Richmond, BC	1,990
6	Montréal, QC	1,355
7	Surrey, BC	1,305
8	Edmonton, AB	1,235
9	Mississauga, ON	1,150
10	Ottawa, ON	1,135
11	Winnipeg, MB	790
12	Coquitlam, BC	645
13	Kelowna, BC	630
14	Markham, ON	530
15	Richmond Hill, ON	525
16	Saanich, BC	520
17	Oakville, ON	440
18	Hamilton, ON	390
19	Langley, BC	380
20	Abbotsford, BC	290
21	London, ON	270
22	Brampton, ON	250
23	Burlington, ON	220
24	Ajax, ON	190
25	Halifax, NS	180
26	Kitchener, ON	175
27	Cambridge, ON	160
28	Barrie, ON	150
28	Whitby, ON	150
30	Saskatoon, SK	145
31	Vaughan, ON	140
32	Kingston, ON	135
32	St. Catharines, ON	135
34	Longueuil, QC	125
35	Québec, QC	105
36	Gatineau, QC	100
37	Thunder Bay, ON	90
38	Regina, SK	80
39	Guelph, ON	70
40	Chatham-Kent, ON	60
40	Laval, QC	60
42	Windsor, ON	55
43	Oshawa, ON	50
44	Trois-Rivières, QC	25
45	Greater Sudbury, ON	15
45	St. John's, NL	15
47	Lévis, QC	0
47	Saguenay, QC	0
47	Sherbrooke, QC	0
47	Terrebonne, QC	0
–	Canada	48,990

Note: The Employment Equity Act defines visible minorities as 'persons, other than Aboriginal peoples, who are non-Caucasian in race or non-white in colour.'
Source: Statistics Canada. 2013. 2011 National Household Survey. Statistics Canada Catalogue no. 99-004-XWE. Ottawa. Released September 11, 2013.

Cities Ranked by Visible Minority Population: Japanese
By Percent

Total

Rank	City	Percent
1	Richmond, BC	2.0%
2	Burnaby, BC	1.7%
2	Vancouver, BC	1.7%
4	Coquitlam, BC	1.0%
5	Kelowna, BC	0.9%
6	Saanich, BC	0.8%
7	Langley, BC	0.7%
8	Calgary, AB	0.5%
8	Richmond Hill, ON	0.5%
8	Surrey, BC	0.5%
8	Toronto, ON	0.5%
12	Abbotsford, BC	0.4%
12	Markham, ON	0.4%
12	Oakville, ON	0.4%
15	Ajax, ON	0.3%
15	Burlington, ON	0.3%
15	Edmonton, AB	0.3%
15	Mississauga, ON	0.3%
15	Thunder Bay, ON	0.3%
20	Barrie, ON	0.2%
20	Cambridge, ON	0.2%
20	Hamilton, ON	0.2%
20	Kingston, ON	0.2%
20	Ottawa, ON	0.2%
20	St. Catharines, ON	0.2%
20	Whitby, ON	0.2%
20	Winnipeg, MB	0.2%
28	Brampton, ON	0.1%
28	Chatham-Kent, ON	0.1%
28	Gatineau, QC	0.1%
28	Guelph, ON	0.1%
28	Halifax, NS	0.1%
28	Kitchener, ON	0.1%
28	London, ON	0.1%
28	Longueuil, QC	0.1%
28	Montréal, QC	0.1%
28	Oshawa, ON	0.1%
28	Regina, SK	0.1%
28	Saskatoon, SK	0.1%
28	Trois-Rivières, QC	0.1%
28	Vaughan, ON	0.1%
42	Greater Sudbury, ON	0.0%
42	Laval, QC	0.0%
42	Lévis, QC	0.0%
42	Québec, QC	0.0%
42	Saguenay, QC	0.0%
42	Sherbrooke, QC	0.0%
42	St. John's, NL	0.0%
42	Terrebonne, QC	0.0%
42	Windsor, ON	0.0%
–	Canada	0.3%

Male

Rank	City	Percent
1	Richmond, BC	2.0%
2	Burnaby, BC	1.6%
3	Vancouver, BC	1.3%
4	Coquitlam, BC	1.1%
5	Kelowna, BC	0.8%
6	Langley, BC	0.7%
7	Saanich, BC	0.6%
8	Richmond Hill, ON	0.5%
8	Surrey, BC	0.5%
10	Calgary, AB	0.4%
10	Markham, ON	0.4%
10	Oakville, ON	0.4%
10	Thunder Bay, ON	0.4%
10	Toronto, ON	0.4%
15	Abbotsford, BC	0.3%
15	Burlington, ON	0.3%
15	Mississauga, ON	0.3%
15	St. Catharines, ON	0.3%
19	Ajax, ON	0.2%
19	Barrie, ON	0.2%
19	Brampton, ON	0.2%
19	Chatham-Kent, ON	0.2%
19	Edmonton, AB	0.2%
19	Hamilton, ON	0.2%
19	Ottawa, ON	0.2%
19	Whitby, ON	0.2%
19	Winnipeg, MB	0.2%
28	Cambridge, ON	0.1%
28	Gatineau, QC	0.1%
28	Guelph, ON	0.1%
28	Halifax, NS	0.1%
28	Kingston, ON	0.1%
28	Kitchener, ON	0.1%
28	London, ON	0.1%
28	Montréal, QC	0.1%
28	Oshawa, ON	0.1%
28	Regina, SK	0.1%
28	Saskatoon, SK	0.1%
28	St. John's, NL	0.1%
28	Trois-Rivières, QC	0.1%
28	Vaughan, ON	0.1%
42	Greater Sudbury, ON	0.0%
42	Laval, QC	0.0%
42	Longueuil, QC	0.0%
42	Lévis, QC	0.0%
42	Québec, QC	0.0%
42	Saguenay, QC	0.0%
42	Sherbrooke, QC	0.0%
42	Terrebonne, QC	0.0%
42	Windsor, ON	0.0%
–	Canada	0.2%

Female

Rank	City	Percent
1	Vancouver, BC	2.1%
2	Richmond, BC	2.0%
3	Burnaby, BC	1.8%
4	Kelowna, BC	1.1%
5	Coquitlam, BC	1.0%
6	Saanich, BC	0.9%
7	Langley, BC	0.7%
8	Richmond Hill, ON	0.6%
8	Surrey, BC	0.6%
10	Calgary, AB	0.5%
10	Oakville, ON	0.5%
10	Toronto, ON	0.5%
13	Abbotsford, BC	0.4%
14	Ajax, ON	0.3%
14	Cambridge, ON	0.3%
14	Edmonton, AB	0.3%
14	Markham, ON	0.3%
14	Mississauga, ON	0.3%
14	Ottawa, ON	0.3%
20	Barrie, ON	0.2%
20	Burlington, ON	0.2%
20	Hamilton, ON	0.2%
20	Kingston, ON	0.2%
20	Kitchener, ON	0.2%
20	Montréal, QC	0.2%
20	St. Catharines, ON	0.2%
20	Thunder Bay, ON	0.2%
20	Whitby, ON	0.2%
20	Winnipeg, MB	0.2%
30	Brampton, ON	0.1%
30	Chatham-Kent, ON	0.1%
30	Gatineau, QC	0.1%
30	Guelph, ON	0.1%
30	Halifax, NS	0.1%
30	London, ON	0.1%
30	Longueuil, QC	0.1%
30	Oshawa, ON	0.1%
30	Regina, SK	0.1%
30	Saskatoon, SK	0.1%
30	Vaughan, ON	0.1%
30	Windsor, ON	0.1%
42	Greater Sudbury, ON	0.0%
42	Laval, QC	0.0%
42	Lévis, QC	0.0%
42	Québec, QC	0.0%
42	Saguenay, QC	0.0%
42	Sherbrooke, QC	0.0%
42	St. John's, NL	0.0%
42	Terrebonne, QC	0.0%
42	Trois-Rivières, QC	0.0%
–	Canada	0.3%

Note: The Employment Equity Act defines visible minorities as 'persons, other than Aboriginal peoples, who are non-Caucasian in race or non-white in colour.'
Source: Statistics Canada. 2013. 2011 National Household Survey. Statistics Canada Catalogue no. 99-004-XWE. Ottawa. Released September 11, 2013.

Cities Ranked by Visible Minority Population: Multiple Visible Minorities

By Number

Total

Rank	City	Number
1	Toronto, ON	37,920
2	Mississauga, ON	10,435
3	Montréal, QC	10,150
4	Calgary, AB	9,130
5	Vancouver, BC	8,680
6	Brampton, ON	7,385
7	Edmonton, AB	6,665
8	Ottawa, ON	6,100
9	Markham, ON	5,805
10	Richmond, BC	4,305
11	Surrey, BC	4,295
12	Burnaby, BC	3,855
13	Winnipeg, MB	3,770
14	Vaughan, ON	2,865
15	Richmond Hill, ON	2,345
16	Hamilton, ON	2,180
17	Ajax, ON	2,135
18	London, ON	1,870
19	Coquitlam, BC	1,615
20	Oakville, ON	1,440
21	Laval, QC	1,370
22	Kitchener, ON	1,290
23	Whitby, ON	1,180
24	Halifax, NS	1,090
24	Windsor, ON	1,090
26	Saskatoon, SK	910
27	Burlington, ON	845
28	Guelph, ON	655
29	Oshawa, ON	610
30	Abbotsford, BC	575
31	Longueuil, QC	560
32	Langley, BC	530
32	Regina, SK	530
34	Gatineau, QC	525
35	Barrie, ON	500
36	Saanich, BC	450
37	St. Catharines, ON	430
38	Cambridge, ON	385
39	Québec, QC	315
40	Greater Sudbury, ON	225
41	Thunder Bay, ON	220
42	Kelowna, BC	215
43	Kingston, ON	175
44	Sherbrooke, QC	165
45	St. John's, NL	140
46	Chatham-Kent, ON	80
46	Lévis, QC	80
46	Terrebonne, QC	80
49	Trois-Rivières, QC	35
50	Saguenay, QC	30
–	Canada	171,935

Male

Rank	City	Number
1	Toronto, ON	18,130
2	Mississauga, ON	4,950
3	Montréal, QC	4,890
4	Calgary, AB	4,455
5	Vancouver, BC	4,185
6	Brampton, ON	3,680
7	Edmonton, AB	3,300
8	Ottawa, ON	2,950
9	Markham, ON	2,710
10	Richmond, BC	2,200
11	Surrey, BC	2,080
12	Winnipeg, MB	1,850
13	Burnaby, BC	1,805
14	Vaughan, ON	1,295
15	Richmond Hill, ON	1,090
16	Ajax, ON	1,050
17	Hamilton, ON	1,020
18	Coquitlam, BC	845
19	London, ON	835
20	Kitchener, ON	675
20	Oakville, ON	675
22	Whitby, ON	635
23	Laval, QC	630
24	Windsor, ON	475
25	Halifax, NS	450
26	Saskatoon, SK	415
27	Burlington, ON	385
28	Oshawa, ON	340
29	Guelph, ON	330
30	Abbotsford, BC	310
31	Regina, SK	305
32	Barrie, ON	280
33	Longueuil, QC	255
34	Langley, BC	250
35	Saanich, BC	245
36	St. Catharines, ON	230
37	Gatineau, QC	220
38	Cambridge, ON	180
39	Québec, QC	170
40	Greater Sudbury, ON	125
41	Thunder Bay, ON	115
42	Kelowna, BC	100
43	Kingston, ON	90
44	Sherbrooke, QC	85
45	St. John's, NL	70
46	Chatham-Kent, ON	55
47	Lévis, QC	45
48	Terrebonne, QC	30
49	Trois-Rivières, QC	25
50	Saguenay, QC	0
–	Canada	83,335

Female

Rank	City	Number
1	Toronto, ON	19,785
2	Mississauga, ON	5,490
3	Montréal, QC	5,265
4	Calgary, AB	4,675
5	Vancouver, BC	4,495
6	Brampton, ON	3,705
7	Edmonton, AB	3,370
8	Ottawa, ON	3,150
9	Markham, ON	3,095
10	Surrey, BC	2,210
11	Richmond, BC	2,105
12	Burnaby, BC	2,050
13	Winnipeg, MB	1,920
14	Vaughan, ON	1,570
15	Richmond Hill, ON	1,255
16	Hamilton, ON	1,160
17	Ajax, ON	1,090
18	London, ON	1,035
19	Coquitlam, BC	770
20	Oakville, ON	765
21	Laval, QC	740
22	Halifax, NS	640
23	Kitchener, ON	615
23	Windsor, ON	615
25	Whitby, ON	545
26	Saskatoon, SK	500
27	Burlington, ON	455
28	Guelph, ON	330
29	Gatineau, QC	305
30	Longueuil, QC	300
31	Langley, BC	275
32	Abbotsford, BC	270
32	Oshawa, ON	270
34	Regina, SK	225
35	Barrie, ON	210
36	Cambridge, ON	205
36	Saanich, BC	205
38	St. Catharines, ON	200
39	Québec, QC	150
40	Kelowna, BC	120
41	Greater Sudbury, ON	105
42	Thunder Bay, ON	100
43	Kingston, ON	85
43	Sherbrooke, QC	85
45	St. John's, NL	75
46	Terrebonne, QC	55
47	Lévis, QC	35
48	Chatham-Kent, ON	20
49	Saguenay, QC	0
49	Trois-Rivières, QC	0
–	Canada	88,600

Note: The Employment Equity Act defines visible minorities as 'persons, other than Aboriginal peoples, who are non-Caucasian in race or non-white in colour'; "Multiple Visible Minorities" includes respondents who reported more than one visible minority group by checking two or more mark-in circles, e.g., 'Black' and 'South Asian.'

Source: Statistics Canada. 2013. 2011 National Household Survey. Statistics Canada Catalogue no. 99-004-XWE. Ottawa. Released September 11, 2013.

Cities Ranked by Visible Minority Population: Multiple Visible Minorities
By Percent

Total

Rank	City	Percent
1	Richmond, BC	2.3%
2	Ajax, ON	2.0%
3	Markham, ON	1.9%
4	Burnaby, BC	1.8%
5	Mississauga, ON	1.5%
5	Toronto, ON	1.5%
5	Vancouver, BC	1.5%
8	Brampton, ON	1.4%
9	Coquitlam, BC	1.3%
9	Richmond Hill, ON	1.3%
11	Vaughan, ON	1.0%
11	Whitby, ON	1.0%
13	Surrey, BC	0.9%
14	Calgary, AB	0.8%
14	Edmonton, AB	0.8%
14	Oakville, ON	0.8%
17	Ottawa, ON	0.7%
18	Kitchener, ON	0.6%
18	Montréal, QC	0.6%
18	Winnipeg, MB	0.6%
21	Burlington, ON	0.5%
21	Guelph, ON	0.5%
21	Langley, BC	0.5%
21	London, ON	0.5%
21	Windsor, ON	0.5%
26	Abbotsford, BC	0.4%
26	Barrie, ON	0.4%
26	Hamilton, ON	0.4%
26	Oshawa, ON	0.4%
26	Saanich, BC	0.4%
26	Saskatoon, SK	0.4%
32	Cambridge, ON	0.3%
32	Halifax, NS	0.3%
32	Laval, QC	0.3%
32	Regina, SK	0.3%
32	St. Catharines, ON	0.3%
37	Gatineau, QC	0.2%
37	Kelowna, BC	0.2%
37	Longueuil, QC	0.2%
37	Thunder Bay, ON	0.2%
41	Chatham-Kent, ON	0.1%
41	Greater Sudbury, ON	0.1%
41	Kingston, ON	0.1%
41	Lévis, QC	0.1%
41	Québec, QC	0.1%
41	Sherbrooke, QC	0.1%
41	St. John's, NL	0.1%
41	Terrebonne, QC	0.1%
49	Saguenay, QC	0.0%
49	Trois-Rivières, QC	0.0%
–	Canada	0.5%

Male

Rank	City	Percent
1	Richmond, BC	2.4%
2	Ajax, ON	2.0%
3	Markham, ON	1.8%
4	Burnaby, BC	1.7%
5	Toronto, ON	1.5%
5	Vancouver, BC	1.5%
7	Brampton, ON	1.4%
7	Coquitlam, BC	1.4%
7	Mississauga, ON	1.4%
10	Richmond Hill, ON	1.2%
11	Whitby, ON	1.1%
12	Surrey, BC	0.9%
12	Vaughan, ON	0.9%
14	Calgary, AB	0.8%
14	Edmonton, AB	0.8%
14	Oakville, ON	0.8%
17	Ottawa, ON	0.7%
18	Guelph, ON	0.6%
18	Kitchener, ON	0.6%
18	Montréal, QC	0.6%
18	Winnipeg, MB	0.6%
22	Abbotsford, BC	0.5%
22	Burlington, ON	0.5%
22	Langley, BC	0.5%
22	London, ON	0.5%
22	Oshawa, ON	0.5%
22	Saanich, BC	0.5%
22	Windsor, ON	0.5%
29	Barrie, ON	0.4%
29	Hamilton, ON	0.4%
29	Saskatoon, SK	0.4%
29	St. Catharines, ON	0.4%
33	Cambridge, ON	0.3%
33	Laval, QC	0.3%
33	Regina, SK	0.3%
36	Gatineau, QC	0.2%
36	Greater Sudbury, ON	0.2%
36	Halifax, NS	0.2%
36	Kelowna, BC	0.2%
36	Kingston, ON	0.2%
36	Longueuil, QC	0.2%
36	Thunder Bay, ON	0.2%
43	Chatham-Kent, ON	0.1%
43	Lévis, QC	0.1%
43	Québec, QC	0.1%
43	Sherbrooke, QC	0.1%
43	St. John's, NL	0.1%
43	Terrebonne, QC	0.1%
49	Saguenay, QC	0.0%
49	Trois-Rivières, QC	0.0%
–	Canada	0.5%

Female

Rank	City	Percent
1	Richmond, BC	2.1%
2	Markham, ON	2.0%
3	Ajax, ON	1.9%
4	Burnaby, BC	1.8%
5	Mississauga, ON	1.5%
5	Toronto, ON	1.5%
5	Vancouver, BC	1.5%
8	Brampton, ON	1.4%
9	Richmond Hill, ON	1.3%
10	Coquitlam, BC	1.2%
11	Vaughan, ON	1.1%
12	Calgary, AB	0.9%
12	Surrey, BC	0.9%
12	Whitby, ON	0.9%
15	Edmonton, AB	0.8%
15	Oakville, ON	0.8%
17	Ottawa, ON	0.7%
18	Kitchener, ON	0.6%
18	London, ON	0.6%
18	Montréal, QC	0.6%
18	Windsor, ON	0.6%
18	Winnipeg, MB	0.6%
23	Burlington, ON	0.5%
23	Guelph, ON	0.5%
23	Langley, BC	0.5%
23	Saskatoon, SK	0.5%
27	Abbotsford, BC	0.4%
27	Hamilton, ON	0.4%
27	Laval, QC	0.4%
27	Oshawa, ON	0.4%
27	Saanich, BC	0.4%
32	Barrie, ON	0.3%
32	Cambridge, ON	0.3%
32	Halifax, NS	0.3%
32	Longueuil, QC	0.3%
32	St. Catharines, ON	0.3%
37	Gatineau, QC	0.2%
37	Kelowna, BC	0.2%
37	Regina, SK	0.2%
37	Thunder Bay, ON	0.2%
41	Greater Sudbury, ON	0.1%
41	Kingston, ON	0.1%
41	Lévis, QC	0.1%
41	Québec, QC	0.1%
41	Sherbrooke, QC	0.1%
41	St. John's, NL	0.1%
41	Terrebonne, QC	0.1%
48	Chatham-Kent, ON	0.0%
48	Saguenay, QC	0.0%
48	Trois-Rivières, QC	0.0%
–	Canada	0.5%

Note: The Employment Equity Act defines visible minorities as 'persons, other than Aboriginal peoples, who are non-Caucasian in race or non-white in colour'; "Multiple Visible Minorities" includes respondents who reported more than one visible minority group by checking two or more mark-in circles, e.g., 'Black' and 'South Asian.'
Source: Statistics Canada. 2013. 2011 National Household Survey. Statistics Canada Catalogue no. 99-004-XWE. Ottawa. Released September 11, 2013.

Cities Ranked by Religion: Buddhist
By Number

Total

Rank	City	Number
1	Toronto, ON	68,885
2	Vancouver, BC	33,450
3	Montréal, QC	32,205
4	Calgary, AB	22,375
5	Edmonton, AB	16,840
6	Mississauga, ON	15,615
7	Markham, ON	13,280
8	Richmond, BC	12,330
9	Ottawa, ON	11,705
10	Burnaby, BC	10,660
11	Surrey, BC	10,520
12	Vaughan, ON	7,215
13	Brampton, ON	6,715
14	Winnipeg, MB	6,260
15	Laval, QC	5,625
16	Richmond Hill, ON	5,125
17	Hamilton, ON	4,635
18	Kitchener, ON	3,070
19	London, ON	2,760
20	Coquitlam, BC	2,540
21	Windsor, ON	2,390
22	Guelph, ON	2,265
23	Longueuil, QC	1,955
24	Saskatoon, SK	1,670
25	Regina, SK	1,655
26	Halifax, NS	1,590
27	Saanich, BC	1,555
28	Langley, BC	1,445
29	Oakville, ON	1,415
30	Québec, QC	1,325
31	Gatineau, QC	1,085
32	Cambridge, ON	1,050
33	Ajax, ON	785
34	Burlington, ON	760
35	St. Catharines, ON	750
36	Abbotsford, BC	720
37	Oshawa, ON	625
38	Barrie, ON	600
39	Kelowna, BC	570
40	Whitby, ON	505
41	Kingston, ON	375
42	Greater Sudbury, ON	295
43	Lévis, QC	260
43	Sherbrooke, QC	260
45	St. John's, NL	240
46	Thunder Bay, ON	210
47	Trois-Rivières, QC	165
48	Chatham-Kent, ON	130
49	Terrebonne, QC	105
50	Saguenay, QC	60
–	Canada	366,830

Male

Rank	City	Number
1	Toronto, ON	30,910
2	Montréal, QC	15,175
3	Vancouver, BC	14,505
4	Calgary, AB	10,265
5	Edmonton, AB	8,065
6	Mississauga, ON	7,445
7	Markham, ON	5,895
8	Richmond, BC	5,415
9	Ottawa, ON	5,370
10	Surrey, BC	4,915
11	Burnaby, BC	4,615
12	Brampton, ON	3,355
13	Vaughan, ON	3,335
14	Winnipeg, MB	3,010
15	Laval, QC	2,645
16	Richmond Hill, ON	2,360
17	Hamilton, ON	2,140
18	Kitchener, ON	1,545
19	London, ON	1,310
20	Windsor, ON	1,255
21	Coquitlam, BC	1,160
22	Guelph, ON	1,080
23	Longueuil, QC	920
24	Halifax, NS	825
25	Saskatoon, SK	820
26	Regina, SK	790
27	Langley, BC	720
28	Saanich, BC	705
29	Québec, QC	650
30	Oakville, ON	600
31	Cambridge, ON	535
32	Gatineau, QC	510
33	Ajax, ON	350
34	Abbotsford, BC	335
34	St. Catharines, ON	335
36	Burlington, ON	315
37	Oshawa, ON	295
38	Kelowna, BC	250
38	Whitby, ON	250
40	Barrie, ON	230
41	Greater Sudbury, ON	195
41	Kingston, ON	195
43	St. John's, NL	150
44	Sherbrooke, QC	115
45	Lévis, QC	105
46	Trois-Rivières, QC	95
47	Thunder Bay, ON	80
48	Chatham-Kent, ON	75
49	Terrebonne, QC	50
50	Saguenay, QC	40
–	Canada	168,465

Female

Rank	City	Number
1	Toronto, ON	37,975
2	Vancouver, BC	18,950
3	Montréal, QC	17,030
4	Calgary, AB	12,110
5	Edmonton, AB	8,775
6	Mississauga, ON	8,170
7	Markham, ON	7,385
8	Richmond, BC	6,915
9	Ottawa, ON	6,330
10	Burnaby, BC	6,050
11	Surrey, BC	5,610
12	Vaughan, ON	3,880
13	Brampton, ON	3,365
14	Winnipeg, MB	3,250
15	Laval, QC	2,985
16	Richmond Hill, ON	2,760
17	Hamilton, ON	2,495
18	Kitchener, ON	1,525
19	London, ON	1,455
20	Coquitlam, BC	1,385
21	Guelph, ON	1,190
22	Windsor, ON	1,135
23	Longueuil, QC	1,035
24	Regina, SK	870
25	Saskatoon, SK	855
26	Saanich, BC	850
27	Oakville, ON	810
28	Halifax, NS	765
29	Langley, BC	730
30	Québec, QC	670
31	Gatineau, QC	575
32	Cambridge, ON	520
33	Burlington, ON	440
34	Ajax, ON	435
35	St. Catharines, ON	415
36	Abbotsford, BC	380
37	Barrie, ON	365
38	Oshawa, ON	330
39	Kelowna, BC	320
40	Whitby, ON	250
41	Kingston, ON	185
42	Lévis, QC	150
43	Sherbrooke, QC	145
44	Thunder Bay, ON	130
45	Greater Sudbury, ON	100
46	St. John's, NL	90
47	Trois-Rivières, QC	70
48	Chatham-Kent, ON	60
48	Terrebonne, QC	60
50	Saguenay, QC	20
–	Canada	198,365

Note: Religion refers to the person's self-identification as having a connection or affiliation with any religious denomination, group, body, sect, cult or other religiously defined community or system of belief. Religion is not limited to formal membership in a religious organization or group. Persons without a religious connection or affiliation can self-identify as atheist, agnostic or humanist, or can provide another applicable response.
Source: Statistics Canada. 2013. 2011 National Household Survey. Statistics Canada Catalogue no. 99-004-XWE. Ottawa. Released September 11, 2013.

Cities Ranked by Religion: Buddhist
By Percent

Total

Rank	City	Percent
1	Richmond, BC	6.5%
2	Vancouver, BC	5.7%
3	Burnaby, BC	4.8%
4	Markham, ON	4.4%
5	Richmond Hill, ON	2.8%
6	Toronto, ON	2.7%
7	Vaughan, ON	2.5%
8	Surrey, BC	2.3%
9	Mississauga, ON	2.2%
10	Calgary, AB	2.1%
10	Edmonton, AB	2.1%
12	Coquitlam, BC	2.0%
12	Montréal, QC	2.0%
14	Guelph, ON	1.9%
15	Kitchener, ON	1.4%
15	Langley, BC	1.4%
15	Laval, QC	1.4%
15	Saanich, BC	1.4%
19	Brampton, ON	1.3%
19	Ottawa, ON	1.3%
21	Windsor, ON	1.1%
22	Winnipeg, MB	1.0%
23	Hamilton, ON	0.9%
23	Longueuil, QC	0.9%
23	Regina, SK	0.9%
26	Cambridge, ON	0.8%
26	London, ON	0.8%
26	Oakville, ON	0.8%
26	Saskatoon, SK	0.8%
30	Ajax, ON	0.7%
31	St. Catharines, ON	0.6%
32	Abbotsford, BC	0.5%
32	Barrie, ON	0.5%
32	Kelowna, BC	0.5%
35	Burlington, ON	0.4%
35	Gatineau, QC	0.4%
35	Halifax, NS	0.4%
35	Oshawa, ON	0.4%
35	Whitby, ON	0.4%
40	Kingston, ON	0.3%
40	Québec, QC	0.3%
42	Greater Sudbury, ON	0.2%
42	Lévis, QC	0.2%
42	Sherbrooke, QC	0.2%
42	St. John's, NL	0.2%
42	Thunder Bay, ON	0.2%
47	Chatham-Kent, ON	0.1%
47	Terrebonne, QC	0.1%
47	Trois-Rivières, QC	0.1%
50	Saguenay, QC	0.0%
–	Canada	1.1%

Male

Rank	City	Percent
1	Richmond, BC	5.9%
2	Vancouver, BC	5.0%
3	Burnaby, BC	4.3%
4	Markham, ON	4.0%
5	Richmond Hill, ON	2.6%
6	Toronto, ON	2.5%
7	Vaughan, ON	2.4%
8	Mississauga, ON	2.1%
8	Surrey, BC	2.1%
10	Edmonton, AB	2.0%
11	Calgary, AB	1.9%
11	Coquitlam, BC	1.9%
11	Montréal, QC	1.9%
14	Guelph, ON	1.8%
15	Kitchener, ON	1.4%
15	Langley, BC	1.4%
15	Laval, QC	1.4%
18	Brampton, ON	1.3%
18	Ottawa, ON	1.3%
18	Saanich, BC	1.3%
21	Windsor, ON	1.2%
22	Winnipeg, MB	1.0%
23	Cambridge, ON	0.9%
23	Hamilton, ON	0.9%
23	Regina, SK	0.9%
26	Longueuil, QC	0.8%
26	Saskatoon, SK	0.8%
28	Ajax, ON	0.7%
28	London, ON	0.7%
28	Oakville, ON	0.7%
31	Abbotsford, BC	0.5%
31	Kelowna, BC	0.5%
31	St. Catharines, ON	0.5%
34	Barrie, ON	0.4%
34	Burlington, ON	0.4%
34	Gatineau, QC	0.4%
34	Halifax, NS	0.4%
34	Oshawa, ON	0.4%
34	Whitby, ON	0.4%
40	Greater Sudbury, ON	0.3%
40	Kingston, ON	0.3%
40	Québec, QC	0.3%
40	St. John's, NL	0.3%
44	Chatham-Kent, ON	0.2%
44	Lévis, QC	0.2%
44	Sherbrooke, QC	0.2%
44	Thunder Bay, ON	0.2%
44	Trois-Rivières, QC	0.2%
49	Saguenay, QC	0.1%
49	Terrebonne, QC	0.1%
–	Canada	1.0%

Female

Rank	City	Percent
1	Richmond, BC	7.0%
2	Vancouver, BC	6.3%
3	Burnaby, BC	5.4%
4	Markham, ON	4.8%
5	Richmond Hill, ON	2.9%
6	Toronto, ON	2.8%
7	Vaughan, ON	2.7%
8	Surrey, BC	2.4%
9	Mississauga, ON	2.3%
10	Calgary, AB	2.2%
10	Coquitlam, BC	2.2%
10	Edmonton, AB	2.2%
13	Montréal, QC	2.1%
14	Guelph, ON	1.9%
15	Laval, QC	1.5%
15	Saanich, BC	1.5%
17	Kitchener, ON	1.4%
17	Langley, BC	1.4%
17	Ottawa, ON	1.4%
20	Brampton, ON	1.3%
21	Windsor, ON	1.1%
22	Hamilton, ON	1.0%
22	Winnipeg, MB	1.0%
24	Longueuil, QC	0.9%
24	Oakville, ON	0.9%
24	Regina, SK	0.9%
27	Ajax, ON	0.8%
27	Cambridge, ON	0.8%
27	London, ON	0.8%
27	Saskatoon, SK	0.8%
31	Abbotsford, BC	0.6%
31	St. Catharines, ON	0.6%
33	Barrie, ON	0.5%
33	Burlington, ON	0.5%
33	Kelowna, BC	0.5%
36	Gatineau, QC	0.4%
36	Halifax, NS	0.4%
36	Oshawa, ON	0.4%
36	Whitby, ON	0.4%
40	Kingston, ON	0.3%
40	Québec, QC	0.3%
42	Lévis, QC	0.2%
42	Sherbrooke, QC	0.2%
42	St. John's, NL	0.2%
42	Thunder Bay, ON	0.2%
46	Chatham-Kent, ON	0.1%
46	Greater Sudbury, ON	0.1%
46	Terrebonne, QC	0.1%
46	Trois-Rivières, QC	0.1%
50	Saguenay, QC	0.0%
–	Canada	1.2%

Note: Religion refers to the person's self-identification as having a connection or affiliation with any religious denomination, group, body, sect, cult or other religiously defined community or system of belief. Religion is not limited to formal membership in a religious organization or group. Persons without a religious connection or affiliation can self-identify as atheist, agnostic or humanist, or can provide another applicable response.

Source: Statistics Canada. 2013. 2011 National Household Survey. Statistics Canada Catalogue no. 99-004-XWE. Ottawa. Released September 11, 2013.

Cities Ranked by Religion: Christian
By Number

Total

Rank	City	Number
1	Toronto, ON	1,394,210
2	Montréal, QC	1,061,605
3	Calgary, AB	594,270
4	Ottawa, ON	567,485
5	Edmonton, AB	444,560
6	Québec, QC	428,380
7	Mississauga, ON	424,715
8	Winnipeg, MB	414,270
9	Hamilton, ON	344,625
10	Laval, QC	316,010
11	Halifax, NS	274,780
12	Brampton, ON	263,385
13	London, ON	226,615
14	Vancouver, BC	213,855
15	Gatineau, QC	209,910
16	Longueuil, QC	181,230
17	Surrey, BC	177,020
18	Vaughan, ON	173,565
19	Saskatoon, SK	144,200
20	Windsor, ON	143,945
21	Kitchener, ON	142,360
22	Saguenay, QC	132,335
23	Markham, ON	132,230
24	Regina, SK	128,755
25	Greater Sudbury, ON	127,090
26	Oakville, ON	126,570
27	Sherbrooke, QC	126,220
28	Lévis, QC	122,425
29	Burlington, ON	121,505
30	Trois-Rivières, QC	114,210
31	Oshawa, ON	100,785
32	Burnaby, BC	94,475
33	St. Catharines, ON	92,410
34	Richmond Hill, ON	92,195
35	Terrebonne, QC	92,085
36	St. John's, NL	90,225
37	Barrie, ON	88,365
38	Cambridge, ON	86,170
39	Whitby, ON	85,125
40	Chatham-Kent, ON	79,145
41	Kingston, ON	78,880
42	Thunder Bay, ON	76,245
43	Guelph, ON	74,495
44	Ajax, ON	72,775
45	Richmond, BC	71,030
46	Abbotsford, BC	65,055
47	Kelowna, BC	62,410
48	Coquitlam, BC	61,075
49	Langley, BC	54,550
50	Saanich, BC	48,640
–	Canada	22,102,745

Male

Rank	City	Number
1	Toronto, ON	637,595
2	Montréal, QC	494,940
3	Calgary, AB	280,400
4	Ottawa, ON	263,940
5	Edmonton, AB	210,590
6	Québec, QC	202,470
7	Mississauga, ON	200,575
8	Winnipeg, MB	192,570
9	Hamilton, ON	161,670
10	Laval, QC	151,770
11	Halifax, NS	127,320
12	Brampton, ON	125,860
13	London, ON	104,125
14	Gatineau, QC	99,745
15	Vancouver, BC	96,175
16	Longueuil, QC	85,870
17	Vaughan, ON	83,600
18	Surrey, BC	82,645
19	Kitchener, ON	67,570
20	Windsor, ON	67,425
21	Saskatoon, SK	66,865
22	Saguenay, QC	64,580
23	Markham, ON	62,090
24	Sherbrooke, QC	60,210
25	Greater Sudbury, ON	60,120
26	Regina, SK	59,865
27	Oakville, ON	59,570
28	Lévis, QC	59,195
29	Burlington, ON	56,185
30	Trois-Rivières, QC	54,435
31	Oshawa, ON	46,755
32	Terrebonne, QC	45,220
33	Burnaby, BC	43,345
34	Richmond Hill, ON	43,315
35	St. Catharines, ON	42,340
36	St. John's, NL	41,820
37	Barrie, ON	41,345
38	Cambridge, ON	40,800
39	Whitby, ON	40,305
40	Chatham-Kent, ON	37,525
41	Kingston, ON	35,620
42	Thunder Bay, ON	35,490
43	Ajax, ON	34,375
44	Guelph, ON	34,070
45	Richmond, BC	31,975
46	Abbotsford, BC	30,380
47	Coquitlam, BC	28,345
48	Kelowna, BC	28,090
49	Langley, BC	25,120
50	Saanich, BC	21,650
–	Canada	10,497,775

Female

Rank	City	Number
1	Toronto, ON	756,610
2	Montréal, QC	566,660
3	Calgary, AB	313,870
4	Ottawa, ON	303,545
5	Edmonton, AB	233,970
6	Québec, QC	225,910
7	Mississauga, ON	224,145
8	Winnipeg, MB	221,695
9	Hamilton, ON	182,955
10	Laval, QC	164,235
11	Halifax, NS	147,460
12	Brampton, ON	137,520
13	London, ON	122,490
14	Vancouver, BC	117,680
15	Gatineau, QC	110,165
16	Longueuil, QC	95,365
17	Surrey, BC	94,380
18	Vaughan, ON	89,965
19	Saskatoon, SK	77,335
20	Windsor, ON	76,520
21	Kitchener, ON	74,795
22	Markham, ON	70,135
23	Regina, SK	68,890
24	Saguenay, QC	67,755
25	Oakville, ON	67,000
26	Greater Sudbury, ON	66,970
27	Sherbrooke, QC	66,010
28	Burlington, ON	65,315
29	Lévis, QC	63,230
30	Trois-Rivières, QC	59,775
31	Oshawa, ON	54,025
32	Burnaby, BC	51,135
33	St. Catharines, ON	50,075
34	Richmond Hill, ON	48,875
35	St. John's, NL	48,410
36	Barrie, ON	47,015
37	Terrebonne, QC	46,865
38	Cambridge, ON	45,370
39	Whitby, ON	44,815
40	Kingston, ON	43,250
41	Chatham-Kent, ON	41,620
42	Thunder Bay, ON	40,750
43	Guelph, ON	40,425
44	Richmond, BC	39,050
45	Ajax, ON	38,405
46	Abbotsford, BC	34,675
47	Kelowna, BC	34,325
48	Coquitlam, BC	32,730
49	Langley, BC	29,430
50	Saanich, BC	26,990
–	Canada	11,604,975

Note: Religion refers to the person's self-identification as having a connection or affiliation with any religious denomination, group, body, sect, cult or other religiously defined community or system of belief. Religion is not limited to formal membership in a religious organization or group. Persons without a religious connection or affiliation can self-identify as atheist, agnostic or humanist, or can provide another applicable response.

Source: Statistics Canada. 2013. 2011 National Household Survey. Statistics Canada Catalogue no. 99-004-XWE. Ottawa. Released September 11, 2013.

Cities Ranked by Religion: Christian
By Percent

Total

Rank	City	Percent
1	Saguenay, QC	93.6%
2	Lévis, QC	90.1%
3	Trois-Rivières, QC	89.9%
4	Terrebonne, QC	87.2%
5	St. John's, NL	86.8%
6	Québec, QC	85.2%
7	Sherbrooke, QC	84.0%
8	Greater Sudbury, ON	80.6%
9	Laval, QC	80.5%
10	Gatineau, QC	80.2%
11	Longueuil, QC	79.5%
12	Chatham-Kent, ON	77.8%
13	Thunder Bay, ON	72.0%
14	St. Catharines, ON	71.8%
15	Halifax, NS	71.5%
16	Whitby, ON	70.8%
17	Oakville, ON	70.1%
18	Burlington, ON	70.0%
19	Windsor, ON	69.2%
20	Cambridge, ON	68.9%
21	Oshawa, ON	68.2%
22	Regina, SK	67.9%
23	Hamilton, ON	67.6%
24	Ajax, ON	66.6%
25	Barrie, ON	66.3%
25	Kingston, ON	66.3%
27	Saskatoon, SK	66.0%
28	Kitchener, ON	65.9%
29	Montréal, QC	65.8%
30	Ottawa, ON	65.4%
31	Winnipeg, MB	63.7%
32	London, ON	62.8%
33	Guelph, ON	61.8%
34	Vaughan, ON	60.6%
35	Mississauga, ON	59.9%
36	Edmonton, AB	55.9%
37	Calgary, AB	54.9%
38	Kelowna, BC	54.5%
39	Toronto, ON	54.1%
40	Langley, BC	52.9%
41	Brampton, ON	50.5%
42	Richmond Hill, ON	50.0%
43	Abbotsford, BC	49.7%
44	Coquitlam, BC	48.9%
45	Saanich, BC	45.1%
46	Markham, ON	44.1%
47	Burnaby, BC	42.9%
48	Surrey, BC	38.2%
49	Richmond, BC	37.5%
50	Vancouver, BC	36.2%
–	Canada	67.3%

Male

Rank	City	Percent
1	Saguenay, QC	92.4%
2	Lévis, QC	88.5%
2	Trois-Rivières, QC	88.5%
4	Terrebonne, QC	86.0%
5	St. John's, NL	84.5%
6	Québec, QC	83.1%
7	Sherbrooke, QC	82.2%
8	Laval, QC	79.4%
9	Gatineau, QC	78.5%
10	Greater Sudbury, ON	77.9%
11	Longueuil, QC	77.5%
12	Chatham-Kent, ON	75.5%
13	St. Catharines, ON	68.9%
14	Thunder Bay, ON	68.8%
15	Whitby, ON	68.5%
16	Halifax, NS	68.4%
17	Oakville, ON	68.1%
18	Burlington, ON	67.1%
19	Windsor, ON	66.6%
20	Cambridge, ON	66.2%
21	Ajax, ON	65.1%
22	Oshawa, ON	64.9%
23	Hamilton, ON	64.7%
24	Regina, SK	64.6%
25	Barrie, ON	63.8%
26	Kitchener, ON	63.3%
27	Montréal, QC	62.9%
28	Ottawa, ON	62.6%
29	Kingston, ON	62.5%
30	Saskatoon, SK	62.4%
31	Winnipeg, MB	60.8%
32	London, ON	59.6%
32	Vaughan, ON	59.6%
34	Guelph, ON	58.1%
35	Mississauga, ON	57.7%
36	Edmonton, AB	53.1%
37	Calgary, AB	51.8%
38	Toronto, ON	51.5%
39	Kelowna, BC	50.8%
40	Langley, BC	49.6%
41	Brampton, ON	48.9%
42	Richmond Hill, ON	48.1%
43	Abbotsford, BC	47.1%
44	Coquitlam, BC	46.0%
45	Markham, ON	42.3%
46	Saanich, BC	41.4%
47	Burnaby, BC	40.1%
48	Surrey, BC	36.0%
49	Richmond, BC	35.1%
50	Vancouver, BC	33.4%
–	Canada	64.9%

Female

Rank	City	Percent
1	Saguenay, QC	94.9%
2	Lévis, QC	91.7%
3	Trois-Rivières, QC	91.3%
4	St. John's, NL	89.0%
5	Terrebonne, QC	88.4%
6	Québec, QC	87.2%
7	Sherbrooke, QC	85.7%
8	Greater Sudbury, ON	83.1%
9	Gatineau, QC	81.9%
10	Laval, QC	81.5%
11	Longueuil, QC	81.4%
12	Chatham-Kent, ON	80.1%
13	Thunder Bay, ON	75.0%
14	Halifax, NS	74.4%
14	St. Catharines, ON	74.4%
16	Whitby, ON	72.9%
17	Burlington, ON	72.8%
18	Oakville, ON	72.1%
19	Windsor, ON	71.7%
20	Cambridge, ON	71.5%
21	Oshawa, ON	71.4%
22	Regina, SK	71.0%
23	Hamilton, ON	70.4%
24	Kingston, ON	69.8%
25	Saskatoon, SK	69.6%
26	Barrie, ON	68.7%
27	Montréal, QC	68.6%
28	Kitchener, ON	68.5%
29	Ajax, ON	68.1%
29	Ottawa, ON	68.1%
31	Winnipeg, MB	66.5%
32	London, ON	65.9%
33	Guelph, ON	65.3%
34	Mississauga, ON	62.0%
35	Vaughan, ON	61.6%
36	Edmonton, AB	58.7%
37	Calgary, AB	58.0%
38	Kelowna, BC	57.9%
39	Toronto, ON	56.6%
40	Langley, BC	56.1%
41	Abbotsford, BC	52.2%
42	Brampton, ON	52.1%
43	Richmond Hill, ON	51.8%
44	Coquitlam, BC	51.6%
45	Saanich, BC	48.6%
46	Markham, ON	45.7%
47	Burnaby, BC	45.6%
48	Surrey, BC	40.4%
49	Richmond, BC	39.7%
50	Vancouver, BC	39.0%
–	Canada	69.5%

Note: Religion refers to the person's self-identification as having a connection or affiliation with any religious denomination, group, body, sect, cult or other religiously defined community or system of belief. Religion is not limited to formal membership in a religious organization or group. Persons without a religious connection or affiliation can self-identify as atheist, agnostic or humanist, or can provide another applicable response.
Source: Statistics Canada. 2013. 2011 National Household Survey. Statistics Canada Catalogue no. 99-004-XWE. Ottawa. Released September 11, 2013.

RANKINGS / Cities Ranked by Religion: Hindu

Cities Ranked by Religion: Hindu

By Number

Total

Rank	City	Number
1	Toronto, ON	145,035
2	Brampton, ON	63,390
3	Mississauga, ON	49,325
4	Markham, ON	29,540
5	Montréal, QC	22,580
6	Calgary, AB	17,410
7	Surrey, BC	16,790
8	Edmonton, AB	14,865
9	Vaughan, ON	12,880
10	Ottawa, ON	11,965
11	Vancouver, BC	8,220
12	Winnipeg, MB	6,795
13	Ajax, ON	6,490
14	Burnaby, BC	4,895
15	Richmond Hill, ON	4,390
16	Hamilton, ON	3,910
17	Oakville, ON	3,700
18	London, ON	2,790
19	Richmond, BC	2,675
20	Kitchener, ON	2,580
21	Windsor, ON	2,510
22	Laval, QC	2,425
23	Burlington, ON	1,995
24	Abbotsford, BC	1,955
25	Whitby, ON	1,905
26	Cambridge, ON	1,850
27	Guelph, ON	1,800
28	Saskatoon, SK	1,575
29	Regina, SK	1,545
30	Halifax, NS	1,540
31	Coquitlam, BC	1,115
32	Oshawa, ON	710
33	Saanich, BC	650
34	Longueuil, QC	545
35	Kingston, ON	520
36	St. John's, NL	505
37	Kelowna, BC	455
38	Barrie, ON	410
39	St. Catharines, ON	370
40	Québec, QC	360
41	Greater Sudbury, ON	340
42	Gatineau, QC	295
42	Sherbrooke, QC	295
44	Langley, BC	215
45	Chatham-Kent, ON	155
46	Thunder Bay, ON	125
47	Lévis, QC	0
47	Saguenay, QC	0
47	Terrebonne, QC	0
47	Trois-Rivières, QC	0
–	Canada	497,965

Male

Rank	City	Number
1	Toronto, ON	72,750
2	Brampton, ON	31,760
3	Mississauga, ON	24,390
4	Markham, ON	14,860
5	Montréal, QC	11,505
6	Calgary, AB	9,080
7	Surrey, BC	8,470
8	Edmonton, AB	7,630
9	Vaughan, ON	6,525
10	Ottawa, ON	6,165
11	Vancouver, BC	4,260
12	Winnipeg, MB	3,385
13	Ajax, ON	3,055
14	Burnaby, BC	2,385
15	Richmond Hill, ON	2,250
16	Hamilton, ON	1,970
17	Oakville, ON	1,840
18	Windsor, ON	1,335
19	Kitchener, ON	1,315
19	London, ON	1,315
21	Richmond, BC	1,280
22	Laval, QC	1,195
23	Burlington, ON	1,025
24	Abbotsford, BC	960
25	Whitby, ON	950
26	Cambridge, ON	895
27	Regina, SK	880
28	Saskatoon, SK	810
29	Guelph, ON	800
29	Halifax, NS	800
31	Coquitlam, BC	495
32	Oshawa, ON	400
33	Saanich, BC	360
34	Longueuil, QC	310
35	Kingston, ON	300
36	St. John's, NL	265
37	Barrie, ON	235
38	Kelowna, BC	195
39	Greater Sudbury, ON	185
39	Québec, QC	185
41	Gatineau, QC	170
42	St. Catharines, ON	165
43	Sherbrooke, QC	150
44	Langley, BC	120
45	Chatham-Kent, ON	80
46	Thunder Bay, ON	65
47	Lévis, QC	0
47	Saguenay, QC	0
47	Terrebonne, QC	0
47	Trois-Rivières, QC	0
–	Canada	250,435

Female

Rank	City	Number
1	Toronto, ON	72,285
2	Brampton, ON	31,630
3	Mississauga, ON	24,940
4	Markham, ON	14,680
5	Montréal, QC	11,080
6	Calgary, AB	8,330
7	Surrey, BC	8,325
8	Edmonton, AB	7,230
9	Vaughan, ON	6,355
10	Ottawa, ON	5,805
11	Vancouver, BC	3,960
12	Ajax, ON	3,440
13	Winnipeg, MB	3,405
14	Burnaby, BC	2,510
15	Richmond Hill, ON	2,140
16	Hamilton, ON	1,940
17	Oakville, ON	1,865
18	London, ON	1,470
19	Richmond, BC	1,390
20	Kitchener, ON	1,265
21	Laval, QC	1,235
22	Windsor, ON	1,175
23	Guelph, ON	1,000
24	Abbotsford, BC	995
25	Burlington, ON	965
26	Whitby, ON	955
27	Cambridge, ON	950
28	Saskatoon, SK	770
29	Halifax, NS	740
30	Regina, SK	665
31	Coquitlam, BC	620
32	Oshawa, ON	310
33	Saanich, BC	290
34	Kelowna, BC	265
35	Longueuil, QC	240
35	St. John's, NL	240
37	Kingston, ON	225
38	St. Catharines, ON	210
39	Québec, QC	175
40	Barrie, ON	165
41	Greater Sudbury, ON	155
42	Sherbrooke, QC	145
43	Gatineau, QC	125
44	Langley, BC	95
45	Chatham-Kent, ON	75
46	Thunder Bay, ON	55
47	Lévis, QC	0
47	Saguenay, QC	0
47	Terrebonne, QC	0
47	Trois-Rivières, QC	0
–	Canada	247,525

Note: Religion refers to the person's self-identification as having a connection or affiliation with any religious denomination, group, body, sect, cult or other religiously defined community or system of belief. Religion is not limited to formal membership in a religious organization or group. Persons without a religious connection or affiliation can self-identify as atheist, agnostic or humanist, or can provide another applicable response.

Source: Statistics Canada. 2013. 2011 National Household Survey. Statistics Canada Catalogue no. 99-004-XWE. Ottawa. Released September 11, 2013.

Cities Ranked by Religion: Hindu
By Percent

Total

Rank	City	Percent
1	Brampton, ON	12.2%
2	Markham, ON	9.8%
3	Mississauga, ON	7.0%
4	Ajax, ON	5.9%
5	Toronto, ON	5.6%
6	Vaughan, ON	4.5%
7	Surrey, BC	3.6%
8	Richmond Hill, ON	2.4%
9	Burnaby, BC	2.2%
10	Oakville, ON	2.1%
11	Edmonton, AB	1.9%
12	Calgary, AB	1.6%
12	Whitby, ON	1.6%
14	Abbotsford, BC	1.5%
14	Cambridge, ON	1.5%
14	Guelph, ON	1.5%
17	Montréal, QC	1.4%
17	Ottawa, ON	1.4%
17	Richmond, BC	1.4%
17	Vancouver, BC	1.4%
21	Kitchener, ON	1.2%
21	Windsor, ON	1.2%
23	Burlington, ON	1.1%
24	Winnipeg, MB	1.0%
25	Coquitlam, BC	0.9%
26	Hamilton, ON	0.8%
26	London, ON	0.8%
26	Regina, SK	0.8%
29	Saskatoon, SK	0.7%
30	Laval, QC	0.6%
30	Saanich, BC	0.6%
32	Oshawa, ON	0.5%
32	St. John's, NL	0.5%
34	Halifax, NS	0.4%
34	Kelowna, BC	0.4%
34	Kingston, ON	0.4%
37	Barrie, ON	0.3%
37	St. Catharines, ON	0.3%
39	Chatham-Kent, ON	0.2%
39	Greater Sudbury, ON	0.2%
39	Langley, BC	0.2%
39	Longueuil, QC	0.2%
39	Sherbrooke, QC	0.2%
44	Gatineau, QC	0.1%
44	Québec, QC	0.1%
44	Thunder Bay, ON	0.1%
47	Lévis, QC	0.0%
47	Saguenay, QC	0.0%
47	Terrebonne, QC	0.0%
47	Trois-Rivières, QC	0.0%
–	Canada	1.5%

Male

Rank	City	Percent
1	Brampton, ON	12.3%
2	Markham, ON	10.1%
3	Mississauga, ON	7.0%
4	Toronto, ON	5.9%
5	Ajax, ON	5.8%
6	Vaughan, ON	4.7%
7	Surrey, BC	3.7%
8	Richmond Hill, ON	2.5%
9	Burnaby, BC	2.2%
10	Oakville, ON	2.1%
11	Edmonton, AB	1.9%
12	Calgary, AB	1.7%
13	Whitby, ON	1.6%
14	Abbotsford, BC	1.5%
14	Cambridge, ON	1.5%
14	Montréal, QC	1.5%
14	Ottawa, ON	1.5%
14	Vancouver, BC	1.5%
19	Guelph, ON	1.4%
19	Richmond, BC	1.4%
21	Windsor, ON	1.3%
22	Burlington, ON	1.2%
22	Kitchener, ON	1.2%
24	Winnipeg, MB	1.1%
25	Regina, SK	0.9%
26	Coquitlam, BC	0.8%
26	Hamilton, ON	0.8%
26	London, ON	0.8%
26	Saskatoon, SK	0.8%
30	Saanich, BC	0.7%
31	Laval, QC	0.6%
31	Oshawa, ON	0.6%
33	Kingston, ON	0.5%
33	St. John's, NL	0.5%
35	Barrie, ON	0.4%
35	Halifax, NS	0.4%
35	Kelowna, BC	0.4%
38	Longueuil, QC	0.3%
38	St. Catharines, ON	0.3%
40	Chatham-Kent, ON	0.2%
40	Greater Sudbury, ON	0.2%
40	Langley, BC	0.2%
40	Sherbrooke, QC	0.2%
44	Gatineau, QC	0.1%
44	Québec, QC	0.1%
44	Thunder Bay, ON	0.1%
47	Lévis, QC	0.0%
47	Saguenay, QC	0.0%
47	Terrebonne, QC	0.0%
47	Trois-Rivières, QC	0.0%
–	Canada	1.5%

Female

Rank	City	Percent
1	Brampton, ON	12.0%
2	Markham, ON	9.6%
3	Mississauga, ON	6.9%
4	Ajax, ON	6.1%
5	Toronto, ON	5.4%
6	Vaughan, ON	4.3%
7	Surrey, BC	3.6%
8	Richmond Hill, ON	2.3%
9	Burnaby, BC	2.2%
10	Oakville, ON	2.0%
11	Edmonton, AB	1.8%
12	Guelph, ON	1.6%
12	Whitby, ON	1.6%
14	Abbotsford, BC	1.5%
14	Calgary, AB	1.5%
14	Cambridge, ON	1.5%
17	Richmond, BC	1.4%
18	Montréal, QC	1.3%
18	Ottawa, ON	1.3%
18	Vancouver, BC	1.3%
21	Kitchener, ON	1.2%
22	Burlington, ON	1.1%
22	Windsor, ON	1.1%
24	Coquitlam, BC	1.0%
24	Winnipeg, MB	1.0%
26	London, ON	0.8%
27	Hamilton, ON	0.7%
27	Regina, SK	0.7%
27	Saskatoon, SK	0.7%
30	Laval, QC	0.6%
31	Saanich, BC	0.5%
32	Halifax, NS	0.4%
32	Kelowna, BC	0.4%
32	Kingston, ON	0.4%
32	Oshawa, ON	0.4%
32	St. John's, NL	0.4%
37	St. Catharines, ON	0.3%
38	Barrie, ON	0.2%
38	Greater Sudbury, ON	0.2%
38	Langley, BC	0.2%
38	Longueuil, QC	0.2%
38	Sherbrooke, QC	0.2%
43	Chatham-Kent, ON	0.1%
43	Gatineau, QC	0.1%
43	Québec, QC	0.1%
43	Thunder Bay, ON	0.1%
47	Lévis, QC	0.0%
47	Saguenay, QC	0.0%
47	Terrebonne, QC	0.0%
47	Trois-Rivières, QC	0.0%
–	Canada	1.5%

Note: Religion refers to the person's self-identification as having a connection or affiliation with any religious denomination, group, body, sect, cult or other religiously defined community or system of belief. Religion is not limited to formal membership in a religious organization or group. Persons without a religious connection or affiliation can self-identify as atheist, agnostic or humanist, or can provide another applicable response.
Source: Statistics Canada. 2013. 2011 National Household Survey. Statistics Canada Catalogue no. 99-004-XWE. Ottawa. Released September 11, 2013.

Cities Ranked by Religion: Jewish
By Number

Total

Rank	City	Number
1	Toronto, ON	98,690
2	Vaughan, ON	43,760
3	Montréal, QC	35,785
4	Ottawa, ON	10,615
5	Winnipeg, MB	10,535
6	Vancouver, BC	10,350
7	Richmond Hill, ON	10,125
8	Markham, ON	7,330
9	Calgary, AB	5,995
10	Edmonton, AB	3,445
11	Hamilton, ON	3,335
12	Laval, QC	2,915
13	Richmond, BC	2,885
14	Mississauga, ON	1,830
15	London, ON	1,715
16	Halifax, NS	1,340
17	Surrey, BC	1,105
18	Windsor, ON	925
19	Oakville, ON	910
20	Brampton, ON	830
21	Kingston, ON	785
22	Barrie, ON	665
23	Burlington, ON	660
24	Kitchener, ON	620
25	Burnaby, BC	605
26	Coquitlam, BC	560
27	Saanich, BC	555
28	Guelph, ON	490
29	St. Catharines, ON	480
30	Whitby, ON	445
31	Oshawa, ON	440
32	Saskatoon, SK	420
33	Ajax, ON	410
34	Regina, SK	335
35	Kelowna, BC	215
36	Abbotsford, BC	210
36	Gatineau, QC	210
38	Longueuil, QC	185
39	Langley, BC	170
40	Cambridge, ON	145
41	Québec, QC	140
42	Thunder Bay, ON	135
43	Greater Sudbury, ON	120
44	St. John's, NL	110
45	Sherbrooke, QC	85
46	Chatham-Kent, ON	65
47	Terrebonne, QC	50
48	Lévis, QC	25
49	Trois-Rivières, QC	15
50	Saguenay, QC	0
–	Canada	329,495

Male

Rank	City	Number
1	Toronto, ON	47,925
2	Vaughan, ON	21,405
3	Montréal, QC	17,550
4	Ottawa, ON	5,400
5	Winnipeg, MB	5,170
6	Richmond Hill, ON	5,010
7	Vancouver, BC	4,995
8	Markham, ON	3,520
9	Calgary, AB	2,925
10	Hamilton, ON	1,710
11	Edmonton, AB	1,695
12	Richmond, BC	1,520
13	Laval, QC	1,475
14	Mississauga, ON	955
15	London, ON	815
16	Halifax, NS	630
17	Surrey, BC	565
18	Windsor, ON	445
19	Oakville, ON	415
20	Brampton, ON	380
21	Kingston, ON	360
22	Barrie, ON	355
23	Burlington, ON	330
23	Kitchener, ON	330
25	St. Catharines, ON	300
26	Burnaby, BC	295
27	Coquitlam, BC	280
27	Guelph, ON	280
29	Whitby, ON	275
30	Oshawa, ON	230
31	Saanich, BC	225
31	Saskatoon, SK	225
33	Regina, SK	190
34	Ajax, ON	180
35	Gatineau, QC	125
36	Kelowna, BC	115
37	Longueuil, QC	110
38	Abbotsford, BC	100
39	Langley, BC	85
39	Québec, QC	85
41	Thunder Bay, ON	80
42	Cambridge, ON	75
42	Greater Sudbury, ON	75
44	St. John's, NL	50
45	Sherbrooke, QC	35
45	Terrebonne, QC	35
47	Lévis, QC	20
48	Chatham-Kent, ON	0
48	Saguenay, QC	0
48	Trois-Rivières, QC	0
–	Canada	161,265

Female

Rank	City	Number
1	Toronto, ON	50,765
2	Vaughan, ON	22,355
3	Montréal, QC	18,235
4	Winnipeg, MB	5,365
5	Vancouver, BC	5,355
6	Ottawa, ON	5,210
7	Richmond Hill, ON	5,115
8	Markham, ON	3,815
9	Calgary, AB	3,075
10	Edmonton, AB	1,750
11	Hamilton, ON	1,620
12	Laval, QC	1,440
13	Richmond, BC	1,365
14	London, ON	900
15	Mississauga, ON	875
16	Halifax, NS	715
17	Surrey, BC	540
18	Oakville, ON	490
19	Windsor, ON	480
20	Brampton, ON	450
21	Kingston, ON	420
22	Burlington, ON	335
23	Saanich, BC	330
24	Barrie, ON	305
24	Burnaby, BC	305
26	Kitchener, ON	290
27	Coquitlam, BC	280
28	Ajax, ON	235
29	Guelph, ON	210
29	Oshawa, ON	210
31	Saskatoon, SK	190
32	St. Catharines, ON	175
33	Whitby, ON	165
34	Regina, SK	140
35	Abbotsford, BC	115
36	Kelowna, BC	100
37	Gatineau, QC	80
37	Langley, BC	80
39	Longueuil, QC	75
40	Cambridge, ON	70
41	St. John's, NL	60
42	Québec, QC	55
42	Thunder Bay, ON	55
44	Sherbrooke, QC	50
45	Greater Sudbury, ON	45
46	Chatham-Kent, ON	35
47	Terrebonne, QC	20
48	Lévis, QC	0
48	Saguenay, QC	0
48	Trois-Rivières, QC	0
–	Canada	168,235

Note: Religion refers to the person's self-identification as having a connection or affiliation with any religious denomination, group, body, sect, cult or other religiously defined community or system of belief. Religion is not limited to formal membership in a religious organization or group. Persons without a religious connection or affiliation can self-identify as atheist, agnostic or humanist, or can provide another applicable response.
Source: Statistics Canada. 2013. 2011 National Household Survey. Statistics Canada Catalogue no. 99-004-XWE. Ottawa. Released September 11, 2013.

Cities Ranked by Religion: Jewish
By Percent

Total

Rank	City	Percent
1	Vaughan, ON	15.3%
2	Richmond Hill, ON	5.5%
3	Toronto, ON	3.8%
4	Markham, ON	2.4%
5	Montréal, QC	2.2%
6	Vancouver, BC	1.8%
7	Winnipeg, MB	1.6%
8	Richmond, BC	1.5%
9	Ottawa, ON	1.2%
10	Hamilton, ON	0.7%
10	Kingston, ON	0.7%
10	Laval, QC	0.7%
13	Calgary, AB	0.6%
14	Barrie, ON	0.5%
14	London, ON	0.5%
14	Oakville, ON	0.5%
14	Saanich, BC	0.5%
18	Ajax, ON	0.4%
18	Burlington, ON	0.4%
18	Coquitlam, BC	0.4%
18	Edmonton, AB	0.4%
18	Guelph, ON	0.4%
18	St. Catharines, ON	0.4%
18	Whitby, ON	0.4%
18	Windsor, ON	0.4%
26	Burnaby, BC	0.3%
26	Halifax, NS	0.3%
26	Kitchener, ON	0.3%
26	Mississauga, ON	0.3%
26	Oshawa, ON	0.3%
31	Abbotsford, BC	0.2%
31	Brampton, ON	0.2%
31	Kelowna, BC	0.2%
31	Langley, BC	0.2%
31	Regina, SK	0.2%
31	Saskatoon, SK	0.2%
31	Surrey, BC	0.2%
38	Cambridge, ON	0.1%
38	Chatham-Kent, ON	0.1%
38	Gatineau, QC	0.1%
38	Greater Sudbury, ON	0.1%
38	Longueuil, QC	0.1%
38	Sherbrooke, QC	0.1%
38	St. John's, NL	0.1%
38	Thunder Bay, ON	0.1%
46	Lévis, QC	0.0%
46	Québec, QC	0.0%
46	Saguenay, QC	0.0%
46	Terrebonne, QC	0.0%
46	Trois-Rivières, QC	0.0%
–	Canada	1.0%

Male

Rank	City	Percent
1	Vaughan, ON	15.3%
2	Richmond Hill, ON	5.6%
3	Toronto, ON	3.9%
4	Markham, ON	2.4%
5	Montréal, QC	2.2%
6	Richmond, BC	1.7%
6	Vancouver, BC	1.7%
8	Winnipeg, MB	1.6%
9	Ottawa, ON	1.3%
10	Laval, QC	0.8%
11	Hamilton, ON	0.7%
12	Kingston, ON	0.6%
13	Barrie, ON	0.5%
13	Calgary, AB	0.5%
13	Coquitlam, BC	0.5%
13	Guelph, ON	0.5%
13	London, ON	0.5%
13	Oakville, ON	0.5%
13	St. Catharines, ON	0.5%
13	Whitby, ON	0.5%
21	Burlington, ON	0.4%
21	Edmonton, AB	0.4%
21	Saanich, BC	0.4%
21	Windsor, ON	0.4%
25	Ajax, ON	0.3%
25	Burnaby, BC	0.3%
25	Halifax, NS	0.3%
25	Kitchener, ON	0.3%
25	Mississauga, ON	0.3%
25	Oshawa, ON	0.3%
31	Abbotsford, BC	0.2%
31	Kelowna, BC	0.2%
31	Langley, BC	0.2%
31	Regina, SK	0.2%
31	Saskatoon, SK	0.2%
31	Surrey, BC	0.2%
31	Thunder Bay, ON	0.2%
38	Brampton, ON	0.1%
38	Cambridge, ON	0.1%
38	Gatineau, QC	0.1%
38	Greater Sudbury, ON	0.1%
38	Longueuil, QC	0.1%
38	St. John's, NL	0.1%
38	Terrebonne, QC	0.1%
45	Chatham-Kent, ON	0.0%
45	Lévis, QC	0.0%
45	Québec, QC	0.0%
45	Saguenay, QC	0.0%
45	Sherbrooke, QC	0.0%
45	Trois-Rivières, QC	0.0%
–	Canada	1.0%

Female

Rank	City	Percent
1	Vaughan, ON	15.3%
2	Richmond Hill, ON	5.4%
3	Toronto, ON	3.8%
4	Markham, ON	2.5%
5	Montréal, QC	2.2%
6	Vancouver, BC	1.8%
7	Winnipeg, MB	1.6%
8	Richmond, BC	1.4%
9	Ottawa, ON	1.2%
10	Kingston, ON	0.7%
10	Laval, QC	0.7%
12	Calgary, AB	0.6%
12	Hamilton, ON	0.6%
12	Saanich, BC	0.6%
15	London, ON	0.5%
15	Oakville, ON	0.5%
17	Ajax, ON	0.4%
17	Barrie, ON	0.4%
17	Burlington, ON	0.4%
17	Coquitlam, BC	0.4%
17	Edmonton, AB	0.4%
17	Halifax, NS	0.4%
17	Windsor, ON	0.4%
24	Burnaby, BC	0.3%
24	Guelph, ON	0.3%
24	Kitchener, ON	0.3%
24	Oshawa, ON	0.3%
24	St. Catharines, ON	0.3%
24	Whitby, ON	0.3%
30	Abbotsford, BC	0.2%
30	Brampton, ON	0.2%
30	Kelowna, BC	0.2%
30	Langley, BC	0.2%
30	Mississauga, ON	0.2%
30	Saskatoon, SK	0.2%
30	Surrey, BC	0.2%
37	Cambridge, ON	0.1%
37	Chatham-Kent, ON	0.1%
37	Gatineau, QC	0.1%
37	Greater Sudbury, ON	0.1%
37	Longueuil, QC	0.1%
37	Regina, SK	0.1%
37	Sherbrooke, QC	0.1%
37	St. John's, NL	0.1%
37	Thunder Bay, ON	0.1%
46	Lévis, QC	0.0%
46	Québec, QC	0.0%
46	Saguenay, QC	0.0%
46	Terrebonne, QC	0.0%
46	Trois-Rivières, QC	0.0%
–	Canada	1.0%

Note: Religion refers to the person's self-identification as having a connection or affiliation with any religious denomination, group, body, sect, cult or other religiously defined community or system of belief. Religion is not limited to formal membership in a religious organization or group. Persons without a religious connection or affiliation can self-identify as atheist, agnostic or humanist, or can provide another applicable response.
Source: Statistics Canada. 2013. 2011 National Household Survey. Statistics Canada Catalogue no. 99-004-XWE. Ottawa. Released September 11, 2013.

Cities Ranked by Religion: Muslim
By Number

Total

Rank	City	Number
1	Toronto, ON	212,345
2	Montréal, QC	154,540
3	Mississauga, ON	84,325
4	Ottawa, ON	58,415
5	Calgary, AB	56,785
6	Edmonton, AB	43,645
7	Brampton, ON	36,960
8	Laval, QC	25,740
9	Markham, ON	22,415
10	Richmond Hill, ON	21,245
11	Hamilton, ON	19,025
12	Surrey, BC	18,345
13	London, ON	15,780
14	Windsor, ON	14,305
15	Vaughan, ON	14,080
16	Vancouver, BC	13,255
17	Winnipeg, MB	11,230
18	Kitchener, ON	10,590
19	Burnaby, BC	9,900
20	Longueuil, QC	9,565
21	Ajax, ON	7,550
22	Halifax, NS	7,535
23	Gatineau, QC	7,190
24	Oakville, ON	7,180
25	Coquitlam, BC	6,475
26	Québec, QC	6,125
27	Saskatoon, SK	5,655
28	Richmond, BC	5,530
29	Cambridge, ON	3,760
30	Regina, SK	3,545
31	Whitby, ON	3,485
32	Burlington, ON	3,435
33	Guelph, ON	3,185
34	St. Catharines, ON	2,630
35	Sherbrooke, QC	2,515
36	Oshawa, ON	1,895
37	Kingston, ON	1,735
38	Terrebonne, QC	1,580
39	Barrie, ON	1,405
40	Saanich, BC	1,120
41	St. John's, NL	960
42	Trois-Rivières, QC	910
43	Abbotsford, BC	715
44	Greater Sudbury, ON	650
45	Langley, BC	575
46	Kelowna, BC	480
47	Lévis, QC	420
48	Thunder Bay, ON	345
49	Chatham-Kent, ON	335
49	Saguenay, QC	335
–	Canada	1,053,945

Male

Rank	City	Number
1	Toronto, ON	106,425
2	Montréal, QC	82,235
3	Mississauga, ON	43,205
4	Ottawa, ON	29,460
5	Calgary, AB	29,225
6	Edmonton, AB	22,755
7	Brampton, ON	18,430
8	Laval, QC	12,820
9	Markham, ON	11,165
10	Richmond Hill, ON	10,325
11	Hamilton, ON	9,905
12	Surrey, BC	9,200
13	London, ON	7,980
14	Windsor, ON	7,295
15	Vaughan, ON	7,080
16	Vancouver, BC	6,865
17	Winnipeg, MB	5,715
18	Kitchener, ON	5,175
19	Longueuil, QC	4,945
20	Burnaby, BC	4,935
21	Halifax, NS	4,205
22	Gatineau, QC	3,865
23	Ajax, ON	3,760
24	Oakville, ON	3,600
25	Québec, QC	3,320
26	Coquitlam, BC	3,230
27	Saskatoon, SK	2,930
28	Richmond, BC	2,860
29	Cambridge, ON	2,010
30	Regina, SK	1,805
31	Whitby, ON	1,745
32	Burlington, ON	1,710
33	Guelph, ON	1,690
34	Sherbrooke, QC	1,410
35	St. Catharines, ON	1,365
36	Kingston, ON	955
36	Oshawa, ON	955
38	Terrebonne, QC	850
39	Barrie, ON	760
40	St. John's, NL	570
41	Saanich, BC	565
42	Trois-Rivières, QC	495
43	Abbotsford, BC	400
44	Greater Sudbury, ON	375
45	Langley, BC	285
46	Lévis, QC	275
47	Kelowna, BC	235
48	Thunder Bay, ON	205
49	Chatham-Kent, ON	165
50	Saguenay, QC	160
–	Canada	540,555

Female

Rank	City	Number
1	Toronto, ON	105,920
2	Montréal, QC	72,310
3	Mississauga, ON	41,120
4	Ottawa, ON	28,955
5	Calgary, AB	27,560
6	Edmonton, AB	20,890
7	Brampton, ON	18,530
8	Laval, QC	12,920
9	Markham, ON	11,255
10	Richmond Hill, ON	10,920
11	Surrey, BC	9,145
12	Hamilton, ON	9,120
13	London, ON	7,805
14	Windsor, ON	7,010
15	Vaughan, ON	7,000
16	Vancouver, BC	6,395
17	Winnipeg, MB	5,520
18	Kitchener, ON	5,415
19	Burnaby, BC	4,965
20	Longueuil, QC	4,625
21	Ajax, ON	3,790
22	Oakville, ON	3,580
23	Halifax, NS	3,330
24	Gatineau, QC	3,325
25	Coquitlam, BC	3,245
26	Québec, QC	2,805
27	Saskatoon, SK	2,725
28	Richmond, BC	2,675
29	Cambridge, ON	1,745
30	Regina, SK	1,740
31	Whitby, ON	1,735
32	Burlington, ON	1,730
33	Guelph, ON	1,495
34	St. Catharines, ON	1,255
35	Sherbrooke, QC	1,100
36	Oshawa, ON	940
37	Kingston, ON	780
38	Terrebonne, QC	735
39	Barrie, ON	645
40	Saanich, BC	555
41	Trois-Rivières, QC	415
42	St. John's, NL	390
43	Abbotsford, BC	315
44	Langley, BC	290
45	Greater Sudbury, ON	270
46	Kelowna, BC	240
47	Saguenay, QC	180
48	Chatham-Kent, ON	165
49	Lévis, QC	145
50	Thunder Bay, ON	140
–	Canada	513,395

Note: Religion refers to the person's self-identification as having a connection or affiliation with any religious denomination, group, body, sect, cult or other religiously defined community or system of belief. Religion is not limited to formal membership in a religious organization or group. Persons without a religious connection or affiliation can self-identify as atheist, agnostic or humanist, or can provide another applicable response.
Source: Statistics Canada. 2013. 2011 National Household Survey. Statistics Canada Catalogue no. 99-004-XWE. Ottawa. Released September 11, 2013.

Cities Ranked by Religion: Muslim
By Percent

Total

Rank	City	Percent
1	Mississauga, ON	11.9%
2	Richmond Hill, ON	11.5%
3	Montréal, QC	9.6%
4	Toronto, ON	8.2%
5	Markham, ON	7.5%
6	Brampton, ON	7.1%
7	Ajax, ON	6.9%
7	Windsor, ON	6.9%
9	Ottawa, ON	6.7%
10	Laval, QC	6.6%
11	Edmonton, AB	5.5%
12	Calgary, AB	5.2%
12	Coquitlam, BC	5.2%
14	Kitchener, ON	4.9%
14	Vaughan, ON	4.9%
16	Burnaby, BC	4.5%
17	London, ON	4.4%
18	Longueuil, QC	4.2%
19	Oakville, ON	4.0%
19	Surrey, BC	4.0%
21	Hamilton, ON	3.7%
22	Cambridge, ON	3.0%
23	Richmond, BC	2.9%
23	Whitby, ON	2.9%
25	Gatineau, QC	2.7%
26	Guelph, ON	2.6%
26	Saskatoon, SK	2.6%
28	Vancouver, BC	2.2%
29	Burlington, ON	2.0%
29	Halifax, NS	2.0%
29	St. Catharines, ON	2.0%
32	Regina, SK	1.9%
33	Sherbrooke, QC	1.7%
33	Winnipeg, MB	1.7%
35	Kingston, ON	1.5%
35	Terrebonne, QC	1.5%
37	Oshawa, ON	1.3%
38	Québec, QC	1.2%
39	Barrie, ON	1.1%
40	Saanich, BC	1.0%
41	St. John's, NL	0.9%
42	Trois-Rivières, QC	0.7%
43	Langley, BC	0.6%
44	Abbotsford, BC	0.5%
45	Greater Sudbury, ON	0.4%
45	Kelowna, BC	0.4%
47	Chatham-Kent, ON	0.3%
47	Lévis, QC	0.3%
47	Thunder Bay, ON	0.3%
50	Saguenay, QC	0.2%
–	Canada	3.2%

Male

Rank	City	Percent
1	Mississauga, ON	12.4%
2	Richmond Hill, ON	11.5%
3	Montréal, QC	10.5%
4	Toronto, ON	8.6%
5	Markham, ON	7.6%
6	Brampton, ON	7.2%
6	Windsor, ON	7.2%
8	Ajax, ON	7.1%
9	Ottawa, ON	7.0%
10	Laval, QC	6.7%
11	Edmonton, AB	5.7%
12	Calgary, AB	5.4%
13	Coquitlam, BC	5.2%
14	Vaughan, ON	5.1%
15	Kitchener, ON	4.8%
16	Burnaby, BC	4.6%
16	London, ON	4.6%
18	Longueuil, QC	4.5%
19	Oakville, ON	4.1%
20	Hamilton, ON	4.0%
20	Surrey, BC	4.0%
22	Cambridge, ON	3.3%
23	Richmond, BC	3.1%
24	Gatineau, QC	3.0%
24	Whitby, ON	3.0%
26	Guelph, ON	2.9%
27	Saskatoon, SK	2.7%
28	Vancouver, BC	2.4%
29	Halifax, NS	2.3%
30	St. Catharines, ON	2.2%
31	Burlington, ON	2.0%
32	Regina, SK	1.9%
32	Sherbrooke, QC	1.9%
34	Winnipeg, MB	1.8%
35	Kingston, ON	1.7%
36	Terrebonne, QC	1.6%
37	Québec, QC	1.4%
38	Oshawa, ON	1.3%
39	Barrie, ON	1.2%
39	St. John's, NL	1.2%
41	Saanich, BC	1.1%
42	Trois-Rivières, QC	0.8%
43	Abbotsford, BC	0.6%
43	Langley, BC	0.6%
45	Greater Sudbury, ON	0.5%
46	Kelowna, BC	0.4%
46	Lévis, QC	0.4%
46	Thunder Bay, ON	0.4%
49	Chatham-Kent, ON	0.3%
50	Saguenay, QC	0.2%
–	Canada	3.3%

Female

Rank	City	Percent
1	Richmond Hill, ON	11.6%
2	Mississauga, ON	11.4%
3	Montréal, QC	8.8%
4	Toronto, ON	7.9%
5	Markham, ON	7.3%
6	Brampton, ON	7.0%
7	Ajax, ON	6.7%
8	Windsor, ON	6.6%
9	Ottawa, ON	6.5%
10	Laval, QC	6.4%
11	Edmonton, AB	5.2%
12	Calgary, AB	5.1%
12	Coquitlam, BC	5.1%
14	Kitchener, ON	5.0%
15	Vaughan, ON	4.8%
16	Burnaby, BC	4.4%
17	London, ON	4.2%
18	Longueuil, QC	3.9%
18	Oakville, ON	3.9%
18	Surrey, BC	3.9%
21	Hamilton, ON	3.5%
22	Cambridge, ON	2.8%
22	Whitby, ON	2.8%
24	Richmond, BC	2.7%
25	Gatineau, QC	2.5%
25	Saskatoon, SK	2.5%
27	Guelph, ON	2.4%
28	Vancouver, BC	2.1%
29	Burlington, ON	1.9%
29	St. Catharines, ON	1.9%
31	Regina, SK	1.8%
32	Halifax, NS	1.7%
32	Winnipeg, MB	1.7%
34	Sherbrooke, QC	1.4%
34	Terrebonne, QC	1.4%
36	Kingston, ON	1.3%
37	Oshawa, ON	1.2%
38	Québec, QC	1.1%
39	Saanich, BC	1.0%
40	Barrie, ON	0.9%
41	St. John's, NL	0.7%
42	Langley, BC	0.6%
42	Trois-Rivières, QC	0.6%
44	Abbotsford, BC	0.5%
45	Kelowna, BC	0.4%
46	Chatham-Kent, ON	0.3%
46	Greater Sudbury, ON	0.3%
46	Saguenay, QC	0.3%
46	Thunder Bay, ON	0.3%
50	Lévis, QC	0.2%
–	Canada	3.1%

Note: Religion refers to the person's self-identification as having a connection or affiliation with any religious denomination, group, body, sect, cult or other religiously defined community or system of belief. Religion is not limited to formal membership in a religious organization or group. Persons without a religious connection or affiliation can self-identify as atheist, agnostic or humanist, or can provide another applicable response.
Source: Statistics Canada. 2013. 2011 National Household Survey. Statistics Canada Catalogue no. 99-004-XWE. Ottawa. Released September 11, 2013.

Cities Ranked by Religion: Sikh
By Number

Total

Rank	City	Number
1	Surrey, BC	104,720
2	Brampton, ON	97,790
3	Calgary, AB	28,565
4	Abbotsford, BC	26,145
5	Mississauga, ON	23,995
6	Toronto, ON	20,405
7	Edmonton, AB	19,555
8	Vancouver, BC	16,815
9	Winnipeg, MB	9,800
10	Richmond, BC	7,155
11	Burnaby, BC	6,395
12	Montréal, QC	5,415
13	Vaughan, ON	5,030
14	Markham, ON	4,335
15	Hamilton, ON	4,260
16	Ottawa, ON	3,410
17	Oakville, ON	2,610
18	Saanich, BC	2,380
19	Langley, BC	1,965
20	Burlington, ON	1,655
21	Kelowna, BC	1,525
22	Windsor, ON	1,500
23	Cambridge, ON	1,430
23	Coquitlam, BC	1,430
25	Kitchener, ON	1,360
26	Guelph, ON	1,195
27	Laval, QC	1,015
28	Regina, SK	925
29	Richmond Hill, ON	910
30	London, ON	715
31	Ajax, ON	590
32	Saskatoon, SK	580
33	Halifax, NS	350
34	Whitby, ON	245
35	Oshawa, ON	195
36	Barrie, ON	140
37	Kingston, ON	125
38	St. John's, NL	85
39	Greater Sudbury, ON	75
40	Longueuil, QC	65
41	Thunder Bay, ON	60
42	St. Catharines, ON	35
43	Chatham-Kent, ON	30
44	Gatineau, QC	25
45	Lévis, QC	0
45	Québec, QC	0
45	Saguenay, QC	0
45	Sherbrooke, QC	0
45	Terrebonne, QC	0
45	Trois-Rivières, QC	0
–	Canada	454,965

Male

Rank	City	Number
1	Surrey, BC	52,380
2	Brampton, ON	49,345
3	Calgary, AB	14,620
4	Abbotsford, BC	13,020
5	Mississauga, ON	12,190
6	Toronto, ON	10,185
7	Edmonton, AB	10,050
8	Vancouver, BC	8,575
9	Winnipeg, MB	4,910
10	Richmond, BC	3,640
11	Burnaby, BC	3,275
12	Montréal, QC	3,090
13	Vaughan, ON	2,500
14	Markham, ON	2,240
15	Hamilton, ON	2,175
16	Ottawa, ON	1,855
17	Oakville, ON	1,220
18	Saanich, BC	1,150
19	Langley, BC	975
20	Kelowna, BC	820
21	Burlington, ON	815
22	Windsor, ON	765
23	Coquitlam, BC	695
24	Kitchener, ON	680
25	Cambridge, ON	670
26	Laval, QC	550
27	Guelph, ON	535
28	Richmond Hill, ON	510
29	Regina, SK	490
30	Saskatoon, SK	360
31	London, ON	345
32	Ajax, ON	285
33	Halifax, NS	180
34	Oshawa, ON	110
34	Whitby, ON	110
36	Barrie, ON	80
37	St. John's, NL	60
38	Longueuil, QC	55
39	Kingston, ON	50
40	Greater Sudbury, ON	45
41	Thunder Bay, ON	30
42	Chatham-Kent, ON	25
43	St. Catharines, ON	20
44	Gatineau, QC	0
44	Lévis, QC	0
44	Québec, QC	0
44	Saguenay, QC	0
44	Sherbrooke, QC	0
44	Terrebonne, QC	0
44	Trois-Rivières, QC	0
–	Canada	229,435

Female

Rank	City	Number
1	Surrey, BC	52,345
2	Brampton, ON	48,445
3	Calgary, AB	13,945
4	Abbotsford, BC	13,125
5	Mississauga, ON	11,810
6	Toronto, ON	10,220
7	Edmonton, AB	9,510
8	Vancouver, BC	8,235
9	Winnipeg, MB	4,890
10	Richmond, BC	3,515
11	Burnaby, BC	3,115
12	Vaughan, ON	2,540
13	Montréal, QC	2,330
14	Markham, ON	2,095
15	Hamilton, ON	2,090
16	Ottawa, ON	1,555
17	Oakville, ON	1,390
18	Saanich, BC	1,235
19	Langley, BC	990
20	Burlington, ON	840
21	Cambridge, ON	765
22	Coquitlam, BC	735
23	Windsor, ON	730
24	Kelowna, BC	700
25	Kitchener, ON	680
26	Guelph, ON	660
27	Laval, QC	465
28	Regina, SK	435
29	Richmond Hill, ON	400
30	London, ON	370
31	Ajax, ON	305
32	Saskatoon, SK	220
33	Halifax, NS	170
34	Whitby, ON	135
35	Oshawa, ON	85
36	Kingston, ON	80
37	Barrie, ON	60
38	Thunder Bay, ON	30
39	Greater Sudbury, ON	25
39	St. John's, NL	25
41	Gatineau, QC	20
41	St. Catharines, ON	20
43	Chatham-Kent, ON	0
43	Longueuil, QC	0
43	Lévis, QC	0
43	Québec, QC	0
43	Saguenay, QC	0
43	Sherbrooke, QC	0
43	Terrebonne, QC	0
43	Trois-Rivières, QC	0
–	Canada	225,530

Note: Religion refers to the person's self-identification as having a connection or affiliation with any religious denomination, group, body, sect, cult or other religiously defined community or system of belief. Religion is not limited to formal membership in a religious organization or group. Persons without a religious connection or affiliation can self-identify as atheist, agnostic or humanist, or can provide another applicable response.
Source: Statistics Canada. 2013. 2011 National Household Survey. Statistics Canada Catalogue no. 99-004-XWE. Ottawa. Released September 11, 2013.

Cities Ranked by Religion: Sikh
By Percent

Total

Rank	City	Percent
1	Surrey, BC	22.6%
2	Abbotsford, BC	20.0%
3	Brampton, ON	18.8%
4	Richmond, BC	3.8%
5	Mississauga, ON	3.4%
6	Burnaby, BC	2.9%
7	Vancouver, BC	2.8%
8	Calgary, AB	2.6%
9	Edmonton, AB	2.5%
10	Saanich, BC	2.2%
11	Langley, BC	1.9%
12	Vaughan, ON	1.8%
13	Winnipeg, MB	1.5%
14	Markham, ON	1.4%
14	Oakville, ON	1.4%
16	Kelowna, BC	1.3%
17	Cambridge, ON	1.1%
17	Coquitlam, BC	1.1%
19	Burlington, ON	1.0%
19	Guelph, ON	1.0%
21	Hamilton, ON	0.8%
21	Toronto, ON	0.8%
23	Windsor, ON	0.7%
24	Kitchener, ON	0.6%
25	Ajax, ON	0.5%
25	Regina, SK	0.5%
25	Richmond Hill, ON	0.5%
28	Ottawa, ON	0.4%
29	Laval, QC	0.3%
29	Montréal, QC	0.3%
29	Saskatoon, SK	0.3%
32	London, ON	0.2%
32	Whitby, ON	0.2%
34	Barrie, ON	0.1%
34	Halifax, NS	0.1%
34	Kingston, ON	0.1%
34	Oshawa, ON	0.1%
34	St. John's, NL	0.1%
34	Thunder Bay, ON	0.1%
40	Chatham-Kent, ON	0.0%
40	Gatineau, QC	0.0%
40	Greater Sudbury, ON	0.0%
40	Longueuil, QC	0.0%
40	Lévis, QC	0.0%
40	Québec, QC	0.0%
40	Saguenay, QC	0.0%
40	Sherbrooke, QC	0.0%
40	St. Catharines, ON	0.0%
40	Terrebonne, QC	0.0%
40	Trois-Rivières, QC	0.0%
–	Canada	1.4%

Male

Rank	City	Percent
1	Surrey, BC	22.8%
2	Abbotsford, BC	20.2%
3	Brampton, ON	19.2%
4	Richmond, BC	4.0%
5	Mississauga, ON	3.5%
6	Burnaby, BC	3.0%
6	Vancouver, BC	3.0%
8	Calgary, AB	2.7%
9	Edmonton, AB	2.5%
10	Saanich, BC	2.2%
11	Langley, BC	1.9%
12	Vaughan, ON	1.8%
13	Winnipeg, MB	1.6%
14	Kelowna, BC	1.5%
14	Markham, ON	1.5%
16	Oakville, ON	1.4%
17	Cambridge, ON	1.1%
17	Coquitlam, BC	1.1%
19	Burlington, ON	1.0%
20	Guelph, ON	0.9%
20	Hamilton, ON	0.9%
22	Toronto, ON	0.8%
22	Windsor, ON	0.8%
24	Kitchener, ON	0.6%
24	Richmond Hill, ON	0.6%
26	Ajax, ON	0.5%
26	Regina, SK	0.5%
28	Montréal, QC	0.4%
28	Ottawa, ON	0.4%
30	Laval, QC	0.3%
30	Saskatoon, SK	0.3%
32	London, ON	0.2%
32	Oshawa, ON	0.2%
32	Whitby, ON	0.2%
35	Barrie, ON	0.1%
35	Chatham-Kent, ON	0.1%
35	Greater Sudbury, ON	0.1%
35	Halifax, NS	0.1%
35	Kingston, ON	0.1%
35	St. John's, NL	0.1%
35	Thunder Bay, ON	0.1%
42	Gatineau, QC	0.0%
42	Longueuil, QC	0.0%
42	Lévis, QC	0.0%
42	Québec, QC	0.0%
42	Saguenay, QC	0.0%
42	Sherbrooke, QC	0.0%
42	St. Catharines, ON	0.0%
42	Terrebonne, QC	0.0%
42	Trois-Rivières, QC	0.0%
–	Canada	1.4%

Female

Rank	City	Percent
1	Surrey, BC	22.4%
2	Abbotsford, BC	19.8%
3	Brampton, ON	18.4%
4	Richmond, BC	3.6%
5	Mississauga, ON	3.3%
6	Burnaby, BC	2.8%
7	Vancouver, BC	2.7%
8	Calgary, AB	2.6%
9	Edmonton, AB	2.4%
10	Saanich, BC	2.2%
11	Langley, BC	1.9%
12	Vaughan, ON	1.7%
13	Oakville, ON	1.5%
13	Winnipeg, MB	1.5%
15	Markham, ON	1.4%
16	Cambridge, ON	1.2%
16	Coquitlam, BC	1.2%
16	Kelowna, BC	1.2%
19	Guelph, ON	1.1%
20	Burlington, ON	0.9%
21	Hamilton, ON	0.8%
21	Toronto, ON	0.8%
23	Windsor, ON	0.7%
24	Kitchener, ON	0.6%
25	Ajax, ON	0.5%
26	Regina, SK	0.4%
26	Richmond Hill, ON	0.4%
28	Montréal, QC	0.3%
28	Ottawa, ON	0.3%
30	Laval, QC	0.2%
30	London, ON	0.2%
30	Saskatoon, SK	0.2%
30	Whitby, ON	0.2%
34	Barrie, ON	0.1%
34	Halifax, NS	0.1%
34	Kingston, ON	0.1%
34	Oshawa, ON	0.1%
34	Thunder Bay, ON	0.1%
39	Chatham-Kent, ON	0.0%
39	Gatineau, QC	0.0%
39	Greater Sudbury, ON	0.0%
39	Longueuil, QC	0.0%
39	Lévis, QC	0.0%
39	Québec, QC	0.0%
39	Saguenay, QC	0.0%
39	Sherbrooke, QC	0.0%
39	St. Catharines, ON	0.0%
39	St. John's, NL	0.0%
39	Terrebonne, QC	0.0%
39	Trois-Rivières, QC	0.0%
–	Canada	1.4%

Note: Religion refers to the person's self-identification as having a connection or affiliation with any religious denomination, group, body, sect, cult or other religiously defined community or system of belief. Religion is not limited to formal membership in a religious organization or group. Persons without a religious connection or affiliation can self-identify as atheist, agnostic or humanist, or can provide another applicable response.
Source: Statistics Canada. 2013. 2011 National Household Survey. Statistics Canada Catalogue no. 99-004-XWE. Ottawa. Released September 11, 2013.

Cities Ranked by Religion: Traditional (Aboriginal) Spirituality

By Number

Total

Rank	City	Number
1	Winnipeg, MB	1,775
2	Edmonton, AB	1,240
3	Saskatoon, SK	1,080
4	Calgary, AB	915
5	Regina, SK	885
6	Toronto, ON	850
7	Vancouver, BC	545
8	Thunder Bay, ON	535
9	Hamilton, ON	450
10	Ottawa, ON	310
11	Greater Sudbury, ON	300
12	London, ON	280
13	Surrey, BC	180
14	Montréal, QC	105
15	Kitchener, ON	85
16	Kelowna, BC	70
16	Kingston, ON	70
18	Mississauga, ON	65
19	Gatineau, QC	60
19	St. Catharines, ON	60
19	Windsor, ON	60
22	Chatham-Kent, ON	55
23	Halifax, NS	45
24	Barrie, ON	40
25	Oshawa, ON	35
25	Richmond, BC	35
27	Abbotsford, BC	25
27	Saanich, BC	25
27	Vaughan, ON	25
27	Whitby, ON	25
31	Burnaby, BC	20
31	Markham, ON	20
31	Québec, QC	20
34	Coquitlam, BC	15
34	Guelph, ON	15
36	Cambridge, ON	10
36	Sherbrooke, QC	10
38	Ajax, ON	0
38	Brampton, ON	0
38	Burlington, ON	0
38	Langley, BC	0
38	Laval, QC	0
38	Longueuil, QC	0
38	Lévis, QC	0
38	Oakville, ON	0
38	Richmond Hill, ON	0
38	Saguenay, QC	0
38	St. John's, NL	0
38	Terrebonne, QC	0
38	Trois-Rivières, QC	0
–	Canada	64,935

Male

Rank	City	Number
1	Winnipeg, MB	695
2	Edmonton, AB	490
3	Regina, SK	460
4	Calgary, AB	435
4	Saskatoon, SK	435
6	Toronto, ON	400
7	Vancouver, BC	285
8	Thunder Bay, ON	195
9	Greater Sudbury, ON	190
10	London, ON	170
11	Hamilton, ON	130
12	Ottawa, ON	125
13	Surrey, BC	90
14	Kingston, ON	45
15	Kelowna, BC	40
15	Kitchener, ON	40
17	Montréal, QC	35
18	Chatham-Kent, ON	30
18	Mississauga, ON	30
20	Barrie, ON	20
20	Gatineau, QC	20
20	Windsor, ON	20
23	Halifax, NS	15
23	Markham, ON	15
25	Vaughan, ON	10
26	Abbotsford, BC	0
26	Ajax, ON	0
26	Brampton, ON	0
26	Burlington, ON	0
26	Burnaby, BC	0
26	Cambridge, ON	0
26	Coquitlam, BC	0
26	Guelph, ON	0
26	Langley, BC	0
26	Laval, QC	0
26	Longueuil, QC	0
26	Lévis, QC	0
26	Oakville, ON	0
26	Oshawa, ON	0
26	Québec, QC	0
26	Richmond, BC	0
26	Richmond Hill, ON	0
26	Saanich, BC	0
26	Saguenay, QC	0
26	Sherbrooke, QC	0
26	St. Catharines, ON	0
26	St. John's, NL	0
26	Terrebonne, QC	0
26	Trois-Rivières, QC	0
26	Whitby, ON	0
–	Canada	31,805

Female

Rank	City	Number
1	Winnipeg, MB	1,080
2	Edmonton, AB	755
3	Saskatoon, SK	645
4	Calgary, AB	480
5	Toronto, ON	450
6	Regina, SK	420
7	Thunder Bay, ON	340
8	Hamilton, ON	315
9	Vancouver, BC	265
10	Ottawa, ON	190
11	Greater Sudbury, ON	115
11	London, ON	115
13	Surrey, BC	85
14	Montréal, QC	65
15	Kitchener, ON	45
16	Windsor, ON	40
17	Gatineau, QC	35
17	Mississauga, ON	35
19	Halifax, NS	30
19	Kelowna, BC	30
19	Kingston, ON	30
22	Chatham-Kent, ON	20
22	Saanich, BC	20
22	St. Catharines, ON	20
25	Barrie, ON	15
25	Burnaby, BC	15
25	Guelph, ON	15
28	Coquitlam, BC	10
28	Oshawa, ON	10
28	Sherbrooke, QC	10
28	Vaughan, ON	10
32	Abbotsford, BC	0
32	Ajax, ON	0
32	Brampton, ON	0
32	Burlington, ON	0
32	Cambridge, ON	0
32	Langley, BC	0
32	Laval, QC	0
32	Longueuil, QC	0
32	Lévis, QC	0
32	Markham, ON	0
32	Oakville, ON	0
32	Québec, QC	0
32	Richmond, BC	0
32	Richmond Hill, ON	0
32	Saguenay, QC	0
32	St. John's, NL	0
32	Terrebonne, QC	0
32	Trois-Rivières, QC	0
32	Whitby, ON	0
–	Canada	33,135

Note: Religion refers to the person's self-identification as having a connection or affiliation with any religious denomination, group, body, sect, cult or other religiously defined community or system of belief. Religion is not limited to formal membership in a religious organization or group. Persons without a religious connection or affiliation can self-identify as atheist, agnostic or humanist, or can provide another applicable response.
Source: Statistics Canada. 2013. 2011 National Household Survey. Statistics Canada Catalogue no. 99-004-XWE. Ottawa. Released September 11, 2013.

Cities Ranked by Religion: Traditional (Aboriginal) Spirituality

By Percent

Total

Rank	City	Percent
1	Regina, SK	0.5%
1	Saskatoon, SK	0.5%
1	Thunder Bay, ON	0.5%
4	Winnipeg, MB	0.3%
5	Edmonton, AB	0.2%
5	Greater Sudbury, ON	0.2%
7	Calgary, AB	0.1%
7	Chatham-Kent, ON	0.1%
7	Hamilton, ON	0.1%
7	Kelowna, BC	0.1%
7	Kingston, ON	0.1%
7	London, ON	0.1%
7	Vancouver, BC	0.1%
14	Abbotsford, BC	0.0%
14	Ajax, ON	0.0%
14	Barrie, ON	0.0%
14	Brampton, ON	0.0%
14	Burlington, ON	0.0%
14	Burnaby, BC	0.0%
14	Cambridge, ON	0.0%
14	Coquitlam, BC	0.0%
14	Gatineau, QC	0.0%
14	Guelph, ON	0.0%
14	Halifax, NS	0.0%
14	Kitchener, ON	0.0%
14	Langley, BC	0.0%
14	Laval, QC	0.0%
14	Longueuil, QC	0.0%
14	Lévis, QC	0.0%
14	Markham, ON	0.0%
14	Mississauga, ON	0.0%
14	Montréal, QC	0.0%
14	Oakville, ON	0.0%
14	Oshawa, ON	0.0%
14	Ottawa, ON	0.0%
14	Québec, QC	0.0%
14	Richmond, BC	0.0%
14	Richmond Hill, ON	0.0%
14	Saanich, BC	0.0%
14	Saguenay, QC	0.0%
14	Sherbrooke, QC	0.0%
14	St. Catharines, ON	0.0%
14	St. John's, NL	0.0%
14	Surrey, BC	0.0%
14	Terrebonne, QC	0.0%
14	Toronto, ON	0.0%
14	Trois-Rivières, QC	0.0%
14	Vaughan, ON	0.0%
14	Whitby, ON	0.0%
14	Windsor, ON	0.0%
–	Canada	0.2%

Male

Rank	City	Percent
1	Regina, SK	0.5%
2	Saskatoon, SK	0.4%
2	Thunder Bay, ON	0.4%
4	Greater Sudbury, ON	0.2%
4	Winnipeg, MB	0.2%
6	Calgary, AB	0.1%
6	Chatham-Kent, ON	0.1%
6	Edmonton, AB	0.1%
6	Hamilton, ON	0.1%
6	Kelowna, BC	0.1%
6	Kingston, ON	0.1%
6	London, ON	0.1%
6	Vancouver, BC	0.1%
14	Abbotsford, BC	0.0%
14	Ajax, ON	0.0%
14	Barrie, ON	0.0%
14	Brampton, ON	0.0%
14	Burlington, ON	0.0%
14	Burnaby, BC	0.0%
14	Cambridge, ON	0.0%
14	Coquitlam, BC	0.0%
14	Gatineau, QC	0.0%
14	Guelph, ON	0.0%
14	Halifax, NS	0.0%
14	Kitchener, ON	0.0%
14	Langley, BC	0.0%
14	Laval, QC	0.0%
14	Longueuil, QC	0.0%
14	Lévis, QC	0.0%
14	Markham, ON	0.0%
14	Mississauga, ON	0.0%
14	Montréal, QC	0.0%
14	Oakville, ON	0.0%
14	Oshawa, ON	0.0%
14	Ottawa, ON	0.0%
14	Québec, QC	0.0%
14	Richmond, BC	0.0%
14	Richmond Hill, ON	0.0%
14	Saanich, BC	0.0%
14	Saguenay, QC	0.0%
14	Sherbrooke, QC	0.0%
14	St. Catharines, ON	0.0%
14	St. John's, NL	0.0%
14	Surrey, BC	0.0%
14	Terrebonne, QC	0.0%
14	Toronto, ON	0.0%
14	Trois-Rivières, QC	0.0%
14	Vaughan, ON	0.0%
14	Whitby, ON	0.0%
14	Windsor, ON	0.0%
–	Canada	0.2%

Female

Rank	City	Percent
1	Saskatoon, SK	0.6%
1	Thunder Bay, ON	0.6%
3	Regina, SK	0.4%
4	Winnipeg, MB	0.3%
5	Edmonton, AB	0.2%
6	Calgary, AB	0.1%
6	Greater Sudbury, ON	0.1%
6	Hamilton, ON	0.1%
6	Kelowna, BC	0.1%
6	London, ON	0.1%
6	Vancouver, BC	0.1%
12	Abbotsford, BC	0.0%
12	Ajax, ON	0.0%
12	Barrie, ON	0.0%
12	Brampton, ON	0.0%
12	Burlington, ON	0.0%
12	Burnaby, BC	0.0%
12	Cambridge, ON	0.0%
12	Chatham-Kent, ON	0.0%
12	Coquitlam, BC	0.0%
12	Gatineau, QC	0.0%
12	Guelph, ON	0.0%
12	Halifax, NS	0.0%
12	Kingston, ON	0.0%
12	Kitchener, ON	0.0%
12	Langley, BC	0.0%
12	Laval, QC	0.0%
12	Longueuil, QC	0.0%
12	Lévis, QC	0.0%
12	Markham, ON	0.0%
12	Mississauga, ON	0.0%
12	Montréal, QC	0.0%
12	Oakville, ON	0.0%
12	Oshawa, ON	0.0%
12	Ottawa, ON	0.0%
12	Québec, QC	0.0%
12	Richmond, BC	0.0%
12	Richmond Hill, ON	0.0%
12	Saanich, BC	0.0%
12	Saguenay, QC	0.0%
12	Sherbrooke, QC	0.0%
12	St. Catharines, ON	0.0%
12	St. John's, NL	0.0%
12	Surrey, BC	0.0%
12	Terrebonne, QC	0.0%
12	Toronto, ON	0.0%
12	Trois-Rivières, QC	0.0%
12	Vaughan, ON	0.0%
12	Whitby, ON	0.0%
12	Windsor, ON	0.0%
–	Canada	0.2%

Note: Religion refers to the person's self-identification as having a connection or affiliation with any religious denomination, group, body, sect, cult or other religiously defined community or system of belief. Religion is not limited to formal membership in a religious organization or group. Persons without a religious connection or affiliation can self-identify as atheist, agnostic or humanist, or can provide another applicable response.
Source: Statistics Canada. 2013. 2011 National Household Survey. Statistics Canada Catalogue no. 99-004-XWE. Ottawa. Released September 11, 2013.

Cities Ranked by Religion: Other Religions
By Number

Total

Rank	City	Number
1	Toronto, ON	12,950
2	Calgary, AB	6,085
3	Vancouver, BC	5,275
4	Ottawa, ON	5,255
5	Edmonton, AB	4,375
6	Montréal, QC	4,195
7	Mississauga, ON	3,185
8	Winnipeg, MB	2,835
9	Hamilton, ON	2,705
10	London, ON	2,080
11	Surrey, BC	2,015
12	Richmond Hill, ON	1,695
13	Burnaby, BC	1,635
14	Halifax, NS	1,515
15	Coquitlam, BC	1,485
16	Brampton, ON	1,340
17	Markham, ON	1,290
18	Kitchener, ON	1,160
19	Saanich, BC	1,105
20	Vaughan, ON	1,010
21	Kingston, ON	1,000
22	Kelowna, BC	960
23	Richmond, BC	860
24	Saskatoon, SK	850
25	Oakville, ON	820
26	Québec, QC	800
27	Windsor, ON	785
28	Regina, SK	675
29	Abbotsford, BC	665
30	Gatineau, QC	600
30	Guelph, ON	600
32	Oshawa, ON	535
33	Langley, BC	530
34	Laval, QC	490
35	St. Catharines, ON	485
36	Burlington, ON	425
37	Longueuil, QC	415
38	Greater Sudbury, ON	405
39	Barrie, ON	355
40	Thunder Bay, ON	350
41	Whitby, ON	340
42	Cambridge, ON	280
43	St. John's, NL	270
44	Ajax, ON	250
45	Sherbrooke, QC	195
46	Chatham-Kent, ON	170
47	Saguenay, QC	150
48	Lévis, QC	120
49	Trois-Rivières, QC	80
50	Terrebonne, QC	30
–	Canada	130,835

Male

Rank	City	Number
1	Toronto, ON	5,945
2	Calgary, AB	2,775
3	Vancouver, BC	2,340
4	Ottawa, ON	2,235
5	Montréal, QC	2,110
6	Edmonton, AB	1,850
7	Mississauga, ON	1,555
8	Hamilton, ON	1,240
9	Winnipeg, MB	1,215
10	London, ON	940
11	Surrey, BC	835
12	Richmond Hill, ON	800
13	Burnaby, BC	720
14	Coquitlam, BC	650
15	Halifax, NS	620
15	Markham, ON	620
17	Brampton, ON	585
18	Vaughan, ON	565
19	Kitchener, ON	540
20	Saskatoon, SK	445
21	Québec, QC	430
21	Windsor, ON	430
23	Kingston, ON	405
24	Saanich, BC	385
25	Kelowna, BC	375
25	Richmond, BC	375
27	Regina, SK	325
28	Gatineau, QC	300
29	Oakville, ON	295
30	Laval, QC	265
31	Guelph, ON	240
32	Abbotsford, BC	205
32	St. Catharines, ON	205
34	Greater Sudbury, ON	200
35	Longueuil, QC	185
35	Oshawa, ON	185
37	Langley, BC	175
38	Burlington, ON	160
38	St. John's, NL	160
40	Cambridge, ON	155
40	Thunder Bay, ON	155
42	Ajax, ON	130
43	Barrie, ON	115
44	Sherbrooke, QC	100
44	Whitby, ON	100
46	Chatham-Kent, ON	80
47	Saguenay, QC	75
48	Lévis, QC	45
49	Trois-Rivières, QC	40
50	Terrebonne, QC	10
–	Canada	57,745

Female

Rank	City	Number
1	Toronto, ON	7,005
2	Calgary, AB	3,310
3	Ottawa, ON	3,025
4	Vancouver, BC	2,930
5	Edmonton, AB	2,525
6	Montréal, QC	2,090
7	Mississauga, ON	1,630
8	Winnipeg, MB	1,620
9	Hamilton, ON	1,460
10	Surrey, BC	1,180
11	London, ON	1,140
12	Burnaby, BC	920
13	Halifax, NS	895
13	Richmond Hill, ON	895
15	Coquitlam, BC	830
16	Brampton, ON	755
17	Saanich, BC	720
18	Markham, ON	665
19	Kitchener, ON	625
20	Kingston, ON	595
21	Kelowna, BC	590
22	Oakville, ON	520
23	Richmond, BC	485
24	Abbotsford, BC	465
25	Vaughan, ON	445
26	Saskatoon, SK	410
27	Québec, QC	370
28	Guelph, ON	360
29	Langley, BC	355
29	Windsor, ON	355
31	Oshawa, ON	345
31	Regina, SK	345
33	Gatineau, QC	300
34	St. Catharines, ON	280
35	Burlington, ON	265
36	Barrie, ON	240
37	Whitby, ON	235
38	Longueuil, QC	230
39	Laval, QC	225
40	Greater Sudbury, ON	205
41	Thunder Bay, ON	195
42	Cambridge, ON	130
43	Ajax, ON	120
44	St. John's, NL	110
45	Sherbrooke, QC	95
46	Chatham-Kent, ON	90
47	Lévis, QC	75
48	Saguenay, QC	70
49	Trois-Rivières, QC	45
50	Terrebonne, QC	20
–	Canada	73,090

Note: Religion refers to the person's self-identification as having a connection or affiliation with any religious denomination, group, body, sect, cult or other religiously defined community or system of belief. Religion is not limited to formal membership in a religious organization or group. Persons without a religious connection or affiliation can self-identify as atheist, agnostic or humanist, or can provide another applicable response.
Source: Statistics Canada. 2013. 2011 National Household Survey. Statistics Canada Catalogue no. 99-004-XWE. Ottawa. Released September 11, 2013.

Cities Ranked by Religion: Other Religions
By Percent

Total

Rank	City	Percent
1	Coquitlam, BC	1.2%
2	Saanich, BC	1.0%
3	Richmond Hill, ON	0.9%
3	Vancouver, BC	0.9%
5	Kelowna, BC	0.8%
5	Kingston, ON	0.8%
7	Burnaby, BC	0.7%
8	Calgary, AB	0.6%
8	London, ON	0.6%
8	Ottawa, ON	0.6%
11	Abbotsford, BC	0.5%
11	Edmonton, AB	0.5%
11	Guelph, ON	0.5%
11	Hamilton, ON	0.5%
11	Kitchener, ON	0.5%
11	Langley, BC	0.5%
11	Oakville, ON	0.5%
11	Richmond, BC	0.5%
11	Toronto, ON	0.5%
20	Halifax, NS	0.4%
20	Markham, ON	0.4%
20	Mississauga, ON	0.4%
20	Oshawa, ON	0.4%
20	Regina, SK	0.4%
20	Saskatoon, SK	0.4%
20	St. Catharines, ON	0.4%
20	Surrey, BC	0.4%
20	Vaughan, ON	0.4%
20	Windsor, ON	0.4%
20	Winnipeg, MB	0.4%
31	Barrie, ON	0.3%
31	Brampton, ON	0.3%
31	Greater Sudbury, ON	0.3%
31	Montréal, QC	0.3%
31	St. John's, NL	0.3%
31	Thunder Bay, ON	0.3%
31	Whitby, ON	0.3%
38	Ajax, ON	0.2%
38	Burlington, ON	0.2%
38	Cambridge, ON	0.2%
38	Chatham-Kent, ON	0.2%
38	Gatineau, QC	0.2%
38	Longueuil, QC	0.2%
38	Québec, QC	0.2%
45	Laval, QC	0.1%
45	Lévis, QC	0.1%
45	Saguenay, QC	0.1%
45	Sherbrooke, QC	0.1%
45	Trois-Rivières, QC	0.1%
50	Terrebonne, QC	0.0%
–	Canada	0.4%

Male

Rank	City	Percent
1	Coquitlam, BC	1.1%
2	Richmond Hill, ON	0.9%
3	Vancouver, BC	0.8%
4	Burnaby, BC	0.7%
4	Kelowna, BC	0.7%
4	Kingston, ON	0.7%
4	Saanich, BC	0.7%
8	Calgary, AB	0.5%
8	Edmonton, AB	0.5%
8	Hamilton, ON	0.5%
8	Kitchener, ON	0.5%
8	London, ON	0.5%
8	Ottawa, ON	0.5%
8	Toronto, ON	0.5%
15	Guelph, ON	0.4%
15	Markham, ON	0.4%
15	Mississauga, ON	0.4%
15	Regina, SK	0.4%
15	Richmond, BC	0.4%
15	Saskatoon, SK	0.4%
15	Surrey, BC	0.4%
15	Vaughan, ON	0.4%
15	Windsor, ON	0.4%
15	Winnipeg, MB	0.4%
25	Abbotsford, BC	0.3%
25	Cambridge, ON	0.3%
25	Greater Sudbury, ON	0.3%
25	Halifax, NS	0.3%
25	Langley, BC	0.3%
25	Montréal, QC	0.3%
25	Oakville, ON	0.3%
25	Oshawa, ON	0.3%
25	St. Catharines, ON	0.3%
25	St. John's, NL	0.3%
25	Thunder Bay, ON	0.3%
36	Ajax, ON	0.2%
36	Barrie, ON	0.2%
36	Brampton, ON	0.2%
36	Burlington, ON	0.2%
36	Chatham-Kent, ON	0.2%
36	Gatineau, QC	0.2%
36	Longueuil, QC	0.2%
36	Québec, QC	0.2%
36	Whitby, ON	0.2%
45	Laval, QC	0.1%
45	Lévis, QC	0.1%
45	Saguenay, QC	0.1%
45	Sherbrooke, QC	0.1%
45	Trois-Rivières, QC	0.1%
50	Terrebonne, QC	0.0%
–	Canada	0.4%

Female

Rank	City	Percent
1	Coquitlam, BC	1.3%
1	Saanich, BC	1.3%
3	Kelowna, BC	1.0%
3	Kingston, ON	1.0%
3	Vancouver, BC	1.0%
6	Richmond Hill, ON	0.9%
7	Burnaby, BC	0.8%
8	Abbotsford, BC	0.7%
8	Langley, BC	0.7%
8	Ottawa, ON	0.7%
11	Calgary, AB	0.6%
11	Edmonton, AB	0.6%
11	Guelph, ON	0.6%
11	Hamilton, ON	0.6%
11	Kitchener, ON	0.6%
11	London, ON	0.6%
11	Oakville, ON	0.6%
18	Halifax, NS	0.5%
18	Mississauga, ON	0.5%
18	Oshawa, ON	0.5%
18	Richmond, BC	0.5%
18	Surrey, BC	0.5%
18	Toronto, ON	0.5%
18	Winnipeg, MB	0.5%
25	Barrie, ON	0.4%
25	Markham, ON	0.4%
25	Regina, SK	0.4%
25	Saskatoon, SK	0.4%
25	St. Catharines, ON	0.4%
25	Thunder Bay, ON	0.4%
25	Whitby, ON	0.4%
32	Brampton, ON	0.3%
32	Burlington, ON	0.3%
32	Greater Sudbury, ON	0.3%
32	Montréal, QC	0.3%
32	Vaughan, ON	0.3%
32	Windsor, ON	0.3%
38	Ajax, ON	0.2%
38	Cambridge, ON	0.2%
38	Chatham-Kent, ON	0.2%
38	Gatineau, QC	0.2%
38	Longueuil, QC	0.2%
38	St. John's, NL	0.2%
44	Laval, QC	0.1%
44	Lévis, QC	0.1%
44	Québec, QC	0.1%
44	Saguenay, QC	0.1%
44	Sherbrooke, QC	0.1%
44	Trois-Rivières, QC	0.1%
50	Terrebonne, QC	0.0%
–	Canada	0.4%

Note: Religion refers to the person's self-identification as having a connection or affiliation with any religious denomination, group, body, sect, cult or other religiously defined community or system of belief. Religion is not limited to formal membership in a religious organization or group. Persons without a religious connection or affiliation can self-identify as atheist, agnostic or humanist, or can provide another applicable response.
Source: Statistics Canada. 2013. 2011 National Household Survey. Statistics Canada Catalogue no. 99-004-XWE. Ottawa. Released September 11, 2013.

Cities Ranked by Religion: No Religious Affiliation
By Number

Total

Rank	City	Number
1	Toronto, ON	622,655
2	Calgary, AB	349,830
3	Montréal, QC	296,215
4	Vancouver, BC	288,435
5	Edmonton, AB	247,150
6	Ottawa, ON	197,930
7	Winnipeg, MB	186,510
8	Surrey, BC	132,635
9	Hamilton, ON	126,700
10	London, ON	107,975
11	Mississauga, ON	105,660
12	Halifax, NS	95,630
13	Burnaby, BC	91,670
14	Markham, ON	89,695
15	Richmond, BC	86,805
16	Québec, QC	65,450
17	Saskatoon, SK	62,285
18	Kitchener, ON	54,125
19	Saanich, BC	51,825
20	Regina, SK	51,420
21	Brampton, ON	50,885
22	Coquitlam, BC	50,315
23	Richmond Hill, ON	48,690
24	Kelowna, BC	47,885
25	Langley, BC	43,680
26	Burlington, ON	43,045
27	Oshawa, ON	42,460
28	Gatineau, QC	42,300
29	Windsor, ON	41,605
30	Barrie, ON	41,275
31	Laval, QC	38,500
32	Oakville, ON	37,210
33	Guelph, ON	36,500
34	Abbotsford, BC	35,465
35	Kingston, ON	35,435
36	Longueuil, QC	34,000
37	St. Catharines, ON	31,550
38	Cambridge, ON	30,355
39	Vaughan, ON	28,735
40	Greater Sudbury, ON	28,490
41	Whitby, ON	28,225
42	Thunder Bay, ON	27,950
43	Chatham-Kent, ON	21,600
44	Sherbrooke, QC	20,670
45	Ajax, ON	20,365
46	Lévis, QC	12,585
47	Terrebonne, QC	11,740
48	Trois-Rivières, QC	11,585
49	St. John's, NL	11,505
50	Saguenay, QC	8,420
–	Canada	7,850,605

Male

Rank	City	Number
1	Toronto, ON	327,085
2	Calgary, AB	191,330
3	Montréal, QC	160,105
4	Vancouver, BC	150,235
5	Edmonton, AB	133,785
6	Ottawa, ON	106,770
7	Winnipeg, MB	99,995
8	Surrey, BC	70,710
9	Hamilton, ON	68,845
10	London, ON	57,800
11	Mississauga, ON	56,985
12	Halifax, NS	51,575
13	Burnaby, BC	48,515
14	Markham, ON	46,380
15	Richmond, BC	43,925
16	Québec, QC	36,480
17	Saskatoon, SK	34,330
18	Kitchener, ON	29,630
19	Regina, SK	27,890
20	Brampton, ON	27,730
21	Saanich, BC	27,235
22	Coquitlam, BC	26,710
23	Richmond Hill, ON	25,455
24	Kelowna, BC	25,210
25	Burlington, ON	23,195
26	Langley, BC	23,180
27	Oshawa, ON	23,100
28	Gatineau, QC	22,375
29	Windsor, ON	22,290
30	Barrie, ON	21,665
31	Laval, QC	20,505
32	Oakville, ON	19,950
33	Guelph, ON	19,930
34	Abbotsford, BC	19,135
35	Kingston, ON	19,080
36	Longueuil, QC	18,450
37	St. Catharines, ON	16,695
38	Cambridge, ON	16,480
39	Greater Sudbury, ON	15,805
40	Thunder Bay, ON	15,320
41	Vaughan, ON	15,165
42	Whitby, ON	15,095
43	Chatham-Kent, ON	11,715
44	Sherbrooke, QC	11,245
45	Ajax, ON	10,680
46	Lévis, QC	7,215
47	Trois-Rivières, QC	6,450
48	Terrebonne, QC	6,420
49	St. John's, NL	6,415
50	Saguenay, QC	5,045
–	Canada	4,225,645

Female

Rank	City	Number
1	Toronto, ON	295,570
2	Calgary, AB	158,505
3	Vancouver, BC	138,205
4	Montréal, QC	136,110
5	Edmonton, AB	113,365
6	Ottawa, ON	91,160
7	Winnipeg, MB	86,510
8	Surrey, BC	61,925
9	Hamilton, ON	57,845
10	London, ON	50,175
11	Mississauga, ON	48,675
12	Halifax, NS	44,055
13	Markham, ON	43,315
14	Burnaby, BC	43,155
15	Richmond, BC	42,875
16	Québec, QC	28,970
17	Saskatoon, SK	27,950
18	Saanich, BC	24,585
19	Kitchener, ON	24,490
20	Coquitlam, BC	23,605
21	Regina, SK	23,535
22	Richmond Hill, ON	23,240
23	Brampton, ON	23,155
24	Kelowna, BC	22,680
25	Langley, BC	20,495
26	Gatineau, QC	19,920
27	Burlington, ON	19,850
28	Barrie, ON	19,610
29	Oshawa, ON	19,360
30	Windsor, ON	19,315
31	Laval, QC	17,995
32	Oakville, ON	17,265
33	Guelph, ON	16,575
34	Kingston, ON	16,350
35	Abbotsford, BC	16,325
36	Longueuil, QC	15,550
37	St. Catharines, ON	14,855
38	Cambridge, ON	13,870
39	Vaughan, ON	13,570
40	Whitby, ON	13,130
41	Greater Sudbury, ON	12,685
42	Thunder Bay, ON	12,630
43	Chatham-Kent, ON	9,890
44	Ajax, ON	9,680
45	Sherbrooke, QC	9,430
46	Lévis, QC	5,375
47	Terrebonne, QC	5,315
48	Trois-Rivières, QC	5,140
49	St. John's, NL	5,090
50	Saguenay, QC	3,375
–	Canada	3,624,965

Note: Religion refers to the person's self-identification as having a connection or affiliation with any religious denomination, group, body, sect, cult or other religiously defined community or system of belief. Religion is not limited to formal membership in a religious organization or group. Persons without a religious connection or affiliation can self-identify as atheist, agnostic or humanist, or can provide another applicable response.
Source: Statistics Canada. 2013. 2011 National Household Survey. Statistics Canada Catalogue no. 99-004-XWE. Ottawa. Released September 11, 2013.

Cities Ranked by Religion: No Religious Affiliation
By Percent

Total

Rank	City	Percent
1	Vancouver, BC	48.9%
2	Saanich, BC	48.0%
3	Richmond, BC	45.9%
4	Langley, BC	42.3%
5	Kelowna, BC	41.8%
6	Burnaby, BC	41.6%
7	Coquitlam, BC	40.2%
8	Calgary, AB	32.3%
9	Edmonton, AB	31.1%
10	Barrie, ON	31.0%
11	Guelph, ON	30.3%
12	London, ON	29.9%
12	Markham, ON	29.9%
14	Kingston, ON	29.8%
15	Oshawa, ON	28.8%
16	Winnipeg, MB	28.7%
17	Surrey, BC	28.6%
18	Saskatoon, SK	28.5%
19	Abbotsford, BC	27.1%
19	Regina, SK	27.1%
21	Richmond Hill, ON	26.4%
21	Thunder Bay, ON	26.4%
23	Kitchener, ON	25.1%
24	Halifax, NS	24.9%
24	Hamilton, ON	24.9%
26	Burlington, ON	24.8%
27	St. Catharines, ON	24.5%
28	Cambridge, ON	24.3%
29	Toronto, ON	24.2%
30	Whitby, ON	23.5%
31	Ottawa, ON	22.8%
32	Chatham-Kent, ON	21.2%
33	Oakville, ON	20.6%
34	Windsor, ON	20.0%
35	Ajax, ON	18.6%
36	Montréal, QC	18.4%
37	Greater Sudbury, ON	18.1%
38	Gatineau, QC	16.2%
39	Longueuil, QC	14.9%
39	Mississauga, ON	14.9%
41	Sherbrooke, QC	13.8%
42	Québec, QC	13.0%
43	St. John's, NL	11.1%
43	Terrebonne, QC	11.1%
45	Vaughan, ON	10.0%
46	Brampton, ON	9.8%
46	Laval, QC	9.8%
48	Lévis, QC	9.3%
49	Trois-Rivières, QC	9.1%
50	Saguenay, QC	6.0%
–	Canada	23.9%

Male

Rank	City	Percent
1	Saanich, BC	52.1%
1	Vancouver, BC	52.1%
3	Richmond, BC	48.3%
4	Langley, BC	45.8%
5	Kelowna, BC	45.6%
6	Burnaby, BC	44.9%
7	Coquitlam, BC	43.4%
8	Calgary, AB	35.4%
9	Guelph, ON	34.0%
10	Edmonton, AB	33.7%
11	Kingston, ON	33.5%
12	Barrie, ON	33.4%
13	London, ON	33.1%
14	Oshawa, ON	32.1%
15	Saskatoon, SK	32.0%
16	Markham, ON	31.6%
16	Winnipeg, MB	31.6%
18	Surrey, BC	30.8%
19	Regina, SK	30.1%
20	Thunder Bay, ON	29.7%
21	Abbotsford, BC	29.6%
22	Richmond Hill, ON	28.3%
23	Burlington, ON	27.7%
23	Halifax, NS	27.7%
23	Kitchener, ON	27.7%
26	Hamilton, ON	27.6%
27	St. Catharines, ON	27.2%
28	Cambridge, ON	26.7%
29	Toronto, ON	26.4%
30	Whitby, ON	25.6%
31	Ottawa, ON	25.3%
32	Chatham-Kent, ON	23.6%
33	Oakville, ON	22.8%
34	Windsor, ON	22.0%
35	Greater Sudbury, ON	20.5%
36	Montréal, QC	20.4%
37	Ajax, ON	20.2%
38	Gatineau, QC	17.6%
39	Longueuil, QC	16.6%
40	Mississauga, ON	16.4%
41	Sherbrooke, QC	15.3%
42	Québec, QC	15.0%
43	St. John's, NL	13.0%
44	Terrebonne, QC	12.2%
45	Brampton, ON	10.8%
45	Lévis, QC	10.8%
45	Vaughan, ON	10.8%
48	Laval, QC	10.7%
49	Trois-Rivières, QC	10.5%
50	Saguenay, QC	7.2%
–	Canada	26.1%

Female

Rank	City	Percent
1	Vancouver, BC	45.8%
2	Saanich, BC	44.2%
3	Richmond, BC	43.6%
4	Langley, BC	39.1%
5	Burnaby, BC	38.5%
6	Kelowna, BC	38.3%
7	Coquitlam, BC	37.2%
8	Calgary, AB	29.3%
9	Barrie, ON	28.7%
10	Edmonton, AB	28.4%
11	Markham, ON	28.2%
12	London, ON	27.0%
13	Guelph, ON	26.8%
14	Surrey, BC	26.5%
15	Kingston, ON	26.4%
16	Winnipeg, MB	26.0%
17	Oshawa, ON	25.6%
18	Saskatoon, SK	25.2%
19	Abbotsford, BC	24.6%
19	Richmond Hill, ON	24.6%
21	Regina, SK	24.3%
22	Thunder Bay, ON	23.2%
23	Kitchener, ON	22.4%
24	Hamilton, ON	22.3%
25	Halifax, NS	22.2%
26	Burlington, ON	22.1%
26	St. Catharines, ON	22.1%
26	Toronto, ON	22.1%
29	Cambridge, ON	21.9%
30	Whitby, ON	21.4%
31	Ottawa, ON	20.4%
32	Chatham-Kent, ON	19.0%
33	Oakville, ON	18.6%
34	Windsor, ON	18.1%
35	Ajax, ON	17.2%
36	Montréal, QC	16.5%
37	Greater Sudbury, ON	15.7%
38	Gatineau, QC	14.8%
39	Mississauga, ON	13.5%
40	Longueuil, QC	13.3%
41	Sherbrooke, QC	12.2%
42	Québec, QC	11.2%
43	Terrebonne, QC	10.0%
44	St. John's, NL	9.4%
45	Vaughan, ON	9.3%
46	Laval, QC	8.9%
47	Brampton, ON	8.8%
48	Trois-Rivières, QC	7.9%
49	Lévis, QC	7.8%
50	Saguenay, QC	4.7%
–	Canada	21.7%

Note: Religion refers to the person's self-identification as having a connection or affiliation with any religious denomination, group, body, sect, cult or other religiously defined community or system of belief. Religion is not limited to formal membership in a religious organization or group. Persons without a religious connection or affiliation can self-identify as atheist, agnostic or humanist, or can provide another applicable response.
Source: Statistics Canada. 2013. 2011 National Household Survey. Statistics Canada Catalogue no. 99-004-XWE. Ottawa. Released September 11, 2013.

Cities Ranked by Mother Tongue: English
By Number

Total

Rank	City	Number
1	Toronto, ON	1,317,025
2	Calgary, AB	752,525
3	Edmonton, AB	545,840
4	Ottawa, ON	544,045
5	Winnipeg, MB	468,305
6	Hamilton, ON	378,590
7	Halifax, NS	348,515
8	Mississauga, ON	338,280
9	Vancouver, BC	299,290
10	London, ON	281,995
11	Brampton, ON	269,790
12	Surrey, BC	240,485
13	Montréal, QC	206,210
14	Saskatoon, SK	178,470
15	Regina, SK	162,475
16	Kitchener, ON	154,125
17	Windsor, ON	142,795
18	Burlington, ON	140,590
19	Vaughan, ON	131,770
20	Oshawa, ON	128,555
21	Oakville, ON	126,220
22	Barrie, ON	117,135
23	Markham, ON	115,750
24	St. Catharines, ON	103,640
25	Kingston, ON	102,845
26	Greater Sudbury, ON	102,320
27	Whitby, ON	101,320
28	Cambridge, ON	100,075
29	St. John's, NL	99,745
30	Kelowna, BC	98,145
31	Guelph, ON	95,845
32	Burnaby, BC	93,425
33	Thunder Bay, ON	90,145
34	Chatham-Kent, ON	89,795
35	Abbotsford, BC	86,660
36	Saanich, BC	86,590
37	Langley, BC	85,820
38	Ajax, ON	83,200
39	Richmond Hill, ON	75,125
40	Richmond, BC	69,460
41	Coquitlam, BC	68,700
42	Gatineau, QC	29,060
43	Laval, QC	27,680
44	Longueuil, QC	14,155
45	Québec, QC	7,370
46	Sherbrooke, QC	6,235
47	Terrebonne, QC	2,190
48	Trois-Rivières, QC	1,480
49	Lévis, QC	1,350
50	Saguenay, QC	1,185
–	Canada	18,858,980

Male

Rank	City	Number
1	Toronto, ON	645,720
2	Calgary, AB	380,205
3	Edmonton, AB	275,805
4	Ottawa, ON	270,365
5	Winnipeg, MB	230,515
6	Hamilton, ON	186,285
7	Mississauga, ON	167,990
8	Halifax, NS	167,925
9	Vancouver, BC	154,040
10	London, ON	136,650
11	Brampton, ON	133,185
12	Surrey, BC	120,785
13	Montréal, QC	102,495
14	Saskatoon, SK	87,795
15	Regina, SK	79,230
16	Kitchener, ON	76,450
17	Windsor, ON	69,685
18	Burlington, ON	68,285
19	Vaughan, ON	66,225
20	Oshawa, ON	62,860
21	Oakville, ON	61,880
22	Markham, ON	58,175
23	Barrie, ON	57,065
24	Greater Sudbury, ON	50,925
25	St. Catharines, ON	50,055
26	Whitby, ON	49,670
27	Kingston, ON	49,485
28	Cambridge, ON	49,410
29	Burnaby, BC	48,175
30	Kelowna, BC	47,595
31	St. John's, NL	47,315
32	Guelph, ON	46,635
33	Thunder Bay, ON	44,095
34	Chatham-Kent, ON	43,925
35	Abbotsford, BC	43,000
36	Langley, BC	42,320
37	Saanich, BC	42,265
38	Ajax, ON	40,330
39	Richmond Hill, ON	37,895
40	Richmond, BC	34,995
41	Coquitlam, BC	34,620
42	Gatineau, QC	14,520
43	Laval, QC	14,235
44	Longueuil, QC	6,965
45	Québec, QC	3,855
46	Sherbrooke, QC	2,995
47	Terrebonne, QC	1,130
48	Trois-Rivières, QC	730
49	Lévis, QC	680
50	Saguenay, QC	625
–	Canada	9,345,225

Female

Rank	City	Number
1	Toronto, ON	671,305
2	Calgary, AB	372,315
3	Ottawa, ON	273,680
4	Edmonton, AB	270,035
5	Winnipeg, MB	237,790
6	Hamilton, ON	192,300
7	Halifax, NS	180,590
8	Mississauga, ON	170,290
9	London, ON	145,340
10	Vancouver, BC	145,250
11	Brampton, ON	136,605
12	Surrey, BC	119,705
13	Montréal, QC	103,710
14	Saskatoon, SK	90,675
15	Regina, SK	83,245
16	Kitchener, ON	77,675
17	Windsor, ON	73,115
18	Burlington, ON	72,305
19	Oshawa, ON	65,695
20	Vaughan, ON	65,535
21	Oakville, ON	64,340
22	Barrie, ON	60,065
23	Markham, ON	57,570
24	St. Catharines, ON	53,590
25	Kingston, ON	53,365
26	St. John's, NL	52,430
27	Whitby, ON	51,645
28	Greater Sudbury, ON	51,400
29	Cambridge, ON	50,665
30	Kelowna, BC	50,550
31	Guelph, ON	49,215
32	Thunder Bay, ON	46,050
33	Chatham-Kent, ON	45,865
34	Burnaby, BC	45,250
35	Saanich, BC	44,320
36	Abbotsford, BC	43,670
37	Langley, BC	43,505
38	Ajax, ON	42,865
39	Richmond Hill, ON	37,230
40	Richmond, BC	34,465
41	Coquitlam, BC	34,075
42	Gatineau, QC	14,535
43	Laval, QC	13,450
44	Longueuil, QC	7,190
45	Québec, QC	3,510
46	Sherbrooke, QC	3,245
47	Terrebonne, QC	1,070
48	Trois-Rivières, QC	745
49	Lévis, QC	665
50	Saguenay, QC	560
–	Canada	9,513,750

Note: Figures cover total population excluding institutional residents.
Source: Statistics Canada. 2012. Census Profile. 2011 Census. Statistics Canada Catalogue no. 98-316-XWE. Ottawa. Released October 24 2012.
http://www12.statcan.gc.ca/census-recensement/2011/dp-pd/prof/index.cfm?Lang=E

Cities Ranked by Mother Tongue: English
By Percent

Total

Rank	City	Percent
1	St. John's, NL	95.3%
2	Halifax, NS	90.2%
3	Chatham-Kent, ON	87.7%
4	Barrie, ON	87.3%
5	Oshawa, ON	86.7%
6	Kingston, ON	85.5%
7	Regina, SK	85.1%
8	Kelowna, BC	84.9%
9	Thunder Bay, ON	84.5%
10	Whitby, ON	83.7%
11	Langley, BC	83.0%
12	Saskatoon, SK	81.6%
13	Burlington, ON	80.7%
14	St. Catharines, ON	80.3%
15	Cambridge, ON	79.7%
16	Saanich, BC	79.6%
17	Guelph, ON	79.2%
18	London, ON	77.8%
19	Ajax, ON	76.1%
20	Hamilton, ON	73.8%
21	Winnipeg, MB	71.4%
22	Kitchener, ON	71.2%
23	Oakville, ON	69.6%
24	Calgary, AB	69.2%
25	Windsor, ON	68.4%
26	Edmonton, AB	68.1%
27	Abbotsford, BC	65.7%
28	Greater Sudbury, ON	64.5%
29	Ottawa, ON	62.4%
30	Coquitlam, BC	54.9%
31	Brampton, ON	51.7%
31	Surrey, BC	51.7%
33	Toronto, ON	50.9%
34	Vancouver, BC	50.2%
35	Mississauga, ON	47.6%
36	Vaughan, ON	45.9%
37	Burnaby, BC	42.2%
38	Richmond Hill, ON	40.7%
39	Markham, ON	38.5%
40	Richmond, BC	36.6%
41	Montréal, QC	12.7%
42	Gatineau, QC	11.0%
43	Laval, QC	7.0%
44	Longueuil, QC	6.2%
45	Sherbrooke, QC	4.1%
46	Terrebonne, QC	2.1%
47	Québec, QC	1.4%
48	Trois-Rivières, QC	1.1%
49	Lévis, QC	1.0%
50	Saguenay, QC	0.8%
–	Canada	56.9%

Male

Rank	City	Percent
1	St. John's, NL	94.8%
2	Halifax, NS	89.8%
3	Chatham-Kent, ON	87.8%
4	Barrie, ON	87.6%
5	Oshawa, ON	87.0%
6	Kelowna, BC	85.7%
7	Kingston, ON	85.5%
8	Thunder Bay, ON	85.1%
9	Regina, SK	85.0%
10	Whitby, ON	84.2%
11	Langley, BC	83.4%
12	Saskatoon, SK	81.9%
13	Burlington, ON	81.2%
14	St. Catharines, ON	80.9%
15	Saanich, BC	80.6%
16	Cambridge, ON	80.0%
17	Guelph, ON	79.4%
18	London, ON	78.1%
19	Ajax, ON	76.4%
20	Hamilton, ON	74.2%
21	Winnipeg, MB	72.3%
22	Kitchener, ON	71.6%
23	Oakville, ON	70.5%
24	Calgary, AB	70.0%
25	Edmonton, AB	69.0%
26	Windsor, ON	68.6%
27	Abbotsford, BC	66.1%
28	Greater Sudbury, ON	65.6%
29	Ottawa, ON	63.8%
30	Coquitlam, BC	56.2%
31	Vancouver, BC	52.8%
32	Surrey, BC	52.5%
33	Toronto, ON	51.9%
34	Brampton, ON	51.7%
35	Mississauga, ON	48.3%
36	Vaughan, ON	47.1%
37	Burnaby, BC	44.4%
38	Richmond Hill, ON	42.1%
39	Markham, ON	39.6%
40	Richmond, BC	38.5%
41	Montréal, QC	13.0%
42	Gatineau, QC	11.4%
43	Laval, QC	7.4%
44	Longueuil, QC	6.3%
45	Sherbrooke, QC	4.0%
46	Terrebonne, QC	2.1%
47	Québec, QC	1.6%
48	Trois-Rivières, QC	1.2%
49	Lévis, QC	1.0%
50	Saguenay, QC	0.9%
–	Canada	57.5%

Female

Rank	City	Percent
1	St. John's, NL	95.7%
2	Halifax, NS	90.7%
3	Chatham-Kent, ON	87.6%
4	Barrie, ON	87.0%
5	Oshawa, ON	86.5%
6	Kingston, ON	85.5%
7	Regina, SK	85.2%
8	Kelowna, BC	84.2%
9	Thunder Bay, ON	83.9%
10	Whitby, ON	83.2%
11	Langley, BC	82.6%
12	Saskatoon, SK	81.4%
13	Burlington, ON	80.2%
14	St. Catharines, ON	79.7%
15	Cambridge, ON	79.4%
16	Guelph, ON	79.0%
17	Saanich, BC	78.6%
18	London, ON	77.6%
19	Ajax, ON	75.8%
20	Hamilton, ON	73.3%
21	Kitchener, ON	70.8%
22	Winnipeg, MB	70.6%
23	Oakville, ON	68.7%
24	Calgary, AB	68.4%
25	Windsor, ON	68.1%
26	Edmonton, AB	67.3%
27	Abbotsford, BC	65.4%
28	Greater Sudbury, ON	63.4%
29	Ottawa, ON	61.0%
30	Coquitlam, BC	53.5%
31	Brampton, ON	51.7%
32	Surrey, BC	51.0%
33	Toronto, ON	49.9%
34	Vancouver, BC	47.7%
35	Mississauga, ON	47.0%
36	Vaughan, ON	44.7%
37	Burnaby, BC	40.0%
38	Richmond Hill, ON	39.4%
39	Markham, ON	37.5%
40	Richmond, BC	34.9%
41	Montréal, QC	12.4%
42	Gatineau, QC	10.7%
43	Laval, QC	6.6%
44	Longueuil, QC	6.1%
45	Sherbrooke, QC	4.1%
46	Terrebonne, QC	2.0%
47	Québec, QC	1.3%
48	Trois-Rivières, QC	1.1%
49	Lévis, QC	1.0%
50	Saguenay, QC	0.8%
–	Canada	56.4%

Note: Figures cover total population excluding institutional residents.
Source: Statistics Canada. 2012. Census Profile. 2011 Census. Statistics Canada Catalogue no. 98-316-XWE. Ottawa. Released October 24 2012.
http://www12.statcan.gc.ca/census-recensement/2011/dp-pd/prof/index.cfm?Lang=E

Cities Ranked by Mother Tongue: French
By Number

Total

Rank	City	Number
1	Montréal, QC	818,970
2	Québec, QC	478,395
3	Laval, QC	241,615
4	Gatineau, QC	203,360
5	Longueuil, QC	181,800
6	Saguenay, QC	140,915
7	Sherbrooke, QC	135,790
8	Lévis, QC	133,905
9	Trois-Rivières, QC	124,970
10	Ottawa, ON	123,925
11	Terrebonne, QC	95,940
12	Greater Sudbury, ON	42,805
13	Toronto, ON	32,665
14	Winnipeg, MB	23,455
15	Calgary, AB	16,900
16	Edmonton, AB	16,180
17	Halifax, NS	10,155
18	Vancouver, BC	8,905
19	Mississauga, ON	7,400
20	Hamilton, ON	6,765
21	Windsor, ON	5,405
22	London, ON	4,780
23	Brampton, ON	4,375
24	Kingston, ON	4,315
25	Surrey, BC	3,475
26	Oakville, ON	3,280
27	Saskatoon, SK	3,240
28	Oshawa, ON	3,205
29	Barrie, ON	3,120
30	Burlington, ON	3,080
31	Chatham-Kent, ON	2,915
32	St. Catharines, ON	2,890
33	Kitchener, ON	2,860
34	Thunder Bay, ON	2,515
35	Regina, SK	2,355
36	Whitby, ON	2,050
37	Markham, ON	2,035
38	Kelowna, BC	1,930
39	Vaughan, ON	1,795
40	Cambridge, ON	1,705
41	Burnaby, BC	1,680
42	Guelph, ON	1,605
43	Ajax, ON	1,580
44	Coquitlam, BC	1,420
45	Saanich, BC	1,360
46	Richmond Hill, ON	1,335
47	Richmond, BC	1,115
48	Abbotsford, BC	1,095
49	Langley, BC	1,025
50	St. John's, NL	500
–	Canada	7,054,975

Male

Rank	City	Number
1	Montréal, QC	393,470
2	Québec, QC	229,785
3	Laval, QC	115,405
4	Gatineau, QC	97,825
5	Longueuil, QC	87,680
6	Saguenay, QC	69,260
7	Sherbrooke, QC	65,720
8	Lévis, QC	65,545
9	Trois-Rivières, QC	60,115
10	Ottawa, ON	56,845
11	Terrebonne, QC	47,590
12	Greater Sudbury, ON	20,290
13	Toronto, ON	15,305
14	Winnipeg, MB	10,710
15	Calgary, AB	8,430
16	Edmonton, AB	8,425
17	Halifax, NS	5,015
18	Vancouver, BC	4,575
19	Mississauga, ON	3,275
20	Hamilton, ON	3,120
21	Windsor, ON	2,455
22	Kingston, ON	2,155
23	London, ON	2,110
24	Brampton, ON	2,055
25	Surrey, BC	1,710
26	Oshawa, ON	1,530
27	Saskatoon, SK	1,480
28	Barrie, ON	1,420
29	Oakville, ON	1,410
30	Chatham-Kent, ON	1,390
31	Burlington, ON	1,320
31	Kitchener, ON	1,320
31	St. Catharines, ON	1,320
34	Thunder Bay, ON	1,220
35	Regina, SK	1,080
36	Markham, ON	955
37	Whitby, ON	950
38	Kelowna, BC	890
39	Burnaby, BC	885
40	Vaughan, ON	820
41	Cambridge, ON	815
42	Guelph, ON	720
43	Ajax, ON	710
44	Coquitlam, BC	655
45	Saanich, BC	650
46	Richmond Hill, ON	575
47	Abbotsford, BC	555
48	Richmond, BC	540
49	Langley, BC	500
50	St. John's, NL	250
–	Canada	3,452,380

Female

Rank	City	Number
1	Montréal, QC	425,500
2	Québec, QC	248,610
3	Laval, QC	126,215
4	Gatineau, QC	105,535
5	Longueuil, QC	94,120
6	Saguenay, QC	71,650
7	Sherbrooke, QC	70,065
8	Lévis, QC	68,350
9	Ottawa, ON	67,075
10	Trois-Rivières, QC	64,855
11	Terrebonne, QC	48,350
12	Greater Sudbury, ON	22,515
13	Toronto, ON	17,365
14	Winnipeg, MB	12,745
15	Calgary, AB	8,470
16	Edmonton, AB	7,750
17	Halifax, NS	5,145
18	Vancouver, BC	4,330
19	Mississauga, ON	4,125
20	Hamilton, ON	3,640
21	Windsor, ON	2,945
22	London, ON	2,670
23	Brampton, ON	2,325
24	Kingston, ON	2,165
25	Oakville, ON	1,865
26	Burlington, ON	1,760
26	Saskatoon, SK	1,760
26	Surrey, BC	1,760
29	Barrie, ON	1,705
30	Oshawa, ON	1,670
31	St. Catharines, ON	1,570
32	Kitchener, ON	1,540
33	Chatham-Kent, ON	1,525
34	Thunder Bay, ON	1,295
35	Regina, SK	1,275
36	Whitby, ON	1,110
37	Markham, ON	1,075
38	Kelowna, BC	1,045
39	Vaughan, ON	975
40	Guelph, ON	890
41	Cambridge, ON	885
42	Ajax, ON	875
43	Burnaby, BC	795
44	Coquitlam, BC	765
45	Richmond Hill, ON	760
46	Saanich, BC	705
47	Richmond, BC	570
48	Abbotsford, BC	540
49	Langley, BC	520
50	St. John's, NL	250
–	Canada	3,602,590

Note: Figures cover total population excluding institutional residents.
Source: Statistics Canada. 2012. Census Profile. 2011 Census. Statistics Canada Catalogue no. 98-316-XWE. Ottawa. Released October 24 2012.
http://www12.statcan.gc.ca/census-recensement/2011/dp-pd/prof/index.cfm?Lang=E

Cities Ranked by Mother Tongue: French
By Percent

Total

Rank	City	Percent
1	Saguenay, QC	98.2%
2	Lévis, QC	97.6%
3	Trois-Rivières, QC	96.3%
4	Québec, QC	93.8%
5	Terrebonne, QC	90.5%
6	Sherbrooke, QC	89.1%
7	Longueuil, QC	79.2%
8	Gatineau, QC	77.2%
9	Laval, QC	60.8%
10	Montréal, QC	50.3%
11	Greater Sudbury, ON	27.0%
12	Ottawa, ON	14.2%
13	Kingston, ON	3.6%
13	Winnipeg, MB	3.6%
15	Chatham-Kent, ON	2.8%
16	Halifax, NS	2.6%
16	Windsor, ON	2.6%
18	Thunder Bay, ON	2.4%
19	Barrie, ON	2.3%
20	Oshawa, ON	2.2%
20	St. Catharines, ON	2.2%
22	Edmonton, AB	2.0%
23	Burlington, ON	1.8%
23	Oakville, ON	1.8%
25	Kelowna, BC	1.7%
25	Whitby, ON	1.7%
27	Calgary, AB	1.6%
28	Saskatoon, SK	1.5%
28	Vancouver, BC	1.5%
30	Ajax, ON	1.4%
30	Cambridge, ON	1.4%
32	Guelph, ON	1.3%
32	Hamilton, ON	1.3%
32	Kitchener, ON	1.3%
32	London, ON	1.3%
32	Toronto, ON	1.3%
37	Regina, SK	1.2%
37	Saanich, BC	1.2%
39	Coquitlam, BC	1.1%
40	Langley, BC	1.0%
40	Mississauga, ON	1.0%
42	Abbotsford, BC	0.8%
42	Brampton, ON	0.8%
42	Burnaby, BC	0.8%
45	Markham, ON	0.7%
45	Richmond Hill, ON	0.7%
45	Surrey, BC	0.7%
48	Richmond, BC	0.6%
48	Vaughan, ON	0.6%
50	St. John's, NL	0.5%
–	Canada	21.3%

Male

Rank	City	Percent
1	Saguenay, QC	98.0%
2	Lévis, QC	97.5%
3	Trois-Rivières, QC	96.1%
4	Québec, QC	93.4%
5	Terrebonne, QC	90.3%
6	Sherbrooke, QC	88.8%
7	Longueuil, QC	78.8%
8	Gatineau, QC	76.7%
9	Laval, QC	59.8%
10	Montréal, QC	49.7%
11	Greater Sudbury, ON	26.1%
12	Ottawa, ON	13.4%
13	Kingston, ON	3.7%
14	Winnipeg, MB	3.4%
15	Chatham-Kent, ON	2.8%
16	Halifax, NS	2.7%
17	Thunder Bay, ON	2.4%
17	Windsor, ON	2.4%
19	Barrie, ON	2.2%
20	Edmonton, AB	2.1%
20	Oshawa, ON	2.1%
20	St. Catharines, ON	2.1%
23	Burlington, ON	1.6%
23	Calgary, AB	1.6%
23	Kelowna, BC	1.6%
23	Oakville, ON	1.6%
23	Vancouver, BC	1.6%
23	Whitby, ON	1.6%
29	Saskatoon, SK	1.4%
30	Ajax, ON	1.3%
30	Cambridge, ON	1.3%
32	Guelph, ON	1.2%
32	Hamilton, ON	1.2%
32	Kitchener, ON	1.2%
32	London, ON	1.2%
32	Regina, SK	1.2%
32	Saanich, BC	1.2%
32	Toronto, ON	1.2%
39	Coquitlam, BC	1.1%
40	Langley, BC	1.0%
41	Abbotsford, BC	0.9%
41	Mississauga, ON	0.9%
43	Brampton, ON	0.8%
43	Burnaby, BC	0.8%
45	Surrey, BC	0.7%
46	Markham, ON	0.6%
46	Richmond, BC	0.6%
46	Richmond Hill, ON	0.6%
46	Vaughan, ON	0.6%
50	St. John's, NL	0.5%
–	Canada	21.2%

Female

Rank	City	Percent
1	Saguenay, QC	98.3%
2	Lévis, QC	97.7%
3	Trois-Rivières, QC	96.5%
4	Québec, QC	94.2%
5	Terrebonne, QC	90.8%
6	Sherbrooke, QC	89.3%
7	Longueuil, QC	79.6%
8	Gatineau, QC	77.8%
9	Laval, QC	61.7%
10	Montréal, QC	50.8%
11	Greater Sudbury, ON	27.8%
12	Ottawa, ON	15.0%
13	Winnipeg, MB	3.8%
14	Kingston, ON	3.5%
15	Chatham-Kent, ON	2.9%
16	Windsor, ON	2.7%
17	Halifax, NS	2.6%
18	Barrie, ON	2.5%
19	Thunder Bay, ON	2.4%
20	St. Catharines, ON	2.3%
21	Oshawa, ON	2.2%
22	Burlington, ON	2.0%
22	Oakville, ON	2.0%
24	Edmonton, AB	1.9%
25	Whitby, ON	1.8%
26	Kelowna, BC	1.7%
27	Calgary, AB	1.6%
27	Saskatoon, SK	1.6%
29	Ajax, ON	1.5%
30	Cambridge, ON	1.4%
30	Guelph, ON	1.4%
30	Hamilton, ON	1.4%
30	Kitchener, ON	1.4%
30	London, ON	1.4%
30	Vancouver, BC	1.4%
36	Regina, SK	1.3%
36	Saanich, BC	1.3%
36	Toronto, ON	1.3%
39	Coquitlam, BC	1.2%
40	Mississauga, ON	1.1%
41	Langley, BC	1.0%
42	Brampton, ON	0.9%
43	Abbotsford, BC	0.8%
43	Richmond Hill, ON	0.8%
45	Burnaby, BC	0.7%
45	Markham, ON	0.7%
45	Surrey, BC	0.7%
45	Vaughan, ON	0.7%
49	Richmond, BC	0.6%
50	St. John's, NL	0.5%
–	Canada	21.4%

Note: Figures cover total population excluding institutional residents.
Source: Statistics Canada. 2012. Census Profile. 2011 Census. Statistics Canada Catalogue no. 98-316-XWE. Ottawa. Released October 24 2012.
http://www12.statcan.gc.ca/census-recensement/2011/dp-pd/prof/index.cfm?Lang=E

Cities Ranked by Mother Tongue: Non-official Language
By Number

Total

Rank	City	Number
1	Toronto, ON	1,154,245
2	Montréal, QC	536,560
3	Mississauga, ON	334,060
4	Calgary, AB	292,540
5	Vancouver, BC	270,490
6	Brampton, ON	225,065
7	Edmonton, AB	219,195
8	Surrey, BC	205,815
9	Ottawa, ON	178,120
10	Markham, ON	171,875
11	Winnipeg, MB	146,340
12	Vaughan, ON	143,250
13	Burnaby, BC	119,440
14	Hamilton, ON	118,420
15	Laval, QC	113,160
16	Richmond, BC	112,895
17	Richmond Hill, ON	101,945
18	London, ON	69,650
19	Kitchener, ON	55,620
20	Windsor, ON	55,320
21	Coquitlam, BC	51,790
22	Oakville, ON	47,935
23	Abbotsford, BC	41,670
24	Saskatoon, SK	33,410
25	Longueuil, QC	28,115
26	Burlington, ON	28,025
27	Gatineau, QC	23,855
27	Halifax, NS	23,855
29	Regina, SK	23,500
30	Cambridge, ON	21,940
31	Guelph, ON	21,890
32	Ajax, ON	21,680
33	St. Catharines, ON	20,755
34	Québec, QC	19,790
35	Saanich, BC	19,285
36	Whitby, ON	15,885
37	Langley, BC	15,390
38	Oshawa, ON	14,825
39	Kelowna, BC	14,215
40	Thunder Bay, ON	12,710
41	Barrie, ON	12,410
42	Kingston, ON	11,750
43	Greater Sudbury, ON	10,290
44	Chatham-Kent, ON	8,735
45	Sherbrooke, QC	8,580
46	Terrebonne, QC	6,310
47	St. John's, NL	3,960
48	Trois-Rivières, QC	2,485
49	Lévis, QC	1,285
50	Saguenay, QC	975
–	Canada	6,567,680

Male

Rank	City	Number
1	Toronto, ON	542,440
2	Montréal, QC	262,135
3	Mississauga, ON	161,610
4	Calgary, AB	141,685
5	Vancouver, BC	124,825
6	Brampton, ON	111,165
7	Edmonton, AB	105,940
8	Surrey, BC	100,120
9	Ottawa, ON	84,250
10	Markham, ON	82,505
11	Winnipeg, MB	69,440
12	Vaughan, ON	68,580
13	Hamilton, ON	56,945
14	Burnaby, BC	56,095
15	Laval, QC	55,780
16	Richmond, BC	52,475
17	Richmond Hill, ON	48,655
18	London, ON	33,395
19	Kitchener, ON	27,095
20	Windsor, ON	26,835
21	Coquitlam, BC	24,685
22	Oakville, ON	22,615
23	Abbotsford, BC	20,280
24	Saskatoon, SK	16,270
25	Longueuil, QC	13,860
26	Burlington, ON	13,280
27	Halifax, NS	12,305
28	Gatineau, QC	11,815
29	Regina, SK	11,635
30	Cambridge, ON	10,615
31	Guelph, ON	10,560
32	Ajax, ON	10,375
33	Québec, QC	10,010
34	St. Catharines, ON	9,675
35	Saanich, BC	8,780
36	Whitby, ON	7,535
37	Langley, BC	7,365
38	Oshawa, ON	7,070
39	Kelowna, BC	6,495
40	Barrie, ON	5,945
41	Thunder Bay, ON	5,880
42	Kingston, ON	5,610
43	Greater Sudbury, ON	4,895
44	Sherbrooke, QC	4,340
45	Chatham-Kent, ON	4,260
46	Terrebonne, QC	3,205
47	St. John's, NL	2,100
48	Trois-Rivières, QC	1,280
49	Lévis, QC	645
50	Saguenay, QC	500
–	Canada	3,157,785

Female

Rank	City	Number
1	Toronto, ON	611,800
2	Montréal, QC	274,430
3	Mississauga, ON	172,445
4	Calgary, AB	150,855
5	Vancouver, BC	145,670
6	Brampton, ON	113,900
7	Edmonton, AB	113,255
8	Surrey, BC	105,695
9	Ottawa, ON	93,875
10	Markham, ON	89,370
11	Winnipeg, MB	76,895
12	Vaughan, ON	74,670
13	Burnaby, BC	63,340
14	Hamilton, ON	61,475
15	Richmond, BC	60,415
16	Laval, QC	57,385
17	Richmond Hill, ON	53,285
18	London, ON	36,260
19	Kitchener, ON	28,525
20	Windsor, ON	28,485
21	Coquitlam, BC	27,100
22	Oakville, ON	25,320
23	Abbotsford, BC	21,390
24	Saskatoon, SK	17,135
25	Burlington, ON	14,745
26	Longueuil, QC	14,250
27	Gatineau, QC	12,050
28	Regina, SK	11,865
29	Halifax, NS	11,550
30	Guelph, ON	11,330
31	Cambridge, ON	11,320
32	Ajax, ON	11,305
33	St. Catharines, ON	11,085
34	Saanich, BC	10,510
35	Québec, QC	9,780
36	Whitby, ON	8,350
37	Langley, BC	8,025
38	Oshawa, ON	7,755
39	Kelowna, BC	7,715
40	Thunder Bay, ON	6,825
41	Barrie, ON	6,470
42	Kingston, ON	6,140
43	Greater Sudbury, ON	5,395
44	Chatham-Kent, ON	4,475
45	Sherbrooke, QC	4,240
46	Terrebonne, QC	3,110
47	St. John's, NL	1,860
48	Trois-Rivières, QC	1,205
49	Lévis, QC	640
50	Saguenay, QC	475
–	Canada	3,409,895

Note: Figures cover total population excluding institutional residents.
Source: Statistics Canada. 2012. Census Profile. 2011 Census. Statistics Canada Catalogue no. 98-316-XWE. Ottawa. Released October 24 2012.
http://www12.statcan.gc.ca/census-recensement/2011/dp-pd/prof/index.cfm?Lang=E

Cities Ranked by Mother Tongue: Non-official Language

By Percent

Total

Rank	City	Percent
1	Richmond, BC	59.5%
2	Markham, ON	57.2%
3	Richmond Hill, ON	55.3%
4	Burnaby, BC	53.9%
5	Vaughan, ON	49.9%
6	Mississauga, ON	47.0%
7	Vancouver, BC	45.4%
8	Toronto, ON	44.6%
9	Surrey, BC	44.3%
10	Brampton, ON	43.1%
11	Coquitlam, BC	41.4%
12	Montréal, QC	33.0%
13	Abbotsford, BC	31.6%
14	Laval, QC	28.5%
15	Edmonton, AB	27.4%
16	Calgary, AB	26.9%
17	Windsor, ON	26.5%
18	Oakville, ON	26.4%
19	Kitchener, ON	25.7%
20	Hamilton, ON	23.1%
21	Winnipeg, MB	22.3%
22	Ottawa, ON	20.4%
23	Ajax, ON	19.8%
24	London, ON	19.2%
25	Guelph, ON	18.1%
26	Saanich, BC	17.7%
27	Cambridge, ON	17.5%
28	Burlington, ON	16.1%
28	St. Catharines, ON	16.1%
30	Saskatoon, SK	15.3%
31	Langley, BC	14.9%
32	Whitby, ON	13.1%
33	Kelowna, BC	12.3%
33	Regina, SK	12.3%
35	Longueuil, QC	12.2%
36	Thunder Bay, ON	11.9%
37	Oshawa, ON	10.0%
38	Kingston, ON	9.8%
39	Barrie, ON	9.3%
40	Gatineau, QC	9.1%
41	Chatham-Kent, ON	8.5%
42	Greater Sudbury, ON	6.5%
43	Halifax, NS	6.2%
44	Terrebonne, QC	6.0%
45	Sherbrooke, QC	5.6%
46	Québec, QC	3.9%
47	St. John's, NL	3.8%
48	Trois-Rivières, QC	1.9%
49	Lévis, QC	0.9%
50	Saguenay, QC	0.7%
–	Canada	19.8%

Male

Rank	City	Percent
1	Richmond, BC	57.7%
2	Markham, ON	56.1%
3	Richmond Hill, ON	54.0%
4	Burnaby, BC	51.7%
5	Vaughan, ON	48.8%
6	Mississauga, ON	46.5%
7	Toronto, ON	43.6%
8	Surrey, BC	43.5%
9	Brampton, ON	43.1%
10	Vancouver, BC	42.8%
11	Coquitlam, BC	40.1%
12	Montréal, QC	33.1%
13	Abbotsford, BC	31.2%
14	Laval, QC	28.9%
15	Edmonton, AB	26.5%
16	Windsor, ON	26.4%
17	Calgary, AB	26.1%
18	Oakville, ON	25.8%
19	Kitchener, ON	25.4%
20	Hamilton, ON	22.7%
21	Winnipeg, MB	21.8%
22	Ottawa, ON	19.9%
23	Ajax, ON	19.7%
24	London, ON	19.1%
25	Guelph, ON	18.0%
26	Cambridge, ON	17.2%
27	Saanich, BC	16.7%
28	Burlington, ON	15.8%
29	St. Catharines, ON	15.6%
30	Saskatoon, SK	15.2%
31	Langley, BC	14.5%
32	Whitby, ON	12.8%
33	Longueuil, QC	12.5%
33	Regina, SK	12.5%
35	Kelowna, BC	11.7%
36	Thunder Bay, ON	11.4%
37	Oshawa, ON	9.8%
38	Kingston, ON	9.7%
39	Gatineau, QC	9.3%
40	Barrie, ON	9.1%
41	Chatham-Kent, ON	8.5%
42	Halifax, NS	6.6%
43	Greater Sudbury, ON	6.3%
44	Terrebonne, QC	6.1%
45	Sherbrooke, QC	5.9%
46	St. John's, NL	4.2%
47	Québec, QC	4.1%
48	Trois-Rivières, QC	2.0%
49	Lévis, QC	1.0%
50	Saguenay, QC	0.7%
–	Canada	19.4%

Female

Rank	City	Percent
1	Richmond, BC	61.2%
2	Markham, ON	58.1%
3	Richmond Hill, ON	56.5%
4	Burnaby, BC	56.1%
5	Vaughan, ON	51.0%
6	Vancouver, BC	47.9%
7	Mississauga, ON	47.6%
8	Toronto, ON	45.5%
9	Surrey, BC	45.0%
10	Brampton, ON	43.1%
11	Coquitlam, BC	42.6%
12	Montréal, QC	32.8%
13	Abbotsford, BC	32.0%
14	Edmonton, AB	28.2%
15	Laval, QC	28.0%
16	Calgary, AB	27.7%
17	Oakville, ON	27.0%
18	Windsor, ON	26.5%
19	Kitchener, ON	26.0%
20	Hamilton, ON	23.4%
21	Winnipeg, MB	22.8%
22	Ottawa, ON	20.9%
23	Ajax, ON	20.0%
24	London, ON	19.4%
25	Saanich, BC	18.6%
26	Guelph, ON	18.2%
27	Cambridge, ON	17.7%
28	St. Catharines, ON	16.5%
29	Burlington, ON	16.4%
30	Saskatoon, SK	15.4%
31	Langley, BC	15.2%
32	Whitby, ON	13.5%
33	Kelowna, BC	12.8%
34	Thunder Bay, ON	12.4%
35	Regina, SK	12.1%
36	Longueuil, QC	12.0%
37	Oshawa, ON	10.2%
38	Kingston, ON	9.8%
39	Barrie, ON	9.4%
40	Gatineau, QC	8.9%
41	Chatham-Kent, ON	8.5%
42	Greater Sudbury, ON	6.7%
43	Halifax, NS	5.8%
43	Terrebonne, QC	5.8%
45	Sherbrooke, QC	5.4%
46	Québec, QC	3.7%
47	St. John's, NL	3.4%
48	Trois-Rivières, QC	1.8%
49	Lévis, QC	0.9%
50	Saguenay, QC	0.7%
–	Canada	20.2%

Note: Figures cover total population excluding institutional residents.
Source: Statistics Canada. 2012. Census Profile. 2011 Census. Statistics Canada Catalogue no. 98-316-XWE. Ottawa. Released October 24 2012.
http://www12.statcan.gc.ca/census-recensement/2011/dp-pd/prof/index.cfm?Lang=E

Sources for City Backgrounds

"2011 Annual Financial Report," City of Kelowna, accessed October 12, 2012, http://www.kelowna.ca/CM/Page626.aspx.

"2011 Annual Report," City of Kelowna, accessed October 12, 2012, http://www.kelowna.ca/CityPage/Docs/PDFs//Communications/2011_AnnualReport.pdf.

"2012 News Releases," City of Surrey, accessed October 16, 2012, http://www.surrey.ca/city-government/10412.aspx.

"5 Cultures that Helped Shape Vancouver," The Greater Vancouver Visitors and Convention Bureau, accessed October 16, 2012, http://www.tourismvancouver.com/vancouver/about-vancouver/5-cultures-that-shape-vancouver/.

"A Brief History of the City of Oshawa," The City of Oshawa, accessed October 23, 2012, http://www.oshawa.ca/tourism/history3.asp.

"Abbotsford Community Profile 2010," City of Abbotsford, accessed October 12, 2012, http://viewer.zmags.com/publication/851986af#/851986af/12.

"Abbotsford," Destination British Columbia, accessed October 12, 2012, http://www.hellobc.com/abbotsford.aspx.

"Aboriginal Place Names," Aboriginal Affairs and Northern Development Canada, July 2001, http://www.aadnc-aandc.gc.ca/eng/1100100016346/1100100016350.

"About Brampton," City of Brampton, accessed October 22, 2012, http://www.brampton.ca/en/City-Hall/Pages/About-Brampton.aspx.

"About Burnaby," City of Burnaby, accessed October 12, 2012, http://www.burnaby.ca/About-Burnaby.html.

"About the Town," The Town of Richmond Hill, accessed November 1, 2012, http://www.town.richmond-hill.on.ca/subpage.asp?textonly=&pageid=townhall_about_the_town.

"About UOIT," University of Ontario Institute of Technology, accessed October 23, 2012, http://uoit.ca/about/index.php.

"About," Tourism Burlington, accessed October 22, 2012, http://www.tourismburlington.com/about/.

Adach, Kate, "New Hamilton restaurant hopes to bring elegance to waterfront," *CBC News,* July 24, 2012, http://www.cbc.ca/news/canada/hamilton/news/new-hamilton-restaurant-hopes-to-bring-elegance-to-waterfront-1.1157255.

"Advanced Manufacturing," Hamilton Economic Development Office, accessed October 18, 2012, http://www.investinhamilton.ca/key-industries/advanced-manufacturing/.

"Agriculture," Fraser Valley Regional District, accessed October 12, 2012, http://www.fvrd.bc.ca/InsidetheFVRD/RegionalPlanning/Pages/Agriculture.aspx.

"Agriculture," Richmond City Hall, accessed October 16, 2012, http://www.richmond.ca/plandev/planning2/agriculture.htm.

"Attractions," Tourism Regina, accessed November 5, 2012, http://tourismregina.com/attractions/.

Bailie, Alison, "Canada's Coolest Cities—Montreal: Montreal Case Study," Pembina Institute, May 26, 2010, http://www.pembina.org/pub/2026.

"Barrie Ski Hills & Resorts," WorldWeb.com, accessed October 22, 2012, http://www.barrie-on.worldweb.com/ToursActivities/SkiHillsResorts/.

"Barrie's Festivals Listing," FoundLocally.com, accessed October 22, 2012, http://barrie.foundlocally.com/entertainment/FestivalsList-Barrie.htm.

"Blenkinsop Active Planning Applications," District of Saanich, accessed October 16, 2012, http://www.saanich.ca/business/development/blenkinsop.html.

"Burnaby," Destination British Columbia, accessed October 12, 2012, http://www.hellobc.com/burnaby.aspx.

"Business & Economic Development," City of Surrey, accessed October 16, 2012, http://www.surrey.ca/3463.aspx.

"Business Attraction," London Economic Development Corporation, accessed October 23, 2012, http://www.ledc.com/main/term/about-us/business-attraction.

"Business plans and budgets 2012-2014: Transportation," The City of Calgary, accessed October 12, 2012, http://calgary.ca/CA/fs/Pages/Plans-Budgets-and-Financial-Reports/Business-Plans-and-Budgets-2012-2014/Business-Plans-and-Budgets-2012-2014-Transp

"Calgary: Heart of the North West," Tourism Calgary, accessed October 12, 2012, http://www.visitcalgary.com/sites/default/files/pdf/Leisure%20Sales%20Sheet_English_V2.pdf.

Cambridge Visitor Information Centre, Cambridge Chamber of Commerce, accessed October 23, 2012, http://www.visitcambridgeontario.com/.

Sources for City Backgrounds

"Canada's Coolest Cities—Ottawa—Ottawa Case study," Pembina Institute, May 26, 2010, http://www.pembina.org/pub/2025.

"Canada's Top Ten Weather Stories of 1997," Environment Canada, accessed Oct. 10, 2012, http://www.ec.gc.ca/meteo-weather/default.asp?lang=En&n=3AA35C31-1.

"Canada-Quebec partnership benefits City of Trois-Rivières," Canada Economic Development for Quebec Regions, accessed October 18, 2012, http://www.dec-ced.gc.ca/eng/media-room/news-releases/2012/07/3283.html.

City of Abbotsford, City of Abbotsford, accessed October 12, 2012, http://www.abbotsford.ca/home.

City of Burnaby, City of Burnaby, accessed October 12, 2012, http://www.burnaby.ca/About-Burnaby/About/Population---Quick-Stats/2011-Census-Data.html.

City of Edmonton, City of Edmonton, accessed Oct. 10, 2012, http://www.edmonton.ca.

City of Guelph, City of Guelph, accessed October 23, 2012, http://guelph.ca/.

City of Langley Community Profile & Site Selector Database," City of Langley, 2009, accessed October 16, 2012, http://www.city.langley.bc.ca/images/Profile/community_profile.pdf.

City of London, City of London, accessed October 23, 2012, http://www.london.ca/Pages/Default.aspx.

City of Toronto website. http://www1.toronto.ca/wps/portal/toronto/portal?vgnextoid=b0898622e011c210VgnVCM10000067d60f89RCRD. Accessed Oct. 10, 2012.

City of Vaughan, City of Vaughan, accessed Oct. 10, 2012, http://www.vaughan.ca/Pages/default.aspx.

Coates, Jim, "History of Calgary, Alberta," Discover Calgary, accessed October 12, 2012, http://www.discovercalgary.ca/history/.

"Communities in Halifax," Greater Halifax Partnership, accessed October 22, 2012, http://www.greaterhalifax.com/en/home/livinginhalifax/communities.aspx.

"Community Highlights," City of Cambridge, accessed October 23, 2012, http://www.cambridge.ca/economic_development/stats_facts_and_profiles.

"Community Profile," Town of Ajax, accessed October 22, 2012, http://www.ajax.ca/en/doingbusinessinajax/communityprofile.asp.

Cotroneo, Christian, "General Motors Automotive Centre For Excellence In Oshawa Boasts One Of The World's Biggest Wind Tunnels," The Huffington Post Canada, August 13, 2011, http://www.huffingtonpost.ca/2011/06/13/general-motors-automotive-centre-ex

Daniszewski, Hank, "Wind dome in the works," *The London Free Press,* March 2, 2011, http://www.lfpress.com/news/london/2011/03/01/17455766.html.

"Days of Sail and Steam," Town of Oakville, accessed Oct. 10, 2012, http://www.oakville.ca/culturerec/harbourheritage-essay3.html.

"Detroit River International Crossing," Prime Minister of Canada, accessed Oct. 10, 2012, http://pm.gc.ca/eng/media.asp?id=4865.

"Detroit-Windsor Tunnel: Save Time. Save Gas," Detroit-Windsor Tunnel: An American Roads company, accessed Oct. 10, 2012, http://www.dwtunnel.com/AboutUs.aspx.

"Discover Brampton's History," City of Brampton, accessed October 22, 2012, http://www.brampton.ca/en/Arts-Culture-Tourism/heritage/Pages/Brampton%27s-History.aspx.

Economic Development Burlington, Burlington Economic Development Corporation, accessed October 22, 2012, http://www.bedc.ca/.

"Economic Development: Heritage & History," City of Coquitlam, accessed October 12, 2012, http://www.coquitlam.ca/economic-development/heritage.aspx.

"Economic Development: Overview," City of Coquitlam, accessed October 12, 2012, http://www.coquitlam.ca/economic-development/overview.aspx.

"Economic Highlights," Economic Development Winnipeg, accessed Oct. 10, 2012, http://www.economicdevelopmentwinnipeg.com/winnipegs-economy/economic-highlights.

"Edmonton Census 2012," The City of Edmonton, accessed Oct. 10, 2012, http://www.edmonton.ca/city_government/municipal-census.aspx.

English, John, "Kitchener meets its Waterloo," *Maclean's.ca,* July 28, 2011, http://www2.macleans.ca/2011/07/28/kitchener-meets-its-waterloo/.

Evergreen Line, British Columbia Ministry of Transportation and Infrastructure, accessed October 12, 2012, http://www.evergreenline.gov.bc.ca/.

"Factoids: Made in Winnipeg," Vol. 4. Economic Development Winnipeg, accessed Oct. 10, 2012, http://www.economicdevelopmentwinnipeg.com/uploads/files/Factoids%20Volume%204%20WEB%20FNL.pdf.

"Fast facts about Kitchener," City of Kitchener, January 2011, http://www.kitchener.ca/en/insidecityhall/resources/2011_01_Fast_Facts.pdf.

Sources for City Backgrounds

"Fast Facts," The Greater Vancouver Visitors and Convention Bureau, accessed October 16, 2012, http://www.tourismvancouver.com/vancouver/fast-facts/.

"Fort George National Historic Site of Canada," Parks Canada, accessed Oct. 10, 2012, http://www.pc.gc.ca/lhn-nhs/on/fortgeorge/edu/edua1.aspx.

"Geography," City of Vancouver, accessed October 16, 2012, http://vancouver.ca/green-vancouver/geography.aspx.

"Getting Here," Newfoundland and Labrador Tourism, accessed October 18, 2012, http://www.newfoundlandlabrador.com/PlanYourTrip/GettingHere.

"GM Canada to invest $850-million in R&D at Oshawa facility," *Financial Post,* July 24, 2012, http://business.financialpost.com/2012/07/24/gm-canada-to-invest-850-million-in-rd-at-oshawa-facility/.

"Going to a University or College in Sudbury, Ontario," Campus Starter, accessed October 23, 2012, http://www.campusstarter.com/Sudbury.cfm.

"Greenest City 2020," City of Vancouver, 2012, accessed October 16, 2012, http://vancouver.ca/files/cov/Greenest-city-action-plan.pdf.

"Guided Tours," Tourisme Lévis, accessed November 1, 2012, http://www.tourismelevis.com/en/service/guided-tours/guided-tours/.

"Halifax Quick Facts, 2011," Greater Halifax Partnership, accessed October 22, 2012, http://www.greaterhalifax.com/site-ghp2/media/greaterhalifax/Halifax%20Quick%20Facts%202011.pdf.

"Happy Simcoe Day," Spacing Toronto: Canadian Urbanism Uncovered. http://spacingtoronto.ca/2007/08/06/happy-simoce-day-celebrate-the-man-who-founded-toronto. Accessed Oct 10, 2012.

"Harper Government Invests in Festival JAZZ etcetera Lévis," CNW Group Ltd., July 20, 2012, http://www.newswire.ca/en/story/1010305/harper-government-invests-in-festival-jazz-etcetera-levis.

"Health and Wellness," The Corporation of the City of St. Catharines, accessed November 1, 2012, http://www.stcatharines.ca/en/investin/GreenIndustry.asp.

"Heritage Driving Tour," City of Kelowna, accessed October 12, 2012, http://www.kelowna.ca/CityPage/Docs/PDFs//Strategic%20Planning/Heritage_Driving_Tour_Brochure.pdf.

"Heritage," City of Mississauga, accessed October 23, 2012, http://www.mississauga.ca/portal/residents/heritage.

"History of Hamilton," HamiltonKiosk, accessed October 18, 2012, http://www.hamiltonkiosk.ca/history.php.

"History of Laval," ProvinceQuebec.com, accessed November 1, 2012, http://www.provincequebec.com/laval/history-of-laval/.

"History of Montreal," Best-of-Montreal.com, accessed November 5, 2012, http://www.best-of-montreal.com/history/.

"History of Vaughan," City of Vaughan, accessed Oct. 10, 2012, http://www.vaughan.ca/services/vaughan_archives/historyofvaughan/Pages/default.aspx.

"History," Québec Winter Carnival, accessed October 18, 2012, http://carnaval.qc.ca/en/about/history/.

"Invest," City of Mississauga, accessed October 23, 2012, http://www.mississauga.ca/portal/business/Locate.

"JBMH Expansion," Burlington Chamber of Commerce, October 26, 2011, http://www.burlingtonchamber.com/index.php/category/hot-topics.html.

"Key Sectors," City of Mississauga, accessed October 23, 2012, http://www.mississauga.ca/portal/business/keysectors.

"Langley," Destination BC Corp., accessed October 16, 2012, http://www.hellobc.com/langley/geography.aspx.

"Laurentian University of Sudbury," Uopoly.com, accessed October 23, 2012, http://www.uopoly.com/ontario-universities/laurentian-university-of-sudbury/.

"Le FestiVoix de Trois-Rivières," Tourisme Québec, accessed October 18, 2012, http://www.bonjourquebec.com/qc-en/events-directory/festival-special-event/le-festivoix-de-trois-rivieres_5789232.html.

"Le parc national du Fjord-du-Saguenay," Sépaq, accessed November 5, 2012, www.sepaq.com/pq/sag/index.dot.

"Living in Halifax, Nova Scotia," *Canadian Immigrant,* May 25, 2011, http://canadianimmigrant.ca/settling-in-canada/living-in-halifax-nova-scotia.

"Living in Toronto," University of Toronto John H. Daniels Faculty of Architecture, Landscape, and Design, accessed Oct. 10, 2012, http://www.daniels.utoronto.ca/about/living-toronto.

"Local: Sudbury History—Railway and Mining Boom," FoundLocally.com, accessed October 23, 2012, http://sudbury.foundlocally.com/local/Info-CityHistoryRailwayMiningBoom.htm.

"Location Advantage," Hamilton Economic Development Office, accessed October 18, 2012, http://www.investinhamilton.ca/why-hamilton/location-advantage/.

Sources for City Backgrounds

"Location and Downtown Facts," City of Brampton, accessed October 22, 2012, http://www.brampton.ca/en/Business/edo/Downtown-Queen-Street/Pages/LocationDowntownFacts.aspx.s

"Location," City of Greater Sudbury, accessed October 23, 2012, http://www.city.greatersudbury.on.ca/keyfacts/index.cfm?app=keyfacts&lang=en&ct=350.

"Location," The City of Oshawa, accessed October 23, 2012, http://www.oshawa.ca/eco_dev/locationoe.asp.

London Economic Development Corporation, London Economic Development Corporation, accessed October 23, 2012, http://www.ledc.com/.

"Longueuil," The Canadian Encyclopedia, accessed November 1, 2012, http://www.thecanadianencyclopedia.com/articles/longueuil.

"Lévis Forts National Historic Site," Parks Canada, accessed November 1, 2012, http://www.pc.gc.ca/lhn-nhs/qc/levis/index.aspx.

"Lévis Tourist Guide 2012-2013," Tourisme Lévis, accessed November 1, 2012, http://issuu.com/villedelevis/docs/villedelevis_touristguide_eng_2012.

Macaluso, Grace, "Oshawa automotive capital of Canada," *The Windsor Star,* February 7, 2012, http://blogs.windsorstar.com/2012/02/07/oshawa-automotive-capital-of-canada/.

"Maritime Services—Québec-Lévis," Société des traversiers du Québec, accessed November 1, 2012, http://traversiers.com/ferries/quebeclevis_16.php.

"Markham," York Region Economic Strategy, accessed October 23, 2012, http://www.investinyork.ca/our-communities/markham.

"Montreal a city of design," *Gazette (Montreal),* May 5, 2007, http://www.canada.com/montrealgazette/story.html?id=3b345e23-1c16-4b82-839c-d5fdc9d3d8e3&k=79136.

"Montreal Parks," montreal.com, accessed November 5, 2012, http://www.montreal.com/parks/mtroyal.html.

"Montréal," The Canadian Trade Commissioner Service," accessed November 5, 2012, http://www.international.gc.ca/investors-investisseurs/cities-villes/montreal.aspx.

"News," IBM Data Centre information, September 21, 2012, http://www.ibm.com/news/ca/en/2012/09/21/f442801w72056a83.html.

"Official Words," Cultural Capital of Canada, accessed October 18, 2012, http://www.capitaleculturelle.ca/en/node/35.

"Old Port of Montréal/Longueuil crossing," Tourisme Québec, accessed November 1, 2012, http://www.bonjourquebec.com/qc-en/tourist-services-directory/ferry/old-port-of-Montr%C3%A9al-longueuil-crossing_6685657.html.

"Ottawa-Gatineau Population Outpaced National Growth," The Canadian Press, accessed Oct. 10, 2012, http://www.cbc.ca/news/canada/ottawa/story/2012/02/08/ottawa-gatineau-census-population-growth.html.

"Our History," Western University, accessed October 23, 2012, http://www.uwo.ca/about/whoweare/history.html.

"Outaouais. Near and Dear," Tourisme Outaouais, accessed Oct. 10, 2012, http://www.tourismeoutaouais.com/en-ca/_pages/Outaouais.aspx.

"Programs and Activities," The Corporation of the City of Markham, accessed October 23, 2012, http://www.markham.ca/wps/portal/Markham/RecreationCulture/ProgramsActivities.

"Projects and Initiatives," City of Burlington, accessed October 22, 2012, http://cms.burlington.ca/Page150.aspx.

"Quality of Life," Chatham-Kent, accessed October 23, 2012, http://www.chatham-kent.ca/EconomicDevelopment/QualityofLife/Pages/CommunityProfile.aspx.

"Quick Facts," City of Saskatoon, accessed Oct. 10, 2012, http://www.saskatoon.ca/QUICK%20FACTS/Pages/Quick%20Facts.aspx.

"Québec City," The Canadian Encyclopedia, accessed October 18, 2012, http://www.thecanadianencyclopedia.com/articles/quebec-city.

"Québec," Tourisme Québec, accessed October 18, 2012, http://www.bonjourquebec.com/qc-en/quebec0.html.

"Regina," Tourism Saskatchewan, accessed November 5, 2012, http://www.sasktourism.com/places-to-go/regions/regina.

Richmond City Hall, Richmond City Hall, accessed October 16, 2012. http://www.richmond.ca/home.htm.

"Richmond Hill," York Region Economic Strategy, accessed November 1, 2012, http://www.investinyork.ca/our-communities/richmond-hill.

"Richmond, British Columbia—Did You Know?," Tourism Richmond, accessed October 16, 2012, http://www.tourismrichmond.com/media/news-releases/richmond-british-columbia-did-you-know .

Roy-Sole, Monique, "Trois-Rivières—A tale of tenacity," Canadian Geographic Magazine, April 2009, http://www.canadiangeographic.ca/magazine/apr09/trois_rivieres4.asp.

"Saanich," VancouverIsland.com, accessed October 16, 2012, http://www.saanichbc.com/.

Sources for City Backgrounds

"Saskatoon," Saskbiz.ca, accessed Oct. 10, 2012, http://www.saskbiz.ca/communityprofiles/communityprofile.asp?CommunityID=10.

"Self-guided Walking Tour," Local Architectural Conservation Advisory Committee, accessed Oct. 10, 2012, http://www.whitby.ca/en/resources/walking_tour.pdf.

Shantz, Hilary, "A Little Oakville (Ontario) History Lesson: Understanding Our Roots as a Community," The Oakville Buzz, accessed October 4, 2012, http://theoakvillebuzz.com/2008/01/29/a-little-oakville-ontario-history-lesson-understanding-our-roots

"Sherbrooke Parks & Gardens," WorldWeb.com, accessed November 5, 2012, http://www.sherbrooke-qc.worldweb.com/SightsAttractions/ParksGardens/.

"Sherbrooke," Encyclopedia Britannica, accessed November 5, 2012, http://www.britannica.com/EBchecked/topic/540023/Sherbrooke.

"Sherbrooke," Tourism Eastern Townships, accessed November 5, 2012, http://www.easterntownships.org/city/43025/sherbrooke.

"St. John's-City of Legends," Memorial University of Newfoundland, accessed October 18, 2012, http://www.mun.ca/folklore/about/st.php.

"Statistics and Demographics," The Corporation of the City of Markham, accessed October 23, 2012, http://www.markham.ca/wps/portal/Markham/AboutMarkham/FactsStats.

"Sudbury is business centre of Northern Ontario and Canada's mining capital," *Sudbury Northern Life,* April 7, 2009, http://www.northernlife.ca/sudbury/default.aspx.

"Terrebonne (Quebec)," Canadian Travel Guide, accessed November 5, 2012, http://www.canadiantravelguide.net/cities/TERREBONNE/.

"Terrebonne," Authentic Québec, accessed November 5, 2012, http://www.quebecauthentique-pro.org/member/302_Terrebonne.

"Terrebonne," The Canadian Encyclopedia, accessed November 5, 2012, http://www.thecanadianencyclopedia.com/articles/terrebonne.

"The Laval region at a glance," Gouvernement du Québec, Ministre de l'Immigration et des Communautés culturelles, accessed November 1, 2012, http://www.immigration-quebec.gouv.qc.ca/en/settle/laval.html.

"The Liveabililty Ranking and Overview August 2012," The Economist Group, accessed October 12, 2012, https://www.eiu.com/public/topical_report.aspx?campaignid=Liveability2012.

The Official Website of Tourism Toronto. Media Toolkit. http://www.seetorontonow.com/Media/MediaKit.aspx. Accessed Oct. 10, 2012.

"The Parliament Buildings," Library of Parliament, accessed October 23, 2013, http://www.parl.gc.ca/About/Parliament/Publications/ParliamentBuildings/ParlBlgs-e.asp.

"The Welland Canal Section of the St. Lawrence Seaway," The St. Lawrence Seaway Management Corporation, March 2003, http://www.greatlakes-seaway.com/en/pdf/welland.pdf .

Thiessen, Carol, "Calgary Rankings," Calgary Economic Development, accessed October 12, 2012, http://www.calgaryeconomicdevelopment.com/economic-research/calgary-rankings.

"Things to See," Chatham-Kent, accessed October 23, 2012, http://www.chatham-kent.ca/tourism/ThingstoSee/Pages/Things%20to%20See.aspx.

"Thunder Bay History," City of Thunder Bay, accessed Oct. 10, 2012, http://www.thunderbay.ca/Living/culture_and_heritage/tbay_history.htm.

"Top Ten—Canada's Top 10 Most Populous Cities," *Business Review Canada,* April 13, 2011, http://www.businessreviewcanada.ca/top_ten/top-10-people/canadas-top-10-most-populous-cities.

Tourism Burlington, Tourism Burlington, accessed October 22, 2012, http://www.tourismburlington.com.

"Tourism Information—Top Ten Reasons To Visit Richmond Hill," The Town of Richmond Hill, accessed November 1, 2012, http://richmondhill.ca/printpage.asp?pageid=hotnews_top_ten_reasons.

Tourism Kingston, Tourism Kingston Corporate, accessed October 23, 2012, http://tourism.kingstoncanada.com/en/index.asp.

Tourism Richmond, Tourism Richmond, accessed October 16, 2012, http://www.tourismrichmond.com/.

Town of Whitby, Town of Whitby, accessed Oct. 10, 2012, http://www.whitby.ca/en.

"Travel to Sherbrooke," Université de Sherbrooke, accessed November 5, 2012, http://www.mednuc.usherb.ca/dosgel2006/travel.htm.

Vaughan: A City on the Move, City of Vaughan, accessed Oct 10, 2012, https://www.vaughan.ca/business/international_business_development/General%20Documents/World_of_Opportunity_Vaughan_promo_brochure_2013.pdf.

"Ville de Terrebonne," Tourisme Lanaudière, accessed November 5, 2012, http://www.lanaudiere.ca/en/members/5112.

"Visitors," City of Winnipeg, accessed Oct. 10, 2012, http://winnipeg.ca/interhom/toc/visitors.asp.

Sources for City Backgrounds

"War of 1812 Bicentennial," City of Windsor, accessed Oct. 10, 2012, http://www.citywindsor.ca/residents/Culture/Windsors-Community-Museum/Pages/War-of-1812-Bicentennial.aspx.

"Waterloo Regional Tourism Marketing Corporation (WRTMC)," Explore Waterloo Region, accessed October 18, 2012, http://www.explorewaterlooregion.com/about/kitchener.

Weaver, Grant, "History of Markham, Ontario, Canada," GuidingStar.ca, accessed October 23, 2012, http://www.guidingstar.ca/Markham_Ontario_History.htm.

Welling, Dominic, "Kelowna Airport kick-starts $50m expansion programme," *Airport World*, September 27, 2011, http://www.airport-world.com/home/general-news/item/1020-kelowna-airport-kick-starts-$50m-expansion-programme.

"What's on Where—Oshawa and Ajax, Ontario," HOToronto, accessed October 22, 2012, http://www.hotoronto.com/oshawa/index.htm.

"Who is Metro Vancouver," Metro Vancouver, accessed October 16, 2012, http://www.metrovancouver.org/about/Pages/default.aspx.

"Why choose Laval?," Tourisme Laval, accessed November 1, 2012, http://www.tourismelaval.com/en/tour-and-travel/choose-laval.

"Windsor," Tourism Windsor-Essex-Pelee Island, accessed Oct. 10, 2012, http://www.visitwindsoressex.com/wps/wcm/connect/TWEPI/TWEPI/LEFT+NAV/COMMUNITIES/Windsor.

"Workforce Development," The City of Edmonton, accessed Oct. 10, 2012, http://www.edmonton.com/for-business/3377.aspx.

CANADA'S INFORMATION RESOURCE CENTRE (CIRC)

Access all these great resources Online, all the time, at Canada's Information Resource Centre (CIRC)
http://circ.greyhouse.ca

Canada's Information Resource Centre (CIRC) integrates all of Grey House Canada's award-winning reference content into one easy-to-use online resource. With over 100,000 Canadian organizations, contacts, facts and figures, it is the most comprehensive resource for specialized database content in Canada!

KEY ADVANTAGES OF CIRC:

- seamlessly cross-database search content from select databases
- save search results for future reference
- link directly to websites or email addresses
- clear display of your results make compiling and adding to your research easier than ever before

DESIGN YOUR OWN CUSTOM CONTACT LISTS!

CIRC gives you the option to define and extract your own lists in seconds. Whether you need contact, mail or e-mail lists, CIRC can pull together the information quickly and export it in a variety of formats.

CHOOSE BETWEEN QUICK AND EXPERT SEARCH!

With CIRC, you can choose between Expert and Quick search to pinpoint information. Designed for both novice and advanced researchers, you can conduct simple text searches as well as powerful Boolean searches.

SEARCH THE DATABASE USING COMMON OR UNIQUE FIELDS SUCH AS:

- organization type - area code - number of employees
- affiliations - founding year - language
- category - city - branch name
- contact name - contact title - postal code

ONLY GREY HOUSE DIRECTORIES PROVIDE SPECIAL CONTENT YOU WON'T FIND ANYWHERE ELSE!

- **Associations Canada:** finances/funding sources, activities, publications, conferences, membership, awards, member profile
- **Canadian Parliamentary Guide:** private and political careers of elected members, complete list of constituencies and representatives
- **Canadian Environmental Resouce Guide:** products/services/areas of expertise, working languages, domestic markets, type of ownership, revenue sources
- **Financial Services:** type of ownership, number of employees, year founded, assets, revenue, ticker symbol
- **Libraries Canada:** staffing, special collections, services, year founded, national library symbol, regional system
- **Governments Canada:** municipal population
- **Canadian Who's Who:** birth city, publications, education (degrees, alma mater), career/occupation and employer
- **Major Canadian Cities:** demographics, ethnicity, immigration, language, education, housing, income, labour and transportation
- **Health Guide Canada:** chronic and mental illnesses, general resources, appendices and statistics

Health Guide Canada now available on CIRC!

Health Guide Canada now available on CIRC! With just a few clicks, you'll have access to information on 99 chronic and mental illnesses, relevant resources and statistics.

CIRC provides easier searching and faster, more pinpointed results of all of our great resources in Canada, from Associations and Government to Major Companies to Zoos and everything in between. Whether you need fully detailed information on your contact or just an email address, you can customize your search query to meet your needs. Contact us now for a free trial subscription or visit http://circ.greyhouse.ca. You'll be amazed at how much data can be right at your fingertips 24/7!

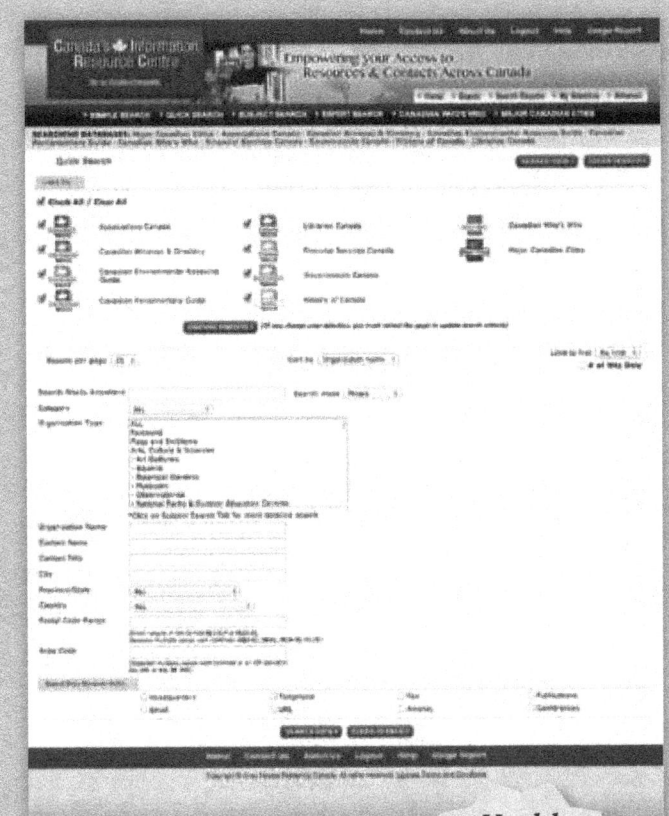

GREY HOUSE PUBLISHING CANADA

For more information please contact Grey House Publishing Canada
Tel.: (866) 433-4739 or (416) 644-6479 Fax: (416) 644-1904 | info@greyhouse.ca | www.greyhouse.ca

CENTRE DE DOCUMENTATION DU CANADA (CDC)

Consultez en tout temps toutes ces excellentes ressources en ligne grâce au Centre de documentation du Canada (CDC) à http://circ.greyhouse.ca

Le Centre de documentation du Canada (CDC) regroupe sous une seule ressource en ligne conviviale tout le contenu des ouvrages de référence primés de Grey House Canada. Répertoriant plus de 100 000 entreprises canadiennes, personnes-ressources, faits et chiffres, il s'agit de la ressource la plus complète en matière de bases de données spécialisées au Canada.

PRINCIPAUX AVANTAGES DU CDC

- Recherche transversale efficace dans le contenu des bases de données
- Sauvegarde des résultats de recherche pour consultation future
- Lien direct aux sites Web et aux adresses électroniques
- Grâce à l'affichage lisible de vos résultats, il est dorénavant plus facile de compiler les résultats ou d'ajouter des critères à vos recherches.

CONCEPTION PERSONNALISÉE DE VOS LISTES DE PERSONNES-RESSOURCES!

Le CDC vous permet de définir et d'extraire vos propres listes, et ce, en quelques secondes. Que vous ayez besoin d'une liste de coordonnées, de distribution ou de courriels, le CDC peut rassembler l'information rapidement et l'exporter en plusieurs formats.

CHOISISSEZ ENTRE LA RECHERCHE RAPIDE ET CELLE D'EXPERT!

Grâce au CDC, vous pouvez choisir entre une recherche d'expert ou rapide pour localiser l'information avec précision. Vous avez la possibilité d'effectuer des recherches en texte simple ou booléennes puissantes – les recherches sont conçues à l'intention des chercheurs débutants et avancés.

RECHERCHE DANS LA BASE DE DONNÉES À L'AIDE DE CHAMPS COMMUNS OU SPÉCIAUX

- Type d'organisation – indicatif régional – nombre d'employés
- Affiliations – année de la fondation – langue
- Catégorie – ville – nom de la succursale
- Nom de la personne-ressource – titre de la personne-ressource – code postal

SEULS LES RÉPERTOIRES DE GREY HOUSE VOUS OFFRENT UN CONTENU PARTICULIER QUE VOUS NE TROUVEREZ NULLE PART AILLEURS!

- **Le répertoire des associations du Canada:** sources de financement, activités, publications, congrès, membres, prix, profil de membre
- **Guide parlementaire canadien:** carrières privées et politiques des membres élus, liste complète des comtés et des représentants
- **Guide des ressources environnementales canadiennes:** produits/services/domaines d'expertise, langues de travail, marchés nationaux, type de propriétaire, sources de revenus
- **Services financiers:** type de propriétaire, nombre d'employés, année de la fondation, immobilisations, revenus, symbole au téléscripteur
- **Bibliothèques Canada:** personnel, collections particulières, services, année de la fondation, symbole de bibliothèque national, système régional
- **Gouvernements du Canada:** population municipale
- **Canadian Who's Who:** ville d'origine, publication, formation (diplômes et alma mater), carrière/emploi et employeur
- **Major Canadian Cities:** données démographiques, ethnicité, immigration, langue, éducation, logement, revenu, main-d'œuvre et transport
- **Health Guide Canada:** maladies chroniques et mentales, ressources generales, annexes et statistiques.

Health Guide Canada est désormais offert dans le CDC! Il vous suffira quelques clics de souris pour avoir accès à l'information de 99 maladies chroniques et mentales, ainsi que des ressources et statistiques pertinentes.

Le nouveau CDC facilite la recherche au sein de toutes nos ressources au Canada et procure plus rapidement des résultats plus poussés – des associations au gouvernement en passant par les principales entreprises et les zoos, sans oublier tout un éventail d'organisations! Que vous ayez besoin d'information très détaillée au sujet de votre personne-ressource ou d'une simple adresse électronique, vous pouvez personnaliser votre requête afin qu'elle réponde à vos besoins. Communiquez avec nous pour obtenir une inscription d'essai GRATUITE ou visitez le http://circ.greyhouse.ca. Vous serez agréablement surpris de constater que les renseignements sont à portée de main, et ce, 24 heures sur 24, 7 jours sur 7!

Health Guide Canada est désormais offert dans le CDC!

GREY HOUSE PUBLISHING CANADA

Pour obtenir plus d'information, veuillez contacter Grey House Publishing Canada par tél. : 1 866 433-4739 ou 416 644-6479 par téléc. : 416 644-1904 | info@greyhouse.ca | www.greyhouse.ca

Canadian Almanac & Directory
The Definitive Resource for Facts & Figures About Canada

The *Canadian Almanac & Directory* has been Canada's most authoritative sourcebook for 166 years. Published annually since 1847, it continues to be widely used by publishers, business professionals, government offices, researchers, information specialists and anyone needing current, accessible information on every imaginable topic relevant to those who live and work in Canada.

A directory and a guide, the *Canadian Almanac & Directory* provides the most comprehensive picture of Canada, from physical attributes to economic and business summaries, leisure and recreation. It combines textual materials, charts, colour photographs and directory listings with detailed profiles, all verified and organized for easy retrieval. The *Canadian Almanac & Directory* is a wealth of general information, displaying national statistics on population, employment, CPI, imports and exports, as well as images of national awards, Canadian symbols, flags, emblems and Canadian parliamentary leaders.

For important contacts throughout Canada, for any number of business projects or for that once-in-a-while critical fact, the *Canadian Almanac & Directory* will help you find the leads you didn't even know existed—quickly and easily!

ALL THE INFORMATION YOU'LL EVER NEED, ORGANIZED INTO 17 DISTINCT CATEGORIES FOR EASY NAVIGATION!

Almanac—a fact-filled snapshot of Canada, including History, Geography, Economics and Vital Statistics.

Arts & Culture—includes 9 topics from Galleries to Zoos.

Associations—thousands of organizations arranged in 139 different topics, from Accounting to Writers.

Broadcasting—Canada's major Broadcasting Companies, Provincial Radio and Television Stations, Cable Companies, and Specialty Broadcasters.

Business & Finance—Accounting, Banking, Insurance, Canada's Major Companies and Stock Exchanges.

Education—arranged by Province and includes Districts, Government Agencies, Specialized and Independent Schools, Universities and Technical facilities.

Government—spread over three sections, with a Quick Reference Guide, Federal and Provincial listings, County and Municipal Districts and coverage of Courts in Canada.

Health—Government agencies, hospitals, community health centres, retirement care and mental health facilities.

Law Firms—all Major Law Firms, followed by smaller firms organized by Province and listed alphabetically.

Libraries—Canada's main Library/Archive and Government Departments for Libraries, followed by Provincial listings and Regional Systems.

Publishing—Books, Magazines and Newspapers organized by Province, including frequency and circulation figures.

Religion—broad information about religious groups and associations from 21 different denominations.

Sports—Associations for 93 single sports, with detailed League and Team listings.

Transportation—complete listings for all major modes.

Utilities—Associations, Government Agencies and Provincial Utility Companies.

PRINT OR ONLINE—QUICK AND EASY ACCESS TO ALL THE INFORMATION YOU NEED!

Available in hardcover print or electronically via the web, the *Canadian Almanac & Directory* provides instant access to the people you need and the facts you want every time.

Canadian Almanac & Directory print edition is verified and updated annually. Regular ongoing changes are added to the web version on a monthly basis. The web version allows you to narrow your search by using index fields such as name or type of organization, subject, location, contact name or title and postal code.

Online subscribers have the option to instantly generate their own contact lists and export them into spreadsheets for further use—a great alternative to high cost list broker services.

GREY HOUSE PUBLISHING CANADA

For more information please contact Grey House Publishing Canada
Tel.: (866)-433-4739 or (416) 644-6479 Fax: (416) 644-1904 | info@greyhouse.ca | www.greyhouse.ca

Répertoire et almanach canadien
La ressource de référence au sujet des données et des faits relatifs au Canada

Le *Répertoire et almanach canadien* constitue le guide canadien le plus rigoureux depuis 166 ans. Publié annuellement depuis 1847, il est toujours grandement utilisé dans le monde des affaires, les bureaux gouvernementaux, par les spécialistes de l'information, les chercheurs, les éditeurs ou quiconque est à la recherche d'information actuelle et accessible sur tous les sujets imaginables à propos des gens qui vivent et travaillent au Canada.

À la fois répertoire et guide, le *Répertoire et almanach canadien* dresse le tableau le plus complet du Canada, des caractéristiques physiques jusqu'aux revues économique et commerciale, en passant par les loisirs et les activités récréatives. Il combine des documents textuels, des représentations graphiques, des photographies en couleurs et des listes de répertoires accompagnées de profils détaillés. Autant d'information pointue et organisée de manière à ce qu'elle soit facile à obtenir. Le *Répertoire et almanach canadien* foisonne de renseignements généraux. Il présente des statistiques nationales sur la population, l'emploi, l'IPC, l'importation et l'exportation ainsi que des images des prix nationaux, des symboles canadiens, des drapeaux, des emblèmes et des leaders parlementaires canadiens.

Si vous cherchez des personnes-ressources essentielles un peu partout au Canada, peu importe qu'il s'agisse de projets d'affaires ou d'une question factuelle anecdotique, le Répertoire et almanach canadien vous fournira les pistes dont vous ignoriez l'existence – rapidement et facilement!

TOUTE L'INFORMATION DONT VOUS AUREZ BESOIN, ORGANISÉE EN 17 CATÉGORIES DISTINCTES POUR UNE CONSULTATION FACILE!

Almanach—un aperçu informatif du Canada, notamment l'histoire, la géographie, l'économie et les statistiques essentielles.

Arts et culture—comprends 9 sujets, des galeries aux zoos.

Associations—des milliers d'organisations classées selon 139 sujets différents, de l'actuariat au zoo.

Radiodiffusion—les principales sociétés de radiodiffusion au Canada, les stations radiophoniques et de télévision ainsi que les entreprises de câblodistribution et les diffuseurs thématiques.

Commerce et finance—comptabilité, services bancaires, assurances, principales entreprises et bourses canadiennes.

Éducation—organisé par province et comprend les arrondissements scolaires, les organismes gouvernementaux, les écoles spécialisées et indépendantes, les universités et les établissements techniques.

Gouvernement—s'étend sur trois sections et comprend un guide de référence, des listes fédérales et provinciales, les comtés et arrondissements municipaux ainsi que les cours canadiennes.

Santé—organismes gouvernementaux, hôpitaux, centres de santé communautaires, établissements de soins pour personnes retraitées et de soins de santé mentale.

Sociétés d'avocats—toutes les principales sociétés d'avocats, suivies des sociétés plus petites, classées par province et en ordre alphabétique.

Bibliothèques—la bibliothèque et les archives principales du Canada ainsi que les bibliothèques des ministères, suivis des listes provinciales et des systèmes régionaux.

Édition—livres, magazines et journaux classés par province, y compris leur fréquence et les données relatives à leur diffusion.

Religion—information générale au sujet des groupes religieux et des associations religieuses de 21 dénominations.

Sports—associations de 93 sports distincts; comprend des listes de ligues et d'équipes.

Transport—des listes complètes des principaux modes de transport.

Services publics—associations, organismes gouvernementaux et entreprises de services publics provinciales.

FORMAT PAPIER OU EN LIGNE— ACCÈS RAPIDE À TOUS LES RENSEIGNEMENTS DONT VOUS AVEZ BESOIN!

Offert sous couverture rigide ou en format électronique grâce au web, le *Répertoire et almanach canadien* offre invariablement un accès instantané aux représentants du gouvernement et aux faits qui font l'objet de vos recherches.

La version imprimée du Répertoire et almanach canadien est vérifiée et mise à jour annuellement. La version en ligne est mise à jour mensuellement. Cette version vous permet de circonscrire la recherche grâce aux champs de l'index comme le nom ou le type d'organisme, le sujet, l'emplacement, le nom ou le titre de la personne-ressource et le code postal.

Les abonnés au service en ligne peuvent générer instantanément leurs propres listes de contacts et les exporter en format feuille de calcul pour une utilisation approfondie – une solution de rechange géniale aux services dispendieux d'un commissionnaire en publipostage.

GREY HOUSE PUBLISHING CANADA

Pour obtenir plus d'information, veuillez contacter Grey House Publishing Canada
par tél. : 1 866 433-4739 ou 416 644-6479 par téléc. : 416 644-1904 | info@greyhouse.ca | www.greyhouse.ca

Health Guide Canada
An Informative Handbook on Health Services in Canada

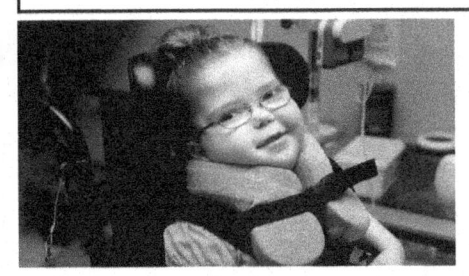

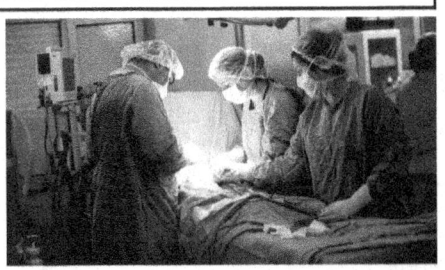

Health Guide Canada: An informative handbook on chronic and mental illnesses and health services in Canada offers a comprehensive overview of 99 chronic and mental illnesses, from Addison's to Wilson's disease. Each chapter includes an easy-to-understand medical description, plus a wide range of condition-specific support services and information resources that deal with the variety of issues concerning those with a chronic or mental illness, as well as those who support the illness community.

Health Guide Canada contains thousands of ways to deal with the many aspects of chronic or mental health disorder. It includes associations, government agencies, libraries and resource centres, educational facilities, hospitals and publications. In addition to chapters dealing with specific chronic or mental conditions, there is a chapter relevant to the health industry in general, as well as others dealing with charitable foundations, death and bereavement groups, homeopathic medicine, indigenous issues and sports for the disabled.

Specific sections include:

- Educational Material
- Section I: Chronic & Mental Illnesses
- Section II: General Resources
- Section III: Appendices
- Section IV: Statistics

Each listing will provide a description, address (including website, email address and social media links, if possible) and executives' names and titles, as well as a number of details specific to that type of organization.

In addition to patients and families, hospital and medical centre personnel can find the support they need in their work or study. *Health Guide Canada* is full of resources crucial for people with chronic illness as they transition from diagnosis to home, home to work, and work to community life.

PRINT OR ONLINE—QUICK AND EASY ACCESS TO ALL THE INFORMATION YOU NEED!

Available in softcover print or electronically via the web, *Health Guide Canada* provides instant access to the people you need and the facts you want every time. Whereas the print edition is verified and updated annually, ongoing changes are added to the web version on a monthly basis. The web version allows you to narrow your search by using index fields such as name or type of organization, subject, location, contact name or title and postal code.

HEALTH GUIDE CANADA HELPS YOU FIND WHAT YOU NEED WITH THESE VALUABLE SOURCING TOOLS!

Entry Name Index—An alphabetical list of all entries, providing a quick and easy way to access any listing in this edition.

Tabs—Main sections are tabbed for easy look-up. Headers on each page make it easy to locate the data you need.

Create your own contact lists! Online subscribers have the option to instantly generate their own contact lists and export them into spreadsheets for further use—a great alternative to high cost list broker services.

GREY HOUSE PUBLISHING CANADA For more information please contact Grey House Publishing Canada
Tel.: (866)-433-4739 or (416) 644-6479 Fax: (416) 644-1904 | info@greyhouse.ca | www.greyhouse.ca

Guide canadien de la santé
Un manuel informatif au sujet des services en santé au Canada

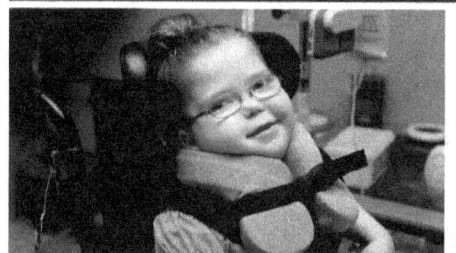

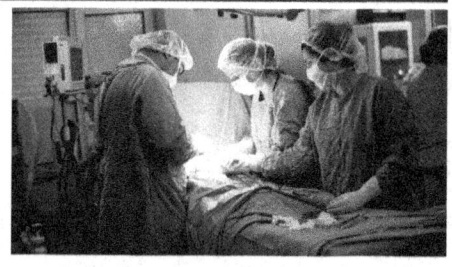

Le *Guide canadien de la santé : un manuel informatif au sujet des maladies chroniques et mentales de même que des services en santé au Canada* donne un aperçu exhaustif de 99 maladies chroniques et mentales, de la maladie d'Addison à celle de Wilson. Chaque chapitre comprend une description médicale facile à comprendre, une vaste gamme de services de soutien particuliers à l'état et des ressources documentaires qui portent sur diverses questions relatives aux personnes qui sont aux prises avec une maladie chronique ou mentale et à ceux qui soutiennent la communauté liée à cette maladie.

Le *Guide canadien de la santé* contient des milliers de moyens pour composer avec divers aspects d'une maladie chronique ou d'un problème de santé mentale. Il comprend des associations, des organismes gouvernementaux, des bibliothèques et des centres de documentation, des services d'éducation, des hôpitaux et des publications. En plus des chapitres qui portent sur des états chroniques ou mentaux, un chapitre traite de l'industrie de la santé en général; d'autres abordent les fondations qui réalisent des rêves, les groupes de soutien axés sur le décès et le deuil, la médecine homéopathique, les questions autochtones et les sports pour les personnes handicapées. Les sections incluent

- Matériel didactique
- Section I : Les maladies chroniques ou mentales
- Section II : Les ressources génériques
- Section III : Les annexes
- Section IV : Les statistiques

Chaque entrée comprend une description, une adresse (y compris le site Web, le courriel et les liens des médias sociaux, lorsque possible), les noms et titres des directeurs de même que plusieurs détails particuliers à ce type d'organisme.

Les membres du personnel des hôpitaux et des centres médicaux peuvent trouver, au même titre que parents et familles, le soutien dont ils ont besoin dans le cadre de leur travail ou de leurs études. Le *Guide canadien de la santé* est rempli de ressources capitales pour les personnes qui souffrent d'une maladie chronique alors qu'elles passent du diagnostic au retour à la maison, de la maison au travail et du travail à la vie au sein de la communauté.

OFFERT EN FORMAT PAPIER OU EN LIGNE—UN ACCÈS RAPIDE ET FACILE À TOUS LES RENSEIGNEMENTS DONT VOUS AVEZ BESOIN!

Offert sous couverture souple ou en format électronique grâce au web, le *Guide canadien de la santé* donne invariablement un accès instantané aux personnes et aux faits dont vous avez besoin. Si la version imprimée est vérifiée et mise à jour annuellement, des changements continus sont apportés mensuellement à la base de données en ligne. Servez-vous de la version en ligne afin de circonscrire vos recherches grâce à des champs spéciaux de l'index comme le nom de l'organisation ou son type, le sujet, l'emplacement, le nom de la personne-ressource ou son titre et le code postal.

LE GUIDE CANADIEN DE LA SANTÉ VOUS AIDERA À TROUVER CE DONT VOUS AVEZ BESOIN GRÂCE À CES OUTILS DE REPÉRAGE PRÉCIEUX!

Répertoire nominatif—une list alphabétique offrant un moyen rapide et facile d'accéder à toute liste de cette edition.

Onglets—les sections principals possèdent un onglet pour une consultation facile. Les notes en tête de chaque page vous aident à trouver les données voulues.

Créez vos propres listes! Les abonnés au service en ligne peuvent générer instantanément leurs propres listes de contacts et les exporter en format feuille de calcul pour une utilisation approfondie – une solution de rechange géniale aux services dispendieux d'un commissionnaire en publipostage.

GREY HOUSE PUBLISHING CANADA

Pour obtenir plus d'information, veuillez contacter Grey House Publishing Canada
par tél. : 1 866 433-4739 ou 416 644-6479 par téléc. : 416 644-1904 | info@greyhouse.ca | www.greyhouse.ca

Associations Canada
Makes Researching Organizations Quick and Easy

Associations Canada is an easy-to-use compendium, providing detailed indexes, listings and abstracts on over 19,000 local, regional, provincial, national and international organizations (identifying location, budget, founding date, management, scope of activity and funding source—just to name a few).

POWERFUL INDEXES HELP YOU TARGET THE ORGANIZATIONS YOU WANT

There are a number of criteria you can use to target specific organizations. Organized with the user in mind, *Associations Canada* is broken down into a number of indexes to help you find what you're looking for quickly and easily.

- **Subject Index**—listing of Canadian and foreign association headquarters, alphabetically by subject and keyword
- **Acronym Index**—an alphabetical listing of acronyms and corresponding Canadian and foreign associations, in both official languages
- **Budget Index**—Canadian associations, alphabetical within eight budget categories
- **Conferences & Conventions Index**—meetings sponsored by Canadian and foreign associations, listed alphabetically by conference name
- **Executive Name Index**—alphabetical listing of key contacts of Canadian associations, for both headquarters and branches
- **Geographic Index**—listing of headquarters, branch offices, chapters and divisions of Canadian associations, alphabetical within province and city
- **Mailing List Index**—associations that offer mailing lists, alphabetical by subject
- **Registered Charitable Organizations Index**—listing of associations that are registered charities, alphabetical by subject

PRINT OR ONLINE—QUICK AND EASY ACCESS TO ALL THE INFORMATION YOU NEED!

Available in hardcover print or electronically via the web, *Associations Canada* provides instant access to the people you need and the facts you want every time. Whereas the print edition is verified and updated annually, ongoing changes are added to the web version on a monthly basis. The web version allows you to narrow your search by using index fields such as name or type of organization, subject, location, contact name or title and postal code.

Create your own contact lists! Online subscribers have the option to instantly generate their own contact lists and export them into spreadsheets for further use—a great alternative to high cost list broker services.

ASSOCIATIONS CANADA PROVIDES COMPLETE ACCESS TO THESE HIGHLY LUCRATIVE MARKETS:

Travel & Tourism
- Who's hosting what event...when and where?
- Check on events up to three years in advance

Journalism and Media
- Pure research—What do they do? Who is in charge? What's their budget?
- Check facts and sources in one step

Libraries
- Refer researchers to the most complete Canadian association reference anywhere

Business
- Target your market, research your interests, compile profiles and identify membership lists
- Warm up your cold calls with all the background you need to sell your product or service
- Preview prospects by budget, market interest or geographic location

Association Executives
- Look for strategic alliances with associations of similar interest
- Spot opportunities or conflicts with convention plans

Research & Government
- Scan interest groups or identify charities in your area of concern
- Check websites, publications and speaker availability
- Evaluate mandates, affiliations and scope

GREY HOUSE PUBLISHING CANADA
For more information please contact Grey House Publishing Canada
Tel.: (866) 433-4739 or (416) 644-6479 Fax: (416) 644-1904 | info@greyhouse.ca | www.greyhouse.ca

Associations du Canada
La recherche d'organisations simplifiée

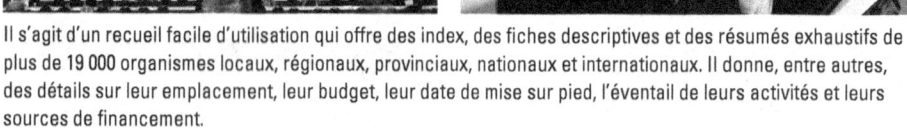

Il s'agit d'un recueil facile d'utilisation qui offre des index, des fiches descriptives et des résumés exhaustifs de plus de 19 000 organismes locaux, régionaux, provinciaux, nationaux et internationaux. Il donne, entre autres, des détails sur leur emplacement, leur budget, leur date de mise sur pied, l'éventail de leurs activités et leurs sources de financement.

En plus d'affecter plus d'un milliard de dollars annuellement aux frais de transport, à la participation à des congrès et à la mise en marché, *Associations du Canada* débourse des millions de dollars dans sa quête pour répondre aux intérêts de ses membres.

DES INDEX PUISSANTS QUI VOUS AIDENT À CIBLER LES ORGANISATIONS VOULUES

Vous pouvez vous servir de plusieurs critères pour cibler des organisations précises. C'est avec l'utilisateur en tête qu'*Associations du Canada* a été divisé en plusieurs index pour vous aider à trouver, rapidement et facilement, ce que vous cherchez.

- **Index des sujets**—liste des sièges sociaux d'associations canadiennes et étrangères; sujets classés en ordre alphabétique et mot-clé.
- **Index des acronymes**—liste alphabétique des acronymes et des associations canadiennes et étrangères équivalentes; présenté dans les deux langues officielles.
- **Index des budgets**—associations canadiennes classées en ordre alphabétique parmi huit catégories de budget.
- **Index des congrès**—rencontres commanditées par des associations canadiennes et étrangères; classées en ordre alphabétique selon le titre de l'événement.
- **Index des directeurs**—liste alphabétique des principales personnes-ressources des associations canadiennes, aux sièges sociaux et aux succursales.
- **Index géographique**—liste des sièges sociaux, des succursales, des sections régionales et des divisions des associations canadiennes; ordre alphabétique au sein des provinces et des villes.
- **Index des listes de distribution**—liste des associations qui offrent des listes de distribution; en ordre alphabétique selon le sujet.
- **Index des œuvres de bienfaisance enregistrées**—liste des associations enregistrées en tant qu'œuvres de bienfaisance; en ordre alphabétique selon le sujet.

OFFERT EN FORMAT PAPIER OU EN LIGNE—UN ACCÈS RAPIDE ET FACILE À TOUS LES RENSEIGNEMENTS DONT VOUS AVEZ BESOIN!

Offert sous couverture rigide ou en format électronique grâce au web, *Associations du Canada* donne invariablement un accès instantané aux personnes et aux faits dont vous avez besoin. Si la version imprimée est vérifiée et mise à jour annuellement, des changements continus sont apportés mensuellement à la base de données en ligne. Servez-vous de la version en ligne afin de circonscrire vos recherches grâce à des champs spéciaux de l'index comme le nom de l'organisation ou son type, le sujet, l'emplacement, le nom de la personne-ressource ou son titre et le code postal.

Créez vos propres listes! Les abonnés au service en ligne peuvent générer instantanément leurs propres listes de contacts et les exporter en format feuille de calcul pour une utilisation approfondie – une solution de rechange géniale aux services dispendieux d'un commissionnaire en publipostage.

ASSOCIATIONS DU CANADA OFFRE UN ACCÈS COMPLET À CES MARCHÉS HAUTEMENT LUCRATIFS

Voyage et tourisme
- Renseignez-vous sur les hôtes des événements... sur les dates et les endroits.
- Consultez les événements trois ans au préalable.

Journalisme et médias
- Recherche authentique—quel est leur centre d'activité? Qui est la personne responsable? Quel est leur budget?
- Vérifiez les faits et sources en une seule étape.

Bibliothèques
- Orientez les chercheurs vers la référence la plus complète en ce qui concerne les associations canadiennes.

Commerce
- Ciblez votre marché, faites une recherche selon vos sujets de prédilection, compilez des profils et recensez des listes des membres.
- Préparez votre sollicitation au hasard en obtenant les renseignements dont vous avez besoin pour offrir votre produit ou service.
- Obtenez un aperçu de vos clients potentiels selon les budgets, les intérêts au marché ou l'emplacement géographique.

Directeurs d'associations
- Recherchez des alliances stratégiques avec des associations partageant vos intérêts.
- Repérez des occasions ou des conflits dans le cadre de la planification des congrès.

Recherche et gouvernement
- Parcourez les groupes d'intérêts ou identifiez les organismes de bienfaisance de votre domaine d'intérêt.
- Consultez les sites Web, les publications et vérifiez la disponibilité des conférenciers.
- Évaluez les mandats, les affiliations et le champ d'application.

GREY HOUSE PUBLISHING CANADA

Pour obtenir plus d'information, veuillez contacter Grey House Publishing Canada
par tél. : 1 866 433-4739 ou 416 644-6479 par téléc. : 416 644-1904 | info@greyhouse.ca | www.greyhouse.ca

Canadian Parliamentary Guide
Your Number One Source for All General Federal Elections Results!

Published annually since before Confederation, the *Canadian Parliamentary Guide* is an indispensable directory, providing biographical information on elected and appointed members in federal and provincial government. Featuring government institutions such as the Governor General's Household, Privy Council and Canadian legislature, this comprehensive collection provides historical and current election results with statistical, provincial and political data.

THE CANADIAN PARLIAMENTARY GUIDE IS BROKEN DOWN INTO FIVE COMPREHENSIVE CATEGORIES

Monarchy—biographical information on Her Majesty Queen Elizabeth II, The Royal Family and the Governor General

Federal Government—a separate chapter for each of the Privy Council, Senate and House of Commons (including a brief description of the institution, its history in both text and chart format and a list of current members), followed by unparalleled biographical sketches*

General Elections

1867–2008

- information is listed alphabetically by province then by riding name
- notes on each riding include: date of establishment, date of abolition, former division and later divisions, followed by election year and successful candidate's name and party
- by-election information follows

2011

- information for the 2011 elections is organized in the same manner but also includes information on all the candidates who ran in each riding, their party affiliation and the number of votes won

Provincial and Territorial Governments—Each provincial chapter includes:

- statistical information
- description of Legislative Assembly
- biographical sketch of the Lieutenant Governor or Commissioner
- list of current Cabinet Members
- dates of legislatures since confederation
- current Members and Constituencies
- biographical sketches*
- general election and by-election results

Courts: Federal—each court chapter includes a description of the court (Supreme, Federal, Federal Court of Appeal, Court Martial Appeal and Tax Court), its history and a list of its judges followed by biographical sketches*

* Biographical sketches follow a concise yet in-depth format:

Personal Data—place of birth, education, family information

Political Career—political career path and services

Private Career—work history, organization memberships, military history

AVAILABLE IN PRINT AND NOW ONLINE!

Available in hardcover print, the *Canadian Parliamentary Guide* is also available electronically via the Web, providing instant access to the government officials you need and the facts you want every time. Whereas the print edition is verified and updated annually, the web version is updated on a monthly basis. Use the web version to narrow your search with index fields such as institution, province and name.

Create your own contact lists! Online subscribers can instantly generate their own contact lists and export information into spreadsheets for further use. A great alternative to high cost list broker services!

GREY HOUSE PUBLISHING CANADA

For more information please contact Grey House Publishing Canada

Tel.: (866) 433-4739 or (416) 644-6479 Fax: (416) 644-1904 | info@greyhouse.ca | www.greyhouse.ca

Guide parlementaire canadien

Votre principale source d'information en matière de résultats d'élections fédérales!

Publié annuellement depuis avant la Confédération, le *Guide parlementaire canadien* est une source fondamentale de notices biographiques des membres élus et nommés aux gouvernements fédéral et provinciaux. Il y est question, notamment, d'établissements gouvernementaux comme la résidence du gouverneur général, le Conseil privé et la législature canadienne. Ce recueil exhaustif présente les résultats historiques et actuels accompagnés de données statistiques, provinciales et politiques.

LE GUIDE PARLEMENTAIRE CANADIEN EST DIVISÉ EN CINQ CATÉGORIES EXHAUSTIVES:

La monarchie—des renseignements biographiques sur Sa Majesté la reine Elizabeth II, la famille royale et le gouverneur général.

Le gouvernement fédéral—un chapitre distinct pour chacun des sujets suivants: Conseil privé, sénat, Chambre des communes (y compris une brève description de l'institution, son historique sous forme de textes et de graphiques et une liste des membres actuels) suivi de notes biographiques sans pareil.*

Les élections fédérales

1867–2008

- Les renseignements sont présentés en ordre alphabétique par province puis par circonscription.
- Les notes de chaque circonscription comprennent : La date d'établissement, la date d'abolition, l'ancienne circonscription, les circonscriptions ultérieures, etc. puis l'année d'élection ainsi que le nom et le parti des candidats élus.
- Viennent ensuite des renseignements sur l'élection partielle.

2011

- Les renseignements de l'élection 2011 sont organisés de la même manière, mais comprennent également de l'information sur tous les candidats qui se sont présentés dans chaque circonscription, leur appartenance politique et le nombre de voix récoltées.

Gouvernements provinciaux et territoriaux—Chaque chapitre portant sur le gouvernement provincial comprend :

- des renseignements statistiques
- une description de l'Assemblée législative
- des notes biographiques sur le lieutenant-gouverneur ou le commissaire
- une liste des ministres actuels
- les dates de périodes législatives depuis la Confédération
- une liste des membres et des circonscriptions
- des notes biographiques*
- les résultats des élections générales et partielles

Cours : fédérale—chaque chapitre comprend : une description de la cour (suprême, fédérale, cour d'appel fédérale, cour d'appel de la cour martiale et cour de l'impôt), son histoire, une liste des juges qui y siègent ainsi que des notes biographiques.*

* Les notes biographiques respectent un format concis, bien qu'approfondi :

Renseignements personnels—lieu de naissance, formation, renseignements familiaux

Carrière politique—cheminement politique et service public

Carrière privée—antécédents professionnels, membre d'organisations, antécédents militaires

OFFERT EN FORMAT PAPIER ET DÉSORMAIS ÉLECTRONIQUE!

Offert sous couverture rigide ou en format électronique grâce au web, le *Guide parlementaire canadien* donne invariablement un accès instantané aux représentants du gouvernement et aux faits qui font l'objet de vos recherches. Si la version imprimée est vérifiée et mise à jour annuellement, des changements continus sont apportés mensuellement à la base de données en ligne. Servez-vous de la version en ligne afin de circonscrire vos recherches grâce aux champs spéciaux de l'index comme l'institution, la province et le nom.

Créez vos propres listes! Les abonnés au service en ligne peuvent générer instantanément leurs propres listes de contacts et les exporter en format feuille de calcul pour une utilisation approfondie – une solution de rechange géniale aux services dispendieux d'un commissionnaire en publipostage!

GREY HOUSE PUBLISHING CANADA

Pour obtenir plus d'information, veuillez contacter Grey House Publishing Canada

par tél. : 1 866 433-4739 ou 416 644-6479 par téléc. : 416 644-1904 | info@greyhouse.ca | www.greyhouse.ca

Governments Canada

The Most Complete and Comprehensive Guide to Locating People and Programs in Canada

Governments Canada provides regularly updated listings on federal, provincial/territorial and municipal government departments, offices and agencies across Canada. Branch and regional offices are also included, along with all associated agencies, boards, commissions and Crown corporations.

Listings include contact name, full address, telephone and fax numbers, as well as e-mail addresses. You can be sure of our commitment to superior indexing and accuracy.

ACCESS IS PROVIDED TO THE KEY DECISION-MAKERS IN ALL LEVELS OF THE GOVERNMENT INCLUDING:

- Cabinets/ Executive Councils
- Elected Officials
- Governors General/ Lieutenant Governors/ Territorial Commissioners
- Prime Ministers/ Premiers/ Government Leaders
- Auditor General/ Provincial Auditors
- Electoral Officers
- Departments/ Agencies and Administration

THESE POWERFUL AND EASY-TO-USE INDEXES WERE DESIGNED TO HELP FIND QUICK AND AUTHORITATIVE RESULTS FOR ANY RESEARCH QUERY.

- **Topical Table of Contents**—a single unified index to all jurisdictions
- **Quick Reference Topics**—a detailed list with references to over 170 topics of interest
- **Highlights of Significant Changes**—a list of highlights of major changes that have recently occurred in government.
- **Contacts**—an invaluable networking and sales tool with over 130 pages of full contact information
- **Website/ Email listings**—organized by government and department or ministry
- **Acronyms**—an alphabetical list of the most commonly used acronyms

GOVERNMENTS CANADA IS AN ESSENTIAL FINDING TOOL FOR:

Lobbyists—Locate the right person for productive conversation on key issues

Lawyers, Accountants and Consultants—Access the most current names and addresses of key contacts in every government office

Librarians—Reduce research time with this all-in-one reference tool

Embassies & Consulates—Find the right referral contact or official from across Canada

Government Employees—Peruse the easy-to-find facts and information on all levels of government

Suppliers to Government—Locate the decision-makers to target your products or services

---

GREY HOUSE PUBLISHING CANADA For more information please contact Grey House Publishing Canada
Tel.: (866)-433-4739 or (416) 644-6479 Fax: (416) 644-1904 | info@greyhouse.ca | www.greyhouse.ca

Gouvernements du Canada

Le guide le plus complet et exhaustif pour trouver des personnes et des programmes au Canada

Ce répertoire offre des fiches descriptives mises à jour régulièrement au sujet des ministères fédéraux, provinciaux et territoriaux, des bureaux et des agences du gouvernement de partout au pays. Les directions générales et les bureaux régionaux en font également partie, tout comme les organismes associés, les conseils, les commissions et les sociétés de la Couronne.

Les fiches descriptives comprennent les noms de personnes-ressources, l'adresse complète, les numéros de téléphone et de télécopieur de même que les courriels. Vous pouvez compter sur notre engagement envers la précision et l'indexation de qualité supérieure.

VOUS AVEZ AINSI ACCÈS AUX DÉCIDEURS CLÉS À TOUS LES PALIERS DE GOUVERNEMENT, NOTAMMENT :

- Conseils des ministres/conseils exécutifs
- Représentants élus
- Gouverneur général/lieutenants gouverneurs/ commissaires territoriaux
- Premiers ministres/premiers ministres provinciaux/ leaders du gouvernement
- Vérificateur général du Canada/vérificateurs provinciaux
- Fonctionnaires électoraux
- Ministères/organismes et administration publique

CES INDEX PUISSANTS ET FACILES D'UTILISATION SONT CONÇUS POUR VOUS AIDER À OBTENIR DES RÉSULTATS RAPIDES ET DIGNES DE FOI, PEU IMPORTE VOTRE RECHERCHE.

- **Table des matières de noms communs**—un seul index unifié pour toutes les juridictions.
- **Guide éclair des sujets**—une liste détaillée accompagnée de références sur plus de 170 sujets d'intérêt.
- **Faits saillants des changements importants**—une liste des principaux changements importants récemment apportés au sein du gouvernement.
- **Personnes-ressources**—un outil irremplaçable de réseautage et de ventes grâce à plus de 130 pages de coordonnées complètes.
- **Listes de sites Web et de courriels**—classées par gouvernement et ministère.
- **Acronymes**—une liste alphabétique des acronymes les plus utilisés.

GOUVERNEMENTS DU CANADA EST L'OUTIL ESSENTIEL DES PROFESSIONNELS POUR TROUVER:

Des groupes de revendication—trouvez les bonnes personnes pour avoir une conversation productive sur des questions-clés.

Des avocats, des comptables et des conseillers—obtenez les noms et les adresses les plus courants des personnes-ressources clés de chaque bureau gouvernemental.

Des bibliothécaires—épargnez du temps de recherche grâce à cet outil de référence complet.

Des ambassades et des consulats—trouvez la bonne personne-ressource ou le bon fonctionnaire en matière de présentation partout au Canada.

Des employés du gouvernement—consultez les faits et renseignements faciles à obtenir à tous les paliers gouvernementaux.

Des fournisseurs du gouvernement—trouvez les décideurs afin de cibler vos produits et services.

GREY HOUSE PUBLISHING CANADA

Pour obtenir plus d'information, veuillez contacter Grey House Publishing Canada
par tél. : 1 866 433-4739 ou 416 644-6479 par téléc. : 416 644-1904 | info@greyhouse.ca | www.greyhouse.ca

Canadian Environmental Resource Guide
The Only Complete Guide to the Business of Environmental Management

The *Canadian Environmental Resource Guide* provides data on every aspect of the environment industry in unprecedented detail. It's one-stop searching for details on government offices and programs, information sources, product and service firms and trade fairs that pertain to the business of environmental management. All information is fully indexed and cross-referenced for easy use. The directory features current information and key contacts in Canada's environmental industry including:

ENVIRONMENTAL UP-DATE

- A one-year summary of environmental events, including articles, tradeshows, conferences and seminars
- Overview of government acts and regulations, environmental abbreviations, prominent environmentalists and statistics

ENVIRONMENTAL PRODUCTS & SERVICES

- Comprehensive listings for companies and firms producing and selling products and services in the environmental sector, including markets served, working language and percentage of revenue sources: public and private
- Detailed indexes by subject, geography and ISO

ENVIRONMENTAL INFORMATION RESOURCES

- An all inclusive list of environmental associations, organizations, special libraries and resource centres, environmental publications

ENVIRONMENTAL GOVERNMENT LISTINGS

- Information for every department and agency influencing environmental initiatives and purchasing policies, including federal and provincial government, municipal government, inter-government offices and councils and environmental trade representatives abroad

Available in softcover print or electronically via the web, the *Canadian Environmental Resource Guide* provides instant access to the people you need and the facts you want every time. The *Canadian Environmental Resource Guide* is verified and updated annually. Regular ongoing changes are added to the web version on a monthly basis.

CANADIAN ENVIRONMENTAL RESOURCE GUIDE NOW OFFERS THESE VALUABLE INDEXING AND SOURCING TOOLS TO AID YOUR SEARCH!

Entry Name Index—An alphabetical list of all entries, providing a quick and easy way to access any listing in this edition.

Associations—Complete subject and key word index to environmental associations everywhere, plus an acronym index.

Directory of Products and Services—Indexed by the industry's best product/service classifications PLUS a separate geographic index for sources in your region. All companies listed alphabetically.

Tabs—Main sections are tabbed for easy look-up. Headnotes on each page make it easy to locate the data you need.

The web version allows you to narrow your search by using index fields such as name or type of organization, subject, location, contact name or title and postal code.

Create your own contact lists! Online subscribers have the option to instantly generate their own contact lists and export them into spreadsheets for further use—a great alternative to high cost list broker services.

GREY HOUSE PUBLISHING CANADA For more information please contact Grey House Publishing Canada
Tel.: (866) 433-4739 or (416) 644-6479 Fax: (416) 644-1904 | info@greyhouse.ca | www.greyhouse.ca

Guide des ressources environnementales canadiennes
Le seul guide complet dédié à la gestion de l'environnement

Le *Guide des ressources environnementales canadiennes* offre de l'information relative à tous les aspects de l'industrie de l'environnement dans les moindres détails. Il permet d'effectuer une recherche de données complètes sur les bureaux et programmes gouvernementaux, les sources de renseignements, les entreprises de produits et de services et les foires commerciales qui portent sur les activités de la gestion de l'environnement. Toute l'information est entièrement indexée et effectue un double renvoi pour une consultation facile. Le répertoire présente des renseignements actualisés et les personnes-ressources clés de l'industrie de l'environnement au Canada, y compris les suivants.

MISE À JOUR SUR L'INDUSTRIE DE L'ENVIRONNEMENT

- Un sommaire annuel des activités environnementales, y compris des articles, des salons professionnels, des congrès et des colloques
- Un aperçu des lois et règlements gouvernementaux, des abréviations liées à l'environnement, les environnementalistes éminents et les statistiques

PRODUITS ET SERVICES ENVIRONNEMENTAUX

- Des listes exhaustives des entreprises et des cabinets qui fabriquent ou offrent des produits et des services dans le domaine de l'environnement, y compris les marchés desservis, la langue de travail et la ventilation des sources de revenus – publics et privés
- Des index selon le sujet, la géographie et la certification ISO

RESSOURCES D'INFORMATION ENVIRONNEMENTALE

- Une liste exhaustive d'associations environnementales, d'organismes, de bibliothèques spécialisées et de centres de ressources, de publications portant sur l'environnement

LISTES GOUVERNEMENTALES RELATIVES À L'ENVIRONNEMENT

- Des renseignements sur tous les ministères et organismes qui influent les initiatives environnementales et les politiques d'approvisionnement, y compris les gouvernements fédéral et provinciaux, les administrations municipales, les bureaux et conseils interministériels ainsi que les représentants au commerce environnemental à l'étranger

Offert sous couverture rigide ou en format électronique grâce au Web, le *Guide des ressources environnementales canadiennes* offre invariablement un accès instantané aux représentants du gouvernement et aux faits qui font l'objet de vos recherches. Il est vérifié et mis à jour annuellement. La version en ligne est mise à jour mensuellement.

LE GUIDE DES RESSOURCES ENVIRONNEMENTALES CANADIENNES OFFRE DÉSORMAIS CES PRÉCIEUX OUTILS D'INDEXATION ET DE SOURÇAGE POUR VOUS AIDER DANS VOS RECHERCHES!

Répertoire nominatif—une liste alphabétique offrant un moyen rapide et facile d'accéder à toute liste de cette édition.

Associations—un index complet par sujet et mot-clé des associations environnementales, où qu'elles se trouvent, plus un index d'acronymes.

Répertoire des produits et des services—catalogué selon les meilleures classifications de produits et de services de l'industrie PLUS un index géographique indépendant pour trouver les sources de votre région. Toutes les entreprises sont énumérées en ordre alphabétique.

Onglets—les sections principales possèdent un onglet pour une consultation facile. Les notes en tête de chaque page vous aident à trouver les données voulues.

Format papier ou en ligne—un accès rapide à tous les renseignements dont vous avez besoin!

Servez-vous de la version en ligne afin de circonscrire vos recherches grâce à des champs spéciaux de l'index comme le nom de l'organisation ou son type, le sujet, l'emplacement, le nom de la personne-ressource ou son titre et le code postal.

Créez vos propres listes! Les abonnés au service en ligne peuvent générer instantanément leurs propres listes de contacts et les exporter en format feuille de calcul pour une utilisation approfondie—une solution de rechange géniale aux services dispendieux d'un commissionnaire en publipostage.

GREY HOUSE PUBLISHING CANADA

Pour obtenir plus d'information, veuillez contacter Grey House Publishing Canada
par tél. : 1 866 433-4739 ou 416 644-6479 par téléc. : 416 644-1904 | info@greyhouse.ca | www.greyhouse.ca

Libraries Canada

Gain Access to Complete and Detailed Information on Canadian Libraries

Libraries Canada brings together the most current information from across the entire Canadian library sector, including libraries and branch libraries, educational libraries, regional systems, resource centres, archives, related periodicals, library schools and programs, provincial and governmental agencies and associations.

As the nation's leading library directory for over 25 years, *Libraries Canada* gives you access to almost 10,000 names and addresses of contacts in these institutions. Also included are valuable details such as library symbol, number of staff, operating systems, library type and acquisitions budget, hours of operation—all thoroughly indexed and easy to find.

INSTANT ACCESS TO CANADIAN LIBRARY SECTOR INFORMATION

Developed for publishers, advocacy groups, computer hardware suppliers, internet service providers and other diverse groups which provide products and services to the library community; associations that need to maintain a current list of library resources in Canada; and research departments, students and government agencies which require information about the types of services and programs available at various research institutions, *Libraries Canada* will help you find the information you need—quickly and easily.

EXPERT SEARCH OPTIONS AVAILABLE WITH ONLINE VERSION...

Available in print and online, *Libraries Canada* delivers easily accessible, quality information that has been verified and organized for easy retrieval. Five easy-to-use indexes assist you in navigating the print edition while the online version utilizes multiple index fields that help you get results.

Available on Grey House Publishing Canada's CIRC interface, you can choose between Expert and Quick search to pinpoint information. Designed for both novice and advanced researchers, you can conduct simple text searches as well as powerful Boolean searches, plus you can narrow your search by using index fields such as name or type of institution, headquarters, location, area code, contact name or title and postal code. Save your searches to build on at a later date or use the mark record function to view, print, e-mail or export your selected records.

Online subscribers have the option to instantly generate their own contact lists and export them into spreadsheets for further use. A great alternative to high cost list broker services.

LIBRARIES CANADA GIVES YOU ALL THE ESSENTIALS FOR EACH INSTITUTION:

Name, address, contact information, key personnel, number of staff

Collection information, type of library, acquisitions budget, subject area, special collection

User services, number of branches, hours of operation, ILL information, photocopy and microform facilities, for-fee research, Internet access

Systems information, details on electronic access, operating and online systems, Internet and e-mail software, Internet connectivity, access to electronic resources

Additional information including associations, publications and regional systems

With almost 60% of the data changing annually it has never been more important to have the latest version of *Libraries Canada*.

GREY HOUSE PUBLISHING CANADA For more information please contact Grey House Publishing Canada
Tel.: (866) 433-4739 or (416) 644-6479 Fax: (416) 644-1904 | info@greyhouse.ca | www.greyhouse.ca

Bibliothèques Canada

Accédez aux renseignements complets et détaillés au sujet des bibliothèques canadiennes

Bibliothèques Canada combine les renseignements les plus à jour provenant du secteur des bibliothèques de partout au Canada, y compris les bibliothèques et leurs succursales, les bibliothèques éducatives, les systèmes régionaux, les centres de ressources, les archives, les périodiques pertinents, les écoles de bibliothéconomie et leurs programmes, les organismes provinciaux et gouvernementaux ainsi que les associations.

Principal répertoire des bibliothèques depuis plus de 20 ans, *Bibliothèques Canada* vous donne accès à près de 10 000 noms et adresses de personnes-ressources pour ces établissements. Il comprend également des détails précieux comme le symbole d'identification de bibliothèque, le nombre de membres du personnel, les systèmes d'exploitation, le type de bibliothèque et le budget attribué aux acquisitions, les heures d'ouverture – autant d'information minutieusement indexée et facile à trouver.

Offert en version imprimée et en ligne, *Bibliothèques Canada* offre des renseignements de qualité, facile d'accès, qui ont été vérifiés et organisés afin de les obtenir facilement. Cinq index conviviaux vous aident dans la navigation du numéro imprimé tandis que la version en ligne vous permet de saisir plusieurs champs d'index pour vous aider à découvrir l'information voulue.

ACCÈS INSTANTANÉ AUX RENSEIGNEMENTS DU DOMAINE DES BIBLIOTHÈQUES CANADIENNES

Conçu pour les éditeurs, les groupes de revendication, les fournisseurs de matériel informatique, les fournisseurs de services Internet et autres groupes qui offrent produits et services aux bibliothèques; les associations qui ont besoin de conserver une liste à jour des ressources bibliothécaires au Canada; les services de recherche, les organismes étudiants et gouvernementaux qui ont besoin d'information au sujet des types de services et de programmes offerts par divers établissements de recherche, *Bibliothèques Canada* vous aide à trouver l'information nécessaire – rapidement et simplement.

LA VERSION EN LIGNE COMPREND DES OPTIONS DE RECHERCHE POUSSÉES…

À partir de l'interface du Centre de documentation du Canada de Grey House Publishing Canada, vous pouvez choisir entre la recherche poussée et rapide pour cibler votre information. Vous pouvez effectuer des recherches par texte simple, conçues à la fois pour les chercheurs débutants et chevronnés, ainsi que des recherches booléennes puissantes. Vous pouvez également restreindre votre recherche à l'aide des champs d'index, comme le nom ou le type d'établissement, le siège social, l'emplacement, l'indicatif régional, le nom de la personne-ressource ou son titre et le code postal. Enregistrez vos recherches pour vous en servir plus tard ou utilisez la fonction de marquage pour afficher, imprimer, envoyer par courriel ou exporter les dossiers sélectionnés.

Les abonnés au service en ligne peuvent générer instantanément leurs propres listes de contacts et les exporter en format feuille de calcul pour une utilisation approfondie – une solution de rechange géniale aux services dispendieux d'un commissionnaire en publipostage.

BIBLIOTHÈQUES CANADA VOUS DONNE TOUS LES RENSEIGNEMENTS ESSENTIELS RELATIFS À CHAQUE ÉTABLISSEMENT :

Leurs nom et adresse, les coordonnées de la personne-ressource, les membres clés du personnel, le nombre de membres du personnel

L'information relative aux collections, le type de bibliothèque, le budget attribué aux acquisitions, le domaine, les collections particulières

Les services aux utilisateurs, le nombre de succursales, les heures d'ouverture, les renseignements relatifs au PEB, les services de photocopie et de microforme, la recherche rémunérée, l'accès à Internet

L'information relative aux systèmes, des détails sur l'accès électronique, les systèmes d'exploitation et ceux en ligne, Internet et le logiciel de messagerie électronique, la connectivité à Internet, l'accès aux ressources électroniques

L'information supplémentaire, y compris les associations, les publications et les systèmes régionaux

Alors que près de 60 % des données sont modifiées annuellement, il est plus important que jamais de posséder la plus récente version de *Bibliothèques Canada*.

GREY HOUSE PUBLISHING CANADA

Pour obtenir plus d'information, veuillez contacter Grey House Publishing Canada
par tél. : 1 866 433-4739 ou 416 644-6479 par téléc. : 416 644-1904 | info@greyhouse.ca | www.greyhouse.ca

Financial Services Canada
Unparalleled Coverage of the Canadian Financial Service Industry

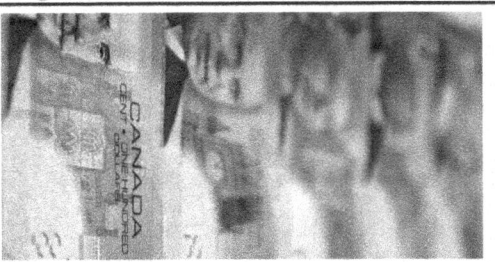

With corporate listings for over 17,000 organizations and hard-to-find business information, *Financial Services Canada* is the most up-to-date source for names and contact numbers of industry professionals, senior executives, portfolio managers, financial advisors, agency bureaucrats and elected representatives.

Financial Services Canada is the definitive resource for detailed listings—providing valuable contact information including: name, title, organization, profile, associated companies, telephone and fax numbers, e-mail and website addresses. Use our online database and refine your search by stock symbol, revenue, year founded, assets, ownership type or number of employees.

POWERFUL INDEXES HELP YOU LOCATE THE CRUCIAL FINANCIAL INFORMATION YOU NEED.

Organized with the user in mind, *Financial Services Canada* contains categorized listings and 4 easy-to-use indexes:

Alphabetic—financial organizations listed in alphabetical sequence by company name

Geographic—financial institutions and their branches broken down by town or city

Executive Name—all officers, directors and senior personnel in alphabetical order by surname

Insurance class—lists all companies by insurance type

Reduce the time you spend compiling lists, researching company information and searching for e-mail addresses. Whether you are interested in contacting a finance lawyer regarding international and domestic joint ventures, need to generate a list of foreign banks in Canada or want to contact the Toronto Stock Exchange—*Financial Services Canada* gives you the power to find all the data you need.

PRINT OR ONLINE—QUICK AND EASY ACCESS TO ALL THE INFORMATION YOU NEED!

Available in softcover print or electronically via the web, *Financial Services Canada* provides instant access to the people you need and the facts you want every time.

Financial Services Canada print edition is verified and updated annually. Regular ongoing changes are added to the web version on a monthly basis. The web version allows you to narrow your search by using index fields such as name or type of organization, subject, location, contact name or title and postal code.

Create your own contact lists! Online subscribers have the option to instantly generate their own contact lists and export them into spreadsheets for further use—a great alternative to high cost list broker services.

ACCESS TO CURRENT LISTINGS FOR...

Banks and Depository Institutions
- Domestic and savings banks
- Foreign banks and branches
- Foreign bank representative offices
- Trust companies
- Credit unions

Non-Depository Institutions
- Bond rating companies
- Collection agencies
- Credit card companies
- Financing and loan companies
- Trustees in bankruptcy

Investment Management Firms, including securities and commodities
- Financial planning / investment management companies
- Investment dealers
- Investment fund companies
- Pension/money management companies
- Stock exchanges
- Holding companies

Insurance Companies, including federal and provincial
- Reinsurance companies
- Fraternal benefit societies
- Mutual benefit companies
- Reciprocal exchanges accounting and law
- Accountants
- Actuary consulting firms
- Law firms (specializing in finance)
- Major Canadian companies
- Key financial contacts for public, private and Crown corporations
- Government
- Federal, provincial and territorial contacts

Publications Appendix
- Leading publications serving the financial services industry

---

GREY HOUSE PUBLISHING CANADA For more information please contact Grey House Publishing Canada
Tel.: (866)-433-4739 or (416) 644-6479 Fax: (416) 644-1904 | info@greyhouse.ca | www.greyhouse.ca

Services financiers au Canada

Une couverture sans pareille de l'industrie des services financiers canadiens

Grâce à plus de 17 000 organisations et renseignements commerciaux rares, *Services financiers du Canada* est la source la plus à jour de noms et de coordonnées de professionnels, de membres de la haute direction, de gestionnaires de portefeuille, de conseillers financiers, de fonctionnaires et de représentants élus de l'industrie.

Services financiers du Canada intègre les plus récentes modifications à l'industrie afin de vous offrir les détails les plus à jour au sujet de chaque entreprise, notamment le nom, le titre, l'organisation, les numéros de téléphone et de télécopieur, le courriel et l'adresse du site Web. Servez-vous de la base de données en ligne et raffinez votre recherche selon le symbole, le revenu, l'année de création, les immobilisations, le type de propriété ou le nombre d'employés.

DES INDEX PUISSANTS VOUS AIDENT À TROUVER LES RENSEIGNEMENTS FINANCIERS ESSENTIELS DONT VOUS AVEZ BESOIN.

C'est avec l'utilisateur en tête que Services financiers au Canada a été conçu; il contient des listes catégorisées et quatre index faciles d'utilisation :

Alphabétique—les organisations financières apparaissent en ordre alphabétique, selon le nom de l'entreprise.

Géographique—les institutions financières et leurs succursales sont détaillées par ville.

Nom de directeur—tous les agents, directeurs et cadres supérieurs sont classés en ordre alphabétique, selon leur nom de famille.

Classe d'assurance—toutes les entreprises selon leur type d'assurance.

Passez moins de temps à préparer des listes, à faire des recherches ou à chercher des contacts et des courriels. Que vous soyez intéressé à contacter un avocat en droit des affaires au sujet de projets conjoints internationaux et nationaux, que vous ayez besoin de générer une liste des banques étrangères au Canada ou que vous souhaitiez communiquer avec la Bourse de Toronto, *Services financiers au Canada* vous permet de trouver toutes les données dont vous avez besoin.

OFFERT EN FORMAT PAPIER OU EN LIGNE – UN ACCÈS RAPIDE ET FACILE À TOUS LES RENSEIGNEMENTS DONT VOUS AVEZ BESOIN!

Offert sous couverture rigide ou en format électronique grâce au Web, Services financiers du Canada donne invariablement un accès instantané aux personnes et aux faits dont vous avez besoin. Si la version imprimée est vérifiée et mise à jour annuellement, des changements continus sont apportés mensuellement à la base de données en ligne. Servez-vous de la version en ligne afin de circonscrire vos recherches grâce à des champs spéciaux de l'index comme le nom de l'organisation ou son type, le sujet, l'emplacement, le nom de la personne-ressource ou son titre et le code postal.

Créez vos propres listes! Les abonnés au service en ligne peuvent générer instantanément leurs propres listes de contacts et les exporter en format feuille de calcul pour une utilisation approfondie – une solution de rechange géniale aux services dispendieux d'un commissionnaire en publipostage.

ACCÉDEZ AUX LISTES ACTUELLES...

Banques et institutions de dépôt
- Banques nationales et d'épargne
- Banques étrangères et leurs succursales
- Bureaux des représentants de banques étrangères
- Sociétés de fiducie
- Coopératives d'épargne et de crédit

Établissements financiers
- Entreprises de notation des obligations
- Agences de placement
- Compagnies de carte de crédit
- Sociétés de financement et de prêt
- Syndics de faillite

Sociétés de gestion de placements, y compris les valeurs et marchandises
- Entreprises de planification financière et de gestion des investissements
- Maisons de courtage de valeurs
- Courtiers en épargne collective
- Entreprises de gestion de la pension/de trésorerie
- Bourses
- Sociétés de portefeuille

Compagnies d'assurance, fédérales et provinciales
- Compagnies de réassurance
- Sociétés fraternelles
- Sociétés de secours mutuel
- Échanges selon la formule de réciprocité — comptabilité et droit
- Comptables
- Cabinets d'actuaires-conseils
- Cabinets d'avocats (spécialisés en finance)
- Principales entreprises canadiennes
- Principaux contacts financiers pour les sociétés de capitaux publiques, privées et de la Couronne
- Gouvernement
- Personnes-ressources aux paliers fédéral, provinciaux et territoriaux

Annexe de publications
- Principales publications qui desservent l'industrie des services financiers

GREY HOUSE PUBLISHING CANADA

Pour obtenir plus d'information, veuillez contacter Grey House Publishing Canada
par tél. : 1 866 433-4739 ou 416 644-6479 par téléc. : 416 644-1904 | info@greyhouse.ca | www.greyhouse.ca

Mailing List Services

As a boutique provider of mailing lists, Grey House Publishing Canada specializes in the areas below to ensure a high level of accuracy. Our clients return to us time and time again because of the reliability of our information and great customer service. We'll work with you to develop a campaign that provides results. No other list services will work as closely as we do to meet your unique needs.

GREY HOUSE CANADA CUSTOM MAILING LISTS

Associations—the most extensive list of Canadian associations available, featuring all professional, trade and business organizations together with not-for-profit groups.

Arts & Culture—the definitive source of key prospects in various Canadian arts and cultural outlets.

Education—the most comprehensive list of educational institutions and organizations in Canada.

Health Care / Hospitals—includes all major medical facilities with chief executives.

Lawyers—key prospects for a number of direct mail offers.

Media—the definitive source of key prospects in various Canadian media outlets, offering the top business managers and/or publishers.

Environmental—a complete profile of the Canadian Environmental scene, constantly revised for the annual Canadian Environmental Resource Guide.

Financial Services—a list of key contacts from the full range of Canada's financial services industry.

Government Key Contacts—a list of key Government contacts, maintained by the Canadian Almanac & Directory, Canada's standard institutional reference for 165 years.

Libraries—the most unique and complete list of government, special and public libraries available.

Major Canadian Companies—listings of Canada's largest private, public and Crown corporations with major key contacts of the top business decision-makers.

AVAILABILITY

Lists are available on CD, labels and via e-mail. They are provided on a one-time use basis or for a one-year lease. For a quotation on tailor-made lists to suit your needs, inquire using the contact information listed below.

GREY HOUSE PUBLISHING CANADA

For more information please contact Grey House Publishing Canada
Tel.: (866) 433-4739 or (416) 644-6479 Fax: (416) 644-1904 | info@greyhouse.ca | www.greyhouse.ca

Services de liste de distribution

En tant que point de service fournisseur de listes de distribution, Grey House Canada se spécialise dans les domaines ci-dessous pour assurer un degré supérieur de précision. Nos clients nous sont fidèles, car ils souhaitent bénéficier de notre fiabilité et de notre service à la clientèle. Nous collaborerons avec vous pour développer une campagne qui produit des résultats. Aucun autre service de création de listes ne collabore aussi étroitement que nous avec leurs clients pour satisfaire leurs besoins particuliers.

GREY HOUSE CANADA
LISTES DE DISTRIBUTION PERSONNALISÉES

Associations—la liste la plus complète des associations canadiennes qui énumère toutes les associations professionnelles, corporatives et commerciales ainsi que les groupes sans but lucratif.

Arts et culture—la source manifeste des candidats clés des divers vecteurs artistiques et culturels au Canada.

Éducation—la liste la plus complète des établissements et des organismes d'enseignement au Canada.

Soins de santé/hôpitaux—comprend les principaux établissements médicaux et leurs directeurs.

Avocats—les principaux clients potentiels pour nombre d'offres de publipostage direct.

Médias—la source certaine des clients potentiels clés dans divers points de vente de médias canadiens; elle comprend les principaux dirigeants et éditeurs.

Environnement—un profil complet de la scène environnementale canadienne; constamment mis à jour pour le Guide des ressources environnementales canadiennes.

Services financiers—une liste des personnes-ressources clés de tout l'éventail de l'industrie des services financiers du Canada.

Coordonnées gouvernementales clés—une liste des contacts essentiels, entretenue par le Répertoire et almanach canadien, la référence institutionnelle au Canada depuis 165 ans.

Bibliothèques—la liste la plus unique et la plus complète des bibliothèques gouvernementales, spécialisées et publiques disponible.

Principales entreprises canadiennes—une liste des plus grandes sociétés privées, publiques et de la Couronne au Canada, y compris les coordonnées des principaux décideurs du monde des affaires.

DISPONIBILITÉ

Les listes sont offertes sur disque, étiquettes et par courriel. Elles sont fournies sur la base d'une utilisation unique ou d'un abonnement d'un an. Pour obtenir un devis pour une liste personnalisée selon vos besoins, contactez-nous.

GREY HOUSE PUBLISHING CANADA

Pour obtenir plus d'information, veuillez contacter Grey House Publishing Canada
par tél. : 1 866 433-4739 ou 416 644-6479 par téléc. : 416 644-1904 | info@greyhouse.ca | www.greyhouse.ca